Mexico

John Noble

Daniel Schechter, Suzanne Plank, Sandra Bao, Ben Greensfelder,
Alan Tarbell, Michael Read, Iain Stewart, Andrew Dean Nystrom,
Beth Greenfield and Ray Bartlett

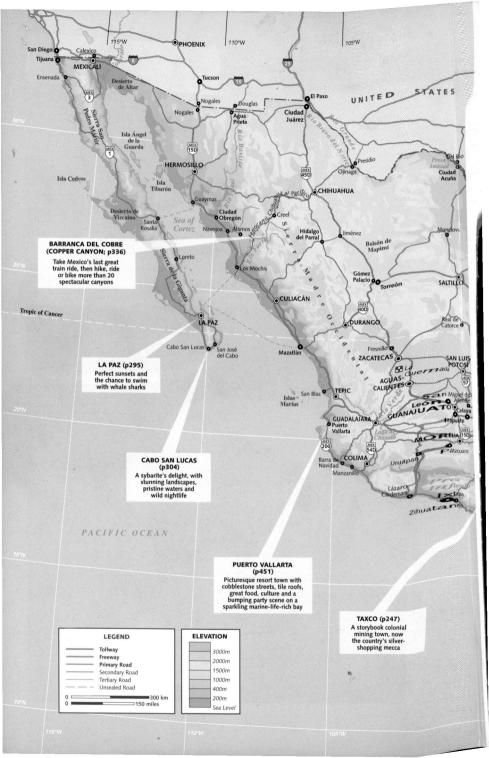

**BARRANCA DEL COBRE
(COPPER CANYON; p336)**
Take Mexico's last great train ride, then hike, ride or bike more than 20 spectacular canyons

LA PAZ (p295)
Perfect sunsets and the chance to swim with whale sharks

**CABO SAN LUCAS
(p304)**
A sybarite's delight, with stunning landscapes, pristine waters and wild nightlife

**PUERTO VALLARTA
(p451)**
Picturesque resort town with cobblestone streets, tile roofs, great food, culture and a bumping party scene on a sparkling marine-life-rich bay

TAXCO (p247)
A storybook colonial mining town, now the country's silver-shopping mecca

LEGEND

	Tollway
	Freeway
	Primary Road
	Secondary Road
	Tertiary Road
	Unsealed Road

0 ———— 300 km
0 ———— 150 miles

ELEVATION

3000m
2000m
1500m
1000m
400m
200m
Sea Level

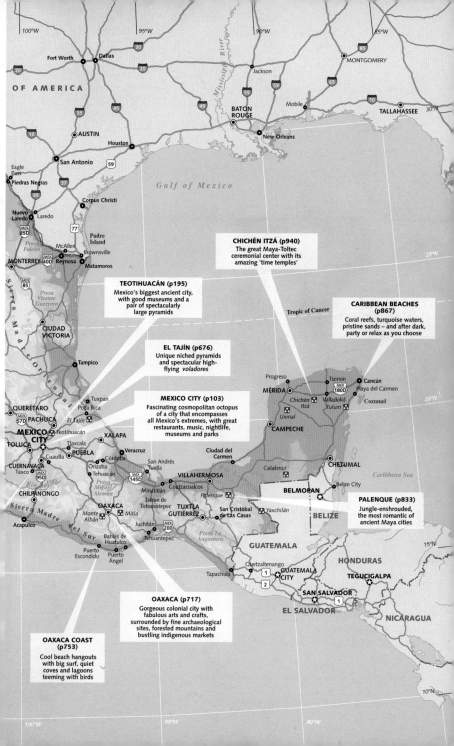

CHICHÉN ITZÁ (p940)
The great Maya-Toltec ceremonial center with its amazing 'time temples'

TEOTIHUACÁN (p195)
Mexico's biggest ancient city, with good museums and a pair of spectacularly large pyramids

CARIBBEAN BEACHES (p867)
Coral reefs, turquoise waters, pristine sands – and after dark, party or relax as you choose

EL TAJÍN (p676)
Unique niched pyramids and spectacular high-flying *voladores*

MEXICO CITY (p103)
Fascinating cosmopolitan octopus of a city that encompasses all Mexico's extremes, with great restaurants, music, nightlife, museums and parks

PALENQUE (p833)
Jungle-enshrouded, the most romantic of ancient Maya cities

OAXACA (p717)
Gorgeous colonial city with fabulous arts and crafts, surrounded by fine archaeological sites, forested mountains and bustling indigenous markets

OAXACA COAST (p753)
Cool beach hangouts with big surf, quiet coves and lagoons teeming with birds

Day of the Dead celebrations bring all of Mexico to life in November
CHRISTIAN ÅSLUND

Mi Querido Mexico

my beloved mexico

To explore Mexico is to walk through rain forests and along tropical beaches, to traverse vast deserts and gaze at snow-capped volcanoes, and to wander the streets of bustling cities, sleepy villages, chic resorts and the ruined cities of the Maya, the Aztecs and other great civilizations that flourished here long ago.

Mexico is a kaleidoscope of cultures, cuisines, landscapes, adventures, music, languages, arts and history. When asked to describe the country, its Spanish conqueror, Hernán Cortés, simply crumpled a piece of paper and set it on a table. The rugged, mountainous topography he was indicating has yielded a colorful variety of distinct places, people and traditions – which today are more accessible than ever before. Thanks to modern communications and innovative tourism initiatives, it has never been easier to hike Mexico's remote canyons or cloud forests, watch whales or flamingos, climb volcanoes, dive waters teeming with tropical fish, or ride on horseback to remote indigenous villages.

If you're slightly less activity-minded, delight your senses with Mexico's endless palm-fringed beaches, world-class museums and galleries, superb handicrafts, hectic markets, flavorsome food, friendly hotels and beautiful colonial cities.

At the end of the day, sit back and take it all in with a margarita or an ice-cold Mexican beer at a beach bar or in a plaza with splashing fountains. After dark, indulge in the bars, music and stylish clubs of Mexico's cities and resorts, or lose yourself in the fun, fireworks and spectacle of one of the country's noisy fiestas: there's one happening almost every day, not far from you! JOHN NOBLE

See the sun set over svelte sand dunes in Baja California (p264)
RALPH LEE HOPKINS

Color Illuminating Life

NAME	Beatriz Narváez
AGE	Timeless
OCCUPATION	Painter, gallery owner
RESIDENCE	Puerto Vallarta

We are so deeply involved in the world of color. It's what gives us life…my world is color. When I stand before my white canvas I may not know what I'm going to paint, but I know what color it will be. You let your hand go, and everything that you imagined – and all that your creativity and imagination wanted – just comes out. And this is the beauty of art.

As Mexicans we have many famous muralists – Orozco, Tamayo – and a lot of artists who paint with a beauty that I love, and that nobody will ever surpass.

Here color illuminates life – this is the seal of Vallarta. It is life, Vallarta, and it is movement. I've been living here for 14 years, and I wouldn't leave it for anything. Puerto Vallarta *es muy bonito, muy bonito* Vallarta.

AS RELATED TO GREG BENCHWICK

Check out the rhythm and hues in Cabo San Lucas (p304)

RICHARD CUMMINS

Even church facades are covered in brightly colored artwork (p67)

JEFFREY BECOM

Face José Clemente Orozco's fiery *Miguel Hidalgo* mural in the Palacio de Gobierno, Guadalajara (p527)

WITOLD SKRYPCZAK

Make a date with Maya history at the giant stone calendar at El Castillo (p941)

RICHARD NEBESKY

Maya ruins abound in hilly Uxmal (p930)

JOHN ELK III

Palm beaches, turquoise waters and 600-year-old ruins attract explorers to Tulum (p900)

LEE FOSTER

Adventure into History

NAME	Jaime Suchlicki, PhD
AGE	66
OCCUPATION	Mexican historian at the University of Miami, author of *Mexico: From Montezuma to the Fall of the PRI* (2001)
RESIDENCE	Miami, Florida

I think Mexico is a land of contrasts. It is a country of poor people and rich people; a mix of various groups and civilizations. Mexico also has a very turbulent past – a vivid history with great variety, violence and surprises.

Originally the indigenous Mexicans saw the conquest by the Spaniards as a liberation from the Aztecs. Many of the tribes in the Valle de México feared and disliked the Aztecs. After the colonization, they realized they had changed one master, the Aztecs, for another, the Spaniards.

Because it is the cradle of the Classic Maya civilization, the Yucatán is also a very important area. There are two major centers of Maya civilization in Mexico: Chichén Itzá and Uxmal. The pyramids here rival those found in Egypt – as a matter of fact, I find them more beautiful. But the seminal moment in Mexican history is the Mexican Revolution of 1910. Among other things, this gave rise to putting the mestizos into power, which has come to dominate the politics of the 20th century.

AS RELATED TO GREG BENCHWICK

Discover the exquisite Maya ruins of Palenque (p835) set amid dense, green jungle

JON DAVISON

Unraveling Artistic Traditions

NAME	Maria Concepcion Abalos Acosta*
AGE	66
OCCUPATION	Artisan, ceramacist
RESIDENCE	Tonalá

* WHILE DOÑA MARIA DID NOT WANT HER PHOTO TAKEN – SOMETHING QUITE COMMON AMONG MEXICO'S INDIGENOUS POPULATIONS – HER HANDICRAFTS CERTAINLY SPEAK FOR THEMSELVES

'It's beautiful to be Mexican. Working relaxes you – we are very hard workers '

I'm from an area near Guadalajara. I've been working with clay since I was 15 years old – now I'm 66. We've always done *artesanía* – it's part of the culture from my *pueblo*. Almost everybody from my town is an artisan. I've made all of these sculptures – with my own hands. They are made from clay, all by hand.

It's beautiful to be Mexican. Working relaxes you – we are very hard workers – and we are so used to it. When people don't work, it means they will be leaving this world earlier than the rest of us. God gave us the mandate to work. That's how it is, all our lives we have worked in *la artesanía*. We all work. There in my town of Tonalá, we all work.

AS RELATED TO GREG BENCHWICK

Marvel at the craft work of the Huichol people (p615)

DAVID PEEVERS

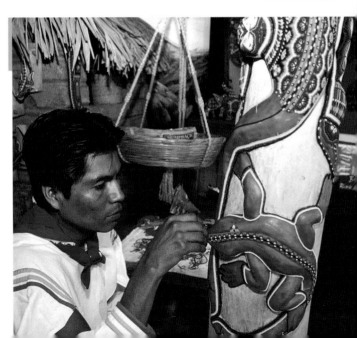

Cancún has more than one face, as the 1000-year-old masks and jewelry at Museo INAH (p870) reveal
CHRISTINA LEASE

San Miguel de Allende (p635) has some of the finest textiles and handicrafts from all over Mexico
FRANK WING

Share local drinks with the local people in Guadalajara (p521)
GREG ELMS

Feeling chili? Give your tastebuds a temperature test in San Cristóbal de Las Casas (p812)
RICHARD I'ANSON

Chapulinas (grasshoppers) fried in chili – try them if you dare – in Oaxaca city (p89)
GREG ELMS

Rescuing Mexico's Culinary Traditions

NAME	Oscar Galvan
AGE	24
OCCUPATION	Chef, Agave Grill
RESIDENCE	Puerto Vallarta

Mexican food is one of the most varied forms of cuisine in the world. We have 31 states, and in each part it's a totally different world when it comes to cooking.

Talking about the Pacific Coast, the ingredients are a little bit different – we include more acidic and piquant flavors. On the other side, on the Gulf Coast, they don't eat as much *ceviche*, they eat things that are a bit more cooked. Like the dishes from Veracruz or from the Yucatán, the flavors for these dishes require more spices and a bit more preparation – this food is very different. And in the center of the country, the food doesn't have anything to do with what is found along the coasts.

What I want to show people is that Mexican food isn't simply guacamole, tacos, burritos. In my restaurant, flavor is what's important for my dishes. I base these on the most tried-and-true traditions and recipes. These traditions are what I want to rescue and teach visitors about.

AS RELATED TO GREG BENCHWICK

You'll be amazed at the variety of food (p88) and cooking methods throughout Mexico

JEFFREY BECOM

'La Música' follows its own course

NAME	Ascensíon Ulloa Contrera
AGE	Older than he looks
OCCUPATION	Mariachi
RESIDENCE	El Tuito

Being a mariachi, well just imagine, I've suffered a lot – in 'la música.'

I was born in a ranch in Río Alto near San Sebastían. That's where I began to learn about music, just on my own, following my own course. Then I started to learn my scales, and I started to learn about the beauty of music… I play the trumpet, which forms a very important part of *mariachi* music.

From my point of view, as a Mexican, it's just incredibly beautiful here in my country. The sea is beautiful. You also have a sea in your country, right? It's the same thing. When you are on the ocean, it's the same here as it is there. Our cities are also unique – cities like Guadalajara and Mexico City.

There are noble people here, but there are also people that aren't so noble. There's a bit of everything. I'm speaking from the bottom of my heart, as a human being.

AS RELATED TO GREG BENCHWICK

Listen to the myriad beats of the streets of Mexico City (p103)

CONOR CAFFREY

Party on at the lively festivals held in Oaxaca city (p726)
GREG ELMS

BLUELIST* (BLU,LIST) V.

TO RECOMMEND A TRAVEL EXPERIENCE

Mexico is all about living life to its fullest. The country's unique and often uproarious fiestas merit two spots in Lonely Planet's Bluelist for 'Most Extraordinary Festivals.'

Noche de los Rábanos (Oaxaca, December)

The 'Night of the Radishes' began as a marketing gimmick in the 16th century, when radishes were carved into fanciful shapes to attract buyers. Today it is a competition between local artisans.

Día de Los Muertos (Anywhere in Mexico, November)

Mexico's 'Day of the Dead' is a two-day festival celebrating the reunion of relatives with their dear departed. Expect colorful costumes, skeletons on stilts, parties in cemeteries and mariachi bands performing next to graves.

* To learn more about Bluelists or to make your own, head on over to www.lonelyplanet .com/bluelist. Turns out all this partying won't cost you a load of cash either – Mexico also garnered Bluelist status as a 'Best Bang for your Buck' locale.

Explore the many
islands of Baja
California, in a canoe
or kayak
RALPH LEE HOPKINS

Contents

Regional Map Contents

The Authors

JOHN NOBLE
Coordinating Author, History, The Culture, Environment, Tabasco & Chiapas, Directory, Transport

John has felt the pull of Mexico ever since reading the barely credible story of Cortés and the Aztecs as a teenager. A backpacking trip many moons ago took him to Mexico and he has returned for extended visits ever since. As an author on eight editions of this guide (six as coordinating author), he has explored almost every part of the country. He loves Mexico's art, archaeology, history, music, ethnic diversity, languages, food, drinks, traditional culture, beaches, wildlife and stunningly varied landscapes. John now lives in Spain – which provides yet another angle on what makes Mexico tick.

My Favorite Trip

I always return to beautiful, mysterious Chiapas. My trip starts with some preparatory beach time at super-relaxed Puerto Arista (p857). Then I head up into the misty mountains to cool off at San Cristóbal de Las Casas (p812), a romantic town at the heart of Mexico's most deep-rootedly indigenous region. I descend northward to the Maya ruins of Toniná (p830). Next stop, the even more magical Maya ruins of Palenque (p833), then I'm off to Frontera Corozal (p846) for a boat along the jungle-lined Río Usumacinta to Yaxchilán (p847), another marvelous Maya site, where I climb Building 41 and look across the tops of the rainforest to the hills of Guatemala, with the roars of howler monkeys echoing through the trees around me.

SANDRA BAO
Western Central Highlands

Sandra is a Chinese-American born in Argentina. She's traveled in over 50 countries, has been a Lonely Planet author for almost five years and grows tomatoes on the side. The first time Sandra went to Mexico, she almost gave her then-boyfriend a heart attack by passing a slow car on a blind hill. Her now-husband and co-author Ben Greensfelder (that same terrified boyfriend) has never quite forgiven her – and does all the driving in Mexico now. Despite this shaky beginning, Mexico has drawn Sandra back repeatedly, and she's seen what diversity this country has to offer. It is one of her favorite places, especially the magical western central highlands.

LONELY PLANET AUTHORS

Why is our travel information the best in the world? It's simple: our authors are independent, dedicated travelers. They don't research using just the Internet or phone, and they don't take freebies in exchange for positive coverage. They travel widely, to all the popular spots and off the beaten track. They personally visit thousands of hotels, restaurants, cafés, bars, galleries, palaces, museums and more – and they take pride in getting all the details right, and telling it how it is. For more, see the authors section on www.lonelyplanet.com.

RAY BARTLETT
Baja California, Central North Mexico

Ray Bartlett fell in love with Mexico in college, camping on the beach for a week in Guaymas, then returning to study in Cuernavaca for part of his senior year. His travel writing career began at age 18, when he jumped a freight train for 1300 miles and wrote about the experience for a local newspaper. In 1999 he received his MA in Fiction from Boston University, where he taught writing full time. Bartlett's travel writings have appeared in various places, including *Travelers' Tales* and *Cape Cod Life*, where he is a regular contributor of photos and articles. When not on assignment, he lives on Cape Cod.

BETH GREENFIELD
Northwest Mexico

Of the many far-flung places Beth has visited around the globe, Mexico remains one of her favorites, and is the place she has returned to more than any other foreign country. For this edition she researched and wrote the northwest chapter, which allowed her to explore and fall in love with the gorgeous Copper Canyon and the untouristy shores of the Sea of Cortez. Beth lives with her partner, Kiki, in New York City, where she is a part-time editor and writer for *Time Out New York* magazine and a freelance writer for publications that have included the *New York Times, Out Traveler, Esquire* and *Budget Travel*.

BEN GREENSFELDER
Central Pacific Coast, Oaxaca State

Ben was born and raised in California; his first experience with Mexico was a family road trip to Álamos, Sonora, in 1964. Since then he has returned over a dozen times, including six visits in as many years for Lonely Planet projects. Each time, the country reveals more of itself and, each time, Ben finds himself drawn ineluctably back to explore further. Now living in Oregon with his wife, the inveterate Lonely Planet author Sandra Bao, Ben is always happy to head south, whether it's to help Sandra with research, do his own or just knock around.

ANDREW DEAN NYSTROM
Around Mexico City

Born a mile high in Colorado, Andrew has always gravitated toward geographic extremes. He has contributed to two dozen books, including Lonely Planet's *Argentina, Bolivia* and *South America*. As a syndicated columnist, he has surveyed the Americas' surreal landscapes for the *Chicago Tribune, Los Angeles Times, San Francisco Chronicle* and Yahoo! Travel. His *Top Trails Yellowstone & Grand Teton National Parks* book won the 2005 National Outdoor Book Award for Best Outdoor Adventure Guidebook. Based in northern California, Andrew is an advisor to the National Geographic Society's Sustainable Tourism Initiative and works as an adventure travel consultant for Mountain Travel Sobek.

SUZANNE PLANK   Yucatán Peninsula

Suzanne was five when she first road-tripped through Mexico with her family. Somewhere between the cobblestones of Taxco and the grandeur of Paseo de la Reforma, Mexico captured her imagination and has held on tight. Over the years Suzanne has returned to Mexico to travel, live and work. She first discovered the Maya world of the Yucatán Peninsula in 1990. Apparently she was not the only one captivated; the peninsula has since become Mexico's most visited region. This is the second edition of *Mexico* for which Suzanne has had the thrilling opportunity to research and explore the Yucatán…this time with her sweetheart by her side and Hurricane Wilma at her heels.

MICHAEL READ   Central Pacific Coast

Having never made good on his threat to set up housekeeping south of the border, Michael Read takes every opportunity to head south from his Oakland, California home to delve deeper into Mexico's marvelous mysteries. A three-year veteran of Lonely Planet's web team, in 2003 Michael succumbed to a burning case of wanderlust and hit the road as a full-time travel writer. Since then he's contributed nearly half a million words to Lonely Planet guidebooks, including the previous edition of *Mexico, Jamaica,* and the forthcoming *Puerto Vallarta & Pacific Mexico*.

DANIEL C SCHECHTER   Mexico City

Definitely swimming against the tide, native New Yorker Daniel C Schechter migrated *al otro lado* southward in 1994 to take a peso-salaried teaching post at a university in Mexico City. Shortly afterward, Mexico experienced its worst peso devaluation in decades. Rather than cut and run, Daniel found an even less lucrative job as an editor at Mexico's English-language daily newspaper, launching a midlife career as a writer/translator. After a decade in the capital, Daniel and wife Myra have adopted the less hectic climes of San Miguel de Allende in the northern state of Guanajuato, returning now and then to their old neighborhood for a breath of fresh smog.

IAIN STEWART   Northeast Mexico, Central Gulf Coast

Iain Stewart is based in Brighton, UK, but daydreams of swapping the city's pebble beach for a palm-fringed version. He first visited Mexico in the early 1990s, and has returned to the region regularly since then. Iain has written and cowritten several guidebooks about Central America and the Maya region for other publishers. An offer from Lonely Planet to revisit subtropical Mexico for another bout of temple trampling and mosquito slapping was far too tempting to turn down.

ALAN TARBELL Northern Central Highlands

Growing up in California, Alan's contact with Mexico began with frequent trips to Baja. The allure of the color, smells, sounds and movement was enough to enrapture the senses and leave a permanent impression. A summer in Spain during high school cemented the language, and studying geography at UC Davis furthered his cultural aspirations. After other ventures abroad, a return to California brought a reflection about the synthesis of Mexican and American cultures. In 2002 he decided to study his MFA at the Instituto Allende, in San Miguel de Allende, Guanajuato, where he teaches painting and finds a base for updating the northern central highlands.

CONTRIBUTING AUTHORS

Dale Hoyt Palfrey provided some material for the Western Central Highlands chapter. She is a bilingual journalist and translator residing in the Lake Chapala area since 1973. Dale is the Chapala area news correspondent for the *Guadalajara Colony Reporter*, an English-language weekly, a credited writer in *Mexico's Lake Chapala & Ajijic: The Insider's Guide* and a frequent contributor to www.mexico-insights .com and www.mexconnect.com.

James W Peyton (Food & Drink) has written three books on Mexican cooking as well as articles for magazines such as *Fine Cooking*, *Texas Highways* and *Food & Wine*. He appears on television, conducts cooking classes and lectures on Mexican cuisine. In addition Jim maintains a website, Jim Peyton's Lo Mexicano at www.lomexicano.com, providing information about Mexico and Mexican cooking. Jim also consults on recipe development and menu design for the Mexican food industry. Jim's recipes were selected to appear in the 2000 and 2001 issues of Houghton Mifflin's *The Best American Recipes*. His latest book is *Jim Peyton's New Cooking from Old Mexico*.

David Goldberg MD (Health) completed his training in internal medicine and infectious diseases at Columbia-Presbyterian Medical Center in New York City, where he has also served as voluntary faculty. At present, he is an infectious diseases specialist in Scarsdale, NY and the editor-in-chief of the website MDTravelHealth.com.

Getting Started

Mexico requires as little planning as you like. You can just grab your passport, get on the plane or bus or into your car and go! Traveling by road or plane within Mexico is easy and you'll discover so much to do and see that any plans you have may change in any case. You'll rarely have trouble finding suitable accommodation, on any budget. Equally, if you have limited time and specific goals, you can work out a detailed itinerary and reserve accommodations in advance. If this is your first trip to Mexico, especially if it's your first trip outside the developed world, be ready for more crowds, noise, bustle and poverty than you're accustomed to. But don't worry – most Mexicans will be only too happy to help you feel at home in their country. Invest a little time before your trip in learning even just a few phrases of Spanish – every word you know will make your trip that little bit easier and more enjoyable.

WHEN TO GO

Any time is a good time to visit Mexico, though the coastal and low-lying regions, especially in the southern half of the country, are fairly hot and humid from May to September (these are the months of highest rainfall and highest temperatures almost everywhere). The interior of the country has a more temperate climate than the coasts. In fact, it's sometimes decidedly chilly in the north and in the central highlands from November to February.

July and August are peak holiday months for both Mexicans and foreigners. Other big holiday seasons are mid-December to early January (for both foreigners and Mexicans), and a week either side of Easter (for Mexicans). At these times the coastal resorts attract big tourist crowds, room prices go up in popular places, and rooms and public transportation can be heavily booked, so advance reservations are advisable.

See Climate Charts (p970), Festivals & Events (p976) and Holidays (p977) for information to help you decide when to go.

DON'T LEAVE HOME WITHOUT...

- checking your foreign ministry's Mexico travel information (p972)
- all the necessary paperwork if you're driving (p992)
- clothes to cope with Mexico's climatic variations and air-conditioned rooms (and buses)
- any necessary immunizations or medications (p1005), and any special toiletries you require, including contact-lens solution and contraceptives
- a flashlight (torch) for some of those not-so-well-lit Mexican streets and stairways – and for power outages
- an inconspicuous container for money and valuables, such as a small, slim wallet or an under-the-clothes pouch or money belt (p972)
- your favorite sunglasses
- a small padlock
- a small Spanish dictionary and/or phrasebook
- adequate insurance (p977)
- mosquito repellent
- a mosquito net if you plan to sleep outdoors
- sun screen and aloe vera (often overpriced in beach resorts)

TOP TENS

Adventures

See the regional chapters for details on these adrenalin rushes.

- Surfing the big Pacific waves at Puerto Escondido (p754)
- Volcano hiking on Pico de Orizaba (p703)
- Diving and snorkeling the crystal-clear Caribbean reef waters (p888)
- Canyon hiking in the Barranca del Cobre (p336)
- Watching whales at Laguna Ojo de Liebre (p285)
- Cloud-forest hiking in Oaxaca's Sierra Norte (p746)

- Snorkeling and kayaking with sea lions around Isla Espíritu Santo (p297)
- Hanging from a ledge in the rock-climbing mecca Potrero Chico (boxed text, p412)
- Kayaking the islands and shores of the Parque Marino Nacional Bahía de Loreto (p292)
- Sportfishing at Mazatlán (p430)

Fiestas

You'll really catch the Mexican mood at these events (see p976 for further information).

- Carnaval (Carnival), week leading up to Ash Wednesday (late February or early March), celebrated most wildly in Veracruz (p693), Mazatlán (p432) and La Paz (p297)
- Semana Santa (Holy Week), Palm Sunday to Easter Sunday, particularly colorful in San Miguel de Allende (p641) and Pátzcuaro (p572)
- Feria de San Marcos, mid-April to mid-May, Aguascalientes (p604)
- Guelaguetza, last two Mondays of July, Oaxaca (p726)
- La Morisma, last weekend of August, Zacatecas (p594)

- Grito de la Independencia (Cry for Independence), September 15, Mexico City (p152)
- Fiestas de Octubre, October, Guadalajara (p532)
- Festival Internacional Cervantino, October, Guanajuato (p626)
- Día de Todos los Santos (All Saints' Day), November 1, and Día de Muertos (Day of the Dead), on November 2, celebrated nationwide (p152)
- Día de Nuestra Señora de Guadalupe (Day of Our Lady of Guadalupe), December 12, Mexico City (p152)

COSTS & MONEY

Travel in Mexico is still fairly inexpensive. Midrange travelers can live well in most parts of the country on $60 to $100 per person per day. Two people can usually find a clean, comfortable room with private bathroom and fan or air-conditioning for $35 to $60, and have the rest to pay for food (a full lunch or dinner in a typical decent restaurant costs around $12 to $15), admission fees, transport and incidentals. Budget travelers should allot $25 to $40 a day to cover accommodation and two meals a day in restaurants. Add in other costs and you'll spend $40 to $60.

The main exceptions to this are the Caribbean coast, parts of Baja California and some Pacific coast resorts, where rooms can easily cost 50% more than elsewhere.

Extra expenses such as internal airfares, car rentals and shopping will, of course, push your expenses up, but if there are two or more of you, costs per person drop considerably. Double rooms often cost only a few dollars more than singles, and triple or family rooms only a few dollars more than doubles. A rented car (costs start at around $50 to $60 per day, plus fuel) costs no more for four people than for one. Children under 13 pay reduced prices on many buses and flights, and at some sights and attractions.

See Accommodations (p964) and Getting Around (p995) for tips on places to stay and how to travel around in Mexico.

TOP TENS

Movies

Mexicans and non-Mexicans alike have been inspired to make great films set in Mexico.

- *Traffic* – Steven Soderbergh's four-Oscar, cross-border drug movie with Michael Douglas, Catherine Zeta-Jones and Benicio del Toro (2000); don't watch it the night before you leave for Mexico

- *Frida* – the atmospheric 2002 Hollywood Kahlo biopic, starring Salma Hayek

- *Amores Perros* (Love's a Bitch) – Alejandro González Iñárritu's raw, ground-breaking movie of modern Mexico City life (2000)

- *Y Tu Mamá También* (And Your Mother Too) – Alfonso Cuarón's 2002 road movie and the most successful Mexican film ever

- *7 Days* – a big Mexican hit in 2005, Fernando Kalife's movie tells how a lowly music promoter pulls off the miraculous coup of getting U2 to play in his home town, Monterrey

- *El Crimen del Padre Amaro* (The Crime of Father Amaro) – Carlos Carrera's 2002 tale of the corrupt church

- *Los Olvidados* (The Forgotten Ones) – Luis Buñuel's 1950 condemnation of Mexico City poverty portrays a gang of nasty teenage thugs, with haunting dream sequences adding a surreal touch

- *El Mariachi* – legendary low-budget 1992 action film, shot by Robert Rodriguez in two weeks for $7000, about a wandering musician (Carlos Gallardo) who gets mixed up in mob violence

- *Man on Fire* – in this 2004 thriller, Denzel Washington plays a burned-out ex-CIA operative who comes to Mexico City to protect a family against a wave of kidnappings

- *The Wild Bunch* – Sam Peckinpah's landmark 1969 Western, with Texas outlaws escaping to pre-revolutionary north Mexico, has a feel for Mexican rituals and generosity despite all the violence

---

At the top end of the scale are a few hotels and resorts that charge over $200 for a room, and restaurants where you can pay $50 per person. But you can also stay in classy smaller hotels for $60 to $100 a double and eat extremely well for $30 to $45 per person per day.

TRAVEL LITERATURE

In *True Tales from Another Mexico* (2001), US journalist Sam Quiñones uncovers countless weird and little-known facets of Mexican life and death – drug traffickers to cult religions, cross-dressers to rural lynchings. It is well-told and endlessly surprising.

Travels to Oaxaca with a group of pteridologists (fern fanatics) provide scientist Oliver Sacks with food for many quirky, amusing observations, not only of a scientific nature but also on his botanist companions, in *Oaxaca Journal* (2002).

British writer Isabella Tree takes peyote with the Huicholes and meets the matriarchs of Juchitán in *Sliced Iguana: Travels in Unknown Mexico* (2001), a warm, perceptive account of Mexico and its indigenous cultures.

Ronald Wright offers insight into the cultures of southeast Mexico, Belize and Guatemala in *Time Among the Maya* (1989), an investigation of the Maya concept of time and their tragic modern history.

In the 1930s, a time of conflict between Catholics and an atheistic state, Graham Greene wandered down eastern Mexico to Chiapas. *The Lawless Roads* (1939) traces his journey and gives Greene's insights into what makes Mexicans tick.

Elijah Wald's fascinating *Narcocorrido* (2001) is a travel narrative and an investigation of a popular Mexican song genre built around the travails of ordinary folk involved in drug-running on Mexico's northern border.

See the Language chapter (p1014) for some basic Spanish words and phrases.

There's a Word for It in Mexico by Boyé Lafayette De Mente (1998) is less literature than cultural primer in the form of brief, snippet-like essays on 139 key Mexican concepts – *simpático, siesta, tu/usted* and others less expected. The concept of *igualdad* (equality), he writes, 'has never been part of the Mexican experience.'

Beyond the Deep: The Deadly Descent into the World's Most Treacherous Cave by William Stone and Barbara am Ende tells the hair-raising tale of the deepest-ever Western Hemisphere cave dive in the Sótano de San Agustín sinkhole near Huautla, Oaxaca in 1994.

INTERNET RESOURCES

Lanic (http://lanic.utexas.edu/la/mexico) Best broad collection of Mexico links, from the University of Texas.

Lonely Planet (www.lonelyplanet.com) Succinct summaries on travel in Mexico; the popular Thorn Tree bulletin board; travel news; and great links to the best travel resources elsewhere on the Web.

Mexican Wave (www.mexicanwave.com) 'Europe's gateway to Mexico' is a fund of travel, culture and food-related material.

Mexico (www.visitmexico.com) Colorful and informative site of Mexico's tourism ministry – a useful place to start.

Mexico Connect (www.mexconnect.com) Goldmine fund of articles, forums and information on everything under the Mexican sun.

Mexico Online (www.mexonline.com) News, bulletin boards and a huge variety of other content and links.

Planeta.com (www.planeta.com) Great articles and listings for anyone interested in Mexican travel or the Mexican environment.

Itineraries
CLASSIC ROUTES

CENTRAL OVERLAND ROUTE
Two Weeks

Don't rush the top half of Mexico. The journey from the border to the nation's capital shows you the contrast and fascination of a slice of the real Mexico: the northern deserts and the colonial silver cities. Start by crossing the Río Barvo del Norte from El Paso to **Ciudad Juárez** (p353). Head south to lively **Chihuahua** (p363) and peaceful **Hidalgo del Parral** (p370), old stamping grounds of revolutionary Pancho Villa. Continue via friendly **Durango** (p375) to **Zacatecas** (p589), one of the fabled silver cities and a surprisingly cultured town amid the arid deserts. Continue to the fertile Bajío region and gorgeous **Guanajuato** (p619) where cultural attractions are piled on top of each other. Divert eastward to **San Miguel de Allende** (p635), an oasis of culture and colonial architecture, with more galleries than you can shake a *churro* at.

Explore the charms of **Querétaro** (p648), where history looms large and tradition still holds sway in the cafés around its tranquil plazas. Then give way to the magnetic pull of **Mexico City** (p103), the crucible of all things Mexican – a must-see or unavoidable, depending on your perspective. If you can't stay long enough to hook into its culture, history and entertainment scene, at least hope for a smog-free stint and try not to get stuck in traffic.

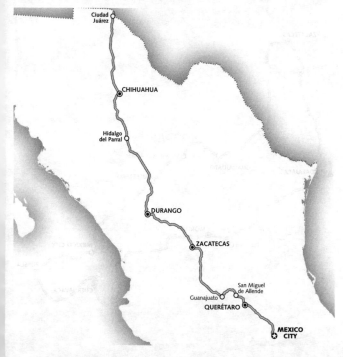

This 1740km trip from the US border to the Mexican capital crosses the northern deserts and passes through the fertile Bajío region with its colonial cities. With adequate time to enjoy the best stops along the way, it takes around two weeks.

COLONIAL HEARTLAND   Three Weeks

The nation's capital is ringed by a necklace of colonial cities blessed with gorgeous architecture of carved stone and colorful tiles, broad plazas, splashing fountains and lively modern cultural scenes – Mexico's historic, architectural and artistic gems.

After checking out the colonial center of **Mexico City** (p103) itself, head east for **Puebla** (p212), which has the country's greatest concentration of restored colonial architecture. Southward, **Cuernavaca** (p237) has been a retreat from Mexico City ever since Cortés built his fortress-palace there in the 1520s. Continue south to charming, hillside **Taxco** (p247), which harbors many surprises in its lovely cobblestone alleyways.

Go west to Michoacán's capital **Morelia** (p558), home to an imposing cathedral and many well-preserved buildings. **Pátzcuaro** (p568) is a handsome highland town where the indigenous Purépecha sell their wares around one of Mexico's loveliest central plazas. Further west, *muy mexicano* **Guadalajara** (p521) is less quaint than its neighbors but retains beautiful plazas and plenty of fine architecture, not to mention fabulous shopping and nightlife.

To the north, trip up to prosperous **Zacatecas** (p589), a stylish silver city with a stupendous cathedral. Back toward Mexico City, in the Bajío region, lively **Guanajuato** (p619) awaits in a ravine awash with quixotic *callejones* (alleys) and vibrant student life. The lack of stoplights is only part of the charm in the festive expat capital **San Miguel de Allende** (p635). En route back to Mexico City, stop off in historic **Querétaro** (p648) which has several fine museums and a very walkable historic center.

The entire loop around all the finest colonial cities, starting and finishing in Mexico City, is 2200km and takes around three weeks with a few days at each stop en route. Many travelers are selective and cover only chosen parts of the route.

DEEP SOUTH
One Month

This magnificent classic journey leads travelers from Mexico's colonial heartland to its glorious Caribbean beaches. Start by exploring fascinating **Mexico City** (p103), including a visit to the awesome pyramids of **Teotihuacán** (p195). Then head east to colonial **Puebla** (p212) before crossing the mountains southward to **Oaxaca** (p717), a lovely and lively colonial city with Mexico's finest handicrafts, at the heart of a beautiful region with a high indigenous population.

If you have time, divert south to one of the sun-baked Pacific beach spots south of Oaxaca, such as **Puerto Escondido** (p754), **Zipolite** (p770) or **Bahías de Huatulco** (p776). Then move east to **San Cristóbal de Las Casas** (p812), a beautiful highland town surrounded by intriguing indigenous villages, and **Palenque** (p833), perhaps the most stunning of all ancient Maya cities, set against a backdrop of emerald-green jungle.

Head northeast to the Yucatán Peninsula, with a stop at historic **Campeche** (p951) before you reach colonial, cultural **Mérida** (p917), the base for visiting **Uxmal** (p930) and other fine Maya ruins nearby. Next stop is **Chichén Itzá** (p940), the Yucatán's most awesome ancient Maya site. Now head directly to **Tulum** (p899) on the Caribbean coast, a Maya site with a glorious beachside setting, and then make your way northward along the 'Riviera Maya' toward Mexico's glitziest resort, **Cancún** (p867). On the way, halt at lively **Playa del Carmen** (p892) or take a side trip to **Cozumel** (p884) for a spot of world-class snorkeling and diving.

This 2800km, one-month adventure takes you from Mexico's geographic and cultural center through the states of Oaxaca and Chiapas – with their colorful indigenous populations, pre-Hispanic ruins and dramatic scenery – to the ancient Mayan cities and beaches of the Yucatán Peninsula.

BARRANCA DEL COBRE & PACIFIC COAST   Four to Six Weeks

Mexico's Pacific coast is a glittering sequence of large, famous resorts, pristine, empty, jungle-lined beaches and every grade of coastal dream in between. A great approach to the coast is from **Chihuahua** (p363) via the awesome **Barranca del Cobre** (Copper Canyon; p336) with its dramatic railroad and spectacular hiking.

Spend an evening sipping margaritas on the lively plaza in **Mazatlán** (p426) before venturing to the ancient island of **Mexcaltitán** (p439) and the wildlife-rich lagoons of laid-back **San Blas** (p440). Hang ten in **Sayulita** (p449), then it's on to nightclubs, gourmet food, whale-watching and shopping in **Puerto Vallarta** (p451).

Isolated beaches abound on the Costalegre, home to some of the world's most luxurious resorts. Spend a day snorkeling here at **Playa Tenacatita** (p468) and don't miss the street tacos in **Melaque** (p468). Rent a beach-bum bungalow on the internationally renowned surf beach **Barra de Nexpa** (p481); novice surfers should head to **Caleta de Campos** (p482). Surf, snorkel and take romantic sunset walks in **Troncones** (p483) before hiring a fishing boat in **Zihuatanejo** (p489).

Pick up the pace to hit the discos, go bungee jumping and learn a little Mexican history in **Acapulco** (p501). **Puerto Escondido** (p754) has A-grade surf and a lively little after-dark scene. To end your trip, lie back in a hammock at the low-budget paradise beaches of **Mazunte** (p774) or **Zipolite** (p770), or relax at the resort of **Bahías de Huatulco** (p776), set along a string of beautiful, sheltered bays.

The entire trip from Chihuahua to Huatulco involves 3200km of travel, including 670km by rail at the outset, and can take up to six weeks if you stop in every recommended place. Some travelers approach the coast through Nogales and Hermosillo instead of Chihuahua. Several cities along the way have airports, so it's easy to shorten the route if you wish.

ROADS LESS TRAVELED

SOUTHEASTERN JUNGLES   Three Weeks

This trip from highland Chiapas to the Caribbean coast provides close encounters with exotic wildlife and visits some of Mexico's most exciting archaeological sites. Starting at graceful **San Cristóbal de Las Casas** (p812), head north to the jungle-backed Maya ruins of **Toniná** (p830) and on to the thundering waterfalls of **Agua Azul** (p832) and **Misol Ha** (p833), and jungle-clad **Palenque** (p833), arguably the most exquisite of all Maya cities. A fascinating side-trip leads southeast to **Bonampak** (p844) and **Yaxchilán** (p847), two fine Maya sites situated in dense forest where you stand a good chance of spotting toucans, monkeys and other wildlife, then on to **Las Guacamayas** (p849), a scarlet-macaw reserve.

Return to Palenque and make your way east across the base of the Yucatán Peninsula to the huge **Reserva de la Biosfera Calakmul** (p962), which protects hundreds of species of rainforest wildlife and shelters important archaeological sites including the awesome ancient metropolis of **Calakmul** (p962). A visit here provides a good chance to spot a variety of exotic birds and animals. To the northeast, on the Caribbean coast, the jungle, marshes and islands of the **Reserva de la Biosfera Sian Ka'an** (p906) are home to a huge variety of land, air and water wildlife, best seen with an expert local guide.

This route offers the best opportunities to access the tropical forests of Chiapas and the Yucatán Peninsula, covering 1800km in about three weeks.

INDIGENOUS MEXICO

Three Weeks

Mexico possesses some of the American continent's most colorful and unusual traditional cultures, all directly descended from people who were here long before Europeans arrived. One place you can make contact with central Mexico's Nahua people, related to the ancient Aztecs, is the hill village of **Cuetzalan** (p228), north of Puebla. The largest indigenous populations tend to be concentrated in the south of the country, especially the states of Oaxaca and Chiapas. The Zapotecs and Mixtecs of **Oaxaca** (boxed text, p752) are wonderful artisans in ceramics, textiles, wood and much more – see their wares at bustling markets and in city stores. **Oaxaca City** (p726) stages the country's most exciting celebration of indigenous dance, the annual Guelaguetza festival in July. In the remote **Chiapas Highlands** (boxed text, p825), Maya groups such as the Tzotziles and Tzeltales cling to mysterious, age-old religious, social and medical practices, and their colorful traditional costumes, still worn daily, are complex works of art and symbolism.

In Veracruz state, the Totonac people regularly re-enact ancient rituals with their spectacular *voladores* rite, 'flying' from a tall pole at places like **El Tajín** (p678). The Huicholes from the borders of Jalisco, Nayarit and Zacatecas in western Mexico make an annual pilgrimage across the mountains and deserts to seek the cactus that bears the powerful hallucinogen peyote, essential to their religion and art, near the remote town of **Real de Catorce** (boxed text, p615).

In the northwest the Tarahumara who dwell in the rugged canyons of the **Barranca del Cobre** (Copper Canyon; boxed text, p342) are famed for their amazing long-distance running feats.

Anthropologically-minded travelers who follow this whole itinerary will cover around 4000km and will need a good three weeks to take it all in.

Barranca del Cobre
(Copper Canyon)

Real de Catorce

El Tajín
Cuetzalan
MEXICO CITY

OAXACA

Chiapas
Highlands

NORTHERN DESERTS, CANYONS & FORESTS   One Month

Awesome natural configurations and bizarre discoveries await adventurous travelers in the more remote reaches of Mexico's north. Make the pre-Hispanic, desert trading settlement **Paquimé** (p359) your first goal. From here visit the renowned potters' village **Mata Ortiz** (boxed text, p361). Then head south along winding roads to the pre-Hispanic cliff dwellings at **Cuarenta Casas** (p362) and the town of **Madera** (p362), set amid the forests of the Sierra Madre Occidental.

Move southeast to **Cuauhtémoc** (p369), where you can board the **Ferrocarril Chihuahua al Pacífico** (p337) to explore the spectacular **Barranca del Cobre** (Copper Canyon; p336). Next, follow the footsteps of legendary revolutionary Pancho Villa through **Chihuahua** (p363), **Hidalgo del Parral** (p370), **Canutillo** (p372) and **Torreón** (p373).

En route to Torreón, visit **Mapimí** (p374) and the ghost town of **Ojuela** (p374), at the heart of a once-booming mining area. Head northeast across the deserts from Torreón for (what else?) a spot of swimming and snorkeling at the bizarrely beautiful oasis of **Cuatro Ciénegas** (p414), then go south to quaff a *copa* of desert wine at **Parras** (p420). Move on to laid-back **Saltillo** (p415) with its Churrigueresque cathedral and first-class desert museum. Then turn south to the magical ex–ghost town of **Real de Catorce** (p614), a former silver-mining center coming back to life with annual floods of Catholic pilgrims and indigenous Huichol people (and others) seeking the hallucinogenic cactus peyote, and artists, filmmakers and other creative types. For one more natural marvel, head east for some hiking and bird-watching in the cloud forests of **Reserva de la Biosfera El Cielo** (p396).

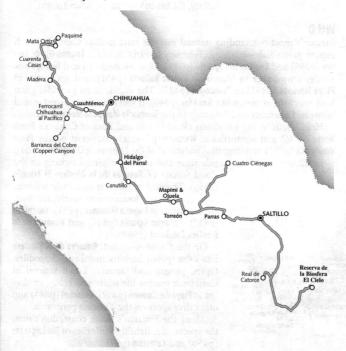

Running in a northwest-to-southeast direction across some remote areas of northern Mexico, this trip needs a month if you are to enjoy every major attraction along the 3200km route from Paquimé to El Cielo.

TAILORED TRIPS

RUINED

The mysterious and awe-inspiring cities and temple complexes left behind by Mexico's pre-Hispanic cultures are unforgettable. Excellent museums at or near many sites help interpret what you see. Begin at the center of the Aztecs' universe, the **Templo Mayor** (p129) of their capital Tenochtitlán, today in downtown Mexico City, followed by the capital's comprehensive **Museo Nacional de Antropología** (p138).

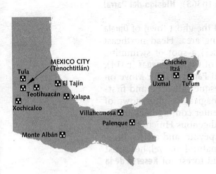

Then visit some of the fine sites within day-trip distance of the capital: awesome **Teotihuacán** (p195) with its gigantic pyramids; **Tula** (p193), the Toltec capital; and hilltop **Xochicalco** (p246).

Journey east to **El Tajín** (p676), the highest architectural achievement of the Classic Veracruz civilization, and see the awesome sculptures of the mysterious Olmecs of the Gulf coast in **Xalapa's Museo de Antropología** (p682) and **Villahermosa's Parque-Museo La Venta** (p793). Don't miss **Monte Albán** (p739), the ancient Zapotec capital, situated on a hilltop overlooking Oaxaca city.

Southeast Mexico was the land of the Maya, whose architectural legacy is one of unmatched beauty. Don't miss **Palenque** (p833), **Uxmal** (p930), **Chichén Itzá** (p940) or **Tulum** (p899).

WILD

Mexico's most outstanding natural marvels start in Baja California with superb gray whale–watching (February to early April) at **Laguna Ojo de Liebre** (p285) and **Laguna San Ignacio** (p287). Observe dolphins and humpback whales (November to March) at **Puerto Vallarta** (p451), and sea turtles at **Playa Maruata** (p481) or **Troncones** (p483). The Pacific coast provides great bird-watching at places like **San Blas** (p440). If you have time, divert inland between December and February to the **Santuario Mariposa Monarca** (p566).

Head south to the wondrous cloud forests and flora of Oaxaca's **Sierra Norte** (p746) and see turtles at **Mazunte** (p774), crocodiles at nearby **Playa Ventanilla** (p775) and countless waterfowl at the **Lagunas de Chacahua** (p764).

In Chiapas try to set aside time and funds for bird-watching in the cloud forests of **Reserva de la Biosfera El Triunfo** (p856). Tropical rainforests and their wildlife, such as monkeys, toucans and scarlet macaws, are accessible at **Laguna Miramar** (p831), **Yaxchilán** (p847), **Reforma Agraria** (p849) and **Reserva de la Biosfera Calakmul** (p962).

On the Caribbean coast, **Reserva de la Biosfera Sian Ka'an** (p906) harbors monkeys, crocodiles, tapirs, pumas and jaguars. You'll marvel at Caribbean marine life while snorkeling or diving at **Playa del Carmen** (p892), **Cozumel** (p884) and other dive spots on the Yucatán peninsula.

Along the Yucatán's north coast, don't miss the spectacular flamingo colonies of **Río Lagartos** (p950) and **Celestún** (p938).

BEACHED

For an end-to-end trip encompassing Mexico's most peerless *playas,* start in Baja California by picking your own pristine beach **south of Mulegé** (p290), then head to **Loreto** (p291), Baja's water-sports paradise, for more action.

Over on the mainland, make a beeline for the lagoon-backed beaches of **San Blas** (p440) and the popular surf village **Sayulita** (p449) before hitting **Puerto Vallarta** (p451) with its beach parties and marine wildlife. Slow down on the nearly empty beaches of the **Costalegre** (p467) before soaking in the rolling waves of **Melaque** (p468).

Zip down to **Barra de Nexpa** (p481) where international surfers rule, and don't miss the crashing waves of **Troncones** (p483). Revive on the soothing bay at **Zihuatanejo** (p489) before taking on high-energy **Acapulco** (p501).

On the Oaxaca coast, the 'Mexican Pipeline' challenges experienced surfers at lively **Puerto Escondido** (p754), or you can simply stroll the sands and lie back in a hammock at backpackers' haven **Zipolite** (p770).

Move over to the Caribbean for party time at **Cancún** (p867) followed by a spot of snorkeling and relaxation at nearby **Isla Mujeres** (p877). **Tulum** (p899), with beachside Maya ruins and palm-fringed white sand, is a highly popular place to end a trip, but the pretty beaches around **Xcalak** (p910), to the south, are less developed.

CULTURED

Food for the mind? You can't go far in Mexico without bumping into a top-class museum, vibrant arts festival or a city full of World Heritage colonial architecture. **Mexico City** (p127) boasts not only one of the country's finest colonial centers but also ground-breaking modern architecture, top museums such as the **Museo Nacional de Antropología** (p138) and a vibrant modern-art heritage from the work of Frida Kahlo and the great muralists onwards.

North of the capital, **Guanajuato** (p619) is another World Heritage city, chock full of history and beautiful buildings, and home to Mexico's biggest arts festival, the **Festival Internacional Cervantino** (p626), every October. Nearby **San Miguel de Allende** (p635) is another vibrant artistic center. Aguascalientes' **Feria de San Marcos** (April to May; p604) is Mexico's biggest regional fair, with many cultural events. Still further north, World-Heritage **Zacatecas** (p589) boasts perhaps the country's most spectacular cathedral and several excellent art museums. **Monterrey** (p397) has some of Mexico's most daring modern architecture and a slew of top-notch museums ranging from contemporary art to science to Mexican history.

West of the center, Mexico's second city, **Guadalajara** (p521), has a buzzing cultural and entertainment scene and is earning a name as the country's contemporary style capital.

Down south, beautiful **Oaxaca** (p717), another World Heritage city, has a thriving art and culture scene and several classy museums. Over on the Yucatán Peninsula, the historic fortified center of **Campeche** (p951) is a World Heritage architectural site, but **Mérida** (p917) is the peninsula's most beautiful and cultured city.

Snapshot

Mexico stands at a curious and typically contradictory crossroad. Politically, the genuinely democratic electoral structures installed at the dawn of the 21st century were consolidated by the 2006 presidential elections. Economically, overall standards of living are climbing gradually. Socially, Mexicans are now more confident about asserting their rights and opinions, while in the arts they're expressing their dreams and imaginations, as well as the gritty realities of 21st-century life, with waves of innovative, successful music, films and art (see p67). Yet the lot of the poor (especially the rural, often indigenous, poor) gets worse, emigration to the US continues unabated and Mexico's vicious drug gangs display more contempt than ever for civilized society.

Vicente Fox of the right-of-center PAN (National Action Party) reached the end of his six-year presidential term in 2006. As this book went to press, a close battle to succeed him was being fought between Andrés Manuel López Obrador of the left-of-center PRD (Party of the Democratic Revolution) and the PAN's Felipe Calderón. López Obrador was courting poorer Mexicans with promises of increased welfare spending but still seemed a responsible social democrat somewhat in the mold of Brazil's Lula da Silva.

Whoever wins faces big challenges. Mexico's economy, though growing at 3% to 4% annually, still disappoints. Most Mexicans like to blame Nafta, the North American Free Trade Agreement, which came into force in 1994. In fact, trade and investment with the US have both doubled under Nafta, but imports of cheap US corn (maize) have undoubtedly accelerated the decline in small-scale Mexican agriculture. Meanwhile Mexican exports to the vital US market are threatened by cheaper products from China, and the flow of oil from the Gulf of Mexico (which provides one-third of Mexico's government revenue) will slow drastically unless enormous sums are spent on developing deep-water reserves.

Also vital to the Mexican economy are the estimated 15 million Mexicans in the US. While farms, construction sites and restaurants in the US depend on migrant labor, Mexicans working in the US send home some $16 billion a year. A further 1.5 million Mexicans try to join them illegally each year (a quarter of them successfully). But the two countries cannot agree any joint approach to the border problem.

Mexico's violent, powerful and uncontrolled drug mobs, coining vast fortunes from satisfying the USA's craving for Colombian cocaine and indulging in astonishingly violent turf wars, bring Mexico a lot of bad publicity. Hundreds of people were killed in drug-related murders in northern Mexico in 2005 (see boxed text, p384) The drug gangs are just too powerful to be easily controlled or quickly defeated – a situation not helped by the fact that Mexican police often work for, not against, drug gangs and other criminal organizations.

Visitors don't need to be alarmed, however. The overall tenor of Mexican life remains as humane and relaxed as ever, and tourists are very rarely caught up in criminal violence. In fact, tourism is on a roll, largely thanks to the US perception of Mexico as a safe destination. Twenty million foreign visitors brought a record US$11 billion into Mexico in 2004. Hurricane Wilma, which devastated Cancún and other Caribbean resorts in October 2005, caused over $2 billion of damage and took a big bite out of tourism earnings, but business should be back to normal within a year.

FAST FACTS

Population: 105 million

Annual population growth: 1.2%

Area: 1.9 million sq km

GDP per person: US$7100

US share of Mexican exports: 87%

Adult literacy: 90%

Tortillas eaten daily: 1200 million

Share of world carbon-dioxide emissions: 1.8% (US: 24%)

Routine bribe to traffic police: US$5

Number of languages spoken: 50

History

Mexico's story is always extraordinary, and at times is barely credible. How could a 2700-year-long tradition of ancient civilization, involving the Olmecs, the Maya and the Aztecs – all intellectually sophisticated and aesthetically gifted, yet at times astoundingly bloodthirsty – crumble in two short years at the hands of a few hundred adventurers from Spain? How could Mexico's 11-year war for independence from Spain lead to three decades of dictatorship by Porfirio Díaz? How could the people's revolution that ended that dictatorship yield 70 years of one-party rule? And how was one-party rule finally ended in 2000?

Travel in Mexico is a fascinating encounter with this unique story and the modern country that it has produced. From the awesome ancient cities to the gorgeous colonial palaces, through the superb museums and the deep-rooted traditions and beliefs of the Mexicans themselves – both the mixed-ancestry mestizos and the millions of indigenous people who are direct descendants of the ancient civilizations – Mexico's ever-present past will never fail to enrich your journey.

BEGINNINGS

It's accepted that, barring a few Vikings in the north and some possible direct transpacific contact with Southeast Asia, the pre-Hispanic inhabitants of the Americas arrived from Siberia. They came in several migrations during the last Ice Age, between perhaps 60,000 and 8000 BC, crossing land now submerged beneath the Bering Strait. The earliest human traces found in Mexico date from about 20,000 BC. These first Mexicans hunted big animal herds in the grasslands of the highland valleys. When temperatures rose at the end of the Ice Age, the valleys became drier, ceasing to support such animal life and forcing the people to derive more food from plants.

Archaeologists have traced the slow beginnings of agriculture to the Tehuacán valley in Puebla state where, soon after 6500 BC, people were planting seeds of chili and a kind of squash. Between 5000 and 3500 BC they started to plant mutant forms of a tiny wild maize, and to grind the maize into meal. After 3500 BC a much better variety of maize, and also beans, enabled the Tehuacán valley people to live semipermanently in villages and spend less time in seasonal hunting camps. Pottery appeared by 2300 BC.

For concise but pretty complete accounts of the ancient cultures of Mexico and Guatemala, read *Mexico: From the Olmecs to the Aztecs* and *The Maya*, both by Michael D Coe.

OLMECS

Mexico's ancestral civilization arose near the Gulf Coast in the humid lowlands of southern Veracruz and neighboring Tabasco. These were the Olmecs, a name coined in the 1920s meaning 'People from the Region of Rubber.' Their civilization is famed for the awesome 'Olmec heads', stone sculptures up to 3m high with grim, pug-nosed faces and wearing curious helmets. You can view Olmec heads and other artifacts at Mexico City's Museo Nacional de Antropología (p138), Xalapa's Museo de Antropología (p682) and Villahermosa's Parque-Museo La Venta (p793).

TIMELINE	20,000 BC or earlier	6500 BC
	First humans in Mexico	Beginning of agriculture – chili seeds are planted

The first known great Olmec center, San Lorenzo in Veracruz state (p713), flourished from about 1200 to 900 BC. The basalt material for eight Olmec heads, and many other stone monuments known to have been carved here, was probably dragged, rolled or rafted from 60km to 80km away. Finds at San Lorenzo of such faraway objects as obsidian (volcanic glass) from Guatemala and the Mexican highlands suggest that San Lorenzo was involved in trade over a large region.

The second great Olmec center was La Venta, Tabasco (p802), which flourished from about 800 to 400 BC. Several tombs were found here, with jade (a favorite pre-Hispanic ornamental material) making an early appearance in one of them. La Venta produced at least five Olmec heads.

Olmec sites found in central and western Mexico, far from the Gulf Coast, may well have been trading posts or garrisons to ensure the supply of jade, obsidian and other luxuries for the Olmec elite. Both San Lorenzo and La Venta were destroyed violently, but Olmec art, religion and society strongly influenced later Mexican civilizations. Olmec gods included fire and maize deities, and the feathered serpent, all of which persisted throughout the pre-Hispanic era.

TEOTIHUACÁN

Teotihuacán's Pirámide del Sol (Pyramid of the Sun) is the third biggest pyramid in the world. The biggest is Egypt's Pyramid of Cheops. And the second biggest is Mexico's little-known Pirámide Tepanapa, or the Great Pyramid of Cholula.

The first great civilization in central Mexico emerged in a valley about 50km northeast of the center of modern Mexico City. Teotihuacán grew into a city of an estimated 125,000 people during its apogee, between AD 250 and 600, and it controlled what was probably the biggest pre-Hispanic Mexican empire. Teotihuacán had writing and books, the bar-and-dot number system and the 260-day sacred year.

The building of a magnificent planned city began about the time of Christ. The greatest of its buildings, the huge Pirámide del Sol (Pyramid of the Sun; p197), was constructed by AD 150. Most of the rest of the city, including the almost-as-big Pirámide de la Luna (Pyramid of the Moon; p198), was built between AD 250 and 600.

Teotihuacán probably became an imperialistic state some time after AD 400. It may have controlled the southern two-thirds of Mexico, all of Guatemala and Belize, and bits of Honduras and El Salvador, but it was an empire seemingly geared toward tribute-gathering rather than full-scale occupation.

Within Teotihuacán's cultural sphere was Cholula, near Puebla, with a pyramid even bigger than the Pirámide del Sol. Teotihuacán may also have had hegemony over the Zapotecs of Oaxaca, whose capital, Monte Albán, grew into a city of perhaps 25,000 in the years between AD 300 and 600. In about 400, Teotihuacán invaders reached what is now Guatemala.

Teotihuacán The City of the Gods (http://archae ology.la.asu.edu/TEO) is a welcome website on this grand city.

In the 8th century, Teotihuacán was burned, plundered and abandoned. It is likely that the state had already been weakened by the rise of rival powers in central Mexico.

Teotihuacán's influence on Mexico's later cultures was huge. Many of its gods, such as the feathered serpent Quetzalcóatl (an all-important symbol of fertility and life, itself inherited from the Olmecs) and Tláloc (the rain and water deity) were still being worshipped by the Aztecs a millennium later.

2300 BC	**1200 BC–400 BC**
First pottery appears	Olmec civilization flourishes along Gulf coast

CLASSIC MAYA

By the close of the Preclassic period (around AD 250), the Maya people of the Yucatán Peninsula and the Petén forest of Guatemala were already building stepped temple pyramids. During what's known as the Classic period (about AD 250 to 900), these and adjacent regions produced pre-Hispanic America's most brilliant civilization, the Classic Maya.

The Classic Maya region comprised three areas: the Yucatán Peninsula in the north; the central area, made up of the Petén forest of present day northern Guatemala and the adjacent lowlands in Chiapas and Tabasco in Mexico (to the west) and Belize (to the east); and the southern area which consisted of the highlands of Guatemala and a small section of Honduras. It was in the northern and central areas that Maya civilization flowered most brilliantly.

The Classic Maya were divided among many independent, often warring city-states, but most of these appear to have been grouped into two loose military alliances, centered on Tikal (Guatemala) and Calakmul (in Mexico's Campeche state). Tikal is believed to have conquered Calakmul in 695, but to have been unable to exert unified control over Calakmul's former subject states.

Joyce Kelly's *Archaeological Guide to Central and Southern Mexico* gives visitors both practical and background information on 70 sites.

WHY THE MAYA COLLAPSED

In the second half of the 8th century, trade between the Maya city-states started to shrink and conflict began to grow. By the early 10th century, the several million inhabitants of the flourishing central Maya heartland had virtually disappeared, and the Classic era was at an end – a cataclysm known as the Maya collapse.

Over the years expert and amateur Mayanists have expended much effort in trying to explain this mysterious phenomenon. Overpopulation and consequent ecological and political crises rank high among the theories. The Maya heartland underwent a big population explosion between AD 600 and 800. This seems to have led to greater competition and conflict between the city-states for control of the area's resources. At the same time deforestation followed by a sequence of erosion, higher temperatures and scarce water may have been disastrous for a people who had few sources of running water and depended on water stored in pools and reservoirs for their survival.

In 2003 scientists analyzing sea-bed sediments off Venezuela came up with new data that made the jigsaw a lot more complete. The sediments were composed of thin light and dark layers, each about 1mm deep, the dark layers containing titanium which was washed into the sea during rainy seasons. Unusually thin dark layers therefore indicated unusually dry rainy seasons. The investigators worked out that the weather in the region in the 9th and 10th centuries was unusually dry, and that there had been three or four periods of particularly intense drought, each lasting several years, during the period that saw the collapse of Classic Maya civilization. Climatic change thus became a likely cause of the exceptional dryness that probably drove the Maya out of their heartland.

The inhabitants of these areas did not just completely disappear in a puff of dust, of course; many of them probably migrated to the northern Maya area (the Yucatán Peninsula) or the highlands of Chiapas, where their descendants live on today. And small numbers, it seems, managed to stay on in the central lowlands, eking out an existence at a far lower cultural level than that of their ancestors. The jungle grew back up around the ancient cities, and only now is it being cut down again.

AD 150	AD 250–900
World's third-biggest pyramid, the Pirámide del Sol, completed at Teotihuacán	Classic Maya civilization flourishes

Cities

A typical Maya city functioned as the religious, political and market hub for surrounding farming hamlets. Its ceremonial center focused on plazas surrounded by tall temple pyramids (usually the tombs of deified rulers) and lower buildings – so-called palaces, with warrens of small rooms. Steles and altars were carved with dates, histories and elaborate human and divine figures. Stone causeways called *sacbeob,* probably for ceremonial use, led out from the plazas.

Classic Maya centers in Mexico fall into four main zones, one in Chiapas in the central Maya area, and three on the Yucatán Peninsula.

The chief Chiapas sites are Yaxchilán (p847), Bonampak (p844), Toniná (p830) and Palenque (p835). For many people the most beautiful of all Maya sites, Palenque rose to prominence under the 7th-century ruler Pakal, whose treasure-loaded tomb deep inside the fine Templo de las Inscripciones was discovered in 1952.

In the southern Yucatán, the Río Bec and Chenes zones, noted for their lavishly carved buildings, are in a wild area, still little-investigated. The archaeological sites here, which include Calakmul (p962), draw relatively few visitors.

The other focus of northern Classic Maya culture was the Puuc zone, whose most important city was Uxmal (p930), south of Mérida. Puuc ornamentation, which reached its peak on the Governor's Palace at Uxmal, featured intricate stone mosaics, often incorporating faces of the hook-nosed sky-serpent/rain-god, Chac. The amazing Codz Pop (Palace of Masks) at Kabah (p933), south of Uxmal, is covered with nearly 300 Chac faces. Chichén Itzá (p940), east of Mérida, is another Puuc site, though it owes more to the later Toltec era (see opposite).

Calendar & Religion

The Maya developed a complex writing system – partly pictorial, partly phonetic – with 300 to 500 symbols, whose decipherment in the 1980s enabled huge advances in the understanding of their culture. They also refined a calendar used by other pre-Hispanic peoples into a tool for the exact recording of earthly and heavenly events. They could predict eclipses of the sun and the movements of the moon and Venus. They measured time in various interlocking cycles, ranging from 20 to 144,000 days, and believed the current world to be just one of a succession of worlds destined to end in cataclysm and be succeeded by another. This cyclical nature of things enabled the future to be predicted by looking at the past.

Religion permeated every facet of Maya life. The Maya believed in predestination and followed complex astrology. To win the gods' favors they carried out elaborate rituals involving the consumption of the alcoholic drink *balche;* bloodletting from ears, tongues or penises; and dances, feasts and sacrifices. The Classic Maya seem to have practiced human sacrifice on a small scale, the Postclassic on a larger scale. Beheading was probably the most common method. At Chichén Itzá, victims were thrown into a deep cenote (well) to bring rain.

The Maya inhabited a universe with a center and four directions (each with a color: east was red; north, white; west, black; south, yellow; the

---

Mesoweb (www .mesoweb.com), Maya Exploration Center (www .mayaexploration.org) and goMaya (www .gomaya.com) are all fabulous resources on the Maya, past and present.

Chronicle of the Maya Kings and Queens (2000) by Simon Martin and Nikolai Grube tells in superbly illustrated detail the histories of 11 of the most important Mayan city-states and their rulers.

Around 1325	1487
Aztec capital Tenochtitlán founded at site of present-day Mexico City	20,000 human captives sacrificed for dedication of Tenochtitlán's Great Temple

center, green), 13 layers of heavens, and nine layers of underworld to which
the dead descended. The earth was the back of a giant reptile floating on
a pond. (It's not *too* hard to imagine yourself as a flea on this creature's
back as you look across a lowland Maya landscape!) Maya gods included
Itzamná, the fire deity and creator; Chac, the rain god; Yum Kaax, the
maize and vegetation god; and Ah Puch, the death god. The feathered serpent, known to the Maya as Kukulcán, was introduced from central Mexico
in the Postclassic period. Also worshiped were dead ancestors, particularly
rulers, who were believed to be descended from the gods.

According to the
traditional Maya calendar,
the current world is
scheduled to come to an
end in December 2012.
Stay alert!

CLASSIC VERACRUZ CIVILIZATION

Along Mexico's Gulf coast, in what is now central and northern Veracruz,
the Classic period saw the rise of a number of statelets with a shared culture, together known as the Classic Veracruz civilization. Their hallmark
is a style of abstract carving, featuring pairs of curved and interwoven
parallel lines. Classic Veracruz appears to have been particularly obsessed
with the ball game (see boxed text, p65); its most important center, El
Tajín (p676), which flourished from about AD 600 to 900, contains at
least 11 ball courts.

TOLTECS

In central Mexico, one chief power center after the decline of Teotihuacán
was Xochicalco (p246), a hilltop site in Morelos state, with Maya influences and impressive evidence of a feathered-serpent cult. Tula, 65km
north of Mexico City, is thought to have been the capital of an empire
referred to by later Aztec 'histories' as that of the Toltecs (Artificers).

Tula

It's hard to disentangle myth and history in the Tula/Toltec story, but a
widely accepted version is that the Toltecs were one of many semicivilized
tribes from the north who moved into central Mexico after the fall of Teotihuacán. Tula became their capital, probably in the 10th century, growing
into a city of about 35,000. The Tula ceremonial center is dedicated to the
feathered-serpent god Quetzalcóatl, but annals relate that Quetzalcóatl was
displaced by Tezcatlipoca (Smoking Mirror), a newcomer god of warriors
and sorcery who demanded a regular diet of the hearts of sacrificed warriors. A king identified with Quetzalcóatl, Topiltzin, fled to the Gulf Coast
and set sail eastward on a raft of snakes, promising one day to return.

Tula seems to have become the capital of a militaristic kingdom that
dominated central Mexico, with warriors organized in orders dedicated
to different animal-gods: the coyote, jaguar and eagle knights. Mass
human sacrifice may have started at Tula.

Tula's influence was great. It is seen at Paquimé (p359) in Chihuahua
and at Gulf Coast sites such as Castillo de Teayo (p674), and is even suspected in temple mounds and artifacts found in Tennessee and Illinois.
Pottery from as far south as Costa Rica has been found at Tula.

Tula was abandoned around the start of the 13th century, seemingly
destroyed by Chichimecs, as the periodic hordes of barbarian raiders
from the north came to be known. But later Mexican peoples revered the
Toltec era as a golden age.

1519–21	1534–58
Spaniard Hernán Cortés lands on Gulf coast, captures Aztec god-king Moctezuma II and conquers Tenochtitlán	The Spanish find huge lodes of silver at Pachuca, Zacatecas and Guanajuato

Chichén Itzá

Maya scripts relate that toward the end of the 10th century much of the northern Yucatán Peninsula was conquered by one Kukulcán, who bears many similarities to Quetzalcóatl. The Yucatán site of Chichén Itzá (p940) contains many Tula-like features, from flat beam-and-masonry roofs (contrasting with the Maya corbeled roof) to gruesome *chac-mools*, reclining human figures holding dishes for sacrificial human hearts. Tiers of grinning skulls engraved on a massive stone platform suggest sacrifice on a massive scale. And there's a resemblance that can hardly be coincidental between Tula's Pirámide B (Pyramid B) and Chichén Itzá's Temple of the Warriors. Many writers therefore believe Toltec exiles invaded the Yucatán and created a new, even grander version of Tula at Chichén Itzá.

AZTECS

The Aztecs' legends related that they were the chosen people of their tribal god, Huizilopochtli. Originally nomads from somewhere to the west or north, they were led by their priests to the Valle de México (site of present-day Mexico City), where they settled on islands in the lakes that then filled much of the valley.

> Richard F Townsend's *The Aztecs* is the best introduction to this enigmatic empire.

The Aztec capital, Tenochtitlán, was founded on one of those islands around 1325. A century later the Aztecs rebelled against Azcapotzalco, then the strongest statelet in the valley, and themselves became the most powerful.

In the mid-15th century the Aztecs (also known as the Mexica) formed the Triple Alliance with two other valley states, Texcoco and Tlacopan, to wage war against Tlaxcala and Huejotzingo, east of the valley. The prisoners they took formed the diet of sacrificed warriors that their voracious god Huizilopochtli demanded to keep the sun rising every day.

The Triple Alliance brought most of central Mexico – from the Gulf Coast to the Pacific, though not Tlaxcala – under its control. The total population of the empire's 38 provinces may have been about five million. The empire's purpose was to exact tributes of resources absent from the heartland. Jade, turquoise, cotton, paper, tobacco, rubber, cacao and precious feathers were needed for the glorification of the Aztec elite, and to support the many nonproductive servants of its war-oriented state.

Ahuizotl's successor was Moctezuma II Xocoyotzin, a reflective character who believed, perhaps fatally, that the Spaniard Hernán Cortés, who arrived on the Gulf Coast in 1519, might be Quetzalcóatl, returned from the east to reclaim his throne.

Economy & Society

> For a wealth of information about the Aztecs and their modern descendants, and other indigenous Mexicans, see the US-based Azteca Web Page (www.mexica .net). The site includes a Nahuatl dictionary and lessons in the language.

By 1519 Tenochtitlán and the adjoining Aztec city of Tlatelolco (p147) probably had more than 200,000 inhabitants, and the Valle de México as a whole, over a million. They were supported by a variety of intensive farming methods that used only stone and wooden tools, and involved irrigation, terracing and swamp reclamation.

The basic unit of Aztec society was the *calpulli*, consisting of a few dozen to a few hundred extended families, who owned land communally. The king held absolute power but delegated important roles such as priest or tax collector to members of the *pilli* (nobility). Military leaders were

1537	1767
Pope declares indigenous Mexicans to be human	Jesuits expelled from all Spanish dominions, fomenting discontent in Mexico

usually *tecuhtli*, elite professional soldiers. Another special group was the *pochteca*, militarized merchants who helped extend the empire, brought goods to the capital and organized the large markets that were held daily in big towns. At the bottom of society were pawns (paupers who could sell themselves for a specified period), serfs and slaves.

Culture & Religion

Tenochtitlán-Tlatelolco had hundreds of temple complexes. The greatest, set on and around modern Mexico City's *zócalo*, was, to the Aztecs, the center of the universe. Its main temple pyramid was dedicated to Huizilopochtli and the rain god, Tláloc.

Much of Aztec culture was drawn from earlier Mexican civilizations. They had writings, bark-paper books and the Calendar Round (the dating system used by the Maya, Olmecs and Zapotecs). They observed the heavens for astrological purposes. Celibate priests performed cycles of great ceremonies, typically including sacrifices and masked dances or processions enacting myths.

The Aztecs believed they lived in the 'fifth world,' whose four predecessors had each been destroyed by the death of the sun and of humanity. Aztec human sacrifices were designed to keep the sun alive. Like the Maya, the Aztecs saw the world as having four directions, 13 heavens and nine hells. Those who died by drowning, leprosy, lightning, gout, dropsy or lung disease went to the paradisiacal gardens of Tláloc, the god who had killed them. Warriors who were sacrificed or died in battle, merchants killed while traveling far away, and women who died giving birth to their first child all went to heaven as companions of the sun. Everyone else traveled for four years under the northern deserts in the abode of the death god Mictlantecuhtli, before reaching the ninth hell, where they vanished altogether.

Bernal Díaz del Castillo gives a detailed first-hand account of the conquest of Mexico in *History of the Conquest of New Spain*, while *The Broken Spears: Aztec Account of the Conquest of Mexico*, edited by Miguel Leon-Portilla, is a rare piece of history from the losers' point of view.

OTHER POSTCLASSIC CIVILIZATIONS

On the eve of the Spanish conquest, most Mexican civilizations shared deep similarities. Each was politically centralized and divided into classes, with many people occupied in specialist tasks, including professional priests. Agriculture was productive, despite the lack of draft animals, metal tools and the wheel. Maize tortillas, *pozol* (maize gruel) and beans were staple foods, and a great variety of other crops were grown in different regions, such as squash, tomatoes, chilies, avocados, peanuts, papayas and pineapples. Luxuries for the elite included turkey, domesticated hairless dog, game and chocolate drinks. War was widespread, and often connected with the need for prisoners to sacrifice to a variety of gods.

The Toltec phase at Chichén Itzá lasted until about 1200. After that, the city of Mayapán (p930) dominated most of the Yucatán Peninsula until the 15th century, when it became a quarreling-ground for numerous city-states, with a culture much decayed from Classic Maya glories.

After 1200 the remaining Zapotec settlements in Oaxaca, such as Mitla (p744) and Yagul (p744), were increasingly dominated by the Mixtecs, who were metalsmiths and potters from the uplands around the Oaxaca–Puebla border. Mixtec and Zapotec cultures became entangled before much of the territory fell to the Aztecs in the 15th and 16th centuries.

1810–21	1824
War of Independence from Spain	Constitution of 1824 establishes a Mexican republic of 19 states and four territories

SOME WE LOVE, SOME WE LOVE TO HATE

Mexicans have strong opinions about some of their historical characters. Some are held up as shining examples for every Mexican to be proud of, with statues in every city and streets named for them all over the country. Others, just as influential, are considered objects of shame and ridicule.

Mexico's Top 10 Heroes

- Cuauhtémoc – Aztec leader who resisted the Spanish invaders (p48)
- Benito Juárez – reforming, liberal, indigenous president who fought off French occupiers (p753)
- Miguel Hidalgo – the priest who launched the war for independence (see boxed text, p633)
- José María Morelos – the priest who took up the independence sword after Hidalgo's death (p50 and p559)
- Pancho Villa – larger-than-life revolutionary (see boxed text, p371)

- Emiliano Zapata – Land and Liberty! (see boxed text, p238)
- Niños Héroes de Chapultepec – cadet soldiers who died defending Chapultepec castle against US invaders (p137)
- Lázaro Cárdenas – 1930's president adored for boldly expropriating foreign oil operations (p53)
- Bartolomé de Las Casas – early bishop of Chiapas who fought for the humane treatment of indigenous Mexicans (p813)
- Vasco de Quiroga – bishop who founded indigenous villages on Utopian lines in Michoacán (p569)

Mexico's Top 10 Villains

- Hernán Cortés – the original evil Spanish conqueror (opposite)
- Carlos Salinas de Gortari – president 1988–94, blamed for peso crisis, drugs trade, corruption, Nafta, you name it… (p54)
- Santa Anna – he won the Alamo, but lost Texas, and California, and Arizona, and… (p51)
- Porfirio Díaz – 19th-century dictator (p51)
- Nuño de Guzmán – conquistador of legendary cruelty (p520)
- Gustavo Díaz Ordaz – authoritarian president at time of the Tlatelolco massacre (see boxed text, p106)

- Victoriano Huerta – turncoat revolutionary general (p52)
- La Malinche – Hernán Cortés' indigenous Mexican translator and lover (opposite)
- Henry Lane Wilson – US ambassador involved in the 1913 plot to depose elected president Francisco Madero (p52)
- Miguel de la Grúa Talamanca y Branciforte – Spanish viceroy of the 1790s whose corruption helped spur the independence movement (p49)

The Totonacs established themselves in much of Veracruz state. To their north, the Huastecs, who inhabited a group of probably independent statelets, flourished between 800 and 1200. Later, in the 15th century, the Aztecs subdued most of these areas.

One group who managed to avoid conquest by the Aztecs were the Tarascos. They were skilled artisans and jewelers who ruled modern Michoacán from their capital, Tzintzuntzan (p577), about 200km west of Mexico City.

1836	1842
President Santa Anna attacks the Alamo in February, and suffers defeat on the San Jacinto River in April	Santa Anna disinters his amputated leg and parades it through Mexico City

SPANISH CONQUEST

Ancient Mexican civilization, nearly 3000 years old, was shattered in the two years from 1519 to 1521 by a tiny group of invaders who destroyed the Aztec empire, brought a new religion to Mexico and reduced the native people to second-class citizens and slaves. So alien to each other were the newcomers and indigenous people, that each doubted whether the other was human.

From this traumatic encounter arose modern Mexico. Most Mexicans are mestizo, of mixed indigenous and European blood, and thus descendants of both cultures. But while Cuauhtémoc, the last Aztec emperor, is now an official hero, Cortés, the leader of the Spanish conquerors, is considered a villain and his indigenous allies as traitors.

Early Expeditions

The Spaniards had been in the Caribbean since Columbus arrived in 1492, with their main bases on the islands of Hispaniola and Cuba. Realizing that they had not reached the East Indies, they began looking for a passage through the land mass to their west, but were distracted by tales of gold, silver and a rich empire there.

Early expeditions from Cuba, led by Francisco Hernández de Córdoba in 1517 and Juan de Grijalva in 1518, were driven back from Mexico's Gulf Coast by hostile locals. In 1518 the governor of Cuba, Diego Velázquez, asked Hernán Cortés, a Spanish colonist on the island, to lead a new expedition westward. As Cortés gathered ships and men, Velázquez became uneasy about the costs and Cortés' loyalty. He tried to cancel the expedition, but Cortés ignored him and set sail on February 15, 1519, with 11 ships, 550 men and 16 horses.

The confrontation between the Machiavellian Cortés and the Aztecs, no shabby players of military politics themselves, would be one of the most bizarre in history.

Cortés & the Aztecs

The Spaniards landed first at Cozumel, off the Yucatán, then sailed around the coast to Tabasco, where they defeated inhospitable locals, and Cortés delivered the first of many lectures to Mexicans on the importance of Christianity and the greatness of King Carlos I of Spain. The locals gave him 20 maidens, among them Doña Marina (La Malinche), who became his interpreter, aide and lover.

At 17 years of age, Moctezuma's only surviving heir, Tecuichpo, bore Cortés' illegitimate daughter, Doña Leonor Cortés y Moctezuma.

The expedition next put in near the present city of Veracruz. In the Aztec capital Tenochtitlán, tales of 'towers floating on water,' bearing fair-skinned beings, reached Moctezuma II. Lightning struck a temple, a comet sailed through the night skies and a bird 'with a mirror in its head' was brought to Moctezuma, who saw warriors in it. According to the Aztec calendar, 1519 would also see the legendary god-king Quetzalcóatl return from the east. Unsure if Cortés really was the god returning, Moctezuma sent messengers to attempt to discourage Cortés from traveling to Tenochtitlán.

The Spaniards were well received at the Gulf Coast communities of Zempoala and Quiahuiztlán, which resented Aztec dominion. Cortés set up a coastal settlement, Villa Rica de la Vera Cruz, then scuttled his ships

1846-48	**Late 1840s**
Mexican-American War: Mexico cedes California, Texas, Utah, Colorado and most of New Mexico and Arizona to the US	Mexico almost loses the Yucatán to the indigenous Maya in the War of the Castes

to stop his men from retreating. Leaving about 150 men at Villa Rica, Cortés set off for Tenochtitlán. On the way he won over the Tlaxcalan people, who became valuable allies.

After considerable vacillation, Moctezuma finally invited Cortés to meet him, denying responsibility for an ambush at Cholula that had resulted in the Spanish massacring many of that town's inhabitants. On November 8, 1519 the Spaniards and 6000 indigenous allies entered Tenochtitlán, a city bigger than any in Spain, by one of the causeways that linked it to the lakeshore. Cortés was met by Moctezuma who was carried by nobles in a litter with a canopy of feathers and gold. The Spaniards were lodged, as befitted gods, in the palace of Moctezuma's father, Axayácatl.

Though entertained in luxury, the Spaniards were trapped. But Moctezuma continued to behave hesitantly, and the Spaniards took him hostage. Believing Cortés a god, Moctezuma told his people he went willingly but hostility rose in the city, aggravated by the Spaniards' destruction of Aztec idols.

Fall of Tenochtitlán

When the Spaniards had been in Tenochtitlán about six months, Moctezuma informed Cortés that another fleet had arrived on the Veracruz coast. This was led by Pánfilo de Narváez, sent by Diego Velázquez to arrest Cortés. Cortés left 140 Spaniards under Pedro de Alvarado in Tenochtitlán and sped to the coast with the others. They routed Narváez' much bigger force, and most of the defeated men joined Cortés.

But in Cortés' absence things had boiled over in Tenochtitlán. Apparently fearing an attack, the Spaniards struck first and killed about 200 Aztec nobles trapped in a square during a festival. Cortés and his enlarged force returned to the Aztec capital and were allowed to rejoin their comrades – only then to come under fierce attack. Trapped in Axayácatl's palace, Cortés persuaded Moctezuma to try to pacify his people. According to one version of events, the king went up to the roof to address the crowds but was wounded by missiles and died soon afterward; other versions say the Spaniards killed him.

The Spaniards fled on June 30, 1520, but several hundred of them, and thousands of their indigenous allies, were killed on what's known as the Noche Triste (Sad Night). The survivors retreated to Tlaxcala, where they prepared for another campaign by building boats in sections, to be carried across the mountains for a waterborne assault on Tenochtitlán. When the 900 Spaniards re-entered the Valle de México they were accompanied by some 100,000 native allies. For the first time, the odds were in their favor.

Moctezuma had been succeeded by his nephew, Cuitláhuac, who then died of smallpox (brought to Mexico by one of Narváez' soldiers). He was succeeded by another nephew, the 18-year-old Cuauhtémoc. The Spanish attack began in May 1521. Cortés had to resort to razing Tenochtitlán building by building, but by August 13, 1521, the resistance had ended. The captured Cuauhtémoc asked Cortés to kill him, but was kept alive until 1525 as a hostage, undergoing occasional foot-burning as the Spanish tried to make him reveal the whereabouts of Aztec treasure.

You can still see the ruins of Tenochtitlán's main temple and there's a model of Tenochtitlán at the Museo Nacional de Antropología (p138).

Indigenous slavery was abolished in the 1550s, but partly replaced by Black slavery.

As a warning to other rebels, Miguel Hidalgo's head was put on public display for 10 years in Guanajuato. His skull is now inside Mexico City's Monumento a la Independencia.

1861	1862
Benito Juárez becomes the first indigenous Mexican president	Mexican forces defeat French invaders at Puebla

COLONIAL ERA

The Spaniards renamed Tenochtitlán 'México' and rebuilt it as the capital of Nueva España (New Spain), as they named their new colony. Cortés granted his soldiers *encomiendas*, which were rights to the labor or tribute of groups of indigenous people.

By 1524, virtually all the Aztec empire, plus other Mexican regions such as Colima, the Huasteca area and the Isthmus of Tehuantepec, had been brought under at least the loose control of the colony. In 1527 Spain set up Nueva España's first *audiencia*, a high court with government functions.

Central America too was conquered in the 1520s by Spanish forces from Mexico and Panama, and in the 1540s the subjection of the Yucatán Peninsula was accomplished. Nueva España's northern border ran roughly from modern Tampico to Guadalajara; beyond it dwelt fierce semi-nomads.

Big finds of silver in Zacatecas in the mid-1540s, and further finds at Guanajuato, San Luis Potosí and Pachuca, spurred Spanish attempts to subdue the north. The northern borders were slowly extended by missionaries and a few settlers, and by the early 19th century Nueva España included (albeit loosely) most of the modern US states of Texas, New Mexico, Arizona, California, Utah and Colorado.

The populations of the conquered peoples of Nueva España declined disastrously, from an estimated 25 million at the conquest to little over a million by 1605, mainly from epidemics of new diseases brought by the Spaniards. The indigenous peoples' only real allies were some of the monks who started arriving in 1523. The monks' missionary work helped extend Spanish control over Mexico – by 1560 they had carried out millions of conversions and built more than 100 monasteries (some fortified), as at Acolman (p195) – but many of them were compassionate and brave men, who protected local people from the colonists' worst excesses. Indigenous slavery was abolished in the 1550s, but partly replaced by black slavery.

A person's place in colonial Mexican society was determined by skin color, parentage and birthplace. Spanish-born colonists *(peninsulares)* were a minuscule part of the population, but were at the top of the tree and considered nobility in Nueva España, however humble their origins in Spain.

Next were the criollos, people born of Spanish parents in Nueva España. By the 18th century some criollos had made fortunes in mining, commerce or agriculture. Haciendas (large estates) began to spring up. Not surprisingly, criollos sought political power commensurate with their wealth.

Below the criollos were the mestizos (people of mixed ancestry), and at the bottom of the pile were the indigenous people and African slaves. Though the poor were paid for their labor by the 18th century, they were paid very little. Many were *peones*, bonded laborers tied by debt to their employers, and indigenous people still had to pay tribute to the crown.

Criollo discontent with Spanish rule began to stir in the 18th century, following the 1767 expulsion of the Jesuits (many of whom were criollos) from the Spanish empire, and the replacement in 1794 of the popular Conde de Revillagigedo as viceroy by the corrupt Marqués de Branciforte. When the crown confiscated church assets in 1804, the church had to call in many debts, which hit criollos hard. The catalyst for rebellion came in 1808 when Napoleon occupied Spain, and direct Spanish control over Nueva España evaporated. Rivalry between *peninsulares* and criollos intensified.

The most readable and useful tellings of the whole story include *The Course of Mexican History* by Michael C Meyer and William L Sherman, Lynn V Foster's *A Brief History of Mexico*, Kenneth Pearce's *Traveller's History of Mexico* and Brian R Hamnett's *A Concise History of Mexico*.

1863	1867
French invaders take Puebla – and Mexico City	Napoleon's puppet–Mexican emperor Maximilian is executed

INDEPENDENCE

In 1810, a criollo coterie based in Querétaro, north of Mexico City, began planning a rebellion. News of the plans leaked to the colonial authorities, so the group acted immediately. On September 16 one of its members, Miguel Hidalgo y Costilla, priest of the town of Dolores (p632), summoned his parishioners and issued his now-famous call to rebellion, the Grito de Dolores (basically 'Death to the Spaniards!').

A mob formed and marched on San Miguel, Celaya and Guanajuato, massacring *peninsulares* in Guanajuato. Over the next month and a half, the rebels captured Zacatecas, San Luis Potosí and Morelia. On October 30 their army, numbering about 80,000, defeated loyalist forces at Las Cruces outside Mexico City, but Hidalgo was hesitant to attack the capital. The rebels occupied Guadalajara, but then were pushed northward. Their numbers shrank, and in 1811 their leaders, including Hidalgo, were captured and executed. As a warning to other potential rebels, Hidalgo's head was put on public display for 10 years in Guanajuato.

José María Morelos y Pavón, a former student of Hidalgo and also a parish priest, assumed the rebel leadership, blockading Mexico City for several months. He convened a congress at Chilpancingo that adopted guiding principles for the independence movement, including universal male suffrage, popular sovereignty and the abolition of slavery. But Morelos was captured and executed in 1815, and his forces split into several guerrilla bands, the most successful of which was led by Vicente Guerrero in the state of Oaxaca.

In 1821 the royalist general Agustín de Iturbide defected during an offensive against Guerrero, and conspired with the rebels to declare independence from Spain. Iturbide and Guerrero worked out the *Plan de Iguala*, which established three guarantees – religious dominance by the Catholic Church, a constitutional monarchy and equal rights for criollos and *peninsulares*. The plan won over all influential sections of society, and the incoming Spanish viceroy in 1821 agreed to Mexican independence. Iturbide, who had command of the army, took the new Mexican throne as Emperor Agustín I in 1822.

> UNAM, the national university in Mexico City, has the world's largest mosaic mural. Created by Juan O'Gorman, the 4000 sq meters of mural on the university's library depict scenes of Mexican history.

MEXICAN REPUBLIC

Iturbide was deposed in 1823 by a rebel army led by another opportunistic soldier, Antonio López de Santa Anna. A new constitution in 1824 established a federal Mexican republic of 19 states and four territories. In the north, Mexico included much of what is now the southwestern USA; in the south, its boundary was the same as it is today (Central America set up a separate federation in 1823). Guadalupe Victoria, a former independence fighter, became Mexico's first president.

Vicente Guerrero stood as a liberal candidate in the 1828 presidential elections and was defeated, but was eventually awarded the presidency after another Santa Anna–led revolt. Guerrero abolished slavery but was then deposed and executed by his conservative vice president, Anastasio Bustamante. The struggle between liberals, who favored social reform, and conservatives, who opposed it, would be a constant theme in 19th-century Mexican politics.

1876–1911	1910
The Porfiriato, the era of despotic rule by President Porfirio Díaz, brushing aside 'no re-election' laws	Francisco Madero launches revolution against Díaz

Texas & War

Intervention in politics by ambitious military men was also becoming a habit. Santa Anna, a national hero after defeating a small Spanish invasion force at Tampico in 1829, overthrew Bustamante in 1829, overthrew Bustamante and was elected president in 1833. Thus began 22 years of chronic instability, in which the presidency changed hands 36 times – going 11 times to Santa Anna. Economic decline and corruption became entrenched, and Santa Anna quickly turned into a conservative.

Santa Anna is remembered for helping to lose large chunks of Mexican territory to the USA. North American settlers in Texas, initially welcomed by the Mexican authorities, grew restless and declared Texas independent in 1836. Santa Anna led an army north and wiped out the defenders of an old mission called the Alamo in San Antonio, but he was routed on the San Jacinto River a few weeks later.

In 1845 the US Congress voted to annex Texas, and US president James Polk demanded further Mexican territory. That led to the Mexican-American War (1846–48), in which US troops captured Mexico City. At the end of the war, by the Treaty of Guadalupe Hidalgo (1848), Mexico ceded Texas, California, Utah, Colorado, and most of New Mexico and Arizona to the USA. A Santa Anna government sold the remainder of New Mexico and Arizona to the USA in 1853 for $10 million in the Gadsden Purchase. This loss precipitated the liberal-led Revolution of Ayutla that ousted Santa Anna for good in 1855.

Mexico almost lost the Yucatán Peninsula too, in the so-called War of the Castes in the late 1840s, when the Maya people rose up against their criollo overlords and narrowly failed to drive them off the peninsula.

Mexico Online (www .mexonline.com) has good history links, among much other information.

Benito Juárez, the French & Porfirio Díaz

The new liberal government ushered in an era known as the Reform, in which it set about dismantling the conservative state that had developed in Mexico. The key figure was Benito Juárez, a Zapotec from Oaxaca, and a leading lawyer and politician. Laws requiring the church to sell much of its property helped precipitate the internal War of the Reform (1858–61) between the liberals (with their 'capital' at Veracruz) and the conservatives (based in Mexico City). The liberals eventually won and Juárez became president in 1861. But Mexico was in disarray and heavily in debt to Britain, France and Spain. These three countries sent a joint force to collect their debts, and France's Napoleon III decided to go further and take over Mexico, leading to yet another war.

The French were defeated at Puebla in 1862, but then took Puebla and Mexico City a year later. Napoleon sent Maximilian of Hapsburg over to rule as emperor in 1864, but he didn't last long. In 1867 he was executed by Juárez loyalists.

Juárez immediately set an agenda of economic and educational reform. Schooling was made mandatory, a railway was built between Mexico City and Veracruz, and a rural police force, the *rurales*, was organized to secure the transport of cargo through Mexico.

Juárez died in 1872. Porfirio Díaz, elected president in 1876, ruled for 31 of the next 35 years, a period known as the *Porfiriato*. Díaz brought Mexico into the industrial age, launching public-works projects throughout the

1910–20   **1917**

| Almost two million people die and the economy is shattered in the Mexican Revolution | The Constitution of 1917 guarantees civil rights, introduces election reforms and protects Mexico from foreign exploitation |

country, particularly in Mexico City. Telephone and telegraph lines were strung and the railway network spread.

Díaz kept Mexico free of the civil wars that had plagued it for over 60 years, but at a cost. Political opposition, free elections and a free press were banned. Many of Mexico's resources went into foreign ownership, peasants were cheated out of their land by new laws, workers suffered appalling conditions, and the country was kept quiet by a ruthless army and the now-feared *rurales*. Land and wealth became concentrated in the hands of a small minority. All this led, in 1910, to the Mexican Revolution.

MEXICAN REVOLUTION

The revolution was a 10-year period of shifting allegiances between a spectrum of leaders of all political stripes, in which successive attempts to create stable governments were wrecked by new outbreaks of devastating fighting.

Francisco Madero, a wealthy liberal from Coahuila, would probably have won the presidency in 1910 if Díaz hadn't jailed him. On his release, Madero called for the nation to rise in revolution on November 20, 1910. The call was heard, and revolution spread quickly across the country. When revolutionaries under the leadership of Francisco 'Pancho' Villa (see boxed text, p371) took Ciudad Juárez in May 1911, Díaz resigned. Madero was elected president in November 1911.

The best movie of the Mexican Revolution is Elia Kazan's *Viva Zapata!* (1952), starring Marlon Brando. John Steinbeck's script is historically sound for the first phase of the revolution, up to the meeting between Pancho Villa and Emiliano Zapata in Mexico City. Beyond that point it flounders until Zapata is assassinated.

But Madero was unable to contain the factions fighting for power throughout the country. The basic divide was between liberal reformers like Madero and more radical leaders such as Emiliano Zapata (see boxed text, p238), who was fighting for the transfer of hacienda land to the peasants with the cry '*¡Tierra y Libertad!*' (Land and Freedom!). Madero sent federal troops to disband Zapata's forces, and the Zapatista movement was born.

Madero's government was brought down in 1913, partly thanks to the machinations of US ambassador Henry Lane Wilson who, in pursuit of what he considered to be US interests, negotiated the switch of Madero's top general in Mexico City, Victoriano Huerta, to the side of conservative rebels fighting against Madero. Madero was executed and Huerta became president, only to foment greater strife around the country. In March 1913, three revolutionary leaders in the north united against him under the Plan de Guadalupe: Venustiano Carranza, a Madero supporter, in Coahuila; Pancho Villa in Chihuahua; and Álvaro Obregón in Sonora. Zapata was also fighting against Huerta. Terror reigned in the countryside as Huerta's troops fought, pillaged and plundered. Finally he was defeated and forced to resign in July 1914.

War then broke out between the victorious factions, with Carranza eventually emerging the victor. A new reformist constitution, still largely in force today, was enacted in 1917.

In the state of Morelos, south of Mexico City, the Zapatistas continued to demand reforms. Carranza had Zapata assassinated in 1919, but the following year Carranza was in turn assassinated on Obregón's orders. Pancho Villa was killed in 1923.

The 10 years of violent civil war had cost between 1.5 and two million lives (roughly one in eight Mexicans) and shattered the economy.

1920–24	1929
President Alvaro Obregón presides over a reconstruction period, with rural schools built and land redistributed to peasants	The Partido Nacional Revolucionario (PNR) is founded

---

TOP FIVE REVOLUTIONARY BULLET HOLES

- La Ópera Bar, Mexico City (p166) – hole in the ceiling made by Pancho Villa
- Museo de la Revolución Mexicana, Chihuahua (p365) – the bullet-riddled black Dodge in which Villa was assassinated
- Ex-Hacienda de San Juan Chinameca (see boxed text, p238) – where Emiliano Zapata was assassinated

- Museo de la Revolución, Puebla (p215) – pockmarked house where the revolution's first battle was fought out
- Cuartel General de Zapata, Tlaltizapán (p238) – the bullet-torn, bloodstained clothes in which Zapata died

---

FROM REVOLUTION TO WWII

As president from 1920 to 1924, Álvaro Obregón turned to national reconstruction. More than a thousand rural schools were built and some land was redistributed from big landowners to the peasants. Top artists, such as Diego Rivera, were commissioned to decorate important public buildings with large, vivid murals on social and historical themes. Many of these can be seen in Mexico City.

Plutarco Elías Calles, president from 1924 to 1928, closed monasteries, convents and church schools, and prohibited religious processions. These measures precipitated the bloody Cristero Rebellion by Catholics, which lasted until 1929 and included the assassination of Álvaro Obregón after he was elected president again in 1928. Calles reorganized his supporters to found the Partido Nacional Revolucionario (PNR, National Revolutionary Party), a precursor of today's Partido Revolucionario Institucional (PRI) and initiator of a long tradition of official acronyms.

Lázaro Cárdenas won the presidency in 1934 with the PNR's support and stepped up the reform program. Cárdenas redistributed almost 200,000 sq km of land – nearly double the amount distributed before him – mostly through the establishment of *ejidos* (peasant landholding cooperatives). Thus, most of Mexico's arable soil was redistributed, and nearly one-third of the population received land. Cárdenas also set up the million-member labor union Confederación de Trabajadores Mexicanos (CTM, Confederation of Mexican Workers), reorganized the PNR into the Partido de la Revolución Mexicana (PRM, Party of the Mexican Revolution), and boldly expropriated foreign oil-company operations in Mexico in 1938, forming Petróleos Mexicanos (Pemex, the Mexican Petroleum Company). After the oil expropriation, foreign investors avoided Mexico, slowing the economy.

Cárdenas' successor, Manuel Ávila Camacho (1940–46), marked a transition toward more conservative government. He sent Mexican troops to help the WWII Allies in the Pacific and supplied raw materials and labor to the USA. The war boosted Mexican industry and exports.

MODERN MEXICO

As the Mexican economy expanded, new economic and political groups demanded influence in the ruling PRM. To recognize their inclusion, the party was renamed the Partido Revolucionario Institucional (PRI, 'El Pree'). President Miguel Alemán (1946–52) continued development by extending

---

1938

President Lázaro Cárdenas nationalizes foreign oil operations in Mexico, forming the national oil company Pemex

1968

Government troops kill hundreds of protesters during the Tlatelolco massacre one week before the Olympic Games in Mexico City

the road system and building hydroelectric stations, irrigation projects and UNAM, the National Autonomous University of Mexico (p143). Pemex grew dramatically and spawned some of Mexico's worst corruption.

A contingent of 250,000 Mexican and Mexican-American men fought in WWII. One thousand were killed in action, 1500 received purple hearts and 17 received the Congressional Medal of Honor.

By the 1950s, Mexico was having to confront a new problem: explosive population growth. In two decades the national population had doubled, and many people began migrating to urban areas to search for work. Adolfo López Mateos (1958–64), one of Mexico's most popular post-WWII presidents, benefiting from strong growth in tourism and exports, nationalized foreign utility concessions, implemented social welfare and rural education programs, and redistributed 120,000 sq km of land to small farmers.

Unrest, Boom & Bust

Though the economy continued to grow through the 1960s, President Gustavo Díaz Ordaz (1964–70) is better remembered for his repression of civil liberties. University students in Mexico City were the first to express their outrage with his administration. Discontent came to a head in the months preceding the 1968 Olympic Games in Mexico City, the first Olympics ever held in a developing nation. Single-party rule and restricted freedom of speech were among the objects of protest. On October 2, with the Olympics only a few days away, a rally was organized in Tlatelolco, Mexico City. The government sent in heavily armed troops and police, and several hundred people died in the ensuing massacre (see boxed text, p106).

The 1970s saw Mexico suddenly riding the crest of an economic wave, following the jump in world oil prices caused by an OPEC (Organization of the Petroleum Exporting Countries) embargo. On the strength of the country's vast oil reserves, international institutions began lending Mexico billions of dollars. Then, just as suddenly, a world oil glut sent prices plunging. Mexico's worst recession for decades began. The national gloom was deepened by the 1985 Mexico City earthquake, which killed at least 10,000 people, destroyed hundreds of buildings and caused more than $4 billion in damage.

In a climate of economic helplessness and rampant corruption, dissent grew, even inside the PRI. There were sometimes violent protests over the PRI's now routine electoral fraud and strong-arm tactics.

Salinas & Zedillo

Harvard-educated Carlos Salinas de Gortari (1988–94) came to power in a disputed election, in which he had been heading for defeat by Cuauhtémoc Cárdenas of the left-of-center Partido de la Revolución Democrática (PRD, Party of the Democratic Revolution) until a mysterious computer failure interrupted vote-tallying. Salinas transformed Mexico's state-dominated economy into one of private enterprise and free trade. The apex of this program was the North American Free Trade Agreement (Nafta), which came into effect on January 1, 1994. Salinas did not go out in a blaze of glory, however – far from it. January 1, 1994 also saw the start of the left-wing Zapatista uprising in Mexico's southernmost state, Chiapas (see boxed text, p828). Then in March 1994 Luis Donaldo Colosio, Salinas' chosen successor as PRI presidential candidate, was assassinated in Tijuana. Conspiracy theories abound as to who was responsible.

1985	1994, Jan 1
Magnitude 8.0 earthquake strikes Mexico City, killing more than 10,000 people	The North American Free Trade Agreement (Nafta) comes into effect

During Salinas' term, drug trafficking grew into a huge business in Mexico (many believe Salinas himself was deeply involved in it), and within days of his leaving office in late 1994, Mexico's currency, the peso, suddenly collapsed. This brought on a rapid and deep economic recession that hit hard at everyone, especially the poor. Salinas ended up as the ex-president that Mexicans most love to hate.

The slump led to, among other things, a big increase in crime, intensified discontent with the PRI, and much more Mexican emigration to the USA. It was estimated that by 1997, more than 2.5 million Mexicans a year were entering the USA illegally. President Ernesto Zedillo (1994–2000) of the PRI, an uncharismatic economist, pulled Mexico gradually out of recession and by the end of his term in 2000, Mexicans' purchasing power was again approaching what it had been in 1994. Zedillo also transformed the country's politics so that at the end of his term power could be peacefully transferred to an elected non-PRI successor – the first ever peaceful change of regime in Mexican history. Zedillo was, however, unable to make many inroads into the burgeoning power of Mexico's drug mobs.

By 2000, thanks to Zedillo's efforts to set up a new, independent electoral system, 11 of Mexico's 31 states had elected non-PRI governors and half the population (including Mexico City) had non-PRI mayors.

Opening Mexico: The Making of a Democracy, by New York Times journalists Samuel Dillon and Julia Preston, is the best (if over-optimistic) read on modern Mexican history and politics, focusing on the Zedillo presidency (1994–2000) and the changes that culminated in the election of Vicente Fox.

The Drug Trade

Mexico has long been a marijuana- and heroin-producer, but a mid-1980s US crackdown on drug shipments from Colombia through the Caribbean to Florida, gave a huge impetus to its drug gangs. As a result, drugs being transported from South America to the USA went through Mexico instead.

Three main Mexican cartels emerged, each controlling different sectors of the Mexico–US border: the Pacific (or Tijuana) cartel, the (Ciudad) Juárez cartel and the Matamoros-based Gulf cartel. Later a fourth mob, the Sinaloa cartel, muscled in on the Sonora border between the Pacific and Juárez mobs. These cartels bought up politicians, top antidrug officials, and whole police forces. Many Mexicans believe organized crime in the early 1990s was actually controlled by the PRI, with President Carlos Salinas and his brother Raúl deeply involved.

By 1997, most illegal drugs entering the USA were going through Mexico. President Zedillo brought the armed forces into the fight against the drug mobs, but in 1997 his trusted top drug fighter was arrested on charges of being in the pay of the Juárez mob. In the late 1990s Tijuana was the scene of literally hundreds of drug-related murders, including those of judges, witnesses, honest police and journalists. President Vicente Fox (2000–06) had some successes against the drug mobs, including several high-profile arrests of cartel leaders and the sacking of the entire Morelos state police force in 2004, but by then 92% of the cocaine entering the US was coming through Mexico, according to US government figures. In 2003, Fox even called in the army to dismantle Mexico's deeply corrupt antidrug police. But there were also high-profile jail escapes by cartel leaders and outbreaks of exceptionally vicious turf wars between rival mobs. The latter claimed over 500 deaths in the first half of 2005 alone, with more than 100 of those murders happening in the border city of Nuevo Laredo, where the US consulate briefly closed

1994, Jan 1	2000
Zapatista uprising starts in Chiapas	Vicente Fox is elected president; the PRI, descendant of the PNR, loses 70-year grip on presidency

down for safety reasons. Later in 2005, Fox's public-security minister and leader of the struggle against the drug trade, Ramón Martín Huerta, was killed in an air crash that many refuse to believe was an accident. The mobs are just too powerful and dangerous to be easily defeated.

You'll certainly get a feel for the scary brutality and corruption of the cross-border narco world from Steven Soderbergh's 2000 movie Traffic.

The Fox Presidency

The independent electoral system set in place by Zedillo ensured that his party, the PRI, lost its 70-year grip on power in the 2000 presidential election. The winner was Vicente Fox of the right-of-center Partido Acción Nacional (PAN, National Action Party), a former state governor of Guanajuato and former chief of Coca-Cola's operations in Mexico (which drinks more Coke per person than any other country in the world). A 6ft 5in (nearly 2m) tall rancher, with a penchant for jeans and cowboy boots, Fox entered office with the goodwill of a wide range of Mexicans, who hoped a change of ruling party would bring real change in the country. Pledging to tackle corruption and crime, and to work for a fairer distribution of income, he picked a broad-based ministerial team ranging from ex-PRI officials to left-wing academics, and did not, as incoming Mexican administrations had traditionally done, replace the entire governing apparatus with his own friends and hangers-on.

Though Fox remained personally popular and was perceived as honest and well-intentioned, in the end his presidency disappointed many – largely because his party did not have a majority in Mexico's national Congress. Things got worse when the PAN lost more seats to the PRI in mid-term congressional elections in 2003. Fox was thus unable to enact the reforms that he believed key to stirring Mexico's slumbering economy, such as raising taxes or introducing private investment into the energy sector. His government consequently lacked money to improve education, social welfare or roads. By the end of Fox's term of office in 2006, Mexicans' overall standard of living was only a little higher than when he took power. Peasants and small farmers felt the pinch of Nafta, as subsidized corn (maize) from the USA was sold cheaper in Mexico than Mexican corn.

Fox failed to achieve a deal with the indigenous Zapatista rebels in the southern state of Chiapas (see boxed text, p828), but his government did pass a law on indigenous-language rights. Crime in general, a major pre-occupation of late-1990s Mexico, did perhaps become a little less rampant. Mexico City feels like a safer city today than a few years ago, even though in 2004 citizens were still staging large protest marches against crime levels (especially kidnappings, running at a rate of 3000 a year by 2003).

Mexicans did enjoy a certain social liberation after the PRI's grip was prized loose. Government became more transparent, honest and ac-countable, and Mexicans have become more confident about expressing their opinions and asserting their rights, aware that their rulers are now subject to more or less fair elections. As the time to elect Fox's successor approached, the PAN and the PRI colluded in a bizarre attempt to derail the election favorite, Andrés Manuel López Obrador of the PRD, over a legal technicality, but backed off after an enormous Mexico City demon-stration in López Obrador's favor. At least it seemed that Fox's successor would be elected, as he was, by a free and fair popular vote – something few Mexicans would have believed likely 12 years before.

2003	2006
Population passes 100 million	Fox presidency ends; Zapatistas stage unarmed tour of Mexico, launching peaceful, anticapitalist politics of 'liberation from below'

The Culture

THE NATIONAL PSYCHE

The last thing you could do with Mexicans is encapsulate them in simple formulae. They adore fun, music and a fiesta, yet in many ways are deeply serious. They work hard but relax and enjoy life to the full in their time off. They're hospitable and warm to guests, yet are most truly themselves only within their family group. They will laugh at death, but have a profound vein of spirituality. You may read about anti-gringo sentiment in the media, but Mexicans will treat you, as a visitor to their country, with refreshing warmth and courtesy. (The word 'gringo,' incidentally, isn't exactly a compliment, but nor is it necessarily an insult: the term is often simply a neutral synonym for 'American.')

Mexico is, of course, the home of machismo, that exaggeration of masculinity whose manifestations may range from a certain way of trimming a moustache to aggressive driving, heavy drinking or the carrying of weapons. The other side of the machismo coin is the exaggeratedly feminine female. But gender equalization has come a long way in a few decades: you'll find most Mexicans, especially among the increasingly educated and worldly younger generations, ready to relate simply as one person to another – even if there's still a grain of truth in the cliché Mexican family dynamic (son idolizes mother and must protect virtue of sisters and daughters, but other women are fair game).

Mexico's 'patron saint' – not actually a saint but a manifestation of the Virgin Mary – is the dark-skinned Virgin of Guadalupe, who made her appearance before an Aztec potter in 1531 on a hill near Mexico City. Universally revered, she's both the archetypal mother and the pre-eminent focus of Mexicans' inborn spirituality, which has its roots both in Spanish Catholicism and in the complex belief systems of Mexico's pre-Hispanic civilizations. Elements of ancient nature-based beliefs survive alongside Catholicism among the country's many indigenous people, and most Mexicans still inhabit a world where – as in pre Hispanic times – omens, portents, coincidences, and curious resemblances and repetitions and parallels loom large in importance. The ancient belief in the cyclical, repetitive nature of time persists too, somewhere in most Mexicans' subconscious. Mexicans have certainly not lost that awareness of death and afterlife that was so central to the pre-Hispanic cultures. The famous Día de Muertos festival (Day of the Dead, November 2), when the departed are believed to revisit the living, is one key way of bridging the gap between this life and whatever follows it.

On a more mundane level, you'll find most Mexicans are chiefly concerned with earning a crust for themselves and their strongly knit families – and also with enjoying the leisure side of life, whether it be partying at clubs, bars or fiestas or relaxing over a long, extended-family Sunday lunch at a beachside restaurant. Nobel Prize–winning Mexican writer Octavio Paz argued in *The Labyrinth of Solitude* that Mexicans' love of noise, music and crowds is no more than a temporary escape from a deeper personal isolation and gloom – but make your own judgment!

On a political level, the country is becoming democratized, but most Mexicans still despair of it ever being governed well. They mock their country's failings – but at the same time are a proud people, proud of their families, their villages and towns, proud of Mexico. They don't like perceived slurs or any hint of foreign interference. So close to the US,

Many Mexicans, when sick, prefer to visit a traditional *curandero* – a kind of cross between a naturopath and a witch doctor – rather than resort to a modern *médico*.

where millions of Mexicans have spent years of their lives, they take on board a certain amount of US technology, fashion and products, but they also strongly value the positives they see in Mexican life – a more human pace, a stronger sense of community and family, their own very distinctive cuisine, their unique heritage and their thriving national culture.

LIFESTYLE

Around three-quarters of Mexicans now live in cities and towns, and this percentage continues to increase as rural folk are sucked in by the hope of raising their income. Most urban dwellers inhabit crowded, multigenerational, family homes on tightly packed streets in crowded neighborhoods, with few parks or open spaces. Fly into Mexico City and you'll get a bird's-eye view of just how little space is not occupied by housing or roads. Around the edges of the city, new streets climb the steep slopes of extinct volcanoes, while the city's poorest new arrivals inhabit shacks on the city's fringes made of whatever they can lay hands on – a few concrete blocks, wooden boards, sheets of corrugated tin. Many of these people barely scrape a living in the 'informal economy,' as street hawkers, buskers or home workers, rarely earning much more than $5 a day.

More affluent city neighborhoods often have blocks of relatively spacious, well-provided apartments. In the wealthiest quarters, imposing detached houses with well-tended gardens and satellite dishes sit behind high walls with strong security gates. Domestic staff can be seen walking dogs or babies, while tradespeople and delivery drivers talk through intercoms to gain admittance to the fortresses of the privileged. The owners of these homes will often have other properties too – a ranch in the country or a coastal holiday villa.

At the other extreme, out in the villages people work the land and often live in homes comprising a yard surrounded by a few separate small buildings for members of an extended family – buildings of adobe, wood or concrete, often with earth floors, and with roofs sometimes of tile but more likely of cheaper tin. Inside these homes are few possessions – beds, a cooking area, a table with a few chairs and a few aging photos of departed relatives. These villages may or may not be reached by paved roads, but will nearly always be accessed by decrepit buses, pickups or some other public transport, because few of their inhabitants own cars.

The contrasts between poor and rich couldn't be greater: while kids from rich families go clubbing in flashy cars and attend private universities (or go to school in the US), poor villagers may dance only at local fiestas and are lucky to complete primary education.

Family and hometown ties remain strong among Mexicans. Even if they are not actually living together, large family groups take holidays or spend Sunday lunches together, while Mexicans in the US send money back to their families or to fund projects, like schools and clinics, in their hometowns.

Mexico is more broad-minded about sexuality than you might expect. Gays and lesbians rarely attract open discrimination or violence and there are large, growing and confident gay communities in Guadalajara, Mexico City and Puerto Vallarta.

Tradition remains powerful. Holidays for saints' days, patriotic anniversaries and festivals such as Semana Santa (Holy Week), Día de Muertos (Day of the Dead, November 2), the Día de la Virgen de Guadalupe (December 12) and Christmas are essential to the rhythm of Mexican life, ensuring that people get a break from work every few weeks and bringing them together for the same processions and rituals year after year.

The secrets of physical and spiritual health of a Nahua *curandera* are revealed in *Woman Who Glows in the Dark* by Elena Ávila with Joy Parker (1999).

A United Nations Development Programme study in 2004 reported that while the wealthiest zones of Mexico City and Monterrey could be compared to rich European cities, other parts of the capital and rural areas in the south of Mexico were more like parts of Africa.

POPULATION
In 2006 Mexico's population was estimated at 105 million. About 75% of these people live in towns or cities, and one-third are aged under 15. The biggest cities are Mexico City (with around 18 million people), Guadalajara (with a conurbation estimated at four million) and Monterrey (conurbation estimated at 3.6 million). Tijuana, Puebla, Ciudad Juárez, León and the Torreón and San Luis Potosí conurbations all have populations above one million. The most populous state is the state of México, which includes the rapidly growing outer areas of Mexico City, though not the city itself, and has nearly 15 million people.

MULTICULTURALISM
Mexicans are not a uniform people (far from it!) and their ethnic diversity is one of the most fascinating aspects of traveling around the country. In ethnic terms the major distinction is between mestizos and *indígenas*. Mestizos are people of mixed ancestry – usually a compound of Spanish and indigenous, although African slaves and other Europeans were also significant elements. *Indígenas* (indigenous people; less respectfully called *índios,* meaning 'Indians') are descendants of Mexico's pre-Hispanic inhabitants – the Maya, the Zapotecs, the Nahua, the Mixtecs and other peoples there before the Spanish arrived – who have retained a distinct ethnic identity. Mestizos make up the great majority of the population, and together with the few people of supposedly pure Spanish ancestry they hold most positions of power and influence in Mexican society.

Researchers have listed at least 139 vanished indigenous languages (and thus, 139 vanished indigenous cultures). The 60 or so that remain have survived primarily because of their rural isolation. Each group has its own language and traditions and, often, its own unique costumes. But

Anthropologist Guillermo Bonfil Batalla argues in *México Profundo: Reclaiming a Civilization* that Mexico's urban and rural poor, mestizo and indigenous, constitute a uniquely mesoamerican civilization quite distinct from Mexico's European- and American-influenced middle class.

MANNERS FOR MEXICO
In most places in Mexico that are frequented by travelers, the locals are accustomed to foreign visitors and tolerant of their strange ways. But it's still recommended that women dress conservatively in small towns and in places off the beaten track (avoid shorts, skimpy tops etc). Everyone should lean toward the respectful end of the dress spectrum when visiting churches. It's also appreciated if you start off any conversation with a few words of Spanish. If the person you're talking with speaks better English than your Spanish, then you can slip into English.

Mexicans love to hear that you're enjoying their country. As a rule they are slow to criticize or argue, expressing disagreement more by nuance than blunt assertion. An invitation to a Mexican home is an honor for an outsider; as a guest you will be treated hospitably and will enter a part of the real Mexico to which few outsiders are admitted. Take a small gift if you can.

Away from tourist destinations, your presence may evoke any reaction from curiosity to shyness or, very occasionally, brusqueness. But any negative response will usually evaporate as soon as you show that you're harmless and friendly. Just a few words of Spanish will often bring smiles and warmth, probably followed by questions. Then someone who speaks a few words of English will dare to try them out.

Some indigenous people adopt a cool attitude toward visitors: they have come to mistrust outsiders after five centuries of rough treatment. They don't like being gawked at by tourists and can be very sensitive about cameras. If in any doubt at all about whether it's OK to take a photo, ask first.

Ways you can help poor communities are to give business to community organizations – ecotourism initiatives, crafts cooperatives and the like – and to buy crafts and commodities direct from villages or from the artisans themselves, rather than through urban entrepreneurs.

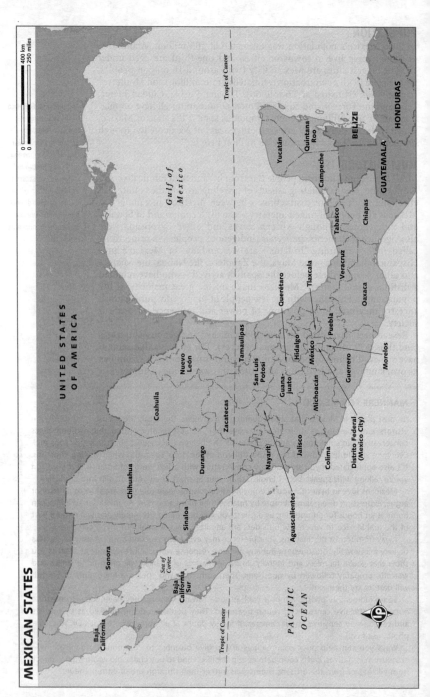

indigenous people generally remain second-class citizens, often restricted to the worst land or forced to migrate to city slums or the USA in search of work. Their main wealth is traditional and spiritual, and their way of life is imbued with communal customs, beliefs and rituals bound up with nature.

Since 1994 the Zapatista rebels in Chiapas have spearheaded a campaign for indigenous rights. The San Andrés Accords of 1996, agreed between Zapatista and government negotiators, promised a degree of autonomy to Mexico's indigenous peoples, but the government of the day, under President Ernesto Zedillo, failed to turn the accords into law. In 2001 President Vicente Fox presented Mexico's Congress with a bill closely based on the San Andrés Accords, but Congress passed only a watered-down version, which the Zapatistas rejected as a basis for peace talks, and which most Mexican state governments with large indigenous populations refused to accept in any case.

At least the cause of indigenous languages took a step forward with the passing of a Law of Linguistic Rights in 2002. This recognizes indigenous tongues as 'national' languages and aims to develop, through teaching, Mexico's linguistic plurality. A National Institute of Indigenous Languages (Inali) has been set up to promote the use of indigenous languages in the media, on signs and in government propaganda, and to offer language options for official purposes.

In the most recent national census (in 2000), just 7% of Mexicans listed themselves as speakers of indigenous languages, but people of predominantly indigenous ancestry may actually total as many as 15% – around 16 million people. The biggest indigenous group is the Nahua, descendants of the ancient Aztecs. Over two million Nahua are spread around central Mexico, chiefly in the states of Puebla, Veracruz, Hidalgo, Guerrero and San Luis Potosí. Southeastern Mexico has a particularly high indigenous population. The approximately 1.5 million Yucatec Maya speakers on the Yucatán Peninsula are direct descendants of the ancient Maya, and the Tzotziles and Tzeltales of Chiapas (400,000 to 500,000 of each) are probably descendants of Maya who migrated there at the time of the Classic Maya downfall.

Also directly descended from well-known pre-Hispanic peoples are the estimated 800,000 Zapotecs, mainly in Oaxaca; the 770,000 Mixtecs, mainly in Oaxaca, Guerrero and Puebla; the 400,000 Totonacs, in Veracruz and Puebla; and the 150,000 Purépecha in Michoacán (descendants of the pre-Hispanic Tarascos). There are 50 or so other indigenous peoples, some now comprising only a few hundred people.

Mel Gibson has turned his beady eye on Mexican ethnic history with a film entitled *Apocalypto*, which is set during the mysterious ancient Maya collapse, and began shooting in Mexico in 2005 with dialogue in the Yucatecan Maya language. Early reports suggest it presents a rather sensationalized representation of Maya history.

THE LESS THE MERRIER?

Overpopulation still looms as perhaps Mexico's greatest problem. The population in 1940 was 20 million, and in 2003 it passed 100 million. The situation seemed hopeless in 1968 when the Vatican banned all methods of contraception. In 1970, more than 600,000 Mexican women underwent illegal abortions, and 32,000 died.

Government-sponsored clinics were established to offer birth-control literature, and by 1992 more than 6000 family-planning centers were established. Mexifam is the largest nongovernment family-planning service, concentrating on the poorest areas of the country; it does not advocate abortion but does provide information on 'morning after' pills to prevent pregnancy. The goal of government and privately funded programs was to reach a balance between births and deaths by 2005. This has not quite been achieved, but population growth has been reduced from 3.4% in 1970 to 1.2% in 2005 – from seven children per woman to 2.4.

NORTH OF THE BORDER

An estimated 15 million Mexicans live in the US, where average wages are six times higher than in Mexico. Mexicans in the US each send back, on average, $1000 a year to Mexico, making them the country's second biggest source of foreign exchange (after oil). Some 400,000 more Mexicans move north each year, many of them paying an average $1200 to be smuggled across the border by 'coyotes.' A million or more are apprehended annually in the attempt, and hundreds die from drowning or thirst (in the deserts straddling the border) or from being hit by vehicles on US highways.

In 2006 it was estimated that about one in three of the Mexicans in the US was there illegally. In 2004 US president George W Bush proposed allowing undocumented immigrants to apply for three-year temporary work permits (renewable once), which would give them full legal rights and entitlement to minimum wages. But by 2006 this idea remained unlegislated, and Congress was debating plans for 1130km of fence along parts of the 3326km US–Mexico border to keep illegals out.

RELIGION
Roman Catholicism

Nearly 90% of Mexicans profess Catholicism – a remarkable figure considering the rocky history that the Catholic church has had in Mexico.

The church was present in Mexico from the very first days of the Spanish conquest. Enlightened churchmen such as Bartolomé de Las Casas, bishop of Chiapas, and Vasco de Quiroga in Michoacán helped to protect indigenous Mexicans from the excesses of early colonial rule. Until Mexico's independence it was really the only unifying force in Mexican society and was the principal provider of social services and education. The Jesuits were among the foremost providers and administrators, establishing missions and settlements throughout Mexico. Their expulsion from Mexico in 1767 marked the beginning of stormy church–state relations. From then until 1940, Mexico passed numerous measures restricting the church's power and influence. The bottom line was money and property, both of which the church amassed more successfully than the generals and political bosses. The 1917 Mexican constitution prevented the church from owning property or running schools or newspapers, and banned clergy from voting or wearing clerical garb. Church–state relations bottomed in the 1920s, when the Cristeros (Catholic rebels) burned government schools, murdered teachers and assassinated a president, while government troops killed priests and looted churches. But most of the anti-church provisions in the constitution ceased to be enforced during the second half of the 20th century, and in the 1990s President Salinas had them removed from the constitution. In 1992 Mexico established diplomatic relations with the Vatican.

For more on Nuestra Señora de Guadalupe, check out www.interlupe.com.mx.

The Mexican Catholic Church is one of Latin America's more conservative. Only in the south of the country have its leaders become involved in political issues such as human rights and poverty, most notably Samuel Ruiz, long-time bishop of San Cristóbal de Las Casas, who retired in 1999.

The Mexican church's most binding symbol is Nuestra Señora de Guadalupe, the dark-skinned manifestation of the Virgin Mary who appeared to an Aztec potter, Juan Diego, near Mexico City in 1531. The Virgin of Guadalupe became a crucial link between Catholic and indigenous spirituality, and as Mexico grew into a mestizo society she became the most potent symbol of Mexican Catholicism. Today the Virgin of Guadalupe is the country's patron, her blue-cloaked image is ubiquitous, and her name is invoked in religious ceremonies, political speeches and literature.

Indigenous Religion

The missionaries of the 16th and 17th centuries won the indigenous people over to Catholicism by grafting it onto pre-Hispanic religions. Often old gods were simply renamed as Christian saints, and the old festivals continued to be celebrated much as they had been in pre-Hispanic times, but on the nearest saint's day. Acceptance of the new religion was greatly helped by the appearance of the Virgin of Guadalupe in 1531.

WHEN THE DEAD RETURN

Mexico's most characteristic and perhaps oddest fiesta, Día de Muertos (Day of the Dead), has its origins in the belief of the pre-Hispanic Tarasco people of Michoacán that the dead could return to their homes on one day each year.

The underlying philosophy is that death does not represent the end of a life, but the continuation of life in a parallel world. This day when the dead could return was a month after the autumn equinox. The occasion required preparations to help the spirits find their way home and make them welcome. An arch made of bright yellow marigold flowers was put up in each home, as a symbolic doorway from the underworld. *Tamales*, fruits, corn and salt were placed in front of the arch on an altar, along with containers of water because spirits always arrived thirsty after their journey. Traditionally, the spirits of departed children visited on the first night and the spirits of dead adults came on the following night, when they joined their living relatives to eat, drink, talk and sing.

Come the Spanish conquest, the Catholic celebrations of All Saints' Day (November 1) and All Souls' Day (November 2) were easily superimposed on the old 'day of the dead' traditions, which shared much of the same symbolism – flowers for the dead, offerings of food and drink, and the burning of candles. All Souls' Day is the Catholic day of prayers for those in purgatory; All Saints' Day was understood as a visit by the spirits of children who immediately became *angelitos* (little angels) when they died. The growing mestizo community evolved a new tradition of visiting graveyards and decorating graves of family members.

Día de Muertos persisted in the guise of Catholic celebration throughout the colonial period, when the idea of death as a great leveler and release from earthly suffering must have provided comfort for the overwhelmingly poor populace. After independence, poets used the occasion to publish verses ridiculing members of the social elite by portraying them as dead, with all their wealth and pretensions rendered futile. The great Mexican engraver José Guadalupe Posada (1852–1913) expressed similar sentiments in his famous *calaveras* – skeletal figures of death cheerfully engaging in everyday life, working, dancing, courting, drinking and riding horses into battle. One of his most enduring characters is La Calavera Catrina, a female skeleton in an elaborate low-cut dress and flamboyant flower-covered hat, suggestively revealing a bony leg and an ample bust that is all ribs and no cleavage.

In indigenous communities, most notably the Purépecha of Michoacán, Día de Muertos is still very much a religious and spiritual event today. For them, the observance is more appropriately called Noche de Muertos (Night of the Dead) because families will actually spend whole nights at the graveyard – the night of October 31/November 1 with the sprits of dead children, the following night with the spirits of dead adults.

For Mexico's mestizo majority, Día de Muertos is more of a popular folk festival and family occasion. People may visit a graveyard to clean and decorate family graves, but they do not usually maintain an all-night vigil. And though they may pray for the souls of the departed and build altars in their homes to welcome them back, the Catholic belief is that those souls are in heaven or in purgatory, not actually back on a visit to Earth. Sugar skulls, chocolate coffins and toy skeletons are sold in markets everywhere as gifts for children as well as graveyard decorations; they derive as much from Posada's work as from the icons of the ancient death cults.

Many Mexicans today are concerned that the American Halloween tradition, whose pumpkin heads, friendly ghosts and kids' costume parties are increasingly evident in Mexico, may be a threat to the continuance of Día de Muertos traditions. But the uniquely Mexican attitude to life and death expressed by Día de Muertos – profoundly fatalistic yet eternally optimistic – is very deeply rooted. It will probably absorb the pagan festival of Halloween just as it adapted to Catholicism over 400 years ago.

Indigenous Christianity is still fused with ancient beliefs today. In some remote regions Christianity is only a veneer at most. The Huichol people of Jalisco have two Christs, but neither is a major deity. Much more important is Nakawé, the fertility goddess. The hallucinogen peyote is a crucial source of wisdom in the Huichol world. Elsewhere, among peoples such as the Tarahumara and many Tzotzil people in highland Chiapas, intoxication is an almost sacred element at festival times. In a visit to the church at the Tzotzil village of San Juan Chamula (p826), you may see chanting *curanderos* (healers) carrying out shamanic rites.

Even among the more orthodox Christian indigenous peoples, spring saints' festivals, or the pre-Lent carnival, may still be accompanied by remnants of fertility rites. The famous flying Totonac *voladores* (see p678) enact one such ritual. The Guelaguetza dance festival, which draws thousands of visitors to Oaxaca every summer, has roots in pre-Hispanic maize-god rituals.

In the traditional indigenous world almost everything has a spiritual dimension – trees, rivers, plants, wind, rain, sun, animals and hills have their own gods or spirits. Witchcraft, magic and traditional medicine survive. Illness may be seen as a 'loss of soul' resulting from the sufferer's wrongdoing or from the malign influence of someone with magical powers. A soul can be 'regained' if the appropriate ritual is performed by a *brujo* (witch doctor) or *curandero*.

Other Christian Faiths

Around 7% of Mexicans practice other varieties of Christianity. Some are members of the Methodist, Baptist, Presbyterian or Anglican churches set up by US missionaries in the 19th century. Others have been converted since the 1970s by a wave of American Pentecostal, Evangelical, Mormon, Seventh-Day Adventist and Jehovah's Witness missionaries. These churches have gained millions of converts, particularly among the rural and indigenous peoples of southeast Mexico, some of whom have come to view Catholicism as just another part of a political apparatus that has subjugated them for centuries. This has led to some serious strife with Catholics, notably in and around San Juan Chamula in Chiapas.

WOMEN IN MEXICO

Hollywood turned its attention to the Ciudad Juárez feminicides with *Bordertown*, filmed in 2005, with Jennifer Lopez playing a US reporter sent to investigate the killings.

Mexico may be the home of machismo, but machismo is no longer the norm among the younger and more educated generations. Education and jobs are more accessible for young women, with enrolment rates for women at all levels of education similar to those for men, and 40% of the country's professional and technical jobs held by women. But women's wages overall still trail far behind men's, averaging less than half of what men earn. Among the poor, women still tend to play out traditional domestic and mothering roles, though they may also have part-time jobs or sell produce at market.

Women have had the vote since 1947 and currently hold 21% of seats in the national Congress.

Violence against women, especially among the poor and the socially dislocated, remains a serious problem. The hundreds of murders of women in Ciudad Juárez have gained much publicity (see boxed text, p355), but violence against women may actually be more widespread, though less reported, in impoverished southern rural areas such as Guerrero and Chiapas.

SPORTS
Soccer (Football)

No sport ignites Mexicans' passions as much as *fútbol*. Games in the 20-team national Primera División (First Division) are watched by large crowds and followed by millions on TV. Mexico City's Estadio Azteca (Aztec Stadium) hosted the 1970 and 1986 World Cup finals. Attending a game is fun; rivalry between opposing fans is generally good-humored. Tickets are sold at the entrance for anything from $5 to $25, depending on the quality of the seat.

The two most popular teams in the country are América, of Mexico City, known as the Águilas (Eagles), and Guadalajara (Chivas – the Goats). They have large followings wherever they play and matches between the two, known as 'Los Clásicos,' are the biggest games of the year. Other leading clubs are: Cruz Azul (known as La Máquina – The Machine) and UNAM (Universidad Autónoma de Mexico, known as Pumas), both from Mexico City; Universidad Autónoma de Guadalajara (Los Tecos) and Atlas, both from Guadalajara; Monterrey and Universidad Autónoma de Nuevo León (Los Tigres), both from Monterrey; Toluca, Pachuca, Necaxa of Aguascalientes and Santos of Torreón. It was at Pachuca that soccer was introduced to Mexico by miners from Cornwall, England, in the 19th century.

Crowds at Primera División games normally range from a few thousand to 70,000. Games are spaced over the weekend from Friday to Sunday; details are printed in the newspapers. The Primera División's season is divided into the Torneo de Apertura (Opening Tournament, August to December) and the Torneo de Clausura (Closing Tournament, January to June), each ending in eight-team play-offs (La Liguilla) and eventually a two-leg final to decide the champion. There's a uniquely complicated system of promotion and relegation with the Primera División A,

> The Spanish-language Mundo Soccer (www .mundosoccer.com) and FutMex (www.futmex .com) give Mexican soccer scores, standings, and upcoming games. FutMex also has links to club websites.

THE BALL GAME, THEN & NOW

Probably all pre-Hispanic Mexican cultures played some version of the mesoamerican ritual ball game, the world's first-ever team sport. The game varied from place to place and era to era, but had certain lasting features. Over 500 ball courts have survived at archaeological sites around Mexico and Central America. The game seems to have been played between two teams, and its essence was to keep a rubber ball off the ground by flicking it with hips, thighs, knees or elbows. The vertical or sloping walls alongside the courts were likely part of the playing area. The game had (at least sometimes) deep religious significance, serving as an oracle, with the result indicating which of two courses of action should be taken. Games could be followed by the sacrifice of one or more of the players – whether winners or losers, no one is sure.

The ancient ball game survives in Mexico today, somewhat modified (and without human sacrifice), in at least three areas and several different forms. All are team sports of around five a side, played on whatever open ground is available. The Pelota Mixteca (Mixtec Ball Game) is played regularly in numerous towns and villages in Oaxaca state, including Ejutla, Nochixtlán and Bajos de Chila near Puerto Escondido. Participants hit the ball with a thick heavy glove. A competition is held in Oaxaca city at the time of the Guelaguetza festival in late July. Oaxacan migrants have exported the game to other parts of Mexico and even to Santa Barbara and Fresno, California.

The Juego de Pelota Purépecha (Purépecha Ball Game) is played in the state of Michoacán, chiefly around the Lago de Pátzcuaro and in Angahuan, Zacán and Aranza. Participants use a stick to hit the ball. In Sinaloa the game is known as *ulama* and has some resemblance to volleyball in that the playing area is divided into two halves, with teams trying to return the ball back to the opposing half.

which you need the astrological capabilities of an ancient Aztec priest to understand.

Mexico's national team, known as El Tri (short for Tricolor, the name for the national flag), reached the last 16 of the World Cup in 1994, 1998 and 2002 – though it will take Mexicans a long time to get over the disappointment of being eliminated by the US in Korea in 2002!

Bullfighting

Bullfighting is another Mexican passion, though less widespread than soccer. Fights take place chiefly in the larger cities, often during local festivals.

To many gringo eyes, the *corrida de toros* (bullfight; literally, running of the bulls) hardly seems to be sport. To Mexicans it's as much a ritualistic dance as a fight, and it's said that Mexicans arrive on time for only two events – funerals and bullfights.

The *corrida de toros* begins promptly at an appointed time in the afternoon, usually on a Sunday. To the sound of a Spanish *paso doble*, the matador (literally, 'killer'), in his *traje de luces* (suit of lights), and the *toreros* (his assistants) give the traditional *paseillo* (salute) to the fight authorities and the crowd. Then the first of the day's bulls (there are usually six in an afternoon) is released from its pen.

Each bull is fought in three *suertes* (acts) or *tercios* (thirds). In the first, the cape-waving *toreros* spend a few minutes tiring the bull by luring him around the ring, then two *picadores*, on heavily padded horses, enter and jab long *picas* (lances) into the bull's shoulders to weaken him. Somehow this is often the most gruesome part of the whole process.

After the *picadores* leave the ring the *suerte de banderillas* begins, as the *toreros* attempt to stab three pairs of elongated darts into the bull's shoulders without getting impaled on his horns. Finally comes the *suerte de muleta*, the climax in which the matador has exactly 16 minutes to kill the bull. Starting with fancy cape work to tire the animal, the matador then exchanges his large cape for the smaller *muleta* (a small piece of cloth attached to the end of a short stick) and takes sword in hand, baiting the bull to charge before delivering the fatal *estocada* (lunge) with his sword. This must be done into the neck from a position directly in front of the animal.

If the matador succeeds, and he usually does, the bull collapses and an assistant dashes into the ring to slice its jugular. If the applause from the crowd warrants it, he will cut off an ear or two and sometimes the tail for the matador. The dead bull is dragged from the ring to be butchered for sale.

A 'good' bullfight depends not only on the skill and courage of the matador but also the spirit of the bulls. Animals lacking heart for the fight bring shame on the ranch that bred them. Very occasionally, a bull that has fought outstandingly is *indultado* (spared) – an occasion for great celebration – and will then retire to stud.

In northern Mexico the bullfighting season generally runs from March or April to August or September. In Mexico City's Monumental Plaza México, one of the world's biggest bullrings, and other rings in central and southern Mexico, the main season is from October or November to March. The veteran Eloy Cavasos, from Monterrey, is often acclaimed as Mexico's top matador. Eulalio 'Zotoluco' López is another major established name. Ignacio Garibay, José Luis Angelino and José María Luévano are younger stars in their 20s and early 30s. Bullfights featuring star matadors from Spain, such as Enrique Ponce, El Juli or José Tomás, have extra spice.

The Mesoamerican Ballgame (www.ballgame .org) is an interesting educational website about the indigenous ball game, with film of a contest in action.

For details of upcoming fights, biographies of matadors and much more on bullfighting, visit Portal Taurino (www .portaltaurino.com /mexico/mexico.htm), in Spanish and (sort of) English.

Baseball

Professional *béisbol* has a strong following. The winner of the October-to-January Liga Mexicana del Pacífico (www.ligadelpacifico.com.mx in Spanish), with teams from northwest Mexico, represents Mexico in the February Serie del Caribe (the biggest event in Latin American baseball) against the champions of Venezuela, Puerto Rico and the Dominican Republic. The two strongest clubs are the Tomateros of Culiacán and the Naranjeros of Hermosillo. Younger American players on the way up often play in the Pacific league. The Liga Mexicana de Beisbol (www.lmb .com.mx in Spanish), with 16 teams spread down the center and east of the country from Monclova to Cancún, plays from March to September – the Tigres of Puebla is its strongest club.

Other Sports

Charreadas (rodeos) are held, mainly in the northern half of Mexico, during fiestas and at regular venues often called *lienzos charros*.

The highly popular *lucha libre* (wrestling) is more showbiz than sport. Participants in this pantomime-like activity give themselves names like Shocker, Tarzan Boy, Virus and Heavy Metal, then clown around in Day-Glo tights and lurid masks. For the audience it provides a welcome change from real life because the good guys win. Most bouts pit *técnicos* (craftsmen) against *rudos* (rule-breakers). The *rudos,* who usually wear black and adopt dirty tactics, usually get the upper hand early on, only to be pounded by the *técnicos* in a stunning reversal of fortune towards the end of the bout.

Also popular is boxing, in which Mexico has produced many world champions. The legendary Julio César Chávez won five world titles at three different weights, and achieved an amazing 90 consecutive wins after turning pro in 1980. Chávez was a classic Mexican boxer – tactically astute but also able to take punishment and hand out even more.

One variant of the Purépecha ball game, Juego de la Pelota Encendida (Game of the Burning Ball), is played with a ball in flames, symbolizing the sun. Players need sufficient dexterity to avoid being burned!

ARTS
Painting & Sculpture

Mexicans have had an exciting talent for painting since pre-Hispanic times. The wealth of modern and historic art in mural form and in the country's many galleries are highlights of Mexico.

PRE-HISPANIC

Mexico's first civilization, the Olmecs of the Gulf coast, produced remarkable stone sculptures depicting deities, animals and wonderfully lifelike human forms. Most awesome are the huge Olmec heads, which combine the features of human babies and jaguars. The earliest outstanding Mexican murals are found at Teotihuacán, where the colorful *Paradise of Tláloc* depicts the delights awaiting those who died at the hands of the water god, Tláloc.

The Classic Maya of southeast Mexico, at their cultural height from about AD 250 to 800, were perhaps ancient Mexico's most artistically gifted people. They left countless beautiful stone sculptures, complicated in design but possessing great delicacy of touch. Subjects are typically rulers, deities and ceremonies. The art of the later Aztecs reflects their harsh worldview, with many carvings of skulls and complicated symbolic representations of gods.

COLONIAL PERIOD

Mexican art during Spanish rule was heavily Spanish-influenced and chiefly religious in subject, though portraiture grew in popularity under wealthy patrons. The influence of indigenous artisans is seen in the elaborate altarpieces and sculpted walls and ceilings, overflowing with tiny detail, in churches and monasteries, as well as in fine frescoes such as those at Actopan monastery in Hidalgo state (p203). Miguel Cabrera (1695–1768), from Oaxaca, was arguably the most talented painter of the era; his scenes and figures have a sureness of touch lacking in others' more labored efforts. They can be seen in churches and museums all over Mexico.

INDEPENDENT MEXICO

The landscapes of José María Velasco (1840–1912) capture the magical qualities of the countryside around Mexico City and areas farther afield, such as Oaxaca.

The years before the 1910 revolution saw a break from European traditions and the beginnings of socially conscious art. Slums, brothels and indigenous poverty began to appear on canvases. The cartoons and engravings of José Guadalupe Posada (1852–1913), with their characteristic *calavera* (skull) motif, satirized the injustices of the Porfiriato period. Gerardo Murillo (1875–1964), also known as Dr Atl, displayed some scandalously orgiastic paintings at a 1910 show marking the centenary of the independence movement.

THE MURALISTS

In the 1920s, immediately following the Mexican Revolution, education minister José Vasconcelos commissioned leading young artists to paint a series of public murals to spread a sense of Mexican history and culture and awareness of the need for social and technological change. The trio of great muralists were Diego Rivera (1886–1957), José Clemente Orozco (1883–1949) and David Alfaro Siqueiros (1896–1974).

Rivera's work carried a clear left-wing message, emphasizing past oppression of indigenous people and peasants. His art pulled the country's indigenous and Spanish roots together in colorful, crowded tableaus depicting historical people and events, or symbolic scenes of Mexican life, with a simple moral message. Many of Rivera's greatest works are in and around Mexico City (see boxed text, p145).

Siqueiros, who fought on the Constitutionalist side in the revolution (while Rivera was in Europe), remained a political activist afterward. His murals lack Rivera's realism but convey a more clearly Marxist message through dramatic, symbolic depictions of the oppressed, and grotesque caricatures of the oppressors. Some of his best works are at the Palacio de Bellas Artes, Castillo de Chapultepec and Ciudad Universitaria, all in Mexico City.

Orozco, from Jalisco, focused more on the universal human condition than on historical specifics. He conveyed emotion, character and atmosphere. By the 1930s Orozco grew disillusioned with the revolution. His work reached its peak in Guadalajara between 1936 and 1939, particularly in the 50-odd frescoes in the Instituto Cultural Cabañas.

Among their successors, Rufino Tamayo (1899–1991) from Oaxaca (also represented in Mexico City's Palacio de Bellas Artes) was absorbed by abstract and mythological scenes and effects of color. Many of his works are easily identified by his trademark watermelon motif (his father was a fruit seller). Juan O'Gorman (1905–82), a Mexican of Irish ancestry, was even more realistic and detailed than Rivera. His multicolored mosaic interpretation of Mexican culture on the Biblioteca Central at Mexico City's Ciudad Universitaria is his best-known work.

The best books on Mexican artists include Diego Rivera's autobiography *My Art, My Life*; Patrick Marnham's biography of Rivera, *Dreaming with his Eyes Open*; Hayden Herrera's *Frida: A Biography of Frida Kahlo*; *Frida Kahlo* by Malka Drucker; and *Mexican Muralists* by Desmond Rochfort.

OTHER 20TH-CENTURY ARTISTS

Frida Kahlo (1907–54), physically crippled by a road accident and mentally tormented in her tempestuous marriage to Diego Rivera, painted anguished self-portraits and grotesque, surreal images that expressed her left-wing views and externalized her inner tumult. Kahlo's work suddenly seemed to strike an international chord in the 1980s, almost overnight becoming as renowned as Rivera's. Thanks to the 2002 Hollywood biopic *Frida*, she's now better known worldwide than any other Mexican artist.

After WWII, the young Mexican artists of La Ruptura (The Rupture) reacted against the muralist movement, which they saw as too didactic and too obsessed with *mexicanidad* (Mexicanness). They opened Mexico up to world trends such as abstract expressionism and pop art. One leader of La Ruptura was José Luis Cuevas (b 1934), some of whose work you can see at the Mexico City art museum founded by and named for him. Other interesting artists to look for include Zacatecan Francisco Goitia (1882–1960), who conveyed the hardships of indigenous life; brothers Pedro (1923–85) and Rafael (b 1931) Coronel, also from Zacatecas; and Oaxacans Francisco Toledo (b 1940) and Rodolfo Morales (1925–2001).

Despite faint critical praise, *Frida*, Julie Taymor's 2002 factually informative movie biography, shouldn't be missed for its strong Mexican period atmosphere and a fine performance by Mexican Salma Hayek as Ms Kahlo.

CONTEMPORARY ART

The unease and irony of postmodernism found fertile ground among Mexico's ever-questioning intelligentsia from the late 1980s onward. The many privately owned galleries that have sprung up display an enormous diversity of attempts to interpret the uncertainties of the early 21st century. Frida Kahlo, with her unsettling, disturbing images from a 'pre-modern' era from which many postmodernists drew inspiration, stands as a kind of mother figure amid the maelstrom. Contemporary Mexican artists are mostly ironic individualists who can't be categorized into movements or groups. A few artists who incorporate Mexican themes, such as Dulce María Núñez and Nahum B Zenil, are labeled 'neo-Mexicanists.' The colorful canvases of Núñez juxtapose popular icons such as saints, sports figures and cacti to show their impact on the everyday lives and psyches of Mexicans. Zenil, perhaps emulating Kahlo, is best known for his self-portraits, which confront contemporary social issues including homosexuality and AIDS. Sergio Hernández incorporates the indigenous iconography and popular culture of his native Oaxaca state into his abstract, colorful canvases and sculptures.

The abstract painting of Francisco Castro Leñero is an extension of La Ruptura. Castro Leñero is a minimalist who employs collage and geometric forms and uses color sparingly; his works have been likened to musical compositions. In general, however, the pendulum has swung away from abstraction to hyper-representation and photo-realism. In the work of Rocío Maldonado, Rafael Cauduro and Roberto Cortázar you'll see classically depicted figures against amorphous, bleak backgrounds. Cauduro paints photo-realistic landscapes of eroded, urban surfaces, often populated by prostitutes and other street characters, the cast-off remains of civilization.

The best way to catch up on the art scene is simply to visit some of the better contemporary galleries. See the city sections in this guide for recommendations. The current epicenters of contemporary Mexican art are Mexico City and Oaxaca. Monterrey, with its Museo de Arte Contemporáneo (Marco) is another focus. *La Jornada* newspaper has a great cultural section with daily listings of exhibitions and culture of all kinds.

Architecture

Mexico's beautiful and awe-inspiring architectural heritage ranks among its biggest attractions.

PRE-HISPANIC

Hook into the Mexico City art scene and get a glimpse of its stunning colors and images through Arte Mexico (www.arte-mexico .com in Spanish), with a calendar of exhibitions, data on artists and galleries, maps and more.

The ancient civilizations produced some of the most spectacular, eye-pleasing architecture ever built. At Teotihuacán, Monte Albán, Chichén Itzá and Uxmal you can still see fairly intact pre-Hispanic cities. Their spectacular ceremonial centers were designed to impress, with great stone pyramids, palaces and ball courts. Pyramids usually functioned as the bases for small shrines on their summits. Mexico's three biggest pyramids are the Pirámide del Sol and Pirámide de la Luna, both at Teotihuacán, and the Pirámide Tepanapa at Cholula, near Puebla.

There were many differences in style between the pre-Hispanic civilizations: while Teotihuacán, Monte Albán and Aztec buildings were relatively simple in design, intended to awe with their grand scale, Maya architecture paid more attention to aesthetics, with intricately patterned facades, delicate 'combs' (grid-like arrangements of stone with multiple gaps) on temple roofs, and sinuous carvings. Buildings at Maya sites such as Uxmal, Chichén Itzá and Palenque are among the most beautiful human creations in the Americas. Maya buildings are characterized by the corbeled vault, their version of the arch: two stone walls leaning toward one another, nearly meeting at the top and surmounted by a capstone.

COLONIAL

Many of the fine mansions, churches, monasteries and plazas that today contribute so much to Mexico's beauty were created during the 300 years of Spanish rule. Most were in basic Spanish styles, but with unique local variations.

Gothic and renaissance styles dominated colonial building in Mexico in the 16th and early 17th centuries. Gothic is typified by soaring buttresses, pointed arches, clusters of round columns and ribbed ceiling vaults. The renaissance saw a return to the disciplined ancient Greek and Roman ideals of harmony and proportion, with shapes such as the square and the circle predominating. In Mexico, it usually took the form of plateresque (from *platero,* meaning 'silversmith,' because its decoration resembled ornamented silverwork). Plateresque commonly appears on the facades of buildings, particularly church doorways, which have round arches bordered by classical columns and stone sculpture. A later, more austere renaissance style was called Herreresque, after the Spanish architect Juan de Herrera. Mérida's cathedral and Casa de Montejo are outstanding renaissance buildings. The cathedrals of Mexico City and Puebla mingle renaissance and baroque styles.

Gothic and renaissance influences were combined in many of the fortified monasteries that were built as Spanish monks carried their missionary work to all corners of Mexico. Monasteries usually had a large church, a cloister and often a *capilla abierta* (open chapel), from which priests could address large crowds of indigenous people. The many notable monasteries include Actopan and Acolman in central Mexico, and Yanhuitlán, Coixtlahuaca and Teposcolula in Oaxaca.

The Spanish Muslim–influenced style known as Mudejar can be seen in some beautifully carved wooden ceilings and in the decorative feature known as the *alfiz,* a rectangle framing a round arch. The 49 domes of the Capilla Real in Cholula almost resemble a mosque.

Baroque style, which reached Mexico from Spain in the early 17th century, combined renaissance influences with other elements aimed at a dramatic effect – curves, color, contrasts of light and dark, and increasingly elaborate decoration. Painting and sculpture were integrated with architecture, most notably in ornate, often enormous *retablos* (altarpieces). Fine baroque buildings in Mexico include the marvelous facade of Zacatecas' cathedral and the churches of Santiago Tlatelolco in Mexico City, San Felipe Neri in Oaxaca, and San Francisco in San Luis Potosí. Mexican baroque reached its final form, Churrigueresque, between 1730 and 1780. This was characterized by spectacularly out-of-control ornamentation – witness the Sagrario Metropolitano in Mexico City, the Ocotlán sanctuary at Tlaxcala and the churches of San Francisco Javier in Tepotzotlán, Santa Prisca in Taxco, and San Francisco, La Compañía and La Valenciana in Guanajuato.

Indigenous artisans added profuse sculpture in stone and colored stucco to many baroque buildings, such as the Capilla del Rosario in Puebla's Templo de Santo Domingo, and the nearby village church of Tonantzintla. Arabic influence continued with the popularity of *azulejos* (colored tiles) on the outside of buildings, particularly in and around Puebla.

Neoclassical style, dominant in Mexico from about 1780 to 1830, was another return to sober Greek and Roman ideals. Outstanding examples include the Palacio de Minería in Mexico City and the Alhóndiga de Granaditas in Guanajuato; the most prominent neoclassical architects were Eduardo Tresguerras and Spanish-born Manuel Tolsá.

19TH TO 21ST CENTURIES
Independent Mexico in the 19th and early 20th centuries saw revivals of Gothic and colonial styles and imitations of contemporary French or Italian styles. Mexico City's semi–art nouveau Palacio de Bellas Artes is one of the finest buildings from this era.

After the revolution of 1910–21, art deco made an appearance but more importantly was an attempt to return to pre-Hispanic roots in the search for a national identity. This trend was known as Toltecism, and many public buildings exhibit the heaviness of Aztec or Toltec monuments. Toltecism culminated in the 1950s with the UNAM campus in Mexico City, where many buildings are covered with colorful murals.

Modern architects have provided some cities with a few eye-catching and adventurous buildings as well as a large quota of dull concrete blocks. The icon is Luis Barragán (1902–88), who was strongly influenced by the functionalists Le Corbusier and Alvar Aalto, but also exhibited a strong Mexican strain in his use of vivid colors, textures, scale, space, light and vegetation, with small interior gardens. His own Mexico City home was made a Unesco World Heritage site in 2004 (see boxed text, p140).

Pedro Ramírez Vásquez (b 1919) is a modernist who designed three vast public buildings – the 1960s Estadio Azteca and Museo Nacional de Antropología and the 1970s Basílica de Guadalupe – in Mexico City. His work more or less ignores Mexican traditions. The two biggest names in contemporary Mexican architecture are Ricardo Legorreta (b 1931), who has designed a slew of large buildings in bold concrete shapes and 'colonial' orangey-brown hues, and Enrique Norton (b 1954), of TEN Arquitectos (www.ten-arquitectos.com), who works on a smaller scale with a lot of glass and an emphasis on the verticality of his buildings. Both have worked in the US and other countries as well as Mexico. Legorreta is responsible for Mexico City's Camino Real hotel and Centro Nacional

Bacaanda (www .bacaanda.org.mx in Spanish) is a collective of pioneering creative folk who stage a broad range of arts and multimedia events in and around Mexico City.

de las Artes, Monterrey's Museo de Arte Contemporáneo and much of the new south side of the Alameda Central in Mexico City.

The Art of Mesoamerica by Mary Ellen Miller is an excellent survey of pre-Hispanic art and architecture.

Music

In Mexico live music may start up at any time on streets, plazas or even buses. These musicians are playing for a living and range from marimba (wooden xylophone) teams and mariachi bands (trumpeters, violinists, guitarists and a singer, all dressed in smart wild-west-like costumes) to ragged lone buskers with out-of-tune guitars and sandpaper voices. Mariachi music (perhaps the most 'typical' Mexican music of all) originated in the Guadalajara area but is played nationwide (see boxed text, p540). Marimbas are particularly popular in the southeast and on the Gulf coast.

Such performers are just among the most visible actors of a huge and vibrant popular music scene in Mexico, which encompasses great stylistic and regional variety. Its outpourings can be heard live at fiestas, nightspots and concerts, or bought from music shops. Finding out who's playing where and when is mainly a matter of keeping an eye on posters and the entertainment pages of the press. Ticketmaster Mexico (www.ticketmaster.com.mx in Spanish) has a certain amount of information.

ROCK & HIP-HOP

So close to the big US Spanish-speaking market, Mexico can claim to be the most important hub of *rock en español*. Talented Mexico City bands such as Café Tacuba and Maldita Vecindad have taken their music to new heights and new audiences (well beyond Mexico), mixing a huge range of influences – from rock, hip-hop and ska to traditional Mexican *son* (folk music), bolero or mariachi. Café Tacuba's exciting handling of so many styles, yet with their own very strong musical identity, keeps them at the forefront of Mexican rock today. The albums *Re* (1994), *Avalancha de Éxitos* (1996), *Tiempo Transcurrido* (2001) and *Cuatro Caminos* (2003) are all full of great songs.

The city of Monterrey has produced hip-hop twosome Plastilina Mosh (a kind of Mexican Beastie Boys whose 1998 debut album *Aquamosh* was a huge success), hip-hoppers Control Machete, the Britpop-like Zurdok and metal-hip-hop band Molotov, who attract controversy with their expletive-laced lyrics in a mix of Spanish and English. They're angry about everything. Listen to *Frijolero,* an aggressive attack on US attitudes to Mexicans, from their album *Dance and Dense Denso* (2003).

Still one of the country's most popular bands is Jaguares, mystical Def Leppard–type rockers who spearheaded the coming of age of Mexican rock in the 1980s under the earlier name Caifanes.

Probably best known worldwide of all Mexican bands is Maná, which is from Guadalajara, and is an unashamedly commercial band with British and Caribbean influences, reminiscent of the Police. Not to be forgotten are El Tri, the grandfathers of Mexican rock, who after more than 30 years are still pumping out energetic rock and roll.

POP

Skinny Paulina Rubio is Mexico's answer to Shakira and Britney Spears. She has also starred in several Mexican films and TV series. Balladeer Luis Miguel (born in Veracruz in 1970), meanwhile, is Mexico's Julio Iglesias. Even if you don't know his voice you've probably heard about his love life.

Natalia Lafourcade, a young singer with a strong voice able to tackle varied styles, made her name with the title track on the 2002 film *Amar te Duele,* a romanticized Romeo and Juliet story set in contemporary Mexico City. Sometimes compared with Canada's Nelly Furtado, Lafourcade released *Natalia Lafourcade* in 2003. *Casa,* performed with her band Natalia y la Forquetina, followed in 2005.

ELECTRONIC MUSIC

Mexico has a big *punchis-punchis* (as they accurately call it) scene: almost every weekend there's a big event in or around one of the big cities, where you can check out the country's top DJs and also international guests from countries such as Germany or Israel. Top names include DJ Vazik (psychedelic) and DJ Klang (house and trance).

The Tijuana-based Nortec Collective is a group of northern DJs, centered on DJ Bostich and chemical engineer Pepe Mogt, that has melded traditional Mexican music with electronica into a unique, fun genre known as Nortec. Look for *The Nortec Sampler* (2000), *Tijuana Sessions Vol 1* (2001) or *Tijuana Sessions Vol 3* (2005). (There's no *Vol 2!*) Also a big success is Murcof, an ambient Nortec offshoot that uses elements of classical music to create some pretty moody tracks – try *Martes* (2001) or *Utopía* (2004).

Kinky, from Monterrey, successfully fuses Latin rock with electronics and are great live performers. Their albums are *Kinky* (2002) and *Atlas* (2003).

> Foreign rock acts were not allowed to play in Mexico until the late 1980s.

REGIONAL & FOLK MUSIC

The deepest-rooted Mexican folk music is *son* (literally, 'sound'), a broad term covering a range of country styles that grew out of the fusion of indigenous, Spanish and African musical cultures. *Son* is essentially guitars plus harp or violin, often played for a foot-stamping dance audience, with witty, frequently improvised lyrics. The independent Mexican label Discos Corasón has done much to promote these most traditional of Mexican musical forms.

The most celebrated brands of Mexican *son* come from four areas. Around Huasteca, inland from Tampico, *son huasteco* trios feature a solo violinist and two guitarists singing falsetto between soaring violin passages. Keep an eye open for *son* festivals or performances by top group Camperos de Valles. In Jalisco *sones jaliscenses* originally formed the repertoire of many mariachi bands.

The baking-hot region of the Río Balsas basin, southwest of Mexico City, produced perhaps the greatest *son* musician of recent decades, violinist Juan Reynoso. Around Veracruz, the exciting local *son jarocho* is particularly African-influenced; its principal instruments are harp, guitars and the *jarana,* a small guitar-shaped instrument. Harpist La Negra Graciana is one of the greats; Grupo Mono Blanco lead a revival of the genre with contemporary lyrics; also listen out for the groups Yndios Verdes and Los Utrera. *La Bamba* is a *son jarocho!*

Modern Mexican regional music is rooted in a strong rhythm from several guitars, with voice, accordion, violin or brass providing the melody. *Ranchera* is Mexico's urban 'country music.' This is mostly melodramatic stuff with a nostalgia for rural roots – vocalist-and-combo music, maybe with a mariachi backing. The hugely popular Vicente Fernández, Ana Bárbara, Juan Gabriel and Alejandro Fernández (Vicente's son) are among the leading *ranchera* artists now that past generations of beloved stars like Lola Beltrán, Lucha Reyes, Chavela Vargas and Pedro Infante have died or retired.

Norteño is country ballad and dance music, originating in northern Mexico but nationwide in popularity. Its roots are in *corridos,* heroic ballads with the rhythms of European dances such as the polka or waltz, which were brought to southern Texas by 19th-century German and Czech immigrants. Originally the songs were tales of Latino-Anglo strife in the borderlands or themes from the Mexican Revolution. The gritty modern ballads known as *narco-corridos* deal with drug-runners, coyotes and other small-time crooks trying to survive amid big-time corruption and crime, and with the injustices and problems faced by Mexican immigrants in the US. The superstars of *norteño* are Los Tigres del Norte, originally from Sinaloa but long based in California. They play to huge audiences on both sides of the frontier. *Norteño* groups *(conjuntos)* go for 10-gallon hats, with backing centered on the accordion and the *bajo sexto* (a 12-string guitar), along with bass and drums. Los Tigres del Norte added saxophone and absorbed popular *cumbia* rhythms from Colombia. Other leading *norteño* exponents include Los Tucanes de Tijuana, Los Huracanes del Norte, Los Pingüinos del Norte, vocalist Marco Antonio Solis and accordionist Flaco Jiménez.

Banda is Mexican big-band music, with large brass sections replacing *norteño's* guitars and accordion. Popular since the 1970s in the hands of Sinaloa's Banda el Recodo, it exploded in popularity nationwide and among Hispanics in the US in the 1990s.

Kinetik.tv (www.kinetik .tv in Spanish) has details of upcoming raves and parties.

An exciting talent is Oaxaca-born Lila Downs, who has an American father and Mexican Mixtec mother from Oaxaca. At one stage a Deadhead (Grateful Dead–camp follower), and also influenced by her relationship with US jazz-pianist Paul Cohen, Lila has emerged as a passionate and original reinterpreter of traditional Mexican folk songs. Her major albums are *La Sandunga* (1997), *Tree of Life* (2000) and *Border* (2001). She sang several songs on the soundtrack of the 2002 movie *Frida.* Another powerful interpreter of mainly Oaxacan songs is Susana Harp (*Mi Tierra,* 2002).

MÚSICA TROPICAL

Though its origins lie in the Caribbean and South America, several brands of *música tropical* or *música afroantillana* have become integral parts of the Mexican musical scene. Two types of dance music – *danzón,* originally from Cuba, and *cumbia,* from Colombia – both took deeper root in Mexico than in their original homelands (see p77). Some *banda* and *norteño* groups throw in a lot of *cumbia.* The leading Mexican exponents were probably Los Bukis (who split in 1995). Kumbia Kings, though based in Texas, are hugely popular in Mexico with their *cumbia*-rap-pop mix. Also listen out for lively Junior Klan from Tabasco.

TROVA

This genre of troubadour-type folk music has roots in 1960s and '70s songs. Typically performed by singer-songwriters *(cantautores)* with a solitary guitar, it's still popular. Nicho Hinojosa, Fernando Delgadillo and Alberto Escobar are leading artists.

Many *trova* singers are strongly inspired by Cuban political singer-songwriter Silvio Rodríguez. Powerful and popular singers like Eugenia León, Tania Libertad and the satirical cabaret artist Astrid Hadad are sometimes categorized under *trova* but they actually range widely over Mexican song forms – and are all well worth hearing.

Cinema

A clutch of fine, gritty movies by young directors thrust Mexican cinema into the limelight in the 1990s and early 2000s, garnering commercial success as well as critical acclaim after decades in the doldrums. These films confronted the ugly and the absurd in Mexican life as well as the beautiful, comical and sad. Alfonso Arau's *Como Agua para Chocolate* (Like Water for Chocolate; 1992) and Guillermo del Toro's 1993 horror movie *Cronos* set the ball rolling, then in 1999 Mexicans flocked to see Antonio Serrano's *Sexo, Pudor y Lágrimas* (Sex, Shame and Tears), a comic but sad tale of young couples' relationships, and Luis Estrada's black comedy of political corruption *La Ley de Herodes,* a damning indictment of the Partido Revolucionario Institucional (PRI).

> Fearful of *narco-corridos'* tendency to glorify the activities of drug runners, several Mexican state governments have encouraged radio stations to ban them.

But the one to really catch the world's eye, in 2000, was *Amores Perros* (Love's a Bitch), directed by Alejandro González Iñárritu and starring Gael García Bernal. Set in contemporary Mexico City, with three plots connected by one traffic accident, it's a raw, honest movie with its quota of graphic blood, violence and sex.

Y Tu Mamá También (And Your Mother Too), Alfonso Cuarón's 2002 'growing up' tale of two teenagers from privileged Mexico City circles, became the biggest grossing Mexican film ever, netting $11 million in Mexico and $13.6 million in the US. The teenagers (Gael García Bernal and Diego Luna) venture out of the city with an older woman in search of a paradisiacal beach called Boca del Cielo (Heaven's Mouth). On the way they discover lots of things about themselves and their country, raising themes such as class, sexuality and loyalty.

In Carlos Reygadas' 2002 movie *Japón* (Japan) a middle-aged Mexico City man goes to a village in Hidalgo state to commit suicide – and finds that the change of scene and society upsets all his certainties. It's a slow, meditative, no-easy-explanations film that some people love and others find frustrating (not least because it has nothing to do with Japan).

The 2002 success *El Crimen del Padre Amaro* (The Crime of Father Amaro), directed by Carlos Carrera and again starring Gael García Bernal, paints an ugly picture of corruption in the Catholic church in a small Mexican town.

Would Mexico's new cinematic talents continue to film in, and about, Mexico? Yes and no, it seems. After *Amores Perros,* Alejandro González Iñárritu moved to Hollywood to direct *21 Grams* with Sean Penn, Benicio del Toro and Naomi Watts – another great movie with multiple plots weirdly connected, but nothing to do with Mexico. But at the time of writing González Iñárritu was working from Tijuana on a multilingual trilogy starring Brad Pitt and Gael García Bernal. Alfonso Cuarón stepped from *Y Tu Mamá También* to directing *Harry Potter and the Prisoner of Azkaban* (2004), and García Bernal played Che Guevara in the 2004 US production *The Motorcycle Diaries*. Carlos Reygadas however stayed firmly at home with *Batalla en el Cielo* (Battle in Heaven; 2005), a graphic tale of kidnapping, prostitution and brutal Mexico City realities.

Meanwhile the latest Mexican director to emerge was Fernando Kalife, whose *7 Días* (7 Days), the story of a lowly music promoter's miraculous coup of getting U2 to play in his home town, Monterrey, was the country's big hit of 2005.

The golden age of Mexican movie-making was WWII, when the country was turning out up to 200 films a year, typically epic, melodramatic productions. Hollywood reasserted itself after the war and Mexican filmmakers have struggled for funds ever since. But Mexico has the world's seventh-biggest cinema-audience figures and locally made films attract around 10% of the audience. Mexico still has a high-class movie-making infrastructure, with plenty of technical expertise and up-to-the-minute equipment. By 2005 the country was producing around 50 films a year, a big increase since a few years before. Since 2003 the city of Morelia has held an annual international film festival (www.moreliafilmfest.com), intended to further promote Mexican cinema in international circles.

Literature

Mexicans such as Carlos Fuentes, Juan Rulfo and Octavio Paz produced some of the great Spanish-language writing of the 20th century.

Prolific novelist and commentator Carlos Fuentes (b 1928) is the best-known internationally. His first and one of his best novels, *Where the Air Is Clear* (1958), traces the lives of various Mexico City dwellers through Mexico's post-revolutionary decades in a critique of the revolution's failure. *The Death of Artemio Cruz* (1962) takes another critical look at the post-revolutionary era through the eyes of a dying, corrupted press baron and landowner. Fuentes' *Aura* (1962) is a magical book with one of the most stunning endings of any novel. *La Silla del Águila* (The Eagle Throne; 2003) again deals with political corruption and cynicism. It's set in 2020 at a time when an all-powerful USA has cut off Mexico's access to telecommunications and computers, Condoleezza Rice is US president, Fidel Castro is still in power, and a vicious struggle is being played out for the lifetime presidency of Mexico.

In Mexico, Juan Rulfo (1918–86) is widely regarded as the supreme novelist. His *Pedro Páramo* (1955), about a young man's search for his lost father among ghostlike villages in western Mexico, is a scary, desolate work with confusing shifts of time – a kind of Mexican *Wuthering Heights* with a spooky, magical-realist twist. Some acclaim it as the ultimate expression of Latin American existence – and Rulfo certainly never felt the need to write anything else afterward. His only other book, *The Burning Plain* (1953), is a collection of short stories of Jalisco peasant life.

Octavio Paz (1914–98), poet, essayist and winner of the 1990 Nobel Prize in Literature, wrote a probing, intellectually acrobatic analysis of Mexico's myths and the Mexican character in *The Labyrinth of Solitude* (1950). Decide for yourself whether you agree with his pessimistic assessments of his fellow Mexicans. Paz's *Sor Juana* (1982) reconstructed the life of Mexico's earliest literary giant, Sister Juana Inés de la Cruz, a 17th-century courtesan-turned-nun (and proto-feminist) whose love poems, plays, romances and essays were aeons ahead of their time (see p133).

The 1960s-born novelists who form the *movimiento crack* have nothing to do with drugs but takes their name from the sound of a limb falling off a tree – an image that represents these writers' desire to break with Mexico's literary past. Their work tends to adopt global themes and international settings. Best known is Jorge Volpi, whose *In Search of Klingsor* (1999) has been an international best-seller. With an exciting plot around post-WWII efforts to unmask the scientist in charge of Nazi Germany's atomic weapons program, it also weaves in a good deal of scientific theory to make sure your brain cells don't rest. The follow-up *El Fin de la Locura* (The End of Madness; 2003) deals with psychoanalysis and Marxism, and the third in the trilogy will be concerned with the fall of the Berlin Wall. Ignacio Padilla, too, takes Nazism as a theme in his sophisticated *Shadow Without a Name* (2000; published in Spanish as *Amphitryon*).

Northern Mexican writers, mostly born in the 1960s and focusing on themes like violence, corruption, drug trafficking, the border and conflicts of identity, are producing some of the most immediate and gritty Mexican writing today. Juan José Rodríguez (*Mi Nombre es Casablanca;* 2003), Raúl Manríquez (*La Vida a Tientas;* 2003) and Élmer Mendoza (*Un Asesino Solitario;* 1999) tell of explosive violence provoked by drug conflicts.

Arguably the most famous of all Mexican film actors was Zorba the Greek – Anthony Quinn (1915–2001), born Antonio Quiñones in Chihuahua. His family moved to the US when he was four months old.

The Mexican Revolution yielded a school of novels: the classic is *The Underdogs,* the story of a peasant who becomes a general, by Mariano Azuela (1873–1952). Modern writers have also been inspired by the revolution and its aftermath: Ángeles Mastretta (b 1949) views the era through a woman's eyes in the amusing *Tear This Heart Out* (1985), written as the memoir of the wife of a ruthless political boss. Laura Esquivel (b 1950) made her name with *Like Water for Chocolate* (1989), a love story interwoven with both fantasy and cooking recipes set in rural Mexico during the revolution.

Rosario Castellanos (1925–74), from Chiapas, an early champion of women's and indigenous rights, wrote of the injustices that provoked the 1994 Zapatista rebellion decades before it happened. *The Book of Lamentations* (1962) draws on earlier historical events for its story of an indigenous uprising in the 1930s.

In poetry, the great figures are Octavio Paz and a reclusive figure from Chiapas, Jaime Sabines (1925–99), who both treated themes of love and death with stark, vivid imagery.

Dance

INDIGENOUS DANCE

Colorful traditional indigenous dances are an important part of Mexican fiestas. There are hundreds of them, some popular in several parts of the country, others danced only in a single town or village. Many bear traces of pre-Hispanic ritual, having evolved from old fertility rites and other ancient practices. Other dances tell stories of Spanish or colonial origin – Oaxaca's Danza de las Plumas (Feather Dance) represents the Spanish conquest of Mexico, while the fairly widespread Moros y Cristianos re-enacts the victory of Christians over Muslims in 15th-century Spain.

Nearly all traditional dances require special colorful costumes, sometimes this includes masks. The Danza de las Plumas and the Danza de los Quetzales (Quetzal Dance), from Puebla state, both feature enormous feathered headdresses or shields.

Today some of these dances are performed outside their sacred context, as simple spectacles. The Ballet Folklórico in Mexico City brings together traditional dances from all over the country in a spectacular stage show. Other folkloric dance performances can be seen in several cities and at festivals such as the Guelaguetza, in Oaxaca on the last two Mondays of July.

LATIN DANCE

Caribbean and South American dances are popular in Mexico. This is tropical ballroom dancing, to percussion-heavy, infectiously rhythmic music. Mexico City has over a dozen clubs and large dance halls devoted to this scene: aficionados can go to a different hall each night of the week (see p173), often with big-name bands from the Caribbean or South America. One of the more formal, old-fashioned varieties of Latin dance is the elegant *danzón,* originally from Cuba and associated mostly with the port city of Veracruz. *Cumbia,* from Colombia but now with its adopted home in Mexico City, is livelier, more flirtatious and less structured. It rests on thumping bass lines with brass, guitars, mandolins and sometimes marimbas.

Salsa developed in New York when jazz met *son,* and cha-cha and rumba came from Cuba and Puerto Rico. Musically it boils down to brass (with trumpet solos), piano, percussion, singer and chorus – the dance is a hot one with a lot of exciting turns. Merengue, mainly from the Dominican Republic, is a *cumbia*-salsa blend with a hopping step; the rhythm catches the shoulders, the arms go up and down. The music is strong on maracas, and the musicians go for puffed-up sleeves.

Chronicle Books publish beautiful softback photo essays on Mexican style and crafts, including *Mexicolor* by Melba Levick, Tony Cohan and Masako Takahashi (on Mexican design), and *In a Mexican Garden* by Melba Levick and Gina Hyams.

Folk Art

Mexicans' skill with their hands and love of color, beauty, fun and tradition are expressed most ubiquitously in their myriad appealing *artesanías* (handicrafts). The highly decorative crafts that catch the eye in shops and markets today are counterparts to the splendid costumes, beautiful ceramics and elaborate jewelry used by the ancient Aztec and Maya nobility, and many modern craft techniques, designs and materials are easily traced to pre-Hispanic origins. The areas producing the most exciting *artesanías* are still mostly those with prominent indigenous populations, in states such as Chiapas, Guerrero, México, Michoacán, Nayarit, Oaxaca, Puebla and Sonora. Selling folk art to tourists and collectors has been a growing business for Mexican artisans since before WWII.

Diamond shapes on some *huipiles* from San Andrés Larrainzar, in Chiapas, represent the universe of the villagers' Maya ancestors, who believed that the earth was a cube and the sky had four corners.

TEXTILES

If you get out to some of Mexico's indigenous villages you'll be intrigued by the variety of intensely colorful, intricately decorated everyday attire, differing from area to area and often village to village. Traditional costume – more widely worn by women than men – serves as a mark of the community to which a person belongs. Some garments are woven or embroidered with a web of stylized animal, human, plant and mythical shapes that can take months to complete.

Four main types of women's garments have been in use since long before the Spanish conquest. A long, sleeveless tunic *(huipil)* is found mainly in the southern half of the country. The *enredo* is a wraparound skirt, almost invisible if worn beneath a long *huipil*. The *enredo* is held in place by a *faja* (waist sash). The *quechquémitl* is a shoulder cape with an opening for the head, found mainly in the center and north of Mexico.

Blouses, introduced by Spanish missionaries, are now often embroidered with just as much care and detail as the more traditional garments. The *rebozo,* which probably appeared in the Spanish era, is a long shawl that may cover the shoulders or head or be used for carrying. The male equivalent of the *rebozo,* also dating from the Spanish era, is the sarape, a blanket with an opening for the head.

The basic materials of indigenous weaving are cotton and wool, though synthetic fibers are now common too. Dye, too, is often synthetic today, but some natural dyes are still in use or are being revived – deep blues from the indigo plant; reds and browns from various woods; reds, pinks and purples from the cochineal insect (chiefly used in Oaxaca state).

The basic indigenous weaver's tool – used only by women – is the back-strap loom *(telar de cintura),* on which the warp (long) threads are stretched between two horizontal bars, one of which is fixed to a post or tree, while the other is attached to a strap that goes around the weaver's lower back; the weft (cross) threads are then woven in. A variety of sophisticated techniques is used to weave amazing patterns into the cloth. *Huipiles* in the southern states of Oaxaca and Chiapas are among Mexico's most intricate and eye-catching garments.

Indigenous costume and its patterning may have a magical or religious role, usually of pre-Hispanic origin. Among the Huichol people, who live in a remote region on the borders of Nayarit, Jalisco and Durango states, waist sashes are identified with snakes, which are themselves symbols of rain and fertility, so the wearing of a waist sash can be a symbolic prayer for rain.

One textile art that's practised by men is weaving on a treadle loom, which is operated by foot pedals. The treadle loom can weave wider cloth than the back-strap loom and tends to be used for blankets, rugs, wall hangings, *rebozos,* sarapes and skirt material. It allows for great intricacy in design. Mexico's most famous rug-weaving village is Teotitlán del Valle, Oaxaca.

The 'yarn paintings' of the Huichol people – created by pressing strands of wool or acrylic yarn onto a wax-covered board – make colorful and unique decorations. The scenes resemble visions experienced under the influence of the drug peyote, which is central to Huichol culture.

CERAMICS

Because of its durability, pottery tells us much of what we know about Mexico's ancient cultures. Today the country still has many small-scale potters' workshops, turning out everything from plain cooking pots to elaborate decorative pieces that are true works of art.

One highly attractive variety of Mexican pottery is Talavera, made chiefly in Puebla and Dolores Hidalgo and characterized by bright colors (blue and yellow are prominent) and floral designs. Another very distinctive Mexican ceramic form is the *árbol de la vida* (tree of life). These elaborate candelabra-like objects, often a meter or more high, are molded by hand and decorated with numerous tiny figures of people, animals, plants and so on. The Garden of Eden is a common subject, but trees of life may be devoted to any theme. Some of the best are made in Acatlán de Osorio and Izúcar de Matamoros, Puebla, and Metepec, in the state of México. Metepec is also the source of colorful clay suns.

The Guadalajara suburbs of Tonalá and Tlaquepaque are also renowned pottery centers, producing a wide variety of ceramics. In northern Mexico the villagers of Mata Ortiz produce a range of beautiful earthenware, drawing on the techniques and designs of pre-Hispanic Paquimé – similar to some of the native American pottery of the US southwest.

MEXICO THROUGH OTHERS' EYES

Mexico has inspired much fine writing from non-Mexicans. Graham Greene's *The Power and the Glory* dramatizes the state–church conflict that followed the Mexican Revolution. *Under the Volcano* (1938) by Malcolm Lowry follows a dipsomaniac British diplomat in Mexico who drinks himself to death on the Day of the Dead.

B Traven is perhaps best known as the author of the 1935 adventure story of gold and greed in northwest Mexico, *The Treasure of the Sierra Madre.* But he wrote many other novels set in Mexico, chiefly the six of the Jungle series – among them *The Rebellion of the Hanged, General from the Jungle* and *Trozas* – focusing on pre-revolutionary oppression in Chiapas. The identity of Traven himself is one of literature's great mysteries. Was he really a Bavarian anarchist called Ret Marut, or a Norwegian American living reclusively in Acapulco called Traven Torsvan? Quite likely he was both.

The beat generation too spent plenty of time in Mexico: William Burroughs' early novel *Queer* chronicles the guilt, lust and drug excesses of an American in Mexico City in the 1940s. The city was also the scene of parts of Burroughs' *Junky* and Jack Kerouac's *On the Road* and *Tristessa,* and was where Kerouac wrote his long work of jazz poetry *Mexico City Blues* and two other novels.

The 1990s brought some fine new English-language novels set in Mexico. Cormac McCarthy's marvelous *All the Pretty Horses* is the laconic, tense, poetic tale of three young latter-day cowboys riding south of the border. *The Crossing* and *Cities of the Plain* completed McCarthy's Border Trilogy. James Maw's *Year of the Jaguar* (1996) catches the feel of Mexican travel superbly, taking its youthful English protagonist from the US border to Chiapas in an exciting search for a father he has never met.

For nonfiction travel writing set in Mexico, see p27.

MASKS

For millennia Mexicans have worn masks for magical purposes in dances, ceremonies and shamanistic rites: the wearer temporarily becomes the creature, person or deity represented by the mask. Today, these dances often have a curious mixture of pre-Hispanic and Christian or Spanish themes. A huge range of masks exists and you can admire their artistry at museums in cities such as San Luis Potosí, Zacatecas, Morelia and Colima, and at shops and markets around the country. The southern state of Guerrero has produced probably the broadest range of fine masks.

Wood is the basic material of most masks, but papier-mâché, clay, wax and leather are also used. Mask-makers often paint or embellish their masks with real teeth, hair, feathers or other adornments. 'Tigers,' often looking more like jaguars, are fairly common, as are other animals and birds, actual and mythical, and masks depicting Christ, devils, and Europeans with comically pale, wide-eyed, mustachioed features.

Today, masks are also made for hanging on walls.

Chloe Sayer's fascinating Arts and Crafts of Mexico *traces the evolution of crafts from pre-Hispanic times to the present, with many fine photos.*

LACQUERWARE & WOODWORK

Gourds, the hard shells of certain squash-type fruits, have been used in Mexico since antiquity as bowls, cups and small storage vessels. Today they serve many other uses, including children's rattles, maracas and even hats. The most eye-catching gourd decoration technique is the lacquer process, in which the outside of the gourd is coated with layers of paste or paint, each left to harden before the next is applied. The final layer is painted with the artisan's chosen design, then coated with oil varnish to seal the lacquer. All this makes the gourd nonporous and, to some extent, heat resistant.

Wood, too, can be lacquered, and most lacquerware you'll see in Mexico today is pine or a sweetly scented wood from the remote town of Olinalá, Guerrero. Olinalá boxes, trays, chests and furniture are lacquered by the *rayado* method, in which designs are created by scraping off part of the top coat of paint to expose a different-colored layer below.

Among Mexico's finest wooden crafts are the polished *palo fierro* (ironwood) carvings of the Seri people of Sonora, who work the hard wood into dramatic human, animal and sea-creature shapes. Also attractive are the brightly painted copal dragons and other imaginary beasts produced by villagers around Oaxaca city.

Paracho, in Michoacán, turns out Mexico's finest guitars, as well as violins, cellos and other musical instruments.

The Crafts of Mexico is a gorgeously illustrated coffee-table volume focusing on ceramics and textiles, by Margarita de Orellana and Albertio Ruy Sánchez, editors of the superb magazine Artes de México.

BARK PAINTINGS

Colorful paintings on *amate* (paper made from tree bark) are sold in countless souvenir shops. Many are humdrum touristic productions, but others qualify as genuine art, showing village life in skillful detail. Bark paper has been made in Mexico since pre-Hispanic times, when some codices (pictorial manuscripts) were painted on it. The skill survives only among women in one small, remote area of central Mexico, where the states of Hidalgo, Puebla and Veracruz converge. One chief source of the paper is the village of San Pablito. Most of the product is bought by Nahua villagers from the state of Guerrero, who have been creating bark paintings since the 1960s.

JEWELRY & METALWORK

Some ancient Mexicans were expert metalsmiths and jewelers, but the Spanish banned indigenous people from working gold and silver for a time during the colonial period. Indigenous artisanship was revived in the 20th century – most famously in Taxco, by the American William Spratling, who initiated a silver-craft industry that now supplies more than 300 shops in the town. Silver is much more widely available than gold in Mexico, and is fashioned in all manner of styles and designs, with artistry ranging from the dully imitative to the superb.

Precious stones are less common than precious metals. True jade, beloved of ancient Mexicans, is a rarity; most 'jade' jewelry is actually jadeite, serpentine or calcite.

Oaxaca city is the center of a thriving craft of tinplate, stamped into low relief and painted in hundreds of colorful designs.

RETABLOS

An engaging Mexican custom is to adorn the sanctuaries of saints or holy images with *retablos* (also called *exvotos*), small paintings giving thanks to a saint for answered prayers. Typically done on small sheets of tin, but sometimes on glass, wood or cardboard, these *retablos* depict these miracles in touchingly literal images painted by their beneficiaries. They may show a cyclist's hair's-breadth escape from a hurtling bus, or an invalid rising from a sickbed, beside a representation of the saint and a brief message along the lines of 'Thanks to San Milagro for curing my rheumatism – María Suárez, June 6, 1999.' The Basílica de Guadalupe in Mexico City, the Santuario de Plateros near Fresnillo in Zacatecas and the church at Real de Catorce in San Luis Potosí state all have fascinating collections of *retablos*.

See a great collection of modern *retablos* and *exvotos* in *Contemporary Mexican Votive Painting* by Alfredo Vilchis Roque.

MEDIA

Mexican TV is still dominated by the Televisa group, which is the biggest TV company in the Spanish-speaking world, and runs four national networks and has many local affiliates, and is strongly linked with the PRI, the political party that ran Mexico as a virtual one-party state for 70 years until 2000. Since the PRI's grip was loosened, the rival Azteca group (two networks) and foreign satellite and cable operators have started to undermine Televisa's dominance. Network programming continues to comprise mainly soap operas *(telenovelas)*, ads, game shows, comedy, soccer and a bit of reality TV. However many hotel rooms are now endowed with multichannel cable or satellite systems giving access to international TV. Two good noncommercial Mexican channels, with plenty of arts and documentaries, are Once TV (11 TV), run by Mexico City's Instituto Politécnico Nacional, and Canal 22, run by Conaculta, the National Culture & Arts Council.

Mexico has around 1400 regional and local radio stations, with a good quota of local news and perky talk, as well as some often pretty bland music.

Newspaper and magazine journalism reflects the country's political and regional variety, with a spectrum of national dailies and hundreds of local dailies, and some serious magazine journalism. But the most popular press still lives on a diet of crime and road accidents, with gory photos of the victims. In many cases journalists remain constrained by the commercial requirements of their publishers – and can be subject to political pressures and the threat of violence from drug gangs or others if they make unwelcome revelations. The international watchdog group Reporters Without Borders declared Mexico to be Latin America's most dangerous country for journalists in 2005, a year in which at least six journalists were murdered.

For the online editions of about 300 Mexican newspapers and magazines, and links to hundreds of Mexican radio and TV stations and other media sites, visit www.zonalatina.com.

Environment

From the parched painted deserts of Sonora and Chihuahua, embroidered with a stubble of cactus and scrub and where only the toughest creatures survive, across alpine meadows and lava-spitting volcanoes, past coral reefs and teeming lagoons, and into the luxuriant greenery of the cloud forests and jungle-covered lowlands of the south, Mexico is one of the most biologically and geographically diverse countries on the planet. Just 1.4% of the Earth's land mass cradles 10% of its species, and more than 1000 birds, 400 mammals and 700 reptiles (a world record) move among the 26,000 different plants that carpet this spectacular country.

THE LAND

Covering almost two million sq km, Mexico is big: it's nearly 3500km as the crow flies (or 4600km by road) from Tijuana in the northwest to Cancún in the southeast. Mexico's spectacularly rugged topography helps to delimit travel routes and has yielded a diversity of cultures and ecosystems that makes travel here all the more fascinating.

High Plains & Sierras

The northern half of Mexico is dominated by extensions of the mountains and uplands of the western half of the US. A group of broad plateaus strung down the middle of the country, the Altiplano Central, is fringed by two long mountain chains – Sierra Madre Occidental on the west and Sierra Madre Oriental on the east. The altiplano rises in altitude from about 1000m in the north to more than 2000m in central Mexico. Most of the northern altiplano is occupied by the sparsely vegetated Desierto Chihuahuense (Chihuahuan Desert), which extends north into Texas and New Mexico. The southern altiplano is mostly rolling hills and broad valleys, and includes some of the best Mexican farm- and ranchland north of Mexico City.

Routes through the mountain chains fringing the Altiplano Central are tortuous and rare. Only two make it across the whole wide and rugged Sierra Madre Occidental: the Ferrocarril Chihuahua al Pacífico (Chihuahua Pacific Railway), which runs through the awesome canyon country of the Barranca del Cobre (Copper Canyon); and dramatic Hwy 40 from Durango to Mazatlán.

RJ Secor's *Mexico's Volcanoes: A Climbing Guide* is invaluable for those planning to pit themselves against the might of Mexico's central volcanic belt.

The two *sierras madre* meet where they run into the Cordillera Neovolcánica. This spectacular volcanic chain, strung east to west across the middle of Mexico, includes the active volcanoes Popocatépetl (5452m) and Volcán de Fuego de Colima (3820m), as well as the nation's other highest peaks – Pico de Orizaba (5611m) and Iztaccíhuatl (5286m). Mexico City lies in the heart of volcanic country, in a broad valley surrounded by extinct and active volcanoes including Popocatépetl and Iztaccíhuatl.

Coastal Plains

Narrow coastal plains lie between the *sierras madre* and the sea. The Gulf coast plain, an extension of a similar plain in Texas, is crossed by many rivers flowing down from the Sierra Madre Oriental. On the west side of Mexico, a relatively dry coastal plain stretches south from the US border almost to Tepic, in Nayarit state. Its northern end is part of a second great desert straddling the Mexico–US border – the Desierto Sonorense (Sonoran Desert). This desert also extends down onto the 1300km peninsula Baja California, which is divided from 'mainland' Mexico by the Sea of

Cortez (Golfo de California). Baja California's mountainous spine is a southward extension of the coastal ranges of California, USA.

South of the resort of Puerto Vallarta, the Pacific plain narrows to a thin strip as the coast turns more east than south. Another mountain chain, the Sierra Madre del Sur, stretches from west to east across the states of Guerrero and Oaxaca, ending at the Isthmus of Tehuantepec, the narrowest part of Mexico at just 220km wide. The north side of the isthmus is a wide, marshy plain, strewn with meandering rivers.

The Far South

East of the isthmus, Mexico's southernmost state, Chiapas, rises sharply from a fertile Pacific plain, El Soconusco, to highlands almost 3000m high, then falls away to lowland jungles that stretch into northern Guatemala. The jungle melts into a region of tropical savanna on the Yucatán Peninsula, a flat, low limestone platform separating the Gulf of Mexico from the Caribbean Sea. The tip of the peninsula is arid, almost desertlike.

> Mexico's youngest volcano, Paricutín (2800m), in Michoacán, only arose in 1943.

WILDLIFE

From the whales and giant cacti of Baja California to the big cats and scarlet macaws of the southeastern jungles, Mexico has exotic and fascinating fauna and flora. You need to make an effort to see the best of it; sometimes you have to head for some pretty remote areas. Fortunately the possibilities of doing just this are growing, with a number of ecotourism and active tourism firms ready to take you out to the most exciting natural sites Mexico has to offer.

Animals

In the north, domestic grazing animals have pushed the puma (mountain lion), bobcat, wolf, deer and coyote into isolated, often mountainous, pockets. Raccoons, armadillos and skunks are still fairly common, however. The Cuatro Ciénegas valley (p414), a strange and hauntingly beautiful oasis in the northern deserts, is renowned for its endemic species including several kinds of turtle and fish.

Baja California is famous for whale-watching in the early months of the year – gray whales swim 10,000km from the Arctic to breed in its coastal waters – but it's also a breeding ground for other big sea creatures such as sea lions and elephant seals. More than one-third of all the world's marine mammal species have been found in the Sea of Cortez. For a roundup of whale-watching hot spots, see boxed text, p284.

Mexico's coasts, from Baja to Chiapas and from the northeast to the Yucatán Peninsula, are among the world's chief breeding grounds for sea turtles. All the world's eight species are in danger of extinction, and seven of them inhabit Mexican waters, with some female turtles swimming unbelievable distances (right across the Pacific Ocean in the case of some loggerhead turtles) to lay eggs on the beaches where they were born. Killing sea turtles is illegal in Mexico, which has over a hundred protected nesting beaches. Even so, an estimated 400,000 eggs are taken illegally each year. The beaches of the smallest and most endangered sea turtle, the Kemp's ridley, are nearly all in the northeastern Mexican state of Tamaulipas (see p393). By contrast, Playa Escobilla, near the Oaxaca town of Puerto Escondido, is one of the world's main nesting grounds for the least endangered turtle, the olive ridley. Some 700,000 turtles come ashore here in a dozen *arribadas* (landfalls) between May and January.

Dolphins play along much of the Pacific coast, while many coastal wetlands, especially in the south of the country, harbor crocodiles *(caimans)*.

Underwater life is richest of all on the coral reefs off the Yucatán Peninsula's Caribbean coast, where there's world-renowned diving and snorkeling at places like Cozumel (p884).

Back on land, the surviving tropical forests of the southeast still harbor jaguars, ocelots, spider monkeys, two types of howler monkey (all endangered), tapirs, anteaters, peccaries (a type of wild pig), deer and some mean tropical reptiles, including boa constrictors. The big cats are reduced to isolated pockets mainly in eastern Chiapas, though they also survive in Tabasco and around Celestún in Yucatán. You may well see howler monkeys, or hear their eerie growls, near the Maya ruins at Palenque (p835) and Yaxchilán (p847).

In all warm parts of Mexico you'll meet two colorful and harmless, though occasionally alarming, lizards: the iguana, which can grow a meter or so long and comes in many different colors; and the tiny, usually green gecko, which has a habit of shooting out from behind a curtain or cupboard when disturbed. Geckos can startle you, but they're good news because they eat mosquitoes.

Lacantunia enigmatica, a catfish found in the Usumacinta basin in 2005, represents only the second newly discovered fish family since 1938, the Lacantuniidae.

Coastal Mexico is a marvelous bird habitat, especially on the estuaries, lagoons and islands of the northeast, on the Yucatán Peninsula and along the Pacific coast. Inland Mexico abounds with eagles, hawks and buzzards, and innumerable ducks and geese winter in the northern Sierra Madre Occidental.

Tropical species such as trogons, hummingbirds, parrots, parakeets and tanagers start to appear south of Tampico in the east of the country and from around Mazatlán in the west. The southeastern jungles and cloud forests are home to colorful macaws, toucans, guans and even a few resplendent quetzals. Yucatán has spectacular flamingo colonies at Celestún and Río Lagartos. Twenty of Mexico's 22 parrot and macaw species are at risk.

The most unforgettable insect marvel is Michoacán's Santuario Mariposa Monarca (p566), where the trees and earth turn orange when millions of monarch butterflies arrive every winter.

Plants

Northern Mexico's deserts are sparsely vegetated with cacti, agaves, yucca, scrub and short grasses. Between the deserts and the mountains a lot of land has been turned over to irrigation or grazing, or has become wasteland, but there are still natural grasslands dotted with mesquite, a hardy bush of the bean family. Baja California, because of its isolation, has a specialized and diverse flora, from the 20m-high cardón, the world's tallest cactus, to the bizarre boojum tree (see boxed text, p266).

The Sierras Madre Occidental and Oriental, the mountains of central Mexico, and the Sierra Madre del Sur still have big stretches of pine forest and (at lower elevations) oak forest. In the southern half of Mexico, high-altitude pine forests are often covered in clouds, turning them into cloud forests, an unusual environment with lush, damp vegetation, an enormous variety of colorful wildflowers, and epiphytes growing on tree branches. Oaxaca's Sierra Norte (p746) and El Triunfo Biosphere Reserve in Chiapas (p856) preserve outstanding cloud forests.

The natural vegetation of the low-lying areas of southeast Mexico is predominantly evergreen tropical forest (rain forest in parts). This forest is dense and diverse, with ferns, epiphytes, palms, tropical hardwoods such as mahogany, and fruit trees such as the mamey and the *chicozapote* (sapodilla), which yields *chicle* (natural chewing gum). Despite ongoing destruction, the Selva Lacandona (Lacandón Jungle) in Chiapas is the largest remaining tropical-forest area in the country, containing a large number of Chiapas' 10,000 plant species. The Yucatán Peninsula changes from rain forest in the south to dry forest in the north, with thorny bushes and small trees (including many acacias) resembling the vegetation of the drier parts of the Pacific coastal plain.

PARKS & RESERVES

Mexico has some spectacular national parks and other protected areas – about 10% (187,000 sq km) of its territory is under some kind of federal, state or municipal protection. Sadly, governments have never had the money for effective protection of these areas against unlawful hunting, logging, farming, grazing and species collection.

National Parks

Mexico's 67 national parks *(parques nacionales)* total 14,570 sq km. Many are tiny (smaller than 10 sq km) and around half of them were created between 1934 and 1940, often for their archaeological, historical or recreational value rather than for ecological reasons. Most recently created national parks protect offshore islands or coral reefs. Some national parks have no visitor infrastructure and draw few people; others are alive with weekend picnickers. Despite illegal logging, hunting and grazing, national parks have succeeded in protecting some big tracts of forest, especially the high coniferous forests of central Mexico.

Biosphere Reserves

Biosphere reserves *(reservas de la biosfera)* are based on the recognition that it is impracticable to put a complete stop to economic exploitation of many ecologically important areas. Instead, these reserves encourage sustainable local economic activities within their territory, except in strictly protected core areas *(zonas núcleo)*. Today Mexico has 35 biosphere reserves, covering 109,565 sq km. Sixteen of these are included in the Unesco biosphere reserves network; the others are recognized only at a national level. They range from deserts through dry and temperate forests to tropical forests and coastal areas. All focus on whole ecosystems with genuine biodiversity. Controlled tourism is seen as an important source of income in several of them, though they tend to be harder to access than national parks.

Mexican biosphere reserves have had varied success. Sian Ka'an, on the Caribbean coast, is one of the most successful, with lobster fishers accepting a two-month off-season for egg-laying, and some villagers turning from slash-and-burn farming and cattle grazing to drip irrigation and multiple crops, thus conserving the forest and increasing food yields. Sian Ka'an is also one of three Mexican natural sites with Unesco World Heritage listing: the others are El Vizcaíno whale sanctuary in Baja California, and the islands and protected areas of the Sea of Cortez (Golfo de California).

Planeta (www.planeta .com) brims with information and links for those wanting to delve deeper into Mexico's flora, fauna and environment.

Tropical Mexico – The Ecotravellers' Wildlife Guide by Les Beletsky is a well illustrated, informative guide to the land, air and sea life of southeastern Mexico.

YOU CAN HELP

You can do your bit for Mexico's fragile environment by not buying turtle, iguana, crocodile or black-coral products; by not disturbing coral or nesting turtles; and by not collecting wild cacti, their seeds or wild orchids. You can also support projects that promote sustainable development. If the human inhabitants of forests and wetlands can earn a living from hosting low-impact eco-tourism, then they may not cut down their forests or fish their lagoons dry. Many eco-conscious enterprises in Mexico are community-run, which ensures that any profit made from your visit goes to locals (who are often poor), and not to entrepreneurs from elsewhere.

ENVIRONMENTAL ISSUES

From the early 20th century, Mexican governments saw urban industrial growth, chemical-based agriculture, and the destruction of forests for logging and development as the way to prosperity. Growth in awareness since the 1970s has achieved only limited change. Even if they have the will, governments rarely have funds to implement major environment programs.

Mexico's most infamous environmental problem is Mexico City itself, a high-altitude metropolis that is now spreading over the mountainous rim of the Valle de México and threatening to fuse with the cities of Puebla and Toluca. The ring of mountains traps polluted air in the city, causing health problems for residents. In an effort to limit pollution levels, many vehicles are banned from the roads one day a week. Mexico City consumes two-thirds of Mexico's electricity and, despite extracting groundwater at a rate that causes the earth to sink all over the city, it still has to pump up about a quarter of its water needs from outside the Valle de México. One of the rivers that provides the capital with water is the Lerma, which then receives sewage and industrial effluent from many other towns on its way into poor Lago de Chapala (see p546), Mexico's biggest natural lake, near Guadalajara.

Waste water leaves Mexico City by a system of pumps and tunnels. Liquids from a 50km tunnel eventually feed into the Río Pánuco, which enters the Gulf of Mexico at Tampico carrying about 2000 tons of sewage a day.

From the city of Tijuana, raw sewage flows down the Río Tijuana into southern California, where the existing treatment plant is insufficient to stop toxic water entering the ocean. The US government and businesses are considering building a second plant in Mexico. Further east along the border, the Río Barvo del Norte receives huge amounts of sewage and industrial wastes, but farmers and cities still extract so much water that it dries up before reaching the Gulf of Mexico. Ciudad Juárez is one of the few cities on the Mexican side of the river to have a sewage treatment plant.

Urban growth is not only problematic in the capital. In some expanding towns near the US border, little more than half the population has running water or sewerage.

In rural areas, a crucial issue is forest conservation. Before the Spanish conquest, about two-thirds of Mexico was forested, from cool pine-clad highlands to tropical jungle. Today only around 15% of this (300,000 sq km) remains, and this is being reduced by around 10,000 sq km a year for grazing, logging and farming. The southern states of Chiapas and Tabasco have probably lost more than half their tropical jungles since 1980, a devastating loss of habitat for many of Mexico's wildlife species. Deforestation followed by cattle grazing or intensive agriculture on unsuitable terrain often leads to erosion. Around 13% of Mexican land is considered severely eroded, with an estimated 2000 sq km of fertile land lost annually.

The US Sierra Club's prestigious Chico Mendes Prize, for bravery and leadership in environmental protection, was awarded in 2005 to Felipe Arreaga and two other leaders of the Organización Ecologista de la Sierra de Petatlán, a peasant organization battling logging in the state of Guerrero. Arreaga was unable to collect the award because he was in jail on what he said was a trumped-up murder charge. One of the other recipients was in hiding after an attack in which two of his children were murdered.

Some tourism projects threaten fragile ecosystems. Developments along the 'Riviera Maya,' south of Cancún, threaten to kill off coral reefs, swamps and turtle-nesting beaches. Rampant development in Baja California endangers local water resources. In a few places, like the Pueblos Mancomunados of Oaxaca (p746), local ecotourism projects are trying to preserve environments by providing alternative, sustainable income for local people.

More than 900 of the world's 1500 or so cactus species are found in Mexico; 118 of them are threatened or endangered.

Birders should carry *Mexican Birds* by Roger Tory Peterson and Edward L Chalif or *Birds of Mexico & Adjacent Areas* by Ernest Preston Edwards.

Bioplanet@ (www .bioplaneta.com) is a broad grouping of community projects, companies, organizations and institutions committed to environmentally sustainable development in Mexico; it has an online purchasing facility for ecological products.

Park/Reserve	Features	Activities	Best Time to Visit
Parque Marino Nacional Arrecifes de Cozumel (p888)	coral reefs, clear waters, awesome variety of marine life, beaches	diving, snorkeling	year-round
Parque Marino Nacional Bahía de Loreto (p291)	islands, shores & waters of the Sea of Cortez	snorkeling	year-round
Parque Nacional Cañón del Sumidero (p812)	800m-deep flooded canyon	boat trips, wildlife spotting, adventure sports	year-round
Parque Nacional Iztaccíhuatl-Popocatépetl (p204)	live & extinct volcanic giants on rim of Valle de México	hiking, climbing	Nov-Feb
Parque Nacional Lagunas de Chacahua (p764)	coastal lagoons, beaches, waterbirds	bird-watching, boat trips	year-round
Parque Nacional Pico de Orizaba (p703)	Mexico's highest peak (5611m)	volcano hiking & climbing	Oct-Mar
Parque Nacional Volcán Nevado de Colima (p557)	live & extinct volcanoes; pumas, coyotes, pine forests	volcano hiking	Dec-May
Reserva de la Biosfera Calakmul (p962)	rain forest with major Maya ruins	visiting ruins, wildlife spotting	year-round
Reserva de la Biosfera El Cielo (p396)	mountainous transition zone btwn tropical & temperate ecosystems; birds, bats, orchids	hiking, birding, fishing, 4WD trips	year-round
Reserva de la Biosfera El Triunfo (p856)	cloud forests; many rare birds including resplendent quetzals	guided hiking, birding, wildlife-spotting	Jan-May
Reserva de la Biosfera El Vizcaíno (p284 & p287)	deserts & coastal lagoons where gray whales calve	whale-watching, treks to pre-Hispanic rock art	Feb-early Apr
Reserva de la Biosfera Montes Azules (p831, p845, p849)	tropical jungle, lakes, rivers; jungle	wildlife hikes, birding, canoeing/rafting, boat trips, wildlife-watching	year-round
Reserva de la Biosfera Pantanos de Centla (p804)	Large wetland region of rivers, lakes, marshes & mangroves; important wildlife sanctuary	Birding, boat & canoe trips, wildlife observation	Mar-May
Reserva de la Biosfera Ría Celestún (p938)	Estuary with petrified forest & plentiful bird life including flamingos	Bird-watching, boat trips	Mar-Sep
Reserva de la Biosfera Ría Lagartos (p950)	estuary with large flamingo colony & other water birds	bird-watching	year-round
Reserva de la Biosfera Sian Ka'an (p906)	Caribbean coastal jungle, wetlands & islands with incredibly diverse wildlife	birding, snorkeling & nature tours, mostly by boat	year-round
Santuario Mariposa Monarca (p566)	forests festooned with millions of monarch butterflies	butterfly observation	Dec-Feb

Environmental campaigning today is carried out mainly by small organizations working on local issues, though some successful campaigns in recent years have rested on broader-based support, even from outside Mexico. One was the defeat in 2000 of the plan for a giant saltworks at Laguna San Ignacio in Baja California, a gray-whale breeding ground. Another was the annulment in 2001 of a large hotel project at the Caribbean turtle-nesting beach of Xcacel. Ideas for hydroelectric dams on the Río Usumacinta, along Mexico's border with Guatemala, attract broad opposition whenever they resurface, owing to their consequences for the huge watershed of what is Mexico's biggest river and for the area's many Maya archaeological sites.

Food & Drink James Peyton

Regardless of your principal reason for visiting Mexico, if you delight in finding new and delicious foods, your culinary discoveries here will be etched in your memory beside a bright gold star. You can dine in an elegant restaurant in Mexico City where the meal's presentation is designed by an artist; you can sample local specialties in colorful, out-of-the-way villages; or you can time-travel with chefs who are rediscovering the cuisines of pre-Columbian Mexico. So vast and regional is Mexican cooking, your only problem will be getting beyond the highlights.

For those whose culinary tastes run to the tried and true, and for whom a sprinkling of black pepper is enough heat, hotel dining rooms and restaurants catering to tourists offer delicious renditions of familiar salads, steaks, seafood and pasta, with the heat confined to little bowls on the side. Whatever your tastes, you will quickly learn that Mexicans, from all walks of life, are extremely knowledgeable about their cuisine, and ever conscious of its cultural importance. More importantly, you will discover that they are anxious to share it with you.

When the Spanish arrived in Mexico, they found a diet based on corn, beans, squash, chilies, wild game and fish. While Spanish soldiers brought meats, nuts, fruits, cheese and spices, they forgot to bring cooks! So, in the time-honored tradition of invading armies, they enlisted local women who promptly mixed the new ingredients with their own, then either misunderstood or ignored their conqueror's instructions. The result was that the Spanish ingredients, instead of being made into Spanish foods, were used to create new versions of native Mexican dishes.

During the next 500 (almost) years, the two food cultures – with contributions from France, Africa, and Spain's outposts in Asia – continued to fuse, creating the cuisine, with its countless regional variations, that you will enjoy during your stay. People from all cultures will find the vast majority of Mexican food appealing, partly because it has been influenced by so many of their own traditions.

Many people visiting Mexico, especially from the US, expect to find some variation on the menus of their favorite Mexican restaurants – margaritas, nachos, sizzling fajita platters, the Number 1 combination plate etc. What they discover is that Tex-Mex, and the other styles found outside Mexico, are but simple regional variations of a cuisine that is far more varied and sophisticated than they ever dreamed. The truth is that most restaurants outside of Mexico serve only one aspect of the cuisine. Called *antojitos mexicanos* (little Mexican whims) it is roughly the equivalent of American hamburgers and hotdogs, or Britain's fish and chips, although with far more cultural significance. In Mexico's interior they consist of a nearly endless array of casual, universally beloved dishes like tacos, enchiladas, quesadillas, *tamales*, burritos, and a unique genre of sandwiches called *tortas*.

Today, Mexican cooking includes many fascinating aspects. In addition to *antojitos*, you will encounter Mexico's traditional dishes, including soups, *moles* and *pipianes* – special stews, often with more than 30 ingredients (see boxed text, p91). Along Mexico's Gulf and Pacific coasts you will discover an amazing variety of creative seafood dishes. For those who enjoy sophisticated upscale dining, Mexico's contemporary cooking style, *nueva cocina mexicana*, ('new Mexican cooking', which mixes and matches Mexican regional cooking in new and elegant ways) will be a gift from the food gods.

Cooking with Baja Magic (1997), by Ann Hazard, presents the favorite regional recipes of an experienced Baja traveler.

Diana Kennedy is the acknowledged doyenne of Mexican food. Her latest book, *From My Mexican Kitchen: Techniques and Ingredients* (2003), captures the essence of Mexico's complex food, and makes it available to cooks outside the country.

STAPLES & SPECIALTIES

Mexicans traditionally eat three meals each day, but not always at the time some visitors are accustomed to. *Dasayuno* (breakfast) conforms to the normal schedule, and is eaten anytime between about 7am and 10:00am. It consists of anything from coffee and *pan dulce* (delicious, 'sweet breads'), to the ever present *huevos rancheros* (a corn tortilla with fried eggs and a sauce of tomato, chili and onion) and a large selection of omelettes, filled with everything from squash blossoms to *chorizo* (a Mexican-style sausage). You will also find *chilaquiles,* made by heating meat or chicken in a red or green chili sauce with crispy, tortilla chips, and topping it with cheese and often with either a fried egg or dollop of cream. Tropical fruits, yogurt and granola are also popular all over Mexico, and the latter two have a delightfully rich, homemade quality. Coffee, tea, milk, and fresh-squeezed juices are commonly served with breakfast, as is *pan tostado* (toast).

The *comida* (lunch) is the main meal of the day, and is usually taken between about 1:30pm and 4:00pm. Nevertheless, restaurants catering to tourists often open by 11:30am or noon. (A terrific way to beat the crowds is to arrive before 1:30pm.) This meal usually consists of an appetizer, soup or salad, a main course of meat, poultry or seafood, usually served with rice and/or beans, and steaming hot tortillas. Dessert can be anything from pastry to flan, other confections and fresh fruit. While Mexicans prefer to spend a relaxing two or more hours over this meal, they have not escaped the stress of modern life, and there are ample coffee shops and fast-food outlets available for quick meals at nearly any time.

The *cena* (supper) in Mexico usually consists of a light meal, perhaps some soup or a few tacos around 8:00pm or 9:00pm. However, most restaurants are happy to serve the larger dinner that so many visitors desire throughout the normal evening hours.

Notwithstanding the above, please note that in resort areas meals often conform more to *norte americano* meal schedules, and lunch is commonly served by noon. Some of the better restaurants do not open for the main meal until 6:00pm.

Regional Specialties

If you are at all adventurous in culinary matters, what you eat in Mexico will depend to a large extent on where you are. The country has nearly every imaginable climate. Each produces different foods, and has

Restaurateur and chef Zarela Martinez has provided the perfect guide to the regional cooking of Veracruz. Zarela's *Veracruz: Mexico's Simplest Cuisine* (2004) is part travelogue, and is filled with anecdotes and recipes from places you can actually visit.

WE DARE YOU

A current culinary renaissance in Mexico features pre-Hispanic foods that are often accompanied by copious amounts of tequila's fiery cousin, *mezcal*. One of the most popular foods is *chapulines*, which are grasshoppers (purged of digestive matter and dried, you will be happy to hear). They come in large and small sizes, with the latter often being smoked, and are served in many ways, from a taco-filling to sautéed in butter and flamed in brandy. The small, smoked variety are actually quite tasty, and are less likely to leave bits of carapace and feelers protruding from your teeth!

Jumiles are beetles – actually a type of stink bug – esteemed in central Mexico during their season in late fall and early winter. They are usually either ground with chilies, tomatoes and *tomatillos* to make a sauce, or are used as a taco-filling, either toasted or live. In discussing the latter, Diana Kennedy says in *My Mexico*: 'The more fleet-footed ones have to be swept back into the mouth and firmly crunched to prevent them from escaping.' The flavor is unforgettable by nature and forgettable by choice.

Other favorites include stewed iguana, which tastes like a cross between chicken and pork, as does armadillo, whose copious small bones are their most irritating quality.

developed a distinctive regional cuisine. The following are some of the most famous and interesting.

IN & AROUND MEXICO CITY

Tlacoyos are turnover-shaped *antojitos* made with smooth, fragrant corn dough – sometimes from blue or green corn – filled with everything from squash blossoms to *huitlacoche,* and cooked to a crispy, golden perfection on ungreased griddles. A fixture of street stalls, they are now sometimes found in upscale restaurants.

Sábana means 'sheet,' and that perfectly describes these fork-tender tenderloin steaks, which are pounded until they have a diameter of up to one foot and are less than one-eighth of an inch thick, and are then quickly seared and often served with mushrooms, mild chilies and melted cheese.

Crepas de flor de calabaza and *huitlacoche* are similar to French dinner crepes, but are made into exotic temptations by their fillings of squash blossoms and inky *huitlacoche.* They are usually complemented with a rich sauce of cream and very mild chilies.

Barbacoa (Mexican-style barbecue food) is often still smoked in earthen pits. Around Mexico City it is usually made by smoking seasoned lamb that is wrapped in leaves of the maguey plant, the agave from which both tequila and *mezcal* are made. The fragrant, steaming packages are opened at the table and served with fresh-baked corn tortillas, guacamole and a *salsa borracha,* or drunken sauce that is made with chilies, pulque, beer or tequila.

Mexico City is full of *torterías,* where Mexico's unique sandwiches are served. Made with crusty French-style rolls called either *bolillos* or *teleras* (depending on their shape) with much of the inside crumb removed, they are filled with everything from *chorizo* and avocado (these are often called *pambazos or pambacitos*) to *tamal* smothered in chili sauce (called the *tamal-torta*). The *torta cubana* is Mexico's rendition of the famous Cuban sandwich.

PUEBLA

Puebla is the home of *mole poblano,* Mexico's most famous dish, and one that represents the mixing of Spanish and indigenous cultures. It is a must-try dish for visitors (see boxed text, opposite). Mexico's second most-famous dish (and the most expensive in restaurants), *chiles en nogada,* is also from Puebla. Invented to honor General and Emperor Iturbide for his leadership in achieving independence from Spain, it consists of large, mild *poblano* chilies stuffed with a *picadillo* (ground meat filling) containing fruits nuts and spices, and covered with a unique, perfectly smooth sauce of cream, cheese and walnuts, garnished with pomegranate seeds. The dish's colors—red, white and green—were designed to represent the nation's new flag. It is usually served only from September into November, when the walnut and *poblano* chili crops are at their best. More casual specialties from Puebla include *tacos arabes* and

MEXICAN TRUFFLES

Huitlacoche, sometimes spelled *cuitlacoche* (pronounced 'wheat-lah-coach-ay' or 'cweet-lah-coach-ay'), is a delicacy that is virtually unknown outside of Mexico. It's actually an inky-black fungus that grows on corn kernels and is used as a filling for everything from crepes to quesadillas. Its promoters often refer to it as 'Mexican truffles,' or 'corn mushrooms.' *Huitlacoche* imparts both its enchanting flavor and striking color to everything it touches, and is found most often around Mexico City and Puebla.

MOLE

Because they incorporate both New and Old World ingredients in original ways, *moles* are considered the most distinctive and important dishes in traditional Mexican cooking. They are also the least understood outside of Mexico, where only one version is usually served: *mole poblano* (Puebla-style *mole*). While it is the most famous dish in Mexico, and several other *moles* are similar, it is far from the only one. For example, Oaxaca is known as the 'Land of Seven Moles.' The most famous of these is *mole negro* (black *mole*), which is made special by the use of the *chilhuacle negro* chili, one that is rarely available elsewhere in Mexico. Other Oaxacan *moles* that many visitors enjoy include *mole colorado* (red *mole*), *coloradito* (a lighter red *mole*), and *verde* (green), which is made with chicken or pork, *tomatillos*, fresh green chilies, and served with corn dumplings. Particularly popular with visitors is *mancha-manteles* (tablecloth-stainer), made with pork in a dark red sauce of chilies, fruits and nuts. Versions of some of the above and many other *moles* are found throughout Mexico.

All *moles* have at least two things in common: they are made with many ingredients, each of which is cooked separately – fried, toasted, or broiled – before being combined, ground into a paste and then cooked again in oil or lard, then thinned with broth into a sauce. For example, *mole poblano* usually consists of 30 or more ingredients, including three or four different chilies (*anchos*, *mulatos*, *pasillas* and sometimes *chipotles*), oregano, thyme, marjoram, onions, garlic, tomatoes, *tomatillos*, plantains, raisins, cinnamon, coriander, cloves, sesame seeds, aniseed, pumpkin seeds, peanuts, almonds and, of course, chocolate – but only a small quantity, and never enough to do more than add a subtle dimension to the dish. This time-consuming process creates multiple layers of flavor and produces a complex, sophisticated result. It is the sauces that are the stars, and the turkey, chicken, pork, lamb or goat, with which the *moles* are served, play second fiddle. Another similarity is that, although *moles* resemble stews, they are thickened with their ingredients rather than with flour or another starch.

---

cemitas. The former are tacos made with thin, tortilla-like Arab bread and filled with pork that is grilled on huge vertical skewers, then served with *jocoque* (a type of yoghurt), honey and sometimes herb-infused olive oil. *Cemitas* are *tortas* (sandwiches) made with hollowed-out brioche-type rolls that are filled with *milanesa*, (breaded and fried pork, veal or beef), or roast turkey, avocado and Mexican-style string cheese.

OAXACA

In the Land of Seven Moles, *mole negro* (black *mole*) is by far the most well-known, and for good reason: its complexity rivals that of the best *mole poblanos*. *Chiles rellenos* (stuffed chilies) are very popular in Oaxaca, and are often filled with fruit and nut-laced ground meat fillings. One of the most interesting is made with the smoke-dried *pasilla de Oaxaca* chili, which can be served either fried in batter or simply heated with a salsa on the side. *Tasajo* is a very thin cut of meat rubbed with chili paste (which can be a bit tough). A little less fancy on the gastronomic scale, you will see outsized corn tortillas in the markets that have been cooked nearly crisp; called *tlayudas*, these make delicious snacks that are topped, pizza-style, with beans, cheese and other delights. Other special items you will discover in Oaxaca are *quesillo*, a delicious string-like cheese, and, of course, the regional favorite, *chapulines* (grasshoppers; see boxed text, p89).

Jim Peyton's *New Cooking from Old Mexico* (1999) includes a history of Mexican cooking, illustrated with traditional recipes. It also introduces Mexico's unique new contemporary cuisine, *nueva cocina mexicana*, a fusion between Mexico's traditional and regional cuisines with an emphasis on elegance and presentation.

THE YUCATÁN

The Yucatán's cuisine has its roots with the Maya, rather than the Aztecs or other tribes. It is quite distinct, and is often thought of as being less rich than the cooking of other areas. Defying this generality is the area's special version of *barbacoa*, and probably its best-known dish, *cochinita pibil*,

www.mexconnect.com
does a comprehensive job
of covering both Mexico
and its foods. Some
portions of the site are
free, but most require
a yearly subscription
of $30.

which literally means pit-style pork. To make this spectacular dish, pork is marinated in a *recado* (or spice-rub, featuring the ground red seeds of the *annato* tree), then wrapped in banana leaves and smoked or baked. It is served with a salsa made from Seville (sour) oranges, and the region's special *habanero* chilies – by far the world's hottest variety, but they are typically used with great moderation. A chicken version of the dish, called *pollo pibil*, is equally delicious and not as rich. Consider beginning your main meal or supper with a bowl of *sopa de lima* – lime soup made with a flavorful broth, shredded chicken, special limes found only in the Yucatán, and sizzling hot, fried corn tortilla strips. For breakfast, do not miss *huevos motuleños*, fried eggs sandwiched between quickly seared corn tortillas and topped with ham, green peas, tomato salsa and grated cheese. One of the Yucatán's greatest treats is *papadzules*, a light and tasty cross between enchiladas and soft tacos. Corn tortillas are dipped in a pumpkin-seed sauce, rolled around chopped hard-boiled egg, and garnished with a mild tomato sauce and pumpkin-seed oil. Other foods commonly found in the Yucatán are *pavo* (turkey), *venado* (venison) and *salbutes*, which are very small *tostadas*, topped with tomato, cabbage, onion and shredded chicken, turkey, venison or pork. All the above are often served with *salsa xnipec*, made with tomato, purple onion, sour orange juice and a touch of fiery *habanero* chili.

MICHOACÁN

The cities of Morelia and Patzcuaro are popular destinations within the state of Michoacán. The former is famous for *enchiladas de plaza*, which are cheese enchiladas served with chicken that is first poached then fried and garnished with potatoes carrots, onions and chilies. Patzcuaro is known for its lake, from which seemingly unlimited amounts of *pescado blanco* (white fish) are pulled. Sautéed in a filmy coating of egg and often served *al mojo de ajo* (with minced garlic sautéed in olive oil), the tender and mild fish filets are exquisite. A bit more ethnic in character are *charales*, tiny dried fish used in appetizers, tacos and soup. Michoacán is also famous for *carnitas*, chunks of pork simmered in lard until crisp and

THE MAGIC OF MEXICAN MAIZE

The fact that maize (otherwise known as corn) does not reseed itself leads us to conclude that corn was *developed* rather than discovered.

Although maize was a dietary staple in Mexico and the Americas for years, when the rest of the world – including Italy, Romania, Africa and later the US South – introduced it to their diets, people became seriously ill and often died. They called the malady 'corn sickness,' and we now call it pellagra.

It was not until the 1970s that scientists discovered why the people of Mexico were able to live on maize when nobody else could. The secret turned out to be a chemical process developed by the ancients. To make the *masa* (or dough) used to prepare their tortillas and other maize-based foods, the people dried it, then boiled it in water made alkaline with lime, seashells or ashes, and soaked it overnight. The next day the skins of the kernels were easily removed. Without this step, the dough would have been unpleasantly rough and difficult to shape. What the people probably did not realize was that this process did much more than permit a smooth dough. Now referred to as nixtamalization, it allowed the human body to absorb maize's essential nutrients, without which life could not be sustained. If not now, certainly until a few years ago, Mexican corn was indeed magic in that it possessed distinctive qualities that produced unaccountable or baffling effects. To this day, the nearly infinite, delightful ways corn is used by Mexican cooks remains a sort of magic at its very best!

meltingly tender, then served with corn tortillas and guacamole. They are lighter than they sound but don't tell your cardiologist! Consider beginning your meal with a bowl of *sopa tarasca*. Named for the local Tarascan Indians, it is made by pouring a tomato broth into each bowl over cheese, mild and fruity *ancho* chilies, and crisp fried tortilla strips, followed by a garnish of Mexican-style *creme fraiche*. This could be the original and best version of tortilla soup! Do not pass up the opportunity to savor *uchepos*, the area's incredibly delicious *tamales*, made with fresh rather than dried corn.

The owners of www .mexgrocer.com have in-depth experience with Mexican food products, and offer a large selection at reasonable prices.

VERACRUZ

To this day, Veracruz, where most Spanish conquerors and settlers first arrived in Mexico, maintains strong Spanish food traditions. Being Mexico's principal Caribbean port, it also combines the islands Afro-based food ways with those of the original inhabitants, so you are liable to find olives, capers, vinegar and tomatoes mixed with plantains and jalapeño chilies (named for Veracruz's city of Xalapa, sometimes spelled Jalapa). Perfectly fresh seafood is the order of the day, and by far the area's most famous dish is *huachinango veracruzana* (red snapper Veracruz style). Red snapper is broiled or sautéed and covered in a sauce with items similar to those mentioned above. You will also discover an infinity of delightful tomato- and chili-based seafood stews and soups. Additionally, some of the world's best coffee is grown in Veracruz, and its jungles are the source of the orchid from which vanilla is made.

www.fronterakitchens .com, by noted chef and restaurateur Rick Bayless, is partially promotional, but has a very nice selection of recipes and other information on Mexican food.

GUADALAJARA

Guadalajara is often said to be the most Mexican of cities, in that it embodies the mestizo (or combination of Spanish and indigenous influences); it certainly does so with its food. Two famous regional dishes include *pozole* and *birria*. *Pozole* is made by simmering hominy with meat (usually pork), chilies and herbs to make a stew or thick soup. *Birria* is a regional *barbacoa* where lamb or sometimes goat, seasoned with chili, is smoked then steamed, and served with a very special broth.

NORTHERN MEXICO

This region stretches from the Pacific to the Gulf of Mexico along the US border. Although it encompasses a vast and diverse area, it has many similar foods, several of which are prepared *al carbón* (char-broiled) over mesquite coals, and served as often with flour tortillas as corn. *Tacos al carbón* (tortillas filled with char-broiled meats, poultry or fish) are a specialty throughout the north. In Tijuana you will find them made from New York cut steak, and in other areas from different cuts of meat, chicken, fish or shrimp. The steaks, ribs and other cuts, such as *mollejas* (sweetbreads) are also broiled over mesquite, and have the incomparable flavor of grass-fed beef. In the state of Sonora you will find burritos and *chimichangas* (deep-fried burritos) where their huge, paper-thin *tortillas de agua* (water tortillas) are filled with minced, sun-dried beef called either *carne seca* or *machacado*. In Chihuahua, a state of huge *ranchos*, T-bone steaks are served with mild, ripe chilies fried with onions. Perfectly fresh black bass (referred to by its English name) comes from nearby reservoirs and rivals the popularity of beef. It is delicious when broiled over mesquite and served *al mojo de ajo*, (with garlic sauce). In Monterrey the specialty is *cabrito al pastor*, (shepherd-style kid) where the whole animal is cooked on a spit over glowing coals. The *pierna* (leg) and *riñones* (kidneys) are the most esteemed cuts, with the former the most popular with visitors.

Jim Peyton's www .lomexicano.com is updated quarterly and offers regional Mexican recipes, food-related travel articles and a large glossary of Mexican food terms.

http://mexicanfood.
about.com provides many
recipes for Mexican foods.

In the state of Coahuila you will find broiled and deep-fried quail, and *parrilladas*, which are platters heaped with a selection of char-broiled beef and poultry, often including sweetbreads and *chorizo* – the ultimate mixed grill! In this area you will also find the original fajitas (char-broiled skirt steak), usually called *arracheras*. Another prized steak is called *agujas,* a thin cut from the eye of the chuck.

DRINKS
Alcoholic

Before the Spanish Conquest, two of Mexico's most important drinks were tapped from maguey (agave) plants. *Aguamiel* is non-alcoholic sweet juice, which comes straight from the plant. After fermentation it becomes pulque, a delicious beverage, with around the alcohol content of beer, which was consumed by indigenous Mexicans for over 5000 years. Now it's often flavored with coconut and other fruits. It is not bottled, and is found almost exclusively in special (often seedy) bars called *pulquerías.*

After their arrival in Mexico, Spaniards quickly discovered that by roasting the hearts of agaves, then extracting, fermenting and distilling the liquids, they could produce fiery alcoholic beverages called tequila and *mezcal* (see boxed text, p546 and p736).

Contrary to popular belief, the margarita is not the most popular way to drink tequila in Mexico. That ubiquitous cocktail, whose origin is the subject of several legends, is largely an American invention whose popularity has recently spread south of the border. Besides establishments that are accustomed to tourists, finding a properly made margarita can still be problematic, and a tequila sour is often a safer bet. Tequila is customarily imbibed straight, followed either by a lick of salt and a bite of lime wedge, or by a chaser of *sangrita* – a mixture of orange juice, grenadine, a dash of chili, and sometimes a dollop of tomato juice. *Mezcal,* whose finest examples are produced in Oaxaca, is traditionally taken neat.

Another popular drink in all parts of Mexico is rum and coke, served with a wedge of lime and referred to as a 'Cuba libre.'

During the 19th century, beer made by immigrants with roots in Germany and Switzerland became popular in Mexico. To this day, the country produces some of the world's best examples, with Bohemia, Corona, Dos Equis, Pacifica, Tecate and Modelo being favorite brands.

Brandy is popular all over Mexico. Although not of the quality of the better French cognacs, Presidente, Madero and Viejo Vergel produce decent renditions at very reasonable prices.

Spain, in an effort to reduce competition to its home industry, carefully controlled the production and use of wine in Mexico, much of which was restricted to use for Catholic communion. Nevertheless, the family of President Madero (also of brandy fame) operated a winery for many years, originally begun in 1597 near Parras. Although its production has either dwindled or ceased, there has been a renaissance of wine-making in Mexico, particularly in Baja near Ensenada, and near Fresnillo in Zacatecas. Often run by international corporations, the quality of Mexican wines is making great leaps. Ask your waiter for recommendations, and conduct your own taste test! But be aware that wine-drinking in Mexico is still pretty much restricted to upper-class establishments, and that in other spots the word for wine, *vino,* is often used to include distilled alcoholic drinks in general.

Mexico is full of lesser-known alcoholic drinks, many of them generically called *aguardiente* and a bit on the crude side, but also others that are quite interesting. There is *rompope*, a type of eggnog originally developed in monasteries and convents, which is bottled throughout the country. In

Baja, a sweet liqueur called *damiana* is made from an herb with purported aphrodisiacal qualities, which makes a terrific addition to margaritas.

Non-alcoholic

Mexico has a long tradition of non-alcoholic drinks. Many of them are either teas made from herbs and other items, steeped in boiling water and mixed with sugar. The most popular include *tamarindo*, made with tamarind pods, and *jamaica,* made with dried hibiscus leaves.

Aguas frescas, or 'fresh waters', are a mix of pulped fruits, cornmeal or rice, blended with water. *Horchata* is one made with melon fruit and seeds and/or rice, and limeaid is ubiquitous. These delicious, fruity drinks are sold from large, keg-shaped, glass containers, often garnished with mint leaves. Note that although these are prepared with boiled water, sometimes the ice is untreated.

Mexicans also enjoy a variety of smoothies and milk shakes called *licuados*, made with milk, fruits, yogurt and honey. Orange juice, nearly always fresh-squeezed, is available everywhere, as are juices of other fruits and vegetables. Many of these items are found in street *puestos* (stalls) and larger, bar-like establishments.

Some of the best coffee in the world is grown in Mexico, especially in Veracruz. Mexicans have a unique way of making it called *café de olla,* where it is brewed in a special clay vessel with a raw sugar called *piloncillo* and cinnamon. *Café con leche* (coffee with milk), is very popular. Waiters will often pour both items at the table according to your instructions. For ordinary coffee, with cream on the side, simply ask for *café con crema.*

Chocolate originated in Mexico, and Moctezuma, the Aztec king, finished nearly every meal with cup of it. Mexican chocolate often includes cinnamon and some crushed almonds, and has a unique flavor and texture. As a drink, it is mixed with milk or water and sugar, and whipped to a cappuccino-like froth with a decorative wooden implement called a *molinillo.* Sometimes a little ground cornmeal is added to create a delicious pre-Hispanic drink called *champurrado.*

Like Water for Chocolate, besides being a great book and film, also shows the importance of food in Mexico, and the use of magic-realism showcases the way so many Mexicans view life.

CELEBRATIONS

The importance of food in Mexican celebrations cannot be overemphasized. When the Spanish arrived they were surprised to find many similarities between their own religious fasts and food traditions, and those of the Aztecs. They were horrified to find ceremonies where blood mixed with ground amaranth was eaten in a manner resembling their own communions. One result was that amaranth, which was of great importance as the earliest ripening crop, was banned. To this day it is seldom used except in the famous *alegría* candies where amaranth seeds are mixed with honey.

Food is a vital aspect of virtually every celebration in Mexico, perhaps the most important being Día de Muertos (see p976). In the week leading up to it, people bake and buy a special, sweet bread, called *pan de muertos* (bread of the dead) and make *tamales,* which are part of nearly every other celebration, as they were in pre-Hispanic times.

During Lent, special meatless menus appear in restaurants. Favorite items include *romeritos, revoltijo* and *tortas de camarón,* all of which are made with the special green vegetable, *romeritos,* and dried shrimp. These same dishes are also popular during Holy Week and at Christmas. Another Easter favorite is *capirotada,* an elaborate pudding made with bread, cream, fruit, cinnamon, cheese and brandy or rum. *Bacalao,* Spanish-style, dried codfish, is traditionally served at Christmas, as are the ubiquitous celebratory *tamales,* and turkey is a New Year's favorite.

WHERE TO EAT & DRINK

You will have a nearly dizzying array of places to eat in Mexico, from simple street-vendor stalls, called *puestos*, to fine restaurants rivaling the world's best in both food and decor.

Hotel restaurants and cafés are good for breakfast, with the former often offering opulent buffets. In the afternoon, you can chose anything from a *taquería* (a place specializing in tacos, sometimes with twenty or more different varieties) to upscale restaurants. In between are small restaurants offering reasonably priced *comidas corridas* (prix-fixe menus). There are also *torterías* specializing in sandwiches, *loncherías* offering light meals like sandwiches and tacos, and cafés resembling American coffee shops.

Most top hotels have restaurants that serve a combination of Mexican dishes and international favorites. Even restaurants catering mostly to tourists will usually serve authentic Mexican food, albeit a bit blander than usual. Most restaurants that offer meals throughout the day are open from 7am or 8am, until between 10pm and midnight. However, be aware that some of them may not begin serving what we consider lunch until 1:30pm.

Both *cantinas* and bars serve alcoholic beverages. *Cantinas* are the traditional gathering place for men (women were barred from them by law until recently), and each one has its own culture: think *Cheers* with an edge. They are famous for the *botanas* (appetizers) which include things like pickled pigs feet. While women may now be allowed in *cantinas*, it is not recommended unless you are with a regular. Bars fit the typical definition of drinking places, and range from upscale establishments with leather, brass and stained glass, to the just plain sleazy. Instead of the more elaborate food items found in *cantinas*, bars usually serve only salty snacks.

QUICK EATS

Within the central *mercados* (markets) you will find numerous, small eating places, called either *fondas* or *comedores*, which serve everything from sandwiches to *comidas corridas*, and sweets. Most cities also have branches of US fast-food outlets. You will find *panaderías* (bakeries) selling traditional items all over Mexican towns; for a terrific light breakfast, dessert or snack, stop and pick up a selection. The system requires you to grab an aluminum tray and a pair of tongs, place your treats on the tray, and bring it to the cashier. You will be amazed at how much you get for so little cost.

If you have adventurous food tastes you will be attracted to the countless *puestos*, or street stalls. They offer tacos and other *antojitos* in every imaginable form – steamed or char-broiled corn, rotisserie-broiled chicken, creative hot dogs, seafood cocktails, ice cream, and just about anything else you can imagine. Many are popular and well-patronized, but hygiene can be a risk. Deciding whether to use them is a matter of judgment; those with a lot of customers are likely to be the best and safest. It is a good idea to avoid things that spoil easily (like mayonnaise), salads that may not have been properly washed, and fruit that has not been recently washed and peeled. With a common-sense approach you should have no problems, other than what might be expected when you introduce new foods into your system.

TIPPING, TAXES & ETIQUETTE

While a 15% IVA (or value-added tax) is added to restaurant checks in Mexico by law, but gratuities are not. Expected tips are about the same as those in the United States, with 15% being the average. People from some European countries where tips are included, are often not aware of this. Also, unless given great provocation, it is *de rigeur* to treat waiters with respect.

MEXICO'S TOP FIVE

■ Located in the heart of Tijuana's tourist district, at the corner of Revolución and Third, Los Panchos serves possibly the best *tacos al carbón* around, made with char-broiled New York steak and nearly perfect corn tortillas. Grab a taco-to-go at the stall outside the small restaurant, or go inside for a greater selection of regional items at terrific prices.

■ Águila y Sol is considered by some to be Mexico's best contemporary-style restaurant. Located in Mexico City's Polanco district, it is owned by the daughter of famous artist and cookbook-writer Martha Chapa, and shows that both talents can be inherited.

■ A few years ago, when the original Café de Tacuba – located in Mexico City's central historic district – was destroyed by fire, much of the city wept. It has been rebuilt and still serves traditional and a few unique dishes to people of all classes at reasonable prices. Try the *Especiales Tacuba enchiladas!*

■ Located in Mexico City's Coyoacán district, El Tajín is owned and managed by Alicia and Jorge De'Angelli, authors of many cookbooks, and culinary icons in their own right. The restaurant specializes in pure *cocina mexicana*, served in just the right atmosphere.

■ Saltillo's La Canasta restaurant serves some of the best food in northern Mexico. Nearly across from the University on the city's main street, it is located in a beautiful building, constructed with materials from all over Mexico, and furnished from the owner's extensive collection of Mexican art and antiques.

VEGETARIANS & VEGANS

There is good and bad news for vegetarians traveling in Mexico, but ultimately it is mostly good. Before the Spanish arrived the people had a very low fat, nearly totally vegetarian diet. However, following the Conquest they became committed carnivores. These days, even medium-sized towns will usually have at least one vegetarian establishment, and most restaurants have a fine selection of salads and vegetable side dishes, including beans and rice, that can be combined for a terrific meal.

More good news is that Mexico has many interesting vegetables, such as the broccoli-like *huauzontles* and chewy greens called *romeritos*. *Nopalitos* (cactus paddles) are prepared many ways, and are both delicious and a folk treatment for diabetes. Other common vegetables are *verdolagas* (purslane), Swiss chard and a variety of both domestic and wild mushrooms. *Chiles rellenos*, stuffed with cheese, can be a good bet if they have not been cooked in animal fat. There is also a plethora of both familiar and exotic fruits.

Mexican waiters are generally knowledgeable and anxious to please. However, they are often not aware of the requirements of vegetarians, and especially vegans, and may find the concept hard to understand. Most Mexicans do without meat only when they cannot afford it, and many Mexican vegetarians eat vegetables because they're healthy, not for ethical reasons. So you must make your requirements clear. One problem is that your server may think he is bringing you a vegetarian meal when it has been flavored with beef or chicken broth. The more upscale the restaurant, the better your chances of being understood and accommodated.

> In addition to many other items, such as corn and turkey, two of the world's most beloved edibles, chocolate and vanilla, originally came from Mexico.

EATING WITH KIDS

Mexicans adore children, and the country is a child-friendly place. Most waiters will cheerfully do anything special (within reason) to please your child, and most restaurants have high chairs – just ask for a *silla para niños*. Mexican supermarkets carry a full range of international brands of baby food. For more on children, see the Directory chapter (p969).

HABITS & CUSTOMS

With a couple of exceptions, you will find that Mexican eating customs are similar to those in other western countries. The *comida* is traditionally taken between 1:30pm and 4:00pm. It is meant to be a leisurely family or business affair, and usually takes at least two hours, but can last up to three or four. However, modern life mean that not everyone can do this; many families are only able to follow this tradition on Sundays. As previously noted, you will find more familiar lunch and dinner hours in most resort areas, but try the Mexican schedule, and after a few days you may love it!

To obtain the full experience, plan on arriving about 2pm, and staying until at least 4pm. But no one will look askance if you order nothing but a small entrée or appetizer, or grab a few tacos at a nearby *taquería,* and save your main meal for the evening. Nearly every meal is accompanied by a basket of hot tortillas; diners take one, usually the second from the top, and request a refill when the basket is nearly empty.

Mexico's attitude toward liquor is usually quite liberal. However, be aware that in many communities liquor cannot be sold on election days or when the President is visiting. Also, while alcoholic beverages are usually considered a normal part of life, some towns frown on drinking in their streets, and drinking while driving is a serious no-no!

If you are invited to someone's home it is polite to bring a gift; chocolates or a bottle of wine or tequila is perfect. Most people are aware that Mexicans are not always prompt, and being half an hour late, or even more, rarely causes notice, especially in Mexico City where traffic can be a serious problem. Punctuality, however, is expected at restaurant meetings.

During Lent you will find restaurants offering special menus, many with interesting and delicious items that will appeal to vegetarians. During Holy Week, Mexicans often visit family or take vacations, and you may find smaller restaurants closed for the week.

> English sailors coined the term 'cocktail' upon discovering that their drinks in the Yucatan port of Campeche were stirred with the thin, dried roots of a plant called *cola de gallo,* which translates as 'cock's tail.'

COOKING COURSES

Two cooking schools, which offer quite different experiences, are heartily recommended. In Oaxaca, Seasons of my Heart is operated by well-known cookbook-author Susana Trilling. She also conducts culinary tours in Oaxaca and other selected regions of Mexico. See p726 for more information.

Owned and operated by transplanted New Yorker Magda Bogin, **Cocinar Mexicano** (www.cocinarmexicano.com) is located in the enchanting village of Tepoztlán, near Mexico City. The program offers weeklong classes that include most meals, a market tour, attendance at a local fiesta, cooking lectures, workshops by guest chefs, five hands-on cooking classes, Margaritas 101 and a Mexican wine-tasting for $1,895 per week (air and hotel are separate). Spanish language instruction is also available.

Set in a colonial mansion in downtown Mérida, **Los Dos** (Calle 68 No 517, Mérida, Mexico, Yucatán 97000; in US ☎ 212-400-1642, in Mexico ☎ 999-928-1116; www.los-dos .com) offers a Culinary Overview as well as one-, two- and three-day classes taught by Chef David Sterling. Classes include meals and market tours. Rates range from $25 to $300. Contact the school for specific details.

THE CHECK PLEASE!

Do not expect your meal check to be brought until you ask for it. That would be considered impolite, and serving staff will often remain open long after normal hours to accommodate guests taking time over coffee and brandy. When you're ready, simply say *La cuenta por favor* (lah-cwenta pour fah-vor) or make the universal scribbling sign.

EAT YOUR WORDS

Knowing at least a few words in Spanish indicate a respect for the locals and their culture, not to mention a willingness to risk embarrassment, and that can make a huge difference.

Useful Phrases

Are you open?
¿Está abierto?   e·sta a·byer·to
When are you open?
¿Cuando está abierto?   kwan·do e·sta a·byer·to
Are you now serving breakfast/lunch/dinner?
¿Ahora, está sirviendo desayuno/   a·o·ra e·sta ser·vyen·do de·sa·yoo·no/
la comida/la cena?   la ko·mee·da/la se·na
I'd like to see a menu.
Quisiera ver la carta/el menu.   kee·sye·ra ver la kar·ta/el me·noo
Do you have a menu in English?
¿Tienen un menú en inglés?   tye·nen oon me·noo en een·gles
Can you recommend something?
¿Puede recomendar algo?   pwe·de re·ko·men·dar al·go
I'm a vegetarian.
Soy vegetariano/a. (m/f)   soy ve·khe·te·rya·no/a
I can't eat anything with meat or poultry products, including broth.
No puedo comer algo de carne o aves, no pwe·do ko·mer al·go de kar·ne o a·ves
incluyendo caldo.   een·kloo·yen·do kal·do
I'd like mineral water/natural bottled water.
Quiero agua mineral/agua purificada. kee·ye·ro a·gwa mee·ne·ral/a·gwa poo·ree·fee·ka·da
Is it (chili) hot?
¿Es picoso?   es pee·ko·so
The check, please.
La cuenta, por favor.   la kwen·ta por fa·vor

Glossary

a la parilla	a la pa·ree·ya	grilled
a la plancha	a la plan·cha	pan-broiled
adobada	a·do·ba·da	marinated with adobo (chili sauce)
agua mineral	a·gwa mee·ne·ral	mineral water or club soda
agua purificado	a·gwa poo·ree·fee·ka·do	bottled, uncarbonated water
al albañil	al al·ba·nyeel	'bricklayer style' – served with a hot chili sauce
al carbón	al kar·bon	char-broiled
al mojo de ajo	al mo·kho de a·kho	with garlic sauce
al pastor	al pas·tor	cooked on a pit, shepherd's style
albóndigas	al·bon·dee·gas	meatballs
antojitos	an·to·khee·tos	'little mexican whims,' and tortilla-based snacks like tacos and gorditas
arroz mexicana	a·ros me·khee·ka·na	pilaf-style rice with a tomato base
ate	a·te	jam, preserves
atole	a·to·le	gruel made with ground corn
avena	a·ve·na	oatmeal
aves	a·ves	poultry
azucar	a·soo·kar	sugar
barbacoa	bar·ba·ko·a	pit-smoked barbecue
biftec	beef·tek	steak
bolillo	bo·lee·yo	French-style roll
brocheta	bro·che·ta	shishkabob

buñuelos	boo-*nywe*-los	tortilla-size fritters with a sweet, anise sauce
burrito	boo-*ree*-to	a filling in a large flour tortilla
cabra	ka-bra	goat
cabrito	ka-*bree*-to	kid goat
café con crema/leche	ka-*fe* kon *kre*-ma/*le*-che	coffee with cream/milk
cajeta	ka-*khe*-ta	goat's milk and sugar boiled to a paste
calabacita	ka-la-ba-*see*-ta	squash
calamar	ka-la-*mar*	squid
caldo	*kal*-do	broth or soup
camarones	ka-ma-*ro*-nes	shrimp
cangrejo	kan-*gre*-kho	crab
carne de puerco	*kar*-ne de *pwer*-ko	pork
carne de res	*kar*-ne de res	beef
carne	*kar*-ne	meat
carnero	kar-*ne*-ro	mutton
carnitas	kar-*nee*-tas	pork simmered in lard
cebolla	se-*bo*-ya	onion
cecina	se-*see*-na	thin cut of meat, flavored with chili and sautéed or grilled
cerdo	*ser*-do	pork
chalupas	cha-*loo*-pas	open-faced, canoe-shaped cooked corn dough, topped with meat and chilies
chicharrones	chee-cha-*ro*-nes	fried pork skins
chilaquiles	chee-la-*kee*-les	fried tortilla strips cooked with a red or green chili sauce, and sometimes meat and eggs
chile relleno	*chee*-le re-*ye*-no	chili stuffed with meat or cheese, usually fried with egg batter
chiles en nogada	*chee*-les en no-*ga*-da	mild green chilies stuffed with meat and fruit, fried in batter and served with a sauce of cream, ground walnuts and cheese
chorizo	cho-*ree*-so	Mexican-style bulk sausage made with chili and vinegar
chuleta de puerco	choo-*le*-ta de *pwer*-ko	pork chop
churros	choo-*ros*	doughnut-like fritters
cochinita pibil	ko-chee-*nee*-ta pee-*beel*	pork, marinated in chilies, wrapped in banana leaves, and pit-cooked or baked
coco	*ko*-ko	coconut
coctel de frutas	kok-*tel* de *froo*-tas	fruit cocktail
cordero	kor-*de*-ro	lamb
costillas de res	kos-*tee*-yas de res	beef ribs
crema	*kre*-ma	cream
crepas	*kre*-pas	crepes or thin pancakes
elote	e-*lo*-te	fresh corn
empanada	em-pa-*na*-da	pastry turnover filled with meat, cheese or fruits
empanizado	em-pa-nee-*sa*-do	sautéed
enchilada	en-chee-*la*-da	corn tortilla dipped in chili sauce, wrapped around meat or poultry, and garnished with cheese
ensalada	en-sa-*la*-da	salad
filete al la tampiqueña	fee-*le*-te a la tam-pee-*ke*-nya	steak, tampico style, a thin tenderloin, grilled and served with chili strips and onion, a quesadilla and enchilada
filete	fee-*le*-te	filet

flor de calabaza	flor de ka·la·*ba*·sa	squash blossom
fresa	*fre*·sa	strawberry
frijoles a la charra	free·*kho*·les a la *cha*·ra	beans cooked with tomatoes, chilies and onions (also called *frijoles rancheros*)
frijoles negros	free·*kho*·les *ne*·gros	black beans
frijoles refritos	free·*kho*·les re·*free*·tos	refried beans
frito	*free*·to	fried
galleta	ga·*ye*·ta	cookie
gelatina	khe·la·*tee*·na	gelatin; also Jello (English jelly)
gorditas	gor·*dee*·tas	small circles of tortilla dough, fried and topped with meat and/or cheese
guacamole	gwa·ka·*mo*·le	mashed avocado, often with lime juice, onion, tomato and chili
helado	e·*la*·do	ice cream
hígado	ee·ga·do	liver
horchata	hor·*cha*·ta	a soft drink made with melon
huachinango *veracruzana*	wa·chee·*nan*·go ve·ra·kroo·*sa*·na	Veracruz-style red snapper with a sauce of tomatoes, olives, vinegar and capers
huevos fritos	*hwe*·vos *free*·tos	fried eggs
huevos motuleños	*hwe*·vos mo·too·*le*·nyos	fried eggs sandwiched between corn tortillas, and topped with peas, tomato, ham and cheese
huevos rancheros	*hwe*·vos ran·*che*·ros	fried eggs served on a corn tortilla, topped with a sauce of tomato, chilies, and onions, and served with refried beans
huevos revueltos	*hwe*·vos re·*vwel*·tos	scrambled eggs
huitlacoche	weet·la·*ko*·che	corn mushrooms — a much esteemed fungus that grows on corn
jaiba	*khay*·ba	crab
jamón	kha·*mon*	ham
jitomate	khee·to·*ma*·te	red tomato
jugo de manzano	*khoo*·go de man·*sa*·na	apple juice
jugo de naranja	*khoo*·go de na·*ran*·kha	orange juice
jugo de piña	*khoo*·go de *pee*·nya	pineapple juice
langosta	lan·*gos*·ta	lobster
leche	*le*·che	milk
lengua	*len*·gwa	tongue
licuado	lee·*kea*·do	smoothie
limón	lee·*mon*	lime (lemons are rarely found in Mexico)
lomo de cerdo	*lo*·mo de *ser*·do	pork loin
machacado	ma·cha·*ka*·do	pulverized jerky, often scrambled with eggs
mantequilla	man·te·*kee*·ya	butter
mariscos	ma·*rees*·kos	seafood
menudo	me·*noo*·do	stew of tripe
milanesa	mee·la·*ne*·sa	thin slices of beef or pork, breaded and fried
mixiote	mee·*shyo*·te	chili-seasoned lamb steamed in agave membranes or parchment
mole negro	*mo*·le *ne*·gro	chicken or pork in a very dark sauce of chilies, fruits, nuts, spices and chocolate
mole poblano	*mo*·le po·*bla*·no	chicken or turkey in a sauce of chilies, fruits, nuts, spices and chocolate

mole	*mo*·le	a traditional stew
mollejas	mo·*ye*·khas	sweetbreads (thymus or pancreas)
nieve	*nye*·ve	sorbet
nopalitos	no·pa·*lee*·tos	sautéed or grilled, sliced cactus paddles
ostras/ostiones	*os*·tras/os·*tyo*·nes	oysters
pan	pan	bread
papas fritas	*pa*·pas *free*·tas	French fries
papas	*pa*·pas	potatoes
pastel	pas·*tel*	cake
pato	*pa*·to	duck
pay	*pa*·ee	pie
pechuga	pe·*choo*·ga	breast
picadillo	pee·ka·*dee*·yo	a ground beef filling that often includes fruit and nuts
piña	*pee*·nya	pineapple
pipian verde	pee·*pyan ver*·de	a stew of chicken, with ground squash seeds, chilies and *tomatillos*
platano macho	*pla*·ta·no *ma*·cho	plantain
platano	*pla*·ta·no	banana
pollo	*po*·yo	chicken
postre	*pos*·tre	dessert
pozole	pa·*so*·le	a soup or thin stew of hominy, meat, vegetables and chilies
pulpo	*pool*·po	octopus
puntas de filete al a lbañil	*poon*·tas de fee·*le*·te al al·ba·*nyeel*	beef tips stewed with smokey chipotle chilies
quesadilla	ke·sa·*dee*·ya	cheese folded between a tortilla and fried or grilled
queso fundido	*ke*·so foon·*dee*·do	cheese melted, often with chorizo or mushrooms, and served as an appetizer with tortillas
rajas	*ra*·khas	strips of mild green chili fried with onions
sábana	*sa*·ba·na	filet mignons pounded paper thin and seared
sopa de ajo	*so*·pa de *a*·kho	garlic soup
sopa de cebolla	*so*·pa de se·*bo*·ya	onion soup
sopa de pollo	*so*·pa de *po*·yo	chicken soup
sopa	*so*·pa	soup, either 'wet' or 'dry' — as in rice and pasta
sope	*so*·pe	a type of *gordita*
taco	*ta*·ko	filling of meat, poultry or vegetables wrapped in a tortilla
té de manzanillo	te de man·sa·*nee*·ya	chamomile tea
té negro	te *ne*·gro	black tea
tinga poblana	*teen*·ga po·*bla*·na	a stew of pork, vegetables and chilies
tocino	to·*see*·no	bacon
tomates verdes	to·*ma*·tes *vair*·des	tomatillos
toronja	to·*ron*·kha	grapefruit
tuna	*too*·na	cactus fruit
venado	ve·*na*·do	venison
verduras	ver·*doo*·ras	vegetables

Mexico City

When people first arrive in the Distrito Federal, they find a civilized, likeable destination, with serene parks, delightful plazas and vibrant street life, brimming with history, architecture and culture. Like any great metropolis, Mexico City presents a mosaic of scenes. One easily shifts from *lucha libre* to experimental theater, street markets to sleek shopping malls, *tamales* to fusion cuisine. Compared with many North American cities, streets feel safe for strolling, and the residents are remarkably patient and accommodating.

Mexico City is the political, financial and cultural nerve center, and to understand Mexico one should spend some time here. People continue to move to Mexico City and it has become a more livable place. Strict emission controls have reduced pollution, and mass-transit solutions have addressed traffic problems. The Condesa and Roma neighborhoods have blossomed as nightlife zones, while the Centro Histórico is being made over as a vibrant cultural quarter.

Part modern metropolis, part monstrosity, Mexico City encapsulates the contemporary urban experience. Perhaps more than any city on earth, it is at the intersection of the first and third worlds, with all the ills and thrills that suggests. The modern heir to one of the ancient world's most remarkable cities – Tenochtitlán – it remains a city of epic proportions.

TOP FIVE

- Surveying the incredible architectural catalogue of the **Centro Histórico** (p128)

- Ambling through **Parque México** (p136) in spring, when the are jacarandas in bloom

- Enjoying a dish of roasted peanuts and *caballito* of tequila at **El Nivel** (p166), the nation's first registered cantina

- Cheering on the 'good guys' at the *lucha libre* bouts of **Arena Coliseo** (p175)

- Cruising Xochimilco's back canals to the **Isla de las Muñecas** (Island of the Dolls; p150)

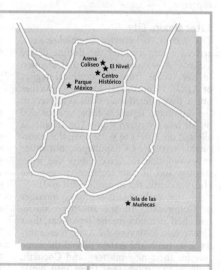

- TELEPHONE CODE: 55
- POPULATION: 18 MILLION

- JANUARY DAILY HIGH: 21°C | 70.3°F
- JULY DAILY HIGH 23°C | 73.8°F

- ELEVATION: 2240 M

HISTORY

As early as 10,000 BC, humans were attracted to the Lago de Texcoco, the lake that then covered much of the floor of the Valle de México. After 7500 BC the lake started shrinking, hunting became more difficult, and the inhabitants turned to agriculture. A loose federation of farming villages had evolved around Lago de Texcoco by 200 BC. The biggest, Cuicuilco, was destroyed by a volcanic eruption about AD 100.

Breakthroughs in irrigation techniques and the development of an economy based on the cultivation of maize contributed to the rise of a civilization at Teotihuacán, 40km northeast of the lake. For centuries Teotihuacán was the capital of an empire whose influence was felt as far away as Guatemala. However, unable to sustain its burgeoning population, it fell in the 8th century. The Toltecs, possibly descended from the nomadic tribes who invaded Teotihuacán, arose as the next great civilization, building their capital at Tula, 65km north of modern-day Mexico City. By the 12th century the Tula empire had collapsed as well, leaving a number of small statelets to compete for control of the Valle de México. It was the Aztecs who emerged supreme.

Aztec Mexico City

The Aztecs, or Mexica (meh-*shee*-kah), arrived a century after the decline of the Toltecs. A wandering tribe that claimed to have come from the mythical region of Aztlán in northwest Mexico or further north, they offered their skills as fighters to the dominant Tepaneca tribe who resided on the lake's western shore. The Tepanecas allowed the Aztecs to settle upon the inhospitable terrain of Chapultepec, but other tribes objected to Aztec habits like wife-stealing and human sacrifice (to appease Huizilopochtli, the hummingbird god).

In the early 14th century, warriors of Culhuacán, on the southern shore, launched an attack on the Tepanecas, their chief rivals, enslaving the Aztec mercenaries. Eventually the Aztecs played the same role for their new masters, and Cocoxtli, Culhuacán's ruler, sent them into battle against nearby Xochimilco. The Aztecs delivered over 8000 human ears to Cocoxtli as proof of their victory. When the Aztecs

sought a marriage alliance with Culhuacán, Cocoxtli rashly offered his own daughter's hand to the Aztec chieftain. But when he arrived at the wedding banquet, his pride turned to horror: a dancer was garbed in the flayed skin of his daughter, who had been sacrificed to Huizilopochtli. Fleeing from the wrath of Culhuacán, the Aztecs wandered around the swampy fringes of the lake, finally reaching an island near the western shore around 1325. There, according to legend, they witnessed an eagle standing on a cactus and eating a snake, which they interpreted as a sign to stop and build a city, Tenochtitlán. (The eagle depicted on the Mexican flag refers to this event.)

Tenochtitlán rapidly became a sophisticated city-state whose empire would, by the early 16th century, span most of modern-day central Mexico from the Pacific to the Gulf of Mexico and into far southern Mexico. The Aztecs built their city on a grid plan, with canals as thoroughfares and causeways to the lakeshore. At the city's heart stood the main *teocalli* (sacred precinct), with its temple dedicated to Huizilopochtli and the water god, Tláloc. In the marshier parts of the island, they created raised gardens by piling up vegetation and mud, and planting willows. These *chinampas* (versions of which can still be seen at Xochimilco in southern Mexico City) gave three or four harvests yearly but were still not enough to feed the growing population.

To supplement their resources, the Aztecs extracted tribute from conquered tribes. In the mid-15th century they formed the Triple Alliance with the lakeshore states Texcoco and Tlacopan to conduct wars against Tlaxcala and Huejotzingo, which lay east of the valley. The purpose was to gain a steady supply of prisoners to sate Huizilopochtli's vast hunger for sacrificial victims, so that the sun would rise each day.

When the Spanish arrived in 1519, Tenochtitlán's population was an estimated 200,000 to 300,000, and that of the whole Valle de México was perhaps 1.5 million, already making it one of the world's densest urban areas. For an account of the Spanish conquest of Tenochtitlán, see p48.

Capital of Nueva España

So assiduously did the Spanish raze Tenochtitlán that only a handful of Aztec structures remain standing in Mexico City today. Having wrecked the Aztec capital, they chose to rebuild it as their own. The conquistador Hernán Cortés hoped to preserve the arrangement whereby Tenochtitlán siphoned off the bounty of its vassal states.

Ravaged by disease, the population of the Valle de México shrank drastically – by some estimates, from 1.5 million to fewer than 100,000 within a century of the conquest. But the city emerged by 1550 as the prosperous, elegant capital of Nueva España. Broad, straight streets were laid out, and buildings were constructed to Spanish designs with local materials such as *tezontle*, a red volcanic rock that the Aztecs had used for their temples. Hospitals, churches, palaces and a university were built. But, lacking natural drainage, the city suffered floods caused by the partial destruction in the 1520s of the Aztecs' canals. Lago de Texcoco often overflowed, damaging buildings, bringing disease and forcing thousands of people to relocate.

Independence

On October 30, 1810, some 80,000 independence rebels, fresh from victory at Guanajuato, overpowered Spanish loyalist forces just west of the capital. But they were not sufficiently equipped to capitalize on this triumph, and their leader Miguel Hidalgo chose not to advance on the city – a decision that cost Mexico 11 more years of fighting before independence was achieved. By 1821 the city's population had swelled to 160,000, making it the biggest in the Americas.

Mexico City entered the modern age under the despotic Porfirio Díaz, who ruled Mexico for most of the period from 1877 to 1911 and attracted much foreign investment. Díaz ushered in a construction boom, building Parisian-style mansions and theaters to serve the city's elite. Some 150km of electric tramways threaded the streets, industry grew, and by 1910 the city had 471,000 inhabitants. A drainage canal and tunnel finally succeeded in drying up much of Lago de Texcoco, allowing further expansion.

Modern Megalopolis

After Díaz fell in 1911, the Mexican Revolution (see p52) brought war, hunger and disease to the streets of Mexico City. Following the Great Depression, a drive to industrialize attracted more money and people to the city. By 1940 the population had reached 1.7 million. In the 1940s and '50s, factories and skyscrapers rose almost as quickly. The supply of housing, jobs and services could not keep pace with the influx of people; shantytowns appeared on the city's fringes, and Mexico City began to grow uncontrollably.

Despite continued economic growth into the 1960s, political and social reform lagged behind, as was made painfully evident by the massacre of hundreds of students in the lead-up to the 1968 Olympic Games (see the boxed text, p106).

In the 1970s Mexico City continued to grow at an alarming rate, spreading beyond the Distrito Federal (DF) into the adjacent state of México and developing some of the world's worst traffic and pollution, only partly alleviated by the metro system (opened in 1969) and by attempts in the 1990s to limit traffic. On September 19, 1985, an earthquake measuring over eight on the Richter scale hit Mexico City, killing at least 10,000, displacing thousands more and causing more than $4 billion in damage. But people continued to pour in.

Since 1940 Mexico City has multiplied in area over 10 times, yet it's still one of the world's most crowded metropolitan areas. Today the city counts 18 million inhabitants, around a sixth of the country's population. Though growth has slowed in the last decade, there are still some 600 newcomers daily and the population is expected to top 20 million by 2010. It is the industrial, financial and communications center of the country; its industries generate more than one-third of Mexico's wealth, and its people consume two-thirds of Mexico's energy. Its cost of living is the highest in the nation.

Heavy subsidies are needed to keep the city from seizing up. Water extraction from the subsoil makes the city sink steadily – parts of the center sank 10m in the 20th century. Even so, one-third of the city's water must be pumped in at great cost from outside the Valle de México; and because

MEXICO CITY

there is no natural drainage, waste water must be pumped back out.

From 1928 to 1997 the federal government ruled DF directly, with federally appointed 'regents' heading notoriously corrupt administrations. Since 1997 the DF has had political autonomy and the chance to elect its own mayor. In 2000 Andrés Manuel López Obrador, a member of the left-leaning PRD (Party of the Democratic Revolution), was elected. *Capitalinos* generally approved of the mayor's initiatives, which included an ambitious makeover of the Centro Histórico. In 2005, the Fox administration attempted to have 'AMLO' removed from his post – and from political life – by prosecuting him on tenuous contempt-of-court charges. But the plan backfired: when the mayor handed the reins over to Alejandro Encinas, his chief cabinet minister, to launch a presidential campaign, he found himself more popular than ever. Elections in 2006 were expected to determine Encinas' successor.

ORIENTATION

Mexico City's 350 *colonias* (neighborhoods) sprawl across the ancient bed of Lago de Texcoco and beyond. Though this vast urban expanse appears daunting, the main areas of interest to visitors are fairly well defined and easy to traverse.

Note that some major streets, such as Av Insurgentes, keep the same name for many kilometers, but the names (and numbering) of many lesser streets switch every few blocks.

Full addresses normally include the *colonia*. Often the easiest way to find an address is by asking for the nearest metro station.

Centro Histórico & Alameda Central

The historic heart of the city is the wide plaza known as the Zócalo, surrounded by the presidential palace, the metropolitan cathedral and the excavated site of the Templo Mayor, the main temple of Aztec Tenochtitlán. The Zócalo and its surround-

---

ECHOES OF TLATELOLCO

Nineteen sixty-eight marked a pivotal moment for Mexican democracy. Perhaps due to the subversive mood of the era, unrest was rife and students took to the streets to denounce political corruption and authoritarianism. Mexico had been chosen that year to host the Olympics, and President Gustavo Díaz Ordaz was anxious to present an image of stability to the world. Known for his authoritarian style, Díaz Ordaz employed heavy-handed tactics to stop the protests, in turn generating further unrest, with the mantle now being taken up by a broader coalition of middle-class *capitalinos*.

On the afternoon of October 2, a week before the Olympics were to begin, a demonstration was held on Tlatelolco's Plaza de las Tres Culturas. Helicopters hovered overhead and a massive police contingent cordoned off the zone. Suddenly a flare dropped from one of the choppers and shots rang out, apparently from the balcony which the protestors had made into a speakers platform. Police then opened fire on the demonstrators and mayhem ensued. Later, government-authorized newspaper accounts blamed student snipers for igniting the incident and reported 20 protesters killed, although the real number is acknowledged to be closer to 400. News of the massacre was swept under the rug and the Olympic games went on without a hitch.

There are numerous theories as to what actually occurred that October day. But the generally accepted version is that the government staged the massacre, planting snipers on the balcony to make it seem as if the students had provoked the violence. Many Mexicans viewed the killings as a premeditated tactic by the government to suppress dissent, permanently discrediting the post-revolutionary regime.

More than 30 years later, the Tlatelolco massacre was still recalled bitterly by a generation of Mexicans when President Vicente Fox took office, pledging to bring human-rights abusers to justice, and it appeared some light would finally be shed on the matter. A special investigator was appointed and secret files were released for scrutiny. Luis Echeverría, who as minister of the interior under Díaz Ordaz controlled internal security, was questioned. But, whether because the authorities under investigation stonewalled or because the prosecutor mishandled matters, results were inconclusive and no convictions were made. Skeptical Mexicans have given up hope the case will be resolved – unless the next administration picks it up again.

ing neighborhoods are known as the Centro Histórico (Historic Center) and are full of notable old buildings and interesting museums. North, west and south of the Zócalo are many good, economical hotels and restaurants.

Av Madero and Av 5 de Mayo (or Cinco de Mayo) link the Zócalo with the Alameda Central park, eight blocks to the west. On the east side of the Alameda stands the magnificent Palacio de Bellas Artes. The landmark Torre Latinoamericana (Latin American Tower) pierces the sky a block south of Bellas Artes, beside one of the city's main north–south arterial roads, the Eje Central Lázaro Cárdenas.

Plaza de la República

Some 750m west of the Alameda, across Paseo de la Reforma, is the Plaza de la República, marked by the somber, domed Monumento a la Revolución. This is a fairly quiet, mostly residential area with many budget and midrange hotels. The districts called San Rafael and Juárez are respectively west and south of here.

Paseo de la Reforma

Mexico City's grandest boulevard runs through the city's heart, connecting the Alameda to the Bosque de Chapultepec. Along the way, the Monumento a la Independencia (aka 'El Ángel'), the capital's signature monument, marks the northern side of the Zona Rosa, while the sleek Torre Mayor, the city's tallest building, stands at the eastern end of Chapultepec Park.

Zona Rosa

The Zona Rosa (Pink Zone) is a glitzy shopping, eating, hotel and nightlife district bound by Paseo de la Reforma to the north, Av Insurgentes to the east and Av Chapultepec to the south.

Bosque de Chapultepec

The woods of Chapultepec, known to gringos as Chapultepec Park, are to the west of the Zona Rosa. This large expanse of greenery and lakes is Mexico City's 'lungs,' and holds many major museums, including the renowned Museo Nacional de Antropología. North of the park is the swanky Polanco district, filled with embassies and upscale shopping and dining establishments.

North of the Centro

Five kilometers north of the center is the Terminal Norte, the largest of the four bus terminals. Six kilometers north is the Basílica de Guadalupe, Mexico's most revered shrine.

South of the Centro

Av Insurgentes Sur connects Paseo de la Reforma to most points of interest in the south. Just south of the Zona Rosa is Colonia Roma, a quaint area of Porfiriato-era architecture, art galleries and plazas. West of Roma, 1km to 2km south of the Zona Rosa, is Colonia Condesa, a trendy neighborhood with pleasant parks, quiet streets, and plentiful restaurants and cafés. Five to 10km further south are the atmospheric former villages of San Ángel and Coyoacán and the vast campus of the national university. In the southeast of the city are the canals and gardens of Xochimilco.

The Eje System

Besides their regular names, many major streets are termed Eje (axis). The Eje system establishes a grid of priority roads across the city, supposedly speeding up transport. The key north–south Eje Central Lázaro Cárdenas, running from Coyoacán in the south to Tenayuca in the north, passes just east of the Alameda Central. Major north–south roads west of the Eje Central are termed Eje 1 Poniente, Eje 2 Poniente etc, while roads to the east of Eje Central are labeled Eje 1 Oriente, Eje 2 Oriente and so on. The same goes for major east–west roads to the north and south of the Alameda Central and Zócalo – Rayón is Eje 1 Norte, Fray Servando Teresa de Mier is Eje 1 Sur.

Maps

Mexico City tourist modules hand out useful color maps with enlargements of the Centro Histórico, Coyoacán and San Ángel. Those needing more detail should pick up a Guía Roji fold-out map of Mexico City ($4), or a Guía Roji Ciudad de México street atlas ($18), updated annually, with a comprehensive index. Find them at Sanborns stores, Librería Sama (see p125) and at larger newsstands.

Inegi (Map pp114-15; ☎ 5512-1873; Balderas 71, Juárez; ⏰ 9am-4:30pm Mon-Fri; Ⓜ Juárez), Mexico's

MEXICO CITY IN...

Two Days

Day one dawns and you're overlooking the Zócalo from one of the rooftop restaurants on the plaza's west side. For a different angle, climb the bell tower of the **Catedral Metropolitana** (p128), then admire Diego Rivera's cinematic murals at the **Palacio Nacional** (p128). Take the **Turibús** (p151) for a survey of the city's neighborhoods, getting off in **Polanco** (p140) or the **Zona Rosa** (p136) for lunch and shopping. Spend the evening relaxing at a café near your hotel, or if you're up for it, tequila tasting with the mariachis at Plaza Garibaldi. Day two, delve into Mexico's past at the **Museo Nacional de Antropología** (p138) and **Castillo de Chapultepec** (p137).

Four Days

With a couple more days, head out to the pyramids at **Teotihuacán** (p195). Spend a morning roaming around the **Alameda Central** (p134), making time to acquaint yourself with the **Palacio de Bellas Artes** (p134) and **Museo Franz Mayer** (p134). Have the quintessential Mexican *comida* (lunch) at **Los Girasoles** (p158), then do some *artesanías* (crafts) shopping at **La Ciudadela** (p133). In the evening plug into the lively **Condesa** (p170) scene.

One Week

Get to know the southern districts: Visit **Frida Kahlo's Blue House** (p144) in Coyoacán; hire a *trajinera* (gondola) for a cruise along the ancient canals of **Xochimilco** (p141); shop for quality crafts at **San Ángel's Bazar Sábado market** (p177). Reserve Wednesday or Sunday evening for the **Ballet Folclórico** (p171) at the Palacio de Bellas Artes.

national geographical institute, publishes topographical maps covering the whole country (subject to availability). There is also an outlet at the **airport** (☎ 5786-0212; Sala C; ⏰ 8:30am-8pm) and their headquarters are in **Colonia Mixcoác** (Map pp110-11; ☎ 5278-1000, ext 1207; Patriotismo 711; ⏰ 9am-9pm Mon-Fri; Ⓜ Mixcoác).

INFORMATION
Bookstores

Books in English and other languages can be found in top-end hotels and major museums, as well as most of the following bookstores.

CENTRO HISTÓRICO

American Bookstore (Map pp114-15; ☎ 5512-0306; Bolívar 23; ⏰ 10am-7pm Mon-Sat; Ⓜ Allende) Has novels and books on Mexico in English, and Lonely Planet guides.

Gandhi (Map pp114-15; ☎ 5512-4360; Juárez 4; ⏰ 10am-9pm Mon-Fri, 11am-8pm Sat & Sun; Ⓜ Bellas Artes) Good source of books about Mexico and Mexico City, and novels in English, plus a worthwhile music section.

Librería Madero (Map pp114-15; ☎ 5510-2068; Madero 12; ⏰ 10am-6:30pm Mon-Fri, 10am-2pm Sat; Ⓜ Allende) Great selection of Mexican history, art and architecture, including many secondhand books.

OTHER AREAS

Rare-book aficionados can dig up some gems in the used bookstores along Av Álvaro Obregón in Colonia Roma.

Cenca (Map pp120–1; ☎ 5399-5821; Temístocles 73B, Polanco; ⏰ 8am-10pm Mon-Fri, 8am-9pm Sat & Sun; Ⓜ Polanco) Wide variety of foreign magazines, plus best-sellers in English.

Gandhi (Map p122; ☎ 5661-0911; Miguel Ángel de Quevado 121; ⏰ 9am-10pm Mon-Fri, 10am-10pm Sat & Sun; Ⓜ Migeul Angel de Quevado) The large San Ángel branch has outlets on both sides of Quevedo.

La Bouquinerie Zona Rosa (Map pp118-19; ☎ 5514-0838; Casa de Francia, Havre 15; ⏰ 10am-7pm Mon-Fri, until 6pm Sat; Ⓜ Insurgentes); San Ángel (Map p122; ☎ 5616-6066; Camino al Desierto de los Leones 40; ⏰ 10am-8pm Mon-Sat, noon-6pm Sun; Ⓜ Migeul Angel de Quevado) French bookstore with *Le Figaro* and *Libération*.

Librería Alemana (Map pp118-19; ☎ 5533-1002; Orizaba 6, Colonia Roma; ⏰ 10am-7pm Mon-Fri, 11am-4pm Sun; Ⓜ Insurgentes) German pop fiction and literature.

Librería Pegaso (Map pp118-19; ☎ 5208-0174; Álvaro Obregón 99; ⏰ 11am-8pm Mon-Sat, 10am-7pm Sun; Ⓜ Insurgentes) Inside the Casa Lamm; carries mostly Spanish-language titles with a small English literature section, plus a few Lonely Planet guides.

Emergency

The Policía Turística, recognizable by the heart-shaped patch on their sleeve, patrol Paseo de la Reforma and the Centro Histórico. Their function is to help tourists. They supposedly speak English.

Report crimes and get legal assistance through the **Unidad Ministerial Especializada para Atención al Turista** (Map pp114-15; ☎ 5592-2665, ext 1114; Paseo de la Reforma 42; ☼ 9am-2pm & 4-6pm Mon-Fri; Ⓜ Hidalgo). You fill out a form, possibly available at hotels and embassies, in English, Spanish and French, describing the incident and submit it to the office, which will address it to the proper authorities. Mobile units of the PGJDF (Federal District Attorney General's Office) can assist crime victims on the spot; call ☎ 061.

Other useful numbers:

Ambulance, Fire (☎ 080)
Cruz Roja (Red Cross; ☎ 5395-1111)
Hospital ABC (emergency ☎ 5230-8161; Sur 136 No 16, Colonia Las Américas; Ⓜ Observatorio)
Hospital Ángeles Clínica Londres (emergency ☎ 5229-8445; Durango 64, Colonia Roma; Ⓜ Cuauhtémoc)
Missing persons & vehicles (☎ 5658-1111)

Internet Access

Public Internet services are easily found throughout town. Rates range from $1 to $2 per hour, unless otherwise noted. In addition, many cafés offer wireless Internet (though oddly, not Starbucks).

CENTRO HISTÓRICO

C&X (Map pp114-15; Humboldt 62; ☼ 8am-10:30pm Mon-Fri, 10am-6pm Sun; Ⓜ Juárez) Adjacent to the YWCA.
Esperanto (Map pp114-15; ☎ 5512-4123; Independencia 66; ☼ 8am-10pm Mon-Sat, noon-6pm Sun; Ⓜ Juárez)
Keep in Touch (Map pp114-15; ☎ 5512-4186; Gante 6, Pasaje Iturbide; ☼ 9am-8:30pm Mon-Sat, 11am-6pm Sun; Ⓜ Allende) Wireless access and X-Box available, plus frappuccinos and sandwiches.

COYOACÁN

Papelería Dabo (Map p123; ☎ 5659-5547; Allende 45, cnr Cuauhtémoc, Coyoacán; ☼ 9am-8pm Mon-Sat, 10am-7pm Sun; Ⓜ Viveros)

ZONA ROSA

Plenty of cybercafés occupy the big Insurgentes roundabout.

C@lling Home (Map pp118-19; ☎ 5207-2586; Jalapa 51, Colonia Roma; ☼ 9am-9pm Mon-Fri, 11am-4pm Sat, 11am-3pm Sun; Ⓜ Insurgentes)

Cafenauta (Map pp118-19; ☎ 5553-1517; Ensenada 6, Colonia Condesa; ☼ 10am-10pm Mon-Sat, noon-8pm Sun; Ⓜ Patriotismo)
Conecte Café (Map pp118-19; Génova 71, cnr Londres; ☼ 10am-midnight Mon-Sat, 10am-9pm Sun; Ⓜ Insurgentes)
Mac Coffee (Map pp118-19; ☎ 5525-4391; 1st fl, Londres 152; ☼ 10am-9pm Mon-Sat, 11am-6pm Sun; Ⓜ Insurgentes) Haven for Macheads.

Internet Resources

The following sites compile oodles of information on the capital. Some offer their pages in English, but the English pages are often not as thorough or are barely comprehensible.
Artes Visuales (www.artesvisuales.com.mx in Spanish) Covers DF galleries and museums.
Consejo Nacional Para la Cultura y las Artes (www.cnca.gob.mx in Spanish) Up-to-date guide to DF museums, theaters and other cultural institutions.
DFiesta en el DF (www.defiestaeneldf.com) Tourism department's exhaustive listings with plenty of practical information.
Secretaría de Cultura del Distrito Federal (www.cultura.df.gob.mx in Spanish) DF festivals and museum events.
Sistema de Transporte Colectivo (www.metro.df.gob.mx in Spanish) All about the Mexico City metro.
Vive el Centro (www.viveelcentro.com in Spanish) Excellent overview of Centro Histórico places and happenings, maintained by the downtown restoration foundation.

Laundry

Self-service laundromats have yet to catch on here. The following *lavanderías* charge $4 to $6 to wash and dry a 3kg load for you, and only slightly less if you do it yourself.
Acqualav (Map pp118-19; ☎ 5514-7348; Orizaba 42, Colonia Roma; ☼ 8:30am-7pm Mon-Fri, 9am-5pm Sat, 9am-3pm Sun; Ⓜ Insurgentes)
Lavajet (Map pp118-19; ☎ 5207-3032; Río Danubio 119B; ☼ 8:15am-5:30pm Mon-Fri, 8:15am-4pm Sat; Ⓜ Insurgentes)
Lavandería Automática Édison (Map pp114-15; Édison 91; ☼ 10am-7pm Mon-Sat; Ⓜ Revolución) Near Plaza de la República.

Libraries & Cultural Centers

Biblioteca Benjamín Franklin (Map pp118-19; ☎ 5080-2733; Liverpool 31; ☼ 11am-7pm Mon-Fri; Ⓜ Cuauhtémoc) Housed in the US Trade Center, the library subscribes to a wide range of periodicals, from *Foreign Affairs* to *Mad*. Leave your ID at the gate.

(Continued on page 125)

Estado de México
Distrito Federal

Vía Bar Prada
Blvd Ávila Camacho
Calz de las Armas

Comité Olímpico Mexicano

Lomas de Chapultepec

Los Morales

Polanco

See Bosque de Chapultepec & Polanco Map (pp120–1)

Bosque de Chapultepec 1a Sección
Bosque de Chapultepec 2a Sección
Bosque de Chapultepec 3a Sección

Paseo de la Reforma
Paseo de las Palmas

To Santa Fe (4km); Netherlands Embassy (4km); Parque Nacional Desierto de los Leones (13km); Toluca (66km)

To Tepotzotlán (30km); Tula (88km); Querétaro (199km)
To Teotihuacán (55km)
To Villa
La Villa de Guadalupe

Insurgentes Norte
Calz de Guadalupe
Calz de los Misterios
Calz Ticomán
Eje Central
Av Montevideo

Calz Vallejo
To Tenayuca (6km)
Av Cuitláhuac
To Ceylán

Calz Gral Escobedo
Calz México Tacuba
Av de las Granjas
Av Inst Téc Industrial

Aquiles Serdán
Blvd Ávila Camacho

San Rafael
Plaza de la República
Estación Buenavista

Tlatelolco
Lázaro Cárdenas (Eje Central)

Insurgentes Norte

Alameda Central
Juárez
Centro Histórico

See Centro Histórico, Plaza de la República & Juárez Map (pp114–16)

Zona Rosa
Roma Norte
Roma Sur
Condesa

See Zona Rosa, Condesa & Roma Map (pp117–19)

Av Chapultepec
Av Cuauhtémoc
Av Insurgentes Sur
Av Revolución
Av San Antonio
Av Patriotismo

Río Mixcoac
Av Sur 122
Anillo Periférico
To Constituyentes

Estado de México
Distrito Federal

Av Central
Anillo Periférico
Autopista Texcoco
To Texcoco (20km)

Bosque de San Juan de Aragón

Av San Aragón

Aeropuerto Internacional Benito Juárez
Alameda Oriente
Blvd Puerto Aéreo

Nezahualcóyotl
Av Xochiaca
Av Chimalhuacán
Av Pantitlán

To Puebla (123km)
Calz Zaragoza
Parque Santa Cruz Meyehualco
Cuitáhon

Canal de San Juan
Iztapalapa

Viaducto Río de la Piedad
Autódromo Hermanos Rodríguez
Ferrocarril Río Frío

Av Río Churubusco (Circuito Interior)
Paseo y Troncoso

Purísima
Calz de la Viga
Calz Ermita Iztapalapa
Av Morelos (Eje 3 Sur)
Av Presidente Calles (Eje 4 Sur)
Calz San Antonio Abad
Viaducto Miguel Alemán
Av Molina Enríquez
Av Presidente Calles
Calz de Tlalpan
Av Cuauhtémoc

Estado de México

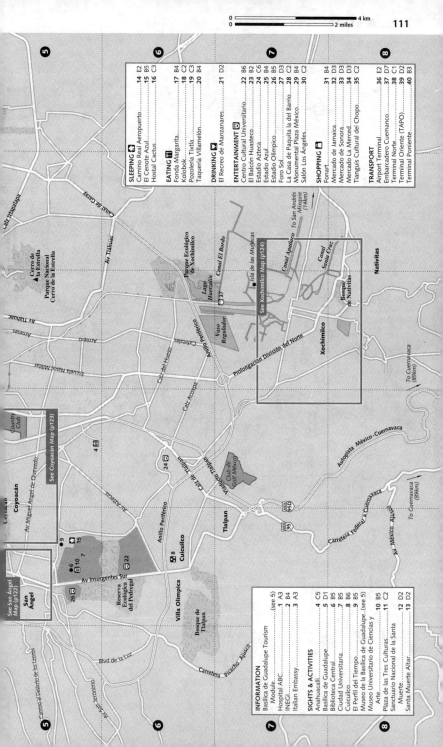

0 _____ 4 km
0 _____ 2 miles

SLEEPING 🛏
Camino Real Aeropuerto...............14 E2
El Cenote Azul..............................15 B5
Hostal Cactus................................16 C3

EATING 🍴
Fonda Margarita.............................17 B4
Kolobok..18 C2
Pozolería Tixtla...............................19 C3
Taquería Villamelón........................20 B4

DRINKING 🍷
El Recreo de Manzanares................21 D2

ENTERTAINMENT 🎭
Centro Cultural Universitario...........22 B6
El Balcón Huasteco.........................23 B2
Estadio Azteca................................24 C6
Estadio Azul...................................25 B4
Estadio Olímpico.............................26 B5
Foro Sol..27 D3
La Casa de Paquita la del Barrio......28 C2
Monumental Plaza México................29 B4
Salón Los Angeles..........................30 C2

SHOPPING 🛍
Fonart...31 B4
Mercado de Jamaica.......................32 D3
Mercado de Sonora..........................33 D3
Mercado La Merced.........................34 D3
Tianguis Cultural del Chopo.............35 C2

TRANSPORT
Airport Terminal..............................36 E2
Embarcadero Cuemanco...................37 D7
Terminal Norte................................38 C1
Terminal Oriente (TAPO)..................39 D2
Terminal Poniente...........................40 B3

INFORMATION
Basílica de Guadalupe Tourism
Module..(see 5)
Hospital ABC.....................................1 A3
INEGI...2 B4
Italian Embassy................................3 A3

SIGHTS & ACTIVITIES
Anahuacalli......................................4 C5
Basílica de Guadalupe......................5 D1
Biblioteca Central.............................6 B5
Ciudad Universitaria.........................7 B5
Cuicuilco..8 B6
El Perfil del Tiempo..........................9 B5
Museo de la Basílica de Guadalupe..(see 5)
Museo Universitario de Ciencias y
Arte...10 B5
Plaza de las Tres Culturas...............11 C2
Santuario Nacional de la Santa
Muerte...12 D2
Santa Muerte Altar.........................13 D2

To Ciudad Azteca

To Texcoco

Bosque de Aragón

Aeropuerto Internacional Benito Juárez

Líneas 1, 5, 9, A

Pantitlán

Agrícola Oriental

Deportivo Oceanía

Oceanía

Romero Rubio

Aragón

Terminal Aérea

Hangares

Calz. Zaragoza

Zaragoza

Gómez Farías

Ricardo Flores Magón

Moctezuma

Boulevard Puerto Aéreo

Balbuena

Velódromo

Mixhuca

Líneas 4, 6

Martín Carrera

Calz. San Juan de Aragón

Talismán

Bondojito

Eduardo Molina

Av. Eduardo Molina

San Lázaro

TAPO

Fray Servando

Canal del Norte

Morelos

Candelaria

Merced

Jamaica

Santa

Parque Nacional El Tepeyac

Línea 3

Indios Verdes

La Villa-Basílica

Deportivo 18 de Marzo

Potrero

Lindavista

Av. Insurgentes Norte

Valle Gómez

Consulado

Misterios

Manuel González

Plaza de las Tres Culturas

Lagunilla

Garibaldi

Tepito

Línea 8

Bellas Artes

Allende

Zócalo

Pino Suárez

San Antonio Abad

Chabacano

Obrera

Instituto Politécnico Nacional

Politécnico

Instituto del Petróleo

Eje Central Lázaro Cárdenas

La Raza

Tlatelolco

Guerrero

San Juan de Letrán

Isabel la Católica

Salto del Agua

Doctores

Línea 5

Autobuses del Norte

Terminal Norte

(Circuito Interior)

Av. Cuitláhuac

Línea B

Buenavista

San Cosme

Revolución

Hidalgo

Juárez

Alameda Central

Balderas

Niños Héroes

Cuauhtémoc

Hospital General

Centro Médico

Vallejo

Calz. Vallejo

Norte 45

Av. Ceylán

Normal

Insurgentes

Sevilla

Ferrería

Av. de las Granjas

Azcapotzalco

Popotla

Cuitláhuac

Colegio Militar

Chapultepec

Juanacatlán

Tezozómoc

Camarones

Refinería

Tacuba

San Joaquín

Bosque de Chapultepec 1a Sección

Aquiles Serdán

Panteones

San Cosme

Polanco

Auditorio

Paseo de la Reforma

Constituyentes

Bosque de Chapultepec 2a Sección

El Rosario

Líneas 6, 7

Parque Tezozómoc

Cuatro Caminos

Línea 2

Av. Río San Joaquín

Panteón Civil de Dolores

Bosque

CENTRO HISTÓRICO, PLAZA DE LA REPÚBLICA & JUÁREZ

0 ——————— 2 km
0 ——————— 1 mile

See inset below for
continuation of Linea A

Continuation of Linea A

0 ——— 2 km
0 ——— 1 mile

Linea A

La Paz
Los Reyes
Santa Martha
Acatitla
Peñón Viejo
Guelatao
Tepalcates
Canal de San Juan
Calz Ignacio Zaragoza
Av Juárez
Parque Santa Cruz Meyehualco
Canal De San Juan

Canal de San Juan

Reja Gómez

Lázaro Rodríguez

Leyes de Reforma

Av Jalisco

UAM-1
Constitución de 1917
Linea 8

Cerro de la Estrella
Iztapalapa
Atlalilco
Parque Nacional Cerro de la Estrella

Av Río Churubusco (Circuito Interior)

Escuadrón 201
Calz Ermita Iztapalapa

Coyuya
Iztacalco
Apatlaco
Aculco

Calz de la Viga

Av Molina Enríquez

Viaducto
Xola
Villa de Cortés
Nativitas
Portales
Ermita
Tasqueña
Terminal Sur
Av Presidente Calles
Calz de Tlalpan

Country Club

Linea 2
Las Torres
Ciudad Jardín
La Virgen
Xotepingo
Nezahualpilli
Registro Federal
Nezahualpilli
Textitlán

El Vergel

To Xochimilco

Etiopía
Av Cuauhtémoc
Eugenia
División del Norte
Av División del Norte
Zapata
Coyoacán
Av Río Churubusco (Circuito Interior)
Viveros de Coyoacán
General Anaya

Av Coyoacán
Av Universidad

Av Miguel Ángel de Quevedo

Henríquez Ureña

Av Antena

Linea 3
Universidad

Terminal Poniente
Linea 1
Observatorio
San Pedro de los Pinos
San Antonio
Mixcoac
Linea 7
Barranca del Muerto

Viaducto Miguel Alemán

Av Insurgentes Sur

Viveros
MA de Quevedo

Copilco
Ciudad Universitaria
Ciudad Universitaria

Reserva Ecológica del Pedregal

Av Insurgentes Sur

Paseo del Pedregal

Blvd López Mateos

Linea 3   Metro Line Terminus
Ⓜ   Metro Station
Ⓣ   Tren Ligero Station

A

B Buenavista

To Kolobok (150m);
Alameda de Santa
María (150m)

Línea B

Triángulos
Cultural
del Chopo

C

D To La Casa e
Paquita la d
Barrio (200n

Mosqueta

Guerrero

Sor Juana Inés de la Cruz
To El Balcón
Huasteco
(400m)

1

Guerrero

Gómez Bodet
Santa María La Ribera
Dr Atl
González Martínez

Moctezuma

Magnolia

Pedro Moreno

Línea 2

San Cosme
Ribera de San Cosme

147
156

Mina

Metrobus Stop

Revolución

Violeta

Héroes

Mina

Guerrero (Eje 1 Poniente)

110
104

del Castillo
Sadi Carnot

179

Orozco y Berra

Panteón de
San Fernando

Plaza
de San
Fernando

SAN RAFAEL

Altamirano
Rosas Moreno
Miguel Schultz
Serapio Rendón
Gómez Farías
Montes

Edison

Av Insurgentes Centro

Puente de Alvarado

Mariscal
20
Iglesias
66
16

179

Ramos Arizpe
Arista

52
Plaza
Buenavista
92

84

65

Hidalgo

79

2

3 Frontón de
México

91
Edison
Aldama
Zarco
Terán
Rosales
Vadillo

Colón

39
149
48
107
124

Dr Mora

Jardín
de la
Solidaridad

43
Plaza de
la República

50

34
Lotería
Lotería
Nacional

167

178

97

Av de la República

Av Juárez

148

73

Antonio Caso

102

76
Lafragua

Paseo de la Reforma

Iturbide
Humboldt
Balderas

162
90
11

87

123

89

26

177

Guerra

Bucareli

Juárez
14

9

80

78
95

Sullivan

Monumento
a la Madre
Plaza

Metrobus
Stop

96
7

41

82
Av Morelos

133

2

4

Jardín
del Arte

Villalongín
Río Neva
Río Marne

Vía Lassa

Jardín
Luis
Pasteur

42

176

Atenas

Ayuntamiento

164

111

Ignacio Mariscal
Ramírez
Madrid
Ponciano Arriaga
Parra

Paseo de la Reforma

Mullin
Roma
Viena

General Prim
Milán
Lisboa
Lucerna

93

Plaza de
Danzón

Donde
Plaza José
María Morelos

Pugibet

Abraham González

Márquez Sterling

126

112

JUÁREZ

Bruselas
Versalles

28
32

La Ciudadela

Luis Moya
Revillagigedo

Hamburgo

Bucareli (Eje 1 Poniente)

Tolsá

Arcos de B

5

Metrobus
Stop

Nilo
Havre
Nápoles
Liverpool

Londres
Dinamarca
Berlín

Turín

Trespuentes
Enrico Martínez
Balderas

Balderas

Av Insurgentes Centro

Cuauhtémoc

Av Chapultepec

Niños Héroes

Dr Río de la Loza

Dr Jiménez
Dr Vertiz

Av Chapultepec

Línea 1

Ciclovía

Cuajimalpa

See Zona Rosa, Condesa & Roma Map (pp117–19)

Av Cuauhtémoc

Dr Lucio

144

Dr Lavista

Dr Carmona y Valle
Dr Bernard

Línea 3

6

Niza
Orizaba
Puebla
Córdoba

Flora
Frontera
Mérida
Morelia
Real de
Romita

Durango

ROMA

Dr Liceaga

Jardín
Dr Chávez

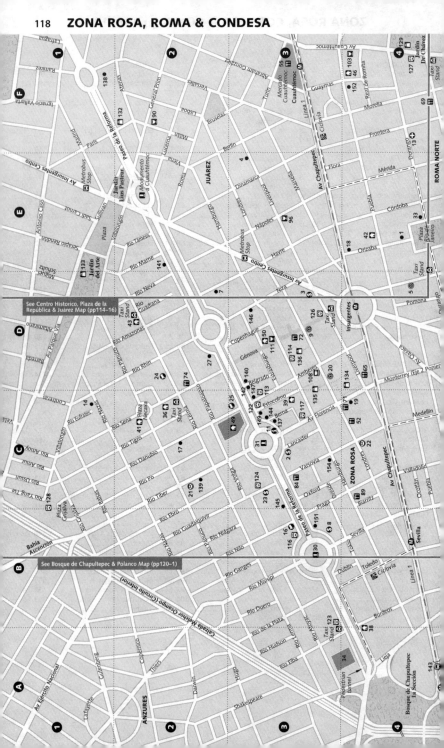

INFORMATION
Antropología Tourism Module......1 F4
Australian Embassy....................2 G3
Belize Embassy.........................3 C5
Canadian Embassy & Library.......4 F3
Cenca.....................................5 E3
Cuban Embassy.........................6 C3
French Embassy.........................7 D3
German Embassy.........................8 E3
Guatemalan Embassy..................9 B5
Instituto Nacional de Migración..10 C2
Irish Embassy............................11 C3
Mundo Joven...........................12 E2
New Zealand Embassy............(see 52)
Sectur....................................13 F3
Spanish Embassy.......................14 E2

SIGHTS & ACTIVITIES
Cárcamo del Río Lerma...........(see 17)
Casa de Los Espejos (Hall of
  Mirrors)..............................15 G4
Casa Luis Barragán..................16 E6
Castillo de Chapultepec..........(see 27)
Fuente de Tlaloc (Murals)........17 D6
Fuente de Xochipilli.................18 D5
Galería Abierta de las Rejas de
  Chapultepec........................19 F4
La Feria...................................20 E5
Los Pinos Presidential Residence.21 E6
Monumento a los Niños Héroes..22 G4
Museo de Arte Moderno...........23 G4
Museo de Historia Natural.........24 D6
Museo del Caracol....................25 F5
Museo Nacional de
  Antropología........................26 F4
Museo Nacional de Historia.......27 G5
Museo Rufino Tamayo..............28 G4
Museo Tecnológico..................29 E6
Papalote Museo del Niño..........30 E6
Zoológico de Chapultepec........31 F4

SLEEPING
Camino Real México..................32 G3
Habita Hotel............................33 E3
Hotel Park Villa........................34 F5
W Mexico City Hotel.................35 E3

EATING
Caldos d'Leo............................36 C2
Klein's....................................37 D3
La Hacienda de los Morales........38 B2
Villa María...............................39 E2

DRINKING
Área....................................(see 33)
Moon Bar.............................(see 32)
Pink..40 E3
Segafredo................................41 E3
Terra de Galicia........................42 D3

ENTERTAINMENT
Auditorio Nacional....................43 E4
Cafebrería El Péndulo................44 E3
Centro Cultural del Bosque........45 E4
Cinemex Casa de Arte...............46 D3

Liverpool Polanco (Ticketmaster)..47 G3
Salón 21..................................48 D1
Teatro de la Danza....................49 E4

SHOPPING
Plaza Moliere............................50 C2

TRANSPORT
Air Canada...............................51 C3
Air France.............................(see 52)
British Airways..........................52 B2
Continental Airlines...................53 E3
Cubana....................................54 E2
Iberia......................................55 F2
KLM/Northwest......................(see 53)
Lufthansa................................56 B3
Mexicana.................................57 C2
Ticketbus Polanco....................58 F3

0 1 km
0 0.5 miles

E **F** **G** **H**

①

Río San Joaquín

vantes Saavedra

Cervecería Modelo
(Modelo Brewery)

Lago Alberto

Av Río San Joaquín

Av Ejército Nacional

Av Marina Nacional

Calz Gral Escobedo

Lago Xochimilco

Av Ejército Nacional

Bahía Ascensión

②

55

Newton

Homero

Hegel

Schiller

Petrarca

Taine

Sudermann

Tasso

Thiers (Eje 3 Poniente)

Calz Mariano Escobedo

Rousseau

Lafayette

Gutenberg

Copérnico

Thiers (Eje 3 Poniente)

Río Nazas

③

12

39 54

14

Eugenio Sue

Aristóteles

Temístocles

M Polanco

Emerson

Lope de Vega

Plaza
Uruguay

Río Nilo

Galileo

Horacio

Tennyson

5

33

Arquímedes

Heráclito

Lamartine

13 ① 58

Av Presidente Masaryk

47 🚻

ANZURES

Copérnico

Darwin

Kant

Hugo

Shakespeare

Río Guadiana

Río Danubio

Río Misisipi

Río de la Plata

Río Hudson

Río Duero

Río Lerma

Calzada Melchor Ocampo (Circuito Interior)

40

Castelar

Newton

Polanco

Campos Elíseos

Tres Picos

4 🅿

Rincón del Bosque

Spencer

Schiller

2

④

35 53

Zona
Hotelera

Andrés Bello

8 🅿

Rubén Darío

Calz Gandhi

Río Atoyac

Río Elba

To Alameda
Central (3km)

Paseo de la Reforma

M Auditorio

43

26 🏛

1 ①

Ciclovía

28 🏛

Paseo de la Reforma

Torre
Mayor

Toledo

Tíber

Burdeos

Tokio

④

45 49

Calz Chivatito

19

Lago de
Chapultepec

31

23 🏛

22 🚹

Public Bus
Terminal

Av Chapultepec

Guadalajara

M

Av Colegio Militar

Calz Gandhi

15

27 🏛

25 🏛

M Chapultepec

Acapulco

Sonora

**ROMA
NORTE**

Melgar

Tampico

Durango

Veracruz

⑤

(Anillo Periférico)

Calz Molino del Rey

Calz del Rey

Gran Avenida

**Bosque de
Chapultepec
1a Sección**

Calz de Cerro

Vasconcelos (Circuito Interior)

Av Chapultepec

Zamora

Juan de la Barrera

Antonio Solá

Cuauhtémoc (Eje 2 Sur)

Escuela

Aguascalientes

Jojutla

Montes de Oca

Amatlán

Guerrero

Atlixco

Parque
España

See Zona Rosa, Condesa & Roma Map (pp117–19)

CONDESA

29

30

21

34

Av Constituyentes

General Gómez Pedraza

Alumnos

Fagoaga

General Monfler

General León

Lagie

Tornel

M Juanacatlán

Vicente Suárez

Márquez

Av Mazatlán

Tamaulipas

Tabasco

Av Tamaulipas

Culiacán

Tlacotalpan

Ensenada

Cholula

Saltillo

⑥

Gral Ramírez

16

Muzquiz

M Constituyentes

General Cano

Rebollar

Reyes

Ceballos

Av Michoacán

Campeche

Ciclovía

0 — 500 m
0 — 0.3 miles

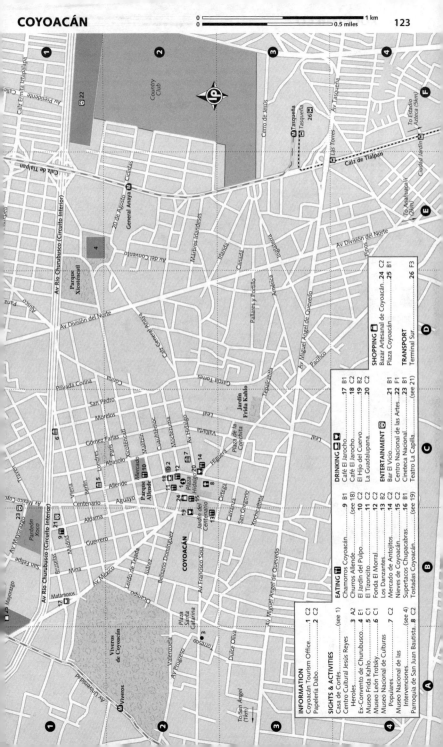

0 _____ 1 km
0 _____ 0.5 miles

INFORMATION
Coyoacán Tourism Office............	1 C2
Papelería Dabo.........................	2 C2

SIGHTS & ACTIVITIES
Casa de Cortés.........................	(see 1)
Centro Cultural Jesús Reyes	
Heroles..................................	3 A2
Ex-Convento de Churubusco......	4 E1
Museo Frida Kahlo...................	5 C1
Museo León Trotsky.................	6 C1
Museo Nacional de Culturas	
Populares...............................	7 C2
Museo Nacional de las	
Intervenciones.......................	(see 4)
Parroquia de San Juan Bautista..8 C2	

EATING
Chamorros Coyoacán................	9 B1
Churros Allende......................	(see 18)
El Jardín del Pulpo...................	10 C2
El Tizoncito...........................	11 C2
Fonda El Morral......................	12 C2
Los Danzantes........................	13 B2
Mercado de Antojitos..............	14 C2
Nieves de Coyoacán................	15 C2
Supertacos Chupacabras...........	16 B1
Tostadas Coyoacán..................	(see 19)

DRINKING
Café El Jarocho.......................	17 B1
Café El Jarocho.......................	18 C2
El Hijo del Cuervo....................	19 B2
La Guadalupana......................	20 C2

ENTERTAINMENT
Bar El Vicio............................	21 B1
Centro Nacional de las Artes.....	22 F1
Cineteca Nacional...................	23 B1
Teatro La Capilla....................	(see 21)

SHOPPING
Bazar Artesanal de Coyoacán....	24 C2
Plaza Coyoacán......................	25 B1

TRANSPORT
Terminal Sur..........................	26 F3

0 ———————— 1 km
0 ———————— 0.5 miles

INFORMATION
Xochimilco Tourism Module...........1 E3
Xochimilco Tourist Office................2 D2

SIGHTS & ACTIVITIES
Mercado de Xochimilco...................3 D2
Museo Dolores Olmedo Patiño........4 A2
Parroquia de San Bernardino de Siena.5 D2

TRANSPORT
Embarcadero Caltongo..................6 E2
Embarcadero Fernando Celada........7 C2
Embarcadero Nativitas...................8 E3
Embarcadero Salitre.......................9 D2
Embarcadero San Cristóbal............10 D2

To Parque Ecológico de Xochimilco (1.8km)

(Continued from page 109)

Canadian Embassy Library (Map pp120–1; ☎ 5724-7960; Schiller 529, Polanco; ⏰ 9am-12:30pm Mon-Fri; Ⓜ Auditorio)

Casa de Francia (Map pp118-19; ☎ 5511-3151; Havre 15, Zona Rosa; ⏰ 10am-8pm Mon-Sat; Ⓜ Insurgentes) The complex includes an art gallery, French bookstore and restaurant, plus a *mediateca* for watching videos or browsing the Internet.

Centro Cultural de España (Spanish Cultural Center; Map pp114-15; ☎ 5521-1925; www.ccemx.org; República de Guatemala 18; admission free; ⏰ 10am-8pm Tue & Wed, 10am-11pm Thu-Sat, 10am-4pm Sun; Ⓜ Zócalo) Dedicated to promoting Spanish culture in Mexico. See p130 for more details.

Instituto Francés de América Latina (IFAL; Map pp118-19; ☎ 5566-0777; www.francia.org.mx/ifal; Río Nazas 43, Colonia Cuauhtémoc) Films, concerts and other events take place here.

Instituto Goethe (Map pp118-19; ☎ 5207-0487; www.goethe.de/hn/mex in German; Tonalá 43, Colonia Roma; ⏰ 9am-1:30pm & 4-7:30pm Tue-Thu, 10am-1:45pm Sat; Ⓜ Insurgentes) Subscribes to *Die Zeit* and other German periodicals.

Media

Tiempo Libre, the city's Spanish-language what's-on weekly, comes out on Thursday and is sold at newsstands everywhere.

Recommended Spanish-language daily newspapers include *La Jornada*, with excellent cultural coverage, and *Reforma*, the latter available at convenience stores and some metro stations.

English-language newspapers and magazines can be found at these locations:

La Torre de Papel (Map pp114-15; ☎ 5512-9703; Filomena Mata 6A; ⏰ 8am-7pm Mon-Fri, 8:30am-2:30pm Sat; Ⓜ Allende) Also stocks newspapers from around Mexico.

Librería Sama (Map pp118-19; ☎ 5525-0647; Florencia 57; ⏰ 7am-9pm Mon-Fri, 8am-6pm Sat & Sun; Ⓜ Insurgentes)

Medical Services

For recommendation of a doctor, dentist or hospital, call your embassy or **Sectur** (☎ 5212-0260), the tourism ministry. An extended list of Mexico City hospitals and English-speaking physicians (with their credentials), in PDF format, is on the website of the **US embassy** (www.usembassy-mexico.gov/medical_lists.html). A private doctor's consultation generally costs between $35 and $50.

Dalinde Centro Médico (Map pp118-19; ☎ 5265-2805, emergency dial 9; Tuxpán 25, Colonia Roma Sur; Ⓜ Chilpancingo) Less expensive and often with a doctor on-call who speaks English.

Hospital ABC (American British Cowdray Hospital; Map pp110-11; ☎ 5230-8000, emergency ☎ 5230-8161; Sur 136 No 16, Colonia Las Américas; Ⓜ Observatorio) One of the best (and most expensive) hospitals in Mexico. There's an outpatient section and English-speaking staff.

Hospital Ángeles Clínica Londres (Map pp118-19; ☎ 5229-8400, emergency ☎ 5229-8445; Durango 64, Colonia Roma; Ⓜ Cuauhtémoc)

The pharmacies that are found inside Sanborns stores are among the most reliable, as are the following.

Farmacia de Ahorros (Map pp118-19; ☎ 5264-3128; Yucatán 40; ⏰ 24hr; Ⓜ Insurgentes) Take metrobus 'Álvaro Obregón.'

Farmacia París (Map pp114-15; ☎ 5709-5349; República de El Salvador 97, Centro; ⏰ 8am-11pm Mon-Sat, 10am-9pm Sun; Ⓜ Isabel La Católica)

Médicor (Map pp114-15; ☎ 5512-0431; Independencia 66; ⏰ 10am-8pm Mon-Fri, 10am-6:30pm Sat; Ⓜ Juárez) Specializing in homeopathic medicines.

Money

Most banks and *casas de cambio* (exchange offices) will change both cash and traveler's checks – but some will change only Euros and US or Canadian dollars. Exchange rates vary, so check one or two beforehand.

The greatest concentration of ATMs, banks and *casas de cambio* is on Paseo de la Reforma between the Monumento a Cristóbal Colón and the Monumento a la Independencia, but there are others all over town, including 24-hour branches at the airport.

AMERICAN EXPRESS

American Express (Map pp118-19; ☎ 5207-7282; Paseo de la Reforma 350; ⏰ 9am-6pm Mon-Fri, 9am-1pm Sat; Ⓜ Insurgentes)

CASAS DE CAMBIO

Casa de Cambio Puebla (Map pp118-19; ☎ 5207-9485; Paseo de la Reforma 308A; ⏰ 9am-5pm Mon-Fri, 10am-2pm Sat; Ⓜ Insurgentes)

Centro de Cambios y Divisas (Map pp114-15; ☎ 5705-5656; Paseo de la Reforma 87-F; ⏰ 8:30am-7:30pm Mon-Fri, 9am-5pm Sat, 9am-2:30pm Sun; Ⓜ Hidalgo)

Mexcambios (Map pp114-15; ☎ 5510-9690; Madero 13; ⏰ 9:30am-7pm Mon-Sat, 10am-6pm Sun; Ⓜ Bellas Artes)

MEXICO CITY

WIRE TRANSFERS

Western Union's 'Dinero en Minutos' wiring service is available at several locations, including Banamex branches.

Elektra (☼ 9am-9pm) Alameda Central (Map pp114-15; ☎ 5510-2185; Balderas 62; Ⓜ Juárez); Zócalo (Map pp114-15; ☎ 5522-5567; República de El Salvador 225 at Pino Suárez; Ⓜ Pino Suárez)

Telecomm (Map pp118-19; ☎ 5511-7495; Guadalquivir 109, Colonia Cuauhtémoc; ☼ 8am-7pm Mon-Fri, 9am-4pm Sat, 9am-noon Sun; Ⓜ Sevilla)

The US Postal Service's **'Dinero Seguro' service** (in the US ☎ 888-368-4669; www.usps.com) sends cash within 15 minutes to any branch of **Bancomer** Alameda Central (Map pp114-15; ☎ 5512-9511; Balderas 92; Ⓜ Juárez); Zona Rosa (Map pp118-19; ☎ 5208-4243; Liverpool 109; Ⓜ Insurgentes); Centro Histórico (Map pp114-15; ☎ 5226-8495; Bolívar 38; Ⓜ Allende).

Post

The **Palacio Postal** (Map pp114-15; ☎ 5521-1408; Tacuba 1; Ⓜ Bellas Artes), across from the Palacio de Bellas Artes, is not just Mexico City's central post office, but an architectural masterpiece. The early-20th-century building was designed in Italian renaissance style by Adamo Boari, the original author of Bellas Artes. Note in particular the marble stairway with bronze banisters.

The stamp windows, marked *'estampillas,'* stay open beyond normal post office hours (until 7:30pm Monday to Friday, and on Sunday). The *lista de correos* window (similar to poste restante) is on the right side.

Other post-office branches, scattered around town, open 9am to 3pm Monday to Friday, 9am to 1pm Saturday, unless noted otherwise.

Cuauhtémoc (Map pp118-19; ☎ 5207-7666; Río Tiber 87; Ⓜ Insurgentes)

Plaza de la República (Map pp114-15; ☎ 5592-1783; Arriaga 11; Ⓜ Revolución)

Zócalo (Map pp114-15; ☎ 5512-3661; Plaza de la Constitución 7; Ⓜ Zócalo) On the west side of the Zócalo.

Zona Rosa (Map pp118-19; ☎ 5514-3029; Londres 208; ☼ 9am-5pm Mon-Fri, 9am-1pm; Ⓜ Sevilla)

Telephone & Fax

There are thousands of Telmex card phones scattered around town. Pick up cards at shops or newsstands bearing the blue-and-yellow 'Ladatel' sign.

Some Internet cafés let you make reduced-rate international calls via an Internet server line. Typical rates are $0.20 per minute to the US or Europe.

Some stationery stores, copy shops and Internet cafés offer fax service; look for *'fax público'* signs. Sending one page to the US or Canada costs about $1; receiving a fax costs $0.50.

Toilets

Use of the bathroom is free at Sanborns stores. Public toilets are also found inside most market buildings and at some other locations in the Centro Histórico area; look for the 'WC' signs. Standards of hygiene may vary at these latter facilities, and a fee of two or three pesos is usually charged. Toilet paper is dispensed by an attendant on request, or may be taken from a common roll outside the stalls.

Tourist Information

The Mexico City Ministry of Tourism has modules in key areas, as well as at the airport and four bus stations. They can answer your queries on Mexico City and distribute a decent map and practical guide, free of charge. At least one staff member should speak English.

The following offices are all open from 9am to 6pm daily, unless otherwise noted.

Antropología (Map pp120–1; ☎ 5286-3850; Paseo de la Reforma; Ⓜ Auditorio) At the entry to the Museo Nacional de Antropología.

Basílica de Guadalupe (Map pp110-11; ☎ 5748-2085; Plaza de las Américas 1; Ⓜ La Villa-Basilica)

Bellas Artes (Map pp114-15; ☎ 5518-2799; cnr Juárez & Peralta; Ⓜ Bellas Artes)

Catedral (Map pp114-15; ☎ 5518-1003; Monte de Piedad; Ⓜ Zócalo) West of the Catedral Metropolitana.

Del Ángel (Map pp118-19; ☎ 5208-1030; Paseo de la Reforma & Florencia; Ⓜ Insurgentes) On the Zona Rosa side of Monumento a la Independencia.

San Ángel (Map p122; Revolución at Madero; ☼ 10am-6pm Sat & Sun; Ⓜ Miguel Angel de Quevado) In front of Centro Cultural.

Templo Mayor (Map pp114-15; ☎ 5512-8977; Seminario; Ⓜ Zócalo) On the east side of Catedral Metropolitana.

Xochimilco (Map p124; ☎ 5653-5209; Mercado) At the Nativitas boat landing. There are additional tourism modules at other landings, open Saturday and Sunday only.

Additionally, these city *delegaciones* (urban governmental subdivisions) operate information offices:

Coyoacán (Map p123; ☎ 5658-0221; Jardín Hidalgo 1; ⊙ 9am-6pm Mon-Fri, 8am-8pm Sat & Sun; Ⓜ Viveros) Inside the Casa de Cortés.

Xochimilco (Map p124; ☎ 5676-0810; Pino 36; ⊙ 9am-9pm Mon-Fri, 8am-8pm Sat & Sun) Just off the Jardín Juárez.

The office of **Corazón de México** (Map pp114-15; ☎ 5518-1869; www.elcorazondemexico.com.mx; Gante 15; ⊙ 10am-6pm; Ⓜ San Juan de Letrán) provides information on these Mexican states: Hidalgo, Morelos, Michoacán, Guerrero and Estado de México.

The national tourism ministry, **Sectur** (Map pp120-1; ☎ 3002-6300; Presidente Masaryk 172; ⊙ 9am-6pm Mon-Fri, 9am-2pm Sat; Ⓜ Polanco), hands out stacks of brochures on the entire country, though you're better off at the above modules for up-to-date information about the capital.

Travel Agencies

A number of midrange and top-end hotels have an *agencia de viajes* on-site or can recommend one nearby.

Mundo Joven (www.mundojoven.com in Spanish; ⊙ 9am-8pm Mon-Fri, 10am-5pm Sat) airport (Map pp110-11; ☎ 2599-0155; Sala E2, international arrivals; ⊙ 8am-10pm Mon-Fri, 9am-8pm Sat, 10am-7pm Sun); Polanco (Map pp120-1; ☎ 5250-7191; Eugenio Sue 342, cnr Homero; Ⓜ Polanco); Zócalo (Map pp114-15; ☎ 5518-1755; República de Guatemala 4; Ⓜ Zócalo) Specializes in cheap travel for students and teachers, with reasonable airfares from Mexico City. Issues ISIC, ITIC and IYTC and HI cards.

Turismo Zócalo (Map pp114-15; ☎ 5518-3606; www .agenciazocalo.com; Venustiano Carranza 67, Local 3, Centro; ⊙ 10am-7pm Mon-Fri, 10am-2pm Sat; Ⓜ Zócalo) Also functions as a Ticketbus outlet.

DANGERS & ANNOYANCES

Mexico City is often portrayed as an extremely crime-ridden city, so first-time visitors can be astonished to find how safe and human it feels. While the incidence of street crime remains too significant to deny the risks – four express kidnappings, 84 car thefts and 55 muggings a day in 2004 – there is no need to walk in fear whenever you step outside. A few precautions greatly reduce any dangers. See p972 for some general hints.

Robberies happen most often in areas frequented by foreigners, including the Bosque de Chapultepec, around the Museo Nacional de Antropología and the Zona Rosa. Be on your guard at the airport and bus stations, and remember to keep your bag between your feet when checking in. Avoid pedestrian underpasses that are empty or nearly so. Crowded metro cars and buses are favorite haunts of pickpockets. Stay alert and keep your hand on your wallet and you'll be fine.

Unless absolutely necessary, avoid carrying ATM cards, credit cards or large amounts of cash. Most importantly, if you become a robbery victim, don't resist. Give the perpetrator your valuables rather than risking injury or death.

A far more immediate danger than muggings is traffic, which statistically takes more lives in the capital than street crime. Obvious as it sounds, always look both ways when crossing streets. Some one-way streets have bus lanes running counter to the traffic flow, and traffic on some divided streets runs in just one direction. Never assume that a green light means it's safe to cross, as cars may turn left into your path. It is useful to take the 'safety in numbers' approach, crossing with other pedestrians.

Ambulantes (mobile street vendors) clog many downtown streets, impeding movement along the sidewalk and forcing you to walk in the street. Attempting to move through the throngs makes you more susceptible to pickpockets.

Taxi Crime

Although not as prevalent a danger as in the 1990s, taxi assaults still do occur and visitors are strongly advised to take precautions. Many victims have hailed a cab on the street and been robbed by armed accomplices of the driver. In particular, taxis parked in front of nightclubs or restaurants should be avoided, unless specifically authorized by the management. Rather than taking the risk of hailing cruising cabs, phone a radio *sitio* (taxi service). See p186 for a list of recommended companies.

SIGHTS

One could spend months exploring all the museums, monuments, plazas, colonial buildings, monasteries, murals, galleries, archaeological finds, statuary, shrines and religious relics this encyclopedia of a city has to offer.

Centro Histórico

A good place to start your exploration of Mexico City is where it all began. Declared a Unesco World Heritage site in 1987, the 34-block area defined as the Historic Center presents an array of sites from the Aztec, colonial and prerevolutionary eras, and the legacy of the incomparable wealth and importance the city has enjoyed, and is home to numerous absorbing museums. It also bustles with modern-day street life. The focus of this historic core, and indeed of all Mexico, is the Zócalo, the vast main plaza.

Under the administration of Mayor Andrés Manuel López Obrador, investments were poured into upgrading the image and infrastructure of the Centro. Streets were repaved, buildings refurbished, lighting and traffic flow improved and security bolstered.

ZÓCALO

The heart of Mexico City is the Plaza de la Constitución, though city residents began calling it the Zócalo (Map pp114–15), meaning 'base,' in the 19th century when plans for a major monument to independence went unrealized, leaving only the pedestal.

The ceremonial center of Aztec Tenochtitlán, known as the Teocalli, lay immediately northeast of the Zócalo. Today *conchero* dancers in feathered headdresses and *concha* (shell) anklets and bracelets remind everyone of this heritage with daily gatherings in the Zócalo for a sort of pre-Hispanic aerobics, carried out to the rhythm of booming drums.

In the 1520s Cortés paved the plaza with stones from the ruined Teocalli and other Aztec buildings. Until the early 20th century, the Zócalo was more a maze of market stalls than an open plaza. Measuring more than 220m from north to south, 240m from east to west, it's one of the world's largest city squares.

The Zócalo is home to the powers-that-be in Mexico City. On its east side is the Palacio Nacional (the presidential palace), on the north the Catedral Metropolitana,

and on the south the offices of the Distrito Federal government. The plaza is also a place for political protesters to make their point, and it's often occupied by makeshift camps of strikers. Lately it's also been a venue for free concerts and other popular entertainment.

PALACIO NACIONAL

Home to the offices of the president of Mexico, the Federal Treasury and dramatic murals by Diego Rivera, the **National Palace** (Map pp114-15; ☎ 9158-1259; Plaza de la Constitución; admission free, ID required; ⏰ 10am-5pm; Ⓜ Zócalo) fills the entire east side of the Zócalo.

The first palace on this spot was built by Aztec emperor Moctezuma II in the early 16th century. Cortés destroyed the palace in 1521, rebuilding it as a fortress with three interior courtyards. In 1562 the crown bought the palace from Cortés' family to house the viceroys of Nueva España. Destroyed during riots in 1692, it was rebuilt and remained the vice-regal residence until Mexican independence.

As you face the palace you will see three portals. On the right (south) is the guarded entrance for the president and other officials. High above the center door hangs the **Campana de Dolores**, the bell rung in the town of Dolores Hidalgo by Padre Miguel Hidalgo in 1810 at the start of the Mexican War of Independence. From the balcony underneath it, the president delivers the *grito* (shout) – *Viva México!* – on September 15 to commemorate independence.

Enter the palace through the center door. The **Diego Rivera murals** along the main staircase, painted between 1929 and 1935, depict Mexican civilization from the arrival of Quetzalcóatl (the Aztec plumed serpent god) up to the post-revolutionary period. The nine murals covering the north and east walls of the first level above the patio deal with indigenous life before the Spanish Conquest; Rivera's vision of Tenochtitlán is incredibly detailed.

Beyond the main patio is a botanical garden containing plants from around Mexico.

CATEDRAL METROPOLITANA

Construction of the **Metropolitan Cathedral** (Map pp114-15; ☎ 5510-0440, ext 123; admission free; ⏰ 8am-7pm; Ⓜ Zócalo) began in 1573 under the direction of the architect Claudio de Arciniega and remained a work in progress during the entire colonial period. Because of its placement atop the ruins of the Aztec temple complex, the massive building has been sinking unevenly since its construction, resulting in fissures and cracks in the structure.

Visitors may wander freely, though they are asked not to do so during Mass. A $1 donation is requested to enter the **sacristy** or **choir**, where docents provide commentary. You can climb the **bell tower** (admission $1.25; 10:30am-6pm). Sunday evenings at 7pm, Mass is accompanied by mariachis.

With a five-nave basilica design of vaults on semicircular arches, the cathedral was built to resemble that of Seville. The baroque portals facing the Zócalo, built in the 17th century, have two levels of columns and marble panels with bas-reliefs. The central panel shows the Assumption of the Virgin Mary, to whom the cathedral is dedicated.

The upper levels of the towers, with unique bell-shaped tops, were added in the late 18th century. The exterior was completed in 1813, when architect Manuel Tolsá added the clock tower – topped by statues of Faith, Hope and Charity – and a great central dome.

The first thing you notice upon entering from the Zócalo is the elaborately carved and gilded Altar de Perdón (Altar of Pardon). Invariably there is a line of worshippers at the foot of the Señor del Veneno (Lord of the Poison), the dusky Christ figure on the right. Legend has it that the figure attained its color when it miraculously absorbed a dose of poison through its feet from the lips of a clergyman, to whom an enemy had administered the lethal substance.

The cathedral's chief artistic treasure is the gilded 18th-century **Altar de los Reyes** (Altar of the Kings), behind the main altar. It's a masterly exercise in controlled elaboration and a high point of Churrigueresque style. The two side naves are lined with 14 richly decorated chapels. At the southwest corner, the **Capilla de los Santos Ángeles y Arcángeles** (Chapel of the Holy Angels and Archangels) is another example of baroque sculpture and painting, with altarpieces embellished by the 18th-century painter Juan Correa.

Also worthy of admiration are the intricately carved late-17th-century wooden choir stalls by Juan de Rojas in the central nave, and the sacristy, the first component of the cathedral to be built, with a pair of enormous painted panels. *La Asunción de la Virgen,* by Correa, depicts the ascension of Mary, while *La Mujer del Apocalípsis,* by Cristóbal de Villalpando, portrays the apocalyptic vision of St John the Apostle.

Adjoining the east side of the cathedral is the 18th-century **Sagrario Metropolitano** (Map pp114-15; 7:30am-7:30pm). Originally built to house the archives and vestments of the archbishop, it is now the city's main parish church. Its front entrance and mirror-image eastern portal are superb examples of the ultra-decorative Churrigueresque style.

TEMPLO MAYOR

The Teocalli of Tenochtitlán, demolished by the Spaniards in the 1520s, stood on the site of the cathedral and the blocks to its north and east. It wasn't until 1978, after electricity workers happened on an eight-ton stone-disc carving of the Aztec goddess Coyolxauhqui, that the decision was taken to demolish colonial buildings and excavate the **Templo Mayor** (Map pp114-15; ☎ 5542-4943; Seminario 8; admission $3.50; 9am-5pm Tue-Sun; Ⓜ Zócalo). The temple is thought to be on the exact spot where the Aztecs saw their symbolic eagle, perching on a cactus with a snake in its beak – the symbol of Mexico today. In Aztec belief this was, literally, the center of the universe.

The entrance to the temple site and museum is east of the cathedral, across the hectic Plaza Templo Mayor, with a model of Tenochtitlán. Authorized tour guides (with Sectur ID) offer their services by the entrance. Alternatively, rent a recorded audio-guide inside the museum, available in English ($5.50).

Like other sacred buildings in Tenochtitlán, the temple, begun in 1325, was enlarged several times, with each rebuilding accompanied by the sacrifice of captured warriors. In 1487 these rituals were performed at a frenzied pace to rededicate the temple after one major reconstruction. By some estimates, as many as 20,000 sacrificial victims went under the blade in one ghastly four-day ceremony.

What we see today are sections of the temple's different phases. (Little is left of the seventh and last version seen by the Spanish conquistadors, built around 1500.) At the center is a platform dating from about 1400; on its southern half, a sacrificial stone stands in front of a shrine to Huizilopochtli, the Aztec war god. On the northern half is a *chac-mool* (a Maya reclining figure that served as a messenger to the gods) before a shrine to the water god, Tláloc. By the time the Spanish arrived, a 40m-high double pyramid towered above this spot, with steep twin stairways climbing to shrines of the two gods.

As you approach the museum, notice the large-scale quotes chiseled on its west walls. These are awe-struck descriptions of Tenochtitlán from three of its earliest European visitors – Hernán Cortés, Bernál Díaz del Castillo and Motolinía.

The **Museo del Templo Mayor** houses artifacts from the site and gives a good overview of Aztec civilization, including *chinampa* agriculture, systems of government and trade, and beliefs, wars and sacrifices. Pride of place is given to the great wheel-like stone of Coyolxauhqui (She of Bells on her Cheek), best viewed from the top floor vantage point. She is shown decapitated – the result of her murder by Huizilopochtli, her brother, who also killed his 400 brothers en route to becoming top god. Other outstanding exhibits include full-size terracotta eagle warriors.

CALLE MONEDA
Just to the north of the Palacio Nacional, Moneda is a pedestrian thoroughfare lined with *tezontle* buildings and often clogged with *ambulantes*. The **Museo de la Secretaría de Hacienda y Crédito Público** (Museum of the Finance Secretariat; Map pp114-15; ☎ 9158-1245; Moneda 4; admission $0.80, free Sun; ✆ 10am-5:30pm Tue-Sun; Ⓜ Zócalo) shows off its vast collection of Mexican art, with an emphasis on 20th-century painters. The former colonial archbishop's palace also hosts a full program of cultural events (many free), from puppet shows to chamber music recitals.

Constructed in 1567 as the colonial mint, the **Museo Nacional de las Culturas** (National Museum of Cultures; Map pp114-15; ☎ 5542-0165; Moneda 13; admission free; ✆ 9:30am-6pm Tue-Sun; Ⓜ Zócalo) exhibits art, dress and handicrafts of the world's cultures. A block further east, then a few steps north, is a former

convent housing the **Museo José Luis Cuevas** (Map pp114-15; ☎ 5522-0156; Academia 13; admission $1, Sun free; ✆ 10am-5:30pm Tue-Sun; Ⓜ Zócalo). A haven for Mexico's fringe art scene, the museum showcases the works of Cuevas, a leading modern Mexican artist, and his contemporaries. Cuevas' *La Giganta*, a 9m-high bronze figure with male and female features, dominates the central patio, while the Sala de Arte Erótico is an intriguing gallery of the artist's sexual themes.

CENTRO CULTURAL DE ESPAÑA
The **Spanish Cultural Center** (Map pp114-15; ☎ 5521-1925; www.ccemx.org; República de Guatemala 18; admission free; ✆ 10am-8pm Tue & Wed, 10am-11pm Thu-Sat, 10am-4pm Sun; Ⓜ Zócalo), dedicated to promoting Spanish culture in Mexico, is one of the more happening spaces in the Centro, with various cutting-edge exhibitions going on at once, plus frequent concerts by Spanish bands. The splendidly restored building, which conquistador Hernán Cortés once awarded to his butler, has a rooftop terrace for tapas-munching and, on weekends, late-night DJ sessions.

MUSEO DE LA CIUDAD DE MÉXICO
For a good overview of the megalopolis, visit the **Museum of Mexico City** (Map pp114-15; ☎ 5542-0083; Pino Suárez 30; admission $2, Wed free; ✆ 10am-6pm Tue-Sun; Ⓜ Pino Suárez). The innovative permanent exhibit, 'It All Fits in a Basin,' conveys a sense of the capital's epic sweep while providing all kinds of fascinating details along the way. There's a concise history of the city with models and maps, a photo gallery of nocturnal life and a sort of hall of fame of DF entertainers. One room is devoted exclusively to the Zócalo and its role as a stage for social movements. The 18th-century Palace of the Counts of Santiago de Calimaya that houses the museum is a piece of history itself: check out the serpent's head embedded into the outside corner at Calle República de El Salvador, probably a leftover from the wall that once surrounded Tenochtitlán's sacred precinct.

PLAZA SANTO DOMINGO
Two blocks north of the Zócalo is this smaller, less formal plaza. Printers, with ancient machines, work beneath the **Portal**

de Evangelistas, along its west side. They are the descendants of the scribes who once did paperwork for the merchants who came to register their wares at the customs building (now the Education Ministry) across the square. The maroon stone **Iglesia de Santo Domingo** (Map pp114–15), dating from 1736, is a beautiful baroque church. The three-tiered facade deserves a close look: statues of St Francis and St Augustine stand in the niches alongside the doorway. The middle panel shows Saint Dominic de Guzmán receiving a staff and the Epistles from St Peter and St Paul, respectively; the dove above them represents the Holy Spirit. At the top is a bas-relief of the Assumption of the Virgin Mary.

Opposite the big church, the 18th-century Palacio de la Inquisición was headquarters of the Holy Inquisition in Mexico until 1820.

MURALS

In the 1920s the post-revolution Minister of Education, José Vasconcelos, commissioned talented young artists – among them Diego Rivera, David Alfaro Siqueiros and José Clemente Orozco – to decorate numerous public buildings with dramatic, large-scale murals conveying a new sense of Mexico's past and future. One was the former convent that housed the newly established **Secretaría de Educación Pública** (Secretariat of Education; Map pp114–15; ☎ 5328-1097; República de Brasil 31; admission free; ☉ 9am-5pm Mon-Fri; Ⓜ Zócalo). The entrance is on the east side of Plaza Santo Domingo.

The two front courtyards (on the opposite side of the building from the entrance) are lined with 120 fresco panels painted by Diego Rivera in the 1920s. Together they form a tableau of 'the very life of the people,' in the artist's words. Each courtyard is thematically distinct: the one nearest the República de Argentina entrance deals with labor, industry and agriculture, and the top floor holds portraits of Mexican heroes. The second courtyard depicts traditions and festivals. On its top level is a series on capitalist decadence and proletarian and agrarian revolution, underneath a continuous red banner emblazoned with a Mexican *corrido* (folk song). The likeness of Frida Kahlo appears in the first panel, as an arsenal worker.

A block back toward the Zócalo, then east, is the **Antiguo Colegio de San Ildefonso** (Map pp114–15; ☎ 5789-6845; www.sanildefonso.org.mx in Spanish; Justo Sierra 16; admission $3.25, free Tue; ☉ 10am-5:30pm Tue-Sun; Ⓜ Zócalo). Built in the 16th century as a Jesuit college, it later became a prestigious teacher training institute. In the 1920s, Rivera, Orozco, Siqueiros and others were brought in to adorn it with murals. Most of the work on the main patio and staircase is by Orozco, whose caustic interpretation of prerevolutionary Mexico suggests a grotesque pageant of exploitation and brutality. The amphitheater, off the lobby, holds Rivera's first mural, *La Creación,* commissioned by Vasconcelos upon Rivera's return from Europe in 1923. Mural tours (in Spanish) are given at 1pm and 4pm. Nowadays, the San Ildefonso hosts outstanding temporary exhibitions, as well as the Filmoteca of the national university.

PLAZA TOLSÁ

Several blocks west of the Zócalo is this handsome square, named after the illustrious late-18th-century sculptor and architect who completed the Catedral Metropolitana.

Manuel Tolsá also created the bronze equestrian statue of the Spanish king Carlos IV (who reigned from 1788 to 1808) that is the plaza's centerpiece. It originally stood in the Zócalo, then on Paseo de la Reforma, before being moved here in 1979 ('as a work of art,' a chiseled plaque emphasizes).

King Carlos rides in front of the **Museo Nacional de Arte** (National Art Museum; Map pp114–15; ☎ 5130-3400; www.munal.com.mx in Spanish; Tacuba 8; admission $2.75, free Tue; ☉ 10:30am-5:30pm Tue-Sun; Ⓜ Bellas Artes). Built around 1900 in the style of an Italian renaissance palace, it holds collections representing every school of Mexican art until the early 20th century. A highlight is the work of José María Velasco, depicting the Valle de México in the late 19th century – with Guadalupe and Chapultepec far outside the city.

Opposite the art museum is the **Palacio de Minería** (Palace of Mining; Map pp114–15; ☎ 5623-2981; Tacuba 5; admission $2.50; tours ☉ 11am & 1pm Sat & Sun; Ⓜ Bellas Artes), where mining engineers were trained in the 19th century. Today it houses a branch of the national university's engineering department. A neoclassical masterpiece, the palace was designed by Tolsá and built between 1797 and 1813. Visits are by guided tour only. The palace contains a small **museum** (admission $1; 🕙 10am-6pm Wed-Sun) on Tolsá's life and work.

AVENIDA MADERO

A landmark for disoriented visitors since 1952, the **Torre Latinoamericana** (Latin American Tower; Map pp114-15; ☎ 5518-7423; Eje Central Lázaro Cárdenas 2; adult/child $3.75/2.75; 🕙 9am-10pm; Ⓜ Bellas Artes) was Latin America's tallest building when constructed. (Today it's Mexico City's fifth tallest.) Views from the 44th-floor observation deck are spectacular, smog permitting. Also worth checking out is the 37th-floor **museum** (admission $1) with exhibits on the history of the building, plus vintage photos of the Centro.

A block east toward the Zócalo stands one of the city's gems, the **Casa de Azulejos** (House of Tiles; Map pp114-15; ☎ 5518-6676; Madero 4; 🕙 7am-1am; Ⓜ Bellas Artes). Dating from 1596, it was built for the Condes (Counts) del Valle de Orizaba. Although the superb tile work that has adorned the outside walls since the 18th century is Spanish and Moorish in style, most of the tiles were actually produced in China and shipped to Mexico on the Manila *naos* (Spanish galleons used up to the early 19th century). The building now houses a Sanborns restaurant in a covered courtyard around a Moorish fountain. The staircase has a 1925 mural by Orozco.

Continuing eastward you'll encounter the baroque facade of the late-18th-century **Palacio de Iturbide** (Map pp114-15; ☎ 1226-0011; Madero 17; admission free; 🕙 10am-7pm Wed-Mon; Ⓜ Allende). Built for colonial nobility, in 1821 it became the residence of General

---

HIDDEN MURALS

So broad was the muralist movement's canvas that it sometimes seems not a wall has gone uncovered. With murals showing up in markets, libraries, metro stations and restaurants, Chilangos naturally grow indifferent to the presence of these grandiose artistic statements in their midst. Sure, you've seen the tableaux at the Palacio Nacional and Bellas Artes, but some lesser-known murals are just as worthy of viewing, and tracking them down is half the fun.

■ **El Agua, El Origen de la Vida** (*Water, Origin of Life*; Map pp120-1; Cárcamo del Río Lerma, 2a Sección Bosque de Chapultepec; Ⓜ Constituyentes) Diego Rivera painted these murals inside the Chapultepec water works, built in the 1940s to channel the waters of the Río Lerma, 62km west, into giant cisterns to supply the city. Experimenting with waterproof paints, the artist covered the collection tank, sluice gates and part of the pipeline with images of amphibious beings and the workers involved in the project. The murals are housed in a pavilion behind the Tlaloc fountain, another Rivera work. Though not technically open, the guard can be persuaded to let you in for a tip.

■ **Velocidad** (*Speed*; Map pp114-15; Plaza Juárez, Av Juárez; Ⓜ Bellas Artes) Originally designed for a Chrysler factory, this 1953 work by David Siqueiros represents the notion of speed through the kinetic figure of a female runner. The mosaic canvas was transplanted to the entrance of the new Plaza Juárez shopping mall as part of the Alameda development project.

■ **Historia de México** (*History of Mexico*; Map pp114-15; Mercado Abelardo Rodríguez, República de Venezuela, cnr Rodríguez Puebla; Ⓜ Zócalo) The large Abelardo Rodríguez public market, east of the Zócalo, became a canvas for a group of young international artists in the 1930s. Sadly many of these paintings are decaying from neglect. One of the most intriguing (and best preserved) works, created by the Japanese artist Isama Noguchi, is a dynamic three-dimensional mural sculpted of cement and plaster that symbolizes the struggle against fascism. It's located in the community center, upstairs from the southeast corner of the market.

■ **El Perfil del Tiempo** (*The Profile of Time*; Map pp110-11; Metro Copilco, línea 3 platform; Ⓜ Copilco) As any metro rider is aware, the walls of many stations were illustrated by major artists during the 1980s. The Copilco station, at the eastern entrance to UNAM, features this work by Durango artist Guillermo Cenicero. Covering 1000 sq meters – the largest of any metro murals – it surveys the history of world painting, from Spain's Altamira cave paintings to Mexico's modern masters, and also includes scenes from the conquest of Mexico.

THROW A PESO IN THE HAT

Dressed in khaki uniforms, they stand on street corners, in front of theaters, at busy traffic intersections – anywhere that people congregate. They work in pairs: the organ grinder and the tip collector, who extends an upturned cap at any pedestrian or driver in sight. The music-maker cranks the handle of a varnished wooden box, manufactured in Berlin in the late 19th century, to produce a carnivalesque string of tunes that echo Mexico's distant past. The jukeboxes of their era, these 'organs' generally play eight tunes of a minute each. Though some passersby consider them a mere annoyance, the 100 or so organ grinders who work the city are actually heirs to a tradition dating back to before the Revolution. Brought over by Italian immigrants who earned their living as itinerant carnival performers, the instrument became fashionable during the Porfirio Díaz regime. Later the old European ditties were replaced by Mexican tunes. If you'd like to see the tradition continue, drop a few pesos in the hat.

Agustín Iturbide, a hero of the Mexican struggle for independence. To the cheers of a rent-a-crowd, Iturbide was proclaimed Emperor Agustín I here in 1822. (He abdicated less than a year later, after General Santa Anna announced the birth of a republic.) Acquired and restored by Banamex bank in 1965, the palace now functions as the Palacio de Cultura Banamex, with exhibits drawn from the bank's vast Mexican art collection, as well as contemporary Mexican handicrafts. Some of the palace's original salons are displayed on the upper level, along with exhibits on its eventful history. Guided tours are offered (in Spanish) at noon, 2pm and 4pm.

UNIVERSIDAD DEL CLAUSTRO DE SOR JUANA

Considered the greatest Spanish-language poet of the 17th century, Sister Juana Inés de la Cruz composed many of her sonnets in the former convent of San Jerónimo, today the **University of the Cloister of Sor Juana** (Map pp114-15; ☎ 5130-3336; www.ucsj.edu .mx; Izazaga 92; admission free; ☉ 7am-8pm Mon-Fri, 7am-3pm Sat; Ⓜ Isabel la Católica). Its magnificent two-level cloister, dating from 1585, now buzzes with students of gastronomy, literature and philosophy. To the east is the painstakingly restored Iglesia de San Jerónimo containing Sor Juana's tomb and a 1750 portrait of the poetess. The series of tiled niches on its south wall is what remains on the confessional. The adjacent **Museo de la Indumentaria Mexicana** (Map pp114-15; admission free; ☉ 10am-5pm Mon-Fri) displays regional outfits from around Mexico.

The university also hosts a dynamic range of cultural activities, including films, plays, book presentations and conferences.

LA CIUDADELA

The formidable compound now known as 'The Citadel' started off as a tobacco factory in the late 18th century. Later it was converted to an armory and political prison, but is best known as the scene of the Decena Trágica (Tragic Ten Days), the coup that brought down the Madero government in 1913. Today it is home to the **Biblioteca Nacional José Vasconcelos** (National Library; Map pp114-15; ☎ 5510-2591; Plaza de la Ciudadela 4; ☉ 7:30am-7:30pm; Ⓜ Balderas), with holdings of over 260,000 volumes and a good periodicals collection. The central halls are given over to art exhibits.

At the Calle Balderas entrance is the **Centro de la Imagen** (Map pp114-15; ☎ 9172-4724; www .conaculta.gob.mx/cimagen; admission free; ☉ 11am-6pm Tue-Sun; Ⓜ Balderas), the city's photography museum. This innovatively curated museum stages compelling exhibitions, often focusing on documentary views of Mexican life by some of the country's sharpest observers. Pick up a copy of *Luna Córnea*, the photography journal published by the center, at the excellent bookstore.

Alameda Central & Around

The only sizable downtown park, the Alameda Central is surrounded by some of the city's most interesting buildings and museums. Less than 1km from the Zócalo, it is near two metro stations, Bellas Artes on its east, and Hidalgo on its northwest corner.

Under the administration of Mayor López Obrador, the Alameda and adjacent Av Juárez have undergone ambitious redevelopment. The Foreign Relations Secretariat towers, designed by leading architect Ricardo Legorreta, and Sheraton Centro Histórico have transformed the look of the corridor, much of which was destroyed in the 1985 earthquake. Opened in 2006 to occupy the art-deco structure at the corner of Independencia and Revillagigedo, the Museo de Arte Popular should have a galvanizing effect on the moribund zone south of Juárez. The museum will be a major showcase for Mexico's folk arts and traditions.

ALAMEDA CENTRAL

Created in the late 1500s by mandate of then-Viceroy Luis de Velasco, the Alameda (Map pp114–15) took its name from the *álamos* (poplars) planted over its rectangular expanse. By the late 19th century, the park was graced with European-style statuary and a bandstand and lit by gas lamps. It became the place to be seen for the city's elite. Today the Alameda is a popular refuge, particularly on Sunday when families stroll its broad pathways and gather for open-air concerts.

PALACIO DE BELLAS ARTES

Dominating the east end of the Alameda is the splendid white-marble **Palace of Fine Arts** (Map pp114-15; ☎ 5512-2593; Hidalgo 1; admission $3.25, free Sun; ☼ 10am-6pm Tue-Sun; Ⓜ Bellas Artes), a concert hall and arts center commissioned by President Porfirio Díaz. Construction began in 1905 under Italian architect Adamo Boari, who favored neoclassical and art-nouveau styles. The project became more complicated than anticipated as the heavy marble shell sank into the spongy subsoil, and then the Revolution intervened. Work was halted and Boari returned to Italy. Architect Federico Mariscal eventually finished the interior in the 1930s, utilizing the more modern art-deco style.

Immense murals dominate the upper floors. On the 2nd floor are two early-1950s works by Rufino Tamayo: *México de Hoy* (Mexico Today) and *Nacimiento de la Nacionalidad* (Birth of Nationality), a symbolic depiction of the creation of the mestizo (person of mixed indigenous and Spanish ancestry) identity.

At the west end of the 3rd floor is Diego Rivera's famous *El Hombre En El Cruce de Caminos* (Man at the Crossroads), originally commissioned for New York's Rockefeller Center. The Rockefellers had the original destroyed because of its anti-capitalist themes, but Rivera re-created it

here in 1934. Capitalism, accompanied by war, is shown on the left; socialism, with health and peace, on the right.

On the north side are David Alfaro Siqueiros' three-part *La Nueva Democracía* (New Democracy) and Rivera's four-part *Carnaval de la Vida Mexicana* (Carnival of Mexican Life); to the east is José Clemente Orozco's eye-catching *La Katharsis* (Catharsis), depicting the conflict between humankind's 'social' and 'natural' aspects.

The 4th-floor **Museo Nacional de Arquitectura** (admission $2.75, free Sun; ☼ 10:30am-5pm Tue-Sun) features changing exhibits on contemporary architecture.

The Bellas Artes theater (only available for viewing at performances) is itself an architectural gem, with a stained-glass curtain depicting the Valle de México. Based on a design by Mexican painter Gerardo Murillo (aka Dr Atl), it was assembled by New York jeweler Tiffany & Co from almost a million pieces of colored glass.

In addition, the palace stages outstanding temporary art exhibitions and the Ballet Folclórico de México (see p171). A worthwhile bookstore and elegant café are on the premises too.

MUSEO FRANZ MAYER

An oasis of calm and beauty north of the Alameda, the **Franz Mayer Museum** (Map pp114-15; ☎ 5518-2266; Hidalgo 45; admission $2.75, Tue free; ☼ 10am-5pm Tue & Thu-Sun, until 7pm Wed; Ⓜ Bellas Artes) is the fruit of the efforts of Franz Mayer, born in Mannheim, Germany, in 1882. Prospering as a financier in his adopted Mexico, Mayer amassed the collection of Mexican silver, textiles, ceramics and furniture masterpieces that is now on display at the museum.

Taking up the west side of the compact Plaza de Santa Veracruz, the museum is housed in the old hospice of the San Juan de Dios order. Under the brief reign of Maximilian it became a halfway house for prostitutes.

The exhibit halls open off a superb colonial patio; along its west side is a suite of rooms decorated in antique furnishings, on the north side the Cloister Café.

MUSEO MURAL DIEGO RIVERA

Among Diego Rivera's most famous works is *Sueño de una Tarde Dominical en la*

Alameda (Dream of a Sunday Afternoon in the Alameda), painted in 1947. In the 15m-long by 4m-high mural, the artist imagined many of the figures who walked in the city from colonial times onward, among them Cortés, Juárez, Emperor Maximilian, Porfirio Díaz, and Francisco Madero and his nemesis, General Victoriano Huerta. All are grouped around a *Catarina* (skeleton in prerevolutionary women's garb). Rivera himself, as a pug-faced child, and Frida Kahlo stand beside the skeleton. Charts identify all the characters.

Just west of the Alameda, the **Diego Rivera Mural Museum** (Map pp114-15; ☎ 5512-0754; cnr Balderas & Colón; admission $1.50, free Sun; ◷ 10am-6pm Tue-Sun; Ⓜ Hidalgo) was built in 1986 to house the mural, after its original location, the Hotel del Prado, was wrecked by the 1985 earthquake.

LABORATORIO DE ARTE ALAMEDA

As is often the case with museums in the Centro Histórico, the building that contains the **Alameda Art Laboratory** (Map pp114-15; ☎ 5510-2793; www.artealameda.inba.gob.mx; Dr Mora 7; admission $1.50, free Sun; ◷ 9am-5pm Tue-Sun; Ⓜ Hidalgo) is as interesting as its contents. The former church is just a fragment of the 17th-century Convento de San Diego that was dismantled under the post-independence reform laws. As the museum's name suggests, it hosts installations by leading experimental artists from Mexico and abroad, with an emphasis on current electronic, virtual and interactive media. They could not have asked for a grander exhibition space.

Plaza de la República & Around

This plaza, west of the Alameda Central, is dominated by the imposing, domed Monumento a la Revolución. The grand art-deco building northeast of the plaza is the Frontón de México, a now-defunct jai-alai arena.

MONUMENTO A LA REVOLUCIÓN

Begun in the 1900s under Porfirio Díaz, the **Monumento a la Revolución** (Map pp114–15) was originally meant to be a meeting chamber for legislators. But construction (not to mention Díaz' presidency) was interrupted by the Revolution. The structure was modified and given a new role in the 1930s: the tombs of the revolutionary and post-revolutionary heroes Pancho Villa, Francisco Madero, Venustiano Carranza, Plutarco Elías Calles and Lázaro Cárdenas are inside its wide pillars.

Underlying the monument, the **Museo Nacional de la Revolución** (National Museum of the Revolution; Map pp114-15; ☎ 5546-2115; Plaza de la República; admission $1.25, free Sun; ◷ 9am-5pm Tue-Sun; Ⓜ Revolución) covers an 80-year period, from the implementation of the constitution guaranteeing human rights in 1857 to the nationalization of Mexico's oil reserves by President Lázaro Cárdenas in 1938. Enter from the northeast quarter of the plaza.

MUSEO NACIONAL DE SAN CARLOS

The **Museum of San Carlos** (Map pp114-15; ☎ 5566-8342; Puente de Alvarado 50; admission $2.50, Mon free; ◷ 10am-6pm Wed-Mon; Ⓜ Revolución) exhibits a formidable collection of European art from the 16th to the early 20th century, including works by Rubens, Van Dyck and Goya. Occupying the former mansion of the Conde de Buenavista, the unusual rotunda structure was designed by Manuel Tolsá in the late 18th century. It later became home to Alamo-victor Santa Anna, and subsequently served as a cigar factory, lottery headquarters and school before being reborn as a museum in 1968.

Paseo de la Reforma

Mexico City's main boulevard runs southwest past the Alameda Central and through the Bosque de Chapultepec. Emperor Maximilian of Hapsburg laid out the boulevard to connect his castle on Chapultepec Hill with the old city center. You'll almost certainly pass along Reforma at some point during your stay, to call at one of the nearby banks, shops, hotels, restaurants or embassies.

The López Obrador administration undertook a thorough restoration of Paseo de la Reforma, paving the broad esplanades with mosaic cobblestones and planting attractive gardens along its length.

Paseo de la Reforma links a series of monumental *glorietas* (traffic circles) and is studded with impressive architecture. A couple of blocks west of the Alameda Central is **El Caballito** (Map pp114–15), a bright yellow representation of a horse's head by the sculptor Sebastián. It commemorates another equestrian sculpture that stood here for 127 years and today fronts the Museo Nacional de Arte (p131). A few blocks southwest on Reforma is the **Monumento a Cristóbal Colón** (Map pp114–15), an 1877 statue by French sculptor Enrique Cordier of Columbus gesturing toward the horizon.

Reforma's busy intersection with Av Insurgentes is marked by the **Monumento a Cuauhtémoc** (Map pp118–19), memorializing the last Aztec emperor. Two blocks northwest is the **Jardín del Arte**, site of a lovely Sunday art market (p176).

The **Centro Bursátil** (Map pp118–19), a glass arrow housing the nation's stock exchange (Bolsa), marks the northeast corner of the Zona Rosa. Continuing west past the US embassy, you reach the symbol of Mexico City, the **Monumento a la Independencia** (Map pp118-19; admission free; 🕙 10am-6pm; Ⓜ Insurgentes). Known as 'El Ángel' (The Angel), this gilded statue of Victory on a 45m pillar was sculpted for the independence centennial of 1910. The female figures around the base portray Law, Justice, War and Peace; the male ones are Mexican independence heroes. Inside the monument are the remains of Miguel Hidalgo, Ignacio Allende, Juan Aldama and nine other notables.

At Reforma's intersection with Sevilla is the monument commonly known as **La Diana Cazadora** (Diana the Huntress; Map pp118–19), a 1942 bronze sculpture actually meant to represent the Archer of the North Star. The League of Decency under the Ávila Camacho administration had the sculptor add a loincloth to the female figure, which wasn't removed until 1966.

Southwest from here stands the newest addition to the Mexico City skyscape, the **Torre Mayor** (Map pp118–19). Designed by Canadian architect Heberhard Zeidler, the green-glass tower rises 225m above the capital, making it Latin America's tallest building. Inaugurated in 2003, the 59-storey structure contains 43 floors of offices, 13 parking levels and a shopping mall. A 52nd-floor **Skydeck** (☎ 5283-9000; adult/child 3-12 $6.50/3.25; 🕙 7-10pm Tue-Fri, 11am-9pm Sat & Sun) affords mesmerizing views of the Reforma corridor, Bosque de Chapultepec and beyond. Sharing this level is a museum with changing exhibits, so plan on spending a few hours.

GETTING THERE & AWAY

Metro Hidalgo is on Reforma at the Alameda Central; Insurgentes station marks the southern edge of the Zona Rosa, 500m south of Reforma. Any 'Metro Auditorio' bus heading southwest on Reforma continues through the Bosque de Chapultepec, while 'Metro Chapultepec' buses terminate just south of Reforma at the east end of the Bosque de Chapultepec. In the opposite direction, 'Metro Hidalgo' and 'La Villa' buses head northeast up Reforma to the Alameda Central and beyond.

A metrobus, similar to the one along Av Insurgentes, is planned to run the length of Reforma.

Zona Rosa

Both glossy and sleazy, the Pink Zone is an integral piece of the Mexico City jigsaw. People-watching from its sidewalk cafés reveals a higher degree of diversity than elsewhere: it's the city's principal gay and lesbian district and an expat haven, with a significant Korean population.

Condesa & Roma

Colonia Condesa's architecture, palm-lined esplanades and idyllic parks echo its early-20th-century origins as a haven for a newly emerging elite. La Condesa is now a trendy neighborhood of informal restaurants and sidewalk cafés. Amsterdam, Tamaulipas and Mazatlán, with pedestrian paths, are worth strolling to admire the art-deco and California colonial–style buildings. A focus is the peaceful **Parque México** (Map pp118–19), with an oval shape that reflects its earlier use as a horse-racing track. It makes for a delightful ramble, especially in spring when lavender jacaranda blossoms carpet the paths. Two blocks northwest is **Parque España** (Map pp118–19), with a children's fun fair.

Parque México is a 200m walk west from the Av Insurgentes Metrobus Campeche station. The main cluster of bistro-type eateries in Condesa is about 500m west of Parque México, near the intersection of Michoacán and Tamaulipas. Patriotismo and Chapultepec metro stations are also within walking distance.

Colonia Roma, home to numerous artists and writers, was established in the late 19th century on the hacienda lands

Aztec performers in the Zócalo, Mexico City (p128)

Crowded public transport, Mexico City (p183)

Tacos and tortillas, Oaxaca (p730)

Food stalls, Mexico City (p159)

RICHARD I'ANSON

Murals abound in Mexico City (p131)

NEIL SETCHFIELD

Crazy restaurant sign, Cabo San Lucas (p304)

RICHARD CL

surrounding the center. Northeast of Condesa, its Parisian-style buildings (many damaged in the 1985 earthquake) are a reminder of the Porfiriato era's admiration for all things French. Two lovely plazas – Río de Janeiro, with a giant statue of David, and Luis Cabrera with dancing fountains – reinforce the old-world character. When in Roma, browse the secondhand-book stores, linger in the cafés and check out a few art galleries. On weekends inspect the **antique market** along Av Álvaro Obregón, the main thoroughfare. The neighborhood holds literary notoriety as the site of William S Burroughs' William Tell incident, in which the beatnik novelist fatally shot his wife Joan while aiming for a martini glass on her head.

GALLERIES

The Roma neighborhood is dotted with art galleries – see www.arte-mexico.com (in Spanish) for a map.

Centro de Cultura Casa Lamm (Map pp118-19; ☎ 5511-0899; www.casalamm.com.mx in Spanish; Álvaro Obregón 99; admission free; 🕙 10am-6pm Tue-Sun; Ⓜ Insurgentes) houses a contemporary-art gallery, plus the Manuel Álvarez Bravo photo collection, with more than 2000 original images by masters like Henri Cartier-Bresson, Edward Weston and Tina Modotti.

Other galleries of note:

Galería Nina Menocal (Map pp118-19; ☎ 5564-7209; www.ninamenocal.com; Zacatecas 93; 🕙 9am-7pm Mon-Fri, 10am-3pm Sat; Ⓜ Insurgentes) Highlights emerging Latin American artists.

MUCA Roma (Map pp118-19; ☎ 5511-0925; Tabasco 73; 🕙 10am-6pm; Ⓜ Cuauhtémoc) Roma branch of the university museum (p143).

OMR (Map pp118-19; ☎ 5511-1179; www.galeriaomr .com; Plaza Río de Janeiro 54; 🕙 10am-3pm & 4-7pm Mon-Fri, 10am-2pm Sat; Ⓜ Insurgentes) Showcases cutting-edge painting, photography and sculpture by international artists. It hosts six to eight exhibitions per year.

Bosque de Chapultepec

Chapultepec – 'Hill of Grasshoppers' in Náhuatl – served as a refuge for the wandering Aztecs before becoming a summer residence for their noble class. It was the nearest freshwater supply for Tenochtitlán and an aqueduct was built to channel its waters over Lago de Texcoco to the pre-Hispanic capital. In the 15th century,

Nezahualcóyotl, ruler of nearby Texcoco, designated the area a forest reserve.

The Bosque de Chapultepec, Mexico City's largest park, now covers more than 4 sq km and has lakes, a zoo and several excellent museums. It also remains an abode of Mexico's high and mighty, containing the current presidential residence, **Los Pinos** (Map pp120–1) and a former imperial and presidential palace, the Castillo de Chapultepec.

The park is busiest on Sunday, when vendors line its main paths and throngs of families come to picnic and crowd into the museums. It is divided into two main sections by two major north–south roads, Calz Chivatito and the Anillo Periférico. Most of the major attractions are in or near the eastern **1a Sección** (First Section; Map pp120-1; 🕙 5am-5pm Tue-Sun), while a large amusement park and children's museum dominate the **2a Sección**.

Photo exhibitions are staged at the **Galería Abierta de las Rejas de Chapultepec**, an outdoor gallery that lines the park's northern fence along Reforma, from the zoo entrance to the Rufino Tamayo museum. These giant photo enlargements, which often cover some fascinating aspects of DF history, can be viewed during the day, or by night when they're amply illuminated.

MONUMENTO A LOS NIÑOS HÉROES

The six asparagus-shaped columns marking the eastern entrance to the park (Map pp120–1), near Chapultepec metro, commemorate the 'boy heroes,' six brave cadets who perished in battle. On September 13, 1847, more than 8000 American troops stormed Chapultepec Castle, which then housed the national military academy. Mexican General Santa Anna retreated before the onslaught, excusing the cadets from fighting, but the youths, aged 13 to 20, chose to defend the castle. Legend has it that one of them, Juan Escutia, wrapped himself in a Mexican flag and leapt to his death rather than surrender.

CASTILLO DE CHAPULTEPEC

The castle atop Chapultepec Hill was built in 1785 as a residence for the viceroys of Nueva España. After independence it became the national military academy. When Emperor Maximilian and Empress Carlota arrived in 1864, they refurbished it as their residence. The castle became home to Mexico's presidents until 1939 when President Lázaro Cárdenas converted it into the **Museo Nacional de Historia** (National History Museum; Map pp120-1; ☎ 5241-3100; admission $3.50; ☻ 9am-4:30pm Tue-Sun; Ⓜ Chapultepec).

Historical exhibits, chronicling the period from the rise of colonial Nueva España to the Mexican Revolution, occupy the museum. The east end of the castle preserves the palace occupied by Maximilian and Carlota, flanked by a patio with expansive views. On the upper floor are Porfirio Díaz' sumptuous rooms, opening onto a patio where a tower marks the top of Chapultepec Hill, 45m above street level. The lower southwest room covers the battle of Chapultepec, with portraits of the six heroic boys (see p137)

In addition to displaying such iconic objects as Santa Anna's wooden leg and the Virgin of Guadalupe banner borne by Miguel Hidalgo in his march for independence, the academy features a number of dramatic interpretations of Mexican history by leading muralists including Juan O'Gorman's *Retablo de la Independencia* (Panel of Independence) in room 5, and David Alfaro Siqueiros' *Del Porfiriato a la Revolución* (From Porfirism to the Revolution) in room 13.

To reach the castle, follow the road that curves up the hill behind the Monumento a los Niños Héroes. Alternatively, a little road-train ($1 round-trip) runs up every 10 minutes while the castle is open.

At the base of the castle is one of the park's perennial attractions, the **Casa de los Espejos** (Map pp120-1; admission $0.30; Ⓜ Chapultepec), housing 16 fun-house mirrors imported from Spain in 1932.

MUSEO DEL CARACOL

From the Castillo de Chapultepec, the **Museo del Caracol** (Map pp120-1; ☎ 5241-3145; admission $3; ☻ 10am-4:15pm Tue-Sun; Ⓜ Chapultepec) is a short distance back down the road. Shaped somewhat like a snail shell, this 'gallery of history' traces the origins of Mexico's present-day institutions, identity and values through a series of audio-enhanced dioramas re-enacting key moments in the country's struggle for liberty. The 12 exhibit halls spiral downward, along the

way depicting the cry for independence at Dolores Hidalgo, the May 5 battle of Puebla, the execution of Maximillian, and the triumphant entrance of Madero into Mexico City. The tour ends at a circular hall that contains only one item – a replica of the 1917 Constitution of Mexico.

MUSEO DE ARTE MODERNO

The **Museum of Modern Art** (Map pp120-1; ☎ 5211-8331; cnr Paseo de la Reforma & Gandhi; admission $2, Sun free; ☻ 10am-6pm Tue-Sun; Ⓜ Chapultepec) exhibits work by noteworthy 20th-century Mexican artists. The main building consists of four skylit rotundas, housing canvasses by Dr Atl, Rivera, Siqueiros, Orozco, Kahlo, Tamayo and O'Gorman, among others. *Las Dos Fridas*, possibly Frida Kahlo's most well-known painting, is in the Sala Xavier Villarrutia. Temporary exhibitions feature prominent Mexican and foreign artists. Just northwest of the Monumento a los Niños Héroes (access is via Paseo de la Reforma), the museum has a pleasant café beside a sculpture garden.

ZOOLÓGICO DE CHAPULTEPEC

The **Chapultepec Zoo** (Map pp120-1; ☎ 5553-6263; admission free; ☻ 9am-4:30pm Tue-Sun; Ⓜ Auditorio) houses a wide range of the world's creatures in large open-air enclosures. The first place outside China where pandas were born in captivity, the zoo has three of these rare bears, descendants of the original pair donated by the People's Republic in 1975. Endangered Mexican species include the Mexican grey wolf and the hairless xoloitzcuintle, the only surviving dog species from pre-Hispanic times.

Part of Chapultepec forest was given over to a bird sanctuary back during Moctezuma's reign; today, parrots, macaws, toucans, flamingos and other Mexican species swoop around the Aviario Moctezuma (only 20 visitors allowed in at a time).

There are various fast-food franchises on the premises.

MUSEO NACIONAL DE ANTROPOLOGÍA

The **National Museum of Anthropology** (Map pp120-1; ☎ 5553-6381; www.mna.inah.gob.mx; cnr Paseo de la Reforma & Gandhi; admission $3.50; ☻ 9am-7pm Tue-Sun; Ⓜ Auditorio), among the finest of its kind, stands in an extension of the Bosque de Chapultepec.

The vast museum offers more than most people can absorb in a single visit. Concentrate on the regions you plan to visit or have visited, with a quick look at some of the other eye-catching exhibits. Everything is superbly displayed, with much explanatory text translated into English. Audio-guide devices, in English, are available at the entrance ($6).

The spacious complex, constructed in the 1960s, is the work of Mexican architect Pedro Ramírez Vázquez. Its long, rectangular courtyard is surrounded on three sides by two-storey display halls. An immense umbrella-like stone fountain rises up from the center of the courtyard.

The 12 ground-floor *salas* (halls) are dedicated to pre-Hispanic Mexico. The upper level shows how Mexico's indigenous descendants live today. Here's a brief guide to the ground-floor halls, proceeding counterclockwise around the courtyard:

Culturas Indígenas de México Currently serves as a space for temporary exhibitions.

Introducción a la Antropología Introduces visitors to the field of anthropology and traces the emergence of *homo sapiens* from its hominid ancestors.

Poblamiento de América Demonstrates how the hemisphere's earliest settlers got here and survived in their new environment.

Preclásico en el Altiplano Central Focuses on the Pre-classic period, approximately 2300 BC to AD 100. These exhibits highlight the transition from a nomadic hunting life to a more settled farming life in Mexico's Central Highlands.

Teotihuacán Displays models and objects from the Americas' first great and powerful state. The exhibit includes a full-size replica of part of the Templo de Quetzalcóatl.

Los Toltecas y Su Época Covers cultures of central Mexico between about AD 650 and 1250 and is named for one of the most important, the Toltecs. On display is one of the four basalt warrior columns from Tula's Temple of Tlahuizcalpantecuhtli.

Mexica Devoted to the Mexicas, aka Aztecs. Come here to see the famous sun stone, unearthed in a fractured state beneath the Zócalo in 1790. Though often erroneously identified as a representation of the Aztec calendar, it is probably a sacrificial altar. It depicts the face of the fire god, Xiuhtechtli, at the center of a web of symbols representing the Mexica vision of the cosmos. Other exhibits include a model of the Tlatelolco market, an 'aerial view' painting of Tenochtitlán, and more magnificent sculptures from the pantheon of Aztec deities.

Culturas de Oaxaca Devoted to that state's cultural heights, scaled by the Zapotec and Mixtec peoples. A tomb from the hilltop site of Monte Albán is reproduced full-size below the main exhibit hall.

Culturas de la Costa del Golfo Spotlights the important civilizations along the Gulf of Mexico including the Olmec, Classic Veracruz, Totonac and Huastec. Stone carvings here include two Olmec heads weighing in at almost 20 tons.

Maya Has exhibits from southeast Mexico, Guatemala, Belize and Honduras. A full-scale replica of the tomb of King Pakal, discovered deep in the Templo de las Inscripciones at Palenque, is breathtaking. On the outside patio are reproductions of the famous wall paintings of Bonampak and of Edificio II at Hochob, in Campeche, constructed as a giant mask of the rain god, Chac.

Culturas del Occidente Profiles cultures of western Mexico from Nayarit, Jalisco, Michoacán, Colima and Guerrero states. Reproductions of the region's characteristic shaft tombs are on display.

Culturas del Norte Covers the Casas Grandes (Paquimé) site and other cultures from arid northern Mexico, and traces their links with indigenous groups of the US southwest.

In a clearing about 100m in front of the museum's entrance, indigenous Totonac people perform their spectacular *voladores* rite – 'flying' from a 20m-high pole (see p678) – several times a day.

MUSEO RUFINO TAMAYO

A multilevel concrete and glass structure east of the Museo Nacional de Antropología, the **Tamayo Museum** (Map pp120-1; ☎ 5286-6519; www .museotamayo.org in Spanish; cnr Paseo de la Reforma & Gandhi; admission $1.50, free Sun; ☽ 10am-6pm Tue-Sun; Ⓜ Auditorio) was built to house international modern art donated by Oaxaca-born Rufino Tamayo and his wife, Olga, to the people of Mexico. Exhibitions of cutting-edge modern art from around the globe alternate with thematically arranged shows from the Tamayo collection.

SEGUNDA (2ª) SECCIÓN

The second section of the Bosque de Chapultepec lies west of the Periférico. In addition to family attractions, there is a pair of upscale lake-view restaurants on the Lago Mayor and Lago Menor.

Kids will enjoy **La Feria** (Map pp120-1; ☎ 5230-2121; passes from $2.75; ☽ 10am-6pm Mon-Fri, 10am-9pm Sat & Sun; Ⓜ Constituyentes), an old-fashioned amusement park with some hair-raising rides. A 'Super Ecolín' passport ($7.50) is good for all the rides except the roller-coaster and a few others; a 'pase mágico' ($2.75) includes two dozen children's rides and five big kids' rides. There is separate admission for the white-whales show.

Your children won't want to leave **Papalote Museo del Niño** (Map pp120-1; ☎ 5237-1700; www .papalote.org.mx; adult/child 2-11yr & seniors $9/8; 🕙 9am-6pm Mon-Wed & Fri, 9am-11pm Thu, 10am-7pm Sat & Sun; Ⓜ Constituyentes). At this innovative, hands-on museum, kids can put together a radio program, lie on a bed of nails, join an archaeological dig and try out all manner of technological gadget-games. Everything is attended by child-friendly supervisors. The museum also features a 3-D IMAX movie theater.

Just north of Papalote, the **Museo Tecnológico** (Map pp120-1; ☎ 5516-0964; admission free; 🕙 9am-5pm; Ⓜ Constituyentes), managed by the Federal Electricity Commission, showcases Mexico's technological developments, with interactive exhibits on electricity and transportation as well as a planetarium. The **Museo de Historia Natural** (Natural History Museum; Map pp120-1; ☎ 5515-6304; admission $1.75, Tue free; 🕙 10am-5pm Tue-Sun; Ⓜ Constituyentes), a 10-minute walk west of Papalote, presents the evolution of life on earth under a series of colored domes.

Circling around the Lago Menor, you'll find the **Fuente de Tlaloc** by Diego Rivera, a huge mosaic-skinned sculpture of the rain god lying in an oval pool in front of the old Chapultepec water works. To the north is the beautiful **Fuente de Xochipilli**, dedicated

to the Aztec 'flower prince,' with terraced fountains around a *talud tablero*–style pyramid (a steep building style typical of Teotihuacán).

GETTING THERE & AWAY
Chapultepec metro station is at the east end of the Bosque de Chapultepec, near the Monumento a los Niños Héroes and Castillo de Chapultepec. Auditorio metro station is on the north side of the park, 500m west of the Museo Nacional de Antropología.

From anywhere on Paseo de la Reforma west of the Alameda Central, buses saying 'Metro Chapultepec' reach Chapultepec metro station, while 'Metro Auditorio' buses pass right outside the Museo Nacional de Antropología. Returning downtown, any 'Metro Hidalgo/La Villa', 'Alameda' or 'Garibaldi' bus, from either metro Chapultepec or heading east on Reforma, follows Reforma at least as far as metro Hidalgo.

To get to the 2a Sección and La Feria, from metro Chapultepec take the 'Paradero' exit and catch a 'Feria' bus at the top of the stairs. These depart continuously and travel nonstop to the 2a Sección, dropping off riders at the Papalote Museo del Niño, Museo Tecnológico and La Feria.

Polanco
This affluent residential quarter north of Bosque de Chapultepec (Map pp120–1), where the streets are named after writers

---

BARRAGÁN'S MEXICAN WORLDVIEW

Luis Barragán (1902–88) led Mexico to the forefront of international modern architecture through a very personal view about living space. Born into an *hacendado* family in Jalisco state, he developed a passion for horse riding from an early age. Trained as a civil engineer, he taught himself architecture, making his name as a modernist designer of urban dwellings. His most visible work is the group of colorful skyscraper sculptures at the gateway to Ciudad Satélite, on Bulevar Ávila Camacho (aka the Periférico) north of downtown Mexico City. His works were both informed by the currents of modernism and imbued with the light and colors of Mexico's landscapes, villages and colonial architecture. Barragán received the Pritzer Prize, international architecture's highest honor, in 1980.

South of the Bosque de Chapultepec's 2a Sección, Barragán's home – which he inhabited from 1948 until his death 40 years later – was designated a Unesco World Heritage site in 2004 'as a masterpiece of human creative genius.' With its purposely circuitous passageways, seamless integration of outdoor and indoor spaces, bold swathes of Mexican folk tones, and a rooftop terrace that has the sky as its canopy, the **Casa Luis Barragán** (Map pp120-1; ☎ 5272-4945; www.casaluis barragan.org; General Francisco Ramírez 12; admission $7.50; 🕙 10am-1pm & 4-5pm by guided tour only; Ⓜ Constituyentes) is a monument to both Barragán's vision and the Mexican worldview.

and scientists, contains lots of restaurants, art galleries and embassies, some luxury hotels and the Sectur tourist office (p127). Much of the architecture is in the California Colonial style of the 1930s and 1940s, with carved stone doorways and window surrounds. A tour of Polanco could be combined with a visit to the nearby Museo Nacional de Antropología (p138).

Xochimilco & Around

About 20km south of downtown Mexico City, the urban sprawl is strung with a network of canals lined by gardens. These are the so-called 'floating gardens' of Xochimilco (so-chi-*meel*-co), remnants of the *chinampas* where the indigenous inhabitants grew their food. Gliding along the canals in a *trajinera* (gondola) is an alternately tranquil and festive experience. Nearby attractions include an ecological theme park and one of the city's best art museums.

MUSEO DOLORES OLMEDO PATIÑO

Set in a peaceful 17th-century hacienda, the **Olmedo Patiño museum** (Map p124; ☎ 5555-1221; Av México 5843; admission $2.75, free Tue; ⊙ 10am-6pm Tue-Sun), 2km west of Xochimilco, has perhaps the biggest and most important Diego Rivera collection of all. You'll see xoloitzcuintles, a pre-Hispanic hairless canine breed, roaming the estate's extensive gardens.

Dolores Olmedo Patiño, who resided here until her death in 2002, was a socialite and a patron of Rivera. The museum's 137 Rivera works – including oils, watercolors and lithographs from various periods – are displayed alongside pre-Hispanic figurines and folk art. Another room is reserved for Frida Kahlo's paintings.

To get there take the Tren Ligero (light rail) from metro Tasqueña and get off at La Noria. Leaving the station, turn left at the top of the steps, walk down to the street and continue to an intersection with a footbridge. Here turn a sharp left, almost doubling back on your path, onto Antiguo Camino a Xochimilco. The museum is 300m down this street.

XOCHIMILCO

Xochimilco, Náhuatl for 'Place where Flowers Grow,' was an early target of Aztec hegemony, probably due to its inhabitants' farming skills. The Xochimilcas piled up vegetation and mud in the shallow waters of Lake Xochimilco, a southern offshoot of Lago de Texcoco, to make fertile gardens called *chinampas*, which later became an economic base of the Aztec empire. As the *chinampas* proliferated, much of the lake was transformed into a series of canals. Approximately 180km of these waterways remain today and provide a favorite weekend destination for *defeños* (residents of Mexico City). The *chinampas* are still under cultivation, mainly for garden plants and flowers such as poinsettias and marigolds.

On weekends a fiesta atmosphere takes over as the town and waterways become jammed with people arranging boats to cruise the canals. Local vendors and musicians hover alongside the partygoers serving food and drink, playing marimbas and taking photos with old box cameras. (For a more relaxed atmosphere, come on a weekday.)

Hundreds of colorful *trajineras* await passengers at the village's nine *embarcaderos* (boat landings). Nearest to the center are Salitre and San Cristóbal *embarcaderos*, both 400m east of the plaza; and Fernando Celada, 400m west on Guadalupe Ramírez. Boats seat 14 to 20 persons; official cruise prices ($13 to $15 per hour) are posted at the *embarcaderos*. On Saturday, Sunday and holidays, 60-person *lanchas colectivos* run between the Salitre, Caltongo and Nativitas *embarcaderos* charging $1 per passenger.

You can get a taste of Xochimilco in one hour, but it's worth going for longer; you'll see more and get a proper chance to relax. You can arrange for your *trajinera* to stop at Nativitas *embarcadero* for some shopping at its large *artesanías* market.

Though the canals are definitely the main attraction, Xochimilco village is also worthy of exploration. East of Jardín Juárez stands the 16th-century **Parroquia de San Bernardino de Siena** (Map p124), with elaborate gold-painted *retablos* (altarpieces) and a large tree-studded atrium. To the south is the bustling **Mercado de Xochimilco**.

To reach Xochimilco, take the metro to Tasqueña station, then continue on the Tren Ligero ($0.20) to its last stop. Upon exiting the station, turn left (north) and follow Av Morelos to the market, plaza and church. If you don't feel like walking, bicycle taxis will shuttle you to the *embarcaderos* ($3).

PARQUE ECOLÓGICO DE XOCHIMILCO

Owing to its cultural and historical significance, Xochimilco was designated a Unesco World Heritage site in 1987. However, encroaching urbanization and illegal settlement along the canals have put a strain on this unique habitat, and at least one endemic species of the zone, the *axolotl* – a fish-like salamander – is in danger of extinction. Thus in 1991 the **Ecological Park of Xochimilco** (☎ 5673-8061; Periférico Oriente 1; adult/senior/child $1.50/0.50/0.20; ✆ 9am-6pm) was established, about 3km northeast of downtown Xochimilco, both to recover the zone's fragile ecosystem and to provide a retreat for stressed-out urbanites.

Covering some 2 sq km, the protected area comprises a botanical garden, artificial lakes and a variety of waterbirds. Stroll the pleasant pathways, or rent a bicycle or pedal boat for more extensive exploration. In the park's southeast corner, *chinampas* have been set aside to demonstrate traditional indigenous cultivation techniques. A visitors center has displays on plants and birds.

Trajineras departing from Embarcadero Cuemanco, 2km west of the park entrance, ply this lower-key section of the canals. This is also the best point of departure for an excursion to the Isla de las Muñecas (p150).

To reach Parque Ecológico de Xochimilco, take the Tren Ligero to the Periférico station. Exit on the Xochimilco-bound side, then go through the tunnel that underpasses the Periférico freeway. Emerging from the tunnel, turn right and walk to where you catch a 'Cuemanco' pesero (*colectivo;* minibus); the park entrance is a 10-minute ride.

San Ángel

Just a little over 60 years ago, San Ángel was a village separated from Mexico City by open fields. Today it's one of the city's most charming suburbs, with quiet cobblestoned streets lined by both old colonial and expensive modern houses, and a variety of things to see and do.

Av Insurgentes Sur and Av Revolución run north to south through eastern San Ángel.

PLAZA SAN JACINTO

Every Saturday the **Bazar Sábado** (p177) brings masses of color and crowds of people to San Ángel's Plaza San Jacinto.

The **Museo Casa del Risco** (Map p122; ☎ 5616-2711; Plaza San Jacinto 15; admission free; ✆ 10am-5pm Tue-Sun; Ⓜ Miguel Angel de Quevedo) occupies a 17th-century mansion. As compelling as the treasure trove of Mexican baroque and medieval European paintings is the elaborate fountain in the courtyard, a mosaic of Talavera tile and Chinese porcelain.

About 50m west from the plaza is the 16th-century **Iglesia de San Jacinto** and its peaceful gardens.

MUSEO CASA ESTUDIO DIEGO RIVERA Y FRIDA KAHLO

One kilometer northwest of Plaza San Jacinto is the **Diego Rivera & Frida Kahlo Studio Museum** (Map p122; ☎ 5550-1518; Diego Rivera 2, cnr Av Altavista; admission $1, free Sun; ✆ 10am-6pm Tue-Sun). Designed by their friend, the architect and painter Juan O'Gorman, the innovative abode was the home of the artistic couple from 1934 to 1940, with a separate house for each of them. If you saw *Frida,* you'll recognize the building, which served as a location in the film.

Though the museum has only a few examples of Rivera's art and none of Kahlo's, it does hold a lot of memorabilia. Rivera's house (the pink one) has an upstairs studio. Across the street is the San Ángel Inn (p164), in the 17th-century Ex-Hacienda de Goicoechea, once the home of the marquises of La Selva Nevada and the count of Pinillas. The former pulque hacienda is where Pancho Villa and Emiliano Zapata agreed to divide control of the country.

TEMPLO Y MUSEO DE EL CARMEN

The austere Templo de El Carmen houses a **museum** (Map p122; ☎ 5616-2816; www.museo deelcarmen.org in Spanish; Av Revolución 4; admission $3, free Sun; ✆ 10am-5pm Tue-Sun) in the former monastic quarters of the Carmelite order. Irrigated by the waters of the Río de la Magdalena, its orchard was once a source of cuttings and seeds for much of colonial Mexico. The convent is a storehouse of magnificent sacred art, including eight oils by Mexican master Cristóbal Villalpando. The polychrome and gilt ceiling decoration are unique examples of this type of work in Mexico. The big draw, however, is the dozen mummies in the crypt. Thought to be the bodies of 17th-century benefactors of the order, they were uncovered during the revolution by Zapatistas looking for buried treasure.

JARDÍN DE LA BOMBILLA

Popular with Chilango families, this pleasant park spreading east of Av Insurgentes has pedal-driven carts and motorized buggies for the kids. The **Monumento a Álvaro Obregón** (Map p122) marks the spot where the Mexican president was assassinated during a banquet in 1928. Obregón's killer, José de León Toral, was involved in the Cristero rebellion against the government's anti-Church policies.

GETTING THERE & AWAY

The La Bombilla station of the Av Insurgentes Metrobus is about 500m east of the Plaza San Jacinto. To Coyoacán, catch a 'Metro General Anaya' bus from in front of the flower market on the east side of Av Revolución; this will drop you by the Coyoacán market.

Ciudad Universitaria

The **University City** (Map pp110-11; Ⓜ Universidad), 2km south of San Ángel, is the main campus of Latin America's largest university, the Universidad Nacional Autónoma de México (UNAM), and a modern architectural showpiece. To see a map go to www .mapa.unam.mx.

Founded in 1553 as the Royal and Papal University of Mexico, the institution was modeled after Spain's University of Salamanca. Most of the modern campus was built between 1949 and 1952 by a team of 150 young architects and technicians. It's a monument to both national pride and an educational ideal in which almost anyone is entitled to university tuition. And its prestige remains solid: in an international survey conducted in 2005 by *The Times Higher Education Supplement*, UNAM was ranked as the No 1 university in Latin America and among the top 100 higher-education institutions in the world.

UNAM has over 260,000 students and 31,000 teachers. It has often been a center of political dissent, most notably prior to the 1968 Mexico City Olympics (see the boxed text, p106).

Most of the faculty buildings are scattered over an area about 1km square at the north end. As you enter from Av Insurgentes, it's easy to spot the **Biblioteca Central** (Central Library), 10 storeys high and covered with mosaics by Juan O'Gorman. The south wall, with two prominent zodiac wheels, covers colonial times, while the north wall deals with Aztec culture. The east wall shows the creation of modern Mexico; and the more abstract west wall may be dedicated to Latin American culture as a whole.

La Rectoría, the administration building at the west end of the wide, grassy Jardín Central, has a vivid, three-dimensional Siqueiros mosaic on its south wall, showing students urged on by the people. Fanciful animal sculptures by José Luis Cuevas dot the vast lawn, where students cram for exams or coo to sweethearts.

South of the Rectoría stands the **Museo Universitario de Ciencias y Arte** (☎ 5622-0305; www.muca.unam.mx; admission free; ☉ 10am-7pm Tue-Fri, 10am-6pm Sat & Sun), with eclectic exhibits from the university collection and some contemporary art.

Further east, illustrating the **Facultad de Medicina**, is an intriguing mosaic by Francisco Eppens in which Spanish and indigenous profiles combine to form a mestizo face.

Rebuilt for the 1968 Olympics, the **Estadio Olímpico**, to the west of Av Insurgentes, seats 80,000. A Rivera mosaic resembling a volcanic cone graces the main entrance.

A second section of the campus, about 2km south, contains the **Centro Cultural Universitario** (see p170), hosting films and the performing arts in its theaters and concert halls; and the **Museo Universitario de Ciencias** (Universum; ☎ 5622-7287; www.universum.unam.mx in Spanish; admission $3.75; ☉ 9am-6pm Mon-Fri, 10am-6pm Sat & Sun), a science museum with kids' activities and workshops. Other attractions include UNAM's botanical gardens; the Unidad Bibliográfica, housing part of Mexico's National Library; and the Espacio Escultórico (Sculptural Space), focused on a striking work by Mathias Goeritz consisting of triangular concrete blocks around a lava bed.

Student cafés, open to everyone during academic sessions, are in both the architecture and philosophy buildings at the Jardín Central's west end, and in the Centro Cultural Universitario.

GETTING THERE & AWAY

Take the metrobus to its southern terminus, where you can catch a 'Perisur' pesero (see map p122) to the west side of the university. For the northern part of the campus, get off at the first yellow footbridge crossing Av Insurgentes, just before the Estadio Olímpico. For the southern section, get off at the second yellow footbridge after the Estadio Olímpico. Returning, catch any pesero marked 'San Ángel-Revolución,' getting off just after it turns left to catch the metrobus.

Otherwise, take the metro to Universidad station, on the east side of the campus. The university runs three bus routes (free) from the metro station between 6:30am and 10:30pm Monday to Friday. Ruta 1 goes west to the main part of the campus; Ruta 3 heads southwest to the Centro Cultural Universitario.

Coyoacán

About 10km south of downtown, Coyoacán ('Place of Coyotes' in the Náhuatl language) was Cortés' base after the fall of Tenochtitlán. It remained a small outlying town until urban sprawl reached it 50 years ago. Close to the university, and once home to Leon Trotsky and Frida Kahlo (whose houses are now fascinating museums), Coyoacán retains its own identity, with narrow colonial- era streets, plazas, cafés and a lively atmosphere. Especially on weekends, assorted musicians, mimes and crafts markets draw large but relaxed crowds from all walks of life to Coyoacán's central plazas.

VIVEROS DE COYOACÁN

A pleasant approach is via the **Viveros de Coyoacán** (Map p123; ☎ 5554-1851; admission free; ☽ 6am-6pm; Ⓜ Viveros), the principal nurseries for Mexico City's parks and gardens. The 390,000-sq-meter swath of greenery, 1km west of central Coyoacán, is popular with joggers and perfect for a stroll, but watch out for belligerent squirrels! From metro Viveros, walk south along Av Universidad and take the first left, Av Progreso; or enter on Av México near Calle Madrid.

A block south of Viveros is the quaint **Plaza Santa Catarina**, with a 17th-century chapel by the same name. The adjacent **Centro Cultural Jesús Reyes Heroles** (Map p123; ☎ 5659-3937; Francisco Sosa 202; 9am-7pm; Ⓜ Viveros) is a colonial estate hosting art exhibits, concerts and culinary demonstrations in a Talavera-tiled kitchen. The 700m walk east along **Av Francisco Sosa** to Plaza Hidalgo passes some beautiful 16th- and 17th-century houses.

PLAZA HIDALGO & JARDÍN DEL CENTENARIO

The focus of Coyoacán life, and scene of most of the weekend fun, is its central plaza – actually two adjacent plazas: the eastern **Plaza Hidalgo**, with a statue of Miguel Hidalgo; and the western **Jardín del Centenario**, with a coyote fountain.

The **Casa de Cortés** (Map p123; ☎ 5658-0221; Jardín Hidalgo 1; admission free; ☽ 8am-8pm; Ⓜ Viveros), on the north side of Plaza Hidalgo, is where conquistador Cortés established Mexico's first municipal seat during the siege of Tenochtitlán, and later had the defeated emperor Cuauhtémoc tortured to make him divulge the location of Aztec treasure (the scene is depicted on a mural inside the chapel). Cortés resided here until 1523 when the colonial government was transferred to Mexico City. In front of the building is a domed gazebo contributed by the Díaz regime in 1910.

The 16th-century **Parroquia de San Juan Bautista** and its adjacent ex-monastery dominate the south side of Plaza Hidalgo. Half a block east, the **Museo Nacional de Culturas Populares** (Map p123; ☎ 5554-8968; Hidalgo 289; admission free; ☽ 10am-6pm Tue-Thu, 10am-8pm Fri-Sun; Ⓜ Viveros) hosts innovative exhibitions on popular culture, covering such topics as *lucha libre* (wrestling) and the role of maize in society. Outside, an amazing tree of life from Metepec marks the 500th anniversary of the meeting of the old and new worlds.

MUSEO FRIDA KAHLO

The **'Blue House'** (Map p123; ☎ 5554-5999; Londres 247; adult/child 6-12yr $3.25/2; ☽ 10am-6pm Tue-Sun; Ⓜ Coyoacán), six blocks north of Plaza Hidalgo, was the longtime home of artist Frida Kahlo (see the boxed text, opposite).

Kahlo and her husband, Diego Rivera, were part of a glamorous but far from harmonious leftist intellectual circle (which included, in the 1930s, Leon Trotsky), and the house is littered with mementos. In addition to their own and other artists' work, it contains pre-Hispanic objects and Mexican crafts collected by the couple.

The Kahlo art expresses the anguish of her existence; one painting, *El Marxismo Dará la Salud* (Marxism Will Give Health), shows her casting away her crutches. In the upstairs studio an unfinished portrait of Stalin stands before a poignantly positioned wheelchair. The folk-art collection includes Mexican regional costumes worn by Kahlo, and Rivera's collection of *retablo* paintings.

MUSEO LÉON TROTSKY

Having come second to Stalin in the power struggle in the Soviet Union, Trotsky was expelled in 1929 and condemned to death in absentia. In 1937 he found refuge in Mexico. At first Trotsky and his wife, Natalia, lived in Frida Kahlo's Blue House, but after falling out with Kahlo and Rivera they moved a few streets away, to Viena 45.

The **Trotsky home** (Map p123; ☎ 5554-0687; Río Churubusco 410; admission $2.75; ☻ 10am-5pm Tue-Sun; Ⓜ Coyoacán), whose main entrance is at the rear of the old residence, remains much as it was on the day when a Stalin agent finally caught up with the revolutionary. The fatal attack took place in Trotsky's study. Assassin Ramón Mercader, a Catalan, had become the lover of Trotsky's secretary and gained the confidence of the household. On August 20, 1940, Mercader approached Trotsky at his desk and asked him to look at a document. He then pulled an ice axe from under his coat

---

FRIDA & DIEGO

Diego Rivera, born in Guanajuato in 1886, first met Frida Kahlo, 21 years his junior, while painting at the Escuela Nacional Preparatoria, where she was a student in the early 1920s. Rivera was already at the forefront of Mexican art and a socialist; his commission at the school was the first of many semi-propagandistic murals on public buildings that he was to execute over three decades. He had already fathered children by two Russian women in Europe and in 1922 married Lupe Marín in Mexico. She bore him two more children before their marriage broke up in 1928.

Kahlo, born in Coyoacán in 1907, contracted polio at age six, leaving her right leg permanently thinner than her left. In 1925 she was horribly injured in a trolley accident that broke her back, right leg, collarbone, pelvis and ribs. She made a miraculous recovery but suffered much pain thereafter and underwent many operations to try to alleviate it. It was during convalescence that she began painting. Pain – physical and emotional – was to be a dominating theme of her art.

Kahlo and Rivera both moved in left-wing artistic circles and met again in 1928; they married the following year. The liaison, described as 'a union between an elephant and a dove,' was always a passionate love-hate affair. Rivera wrote: 'If I ever loved a woman, the more I loved her, the more I wanted to hurt her. Frida was only the most obvious victim of this disgusting trait.' Both had many extramarital affairs.

Kahlo's beauty, bisexuality and unconventional behavior – she drank tequila, told dirty jokes and held wild parties – fascinated many people. In 1934, after a spell in the USA, the pair moved into a new home in San Ángel (see p142), with separate houses for each of them, linked by an aerial walkway. Rivera and Kahlo divorced in 1940 but remarried soon after. She moved into the Blue House and he stayed at San Ángel – a state of affairs that endured for the rest of their lives, though their relationship endured too. Kahlo remained Rivera's most trusted critic, and Rivera was Kahlo's biggest fan.

Kahlo had only one exhibition in Mexico in her lifetime, in 1953. She arrived at the opening on a stretcher. Rivera said of the exhibition, 'Anyone who attended it could not but marvel at her great talent.' She died, at the Blue House, the following year. Rivera called the day of her death 'the most tragic day of my life... Too late I realized that the most wonderful part of my life had been my love for Frida.'

Though Kahlo's work was little appreciated during her lifetime, it has since become the most highly valued of any Mexican painter – or of any female artist – fetching more at international auctions than Rivera's. (Kahlo's *Self-Portrait with Curly Hair* sold for $1.3 million at a Christie's auction in 2003.)

Frida, the 2002 hit biopic, brought the painter even wider recognition. Though the film did very well in Mexico, it got mixed reviews from intellectuals who complained that none of the actors (except Salma Hayek, who played Kahlo) were Mexican – and even worse, that they spoke English, a betrayal of the vocally anti-American Frida.

and smashed the pick end into Trotsky's skull. Mercader was arrested and spent 20 years in prison.

Memorabilia and biographical notes are displayed in outbuildings, and videos on the life of the revolutionary are continuously screened in a room off the patio, where a tomb engraved with a hammer and sickle contains the Trotskys' ashes.

EX-CONVENTO DE CHURUBUSCO

The 17th-century former Monastery of Churubusco, scene of one of Mexico's heroic military defeats, stands east of Av División del Norte.

On August 20, 1847, Mexican troops defended the monastery against US forces advancing from Veracruz in a dispute over the US annexation of Texas. The Mexicans fought until they ran out of ammunition and were beaten only after hand-to-hand fighting. General Pedro Anaya, when asked by US general David Twiggs to surrender his ammunition, is said to have answered, 'If there was any, you wouldn't be here.' Cannons and memorials outside recall these events.

Most of the monastery now houses the **Museo Nacional de las Intervenciones** (National Interventions Museum; Map p123; ☎ 5604-0699; cnr Calle 20 de Agosto & General Anaya; admission $2.75, Sun free; ☑ 9am-6pm Tue-Sun; Ⓜ General Anaya). Displays include an American map showing operations in 1847, material on the French occupation of the 1860s and the plot by US ambassador Henry Lane Wilson to bring down the Madero government in 1913. Parts of the monastery gardens are also open.

To reach Churubusco, catch an eastbound 'M(etro) Gral Anaya' pesero or bus on Xicoténcatl at Allende, a few blocks north of Coyoacán's Plaza Hidalgo. Alternatively, walk 500m from the General Anaya metro station.

ANAHUACALLI

This dramatic **museum** (Map pp110-11; ☎ 5617-4310; Calle del Museo 150; admission $3.25; ☑ 10am-6pm Tue-Sun), 3.5km south of Coyoacán, was designed by Diego Rivera to house his collection of pre-Hispanic art. A fortress-like building made of dark volcanic stone, the 'House of Anáhuac' (Aztec name for the Valle de México) also contains one of

Rivera's studios and some of his work, including a study for 'Man at the Crossroads,' the mural that was commissioned for the Rockefeller Center in 1934.

If the air is clear, there's a great view from the roof. In November elaborate Day of the Dead offerings pay homage to the painter.

To get to Anahuacalli, take the Tren Ligero (from metro Tasqueña) to the Xotepingo station. Exit on the west side and walk 200m to División del Norte; cross and continue 600m along Calle del Museo.

GETTING THERE & AWAY

The nearest metro stations (1.5km to 2km) to central Coyoacán are Viveros, Coyoacán and General Anaya. If you don't fancy a walk, get off at Viveros station, walk south to Av Progreso and catch an eastbound 'M(etro) Gral Anaya' pesero to the market.

Returning, 'Metro Viveros' peseros go west on Malitzin; 'Metro Coyoacán' and 'Metro Gral Anaya' peseros depart from the west side of Plaza Hidalgo.

San Ángel–bound peseros and buses head west on Av MA de Quevedo, five blocks south of Plaza Hidalgo. To Ciudad Universitaria, take a 'CU' pesero west on Belisario Domínguez, from the corner of Centenario.

Cuicuilco

Cuicuilco (Map pp110-11; ☎ 5606-9758; Insurgentes Sur; admission free; ☑ 9am-5pm), between San Fernando and Anillo Periférico, is one of the oldest significant remnants of pre-Hispanic settlement within the DF. The civilization dates as far back as 800 BC, when it stood on the shores of Lago de Xochimilco. In its heyday in the 2nd century BC, the 'place of singing and dancing' counted as many as 40,000 inhabitants and rivaled Teotihuacán in stature. The site was abandoned a couple of centuries later, however, after an eruption of the nearby Xitle volcano covered most of the community in lava.

The principal structure is a huge circular platform of four levels, faced with volcanic stone blocks, that probably functioned as a ceremonial center. Set amid a park studded with cactus and shade trees, the platform can be easily scaled for sweeping views of the southern districts including the formidable Xitle. The site includes a small museum.

To reach Cuicuilco, take the metrobus to the end of the line, then catch a Perisur bus. The site is a five-minute walk south of the Perisur shopping mall.

Tlalpan

Tlalpan is 'what Coyoacán used to be' – an outlying colonial village with a bohemian atmosphere and some impressive 18th-century architecture. Municipal seat of the city's largest *delegación*, Tlalpan sits at the foot of the southern Ajusco range and enjoys a cooler, moister climate. There are some fine restaurants along the arcades of the cute little plaza and a boisterous cantina nearby, **La Jalisciense** (☎ 5573-5586; Plaza de la Constitución 6). The **Capilla de las Capuchinas Sacramentarias** (☎ 5573-2395; Hidalgo 43; admission $4.50; ☾ 9:30-noon & 4-6pm Mon-Thu), the chapel of a convent for Capuchine nuns designed by Luis Barragán in the 1940s, is a modernist gem amid the colonial relics. In addition to its historical collection, the **Museo de Historia de Tlalpán** (☎ 5573-0173; Plaza de la Constitución 10; admission free; ☾ 10am-7pm Tue-Sun) stages eclectic concert series.

A trip out to Tlalpan could be combined with a visit to Cuicuilco (see opposite). From metro Tasqueña, take the Tren Ligero to the Estadio Azteca station, then catch a 'Centro de Tlalpan' pesero.

Parque Nacional Desierto de los Leones

Cool, fragrant pine and oak forests dominate this 20-sq-km **national park** (☾ 6am-5pm) in the hills surrounding the Valle de México. Some 23km southwest of Mexico City and 800m higher, it makes a fine escape from the carbon monoxide and concrete.

The name derives from the **Ex-Convento del Santo Desierto de Nuestra Señora del Carmen** (admission $1; ☾ 10am-5pm Tue-Sun), the 17th-century former Carmelite monastery within the park. The Carmelites called their isolated monasteries 'deserts' to commemorate Elijah, who lived as a recluse in the desert near Mt Carmel. 'Leones' may stem from the presence of wild cats in the area, but more likely refers to José and Manuel de León, who once administered the monastery's finances.

The restored Ex-Convento has exhibition halls and a restaurant. Tours in Spanish (weekends only) are run by guides garbed in cassock and sandals who explore the patios

within and expansive gardens around the buildings, as well as some underground passageways.

The rest of the park has extensive walking trails. (Robberies have been reported, so stick to the main paths.)

GETTING THERE & AWAY

Take one of Flecha Roja's frequent 'Toluca Intermedio' buses from the Terminal Poniente bus station to La Venta, on Hwy 15 ($1, 30 minutes). Tell the driver your destination and you should be dropped at a yellow footbridge near a *caseta de cobro* (toll booth). Cross the footbridge and you'll see the Desierto de los Leones signpost on a side road to the south. On weekends taxis may wait here to take people up the 4km paved road to the Ex-Convento. Other days you'll probably have to walk, but traffic will be light and it's a pleasant, gently rising ascent.

Tlatelolco & Guadalupe
PLAZA DE LAS TRES CULTURAS

So named because it symbolizes the fusion of pre-Hispanic and Spanish roots into the Mexican mestizo identity, the **Plaza of the Three Cultures** (Map pp110-11; ☎ 5583-0295; Eje Central Lázaro Cárdenas, cnr Flores Magón; admission free; ☾ 8am-6pm; Ⓜ Tlatelolco) displays the architectural legacy of three cultural facets: the Aztec pyramids of **Tlatelolco**, the 17th-century Spanish **Templo de Santiago** and the former Foreign Relations Secretariat building on the plaza's south side, planned for conversion into a cultural center. A calm oasis north of the city center, the plaza is nonetheless haunted by echoes of its somber history.

Tlatelolco was founded by an Aztec faction in the 14th century on a separate island in Lago de Texcoco and later conquered by the Aztecs of Tenochtitlán, who built a causeway to connect the two ceremonial centers. In pre-Hispanic times it had the largest market in the Valle de México. Cortés defeated Tlatelolco's defenders, led by Cuauhtémoc, in 1521. An inscription about that battle in the plaza translates: 'This was neither victory nor defeat. It was the sad birth of the mestizo people that is Mexico today.'

Tlatelolco is also a symbol of modern troubles. On October 2, 1968, 300 to 400 student protesters were massacred by government troops on the eve of the Mexico City Olympic Games (see the boxed text, p106). The area subsequently suffered some of the worst damage of the 1985 earthquake when apartment blocks collapsed, killing hundreds.

You can view the remains of Tlatelolco's main pyramid-temple and other Aztec buildings from a walkway around them. Like the Templo Mayor of Tenochtitlán, Tlatelolco's main temple was constructed in stages, with each of seven temples superimposed atop its predecessors. The double pyramid on view, one of the earliest stages, has twin staircases which supposedly ascended to temples dedicated to Tlaloc and Huitzilopochtli. Numerous calendric glyphs are carved into the outer walls.

Recognizing the religious significance of the place, the Spanish erected the **Templo de Santiago** here in 1609, using stones from the Aztec structures as building materials. Just inside the main (west) doors of this church is the **baptismal font of Juan Diego** (see below). Outside the north wall of the church, a monument erected in 1993 honors the victims of the 1968 massacre.

Along Eje Central Lázaro Cárdenas, northbound 'Central Autobuses del Norte' peseros and trolleybuses pass right by the Plaza de las Tres Culturas.

BASÍLICA DE GUADALUPE

In December 1531, as the story goes, an indigenous Christian convert named Juan Diego stood on Cerro del Tepeyac (Tepeyac Hill), site of an old Aztec shrine, and beheld a beautiful lady dressed in a blue mantle trimmed with gold. She sent him to tell the bishop, Juan de Zumárraga, that he had seen the Virgin Mary, and that she wanted a shrine built in her honor. But the bishop didn't believe him. Returning to the hill, Juan Diego had the vision several more times. After her fourth appearance, the lady's image was miraculously emblazoned on his cloak, causing the church to finally accept his story, and a cult developed around the site.

Over the centuries Nuestra Señora de Guadalupe (named after a Spanish manifestation of the Virgin whose cult was particularly popular in early colonial times) came to receive credit for all manner of miracles,

hugely aiding the acceptance of Catholicism by Mexicans. Despite the protests of some clergy, who saw the cult as a form of idolatry with the Virgin as a Christianized version of the Aztec goddess Tonantzin (the basilica was built over a pyramid dedicated to her), in 1737 the Virgin was officially declared the patron of Mexico after she had extinguished an outbreak of plague in Mexico City. Two centuries later she was named celestial patron of Latin America and empress of the Americas. Today her image is seen throughout the country, and her shrines around the Cerro del Tepeyac are the most revered in Mexico, attracting thousands of pilgrims daily and hundreds of thousands on the days leading up to her feast day, December 12 (see p151). Some pilgrims travel the last meters to the shrine on their knees. In 2002 Pope John Paul II canonized Juan Diego.

By the 1970s the old yellow-domed basilica, built around 1700, was swamped by worshipers and was sinking slowly into the soft subsoil. So the new **Basílica de Nuestra Señora de Guadalupe** (Ⓜ La Villa-Basilica) was built next door. Designed by Pedro Ramírez Vázquez, architect of the Museo Nacional de Antropología, it's a vast, round, openplan structure with a capacity for over 40,000 people. The image of the Virgin hangs above and behind the main altar, with moving walkways to bring visitors as close as possible.

The rear of the Antigua Basílica is now the **Museo de la Basílica de Guadalupe** (Map pp110-11; ☎ 5577-6022; admission $0.50; ⓧ 10am-6pm Tue-Sun; Ⓜ La Villa-Basilica), with a fine collection of colonial art interpreting the miraculous vision.

Stairs behind the Antigua Basílica climb about 100m to the hilltop **Capilla del Cerrito** (Hill Chapel), where Juan Diego had his vision, then lead down the east side of the hill to the Parque de la Ofrenda with gardens and waterfalls around a sculpted scene of the apparition. Continue on down to the baroque **Templo del Pocito**, a circular structure with a trio of tiled cupolas, built in 1787 to commemorate the miraculous appearance of a spring where the Virgen de Guadalupe had stood. From there the route leads back to the main plaza, re-entering it beside the 17th-century **Capilla de Indios** (Chapel of Indians).

An easy way to reach the Basílica de Guadalupe is to take the metro to La Villa-Basílica station, then walk two blocks north along Calz de Guadalupe. You can reach the same point on any 'Metro Hidalgo–La Villa' pesero or bus heading northeast on Paseo de la Reforma. To return downtown, walk to Calz de los Misterios, a block west of Calz de Guadalupe, and catch a southbound 'Metro Hidalgo' or 'Metro Chapultepec' pesero.

WALKING TOUR

The historical hub of all Mexico, the Centro Histórico is the most densely packed and fascinating part of the city and worthy of extended exploration. The obvious point of departure is the Zócalo. Take it all in from the terrace of the **Hotel Majestic** (**1**; p154) on the west side of the plaza, then investigate the sites around it: the **Catedral Metropolitana** (**2**; p128) and **Palacio Nacional** (**3**; p128).

Next strike east along Calle Moneda. The first building on the left contains Mexico's first registered cantina, **El Nivel** (**4**; p166), 'The Level.' Next door is the former **Archbishop's Palace** (**5**; p130) and further down Moneda is New Spain's first mint, now home to the **Museo Nacional de las Culturas** (**6**; p130).

> **WALK FACTS**
>
> **Distance:** 2.5km
> **Duration:** 3½ to 5 hours

Circling around the Palacio Nacional, you're engulfed in the frenetic *ambulante* activity of the zone; vendor stalls spread for blocks in every direction. Return via Corregidora to the Zócalo. Crossing Pino Suárez, note the sculpted scene on your left depicting the **foundation of Tenochtitlán** (**7**). Stroll westward through the arcades that front the pair of buildings housing the **Federal District Department** (**8**) and continue along Calle 16 de Septiembre. On the Zócalo's southwest corner stands the Porfiriato cupcake that is now the **Gran Hotel Ciudad de México** (**9**; p153). Turn right on La Palma; to your left is the **Centro Joyero** (**10**) with scores of gold and jewelry vendors.

Take a left up Av Madero, admiring the avenue's panoply of majestic edifices. At the next intersection stands the baroque **Iglesia de la Profesa** (**11**; ☎ 5521-8362; Isabel la Católica 21), headquarters of the Jesuits until their expulsion in 1767. Next in line are the **Palacio de Iturbide** (**12**; p132) and the **Iglesia de San Francisco** (**13**; ☎ 5521-7731; Av Madero 7), a remnant of the vast Franciscan convent built over the site of Moctezuma's private zoo in the 16th century and divvied up under the reform laws of the 1850s. The lion's head at the southwest corner with Motolinía marks the level reached by the flood of 1629. Stop for refreshments at Sanborns inside the beautiful **Casa de Azulejos** (**14**; p132).

Proceed west to the **Torre Latinoamericana** (**15**; p132), where you could zoom up to the observation deck for the big picture.

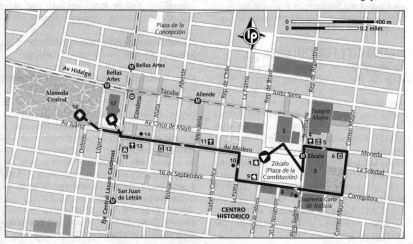

Back at ground level, conclude the tour by taking a bench in the **Alameda Central** (**16**; p134) or attending a chamber music recital at the **Palacio de Bellas Artes** (**17**; p134).

COURSES

A number of institutes can help get your Spanish up to speed.

Alliant International University (Map pp118-19; ☎ 5264-2187; www.alliantmexico.edu; Álvaro Obregón 110, Roma; Ⓜ Insurgentes) Small private US university offering various Spanish courses and activities for travelers and professionals ($120 to $160), plus degree programs with classes taught in English; also hosts guided cultural tours and open lectures and seminars.

Centro de Cultura Mexicana Para Extranjeros, Universidad del Claustro de Sor Juana (Center of Mexican Culture for Foreigners; Map pp114-15; ☎ 5130-3386, toll-free from US or Canada ☎ 866-357-1671; www.ucsj.edu.mx/CCME; Izazaga 92; Ⓜ Isabel la Católica) Two programs are offered at this 17th-century ex-convent turned progressive university (see p133): for beginners, a four-week summer-intensive Spanish course with a history, art and culture component taught in English ($1500 including lunch prepared by the university's gastronomy students); and for those with some knowledge of Spanish, two- to three-month culture courses, taught in Spanish, on an eclectic range of topics, from 20th-century Mexican poetry to gastronomic spaces of Mexico ($250 to $400). Lodging can be arranged.

Centro de Enseñanza Para Extranjeros (Foreigners Teaching Center; ☎ 5622-2467; www.cepe.unam.mx; Universidad 3002, Ciudad Universitaria) The national university (see p143) offers six-week intensive classes meeting three hours daily ($300). Students who already speak Spanish may take courses on Mexican art and culture, which are taught in Spanish and run concurrently with the UNAM semester.

MEXICO CITY FOR CHILDREN

As elsewhere in Mexico, kids take center stage in the capital. Many theaters stage children's plays and puppet shows on weekends and during school holidays, including the **Centro Cultural del Bosque** (p172) and the **Centro Nacional de las Artes** (p172). Cartoons are a staple at cinemas around town, including weekend matinees at the **Cineteca Nacional** (p170) and the hotel **Condesa df** (p157), though keep in mind that children's films are often dubbed in Spanish (unlike other films which are subtitled). Consult the Niños sections of *Tiempo Libre* and *Donde Ir* magazines for current programs.

Museums often organize hands-on activities for kids, and the **Museo Nacional de Arte** (p131) offers children's art workshops Saturday and Sunday.

Mexico City's numerous parks and plazas are usually buzzing with kids' voices. Bosque de Chapultepec is the obvious destination, with the **Papalote Museo del Niño** (p140), **La Feria** (p139) and the **Chapultepec zoo** (p138), not to mention several lakes with rowboat rentals. But also consider Condesa's **Parque México** (p136), where Sunday is family activities day. There are craft workshops and face painting and you can rent bicycles for a spin around the lush grounds. **Plaza Hidalgo** (p144) in Coyoacán is another fun-filled spot with balloons, street mimes and cotton candy.

In **Xochimilco** (p141), kids find the sensation of riding the gondolas through the canals as magical as any theme park. Also in this part of town is the **Museo Dolores Olmedo Patiño** (p141), where peacocks, ducks and a pack of pre-Hispanic dogs roam the gardens, and children's shows are performed in the patio Saturday and Sunday at 1pm.

Be sure to take the kids through a market for an eye-opening tour of local fruits, piñatas and pig's heads.

QUIRKY MEXICO CITY

Anyone who's spent time in Mexico will understand why French poet André Bretón called it 'the surrealist country par excellence.' Though it's hard to pin it down, something strange lurks beneath the surface of everyday life, popping up in the oddest places.

El Cuadrilátero (see p159) Owned by *luchador* (wrestler) Super Astro, it features a wall of wrestlers' masks, many donated by his ring pals and enemies.

Isla de las Muñecas (Island of the Dolls) For a truly surreal experience, head for Xochimilco (p141) and hire a *trajinera* to the Isla de las Muñecas. Whatever festive mood you may have set out with will turn to dread approaching this remote spot, where thousands of dolls, many partially decomposed or missing limbs, hang from trees and rafters. The installation was created by recently deceased island resident don Julián, who fished the playthings from the canals to mollify the spirit of a girl who had drowned nearby. The best departure point for the four-hour round-trip is the Cuemanco landing, near the Parque Ecológico de Xochimilco.

Mercado de Sonora (Map pp110-11; cnr Fray Servando & Rosales; Ⓜ Merced) Has all the ingredients for Mexican witchcraft. Aisles are crammed with stalls hawking things like Lucky Hunchback potion, amulets, voodoo dolls and other esoterica. Located south of Mercado de la Merced, this is also the place for a *limpia* (spiritual cleansing), a ritual that involves clouds of incense and an herbal brushing.

Plaza Sex Capital (Map pp114-15; ☎ 5518-7337; Av 16 de Septiembre 11; ⏲ 11am-9pm; Ⓜ San Juan de Letrán) In a country not usually associated with libidinous expression, Plaza Sex Capital is on the cusp of naughty consumerism. Devoted entirely to the erotic urge, this new shopping mall features scores of sex shops, a 3-D cinema and a sex museum, plus a food court with exotic dancers to spice up your salsa.

Virgen del Metro (Map pp114-15; cnr Paseo de la Reforma & Zarco; Ⓜ Hidalgo) Housed in a small tiled shrine is this evidence of a recent miracle. Metro riders in June 1997 noticed that a water leak in Hidalgo station had formed a stain in the likeness of the Virgin of Guadalupe. Following the discovery, thousands flocked to witness the miraculous image. The stone section was removed and encased in glass at the Zarco entrance to metro Hidalgo.

TOURS

Recorridos Dominicales (☎ 5662-8228, ext 526; www .cultura.df.gob.mx/culturama/visitasguiadas; ⏲ 10:45am-1pm Sun) The DF cultural ministry offers Sunday walking tours. Routes vary weekly with participants divided among 10 guides. The website lists the week's destination and departure point.

Tranvía (☎ 5512-1012, ext 0202; adult/child $3.25/2; ⏲ 10am-5pm) Runs a motorized version of a vintage streetcar around a 45-minute circuit of the Centro Histórico, with guides relating fascinating bits of lore (in Spanish) along the way. On Thursday night there's a special cantina tour ($9.50 including cocktail, reservation required). Tours depart from Av Juárez by Bellas Artes.

Turibús Circuito Turístico (☎ 5133-2488; www .turibus.com.mx in Spanish; adult/child 4-12 $11/6, 2-day pass $15/8; ⏲ 9am-9pm) Provides an overview of the key areas. The total *recorrido* (route) lasts about three hours, but you can get off and back on at any designated stop along the way. Tickets are sold on board for the red double-decker bus. Red banners mark stops along Reforma, at the southwest corner of the Zócalo, and by the Auditorio Nacional, among other places. Buses pass every 30 minutes or so. The fare includes headphones for recorded explanations in English, French, Italian, German or Japanese.

FESTIVALS & EVENTS

Mexico City celebrates some unique local events in addition to all the major nationwide festivals (see p976), which often take on a special flavor in the capital.

Festival de México en el Centro Histórico (www.fch mexico.com; late March) The Centro Histórico's plazas, temples and theaters become venues for a slew of international artists and performers.

Semana Santa (late March or early April) The most evocative events of Holy Week are in the Iztapalapa district,

---

THE SAINT OF TEPITO

Garbed in a gold-trimmed white gown, wearing a wig of dark tresses and clutching the staff of the Grim Reaper in one bony hand, a scale in the other, the skeletal figure bears an eerie resemblance to Mrs Bates from the film *Psycho*. She is Santa Muerte (Saint Death) and she is the object of a fast-growing cult in Mexico, particularly in the rough Barrio Tepito, where the principal **altar** (Map pp110-11; Ⓜ Tepito) stands in a glass booth on Alfarería north of Mineros. Possibly rooted in pre-Hispanic ritual, Santa Muerte has been linked to Mictlantecuhtli, the Mexican god of death.

The cult counts an estimated two million members in Mexico, who tend to come from society's lower economic echelons. On the first day of each month, as many as 6000 devotees line up at the Tepito altar, which is surrounded by candles, cigarettes, jewelry and various relics that can be purchased nearby.

The saint's popularity is feared to be rivaling that of the Virgin of Guadalupe, and for that very reason the Roman Catholic Church has harshly denounced the cult and sought to have its official status removed.

Calling itself the Traditional Catholic Mex-USA Church, the cross-border sect has 15 temples in Los Angeles and one in Mexico City. The **Santuario Nacional de la Santa Muerte** (National Sanctuary of Saint Death; (Map pp110-11; ☎ 5702-8607; Bravo 35; ⏲ 10am-6pm Mon-Sat, 10am-8pm Sun; Ⓜ Morelos), in the Morelos neighborhood near Tepito, sees around 90 worshipers a day. Exorcisms are held Thursday at noon and 6pm.

While the altar and sanctuary are open to the public, travelers who choose to visit either site should be aware that the Tepito neighborhood is notorious among Mexicans as a scene of criminal activity and that church members may not welcome the scrutiny of curious onlookers.

9km southeast of the Zócalo, where more than 150 locals act out a realistic Passion Play. The most emotive scenes begin at noon on Good Friday, when Christ is sentenced, beaten and crowned with real thorns. He then carries his cross up Cerro de la Estrella, where he is 'crucified.'

Grito de la Independencia (September 15) Thousands gather in the Zócalo on the eve of Independence Day to hear the Mexican president's version of the Grito de Dolores (Cry of Dolores), Hidalgo's famous call to rebellion against the Spanish in 1810, from the central balcony of the Palacio Nacional at 11pm. Afterwards, there's a spectacular fireworks display over the cathedral.

Día de Muertos (November 2) In the lead-up to Day of the Dead, elaborate *ofrendas* (offerings) show up everywhere from public markets to metro stations. Some of the best are at Anahuacalli (p146) and the Museo Dolores Olmedo Patiño (p141), while a contest for the most creative *ofrenda* is held at the Zócalo. Major vigils take place in the Panteón Civil de Dolores cemetery, west of Bosque de Chapultepec; and at San Andres Mixquic, in the extreme southeast of the Distrito Federal.

Fiesta de Santa Cecilia (November 22) The patron saint of musicians is honored with special fervor at Plaza Garibaldi (Map pp114–15).

Día de Nuestra Señora de Guadalupe (December 12) At the Basílica de Guadalupe (p148), the Day of Our Lady of Guadalupe caps 10 days of festivities honoring Mexico's religious patron. On December 11 and 12, groups of indigenous dancers and musicians from across Mexico perform on the basilica's broad plaza in uninterrupted succession. The numbers of pilgrims reach the millions by December 12, when religious services go on in the basilica almost around the clock.

SLEEPING

The range of places to stay is enormous, from basic guesthouses to top-flight hotels. Accommodations are described here first by neighborhood, then by price range.

In general, the best moderately priced rooms are in the areas west of the Zócalo, near the Alameda Central and Plaza de la República. These are sometimes in charming old colonial style with high ceilings and attractive balconies. Several hostels geared to international budget travelers provide another economical option.

Midrange accommodations provide comfortable, if sometimes small, rooms in multistorey buildings with restaurants and bars. They often trade character for modern convenience. Hotels in this category are concentrated in the Plaza de la República and Roma neighborhoods, though they're found all over town. Note that places with

the word '*garage*' on the sign generally cater to short-term tryst-seeking guests, but these 'love motels' can be good-value options.

Top-end hotel rooms run from $85 up to the sky and range from comfortable medium-sized, tourist-oriented hotels to modern luxury high-rises for business travelers. Top-end places are most densely concentrated in the Zona Rosa and Polanco.

Centro Histórico

Despite ongoing investment and improvements in the Historic Center, accommodations remain surprisingly affordable. Most of the suitable places are on Av 5 de Mayo and the streets to its north and south.

BUDGET

Hostel Catedral (Map pp114–15; ☎ 5518-1726; www.hostelcatedral.com; República de Guatemala 4; dm HI members/nonmembers $10/13; r incl breakfast $33; M Zócalo; ✕ ⬚) Backpacker central in Mexico City, the capital's only HI affiliate is abuzz with a global rainbow of young travelers. Every facility you might need is here, the location couldn't be more central and the place is cordially managed. Off the guest kitchen, a delightful deck overlooks the cathedral.

Hotel Isabel (Map pp114–15; ☎ 5518-1213; www .hotel-isabel.com.mx; Isabel la Católica 63; s/d $11.50/16, s/d/tr with private bathroom $18/25/33; M Isabel la Católica; ⬚) The Isabel is a long-time budget-traveler's favorite, and it's easy to see why. Just a few blocks from the Zócalo, it offers large, well-scrubbed rooms with old but sturdy furniture, high ceilings and great balconies, plus a hostel-like social scene.

Hostal Virreyes (Map pp114–15; ☎ 5521-4180; www.hostalvirreyes.com.mx; Izazaga 8; dm $10, r $23; M Salto del Agua; ⬚) Once a prestigious hotel, the Virreyes has quite naturally morphed into a hostel–student residence. Dorms are spacious, facilities user-friendly, and the lobby lounge hosts hip events. An ISIC card will get you a 10% discount.

Hotel Rioja (Map pp114–15; ☎ 5521-8333; Av 5 de Mayo 45; s/d from $18/20; M Allende) A superior value, the Rioja is a well-maintained lodging in the middle of everything. Unlike at many hotels in this category, the owners have invested in renovations, and the quality of its facilities matches those of places at twice the price.

Hostel Amigo (Map pp114-15; ☎ 5512-3464; www
.hostelamigo.com; Isabel la Católica 61A; dm $10, r incl
breakfast $30; Ⓜ Isabel la Católica; 🖳) This brand-
new hostel occupies a lovingly preserved
250-year-old former nuns' residence. The
atmosphere is casual, with cozy common
areas, and if you like to party you'll find
plenty of amigos and amigas who share
your interest.

Hostal Moneda (Map pp114-15; ☎ 5522-5821, 800-
221-72-65; www.hostalmoneda.com.mx; Moneda 8; dm
$13, r incl breakfast $27; Ⓜ Zócalo; ✕ 🖳) Sitting
on one of the city's most exuberant and
historic streets, the Moneda is an altogether
more modest affair than the nearby Hostel
Catedral, but it has been established longer,
and has its faithful fans. Chief among its
assets are the well-informed, bilingual staff,
environmentally friendly water and energy systems, and a terrific multi-purpose
rooftop. There are also laundry facilities
and an airport pick-up service.

Hotel Azores (Map pp114-15; ☎ 5521-5220; www
.hotelazores.com; República de Brasil 25; s/d from $24/28;
Ⓜ Zócalo; Ⓟ) Just off the fascinating Plaza
Santo Domingo, the uncharacteristically
modern Azores boasts a cheerily designed
and scrupulously maintained interior. Of
the 65 rooms, just eight overlook the street
through picture windows.

Hotel Washington (Map pp114-15; ☎ 5512-3502;
Av 5 de Mayo 54; s/d $19/24; Ⓜ Allende) If you're
sticking to a budget but don't want to
sacrifice comfort, and prefer to be right in
the middle of things, the Washington will
do nicely, and you'll likely be amid similar-
minded travelers.

Hotel Zamora (Map pp114-15; ☎ 5512-8245;
Av 5 de Mayo 50; s/d $10.50/14, with private bathroom
$18/21; Ⓜ Allende) Absolutely no frills here,
but it's clean, friendly and cheap, with hot
showers and a safe. Ask for a front room:
the balconies over Av 5 de Mayo are worth
the price alone.

Hotel Juárez (Map pp114-15; ☎ 5512-6929;
1a Callejón de 5 de Mayo 17; s/d $15/19; Ⓜ Allende)
Nestled in an L-shaped alley, the Juárez
is another incredibly cheap but perfectly
good choice in the thick of things, though
just out-of-the-way enough to ensure a
tranquilo night's sleep. True, its feng shui
may need an overhaul, but the shoestring
travelers who regularly check in here don't
seem to mind. Try and get a balcony onto
the main street.

MIDRANGE

Hotel Catedral (Map pp114-15; ☎ 5518-5232; www
.hotelcatedral.com; Donceles 95; s/d/tr from $38/52/68;
Ⓜ Zócalo; Ⓟ 🖳) Though short on colonial
charm, this comfortable lodging has clearly
considered its location, directly behind the
Metropolitan Cathedral. Even if you get
an interior room, you can lounge on the
rooftop terraces, with impressive cityscapes
in all directions.

Hotel Gillow (Map pp114-15; ☎ 5518-1440; www
.hotelgillow.com; Isabel la Católica 17; s/d/tr from $39/51/61;
Ⓜ Allende; 🖳) A historic building with stand-
ard midrange facilities, the Gillow boasts
old-fashioned service and spacious carpeted
rooms around a sunlit central courtyard. For
views, request a Av 5 de Mayo or Isabel la
Católica unit.

Tulip Inn Ritz (Map pp114-15; ☎ 5130-0160, 800-
201-52-56; www.tulipinnritzmexico.com; Madero 30; r
$75; Ⓜ Bellas Artes; ✕ 🖳) Popular with Euro
groups on tour who appreciate its prime
location, *simpático* staff and modern
conveniences, the 70-year-old Ritz was
recently spruced up by new overseers from
Holland. About half of the 117 large rooms
overlook Madero or Bolívar, while the rest
face a tranquil patio.

Hotel Capitol (Map pp114-15; ☎ 5512-0460;
República de Uruguay 12; s/d $30/37; Ⓜ San Juan de Letrán;
🖳) Opposite the computer shopping center,
this friendly establishment offers plain
rooms around a central hall with fountain.
Romantically inclined guests often opt for
the Jacuzzi-equipped suites.

TOP END

Gran Hotel Ciudad de México (Map pp114-15; ☎ 1083-
7700; reservaciones@granhotelciudaddemexico.com.mx;
Av 16 de Septiembre 82; s/d $228/269; Ⓜ Zócalo;
Ⓟ ✕ 🖳) The Gran Hotel flaunts the French
art-nouveau style of the pre-revolutionary
era. Crowned high overhead by a stained-
glass canopy crafted by Tiffany in 1908,
the vast atrium is a fin-de-siècle fantasy
of curved balconies, original wrought-iron
elevators and chirping birds in zoo-
sized cages. Rooms do not disappoint in
comparison.

Holiday Inn Zócalo (Map pp114-15; ☎ 5130-5130,
800-009-99-00; www.holidayinnzocalo.com.mx; Av 5 de Mayo
61; r $100, ste from $147; Ⓜ Zócalo; Ⓟ ✕ ✕ 🖳) The
northernmost of three upper-echelon hotels
facing the Zócalo, the Holiday Inn seems
the least pretentious, eschewing colonial

trimmings for contemporary comfort. And its rooftop-terrace restaurant ranks with those of its neighbors.

Hotel Majestic (Map pp114-15; ☎ 5521-8600; www.hotelmajestic.com.mx; Madero 73; r $130, ste from $175; Ⓜ Zócalo; Ⓟ ⊠ ▯) This Best Western franchise has a lot going for it, including an attractive colonial interior, an unbeatable location and perhaps the most panoramic terrace restaurant on the Zócalo. Rooms, however, are less fabulous than you'd expect at these prices.

Alameda Central & Around
BUDGET
Hotel Toledo (Map pp114-15; ☎ 5521-3249; López 22; s/d $17/25; Ⓜ San Juan de Letrán) The area is in transition, but this older establishment remains rooted in another era. Though teetering on the edge of divedom, the place is cozy enough and some may appreciate its retro style.

MIDRANGE
Hotel Monte Real (Map pp114-15; ☎ 5518-1149; www.hotelmontereal.com.mx; Revillagigedo 23; s/d $48/54; Ⓜ Juárez; Ⓟ ▯) This modern option, across the way from the new Museo de Artes Populares, gets high marks for its eager-to-please staff and well-maintained facilities.

Similarly unremarkable but perfectly comfortable places with decent restaurants abound in this zone.

Hotel Fleming (Map pp114-15; ☎ 5510-4530; www.hotelfleming.com.mx; Revillagigedo 35; s/d/tr $30/36/41; Ⓜ Juárez; Ⓟ)

Hotel Marlowe (Map pp114-15; ☎ 5521-9540; www.hotelmarlowe.com.mx in Spanish; Independencia 17; s/d/tr $40/47/62; Ⓜ San Juan de Letrán; Ⓟ ⊠ ▯)

TOP-END
Hotel Sheraton Centro Histórico (Map pp114-15; ☎ 5130-5252, 800-470-70-70; www.sheratonmexico.com; Juárez 70; r from $350; Ⓜ Hidalgo; Ⓟ ⊠ ⊠ ▯ ⛷) A cornerstone in the downtown redevelopment project, the sleek Sheraton towers above quaint Alameda Central. Most travelers are here on business, but anyone desiring a dose of comfort and sublime cityscapes should be more than satisfied. At the time of writing a huge spa was being developed, with saunas, massage clinic and fitness center.

Hotel de Cortés (Map pp114-15; ☎ 5518-2181, 800-509-23-40; www.hoteldecortes.com.mx; Hidalgo 85; s/d $152/217; Ⓜ Hidalgo; ⊠ ▯) Once a hospice

for pilgrims of the Augustinian order, this Best Western property has a long history of sheltering travelers, with rooms encircling a lovely late-18th-century patio. If you don't mind the price tag, staying here will give you a genuine taste of colonial Mexico.

Plaza de la República & Around
Though less convenient, this mainly residential area a few blocks west of the Alameda is relatively tranquil and boasts a number of reasonably priced accommodations options.

BUDGET
Casa de los Amigos (Map pp114-15; ☎ 5705-0521; www.casadelosamigos.org; Mariscal 132; dm $8.50, s/d with shared bathroom $12/24; Ⓜ Revolución; ⊠ ▯) Not technically a hostel, the Quaker-run Casa is primarily a residence for NGOs, researchers and others seeking social change, but welcomes walk-in travelers. It generally attracts a more serious individual than the average hostel and thus has a more low-key atmosphere. Meditation sessions, discussions with community members and Spanish conversation are available to guests, who may volunteer to help run the Casa for a reduced rate. A hearty breakfast ($1.50) is served Monday to Friday in the ground-floor dining room. There's a two-night minimum stay.

THE AUTHOR'S CHOICE

Mexico City Hostel (Map pp114-15; ☎ 5512-3666; www.mexicocityhostel.com; República de Brasil 8; dm $13; private r per person $18; Ⓜ Allende; ▯) Amid a slew of hostel options in the Centro, this just-unwrapped addition stands out. Steps from the Zócalo, the solid colonial structure has been artfully restored, with original wood beams and stone walls as a backdrop for modern energy-efficient facilities. An enormous mural graces the sunlit entry hall, with stone arches framing passages to cafeteria and TV rooms on the upper levels. In the spacious dorms, three or four sturdy bunk beds stand on terracotta floors. Immaculate bathrooms trimmed with azulejo tile amply serve around 100 occupants. Rates include a buffet breakfast.

Hotel Oxford (Map pp114-15; ☎ 5566-0500; Mariscal 67; s/d $10.50/17; Ⓜ Revolución) Some find a special allure in this art-deco remnant of 1940s Mexico City which sits on the delightful Plaza Buenavista behind the Museo de San Carlos. Others just call it a dive. If it's seedy charm you're after, the Oxford's bar will do nicely, and they'll send up drinks until 4am.

Also worth checking is:

Hotel Mallorca (Map pp114-15; ☎ 5566-4833; Serapio Rendón 119; s/d from $23/27; Ⓜ San Cosme; Ⓟ) Doubles come in two sizes.

MIDRANGE

Almost all of the following places have convenient on-site restaurants serving 'international' cuisine.

Palace Hotel (Map pp114-15; ☎ 5566-2400; Ramírez 7; s/d $32/48; Ⓜ Revolución; Ⓟ) The gregarious Asturians who run the Palace have renovated massively, highlighting the spacious rooms with appealing Mexican tones. Broad balconies give terrific views down palm-lined Ramírez to the Plaza de la Revolución. Cash-paying guests get substantial discounts.

Hotel Sevilla (Map pp114-15; ☎ 5566-1866; www .sevilla.com.mx; Serapio Rendón 124; s/d $25/35, 'modern' s/d $41/51; Ⓜ Revolución; Ⓟ Ⓧ 🖳) Opposite the Jardín del Arte this oft-recommended business hotel is divided into 'traditional' and 'modern' sections. Rooms in the latter are air-conditioned with some facing the Monumento a la Madre (Monument to Motherhood).

Hotel New York (Map pp114-15; ☎ 5566-9700; Édison 45; s/d $29/48; Ⓜ Revolución; Ⓟ) A few blocks northeast of Plaza de la República, this is an upscale option in a zone crammed with cut-rate hotels. Rates include breakfast and four Sky channels.

Hotel Casa Blanca (Map pp114-15; ☎ 5096-4500; www.hotel-casablanca.com.mx; Lafragua 7; s/d $64/81; Ⓜ Juárez; Ⓟ Ⓧ Ⓧ 🖳 🖳) Here's a five-star hotel with all the trimmings for much less than the chains. A sexy new lobby bar jazzes up the otherwise '60s ambience, with a pink color scheme in the 270 rooms. Bonus: a rooftop pool with adjacent lounge.

Hotel Mayaland (Map pp114-15; ☎ 5566-6066; www.hotelmayaland.com; Antonio Caso 23; s/d $36/47; Ⓜ Juárez; Ⓟ 🖳) A business-oriented hotel on a rather sterile street, this has well-maintained facilities with a Maya motif.

Hotel Jena (Map pp114-15; ☎ 5097-0277; Terán 12; s/d/tr $64/74/95; Ⓜ Hidalgo; Ⓟ Ⓧ 🖳) Not as tall as it looks (the imposing black tower is strictly for show), the Jena's huge rooms are among the most luxurious in this range, and it's just a block and a half from Reforma.

Hotel Prim (Map pp114-15; ☎ 5592-4600; www.hotelprim.com; Versalles 46; s/d $54/62, ste $77; Ⓜ Cuauhtémoc; Ⓟ 🖳) The hulking Prim does not present an attractive facade, but it's decent value and a quick hike from Reforma, the Zona Rosa or Colonia Roma. The junior suites are the best deal, with cozy living rooms, huge beds and two bathrooms.

The following two lodgings are along Serapio Rendón, just above the Jardín del Arte. What they lack in character they make up for in convenience, comfort and price.

Hotel Compostela (Map pp114-15; ☎ 5566-0733; Sullivan 35; traditional s/d $26/32, modern $35/40; Ⓜ San Cosme; Ⓟ) Friendliest of the two; 'modern' rooms are more luxurious, with bigger bathrooms.

Hotel Astor (Map pp114-15; ☎ 5148-2644; hotel.astor@ mexico.com; Antonio Caso 83; s/d $35/45; Ⓜ San Cosme; Ⓟ Ⓧ 🖳)

TOP END

Hotel Imperial (Map pp114-15; ☎ 5705-4911, 800-714-29-09; Paseo de la Reforma 64; r $152; Ⓜ Hidalgo; Ⓧ 🖳) The century-old Imperial is an immediately recognizable cake wedge of a building, with a gold cupola crowning its front turret. The dictator Porfirio Díaz unwrapped this frenchified confection in 1904, and it remains a refreshingly stylish structure alongside the monolithic chain hotels in the vicinity of the Columbus traffic circle. Unfortunately, room decor fails to match the building's Porfiriato splendor.

Hotel Sevilla Palace (Map pp114-15; ☎ 5566-8877, 800-700-70-70; www.sevillapalace.com.mx; Paseo de la Reforma 105; r $115, ste from $165; Ⓜ Revolución; Ⓟ Ⓧ 🖳 Ⓢ) While it's neither quaint nor cutting edge, this 400-room monolith *is* extremely comfortable and well-run with unusually cordial service, as well as a pretty amazing rooftop pool deck.

Zona Rosa & Around

Accommodations right in the glitzy Pink Zone are expensive, but a couple of popular midrange places are nearby (book ahead). Many of the top-end options offer discounts for walk-ins.

BUDGET

Hostal San Sebastián (Map pp118-19; ☎ 5208-6528; sansebastianhostal@hotmail.com; Estolcomo 29; dm $11, s/d with shared bathroom $22/32; Ⓜ Insurgentes; 🖵) Appropriately for the area, this is a gay-oriented hostel, though any open-minded traveler is welcome. There are plenty of good reasons to stay here, whatever your orientation, among them a great location, stylish decor and well-maintained facilities. On weekends, the hostel's Mitomanía Café turns into a cabaret.

Villa H (Map pp118-19; ☎ 5208-5880; www.geo cities.com/villahmx; Génova 30-H; dm $12, s/d incl breakfast $23/32; Ⓜ Insurgentes; 🖵) Casual but fastidiously maintained, this new hostel in a cul-de-sac off party corridor Génova should appeal to fun-loving travelers and neatness freaks alike. The environment is gay-friendly but open to all.

MIDRANGE

Casa González (Map pp118-19; ☎ 5514-3302; casa .gonzalez@prodigy.net.mx; Río Sena 69; s/d from $32/41; Ⓜ Insurgentes; 🖵) A family-run operation for nearly a century, the Casa is a perennial hit with mature travelers. While rooms are modest, the general ambience is extraordinarily *tranquilo*. Grounds are amply endowed with gardens and plants, and a big breakfast is served on old china in the dining room.

Hotel María Cristina (Map pp118-19; ☎ 5703-1212; Río Lerma 31; s/d from $61/67; Ⓜ Insurgentes or Chilpancingo; Ⓟ 🖵) Guests appreciate the grandeur and tranquility of this facsimile of an Andalusian estate, though most of the colonial charm has been poured into the lobby lounge and adjacent gardens rather than the rooms.

Hotel Bristol (Map pp118-19; ☎ 5208-1717; www.hotelbristol.com.mx; Plaza Necaxa 17; s/d/ste from $52/60/69; Ⓜ Chilpancingo; Ⓟ ✗ 🏊 🖵) A good-value option in the pleasant but central Cuauhtémoc neighborhood, the Bristol caters primarily to business travelers, offering quality carpet, a soothing color scheme and an above-average restaurant.

TOP END

Four Seasons Hotel (Map pp118-19; ☎ 5230-1818; www.fourseasons.com/mexico; Paseo de la Reforma 500; r $363-480; Ⓜ Chapultepec; Ⓟ ✗ 🏊 🖵 🐾) One of the city's most elegant lodgings, the Four Seasons was designed to resemble a French-Mexican late-19th-century structure, with aristocratically furnished rooms facing a beautifully landscaped central courtyard.

Sheraton María Isabel Hotel (Map pp118-19; ☎ 5242-5555, in the US ☎ 800-598-1753; www .sheraton.com/mariaisabel; Paseo de la Reforma 325; r from $299; Ⓜ Insurgentes; Ⓟ ✗ 🏊 🖵 🐾) Overlooking the Independence monument and next door to the US embassy, the Sheraton's two towers have accommodated business-people, diplomats and journalists for over three decades. Among its varied attractions are a rooftop pool, fitness center, Starbucks branch and nightly mariachis. About half of the 755 rooms were redone in 2004.

Condesa & Roma

BUDGET

Hostel Home (Map pp118-19; ☎ 5511-1683; www .hostelhome.com.mx; Tabasco 303; dm student/nonstudent $9.50/10; Ⓜ Insurgentes; 🖵) Housed in a fine Porfiriato-era building, this small (20-bed) hostel is on narrow tree-lined Calle Tabasco, a tranquil gateway to the Roma neighborhood. Managed by youthful, easygoing staff, the Home is a good place to meet other travelers and find out what's going on. Catch metrobus 'Álvaro Obregón.'

Hotel Embassy (Map pp118-19; ☎ 5208-0859; Puebla 115; s/d/tr $25/30/33; Ⓜ Insurgentes; Ⓟ) Despite a charmless location, this well-maintained modern lodging is conveniently placed a couple of blocks from the metro, and right next door to the excellent Cantina Covadonga (see p169).

MIDRANGE

Casa de la Condesa (Map pp118-19; ☎ 5574-3186; reservations@extendedstaymexico.com; Plaza Luis Cabrera 16; s/ste $43/80; Ⓜ Insurgentes; 🖵) Right on the delightful Plaza Luis Cabrera, the Casa makes a tranquil base for visitors on an extended stay, offering 'suites' that are essentially studio apartments with kitchens.

Hotel Milán (Map pp118-19; ☎ 5584-0222; www .hotelmilan.com.mx; Álvaro Obregón 94; s/d $33/40; Ⓜ Insurgentes; Ⓟ 🖵) The Milán makes a good place to land in Mexico City. Though lacking in character, it's comfortable and well maintained and sits on the main corridor of bohemian Colonia Roma.

Hotel Park Villa (Map pp118-19; ☎ 5515-5245; www.hotelparkvilla.com.mx; General Gómez Pedraza 68; s/d $48/64; Ⓜ Juanacatlán; Ⓟ) The Park Villa is the only lodging on the Condesa side of

Bosque de Chapultepec. Just across from the vast swath of greenery, the hotel is in a self-contained compound with its own peaceful garden restaurant and a tiny zoo containing a couple of sleepy lions.

Hotel Roosevelt (Map pp118-19; ☎ 5208-6813; www.hotelroosevelt.com.mx; Insurgentes Sur 287; s/d/ste $36/51/59; Ⓜ Insurgentes; Ⓟ ⌨) On the eastern edge of Condesa, this functional hotel is the only midpriced option near the modish nightlife zone. Also within easy reach of the Cuban club district, it should appeal to nocturnally inclined travelers. Catch metrobus 'Álvaro Obregón.'

Hotel Parque Ensenada (Map pp118-19; ☎ 5208-0052; www.hotelensenada.com.mx; Álvaro Obregón 13; s/d from $54/58; Ⓜ Cuauhtémoc; Ⓧ ⌨) Though accommodations here are of the standard-issue business-class variety, travelers may find it a reassuringly cushy transition stage coming from or going back to their native land.

Hotel Puebla (Map pp118-19; ☎ 5525-3689; www.hotelpuebla.com; Puebla 36; s/d/ste $31/35/36; Ⓜ Cuauhtémoc; Ⓟ) Though not exactly innovative in design, the Puebla, on the eastern edge of Colonia Roma, is squeaky clean, cordially managed and extremely quiet.

TOP END

La Casona (Map pp118-19; ☎ 5286-3001; www.hotellacasona.com.mx; Durango 280; r incl breakfast $150; Ⓜ Sevilla; Ⓧ) This stately mansion was restored to its early-20th-century splendor to become one of the capital's most distinctive boutique hotels. Each of the 29 rooms has been uniquely appointed to bring out its original charm.

Condesa df (Map pp118-19; ☎ 5241-2600; www.condesadf.com; Veracruz 102; r from $182; Ⓜ Chapultepec; Ⓧ ⌨ Ⓐ) Opened in 2005, this c 1920s structure has been quirkily made over in a style that perfectly reflects the hip 'new Condesa.' Every detail has been specially crafted, from the peanut-shaped coffee tables to the globular lampshades over the bar, already one of Condesa's trendiest nightspots (see the boxed text, p168).

Polanco

North of Bosque de Chapultepec, this area has some of the best business accommodations and a couple of excellent boutique hotels.

Camino Real México (Map pp120-1; ☎ 5263-8888; www.caminoreal.com; Calz Mariano Escobedo 700; r $215; Ⓜ Auditorio or Chapultepec; Ⓟ Ⓧ Ⓧ ⌨ Ⓡ) With over 700 rooms and covering 33,000 sq meters of grounds, the Camino Real is a monumental endeavor. It's also a national architectural landmark, boldly designed by Mexican Ricardo Legorreta.

Hábita Hotel (Map pp120-1; ☎ 5282-3100; www.hotelhabita.com; Presidente Masaryk 201; s/d/ste $228/310/369; Ⓜ Polanco; Ⓟ Ⓧ Ⓧ ⌨ Ⓡ) Mexican architect Enrique Norten turned a functional apartment building into one of the city's top boutique hotels. Decor in the 36 rooms is boldly minimal, and the sleek rooftop bar, Área, is Polanco's hottest nightspot (see p169).

W Mexico City Hotel (Map pp120-1; ☎ 9138-1800; www.whotels.com; Campos Elíseos 252; r $397; Ⓜ Auditorio; Ⓟ Ⓧ Ⓧ ⌨ Ⓡ) One of the four sentinels opposite the Auditorio Nacional, Latin America's first W is a 25-floor business hotel that's determined to break away from the stodginess of its neighbors.

Southern Districts

Hostal Cactus (Map pp110-11; ☎ 5530-0839; hostal cactus@yahoo.com; La Quemada 76; dm $10; Ⓜ Etiopia) This homey hostel is in Colonia Narvarte, a pleasant residential zone that is well connected to both the Centro and Coyoacán. Staying here, you're essentially sharing a home with a few dozen other travelers in a very casual setting.

El Cenote Azul (Map pp110-11; ☎ 5554-8730; www.elcenoteazul.com; Alfonso Pruneda 24; dm $9; Ⓜ Copilco) This small, laid-back hostel is one of the only accommodations near the UNAM campus. Conditions are backpacker basic but everything is kept quite clean and comfortable.

Airport

Camino Real Aeropuerto (Map pp110-11; ☎ 5227-7200; www.caminoreal.com/aeropuerto; Puerto México 80; r $210; Ⓟ Ⓧ Ⓐ) For early-morning departures, the hotel is conveniently connected by sky-tunnel to the airport's domestic terminal.

EATING

The capital offers eateries for all tastes and budgets, from taco stalls to exclusive restaurants. Some of the best places are cheap; some of the more expensive ones are well worth the extra money.

The center is a good area to sample *chiles en nogada* (large, mild *poblano* chilies stuffed with a ground-meat filling containing fruits, nuts and spices, and covered with a sauce of cream, cheese and walnuts), *mole poblano* (Puebla-style *mole*; a traditional stew) or other traditional Mexican fare, while Condesa, Polanco and Roma offer plenty of European, Asian and Argentine restaurants (see the boxed text, p165).

Those on a budget will find literally thousands of restaurants and holes-in-the-wall serving a *comida corrida* (set lunch) for as little as $3. Market buildings are good places to look for these while *tianguis* (weekly street markets) customarily have an eating section offering tacos, *barbacoa* (Mexican-style barbecue) and quesadillas (cheese folded between tortillas and fried or grilled). See also the boxed text, opposite.

Certain items can be found all over town. In the evening *tamales* are delivered by bicycle, their arrival heralded by an eerie moan through a cheap speaker. You'll know the *camote* (sweet potato) man is coming by the ear-splitting steam whistle emitting from his cart, heard for blocks around. The same vendor offers delicious baked plantains, laced with cream on request.

The city is also peppered with modern chain restaurants whose predictable menus make a sound, if unexciting, fallback. Branches of VIPS, Sanborns, Wings and California restaurants serve US-style coffee-shop fare and Mexican standards. International chains, from KFC to Starbucks, are well represented, too.

Centro Histórico

Perhaps the quintessential Mexico City experience is dining or sipping cocktails overlooking the vast Zócalo with the Mexican *tricolor* waving proudly over the scene. The three upscale hotels overlooking the plaza offer abundant buffet breakfasts most days, although the food isn't as spectacular as the vista. If it's not too busy you can enjoy the view for the price of a drink.

QUICK EATS

Taquería Beatriz (Map pp114-15; tacos $1; 9am-5pm; M San Juan de Letrán) This unassuming hole-in-the-wall, opposite Uruguay 31, has served outstanding tacos for nearly a century. *Rajas* (sliced peppers), *mole*, *chicharrón* (fried pork skins) in salsa and other items are skillfully stuffed into handmade tortillas.

Tacos de Canasta Chucho (Map pp114-15; ☎ 5521-0280; Av 5 de Mayo 17A; tacos $0.50; 9am-6pm Mon-Fri, 8am-5pm Sat; M Allende) These bite-sized tacos are filled with things like refried beans, *chicharrón* and *mole* (just the sauce), and arranged in a big basket. A couple of pails contain the garnishes: spicy guacamole and marinated carrot chunks and chilies.

BUDGET

Restaurante Dzib (Map pp114-15; ☎ 5709-9402; Regina 54-C; set lunch $2.75; 8am-6pm Mon-Sat; M Isabel la Católica) This deceptively large dining hall must be the ultimate *comida corrida* joint, serving toothsome four-course lunches. Friday is seafood day.

Vegetariano Madero (Map pp114-15; ☎ 5521-6880; Madero 56; 4-course lunches $4; 8am-7pm; M Allende; V) Despite the austere entrance, there's a lively restaurant upstairs where a pianist plinks out old favorites. The meatless menu includes tasty variations on Mexican standards. Balcony seating lets you observe the street activity.

Restaurante Vegetariano (Map pp114-15; ☎ 5521-1895; Mata 13; 8am-10pm; M Allende) This more modern, street-level branch of Vegetariano Madero is near the main restaurant.

Café El Popular (Map pp114-15; ☎ 5518-6081; Av 5 de Mayo 52; breakfast & set lunches $2.50-4; 24hr; M Allende) An amazing number of people squeeze into this tiny split-level café. Fresh pastries and good combination breakfasts (fruit, eggs, *frijoles* – beans – and coffee) are the main attractions. *Café con leche* (coffee with milk; $1) is served *chino* style (ie you specify the strength).

Café La Blanca (Map pp114-15; ☎ 5510-9260; Av 5 de Mayo 40; 3-course lunch $4.75; M Allende) White-coated waiters and orange upholstery set the tone for this 1960s' relic offering hearty breakfasts and daily lunch specials. Sit at the U-shaped counter or grab a table by the window for people-watching over a cappuccino ($1.75). Be sure to sample the *tamales de nata* – sweet with a hint of anise.

MIDRANGE & TOP END

Half the fun of eating in the Centro Histórico is basking in the atmosphere of some extraordinary colonial buildings.

Los Girasoles (Map pp114-15; ☎ 5510-0630; Tacuba 8A; starters from $3, main courses $8.50-13; 1pm-midnight Tue-Sat, 1-9pm Sun & Mon; M Allende; P) Beside the Museo Nacional de Arte, this fine restaurant specializes in *alta cocina mexicana*. The menu boasts an encyclopedic range of Mexican fare, from pre-Hispanic (ant larvae), to colonial (turkey in tamarind *mole*), to innovative (snapper fillet in rose-hip salsa).

La Casa de las Sirenas (Map pp114-15; ☎ 5704-3225; República de Guatemala 32; main courses $12-15, desserts $4; ⏰ 1-6pm Mon, 1-11pm Tue-Fri, 8am-11pm Sat, 8am-6pm Sun; Ⓜ Zócalo) Ensconced in a 17th-century home behind the cathedral, this atmospheric restaurant serves creatively prepared and attractively presented Mexican cuisine. Dinner on the terrace might start with mushrooms sautéed in *chipotle* (a type of chili), followed by a sesame sea bass, then corn flan. And to drink? Some 180 varieties

of tequila ($3 to $10 a shot) are served in the downstairs salons.

El Cuadrilátero (Map pp114-15; ☎ 5521-3060; Luis Moya 73; ⏰ 7am-8pm Mon-Sat; Ⓜ Juárez) Not just wrestlers, but also ordinary denizens of the Centro frequent this shrine to *lucha libre*, famous for its gigantic tortas, versions of which are displayed at the entrance. If you manage to consume a 1.3kg cholesterol-packed Torta Gladiador in 15 minutes, it's free.

La Fonda del Hotentote (Map pp114-15; ☎ 5522-1025; Las Cruces 40-3; dishes $8-12; ⏰ lunch Sun-Fri; Ⓜ Pino Suárez) In the wholesale-paper district southeast of the Palacio Nacional, this lunchtime-only *comedor* (eating place)

MARKET FARE

Some of the best eating in Mexico City is not found in any restaurant but in the big covered *mercados* and *tianguis* (weekly street markets).

- **Mercado San Camilito** (Map pp114-15; Plaza Garibaldi; pozole $3.75; ⏰ 24hr; Ⓜ Garibaldi) The block-long building contains over 70 kitchens serving Jalisco-style *pozole*, a broth brimming with hominy kernels and pork, served with garnishes like radishes and oregano. (Specify *maciza* if pig noses and ears fail to excite you.) Also served are *birria*, a soulful goat stew, and *tepache*, a fermented pineapple drink.

- **Mercado Medellín** (Map pp118-19; Coahuila, btwn Medellín & Monterrey; Ⓜ Chilpancingo) Features an extensive eating area with cheap and filling *comidas corridas*, as well as several excellent seafood restaurants.

- **Parrillada Bariloche** (Map pp118-19; Bazar de Oro; ⏰ Wed, Sat & Sun; Ⓜ Insurgentes) This stall along the southern aisle of an upscale street market grills some of the least-expensive Uruguayan-style steaks and sausages in town, along with excellent side salads. Reach it be metrobus 'Durango.'

- **Caldos de Gallina Vale** (Map pp118-19; Mercado Cuauhtémoc, Av Cuauhtémoc; Ⓜ Cuauhtémoc) A giant pot of chicken broth bubbles away at this simple stall on the east side of the rustic market on the northeastern edge of Colonia Juárez. The friendly proprietors add chicken pieces, giblets and/or hard-boiled eggs to your broth, which you can garnish with some seriously spicy salsas.

- **Tianguis de Pachuca** (Map pp118-19; Agustín Melgar; ⏰ 10am-4pm Tue; Ⓜ Chapultepec) The 'food court' at the north end of the weekly Condesa street market offers many tempting options, but none so mouthwatering as the *mixiotes*, steamed packets of seasoned mutton, whose contents may be rolled into thick tortillas and garnished with fiery *chiles de manzana* (very hot, yellow chili peppers).

- **Mercado de Antojitos** (Map p123; Higuera, cnr Plaza Hidalgo & Caballo Calco; Ⓜ Coyoacán) Near Coyoacán's main plaza, this busy spot has all kinds of snacks, including deep-fried quesadillas, *pozole*, *esquites* (boiled corn kernels served with a dollop of mayo), *tamales* and *flautas* (chicken tacos, rolled long and thin then deep-fried; garnished with lettuce and cream).

- **Tostadas Coyoacán** (Map p123; ☎ 5659-8774; Allende btwn Malitzin & Xicoténcatl; tostadas $1.50-2; ⏰ noon-6pm Ⓜ Viveros) Inside Coyoacán's main market is one of the best places to eat anywhere in town. The attractive array of platters here will stop hungry visitors in their tracks. Tostadas are piled high with things like ceviche, marinated octopus and pig's feet, mushrooms and shredded chicken.

brings a touch of class to Mexican standards without putting on airs. Highlights include red-snapper *tamales*, nopales (cactus paddles) in *chile guajillo* (slightly chili) sauce, and *pollo tocotlán* (chicken steamed in maguey leaves with aromatic herbs). Desserts are equally enticing.

Restaurante Chon (Map pp114-15; ☎ 5542-0873; Regina 160; main dishes $8.50-16; ☯ 10am-7pm Mon-Sat; Ⓜ Pino Suárez) Pre-Hispanic fare is the specialty of this cantina-style restaurant. Sample maguey worms (in season), grasshoppers, wild boar or armadillo in a mango sauce.

Hostería de Santo Domingo (Map pp114-15; ☎ 5526-5276; Domínguez 72; dishes $7-16; ☯ 9am-10:30pm; Ⓜ Allende; Ⓟ) Whipping up classic Mexican fare since 1860, this hugely popular (though not touristy) restaurant has a festive atmosphere, enhanced by chamber music. It's famous for its enormous *chiles en nogada* ($16), an Independence Day favorite, served here year-round.

Casino Español (Map pp114-15; ☎ 5510-2967; Isabel la Católica 29; 4-course lunch $6.50; ☯ lunch Mon-Fri; Ⓜ Allende) The old Spanish social center, housed in a fabulous Porfiriato-era building, has a popular cantina-style eatery downstairs and an elegant restaurant upstairs. Stolid execs loosen their ties here for a long leisurely lunch, and the courses keep coming. Spanish fare, naturally, highlights the menu (Thursday there's *cocido madrilène*, a Madrid-style stew with chick peas and sausage) though *tacos dorados* (chicken tacos, rolled and deep fried) and *chiles en nogada* are equally well-prepared.

Café de Tacuba (Map pp114-15; ☎ 5518-4950; Tacuba 28; 5-course lunch $15; main courses $5-12; Ⓜ Allende; Ⓟ) Before the band there was the restaurant. Way before. A fantasy of colored tiles, brass lamps and oil paintings, this mainstay has served *antojitos* (tortilla-based snacks like tacos and gorditas) since 1912. The food is overrated, but the atmosphere is just right for a plate of *pambazos* (filled roll fried in chili sauce) or *tamales* with hot chocolate.

Alameda Central & Around
QUICK EATS
El Califa de León (Map pp114-15; San Cosme 56-B; tacos from $1.75; ☯ 11am-2am; Ⓜ San Cosme) Practically hidden amid the surrounding *ambulante*

activity, this standing room–only *taquería* is sought out by taco mavens from all over. Unlike at thousands of similar places, the twist here is that the beef is not chopped up but grilled in thin slices. The salsas – *chipotle* and *salsa verde* – are exceptional.

Tacos Xotepingo (Map pp114-15; ☎ 5709-4548; Balderas 42; tacos $1.25-2.50; ☯ 11am-11pm; Ⓜ Balderas) With seating inside the big dining hall, on the sun-dappled patio or alongside the formidable grill, this taco temple makes a great pit stop after shopping at the Ciudadela crafts market, opposite.

Churrería El Moro (Map pp114-15; ☎ 5512-0896; Eje Central Lázaro Cardenas 42; hot drink with 4 churros $3; ☯ 24hr; Ⓜ San Juan de Letrán) A fine respite from the Eje Central crowds, El Moro manufactures long, slender deep-fried *churros* (doughnut-like fritters), just made to be dipped in thick hot chocolate. It's a popular late-night spot, perfect for winding down after hours.

Both the Cloister Café at the **Museo Franz Mayer** (p134) and the more upscale **Café del Palacio at Bellas Artes** (p134) offer sandwiches, salads and pastries between exhibits.

BUDGET
Café Trevi (Map pp114-15; ☎ 5512-3020; Colon 1; breakfast combos $2.75-5, 4-course lunch $3.50; Ⓜ Hidalgo) This remnant of old Alameda culture has a cheery retro vibe. In addition to the great-value *comida del día*, it prepares various pasta dishes.

Mi Fonda (Map pp114-15; ☎ 5521-0002; López 101; paella $2.75; ☯ lunch; Ⓜ San Juan de Letrán) Working-class Chilangos line up for their share of *paella valenciana*, made fresh daily and patiently ladled out by women in white bonnets. Jesús from Cantabria in Spain oversees the proceedings. Space is limited but you can share a table.

MIDRANGE
El Regiomontano (Map pp114-15; ☎ 5518-0196; Luis Moya 115; grilled goat $15; ☯ 11am-10pm; Ⓜ Balderas) Lettered on the window is the message, 'Baby goats very young kids' and there they are, splayed on stakes and grilling over a circle of coals, *norteño*-style. A single platter serves two.

Boca del Río (Map pp114-15; ☎ 5535-0128; Ribeira de San Cosme 42; seafood cocktails from $4.50, fish from $7; ☯ 9am-11pm; Ⓜ San Cosme) This old-fashioned seafood purveyor has its fish delivered daily from the coast. Have a seat at the long stainless-steel counter and enjoy shrimp, oyster or octopus cocktails (or eat all three in one serve, *campechano* style), served with a lemon squeezer, bottle of *habanero* (a fiery chili) salsa and package of Saltines.

Zona Rosa & Around

While the Zona Rosa is packed with places to eat and drink, the culinary offerings tend to disappoint, with one notable exception: the various authentic Asian restaurants aimed primarily at the neighborhood's growing Korean community (see the boxed text, p165). Fast-food junkies can get their fix on Génova between Hamburgo and Liverpool, with all the major franchises.

BUDGET

Beatricita (Map pp118-19; ☎ 5511-4213; Londres 190D; set lunch $4.50; ☒ 10am-6pm; Ⓜ Insurgentes) This popular lunchtime destination has a solid *comida corrida* and friendly service. Friday is *pozole* day.

MIDRANGE

Fonda El Refugio (Map pp118-19; ☎ 5525-8128; Liverpool 166; dishes $8-10; ☒ 1-11pm Mon-Sat, 1-10pm Sun; Ⓜ Insurgentes; Ⓟ) Your best bet for Mexican fine dining in the Zona Rosa, the Fonda El Refugio serves regional specialties like *moles* and *escamoles* (ant larvae) in a charming old house.

Restaurante Vegetariano Yug (Map pp118-19; ☎ 5333-3296; Varsovia 3; buffet lunch $6.50; ☒ 7am-10pm Mon-Fri, 8:30am-8pm Sat, 1-8pm Sun; Ⓜ Insurgentes; Ⓥ) Just south of Reforma, Yug has downtown's best vegetarian fare. Local office workers head upstairs for the generous lunch buffet, served from 1pm to 5pm, with a plethora of salads and fresh whole-wheat bread.

Konditori (Map pp118-19; ☎ 5511-0722; Génova 61; dishes $6-10; Ⓜ Insurgentes) This Scandinavian café is a favorite along the Pink Zone's main pedestrian thoroughfare. Some people make a special trip here for the weekend brunch ($10) accompanied by live jazz.

TOP END

Les Moustaches (Map pp118-19; ☎ 5533-3390; Río Sena 88; main dishes $13-20; ☒ 1-11:30pm Mon-Sat, 1-6pm Sun; Ⓜ Insurgentes; Ⓟ) This is one of the city's most sophisticated French restaurants,

with tables in an elegant patio. Start off with pâté de foie gras, then choose from duck in Grand Marnier sauce, beef Wellington or lobster thermidor. For dessert, there are tempting crepes and soufflés.

Condesa

La Condesa has become the hub of the eating-out scene, and dozens of informal bistros and cafés, many with sidewalk tables, compete for space along several key streets. It must be added, however, that style often triumphs over substance here, and popularity does not necessarily correlate with quality. Most higher-end Condesa restaurants offer valet parking for around $2.50 (plus tip).

QUICK EATS

El Califa (Map pp118-19; ☎ 5271-7666; Altata 22, cnr Alfonso Reyes; tacos $1.50-3; ☒ 1:30pm-3:30am; Ⓜ Chilpancingo; Ⓟ) This very popular *taquería* on Condesa's southern edge puts its own spin on the classic Mexican snack. Tables are set with a palette of savory salsas in sturdy clay bowls.

El Tizoncito (Map pp118-19; ☎ 5286-7321; Tamaulipas 122, cnr Campeche; tacos from $0.70; ☒ noon-3:30am Sun-Thu, until 4:30pm Fri & Sat; Ⓜ Patriotismo) The original branch of the city-wide chain has been going for nearly 40 years. It claims to have invented tacos *al pastor* (ie cooked on a spit, shepherd style), and half the fun is watching the grillmen deftly put them together. If there are no seats, try the bigger location two blocks east on Campeche.

Nevería Roxy (Map pp118-19; Mazatlán 89, cnr Montes de Oca; scoops from $0.80, banana splits $3; ☒ 11am-9pm; Ⓜ Chapultepec) For dessert, try the old-fashioned Roxy which makes fresh sherbet on-site. Another branch is at Tamaulipas 161 at Alfonso Reyes, close to metro Patriotismo.

A **pickup truck** (Map pp118-19; ☒ 11am-3pm Mon-Sat; Ⓜ Chilpancingo), at the corner of Tamaulipas and Alfonso Reyes, has crowds lining up midmorning for tasty quesadillas and *carnitas* (chunks of pork simmered in lard, then served with corn tortillas and guacamole).

BUDGET

El Figonero (Map pp118-19; ☎ 5211-9951; Campeche 429-C; set lunch $3.50; ☒ 8:30am-4pm Mon-Sat; Ⓜ Patriotismo) In the midst of all the trendiness is this little neighborhood place, offering a *comida corrida* that's a bit more creative than usual. Show up before 3pm to avoid the rush.

Green Corner (Map pp118-19; ☎ 5286-3939; Mazatlán 81; breakfast $3, salads & sandwiches $3-4; ✆ 7:30am-10pm; Ⓜ Patriotismo; Ⓥ) Not just a place to purchase natural products like whole-wheat bread and tofu, Green Corner also makes a delightful spot for a healthy breakfast, with sidewalk tables on a laid-back corner.

Frutos Prohibidos (Map pp118-19; ☎ 5264-5808; Amsterdam 244; wraps $4-5; ✆ 8am-10pm Mon-Fri, 10am-6pm Sat & Sun; Ⓜ Chilpancingo) When you need a break from *biftek*, Forbidden Fruits puts together healthy salads, wraps and fruit-juice combos. Consider taking out for a picnic in nearby Parque México. Catch metrobus 'Campeche.'

Don Keso (Map pp118-19; ☎ 5211-3806; Amsterdam 73, cnr Parras; baguettes & salads $3-4; ✆ 10am-midnight Mon-Wed, 10am-2am Thu-Sat, 1-9pm Sun; Ⓜ Insurgentes) This casual, reasonably priced hangout near Parque México has great baguettes and salads, plus an exciting cocktail selection. Crowds rush in for the good-value *comida corrida* ($5).

MIDRANGE & TOP END

Condesa's culinary heart is the intersection of Av Michoacán, Vicente Suárez and Atlixco. After 8pm the following places are often filled to capacity and getting a table means waiting around for a while. More good restaurants and cafés ring Parque México.

El Zorzal (Map pp118-19; ☎ 5273-6023; Alfonso Reyes 39, cnr Tamaulipas; steaks $9.50-19, pasta $5-6.50; ✆ 1-11pm; Ⓜ Patriotismo; Ⓟ) Run by Buenos Aires–native Julio, this is the best of many options for Argentinean fare, with imported cuts, as well as fresh pasta and generous salads. The *parrillada* ($26), a mixed grill served on a chopping board, feeds at least two.

La Sábia Virtud (Map pp118-19; ☎ 5286-6480; Tamaulipas 134B; main courses $7-9; Ⓜ Patriotismo; Ⓟ) Nouvelle cuisine from Puebla is lovingly presented at this cozy spot. *Mole* is prepared in the classic Santa Clara convent style or the restaurant's own *verde* version.

Café La Gloria (Map pp118-19; ☎ 5211-4180; Vicente Suárez 41; pasta & salads $5-6, main dishes $8-10; ✆ 1pm-midnight Mon-Sat, 1-11pm Sun; Ⓜ Patriotismo; Ⓟ) Check out the blackboard specials at

this hip, casual bistro with an international clientele.

Fonda Garufa (Map pp118-19; ☎ 5286-8295; Michoacán 93; pasta $7, steaks $13; ✆ 2pm-midnight Mon, 8am-midnight Tue & Wed, 8am-1am Thu-Sat, 8am-11pm Sun; Ⓜ Patriotismo; Ⓟ) One of the first in the zone to put tables on the sidewalk and fire up a grill, Garufa remains a popular and romantic spot.

Don Asado (Map pp118-19; ☎ 5286-0789; Michoacán 77; steaks from $9; ✆ Tue-Sun; Ⓜ Patriotismo) Perhaps it's the way they grill their steaks and sausages – slowly, over coals – or perhaps it's their affordable prices, but there's often a line outside this cozy Uruguayan place. A *parrillada* (board for two or three) is a good way to sample some of the choicest cuts, such as *tira de asado* (ribs, sliced into strips) or *bife de chorizo* (boneless sections of loin).

Bistrot Mosaico (Map pp118-19; ☎ 5584-2932; Michoacán 10; starters $4-9, main courses $9-16; ✆ noon-11:30pm Mon-Sat, noon-5:30pm Sun; Ⓜ Chilpancingo; Ⓟ) A slice of Paris just west of Av Insurgentes, this unpretentious bistro is the successful creation of French restaurateur Francois Avernin. It's trendy for a reason: the service is stellar, the salads fresh and varied, and the wines well chosen. Picnickers can stock up on pâté and escargots at the deli counter.

Barracuda Diner (Map pp118-19; ☎ 5211-9480; Av Nuevo León 4A, cnr Av Sonora; burgers $6.50-8.50; ✆ 1pm-4am Mon-Thu, 24hr Fri-Sun; Ⓜ Sevilla) This retro-style diner does a fine facsimile of gringo comfort food, including cheeseburgers and macaroni and cheese, fish and chips, plus some pretty far-out milkshakes (mmm, *mamey*).

Roma
QUICK EATS

An unassuming street stall labeled **hamburguesas** (Map pp118-19; cnr Morelia & Colima; burgers $1.50; ✆ 10am-midnight; Ⓜ Cuauhtémoc) does a roaring trade in hamburgers *al carbón* (charcoal-broiled), garnished with lettuce, tomatoes and chilies. Across Morelia, another popular stall produces exquisite deep-fried quesadillas, filled with things like *huitlacoche* (corn mushrooms) and squash blossoms. Mornings before 10:30am, look for superb *tamales oaxaqueños* at the corner of Álvaro Obregón and Tonalá.

THE AUTHOR'S CHOICE

María del Alma (Map pp118-19; ☎ 5553-0403; Cuernavaca 68, Condesa; starters $4-6, main courses $7-12; ⏰ 1:30-11pm Mon-Fri, until 1:30am Sat, until 6pm Sun; Ⓜ Patriotismo; Ⓟ) A culinary escape to the Mexican state of Tabasco, María del Alma is a bit removed from the Condesa hubbub. Dining is in a leafy patio among singing birds and a romantically inclined pianist. Enjoy a guanabana margarita as *tabasqueño* owners Jorge and Fernando describe such regional treats as *tamales de chipilín*. For a main dish, try sea bass steamed in aromatic herbs. Be sure to save room for the mind-blowing desserts, say, *dulce de coco con almendra*, a scoop of sweet, shredded coconut spiked with chocolate.

BUDGET

El 91 (Map pp118-19; ☎ 5208-1666; Valladolid 91; dishes $4-9.50; ⏰ 1-7pm Sun-Fri; Ⓜ Sevilla) Lunch is served to piano accompaniment at this triple-deck restaurant-bar – dumbwaiters deliver the food to the top terrace. It offers a different menu daily, with a long list of homemade soups and main dishes.

Taquería El Jarocho (Map pp118-19; ☎ 5564-4077; Manzanillo 49, cnr Tapachula; tacos $1.75; ⏰ 7am-10pm Mon-Sat, 8am-7pm Sun; Ⓜ Chilpancingo) Scrambled eggs in *salsa verde*, cactus leaves with shrimp cakes, and brains *a la mexicana* are among the two-dozen taco fillings to choose from at this snack bar. Get two tacos for one from 8am to 9:30am and 8:30pm to 10pm.

Non Solo Panino (Map pp118-19; ☎ 3096-5128; Plaza Luis Cabrera, Guanajuato 102; sandwiches & salads $4-6; ⏰ 1pm-midnight Mon-Sat; Ⓜ Insurgentes; Ⓟ) The plaza's dancing fountains make a lovely backdrop for Italian sandwiches stuffed with things like mozzarella, pesto and smoked salmon.

Los Bisquets Obregón (Map pp118-19; ☎ 5584-2802; Álvaro Obregón 60; breakfast $4-5, antojitos $4.50-6; Ⓜ Insurgentes; Ⓟ ✂) The flagship branch of this nationwide chain overflows most mornings; fortunately there are a couple more nearby. Chilangos flock here for the *pan chino* (Chinese pastries) and *café con leche*, dispensed from two pitchers, Veracruz style.

Pozolería Tixtla (Map pp110-11; ☎ 5233-2081; Hernández y Dávalos 35; pozole $3.50; ⏰ 11am-9:30pm;

Ⓜ Lázaro Cárdenas) East of Roma, in working-class Colonia Algarín, this old-fashioned dining hall attracts plenty of families with hefty appetites. The specialty (it's been perfecting for 35 years) is Guerrero-style green *pozole*, a soulful variation on the classic pork and hominy broth, garnished with crackling *chicharrón* and creamy avocado slices.

MIDRANGE & TOP END

Contramar (Map pp118-19; ☎ 5514-3169; Durango 200; starters $5-9, main courses $12-14; ⏰ 1:30-6:30pm; Ⓜ Insurgentes; Ⓟ) Fresh seafood, artfully prepared, is the star attraction at this stylish dining hall with a seaside ambience. The specialty is tuna fillet Contramar style – split, swabbed with red chili and parsley sauces, and grilled to perfection.

Ixchel (Map pp118-19; ☎ 3096-5010; Medellín 65; main dishes $15; ⏰ 1pm-3.30am Mon-Sat; Ⓜ Insurgentes; Ⓟ) 'Fusion' is an overused term among Condesa and Roma bistros, but this late-night supper club takes it seriously. Ixchel's innovative chef deftly fuses Mexican elements (grasshoppers, squash blossoms) with Mediterranean and Asian fare (risotto and tempura). The upstairs Salón Azul adds another dimension (Wednesday to Saturday nights), with DJs supplying the appropriately chilled ambience.

Polanco & Bosque de Chapultepec
BUDGET & MIDRANGE

For moderately priced fare in Polanco, head for Av Presidente Masaryk between Dumas and France; a string of sidewalk cafés lines the south side of the street.

Caldos d'Leo (Map pp120-1; ☎ 5580-0515; Ejército Nacional 1014-B; chicken soup $3-5; ⏰ 8am-8pm; Ⓜ Polanco) In this wealthy zone, mid-level salarymen and women file into this large hall, a modernized version of the market chicken-soup stall. The *sopa especial d'Leo* – packed with hard-boiled egg, sliced avocado, garbanzo beans and chicken giblets – is a meal in itself.

Klein's (Map pp120-1; ☎ 5281-0862; Presidente Masaryk 360-B; antojitos $5-10; Ⓜ Polanco; Ⓟ) With sidewalk seating on Presidente Masaryk, Klein's is a popular hangout for the local Jewish community. Though most of the fare is typically Mexican (enchiladas, *carne a la tampiqueña*), you can also get bagels or a plate of kosher salami and eggs.

TOP END

La Hacienda de los Morales (Map pp120-1; ☎ 5096-3054; Vázquez de Mella 525; main dishes $17-30; ☺ 1pm-1am; Ⓜ Polanco; Ⓟ) Often the setting for banquets and receptions, the 400-year-old hacienda serves sumptuous variations on Mexican and Spanish classics in its elegant dining room. Reservations are advisable and dress is formal.

Villa María (Map pp120-1; ☎ 5203-0306; Homero 704; main dishes $8-15; ☺ 1:30pm-midnight Mon-Sat, 1:30-7pm Sun; Ⓜ Polanco; Ⓟ) A large spread with an invariably celebratory atmosphere, the Villa María makes a good choice for that special meal *a la mexicana*. Original recipes incorporate regional styles from around the Republic. Mega-margaritas come in 10 versions.

Colonia del Valle

Fonda Margarita (Map pp110-11; Adolfo Prieto 1346; main dishes half/full portion $2/2.75; ☺ 5:30-11:30am Mon-Sat) Possibly the capital's premier hangover-recovery spot – witness the line down the street on Saturday mornings – the humble *fonda* (eating place) opposite Parque Tlacoquemécatl whips up big batches of comfort food for the day ahead. Soulful fare like pork back in *chile guajillo* sauce is doled out of giant pots. Don't miss the *huevos refritos* (eggs scrambled with refried black beans). Catch metrobus 'Parque Hundido.'

Taquería Villamelón (Map pp110-11; ☎ 5563-2779; Alberto Balderas 3a; tacos $1; ☺ 9am-6pm Thu-Sun) After the *corrida*, stop by this popular joint just outside the bullring, whose name translates as 'bullfighting neophyte.' There are ample bowls of salsa – the house blend is plenty hot – to spice up your sausage, pork rind or *cecina* (a thin cut of meat, flavored with chili and sautéed or grilled) tacos, or all three combined. Catch metrobus 'Ciudad de los Deportes.'

San Ángel

BUDGET

Bazar Sábado (Map p122; Plaza San Jacinto 11; quesadillas $1.50; ☺ 10am-7pm Sat; Ⓜ Miguel Angel de Quevedo) For a break from shopping, grab a few fresh-made quesadillas in the plaza of the market building; there's also a lunch buffet ($18).

El Convento (Map p122; Plaza del Carmen 4; churros & chocolate $3; Ⓜ Miguel Angel de Quevedo) Next door to the Carmelite ex-convent (see p142), this is a popular stop for *churros*, sprinkled with sugar and served alongside French or Mexican chocolate (spiked with tequila on request).

MIDRANGE & TOP END

Capicua (Map p122; ☎ 5616-5211; Av de la Paz 14-B; tapas & raciones $4-7; Ⓜ Miguel Angel de Quevedo; Ⓟ) One of several restaurants in a little mall off Av Insurgentes, Capicua offers toothsome tapas in sleek surroundings. Served in abundant portions, the *pulpos a la gallega* (octopus boiled with potato, drizzled with olive oil and sprinkled with paprika) and *tortilla de patata* (potato tortilla) are the best you'll find this side of Madrid, and the wine list is equally impressive.

Saks (Map p122; ☎ 5616-1601; Plaza San Jacinto 9; main dishes $8-11.50; ☺ 7:30am-6pm Sun-Thu, 7:30am-midnight Fri & Sat; Ⓜ Miguel Angel de Quevedo; Ⓟ Ⓥ) At this mostly vegetarian restaurant with a splendid terrace, choose from meatless specialties like *poblano* chilies stuffed with corn-fungus, huge salads and squash blossom crepes. Breakfast combos are popular, with plenty of fruit, fresh-baked bread and a half-liter of juice.

Fonda San Ángel (Map p122; ☎ 5550-1641; Plaza San Jacinto 3; main dishes $8.50-11; Ⓜ Miguel Angel de Quevedo; Ⓟ) On weekends, this attractive restaurant by the plaza does an abundant brunch buffet ($10), with all kinds of egg dishes, pastries and fresh-squeezed juices, plus great quesadillas.

San Ángel Inn (Map p122; ☎ 5616-1402; Diego Rivera 50; main dishes $9-19; ☺ 1pm-1am Mon-Sat, 1-10pm Sun; Ⓟ) Next to the Estudio Diego Rivera, this ex-hacienda serves Mexican and European cuisine. Even if you don't splurge for dinner, have one of its renowned margaritas or martinis in the garden. Walk or take a taxi 1km northwest from San Ángel's Plaza San Jacinto. On foot, one pleasant route is west on Galeana, then north on Leandro Valle

Coyoacán

QUICK EATS

Supertacos Chupacabras (Map p123; Mayorazgo, cnr Av Universidad; tacos $0.70; ☺ 7am-3am Mon-Sat, 7am-midnight Sun; Ⓜ Coyoacán) Named after the mythical 'goat sucker' (something like the Loch Ness monster), this mega taco stall provides an ideal stand-up snack between metro Coyoacán and the Cineteca

Nacional. The beef and sausage tacos can be enhanced by availing yourself of the fried onions, *nopales* and other tasty toppings that fill half a dozen huge clay casseroles in front. As the sign says, '*Si es de res aqui es*' (If it's made of beef, here it is).

El Tizoncito (Map p123; ☎ 5554-7712; Aguayo 3; tacos from $0.70; ☯ noon-2:30am Sun-Thu, noon-3:30am Fri & Sat; Ⓜ Viveros) Branch of the popular taco chain that originated in Condesa.

Nieves de Coyoacán (Map p123; Plaza Hidalgo 31; scoops from $1; 8am-10pm or 11pm; Ⓜ Viveros) This obligatory weekend stop has homemade ice cream and popsicles in flavors ranging from corn to Nescafé.

Coyoacán's best deep-fried snacks are found at **Churros Allende** (Map p123; Allende 38; from $0.70; Ⓜ Viveros). Get in line for a bag – cream-filled or straight up – then stroll over to El Jarocho for coffee (p170).

BUDGET
Chamorros Coyoacán (Map p123; ☎ 5659-0340; Madrid 29; main dishes $2.50-3.75; ☯ 1-6pm Mon-Sat; Ⓜ Coyoacán) Office workers fill this barn-like structure at lunchtime. Most patrons

order the *chamorros* ($7.50), Flintstone-size joints of pork, and stuff the morsels into homemade tortillas.

Fonda El Morral (Map p123; ☎ 5554-0298; Allende 2; breakfast $5.50-7.50, antojitos $4-6; Ⓜ Viveros) This large restaurant with tiled arches is good for a traditional breakfast or evening *huchepos* (slightly sweet Michoacán-style *tamales*) and chocolate, served in clay mugs.

MIDRANGE & TOP END
El Jardín del Pulpo (Map p123; cnr Allende & Malitzin; cocktails $3.75-6.50, fish dishes $11-15; ☯ 10:30am-6pm; Ⓜ Viveros) Fresh-fish platters, shrimp and oyster cocktails and *caldos* (broths) are served at this locale on a corner of the main market. Everyone sits on benches at long tables.

Los Danzantes (Map p123; ☎ 5658-6054; Jardín del Centenario 12; dishes $8.50-13; Ⓜ Viveros) Los Danzantes puts a contemporary spin on Mexican cuisine with dishes like *fusilli con chapulines* (grasshopper pasta) and squash blossom salad. You'll also find *mezcal* cocktails and cigars from San Andrés in Veracruz.

ETHNIC EATING

Though Chilangos tend to be conservative in their tastes, the city hosts enough foreign communities to cater to more internationally inclined palates. Note that generally *cafés chinos* (Chinese restaurants) are more likely to serve enchiladas and biscuits than authentic Chinese fare.

■ **Hong King** (Map pp114-15; ☎ 5512-6703; Dolores 25A; dishes $5-7; ☯ 11am-11pm; Ⓜ Bellas Artes) The most popular restaurant in Mexico City's small Chinatown, with set Cantonese meals ($5.50 to $15, minimum two people) and some vegetarian offerings such as the tofu with veggie stir-fry.

■ **King Felafel** (Map pp118-19; ☎ 5514-9030; Londres 178, cnr Florencia; sandwiches $2, salads $3.50; ☯ 9am-8pm Mon-Fri, 9am-6pm Sat; Ⓜ Insurgentes) Middle-Eastern fast-food place with felafel, hummus and tabouleh, run by a Syrian Jew who knows all the family recipes.

■ **U Rae Ok** (Map pp118-19; ☎ 5511-1233; Hamburgo 232; main dishes $6-8; ☯ Mon-Sat; Ⓜ Insurgentes) Core of the Korean community, the Zona Rosa has several authentic restaurants catering to it. This simple upstairs locale has the finest *bul-go-gi* (grilled marinated beef) and *chigae* (hearty soup), at the best prices.

■ **Kolobok** (Map pp110-11; ☎ 5541-7085; Díaz Mirón 87; salads $3.50, combo platters $4; ☯ 9am-8pm; Ⓜ Buenavista) Run by a Russian family, this humble place facing the charming Alameda of the Santa María La Ribera neighborhood has excellent layered salads, tasty 'Russian empanadas' and borscht, of course.

■ **Restaurante Shalala** (Map pp118-19; ☎ 5286-5406; Tamaulipas 93, cnr Alfonso Reyes, Condesa; sushi from $2, noodle & rice dishes $8; ☯ 1-11pm Mon-Sat, 1-8pm Sun; Ⓜ Patriotismo; Ⓟ Ⓥ) Long-standing Japanese deli noted for its authenticity (owner Hiroshi is a Tokyo native) and casual atmosphere. Standouts include the tempura and *negitoro don* (fresh tuna with sesame oil served on a bed of rice).

DRINKING

Cafés, bars and cantinas are all major social venues on the capital's landscape. Starbucks is a latecomer to a long-standing café tradition fueled by beans from Veracruz, Oaxaca and Chiapas. Coyoacán in particular is jammed with java joints. The bar scene is extraordinarily lively with a high degree of specialization, from Irish pubs to martini clubs. Cantinas, Mexico's pubs, are traditionally a male domain but women are welcome nowadays.

Prices for drinks vary quite a bit, but generally beers are around $2 to $3, and mixed drinks range from $4 to $10.

Centro Histórico

CAFÉS

Take a coffee break at any of these charming downtown locales.

Café Jakemir (Map pp114-15; ☎ 5709-7038; Isabel la Católica 74A; ☺ 9am-8pm Mon-Sat; Ⓜ Isabel la Católica) Run by a family of Lebanese coffee traders from Orizaba, this old distribution outlet transformed into a popular café has excellent and inexpensive cappuccinos.

Café La Habana (Map pp114-15; ☎ 5535-2620; Morelos 62; ☺ 8am-11pm Mon-Sat, 8am-10pm Sun; Ⓜ Juárez) This grand coffeehouse is a traditional haunt for writers and journalists, who linger for hours over their café americano. Legend has it that Fidel and Che plotted strategy here prior to the Cuban revolution.

Other options:

La Selva Café (Map pp114-15; ☎ 5521-4111; Bolívar 31; ☺ 8:30am-10pm; Ⓜ Allende) Branch of the Chiapas coffee distributor in the stunning patio of a colonial building.

Café del Passaje (Map pp114-15; ☎ 5521-0683; Pasaje Iturbide; ☺ 8am-9:30pm Mon-Sat, 10am-9:30pm Sun; Ⓜ Allende) Nice journal-writing spot on traffic-free Gante.

Cafe Cordobés (Map pp114-15; ☎ 5512-5545; Ayuntamiento 18; ☺ 8am-8pm Mon-Sat, 10am-6pm Sun; Ⓜ San Juan de Letrán) Good spot for a standup *cortado* (espresso with a little foamed milk) amid a busy shopping district; bulk coffee from Veracruz at reasonable prices.

BARS

La Gioconda (Map pp114-15; ☎ 5518-7823; Filomena Mata 18; ☺ 2-10pm Mon-Thu, 2pm-3am Fri & Sat; Ⓜ Allende) Dark and light draft beer are poured in this happening little pub off a pedestrian thoroughfare.

Bar Mancera (Map pp114-15; ☎ 5521-9755; Venustiano Carranza 49; cover Fri & Sat night $5; ☺ noon-10pm Mon-Thu, noon-2am Fri & Sat; Ⓜ San Juan de Letrán) This ancient gentlemen's salon with ornate wood carving and well-used domino tables has been adopted by young clubbers who set up turntables Friday nights from around 9pm.

Hostería La Bota (Map pp114-15; Callejón de Mesones 7; ☺ 10am-8pm Mon-Wed, 10am-2am Thu-Sat; Ⓜ Isabel la Católica) A cultural beachhead in the rough-and-tumble southern fringe of the Centro, this fun and funky new bar is one component of the Casa Vecina community arts center. The warped bullfighting paraphernalia and mismatched furniture seem attuned to a contemporary Spanish sensibility.

El Nivel (Map pp114-15; ☎ 5522-9755; Moneda 2; ☺ noon-midnight Mon-Sat; Ⓜ Zócalo) The country's first cantina proudly displays its license (No 1), dating from 1855. On the site of the hemisphere's first university, it's within shouting distance of the Palacio Nacional, and since its opening, every Mexican president except Vicente Fox has stopped in for a *trago* (drink). The *botanas* (drinking snacks) here are particularly fine.

Salón Corona (Map pp114-15; ☎ 5512-5725; Bolívar 24; ☺ 9am-midnight; Ⓜ Allende) Punks and suits crowd this boisterous, no-frills bar, running since 1928. Amiable staff serve up *tarros* (mugs) of light or dark *cerveza de barril* (draft beer) and bottles of almost every known Mexican beer for $2.50 each.

Los Portales de Tlaquepaque (Map pp114-15; ☎ 5518-6344; Bolívar 56; ☺ 9am-2am; Ⓜ San Juan de Letrán) Sharing a downtown spot with a number of other straightforward saloons, this two-storey operation has the best-stocked bar and liveliest atmosphere.

La Ópera Bar (Map pp114-15; ☎ 5512-8959; Av 5 de Mayo 10; ☺ 1pm-midnight Mon-Sat, 1-5:30pm Sun; Ⓜ Allende) This early-20th-century watering hole only opened its doors to women in the 1970s. With original booths of dark walnut and an ornate tin ceiling (said to have been punctured by Pancho Villa's bullet on an otherwise slow night), it's a pleasant setting for a tequila (but seek dinner elsewhere).

Zona Rosa & Around

The Pink Zone can seem pretty sleazy with so many dark-suited bouncers and touts trying to lure business into strip joints, but there are plenty of fully clothed establishments, too.

CAFÉS

Sanborns Café (Map pp118-19; ☎ 5207-9760; Londres 149; ⏰ 24hr; Ⓜ Insurgentes) Chilangos customarily meet here for a business breakfast or lunch. After hours, the round-the-clock

coffee shop makes a convenient port-of-call between clubs. Perhaps the fresh-juice combos are the most exciting item on an otherwise bland menu.

Cafetería Gabi's (Map pp118-19; ☎ 5511-7637; Nápoles 55, cnr Liverpool; ⏰ Mon-Sat; Ⓜ Insurgentes) Cluttered with caffeine-related paraphernalia, this family-run coffeehouse in an otherwise nondescript section of Colonia Juárez

---

PULQUERÍAS

Before discotheques, even before cantinas, Mexico had *pulquerías*. Named after the drink they served, these seedy hovels were *the* working-class watering hole for the better part of 400 years, before refrigeration and more conventional beverages starting pushing them to the side.

When the Aztecs ruled Mexico, pulque, extracted from the maguey plant, was used only in rituals and by the elite. Its production was strictly controlled and drunkenness was severely punished. When the Spanish arrived, pulque hit the streets. The milky, low-alcohol brew was sold from open-air stands and the method of service was just as primitive: purveyors would ladle the drink from large basins into earthenware cups. As the day wore on, these cups would be smashed by rowdy patrons once the contents were drained – *¡epa!*

The ancient beverage was widely consumed in Mexico City throughout the colonial period, chiefly among the city's underclasses – statistics of the era show an annual per capita consumption among adults of 187 gallons. In the mid-17th century there were some 200 *pulquerías* operating in the Centro. The government restricted their locations to outlying neighborhoods, a factor that may have contributed to the wicked brew's eventual demise. In the meantime, other potent potables, such as beer brought by German immigrants, as well as *mezcal* and tequila, began to gain greater popularity and supplant pulque as the intoxicant of choice. True pulque is homemade, not bottled, and therefore not viable for large-scale commercial production.

Nowadays just a handful of *pulquerías* still function. They tend to be extremely rustic places, and some remain male-only enclaves. However, they are highly social venues with patrons in a conversant mood. Food is served (often for free) and jukeboxes are normally set just below blast volume. The viscous white liquid may be served straight up or in the somewhat more palatable *curado* (flavored form). Coconut, pineapple and mango are popular, along with some odd variations like beet, oat (sprinkled with cinnamon) and celery.

■ **Las Duelistas** (Map pp114-15; Aranda 30; ⏰ 8:30am-9pm Mon-Sat; Ⓜ Salto del Agua) Behind the swinging doors is this larger *pulquería* alongside the Mercado San Juan. Pulque is dispensed straight out of the barrel in a wide range of flavors, including pistachio and pine nut (and for the brave, in shrimp and oyster cocktails Friday and Saturday).

■ **La Risa** (Map pp114-15; ☎ 5709-4963; Mesones 71; ⏰ 9am-8pm Mon-Sat; Ⓜ Isabel la Católica) Going since 1900, 'The Laugh' is popular among bohemian young men and women who engage in intellectual pursuits like playing chess or reading history while drinking their pulque, and the jukebox features a more contemporary selection than usual.

■ **La Hermosa Hortensia** (Map pp114-15; Plaza Garibaldi 4; ⏰ 10am-midnight; Ⓜ Garibaldi) Opening onto Plaza Garibaldi, this makes a good *pulquería* for beginners: its hygiene is a cut above the norm, they're used to seeing foreigners, and the atmosphere is 100% 'familiar.'

■ **El Recreo de Manzanares** (Map pp110-11; Manzanares 30; ⏰ 9am-7pm Mon-Sat; Ⓜ Zócalo) At this hole-in-the-wall near the Mercado de la Merced, you'll find a group of grizzled characters in a festive mood sitting around a long table sharing pitchers of pulque 'natural,' a scene straight from the Golden Age.

■ **La Hija de los Apaches** (Map pp118-19; ☎ 5511-0071; Cuauhtémoc 39; ⏰ 9am-9:30pm Mon-Sat; Ⓜ Cuauhtémoc) This working-class *pulquería* has long been a haunt of professional boxers.

buzzes with conversation midmornings and early evenings, when the occupants of neighboring offices pour in for a rich *café con leche* (coffee with milk) and a crispy *banderilla* (stick-like glazed pastry).

BARS

Bar Milán (Map pp118-19; ☎ 5592-0031; Milán 18; ☒ 9pm-midnight Tue & Wed, 9pm-3am Thu-Sat; Ⓜ Cuauhtémoc) Tucked away on a quiet backstreet, this cave-like hangout gets as crowded as the metro. Purchase beer tickets, then make your way over to the cactus-trimmed bar. The soundtrack ranges from classic rock to Café Tacuba; don't be surprised when the crowd spontaneously bursts into chorus.

Yuppie's Sports Café (Map pp118-19; ☎ 5533-0919; Génova 34; ☒ 1pm-2am; Ⓜ Insurgentes) For those who need their sports fix, this gringo-style betting and viewing parlor has about 50 TVs showing the big game.

Condesa

CAFÉS

Café La Selva (Map pp118-19; ☎ 5211-5170; Vicente Suárez 38; Ⓜ Patriotismo) The Mexican Starbucks serves organic coffee from Chiapas, produced by small-scale indigenous coffee growers. The Condesa branch is the hippest place in town for a coffee break.

Café Bola de Oro (Map pp118-19; ☎ 5286-5659; Nuevo León 192-B; ☒ 7am-10pm Mon-Fri, 9am-7pm Sat; Ⓜ Chilpancingo) An outlying branch of the Xalapa coffee purveyor, this is a good place to score a bag of Coatepec beans or simply enjoy a cup of Veracruz' fine, full-bodied blends.

Caffé Toscano (Map pp118-19; ☎ 5584-3681; Michoacán 30; ☒ 7:30am-11pm; Ⓜ Chilpancingo) This sidewalk café sits on a delightful corner of Parque México, making a fine setting for a latte and the morning paper – grab one off the rack.

BARS

Condesa's bar scene continues to thrive, and new places are popping up (and shutting down) all the time. The following are relatively well established and filled beyond capacity Thursday through Saturday evenings. The confluence of Tamaulipas and Nuevo León has emerged as a major bar zone, earning a reputation as a haven for

fresas (literally 'strawberries,' a derogatory term for upper-class youth).

Black Horse (Map pp118-19; ☎ 5211-8740; Mexicali 85, cnr Tamaulipas; ☒ 6pm-2am Tue-Sat; Ⓜ Patriotismo) This authentic British pub is a useful addition to the Condesa scene, and not just because you can get bangers and mash and watch the soccer match (projected on one wall). It also boasts an international social scene and has excellent bands playing the back room most nights.

El Centenario (Map pp118-19; ☎ 5553-4454; Vicente Suárez 42; ☒ noon-midnight Mon-Sat; Ⓜ Patriotismo) An enclave of tradition in the heart of modish Condesa, this little gem is jammed most evenings.

THE AUTHOR'S CHOICE

Condesa df (Map pp118-19; ☎ 5241-2600; Veracruz 102, cnr Guadalajara; ☒ 1pm-midnight Mon-Wed, 1pm-1:30am Thu-Sat, 1-11pm Sun; Ⓜ Chapultepec) The bar of the fashionable new boutique hotel (see p157) has fast become an essential stop on the Condesa nightlife circuit. Action focuses on the triangular atrium and wackily decorated alcoves around it, where businessfolk, artists and the occasional film star gather before moving on to still hotter spots. Up on the roof terrace, guests lounge on big-wheel wicker sofas, nibble on sushi and enjoy views of verdant Parque España across the way.

Mitote (Map pp118-19; ☎ 5211-9150; Amsterdam 53; ☒ 8pm-2am Tue-Sat; Ⓜ Chilpancingo) Mitote (Náhuatl for 'ruckus'), a lively little joint near Parque España, lives up to its name. Owner Walter works the quirkily decorated lounge like a good host. If you're hungry, try the tasty tapas.

Malafama (Map pp118-19; ☎ 5553-5138; Av Michoacán 78; tables per hr $7.50; Ⓜ Patriotismo) Not an exclusively male domain by any means, Condesa's billiard hall is as trendy as its bars and cafés. The well-maintained tables are frequented by both pool sharks and novices.

Hookah Lounge (Map pp118-19; ☎ 5264-6275; Campeche 284; ☒ 1pm-12:30am Mon-Wed, until 2am Thu-Sat; Ⓜ Chilpancingo) Moroccan tapestries and pillows set the tone for this North African fantasy augmented by house music. Bring friends and share a water pipe (from $10),

Huastecan guitar seller, Tampico (p661)

Festivities in Tijuana (p267)

Volkswagon taxis, Taxco (p247)

CHRISTIAN ASLUND

Visit a *cantina* (p96) and live local history
through the eyes of those who really know

JIM WARK

Barranca del Cobre (p336)

Paddling in the Sea of Cortez, Puerto Peñasco (p315)

RALPH LEE

available in a bewildering array of flavors. Belly dancers perform Wednesdays.

Pata Negra (Map pp118-19; ☎ 5211-5563; Tamaulipas 30; ☯ 1:30pm-2am; Ⓜ Patriotismo) Nominally a tapas bar, this oblong salon draws a friendly, clean-cut crowd of 20-something Chilangos and expats. There's live music on both levels, with the upper Salón Pata Negra striking a more bohemian tone.

Cafeina (Map pp118-19; ☎ 5212-0090; Nuevo León 73; ☯ 1pm-2am; Ⓜ Patriotismo) This sleek café-bar hybrid has crushed-velvet armchairs and a narrow terrace, and is a good vantage point for gawking at gorgeous arrivals over a latte or Cafeini (espresso martini). Star DJs work the room from a central module.

Celtics (Map pp118-19; ☎ 5211-9081; Tamaulipas 36; ☯ 1:30pm-3am Mon-Sat; Ⓜ Patriotismo) An Argentinian-run facsimile of an Irish pub, Celtics remains hugely popular with young *defeños*. A Guinness will set you back $6 here, a draft Sol, $3. The soundtrack is more U2 than Chieftains; bands play Monday and Tuesday nights.

Roma
CAFÉS

Enanos de Tapanco (Map pp118-19; ☎ 5564-2274; Orizaba 161, cnr Querétaro; ☯ 8am-11:30pm Mon-Fri, 9am-11:30pm Sat, 3:30-10:30pm Sun; Ⓜ Centro Médico) Possibly Mexico City's coolest café, the 'Dwarves of the Loft' also functions as an art gallery. Cappuccinos and quiches are served along with an eclectic music selection. There's live music Friday and story-telling Tuesday evening.

Café de Carlo (Map pp118-19; ☎ 5574-5647; Orizaba 115; ☯ Mon-Sat; Ⓜ Insurgentes) Coffee connoisseurs head for this unassuming sidewalk café, with an aromatic roaster and vintage espresso machine.

La Mediterránea (Map pp118-19; ☎ 5208-7810; Orizaba 87; ☯ 9am-10pm Mon-Fri, 10am-10pm Sat; Ⓜ Insurgentes) Almost hidden on a tree-lined corridor, this Turkish teahouse has sidewalk tables and a small tapestry-draped salon for savoring exotic teas, strong Turkish coffee and fabulously rich desserts.

BARS

La Bodeguita del Medio (Map pp118-19; ☎ 5553-0246; Cozumel 37; ☯ 2pm-2am Tue-Sat, 2pm-midnight Sun & Mon; Ⓜ Sevilla) The walls of various salons are scribbled with verses and messages at this animated branch of the famous Havana joint. Have a *mojito*, a Cuban concoction of rum and mint leaves ($4.50), and enjoy the excellent *son cubano* combos that perform here.

Lamm (Map pp118-19; ☎ 5514-8501; Álvaro Obregón 99; ☯ until 2am Mon-Sat; Ⓜ Insurgentes) In the evening the open-air restaurant of the Casa Lamm turns into a hip lounge where a smart set congregates until the wee hours. There's live *música cubana* and jazz Tuesday and Wednesday.

Taberna Red Fly (Map pp118-19; ☎ 1054-3616; Orizaba 143; ☯ 6pm-midnight Mon-Wed, 6pm-2am Thu-Sat; Ⓜ Centro Médico) An elegantly furnished space in a typical Porfiriato-era residence, the Red Fly gets busy on weekends when a youthful, alternative crowd moves in. The upstairs lounge is reserved for DJ sessions and occasional live music.

Tierra de Vinos (Map pp118-19; ☎ 5208-5133; Durango 197; ☯ 1-8pm Mon & Tue, 1pm-midnight Wed-Sat; Ⓜ Insurgentes) Mexico is not a nation of oenophiles, so this wine-tasting salon is a pleasant surprise. The wine list changes monthly, with most of the world's vineyards represented, and there's classic Spanish fare to complement your choice.

Cantina Covadonga (Map pp118-19; ☎ 5533-2922; Puebla 121; ☯ 1pm-3am Mon-Fri; Ⓜ Insurgentes) Echoing with the sounds of clacking dominoes, the old Asturian social hall is a traditionally male enclave, though hipsters of both sexes have increasingly moved in on this hallowed ground.

Polanco
Though not as cutting-edge as Condesa, this well-heeled neighborhood gets quite lively after dark.

Segafredo (Map pp120-1; ☎ 5281-1203; Dumas 71-C; ☯ 8am-midnight Sun-Wed, 8am-2:30am Thu-Sat; Ⓜ Polanco) The Bologna-based chain expertly prepares all the espresso variations, from *caffé latte fredo* to *macchiato con panna*. Attracted by wireless access, laptop-users often occupy the upper level, which has an open-air terrace attached.

Área (Map pp120-1; ☎ 5282-3100; Presidente Masaryk 201; ☯ 7-11pm Mon-Wed, 7pm-2am Thu-Sat; Ⓜ Polanco) Atop the Hábita Hotel, this rooftop bar does a brisk trade in exotic martinis, as videos are projected on the wall of a nearby building.

Terra de Galicia (Map pp120-1; ☎ 5280-7737; Dumas 7; ☯ 1:30pm-1:30am Mon-Sat, 1:30am-midnight Sun; Ⓜ Auditorio; Ⓟ) Galicia's signature beer is dispensed from copper tanks here, along with authentic Spanish tapas.

Moon Bar (Map pp120-1; ☎ 5263-8887; Mariano Escobedo 700; cover for events; ✆ 9pm-2am Wed-Sat; Ⓜ Auditorio) Inside the Camino Real hotel is this ambient open-air lounge, where a select clientele unwind on canopied beds under the moonlight.

Coyoacán

Café El Jarocho (Map p123; ☎ 5658-5029; Cuauhtémoc 134, cnr Allende; ✆ 6am-1am; Ⓜ Coyoacán) This immensely popular joint churns out $0.70 cappuccinos for long lines of java hounds. As there's no seating inside, people have their coffee standing in the street or sitting on curbside benches. The branch just around the corner makes great tortas, and both branches have terrific doughnuts. An **El Jarocho branch** (Map p123; ☎ 5659-9107; Av México 25-C) is convenient to Viveros park. Get off at Viveros metro stop.

La Guadalupana (Map p123; ☎ 5554-6253; Higuera 2; ✆ noon-12:30am Mon-Sat; Ⓜ Viveros) Serving drinks for over seven decades, this rustic tavern breathes tradition down to the blasé waiters in white coats. There are *botanas* and tortas as well as heartier fare.

El Hijo del Cuervo (Map p123; ☎ 5658-7824; Jardín del Centenario 17; ✆ 5pm-1am Mon-Wed, 1pm-2am Thu-Sun; Ⓜ Viveros) This enormous stone-walled *antro* (den) has a classic rock ambience with groups of friends packing into its various salons and sharing pitchers of beer. Bands rock the house Tuesday and Wednesday nights.

ENTERTAINMENT

There's so much going on in Mexico City on any given evening, it's hard to keep track. *Tiempo Libre*, the city's comprehensive what's-on magazine, will help you sort it all out. Published Thursday, it covers live music, theater, movies, dance, art and nightlife, with lots of family options, and gay venues. Other useful guides include the comprehensive monthlies *Donde Ir* and *Chilango*, the latter with a *Time Out* supplement. *Primera Fila*, a Friday section of the *Reforma* newspaper, has lots of entertainment listings.

Ticketmaster (☎ 5325-9000; www.ticketmaster .com.mx in Spanish) sells tickets for all the major venues via Internet, phone or any of these outlets.

Auditorio Nacional (Map pp120-1; Paseo de la Reforma 50; ✆ 11am-6pm; Ⓜ Auditorio)
Liverpool Centro (Map pp114-15; Venustiano Carranza 92; ✆ 11am-7pm; Ⓜ Zócalo); Polanco (Map pp120-1; Mariano Escobedo 425; ✆ 11am-8pm; Ⓜ Polanco)
Mixup Centro Histórico (Map pp114-15; Madero 51; ✆ 10am-9pm Mon-Sat, 11am-8pm Sun; Ⓜ Zócalo); Calle 16 de Septiembre (Map pp114-15; Calle 16 de Septiembre 14; Ⓜ San Juan de Letrán); Zona Rosa (Map pp118-19; Génova 76; ✆ 9am-9pm; Ⓜ Insurgentes)

Cinemas

Mexico City is a banquet for moviegoers. Almost everything is screened here and ticket prices are around $4, with many places offering discounts on Wednesday. Except for children's fare, movies are in original languages, with Spanish subtitles. *Reforma* and *La Jornada* have daily listings.

The following multiplexes have mostly Hollywood fare, with the odd Mexican hit.

Cine Diana (Map pp118-19; ☎ 2122-6060; Paseo de la Reforma 423; Ⓜ Sevilla) It faces La Diana Cazadora.
Cinemex Palacio (Map pp114-15; ☎ 5512-0348; Iturbide 25; Ⓜ Juárez)
Cinemex Real (Map pp114-15; ☎ 5512-7718; www .cinemex.com.mx; Colón 17; Ⓜ Hidalgo)

There are other theaters offering a more eclectic program.

Cinemex Casa de Arte (Map pp120-1; ☎ 5280-9156; Anatole France 120; admission $4.50; Ⓜ Polanco)
Lumiere Reforma (Map pp118-19; ☎ 5514-0000; Río Guadalquivir 104; admission $4; Ⓜ Sevilla)

In addition, several repertory cinemas cater to film buffs.

Centro Cultural Universitario (Map pp110-11; ☎ 5665-0709; Insurgentes Sur 3000; tickets $2.25) UNAM's two cinemas screen films from its collection of over 35,000 titles. Programming for this and other UNAM-system cinemas can be found at: www.unam.mx/filmoteca /Cines/cines.htm. See p143 for directions on how to get there.

Cinematógrafo del Chopo (Map pp114-15; ☎ 5702-3494; Dr Atl 37, Colonia Santa María La Ribera; tickets $2.25; Ⓜ San Cosme)
Cineteca Nacional (Map p123; ☎ 1253-9390; www .cinetecanacional.net in Spanish; Av México-Coyoacán 389; tickets $3.50; Ⓜ Coyoacán) Thematically focused film series are shown on six screens, with at least one for Mexican cinema. There are cafés and bookstores at the center of the complex, 700m east of metro Coyoacán. In November the Cineteca hosts the Muestra Internacional de Cine, Mexico City's international film festival.

Contempo Cinema (Map pp118-19; ☎ 5208-4044; Londres 161; www.contempocinema.com; Ⓜ Insurgentes) Emphasis on gay and erotic themes; inside the Zona Rosa's Plaza Ángel shopping center.

Salon Cinematográfico Fósforo (Map pp114-15; ☎ 5702-3494; San Ildefonso 43; tickets $2.25; Ⓜ Zócalo) Inside the Antiguo Colegio de San Ildefonso (p131).

Dance, Classical Music & Theater

Orchestral music, opera, ballet, contemporary dance and theater are all abundantly represented in the capital's numerous theaters. Museums, too, serve as performance venues, including the **Museo de la Secretaría de Hacienda y Crédito Público** (p130) and the **Museo Universitario del Chopo** (Map pp114-15; ☎ 5546-5484; www.chopo.unam.mx in Spanish; González Martínez 10; Ⓜ San Cosme). The national arts council (Conaculta) provides a rundown on

its website (www.cnca.gob.mx in Spanish) and in Friday's *La Jornada*.

Palacio de Bellas Artes (Map pp114-15; ☎ 5521-9251; Av Hidalgo 1; box office ☯ 11am-7pm; Ⓜ Bellas Artes) The Orquesta Sinfónica Nacional and prestigious opera and dance companies perform in the palace's ornate theater, while chamber groups appear in the recital halls. It's most famous, though, for the **Ballet Folclórico de México** (tickets $27-46; ☯ 8:30pm Wed, 9:30am & 8:30pm Sun), a two-hour festive blur of costumes, music and dance from all over Mexico. Tickets are usually available the day of the show at the Palacio or from Ticketmaster (see opposite).

Centro Cultural Universitario (Map pp110-11; ☎ 5622-7185; www.agendacultural.unam.mx in Spanish; Av Insurgentes Sur 3000) Ensconced in the woodsy southern section of the national university

---

campus, the complex comprises five theaters, including the Sala Nezahualcóyotl, home of the UNAM Philharmonic; the Teatro Alarcón, which puts on plays; and the Sala Miguel Covarrubias, a contemporary dance venue. See p143 for directions.

Centro Nacional de las Artes (CNA; Map p123; ☎ 1253-9400, ext 1035; www.cenart.gob.mx in Spanish; Río Churubusco 79; Ⓜ General Anaya) This sprawling art institute has events across the artistic spectrum, many free. Exit metro General Anaya (Línea 2) on the east side of Calz de Tlalpan, walk north to the corner and turn right.

Centro Cultural del Bosque (Map pp120-1; ☎ 5280-6228; cnr Paseo de la Reforma & Campo Marte; box office ⓨ noon-3pm & 5-7pm Mon-Fri & prior to events; Ⓜ Auditorio) This complex behind the Auditorio Nacional features six theaters, including the Teatro de la Danza, dedicated to modern dance. On Saturday and Sunday afternoons, children's plays and puppet shows are staged.

If your Spanish is up to it, you might sample Mexico City's lively theater scene. The website www.mejorteatro.com.mx (in Spanish) covers the major venues. Performances are generally Thursday to Sunday evenings with weekend matinees.

Foro Shakespeare (Map pp118-19; ☎ 5553-4642; Zamora 7, Condesa; tickets free-$14; Ⓜ Chapultepec) Small independent theater with eclectic program.

Teatro Blanquita (Map pp114-15; ☎ 5512-8264; Eje Central Lázaro Cárdenas 16, Centro; tickets $8-15; Ⓜ Bellas Artes) Classic variety theater.

Teatro La Capilla (Map p123; ☎ 3095-4077; www .geocities.com/losendebles; Madrid 13, Coyoacán; tickets $8-10; Ⓜ Coyoacán) Highlighting contemporary Mexican playwrights.

Live Music

The variety of music is impressive, with traditional Mexican, Cuban, folk, jazz, rock and other styles being played in concert halls, clubs, bars, museums, on public transportation and on the street. The 'Espectáculos Nocturnos' and 'Espectáculos Populares' sections in *Tiempo Libre* cover events.

Free concerts take place most weekends on the Zócalo. Coyoacán is another good bet most evenings and all day Saturday and Sunday: musicians, comedians and mimes turn its two central plazas into a big open-air party.

Additionally, a number of Colonia Roma and Condesa bars and restaurants turn into live-music venues after dark (see p168).

CONCERTS

Auditorio Nacional (Map pp120-1; ☎ 5280-9250; www.auditorio.com.mx in Spanish; Paseo de la Reforma 50; Ⓜ Auditorio) Major gigs by Mexican and visiting rock and pop artists take the stage at the 10,000-seat Auditorio Nacional (National Auditorium).

Salón 21 (Map pp120-1; ☎ 5255-1496; Andrómaco 17, cnr Moliere; cover varies; Ⓜ Polanco) A warehouse-sized venue for touring salsa stars as well as rock, world and other performers. With excellent sound, wall-length bar and dance floor for thousands, this is one of Mexico's most cutting-edge clubs.

Teatro de la Ciudad (Map pp114-15; ☎ 5510-2942; Donceles 36; Ⓜ Allende) Built in 1918, this lavishly restored 1500-seat hall gets some of the more interesting touring groups.

Teatro Metropolitan (Map pp114-15; ☎ 5510-1035; Independencia 90; Ⓜ Juárez) Artists as diverse as Café Tacuba, Bobby McFerrin and the Russian National Ballet have played this medium-sized hall.

MARIACHIS

Five blocks north of the Palacio de Bellas Artes, Plaza Garibaldi (Map pp114–15) is where the city's mariachi bands gather. Outfitted in fancy costumes, they tootle their trumpets, tune their guitars and stand around with a drink until approached by someone who'll pay for a song (about $10) or whisk them away to entertain at a party.

Plaza Garibaldi gets going by about 8pm and stays busy until around midnight. For food, try the Mercado San Camilito north of the plaza.

El Tenampa (Map pp114-15; ☎ 5526-6176; ⓨ 1pm-3am; Ⓜ Garibaldi) Graced with murals of the giants of Mexican song and enlivened by its own songsters, this festive cantina on the north side of the plaza is an obligatory visit.

ROCK

The street-market **Tianguis Cultural del Chopo** (see the boxed text, p177) has a stage at its north end every Saturday afternoon for young and hungry alternative, metal and punk bands.

Dada X (Map pp114-15; ☎ 2454-4310; www.dadax .com.mx in Spanish; Bolívar 31, cnr Calle 16 de Septiembre;

depending on event, free–$10; ☺ from 9pm Thu-Sat; Ⓜ San Juan de Letrán) Black-clad youth gravitate toward this space on the upper floor of a magnificent colonial building. The varied program includes cult films, poetry readings and live music, which might be anything from ska to electronica.

Multiforo Alicia (Map pp118-19; ☎ 5511-2100; Av Cuauhtémoc 91; cover $5; ☺ 8pm-2am Fri & Sat; Ⓜ Cuauhtémoc) Behind the graffiti-scrawled facade is Mexico City's premier rock club. A suitably smoky, seatless space, the Alicia stages up-and-coming punk, surf and ska bands, who hawk their music at the store downstairs.

Pasagüero (Map pp114-15; ☎ 5521-6112; Motolinía 33; Ⓜ Allende) Some visionary developers took a historic building and transformed its ground level into a space for various cultural happenings, especially rock and electronica gigs. A key venue in the Centro redevelopment scheme, the club only opens for events: phone to find out what's on.

JAZZ
Papa Beto (Map pp118-19; ☎ 5592-1638; www.papa beto.com in Spanish; Villalongín 196, Colonia Cuauhtémoc; cover $7.50; ☺ 1st/2nd set 9:30pm/11pm Tue-Sat; Ⓜ Insurgentes) Run by a Japanese expatriate to highlight the impressive wealth of local talent, this club is the city's top jazz venue. Tuesday night is reserved for jam sessions with surprise guests.

Zinco Jazz Club (Map pp114-15; ☎ 5512-3369; Motolinía 20; cover varies with event; ☺ from 9pm Wed-Sun; ☎ Allende) Another new space in the Centro, Zinco is a subterranean supper club featuring local players and occasional big-name touring artists.

LATIN DANCE
The city's many aficionados have a circuit of clubs and *salones de baile* (dance halls) to choose from. Even if you don't dance, you'll enjoy just listening to the great music and watching the experts on the dance floor. At the clubs listed here, it's customary to go in a group and share a bottle of rum or tequila (around $60, including mixers).

Cuban dance clubs abound in Colonia Roma, particularly near the intersection of Insurgentes and Medellín.

You might learn a few steps at the Plaza de Danzón (Map pp114–15), northwest of La Ciudadela near metro Balderas. Couples crowd the plaza every Saturday afternoon to do the *danzón*, an elegant though complicated Cuban step that infiltrated Mexico in the 19th century. Lessons in *danzón* and other steps are given from noon to 4pm.

Salón Los Ángeles (Map pp110-11; ☎ 5597-5181; Lerdo 206; cover $3.25; ☺ 6-11pm Tue & Sun; Ⓜ Tlatelolco) 'Those who don't know Los Ángeles don't know Mexico' reads the marquee, and for once the hyperbole is well deserved. Cuban-music fans won't want to miss the outstanding orchestras here nor the incredibly graceful dancers who fill the vast floor. Particularly on Tuesday evening, when an older crowd comes for *danzones*, it's like the set of a period film. Salón Los Ángeles is in a rough area so take a taxi.

El Gran León (Map pp118-19; ☎ 5564-7110; Querétaro 225; cover $5.50; ☺ 9pm-3:30am Thu-Sat; Ⓜ Chilpancingo) This club hosts the city's finest Cuban *son* ensembles. Two or three groups take the tropical stage nightly. Unescorted (and escorted) women should expect to be invited up onto the tightly packed dance floor.

Mamá Rumba (cover $6.50; ☺ 9pm-3am Thu-Sat) Roma (Map pp118-19; ☎ 5564-6920; Querétaro 230, cnr Medellín; Ⓜ Chilpancingo); San Ángel (Map p122; ☎ 5550-8099; Plaza San Jacinto 23; Ⓜ Miguel Angel de Quevado) Mamá Rumba features contemporary salsa, attracting a younger, upscale crowd. It's also a gathering place for the local Cuban community. Be sure to arrive early for a table, as the club invariably fills beyond capacity.

Primer Cuadro (Map pp114-15; ☎ 5521-2016; Bolívar 12; ☺ from 9pm Thu-Sat; Ⓜ Allende) At this stylish bookstore-restaurant, the evening's entertainment begins with *trova* (songs), then shifts into dance mode as Cuban *salseros* take the stage and a mostly over-30 set fills the floor.

CABARET
La Casa de Paquita la del Barrio (Map pp110-11; ☎ 5583-8131; Zarco 202; ☺ 8:30pm Fri & Sat; cover $14; Ⓜ Guerrero) Located in the rough-and-tumble Guerrero district, Paquita's house is a bastion of popular culture. Following a series of openers, Paquita la del Barrio, the corpulent TV and recording star, takes the stage and proceeds to run through a sublime set of plaintive ballads, almost all of which express disdain for her suitors – her

asides are deliciously bitter. Phone ahead to find out if Paquita is performing.

El Bataclán (Map pp118-19; ☎ 5511-7390; Popocatépetl 25, cnr Amsterdam; cover $15; 🕑 9pm Tue-Sat; Ⓜ Insurgentes) A theater within a club (La Bodega), this intimate cabaret showcases some of Mexico's most vivid performers, with frequent appearances by the wonderfully surreal Astrid Haddad. Afterwards, catch top-notch Cuban *son* combos in La Bodega's various salons.

Bar El Vicio (Map p123; ☎ 5659-1139; www .lasreinaschulas.com in Spanish; Madrid 13; cover $10-15; ☎ Coyoacán) Alternative cabaret with liberal doses of irreverent comedy and great music.

Hexen-Café (Map pp118-19; ☎ 5514-5969; Jalapa 104; cover free-$7; shows 🕑 8:30pm Thu-Sat; Ⓜ Insurgentes) This pocket of German culture has an eclectic performance program, ranging from poetry marathons to Cuban jazz.

TROVA & TRADITIONAL
Cafebrería El Péndulo (www.pendulo.com in Spanish; cover varies; 🕑 shows from 9:30pm) Condesa (Map pp118-19; ☎ 5286-9493; Av Nuevo León 115; Ⓜ Chilpancingo); Zona Rosa (Map pp118-19; ☎ 5208-2327; Hamburgo 126; Ⓜ Insurgentes); Polanco (Map pp120-1; ☎ 5280-4111; Dumas 81; Ⓜ Polanco) Leading Mexican *trovadores* play each branch of this café-bookstore.

El Balcón Huasteco (Map pp110-11; ☎ 5341-6762; Sor Juana Inés de la Cruz 248, cnr Av de los Maestros; 🕑 from 6pm Thu-Sat; Ⓜ Normal) A center for the Huastec culture of Hidalgo and Veracruz, this old house stages the region's finest trios. There are wooden platforms for traditional *zapateando* dancing and snacks from the area.

Cafe Corazón (Map p122; ☎ 5550-8854; Frontera 4; cover $6-8; 🕑 9:30pm Fri & Sat; Ⓜ Miguel Angel de Quevado) Folk singers in the Silvio Rodríguez mold take the small stage at this temple of *trova* near San Ángel's Plaza San Jacinto. Catch metrobus 'La Bombilla.'

Dance & Electronica
The capital's thriving club scene has become an obligatory stop on the international DJ circuit. To find out what's going on, pick up flyers at Condesa's Malafama billiard hall (p168).

AM (Map pp118-19; ☎ 5286-8572; Nuevo León 67; cover $9.50; 🕑 from 10pm Wed-Sat; Ⓜ Patriotismo) Condesa's super-trendy new nightspot takes

up a floor of the mammoth Plaza Condesa building. A narrow hall eerily enhanced by liquid illumination, it has fast become *the* choice for electronica aficionados, with great sound and an ever-changing cast of DJs.

La Terraza (Map pp114-15; ☎ 5521-1925; www .ccemx.org; 🕑 from 10pm Fri & Sat; Ⓜ Zócalo) The top terrace of the Spanish cultural center has gained a reputation for its excellent weekend DJ sessions.

Continental DJ Club (Map pp118-19; ☎ 5525-6268; www.continentaldjclub.com; Florencia 12; cover $15; 🕑 10pm-10am Wed-Sat; Ⓜ Insurgentes) Mirror balls, pulsing beats, hip dancers and video projections keep after-hours scenemakers hypnotized at this cutting-edge hall, known for its internationally acclaimed guest DJs. Progressive house predominates, but there is variety.

Pink (Map pp120-1; ☎ 5282-1635; Dumas 107; cover $9.50; 🕑 7pm-4am Tue-Sat; Ⓜ Polanco) A less self-consciously hip venue than usual for Polanco, Pink is a party palace. Within a kitschily designed circular lounge, young singles, along with the occasional artist or model, sip Pink martinis and sing along with hits *en español*.

Kubrik (Map p122; ☎ 5616-6972; Av de la Paz 39; 🕑 from 10pm Thu-Sat; cover $9.50; Ⓜ Miguel Angel de Quevado) This state-of-the-art club pulls in close to a thousand well-heeled hedonists who lounge on its numerous sofas or jump around on the levitating dance floor. Take metrobus 'La Bombilla' to San Ángel.

El Colmillo (Map pp114-15; ☎ 5592-6114; Versalles 52; cover $9.50; 🕑 from 11pm Thu-Sat; Ⓜ Cuauhtémoc) DJs crank the volume to coccyx-crunching levels at this hallucinogenic hangout. Gyrate to deep house, psychedelic trance etc; the cocktail list is equally varied. The more subdued upstairs lounge has performance events.

Pervert Lounge (Map pp114-15; ☎ 5510-4457; Uruguay 70; cover $9.50; 🕑 11pm-5am Thu-Sat; Ⓜ Isabel la Católica) A magnet for 20-something hipsters, the garage-like space offers kitschy decor, two turntables and some very large speakers.

Sports
SOCCER
The capital stages two or three *fútbol* (soccer) matches in the national Primera División almost every weekend of the year. There are two seasons: January to June and

August to December. Mexico City has four teams: América, nicknamed Las Águilas (the Eagles), Las Pumas of UNAM, Cruz Azul and Atlante. The newspaper *Esto* has the best coverage.

The biggest match of all is El Clásico, between América and Guadalajara, filling the Estadio Azteca with 100,000 flag-waving fans – an occasion surprising for the friendliness between rival fans. This is about the only game of the year when you should get tickets in advance.

Tickets ($7.50 to $40 for regular season games) are usually available at the gate right up to game time, or from Ticketmaster (see p170). There are several stadiums that host games.

Estadio Azteca (Map pp110-11; ☎ 5617-8080; www .esmas.com/estadioazteca in Spanish; Calz de Tlalpan 3665) The country's biggest stadium (capacity 114,000) is home to both the América and Atlante clubs. Games are played on weekend afternoons; check the website for kickoff times. Take the Tren Ligero from metro Tasqueña to Estadio Azteca station.

Estadio Azul (Map pp110-11; ☎ 5563-9040; www .cruz-azul.com.mx in Spanish; Indiana 260, Colonia Nápoles) The stadium is next door to the Plaza México bullring. Cruz Azul home games kick off at 5pm on Saturday. Catch metrobus 'Ciudad de los Deportes.'

Estadio Olímpico (Map pp110-11; ☎ 5522-0491; www.pumasunam.com.mx in Spanish; Insurgentes Sur 3000, Ciudad Universitaria) Home of the Pumas; games start at noon on Sunday. See p143 for directions.

BASEBALL
Mexico City has one team in the Liga Mexicana de Béisbol, the Diablos Rojos (www.diablos.com.mx). During the regular season (March to July), they play every other week at the **Foro Sol** (Map pp110-11; ☎ 5764-8415; cnr Av Río Churubusco & Viaducto Río de la Piedad; tickets $2-8; ⏰ 7pm Mon-Fri, 4pm Sat, noon Sun). From Ciudad Deportiva station, on metro Línea 9, it's a five-minute walk to the ballpark.

BULLFIGHTS
If you're not put off by the very concept, a *corrida de toros* is quite a spectacle, from the milling throngs and hawkers outside the arena to the pageantry and drama in the ring itself.

One of the largest bullrings in the world, **Monumental Plaza México** (Map pp110-11; ☎ 5563-3961; Rodin 241, Colonia Nochebuena) is a deep concrete bowl holding 42,000 spectators. It's a few blocks west of Av Insurgentes. Catch metrobus 'Ciudad de los Deportes.'

From November to March, professional fights are held on Sunday from 4pm. From June to October, junior matadors fight young bulls. Six bulls are fought in an afternoon, two each by three matadors.

The cheapest seats, less than $5, are in the Sol General section – the top tiers on the sunny side of the arena. Seats in the Sombra General section, on the shady side, cost slightly more. The best seats are in the Barreras, the seven front rows, and cost $50. Between the Barreras and General sections are the Primer (1er) Tendido and Segundo (2o) Tendido.

Except for the biggest *corridas*, tickets are available up to the killing of the third bull, though the best seats may sell out early. You can buy advance tickets from 9:30am to 2pm and 4pm to 7pm Saturday, and from 9:30am onward Sunday.

For more on bullfights, see p66.

LUCHA LIBRE (MEXICAN WRESTLING)
Mexico City's two wrestling venues, the 17,000-seat **Arena de México** (Map pp114-15; Dr Lavista 189, Colonia Doctores; ☎ 5588-0266; tickets $3.50-7; ⏰ 8:30pm Fri; Ⓜ Cuauhtémoc) and the smaller **Arena Coliseo** (Map pp114-15; ☎ 5526-1687; República de Perú 77; tickets $2-4; ⏰ 7:30pm Tue, 5pm Sun; Ⓜ Lagunilla) are taken over by a circus atmosphere each week, with flamboyant *luchadores* (wrestlers) like Shocker and Tarzan Boy going at each other in teams or one-on-one. There are three or four bouts, building up to the most formidable match-ups.

SHOPPING
If you explore the public and street markets, it's common to negotiate a bit on the price. Before you start, consider what you are willing to pay, then offer that or a little less.

Markets
Mexico City's markets are worth visiting, not just for their extraordinarily varied contents, but also for a glimpse of the frenetic business conducted within. Besides the major ones listed here, neighborhood markets (indicated by 'Mi Mercado' signs) also make for an interesting wander.

Mercado Insurgentes (Map pp118-19; Londres, Zona Rosa; ⏰ 9:30am-7:30pm Mon-Sat, 10am-4pm Sun; Ⓜ Insurgentes) Between Florencia and

Amberes, and packed with crafts – silver, textiles, pottery, leather and carved wooden figures – but you'll need to bargain to get sensible prices.

Centro de Artesanías La Ciudadela (Map pp114-15; Balderas, cnr Dondé; 10am-6pm; Balderas) A favorite destination for good stuff from all over Mexico. Worth seeking out are Oaxaca *alebrijes* – whimsical representations of animals in wood (local 6, northernmost aisle, near Balderas entrance); guitars from Paracho (local 64 off central patio); and Huichol beadwork (local 163, off Dondé at parking entrance). Prices are generally fair even before you bargain.

Mercado de Artesanías San Juan (Map pp114-15; Ayuntamiento, cnr Buen Tono; 9am-7pm Mon-Sat, 9am-4pm Sun; San Juan de Letrán) Four blocks east of La Ciudadela, with similar goods and prices. Part of the Mercado San Juan complex, it is noted for its local and specialty foods.

La Lagunilla (Map pp114-15; cnr Rayón & Allende; 9am-8pm Mon-Sat, 10am-7pm Sun; Garibaldi) This enormous co mplex comprises three buildings: building No 1 contains clothes and fabrics, No 2 food, and No 3 furniture.

Mercado de La Merced (Anillo de Circunvalación, cnr General Anaya; 8am-7pm; Merced) This occupies four whole blocks dedicated to the buying and selling of daily needs, and features photogenic food displays.

Mercado de Jamaica (Map pp110-11; cnr Guillermo Prieto & Congreso de la Union, Colonia Jamaica; 8am-7pm; Jamaica) A huge, colorful flower market. The numerous stalls display both baroque floral arrangements and more exotic blooms like tropical orchids and heliconias.

STREET MARKETS
In most neighborhoods, you'll find a *tianguis* (from the Nahua *tianquiztli*) at least once a week selling the freshest fruits and vegetables, with vendors shouting out *'¿Que le damos?'* (What can we give you?). *Tianguis* generally set up by 10am and break down around 5pm.

Bazar Artesanal de Coyoacán (Map p123; Plaza Hidalgo, Coyoacán; Sat & Sun; Viveros) Has handmade hippie jewelry and indigenous crafts, jugglers, fortune-tellers, candles and incense.

Bazar de la Roma (Map pp118-19; Parque Ignacio Chávez & Álvaro Obregón, Colonia Roma; Sat & Sun; Cuauhtémoc) East of Av Cuauhtémoc, this market has used and antique items, large

and small: books, beer trays, posters and furniture. There is also a similar antiques and art market along Álvaro Obregón on the same days

Bazar del Oro (Map pp118-19; Calle de Oro, Roma; Wed, Sat & Sun; Insurgentes) This upscale street market between Insurgentes and Plaza Cibeles has clothing, gifts and an excellent eating section (see the boxed text, p159). You can catch metrobus 'Durango.'

Jardín del Arte (Map pp118-19; btwn Sullivan & Villalongín; Sun) Also known as the Sullivan Market, this one has a large selection of paintings and art supplies, plus some food. Catch metrobus 'Reforma.'

Plaza del Ángel (Map pp118-19; btwn Amberes & Florencia, Zona Rosa; Sun; Insurgentes) Sells antique silverware, jewelry, furniture and art.

Tepito (Map pp114-15; Héroe de Granaditas; Wed-Mon; Lagunilla) The mother of all street markets: maze of semipermanent stalls spreading east and north, between Eje 1 Oriente and Reforma, from La Lagunilla, with miles of clothes, pirated CDs and DVDs and electronics. Also known as the Thieves Market for its black-market goods and pickpockets.

Tianguis Dominical de la Lagunilla (Map pp114-15; cnr González Bocanegra & Rayón; Sun; Garibaldi) Hunt for antiques, old souvenirs and bric-a-brac; books and magazines are alongside the Lagunilla building. Look for exvoto paintings by Alfredo Vilchis & Sons (or have your own miracles depicted).

Shops
The well-heeled residents of Mexico City shop in modern malls with designer-clothing stores and cosmeticians. Among the more accessible are Plaza Loreto (Map p122) in San Ángel; Plaza Insurgentes (Map pp118–19), on Insurgentes at the edge of Colonia Roma; Plaza Coyoacán (Map p123) near metro Coyoacán; and Plaza Molière (Map pp120–1), at Molière and Horacio in Polanco.

Fonart Mixcoác (Map pp110-11; ☎ 5563-4060; Patriotismo 691; 9am-8pm Mon-Sat, 10am-7pm Sun; Mixcoác); Alameda (Map pp114-15; ☎ 5521-0171; Juárez 89; 10am-7pm; Hidalgo); Reforma (Map pp118-19; ☎ 5328-5000, ext 53089; Paseo de la Reforma 116; 10am-7pm Mon-Fri, 10am-6pm Sat; Cuauhtémoc) The government-run handicrafts store sells quality wares from around the country, from Olinalá lacquered boxes to Teotitlán del Valle blankets, as well as pottery and glassware. Prices are fixed and fair. The largest branch is the one in Mixcoác.

Bazar Sábado (Map p122; Plaza San Jacinto 11, San Ángel; 🕒 10am-7pm Sat; 🅜 Miguel Angel de Quevado) The bazaar showcases some of Mexico's best handcrafted jewelry, woodwork, ceramics and textiles. Prices are high but so is quality. Artists and artisans also display work in Plaza San Jacinto itself, and in nearby Plaza del Carmen. Between the two plazas are some interesting boutiques and antique shops, many open daily, including the Casa del Obispo (Map p122).

CENTRO HISTÓRICO

Mexico City's most upscale department chains, **El Palacio de Hierro** (Map pp114-15; ☎ 5728-9905; Av 20 de Noviembre 3; 🅜 Zócalo) and **Liverpool** (Map pp114-15; ☎ 5133-2800; Venustiano Carranza 92; 🅜 Zócalo) both maintain their original c-1930s stores downtown.

The streets around the Zócalo are lined with stores specializing in everyday goods; you'll find clusters of shops selling similar items on the same street. To the west, photography supplies and used books show up on Donceles, sports gear and backpacks on Venustiano Carranza, and perfumes along Tacuba. Jewelry and gold outlets, as well as numismatists shops, are found along La Palma, while opticians are sighted along Madero. To the south, shoes show up on Pino Suárez and Av 20 de Noviembre; and electric guitars and other instruments

along Bolívar. To the north, there's costume jewelry on República de Colombia and Venezuela streets and beauty products along Calle del Carmen. Going east, there are tons of tools along Corregidora. Look for underwear down Correo Mayor, and bicycles on San Pablo west of Mercado La Merced.

Hundreds of computer stores huddle in the **Plaza de la Computación y Electrónica** (Map pp114-15; Eje Central Lázaro Cárdenas; 🅜 San Juan de Letrán), south of Uruguay.

Tucked away in the backstreets are some special items.

Dulcería de Celaya (🕒 10:30am-7pm) Centro Histórico (Map pp114-15; ☎ 5521-1787; Av 5 de Mayo 39; 🅜 Allende); Colonia Roma (Map pp118-19; ☎ 5207-5858; Colima 143; 🅜 Insurgentes) Traditional candy store operating since 1874 with candied fruits and coconut-stuffed lemons; worth a look just for the ornate building.

Hoja Real (Map pp114-15; ☎ 5518-5200; Uruguay 12; 🅜 San Juan de Letrán) Cigars from San Andrés, Veracruz.

La Europea (Map pp114-15; ☎ 5512-6005; Ayuntamiento 25; 🅜 San Juan de Letrán) Big selection of reasonably priced tequilas and wines.

Palacio de las Máscaras (Map pp114-15; ☎ 5529-2849; Allende 84; 🕒 11am-6pm Mon-Sat; 🅜 Garibaldi) More than 5000 masks from all over the country; Lagunilla market area.

ZONA ROSA

This area has a variety of boutiques aimed at tourists. Between Génova and Florencia are a couple of arcades with access from Hamburgo or Londres. Plaza La Rosa is a good place to look for clothes. Plaza del

---

TIANGUIS CULTURAL DEL CHOPO

One of the weirder street markets in town, the **Tianguis Cultural del Chopo** (Map pp110-11; Calle Juan Nepomuceno; 🕒 10am-4pm Sat; 🅜 Buenavista) is a gathering place for the city's various youth subcultures. Punks, goths, metalheads and all the other urban tribes gravitate here each Saturday to buy and trade CDs, hear live bands, find out about upcoming events and exchange ideas. Established in 1980 at the Museo Universitario del Chopo, it moved eight years later to its current location near the now-defunct Buenavista railroad station, and has been thriving ever since. Of the hundreds of vendor stalls that extend along two aisles for several blocks, most are devoted to music CDs, with many specializing in subgenres like progressive rock, hardcore and ska. One vendor, Ramón García Bolaños, on the west side near the entrance to the market, has more than 3000 discs of *rock mexicano* on offer. There's an art gallery, a book club with poetry readings, and a stall for NGOs dealing with the environment and animal rights. At the far end is a concert stage for young-and-hungry bands, plus a trading post where people bring crates of CDs to swap.

Anyone interested in plugging into Mexico's alternative currents should roam amid this 'temple of the counterculture,' as commentator Carlos Monsiváis termed it.

Ángel has a number of classy antique and art shops; more are strung along Amberes and Estocolmo. Insurgentes is the closest metro stop to these plazas.

POLANCO
Designer-clothing houses line Presidente Masaryk in the blocks west of Anatole France. More boutiques occupy the Pasaje Polanco (Map pp120–1) and nearby streets.

GETTING THERE & AWAY
Drop into the **Instituto Nacional de Migración** (Map pp120-1; ☎ 2581-0000, ext 32005; Ejército Nacional 862, Polanco; ☒ 9am-1:30pm Mon-Fri; Ⓜ Polanco) to get your tourist card stamped or check what other documents are needed.

Note that all passenger train services from Mexico City have been discontinued.

Air
Aeropuerto Internacional Benito Juárez (Map pp110-11; ☎ 5571-3600; www.aicm.com.mx in Spanish), 6km east of the Zócalo, is Mexico City's only passenger airport. Recent renovations have expanded its capacity to 30 million passengers annually, making it the largest airport in Latin America. See p988 for information on international flights and p996 for information on domestic flights. See p989 for airlines serving Mexico City.

The single terminal is divided into eight *salas* (halls):

Sala A Domestic arrivals.
Sala B Check-in for Aeroméxico, Mexicana and Aero California; Hotel Camino Real access.
Sala C Check-in for Aviacsa.
Sala D Check-in for Azteca and Magnicharters.
Sala E2 International arrivals.
Sala F & J Check-in for international flights.
Sala G International departures.

The terminal's shops and facilities include numerous *casas de cambio*; **Tamibe** (☎ 5726-0578) in Sala E2 stays open 24 hours. Peso-dispensing ATMs on the Cirrus and Plus networks are easily found.

Telmex card phones and Internet terminals abound; cards are available from shops and machines. Car-rental agencies and **luggage lockers** (up to 24hr $5; ☒ 24hr) are in Salas A and E2.

Direct buses to Cuernavaca, Querétaro, Toluca, Puebla and Córdoba depart from

platforms adjacent to Sala E (see the table, p180). Ticket counters are on the upper level, off the food court.

AIRLINE OFFICES
Aero California (Map pp118-19; ☎ 5207-1392; Paseo de la Reforma 332, Zona Rosa; Ⓜ Insurgentes)
Aeromar (Map pp118-19; ☎ 5514-2248, 800-237-66-27; Sheraton María Isabel Hotel, Paseo de la Reforma 325; Ⓜ Insurgentes)
Aeroméxico (☎ 5133-4010) Juárez (Map pp114-15; Paseo de la Reforma 80; Ⓜ Juárez); Zona Rosa (Map pp118-19; Paseo de la Reforma 445; Ⓜ Cuauhtémoc)
Air Canada (Map pp120-1; ☎ 9138-0289, ext 2228, 800-719-28-27; 13th fl, Blvd Ávila Camacho 1, Colonia Lomas de Chapultepec; Ⓜ Auditorio)
Air France (Map pp120–1; ☎ 2122-8200, 800-123-46-60; 8th fl, Jaime Balmes 8, Colonia Los Morales; Ⓜ Polanco)
Alitalia (Map pp118-19; ☎ 5533-1240, 800-012-59-00; 6th fl, Río Tíber 103, Colonia Cuauhtémoc; Ⓜ Insurgentes)
American Airlines (Map pp118-19; ☎ 5209-1400; Paseo de la Reforma 300, Zona Rosa; Ⓜ Insurgentes)
Aviacsa (☎ 5716-9005, 800-006-22-00; Airport)
Avianca (Map pp118-19; ☎ 5546-3073, 800-705-79-00; Paseo de la Reforma 195; Ⓜ Insurgentes)
British Airways (Map pp120–1; ☎ 5387-0300; 14th fl, Jaime Balmes 8, Colonia Los Morales; Ⓜ Polanco)
Continental Airlines (Map pp120–1; ☎ 5283-5500, 800-900-50-00; Andrés Bello 45, Polanco; Ⓜ Auditorio)
Copa Airlines (Map pp118-19; ☎ 5241-2000; Berna 6; Ⓜ Insurgentes)
Cubana (Map pp120–1; ☎ 5250-6355; Sol y Son Viajes, Homero 613, Polanco; Ⓜ Polanco)
Delta Airlines (Map pp118-19; ☎ 5279-0909, 800-123-47-78; Paseo de la Reforma 381; Ⓜ Sevilla)
Iberia (Map pp120–1; ☎ 1101-1515; Ejército Nacional 436, Colonia Chapultepec Morales; Ⓜ Polanco)
Japan Air Lines (Map pp118-19; ☎ 5242-0150, 800-024-01-50; 36th fl, Torre Mayor, Paseo de la Reforma 505; Ⓜ Chapultepec)
KLM/Northwest (Map pp120–1; ☎ 5279-5390; 11th fl, Andrés Bello 45, Polanco; Ⓜ Auditorio)
Lineas Aéreas Azteca (Map pp118-19; ☎ 5716-8989, 800-229-83-22; Niza 17, Zona Rosa; Ⓜ Insurgentes)
Lufthansa (Map pp120–1; ☎ 5230-0000; Paseo de las Palmas 239, Colonia Lomas de Chapultepec; Ⓜ Auditorio)
Magnicharters (Map pp114-15; ☎ 5141-1351; Donato Guerra 9, cnr Bucareli; Ⓜ Juárez)
Mexicana (☎ 5448-0990, 800-502-20-00) Juárez (Map pp114-15; Juárez 82, cnr Balderas; Ⓜ Juárez); Zona Rosa (Map pp118-19; Paseo de la Reforma 312, cnr Amberes; Ⓜ Insurgentes) Los Morales (Map pp120-1; Pabellón Polanco Shopping Mall, Ejército Nacional 980)

United Airlines (Map pp118-19; ☎ 5627-0222, 800-00-30-777; Hamburgo 213, Zona Rosa; Ⓜ Sevilla)

Bus

Mexico City has four long distance–bus terminals serving the four compass points: Terminal Norte (north), Terminal Oriente (called TAPO, east), Terminal Poniente (west) and Terminal Sur (south). All terminals have baggage-check services or lockers ($1 to $5 per item), as well as tourist information modules, newsstands, card phones, Internet, ATMs and snack bars. For directions to the bus stations, see p184.

There are also buses to nearby cities from the airport (see the table, p180).

For trips up to five hours, it usually suffices to go to the bus station, buy your ticket and go. For longer trips, many buses leave in the evening and may well sell out, so buy your ticket beforehand.

One helpful resource is **Ticketbus** (☎ 5133-2424, 800-702-80-00, from US ☎ 800-95-00-287; www .ticketbus.com.mx), an agency that reserves and sells tickets for more than a dozen bus lines out of all four stations. For ADO GL, UNO and ETN, Ticketbus offers purchase by phone or Internet with Visa or MasterCard (plus $4 service fee per ticket). In addition to the Ticketbus locations below, a couple more are inside the airport international departures terminal. Outlets open 9am or 10am to 2:30pm, and 3:30pm to 7pm or 8pm Monday to Friday, and 9am or 10am to 2pm or 3pm Saturday.

Buenavista(Map pp114-15; Buenavista 9; Ⓜ Revolución)
Centro Histórico (Map pp114-15; Isabel la Católica 83E; Ⓜ Isabel la Católica)
Condesa (Map pp118-19; Iztaccíhuatl 6, cnr Insurgentes; Ⓜ Chilpancingo)
Polanco (Map pp120–1; Presidente Masaryk, cnr Hegel; Ⓜ Polanco)
Reforma (Map pp118-19; Paseo de la Reforma 412; Ⓜ Sevilla) Across from La Diana Cazadora.
Roma Norte (Map pp118-19; Puebla 46; Ⓜ Cuauhtémoc)
Roma Norte (Map pp118-19; Mérida 156; Ⓜ Hospital General)
Zócalo (Map pp114-15; Turismo Zócalo, Venustiano Carranza 67; Ⓜ Zócalo)

For certain destinations you have a choice of terminals, thus avoiding the need to travel across town for connections. Oaxaca, for example, is served by TAPO, Sur and Norte terminals.

See the table, p180 for a list of daily services from Mexico City. More information can be found in other town and city sections of this book. It's all subject to change, of course.

Check schedules by phoning the bus lines or by visiting their (sometimes functional) websites.

ADO Group (☎ 5133-2424, 800-702-80-00; www .ticketbus.com.mx) Includes ADO, ADO GL, UNO, OCC, AU.
Autovías, Herradura de Plata (☎ 5567-4550)
Estrella Blanca Group (☎ 5729-0707) Includes Futura, Elite, Turistar.
Estrella de Oro (☎ 5689-3955; www.estrelladeoro .mx in Spanish)
Estrella Roja (☎ 5130-1800, 800-712-22-84; www .estrellaroja.com.mx in Spanish)
ETN (☎ 5089-9200, 800-800-0386; www.etn.com.mx)
Omnibus de México (☎ 5141-4300, 800-765-6636; www.odm.com.mx in Spanish)
Primera Plus, Flecha Amarilla (☎ 5567-7176, 800-375-7587; www.primeraplus.com.mx in Spanish)
Pullman de Morelos (☎ 5549-3505; www.pullman .com.mx in Spanish)

TERMINAL NORTE
Largest of the four, the **Terminal Central de Autobuses del Norte** (Map pp110-11; ☎ 5587-1552) serves points north, including cities on the US border, plus some points west (Guadalajara, Puerto Vallarta), east (Puebla, Veracruz) and south (Acapulco, Oaxaca). Over 30 bus companies have services here. Deluxe and 1st-class counters are mostly in the southern half of the terminal. Luggage-storage services are at the far south end (open 24 hours) and in the central passageway; the latter section contains a hotel-booking agency.

TERMINAL ORIENTE
Terminal de Autobuses de Pasajeros de Oriente (Map pp110-11; ☎ 5762-5977), usually called TAPO, serves points east and southeast, including Puebla, Veracruz, Yucatán, Oaxaca and Chiapas. Bus-line counters are arranged around a rotunda with a restaurant and Internet terminals at the center. There's an ATM outside the AU counters and luggage lockers in Tunnel 3 beside Estrella Roja.

TERMINAL PONIENTE
Terminal Central de Autobuses del Poniente (Map pp110-11; ☎ 5271-4519) is the departure point for buses heading to Michoacán and shuttle services running to nearby Toluca. In addition, ETN offers service to Guadalajara.

BUSES FROM MEXICO CITY

Destination	Duration	Terminal in Mexico City	Class	Bus Company	Daily Departures	Price
Acapulco	5hr	Sur	executive	Estrella de Oro	7	$41
			deluxe	Estrella de Oro	every 30min	$29
			1st	Futura	every 30min 5am-8pm	$28
		Norte	1st	Futura	hourly	$28
Bahías de	14-15hr	Oriente (TAPO)	deluxe	ADO GL	1	$62
Huatulco		Norte	1st	OCC	1	$46
		Sur	1st	Futura	2	$44
Campeche	16-17hr	Oriente (TAPO)	deluxe	ADO GL	1	$82
			1st	ADO	5	$69
		Norte	1st	ADO	1	$69
Cancún	24hr	Oriente (TAPO)	deluxe	ADO GL	1	$111
			1st	ADO	4	$92
		Norte	1st	ADO	2	$92
Chetumal	20hr	Oriente (TAPO)	1st	ADO	3	$75
Chihuahua	18hr	Norte	1st	Ómnibus de México	10	$100
Ciudad Juárez	24hr	Norte	1st	Ómnibus de México	10	$115
Cuernavaca	1¼hr	Sur	executive	Pullman de Morelos	every 30min to 8:30pm	$6.50
			deluxe	Pullman de Morelos	every 15min to 11pm	$5.50
		Airport	1st	Pullman de Morelos	every 30min or 40min to 8pm	$10
Guadalajara	7hr	Norte	deluxe	ETN	23	$51
			1st	Primera Plus	28	$40
		Poniente	deluxe	ETN	6	$51
Guanajuato	5hr	Norte	deluxe	ETN	9	$30
			1st	Primera Plus	11	$25
Matamoros	14hr	Norte	1st	Transportes del Norte	4	$65
Mazatlán	14½hr		1st	Elite	hourly	$74
Mérida	19½hr	Oriente (TAPO)	deluxe	ADO GL	1	$91
			1st	ADO	4	$78
		Norte	1st	ADO	2	$78
Mexicali	37hr	Norte	1st	Elite	19	$139
Monterrey	12hr	Norte	deluxe	Turistar	7	$80
			1st	Transportes del Norte	20	$61
Morelia	4hr	Poniente	deluxe	ETN	every 30min	$27
		Norte	1st	Primera Plus	19	$21
Nogales	36hr	Norte	1st	Elite	13	$131
Nuevo Laredo	15hr	Norte	deluxe	Turistar	4	$97
			1st	Futura	10	$75
Oaxaca	6½hr	Oriente (TAPO)	deluxe	UNO	5	$46
			deluxe	ADO GL	7+	$33
			1st	ADO	16+	$28
		Sur	1st	OCC	3	$28
		Norte	1st	ADO	5+	$26
			deluxe	ADO GL	1	$33
Palenque	13½hr	Oriente (TAPO)	1st	ADO	1+	$55
		Norte	1st	ADO	1	$55
Papantla	5hr	Norte	1st	ADO	7	$16

Destination	Duration	Terminal in Mexico City	Class	Bus Company	Daily Departures	Price
Pátzcuaro	5hr	Poniente	1st	Autovías	11	$24
		Norte	1st	Primera Plus	2	$24
				Autovías	2	$24
Puebla	2hr	Oriente (TAPO)	deluxe	Estrella Roja	every 40min	$9
			1st	Estrella Roja	every 20min	$8.50
		Norte	1st	ADO	every 30min	$8.50
		Airport	deluxe	Estrella Roja	hourly	$12
Puerto Escondido	18hr	Sur	1st	OCC	1	$46
			1st	Futura	3	$41
		Norte	1st	OCC	1	$46
Puerto Vallarta	12hr	Norte	1st	Futura	4	$66
Querétaro	3hr	Norte	deluxe	ETN	every 20min or 30min	$18
			1st	Primera Plus	every 20min	$16
		Poniente	1st	Primera Plus	5	$15
		Airport	1st	Primera Plus	21	$20
San Cristóbal de Las Casas	14hr	Oriente (TAPO)	deluxe	UNO	1	$91
			deluxe	ADO GL	2	$73
		Norte	deluxe	ADO GL	1	$73
			1st	OCC	1	$61
San Luis Potosí	5hr	Norte	deluxe	ETN	hourly	$35
			1st	Primera Plus	10	$29
San Miguel de Allende	4hr	Norte	deluxe	ETN	4	$23
			1st	Primera Plus	3	$19
Tapachula	16-18hr	Oriente (TAPO)	deluxe	UNO	1 (Fri-Sun)	$91
			deluxe	ADO GL	2	$74
		Sur	1st	OCC	1	$64
Taxco	2½hr	Sur	1st	Estrella de Oro	2	$10
			1st	Futura	hourly	$10
Teotihuacán	1hr	Norte	2nd	Autobuses Teotihuacán	every 15min 7am-6pm	$2.50
Tepoztlán	1¼hr	Sur	1st	OCC	every 40min	$5.50
			1st	Estrella Roja (to caseta)	every 20min 7am-10pm	$5
Tijuana	41hr	Norte	1st	Elite	17	$155
Toluca	1hr	Poniente	deluxe	ETN	every 20min or 30min	$4.50
			2nd	Flecha Roja	every 10min to 11:30pm	$3
		Airport	deluxe	TMT Caminante	hourly	$9.50
Tula	1½hr	Norte	1st	AVM	every 40min	$4.50
Tuxtla Gutiérrez	12-13hr	Oriente (TAPO)	deluxe	UNO	1+	$83
			deluxe	ADO GL	3+	$68
			1st	ADO	1+	$57
		Norte	1st	OCC	1+	$57
Uruapan	6hr	Poniente	deluxe	ETN	8	$34
			1st	Autovías	12	$29
		Norte	1st	Primera Plus	5	$30
Veracruz	5½hr	Oriente (TAPO)	deluxe	UNO	5	$39
			deluxe	ADO GL	10+	$28

BUSES FROM MEXICO CITY (CONTINUATION)

Destination	Duration	Terminal in Mexico City	Class	Bus Company	Daily Departures	Price
Veracruz (continued)			1st	ADO	hourly	$24
	7hr		2nd	AU	hourly	$20
		Norte	1st	ADO	6+	$24
Villahermosa	10hr	Oriente (TAPO)	executive	UNO	2	$80
			deluxe	ADO GL	7	$57
			1st	ADO	19+	$48
		Norte	deluxe	ADO GL	1	$57
			1st	ADO	8+	$48
Xalapa	4½hr	Oriente (TAPO)	deluxe	UNO	5	$28
			deluxe	ADO GL	7+	$20
			1st	ADO	19+	$17
		Norte	1st	ADO	3+	$17
Zacatecas	8hr	Norte	1st	Ómnibus de México	18	$40
Zihuatanejo	9hr	Sur	executive	Estrella de Oro	1	$50
			deluxe	Estrella de Oro	4	$40
			1st	Futura	4	$40
		Poniente	1st	Autovías	2	$37

Note: + indicates additional departures on weekends

TERMINAL SUR
Terminal Central del Sur (Map p123; ☎ 5689-9745) serves Tepoztlán, Cuernavaca, Taxco, Acapulco and other southern destinations, as well as Oaxaca, Huatulco and Ixtapa-Zihuatanejo. Estrella de Oro (Acapulco, Taxco) and Pullman de Morelos (Cuernavaca) counters are on the right side of the terminal, while OCC and Estrella Roja (Tepoztlán) are on the left side of the termial. In Sala 1, you'll find a left-luggage service, agents booking Acapulco hotels and an ATM.

Car & Motorcycle
RENTAL
Car-rental companies have offices at the airport and in the Zona Rosa. Rates generally start at about $50 per day, but you will often do better by booking ahead via the Internet.
Avis (Map pp118-19; ☎ 5511-2228; Paseo de la Reforma 308; Ⓜ Insurgentes)
Thrifty (Map pp118-19; ☎ 5207-1100; Paseo de la Reforma 322; Ⓜ Insurgentes)

ROADSIDE ASSISTANCE
The *Ángeles Verdes* (Green Angels) can provide assistance from 8am to 8pm. Phone

☎ 5250-8221 and tell them your location. For more information, see p1002.

ROUTES IN & OUT OF THE CITY
Whichever way you come in, once past the last *caseta* (toll booth) you enter a no-man's land of poorly marked lanes and chaotic traffic. These *casetas* are also the points from which 'Hoy No Circula' rules take effect (see p186).

East
From Puebla, the highway eventually feeds traffic left into Ignacio Zaragoza. Stay on Zaragoza for about 10km, then move left and follow signs for Río de la Piedad (aka Viaducto Miguel Alemán), exiting left after the metro crosses the highway. From the Viaducto, exits access all the key areas. Get off at Viaducto Tlalpan to reach the Zócalo. Av Monterrey goes through Colonia Roma and the Zona Rosa.

Coming out of the airport, head south along Blvd Puerto Aéreo. After you cross Zaragoza, watch for signs to Río de la Piedad and Viaducto Alemán.

Heading for Puebla, Oaxaca or Veracruz, take the Viaducto Alemán east. This is most conveniently accessed off Av Cuauhtémoc, the southern extension of Bucareli (Eje 1 Poniente). Immediately after crossing over the Viaducto – just before the Liverpool department store – turn left for the access ramp. Take the Viaducto to Av Zaragoza, then follow the signs for Oaxaca until you join the Puebla highway.

North

From Querétaro, the last toll booth as you approach the city is at Tepotzotlán. Continue south, following signs for Cd Satélite and Toreo. Beyond the skyscraper sculptures marking the gateway to Satélite, move into the lateral at the first signs indicating the 'Río San Joaquín' exit, which appears just north of the giant dome of the Toreo arena. Take this exit; the ramp curves left over the Periférico. Keep right as you go over, then follow signs for 'Circuito Interior.' After passing the Corona factory, take the Thiers exit. Keep left, following signs for Reforma, and you'll end up on Río Misisipi, which intersects Reforma at the La Diana roundabout. Turn left on Reforma to get to the Centro Histórico, or continue straight ahead for Colonia Roma.

Leaving the city, the simplest option is to take Reforma to the west end of Bosque de Chapultepec, then a right exit to pick up the Periférico northbound.

From Pachuca, Hidalgo and northern Veracruz, the inbound route is one of the easiest, if no less chaotic, since the highway feeds into Av Insurgentes; follow signs for the Centro Histórico and Zona Rosa. Leaving the city, take Insurgentes north (also the route to Teotihuacán).

South

After the last *caseta* on the autopista from Cuernavaca, continue straight, taking a right exit for Calz Tlalpan (some signs are hidden behind trees). Calz Tlalpan eventually feeds into Av 20 de Noviembre, which ends at the Zócalo. Leaving town, turn right (south) at the Zócalo onto Pino Suárez, which becomes Calz Tlalpan. Follow Tlalpan about 20km south, then watch for a Y where signs point left for the autopista.

West

Coming from Toluca, about 4km past the high-rises of Santa Fe, keep right and follow signs for Av Constituyentes (don't

take the exit for Reforma). Constituyentes passes under the Circuito Interior near the eastern end of Bosque de Chapultepec. Turn left after the underpass to pick up the Circuito, then follow signs for Reforma to get to the Zona Rosa and downtown. Or, continue straight ahead on Juan Escutia (Eje 2 Sur) right into Condesa. Heading west out of the city, take Av Chapultepec to Constituyentes, then follow the signs for the *cuota* (toll highway) or *libre* to Toluca.

GETTING AROUND

Mexico City has an inexpensive, easy-to-use metro and an equally cheap and practical bus system plying all the main routes. Taxis are plentiful, but some are potentially hazardous (see p127).

To/From the Airport

The metro is convenient to the airport, though hauling luggage amid rush-hour crowds can be a Herculean task. Authorized taxis provide a painless, relatively inexpensive alternative.

METRO

The airport metro station is Terminal Aérea, on Línea 5 (yellow). It's 200m from the terminal: leave by the exit at the end of Sala A (domestic arrivals) and continue past the taxi stand, to the station.

To the city center, follow signs for 'Dirección Politécnico'; at La Raza (seven stops away) change for Línea 3 (green) toward 'Dirección Universidad.' Metro Hidalgo, at the west end of the Alameda, is three stops south; it's also a transfer point for Línea 2 (blue) to the Zócalo.

To get to the Zona Rosa from the airport, take Línea 5 to 'Pantitlán' the end of the line. Change for Línea 1 (pink) and get off at metro Insurgentes.

Going to the airport, take the Av Aeropuerto Municipal exit on the Dirección Politécnico side, and proceed directly to the terminal.

TAXI

Steer clear of street cabs outside the airport. Safe and reliable 'Transporte Terrestre' taxis, recognizable by their yellow doors and airplane logos, are controlled by a fixed-price ticket system.

Purchase taxi tickets from booths labeled 'Sitio 300' (those labeled 'ProTaxi' sell tickets for Suburban van taxis), located in Sala E2 (international arrivals), on your left as you exit customs, and by the Sala A (domestic arrivals) exit. Fares are determined by zones (shown on a map next to the booth). A ride to the Zócalo or Alameda Central is $12, to the Zona Rosa or Plaza de la República $15. One ticket is valid for up to four passengers and luggage that will fit in the trunk.

Taxi stands for the Sitio 300 taxis are outside Salas A and E. Porters may offer to take your ticket and luggage the few steps to the taxi, but hold on to the ticket and hand it to the driver. Drivers won't expect a tip for the ride, but will of course welcome one.

To reserve a Transporte Terrestre taxi to the airport call ☎ 5571-9344; fares are slightly higher in this direction.

To/From the Bus Terminals

The metro is the fastest and cheapest way to any bus terminal, but it's tricky to maneuver through crowded stations and cars. Taxis are an easier option, but avoid street cabs outside the terminals. Fortunately, all terminals have ticket booths for 'taxis autorizados,' with fares set by zone ($2 from 9pm or 10pm to 6am). An agent at the exit will assign you a cab. Ignore hustlers who tell you there are no authorized cabs left, or who try to take your ticket before you reach the taxi.

TERMINAL NORTE

Metro Línea 5 (yellow) stops at Autobuses del Norte, just outside the terminal. To the center, follow signs for 'Dirección Pantitlán,' then change at La Raza for Línea 3 (green) toward 'Dirección Universidad.' (The La Raza connection is a six-minute hike through a 'Tunnel of Science.')

The taxi kiosk is in the central passageway; a cab for up to four people to the Alameda or Zócalo costs $8; to Colonia Roma, $7.50.

TERMINAL ORIENTE (TAPO)

This bus terminal is next door to metro San Lázaro. To the center or Zona Rosa, take Línea 1 (pink) toward 'Dirección Observatorio.'

The authorized taxi booth is at the top (metro) end of the main passageway from the rotunda. The fare to the Zócalo is $5.50; to the Zona Rosa, $6.50.

ADO Group's deluxe lines (UNO, ADO GL) run a shuttle service, called Citibus, to/from area hotels and to (not from) the airport. There are six departures from Monday to Friday to the **Hotel del Ángel** (Río Lerma 154) and eight to the airport (fewer on weekends). Purchase tickets ($3.75) at TAPO or the hotel. Contact Ticketbus (p179) for schedules and other pickup locations.

TERMINAL PONIENTE

Observatorio metro station, the eastern terminus of Línea 1 (pink), is a couple of minutes' walk across a busy street (the pedestrian bridge has been closed until further notice). A taxi ticket to Colonia Roma costs $6.50; to the Zócalo it's $9.

TERMINAL SUR

Terminal Sur is a two-minute walk from metro Tasqueña, the southern terminus of Línea 2 which stops at the Zócalo. For the Zona Rosa, transfer at Pino Suárez and take Línea 1 to Insurgentes (Dirección Observatorio). Going to the terminal, take the 'Autobuses del Sur' exit, which leads upstairs to a footbridge. Descend the last staircase on the left to reach the terminal.

Authorized taxis from Terminal Sur cost $9 to the Zona Rosa; $8 to the Centro Histórico. Ticket booths are by the main exit and in Sala 3.

Bicycle

Though not commonly used as transport in Mexico City (except by delivery boys), bicycles are a viable way to get around and are often quicker and more pleasant than riding on overcrowded, recklessly driven buses. Although careless drivers and potholes can make DF cycling an 'extreme sport,' if you stay alert and keep off the major thoroughfares, it's manageable.

The recently completed *ciclovía* is an extensive bike trail that follows the old bed of the Cuernavaca railroad as far as the Morelos border. It extends from Av Ejército Nacional in Polanco through the Bosque de Chapultepec, skirting the Periférico freeway from La Feria to Av San Antonio, with several steep bridges passing over the freeways. The trail then continues south to the Parque Ecológico de la Ciudad de México, for a total distance of 90km.

Another path follows Av Chapultepec along a protected median from Bosque de Chapultepec to the Centro Histórico, though a detour through the streets of Colonia Roma is ignored by motorists. A third route runs along Paseo de la Reforma from the Auditorio Nacional to the Museo Rufino Tamayo. Follow the red stripe.

Bicitekas (www.bicitekas.org in Spanish) is an urban cycling group that organizes rides starting from the Monumento a la Independencia at 9pm every Wednesday, and from the Zócalo at 10am Sunday. Groups of up to 100 cyclists ride to destinations like Coyoacán and Ciudad Satélite. Participants must be sufficiently robust to handle treks of up to 40km. Helmets and rear lights are required.

The website **Bicimapas** (www.bicimapas.com.mx in Spanish) has maps for bicycling in the Valle de México.

Rent bicycles at **Taller de Bicicletas Orozco** (Map pp118-19; ☎ 5286-3582; Av México 13A; ☾ 10:30am-8pm Tue-Sun; Ⓜ Sevilla), at Parque México in Condesa. Prices are $2.75 per hour or $19 per day (ID plus deposit required), with better rates for longer periods.

Bus, Pesero & Trolleybus

Mexico City's thousands of buses and peseros (also called microbuses or combis) operate from around 5am till 8pm or 9pm daily; electric trolleybuses until 11:30pm. Only a few routes run all night, notably those along Paseo de la Reforma and the new metrobus along Av Insurgentes. This means you'll get anywhere by bus and/or metro during the day but will probably have to take a few taxis after hours.

Peseros are generally gray-and-green minibuses operated by private firms. They follow fixed routes, often starting or ending at metro stations, and will stop at virtually any street corner. Route information is randomly displayed on cards attached to the windshield. Fares are $0.25 for trips of up to 5km, $0.30 for 5km to 12km and $0.40 for more than 12km. Add 20% to all fares between 11pm and 6am. Municipally operated full-size orange buses (labeled 'RTP') and trolleybuses only pick up at bus stops; fares are $0.20 (exact change only) regardless of distance traveled.

Seeking to alleviate traffic along one of the capital's most congested thorough-fares, in 2005 the city installed the metrobus on Av Insurgentes. Where once a motley assortment of smoke-belching buses competed for passengers along this north–south artery, now a uniform fleet of 24m-long Volvo vehicles plies a dedicated inner lane. The metrobus stops at metro-style stations amid the traffic, spaced at three- to four-block intervals. Access is by prepaid card, issued by machines at the entrance to the platforms, and rides cost $0.30. Rechargeable cards ($0.80) are placed on a sensor device for entry. The metrobus runs round the clock, though frequency is reduced to every 20 minutes between midnight and 5am, when the fare increases to $0.50.

Pesero routes ply practically every street that crisscrosses the Centro Histórico grid, while trolleybuses follow a number of the key *ejes* (priority roads) throughout the rest of the city.

Some useful routes are listed below.
'Autobuses del Sur' & 'Autobuses del Norte' trolleybus: Eje Central Lázaro Cardenas between north and south bus terminals (stops at Plaza de las Tres Culturas; Plaza Garibaldi; Bellas Artes/Alameda; metro Hidalgo)
'Metro Hidalgo-La Villa' bus or pesero: Paseo de la Reforma between Auditorio Nacional or metro Chapultepec and Basílica de Guadalupe (stops at Zona Rosa; Av Insurgentes; Alameda/metro Hidalgo; Plaza Garibaldi; Plaza de las Tres Culturas)
'Metro Sevilla-P Masaryk' pesero: Between Colonia Roma and Polanco via Av Álvaro Obregón and Av Presidente Masaryk (stops at metro Niños Héroes; Av Insurgentes; metro Sevilla; Leibnitz)
'Metro Tacubaya-Balderas-Escandón' pesero: Between Centro Histórico and Condesa, westbound via Puebla, eastbound via Durango (stops at Plaza San Juan; metro Balderas; metro Insurgentes; Parque España; Av Michoacán)

Car & Motorcycle

Touring Mexico City by car is strongly discouraged, unless you have a healthy reserve of stamina and patience. Even more than elsewhere in the country, traffic rules are seen as suggested behavior. Red lights may be run at will, no-turn signs are ignored and signals are seldom used. On occasion you may be hit by the bogus traffic fine, a routine means for traffic cops to increase their miserly salaries. Nevertheless, you may want to rent a car here for travel outside the city. Avoid parking on the street; most midrange and top-end hotels have guest garages.

DRIVING RESTRICTIONS
To help combat pollution, Mexico City operates its 'Hoy No Circula' (Don't Drive Today) program, banning many vehicles from being driven in the city between 5am and 10pm on one day each week. Cars under 10 years old (supposedly less polluting) with a calcomanía de verificación (verification hologram sticker) are exempted. This sticker is obtained under the city's vehicle-pollution assessment system.

For other vehicles (including foreign-registered ones), the last digit of the license plate numbers determine the day when they cannot circulate. Any car may operate on Saturday and Sunday.

Day	Prohibited last digits
Monday	5, 6
Tuesday	7, 8
Wednesday	3, 4
Thursday	1, 2
Friday	9, 0

Metro

The metro system offers the quickest way to get around Mexico City. About 3.9 million people ride the metro on an average weekday, making it the world's fourth-busiest subway. It has 175 stations and 177km of track on 11 lines. Trains arrive every two to three minutes during rush hours. At $0.20 a ride, including transfers, it's also one of the world's cheapest subways.

All lines operate from 5am to midnight weekdays, 6am to midnight Saturday, and 7am to midnight Sunday. Platforms and cars can become alarmingly packed during rush hours (roughly 7:30am to 10am and 3pm to 8pm). At these times the forward cars are reserved for women and children, and men may not proceed beyond the 'Solo Mujeres y Niños' gate.

With such crowded conditions, it's not surprising that pickpocketing occurs, so watch your belongings.

Nevertheless, the metro is easy to use. Lines are color-coded and each station is identified by a unique logo. Signs reading 'Dirección Pantitlán,' 'Dirección Univer-

sidad' and so on name the stations at the ends of the lines. Check a map for the direction you want. Buy a boleto (ticket), or several, at the taquilla (ticket window), feed it into the turnstile, and you're on your way. When changing trains, look for 'Correspondencia' (Transfer) signs. Maps of the vicinity around each station are posted near the exits.

Taxi

Mexico City has several classes of taxi. Cheapest are the cruising street cabs, mostly Volkswagen Beetles but also Nissans and other Japanese models. These are not recommended due to the risk of assaults (see p127). If you must hail a cab off the street, check that it has actual taxi license plates: numbers begin with the letter L (for libre, or free), and a green stripe runs along the bottom. Check that the number on them matches the number painted on the bodywork. Also look for the carta de identificación (also called the tarjetón), a postcard-sized ID that should be displayed visibly inside the cab, and ensure that the driver matches the photo. If the cab you've hailed does not pass these tests, get another.

In libre cabs, fares are computed by taxímetro (meter), which should start at 5.8 to 6.4 pesos ($0.50 to $0.60). The total cost of a 2km or 3km ride in moderate traffic – say, from the Zócalo to the Zona Rosa – should be $2 to $2.50. Between 11pm and 6am, add 20%.

A radio taxi costs two or three times as much, but the extra cost adds an immeasurable degree of security. Their plates begin with S – for sitio (taxi stand) – and bear an orange stripe. When you phone, the dispatcher will tell you the cab number and the type of car. Hotels and restaurants can call a reliable cab for you.

Some reliable radio-taxi firms, available 24 hours, are listed below. Maps in this chapter show the locations of some key sitios.

Servitaxis (☎ 5516-6020, 5516-6034)
Sitio Parque México (☎ 5286-7129, 5286-7164)
Taxi-Mex (☎ 9171-8888, 5634-9912)
Taxis Radio Unión (☎ 5514-8124)

Around Mexico City

Wondering where Chilangos (Mexico City's residents) go to maintain their sanity? Look no further than the picturesque *pueblos mágicos* (magical villages) that surround the world's largest and fastest growing megalopolis. Several of Mexico's highlights are within a day's travel of the capital, and many of them – such as the picturesque and artsy village of Tepoztlán, or the ancient city of Teotihuacán – are easy day trips. Other destinations, such as the colonial cities of Taxco and Puebla, merit several days exploration. Another intriguing, less-touristed option, is to circumnavigate the capital.

South of Mexico City, the east–west-trending Cordillera Neovolcánica, home to the country's highest volcanoes, stretches from the Pico de Orizaba to the Nevado de Toluca. North of this imposing range is the Altiplano Central (Central Plateau). This topographic diversity harbors a variety of landscapes, from dramatic gorges and fertile plains to fragrant pine forests and prominent snow peaks. The altitude makes for a very salubrious climate. Geologically, the region remains quite active and it's riddled with hot springs and still-smoking volcanoes.

On weekends, most getaways cater to visitors from the capital. Generally, this means that there are ample facilities and often generous discounts available midweek, and if a place is crowded it won't be with foreigners.

TOP FIVE

- Clambering around a pair of spectacular pyramids at **Teotihuacán** (p195), Mexico's biggest and most beguiling ancient city

- Munching your way around **Puebla** (p212), a scrumptious metropolis where the eminently strollable Centro Historíco faithfully preserves the charming Spanish imprint

- Learning how to cook up a savory storm at a rustic country kitchen in a village near **Tlaxcala** (p208)

- Shopping for unique silver designs in picturesque **Taxco** (p254), a gorgeous colonial gem that's perfect for getting lost in

- Wandering cobbled side streets in magical villages like far-flung **Cuetzalan** (p228), artsy **Tepoztlán** (p231), devout **Tepoztlán** (p192) and easy-going **Malinalco** (p261)

- PUEBLA JANUARY DAILY HIGH 24°C | 75°F
- PUEBLA JULY DAILY HIGH 27°C | 80°F

AROUND MEXICO CITY

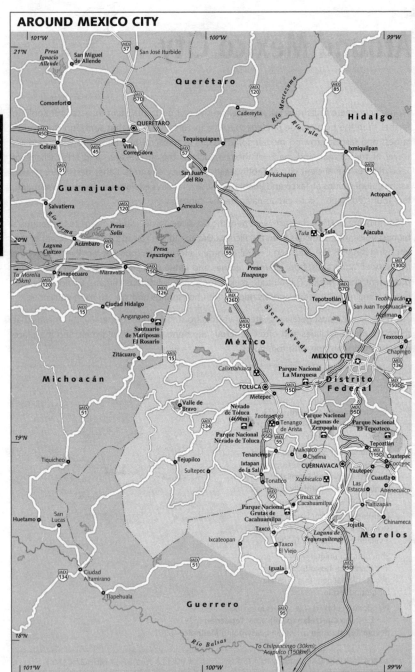

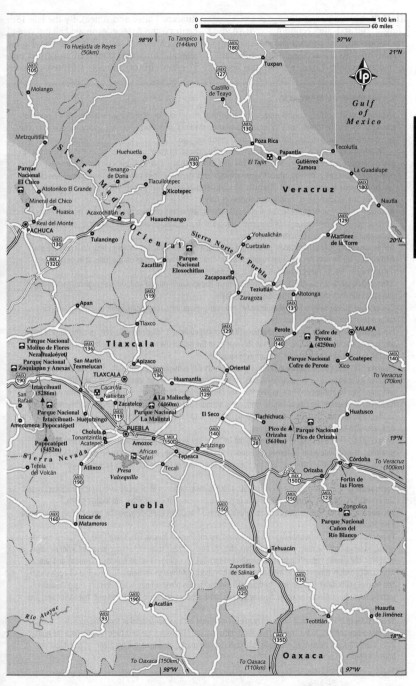

History

Long a cultural and economic crossroads, the region around present-day Mexico City played host to a succession of important indigenous civilizations (notably the Teoti-huacán, Toltec and Aztec). By the late 15th century, the Aztecs dominated all but one of central Mexico's states. Many archaeological sites and museums preserve remnants of pre-Hispanic history; Puebla's Museo Amparo

---

TO MARKET, AL MERCADO...

Mexico's most enduring and endearing tradition may well be the *tianguis* (indigenous people's market). In many towns and villages, hawking, trading and bartering for everything under the sun carries on to this day much as it did centuries ago.

Much more than a simple economic venue, these engaging places of commerce offer an intimate glimpse at Mexico's robust social fabric. What's more, their convivial eateries, called *comedores* (literally 'eating places'), are cheap and inviting spots to sample regional specialties. So, hone your bartering (and Spanish or sign-language) skills, prime your palate for adventure, and join the stimulating, open-air shopping fray.

Actopan (p203) The recipe for succulent pit-roasted lamb, still served traditionally wrapped in maguey leaves here, was perfected centuries ago. Embroidered tablecloths, leather sandals and Otomí handicrafts skillfully woven from maguey fiber are also on offer (Wednesday).

Amecameca (p204) In the shadow of an active volcano, a lively local market convenes here daily near the plaza.

Atlixco (p230) An easy day trip from Puebla, this mid-size colonial town shows off the fruits of its near-perfect climate twice a week (Tuesday and Saturday) at its colorful markets.

Atotonilco el Grande (p203) This welcoming town boasts a mild climate and a unique regional gastronomy – don't miss the barbecued lamb (Thursday and Sunday).

Cuetzalan (p228) Besides high-altitude coffee and ever-present mist, this mountainous colonial town is most famous for its colorful Sunday *tianguis*.

Ixmiquilpan (p203) On Monday, indigenous Otomí craftspeople cart unique reed baskets, pottery, musical instruments and colorful maguey-fiber textiles to this market in the hub of the arid Mezquital Valley. The rest of the week, you can seek out the same artisans in nearby communities.

Puebla (p212) In Puebla's bustling Centro Histórico, every day is market day along Calle 5 Nte near Mercado Cinco de Mayo. All manner of fresh fruits, vegetables, steaming-hot street food and seasonal treats like wild mushrooms and *chapulines* (grasshoppers) turn up here from the fertile surrounding countryside. The charming Plazuela de los Sapos, the heart of the City of Angels' world-class antiques district, transforms into a lively outdoor market on Sunday, featuring an eclectic assortment of goods, from junk to 16th-century finery. Within walking distance, Barrio de Analco also hosts a major outdoor market.

Taxco (p247) The crafts tend to get drowned out by the sheer weight of produce and whatsit vendors at this sprawling, labyrinthine affair (Saturday and Sunday). On Friday and Saturday it's easy to get lost (that's sort of the point, no?) while clambering around the stairways, but midweek there's still plenty to buy and things are less chaotic.

Tehuacán (p230) A short detour off Hwy 135D, about halfway between Mexico City and Oaxaca, the Saturday and Sunday market is a good excuse to stretch your legs while shopping for carved onyx and leather goods.

Tepeaca (p230) Another easy day trip from Puebla, with a Franciscan monastery, nearby onyx-carving villages and a big Friday market.

Tepotzotlán (p192) A favorite day trip just beyond the madness of Mexico City, there's a lively, varied *comedor* eating scene just off the main plaza, the perfect place to enjoy a fresh-squeezed orange juice and a *flor de calabaza* or *huitlacoche gordita* (squash blossom or mushroom tortilla). Shopping is best on holidays, Saturday and Sunday, when craft vendors congregate in front of the church – check out the woolen items. This magical village's shops and market stalls hawk a mélange of traditional handicrafts, plus plenty of neo-hippie jewelry and patchouli-scented home furnishings. For crafts, Sunday attracts more vendors and is the most crowded, but Saturday is just as enjoyable.

Tepoztlán (p231) Tepoz' local Wednesday market is blessed with a smorgasbord of tempting *comedores*. It also provides a fine contrast to the crowded weekend crafts market: Midweek is the best time to appreciate the quirky town's laid-back yet creative vibe. Unique local crafts include masks, glass accented with leather, and miniature houses fashioned from tree spines.

(p213) provides an excellent overview of the region's history and cultures.

Post-conquest, the Spanish transformed central Mexico, establishing ceramic industries at Puebla, mines at Taxco and Pachuca, and wheat-, sugar- and cattle-producing haciendas. The Catholic church used the region as a base for its missionary activities, and left a series of imposing churches and fortified monasteries. Today, most towns retain a central plaza surrounded by colonial buildings.

Climate

The extra altitude outside Mexico City makes for a very agreeable climate – cooler and less humid than the lowlands, with most rain falling in brief summer downpours. Snow tops the highest peaks (nevados) for several months a year (November through March), but the populated areas in the foothills continue to enjoy a mild climate, while cross-country skiers glide about up in the clouds.

Parks & Reserves

Several national parks within a day's drive of Mexico City are delightfully crowd-free and, with a bit of effort, are accessible via public transport.

El Chico Rock formations attract climbers and pine forests make for cool day hiking at this diminutive, mountainous park outside Pachuca (p202).

El Tepozteco Near Cuernavaca, a short but steep and stunning ascent leads to an Aztec pyramid overlooking the artsy village of Tepoztlán (p232).

Grutas de Cacahuamilpa Near Taxco, the region's most popular park preserves a staggering network of gaping caverns (p255).

Iztaccíhuatl-Popocatépetl The foothills around Amecameca offer some fine hiking. Popo remains off-limits due to volcanic activity; only experienced climbers should attempt to summit Izta (p204).

La Malintzi Near Puebla, the towering peak La Malinche is a challenging nontechnical goal for day hikers (p211).

Molino de Flores Nezahualcóyotl Near Texcoco, this small park preserves a pulque (alcohol brewed from agave) hacienda and a little-known archaeological site (p206).

Nevado de Toluca Drive right up to, or cross-country ski around, the extinct crater within easy reach of Toluca (p260).

Getting There & Around

Most visitors access destinations around Mexico City by bus or private vehicle. There are several regional airports, but for international flights it's easiest to use the express-bus services that link the region's major cities to Mexico City's airport. Within the region, a car comes in handy if visiting out-of-the-way attractions. With enough patience, however, you can get almost anywhere by bus.

NORTH OF MEXICO CITY

Two main escape routes head north from Mexico City to impressive, well-preserved archaeological sites, colonial relics and wide-open landscapes. The modern but often congested toll road, Hwy 57D, skirts the colonial religious center of Tepotzotlán, then swings northwest past the turnoff for Tula's Toltec ruins and continues to charismatic Querétaro (p648). Equally modern, Hwy 185D beelines northeast, linking the capital to Pachuca, a colonial mining town

AROUND MEXICO CITY

TOP FIVE QUIRKY ATTRACTIONS

Quirky things come in cute little packages at the following Lilliputian museums:

- When visiting the must-see ruins, budget time for a detour to see the authentic replica of a *pulquería* (pulque distillery) at Teotihuacán's **Centro de Estudios Teotihuacanos** (p197), en route to La Gruta restaurant.

- Pachuca's worthwhile **Museo Nacional de la Fotografía** and **Museo de Minería** (p200) provide fascinating flashbacks to a then-modernizing 19th-century Mexico.

- Tlaxcala's **Museo Vivo de Artes y Tradiciones Populares** (p208) proves that Mexico's tiniest state is big on preserving living folk arts and popular traditions.

- Tehuacán's **Peñafiel mineral-water bottling plant** and nearby competitor **Garci-Crespo** (p230) both open their bubbly underground springs to visitors.

- Toluca's trippy **Cosmo Vitral Jardín Botánico** (p256) houses some lovely gardens inside an impressive stained-glass structure that originally served as the city's central marketplace.

and fast-growing capital of Hidalgo state. From Pachuca, well-paved routes snake north into the lush Huasteca and east to the Gulf coast, traversing some spectacular country as the fringes of the Sierra Madre tumble to the coastal plain.

Outside the Distrito Federal, Hwy 132D branches off 85D and continues past exits for the old monastery at Acolman, and the vast archaeological zone of Teotihuacán, then cuts across a stark plateau before reaching Tulancingo, Hidalgo's second largest city.

TEPOTZOTLÁN
☎ 55 / pop 45,000 / elevation 2300m

Just beyond Mexico City's urban sprawl, the primary attraction in Tepotzotlán (teh-po-tzot-*lan*) is the **Museo Nacional del Virreinato** (National Museum of the Viceregal Period; ☎ 5876-0245; Plaza Hidalgo 99; admission $3.50; ☻ 9am-6pm Tue-Sun), comprised of the restored Jesuit **Iglesia de San Francisco Javier** and an adjacent **monastery**.

Among the folk art and fine art on display are silver chalices, pictures created from inlaid wood, porcelain, furniture and fine religious paintings and statues.

Don't miss the **Capilla Doméstica**, whose Churrigueresque main altarpiece boasts more mirrors than a carnival fun house. The biggest crowds arrive on Sunday, when a crafts market convenes out front. The church, an extreme example of Churrigueresque architecture, was originally built between 1670 and 1682; elaborations carried out in the 18th century made it one of Mexico's most lavish places of worship. The facade is a phantasmagoric array of carved saints, angels, plants and people, while the interior walls and the Camarín del Virgen adjacent to the altar are swathed with a circus of gilded ornamentation.

Tepotzotlán's highly regarded Christmas *pastorelas* (nativity plays) are performed inside the former monastery in the weeks leading up to December 25. Tickets, which include Christmas dinner and piñata smashing, can be purchased at La Hostería de Tepotzotlán (see right), or via **Ticketmaster** (☎ 5325-9000; www.ticketmaster.com.mx in Spanish).

Sleeping
Tepotzotlán is geared towards day-trippers, but there are a few good-value hotels.

Hotel Posada San José (☎ /fax 5876-0520/0835; Plaza Virreinal 13; r $17, with view $23) On the south side of the *zócalo* (main plaza), this colonial-style hotel has a good restaurant and 14 comfortable rooms with TV and private bathrooms. Avoid rooms 8 and 9, which are directly below the building's noisy water pump.

Hotel Posada del Virrey (☎ /fax 5876-1864; Av Insurgentes 13; s/d $26/41; P) This cheery option is midway between the *zócalo* and the tollbooth on the autopista. Pluses include easy parking, a restaurant, and 55 clean, colorful rooms (a few with Jacuzzis) with cable TV on two arcaded levels.

Posada del Cid (☎ 5876-0064; Av Insurgentes 12; s/d $15/23; P) Opposite Posada del Virrey, the Cid's 14 no-frills rooms are well-tended, but darker and noisier. Only some rooms have cable TV, but they all cost the same.

Eating
La Hostería de Tepotzotlán (☎ 5876-0243, 5876-1646; Plaza Virreinal 1; mains $7-11; ☻ 12:30-6pm Tue-Sun) In a pretty little courtyard within the monastery museum, this appealing bar-restaurant serves hearty soups along with original main courses like *huitlacoche* (earthy corn mushroom) crepes for brunch and lunch.

On the north side of the *zócalo*, touting waiters await at three nearly indistinguishable restaurants under the arcades: **Los Virreyes** (☎ 5876-0235), **Montecarlo** (☎ 5876-0586) and **Casa Mago** (☎ 5876-0229), which has a Saturday buffet breakfast spread. All serve traditional Mexican favorites at inflated prices – soup and salad $3.50 to $5, mains $7 to $15. You're paying for the festive ambience, generated by roving *ranchera* (urban country music) performers playing Mexican-style country music.

Posada San José's **Restaurant-Bar Pepe** (☎ 5876-0520; mains $7-14) is similarly priced but smaller and more intimate, with friendly service, more romantic music and complimentary appetizers like warm cactus salad.

Alternatively, join the locals at the *taquerías* (taco stalls) west of the plaza, or in the market behind the Palacio Municipal, where food stalls serve rich *pozole* (a thin stew of hominy, pork or chicken, and avocado), *gorditas* (fried stuffed tacos in fat handmade blue corn tortillas), and fresh-squeezed juices all day long.

Getting There & Away

Tepotzotlán is en route from Mexico City to Querétaro, 1.5km west of the first tollbooth on Hwy 57D.

From Mexico City's Terminal Norte, Autotransportes Valle de Mezquital (AVM) buses stop at the tollbooth every 15 minutes en route to Tula. From there, catch a local bus ($0.40) or taxi ($2), or walk west for about 20 minutes along Av Insurgentes. You can also catch a *colectivo* (minibus or car that picks up and drops off passengers along a predetermined route) to Tepotzotlán from Mexico City's Rosario metro station ($1.25). In Tepotzotlán, returning 'Rosario' buses depart from Av Insurgentes opposite Posada San José.

TULA

☎ 773 / pop 27,000 / elevation 2060m

The probable capital of the ancient Toltec civilization is best known for its fearsome 4.5m-high stone warrior figures. Though less spectacular than Teotihuacán, Tula is still an absorbing site. The modern town is surrounded by a Pemex refinery and an odoriferous petrochemical plant, but the center is serviceable enough for an overnight stay if you don't want to make the 75km trip back to Mexico City.

History

Tula was an important city from about AD 900 to 1150, reaching a peak population of 35,000. Aztec annals tell of a king called Topiltzin – fair-skinned, black-bearded and long-haired – who founded a Toltec capital in the 10th century. There's debate however about whether Tula was this capital.

The Toltecs were mighty empire-builders whom the Aztecs looked upon with awe, claiming them as royal ancestors. Topiltzin was supposedly a priest-king, dedicated to peaceful worship (which only included sacrifices of animals) of the feathered serpent god Quetzalcóatl. Tula is known to have housed followers of the less likable Tezcatlipoca (Smoking Mirror), god of warriors, witchcraft, life and death; worshiping Tezcatlipoca required human sacrifices. The story goes that Tezcatlipoca appeared in various guises in order to provoke Topiltzin. As a naked chili-seller, he aroused the lust of Topiltzin's daughter and eventually married her; as an old man,

he persuaded the teetotaling Topiltzin to get drunk.

Eventually, the humiliated leader left for the Gulf coast, where he set sail eastward on a raft of snakes, promising one day to return and reclaim his throne. (This caused the Aztec emperor Moctezuma much consternation when Hernán Cortés appeared on the Gulf coast in 1519.) The conventional wisdom is that Topiltzin set up a new Toltec state at Chichén Itzá in Yucatán, while the Tula Toltecs built a brutal, militaristic empire that dominated central Mexico.

Tula was evidently a place of some splendor – legends speak of palaces of gold, turquoise, jade and quetzal feathers, of enormous corn cobs and colored cotton that grew naturally. Possibly its treasures were looted by the Aztecs or Chichimecs.

In the mid-12th century, the ruler Huémac apparently moved the Toltec capital to Chapultepec after factional fighting at Tula, then committed suicide. Tula was abandoned in the early 13th century, seemingly after violent destruction by the Chichimecs.

Orientation & Information

The Zona Arqueológica (Archaeological Zone) is 2km north of the center. Tula's principal avenue, Av Zaragoza, links the *zócalo* with the outskirts. Av Hidalgo, the other main drag, has essential services like Internet and ATMs.

Sights

TOWN CENTER

On Av Zaragoza, Tula's fortress-like **cathedral** was part of the 16th-century monastery of San José. Inside, its vault ribs are picked out in gold. On the library wall opposite the *zócalo* is a colorful **mural** of Tula's history.

ZONA ARQUEOLÓGICA

The old settlement of Tula covered nearly 16 sq km and stretched to the modern town's far side, but the present focus is the **ruins** (admission $3; ☉ 10am-5pm Tue-Sun) of the main ceremonial center, perched on a hilltop with good views over rolling countryside.

About half a kilometer from the entrance, there's a **museum** (signs are in Spanish only) displaying pottery and large sculptures. After another 700m, you'll reach the center of the ancient city. Explanatory signs at the site are in English, Spanish and Náhuatl.

From the museum, the first large structure you'll reach is the **Juego de Pelota No 1**, a copy of an I-shaped ball court from Xochicalco. Archaeologists believe its walls were decorated with sculpted panels that were removed under Aztec rule.

Also known as the temple of Quetzalcóatl or Tlahuizcalpantecuhtli (Morning Star), **Pirámide B** can be scaled via steps on its south side. At the top of the stairway, the remains of two columnar roof supports – that once depicted feathered serpents with their heads on the ground and their tails in the air – remain standing. The four basalt warrior-telamones at the top and the pillars behind supported the temple's roof. Wearing headdresses, butterfly-shaped breastplates and short skirts held in place by sun disks, the warriors hold spear-throwers in their right hands, and knives and incense bags in their left. The telamon on the left side is a replica of the original, now in Mexico City's Museo Nacional de Antropología (p138). The columns behind the telamones depict crocodile heads (which symbolize the Earth), warriors, symbols of warrior orders, weapons and Quetzalcóatl's head.

On the pyramid's north wall are some of the carvings that once surrounded the structure. These show the symbols of the warrior orders: jaguars, coyotes, eagles eating hearts, and what may be a human head in Quetzalcóatl's mouth.

Now roofless, the **Gran Vestíbulo** (Great Vestibule) extends along the front of the pyramid, facing the plaza. The stone bench carved with warriors originally ran the length of the hall, possibly to seat priests and nobles observing ceremonies in the plaza.

Near the north side of Pirámide B is the **Coatepantli** (Serpent Wall), 40m long, 2.25m high, and carved with rows of geometric patterns and a row of snakes devouring human skeletons. Traces remain of the original bright colors with which most of Tula's structures were painted.

Immediately west of Pirámide B, the **Palacio Quemado** (Burnt Palace) is a series of halls and courtyards with more low benches and relief carvings, one depicting a procession of nobles. It was probably used for ceremonies or reunions meetings.

The **plaza** in front of Pirámide B would have been the scene of religious and military displays. At its center is the *adoratorio* (ceremonial platform). On the east side of the plaza, **Pirámide C** is Tula's biggest structure, but remains largely unexcavated. To the west is **Juego de Pelota No 2**, central Mexico's largest ball court at more than 100m in length.

Sleeping & Eating

Hotel Casa Blanca (☎ 732-11-86; www.casablancatula .com; Pasaje Hidalgo 11; s/d $23/27; **P** **⌨**) The family-run 'White (actually rather tangerine-pink) House' is Tula's best budget bet. The 36 tiled rooms are bright, clean and quiet, and have cable TV. It's on a narrow pedestrian street opposite the restaurant of the same name. Parking access is around back, via Zaragoza.

Hotel Sharon (☎ 732-09-76/35-00; www.hotel sharon.com.mx in Spanish; Blvd Tula, Iturbe 1; s/d from $41/49, ste $57-87; **P** **⌨**) This modern four-star place is Tula's most business-friendly in-town hotel, with wireless Internet and in-room satellite radio. It's conveniently located at the turnoff to the Zona Arqueológica.

Hotel Lizbeth (☎ 732-00-45; www.tulaonline.com /hotellizbeth; Ocampo 200; s/d/ste $28/32/43; **P** **⌨**) This modern hotel has a gaggle of clean and comfortable rooms, with shared balconies and free wi-fi Internet. The tiled rooms smell much better than carpeted ones. It's a couple of blocks from the bus station (turn right at the station entrance).

Restaurant Casablanca (☎ 732-22-74; Hidalgo 114; mains $4-10) Near the cathedral, this popular warehouse-like feeding hall features a traditional buffet-style lunch ($10), decent regional à la carte meals, and a breakfast buffet on Saturday and Sunday.

Fonda Naturística Maná (Pasaje Hidalgo; mains $1.50-3; **V**) A friendly vegetarian hole-in-the-wall, adjacent the Hotel Casa Blanca entrance, that's great for fruit salads, juices, towering veggie burgers and other meatless fare, both solid and liquid.

Getting There & Away

Tula's stadium-like bus depot is on Xicoténcatl, three blocks downhill from the cathedral: departing from the main entrance, turn right, then immediately left on Rojo del Río and look for the church steeple atop the hill. First-class Ovnibus buses go to/from Mexico City's Terminal Norte ($4.50, 1¾ hours, every 30 to 40 minutes) and to/from Pachuca ($4.50, 1¾ hours, hourly). Autotransportes Valle de Mezquital (AVM) runs 2nd-class buses ($3.75) to the same destinations every 15 minutes. **Flecha Amarilla** (☎ 01-800-375-7587; www.flecha-amarilla .com) has daily service to Querétaro ($8), Guanajuato ($18) and León ($19).

Getting Around

If you arrive in Tula by bus, the easiest way to get to the Zona Arqueológica is to catch a taxi ($2) outside the depot. From the center, 'Actopan' microbuses ($0.50) depart from the corner of Calle 5 de Mayo and Zaragoza, and pass within 100m of the site entrance. Alternatively, all Pachuca-bound buses will also stop outside the site on request.

ACOLMAN

☎ 957 / pop 4000 / elevation 2250m

Beside Hwy 132D, 32km northeast of Mexico City, you'll see what look like battlements surrounding the **Ex-Convento de San Agustín Acolman**. The historic complex, with its massive walls, carved stonework and colonnaded courtyards, harbors many frescoes. The adjacent **Iglesia de San Agustín**, built between 1539 and 1560, has a spacious Gothic interior and one of Mexico's earliest plateresque facades. The old monastery now houses a **museum** (☎ 957-16-44; admission $2.75; ☺ 9am-6pm) with paintings and artifacts from the early Christian missionary period.

It's a good leg-stretching stop en route to and from Teotihuacán, especially during the annual mid-December **Feria de la Piñata**, which features music, art, dance, handicrafts and heaps of colorful papiermâché creations bursting with candy.

Buses link Acolman ($1.50) with Mexico City's Indios Verdes metro station. Acolman is not far from Teotihuacán; if there's no convenient bus, taxis ask around $4 oneway from there. Frequent *colectivos* ($0.50) also make the journey from Av Guerrero in San Juan Teotihuacán.

TEOTIHUACÁN

☎ 594 / pop 25,000 / elevation 2300m

If there is a must-see attraction near Mexico City, it is the archaeological zone Teotihuacán (teh-oh-tee-wah-*kahn*), 50km

northeast of Mexico City in a mountain-ringed offshoot of the Valle de México. Site of the huge Pirámides del Sol y de la Luna (Pyramids of the Sun and Moon), Teotihuacán was Mexico's biggest ancient city and the capital of what was probably Mexico's largest pre-Hispanic empire. (See p40 for an outline of its importance.) Exploring the site can be awesome, if you don't let the hawkers get you down.

The city's grid plan was platted in the early part of the 1st century AD, and the Pirámide del Sol was completed – over an earlier cave shrine – by AD 150. The rest of the city was developed between about AD 250 and 600. Social, environmental and economic factors hastened its decline and eventual collapse in the 8th century AD.

The city was divided into quarters by two great avenues that met near La Ciudadela (the Citadel). One, running roughly north–south, is the famous Calzada de los Muertos (Avenue of the Dead) – so called because the later Aztecs believed the great buildings lining it were vast tombs, built by giants for Teotihuacán's first rulers. The major structures are typified by a *talud-tablero* style, in which the rising portions of stepped, pyramid-like buildings consist of both sloping (*talud*) and upright (*tablero*) sections. They were often covered in lime and colorfully painted. Most of the city was made up of residential compounds, some of which contained elegant frescoes.

Centuries after its fall, Teotihuacán remained a pilgrimage site for Aztec royalty, who believed that all of the gods had sacrificed themselves here to start the sun moving at the beginning of the 'fifth world,' inhabited by the Aztecs. It remains an important pilgrimage site: thousands of New Age devotees flock here each year to celebrate the vernal equinox (March 21) and soak up the mystical energies believed to converge here.

Orientation

Though ancient Teotihuacán covered more than 20 sq km, most of what there is to see today lies along nearly 2km of the Calzada de los Muertos. Buses arrive at a traffic circle by the southwest entrance (Gate 1); four other entrances are reached by the ring road around the site. There are parking lots and ticket booths at each entrance. Your

AROUND MEXICO CITY

ticket allows you to re-enter via any of them on the same day. The site museum is just inside the main east entrance (Gate 5).

Information

There's an **information booth** (☎ 956-02-76; ☼ 9am-4pm) near the southwest entrance (Gate 1). Free site tours by authorized guides (in Spanish only) may be available here if a sizable group forms.

Crowds at the **ruins** (admission $3.50; ☼ 7am-6pm) are thickest from 10am to 2pm, and it is busiest on Sunday, holidays and around the vernal equinox (between March 19 and March 21). Due to the heat and altitude, it's best to take it easy while exploring the

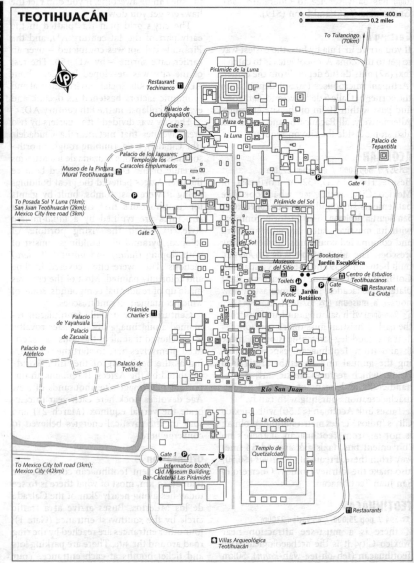

TEOTIHUACÁN

0 ————— 400 m
0 ————— 0.2 miles

To Tulancingo (70km)

Restaurant Techinanco

Pirámide de la Luna

Palacio de Quetzalpapálotl

Gate 3

Plaza de la Luna

Palacio de los Jaguares;
Templo de los Caracoles Emplumados

Museo de la Pintura Mural Teotihuacana

Palacio de Tepantitla

Gate 4

To Posada Sol Y Luna (1km);
San Juan Teotihuacán (2km);
Mexico City free road (3km)

Calzada de los Muertos

Pirámide del Sol

Gate 2

Plaza del Sol

Bookstore
Jardín Escultórica

Museum del Sitio

Toilets

Picnic Area

Centro de Estudios Teotihuacanos

Restaurant La Gruta

Gate 5

Jardín Botánico

Pirámide Charlie's

Palacio de Yayahuala

Palacio de Zacuala

Palacio de Atetelco

Palacio de Tetitla

Río San Juan

La Ciudadela

To Mexico City toll road (3km);
Mexico City (42km)

Gate 1

Information Booth;
Old Museum Building;
Bar-Cafetería Las Pirámides

Templo de Quetzalcóatl

Restaurants

Villas Arqueológica Teotihuacán

expansive ruins. Bring a hat and water – most visitors walk several kilometers, and the midday sun can be brutal. Afternoon rain showers are common from June to September.

Full-day tours to Teotihuacán are offered from Mexico City by several operators for around $30.

Sights

CALZADA DE LOS MUERTOS

Centuries ago the 'Avenue of the Dead,' Teotihuacán's main drag, must have seemed incomparable to its inhabitants, who saw its buildings at their best. Gate 1 brings you to the avenue in front of La Ciudadela. For 2km to the north, the avenue is flanked by former palaces of Teotihuacán's elite, and other major structures such as the Pirámide del Sol. The Pirámide de la Luna looms large at the northern end.

LA CIUDADELA

The expansive, square complex called the Citadel is believed to have been the residence of the city's supreme ruler. Four wide walls, 390m long and topped by 15 pyramids, enclose a huge open space, of which the main feature, to the east, is a pyramid called the **Templo de Quetzalcóatl**. The temple is flanked by two large, ruined complexes of rooms and patios, which may have been the city's administrative center.

The temple's most fascinating feature is the facade of an earlier structure (from around AD 250 to 300), which was revealed by excavating the more recent pyramid that had been superimposed on it. The four surviving steps of this facade (there were originally seven) are adorned with striking carvings. In the *tablero* panels the sharp-fanged feathered serpent deity, its head emerging from a necklace of 11 petals, alternates with a four-eyed, two-fanged creature often identified as the rain god Tláloc, but perhaps more authoritatively considered to be the fire serpent, bearer of the sun on its daily journey across the sky. On the sloping panels are side views of the plumed serpent.

MUSEO DEL SITIO

Continuing north along Calzada de los Muertos across the river toward the pyramids, a path to the right leads to the **site** **museum** (958-20-81; admission free with site ticket; 7am-6pm), just south of the Pirámide del Sol. It's a refreshing stop midway through a site visit. Nearby are the Jardín Escultórica (a lovely sculpture garden with Teotihuacán artifacts), the Jardín Botánico (Botanic Garden), public toilets, a snack bar, picnic tables and a bookstore.

The museum is thematically divided, with explanations in English and Spanish. There are excellent displays of artifacts, fresco panels, and an impressive large-scale model of the city set under a transparent walkway, from where the real Pirámide del Sol can be viewed through a wall-size window.

CENTRO DE ESTUDIOS TEOTIHUACANOS

Situated just outside the east entrance (Gate 5), this research center is home to the interesting **Museo Manuel Gamio** (965-15-99; admission free; 7am-4pm Mon-Fri, 9am-4pm Sat & Sun), sponsored by the Instituto de Antropología e Historia (INAH), which presents bimonthly cultural exhibitions, and has a permanent exhibition exploring the history of pulque, complete with a full-scale replica of a traditional *pulquería*. (See p167 for more on these age-old Mexican drinking dens.)

PIRÁMIDE DEL SOL

The world's third-largest pyramid, surpassed in size only by Egypt's Cheops and the pyramid of Cholula (p224), overshadows the east side of Calzada de los Muertos. The base is 222m long on each side, and it's now just over 70m high. The pyramid was cobbled together around AD 100, from three million tons of stone, without the use of metal tools, pack animals or the wheel.

The Aztec belief that the structure was dedicated to the sun god was validated in 1971, when archaeologists uncovered a 100m-long underground tunnel leading from the pyramid's west flank to a cave directly beneath its center, where they found religious artifacts. It's thought that the sun was worshiped here before the pyramid was built and that the city's ancient inhabitants traced the very origins of life to this grotto.

At Teotihuacán's height, the pyramid's plaster was painted bright red, which must have been a radiant sight at sunset.

AROUND MEXICO CITY

Clamber up the pyramid's 248 steps – yes, we counted – for an inspiring overview of the ancient city.

PALACIO DE TEPANTITLA

Teotihuacán's most famous fresco, the worn **Paradise of Tláloc**, is in the Tepantitla Palace, a priest's residence 500m northeast of Pirámide del Sol. The mural flanks a doorway in a covered patio, in the building's northeast corner. The rain god Tláloc, attended by priests, is shown on both sides. To the right of the door appears his paradise, a garden-like Eden with people, animals and fish swimming in a mountain-fed river. To the left of the door, tiny human figures are engaged in a unique ball game. Frescoes in other rooms show priests with feather headdresses.

PIRÁMIDE DE LA LUNA

The Pyramid of the Moon, at the north end of Calzada de los Muertos, is smaller than Pirámide del Sol, but it's more gracefully proportioned. Completed around AD 300, its summit is nearly the same height, because it's built on higher ground.

The Plaza de la Luna, located just in front of the Luna pyramid, is a handsome arrangement of 12 temple platforms. Some experts attribute astronomical symbolism to the total number of 13 (made up of the 12 platforms plus the pyramid), a key number in the day-counting system of the mesoamerican ritual calendar. The altar in the plaza's center is thought to have played host to religious dancing.

PALACIO DE QUETZALPAPÁLOTL

Off the Plaza de la Luna's southwest corner is the Palace of the Quetzal Butterfly, reckoned to be the home of a high priest. A flight of steps leads up to a roofed portico with an abstract mural, and nearby a well-restored patio has columns carved with images of the quetzal bird or a hybrid quetzal butterfly.

The **Palacio de los Jaguares** (Jaguar Palace) and **Templo de los Caracoles Emplumados** (Temple of the Plumed Conch Shells) are behind and below the Palacio de Quetzalpapálotl. On the lower walls of several of the chambers off the patio of the Jaguar Palace, are parts of murals showing the jaguar god in feathered headdresses,

blowing conch shells and apparently praying to the rain god Tláloc.

The Temple of the Plumed Conch Shells, entered from the Palacio de los Jaguares' patio, is a now-subterranean structure of the 2nd or 3rd century AD. Carvings on what was its facade show large shells – possibly used as musical instruments – decorated with feathers and four-petal flowers. The base on which the facade stands has a rainbow-colored mural of birds with water streaming from their beaks.

MUSEO DE LA PINTURA MURAL TEOTIHUACANA

On the ring road between Gates 2 and 3, this impressive **museum** (☎ 958-20-81; admission free with site ticket, parking $2; ☼ 9am-6pm) showcases murals from Teotihuacán, as well as reconstructions of murals you'll see at the ruins. Explanations of the exhibits are in Spanish only, but it's definitely worth a stop.

PALACIO DE TETITLA & PALACIO DE ATETELCO

Another group of palaces lies west of the site's main area, several hundred meters northwest of Gate 1. Many of the murals, discovered in the 1940s, are well-preserved or restored, and perfectly intelligible. Inside the sprawling Tetitla Palace, no fewer than 120 walls are graced by murals, with Tláloc, jaguars, serpents and eagles among the easiest figures to make out. Some 400m west is the Atetelco Palace, whose vivid jaguar or coyote murals – a mixture of originals and restorations – are in the Patio Blanco (White Patio) in the northwest corner. Processions of these creatures in shades of red perhaps symbolize warrior orders.

About 100m further northeast are Zacuala and Yayahuala, a pair of enormous walled compounds that probably served as communal living quarters. Separated by the original alleyways, the two structures are made up of numerous rooms and patios, but few entranceways – perhaps to discourage unwanted visits from in-laws.

Sleeping

The town of San Juan Teotihuacán, 2km west of the archaeological zone, has a few good overnight options.

Villas Arqueológica Teotihuacán (☎ 956-09-09, in Mexico City ☎ 55-5836-9020; www.teotihuacaninfo.com;

r/tr/f $64/79/125; (P X Q) There's no beach, but this well-located, 39-room Club Med–run complex, at the south end of the road that encircles the ancient city, has cozy yet charming rooms, with all the standard midrange features. Amenities include a heated outdoor pool, a lit tennis court, a playground, a billiards table, nice gardens and a refined French-Mexican bar-restaurant. A couple of one-bedroom suites have in-room whirlpools. Rates rise $10 Thursday to Saturday night.

Hotel Posada Sol y Luna (☎ 956-23-68/71; www .posadasolyluna.com in Spanish; Cantú 13; s/d/ste from $27/35/45; P) This superior-value option has attentive staff (some English-speaking), an optional $5 breakfast and 16 spacious, carpeted rooms – including a few Jacuzzi suites – each with on-demand hot water, individual heating and cable TV. Reserve ahead or risk finding only the most expensive rooms available. It's at the east end of town, en route to the pyramids.

Hotel Posada Teotihuacán (☎ 956-04-60; Canteroco 5; s/d/q $17/22/28; P) Two blocks south and east of the central plaza, this friendly, ever-expanding place offers clean rooms with TVs – follow the signs for Posada Sol y Luna from the plaza or the ruins.

Teotihuacán Trailer Park (☎ 956-03-13; teotipark@prodigy.net.mx; López Mateos 17; camp sites per person $5, full RV hookups per vehicle $10; P) Pitch a tent in town, on a peaceful street behind the 16th-century Jesuit church, a couple of blocks southwest of San Juan's plaza and bus depot. The large, grassy park has 24/7 hot showers, and the helpful English-speaking owners have plans for a new dormitory.

Hotel & Motel Quinto Sol (☎ 956-18-81; www .hotelquintosol.com.mx in Spanish; Av Hidalgo 26; s/d/ste from $55/66/74; P 🖳 🖭) This modern, if sterile, tour bus favorite, near the toll-road exit, has 34 well-equipped rooms and four Jacuzzi suites with most every mod con, including coffeemakers, phones and cable TV. The breakfast buffet ($7.50) will keep you going all day, and there's live music and the occasional 'pre-Hispanic show' in the bar Thursday to Saturday nights.

Behind the hotel, an anonymous drive-in **motel** (r/ste $28/37) has modern rooms with king-size beds above private garages. The suites have Jacuzzis and you can use the hotel's pool. On Friday and Saturday nights, rooms rent in six-hour blocks, giving you some idea of the target clientele. Not quite seedy, but clean and discreet.

Eating

Except for the rank of dusty numbered eateries along the ring road on the southeast side of the archaeological site, meals in the vicinity of the ruins are pricey. The most convenient place is on the 3rd floor of the old museum building near Gate 1, where the busy Bar-Cafetería Las Pirámides has panoramic views of La Ciudadela.

Restaurant La Gruta (☎ 956-01-04/27; 75m east of Gate 5; mains $5-15; ⏲ 11am-7pm) Gourmet meals have been served in this huge, cool cavern – originally a Toltec granary – for at least a century; Porfirio Díaz (Mexican president for 33 years prior to the Mexican Revolution) ate here in 1906. Service is attentive and the authentic food is quite good. On Saturday and Sunday afternoons, there's live music and folkloric ballet (cover $2). All major credit cards accepted.

Pirámide Charlie's (☎ 956-04-72; ring road btwn Gates 1 & 2; mains $5-20; ⏲ 11am-7pm) Welcome amigos! This super-kooky tourist trap translates its menu into four languages and serves a bold hotchpotch of 'cheese chowder,' 'cilantro chicken and breast breaded with green sauce,' 'no traslation

---

THE AUTHOR'S CHOICE

Restaurant Techinanco (☎ 958-23-06; ring road opposite Pirámide de la Luna; mains $3-7; ⏲ 10am-5:30pm) This friendly home-cooking eatery concentrates its energy in the kitchen, rather than touting for customers, and thus is the best bet for miles around. It serves a limited menu of authentic homemade *moles* (chili-based sauces made with a variety of herbs and spices) and other flavorful traditional dishes. The *mole de huitlacoche* (corn mushroom *mole*, freshest in August and September), *caldo de hongos* (mushroom soup) and *huarache con carne asada* (grilled beef sandwich) are all delectable. Ask ebullient owner, Emma (nicknamed Maya), about her curative massage (from $30); call 24 hours in advance to arrange a *temazcal* (indigenous Mexican steam bath) for up to 15 people (around $200).

AROUND MEXICO CITY

molcajete beef & chicken,' 'moo…cheese and chile steak,' 'spaguetti sailor shrimps' and 'calories: frozzen lime pie.' Stop by for a few laughs over a 'margarita de tuna'?!?

Getting There & Away

During daylight hours, Autobuses México–San Juan Teotihuacán runs buses from Mexico City's Terminal Norte to the ruins ($2.50, one hour), every 15 minutes from 7am to 6pm. The ticket office is at the terminal's north end. Make sure your bus is headed for 'Los Pirámides,' not the nearby town of San Juan Teotihuacán.

Buses arrive and depart from near Gate 1, also making stops at Gates 2 and 3. Return buses are more frequent after 1pm. The last bus back to Mexico City leaves around 6:30pm; some terminate at Indios Verdes metro station, but most continue to Terminal Norte.

Getting Around

To reach the pyramids from San Juan Teotihuacán, take a taxi ($1.50) or any combi ($0.40) labeled 'San Martín' departing from Av Hidalgo, beside the central plaza. Combis returning to San Juan stop at Gates 1, 2 and 3.

PACHUCA

☎ 771 / pop 320,000 / elevation 2425m

Brightly painted houses blanketing the arid hillsides around untouristed Pachuca, capital of Hidalgo state, are evidence of the region's rapid growth in recent times. The town itself, 90km northeast of Mexico City, is friendly for its largish size, has several noteworthy sights, and is a good jumping-off point for forays north and east into the dramatic Sierra Madre Oriental. Pachuca's mines have slowed considerably, due to water-logged shafts and low silver prices, but hints of former mining wealth abound.

Silver was unearthed nearby as early as 1534, and Real del Monte's mines still produce quite a respectable amount of ore, even today. Pachuca was also the gateway through which *fútbol* (soccer) entered Mexico, introduced in the 19th century by miners from Cornwall, England. The savory Cornish meat pies known as *pastes* (pasties) remain a favorite staple form of sustenance.

Orientation

The 40m-high Reloj Monumental (Clock Tower), built between 1904 and 1910 to commemorate the independence centennial, overshadows the north end of Pachuca's Plaza de la Independencia (*zócalo*), which is flanked by Av Matamoros on the east and Av Allende on the west. Guerrero runs parallel to Av Allende, 100m to the west. Some 700m to the south, Guerrero and Av Matamoros converge at the modern Plaza Juárez.

Information

Banks ATMs are numerous around Plaza de la Independencia.

Café Internet (cnr Hidalgo & Leandro Valle; per hr $1; ☻ 10am-10pm) Two blocks east of the southeast corner of the *zócalo*.

State Tourism Authority (☎ 800-718-26-00; turismo. hidalgo.gob.mx in Spanish; Av Revolución 1300)

Tourist Module (☎ 715-14-11; www.pachuca.gob.mx; Plaza de la Independencia; ☻ 10am-6pm) Inside the clock tower; may have free city maps.

Sights

CENTRO CULTURAL DE HIDALGO

The Ex-Convento de San Francisco is now the **Hidalgo Cultural Center** (cnr Hidalgo & Arista; admission free; ☻ 10am-6pm Tue-Sun), which embodies two museums and a gallery, a theater, a library and several lovely plazas. It's two blocks east and four long blocks south of Plaza Juárez. Upstairs, the **Museo Nacional de la Fotografía** (admission free; ☻ 10am-6pm Tue-Sun) displays early imaging technology and selections from the 1.5 million photos in the INAH archives. The images – some by Europeans and Americans, many more by pioneer Mexican photojournalist Agustín Victor Casasola – provide fascinating glimpses of Mexico from 1873 to the present.

MUSEO DE MINERÍA

Two blocks south and half a block east of the *zócalo*, Pachuca's **mining museum** (Mina 110; admission $1.50; ☻ 10am-2pm & 3-6pm Wed-Sun) provides a good overview of the industry that shaped the region. Headlamps, miner's shrines and old mining maps are on display, and photos depict conditions in the shafts from the early years to the present. There's a 20-minute English-language video program and engaging ex-miners give tours hourly in Spanish.

LOOKOUT POINTS
For jaw-dropping vistas, catch a 'Mirador' bus ($0.40) from Plaza de la Constitución a few blocks northeast of the *zócalo* to the **mirador** on the road to Real del Monte. Even better panoramas can be seen from north of town, at the **Cristo Rey monument** on Cerro de Santa Apolonia.

Tours
Trolley tours (Tranvía Turístico; ☎ 718-71-20; per person $3.75) depart hourly from the plaza's west side from Wednesday to Sunday. Guided 4½hr trips to Real de Monte leave at noon on Saturday and Sunday.

Sleeping
Hotel Emily (☎ 715-08-28, 800-501-63-39; www.hotelemily.com.mx; Plaza Independencia; s/d/ste $41/50/63; P ✕ ▯) On the southern side of the *zócalo*, the recently upgraded Hotel Emily has free wi-fi Internet, cable TV, and large, comfortable rooms – some facing a back patio, others with balconies overlooking the busy plaza.

Hotel Ciro's (☎ 715-40-83; www.hotelciros.com in Spanish; Plaza Independencia 110; s/d $36/39; P) Run by the same family as the Emily, it is on the opposite side of the plaza, where similar but older rooms go for a bit less.

Hotel de los Baños (☎ 713-07-00/01; Av Matamoros 205; s/d $22/27; P) The Baños has a restaurant with cheap set meals and a handsome enclosed courtyard. The 56 rooms vary in size and quality, but all have cable TV, phones and clean bathrooms. Parking is an extra $2.75. It's a block southeast of the *zócalo*.

Hotel Noriega (☎ 715-15-55; Av Matamoros 305; s/d $20/25; P) This colonial-style option, a block south of Los Baños, has a leafy courtyard, stately staircase and decent restaurant. Have a look at a few rooms before checking in – some are tiny and claustrophobic, while others are large and airy. TV is $2 extra, or you can watch *lucha libre* (wrestling) in the courtyard with the staff.

Gran Hotel Independencia (☎ 715-05-15; Plaza Independencia 116; s/d $37/39; P) This hotel occupies an imposing building on the west side of the *zócalo*, but is much less impressive inside, with big, but austere, rooms around an interior courtyard. Rates rise a couple of dollars on Friday and Saturday night.

Eating
Pasties are available all over town, including at the bus station. Baked in pizza ovens, they contain a variety of fillings probably never imagined by Cornish miners, such as beans, pineapple and rice pudding. Especially popular is Pastes Kiko's, near Gran Hotel Independencia. Pick up *tamales* (steamed cornmeal dough), *tortas* (sandwiches) and take-out chicken at the **Trico grocery store** (Av Matamoros 205), next door to Hotel de Los Baños.

Mi Antiguo Café (Matamoros 115; mains $3-6) This charming, modern seven-table café, on the east side of the *zócalo*, serves crepes, good espresso, breakfasts and a decent four-course set lunch ($5).

Mina La Blanca Restaurant Bar (☎ 715-19-64; Av Matamoros 201; mains $5-10) Facing the southwest corner of the *zócalo*, this atmospheric place serves 'authentic' pasties, stuffed with potatoes, leeks, parsley, ground beef and black pepper. Decorated with stained-glass panels of mining scenes, the cavernous dining hall also offers set breakfasts, salads and seasonal regional *antojitos* ('little Mexican whims' – tortilla-based snacks like tacos and *gorditas*) such as *gusanos de maguey* (maguey worms).

Getting There & Away
There's daily 1st-class bus service to/from Mexico City (Terminal Norte, $6, 1¼ hours, every 15 minutes); Poza Rica ($10, five hours, seven daily); and Tampico ($25, eight hours, two daily).

Three scenic roads (Hwys 85, 105 and 130/132D) climb north into the forested, often foggy, Sierra Madre Oriental. Buses serving nearby destinations, nearly all of which are 2nd-class, go frequently to and from Tula, Tulancingo and Tamazunchale (say *that* three times, fast to tie your tongue– *horale!*), while several also go daily to and from Querétaro and Huejutla de Reyes.

Getting Around
Pachuca's bus station is 5km southwest of downtown, on the road to Mexico City. Green-striped *colectivos* marked 'Centro' pass by Plaza de la Constitución ($0.40), a short walk from the *zócalo*; in the reverse direction, hop on along Av Allende. The trip by taxi costs around $2.

HIGHWAY 105

Serpentine Hwy 105 wends its way north past several worthwhile stops en route to Huejutla de Reyes (p671), Tampico (p661) and the Gulf coast.

Parque Nacional El Chico

☎ 771

Nine kilometers north of Pachuca, a road branches northwest (left) off Hwy 105 and snakes 20km to the picturesque old mining town of **Mineral del Chico**, inside El Chico National Park – a reserve since 1898. The small park has pine forests with lovely day hikes, spectacular rock formations (popular with climbers), waterfalls, rivers and an abundance of fresh air, making it a popular weekend retreat. Ask at the hotels or park's visitor centers for details about possible guided outdoor activities.

SLEEPING & EATING

In Mineral del Chico there are many cafés and eateries, both fancy and humble. Near the plaza are a couple of nice hotels that fill up fast on Friday and Saturday, but are empty during the week.

Hospedaje El Chico (☎ 715-47-41; Corona del Rosal 1; s/d $25/43) Ring the bell to the right of Casa Brisa to access these 10 squeaky clean and comfortable rooms, each holding up to four people. Rates here are per bed, not per person.

La Cabaña del Lobo/Gotcha! (☎ 791-913-61-93, in Mexico City 55-5776-2222; s/d $35/45; **P**) Five kilometers from Hwy 105 (on the road toward Mineral del Chico), a right turn leads 1km down a bumpy dirt road to the 'Wolf's Cabin', in a remote valley ringed by pine-covered mountains. The hotel features a row of cozy rooms with hot water and clean bathrooms, overlooking a restaurant and campfire-playground area. Some of the rooms have fireplaces – a nice touch since it gets chilly up here.

Hotel Posada del Amanacer (☎ 715-01-90; www .hotelesecoturisticos.com.mx in Spanish; Morelos 3; r Sun-Thu $46, Fri & Sat $73) This 11-room adobe complex has spacious rooms on two levels beside a lovely patio. Since there are no phones or TVs, it's a peaceful getaway. Fireplaces cost $10 extra and full Mexican meal plans are available for $30 per person; children under 12 stay free. Low-season rates are 25% less and all rates include guided hiking and cycling tours. Massage, spa treatments and adventure activities like rock climbing are offered for an extra fee.

The same chain also runs the fancier 26-room **Hotel El Paraíso** (☎ 715-56-54; www .hotelesecoturisticos.com.mx in Spanish; r Sun-Thu from $69, Fri & Sat from $119; **P**), down the hill from Posada del Amanacer; and the more traditional, 15-room **Hotel Real del Monte** (☎ 797-12-02/03; www .hotelesecoturisticos.com.mx in Spanish; r Sun-Thu from $46, Fri & Sat from $70; **P**) in Mineral del Monte.

There are several **campgrounds** (per car/camp-site $2.50, plus per person $1) with rudimentary facilities en route to Mineral del Chico between Km 7 and Km 10, plus a **trailer park** (full RV hookups per vehicle $10) just inside the park's main entrance gate.

GETTING THERE & AWAY

From Pachuca, *colectivos* ($1) depart frequently from Galeana (west of the market, and through an arch labeled 'Barrio el Arbolito'). From Pachuca's bus station, Flecha Roja (☎ 01-800-507-5500; www.estrella blanca.com.mx) runs regular 2nd-class buses to Mineral del Chico ($1.25, one hour, three daily).

Mineral del Monte

Two kilometers past the turnoff for Parque Nacional El Chico, **Real del Monte** (also known as Mineral del Monte) was the scene of a miners' strike in 1776 – commemorated as the first strike in the Americas. Most of the town was settled in the 19th century, after a British company commandeered the mines. Cornish-style cottages line many of the steep cobbled streets.

Mine tours (☎ 771-715-27-63; adult/child $13.50/9) descend 250m into some abandoned workings on Saturday and Sunday. The field opposite the Dolores mine was the site of Mexico's first soccer match; there's an English cemetery nearby.

Second-class buses depart Pachuca's terminal for Mineral del Monte ($0.80, 30 minutes) every 30 minutes.

Huasca & Atotonilco el Grande

Eleven kilometers north of Mineral del Monte, a well-signed turnoff leads east to **Huasca** (or Huasca de Ocampo), which has a 17th-century church, *balnearios* (bathing places) and a variety of local crafts. A few old haciendas have been converted into attractive hotels. Nearby is a canyon with a waterfall and imposing basalt columns.

At **Atotonilco el Grande**, 34km northeast of Pachuca, there's a 16th-century fortress-monastery and a *balneario* beside some hot springs. Thursday is market day.

Soon after, Hwy 105 descends to scenic **Metzquititlán**, in the fertile Río Tulancingo Valley. For coverage of places of interest further along this little-explored but rewarding route, see p671 and p671.

HIGHWAY 85

An original part of the fabled Pan-American Highway, this dual carriageway heads northwest of Pachuca for 37km to Actopan. Beyond Ixmiquilpan, 75km northwest of Pachuca, the route becomes an undivided two-lane road, eventually reaching Tamazunchale and Ciudad Valles in the verdant Huasteca region (p666).

Actopan

☎ 772 / pop 26,000 / elevation 2400m

Founded in 1548, Actopan's well-preserved **Convento de San Nicolás de Tolentino** is one of the finest of Hidalgo's 16th-century fortress-monasteries. Its church has a lovely plateresque facade and a single tower showing Moorish influence. Mexico's best 16th-century frescoes are in the cloister: hermits in the Sala De Profundis, and saints, monks and a meeting between Fray Martín de Acevedo (an important early monk at Actopan) and two indigenous nobles (Juan Inica Actopa and Pedro Ixcuincuitlapilco) are shown on the stairs. To the left of the church, a vaulted *capilla abierta* (open-air chapel) is also adorned with frescoes.

The more things change, the more they stay the same: Wednesday has been market day in Actopan for at least 400 years. Local handicrafts are sold, alongside regional dishes like succulent barbecued lamb, wrapped in maguey leaves and then pit roasted. Several nearby water parks allow camping and provide secure RV parking.

PAI (Pachuca-Actopan-Ixmiquilpan) runs 1st-class buses from Pachuca to Actopan ($2.25, 20 minutes, every 15 minutes).

Ixmiquilpan

☎ 759 / pop 35,000 / elevation 1700m

The arid Mezquital Valley is a modern-day ethnic enclave; around half of Mexico's

several hundred thousand Otomí people, descendants of ancient inhabitants, call the state of Hidalgo home. Ixmiquilpan is the former Otomí capital and the valley's modern day commercial hub.

The valley is well known for Mexico's finest *ayates*, cloths woven from *ixtle* (maguey fiber). Traditional Otomí women's dress is a *quechquémitl*, an embroidered shoulder cape worn over an embroidered cloth blouse.

The hustle-bustle of the Monday market is the best place to find Otomí crafts, such as miniature musical instruments made of juniper wood with shell or pearl inlay, colorful drawstring bags, or embroidered textiles. The rest of the week, you can find such items in the nearby community of **El Nith** (east of Ixmiquilpan). Combis depart from Jesús del Rosal near the market; taxis ask around $3 for the trip.

Ixmiquilpan's **monastery** was founded by Augustinians in the mid-16th century. The church's nave, crowned by a huge Gothic vault, is unusual for its band of frescoes depicting indigenous warriors in combat. These depict a clash between soldiers in Aztec military garb and scantily clad warriors wielding obsidian swords. Experts speculate the murals were painted by Mexica (Aztec) artists as propaganda against Chichimec invaders.

PAI runs 1st-class buses from Pachuca to Ixmiquilpan ($4, 1½ hours, every 15 minutes).

HIGHWAY 130 & 132D

Two-lane Hwy 130 goes 46km east of Pachuca to the city of **Tulancingo** (pop 103,000; elevation 2140m), briefly the Toltec capital before Tula. There's a Toltec pyramid at the foot of a cliff at **Huapalcalco**, 3km north. Thursday is market day.

The Otomí village of **Tenango de Doria** is 40km northeast of Tulancingo, by sometimes impassable roads. Skillful residents fashion cotton fabric, colorfully embroidered with plants and animals. **Huehuetla**, 50km northeast of Tulancingo, is one of the few communities of the tiny Tepehua indigenous group, who embroider floral and geometric patterns on their *enredos* (wraparound skirts) and *quechquémitls*.

Beyond Tulancingo, Hwy 130 descends toward the market towns of Acaxochitlán and Huauchinango (p674). Alternatively, the new super-fast toll road, Hwy 132, zips northeast and will eventually reach all the way to Poza Rica (p674).

EAST OF MEXICO CITY

Toll road 150D speeds east to Puebla, across a high and dry region studded with towering volcanic peaks, including Popocatépetl, Iztaccíhuatl and La Malinche. The rugged Sierra Nevada offers scope for anything from invigorating alpine strolls to demanding technical climbs – moody Popocatépetl, however, remains off-limits due to volcanic activity. Just north of the highway, the tiny state of Tlaxcala boasts a charming capital and relics from a rich pre-Hispanic and colonial history.

Puebla is one of Mexico's best preserved colonial cities, a pivot of its history and a lively modern metropolis with much to taste and experience. Nevertheless, the state of Puebla is predominantly rural, and is home to approximately half a million indigenous people. This enduring presence lends Puebla a rich handicraft legacy, with products including pottery, carved onyx and fine handwoven and embroidered textiles.

From Puebla, you can continue east on Hwy 150D, past Mexico's tallest peak, Pico de Orizaba (p703), and descend from the verdant highlands to the beach and hedonistic port of Veracruz (p687). Alternatively, you can swing north on Hwy 140 toward the remote Sierra Norte de Puebla, wend your way to the tropical Gulf coast via Veracruz' cultured capital of Xalapa (p682), or follow scenic Hwy 135D southeast across the rugged Sierra Madre Oriental to the spectacular state and city of Oaxaca (p717).

POPOCATÉPETL & IZTACCÍHUATL

Mexico's second- and third-highest peaks – Popocatépetl (po-po-ka-*teh*-pet-l; Náhuatl for 'Smoking Mountain,' also known as Don Goyo; 5452m) and Iztaccíhuatl (iss-ta-*see*-wat-l; 5220m) – form the eastern rim of the Valle de México, which is 43km west of Puebla and 72km southeast of Mexico City. While the craterless Iztaccíhuatl is dormant, 'Popo,' as the volcano is affec-

tionately known, has been signaling the arrival of the new Pope recently via plumes of gas and steam, including a December 2005 explosion that catapulted ash 5km into the sky. Between 1994 and 2001, Popo's major bursts of activity triggered evacuations of 16 villages and warnings to the 30 million people who live within striking distance of the volatile crater.

Mexico's **National Disaster Prevention Center** (Cenapred; 24hr hotline ☎ 55-5205-1036; www.cena pred.unam.mx in Spanish) monitors volcanic activity via variations in gas emissions and seismic intensity. Though almost entirely in Spanish, the website posts daily webcam photo captures and updates on conditions in English.

Historically, Popo has been relatively tranquil, with most activity occurring in the cooler winter months when ice expands and cracks the solidified lava around the crater rim. It's had 20 eruptive periods during the past 600 years, but none has caused a major loss of life or property. The last really big blast occurred over a thousand years ago, but volcanologists estimate that there's a 10% chance of one in the near future. At the time of writing, a crack team of scientists were continuing to observe Popo's increasingly predictable outbursts with great interest. The good news is that fetching Iztaccíhuatl (White Woman), 20km north of Popo from summit to summit, remains open to climbers.

Amecameca
☎ 597 / pop 32,000 / elevation 2480m
The sleepy town of Amecameca, 60km east of Mexico City by road, is the key staging

---

POPO & IZTA: AN EXPLOSIVE DUO

Legend has it that Popo was a warrior who fell in love with Izta, the emperor's daughter. As the story goes, Izta died of grief while Popo was away at war. Upon his return, he created the two mountains, laid her body on one and stood holding her funeral torch on the other. With some imagination, Izta does resemble a woman lying on her back. From the Mexico City side, you can, when the sky is clear, make out four peaks from left to right: La Cabeza (Head), El Pecho (Breast), Las Rodillas (Knees) and Los Pies (Feet).

point for an Izta climb. With volcanoes and 16th-century churches as a backdrop, it makes an appealing destination in itself. A lively market convenes daily next to the church and there are ATMs and Internet cafés around the plaza. The best way to get around town is by bicycle-taxi ($0.40).

The 450,000-sq-meter **Parque Nacional Sacromonte**, 90m above Amecameca to the west, protects an important pilgrimage site built over a cave that was the retreat of the Dominican friar Martín de Valencia in the early 16th century. It makes a delightful acclimatization walk, with awesome views of the town spread out beneath the volcanoes. From the southwest side of the plaza, head out through the arch and walk down Av Fray Martín for two blocks until you see the stairs ascending the hill on your right. After hailing Mary, follow the stations of the cross uphill to the sanctuary.

Most climbers sack out at the unassuming **Hotel San Carlos** (☎ 978-07-46; Plaza de la Constitución 10; s/d $9/18), facing the plaza's southwest corner, where the rooms are clean and spartan but comfortable, and cost $5 more with TV.

From Mexico City's Terminal de Autobuses de Pasajeros de Oriente (TAPO), Volcanes and Sur run 2nd-class buses to/from Amecameca ($2, 1½ hours, every 15 minutes). To reach the plaza from Amecameca's bus station, turn right and walk two blocks.

Hiking

Izta's highest peak is **El Pecho** (5286m). All routes require a night on the mountain and between the staging point at La Joya and Las Rodillas, there's a shelter hut that can be used during an ascent of El Pecho. On average, it takes at least five hours to reach the hut from La Joya, another six hours from the hut to El Pecho, and six hours back to the base.

Before making the ascent, all climbers should contact the **Parque National Iztaccíhuatl-Popocatépetl** (☎ /fax 597-978-38-29/30; http://iztapopo.conanp.gob.mx; Plaza de la Constitución 9B; ☺ 9am-6pm Mon-Fri, 9am-3pm Sat), on the southeast side of Amecameca's *zócalo*. To arrange permission, call the office or submit a form that's available online. Technically, you do not need permission to climb Izta, but if you're starting from Amecameca, you'll need the permit to

pass the military checkpoint near Paso de Cortés, in the saddle approximately halfway between Popo and Izta. Alternatively, you can depart from the village of San Rafael, 8km north of Amecameca, a longer and more rigorous climb.

Near Paso de Cortés there are plenty of lower-altitude trails through pine forests and grassy meadows, some offering breathtaking glimpses of nearby peaks. Trails begin at the La Joya parking lot, 2km beyond the Altzomoni Lodge (4000m). Again, you need to arrange a permit, which may be available on Sundays at the checkpoint when the in-town office is closed. *Colectivos* departing from Amecameca's plaza for Paso de Cortés cost around $3. From the national park office, taxis will take groups to La Joya (40 minutes) for a negotiable $20 to $30.

Basic shelter is available at the **Altzomoni Lodge** (beds per person $2), by a microwave station roughly halfway between Paso de Cortés and La Joya. Request the keys at Paso de Cortés before hiking up, and bring bedding, warm clothes and drinking water. All visitors must pay the $1 per day parkentrance fee in advance at the national park office in Amecameca, or on Sunday at Paso Cortés.

CLIMATE & CONDITIONS
It can be windy and well below freezing any time of year on Izta's upper slopes, and it's nearly always below freezing near the summit at night. Ice and snow are fixtures here; the average snow line is 4200m. The ideal months for ascents are November to February, when there is hard snowpack for crampons. The rainy season (April to October) brings with it the threat of whiteouts, thunderstorms and avalanches.

Anyone can be affected by altitude problems, including life-threatening altitude sickness. Even Paso de Cortés (3650m), the turnoff for Izta, is at a level where you should know the symptoms (see p1011).

GUIDES
Iztaccíhuatl should *only* be attempted by experienced climbers. Because of hidden crevices on the ice-covered upper slopes, a guide is advisable. Besides the following reader recommendations, the national park office may have other suggestions.

Amecameca-based **José Luis Ariza** (☎ 597-978-13-35), a rescue-squad member who has scaled peaks throughout Latin America, leads climbers up Izta year-round. He charges $100 for one person and $50 for each additional person (transportation and equipment rental cost extra).

Mexico City–based **Mario Andrade** (☎ 55-1038-4008, 55-1826-2146; mountainup@hotmail.com), an authorized, English-speaking guide, has led many Izta ascents. His Izta fee is $350 for one person, less per person for groups. The cost includes round-trip transportation from Mexico City, lodging, mountain meals and rope usage.

TEXCOCO & AROUND
☎ 595 / pop 116,000 / elevation 2778m

Some of Diego Rivera's finest murals are at the agriculture school of the **Universidad Autónoma de Chapingo** just outside Texcoco, 67km northeast of Mexico City via Hwy 136. The former hacienda is now part of the university's administration building. Inside the **Capilla Riveriana** (admission $3; ⏰ 10am-3pm Mon-Fri, 10am-5pm Sat & Sun), sensual murals intertwine images of the Earth's fertility cycles and the Mexican struggle for agrarian reform. One of the 24 panels depicts buried martyrs of reform symbolically fertilizing the land, and thus the future. From Mexico City, take a local bus from the Zaragoza metro station or a direct bus from TAPO to downtown Texcoco, then flag down a 'Chapingo' combi.

Also worth visiting is the **Parque Nacional Molino de Flores Nezahualcóyotl**, 3km east of Texcoco. Established in 1585 as the region's first wheat mill, the Molino later served as a pulque hacienda before being expropriated by the government in 1937. Today, many of the buildings are in ruins, and works of local artists are exhibited in the *tinacal*, where pulque was processed. To get here, hop on a 'Molino de Flores' combi from downtown Texcoco.

About 5km further east, the little known but interesting archaeological site, **Baños de Nezahualcóyotl**, contains the remains of temples, a palace, fountains, baths and spring-fed aqueducts built by the Texcocan poet-king, Nezahualcóyotl. He was perhaps the only mesoamerican ruler to observe a type of monotheistic religion, worshiping an abstract god with masculine and feminine qualities. When the pollution isn't too bad, the hilltop site has a view as far as Xochimilco. Take a 'Tlamincas' combi from downtown Texcoco, or just outside the national park's entrance, and get off at the sign pointing to the site; it's an easy 1km stroll to the summit.

TLAXCALA
☎ 246 / pop 85,000 / elevation 2250m

About 32km north of Puebla and 120km east of Mexico City, Tlaxcala (tlas-*ca*-la) is a sleepy colonial town, and the capital of Mexico's smallest state. It's an easy day trip or relaxing overnight visit from either city. The unhurried pace is most appreciated by visitors specifically looking for an untouristy small-town experience.

History
In the last centuries before the Spanish conquest, numerous small warrior kingdoms *(señoríos)* arose in and around Tlaxcala. Some of them formed a loose federation that remained independent of the Aztec empire as it spread from the Valle de México in the 15th century. The most important kingdom seems to have been Tizatlán, now on the northeast edge of Tlaxcala city.

When the Spanish arrived in 1519, the Tlaxcalans fought fiercely at first, but ultimately became Cortés' staunchest allies against the Aztecs (with the exception of one chief, Xicoténcatl the Younger, who tried to rouse his people against the Spanish and is now a Mexican hero). The Spanish rewarded the Tlaxcalans with privileges and used them to help pacify and settle Chichimec areas to the north. In 1527, Tlaxcala became the seat of the first bishopric in Nueva España, but a plague in the 1540s decimated the population and the town has played only a supporting role ever since.

Orientation
Two large central plazas converge at the corner of Independencia and Muñoz. The northern one, surrounded by colonial buildings, is the *zócalo*, called Plaza de la Constitución. The other, Plaza Xicoténcatl, hosts a crafts market on Saturday and Sunday.

Information
Several banks around the *zócalo* exchange dollars and have ATMs.

Cruz Roja (Red Cross; ☎ 462-09-20)
Farmacia Cristo Rey (Lardizabal 15; ☻ 24hr)
Hospital General (☎ 462-00-30/34-00)
Internet Millenium (Av Morelos 6; per hr $1; ☻ closed Sun) Fast connections, but small monitors.
Police (☎ 464-52-56/57)
Post Office (cnr Avs Muñoz & Díaz)
State Tourist Office (☎ 465-09-60 ext 1519, 800-509-65-57; www.tlaxcala.gob.mx in Spanish; cnr Avs Juárez & Lardizabal; ☻ 9am-6pm Mon-Fri, 10am-6pm Sat & Sun) English-speaking staff run $2 guided bus and trolley tours of the city and most outlying areas on Friday, Saturday and Sunday, with departures from Hotel Posada San Francisco starting at 11am.

Sights
PLAZA DE LA CONSTITUCIÓN
Tlaxcala's shady, spacious *zócalo* is one of Mexico's most fetching. The 16th-century **Palacio Municipal**, a former grain storehouse, and the **Palacio de Gobierno** occupy most of its north side. Inside the latter there are vivid murals of Tlaxcala's history by Desiderio Hernández Xochitiotzin. The 16th-century building on the plaza's northwest side is the **Palacio de Justicia**, the former Capilla Real de Indios, built for the use of indigenous nobles. The handsome mortar bas-reliefs around its doorway include the seal of Castilla y León and a two-headed eagle, symbol of the Hapsburg monarchs who ruled Spain in the 16th and 17th centuries.

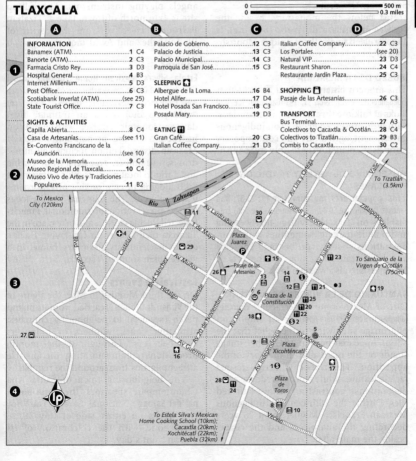

TLAXCALA

0 — 500 m
0 — 0.3 miles

Off the northwest corner of the *zócalo* is the pretty-in-pink tile, brick and stucco **Parroquia de San José**. As elsewhere in the Centro Histórico, bilingual signs explain the significance of the church and its many fountains.

EX-CONVENTO FRANCISCANO DE LA ASUNCIÓN

This former monastery is up along a shaded path from the southeast corner of Plaza Xicohténcatl. Built between 1537 and 1540, it was one of Mexico's earliest monasteries, and its church – the city's cathedral – has a beautiful Moorish-style wooden ceiling. Next door is the **Museo Regional de Tlaxcala** (☎ 462-02-62; admission $3; ⌚ 10am-5pm Tue-Sun), with a large collection of religious paintings and a few pre-Columbian artifacts.

Just below the monastery, beside the 19th-century Plaza de Toros (bullring), is a **capilla abierta** with three unique Moorish-style arches.

MUSEO DE LA MEMORIA

This modern **history museum** (☎ 466-07-91; Av Independencia 3; admission $1; ⌚ 10am-5pm Tue-Sun) looks at folklore through a multimedia lens, with well-presented exhibits on indigenous government, agriculture and contemporary festivals. Explanations are only in Spanish.

MUSEO VIVO DE ARTES Y TRADICIONES POPULARES

This **popular arts museum** (☎ 462-23-37; Blvd Sánchez 1; admission $0.80; ⌚ 10am-6pm Tue-Sun) has displays on Tlaxcalan village life, weaving and pulque-making, sometimes with demonstrations – sorry, no tasting! The café and handicrafts next door at the **Casa de Artesanías** are also worth a look.

SANTUARIO DE LA VIRGEN DE OCOTLÁN

One of Mexico's most spectacular **churches** (admission free; ⌚ 9am-6pm) is an important pilgrimage site owing to the belief that the Virgin appeared here in 1541 – her image stands on the main altar in memory of the apparition. The classic Churrigueresque facade features white stucco 'wedding cake' decorations, contrasting with plain red tiles. During the 18th century, indigenous Mexican Francisco Miguel spent 25 years decorating the altarpieces and the chapel beside the main altar.

Visible from most of town, the hilltop church is 1km northeast of the *zócalo*. Walk north on Av Juárez for three blocks, then turn right onto Zitlalpopocatl. Alternatively, catch a 'Ocotlán' *colectivo* from near the corner of Avs Guerrero and Independencia.

TIZATLÁN

All that's left of Xicoténcatl's palace is preserved under a humble shelter: two altars with some faded frescoes of the gods Tezcatlipoca (Smoking Mirror), Tlahuizcalpantecuhtli (Morning Star) and Mictlantecuhtli (Underworld). Next to the **ruins** (☎ 412-41-69; admission free; ⌚ 10am-5pm Tue-Sun), Templo San Esteban has a 16th-century Franciscan *capilla abierta* and frescoes of angels playing instruments. The hilltop site is 4km north of town; take a 'Tizatlán Parroquia' *colectivo* from the corner of Blvd Sánchez and Av Muñoz.

Courses

Estela Silva's Mexican Home Cooking School (☎ /fax 468-09-78; mexicanhomecooking@yahoo.com, www.mexicanhomecooking.com; courses $1080, non-student guests $500) offers an intimate five-day gastronomic course, with hands-on instruction in the preparation of classic Mexican dishes. Tuition includes all meals, drinks, live music, transfers from Puebla and a trip to local markets, plus six nights of B&B lodging in comfortable private rooms with fireplaces. The bilingual lessons focus on the preservation of traditional French-inflected Puebla cuisine, and take place in the Talavera-tiled kitchen of fun-loving Estela's quaint hacienda-style country home, in a village 10km south of Tlaxcala.

Festivals & Events

On the third Monday in May, the figure of the **Virgen de Ocotlán** is carried from its hilltop perch (see left) to neighboring churches, attracting equal numbers of onlookers and believers. Throughout the month, processions commemorating the miracle attract pilgrims from around the republic.

The neighboring town of Santa Ana Chiautempan sponsors the **Feria Nacional del Sarape** (National Sarape Fair) for two weeks on either side of July 26, to correspond with the celebration of its patron saint's day.

Tlaxcala's Teatro Xicohténcatl hosts dancers from around the country every September during the vibrant month-long **Nacional de Danza Folklórica** celebration.

Tlaxcala's **feria** (fair) draws participants from around the state between late October and mid-November, when *charrería* (horsemanship), bullfights and other rodeo-inspired pageantry take center stage. The festival kicks off with a *pamplonada* (running of the bulls) and includes Día de Muertos activities.

Sleeping

Hotel Posada San Francisco (☎ 462-60-22; www .posadasanfrancisco.com; Plaza de la Constitución 17; s/d/ ste $80/90/130; P ⊒ ⊠) Occupying a restored colonial mansion called Casa de Piedra (after its locally quarried facade), the full-service San Francisco is the classiest place in town. Besides 68 heated rooms with bathtubs, there's a bar with live music in the evening, and a good restaurant serving traditional Tlaxcalan cuisine, tennis courts, a cozy library, wi-fi Internet and an inviting outdoor pool. Enter the parking lot around the back of Av Guerrero.

Hotel Alifer (☎ 462-56-78; www.hotelalifer.com in Spanish; Av Morelos 11; s/d $32/46; P) The cheery hillside Alifer has firm beds, ample carpeted rooms, plenty of hot water and cable TV. Parking is free, there's a good restaurant for breakfast and bath towels are arranged like swans. Avoid bottom-floor rooms that face echo-chamber hallways and lack exterior windows.

Albergue de la Loma (☎ 462-04-24; Av Guerrero 58; s/d $21/26; P) This modernish if bland hotel, perched atop 61 steep steps, has an unsecured parking lot down below and big carpeted rooms with tiled bathrooms, some with good city views.

Posada Mary (☎ 462-96-55; Xicohténcatl 19; s/d with bathroom $9.50/16; P) Within stumbling distance of the *zócalo*, Tlaxcala's cheapest option is a basic, but clean and friendly, concrete crash pad down a well-lit street.

Eating

Under the arcades on the east side of the *zócalo*, several bar-restaurants compete for attention with regional and national Mexican meals, plus live music on Friday and Saturday nights. **Restaurante Jardín Plaza** (☎ 462-48-91; mains $4-8) is the best of the bunch,

with an espresso machine and good regional specialties like anise-flavored *tamales*. **Gran Café** (☎ 462-18-54) and **Los Portales** (☎ 462-54-19) both offer popular dinner buffets ($8) featuring a wide variety of traditional dishes. Students fuel up on top-peso espresso, proper teas, sandwiches and decadent desserts at the slick **Italian Coffee Company** (drinks & snacks $1-4) before heading upstairs to the thumping disco. There's another branch a few doors down the street.

The health-focused café **Natural VIP** (Av Juárez 12; mains $2-5; Ⓥ) pumps out fresh juices and sandwiches. For scrumptious tacos and *rica carne asada* (savory grilled steak) try **Restaurant Sharon** (Av Guerrero 14; 3 tacos $2.50; ☾ 1-7pm Sun-Fri), an unpretentious *mama-y-papa* hole-in-the-wall.

Shopping

Embroidered *huipiles* (sleeveless tunics) from Santa Ana Chiautempan, carved canes from Tizatlán, and amaranth candies from San Miguel del Milagro are sold along the pedestrian-only Pasaje de las Artesanías alley, which forms an arc northeast of the Muñoz/Allende intersection.

Getting There & Away

Tlaxcala's sprawling **bus terminal** (☎ 462-03-62) is just under 1km west of the central plazas. For Mexico City's TAPO terminal, ATAH runs 1st-class 'expresso' buses ($7.50, two hours) every 20 minutes. Frequent 2nd-class Flecha Azul buses rumble to Puebla ($1).

Getting Around

Most *colectivos* ($0.30) passing the bus terminal are heading into town. To reach the terminal from the center, catch a blue-and-white *colectivo* on the east side of Blvd Sánchez.

CACAXTLA & XOCHITÉCATL

The impressive hilltop ruins at Cacaxtla (ca-*casht*-la) feature well-preserved, vividly colored frescoes depicting, among many other scenes, nearly life-size jaguar and eagle warriors engaged in battle. The ruins were discovered in 1975, when men from the nearby village of San Miguel del Milagro, looking for a reputedly valuable cache of relics, dug a tunnel and uncovered a mural.

The much older ruins at Xochitécatl (so-chi-*teh*-catl), 2km away and reachable from

Cacaxtla on foot, include an exceptionally wide pyramid as well as a circular pyramid. A German archaeologist led the first systematic exploration of the site in 1969, but it wasn't until 1994 that the pyramids were opened to the public. The two archaeological sites, 20km southwest of Tlaxcala and 32km northwest of Puebla, are among Mexico's most intriguing.

Both sites can be toured without a guide, but the bilingual explanatory signs tend to be either sketchy or overly technical. A good, if rushed, alternative is the guided Sunday tour conducted by the Tlaxcala state tourist office (p207). From Thursday to Sunday, it may be possible to hire a guide at the sites.

History

Cacaxtla was the capital of a group of Olmeca-Xicallanca, or Putún Maya (see boxed text, p801), who arrived in central Mexico as early as AD 450. After the decline of Cholula (which they probably helped bring about) in around AD 600, they became the chief power in southern Tlaxcala and the Puebla valley. Cacaxtla peaked from AD 650 to 950, before being abandoned by AD 1000 in the face of possibly Chichimec newcomers.

Two kilometers west of Cacaxtla, atop a higher hill, the ruins of Xochitécatl predate Christ by a millennium. Just who first occupied the spot is a matter of dispute, but experts agree that whereas Cacaxtla primarily served as living quarters for the ruling class, Xochitécatl was chiefly used for gory ceremonies honoring Quecholli, the fertility god. That isn't to say Cacaxtla didn't hold similar ceremonies; the discovery of the skeletal remains of hundreds of mutilated children attest to Cacaxtla's bloody past.

Cacaxtla

From the parking lot opposite the **site entrance** (☎ 246-416-00-00; admission $3.50; ☒ 10am-5pm Tue-Sun), it's a 200m walk to the ticket office, museum and restaurant.

From the ticket office, it's another 600m downhill to the main attraction – a natural platform, 200m long and 25m high, called the **Gran Basamento** (Great Base), now sheltered under an expansive metal roof. Here stood Cacaxtla's main civic and religious buildings, and the residences of

its ruling priestly classes. At the top of the entry stairs is the **Plaza Norte**. From here, the path winds clockwise around the ruins until you reach the **murals**.

Archaeologists have yet to determine the muralists' identity; many of the symbols are clearly from the Mexican highlands, and yet a Mayan influence from southeastern Mexico appears in all of them. The combined appearance of Mayan style and Mexican-highlands' symbols in a mural is unique to Cacaxtla, and the subject of much speculation.

Before reaching the first mural you come to a small patio, whose main feature is an **altar** fronted by a small square pit, in which numerous human remains were discovered. Just beyond the altar, you'll find the **Templo de Venus**, which contains two anthropomorphic figures in blue – a man and a woman – wearing jaguar-skin skirts. The temple's name is attributed to the appearance of numerous half-stars around the female figure, which are associated with the Earth's sister planet, Venus.

On the opposite side of the path toward the Plaza Norte, **Templo Rojo** contains four murals, only one of which is currently visible. Its vivid imagery is dominated by a row of corn and cacao crops, whose husks contain human heads.

Facing the north side of Plaza Norte is the long **Mural de la Batalla** (Battle Mural), dating from before AD 700. It shows two warrior groups, one wearing jaguar skins and the other bird feathers, engaged in ferocious battle. The Olmeca-Xicallanca (the jaguar-warriors with round shields) are clearly repelling invading Huastecs (the bird-warriors with jade ornaments and deformed skulls).

Beyond the Mural de la Batalla, turn left and climb the steps to see the second major **mural group**, behind a fence to your right. The two main murals (c AD 750) show a figure in a jaguar costume and a black-painted figure in a bird costume (believed to be the Olmeca-Xicallanca priest-governor) standing atop a plumed serpent.

Xochitécatl

From the parking lot at the **site entrance** (☎ 246-462-41-69; admission $3.50; ☒ 10am-5pm Tue-Sun), follow a path to the circular **Pirámide de la Espiral**. Because of its outline and the materials used, archaeologists believe the pyramid was built between 1000 and 800 BC. Its form and hilltop location suggest it may have been used as an astronomical observation post or as a temple to Ehecatl, the wind god. From here, the path passes three other pyramids.

Basamento de los Volcanes, all that remains of the first pyramid, is the base of the Pirámide de los Volcanoes, and it's made of materials from two periods. Cut square stones were placed over the original stones, visible in some areas, and then stuccoed over. In an interesting twist, the colored stones used to build Tlaxcala's municipal palace appear to have come from this site.

The **Pirámide de la Serpiente** gets its name from a large piece of carved stone with a snake head at one end. Its most impressive feature is the huge pot found at its center, carved from a single boulder, which was hauled from another region. Researchers surmise it was used to hold water.

Experts speculate that rituals honoring the fertility god were held at the **Pirámide de las Flores**, due to the discovery of several sculptures and the remains of 30 sacrificed infants. Near the pyramid's base – Latin America's fourth widest – is a pool carved from a massive rock, where the infants were believed to have been washed before being killed.

Getting There & Away

Cacaxtla is 1.5km uphill from a back road between San Martín Texmelucan (near Hwy 150D) and Hwy 119, the secondary road between Tlaxcala and Puebla. If driving from Tlaxcala, turn west off Hwy 119 just south of town and watch for a sign pointing towards Cacaxtla, 1.5km west of the village of Nativitas.

By public transport from Tlaxcala, catch a 'San Miguel del Milagro' *colectivo* near the northwest corner of Av 20 de Noviembre and Av Lardizabal, which will drop you off about 500m from Cacaxtla. Alternatively, a 'Nativitas–Texoloc–Tlaxcala' *colectivo*, which departs from the same corner, goes to the town of Nativitas, 3km east of Cacaxtla; from there, catch a 'Zona Arqueológica' *colectivo* directly to the site. Flecha Azul buses go direct from Puebla's Central de Autobuses de Puebla (CAPU) terminal to Nativitas. Between Cacaxtla and Xochitécatl, take a taxi ($3), or walk the 2km.

LA MALINCHE

The long, sweeping slopes of this dormant 4460m volcano, named after Cortés' interpreter and indigenous lover, dominate the skyline northeast of Puebla.

The main route to the summit is via Hwy 136; turn southwest at the 'Centro Vacacional Malintzi' sign. Before you reach the center, you must register at the entrance of the **Parque Nacional La Malintzi**. La Malinche, Mexico's fifth tallest peak, is snowcapped only a few weeks each year, typically in May.

Run by the Mexican Social Security Institute, the **Centro Vacacional IMSS Malintzi** (☎ 246-462-40-98, in Mexico City 55-5627-6900, 800-001-09-00; up to 6 people $40-46, up to 9 people $65-75; **P** 🛁) has a handful of rustic cabins at a frosty 3333m. This family-oriented resort has woodsy grounds and fine views of the peak. The recently remodeled cabins are basic but include TVs, fireplaces, hot water and kitchens with refrigerators. It gets crowded from Friday to Sunday but is quiet midweek. Those not staying overnight can park here for $3; camping is also a possibility.

Beyond the vacation center, the road becomes impassable by car. Then it's 1km by footpath to a ridge, from where it's an arduous five-hour round-trip hike to the top. Hikers should take precautions against altitude sickness (see p1011).

Buses to the Centro Vacacional ($1, 8am, noon and 4pm daily) make the 26km run from downtown Apizaco (served by frequent buses from Puebla and Tlaxcala), departing from the corner of Av Hidalgo and Aquiles Serdán.

HUAMANTLA

☎ 247 / pop 46,000 / elevation 2500m

Quaint Huamantla is a national historic monument dating from around 1534. Besides La Malinche looming over the town, the most notable attractions are the 16th-century **Ex-Convento de San Francisco** and the 17th-century baroque **Parroquia de San Luis Obispo de Tolosa**. Opposite the church, the **Museo de Títere** (National Puppet Museum; ☎ 472-10-33; Parque Juárez 15; 🕙 10am-2pm & 4-7pm Tue-Sat, 10am-3pm Sun; 🛁) is a fun stop for the young and young at heart, displaying dolls and marionettes from all around the world.

During August, Huamantla sees a few sleepless nights during its annual **feria**. The day before the Feast of the Assumption (August 15), locals blanket the town's streets with beautiful carpets crafted from flowers and colored sawdust. The Saturday following this event, there's a Pamplonaesque running of the bulls, similar to that in Spain – but more dangerous since the uncastrated males charge from two directions!

During the *feria*, rates double and rooms are reserved well in advance. If everything is reserved, you can always find a room in Puebla or Tlaxcala.

Hotel Mesón del Portal (☎ 472-26-26; Parque Juárez 9; s/d $17/22) faces the central plaza. This basic place is Huamantla's best in-town option, with clean, cheery rooms and cable TV.

Hotel Cuamanco (☎ 472-22-09/11; Carretera 136, Km 146.5; s/d $19/23; P) is a couple of kilometers east of town. Surprisingly tasteful, this three-star motel has a bar-restaurant, satellite TV and 20 clean, sizable rooms, some of which have balconies affording glimpses of La Malinche.

Oro and Suriano run frequent buses from Puebla. ATAH runs frequent buses from Tlaxcala.

PUEBLA
☎ 222 / pop 1.9 million / elevation 2160m

Few major Mexican cities preserve the Spanish imprint as faithfully as the City of Angels. There are 70 churches and, in the historic center alone, more than a thousand colonial buildings – many adorned with the *azulejos* (painted ceramic tiles) for which the city is justly famous.

Strongly Catholic, conservative and criollo, Puebla's citizens *(poblanos)* maintained Spanish affinities longer than most Mexicans. In the 19th century their patriotism was regarded as suspect, and today Puebla's Spanish-descended families have a reputation for snobbishness. Nevertheless, it's a lively city with much to taste, see and explore.

A great deal of conservation and restoration has taken place in the Centro Histórico in the wake of the 1999 earthquake, which measured 6.9 on the Richter scale. Inscribed by Unesco as a World Heritage Site in 1987, Puebla's city center has a prosperous modern dimension, including its share of fancy boutiques and fast-food outlets. Nearby, Cerro de Guadalupe is a peaceful retreat

from the hubbub, as well as the site of a clutch of museums and a celebrated Mexican military victory.

History
Founded by Spanish settlers in 1531, as Ciudad de los Ángeles, with the aim of surpassing the nearby pre-Hispanic religious center of Cholula, the city became known as Puebla de los Ángeles ('La Angelópolis') eight years later, and quickly grew into an important Catholic center. Fine pottery had long been crafted from the local clay, and after the colonists introduced new materials and techniques, Puebla pottery evolved as both an art and an industry. By the late 18th century, the city emerged an important glass and textile producer. With 50,000 residents by 1811, Puebla remained Mexico's second-biggest city until Guadalajara overtook it in the late 19th century.

Puebla's French invaders expected a warm reception in 1862, but General Ignacio de Zaragoza fortified the Cerro de Guadalupe, and on May 5, his 2000 men defeated a frontal attack by 6000 French, many handicapped by diarrhea. This rare Mexican military success is the excuse for annual (and increasingly drunken and corporate-sponsored) national celebrations, and hundreds of streets named Cinco de Mayo. Few seem to remember that the following year the reinforced French took Puebla and occupied the city until 1867. *Touché!*

Orientation
The heart of the city is the spacious and shady *zócalo*, with the cathedral flanking its south side. Most attractions, hotels and restaurants are within a few blocks of here. The upscale area of smart shops and refined restaurants along Av Juárez, 2km west of the *zócalo*, is called the Zona Esmeralda.

The crucial intersection for the naming system of Puebla's grid plan is the northwest corner of the *zócalo*. From here, Av 5 de Mayo heads more or less north, Av 16 de Septiembre shoots south, Av Reforma beelines west, and Av Palafox y Mendoza goes east. Other north–south streets are suffixed Norte (Nte) or Sur, and west–east streets Poniente (Pte) or Oriente (Ote). These are designated with rising sequences of either odd or even numbers as you move away from the center.

Information

EMERGENCY
Ambulance, Fire & Police (☎ 066)
Cruz Roja (Red Cross; ☎ 235-86-31, 235-82-44)
Fire (☎ 245-73-92/77-99)
Tourist Police (☎ 800-903-92-00)

INTERNET ACCESS
Places to get online are abundant; most charge around $1 per hour.
Cyberbyte (Map p216; Calle 2 Sur 505B) Cheap international VoIP (Voice over Internet Protocol) phone calls.
Red Cup (Map p216; cnr Av 2 Ote & Calle 4 Nte) Next to Holiday Inn. Hip and fast. Good coffee.
Vité Cafe (Map p216; Calle 8 Sur 204) Off Plaza Parián, with VoIP phone calls.

MEDICAL SERVICES
Hospital UPAEP (Hospital Universidad Popular Autónoma del Estado de Puebla; Map p216; ☎ 229-81-00/02/03; Av 5 Pte 715)

MONEY
Banks on the *zócalo* and Av Reforma have ATMs and change cash and travelers checks.

POST & TELEPHONE
Main Post Office & Telecomm (Map p216; Av 16 de Septiembre)

TOURIST INFORMATION
Municipal Tourist Office (Map p216; ☎ 404-50-08/47; www.puebla.gob.mx in Spanish; Portal Hidalgo 14; ☽ 9am-8pm Mon-Fri, 9am-5pm Sat, 9am-3pm Sun) English- and French-speaking office.
State Tourist Office (Sectur; Map p216; ☎ 246-20-44; www.turismopuebla.com.mx in Spanish; Av 5 Ote 3; ☽ 8am-8pm Mon-Sat, 8am-2pm Sun) Faces the cathedral yard. English-speaking staff.

Sights
ZÓCALO
Puebla's central plaza (Map p216) was originally a marketplace where bullfights, theater and hangings transpired, before it assumed its current arboretum-like appearance in 1854. The surrounding arcades date from the 16th century. The plaza fills with an entertaining mix of clowns, balloon hawkers and ambulatory snack vendors on Sunday evenings. If you're in town on Thursday around 6pm, don't miss the patriotic changing of the flag ceremony, animated by the city's marching band.

CATEDRAL
Puebla's impressive **cathedral** (Map p216; cnr Avs 3 Ote & 16 de Septiembre; ☽ 7am-12:30pm, 4:15-7.30pm), whose image appears on Mexico's 500-peso bill, occupies the entire block south of the *zócalo*. It blends early baroque and severe Herreresque-renaissance styles. Construction began in 1550 but most of it took place under Bishop Juan de Palafox in the 1640s. At 69m the towers are Mexico's highest. Inside, bilingual signs explain the main features; free introductory talks (in Spanish only) are given inside the north entrance as demand dictates.

MUSEO AMPARO
This superb private **museum** (Map p216; ☎ 246-38-50; www.museoamparo.com; Calle 2 Sur 708; adult/student $2.25/1.50, free Mon; ☽ 10am-6pm Wed-Mon), housed in two linked 16th- and 17th-colonial buildings, is a must-see. The first has eight rooms loaded with pre-Hispanic artifacts, which are well displayed, with explanations (in English and Spanish) of their production techniques, regional and historical context, and anthropological significance. Crossing to the second building, you enter a series of rooms rich with the finest colonial art and furnishings from all over Mexico.

An audiovisual system (headset rental $1) delivers details about the pre-Hispanic area in Spanish, English, French, German and Japanese. Two-hour guided group tours are offered in English ($17) by request, and free two-hour tours are given at noon on Sunday. The complex also houses a library, good bookstore, café with set lunches ($4) and an upmarket Talavera gift shop.

MUSEO POBLANO DE ARTE VIRREINAL
Inaugurated in 1999, this top-notch **museum** (Map p216; ☎ 246-58-58; Calle 4 Nte 203; admission $1.50, incl Museo Casa del Alfeñique, free Tue; ☽ 10am-5pm Tue-Sun) is housed in the 16th-century Hospital de San Pedro. One gallery displays temporary exhibits on the art of the viceregal period (16th to 19th centuries); another has temporary exhibits of contemporary Mexican art; and the last houses a fascinating permanent exhibit on the hospital's history, including a fine model of the building. The excellent library and bookstore have many art and architecture books in English.

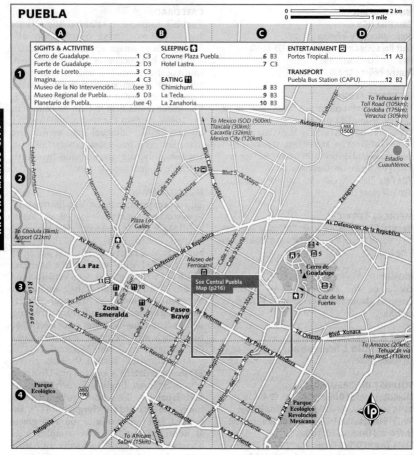

PUEBLA

SIGHTS & ACTIVITIES
Cerro de Guadalupe......................1 C3
Fuerte de Guadalupe....................2 D3
Fuerte de Loreto..........................3 C3
Imagina......................................4 C3
Museo de la No Intervención..........(see 3)
Museo Regional de Puebla.............5 D3
Planetario de Puebla....................(see 4)

SLEEPING
Crowne Plaza Puebla....................6 B3
Hotel Lastra................................7 C3

EATING
Chimichurri.................................8 B3
La Tecla.....................................9 B3
La Zanahoria..............................10 B3

ENTERTAINMENT
Portos Tropical............................11 A3

TRANSPORT
Puebla Bus Station (CAPU).............12 B2

CASA DE LA CULTURA

Occupying the entire block facing the south side of the cathedral, the former bishop's palace is a classic 17th-century brick-and-tile edifice, which now houses government offices, including the **Casa de la Cultura** (Map p216; ☎ 232-12-27; Av 5 Ote 5; ☻ 10am-8pm) and the state tourist office (p213). Inside are art galleries, a bookstore and cinema, and a congenial café out back in the courtyard.

Upstairs is the **Biblioteca Palafoxiana** (☎ 246-56-13; www.bpm.gob.mx; adult/child $1/0.50, Tue free; ☻ 10am-5pm Tue-Fri, 10am-4pm Sat & Sun), housing thousands of rare books, including the 1493 *Nuremberg Chronicle*, with more than 2000 engravings.

IGLESIA DE LA COMPAÑÍA

This **Jesuit church** (Map p216; cnr Av Palafox y Mendoza & Calle 4 Sur) with a 1767 Churrigueresque facade is also called Espíritu Santo. Beneath the altar is a tomb said to be that of a 17th-century Asian princess, who was sold into slavery in Mexico and later freed. She was supposedly responsible for the colorful *china poblana* costume – a shawl, frilled blouse, embroidered skirt, and gold and silver adornments. This costume became a kind of 'peasant chic' in the 19th century. But *china* (*chee*-nah) also meant 'maidservant,' and the style may have evolved from Spanish peasant costumes.

Next door is the 16th-century **Edificio Carolino**, now the main building of Universidad Autónoma de Puebla.

TEATRO PRINCIPAL & BARRIO DEL ARTISTA

Puebla's main **theater** (Map p216; ☎ 232-60-85; Av 8 Ote at Calle 6 Nte; ⊙ 10am-5pm) dates from 1759, making it one of the oldest in the Americas – sort of. It went up in flames in 1902 and was rebuilt in the 1930s. You can peek inside when it's not in use. Nearby is the **Barrio del Artista**, which takes up a whole block between Av 4 Norte and Av 6 Norte on Calle 6 Norte, where you can visit artists in their studios fronting the shaded pedestrian street, and buy their work – mostly classical oil paintings, with a few modernist flairs. On Saturday and Sunday, there's often folkloric dancing and live music in the plaza adjacent to Café-Galeria Amparo.

TEMPLO DE SAN FRANCISCO

The north doorway of the **San Francisco church** (Map p216; Av 14 Ote, east of Blvd 5 de Mayo; ⊙ 8am-8pm) is a good example of 16th-century plateresque; the tower and fine brick-and-tile facade were added in the 18th century. In the north chapel is the mummified body of San Sebastián de Aparicio, a Spaniard who emigrated to Mexico in 1533, and planned many of Mexico's roads before becoming a monk. Since he's now the patron saint of drivers, merchants and farm workers, his canonized corpse attracts a dutiful stream of thankful worshipers.

MUSEO DE LA REVOLUCIÓN

This pockmarked 19th-century **house** (Map p216; ☎ 242-10-76; Av 6 Ote 206; admission $1, free Tue; ⊙ 10am-4:30pm Tue-Sun) was the scene of the first battle of the 1910 revolution. Betrayed only two days before a planned uprising against Porfirio Díaz' dictatorship, the Serdán family (Aquiles, Máximo, Carmen and Natalia) and 17 others fought 500 soldiers until only Aquiles, their leader, and Carmen were left alive. Aquiles, hidden under the floorboards, might have survived if the damp hadn't provoked a cough that gave him away. Both were subsequently killed. The house retains its bullet holes and some revolutionary memorabilia, including a room dedicated to female insurgents. Tours are available in English, German and Spanish.

TEMPLO DE SANTO DOMINGO

Santo Domingo (Map p216; cnr Av 5 de Mayo & Av 4 Pte; ⊙ closed 1-4pm Mon-Sat) is a fine Dominican church, and its **Capilla del Rosario** (Rosary Chapel), south of the main altar, is a real gem. Built between 1650 and 1690, it has a sumptuous baroque proliferation of gilded plaster and carved stone, with angels and cherubim seemingly materializing from behind every leaf. See if you can spot the heavenly orchestra.

EX-CONVENTO DE SANTA ROSA & MUSEO DE ARTE POPULAR POBLANO

This 17th-century **ex-convent** (Map p216; ☎ 232-77-92; enter at Av 14 Pte 305; admission $1, free Tue; ⊙ 10am-5pm Tue-Sun) houses an extensive collection of Puebla state handicrafts. You must join one of the hourly guided tours to see the fine displays of traditional indigenous costumes, pottery, onyx, glass and metal work. Tours are in Spanish, but there are occasionally English-speaking guides available. *Mole poblano* is said to have originated in the nunnery's kitchen (see p90).

MUSEO CASA DEL ALFEÑIQUE

This colonial **house** (Map p216; ☎ 232-42-96; Av 4 Ote 416; admission $1.50, incl Museo Poblano de Arte Virreinal, free Tue; ⊙ 10am-5pm Tue-Sun) is an outstanding example of the over-the-top 18th-century decorative style, *alfeñique*, characterized by elaborate stucco ornamentation and named after a candy made from sugar and egg whites. The museum exhibits colonial Puebla household paraphernalia, such as paintings, furniture and China Poblana gear.

MUSEO BELLO

This **house** (Map p216; ☎ 232-94-75; Av 3 Pte 302; admission $2, free Tue; ⊙ 10am-5pm Tue-Sun) is filled with the diverse art and crafts collection of a 19th-century industrialist family. There is exquisite French, English, Japanese and Chinese porcelain, and a large collection of *Puebla Talavera*. Optional tours are available in English and Spanish for no charge.

CASA DE LOS MUÑECOS

The tiles on the facade of the 'House of Puppets' (Map p216), just off the northeast corner of the *zócalo*, caricature the city fathers who took the house's owner to court because his home was taller than theirs. Inside are the **Museo Universitario** (☎ 246-28-99; Calle 2 Nte 2; admission $0.50; ⊙ 10am-5pm Tue-Sun), which recounts the story of education in Puebla.

AROUND MEXICO CITY

CENTRAL PUEBLA

| 0 | 500 m |
| 0 | 0.3 miles |

CERRO DE GUADALUPE
This rambling hilltop park (Map p214), 2km northeast of the *zócalo*, contains a trio of museums and the historic forts of Loreto and Guadalupe. Fresh air and good views of the volcanoes Popo and Izta add to the appeal. Catch any 'Plaza de Loreto' bus ($0.40) heading north on Blvd 5 de Mayo.

At the west end of the hilltop, **Fuerte de Loreto** was one of the key Mexican defense points on May 5, 1862, during the victory over the invading French. Today, it houses **Museo de la No Intervención** (admission $3; ☺ 10am-5pm Tue-Sun), which has displays of uniforms and documents relating to the French occupation of Mexico.

A short walk east of the fort, beyond the domed auditorium, are the **Museo Regional de Puebla** (☎ 235-97-20; admission $3; ☺ 10am-5pm Tue-Sun), which traces human history in the state; the **Imagina** (☎ 235-34-19; adult/child $3.25/2.75; ☺ 9am-1pm & 2-6pm Mon-Fri, 10am-2pm & 3-7pm Sat & Sun; ♿) interactive science museum; and the pyramid-shaped **Planetario de Puebla** (☎ 235-20-99; admission $2.75; ♿), which screens IMAX movies (at 10am, noon, 4pm and 6pm, daily except Monday) and hosts evening light shows. At the far end of the hilltop is **Fuerte de Guadalupe** (admission $3; ☺ 10am-5pm Tue-Sun), which played a starring role in the 1862 battle.

Tours
El Ángel trolley (☎ 273-83-00, 800-712-22-84; adult/child $3.25/2.35) loops around Puebla's Centro Histórico hourly between 10am and 6pm every day, with separate trips to Cholula (adult/child $7/4) departing daily from the southeast corner of the *zócalo* around 11am. The ticket kiosk is opposite the cathedral on the south side of the plaza. Other full-day bus trips depart for Teotihuacán ($23), and Mexico City's Chapultepec Zoo ($16) via Acolman every Sunday at 7am.

Ninety-minute double-decker **Turibus** tours (adult/child $8.50/4, Sat, Sun & holidays $9/4.50) of Puebla's Centro Histórico depart every half hour daily between 9am and 7pm from in front of the State Tourist Office (p213). Multilingual commentary (in English, French, German, Italian, Japanese and Spanish) is delivered via audio headphones. Buy tickets on board; you can hop on and off all day long.

Festivals & Events
Starting in late April, the monthlong **Feria de Puebla** honors the state's cultural and economic achievements with cultural and music events. In early June, the **Festival del Mole Poblano** fetes culinary triumphs at several of the city's storied eateries. Leaving no culinary stone unturned, the city's savvy restaurateurs promote a **Festival del Chile en Nogada** in late August. Puebla has also jumped on the **Día de Muertos** bandwagon, with a four-day citywide cultural program starting in late October.

Sleeping
Despite Puebla's abundance of hotels (designated by the illuminated red 'H' signs over their entrances), the most budget-conscious options fill up fast. Midrange and top-end options tend to offer much better value. It's worth searching online for special last-minute, seasonal and weekend package rates.

Most colonial buildings have two types of rooms, interior and exterior, with the former often lacking windows and the latter often having balconies exposed to a noisy street. All places mentioned here that lack on-site parking have an arrangement with nearby garages.

BUDGET
Bottom-end choices, most of which are several stories tall and lack elevators, are concentrated west of the cathedral.

Hotel San Miguel (Map p216; ☎ 242-48-60/61; Av 3 Pte 721; s/d $24/30; ℗) The almost-retro San Miguel – give it a couple of years of deferred maintenance – has 65 plain, clean, respectably sized rooms, with TVs and an early 1970s dorm feel. The three-bed rooms with balconies overlooking the street are the best deal.

Hostal Santo Domingo (Map p216; ☎ 232-16-71; Av 4 Pte 312; dm $7, interior/exterior r $18/23; ℗ ✗) Short of a flophouse, beds in the mixed-sex dorms here are the cheapest in town. Private rooms are spare but clean, with high beamed ceilings and TV available for an extra $2.25. Exterior rooms have balconies. The large but underutilized interior courtyard exudes potential as a common meeting space.

Hotel Reforma 2000 (Map p216; ☎ 242-33-63; Av 4 Pte 916; s/d $18/23; ℗) Set an alarm or you may never wake up at this basic colonial option overlooking a busy intersection. The ample, carpeted rooms have cable TV and surround a fountain-filled interior courtyard, but many are dungeon-like and lack windows. Upstairs, exterior rooms with balconies are less dark but noisy. Seek solace downstairs with locals in the popular bar or restaurant.

Hotel Teresita (Map p216; ☎ 232-70-72; Av 3 Pte 309; s/d $17/20; **P**) Basic but central, this musty old dame has 46 carpeted rooms with unyielding mattresses and, thankfully, cable TV. Avoid the tiny windowless interior single chamber of horrors; it's worth plunking down a bit more ($27) for two beds or windows facing the street. Parking is an extra $6.

Gran Hotel San Agustín (Map p216; ☎ 232-50-89, 800-849-27-93; Av 3 Pte 531; s/d incl breakfast $18/26; **P**) Hardly grand, the San Agustín has a cheap restaurant with $2 set meals and 74 small, rather stuffy rooms, brightened only by unreliable fluorescent lighting and cable TV. Top-floor rooms are best and you save $3.75 if you forgo TV.

MIDRANGE

Hotel Colonial (Map p216; ☎ 246-41-99, 800-013-00-00; www.colonial.com.mx; Calle 4 Sur 105; s/d/tr/q $50/59/66/73; 🖳) Originally part of a 17th-century Jesuit monastery, this long-running hotel near the university retains a hearty colonial atmosphere despite extensive renovations. Most rooms are big and tiled, many have bathtubs, and all have direct-dial phones and cable TV. Half of the 67 rooms are modern and half have colonial decor. If you don't mind street noise, exterior rooms with balconies are best. Naysayers complain of thin pillows, hard twin beds and noisy rooms. There's a coin-op laundry and sunset views on the roof – good excuses for a ride in the antique French elevator. Reserve ahead as it's often full of tour groups and foreign exchange students. The popular courtyard restaurant often features live music.

Hotel Royalty (Map p216; ☎ 242-47-40, 800-638-99-99; www.hotelr.com; Portal Hidalgo 8; s/d $50/67, ste $85-93; **P**) On the *zócalo*'s north side, with an entrance off the arcade, the 45-room Royalty is a friendly, well-kept colonial-style place. The carpeted rooms are colorful and comfortable, and all are blessed with

satellite TV. The junior suites with cathedral views merit the extra pesos. Downstairs, the sidewalk restaurant-café is perfect for people-watching.

Hostal Santa María (Map p216; ☎ 298-82-40; www.hostalsantamaria.com.mx in Spanish; Av 3 Ote 603; s/d/ste incl breakfast $40/50/55; **P**) There are only five rooms at this restored 18th-century home, making it an intimate choice in a good central location. All the well-kept rooms have phones, cable TV, tiled bathrooms and rustic furnishings, and all but one have balconies facing the street below (very loud on Friday and Saturday nights). Rates include parking and continental breakfast.

Hotel Puebla Plaza (Map p216; ☎ 246-31-75, 800-926-2703; www.hotelpueblaplaza.com.mx in Spanish; Av 5 Pte 111; s/d $35/46; **P** 🖳) Just west of the cathedral, this attractively remodeled hotel offers 48 rooms with wood-beamed ceilings, colonial-style furniture, tiled baths, phones, wi-fi Internet and cable TV. There's no elevator, but there's only three floors. Some rooms are larger than others; the biggest shortcoming is the lack of daylight and exterior windows. If you're not prepared to splash out elsewhere to overlook the plaza, the central location is tough to beat.

Hotel Imperial (Map p216; ☎ 242-49-80, 800-874-49-80; http://travelbymexico.com/pueb/imperial; Av 4 Ote 212; s/d $33/42; **P** 🖳) The Imperial charges a bit more for comfortable units in the newer 'executive' wing, and tiled, rustically furnished, colonial-style suites on the upper levels. Older rooms range from windowless interior cubbyholes in the noise-prone courtyard, to spacious suites with soaring 20-foot ceilings overlooking the street. All rooms have coffeemakers, phones and purified drinking water. Extras include a free basic breakfast and light evening snack, self-service laundry machines, Internet access (9am to 5pm) and a pool table.

Hotel del Portal (Map p216; ☎/fax 404-62-00, ☎ 800-087-01-07; www.hoteldelportal.com; Av Palafox y Mendoza 205; s/d $45/49, with balcony $54/59; **P**) This outwardly colonial hotel sports a surprisingly modern interior. The 100 good-value rooms are modest, carpeted and 1980s in style, but well appointed. Exterior rooms with small balconies face either the plaza or busy avenue below. Its entrance is half a block east of the *zócalo*.

Hotel Lastra (Map p214; ☎ 235-97-55, 800-713-45-00; www.travelbymexico.com/pueb/lastra; Calz de los

Fuertes 2633; r from $75; (P 🖵 🐾) The business-friendly Lastra, 2km northeast of the center on Cerro de Guadalupe, boasts good views, a peaceful yet accessible location, a well-groomed garden and easy parking. The 51 rooms come in various shapes and sizes, but all are quite comfortable.

Hotel Palace (Map p216; ☎ 232-24-30; hot palace@prodigy.net.mx; Av 2 Ote 13; s/d $40/50; P 🖵) The serviceable, if somewhat optimistically named, Palace caters to business travelers with ramped up wi-fi Internet. The 60 remodeled rooms have cable TV and promo rates often start around $30 for a couple sharing a double bed (ask for a matrimonial bed). Parking costs $4 extra.

Gilfer Hotel (Map p216; ☎ 246-06-11; www .gilferhotel.com.mx; Av 2 Ote 11; s/d/ste $39/47/71; P 🖵) Next door to the Palace, the Gilfer is yet another centrally located, business-focused favorite, offering 92 simple yet comfortable rooms with safes, phones and satellite TV.

TOP END

El Sueño Hotel & Spa (Map p216; ☎ 232-64-23/89, 800-690-84-66; www.elsueno-hotel.com in Spanish; Av 9 Ote 12; s/d $105/115, ste incl breakfast $140-175; P 🐾 🖵) This dreamy minimalist oasis, a block from the Museo Amparo, occupies an 18th-century colonial mansion and blends restored antique details with thoughtful contemporary touches. The 11 suites, with air-con, pay homage to famous female Mexican artists; the best are upstairs, perched above the courtyards calmed by effervescent fountains. All rooms have tall ceilings and are removed from the street, but some have only tiny windows. Mod cons include flat-panel TVs, wi-fi Internet, minibars, plush bath robes and full entertainment systems. Rates include use of the terrace hot tub (with a view of the cathedral) and the spa's steam bath. Even if you're not staying here, check out the indulgent massage packages, intimate La Tentación lounge and Mediterranean restaurant.

Mesón Sacristía de la Compañía (Map p216; ☎ 242-35-54, 800-712-40-28, in USA 800-728-9098; www .mesones-sacristia.com; Calle 6 Sur 304; ste incl full breakfast $150-190; P) This 18th-century retreat, in the heart of the charming Barrio de los Sapos antiques district, blends modern comfort with rustic colonial grandeur. The small but splendid rooms and spacious suites are outfitted with dramatic vintage furnishings (all for sale), such as wooden prison doors complete with skeleton keys. In the charming courtyard, there's an intimate piano bar, Talavera salon and the fine Restaurant Sacristía (p221), which serves aromatic American breakfasts and refined *poblano* cuisine. The service epitomizes the concept of personal and attentive.

Hotel Posada San Pedro (Map p216; ☎ 246-50-77, 800-712-28-08; Av 2 Ote 202; r/ste $89/115; P 🐾 🖵 🐾) This tastefully decorated inn, A block from the *zócalo*, has a restaurant, wi-fi Internet, a full-service business center, and a bar with foosball and a pool table. The heated pool is surrounded by a quiet central garden courtyard. The 80 large rooms are comfortable, if not elegant. Suites have hot tubs, most rooms have balconies and special off-season rates start around $55, including breakfast and parking.

Crowne Plaza Puebla (Map p214; ☎ 248-60-55, 800-226-76-00; www.crowneplazapuebla.com.mx; Blvd Hermanos Serdán 141; r/ste from $182/214; P 🐾 🐾 🖵 🐾) Geared toward business travelers, this full-service luxury chain property is 3km northwest of the center (there's free shuttle service) and convention center, and 30 minutes from the airport. Last renovated in 2000, its 214 spacious and well-appointed, if slightly worn, rooms surround a courtyard pool.

THE AUTHOR'S CHOICE

Mesón Sacristía de Capuchinas (Map p216; ☎ 232-80-88, 800-712-40-28, in USA ☎ 800-728-9098; www.mesones-sacristia.com; Av 9 Ote 16; ste incl full breakfast $150-190; P) Only steps from the Museo Amparo, the stylish renovation of an aristocratic 16th-century residence created this delightful antique-meets-avant-garde boutique B&B hide-away, where the assiduous service makes everyone feel like royalty. In the six spacious interior suites, the decor is elegant, the high-vaulted ceilings are wood beamed, and, since the gracious owners are antique dealers, all the unique furnishings are for sale. The romantic El Santuario Restaurant is open on guests' request and crafts inspired contemporary takes on traditional Mexican cuisine. Breakfast in bed is simply divine.

Eating

Note that many *poblanos* still enjoy their main meal of the day around 2pm. See p90 for insights into Puebla's rich gastronomy.

RESTAURANTS
Around the Zócalo

Half the pleasure of eating in Puebla's Centro Histórico is having a wander around the sidewalk tables facing the *zócalo*, browsing the menus to see what catches your fancy. The other half is grazing at the amazing variety of snacks stalls and street carts in the surrounding blocks.

Restaurant La Princesa (Map p216; ☎ 232-11-95; Av 16 de Septiembre 101; mains $3-8) Facing the *zócalo*, this old-school dining hall – think cordial bow-tied waiters – is packed at midday for its generous five-course set meals ($6); from late afternoon there's a popular taco stand out front.

Restaurant Royalty (Map p216; ☎ 242-47-40; Portal Hidalgo 8; mains $4-15) Hotel Royalty's smart café-eatery has a breakfast buffet and popular outdoor tables where you can watch the world go by for the price of a cappuccino. It also does well-prepared

meat and fish dishes, and seasonal *poblano* treats such as *gusanos de maguey* (maguey worms).

Vittorio's (Map p216; ☎ 232-79-00; Morelos 106; mains $5-15) This Italian-run bar-restaurant is one of the culinary highlights of the *zócalo*. The pizzas are authentic, there's sidewalk seating and live music on Friday and Saturday…and they claim to have Mexico's biggest knife collection.

North of the *zócalo*, two architecturally noteworthy department stores have reliable coffee shops: **Sanborns** (Map p216; Av 2 Ote 6) does mains for between $4.50 and $10, and the newsstand stocks English-language paperback best-sellers, while **VIPS** (Map p216; Calle 2 Nte 8; mains $4-9) has the best English-language magazine selection in town.

Zona Esmeralda

Between Paseo Bravo and the La Paz area, the upscale stretch of Av Juárez is lined with international-style restaurants.

La Tecla (Map p214; ☎ 246-60-66; Av Juárez 1909 near Calle 21 Sur; mains $5-10; ⏰ 1:30pm-2am Mon-Sat, 1:30-6pm Sun) 'The Key' here is an enticing array of *alta cocina mexicana*, served up in a stylish setting. Try the house specialty, *filete tecla*, a tender steak graced with Roquefort cheese and a rich white *huitlacoche* (corn mushroom) sauce.

Chimichurri (Map p214; ☎ 249-15-34; Calle 27 Sur 701; mains $8-20; ⏰ 1:30pm-2am Mon-Sat, 1:30-6pm Sun) This sleek Argentine restaurant features live piano music and caters to a jet-setting crowd with pastas, generous pours of fine wine and big thick 'n' juicy steaks.

POBLANO SPECIALTIES

Food court (Zona Gastronómica; Map p216; upper level, Centro Comercial La Victoria; mains $1-5; ⏰ 9am-9pm) This is a cheap place to sample Puebla specialties like *mole* and *chalupas* (tostada topped with meat, chilies, beans, cheese… whatever!) in a less-chaotic, cleaned-up, market-style *comedor* setting.

La Poblanita (Map p216; Av 5 Pte near Av 16 de Septiembre; mains $1; Ⓥ) At night don't pass on the chance to sample authentic snacks at food stands like this one, where *huitlacoche* and a dozen other authentic *gordita* fillings are served up until 11pm.

Fonda de Santa Clara (Map p216; ☎ 246-19-19; Av 3 Pte 920; mains $6-10) This popular tour-group stop is a reliable if clichéd place to

---

PUEBLA'S SEASONAL TASTE TREATS

When in season, don't miss the following unique *poblano* treats:

- *Escamoles* (March–June) Ant larvae, a delicacy that looks like rice, usually sautéed in butter.

- *Gusanos de maguey* (April–May) Worms that inhabit maguey agave plants, fried in a drunken chili-and-pulque sauce.

- *Huitlacoche* (June–October) Also spelt *cuitlacoche* (kweet-lah-koh-chay). Corn mushrooms are an inky black fungus delicacy with an enchanting, earthy flavor.

- *Chiles en nogada* (July–September) Large green chilies stuffed with dried fruit and meat, covered with a creamy walnut sauce and sprinkled with red pomegranate seeds.

- *Chapulines* (October–November) Grasshoppers purged of digestive matter, then dried, smoked or fried in lime and chili powder.

sample exotic seasonal regional special-ties and typical *comida poblana* (Pueblan food). Standbys include enchiladas and chicken *mole*. Note that the *mixiote* (lamb stew served with guacamole) is cooked in bundles of wax paper, rather than the cus-tomary maguey leaf – indicative of how tradition is falling by the wayside. Service is friendly but brisk, and the menu is bi-lingual. The large Paseo Bravo branch, in a well-restored colonial mansion, is very festive since it attracts locals celebrating special occasions. It also has a gift shop full of Talavera items and typical sweets. There is also a second smaller **branch** (Map p216; ☎ 242-26-59, Av 3 Pte 307).

Fonda La Mexicana (Map p216; ☎ 232-67-47; Av 16 de Septiembre 706; mains $5-9; ◷ 11am-8pm) This unassuming eatery serves a great *mole poblano*, plus a set lunch ($4.50) with a few options and other good-value Puebla and Oaxaca specialties.

La Poblana (Map p216; ☎ 246-09-93; Av 7 Ote 17; mains $1.25-2.50; ◷ 10am-6pm) Around the cor-ner from the Museo Amparo, this cubby-hole whips up (and delivers) a dozen styles of authentic Puebla *cemitas* (a type of sand-wich with meat and cheese).

CHEAP EATS
Tacos Tony (Map p216; ☎ 240-94-31; Av 3 Pte 149; tacos $1-2) Follow your nose – or ring for delivery – for a *torta* or *pan árabe* taco (made with pita bread instead of tortillas), stuffed with seasoned pork sliced from a trio of enor-mous grilling cones.

Café Aroma (Map p216; ☎ 232-60-77; Av 3 Pte 520; drinks $1-2; breakfast $3; ◷ closed Sun) Opposite

---

THE AUTHOR'S CHOICE

Restaurant Sacristía (Map p216; ☎ 242-45-13; Calle 6 Sur 304; mains $6-10; ◷ 8am-11:30pm Mon-Sat, 8am-6pm Sun) This award-winning restaurant, in the delightful colonial patio of the Mesón Sacristía de la Compañía (p219), is an elegant place for a meal of authentic *mole* and creative twists on rich *poblano* cuisine, or a cocktail or coffee and des-sert in the intimate Confesionario bar. Live piano and violin soloists lend a romantic ambience most nights from around 9pm. If you like what you taste, inquire about their small-group cooking classes.

Gran Hotel San Agustín, this is the spot for good coffee, breakfast and light snacks. The top-notch beans are roasted on-site and sold in bulk. The downside? All six tables are usually spoken for.

Super Tortas Puebla (Map p216; ☎ 298-25-05; Av 3 Pte 311; tortas $1.50-4) Tabletops at this cozy nook are set with dishes of marinated chilies, carrots and onions to spice up the basic breakfasts and super sandwiches. Feeling lazy? Call for delivery.

Café Plaza (Map p216; ☎ 237-25-05; Av 3 Pte 145; mains $4-8; ◷ 8am-9pm) Just off the *zócalo*, this modern café serves full meals and fresh-squeezed juices, and brews a mean cup of java from a fresh-ground blend of local beans.

VEGETARIAN
La Zanahoria (Map p216; ☎ 232-48-13; Av 5 Ote 206; set meals $4-6; ✗ Ⓥ) Occupying a spacious interior colonial courtyard – with a juice bar and health food shop up front – the nonsmoking, vegetarian place has generous set meals, a Sunday brunch buffet and a lengthy menu of meatless dishes like *chiles rellenos* (stuffed chilies), *enchiladas suizas* (cheese enchiladas) and *nopales rellenos* (stuffed cactus paddles). Add a salad, soup and drink to any entrée for $1.50. Its sister **Zona Esmeralda branch** (Map p214; ☎ 246-29-90; Av Juárez 2104) has the same good service and reliable menu.

Drinking
By day, students pack the sidewalk tables near the university, along the pedestrian-only block of Av 3 Ote. At night, macho mariachis lurk around Callejón de los Sapos – Calle 6 Sur between Avs 3 and 7 Ote – but they're being crowded out by the bars on nearby Plazuela de los Sapos (Map p216). These rowdy watering holes, especially **La Bella** (Plazuela de los Sapos s/n), are packed most every night of the week. After dark, many of these places become live-music venues. The best bet is to wander around, chat with the doormen, compare two-for-one drink specials and see what gets your booty shaking.

Entertainment
Check the online monthly **A dónde Puebla** (www.adondepuebla.com in Spanish) for the low-down on cultural events. Or pick up the free biweekly *Andanzas* cultural guide at a

AROUND MEXICO CITY

tourist office. The weekly *Los Subterráneos*, a free tabloid supplement to the newspaper *Síntesis*, reviews alternative music in Puebla, Tlaxcala and Hildago.

Librería Cafetería Teorema (Map p216; ☎ 242-10-14; Av Reforma 540; cover $1.50; ☺ 10am-2:30pm & 4:30pm-3am) This bookstore-café fills up in the evenings with a mixed arty-student-professor crowd. There's live music – *trova* (troubadour-style folk music) Monday to Thursday, and rock Friday to Sunday – from 9:30pm to 1am.

La Bella Epoca/La Probadita (Map p216; Av 5 Ote 209; cover $2-3) This eclectic hangout attracts a diverse crowd with live music most nights, ranging from dub, reggae and drum'n'bass to Gothic and heavy metal.

La Batalla (Calle 6 Sur 506) favors karaoke and thumping dance music, while **La Boveda** (Calle 6 Sur 503) and La Serenata, a large hall with a good sound system, feature rock and *rock en español*.

In the Zona Esmeralda, a number of cinemas, trendy discos and *antros* (music bars) line Av Juárez near Blvd Norte; surf www .antrito.com for current listings. Things rarely get going before 10pm, but Friday and Saturday night dancing hot spots include the disco **Portos Tropical** (Map p214; ☎ 284-06-11; Av Juárez 2923; cover $2-4; ☺ 10pm-5am Wed-Sat), for salsa and merengue. Puebla students also frequently go clubbing in Cholula (p227).

Shopping

Several shops along Av 18 Pte, west of Ex-Convento de Santa Mónica (Map p216), sell colorful, hand-painted ceramics, known as Talavera. Designs reveal Asian, Spanish-Arabic and Mexican indigenous influences. Bigger pieces are expensive, delicate and difficult to transport. Smaller tiles fetch up to $5, quality plates upwards of $10. The finest Puebla pottery of all is the white ceramic dishware called *majolica*.

Along Av 6 Ote, east of Av 5 de Mayo (Map p216), a number of shops sell traditional handmade Puebla sweets, such as *camotes* (candied sweet potato sticks) and *jamoncillos* (bars of pumpkin seed paste). Stay away if you're allergic to bees!

Antique shops dominate Callejón de los Sapos (Map p216), around the corner of Av 5 Ote and Calle 6 Sur. Most shops open from 10am to 7pm. On Sunday the Plazuela

> **THE AUTHOR'S CHOICE**
>
> **El Convento de las Carolinas** (Map p216; ☎ 242-76-53; Av 3 Ote 407; cover $1-2) Near Callejón de los Sapos, this youthful indoor-outdoor café serves up live jazz, folk, blues… and a spot of karaoke just to keep things interesting. Examining the university crowd of psychology students, you'd think they were majoring in beer, smokes and flirting! Nearby, several similar cafés compete with two-for-one drink specials.

de los Sapos is the site of a lively outdoor antiques market. It's great for browsing, with a wonderful variety of old books, furniture, bric-a-brac and plain olde junque.

Talavera Uriarte (Map p216; ☎ 232-15-98; Av 4 Pte 911; www.uriartetalavera.com.mx; ☺ 9am-7pm Mon-Fri, 10:30am-5:30pm Sat, 11:30am-4:30pm Sun) Few of Puebla's Talavera shops make pottery on site anymore, but Uriarte still does, and it has a factory and showroom. Factory tours ($5) are offered Monday to Friday until 1pm in English and French, and later in Spanish as groups arrive.

El Parián crafts market (Map p216; btwn Calles 6 & 8 Nte & Avs 2 & 4 Ote) Browse local Talavera, onyx and trees of life, as well as the sorts of leather, jewelry and textiles that you find in other cities. Some of the work is shoddy, but there is also some quality handiwork and prices are reasonable.

Barrio de Analco market (Map p216; east side of Blvd 5 de Mayo) Held on Sunday, this major market across town is where flowers, sweets, paintings and other items are sold.

Getting There & Away

AIR

Aeropuerto Hermanos Serdán (PBC; ☎ 232-00-32; http://aeropuerto.pue.gob.mx in Spanish), 22km west of Puebla off Hwy 190, has daily flights to/from Guadalajara and Tijuana by Aero California; to/from Mexico City (except Sunday) and Monterrey (except Saturday) with Aeromar; direct daily flights to Houston, Texas with Continental; plus short high-season puddle-jumper Cessna hops twice weekly (usually Friday and Sunday) to/from Puerto Escondido and Huatulco with Aero Tucán.

Líneas Aéreas Azteca (☎ 240-98-20, 240-01-25, 800-229-83-22, in US ☎ 1-888-754-0066;

http://aazteca.com.mx) has announced a new Puebla–Monterrey–New York (JFK) route, scheduled to depart three times a week. At the time of research, the upstart airline was also contemplating a Puebla–Guadalajara–Los Angeles flight.

BUS

Puebla's full-service **Central de Autobuses de Puebla** (Map p214; CAPU; ☎ 249-72-11; Blvd Norte 4222) is 4km north of the *zócalo* and 1.5km off the autopista. Tickets for most routes can also be purchased via **Ticketbus** (Map p216; ☎ 232-19-52; www.ticketbus.com.mx; Av Palafox y Mendoza 604; ☼ 9:30am-6:30pm) inside the Multipack office.

Most buses to and from Puebla use Mexico City's TAPO, with additional half-hourly services to Terminal Norte. The trip takes about two hours. Three bus lines have frequent services: the deluxe line **ADO GL** (☎ 800-702-80-00; www.ado.com.mx) runs buses every 40 minutes ($9.50); **Estrella Roja** (ER; ☎ 800-712-22-84; www.estrellaroja.com.mx) runs 1st-class buses every 20 minutes ($8.50) and 2nd-class buses every 10 minutes ($7); and **AU** (☎ 800-702-80-00; www.ticketbus.com.mx) offers 2nd-class trips every 12 minutes ($7). Other companies that service this area are **Estrella de Oro** (Oro; ☎ 55-5689-3955; www.estrelladeoro.com.mx) and **UNO** (☎ 800-702-80-00; www.ado.com.mx)

From Puebla's CAPU, there's daily service to most everywhere to the south and east:

Destination	Price	Duration	Frequency
Cuernavaca	$12.50	3hr	4 deluxe Oro & ER
	$11.50	3½hr	8 1st-class Oro & ER
	$9.50	3½hr	hourly 2nd-class Oro & ER
Oaxaca	$25	4hr	1 deluxe ADO
	$21	4¼hr	12 1st-class ADO
	$18	4¼hr	2 2nd-class ADO
Tuxtla Gutiérrez	$82	12hr	2 deluxe UNO
	$59	13hr	3 directo ADO GL
	$50	12hr	3 1st-class OCC
Veracruz	$20	3½hr	6 deluxe ADO GL
	$17	3½hr	9 1st-class ADO
	$15	4¾hr	hourly 2nd-class ADO
Xalapa	$12	3hr	9 1st-class ADO
	$8.50	3hr	hourly 2nd-class 7am-8pm ADO

Frequent 'Cholula' *colectivos* ($0.50, 30 minutes) stop at the corner of Av 6 Pte and Calle 13 Nte in Puebla.

CAR & MOTORCYCLE

Puebla is 123km east of Mexico City by a *super-carretera*, Hwy 150D (tolls total about $10). East of Puebla, 150D continues to Orizaba (negotiating a cloudy, winding 22km descent from the 2385m-high Cumbres de Maltrata en route), Córdoba and Veracruz.

Getting Around

Most hotels and places of interest are within walking distance of Puebla's *zócalo*. From the CAPU bus station, take a taxi to the city center (ticket from the kiosk, flat rate $3.50 – $4.50 after 10pm – beware overpriced touts); or exit the station at the 'Autobuses Urbanos' sign and go up a ramp leading to the bridge over Blvd Norte. Once across the bridge, walk west (toward VIPS coffee shop) and stop in front of the Chedraui supermarket. From there, catch combi No 40 to Av 16 de Septiembre, four blocks south of the *zócalo*. The ride takes 15 to 20 minutes.

From the city center to the bus station, catch any northbound 'CAPU' *colectivo* from Blvd 5 de Mayo at Av Palafox y Mendoza, three blocks east of the *zócalo*, or from the corner of Calle 9 Sur and Av Reforma. All city buses and *colectivos* cost $0.40 (four pesos; exact change not required).

Several bus companies offer express service to Mexico City's international airport, including **Estrella Roja** (☎ 273-83-00, 800-712-2284), departing from Av 4 Pte 2110 in the Zona Esmerelda, hourly between 2:30am and 10:30pm ($14), and daily from 3am to 10pm from Puebla's CAPU terminal.

AFRICAM SAFARI

One of Mexico's best places to see both native and exotic wildlife is this drive-through **safari park** (☎ 222-281-70-00, in Mexico City ☎ 55-5575-2731; www.africamsafari.com.mx in Spanish; Km 16.5 on road to Presa Valsequillo; adult/child $11.50/11; ☼ 10am-5pm; ⊕). More than 3000 animals – among them rhinoceroses, bears and tigers – live in spacious 'natural' settings, and you can view them up close from within your car, a taxi or an Africam bus. It's best to visit first thing in the morning, when the animals are most active. **Estrella Roja** (☎ 222-273-83-00) runs daily round-trip buses from CAPU to Africam (adult/child $15/14, including admission and a four-hour park tour). Similarly priced tours also depart from Puebla's *zócalo* daily at 11:30am and 2:30pm (and at night during winter).

CHOLULA

☎ 222 / pop 152,000 / elevation 2170m

Ten kilometers west of Puebla stands the widest pyramid ever built, Pirámide Tepanapa – the Great Pyramid of Cholula. By the 4th century AD, it measured 450m along each side of the base, and was 65m high, making it larger in volume than Egypt's Pyramid of Cheops. Now overgrown and topped by a church, it's difficult to even recognize the huge grassy mound as a pyramid.

The tidy town of Cholula feels far removed from the incessant buzz of neighboring Puebla. Its private University of the Americas, home to many foreign students, adds a youthful touch and fuels a lively nightlife on Friday and Saturday. Otherwise, it's a fine relaxing overnight alternative. Nearby, the colonial villages of Acatepec and Tonantzintla (p227) have splendid churches.

History

Between around AD 1 and 600, Cholula grew into an important religious center, while powerful Teotihuacán flourished 100km to the northwest. The Great Pyramid was built over several times. Around AD 600, Cholula fell to the Olmeca-Xicallanca, who built nearby Cacaxtla. Sometime between AD 900 and 1300, Toltecs and/or Chichimecs took over, and it later fell under Aztec dominance. There was also artistic influence from the Mixtecs to the south.

By 1519, Cholula's population had reached 100,000, and the Great Pyramid was already overgrown. Cortés, having befriended the neighboring Tlaxcalans, traveled here at Moctezuma's request. Aztec warriors set an ambush, but unfortunately for them, the Tlaxcalans tipped off Cortés about the plot and the Spanish struck first. Within a day, they killed 6000 Cholulans before the city

was looted by the Tlaxcalans. Cortés vowed to build a church here for each day of the year, or one on top of every pagan temple, depending on which legend you prefer. Today there are 39 churches – far from 365, but still plenty for a small town.

The Spanish developed nearby Puebla to overshadow the old pagan center, and Cholula never regained its importance, especially after a severe plague in the 1540s decimated its indigenous population.

Orientation & Information

Buses and *colectivos* stop two or three blocks north of the *zócalo*. Two long blocks to the southeast, the pyramid, with its domed church on top, is a tough-to-miss landmark.

Banks (Facing *zócalo's* south side) All change cash and have ATMs.

Internet Inalambrico (cnr Calles 2 Sur & 5 Ote; per hr $1.50)

El Globo Lavandería (Calle 5 Ote 9) per kilo $1 – minimum 3kg – for machine wash-and-dry service.

Tourist Office (☎ 261-23-93; cnr Calles 12 Ote & Av 4 Nte; ☺ 9am-7pm Mon-Fri, 9am-2pm Sat & Sun)

Sights

ZÓCALO

The **Ex-Convento de San Gabriel** (also known as Plaza de la Concordia, facing the east side of Cholula's huge *zócalo*, includes a **Franciscan library**, the **Museo de la Ciudad de Cholula** and three fine churches, all of which will appeal to travelers interested in antique books, and early religious and Franciscan history. On the left, as you face the ex-convent, is the Arabic-style **Capilla Real**, which has 49 domes and dates from 1540. In the middle is the 19th-century **Capilla de la Tercera Orden**, and on the right is the **Templo de San Gabriel**, founded in 1530 on the site of a pyramid.

ZONA ARQUEOLÓGICA

Probably originally dedicated to Quetzalcóatl, Cholula's Pirámide Tepanapa is topped by the **Santuario de Nuestra Señora de los Remedios.** It's a classic symbol of conquest, but possibly an inadvertent one, as the church may have been built before the Spanish realized the mound contained a pagan temple. You can climb to the church for free via a path starting near the northwest corner of the pyramid.

The **Zona Arqueológica** (☎ 235-94-24, 235-97-20; admission $2.75; ⊙ 9am-6pm Tue-Sun) comprises the excavated areas around the pyramid and the tunnels underneath. Enter via the tunnel on the north side. A small **museum** (Calz San Andrés; admission free with site ticket), across the road from the ticket office and down some steps, provides the best introduction to the site – a cutaway model of the pyramid mound shows the various superimposed structures.

Several pyramids were built on top of each other during various reconstructions. Over 8km of tunnels have been dug beneath the pyramid by archaeologists to penetrate each stage. From the access tunnel, a few hundred meters long, you can see earlier layers of the building. At the tunnel entrance, guides (some English-speaking) charge around $7 for a one-hour tour, or $3 for a 15-minute tour of just the tunnels. You don't need a guide to follow the tunnel through to the structures on the pyramid's south and west sides, but since nothing is labeled, they can be helpful in pointing out and explaining various features.

The access tunnel emerges on the east side of the pyramid, from where you can follow a path around to the **Patio de los Altares** on the south side. Ringed by platforms and unique diagonal stairways, this Great Plaza was the main approach to the pyramid. Three large stone slabs on its east, north and west sides are carved in the Veracruz interlocking-scroll design. At its south end

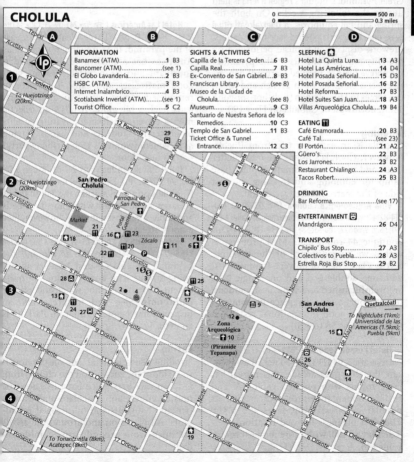

CHOLULA

0 ____ 500 m
0 ____ 0.3 miles

INFORMATION
Banamex (ATM).....................1 B3
Bancomer (ATM)...............(see 1)
El Globo Lavandería...............2 B3
HSBC (ATM)..........................3 B3
Internet Inalámbrico..............4 B3
Scotiabank Inverlat (ATM)....(see 1)
Tourist Office.......................5 C2

SIGHTS & ACTIVITIES
Capilla de la Tercera Orden.....6 B3
Capilla Real...........................7 B3
Ex-Convento de San Gabriel...8 B3
Franciscan Library..............(see 8)
Museo de la Ciudad de
Cholula.............................(see 8)
Museum...............................9 C3
Santuario de Nuestra Señora de los
Remedios.........................10 C3
Templo de San Gabriel.........11 B3
Ticket Office & Tunnel
Entrance...........................12 C3

SLEEPING
Hotel La Quinta Luna...........13 A3
Hotel Las Américas..............14 D4
Hotel Posada Señorial..........15 D3
Hotel Posada Señorial..........16 B2
Hotel Reforma.....................17 B3
Hotel Suites San Juan...........18 A3
Villas Arqueológica Cholula....19 B4

EATING
Café Enamorada....................20 B3
Café Tal............................(see 23)
El Portón.............................21 A2
Güero's................................22 B3
Los Jarrones........................23 B2
Restaurant Chialingo............24 A3
Tacos Robert.......................25 B3

DRINKING
Bar Reforma......................(see 17)

ENTERTAINMENT
Mandrágora.........................26 D4

TRANSPORT
Chipilo' Bus Stop.................27 A3
Colectivos to Puebla............28 A3
Estrella Roja Bus Stop..........29 B2

is an Aztec-style altar in a pit, dating from shortly before the Spanish conquest. On the mound's west side is a reconstructed section of the latest pyramid, with two earlier exposed layers.

Tours

Three-and-a-half-hour **trolley tours** (adult/child $7/4; ⊙ 11am Tue-Sun) of Cholula and the pyramid zone depart daily from Puebla; see p217 for details.

Festivals & Events

Of Cholula's many festivals, perhaps the most important is the **Festival de la Virgen de los Remedios**, celebrated the week of September 1, with daily traditional dances atop the Great Pyramid. Cholula's **regional feria** is held during the following weeks. On both the spring and fall equinoxes, a **Quetzalcóatl ritual** is re-enacted, with poetry, sacrificial dances, firework displays and music performed on pre-Hispanic instruments at the pyramids. On **Shrove Tuesday**, masked Carnaval dancers re-enact a battle between French and Mexican forces in Huejotzingo (weh-hot-*sin*-goh), 14km northwest of Cholula off Hwy 190.

Sleeping

Cholula is an easy day trip from Puebla. However, Cholula's hotels are often better value and it's an increasingly popular base camp for climbing and trekking the east side of the Sierra Madre Occidental.

Villa Arqueológica Cholula (☎ 273-79-00, 800-514-82-44; www.clubmedvillas.com/cholula; Calle 2 Pte 601; r Sun-Wed $77, Thu-Sat $88, ste $139; P 🏊) This boutique 44-room Club-Med property is within walking distance of the pyramid, across a large field of flowers. Rooms (most with one double bed and one single bed) are well-furnished and it has lush gardens, tennis courts, cozy fireplace-lit common areas and a good international restaurant (dinner mains $8 to $20).

Hotel Posada Señorial (☎ 247-03-41, 247-77-19; Portal Guerrero 5; s/d $29/33; P) Tucked away inside the shopping arcade, this retreat has large rooms with phones, cable TV and rustic wooden furniture. Downstairs, its popular café-restaurant faces the plaza. There's a business-focused location at Av 5 de Mayo 1400, with more modern rooms from $48.

Hotel Las Américas (☎ /fax 247-09-91; Calle 14 Ote 6; s/d $16/19; P 🏊) Three bleak blocks east of the pyramid, the sprawling 60-room Las Américas has a small pool in the garden courtyard and clean, sizable rooms with good mattresses and cable TV. Recently remodeled rooms with two matrimonial beds fetch a bit more. It hosts an eclectic mix of traveling salesmen, visiting parents of university students and bands playing *quinceañera* (women's 15th birthday party) parties next door.

Hotel Suites San Juan (☎ 247-02-78; Calle 5 Sur 103; s/d $32/38; P) Half a block southwest of Cholula's principal market, the San Juan has 14 large, clean rooms with enormous beds and cable TV; most windows, however, face a noisy street.

Hotel Reforma (☎ 247-01-49; Calle 4 Sur 101; s/d $16.50/20; P) Between the *zócalo* and the pyramid, Cholula's oldest hostelry is still going strong. The dozen rooms are quite decent and all have hot water and private bathrooms. Size and features vary, so inspect a few before settling in. Parking is an extra $2.

Eating

Strolling beneath the arcade on the northwest side of the *zócalo*, you can choose from a dozen café-bars, juice bars, live acoustic music venues, hot chocolate and *churros* (fritters) hangouts and full-fledged restaurants. All places on and around the *zócalo* are open from around 9am to midnight daily.

Café Enamorada (mains $2.50-5) Facing the *zócalo*, this café is one of the most popular places in town, at least on weeknights and for its Sunday brunch buffet. There's live music most nights (when minimum consumption is $5) and decent doses of the usual sandwiches, tacos and quesadillas.

Los Jarrones (mains $4-8) Underneath the plaza's attractive arcade, this casual indoor-outdoor eatery serves set breakfasts and a wide menu of good-value regional dishes.

Café Tal (snacks & drinks $2-5) Next to Los Jarrones, this more intimate café is a favorite for coffee and a snack – perfect for watching the action on the plaza.

Restaurant Chialingo (☎ 247-28-31; Calle 7 Pte 113; mains $5-10; ☺ 1-9pm) Around the corner from La Quinta Luna, Chialingo, one of the fancier places in town, looks out on a lovely courtyard and specializes in salads, steaks and seafood.

Güero's (☎ 247-00-11; Av Hidalgo 101; mains $3-9) Decorated with antique photos of Cholula, Whitey's is a lively family-friendly hangout. Besides pizza, pasta and burgers, hearty Mexican choices include *pozole, cemitas* and quesadillas, all served with a delicious *salsa roja*.

El Portón (Av Hidalgo 302; set menu $3.50; ☺ 10am-6pm) The Portal is popular for its daily set menu, which includes a choice of three soups, a main course (chicken, beef or vegetables), coffee and dessert.

Drinking & Entertainment

Bar Reforma (cnr Av 4 Nte & Calz San Andrés; drinks $1-3) Attached to Hotel Reforma, Cholula's oldest drinking spot is a classic, smoky corner abode with swinging doors, specializing in iceless margaritas and freshly prepared sangrias. After 9pm, it's popular with the pre-clubbing university crowd.

Tacos Robert (cnr 14 Oriente & Av 5 de Mayo) Across the street, this place, where the beer is cold and *fútbol* is always on the *tele*, is also popular with the pre-clubbing university crowd.

East of the pyramid on Calle 14 Pte, around the Av 5 de Mayo intersection, bars and discos compete for the short attention span of the university students (who live across the street in a gated complex) after 10pm Thursday to Saturday. Sporting names like Pimp and Sins Cocktails-to-Go, these short-lived places often vanish with the end of each semester.

At last look, most places were boarded up and, with the notable exception of **Mandrágora** (cnr Calz San Andrés & Calle 3 Sur; no cover), a cavernous dance hall, the action had moved to warehouse-like *antros* and discos (where cover averages $5 to $10), a couple of kilometers east, near the university exit of the 'Recta,' as the Cholula–Puebla highway is known.

Your best bet is to quiz students or ask a cab driver where the current hot spots are. Wherever you end up, dress to impress and come prepared to wait out in the street behind the velvet rope with the pretty young thangs…if you're not on the VIP list.

Getting There & Away

Frequent *colectivos* to Puebla ($0.50, 20 to 30 minutes) leave from the corner of Calle 5 Pte and Calle 3 Sur. Estrella Roja runs frequent buses between Mexico City's TAPO and Puebla ($5) that stop in Cholula ($5) on Calle 12 Pte.

TONANTZINTLA & ACATEPEC

Tonantzintla is a few kilometers south of Cholula, off Hwy 190. The interior of Tonantzintla's **Templo de Santa María** (☺ 7am-2pm & 4-8pm) is among Mexico's most exuberant. Under the dome, the surface is plastered with colorful stucco saints, devils, flowers, fruit, birds and more – a great example of indigenous artisanship applied to Christian themes. Tonantzintla celebrates the **Festival de la Asunción** (Festival of the Assumption) on August 15 with a procession and traditional dances.

Acatepec's **Templo de San Francisco** (☺ 7am-2pm & 4-8pm), 1.5km southeast of Tonantzintla, dates from the 1730s. The brilliant exterior is beautifully decorated with blue, green and yellow Talavera tiles, set in red brick on an ornate Churrigueresque facade.

Autobuses Puebla–Cholula runs 'Chipilo' buses ($0.80) from Puebla's CAPU bus terminal to Tonantzintla and Acatepec. In Cholula, pick them up on the corner of Calle 7 Pte and Blvd Miguel Alemán. Between the two villages, you can either walk or wait for the next bus.

SIERRA NORTE DE PUEBLA

The mountains that dominate much of remote northern Puebla state rise to over 2500m before falling away to the Gulf coastal plain. Despite deforestation, it's fetching country, with pine forests and, at lower altitudes, semitropical vegetation. When the fog settles in after a serious downpour, there's often a palpable hint of magical realism in the air.

The Sierra Norte is home to most of Puebla state's approximately 400,000 indigenous Nahua people. The Nahua are one of Mexico's largest indigenous groups and more of them live in Puebla than in any other state. Another 200,000 Nahua reside in western parts of Veracruz state. The Nahua language (Náhuatl) was spoken by the Aztecs and, like the Aztecs, the Nahua were probably of Chichimec origin. Many Nahua are now Christian but often also believe in a pantheon of supernatural beings, including *tonos* (people's animal 'doubles') and witches who can become blood-sucking birds and cause illness.

Traditional Nahua women's dress consists of a black wool *enredo*, an embroidered blouse and *quechquémitl* (shoulder cape). Sierra Norte handicrafts, such as baskets, carved wooden masks, woolen textiles, woven belts and fireworks, are sold in markets at Cuetzalan, Zacapoaxtla, Teziutlán and elsewhere.

Cuetzalan

☎ 233 / pop 6000 / elevation 980m

The commercial center of a lush coffee-, pepper- and vanilla-growing region riddled with rivers, caves and waterfalls, colonial Cuetzalan (Place of the Quetzals) is famed for its vibrant festivals and Sunday *tianguis,* which attracts scores of indigenous people in traditional dress. It's a favorite *telenovela* (TV series) filming location, and there's a smaller market on Thursday, plus plenty of bartering for flowers, chickens, and *tamales* on the days in between. The humidity hovers around 90%, and on the clearest days, you can see all the way from the hilltops to the Gulf coast – 70km away, as the quetzal flies.

ORIENTATION & INFORMATION

From the south, the main road into town (an extension of Hwy 129) passes the bus depot before hitting the *zócalo*. The center is on a hillside, and from the *zócalo* most hotels and restaurants are uphill. None-too-shy kids will offer to guide you around the slick, marble-cobbled streets for a small fee.

No English is spoken at the **tourist office** (☎ 331-05-27/62, 800-000-11-22; 9am-4pm Wed-Sun), at the Palacio Municipal on the east side of the *zócalo*, but it's got town maps. The **information kiosk** (Thu-Tue) at the entrance to town keeps slightly longer, if irregular, hours. Just west of the *zócalo*, **Banamex** (Alvarado) has an ATM. There's a cyber-lair called **Internet** (per hr $1.25) on the west side of the *zócalo*, and several others nearby.

SIGHTS & ACTIVITIES

Three towers rise above Cuetzalan: the plaza's free-standing **clock tower**, the Gothic spire of the **Parroquia de San Francisco** and, to the west, the tower of the French-Gothic **Santuario de Guadalupe**, with its highly unusual decorative rows of clay vases *(los jarritos).* Between Banamex and the bus depot, the **Casa de Cultura** (Alvarado) houses a free regional **museum**.

Two lovely waterfalls, collectively called **Las Brisas**, are 4km and 5km northeast of town. Hail a *colectivo* behind the Parroquia de San Francisco heading for the village of San Andrés Tziculian, or walk west along the dirt road from the bus depot, keeping to the right when it forks, until you reach San Andrés. Kids will offer to guide you to the falls for a few pesos. You should accept since there are no signs and many trails in the forest. The **natural swimming pools** beneath the falls are enticing – bring your bathing kit. Parts of a 32km network of caves can be explored at **Atepolihui**, accessible from the village of San Miguel, a half-hour walk from the end of Calle Hidalgo.

FESTIVALS & EVENTS

For several lively days around October 4, Cuetzalan celebrates both its patron saint, St Francis of Assisi, and the start of the coffee harvest, with the **Feria del Café y del Huipil** (Festival of Coffee and Huipiles), featuring hearty drinking, traditional quetzal dancing, and airborne *voladores* (literally 'fliers'), the Totonac ritual in which men, suspended by their ankles, whirl around a tall pole.

SLEEPING

Hotel Posada Cuetzalan (☎ 331-01-54; www.posada cuetzalan.com; Zaragoza 12; s/d $32/41;) This sprawling hotel has a swimming pool, a good restaurant featuring local fruit wines and liqueurs, two lovely courtyards full of chirping birds, and 35 well-kept rooms with tropical colors, tiled floors, lots of lightly stained wood and cable TV. A new wing will add 16 rooms and two family-friendly suites. Parking is accessed from the back side of the hotel. It's uphill 100m from the *zócalo*.

Posada Jaqueline (☎ 331-03-54; Calle 2 de Abril 2; s/d $9/14.50) Jaqueline's 20 basic but clean rooms, overlooking the uphill side of the *zócalo*, are Cuetzalan's best in-town value. Some upstairs rooms share a balcony and have views over town.

Taselotzin (☎ /fax 331-04-80; www.laneta.apc .org/maseualsiua/hotel1.htm in Spanish; Yoloxóchitl, Barrio Zacatipan; dm/s/d $8.50/19/30; P ♿) Just outside Cuetzalan, this *albergue* (hostel) is run by local Nahua craftswomen, who offer traditional massage and sell their fair-traded handicrafts and herbal medicines. It has five fusty but cozy private rooms, with good views amid peaceful gardens, plus a surplus of dormitory-style cabins. The restaurant serves traditional local dishes, and horseback rides to waterfalls, caves and the pyramids can be arranged. Follow the right-hand fork past Cuetzalan's info kiosk off the Puebla road; watch for an inconspicuous sign on the right-hand side, about 300m downhill.

Centro Vacacional Ecológico Metzintli (☎ 231-319-00-51, in Puebla 222-249-04-72; camping per person $7, r $37, 4–6-person cabins $64-73; P ♿) This vacation center has a bar-restaurant, lovely rooms and rustic cabins. The grounds include a soccer field and basketball court. Horses and all-terrain vehicles – so much for the

---

THE AUTHOR'S CHOICE

Hotel La Casa de la Piedra (☎ 331-00-30, in Puebla 222-249-40-89; www.lacasadepiedra.com; García 11; s/d/ste $30/40/60; P 🚲) Two blocks below the *zócalo*, the 'House of the Stone' is Cuetzalan's most atmospheric hostelry, hands down. All 16 rooms in the renovated yet rustic former *beneficio* (coffee-processing warehouse) have large picture windows and refinished wood floors. Upstairs, the two-level suites accommodate up to four people and boast expansive views of the valley; downstairs rooms are equally well-decorated, with tiled bathrooms, rough stone walls, and one or two beds.

---

tranquility – are rearin' for hire. It's about 2km north of the turnoff for Cuetzalan on the road to Yohualichán.

EATING & DRINKING

Regional specialties, sold at many roadside stands, include fruit wines, smoked meats and herbal liqueurs.

La Terraza (☎ 331-02-62; Hidalgo 33; mains $2-5.50) West of the plaza, the Terrace is the best of several inviting restaurants along Calle Hidalgo. It's open all day and serves midweek set meals, plus an à la carte assortment of salads, pasta and seafood (crawfish are a specialty).

Restaurant Yoloxochitl (☎ 331-03-35; 2 de Abril; mains $2.50-4) Opposite Posada Jaqueline, this charming restaurant has lovely plaza views. Besides salads, *antojitos* and meat dishes, it offers wild mushrooms pickled in *chile de chipotle* sauce year-round.

Bar El Calate (☎ 331-05-66; Morelos 9B; shots from $0.50) On the west side of the *zócalo*, this is *the* place to sup homemade hooch – flavored with coffee, limes, berries, you name it – orange wine, and the all-curing *yolixpán*, a medicinal herbal brew consisting of *aguardiente* (fire water) tempered by honey.

Restaurant Peña Los Jarritos (☎ 331-05-58, in Puebla 222-249-40-89; Plazuela López Mateos 7; mains $3-7; ⏰ 8:30am-1am) Just uphill from Posada Cuetzalan, this otherwise sleepy place hosts a *peña* (evening of Latin American folk music, often with a political protest theme) on Saturday nights. These feature drinks and regional dishes, and from 8:30pm quetzal dancers, *huapango* (folk music from the Huastec region) bands, and, in high season, high-flying *voladores* in the parking lot.

GETTING THERE & AWAY

First-class buses ($12, four hours) depart Puebla for Cuetzalan at 3pm, and Cuetzalan for Puebla at around 5:30am. Second-class Vía buses ($10) make the same run hourly from 5am to 7:30pm, with extra services on Sunday and the last bus to Puebla at 5:30pm. During the rainy season, it pays to double-check road conditions and buy your return bus tickets in advance.

Yohualichán

About 8km northeast of Cuetzalan, the last 2km via a cobblestone road, this ceremonial **pre-Hispanic site** (admission $2.50; ⏰ 10am-5pm

Tue–Sun) has niche pyramids similar to El Tajín. The entrance is adjacent to Yohualichán's church and town plaza. To get here, board any *colectivo* ($0.50) out of Cuetzalan and walk 20 minutes down from the stop where there's a blue sign with a pyramid on it. Alternatively, ask around the bus depot for a *camión* (truck) passing by the pyramids.

SOUTHERN PUEBLA

The main route from Puebla to Oaxaca is Hwy 135D, a modern toll road that turns south off Hwy 150D, 83km east of Puebla. Two older roads, Hwys 150 and 190, ramble through southern Puebla state toward Oaxaca (p717).

Highway 150

Heading east from Puebla, this road parallels Hwy 150D, but it's slower and more congested. Second-class buses stop at the towns en route. **Amozoc** (population 58,000), 18km east of Puebla, produces pottery, leather goods and many of the fancy silver decorations flaunted by *charros* (Mexican cowboys). **Tepeaca** (population 25,000), 38km southeast of Puebla, has a 16th-century Franciscan monastery and a big Friday market. The tranquil village of **Tecali**, 11km southwest of Tepeaca, is an onyx-carving center.

Highway 190

Hwy 190 swings 31km southwest from Puebla to colonial **Atlixco** (population 86,000), known for its avocados, cool mineral springs, near-perfect climate and colorful Tuesday and Saturday markets. It's also known for its September weeklong **Atlixcáyotl festival** of traditional indigenous culture, which celebrates the harvest and culminates in spectacular dance displays on the last Sunday of September. Another 36km brings you to **Izúcar de Matamoros** (population 45,000), which also has therapeutic spas, but is best known for ceramic handicrafts. Eventually, the serpentine route emerges in Oaxaca.

Tehuacán

☎ 238 / pop 242,000 / elevation 1640m

Tehuacán, a regional commercial center just east of Hwy 135D and 120km southeast of Puebla, is a pretty town with a fine, shady *zócalo*. About halfway between Mexico City and Oaxaca, it makes a good pit stop,

especially if shopping for handicrafts at the Saturday market, but otherwise doesn't see many foreign visitors.

ORIENTATION & INFORMATION

Coming from Puebla, the main road into town, Av Independencia, passes by the ADO bus station before reaching the north side of the *zócalo*, Parque Juárez. The main north–south road is Av Reforma.

Essential services surround the *zócalo*. On the northwest corner of the *zócalo*, the sleepy **tourist information kiosk** (☽ 10am-2pm & 4-7pm) may have city maps.

SIGHTS

Tehuacán is best known for its mineral water, which is sold in bottles all over Mexico; there are free tours of the **Peñafiel plant** (☽ 9am-noon & 4-6pm Sat-Thu; Av José Garci-Crespo), 100m north of the Casas Cantarranas hotel (see below). Just up the road, competitor **Garci-Crespo** (☽ 10am-4pm; Av José Garci-Crespo) also offers tours of its bubbly underground springs.

The arid Tehuacán Valley was the site of some of Mexico's earliest agriculture. By 7000 to 5000 BC, people were harvesting avocados, chilies, corn and cotton. Pottery, the sign of a truly settled existence, appeared around 2000 BC.

The **Museo del Valle de Tehuacán** (admission $1; ☽ 10am-6pm Tue-Sun), three blocks northwest of the *zócalo* and inside the imposing Ex-Convento del Carmen, explains in Spanish some of the archaeological discoveries, and exhibits tiny preserved corn cobs thought to be among the first ever cultivated.

FESTIVALS & EVENTS

The Sunday closest to October 15 marks the start of the two-week **La Matanza** festival, when goats are slaughtered en masse. *Mole de caderas* (goat stew) is the regional specialty that results from the carnage (you can try it year-round at Restaurant Danny Richard, opposite Ex-Convento del Carmen).

SLEEPING & EATING

Casas Cantarranas (☎ 383-49-22; www.cantarranas .com.mx; Av José Garci-Crespo 2215; s/d/ste $64/73/89; P ⊠ ⊠) This good-value business-friendly resort, 2km northwest of the *zócalo*, features expansive gardens, an upscale international restaurant, a spa, a gym, a bar and 55 refined rooms with hardwood floors and amenities like air-con and satellite TV.

Hotel México (☎ 382-00-19; cnr Reforma Nte & Independencia Pte; s/d $40/46; P ⛽) This central hotel is quite tranquil, with 86 large comfortable rooms and suites, several courtyards, mineral water–fed pools and a good restaurant. It's a block northwest of the zócalo.

Bogh Suites Hotel (☎ 382-44-88; Calle 1 Nte 102; s/d/ste $31/37/50; P) The Bogh, off the zócalo's northwest side, has small but attractive rooms with TVs, fans and phones. Fourth floor rooms (no elevator) are a bit cheaper, and the downstairs restaurant has hearty set meals for $4.

Hotel Monroy (☎ 382-04-91; Reforma Nte 217; s/d $19/25) The no-frills Monroy, opposite the convent, maintains clean and spacious standard rooms.

Peñafiel Restaurant (☎ 383-24-90; Av López Rayon 2; mains $3-7) One of the city's most popular eateries, near the zócalo.

GETTING THERE & AWAY
ADO (☎ 800-702-80-00; www.ado.com.mx; Independencia 137) has 1st-class buses to/from Puebla ($6.50, two hours, every 30 minutes), hourly service to/from Mexico City ($13.50, four hours), a daily 6:30pm bus to Veracruz ($12, four hours) and two daily buses to Oaxaca ($13, three hours).

SOUTH OF MEXICO CITY

Heading south from Mexico City, parallel Hwy 95 and toll Hwy 95D climb from the smog-choked Valle de México into refreshing pine forests above 3000m, then descend to Cuernavaca, a long-time popular escape from Mexico City. Along the way, Hwy 115D branches southeast to Tepoztlán, nestled beneath high cliffs, and to balnearios at Cuautla and Oaxtepec.

The state of Morelos, which encompasses all of the towns mentioned above, is one of Mexico's smallest and most densely populated states. Valleys at different elevations have a variety of microclimates, and many fruits, grains and vegetables have been cultivated here since pre-Hispanic times. The archaeological sites at Cuernavaca, Tepoztlán and Xochicalco show signs of the

agricultural Tlahuica civilization and the Aztecs who subjugated them. During the colonial era, most of the region was controlled by a few families, including descendants of Cortés. You can visit their palaces and haciendas, along with 16th-century churches and monasteries. Unsurprisingly, the campesinos (farmers) of Morelos were fervent supporters of the Mexican Revolution, and local lad Emiliano Zapata (see p238) is the state's hero.

South of Cuernavaca, spurs of Hwy 95D lead to the remarkable silver town of Taxco and the industrial city of Iguala, both in mountainous Guerrero state. The Iguala branch continues south as Hwy 95 to Chilpancingo (p517) and Acapulco (p501). Locals claim they can navigate the 400km between Mexico City and Acapulco via the Hwy 95D expressway in under three hours; depending on your risk tolerance, your mileage may vary. The alternative free roads are heavily used, slow and dangerous.

TEPOZTLÁN
☎ 739 / pop 15,000 / elevation 1700m
Magical Tepoztlán lies in a valley that is surrounded by high, jagged cliffs, 80km south of Mexico City. It was the legendary birthplace, more than 1200 years ago, of Quetzalcóatl, the omnipotent serpent god of the Aztecs. Despite a recent New Age onslaught, the town retains indigenous traditions, with some elders still speaking Náhuatl, and younger generations learning it in school. As something of an international post-hippie mecca, Tepoztlán attracts writers, artists and astrologers – who, encouraged by UFO sightings, claim the place has a creative energy – plus a steady stream of more straight-laced weekenders from Mexico City.

Orientation & Information
Everything in Tepoztlán is easily accessible on foot, except the cliff-top Pirámide de Tepozteco, 2.5km away. Street names change in the center of town; for example, Av 5 de Mayo becomes Av Tepozteco north of the plaza.

On the west side of the plaza, Bancomer and HSBC have ATMs. **Internetepoz** (Av Revolución 1910 22; per hr $1) offers broadband access. There's no official tourist office, but shopkeepers and the knowledgeable archaeology museum staff can answer most questions.

Sights

EX-CONVENTO DOMÍNICO DE LA NATIVIDAD

This **monastery** (admission free; 🕑 10am-5pm Tue-Sun) and the attached church were built by Dominican priests between 1560 and 1588. The plateresque church facade has Dominican seals interspersed with indigenous symbols, floral designs and various figures, including the sun, moon and stars, animals, angels and the Virgin Mary.

The monastery's arched entryway is adorned with an elaborate **seed mural** of pre-Hispanic history and symbolism. Every year, during the first week of September, local artists sow a new mural from 60 varieties of seeds.

The 400-year-old complex is undergoing a major restoration; many murals from the 16th and 17th centuries have been meticulously restored. Upstairs, various cells house a bookstore, galleries and a **regional history museum**.

MUSEO ARQUEOLÓGICO CARLOS PELLICER

Behind the Dominican church, this **archaeology museum** (☎ 395-10-98; González 2; admission $1; 🕑 10am-6pm Tue-Sun) has a small but interesting collection of pieces from around the country, donated by Tabascan poet Carlos Pellicer Cámara. The objects on display here are lively and vibrant, with an emphasis on human figures, but also including some animals. The stone fragments depicting a pair of rabbits – the symbol for Ometochtli, one of the 400 pulque gods – were discovered at the Tepozteco pyramid site.

PIRÁMIDE DE TEPOZTECO

The 10m-high **Pyramid of Tepozteco** (admission $2.75; 🕑 9am-5:30pm) was built on a cliff 400m above Tepoztlán in honor of Tepoztécatl, the Aztec god of the harvest, fertility and pulque. It's accessible by a steep path; the 2km one-way walk can take as little as half an hour or up to 90 minutes, and may be too strenuous if you have any physical ailments. At the top, depending on haze levels, you may be rewarded with a panorama of the valley. Hiking boots, or at least good tennis shoes, are highly recommended.

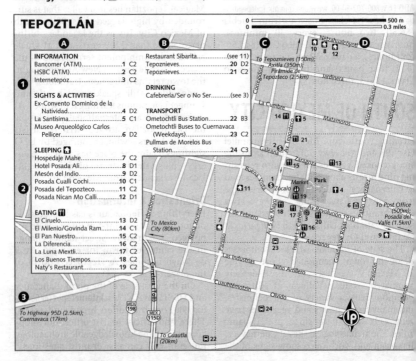

TEPOZTLÁN

0 ——— 500 m
0 ——— 0.3 miles

INFORMATION
Bancomer (ATM)..................1 C2
HSBC (ATM)........................2 C2
Internetepoz......................3 C2

SIGHTS & ACTIVITIES
Ex-Convento Dominico de la
 Natividad.......................4 D2
La Santísima......................5 C1
Museo Arqueológico Carlos
 Pellicer.........................6 D2

SLEEPING
Hospedaje Mahe..................7 C2
Hotel Posada Ali.................8 D1
Mesón del Indio..................9 D2
Posada Cualli Cochi..............10 C1
Posada del Tepozteco............11 C2
Posada Nican Mo Calli...........12 D1

EATING
El Ciruelo........................13 D2
El Milenio/Govinda Ram..........14 C1
El Pan Nuestro...................15 C2
La Diferencia.....................16 C2
La Luna Mextli....................17 C2
Los Buenos Tiempos..............18 C2
Naty's Restaurant................19 C2
Restaurant Sibarita.............(see 11)
Tepoznieves.......................20 D2
Tepoznieves.......................21 C2

DRINKING
Cafebrería/Ser o No Ser.........(see 3)

TRANSPORT
Ometochtli Bus Station..........22 B3
Ometochtli Buses to Cuernavaca
 (Weekdays).....................23 C2
Pullman de Morelos Bus
 Station.........................24 C3

Festivals & Events

Tepoztlán is a hyper-festive place, with many Christian feasts superimposed on pagan celebrations. With eight *barrios* (neighborhoods) and an equal number of patron saints, there always seems to be some excuse for fireworks.

During the five days preceding Ash Wednesday (46 days before Easter Sunday), **Carnaval** features the colorful dances of the Huehuenches and Chinelos with feather headdresses and beautifully embroidered costumes. On **September 7** an all-night celebration goes off on Tepozteco hill near the pyramid, with copious consumption of pulque in honor of Tepoztécatl. The following day is the **Fiesta del Templo**, a Catholic celebration featuring theater performances in Náhuatl. The holiday was first intended to coincide with – and perhaps supplant – the pagan festival, but the pulque drinkers get a jump on it by starting the night before.

Sleeping

It can be difficult to find decent inexpensive accommodations during festivals and on weekends, when 'hospedaje económico' signs spring up around town faster than tarot card readers. Nicer places, catering mainly to Mexico City escapees, discount rates by up to 30% Sunday through Thursday.

Hotel Posada Ali (☎ 395-19-71; Netzahualcóyotl 2C; r $37-55; P 🔊) The homey Ali has a sitting room, *frontón* (jai alai, a court game like handball) court and a small pool. Its 13 spacious, attractive rooms come in various shapes and sizes; the most expensive have king-size beds and cable TV.

Posada Cualli Cochi (☎ 395-03-93; Netzahualcóyotl 2; r $39, d $40-65; P 🖳 🔊) Next to Posada Ali, this newer hotel has a small pool out back under a lemon tree, and 10 sparsely furnished, clean but cramped rooms with cable TV.

Posada Nican Mo Calli (☎ 395-31-52; www .travelbymexico.com/more/nican; Netzahualcóyotl 4A; r $78-95; P 🔊) One of the newer in-town places, this has lots of friendly pets, a large shared living room, and 11 rooms, all with great views and cable TV. There's a squash court, heated pool and Jacuzzi; the larger rooms have private terraces.

Hospedaje Mahe (☎ 395-32-92; www.tepoz.com .mx/hospedajemahe; Paraíso 12; r $32-41, with shared bathroom $20-28; P 🔊) This colorful, if a bit dank, six-room place is the best budget choice.

There's a Ping-Pong table, a guayaba tree, cable TV and laundry possibilities. The friendly owners live downstairs.

Mesón del Indio (☎ 395-02-38; Av Revolución 1910 44; r $20) Guarded by a hyperactive hairless dog with a perma-smile, named Sweet Like Honey, the Indio is Tepoz' most basic passable option, with eight small, damp rooms (each with hot water) beside a garden and a five-person apartment.

Posada del Valle (☎ 395-05-21; www.posadadel valle.com.mx; Camino a Mextitla 5; r Mon-Thu only $80, spa packages for 2 daily $369; P 🔊) Posada del Valle has quiet, romantic rooms and a good Argentine restaurant. Spa packages include two nights at the hotel, breakfast, massages and a visit to the *temascal* (indigenous Mexican steam bath). Children under 16 are not allowed. It's 2km east of town: take Av Revolución 1910 east and follow the signs for the final 100m to the hotel.

Eating & Drinking

La Diferencia (☎ 393-13-71; Isabel La Católica 3; mains $5-10; 🕙 1-9pm Fri-Mon) Fresh gourmet ingredients and a reasonably-priced wine list ($10 to $25) make all the difference at this enticing little French-inspired bistro. Tuck into a serrano ham baguette or vichyssoise soup, and save room for a homemade dessert. The set lunch ($10) inspires much bonhomie.

El Pan Nuestro (☎ 395-03-10; Av Tepozteco; mains $3-6; V) Homemade bread and market-fresh ingredients star at this health-conscious café, open all day for breakfast, big salads, sandwiches, coffee and dessert.

THE AUTHOR'S CHOICE

Posada del Tepozteco (☎ 395-00-10; www .posadadeltepozteco.com; Paraíso 3; r/ste from $173/240; P 🗶 🖳 🔊) This gorgeous hotel was built as a hillside hacienda in the 1930s. It features lovely, well-manicured grounds, two solar-heated pools, 20 well-done rooms, and terraces with spectacular views surveying town. The airy suites come with private spa baths and the attractive restaurant-bar, La Sibarita, is worth a visit even if you aren't staying here, especially for the weekend brunch. Service is top-notch and rates are discounted up to 20% from Sunday to Thursday.

AROUND MEXICO CITY

El Milenio/Govinda Ram (cnr Av Tepozteco & La Cumbre; snacks & set meals $2-4.50; (V)) This Hindu-inspired vegetarian café is a nice place to stop for coffee, juice or a healthy snack before climbing up to the pyramid, or for an Ayurvedic-style buffet on your way down.

El Ciruelo (☎ 395-12-03; Zaragoza 17; mains $5-15; (✦) 1-6pm Mon-Thu, 1-11pm Fri & Sat, 1-6pm Sun) Te-poztlán's most elegant restaurant-bar, with a lovely courtyard under a soaring band shell, serves good pizzas, salads and international dishes, and boasts picture-perfect views of the pyramid. Try the curry shrimp or steak in tequila sauce. Reservations recommended.

Axitla (☎ 395-05-19; mains $5-15; (✦) 10am-7pm Wed-Sun) At the beginning of the trail to the archaeological site, Axitla offers abundant portions of fine Mexican and international cuisine in a jungle-like setting.

La Luna Mextli (☎ 393-11-14; Av Revolución 1910 16; mains $5-10) This combo restaurant, bar and art gallery serves Mexican standards, plus grilled steaks and Argentine-style *parillada* (mixed grill), in an inviting interior courtyard.

Naty's Restaurant (☎ 395-02-67; Av Revolución 1910 7; mains $3-10) Naty's is the best place to watch the market action over breakfast.

Tepoznieves (Av Revolución 1910 s/n; scoops $1-2) This homegrown ice-cream emporium scoops out some 200 heavenly flavors, including exotics like cactus and pineapple-chili. It's an obligatory stop and has a couple more branches on the road to the pyramid, plus many imitators around town.

Los Buenos Tiempos (☎ 395-05-19; Av Revolución 1910 10; mains $1-3) Tepoz' best espresso fuels lively conversations at this cozy café that also serves light meals. Try the homemade strudel.

Cafebrería/Ser o No Ser (upstairs, Av Revolución 1910 22; snacks $1-2; (♿)) With any luck – the hours vary widely – you'll encounter a few used English-language paperbacks, snacks and *simpático* folks at this community-minded coffeehouse.

Shopping

The local market is most animated on Wednesday and Sunday. In addition, on Saturday and Sunday, stalls around the plaza sell a mélange of handicrafts, including sarapes (blanket-like shawls), carvings, weavings, baskets and pottery. Shops lining adjacent streets also have interesting wares (some from Bali and India) at more upmarket prices. Popular local craft products are miniature villages carved from the cork-like spines of the pochote tree.

Getting There & Away

Pullman de Morelos/OCC (☎ 395-05-20; www .pullman.com.mx; Av 5 de Mayo 35) runs 1st-class buses to/from Mexico City's Terminal Sur ($5.50, 1½ hours, hourly 5am to 8pm). Frequent buses to Cuautla ($1.50, 15 minutes) depart from the Hwy 115D tollbooth just outside town. Pullman de Morelos runs free combis between the Av 5 de Mayo terminal and the gas station near the autopista entrance; from there, walk down the left (exit) ramp to the tollbooth.

Ometochtli direct ($1.50, 45 minutes) and 'ordinario' ($1, one hour) buses run to Cuernavaca every 10 minutes, 5am to 9pm. On Monday to Friday mornings, you can catch the bus downtown.

If driving north from Cuernavaca on Hwy 95D, don't get off at the Tepoztlán exit, which will dump you on the slow federal highway. Instead, take the subsequent Cuautla/Oaxtepec exit.

CUAUTLA

☎ 735 / pop 147,000 / elevation 1300m

Cuautla's (*kwout*-la) agreeable year-round climate and *balnearios* have been attractions since the time of Moctezuma. These days, the city is spread out and uninspiring though walking the streets around the central plazas is enjoyable enough. The main reason locals detour here, or stop over en route to points further south, is to sample the popular sulfur springs.

José María Morelos y Pavón, one of Mexico's first leaders in the independence struggle, based himself in Cuautla; the royalist army besieged the city in 1812, and Morelos and his army were forced to evacuate when their rations ran out. A century later, Cuautla was a center of support for Emiliano Zapata's revolutionary army. Now, every April 10, the Agrarian Reform Minister lays a wreath at Zapata's monument in Cuautla, quoting the revolutionary's principles of land reform.

Orientation

Cuautla spreads north to south roughly parallel to the Río Cuautla. The two main plazas – Plaza Fuerte de Galeana, more commonly known as the Alameda (a favorite haunt of mariachis-for-hire on weekends), and the *zócalo* – are along the main north-south avenue, whose name changes from Av Insurgentes to Batalla 19 de Febrero, then to Galeana, Los Bravos, Guerrero and Ordiera, on its way through town.

The *zócalo*, which comes alive on Sunday, has arcades with restaurants on the north side, a church on the east, the Palacio Municipal on the west and the Hotel Colón on the south. Bus lines have separate terminals in the blocks east of the plaza.

Information

Banks ATMs are plentiful around the plazas.

No-name Internet (cnr Niño Artillero & Bollas; per hr $1)

Tourist office (☎ 352-52-21; 🕑 9am-8pm) On the platform of the old train station. Upstairs, the Casa de Cultura runs a museum and hosts a full calendar of cultural events.

Sights

In 1911, presidential candidate Francisco Madero embraced Emiliano Zapata at Cuautla's old **railroad station** (in the Ex-Convento de San Diego). Currently, Mexico's only steam-powered train fires up for special occasions only.

The former residence of José María Morelos houses the **Museo Histórico del Oriente** (☎ 352-83-31; Callejón del Castigo 3; admission $2.25, free Sun; 🕑 9am-6pm Tue-Sun). Each room covers a different historical period with displays of pre-Hispanic pottery, good maps and early photos of Cuautla and Zapata.

The iconic rebel's remains lie beneath the imposing **Zapata monument** in the middle of Plazuela Revolución del Sur.

Cuautla's best-known *balneario* is riverside **Agua Hedionda** (Stinky Water; ☎ 352-00-44; end of Av Progreso; adult/child $4.50/2.25, Mon-Fri $3.25/1.75; 🕑 6:30am-5:30pm; ♿). Waterfalls replenish two lake-sized pools with sulfur-scented 27°C waters. Take an 'Agua Hedionda' bus ($0.40) from Plazuela Revolución del Sur.

Other *balnearios* worth visiting include **El Almeal** (Hernández; adult/child $3.25/2.25; Mon-Fri $3/2; 🕑 9am-6pm; ♿) and the nicer **Los Limones** (Gabriel Teppa s/n; adult/child $3.75/2.75; 🕑 8:30am-6pm; ♿). Both places are served by the same spring (no sulfur) and have extensive shaded picnic grounds.

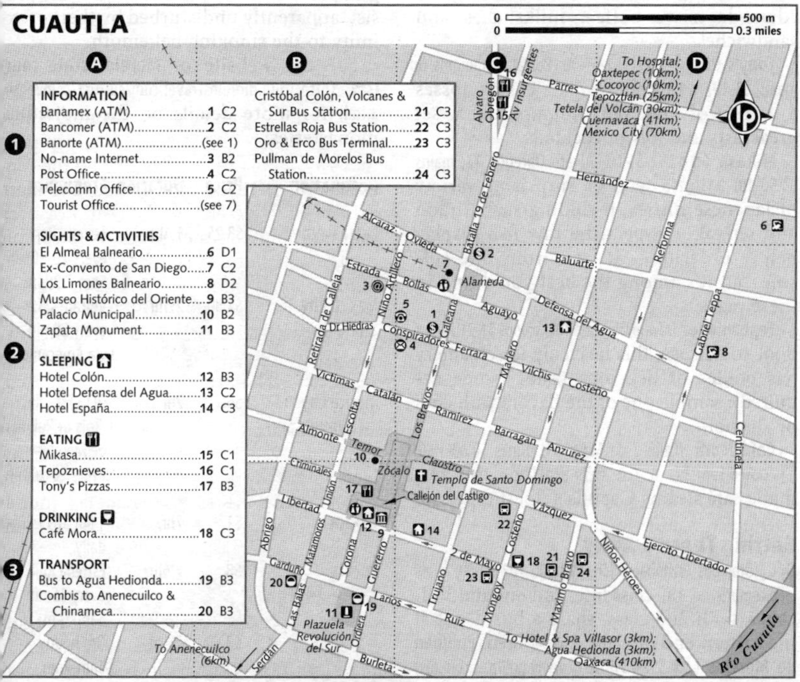

AROUND MEXICO CITY

Sleeping

Hotel Defensa del Agua (☎ 352-16-79; Defensa del Agua 34; s/d $28/37; P ⊠) Surrounding a small garden courtyard and pool, the inviting colonial-style rooms here have cable TV, phones and ceiling fans. Avoid rooms with windows facing the street. Weekend specials lower rates by up to $10.

Hotel & Spa Villasor (☎ 352-65-21/61; www.hotel villasor.com.mx; Av Progreso; s/d $34/44; P ⊠ ⊠) This modern hotel, opposite Agua Hedionda, has a large pool and comfortable rooms equipped with phones, fans and cable TV.

Hotel España (☎ 352-21-86; Calle 2 de Mayo 22; s/d $12/16; P) The central, though average, España has 30 spacious remodeled rooms, with hot water and TV.

Hotel Colón (☎ 352-29-90; Portal Guerrero 48; s/d $11/15) The Colón's 20 rooms are basic (some interior, some exterior) but clean and nice enough for the price. The restaurant downstairs is popular with locals for set meals on the shaded patio. It faces the *zócalo*.

Eating & Drinking

Several popular outdoor cafés facing the Alameda serve coffee, milkshakes and sandwiches.

Tony's Pizzas (☎ 352-67-30; Portal Matamoros 6; mains $3-10) On the *zócalo*, Tony's tosses a variety of pies, plus burgers, pasta, set breakfasts and lots of cocktails.

Mikasa (☎ 352-51-02; Alvaro Obregón 12; mains $3.50-10) Mikasa serves a surprising variety of Japanese dishes, including sushi, udon and teriyaki. Inspect the raw fish display before ordering – it's far from fine cuisine, but it's among the best you'll find in these parts.

Tepoznieves (Alvaro Obregón 10E; scoops $1-2) Next door to Mikasa, this heavenly ice creamery has oodles of delicious tastes (some acquired); sample one of the flavors with chili or alcohol.

Café Mora (Calle 2 de Mayo 91; drinks $0.80-1.50; ⏱ closed Sun) Near the bus stations, this aromatic café steams Cuautla's finest espresso.

Getting There & Away

OCC (Ómnibus Cristóbal Colón; ☎ 800-702-80-00; www .ado.com.mx), a 1st-class line, and Sur and Volcanes, both 2nd-class, share a bus depot at the eastern end of Calle 2 de Mayo. **Pullman de Morelos** (☎ 352-73-71/81; www.pullman.com.mx)

is across the street, with 1st-class service to Tepoztlán ($1.75, every 15 minutes 9am to 9:30pm). **Estrella Roja** (☎ 800-712-22-84; www .estrellaroja.com.mx), a 2nd-class line, is a block west and **Estrella de Oro** (Oro; ☎ 55-5689-3955; www .estrelladeoro.com.mx) is a block south.

AROUND CUAUTLA

The road south of Cuautla leads through some significant revolutionary territory, where General Emiliano Zapata (see the boxed text, p238) was born, fought and met his death at the hands of treacherous federalists.

North of Cuautla, off Hwy 115 to Amecameca, a road heads east along the southern slopes of Popocatépetl (p204), passing a remarkable series of villages with well-conserved 16th-century monasteries along the developing **Ruta de los Conventos** – named by Unesco as World Heritage Site in 1994.

Worthwhile stops along the way with basic places to stay include Yecapixtla, Ocuituco, Tetela del Volcán and Hueyapan. The little-visited route offers a rewarding glimpse of how traditional ways of life persist, apparently undisturbed by their proximity to the smoking behemoth.

See the website of **Morelos state tourism** (http://ing.morelostravel.com/cultura/cmventos .html) for more details on the individual monasteries.

Destination	Price	Duration	Frequency
Cuernavaca	$3.25	1¼hr	Estrella Roja every 20-30min 5am-7:30pm
Mexico City (TAPO)	$3.50	2½hr	Volcanes/Sur every 20min via Amecameca
Mexico City (Terminal Sur)	$6	2hr	OCC, Estrella Roja or Pullman de Morelos every 10-20min
Oaxaca	$17	7hr	1 Sur at 11:30pm daily
Puebla	$8	2½hr	Estrella Roja every 15min 5am-7pm)
	$8.50	2½hr	Oro hourly 6am-7pm

CUERNAVACA

777 / pop 1 million / elevation 1480m

Thanks to its mild climate, Cuernavaca (kwehr-nah-*vah*-kah) has been a relaxing escape from Mexico City since colonial times. It attracts the wealthy from Mexico and abroad, many of whom have stayed on to become temporary or semipermanent residents. A number of their residences have become attractions in themselves, now housing hotels, fine restaurants and museums. As its outskirts swell with commuting refugees from the Distrito Federal, the City of Eternal Spring is acquiring the problems that everyone is trying to flee – traffic, smog and crime. Mexico City's elite are now just as likely to vacation in Acapulco or Miami, but many still maintain magnificent properties in Cuernavaca's sprawling suburbs.

Much of Cuernavaca's elegance is hidden in colonial courtyards, and is largely inaccessible to most visitors. A stroll around the charming *zócalo* costs nothing, but allow some extra pesos to savor the ambience at some of the better restaurants. The city is also worth visiting for the Palacio de Cortés, and its nearby *balnearios* and pre-Hispanic sites. Longer-term visitors often enroll at one of the many Spanish-language schools.

History

Around AD 1200, the first settlers in the valleys of modern Morelos developed a highly productive agricultural society based at Cuauhnáhuac (Place at the Edge of the Forest). The dominant Mexica (Aztecs) called them 'Tlahuica,' which means 'people who work the land.' In 1379 a Mexica war-

---

¡QUE VIVA ZAPATA!

A peasant leader from Morelos state, Emiliano Zapata (1879–1919) was the most radical of Mexico's revolutionaries, fighting for the return of hacienda land to the peasants with the cry '*¡Tierra y Libertad!*' (Land and Freedom!). The Zapatista movement was at odds both with the conservative supporters of the old regime and their liberal opponents. In November 1911, Zapata disseminated his *Plan de Ayala*, calling for restoration of all land to the peasants. After winning numerous battles against government troops in central Mexico (some in association with Pancho Villa), he was ambushed and killed in 1919. The following route traces some of Zapata's defining moments.

Ruta de Zapata

In Anenecuilco, 6km south of Cuautla, what's left of the adobe cottage where Zapata was born (on August 8, 1879), is now the **Museo de la Lucha para la Tierra** (Av Zapata; donation requested; 8am-9pm) featuring photographs of the rebel leader. Outside is a mural by Roberto Rodríguez Navarro that depicts Zapata exploding with the force of a volcano into the center of Mexican history, sundering the chains that bound his countrymen.

About 20km south of Anenecuilco is the Ex-Hacienda de San Juan Chinameca, where in 1919 Zapata was lured into a fatal trap by Colonel Jesús Guajardo, following the orders of President Venustiano Carranza, who was eager to dispose of the rebel leader and consolidate the post-revolutionary government. Pretending to defect to the revolutionary forces, Guajardo set up a meeting with Zapata, who arrived at Chinameca accompanied by a guerrilla escort. Guajardo's men gunned down the general before he crossed the abandoned hacienda's threshold.

The hacienda, with a small **museum** (Cárdenas; donation requested; 9:30am-5pm), is on the left at the end of the town's main street, where there's a statue of Zapata astride a rearing horse. The exhibits (photos and newspaper reproductions) are pretty meager, but you can still see the bullet holes in the walls – *olé!*

From Chinameca, Hwy 9 heads 20km northwest to Tlaltizapán, site of the **Cuartel General de Zapata** (Guerrero 67; donation requested; 9am-5pm Tue-Sun), the main barracks of the revolutionary forces. It contains relics from General Zapata's time, including the bed where he slept, his rifle (the trigger retains his fingerprints) and the outfit he was wearing at the time of his death (riddled with bullet holes and stained with blood).

From Cuautla, yellow 'Chinameca' combis traveling to Anenecuilco and Chinameca ($0.50) leave from the corner of Garduño and Matamoros every 10 minutes.

lord conquered Cuauhnáhuac, subdued the Tlahuica and exacted an annual tribute that included 16,000 pieces of *amate* (bark paper) and 20,000 bushels of corn. The tributes payable by the subject states were set out in a register the Spanish later called the Códice Mendocino, in which Cuauhnáhuac was represented by a three-branch tree; this symbol now graces Cuernavaca's coat of arms.

The Mexican lord's successor married the daughter of the Cuauhnáhuac leader, and from this marriage was born Moctezuma I Ilhuicamina, the 15th-century Aztec king who was a predecessor of the Moctezuma II Xocoyotzin encountered by Cortés. Under the Aztecs the Tlahuica traded extensively and prospered. Their city was a learning and religious center, and archaeological remains suggest they had a considerable knowledge of astronomy.

When the Spanish arrived, the Tlahuica were fiercely loyal to the Aztecs. In April 1521 they were finally overcome and Cortés torched the city. After destroying the city pyramid, Cortés used the stones to build a fortress-palace, Palacio de Cortés, on the pyramid's base (see p240). He also erected the fortress-like Catedral de la Asunción from the rubble. Soon the city became known as Cuernavaca, a more Spanish-friendly version of its original appellation.

In 1529, Cortés received his somewhat belated reward from the Spanish crown when he was named Marqués del Valle de Oaxaca, with an estate that covered 22 towns, including Cuernavaca and 23,000 indigenous Mexicans. After he introduced sugar cane and new farming methods, Cuernavaca became a Spanish agricultural center, as it had been for the Aztecs. Cortés' descendants dominated the area for nearly 300 years.

With its salubrious climate, rural surroundings and colonial elite, Cuernavaca became a refuge for the rich and powerful, including José de la Borda, the 18th-century Taxco silver magnate. Borda's lavish home was later a retreat for Emperor Maximilian and Empress Carlota. Cuernavaca also attracted many artists, and achieved literary fame as the setting for Malcolm Lowry's 1947 novel, *Under the Volcano*.

Orientation

Most important sites, bus terminals and budget-conscious hotels are near Cuer-

navaca's Plaza de Armas. Hwy 95D, the Mexico City–Acapulco toll road, skirts the city's east side. If driving from the north, take the Cuernavaca exit and cross to Hwy 95 (where you'll see a statue of Zapata on horseback). Hwy 95 becomes Blvd Zapata, then Av Morelos as you descend south into town; south of Av Matamoros, Morelos is one-way, northbound only. To reach the center, veer left and go down Matamoros.

Information

BOOKSTORES
Sanborns (cnr Juárez & Abasolo) Upscale department store with a bilingual newsstand, popular bar and coffeeshop.

EMERGENCY
Ambulance (☎ 318-38-82)
Cruz Roja (Red Cross; ☎ 315-35-05/55)
Fire (☎ 317-14-89)
Tourist Police (☎ 800-903-92-00)

INTERNET ACCESS
Other ephemeral places around town charge as little as $0.50 an hour.
Copy@net (Av Morelos 178; per hr $1.25; ☯ 8am-9pm Mon-Sat, 11am-5pm Sun; ▨)

LAUNDRY
Nueva Tintorería Francesa (Juárez 2; ☯ 9am-7pm Mon-Fri, 9am-2:30pm Sat) Per kg $1.

MEDICAL SERVICES
Hospital Cuernavaca (☎ 311-24-82/83; Cuauhtémoc 305) In Colonia Lomas de la Selva, 1km north of town.

POST
Main post office (south side Plaza de Armas; ☯ 8am-6pm Mon-Fri, 9am-1pm Sat)

TELEPHONE
Telecomm (south side Plaza de Armas; ☯ 8am-6pm Mon-Fri, 9am-1pm Sat)

TOURIST INFORMATION
There's an information booth in the cathedral and other kiosks around town, including at most bus stations. Ask at these places for maps.
Municipal tourist office (☎ 318-75-61, 318-64-98; www.cuernavaca.gob.mx in Spanish; Av Morelos 278; ☯ 9am-5pm)
State tourist office (☎ /fax 314-38-72/81, 800-987-82-24; www.morelostravel.com; Av Morelos Sur 187; ☯ 8am-5pm Mon-Fri, Sat 10am-1pm)

CUERNAVACA

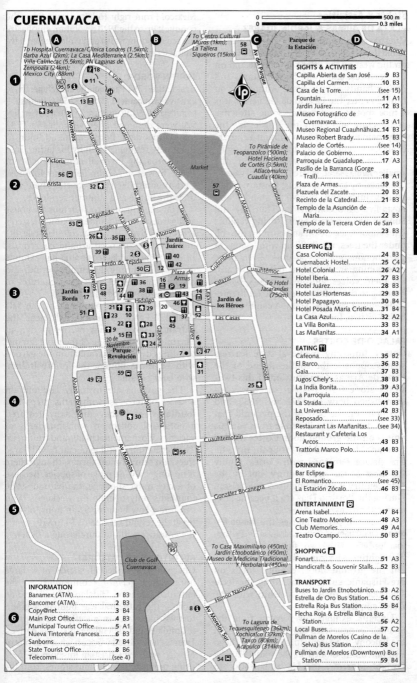

To Centro Cultural
Muros (1km);
La Tallera
Siqueiros (15km)

To Hospital Cuernavaca/Clínica Londres (1.5km);
Barba Azul (2km); La Casa Mediterránea (2.5km);
Villa Calmecac (5.5km); PN Lagunas de
Zempoala (24km);
Mexico City (88km)

Parque de
la Estación

De La Ronda

To Pirámide de
Teopanzolco (500m);
Hotel Hacienda
de Cortés (3.5km);
Atlacomulco;
Cuautla (40km)

To Hotel
Jacarandas
(750m)

To Casa Maximiliano (450m);
Jardín Etnobotánico (450m);
Museo de Medicina Tradicional
Y Herbolaria (450m)

To Laguna de
Tequesquitengo (36km);
Xochicalco (37km);
Taxco (80km);
Acapulco (314km)

AROUND MEXICO CITY

Jardín
Juárez

Plaza de
Armas

Jardín de
los Héroes

Jardín
Borda

Parque
Revolución

Club de Golf
Cuernavaca

500 m
0.3 miles

Sights & Activities

PLAZA DE ARMAS & JARDÍN JUÁREZ

Cuernavaca's *zócalo*, Plaza de Armas, is flanked on the east by the **Palacio de Cortés**, on the west by the **Palacio de Gobierno** and on the northeast and south by restaurants and roving bands of mariachis. Although you can't go enter the Palacio de Gobierno, it is a nice spot to contemplate some attractive architecture and enjoy the music. It's the only main plaza in Mexico without a church, chapel, convent or cathedral overlooking it.

Adjoining the northwest corner is the smaller **Jardín Juárez**, where the central gazebo (designed by tower specialist Gustave Eiffel) houses juice and sandwich stands, and hosts live band concerts on Thursday and Sunday evening from 6pm. Roving vendors sell balloons, ice cream and corn on the cob under the trees, which fill up with legions of cacophonous grackles at dusk. Even more entertaining are the guitar *trios* who warm up their voices and instruments before heading to the cafés across the street to serenade willing patrons. You too can request a ballad or two, for around $7.

PALACIO DE CORTÉS

Cortés' imposing medieval-style fortress stands opposite the southeast end of the Plaza de Armas. Construction of this two-storey stone fortress-style palace was accomplished between 1522 and 1532, and was done on the base of the pyramid that Cortés destroyed, still visible from various points on the ground floor. Cortés resided here until he turned tail for Spain in 1540. The palace remained with Cortés' family for most of the next century, but by the 18th century it was being used as a prison. During the Porfirio Díaz era it became government offices.

Today the palace houses the **Museo Regional Cuauhnáhuac** (Salazar; admission $3; 9am-6pm Tue-Sun), with two floors of exhibits highlighting Mexican cultures and history. On the ground floor, exhibits focus on pre-Hispanic cultures, including the local Tlahuica and their relationship with the Aztec empire.

Upstairs, exhibits cover events from the Spanish conquest to up the present. On the balcony is a fascinating mural by Diego Rivera, commissioned in the mid-1920s by Dwight Morrow, the US ambassador to Mexico. From right to left, scenes from the conquest up to the 1910 revolution emphasize the cruelty, oppression and violence that have characterized Mexican history.

JARDÍN BORDA

Beside the 1784 **Parroquia de Guadalupe**, these extravagant **gardens** (318-82-50; Av Morelos 271; adult/child $2.75/1.50, free Sun; 10am-5:30pm Tue-Sun) were designed after Versailles in 1783 for Manuel de la Borda, as an addition to the stately residence built by his father, José de la Borda, the Taxco silver magnate. From 1866, Emperor Maximilian and Empress Carlota entertained their courtiers here, and used the house as a summer residence.

From the entrance, you can tour the house and gardens to get an idea of how Mexico's aristocracy lived. In typical colonial style, the buildings are arranged around courtyards. In one wing, the **Museo de Sitio** has exhibits on daily life during the empire period, and original documents with the signatures of Morelos, Juárez and Maximilian.

Several romantic paintings in the **Sala Manuel M Ponce**, a recital hall near the entrance, show scenes of the garden in Maximilian's time. One of the most famous paintings depicts Maximilian in the garden with La India Bonita, the 'pretty Indian' who later became his lover.

The gardens are formally laid out on a series of terraces, with paths, steps and fountains, and they originally featured a botanical collection with hundreds of varieties of ornamental plants and fruit trees. The vegetation is still exuberant, with large trees and semitropical shrubs, though there is no longer a wide range of species. Because of a city water shortage, the baroque-style fountains only operate on weekends. You can hire a row boat for $2 an hour, or take tea at the restaurant (mains $4 to $10) inside the entrance without purchasing a ticket.

RECINTO DE LA CATEDRAL

Cuernavaca's cathedral stands in a large high-walled *recinto* (compound) – the entrance gate is on Hidalgo. Like Palacio de Cortés, the cathedral was built in a grand fortress-like style, in an effort to impress, intimidate and defend against the natives. Franciscans started work on what was one of Mexico's earliest Christian missions in 1526, using indigenous labor and stones from the rubble of Cuauhnáhuac. The first construction was the **Capilla Abierta de San José**, an open chapel on the cathedral's west side.

The cathedral itself, the **Templo de la Asunción de María**, is plain and solid, with an unembellished facade. The side door, which faces north to the compound's entrance, shows a mixture of indigenous and European features – the skull and crossbones above it is a symbol of the Franciscan order. Inside are frescoes re-discovered early in the 20th century. Cuernavaca was a center for Franciscan missionary activities in Asia, and the frescoes – said to show the persecution of Christian missionaries in Japan – were supposedly painted in the 17th century by a Japanese convert to Christianity.

The cathedral compound also holds two smaller churches. On the right as you enter is the **Templo de la Tercera Orden de San Francisco**; its exterior was carved in 18th-century baroque style by indigenous artisans, and its interior has ornate, gilded decorations. On the left as you enter is the 19th-century **Capilla del Carmen**, where believers seek cures for illness.

MUSEO ROBERT BRADY

American artist and collector Robert Brady (1928–86) lived in Cuernavaca for 24 years. His home, **Casa de la Torre** (☎ 316-85-54; www .bradymuseum.org; Netzahualcóyotl 4; admission $2.75; ☽ 10am-6pm Tue-Sun), was originally part of the monastery within the Recinto de la Catedral. After an extensive renovation, Brady decorated it with paintings, carvings, textiles, antiques and folk arts he'd acquired in his world travels. Now a museum, it boasts several paintings by well-known Mexican artists, including Tamayo, Kahlo and Covarrubias. The main attraction, however, is the sheer size and diversity of the collection, and the way it's arranged with delightful contrasts of styles, periods and places.

CENTRO CULTURAL MUROS

Contemporary Mexican culture is celebrated at this intriguing new **arts complex** (☎ 310-38-48/53; www.muros.com.mx in Spanish; Guerrero 205, Colonia Lomas de la Selva; admission $2.75, free Tue & Sun; ☽ 10am-6pm Tue-Sun), home to restored murals from Cuernavaca's Hotel Casino de la Selva, and a private collection of more than 320 paintings, sculptures, videos and photographs. Highlights include Frida Kahlo's *Diego en mi Pensamiento*, and

works by Rivera, Siquerios, Orozco, Tamayo and emerging 21st-century artists.

MUSEO DE MEDICINA TRADICIONAL Y HERBOLARIA

In Cuernavaca's suburbs, 1.5km southeast of the center, **Casa Maximiliano** was once a rural retreat for the Emperor Maximilian, where he would meet his Mexican lover. It was called La Casa del Olvido (the House of Forgetfulness), because Maximilian 'forgot' to include a room for his wife here. He did remember to include a small house in the back for his lover, which is now a **museum of traditional herbal medicine** (☽ 312-31-08; Matamoros 14, Colonia Acapantzingo; admission free; ☽ 9am-5pm).

Surrounding the museum, the **Jardín Etnobotánico** has a well-curated collection of herbs and medicinal plants from around the world. To get here, catch a Ruta 6 'Jardines' bus from the corner of Av Morelos and Degollado. Catch the return bus on 16 de Septiembre behind the garden.

PIRÁMIDE DE TEOPANZOLCO

This small **archaeological site** (☎ 314-40-46/48; cnr Río Balsas & Ixcateopan, Colonia Vista Hermosa; admission $2.75; ☽ 9am-5:30pm) is 1km northeast of the center. There are actually two pyramids, one inside the other. You can climb on the outer base and see the older pyramid within, with a double staircase leading up to the remains of a pair of temples. Tlahuicas built the older pyramid over 800 years ago; the outside one was under construction by the Aztecs when Cortés arrived, and was never completed. The name Teopanzolco means 'Place of the Old Temple,' and may relate to an ancient construction to the west of the current pyramid, where artifacts dating from around 7000 BC have been found, as well as others with an Olmec influence.

Several other smaller platform structures surround the double pyramid. Near the rectangular platform to the west, a tomb was discovered, containing the remains of 92 men, women and children mixed with ceramic pieces. They are believed to be victims of human sacrifice in which decapitation and dismemberment were practised.

Catch a Ruta 4 'Barona' bus at the corner of Degollado and Guerrero, get off at Río Balsas, turn right and walk four blocks; or take a taxi to the site.

OTHER ATTRACTIONS

The great Mexican muralist, David Alfaro Siqueiros, had his *taller* (workshop) and home in Cuernavaca from 1964 until his death in 1974. **La Tallera Siqueiros** (☎ 315-11-15; Venus 52; admission free; ☉ 10am-5pm Tue-Sun) is 2km north of the center. On display are four unfinished murals and some mementos of his life.

In a miniature 1897 castle, the **Museo Fotográfico de Cuernavaca** (☎ 312-70-81; Gómez Farías 1; admission free; ☉ 10am-5pm Tue-Sun) has early maps upstairs, and photographs of the city in the basement. Just downhill is the **Pasillo de la Barranca** (☉ 8am-6pm), a walkway that follows a deep gorge bursting with flowers and butterflies, well below the roar of traffic. There are a few waterfalls along the 500m trail, which emerges by the arches at the corner of Guerrero and Gómez Farías.

Courses

Many foreigners come to Cuernavaca to study Spanish, and it has dozens of language schools. The best offer small-group or individual instruction, at all levels, with four to five hours per day of intensive instruction plus a couple of hours' conversation practice. Classes begin each Monday, and most schools recommend a minimum enrollment of four weeks.

Tuition fees range from $150 to $300 per week for small group classes, usually payable in advance. Ask about discounts outside the peak months of January, February, July, August and December; some schools offer discounts if you stay more than four weeks. Most schools also charge a nonrefundable one-time enrollment fee of around $100. Schools can arrange for students to live with a Mexican host family for $20 to $30 per day, including meals.

With so many teaching styles and options, prospective students should research the choices carefully. Contact Morelos' state tourist office (p238) for an extensive list of schools. The following are among the most frequently and highly recommended:

Cemanahuac (☎ 318-64-07; www.cemanahuac .com) Emphasis is on language acquisition and cultural awareness.

Center for Bilingual Multicultural Studies (☎ 317-10-87, in USA 800-932-2068, 800-574-1585; www.bilingual-center.com) Accredited by the Universidad Autónoma del Estado de Morelos and affiliated with many foreign universities.

Cetlalic (☎ /fax 313-26-37; www.cetlalic.org.mx) Emphasizes language learning, cultural awareness and social responsibility. Offers special gay and lesbian programs.

Cuauhnáhuac Spanish Language Institute (☎ 312-36-73; www.cuauhnahuac.edu.mx) Helps students earn university language credits, and members of the business and medical communities develop language interests.

Encuentros (☎ 312-50-88; www.learnspanishinmexico .com) Focuses on professionals and travelers wanting to learn Spanish.

Ideal Latinoamerica (☎ 311-75-51; www.ideal-l.com) Program immerses students in Spanish language and Mexican culture, while respecting the individual's pace and style of learning.

Spanish Language Institute (SLI; ☎ 311-00-63; www.sli-spanish.com.mx) Cultural courses include Mexican customs and Latin American literature.

Universal Centro de Lengua y Comunicación (☎ 318-29-04; www.universal-spanish.com) Mixes language study with trips to local communities and visits from local politicians, scholars and community leaders.

Universidad Autónoma del Estado de Morelos (☎ 316-16-26; www.uaem.mx/espanolparaextranjeros /english.html) The state university's Centro de Lengua, Arte e Historia para Extranjeros uses a communicative approach augmented by audio, video and print source materials.

Festivals & Events

In the five days before Ash Wednesday (late February or early March), Cuernavaca's colorful **Carnaval** celebration features parades, art exhibits and street performances by Tepoztlán's Chinelo dancers. In late March and early April, the **Feria de la Primavera** (Spring Fair) includes cultural and artistic events, concerts and a beautiful exhibit of the city's spring flowers.

Sleeping

Good-value accommodations are scarce in Cuernavaca. Cheap places tend to be depressingly basic, while charming midrange ones are few and far between. Top-end hotels, of course, are wonderful but expensive. On Friday and Saturday nights and holidays, the town fills up with visitors from Mexico City, so it's best to arrive with prior reservations.

BUDGET

Cuernaback Hostel (☎ 310-10-50, 800-221-7265; www.cuernabackhostel.com; Humboldt 46; dm $11-13, d $28-32; ☐ ☒) Affiliated with Mexico City's Hostal Moneda, this new offering occupies a sprawling hacienda-style complex, with a large pool surrounded by lawns and gardens.

The spacious mixed-sex dorms have three to five beds; the nicest private rooms are upstairs. Rates include linen, Internet, and a breakfast and dinner buffet. Pluses include the sunny terrace, rooftop patios, a bar, hammocks and laundry facilities. It's within walking distance of the *zócalo* and near the bus stations.

Hotel Juárez (☎ 314-02-19; Netzahualcóyotl 19; r $28; Ⓟ Ⓡ) Next to the cathedral (with sing-song bells ding-donging all night long) on an otherwise quiet street, this old-fashioned option has a dozen simple but spacious and airy rooms, plus a pool encircled by a lawn. Except for one slightly cheaper room, all habitations have fans and non-cable TVs.

Hotel Iberia (☎ 314-13-24; www.hoteliberia.com.mx; Rayón 7; s/d $28/32; Ⓟ) With a Talavera-tiled reception area, this long-time foreign student favorite is a short walk from the *zócalo*. Recently remodeled rooms are tidy but cramped, and all have cable TV. Bigger rooms upstairs are worth the few extra pesos.

Hotel Colonial (☎ 318-64-14; Aragón y León 17; s/d with bathroom $19/23) Most rooms here, at the best of the backpacker ghetto places, face the well-kept garden. Two people sharing one bed is slightly cheaper that the prices listed, and upstairs rooms with balconies and tall ceilings are best.

Hotel Las Hortensas (☎ 318-52-65; Hidalgo 13; s/d with bathroom $21/25) The mostly tiny, dark rooms with cable TV are clean enough, but price and location are the main reasons to stay here. Upstairs veranda rooms are most desirable: single No 23, on the roof, is bright and breezy.

MIDRANGE

La Casa Mediterranea B&B (☎ 317-11-53; www.lacasamediterranea.com; Acacias 207, Colonia La Pradera; s/d incl breakfast $30/44; Ⓟ Ⓡ) Tired of staying in impersonal, run-down hotels? Try this comfortable, seven-room family residence that's a 3km uphill walk from the center, and just minutes from a bus stop. The helpful owners have been hosting foreign language students for years and offer discounts for longer stays.

Casa Colonial (☎ 312-70-33, 800-623-08-43; www.casacolonial.com in Spanish; Netzahualcóyotl 37; r incl breakfast Sun-Thu $69, Fri & Sat $87, ste $115-225; Ⓟ Ⓛ Ⓡ) Near Museo Robert Brady, this immaculately updated 18th-century colonial

home has sumptuous common areas and 16 spacious rooms with rustic yet refined furnishings, including some period antiques. TVs are by request only, but all rooms have wi-fi and hard-wired Internet; some suites have saunas and fireplaces. The central pool is surrounded by shady palms, lush gardens and an inviting bar-lounge. Smaller bungalows are tucked away in the back of the deep lot.

La Villa Bonita (☎ 169-72-32; www.lavillabonita.com; Netzahualcóyotl 33; r Sun-Thu $60-85, Fri & Sat $75-105; Ⓟ Ⓡ) With only three rooms upstairs, this secluded hideaway occupies a charming, ivy-draped, 16th-century compound. Bathrooms are rustically tiled and modern art is for sale everywhere. Thoughtful touches include minibars and an English-language lending library. Guests read while relaxing on the small terrace overlooking gardens shaded by an ancient laurel tree. If the sweet scents emanating from Reposado restaurant below pique your interest, inquire about their one-day cooking classes ($150).

Hotel Papagayo (☎ 314-17-11; www.tourbymexico.com/hpapagayo, Motolinía 13; s/d $43/54, ste from $49; Ⓟ Ⓟ Ⓖ) Welcome to Miami Beach, circa the swinging 1960s: this sprawling family-oriented place has tons of funky

THE AUTHOR'S CHOICE

La Casa Azul (☎ 314-21-41, 314-36-34; www.tourbymexico.com/lacasaazul; Arista 17; s/d/tr incl breakfast $41/59/73; Ⓟ Ⓛ Ⓡ) Finally, a midrange charmer in central Cuernavaca. The thoughtfully updated 19th-century Blue House, originally part of the Guadalupe Convent, has soothing fountains and nine comfortable rooms (a few with rustically tiled bathtubs) with modern amenities like plush towels and cable TV/VCRs. The staff are delightful, the setting is tranquil and the decor is classic Mexican. In 2006, 15 new upscale rooms will open next door, in a painstakingly restored home. The decor will reflect the French owner's keen interest in traditional Mexican handicrafts: each room will showcase a different type of marble and original decorations from the country's most notable crafts regions. The rooftop terrace has fine panoramic views, and the air-conditioned suites will have Jacuzzi tubs.

rooms – spring $2 for a 'new-era' one – with ceiling fans and TVs, a big swimming pool, a leafy playground (bordered by mango trees) and ample parking. Rates include breakfast and complimentary weekend lounge music.

Villa Calmecac (☎ 313-29-18; www.villacalmecac.com; Zacatecas 114, Colonia Buenavista; dm/d incl breakfast $20/53; P ⊕) Crafted from adobe and surrounded by organic gardens, this eco-friendly hostel, affiliated to Hostelling International (HI), is 7km from Cuernavaca's center. Yoga classes are offered, breakfast is an all-natural buffet and the bunks are in rustic-style rooms. It's 800m west of Hwy 95, a 20-minute ride from the corner of Av Morelos and Degollado on a Ruta 1, 2 or 3 bus. Zacatecas is two blocks past the Zapata monument on the left. Visitors must check in before 9pm.

TOP END

Hotel Posada María Cristina (☎ 318-57-67, 800-713-74-07; www.maria-cristina.com; Juárez 300; r/ste from $135/170; P ⬚) This centrally-located 16th-century estate is one of Cuernavaca's long-time favorites. Highlights include 20 tastefully appointed rooms in a nicely restored colonial building, the charming *nueva cocina mexicana* restaurant and bar Calandria with its popular Sunday champagne buffet, and an inviting pool and Jacuzzi amidst lovely hillside gardens.

Las Mañanitas (☎ 314-14-66, in Mexico City 800-221-52-99, in USA ☎ 888-413-91-99; www.lasmananitas.com.mx; Linares 107; ste incl breakfast $210-469; P ⬚ ⬚ ⬚) Renowned for its private gardens, where peacocks strut their plumed stuff while the guests luxuriate in the heated pool, this is one of Mexico's finest (if overhyped) boutique hotels. The 22 rooms range from original terrace suites and newer rooms with private patios, to the master fireplace suite with a full living room. The restaurant is also justly famous.

Hotel Hacienda de Cortés (☎ 316-08-67, 800-220-76-97; www.hotelhaciendadecortes.com; Plaza Kennedy 90; s/d/ste from $79/99/115; P ⬚) Built in the 16th century by Martín Cortés, who succeeded Hernán Cortés as Marqués del Valle de Oaxaca, this former sugar mill was renovated in 1980. It boasts 23 luxurious suites, each with its own private garden and terrace. There's a swimming pool built around old stone columns. In Atlacomulco, 4km

southeast of the center, it's worth visiting even if you're not a guest, if only to stroll the lovely grounds or lunch underneath the restaurant's magnificent colonial arches.

Hotel Jacarandas (☎ 315-77-77, in Mexico City ☎ 55-5544-3098; www.jacarandas.com.mx; Cuauhtémoc 133, Colonia Chapultepec; r/ste from $165/200; P ⬚) The 80 rooms at the Jacarandas are not large or fancy, but the rambling grounds are graced with lots of trees, exuberant gardens, a good restaurant, and three pools of varying temperatures. It's 2km east of the center.

Eating

For a simple snack of yogurt with fruit, boiled corn on the cob or ice cream, visit one of the booths in the Jardín Juárez, then savor your treat on one of the park's benches.

BUDGET

Cafeona (☎ 318-27-57; Morrow 6; mains $2-6; ☺ 8am-9pm Mon-Sat) This taste of Chiapas is a cool hangout, decorated with handicrafts and serving organic coffee, as well as cheap beer, cocktails, pies, *tamales* and fruit salads with granola. Drop by for the daily buffet breakfast, a generous set midday meal, or to browse its small gift shop.

Jugos Chely's (Galeana; mains $1-3; ☺ 7am-9pm; Ⓥ) Near the Jardín Juárez, Chely's prepares fresh fruit-juice combos such as *toronjil* (grapefruit, pineapple and parsley) and *zanayogui* (carrot and orange), as well as breakfast, burgers and *antojitos*.

MIDRANGE

El Barco (☎ 313-21-31; Rayón 5F; mains $3-7; ☺ 11am-midnight) This popular, no-nonsense joint specializes in Guerrero-style *pozole* (shredded meat and hominy in a delicious pork-based broth), the all-curing Mexican version of matzo-ball soup. Small or heaping clay bowls are accompanied by fine oregano, mildly hot red chili, shredded lettuce, limes and chopped onions. Specify *pollo* (chicken), *maciza* unless you'd like your soup to include bits of fat, and *especial* if you enjoy avocado. For refreshment, there's ice-cold beer, pitchers of *agua de jamaica* (hibiscus water) and top-shelf tequilas.

Restaurant y Cafetería Los Arcos (☎ 312-15-10; Jardín de los Héroes 4; mains $3-9) The Arches is a popular meeting place among the international student set. Grab a seat at an outdoor table, sip a coffee or a cold beer and watch the action on the plaza. The varied bilingual menu has something for everyone; there's a separate seafood menu. On Friday and Saturday night live salsa music inspires dancing in the aisles.

Trattoria Marco Polo (☎ 318-40-32; Hidalgo 30; mains $5-10, pizza $5-25; ☯ 1-10:30pm Sun-Thu, 1pm-midnight Fri & Sat) This energized trattoria has homemade pasta and a decent wine list, and tosses superior pizzas, from single serving to family size. There's a perfect view of the cathedral compound from the balcony and breezy courtyard tables out back.

La Parroquia (☎ 318-58-20; Guerrero 102; mains $4.50-9) Overlooking Jardín Juárez, this is a favorite with Cuernavaca's elder statesmen for its set meals. Come for the conviviality and location – the traditional Mexican food is nothing special.

La Universal (☎ 318-59-70; cnr Gutenberg & Guerrero; mains $4.50-11) The Universal enjoys a strategic position on the corner of the two central plazas, with tables under an awning facing the Plaza de Armas. Like La Parroquia, this popular place is all about location. The people-watching is great, but you can find better eats elsewhere.

TOP END

Restaurant Las Mañanitas (☎ 314-14-66; Linares 107; breakfast $5-15, mains $15-30; ☯ 1-5pm & 7-11pm) For a memorable breakfast, a romantic cocktail or an evening indulgence, try one of Mexico's most famous restaurants at the hotel of the same name. Choose between tables inside the mansion or on the terrace, where you can watch the wildlife wander around the emerald-green garden among fine modern sculptures. The menu, presented at your table on a blackboard, changes daily and features international dishes with Mexican influences. Reservations are recommended.

Reposado (☎ 169-72-32; www.reposado.com.mx; Netzahualcóyotl 33; mains $7-15; ☯ 7pm-1am Tue-Sat, 4-11pm Sun) The dramatic menu of traditional Mexican dishes inflected with *nouvelle* sensibilities is presented in a grand picture frame at this cosmopolitan hideaway. It's also the best bet in town for poolside tapas and cocktails. Tables are scattered throughout the colonial complex and romantically candlelit. There's a stylish sofa-bed cocktail lounge in a loft overlooking the pool.

Gaia (☎ 312-36-56; Juárez 102; mains $10-20; ☯ 1pm-midnight Mon-Sat, 1-8pm Sun) In the former mansion of actor Mario Moreno (aka Cantinflas), this creative restaurant fuses Mexican and Mediterranean ingredients in fabulous signature dishes like duck *taquitos* (mini-tacos) with plum salsa – anything featuring seafood is a winner. Reserve a table with a view of the Diego Rivera mosaic that adorns the bottom of the swimming pool.

La India Bonita (☎ 318-69-67; Morrow 115; mains $6-13; ☯ 8:30am-10:30pm Tue-Fri, 9am-10pm Sat, 9am-8pm Sun) In the former US ambassador's home, this lovely garden courtyard restaurant delivers good breakfasts and well-prepared traditional Mexican cuisine. House specialties include chicken *mole*, and chicken breast stuffed with squash flowers and *huitlacoche* sauce. There's an elaborate Sunday buffet brunch, full bar and live folkloric ballet Saturdays from 7pm.

La Strada (☎ 318-60-85; Salazar 38; mains $9-15) On the walking street also known as Callejon del Cubo, this inviting slice of Rome presents authentic Italian-Mediterranean cuisine in a covered interior courtyard. The napkins are linen, the wine cellar is well-stocked, the lettuce is organic and service is attentive. Considering its location near the Palacio de Cortés, it's not too touristy. Romance fills the air Friday and Saturday nights, when there's live violin music and opera singing.

Drinking

Plazuela del Zacate and the adjacent alley Las Casas come alive most evenings, when bars feature karaoke and live sing-along music. There are plenty of outdoor tables and the crowd is young and friendly. Don't like what you hear? Follow your ears and stumble around to compare the numerous two-for-one drink deals. The worse the music, the cheaper the beer, it seems. These places all open around sunset and typically don't shut their doors until around sunrise. There are no cover charges.

Bar Eclipse (Plazuela del Zacate) Has performers on two levels, folk on the bottom and rock on top.

El Romántico (Plazuela del Zacate) As the name implies, this bar is a venue for ballad singers. It is entertaining enough, if karaoke is your thing.

La Estación Zócalo (☎ 312-13-37; cnr Blvd Juárez & Hidalgo) Opposite the Palacio de Cortés, this popular bar attracts an even younger crowd with blaring rock music and two brightly colored but dimly lit dance floors. Tuesday is ladies night, and things get so loud on Friday and Saturday that the adjacent hotel refuses to accept customers.

Entertainment

Hanging around the central plazas is a popular activity, especially Sundays from 6pm, when open-air concerts are often staged. Jardín Borda (p240) hosts recitals (tickets $6) most Thursdays at 7pm.

DISCOS

Better discos charge a cover of at least $5, but women often get in free. Some discos enforce dress codes, and trendier places post style police at the door. Things really get going after 11pm.

Barba Azul (☎ 311-55-11/55; Prado 10, Colonia San Jerónimo; ☽ Fri & Sat 10pm-late), with fab indoor gardens, and upscale **Club Memories** (☎ 318-43-80; Av Morelos 241; ☽ Wed, Fri & Sat 10pm-late) are two hot spots.

The tropical-themed **Mambo Cafe** (☎ 313-58-13; cnr Guerrero & Nueva Italia, Colonia San Cristóbal; ☽ 10pm-5am Wed-Sat) is best for dancing to live salsa music. You'll need to take a taxi there and back.

THEATER

If your *español* is up to it, sample Cuernavaca's theater scene.

Cine Teatro Morelos (☎ 318-10-50; Av Morelos 188; tickets from $2) Morelos' state theater hosts quality film series, plays and dance performances. There's a full schedule posted out front and a bookstore and café inside.

Teatro Ocampo (☎ 318-63-85; Jardín Juárez 2) Near Jardín Juárez, this theater stages contemporary plays; a calendar of cultural events is posted at its entrance.

LUCHA LIBRE

Arena Isabel (☎ 318-59-16; cnr Juárez & Abasolo; adult/child $5/3; ♿) Are you ready to rumble, *amigo*? Less highbrow diversions, namely *lucha libre* (a form of wrestling), go down here in the squared ring. Check out the good-versus-evil line-ups on posters pasted up around town.

Shopping

Cuernavaca lacks distinctive handicrafts, but if you crave an onyx ashtray, a leather belt or some second-rate silver, peruse the souvenir stalls adjacent to Palacio de Cortés or around the Plaza de Armas on weekends. The **Fonart** (☎ 318-10-50 ext 226; Av Morelos 271; ☽ 10am-3pm & 4-6pm Tue-Sun) outlet inside Jardín Borda has a good selection of fair-traded folk art from around the country.

Getting There & Away

BUS

Cuernavaca's main-line bus companies operate the following five separate long-distance terminals:

Estrella de Oro (EDO; ☎ 55-5689-3955; www.estrelladeoro.com.mx; Av Morelos Sur 900)

Estrella Roja (ER; ☎ 800-712-22-84; www.estrellaroja.com.mx; cnr Galeana & Cuauhtemotzin)

Flecha Roja & Estrella Blanca (FR & EB; ☎ 800-507-55-00; www.estrellablanca.com.mx; Av Morelos 503, btwn Arista & Victoria)

Pullman de Morelos (PDM; ☎ 55-5549-3505; www.pullman.com.mx); Downtown (cnr Abasolo & Netzahualcóyotl); Casino de la Selva (Av del Parque s/n)

CAR & MOTORCYCLE

Cuernavaca is 89km south of Mexico City, a 1½-hour drive on Hwy 95 or a one-hour trip via Hwy 95D. Both roads continue south to Acapulco; Hwy 95 detours through Taxco, Hwy 95D is more direct and much faster.

Getting Around

You can walk to most places of interest in central Cuernavaca. Local buses ($0.40) advertise their destinations on their windshields. Many local buses, and those to nearby towns, leave from the southern corner of the city's labyrinthine market. Taxis serve most places in town for under $3.

To get to the Estrella de Oro bus terminal, 1km south (downhill) of the center, hop on a Ruta 20 bus down Galeana; in the other direction, catch any bus heading up Av Morelos. Ruta 17 buses head up Av Morelos, and stop within one block of the Pullman de Morelos terminal at Casino de la Selva. All other depots are within walking distance of the *zócalo*.

XOCHICALCO

Atop a desolate plateau – 15km southwest of Cuernavaca as the crow flies, but about 38km by road – is the ancient ceremonial center of **Xochicalco** (☎ 777-379-74-16; admission $3; ☽ 9am-6pm), a Unesco World Herit-

CUERNAVACA BUS SCHEDULE

Daily 1st-class and deluxe services from Cuernavaca include the following:

Destination	Price	Duration	Frequency
Acapulco	$21	4hr	1st-class EDO hourly
	$23	4hr	4 daily EDO deluxe
	$22	4hr	7 Estrella Blanca /Futura daily
Cuautla	$3.25	1¼hr	ER every 15min 6am-8pm
Grutas de Cacahuamilpa	$3	2hr	6 FR daily
Mexico City	$5.50	1¼hr	PDM deluxe every 15min 5am-11:15pm from downtown terminal
	$6.50	1¼hr	deluxe every 25min from Casino de la Selva, also at 7:30am & 8:30am from downtown
	$5	1¼hr	frequent Estrella Blanca/Futura
Mexico City Airport	$10*	2hr	PDM deluxe every 30min from Casino de la Selva
Puebla	$12.50	2¾hr	hourly ER & Oro via Autopista Siglo XXI
Taxco	$3.75	1½hr	15 FR daily
	$4.50	1½hr	5 Estrella Blanca daily
Tepoztlán	$1.35	30min	ER every 15min 6am-8pm. Also departs a bit later from the local bus terminal at the city market.
Toluca	$4	2½hr	FR every 30min
Zihuatanejo	$32	7hr	2 EDO at 8:20pm & 10:15pm daily

* tickets may be purchased at PDM's downtown terminal

age Site and one of central Mexico's most important archaeological sites. *Xochicalco* (so-chee-*cal*-co') is Náhuatl for 'place of the house of flowers.'

The collection of white stone ruins, many still yet to be excavated, covers approximately 10 sq km. They represent the various cultures – Toltec, Olmec, Zapotec, Mixtec and Aztec – for which Xochicalco was a commercial, cultural or religious center. When Teotihuacán began to weaken around AD 650–700, Xochicalco began to rise in importance, achieving its maximum splendor between AD 650 and 900, with far-reaching cultural and commercial relations. Around AD 650, Zapotec, Mayan and Gulf Coast spiritual leaders convened here to correlate their respective calendars.

The site's most famous monument is the **Pirámide de Quetzalcóatl** (Pyramid of the Plumed Serpent). Archaeologists have surmised from its well-preserved bas-reliefs, that astronomer-priests met here at the beginning and end of each 52-year cycle of the pre-Hispanic calendar. Xochicalco

remained an important center until around 1200, when its excessive growth precipitated a demise similar to that of Teotihuacán. Site signs are in English and Spanish, but information at the impressive, ecologically-sensitive **museum**, 200m from the ruins, is in Spanish only.

GETTING THERE & AWAY

From Cuernavaca's market, 'Cuautepec' buses ($1) depart every 30 minutes for the site entrance. The last return bus leaves around 6pm. Alternatively, Pullman de Morelos runs hourly buses that will drop you off within 4km of the site. Flecha Roja runs buses by the same intersection every two hours. From there, you can walk (uphill) or catch a taxi (if you're lucky enough to find one).

TAXCO

☎ 762 / pop 90,000 / elevation 1800m

The boom-and-bust silver-mining town of Taxco (*tahss*-ko), 160km southwest of Mexico City, is a gorgeous colonial antique, and one of interior Mexico's most picturesque and endearing places. Clinging to a steep hillside, its narrow cobblestone streets twist between well-worn buildings and open unexpectedly onto pretty plazas, revealing enchanting vistas at every turn. Unlike many colonial-era Mexican towns, Taxco has not become engulfed by industrial suburbs.

The Mexican government has declared Taxco a national historical monument, and local laws help preserve the colonial architecture. Old buildings are restored wherever possible, and new construction must conform to the old in scale, style and materials – for an example check out the colonial Pemex station. Though Taxco's silver mines are nearly exhausted, handmade silver jewelry and tourism are the town's principal industries. There are hundreds of *platerías* (silver shops) and visiting them is the perfect excuse to wander the streets.

History

Taxco was called Tlachco (Ball Playing Place) by the Aztecs, who dominated the region from 1440 until the Spanish arrived. The colonial city was founded by Rodrigo de Castañeda in 1529, with a mandate from Hernán Cortés. Among the town's first Spanish residents were three miners – Juan de Cabra, Juan Salcedo and Diego de Nava – and the carpenter Pedro Muriel. In 1531, they established the first Spanish mine in North America.

The Spaniards came searching for tin, which they found in small quantities, but by 1534 they had discovered tremendous lodes of silver. That year the Hacienda El Chorrillo was built, complete with water wheel, smelter and aqueduct – the remains of which form the old arches (Los Arcos) over Hwy 95 at the north end of town.

The prospectors quickly depleted the hacienda's first silver veins and fled Taxco. Further quantities of ore were not discovered until 1743. Don José de la Borda, who had arrived in 1716 from France at the age of 16 to work with his miner brother, accidentally unearthed one of the region's richest veins. According to legend, Borda was riding near where the Templo de Santa Prisca now stands, when his horse stumbled, dislodged a stone and exposed the precious metal.

Borda went on to make three fortunes and lose two. He introduced new techniques of draining and repairing mines,

and he reportedly treated his indigenous workers better than most colonial mines. The Templo de Santa Prisca was the devout Borda's gift to Taxco. His success attracted more prospectors, and new silver veins were found and played out. With most of the silver gone, Taxco became a quiet town with a dwindling population and economy.

In 1929, an American architect and professor named William (Guillermo) Spratling arrived and, at the suggestion of then US ambassador Dwight Morrow, set up a silver workshop as a way to rejuvenate the town. (Another version has it that Spratling was writing a book and resorted to the silver business because his publisher went bust. A third has it that Spratling had a notion to create jewelry that synthesized pre-Hispanic motifs with art deco modernism.) The workshop evolved into a factory, and Spratling's apprentices began establishing their own shops. Today, Taxco is home to hundreds of silver shops, many producing for export.

Orientation

Taxco's serpentine streets may make you feel like a mouse in a maze; in any case, it's a great place to get lost. The *zócalo*, Plaza Borda, is the heart of town, and its church, the Parroquia de Santa Prisca, is your best landmark. Both bus stations are on Av de los Plateros. The basic minibus route is a counterclockwise loop going north on Av de los Plateros and south through the center of town. Several side roads go east back to Av de los Plateros, which is two-way and therefore the only way a vehicle can get back to the north end of town.

Information

EMERGENCY
Cruz Roja (Red Cross; ☎ 622-32-32)
Police (☎ 622-00-77)

INTERNET ACCESS
Cybercafes come and go like the clouds; most charge around $1 an hour.
Net X Internet (Ruíz de Alarcón 11) Fast connections, with a good nighttime *gordita* stand out front.

LAUNDRY
Lavandería Los Pinos (☎ 627-24-87; 1st fl, Juárez 11; ☎ 11am-1pm & 4-8pm Mon-Sat) Costs $1.25 per kg ($1.65 for express service), with a 3kg minimum.

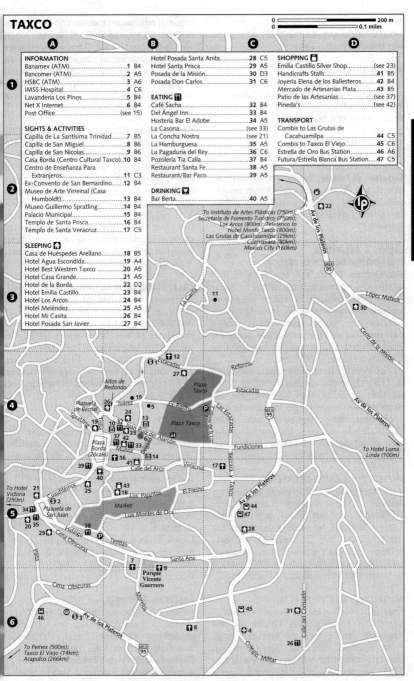

TAXCO

| | 0 | 200 m |
| | 0 | 0.1 miles |

INFORMATION
Banamex (ATM)............................1 B4
Bancomer (ATM)..........................2 A5
HSBC (ATM)................................3 A6
IMSS Hospital..............................4 C6
Lavandería Los Pinos....................5 B4
Net X Internet.............................6 B4
Post Office...............................(see 15)

SIGHTS & ACTIVITIES
Capilla de La Santísima Trinidad.......7 B5
Capilla de San Miguel...................8 B6
Capilla de San Nicolas...................9 B6
Casa Borda (Centro Cultural Taxco).10 B4
Centro de Enseñanza Para
   Extranjeros.............................11 C3
Ex-Convento de San Bernardino...12 B4
Museo de Arte Virreinal (Casa
   Humboldt)..............................13 B4
Museo Guillermo Spratling...........14 B4
Palacio Municipal........................15 B4
Templo de Santa Prisca................16 B4
Templo de Santa Veracruz............17 C5

SLEEPING
Casa de Huéspedes Arellano..........18 B5
Hotel Agua Escondida..................19 A4
Hotel Best Western Taxco 20 A5
Hotel Casa Grande.......................21 A5
Hotel de la Borda........................22 D2
Hotel Emilia Castillo.....................23 B4
Hotel Los Arcos...........................24 B4
Hotel Meléndez...........................25 A5
Hotel Mi Casita...........................26 B4
Hotel Posada San Javier................27 B4

Hotel Posada Santa Anita.............28 C5
Hotel Santa Prisca.......................29 A5
Posada de la Misión.....................30 D3
Posada Don Carlos.......................31 C6

EATING
Café Sacha.................................32 B4
Del Ángel Inn..............................33 B4
Hostería Bar El Adobe...................34 A5
La Casona...............................(see 33)
La Concha Nostra.....................(see 21)
La Hamburguesa.........................35 A5
La Pagaduría del Rey....................36 C6
Pozolería Tia Calla.......................37 B4
Restaurant Santa Fe.....................38 A5
Restaurant/Bar Paco....................39 A5

DRINKING
Bar Berta...................................40 A5

SHOPPING
Emilia Castillo Silver Shop..........(see 23)
Handicrafts Stalls.........................41 B5
Joyería Elena de los Ballesteros......42 B4
Mercado de Artesanías Plata.........43 B5
Patio de las Artesanías ....(see 37)
Pineda's.................................(see 42)

TRANSPORT
Combis to Las Grutas de
   Cacahuamilpa..........................44 C5
Combis to Taxco El Viejo...............45 C6
Estrella de Oro Bus Station...........46 A6
Futura/Estrella Blanca Bus Station....47 C5

AROUND MEXICO CITY

To Instituto de Artes Plásticas (750m);
Secretaría de Fomento Turístico (750m);
Los Arcos (800m); Teleférico to
Hotel Monte Taxco (800m);
Las Grutas de Cacahuamilpa (29km);
Cuernavaca (80km);
Mexico City (160km)

López Mateos

Cerro de la Misión

To Hotel Loma
Linda (100m)

Altos de
Redondo

Plaza
Taxco

Reforma

Estacadas

Av de los Plateros

Plazuela
de Bernal

Juárez

Ex-Rastro

Plaza Taxco

Fundiciones

Spratling

Plaza
Borda
(Zócalo)

Ruiz del Alarcón

Muñoz

Veracruz

Calle del Arco

Callejón de la Luz

Las Estacadas

Bedueria y Turco

Av de los Plateros

Cuauhtémoc

To Hotel
Victoria
(250m)

Plazuela de
San Juan

Market

Los Pajaritos

El Fresno

Luis Montes de Oca

Av de los Plateros

Hidalgo

Cena Obscuras

Tetitlán

Pilita

Cena Obscuras

Santa Ana

Parque
Vicente
Guerrero

Morelos

Av de los Plateros

Calle del Consuelo

To Pemex (500m);
Taxco El Viejo (14km);
Acapulco (266km)

Colegio Militar

MONEY

Several banks around the main plazas and bus stations have ATMs.

POST & TELEPHONE

There are card phones near Plaza Borda, and quieter ones in nicer hotel lobbies.

Post office (Av de los Plateros 382) At the south end of town, with a branch at Palacio Municipal.

TOURIST INFORMATION

The tourist info stand at the Futura bus station has free city maps.

Secretaría de Fomento Turístico (☎ 622-50-73; Av de los Plateros; 9am-3pm & 4-6pm) At north end of town. English- and French-speaking staff arrange guided tours of Taxco. Don't confuse it with an unofficial office 1km south.

Sights & Activities

PARROQUIA DE SANTA PRISCA

Facing Plaza Borda, this landmark church of rose-colored stone is a baroque treasure; its Churrigueresque facade is decorated with elaborately sculpted figures. Above the doorway, the oval bas-relief depicts Christ's baptism. Inside, the intricately sculpted, gold-covered altarpieces are equally fine Churrigueresque specimens.

The local Catholic hierarchy allowed José de la Borda to donate this church to Taxco on the condition that he mortgage his mansion and other assets to guarantee its completion; the project nearly bankrupted Borda. It was designed by Spanish architects Juan Caballero and Diego Durán, and was constructed between 1751 and 1758.

MUSEO GUILLERMO SPRATLING

This three-storey **history and archaeology museum** (☎ 622-16-70; Delgado 1; admission $2.25; 9am-6pm Tue-Sat, 9am-3pm Sun) is off an alley behind Templo de Santa Prisca. On the upper floors, pre-Hispanic art exhibits include jade statuettes, Olmec ceramics and other sterling pieces from William Spratling's private collection.

MUSEO DE ARTE VIRREINAL

One of Taxco's oldest colonial homes is somewhat optimistically known as **Casa Humboldt**: the German explorer and naturalist Friedrich Heinrich Alexander von Humboldt slept here for only one night in 1803. The restored building now houses a colonial **religious art museum** (☎ 622-55-01; Ruiz de Alarcón 12; admission $1.75; 10am-6pm Tue-Sat, 10am-3pm Sun), with a small but well-displayed collection, labeled in English and Spanish. The most interesting exhibit describes restoration work on the Templo de Santa Prisca, during which some fabulous material was discovered in the basement.

CASA BORDA (CENTRO CULTURAL TAXCO)

Built by José de la Borda in 1759, the **Casa Borda** (☎ 622-66-34; Plaza Borda; admission free; 10am-5pm Tue-Sun) serves as a cultural center hosting experimental theater and exhibiting contemporary sculpture, painting and photography by Guerrero artists. The building, however, is the main attraction. Due to the unevenness of the terrain, the rear window looks out on a precipitous four-storey drop, even though the entrance is on the ground floor.

TELEFÉRICO (AERIAL CABLE CAR)

From the north end of Taxco, near Los Arcos, a Swiss-made **cable car** (round-trip adult/child $2.75/1.75; 7:45am-7pm) ascends 173m to the Hotel Monte Taxco resort (p252), affording fantastic views of Taxco and the surrounding mountains. To find the entrance, walk uphill from the south side of Los Arcos and turn right through the Instituto de Artes Plásticas gate.

Courses

Centro de Enseñanza Para Extranjeros (CEPE; ☎ 622-34-10; www.cepe.unam.mx/ingles; courses from $450) This branch of Mexico City's Universidad Nacional Autónoma de México (UNAM) offers intensive Spanish language courses in the atmospheric Ex-Hacienda El Chorrillo. Advanced students may take additional courses in Mexican art history, geography and literature. CEPE can arrange lodging with local host families for $150 to $250 per month.

Escuela Nacional de Artes Plásticas (☎ 622-36-90; www.enap.unam.mx in Spanish) Next door, this school offers arts workshops from $150 per month or $800 per semester.

Festivals & Events

Be sure to reserve your hotel in advance if your visit coincides with one of Taxco's annual festivals. Double-check exact dates of moveable feasts with the tourist office.

Fiestas de Santa Prisca & San Sebastián Taxco's patron saints are feted on January 18 (Santa Prisca) and

January 20 (San Sebastián), when locals parade by the Templo de Santa Prisca, with their pets and farm animals in tow, for an annual blessing.

Jueves Santo The Thursday before Easter, the Eucharist is commemorated with street processions of hooded penitents who flagellate themselves with thorns as the procession winds through town.

Jornadas Alarconianas During this summertime cultural festival, which honors Taxco-born playwright Juan Ruiz de Alarcón, Taxco's plazas and churches host concerts and dance performances by internationally renowned performing artists.

Día del Jumil The Monday after Day of the Dead (November 2), the *jumil* – the savory beetle said to represent the giving of life and energy to Taxco residents for another year – is celebrated. Many families camp on the Cerro de Huixteco over the preceding weekend, and townsfolk climb the hill to collect *jumiles* and share food and camaraderie (see boxed text, p253).

Feria de la Plata The weeklong national silver fair convenes in late November or early December. Competitions are held in various categories (such as jewelry and statuary), and some of Mexico's best silverwork is on display. Other festivities include rodeos, concerts, dances and *burro* (donkey) races.

Las Posadas From December 16 to 24, nightly candlelit processions fill Taxco's streets with door-to-door singing. Children are dressed up to resemble Biblical characters; at the end of the night, they attack piñatas.

Sleeping

Taxco's lodging options are pricier than elsewhere in central Mexico, but they are generally so appealing that they're good value anyway. Few places have on-site parking, but most have a deal (around $4 for 24 hours) with the central Plaza Taxco lot.

BUDGET

Casa de Huéspedes Arellano (☎ 622-02-15; Los Pajaritos 23; dm $12, s with/without bathroom $19/15, d $27/25) Overlooking Taxco's lively market, this popular place has 15 simple but clean rooms, and four shared showers. It's well tended, with lots of flowers, caged birds, a variety of rooms and ample terraces for relaxing. From the Futura bus station, cross Av de los Plateros and head up Luis Montes de Oca (Calle Nueva) for a long block; turn right on the first street, then left up Los Pajaritos. The entrance is on your right-hand side, at the end of Pajaritos.

Hotel Casa Grande (☎ 622-09-69; www.casagran detaxco.com in Spanish; Plazuela de San Juan 7; s with/without bathroom $19/14, d $28/24; 🖵) Occupying the upper level of an old mining building (with a great rooftop terrace), the 'Big House' has 26 clean rooms, with new paint jobs, around an inner courtyard. The shared bathroom is tiny and often overworked. Rooms can be noisy: La Concha Nostra bar blasts loud live music on Saturday nights, when rates inexplicably rise a few dollars.

Hotel Posada Santa Anita (☎ 622-07-52; Av de los Plateros 320; s/d $19/28; 🅿) A few taco stands over from the Futura bus station, this clean, family-run retreat has 25 small, quiet rooms. Rooms with cable TV cost a couple of dollars extra. Go for one of the rooftop rooms, where the sunny terrace has good views.

MIDRANGE

Hotel Posada San Javier (☎ 622-31-77; posadas anjavier@hotmail.com; Estacadas 32; s/d/ste from $39/42/51; 🅿 🛠) This is one of Taxco's most attractive places to stay at any price. Though centrally located, it's peaceful, with a lovely enclosed garden around a big swimming pool. Many of its 18 comfortable, high-ceilinged rooms face the courtyard and have terraces with private views. A couple of good-value, family-size 'mini casas' with living rooms and kitchenettes fetch up to $78. Reservations recommended.

Hotel Los Arcos (☎ 622-18-13/36; www.hotel losarcos.net; Juan Ruiz de Alarcón 4; s/d/ste $35/40/57; 🖵) This former 17th-century monastery retains plenty of colonial character in its wonderful courtyard, lounging areas and spectacular rooftop terrace. The 26 well-located rooms, all with fans and cable TV, are clean and spacious. The two-floor suite is perfect for a family.

THE AUTHOR'S CHOICE

Hotel Mi Casita (☎ 627-17-77; www.mycasita .com; Altos de Redondo 1; s/d/ste/apt incl breakfast from $37/46/64/73; ✗) In an inviting home restored by a family of jewelry designers, this lovely 12-room charmer provides great views of the cathedral at every turn. The comfortable rooms feature original hand-painted bathroom tiles and some have private terraces. Three rooms have rustic Talavera bathtubs, and all have fans and cable TV. Upstairs in room No 4, Secreto de Amor, a special treat awaits at the top of the spiral wooden staircase.

Hotel Santa Prisca (☎ 622-09-80; htl_staprisca@ yahoo.com; Cena Obscuras 1; s/d/f $32/46/62; **P**) Perched high above Plazuela de San Juan, the long-running Santa Prisca has a quiet, leafy interior patio – no TVs or telephones here – a bar, gracious staff, and a breakfast-only restaurant. Rooms are smallish but most have breezy private balconies with good views. All have two beds and newer, sunnier ones fetch a bit more. The parking lot is reached via a tunnel at the hotel's uphill end.

Posada Don Carlos (☎ 622-00-75; Calle del Consuelo 8; r from $60; **P 🏊**) Removed from the hustle and bustle in a residential neighborhood, this eight-room hotel has tastefully appointed rooms, most with balconies offering superb views. There's a small pool on a terrace facing town. The last bit is an uphill slog – take a taxi for $1.50.

Hotel Agua Escondida (☎ 622-07-26, 800-504-03-11; www.aguaescondida.com; Plaza Borda 4; s/d $45/62; **P 🖥 🏊**) Facing the *zócalo*, the 'Hidden Water' has a couple of pools and a café-bar on a high terrace with great views, if you don't mind climbing stairs. Favored by silver buyers, the 60 comfy, if sterile, rooms (some remodeled, some not) have Mexican furnishings, cable TVs and phones. Rooms with balconies overlooking the street suffer much traffic noise.

Hotel Loma Linda (☎ 622-02-01/06; www.hotellomalinda.com; Av de los Plateros 52; s/d $33/39, Fri & Sat r $55; **P 🏊**) Perched on the edge of a vast chasm, 1km north of town, the back rooms at this well-run motel have vertigo-inducing views of a lush green valley. There's a restaurant, a heated pool, easy parking and cable TV in the 71 rooms.

Hotel Victoria (☎ 622-00-04; www.victoriataxco .com in Spanish; Nibbi 5-7; r/ste from $46/66; **P 🏊**) For a fading-fast taste of old-time Taxco, try this sprawling place that dominates the town's southern hills. The paint is fresh, but it retains the fusty feel of a colonial village, wrapped around a bend in the mountainside and complete with cobblestone streets and unexpected overgrown nooks.

Hotel Emilia Castillo (☎ /fax 622-13-96/67-17; www.hotelemiliacastillo.com; Juan Ruiz del Alarcón 7; s/d $32/37) Owned by a famous family of silver workers, this intimate place opposite Hotel Los Arcos offers colonial charm at reasonable rates. Rooms without TV are cheaper, and all have finely carved wood

furnishings. Don't miss the views from the rooftop terrace. A shop downstairs displays the family's unique silver designs.

Hotel Meléndez (☎ 622-00-06; Cuauhtémoc 6; s/d $30/37) Because of its location, street noise penetrates the exterior rooms at this reliable family-run favorite. Upsides include sunny terrace sitting areas, great views from larger upper-level rooms and an unbeatable central location.

TOP END

Hotel Best Western Taxco (☎ 622-34-16, 800-561-2663; www.bestwesterntaxco.com; Nibbi 2; s/d/ste $82/91/138; **P 🎱 🖥**) Care less about a colonial vibe? *Bueno:* this business-friendly chain in a former silver gallery is your best bet. The spic-'n'-span all-white rooms and larger suites sport mod cons, like coffeemakers and hard-wired Internet. Upstairs rooms are larger but lack balconies. No matter, everyone enjoys access to the rooftop sun deck with 360-degree city views.

Posada de la Misión (☎ 622-00-63, 800-008-29-20; www.posadamision.com; Cerro de la Misión 32; s/d/ste incl breakfast $137/169/319; **P 🖥 🏊**) This upmarket colonial-style hotel is a superior option to other in-town hotels within walking distance of the center. The breakfast buffet, however, is often overrun by tour-bus crowds. Most of its large rooms have private terraces with fine views, and two-bedroom suites have fireplaces and kitchenettes. Adjacent to the pool is one of the better restaurants in town, El Mural, and a mosaic mural of the Aztec emperor Cuauhtémoc, designed by Mexican artist Juan O'Gorman.

Hotel Monte Taxco (☎ 622-13-00, 800-980-0000; www.montetaxco.com.mx; Lomas de Taxco; r/ste from $119/199; **P 🎱 🏊**) Way up atop the mountain, this self-contained resort is considered Taxco's finest hostelry, but nicer rooms and breathtaking views can be had in town for less. Rates, which rise on Friday and Saturday nights, include use of the pool but not of the tennis courts, nine-hole golf course, under-equipped gym or steam baths. There are also unremarkable restaurants, bars and a popular disco. It can be reached by car, *teleférico* (cable car) or a 15-minute taxi ride.

Eating & Drinking

RESTAURANTS & BARS

Del Ángel Inn (☎ 622-55-25; Muñoz 4; mains $5-20) Alongside the Templo de Santa Prisca, the

Del Ángel has a spectacular rooftop terrace bar. It's definitely tourist-orientated, but the food isn't bad. The set lunch ($10) consists of fresh bread with herbed butter, soup, a main course and dessert. Main courses include salads, pastas, surf-and-turf and standby Mexican favorites.

La Casona (☎ 622-10-71; Muñoz 4; mains $4-10) Adjacent to Del Ángel, the less formal La Casona features similar fare for less, as well as an excellent balcony with views down Taxco's hillsides.

Restaurant/Bar Paco (☎ 622-00-64; Plaza Borda 7; mains $6-14) Overlooking Plaza Borda through large picture windows, Paco's is great for people-watching. The food is decent too, but you pay dearly for the view. Try the delicious *mole* enchiladas. The bar hosts live music on Friday and Saturday evenings.

Restaurant Santa Fe (☎ 622-11-70; Hidalgo 2; mains $3-8) Frequently recommended by locals, the Santa Fe serves fairly priced traditional Mexican fare, such as *conejo en chile ajo* (rabbit in garlic chili). It offers set breakfasts, a hearty four-course *comida corrida* (set menu; $6) and three styles of *pozole* daily after 6pm.

Hostería Bar El Adobe (☎ 622-14-16; Plazuela de San Juan 13; mains $4-11) Views here are less captivating than at neighboring touristy eateries, but the interior decor is lovely and there's a bar full of cocktails. Specialties include Taxco-style *cecina* (salted strip steak) and shrimp-spiked garlic soup.

Bar Berta (Cuauhtémoc; drinks $2-5; ⏰ 11am-8pm) Just off Plaza Borda, Berta's is a fine place for a stiff drink. Hemingway would have felt at

---

BEETLES...YUM!

Taxco's most noteworthy culinary delicacy are *jumiles*, 1cm-long beetles that migrate annually to the hills behind town to reproduce. They start arriving around September and remain until January or February. The iodine-rich little roly-pollies are a great delicacy, eaten alone or mixed in salsa with tomatoes, garlic, onion and chilies, or even alive, rolled into tortillas. You can buy live *jumiles* in the market (Saturday and Sunday are the main days) from $0.50 per plastic sack. In season, Restaurant Santa Fe harvests their own supply and serves traditionally-prepared *salsa de jumil*.

THE AUTHOR'S CHOICE

Pozolería Tia Calla (☎ 622-56-02; Plaza Borda 1; mains $1.50-4; ⏰ 1:30-11pm Wed-Mon) When in Guerrero, do as the *guerrerenses*: share *pozole* with family and friends. No fine vistas or breezy *terrazas* here...just authentic, no-nonsense white Guerrero-style stew, served up in Auntie Calla's basement. Pick your poison: chicken or pork. Pork comes loaded with *chicharrón* (fried pork skin), avocado and all the fixings. No matter your meat choice, the broth is always pork-based. The beer steins are chilled and there's *fútbol* on the *tele*. What more could you ask for? A shot of *mezcal* (alcohol brewed from maguey plant), perhaps? Besides the namesake dish, there's *chalupas*, tacos, tostadas, enchiladas and *flan* for dessert.

---

home here, with its simple green tables and bullfighting posters on the walls. Papa would have quaffed a *Berta* (tequila, honey, lime and mineral water), the house specialty.

La Concha Nostra (☎ 622-79-44; Plazuela de San Juan 5; mains $3-7) This laid-back bar inside the Casa Grande Hotel serves set breakfast, pizza, salads and snacks until 1am. You can watch the action on Plazuela San Juan from the balcony. Live rock music shakes the house every Saturday night.

La Pagaduría del Rey (☎ 622-00-75; Colegio Militar 8; mains $7-13; ⏰ closed Mon) In Barrio Bermeja, this tranquil retreat offers salads, pastas and classic Mexican dishes. It's also a nice spot to sip a drink and admire the view.

Taxco's best restaurants are in the hills facing the city, and are best reached by taxi. **El Mural at Posada de la Misión** (opposite) is recommended more for its atmosphere than its international cuisine.

CAFÉS & QUICK EATS

Café Sacha (☎ 628-51-50; Juan Ruiz de Alarcón 1A; mains $4-8; Ⓥ) This cozy little bohemian café serves a variety of international snacks and vegetarian dishes, like curry and falafel. It's a great place to have breakfast, or to sip coffee or a romantic cocktail at a candle-lit balcony table.

La Hamburguesa (☎ 622-09-41; Plazuela de San Juan 5; mains $2-4; ⏰ closed Wed) For late-night snacks, try this popular place on the west side of Plazuela San Juan. It slings burger-and-fries combos and excellent enchiladas.

Shopping

SILVER

There are several shops in the **Patio de las Artesanías** (Plaza Borda) building. **Pineda's** (☎ 622-32-33; Muñoz 1) is justly famous; next door, **Joyería Elena de los Ballesteros** (☎ 622-37-67; Muñoz 4) is another worthwhile shop.

Inside Hotel Emilia Castillo, the tableware in the showroom of **Emilia Castillo** (☎ 622-34-71; Ruiz de Alarcón 7) is a unique blend of silver and porcelain. For quantity rather than quality, trawl the vast, poorly-displayed masses of rings, chains and pendants at the **Mercado de Artesanías Plata** (⏱ 11am-8pm).

HANDICRAFTS

It's easy to overlook them among the silver, but there are other things to buy in Taxco. Finely painted wood and papier-mâché trays, platters and boxes are sold along Calle del Arco, on the south side of Santa Prisca, as well as wood carvings and bark paintings. Quite a few shops sell semiprecious stones, fossils and mineral crystals, and some have a good selection of ceremonial masks, puppets and semi-antique carvings.

Getting There & Away

Combis pass both bus terminals on Av de los Plateros every few minutes and will take you up the hill to Plaza Borda. The shared 1st-class Futura/Estrella Blanca and 2nd-class terminal, downhill from the main market, offers luggage storage. The 1st-class Estrella de Oro (EDO) terminal is at the south end of town. Buy outbound tickets early since it can be difficult to secure a seat.

Directo 1st-class departures include the following:

Destination	Price	Duration	Frequency
Acapulco	$15	4-5hr	9 EDO & EB daily
Chilpancingo	$9.50	2-3hr	8 EDO daily
Cuernavaca	$5	1½hr	3 EDO daily)
	($4.50	1½hr	hourly Estrella Blanca 5am-8pm
Mexico City	$10	3hr	7 EDO daily
(Terminal Sur)	$10	3hr	1st-class hourly Futura 5am-8pm

Getting Around

Apart from walking, combis (white Volkswagen minibuses) and taxis are the best way to navigate Taxco's steep and narrow cobbled streets.

Combis ($0.30) are frequent and operate from 7am to 8pm. 'Zócalo' combis depart from Plaza Borda, go down Cuauhtémoc to Plazuela de San Juan, then head down the hill on Hidalgo. They turn right at Morelos, left at Av de los Plateros, and go north until La Garita, where they turn left and return to the *zócalo*. 'Arcos/Zócalo' combis follow the same route except that they continue past La Garita to Los Arcos, where they do a U-turn and head back to La Garita. Combis marked 'PM' (for Pedro Martín) go to the south end of town, past the Estrella de Oro bus station. Taxis cost $1 to $2 for trips around town.

Plaza Taxco shopping center has a large parking garage ($1.50 an hour, with cheaper 24-hour rates via most hotels). Access is off Av de los Plateros, via Estacadas. An elevator takes you up to the shopping center, on Ruiz de Alarcón next door to the Casa Humboldt.

AROUND TAXCO

Taxco El Viejo

Taxco's original town site was 12km south at Taxco El Viejo, where the indigenous Tlahuica mined tin and silver deposits, which were later heavily exploited by the Spaniards. Today, the area's principal attraction is a pair of ranches where silver is crafted in peaceful settings.

RANCHO CASCADA LOS CASTILLO

Just north of Taxco El Viejo, the famed Castillo family's metal **workshops** (☎ 622-19-88; www.silverzeal.com; ⏱ 8am-6pm Mon-Fri, 8am-3pm Sat) occupy lovely ranch grounds. En route to the workshops, a museum displays the antiquities collection of Antonio Castillo, a master craftsman and contemporary of William Spratling. In the workshops, craftspeople create unique silver, copper, tin and *alpaca* (nickel silver) objects. There's no shop on the premises, but you can buy their products online or in town at the shop in front of Posada de la Misión (p252).

RANCHO SPRATLING

Just south of the Ex-Hacienda San Juan Bautista, William Spratling's former **workshop**

PURA PLATA: HOW TO SHOP FOR SILVER

With hundreds of shops, Taxco's silverwork selection is mind-boggling. Look at some of the best places first, to gauge what's available, then focus on the things you're really interested in and shop around for those. If you are careful and willing to bargain – ask if the price is 'fixed' – you can find wonderful pieces at reasonable prices. Most shopkeepers speak English and sell both *menudeo* (retail) and *mayoreo* (wholesale); to get the wholesale price you will have to buy at least 1kg.

The price of a piece is principally determined by its weight; the creative work serves mainly to make it salable, though items with exceptional artisanship command a premium. Serious silver buyers know the current peso-per-gram rate and weigh pieces before talking prices. All reputable silver shops have electronic scales. If a piece costs less than the going price per gram, it's not real silver. High-pressure sales tactics tend to be heaviest in lower-quality shops.

Most pieces also bear a set of initials identifying their workshop of origin. Avoid anything that doesn't have the Mexican government '.925' stamp, which certifies that the piece is 92.5% sterling silver, blended with copper or zinc. If a piece is too small or delicate to stamp, reputable shops will supply a certificate confirming its purity. Anyone caught selling forged .925 pieces is supposed to be sent to prison.

The shops in and around Plaza Borda tend to have higher prices than those out of the center, but they also tend to have more interesting work. Most of the shops on Av de los Plateros are branches of downtown galleries, situated for the tourist buses that can't negotiate Taxco's narrow streets.

(☎ 762-622-61-08; ☒ by appointment, closed Sun) continues to produce some of Mexico's finest silver and employs the same handcrafted methods and classic designs that make Spratling pieces collectibles. Also on the premises is a showroom displaying work designed by Spratling; a second room features new designs by a new generation of apprentices.

GETTING THERE & AWAY

Taxco El Viejo is 25 minutes south of Taxco on Hwy 95. From Taxco, catch any of the frequent 2nd-class buses heading for Iguala at the Futura terminal, or a combi to Taxco El Viejo from just north of Taxco's IMSS hospital.

Parque Nacional Grutas de Cacahuamilpa

Thirty kilometers northeast of Taxco, the **Cacahuamilpa caverns** (tours adult/child $2.75/2; ☒ 10am-7pm, last ticket sold at 5pm) are a beautiful natural wonder of stalactites, stalagmites and twisted rock formations, with huge chambers up to 82m high.

The only way that would-be speleologists can tour the caves is with a guide, through 2km of an illuminated walkway. Many of the formations are named for some fanciful resemblance – 'the

elephant,' 'Dante's head' and so on – and the artificial lighting is used to enhance these features. Much of the guide's commentary focuses on these; actual geological information (and guides' English) is minimal. Thankfully, after the two-hour tour, you can wander back to the entrance at your own pace. You can also walk down to Río Dos Bocas, which flows nearby.

Tours depart the visitor center every hour on the hour between 10am and 5pm; Saturday and Sunday can be very crowded. There are restaurants, snacks and souvenir shops near the entrance.

GETTING THERE & AWAY

From Taxco, blue-striped 'Grutas' combis ($1.75, 45 minutes) depart hourly from the Futura bus terminal and stop at the visitor center. Alternatively, you can take any bus heading for Toluca or Ixtapan de la Sal, then get off at the crossroads and walk 1km down to the entrance. The last combis leave the site around 5pm midweek, and 6pm on Saturday and Sunday; afterwards you may be able to catch a bus to Taxco at the crossroads, but it's an expensive taxi ride.

Estrella Blanca/Futura (☎ 800-507-55-00; www .estrellablanca.com.mx) 1st-class buses arrive and depart the national park six times daily to and from Cuernavaca.

WEST OF MEXICO CITY

The toll road west from the capital, Hwy 15D, leads to the industrial and administrative center of Toluca, which has a foodie-friendly center, plus several art galleries and noteworthy museums. There are ruins nearby, and several close by villages are known for their handicrafts. The countryside surrounding Toluca is scenic, with pine forests, rivers and a huge volcano. Valle de Bravo, a lakeside resort and colonial gem 70km west of Toluca, is a popular weekend getaway for wealthy Mexicans.

There are two highways heading south from Toluca: Hwy 55 passes handicraft centers, impressive pyramids and spas at Ixtapan de la Sal and Tonatico, then continues on to Taxco; Hwy 55D is the fastest route to Ixtapan de la Sal.

TOLUCA

☎ 722 / pop 505,000 / elevation 2660m

The extra altitude in Toluca, 64km west of Mexico City and 400m higher than the capital, is palpable. Beneath its humdrum surface, this administrative center is quite congenial. The eastern outskirts are industrial, but the colonial-era city center has attractive plazas, lively shopping arcades and a number of art galleries and museums.

Toluca was an indigenous settlement from at least the 13th century. The Spanish founded the modern city in the 16th century, after defeating the resident Aztecs and Matlazincas, and it became part of Hernán Cortés' expansive domain, the Marquesado del Valle de Oaxaca. Since 1830, it's been capital of the state of México, which surrounds the Distrito Federal on three sides, like an upside-down U.

Orientation

The main road from Mexico City becomes Paseo Tollocan on Toluca's eastern edge, before bearing southwest and becoming a ring road around the city center's southern edge. Toluca's bus station and the huge Mercado Juárez are 2km southeast of the center, off Paseo Tollocan.

The vast Plaza de los Mártires, with the cathedral and Palacio de Gobierno, marks the town center. Most of the action, however, is concentrated a block south in the

pedestrian precinct. Shady Parque Alameda is three blocks west along Hidalgo.

Information

The free Spanish-language monthly *Agenda Cultural* publishes a schedule of art, music and theater events.

Banks There are many with ATMs near Portal Madero.

Comunic@tel (Bravo; per hr $1.25) Internet and long-distance phone service.

Cruz Roja (Red Cross; ☎ 217-33-33)

Everything Online (Galeana 209; per hr $0.50) Open until 10pm, after the rest of the city shuts down; there's a taco stand next door.

State Tourist Office (☎ 212-59-98; http://turismo .edomex.gob.mx; cnr Urawa & Paseo Tollocan) Inconveniently 2km southeast of the center, but with English-speaking staff and good maps.

Tourist Information Kiosk (Palacio Municipal) Helpful kiosk with free city map.

Sights

CITY CENTER

The 19th-century **Portal Madero**, running 250m along Av Hidalgo, is lively, as is the commercial arcade along the pedestrian street to the east, which attracts mariachis after 9pm. A block north, the large, open expanse of **Plaza de los Mártires** is surrounded by fine old government buildings; the 19th-century **cathedral** and the 18th-century **Templo de la Santa Veracruz** are on its south side.

Just northeast of Plaza de los Mártires is **Plaza Garibay**; at the east end stands the unique **Cosmo Vitral Jardín Botánico** (Cosmic Stained-Glass Window Botanical Garden; ☎ 214-67-85; cnr Juárez & Lerdo de Tejada; admission $1; ◷ 10am-6pm Tue-Sun). Built in 1909 as a market, the building now houses 3500 sq meters of lovely gardens, lit through 48 stained-glass panels by the Tolucan artist Leopoldo Flores. On Plaza Garibay's north side is the 18th-century **Templo del Carmen**.

MERCADO JUÁREZ & CASART

The gigantic daily **Mercado Juárez** (cnr Fabela & Calle 5 de Mayo) is behind the bus station. On Friday, villagers swarm in to exchange fruit, flowers, pots, clothes and plastic goods. The market may be colorful, but it's also chaotic and not a great place to buy local handicrafts.

Nearby, you'll find quality arts and crafts in more peaceful surroundings at the state crafts store, **Casart** (Casa de Artesanía; ◷ 10am-7pm). There's a big range, and the

TOLUCA

0 — 500 m
0 — 0.3 miles

To Centro Cultural Mexiquense (4km);
Nevado de Toluca (48km);
Valle de Bravo (75km)

To Mercado Juárez (1.5km);
Bus Station (1.5km);
Casart (1.5km);
State Tourist
Office (1.5km);
Hwy 15 to
Mexico City
(66km)

INFORMATION	
Bancomer (ATM)	1 C2
Banorte (ATM)	2 C2
Comunic@tel	3 B1
Everything Online	4 B3
Santander Serfin (ATM)	5 B2
Tourist Information Kiosk	(see 8)

SIGHTS & ACTIVITIES	
Cathedral	6 B1
Cosmo Vitral Jardín Botánico	7 C1
Ex-Sacristía del Convento Franciscano	
de la Asunción	8 B1
Museo de Bellas Artes	(see 12)
Palacio de Gobierno	9 B1
Palacio Municipal	(see 8)

Portal Madero	10 B2
Templo de la Santa Veracruz	11 C1
Templo del Carmen	12 C1
Velasco, Gutiérrez & Nishizawa	
Museums	13 B1

SLEEPING	
Hotel Colonial	14 C2
Hotel La Hacienda	15 B2
Hotel San Carlos	16 B1
Hotel San Francisco	17 C2

EATING	
Caffé Espresso	(see 18)
Hostería Las Ramblas	18 C2
Jugos El Bajío	19 C1
La Gloria Chocolatería y Pan 1876	20 A2
La Vaquita Negra del Portal	21 B1
Mariachis	(see 18)
Super Soya	(see 18)
Taco & Sweets Stalls	22 B1

TRANSPORT	
Buses to Bus Terminal	23 C2
Buses to Centro Cultural	
Mexiquense	24 C1

crafts are often top-end pieces from the villages where the crafts originate. Prices are fixed, and higher than you can get with some haggling in markets; gauge prices and quality here before going elsewhere to buy. Craftspeople, such as basket weavers from San Pedro Actopan, often work in the store.

CENTRO CULTURAL MEXIQUENSE

The impressive **State of México Cultural Center** (☎ 274-1200; Blvd Reyes Herdes 302; admission $2, free Sun; ☯ 10am-6pm Mon-Sat, 10am-3pm Sun), 4.5km west of the city center, houses three good museums (which all keep the same hours).

The **Museo de Culturas Populares** has superb examples of the state of México's traditional arts and crafts, with some astounding 'trees of life' from Metepec, whimsical Day of the Dead figures and a fine display of *charro* gear.

The **Museo de Antropología e História** presents exhibits on the state's history from prehistoric times to the 20th century, with a good collection of pre-Hispanic artifacts.

The **Museo de Arte Moderno** traces the development of Mexican art from the late-19th-century Academia de San Carlos to the Nueva Plástica, and includes paintings by Tamayo, Orozco and many others. 'Centro Cultural' buses ($0.50) ply Lerdo de Tejada, passing Plaza Garibay.

OTHER MUSEUMS

The ex-convent buildings adjacent to the Templo del Carmen, on the north side of Plaza Garibay, house Toluca's **Museo de Bellas Artes** (☎ 215-53-29; Degollado 102; admission $1; ☯ 10am-6pm Tue-Sat, 10am-3pm Sun), which exhibits paintings from the colonial period to the early 20th century. On Bravo, opposite the Palacio de Gobierno, are three museums: one dedicated to landscape painter **José María Velasco** (Lerdo de Tejada 400), another to painter **Felipe Santiago Gutiérrez** (Bravo Nte 303) and the last to multifaceted Mexican-Japanese artist **Luis Nishizawa** (Bravo Nte 305).

Sleeping

The cheapest places lack on-site parking. The lot on Hidalgo, opposite Hotel Colonial, charges $5.50 per night (9pm to 8am). Modern, upscale chain hotels are concentrated along the ring road near the airport.

Hotel Colonial (☎ 215-97-00; Hidalgo Ote 103; s/d $32/37; **P**) For true colonial ambience (minus the typical darkness) try this well-maintained place, with spacious rooms around an interior courtyard. Rates include free parking nearby in a lot on Juárez.

Hotel San Francisco (☎ 213-44-15; Rayón 104; s/d/ste $57/64/73; **P**) This business-friendly favorite has comfortable modern rooms and luxury pretensions, like a glass-walled elevator for viewing the skylit atrium restaurant. Business travelers receive a significant discount off rack rates listed here (around 20%).

Hotel San Carlos (☎ 214-43-36, 800-201-98-47; hotelsancarlos@prodigy.net.mx; Portal Madero 210; s/d $28/37; **P**) The 100 rooms at this friendly place are a bit shabby, but still clean, and have large bathrooms and cable TV. Pet birds and fish await in the lobby. Kick down $9 extra for a king-size bed.

Hotel La Hacienda (☎ 214-36-34; Hidalgo Pte 508; s/d $19/23; **P**) The 19 rooms here have cable TV and colonial touches, both positive (high wood-beam ceilings upstairs) and negative (dark downstairs, unreliable hot water). We're hoping whomever picked the mismatched color schemes (Pepto-Bismol pink with mustard yellow?!?) was color-blind.

Eating & Drinking

Toluqueños take snacking and sweets very seriously; join them in the arcades around Plaza Fray Andrés de Castro. Stalls selling *tacos de Obispo* (a sausage from Tenancingo) are easily found by following the crowds that flock around them. The contents of the arm-width sausages – barbecued chopped beef spiced with *epazote* (wormseed, a pungent herb similar to cilantro), almonds and raisins – are stuffed into tortillas. Other stalls sell candied fruit and *jamoncillos*, and *mostachones* (sweets made of burned milk). Most eateries in the center are open from around 8am to 9pm.

La Vaquita Negra del Portal (sandwiches $1-3) On the northwest corner of the arcades, smoked hams and huge green and red sausages hanging over the deli counter signal first-rate *tortas*. Try a messy *toluqueña* (red pork chorizo sausage, white cheese, cream,

tomato and *salsa verde*) and don't forget to garnish your heaping sandwich with spicy pickled peppers and onions.

Hostería Las Ramblas (☎ 215-54-88; Calle 20 de Noviembre 107D; mains $4-10) On a pedestrian mall, one of Toluca's best and most atmospheric places to eat and drink (there's a full bar) serves full breakfasts and a variety of ambrosial *antojitos*, including *sopes* (soup), *mole verde* and *conejo al ajillo* (liberally garlicked rabbit).

Jugos El Bajío (mains $1.50-3; **V**) In the arcade opposite the Templo de la Santa Veracruz, this soda fountain does good *tortas*, fruit cocktails and fresh fruit juices.

Caffé Espresso (☎ 215-54-43; Calle 20 de Noviembre 109D; drinks $1-3) This relaxing café serves espresso, hot chocolate, and hot and cold cappuccinos. There are pastries for breakfast and live music most evenings.

Super Soya (Portal Madero s/n; mains $1-2.50; **V**) Only in Mexico: A neon riot of a 'health' food' shop that sells cup-o'-noodles, diet pills *and* chocolate-dipped frozen yogurt. Also popular are the *tortas*, juices and heaping fruit salad concoctions. The sexy posters advertising herbal supplements are priceless.

Getting There & Away

Toluca's Aeropuerto Adolfo López Mateos is conveniently located off Hwy 15, near downtown, adjacent to the industrial zone and a group of business-friendly chain hotels. Upstart domestic airlines like Click

---

THE AUTHOR'S CHOICE

La Gloria Chocolatería y Pan 1876 (Quintana Roo; snacks $1-3; ⏰ 10am-11:30pm Mon-Sat, 10am-10:30pm Sun; ♿) Occupying a rustic colonial warehouse complex, this 100% Mexican hangout is a favorite after-work rendezvous spot. Families crowd wood benches at the long shared tables, while kids eagerly await their frothy, hand-ground hot chocolate, steamed with milk and spiked with a slight hint of cinnamon. Pair your drink with a basket of three crispy *churros* or an assortment of sweet breads. There's also coffee, *tacos al pastor* (spicy pork tacos) and *tortas* stuffed with oven-baked pork or shredded chicken bathed in red or green *mole poblana*. Heavenly!

Mexicana (☎ 800-122-54-25; www.clickmx.com) and **Interjet** (www.interjet.com.mx) are rapidly expanding service to Toluca from major cities like Guadalajara, Monterrey and Cancún. **Magnicharters** (☎ 55-5756-9807; www.magnicharters.com.mx) offers regular service to Cancún, **Continental Express** (☎ 800-900-50-00, in US ☎ 800-523-3273; www.continental.com) shuttles to Houston, and **Air Madrid** (☎ 55 5093-4668; www.airmadrid.com) started regular Toluca–Madrid flights in mid-2005. There are frequent buses from Mexico City and the capital's Aeropuerto Internacional, which take an hour or two, depending on traffic. A taxi from the airport to downtown Toluca runs around $10.

Toluca's **bus station** (Berriozábal 101) is 2km southeast of the center. Ticket offices for many destinations are on the platforms or at the gate entrances. There are frequent departures to Querétaro (gate 2), Morelia (gate 5), Valle de Bravo (gate 6), Malinalco/Chalma (gate 9) and Cuernavaca, Taxco and Ixtapan de la Sal (platform 12).

In Mexico City, Toluca buses use Terminal Poniente. The 1st-class **TMT** (☎ 219-50-07; www.tmt-caminante.com.mx) line links the two cities ($3.50, one hour) every five minutes from 5:30am to 10pm. From Toluca, TMT runs hourly direct service to the Mexico City airport from 4am to 10pm.

Getting Around

'Centro' buses go from outside Toluca's bus station to the town center along Lerdo de Tejada. From Juárez in the center, 'Terminal' buses go to the bus station ($0.50). Taxis from the bus station to the city center cost around $4; fares around town are considerably cheaper.

AROUND TOLUCA
Calixtlahuaca

This partly excavated and restored **Aztec site** (admission $2.50; ☺ 10am-5pm) is 9km northwest of Toluca, and 2km west of Hwy 55. The site has some unusual features, such as a circular pyramid that supported a temple to Calmecac and Quetzalcóatl, thought to have been a school for the children of priests and nobles. From Toluca, catch a bus in front of the department store Suburbia (near Mercado Juárez) and the driver will drop you off within a short walk of the site.

Metepec

Basically a suburb of Toluca, 7km south on Hwy 55, Metepec (population 173,000) is the center for producing elaborate and symbolic pottery, such as *árboles de la vida* (trees of life) and Metepec suns (earthenware discs brightly painted with sun and moon faces). There are a number of shops along the Corredor Artesanal, on Comonfort south of Paseo San Isidro. Prices for the *árboles de la vida* range from $5 for a miniature, up to $150 for a meter-high tree. Just north of Paseo San Isidro is the Corral Artesanal, a series of small shops along an arcade selling local crafts.

The potters' workshops *(alfarerías)* are spread all over town; there's a map of them painted on the wall of the triangular tourism office in front of the Cerro del Calvario.

The workshop of **Beto Hernández** (Altamirano 58) is itself a work of art, with fountains, altars and designs embedded in the cobblestone walkway, and a sort of chapel built around the lavishly decorated kiln. Within the various display rooms are some amazing trees, many unpainted, at reasonable prices. The most elaborate and expensive trees are in the front gallery.

A few doors down, the workshop of **Adrián Luis González** (Altamirano 212) is equally remarkable; upstairs the floor is adorned with suns and butterflies. A fascinating genealogical tree shows members of the González family (Adrián himself is near the top) with their accoutrements. The tree demonstrates the process of its own creation, with subsequent levels at different stages of production – from unbaked clay at the bottom to a bright paint finish at the top.

A nice hike with great views can be taken to the top of **Cerro del Calvario**, a hill decorated with a huge pottery mural.

Frequent 2nd-class buses link Metepec with Toluca's bus station.

TEOTENANGO

Tenango de Arista, 25km south of Toluca on Hwy 55, is overlooked from the west by the large, well-restored hilltop ruins of **Teotenango** (☎ 717-144-13-44; admission $1.50, Wed free; ☺ 9am-5pm Tue-Sun), a Matlazinca ceremonial center dating from the 9th century. The site is quite extensive – several pyramids, plazas and a ball court – and has great views. Near the entrance, the **Museo Arqueológico del Estado de México** features Teotenango pottery and sculpture, as well as a section devoted to the prehistory of the region.

From Toluca's bus station, buses run every 10 minutes to the center of Tenango; from here you can walk to the site in 20 to 30 minutes or take a taxi ($1.50). Driving south from Toluca on Hwy 55, pass the toll highway and turn right into Tenango; signs indicate where to make a right turn on to a road that passes closest to the ruins.

NEVADO DE TOLUCA

The long-extinct volcano Nevado de Toluca (also known as Xinantécatl), Mexico's fourth tallest peak at 4690m, lies across the horizon south of Toluca. A road runs 48km up to its crater, which contains two lakes, El Sol and La Luna. The earlier you reach the summit, the better the chance of clear views. The summit area can be snowy from November to March, and is sometimes good for off-piste cross-country skiing, but **Parque Nacional Nevado de Toluca** is closed during the heaviest snowfalls.

Buses on Hwy 134, the Toluca–Tejupilco road, will stop at the turnoff for Hwy 10 to Sultepec, which passes the park entrance 7km to the south. On Saturday and Sunday, you should be able to hitch a ride for the 28km from the junction of Hwys 134 and 10 to the crater. From Toluca, taxis will take you to the top for upwards of $20, or there and back (including time for a look around) for a negotiable $40. Be sure to hire a newer taxi; the road up is very rough and dusty.

From the park entrance, a road winds 3.5km up to the main gate at an area called **Parque de los Venados** (entrance per vehicle $1.75; ☺ 8am-5pm, last entrance at 3pm). From there it's a 17km drive along an unsurfaced road up to the crater. Six kilometers from the crater, there's a gate, café and basic *refugio* (rustic shelter). From that point, the crater can also be reached by a 2km hike via **Paso del Quetzal** (fee $0.20), a very scenic walking track. Dress warmly; it gets chilly up top.

Sleeping & Eating

Posada Familiar (dm $9, camp site $4.50) Just beyond the Parque de los Venados gate, this basic, heavily used refuge has shared hot showers, a kitchen (without utensils) and a

common area with a fireplace. Bring extra blankets.

Albergue Ejidal (dm $6.50, camp site $4.50) Two kilometers beyond Parque de los Venados, this community-run hostel has 64 bunk beds (sleeping bag required), hot water, a huge fireplace and a generator that runs on Saturday night. Ask an attendant at Parque de los Venados to open it up for you.

Just below the summit (at 4050m), the basic **state-run shelter** (dm $5) has foam mattresses but no bathrooms.

On Saturday and Sunday, food is served at stalls around Parque de los Venados and at the gate near the summit. Midweek, bring your own food and water.

VALLE DE BRAVO

☎ 726 / pop 28,000 / elevation 1800m

Some 85km west of Toluca, and a sinuous two-hour drive from Mexico City, Valle de Bravo was a quiet colonial-era village in the hills until the 1940s, when it became a base for the construction of a dam and hydroelectric station. The resulting 21 sq km reservoir gave the town a waterside location and 'Valle' soon became an elite weekend getaway. Nevertheless, the vibrant country community still retains its colonial charm. There's a tourist info kiosk on the wharf, and essential services, including ATMs and Internet, are found around the main plaza, a 10-minute walk uphill from the waterfront.

Boating is the main activity here – there are hour-long **cruises** (per person $2.75-3.25) on *colectivo* boats. You can rent a private boat for $20 to $35 per hour. Nighttime cruises featuring live music depart on Saturday from 9pm. Waterskiing, paragliding, windsurfing, fishing and horseback riding are also popular. You can hike and camp in the hills around town, which attract monarch butterflies from December to March. A climb up the rock promontory La Peña, northwest of the center, provides a panorama of the entire lake.

In late October or early November, the weeklong **Festival de las Almas** international arts and culture extravaganza brings in music and dance troupes from all over Europe and Latin America.

Sleeping

Budget hotels here are a cut above those elsewhere in Mexico. Fancier places may discount rates Sunday to Thursday.

Posada Casa Vieja (☎ 262-03-18; posadacasavieja@ yahoo.com.mx; Juárez 101, near Independencia; r from $38; P) This intriguing, centuries-old hotel, catercorner from the lively market, has good-value rooms (most with TV) around an idyllic courtyard with a fountain and chirping birds. There's parking in the courtyard, but the entranceway is a tight squeeze.

Posada Los Girasoles (☎ 262-29-67; girasoles@ valledelbravo.com.mx; Plaza Independencia 1; s/d/f $28/37/46) Facing the convivial central plaza, the simple, clean rooms have TVs and small bathrooms. The bookstore next door, Arawi, has a big newsstand with some English-language magazines.

Centro Vacacional ISSEMYM (☎ 262-00-04/68; Independencia 404; d/ste/f incl breakfast $63/81/86; P ⚹ ♿) This well-kept holiday center for state workers also accepts nonmember guests. There are a couple pools and 48 rooms from various eras, the oldest ones (circa the 1960s) being the cheapest. Rates are discounted 15% from Monday to Thursday. It's a long block uphill from the market.

Eating & Drinking

There are scores of restaurants and cafés along the wharf and around the *zócalo*; most upscale places only open Friday to Sunday.

Los Veleros (☎ 262-03-70; Salitre 104; mains $8-18; ☺ noon-midnight Fri-Sun) Specializing in grilled surf-and-turf fare, elegant Los Veleros occupies an adobe complex with tables on a balcony overlooking a large garden just uphill from the wharf.

El Lobo (Salitre s/n; mains $3-10; ☺ 10am-8pm) More humble, but equally satisfying, this al fresco grouping of tables across from the wharf specializes in super-fresh seafood cocktails. Choose from three sizes and 10 degrees of hot sauce, and mix several ingredients: shrimp, octopus, oyster, crab and sea snail. The beer is cold and they also fry up fresh fish fillets a dozen ways.

For a nice, breezy, equilibrium-challenging ambience, try a drink or a meal at the floating lakefront bar-restaurant **La Balsa** (☎ 262-25-53; mains $6-14; ☺ 9am-10pm Wed-Mon), or the larger **Los Pericos** (☎ 262-05-58; mains $6-13; ☺ 8am-11pm Thu-Tue).

Getting There & Away

Valle's remodeled bus terminal is on Calle 16 de Septiembre. Autobuses Zinacantepec runs hourly 2nd-class *directos* until 5:30pm

to Mexico City's Terminal Poniente ($8, three hours), all of which make a stop near Toluca's terminal. There is also frequent service to Zitácuaro ($4). If driving between Toluca and Valle de Bravo, the southern route via Hwy 134 is quicker and more scenic than Hwy 1.

MALINALCO

☎ 714 / pop 7500 / elevation 1740m

One of Mexico's few reasonably well-preserved **Aztec temples** (admission $3; ☺ 9am-6pm Tue-Sun) persists high above beautiful, but little-visited, Malinalco – 22km east of Tenancingo. The site entrance is 1km west of the plaza, approached by a well-maintained footpath with signs in Spanish, English and Náhuatl. The views over the valley from the summit have inspired legions of painters. Near the site entrance, the **Universidad Autónoma del Estado de México museum** (☎ 147-12-88; admission $1, free Wed; ☺ 10am-6pm Tue-Sun) explores the region's history and archaeology. Next door, the good Café La Fé only opens Wednesday through Sunday.

The Aztecs conquered the region in 1476 and were busy building a ritual center here when they were themselves conquered by the Spanish. El Cuauhcalli, thought to be the Temple of Eagle and Jaguar Warriors – where sons of Aztec nobles were initiated into warrior orders – survived because it's hewn from the mountainside itself. The entrance is carved in the form of a fanged serpent.

A well-restored 16th-century **Augustinian convent** (admission free), fronted by a tranquil tree-lined yard, faces the central plaza. Impressive frescoes fashioned from herb- and flower-based paint adorn its cloister. Just uphill from the plaza, the **tourist office** (☎ 147-13-11; www .malinalco.net in Spanish; ☺ 9am-3pm Mon-Sat) is inside the Palacio Municipal. There's an ATM on Hidalgo, on the convent's north side.

Sleeping

Like other destinations near Mexico City, Malinalco is geared toward weekend visitors, which means you'll have no trouble finding a room Sunday to Thursday nights, but your dining options may be limited. Conversely, hotel reservations are recommended for Friday and Saturday.

A spate of stylish, adult-only boutique B&Bs catering to weekenders has sprung up in the last couple of years – most notably the five-room, artist-owned **Casa Mora** (☎ 147-05-72, in Mexico City 5635-4426; www.casamora.net; Calle de la Cruz 18; ste $130-210; **P** **⚡**) and the 10-room **Casa Limón** (☎ 147-02-56; www.casalimon.com in Spanish; Río Lerma 103; ste from $135; **P** **⚡**). However, things remain pretty sedate midweek.

El Asoleadero (☎ 147-01-84; cnr Aldama & Comercio; s/d from $24/28; **P** **⚡**) This very blue place has a small pool and 15 big clean rooms, with balconies and good views down-valley over the convent. It's a couple of blocks uphill (north) of the plaza.

Hotel Marmil (☎ 147-09-16; Progreso 67; s/d/f $19/28/50; **P** **⚡**) In the ochre-colored complex near the town's north entrance, the Marmil is one of Malinalco's better-value places to stay in town. The 28 standard rooms have large comfy beds. Both guests and nonguests must pay $1.35 to use the pool.

Villa Hotel (☎ 147-00-01; Guerrero 101; s/d $18/37) Facing the plaza's south side, the friendly Villa has 15 rooms: some have cliff views while others (some with better beds) face the plaza. Cable TV costs $4.50. If the gate is closed, try the *panadería* (bakery) next door.

Eating & Drinking

Malinalco has several good restaurants serving a wide variety of cuisines, but only a few of the nicer ones are open during the week. There are, however, plenty of eateries around the plaza patronized by locals which are open daily.

Beto's (☎ 147-03-11; Morelos 8; mains $3-7; ⊙ noon-8pm Tue-Sun) This friendly, owner-attended hangout behind the convent has a full bar and serves surprisingly fresh seafood, including baby shark empanadas and terrific shrimp cocktails. Afterwards, try a *beso de ángel* (coffee liqueur and condensed milk on ice, dusted with cinnamon).

Los Placeres (☎ 147-08-55; west side of the plaza; mains $4-8; ⊙ 9am-midnight Fri-Sun; **V**) This is Malinalco's *simpático* (friendly) choice, with a laid-back atmosphere, good music, occasional movie nights and great views out back. Its varied menu includes hearty breakfasts with proper tea and coffee, bagels with cheese or salmon, original salads, crepes and exotic specials.

Las Palomas (☎ 147-01-22; Guerrero 104; mains $4-8; ⊙ 10am-6pm Tue-Thu, 10am-10pm Fri-Sun; **V**) This inviting place has an open-air country kitchen, citrus and mango trees around the patio, and a *palapa* bar mixing generous cocktails. The reasonably priced menu features all-natural Mexican originals, with healthy, creative salads and meat and trout dishes.

Les Chefs (☎ 147-04-01; Morelos 107; mains from $3-9; ⊙ Fri-Sun) Opposite Beto's, this is a bipolar restaurant: one serves pizzas, the other serves Breton cuisine with a strong Mexican flavor. The gregarious owner, Alain, has at least seven delicious ways of preparing trout. There's no sign; look for the cross above the door.

Don't miss sampling the divine ice cream at Malinalli Nieves, either at the shop on the plaza's west side or at the stand on the plaza. Hip bars catering to weekenders come and go near the plaza – follow your ears and intuition to find them.

Getting There & Away

You can reach Malinalco by bus from Toluca or Tenancingo. There are a couple of direct buses daily from Mexico City's Terminal Poniente; alternatively, take one of many buses to Jajalpa (en route to Tenancingo), then catch a local bus. If driving from Mexico City, turn south at La Marquesa and follow the signs to Malinalco.

Direct buses back to Mexico City depart around 5pm daily. There's a frequent *colectivo* service to Tenango, from where you can catch a Toluca or Mexico City bus.

CHALMA

One of Mexico's most important shrines is in the village of Chalma, 10km east of Malinalco. In 1533 an image of Christ, El Señor de Chalma, miraculously appeared in a cave to replace one of the local gods, Oxtéotl, and proceeded to stamp out dangerous beasts and do other wondrous things. The Señor now resides in Chalma's 17th-century church. The biggest of many annual pilgrimages here is for **Pentecost** (the seventh Sunday after Easter) when thousands of people camp out and perform traditional dances.

Tres Estrellas del Centro runs hourly 2nd-class buses from Toluca to Chalma ($3). Several companies run 2nd-class buses from Mexico City's Terminal Poniente. There's also frequent bus service from Malinalco.

IXTAPAN DE LA SAL

☎ 721 / pop 20,000 / elevation 1880m

Easy-going Ixtapan is an unashamedly tourist town, but it's worth a stop to take to the waters or for a splash with your kids. The principal attraction is the **Ixtapan Balneario, Spa y Parque Acuático** (☎ 143-30-00; adult/child $14/6.50; ☽ spa 8am-7pm, aquatic park 9am-6pm; ✤), a sprawling water park mixing curative thermal water pools with waterfalls, water slides, a wave pool and a miniature railway.

Hotels are clustered along Av Juárez, south of the aquatic park, with a good range of lodging. Most foreign visitors stay adjacent to the *balneario* at the recently renovated **Ixtapan Spa Hotel & Golf Resort** (☎ 143-24-40, 800-904-7200, in Mexico City ☎ 55-5264-2613, in USA ☎ 800-638-7950; www.spamexico.com; s/d with meals from $120/150), where frequent all-inclusive spa promotions make it popular with expat retirees, YMCA group tours and, especially on Saturday and Sunday, Mexican families from the Distrito Federal.

About 5km further south on Hwy 55 is the town of **Tonatico** (population 10,000) with its own public water park, the well-signed **Balneario Municipal Tonatico** (adult/child $4.50/3.25; ☽ 7am-6pm). It's about a tenth of the size of Ixtapan de la Sal's and consequently more relaxed. There's a decent state-run **Hotel Balneario** (r per person incl balneario entrance $12) and restaurant with set meals on the grounds. At the south end of town is a spectacular **waterfall** (El Salto).

From the bus terminal on Hwy 55, between Ixtapan and Tonatico, Tres Estrellas runs frequent buses to Toluca ($2.75), Taxco ($3.25) and Cuernavaca ($4). There's also an hourly express service to Mexico City ($8) until 7pm. Buses to and from the terminal ply Av Juárez in Ixtapan ($0.30); taxis charge $1.25.

Heading north to Toluca, toll Hwy 55D parallels part of Hwy 55, bypassing Tenango and Tenancingo. Heading south towards Taxco, the Grutas de Cacahuamilpa (p255) are a must-see.

AROUND MEXICO CITY

Baja California

Baja. Just the word itself conjures up images of bleach-blond surfers and fiery sunsets, of sun-tortured deserts and wild sierras, of twisted boojum trees and surreal rock formations. Whales, wildlife, wild nightlife and everything in between. Some come here to escape from the hustle-bustle of the city, others need the rush of a 30-knot wind tearing at a kite sail; still others visit to lose themselves in giant parties that make college-frat Fridays seem like Sunday brunch with grandma. The strange thing is that it's *all* here. Baja lives up to any of these expectations.

One way to take it all in is by car. The Transpeninsular Hwy will challenge the driver and reward the passenger with marvelous scenery all along the way. Forests of towering cardón cacti, in an endless variety of shapes and sizes, provide foreground to far-off mountains and the intermittent flash of shocking azure sea. Few who have made the journey will deny that it is one of the planet's great driving adventures. Avoiding cattle, goats and vehicles passing around blind corners only adds to the fun.

To the east are the rugged beauty and fish-rich waters of the Sea of Cortez, inspiration for writers John Steinbeck and Edward Abbey and home to 875 fish species and 30 species of marine mammals. Wherever your journey takes you, Baja's wide-open frontier and its more civilized charms will capture your imagination and hold you in its sway.

TOP FIVE

- Swimming with whale sharks at **La Paz** (p295) as the big Baja sun drops into the bay

- Scratching a gray whale on the nose at **Laguna Ojo de Liebre** (p285) as they arrive after a 9700km journey from the Bering Sea

- Kayaking, diving or snorkeling in the marine-rich waters of the Sea of Cortez near **Loreto** (p291), Baja's water-sports paradise

- Windsurfing along **La Ventana**'s (p300) unspoiled, cactus-lined coast.

- Sipping drinks on a sunset sailing cruise in **Cabo San Lucas** (p304), the quint-essential party town

- TIJUANA JANUARY DAILY HIGH: 20°C/68°F
- TIJUANA JULY DAILY HIGH: 29°C/84°F

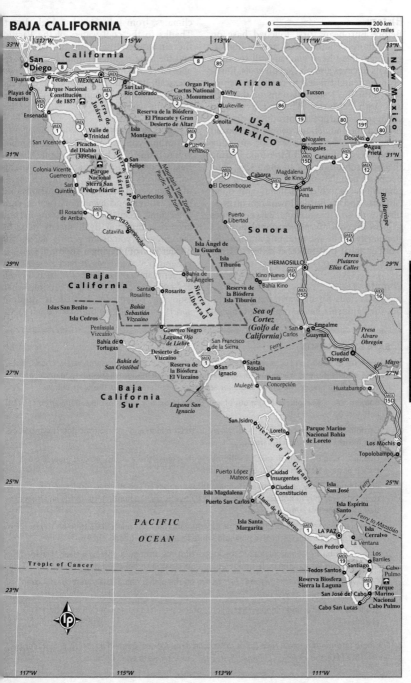

History

Before Europeans first touched base on these shores, about 48,000 mobile hunter-gatherers lived here; you can still see their murals in caves and on canyon walls. European settlement failed to reach the peninsula until the Jesuit missions of the 17th and 18th centuries. The missions soon collapsed as European-introduced diseases ravaged the indigenous people (see boxed text, p290), clearing the way for an influx of ranchers, miners and fisherfolk. During the US prohibition era of the 1920s, Baja became a popular south-of-the-border destination for gamblers, drinkers and other 'sinners,' and the border towns remain popular for those same reasons. Baja continues to grow in economic power, population and popularity, while still retaining much of the frontier spirit that makes it different from mainland Mexico.

Climate

Baja is famous for its warm temperatures, but the peninsula has a surprising range of climates, from subtropical to high desert. Thanks to the cool waters of the Pacific, the air temperature along the west coast and the cape region is humid but comfortable all year. Along the Sea of Cortez or in Mexicali, it's a different story. Here, in the summer, you will be reminded of the meaning of the word 'hot.'

Dangers & Annoyances

Assuming you're not looking for trouble, you're unlikely to have a problem. Most of Baja's cities and towns are mellow places with little violent crime. The border towns of Tijuana and Mexicali are notorious, but basic caution and awareness (watch your bags, don't accept rides from strangers) will keep risks minimal. By all means, don't let fear prevent you from getting across the border or from having a good time.

Sanitation standards in Baja are generally higher than in other parts of Mexico. Travelers' main concerns should be cautious when enjoying potentially hazardous outdoor sports and driving on obstacle-ridden roads.

BAJA BIODIVERSITY

A weekend in Cabo San Lucas will quickly convince you that Baja's got some wacky characters, but the wildlife is pretty wacky as well. The harsh deserts, rich mangrove swamps and underwater reefs make Baja one of the prime spots for seeing cool critters such as the ones below:

- Boojum tree – As if plucked right out of a Dr Seuss book, this tree looks like an inverted carrot and gets up to 20m tall.

- Cardón – The largest cactus on earth grows up to 20m high and is a majestic desert symbol that houses owls and cactus wrens.

- Ocotillo – Like the boojum tree, this thorny shrub seems otherworldly, looking more like a bunch of pipe cleaners stuck into the ground.

- Roadrunner – Aptly named, these stunning birds are easy to see along roadsides and in riverbeds. No, they're not escaping from Wile E Coyote, they're hunting for lizards and insects basking in the hot sun.

- Caracara – For some reason, these large, carrion-eating falcons really like sitting on top of cardóns. Look for the distinctive pink-and-white face patch to identify them.

- Man-o'-war bird – Commonly called the frigate bird, it's distinguishable by a clear, V-shaped tail. In mating season, the male's bubblegum-pink balloon throat stuns potential mates.

- Gray whales – The largest creatures *ever* to live on the planet enjoy Baja's west coast (boxed text, p284) as much as you do.

- Sea lions – Comical and friendly, these 'lions' of the sea often come right up for a close look at you.

For more information, see *A Field Guide to Mexican Birds: Mexico, Guatemala, Belize, El Salvador* by Roger Tory Peterson or *Baja California Plant Field Guide* by Norman C Roberts.

Getting There & Around

There are six official border crossings from the US state of California to Baja. At any crossing, Mexican authorities will issue and stamp tourist cards and process car permits. If you are going further south than Ensenada or San Felipe you *must* remember to get a tourist card.

Several carriers fly to San José del Cabo, at Baja's southern tip. Three major domestic air carriers and several smaller ones connect larger towns with mainland Mexico. Ferries from Santa Rosalía and La Paz connect Baja California to mainland Mexico by sea.

Air-conditioned buses operate daily between towns all along the peninsula. They are nonsmoking and reasonably priced. Except where noted, they run on a two-hour schedule from early morning until around 11pm.

Car travel is often the only way to reach isolated villages, mountains and beaches. Rent in larger cities and major tourist destinations, such as Los Cabos, La Paz, Loreto and the border towns; many US agencies specify that you cannot go further south than Ensenada.

NORTHERN BAJA

Known as La Frontera, this region includes Tijuana and Tecate and extends south to San Quintín. La Frontera corresponds roughly to the area colonized by the Dominicans, who established nine missions north of El Rosario from 1773 to 1821. Many view northern Baja's cities and beaches as hedonistic enclaves, but Tijuana and Mexicali are major manufacturing centers, and Mexicali's Río Colorado hinterland is a key agricultural zone.

TIJUANA

☎ 664 / pop 1.2 million

Tijuana has a reputation that precedes it. Yes, it's true that bars and brothels, prescription meds and strip clubs can all be found here. It's also true that many inebriated visitors pay good money to be photographed sitting upon a zebra-striped donkey holding a sign that reads 'Sitting on My Ass!' The easy way to avoid hassles is to just say 'no.'

That said, go there: cross the border, wander Av Revolución. You'll find yourself wide-eyed and marveling at the fascinating, vibrant cocktail of cultures. And Tijuana has witnessed a renaissance in recent years. Nortec music, with its hybrid blend of techno dance rhythms melded with the traditional sounds of *norteño* (country and dance music originating in northern Mexico) – think souped-up tuba and accordion with a break beat – has given Tijuana a sound that's all its own. Filmmakers, fashion designers and visual artists have taken the DJs' lead, and suddenly TJ has a new creative movement extending to other arts as well.

At the end of WWI Tijuana had fewer than 1000 inhabitants, but it soon drew US tourists with gambling, greyhound racing, boxing and cockfights. Tijuana's population increased to 180,000 by 1960, and with that growth has come severe social and environmental problems. Migrants still inhabit hillside dwellings of scrap wood and cardboard; however, on a positive note, a large and stable middle class is on the rise. While several well-publicized crimes have put TJ in the spotlight as a dangerous travel destination, those are isolated incidents that do not reflect the city as a whole. Exercise the usual caution you would in any larger city and you'll discover that TJ is a fun, fascinating place to visit. Chances are, you'll wish you had more time here.

Orientation

Tijuana is south of the US border post of San Ysidro, California, which is 19km south of downtown San Diego. Tijuana's central grid consists of north–south *avenidas* and east–west *calles*. South of Calle 1A, Av Revolución (La Revo) is the main commercial center.

East of the Frontón Palacio Jai Alai (no longer used), La Revo's major landmark, Tijuana's 'new' Zona Río commercial center straddles the river. Mesa de Otay, to the northeast, has another border crossing, the airport, *maquiladoras* (foreign-owned assembly-plant operations), neighborhoods and shopping areas.

Information
BOOKSTORES

Sanborns (☎ 688-14-62; Av Revolución 1102) This department store has a large selection of US and Mexican newspapers and magazines.

TIJUANA

To California Baja Rent-A-Car (24km);
Hostelling International
San Diego Downtown (25km)

INFORMATION
Canadian Consulate........................1 E5
Central Post Office..........................2 B4
Cotuco Head Office........................3 C3
Cotuco Pedestrian Border Entrance Visitor's
   Center.......................................4 B1
Cotuco Tourist Office......................5 A3
Fire Station.............................(see 9)
Hospital General............................6 F4
Lavamaticas 'Danny'......................7 A4
Mexican Customs & Immigration....8 B1
Police Station.................................9 A4
Secture Office...............................10 B1
US Customs & Immigration......(see 59)
World Net....................................11 A2

SIGHTS & ACTIVITIES
Centro Cultural Tijuana (CECUT)......12 C3
Cine Omnimax.........................(see 12)
Frontón Palacio Jai Alai.................13 A3
Librería El Día...............................14 D5
Monument to Abraham Lincoln......15 E4
Monument to Cuauhtémoc............16 D4
Monument to Diana Cazadora........17 C2
Monument to General Ignacio
   Zaragoza..................................18 E5
Monument to Padre Miguel Hidalgo..19 D3

Monumento México........................20 C3
Mundo Divertido Río......................21 E4
Museo de Cera..............................22 A2
Museo de Las Californias..........(see 12)
Vinicola LA Cetto..........................23 A4

SLEEPING
Grand Hotel Tijuana......................24 F6
Hotel Caesar.................................25 A3
Hotel Catalina...............................26 A3
Hotel El Conquistador....................27 F6
Hotel La Villa de Zaragoza.............28 B3
Hotel Lafayette..............................29 A2
Hotel Nelson.................................30 A2
Hotel Real del Rió.........................31 E4
Motel Plaza Hermosa....................32 A4

EATING
Café La Especial.....................(see 29)
Chiki Jai.......................................33 A3
Cien Años.....................................34 E4
D'Tony Restaurante Argentino........35 B3
La Costa.......................................36 A3
México Lindo.................................37 B3
Panaderia 'La Mejor'.....................38 A4
Restaurant Ricardo's......................39 B3
Vittorio's......................................40 A4

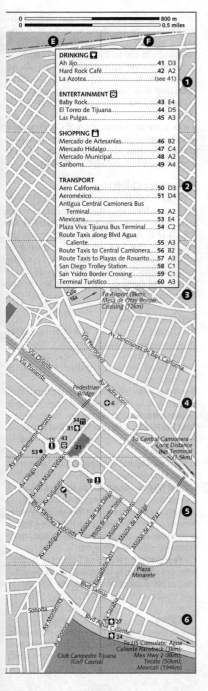

BAJA CALIFORNIA

Fire department (☎ 068)
Police (☎ 066)
Tourist Assistance hotline (☎ 078)

INTERNET ACCESS
Internet access is available in many places
along Av Revolución and its side streets.
World Net (☎ 685-65-14; Calle 2A No 8174; per hr
$1.20; ⏰ 24hr) Cheapest, with lots of computers and
English-speaking staff. Fills up fast.

INTERNET RESOURCES
See Tijuana (www.seetijuana.com) Tijuana's tourism
site.

LAUNDRY
Lavamaticas 'Danny' (☎ 638-50-69; Av Constitución
1821; ⏰ 7am-10pm) Self and wash-and-fold service.

MEDICAL SERVICES
Hospital General (☎ 684-00-78; Av Padre Kino, Zona
Río) Northwest of the junction with Av Rodríguez.

MONEY
Use caution when changing money, especially at night. Everyone accepts US
dollars. Travelers heading south or east by
bus can use the *casa de cambio* at the Central Camionera. Most banks have ATMs,
which is often the quickest and easiest way
to get cash.

POST
Central post office (☎ 684-00-78; cnr Av Negrete &
Calle 11A)

TOURIST INFORMATION
Cotuco (Comité de Turismo y Convenciones, Committee
on Tourism & Conventions) head office (☎ 684-05-37;
convistj@omnitec.com; Suite 201, Paseo de los Héroes
9365; ⏰ 9am-6pm Mon-Fri); pedestrian border-entrance
visitors center (☎ 683-49-87; ⏰ 9am-5pm Mon-Sat,
8am-3pm Sun); Av Revolución visitors center (☎ 685-22-10;
Av Revolución btwn Calle 3A & Calle 4A; ⏰ 10am-4pm
Mon-Thu, Fri-Sun 10am-7pm); airport visitors center
(☎ 683-82-44; airport baggage claim; ⏰ 8am-3pm)
Secture office (Secretaría de Turismo del Estado;
☎ 973-04-24, 973-04-30; Plaza Viva Tijuana; ⏰ 8am-
8pm Mon-Fri, 9am-1pm Sat & Sun) Has a friendly, English-
speaking staff.

Dangers & Annoyances
Tijuana has trouble if you look for it, but
it's also the most visited border city in the

world, a place where thousands of people enter and leave every day without hassles. People approaching you are generally not dangerous – they want you to buy something. That something could be a souvenir, a taxi ride, illegal drugs, an hour of passion…anything. No one will force anything on you. Keep walking and say '*no necesito*' (I don't need it), more effective than *no, gracias*.

Drinking on the streets is prohibited and heavy fines are regularly imposed on offenders. Mexico plays hardball with casual drug users; the possession of even a few grams of contraband can result in eight years or more in prison. US customs still expect you to possess a prescription if you're crossing the border with drugs that aren't the over-the-counter type.

Coyotes and *polleros* (both mean 'people smugglers') congregate along the river west of the San Ysidro crossing. After dark, avoid this area and Colonia Libertad, east of the crossing. Don't panic if you end up here, however – more than likely people will do what they can to help the lost gringo and point you back towards the pedestrian bridges.

Sights & Activities

South of Calle 1A, **La Revo** (Av Revolución) is the heart of Tijuana's tourist area. Take at least a brief stroll to see the crowded discos, fine restaurants, bars, loud hawkers, brash taxi drivers and souvenir shops that proudly claim to be 'Almost free.' You'll either love it or hate it, but this is the heart of TJ.

Until 1998 *frontón* (jai alai, type of handball) tournaments were held at the **Frontón Palacio Jai Alai**. The oddly attractive building, built over two decades from 1926 to 1947, remains a landmark and centerpiece for La Revo.

A modern landmark, Tijuana's **Centro Cultural Tijuana** (Cecut; ☎ 687-96-00; www.cecut.gob.mx in Spanish; cnr Paseo de los Héroes & Av Independencia) is a cultural center of which any comparably sized city north of the border would be proud. It houses an art gallery, the **Museo de las Californias** (admission $2; ☯ 10am-7pm Tue-Sun), a theater and the globular **Cine Omnimax** (tickets from $3.75; ☯ 1-9pm Tue-Fri, 10am-9pm Sat & Sun).

Vinícola LA Cetto (LA Cetto Winery; ☎ 685-30-31; Cañón Johnson 2108; ☯ 10am-6:30pm Mon-Fri, 10am-5pm Sat), southwest of Av Constitución,

offers tours and tasting, and has an English-language video for those who want to disrupt their tasting with a virtual tour. With vineyards in the fertile Valle de Guadalupe between Tecate and Ensenada, LA Cetto produces a range of tasty varietals, as well as sparkling wines and a decent brandy.

Museo de Cera (Wax Museum; ☎ 688-24-78; Calle 1A No 8281; admission $1.50; ☯ 10am-7pm) Okay, it's a wax museum. On view are about 90 waxen figures including an uncanny Frida Kahlo and a really bad Elvis. Bill Clinton, Ghandi and Vicente Fox are also on display.

Tijuana for Children

If Av Revolución is too intense for the kiddies, consider taking them to the American-style amusement park **Mundo Divertido Río** (☎ 634-32-13; Av José Maria Velasco 2578; ☯ noon-9pm Mon-Fri, 11am-10pm Sat & Sun) for miniature golf, a huge arcade, batting cages, rides and the essential snack bar. Or just skip TJ completely and head directly to the beaches of Rosarito (p273).

Festivals & Events

As Tijuana's reputation as a cultural center continues to grow, so does its annual calendar of cultural events. These and other listings can be found online at www.see tijuana.com.

Muestra Internacional de Danza International Dance Festival in April. Local and international groups compete to celebrate and demonstrate contemporary dance.

Feria Del Platillo Mexicano Mexican Food Festival in September. Plates are piled high with goodies – and gobbled down.

Festival del Tequila The Tequila Festival is held in October. Mmmm. Tequila…!

Festival Hispano-Americano de Guitarra Hispanic-American Guitar Festival in November. National guitar graduates and professional players from around the world demonstrate the richness and beauty of the guitar. Rock bands do their best to remind people that the instrument can also just make a lot of noise, too.

Día de Muertos Day of the Dead in November. Families honor their loved ones by visiting family graves. Decorative altars are put up around the city, often with skeletons – some macabre, some quite comical.

Sleeping

Ask to see a room before you slap down dough for a night's stay; the cheapest places are often shabbier than most folks are ready for. The side streets off Revo can be a bit quieter, but the cheapest are usually shared with hourly-rate clientele.

BUDGET

Hostelling International San Diego Downtown (☎ 617-525-15-31; www.sandiegohostels.org; 521 Market St, San Diego; dm $27) Across the border, but only a 30-minute trolley ride away, this spick-and-span hostel boasts easy access to everything – the fracas of the San Diego Gas Lamp district, TJ, even the beaches at Rosarita. Friendly and safe, it's a great option for those on the US side of the border.

Hotel Lafayette (☎ 685-39-40; Av Revolución 325; s/d $25/32) Downtown's most popular budget hotel is the Lafayette, above Café La Especial. The rooms overlooking the cacophonous Av Revolución are not tranquil havens; request one in the back.

Hotel Catalina (☎ 685-97-48; Calle 5A (Zapata) 2039; s/d $18/26) This clean and secure hotel, a block away from Av Revolución, is comparable to the Lafayette but quieter. An adjacent restaurant provides quick eats if you're not up for Av Revo.

Motel Plaza Hermosa (☎ 685-33-53; Av Constitución 1821; s/d/tr $33/33/44; P) Thirty-eight shockingly pink rooms are quiet, cozy and have a TV and fan. Skylights and potted palms brighten up the (pink!) hallways.

MIDRANGE

Hotel La Villa de Zaragoza (☎ 685-18-32; www.hotel lavilla.biz; Av Madero 1120; r/ste $43/72; P ✕ ⌷) Rooms at this modern hotel, directly behind the Frontón, include TV and telephone. There's laundry, childcare, a restaurant and room service.

Hotel El Conquistador (☎ 681-79-55; fax 686-13-40; Blvd Agua Caliente 10750; s/d $62/67; P ⌷ ⌷) This four-star Zona Río hotel has spacious rooms with cable TV and a distinctive restaurant dedicated to Don Quijote. Tiled staircases and lush greenery in the parking lot add to the ambience.

Hotel Nelson (☎ 685-43-02; Av Revolución 721; s/d $45/48) The friendly Nelson Hotel is a long-time favorite with high ceilings and 1950s-era touches that, most likely, haven't been touched. Tidy, carpeted rooms come with color TV, a view and the less-than-soothing sounds of La Revo. The bar has incredibly cheap drink specials.

Hotel Caesar (☎ 685-16-06; fax 685-34-92; Av Revolución & Calle 5A No 1079; s/d $35/45) Hotel Caesar's long reign is evoked by the vintage bullfight posters and photographs that adorn its walls. Rooms are small and clean, and the restaurant (now a sports bar) claims to have created the Caesar salad in 1924. Prices drop in the off-season.

TOP END

Grand Hotel Tijuana (☎ 681-70-00; www.grandhotel tij.com.mx/english/index.htm; Blvd Agua Caliente 4500; r $140, ste from $272; P ⌷ ⌷ ⌷) Asian flute music wafts through the lobby and makes for a soothing check-in, though the hallways are a bit dark. The two 23-story buildings that include the luxurious Grand Hotel Tijuana also have a shopping mall, offices, restaurants and convention facilities, and there's an adjacent golf-course.

Hotel Real del Río (☎ 634-31-00; www.realdelrio .com/index_english.html; Av Velasco 1409A; r/ste $120/168; P ⌷ ⌷ ⌷) The modern and efficient Real del Río provides excellent service and well-appointed, comfortable rooms. It's a high-end option that doesn't have much character but is more than adequate.

Eating

Tijuana's cuisine scene is one of the city's big surprises. You'll find everything from traditional *antojitos* (small plates of basic regional fare) to haute-mexicano miracles, as well as international specialties from around the globe. Avoid the 'free' drink offers from hawkers on the street and head to the real deals listed below.

Café La Especial (☎ 685-66-54; Av Revolución 325; dinner mains $3-6) A mainstay since 1952, this restaurant offers decent Mexican food at reasonable prices and is far quieter than the average eatery on La Revo.

Panadería 'La Mejor' (☎ 685-21-88; Av Constitución 1727; meals $2; ☼ 6am-8pm) Mexican bakery with a myriad of mouthwatering choices and English-speaking staff.

Restaurant Ricardo's (☎ 685-31-46; Av Madero 1410; breakfasts $3-8.50, tortas $2.75-4.50; ☼ 24hr) One of Tijuana's best values is this bright and cheerful diner-style place. Excellent breakfasts and tortas (sandwiches), among the best in town, are served around the clock. The waterfall adds to the ambience.

Mexico Lindo (cnr Av Madero & Hidalgo; tacos $1, dinner mains $3-5) In addition to tacos and quesadillas served with all the accoutrements, this family-run place also serves an excellent *pozole*, a filling soup dish made from pork, corn hominy and plenty of lime and cilantro.

Cien Años (☎ 634-30-39; Av José Maria Velasco 1407; dinner mains $9-15) Giant water vases preside over the patrons at this famous restaurant. Manta-ray quesadillas are exotic, as are some of the specials. A tequila-bottle library at the entrance makes waiting for a table much less of a chore.

La Costa (☎ 685-31-24; Calle 7A No 8131; dinner mains $12-30) The seafood combination plate ($34) provides two people with a huge platter of crab, shrimp, lobster, octopus and fish fillet. Made at your table, La Costa's flaming Mexican coffee is spectacular.

Chiki Jai (☎ 685-49-55; Av Revolución 1388; dinner mains $15; ☷ 11am-9pm) Gorgeous tiled walls and a spectacular painted ceiling make this small eatery stand out from other La Revo options. Try the salmon or the paella if you're in a seafood mood.

Vittorio's (☎ 685-17-29; Av Revolución 1687; pizzas $5-13.50, pastas $7-9.50) For years this cozy Italian restaurant has been serving generous portions of reasonably priced pizza and pasta. Head to the back and you'll feel like the Godfather in the plush leather booths and dim lighting.

Drinking

If you've come here just to get plastered you'll feel like a dog that's found too many fire hydrants: so many choices, so little time. Don't be afraid to wander. The **Hard Rock Café** (☎ 685-02-06; Av Revolución 520) is a safe bet. Look to the hotel bars if you just want to sip a Tecate (Mexican beer) without a Britney wanna-be dancing on the bar and upsetting your dish of peanuts. Head to Plaza Fiesta at Zona Río for the local club scene, where you'll also encounter a dozen or so restaurants and bars – try Ah Jijo or La Azotea, and go from there.

Entertainment

If you get sick of stumbling down La Revo, try some of the city's diverse sporting and cultural offerings. Entertainment listings are readily available at www.seetijuana.com. Most fancier discos are in the Zona Río.

Baby Rock (☎ 634-24-04; Av Diego Rivera 1482; Sat cover $10). Look for the giant fake rock and you'll know you've arrived. Petroglyphs make it only slightly less tacky.

Centro Cultural Tijuana (☎ 687-96-00; www .cecut.gob.mx; cnr Paseo de los Héroes & Av Independencia) The theater here is the city's apex of drama, dance and musical performance with several events scheduled each month.

Las Pulgas (☎ 685-95-94; Av Revolución 1127) Tuba is played with wild abandon here. The cover charge is usually $3.75 but women are frequently admitted free of charge.

Shopping

Jewelry, blankets, furniture, baskets, silver, pottery and leather goods are available in stores on Av Revolución and Av Constitución, at the **Mercado Municipal** (Av Niños Héroes; ☷ 8am-6pm) and the sprawling **Mercado de Artesanías** (Av Ocampo) just south of Comercio (Calle 1A).

Mercado Hidalgo (Blvd Taboada & Av Independencia) is where locals come to buy spices, dried chilies, exotic produce, fresh tortillas and seasonal specialties made from Aztec grains. Be sure to check with customs if you're taking fruits or vegetables over the border.

Getting There & Away

Mexican tourist cards are available 24 hours a day at the San Ysidro–Tijuana border in the **immigration office** (☎ 682-64-39). They are also available – although less dependably – at a small office in the main bus terminal (Central Camionera; below). Be sure to get one if you plan to head further south than Ensenada.

AIR

Aeropuerto Internacional Abelardo L Rodríguez (☎ 683-24-18) is in Mesa de Otay, east of downtown.

Airlines

Aero California (☎ 684-21-00; Plaza Río Tijuana) Flies to La Paz and serves many mainland destinations from Mexico City northward.

Aeroméxico (☎ 683-84-44, 684-92-68; Local A 12-1, Plaza Río Tijuana) Serves many mainland Mexican destinations, and has nonstop flights to La Paz and flights to Tucson and Phoenix, both via Hermosillo.

Mexicana (☎ 634-65-66; Av Diego Rivera 1511, Zona Río) Flies daily to Los Angeles (but not from Los Angeles) and also serves many mainland Mexican cities.

BUS

About 5km southeast of downtown, the main bus terminal is the **Central Camionera**

(☎ 621-29-82), where **Elite** (☎ 688-19-79; www .estrellablanca.com.mx) and **Estrella** (☎ 621-29-55; www.estrellablanca.com.mx) offer 1st-class buses wit h air-con and toilets. Destinations on mainland Mexico include Guadalajara ($105, 36 hours) and Mexico City ($151, 40 hours). All lines stop at major mainland destinations. Autotransportes del Pacífico, Norte de Sonora and ABC leave from Central Camionera and operate mostly 2nd-class buses to mainland Mexico's Pacific coast and around Baja California. ABC's Servicio Plus resembles Elite's and Crucero's. **ABC** (☎ 683-56-81) offers buses to the following destinations:

Destination	Price	Duration
Ensenada	1st/2nd class $10/8	1½hr
Guerrero Negro	$69	12hr
La Paz	$105	22hr
Loreto	$98	16hr
Mexicali	1st/2nd class $25/16	3hr
San Felipe	$34	5hr
Tecate	$4.50	1½hr

Tijuana has two bus departure locations near the border crossing that might prove more convenient than the outlying Central Camionera. **Suburbaja** (☎ 688-00-82), **Elite** (☎ 621-29-82) and the US-based **Greyhound** (☎ 688-19-79) use the handy downtown **Antigua Central Camionera** (☎ 686-06-95; Av Madero & Calle 1A). Suburbaja buses leave for Tecate every 20 minutes ($3, 1½ hours); these are local buses that make many stops. Greyhound buses leave every hour for Los Angeles ($23, four hours). Elite has four 1st-class buses each day to Mexico City ($151, 42 hours) and Guadalajara ($105, 32 hours).

Between 8am and 9pm, **Mexicoach** (www .mexicoach.com) runs frequent buses ($2) from its **San Ysidro terminal** (☎ 619-428-95-17; 4570 Camino de la Plaza) to the **Terminal Turístico** (☎ 685-14-70; Av Revolución 1025).

Between 5:40am and 9:50pm, buses leave from the **San Diego Greyhound terminal** (☎ 619-239-32-66, in the USA ☎ 800-231-22-22; 120 West Broadway, San Diego) and stop at **San Ysidro** (in US ☎ 619-428-11-94; 799 East San Ysidro Blvd), en route to Tijuana's Antigua Central Camionera bus terminal or the Central Camionera. Fares to both locations are $5 one-way, $8 round-trip.

TROLLEY
San Diego's popular **light-rail trolley** (☎ 619-233-30-04) runs from downtown San Diego to San Ysidro ($2.50) every 15 minutes from about 5am to midnight. From San Diego's Lindbergh Field airport, city bus 992 ($2.25) goes to the Plaza America trolley stop in downtown San Diego, across from the Amtrak depot.

CAR & MOTORCYCLE
The San Ysidro border crossing, which is a 10-minute walk from downtown Tijuana, is open 24 hours, but motorists may find the Mesa de Otay crossing (also open round the clock) less congested; it's 8km to the east of San Ysidro.

For rentals, agencies in San Diego are the cheapest option, but most of them allow rentals only as far as Ensenada. **California Baja Rent-A-Car** (☎ 619-470-7368; www.cabaja.com), in Spring Valley, California, 32km from downtown San Diego and 24km from San Ysidro, is a good option if you plan to continue driving beyond Ensenada.

Getting Around
BUS & TAXI
For about $0.40, local buses pretty much go everywhere, but the slightly pricier route taxis are much quicker. To get to the Central Camionera take any 'Buena Vista,' 'Centro' or 'Central Camionera' bus from Calle 2A, east of Av Constitución. For a quicker and more convenient option, take a gold-and-white 'Mesa de Otay' route taxi from Av Madero between Calles 2A and 3A ($0.80).

To get to the airport, take any 'Aeropuerto' blue-and-white bus (about $0.40) from the street just south of the San Ysidro border taxi stand; from downtown, catch it on Calle 5a between Avs Constitución and Niños Héroes. Sharing can reduce the cost of a taxi which is about $15, if hailed on the street.

Tijuana taxis lack meters, but most rides cost about $5 or less. However, beware of the occasional unscrupulous taxi driver, and make sure to agree to a fare beforehand to avoid misunderstandings.

AROUND TIJUANA
Playas de Rosarito
☎ 661 / pop 63,400
South of Tijuana, the valley of Rosarito marks the original boundary between

BAJA CALIFORNIA

mainland California and Baja California. The town of Playas de Rosarito dates from 1885, but the Hotel Rosarito (now the landmark Rosarito Beach Hotel) and its long, sandy beach pioneered local tourism in the late 1920s. These days, the town has taken on a distinctly Hollywood sheen: Fox Studios Baja, built in 1996 for the filming of *Titanic*, has since served as a primary filming location for *Pearl Harbor* and, most recently, *Master and Commander: The Far Side of the World.*

The amphitheater at the beachfront **Parque Municipal Abelardo L Rodríguez** contains Juan Zuñiga Padilla's impressive 1987 mural *Tierra y Libertad* (Land and Liberty).

Rosarito's main street – the noisy commercial strip of Blvd Juárez (part of the Carretera Transpeninsular, Hwy 1) – has many good restaurants and affordable accommodations. There's quick Internet access at **www.bajachat.com** (☎ 612-09-54; Juárez 23; per hr $3; ☻ 9am-10pm) seven days a week.

Rooms at **Festival Plaza Hotel** (☎ 800-027-37-71; www.festivalplazahotel.com; Juárez 1207; r $149; ⓟ ⓧ ⌨ ⓡ) are small and bland, but the location is as central as can be, and if you're facing the ocean it's a spectacular view. The website offers package discounts as low as $39 per person

Friendly and fun, **Rosarito Beach Hostel** (☎ 613-11-79; www.alamo-hostel.com; Calle Alamo 148; dm $15; ⓟ) has free pickup in San Diego and Internet access. Only a quick walk from the clubs or beaches, this a great low-cost option.

The scent of fresh-baked rolls, sweets and breads will have your mouth watering long before you enter **Panaderia La Espiga** (☎ 612-14-59; Juárez 298; ☻ 7am-9pm Mon-Sun). Try the flan Neapolitan or *conos* (cones) filled with crème.

LOBSTER, LOBSTER, EVERYWHERE...

Lobster lovers will want to head 12km south from Playas de Rosarito to lobster-lovers' mecca: Puerto Nuevo. 'New Port' is notable for its small, cluttered streets and good shopping, but mainly for its lobster shacks: there are dozens of them. Find a good one by the crowds – or just stop someone and ask them. Either way, be sure to bring your appetite.

The delicious taco stand, **Tacos El Yaqui** (cnr Palma & Mar del Norte; tacos $2.50; ☻ 10am-4pm Mon, Tue, Thu & Fri, 10am-11pm Sat & Sun), is so popular that they often close early when the ingredients run out.

Come to **Papas & Beer** (☻ 11-3am) for foam dances, a mechanical bull and drunken reveling. If you're tired of partying or it's the morning after, try a hot cuppa joe and a homemade pastry at **Capuchino's** (☎ 612-29-79; Juárez 890; pastries $3).

From downtown Tijuana, route taxis for Playas de Rosarito ($1.10) leave from Av Madero between Calles 3A and 4A. Look for a yellow station wagon with a triangular white patch on the door. You can also catch a shuttle from the Terminal Turístico on Av Revolución between Calles 6A and 7A ($10 round-trip); they leave every two hours between 9am and 7pm.

Tecate
☎ 665 / pop 77,800

Tecate resembles more of a mainland Mexican village than a border town, but hosts several popular tourist events, such as bicycle races. Its landmark **Cuauhtémoc Moctezuma Brewery** (☎ 654-94-78; Hidalgo & Obregón; tours ☻ noon & 3pm Mon-Fri) produces two of Mexico's best-known beers, Tecate and Carta Blanca, but *maquiladoras* drive the local economy.

For lodging, the best value in town is offered by **Motel La Hacienda** (☎ 654-12-50; Av Juárez 861; d $45; ⓟ ⓧ ⓡ), which has clean, carpeted rooms and a magnificent flower-festooned courtyard.

Tecate is 55km east of Tijuana by Hwy 2, the east–west route linking Tijuana and Mexicali. The **border crossing** (☻ 6am-midnight) is less congested than either Tijuana or Mesa de Otay.

ENSENADA
☎ 646 / pop 370,000

Ensenada, 108km south of the border and presided over by perhaps the largest Mexican flag in the world, is a cosmopolitan city. In the tourist zone you can find ceramics, hammocks, textiles and other treasures – even that toothpick holder in the shape of a rear end you've been searching for.

Ensenada enjoys great popularity among tourists; about four million of them descend upon the city each year: 350,000 float in by

ENSENADA

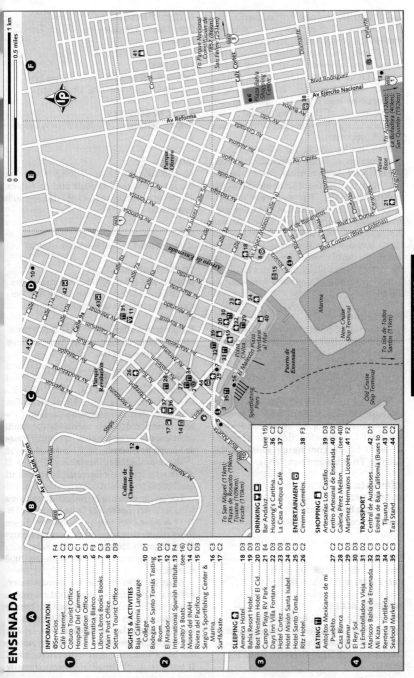

INFORMATION
@Servicios..........................1 F4
Café Internet......................2 C3
Cotuco Tourist Office.........3 C3
Hospital Del Carmen..........4 C1
Immigration Office.............5 C3
Lavematica Blanco..............6 F3
Libros Libros Books Books....7 C3
Main Post Office.................8 D3
Secture Tourist Office.........9 D3

SIGHTS & ACTIVITIES
Baja California Language
College............................10 D1
Bodegas de Santo Tomás Tasting
Room..............................11 D2
El Mirador.........................12 C2
International Spanish Institute.13 F4
Juanito's Boats...................(see 16)
Museo del INAH.................14 C2
Riviera del Pacífico.............15 D3
Sergio's Sportfishing Center &
Marina.............................16 C3
Surf&Skate........................17 C2

SLEEPING
America Hotel.....................18 D3
Bahía Resort Hotel..............19 D3
Best Western Hotel El Cid....20 D3
Campo Playa RV Park..........21 D3
Days Inn Villa Fontana.........22 D3
Hotel Cortez......................23 D3
Hotel Misión Santa Isabel.....24 D3
Hotel Santo Tomás.............25 C2
Ritz Hotel..........................26 C2

EATING
Antojitos Mexicanos de mi
Pueblito...........................27 C2
Casa Blanca.......................28 C2
Casamar............................29 D3
El Rey Sol..........................30 D3
La Embotelladora Vieja........31 D2
Mariscos Bahía de Ensenada.32 C3
Mi Kaza............................33 C3
Rentería Tortillería..............34 C2
Seafood Market..................35 C3

DRINKING
Bar Andaluz.......................(see 15)
Hussong's Cantina..............36 C2
La Casa Antiqua Café...........37 C2

ENTERTAINMENT
Cinemas Gemelos................38 F3

SHOPPING
Artesanías Los Castillo..........39 D3
Centro Artesanal de Ensenada.40 D3
Galería Pérez Meillon...........(see 40)
Martínez Hermanos Licores...41 F2

TRANSPORT
Central de Autobuses...........42 D1
Estrella de Baja California (Buses to
Tijuana)...........................43 D1
Taxi Stand........................44 C2

cruise ship from southern California, the others drive. Most are drawn to Av López Mateos, a landscaped, pedestrian-oriented artery lined with interesting shops, cafés, restaurants, sidewalk seating and many hotels. Outdoor activities such as fishing and surfing are popular, and Ensenada is the locus of Baja's wine industry. Singer Jim Morrison, of Doors fame, used to sip tequila and watch surfers just north at San Miguel (opposite).

Even further back, in colonial times, Ensenada occasionally sheltered Acapulco-bound galleons returning from Manila, but the first permanent settlement was established in 1804. The discovery of gold in 1870 at Real del Castillo, 35km inland, brought a short-lived boom. Ensenada was the capital of Baja territory from 1882 to 1915, but the capital shifted to Mexicali during the revolution. After the revolution the city catered to 'sin' industries until the federal government outlawed gambling in the 1930s.

Orientation

Near the water, hotels and restaurants line Blvd Costero, also known as Blvd Cárdenas. Av López Mateos (Calle 1A) lies parallel to Blvd Costero for a short distance inland (north). The tourist district is between Av Ryerson and Av Castillo.

North of town, Hwy 3 heads northeast to Tecate; at the southeast edge of town it leads east toward Ojos Negros and Parque Nacional Constitución de 1857 (Laguna Hanson) before continuing south to the Valle de Trinidad and San Felipe.

Information

BOOKSTORES
Libros Libros Books Books (☎ 178-84-48; Av López Mateos 690) Good selection of books in Spanish and English.

EMERGENCY
Municipal Police (☎ 060, 176-43-43)
State Police (☎ 061, 176-36-36)

INTERNET ACCESS
@Servicios (☎ 176-16-58; Delante 169-1; per hr $1; 🕑 9am-10pm) A bit of a hike, but the cheapest option; serves pastries and coffee as well.
Café Internet (☎ 175-70-11; Av López Mateos 582; per hr $2)

INTERNET RESOURCES
Enjoy Ensanada (www.enjoyensenada.com) Ensenada's tourism site.

LAUNDRY
Lavematica Blanco (☎ 176-25-48; Plaza Bahía Shopping Center, cnr Calz Cortez & Av Reforma)

MEDICAL SERVICES
Hospital Del Carmen (☎ 178-34-77; cnr Av Obregón & Calle 11)

MONEY
Most banks and *casas de cambio* are near the intersection of Av Ruiz and Av Juárez. There are numerous ATMs throughout Ensenada.

POST
Main post office (cnr Avs López Mateos & Riviera)

TOURIST INFORMATION
Cotuco tourist office (☎ 178-24-11; cotucoe@telnor .net; Blvd Costero 540; 🕑 9am-5pm Sun-Tue, 9am-7pm Wed-Fri) Dispenses maps, brochures and current hotel information.
Secture tourist office (☎ 172-30-22; Blvd Costero 1477; 🕑 8am-8pm Mon-Fri, 9am-1pm Sat & Sun) Carries similar information as the Cotuco office.

Sights

Opened in the early 1930s as Hotel Playa Ensenada, the extravagant **Riviera del Pacífico**, a Spanish-style former casino on Blvd Costero, is rumored to have been a regular haunt of Al Capone. It now houses the small **Museo de Historia de Ensenada** (☎ 177-05-94; admission $1; 🕑 9am-5pm) and Bar Andaluz (p278), and offers retrospective film screenings and art exhibitions.

For an informative introduction to Baja's wine industry, **Bodegas de Santo Tomás** (☎ 178-33-33; Av Miramar 666; tours $5; 🕑 8am-5pm) holds tours of its cellars and wine tastings hourly from 10am to 1pm and at 3pm. Sample its signature big red, the award-winning 2000 Cabernet.

Built in 1886 by the US-owned International Company of Mexico, Ensenada's oldest public building, **ex-Aduana Marítima de Ensenada**, houses the **Museo del Instituto Nacional de Antropología e Historia** (Museo del INAH; ☎ 178-25-31; Av Ryerson 1; admission free; 🕑 9am-5pm Mon-Fri), a historical and cultural museum. It has a relatively small but comprehensive collection of artifacts, and discusses (mainly in Spanish) the area's history from prehistoric times up to now.

Atop the Colinas de Chapultepec, **El Mirador** offers panoramic views of the city and Bahía de Todos Santos. Climb or drive to this highest point in town, up Av Alemán from the western end of Calle 2A in central Ensenada.

Activities

The beach at **San Miguel**, 11km to the north of town, has a wonderful right to left break and often hosts **surfing** contests. Camping ($5 per car) is available. For something a little less predictable, head west of Ensenada by boat to the **Islas de Todos Santos**, where you'll find a legendary spot called **El Martillo** (The Hammer) with swells rising 4m to 5m. Boats run out to the breaks every day; check at the harbor. **Surf&Skate** (☎ 172-50-31; Av Ryerson 59; ☼ 10am-8pm Mon-Sat, 11am-6pm Sun), in the tourist zone downtown, rents boards and wetsuits for a pricey $40 per day.

Ensenada is known the world over for its excellent **sportfishing**. Most charter companies also offer **whale-watching tours** from late December to March. The following options are well regarded, and can be found on the sportfishing pier off El Malecón.

Juanito's Boats (☎ 174-09-53; www.sailorschoice .com/juanitos) Rates start at $200 for up to four people, not including fishing tackle or park admission.

Sergio's Sportfishing Center & Marina (☎ 178-21-85; www.sergios-sportfishing.com) Expect to pay $55 per person for fishing trip, including gear. Private charter boats start at $250.

Courses

The following language schools offer similar immersion programs with homestay opportunities.

Baja California Language College (☎ 174-17-21; www.bajacal.com; Av Riveroll 1287) Courses cost from $25 per hour or $265 per week.

International Spanish Institute (☎ 176-01-09; www.sdro.com/spanishinstitute/index.html; Blvd Rodríguez 377) Costs start at $125 for a week or $80 per weekend.

Festivals & Events

The events listed below constitute a tiny sample of the 70-plus sporting, tourist and cultural happenings that take place each year. Dates change, so contact tourist offices for details.

Carnaval Mardi Gras celebration, late February to early March. The streets flood with floats and dancers.

Baja 500 Off-road car race in early June.

Fiesta de la Vendimia Wine harvest, mid-August.

Fiestas Patrias Mexican independence days, mid-September. Three days of dancing and parades.

Mexican Surf Fiesta Grand finals of local surf competition, mid-October. Everyone just hangs loose.

Fiesta del Tequila Last week in October.

Sleeping

Although Ensenada has many hotels, demand can exceed supply at times, particularly on Saturday and Sunday and in summer. Rates vary both seasonally, and between weekdays (Monday to Friday) and weekends (Saturday and Sunday).

BUDGET

America Motel (☎ 176-13-33; Av López Mateos 1309; s/d $25/32; P) A friendly motor lodge that is quiet and yet only a five-minute walk from the tourist zone. Carpeted rooms are clean and simple, and many have kitchenettes.

Campo Playa RV Park (☎ 176-29-18; cnr Blvd Las Dunas & Sanginés; car or camp sites $15, motor homes $22) A bit of a walk from downtown but only a short drive away, this place is a bit spartan and is dusty when the wind blows. It offers secure, well-maintained facilities and some palm trees for shade.

MIDRANGE

Hotel Santo Tomás (☎ 178-15-03; hst@bajainn.com; Blvd Costero 609; d $80; P) Clean and snazzy, with satellite TV in each room, this is at the high end of midrange. The lobby elevator, on a raised platform, will make you feel like you're stepping into a Star Trek teleportation device. Rates increase by 15% on Friday and Saturday. Beam me up, Scottie.

Hotel Cortez (☎ 178-23-07; fax 178-39-04; Av López Mateos 1089; s/d $70/80; P ✕ ☎) This large, family-friendly hotel has a gym, a basketball court and a popular bar and restaurant.

Days Inn Villa Fontana (☎ 178-34-34; www .villafontana.com.mx; Av López Mateos 1050; s/tr $60/82; ✕ ☎) Pink paint and blue tiles make it cheery, though the air freshener is a bit thick in some rooms. Has tidy, comfortable rooms with views and cable TV. Prices increase by 20% on Friday and Saturday.

Ritz Hotel (☎ 174-05-01; explotur@prodigy.net.mx; Calle 4A 379; s/d/tr $28/35/40; ✕) Not at all ritzy, but clean, friendly and inexpensive. Rooms

BAJA CALIFORNIA

are small and dark, but friendly staff and easy access to the tourist zone, restaurants and the bus station make up for it.

Bahía Resort Hotel (☎ 178-21-03; www.hotelbahia .com.mx; Av López Mateos 850; s/d $60/85; P 🅿 🔁) Welcome margaritas, a nice pool and balconies that look out at the port are why folks keep coming here. Psychedelic hallways only add to the fun.

TOP END

Best Western Hotel El Cid (☎ 178-24-01; www.mex online.com/elcid.htm; Av López Mateos 993; s/d $70/96; P 🅿 🔁 🅿) This four-star hotel has unique rooms, an outstanding restaurant and a lively bar featuring Cuban music on weekends. Prices include continental breakfast. WLAN (wireless local-area network) helps those with laptops stay connected.

Hotel Misión Santa Isabel (☎ 178-33-45; hmision@telnor.net; Blvd Costero 1119; s/d Sun-Thu from $49/86, Fri & Sat $75/95; P 🔁 🅿) This striking hotel, restaurant and bar offers comfortable rooms decorated with tasteful tile work reminiscent of an old Baja mission. The Z-shaped pool is an attractive centerpiece to the airy, quiet courtyard. Prices may rise during holidays.

Eating

Ensenada has eateries ranging from corner taco stands to places serving the best of Mexican and international cuisine. Seafood lovers, in particular, will leave sated and smiling.

Renteria Tortilleria (☎ 178-35-79; Calle 2A No 558; 🕒 5am-4pm) Tiny little grocery store with freshly made flour tortillas for $0.90 per kg. Enjoy both smells and smiles as you watch them being made.

Casa Blanca (☎ 174-03-16; Av Ruiz 254; plates $7) The Casa Blanca serves tasty, traditional fixed-price lunches, in a cute 2nd-floor setting away from the main drag.

El Rey Sol (☎ 178-17-33; Av López Mateos 1000; dinner mains $15-20) This venerable Franco-Mexican institution has elegant French food with unusual fusion delicacies such as crocodile in *tamarindo* sauce with wine, or salmon in champagne. The 'Chocolate Volcano' is their most popular dessert.

Mi Kaza (☎ 178-82-11; Av Riveroll 87-2; breakfasts $3-6, dinner mains $5-10; 🕒 6:30am-10pm) No smoking here please, as you enjoy inexpensive Mexican or American dishes at this not-so-

greasy greasy spoon. Princess Diana lovers (or haters) will enjoy the tribute wall of photos at the back; blue ceramic lamps and bright paint give it quiet cheer.

La Embotelladora Vieja (☎ 178-16-60; cnr Av Miramar & Calle 7A; dinner mains $15-25; 🕒 Mon-Sat) Both rustic and elegant, this place was once a wine-aging warehouse. Beautiful brick arches, simple white tablecloths and an outstanding wine selection make this a great spot to celebrate. The delicious *filet mignon Embotelladora*, marinated in port, is a treat.

Antojitos Mexicanos de mi Pueblito (☎ 156-51-92; Av Gastélium 168; dinner mains $6; 🕒 8am-8pm Tue-Sun) Great enchiladas, quesadillas, burritos, *agua de jamaica* (hibiscus water) and friendly service make this perfect for anyone watching their wallet. Also has breakfast specials and daily set menus.

Casamar (☎ 174-04-17; Blvd Costero 987; dinner mains $8-15, lobster dishes $30) This family-owned restaurant features elegant seafood dining and a full bar that offers great views of the port. Try the signature dish, *fillet casamar* (sea bass stuffed with seafood and spinach covered with clam sauce).

Drinking

Ensenada is a perfect place to start (or continue) that long-awaited vacation bender. On weekends, most bars and cantinas along Av Ruiz are packed from noon to early morning. If that's not your scene, head for one of the many quality hotels and fine restaurants where you're likely to find a laid-back spot to sip a top-shelf tequila.

Hussong's Cantina (☎ 178-32-10; Av Ruiz 113; 🕒 10am-1am) The oldest and perhaps liveliest cantina in the Californias has been serving tequila since 1892. It's also a raucous palace of mariachi music.

Bar Andaluz (☎ 177-17-30; Blvd Costero; 🕒 11am-11pm) For a complete change in ambience, visit the cultured inside the Riviera del Pacífico (p276), where having a drink is an exercise in nostalgia. You can almost visualize Lana Turner sipping a martini at the polished walnut bar.

La Casa Antiqua Café (☎ 175-73-20; lacasaantigua café@hotmail.com; Av Obregón 110; coffee $3, sandwiches $3-6; 🕒 8am-10:30pm Mon-Sat) Vintage photos and clapboards separate this place from the coffee megachains. Delicate pastries, good bagels and sandwiches, and rich coffee are all worth ducking away from the strip for.

Entertainment

Entertainment opportunities in Ensenada are primarily of the drinking, eating, shopping and sporting variety. **Cinemas Gemelos** (☎ 176-36-16; cnr Avs López Mateos & Balboa) has recent Hollywood fare, often dubbed into Spanish.

Shopping

Galería Pérez Meillon (☎ 171-61-27; Blvd Costero 1094; ⏰ 9am-6pm) In the Centro Artesanal de Ensenada, this gallery sells authenticated pottery from the Paipai (one of Baja California's indigenous people known for fine craftwork, particularly pottery and baskets) and Mata Ortiz, a major pottery center in the north of Mexico. Also for sale are baskets woven from aromatic materials such as sage by the Kumiai people. Kumiai are also indigenous to Baja and are becoming well known for their fine artisanship. When shopping, always consider whether you will be able to take the items into your home country.

Artesanías Los Castillo (☎ 178-29-62; Av López Mateos 815; ⏰ 10am-7pm) Taxco silver is available here.

Martínez Hermanos Licores (☎ 177-39-08; Coral 768; ⏰ 10am-midnight) Known for the widest tequila selection in the surrounding area with over 400 brands on the shelves. Sorry, no tasting.

Getting There & Away

The **immigration office** (☎ 174-01-64; Blvd Azueta 101; document delivery ⏰ 8:30am-1pm, document pickup 1-3pm) is open daily.

AIR

Primarily a military airport, **Aeropuerto El Ciprés** (☎ 177-45-03; Carreterra Tranpenisular Km 114.5) is just south of town off the Transpeninsular. The only regularly scheduled flights serving Ensenada are by **Aerocedros** (☎ 177-35-34), which flies to Guerrero Negro and Isla Cedros.

BUS

Ensenada's **Central de Autobuses** (☎ 178-66-80; Av Riveroll 1075) is 10 blocks north of Av López Mateos. **Elite** (☎ 178-67-70) serves mainland Mexican destinations as far as Guadalajara ($110, 36 hours) and Mexico City ($156, 44 hours). **ABC** (☎ 178-66-80) is the main peninsular carrier, and offers buses to the following destinations.

Destination	Price	Duration
Guerrero Negro	$49	9hr
La Paz	$105	20hr
Mexicali	1st/2nd class $25/18	4hr
San Felipe	$22	4hr
Tecate	$7	2hr
Tijuana	1st/2nd class $10/8	1½hr

Estrella de Baja California (☎ 178-85-21; Av Riveroll 861) goes to Tijuana ($8, 1½ hours) hourly from 5am to 9am, and at 11am, 2pm, 4pm and 6pm. Make sure you specify whether you want to go to the Tijuana's main terminal or to La Línea (the border).

Getting Around

The main taxi stand is at the corner of Avs López Mateos and Miramar; taxis also congregate along Av Juárez. Most fares within the city cost from $4 to $8.

The asking price for a taxi trip to the airport is $15 for one to four passengers. Surfers can get a trip out to San Miguel and a pickup later in the day for $10 each way. Ensenada's main avenues are well served by buses and vans; most routes are designated by street name and charge $0.50.

AROUND ENSENADA

If you like getting wet (amid cheering crowds of onlookers), head to **La Bufadora**. This magnificent tidewater blowhole 40km south of Ensenada periodically sends a jet of water 30m into the sky. To get there, drive south on the Transpeninsular and enter the town of Maneadero then head west at the junction. From here the road meanders through farmlands and skirts rocky shorelines and craggy cliffs. Alternately, you can catch a taxi from the stand in Ensenada ($12 per person, minimum four people). After parking, you'll pass a gauntlet of souvenir stands and vendors before getting to the observation decks. Don't pick the middle (closest) one unless you don't mind getting drenched.

PARQUE NACIONAL CONSTITUCIÓN DE 1857

From Ojos Negros, east of Ensenada at Km 39 on Hwy 3, a 43km dirt road climbs to the Sierra de Juárez and Parque Nacional Constitución de 1857. Its highlight is the marshy, pined **Laguna Hanson** (also

BAJA CALIFORNIA

known as Laguna Juárez, 1200m). The lake abounds with migratory birds from August to November.

It's a great area for mountain biking or and camping, but livestock contaminate the water so bring your own. Pit toilets are available. Nearby granite outcrops offer stupendous views but tiring ascents through dense brush and massive rock falls – beware of both ticks and rattlesnakes. Technical climbers will find short but challenging routes.

The park is also accessible by a steeper road east of Km 55.2, 16km southeast of the Ojos Negros junction.

PARQUE NACIONAL SIERRA SAN PEDRO MÁRTIR

You'll need a car, preferably a 4WD, to head into the Sierra San Pedro Mártir, east of San Telmo de Abajo and west of San Felipe, Baja's most notable national park. Bighorn sheep, bobcats, coyotes and eagles are only a few of the animals and birds that can be viewed in the park, which covers 650 sq km. Its forests, granite peaks exceeding 3000m and canyons cutting into its eastern scarp make rewarding views for hikers and climbers. Below 1800m, beware of rattlesnakes.

The **Observatorio Astronómico Nacional** (☎ 646-174-45-80 ext 302; ☽ 11am-1pm Sat, by reservation) is Mexico's national observatory. It's 2km from the parking area at the end of the San Telmo de Abajo road. You're sure to enjoy the jaw-dropping view of the multi-colored desert mountains receding all the way to the Pacific to the west. To the east the Sea of Cortez and, on an especially clear day, the Mexican mainland.

To reach San Pedro Mártir from San Telmo de Abajo, watch for the sign just south of Km 140 on the Transpeninsular (Hwy 1), about 52km south of San Vicente. A graded dirt road climbs 80km to the east through an ever-changing desert landscape, affording satisfying vistas all along the way. Though passable even for passenger vehicles, this is a rough road and washes may be hazardous if filled with water, so take care.

MEXICALI

☎ 686 / pop 764,000

A unique border city, Mexicali is gritty and authentic, scary in places; one gets the feel-

ing that it's what Tijuana was 20 years ago before being turned into a party destination. Exercise particular caution, especially at the border areas after dark. Better yet, slip across the border to Calexico or just keep going south to San Felipe. The Zona Hotelera is on the east side, primarily along Calle Juárez from Plaza Azteca to Independencia and beyond.

Information

EMERGENCY
Asistencia Turística (☎ 078)
Cruz Roja (Red Cross; ☎ 066)

INTERNET ACCESS
DirectNet Internet Cafe (☎ 554-55-68; Calz Justo Sierra 820; per hr $2) Also has coffee and sweets.

MEDICAL SERVICES
On Av Reforma and Av Obregón, near the US border, are many health-care providers offering quality services at a fraction of the cost north of the border.
Hospital México-Americano (☎ 552-23-00; fax 552-29-42; Av Reforma 1000)

MONEY
Casas de cambio are abundant and keep long hours, while banks offer exchange services Monday to Friday mornings only. Most banks in Mexicali and Calexico have ATMs. Exercise caution if withdrawing money at night.
Banamex (cnr Altamirano & Av Tejada)
Bancomer (cnr Azueta & Av Madero)

POST
Main post office (Av Madero; ☽ 7am-6:30pm Mon-Fri, 8am-3pm Sat & Sun)

TOURIST INFORMATION
Mexican Tourism and Convention Bureau (☎ 557-25-61; cnr Calz López Mateos & Camelias; ☽ 8am-6pm Mon-Fri) Similar offerings are available at this office, opposite the Teatro del Estado 3km southeast of the center.
Secture tourist office (☎ 566-12-77; Calz Montejano 1, Zona Hotelera; ☽ 8am-8pm Mon-Fri, 9am-1pm Sat) Patient, bilingual staff and plenty of information about regional attractions and events.

Sights & Activities
Plaza Constitución is a good place to hear *banda* groups rehearse in the late afternoon (hence its nickname: Plaza del Mariachi).

Most of Mexicali's historic buildings are northeast of Calz López Mateos. **Catedral de la Virgen de Guadalupe** (cnr Av Reforma & Morelos) is the city's major religious landmark. Now the rectory of the **Universidad Autónoma de Baja California**, the former Palacio de Gobierno, built between 1919 and 1922, interrupts Av Obregón just east of Calle E.

Sleeping

If you don't fancy sleeping in a hotel that has iron bars on the reception windows and hourly rate customers, you're better off in the pricier Zona Hotelera.

Araiza (☎ 564-11-00; www.araizahotels.com; Calz Juárez 2220; d $130; P ⚡ 🖳 📶 🏊) This family-friendly deluxe hotel has well-appointed rooms, two excellent restaurants, a gym, tennis courts, a fountain and a convention center. There are lobby computers for guests who need them. Large discounts on weekends bring the price to more affordable levels.

Hotel del Norte (☎ 552-81-01; Av Madero 205; s/d $43/49; ⚡ 🖳) The most pleasant of the border options, the landmark Hotel del Norte has 52 carpeted rooms, some with color TV, and friendly, English-speaking staff.

Hotel Cosmos (☎ 568-11-55; Calz Justo Sierra 1493; s/d $50/60; P ⚡) Continental breakfast is included at this motel, with attractive wide banisters and ochre tile. Rooms have TV and telephones.

Eating

Mexicali's best strength is the variety of its restaurants. Almost any kind of food can be found here, and it's all good.

Los Arcos (☎ 556-09-03; Av Calafia 454; dinner mains $10-20) Mexicali's most popular seafood restaurant is near the Plaza de Toros and the Centro Cívico-Comercial. The *shrimp culichi* (shrimp in a creamy green chili sauce) is spectacular. Toasted tortillas and fresh salsa also hit the spot, and live music brightens the night every night except Tuesday and Sunday.

Petunia 2 (☎ 552-69-51; Av Madero 436; breakfast $4.50, lunch $5) Huge *jugo natural* (fresh squeezed juice) and delicious quesadillas are a great way to start the day at this cheap eat close to the border.

El Sarape (☎ 554-22-87; Bravo 140; dinner mains $5-10.50) Mariachi band at the ready, this traditional Mexican restaurant has a menu

that will delight carnivores and margaritas that, though small, pack a punch.

Entertainment

Night owls should head straight for the Zona Hotelera and its growing selection of late-night diversions. Be cautious about walking home alone even if you're only going a short distance – even the locals take taxis.

Kalia Discoteque (☎ 565-64-01; Calz Justo Sierra 190) Popular dance club with all-you-can-drink specials. Take a taxi home.

Menealo (☎ 557-03-95; Calz Justo Sierra; 🕙 9pm-4am Thu-Sat) Raucous nightclub with themes: Thursday is Salsa and Merengue night; lessons are offered from 8pm to 11pm.

Getting There & Away

AIR

Aeroméxico (☎ 557-25-51; Pasaje Alamos 1008D, Centro Cívico-Comercial) Flies to La Paz, Mexico City, Mazatlán and other mainland points.

Mexicana (☎ 553-59-20; Obregón 1170) Flies daily to Guadalajara, Mexico City and intermediate points.

BUS

Long-distance bus companies leave from the **Central de Autobuses** (☎ 557-24-15; Calz Independencia), near Calz López Mateos. Autotransportes del Pacífico, Norte de Sonora and Elite serve mainland Mexican destinations, while ABC serves the Baja peninsula. Destinations and sample fares include the following.

Destination	Price	Duration
Ensenada	$25	3½hr
Guadalajara	$110	32hr
Guerrero Negro	$85	12hr
La Paz	$114	24hr
Loreto	$106	18hr
Mazatlán	$68	24hr
Mexico City	$139	41h
San Felipe	$34	5hr
Tijuana	1st/2nd class $19/15	2½hr

In Calexico, **Greyhound** (☎ 760-357-18-95; 121 1st St) is directly across from the border. Daily there are five departures to Los Angeles (one-way/round-trip $32/60), four to San Diego ($24/40) and four to Tucson ($49/88).

CAR & MOTORCYCLE

The main Calexico–Mexicali border crossing is open 24 hours. Vehicle permits are

BAJA CALIFORNIA

BAJA CALIFORNIA

MEXICALI

available at the border, as are tourist cards for those traveling beyond Ensenada or San Felipe. US and Mexican authorities have opened a second border complex east of downtown to ease congestion. It's open 6am to 10pm.

Getting Around

Cabs to **Aeropuerto Internacional General Rodolfo Sánchez Taboada** (☎ 553-67-42), 18km east of town, cost $16 but may be shared.

Most city buses start from Av Reforma, just west of Calz López Mateos; check the placard for the destination. Local fares are about $1.

A taxi to the Centro Cívico-Comercial or Zona Hotelera from the border averages about $5; agree on the fare first.

SAN FELIPE

☎ 686 / pop 15,400

Between Mexicali and San Felipe you'll see some of the best scenery Baja has to offer: jagged Tolkienesque sierras, blindingly azure ocean and stark, barren deserts. This fishing community on the Sea of Cortez (Golfo de California), 200km south of Mexicali, has become a major snowbird spot in recent years. Beachcombers will love the tides here – they go way, way out, leaving miles of smooth sands to peck around on. If you're a motorhead, come here to watch (or join) the Baja 250, one of the biggest motorcycle races in Mexico.

Bancomer (160 Av Mar de Cortez; ☯ 8:30am-4pm Mon-Fri, 10am-2pm Sat) exchanges traveler's checks and has an ATM. Head to **B@nditos** (☎ 577-10-12; Av Mar de Cortez 301; per hr $2; ☯ 9am-9pm) for Internet access.

Motel El Pescador (☎ 577-03-77; Av Mar de Cortez 101; d $50; **P** **⊠**) has basic rooms that are clean and comfortable. Its beachside bar has large but watery margaritas. Prices are 30% higher in peak season. **Costa Azul Hotel** (☎ 577-15-48; cnr Av Mar de Cortez & Calle Ensenada; r $82; **P** **⊠** **⊠**) is a midrange family option – up to two children can stay for free. Has a swim-up bar and a cheery pastel blue and white theme.

Good seafood and drinks are served in a sublime location at **Mariscos Conchita's** (☎ 577-02-67; Malecon 202; entrées $2.50-10; ☯ 10am-8pm Tue-Sun). **El Nido Seafood and Steak** (☎ 577-10-28; Av Mar de Cortez 348; dinner mains $8-20; ☯ noon-9pm Thu-Tue) serves well-prepared seafood and

BAJA CALIFORNIA

carne asada (grilled beef) in a rustic stone building.

Doña Chuy (cnr Mananillo & Mar Negro; snacks $2) has great cheap eats, such as tortas and quesadillas, near the bus station.

By Hwy 5, San Felipe is 2½ hours from the Mexicali border crossing. At the **bus terminal** (☎ 577-15-16; Av Mar Caribe), **ABC** (www.abc.com.mx) operates to the following destinations.

Destination	Price	Duration
Ensenada	$22	4hr
Mexicali	$16	2½hr
Tijuana	$34	5½hr

AROUND SAN FELIPE

The 85km road from San Felipe to the scenic, quiet village of **Puertecitos** is passable but only if you go slow, and avoid transmission-destroying potholes. It's much faster to use the Transpeninsular.

SOUTHERN BAJA

Boojum trees and cardón cacti are the most noticeable features of one of the world's most unique deserts. Baja's colonial and historical heritage, date palms, coconuts and mangrove swamps are all items to look for.

Be sure to look at your watch as you head southward, too: south of the 28th parallel, the hour changes; mountain time (to the south) is an hour ahead of Pacific time (to the north). Here you also enter the 25,000-sq-km Reserva de la Biosfera El Vizcaíno, Latin America's largest single protected area. It sprawls from the Península Vizcaíno across to the Sea of Cortez and includes the major gray-whale calving areas of Laguna San Ignacio and Laguna Ojo de Liebre, and the Sierra de San Francisco with its stunning pre-Hispanic rock art.

Beyond Guerrero Negro the Desierto de Vizcaíno is flat and desolate, punctuated by the surprisingly Saharan oasis of San Ignacio. Paralleling the gulf, the Sierra de la Giganta divides the region into an eastern subtropical zone and a western zone of elevated plateaus and dry lowlands. Mulegé is considered by many to be the most beautiful town in Baja. Santa Rosalía and Loreto each have similar, though slightly different charms.

The southernmost part of the peninsula contains La Paz, La Ventana, Cabo Pulmo, Todos Santos, and the popular resorts of Los Cabos, the towns of San José del Cabo and Cabo San Lucas. After the quiet isolation of the north, Los Cabos and the Los Cabos Corridor (the strip of giant resorts

CALIFORNIA GRAY WHALES

The migration of gray whales from Siberian and Alaskan waters to the lagoons of Baja is one amazing animal event. The whales will have swum 6250km to 9700km before reaching the sanctuary of Baja's warm and protected shallow waters. There, in calving grounds such as Laguna Ojo de Liebre (Scammon's Lagoon; opposite), southwest of Guerrero Negro, and Laguna San Ignacio, southwest of San Ignacio, 700kg calves will draw their first breath and begin learning the lessons of the sea from their ever-watchful mothers.

Peak months to see mothers and calves in the lagoons are February to early April, but the official whale-watching season begins December 15 and lasts until April 15. During the later days of their stay in Baja, the calves will have grown strong enough to slip the parental guidance of their leviathan moms. This can result in a curious calf swimming directly up to a rolling *panga* (fiberglass skiff for whale-watching) to have its snout scratched and petted – an awesome close encounter. After two to three months in these sheltered waters and nearly doubling in their birth weight, the calves and mothers head back to the open sea to begin the three-month glide home to their rich feeding grounds in the frozen north. The following year, they will return.

If you've got *ballena* (whale) fever, one of these destinations will provide a cure:

■ Laguna Ojo de Liebre (Scammon's Lagoon) (opposite)

■ Laguna San Ignacio (p287)

■ Puerto López Mateos (p294)

■ Puerto San Carlos (p294)

between the two towns) will either be a jarring shock or a welcome relief.

GUERRERO NEGRO
☎ 615 / pop 11,500

Come here for whale-watching – there's nothing else here unless you want to watch salt dry (literally – they have tours!). The nearby Laguna Ojo de Liebre (known in English as Scammon's Lagoon), which annually becomes the mating and breeding ground of California gray whales, is the prime attraction. Each year between mid-December and March, the whales migrate 9700km from the Bering Sea to the lagoon, where their numbers sometimes exceed 1500.

One of the more curious whale-watching regulations stipulates that one may not take home any *mascotas* (pets). One can only assume they mean whales…and did they really have to make a law about it?

Orientation & Information
The town comprises two sectors: a strip along Blvd Zapata, west of the Transpeninsular, and an orderly company town further west, run by Exportadora de Sal (ESSA). Nearly all accommodations, restaurants and other services are along Blvd Zapata; places in Guerrero Negro do not have street numbers.

There's a Banamex with an ATM at the far end of the commercial district on Blvd Zapata, just at the start of the company town. Get money here if you'll need it in San Ignacio, as that town has no bank.

C@fe Internet (☎ 157-25-34; Victoria Sanchez 10; per hr $2; ☼ 9am-9pm), off Zapata, is just a few streets down from the bus station.

Guerrero Negro's only medical facility is the **Clínica Hospital IMSS** (☎ 157-04-33; Blvd Zapata), located where the road curves southwest.

Whale-Watching
Agencies arrange whale-watching trips on Laguna Ojo de Liebre's shallow waters, where visitors are guaranteed to view whales in their natural habitat. **Malarrimo Eco Tours** (☎ 157-01-00; www.malarrimo.com; Blvd Zapata), at the beginning of the strip, offers four-hour tours (adult/child $45/35). A bit further south *pangueros* (boatmen) from Ejido Benito Juárez take visitors for whale-

watching excursions (adult/child $30/25). If the whales aren't around, they can organize trips for bird watching, cave paintings or the salt factory (one to two hours; $15 per person). Head to the Old Pier if you're a bird watcher, as there are 11km of prime territory for spotting ducks, coots, eagles and other birds.

Sleeping
The whale-watching season can strain local accommodations; reservations are advisable from January through March.

Motel Las Ballenas (☎ 157-01-16; jcachur@hotmail.com; Victoria Sánchez 10; s/d $21/25; ℗) Fourteen clean and comfortable rooms with color TV. Not fancy, but a good budget option.

Cabañas Malarrimo (☎ 157-22-50; www.malarrimo.com; cnr Blvd Zapata & Guerrero; d $40-52; ℗) Hot, strong showers and a lot more ambience than the other options in town. Same ownership as the Malarrimo Trailer Park. Whale headboards and a general whale theme make it impossible to forget why you've come here.

Malarrimo Trailer Park (☎ 157-22-50; www.malarrimo.com; cnr Blvd Zapata & Guerrero; camp sites per person $5, RV sites 10-16; ℗) This park, at the eastern entrance to town, has 45 camp sites with full hookups, plenty of hot water and clean toilets.

Hotel El Morro (☎ 157-04-14; Blvd Zapata; s/d $28/33; ℗) Convenient to the bus station on the north side of Blvd Zapata, this hotel has 36 comfortable, basic rooms.

Eating
Cafeteria del Motel El Morro (☎ 157-04-14; Blvd Zapata; dinner mains $4-6) Adjacent to the Hotel El Morro, this place serves up inexpensive Mexican fare, including great breakfasts and a near perfect *chile relleno*.

Malarrimo (☎ 157-01-00; cnr Blvd Zapata & Guerrero; dinner mains $10-15) Specializing in seafood, both as *antojitos* and sophisticated international dishes, the Malarrimo serves good food and generous portions.

About 8km south of Guerrero Negro, a good graded road leads 25km west to the Campo de Ballenas (Whale-watching Camp) on the edge of the lagoon. Here a $5 parking fee includes the right to camp, and the *ejido* (communal landholding) runs a simple but good restaurant (open in the whale season only).

BAJA CALIFORNIA

Getting There & Away

Guerrero Negro's airport is 2km north of the state border, west of the Transpeninsular.

The Aeroméxico subsidiary **Aerolitoral** (☎ 157-17-45; Blvd Zapata), on the north side of Blvd Zapata, flies Tuesday, Thursday and Saturday to Hermosillo connecting to mainland Mexican cities.

Aerocedros (☎ 157-16-26; Blvd Zapata) flies to Isla Cedros and Ensenada Monday, Wednesday and Friday.

The **bus station** (☎ 157-06-11; Blvd Zapata) is served by **ABC** (www.abc.com.mx) and Autotransportes Águila, one of its subsidiaries. Destinations include the following.

Destination	Price	Duration
Ensenada	$49	9hr
La Paz	$64	11hr
Loreto	$35	6hr
Mulegé	$26	4hr
Tijuana	$62	11hr

SAN IGNACIO

☎ 615 / pop 2000

Shockingly lush after the landscape of the Desierto de Vizcaíno, the village of San Ignacio seems Saharan with its date palms, coconuts and lake. Come here for lazy mornings, for whale-watching day trips and for excursions to the spectacular pre-Hispanic, rock-art sites in the Sierra de San Francisco (opposite). Its central location makes this a great travel hub.

Jesuits located the **Misión San Ignacio de Kadakaamán** here, but Dominicans supervised construction of the striking church (finished in 1786) that still dominates the cool, laurel-shaded plaza. With lava-block walls nearly 1.2m thick and surrounded by bougainvillea, this is one of Baja's most beautiful churches.

Most services are around the plaza, including public telephones, but there is no bank. International calls can be made from the Hotel La Pinta (right). Internet access ($3 per hour) is available at Rice & Beans RV Park (right).

Sleeping & Eating

For such a small town, San Ignacio has a rather surprising number of accommodation choices tucked away beneath its swaying palms.

Casa Lereé (☎ 154-01-58; www.prodigynet.net.mx /janebames/index.html; Madero s/n; r with/without bathroom $65/35) Part guesthouse, part museum, this beautiful old building sits around a verdant garden with all kinds of tropical fruit trees. Rooms are small but very tastefully decorated, and the owner is a wealth of information about all aspects of San Ignacio.

Rice & Beans RV Park (☎ 154-02-83; RV sites $20; P 🖳) Rice and beans – the most basic of meals – is an apt name for this spartan RV park just off the Transpeninsular west of town. The real reason to come here is the on-site restaurant with its cantina ambience and well-prepared seafood dishes for $6 to $13. Also offers whale-watching trips for 3 people ($150).

Ignacio Springs Bed & Breakfast (☎ 154-03-33; www.ignaciosprings.com; d yurts $53-81; P ✂ 🐾 🖳) With air-con and palm-shaded views of the river, and 500m from the highway on the road into town, these yurts (yes, yurts!) provide welcome escape from the heat. With kayaks and good river swimming, this kid-friendly place can also arrange trail riding and generous breakfasts and dinners. Only one of the yurts has a private bathroom; the others are served by a clean, pleasant bathhouse. Backpackers can camp in a tent for $20. Breakfast is served all day; dinners are by reservation (and cost extra).

Hotel La Pinta (☎ 154-03-00; r Apr-Nov $69, Dec-Mar $77; P 🐾 🖳) This service-oriented hotel one mile south of Hwy 1 on the paved road to San Ignacio offers well-appointed rooms with large mirrors. The restaurant serves local beef, good *antojitos* and seafood ($8 to $10). A beautiful pool and hummingbirds buzzing in the courtyard make this a relaxing escape from the ordinary.

Ricardo's Hotel (☎ 154-02-83; s/d $40/60; P 🐾) In the same complex as Rice & Beans RV Park, this is a squeaky-clean hotel offering satellite TV and two queen-sized beds per room.

Tota's (☎ 154-02-30; Penã s/n; meals $3-18; 🕒 6:30am-10pm) An unassuming greasy spoon run by Tota herself. Try the lobster with *mojo de ajo* (garlic sauce), or any of the breakfasts. Everything is good.

Buy a bag of dates, available everywhere in season, for a buck or two if you want a quick snack or energy for the road. If dates aren't your thing, try the hotel eateries.

Getting There & Away

Buses pick up passengers at the bus station near the San Lino junction outside of town, arriving about every two hours from 5am to 11pm.

AROUND SAN IGNACIO

Sierra de San Francisco

The petroglyphs here are impressive: ochre, red, black and white paintings depict what may be religious rites, hunting rituals or warfare. The fact that some of the sites depict fish and whales indicates that the peoples had contact with oceans despite living far from them. In recognition of its cultural importance, the Sierra de San Francisco has been declared a Unesco World Heritage Site. It is also part of the Reserva de la Biosfera El Vizcaíno.

Cueva del Ratón, named for an image of what inhabitants once thought was a rat (or mouse) but is more likely a deer, is the most easily accessible petroglyph. Excursions to Cueva del Ratón require hiring a guide ($5 to $9 for four people, plus a $3 ticket fee and $3 per camera). Guides can be hired through the **Instituto Nacional de Antropología e Historia** (INAH; ☎ 154-02-22; ☜ 8am-3pm Mon-Sat) Adjacent to the Misión San Ignacio on the plaza, be sure to phone ahead several days in advance – otherwise you may have to wait 24 hours for a guide to become available.

The dramatic Cañón San Pablo has sites that are better preserved. At **Cueva Pintada**, Cochimí painters and their predecessors decorated 150m of high rock overhangs with vivid red-and-black representations of human figures, bighorn sheep, pumas and deer, as well as with more abstract designs. **Cueva de las Flechas**, across Cañón San Pablo, has similar paintings, but curiously, some of the figures have arrows through them. One interpretation is that these paintings depict a period of warfare. Similar opinions suggest that they record a raid or an instance of trespass on tribal territory. The images may constitute a warning against trespass.

The beautiful mule-back descent of **Cañón San Pablo** requires at least two days, preferably three. Excursions to Cañón San Pablo involve hiring a guide with a mule through INAH for $15 per day, plus a mule for each individual in the party for $12 per day, and an additional pack animal for each person to carry supplies. Interestingly, visitors should also provide food for the guide. The costs can add up fast, so be sure to get an itemized schedule of fees before departing. If you wish to leave the logistics to a tour operator, Kuyimá (see below) will arrange the three-day trip for $270 to $440 per person per day, depending on the size of the group. Backpacking is permitted, but you still must hire a guide and mule.

Laguna San Ignacio

Along with Laguna Ojo de Liebre and Bahía Magdalena, Laguna San Ignacio is one of the Pacific coast's major winter whale-watching sites, with three-hour excursions costing around $40 per person. **Kuyimá** (☎ 154-00-70; www.kuyima.com; Morelos 23), a cooperative based at the east end of the plaza in San Ignacio, can arrange transport and accommodations. The 65km drive to the camping ground (where cabins are also available) takes about two hours over rough roads.

SANTA ROSALÍA

☎ 615 / pop 14,000

Its mining history makes Santa Rosalía different from other mid-Baja towns. Brightly painted clapboard-sided houses, the prefab church, a port and *malecón* (waterfront boulevard), black sand beaches, lazy pelicans and great views from the surrounding hills are all attractions. For southbound travelers, Santa Rosalía offers the first glimpse of the Sea of Cortez after a long, dry crossing of the Desierto de Vizcaíno.

Orientation & Information

Nestled in the narrow canyon of its namesake *arroyo* (stream), west of the Transpeninsular, central Santa Rosalía is a cluster of densely packed houses, restaurants, inns and stores. Santa Rosalía's narrow *avenidas* run east–west, while its short *calles* run north–south; one-way traffic is the rule. Plaza Benito Juárez, four blocks west of the highway, is the town center.

Travelers bound for Mulegé, which has no banks or ATMs, should be sure to change US cash or traveler's checks here, where Banamex also has an ATM. The post office is on Avenida Constitución at Calle 2. Hotel del Real, on the exit road from town, has long-distance *cabinas* (call centers). Check your email at **Cafe Internet PC Vision** (☎ 152-28-75; cnr 6th & Obregón; per hr $2.50; ✆ 10am-10pm).

Sights

Built in 1885 by the French to house the offices of the Boleo Company, the **Museo Histórico Minero de Santa Rosalía** (admission $1.25; ✆ 8am-3pm Mon-Fri, 9am-1pm Sat) watches over the town and the rusting copper works from its perch on the hill near the Hotel Francés.

Designed and erected for Paris' 1889 World's Fair, disassembled and stored in Brussels, intended for West Africa, Gustave Eiffel's (Yes, of Eiffel Tower fame) prefabricated **Iglesia Santa Bárbara** was shipped here when a Boleo Company director signed for its delivery to the town in 1895. Many travelers agree that the church is interesting more as an example of early prefabricated architecture than for its beauty.

Sleeping

Of all the towns in central Baja, Santa Rosalía has perhaps the best variety of well-priced accommodation choices, from the historic to the picturesque.

BUDGET

Hotel San Victor (☎ 152-01-16; cnr Progresso 36 & Calle 9A; r $15) Rooms are dark and simple, but the quiet, shaded courtyard and off-street parking are nice.

Hotel del Real (☎ 152-00-68; Av Montoya 7; r $25-35; ✖) Has a recently added new wing of tidy new rooms with two beds.

MIDRANGE & TOP END

Hotel Las Casitas (☎ 152-30-23; www.santarosalia casitas.com; Transpeninsular, Km 195; d $45; P ✖) This hotel, 3km south of town, has only five rooms, but each is tastefully appointed and affords private balconies and sublime views of the sea from the queen-sized beds. The hot tub makes for a relaxing evening after a hard day.

Eating

Playas Negras (☎ 152-06-85; breakfast $4, dinner mains $6-14) South of downtown and with a gorgeous view, this waterfront restaurant serves sumptuous seafood as well as steak, chicken and pizza.

> **THE AUTHOR'S CHOICE**
>
> **Hotel Francés** (☎ 152-20-52; Cousteau 15; r $55; ✖ ✆) Overlooking the Sea of Cortez and curious rusting hulks of mine machinery, the Hotel Francés is charming and historic. Built in 1886 and originally the dormitory for 'working girls' of a brothel near the mine, the hotel features beautiful rooms with high ceilings, cloth-covered walls and charming stained-wood details. On site is a restaurant open Monday to Saturday, for breakfast.

Miramar (☎ 152-09-32; Av Montoya 6; breakfasts $5, lunches $5-10) The expansive veranda lets you eat basic Mexican fare and watch the world go by, while the world's noisiest parrot squawks amicably but vociferously off to your left.

Panadería El Boleo (☎ 152-03-10; Obregón 30) Since 1901, this has been an obligatory stop for the rare find of good French bread in Baja. Also on board is a mouth-watering display of Mexican sweetbreads. A loaf of French bread costs about $0.25. Find it between Calles 3 and 4.

Restaurant Don Pedro (☎ 152-01-55; Calle 5 No 3; antojitos $3-4.50) This restaurant, just north of Obregón, serves reasonably priced tacos, *antojitos* and a delicious *caldo de res* (beef stew).

For cheap eats or something different, check out the small **fruit market** (✆ 6am-6pm) on Montoya between Hotel del Real and the highway, or hit one of the many taco stands of high quality along Av Obregón. Most charge $0.80 for a fish taco.

Getting There & Around

AIR

Aéreo Servicio Guerrero (☎ 615-152-31-81) has flights daily to Guaymas ($81) on the Mexican mainland. The ticket office, on the highway 300m south of the ferry terminal on the opposite side of the street, offers free transport to the airport.

BOAT

The passenger/auto ferry *Santa Rosalía*, operated by Operadora Rotuaria del Noroeste, sails to Guaymas at 8pm Tuesday, Friday and Sunday, arriving at 7am the next morning; the return ferry from Guaymas sails at 8pm Monday, Thursday and Saturday, arriving at 6am. Strong winter winds may cause delays.

The ticket office is at the **ferry terminal** (in Santa Rosalía ☎ 152-12-46; www.ferrysantarosalia .com; ⏰ 8am-7pm Mon-Sat), on the highway. Passenger fares are $55 in general seating, $40 for cabins. Advance reservations are recommended. Vehicle rates vary with vehicle length. See the accompanying chart for vehicle fares.

Vehicle	Length	Rate
car or pickup	up to 5m	$250, additional $99 per extra meter
car with trailer	up to 15m	$255
motorcycle		$135
motor home		$850

Before shipping any vehicle to the mainland, officials require a vehicle permit. These can be obtained in Santa Rosalía at Banjército, or in Tijuana, Ensenada, Mexicali or La Paz.

BUS

At least six buses daily in each direction stop at the **bus terminal** (☎ 152-14-08), which is in the same building as the ferry terminal on the highway just south of the entrance to town. Destinations include the following:

Destination	Price	Duration
Ensenada	$62	12hr
Guerrero Negro	$18	3hr
La Paz	$43	8hr
Loreto	$18	3hr
Mulegé	$8	1hr
San Ignacio	$7	1hr
San José del Cabo	$56	12hr
Tijuana	$74	14hr

MULEGÉ

☎ 615 / pop 3900

Some like to say that Mulegé is the prettiest town in all of Baja. It's surely *one* of the prettiest, with its far off mountains, an ancient mission presiding over the date palm–lined Arroyo de Santa Rosalía (Río Mulegé) and its access to kayaking and snorkeling. The town boasts undeveloped charm that is slipping away from the cities to the south. Divers flock to Mulegé for the

dozens of outstanding dive sites just beyond the mangrove-walled river delta.

Most services are on or near Jardín Corona, the town plaza. Mulegé has no bank, but merchants change cash dollars or accept them for payment. To get online try **Prodigy Infinito** (☎ 153-03-77; per hr $2; ⏰ 9am-10pm Mon-Sat), just off the plaza. Hotel Mulegé (below) is another option.

Sights

Come to the hilltop **Misión Santa Rosalía de Mulegé** (founded in 1705, completed in 1766 and abandoned in 1828), for great photos of the mission and river valley.

The former territorial prison is now the **Museo Mulegé** (Barrio Canenea; admission free; ⏰ 8:30am-3pm Mon-Fri). Its eclectic holdings include objects from the Mission de Santa Rosalía and prehistoric artifacts.

Diving

Mulegé's best diving spots can be found around the Santa Inés Islands (north of town) and just north of Punta Concepción (south of town). **Cortez Explorers** (☎ 153-05-00; www.cortez-explorer.com; Moctezuma 75A; ⏰ 10am-1pm, 3-6pm Mon-Sat) offers diving instruction and excursions, and snorkeling equipment and bicycle rental. Book trips one day in advance. Diving excursions cost $60 to $80 per person, snorkeling $35. There's a $120/80 minimum for the scuba/snorkeling charters.

Sleeping

Mulegé's lodging options are limited in number but of great variety.

Hotel Las Casitas (☎ 153-00-19; lascasitas 1962@hotmail.com; Madero 50; s/d $31/37; ☒) Beloved Mexican poet Alán Gorosave once inhabited this well-run hotel near Martínez, perhaps inspired by its beautiful courtyard shaded by a well-tended garden of tropical plants. Breakfasts are wonderful, and Drew Barrymore is rumored to have stayed here.

Hotel Hacienda (☎ 153-00-21; hotelhacienda _mulege@hotmail.com; Madero 3; s/d $25/30; ☒ ☒) The oldest hotel in town, the atmospheric Hacienda offers rooms with twin beds and a fridge, and there's a small pool. It even has its own old well that, though unused, still contains water.

Hotel Mulegé (☎ 153-04-16; Moctezuma s/n; s/d $32/38; ℗ ☒ ☒) Mulegé's only business-style hotel has clean doubles with carpeted floors, bottled water and cable TV. Internet access ($2 per hour) in the lobby is an additional plus.

Casa de Huéspedes Manuelita (☎ 153-01-75; Moctezuma; r with/without air-con $24/15) Rooms are tucked behind a beautiful grape arbor and, while basic, they are clean and have good hot showers.

Hotel Cuesta Real (☎ 153-03-21; Transpeninsular, Km 132; s/d $39/49, RV hookups $18; ✗ ☐ ☎) South of town, Hotel Cuesta Real offers large, spotless rooms and easy access to Río Mulegé as it empties into the sea (very convenient for kayakers). The grounds also boast a pleasant restaurant, and bikes or mopeds to get around. Take in scenic mangrove swamps and pelicans on the way into town. Internet costs $2.50 per hour.

Eating & Drinking

They roll up the sidewalks early in Mulegé, so dine expediently and get some sleep! Alternatively, you can always hit a bar. Or, you can hit the other bar.

Los Equipales (☎ 153-03-30; Moctezuma; mains $5-15) Just west of Zaragoza, this restaurant and bar has outstanding, well-priced meals and a breezy balcony seating that's perfect for an afternoon margarita or an evening chat with friends. Shrimp are snapped up as soon as they are served.

Taqueria Doney (☎ 153-00-95; mulege doney@hotmail.com; Moctezuma s/n; tacos & snacks $1-6) There's counter or table seating here and good, simple enchiladas, burritos and tacos.

Restaurante Bar Candil (Zaragoza s/n; mains $4-8; ☺ 7am-10pm) Nice brick building with open courtyard in the back and arched windows onto Zaragoza for those who want to watch the world (or at least Mulegés' portion of it!) pass by. *Chile rellenos* are delicious, less spicy than some, perfect for those wanting to ease their way into Mexican cuisine.

El Mezquite (Zaragoza; admission free; ☺ until 3am) On the plaza, this place has sweaty mariachis one night and a DJ playing the latest regional grooves the next.

Getting There & Away

Mulegé has no bus terminal. Buses going north and south stop at the Y-junction (La Y Griega) on the Transpeninsular at the western edge of town. Northbound buses

to Santa Rosalía ($8, one hour) stop about every two hours. Southbound buses pass daily to destinations including Loreto ($10, 2½ hours) and La Paz ($36, seven hours).

AROUND MULEGÉ
Cañón La Trinidad

For a day-trip to the beautiful Trinity Canyon to see the pre-Hispanic cave paintings, 29km southwest of town via a challenging dirt road, your best bet is with Mulegé native Salvador Castro of **Mulegé Tours** (☎ 153-02-32; day excursions per person $40). To access the caves, light swimming is required. Rendered in shades of ochre and rust, the paintings feature shamans, manta rays, whales and the famous Trinity Deer, which leaps gracefully from the walls of the cave as arrows pass harmlessly over its head.

Beaches

Mulegé is a gateway to some of Baja's most pristine *playas* (beaches). As you travel south from town there is a quick succession of turnoffs to *playas* (with and without facilities), where you can string up a hammock and watch the pelicans dive-bomb the fish. The following spots are the most

---

ON A MISSION FROM GOD

Baja's missions, built initially to bring salvation to the native people, instead brought death: thriving populations of indigenous people, who had subsisted happily in this wild, harsh climate for thousands of years, were decimated in mere decades by diseases introduced by missionaries. Most missions were subsequently abandoned or destroyed.

A few, such as the ones in San Ignacio (p286), Mulegé (p288) and Loreto (p292), have remained intact. Loreto's **Misión Nuestra Señora de Loreto** is the oldest, an impressive monument still in use today. Others to visit include the remote and beautifully preserved **Misión San Francisco Javier** (p293) and **Misión Santa Rosalía de Mulegé** (p289), accessible by car, and offering a beautiful valley view from a trail in back.

Resources for further reading include *Las Misiones Antiguas*, by Edward W Vernon, and www.vivabaja.com/bajamissions; both feature beautiful photos of these interesting ruins.

easily accessible, but are by no means an exhaustive list.

Playa Buenaventura (Km 94-95) Restaurant and hotel, with beach camping and *cabañas*.

Playa Concepción (Km 111-12) The home of EcoMundo kayaking and natural history center.

Playa Coyote (Km 107-8) A busy RV park makes this place occasionally overcrowded.

Playa El Burro (Km 108-9) This popular beach has large *palapas* (thatched-roof shelters on the beach) for $7, and Bertha's Restaurant and Bar (☎ 615-155-40-55).

LORETO

☎ 613 / pop 11,800

With a history that goes back nearly 12,000 years, Loreto is considered by anthropologists to be the oldest human settlement on the Baja Peninsula. In 1697 Jesuit Juan María Salvatierra established the peninsula's first permanent mission at this modest port some 135km south of Mulegé. These days, Loreto has settled into its reputation as Baja's water-sports paradise. It's home to the Parque Marino Nacional Bahía de Loreto, with 2065 sq km of shoreline, ocean and offshore islands protected from pollution and uncontrolled fishing.

Orientation

Most hotels and services are near the landmark mission church on Salvatierra, while the attractive *malecón* is ideal for evening strolls. The Plaza Cívica is just north of Salvatierra, between Madero and Davis.

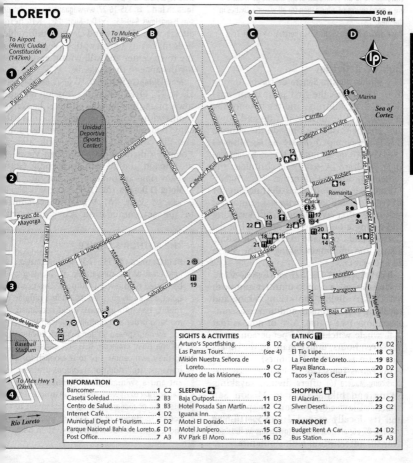

LORETO

0 ───── 500 m
0 ───── 0.3 miles

To Airport (4km); Ciudad Constitución (147km)

To Mulegé (134km)

Marina
Sea of Cortez

Unidad Deportiva (Sports Center)

Plaza Cívica

Baseball Stadium

To Mex Hwy 1 (2km)

Río Loreto

BAJA CALIFORNIA

INFORMATION
Bancomer......................................1	C2
Caseta Soledad...........................2	B3
Centro de Salud.........................3	B3
Internet Café..............................4	D2
Municipal Dept of Tourism.....5	D2
Parque Nacional Bahía de Loreto.6	D1
Post Office..................................7	A3

SIGHTS & ACTIVITIES
Arturo's Sportfishing...................8	D2
Las Parras Tours.....................(see 4)	
Misión Nuestra Señora de Loreto.................................9	C2
Museo de las Misiones..............10	C2

SLEEPING 🛏
Baja Outpost...............................11	D3
Hotel Posada San Martín.........12	C2
Iguana Inn..................................13	C2
Motel El Dorado........................14	D3
Motel Junípero..........................15	C3
RV Park El Moro.........................16	D2

EATING 🍴
Café Olé......................................17	D2
El Tío Lupe.................................18	C3
La Fuente de Loreto..................19	B3
Playa Blanca...............................20	D2
Tacos y Tacos Cesar...................21	C3

SHOPPING 🛍
El Alacrán...................................22	C2
Silver Desert..............................23	C2

TRANSPORT
Budget Rent A Car....................24	D2
Bus Station.................................25	A3

Information

Bancomer (cnr Salvatierra & Madero) Has an ATM and changes US cash and traveler's checks Monday to Friday.

Caseta Soledad (☎ 135-08-22; Salvatierra s/n; per hr $2; ☯ 8am-9pm Mon-Sat, 9am-1pm Sun) Cheap and open on Sunday, with fast computers and USB connections for cameras.

Centro de Salud (☎ 133-00-39; Salvatierra 68; ☯ 24hr)

Internet Café (☎ 135-08-02; Madero s/n; per hr $3; ☯ 9am-8pm Mon-Fri, 9am-5pm Sat) Next to Café Olé and convenient to the town center.

Municipal Department of Tourism (☎ 135-04-11; turismoloreto@hotmail.com; ☯ 8am-3pm Mon-Fri) On the west side of the Plaza Cívica, has a good selection of brochures and flyers.

Parque Nacional Bahía de Loreto (☎ 135-04-77; ☯ 9am-1pm Mon-Sat) This is where you pay the $6 entrance fee to the park. Staff at the marine park office are a good source of information for all water activities in the area.

Post office (☎ 135-06-47; Deportiva; ☯ 8am-3pm Mon-Fri)

Sights & Activities

The **Misión Nuestra Señora de Loreto**, dating from 1697, was the first permanent mission in the Californias and the base for the expansion of Jesuit missions up and down the Baja peninsula. Alongside the church, INAH's revamped **Museo de las Misiones** (☎ 135-04-41; cnr Salvatierra & Misioneros; admission $3; ☯ 9am-1pm & 1:45-6pm Tue-Fri) chronicles the settlement of Baja California.

Loreto is a world-class destination for all types of outdoor activities; a number of outfitters offer everything from kayaking and diving along the reefs around Isla del Carmen and Coronado to horseback riding, hiking and mountain biking in the Sierra de la Giganta.

Baja Outpost (☎ 135-12-29; www.bajaoutpost.com; Blvd López Mateos), a combo outfitter and posh B&B, offers diving, snorkeling, biking and kayaking expeditions in addition to accommodations (see right). Also of note is that their whale-watches ($225 per person) run a full seven hours, unlike many of the others (some are as short as 1½ hours).

Las Parras Tours (☎ 135-10-10; www.lasparras tours.com; Madero 16) offers diving, kayaking, biking and hiking trips to Misión San Francisco Javier (opposite). For sportfishing, try locally owned **Arturo Sportfishing** (☎ 135-07-66; arturosport@loretoweb.mx; Av Hidalgo), near the intersection with Romanita.

Sleeping

Most of Loreto's accommodation choices are on or near the picturesque *malecón*.

BUDGET

Hotel Posada San Martín (☎ 135-11-07; cnr Juárez & Davis; s/d $20/30, r without air-con $15; ☒) The best value in town and probably the cleanest $15 place in all of Baja, this hotel has large rooms and a great location near the plaza.

RV Park El Moro (☎ 135-05-42; Rosendo Robles 8; RV sites $12, s/d $30/40) Half a block from the beach, the friendly Park El Moro has 12 sites with full hookups, clean facilities and comfortable rooms that are color-coded in easy-to-remember red, green, blue and so on.

MIDRANGE & TOP END

Iguana Inn (☎ 135-16-27; www.iguanainn.com; Juarez s/n; bungalows $40-45; ☯ Oct-Aug; ☒) Kitchenettes, a video library and clean, comfortable beds make this a great option. Very close to the town center and still within easy walking distance of the *malecón*.

Motel Junípero Sierra (☎ 135-01-22; Av Hidalgo; s/d $30/40; ☒) Overlooking the mission and the town plaza, this family-run hotel has large rooms with refrigerators and a spacious balcony. Bougainvillea spills over a white-paint-and-tile courtyard with beautiful arches. Rooms in the back have excellent views of the mission, and the staff are friendly. Golf-ball key rings are out of place, but fun.

Motel El Dorado (☎ 135-15-00; cnr Av Hidalgo & El Pipila; s/d $35/50; ☒) A relative newcomer to the accommodation scene in town,

---

THE AUTHOR'S CHOICE

Baja Outpost (☎ 135-11-34; Blvd López Mateos; r incl breakfast $85, palapas $96; ☐ ☒) Don't be misled by the word 'outpost'; this posh, quiet, tastefully finished B&B offers regular rooms, beautiful *palapas*, great breakfasts made to order and multilingual staff (Leon, the owner, speaks six languages). Located off the busy *malecón*, it is still convenient to the town center – or to the beach for a romantic stroll. Additional *palapas*, a restaurant and a swimming pool (with swim-up bar and Jacuzzi) were under construction at the time of research. Lastly, a testament to Leon's sainthood or his faith in guestkind, there is a well-stocked, honor-system bar.

this pleasant motel offers 10 spacious, basic rooms with satellite TV and laundry service. Soccer fans will feel very much at home. Fishing trips can be directly chartered at the front desk.

Eating & Drinking

Loreto has a good selection of restaurants preparing the regional standards: excellent seafood with plenty of lime and cilantro, potent margaritas and fruity *aguas frescas* (ice drinks). Dig in! Most are right in the center, near the mission.

Café Olé (☎ 135-04-96; Madero 14; dinner mains $4-10) The inexpensive Café Olé is the place to stop for breakfast and good, basic Mexican lunches and dinners. Leave a business card in the wicker wall to the right of the counter, or peruse the many odd cards left by others.

El Tío Lupe (☎ 135-18-82; cnr Hidalgo & Colegio s/n; dinner mains $7-12, lobster dishes $23) Dine beneath a surfboard monolith in a relaxed atmosphere with good food. Cream of scallop salsa is unusual and delicious, as is the Mexican fondue. Service is slow, but potent margaritas make up for it. Will also cook your catch of the day for you.

La Fuente de Loreto (Salvatierra 88; mains $4-12; ☼ 7am-9pm Mon-Fri, 7am-5pm Sat) Great *antojitos* and Mexican dishes as well as a variety of western options. Chicken *chilaquiles* (corn tortillas and spicy chili paste) are fantastic.

Tacos y Tacos César (☎ 135-17-45; cnr Hidalgo & Colegio; mains $1-6) Look for the charcoal grill (often in use). Great tacos and other Mexican specialties in a festive outdoor patio. Passing mariachis can be flagged down if you're in the mood for some *música romántica*.

Shopping

The pedestrian mall between Madero and Independencia has many shops selling jewelry and souvenirs.

El Alacrán (☎ /fax 135-00-29; Salvatierra 47; ☼ 9:30am-1pm & 2:30-7pm Mon-Sat) This is the place to try for varied handicrafts.

Silver Desert (☎ 135-06-84; Salvatierra 36; ☼ 9am-2pm & 3-8:30pm Mon-Sat, 9am-2pm Sun) Has a large selection of sterling silver jewelry of good quality from the Taxco mines.

Getting There & Away

Aeropuerto Internacional de Loreto (☎ 135-04-54) is served by only one international airline

and several domestic airlines. **Aero California** (☎ 135-05-00) has daily nonstop flights to La Paz and Los Angeles. **Aerolitoral** (☎ 135-09-99), also with an office at the airport, flies daily to and from La Paz.

Loreto's **bus station** (☎ 135-07-67; ☼ 24hr) is near the convergence of Salvatierra, Paseo de Ugarte and Paseo Tamaral. There are services to the following destinations.

Destination	Price	Duration
Guerrero Negro	$35	6hr
La Paz	$29	5hr
Mexicali	$109	20hr
Santa Rosalía	$18	3hr
Tijuana	$97	17hr

The car-rental agency **Budget** (☎ 135-10-90; Av Hidalgo) has economy models starting at about $55 per day, including appropriate insurance.

Getting Around

Airport taxis, 4km south of Loreto off the highway, cost $10.

AROUND LORETO

About 2km south of Loreto, on the Transpeninsular, is the junction for the rugged 35km mountain road to remote **Misión San Francisco Javier de Viggé-Biaundó**. A spectacular, challenging drive, it is usually passable even for passenger cars. After enjoying the beautifully preserved mission, take a walk on the path behind to find a magnificently gnarled 300-year-old olive tree, planted at the mission's founding in 1699. On December 3, pilgrims celebrate the saint's fiesta here.

Restaurant Palapa San Javier (meals $2-5), on the main street just before the mission, serves simple fare, cold sodas and beer, and offers simple accommodations.

CIUDAD CONSTITUCIÓN

☎ 613 / pop 39,900

Like Guerrero Negro, Ciudad Constitución is a hub for travelers who wish to cavort with whales, which they can do in Puerto San Carlos (p294) or Puerto López Mateos (p294). Similarly, there's not much to do after the whales leave. Most services are within a block or two of the north–south Transpeninsular, commonly known as Blvd Olachea.

Information

Ciudad Constitución has no *casas de cambio*, but three banks on Blvd Olachea change US dollars or traveler's checks, and have ATMs: **Banca Serfin** (cnr of Galeana), **Banamex** (southwestern cnr of Mina), and **Bancomer** (Pino Suárez), just west of Blvd Olachea.

The **post office** (☎ 132-05-84; Galeana; ☙ 8am-3pm Mon-Fri) is just west of Blvd Olachea. For phone service, try the *cabinas* on the east side of Blvd Olachea, between Matamoros and Mina.

Supercom (☎ 132-54-72; Olachea 156; per hr $2; ☙ 9am-1pm, 4-8pm, Mon-Sat) is a small computer-only café.

Taxis line up on Blvd Olachea adjacent to the Plaza Zaragoza, and across from the bus station.

Sleeping

Ciudad Constitución's lodging options are limited; none of them are fancy.

Posadas del Ryal (☎ 132-48-00; Victoria s/n; s/d $34/39; Ⓟ ☢) New, spotless, and peach pink all over, this hotel, just off Olachea, has dark rooms with cable TV.

Hotel Conquistador (☎ 132-15-55; Bravo 161; s/d $33/41) It's somewhat dark and formal, but the adjacent restaurant serves good, cheap meals. If you're a guest, they'll let you quickly check email on their desk computer.

Hotel Conchita (☎ 132-02-66; Olachea 180 at Hidalgo; s/d $22/28; ☢) Offers basic rooms with TV and a very uneven staircase. Watch your step.

Hotel Maribel (☎ 132-01-55; Guadalupe Victoria 156; s with/without phone $34/26, d $37/29; ☢) This place is more expensive, but the rooms are just as spartan. Small balconies brighten the rooms a bit.

Eating

Constitución's many taco stands on Blvd Olachea have the cheapest eats with tacos costing around $1.

Taquería Karen (cnr Blvd Olachea & Hidalgo) This is a particularly good taco stand.

El Nuevo Dragon (☎ 132-29-22; Blvd Olachea 1134; dishes $6-9) A popular greasy spoon with surprisingly good Chinese food.

El Taste (☎ 132-67-71; Blvd Olachea; dinner mains $8-20) A branch of the chain, this place serves thick-cut rib eye and a variety of seafood dishes, including a delicious *brocheta de ostíon* (oyster).

Getting There & Away

At the **bus terminal** (☎ 132-03-76; cnr Zapata & Juárez), destinations include the following.

Destination	Price	Duration	Frequency
La Paz	$15	2½hr	hourly
Mexicali	$102	19hr	2 daily
Puerto López Mateos	$5	45min	2 daily
Puerto San Carlos	$4	45min	2 daily
Tijuana	$79	19hr	2 daily

AROUND CIUDAD CONSTITUCIÓN
Puerto López Mateos
☎ 613 / pop 2400

Shielded from the open Pacific by the offshore barrier of Isla Magdalena, Puerto López Mateos is one of Baja's best whale-watching sites. During the season, the narrow waterway that passes by town becomes a veritable *ballena* cruising strip. Curva del Diablo (The Devil's Bend), 27km south of town, is reported to be the best viewing spot. Three-hour *panga* (skiff) excursions from Puerto López Mateos ($55 per hour for up to six people) are easy to arrange.

Free camping (bring water), with pit toilets only, is possible at tidy Playa Soledad, which is near Playa El Faro, 1.6km east of town (turn left at the water tower). The only other accommodations in Puerto López Mateos are at the small but tidy **Posada Ballena López** (s/d $14/18).

Besides a couple of so-so taco stands, López Mateos has only a smattering of decent restaurants. **Restaurant California** (☎ 131-52-08; meals $5-8) is a decent restaurant across from the church. At the entrance to town, La Ballena Gris (The Gray Whale) serves seafood (not whale).

Puerto López Mateos is 34km west of Ciudad Insurgentes by a paved road; watch for hazardous potholes. Autotransportes Águila has buses from Ciudad Constitución ($5) at noon and 6pm daily; return service to Constitución leaves at 6:30am and 2:30pm.

Puerto San Carlos
☎ 613 / pop 4400

On Bahía Magdalena, 56km west of Ciudad Constitución, Puerto San Carlos is a deepwater port and fishing town. The *ballenas* arrive in January to calve in the warm lagoon and the town turns its attention to both whales and travelers. From January through March, *pangueros* take up to six passengers for whale-watching excursions ($50 per hour).

With several hotels and restaurants to choose from, San Carlos is a good choice from which to base your whale-watching adventure. Accommodations can be tougher to find during the high season, but free camping is possible north of town on the public beach. There are no toilets at the beach. Another budget option is the **Motel Las Brisas** (☎ 136-01-52; Puerto Madero; s/d $14/16), which has rooms that are basic and dark but clean and inexpensive.

The **Hotel Brennan** (☎ 136-02-88; Puerto La Paz; s/d $35/45) strikes just the right balance with intimate rooms and plentiful patio space. With similar amenities, the **Hotel Alcatraz** (☎ 136-00-17; Puerto Acapulco; s/d $40/55) offers 25 comfortable rooms with satellite TV, parking and laundry service.

At the Hotel Alcatraz, **Restaurant Bar El Patio** (☎ 136-00-17; mains $5-15) is the town's best eatery, with – you guessed it – patio seating and seafood. Not to be outdone, **Mariscos Los Arcos** (Puerto La Paz; tacos $2, dinner mains $5-14) has tremendous shrimp tacos and seafood soup, and a full breakfast menu.

From a small house on Calle Puerto Morelos, Autotransportes Águilar runs buses at 7:30am and 1:45pm daily to Ciudad Constitución ($4) and La Paz ($15). This is the only public transport from Puerto San Carlos.

LA PAZ
☎ 612 / pop 197,000
Sit beneath a *palapa* on La Paz' white beaches and you'll swear you're in a Corona commercial. Few places are finer for watching a Baja sunset than on La Paz' splendid *malecón*. La Paz's port of Pichilingue receives ferries from the mainland ports of Topolobampo and Mazatlán, and the airport is served by several North American carriers.

Hernán Cortés established Baja's first European outpost near La Paz, but permanent settlement waited until 1811. La Paz's quirky history includes American occupation and even being temporarily declared its own republic. Its rich pearl industry disappeared during the revolution of (1910–20).

Orientation
As you approach La Paz from the southwest, the Transpeninsular becomes Abasolo as it runs parallel to the bay. Four blocks east of Calle 5 de Febrero, Abasolo becomes Paseo Obregón, leading along the palm-lined *malecón* in the direction of Península Pichilingue.

La Paz' grid makes basic orientation easy, but the center's crooked streets and alleys change names almost every block. The city's heart is Jardín Velasco (Plaza Constitución), three blocks southeast of the tourist pier.

Information
BOOKSTORES
Libros Libros Books Books (☎ 122-14-10; Constitución 195; ☯ 9am-8:45pm) Stocks books in English and Spanish.
Museo Regional de Antropología e Historia (p297) Museum store with good selection of Spanish-language books on Baja California and mainland Mexico.

EMERGENCY
Cruz Roja (Red Cross; ☎ 066)
Fire Department (☎ 066)
Police (☎ 066)
Tourist Police (☎ 122-59-39)

INTERNET ACCESS
Cafe Exquisito (☎ 128-59-91; Obregón; per hr $3) A coffee here includes 15 minutes free use of their two new computers.
Don Tomás (☎ 128-55-07; Paseo Obregón; per hr $2; ☯ 7am-11pm) Near Constitución, this place has Web access, local art, simple drinks, donuts and information.

INTERNET RESOURCES
Viva La Paz (www.vivalapaz.com) La Paz' official tourism site.

LAUNDRY
La Paz Lava (☎ 122-31-12; cnr Ocampo & Mutualismo) Self-service machines and delivery service to hotels or homes.

MEDICAL SERVICES
Hospital Salvatierra (☎ 122-14-96; Bravo; ☯ 24hr) English-speaking staff.

MONEY
Most banks (many with ATMs) and *casas de cambio* are on or around Calle 16 de Septiembre.

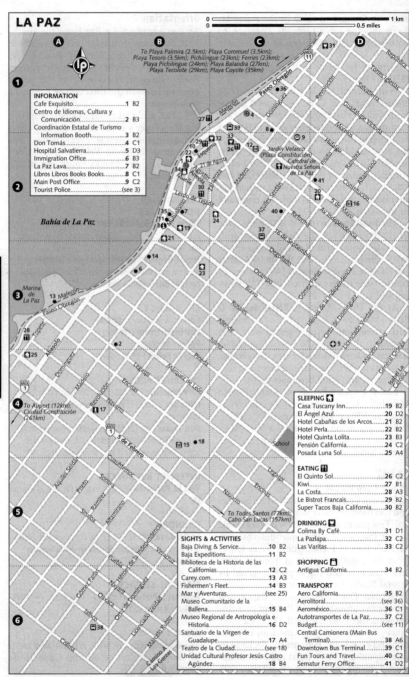

LA PAZ

0 — 1 km
0 — 0.5 miles

BAJA CALIFORNIA

To Playa Palmira (2.5km); Playa Coromuel (3.5km);
Playa Tesoro (3.5km); Pichilingue (23km); Ferries (23km);
Playa Pichilingue (24km); Playa Balandra (27km);
Playa Tecolote (29km); Playa Coyote (35km)

Bahía de La Paz

Marina
de
La Paz

To Airport (12km);
Ciudad Constitución
(261km)

To Todos Santos (77km);
Cabo San Lucas (157km)

INFORMATION
Cafe Exquisito...........................1 B2
Centro de Idiomas, Cultura y
  Comunicación.......................2 B3
Coordinación Estatal de Turismo
  Information Booth.................3 B2
Don Tomás................................4 C1
Hospital Salvatierra...................5 D3
Immigration Office....................6 B3
La Paz Lava...............................7 B2
Libros Libros Books Books........8 C1
Main Post Office.......................9 C2
Tourist Police......................(see 3)

SIGHTS & ACTIVITIES
Baja Diving & Service..............10 B2
Baja Expeditions.....................11 B2
Biblioteca de la Historia de las
  Californias...........................12 C2
Carey.com...............................13 A3
Fishermen's Fleet....................14 B3
Mar y Aventuras.................(see 25)
Museo Comunitario de la
  Ballena...............................15 B4
Museo Regional de Antropología e
  Historia...............................16 D2
Santuario de la Virgen de
  Guadalupe...........................17 A4
Teatro de la Ciudad...........(see 18)
Unidad Cultural Profesor Jesús Castro
  Agúndez...............................18 B4

SLEEPING
Casa Tuscany Inn.....................19 B2
El Ángel Azul...........................20 D2
Hotel Cabañas de los Arcos.....21 B2
Hotel Perla..............................22 B2
Hotel Quinta Lolita.................23 B3
Pensión California....................24 C2
Posada Luna Sol......................25 A4

EATING
El Quinto Sol...........................26 C2
Kiwi.......................................27 B1
La Costa..................................28 A3
Le Bistrot Francais...................29 B2
Super Tacos Baja California.......30 B2

DRINKING
Colima By Café........................31 D1
La Pazlapa...............................32 C2
Las Varitas..............................33 C2

SHOPPING
Antigua California....................34 B2

TRANSPORT
Aero California.........................35 B2
Aerolitoral.........................(see 36)
Aeroméxico............................36 C1
Autotransportes de La Paz.......37 C2
Budget...............................(see 11)
Central Camionera (Main Bus
  Terminal)............................38 A6
Downtown Bus Terminal..........39 C1
Fun Tours and Travel...............40 C2
Sematur Ferry Office................41 D2

POST

Main post office (cnr Constitución & Revolución; ⏱ 8am-3pm Mon-Fri, 9am-1pm Sat)

TOURIST INFORMATION

Coordinación Estatal de Turismo information booth (☎ 124-01-03; Paseo Obregón; ⏱ 8am-3pm Mon-Sat) Brochures and pamphlets are available in English. Some of the staff speak English too.

Sights

The **Museo Regional de Antropología e Historia** (☎ 122-01-62; cnr Calle 5 de Mayo & Altamirano; admission free; ⏱ 9am-6pm) is a large, well-organized museum chronicling the peninsula's history from prehistory to the revolution of 1910 and its aftermath.

Across from the Jardín Velasco, La Paz' former Casa de Gobierno is now the **Biblioteca de la Historia de las Californias** (cnr Madero & Av Independencia; ☎ 8am-3pm Mon-Fri), a history library.

A sprawling concrete edifice, the **Teatro de la Ciudad** is the most conspicuous element of the **Unidad Cultural Profesor Jesús Castro Agúndez** (☎ 125-02-07; ⏱ 8am-3pm Mon-Fri), a cultural center that takes up most of the area bounded by Altamirano, Navarro, Héroes de la Independencia and Legaspi. At the periphery of the grounds, at Navarro and Altamirano, is the small **Museo Comunitario de la Ballena** (Community Whale Museum; admission free; ⏱ 9am-1pm Tue-Sat). A few blocks west, the **Santuario de la Virgen de Guadalupe** (☎ 122-15-18; cnr Calle 5 de Febrero & Aquiles Serdán) is La Paz' biggest religious monument. Its altar, 12m tall, is impressive.

Activities

Festivals and other seasonal events often take place at the Plaza Constitución, between Revolución and Madero at Calle 5 de Mayo. You can rent water-sports equipment and arrange single or multiday excursions at family-run, helpful **Carey.com** (☎ 128-40-48; www.carey.com.mx; cnr Topete & Legaspi 3040), who even include a free snorkel, yours to keep. Kayakers should check out **Mar y Aventuras** (☎ 122-70-39; www.kayakbaja.com; cnr Calle 5 de Febrero & Topete), where you can book an expedition or outfit a self-guided trip. The one-day excursion to Isla Espíritu Santo ($75), where you can snorkel with sea lions and paddle the coast, is an experience you are unlikely to forget. Renting a *panga* for trips around

the point to look at whale sharks will cost about $60 for two hours. Bargain at the beach along the *malecón*.

For sportfishing, try the **Fishermen's Fleet** (☎ 122-13-13; david@lapaz.cromwell.com.mx; Paseo Obregón).

Courses

Centro de Idiomas, Cultura y Comunicación (☎ 125-75-54; www.cicclapaz.com; Madero 2460) offers intensive Spanish classes and will help coordinate homestay lodging.

Festivals & Events

La Paz' pre-Lent **Carnaval** is among the country's best. In early May, *paceños* (person from La Paz) celebrate the **Fundación de la Ciudad** (Hernán Cortés' 1535 landing).

Sleeping

Accommodations in La Paz run the gamut from budget digs to big swanky hotels. Midrange accommodations here are varied and of good quality.

BUDGET

Pensión California (☎ 122-28-96; fax 122-23-98; pensioncalifornia@prodigy.net.mx; Degollado 209; s/d $15/20) Colorfully done in primary blue and bright yellow, this friendly, quirky pension is popular and often full. Cement furniture and padlocks give it a storage-locker feel, but the youth hostel–like ambience is fun and the plant-filled courtyard and plastic furniture lend themselves to good conversations.

Hotel Quinta Lolita (☎ 125-30-31; Revolución s/n; s/d $25/30; 🅿) Simple, small, clean – a nice alternative if Pensión California is full. Say 'hi' to the parakeet as you walk by.

MIDRANGE

Hotel Cabañas de los Arcos (☎ 122-27-44; fax 125-43-13; cnr Rosales & Mutualismo; d/cabaña $84/106; 🅿 🅿 🖳) Rooms set around a lush garden have fireplaces, thatched roofs, tiled floors, TV, air-con and minibars. If you feel like splurging, this is not a bad way to go.

Casa Tuscany Inn (☎ 128-81-03; www.tuscanybaja.com; Bravo 110; r incl breakfast $60-90; 🅿 🅿 🖳) Tasteful mix of Guatemalan and Tuscan furnishings, with lots of lush greens and interesting ironwork in the courtyard. The terrace is a great place to 'bay watch' and sip a beverage of your choice. Nonsmokers

BAJA CALIFORNIA

will appreciate the 'only outdoors' smoking policy.

Posada Luna Sol (☎ 120-70-39; cnr Calle 5 de Febrero & Topete; r $60; **P** **X** **🖳**) Pleasant hotel run by the folks at Mar y Aventuras (p297), with well-decorated rooms and an excellent rooftop terrace with bay views.

TOP END

El Ángel Azul (☎ 125-51-30; cnr Av Independencia & Prieto; d incl breakfast from $95; **X**) Possibly the loveliest of La Paz' lodging options, El Ángel Azul offers elegantly appointed rooms and beautifully landscaped grounds in a historic building.

Hotel Perla (☎ 122-07-77; fax 125-53-63; www.hotel perlabaja.com; Paseo Obregón 1570; r $87) Supposedly the first hotel in La Paz, this yellow standby offers clean rooms and a popular restaurant and nightclub as well. Some rooms have nice balconies – ask.

Eating

La Paz' restaurant scene has become increasingly sophisticated over the past 10 years and now offers much more than the typical *antojitos* and seafood.

Le Bistrot Francais (☎ 125-60-80; bistrot@prodigy .net.mx; Esquerro 10; lunch mains $4-8, dinner mains $8-14; **🕓** 11am-11pm) Excellent crêpes, warm, sweet or savory, make for an unusual treat. The verdant, multilevel courtyard is perfect for a pre-dinner glass of red with friends.

Super Tacos Baja California (Hermanos Gonsales; Lerdo de Tejada; tacos $1-2) The delicious fish, shrimp, and manta ray tacos at this popular stand, between Constitución and Zaragoza, are served with freshly made salsas. Like potato chips, it's hard to eat just one. Also has a stand conveniently located outside the Pensión California.

El Quinto Sol (☎ 122-16-92; cnr Av Independencia & Domínguez; breakfasts $3-4; **V**) In addition to healthy breakfasts and meat-substitute dishes for lunch and dinner, this vegetarian restaurant also sells health foods, fresh breads, teas and tonics.

Kiwi (☎ 123-32-82; dinner mains $9-18) The only restaurant on the ocean side of the *malecón*, between Calle 5 de Mayo and Constitución, Kiwi offers great views you can enjoy while eating decent Mexican and American fare. Open until midnight, it's a nice place for a quiet drink after dinner or to listen to live music on weekends.

La Costa (☎ 122-88-08; cnr Topete & Navarro; dinner mains $7-10, lobster dishes $20) La Costa offers excellent seafood, and in Baja that's saying a lot. The menu is replete with delicious choices such as *chile rellenos*.

Drinking & Entertainment

The following watering holes are within stumbling distance of the *malecón*, where many travelers have been known to practice their drunken-sailor routine.

Las Varitas (☎ 125-20-25; Av Independencia 111, cover $4; **🕓** 9pm-3am Tue-Sun) Featuring live music that often plays to a packed house, this disco is a hit with the under-35 crowd.

Colima By Café (☎ 125-33-11; Malecón 755; **🕓** 6pm-3am) Live music every night, a cramped pool table and a tropical theme make this mellow place a hit.

La Pazlapa (☎ 122-92-90; cnr Paseo Obregón & Calle 16 de Septiembre; **🕓** 10pm-3am) See and be seen at this dimly lit, smoky, popular disco.

Shopping

Local stores that cater to tourists have plenty of junk and a smattering of good stuff. **Antigua California** (☎ 125-52-30; Paseo Obregón 220) features a wide selection of crafts from throughout the country.

Getting There & Away

AIR

The airport, **Manuel Marquez De Leon** (☎ 122-14-86; Transpeninsular Hwy Km 9) is about 9km southwest of the city. There's an **immigration office** (☎ 124-63-49; **🕓** 7am-11pm) at the airport.

Aeroméxico (☎ 124-63-66; Paseo Obregón) has flights every day but Sunday between La Paz and Los Angeles, and daily flights to Tijuana and mainland Mexican cities. Aerolitoral, at the same address and phone number, flies daily to Loreto and Tucson.

Aero California (☎ 125-10-23; Paseo Obregón 550) operates daily nonstop flights to Los Angeles and Tijuana and to mainland Mexican destinations, including Los Mochis (for the Copper Canyon Railway), Mazatlán and Mexico City. It also has branch at the airport.

BOAT

Ferries to Mazatlán and Topolobampo leave from the ferry terminal at Pichilingue, 23km north of La Paz. The Mazatlán ferry is operated by **Sematur** (☎ 125-23-46; cnr Prieto & Calle 5 de Mayo, La Paz). Since 2003, **Baja Ferries** (☎ 123-13-13; www.bajaferries.com) has been operating the La Paz–Topolobampo line; tickets and information can be obtained in La Paz at **Fun Tours and Travel** (☎ 124-23-46; cnr Reforma & Prieto). Tickets for both Sematur and Baja Ferries can also be obtained in Pichilingue.

The ferry to Mazatlán departs at 4pm Tuesday, Thursday and Saturday, arriving at 10am the following day; return ferries leave Mazatlán at 3pm Monday, Wednesday and Friday, to arrive in La Paz at 9am. Passenger fares are $75 in *salón* (numbered seats), or for an extra $40 four people can have a cabin with a shared bathroom, or $112 for a two-person cabin with private bathroom.

The Topolobampo ferry sails at 3pm Monday through Sunday, arriving at 9pm. The return ferry leaves at 11pm Monday through Sunday, arriving at 5am. Passenger fares are $65 in *salón*; *cabina* passengers pay the same rate with an additional $76 fee for a group of up to four. You are asked to arrive at the pier three full hours prior to departure.

Vehicle rates, which are paid in addition to passenger fares, vary with vehicle length.

Vehicle	Length	La Paz–Mazatlán (Sematur)
car	5m or less	$200, additional $65 for each extra meter
motor home		$800
motorcycle		$120

Vehicle	Length	La Paz–Topolobampo (Baja Ferries)
car	5m or less	$97, additional $52 for each extra meter
motor home		$450
motorcycle		$55

Before shipping any vehicle to the mainland, officials require a vehicle permit. You can obtain a permit at **Banjército** (☑ 9am-1:30pm Mon-Sat, 9am-noon Sun), at the ferry terminal.

BUS
ABC (☎ 122-78-98) and **Autotransportes Águila** (☎ 122-78-98) both leave from the **downtown** **bus terminal** (☎ 122-78-98; cnr Malecón & Av Independencia) along the *malecón*. Buses leave for the following destination.

Destination	Price	Duration
Cabo San Lucas	$13	3hr
Ciudad Constitución	$15	2hr
Ensenada	$105	18hr
Guerrero Negro	$64	11hr
Loreto	$29	5hr
Mulegé	$36	6hr
San Ignacio	$50	9hr
San José del Cabo	$16	3hr
Tijuana	$117	22hr
Todos Santos	$7	2hr

Autotransportes Águila also operates two buses which leave daily for Playa Tecolote ($2.50, 1½ hours) and six for Playa Pichilingue ($1.50, one hour).

There's an **immigration office** (☎ 122-04-29; Paseo Obregón; ☑ 8am-8pm Mon-Fri, 9am-3pm Sat) near the center.

Getting Around
The government-regulated minivan service **Transporte Terrestre** (☎ 125-11-56) charges $15 per person to/from the airport. Private taxis cost approximately $25, but they may be shared.

Car-rental rates start around $50 per day. **Budget** (☎ 125-47-47; cnr Paseo Obregón & Bravo) is one of several agencies. All have locations both at the airport and along the *malecón*.

AROUND LA PAZ
Beaches
On Península Pichilingue, the beaches nearest to La Paz are **Playa Palmira** (with the Hotel Palmira and a marina), **Playa Coromuel** and **Playa Caimancito** (both with restaurant-bars, toilets and *palapas*). **Playa Tesoro**, the next beach north, has a restaurant.

Camping is possible at **Playa Pichilingue**, 100m north of the ferry terminal, and it has a restaurant and bar, toilets and shade. The road is paved to **Playa Balandra** and **Playa Tecolote**. Balandra is problematic for camping because of insects in the mangroves, but it's one of the more beautiful beaches, with an enclosed cove. Lovely Playa Tecolote has plenty of private spots for car camping and two beachfront restaurants, and is often thought of as the 'best' beach. **Playa Coyote**, on the gulf, is more isolated. It's always a good idea to avoid bringing valuables, as thieves have been known to break into cars.

LA VENTANA
☎ 612 / pop 320

Only 45 minutes from La Paz, tiny La Ventana has spectacular snorkeling, diving and windsurfing. See whale sharks, sea lions, whales, sea turtles and a myriad of fish – without the crowds. Diving is best in the summer when the water visibility reaches 25m or 30m (80ft or 100ft). In winter, the same winds that made Los Barriles (below) a windsurfing mecca also blow here.

Enjoy unparalleled views of the Sea of Cortez from quiet, *palapa*-style *cabañas* at **Palapas Ventana** (☎ 114-01-98; www.palapasventana .com; cabañas $123-174; P X X Q). Hearty, home-style breakfasts hit the spot. Outfits for diving, snorkeling, windsurfing, kitesurfing, petroglyph hikes and just about anything else are available.

Rafa's Tacos (☎ 114-01-82; 9am-9:30pm, Nov-Mar) is a roadside taco stand that has plastic chairs and surfboards, and serves up great *antojitos*. Try the 'Melissa Special' – melt-on-the-tongue parrotfish, fried in garlic and oil.

LOS BARRILES
☎ 624 / pop 700

South of La Paz, the Transpeninsular brushes the gulf at Los Barriles, where brisk westerlies, averaging 20 to 25 knots, descend the 1800m cordillera, making this Baja's windsurfing capital. From April to August the winds die down and windsurfing becomes pretty much impossible.

Several fairly good dirt roads follow the coast south. Beyond Cabo Pulmo (right) and Bahía Los Frailes, they are rough but passable for vehicles with good clearance. However, the road continuing south beyond Cabo Pulmo and Bahía Los Frailes is impassable for RVs and difficult for most other vehicles, particularly after rainstorms.

Get online at the **Office** (☎ 141-01-42; theoffice@prodigy.net.mx; 8am-8pm Mon-Sat, 10am-6pm Sun) for a wallet-busting $4.50 per hour.

Martín Verdugo's Beach Resort (☎ 141-00-54; Calle 20 de Noviembre; camp/RV sites $12/15, d $50-60) is a crowded 'resort' offering hot showers, full hookups, laundry and a sizable paperback-book exchange. Some rooms have their own kitchenettes.

Hotel Los Barriles (☎ 141-00-24; losbarriles hotel@prodigy.net.mx; s/d $50/62) A laid-back place offering clean, comfortable rooms. It also rents out scuba, snorkeling and windsurfing gear.

Don't be fooled by the plastic chairs at **Los Barrilitos** (☎ 121-58-56; Los Barriles s/n; mains $6-11) at the town's only corner; this is spectacular food. Try the 'Fish Barrilitos Style' or the seafood salad. While you wait, be sure to ask Francisco for the photo album (he used to be a bullfighter), but *don't turn to the back*.

CABO PULMO
☎ 624 / pop 150

Home to the only Pacific coral reef in North America, Cabo Pulmo is a prime snorkeling and diving spot, southward from Barriles along Baja's curvaceous eastern shore. The beautiful desert drive, while bumpy, should be passable for all vehicles except after heavy storms. Begin at **Los Arbolitos**, where snorkeling (not diving) can be done right from the beach. To the right of the parking lot, an easy-to-moderate **hiking trail** (20 minutes) leads to the sea-lion colony of Las Sirenitas, which offers better reefs and chances to interact with sea lions.

Offshore snorkeling and diving trips can be booked through **Pepe's Dive Center** (☎ 141-00-01; pepesfoundation@hotmail.com; 9am-5pm), which also offers Internet access for a budget-busting $5 per 20 minutes.

Nancy's B&B (in USA only ☎ 1-617-524-44-40; cabañas with/without bathroom $50/40; P) is simply furnished, quiet and has great mattresses. It also has a restaurant that serves gourmet Mexican and seafood, such as the popular 'Scallops Nancy.'

RESERVA DE LA BIOSFERA SIERRA DE LA LAGUNA

South of where the Transpeninsular and Hwy 19 meet, the precipitous heart of the cape region begins. Here, the uninterrupted wilds of the lush and rugged Sierra de la Laguna are a draw for stalwart backpackers. Foothill villages provide access to unique interior mountains and steep canyons.

Tranquil **Santiago**, 10km south of the junction for La Rivera and 2.5km west of the Transpeninsular, once witnessed a bloody revolt by the indigenous Pericú against the Jesuits. **Cañón San Dionisio**, about

25km west of Santiago, is the northern-most of three major east–west walking routes across the sierra; the others are **Cañón San Bernardo**, west of Miraflores, and **Cañón San Pedro**, west of Caduaño, which is about 10km south of Santiago. The terrain is difficult and unpredictable, and should only be attempted by experienced hikers. For more information, read Walt Peterson's *Baja Adventure Book*.

Just south of the plaza in Santiago, **Casa de Huéspedes Palomar** (☎ 612-122-06-04; s/d $30/60, camp sites $7) has basic rooms amid fruit tree–covered grounds. Palomar's restaurant is well-known for its seafood, and its English-speaking owner is a good source of information on the Sierra de la Laguna.

SAN JOSÉ DEL CABO
☎ 624 / pop 35,000
Unlike it's party-hearty neighbor, Cabo San Lucas, San José del Cabo is quiet and laid-back. Its narrow streets, Spanish-style buildings and shady plazas make for fun, relaxing shopping, and a variety of restaurants make evenings a treat.

Orientation
San José del Cabo consists of San José proper, about 1.5km inland, and a Zona Hotelera with large beachfront hotels, condos and time-shares. Linking the two areas, just south of shady Plaza Mijares, Blvd Mijares is a gringolandia of restaurants and souvenir shops.

Information
BOOKSTORES
Libros Libros Books Books (☎ 142-44-33; Blvd Mijares 41) A small bookstore with items in English and Spanish.

EMERGENCY
Ambulance (066)
Hospital (☎ 142-01-80)
Police (060)
Fire (068)

INTERNET ACCESS
Trazzo Digital (☎ 142-03-03; Zaragoza; per hr $4) This Internet café has a fast connection and large monitors.

MEDICAL SERVICES
IMSS Hospital (nonemergency ☎ 142-00-76, emergency 142-01-80; cnr Hidalgo & Coronado)

MONEY
Several *casas de cambio* keep long hours. Banks pay better rates but keep shorter hours.
Bancomer (cnr Zaragoza & Morelos) Cashes traveler's checks and has an ATM.

POST
Post office (Blvd Mijares 1924; ✆ 8am-6pm Mon-Fri)

TOURIST OFFICE
Secretaria Municipal de Turismo (☎ 142-29-60 ext 150; Transpeninsular Hwy; ✆ 8am-5pm Mon-Sat) Has a stock of brochures and maps on hand.

Sights & Activities
The colonial-style **Iglesia San José**, built on the site of the 1730 Misión San José Del Cabo, faces the spacious Plaza Mijares.

Between raids on Spanish galleons, 18th-century pirates took refuge at the **Arroyo San José**, now a protected wildlife area replenished by a subterranean spring. A palm-lined **Paseo del Estero** (Marshland Trail) runs parallel to Blvd Mijares all the way to the Zona Hotelera. The best beaches for swimming are along the road to Cabo San Lucas. **Playa Santa María** at Km 13 is one of the nicest beaches in Los Cabos. **Victor's Sportfishing** (☎ 142-10-92; Hotel Posada Real, Paseo San José) arranges fishing excursions, and sells and rents out tackle.

The **Fiesta de San José**, on March 19, celebrates the town's patron saint.

Sleeping
During the peak winter months, it's a good idea to make reservations.

BUDGET
Free camping is possible at Pueblo La Playa, east of the center.

Hotel Nuevo San José (☎ 142-17-05; cnr Obregón & Guerrero; s/d $20/28; ✖) This budget option has dingy rooms, but it's as cheap as the Cabos gets. Some rooms have air-con; most are missing toilet seats. Despite this, it's often full in the peak season.

Hotel Cecci (☎ 142-00-57; Zaragoza s/n; r $33; P ✖) The rooms and lobby here are a bit old, but it's very conveniently located right in the center of town.

MIDRANGE
Hotel Colli (☎ 142-07-25; Hidalgo; r $42; ✖) Cozy, tidy rooms and a sunny terrace characterize

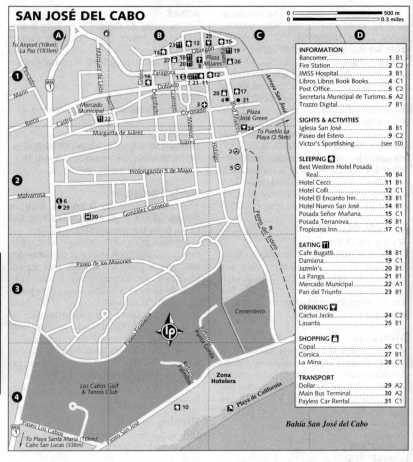

this family-run hotel, near Zaragoza. It also has nice views of the church.

Posada Señor Mañana (☎ 142-04-62; Obregón 1; d $38-42; P ⚊) This casual hotel has a fountain and swimming pool. Overlooking the *arroyo* just north of Plaza Mijares, it offers rooms of many styles as well as a community kitchen. There's a small discount if you pay in dollars.

Posada Terranova (☎ 142-05-34; fax 142-09-02; Degollado s/n; d $55) There's art on the walls, it's very clean and it has nice views of the pueblo from some of the rooms. It also has a good restaurant, and kind English-speaking staff.

Tropicana Inn (☎ 142-15-80; www.tropicanacabo .com; Blvd Mijares 30; s/d/tr $82/82/93; ⚊ ⚊) Charm-

ing place with spacious rooms that have satellite TV, and a big, bucolic courtyard. Rates are 20% higher between January and April. There's a swim-up bar and a replica Olmec head add to the ambience. Love that clay frog.

TOP END
Best Western Hotel Posada Real (☎ 142-01-55; fax 142-04-60; Paseo San José; s/d/tr from $210/240/300; P ⚊ ⚊ ⚊ ⚊) Ocean-view rooms are in a tasteful three-floor structure wrapped around a stately cactus garden. Prices are all inclusive – even drinks – and increase by 30% from October to April.

Hotel El Encanto Inn (☎ 142-03-88; Morelos 133; d $89, ste $116-150; ⚊ ⚊) Beautiful landscaped gardens, interesting pottery, a fountain and clean, well-decorated rooms. Prices increase between October and April.

Eating

Most restaurants are in Plaza Mijares and its side streets, and quality is very high.

Pan del Triunfo (☎ 142-57-20; cnr Morelos & Obregón) An excellent bakery with delicious pastries, baguettes and whole-grain loaves of bread for around $1 or $2 each.

Cafe Bugatti (☎ 142-30-68; cnr Obregón & Morelos; dinner mains $20) Nice 2nd-floor restaurant serving Italian selections with pride. Margaritas here are made with fresh-squeezed orange juice instead of the usual mix.

Damiana (☎ 142-04-99, Plaza Mijares 8; dinner mains $20-30) A romantic seafood restaurant in a restored 18th-century house.

Mercado Municipal (Ibarra) Between Coronado and Castro, this clean market has numerous stalls offering simple and inexpensive but good, filling meals.

Drinking

Head to Cabo San Lucas if you're looking for nightlife. San Jose del Cabo is almost mousy in comparison. **Lasanta** (☎ 142-67-67; www.lasanta.com.mx; Obregón 1732) is a new, upscale wine bar with tastings (not free) on Wednesday and Thursday. **Cactus Jacks** (☎ 142-56-01; cnr Blvd Mijares & Juárez) hosts the occasional live band.

Shopping

San José del Cabo has a wide range of shops to appeal to the interior decorator in you. Wander the plaza and its many side streets

and you're sure to find something fun… or funny. Blvd Mijares is a good place to start.

Copal (☎ 142-30-70; Plaza Mijares 10) On the east side of Plaza Mijares, Copal has an interesting assortment of crafts, jewelry, rugs and masks.

La Mina (☎ 142-37-47; Blvd Mijares 33C) Get your silver, gems and gold from this cave-inspired, creative jewelry store.

Corsica (☎ 146-91-77; corsicacabo@yahoo.fr; Obregón 15) Real art, not the tourist kind, from various local and not-so-local artists.

Getting There & Away

AIR

All airline offices are at **Los Cabos airport** (☎ 146-50-13), north of San José del Cabo, which serves both San José del Cabo and Cabo San Lucas.

Aero California (☎ 146-52-52) Flies daily to/from Los Angeles and Guadalajara.

Aeroméxico (☎ 146-50-97) Flies daily to/from San Diego and to many mainland Mexican destinations, with international connections via Mexico City.

Alaska Airlines (☎ 146-51-06) Flies to/from Los Angeles, Phoenix, San Diego, San Francisco and San Jose, California (USA).

American (☎ 146-53-00) Flies daily to Los Angeles and Dallas.

Continental Airlines (☎ 146-50-50, in USA ☎ 800-900-50-00) Flies to/from Houston and, during the high season, Newark.

Mexicana (☎ 143-53-53) Flies daily to Los Angeles and to mainland destinations such as Mexico City, Guadalajara and Mazatlán.

BUS

From the main **bus terminal** (☎ 142-11-00; González Conseco), east of the Transpeninsular, buses depart for the following destinations.

Destination	Price	Duration	Frequency
Cabo San Lucas	$3	1hr	frequent
La Paz	$16	3hr	frequent
Ensenada	$148	22hr	frequent
Pichilingue's ferry terminal	$11	3½hr	3 daily
Tijuana	$158	24hr	frequent

CAR & MOTORCYCLE

Offering car rental, **Dollar** (☎ 142-01-00, 142-50-60) is on the Transpeninsular just north of the intersection with González Conseco,

---

THE AUTHOR'S CHOICE

La Panga (☎ 142-40-41; www.lapanga.com; Zaragoza 20; dinner mains $20-40) Named after the Mexican word for a boat carved from a single tree, this new restaurant offers mouthwatering fusion entreés, such as succulent tamarind scallops, or a very tender lamb in annato-mint rub. For dessert, try the chocolate *tamal* in tequila. Dim lighting and a multilevel courtyard make it especially romantic; ask for a table near the open-air grill and watch as they prepare your specialty.

and also at the airport. Also try **Payless Car Rental** (☎ 142-55-00; Blvd Mijares). Prices start from about $55 per day.

Getting Around

Taxi drivers are required by law to display a sanctioned price list. The official, government-run company **Aeroterrestre** (☎ 142-05-55) runs bright yellow taxis and minibuses to Aeropuerto Internacional Los Cabos, 10km north of San José, for about $15. Local buses from the main bus terminal to the airport junction cost less than $2, but taking one means a half-hour walk to the air terminal.

LOS CABOS CORRIDOR

West of San José del Cabo, all the way to Cabo San Lucas, a string of luxury resorts lines the once-scenic coastline. Along this stretch of the Transpeninsular, commonly referred to as 'the Corridor,' there are choice **surfing beaches** at Km 27, at Punta Mirador near Hotel Palmilla and at Km 28. Experienced surfers claim that summer reef and point breaks at Km 28 (popularly known as **Zipper's**) match Hawaii's best. The reefs off **Playa Chileno** are excellent for diving.

The best beaches for swimming are along the road to Cabo San Lucas. **Playa Santa Maria**, at Km 13, is one of the nicest.

SURF'S UP

Baja has always been a prime surfer's paradise with swells coming in off the Pacific that, even on bad days, will give beginners challenging fun. Boards can usually be rented from nearby surf shops. Check out the following surf spots for starters, then ask around if you're wanting more.

- San Miguel (p277) Right point break and nice swell, though the rocky shore makes it challenging for beginners

- Los Cerritos (p308) Beautiful sand, nice waves, this is a great beginner beach

- San Pedrito (p308) Similar to Los Cerritos, but requires a bit more finesse

- Zipper's (above) Not a beginner beach, but a whole lot of fun

For more info on surfing, check out the simple, no-nonsense, brown-and-black covered *Surfer's Guide to Baja* by Mike Parise.

CABO SAN LUCAS

☎ 624 / pop 42,600

If you've been looking for clubs that round everyone up into a conga line so that waiters can pour tequila down your throat, well, Cabo San Lucas is the place for you. Get ready to party. Sportfishing and golf are daytime attractions, and many head to the beaches for fun in the sun, ranging from parasailing and jet-skiing, to just laying around and catching rays. All of the action is centered at the waterfront, but rent a car, drive outside the city limits and you'll be awestruck. Majestic cardón cacti, caracara birds, pink hillsides, perfect surfing and mystical *arroyos* will impress you far more than that watery nightclub tequila.

Orientation

Northwest of Cárdenas, central Cabo has a fairly regular grid, while southeast of Cárdenas, Blvd Marina curves along the Harbor Cabo San Lucas toward Land's End (Finisterra), the tip of the peninsula where the Pacific Ocean and the Sea of Cortez meet. Few places have street addresses, so you will need to refer to the map to locate them.

Information

BOOKSTORES

Libros Libros Books Books (☎ 105-09-54; Plaza de la Danza, Blvd Marina) Books in English and Spanish.

EMERGENCY

Cruz Roja (Red Cross; ☎ 066)
Fire (☎ 068)
Police (☎ 060)

INTERNET ACCESS

Café Cabo Mail (☎ 143-77-97; Plaza Arámburo, cnr Cárdenas & Zaragoza; per hr $8)
InternetPuntoCom (☎ 144-41-90; cnr Leona Vicarío & Calle 20 de Noviembre; per hr $2.50)

INTERNET RESOURCES

About Cabo (www.aboutcabo.net) A useful site for visitors.

MEDICAL SERVICES

AmeriMed American Hospital (☎ 143-96-70; Blvd Cárdenas) Near Paseo de la Marina.

MONEY

Several of the downtown banks will cash traveler's checks and have ATMs, including the following:

American Express (☎ 143-57-88; Plaza Bonita;
☺ 9am-6pm Mon-Fri, 9am-1pm Sat)
Banca Serfin (cnr Blvd Cárdenas & Zaragoza)

POST
Main post office (Blvd Cárdenas; ☺ 8am-4pm Mon-Fri)
Near Calle 20 de Noviembre.

TOURIST INFORMATION
Cabo has no government-sanctioned
tourist offices or information booths, but
there are many time-share sellers on Blvd
Marina who distribute town maps and
happily provide information (along with
an aggressive sales pitch). Avoid accepting
the 'free' offers, as they may waste your
entire afternoon.

Sights
Land's End is by far the biggest, and most
impressive, attraction Cabo San Lucas has
to offer. Get on a *panga* ($10) and head to
El Arco (the Arch), a jagged natural feature
which partially fills with the tide. Pelicans,
sea lions, sea, sky – this is what brought
people to Cabo in the first place and it's still
magical, despite the mammoth cruise ship
towering behind it.

For sunbathing and calm waters **Playa
Médano**, in front of what once was the
Hacienda Beach Resort on the Bahía de
Cabo San Lucas, is ideal. **Playa Solmar**, on the
Pacific, has a reputation for dangerous break-
ers and rip tides. Nearly unspoiled **Playa del
Amor** shouldn't be missed; near Land's End,

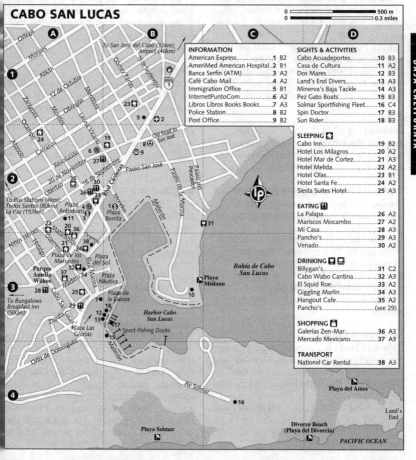

CABO SAN LUCAS

| 0 | 500 m |
| 0 | 0.3 miles |

INFORMATION
American Express.....................**1** B2
AmeriMed American Hospital...**2** B1
Banca Serfin (ATM)..................**3** A2
Café Cabo Mail........................**4** A2
Immigration Office...................**5** B1
InternetPuntoCom....................**6** A2
Libros Libros Books Books........**7** A3
Police Station..........................**8** B2
Post Office..............................**9** B2

SIGHTS & ACTIVITIES
Cabo Acuadeportes.................**10** B3
Casa de Cultura......................**11** A2
Dos Mares.............................**12** B3
Land's End Divers...................**13** A3
Minerva's Baja Tackle..............**14** A3
Pez Gato Boats......................**15** B3
Solmar Sportfishing Fleet.........**16** C4
Spin Doctor...........................**17** B3
Sun Rider..............................**18** B3

SLEEPING
Cabo Inn...............................**19** B2
Hotel Los Milagros..................**20** A2
Hotel Mar de Cortez...............**21** A3
Hotel Melida..........................**22** A2
Hotel Olas.............................**23** B1
Hotel Santa Fe.......................**24** A2
Siesta Suites Hotel..................**25** A3

EATING
La Palapa..............................**26** A2
Mariscos Mocambo.................**27** A2
Mi Casa................................**28** A3
Pancho's...............................**29** A3
Venado.................................**30** A2

DRINKING
Billygan's..............................**31** C2
Cabo Wabo Cantina................**32** A2
El Squid Roe..........................**33** A2
Giggling Marlin......................**34** A3
Hangout Cafe........................**35** A2
Pancho's..........................(see 29)

SHOPPING
Galerías Zen-Mar...................**36** A3
Mercado Mexicano.................**37** A3

TRANSPORT
National Car Rental.................**38** A3

BAJA CALIFORNIA

it is accessible by boat. Appropriately, **Playa del Divorcio** (Divorce Beach) is nearby, across the point on the Pacific side.

Activities

The best **diving** areas are Roca Pelícano, the sea-lion colony off Land's End, and the reef off Playa Chileno, at Bahía Chileno east of town. At most shops, two-tank dives cost around $60, introductory courses around $80 and full-certification courses $375 to $450. Rental equipment is readily available. **Land's End Divers** (☎ 143-22-00) is on the marina at the Plaza Las Glorias. **Cabo Acuadeportes** (☎ 143-01-17), in front of what once was the Hacienda Beach Resort, is the largest water-sports outfitter.

Minerva's Baja Tackle (☎ 143-12-82; www .minervas.com; cnr Madero & Blvd Marina) offers charter boats and fishing tackle. Five or six people can go on 9.3m and 9.9m sport-fishing boats for $465 and $500 per day, respectively. The **Solmar Sportfishing Fleet** (☎ 143-06-46; www.solmar.com; Av Solmar) offers similar trips, charging from $295 for a 7.8m boat to $750 for a 12.6m one.

Tours

Dos Mares (☎ 143-89-71; Plaza Las Glorias) Runs three-hour, glass-bottomed boat tours ($10) to Playa del Amor, near Land's End. Departures take place every hour from 9am to 5pm. It also offers snorkeling tours to Santa Maria ($35).

Pez Gato I & Pez Gato II (☎ 143-37-97) Offers two-hour sunset sailings on catamarans (adult/child $30/15), and segregate their clientele into 'booze cruises' and 'romantic cruises.'

Sun Rider (☎ 143-22-52) Sunset dinner cruises (adults $40) are available. The boats leave at 5:30pm from the Plaza Las Glorias dock; reservations required.

Spin Doctor (☎ 143-76-76; info@cabosports.com; dock M-O; tours $40) Found behind Hotel Costa Real, this outfit offers sunset booze trips along with other daytime packages.

Festivals & Events

Cabo San Lucas is a popular staging ground for fishing tournaments in October and November. The main events are the **Gold Cup**, **Bisbee's Black & Blue Marlin Jackpot**, and the **Cabo Tuna Jackpot**.

One local celebration is **Día de San Lucas**, honoring the town's patron saint, on October 18, with fireworks displays, food stalls, dancing and partying.

THE AUTHOR'S CHOICE

Bungalows Breakfast Inn (☎ 143-50-35; www.cabobungalows.com; cnr Libertad & Herrera; bungalows incl breakfast $135-165, ste $115-175; P ⊠ ⊠ ⊡) Extremely attentive service, delicious breakfasts, very tastefully furnished rooms, fragrant palm-thatched *palapas*, and a noncaustic, salt-cleansed swimming pool set this B&B apart. Breakfasts are different each day: hearty, egg-filled burritos or apple-walnut waffles are two possible options. Fresh-fruit smoothies, fruit juices and excellent coffee all help to make breakfast a great start to the day. The bilingual staff are warm and welcoming and bungalows almost instantly feel like home. Or how you wish home could be. Beautiful handmade soaps are one of the many tiny details that makes this *the* place to splurge.

Sleeping

Prices fluctuate significantly by season. Rates quoted here apply to peak season (November to May). Cabo has plenty of accommodations in all price categories, starting at pricey and ending with 'It-costs-WHAT-per-night?!!' If you want something on a backpacker budget you'll need to sleep in an unlocked car.

MIDRANGE

Hotel Olas (☎ 143-17-80; cnr Revolución & Gómez Farias; s/d/tr $38/38/47; P ⊠) Quiet, yet still close to the action, the Olas has clean, simple rooms. The friendly, grandfatherly owner is a wealth of information about Baja and speaks some English. Giant clam shells arranged like angel's wings and other maritime items add to the courtyard decor.

Hotel Melida (☎ 143-65-64; cnr Niños Heroes & Mata-moros; s/d $35/45) Has 14 very basic rooms with tile floors and TV. Not the best option, but a clean, alternative if the Olas is booked.

Hotel Los Milagros (☎ 143-45-66; www.losmilagros .com.mx; Matamoros 116; d $72; ⊠ ⊡ ⊠) The tranquil courtyard and 11 unique rooms provide a perfect escape from Cabo's excesses. A desert garden (complete with resident iguanas), a beautiful deep blue pool, friendly and courteous service, and no TVs make this stay unforgettable. The place can also be rented in its entirety for groups, such as weddings or birthday parties.

Cabo Inn (☎ 143-08-19; cnr Calle 20 de Noviembre & Leona Vicarío; d/rooftop r $64/132; ❄) This former brothel still retains an aura of sensual languor, and its courtyard, bursting with almond trees, has a lush, tropical feel. Open-air rooms on the roof are particularly romantic; one has a beautiful tiled Jacuzzi.

Hotel Mar de Cortez (☎ 143-00-32; www.mar decortez.com; cnr Cárdenas & Guerrero; old/new r $49/59, ste $63-73; ❄ ☎) This quiet, colonial-style hotel has an outdoor restaurant-bar and a large family-friendly pool area. Rooms are ample, clean and quiet.

Siesta Suites Hotel (☎ 143-27-73; www.cabosiesta suites.com; cnr Zapata & Guerrero; r $55; ❄) This hotel has clean suites, each with a small kitchen, and is very centrally located.

TOP END

Playa Grande (www.playagranderesort.com; d $170-268, ste $240-915; Ⓟ ❌ ❄ ☐ ☎) What sets this high-end resort apart is its saltwater spa, the only one in Baja that uses fresh Pacific sea water for all its services. Indulgences include relaxing facials, massages, even a sea-water sauna. Great beach access, multiple pools and deluxe rooms will make you feel very well taken care of here.

Hotel Santa Fe (☎ 143-44-01; fax 143-44-03; cnr Obregón & Zaragoza; s & d/tr $97/110; Ⓟ ❄ ☐ ☎) Somewhat removed from the action of the strip, this place is good value with its clean, modern rooms that have well-stocked kitchens. Spiral staircases and a well-kept pool are nice additions.

Eating

Cabo's culinary scene features a great variety of eateries, from humble taco stands to gourmet restaurants.

Venado (☎ 147-69-21; Niños Heroes btwn Zaragoza & Morelos; dinner mains $2-5; ☼ noon-7am) Open all night and packed from 3am until dawn, Venado has delicious fish tacos, fresh salsas and other *antojitos*. If it's slow, the friendly waitresses might drop a coin in the jukebox and invite you to dance.

Pancho's (☎ 143-28-91; www.panchos.com; cnr Hidalgo & Zapata; dinner mains $20, with tequila tasting $70) Offers 'all you want to know about tequila,' in a fun, festive Mexican atmosphere. Aromas from the open grill waft along with notes from the mariachi band. The pricey tequila tasting is like an intensive tequila class – but you can get drunk during the lecture instead of taking notes.

Mariscos Mocambo (☎ 143-21-22; cnr Vicario & Calle 20 de Noviembre; dinner mains $10-20) The lobster cream soup keeps people coming back, as do the shrimp and seafood platters.

Drinking

Hangout Cafe (☎ 172-03-08; www.cabohangout.com; cnr Calle 16 de Septiembre & Zaragoza) Good lattes (as well as breakfast and lunch items) can be found where, there's also free use of their Apple laptops or a fifteen-minute international call, if you buy a drink.

That said, coffee and Cabo are not synonymous. This is a proud party town, and alcoholic revelry is encouraged all day long. The following places are all open well past midnight.

Giggling Marlin (☎ 143-11-82; cnr Matamoros & Blvd Marina) Wildly popular bar in the center.

El Squid Roe (☎ 143-12-69; cnr Cárdenas & Zaragoza) Crazy. Just crazy.

Cabo Wabo Cantina (☎ 143-11-88; cnr Guerrero & Madero) Much like a college frat party, only everyone's older. And drunker.

Pancho's (see left) Claims Mexico's largest selection of quality tequilas, some of it even 'smooth, like mother used to make.'

Billygan's (☎ 143-04-02; Playa Médano) Great for people-watchers and a sunset margarita.

Shopping

Mercado Mexicano (cnr Madero & Hidalgo) Cabo's most comprehensive shopping area is this sprawling market, that contains dozens of stalls with crafts from all around the country.

THE AUTHOR'S CHOICE

Mi Casa (☎ 143-19-33; Parque Amelia Wilkes, Cabo San Lucas; dinner mains $18-35) The sensational Mi Casa serves refined, authentic Mexican dishes in its vibrant courtyard. There's an attractive fountain, lots of seating both inside and out on a palm-covered outdoor patio. Diners are happy, waiters helpful and the food is fantastic. *Chiles en nogada* (green chilies stuffed with beef and pork and covered in a walnut cream sauce) is one of many traditional favorites. Delicious, strong margaritas are a nice way to begin – or continue – the meal.

BAJA CALIFORNIA

Galerías Zen-Mar (☎ 143-06-61; Cárdenas) Offers Zapotec weavings, bracelets and masks, as well as traditional crafts from other mainland indigenous peoples.

Getting There & Away

AIR

The closest airport is Los Cabos (p303), north of San José del Cabo.

BUS & CAR

Long-distance bus service to/from Cabo is provided by **Águila** (☎ 143-78-80; Hwy 19), which is located at the Todos Santos crossroad, north of downtown.

Destination	Price	Duration
La Paz	$13	2½-4hr depending on route
Loreto	$40	8hr
San José del Cabo	$3	1hr
Tijuana	$130	24hr
Todos Santos	$6	1hr

From a small terminal near the Águila station, **Autotransportes de La Paz** (cnr Calle 5 de Febrero & Hidalgo) has eight buses daily to La Paz ($10, 2½ hours).

Numerous car-rental agencies have booths along Blvd Marina and elsewhere in town. **National** (☎ 143-14-14; cnr Blvd Marina & Matamoros) offers rentals starting at $60 per day.

There's an **immigration office** (☎ 143-01-35; cnr Cárdenas & Gómez Farías; ⊗ 9am-1pm Mon-Sat) near the center.

Getting Around

The government-regulated **airport minibus** (☎ 146-53-93; per person $14) leaves every two hours from 10am to 4pm, from Plaza Las Glorias. For $60, shared taxis are another option. Cabs are plentiful but not cheap; fares within town range from $5 to $7.

TODOS SANTOS

☎ 612 / pop 4400

Over the past 20 years, Todos Santos has witnessed an invasion from the north as well-heeled New Mexico artists, organic farmers and even some Hollywood types have snapped up property and put down roots.

Todos Santos' newfound prosperity does not reflect its history. Founded in 1723, but nearly destroyed by the Pericú rebellion in 1734, Misión Santa Rosa de Todos los Santos limped along until its abandonment in 1840. In the late 19th century Todos Santos became a prosperous sugar town with several brick *trapiches* (mills), but depleted aquifers have nearly eliminated this thirsty industry.

Orientation & Information

Todos Santos has a regular grid, but residents rely more on landmarks than street names for directions. The plaza is surrounded by Márquez de León, Legaspi, Av Hidalgo and Centenario.

Todos Santos lacks an official tourist office, but **El Tecolote** (☎ 145-02-95; cnr Juárez & Av Hidalgo), an English-language bookstore, distributes a very detailed town map and a sketch map of nearby beach areas.

Banorte (cnr Juárez & Obregón) Exchanges cash and traveler's checks and has an ATM.

Internet café (☎ 145-02-03; Av Hidalgo; per hr $5) In the Los Adobes de Todos Santos restaurant, between Juárez and Heróico Colegio Militar.

Post office (Heróico Colegio Militar) Between Av Hidalgo and Márquez de León.

Sights & Activities

Scattered around town are several former *trapiches* (mills), including **Molino El Progreso**, the ruin of what was formerly El Molino restaurant and **Molino de los Santana** on Juárez, opposite the hospital. The restored **Teatro Cine General Manuel Márquez de León** (⊗ for events) is on Legaspi, facing the plaza.

Housed in a former schoolhouse, the **Casa de la Cultura** (☎ 145-00-51; Juárez; admission free; ⊗ 8am-6pm Mon-Fri, 10am-1pm Sat & Sun), near Topete, is home to some interesting nationalist and revolutionary murals dating from 1933. Also on display is an uneven collection of artifacts evoking the history of the region.

Surfers come here for some of the nicest swells in all of Baja. Catch that perfect wave as eagle rays glide below you on the smooth sand, or just hang out with the relaxed crowd on **Los Cerritos** or **San Pedrito** and watch the coral sun plunge into the Pacific. Boards can be rented at **Pescadero Surf Camp** (opposite), near the beaches. Just down the road from the surf camp is a competition-grade skateboard park.

Festivals & Events

Todos Santos' two-day **Festival de Artes** (Arts Festival) is held in late January. At other times it's possible to visit local artists in their home studios.

Sleeping

Pescadero Surf Camp (☎ 130-30-32; www.pescadero surf.com; cabañas $40, walapas $25-40, camp sites per person $10). Friendly and helpful, Pescadero Surf Camp has everything a surfer could need – rentals, lessons, advice, a community kitchen and even a BYOB swim-up bar.

B&B Las Casitas (☎ 145-02-55; www.mexonline .com/lascasitas.htm; Rangel; s/d/ste incl breakfast $52/67/78) This Canadian-run B&B, between Obregón and Hidalgo, has a superb breakfast, breezy attractive rooms and inexpensive camp sites.

Motel Guluarte (☎ 145-00-06; cnr Juárez & Morelos; s/d $25/30; P ☲) This good budget option has small rooms with refrigerators and a common balcony. No pets, please.

Todos Santos Inn (☎ 145-00-40; todossantosinn@ yahoo.com; Legaspi 33; d $90-130) This 19th-century building has been converted into a swanky hotel with gorgeous interiors and an excellent restaurant. Rates include a simple breakfast.

Eating

Taco stands, along Heróico Colegio Militar between Márquez de León and Degollado, offer fish, chicken, shrimp and beef cheaply.

Los Adobes de Todos Santos (☎ 145-02-03; www .losadobesdetodossantos.com; Hidalgo s/n; lunch mains $15, dinner mains $20-35) Delicious fusion meals such

---

THE AUTHOR'S CHOICE

Posada La Posa (☎ 145-04-00; www.lapoza .com; ste $140-480; P ☒ ☒ ☲ ☲) Boasting 'Mexican hospitality combined with Swiss quality,' this beautiful boutique retreat is right on the Pacific. A saltwater swimming pool, freshwater lagoon, lush garden and superb restaurant with excellent Mexican wines set it apart. A Mexican sweat lodge was under construction at the time of writing. There are no TVs or phones in the rooms, however, you will find a pair of binoculars and even a bird book. Kayak use, bikes and fishing gear are always included.

THE AUTHOR'S CHOICE

Café Santa Fe (☎ 145-03-40; Centenario 4; dinner mains $20-40; ☺ Wed-Mon) The *insalata Mediterranea* (steamed fruits of the sea drizzled in lemon juice and oil) will make even seafood haters change their evil ways. Everything here is prepared with an eye for taste, and the open-air kitchen, designed by the owner himself, allows you to see the food as it's being prepped for your table. Salads are made with organic produce; in season, it's from the owner's own garden. Anything on the menu will delight, surprise, tantalize, but if you need suggestions go for the mussels in wine or any one of the various handmade raviolis: lobster, *carne* (meat) or just spinach and ricotta cheese. This is surely one of the best restaurants in Baja and is well worth the splurge.

---

as *pescado al Cilantro* (fish with cilantro) or *camarones al ajillo* (shrimp in garlic and chili) are served beside a landscaped cactus garden. *Chiles en nogada* (meat-filled green chilies topped with walnut sauce and pomegranate seeds), a Mexican fall specialty, is available year-round.

Caffé Todos Santos (☎ 145-03-00, Centenario 33; breakfast $5-9, dinner mains $9-17) Coffee-conscious travelers can consume cappuccinos with savory pastries, mammoth muffins or enticing fruit salads here. For dinner, it's well-prepared Mexican favorites.

Las Fuentes (☎ 145-02-57; Degollado at Heróico Colegio Militar; antojitos $5-10, seafood mains $15) This moderately priced restaurant with delicious *antojitos* and seafood specialties in a bougainvillea-shaded patio has three refreshing fountains.

Shopping

Galería de Todos Santos (☎ 145-05-00; Legaspi 33) Contemporary artworks by Mexican and North American artists.

Manos Mexicanas (☎ 145-05-38; cnr Topete & Centenario) Wide selection of well-designed jewelry and *artesanías* (handcrafts).

Getting There & Away

About every two hours, regular buses head to La Paz ($7, two hours) and to Cabo San Lucas ($6, one hour) from the bus stop at Heróico Colegio Militar and Zaragoza.

BAJA CALIFORNIA

Northwest Mexico

North of the white beaches and azure waters is a region of deep canyons, dusty deserts, and colonial villages paved with cobblestone streets. Extreme landscapes and mountain villages are the intense soul of the region. The main attractions are the gorgeous Barranca del Cobre – spectacular gorges and mountain cliffs that comprise a system of canyons that surpasses the Grand Canyon in mass, depth and accessibility – and the thrilling railway that runs through it.

Accessibility to this region is a strong pull for visitors from the southwestern US who think nothing of driving over the border to the breezy Sea of Cortez beaches. But while these folks may lend a conspicuously Americanized feel to many communities here – especially Puerto Peñasco and San Carlos, where vacation condos and burger joints may soon outnumber beach shacks and taco stands – nearby communities have rich indigenous roots. The area around Bahía Kino, for example, is known for its still-present Seri culture, while the Barranca del Cobre is alive with colorfully clad, cave-dwelling Tarahumarans.

Beyond the canyons are a couple of major cities, including Sonora's capital of Hermosillo, plus some charming, architecturally rich villages such as Álamos and El Fuerte. Then there's the 12,950-sq-km Desierto Sonorense (Sonoran Desert), an ecological treasure filled with biological riches and shores that hug the Sea of Cortez. Expect surreal vistas of cacti, swirling sand and gentle blue water – and, if you're lucky, the golden glow of a desert sunset.

TOP FIVE

- Sipping a Sol at your waterfront room in the mellow village of **Bahía Kino** (p321)
- Strolling along the hushed, cobblestone streets in the colonial gem of **Álamos** (p328)
- Sticking your face out of the window for a gulp of brisk breeze as you ride the **Ferrocarril Chihuahua al Pacífico** (p337) through the breathtaking Barranca del Cobre
- Riding nimble horses along the steep rim of the Barranca del Cobre at **Posada Barrancas** (p343)
- Traversing the winding road down into deep canyon country, to the lovable mining town of **Batopílas** (p349)

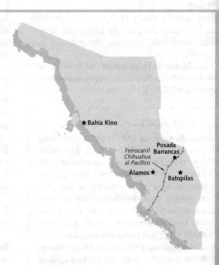

★ Bahía Kino

Posada
Ferrocarril Barrancas ★
Chihuahua
al Pacífico

Álamos ★ ★ Batopílas

■ HERMOSILLO JANUARY DAILY HIGH: 15.5°C | 60°F   ■ HERMOSILLO JULY DAILY HIGH: 31.6°C | 89°F

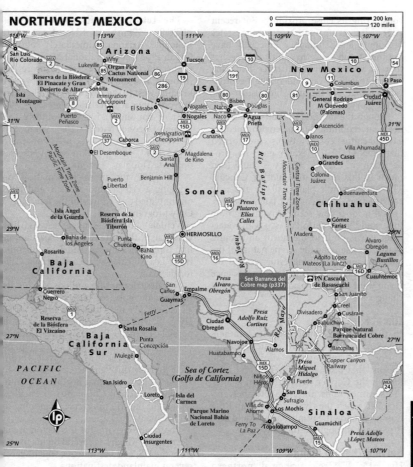

NORTHWEST MEXICO

History

The lands that stretch south from modern-day Nogales have served as a gateway to Mexico ever since the first explorers passed this way some 30,000 years ago. The Pimas – who are direct descendants of those early visitors – established an elaborate system of irrigation that transformed the desert into fruitful agricultural lands. The region's colonial history dates from 1687, when the Italian Jesuit missionary Father Eusebio Francisco Kino began establishing missions and making inroads with the indigenous peoples, ultimately tying their destinies to the rest of Nueva España.

In the 19th century, the coastal waters of the Sea of Cortez (Golfo de California) were witness to naval battles large and small, with most of the action centered on the port jewel of Guaymas, as various world powers challenged Mexico's fledgling independence and coveted its mineral wealth. Between Guaymas and Ciudad Obregón is the ancestral home of the fiercely independent Yaqui tribe, which aggressively resisted the forces of colonialism up until its last rebellion in 1901. The nomadic Seris of the central Sonoran coastal and desert lands fought a losing battle for their way of life, though their population is now steadily increasing.

In recent years, the northwest region of Mexico has been gaining a stronger following from tourists around the world – including from the US, which is ironic, considering its close proximity. But recent advertising campaigns touting the states of Sonora and Chihuahua especially have reminded folks of the glorious beaches that sit within driving distance from the American southwest, and of the beautiful canyons that rival the one which usually gets all the glory.

Though the increase in tourism here has been an economic boom, environmentalists and culture conservationists are worried that FONATUR – Mexico's gung-ho, prodevelopment tourism agency – could turn much of this region into another Cancún. The government's plans call for the new construction of condos and fancy marinas, and also for a new scenic coastal highway that would link Puerto Peñasco with waterfront towns both to the north and south, drastically changing the serene nature of the coastline and disturbing estuaries and diverse marine life. So time is of the essence if you want to see the place before sweeping changes set in.

Climate

In the Desierto Sonorense the summers are extremely hot, and the winters benign. Spring and autumn are similar to the seasons that precede them. The best time to visit the Copper Canyon region is after the summer rains, in late September and October, when the rivers are swift and the flowers abundant. Spring – as it should be – is pleasant throughout the canyons.

Getting There & Around

Hwy 15, Mexico's principal northern Pacific coast highway, begins at the border town of Nogales, Sonora, about 1½ hours (67 miles/107.8km) south of Tucson. This is one of the most convenient border crossings between western Mexico and the US. From Nogales, Hwy 15/15D heads south through the Desierto Sonorense for about four hours (260km) to Hermosillo and then cuts over to the coast at Guaymas. From Guaymas the highway parallels the beautiful Pacific coast for about 1000km, finally turning inland at Tepic (see p444) and heading on to Guadalajara and Mexico City. There are regular toll booths along Hwy 15 (including two between Nogales and Hermosillo that charge around $7.50 in total).

The **Lukeville–Sonoita crossing** (8am-midnight) – 357km west of Nogales opposite Lukeville, Arizona, immediately south of Organ Pipe Cactus National Monument – is the quickest and easiest in the region (though it's only convenient, if you're heading west to Puerto Peñasco). There are also crossings at **San Luis Río Colorado** (24hr) west of Sonoita and 42km southwest of Yuma, Arizona; **Naco** (24hr), 90km east of Nogales, opposite Naco, Arizona; and **Agua Prieta** (24hr), 130km east of Nogales opposite Douglas, Arizona.

See p992 for more information on bringing a vehicle into Mexico, and p994 on simplified procedures for the free Sonora Only program.

Vehicle and passenger ferries link Guaymas with Santa Rosalía (Baja California) three times a week, and Topolobampo (near Los Mochis) with La Paz (Baja California) daily.

Nogales, Hermosillo and Los Mochis are the primary hubs for bus travel. Buses of all classes ply the cities and towns along Hwy 15 with great frequency, making it possible to travel from northwest Mexico to destinations throughout the mainland or to the US with ease. Many travelers begin their journey through the Copper Canyon at Los Mochis, traveling northeast by train on the Ferrocarril Chihuahua al Pacífico. Others do the trip in reverse, beginning in Chihuahua (p363).

The major airports for the region are at Hermosillo, which has several flights to and from the US, and Los Mochis, which serves several mainland destinations.

SONORA

The second largest state in Mexico (nearby Chihuahua is first), Sonora borders the US to the north but shows remarkable cultural diversity within its 185,000 sq km. From island excursions and desert treks to beach resorts and intact colonial villages, the state is like a microcosm of the country wrapped up into one neat package.

NOGALES

 631 / pop 185,882 / elevation 1170m

Like its border-city cousins Tijuana, Ciudad Juárez and Nuevo Laredo, Nogales is a major transit point between the US and Mexico. Yet, though it presents an easier introduction to Mexico than the larger border cities, with its tangle of souvenir shops, bars and pharmacies on a smaller scale, there's no real reason to linger here.

Note that there's another Nogales – a smaller, calmer one – just on the northern side of the border in Arizona. The name, by the way, means 'walnuts,' because these trees were abundant in the 1800s.

Orientation

The commercial section of Nogales is only a few blocks wide, being hemmed in by hills. The main commercial street is Obregón, two blocks west of the border crossing, which eventually runs south into Mexico's Hwy 15. Almost everything you'll need is within walking distance of the border crossing.

Information

INTERNET ACCESS
Cyber Flash (Internacional 67; per hr $1.50; ☺ 10am-10pm)

MEDICAL SERVICES
Cardonelet Holy Cross Hospital (☎ 520-285-3000; 1171 W Target Range Rd, Nogales, AZ) On the US side of the border, this small regional hospital offers emergency and walk-in care.

MONEY
You will find there are plenty of *casas de cambio* (exchange offices) in the area, where

you can change US dollars to pesos or vice versa, on both sides of the border crossing. Dollars and pesos are used interchangeably on the Mexican side. There's a Bancomer on Campillo.

POST
Mexican post office (Cnr Juárez & Campillo; ☺ 9am-3pm Mon-Fri)
US post office (300 N Morley Ave; ☺ 9am-5pm Mon-Fri) Three blocks north of the border crossing.

TOURIST INFORMATION
Border tourist office (☎ 312-06-66; ☺ 9am-5pm Sun-Mon) Beside the border immigration office, this station dispenses information about Sonora and beyond.

Sleeping

Althought staying in Nogales voluntarily would be an unusual choice, you never know when an untimely case of narcolepsy could set in. There's nothing fancy here, but you won't lack for choices if it's just a bed you're after.

Hotel San Carlos (☎ 312-13-46; Juárez 22; s/d $33/42; P ⊠ 🖵) A stone's throw from the border, the well-priced San Carlos offers very clean, basic quarters.

Hotel Granada (☎ 312-29-11; cnr López Mateos & González; s/d $38/42; ⊠) Seven blocks south of the border crossing, the Granada is further from the action and a bit more peaceful. Rooms have TV and phone. Its Parador Restaurant has a tasty selection of Mexican dishes.

NORTHWEST MEXICO

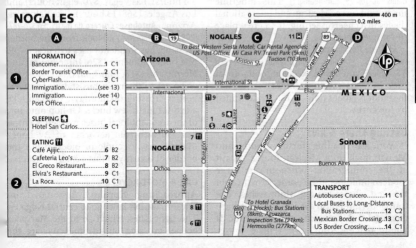

NOGALES

INFORMATION	
Bancomer	1 C1
Border Tourist Office	2 C1
CyberFlash	3 C1
Immigration	(see 13)
Immigration	(see 14)
Post Office	4 C1

SLEEPING 🛏	
Hotel San Carlos	5 C1

EATING 🍴	
Café Ajijic	6 B2
Cafeteria Leo's	7 B2
El Greco Restaurant	8 B2
Elvira's Restaurant	9 C1
La Roca	10 C1

TRANSPORT	
Autobuses Crucero	11 C1
Local Buses to Long-Distance Bus Stations	12 C2
Mexican Border Crossing	13 C1
US Border Crossing	14 C1

Mi Casa RV Travel Park (in the US ☎ 520-281-1150; 2901 N Grand Ave; RV sites $18) On the US side at exit 8, this standard RV park offers spaces with weekly and monthly discounts.

Best Western Siesta Motel (in the US ☎ 520-287-4671; www.bestwesternarizona.com; 673 N Grand Ave; s/d $68/77; P ❌ ❌ ▣ ❑) On the US side, the standard, spic-and-span motel rooms here have free wireless Internet, cable TV, microwaves and refrigerators. The rate includes a continental breakfast.

Eating

Café Ajijic (☎ 312-50-74; Obregón 182; mains $5-14; ☽ 8am-midnight) A favorite among American day-trippers, this spot has festive sidewalk seating, complete with caged birds that sing, and a menu featuring enchiladas (corn tortillas dipped in chili sauce, wrapped around meat or poultry, and garnished with cheese), *antojitos* (tortilla-based snacks like tacos and *gorditas*) and massive frozen margaritas.

La Roca (☎ 312-08-91; www.larocarestaurant.com; Elias 91; mains $8-19; ☽ 11am-midnight) A surprisingly upscale spot for a border town, La Roca has a colonial elegance, live music, and a diverse menu that highlights many regions of Mexico, from Oaxacan *mole* (chicken in a sauce of chilies, fruits, nuts, spices and chocolate) to Guaymas shrimp.

Cafeteria Leo's (cnr Obregón & Campillo; mains $3-6; ☽ 8am-11pm) A bright, clean and cute spot for cheap, fast meals.

Elvira's Restaurant (☎ 312-47-73; Obregón 1; mains $6-16; ☽ 8am-midnight) This longtime institution serves Mexican and international dishes in a cheerful setting. It's a great place to sample *mole*.

El Greco Restaurant (☎ 312-43-58; Obregón 152; mains $7-29; ☽ 11am-midnight Sun-Thu, 11am-1am Fri & Sat) Here you'll find excellent food – from *chile rellenos* (stuffed chilies) to lobster thermidor – that's only slightly undermined by the corny decor.

Getting There & Away

If you are heading further south into Mexico, pick up a Mexican tourist permit at the immigration office in the large modern building at the border crossing, on the west side of the big white arches. The tourist permit is also available at the vehicle checkpoint 21km south of the border. If you're driving your own vehicle (buses

don't stop there), it is more convenient to get it at this checkpoint at the same time as your vehicle permit (see p992). Both offices are open 24 hours a day.

AIR

Nogales doesn't have a local airport. The nearest airport is in Tucson, Arizona, about 100km (1½ hours) north.

BUS

From Nogales' **main bus station** (Hwy 15), 8km south of the city center, **Elite** (☎ 313-16-03) and **TAP** (Transportes y Autobuses del Pacífico; ☎ 662-212-68-70, 313-92-75) have 1st-class air-conditioned buses that head south along Hwy 15 to Guadalajara, and on to Mexico City. Mexican destinations include Chihuahua ($55, 12 hours), Guaymas ($19, five hours) and Hermosillo ($12, 3½ hours, every half-hour).

Tufesa (☎ 662-213-04-42, 631-313-38-62; www .tufesa.com.mx) has its own station, two blocks north of the main station, with hourly 1st-class buses that go south as far as Culiacán. Next door, **Transportes Baldomero Corral** (☎ 903-28-01) serves the major cities along Hwy 15, with a 1st-class bus departing every two hours from 10:30am; stops include Hermosillo ($12, 3½ hours) and Álamos ($30, nine hours).

Autobuses Crucero (☎ 313-54-24) buses also leave from the main bus station, stopping at the station on the Arizona side and going to Tucson ($12, 1½ hours), Phoenix ($27, 3½ hours), Las Vegas ($70, eight hours) and Los Angeles ($68, 13 hours). From Nogales, Arizona, **Autobuses Crucero** (in the US ☎ 520-287-5628; 35 N Terrace Ave), a block from the border crossing, has frequent buses to Tucson ($9, one hour), Phoenix ($26, three hours) and Hermosillo ($18, four hours).

To get to the main bus station from the border crossing (8km away), you can take a taxi for just a few bucks. Or hop onto one of the frequent local buses marked 'Central Camionera,' from a corner of Av López Mateos, just a couple of blocks from the border. It'll cost you just $0.40.

CAR & MOTORCYCLE

Approaching Nogales, Arizona, from Tucson, the left lanes go to central Nogales. The right lanes, which go to the Mariposa border crossing outside the city, are the quickest way to enter Mexico. Both border crossings are open 24 hours a day. As you approach Nogales, you'll see plenty of signs for Mexican auto insurance, which you'll need if you're bringing a vehicle into Mexico.

Temporary vehicle import procedures are dealt with at the Aguazarca inspection site at the 21km point on the highway south of Nogales.

Enterprise Rent-A-Car (in the US ☎ 520-281-0425, 800-325-8007; www.enterprise.com), at multiple locations, allows you to take its rental vehicles to Mexico from the US. You can pick up the vehicle in either Nogales or Tucson (including the Tucson airport), and must return it where you got it. Be forewarned that you must purchase Mexican auto insurance through the rental agency, which costs a hefty $25 per day. Day-trippers – note that several attended lots near the border crossing offer parking on the US side for $7 per day.

With more than 11,000 vehicles crossing into the US at Nogales each day, getting through the border quickly when heading north requires luck, or perhaps some foresight. The **US Department of Homeland Security** (http://apps.cbp.gov/bwt) posts estimated wait times online.

PUERTO PEÑASCO
☎ 638 / pop 33,875 / elevation 48m
On the northeast coast of the Sea of Cortez (Golfo de California), this town has for years been a popular destination for the beach-craving residents of Arizona's desert cities. But Rocky Point, as the US visitors call it, is not the quaint little seaside town it used to be. Its main stretch of waterfront, Sandy Beach (also known as Sandy Point) – which was a favorite camping site – has been the site of extreme overdevelopment in the past couple of years. It's now home to a dozen massive condo-hotel resorts, which offer luxury rooms with views, sports bars, expensive restaurants, and not a hint of Mexican culture. Fans like to call it 'the new Cancún.'

Still, the place has some charms, as long as you stick to the festive *malecón* (Old Port), the non-Americanized downtown areas surrounding it, and the desert-meets-beach residential region known as Las Conchas. The water here has one of the most dramatic tide charts in the world; for a real treat, grab a flashlight and go for a nighttime stroll across the salty tidal flats.

Orientation
Just an hour south of the Arizona border (from the no-fuss Lukeville–Sonoita crossing), Puerto Peñasco sits at the end of Mexico's Hwy 8. After driving through the general downtown and residential blocks, you'll reach the Old Port district to the west, and, west of that, the resort-filled stretch of Sandy Beach. Las Conchas and CEDO are to the east.

Information
BOOKSTORES
CEDO (Freemont Blvd; ☽ 10am-5pm Sun-Sat) This nature center (p316) has a small gift shop with some good books about the region, in both English and Spanish.

EMERGENCY
Ambulance, Fire & Police (☎ 065)
Fire (☎ 383-28-28)
Police (☎ 383-26-26)

INTERNET ACCES
Max's Café (La Marina Center; ☽ 8am-10pm) Has free Internet on two computers.

MEDICAL SERVICES
Santa Fe Clinic (☎ 383-24-47; Av Morua; ☽ 24hr)

MONEY
Serfin and Bancomer, both on Blvd Juárez, have ATMs.

POST
Post office (1285 Av Chiapas; ☽ 9am-5pm Mon-Fri)

TOURIST INFORMATION
Rocky Point Convention and Visitors Bureau (☎ 388-04-44, in the US 877-843-3717; www.cometo rockypoint.net; Benito Juárez & Calle 111)
Rocky Point Reservations (in the US ☎ 602-439-9004, 800-427-6259; www.rockypointres.com) A good source for arranging stays before you arrive
Tourism office (☎ 383-50-10; Blvd Juárez 320B; ☽ 9am-5pm Mon-Fri, 9am-2pm Sat)

Sights & Activities
The **Acuario Cet-Mar** (☎ 382-00-10; Av Freeman, Las Conchas; admission $3; ☽ 10am-3pm Mon-Fri, 10am-6pm Sat & Sun), an aquarium, features educational

tanks filled with various regional fish, turtles, sea lions and other creatures, all accompanied by bilingual explanations.

Just down the road, **CEDO** (Intercultural Center for the Study of Desert and Oceans; ☎ 382-01-13; www .cedointercultural.org; Freemont Blvd, Las Conchas; admission free; ⏰ 9am-5pm Mon-Sat, 10am-2pm Sat) is a wonderful source of information about the fascinating desert-meets-the-sea ecosystem of Rocky Point. It has a museum, library, whale-skeleton exhibit, history displays and free natural-history talks (in English) on Tuesday at 2pm and Saturday at 4pm. The place also offers guided tours of the local ecosystems, from a two-hour **Tidepool Tour** (adult/child $15/10) to a six-hour **Kayak Caper** ($85, adults only).

Festivals & Events

Spring Break (March) Probably a good time to stay away, as this is when the town is overtaken by margarita-chugging college students from the US.

Bathtub Races (October) This odd event has expats racing down the street in bathtubs-on-wheels. Oh those silly Americans!

Shrimp Festival (early December) Get back to the real roots of commerce here, by tasting some fat, local *mariscos* (shrimp).

Sleeping

While the most visible of accommodations these days are the new resorts, there are some great down-to-earth options too (though it's slim pickings for those on tight budgets).

BUDGET & MIDRANGE

Hacienda Del Mar Bed & Breakfast (☎ 083-08-00; www.haciendabnb.com; Freemont Blvd, Las Conchas; r $70-95, ste $105-120; P ⊠ ⊠ ⏰) A wonderful respite from the resorts, this B&B is in a quiet residential development just a block from the ocean. The most affordable rooms are small and sit around a courtyard, while the bigger ones have great views of both desert and sea. All guests have use of a common kitchen, a peaceful backyard barbecue and wet-bar area, and prices include breakfast.

Hotel Viña Del Mar (☎ 383-01-00; www.vinadel marhotel.com; Av Primero de Junio y Malecón Kino; s/d/tr/ste $67/77/97/120; P ⊠ ⊡ ⏰) In the Old Port, this motel-style option has a variety of basic, wood-beam-ceiling rooms, the best being those that surround the pool – a large oasis

that features a swim-up bar and a palm-tree shaded deck.

Posada La Roca Hotel (☎ 383-31-99; Primero de Junio 2; s/d $30/40; ⊠) Located right in the Old Port, this 1927 inn – supposedly a hideout for Al Capone during the US Prohibition – is a stately old stone building. The 10 rooms, all with private bathroom, are a bit dark and musty, but they're off a long and beautiful light-filled hallway.

Playa Elegante RV Resort (☎ 383-37-12; www .elegantervpark.com; Av Matamoros; RV & camp sites beachfront/nonbeachfront $25/19, 2-night minimum; P ⊡ ⏰) One of the last remaining old-school camping spots, this sandy spit on the water is mostly an RV scene, though tent campers are welcome.

TOP END

Playa Bonita Hotel (☎ 383-25-86, in the US ☎ 888-232-8142; www.playabonitaresort.com; Paseo Balboa; r $90-145, ste $135-230; P ⊠ ⊠ ⊡) This large cement-block complex features 128 clean and basic rooms, a private beach and connecting Mexican restaurant.

Sonoran Resorts (☎ 383-02-04; www.sonoran -resorts.com; Sandy Beach; apt $124-327; P ⊠ ⊠ ⊡ ⊡ ⏰) With three gargantuan properties on Peñasco's Sandy Beach, the Sonora Spa, Sea and Sun own a big corner of the resort market. These are condos with units (one-, two- and three-bedroom) that are rented out like hotel rooms, with restaurants, pools, private beaches, bars and game rooms all on the property.

Eating & Drinking

Tacos el Grillo (Av Ruiz Cortínez & Benito Juárez; mains $2-5; ⏰ 10am-9pm) Among the cluster of taco and seafood stands at the Mexican center of town is this delicious, open-air option. Try the fresh beef and fish tacos, or fresh cheese quesadillas (cheese folded between tortillas and fried or grilled).

Lapa Lapa (☎ 388-05-99; Malecón Kino & Zaragoza; mains $9-14; ⏰ noon-9pm) This *palapa*-topped (thatched roofed) 2nd-floor dining room has a view of the sea, a festive bar area and eclectic dishes, such as chicken with tamarind sauce and jicama salad with grilled shrimp. Service is slow but the breezy locale is refreshing.

Blue Marlin (☎ 383-65-64; Zaragoza; mains $5-14; ⏰ noon-9pm) Tucked just off the Old Port's main drag, this cozy joint specializes in smoked fish but also has T-bone steak and *chiles rellenos*.

Coffee's Haus (☎ 388-10-65; www.coffeeshaus.com; Blvd Benito Juárez 216B; mains $9-14; ☻ 8am-4pm Tue-Sat, 8-2pm Sun) An airy new German-owned café, this is the place for good coffee, breakfast items from Belgian waffles to *huevos* (eggs) and *chorizo* (sausage), and lunches like salmon filet and fresh mozzarella salad.

Manny's Beach Club (☎ 383-54-50; www.mannys beachclub.net; Blvd Matamoros, Playa Miramar; ☻ 10am-1am) There's a full restaurant here, but the star attraction is the mega-popular beachfront bar, where you'll find a wide array of tequilas and margaritas, frequent karaoke sessions, and a mob of partiers of all ages – locals and visitors alike.

Getting There & Around

Driving south from Arizona, cross at the Lukeville–Sonoita border (closed from midnight to 6am) and follow Hwy 8 to Puerto Peñasco. Though an international airport is scheduled to open by 2008, you can now fly by private charter to a smaller local airport; check with **West Wind Air Service** (in Phoenix, Arizona ☎ 888-869-0866; www.west windairservice.com) for details. There are a few companies offering shuttle-bus service from Phoenix and Tucson, including **Head Out to Rocky Point** (in the US ☎ 866-443-2368, 602-971-0166; www.headouttorockypoint.com), which transports you for $150 per person return (discounts for groups) and **Kona Shuttle** (in the US ☎ 602-956-5696; www.konashuttle.com), for $179 return. You can travel by bus to Puerto Peñasco from Hermosillo via **TBC** (☎ 662-217-39-61) for about $20. Also, **ABC** (www.abc.com.mx) makes trips here from Tijuana for about $48 one way

Once you're in town, it's best to have a car, as there is no public transportation. Taxis are cheap and plentiful, though, with most cross-town rides costing no more than $5.

AROUND PUERTO PEÑASCO

Northwest of Rocky Point is the **Reserva de la Biosfera El Pinacate y Gran Desierto de Altar** (Pinacate Biosphere Reserve), containing extinct volcanic craters, a large lava flow, vast sand dunes and other surreal landscapes. To get there for a hiking adventure, head 45km northeast (in a high-clearance, 4WD vehicle

only) on Hwy 8 and register at the white **ranger station** (☎ 638-384-90-07). From there, you'll really be on your own, as there's no food, water or fuel. The best way to approach this otherworldly region is to join one of the guided, day-long tours offered by **CEDO** (see opposite; tours $65).

HERMOSILLO

☎ 662 / pop 595,811 / elevation 238m

Many travelers simply pass through Hermosillo, a prosperous agricultural center and the capital of Sonora, without stopping. And really, there's not much reason to linger here – a place where commerce and government rule, where driving is tricky and where the heat gets unbearable most afternoons. It's a true city, after all, that's located smack dab in the middle of the Desierto Sonorense. But if you're driving through this region, chances are you'll spend at least a night here to break the trip.

Many of the streets in Hermosillo, founded in 1700 by Juan Bautista Escalante, have names that acknowledge the city's debt to the native revolutionary heroes, including General Álvaro Obregón. High points include some delicious food, great opportunities for buying cowboy boots and a well-placed *mirador* (viewpoint), where you'll get a lovely overview of the city and its surrounding area. Hermosillo is also *the* place to find a large selection of ironwood carvings made by the Seri people; various friendly vendors hawk them in front of the post office.

Orientation

Hwy 15 enters Hermosillo from the northeast and becomes Blvd Francisco Eusebio Kino, a wide street lined with orange and laurel trees. Blvd Kino (much of which is known as the Zona Hotelera, or Hotel Zone) continues west through the city, curves southwest and becomes Rodríguez, then Rosales as it passes through the city center, then Vildosola before becoming Hwy 15 again south of the city.

MAPS

The tourist office (see p319) offers a good free city map – though you may need a map to find the office! Luckily, many of the city's nicer hotels and restaurants hand out the slick Hermosillo guide, which has a good

HERMOSILLO

0 — 500 m
0 — 0.3 miles

INFORMATION
Centro Medico Del Noreste...............**1** C3
Librerías de Cristal...............**2** B4
Post Office...............**3** B4
State of Sonora Tourist Office...............**4** B6
US Consulate...............**5** A4
Veta Papelería...............**6** B4

SIGHTS & ACTIVITIES
Catedral de Nuestra Señora de la
Ascensión...............**7** A5
Museo de Sonora...............**8** D5
Palacio de Gobierno...............**9** A5

SLEEPING
Colonial Hotel...............**10** B6
Hotel Washington...............**11** C3

EATING
Está Cabral...............**12** B4
La Galería Café...............**13** A4
Verde Olivo...............**14** C2

TRANSPORT
Buses to Bahía Kino...............**15** D3

To Blvd Kino; Hotel San Martín;
La Siesta Motel;
Fiesta Inn; Sonora Steak;
Farmacia Kino (1km);
Mediterraneos Restaurante (3km);
Highway Tourist Office (15km);
Hotels; Nogales (277km)

To San Ángel Hotel (5km);
Airport (10km);
Bahía Kino (110km)

Blvd Encinas

Blvd Rosales

Puebla

Jalisco

Niños Héroes

Oaxaca

Universidad de Sonora

Sonora

Blvd Encinas

To Bus Stations
(2km)

Jardín
Juárez

To Mundo
Divertido
(2km)

Noriega

Blvd Colosio

Pino Suárez

Yáñez

García Morales

Carmenta

Guerrero

Matamoros

Juárez

González

Jesús García

Noriega

Morella

Monterrey

Elías Calles

Mercado
Municipal

Parque Infantil

Serdán

Chihuahua

Villegas

Pesqueira

No Reelección

Ángel Flores

Guadalupe

Blvd Hidalgo

Obregón

Pino Suárez

Plaza
Zaragoza

Velazco

Av Paliza

Allende

Moreno

Salido

Bavispe

California

Bravo

Ocampo

Plaza
Tehuantepec

Oposura

Cucurpe

▲ Cerro de la
Campana

Comonfort

Cubillas

Michel

Blvd Rosales

Blvd Francisco Serna

Paseo Río Sonora Norte

Paseo Río Sonora Sur

To Jardines de Xochimilco (2km);
Centro Ecológico de Sonora (5km);
Guaymas (136km)

To La Sauceda (2km)

NORTHWEST MEXICO

map within its shiny pages. Most hotels in the Zona Hotelera also have an ATM-like machine in their lobbies – cool, interactive city guides that locate attractions and eateries on their computer screens.

Information

BOOKSTORES
Librerías de Cristal (☎ 213-71-97; Serdán 178; ☯ 9am-7:45pm) Wide selection of books in Spanish.

EMERGENCY
Cruz Roja (Red Cross; ☎ 065, 214-00-10)
Police (☎ 066)
Tourist emergency assistance (☎ 800-903-92-00)

INTERNET ACCESS
Veta Papelería (Monterrey 86; per hr $1.50; ☯ 6:30am-7:30pm) Also a place to buy envelopes, not available at the nearby post office.

MEDICAL SERVICES
Centro Médico Del Noroeste (☎ 217-45-21; Colosio 23 Ote; ☯ 24hr)
Farmacia Kino (☎ 215-53-00; Blvd Morelos 15-2; ☯ 24hr) 24-hour pharmacy.

MONEY
Banks and *casas de cambio* are scattered along Blvds Rosales and Encinas.

POST
Main post office (cnr Blvd Rosales & Serdán; ☯ 8am-4pm Mon-Fri, 9am-1pm Sat)

TOURIST INFORMATION
State of Sonora Tourist Office (☎ 217-00-76; in the US ☎ 800-476-6672; www.sonoraturismo.gob .mx; Edificio Sonora Norte, 3rd fl, Comonfort & Paseo Canal; ☯ 8am-9pm Mon-Fri) Located in a massive governmental office building, this isn't the most tourist-friendly place to visit. On-street parking can be a challenge, so opt for one of the area's pay lots ($1.80 for two hours).

Sights

PLAZA ZARAGOZA
Not to be confused with the grittier Jardín Juárez, this **plaza** (btwn Blvd Hidalgo & Av Paliza) is shaded by beautiful orange trees, drawing government workers on lunch breaks and creating a peaceful place to hang. Its majestic **Catedral de Nuestra Señora de la Asunción**, also called the Catedral Metropolitana, was constructed between the years

of 1877 and 1912. The **Palacio de Gobierno**, completed in 1906, is on the east side of the plaza, and features an airy courtyard with colorful, dramatic murals depicting the history of Sonora.

CERRO DE LA CAMPANA
This prominent 'Hill of the Bell' is the most prominent landmark in the area, and an easy point of reference night or day. The panoramic view from the *mirador* on top is beautiful and well worth the walk or drive to get up there.

MUSEO DE SONORA
Hugging the east side of the Cerro de la Campana, this **museum** (☎ 217-27-14; www .inahsonora.gob.mx/xmuseodesonora.htm; Jesús García s/n; admission $3, free Sun & holidays; ☯ 10am-5pm Tue-Sat, 9am-4pm Sun) has fine exhibits on the history and anthropology of Sonora.

CENTRO ECOLÓGICO DE SONORA
This **zoo and botanical garden** (☎ 250-12-25; www.ecol-son.unam.mx; admission $3; ☯ 8am-5pm Tue-Sun) is about 5km south of central Hermosillo. Like a massive park, it features plants and animals of the Desierto Sonorense, as well as an **observatory** (admission $1.50; ☯ 7:30-11pm Fri & Sat) with telescope viewing sessions. To get there by public transit, watch for the 'Luis Orcí' bus at the west side of Jardín Juárez, which departs about every 15 minutes. Ask the driver when to get off, as it's not clearly marked.

Sleeping
You'll find most of Hermosillo's better hotels in the Zona Hotelera (budget travelers will need to stick to places in the city center). If you spend a night here in summer, do yourself a favor and make sure that the air-con works.

BUDGET & MIDRANGE
Hotel San Martín (☎ 289-05-50; in the US ☎ 877-225-2987; www.hotelsanmartin.net; Blvd Kino 498; s/d $48/53; ❏ ✕ ❄ ⬛ ☕) The best bargain in the hotel zone, this place has tile-floored rooms with fridges, coffeemakers, great water pressure and ambient lighting. There's also a 24-hour restaurant, an airport-pickup shuttle, a peaceful pool area and room service. It's a big hit more with Mexican than foreign tourists.

San Ángel Hotel (☎ 289-98-50; www.hotelsan angel.com; Blvd García Morales 104; s/d $55/60; P 🖀 🖾 🖾) This relatively new hotel, on the road that leads out of town toward Bahía Kino, has clean and basic rooms with tile floors, pleasant sconce lighting and coffeemakers.

La Siesta Motel (☎ 289-19-50; www.lasiesta motel.com; Blvd Kino; s/d/ste $53/65/75; P 🖾 🖾) Another spot popular with Mexican tourists, most of the standard motel-style rooms are newly renovated. There is an excellent steak restaurant, plus a popular diner (with great breakfasts) on the property.

Hotel Washington (☎ 213-11-83; Noriega 68 Pte; s/d $18/20; 🖾) Hotel Washington has a cheerfully decorated lobby, vending machines and free coffee. Rooms are on the dark and stuffy side, but hey, it's the cheapest deal in town.

TOP END

Colonial Hotel (☎ 259-00-00; www.hotelescolonial .com; Vado del Río 9; r/ste $93/125; P 🖾 🖾 🖾 🖾) The most stylish hotel in the city, the Colonial, on Hermosillo's south edge, has a colorful lobby with a coffee lounge, fresh-flower arrangements, and brightly tiled murals and flooring. Rooms have nice firm beds, brand-new carpets, marble bathrooms and modern artwork and furniture.

Fiesta Inn (☎ 259-22-00; www.fiestainn.com; Blvd Kino 375; r $120-200; P 🖾 🖾 🖾 🖾 🖾) While most of the 'luxury' accommodations in the hotel zone are hardly worth their price tags, the Fiesta Inn stands above them. The almost-stylish rooms have colorful paint jobs and good lighting, and the property boasts a gym, bar and good restaurant.

Eating

Está Cabral (☎ 213-74-74; cnr Velazco & Allende; antojitos $1-5; ⏲ 5pm-midnight) This large, openair café occupies the interior of a stately ruined building and features romantic live music every night, attracting its fair share of hipsters.

Sonora Steak (☎ 210-03-13; Blvd Kino 914; mains $8-20; ⏲ noon-2am) Located in the hotel zone, this tranquil house has tables on its front yard, back deck and throughout its three rambling, art-filled dining rooms. It's a great place to try the famed Sonora

---

> **THE AUTHOR'S CHOICE**
>
> **Verde Olivo** (☎ 213-28-81; Niños Héroes 75D; buffets $6-9, mains $3-10; ⏲ 7:30am-9pm Mon-Sat, 9:30am-7pm Sun; 🖾) This popular vegetarian restaurant is quite a find in the middle of beef country. Choose from a menu featuring soy burgers, pasta dishes, salads and smoothies, or head right up to the excellent buffet, which has a salad-bar section and many hot meals, from *huitlacoche* (corn mushrooms) crepes to vegetable lasagne. The restaurant is attached to a small health-food store, Jung, where you can grab whole-grain cookies or patchouli candles to go.

---

steak – which waiters cut and weigh for you tableside – while herbivores can choose from hearty pasta, soup and salad options.

La Galería Café (☎ 212-15-16; Blvd Hidalgo 54A; desserts $2-4; ⏲ noon-midnight Sun-Fri) This lively hangout, not far from the cathedral, offers a nice selection of coffees and pastries.

Getting There & Away

AIR

The airport, about 10km from central Hermosillo on the road to Bahía Kino, is served by Aero California, Aeroméxico, America West, Aviacsa and Mexicana. Daily direct flights, all with connections to other centers, go to cities including Chihuahua, Ciudad Juárez, Ciudad Obregón, La Paz, Los Angeles, Los Mochis, Mexicali, Mexico City, Monterrey, Phoenix, Tijuana and Tucson.

BUS

From the **main bus terminal** (☎ 213-44-55; Blvd Encinas), 2km southeast of the city center, 1st-class service is offered by Crucero, Elite, Estrella Blanca (EB), Transportes del Pacífico (TP), Transportes Norte de Sonora (TNS) and others. More companies have separate terminals nearby – Transportes Baldomero Corral (TBC) is next door. Across the street is Tufesa, and about a block west of Blvd Encinas is Estrellas del Pacífico (EP). Services to many destinations depart around the clock. Frequent daily 1st-class departures are shown on the next page.

Destination	Price	Duration
Guaymas	$6	1¾hr
Mexico City	$115	30hr
Nogales	$13	4hr
Phoenix	$42	8hr, 5hr with Crucero, 4hr with TBC
Puerto Peñasco	$13	6½hr, 4hr with TBC

Second-class buses to Bahía Kino ($9, two hours) depart from the AMH and TCH bus terminal in central Hermosillo, on Sonora between González and Jesús García, 1½ blocks east of Jardín Juárez. They leave hourly from 5:30am to 11:30am, and from 3:30pm to 6:30pm.

Getting Around

Local buses operate from 5:30am to 10pm daily ($0.45). To get to the main bus terminal, take any 'Central,' 'Central Camionera' or 'Ruta 1' bus from Juárez on the east side of Jardín Juárez. A taxi to the airport costs about $11.

BAHÍA KINO

☎ 740 / pop 4050

Named for Father Eusebio Kino – a Jesuit missionary who established a small mission here for the indigenous Seri people in the late 17th century – Kino, 110km west of Hermosillo, is the most peaceful waterfront town in this region. It's divided into old and new parts, which sharply underscore the differences between how locals and second-home owners live.

Kino Viejo, the old quarter, is a dusty, run-down fishing village with a skinny little pier that juts out into the bay. Though the town hops with school kids and shrimpers during the day, it turns sleepy at dusk, and most businesses are closed by 8pm. Kino Nuevo, further west, is where you'll most likely spend most of your time. It's also where you'll find the 'snowbirds,' (retired Americans who head south for the winter, when their northern residences turn chilly) who live along this single beachfront road in either spiffy holiday homes or hulking RVs. Its beach is soft, with plenty of *palapas* providing shade, and the water is warm and safe for swimming. High season is November to March; at other times, you may find yourself blissfully alone in any one of the hotels or campgrounds.

Orientation

Route 16 runs west to both parts of town. To get to Viejo, turn left at the Pemex station and you'll be heading directly toward the Sea of Cortez, and will be within the small grid that makes up the old portion of town. Bypass the Pemex and keep heading north to venture into Nuevo. You'll soon be able to see the sea from this main road, and will eventually come to the strip of hotels and restaurants.

Information

Hospital Cruz Roja (Red Cross Hospital; ☎ 242-00-32; Blvd Eusebio Kino, Kino Viejo)

Police (Kino Nuevo ☎ 242-00-67; Kino Viejo ☎ 242-00-32)

Sights & Activities

Museo de los Seris (admission $0.60; ☯ 8am-3pm Tue-Fri), about halfway along the beachfront road in Kino Nuevo, is a tiny spot that features illuminating exhibits (with all-Spanish texts) about the Seri (see the boxed text, p323).

Punta Chueca is a small village about 25km north of Bahía Kino. In fact, it's more like a living museum, as it's where most members of the area's Seri tribe live. You'll need a sturdy 4WD vehicle with high clearance to make the journey along the dirt road; once you arrive, be prepared to be pounced upon by several Seri women who will want to sell you hand-crafted jewelry, baskets or ironwood carvings. If you're interested in making the boat trip out to **Isla del Tiburón** – a peaceful, uninhabited ecological preserve owned by the Seri tribe – this is where you'll have the best chance of finding a willing guide for hire, as the official Seri government office, in Kino Viejo, has closed until further notice.

Sleeping

Las Toninas Condominiums (☎ 242-08-92; Blvd Mar de Cortez; condos $85; ℗ ☒) A great option for families with kids, or large groups of friends, these rentable condos are large and airy (but with a cheesier style than La Playa), and have beachfront terraces, large kitchens, ceiling fans and room to sleep up to six.

Kino Bay RV Park (☎ 242-02-16; www.kinobayrv.com; Blvd Mar de Cortez; sites $20; ℗ ☐) At the far north end of Kino Nuevo, across the street from the beach, this is large and well

THE AUTHOR'S CHOICE

La Playa RV & Hotel (☎ 242-02-74; www
.laplayarvhotel.com; Blvd Mar de Cortez; trailer
sites/r $20/85; P ❄ ♿) Hands-down
the best accommodations in town, this
beachfront-paradise spot has 20 tastefully
designed rooms, all with perfect views of
the sea, and featuring stone floors, firm
beds, mini-kitchen areas with sinks and
fridges, large marble bathrooms and private
front decks. RV travelers will find innovative
trailer sites with enclosures (and full water/
electric hookups).

equipped with 200 spots, laundry facilities
and fishing tackle.

Hotel Posada del Mar (☎ 242-01-55; www.ho
telposadadelmar.com; r $38-45; P ❄ ♨) Directly
across the street from the beach (and the
lovely La Playa), this hotel has lovely, shady
grounds. Unfortunately, its rooms are dark
and musty and have thin mattresses. But if
you're on a budget and don't have a tent,
this is where you'll need to lay your head.

Eating

El Pargo Rojo (☎ 242-02-05; Blvd Mar de Cortez 1426;
mains $8-13; ⏰ 7am-10pm) A festive spot with
primary-color walls, floral tablecloths and
a nautical theme, this is the place to enjoy
delicious fish dishes and hearty Mexican
breakfasts in the midst of Kino Nuevo. Try
to use the Spanish menu, as the poorly
translated English one has various errors,
turning the shrimp stuffed with ham and
cheese, for example, into shrimp stuffed
with cream cheese and jam!

Jorge's Restaurant (☎ 242-00-49; Blvd Mar de Cortez at Alecantres; mains $4-10; ⏰ 8am-9pm) Topped
with a *palapa* roof, this airy spot sits on the
beach at the far end of Kino Nuevo. Tasty
breakfasts of *huevos rancheros* (fried eggs
served on a corn tortilla, topped with a sauce
of tomato, chilies and onions, and served
with refried beans) and late-day options
including garlic shrimp, hamburgers and
tortilla soup, pack in a devoted crowd.

Restaurant Marlin (☎ 242-01-11; Tastiota at
Guaymas; mains $8-15; ⏰ 5-9pm) This popular
Kino Viejo spot serves fat margaritas and
creative fish and seafood meals.

Mexicanos Luis (Ensenada at Guaymas; antojitos
$2-4; ⏰ noon-10pm) Nicknamed the 'plywood

palace,' this open-air spot has good, late-
night *antojitos*, like quesadillas and tacos,
in Kino Viejo.

Getting There & Away

Buses to Hermosillo leave from Kino Nuevo
roughly every hour on the half-hour, with
the last bus departing from Kino Nuevo
at 7:15pm and Kino Viejo at 7:30pm. In
season, if you come at a busy time (on a
Sunday, for example, when lots of families
are there) and you want to get the last bus
of the day, catch it at the first stop, at the
north end of Kino Nuevo, while there is still
space. Be aware that this is the only public
transportation in Kino; there are no local
buses or taxis.

If you're driving, you can make the trip
from Hermosillo to Bahía Kino in about
an hour – *if* there is no road construction
going on. That said, the road is currently
undergoing a disorganized repair process
with no end in sight, so be prepared for
serious delays (the trip could easily take two
hours or more), and along some portions
you'll be forced to drive off-road through
sand and dirt. It's best done in a truck or
SUV, and definitely during daylight hours.
From central Hermosillo, head northwest
out of town on Blvd Encinas and just keep
going.

GUAYMAS

☎ 622 / pop 120,000

Guaymas, Sonora's main port, is inextricably linked to the sea – something you'll
have a hard time forgetting as you stroll
the edge of the harbor, watching fishing
boats return with catches including the
camarones gigantes (massive shrimp) that
Guaymas is known for – be sure not to leave
without sampling these.

This city, founded in 1769 by Spaniards
at the site of Yaqui and Guaymenas indigenous villages, later saw its bay become
the locus of military campaigns by would-
be invaders ranging from the US Navy to
French pirates.

Today Guaymas is a bustling port and
naval supply center, with a thriving fishing industry and lots of city traffic. It's not
much of a tourist magnet – especially with
the resort of San Carlos just 20km to the
northwest – but it's got some great restaurants for shrimp-tasting, plus a selection of

cheap inns geared more to budget travelers than those of San Carlos.

Orientation

Hwy 15 becomes Blvd García López as it passes along the northern edge of Guaymas. Central Guaymas and the port area are along Av Serdán, the town's main drag, running parallel to and just south of García López; everything you'll need is on or near Av Serdán. García López and Serdán intersect a few blocks west of the Guaymas map's extents.

Information

INTERNET ACCESS

Casa Blanquita (Calle 19 at Av 11; per hr $1.50; ☺ 9am-9pm Mon-Sat, 9am-3pm Sun)

MEDICAL SERVICES

Farmacia León (Av Serdán & Calle 19; ☺ 8am-6pm)
General Hospital Guaymas (☎ 224-01-38; Calle 12 at Av 6)

MONEY

All of these banks have ATMs and exchange travelers' checks.
Banamex (Calle 20)
Bancomer (Calle 18)
BanCrecer (Calle 15)
HSBC (Calle 22)

POST

Post Office (Av 10; ☺ 9am-3pm Mon-Fri, 9am-1pm Sat) Between Calles 19 and 20.

TOURIST INFORMATION

Tourist Office (☎ 224-41-14; Av 6 at Calle 19; ☺ 9am-3pm Mon-Fri) Note that plans to move to a new location are in the works.

Sights & Activities

The town's notable features include the **Plaza de los Tres Presidentes**, which commemorates the three Mexican presidents hailing from Guaymas; the 19th-century **Iglesia de San Fernando** and its Plaza 13 de Julio; the **Palacio Municipal** (built in 1899); and the **old jail** (1900). For a pleasant evening stroll, head to the **Plaza del Pescador** to pay your respects to the **fisherman statue** and to take in a good view of the city and its environs.

The **Museo de Guaymas** (☎ 222-55-27; cnr Calle 25 & Av Iberri; admission free; ☺ 8am-2pm & 3:30-5pm Mon-Fri, 9am-1pm Sat) is a peculiar place, with holdings that seem more like the inventory of someone's attic than a museum collection. Displays include photographs and old cameras, archaeological artifacts and a bathtub.

Sleeping

Accommodations choices in Guaymas favor budget-minded travelers, but folks looking for atmosphere should continue on to San Carlos.

BUDGET

Casa de Huéspedes Martha (☎ 222-83-32; Av 9; s/d $14/16; P) This small hotel, a short walk

---

THE SERIS

The Seris are the least numerous indigenous people in Sonora – by the 1930s their population had decreased to 300 due to hunger and the introduction of foreign disease. But they are hardy, and have existed in the same region for more than 500 years. Traditionally a nomadic people living by hunting, gathering and fishing – not agriculture, despite the attempts of Christian missionaries to turn them into farmers over the centuries – the Seris roamed along the Sea of Cortez, from roughly El Desemboque in the north to Bahía Kino in the south, and inland to Hermosillo.

The Seris are one of the few indigenous peoples who do not work for outsiders, preferring to live by fishing, hunting and making handicrafts such as their ubiquitous ironwood carvings of animals, humans and other figures (including some oddly modern choices, such as microscopes and baseball bats). They are no longer strictly nomadic, but still often move from place to place in groups; sometimes you can see numbers camped at Bahía Kino, or traveling up and down the coast. You will also see Seris in Hermosillo – dark-haired men in Western clothing who sell ironwood carvings in front of the post office. Most, though, live in villages north of Bahía Kino, including Punta Chueca (see p321).

You can learn more at the small Museo de los Seris in Kino Nuevo (see p321), with exhibits of the Seris' distinctive clothing, traditional houses with frames of ocotillo cactus, musical instruments and nature-based religion.

GUAYMAS

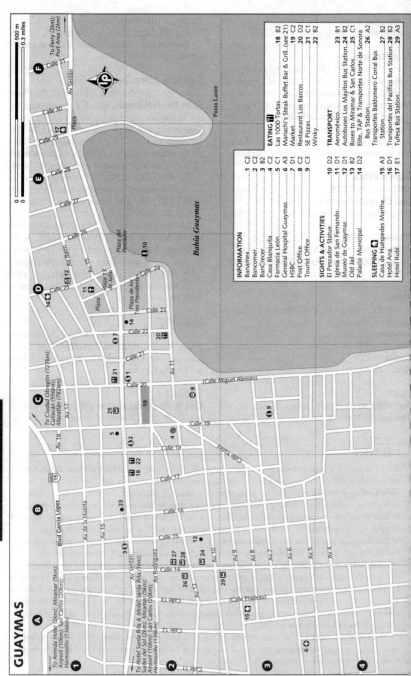

To Armida Hotel (2km); Miramar (5km);
Airport (10km); San Carlos (20km);
Hermosillo (136km)

To Hotel Santa Rita & Motel Santa Rita (1km);
Suites del Sol (2km); Miramar (5km);
Airport (10km); San Carlos (20km);
Hermosillo (136km)

To Ciudad Obregón (127km);
Culiacán (556km);
Mazatlán (782km)

To Ferry (2km);
Port Area (2km)

INFORMATION
Banamex...............................	1 C2
Bancomer.............................	2 C2
BanCrecer............................	3 B2
Casa Blanquita......................	4 C2
Farmacia León.......................	5 C1
General Hospital Guaymas.......	6 A3
HSBC...................................	7 D1
Post Office...........................	8 C2
Tourist Office.......................	9 C3

SIGHTS & ACTIVITIES
El Pescador Statue.................	10 D2
Iglesia de San Fernando.........	11 D1
Museo de Guaymas................	12 D1
Old Jail...............................	13 B2
Palacio Municipal..................	14 D2

SLEEPING
Casa de Huéspedes Martha......	15 A3
Hotel Ana............................	16 D1
Hotel Rubí...........................	17 E1

EATING
Las 1000 Tortas....................	18 B2
Mariachi's Steak Buffet Bar & Grill...(see 21)
Market................................	19 C2
Restaurant Los Barcos............	20 D2
SE Pizzas.............................	21 C1
Winky.................................	22 B2

TRANSPORT
Aeroméxico..........................	23 B1
Autobuses Los Mayitos Bus Station..	24 B2
Buses to Miramar & San Carlos..	25 C1
Elite, TAP & Transportes Norte de Sonora Bus Station..	26 A2
Transportes Baldomero Corral Bus Station..	27 B2
Transportes del Pacífico Bus Station..	28 B2
Tufesa Bus Station.................	29 A3

500 m
0.3 miles

NORTHWEST MEXICO

from the bus terminals and the central market, is a popular dive, with dark rooms, thin mattresses and an overwhelming smell of cleanser in the air. At least its rooms have floors, not moldy carpeting.

Hotel Ana (☎ 222-30-48; Calle 25 No 135; d/tr $20/27; P ⚒) Offers basic, musty but clean rooms, set around dusty courtyards.

Hotel Rubí (☎ 224-01-69; Av Serdán s/n; s/d $23/26; ⚒) Between Calles 29 and 30, is similarly appointed to Hotel Ana.

MIDRANGE & TOP END
Armida Hotel (☎ 224-30-35; Carretera Internacional Salida Norte; r $50, ste $75-90; P ⚒ ⚒) Rooms in this well-run hotel on the northern edge of town have refrigerators, satellite TV, balconies or terraces, and bathtubs. There's also a café and the popular El Oeste steak house.

Suites del Sol (☎ 221-29-00; Blvd Benito Juárez N 2; s/d $50/55; P ⚒ ⚒) The newest option in Guaymas is at the edge of town, offering clean rooms and a comfortable vibe.

Motel Santa Rita (☎ 224-19-19; Av Serdán 590 Pte; s/d $40/60; P ⚒ ⚒) This three-storey motel has somewhat cheerful rooms with soft beds and cool tile floors; its retro-style diner (mains $5 to $11) has vinyl-clad booths and bright green doors. Prices include complimentary breakfast.

Eating
Restaurant Los Barcos (cnr Av 11 & Calle 22; mains $5-12; �९ noon-10pm) Head to this popular seafood spot, under an enormous *palapa*, where you can sample Guaymas' famous fat shrimp, or choose from steaks, salads or seafood cocktail.

Winky (Av Serdán at Calle 18; drinks $2) A tiny storefront amid fast-food stops, Winky serves healthy and refreshing juices and smoothies.

Other eating options include the following:

Mariachi's Steak Buffet Bar & Grill (cnr Calle 20 & Av Serdán; buffet $4; ☉ noon-11pm) Serves an ample buffet.

Las 1000 Tortas (Av Serdán btwn Calles 17 & 18; tortas $2-4) A good snack shop serving tortas and hamburgers.

SE Pizzas (Av Serdán near Calle 20; buffet from $3) Has an all-you-can-eat pizza and salad buffet, with cheap beer and excited crowds.

As in most Mexican towns, Guaymas supports a market, which has stalls where

you can sit down to eat cheaply. It's a block south of Av Serdán, on Av Rodríguez between Calles 19 and 20, and opens at around 5am.

Getting There & Away
AIR
The airport is about 10km northwest of Guaymas on the highway to San Carlos. **Aeroméxico** (☎ 222-01-23; cnr Av Serdán & Calle 16) offers direct flights to the Baja California destinations of La Paz, Loreto and Santa Rosalía, and to Hermosillo, where you can catch connecting flights to other destinations. **America West** (☎ 221-22-66; www .americawest.com) offers two direct flights to Phoenix each week.

BOAT
Overnight ferries connect Guaymas with Santa Rosalía, Baja California. The passenger/ auto ferry *Santa Rosalía*, operated by Operadora Rotuaria del Noroeste, departs at 8pm on Monday, Thursday and Saturday, and takes about nine hours, though strong winter winds may cause delays.

The ticket office is at the **ferry terminal** (☎ 222-02-04; www.ferrysantarosalia.com; Av Serdán; ☉ 9am-6pm) at the east end of town. Vehicle reservations are accepted by telephone a week in advance. Passenger tickets are sold at the ferry office on the morning of departure, or a few days before. Make reservations at least three days in advance and, even if you have reservations, arrive early at the ticket office. Passenger fares are $55 for seats and $75 for cabins. Advance reservations are recommended. See p289 for vehicle fares.

BUS
Guaymas has five small bus stations, all on Calle 14, about two blocks south of Av Serdán. Elite, TAP and Transportes Norte de Sonora share a terminal at the corner of Calle 14 and Av 12; Transportes del Pacífico is opposite. All these have far-ranging northbound and southbound routes departing hourly, 24 hours.

Also on Calle 14, TBC goes hourly to Hermosillo, Nogales, Ciudad Obregón and Navojoa, and also has a daily bus (3:40pm) direct to Álamos. Autobuses Los Mayitos, between Avs 10 and 12, operates hourly buses north to Hermosillo and south to

NORTHWEST MEXICO

Navojoa, 7am to 9pm. Tufesa, at the corner of Av 10, has hourly buses heading north to Nogales, afternoon buses to Hermosillo, and bi-hourly buses south to Culiacán. Trip times and 1st-class fares include Álamos ($10, four hours), Guadalajara ($54 to $65, 20 hours), Hermosillo ($4 to $6, 1¾ hours), Los Mochis ($10 to $16, five hours) and Tijuana ($42 to $49, 15 hours).

Getting Around

To get to the airport, catch a bus from Av Serdán heading to Itson or San José, or take a taxi (around $12). Local buses run along Av Serdán frequently between 6am and 9pm daily ($0.45). Several eastbound buses stop at the ferry terminal; ask for the 'transbordador' (ferry).

AROUND GUAYMAS

The closest beach is **Miramar** on the Bahía de Bacochibampo, about 5km west of Guaymas. It has a small surrounding residential area and is not a big tourist destination like San Carlos, though it does have an interesting industry – pearl farming – and a classic beachfront inn that has a trippy, stuck-in-time feel: **Hotel Playa de Cortés** (☎ 622-221-01-35; Bahía de Bacochibampo; RV sites $26, r $99, ste $125-228; ⓟ ⌘ ⌘), with stunning views of the bay and large, well-decorated (if dated) quarters, is a sprawling resort and world unto itself. It provides an interesting alternative to touristy San Carlos, and has 120 big clean rooms, a good restaurant, and activities from boating to ping-pong on some dusty tables. A 90-space trailer park with full hookups provides access to all hotel facilities.

SAN CARLOS

☎ 622 / pop 4500

On Bahía San Carlos, about 20km northwest of Guaymas, San Carlos is a beautiful desert-and-bay landscape presided over by the dramatic twin-peaked Cerro Tetakawi. From October to April, the town is overtaken by a massive influx of *norte americanos*, who speak English to everyone and don't bother to change their dollars to pesos, but at other times you'll find it a quiet, beautiful spot that's a respite from the hot, surrounding desert cities. San Carlos is bursting with outdoor activities, from snorkeling and sailing to fishing

and horseback riding – though don't go there looking for sandy beaches, as the accessible public shoreline is mostly rocky and difficult to reach. The view from the *mirador* is spectacular, especially at sunset or during a full moon.

Orientation

San Carlos is based around two marinas: Marina San Carlos, in the heart of town, and the newer Marina Real at Algodones, which is in the northernmost section. Most motels and eateries lie along the skinny strip of Blvd Beltrones, while the larger resorts are toward Algodones.

Information

EMERGENCY

Ambulance (☎ 226-09-11)
Police (☎ 226-14-00)

INTERNET ACCESS

Gary's Internet Connection (☎ 226-00-49; www .garysdiveshop.com; Blvd Manlio Beltrones Km 10; per hr $3; ⓧ 9am-6pm Mon-Sat) Located at the one-stop-shop that is Gary's Dive Shop.
JC's Cafe (☎ 226-00-87; Blvd Manlio Beltrones 158; per hr $3; ⓧ 6:30am-9pm)

INTERNET RESOURCES

www.go2sancarlos.org Makes hotel reservations easy.
www.sancarlosmexico.com Run by American expats, a good source for inns, activities, restaurants and important local phone numbers.

MONEY

Both US dollars and pesos are accepted everywhere. Banamex, next to the Pemex station on Beltrones, has two ATMs that operate in English and Spanish.

TOURIST INFORMATION

Tourist office (☎ 226-02-02; Blvd Beltrones; ⓧ 9am-5pm Mon-Fri, 9am-2pm Sat) In the Edificio Hacienda Plaza, the office has information on local happenings.

Activities

Though it's not especially known for its beaches, San Carlos offers a wealth of beach-related activities. The following companies lead snorkeling, wildlife, fishing and scuba excursions, and also provide scuba certification, outfitting and rentals:
Blue Water Sports (☎ 227-01-71; www.desertdivers .com) Beachside at the San Carlos Plaza Hotel, Algodones.

El Mar Diving Center (☎ 226-04-04; www.elmar.com; 263 Creston)

Gary's Dive Shop (☎ 226-00-49; www.garysdiveshop .com; Blvd Manlio Beltrones Km 10)

The **Centro Cultural de Naturaleza y Arte** (☎ 226-08-18; www.cafenaturarte.com; Gabriel Estrada) leads ecotourism adventures such as camping, hiking and boating.

Sleeping

Hotel Fiesta Real San Carlos (☎ 226-02-29; Blvd Manlio Beltrones Km 8.5; s/d $65/87; **P** ⊠ ≋ ⚐ ⅋)
This wonderful, family-run spot has practically everything you'll find at the pricier resorts (such as the insanely overpriced San Carlos Plaza) – beachfront rooms with balconies, a swimming pool, a *palapa* bar and restaurants – but at a fraction of the cost and with a more down-to-earth vibe.

Marinaterra (☎ 225-20-20; www.marinaterra.com; Gabriel Estrada, Sector La Herradura; r $109-135, ste $170; **P** ⊠ ≋ ⚐ ⅋) Overlooking the San Carlos marina, this resort has large rooms with kitchenettes, and some with excellent balconies that boast wide hammocks. There's also a bar, restaurant, gym, travel agency and business center on-site.

El Mirador RV Park (☎ 227-02-13; www.elmirador rv.com; RV sites $23; **P** ⚐ ⅋) This park, overlooking Marina Real, has great views, many amenities (from tennis courts to a hot tub and rec room) and 90 spaces.

Posada del Desierto (☎ 226-04-67; ste for up to 4 people $35-40; **P** ⊠) The Posada del Desierto, San Carlos' most economical hotel, overlooks Marina San Carlos. It has seven basic air-conditioned studio apartments with kitchen, and cheaper weekly and monthly rates are available. To find it, follow signs to Hotel Marinaterra and keep going – at the convenience store, turn right.

Motel Creston (☎ 226-00-20; Blvd Manlio Beltrones Km 10; s/d $45/50; **P** ⊠ ⚐) This well-run motor lodge has large rooms and retro charm.

Eating

JC's Café (☎ 226-00-87; Blvd Manlio Beltrones 158; mains $3-10; ⏱ 7am-10pm) A restaurant-café-Internet spot, JC's has serious variety. Big breakfasts include pancakes, eggs and waffles, and lunch and dinner offerings include burgers, tuna melts, lasagne and vegetable plates.

Rosa's Cantina (☎ 226-10-00; Blvd Manlio Beltrones Km 9.5; mains $4-12; ⏱ 7am-9pm) A spot popular with snowbirds, who appreciate everyone's well-spoken English. As well as the sugared cereals on the breakfast menu that sate visiting grandkids, you'll also find Mexican favorites for breakfast, lunch and dinner.

El Buen Café (Gabriel Estrada; mains $3-7; ⏱ 8am-8pm Mar-Sep) Enjoy light fare, like a Greek salad, a veggie pita melt or a slice of banana-nut bread under an umbrella at this friendly sidewalk café, part of the Centro Cultural de Naturaleza y Arte (see left).

El Bronco (☎ 226-11-30; Creston 178; mains $5-21; ⏱ noon-9pm) This steakhouse serves the thick cuts of beef for which Sonora is famous.

San Carlos Mariscos Esterito (Bahía San Carlos; dinners $4-10; ⏱ 4am-8pm) If you'd rather not make the nighttime trip to Guaymas, home to the best seafood around, then do yourself a favor and settle on this open-air *palapa*. It's across from the old marina and situated on a scenic estuary where you can bird-watch from your table.

Getting There & Around

Buses to San Carlos from Guaymas run west along Av Serdán (starting from between Calles 19 and 20) from 5:30am to 10pm. Return buses leave San Carlos between 6:30am and 11pm. Buses run every 20 minutes ($1).

NAVOJOA

☎ 642 / pop 102,170

Navojoa, 194km from Guaymas, is small, crowded and unremarkable. However, it is a significant hub for those who live in tiny Álamos, 53km east on Hwy 13, and also for those heading there.

Hwy 15D becomes Av Pesquería as it passes through town; most of the town's five bus stations are on the cross streets Guerrero or Allende. Second-class buses to Álamos depart from the **TBC station** (cnr Guerrero & No Reelección) every half-hour between 6am and 3pm, and hourly between 3:30pm and 10:30pm ($2.50, one hour). TBC also has 1st-class service for longer trips, including 12 daily buses north to Hermosillo ($15, five hours), plus several to Tucson ($37, 11 hours) and Phoenix ($52, 13 hours).

If you're driving to Álamos and can't wait till you get there to eat, make a quick pit stop at **Taquería las Palmas** (mains $2-5;

(🕙 7am-11pm), on the main road into town, across the street from the Pemex. It's a pleasant little orange hut, with Mexican flags and a caged parakeet, and the family in charge churns out delicious plates of tacos, quesadillas and the like.

ÁLAMOS

☎ 647 / pop 8521 / elevation 432m

Set in the forested foothills of the Sierra Madre Occidental, Álamos lies in wait like a buried treasure. It's a small and sleepy oasis – a place to land in for several days, not leaving until you fall into step with the mellow and meandering pace of the town. Strolling along quiet cobblestone streets is the number-one activity here, as there is plenty to take in – facades of restored colonial mansions with lush courtyards, friendly local cowboys gathering at myriad taco stands, towering palms and shady cottonwood trees lining simple plazas. You'll notice a Moorish sensibility in much of the architecture, thanks to the influence of 17th-century Andalucían architects, and won't have to wonder why the town was declared both a national historic monument and one of a handful of Mexico's Pueblos Mágicos.

The town's charms have proven irresistible to a community of American retirees and creative types who, since the '50s, have been snapping up many decaying colonial buildings to renovate and convert to hotels, restaurants and second homes. Now, the well-heeled expats – who comprise a small but influential part of the town population (it stood at 365 in 2005, according to one woman who does an annual count) – entertain each other in their enclosed courtyards, remaining largely segregated from their Mexican neighbors. The upside of all this for the traveler, of course, is that there is a wide range of choices in quality lodgings.

Nature-lovers are attracted by the area's 450 species of birds and animals (including some endangered and endemic species) and over 1000 species of plants. Horseback riding, hunting, fishing, hiking and swimming are popular activities.

From mid-October to mid-April, when the air is cool and fresh, *norte americanos* arrive to take up residence in their winter homes, and the town begins to hum with foreign visitors. Quail and dove hunting season, from November to February, also attracts many foreigners. Mexican tourists come in the scorching hot summer months of July and August, when school is out. At other times you may find scarcely another visitor.

History

In 1540 this was the campsite of Francisco Vázquez de Coronado, future governor of Nueva Galicia (the colonial name for much of western Mexico), during his wars against the indigenous Mayo and Yaqui (the Yaqui resisted all invaders until 1928). If he had known about the vast amounts of gold and silver that prospectors later found, he would have stayed.

In 1683, silver was discovered at Promontorios, near Álamos, and the Europa mine was opened. Other mines soon followed and Álamos became a boom town of more than 30,000, one of Mexico's principal 18th-century mining centers. Mansions, haciendas, a cathedral, tanneries, metalworks, blacksmiths' shops and later a mint were all built. El Camino Real (the King's Highway), a well-trodden Spanish mule trail through the foothills, connected Álamos with Culiacán and El Fuerte to the south.

After Mexican independence, Álamos became the capital of the newly formed province of Occidente, a vast area including all of the present states of Sonora and Sinaloa. Don José María Almada, owner of the richest silver mine in Álamos, was appointed as governor.

During the turmoil of the 19th century, and up to the Mexican Revolution, Álamos was attacked repeatedly, both by rebels seeking its vast silver wealth and by the fiercely independent Yaqui. The years of the revolution took a great toll on the town. By the 1920s, most of the population had left and many of the once-beautiful haciendas had fallen into disrepair. Álamos became practically a ghost town.

In 1948 Álamos was reawakened by the arrival of William Levant Alcorn, a Pennsylvania dairy farmer who bought the 15-room Almada mansion on Plaza de Armas and restored it as the Hotel Los Portales. Alcorn brought publicity to the town and made a fortune selling Álamos real estate. A number of *norte americanos* crossed the border, bought the crumbling old mansions for good prices and set about the task of lovingly restoring them to their former glory. Many of these people still live in Álamos today.

Orientation

The paved road from Navojoa enters Álamos from the west and leads to the green, shady Plaza Alameda. The market is at the east end of Plaza Alameda; the other main square, Plaza de Armas, is two blocks south of the market. The Arroyo La Aduana (Customs House Stream, which is usually dry) runs along the town's northern edge; the Arroyo Agua Escondida (Hidden Waters Stream, also usually dry) runs along the southern edge. Both converge at the east end of town with the Arroyo La Barranca (Ravine Stream), which runs, dryly, from the northwest.

MAPS

Free maps of the town, which note places to eat, sleep and visit, are available at the tourist office (p330), as well as at various shops around town, including Terracotta Tiendas (p330).

Information

BOOKSTORES

El Nicho Artesanías y Curios (Juárez 15; 🕐 9am-6pm) This eclectic gift shop, just behind the cathedral, has various books about Álamos.

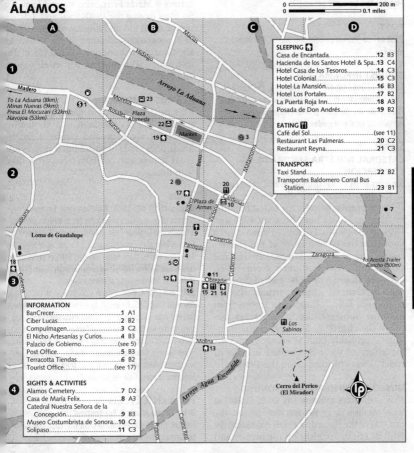

```
ÁLAMOS                          0          200 m
                                0          0.1 miles
```

SLEEPING 🏠
Casa de Encantada.........................12 B3
Hacienda de los Santos Hotel & Spa..13 C4
Hotel Casa de los Tesoros..............14 C3
Hotel Colonial..............................15 C3
Hotel La Mansión..........................16 B3
Hotel Los Portales........................17 B2
La Puerta Roja Inn.........................18 A3
Posada de Don Andrés....................19 B2

EATING 🍴
Café del Sol...............................(see 11)
Restaurant Las Palmeras.................20 C2
Restaurant Reyna..........................21 C3

TRANSPORT
Taxi Stand..................................22 B2
Transportes Baldomero Corral Bus
  Station....................................23 B1

To La Aduana (8km);
Minas Nuevas (9km);
Presa El Mocuzari (32km);
Navojoa (53km)

To Acosta Trailer
Rancho (500m)

INFORMATION
BanCrecer....................................1 A1
Ciber Lucas..................................2 B2
Compulmagen................................3 C2
El Nicho Artesanías y Curios.............4 B3
Palacio de Gobierno....................(see 5)
Post Office...................................5 B3
Terracotta Tiendas.........................6 B2
Tourist Office...........................(see 17)

SIGHTS & ACTIVITIES
Alamos Cemetery............................7 D2
Casa de María Felix........................8 A3
Catedral Nuestra Señora de la
  Concepción................................9 B3
Museo Costumbrista de Sonora.........10 C2
Solipaso....................................11 C3

NORTHWEST MEXICO

Terracotta Tiendas (Juárez 8; ☉ 9am-6pm) This jumble of stores along the west side of Plaza de Armas includes a small bookshop, where you'll find maps, atlases and books about the region, including *The Alamos Guide*, written by shop owners BK Hamma and Donna McGee.

INTERNET ACCESS
Ciber Lucas (Madero 5A; per hr $1; ☉ 8am-9pm)
Compulmagen (Morelos 39; per hr $1; ☉ 7:30am-10:30pm Mon-Sat)

MEDICAL SERVICES
Dr Joaquín Navarro (☎ 428-03-98, 428-03-10) An English-speaking general practitioner who provides an ambulance service.

MONEY
BanCrecer (Madero 37; money exchange ☉ 9am-2pm Mon-Fri) This bank also has an ATM.

POST
Post office (Palacio de Gobierno, Juárez; ☉ 9am-3pm Mon-Fri)

TOURIST INFORMATION
Tourist office (☎ 428-04-50; Juárez 6; ☉ 9am-6pm Mon-Fri) Under the Hotel Los Portales on the west side of Plaza de Armas, the office provides maps, brochures and contacts for local tour guides.

Sights
CATEDRAL NUESTRA SEÑORA DE LA CONCEPCIÓN
Known simply as 'the cathedral', the **Church of the Immaculate Conception** (Plaza de Armas; ☉ daily services 8am & 6pm) is the tallest building in Álamos. It was built between 1786 and 1804, as a copy of a Tucson, Arizona church known as the 'White Dove of the Desert.' Inside, the altar rail, lamps, censers and candelabra were fashioned from silver, but were all ordered to be melted down in 1866 by General Ángel Martínez after he booted out French imperialist troops from Álamos. Subterranean passageways between the church and several of the mansions – probably built as escape routes for the safety of the rich families in time of attack – were blocked off in the 1950s.

MUSEO COSTUMBRISTA DE SONORA
This well-done **museum** (☎ 428-00-53; Plaza de Armas; admission $2; ☉ 9am-6pm Wed-Sun), on the east side of the Plaza de Armas, has extensive exhibits (all in Spanish) on the history and traditions of the people of Sonora. Special attention is paid to the influence of mining on Álamos, and the fleeting prosperity it created.

EL MIRADOR
This lookout, atop a hill on the southeast edge of town, affords a sweeping view of Álamos and its mountainous surroundings, and is a popular hangout spot at sunset. To get there, take the walking trail that ascends from the Arroyo Agua Escondida next to Los Sabinos restaurant. Alternatively, you can walk or drive up the steep, paved road that ascends from its southern approach.

CASA DE MARÍA FELIX
This former home of Mexico's most famous actress – María Felix, who starred in nearly 50 films during the 1940s, '50s and '60s – is now a small inn and kitschy **museum** (☎ 428-09-29; www.casademariafelix.com; Galeana 41; admission $2), filled with hundreds of photos of the icon, along with much of her jewelry, shoes and outfits.

ÁLAMOS CEMETERY
This deliciously ancient **graveyard** (Las Delicias at Posada; ☉ usually 8am-sunset) is a fascinating jumble of above-ground tombs, elaborate headstones made of pastel-hued crosses and angel statues, and tall palm trees, often filled with flocks of crows.

Tours
Grajeda (☎ 428-13-68) A lifelong local, Emiliano Grajeda offers a variety of walking tours: a History Walk, a Ghosts and Legends Tour and the popular House and Garden Tour of the most impressive haciendas in town. Tours last two to three hours and cost $10 per person; the House and Garden Tour starts each Saturday, from October to May, at 10am in front of the museum.
Solipaso (☎ 428-04-66; www.solipaso.com; Obregón 3; day trips $100-250) An excellent resource for nature lovers, this eco-tour company offers nature excursions, including trips on the Río Mayo and Sea of Cortez, and to the nearby former silver mining–town of La Aduana. Its Californian expat owners, David and Jennifer MacKay, also lead birdwatching, hiking and historical tours from October through May, and operate Café del Sol (p332).

Festivals & Events
Ortíz Tirado Music & Art Festival Held in late January, this 10-day festival of orchestra, choir and dance performances attracts thousands of visitors each year.

Traditional Holiday Posadas These processions, which re-enact the journey of Mary and Joseph to Bethlehem, begin on December 16 and continue through Christmas Eve.

Sleeping

Out of all the towns in northwest Mexico, Álamos has the most unique and attractive accommodations, most of which inhabit restored colonial mansions and have rooms encircling flower-filled courtyards. Though budget travelers may have a bit of trouble finding a place, the tourist office keeps a list of *casas particulares* (private homes) that rent out rooms for reasonable rates.

BUDGET & MIDRANGE

La Puerta Roja Inn (☎ 428-01-42; www.lapuertarojainn.com; Galeana 46; r incl breakfast $75-85, casita with kitchen $90; P) This gorgeous 150-year-old home has colorful rooms filled with eclectic art and furnishings, and a breezy garden and courtyard where the proprietor, an expat and trained chef, serves delicious meals (right).

Casa de María Felix (see opposite; ☎ 428-09-29; www.casademariafelix.com; Galeana 41; r $65-90; ✗ ⓛ) Among the exhibits dedicated to Mexico's most famous film actress, 'La Doña,' are several clean and spacious rooms, each with a differently decorated, homey feel.

Posada de Don Andrés (☎ 428-11-10; Rosales 24; d/tr/q $69/80/92; ✗) One of the few Mexican-run hotels in town, this well-priced option on the bustling Plaza Alameda is run by Jorge Álvarez Ramos, an artist and musician whose friends sometimes come around in the early evenings to hang out and make music. Rooms are dark and a bit musty, though the two-storey courtyard is leafy and pleasant.

Acosta Trailer Rancho (☎ 428-02-46; 5 de Mayo at Guadalupe Posada; camp sites $7, trailer sites $10-15, r $60; ✗) About 1km east of the town center, the Acosta has 20 sites with full hookups, barbecue areas, shady trees and two swimming pools. It also has eight comfy rooms (for up to three people). The surrounding woods are a bird-watcher's paradise.

Hotel Los Portales (☎ 428-02-11; Juárez 6; r $30-50) The restored mansion of the Almada family, on the west side of Plaza de Armas, is a dark and dusty place in desperate need of some cheer. Still, it's right in the center of town and could be a necessary choice for folks on a tight budget.

TOP END

Hacienda de los Santos Hotel & Spa (☎ 428-02-17, from the US ☎ 800-525-4800; www.haciendadelossantos.com; Molina 8; r $225-1000; P ✗ ⓛ ⓢ) This sprawling collection of restored mansions is in mint condition, with gorgeous courtyards, antique-filled spacious rooms, three small swimming pools, a lovely restaurant and tequila bar, and a spa with a wide range of treatments. Service is a bit amateurish for such a sophisticated spot, but it's far and away the most romantic and opulent choice in town.

Hotel Colonial (☎ 428-13-71; www.alamoshotelcolonial.com; Obregón 8; r $125-150; ✗) This new inn, with just-renovated rooms around a wide courtyard, is run by a couple of Louisiana expats. Its decor, more New England B&B than Mexican hacienda, is an odd jumble of sleigh beds, Asian wall tapestries and formal artwork. But it's cozy and classy, and just a block from the main square.

Hotel Casa de los Tesoros (☎ 428-00-10; www.tesoros-hotel.com; Obregón 10; r $70-95; P ✗ ⓢ) Formerly an 18th-century convent, this is now a mellow hotel with a breezy, orange-tree shaded courtyard, good restaurant and cozy bar, called Chato's, which is popular with the expat locals. Though quarters are roomy and have small fireplaces, they're a bit dim and musty compared to the property at large. Of similar price and quality are Hotel La Mansión and Casa de Encantada, both within the same block and run by the same owner; you can call Tesoros for reservations.

Eating

Though the dining options aren't overwhelmingly plentiful, there is still some good variety, including the cheap and tasty tacos from the carts that edge the Plaza Alameda and dot the inside of the market. For a gastronomic adventure, **Café la Aduana** (p332) is well worth the 10-minute drive out of town.

La Puerta Roja Inn (☎ 428-01-42; www.lapuertarojainn.com; Galeana 46; lunch mains $4-9, dinner tasting menu $25; ⏱ noon-3pm daily, dinner Wed only) Guests and nonguests alike are welcome to partake in owner Teri Arnold's delicious meals, made with local produce, fish and fowl (courtesy of her hunter husband). Light lunches include grilled artichokes, fresh salads topped with tuna and white beans, and Mexican specialties, while the special Wednesday-night dinners – a major hit with the local expat community – are eclectic and copious delights.

Restaurant Las Palmeras (☎ 428-00-65; Cárdenas 9; meals $3.50-8; ⏰ 7am-10pm) This place, on the north side of Plaza de Armas, is a town favorite. The food is tasty, the prices are good, and the dining rooms are spacious and festive. The diverse dessert menu is icing on the cake.

Café del Sol (☎ 428-04-66; Obregón 3; meals $4-8; ⏰ 7:30am-3pm Tue-Sat) An airy new café, run by the same folks who own the Solipaso tour company (p330), this is the place for great coffee and espresso, along with eclectic fare including chicken salad crepes with sautéed apples, and a range of fresh salads, sandwiches and casseroles.

Restaurant Reyna (Obregón 8; meals $3-7; ⏰ 8am-10pm) A new spot on the now-busy strip of Obregón, this small eatery, with a couple of sidewalk tables, offers Mexican favorites from enchiladas to grilled steaks.

Hacienda de los Santos (dinner mains $10-20) Serves breakfast, lunch, dinner and Sunday brunch, and a trio provides music every evening at this top-end accommodations (see p331).

Shopping

El Nicho Artesanías y Curios (Juárez 15; ⏰ 9am-6pm Mon-Sat, 10am-4pm Sun) Occupying a former silk factory behind the cathedral is this fascinating shop, brimming with antiques, curios, folk art and handicrafts from all over Mexico.

Terracotta Tiendas (Juárez 8; ⏰ 9am-6pm) This is a new collection of boutiques that sell books, maps, freshly brewed espresso and regional crafts, from famed Mata Ortiz pottery to jewelry and embroidered clothing.

A *tianguis* (flea market) is held from about 6am to 2pm Sunday beside the Arroyo La Aduana on the north side of town.

Getting There & Away

Access to Álamos is via Hwy 13 from Navojoa. Transportes Baldomero Corral and other bus companies have frequent service from Navojoa to Álamos (for details see p327).

Álamos' Transportes Baldomero Corral bus station is on the north side of Plaza Alameda. Buses depart for Navojoa ($2,

one hour) at 4am, half-hourly from 6am to 12:30pm, hourly from 12:30pm to 6:30pm and at 9:15pm. A bus to Phoenix ($55, 14 hours) departs nightly at 4pm.

The closest airport is in Ciudad Obregón, about 90 minutes away. You can also take a private jet to town, thanks to Alamos' small landing strip.

AROUND ÁLAMOS

El Chalatón, a park about 2km southwest of town, is popular for swimming in summer. About 10km east of town, **Arroyo de Cuchujaqui** has a delightful swimming hole and is enjoyable for fishing, camping and bird-watching.

Several small historic villages near Álamos make interesting day excursions. Check out **Minas Nuevas**, about 9km from Álamos on the Navojoa–Álamos road; the bus to Navojoa will drop you off there.

La Aduana, the mine that once made Álamos rich, is also worth a visit, and is often included on guided-tour itineraries. It's a tiny little town with a small main plaza and a rustic feel. But **Casa La Aduana Gourmet Restaurant & Inn** (☎ 642-482-25-25; www .casaladuana.com; r/ste with breakfast $65/85, r/ste with meals $100/120) is the real star. It has basic rooms on the plaza, but the big draw is its lauded restaurant (lunch and dinner $17–28), where owner/chef Sam Beardsley turns out lovingly prepared gourmet meals, such as chicken in apple and chipotle cream sauce, and chicken and shrimp with *poblano* peppers.

LOS MOCHIS
☎ 668 / pop 214,600

In the past, most Copper Canyon railway travelers would pass through Los Mochis (Place of Turtles) because it's the train's western terminus, but many now skip the city in favor of starting their journey in small El Fuerte, as it's from that point north that the scenery is best. Those who still choose to include the modern city of Los Mochis on their travel plans have more of it to themselves – which is a good thing, considering the place has a nice selection of inns and eateries, and maintains a great balance of urban bustle and friendly energy.

Orientation

The main street through the city, running southwest from Hwy 15D directly into the center of town, changes names from Calz López Mateos to Leyva as it enters the center. Coming from Topolobampo, you will enter the city center on Blvd Castro, another major artery. Some blocks in the center are split by smaller streets (not shown on the Los Mochis map) running parallel to the main streets.

Information

INTERNET ACCESS

Online Café Internet (Obregón; per hr $1; 🕑 9am-9pm Mon-Sat, 10am-3pm Sun) Next to Corintios.

Tito Café Internet (Blvd Castro 337; per hr $1; 🕑 10am-10pm Mon-Sat)

MEDICAL SERVICES

Centro Médico (☎ 812-33-12; Blvd Castro 639)

Hospital de Fátima (☎ 812-74-26; Blvd Jiquilpan 130)

MONEY

Banks are plentiful around the city center.

Bancomer (cnr Leyva & Juárez) Has an ATM.

Servicio de Cambio (Obregón 423)

POST

Post office (Ordóñez btwn Zaragoza & Prieto; 🕑 8am-3pm Mon-Fri, 8am-noon Sat)

TOURIST INFORMATION

Tourist office (☎ 815-10-90; Av Allende at Calle Ordóñez; 🕑 9am-4pm Mon-Fri)

Sights & Activities

Plazuela 27 de Septiembre is a pleasant, quiet and shady plaza with a classic gazebo. It's

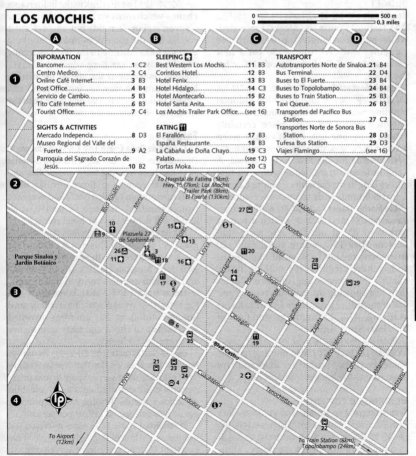

LOS MOCHIS

0 ─────── 500 m
0 ─────── 0.3 miles

INFORMATION	
Bancomer	1 C2
Centro Medico	2 C4
Online Café Internet	3 B3
Post Office	4 B4
Servicio de Cambio	5 B3
Tito Café Internet	6 B3
Tourist Office	7 C4

SIGHTS & ACTIVITIES	
Mercado Indepencia	8 D3
Museo Regional del Valle del Fuerte	9 A2
Parroquia del Sagrado Corazón de Jesús	10 B2

SLEEPING 🏠	
Best Western Los Mochis	11 B3
Corintios Hotel	12 B3
Hotel Fenix	13 B3
Hotel Hidalgo	14 C3
Hotel Montecarlo	15 B2
Hotel Santa Anita	16 B3
Los Mochis Trailer Park Office	(see 16)

EATING 🍴	
El Farallón	17 B3
España Restaurante	18 B3
La Cabaña de Doña Chayo	19 C3
Palatio	(see 12)
Tortas Moka	20 C3

TRANSPORT	
Autotransportes Norte de Sinaloa	21 B4
Bus Terminal	22 D4
Buses to El Fuerte	23 B4
Buses to Topolobampo	24 B4
Buses to Train Station	25 B3
Taxi Queue	26 B3
Transportes del Pacifico Bus Station	27 C2
Transportes Norte de Sonora Bus Station	28 D3
Tufesa Bus Station	29 D3
Viajes Flamingo	(see 16)

To Hospital de Fátima (5km);
Hwy 15 (7km); Los Mochis
Trailer Park (8km);
El Fuerte (130km)

Parque Sinaloa y
Jardín Botánico

To Airport
(12km)

To Train Station (8km);
Topolobampo (24km)

in front of the **Parroquia del Sagrado Corazón de Jesús** (cnr Obregón & Mina), a church with a brilliant white facade and a graceful tower. There is a small museum, the **Museo Regional del Valle del Fuerte** (cnr Blvd Rosales & Obregón; admission $0.50, free Sun; 9am-1pm & 4-7pm Tue-Sat, 10am-1pm Sun), which has somewhat static exhibits (Spanish language only) on the history and culture of northwest Mexico, with more interesting rotating exhibits by local and international artists. The **Mercado Independencia** (Av Independencia), between Degollado and Zapata is an energetic marketplace where vendors hawk everything from cowboy hats to fresh papayas.

Sleeping

BUDGET

Hotel Fenix (812-26-23; Flores 365 Sur; s/d $27/32;) Half of Fenix is nicely renovated, while half is achingly scruffy, with old carpeting and dark rooms. So get a new room and you'll find it's a good choice for the price.

Hotel Montecarlo (812-18-18; Flores 322 Sur; s/d $27/33; P) A cheerful blue colonial building, with basic rooms around a sunny enclosed courtyard, this place certainly evokes a bygone era. But it's quite worn around the edges, unfortunately, making it best suitable for the low-budget crowd. A good little restaurant, along with a lot that allows long-term parking (if you're Copper Canyon bound) adds to its convenience.

Los Mochis Trailer Park (812-68-17; Calz López Mateos; camp/RV sites $15/20; P) Pitch a tent or park your RV at this five-acre park, 1km west of Hwy 15D, where you'll find 120 spaces with full hookups, an all-night guard and laundry facilities. It's nothing fancy, but it's the cheapest gig in town. Rather than just showing up, you can reserve and pay at the trailer park office (812-00-21) at Hidalgo 419C Pte on the ground floor of the Hotel Santa Anita.

Hotel Hidalgo (818-34-53; Hidalgo 260 Pte; r with fan $17, s/d $22/25; P) Also nothing to write home about, the Hidalgo has small and very basic rooms for budget travelers only.

MIDRANGE & TOP END

Best Western Los Mochis (816-30-30; www.bestwestern.com; Obregón 691 Pte; r/ste $110/198; P) New in 2004, this all-amenity chain hotel rises six storeys along

the southern side of the plaza. The very clean, new rooms are tastefully decorated with modern artwork, plus they have coffeemakers and firm beds. Suites have microwaves and two – count 'em – TVs. The lower floors of the hotel are completely nonsmoking, and an on-site restaurant serves three meals a day.

Corintios Hotel (818-22-24, 800-690-30-00; Obregón 580 Pte; s/d $62/70, ste $77-107; P) With its airy courtyard and somewhat dark but cozy rooms (and nicely tiled bathtubs), the Corintios is big on charm. The staff members are friendly, and the hotel's restaurant is good and popular with locals.

Hotel Santa Anita (818-70-46; www.santaanitahotel.com; Leyva at Hidalgo; s/d/ste $115/135/145; P) The first link in the Balderrama chain – which owns six hotels in the Copper Canyon region – has tidy but unspectacular rooms. But the place does make everything easy for folks heading to the train by letting you leave your car here while you travel, making reservations for you at their other hotels along the way, arranging tours and guides in the canyon, and driving you to the train station early in the morning.

Eating

La Cabaña de Doña Chayo (818-54-98; Obregón 99 Pte; mains from $2; 9am-1am) This down-home spot has been serving tasty quesadillas and handmade corn, and flour tortillas filled with *carne asada* (grilled beef) and *machaca* (spiced shredded dried beef) since 1963. Call and it will deliver to your hotel room.

Palatio (818-22-24; Corintios Hotel, Obregón 580 Pte; mains $3-8; 7am-11pm) This spot is a magnet for locals who appreciate the hearty breakfasts, well-done Mexican classics, friendly service and delicious coffee (a rarity in these parts).

Tortas Moka (812-39-41; Independencia 216A Pte; tortas $1-3; noon-9pm) This small and hoppin' storefront has counters crowded with teens and cheap and tasty sandwiches on home-baked bread.

España Restaurante (812-22-21; Obregón 525 Pte; mains from $7-16; 7am-11pm Mon-Sat, 7am-7pm Sun) This restaurant serves Spanish and international cuisine, including a good selection of seafood dishes. Try the house specialty, *paella a la valenciana* ($9.50 per person).

El Farallón (812-12-73; Flores at Obregón; seafood dinners $7-11, sushi $5-7; noon-11pm) This excellent seafood restaurant serves creative sushi, in addition to Mexican favorites, and it has a liquor cart that comes right to your table.

Getting There & Away

AIR
The Los Mochis airport is about 12km southwest of the city. Daily direct flights (all with connections to other cities) are offered by **Aeroméxico/Aerolitoral** (☎ 815-25-70; at the airport) to Chihuahua, Hermosillo, La Paz, Los Cabos and Mazatlán. **Aero California** (☎ 818-16-16; at the airport) flies to Ciudad Obregón, Culiacán, Guadalajara, Hermosillo, La Paz, Mexico City and Tijuana.

BOAT
Ferries go from nearby Topolobampo to La Paz, Baja California Sur; they leave at 11pm daily. Tickets are sold by **Baja Ferries** (www.bajaferries.com.mx) at the ferry terminal in Topolobampo (right). In Los Mochis, **Viajes Flamingo** (☎ 815-61-20; Leyva 121 Sur) sells tickets up to a month in advance.

BUS
Los Mochis has several major bus lines offering hourly buses heading north and south, 24 hours a day. Elite, Futura, Turistar, TAP and Transportes Chihuahuenses (all 1st-class) share a large **bus terminal** (☎ 815-00-62; cnr Blvd Castro & Constitución) several blocks east of the center. Other 1st-class bus lines have their own terminals, such as **Transportes Norte de Sonora** (☎ 812-03-41; Degollado at Juárez) and **Transportes del Pacífico** (☎ 812-57-49; Morelos btwn Zaragoza & Leyva); all serve the same destinations. **Tufesa** (☎ 818-22-22), on Zapata between Juárez and Merlos, goes north to Nogales and south to Culiacán on a limited schedule. **Autotransportes Norte de Sinaloa** (☎ 818-03-57), at Zaragoza and Ordoñez, has 2nd-class buses to Culiacán and Mazatlán.

More destinations (with 1st-class fares) are given below:

Destination	Price	Duration
El Fuerte	$6	2hr
Guadalajara	$42-46	13hr
Guaymas	$13-16	5hr
Hermosillo	$18-24	7hr
Mazatlán	$25-29	6hr
Nogales	$31-37	11hr
Topolobampo	$2	45min

TRAIN
The train station is 8km east of the center on Serrano. The ticket window is open from 5am to 7am daily for the morning's departures toward the Copper Canyon and Chihuahua. Tickets are also sold inside the **office** (☎ 824-11-51; ☙ 9am-5:30pm Mon-Fri, 9am-12:30pm Sat, 9-11:30am Sun).

You can buy *primera express* (1st-class) tickets up to one week in advance of travel. Tickets for *clase económica* (economy-class) trains are sold an hour before the train departs, or the day before. You can also purchase tickets (service fees apply) for either class one day in advance through **Hotel Santa Anita** (☎ 818-70-46; www.santaanita hotel.com; Leyva at Hidalgo).

The *primera express* train leaves Los Mochis at 6am; *clase económica* at 7am. See the boxed text, p338, for fares and schedules.

Getting Around
Nearly everything of interest to travelers in Los Mochis is within walking distance of the city center. Taxis queue up on Obregón, right in front of the Best Western. A taxi to the airport costs approximately $12. One dependable provider is **EcoTaxi** (☎ 817-11-05).

'Estación' buses to the train station ($0.50, 20 minutes) depart every five minutes between 5:30am and 8:30pm from Blvd Castro, between Zaragoza and Prieta. You can take the bus to the station for the *clase económica* train, which departs at 7am, but for the 6am *primera express* departure it is probably safer to fork out $10 for a taxi. If arriving in Los Mochis by train, you can catch a group taxi to the city center for $5.

TOPOLOBAMPO
☎ 668 / pop 7580
Topolobampo, 24km southwest of Los Mochis, used to be the terminus for the Copper Canyon railway train, providing folks who rode the entire way from Chihuahua's desertscape with a lovely glimpse of the sea at the end. Now that the train goes no further than Los Mochis, the main importer of visitors here is the ferry that goes between the mainland and La Paz, in Baja. Locals also love to spend afternoons at the beach here, to soak up some sun and enjoy a fresh-seafood dinner. A quick visit provides a nice break from the bustle of

nearby Los Mochis, but don't expect to be wowed, as the scene is more rough-and-tumble former port than seaside paradise.

For lodging, the only game in town is the **Hotel Marina** (☎ 862-01-00; Albert K Owen 33 Pte; r $35), a clean and comfortable inn with a large pool and restaurant. It's easy to find; just follow the signs to the town center.

A 20-minute bus ride from Topolobampo is **Playa El Maviri**, a popular beach with plenty of seafood restaurants in which to sample some *pescado zarandeado* (charcoal-grilled fish wrapped in foil). On the way to Playa El Maviri, you pass the **Cueva de los Murciélagos** (Cave of Bats); you cannot enter this protected area, but it's beautiful to see the bats emerging at sunset and returning at sunrise.

Inexpensive *lanchas* (small motorized boats) will take you from either Topolobampo or Playa El Maviri to some beautiful natural spots, which attract large populations of the animals for which they are named. **Isla de Pájaros** is home to hundreds of birds, and **Santuario de Delfines** is a dolphin sanctuary. Other spots include **Playa Las Copas**, **Isla Santa María** (with dunes where you can camp), and **Isla El Farallón**, where you'll find seals and sea lions.

To make the five-hour excursion over to Baja, you can buy same-day tickets from **Baja Ferries** (☎ 862-10-03; www.bajaferries .com; Topolobampo ferry terminal, Cerro de las Gallinas s/n; ☺ 9am-10pm Sun-Fri). Seats are $65 for adults and $32 for children. Passenger ferries leave at 11pm daily, arriving in La Paz at 4am. Returning ferries leave La Paz at 3pm, arriving in Topolobampo at 9pm the same night. See p298 for vehicle fares.

BARRANCA DEL COBRE (COPPER CANYON)

The star attraction in northwest Mexico is certainly the Barranca del Cobre (Copper Canyon), a series of more than 20 spectacular canyons, which altogether comprise a region that's four times larger than the Grand Canyon in Arizona, and in several parts much deeper. Curiously, even some of the most traveled folks have never heard of the Barranca del Cobre, but that is swiftly changing, thanks to both a massive international ad campaign that Mexico unleashed in 2005, and also because of the excited word of mouth about this natural wonder which, though commercialized and tour bus–filled in some spots, has remained wondrously unspoiled. The best part about the region is that you can travel right up, over and through some of the steepest areas on the Ferrocarril Chihuahua al Pacífico (Chihuahua–Pacific Railway, also known as the Copper Canyon Railway), which takes passengers on a breathtaking journey over 655km of impressively laid rails. The train, which travels between Los Mochis at its western terminus and Chihuahua in the Midwest, is the most popular way to see the canyons.

The name Copper Canyon refers specifically to the awe-inspiring Barranca de Urique – which, at an altitude of only 500m (but 1879m deep), is the canyons' deepest point – but also generally applies to the rest of the nearby canyons, which are carved out of the Sierra Tarahumara by at least six different rivers. The Barranca de Urique has a subtropical climate, while the peaks high above are 2300m above sea level, and home to conifers and evergreens. The entire region is also home to one of Mexico's largest groups of indigenous people, the Tarahumara, also known as the Raramuri (see the boxed text, p342).

Though many people simply ride the train all the way through and then stop overnight before returning, the best way to truly experience the Barranca del Cobre region is to make a few stops along the way – and there are plenty of excellent places to choose from. Creel (p344), approximately eight hours from Los Mochis, is where most people (especially backpackers) choose to break the journey, as it's near plenty of good spots for exploring, and is a town full of traveler amenities – from affordable inns to experienced travel guides. Overnight stays are also possible at Cerocahui, Urique, Posada Barrancas and Divisadero, allowing you 24 hours before the train passes by again – time enough to get a closer look and explore the canyons.

Many travelers prefer to visit the area in spring or autumn, when the temperatures are not too hot at the bottom of the canyon (as in summer), or too cold at the top (as in winter). A particularly good time to

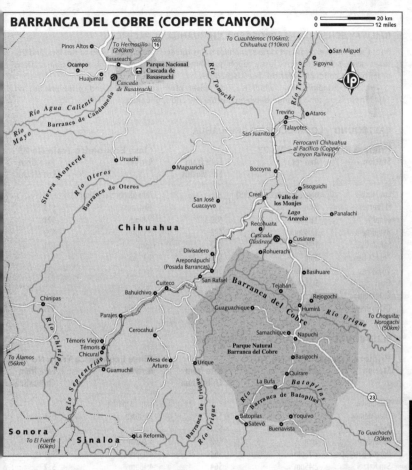

BARRANCA DEL COBRE (COPPER CANYON)

come is late September and October (after the summer rains), when the vegetation is still green. Things dry up from February to June, but you can still glimpse some wildflowers.

FERROCARRIL CHIHUAHUA AL PACÍFICO (COPPER CANYON RAILWAY)

One of the world's most scenic rail journeys, the Ferrocarril Chihuahua al Pacífico is also a considerable feat of engineering: it has 36 bridges and 87 tunnels along its 655km of railway line, and connects the mountainous, arid interior of northern Mexico with a town just 24km shy of the Pacific coast. The line, which was opened in 1961 after many decades of building, is now the major link between Chihuahua and the coast, and is used heavily not only by passengers but also for freight. The beauty of the landscape it traverses – sweeping mountain vistas, sheer canyon walls, sparkling lakes and fields of flowers, most of it free of humans and development of any kind – has made it one of Mexico's prime tourist excursions.

The Ferrocarril Chihuahua al Pacífico (CHEPE, pronounced *che*-pe) operates two trains: the 1st-class *primera express*, which costs twice as much but makes fewer stops and has a restaurant, bar and reclining seats; and the cheaper and slower *clase económica*, which has food provided by vendors as well as a snack bar. Cars on both trains have air-conditioning and

RAILWAY SCHEDULE – FERROCARRIL CHIHUAHUA AL PACÍFICO

Both the *primera express* and *clase económica* trains run every day. Trains tend to run late, and the times given below comprise just a rough guideline. Check with your hotel, at the train stations or with train conductors for the latest schedules.

The *clase económica* train, which is much slower, often arrives at the end of the line around 1am. There is no time change between Los Mochis and Chihuahua.

EASTBOUND – LOS MOCHIS TO CHIHUAHUA

Primera Express Train No 73			Clase Económica Train No 75	
Station	Arrives	Fare from Los Mochis	Arrives	Fare from Los Mochis
Los Mochis	6am (departs Los Mochis)	-	7am (departs Los Mochis)	-
El Fuerte	9am	$25	10:45am	$13
Témoris	11:30am	$39	1:40pm	$21
Bahuichivo	12:40pm	$48	2:15pm	$28
San Rafael	1:35pm	$52	3pm	$31
Posada Barrancas	2pm	$60	3:35pm	$33
Divisadero	2:10pm	$63	4pm	$34
Creel	3:35pm	$69	5pm	$36
Cuauhtémoc	7pm	$85	9:10pm	$49
Chihuahua	8:15pm	$120	midnight	$63

WESTBOUND – CHIHUAHUA TO LOS MOCHIS

Primera Express Train No 74			Clase Económica Train No 76	
Station	Arrives	Fare from Chihuahua	Arrives	Fare from Chihuahua
Chihuahua	6am (departs)	-	7am (departs)	-
Cuauhtémoc	9:30am	$25	10:30am	$13
Creel	12:45am	$52	2pm	$26
Divisadero	2pm	$62	3:30pm	$31
Posada Barrancas	2:15pm	$63	4:05pm	$31
San Rafael	2:45pm	$64	4:15pm	$32
Bahuichivo	3:45pm	$70	5:35pm	$34
Témoris	4:45pm	$77	6:35pm	$38
El Fuerte	7:30pm	$100	9:42pm	$49
Los Mochis	9:05pm	$120	11:25pm	$63

heating. It takes at least 14 hours to make the one-way trip on the *primera express,* and at least two hours longer on the *clase económica,* which stops frequently along the way.

If you're heading toward Los Mochis from Chihuahua, consider taking the *primera express,* as the *clase económica* runs later and is often behind schedule anyway, and passes much of the best scenery

(between Creel and El Fuerte) after dark, especially in winter when the sun sets earlier. Heading in the other direction, you should be able to see the best views on either train, unless the *clase económica* is excessively delayed.

The majority of the good views are on the right side of the carriage heading inland (east), while the left side is best for trips going to the coast (west); if you've been issued an advanced ticket that's not on the side you were hoping for, just ask the conductor to switch you, and they're likely to happily comply. Wherever your seat, it's fun to congregate in the vestibules between cars, where the windows open and you can take unobstructed photos and feel the fresh mountain air whoosh past your face.

Between Los Mochis and El Fuerte, the train passes through flat, gray farmland. Shortly after, it begins to climb through fog-shrouded hills speckled with dark pillars of cacti. It passes over the long Río Fuerte bridge and through the first of 87 tunnels about three hours after leaving Los Mochis. The train cuts through small canyons and hugs the sides of cliffs as it climbs higher and higher through the mountains of the Sierra Tarahumara until the highlight: when the train stops at Divisadero and, after making your way through hordes of vendors, you get your first and only glimpse of the actual Barranca del Cobre.

Note that if you're traveling only between Creel and Chihuahua, you may prefer to take the bus, as it's quicker and more convenient, schedule-wise.

Tickets

Primera express tickets can be purchased up to one week in advance, while tickets for *clase económica* trains can only be purchased one day in advance. You can usually be pretty sure of getting a ticket a day or two before your departure, though you should allow longer than this for travel during *Semana Santa*, July or August, or at Christmas.1

For a same-day *primera express* ticket, it's prudent to go to the ticket office by 5am, if you're at **Los Mochis station** (☎ 668-824-11-51; ticket window ✆ 5-7am & 9-5:30pm Mon-Fri, 5-7am & 9am-12:30pm Sat, 5-7am & 9-11:30am Sun) or **Chihuahua station** (☎ 614-439-72-12; ticket window ✆ 5-7am & 9am-6pm Mon, Wed & Fri, 5-6am & 9am-6pm Tue & Thu, 5-6am & 9am-noon Sat & Sun). It is usually possible to just show up at the other stations, about an hour early, and purchase same-day tickets. Tickets also can be bought on the train, but you run the risk that they might be sold out by then. Alternatively, any of the many **Balderrama Hotels** (☎ 668-712-16-23, www.mexicoscopper

canyon.com), which run **Viajes Flamingo** (☎ 668-815-61-20; Leyva 121 Sur, Los Mochis) travel agency, can assist you in making reservations, as long as you're willing to pay a small percentage fee.

Barranca del Cobre via the Orient Express

If you want to travel the rails in true luxury, the **American Orient Express** (www.americanorientexpress.info/copper_canyon.html), which traverses North America with varied itineraries, has added a Copper Canyon and Colonial Mexico trip to its offerings. Starting in El Paso, Texas, the nine-day journey aboard the opulent vintage Pullman sleeper cars makes stops in Chihuahua, Creel, Divisadero and Álamos, with prices ranging from $3500 to $5900. Check tour dates and find more information on the website.

EL FUERTE

☎ 698 / pop 11,171 / elevation 180m

El Fuerte is a sleepy and picturesque little town, notable for its colonial ambience, its Spanish architecture and, mostly, for being a good starting or ending point for a trip on the Copper Canyon Railway.

Founded in 1564 by the Spanish conqueror Francisco de Ibarra, El Fuerte – named for its 17th-century fort that Spaniards built to protect settlers from various natives – was an important Spanish settlement throughout the colonial period. For more than three centuries it was a major farming and commercial center, and a trading post on El Camino Real, the Spanish mule trail between Guadalajara and Álamos. In 1824 El Fuerte became the capital of the state of Sinaloa, and remained so for several years.

Today there's not a lot to do in town, although strolling the cobblestone streets and people-watching in the main plaza the night before you board your train makes for a wonderfully peaceful evening.

The Palacio Municipal, plaza, church and Hotel Posada del Hidalgo (p340) are El Fuerte's most notable features. You can visit the **Museo de El Fuerte** (☎ 893-15-01; admission $0.50; ✆ 9am-8pm), a replica of the original fort, at the top of the town's small *mirador* – called Cerro de las Pilas. This is an excellent vantage point of the town, its surrounding area and the wide Río Fuerto, home to the delicious river bass you'll find

NORTHWEST MEXICO

on menus all over town. It's an especially dramatic view at sunset. Fishing excursions and riverboat journeys are run by the local **Villa del Pescador** (☎ 893-01-60, 800-796-54-11; www.villadelpescador.com; daily tours per person from $25, all-inclusive trips from $895), a rustic inn and adventure company.

Sleeping

Though its pickings are slimmer than those of the colonial town of Álamos, El Fuerte does have just enough options for every type of traveler, from backpackers to retirees on bus tours. Most spots will agree to keep an eye on your car – which can be safely parked on the street near the inn – while you're off on your Barranca del Cobre rail journey; just remember to tip the employee with whom you strike a deal.

Hotel La Choza (☎ 893-12-74; Cinco de Mayo 101; r $60-85; P ✕ ✕ ✕) This new spot is also the best, as its rooms actually have style: brick domed ceilings (on the top floors), colorful tile work, moody lighting, brightly sponge-painted walls and cool stone floors. Showers are huge, beds are firm and the air-cons are quiet yet powerful. An on-site restaurant (see right) and private parking lot are pluses; if not for the depressingly caged peacock on the property, La Choza would be flawless.

El Fuerte (☎ 893-02-26; Montesclaro 37; r $80-100; ✕) The rooms at this charmer, a 17th-century mansion at the foot of the *mirador,* are set around large, flowering courtyards filled with wonderful antiques. It's a great place to gaze up at the moon before returning to your quarters, which are roomy and comfortable, but awkwardly decorated and lacking the style of the property at large. Still, with an on-site restaurant and particularly friendly staff, El Fuerte is a good pick.

Río Vista Lodge (☎ 893-04-13; Cerro de las Pilas; s/d $37/53; P ✕) This quirky hotel, at the top of the *mirador,* does indeed have a lovely view of the river, especially from its peaceful, high-altitude backyard. The 11 rustic and cozy rooms are individually decorated, and feature varnished stone walls covered with art and curios; bird feeders filled with honey attract scads of adorable hummingbirds (as well as bees) in a small courtyard.

Hotel Posada del Hidalgo (☎ 893-11-92; www.hotelposadadelhidalgo.com; Hidalgo & 5 de Mayo; s/d $110/

120; ✕ ✕) Part of the ubiquitous Balderrama chain, the rooms in this 1890 mansion are comfortable and perfectly attractive, but don't stand up to the charm of the hotel itself (not an unusual problem in these parts). Beware that the place is often filled with large tour groups, and that the restaurant, while good, caters to groups with cheap tricks such as Zorro Happy Hour, which features a live masked man. The hotel can arrange eco-trips in the region, as well as make reservations for you at other Balderrama hotels throughout the Barranca del Cobre.

Casa Pascola (☎ 893-10-68; José Morelos 510; s/d with continental breakfast $20/30) The closest thing El Fuerte has to a hostel, this new 'economy lodging' spot is the best option for budget travelers. It's on a quiet residential street just a few blocks away from the plaza, and has clean and small simple rooms with shared bathrooms, plus a communal kitchen and a lovely communal yard that's home to a friendly dog. Dorm-room beds are coming soon.

Eating

You'll find a line-up of excellent taco stands – as well as storefronts selling delicious *licuados* (fruit-flavored drinks) – near the main market, at around Juárez and 16 de Septiembre, and also on the main road that edges the outskirts of town. Also look for vendors hawking mayo- and chili-smothered corn at the main plaza. But try not to leave town without trying one of the local river specialties: *langostino* (crayfish) and *filete de lobina* (fillet of bass).

Restaurant El Supremo (Rosales at Constitución; mains $3-8; ✕ 8am-9pm) One block off the plaza, this simple, family-run spot offers Mexican classics in a casual atmosphere.

Restaurante Diligencias (☎ 893-12-74; Cinco de Mayo 101; mains $4-10; ✕ 7am-11pm) Whether you're staying at the Hotel La Choza or not, it's worth eating at its on-location restaurant, which serves fresh black bass stuffed, grilled, breaded or smothered in garlic sauce. You'll find lots of tourists in the dining room, but don't let that detract from the topnotch food.

El Mesón del General (☎ 893-02-60; Juárez 202; mains $4-10; ✕ 10am-noon) This bright restaurant – a favorite of El Fuerte locals and a former residence of revolutionary Don Pablo Valenzuela – serves specialties from the river and sea, including several styles of *pulpo* (octopus).

Getting There & Around

If you're driving from the north, follow the small local roads into town only if you have a high-clearance 4WD, as conditions are rough. Any sort of vehicle will do, however, on the small road to El Fuerte that shoots east off of Hwy 15; it looks small on maps, but it is indeed a paved, safe road that's much better than heading to Los Mochis before going north. Just follow the signs to El Fuerte.

In El Fuerte, buses to Los Mochis ($5, two hours) depart every half-hour between 6am and 7pm from the corner of Juárez and 16 de Septiembre.

The train station is a few kilometers east of town. The departure time for the northbound *primera express* is 8am, though it never arrives before 9am, with the *clase económica* trailing about an hour and half to two hours behind. Tickets are sold on board. You can take a taxi to the station for about $8.

CEROCAHUI

☎ 635 / pop 500 / elevation 1600m

Cerocahui, two stops after El Fuerte and one stop past Témoris, is a hub for local travelers and a place where tourists rarely disembark. Témoris, though, is where you'll get your first glimpse of the Tarahumara (see the boxed text, p342), as the women gather here in droves to sell baskets through the vestibules of stopped trains. Cerocahui is about 16km from the Bahuichivo train stop; make the trip and you'll find a picturesque village in a valley, with apple and peach orchards and fir and madrone trees.

The town's pretty yellow-domed church, San Francisco Javier de Cerocahui, was founded in 1680 by the Jesuit Padre Juan María de Salvatierra. Today, Cerocahui is an *ejido* (communal landholding) dedicated to forestry. It boasts a few good lodging options, an orphanage for Tarahumara children, a peaceful atmosphere and, best of all, proximity to the surrounding countryside, which is excellent for bird-watching; over 168 species of birds have been spotted here. Hikers will enjoy the gentle hills and interesting limestone outcroppings, and can do a memorable 8km round-trip hike to Cerocahui Falls. The trek, which goes uphill for much of

the way, starts out along the river and winds up at the cascade, in a spot called Huicohi (place of many trees) by Tarahumarans. You can also have a guide set you up to make the trip on horseback.

Any of the hotels here can arrange trips into the canyon, as well as pick you up at the train station for the 40-minute drive into town.

Sleeping & Eating

Hotel Paraíso del Oso (in Chihuahua ☎ 614-421-33-72, in the US ☎ 800-844-3107; www.mexicohorse.com; s/d incl meals $110/165, campsite/dm $7/12) Named after a nearby rock formation resembling the Yogi Bear cartoon, Paraíso del Oso occupies a peaceful and picturesque spot just north of Cerocahui village. The down-to-earth scene here is one that emphasizes eco-tourism and cultural exchange; vegetarian meals are available, as are riverside camp sites and eight dorm beds. The management can also arrange horseback or hiking trips throughout the surrounding area.

Margarita's Cerocahui Wilderness Lodge (☎ 456-02-45; http://casamargaritas.tripod.com; s/d incl all meals $150/190) Perched on a cliff about 25 minutes from town, this rustic lodge offers spectacular views, along with basic rooms that have some luxury touches – bright paint jobs, claw-foot tubs, kerosene lamps and colorful tile detailing. It's one of four Margarita hotels in the region, including one in Batopilas and two popular spots in Creel.

Hotel Misión (in Los Mochis ☎ 668-818-70-46; www.hotelmision.com; s/d incl all meals $168/240) Yet another link in the Balderrama chain of Barranca del Cobra hotels, this former hacienda has rustic rooms with fireplaces, a bar, a restaurant, gardens and a small vineyard. It's the oldest and best-known hotel in Cerocahui, and is therefore popular with tour groups.

For the following two basic options, contact the town **caseta** (☎ 456-06-19):

Hotel Raramuri (s/d $15/20) This small hotel on the far side of the church is clean, and is pretty popular with backpackers, but don't expect hot water.

Hotel Plaza (s/d $17/25) Another basic budget place to rest your head, with 11 tidy, comfortable rooms.

Getting There & Away

All the hotels except Raramuri and the Hotel Plaza will pick you up at the Bahuichivo train station, and you can always catch a ride with one of the other hotels' buses, or pick up a lift by thumb. The daily minibus from Bahuichivo to Urique may drop you off in Cerocahui if it's not too full (see below).

URIQUE

☎ 635 / elevation 550m

This village, at the bottom of the impressive Barranca de Urique, is also accessed from the Bahuichivo train stop, and is a good base for all kinds of canyon hikes lasting anywhere from one to several days. The two- to three-day hike between Batopilas and Urique is a popular trek.

A minibus heads down to Urique from Bahuichivo train station once a day after the last train passes the station (around 5pm). The jarring ride ($10, three hours) makes a breathtaking descent into the Barranca de Urique, the deepest of the canyons. It departs for the return trip at around 8am, so you may want to plan on staying for two nights. Alternatively, you may be able to arrange transportation with your hotel in Urique. Hotels in Cerocahui can also arrange for guided trips down into this deep canyon town (see p341). For basic supplies, from toothpaste to batteries, head to the general store, the 1909 La Central.

Urique has only a few accommodations choices, but all will also feed you. **Hotel Estrella del Río** (☎ 456-60-03; r $37) has spacious, bright rooms with electric fans, plenty of hot water and a privileged view of the Río Urique. Inquire about rooms at Restaurant Plaza, across from the plaza. **Hotel Cañón de Urique** (☎ 456-60-24; Principal s/n; s/d $11/16), a favorite with backpackers, is extremely basic but provides a good value. Ask about rooms at Restaurante Gran Cañón de Urique, across the street, where you can also get simple meals all day long. **Hotel Barrancas de Urique** (☎ 456-60-76; Principal 201; r $34) is a tidy establishment, on the main road at the edge of the river. It has basic rooms with fans and TV, plus a small restaurant.

THE TARAHUMARA

At least 50,000 indigenous Tarahumara ('Rarámuri' in their own language) live in the Sierra Tarahumara's numerous canyons, including the Barranca del Cobre. You will see them – mostly women, dressed in colorful skirts and blouses, peddling beautiful hand-woven baskets and carrying infants on their backs – as you travel deeper into this region. The women are known for their bright apparel, while most men wear Western jeans and shirts (except in more remote areas, where you'll still see men in loincloths); both men and women wear sandals hewn from tire-tread and strips of leather.

'Rarámuri' means 'those who run fast' – an appropriate name for a people who are most famous for running long distances swiftly. Traditionally, the Tarahumara hunted by chasing down and exhausting deer, then driving the animals over cliffs to be impaled on wooden sticks strategically placed at the bottom of the canyon. Today, they run grueling footraces of at least 160km through rough canyons, all while kicking a small wooden ball ahead of them (endorsement offers from Nike shouldn't be far off).

Another tradition is that of the *tesquinada*, a raucous social gathering in which Tarahumarans consume copious amounts of *tesquino*, a potent alcoholic beverage made from fermented corn.

Though many are determined to remain isolated within this formidable topography, and do manage to retain many traditions (such as residing in cave dwellings), it will be clear the very first time you see a bargain-happy tourist trying to save 2¢ on a basket that the Tarahumaran way of life is under serious threat. Between the rapid loss of their language and severe degradation of their environment – by logging, mining, drug cultivation and tourist-based development – the line between Tarahumarans and other Mexicans becomes thinner every day. Because of that, their overwhelming poverty (more than 40% have no income) becomes more and more of an issue. Poor health is also problematic; there is a high infant mortality rate and high teenage pregnancy rate among Tarahumarans (it is not uncommon for girls to be taken out of school and married by the age of 14), with some of the only relief coming from Catholic missionaries – who have managed to make improvements without wiping out the Tarahumaran tradition of worshiping ancestral gods.

POSADA BARRANCAS (AREPONÁPUCHI)

☎ 635 / elevation 2220m

About 5km southwest of Divisadero (see right), Posada Barrancas station is next to Areponápuchi, the only village on the train line that is right on the rim of the canyon. Often referred to as Arepo, this village – made up of just a couple of dozen houses, a tiny church and a handful of inns – has magnificent views of the canyon, and is a good point for going into the canyon by foot, car or horseback. Most of the hotels will organize any kind of canyon trip you would like, be it a hike to the rim or a horseback ride down into the deep village Wakajípare, below.

Sleeping & Eating

Hotel Posada Mirador (in Los Mochis ☎ 668-818-70-46, in the US ☎ 800-896-8196; http://mirador.mexicoscopper canyon.com; s/d incl meals $175/250; P) Though it's often overrun with large tour groups, it's worth a splurge to stay here, the jewel in the Balderrama chain's crown – not for the basic tile-floored rooms (with fireplaces that you're not permitted to use), but for the spectacular view from each room's private balcony. Meals, served in a large dining hall with magnificent views, are delicious. Beware of rooms 73 to 78, which are actually in a separate building, otherwise you'll have a steep walk to the dining hall, and a terrace that's set back from the canyon rim and shrouded with foliage, offering a partially blocked vista.

Hotel Posada Barrancas (s/d $79/90) Also run by Balderrama, this hotel is down the hill, right at the train stop. Though rooms have no views, they are a bit more cozy, less expensive, and allow you to have breakfast, with no extra charge, at the Mirador.

Cabañas Díaz (☎ 578-30-08; 1-3-person cabaña with shared/private bathroom $30-60, 3-5-person cabaña with private bathroom $70, large room with 8 bunks $70; meals $6; P) The Díaz family's guest lodge is known for its hospitality, delicious meals and tranquil, relaxing atmosphere. Its various cabins and rooms are basic and cozy, with fireplaces and firm beds, and the family can help arrange custom trips. If no one from the family comes to meet the train, just walk down the main road into the village until you see the sign on the right (about 10 minutes).

Copper Canyon Trailhead Inn (☎ 578-30-07; dm $6, r $27) This family-run spot has several small basic rooms on the trail to the Río Urique, good meals in the home adjacent to the inn, and guide services. To find it, walk from the station to town and turn left at the shop.

Hotel Mansión Tarahumara (in Chihuahua ☎ 614-416-54-44, 800-639-68-45; www.mansiontarahumara.com .mx; s/d incl meals $120/175; P ☎) Near the train station and known as 'El Castillo' because it looks like a medieval stone castle, this full-fledged resort has a variety of cozy, rustic cabins. You'll also find amenities including an indoor pool, steam room, pool tables, bar and restaurant, plus a small private lake. There's a special two-night rate of $205 for a single and $290 for a double.

Karina Barasa-González (per person/cabaña $10/30) Karina rents out rooms in Arepo, just as her mother, Lucy González, used to do. You will find them both selling excellent tacos and *gorditas* at the Divisadero train station; if you get off there, she'll make sure you get a ride to her house.

Cabañas Arepo Barrancas (☎ 578-30-46; r incl breakfast $36) Bargain seekers will find basic, two-bed rooms and a cozy on-site restaurant here, plus various guide services. Call in advance to arrange transportation from the station.

Getting There & Away

See the boxed text on p338 for information on getting to Posada Barrancas by train. Buses between San Rafael and Creel will drop you off in Areponápuchi at the highway entrance (see p348). The bus is much faster and cheaper than the train, but arrange for transportation to the center of town, as there are no taxis.

DIVISADERO

elevation 2240m

Definitely a train stop rather than an actual village, the viewpoint here – about seven hours out of Los Mochis – will be your first and only chance to see into the canyon from the train. Luckily, the train stops for 15 minutes, giving you enough time to jump out, gawk and snap some photos at the rim of the canyon and hop back on. But be prepared to budget your time more carefully, as the place is also a Tarahumaran market, with scads of vendors hawking beautiful handmade baskets, carvings and other crafts, as well as fresh fruit and delicious fare – *gorditas*, tacos and *chiles rellenos* – cooked up in makeshift oil-drum stoves. Gobble them up quickly (or hide them under your shirt), as the conductors won't allow food back onto the train.

If you decide you want to stay longer than 15 minutes, you can check into the **Hotel Divisadero Barrancas** (in Chihuahua ☎ 614-415-11-99; s/d incl meals Jun-Aug $82/121, other times $149/179), right at the train station, which has 52 beautiful rooms with wood-beam ceilings and views of the canyon. The restaurant-bar, with a spectacular view, is open to the public. The hotel will arrange guided tours into the canyon, but you can also arrange a good deal yourself with one of the Tarahumara who work the market at the station. If you hire a guide, you must have your own food for the trip; there are two restaurants and some snack stalls, but no stores in Divisadero. Your guide will lead you 1000m down to the Río Urique. Carry enough water for the descent and be prepared for a change in climate from cool – Divisadero is 2240m high – to warm and humid near the river. Autumn is the best time to come; flash floods and suffocatingly high temperatures are a problem in summer.

You can also spend more time here without spending the night if you switch from a *primera express* to *clase económica* train, which is roughly two hours behind. You will need two separate tickets to do this. Alternatively, you could catch a bus, right next to the train station, to Posada Barranca (Areponápuchi), where there are several well-priced lodging options (p343). Buses also run to Creel – a shorter and slightly cheaper way than continuing on the train (see p348). For information on getting to Divisadero by train, see the boxed text, p338.

CREEL

☎ 635 / pop 5100 / elevation 2338m

Creel, a pleasant small town surrounded by pine forests and interesting rock formations, is a total travelers' scene. Hotels and guesthouses line the main drags, tour-guide companies are aplenty, and backpackers can be seen stalking up and down the streets in search of bargains several times a day after the train comes through. Unlike many of the

towns along the railway, Creel has some fun watering holes, perfect for kicking back with other travelers, plus great bargain accommodations and several opportunities for shopping – be it for Tarahumara crafts and Mata Ortiz pottery, or basics like soap or tampons (which are impossible to find in most mountain villages). This is a great base for exploring the rest of the Barranca del Cobre, whether you want to venture down into the canyon village of Batopilas or rent bicycles for a trip to the nearby Lago Arareko.

Its high elevation means Creel can be very cold in winter, even snowy. In summer, the cool air and pine-tree aroma from the town's surrounding forests are a welcome relief from the heat of the tropical coastal lowlands and the deserts of northern Mexico.

Orientation

Creel is a very small town. Most things you need, including many hotels and restaurants, are on Av López Mateos, the town's main street. This leads south from the town plaza, the site of two churches, the post office, the bank and the Artesanías Misión shop. The train station is one block north of the plaza. Across the tracks are a couple more hotels and restaurants, as well as the bus station.

Av Gran Visión is the highway through town; it heads northeast to Chihuahua and southeast to Guachochi, passing Lago Arareko and Cusárare. There is a paved road that runs southwest from Creel through Divisadero and on to San Rafael. Av López Mateos and Av Gran Visión intersect a couple of kilometers south of the center of town.

MAPS

A large map of Creel is posted on the outside wall of **Tarahumara Tours** (☎ 456-01-21), on the main plaza. Maps of the surrounding area, including a series of topographical maps of the canyons, are sold at the Artesanías Misión shop (p348). You can also find copies of both local and area maps for free at 3Amigos Canyon Expeditions (p346).

Information
BOOKSTORES

Artesanías Misión (p348) Here you can purchase various books about the Barranca del Cobre and the Tarahumara, in Spanish and English.

INTERNET ACCESS

CompuCenter (Av López Mateos 33; per hr $2; 🕒 8:30am-9:30pm)

LAUNDRY

Best Western: The Lodge at Creel (Av López Mateos 61; 🕒 9am-6pm Mon-Sat) Laundry open to the public at the Best Western Hotel (see p347).

MEDICAL SERVICES

Clínica Santa Teresa (☎ 456-01-05; 🕒 24hr) Behind Casa Margarita.

MONEY

Banca Serfin (🕒 9am-4pm Mon-Fri) On the plaza. It changes money and has the town's only ATM.

Divisas La Sierra (Av López Mateos 59) Changes US dollars and traveler's checks.

POST

Post office (🕒 9am-3pm Mon-Fri) On the plaza.

TOURIST INFORMATION

Information about local attractions is available from the tour operators, most accommodations, and the Artesanías Misión shop.

There is fierce competition for tour business, so be sure to compare prices.

3Amigos Canyon Expeditions (p346) A great outlet for information; whether or not you decide to pay for tour services, it provides literature about the region and a good map of the town, all for free.

Sights & Activities

The **Casa de las Artesanías del Estado de Chihuahua y Museo** (☎ 456-00-80; admission $2; 🕒 9am-1pm & 3-6pm Tue-Fri, 10am-6pm Sat, 9am-1pm Sun), overlooking the plaza, contains excellent exhibits with texts in English on Tarahumara culture and crafts. You'll see gorgeous woven baskets, traditional clothing, pottery, black-and-white photos and more.

The **Museo de Paleontología** (admission $1; 🕒 9am-8pm, closed Wed), on the smaller plaza, is less impressive. It has a hodgepodge of exhibits on Chihuahuan history, ranging from fossils and rocks to antiques and Mennonite artifacts.

Tours

Most of Creel's hotels offer tours of the surrounding area, with trips to canyons,

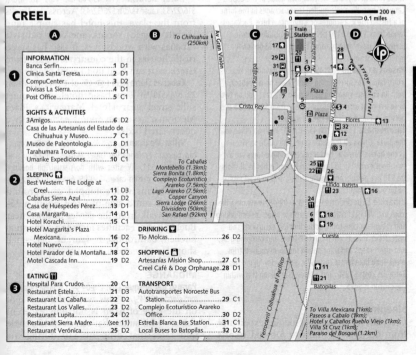

CREEL

Map labels:
To Chihuahua (250km)
Av Gran Visión
Av Raralipa
Train Station
Av Tarahumara
Arroyo del Creel
Cristo Rey
Av Ferrocarril
Villa
Plaza
Av López Mateos
Flores
Plaza
To Cabañas Montebello (1.3km); Sierra Bonita (1.8km); Complejo Ecoturístico Arareko (7.5km); Lago Arareko (7.5km); Copper Canyon Sierra Lodge (26km); Divisadero (50km); San Rafael (92km)
Elfido Batista
Cuesta
Batopilas
Ferrocarril Chihuahua al Pacífico
To Villa Mexicana (1km); Paseos a Cabalo (1km); Hotel y Cabañas Pueblo Viejo (1km); Villa St Cruz (1km); Paraíso del Bosque (1.2km)

rivers, hot springs, waterfalls and other places. Trips range from a seven-hour tour to the bottom of the Barranca de Urique, to an eight-hour excursion to Mennonite settlements in Cuauhtémoc, and overnight excursions to Batopilas, a wonderful canyon village, which descends from an altitude of 2338m at Creel, to 495m, via a winding dirt road. This is also prime riding country, and many of Creel's nearby attractions can be enjoyed from horseback; you can also rent a bicycle and venture out on your own.

All tours require a minimum number of people. The easiest place to get a group together is often at Casa Margarita (right), but any hotel will organize a tour if there are enough people wanting to go – usually four or five – or you could hire your own private guide. Expect to pay around $30 per person, per day – and much more if you are doing a bigger trip that requires a vehicle and driver; to Batopilas, for example, a private driver with an SUV will run you around $250.

3Amigos Canyon Expeditions (☎ 456-05-46; www .the3amigoscanyonexpeditions.com; Av López Mateos 46) These folks help you to 'be your own guide in the Copper Canyon!' by selling self-guided tour packages in the form of a Nissan truck, a scooter or a mountain bike. Packages range from $15 to $100 per day, and include a lunch, maps and travel information. This is a great option for independent souls.

Paseos a Caballo (☎ 456-05-57; www.ridemexico .com) Enjoy the surrounding countryside on horseback, with an English-speaking guide who will take you on two- to seven-hour adventures that range from $12 to $38 per person. It's next to Hotel Pueblo Viejo.

Tarahumara Tours (☎ 456-01-21) With an office on the plaza. Offers all the same tours and guide services as the hotels, often at better prices. Sample tours are a two-hour excursion to Lago Arareko and other local spots for $10 per person, and an eight-hour trip to overlooks at La Bufa and Urique.

Umarike Expediciones (☎ 456-02-48; www.umarike .com.mx; Villa at Cristo Rey) This place offers guided hiking and mountain-bike tours, rock-climbing excursions and instruction. It rents out mountain bikes and camping gear, and offers maps and information for do-it-yourself trips. Week-long bike rental costs $75, a nine-day hiking trip to Batopilas costs $1250, and a three-day hiking trip within the canyon is $425.

Sleeping

Creel offers every kind of lodging experience, from dorm-style bunks to top-end resorts.

A couple of nice new spots round out the offerings in town and, for a truly unique experience, head to the rustic Copper Canyon Sierra Lodge (p349), in nearby Cusárare.

BUDGET

Casa Margarita (☎ 456-00-45; Av López Mateos 11; mattress on fl $5, dm $8, s/d $20/30) With its hawkers, who charge at you with pamphlets when you disembark the train in town, Casa Margarita lures all types to its variety of accommodations – from beds in cramped dorms to nicer private rooms. It's a bustling backpacker scene, where everyone gathers at the table to eat together and swap travel tales, and is also where you can organize many daily tours. It rents out bicycles and has laundry service, and plans to open a juice bar, Internet café and lounge in the near future.

Casa de Huéspedes Pérez (☎ 456-00-47; Flores 257; dm $10) Roomier and more attractive than Margarita's dorms, the Casa has one- to six-person log-walled rooms with wood-stove heating. Also on the premises is a communal kitchen and Café Luly, which serves the ever-elusive good coffee.

Hotel Korachi (☎ 456-00-64; Villa 16; s/d/tr $16/22/33, cabaña s/d/tr $26/32/43) Across the tracks from the plaza, this hotel has simple (and slightly ragged) rooms, and cozy old-style cabañas with woodstoves. It also has seven rustic houses in the countryside, 2km from Creel; each can hold up to eight people.

Cabañas Sierra Azul (☎ 456-01-11; Av López Mateos 29; tr/q $20/25) This basic hotel, on a quiet side street near Hotel Margarita's Plaza Mexicana, has clean rooms each with two queen-sized beds.

Villa Mexicana (☎ 456-06-65; www.vmcopper canyon.com; Prolongación López Mateos s/n; camp sites per person $11, RV sites with no/partial/full hookups $10/15/20, 4-person cabins $50-85, 6-person cabins $75-150; **P**) This well-equipped campground is on the south side of Creel, about a 15-minute walk from the center of town near Pueblo Viejo. Facilities include a communal kitchen, bathrooms, restaurant, bar, small shop, laundry and tours.

MIDRANGE

Paraíso del Bosque (☎ 456-04-44; Carretera Gran Misión; s/d/ste $30/45/75) This wonderful new spot on the edge of town is not only excellent value – with suites that can sleep 10 people and rates that drop by $10 during the low season – it's also got style. Rooms are painted in varying, soothing shades, while furnishings are tasteful and bedspreads are bright and colorful. An on-site restaurant makes it even more convenient.

Villa St Cruz (☎ 456-02-27, 800-570-3277; r/ste/cabaña $40/80/150) Another newcomer, at the edge of town not far from Pueblo Viejo, this squeaky-clean and stylish spot has a variety of options. Its comfortable hotel rooms can sleep four people, while its family-friendly cabañas come stocked with five beds.

Hotel y Cabañas Pueblo Viejo (☎ 456-05-38; s/d incl breakfast $60/70; P) On the edge of town, the family-friendly Pueblo Viejo features several cabins in various sizes and styles, from log cabin to a bank, which make up a kitschy, old-village stage set. There's a large dining room and bar on the property, plus a van that will pick you up at the train station.

Hotel Nuevo (☎ 456-00-22; Villa 121; s/d/cabaña $30/45/75) Across from the train station, the Nuevo offers standard, newly renovated hotel rooms as well as large, log-and-stone cabaña-style rooms. Be sure to say hello to the chatty parrot in the check-in office.

Hotel Margarita's Plaza Mexicana (☎ 456-02-45; Elfido Batista s/n; s/d $38/48; P) If you've outgrown the hostel scene but still want a laid-back bargain, head to this comfortable hotel, run by the same family that runs the Casa Margarita. Rooms, many of which have been recently renovated but all of which are clean and cozy, are set around a charming courtyard. Prices include breakfast and a three-course dinner (though the food is just barely palatable, so it'd be worth it to spring for tacos elsewhere).

Hotel Parador de la Montaña (☎ 456-00-23; Av López Mateos 44; s/tr/q $63/73/83; P) This well-run hotel offers spacious, though spare, rooms with tiled floors, high ceilings and floral bedspreads. There is also a good restaurant and a cozy lounge with a fireplace.

Motel Cascada Inn (☎ 456-02-53; Av López Mateos 49; r $58; P 🐕) The friendly, homey Cascada has a restaurant, a lively bar, a cozy fireplace in its communal lobby and basic rooms each with TV, a tile floor and two double beds.

TOP END

Best Western: The Lodge at Creel (☎ 456-00-71, in the US ☎ 800-528-1234; www.thelodgeatcreel.com; Av López Mateos 61; s & d $100, ste $155; P ✗) The classiest spot in town, designed to look like a hunting

lodge, has well-designed rooms (several in log cabins), each with gas woodstove, two double beds and beautiful wood-beam floors. The honeymoon suite comes with a private Jacuzzi and kitchenette.

Sierra Bonita (☎ 456-06-15; Gran Visión s/n; r/cabañas $64/80; P) A bit removed from the center of town but not lacking in amenities, the Sierra Bonita is a nice, self-contained complex featuring a restaurant, nightclub, bar and large rooms with tile floors and high ceilings. It looks like a white castle and is set atop a dramatic hillside.

Eating

You'll find plenty of restaurants, all pretty similar to one another, on Av López Mateos in the few blocks south of the plaza. Most are open from around 7:30am to 10pm daily.

Hospital Para Crudos (meals $3-6) Also known as Tungar, this place, next to the tracks just south of the train station, specializes in hangover remedies (hence the name) like *menudo* (tripe stew), plus substantial snack foods, including fat burritos.

Restaurant Los Valles (Av López Mateos; meals $2-7) This new place, on the main drag at the corner of Batista, serves excellent *carne asada* and Mexican specialties in generous portions.

Restaurant Sierra Madre (mains $4-15) For more upscale dining, try this festive place at Best Western (left), with stone walls and exposed wood beams, plus good, eclectic food and a full bar. It serves breakfasts, pizza, and a multi-course dinner including soup, salad, main course and dessert.

Restaurant Verónica and Restaurant La Cabaña are popular, serving steak, seafood and Mexican dishes for $4 to $9; Veronica has a good array of vegetarian options. The casual **Restaurant Lupita** (meals $3-5) is popular with locals and serves a delicious breakfast. Homey **Restaurant Estela** (meals $3-5) serves good, economical meals in the same range.

Drinking

As Creel's status as a traveler's mecca continues to grow, its nightlife is starting to pick up. Best Western: The Lodge at Creel (left) has a pool table to help you unwind.

Tío Molcas (Av López Mateos 35) With its wood-heated bar, close tables and good beer options, this is a cozy spot where hip global travelers gather to swap stories.

NORTHWEST MEXICO

Motel Cascada Inn (Av López Mateos) The Cascada has a spacious 2nd-floor bar that keeps late hours for its mix of locals and travelers.

Shopping

Many shops in Creel sell Tarahumara handicrafts, including baskets, colorful dolls, wood carvings, violins and clothing, as well as distinctive Mata Ortiz pottery, all for very reasonable prices.

Artesanías Misión (9:30am-1pm & 3-6pm) On the north side of the plaza, this is a great place to buy handicrafts. All of the store's earnings go to support the Catholic mission hospital, which provides free medical care for the Tarahumara. If you'd rather support individual Tarahumarans directly, then buy straight from the vendors who work the sidewalks.

Creel Café & Dog Orphanage (456-05-58; 9:30am-1pm Mon-Sat) This funky spot next to Casa Margarita has more eclectic offerings; here you'll find a book exchange, camping supplies, dried foods, all sorts of information about Creel and its environs. All proceeds go to feed local children (or any hungry soul) via a daily sidewalk kitchen, and to support a casual street-dog orphanage.

Getting There & Around

BICYCLE

Several places rent out bicycles, and the surrounding countryside has many places accessible by pedal power.

3Amigos Canyon Expeditions (p346) Half/full day $6/11.

Casa Margarita (p346) Full day $8.

Complejo Ecoturístico Arareko (456-01-26; Av López Mateos) Hour/day $2.50/22. See also opposite.

Creel Café & Dog Orphanage (above) Full day $6.

Umarike Expediciones (p346) Half/full day $12/17. Includes map, helmet and tool kit.

BUS

Travel between Creel and Chihuahua, as well as between Creel and Divisadero, may be more convenient via bus than train, as the trips are shorter and the schedules more flexible. The Estrella Blanca bus station, across the tracks from the plaza, has nine daily buses to Chihuahua ($18, 4½ hours), passing through San Juanito ($2.50, 45 minutes), La Junta ($8.50, two hours) and Cuauhtémoc ($12, three hours) on the way. Estrella Blanca also has three daily buses to

San Rafael ($4, 1½ hours) via Divisadero ($4, one hour) and Posada Barrancas (Areponápuchi; $3.50, one hour); they depart Creel daily at 11am, 3pm and 6pm.

Autotransportes Noroeste, just north of Estrella Blanca, is another bus company, with departures for San Rafael ($4.50) at 10:20am, 2:20pm and 6pm, and buses to Chihuahua ($17) at 9am, 11:15am and 3pm.

The local bus to Batopilas ($16, five hours) leaves from outside the Hotel Los Pinos on López Mateos, two blocks south of the plaza, at 7:30am Tuesday, Thursday and Saturday, and at 9:30am Monday, Wednesday and Friday.

CAR & MOTORCYCLE

There's now a paved road all the way from Creel to Divisadero and on to San Rafael. From San Rafael, if you have a sturdy 4WD vehicle, you could go all the way to El Fuerte in the dry season (March to May is the best time) via Bahuichivo, Mesa de Arturo, La Reforma and Choix, crossing the Colosio reservoir in a two-vehicle ferry. Or you could go from San Rafael to Álamos via Bahuichivo, Témoris and Chinipas, crossing the Río Chinipas. Both of these roads are very rough, and have also been the sites of assaults, so travel at your own risk.

TRAIN

Creel's train station is half a block from the main plaza. The westbound *primera express* train departs Creel at about noon, and the *clase económica* at about 1:30pm; the eastbound trains depart at about 3:30pm and 5pm. However, times vary greatly and they are usually late. Check the board inside the train station for the estimated times of arrival that day. See the boxed text, p338, for ticket information.

AROUND CREEL

The area around Creel is rich in natural wonders, offering everything from waterfalls and hot springs to massive speckled boulders and expansive parklands, all of which are only a day's hike, bike ride or drive from town. Local guides offer a variety of guided tours, or you can venture out on your own on a rented bicycle. It's not a good idea to walk into the countryside by yourself, though, as at least one woman has been assaulted while walking alone to Lago Arareko.

Sights & Activities

A popular day trip is to the nearby **Complejo Ecoturístico Arareko**, a Tarahumara *ejido* (communal landholding) that's home to about 400 families who live in caves and small homes among waterfalls, farmlands, deep canyons, hot springs, dramatic rock formations and a 200-sq-km forest of thick pine trees 7.5km from Creel. A lovely lake, **Lago Arareko**, sits on the *ejido* as well.

Just 2km past this area is **Valle de los Monjes**, where vertical rock formations inspired its traditional Tarahumara name, Bisabírachi, meaning the 'Valley of the Erect Penises'. It makes a nice full-day trip on horseback, and takes you past some other animatedly named valleys on the way, including Valle de las Ranas and Valle de los Hongos – 'frogs' and 'mushrooms,' respectively.

The 30m-high **Cascada Cusárare** is a waterfall that's 22km south of Creel, near the Tarahumara village of **Cusárare** (place of eagles). Tour operators offer excursions here, but if you drive to the trailhead yourself from Creel, be sure to pass the first turnoff and wait for the second sign, which brings you to a much more interesting hiking trail. Park at the Copper Canyon Sierra Lodge (right). Also in Cusárare is the **Loyola Museum** (admission $2; ☼ 10am-4:30pm Tue-Sun), dedicated to preserving and displaying its collection of centuries-old paintings that were found wasting away in regional churches and missions.

Though the soothing **Recohuata Aguas Termales** (Recohuata Hot Springs) are only about 35km southwest of Creel, getting there is no easy matter, as the journey, which requires a 1½-hour truck ride, followed by a steep hike to the bottom of Barranca Tararecua, takes a full day with a guide.

Even more dramatic than the waterfall in Cusárare is the **Cascada de Basaseachi**, which at 246m is the highest in Mexico. It's 140km northwest of Creel, and takes a full day to visit, thanks to a bumpy three-hour drive, a two-hour hike to the bottom, three hours to walk back up, and then the return drive. If you're up for the challenge, it's worth it – but keep in mind that, if you'd like to skip the hiking part, the views of the falls are beautiful from up on its rim, too.

For details about bike rides, horseback riding adventures and other treks in the area – such as the backcountry journey to

the 'forgotten canyon' of Wa'Chahuri – 3Amigos Canyon Expeditions (p346) is a great source.

Sleeping & Eating

Once you get out into Creel's natural surroundings for a day trip, you may decide you'd like to spend the night there. The region has several rustic places to choose from – some with campsites, others with cozy bedrooms. Most will feed you too.

Copper Canyon Sierra Lodge (reserve through 3Amigos Canyon Expeditions in Creel, ☎ 635-456-05-46; www.the3amigoscanyonexpeditions.com; r $110) This atmospheric mountain lodge has comfy rooms with beamed ceilings, kerosene lamps (there's no electricity), fluffy white robes, showers with plenty of hot water, and potbelly stoves (one room has a working fireplace). Truly excellent meals – and copious margaritas – are served in a fine old dining room. Just be aware that you won't be completely 'getting away from it all' here, as the lodge, located in a Tarahumaran village, draws groups of women who will set up shop right on your doorstep to hawk beautifully hand-woven pine baskets and other crafts.

Complejo Ecoturístico Arareko (☎ 635-456-01-26; Av López Mateos, Creel) has an office in Creel, where you can reserve a spot at (and arrange for transportation to) one of the *ejido*'s various options. To pitch a tent, head to the campground on the northeast shore of Lago Arareko. It has sites with barbecue pits, picnic areas, water and bathrooms for $1.50 per person. The *ejido* also operates two lodges: **Albergue de Batosárachi** (dm/d $11/21) accommodates 70 people in its three rustic cabins, which contain either bunk beds or individual rooms, plus hot showers and a communal kitchen – you can also arrange to have meals prepared. The more comfortable **Cabaña de Segórachi** (d $25), on the south shore of Lago Arareko, includes the use of a rowboat and holds just 15 people.

BATOPILAS

☎ 649 / pop 1200 / elevation 495m

If you make it down the steep, twisting dirt road to Batopilas, a serene 19th-century silver-mining village 140km south of Creel, you can be satisfied that you have made your way deep into canyon country. The journey is a thrilling ride – from an altitude of 2338m, at Creel, to 495m at Batopilas – with dramatic descents and ascents through several canyons, climates and vegetative zones, ending in a warm little village. On the way you'll pass a dramatic viewpoint, La Bufa, overlooking the town of the same name in a canyon 1750m deep, with a cool river at the bottom.

The biggest activity once you arrive at Batopilas is slowing down and enjoying the stuck-in-time feel of the place – strolling, eating, and chatting with welcoming locals. However, there's plenty of history to explore as well. There are various abandoned mines (bring a flashlight!), plus the nearby ruins of **Hacienda San Miguel**, which housed the Washington DC mayor Alexander Shepherd, who brought technological advances to the mining scene here. One of the most popular excursions is to the **Catedral Perdida** (Lost Cathedral) at Satevó, an elaborate cathedral that was discovered in a remote, uninhabited canyon. It's a long 8km hike along the river, or a 20-minute drive; you can get the key to the church from the house next door . Any hotel can help arrange day trips; the two- to three-day trek to the canyon town of Urique is also a popular journey.

Sleeping

Copper Canyon Riverside Lodge (☎ 456-90-45, in the US 800-776-3942; r $90-120) On the road to the main plaza is this absolute gem – a 19th-century hacienda restored many years ago by American entrepreneur Skip McWilliams. The 15 rooms are all exquisite – high and firm beds, claw-foot bathtubs, stenciled wall paintings, stone floors and carved wooden window shutters – and are set around a series of flowering courtyards. There's a peaceful library and sitting room, too. Reservations can be made through the Real de Minas, or, by calling the Michigan-based sales office.

Real de Minas (☎ 456-90-45; Guerra at Ochoa; r $50) Here you'll find eight brightly decorated rooms around a lovely courtyard with a fountain. A newly built addition, just down the road, has six airy and immaculate rooms with orange doors and a peaceful vibe. Owner Martín Alcaraz-Gastélum, who also co-owns the Riverside Lodge, is a friendly and knowledgeable presence.

La Hacienda Río Batopilas (in Creel ☎ 635-456-02-45; r/tr incl all meals $80/90) The newest spot in town, run by the same folks who own

Casa Margarita in Creel, has pretty rooms decorated with tile and stained-glass windows that overlook the river on the edge of town. An on-site restaurant serves breakfast and dinner, which comes in handy when you consider this place is about a half-hour walk from the center of town.

Hotel Juanita's (☎ 456-90-43; main plaza; s/d $25/35) This clean and basic hotel has rooms decorated with a simple flair, plus a courtyard overlooking the river that's a lovely place to gather in the evening. You'll most likely find Juanita visiting with her neighbors in the plaza, right in front of the hotel's entrance.

Hotel Batopilas (s/d $8/16) The best of the budget-backpacker options is this simple inn run by Florentina DeMachado, on the road to the main plaza. Spare but spotless rooms have firm mattresses, and with a flowering courtyard in the center of it all, it's an unbelievable bargain.

Eating & Drinking

Foraging for good meals is not hard in this tiny town, and eating them is usually an intimate experience, as some 'restaurants' consist of a few tables on the porch of a private home.

Doña Mica (Plaza de la Constitución; meals $3-8) Now run by the late Mica's daughter-in-law, this is an excellent spot for home-cooked Mexican meals; vegetarians are well cared for.

El Puente Colgante (The Hanging Bridge; ☎ 456-90-23; mains $4-8.50) at the far end of the plaza by the bridge over the river, serves a delicious seasoned steak and stuffed trout. Its lively bar is a great place to while away an evening.

Carolina (Plaza de la Constitución; meals $3-8) Across from Mica's is this other rustic spot, with a more seating and delicious breakfasts.

Getting There & Away

There's just one road in and, no matter what mode of transport you choose, getting to and from Batopilas is a bit scary – especially for those with acrophobia. The cheapest trip is on the public bus from Creel, which is usually crowded and takes at least five hours ($16, Monday to Saturday). On Tuesday, Thursday and Saturday the bus from Batopilas goes all the way to Chihuahua ($35, eight hours). You can rent a truck and drive – though it's not recommended as the road is very steep and narrow – join a tour group, or hire a private driver in Creel.

Central North Mexico

Intense desert landscapes are one reason to come here: surreal, magenta mountains of the Sierra Madre Occidental, carpets of rainy-season wildflowers, spectacular thunderstorms, and wide sweeps of cerulean sky make photographers or vista-viewers swoon. The sierras have cave paintings, archaeological ruins and interesting wildlife and birds. History buffs can meander through museums about the revolutionary hero Pancho Villa, or the soft, eroded ruins of Paquimé and Cuarenta Casas – enigmatic remnants of once-flourishing settlements of northern Mexico's indigenous people.

The best part about this region is that it gets so few tourists – Chihuahua sees a trickle of moneyed foreigners passing through to board the deluxe Barranca del Cobre (Copper Canyon) railroad trains, but most of the central north consists of quiet towns that haven't been spruced up for visitors. People here are warm and welcoming.

Come here to enjoy the natural beauty, the quiet villages, and the call of ancient cultures that have long since vanished. Come here to pass through ethereal desertscapes where stark beauty defies description and to see where many important moments of Mexican – and American – history were defined.

Some tourists pass through and wonder what the fuss is all about. For others, the first visit to the Chihuahuan desert becomes the beginning of a whole new journey. Either way, this intense and interesting area is worth a visit.

TOP FIVE

- Staying in the yesteryear-era **Hotel Acosta** (p372) in friendly Hidalgo del Parral
- Shopping for cowboy boots in **Chihuahua** (boxed text, p368), followed by a romantic dinner and live music at **La Casa de los Milagros** (p367)
- Dance until you drop with the friendly cowboys and cowgirls of **Nuevo Casas Grandes** (p360)
- Strolling through Durango's beautiful **Plaza de Armas** (p375)
- Exploring the pre-Hispanic cliffside dwellings at **Cueva Grande** (p363) around mountainous Madera

★ Nuevo Casas Grandes

★ Madera

★ Chihuahua

★ Hidalgo del Parral

Durango ★

CENTRAL NORTH MEXICO

- CHIHUAHUA JANUARY DAILY HIGH: 36°C | 64°F
- CHIHUAHUA JULY DAILY HIGH 34°C | 94°F

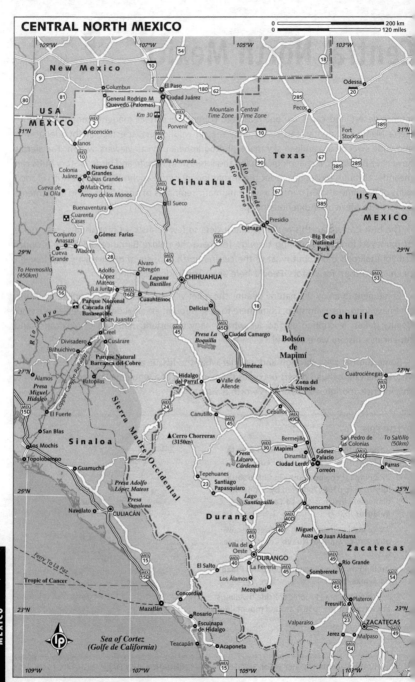

CENTRAL NORTH MEXICO

0 ——————— 200 km
0 ——————— 120 miles

History

his region of Mexico was the subject of ierce battles during the Revolution, giving ise to Pancho Villa's División del Norte. As ou travel through the area, you'll find that 'illa is the most popular hero in these parts. 'ou'll see evidence of early-20th-century nfluence lingering, too – especially at Nuevo Casas Grandes, the site of a no-longer-ctive railway station that has served the Rio irande Company, Sierra Madre Company nd Pacific Railway Company at various mes through history. But the ruins of 'aquimé and Cuarenta Casas show evidence f flourishing settlements of highly sophis-cated peoples long before the Spanish rrived. More recently, the area has become hot spot for Hollywood, with its still-ristine vistas making great backdrops for lms such as John Wayne classics and newer icks like *Fat Man and Little Boy,* starring aul Newman and John Cusack.

Climate

he state of Chihuahua – the main focus f this chapter – is Mexico's largest; and ne Desierto Chihuahuense (Chihuahuan)esert) is North America's largest. That nakes for an awfully huge swath of sandy, rid land (though its western side is broken p by the Sierra Madre Occidental, which orms plenty of fertile valleys). The entire egion is hot and dry, with an average ainfall of less than 102cm and an aver-ge temperature of 28°C. Durango's a bit vetter, with average temperatures going as igh as 28°C in June and 13°C in January. emember that even deserts can be chilly fter dark, and taller mountain peaks will e much, much colder.

Getting There & Around

xcellent bus service makes traveling around nis region easy. Omnibus, Estrella Blanca nd Chihuahuenses companies all have fre-uent services connecting the major cities nd many towns, including Parral, Nuevo Casas Grandes and Madera. When heading nto the region from the US you can cross ne border into Ciudad Juárez on foot (or by axi for about $20 from the El Paso airport), atch a local bus to the major bus depot, nd then continue on from there. Direct bus ourneys – as well as flights – from the US end to be more costly.

CIUDAD JUÁREZ & EL PASO

☎ 656

Ciudad Juárez (population 1.4 million; ele-vation 1145m) and El Paso (population 564,000; elevation 1140m) form two parts of the same whole, and each city has come to depend on the border's constant ebb and flow. El Paso is, despite the University of Texas' El Paso campus (UTEP), pretty quiet, with most stores closing at 5pm and many restaurants at 8pm. Juárez, on the other hand, is the second busiest port of entry on the US–Mexico border. Texas day-trippers come over for bargain shopping or under-age drinking at bustling cantinas and clubs. Most travelers do not linger here, but use the city's excellent bus and road con-nections as a starting point for exploration further south or north.

While high-profile safety concerns like the 'feminicides' (see boxed text, p355) have given the area a bad reputation, crime against tourists is rare. Your wallet is much more likely to disappear if you leave it on top of the phone than by out-right mugging.

History

During the Mexican Revolution, Juárez had a strategic importance beyond its small size. Pancho Villa stormed the town on May 10, 1911, forcing the resignation of the dictator Porfirio Díaz. After the February 1913 coup against legitimately elected President Fran-cisco Madero, Villa sought refuge in El Paso before recrossing the Río Barvo del Norte (Rio Grande) with just eight followers to begin the reconquest of Mexico. Within months, he had recruited and equipped an army of thousands, La División del Norte. In November he conquered Juárez for a se-cond time – this time by loading his troops onto a train, deceiving the defenders into thinking it was one of their own, and steam-ing into the middle of town in a modern version of the Trojan-horse tactic.

After the implementation of the North American Free Trade Agreement (Nafta) in the mid-1990s, industry mushroomed in the city, as US manufacturers took advantage of low-cost labor in Mexico, and markets grew on both sides of the border. Since then, however, the city has lost more than 100,000 jobs, and for the first time since Nafta was introduced, exports to the US dropped in

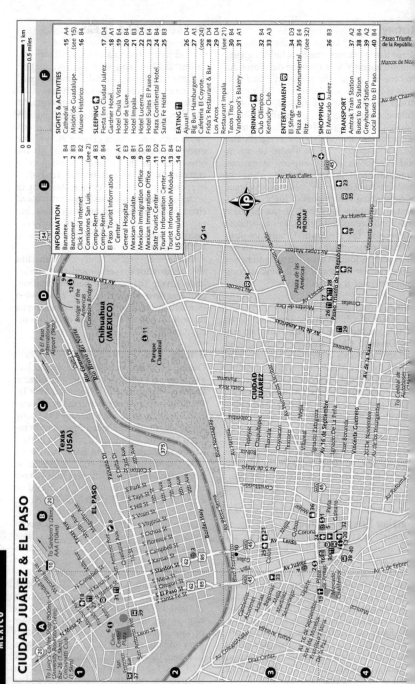

CIUDAD JUÁREZ & EL PASO

INFORMATION	
Banamex	1 B4
Bancomer	2 B3
Click Land Internet	3 B2
Comisiones San Luis	4 B3
Compu-Rent	(see 2)
Compu-Rent	5 B4
El Paso Tourist Information Center	6 A1
General Hospital	7 E3
Mexican Consulate	8 B1
Mexican Immigration Office	9 D1
Mexican Immigration Office	10 B3
State Tourist Center	11 D2
Tourist Information Center	12 D1
Tourist Information Module	13 B4
US Consulate	14 E2

SIGHTS & ACTIVITIES	
Cathedral	15 A4
Misión de Guadalupe	(see 15)
Museo Histórico	16 B4

SLEEPING	
Fiesta Inn Ciudad Juárez	17 D4
Gardner Hotel	18 A1
Hotel Chula Vista	19 E4
Hotel de Luxe	20 B4
Hotel Impala	21 B3
Hotel Lucerna	22 D4
Hotel Suites El Paseo	23 E4
Plaza Continental Hotel	24 B4
Santa Fe Hotel	25 B3

EATING	
Ajuua!	26 D4
Big Bun Hamburgers	27 A1
Cafetería El Coyote	(see 24)
Frida's Restaurant & Bar	28 D4
Los Arcos	29 D4
Restaurant Impala	(see 21)
Tacos Tito's	30 B4
Vanderpool's Bakery	31 A1

DRINKING	
Club Olímpico	32 B4
Kentucky Club	33 A3

ENTERTAINMENT	
El Sfinge	34 D3
Plaza de Toros Monumental	35 E4
Ritz	(see 32)

SHOPPING	
El Mercado Juárez	36 B3

TRANSPORT	
Amtrak Train Station	37 A2
Buses to Bus Station	38 B4
Greyhound Station	39 A2
Local Buses to El Paso	40 B4

002. Juárez is also considered a key transit oint for illicit drugs entering the US. Much f the city's crime is directly drug related; ourists here for legitimate travel will find uárez welcoming and friendly.

rientation

Ciudad Juárez and El Paso sprawl on both ides of the Río Barvo del Norte, but most laces of interest to travelers and locals like are concentrated in the central areas f the two cities, along the streets connected y the international bridges: El Paso's Santa e St, which becomes Av Juárez on the Mexican side; and Stanton St, which becomes v Lerdo. Shooting out to the east of the wer end of Lerdo is Av 16 de Septiembre, hose newer, eastern end is a main strip at caters strictly to tourists who don't ant to mingle with locals; its supply of pscale hotels and nightclubs draws mostly Mexican Texans who have money to burn. orth of here is Av Lincoln, which runs rough Zona Pronaf, located alongside e large Parque Chamizal, and home to ore upscale shopping and a fairly impres- ve fine-arts museum.

You can walk across either the Stanton t–Av Lerdo or Santa Fe St–Av Juárez ridges into Mexico ($0.40), but to return n foot you must use the Av Juárez bridge. y car, you must take Stanton St going south nd Av Juárez going north – the vehicle oll is $2 each way.

About 4km east of the Santa Fe St–Av Juá- ez bridge, the toll-free Bridge of the Americas Cordova Bridge) leads to a bypass road and fwy 45D, which goes south to Chihuahua.

Even further east, the Zaragoza toll bridge entirely avoids both El Paso and Juárez.

Information

BOOKSTORES
University Bookstore (☎ 888-747-5594; www .utepbookstore.com; 500 W University Av; ☻ 8am-7pm Mon-Thurs, 8am-5pm Fri, 10am-5pm Sat, noon-5pm Sun)

EMERGENCY
Ambulance, Fire & Police (☎ 060)

INTERNET ACCESS
Internet cafés are all over Juárez and rates vary between $1.20 and $2 per hour. Rates are much more expensive in the US, and non-wireless access very hard to find.
Click Land Internet Cafe (in the US ☎ 915-351-1782; 714 S Stanton; per hr $2; ☻ 10am-7pm Mon-Sat) The least expensive place to check Internet on the El Paso side, just before the crossing.
Compu-Rent (☎ 612-70-66; Av Juárez 243; per hr $1.50) Glass desks, speedy computers and a hip young vibe. There is another branch on the corner of Av 16 de Septiembre and Corona.

MEDICAL SERVICES
General Hospital (☎ 613-15-71; Paseo Triunfo de la República 2401) Head here for walk-ins.

MONEY
Businesses in Ciudad Juárez generally ac- cept US currency. Banks are clustered along Av 16 de Septiembre, with most open 9am to 5pm Monday to Friday.
Comisiones San Luis (☎ 614-20-33; cnr Juárez & Av 16 de Septiembre) This *casa de cambio* (exchange bureau) changes traveler's checks, as does the one at the bus station.

THE 'FEMINICIDES' OF CIUDAD JUÁREZ

Besides its drug cartels, Ciudad Juárez has another disturbing claim to fame: the brutal murders (dubbed 'feminicides') of more than 350 young women, mainly workers in the city's many *maq- uiladoras* (foreign-owned assembly plants). The first corpse, of a 13-year-old girl, was discovered beaten and strangled in an empty lot back in 1993. It wasn't until years later that the murders received any sort of national or international attention from the media or Mexican government. Recently, thanks to a combination of Juárez-resident Ester Chávez's efforts, *norteño* bands, and international pressure from groups like Amnesty International, the issue has received attention both inside and outside of Mexico.

These murders have not been aimed at tourists, but they have yet to be solved. Urban legends claim the murders are for valuable organs, for rituals, or that they've actually been perpetrated by slow-responding Mexican police. At the time of writing, no sufficient evidence had been found to support any of the theories, but the murders are still happening: about 25 bodies were found in 2005 alone.

POST
Main post office (cnr Lerdo & Peña; ⏰ 8am-5:30pm Mon-Fri, 9am-12:30pm Sat)

TOURIST INFORMATION
El Paso Tourist Information Center El Paso (☎ 915-544-0061; cnr Santa Fe St & Main Dr; ⏰ 8:30am-5pm); Airport (☎ 915-780-4775; ⏰ 9am-6pm)
State Tourist Center (☎ 613-49-39; ⏰ 9am-9pm) This state-run center sits in the Parque Chamizal, and offers information on everything from hotels and transportation to organized tours.
Tourist Information Center (☎ 611-31-74; Av de las Américas 2551; ⏰ 9am-9pm) Bilingual staff; stocks a variety of brochures.
Tourist Information Module (☎ 629-33-40; cnr Villa & Guerrero; ⏰ Mon-Fri, hr erratic) This small brick building that once served as a control point for metals exports is a more conveniently located information module. It offers many of the same materials as the main office.

Dangers & Annoyances

Basic street smarts that might apply anywhere also apply in Ciudad Juárez. Drugs are illegal in Mexico and if you purchase them you risk heavy fines or imprisonment. The main drag along Juárez until it meets Av 16 de Septiembre is fairly well lit and always bustling, but is potentially dangerous later at night. The police presence along the main drag of Av Juárez is visible and law-abiding tourists can expect to be fine until well after dark. After 11pm, however, it's wise to avoid walking alone. Remain vigilant, use taxis to get around after dark if you feel uncomfortable, and don't stray into unlit side streets away from the main drag. Crime is a possibility, but a little caution beforehand will reduce risks to a minimum. Never accept 'free' offers (rides, drinks etc), as they are never free…and can occasionally be dangerous.

Hawkers may seem aggressive and they are certainly an annoyance, but they are generally harmless. Just ignore them or say *'no necesito'* ('I don't need it') and just keep walking if they continue to push for a sale.

Be aware that drinking alcohol in public is illegal, as is crossing into the US without a prescription for any drugs you have that are not over-the-counter.

Sights

Come to Ciudad Juárez to see cultures collide in the crazed neon jungle of Av Juárez.

What better place to people-watch, eat great food, and sip a tequila or two? If that wear thin, consider the following.

The grand **cathedral** (cnr Av 16 de Septiembre & Gue rero; ⏰ 6:30am-10pm), built in 1935 and restore in 1976, is in the central Plaza de Armas. has gorgeous stained-glass windows and a impressive neoclassical facade.

The conical **Museo de Arte e Historia** (☎ 616 74-14; cnr Av Lincoln & Anillo Pronaf; ⏰ 10am-6pm Tue Sun) is an architectural curiosity. Locate within the Zona Pronaf, it houses colorfu eclectic exhibits on Mexico's pre-Hispani civilizations, as well as creations by loca and national artists.

Museo Histórico (☎ 612-4707; cnr Av Juárez & Av 1 de Septiembre; admission free; ⏰ 9am-5pm Tue-Sun), i the city's grand old customs building, ha rather flat and unimpressive exhibits (i Spanish) of local art and regional history.

Sleeping

Be prepared for less than deluxe accommo dations in Juárez, and be aware that man of the cheapest hotels are for hourly rat guests.

BUDGET
Gardner Hotel (☎ 915-532-36-61; epihostl@whc.ne 311 E Franklin; dm $17, plus sheets $2; d with/withou bathroom $45/25; 💀 💻) This El Paso institu tion is within easy walking distance of th border and has both character and charm The elevator (still in use) and the ol switchboard (on display) hearken back to bygone era. The Gardner offers both fou bed dorms and single rooms with cable T\ and the sometimes gruff assistant manage is a wealth of information about history culture, and activities in the area. Room could definitely use some TLC, but locatio and charm make up for it.

Hotel de Luxe (☎ 615-00-82; hoteldeluxe3@hotma .com; Av Lerdo Sur 300; s/d $27/32; 💀) Not exactl 'deluxe,' but this budget option is nicely lo cated and offers access to nightclubs, Lerd and Juárez.

MIDRANGE
Hotel Suites El Paseo (☎ 611-50-00; www.mexguid .net/hpaseo; Paseo Triunfo de la República 4850; s/d/ $56/56/62; 🅿 💀 💻 🔁) A steal, this is a top end hotel with a midrange price that include all the pizzazz of a much more expensiv stay: crystal-clear pool, clean rooms, fre

Internet in the lobby, parking, and details such as origami-folded tissues and kitchenettes.

Hotel Impala (☎ 615-04-31; www.hotel-impala.com /index1.html; Av Lerdo Nte 670; s/d $33/37) Right over the border near the Stanton St bridge is this old standby, with basic, clean rooms and firm beds. It has a restaurant (see right) and a jolly, plant-filled lobby.

Hotel Chula Vista (☎ 617-12-07; Paseo Triunfo de la República 3555; s/d $32/42; P ⍾ ⌨ ⍟) A very solid deal that includes a restaurant, a bar and spacious comfortable rooms, each with two double beds and a color TV. Smaller single rooms are in an older wing by the highway.

Plaza Continental Hotel (☎ 615-00-84; hotelcon@ avantel.net; Av Lerdo Sur 112; s & d/tr $42/45; ⍟) Decent rooms are carpeted and clean; a nice lobby with an ornate chandelier, plus a funky all-night diner, make this a step up.

Santa Fe Hotel (☎ 615-15-58; www.hotel-santafe -juarez.com; Av Lerdo Nte 675; r $34; P ⍟) This hotel is cheery and spotlessly clean. The rooms have cable TV, fans, and tiled floors rather than carpeting.

TOP END

Fiesta Inn Ciudad Juárez (☎ 686-07-00; Paseo Triunfo de la República 3451; r $95; P ⍻ ⍾ ⌨ ⍟) Spiffy, business-class rooms – not to mention the satellite TV, large pool and restaurant-lounge – are more than adequate, particularly for those seeking something less quirky than the cheaper options. Their lobby Internet is available for public use for a pricey $5 per hour.

Hotel Lucerna (☎ 629-99-00; www.lucerna.com.mx; Paseo Triunfo de la República 3976; r Mon-Fri $84, Sat & Sun $72; P ⍻ ⍾ ⌨ ⍟) Catering to Juárez' business-class travelers – hence the cheaper rates on weekends – this luxurious option is a nice escape. The poolside restaurant, palm-studded gardens and classy lounge areas make the seediness of Av Juárez seem far, far away.

Eating

There are lots of cheap eats on both sides of the border and it can be fun to just wander. El Paso's downtown has lots of options, many of which close as early as 5pm. Those in Ciudad Juárez stay open much later. Don't feel pressured to pick one from the following places, unless you're short on time.

Restaurant Impala (☎ 615-04-31; cnr Lerdo & Tlaxcala; main dishes $5-10) A large breakfast buffet has Mexican scrambled eggs, hot and cold mains, and more. Part of the Impala Hotel, it's a great option for those wanting a hearty meal at a decent price.

Lucy's Coffee Shop (☎ 915-534-74-21; 1301 N Mesa; breakfasts $2-4; ◷ 7am-3pm) As humble as El Paso's cheap eats get, but locally famous for flavorful, filling breakfast burritos, *machaca* (eggs mixed with shredded beef and wrapped in a flour tortilla), and other Tex-Mex favorites.

Tacos Tito's (cnr Villa, Peña & Av Juárez) Cheap, excellent tacos – wrapped in fresh tortillas grilled right before your eyes – can be had at this roadside stall grouped with several others, all of which are quite popular with the locals.

Frida's Restaurant & Bar (☎ 639-01-48; Paseo Triunfo de la República; dinners $10-20) *Sopa de tortilla* ($4) here is well worth the hike, and colossal frozen margaritas make it a nice oasis on a hot afternoon.

Ajuua!! (☎ 616-69-35; Ornelas Nte 162; mains $7-15; ◷ 8am-1am Sun-Thu, 8am-2am Fri & Sat) Giant margaritas are a major draw, and while there are touristy gimmicks, this cavernous restaurant-bar offers tasty versions of all the classics, from excellent *chiles rellenos* (chili stuffed with meat or cheese, and usually fried with egg batter) to bowl-sized glasses of frozen margaritas. Plus, it's fun to watch the large tables of Mexican-Texan tourists thrill over the rowdy, flirtatious mariachi band (Friday to Sunday).

Los Arcos (☎ 616-86-08; Paseo Triunfo de la República 2220; mains $6-12) While eating fish in the middle of a desert may feel just plain wrong, you can catch some fine smoked-marlin tacos and fresh fish fillets at this festive spot, a popular place for locals to hold celebratory dinners.

Big Bun Hamburgers (☎ 915-533-39-26; www.big bunhamburgers.com; 500 N Stanton; burgers $2-4.50; ◷ 8am-6:30pm) If you're craving a burger and don't want a megachain, go for Big Bun's cheap, but colossal, selections. The 'Santa Fe chicken with long green chile' is something you won't find elsewhere.

Vanderpool's Bakery (☎ 915-351-10-14; 117 N Stanton; meals $2-5) Skip the chains and come here instead. Fascinating vintage photos of bygone El Paso and inexpensive, freshly made breads, rolls and pastries. While the coffee is 'American style' (weak, with creamer and sweetener packets), the $0.50 bags of day-old goodies are big enough to feed a family of four. Tortas with avocado are $2.50.

Drinking

Take a taxi if you're planning on a late-night stumble home. 'Free' offers are usually going to end up costing you money. That said, if you're here to get plastered you've come to the right place. Close your eyes and walk into the nearest doorway – it's likely a bar. Bars open early, (often at 8am!) in Juarez and close late – 1am or 2am at the earliest.

Kentucky Club (☎ 632-61-13; Av Juárez 629) This polished-wood bar is a fine place to sip a margarita, and while its claim to have invented the cocktail sounds like a publicity ploy, they do make a decent one.

Club Olímpico (☎ 615-57-42; Av Lerdo 210) This watering hole has no live music – just a mellow, mixed crowd of local gays and straights, who are happy enough with the jukebox and the laid-back bartenders.

El Paso's drinking options are fewer and farther between. There are a few bars open in the downtown area, and others near UTEP on North Mesa. Except on a Friday or Saturday there won't be lots going on.

Popular and classic, **Cincinnati Club** (☎ 915-532-5592; 207 Cincinnati) is a typical, fun Western bar. Friendly bartenders, gregarious locals and a well-balanced pool table make it a good bet any day of the week.

Entertainment

Be aware that many of the nightclubs off Av Juárez are seedy; you may be asked to buy drugs or to head to a nearby hotel. Unless specified otherwise, places are open from 8pm until the wee hours.

El Sfinge (☎ 616-23-77; cnr Lincoln & Hermanos Escobar) In the Zona Pronaf, this Egypt-themed dance club is where it's happening.

Bar 26 (☎ 915-542-26-26; www.bar26.com; 2626 N Mesa) It's just DJs, drinks and dancing at this boisterous El Paso club. Drink specials vary nightly, and hotties flock to flirt on the breezy outdoor patio.

Ritz (cnr Peña & Lerdo) Earnest, old-school drag shows are the main draw on weekends at this gay nightclub, which draws a mixed clientele of both women and men.

Ciudad Juárez' bullfighting season is April to August. Events at **Plaza de Toros Monumental**

(☎ 613-16-56; Paseo Triunfo de la República) typically begin at 6pm Sunday. Off-track betting on the bullfighting (and on horse racing in the area) is available at the Juárez Turf Club, a block from the Juárez bridge.

Shopping

El Mercado Juárez (cnr Av 16 de Septiembre & Melgar; ☽ 9am-8pm) is a huge market that has an unfortunate mall-like quality, but its merchandise – blankets, jewelry, cheese and more – is affordable, and much of it is good quality. The hawkers are mellower than they first appear, making strong pitches that quickly become half-hearted as you pass by.

Getting There & Away

AIR

The best option for international arrivals and departures is the **El Paso International Airport** (ELP; ☎ 915-780-47-49; www.elpasointernationalairport .com) where flights from major US cities, including New York, Los Angeles and Chicago, are half the price of those to Ciudad Juárez.

Ciudad Juárez' Aeropuerto Internacional Abraham González is just east of Hwy 45D, about 18km south of the center of town. Direct flights are available to/from Mexico City, Chihuahua, Guadalajara, Mazatlán and Tijuana. Flights to most other major cities go via Chihuahua or Mexico City. The main Mexican carriers are **Aeroméxico** (☎ 800-021-40-00; www.aeromexico.com) and **Aero California** (☎ 55-5207-1392).

BUS

In Ciudad Juárez, the **Central de Autobuses** (☎ 610-64-45; Teófilo Borunda) is about 25 minutes southeast of town and accessible by local bus or taxi. For information on getting there, see opposite. Destinations with daily departures include the following.

Destination	Price	Duration	Frequency
Chihuahua	$25	5hr	frequent
Mexico City (Terminal Norte)	$125	24hr	frequent
Nuevo Casas Grandes	$16	4hr	hourly

Frequent 1st-class buses also go to Durango, Monterrey, San Luis Potosí and Zacatecas. **Autobuses Americanos** (www.autobusesamericanos .com.mx) has buses going direct to US cities eg Albuquerque, Dallas and Denver) that re generally cheaper than Greyhound from El Paso.

The **El Paso Greyhound station** (☎ 915-532-3-65) has its main entrance on Santa Fe St. Several buses a day travel to Los Angeles ($51, 16 hours), Chicago ($125, 34 hours), Miami ($124, 35 hours), New York ($110, 8 hours) and other major US cities.

Tourist cards are available at the Mexican mmigration offices at the ends of the Stanon St bridge and the Bridge of the Americas. Officers are generally friendly.

CAR & MOTORCYCLE

f you're driving into the Mexican interior, you must obtain a vehicle permit (see p992). The only place to do so in the Ciudad Juárez area (even if you're heading in another direction) is at the major customs checkpoint at Km 30 on Hwy 45D south.

Beyond the checkpoint, the highway to Chihuahua is in good condition but it comes with a $15 toll. Hwy 2 to Nuevo Casas Grandes branches west at a traffic circle 25km south of town.

For liability and vehicle insurance coverage while in Mexico, compare the policies of **Sanborn's** (☎ 915-779-3538; 2401 E Missouri Av) and **AAA** (☎ 915-778-9521; 1201 Airway Blvd) in El Paso.

TRAIN

El Paso's **Amtrak train station** (☎ 915-545-2247; 700 San Francisco) is three blocks west of the Civic Center Plaza. Trains run three times a week to Los Angeles ($96, 15 hours), Chicago ($123, 48 hours), Miami ($138, 48 hours) and New York ($204, 60 hours).

Getting Around

Local buses to the Ciudad Juárez bus station leave from Guerrero, west of Villa. Catch a blue-striped 'C Camionera' bus or a green-top 'Permisionarios Unidos' bus ($0.40); it's a 25-minute trip. From the bus station to the town center, turn left and go to the highway; any 'Centro' bus will drop you near the cathedral. Inside the station, a booth sells tickets for authorized taxis into town ($7.75).

In Ciudad Juárez, taxis from the Av Juárez area (where they are plentiful) to the pricier hotels toward Zona Pronaf cost about $8.

From the El Paso bus station to the Juárez bus station, hourly buses run for $5. Autobuses Twin Cities runs a shuttle service

between the Juárez and El Paso downtown areas; the blue vans depart from the corner of Villa and Galeana every 10 minutes ($0.30). It's $0.40 for a ride on a *colectivo* to and from the Zona Pronaf. A taxi over the border from the El Paso airport costs $30, or you can catch one of the frequent Border Jumper trolleys from the El Paso Civic Center, in the center of downtown, accessible by public buses from the airport.

NUEVO CASAS GRANDES & CASAS GRANDES

☎ 636 / combined pop 80,000 / elevation 1463m

Nuevo Casas Grandes, a four-hour bus trip southwest of Ciudad Juárez, is a sleepy, prosperous country town with wide streets and a vibe similar to that of dusty small towns in the US west. The people, a mix of working folk, farming families and Mormon settlers whose presence dates back to the late 19th century, are unhurried and friendly. The biggest social event here is the rodeo and fair, which come for a few weeks in September. Archaeology fans come to see the soft, mysterious ruins of Paquimé in the nearby residential village of Casas Grandes. Artlovers trek from the all over the southern US to purchase pottery in Mata Ortiz.

Information

You'll find banks (ATMs at Banamex and Bancomer), several *casas de cambio* and a post office clustered within blocks of Calle 5 de Mayo and Constitución (the street with railway tracks down the middle).

For Internet and email, video-enabled machines are at Copias Y Fax (☎ 694-24-17; cnr Obregón & Calle 5 de Mayo; per hr $2). **Paquinet** (☎ 694-66-66; Minerva 101; per hr $3) is another option.

Sights & Activities

The **Centro Cultural Paquimé: Museo de las Culturas del Norte & Paquimé Ruins** (☎ 692-41-40; admission to museum & ruins $4, video $3.25; ⏰ 10am-5pm Tue-Sun) are what give Casas Grandes (Big Houses) its name. The maze-like, eroding adobe remnants are from what was the major trading settlement in northern Mexico between AD 900 and 1340. Unfortunately, you're no longer allowed to wander within them, as the passageways have been chained off to protect the walls from damage. Small plaques describe the possible uses of some of the rooms and discuss Paquimé culture; don't miss the clay parrot cages and the distinctive T-shaped door openings, both of which are still clearly visible.

Paquimé was invaded, perhaps by Apaches, in 1340. The city was sacked, burned and abandoned, and its great structures were left alone for more than 600 years. The site was partially excavated in the late 1950s, and subsequent exposure to the elements led to erosion of the walls until their restoration some years later.

The Paquimé were great potters, and produced pieces from black clay as well as cream-colored earthenware with striking red, brown or black geometric designs, examples of which can be seen in the museum. Consider visiting Mata Ortiz (opposite) if you wish to purchase one of these fine wares to bring home.

Each year in mid-September the **rodeo** comes to town, offering rides, calf-roping and shows, along with drinking, dancing and other entertainment. Bars and clubs in town empty out when the rodeo's going on; plan on catching a taxi out to the rings if you're looking for fun. Be sure to wear your dancing shoes, er, boots, and be ready to use them.

Sleeping

Las Guacamayas B&B (☎ 692-41-44; maytelujan@msn .com; s/d incl breakfast $40/50; P) Offering the only accommodations worth getting excited about for miles around, this precious hostel-café sits snuggled on the edge of the small Casas Grandes village, near the entrance of the Paquimé site. While there is absolutely nothing around except small houses and the Paquimé ruins, the pink, adobe-style building has all you need: 11 charming rooms with tiled floors, a lovely garden area with a hammock, and breakfast served in the owner's kitchen. Getting there is easy if you simply follow the signs to the ruins. Then, facing the museum, with the ruins behind you, the pink hotel will be visible to your right. The viewing area on top of the museum may make it easier to locate.

Hotel Hacienda (☎ 694-10-46; hotelhacienda@ paquinet.com.mx; Av Juárez 2603; s/d $57/67; P ✗ ✗ ☎) The Hacienda, 1.5km north of Nuevo Casas Grandes on Hwy 10, is the best option in or near Nuevo Casas Grandes, offering a garden courtyard, swimming pool, restaurant and comfortable rooms. The hotel also organizes guide services to the ruins.

CUEVA DE LA OLLA

Tucked away in the mountains outside of Nuevo Casas Grandes is this unique ruin, named for its shape: a giant pot. Though beautifully preserved, little is known about this place, save that it was clearly connected to the Paquimé culture, as it contains the characteristic T-shaped doors and uses wood frames. About 30 or 40 people must have once lived here, farming the fertile valley and storing their grain beneath these cliffside overhangs. Why the people disappeared remains a mystery.

Getting there is half the fun: the road will challenge all but the hardiest of 4WDs, rewarding the passenger with wonderful views of the desert, the valley, mountain forests, and wildlife. Hire a driver in town for $80 to $100.

Hotel Paquime (☎ 694-47-20; Juárez 401; s/d $32/38; P ✗ ☎) Kids will love the small pool and Jacuzzi, and the modest rooms are clean and comfortable. The desk staff will gladly help answer any questions you have about the town.

Hotel Piñón (☎ 694-06-55; www.hotelpinon.com; Av Juárez 605; s/d $38/42; P ✗ ☎) On Av Juárez as you enter town from the north, this lodge features simple rooms that incorporate Paquimé motifs into the decor. There's a restaurant offering cheap breakfasts, an outdoor pool and a dimly lit bar. See the bartender for driving tours of Paquimé, Mata Ortiz, and other area attractions. Several examples of the local style of pottery are on display.

Hotel Juárez (☎ 694-02-33; Obregón 110; s/d $11/12) This place has dark, dingy rooms but is just south of Calle 5 de Mayo and only a stone's throw from the bus station. There's no heating or air-con (although some rooms have a fan); for those on a real budget, it's the cheapest place around.

Eating & Drinking

Constantino (☎ 694-10-05; cnr Juárez & Minerva; mains $6; ⏰ 7am-midnight) Located just north of the main plaza, the Constantino is popular with locals all day and serves fresh, tasty meals. A $5 set lunch menu is another way to stretch those pesos.

Dinno's Pizza (☎ 694-02-04; cnr Minerva & Constitución; mains $6; ⏰ 8am-9pm) In addition to its good pizzas and super breakfasts, this clean and popular place offers Szechuan-style dishes and good, strong coffee that the locals love.

Chuchy (☎ 694-07-09; Constitución 202; tortas $2; ⏰ 9am-8pm Mon-Sat) Chuchy's classic lunch counter is the perfect place to enjoy cheap, filling fare, from tortas to fries – plus a side of warm chat with Chuchy, the friendly old-timer who has owned the place for two decades.

Tortas Chacon (Av 16 de Septiembre 216; sandwiches $2.50; ⏰ 9am-9pm) This tiny, green-themed sandwich shop makes fantastic tortas with pork, cheese, melt-in-your-mouth avocado, and plenty of hot peppers.

El Capulin (☎ 694-01-80; Minerva 206; ⏰ 9am-7pm) Just a refrigerator and a whole lot of Mennonite cheese. It's cheap (a giant hunk costs only a dollar), sweet, mild and slightly crumbly.

Pollo Express (☎ 661-28-32; Av 16 de Septiembre 216; ⏰ 8am-11pm Tue-Sun) It's hard to beat a whole chicken for just $6. Tortas, *flautas* (delectable rolled up tortillas with meat or chicken that are quickly deep fried and topped with salsas or sour cream) and beer are all in the $2-to-$3 range.

Cerro Grande (alley between Constitution and Obregón) Just north of Av 16 de Septiembre, look where the college and college-plus crowd heads on a Friday or Saturday night. Cheap beers, friendly locals, and a blend of *norteño* favorites make it fun.

Getting There & Away

Daily buses from **Nuevo Casas Grandes bus station** (☎ 694-59-92) run to/from Ciudad Juárez ($16, four hours), Chihuahua ($20, 4½ hours) and Madera ($18, four hours). Other daily buses run to Cuauhtémoc, Monterrey and Zacatecas.

Driving south to Madera, turn right onto Hwy 28 at Buenaventura. This road climbs through scenic mountains dotted with oaks and short stubby cacti on its way to Zaragoza and Gómez Farías before arriving at Madera. It's best driven in daylight, partly for safety but mainly for the beautiful views.

Getting Around

Nuevo Casas Grandes is compact enough to walk everywhere in town, unless you're staying at Hotel Hacienda, where you can get a taxi to take you into the center for about $3.

To reach the ruins, take a 'Casas Grandes/Col Juárez' bus from Constitución in the center of Nuevo Casas Grandes; they run every half hour during the day. The 8km journey takes about 15 minutes ($0.50). You will be let off at the picturesque main plaza of Casas Grandes, and from there signs direct you to the ruins, 15-minutes away. Local taxis wait at Calle 5 de Mayo and Constitución in Nuevo Casas Grandes, charging $8 to take you to Paquimé. For about $35 you can loop through Paquimé, Mata Ortiz, Hacienda de San Diego and Colonia Juárez. Taxi drivers chat near the ATMs and are a good place to bargain for rides to Cueva de la Olla (opposite) or Mata Ortiz (below).

AROUND NUEVO CASAS GRANDES

West and south of Nuevo Casas Grandes are interesting little towns, cool forests and several archaeological sites. Most can be reached by bus, but the ancient rock carvings in rugged **Arroyo de los Monos**, 35km to the south, need a vehicle with good clearance.

A good day trip could include the Mormon village of **Colonia Juárez**, which has very little of tourist value – head to Cuauhtémoc (p369) if you want a guided tour of Mennonite villages – and the **Hacienda de San Diego**, a 1902 mansion owned by the Terrazas family, who controlled most of pre-revolutionary Chihuahua state. Descendants of a servant of the Terrazas still live there and can give a short tour of the building and grounds. While the tour is free, a tip ($2) for the guide is appreciated.

Mata Ortiz

Mata Ortiz, 30km south of Nuevo Casas Grandes, is fast becoming a major pottery center, as the new Acoma (an authentic, now very touristy, town in New Mexico). This tiny village, with its dusty, unpaved streets, loose chickens, and unfinished adobe houses, uses materials, techniques and decorative styles like those of the ancient Paquimé culture, and attracts shoppers worldwide. Juan Quezada, credited with reviving the Paquimé pottery tradition, is the most famous of the village's 300 potters; the best can command $1000 per piece. Both www.ortizpots.com and www.mataortizpottery.com have information on pottery in the area. If you've got your own car, www.4mpc.org is a nice resource for additional points of interest in the Chihuahuan desert.

Accommodation options include **Posada de las Ollas** (☎ 636-691-70-48; s/d incl 3 meals $39/60) and **Adobe Inn** (☎ 636-661-70-82; s/d incl 3 meals $45/75).

Baja's Frontier Tours (in Tucson, Arizona ☎ 800-726-7231; www.bajasfrontierstours.com) runs three-day visits to town, and the **Cultural Arts Tours & Workshops** (in Los Angeles ☎ 323-344-9064) arranges walking tours and pottery classes.

One bus a day makes the journey from Nuevo Casas Grandes to Mata Ortiz ($3.75, 30 minutes), departing at 4pm from the market and returning the next morning at 8am. Try bargaining with mellow taxi drivers in Nuevo Casas Grandes to take you instead.

MADERA

☎ 652 / pop 16,000 / elevation 2092m

Madera is a tiny town with all the good and bad: people are super-friendly and will happily help you out or answer questions, but on the other hand there's not much in the way of nightlife. Don't come here expecting to go out and party…come here expecting some nice food, welcoming people and some gorgeous scenery. The Madera area is lush with mighty pine trees, salmon-colored cliffs, waterfalls and a wealth of archaeological sites. Look for the bright pink building with Garfield the cat painted on it to get online: **SIMS** (cnr Gomez & Calle 5a, ⏰ 10am-9:30pm) has access but may be closed at erratic times.

Sights

The existence of cliff dwellings at **Cuarenta Casas** (Forty Houses; admission $1; ⏰ 9am-3pm) was known to the Spaniards as early as the 16th century, when explorer Álvar Núñez Cabeza de Vaca wrote in his chronicles, '…and here by the side of the mountain we forged our way inland more than 50 leagues and found 40 houses.'

Today about a dozen adobe apartments in the west cliffside of a dramatic canyon are visible at **La Cueva de las Ventanas** (Cave of the Windows); it's the only cave accessible to the public, although others can be viewed from the visitors' hut. Last occupied in the 13th century, Cuarenta Casas is believed to have been an outlying settlement of Paquimé, and perhaps a garrison for defense of commercial routes to the Pacific coast. Though the site is not as well preserved as the dwellings

at Casas Grandes, its natural setting and the hike required to get there make it a worthy outdoor excursion.

Cuarenta Casas is 43km north of Madera via a good paved road through pine forest. From the turnoff, a dirt road leads 1.5km to the entrance, where a trail descends into the Arroyo del Garabato and climbs the western slopes to the cave. Signs provide historical background along the way. The 1.5km hike isn't easy and takes about 80 minutes round-trip. Expect freezing temperatures in winter and be off the premises by 3pm.

From Madera, an 11:30am bus ($4.50) goes by Cuarenta Casas en route to the town of Largo. In the reverse direction, it stops at the site at around 4pm, allowing just enough time to make a day trip from Madera.

Sleeping & Eating

Motel Real del Bosque (☎ 572-05-38; s & d $50; P ﹩) This, the nicest place in town, is on the highway coming in from Chihuahua. The motel's rooms are spacious and carpet-free, and its operators conduct tours of the ruins and natural attractions in the area.

Hotel María (☎ 572-03-23; cnr Calle 5 & Calle 5 de Mayo; s/d $27/54) The bright-yellow rooms here are cramped but comfortable, and 2nd-floor rooms are airier and nicer; the small restaurant has excellent Mexican meals.

Parador de la Sierra (☎ 572-02-77; cnr Calle 3 & Independencia; s/d $23/30) Cute goldfish add some cheer, and the spacious, wood-paneled rooms come with heaters and face a secluded courtyard. The next-door disco can make sleep difficult.

Cueva del Indio (☎ 572-07-11; www.cuevadelindio.qjb.net; cnr Calle 1 & Gonzales; mains $5-10) This new cave-themed grotto offers filling meals of seafood, steak and Mexican food. The owner also arranges cave trips, hiking and fishing tours.

Getting There & Away

Madera's bus station is located on Calle 5. Second-class buses run to/from the following destinations:

Destination	Price	Duration	Frequency
Chihuahua	$17	3hr	hourly
Ciudad Juárez	$33	2hr	3 daily
Cuauhtémoc	$11	2hr	hourly
Nuevo Casas Grandes	$18	2hr	2 daily

Take extreme care if driving the winding, scenic cliff road linking Madera and Nuevo Casas Grandes at night.

AROUND MADERA

About 66km west of Madera, **Cueva Grande** sits behind a waterfall during the rainy season; inside the cave are some ancient adobe buildings in the architectural style of the Mogollón culture, closely associated with Paquimé. More of these cliff dwellings can be seen at **Conjunto Anasazi**, about 35km west of Madera by the same road; a moderately strenuous 4km ascent is required. In the same area as the cliff dwellings is the **Puente Colgante** (Suspension Bridge) over the Río Huápoca, and some **thermal springs**.

The unpaved road to Cueva Grande should be attempted with a 4WD vehicle only; try to find a local guide to take you from Madera. Motel Real del Bosque (opposite) offers guided van excursions that take in the Conjunto Anasazi, Cueva Grande and other points west for $22 per person (minimum of eight). Or you may be able to find English-speaking taxi drivers at the taxi stand opposite the bus station in Madera (from about $60).

CHIHUAHUA

☎ 614 / pop 708,200 / elevation 1455m

Peaceful Chihuahua remains unfettered by the trappings of tourism. It has some beautiful parks and plazas, excellent restaurants, a bustling market and a fine collection of cultural offerings. The bulk of foreigners use the metropolis only as an overnight stop en route to the Barranca del Cobre Railway, so the folks you'll encounter most will be the locals – a pleasing mix of professionals, working-class, students and dapper rancheros decked out in brightly colored cowboy boots.

This capital city of Mexico's largest state, Chihuahua, is a prosperous one, as evidenced by the fine colonial buildings that dot the city's center, and the newer suburbs and industries. Its main attractions are Pancho Villa's old house, Quinta Luz, and the museum of the Mexican Revolution that now occupies it, along with the main market, visited early in the morning by Mennonites and colorfully attired Tarahumaras. There's also a decent club and live-music scene.

CHIHUAHUAS

So what's the connection between Chihuahua and those nervous, yipping little dogs? The puny pups – popular pets averaging about 10cm to 20cm and 2kg in size – were first discovered in this area of Mexico about 100 years ago. While their exact origins are a mystery, it's widely believed that they first came from Asia or Egypt, and were introduced into Mexico by Spanish settlers. The canines were once thought to be indigenous to Mexico because of similar creatures depicted in ancient Toltec and Aztec art and described by explorers, but there exists no archaeological evidence to support this belief. Those beasts, say experts, must have been rodents that disappeared from Mexico not long after the Spanish conquest in the 16th century.

History

The name Chihuahua literally means 'dry and sandy zone' in the indigenous Nahua language, and that's a good description. From the first few Spanish settlers the city grew to become both an administration center for the surrounding territory and a commercial center for cattle and mining interests. In the war of independence, rebel leader Miguel Hidalgo fled here, only to be betrayed, imprisoned by the Spaniards, and shot. President Benito Juárez made Chihuahua his headquarters for a while when forced to flee northward by the French troops of Emperor Maximilian. The city also served as a major garrison for cavalry guarding vulnerable settlements from the incessant raids of the Apaches, until the tribe was subdued by the legendary 'Indian fighter,' Colonel Joaquín Terrazas.

The Porfirio Díaz regime brought railways to Chihuahua and helped consolidate the wealth of the huge cattle fiefdoms – one family held lands the size of Belgium.

After Pancho Villa's forces took Chihuahua in 1913 during the Mexican Revolution, Villa established his headquarters here. He had schools built and arranged other civic works, contributing to his status as a local hero. A statue of Villa graces the intersection of Universidad and División del Norte.

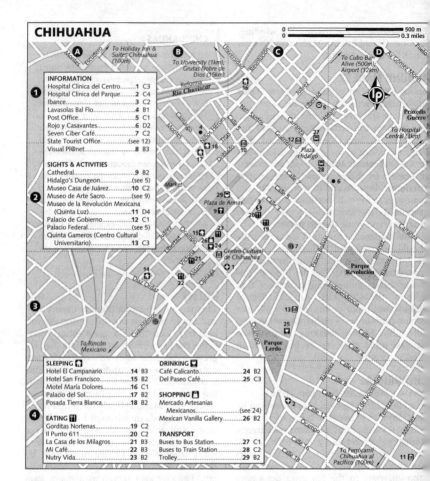

CHIHUAHUA

INFORMATION
Hospital Clínica del Centro.....................**1** C3
Hospital Clínica del Parque......................**2** C4
Ibance...**3** C2
Lavasolas Bal Flo......................................**4** B1
Post Office..**5** C1
Rojo y Casavantes....................................**6** D2
Seven Ciber Café......................................**7** C2
State Tourist Office..........................(see 12)
Visual Pl@net...**8** B3

SIGHTS & ACTIVITIES
Cathedral..**9** B2
Hidalgo's Dungeon.............................(see 5)
Museo Casa de Juárez............................**10** C2
Museo de Arte Sacro..........................(see 9)
Museo de la Revolución Mexicana
  (Quinta Luz)...**11** D4
Palacio de Gobierno...............................**12** C1
Palacio Federal....................................(see 5)
Quinta Gameros (Centro Cultural
  Universitario).......................................**13** C3

SLEEPING
Hotel El Campanario...............................**14** B3
Hotel San Francisco................................**15** B2
Motel María Dolores................................**16** C1
Palacio del Sol...**17** B2
Posada Tierra Blanca..............................**18** B2

EATING
Gorditas Nortenas...................................**19** C2
Il Punto 611..**20** C2
La Casa de los Milagros..........................**21** B3
Mi Café..**22** B3
Nutry Vida..**23** B2

DRINKING
Café Calicanto...**24** B2
Del Paseo Café...**25** C3

SHOPPING
Mercado Artesanias
  Mexicanos.......................................(see 24)
Mexican Vanilla Gallery..........................**26** B2

TRANSPORT
Buses to Bus Station...............................**27** C1
Buses to Train Station.............................**28** C2
Trolley...**29** B2

Orientation

Most areas of interest in Chihuahua are within a dozen blocks of the central Plaza de Armas – sometimes requiring a long walk or quick taxi ride. Independencia, running approximately northwest–southeast, divides the downtown and serves as a sort of 'zero' point for addresses. Streets parallel to it ascend by odd numbers (Calle 3, 5, 7 etc) heading northeast, and by even numbers heading southwest.

Information

EMERGENCY

Ambulance, Fire & Police (☎ 060)
Police (☎ 429-33-82) To report a crime or other nonemergency, call this direct police line.

INTERNET ACCESS

Internet cafés have sprung up all over town. Chances are you'll find one just by wandering.
Seven Ciber Café (☎ 416-69-49; Independencia 1209; per hr $1.20 ☺ 9:30am-8pm Mon-Fri, 11am-8pm Sat) Cheap, fast, Internet access in a small, un-airconditioned space.
Visual Pl@net (☎ 410-20-10; Cuactémoc 1616; per hr $1.50; ☺ 8am-8pm, Mon-Sun) Slick place with fast computers, south of the cathedral.

LAUNDRY

Lavasolas Bal Flo (☎ 415-30-79; Camargo 310; per load $4) Everything is washed, dried and folded in about four hours. Clothes come back fresh, along with a cheerful smile.

EFT LUGGAGE

The Chihuahua bus station has a left-luggage service for $0.30 per hour.

MEDICAL SERVICES

Hospital Central (☎ 415-90-00; Rosales 3302)
Hospital Clínica del Centro (☎ 416-00-22; Ojinaga 816, olonia Centro)
Hospital Clínica del Parque (☎ 439-79-14; Rodríguez)

MONEY

Most of the larger banks are around the Plaza de Armas, and open 9am to 5pm Monday to Friday. You'll find *casas de cambio* on Aldama southwest of the cathedral.
Bance (☎ 416-30-30; Aldama 8, ⊙ 8am-8pm Mon-Sat) changes traveler's checks; the nearby Banco Bital has a foreign-exchange service.

POST

Post office (Palacio Federal, Libertad 1700; ⊙ 8am-5pm Mon-Fri, 9am-1pm Sat)

TELEPHONE

Telmex pay phones, which can be operated with calling cards purchased at newsstands, are plentiful around the city.

TOURIST INFORMATION

State tourist office (☎ 429-33-00, 800-849-52-00; turismo@buzon.chihuahua.gob.mx; cnr Aldama & Guerrero; ⊙ 8:30am-6pm Mon-Fri, 10am-5pm Sat & Sun) On the ground floor of the Palacio de Gobierno, this information outlet has extraordinarily helpful, English-speaking staff and a wide array of brochures.

TRAVEL AGENCIES

Rojo y Casavantes (☎ 439-58-58; www.rojoycasavantes om; Guerrero 1207; ⊙ 9am-7pm Mon-Fri, 9am-noon Sat) This full-service agency can assist you with bus, train and airplane tickets and provide tourist information on other areas in Mexico.

UNIVERSITIES

Universidad de Chihuahua (☎ 439-15-30; Av Escorza 90) The neighborhood surrounding this 52-year-old university is alive with intelligent young folk; programs range from political science to agriculture. There's also an impressive art museum, Centro Cultural Universitario (see p66), which is not on the campus.

Sights

CATHEDRAL

Chihuahua's Plaza de Armas, with its mass of pigeons, shoe shiners, and cowboy-hat sporting local men, is a simple but pretty main plaza. Its majestic **cathedral** (⊙ 10am-8pm) presides over the bustle and fun. Construction began in 1726 but was not completed until 1789 because of frequent raids by indigenous tribes. Its marvelous baroque facade contrasts with the simpler interior, featuring 16 columns and a small cupola. On the southeast side is the entrance to the small **Museo de Arte Sacro** (☎ 413-63-04; admission $1; ⊙ 10am-2pm & 4-6pm Mon-Fri), which displays 38 religious paintings from the 18th century. The painters represented were among the founders of Mexico City's first art schools, notably the Academia de San Carlos. Worthy of at least a peek are the thousands and thousands of swallows that migrate at sunset to the telephone wires on Victoria, just behind the cathedral. They are a free thrill, but a beautiful one.

GRUTAS NOBRE DE DIOS

This cool **grotto** (☎ 400-70-59) has lots to see. Stalagmites and stalactites, caverns and historical figures all make this a fun visit, especially for kids. Don Quixote, the Tower of Pisa, and the Grand Canyon are some of the attractions on this one-hour, 17-room underground journey. In places, the damp walkways can be slippery. Take care! To get there either take a taxi ($10) or a Nombre de Dios Ojo–bound bus ($0.40) from the corner of Calle 4 and Niños Heroes. Ask the driver to tell you when to get off.

MUSEO DE LA REVOLUCIÓN MEXICANA (QUINTA LUZ)

Housed in Quinta Luz, the mansion and former headquarters of Pancho Villa, the **Museum of the Mexican Revolution** (☎ 416-29-58; Calle 10; admission $1; ⊙ 9am-1pm & 3-7pm Tue-Sat, 9am-5pm Sun) is a must-see, not only for history buffs but for anyone who can appreciate a good made-for-Hollywood story of crime, stakeouts and riches.

After his assassination in 1923, a number of Villa's 'wives' (a hilariously long list is displayed at the ticket counter) filed claims for his estate. Government investigations determined that Luz Corral de Villa was the generalissimo's legal spouse; the mansion was awarded to her and became known as Quinta Luz (*quinta* means 'villa' or 'country house'). When Luz died in 1981, the government acquired the estate and made it a museum. You don't need English narratives to understand the bullet-riddled black Dodge that Villa was driving when he was murdered, on morbid display in the back courtyard.

You can walk to the museum from the city center or take any bus designated 'Avaloz' or 'Juárez' running southeast on Ocampo. Get off the bus at the corner of Méndez, cross the street and walk downhill on Méndez for two blocks. Or visit as part of the city's trolley tour (p369), in which case you'll be dropped off at the museum entrance.

QUINTA GAMEROS

Manuel Gameros started building this gorgeous art-nouveau **mansion** (☎ 416-66-84; cnr Paseo Bolívar & Calle 4; adult/child $2/1; ☼ 11am-2pm & 4-7pm Tue-Sun) in 1907 as a wedding present for his fiancée. By the time it was finished, four years later, she had fallen in love with the architect, the Colombian Julio Corredor Latorre, and decided to marry him instead. Despite the wistful feeling this story will elicit when you see the place, the upstairs galleries, holding the Universidad de Chihuahua's art collection **Centro Cultural Universitario**, offer some cultural comfort.

PALACIO DE GOBIERNO

This handsome, 19th-century **palace** (☎ 429-33-00; cnr Aldama & Guerrero; admission free; ☼ 9am-7pm) features colonnades of arches surrounding the classic courtyard, and murals showing the history of Chihuahua cover the walls. Be sure to climb one of the wide staircases to the top and look down at the colorful bustle of visitors and government employees. On one side of the courtyard is a small room with a flickering eternal flame marking the place where Hidalgo was shot.

HIDALGO'S DUNGEON

The cell in which Hidalgo was held prior to his execution is beneath what is now the **Palacio Federal** (Juárez; admission $1; ☼ 9am-6pm Tue-Sun). The entrance to the building is on Juárez between Guerrero and Carranza – look for the cracked eagle's head inscribed 'Libertad.' The creepy quarters contain Hidalgo's crucifix, pistol and other personal effects, and a plaque recalls the verses the revolutionary priest dedicated to his captors in his final hours. There's a cool spiral staircase in the very back.

MUSEO CASA DE JUÁREZ

The home and office of Benito Juárez during the period of French occupation now houses this **museum** (☎ 410-42-58; Juárez 321; admission $0.50; ☼ 9am-7pm Tue-Sun), which maintains an 1850s feel and exhibits documents signed by the great reformer as well as a replica of the carriage he used while in Chihuahua.

Sleeping

Chihuahua's cheapest places may be rougher than you're used to. It pays to look at the rooms before deciding; you may elect to splurge and at least have a toilet that includes a seat.

BUDGET

Hotel Plaza (☎ 415-58-34; Calle 4 No 206; s/d $9/1 ☒) Chihuahua's least expensive is also the best of the budget options: a faded hotel directly behind the cathedral. Rooms aren't bad for the price, with central air-con, TVs, ample hot water and lots of what once was polished wood. Toilet seats and shower heads, unfortunately, are missing.

Motel María Dolores (☎ 410-47-70; motelmadol hotmail.com; Calle 9-A No 304; s/d $25/32; P ☒ ⬜) At the corner of Calle 9, the motel's basic but modern rooms are a very good deal and fill up quickly.

MIDRANGE

Hotel El Campanario (☎ 415-45-45; Díaz Ordaz; s/ $47/50; ☒ ⬜) A fine choice with large comfortable rooms and a nice lobby, El Campanario is your standard type of spot that lacks style but is in a good, central location

Posada Tierra Blanca (☎ 415-00-00; www.posad tierrablanca.com.mx; cnr Niños Héroes & Camargo 100; s/ $65/69; P ☒ ⬜ ⬚) This large motor lodge-style place has stuffy but clean rooms, a nice outdoor pool and friendly staff, though its neighborhood can get a bit dicey after dark.

TOP END

Hotel San Francisco (☎ 439-90-00; www.hotels francisco.com.mx; Victoria 409; s/d Fri-Sun $52/90, Mon-Thu $71/110; P ☒ ☒ ⬜) It's well worth the extra 30 bucks that it costs to stay in this luxury inn – especially on weekends, when rates are lowest. Sitting behind the cathedral and within walking distance of the market and good eateries, it's in a perfect location, and has all the high-end amen ties, from satellite TV to a touristy restaurant and cocktail lounge.

Palacio del Sol (☎ 416-60-00; palacio@infosel.net mx; Independencia 116; s & d/tr $113/123; P ✗ ✗ ⬚) This white cement high-rise looms over the low-level city, but the rooms are positively luxurious and the doting service is welcomed after a long, hot day. The bar has live music in the evenings.

Holiday Inn Hotel & Suites Chihuahua (☎ 439-0-00; suite@holidaychih.com; Escudero 702; s & d $135-250; P ✗ ✗ ⬚ ⬚) Unfortunately, the city's classiest option is part of the Holiday Inn group. But if you're a Barranca del Cobre rider seeking a tranquil escape – with a deluxe suite, a spa and private, well-groomed grounds – you'll find it here, in the hills overlooking downtown. Complimentary shuttle service is available for those without a car.

ating

i Café (☎ 410-12-38; Victoria 1000; mains $5) This classic American-style, greasy-spoon diner caters both to travelers and local cowboys, serving up excellent breakfasts of egg platters and coffee at big, comfy booths. *Chiquiles con huevos* (corn tortillas with chili and eggs) is great – a mouth-blisteringly picy way to start the morning. Unbelievably, it's also traditional Mexican hangover food.

Nutry Vida (☎ 410-96-64; Victoria 420; mains $3-6;) This natural-foods store and bakery, featuring a small café with several tables, a vegetarian's paradise, as well as a good place to stock up for tomorrow's on-the-go meals. You'll find delicious veggie burgers, salads, homemade yogurts, fresh-squeezed juices and a variety of vegan baked goods to eat in or take out.

Il Punto 611 (Independencia 611; $3; 7am-10pm on-Fri, 7am-9pm Sat) If you're sick of Nescafé powder and need a real fix, come here for real lattes and cappuccinos, along with cakes, pastries and friendly smiles.

Rincón Mexicano (☎ 411-15-10; Av Cuauhtémoc 24; mains $10-15; 8pm-midnight) You'll find occasional live music, excellent service, classic *comidas* and a festive ambience in the form of brightly tiled fireplaces, ochre walls and gleaming floors at this dinner ot. Menu highlights include grilled black ass, a succulent T-bone steak with *chipotle* gravy, enchiladas with three types of *mole* and some amazing *huitlacoche* quesadillas.

Gorditas Norteñas (cnr Independencia & Ojinaga; mains $1.50; 9:30am-3:30pm Mon-Sat, 9:30am-2pm Sun) This tiny, casual counter eatery is a don't-miss spot for tasty, cheap, fresh and filling *gorditas* (small circles of tortilla dough), stuffed with treats from cheese and sliced hot peppers to spicy shredded pork. Delicious when you are on the go!

Drinking & Entertainment

Del Paseo Café (☎ 410-32-00; Paseo Bolívar 411, Colonia Centro; 4pm-late) Located along the wide Paseo Bolívar near the university, this bar and eatery has a little something for everyone: live music on weekends, a bustling outdoor patio, luscious cocktails, a good wine list and a full menu, offering everything from salads and tacos to steaks and desserts.

Café Calicanto (☎ 410-44-52; Aldama 411; 4pm-1am Sun-Thu, 4pm-2am Fri & Sat) Enjoy live jazz and folk music, top-shelf cocktails, light snacks and a young trendy crowd on the tree-lined patio of this intimate café.

Hotel San Juan (☎ 410-00-35; Victoria 823; 10am-3am) The bar edging the front courtyard of the San Juan hotel has divey character, a friendly vibe, and entertainment in the form of *norteño* troubadours.

Cubo Bar Alive (☎ 410-68-65; Juárez 3114; cover $5-10; 9pm-2am Fri & Sat) Alive does not even begin to describe this giant stadium-style dance club. Live music gets the crowd crazy: not a chair, table, or pole remains un-danced on.

Shopping
Cowboy-boot shoppers should make a beeline to Libertad between Independencía

and Díaz Ordaz, where stores jammed with a flashy selection of reasonably priced rawhide, ostrich and lizard boots line the avenue. There are some other good buying options:

Mexican Vanilla Gallery (☎ 415-87-07; Victoria 424; ☿ 9am-8pm Mon-Sat) Vanilla lovers rejoice: thy store has been found. Sample a multitude of different kinds of vanilla, including syrups and agave-based sweeteners, then pick up a pint (or gallon) to take back to that vanillaholic friend or family member back home.

Mercado Artesanias Mexicanos (☎ 415-53-07; Aldama 511; ☿ 9am-8pm Mon-Sat, 10am-3pm Sun) You can find anything under the sun here, though most of it the stocking-present souvenir variety – T-shirts, trinkets, guitars, even that fake stuffed ferret you've always wanted.

Getting There & Away

AIR

Chihuahua's **General Fierro Villalobos airport** (☎ 420-26-57) has five flights a day to Mexico City, and daily flights to Los Angeles and to major cities in northern Mexico.

BUS

The **bus station** (☎ 420-01-32; Av Aeropuerto) contains restaurants, a luggage-storage facility and a telephone *caseta* (call station). Chihuahua is a major center for buses in every direction:

Destination	Price	Duration	Frequency
Ciudad Juárez	$25	5hr	1st-class hourly
Creel	$17	5hr	2nd-class hourly
Cuauhtémoc	$7	1½hr	1st-class every 30min
Durango	$40	9hr	1st-class frequen
Hidalgo del Parral	$13	3hr	1st-class frequen
	$9	3hr	5 2nd-class daily
Madera	$17	3hr	2nd-class hourly
Mexico City (Terminal Norte)	$100	18-22hr	frequent 1st-cla
Nuevo Casas Grandes	$20	4½hr	6 1st-class daily
	$16	4½hr	7 2nd-class daily
Zacatecas	$57	12hr	1st-class frequer

Other buses go to Mazatlán, Ojinaga, Mor terrey, Saltillo, San Luis Potosí, Torreó and Tijuana. **Autobuses Americanos** (in the ☎ 713-928-8030) departs daily for Phoeni Los Angeles, Albuquerque and Denver.

TRAIN

Chihuahua is the northeastern terminus the Chihuahua al Pacífico line for Barran del Cobre trains. Tickets are sold from 5a to 7am and 9am to 6pm Monday, Wedne day and Friday; 5am to 6am and 9am 6pm Tuesday and Thursday; 5am to 6a and 9am to noon Saturday and Sunday.

The air-conditioned *primera* (1st-clas express, No 74, departs daily at 6am for th 15-hour run through the canyon count

---

IF THE SHOE FITS, WEAR IT

If you're ever going to get cowboy duds, get them here or in Cuauhtémoc – they're reasonably priced, durable, classy and often made with the tender loving care that you won't find in a department store back home. Best of all, unlike nearby Ciudad Juárez, here you won't get a hard sell.

Cow and snake are common leathers, ostrich (distinguishable by small dots), even eel (actually not made from eel at all, but rather from hagfish, a primitive benthic creature somewhat similar to a lamprey). Colors range from the usual browns, tans and blacks to the more flamboyant hues of blue, green and purple.

Check the fit carefully: you want a snug fit (with room for your toes) that doesn't pinch or cramp after your foot is inside. It'll be tight while it's going on, but it shouldn't be painful afterwards. A pair of good quality boots, well taken care of, can last for decades.

Chihuahua is so proud of its boots and hats that they even have a brochure showing the locations of various stores. You might not need it if you just wander the parallel streets of Victoria and Libertad, but if you're looking for suggestions, pick up a copy at the tourist office. Several shops of Libertad have English-speaking staff and take credit cards. For hats, check out places on Juárez.

Watch out for unusual or exotic leathers, such as alligator, as it's possible that your purchase may increase animal poaching…or even be confiscated by customs upon your return home.

THE MENNONITES

In villages around Cuauhtémoc, Nuevo Casas Grandes and Chihuahua, you're bound to en-counter one of the following curious images: Mennonite men in baggy overalls selling big blocks of cheese, or women in American Gothic dresses and black bonnets speaking a dialect of old German to blonde children. And you may wonder how they got there.

The Mennonite sect, founded by the Dutchman Menno Simonis in the 16th century, maintains a code of beliefs that, from the start, put it at odds with several governments of the world. Members take no oaths of loyalty other than to God and they eschew military service. And so, persecuted for their beliefs, the Mennonites moved from Germany to Russia to Canada – and to post-revolutionary Mexico, where thousands settled in the 1920s.

Even today, these curious figures lead a Spartan existence, speaking little, if any, Spanish, and marrying only among themselves. Their refusal to use machinery has been long forgotten: horse-and-buggy transport has been replaced by tractors and pickup trucks. Several factories are booming, producing stoves, farm equipment and other goods.

Mennonite villages, called *campos* and numbered instead of named, are clustered along Hwy 65, a four-lane highway heading north from Cuauhtémoc's western approach. It feels more like Iowa than Mexico here, where wide unpaved roads crisscross the *campos* through vast cornfields interrupted by the occasional farm building and suburban-type dwellings.

If you are interested in touring the nearby *campos,* prepare for disappointment: most Men-nonites remain firmly uninterested in pandering to shutter-clicking tourists. Don't expect cheerful conversations with gregarious Mennonites; most – on the street or in stores – look at outsiders with disbelief or scorn. John Friessen of Vancouver Travel (p370) in Cuauhtémoc, is the area's only guide. Trilingual and cheery, Friessen will happily arrange a trip to Cuauhtémoc's *campo,* visiting the church, a small farm, a cheese factory, a restaurant and a stove manufacturer. Fries-sen's connections to the Mennonites go back generations, to when his grandfather parted ways with the sect and decided he would offer his children an education.

o Los Mochis. Train No 73 from the coast supposedly arrives in Chihuahua at 8:15pm but is usually late. The fare is $112 each way. The *segunda* (2nd-class) train, No 76, leaves Chihuahua daily at 7am and takes at least two hours longer. Though not as luxurious as the 1st-class train, it's quite comfortable and air-conditioned. This train, in turn, has two fare categories: *turista* for $56 and *subsidio* for much less but available only o locals with identification. For additional information, see p337.

Getting Around

The bus station is a half-hour ride east of own along Av Pacheco. To get there, catch 'Circunvalación 2 Sur' or 'Aeropuerto' bus n Carranza across the street from Plaza Hidalgo ($0.40). From the bus stop in front of the station, the 'Circunvalación Maquilas' us goes back to the center.

For the Ferrocarril Chihuahua al Pacífico tation, take a 'Cerro de la Cruz' bus on Car-anza at Plaza Hidalgo, get off at the prison (it looks like a medieval castle), then walk behind the prison to the station.

Taxis at the taxi stand on Victoria, near the cathedral, charge standard rates to the train station ($3.25), bus station ($5) and airport ($10).

TROLLEY TURÍSTICO

Chihuahua's **trolley** (cnr Libertad & Plaza de Armas; tour $3; ⏰ 9am-1pm & 3-7pm) offers a way to get a peek at the main historic sights (which are not far) if you're too hurried to walk to them; a ride on the loop takes about half an hour.

CUAUHTÉMOC

☎ 625 / pop 90,800 / elevation 2010m

West of Chihuahua, Cuauhtémoc is a center for the Mennonite population of northern Mexico (boxed text, above), and one of the only places where you can get a guided tour of Mennonite settlements. It's less touristy than Chihuahua and has very little night-life. Some good restaurants make a stopover pleasant, as does the quiet town square with its small cathedral. From the town's west end, Hwy 65 runs north through the prin-cipal Mennonite zone, with entrances to the numbered *campos* (villages) along the way.

John Friessen of **Vancouver Travel** (☎ 582-13-22, 625-591-21-63; tours $15-35; ☺ Mon-Sat) has a wealth of information about the local area and is the only person who can arrange a tour of the nearby Mennonite *campos* in your choice of Spanish, English, or German.

Logi-Q Computación (☎ 581-07-87; on the plaza; per hr $3.50; ☺ 9am-2pm & 3:30-7pm Mon-Fri, 9am-3pm Sat) is a small café with Internet connections. Cheaper access can be had at **Discosic** (☎ 581-10-66; cnr Melgar & Guerrero 121; per hr $2; ☺ 9am-8pm Mon-Sat), about 10 minutes' walk from either the plaza or the bus station.

Sleeping & Eating

Hotel San Francisco (☎ 582-31-52; Calle 3 No 132; s/d incl breakfast $16/17; P ☒) This serious bargain was being remodeled at the time of writing, but offers spotless, modern rooms and simple Mexican breakfasts.

Motel Tarahumara Inn (☎ 581-19-19; www.tarahumarainn.com in Spanish; Av Allende 373; s & d $55; P ☒ ☒ ☐) A very comfortable hotel that has clean, unstuffy rooms with tiled floors, plus parking, a restaurant, a bar and a small gym on the premises. If needed, the staff can arrange transport to the airport or bus station.

Nutrivida (☎ 582-33-36; www.nutrivida.com; Allende 556; breads $1-2; ☺ 8am-8pm Sun-Fri) Fresh-baked rolls and other organic selections, plus delicious shakes and smoothies. Vitamins and supplements are available as well.

El Podrino (Allende 17; tortas $2; ☺ noon-midnight) Roadside torta stand with giant-sized portions of beef, pork or chicken. Be sure to ask Jesús to add extra onions, then ask him to tell you why.

Rancho Viejo (☎ 582-43-60; Av Guerrero 333; mains $7-12) Good ol' Mexican food: choose from shrimp, beef and other traditional options at this homey eatery and pub. Apple pie finishes off the meal with style.

St Cruz Cafe (☎ 582-10-61; Hidalgo 1137; ☺ 4:30pm-midnight) As upscale as Cuauhtémoc gets, this is a nicely lit, quiet coffeehouse and bar. Clamato (a brand of clam-tomato juice) drinks are way, way big here.

Getting There & Away

Cuauhtémoc is 1½ hours by bus ($7) or 3½ hours by train from Chihuahua. By car, head west via La Junta to the spectacular Cascada de Basaseachi waterfalls (see p349.)

HIDALGO DEL PARRAL

☎ 627 / pop 101,000 / elevation 1652m

Parral is a pleasantly mellow little town with a bustling main street and friendly residents – its courteous drivers even come to complete halts for pedestrians! Its biggest claim to fame is that it's the town where Pancho Villa was murdered on July 20, 1923 (see boxed text, opposite). A hero to the *campesinos* (country people) of the state of Chihuahua, Villa was buried in Parral, with 30,000 attending his funeral (Unfortunately the story has a sordid postscript: shortly after the general's burial, his corpse was beheaded by unknown raiders.) In 1976, Villa's body was moved to Mexico City.

Founded as a mining settlement in 1631, the town took the 'Hidalgo' tag later but is still commonly called just 'Parral.' Throughout the 17th century, enslaved indigenous people mined the rich veins of silver, copper and lead from La Negrita mine, whose installations still loom above town but are no longer in use.

Orientation

Two main squares, Plaza Principal and Plaza Guillermo Baca, are roughly in a line along the north side of the river, linked by busy Av Herrera (also called Mercaderes). The bus station at the east end of town is connected to the center of town by Av Independencia, which ends at the Hidalgo monument. Though quiet, the town does have a *cholo* (Mexican gangster) presence; buying anything illegal is unwise.

Information

Cámara Nacional de Comercio (☎ 522-00-18; Coleg 28; ☺ 9am-1pm & 3-7pm Mon-Fri, 9am-1pm Sat) is small storefront that functions as a tourist office, distributing maps and brochures.

For financial needs, there are banks and *casas de cambio* around Plaza Principal, including Bancomer, which has an ATM.

Many hotels now include Internet access for free. If yours doesn't, try **Infosel** (Herrer 26, through Iris sewing shop; per hr $2; ☺ 9:30am-1pm 4-7:30pm Mon-Fri, 10am-1pm Sat), the place for fast Internet connections.

The main bus station has left-luggage facilities ($3 per hour), although attendants who keep unpredictable hours, are often nowhere to be found.

PANCHO VILLA: BANDIT-TURNED-REVOLUTIONARY

Best known as a hero of the Mexican Revolution, Francisco 'Pancho' Villa's adulthood was more given to robbing and womanizing than to any noble cause. His years as a bandit are obscured by contradictory claims, half-truths and outright lies. One thing is certain: although an outlaw and ever the bully, Villa detested alcohol. In his *Memorias*, Villa gleefully recalled how he once stole a magnificent horse from a man who was preoccupied with getting drunk in a cantina.

Long after his outlaw years, Pancho Villa had bought a house in Chihuahua. That spring, Chihuahua's revolutionary governor Abraham González began recruiting men to break dictator Porfirio Díaz' grip on Mexico, and among the people he lobbied was Villa. González knew about Villa's past, but he also knew that he needed men like Villa – natural leaders who knew how to fight – if he ever hoped to depose Díaz. Thus, González encouraged Villa to return to marauding, but this time for a noble cause: agrarian reform. The idea appealed to Villa, and a year later he joined the revolution.

When rebels under Villa's leadership took Ciudad Juárez in May 1911, Díaz resigned. Francisco Madero, a wealthy liberal from the state of Coahuila, was elected president in November 1911.

But Madero was unable to contain the various factions fighting for control throughout the country, and in early 1913 he was toppled from power by one of his own commanders, General Victoriano Huerta, and executed. Pancho Villa fled across the US border to El Paso, but within a couple of months he was back in Mexico, one of four revolutionary leaders opposed to Huerta. Villa quickly raised an army of thousands, the División del Norte, and by the end of 1913 he had taken Ciudad Juárez (again) and Chihuahua. His victory at Zacatecas the following year is reckoned to be one of his most brilliant. Huerta was finally defeated and forced to resign in July 1914. With his defeat, the four revolutionary forces split into two camps, with the liberal Venustiano Carranza and Álvaro Obregón on one side and the more radical Villa and Emiliano Zapata on the other, though the latter pair never formed a serious alliance. Villa was defeated by Obregón in the big battle of Celaya (1915).

In July 1920, after 10 years of revolutionary fighting, Villa signed a peace treaty with Adolfo de la Huerta, who had been chosen as the provisional president two months earlier. Villa pledged to lay down his arms and retire to a hacienda called Canutillo, 80km south of Hidalgo del Parral, for which the Huerta government paid 636,000 pesos. In addition, Villa was given 35,926 pesos to cover wages owed to his troops. He also received money to buy farm tools, pay a security guard and help the widows and orphans of the División del Norte.

For the next three years, Villa led a relatively quiet life. He bought a hotel in Parral and regularly attended cockfights. He installed one of his many 'wives,' Soledad Seañez, in a Parral apartment, and kept another at Canutillo. Then, one day while he was leaving Parral in his big Dodge touring car, a volley of shots rang out from a two-storey house. Five of the seven passengers in the car were killed, including the legendary revolutionary. An eight-man assassin team fired the fatal shots, but just who ordered the killings remains a mystery.

ights

ALACIO ALVARADO

ust opened and beautifully restored, his wealthy–silver tycoon's **house** (☎ 522- 2-90; admission $2; ◷ 10am-5pm Mon-Sun) was riginally built for Lady Alvarado, who ied before it was completed. The fabric, urtains and wallpaper are particularly pectacular, but the whole hacienda is full f beautiful period furniture, ceramics and lass. One interesting piece is a table that as specially designed to seat from four o 30 people. A photo display on the 2nd oor has images of the Parral of yesteryear.

Tours are well worth it and free, though a donation is suggested.

MUSEO FRANCISCO VILLA Y BIBLIOTÉCA

Pancho Villa was shot and killed from this building at the west end of town in 1923, and a star just outside the entrance marks the precise spot where he took the fatal bullet. These days it houses the **Pancho Villa Museum & Library** (cnr Juárez & Av Maclovio Herrera; ◷ 9am-4pm), with a small collection of photos, guns and memorabilia. The museum becomes a focal point every year in late July during the Jornadas Villistas festival, when townsfolk re-enact his assassination with guns blazing. The following day, a cavalcade of some 300 riders descend on Parral on horseback after a six-day journey from the north, recalling Villa's famous marathons.

SANTUARIO DE FÁTIMA

This 1953 **church** (Calle Jesús García), located on a hill just beside the town's Prieto mine, was built from chunks of local gold, silver, zinc and copper ore, which sparkle in the thick walls. The congregation sits on short pillar-type stools rather than pews. Hours are unpredictable, so you may only get to see the facade.

Sleeping

Hotel Acosta (☎ 522-02-21; Barbachano 3; s/d/tr $22/28/35; ✗) Centrally located, extremely friendly, spick-and-span Acosta has the most character, with museum-quality, 1950s touches – from the big Pepsi cooler in the green lobby to the bright linoleum floors in the rooms – that have been frozen in time by the third-generation owner, Doña Acosta. It's a treat watching the operator use the ancient switchboard, and be sure to check out the view of Plaza Principal from the roof.

Hotel Fuentes (☎ 522-00-16; Mercaderes 79; s & d/tr $16/28; ✗) The cheapest decent place is the Fuentes, recognizable by its pink-soda facade, opposite the cathedral. The rooms off the cheerful lobby are all clean and basic; they vary in size, and some offer TV and air-con.

Hotel Los Arcos (☎ 523-05-97; Pedro de Lille 5; s/d $40/45; ✗ ✗ ▯) Although it's a bit far from the center of town, this hotel is a stone's throw from the bus station, making it perfect for late-night arrivals. It features a lovely lobby and cozy, clean rooms set around an elegant, flowering courtyard.

Motel El Camino Real (☎ 523-02-02; cnr Av Independencia & Pedro de Lille; s/d/tr 54/61/63; ℗ ✗ ✗ ▯) Also close to the bus station and a trek from town is this comfortable motor lodge, offering a geranium-dotted parking lot, small gym and restaurant. The rooms are clean, but unless you need a safe parking area, go with the nearby Hotel Los Arcos instead.

Eating & Drinking

Restaurant Turista (☎ 523-72-30; Plaza Independencia 14; breakfasts $4) This friendly eatery whips up big, tasty plates of *huevos mexicanos* (Mexican-style eggs).

Restaurant La Fuente (☎ 522-30-88; cnr Av Collegi & Denon; mains $6) Happy yellow walls and bi front windows add to the warm ambience at this local favorite, where you'll find no nonsense dishes including steak, chicken crispy French fries and a fine plate of *chile rellenos*.

La Michoacana (Ramírez 2; ice-cream cones $1 ☺ 9am-9pm) Teens gather around the cloc at this open-air parlor that serves cream homemade ice cream in rich flavors includ ing coffee, caramel, mint and prune.

Antojitos Meny (☎ 522-70-52; Flores Magon 1. mains $2-5; ☺ 8am-9pm Mon-Sun) Great cheap eats *antojitos* and tortas at this restaurant tha gets packed at lunchtime.

Restaurant Bar Calipso (☎ 522-90-66; Paseo Góme Morín 1; mains $7) This slightly upscale, popula spot features international specialties, fron steak to sushi.

Café La Prieta (☎ 522-88-06; Calle del Cerro 3. Sitting on a hill that overlooks the towr this cheerful nightspot offers various cof fees, beers and *antojitos* for an average c $2 a plate.

Getting There & Around

The bus station, on the southeast outskirt of town, is most easily reached by taxi ($3 it's about a 15-minute walk. Regular 1st-clas buses run to Chihuahua ($13, three hours Torreón ($22, four hours), and Durang ($25, six hours). Frequent 2nd-class buse head to Valle de Allende ($1.25, 30 minutes from Independencia, near the bus statio opposite the hospital.

AROUND HIDALGO DEL PARRAL

East of Parral, the village of **Valle de Allend** is lush with trees and surrounded by gree farmland. The stream through the valley fed by mineral springs that start near **O** **de Talamantes**, a few kilometers west, whe there's a small bathing area.

Canutillo, 80km south of Parral and ju over the border of the state of Durango, where Pancho Villa, a Durango native, sper the last three years of his life (see boxe text, p371). His former hacienda, attache to a 200-year-old church, is now a slight dilapidated museum with the unwieldy titl of **Museo Gráfico de la Revolución Mexicana** (admi sion free; ☺ 10am-5pm). It houses a collection c photos, guns and various personal artifact but the surrounding scenery is beautiful

ural. You can get dropped off here by a
us heading from Hidalgo del Parral to
Durango, or take a slow, infrequent local
us from Plaza Guillermo Baca; otherwise,
ou'll need to drive.

ORREÓN

☎ 871 / pop 524,000 / elevation 1150m

f you're a Pancho Villa buff then Torreón is
vorth checking out. However other than the
istorical value it's not much compared to
he much more cosmopolitan cities of Du-
ango or Chihuahua. An attractive central
·laza with several fountains, lots of trees, and
ome good eateries make it a nice base for
xploring the surrounding desert region.

The 1910 battle for Torreón was Pan-
ho Villa's first big victory in the Mexican
Revolution, giving him control of the rail-
vays that radiate from the city. Villa waged
hree more battles for Torreón over the next
ew years. During one, his troops, in their
evolutionary zeal, slaughtered some 200
Chinese immigrants.

·rientation

'orreón is located in the state of Coahuila
nd is contiguous to the cities of Gómez
'alacio and Ciudad Lerdo (both in Du-
ango state); all three together are known
s La Laguna. Torreón itself fans out east
f the Río Nazas, with the central grid lying
t the west end of town and the Plaza de
Armas at the west end of the grid. Avs Juá-
ez and Morelos extend east from the plaza,
·ast the main government plaza and, east
f Colón, past several large shaded parks.
'he Torreón bus station is 6km east of the
enter on Av Juárez.

nformation

'he modern **Protursa tourist office** (☎ 732-22-
4; promotos@prodigy.net.mx; Paseo de la Rosita 308D;
♡ 9am-2pm & 4-7pm Mon-Fri, 9am-2pm Sat), 5km east
f the center, hands out maps and guides of
'orreón and the region. Some staff mem-
ers speak English.

You'll find Internet cafés around the
.lameda park; most are open daily and
·harge about $2.50 per hour.

·angers & Annoyances

'he city center can be fairly seedy after dark,
·articularly along Morelos, so be careful if
·ou're walking around after about 9pm.

CHIHUAHUAN DESERT PLANTS

As you're staring out the window at the
'whole lot of nothing' out there you'll start
to notice that it's actually not nothing at
all. Here are some easily identifiable plants
to look for, all of which have adapted to
thrive in one of the harshest climates on the
planet:

- **Creosote bush** – Olive green, with
  tiny, oily leaves, the most common of
  the desert's plants give the evenings a
  lemony smell as the pores open up for
  the night.
- **Ocotillo** – Looking like a bunch of pipe
  cleaners stuffed into the ground, this
  odd shrub drops its leaves in droughts
  and regains them within days after a
  rainstorm.
- **Yucca** – Creamy white blossoms make
  delicious batter-fried fritters; fabric can
  be made from the thin, fibrous leaves.
- **Agave** – The agave has thick, gel-filled
  leaves and a giant stalk that can be 10m
  high. It's used in tequila, but in non-
  alcoholic drinks as well.
- **Sotol** – Similar to yucca and agave,
  sotols are distinguishable by a fluffy
  tipped stalk, like a giant fox tail. Like
  agave, sotol can also be used to make a
  fiery liquor found only in this region. La
  Casa de los Milagros (boxed text, p367)
  has a wonderful selection of area sotols,
  tequilas and other beverages.

Sights

Pancho Villa's Torreón escapades are docu-
mented in the tiny **Museo de la Revolución** (cnr
Múzquiz & Constitución; donations suggested; ♡ 10am-2pm
Tue-Sun), beside the bridge to Gómez Palacio.

For a panoramic view, take a taxi up to
the **Cerro del Cristo de las Noas** lookout. The
Christ statue, flanked by TV antennas, is the
second-tallest in the Americas.

Sleeping

Hotel Galicia (☎ 716-11-19; Cepeda 273; s & d $11)
This 80-year-old inn is a study in faded
elegance, with beautiful tiled halls, stained
glass and battered furniture. The owners
are very friendly and the place has genuine
character. Toilet seats are missing in most

rooms, so be sure to ask for a *cuello* if that's an issue.

Hotel Alondra (☎ 732-38-38; Juárrez 4691; s & d/tr $45/50) Luxurious red curtains add a flourish to the spotless, sterile rooms. No Internet is a small drawback that can be overlooked by all but the most e-addicted geeks.

Paraíso Del Desierto Grand Hotel (☎ 716-11-22; Blvd Independencia Pte 100; r from $100; P ⊠ ☒ ▯) At the opposite end of the scale, this luxury hotel has an on-site restaurant and gym, plus basic, plush rooms with coffeemakers and data ports; more expensive quarters come with mini bars, full kitchens, fireplaces and hot tubs. A nice buffet breakfast is included as well.

Camino Real Ejecutivo Torreón (☎ 759-16-00; Blvd Independencia 3595; r $142; P ⊠ ☒ ▯) Torreón's newest hotel, located near the airport, offers the finest in business-class amenities, with pink-themed, swanky rooms featuring high-speed Internet access, glass-door showers and marble desks.

Eating
Restaurant Del Granero (☎ 712-91-44; Morelos 444 Pte; mains $5; ⏱ 8am-9pm) Vegetarians and carnivores alike will love this airy café, which serves delicious whole-wheat *gorditas*, burritos and fresh salads.

Casa Alameda (☎ 712-68-88; Guerra 205; mains $7-9) For Spanish and Mexican meals or snacks in a relaxed pub-style with attractive terracotta and tile, try this roomy, bright place across the street from the Alameda park. They have different buffets every day of the week.

Next door to Restaurant Del Granero is a bakery doing whole-wheat versions of standard Mexican pastries.

Getting There & Around
There are bus stations in both Torreón and Gómez Palacio, and long-distance buses will stop at both or transfer you between them without charge if you've paid for a ticket to one or the other. Buses depart regularly for the following:

Destination	Price	Duration
Chihuahua	$30	6hr
Durango	$18	3½hr
Mexico City	$70	14hr
Saltillo	$20	3hr
Zacatecas	$27	6hr

Taxis are the best way to get from the Torreón bus station to downtown (about $3) SOTT, a city-run bus, loops around on a set route to most places and costs $0.35.

The tolls on the highway to Durango total $25. To the León Guzmán Entrance, Hwy 40D costs $16; most vehicles take the slightly slower free road. Drivers, pay attention as you near the sprawling city of Torreón no matter which direction you approach from as the highways, signs and traffic patterns get more confounding the closer you get.

AROUND TORREÓN
The deserts north of La Laguna are starkly beautiful, with strange geological formations around **Dinamita** and many semiprecious stones for gem hunters. Further north, the village of **Mapimí** was once the center of an incredibly productive mining area and served the nearby Ojuela mine between periodic raids by local Cocoyomes and Tobosos tribes. Benito Juárez passed through Mapimí in the mid-19th century during his flight from French forces. The house where he stayed, near the northwest corner of the Mapimí plaza, is now a small **history museum** (⏱ Thu-Tue) displaying some very good sepia photos of Ojuela in its heyday.

At the end of the 19th century, the Ojuela mine supported an adjacent town of the same name with a population of over 3000. Today a cluster of abandoned buildings clings to hillside as a silent reminder of Ojuela town's bonanza years. A spectacular 300m-long suspension bridge, **Puente de Ojuela**, was built over a 100m-deep gorge to carry ore trains from the mine. You can walk across the bridge, fortified with 5cm steel cables, to the mine entrance. A site guide (suggested fee $5) will accompany you through the 800m tunnel and you'll emerge at a point that affords good views of the Bermejillo area.

To reach Mapimí from Torreón, go 40km north on Hwy 49 (stay on Hwy 49 when it splits into Hwy 49 and Hwy 49D) to Bermejillo, then 35km west on Hwy 30. It's easiest to get there with your own transport, but **Agencia Contraste** (☎ 871-715-20-51; Miguel Alemán 12, Torreón) arranges tours of the town and mine. From Torreón's bus station, Autobuses de la Laguna 2nd-class buses depart every half hour for Mapimí ($3.25). To visit Puente de Ojuela, get off 3km before Mapimí, at shop selling rocks and minerals. From there

narrow road winds 7km up to the bridge.
The walk takes about an hour, but you may
be able to hitch a ride. Four kilometers from
the turnoff, the road narrows further as the
surface becomes cobblestone and more suit-
ble for hiking than driving.

At Ceballos, 130km north of Torreón, a
rough road goes 40km east to the **Zona del
Silencio**, so called because conditions in the
area are said to prevent propagation of radio
waves. Peppered with meteorites, Zona del
Silencio is also believed to be a UFO landing site. The mysterious overtones associated
with the region were amplified after a NASA
test rocket crashed here during the 1970s.
The ensuing search for the craft by US teams
was, of course, veiled in secrecy, giving rise
to all manner of suspicions. The Zona del
Silencio is in the **Reserva de la Biosfera Bolsón
de Mapimí**, a desert biosphere reserve dedicated to the study of arid-region plants and
animals, including a very rare tortoise. This
is a remote area with rough roads.

DURANGO
☎ 618 / pop 457,200 / elevation 1912m
Durango is a mellow, pleasant cowboy town
with a delightful Plaza de Armas – one of the
nicest in Mexico – fine colonial architecture,
warm locals and a great selection of hotels
and restaurants. It's a fun place to relax and
unwind in, yet there's also plenty to do both
in town and in the surrounding areas.

Founded in 1563 by conquistador Don
Francisco de Ibarra and named after the
Spanish city of his birth, the city is just
south of the Cerro del Mercado, one of the
world's richest iron-ore deposits; this was
the basis for Durango's early importance,
along with gold and silver from the Sierra
Madre. Other local industries include farming, grazing, timber and paper – as well as
the movie business (see boxed text, p378), as
evidenced by the collection of locations for
westerns just outside the city.

Note that as you cross the border between
Chihuahua and Durango, you enter into a
different time zone; Durango is one hour
ahead of Chihuahua.

Orientation
Durango is a good town to walk around
in, and most of the interesting places to see
and stay are within a few blocks of the two
main squares, the Plaza de Armas and the

Plaza IV Centenario. For some greenery,
go to the extensive Parque Guadiana on the
west side of town.

Information
Several banks with ATMs as well as *casas
de cambio* are on the west side of the Plaza
de Armas.

American Express (☎ 817-00-23; Av 20 de Noviembre
Ote 810; ☑ 9am-7pm Mon-Fri, 10am-5pm Sat) Cashes
traveler's checks.

Cafe Internet (☎ 811-28-06; Av 20 de Noviembre Pte
1003; per hr $1.50) Cheerful Internet café with speedy
terminals right near the center of town.

Hospital General (☎ 813-00-11; cnr Av 5 de Febrero &
Apartado) For emergencies or walk-in medical care.

Main post office (cnr Av 20 de Noviembre & Roncal;
☑ 8am-6pm Mon-Fri, 9am-noon Sat)

State tourist office (☎ 811-11-07; turismor@prodigy
.net.mx; Florida 1006; ☑ 10am-7pm) This tourist office
and small café doubles as the state film board and film
museum. Has friendly staff, some of whom speak English.

Viajes Clatur SA de CV (☎ 813-39-17; Av 20 de
Noviembre Ote 333A) Can hook you up with bus or airplane
reservations.

Sights
The **Catedral Basílica Menor** (Av 20 de Noviembre; admission free; ☑ 8am-7pm), constructed between
1695 and 1750, has an imposing baroque
facade that gives way to a vast Byzantine interior, with fine sculptures and paintings on
the altars, and carved-wood choir stalls.

The **Plaza de Armas** is one of the loveliest in
this region – spotless and shaded, filled with
fountains and intricately carved wooden
benches, and dominated by a domed kiosk.
It's not far from the market, and is a great
place to sit and people-watch, especially in
the late afternoon, when groups of teens
gather to goof around after school lets out.
After dark it becomes a major make-out
spot.

The grand, balcony-topped baroque **Palacio de Gobierno** (Av 5 de Febrero; ☑ 9am-6pm) has
colorful murals depicting the history of the
state. It was built on the estate of a Spanish
mine owner and expropriated by the government after the war of independence.

In its century of existence, the striking,
neoclassical stone **Teatro Ricardo Castro** (cnr Av
20 de Noviembre & Martínez; ☑ 10am-7pm) has served
as a cinema and boxing arena. The entrance
is brimming with decorative carvings and
the French interior has gorgeous lighting

CENTRAL NORTH MEXICO

DURANGO

fixtures, historical murals and a Frederic Chopin medallion in its central balcony.

Museo de Cine (☎ 813-39-17; Florida 1006; admission $0.50; ☼ 10am-7pm) offers a pretty low-budget display, but if you can't make it out to the actual film sets, this tiny museum gives a good overview of how the area has been used in westerns, including *A Man Called Horse* (1969) and *Pat Garrett and Billy the Kid* (1972), starring Bob Dylan.

Museo de Arqueología de Durango Ganot-Peschard (Zaragoza Sur 315; admission $0.50; ☼ 10am-6pm Tue-Fri, 11am-6pm Sat & Sun) is an innovative visual feast presenting the archaeological record of the region's indigenous cultures, from prehistoric times to the Spanish conquest. Highlights include a photographic exhibit on rock paintings and an interesting section demonstrating the archaeological method. All descriptions are in Spanish.

Sleeping

BUDGET

Hotel Plaza Catedral (☎ 813-24-80; Constitución 216 Sur; s & d $20) Right next to the cathedral and the plaza, this cool 120-year-old building is a

labyrinth of stairways, arches, and tile work. Staying here is almost like walking into an MC Escher painting. Rooms are basic an the place could use some TLC, but the staf are very friendly and the location makes the best of the budget options.

Hotel Buenos Aires (☎ 812-31-28; Constitución N 126; s & d $12) In the center of town, the Bueno Aires has tidy little rooms, some with bath rooms and hot water. Curfew is 11:30pm.

Hotel Ana Isabel (☎ 813-45-00; Av 5 de Febrero O 219; s/d $18/20;) Just a stone's throw east o León de la Peña, the rooms here are quain if stuffy; some have balconies over an indoo courtyard. It's an excellent budget option Someone here clearly loves poinsettias.

Villa Deportiva Juvenil (☎ 818-70-71; Colegi Militar; dm $5, plus deposit $5) Durango's cheap est option is a long way from the plaza This purple youth hostel offers clean dorn beds and not much else, and is 400m south of the bus station. Look for the pedestria bridge and you'll have found it.

Hotel Roma (☎ 812-01-22; www.hotelroma.co .mx; Av 20 de Noviembre Pte 705; s/d $25/28;) Th friendly Roma is in a large century-ol building on the opposite corner from the Teatro Ricardo Castro. The rooms here are small but in pretty good shape, with soft beds and access to a lovely roof garden and a nice balcony overlooking the square.

MIDRANGE

Hotel Posada Santa Elena (☎ 812-78-18; Negrete Pte 1007; s/d $38/40; ❇) Friendly, small and quiet, this hotel is a find. It features 10 tastefully furnished rooms, some with their own little courtyard. Beautiful sinks make shaving a luxury.

Hotel Posada San Jorge (☎ 813-32-57; fax 811-50-40; Constitución Sur 102; s/d/tr $45/56/60; ❇) In a handsome 19th-century building with large rooms, this is one of Durango's finest hotels. It offers colonial-style rooms and junior suites, the latter with sofas and walk-in closets, and all with cable TV and small balconies. The restaurant is popular with locals, and the grand stairway and bold mural leading to the sleeping quarters are welcoming sights after a long day of sightseeing.

Hotel Casablanca (☎ 811-35-99; www.hotelcasablancadurango.com; Av 20 de Noviembre Pte 811; s/d/tr $53/58/63; ❇ ❇ ▢) A block west of the Hotel Roma, the Casablanca offers large well-appointed, carpeted rooms with big TVs and small coffeemakers.

TOP END

Hotel Gobernador (☎ 813-19-19; fax 811-14-22; Av 20 de Noviembre Ote 257; s & d $130; ▣ ❇ ❇ ▢ ▣) The Gobernador is the best hotel in town, featuring a pool, lushly landscaped grounds, a banquet hall, good bar and an elegant restaurant. It's the only nonchain luxury hotel in town, and a bargain compared to any US-side counterparts with similar amenities.

Eating

Durango boasts plenty of good restaurants and will provide a thrill for those craving a bit of variety.

Cremería Wallander (☎ 813-86-33; Independencia te 128; items from $3) A great place to stock up on the loaf of bread and jug of wine. You'll also find locally made yogurt, honey and granola, plus extraordinary tortas made with special German cold cuts, and Mennonite cheese on fresh-baked rolls.

Samadhi Vegetarian (Negrete 403; veggie comida 4; Ⓥ) Any herbivore will feel right at home in this small storefront dotted with just a few tables and brightly painted walls. It offers a rotating *menu del día*, with delicious elements including *pozole* (pork and corn hominy soup), *tamales,* soy chorizo and lentil soup. You can also buy tofu and soy milk to go – a real find in these parts!

Gorditas Gabino (☎ 812-11-92; Constitución Nte 100A; gorditas $0.75, mains $5) A cheap-eats haven that bustles with people, all savoring the delicious *gorditas* stuffed with avocados, shredded beef in *salsa verde* and other tasty fillings. Go for the creamy flan to finish things off.

Pampas (☎ 827-61-21; Constitución 102; mains $12-20) This new Brazilian restaurant has a giant salad buffet and offers various pork, beef and chicken delicacies on skewers.

El Zocabón (☎ 811-80-83; Av 5 de Febrero 513; mains $5; Ⓥ 7:30am-11pm) This large, pleasant café with a friendly staff makes a good spot for breakfast, serving big mugs of fresh steaming coffee and well-prepared egg dishes.

Fuente de Sodas (cnr Av 5 de Febrero and Juárez) This old-fashioned sit-down ice-cream parlor serves excellent frozen and baked treats.

Corleone Pizza (☎ 811-69-00; cnr Constitución Nte 110 & Serdán; pizzas $6) You'll find cozy booths, aromatic red sauce, a small wine selection and a European feel inside this dimly lit parlor.

Shopping

You'll find just about everything at **Mercado Gómez Palacio** (cnr Av 20 de Noviembre & Pasteur; Ⓥ 8am-6pm Mon-Sat), a jumbled maze of stalls, including tacos, T-shirts, scorpion key chains, cowboy hats, dried herbs, fresh produce, leather saddles, CDs and homewares.

Getting There & Away

Good bus connections are available from Durango to many of the places that travelers want to go:

Destination	Price	Duration	Frequency
Chihuahua	$40	9hr	6 1st-class daily
Hidalgo del Parral	$25	6hr	9 1st-class daily
Mazatlán	$39	7hr	3 deluxe daily
	$27	7hr	10 1st-class daily
	$24	7hr	6 2nd-class daily
Mexico City (Terminal Norte)	$77	12hr	1 deluxe daily
	$62	12hr	7 1st-class daily
Torreón	$18	3½hr	frequent 1st-class
Zacatecas	$19	4hr	frequent 1st-class

SALOONS, SPITOONS & GUNSLINGERS

Just outside the city limits of Durango is one of Hollywood's prime film sets, but today's young cowboys carry MP3 players on their belts in place of holstered guns. Durango's unspoiled deserts, beautiful rivers and pristine valleys were the staple setting of about 120 westerns in the '60s and '70s. Sam Peckinpah, John Huston and John Wayne are household names who spent many hours filming here. Bob Dylan wrote the soundtrack for and starred in *Pat Garrett and Billy the Kid*. *The Wild Bunch* – purported to signal the end of the Western era – is perhaps the most famous, a classic still popular today.

More recently, *Revenge*, starring Kevin Costner, *Fat Man and Little Boy*, with Paul Newman and John Cusack, and *The Mask of Zorro*, with Antonio Banderas, have all been shot here. *Bandidas*, with Salma Hayek and Penélope Cruz, is in post-production. On a sadder note, late comedic great, John Candy, passed away here while shooting his final film.

Getting Around

The bus station is on the east side of town; white Ruta 2 buses departing from the far side of the parking lot will get you to the Plaza de Armas ($0.30). Taxis, which are metered, charge about $2.25 to the center.

To reach the bus station from downtown, catch a blue-striped 'Camionera' bus from Av 20 de Noviembre beside the plaza. Get off at the intersection of Colegio Militar (a major thoroughfare), then go left toward the Villa monument and take the overpass across Pescador.

AROUND DURANGO
Movie Locations

Villa del Oeste (off Hwy 45; admission $0.50; ☺11am-7pm Sat & Sun) is 12km north of Durango. After its use in a number of westerns, the 'main street,' known locally as Calle Howard, was left undisturbed. When not in production, it's a souvenir-drenched theme park that's open to visitors. You'll either love wandering the replica Wild West or you'll find it pretty cheesy. Either way, it's kinda fun. To get there, take a 2nd-class bus for Chupaderos from the bus station ($1, every half-hour) and tell the driver to drop you at Villa del Oeste. To get back to Durango, just flag down any passing bus headed toward the city. Check with the tourist office in Durango before heading out there, as hours vary. While nothing is open during the week you can still take a taxi there ($5) and walk around.

The small village of **Chupaderos**, 2km north of Villa del Oeste, offers a fascinating look at a former set, now overtaken by the unfazed residents. It's a nice, sleepy, cactus-strewn place to spend a quiet afternoon.

To the southwest of Durango is **Los Álamos**, a '1940s town' where *Fat Man and Little Boy* was filmed in 1989. To get there, take Blvd Arrieta south of town and stay on it for about 30km, past dramatic mesas and a steep river gorge. Watch for a rusty sign on the right announcing the turnoff for the set. From there it's another 1.5km over a rough road. Buses are not an option.

Museo de Arte Guillermo Ceniceros

Originally a British-built ironworks, the Ferrería de las Flores was converted into an **art museum** (☎618-826-03-64; La Ferrería; admission $0.50; ☺10am-6pm Tue-Sun) to display the work of Durango native, Guillermo Ceniceros. Profoundly influenced by his teacher, the formidable muralist David Alfaro Siqueiros, Ceniceros developed his own method of visual expression. Mysterious landscapes and feminine figures are his preferred subjects. La Ferrería is 4km southwest of Durango on the way to Los Álamos. Regular 'Ferrería' buses depart from the Plazuela Baca Ortiz in the center of town.

Durango to Mazatlán

The road west from Durango to the coastal city of Mazatlán (see p426) is particularly scenic, with a number of worthwhile natural attractions. In the vicinity of **El Salto** you can trek to waterfalls, canyons and forests. About 160km from Durango on Hwy 40 is a spectacular stretch of road called **El Espinazo del Diablo** (Devil's Backbone).

You enter a new time zone when you cross the Durango–Sinaloa state border; Sinaloa is one hour behind Durango.

Northeast Mexico

Economically, the northeastern states of Nuevo León, Tamaulipas and Coahuila form one of Mexico's most dynamic and business-driven regions. Most visitors speed through this vast area – stretching nearly 1000km from north to south and 500km from east to west – with magnificent desert scenery, craggy peaks and plenty of cultural interest to merit a diversion off its excellent highways. And perhaps best of all, you can expect a particularly warm welcome from the *norteño* locals, for there is no tourist trail in these parts, and visitors who choose to spend time here are well treated.

Monterrey, a confident progressive city with iconic modern architecture, terrific galleries and museums, and some of the hippest bars and clubs in the country, is certainly well worth a day or two. In the west of the region, the colonial charm of Saltillo, and the atmospheric allure of Parras compete to impress, while for an almost ethereal experience, soak away an afternoon in the idyllic pools of Cuatro Ciénegas, deep in the Chihuahuan desert. The coastal areas, all but neglected by travelers, also have remote beaches, lagoons and wetlands, home to diverse marine life and a winter stopover for many migratory birds.

While the sprawling, heavily industrialized border towns that line the Río Bravo del Norte (Rio Grande) hardly present the best introduction to Mexico, even here there's the odd unexpected sight – a stylish gallery or a historic mansion lurking between the tequila bars and souvenir stalls.

TOP FIVE

- Hiking through the birders' paradise of **Reserva de la Biosfera El Cielo** (p396)
- Wallowing hippo-style in the sublime desert pools of **Cuatro Ciénegas** (p414)
- Discovering the vibrant musical and artistic scenes at **Monterrey** (p397)
- Feasting on fresh fish after swimming in the warm waters of the Gulf around **La Pesca** (p393)
- Dangling over a canyon in the rock-climbing mecca of **Potrero Chico** (boxed text, p412)

- MONTERREY JANUARY DAILY HIGH: 21°C | 69°F
- MONTERREY JULY DAILY HIGH: 37°C | 99°F

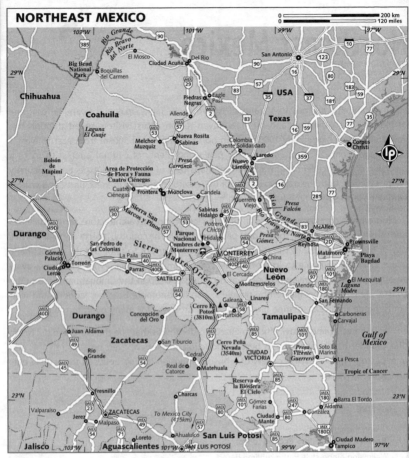

NORTHEAST MEXICO

History

It was here that the two great colonizing movements, Spanish from the south and Anglo-Saxon from the north, confronted each other and displaced the indigenous peoples.

Northeastern Mexico was slow to be developed by Spanish settlers, but became a key area of conflict with the US until the 1846–48 war established the Río Bravo del Norte as the frontier between the two nations. The discovery of petroleum, coal and natural gas accelerated development, and the region emerged as an industrial leader in the late 19th century.

Today this area is perhaps the most Americanized part of the country with money and resources surging back and forth across the border. The Texas economy is particularly dependent on Mexican workers, while American investment was behind most of the *maquiladoras* (assembly-plant operations) that mushroomed here in the 1990s. However, today these factories are suffering the threat of closure, as labor costs are much cheaper in Asia.

Climate

The geographic diversity of northeast Mexico (expansive deserts, remote coastal areas and the highlands of the Sierra Madre Oriental) produces tremendous climatic variation.

Coastal areas along the Gulf of Mexico experience the largest amounts of rain in

September and are generally warm and humid all year round.

August is the hottest month, while winter can bring the occasional 'norther' with cold temperatures and sometimes even snow.

Parks & Reserves

The extraordinarily rich aquatic ecosystem of the **Área de Protección de Flora y Fauna Cuatro Ciénegas** (see p414) is the most impressive reserve in the northern part of this region. In the south, the lush highlands of the **Reserva de la Biosfera El Cielo** (p396) comprise low-altitude rain forest, temperate terrain and cloud forest and are particularly rich in birdlife.

Getting There & Around

Many travelers enter Mexico at one of the region's five main border crossings from the US, and travel full throttle to the colonial towns and beaches in what is perceived as the 'real' Mexico to the south. The towns along the 1000km of international border are also popular for short trips.

Scenic Hwy 2, the Carretera Ribereña, paralleling much of the Río Bravo on the Mexican side, runs between Ciudad Acuña and Matamoros.

The main toll highways running south from the Texas border are Hwy 57, bypassing most mountainous areas, from Piedras Negras to Saltillo and eventually to Mexico City; Hwy 85, also known as the Pan American Highway, beginning at Nuevo Laredo and passing through Monterrey and Ciudad Victoria; and Hwy 40, running southwest from Reynosa to Monterrey, Saltillo and eventually the Pacific coast. Smaller Hwy 180 goes south from Matamoros, continuing all the way down the gulf coast through Tampico and Veracruz.

Very frequent buses leave the cities on the Mexican side of the border to the main destinations in the region and further afield, while numerous international airlines service Monterrey.

TAMAULIPAS

NUEVO LAREDO

☎ 867 / pop 350,000

Nuevo Laredo is Mexico's busiest border town in terms of trade with the US, but due to sporadic violence between rival drug cartels (see boxed text, p384) fewer travelers have been crossing here in recent years. Generally, it's the reputation of the city rather than your safety that is at risk, but because of the ongoing trouble here you may opt to use an alternative border crossing instead. It's also easy to detour around Nuevo Laredo and avoid the city itself, which lacks charm anyway.

Historically the region has always had close connections with Texas, and was part of the independent valley-area republic between 1839 and 1841. Today, ties with Laredo in the US remain very close, and the twin cities are known as Los Dos Laredos, even sharing a professional baseball team, the Tecolotes.

Orientation

Two international bridges link the Laredos. You can walk or drive over Puente Internacional No 1, and there's a toll of $0.50 for pedestrians and $2 for vehicles. This bridge leads you to the north end of Av Guerrero, Nuevo Laredo's main thoroughfare, which stretches for 2km (one-way going south). Northbound traffic heading for Puente Internacional No 1 is directed via Av López de Lara on the western side of the city.

Puente Internacional No 2 is only for vehicles, and enables drivers to bypass Nuevo Laredo's center, feeding into Blvd Luis Colosio on the east of the city. On the US side, Interstate 35 goes north to San Antonio.

A third international bridge, Puente Solidaridad, crosses the border 38km to the northwest, enabling motorists to bypass Laredo and Nuevo Laredo altogether.

Plaza Hidalgo, a pleasant well-kept square with a bandstand and clock tower, and the Palacio Federal on its east side, is seven blocks south of Puente Internacional No 1.

Information

Many businesses accept traveler's checks and US dollars, but the exchange rate can be low.

Ambulance, Fire & Police (☎ 066)
Banamex (Av Guerrero) Has an ATM.
Medical Services (☎ 712 00 49)
Post office (Camargo) Just east of the plaza.
Santander Serfin (Av Guerrero 837) Has an ATM.

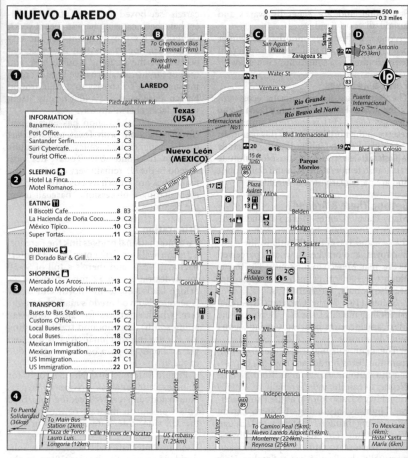

NUEVO LAREDO

INFORMATION
Banamex.....................................1 C3
Post Office..................................2 C3
Santander Serfin..........................3 C3
Suri Cybercafe.............................4 C3
Tourist Office..............................5 C3

SLEEPING
Hotel La Finca.............................6 C3
Motel Romanos............................7 C3

EATING
Il Biscotti Cafe.............................8 B3
La Hacienda de Doña Coco...........9 C3
México Típico.............................10 C3
Super Tortas..............................11 C3

DRINKING
El Dorado Bar & Grill..................12 C2

SHOPPING
Mercado Los Arcos.....................13 C2
Mercado Monclovio Herrera......14 C2

TRANSPORT
Buses to Bus Station...................15 C3
Customs Office...........................16 C3
Local Buses................................17 C2
Local Buses................................18 C3
Mexican Immigration..................19 D2
Mexican Immigration..................20 C2
US Immigration..........................21 C1
US Immigration..........................22 D1

Suri Cybercafé (Canales 3112; per hr $1.75; ☯ 9:30am-10pm)

Tourist office (☎ 712-73-97; www.nuevolaredo.gob.mx in Spanish; ☯ 8am-8pm Mon-Fri) On the ground floor of the Palacio Federal on the east side of Plaza Hidalgo.

www.visitlaredo.com Has useful information about Los Dos Laredos.

Dangers & Annoyances

Sporadic outbreaks of violence, including shootings and kidnappings, have occurred in Nuevo Laredo in recent years. While it's true that most victims had a connection to the city's cocaine gangs, innocent bystanders have also been caught up in the trouble too. That said, homicide levels are actually lower than in many US cities.

Festivals & Events

Nuevo Laredo holds an agricultural, livestock, industrial and cultural fair called **EXPOMEX** from September 6 to 22. The **Celebración del Aniversario de la Ciudad** in 1848 is celebrated June 13 to 15 with music, baseball games and bullfights.

Sleeping

All the hotels reviewed here have air-con (a necessity during Nuevo Laredo's blistering summers) and cable TV. Many international chain hotels are located around where Av Guerrero turns into Av Reforma. Prices are negotiable at all levels. The budget places reduce rates during the week; the luxury hotels at weekends.

Hotel La Finca (☎ 712-88-83; Av Reynosa 811; s/d $28/36; P) First choice in the budget price range, this welcoming and secure brick-fronted hotel is an excellent deal, with three floors of attractive, good-sized rooms with wardrobes and telephones.

Motel Romanos (☎ 712-23-91; Calle Dr Mier 2420; s/d $25/33; P) Gaudy but good value this kitsch Roman-themed hotel has a columned facade, gilded detailing and 32 very well-kept rooms, with chests of drawers and comfortable beds. There's a small store in the lobby.

Camino Real (☎ 711-03-00; Av Reforma 5430; www .caminoreal.com; r/ste $82/121; P). Sumptuous rooms at this modern colossus represent a good deal at this price, and the hotel also has a well-regarded restaurant. It's on the main highway to Monterrey, 6km south of the center.

Eating & Drinking

There are numerous restaurants on and just off Av Guerrero, but many places just south of the bridge are overpriced tourist joints.

La Hacienda de Doña Coco (☎ 713-44-34; Mina 2910B; dishes $2.75-4.50) Looking out over pretty Plaza Juárez, this inexpensive little family-owned *comedor* (eating place) is an enjoyable place for a feed, with set lunches, often including a fish dish, from just $3.

Il Biscotti Caffe (☎ 712-33-79; Calle Canales 3147; breakfast $3, mains $4.50; 8am-9pm Mon-Sat) This small, friendly, wood-paneled neighborhood place offers a pleasant setting for a latte and a piece of carrot cake, though they also serve filling dishes including *nopales rellenos* (stuffed cactus paddles) and *milenesa de res*.

México Típico (☎ 712-15-12; Guererro 934; mains $5-12.50; 8am-1am) An elegant, formal restaurant place that's popular for *chuletas de cerdo* (pork chops), *tacos combinados* and the house specialty, *cabrito* (roasted young goat).

El Dorado Bar & Grill (☎ 712-00-15; cnr Belden & Av Ocampo; starters $3.25-7, mains $7-20; P) This historic, high-ceilinged place has been a haunt for southern Texans since early last century. The sweeping mahogany bar makes a great place to sip a margarita, but avoid the restaurant, which (illegally) has green-turtle soup on its menu.

Super Tortas (Calle Dr Mier 27; tortas $1.50-3) For a quick bite, grab a sandwich here, on the north side of Plaza Hidalgo.

Shopping

Mercado Los Arcos (Plaza Juárez; 8am-6:30pm) This quirky market is on the south side of Plaza Juárez and has some interesting antiques stalls.

Mercado Monclovio (Herrera; 8am-7pm) On the west side of Av Guerrero, this market has an assortment of T-shirts, silver, rugs, liquor, hats, leather and pottery.

Getting There & Away

AIR

Nuevo Laredo airport (☎ 718-07-82) is off the Monterrey road, 14km south of town. **Mexicana** (☎ 719-28-15; Av Obregón 3401) has direct flights twice a day to and from Mexico City. The airport at Laredo, Texas has Continental and American Airlines flights every day to Mexico City, Houston and Dallas.

BUS

Nuevo Laredo's bus station is 3km south of Puente Internacional No 1 on Anáhuac. It has luggage storage ($0.50 per hour) available and telephone facilities. Make sure you use the official, authorized taxi service to get to the bus station, don't grab a cab on the street. There are daily 1st- and 2nd-class buses to most cities in northern Mexico.

Destination	Price	Duration	Frequency
Guadalajara	$66	14hr	3 1st-class
Matamoros	$23	6hr	6 1st-class
Mexico City	$99	15hr	3 deluxe
(Terminal Norte)	$75	14hr	11 1st-class
Monclova	$15	4hr	4 1st-class
Monterrey	$18	3hr	1st-class every 30min
	$12	3hr	2nd-class
Reynosa	$16	4hr	8 1st-class
Saltillo	$22	4½hr	hourly 1st-class
	$22	4½hr	2 2nd-class
San Luis Potosí	$51	10hr	hourly 1st-class
Tampico	$50	10hr	7 buses

Buses also go to Aguascalientes, Ciudad Victoria, Durango and Querétaro, and to most major cities in Texas.

There are also direct buses to various cities in Mexico from the **Greyhound bus terminal** (☎ 956-723-43-24; Av Salinas 610) in Laredo,

'NARCO' LAREDO

Summer 2005 wasn't a great season for the police force of Nuevo Laredo, a city sometimes called 'Narco' Laredo by Mexicans, a place synonymous with violence and drug gangs. First the newly-sworn-in police chief Alejandro Domínguez, ex-president of the city's Chamber of Commerce, lasted just seven hours in his new job before he was riddled with bullets on June 8. Then a crack AFI (Agencia Federal de Investigación) team dispatched to investigate Domínguez's assassination was caught up in a shootout with city police on the outskirts of Laredo – the local cops claimed mistaken identity, while some in the AFI maintained it was a premeditated ambush. Subsequently the entire police force of Nuevo Laredo was suspended from duty, drug-tested and questioned about organized-crime links. Troops replaced police on the streets, and within days they rescued 43 kidnapped people found bound and gagged in safe houses spread across the city. Many of the abducted claimed to have been kidnapped by policemen.

In August, the US ambassador to Mexico closed the city's consulate for a week following a 40-minute gang battle that involved grenades, machine guns and rocket launchers.

Historically, drug running in Nuevo Laredo had been controlled by the Gulf cartel, but when leader Osiel Cárdenas Guillén was jailed in 2003, the rival Sinaloa gang launched a violent bid for supremacy. It's not hard to work out why the city has been so bitterly contested by drug gangs. Over 40% of all Mexican exports (or 9000 trucks per day) enter the US here – the sheer volume of goods making concealed narcotics difficult to detect.

During the first two years of the turf war, Nuevo Laredo's murder rate rose to 80 a year, with the gangs staging ambushes and execution-style killings, often in broad daylight. In 2005, more than 130 killings linked to organized crime were recorded.

Joaquín 'El Chapo' Guzmán-Locra, *capo* (mafia boss) of the Sinaloa cartel, is the man who is thought to have instigated the turf war. 'Shorty' has a reputation as Mexico's most ruthless gang boss, and has been on the run since he escaped from prison, smuggled out in a laundry cart in January 2001. Guzmán is said to have moved 200 men to the city in 2003, and recruited extra muscle from the rival Zetas (ex-commandos employed by the Gulf mob as narco-mercenaries) before unleashing a wave of violence. Priding himself as being a step ahead of the authorities, he even rolled into one of Nuevo Laredo's best-known restaurants in 2005. Whilst his heavies barred the exit door and ordered the 40 diners present to refrain from making cellular calls, Guzmán tucked into some seafood and then picked up the tab for all.

The assassination of several journalists, including Roberto Javier Mora Garcia, editor of *El Mañana* newspaper in 2002, has silenced the local media, which will no longer investigate the gang wars.

While vowing to take on the coke cartels, President Fox called on the US government to do more to stop the import of illegal weapons, including Uzis and AK-47s, most of which are purchased at gun shows in Texas. Many Mexicans also argue that it's the thirst for narcotics north of the border that has provoked the violence in Nuevo Laredo and elsewhere along the border. Drug use within Mexico is relatively low – under 5% of the 18-to-25 age group have used marijuana and less than 1% have used cocaine (compared to 52% and 19% respectively in the US).

Texas, but these will cost you more than services from Nuevo Laredo itself. Bus inspections are often very thorough on this border post, so it's usually quicker to walk across the international bridge and make your way directly to the Nuevo Laredo bus station.

Both of the Puente Internacional bridges have official Mexican immigration offices at the southern end. This is where you need to go to collect your tourist card if you intend to travel further south into Mexico.

CAR & MOTORCYCLE

For a vehicle permit, you must go to the **aduana** (customs office; Internacional Blvd; ◷ 24hr), which is signposted from Puente Internacional No 1; it's about 200m west of the bridge.

The route south via Monterrey is the most direct to central Mexico, the Pacific coast and the Gulf coast. An excellent toll road, Hwy 85D, is fast but expensive (tolls total $18 to Monterrey). The alternative free road (Hwy 85) is longer and slower. Hwy 2 is a rural road following the Río Bravo del Norte to Reynosa and Matamoros.

Getting Around

A good network of city buses ($0.50) means getting around Nuevo Laredo is simple enough. Very regular buses marked 'Mirador' or 'Carretera' leave from the corner of Bravo and Juárez go to the bus station. From the bus station, local buses marked 'Puente-Centro' head to the Puente Internacional No 1 via the city center.

Taxis ask about $10 from the bridge to the bus station; you may be able to get the price down to $7.

Public parking is readily available in Nuevo Laredo – there's a secure **parking garage** (per hr $1.75) four blocks south of the border on Victoria, west of Av Guerrero.

REYNOSA

☎ 899 / pop 499,000

Reynosa is one of northeast Mexico's most important industrial towns, with oil refineries, petrochemical plants, cotton mills, distilleries and *maquiladoras*. Over 200 companies, including some big global brands, employ around 70,000 workers in the city's industrial parks. Pipelines from here carry natural gas to Monterrey and into the US.

As a commercial border crossing, Reynosa rivals Matamoros, but is less important than Nuevo Laredo. It has good road connections into Mexico and Texas, and has become more popular with travelers in recent years. Across the Río Bravo del Norte is the town of McAllen.

The tourist trade is geared to short-term Texan visitors, many of whom are in town to visit the city's surfeit of dentists, plastic-surgery clinics and pharmacies. Restaurants, bars and nightclubs are also thick on the ground, but it's easy to avoid the bawdier side of town if you want to. Reynosa is more attractive and less intimidating than Nuevo Laredo, but not as charming as Matamoros.

The city was founded in 1749 as Villa de Nuestra Señora de Guadalupe de Reynosa, 20km from its present location – flooding forced the move in 1802. Reynosa was one of the first towns to rise up in the independence movement of 1810, but little of historical interest remains.

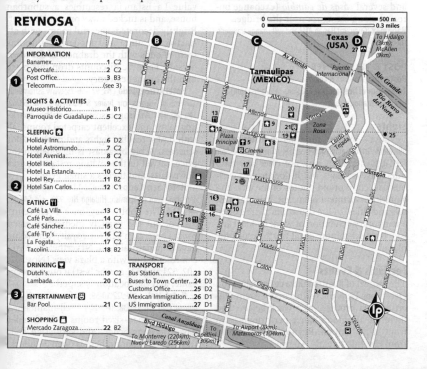

REYNOSA

INFORMATION	
Banamex	1 C2
Cybercafe	2 C2
Post Office	3 B3
Telecomm	(see 3)

SIGHTS & ACTIVITIES	
Museo Histórico	4 B1
Parroquia de Guadalupe	5 C2

SLEEPING	
Holiday Inn	6 D2
Hotel Astromundo	7 C2
Hotel Avenida	8 C2
Hotel Isel	9 C1
Hotel La Estancia	10 C2
Hotel Rey	11 B2
Hotel San Carlos	12 C1

EATING	
Café La Villa	13 C1
Café Paris	14 C2
Café Sánchez	15 C2
Café Tip's	16 C2
La Fogata	17 C2
Tacolini	18 B2

DRINKING	
Dutch's	19 C2
Lambada	20 C1

ENTERTAINMENT	
Bar Pool	21 C1

SHOPPING	
Mercado Zaragoza	22 B2

TRANSPORT	
Bus Station	23 D3
Buses to Town Center	24 D3
Customs Office	25 D2
Mexican Immigration	26 D1
US Immigration	27 D1

Texas (USA)

To Hidalgo (3km); McAllen (9km)

Tamaulipas (MEXICO)

Puente Internacional

Río Grande

Río Bravo del Norte

Zona Rosa

0   500 m
0   0.3 miles

To Monterrey (220km); Nuevo Laredo (256km)

Blvd Hidalgo

Canal Anzalduas

To Capelitui (300m)

To Airport (8km); Matamoros (104km)

Orientation

Reynosa's central streets are laid out on a grid pattern, between the Río Bravo del Norte and the Canal Anzalduas. The Plaza Principal, on a rise a few blocks southwest of the Puente Internacional, is the site of the town hall, banks, hotels, a movie theater and a modern church.

Extending south of the plaza, Hidalgo is a pedestrianized lane lined with shops and cafés. Between the bridge and the center lies the Zona Rosa, with restaurants, bars and nightclubs.

If you're leaving Mexico, follow the signs to the Puente Internacional.

Information

EMERGENCY
Cruz Roja (Red Cross; ☎ 922-13-14)
Police (☎ 060)

INTERNET ACCESS
Cibercafe (Matamoros 735; per hr $1.50)

MONEY
There are banks on and south of the plaza, and several *casas de cambio* (exchange bureaus) along Zaragoza near the bridge.
Banamex (Guerrero) Has an ATM and will change traveler's checks.

POST & TELEPHONES
Post office (cnr Díaz & Colón)
Telecomm office (cnr Díaz & Colón; ☻ 7am-11pm)
Offers international calls

Sights

Reynosa's modest little **Museo Histórico** (cnr Allende & Ortega; admission free; ☻ 9am-2pm & 4-8pm Tue-Sat, 10am-2pm Sun) may not offer any flash interactive displays, but it does have a curious collection of old photos of the city, and a quirky assortment of ancient cameras, pistols and rifles. In the rear room there's often a temporary exhibition of work by local artists. It's a 10-minute stroll northwest of the plaza.

Festivals & Events

The festival of **Nuestra Señora de Guadalupe**, on December 12, is the town's major event. Pilgrims start processions a week before, and there are afternoon dance performances in front of the church. Reynosa's **feria** is held from late July to early August.

Sleeping

BUDGET
Most of the cheap places near the Puente Internacional are very basic. There are much better options available around the plaza for a few dollars more. Virtually every hotel in town has air-con.

Hotel Rey (☎ 922-29-80; Díaz Nte 556; s/d $27/34; P ⊠) This six-storey landmark is now looking slightly worn, but the tariffs are fair, and it offers a secure, central location. The rooms, all with bathrooms, are kept clean, and some offer terrific views.

Hotel Avenida (☎ 922-05-92; Zaragoza Ote 885; s/d $26/31; ⊠) A short walk from the bridge, this two-storey place is reasonable value for money, with modest-sized rooms that have cable TV and phones, and are grouped around a rear courtyard.

MIDRANGE
There are a few good-quality hotels around the center. International chains and business hotels are further outside of town.

Hotel La Estancia (☎ 922-00-77; Guerrero 735; s/d $32/39; P ⊠) The unassuming but superb value La Estancia resembles a suburban house, and is tucked away on a quiet street. Brightly decorated, cheerful rooms with attractive furniture and modern bathrooms seem at odds with the drabness of the town outside. Periodic discounts drop this place into the budget category.

Hotel Astromundo (☎ 922-56-25; www.astromundo .com.mx in Spanish; cnr Juárez & Guerrero ; s/d $53/62; P ⊠ ▯) An impressive place with a sparkling lobby and excellent carpeted rooms, all with desks, reading lights and neutral color schemes. A big breakfast is included in the price, served in the inviting restaurant area downstairs, and there's a small gym.

Hotel San Carlos (☎ 922-12-80; www.sancarlos dereynosa.com in Spanish; Hidalgo Nte 970; s/d $48/53; P ⊠) The lobby may have been refurbished, but the vaguely medieval-themed rooms here aren't fit for royalty, and some have little natural light. Nevertheless, if you can reserve one with a plaza view (Nos 501, 502, 521 and 521 are the best) it offers decent value, and the location is superb.

Hotel Isel (☎ 922-10-59; Chapa s/n; hotel_isel@ hotmail.com; s/d $33/38; P ⊠) Well-maintained place with good-sized rooms – the doubles have two large beds – and very clean hallways. The restaurant here is open 24 hours.

TOP END

Holiday Inn (☎ 921-65-00; Emilio Portes Gil 703; r $112; P ⊠ ⊠ ▢ ⊠) The top luxury choice in town, the Holiday Inn has commodious rooms with full facilities including broadband access. There's a large outdoor pool, Jacuzzi and fitness center. It's about 800m southeast of the plaza.

Eating

In addition to the following listings, you'll find standard-issue taco and fast-food joints on and around Hidalgo.

Café La Villa (☎ 922-02-67; cnr Zaragoza & Hidalgo; breakfasts $4, mains $4.50-7) A dependable, eccentrically styled place, where the back room is decorated like a banquet hall, and the casual front area resembles a Paris café. The good-value menus are standard, however, concentrating on tacos, enchiladas and the rest.

Tacolini (☎ 922-73-94; Hidalgo 560; tacos $5; ✆ 11am-8pm) Easily the most classy taco joint in town, this modish, clean open-fronted place has an extensive menu including wonderfully tasty *chuleta con tocino y queso* (pork, bacon and cheese) tacos.

La Fogata (☎ 922-47-72 Matamoros 750; mains $7-29) Large restaurant with formally attired staff and opulent decor, including an elaborately carved hardwood bar. The huge menu includes Mexican and international cuisine with dishes such as *camarones al tequila* (prawn in tequila sauce; $16) while the wine list offers plenty of choice from Chile and Spain. Favored by Reynosa's high society.

Capellini (☎ 922-09-00; Ejército Nacional 250; mains $6-15) Authentic Italian restaurant where the chef uses imported ingredients, including buffalo mozzarella for pizza toppings. Tuck into pasta, or delicious mains like salmon and chicken dishes. It's located south of the center; head along Chapa and then it's 300m south of the canal.

Café Sánchez (☎ 922-16-65; Morelos 575 Ote; breakfasts $3.50, mains $3.50-7; ✆ 7am-7pm) This venerable place has a daily *comida corrida* ($6) as well as plenty of Mexican fare, including *ternera deshebrada* (shredded beef).

Café Paris (☎ 922-55-35; Hidalgo 815; breakfasts $2.25-3.25, mains $3.25-8) Half a block south of the plaza, this branch of the popular chain features breakfasts and tasty Mexican dishes. Waiters wheel carts of pastries around and serve *café lechero*, pouring coffee and milk from separate pitchers.

Café Tips (☎ 922-60-19; Méndez 640; meals $3) Mexican favorites, including burritos, come in filling portions at this simple place, which also sells beer, unlike most other budget places in the center.

Entertainment

Reynosa's Zona Rosa has a slew of gringo-geared restaurants and bars that which come to life only when the young Texas crowd rolls into town. Popular bars include **Lambada** (Allende 142; ✆ 10pm-2am) and **Dutch's** (Ocampo; ✆ 8pm-3am), while the club **Bar Pool** (cnr Ocampo & Allende; ✆ 10pm-4am) has a huge dance floor with pumping beats. Sleazier entertainment (exotic dancing and prostitution) is the rule at 'boys' town', a few kilometers west, just beyond where Aldama becomes a dirt road.

Shopping

The stores inside **Mercado Zaragoza** (Hidalgo) sell ceramics, leather goods and souvenirs.

Getting There & Away

AIR

Reynosa's own airport, **Aeropuerto General Lucio Blanco** (☎ 958-00-00), is 8km southeast of town, off the Matamoros road. **Aeroméxico** (☎ 926-04-93) has two daily direct flights to/from Mexico City and a daily flight to/from Guadalajara.

BUS

The **bus station** (☎ 922 99-74; Av Colón; ✆ 24hr) is on the southeastern corner of the central grid, opposite the parking lot of the Gigante supermarket. Buses run to dozens of destinations in Mexico. Daily services include the following:

Destination	Price	Duration	Frequency
Aguascalientes	$51	12hr	hourly 1st-class
Ciudad Victoria	$23	4½hr	6 1st-class
Guadalajara	$80	15hr	7 1st-class
Matamoros	$6.50/6	2hr	every 2hr
Mexico City	$86	14hr	2 deluxe
(Terminal Norte)	$67	14hr	6 1st-class
Monterrey	$16	3hr	hourly 1st-class
Saltillo	$20	5hr	5 1st-class
San Luis Potosí	$35	10hr	3 1st-class
Tampico	$34	8hr	2 1st-class
Torreón	$35	9hr	9 1st-class
Zacatecas	$43	10hr	2 1st-class

First-class buses also serve Chihuahua, Ciudad Juárez, Durango, Puebla, Querétaro, Veracruz and Villahermosa, and 2nd-class buses leave here to mainly local destinations. Direct daily buses run to Houston ($29), San Antonio ($27), Austin ($34) and Dallas ($44).

The nearest Texas transportation center, McAllen, is 9km from the border. **Valley Transit Company** (in McAllen ☎ 956-686-54-79) runs buses between the McAllen and Reynosa bus stations every 30 minutes between 6am and 10pm ($6). In Reynosa, purchase tickets at the Greyhound counter at the bus station.

US and Mexican immigration are at their respective ends of the bridge, and there's another Mexican post inside the Reynosa bus station. Get a tourist card stamped at either Mexican post if you're proceeding beyond the border area deeper into Mexico.

CAR & MOTORCYCLE

East of the bridge, there's an *aduana* (customs office) that can issue car permits. To get there, turn left up Av Alemán after clearing immigration, and follow the yellow arrows. Take the first left after the Matamoros turnoff; the entrance is at the end of the street.

Going west to Monterrey (220km), the toll Hwy 40D is excellent and patrolled by Green Angels (bilingual mechanics in green uniforms and green trucks); the tolls total $18. (The less-direct toll-free Hwy 40 follows roughly the same route.) Hwys 97 and 180 south to Tampico are two-lane, surfaced roads, but not too busy. Hwy 101 branches off Hwy 180 to Ciudad Victoria and the scenic climb to San Luis Potosí. Hwy 2 to Nuevo Laredo is in fair shape, but it's quicker to travel on the US side of the Río Bravo del Norte. Side roads off Hwy 2 reach a number of obscure border crossings and the Presa Falcón (Falcon Reservoir), as well as Guerrero Viejo, a town that was submerged after the dam's construction in 1953, and moved to its current site at Nueva Ciudad Guerrero, 33km to the southeast. It's a smooth one-hour drive east to Matamoros via the toll Hwy 2D, which begins just past Reynosa airport ($4.50).

Getting Around

Peseros (battered buses) rattle around Reynosa. From the international bridge to the bus station, catch one of the Valley Transit

Company coaches coming from McAllen with 'Reynosa' on the front ($2).

To get from the bus station to the town center, turn left after exiting the bus station and go half a block, then cross the Gigante parking lot to the bus stop on Colón. Take one of the buses labeled 'Olmo' ($0.40).

Taxis between the bus station and the bridge should not cost more than $4, though you'll have to pay around $6 in the opposite direction. Expect to pay around $14 for a taxi ride to/from the airport.

MATAMOROS

☎ 868 / pop 435,000

While Matamoros could hardly be described as a cultural mecca, it's the most likable of the gritty Mexican border towns that dot the frontier with Texas. With a cluster of historic buildings, a decent contemporary-art museum and a stylish restaurant or two, it makes a relatively easygoing and fairly attractive base, though most visitors here are daytrippers from *el otro lado* (the other side).

The city has a shady plaza dotted with ornate wrought-iron benches, and also a fine blue-tiled Mudejar bandstand. Standing on the west side of the square is a Gothic-style cathedral with twin bell towers and a dusky pink facade. South of the central area is a broad swathe of newer industrial zones.

First settled during the Spanish colonization of Tamaulipas in 1686 as Los Esteros Hermosos (The Beautiful Estuaries), the city was renamed in 1793 after Padre Mariano Matamoros. In 1846, Matamoros was the first Mexican city to be taken by US forces in the Mexican-American War; Zachary Taylor then used it as a base for his attack on Monterrey. During the US Civil War, when sea routes to the Confederacy were blockaded, Matamoros shipped cotton out of Confederate Texas, and supplies and war material in.

Orientation

Matamoros lies across the Río Bravo del Norte from Brownsville, Texas. The river is spanned by the Puente Nuevo (International Gateway Bridge), which is the most convenient for the town center, and the Puente Zaragoza (Veteran's Bridge), 3km to the east which offers a more direct route south into Mexico. Both are open 24 hours and have border controls at each

MATAMOROS

INFORMATION
Banca Afirme	**1** C2
Bancomer	**2** C2
Banorte	**3** C2
Galaxy Ciber Café	**4** C2
Internet Cyber Café	**5** C2
Lavandería Americana	**6** C1
Post Office	**7** B3
Scotiabank Inverlat	**8** C2
Telecomm	(see 7)
US Consulate	**9** C1

SIGHTS & ACTIVITIES
Casa Cross	**10** B1
MACT	**11** C1
Museo Casamata	**12** D2

SLEEPING
Best Western Hotel Plaza Matamoros	**13** B2
Hotel Autel Nieto	**14** B2
Hotel Colonial	**15** C2
Hotel Majestic	**16** B2
Hotel Ritz	**17** B2
Hotel Roma	**18** B2

EATING
Aroma's	**19** C2
Café Latino	**20** C2
Café Paris	**21** C2
Cafetería Deli	**22** C2
Los Norteños	**23** B2
Mi Pueblito	**24** C2
Restaurant Louisiana	**25** B2
Takai	**26** C1

ENTERTAINMENT
Teatro de la Reforma	**27** C2

SHOPPING
Mercado Juárez	**28** B2

TRANSPORT
Aero California	**29** C2
Bus Station	**30** C3
Combi Vans to Playa Bagdad	**31** B2

---

end. The Río Bravo del Norte is a disappointing trickle in this area, as most of its water has been siphoned off upstream for irrigation.

From the southern end of Puente Nuevo, Alvaro Obregón heads down to the town's central grid, 1.5km to the southwest.

Information

EMERGENCY
Cruz Roja (Red Cross; ☎ 812-00-04)
Police (☎ 060)

INTERNET ACCESS
Galaxy Ciber Café (Abasolo 74; per hr $1.25) Between Calles 5 and 6.
Internet Cyber Café (Edificio Adan Lorano 106, cnr Calle 5 & Morelos; per hr $1.50)

INTERNET RESOURCES
Matamoros Punto Com (www.matamoros.com) A visitors' guide to Monterrey with business information and good online city maps.

LAUNDRY
Lavandería Americana (Bustamante 601; per load $3.25)

MONEY
In Brownsville, there are exchange houses, some open 24 hours, on International Blvd, which runs north from Puente Nuevo.
Banca Afirme (Plaza Hidalgo) Has an ATM and will also change cash or traveler's checks.
Banorte (Plaza Hidalgo) Has the same services.

POST
Post office (cnr Calle 11 & Río Bravo) About 1km south of the center.

TOURIST INFORMATION
Tourist office (☎ 812-02-12; www.ocvmatamoros.com in Spanish; Obregón s/n; ☺ 9am-5pm Mon-Fri, 9am-2pm Sat) Just south of Puente Nuevo, this helpful place has piles of useful information about Matamoros and excellent maps. Some staff speak English.

Dangers & Annoyances
Matamoros is one of the more tranquil border towns, but the city is a transit point for both people- and narcotic-smuggling. However visitors are extremely unlikely to be caught up in the violence that can be associated with these activities.

SCAMS

Taxi drivers sometimes ask for extortionate rates for short journeys from the border. Fix the price first; around $6 is an acceptable tariff to central Matamoros, and offer a little more to the bus station.

Sights

MUSEO DE ARTE CONTEMPORANEO DE TAMAULIPAS

Matamoros' excellent contemporary art museum **MACT** (☎ 813-14-99; http://mact.tamaulipas.gob .mx; cnr Calle 5 & Constitución; admission $1.50, Wed free; ☻ 10am-6pm Tue-Sat) showcases first-rate exhibitions of photography, sculptures and paintings. The building itself is a landmark modernist structure, completed in 1968, with a maze-like interior, and walls (some inlaid with pebbles) set at oblique angles to the polished concrete floor. Fine local *artesanías* (handicrafts) are sold in the foyer.

CASA CROSS

This imposing, partly restored **Victorian mansion** (☎ 812-23-25; cnr Calle 7 & Herrera; admission free; ☻ 10am-2pm Mon-Fri), complete with elaborate verandas and dormer windows, has a fascinating history. The three-storey house, finished in 1885, was the home of an Englishman, Meliton Cross, who fell in love with and married a black nurse, against his father's wishes. The couple later settled in Matamoros. Casa Cross is a highly atmospheric place, with some period furnishings, original wallpaper and fireplaces, though there remains a lot of restoration to be done.

MUSEO CASAMATA

Dating from 1845, this **fort** (☎ 816-20-71; cnr Guatemala & Degollado) was part of the original city defenses. Though closed for renovation at the time of research, it should reopen with improved displays of Mexican revolutionary memorabilia and historic photographs of the city.

MUSEO DEL AGRARISMO MEXICANO

This small modern **museum** (☎ 837-05-27; Hwy Playa Bagdad, Km 6.5; admission free; ☻ 9am-5pm Tue-Fri, 9am-2pm Sat & Sun) documents the *ejido* social movement, a campaign for the redistribution of land in Mexico, as well as the history of the Mexican revolution in Tamaulipas. To get here take a Playa Bagdad–bound combi; the museum is 200m north of the highway.

PLAYA BAGDAD

The nearest beach to Matamoros is Playa Bagdad, a scruffy settlement that clings to an expansive stretch of clean sand 37km east of town. A large port prospered on the Mexican bank of the Río Bravo del Norte just north of here until hurricanes destroyed the settlement in the early 20th century. According to local folklore this town was given the name 'Bagdad' by Texans, who were astounded by its wealth (mostly derived from smuggling), though there's nothing left to see of the old port anymore.

Playa Bagdad today consists of a tiny fishing settlement and a row of wind-battered clapboard and concrete beach restaurants, including the clean, hospitable **Costa Azul** (seafood mains $6, beer $1.50; ☻ 8am-11pm). If you head away from the bus stop it's easy to find a peaceful spot on the beach, unless it's a holiday – then the sands are packed with parked cars.

Hwy 2 from Matamoros is a four-lane highway for most of the route to Bagdad. Blue, ramshackle combi vans head here from Calle 10 on the east side of Plaza Allende ($1.75, one hour), leaving hourly during the summer months but only when full at quiet times of the year. The last bus back to Matamoros is at 7pm.

Festivals & Events

Expo Fiesta Matamoros Held every year from late June to early July, and features an amusement park, handicrafts displays and live music.

Festival Internacional de Otoño Cultural events, in October, include chamber music and traditional dance displays, many performed in the beautifully restored Teatro de la Reforma.

Sleeping

Like most border towns in Mexico, accommodation is not great value in Matamoros. Cheap places tend to be very basic but there are several decent midrange options.

BUDGET

Hotel Majestic (☎ 813-36-80; Abasolo 131; s/d with fan $14/21) Clean, if slightly drab, rooms with ceiling fans and tiled floors off a long corridor. Run by a firm señora, it's less dispiriting than the Hotel México next door.

MIDRANGE

Hotel Colonial (☎ 816-66-06; www.hcolonial.com; cnr Calle 6 & Matamoros; s $48, d $53-63; P ✗ ⚛) This place has been pleasingly refurbished and has a welcoming, stylish lobby area. The inviting rooms all come with sturdy wooden beds, Mexican-themed prints on the walls, attractively tiled floors and bathrooms. Breakfast is included.

Hotel Ritz (☎ 812-11-90; www.ritzhotel.org; Matamoros 612; r $53; P ☼ ▣) The Ritz has a garish purple facade but its rooms are much more sober, with attractive wooden beds, reading lights and desks. There's a gym, laundry service and a piano bar. A filling breakfast is gratis.

Best Western Plaza Matamoros (☎ 816-16-96; www.bestwestern.com/mx/hotelplazamatamoros; cnr Calle 4 & Bravo; r $69; P ☼ ▣ ☎) A well-run place, catering mainly to business travelers, where the fairly spacious, carpeted rooms have most mod cons including safes, irons and hairdryers. The ungainly looking central atrium covers a ground-floor snack bar, while the outdoor pool is tiny.

Other possibilities include the following:

Hotel Roma (☎ 813-61-76, 800-112-43-76; cnr Calle 9 & Bravo; r US$41; P ☼) A modern hotel with plain but comfortable, hotel chain-style rooms, all with safes and most with reading lights.

Hotel Autel Nieto (☎ 813-08-57; autelnieto@hotmail.com; Calle 10 No 1508; s/d $34/45; P ☼ ▣ ☎) Old-fashioned but a fair value, all the large rooms have cable TV, and there's a bar-restaurant and a small (unheated) pool.

Hotel Hernández (☎ 812-55-45; www.hotelhernandez.com in Spanish; Laguna Madre 105; $33/40; P ☼) A long-running place 750m southwest of the bus station.

TOP END

Best Western Gran Hotel Residencial (☎ 813-94-40, 00-718-8230; www.bestwestern.com; Obregón 249; r incl breakfast $126; P ☼ ☼ ▣ ☎) Set in large leafy grounds with two pools, this low-rise hotel has 114 fully equipped, comfortable rooms, some with balconies. There's a restaurant and cocktail bar. It's 1.2km south of the Puente Nuevo.

Holiday Inn (☎ 811-50-00, 800-221-97-75; www.hiinnmatamoros.com in Spanish; Av Cárdenes 5001; r/ste $98/124; P ☼ ☼ ▣ ☎) Comfortable and a fair value, but 4km south of the plaza, and the pool is indoors.

Eating

Matamoros has a smattering of fashionable restaurants as well as plenty of down-to-earth places, where the emphasis is more on substance than style.

Aroma's (☎ 812-62-33; Calle 6 No 181; panini $4.50-6, mains $8-11; ☼ 9am-1.30am; P) Matamoros' hippest venue boasts a ground-floor restaurant with exposed brick walls and an intimate garden patio, where you can enjoy breakfasts ($5), salads and well-executed dishes including *scampi de mariscos* (deep-fried seafood; $10.50). The bar area upstairs, with modern booths and avant-garde paintings, is perfect cocktail-quaffing territory and has live music on Saturday nights and DJs spinning house and lounge tunes on Fridays.

Café Latino (☎ 816-90-93; Morelos 84; mains $5-7; ☼ 3-11pm Mon-Fri, 10am-11pm Sat) Café Latino is a stunning setting for a snack or a drink, with elegant colonial-style floor tiles, brick walls and dramatic artwork. There's a selection of dishes, including *tortilla española* ($5), with plenty of healthy eating and vegetarian options. No marks for the coffee prices however – a cappuccino is $3!

Mi Pueblito (☎ 816-05-86; Constitución 13; mains $6-12.50) Positioned opposite MACT, this large atmospheric restaurant is topped by a soaring *palapa* (thatched) roof and has colorful textile tablecloths. It offers a long menu of Mexican favorites, but it's best value is the filling set lunch ($6.75), which includes a drink and soup starter. There's a fine tequila and cigar selection here.

Takai (☎ 812-43-92; Plaza Mexicana, cnr Calle 6 & Herrera; sushi $1.50-2.25, set meals $5.50-11; P). Small informal Japanese place with winsome tempura salads, *teppanyaki* and *yakisoba* dishes and lots of set-meal options.

Cafetería Deli (☎ 812-61-14; Matamoros 82; meals $3-5; ☼ 6am-9pm) Small informal place next to Hotel Ritz with dishes including *chiles rellenos, camarones en salsa* (seafood in salsa) and bargain set lunches ($3.25). It's the best bet in town for an early breakfast.

Café Paris (☎ 816-03-10; González 125; breakfast $3.50, mains $3-8) The decor at this temple to kitsch is a riotous assembly of mirrored walls and chandeliers. The food is much more mundane however: standard-issue Mexican breakfasts and pastries, plus enchiladas ($4), salads and steaks.

Restaurant Louisiana (☎ 812-10-96; Bravo 807; sandwiches $4.50, mains $9-11; P) One of the swankiest places in town, this formal restaurant offers very filling mains including Tampico-style steak ($10.50), quail and frogs' legs – all served with avocado, fries, tostadas and salad.

Los Norteños (☎ 813-00-37; Matamoros 109; mains $4.50-11) A carnivore's delight, head here for authentic north Mexican cuisine like *cabrito* ($8.50) and chicken cooked over huge charcoal pits.

Shopping

The 'new market,' **Mercado Juárez** (☼ 8am-6:30pm Mon-Sat, 9am-5pm Sun), occupies the blocks bordered by Calles 9 and 10, and Abasolo and Matamoros. A lot of the stuff on sale is second-rate but there's plenty of variety.

Getting There & Away

AIR

Matamoros has an **airport** (☎ 812 2163) 17km out of town on the road to Ciudad Victoria. **Aeroméxico** (☎ 812-24-60) operate two daily direct flights, and **Mexicana** (☎ 800-502-20-00; www .mexicana.com) one daily direct flight, to Mexico City.

BUS

Both 1st- and 2nd-class buses run from the **bus station** (☎ 812 0181; Canales; ☼ 24hr) near the corner of Guatemala. There's an immigration office and restaurant here (both open 24 hours a day), post office, left-luggage service and a telephone office (which also sells city maps).

Daily services from Matamoros include the following:

Destination	Price	Duration	Frequency
Ciudad Victoria	$19	4hr	7 1st-class
Dallas	$40	13hr	11 1st-class
Houston	$28	10hr	9 1st-class
Mexico City	$78	15hr	1 deluxe
(Terminal	$66	15hr	8 1st-class
Norte)	$60	15hr	2 2nd-class
Monterrey	$22	5hr	17 1st-class
Reynosa	$6.50	2hr	hourly 1st-class
	$6	2hr	5 2nd-class
Saltillo	$24	7hr	13 1st-class
San Antonio	$32	11hr	5 1st-class
Tampico	$26	7hr	10 1st-class
Torreón	$39	9hr	8 1st-class

Buses go to many other destinations including Chihuahua, Durango, Guadalajara, San Luis Potosí and Veracruz.

You can get buses from Brownsville, Texas direct to several cities inside Mexico, but they cost more than from Matamoros, and they might take up to two hours to get over the international bridge and through customs and immigration. It's quicker to walk across the bridge and take local transport to the Matamoros bus station.

Facing the US from the north end of Puente Nuevo, go left (west) on Elizabeth then two blocks south on 12th for the **Brownsville bus station** (☎ 956-546-71-71; 1134 E St Charles) There are buses to all the major cities in Texas, and connections to other US cities.

The Mexican border post waves most pedestrians through on the assumption that they are visitors over for the day, but some cars will get the red light to be checked. If you're planning to proceed further south into Mexico, get a tourist card from immigration here (or at the other office inside the main bus terminal).

CAR & MOTORCYCLE

Driving across the bridge to/from Brownsville costs $2. At the Mexican end be sure to get your temporary vehicle permit (and cancel it on the way back).

The main routes on into Mexico are Hwy 180 south to Tampico and Hwy 101 southwest to Ciudad Victoria and into the Bajío region (see opposite for more information on Hwys 180 and 101). These two-lane roads are both in fair condition and free of tolls. Officials at various checkpoints will want to see your tourist card and vehicle permit, and might check your vehicle for drugs or firearms. Hwy 2D leads west to Reynosa, from where Hwys 40 and 40D continue to Monterrey.

Getting Around

Matamoros is served by small buses called maxi-taxis, which charge $0.50 to anywhere in town. You can stop them on any street corner. Ruta 2 maxi-taxis pass the bus station on Calle 1 and go to the town center.

To get to the bus station from the Puente Nuevo border, take a city bus marked 'Colonial Verde' or 'Central de Autobuses' from behind the tourist office. From the border to the town center hop aboard one of the free buses (every 15 minutes) that leave from the García crafts shop on Obregón near the bridge; these drop you off by Mercado Juárez. Some taxi drivers ask for a hefty $11 (or more) from the border to the center, though most will accept $6 to $7 if you bargain.

SOUTH OF MATAMOROS

It's 500km to Tampico from Matamoros along Hwy 180, which roughly follows the contours of the Gulf coastline, around 50km or so inland. This route passes through unspectacular lowlands where sugarcane is the chief crop, though there are some more scenic stretches where the foothills of the Sierra Madre Oriental skirt the coast. Budget and midrange hotels are found in **San Fernando** (137km from Matamoros), **Soto La Marina** (267km) and **Aldama** (379km). Side roads go east to the coast, most of which consists of lagoons separated from the gulf by narrow sand spits. The longest is the **Laguna Madre**, extending some 230km along the northern Tamaulipas coast. (The lagoon dried up in the mid-20th century, forcing many to leave the area. When a 1967 hurricane replenished it, the area was resettled by people from Veracruz.) The lagoons, sand dunes and coastal wetlands support a unique ecosystem, with many bird species and excellent fishing.

About 20km south of Matamoros, just past the airport, a side road crosses marshland for 60km before reaching **El Mezquital**, a small fishing village with a lighthouse and beach on the long thin spit of land that divides the Laguna Madre from the Gulf. From San Fernando, 120km further south, a road leads to **Carboneras**, another small fishing village facing the lagoon. There's not much here, but you might be able to get a boat out to the lagoon barrier island, where porpoises can sometimes be seen. Food and gas are available, but there are no rooms for rent in either El Mezquital or Carboneras.

From Soto La Marina, about 130km south of San Fernando, Hwy 70 heads east for 70km, paralleling the Río Soto La Marina, to La Pesca. Further south, a 45km road runs east from Aldama, through the eastern fringes of the Sierra de Tamaulipas, to **Barra el Tordo**, another fishing village with a beach and good sportfishing. Facilities include budget and midrange hotels, restaurants and a campground.

LA PESCA

☎ 835 / pop 1600

If coming directly from the US or a Mexican city to the north, La Pesca feels satisfyingly worlds apart. It maintains the ramshackle and relaxed air of an ordinary fishing village – you'll drive right through if you're

not careful. The long, wide sandy beach, Playa La Pesca, 6km east of town, is dotted with *palapa* shades and has two seaside restaurants. It's all but deserted here during the day, though on weekends families cruise in from Ciudad Victoria and Monterrey. The Río Soto La Marina and the Laguna Morales have abundant rainbow trout, kingfish, sea bass, porgy and sole, while some of the fish offshore include tarpon and baitfish. Most of the hotels can arrange boat rentals with fishing guides for around $65 a day. A fishing tournament for sea bass takes place in November.

One of the world's most endangered sea turtles, Kemp's Ridley, known locally as the *tortuga lora* (parrot turtle) because of its beak-like nose, nests on this coastline from March to July. The Tamaulipas state environmental authority has a **turtle center** (in Ciudad Victoria ☎ 834-312-60-18; ☉ 9am-4.30pm), 800m north of the main beach, dedicated to the species' preservation at La Pesca, the northern limit of the turtle's nesting grounds. Visitors are educated about protection efforts and offered a firsthand glimpse of the hatching process during the months of peak activity.

There are no banks or ATMs and most places do not accept credit cards. You can purchase a phone card to make long-distance calls but sometimes the entire town can run out.

For somewhere to stay, the **Rivera del Río** (☎ 327-06-58; s/d $27/37; P ❄ ☐) makes an excellent choice. Heading west out of town, look to your right for the sign and turnoff at the Km 48 marker. The 34 rooms here are large and quite plain but the well-maintained grounds are lovely, with a swimming pool perched over the river. There's a good **restaurant** (☉ Thu-Sun) attached serving trout and sea bass dishes ($8); and fishing and self-catering facilities are also available here. On your left, just before the Rivera del Río turnoff, the functional rooms of the ordinary **Hotel Titanic** (r $22; P ❄) will do for a base in town. If you have your own transport, there are plenty of riverside hotels along the approach to La Pesca. All are geared to accommodating families for the weekend, and most offer discounts at other times. Many feature piers with lights for night-fishing and grills for cooking your catch. **La Gaviota** (☎ 818-192-01-04; www.lagaviota.info;

Humberto Lobo 161A; bungalows $82; (P) (☒)) is one of the nicest of these, with RV hookups ($18), and attractive brick-built bungalows in a lovely landscaped riverside plot with a pool, a tennis court and a restaurant.

The nondescript village also has a few grocery stores and taco stands. For table service, try **El Barco del Capitán Axel** (☎ 327-07-15; seafood mains $6-8), which accepts some credit cards, and is just before the bridge as you enter La Pesca proper. Or unwind with drinks and a meal at **Posada Restaurant** (seafood mains $7), next to the lighthouse at Playa la Pesca.

Transportes Tamaulipecos De La Costa runs 11 buses a day between Ciudad Victoria's bus terminal and Playa La Pesca ($10, three hours). You can also catch any of these buses from Soto La Marina's central plaza, an hour from La Pesca ($2).

CIUDAD VICTORIA
☎ 834 / pop 270,000 / elevation 230m
Despite its status as the capital of the state of Tamaulipas, Ciudad Victoria is a thoroughly provincial city. It's an unpretentious place, and though it lacks any real sights, it does make a good place to break a journey, and has regular bus connections in every direction. With the Sierra Madre Oriental forming an impressive backdrop to the city, there's just enough altitude to ensure that the climate is a little more bearable than the sticky heat of the coastal plains.

Orientation
Three highways converge at Ciudad Victoria, and a ring road allows through traffic to move between them without entering the city itself. The center is laid out in a grid pattern. The north–south streets have both numbers (Calle 7, Calle 8 etc) and names (Díaz, Tijerina etc). Most of the shops, from the central market to the Centro Cultural Tamaulipas, are on Hidalgo. The Río San Marcos, a small trickle for much of the year, separates the city center from neighborhoods that are steadily creeping up the mountainside to the south.

Information
Copy & Ciber Express (Calle 9 No 202; per hr $1) For Internet access; also offers discounted international phone calls.
Lavandería Burbuja (Matamoros 939; wash & dry $3.50; ☽ 8am-6pm Mon-Sat) A do-it-yourself service, a block north of the plaza.

Main post office (Morelos) Northeast of the plaza in the Palacio Federal building.

Sights & Activities
Ciudad Victoria lacks compelling attractions but there is the **Museo de Antropología e Histori** (☎ 318-18-31; Matamoros; admission free; ☽ 9:30am-7pr Mon-Fri), one block north of Plaza Hidalgo, ru by the University of Tamaulipas. It's a grab bag of Huastec ceramics, mammoth bones colonial memorabilia, revolutionary photo and one vintage carriage. It's a measure o the scarce foot traffic that the attendant o duty is likely to greet you with a warm an somewhat surprised welcome.

Both the **Palacio de Gobierno del Estado** (Juárez between Calles 15 and 16, and the **Teatro Juá rez**, facing the north side of the Plaza Hidalg have large murals. The **Paseo Méndez** has plent of greenery, and a couple of **public pools** (admis sion $1; ☽ 7am-10pm). There is an entrance t Paseo Méndez on Calle 17 (Madero) betwee Berriozabal and Carrera Torres.

About 40km northeast of Ciudad Victori the **Presa Vicente Guerrero** is a huge reservoi that attracts Mexicans and US citizens fo bass fishing. There's a free camping groun here with hookups.

Sleeping
All of these places are within a few block of Plaza Hidalgo.

Hotel Villa de Aguayo (☎ 312-78-18; Calle 10; s/ with fan $18/23 with air-con $21/26; (P) (☒)) A hos pitable place with excellent value, scrupu lously clean, pleasant if smallish rooms, al with firm beds and cable TV.

Hotel Los Monteros (☎ 312-03-00; Plaza Hidalg 962; r with fan/air-con $24/29; (☒)) Good value, i sparsely presented, tiled rooms and a fin courtyard and garden. Rooms No 202 to 20 have views over the plaza.

Best Western Santorín (☎ 318-15-15; www.sa torinhotel.com in Spanish; Colón 349; r $91; (P) (☒) (▢) Large hotel with very spacious, nicely fur nished rooms, each with an iron, a safe an broadband connection. Also has a gym an a stylish restaurant, and offers free airpor transfers and weekend discounts.

Also worth considering:
Howard Johnson Hotel Everest (☎ 318-70-70; ww .howard-johnson-everest.com in Spanish; Colón 126; r $12 (P) (☒) (☒) (▢) (▢)) Luxurious, modern rooms, some with balconies overlooking the plaza. Weekend rates can drop to half the standard rack rate.

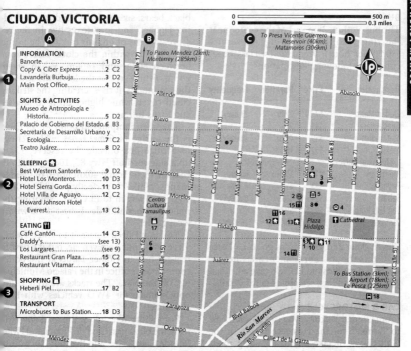

CIUDAD VICTORIA

0	500 m
0	0.3 miles

INFORMATION
Banorte	1 D3
Copy & Ciber Express	2 C2
Lavandería Burbuja	3 D2
Main Post Office	4 D2

SIGHTS & ACTIVITIES
Museo de Antropología e Historia	5 D2
Palacio de Gobierno del Estado	6 B3
Secretaría de Desarrollo Urbano y Ecología	7 C2
Teatro Juárez	8 D2

SLEEPING
Best Western Santorín	9 D2
Hotel Los Monteros	10 D3
Hotel Sierra Gorda	11 D3
Hotel Villa de Aguayo	12 C2
Howard Johnson Hotel Everest	13 C2

EATING
Café Cantón	14 C3
Daddy's	(see 13)
Los Largares	(see 9)
Restaurant Gran Plaza	15 C2
Restaurant Vitamar	16 C2

SHOPPING
Heberli Piel	17 B2

TRANSPORT
Microbuses to Bus Station	18 D3

To Paseo Mendez (2km); Monterrey (285km)

To Presa Vicente Guerrero Reservoir (40km); Matamoros (306km)

To Bus Station (3km); Airport (18km); La Pesca (225km)

---

otel Sierra Gorda (☎ 312-20-10; Plaza Hidalgo 990;
d $44/50; (P) (X)) Garish, aging place with bizarre
unting-lodge decor.

ating

here's not a lot to get excited about on the
ulinary front in Victoria. You'll find more
hoices, including international chains,
orth of the center.

Restaurant Vitamar (☎ 312-62-29; cnr Calle 10
Morelos; mains $4-7; ⏰ 10am-6pm Mon-Sat). Ex-
ellent value, popular seafood restaurant
here a fresh *pulpo* (octopus) starter is just
2, while delicious dishes like *camarones
la diabla* (prawns in tomato, chili and
oriander sauce) or a *filete al mojo de ajo*
ish in garlic sauce) cost $4.

Café Cantón (☎ 312-16-43; Colón 114; breakfast
, dishes $2.75-5.50) A modest café ideal for a
ick-to-your-ribs breakfast. Try the excel-
nt *huevos machacados* (scrambled eggs with
redded beef), a *norteño* classic. There are
everal branches of this chain around town.

Restaurant Gran Plaza (Morelos 202; mains $3.50)
ffers filling food at cheap prices, and is
articularly good at lunchtime, when their

comida corrida ($3) includes soup, a main
dish, rice, salad and dessert.

These hotel restaurants are the fanciest
places to dine:

Los Lagares (Best Western Santorín, Colón 349; mains
$6-14; (P)). Offering a slightly bizarre attempt at *cocina
contemporánea*, this place has designer surrounds and an
over-elaborate menu that includes dishes like *camarones a
la naranja* (prawns in orange sauce; $10).

Daddy's (☎ 312-67-84; Colón 126; mains $6-12; (P))
Under the Howard Johnson Hotel Everest, this place has filling
Mexican and international food including pasta and steaks.

Shopping

Browse for handicrafts in the Centro Cultural
Tamaulipas building. **Heberli Piel** (☎ 312-19-54;
Pino Suárez Sur 402) has an extensive selection of
hand-embroidered leather goods.

Getting There & Away

AIR

Aeropuerto Nacional General Pedro J Méndez
(☎ 31646-48) is 18km east of town off the Soto
La Marina road. There are daily flights to
Mexico City with **Aeromar** (☎ 316-96-96) and
Matamoros with **Aero California** (☎ 315-18-50).

BUS

The bus station, 3km east of the center near the ring road, has a left-luggage service ($0.50 per hour). Frequent 1st-class buses run to the following destinations:

Destination	Price	Duration	Frequency
Ciudad Mante	$7.50	2½hr	23 daily
Guadalajara	$42	9hr	
Matamoros	$19	4¼hr	20 daily
Mexico City (Terminal Norte)	$52	10½hr	
Monterrey	$18	3¾hr	hourly
Reynosa	$23	4¼hr	6 daily
Saltillo	$24	4¾hr	6 daily
San Luis Potosí	$22	5½hr	
Tampico	$15	4hr	26 daily

Eleven daily 2nd-class buses go to La Pesca ($10, three hours). For Gómez Farías and the Reserva de la Biosfera El Cielo take a Ciudad Mante–bound bus, see opposite for details.

CAR & MOTORCYCLE

From Ciudad Victoria, you can go southeast to Tampico for the Huasteca region or the Gulf Coast, or take one of the steep roads heading west ascending into the Sierra Madre Oriental. For San Luis Potosí, take Hwy 101 southwest – an incredibly scenic route. For Mexico City, south along Hwy 85, via Ciudad Mante and Ciudad Valles, is the most direct route.

Getting Around

To get to the center from the bus station take a Ruta 25 bus, which goes down Bravo, three blocks north of Plaza Hidalgo ($0.50). In the other direction, minibuses labeled 'Palmas' depart from Blvd Balboa at the bridge over the Río San Marcos. Taxis charge $3 for the same trip, or from Plaza Hidalgo to the tourist office.

RESERVA DE LA BIOSFERA EL CIELO

☎ 832 / pop 3600

An incredibly rich, UN-listed biosphere reserve, El Cielo encompasses a 1440-sq-km chunk of steep-sided forested sierra and plunging river valleys. Marking a transition zone between tropical, semidesert and temperate ecosystems, its diversity is incredible, including half of all Mexico's bird species and 40 kinds of bats. Though seldom seen, black bears, six species of wild cat (including jaguar), and gray foxes live in the reserve. Dozens of orchids can also be found here, mostly within the cloud-forest zone between 800m and 1400m. When warm gulf moisture crosses the lowlands and hits the mountains, it rises, creating the striking cloud cover, while higher up it condenses and turns to rain.

The main jumping-off point for El Cielo is the village of **Gómez Farías**, which clings to a ridge just outside the reserve, 12km up a side road off Hwy 85, 108km south of Ciudad Victoria and 40km north of Ciudad Mante. While it's perfectly possible to hike your own way in to El Cielo, exploring the remote higher altitudes is best done with a local guide.

You don't need a permit to enter the reserve with your own vehicle, but it's best to register first in Gómez Farías at the police commander's office in the Palacio Municipal just off the plaza. The tracks are rough, and only suitable for 4WD vehicles with high clearance.

For a short hike, follow the road downhill from the plaza past Casa de Piedra and Hotel Posada Campestre, and the route turns into a delightful, fairly level, cobbled track. After an hour the route splits. From here retrace your steps to get back to Gómez. Alternatively, take the right fork to continue a further 6km (around three hours) up to the village of **Alta Cima** (860m), the starting point for hikes into the cloud forest, including lovely 4km trail up a narrow canyon to the waterfall of El Salto. Deeper into the reserve are **San José** (1400m), two large caves 4km further on from Alta Cima, and **El Elefante** (1640m) 6km along the same track.

Some outdoor enthusiasts rave about the hiking, fishing, rafting and crystal-clear water at a handful of spots along tributaries of the Río Sabinas. Turn off the road heading back to the highway from Gómez Farías to go bathing at **El Nacimiento** and **Poza Azul**.

Tours

Casa de Piedra (opposite) can arrange guides (Ricardo Jímenez Ramírez, who has ornithological expertise, is recommended) for $29 a day, and transport to the reserve. It also has a shop with food and hiking supplies.

For transport into the cloud forest by 4WD, speak to the owners of Hotel Posada

Campestre (below), who run day trips for $85 for a truckload of up to 10 passengers. They also offer trips to nearby waterfalls and swimming spots including La Bocatoma and La Poza Azul.

Sleeping & Eating

Casa de Piedra (☎ 236-21-96; www.tourbymexico.com /elcielo_casadepiedra; Hidalgo; s/d incl breakfast $38/48; **P**) Just 150m past the plaza, Piedra has six beautifully built stone-and-timber rooms with bathtubs; try to reserve 'Magnolia,' which comes with a valley-view balcony. Guests are free to browse the hotel's book collection devoted to Mexican birds and butterflies. The cooking is good here, and includes tasty chicken *mole* ($4.50), though portions are not overly generous. Alcohol is not served, but you can bring you own.

Hotel Posada Campestre (☎ 236-22-00; www .posadaenelcielo.com in Spanish; Hidalgo; r $35; **P** **😺**) About 800m down the same road on the right, Campestre doesn't have Casa de Piedra's character but does offer clean, orderly rooms with bunk beds. There's a restaurant here too and trips are offered.

Besides a few small grocery stores and the hotels, food is scarce in Gómez Farías. For a quick lunch of tacos and enchiladas try Karlitas in the plaza.

To fully appreciate how isolated and pristine the reserve is, spend a night or two in the mountains. The two-storey **Hotel Alta Cima** (☎ 831-254-61-17; r up to 3/6 people $29/48) in the village of the same name, has simple but agreeable rooms. Just across from the hotel, **La Fe** (🕐 8am-6pm), run by the women's co-operative of Alta Cima, cooks up basic but filling meals.

A little further up the road is **El Pino** (1–2-person cabins $14, 6-person cabins $48), a group of low-slung dormitory-style buildings run by the men's cooperative of Alta Cima.

Canindo Research Station (☎ 831-254-59-30; cabins $33), just before you reach the village of San José, about another hour on the extremely rough road past Alta Cima, is a rustic choice offering bunks with mattresses. Solar panels provide sporadic electricity. Cabins here can accommodate 36 people; call beforehand to book, and bring your own food.

Getting There & Away

From Ciudad Mante, three daily Lumux buses go directly to/from Gómez Farías.

Buses between Ciudad Victoria and Mante pass by the turnoff for Gómez on Hwy 85 at the village of Ejido Sabinas Mante every half hour. From here pick-ups shuttle people to/from the plaza in Gómez ($1, every half hour).

NUEVO LEÓN

It was the crown's search for silver and slaves, and the church's desire to proselytize, that brought the Spanish to this arid region. There were several abortive attempts to establish settlements in Monterrey and Monclova, but it was not until 1596 and 1644, respectively, that the Spanish established themselves at those sites, with help from native Mexicans from Tlaxcala and other areas to the south.

Silver was never found, but ranching slowly became viable around the small new towns, despite the raids by hostile Chichimecs from the north that continued into the 18th century. Nuevo León had an estimated 1.5 million sheep by 1710.

As the 19th century progressed and the railways arrived, ranching continued to expand and industry developed, especially in Monterrey. By 1900, Nuevo León had 328,000 inhabitants. The population has continued to escalate, but with the vast majority being concentrated in the Monterrey region. Today the state capital city accounts for 85% of Nuevo León's 3.8 million people, making it one of Mexico's most sparsely populated states.

MONTERREY

☎ 81 / pop 3.6 million

Self-confident Monterrey, capital of Nuevo León, is Mexico's second-biggest industrial center and third-biggest city. It's an energetic, commerce-orientated place that ranks as perhaps the most Americanized city in the nation, with sprawling suburbs of gargantuan, air-conditioned malls, corporate headquarters and manicured housing estates that could be straight out of Texas. But despite the importance of business, central Monterrey has plenty of metropolitan élan: iconic modern architecture, world-class museums and emerging artistic enclaves abound, while the Barrio Antiguo bursts with urbane restaurants and hip bars.

The historic heart of the city was radically transformed in the mid-1980s, when a series of interlinked concrete plazas bordered by soaring civic structures, theatres and museums emerged. Ambitious new projects continue to add to Monterrey's appeal, as parkland and cultural quarters replace former industrial zones.

Jagged mountains, including the distinctive saddle-shaped Cerro de la Silla (1288m), make a dramatic backdrop for the city, and provide opportunities for some worthwhile side trips; the surrounding countryside contains caves, canyons, lakes and waterfalls.

Most travelers bypass Monterrey in their haste to get to other parts of Mexico, but the city is well worth a few days of your trip. Most of the main attractions are clustered together in the central zone, where extensive pedestrianized areas connect squares and gardens. The city is also a good place to party, with a dynamic live-music scene, hip-hop and techno clubs, lounge bars and grunge hangouts.

For budget travelers, Monterrey's disadvantage is that lodging is expensive and the cheaper hotels are mainly in an unattractive area north of the cultural center. The character of the city also changes dramatically with the weather; the smog, humidity and rain can be bad, but you are just as likely to find fresh breezes, blue skies and clear, dry desert air.

History

After several unsuccessful attempts to found a city here, Diego de Montemayor christened his 34-person settlement, in 1596, after the Conde de Monterrey, then the viceroy of Mexico. Monterrey struggled as an outpost, but its importance grew with the colonization of Tamaulipas in the mid-18th century, since it was on the trade route to the new settlements. By 1777, Monterrey had about 4000 inhabitants and became the seat of the new bishopric of Linares.

In 1824, Monterrey became the capital of Nuevo León state in newly independent Mexico. During the Mexican-American War, Monterrey was occupied by US troops led by Zachary Taylor, and the city was occupied again in the 1860s by French troops.

Monterrey's proximity to the US gave it advantages in trade and smuggling: first as a staging post for cotton exports during the US Civil War, and later its railway lines and industrial tax exemptions attracted significant inward investment. By 1910 Monterrey was one of Mexico's biggest cities with a population of about 80,000.

The city was the site of the first heavy industry in Latin America, as a vast iron and steel works (now the site of the Parque Fundidora) dominated the cityscape, while the conglomerate Monterrey Group controlled much of the business world.

Economic success and distance from the national power center have given Monterrey's citizens, called *regiomontanos,* an independent point of view. The city resents any 'meddling' in its affairs by the central government, which in turn often accuses the city of being too capitalist or, worse, too friendly with the US. Monterrey has undoubtedly profited considerably from Nafta: over 500 US and Canadian firms base their regional operations in Nuevo León's capital.

Today Monterrey commands an excellent international reputation for education – with four universities and a prestigious technological institute. The city has also been feted by *Fortune* magazine readers as 'the best city in Latin American to get business done.' Monterrey remains the pillar of the Nuevo León state economy, which generates over 8% of Mexico's GDP and attracts over 10% of all foreign investment.

Orientation

Central Monterrey focuses on the Zona Rosa, an area of largely pedestrianized streets housing the more expensive hotels, shops and restaurants. The eastern edge of the Zona Rosa brushes the southern end of the Gran Plaza, a series of plazas and gardens studded with monuments.

South of the city center is the Río Santa Catarina, which cuts across the city from west to east – the dry riverbed is used for sports grounds. The bus station is about 2.5km northwest of the city center, and most of the cheap lodging is in this part of town. Colonia del Valle, 6km southwest of the city center, is one of Monterrey's most exclusive suburbs.

Streets in the center are on a grid pattern. The corner of Juárez and Aramberri, roughly halfway between the Zona Rosa and the bus station, is the center of town – the zero point for addresses in both directions. North of

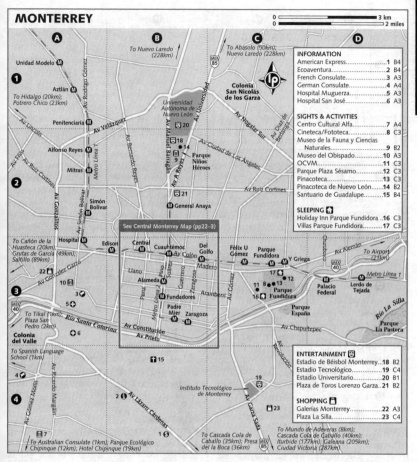

MONTERREY

INFORMATION	
American Express.................**1** B4	
Ecoaventura........................**2** B4	
French Consulate.................**3** A3	
German Consulate................**4** A4	
Hospital Muguerza................**5** A3	
Hospital San José.................**6** A3	

SIGHTS & ACTIVITIES	
Centro Cultural Alfa...............**7** A4	
Cineteca/Fototeca.................**8** C3	
Museo de la Fauna y Ciencias	
Naturales.......................**9** B2	
Museo del Obispado.............**10** A3	
OCVM............................**11** C3	
Parque Plaza Sésamo............**12** C3	
Pinacoteca.......................**13** C3	
Pinacoteca de Nuevo León......**14** B2	
Santuario de Guadalupe.........**15** B4	

SLEEPING	
Holiday Inn Parque Fundidora.**16** C3	
Villas Parque Fundidora..........**17** C3	

See Central Monterrey Map (pp22–3)

ENTERTAINMENT	
Estadio de Béisbol Monterrey..**18** B2	
Estadio Tecnológico.............**19** C4	
Estadio Universitario.............**20** B1	
Plaza de Toros Lorenzo Garza..**21** B2	

SHOPPING	
Galerías Monterrey................**22** A3	
Plaza La Silla......................**23** C4	

Aramberri, north–south streets have the suffix 'Norte' (Nte); south of Aramberri, 'Sur.' West of Juárez, east–west streets have the suffix 'Poniente' (Pte); east of Juárez, 'Oriente' (Ote).

Information
EMERGENCY
Cruz Roja (Red Cross; ☎ 065)
State Public Security (☎ 8328-0606)

INTERNET ACCESS & TELEPHONES
E Connection (Map pp400-1; Escobedo 831; per hr $1.50; Ⓜ Zaragoza) In the heart of the Zona Rosa.
Evertek de Mexico (Map pp400-1; Pino Suárez Nte 930; ⏰ 9:30am-7:30pm Mon-Sat, 10am-2pm Sun; Ⓜ Cuauhtémoc)

Flash Internet (Map pp400-1; 2nd fl, Juárez Sur 164; per hr $1.50; Ⓜ Alameda)
Internet Zone (Map pp400-1; Emilio Carranza 919; per hr $2; Ⓜ Padre Mier) Also offers cheap international calls.

INTERNET RESOURCES
Convention & Visitors Bureau of Monterrey
(☎ 800-832-03-00; www.ocvmty.com.mx in Spanish) Information on hotels, museums and restaurants. Geared towards business travelers.

MEDIA
Acceso (www.accesonet.com in Spanish) A free Spanish-language magazine devoted to the city's music scene.
City News A weekly newspaper with comprehensive cinema, theatre, museum and exhibition listings.

CENTRAL MONTERREY

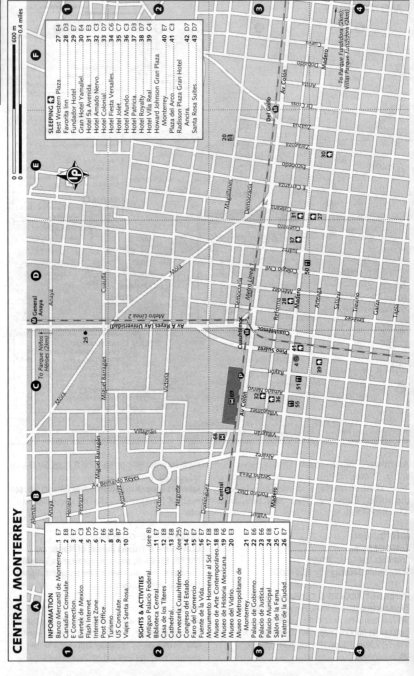

What's On Monterrey A glossy, slightly staid, free quarterly magazine with articles about the city's forthcoming cultural events.

MEDICAL SERVICES
Hospital Muguerza (Map p399; ☎ 8399-3400; Hidalgo 2525)
Hospital San José (Map p399; ☎ 8347-1010; Av Prieto Pte 3000)

MONEY
Numerous city-center banks will change cash, though some do not handle traveler's checks. Almost all have ATMs. Exchange houses are clustered along Ocampo between Emilio Carranza and Escobedo, on the western side of Plaza Zaragoza.
American Express (Map p399; ☎ 8333-0700; Centro Valle Oriente, Av Lázaro Cárdenas 1000) Good rates for Amex traveler's checks, with no commission.

POST
Post office (Map pp400-1; Washington) North of Gran Plaza.

TOURIST INFORMATION
Turismo (Map pp400-1; ☎ 2020-6774, in US ☎ 800-835-24-38; www.turismomonterrey.com; Antiguo Palacio Federal, Zaragoza s/n; ⏱ 8:30am-6:30pm Mon-Fri, 9am-5pm Sat & Sun) A block north of the Palacio Gobierno, most staff here speak fluent English, and they have lots of information about sights and events in Monterrey and the state of Nuevo León. There are also two small tourist information offices at the bus station which are OK for basic stuff.

TRAVEL AGENCIES
Viajes Santa Rosa (Map pp400-1; ☎ 8344-9202; Galeana Sur 940; Ⓜ Zaragoza) Located between Hidalgo and Morelos, and can arrange air tickets.

Sights & Activities
GRAN PLAZA
A grandiose monument to Monterrey's ambition, this city block–wide series of interconnected squares (also known as the Macroplaza; Map pp400–1) was created in the 1980s by the demolition of a prime chunk of city-center real estate. A controversial, but ultimately successful, piece of redevelopment, its charm has increased over the years as once-naked urban space has been softened by parks, trees, fountains and pools. Well-planned vistas of the surrounding mountains open up between a roster of iconic edifices that line the Gran Plaza –

classically designed municipal buildings and cutting-edge modern structures housing some of Mexico's finest museums. For visitors it's a delight to explore by foot, as most traffic is directed away from the heart of the area by underpasses.

At the very southern end, nearest the Río Santa Catarina, the **Monumento Homenaje al Sol** is a soaring sculpture designed by Rufino Tamayo on a traffic island that faces the modern **Palacio Municipal**: a concrete, brutalist-style building raised on legs. Just north of this building there's a shady park, **Plaza Zaragoza**, which is popular with snacking families, smooching lovers, and also the venue for open-air concerts centered on the covered bandstand. Every Sunday the city's *salseros* gather to groove here, and beneath the legs of the *palacio*.

Facing the southeast corner of Plaza Zaragoza is the terrific **Museo de Arte Contemporáneo** (Marco; ☎ 8342-4820; www.mtyol.com /marco in Spanish; cnr Zuazua & Raymundo Jardón; admission $3.25, free Wed; ⏱ 10am-6pm Tue & Thu-Sun, 10am-8pm Wed; Ⓜ Zaragoza), its entrance marked by Juan Soriano's gigantic black dove sculpture. Inside, its idiosyncratic spaces are filled with water and light and major exhibitions of works by Mexican and Latin American artists, including Diego Rivera, Alejandro Colunga and Carlos Mérida. Marco also has a fine bookstore and café-restaurant.

Just north of Marco is the baroque facade of the **cathedral**, built between 1635 and 1770. The south bell tower was not completed until 1899. Facing the cathedral across the plaza is the 19th-century Palacio Municipal, which now houses the small **Museo Metropolitano de Monterrey** (☎ 8344-1971; Zaragoza Sur; admission free; ⏱ 10am-6pm Tue-Sun; Ⓜ Zaragoza). This museum has several upstairs galleries featuring the work of contemporary painters and sculptors. North of the museum, grand banks and modern stores flank the east end of **Morelos**, a bustling pedestrian mall.

The centerpiece of Plaza Zaragoza is a graceless, 174m-long, orange, concrete slab known as the **Faro del Comercio** (Beacon of Commerce), which occasionally looks even more ungainly when green lasers are beamed from its summit at night.

Across Padre Mier is the **Fuente de la Vida** (Fountain of Life) with Neptune riding a chariot. North of here is the bunker-like presence of the concrete **Teatro de la Ciudad**, which sits opposite its brutalist cousin, the lofty **Congreso del Estado**. A concrete leg from the latter extends into a shimmering pool where kids splash about on hot days. Further north again, the **Biblioteca Central** (State Library) and the **Palacio de Justicia** (Courthouse) stand on either side of the **Parque Hundido** (Sunken Garden), a favorite spot for courting couples in daylight hours, and a home for the homeless at night.

North again and down some steps is the **Explanada de los Héroes** (Esplanade of the Heroes), also called the Plaza Cinco de Mayo, with statues of national heroes in each corner. It's the most formal and traditional of the spaces in the Gran Plaza and has the 1908 neoclassical **Palacio de Gobierno** on its north side. Behind the Palacio de Gobierno, a small park faces the 1930s post office and grand facade of the **Antiguo Palacio Federal**, which is now home to the main tourist office.

Just east of the Explanada de los Héroes is yet another wide-open space, the **Plaza 400 Años**. Graced with fountains and pools, it serves as a grand entrance to the sleek modernist **Museo de Historia Mexicana** (Map pp400-1; ☎ 8345-9898; www.museohistoriamexicana .org.mx in Spanish; Plaza 400 Años; admission $1.25, Tue free; ♥ 10am-7pm Wed-Fri, 10am-8pm Sat & Sun; Ⓜ Zaragoza), a 1994 addition to the Gran Plaza. The museum presents an exhaustive chronological survey of Mexican history, dividing its vast subject matter into four periods: ancient Mexico, the colonial era, the 19th century and modern Mexico. Creatively designed and displayed, the museum appeals to kids and adults, with interactive exhibits on the Maya calendar and pre-Hispanic math, as well as excellent models of all the major pre-Conquest cities. All explanations are in Spanish only, but English tours can be arranged by phoning in advance. There's a nice café here too.

Bordering Plaza 400 Años to the southeast is the **Paseo Santa Lucía**, a waterside promenade that's popular with weekend strollers. Development is ongoing and will create a canalside corridor of cafés and greenery from here to the Parque Fundidora (p404).

ZONA ROSA

This upmarket area (Map pp400-1) just west of Plaza Zaragoza contains many of Monterrey's top hotels and restaurants, and is also a prime shopping district with clothing and department stores. It extends towards Padre Mier in the north, Zaragoza in the east, Ocampo to the south, and Juárez to the west. Several of the streets are pedestrianized and usually bustling with life. It's a pleasure to walk around here.

BARRIO ANTIGUO

This is the most atmospheric part of town (Map pp400-1), with cobbled streets and some fine colonial houses, many of which have been converted into cafés, restaurants and art galleries. Its boundaries are the Av Constitución ring road in the south and east, Dr Coss to the west, and Matamoros in the north. On Friday and Saturday nights, the streets around Padre Mier are closed to traffic and it becomes a major party zone with an excellent assortment of bars and clubs.

PARQUE ALAMEDA

Occupying eight city blocks 1km northwest of the city center, this lovely **park** (Map pp400-1) offers fountains, paths and tall shade trees in pleasant contrast to the surrounding chaos of the city. It's a venue for occasional Sunday morning children's concerts.

CERVECERÍA CUAUHTÉMOC

This complex is in the gardens of the **old Cuauhtémoc brewery** (Map pp400-1; Alfonso Reyes 2202; Ⓜ General Anaya), 1km north of the bus station. Brought to you by the maker of Bohemia, Dos Equis and Tecate beer, it now features a baseball hall of fame and brewery tours (and free beer!). From General Anaya station walk south 300m along Av Alfonso Reyes.

Brewery tours (☎ 8328-5355; tours free; ♥ 9am-5pm Mon-Fri, 9am-2pm Sat) are given hourly. Tours in English of the oldest brewery in Mexico (established in 1890) are given in the morning by reservation or any time on Saturday. Or you can join one of the many school groups for tours in Spanish. There is a very pleasant outdoor garden, which is a nice place to sit even if you don't partake of the free mug of Carta Blanca.

The **Salón de la Fama** (Map pp400-1; ☎ 8328-5815; www.salondelafama.com.mx; admission free; ♥ 9:30am-6pm Mon-Fri, 10:30am-6pm Sat & Sun) has photos, memorabilia, facts and figures on Mexican baseball, and features many Mexican and American players. You can also test your throwing arm and batting skills – albeit with a Wiffle ball.

KIDS' MONTERREY

Monterrey has plenty of attractions that will thrill children. Inside the Parque Fundidora, (see below) **Parque Plaza Sésamo** (Map p399; ☎ 8354-5400; www.parqueplazasesamo.com in Spanish; admission $15, after 5pm $7.50, young child free; ☽ 3-8pm Mon-Fri, 11am-8pm Sat & Sun) is a vast Sesame Street theme park complete with dozens of thrilling rides like the Space Shot, which propels you 80m up towards the heavens.

In the Barrio Antiguo, don't miss the fun **Casa de los Títeres** (Map pp400-1; ☎ 8343-0604; www .baulteatro.com in Spanish; Raymundo Jardón 968; admission $1.50; ☽ 2-6pm Sun), which has an extensive collection of antique and modern puppets from all corners of the globe, including European marionettes and Javanese *wayang golek* (stick puppets). An excellent puppet stage show is held here every two weeks on Sunday at 4pm.

The **Museo de la Fauna y Ciencias Naturales** (Map p399; ☎ 8351-7077; admission $0.50; ☽ 9am-6pm), inside Parque Niños Héroes, features life-sized dioramas of stuffed wildlife in natural habitats, from Saharan Africa to the Arctic. Enter the park from Av Alfonso Reyes, about 5km north of the city center.

Some 15km southwest of Monterrey the colossal new theme park **Mundo de Adeveras** (☎ 81-1160-1160; www.deadeveras.com; admission $11.50, young child free; ☽ noon-8pm Tue-Sun), just off Hwy 85, has some good sporting and educational activities; it's geared at children aged between four and 12.

MUSEO DEL VIDRIO

Two blocks north of Av Colón, on the grounds of the former Vitro factory, this **museum** (Map pp400-1; ☎ 8863-1000, tours ext 1107; www.museodelvidrio.com; Magallanes 517; admission $1; ☽ 9am-6pm Tue-Sun; Ⓜ Del Golfo) focuses on the history, manufacturing and artistic use of glass in Mexico. Among the exhibits there are some stunning Spanish glassworks showing a distinct Arabic influence, and a reproduction of a 19th-century stained-glass workshop. Another gallery for temporary exhibitions of glass art is in a restored warehouse opposite the plant, where beer and Coke bottles are made. You can samples of fine glasswork in the gallery shop. Call ahead to schedule a tour in English.

PARQUE NIÑOS HÉROES

A botanical garden, an aviary, a lake and several museums, including the **Museo de la Fauna y Ciencias Naturales** (Map p399; ☎ 8351-7077; admission $0.50; ☽ 9am-6pm), are among the recreational and cultural facilities on offer in this large **park** (admission $1), north of the city center, between Av Alfonso Reyes and Av Manuel Barragán. Most impressive is the permanent collection of paintings and sculpture found at the **Pinacoteca de Nuevo León** (Map p399; ☎ 8331-5462; admission free; ☽ 10am-6pm Tue-Sun), showing the outstanding work of the state's artists since colonial times.

MUSEO DEL OBISPADO

The former **obispado** (bishopric palace), on a hill 2.5km west of the Zona Rosa, gives fine views of the city and surrounding mountains, smog permitting. Initiated in 1787 on the orders of the bishop of Linares, the building has an intricate yellow Churrigueresque facade. Now it's a small historical **museum** (Map p399; ☎ 8346-0404; Verguer; admission $3.25; ☽ 10am-5pm Tue-Sun) with various colonial and revolutionary relics. To get there, take bus No 4 (red and black) heading west along Padre Mier. Get off when the bus turns left at Degollado, head up the hill and turn left, then take the first right (a 10-minute walk).

PARQUE FUNDIDORA

Formally a vast steel-factory complex this once-blighted industrial zone has been transformed into a huge **urban park** (Map p399, ☎ 8343-4143; www.parquefundidora.org in Spanish; ☽ 6am-11pm; Ⓜ Parque Fundidora) that encompasses a dizzying array of attractions, including many that will appeal to children. It's so large you could easily spend a day here taking in the exhibitions and galleries, enjoying a picnic lunch around the lake and finish off by attending a concert at the Arena. Cleverly, the park designers have retained the rusting smoke stacks and furnaces, which now loom above the landscaped grounds and jogging tracks, giving a postmodern, apocalyptic feel to the place.

Occupying the northeast corner of the park is the huge **Parque Plaza Sésamo** (Map p399; ☎ 8354-5400; www.parqueplazasesamo.com in Spanish; admission $15, after 5pm $7.50, young child free; ⊙ 3-8pm Mon-Fri, 11am-8pm Sat & Sun) kids' theme park. Close to the center of the park, the **Pinacoteca** (admission free; ⊙ 10am-9pm Tue-Sun) is a disemboweled factory whose interior has been filled with modern art and exhibitions. Opposite here, the near-identical red-brick building is the **Cineteca-Fototeca** (admission free; ⊙ 10am-10pm), which houses photographic exhibitions and shows art-house films. Towards the western fringes of the park are other facilities including a convention center, an outdoor concert hall, a hotel (p407) and hostel (p406). Oh, and there's also a baseball stadium and a Formula One race track.

Fundidora is a secure environment, patrolled by security staff on mountain bikes. Visitors are not permitted to drink alcohol in the park grounds.

CENTRO CULTURAL ALFA

This extensive **cultural complex** (Map p399; ☎ 8303-0002; www.planetarioalfa.org.mx in Spanish; Av Roberto Garza Sada 1000; admission $6.75; ⊙ 3-7pm Tue-Fri, 11:30am-8pm Sat & Sun) is 7km from the city center in Colonia del Valle. Entirely sponsored by the Alfa industrial group, its striking **museum building** looks like a wonky water tank, with floors that are devoted to computers, astronomy, physics, Mexican antiquities and temporary exhibitions. The scientific displays have lots of educational hands-on exhibits, and everything is labeled (in Spanish). In the center of the building is the **planetarium** and an **IMAX cinema**.

Outside is the **Jardín Prehispánico**, with replicas of some of the great Mexican archaeological finds. Don't miss the striking **Pabellón building**, which resembles a covered wagon and was specially built to showcase a superb glass mural known as **El Universo**. Weighing in at 3.5 tonnes and consisting of 30 panels, the mural was created by artist Rufino Tamayo for the headquarters of the Alfa group.

Special buses leave from the southwest corner of Parque Alameda, at the intersection of Washington and Villagrán, at 3:30pm, 4:30pm, 5:30pm Monday to Friday, and every 30 minutes Saturday and Sunday. The last bus back to central Monterrey departs from the planetarium at 7:45pm on weekdays and 8:45pm on weekends.

PARQUE ECOLÓGICO CHIPINQUE

Several kilometers up the mountainside, and south of Colonia del Valle, this **park** (☎ 8303-0000; www.chipinque.org.mx; pedestrian/cyclist/vehicle $2/2.75/2.75; ⊙ 6am-8pm) is the most accessible section of the **Parque Nacional Cumbres de Monterrey**, offering urbanites ample opportunities for hiking and mountain biking. Trails are well maintained, and it doesn't take long to get into some pretty dense pine and oak forest and to feel far away from the city, though part of the area was burnt in an April 1998 blaze. Butterflies are particularly prolific here, with over 170 species represented, while birdlife includes the bronze-winged woodpecker. Rappel and 'mini-bungee' jumping are also offered.

From the entrance, a 7km drive brings you to the Meseta de Chipinque, where there's the fine **Hotel Chipinque** (☎ 800-849-46-81; www.hotelchipinque.com; r $131; P ⊠ ⚫), which has attractive rooms and *cabañas* with fireplaces, and tennis courts, and from where you can access the park's highest peak, **Copete de las Águilas** (2200m). If you eat at the hotel's restaurant, they will validate your park admission ticket, which will then be refunded at the kiosk on your way out of the park. Maps and snacks are available at the visitors' center, near the park entrance.

Cyclists are required to display an identification badge, which can be purchased at the park entrance. Parking at the visitors' center costs $2.75; to drive up to the mesa, there's an additional charge of $6.50 per car.

Special buses to/from Chipinque leave from the southeast corner of Parque Alameda, at the junction of Washington and Pino Suárez. They run at 9am and 11am, returning at 2pm and 4pm Monday to Friday; and at 8am, 10am and noon, returning at 2pm, 4pm and 6pm Saturday and Sunday.

Courses

Posada El Potrero Chico (boxed text, p412) Offers language classes; near the town of Hidalgo.

Spanish Language School (☎ 8335-7546; http://spanishcenter.tripod.com.mx; Río Potomac 423, Colonia del Valle) It's about 5km southwest of the centre.

Tours

Geo Ecoaventura (Map p399; ☎ 8989-4301; www.geoaventura.com.mx in Spanish; Av Lázaro Cárdenas 2232, Colonia Valle Oriente) offers rafting, rappel, mountain-bike trips and hiking excursions.

Festivals & Events

Festival Internacional de Cine en Monterrey Mexican and international art-house films. Held in mid-August.

Aniversario de Independencia Monterrey's biggest celebrations are held on Mexico's Independence Day, September 16, with fireworks, free tequila and a big parade.

Expo Monterrey The annual trade and cultural fair happens in the Parque Niños Héroes during September.

Festival Cultural del Barrio Antiguo Concerts, art expositions and literary events, all held in venues located in Monterrey's old quarter, during November.

Nuestra Señora de Guadalupe Celebrations of this event, on December 12, begin as early as the last week of November as thousands of pilgrims head for the Santuario de Guadalupe.

Sleeping

Your stay in Monterrey is going to be heavily influenced by the district where your hotel is located. Budget places are grouped together in the streets around the bus station north of the center – a grimy, bustling, traffic-blighted part of town. Most luxury options are in or around the Zona Rosa in the center. Midrange accommodation is in both areas. If you can stretch to more than $45 a night, try to book a hotel in the Zona Rosa and you'll have most of Monterrey's main sights (and shopping areas) on your doorstep.

BUDGET

Budget hotels fill up fast, especially on weekends. All but the most basic places have air-con. There are several decent options around Amado Nervo, in the two blocks running south of the enormous bus station.

Hotel Mundo (Map pp400-1; ☎ 8374-6850; Reforma Pte 736; r $28-33; Ⓜ Cuauhtémoc; ⌘ ▣) An efficiently run, well-maintained and welcoming place that's the best deal in town at this price. The lobby (where the floor is well scrubbed and plastic pot plants are dusted daily) is inviting while the pleasant, spotless rooms all have simple but attractive decor, reading lights, writing tables, cable TV and phones. There's also free Internet access.

Villas Parque Fundidora (Map p399; ☎ 8355-7380; Madero Ote 3500; villa@parquefundidora.org; dm with shared bathroom incl breakfast $7.50; Ⓜ Parque Fundidora; Ⓟ ⌘) Beside the huge Parque Fundidora, this clean functional and cheap hostel has 11 large (up to 36-bed) dorms, each with a TV. Many visitors here are student groups, but travelers are welcome too. Call or email ahead to reserve your bed.

These are reasonable alternatives:

Hotel Villa Real (Map pp400-1; ☎ 8375-0355; Pino Suárez 806; r $27; Ⓜ Cuauhtémoc; Ⓟ ⌘) In a relatively quiet location, and with spacious, clean rooms.

Hotel Amado Nervo (Map pp400-1; ☎ 8375-4632; fax 8372-5488; Amado Nervo Nte 1110; s/d $29/33; Ⓜ Cuauhtémoc; Ⓟ ⌘) It has a gloomy lobby, but acceptable, roomy doubles with TV and telephones.

MIDRANGE
Bus Station Area

The following places near Av Madero. Many offer reduced rates Friday to Sunday.

Best Western Plaza (Map pp400-1; ☎ 8125-4800; Madero Ote 250; s/d $49/53; Ⓜ Cuauhtémoc; Ⓟ ⌘ ▣) Offers large, plush and very comfortable rooms, with polished dark-wood furniture and either a single king-size bed or twin double beds. There's free lobby Internet access, a stylish restaurant and a small gym. The parking-lot entrance is on Galeana.

Hotel Patricia (Map pp400-1; ☎ 8375-0750; Madero Ote 123; s/d incl breakfast $46/51; Ⓜ Cuauhtémoc; ⌘) The Patricia represents a quantum leap in comfort and quality from the budget options nearby. Its rooms may lack a little character, but all have a chest of drawers, a writing table and good-sized beds. Internet access is gratis, and breakfast is served in the great diner-style restaurant.

Plaza del Arco (Map pp400-1; ☎ 8372-4050; www .proximahoteles.com in Spanish; Pino Suárez Nte 935; r/ste $49/62; Ⓜ Cuauhtémoc; Ⓟ ⌘ ▣) An art deco–style landmark, this all-white hotel stands out amid the grayness that pervades Madero. The retro design scheme continues in the modern rooms, which have radio alarm clocks, cable TV and irons.

Also worth considering:

Hotel 5a Avenida (Map pp400-1; Quinta Avenida; ☎ 8375-6565; hotel5aavenida@terra.com.mx; Madero Ote 243; s/d incl breakfast $36/41; M Cuauhtémoc; P ⊠ ▣) Well-kept, tidy if smallish rooms, some with fine views.

Gran Hotel Yamallel (Map pp400-1; ☎ 8375-3500; www.hotelyamallel.com.mx in Spanish; Zaragoza Nte 912; r $43; M Del Golfo; P ⊠) The rooms are looking a tad dated, but stupendous views from the upper floors, and special price promotions keep it competitive.

Gran Plaza

Howard Johnson Gran Plaza Monterrey (Map pp400-1; ☎ 8380-6000, 800-832-4000; www.hojomonterrey.com .mx; Morelos Ote 574; r/ste $73/96; M Zaragoza; P ⊠ ⊠ ▣) A large impressive hotel that has an excellent central location and frequently offers discounts off the rack rate. Rooms are very spacious, many with stunning views over the Gran Plaza, and all have mod cons including irons and safes. There's a tiny indoor pool, gym and business center, and rates include a huge buffet breakfast.

Hotel Jolet (Map pp400-1; ☎ 8150-6500; jolet mty@prodigy.net.mx; Padre Mier Pte 201; r $67; M Padre Mier; P ⊠) Stylish in a 1970s way, this concrete block has classy carpeted rooms, many with panoramic views, with twin double beds, cherry-wood furniture and adjoining marble-floor bathrooms. There's a travel agency and bar downstairs.

Fundador Hotel (Map pp400-1; ☎ 8343-6464; hotelfundador@prodigy.net.mx; Montemayor 802; s $33, d $39-44; M Zaragoza; P ⊠) The sole lodging option in the Barrio Antiguo (east of Gran Plaza), this rambling, slightly shabby, historic hotel has real ambience. It's the antithesis of the sterile, corporate chain hotel, with quirky rooms dotted around a warren of stairways and corridors. Room standards and sizes vary a lot. Some have wood-paneled walls and antique chairs. Room No 221, which is huge and has a fridge and sultan-size bed, is the one to reserve.

Hotel Royalty (Map pp400-1; ☎ 8340-2800; Hidalgo; r incl breakfast $53; M Zaragoza; P ⊠ ⊡) The Royalty is a popular choice for its central location and high service levels. Rooms are not quite as nice as those at the Jolet, but there is a small outdoor pool.

These places have weekend specials and are also worth considering:

Hotel Colonial (Map pp400-1; ☎ 8380-6800; reserv aciones@hotelcolonial.mty.com; Hidalgo Ote 475; r incl breakfast $54; M Zaragoza; P ⊠ ▣) Enjoys a great location, but the rooms are not fancy.

Hotel Fiesta Versalles (Map pp400-1; ☎ 8340-2281; Ramón Pte 360; s/d $45/54; M Fundadores; P ⊠) A small hotel just south of the Parque Alameda, with fair-value, spacious rooms and a café downstairs.

TOP END

All of these luxury places have spacious accommodation, multichannel cable TV and offer special weekend rates.

Radisson Plaza Gran Hotel Ancira (Map pp400-1; ☎ 8150-7023, 800-830-60-00; www.hotel-ancira.com; Ocampo Ote 443; r $176; M Zaragoza; P ⊠ ⊠ ▣ ⊠) Unquestionably the classiest address in the Zona Rosa, this very stylish hotel dates from 1912 and boasts an intricate baroque-style facade, a columned entrance and imposing lobby with a sweeping staircase, shops and a grand piano. It has big rooms with plenty of period elegance and a gym, but the outdoor pool is small. Promotional rates can reduce rooms to below $100 a night.

Santa Rosa Suites (Map pp400-1; ☎ 8342-4200; www.santarosa.com.mx in Spanish; Escobedo Sur 930; ste incl breakfast $98; M Zaragoza; P ⊠ ▣) Much more intimate than the other top-end hotels, the suites here are plush and quite large, each having a separate living area with sofa bed, DVD player, and a dining area with seating for four.

Holiday Inn Parque Fundidora (Map p399; ☎ 8369-6000; Retorno Fundidora 100; r $89; M Zaragoza; P ⊠ ⊠ ▣ ⊠) This striking modern red-and-white oval edifice overlooks the city's green lung, Parque Fundidora, 2km northeast of the Barrio Antiguo. The spacious rooms all have broadband Internet access and full facilities, and there's an outdoor pool, a fitness center and a restaurant.

Eating
BUS STATION AREA

Fast-food restaurants and inexpensive taco outlets proliferate in the streets around the bus station.

Restaurant York (Map pp400-1; ☎ 8125-8400; Madero Ote 243; mains $4-9; M Cuauhtémoc) Good wholesome diner-style place that buzzes with life from early morning. Park yourself in one of the snug vinyl booths and take your pick from the long menu of Mexican favorites.

La Nueva Niza (Map pp400-1; ☎ 8375-1341; Madero 122; mains $3.75-6; 7am-9.45pm; M Cuauhtémoc) Unexpectedly stylish for the location, this very clean, modern, minimalist-style place has tasty food like *tacos piratas con guaca* (beef tacos with guacamole), and the *comida corrida* costs $4.50.

La Zanahoria (Map pp400-1; ☎ 8372-3258; Rayón 932; meals $5; ☺ noon-6pm; M Cuauhtémoc; V) Simple little family-run vegetarian place serving food like *beregena gratinada* (eggplant baked with breadcrumbs and tomato and onion) and *aguacate con queso cottage* (avocado with cottage cheese). All dishes include wholemeal bread, soup and a drink.

Mi Pueblito (Map pp400-1; ☎ 8375-3756; Madero; mains $3; ☺ 24hr; M Cuauhtémoc) Modern, clean Mi Pueblito cooks up filling Mexican standards.

ZONA ROSA

There are surprisingly few good places to eat in the Zona Rosa, which is thick with international and Mexican fast-food places.

Chilo's (Map pp400-1; Hidalgo Ote 110; combo meals $4; M Padre Mier) Packed with Mexican families, this fast food–style place has friendly staff and an air-conditioned upper floor. Dishes include *adobado* (chili dishes) and burgers. Look for the sign of the smiling cactus.

Mi Tierra (Map pp400-1; ☎ 8340-5611; Morelos 350; mains $3.50, set lunches $3.75; M Zaragoza) On the pedestrian mall, open-fronted Mi Tierra serves up tasty *mole* dishes and *chiles rellenos* in a casual setting.

Luisiana (Map pp400-1; ☎ 8343-3753; Hidalgo Ote 530; mains $15-24; M Zaragoza) Tuxedoed waiters and all the trappings of high-end dining are available at Luisiana. It's certainly a swanky setting, though the menu is looking a bit dated – *duck a la orange* even puts in an appearance. Stick to the Spanish dishes like *cazuela de arroz costa brava* (rice casserole) or the seafood. Still, the execution of the cooking can't be faulted and the level of service is high.

Restaurant La Puntada (Map pp400-1; ☎ 8440-6985; Hidalgo Ote 123; mains $3-5; ☺ Mon-Sat; M Padre Mier) A highly popular place with plenty of bustle and a long list of Mexican items, and steaks, at fair prices.

Las Monjitas (Map pp400-1; ☎ 8344-6713; Escobedo 903; mains $3.25-7; M Zaragoza) For good Mexican fare in a bizarre setting, try this restaurant just off Plaza Hidalgo, where the waitresses are dressed as nuns. There's another branch at the corner of Morelos and Galeana.

BARRIO ANTIGUO

A stroll around the *barrio* is the best way to find a place to eat, though it pays to book ahead on Friday and Saturday nights.

La Casa de Maíz (Map pp400-1; ☎ 8340-4332; Abasolo 870; mains $4.50-6; M Zaragoza; V) Bohemian place that specializes in corn-based comfort food from southern Mexico, including *molotes* and *tlacoyos* (croquette-like snacks), plus quesadillas and tostadas, all creatively presented and served on hand-painted tables. There's also some striking artwork on the walls, and the frappés here are delicious, if pricey ($3.75).

El Siciliano (Map pp400-1; ☎ 8675-5784; Morelos Ote 1076; mains $9-12; ☺ 1pm-midnight Mon-Sat, 1-6pm Sun; M Zaragoza) Authentic, intimate little Italian on the eastern edge of the Barrio Antiguo. Great pasta ($8) and stuffed calamari ($9) are served up on gingham tablecloths and there's a good wine selection as well.

Iannilli (Map pp400-1; ☎ 8342-7200; Dr Coss 1221; mains $9.50-18; ☺ 1-11.30pm; M Zaragoza) Seriously elegant and expensive Italian restaurant with intimate dining rooms set off a colonial courtyard, and formal service. The extensive menu includes *tortellini alla crema* ($9.50), gnocchi ($10.50), shrimp dishes and pizza.

El Rey del Cabrito (Map pp400-1; ☎ 8345-3232; cnr Dr Coss & Constitución; mains $9.50-14; M Zaragoza; P) Huge landmark restaurant, complete with a revolving crown on its roof, with hunting lodge–kitsch interior. Your *cabrito* ($12) arrives at the table still sizzling on a bed of onions, with a large salad and tortillas.

THE AUTHOR'S CHOICE

Cafe el Infinito (Map pp400-1; ☎ 8989-5252; Raymundo Jardón Ote 904; www.cafeinfinito.com in Spanish; mains $4-8; ☺ 8am-1am daily Nov-April, 6pm-2am Mon-Sat, 4-11:45pm Sun May-Oct; M Zaragoza; V) Highly enjoyable, tranquil culture café set inside colonial premises with gorgeous tiled floors, high beamed ceilings and walls adorned with art. It offers healthy veggie sandwiches, Oaxacan-style 'pizza,' fruit frappés and properly made espresso coffee. Musically, things are kept tranquil with cinematic sounds, and ambient and classical music on the hi-fi. There are books to browse, and Infinito also shows art-house films and hosts infrequent poetry readings.

Drinking

The best bar (and café) action is in the Barrio Antiguo, where stylish places are thick on the ground.

Café La Galería (Map pp400-1; Morelos 902; 6pm-2am Mon-Sat) A hip, friendly bar, La Galería showcases local house and dance-DJ talent. It's close to the heart of the weekend action in Monterrey, but attracts a slightly more mature crowd than many of the other venues.

Bar 1900 (Map pp400-1; Radisson Plaza Gran Hotel Ancira, Ocampo Ote 443; 5pm-2am) Elegant after-hours cabaret bar that's inside Zona Rosa's Ancira hotel, ideal for a relaxed drink, and has a particularly good selection of whiskeys.

Entertainment

Monterrey has numerous cinemas and an active cultural life including concerts, theater and art exhibitions. The tourist office and local media can tell you what's happening.

LIVE MUSIC & CLUBS

Monterrey's genre-bending, vibrant music scene is diverse and experimental, raiding rhythms from traditional Mexican *norteño* (country ballad and dance music) and Latin *cumbia* (Latin dance originating in Columbia) and fusing it with rock riffs and hip-hop beats. The 1997 release of *Mucho Barato*, the first album by the band Control Machete, marked the beginning of Monterrey's rise to national and international musical acclaim, and the city now has vibrant rock, ska, thrash metal, Nortec and myriad Latin music scenes. Partly because of the city's proximity to the US, and the technology afforded by its relative wealth, bands are much less tied to traditions, and ever more bizarre subgenres emerge, from the dub-*cumbia* of Celso Piña to the techno-tinged funk of Kinky. Groups like Plastilina Mosh, Molotov, El Gran Silencio and Genitallica have all emerged from Monterrey in the last few years. The Barrio Antiguo clubs frequented by Monterrey's affluent younger set are very much the place to catch up with what's going on – Padre Mier east of Dr Coss has loads of venues. The following are just some of the main places.

Café Iguana (Map pp400-1; 8343-0822; Montemayor Sur 927; www.cafeiguana.com.mx in Spanish; admission $3-15; 7pm-2:30am Mon-Sat; Zaragoza) The epicenter of alternative Monterrey, where the pierced, multi-tattooed tribe gather en masse to acclaim the latest local and inter-

national bands. Musically, it's punk, indie and trash bands that tend to dominate, but the odd ska ensemble and trance DJ put in an appearance too.

La Tumba (Map pp400-1; 8345-6860; Padre Mier Ote 827; www.latumba.com in Spanish; admission $5.50; 6pm-2am Tue-Sat; Zaragoza) This venue has live music, *trova* (troubadour-style folk music), blues and Latin American singer-songwriters. There's also a quiet area for chilling where you don't have to pay the admission.

Republika (Map pp400-1; 8342-8822; Morelos 855; 10pm-late Thu-Sat; Zaragoza) Large club where the city's hip-hop crews keep it real to slammin' Latino and American beats.

Achis (Map pp400-1; 8344-3141; Padre Mier 324; admission $2-11; Padre Mier) Hip, happening venue where you can catch some of Monterrey's best indie and alternative rock bands. Also hosts some fearsome techno nights with leading Nortec DJs.

Rincón Antiguo (Map pp400-1; 8379-8299; Raymundo Jardón 1006; 8pm-3am Thu-Sat; Zaragoza) Mustachioed *norteño* groups perform thumping beats with cowboy hats and boots to match.

El Rincón de la Habana (Map pp400-1; 8342-0689; Morelos Ote 887; admission $7; 8:30pm-2:30am Thu-Sat; Zaragoza) Cuban-style salsa, plus a dash of merengue and reggaeton.

SPORT

During the main bullfight season (May to November) *corridas* are held at the **Plaza de Toros Lorenzo Garza** (Map p399; 8374-0450; www.monumentallorenzogarza.com in Spanish; Alfonso Reyes Nte 2401, Colonia del Prado; General Anaya) at 5pm on Sunday.

THE AUTHOR'S CHOICE

Akbal Lounge (Map pp400-1; 8340-4332; Abasolo Ote 870; www.akballounge.com in Spanish; 7pm-3am; Zaragoza) This über-chic lounge bar, an opium den–style mélange of velvet cushions, chandeliers and giant antique mirrors, is a home away from home for metropolitan (and metrosexual) Monterrey's style cats. Sip a cocktail and lose yourself in the mood music – ambient and lounge sounds during the week, revving up to sexy electro and deep house at weekends – spun by live DJs. Outside there's a groovy deck for neon nightscape-gazing. Sunday night is gay night.

The professional soccer season is from August to May. Games are played over the weekend at either the **Estadio Universitario** (Map p399; ☎ 8376-0524; Parque de los Niños Heroes), home of the Tigres (Universidad de Nuevo León) or the **Estadio Tecnológico** (Map p399; ☎ 8358-2000; Instituto Tecnológico de Monterrey, Covarrubias s/n), home of the less successful Monterrey club, nicknamed the Pandilla Rayada (Striped Gang).

Monterrey's Sultanes baseball team plays at **Estadio de Béisbol Monterrey** (Map p399; ☎ 8351-0209; Parque Niños Héroes) from March to August.

There are occasional *charreadas* in which *charros* (cowboys) appear to demonstrate their skills. Contact the tourist information office (see p402) for current venues.

Shopping

Monterrey has some fine stores with quality handicrafts from different parts of Mexico.

Tienda Carápan (Map pp400-1; ☎ 8345-4422; Hidalgo Ote 305; Ⓜ Zaragoza) Zona Rosa's best-quality store for local pottery, silver jewelry, hand-blown glasswork and weavings, sourced from all over the nation by the genial owner.

Tikal (Map p399; ☎ 8335-1740; Río Missouri Pte 316, Colonia del Valle; Ⓨ 9am-6pm Mon-Sat) High-quality Mexican handicrafts, including some interesting textiles.

The two main markets downtown, **Mercado Colón** (Ocampo; Ⓨ 7am-5:30pm Mon-Sat; Ⓜ Padre Mier) and **Mercado Juárez** (Aramberri; Ⓨ 7am-6pm Mon-Sat; Ⓜ Alameda), are large, bustling places that sell everyday items.

The wealthier *regiomontanos* prefer to shop at one of the big air-conditioned malls: **Galerías Monterrey** (Map p399; Av Insurgentes 2500) West of town.

Plaza la Silla (Map p399; Av Garza Sada) South of the city center.

Plaza San Pedro (Humberto Lobo 520) Southwest in the suburb of San Pedro.

Getting There & Away

AIR

There are direct flights, usually daily, to all major cities in Mexico, and connections to just about anywhere else. Most international destinations are best routed via Houston or Mexico City.

Airline offices include the following:

Aero California (☎ 8345-9700)
Aeromexico (☎ 8343-5560)
American Airlines (☎ 8340-3031)
Aviacsa (☎ 8153-4300)

Continental Airlines (☎ 8369-0838)
Mexicana (☎ 8356-6611)
United Airlines (☎ 8356-9582)

BUS

Monterrey's bus station, Central de Autobuses (Map p400-1) occupies three blocks on Av Colón, between Villagrán and Rayón. It's a small city unto itself, with restaurants, phones, an exchange office, and a **left-luggage service** (per hr $0.50; Ⓨ 7:30am-9pm). First-class lines include **Sendor** (☎ 8375-0014), **Ómnibus de México** (☎ 8375-7063) and **Futura** (☎ 8318-3737); deluxe service is provided by **Turistar** (☎ 8318-3737). **Autobuses Americanos** (☎ 8375-0358) is the main company for Texas. Daily services from Monterrey include the following:

Destination	Price	Duration	Frequency
Aguascalientes	$46	8hr	1 deluxe
	$37	8hr	frequent 1st-class
Chihuahua	$64	12hr	2 deluxe
	$53	12hr	frequent 1st-class
Ciudad Acuña	$34		6 daily 1st-class
Ciudad Victoria	$18	3¾hr	hourly 1st-class
	$16	3¾hr	
Dallas	$48		8 daily 1st-class
Durango	$54	9hr	4 deluxe
	$39	9hr	8 1st-class
Guanajuato	$49	9hr	1 daily
Guadalajara	$68	12hr	3 deluxe
	$52	12hr	10 1st-class
Houston	$38		10 daily 1st-class
Matamoros	$22	4½hr	frequent 1st-class
Mexico City	$80	11hr	8 deluxe
(Terminal Norte)	$61	11hr	12 1st-class
Nuevo Laredo	$26	2½hr	4 deluxe
	$18	2½hr	frequent 1st-class
Piedras Negras	$34	7hr	15 daily 1st-class
Reynosa	$16	3hr	1st-class every 30min
Saltillo	$7	1¾hr	1 deluxe
	$5.50		frequent 1st & 2nd-class
San Luis Potosí	$45	7hr	3 deluxe
	$34	7hr	frequent 1st-class
	$27	7hr	frequent 2nd-class
Tampico	$43	7¼hr	2 deluxe
	$36	7¼hr	hourly 1st-class
Torreón	$31	4¾hr	4 deluxe
	$24	4hr	frequent 1st-class
Zacatecas	$27	6hr	frequent 1st-class
	$23	6hr	7 2nd-class

First-class buses also serve Acapulco, Ciudad Juárez, Mazatlán, Puebla and Querétaro.

CAR & MOTORCYCLE

Budget (Map pp400-1; ☎ 8369-0819; Hidalgo Ote 433) Has a desk at the airport as well.

Hertz (Map pp400-1; ☎ 8345-6195 Hidalgo Ote 310)

Payless (Map pp400-1; ☎ 8344-6363; Escobedo Sur 1011; www.paylessmexico.com.mx in Spanish) Also with an airport branch.

Getting Around

TO/FROM THE AIRPORT

Monterrey airport is about 15km northeast of the city center, off Hwy 54 on the way to Ciudad Alemán. A taxi costs around $21 from one of the downtown hotels, or via **radio taxi service** (☎ 8372-4370, 8372-4371). From the airport you can purchase a ticket for an authorized taxi at a booth in the arrivals area.

There is no public transportation that serves the airport directly. However, if money is tight, look for any Pesquería bus with 'airport' indicated on the windshield ($0.50) on Villagrán, just around the corner from the bus station. It will drop you off on the airport access road from where you can flag down a taxi ($2) for the remaining few kilometers.

METRO

Monterrey's has a modern, efficient **metro system** (one-way/return $0.50/0.90; ⏱ 5am-midnight) which consists of two lines. The elevated Línea 1 runs from the northwest of the city across to the eastern suburbs, passing Parque Fundidora (metro Parque Fundidora and Griega). The underground Línea 2 runs north to south from near the Cuauhtémoc brewery (metro General Anaya), past the bus station (metro Cuauhtémoc), and down to the Zona Rosa (metro Padre Mier) and the Gran Plaza (metro Zaragoza). The metro's two lines cross at the intersection of Av Colón and Cuauhtémoc, where the giant, overhead, Cuauhtémoc metro station is located.

A northern extension to Línea 2, due to be completed anytime, will continue the line further 8.5km, up along Avs Reyes and Universidad.

BUS

Frequent buses ($0.40) go almost everywhere in Monterrey, but often by circuitous routes. The following routes might be useful:

Bus station to Center Bus 18, from the corner of Amado Nervo and Reforma, goes down Juárez to the edge of the Zona Rosa at Padre Mier.

Center to Bus Station Bus 1 (blue) can be picked up on Juárez at Padre Mier. It takes you to Av Colón, within two blocks of the bus station.

Center to Del Valle/San Pedro Ruta 131 (orange) from the corner of Juárez and Hidalgo goes to the big traffic circle in Colonia del Valle, then heads west along Av Vasconcelos.

Center to Instituto Tecnológico Take Bus 1 (San Nicolás-Tecnológico) from the corner of Hidalgo and Pino Suárez.

TAXI

Taxis (all have meters) are ubiquitous in Monterrey and very reasonably priced. From the Zona Rosa it costs $2.25 to the bus terminal or $3 to the Parque Fundidora.

CAR & MOTORCYCLE

There are large parking lots underneath the Gran Plaza, charging only $2.25 for the whole night. Another lot, just east of the bus station off Av Colón, is $7.50 for 24 hours.

AROUND MONTERREY

A number of sights near Monterrey are easily reached in your own vehicle, and somewhat less accessible by bus.

Grutas de García

An illuminated, 2.5km route leads through 16 chambers in this **cave system** (☎ 81-8347-1533; admission $7; ⏱ 9am-5pm) discovered by a parish priest in 1843. It's located 1100m up in the Sierra El Fraile. The caves, reached by a spectacular ride in a *teleférico* (cable car), are 50 million years old, with lots of stalactites and stalagmites, and petrified seashells. Admission includes the cable-car ride and a tour.

This is a popular weekend outing. On Saturday and Sunday mornings, Transportes Villa de García runs buses to the *teleférico* (from local platforms No 17 to 19 in the Monterrey bus station), returning in the afternoon. On other days the same line runs frequent buses to Villa de García, 9km from the caves ($0.60); taxis ($10 round-trip) go the rest of the way. Driving from Monterrey, take Hwy 40 toward Saltillo. After 22km a sign points the way to the caves; turn right and go another 18km to the base of the *teleférico*.

No matter how you get to the caves, it might make sense to spend the night in the lovely little town of Villa de García. A block or so from the plaza is the wonderful **Posada De La Villa** (☎ 81-283-19-42; Juan de Dios Treviño 103; r up to 4 people $38), which has six charming antique-furnished rooms and a sunny courtyard. Equally attractive, **Los Vientos de Garcia** (☎ 81-348-87-14; Escobedo Sur 109; ste $49; P 🐾 🖴) has a small pool, a restaurant, a rooftop bar and five spacious suites with living areas and kitchenettes.

Cañón de la Huasteca

About 20km west of Monterrey's city center, this **canyon** (☎ 81-8331-6785; per person/vehicle $0.50/1; 🕙 9am-6pm) is 300m deep and has some dramatic rock formations, as well as cliffside drawings (evidence of its prehistoric inhabitants). The town of Santa Catarina is at one end of the canyon and a playground is in the middle, somewhat reducing its attraction as a wilderness area. Reach the mouth of the canyon by taking a Ruta 206 bus, labeled 'Aurora,' from the corner of Ramón and Cuauhtémoc in Monterrey. If driving, take Av Constitución west out of the city center.

Cascada Cola de Caballo

Six kilometers up a rough road from El Mercado, a village 35km south of Monterrey on Hwy 85, you'll find the **Horsetail Falls** (admission $3; 🕙 9am-7pm). The site has its share of

hawkers and food stalls, but it's quite pretty and attracts a lot of picnickers. Horses and donkeys can be hired for the last kilometer to the falls ($5). Further down the valley, vegetation flourishes on the slopes of the sierra. Autobuses Amarillos runs frequent buses to El Mercado from the Monterrey bus station ($2); you'll have to catch a local bus from there to the falls.

COAHUILA

The state of Coahuila is large, mostly desert and sparsely populated. The border crossings into Coahuila from Texas are less frequently used than those further southeast in Tamaulipas, because the road connections into Mexico and the US are not as convenient for most travelers. Yet the remoteness and the harsh, arid landscape have a raw allure, and the state capital, Saltillo, is definitely worth a visit. For information about the western part of the state, including the city of Torreón and the Zona del Silencio, see the Central North Mexico chapter.

The Spanish came to Coahuila in search of silver, slaves and souls. The region was explored by the Spanish as early as 1535 and the state capital, Saltillo, was founded 42 years after, but incessant attacks by indigenous Chichimecs and, later, Apaches discouraged widespread settlement until the

---

SCALING THE POTRERO CHICO

Crags, spires, steep cliff faces – if you like hanging from these, then climbing the awe-inspiring vertical limestone walls of Potrero Chico is a must. Arguably among the 10 best places in the world for learning rock climbing, Potrero Chico is a towering limestone outcrop, only an hour or so northwest of Monterrey, just west of the town of Hidalgo. Climbs range from 30m to 600m, with attributes that will challenge both beginners and experienced climbers. Expert tuition is available on-site for all levels.

The walls of the canyon currently support over 600 different routes (some requiring an overnight stay) with more being added all the time. In recent years mountain-bike trails have been added, and some terrific hiking paths established, including a 2½-hour trek to the summit of El Toro, which overlooks the canyon. Most of these trails have been set up by a group of American and Mexican climbers who have been developing the area since 1990. Consult the excellent website www.elpotrerochico.com.mx for more information.

Posada El Potrero Chico (☎ 81-8362-6672; posada@elpotrerochico.com.mx; $25, camp site $5), near the canyon, has several modern, comfortable en-suite rooms that can sleep up to three, or you can set up a tent. There are hot-water bathrooms, kitchen and laundry facilities, but no RV hookups. The owners also offer Spanish classes ($10 per hour).

From Monterrey a taxi will cost about $40, or you can catch a 'Mina' bus ($2.50) to Hidalgo and a taxi ($5) from there.

early 19th century. In 1800, Coahuila still had fewer than 7000 people. A few big landowners came to dominate the area. In southeast Coahuila, one holding of 890 sq km was bought from the crown for $33 in 1731, and grew to 58,700 sq km by 1771, becoming the Marquesado de Aguayo, protected by a private cavalry.

After 1821, in the early years of independence, Coahuila and Texas were one state of the new Mexican republic. As the 19th century progressed, ranching grew in importance, helped by the arrival of railways. By 1900, Coahuila had 297,000 inhabitants. In the 20th century, a steel foundry was established in Monclova, giving Coahuila a major industrial center.

From Big Bend National Park in Texas, small boats can ferry you across the river. It's another 1.5km to the small town of Boquillas del Carmen, from where transportation to other parts of Mexico is extremely limited.

CIUDAD ACUÑA
☎ 877 / pop 145,000
Ciudad Acuña, an unremarkable frontier city just across from the US town of Del Rio, is a fairly busy border crossing, open 24 hours a day. The city's main claim to fame is that a number of movies, including *El Mariachi*, have been filmed here. It also regularly registers as the hottest town in Mexico, with temperatures approaching 50°C in summer.

Almost everything of interest is on the main drag, Hidalgo, which runs west from the border. Check out **Crosby's** (☎ 772-20-20; Hidalgo 195; mains $8-13; **P**), where they serve fine international and Mexican dishes and memorable margaritas, or the popular **El Portal** (☎ 722-56-36; Hidalgo 250) whose menu takes in pizzas and burgers as well as Mexican favorites.

About 20km upriver, the **Presa de la Amistad** (Friendship Reservoir) is a joint Mexican–US water-management project, offering good fishing and boating facilities. From Ciudad Acuña to Saltillo it's an eight-hour bus ride ($30) on good two-lane roads.

PIEDRAS NEGRAS
☎ 878 / pop 140,000
The border crossing between Piedras Negras and the US town of Eagle Pass is a major commercial route. Piedras Negras is not a particularly attractive city, but recent

renovation work in the historic center has smartened the place up somewhat, and border-crossing formalities are usually quick and straightforward. Just over the Puente Internacional bridge is the town's attractive *zócalo*, with a bandstand. It's overlooked by the church of **Santuario de Nuestra Señora de Guadalupe**, complete with a fine belltower. You'll find plenty of Mexican leather goods, ceramics and crafts for sale in the Zaragoza market on the corner of Zaragoza and Allende, while the Casa de Cultura has occasional displays of Mexican art, music and dance.

Legend has it that Piedras Negras is the birthplace of the nacho, said to have been invented by Ignacio (Nacho) Anaya, a bar owner, to satisfy the snacking needs of his patrons. The town holds its three-day **International Nacho Festival** in early October.

Most of the hotels are located on Av Carranza, which runs into Allende and the city center. The **California Inn** (☎ 782-77-69; Carranza 1006; s/d $37/42; **P**) makes a very comfortable base, with bright homey rooms, a good restaurant and even a small playground for children. The bus station is 1km from the bridge on Allende, and connected to the border by regular buses. First-class services from here run to many places in northern Mexico:

Destination	Price	Duration	Frequency
Cuatro Ciénegas	$24	6¼hr	3 daily
Mexico City	$86	17hr	6 daily
Monclova	$18	4¼hr	hourly
Monterrey	$34	7hr	15 daily
Saltillo	$32	7hr	10 daily

Buses do run to towns in Texas, including San Antonio, Austin and Houston, but it's usually quicker to cross the border and catch a connection from Del Rio. Heading south by road, Hwy 57 is in good condition, and passes through Allende, Sabinas and Monclova on its way to Saltillo.

MONCLOVA
☎ 866 / pop 196,000
A large industrial city, Monclova is not a place for sightseeing unless you have a predilection for smoke stacks, but it is a convenient stopover for those on their way to the Cuatro Ciénegas protected area. The city's

Altos Hornos iron and steel works (Ahmsa) is one of the largest in Mexico.

The **Monclova tourist office** (☎ 636-27-30; promo torac@prodigy.net.mx; Blvd Harold Pape 455; ☽ 9am-1pm & 4-7pm Mon-Fri, 9am-1pm Sat) has excellent maps of the area. There are several decent, inexpensive hotels near the bus station. Just around the corner, half a block away, are two good places: the very hospitable and well-kept **Hotel San Cristóbal** (☎ 633-20-83; Cuauhtémoc 223; s/d $19/26; P ✖) and directly opposite, the equally good-value **Nuevo Hotel Viena** (☎ 633-09-01; Cuauhtémoc 223; s/d $23/25; P ✖). For more luxury, **Hotel Las Misiones** (☎ 649-68-00; www .monclovalasmisiones.com in Spanish; Blvd Benito Juárez 2005; r $63; P ✖ ⬜ ⬛) fits the bill nicely, with large rooms, a gym and a restaurant.

The main bus terminal is on Carranza, two blocks west of the plaza, with 1st-class service to/from the following destinations:

Destination	Price	Duration	Frequency
Ciudad Acuña	$21	5hr	9 daily
Monterrey	$12.50	3hr	hourly
Nuevo Laredo	$15	4hr	4 daily
Piedras Negras	$18	4hr	hourly
Saltillo	$13	3¼hr	14 daily
Torreón	$19	5½hr	8 daily

Second-class buses to Cuatro Ciénegas depart hourly until 10:30pm ($4.50, two hours). Four luxury ($84) and two first-class ($65) buses serve Mexico City's Terminal Norte (13 hours).

Hwy 57 runs south to Saltillo (192km) and north to Piedras Negras (256km). About 25km south of Monclova, Hwy 53 branches southeast to Monterrey (195km; there are no fuel stations on this highway). Hwy 30 heads west for 82km to Cuatro Ciénegas, then southwest to Torreón.

CUATRO CIÉNEGAS
☎ 869 / pop 9000 / elevation 740m

An astonishing collection of shimmering pools and turquoise streams in the middle of the Chihuahuan desert, the **Área de Protección de Flora y Fauna Cuatro Ciénegas** is unique. Drip-fed by a network of underground springs, it's a desert habitat of extraordinary biological diversity. More than 90 endemic species, including several turtles and eight kinds of fish, thrive in this fragile environment, an 843-sq-km protected reserve.

Some of the pools have been set aside as recreational spots, ideal for swimming and snorkeling. Within the pellucid waters of these desert aquariums is a wide variety of small fish, as well as organisms called *estromatolitos*. These are formed by calcified algae colonies, and biologists believe they are similar to the planet's first oxygen-producing forms of life. Equally impressive is the area called **Las Arenales**, where blinding-white gypsum sand dunes contrast superbly with the six mountain ranges that ring the valley.

The tranquil town of **Cuatro Ciénegas** is the perfect base for exploring the reserve and has a few interesting sights that offer some respite from the punishing desert sun. It's an agreeable place with some adobe buildings, a handful of hotels and restaurants, and you'll find a bank (with ATM) on the corner of Zaragoza and Escobedo, one block north of the plaza.

A block east of the plaza is the excellent little **Acuario y Herpetario Minckley** (☎ 696-11-02; Morelos Sur 112; admission $2; ☽ 10am-1pm & 8pm), where many of the rare snakes, lizards, toads, turtles, fish, spiders and scorpions endemic to the reserve can be viewed. All the creatures in this education center are well looked after by a knowledgeable local scientist. Just north of the plaza, the small **Museo Casa de Carranza** (Carranza s/n; admission free; ☽ 9am-1pm & 3-7pm Tue-Sun) occupies the former home of Venustiano Carranza, a revolutionary leader involved in the overthrow of Porfirio Díaz, and contains many documents and pictures from his life.

You could also pay a visit to a winery. Both **Vinos Vitali** (☎ 696-00-32; ☽ 9am-7pm) and the neighboring **Bodegas Ferriño** (☎ 696-00-33; ☽ 8am-8pm) are just north of town, 1km from the plaza along Carranza. Wine has been made in Cuatro Ciénegas for 150 years, and both places offer tastings and bottles for sale. Call first to arrange a free tour of either winery's vineyards and cellars.

Visiting the Reserve

Access to the reserve is southwest of town along Hwy 30. If you're exploring the area on your own, be aware that not all the desert tracks are signposted, so pick up a map first from the Cuatro Ciénegas **tourist office** (☎ 696-05-74; Juárez; ☽ 9:30am-5pm Mon-Sat). Summer temperatures can be extreme, so bring plenty of water and avoid midday excursions. Using the services of a guide is a good idea, and mandatory if you want to see Las Arenales. **Arturo Contreras** (☎ 100-53-52), a biologist who is also a director of the **Acuario y Herpetario Minckley**, knows the local fauna and environment well, and is highly recommended. Otherwise the tourist office will put you in touch with a licensed local guide. Whoever you go with, all tours are in Spanish and cost $45 to $50 for a half-day trip, including the use of a vehicle.

Six kilometers southwest of town there's a turnoff on the left for the **Río Los Mezquites**. Follow the track for 1.5km past *las salina* (a dried-up salt lake) until you see a sublime stretch of slow-flowing blue water. There's great swimming in the river here, plenty of *palapas* for shade, plus toilets, camping and barbecue areas. It's usually deserted during the week but popular with families at weekends when you may be charged $2.50 per person to use the area. Less than a kilometer further on you come to a not-very-exciting **visitors' center** (Poza Las Tortugas; admission $2.50; ☼ 10am-6pm Tue-Sun) with some maps and illustrated explanations, in Spanish, of the region's natural attractions.

In the reserve area there are over 170 cerulean *pozas* (pools), some up to 13m deep. Wearing suntan lotion is prohibited when swimming in the pools. **Poza La Becerra** (☎ 696-05-74; adult/child $4/2, per tent $5), 15km from Cuatro Ciénegas and just off the highway, is set up as a recreational facility with a diving pier, bathrooms and showers, though there's no restaurant. Swimming here amid the desert landscape is a surreal, revitalizing experience. The water temperature is a balmy, constant 32°C but there are cooler areas where springs feed the pools. Buses run here from town twice daily.

For real solitude, stop by the idyllic **Poza del Churince**, 18km from town on the right side of the highway, where you'll almost certainly have a wonderful, shallow pool to yourself (apart from the endemic fish and odd turtle that is).

Twelve kilometers southeast of Cuatro Ciénegas, there's a white sand beach at **Las Playitas**, a small, shallow lake.

Sleeping & Eating

Camping is permitted within the reserve at Río Los Mezquites, Poza La Becerra and Las Playitas. There are some good midrange hotels in Cuatro Ciénegas, though nothing in the budget category.

Hotel Plaza (☎ 696-00-66; Hidalgo 202; s/d $36/44; P ✖ ☎) This hotel, a well-run and attractive place, a block from the plaza and built in colonial style, is strongly recommended. All rooms face a slim, grassy patio and pool, and have warm colors, high ceilings, comfy beds and stylish bathrooms. Breakfast is included in the attached restaurant La Casona, which matches the hotel for ambience and quality, and offers superb *pinchos* (kebabs; $7.50), club sandwiches ($4.50) and salads.

El Nogalito (☎ 696-00-09; Carranza s/n; www.elnogalito.com in Spanish; r/cabañas $42/91; P ✖ ☎) Highly attractive and well-kept, rustic-style accommodation, set in grassy grounds with a large pool, 1.5km north of the plaza. All the wood *cabañas* have front porches, small kitchenettes and can sleep up to five, while the attractive rooms have two double beds.

Hotel Misión Marielena (☎ 696-11-51; www.hotel misionmarielena.com.mx; Hidalgo 200; s/d $40/51; P ✖ ☐ ☎) Directly opposite the Hotel Plaza, this competitor is not as welcoming or atmospheric, but is a solid choice. The very spacious, sparsely furnished but comfortable rooms, all with two double beds, are set around two rear courtyards.

Hotel Ibarra (☎ 696-01-29; Zaragoza 200; r $30; P ✖) This place, across from the Santander Serfin bank, has large clean rooms (with two double beds and cable TV) that represent fair value.

El Doc (☎ 696-03-69; Zaragoza 103; mains $4-8; ✖) The rather unatmospheric and under-patronized El Doc is on the east side of the plaza.

Getting There & Away

The bus terminal occupies the south side of the plaza. Hourly 2nd-class services go to/from Monclova ($4.50, two hours). First-class buses run to Torreón ($14, 3½ hours, eight daily), Saltillo ($17, 5¼ hours, one daily) and Piedras Negras ($24, 6¼ hours, three daily).

SALTILLO

☎ 844 / pop 621,000 / elevation 1599m

Set high in the arid Sierra Madre Oriental, Saltillo was founded in 1577, making it the oldest city in the northeast. It has a quiet central area with a small-town feel, making it a popular destination, though there are extensive new suburbs and major industries on the city's outskirts. A large student population adds energy and a progressive feel. The city boasts a number of fine colonial buildings, a temperate climate and some good restaurants, and makes a relaxing place to experience northern-Mexican life. It's on the main routes between the northeast border and central Mexico, making it an ideal spot to break a journey.

History

The first mission was established here in 1591 as a center for the education and religious conversion of the local indigenous populations. Native Tlaxcalans were brought to help the Spanish stabilize the area, and they set up a colony beside the Spanish one at Saltillo (the area west of Allende in today's city).

In the late 17th century, Saltillo was the capital of an area that included Coahuila, Nuevo León, Tamaulipas and Texas. The city was occupied by US troops under Zachary Taylor during the Mexican-American War in 1846. At Buenavista, south of Saltillo, the

20,000-strong army of General Santa Anna was repulsed by Taylor's force, a quarter the size, in the decisive battle for control of the northeast during that war.

During the Porfiriato period, agriculture and ranching prospered in the area, and the coming of the railway helped trade and the first industries in the city. Monterrey, however, was quickly overtaking Saltillo in both size and importance.

Today Saltillo is still the center for a large livestock and agricultural area, and in recent decades it has expanded to include automobile and petrochemical plants.

Orientation

Saltillo spreads over a large area, but most places of interest are in the blocks around the two central plazas. Periférico Echeverría, a ring road, enables traffic to bypass the inner city.

The junction of Hidalgo and Juárez, at the southeast corner of Plaza de Armas, serves as a dividing point for Saltillo's street addresses, with those located to the south suffixed 'Sur', those to the east 'Ote' (Oriente), and so on.

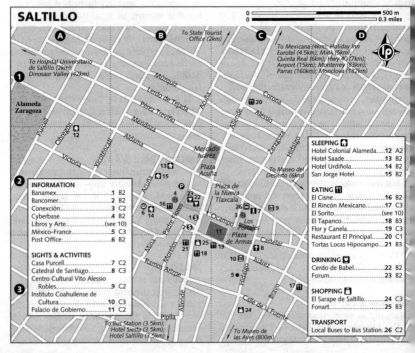

SALTILLO

INFORMATION	
Banamex	1 B2
Bancomer	2 B2
Conexción	3 C2
Cyberbase	4 B2
Libros y Arte	(see 10)
México-France	5 C3
Post Office	6 B2

SIGHTS & ACTIVITIES	
Casa Purcell	7 C2
Catedral de Santiago	8 C3
Centro Cultural Vito Alessio Robles	9 C2
Instituto Coahuilense de Cultura	10 C3
Palacio de Gobierno	11 C2

SLEEPING	
Hotel Colonial Alameda	12 A2
Hotel Saade	13 B2
Hotel Urdiñola	14 B2
San Jorge Hotel	15 B2

EATING	
El Cisne	16 B2
El Rincón Mexicano	17 C3
El Sorito	(see 10)
El Tapanco	18 B3
Flor y Canela	19 C3
Restaurant El Principal	20 C1
Tortas Locas Hipocampo	21 B3

DRINKING	
Cerdo de Babel	22 B2
Forum	23 B2

SHOPPING	
El Sarape de Saltillo	24 C3
Fonart	25 B3

TRANSPORT	
Local Buses to Bus Station	26 C2

0 - 500 m
0 - 0.3 miles

To State Tourist Office (2km)

To Mexicana (4km); Holiday Inn Eurotel (4.5km); Mink (5km); Quinta Real (6km); Hwy 40 (7km); Airport (15km); Monterrey (83km); Parras (160km); Monclova (182km)

To Hospital Universitario de Saltillo (2km); Dinosaur Valley (42km)

Alameda Zaragoza

Múzquiz

Lerdo de Tejada

Pérez Treviño

Corona

Alessio

Mendoza

Obregón

Aldama

Purcell

Xicoténcatl

Victoria

Mercado Juárez

Plaza Acuña

Plaza de la Nueva Tlaxcala

To Museo del Desierto (6km)

Ocampo

Los Portales

Plaza de Armas

Castelar

Juárez

Calle de la Fuente

Bravo

Hidalgo

Zaragoza

Allende

Acuña

Padre Flores

Mina

Morelos

Ramos Arizpe

Pípila

To Bus Station (3.5km); Hotel Siesta (3.5km); Hotel Saltillo (3.5km)

To Museo de las Aves (800m)

The bus station is on the south side of town, on Periférico Echeverría Sur – a 10-minute bus ride from the center.

Information

BOOKSTORES
Libros y Arte (☎ 481-63-51; Instituto Coahuilense de Cultura; Juárez) Has a terrific selection of art, architecture and history titles.

CULTURAL CENTER
México-France (☎ 412-34-62; Hidalgo 140) Shows French films and hosts occasional exhibitions on French culture.

EMERGENCY
Cruz Roja (Red Cross; ☎ 065)
Police (☎ 066)

INTERNET ACCESS
Conexción (Zaragoza 224; per hr $1)
Cyberbase (Padre Flores 159; per hr $1)

MEDIA
S.O.S. is a free monthly magazine with cinema, theatre and live-music coverage and listings.

MEDICAL SERVICES
Hospital Universitario de Saltillo (☎ 412-30-00; Madero 1291)

MONEY
You can change cash and traveler's checks at the banks on Allende (all have ATMs), opposite the Plaza de la Nueva Tlaxcala.

POST
Post office (Victoria Pte 223)

TOURIST INFORMATION
State tourist office (☎ 412-51-22; cnr Blvd Coss & Acuña; www.saltillomexico.org; ⏰ 9am-6:30pm Mon-Fri, 9am-noon Sat, 10am-6pm Sun) In the old train station, about 1.5km north of the center, the office has abundant glossy brochures including multiple-map guides to every region in the state.

Sights

CATEDRAL DE SANTIAGO
Built between 1745 and 1800, Saltillo's cathedral dominates the plaza and has one of Mexico's finest Churrigueresque facades, with columns of elaborately carved pale gray stone. It's particularly splendid when lit up

at night. Inside, the transepts are full of gilt ornamentation – look for the human figure perched on a ledge at the top of the dome.

PALACIO DE GOBIERNO
You can wander into this elegant 19th-century building that houses the state-government headquarters. A mural on its 2nd-floor depicts Coahuila's history and its historical figures, most prominently Venustiano Carranza, who, as governor of the state during the Revolution, led a revolt against the provisional president Victoriano Huerta.

CASA PURCELL
This **cultural center** (☎ 414-50-80; Hidalgo 231; admission free; ⏰ 10am-7pm Tue-Sun) is located in a wonderful 19th-century mansion. Built in an English neo-Gothic style with handsome gray stone, many of its rooms have stately fireplaces, stained-glass windows and parquet floors. Casa Purcell hosts exhibitions of art and photography, and occasional live events with local musicians and DJs.

CENTRO CULTURAL VITO ALESSIO ROBLES
The book collection of the eponymous historian, now estimated at over 13,000 volumes from the 17th to the 19th centuries, anchors this modest **museum** (☎ 412-88-45; cnr Hidalgo & Aldama; admission free; ⏰ 10am-6pm Tue-Sun). On the right side of the central courtyard are temporary art exhibitions, and there's also a striking mural of the city's history.

INSTITUTO COAHUILENSE DE CULTURA
This **cultural center** (☎ 410-20-33; Juárez s/n; admission free; ⏰ 9am-9pm Tue-Sun), on the south side of the plaza, exhibits paintings, sculpture and crafts by artists from Coahuila and beyond. It also hosts occasional concerts and has a terrific bookstore and café.

ALAMEDA ZARAGOZA
Full of shady trees and pathways, this park has a playground, and live music is sometimes on tap on Saturday and Sunday. A pond at the southern end has an island shaped like Mexico.

MUSEO DEL DESIERTO
Deserts cover up to 60% of Mexican territory, and this excellent **museum** (☎ 410-66-33; www.museodeldesierto.org in Spanish; Pérez Treviño 3745; adult/student & senior $6/3; ⏰ 10am-5pm Tue-Sun; **P**),

dedicated to the study of the Desierto Chi-huahuense, the largest in North America, certainly deserves a visit. The displays are entertainingly presented using audiovisual techniques. Illuminating exhibits reveal why sea currents affect rainfall and create deserts, and how sand dunes are formed. Children will also enjoy the collection of extraordinary dinosaur fossils, including winged reptiles and the duck-billed kritosaurus. There's also a reptile house with boas, iguanas and crocodiles, and a botanical garden with over 400 species of cactus.

MUSEO DE LAS AVES

This **museum** (☎ 414-01-67; www.museodelasaves.org in Spanish; cnr Hidalgo & Bolívar; adult/child $1/0.50, Sat free; ☒ 10am-6pm Tue-Sat, 11am-6pm Sun), a few blocks south of the plaza, is devoted to the birds of Mexico, which ranks sixth in the world in terms of avian diversity. Most of the exhibits are birds stuffed and mounted in convincing dioramas of their natural habitat. There are special sections on nesting, territoriality, birdsongs, navigation and endangered species. Over 670 bird species are displayed, along with bird skeletons, fossils and eggs.

Tours

Extrematour (☎ 410-74-11; extrematour@hotmail.com) organizes day and overnight hiking (from $41), climbing, rafting (from $52), rappelling and bird-watching tours.

Festivals & Events

Aniversario de Saltillo A nine-day cultural festival in late July commemorating the city's foundation.
Día del Santo Cristo de la Capilla In honor of Saltillo's patron saint, this festival takes place in the week leading up to August 6. Dance groups from around Coahuila perform in front of the cathedral.
International Festival of the Arts There are artistic and musical events in towns and cities throughout the region in October. Saltillo sees a large share of the more high-profile acts.

Sleeping

There aren't many budget places in Saltillo, and though there's more choice as you enter the midrange category, value for money is not that great.

BUDGET & MIDRANGE

Hotel Urdiñola (☎ 414-09-40; Victoria 251; s/d with fan $33/37; P ☒ ☐) Initial impressions are

excellent at the Urdiñola, which has a stately lobby with a sweeping marble stairway and a stained-glass window. The rooms, mostly set around a rear garden courtyard, are less impressive, with aging decor and the odd chip to the furniture, but they still have character and are kept tidy – those on the upper floor enjoy more natural light.
Hotel Colonial Alameda (☎ 410-00-88; www.hotel colonialalameda.com; Obregón 222; r Sun-Thu $63, Fri & Sat $51; P ☒ ☐) A fine Spanish colonial–style hotel with a plush lobby and elegant, tastefully presented rooms, each containing a pair of huge beds and smart furnishings. There are often substantial weekend discounts offered, when it becomes particularly good value.
Hotel Saltillo (☎ 417-22-00; Echeverría 249; r $28; P ☒) Opposite the bus station on busy Echeverría, the Saltillo is a decent enough place with 24 bright airy rooms, each with cable TV, a phone and a ceiling fan. There's a restaurant here with many seafood choices.
San Jorge Hotel (☎ 412-22-22; Acuña 240; s/d $52/59; P ☒ ☒) Occupying a large concrete block that must have seemed modern in 1972, this hotel has large, carpeted rooms with flowery bedspreads and garish fittings, some with great views. It does boast a small rooftop pool, a restaurant and a central location.

Also worth considering:
Hotel Siesta (☎ 417-07-24; Echeverría 239; r $26-34; P ☐) Fair-value, light rooms, all with fan and TV; located in front of the bus station.
Hotel Saade (☎ 412-91-20; www.hotelsaade.com in Spanish; Aldama 397; s/d $30/34; P) A large place with carpeted rooms, all with a safe and phone.

THE AUTHOR'S CHOICE

Quinta Real (☎ 438-84-50; www.quintareal .com; Blvd Sarmiento 1385; r $129; P ☒ ☒ ☐ ☒) This highly impressive colonial-style palace, 6.5km north of the plaza off the highway to Monterrey, is the best luxury hotel in the region. The decor is more stately home than chain hotel, with antique-lined hallways, while the spacious, commodious accommodation (all rooms are suite-sized) boasts virtually every conceivable amenity, including marble bathrooms with tubs. The hotel's facilities include fitness and business centers, and a restaurant.

TOP END
There are several four- and five-star hotels, aimed at business-class travelers, along the highways heading north and east from Saltillo. Special weekends rates are offered at most luxury places.

Holiday Inn Eurotel (☎ 438-88-88; www.hieurotel com in Spanish; V Carranza 4100; r Mon-Fri $132, Sat & Sun $78; P ✕ ❄ 🖵 ☎) Offers all the modern luxuries including a gym, pool, sauna and Jacuzzi as well as bargain weekend deals. It's 5km from the center, on Hwy 40 to Monterey, just south of the Carranza monument.

Eating
Central Saltillo has an excellent selection of cafés and restaurants within a short walk of Plaza de Armas

El Cisne (☎ 414-68-17; Victoria 178; panini $4-6, mains $4.50-8; ✦ 8am-11pm Mon-Thu, 8am-3am Fri & Sat, 1-10pm un) An enjoyable, stylish café-restaurant with rooms set off a shaded central courtyard, and friendly staff, many of them students. You'll find a good line up of breakfasts, Mexican favorites and pasta dishes, including *espagueti con anchoas y almendras* (spaghetti with anchovies and almonds; $6.50) as well as (overpriced) *panini* and around 40 different types of coffee. On Friday and Saturday nights there's live music, and El Cisne also hosts art exhibitions and films.

El Rincón Mexicano (☎ 481-51-91; Juárez 314; mains $4.50; ✦ 11am-10pm Fri-Wed, until 3am Thu) This likable and informal place has friendly staff and specializes in southern Mexican cuisine: *albutes yucatecos* (small thick tortillas with a spicy topping), *picadas* with salsa, and very filling *huaraches* (thick maize tortillas) smeared with beans and served with toppings such as bacon, cheese, onion and chili. There's live *bohemia* music on Thursdays.

El Sorito (Instituto Coahuilense de Cultura; Juárez s/n; snacks $3-4.50; ✦ 7am-11pm) Tucked away inside a cultural center, this civilized little café grinds its own beans for barista-perfect coffee, and serves snacks like croissants, *panini* and bagels. You can browse the books of the adjoining Libros y Arte while you're here.

Flor y Canela (☎ 414-31-43; Juárez 257; sandwiches 3; ✦ 8am-9:30pm Mon-Fri, 4-9:30pm Sat & Sun) A stylish café ideal for breakfast ($4), a snack, one of their fine *moka*, frappé or espresso coffees, or even a nice cup of tea.

El Tapanco (☎ 414-43-39; Allende 225; mains $13-26) Classy and formal, with attendant prices,

this restaurant has several elegant rooms, or you can dine alfresco on the back patio. The menu majors in European-style cuisine (fish, seafood and meat dishes) but there are also salads and crepes.

Restaurant El Principal (☎ 414-33-84; Allende 702; cabrito dishes $7-12, steak dishes $11; ✖) *Norteño*-style *cabrito* is the specialty at this family restaurant, which offers assorted cuts of goat and beef steak. There are two other Principals, less centrally located.

Tortas Locas Hipocampo (☎ 414-42-26; Allende 146; sandwiches $2-4; ✦ noon-10pm Tue-Sat, noon-9pm Sun) Almost 30 different kinds of sandwiches, freshly prepared to order.

Drinking
Weekdays are generally quiet in the city center except Thursdays, when **El Rincón Mexicano** (see left) has live *música bohemia*. Check out the two pedestrianized lanes just west of Allende where there are a few intimate bars, including the sociable **Cerdo de Babel** (Ocampo 324; ✦ 6:30pm-2am Tue-Sun), and **Forum** (Padre Flores 101; ✦ 7:30pm-2:30am), which have live music. For an altogether different scene, Saltillo's cocktail-quaffing classes gather at **Mink** (Rufino Tamayo 524; ✦ 7pm-2am Tue-Sun), which is a stylish lounge bar with modish decor and a pre-club vibe, off the ring road northeast of the center.

While you're in town try a shot of the locally produced *sotol*, which is similar to *mezcal*.

Shopping
Saltillo is so famous for its sarapes that the local baseball team is known as the Saraperos. These days most items are woven in jarring combinations of colors, but a few less-garish wool ponchos and blankets are usually available.

El Sarape de Saltillo (☎ 414-96-34; Hidalgo 305; ✦ 9am-1pm & 3-7pm Mon-Sat) Sells fine quality sarapes, rugs, ponchos, tablecloths, leather goods and ceramics. Wool is dyed and woven on treadle looms inside the shop.

Mercado Juárez (✦ 7am-5pm), next to Plaza Acuña, Also worth a look, the market has a selection of sarapes, as well as hats, saddles and souvenirs. **Fonart** (Allende 217; ✦ 8am-5pm Mon-Sat), just south of Juárez, is a branch of the government-run crafts shop, with a variety of pottery, textiles and jewelry from around Mexico.

Getting There & Away

AIR

Mexicana (☎ 488-07-70; Europlaza Mall, Venustiano Carranza 4120) has flights between Mexico City and Saltillo. **Continental Airlines** (☎ 488-13-14) flies daily to/from Houston.

BUS

Saltillo's modern bus station is on the ring road at Libertad, 3km south of the center. It has a left-luggage facility ($0.50 per hour).

Lots of buses serve Saltillo but few start their journeys here. This means that on some buses, 2nd-class ones in particular, you often can't buy a ticket until the bus has arrived. The 1st-class lines include **Transportes del Norte** (☎ 417-09-02) and **Ómnibus de México** (☎ 417-03-15), while **Transportes Frontera** (☎ 417-00-76) and Línea Verde are 2nd-class; **Turistar** (☎ 417-09-02) is the deluxe bus line. Daily departures include the following:

Destination	Price	Duration	Frequency
Cuatro Ciénegas	$15	5hr	1 1st-class
Durango	$27	8hr	4 1st-class
Guadalajara	$46	10hr	14 1st-class
Matamoros	$24	7hr	12 1st-class
Mexico City	$68	10hr	3 deluxe
(Terminal Norte)	$56	10hr	10 1st-class
Monclova	$13	3¼hr	14 1st class
Monterrey	$7	1¾hr	3 deluxe
	$5.50	1¾hr	frequent 1st-class
Monterrey airport	$15	2hr	6 daily
Nuevo Laredo	$22	5hr	8 1st-class
Parras	$7.50	2½hr	12 2nd-class
San Luis Potosí	$27	5½hr	12 1st-class
Torreón	$20	3½hr	frequent 1st-class
Zacatecas	$23	5hr	10 1st-class
	$21	5hr	7 2nd-class

Buses also go to Chihuahua, Ciudad Acuña, Ciudad Juárez, Mazatlán, Morelia, Piedras Negras, Reynosa, Querétaro and Tijuana. Autobuses Americanos has services to Chicago, Dallas, Houston and San Antonio.

CAR & MOTORCYCLE

Saltillo is a junction of major roads. Hwy 40, going northeast to Monterrey, is a good four-lane road, with no tolls until you reach the Monterrey bypass. Going west to Torreón (277km), Hwy 40D splits off Hwy 40 after 30km, becoming an over-priced toll road. Hwy 40 is free and perfectly all right.

Hwy 57 goes north to Monclova (192km), penetrating the dramatic Sierra San Marcos y Pinos at Cima de la Muralla (a butterfly-migration zone in the summer months), and onward to Piedras Negras (441km). Going south to Mexico City (852km), recently upgraded Hwy 57 climbs to over 2000m, then descends gradually along the Altiplano Central to Matehuala (260km) and San Luis Potosí (455km), through barren but often scenic country. To the southwest, Hwy 54 crosses high, dry plains toward Zacatecas (363km) and Guadalajara (680km).

Getting Around

The airport is 15km northeast of town on Hwy 40; catch a 'Ramos Arizpe' bus along Xicoténcatl ($1) or a taxi ($14). To reach the city center from the bus station, take minibus No 9 ($0.40), which departs from Libertad, the first street on the right as you leave the station. To reach the bus station from the center, catch a No 9 on Aldama, between Zaragoza and Hidalgo. Taxis between the center and the bus station cost $3.

If you have the time, a convenient way to see the sights is the tourist trolley ($3) which makes the rounds from Friday to Sunday, enabling you to 'hop-on-hop-off' at any of the 14 stops, which include the Museo del Desierto.

PARRAS

☎ 842 / pop 33,000 / elevation 1520m

A graceful oasis town located in the heart of the Coahuilan desert, Parras has a historic center of real colonial character and a delightfully temperate climate. Some 160km west of Saltillo, off the Torreón road, it's most famous for its wine. Underground streams from the sierra surface here as springs, which have been used to irrigate the *parras* (grapevines) since the late 16th century.

An obelisk was erected on Calle Arizpe in memory of Francisco Madero, an important leader in the Mexican Revolution, who was born in Parras. US troops occupied the town in 1846, and French troops took over in 1866.

Orientation & Information

Most restaurants, hotels and shops are found within a short walking distance of the bus station and Plaza Zaragoza.

Bancomer (cnr Reforma & Ramos Arzipe) Has an ATM.

Cafe Internet (Arzipe 121; per hr $1.50) Internet access.

Computo y Linea (Allende 306; per hr $1.50; ☺ 8am-10pm) Internet access.

Tourist office (☎ 422-02-59; www.parrascoahuila.com .mx; ☺ 9:30am-1pm & 3-7pm) On the roadside 3km north of town.

Sights

The first winery in the Americas was established at Parras in 1597, a year before the town itself was founded. Now called **Casa Madero** (☎ 422-00-55; www.madero.com.mx; admission free; ☺ 9am-5pm daily), it's 6km north of the center, in San Lorenzo on the road to the main highway. If you visit, you have to take one of the tours, which are conducted in Spanish and last about an hour. There's a small museum full of old viticulture machinery, and you can buy their quality wine and brandy on-site too.

The town has an old **aqueduct**, some colonial buildings, and three **estanques** (large pools where water from the springs is stored) that are great for swimming. The **Iglesia del Santo Madero**, on the southern edge of town, sits on the plug of an extinct volcano. It is a steep climb, but the expansive views are rewarding.

An important manufacturer of *mezclilla* (denim), Parras is a good place to buy jeans and jackets. Its fig, date and walnut orchards provide the basis for delectable fudgy sweets, on sale around town. Hmm, maybe buy the new jeans after you've tasted the fudge.

Festivals & Events

Perhaps it is not very surprising, the **Feria de la Uva** (Grape Fair) is the biggest festival in town. It goes on for most of the month of August, featuring parades, fireworks, horse races, traditional costumes, religious celebrations on the **Día de la Asunción** (August 15), and traditional dances by descendants of the early Tlaxcalan settlers. And of course, there is lots of wine.

Sleeping

Hostal El Farol (☎ 422-11-13; Ramos Arizpe 301; r $69; P ☻) This excellent colonial-style hotel has 20 spacious, wood-paneled rooms with plenty of period character, that set off a shaded courtyard. Service is friendly and attentive in the bar-restaurant. Reduced rates apply Sunday to Thursday.

Hotel Posada Santa Isabel (☎ 422-04-00; Madero 514; r $34; P) There's plenty of colonial character here too, with accommodations spread out around a graceful and tranquil courtyard. Though clean enough, many rooms are looking a little worn around the edges. There is a decent restaurant here too.

Hotel La Siesta (☎ 422-03-74; Acuña 9; s/d $16/20) The Siesta, around the corner from the bus station, is the best budget option in town. The rooms and beds are smaller than the Santa Isabel, but the lobby and courtyard are inviting.

Rincón del Montero (☎ 422-05-40; www.rincondel montero.com; r $91, cabaña $105, ste $162; P ☻ ☻) About 3km north of the town center, this large resort is set in extensive, leafy grounds and has a choice of accommodation, some with self-catering facilities. There's golf, tennis, a swimming pool and horseback riding, while mountain biking and climbing excursions can also be arranged by the staff.

Eating

Restaurant-Bar La Noria (☎ 422-25-40; Hostal El Farol, Ramos Arizpe 30l; breakfasts $3.50, mains $4-9; P) This hospitable hotel restaurant has a courtyard with tables and makes a good choice for breakfast or Mexican food.

Restaurant Posada (breakfast $4, mains $5) If the hotel of the same name is vacant, you'll most probabaly have the leafy courtyard dining area all to yourself. The food is Mexican standards, but the prices are very affordable.

For an inexpensive meal there are a few places up and down Reforma, including **El Tiburón** (Reforma 29) for tacos and more, and **Pepés** (☎ 422-18-18; Reforma 31-B), which serves up fast food including decent burgers.

Getting There & Away

Only 2nd-class buses serve Parras; there are 12 daily to/from Saltillo ($7.50, 2½ hours). A 1st-class bus from Saltillo or elsewhere might drop you at La Paila, about halfway between Saltillo and Torreón. From La Paila you then have to find local transport. There are six buses daily to/from Torreón ($9.50, 2½ hours) to the west. If you want to head to Cuatro Ciénegas without back-tracking to Saltillo, you can catch a bus to San Pedro Las Colonias ($6, 1½ hours) and then a 1st-class bus from there to Cuatro Ciénegas ($18, two hours). Parras is easy to reach by car; turn off the highway at La Paila and drive 27km south.

Central Pacific Coast

If life is a beach, then hanging out on the central Pacific coast really *is* living. Whether you long to luxuriate undisturbed on a hidden stretch of honeyed sand or to groove until dawn at a cosmopolitan resort-town nightclub, you'll find whatever floats your boat on Mexico's Pacific coast. This is a land of giant sunsets, mangrove-fringed lagoons, pristine bays, ramshackle fishing villages and eminently friendly folks, where sea turtles crawl ashore on moonlit nights to lay their eggs. While just lounging around in the sand you may spot humpback whales breaching on the horizon, or a pod of dolphins surfacing from the waves.

One of the world's top tourist destinations, the coast is also a land of mega-resorts, cruise ships, camera-clad tourists and rowdy spring-breakers on weekend drinking binges. You can snorkel, surf, sail, ride horses, scuba dive, explore lagoons by boat, mountain bike along ocean cliffs and drink yourself silly (all in one day, if you want). Or you can soak up the sun and read a book before indulging in the best spa treatment or full-body massage of your life.

Spend a week in a fabulous beachfront guesthouse, where food and drink are prepared fresh daily, or embark on a harebrained road trip bouncing down back roads to deserted beaches. You can take months exploring the coast on the cheap, roaring along the coastal highway in 2nd-class buses, or hanging onto the back of a pickup packed with locals on your way to a fishing village where they still string fishing nets by hand.

But whatever you do, don't forget your swimsuit.

TOP FIVE

- Enjoying the terrific restaurants and old-town ambience of **Mazatlán's** (p426) lively historic center

- Delving deep into the mangroves and jungles of **La Tovara** (p441) by boat from San Blas

- Luxuriating on the beach, shopping, dancing and dining in **Puerto Vallarta** (p451)

- Thrilling at the fearless cliff-divers of **Acapulco** (p506)

- Reveling in the taste of *tiritas* and handmade tortillas in **Barra de Potosí** (p498)

★ Mazatlán
★ La Tovara
★ Puerto Vallarta
★ Barra de Potosí
★ Acapulco

- **PUERTO VALLARTA JANUARY DAILY HIGH:** 26°C | 78°F
- **PUERTO VALLARTA JULY DAILY HIGH:** 33°C | 91°F

History

Mexico's Pacific coast has a distinct ancient history that is unique in all of Mesoamerica. Archaeologists and art historians treat west Mexico as a unified region, defined by its tradition of shaft or chamber tombs, which are underground burial chambers at the base of a deep shaft. The oldest of these have been dated as far back as 1900 BC, but the most significant were probably built between 1500 BC and 800 BC.

Much of what is known of the cultures of west Mexico is based on the excavation of these tombs and analysis of the clay sculptures and vessels found within. The ceremonial centers around the tombs suggest a fairly developed spiritual and religious life. Shaft tombs are found nowhere else in Mesoamerica, but they *are* found in Ecuador and Colombia. It's therefore quite likely that maritime exchange between west Mexico and northern South America began some 3000 years ago.

Around the close of the Classic period, a metal-working tradition made its appearance in west Mexico and the state of Michoacán. Examination of copper artifacts from both west Mexico and Ecuador shows similarities that are far too striking to be coincidental. Archaeologists conclude that contact between west Mexico and northern South America continued well into the Postclassic period.

The Spanish arrived in Mexico in 1519 and soon traveled to Acapulco, Zihuatanejo, Puerto Vallarta and Manzanillo. In 1564 conquistador Miguel López de Legazpi and Father André de Urdaneta first sailed from Barra de Navidad to the Philippines and soon after claimed it for Spain. Soon after, Acapulco became an established port link in the trade route between Asia and Europe.

It was not until the middle of the 1950s that tourism really hit the coast, starting in Acapulco and Mazatlán, with Puerto Vallarta soon to follow. In recent years more and more foreigners have bought and developed land along the coast, most noticeably around Puerto Vallarta.

Climate

It's hot – very hot – and wet through May and early November. Hurricanes are occasional unwelcome guests in September and October. The high-tourist season understandably coincides with the cooler, dry season from late November to late April.

Dangers & Annoyances

Mexico's central Pacific coast is *tranquilo* (peaceful), with little crime. Acapulco is the grittiest of the coastal cities, where you might find glue-sniffing kids hovering in empty lots behind plush hotels. But for travelers, Acapulco is hardly dangerous.

Avoid driving at night: there are no road lights, many people drive without headlights, checkpoints are more difficult to get through and animals loiter in the middle of the road.

The coastal Hwy 200, which has had an up-and-down safety record, is now mostly safe for travel. The stretch through Michoacán and Guerrero still has a reputation for being unsafe at night, although increased law enforcement has greatly improved the situation.

The route from Iguala to Ixtapa by Hwys 51 and 134 sees a higher-than-normal incidence of highway robbery; take extra precautions here and drive during daylight.

The most likely danger you'll encounter are the powerful undertows that can make swimming deadly. Heed local warnings and swim with caution. Otherwise, kick back; you're on vacation.

Getting There & Around

There are plenty of direct international flights from the US and Canada to Acapulco, Zihuatanejo, Puerto Vallarta and Mazatlán. Playa de Oro International Airport between Manzanillo and Barra de Navidad is popular but requires a bit more land travel.

It's long been popular to drive to Mexico's Pacific coast from the US and Canada. The roads are all tolled between the border and Mazatlán, making it an easy approach. But past Mazatlán the road gets patchy and you'll oscillate between smooth pavement and shock-busting potholes.

If you're driving remember that everything on coastal Hwy 200 – service stations, stores, tire shops – closes around sundown; you do not want to be stranded after dark. The most direct driving routes from Mexico City to the Pacific coast is via Hwy 134 to Ixtapa and Hwy 95 or 95D to Acapulco. All three roads are heavily traveled and for the most part offer smooth sailing.

CENTRAL PACIFIC COAST

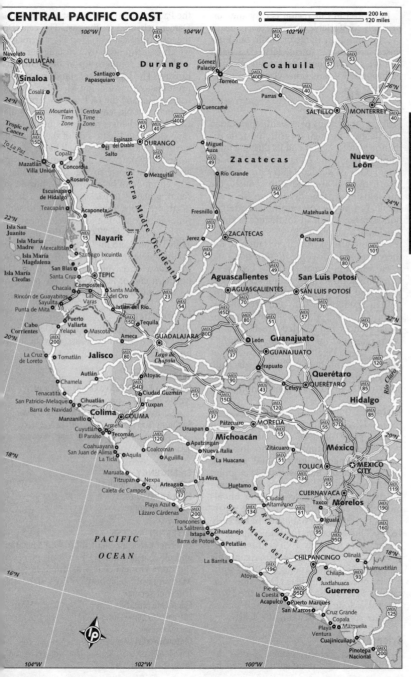

Bus travel in this region is easy and surprisingly comfortable. The buses serve nearly every community, large or small, but nicer buses serve bigger towns. First-class buses all have air-con, comfortable seats, cleanish bathrooms, TVs and other classy comforts.

MAZATLÁN

☎ 669 / pop 328,000

Striking for its many personalities, Mazatlán reveals itself through its gritty port, its romantic historic center and its thriving tourist playground (the Zona Dorada – Golden Zone). One of Mexico's glitzy prototypical resort towns of the mid-20th century, the city remains a prime destination for a no-hassle, fun-in-the-sun vacation. It caters to holidaymakers with an abundance of cheap knickknack stores, taxis, oversized mega-resorts and gringo-friendly restaurants. But there's more to discover in Mazatlán's old town, which in recent years has been revitalized by a flowering cultural scene. Here you'll find a beguiling mixture of cosmopolitan restaurants, bars and art galleries against a backdrop of well-preserved colonial edifices and cobbled streets. Catch a performance at the wonderful refurbished Teatro Ángela Peralta and then a late-night bite at the atmospheric Plazuela Machado and you just may decide to stick around for an extra day to go apartment hunting.

History

In pre-Hispanic times Mazatlán (which means 'place of deer' in Nahuatl) was populated by Totorames, who lived by hunting, gathering, fishing and growing crops. On Easter Sunday in 1531 a group of 25 Spaniards led by Nuño de Guzmán officially founded a settlement here, but almost three centuries elapsed before a permanent colony was established in the early 1820s. 'Old' Mazatlán, the traditional town center, dates from the 19th century. Tourists started coming in the 1930s, mainly for fishing and hunting, and in the 1950s some hotels appeared along Playa Olas Altas, Mazatlán's first tourist beach. From the 1970s onward, a long strip of hotels and tourist facilities spread north along the coast.

Orientation

Old Mazatlán, the city center, is near the southern end of a peninsula, bounded by the Pacific Ocean on the west and the Bahía Dársena channel on the east. The center of the city is the cathedral, on Plaza Principal which is surrounded by a rectangular street grid. At the southern tip of the peninsula El Faro (The Lighthouse) stands on a rocky prominence, overlooking Mazatlán's sport-fishing fleet and the La Paz ferry terminal.

There is a bus-covered, beachside boulevard (which changes names frequently) running along the Pacific side of the peninsula north from Playa Olas Altas. It heads around some rocky outcrops, and around the wide arc of Playa Norte to the Zona Dorada, a concentration of hotels, bars and businesses catering mainly to package tourists. Further north are more hotels, a marina and some time-share condominium developments.

The airport is 27km southeast of the Zona Dorada, and the Central de Autobuses (main bus terminal) is just off Av Ejército Mexicano, three blocks inland from the northern end of Playa Norte; see p438, for details on getting to/from the city center.

Information

The following opening hours reflect winter schedules – summer hours may be more limited.

BOOKSTORES

Mazatlán Book & Coffee Company (Map p427; ☎ 916-78-99; Av Camarón Sábalo s/n; ⏱ 9am-7pm Mon-Sat) Has used books in English for sale and trade.

Sanborns (Map p427; ☎ 992-01-91; La Gran Plaza; ⏱ 7:30am-1am) Spanish-language books, maps and guidebooks.

EMERGENCY

Ambulance (☎ 986-79-11)
Fire (☎ 981-27-69)
Police (☎ 060)

INTERNET ACCESS

Internet cafés are plentiful in Old Mazatlán and all charge about $1 per hour; places in the Zona Dorada charge as much as $2.75 Many private telephone offices also offer Internet service.

Cyber Café Mazatlán (Map p427; Av Camarón Sábalo 204; per hr $2.50; ⏱ 10am-10pm) Pricey but fast, hip and convenient.

Oldtown@ccess (Map p428; Plazuela Machado, Constitución 519; per hr $1; ⏱ 9am-1am) With a bohemian flavor, at Altazor Ars Café.

MAZATLÁN

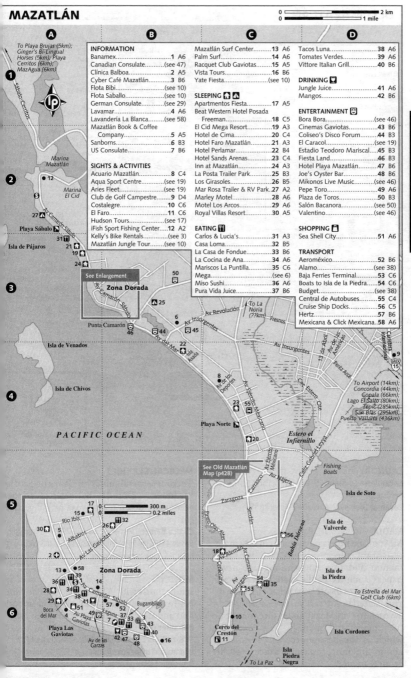

0 — 2 km
0 — 1 mile

INFORMATION
Banamex.............................1 A6
Canadian Consulate...........(see 47)
Clínica Balboa...................2 A5
Cyber Café Mazatlán.........3 B6
Flota Bibi..........................(see 10)
Flota Saballo.....................(see 10)
German Consulate.............(see 29)
Lavamar............................4 A6
Lavandería La Blanca........(see 58)
Mazatlán Book & Coffee
  Company........................5 A5
Sanborns...........................6 B3
US Consulate.....................7 B6

SIGHTS & ACTIVITIES
Acuario Mazatlán...............8 C4
Aqua Sport Centre.............(see 19)
Aries Fleet........................(see 19)
Club de Golf Campestre.....9 D4
Costalegre........................10 C6
El Faro.............................11 C6
Hudson Tours....................(see 17)
iFish Sport Fishing Center....12 A2
Kelly's Bike Rentals...........(see 3)
Mazatlán Jungle Tour........(see 10)

Mazatlán Surf Center.........13 A6
Palm Surf.........................14 A6
Racquet Club Gaviotas.......15 A5
Vista Tours........................16 B6
Yate Fiesta.......................(see 10)

SLEEPING
Apartmentos Fiesta............17 A5
Beat Western Hotel Posada
  Freeman.........................18 C5
El Cid Mega Resort...........19 A3
Hotel de Cima...................20 C4
Hotel Faro Mazatlán..........21 A3
Hotel Perlamar..................22 B4
Hotel Sands Arenas...........23 C4
Inn at Mazatlán.................24 A3
La Posta Trailer Park..........25 B3
Los Girasoles....................26 B5
Mar Rosa Trailer & RV Park...27 A2
Marley Motel....................28 A6
Motel Los Arcos................29 A6
Royal Villas Resort............30 A5

EATING
Carlos & Lucía's................31 A3
Casa Loma.......................32 B5
La Casa de Fondue............33 B6
La Cocina de Ana.............34 A6
Mariscos La Puntilla..........35 C6
Mega...............................(see 6)
Miso Sushi.......................36 A6
Pura Vida Juice.................37 B6

Tacos Luna.......................38 A6
Tomates Verdes.................39 A6
Vittore Italian Grill............40 B6

DRINKING
Jungle Juice.....................41 A6
Mangos...........................42 B6

ENTERTAINMENT
Bora Bora.........................(see 46)
Cinemas Gaviotas..............43 B6
Coliseo's Disco Forum........44 B3
El Caracol........................(see 19)
Estadio Teodoro Mariscal....45 B3
Fiesta Land.......................46 B3
Hotel Playa Mazatlán.........47 B6
Joe's Oyster Bar................48 B6
Mikonos Live Music...........(see 46)
Pepe Toro........................49 A6
Plaza de Toros..................50 B3
Salón Bacanora.................(see 50)
Valentino..........................(see 46)

SHOPPING
Sea Shell City...................51 A6

TRANSPORT
Aeroméxico......................52 B6
Alamo..............................(see 38)
Baja Ferries Terminal..........53 C6
Boats to Isla de la Piedra....54 C6
Budget.............................(see 38)
Central de Autobuses.........55 C4
Cruise Ship Docks..............56 C5
Hertz...............................57 B6
Mexicana & Click Mexicana..58 A6

To Playa Brujas (5km);
Ginger's Bi-Lingual
Horses (5km); Playa
Cerritos (6km);
MazAgua (6km)

Marina
Mazatlán

Marina
El Cid

Playa Sábalo

Isla de Pájaros

Zona Dorada

Punta Camarón

Isla de Venados

Isla de Chivos

PACIFIC OCEAN

Playa Norte

See Old Mazatlán
Map (p428)

Fishing
Boats

Isla de Soto

Isla de
Valverde

Isla de
la Piedra

To Estrella del Mar
Golf Club (6km)

Isla Cordones

Estero el
Infiernillo

To La
Noria
(??km)

Av Insurgentes

To Airport (14km);
Concordia (44km);
Copala (66km);
Lago El Salto (80km);
Tepic (285km);
San Blas (295km);
Puerto Vallarta (436km)

See Enlargement

0 — 300 m
0 — 0.2 miles

Rio Ibis

Río Ibis

Zona Dorada

Boca
del Mar

Playa Las
Gaviotas

Bugambilias

Av Playa
Gaviotas

Av de las
Garzas

Cerro del
Crestón

Isla
Piedra
Negra

To La Paz

CENTRAL PACIFIC COAST

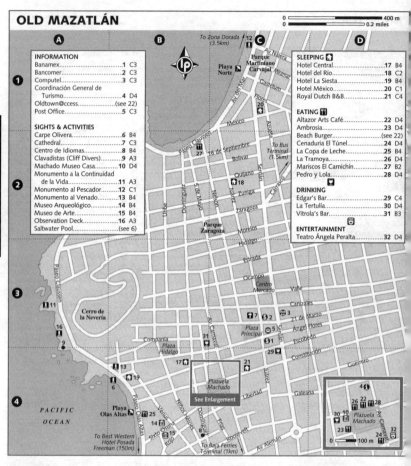

OLD MAZATLÁN

INFORMATION
Banamex..............................1 C3
Bancomer...........................2 C3
Computel............................3 C3
Coordinación General de
  Turismo...........................4 D4
Oldtown@ccess................(see 22)
Post Office..........................5 C3

SIGHTS & ACTIVITIES
Carpe Olivera......................6 B4
Cathedral............................7 C3
Centro de Idiomas..............8 B4
Clavadistas (Cliff Divers)......9 A3
Machado Museo Casa......10 D4
Monumento a la Continuidad
  de la Vida.......................11 A3
Monumento al Pescador....12 C1
Monumento al Venado......13 B4
Museo Arqueológico.........14 B4
Museo de Arte...................15 B4
Observation Deck..............16 A3
Saltwater Pool.................(see 6)

SLEEPING
Hotel Central....................17 B4
Hotel del Río....................18 C2
Hotel La Siesta................19 B4
Hotel México....................20 C1
Royal Dutch B&B.............21 C4

EATING
Altazor Arts Café.............22 D4
Ambrosia.........................23 D4
Beach Burger................(see 22)
Cenaduria El Túnel...........24 D4
La Copa de Leche.............25 D4
La Tramoya......................26 D4
Mariscos El Camichín.......27 B2
Pedro y Lola....................28 D4

DRINKING
Edgar's Bar......................29 C4
La Tertulia.......................30 D4
Vitrola's Bar.....................31 B3

ENTERTAINMENT
Teatro Ángela Peralta.......32 D4

To Zona Dorada
(3.5km)

Parque
Martiniano
Carvajal

Playa
Norte

Playa
Martiniano
Carvajal

Av Nájera

Miramar

Castelum

Flores

Mexico

Arjelia

Paseo Claussen

16 de Septiembre

Bolívar

To Bus
Terminal
(1.5km)

Quijano

Serdán

Carnaval

Juárez

Zúñiga

Zaragoza

Nelson

5 de Mayo

Domínguez

Uribe

Morelos

Parque
Zaragoza

Hidalgo

Estrada

Ocampo

Centro
Mercado

Valle

Canizales

21 de Marzo

Ángel Flores

Escobedo

Constitución

Guerrero

Galeana

Libertad

See Enlargement

Plazuela
Machado

Compaña
Plaza
Hidalgo

Cerro de
la Nevería

Paseo Claussen

PACIFIC
OCEAN

Playa
Olas Altas

Paseo Olas Altas

Niños Héroes

Domínguez

Sixto Osuna

Rojo

Frías

Roosevelt

Av Alemán

To Best Western
Hotel Posada
Freeman (150m)

To Baja Ferries
Terminal (1km)

Plazuela
Machado

0 ──────── 400 m
0 ──────── 0.2 miles

0 ──── 100 m

LAUNDRY
Lavandería La Blanca (Map p427; Camarón Sábalo 357; per 3kg $5)
Lavamar (Map p427; Av Loaiza 214; per kg $5)

MEDIA
Most of the hotels have stacks of city maps, restaurant advertisements, activity information and free English-language newspapers such as **Pacific Pearl** (www.pacificpearl .com), **Welcome Digest** (www.welcomedigest.com.mx) and **Mazatlán Interactivo** (www.mazatlaninterac tivo.com). In Old Mazatlán be sure to pick up the English-and-Spanish *Viejo Mazatlán*, which is the best source of information about the more cultural aspects of life around town.

MEDICAL SERVICES
There are several clinics on Camarón Sábalo in the Zona Dorada, that cater to gringos who come down with a case of indigestion (or worse).
Clínica Balboa (Map p427; ☎ 916-79-33; Av Camarón Sábalo 4480; ⏱ 24hr) English is spoken at this well-regarded, walk-in medical clinic.

MONEY
Banks, most with ATMs, and *casas de cambio* (exchange houses) are plentiful in both Old and new Mazatlán.
Banamex Old Mazatlán (Map p428; Juarez); Zona Dorada (Map p427; Av Camarón Sábalo) Has branches near Plaza Principal and in the Zona Dorada.
Bancomer (Map p428; Juarez)

POST
Main post office (Map p428; Juárez s/n) On the east side of Plaza Principal.

TELEPHONE
Computel (Map p428; Serdán 1516; ☺ 7am-9pm) Friendly and helpful with telephone, fax and limited Internet services.

TOURIST INFORMATION
Coordinación General de Turismo (Map p428; ☎ 981-88-86/87; www.sinaloa-travel.com in Spanish; Carnaval 1317; ☺ 9am-5pm Mon-Fri) Helpful with information about hotel deals as well as what to see and do in Mazatlán and Sinaloa state.

Sights
OLD MAZATLÁN
The old town is a forward-thinking place rooted firmly in the past. It's the cultural heart of the city with well-curated museums, contemporary galleries, colonial architecture and historic monuments. At its center is the soaring 19th-century **cathedral** (Map p428; cnr Juárez & Calle 21 de Marzo) with its high yellow twin towers and a dramatic interior. It was built from 1875 to 1890 and faces the shady, peaceful **Plaza Principal**.

A short southwesterly walk will bring you to the tree-lined **Plazuela Machado** (Map p428; cnr Av Carnaval & Constitución). The plaza and surrounding streets are abuzz with art galleries, cafés and restaurants. Here is the heart of Mazatlán's cultural awakening, and the continuing focus of the city's admirable restoration efforts. The center of attention is the **Teatro Ángela Peralta** (see p436) half a block south of the plaza. All kinds of cultural events are staged here. It's surrounded by historic buildings and attractive sidewalk cafés, restaurants and bars.

At the south end of the peninsula, a particularly prominent rocky outcrop provides the base for **El Faro** (Map p427), 135m above sea level and said to be the second-highest lighthouse in the world (after one in Gibraltar). You can climb up there for a spectacular view of the city and coast. The hill, called Cerro del Crestón, was once an island, but a causeway built in the 1930s now joins it to the mainland. Mazatlán's sportfishing fleet, the ferry to La Paz and some of the tourist boats (see p432) dock at the marina on the east side of the causeway.

MUSEUMS
The **Museo Arqueológico** (Map p428; ☎ 981-14-55; Sixto Osuna 76; admission $2.50; ☺ 10am-6pm Mon-Sat, 10am-3pm Sun) is an interesting little archaeological museum with changing exhibits of artifacts from around Sinaloa and a selection of historical photos of Mazatlán. There are some signs in English. Opposite, the small **Museo de Arte** (Map p428; ☎ 985-35-02; cnr Sixto Osuna & Carranza; admission free; ☺ 10am-2pm & 4-7pm Tue-Sun) has permanent and changing exhibits of work by contemporary Mexican artists. Wall texts are in Spanish.

Also worth a peek is the **Machado Museo Casa** (Map p428; Constitución 79; adult/student $2/1; ☺ 9am-6pm), a beautifully restored 19th-century house filled with a collection of antique French and Austrian furniture, clothing and other items. Some exhibits are in English.

BEACHES & ZONA DORADA
With over 16km of beaches it's easy to find a stretch of sand to call your own in Mazatlán. The following beaches are listed in geographic order, from south to north.

In Old Mazatlán, the crescent-shaped **Playa Olas Altas** (Map p428) is where tourism first flourished in the 1950s. The pebbly beach is not ideal for swimming but it's a grand place to watch the sun drop into the sea or to soak up some regional history.

Flanked by a broad *malecón* (waterfront street) popular with joggers and strollers, the golden sands of **Playa Norte** (Map p428) begin just north of Old Mazatlán. The beach arcs toward **Punta Camarón** (Map p427), a rocky point dominated by the conspicuous castle-like Fiesta Land nightclub complex. The traffic circle here marks the southern end of the **Zona Dorada**, an unashamed tourist precinct of hotels, restaurants, bars and souvenir shops.

The most luxurious hotels face the fine, uncrowded **Playa Las Gaviotas** (Map p427) and **Playa Sábalo** (Map p427), the latter extending north of the Zona Dorada. Sheltered by picturesque islands, here the waters are generally calm and ideal for swimming and water sports; on offer are sailing excursions, waterskiing, banana-boat rides and parasailing (see p430). To reach these beaches from downtown, just hop on a 'Sábalo-Centro' bus; these originate at the market on Juárez and travel along Av del Mar.

Further north, past the ever-evolving **Marina Mazatlán**, are the undeveloped, serene **Playa Bruja** (Witch Beach) and **Playa Cerritos**. Both sport a few excellent seafood restaurants and are well-loved by surfers. To get to these by bus, catch a 'Cerritos Juárez' bus from the Fiesta Land complex or from along Camarón Sábalo in the Zona Dorada.

ISLANDS

The three photogenic land masses (Map p427) jutting from the sea are Mazatlán's signature islands. **Isla de Chivos** (Island of Goats) is on the left and **Isla de Pájaros** (Island of Birds) is on the right. The most visited isle is the one in the middle, **Isla de Venados** (Deer Island). Designated a natural reserve, its secluded beaches are wonderful for a day trip and its limpid waters are ideal for snorkeling.

A five-hour excursion to Isla de Venados from the marina at El Cid Mega Resort (see p434) costs $42 per person. It includes a banana-boat ride, snorkeling equipment, bilingual guide, kayak access, lunch and drinks, and leaves at 9:30am from Tuesday to Saturday. Alternately, from the beach at El Cid you can catch a ride to the island on an amphibious vehicle ($8 per person, leaving at 10am, noon and 2pm).

Isla de la Piedra

Escape artists love **Isla de la Piedra** (Map p427) for its beautiful, long sandy beach bordered by coconut groves, and anyone with an appetite sings the praises of the simple *palapa* (thatched-roof shelter) restaurants. Surfers come for the waves, and on Sunday afternoons and holidays the restaurants draw Mexican families for music and dancing. At other times the beach is nearly empty. It is possible to camp here.

To get here take a small boat (round-trip $1, every 10 minutes from 7am to 6pm) from the Playa Sur *embarcadero* (Map p427) near the ferry terminal. You'll be dropped off at a jetty just a short walk from the Isla de la Piedra beach. 'Playa Sur' buses leave for the boat dock from the north side of the Plaza Principal.

Activities

SURFING

With a season lasting from late March through November, Mazatlán sports several noteworthy surfing sites and a couple of great surf shops to boot. The most famous waves include two that break near downtown. Off **Punta Camarón** is a dependable right-hander, and north of the old fort is a famous lefty known as the **Cannon**. Off **Isla de la Piedra** you'll find a beach break with perfect peaks, but unless there's a decent swell you're better off grabbing a beer and watching from the beach. Rolling in at **Playa Bruja** each morning is a big left that you can set your watch to.

The longest-established surf shop in town is **Mazatlán Surf Center** (Map p427; ☎ 913-18-21; www .mazatlansurfcenter.com; Av Camarón Sábalo 500-4; board rentals per day/week $20/70, 1hr lesson $35; ⏰ 10am-9pm Mon-Sat, 1-9pm Sun), known for its popular surfing lessons and infectious passion for the sport. **Palm Surf** (Map p427; ☎ 914-06-87; www.palm surfshop.com.mx; Av Camarón Sábalo 333; board rentals per day $25, 1hr lesson $35; ⏰ 9:30am-8pm Mon-Sat) is also a contender, with plenty of boards for rent and surf excursions to farther-flung spots like Patolé, Celestinos and Mármol.

OTHER WATER SPORTS

The **Aqua Sport Center** (Map p427; ☎ 913-04-51; El Cid Mega Resort, Av Camarón Sábalo s/n) is the place to go for other water sports, including scuba diving (one-tank dive $60), snorkeling rentals (per day $8), jet skiing (per half-hour $54), parasailing ($30), and kayak rentals ($15 to $25 per hour). Water-sports equipment can also be hired from the beaches of most other large beachfront hotels.

HORSEBACK RIDING

If you love to canter beside the sea – or have dreamed of doing so – your best bet is with **Ginger's Bi-Lingual Horses** (☎ 988-12-54; Playa Bruja; per hr $25; ⏰ 10am-4pm Mon-Sat). Unlike at some other Mexican stables, here the horses are healthy, happy and eager to stretch their legs on the trails leading through coconut plantations and on the open beach. Longer rides into the hills are possible. Take a 'Cerritos Juárez' bus from Zona Dorada, or a taxi to Playa Bruja.

SPORTFISHING

With an excellent location at the confluence of the Sea of Cortez and the Pacific Ocean, Mazatlán is world famous for its sportfishing – especially for marlin, swordfish, sailfish, tuna and *dorado* (dolphinfish). It can be an expensive activity ($400 to $450 for a day in an 11m cruiser with four people fishing), though small-game fishing from a 7m *super panga* (fiberglass skiff) is less expensive ($200 to $240 with up to six people fishing).

Boats leave from the El Cid Mega Resort marina and from Marina Mazatlán, but the best prices are offered by the operators based on the peninsula on Camarena.

Aries Fleet (Map p427; ☎ 916-34-68; www.elcid.com; El Cid Marina)

Flota Bibi (Map p427; ☎ 981-36-40; www.bibifleet.com; Calz Camarena s/n)

Flota Saballo (Map p427; ☎ 981-27-61; Calz Camarena s/n)

Freshwater large-mouth bass fishing is now catching on, particularly at scenic Lago El Salto, one hour north of town. **iFish Sport Fishing Center** (Map p427; ☎ 913-16-21; www.ifishmexico.com; Av Camarón Sábalo 1504) runs day trips ($278 per person) and houses fisher-folk in a comfortable lodge (three nights for $1074 per person). Prices include transport, equipment and all meals.

GOLF & TENNIS
There's golf at the **Club de Golf Campestre** (Map p427; ☎ 980-15-70; www.estrelladelmar.com; Hwy 15; green fees 9/18 holes $18/25), east of town; the **Estrella del Mar Golf Club** (Map p427; ☎ 982-33-00; Isla de la Piedra; green fees $110), south of the airport by the coast; and El Cid Mega Resort (p434) north of the Zona Dorada, with 9/18 holes for $60/75.

Play tennis at the **Racquet Club Gaviotas** (Map p427; ☎ 913-59-39; cnr Ibis & Bravo; per hr US$12) in the Zona Dorada, at El Cid Resort and at almost any of the large hotels north of the center.

Courses
Centro de Idiomas (Map p427; ☎ 985-56-06; www.spanishlink.org; Aurora 203; 2hr/4hr classes per week $142/170) offers Spanish courses from Monday to Friday with a maximum of six students per class. The curriculum is best suited to beginning or intermediate students. Begin any Monday and study for as many weeks as you like; registration is every Saturday morning from 9am to noon. The school also facilitates volunteer work within the community, and homestays (shared/private room $155/170 per week) can be arranged with a Mexican family, which include three meals a day.

Mazatlán for Children
Kids love this town, if only for the many opportunities to get wet.

Saltwater pool (Map p428; bathroom & changing room $0.30) One of the most economical and enjoyable places to get wet is at this delightful, all-natural pool below the Carpe Olivera statue on Paseo Olas Altas. Kids and their adults splash around as waves crash over the pool's seaward edge.

MazAgua (☎ 988-00-41; Entronque Habal-Cerritos s/n; admission $8.50; ⊙ 10am-6pm Mar-Dec) Splashing around is also the featured activity here, where kids can go hog wild with water toboggans, a wave pool and other

---

STUPENDOUSLY STRANGE STATUARY

Puerto Vallarta has its highly surreal *malecón* sculptures, and Manzanillo its epic Swordfish Memorial. But Mazatlán's audacious collection of kitsch statuary is in a category all of its own.

At the waterfront on the western edge of the historic center you'll find several of the town's seafront monuments. At the north end of Playa Olas Altas is **Carpe Olivera** (Map p428), a statue of a buxom mermaid in pike position, drawing passersby irresistibly down the stairs to the rocks below and to a saltwater dipping pool (see above). On a pedestal in the middle of Paseo Olas Altas is the small **Monumento al Venado** (Monument to the Deer; Map p428) depicting a rather forlorn-looking deer on a pedestal in the middle of the street. Further north is the kitsch masterpiece **Monumento a la Continuidad de la Vida** (Monument to the Continuity of Life; Map p428), featuring a nude, gesticulating couple with big hair and nine leaping, rusty dolphins.

Just south of Playa Norte is the **Monumento al Pescador** (Monument to the Fisherman; Map p428). This pigeon perch commissioned in 1958 depicts a nude fisherman with Tintin-type hair and enormous feet. You can tell he's a fisherman as he's clutching a net (although it looks more like a beach towel). To his side is a tawdry muse splayed on a swoosh, looking more like Miss September than fisherman's friend.

Elsewhere are statues of a dapper chap on a motorcycle, a mermaid getting directions from a cherub, a leaky copper beer tank commemorating the first century of Pacífico beer and a memorial to local songbird Lola Beltrán. Take a walk: you can't miss 'em.

amusements. The 'Cerritos-Juárez' bus takes you there from anywhere along the coastal road.

Acuario Mazatlán (Map p427; ☎ 981-78-15; www .acuariomazatlan.gob.mx; Av de los Deportes 111; adult/ child $5/3; ☺ 9:30am-6pm) A block inland from Playa Norte, Acuario Mazatlán has 52 tanks with 250 species of freshwater and saltwater fish and other creatures. Sea lion, diving and bird shows are presented four times daily.

Quirky Mazatlán

From a high platform on Paseo Olas Altas, **clavadistas** (cliff divers; Map p428) cast their bodies into the treacherous ocean swells for your enjoyment. Tip accordingly. They usually perform around lunchtime and in the late afternoon, but they won't risk their necks until a crowd has assembled. Also nearby is an unnamed **observation deck** (Map p428) perched atop a stony precipice. You won't want your kids going anywhere near it. It takes considerable nerve to scale the arching brick stairway – there's no rail and a long drop to open sea on either side – but it's even more unsettling going back down.

Tours

BICYCLE TOURS

Kelly's Bike Rentals (Map p427; ☎ 914-11-87; www .kellys-bikes.com; Av Camarón Sábalo 204; ☺ 10am-2pm & 4:30-8pm Mon-Sat) leads wild and woolly four- to six-hour mountain-bike tours ($28) into the hills, over scenic paved routes and down challenging single track trails. Mountain bikes can be rented for $17 per day.

BOAT TOURS

In addition to trips to Isla de Venados (see p430), several boats take 2½-hour **sightseeing tours** (incl hotel transfers $15), mostly leaving from the marina near El Faro at 11am. Two-hour sunset cruises, sometimes called 'booze cruises,' include hors d'oeuvres and the booze ($15 to $25, depending on your pro-clivities). Look for flyers around town, talk to a tour agent or call the operators of boats such as **Costalegre** (Map p427; ☎ 982-31-30; Calz Joel Montes Camarena s/n) and **Yate Fiesta** (Map p427; ☎ 981-71-54; Calz Joel Montes Camarena s/n). **Mazatlán Jungle Tour** (Map p427; ☎ 914-14-44; Calz Joel Montes Camarena s/n) offers jungle boat tours ($45) into the mangrove swamps of Isla de la Piedra.

BUS TOURS

Several companies offer a variety of tours in and around Mazatlán. Prices are about

the same from company to company for the same tours: a three-hour city tour ($20); a colonial tour ($38 to $48) to the foot-hill towns of Concordia and Copala; and a tequila factory tour ($35) that includes the village of La Noria. Hotel pickups are available.

Recommended agencies:

Hudson Tours (Map p427; ☎ 913-17-64; www.hudson tours.com; Apartamentos Fiesta, Ibis 502) Smaller, person-alized tours including shopping and spearfishing.

Vista Tours (Map p427; ☎ 986-83-83; www.vistatours .com.mx; Av Camarón Sábalo 51) Has a larger range than Hudson Tours, including tours to Cosalá and the San Ignacio Missions.

Festivals & Events

Carnaval Mazatlán has one of Mexico's most flamboy-ant Carnaval celebrations. For the week leading up to Ash Wednesday (the Wednesday 46 days before Easter), the town goes on a nonstop partying spree. It ends abruptly on the morning of Ash Wednesday, when Roman Catholics go to church to receive ash marks on their foreheads for the first day of Lent. Be sure to reserve a hotel room in advance.

Virgen de Guadalupe The day of the Virgen de Guadalupe is celebrated on December 12 at the cathedral. Children come in colorful costumes.

Sleeping

Befitting an old resort town, Mazatlán has an extensive choice of accommodations for any budget. Most cheaper options are found in the historic center and along the beach just north of the center. Midrange hotels rule in the Zona Dorada, with the most sumptuous hotels fronting the beaches fur-ther north.

BUDGET

Hotel Central (Map p428; ☎ 982-18-66; Domínguez 2; s/d $20/23; ⊠) Making up in creature com-forts what it lacks in architectural charm, the Hotel Central is a well-kept, well-run place in the heart of Old Mazatlán. It's en-thusiastically air-conditioned and is popu-lar with Mexican business travelers.

Hotel Perlamar (Map p427; ☎ 985-33-66; cnr Av del Mar & Isla Asada; r $18-20, with air-con & TV $25; P ⊠) Off the main drag near Playa Norte, this lit-tle lemon-yellow, no-frills hotel is cheaply priced. Rooms are perfectly respectable, tidy and clean (albeit rather small).

Hotel del Río (Map p428; ☎ 982-44-30; Juárez 2410; d/q $25/50; P ⊠) This tidy hotel, close to the beach in a working-class neighborhood, is a long-time traveler favorite. Limited English is spoken and cable TV is available for $2 more.

Hotel México (Map p428; ☎ 981-38-06; México 201; s/d $10/15) With colorful tiled floors, dusty curtains and rustic bathrooms, this family-run cheapie a block from the beach still has some colonial charm.

The trailer parks are near the beaches toward the north end of the town, though most of them are not especially attractive for tent camping.

Mar Rosa Trailer & RV Park (Map p427; ☎ 913-61-37; mar_rosa@mzt.megared.net.mx; Av Camarón Sábalo 702; per camp/trailer site $15/30) Lacks sufficient shade but the location is hard to beat.

La Posta Trailer Park (Map p427; ☎ 983-53-10; Av Buelna 7; camp site $18; 🖳 🛋) This place offers more services (broadband Internet, coin-op laundry and a covered party area) than comfort.

MIDRANGE

Apartamentos Fiesta (Map p427; www.mazatlanapartments.com; Ibis 502; studio/1-/2-bedroom apt $32/46/60; 🅿 😃 🛋) Features 12 apartments of different size and layout. All have kitchens and pleasing decor and are peacefully located in or near the leafy garden area. English is spoken.

Hotel La Siesta (Map p428; ☎ 981-26-40, 800-711-52-29; www.lasiesta.com.mx in Spanish; Paseo Olas Altas 11 Sur; r with/without view $47/35; 🅿 😃) La Siesta has a lush courtyard of overgrown plants and creaking stairways covered with much-worn Astroturf. All 51 spacious and tidy rooms have cable TV and a touch of character. Sunset on a private balcony facing the sea is worth the extra bucks.

Los Girasoles (Map p427; ☎ 913-52-88; fax 913-06-86; Av Las Gaviotas 709; apt $60-69; 🅿 🛋) In a pleasant residential area, these comfortable, spacious and sparkling-clean apartments share a well-tended pool and are worth the somewhat inconvenient location.

Marley Motel (Map p427; ☎ 913-55-33; motmarley@mzt.megared.net.mx; Av Playa Gaviotas 226; s & d/tw beds $75/93; 😃 🛋 🅿) This small motel offers exceedingly comfortable seafront apartments with well-equipped kitchens and – best of all – privileged beach access.

Hotel Sands Arenas (Map p427; ☎ 982-00-00; www.sandsarenas.com in Spanish; Av del Mar 1910; d/tr $75/82; 🅿 😃 🛋) If your kids are impressed by swimming pools with a spiraling waterslide, they may well find happiness here.

THE AUTHOR'S CHOICE

Royal Dutch B&B (Map p428; ☎ 981-43-96; www.royaldutchcasadesantamaria.com; Constitución 627; d $45, incl breakfast $75; 😃) Near Plazuela Machada, this cozy inn is a true treasure in a world of ho-hum hotels. The 18th-century house, held by the same family for four generations, conserves its original 4.5m-high ceilings and 80cm-thick walls. Choose from three lovingly and tastefully decorated rooms offered by Alicia and Wim, a welcoming Mexican-Dutch couple. The higher price includes a lavish full European breakfast and 5pm tea time.

Rooms are spotless, modern and large and come with satellite TV and refrigerator. Best of all, the beds are firm.

Hotel de Cima (Map p427; ☎ 985-74-00, 800-696-06-00; Av del Mar 48; r from $34; 🅿 😃 🛋) The paint is peeling in most of the rooms at this wanna-be fancy hotel. It's clean and has a tunnel to the beach but it's only a tiny step up from the budget options. Don't pay a peso more than the semipermanent promotional rate.

TOP END

Rooms at Mazatlán's top-end hotels can be reserved quite economically as part of a holiday package – see your travel agent or poke around online.

Hotel Faro Mazatlán (Map p427; ☎ 913-11-11; Punta de Sábalo s/n; r $110-195, ste $220; 🅿 ✕ 😃 🖳 🛋) All gussied up following a recent renovation, this appealing luxury hotel at Marina Mazatlán offers peace and tranquility in a dramatic cliff-top setting. There's protected swimming in the cove below, two tennis courts, a gym and a heated pool. The rooms are pleasantly bright and welcoming, with full baths and firm mattresses. There's also an all-inclusive plan from $95 per person.

Best Western Hotel Posada Freeman (☎ 985-60-60, from the US 866-638-88-06; www.posadafreeman.com; Paseo Olas Altas 79; incl buffet breakfast r $87-111, ste $140; 🅿 ✕ 😃 🖳 🛋) Perched over Old Mazatlán's historic waterfront, this recently reborn hotel offers character, comfort and grand ocean views. The winning rooftop bar and pool make it exceptional value.

Inn at Mazatlán (Map p427; ☎ 913-55-00; www.innatmaz.com; Camarón Sábalo 6291; r $122-146, ste

$175-281; (P X X R) The 208 bright, cheerful rooms and suites – all with ocean views and private balconies or terraces – are decked out with amenities and are agreeable for longer stays. The three-bedroom, eight-person penthouse ($430) makes for royal digs if you're traveling with a group. The inn is right on the beach.

Motel Los Arcos (Map p427; ☎ 913-50-66; www.motellosarcos.com; Playa Gaviotas 214; s/d $85/95, ste $105-120; (P X R) This attractive hotel features good-value suites with kitchenettes and commanding sea views. They're very comfortable, spacious and clean, and the beach is right there.

El Cid Mega Resort (Map p427; ☎ 913-33-33; www.elcid.com.mx; Av Camarón Sábalo s/n; r $160, ste $200-530; (P X X ☐ R) A behemoth decked out in 1980s-style luxury. This 1068-room, 2.9-sq-km minicity has it all – seven pools, several dive shops, restaurants, travel agencies, kids' areas, gyms and more. If you want to get away from it all and keep the vacation easy but entertaining, this is the place. It's best to reserve ahead of time to get the best deal; discounts are abundant.

Also recommended:

Royal Villas Resort (Map p427; ☎ 916-61-61, 800-696-70-00; www.royalvillas.com.mx; Av Camarón Sábalo 500; ste $95-$450; (P X ☐ R) Excellent rooms sleeping four or more with sea-view balconies.

Pueblo Bonito (Map p427; ☎ 914-37-00; www.pueblobonito.com; Av Camarón Sábalo 2121; ste $135-265; (P X X ☐ R) Luxury amenities overlooking a nearly private stretch of beach.

Aguamarina Hotel (Map p427; ☎ 981-70-80; www.aguamarina.com; Av del Mar 110; r/ste $94/128; (P X X R) Satisfies most picky tourists with very clean, spacious abodes. The rooms aren't fancy but the service is top-notch.

Eating

With all those fishing and shrimping boats heading out to sea every morning, it's no wonder that Mazatlán is famous for fresh seafood. Treat yourself to *pescado zarandeado*, a delicious charcoal-broiled fish stuffed with onion, tomatoes, peppers and spices. A whole kilo, feeding two people well, usually costs around $10.

The restaurants in the Zona Dorada cater mainly to the tourist trade. For something better, head to the heart of Old Mazatlán and Plazuela Machado, a delightful space with old Mexican tropical ambience. It's

sublime in the evening when music plays, kids frolic and the plaza is softly lit to create a very romantic atmosphere.

OLD MAZATLÁN
Budget

Beach Burger (Map p428; ☎ 981-43-56; Constitución 513; burgers $2-4; ☽ noon-midnight) A California-style burger joint that's not really on the beach, but on a beautiful night at one of the sidewalk tables you won't care a whit. The big burgers really stick to the ribs (and they've got the latter, too).

Cenaduria El Túnel (Map p428; Av Carnaval 1207, mains $2-5; ☽ noon-midnight) This atmospheric cheapie has been serving local favorites like *pozole* (a thin stew of hominy meat, vegetables and chilies) and smoked marlin enchiladas for over 50 years.

Mega (Map p427; La Gran Plaza) For serious grocery shopping, head to this superstore.

Midrange

In the vicinity of Plaza Machado are several stylish choices with plenty of ambience and reasonable prices

Altazor Arts Café (Map p428; ☎ 981-55-59; Constitución 519; mains $6-8) This popular, romantically lit cultural spot has great light fare all day, like *marlin ranchero* for breakfast, baguette sandwiches and salads for lunch, and generous seafood cocktails and pasta for dinner. There's live music nightly and movies are screened on Wednesday night.

THE AUTHOR'S CHOICE

Ambrosia (Map p428; ☎ 985-03-33; Sixto Osuna 26; mains $4-8; ☽ 11am-11pm) Never want to see another beef taco? Can't remember what you ever saw in that shrimp? This simple vegetarian mecca has one of the largest and most creative menus in town. Choose from many inventive dishes made with wheat gluten or tofu, or treat yourself to something really special, like *nopales rellenos* (cactus stuffed with goats' cheese and covered with a pumpkin sauce). Want a salad? Oh boy, have they got salads, and good wine, good music and good coffee. The lunch special ($7), available from noon to 4pm Monday to Friday, promises a big, nutritious meal at a bargain.

Pedro y Lola (Map p428; ☎ 982-25-89; Av Carnaval 1303; mains $7-12; ⊙ 10am-2am) Named after beloved Mexican singers Pedro Infante and Lola Beltrán, this very popular sidewalk restaurant-bar serves seafood, burgers and toned-down Mexican favorites.

La Tramoya (Map p428; ☎ 985-50-33; Constitución 509; mains $6-15; ⊙ 11am-2am) Hearty Mexican meat dishes are set out on spacious sidewalk tables. Ravenous? Try the *carne azteca* – a steak stuffed with *huitlacoche* (corn fungus) and served on a bed of *nopales* (prickly pear cactus).

La Copa de Leche (Map p428; ☎ 982-57-53; Paseo Olas Altas 122; mains $6-16) Harkening back to a bygone Mazatlán, this old-timer is prized by the local gentry for its authentic menu. The filling and economical *comida corrida* (prix-fixe menu) is served all day long, but for something really delicious you'd do well to try the hearty *sopa de mariscos*, a soup with squid, shrimp, fish and a wedge of lime.

Mariscos El Camichín (Map p428; ☎ 985-01-97; Paseo Claussen 97; mains $6-12; ⊙ 11am-10pm) Facing Playa Norte, this popular patio restaurant serves delicious seafood and *pescado zarandeado* under a cool *palapa* roof. Suave elderly mariachis are known to play in the back room.

Mariscos La Puntilla (Map p427; ☎ 982-88-77; flota Playa Sur s/n; mains $6-13; ⊙ 8am-7pm) Popular with Mexican families for the weekend breakfast buffet ($8 to $13), this open-air eatery has a relaxed atmosphere and fantastic *pescado zarandeado*. It's near the Isla de la Piedra ferries, on a small point with a view across the water.

ZONA DORADA & AROUND
Budget
Tomates Verdes (Map p427; ☎ 913-21-36; Laguna 42; mains $3-5; ⊙ 9am-5pm Mon-Sat) This cozy and unpretentious lunch spot serves dishes like *pechuga rellena* (stuffed chicken breast) and flavorful soups like *nopales con chipotle* (spicy cactus).

La Cocina de Ana (Map p427; ☎ 916-31-19; Laguna 39; mains $3-7; ⊙ noon-4pm Mon-Sat) Offers buffet lunch fare such as meatball soup, chili con carne and paella in a small and homelike dining area. It's a good antidote for all that fancy tourist junk food.

Also recommended:

Pura Vida Juice (Map p427; ☎ 916-58-15; cnr Bugambilias & Laguna; juices $2-3, snacks $3-6; ⊙ 8am-10:30pm) Fresh juices and vegetarian fare.

Tacos Luna (Map p427; Av Camarón Sábalo 400; tacos $1; ⊙ noon-midnight) Chow down with the locals.

Midrange
La Casa de Fondue (Map p427; ☎ 913-29-59; Av Las Gaviotas 63; mains $8-12; ⊙ 1pm-midnight) If you've been hankering to dip raw meat into hot, creamy sauce – admit it – this recent arrival makes it possible. In addition to classic dishes like cheese or chocolate fondue, staff proudly serve a savory variation made with cheese, tequila and cilantro.

Miso Sushi (Map p427; ☎ 913-02-99; Av Las Gaviotas 17; sushi rolls $3-10; ⊙ 1pm-11pm) Mazatlán has several sushi restaurants, but none as cosmopolitan as this trendy newcomer, recommended for its hipster decor, good music and super-fresh, well-presented fare.

Top End
Casa Loma (Map p427; ☎ 913-53-98; Av Las Gaviotas 104; mains $8-17; ⊙ 1:30-10:30pm; ☒) Escape the tourist scene and enjoy a sophisticated and high-quality meal in a homelike atmosphere. Its devoted clientele rank this secluded restaurant as one of the very best in Mazatlán.

Carlos & Lucia's (Map p427; ☎ 913-56-77; Av Camarón Sábalo s/n; mains $8-18; ⊙ 8am-11pm Tue-Sun) This cheerful Cuban-flavored joint offers exemplary *mojitos* (Cuban cocktails made from rum, mint and lime) and toothsome dishes like *picadillo* (a spaghetti dish with island seasoning, raisins and plenty of garlic).

Vittore Italian Grill (Map p427; ☎ 986-24-24; Av Las Gaviotas 100; mains $8-22; ⊙ noon-midnight) This popular spot is a fine choice for an elegant night out. The service is rather formal and the menu heavy on delicious calorie-rich pasta dishes.

Drinking
Edgar's Bar (Map p428; ☎ 982-72-18; cnr Serdán & Escobedo; ⊙ 9am-midnight) For a taste of Old Mazatlán grab a pint or two at this crusty old bar, a mainstay since 1949. It's adorned with vintage photographs, has a jukebox and, according to the sign on the door, welcomes women.

La Tertulia (Map p428; ☎ 983-16-44; Constitución 1406; ⊙ Mon-Sat) This hip and lively spot is decorated exclusively with bullfighting posters and the stuffed heads of vanquished *toros* (bulls).

Watering holes ideal for heavy partying and youthful exploits:

Mangos (Map p427; ☎ 916-00-44; Playa Las Gaviotas 404) Dancing and drinking in a tropical-themed atmosphere. Gets wild on weekends.

Jungle Juice (Map p427; ☎ 913-33-15; Av de las Garzas 101) A cantina-style place with exotic fruit drinks and a breezy nook upstairs.

Entertainment

There's more on offer than fun in the sun, including throbbing discos, a couple of thriving gay venues and a much-loved theater. For a real Mazatlán experience, blend in with the locals on Sunday afternoon on Isla de la Piedra for live music, hard drinking and hot dancing at one of the *palapa* restaurants.

For entertainment listings check *Pacific Pearl* or *Viejo Mazatlán,* available in hotel lobbies around town.

THEATER

Teatro Ángela Peralta (Map p428; ☎ 982-44-46; www.teatroangelaperalta.com in Spanish; Av Carnaval 47) To feel the pulse of Mazatlán's burgeoning culture scene, a night at the Peralta is a must. Built in 1860, the theater was lovingly restored over five years to reopen in 1990. It has an intimate auditorium with three narrow, stacked balconies. Events of all kinds are presented – movies, concerts, opera, theater and more. A kiosk on the walkway out front announces current and upcoming events.

NIGHTCLUBS

Fiesta Land (Map p427; ☎ 984-16-66; Av del Mar s/n) That ostentatious white castle on Punta Camarón at the south end of the Zona Dorada is home to two of Mazatlán's most popular nightspots. The scene starts percolating around 9pm and boils over after midnight. Valentino (cover $6 to $8) draws well-dressed Mexican and foreign tourists to three throbbing dance floors. If the DJ offends, you can escape to Bora Bora (cover $6), popular for its sand volleyball court, swimming pool, beachside dance floor and lax policy on bar-top dancing.

Joe's Oyster Bar (Map p428; ☎ 983-53-33; Av Loaiza 100; cover $5) This popular spot is OK for a quiet drink in the early evening, but it goes ballistic after 11pm when it's packed with college kids dancing on tables, chairs and each other.

El Caracol (Map p427; ☎ 913-33-33; El Cid Mega Resort, Av Camarón Sábalo s/n; ☼ Tue-Sun) This after-hours favorite attracts a smartly dressed crowd for techno, hip-hop, salsa and *cumbia* music. Things get messy on Saturday nights, when they stage a devil-may-care 'foam party.'

LIVE MUSIC

If you get a chance, try to hear a rousing traditional *banda sinaloense* – a boisterous brass band unique to the state of Sinaloa and especially associated with Mazatlán. Watch for announcements posted around town or broadcasted from slow-moving cars with speakers mounted on top. The following venues host *banda sinaloense* shows.

Coliseo's Disco Forum (Map p427; Av del Mar 406; admission $6-12) This modern dance club and performance hall boasts a state-of-the-art sound system and hosts big shows at least once a month.

Mikono's Live Music (Map p427; ☎ 984-16-66; Fiesta Land, Av del Mar s/n; admission $6-12) Part of the Fiesta Land complex, this venue has a stylish lounge and a diverse roster of live entertainment.

BULLFIGHTS

Tickets for bullfights are available from travel agencies, major hotels and the **Salón Bacanora** (Map p427; ☎ 986-91-55), beside Plaza de Toros.

Plaza de Toros (Map p427; Av Buelna) Just inland from the Zona Dorada traffic circle, Mazatlán's only bullring hosts *corridas de toros* (bullfights) on Sunday at 4pm from mid-December to Easter.

BASEBALL

Estadio Teodoro Mariscal (Map p427; admission to Los Venados games $1-9.50) Mazatlán's baseball team Los Venados (www.venadosdemazatlan.com) makes its home at this large and modern stadium. The season starts in early October and continues through March. The box office opens at 10am on game days.

FIESTAS MEXICANAS

The Fiesta Mexicana is a corny spectacle providing a reductive view of Mexican culture, but it's all in good fun. For three hours guests are treated to a floor show of folkloric dance and music, a generous buffet dinner and an open bar.

GAY MAZATLÁN

Mazatlán's gay scene isn't nearly as effervescent as those of Puerto Vallarta or Guadalajara, but as long as one's expectations are kept in check a reasonably good time is possible.

Forget cruising in Plaza Principal; you'll do much better operating from one of the sidewalk tables at the restaurants lining Plazuela Machado. The beach scene is equally low-key. Bar action is primarily limited to two spots. In the Zona Dorada, **Pepe Toro** (Map p427; ☎ 914-41-76; www.pepetoro.com; Av de las Garzas 18; ⏱ Thu-Sun) is a colorful and lively club attracting a fun-loving mixed crowd. On Saturday night there's a transvestite strip show at 1am. DJs spin a good mix of danceable grooves. For something more elegant, try **Vitrolas's Bar** (Map p428; www.vitrolasbar.com; Frias 1608; ⏱ 5pm-1am Tue-Sun), downtown in a beautifully restored building. It's romantically lit and, overall, more button-down than mesh muscle-shirt.

Hotel Playa Mazatlán (Map p427; ☎ 913-44-44; Av Playa Gaviotas 202; admission $26; ⏱ 7pm Tue, Thu & Sat) Several of the largest luxury hotels stage them, but the hands-down favorite is this one.

CINEMAS
Cinemas Gaviotas (Map p427; ☎ 983-75-45; Av Camarón Sábalo 218; admission Thu-Tue $4, Wed $2) Has six screens showing recent releases, including some in English.

Shopping
Most of your tourist shopping needs will be met in the Zona Dorada, where plenty of clothes, pottery, jewelry and craft stores are located. One noteworthy stop is **Sea Shell City** (Map p427; ☎ 913-13-01; Av Loaiza 407; ⏱ 9am-7pm), packed with an unbelievable assortment of you know what. For something slightly more rarefied, try the shopping complex at Hotel Playa Mazatlán where several high-end shops sell fine crafts including masks from Guerrero, tinware from Oaxaca and Talavera pottery (Talavera tiles are colorful, hand-painted tiles designed with Asian, Spanish-Arabic and Mexican indigenous influences).

In Old Mazatlán at the Centro Mercado (Central Market; Map p428) you can enjoy a classic Mexican market experience, complete with vegetable stands, spice dealers, food stalls and shops selling bargain-priced crafts. In the streets surrounding Plazuela Machado a growing selection of galleries and boutiques gives joy to browsers.

Getting There & Away
AIR
Rafael Buelna International Airport (☎ 928-04-38) is 27km southeast of the Zona Dorada.

Carriers servicing the airport:

Aero California (☎ 913-20-42; Airport) Direct service to Los Angeles and Tijuana.

Aeroméxico (Map p427; ☎ 982-34-44; Av Camarón Sábalo 310) Service to Atlanta, Los Angeles, Phoenix and Tucson, via Mexico City. Direct service to La Paz, Guadalajara and Mexico City.

Alaska Airlines (☎ 913-20-42; Airport) Direct service to Los Angeles, San Francisco and Seattle.

America West (☎ 981-11-84; Airport) Direct service to Los Angeles and Phoenix.

Mexicana (Map p427; ☎ 982-77-22; Av Camarón Sábalo) Service to Chicago, Denver, Los Angeles, Miami and San Antonio, via Mexico City. Direct service to Guadalajara and Mexico City.

BOAT
Baja Ferries (Map p427; ☎ 984-04-71; www.baja ferries.com; tickets adult/child 3-11 $75/38; ⏱ ticket office 8am-4pm Mon-Sat, 9am-1pm Sun), with a terminal at the southern end of town operates ferries between Mazatlán and La Paz in Baja California Sur (actually to the port of Pichilingue, 23km from La Paz). The 16-hour ferry to Pichilingue departs at 5pm (you should be there with ticket in hand at 4pm) on Monday, Wednesday and Friday from the terminal. Tickets are sold from two days in advance until the morning of departure. See p298 for cabin and vehicle prices.

BUS
The full service **Central de Autobuses** (Main Bus Station; Map p427; Av de los Deportes) is just off Av Ejército Mexicano, three blocks inland from the northern end of Playa Norte. All bus lines operate from separate halls in the main terminal. Local buses to small towns nearby (such as Concordia, Copala and Rosario – see Around Mazatlán, p438) operate from a smaller terminal, behind the main terminal.

There are several daily long-distance services:

Destination	Price	Duration	Frequency
Culiacán	$13	2½hr	24 1st class
Durango	$39	7hr	6 1st class
Guadalajara	$35-45	8hr	9 1st class
	$31	9hr	16 2nd class
Manzanillo	$56	12hr	1 1st class
Mexico City	$81-95	8hr	12 1st class
(Terminal Norte)	$70	18hr	13 2nd class
Monterrey	$86	16hr	3 1st class
Puerto Vallarta	$33	7hr	1 1st class, or take bus to Tepic where buses depart frequently for Puerto Vallarta.
Tepic	$15	4½hr	16 1st class
Tijuana	$88	26hr	3 1st class
	$76	28hr	16 2nd class

To get to San Blas (290km), go first to Tepic then get a bus from there – a 2nd-class service from Tepic to San Blas is $4.25 and takes one hour.

CAR & MOTORCYCLE

Shop around for the best rates, which begin at $60 per day during the high season. There are several rental agencies in town:

Alamo (Map p427; ☎ 913-10-10; Av Camarón Sábalo 410)
Budget (Map p427; ☎ 913-20-00; Av Camarón Sábalo 402)
Hertz (Map p427; ☎ 913-60-60; Av Camarón Sábalo 314)

Various companies on Camarón Sábalo in the Zona Dorada rent out motor scooters – you'll see the bikes lined up beside the road. Prices are somewhat negotiable, ranging from $12 per hour to $50 per day. You need a driver's license to hire one; a car license from any country will do.

Getting Around

TO/FROM THE AIRPORT

Colectivo (minibus or car that picks up and drops off passengers along a predetermined route) vans and a bus operate from the airport to town, but not from town to the airport. Taxis do the trip for $20 to $25.

BUS

Local buses run from 6am to 10:30pm. Regular white buses cost $0.45; air-con green buses cost $0.80. Route Sábalo-Centro travels from the Centro Mercado to Playa Norte via Juárez, then north on Av del Mar to the Zona Dorada and further north on Av Camarón

Sábalo. Route Playa Sur travels south along Av Ejército Méxicano, near the bus station and through the city center, passing the market, then to the ferry terminal and El Faro.

To get into the center of Mazatlán from the bus terminal, go to Av Ejército Mexicano and catch any bus going south. Alternatively, you can walk 500m from the bus station to the beach and take a 'Sábalo-Centro' bus heading south (left) to the center.

BICYCLE

Kelly's Bike Rentals (see Tours, p432) can provide mountain bikes for $3.50/17 per hour/day.

SCOOTER

Various companies on Av Camarón Sábalo in the Zona Dorada rent out motor scooters; you'll see the bikes lined up beside the road. Prices are somewhat negotiable – anywhere from $12 per hour to $50 per day. You need a driver's license to hire one.

TAXI

Mazatlán has a special type of taxi called a *pulmonía,* a small open-air vehicle similar to a golf cart. There are also regular red-and-white and green-and-white taxis called 'eco-taxis' that have rates from $2.50 to $5 for trips around town. *Pulmonías* can be slightly cheaper (or much more expensive) depending on your bargaining skills, the time of day and whether or not there is a cruise ship in port.

AROUND MAZATLÁN

Several small, picturesque colonial towns in the Sierra Madre foothills make pleasant day trips from Mazatlán. **Concordia**, founded in 1565, has an 18th-century church with a baroque facade and elaborately decorated columns. The village is known for its manufacture of high-quality pottery and hand-carved furniture. It's about a 45-minute drive east of Mazatlán; head southeast on Hwy 15 for 20km to Villa Unión, turn inland on Hwy 40 (the highway to Durango) and go another 20km.

Also founded in 1565, **Copala**, 40km past Concordia on Hwy 40, was one of Mexico's first mining towns. It still has its colonial church (1748), colonial houses and cobblestoned streets. It's a 1½-hour hour drive from Mazatlán.

Rosario, 76km southeast of Mazatlán on Hwy 15, is another colonial mining town. It was founded in 1655 and its most famous feature is the towering gold-leaf altar in its church, the Nuestra Señora del Rosario. You can also visit the home of beloved songstress Lola Beltrán, whose long recording career made *ranchera* (Mexico's urban 'country music') popular in the mid-20th century.

In the mountains north of Mazatlán, **Cosalá** is a beautiful colonial mining village that dates from 1550. It has a 17th-century church, a historical and mining museum in a colonial mansion on the plaza, and two simple but clean hotels. To get to Cosalá, go north on Hwy 15 for 113km to the turnoff (opposite the turnoff for La Cruz de Alota on the coast) and then go about 45km up into the mountains.

Buses to all of these places depart daily from the small bus terminal at the rear of Mazatlán's main bus station.

Destination	Price	Duration	Frequency
Concordia	$2	1½hr	every 15min 6am-6pm
Copala	$3	2hr	3 1st class
Cosalá	$9	3hr	2 2nd class
Rosario	$3	1½hr	hourly 6am-6pm, take an 'Escuinapa' bus or any heading south on Hwy 15

You can also take tours to any of these towns (see p432).

SANTIAGO IXCUINTLA
☎ 323 / pop 18,000

Despite its charming plaza and impressive gazebo held aloft by eight busty iron muses, Santiago Ixcuintla is mainly of interest as the jumping-off point for Mexcaltitán. It's not a tourist town but there are a couple of hotels near the market. **Hotel Casino Plaza** (☎ 235-08-50; Ocampo & Rayón; s/d $26/30; P ✷) is the modern, pleasant one with a surprisingly good **restaurant** (mains $3-8).

To get to Santiago by car, turn off Hwy 15 63km northwest of Tepic and travel 7km west. Buses to Santiago Ixcuintla leave frequently from Tepic. From Mazatlán you must take a 2nd-class bus to Penas where frequent local buses go to Ixcuintla.

Combis from Santiago Ixcuintla to La Batanga ($1.80, 7am, 10am, noon and 3pm),

the leaving point for boats to Mexcaltitán, go from Terminal de Taxis Foráneos on Juárez at Hidalgo, three blocks north of the market. Transportes del Pacífico also runs a 2nd-class bus to La Batanga ($1.50, one hour, 37km) daily at 4pm.

MEXCALTITÁN
☎ 323 / pop 2000

This ancient island village, settled sometime around the year AD 500, is believed by some experts to be Aztlán, the original homeland of the Aztec people. Today it's foremost a shrimping town. Men head out into the surrounding wetlands in the early evening in small boats, to return just before dawn with their nets bulging. All day long, shrimp are spread out to dry on any available surface throughout the town, making the prospect of an afternoon stroll a pungent, picturesque proposition.

Tourism has scarcely made a mark here. All telephones on the island go through one operator with a **switchboard** (☎ 232-02-11) in her living room. Mexcaltitán has one hotel, a couple of pleasant waterside restaurants and a small museum, making it a pleasant place to visit for a night.

Getting there is half the fun: you must take a *lancha* (a fast, open, outboard boat) through a large mangrove lagoon full of fish and birds (and mosquitoes – bring your repellent!).

Orientation
Mexcaltitán is delightfully free of cars, filled instead with bicycles and handcarts. The main street rings the center of the island, which is a small oval, about 350m from east to west, 400m from north to south. The central *zócalo* has a church on its east side, and the museum on its north side. The hotel is a block behind the museum.

Sights & Activities
The **Museo Aztlán del Origen** (admission $0.50; ◷ 9am-2pm & 4-7pm), on the northern side of the plaza, is small but enchanting. Among the exhibits are many interesting ancient objects and a reproduction of a fascinating long scroll, the *Códice Ruturini*, telling the story of the Aztec peoples' travels, with notes in Spanish. Rendered in a vaguely cartoonish style, the scroll reminds one of an outtake from *The Simpsons*.

AZTEC LAUNCHING PAD?

A visit to ancient Mexcaltitán is undeniably evocative of the distant past. But was it really once Aztlán, the mythical ancestral homeland of the Aztecs? In their origin myths, the Aztec people emerged in what is now northwestern Mexico from the deepest recesses of the earth and embarked on a southerly migration, searching for the one telltale sign that they should settle: a heron clutching a snake. This is what they found at Aztlán, which in the Náhuatl language means, roughly, 'place of herons.' The exact physical location of Aztlán is unknown, but many scholars place it on the estuaries of Pacific Mexico.

The local version of the town's origin contends that the Aztecs left here around AD 1091 to begin the generations-long migration that led them eventually to Tenochtitlán (modern Mexico City) around 1325. Proponents point to the striking similarities between the cruciform design of Mexcaltitán's streets and the urban layout of early Tenochtitlán. A pre-Hispanic bas-relief in stone found in the area is also provided in evidence – it depicts a heron clutching a snake, an allusion to the sign the Aztecs hoped to find in the promised land. (The bas-relief is now on display in the Museo Regional de Nayarit in Tepic – see p445). And then there are the chronicles of reports by Aztecs to Spanish missionaries, including one in which it was related that the ancestors lived happily in beautiful Aztlán, where there were all kinds of ducks, herons and other water birds. Indeed, the name Aztlán means 'place of egrets' – and there are certainly plenty of those milling about.

But not everyone is so sure. Competing theories place Aztlán in the Four Corners area of the United States, in Wisconsin and even in Alaska. 'No serious archeological study has ever been done in Mexcaltitán,' says Jesus Jauregui, an expert in western Mexico at the National Institute of Anthropology and History in Mexico City. 'Aztlán is a mythical place, not a historical one.'

Local opinion goes both ways. One fisherman who considered the facts as they're displayed at the town's museum wasn't buying. 'Why would anyone leave?' he asked.

You can arrange **boat trips** on the lagoon for bird-watching, fishing and sightseeing – every family has one or more boats.

Festivals & Events

Semana Santa Holy Week is celebrated in a big way here. On Good Friday a statue of Christ is put on a cross in the church, then taken down and carried through the streets.

Fiesta de San Pedro Apóstol This raucous festival, celebrating the patron saint of fishing, is on June 29. Statues of St Peter and St Paul are taken out into the lagoon in decorated *lanchas* for the blessing of the waters. Festivities start around June 20, leading up to the big day.

Sleeping & Eating

Hotel Ruta Azteca (☎ 232-02-11, ext 128; Venecia 5; s/d/tr $15/20/30) The town's only hotel. Rooms are simple and marginally clean; ask for one out the back that has a view of the lagoon.

The shrimp *tamales* sold in the morning from a wheelbarrow on the streets are a local culinary highlight. On the east shore, accessible by a rickety wooden walkway, **Restaurant Alberca** (mains $4-6; ⏰ 7am-6pm) has a great lagoon view and a menu completely devoted to shrimp. Don't leave town without trying local specialty of *albóndigas de camarón* (battered and fried shrimp balls served with a savory broth). You'll find it on the menu at Restaurant Alberca, and at every other eatery in town

Getting There & Away

From Santiago Ixcuintla take a bus, taxi or *colectivo* to La Batanga, a small wharf where *lanchas* depart for Mexcaltitán. The arrival and departure times of the *lanchas* are coordinated with the bus schedule. The boat journey takes 15 minutes and costs $0.80 per person. If you miss the *lancha* you can hire a private one for $5 between 8am and 7pm.

SAN BLAS

☎ 323 / pop 9000

The tranquil fishing village of San Blas, 70km northwest of Tepic, was an important Spanish port from the late 16th century to the 19th century. The Spanish built a fortress here to protect their trading galleons from marauding British and French pirates. Later, Romantic poet Henry Wadsworth Longfellow saw fit to honor the town and its bells in a long poem, completed just days before he keeled over. Visitors come to enjoy isolated beaches, fine surfing, abundant bird life, and tropical jungles reached by riverboats. A smattering of entertaining bars and restaurants and an amiable beach scene add to the mix, making for an enjoyable stay.

The bad news: at dusk there's a pernicious proliferation of *jejenes* (sand flies), tiny gnat-like insects with huge appetites for human flesh. Carry insect repellent and check the screens in your hotel room. (If you find this warning to be exaggerated, count yourself lucky.)

Orientation

San Blas sits on a tongue of land situated between Estuario El Pozo and Estuario San Cristóbal, with Playa El Borrego on the Pacific Ocean on the southern side. A 36km paved road connects San Blas with Hwy 15, the Tepic–Mazatlán road. This road goes through town as Av Juárez, the town's main east–west street. At the small *zócalo* (main plaza) it crosses Batallón de San Blas (abbreviated to Batallón), the main north–south street, which goes south to the beach.

Information

Alfa y Omega (Canalizo 194; per hr $1; ☉ 9am-11pm Mon-Sat, noon-11pm Sun) Speedy Internet access.
Banamex (Av Juárez s/n) Has an ATM.
Caseta Telefónica (☎ 285-12-05; Canalizo 5; ☉ 9am-9pm)
Health Clinic (☎ 285-02-32; cnr Canalizo & Guerrero; ☉ 9am-4pm Mon-Sat)
Post office (cnr Sonora & Echeverría)
Tourist office (☎ 285-00-05, 285-03-81; ☉ 9am-3pm Mon-Fri) This basic tourist office, at Casa de Gobierno on the east side of the *zócalo*, has a few maps and brochures about the area and the state of Nayarit.

Sights & Activities

Although the beaches dominate here, everyone loves the boat tours through the estuaries where birds and wildlife abound.

From December to May, **Diving Beyond Adventures** (☎ 285-12-81; www.divingbeyond.com; Av Juárez 187) leads diving, whale-watching and kayaking excursions.

BOAT TRIPS

A boat trip through the jungle to the freshwater spring of **La Tovara** is a real San Blas highlight. Small boats (with a maximum of 13 passengers) go from the *embarcadero* (jetty). The three-hour trips go up Estuario San Cristóbal to the spring, passing thick jungle and mangroves. You'll see exotic birds, turtles and perhaps a few crocodiles. Bring your swimsuit to swim at La Tovara; there's a restaurant here, too.

For a few dollars more you can extend the trip from La Tovara to the **Cocodrilario** (crocodile nursery), where toothy reptiles are reared in captivity for later release in the wild. For a group of up to four people it costs $32 to go to La Tovara (3½ hours) and $40 to the Cocodrilario (four hours). Each extra person costs $8/10 to La Tovara/Cocodrilario. Shorter boat trips to La Tovara can be made from near Matanchén village, further up the river; these boats take an hour less and are a few dollars cheaper.

The mangrove ecosystem surrounding San Blas is a sanctuary for 300 bird species, but you don't have to be a birder to get a thrill from an encounter with the flamingo-like roseate spoonbill. A five-hour bird-watching trip up the Estuario San Cristóbal to the **Santuario de Aves** (Bird Sanctuary) can be arranged at the La Tovara *embarcadero* by the bridge; the cost is $60 for up to four people.

More boat trips depart from a landing on Estuario El Pozo. They include a trip to **Piedra Blanca** ($40, two hours) to visit the statue of the Virgin, to **Isla del Rey** ($1, 10 minutes) just across from San Blas and to **Playa del Rey**, a 20km beach on the other side of the Isla del Rey peninsula. Here you can also hire boatmen to take you on bird-watching excursions for about $15 per hour.

You can make an interesting trip further afield to **Isla Isabel** ($260 for up to five people), also called Isla María Isabelita, four hours northwest of San Blas by boat. You really need a couple of days to appreciate the island, and to visit you'll need permission from the port captain. The island is a bird-watcher's paradise, with colonies of many species and a volcanic crater lake. There are no facilities, so you need to be prepared for self-sufficient camping. For trips to Isla Isabel, ask at the boat landing on Estuario El Pozo.

BEACHES

The beach closest to the town is **Playa El Borrego**, at the end of Azueta. Broad waves roll in with bravado. Stoner's Surf Camp

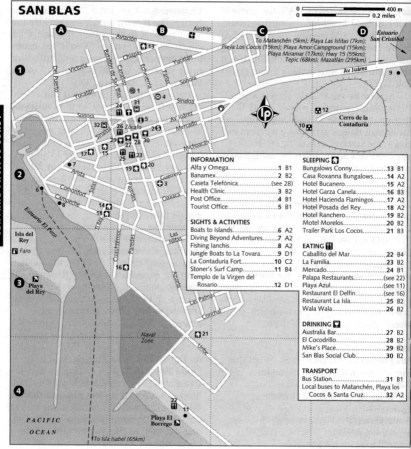

SAN BLAS

0 ——— 400 m
0 ——— 0.2 miles

To Matanchén (5km); Playa Las Islitas (7km);
Playa Los Cocos (15km); Playa Amor Campground (15km);
Playa Miramar (17km); Hwy 15 (55km);
Tepic (68km); Mazatlán (295km)

INFORMATION
Alfa y Omega...........................1 B1
Banamex................................2 B2
Caseta Telefónica..............(see 28)
Health Clinic...........................3 B2
Post Office.............................4 B1
Tourist Office..........................5 B1

SIGHTS & ACTIVITIES
Boats to Islands......................6 A2
Diving Beyond Adventures.........7 A2
Fishing Ianchis........................8 A2
Jungle Boats to La Tovara.........9 D1
La Contaduría Fort.................10 C2
Stoner's Surf Camp.................11 B4
Templo de la Virgen del
Rosario.............................12 D1

SLEEPING
Bungalows Conny...................13 B1
Casa Roxanna Bungalows........14 A2
Hotel Bucanero......................15 A2
Hotel Garza Canela................16 B3
Hotel Hacienda Flamingos.......17 A2
Hotel Posada del Rey.............18 A2
Hotel Ranchero......................19 B2
Motel Morelos.......................20 B2
Trailer Park Los Cocos............21 B3

EATING
Caballito del Mar...................22 B4
La Familia.............................23 B2
Mercado...............................24 B1
Palapa Restaurants............(see 22)
Playa Azul........................(see 11)
Restaurant El Delfin...........(see 16)
Restaurant La Isla.................25 B2
Wala Wala............................26 B2

DRINKING
Australia Bar.........................27 B2
El Cocodrillo.........................28 B2
Mike's Place.........................29 B2
San Blas Social Club..............30 B2

TRANSPORT
Bus Station...........................31 B1
Local buses to Matanchén, Playa los
Cocos & Santa Cruz...........32 A2

(see right) rents out surfboards, boogie boards and bikes. Swimming can be treacherous in some conditions – beware of rip currents and heed locals' warnings.

The best beaches are southeast of town around Bahía de Matanchén, starting with **Playa Las Islitas**, 7km from San Blas. To get here, take the road toward Hwy 15 and turn off to the right after about 4km. This paved road goes east past the village of Matanchén, where a dirt road goes south to Playa Las Islitas. The road continues on to follow 8km of wonderfully isolated beach. Further on, **Playa Los Cocos** and **Playa Miramar**, also popular for surfing, have *palapas* under which you can lounge and drink fresh coconut milk.

SURFING
With many beach and point breaks, beginner and intermediate surfers choose San Blas as the place to hone their skills. The season starts in May, but the waves are fairly mellow until September and October when the south swell brings amazingly long waves curling into Mantanchén Bay. Surf spots include El Borrego, Second Jetty, La Puntilla, Stoner's, Las Islitas and El Mosco.

At Playa El Borrego, **Stoner's Surf Camp** (☎ 285-04-44; www.stonerssurfcamp.com; surfboard rental per hr/day $3/10, lessons per hr $15) is the nexus of the scene. National longboard champion 'Pompis' Cano gives lessons and holds court under the *palapa*, and you can also stay here (see Sleeping, opposite).

CERRO DE LA CONTADURÍA

Just west of the bridge over Estuario San Cristóbal, the road passes the Cerro de la Contaduría. Climb up and see the ruins of the 18th-century Spanish **La Contaduría Fort** and **Templo de la Virgen del Rosario** (admission $0.70); there's a fine view from the top.

Festivals & Events

Father José María Mercado Every year on January 31 the anniversary of Father José María Mercado's death is commemorated with a parade, a march by the Mexican navy and fireworks in the *zócalo*. Mercado lived in San Blas in the early 19th century and helped Miguel Hidalgo with the independence movement by sending him a set of old Spanish cannons from the village.

San Blas On February 3 festivities for San Blas, the town's patron saint, are an extension of those begun on January 31, with dance and musical presentations.

Sleeping

San Blas has plenty of very reasonably priced hotels and one noteworthy fine hotel. In local parlance, a 'bungalow' sleeps more than two and includes a kitchen.

BUDGET

Hotel Ranchero (☎ 285-08-92; Batallón de San Blas 102; r with/without bathroom $15/10) This popular, basic and friendly place has eight rooms and a communal kitchen for guests.

Motel Morelos (Batallón 108; r $15-20) It's stark but homey, with rooms around a central courtyard. An old pelican has made the place home for over a decade, ever since the proprietors nursed him back to health after an injury. He's cute but decidedly not cuddly.

Hotel Bucanero (☎ 285-01-01; Av Juárez 75; s/d/tr $15/25/35; P ▣) It's seen better days but still sparkles with old salty character. The dark, rough-around-the-edges rooms face a big leafy courtyard. There's a lively weekend disco next door.

Tent campers should be prepared for the swarms of insects, especially at sunset. There are a few camping options:

Trailer Park Los Cocos (☎ 285-00-55; Azueta s/n; camp/RV sites $8/13) Pleasant, grassy and very green with just enough trees.

Playa Amor (Playa Los Cocos; camp/RV sites $8/14) A 15-minute drive from town. It's attractive and on the beachfront with sunset views and few mosquitoes.

Stoner's Surf Camp (☎ 285-04-44; cabins $10-15, campsites $3, tent rental $2) There are four rustic cabins at this surf school (see opposite), as well as space to camp.

MIDRANGE & TOP END

Hotel Hacienda Flamingos (☎ 285-09-30; www.sanblas.com.mx; Av Juárez 105; s/d $68/85, ste $76-105; ▣ ▣) This superbly restored colonial gem provides the classiest accommodations in town. All of the spacious rooms around the quaint courtyard have been tastefully modernized with coffeemakers and TVs.

Casa Roxanna Bungalows (☎ 285-05-73; www.casaroxanna.com; El Rey 1; bungalows $50-60; ▣ ▣) This elegant, gay-friendly haven offers five capacious bungalows and a long pool on manicured grounds. English is spoken and discounts are offered for longer stays.

Bungalows Conny (☎ 285-09-86; www.bungalowsconny.com; Chiapas 26; r $35, bungalows $45-50; ▣ ▣) In a quiet part of a quiet town, this new place with only four units rests easy with modern rooms and bungalows. The largest is fresh and feels like a small apartment, with separate bedroom and large kitchen.

Hotel Garza Canela (☎ 285-01-12; www.garzacanela.com; Paredes 106 Sur; s/d $94/120, ste $134-164; P ▣ ▣) Modern, professional and comfortable, the Garza Canela is a reliable top-end choice. Standard rooms are spacious and decorated in colonial style, while the suites are enormous and contemporary with frosted glass and marble floors. It's also home to the best restaurant, Restaurant El Delfín (below), and gift shop in town.

Hotel Posada del Rey (☎ 285-01-23; www.sanblasmexico.com/posadadelrey; Campeche 10; d/tr/ste $35/40/45; ▣ ▣ ▣) Clean, modern rooms surround a cozy courtyard with a swimming pool. It's a family-run business with a low-key but friendly atmosphere. There is a small bar and restaurant in the high season.

Eating

San Blas is a casual town with casual restaurants, all serving fresh seafood. On the beach, *palapa* restaurants are notable for delicious fish cooked in the *campechano* style, with tomatoes, onion, octopus, shrimp and oyster. The cheapest eats can be found at the local *mercado* (market) on the corner of Sonora and Batallón.

Restaurant El Delfín (☎ 285-01-12; Hotel Garza Canela, Paredes 106 Sur; mains $9-18) This, the best choice for fine dining, serves an impressive array of rich, gourmet dishes. Desserts are magnificent and the international wines are reasonably priced.

CENTRAL PACIFIC COAST

Restaurant La Isla (☎ 285-04-07; cnr Paredes & Mercado; mains $5-8; ☺ 2-9pm Tue-Sun) It grills near-perfect seafood, but it's also worth coming in just to check out the overdone seashell decor.

La Familia (☎ 285-02-58; Batallón de San Blas 16; mains $4-8) Decorated in a bottom-of-the-sea spirit, this family restaurant asks moderate prices for delicious seafood and Mexican dishes.

Wala Wala (☎ 285-08-63; Av Juárez 94; mains $6-15; ☺ Mon-Sat) This cheerfully decorated restaurant serves inexpensive, tasty home-style meals. It's mostly basic Mexican and pasta with a few specialties such as lobster and *pollo con naranja* (chicken with orange).

If you're looking to eat near crashing waves, head to Playa El Borrego where *palapas* line the beach. **Caballito del Mar** (☎ 285-04-07; Playa El Borrego; mains $8-15) cooks up remarkably sophisticated seafood dishes and *pescado zarandeado*. At Stoner's Surf Camp, **Playa Azul** (☎ 285-04-44; Playa El Borrego; mains $3.50-5.50) is a traveler hangout with good music, lots of hammocks and well-prepared fare (including vegetarian meals).

Drinking & Entertainment

The nightlife in San Blas is unexciting but pleasant enough, with a good selection of low-key watering holes from which to choose. Most open up at dusk and close late, which, in this town, means midnight.

San Blas Social Club (cnr Av Juárez & Canalizo) Jazz records line the wall; pick one out and the gentleman bartender will slap it on. There's live music Friday and Saturday, movies on Wednesday and good strong coffee every morning.

Mike's Place (Av Juárez 36) This lively bar primes the dance floor with a good mix of blues and rock. There's live music from Friday to Sunday.

El Cocodrilo (Av Juárez 6) This old favorite still attracts gringos in the evening, using well-priced cocktails as bait.

Australia Bar (Av Juárez 34) The long bar of this upstairs pool room, celebrating Down Under chic, is dotted with cool youths and grungy foreigners throwing drinks back.

Getting There & Around

The little **bus station** (cnr Sinaloa & Canalizo) is served by Norte de Sonora and Estrella Blanca 2nd-class buses. For many destin-

ations to the south and east it may be quicker to go to Tepic first. For Mazatlán, transfer in Tepic.

Daily departures:

Destination	Price	Duration	Frequency
Guadalajara	$18	5hr	1 1st class at 7am
Puerto Vallarta	$11	3½hr	4 1st class
Santiago Ixcuintla	$3.50	1hr	frequent 2nd class
Tepic	$4.25	1hr	hourly 2nd class 6am-8pm

Second-class buses also depart from the corner of Sinaloa and Paredes several times a day, serving all the villages and beaches on Bahía de Matanchén.

Taxis will take you around town and to nearby beaches – a good option with two or more people. Rent bicycles from Wala Wala (see left) for $1.50/5 per hour/day or Stoner's Surf Camp (see p442) for $6 per day.

TEPIC

☎ 311 / pop 266,000 / elevation 920m

Founded by the nephew of Hernán Cortés in 1524, Tepic is an old city even by Mexican standards. Today the capital of Nayarit state is a forward-thinking, predominantly middle-class place, retaining few vestiges of the distant past. Many travelers pass through the outskirts of town without looking back, but those that take a day to nose around may come to appreciate the provincial hustle and bustle playing out on its narrow streets. Indigenous Huicholes are often seen here, wearing their colorful traditional clothing, and Huichol artwork is sold on the street and in several shops. Adding interest are an imposing neo-Gothic cathedral and several engrossing museums.

Orientation

Plaza Principal, with the large cathedral at the eastern end, is the heart of the city. Av México, the city's main street, runs south from the cathedral to Plaza Constituyentes, past banks, restaurants, the state museum and other places of interest. The main bus station is on the southeastern side of the city with plenty of buses serving the center. Peripheral roads allow traffic to pass through Tepic without entering the city center.

The airport is 12km southeast of the city.

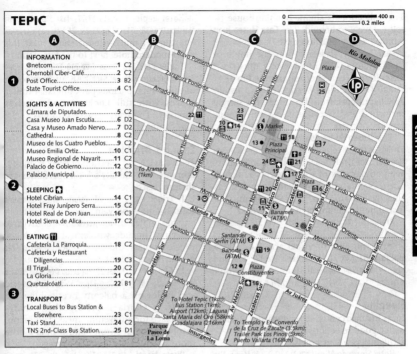

TEPIC

| 0 | 400 m |
| 0 | 0.2 miles |

INFORMATION
@netcom.................................1 C2
Chernobil Ciber-Café..................2 C2
Post Office................................3 B2
State Tourist Office....................4 C1

SIGHTS & ACTIVITIES
Cámara de Diputados................5 C2
Casa Museo Juan Escutia...........6 D2
Casa y Museo Amado Nervo......7 D2
Cathedral.................................8 C2
Museo de los Cuatro Pueblos....9 C2
Museo Emilia Ortiz.................10 C1
Museo Regional de Nayarit.......11 C2
Palacio de Gobierno................12 C2
Palacio Municipal...................13 C2

SLEEPING
Hotel Cibrian..........................14 C1
Hotel Fray Junípero Serra........15 C2
Hotel Real de Don Juan............16 C3
Hotel Sierra de Alica...............17 C2

EATING
Cafetería La Parroquia.............18 C2
Cafetería y Restaurant
  Diligencias...........................19 C3
El Trigal.................................20 C2
La Gloria.................................21 C2
Quetzalcóatl...........................22 B1

TRANSPORT
Local Buses to Bus Station &
  Elsewhere............................23 C1
Taxi Stand...............................24 C2
TNS 2nd-Class Bus Station........25 D1

CENTRAL PACIFIC COAST

Information

Banks and *casas de cambio* line Av México Nte between the two plazas. You'll find the post office at the corner of Durango Sur and Morelos.

@net.com (Av México Sur s/n, Plaza Milenio; Internet access per hr $1)

Chernobil Ciber-Café (☎ 217-69-22; San Luis Nte 46; Internet access per hr $1)

State tourist office (☎ 216-56-61, 212-80-36; www .turismonayarit.gob.mx; cnr Puebla Nte & Amado Nervo Pte; ☻ 8am-8pm) A great resource with free maps and extensive information about everything in Tepic and the state of Nayarit.

Sights

The large **cathedral** on Plaza Principal was dedicated in 1750; the towers were completed in 1885. Opposite the cathedral is the **Palacio Municipal** (city hall), where you'll often find Huicholes under the arches selling handicrafts at very reasonable prices. On Av México, south of the plaza, look inside the **Palacio de Gobierno** and the **Cámara de Diputados** to see some impressive and colorful murals.

The 18th-century **Templo y Ex-Convento de la Cruz de Zacate** (cnr Calz del Ejército & Av México; ☻ 9am-4:30pm Mon-Fri) is about 2km south of the cathedral. It was here in 1767 that Father Junípero Serra organized his expedition that established the chain of Spanish missions in the Californias; you can visit the room where he stayed, but there's not much else to see.

MUSEUMS

Residing in a palatial 18th-century house with a lovely courtyard, **Museo Regional de Nayarit** (☎ 212-19-00; Av México Nte 91; admission $3; ☻ 9am-6pm Mon-Fri, 9am-3pm Sat) concerns itself primarily with pre-Hispanic objects including ancient pottery and tomb artifacts, as well as colonial painting and Huichol culture. Also on hand is an important pre-Hispanic bas-relief found near Mexcaltitán.

A couple of interesting museums are housed in impressive restored colonial residences. The **Casa y Museo Amado Nervo** (☎ 212-29-16; Zacatecas Nte 284; admission free; ☻ 9am-2pm Mon-Fri, 10am-2pm Sat) celebrates the life of poet Amado Nervo, born in this house in 1870.

The collection is slight, but the house itself is lovely to behold. The **Casa Museo Juan Escutia** (☎ 212-33-90; Hidalgo Ote 71; admission free; ⏰ 9am-2pm & 4-7pm Mon-Fri) was the home of Juan Escutia, one of Mexico's illustrious *niños héroes* (child heroes). He died in 1847 at age 17 defending Mexico City's Castillo de Chapultepec from US forces. It's simply furnished and is evocative of early-19th-century Mexico.

The **Museo de los Cuatro Pueblos** (☎ 212-17-05; Hidalgo Ote 60; admission free; ⏰ 9am-2pm & 4-7pm Mon-Thu, 9am-1pm Fri & Sat) displays contemporary popular arts of the Nayarit's Huichol, Cora, Nahua and Tepehuano peoples, including clothing, yarn art, weaving, musical instruments, ceramics and beadwork. **Aramara** (☎ 216-42-46; Allende Pte 329; admission free; ⏰ 9am-2pm & 4-7pm Mon-Sat, 10am-3pm Sun) is a small museum of visual arts. The **Museo Emilia Ortiz** (☎ 212-26-52; Lerdo Pte 192; admission free; ⏰ 9am-7pm Mon-Sat) honors the painter Emilia Ortiz (1917–96) and her work.

Sleeping

In its historic center Tepic rewards travelers with a good selection of comfortable, good-value independent hotels.

Hotel Sierra de Alica (☎ 212-03-22; Av México Nte 180; s/d $44/57; P 🐾) An old hotel that's kept its standards intact, this midrange favorite has 60 bright, spacious rooms with satellite TV and phones. It's so close to Plaza Principal that you can hear the cathedral bells ring.

Hotel Real de Don Juan (☎ /fax 216-18-88; Av México Sur 105; r/ste $73/105) Though it looks old and has some character, this hotel is thoroughly modern. The 48 rooms are done up in appealing pastel colors, with luxurious king beds and marble-accented bathrooms. A good restaurant and classy bar dominate the 1st floor.

Hotel Cibrian (☎ 212-86-98; Amado Nervo Pte 163; s/d $20/25; P) This central hotel provides excellent value with its clean, bright rooms (including TV, telephone and enclosed parking). However, with rooms overlooking a busy street it can get noisy. There's also a good economical restaurant.

Hotel Fray Junípero Serra (☎ 212-25-25; www .frayjunipero.com.mx in Spanish; Lerdo Pte 23; s/d $61/67, ste $80-154; P 🐾) Rooms in this modern hotel are tastefully appointed and come with deluxe amenities; some have a view over the plaza.

Hotel Tepic (☎ 213-17-77; fax 210-05-45; Dr Martinez Ote 438; s $15-18, d $23-28; 🐾) Weary travelers can get much-needed shut-eye at this good modern hotel next to the bus station.

Trailer Park Los Pinos (☎ 210-27-28; Blvd Tepic-Xalisco 150; camp/RV sites $4/15) About 5km south of town, this spacious park offers 24 trailer spaces with full hookups and wireless Internet. The leafy, grassy grounds make tent camping a pleasure.

Eating & Drinking

Tepic has a good selection of vegetarian restaurants, but the city's local specialties are shrimp based.

El Trigal (☎ 216-40-04; Veracruz Nte 112; mains under $3) This good-value vegetarian restaurant has tables in an attractive courtyard. Offerings include wholemeal quesadillas, veggie burgers and an excellent *menú del día* (daily set menu).

La Gloria (☎ 217-04-22; cnr Lerdo Ote & Av México Nte; mains $5-16; ⏰ 7:30am-11pm) With live music and tables on a balcony overlooking the plaza, La Gloria is an especially enjoyable place for an evening meal. The menu, firmly rooted in shrimp and fish, is a little more adventurous than the average.

Quetzalcóatl (☎ 212-99-66; León Nte 224; mains under $4; ⏰ Mon-Sat) A friendly vegetarian restaurant with a pretty courtyard, relaxing music and tasteful decor.

Cafetería y Restaurant Diligencias (☎ 212-15-35; Av México Sur 29; mains $2-4) Popular with locals for its *comida corrida,* Diligencias serves up quality coffee, snacks and full meals all day long in a vintage dining hall.

Cafetería La Parroquia (Amado Nervo 18; snacks $1-3.50) On the northern side of the plaza, upstairs under the arches, this place is very pleasant for breakfasts, drinks and inexpensive light meals, and it does good coffee.

Getting There & Away

AIR

Tepic's **airport** (TPQ; ☎ 214-18-50) is in Pantanal, a 20-minute drive from Tepic, going toward Guadalajara. **Aero California** (☎ 214-23-20; Airport) and **Aeroméxico** (☎ 213-90-47; Airport) offer direct flights to Mexico City and Tijuana, with connections to other centers.

BUS

The main bus station is on the southeastern outskirts of town; local buses marked

'Central' and 'Centro' make frequent trips between the bus station and the city center. The bus station has a cafeteria, left-luggage office, post office, tourist information, card phones, a Telecomm office and an ATM.

The main bus companies are Elite, Estrella Blanca and Ómnibus de México (all 1st class), and Transportes del Pacífico (1st and 2nd class).

Daily departures from Tepic:

Destination	Price	Duration	Frequency
Guadalajara	$20	3½hr	frequent 1st class
	$17	3½hr	frequent 2nd class
Mazatlán	$20	4½hr	hourly 1st class
	$15	4½hr	hourly 2nd class
Mexico City	$57	10hr	hourly 1st class
	$50	11hr	hourly 2nd class
Puerto Vallarta	$15	3½hr	1st class 9pm
	$12	3½hr	hourly 2nd class 1am-10pm
San Blas	$4.25	1hr	TNS hourly 2nd class 5am-7pm
Santiago Ixcuintla	$3	1½hr	TNS 30min 2nd class 6am-7pm

TNS operates a small terminal north of the cathedral near the Río Mololoa, with 2nd-class service to San Blas and Santiago Ixcuintla.

Getting Around

Local buses ($0.30) operate from around 6am to 9pm. Combis ($0.30) operate along Av México from 6am to midnight. There are also plenty of taxis, and a taxi stand opposite the cathedral.

AROUND TEPIC
Laguna Santa María del Oro

Surrounded by steep, forested mountains, idyllic Laguna Santa María del Oro (elevation 730m) fills a volcanic crater 2km around and is thought to be over 100m deep. The clear, clean water takes on colors ranging from turquoise to slate. It's a great pleasure to walk around the lake and in the surrounding mountains, spotting numerous birds (some 250 species) and butterflies along the way. You can also climb to an abandoned gold mine, cycle, swim, row on the lake, kayak or fish for black bass and perch. A few small restaurants serve fresh lake fish.

Koala Bungalows & RV Park (☎ 311-264-36-98; koala@nayarit.com; tent/r/bungalow per person $5/30/43, cabin $57-71), in the village of Santa Maria del Oro, is an attractive, peaceful park with a restaurant, campsites and well-maintained bungalows. It's owned and operated by a friendly Englishman, who's an excellent source of information about the lake.

To get here, take the Santa María del Oro turnoff about 40km from Tepic along the Guadalajara road; from the turnoff it's about 10km to Santa María del Oro, then another 8km from the village to the lake. Buses to the lake ($3, one hour) depart from in front of the bus station in Tepic three times daily.

CHACALA
☎ 327 / pop 500

The tiny coastal fishing village of Chacala is 96km north of Puerto Vallarta and 10km west of Las Varas on Hwy 200. It sits pretty along an amazingly beautiful little cove backed by verdant green slopes and edged by rugged black rocks at either end. With just one main, sandy thoroughfare and a few cobbled side streets, it's a great place to unwind and study the horizon. Camping is possible at several of the beachside *palapa* restaurants, but there are also some unique accommodations from which to choose.

Considerably more than just a hotel, **Mar de Jade** (☎ 219-40-60; www.mardejade.com; Playa Chacala s/n; s/d $138/220, ste $165-275; 🖳) is also a lovely workshop center, spa, Spanish school and organic farm, and it offers a relaxing atmosphere in the company of some very interesting people. Three healthy meals are included and mealtime is something of a thought exchange. Yoga and meditation are typical morning activities.

Super chic and tucked away in the unspoiled jungle overlooking the edge of the cove, **Majahua** (☎ 219-40-54; www.majahua.com; Playa Chacala s/n; incl breakfast r $129-194, ste $355) is an earthy eco-lodge. It offers five beautifully designed rooms, a fantastic outdoor restaurant and spa services. It's a five-minute walk from the parking area located just up the road from Mar de Jade.

Casa Pacífica (☎ 219-40-67; www.casapacificacha cala.com; d incl breakfast $60-70) is a relaxing mid-range option where three large, beautiful suites come with queen-sized beds and a kitchen. The owners are exceptionally knowledgeable about the area and manage eight more vacation rentals in Chacala (from $35 to $100 per night).

Folks interested in getting to know the locals should check out **Techos de Mexico** (☎ 275-02-82; www.playachacala.com/techos.htm; r $18-40), a series of seven homes with room for up to four people. Rooms are separate from the host home and are updated but basic (some come with kitchen).

La Brisa (☎ 291-40-15; mains $5-12; �9 8am-10pm) is the best of the beach restaurants, with good morning coffee and seafood prepared the local way. If you've got a hankering for something decadent, go for the *camarones Costa Azul* (shrimp stuffed with ham, tuna and cheese).

For Chacala, get off a Puerto Vallarta–Tepic bus at Las Varas and take a *colectivo* taxi ($2) from there.

RINCÓN DE GUAYABITOS
☎ 327 / pop 3000

On the coast about 60km north of Puerto Vallarta, Rincón de Guayabitos ('Guayabitos' for short) is a tailor-made beach-resort town catering to Mexican holidaymakers and to winter visitors from Canada and other cold places. It's nothing fancy and shows its weathered age. It gets overrun during Semana Santa, Christmas, and the July and August school holidays. Weekends are busy, but the beautiful beach is practically empty during the rest of the week.

Activities include swimming, fishing, horseback riding and hiking up to the cross on the hill for the fine view. You can also take a boat out to Isla Islote, where you can rent snorkeling gear and eat in the restaurant. Boats take whale-watching trips from November to March.

Orientation & Information

Rincón de Guayabitos is situated on the coast just west of Hwy 200. At the north entrance to town, a high water tower emulates an elongated mushroom. Turn into town here and soon you'll be on Guayabitos' main street, Av del Sol Nuevo. It's lined with shops, restaurants and hotels, and more restaurants and hotels sit along the beach, two blocks over – they're reached by side streets as there's no road along the waterfront.

The nearest bank is in La Peñita, 3km north of Guayabitos, but there's an ATM located at Villas Buena Vida (right).

Delegación de Turismo (☎ /fax 274-06-93; �9 9am-2pm & 4-6pm Mon-Sat, 9am-2pm Sun) Near the water tower; provides information on the local area and the state of Nayarit.
EquiNoxio Internet (Av del Sol Nuevo; per hour $3.50) The only place to log on, with plug-ins for laptops.
Post office (�9 8am-2pm Mon-Fri) Behind the plaza, near the tourist office.

Sleeping

Most hotels in Rincón de Guayabitos are midrange places pitched at Mexican families, offering bungalows with kitchen facilities and accommodations for two, four or more people.

Posada Real (☎ 274-07-07; cnr Av Sol Nuevo & Huanacaxtle; d/q $45/65, bungalows $50-70; P ⊠ ⚲) Drawing attention to itself with the town's most audacious paint job, this cheerful hotel has decent rooms and a good restaurant. The bungalows come complete with kitchens and the hot tub is big enough for you and all of your friends.

Villas Buena Vida (☎ 274-02-31; www.villasbuena vida.com; Retorno Laureles s/n; r $64, villas $91-119; P ⊠ ⚲) This luxurious hotel is a great place to splash out, with its beachfront swimming pool and balconies overlooking the ocean. Villas sleep one to four people; suites sleep five to six. The hotel also presents its guests with sportfishing, snorkeling, biking and horseback-riding opportunities.

Hotel Posada la Misión (☎ 274-03-57; posadala mision@prodigy.net.mx; Retorno Tabachines 6; d/tr $72/78, bungalows $80-128; P ⊠ ⚲) Has a colonial theme going with beautiful tiles lining open halls in front, great sea views out back and a pretty, amoeba-shaped pool in the middle. Rooms are nice and quaint, and bungalows have balconies.

Hotel Guayabitos (☎ 274-09-20; Sol Nuevo 17; d/q $32/45, bungalows $50-70; P ⊠ ⚲) This new hotel offers good value with its large pool, secure parking and comfortable rooms with kitchenettes. Its air-conditioned restaurant (open from 8am to 10pm) is a great place to escape the heat over hearty local dishes like *camarones del diablo*, an exuberantly spiced shrimp dish ($9). Mains range from $4 to $11.

Paraíso del Pescador Trailer Park & Bungalows (☎ 274-00-14; paraisodelpescador@hotmail.com; Retorno Ceibas; camp & RV sites/r/ste $21/55/110, 4/8-person bungalows $65/165) Stark and basic, but right on the beach.

Eating

On the main drag you'll find many economical spots to grab a bite; local tastes tend to gravitate towards *pollo asado* (grilled chicken) and fried fish.

El Campanario (☎ 274-03-57; Hotel Posada la Misión, Retorno Tabachines 6; mains $5-9; ☑ 7am-10pm) Serves up good fish, burgers, enchiladas and omelettes in airy, casual and intimate surroundings. The interior is beautifully tiled and set with hanging ceramic parrots.

Beto's (☎ 274-05-75; Av del Sol Nuevo s/n; mains $3-10; ☑ 7am-9pm) Popular with large families for its simple, no-nonsense Mexican menu. Seafood, *pozole* and other treats help keep everyone happy.

Arthur's 'Los Super' Tacos (Av del Sol Nuevo s/n; tacos $0.80; ☑ 5-11pm) This is the best place in town for a really cheap meal; staff make their own tortillas and salsas.

La Piña Loca (☎ 274-11-81; Retorno Tabachines 7; mains $4-16; ☑ 7am-10pm) It's cute and homelike, colorful and small. It's also totally open and airy, serving breakfast, lunch and dinner from a Mexican menu.

Getting There & Away

Second-class buses coming from Puerto Vallarta ($5.50, 1½ hours) or Tepic ($6, two hours) may drop you on the highway at Rincón de Guayabitos, but sometimes they don't stop here. A couple of kilometers toward Tepic, La Peñita is a sure stop. *Colectivo* vans operate frequently between La Peñita and Guayabitos ($0.50, 10 minutes) or you can take a taxi ($3).

AROUND RINCÓN DE GUAYABITOS

There are many pleasant little beach towns south of Rincón de Guayabitos that make good day trips from either Guayabitos or Puerto Vallarta; they all have places to stay and eat. Visit places like **Playa Los Ayala** (Km 96), about 2km south of Guayabitos, **Lo del Marco** (Km 108) and **San Francisco** (Km 118). First- and 2nd-class buses traveling along Hwy 200 will drop you off about 1km from the edge of each town

SAYULITA

☎ 329 / pop 1600

Sayulita is low-key, but it has definitely been 'discovered' and can feel crowded at times. The beautiful sandy beach, lined with homes and places to stay, is popular with surfers, especially novices. There are a couple of surf shops, two comfortable campgrounds and plenty of tasteful B&Bs. Eating options range from cheap fish tacos on the street to full gourmet Mediterranean dinners on white linen. In addition to playing in the waves, boat trips, horseback riding, trekking and kayaking are all possible.

Note that there's a time difference between Sayulita, which is in Nayarit state, and Puerto Vallarta, which is in Jalisco (Nayarit is one hour behind Jalisco). There are no banks or ATMs in Sayulita and most businesses are closed from May through November.

Information

The nearest bank is in Bucerías, 12km to the south on Hwy 200.

Sayulita Caja de Cambio (☎ 291-30-05; Delfín 44; ☑ 8am-7pm Mon-Sat, 9am-2pm Sun) Near the plaza; offers so-so exchange rates.

SayulitaNet Lounge (Marlín 12; Internet access per hr $4; ☑ noon-midnight) Wireless network and a full bar.

Sayulita Properties (☎ 291-30-76; www.sayulita properties.com; Delfín 9; Internet access per hr $3.25; ☑ 8am-8pm) Has tourist and rental information and Internet service.

Sights & Activities

You can arrange bicycle hire, boat trips, horseback riding, trekking or kayaking from operators on the main street. One popular nearby destination is **Playa Los Muertos**, where picnics and boogie-boarding top the action. It's a 15-minute walk south along the coast road. You can also hire a boat to take your group out to the uninhabited **Islas Marietas** for picnicking, snorkeling and swimming.

Rancho Mi Charrita (☎ 291-31-12; Sanchez 14; ☑ 11am-dusk) offers horseback rides to Los Muertos and Carrisitos beaches ($20, 1½ hours), a zip-line canopy on which thrill seekers can whoosh from tree to tree on zip lines strung high above the forest floor ($40) and boat trips to the Islas Marietas ($150 for up to six people, three to four hours).

SURFING

Surfing is celebrated as a way of life here, and it's a simple matter to join in the fun. With decent-sized waves pouring dependably into the Bahía de Sayulita from both the left and the right, you can practice your well-honed moves or even take up the sport for the first time.

For rentals or lessons:

Sunset Surf Shop (☎ 291-32-96; sunset55@hotmail .com; Marlin 10; board rentals per day $20-25, lessons per hr $30) Also offers fishing and surfing trips to the Islas Marietas ($150 for up to six people, four hours).

Lunazul (☎ 291-20-09; Marlin 4; surfboard/body board rentals per day $20/12, lessons per 90min $40)

Sleeping

The following prices are for the winter high season.

Bungalows Aurinko (☎ 291-31-50; www.sayulita -vacations.com; cnr Marlin & Revolución; 1-/2-bedroom bungalows $68/106, ste $88) Smooth river-stone floors, open-air kitchens, exposed raw beams and well-appointed decor make this a very memorable place to stay. Huichol art adorns the walls while Oaxacan linen covers the beds.

Tia Adriana's B&B (☎/fax 291-30-29, in the US 888-221-92-47; www.tiaadrianas.com; cnr Delfin & Navarrete; ste incl breakfast $65-120) Offers some vibrant suites with kitchenettes; top suites are open to breezes (no walls!) and have privileged views. Other suites also have special touches. The big breakfasts served give occasion for travelers to compare notes and make friends.

Bungalows Las Gaviotas (☎ 291-32-18; Gaviotas 12; r/6-person bungalows $25/50; **P**) Friendly, basic and family-run, Las Gaviotas shows its years but it's only half a block from the beach. At dusk you can expect a thunderous gaggle of boys to use the courtyard as a soccer field.

Bungalows Los Arbolitos (☎ 291-31-46; sayulita bungalows@earthlink.net; Marlin 20; ste $138) Los Arbolitos harbors nine intimate and luxurious suites, two with kitchens. Craftsman touches, creative design and lush gardens add to the paradise.

El Camarón Camping (Del Palmar s/n; campsites per person/huts $4/25) This grassy, kick-back spot on the beach north of town is the heart of the scene for young surfers and hippies. According to the proprietor its beach is the only place in town to enjoy both a left and a right break.

Hotel Diamante (☎ 291-31-91; Miramar 40; s/d/q $35/50/70; 🔁) Has downright small, basic and blah rooms – but there's a pool and outdoor covered kitchen area, both of which attract thrifty backpackers.

Sayulita Trailer Park & Bungalows (☎ 390-27-50; sayupark@prodigy.net.mx; Miramar s/n; camp- & trailer sites with hookups $12-16, r/bungalows $30/70, ste $50-70) Maintains an attractive, palm-shaded property beside the beach, with a restaurant and snack bar. Considerable discounts are offered to those who agree to stick around for a while.

Eating & Drinking

There are plenty of simple cafés near the plaza and lively *palapas* on the beach that offer inexpensive food.

Sayulita Café (☎ 291-35-11; Revolución 37; mains $8-12; 🕓 5pm-11pm) With an atmospheric dining room and candlelit sidewalk tables, this good option serves hearty Mexican fare and splendid fresh seafood dishes. For a special treat, try the Molcajete Azteca ($12), a pre-Hispanic dish combining beef, chicken, chorizo, onions, *panela* cheese, grilled *nopales* and…well, that's enough.

Sayulita Fish Taco (José Mariscal s/n; tacos from $0.50; 🕓 11am-9pm Mon-Sat) Readers agree that these just may be the tastiest fish tacos in Mexico; American owner Albert spent years perfecting his recipe. There are only four outdoor tables and some stools.

Raintree Café (☎ 291-35-23; Revolución 21; mains $6-20; 🕓 8am-11pm Mon-Sat) This new bar and restaurant aims for swanky and hits the mark. The dinner menu proclaims itself to be '*fusión Mexicana*,' with selections like Roquefort fettuccini with shrimp ($7) and tequila shrimp fajitas ($20). It also stages changing exhibitions of local art and employs a very talented bartender.

Don Pedro's (☎ 291-30-90; Marlin 2; mains $11-22; 🕓 upstairs restaurant 6-11pm, downstairs bar & grill noon-11pm) Overlooking the beach, two eateries in one: a fine restaurant offering elegant dining choices, and a bar and grill serving upscale pizza and salads. There's a generous veggie stir-fry on offer for $8. Entertainment includes reggae and rock on Friday night, DJs on Saturday night and Cuban on Monday night.

Rollie's (Revolución 58; breakfast $4-6; 🕓 8am-noon) This is *the* place for breakfast. Rollie and friends lovingly serve Western breakfasts with an occasional Mexican twist. Choose music from Rollie's collection, or sing along with him.

Getting There & Around

Sayulita is about 35km north of Puerto Vallarta just west of Hwy 200. Ten buses per day operate between Sayulita and the Puerto Vallarta bus terminal ($2, one hour); otherwise, any 2nd-class bus headed north from Puerto Vallarta will drop you at the turnoff.

PUERTO VALLARTA

☎ 322 / pop 151,000

Puerto Vallarta – referred to simply as 'Vallarta' by its loyal boosters – is one of Mexico's liveliest and most sophisticated resort destinations. Stretching around the sparkling blue Bahía de Banderas (Bay of Flags) and backed by lush palm-covered mountains, one couldn't ask for a better place to while away a cosmopolitan vacation. Each year millions come to laze on the dazzling sandy beaches, browse in the quaint shops, nosh in the stylish restaurants and wander through the picturesque cobbled streets or along its beautiful *malecón*. If the pretty town beaches aren't enough, you can venture out on cruises, horseback rides, diving trips and day tours – and be back in time for a late dinner and an even later excursion to one of the many sizzling nightspots on offer. Puerto Vallarta is the gay capital of Mexico (see boxed text, p464).

Puerto Vallarta is also one of Mexico's top gay destinations, with a great selection of accommodations, nightspots, and gay-themed activities (see boxed text, p464).

History

Indigenous peoples probably lived in this area, and elsewhere along the coast, for centuries before European settlement. In 1851 the Sánchez family came and made its home by the mouth of the Río Cuale. Farmers and fisherfolk followed, creating a small port north of the Río Cuale. In 1918 the settlement was named 'Vallarta' in honor of Ignacio Luis Vallarta, a former governor of the state of Jalisco.

Tourists began visiting Vallarta in 1954 when the airline Mexicana started a promotional campaign and initiated the first flights here. Planes landed on a dirt airstrip in Emiliano Zapata, an area that is now the center of Vallarta. A decade later John Huston chose the nearby deserted cove of Mismaloya as a location for the film of Tennessee Williams' *The Night of the Iguana*. Hollywood paparazzi descended on the town to report on the tempestuous romance between Richard Burton and Elizabeth Taylor. Vallarta suddenly became world-famous, with an aura of steamy tropical romance. Tourists have been coming ever since.

Orientation

The 'old' town center, called Zona Centro, is the area north of Río Cuale, with the small Isla Cuale in the middle of the river. Two road bridges and a pedestrian bridge allow easy passage between the two sides of town. The city's two principal thoroughfares are Morelos and Juárez, which sandwich the Plaza Principal. Many fine houses, quite a few owned by foreigners, are found further up the Río Cuale valley, also known as Gringo Gulch.

North of the city is a strip of giant luxury hotels called the Zona Hotelera; Marina Vallarta, a large yachting marina (9km from the center); the airport (10km); the bus station (12km); and Nuevo Vallarta, a new resort area of hotel and condominium developments (18km). To the south of the city are a few more large resorts and some of the most beautiful beaches in the area.

South of the river, the Zona Romántica is another tourist district with smaller hotels, restaurants and bars. It has the only two beaches in the city center – Playa Olas Atlas and Playa de los Muertos.

For information on getting to the city center from the airport and bus station, see Getting Around, p467.

MAPS

Guía Roji publishes a detailed *Ciudad de Puerto Vallarta* map, which is available from major Internet booksellers. Basic maps are available at the municipal tourist office (see p453).

Information

Note that any opening hours or days listed for Puerto Vallarta, especially for restaurants or shops, reflect the busy winter season. In other seasons, hours and days of opening tend to be more limited, with some businesses closing down altogether.

BOOKSTORES

Libros Libros Books Books (Map pp454-5; ☎ 222-71-05; Calle 31 de Octubre 127) Has a fair selection of magazines and books (including Lonely Planet guides) in English.

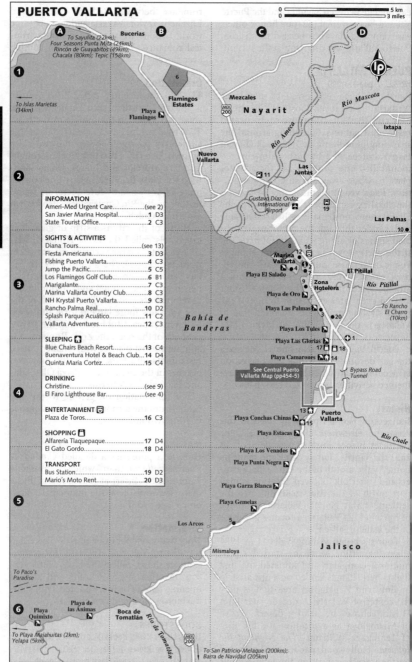

PUERTO VALLARTA

To Sayulita (22km);
Four Seasons Punta Mita (24km);
Rincón de Guayabitos (49km);
Chacala (80km); Tepic (158km)

Bucerías

Nayarit

Río Mascota

Ixtapa

To Islas Marietas
(34km)

6

**Flamingos
Estates**

Mezcales

Playa
Flamingos

**Nuevo
Vallarta**

11

Río Ameca

**Las
Juntas**

Las Palmas

Gustavo Díaz Ordaz
International
Airport

19

10

8 **16**
12
**Marina
Vallarta**
3
4

El Pitillal

Río Pitillal

Playa El Salado

9

**Zona
Hotelera**

To Rancho
El Charro
(10km)

Playa de Oro

**Bahía de
Banderas**

Playa Las Palmas

20

Playa Los Tules

Playa Las Glorias

17 **18**
14

1

Bypass Road
Tunnel

Playa Camarones

See Central Puerto
Vallarta Map (pp454-5)

13
15

**Puerto
Vallarta**

Playa Conchas Chinas

Río Cuale

Playa Estacas

Playa Los Venados

Playa Punta Negra

Playa Garza Blanca

Playa Gemelas

Los Arcos

5

Jalisco

Mismaloya

To Paco's
Paradise

Playa de
las Ánimas

Playa
Quimixto

**Boca de
Tomatlán**

Río Tomatlán

To Playa Majahuitas (2km);
Yelapa (5km)

To San Patricio-Melaque (200km);
Barra de Navidad (205km)

INFORMATION
Ameri-Med Urgent Care	(see 2)
San Javier Marina Hospital	**1** D3
State Tourist Office	**2** C3

SIGHTS & ACTIVITIES
Diana Tours	(see 13)
Fiesta Americana	**3** D3
Fishing Puerto Vallarta	**4** C3
Jump the Pacific	**5** C5
Los Flamingos Golf Club	**6** B1
Marigalante	**7** C3
Marina Vallarta Country Club	**8** C3
NH Krystal Puerto Vallarta	**9** C3
Rancho Palma Real	**10** D2
Splash Parque Acuático	**11** C2
Vallarta Adventures	**12** C3

SLEEPING
Blue Chairs Beach Resort	**13** C4
Buenaventura Hotel & Beach Club	**14** D4
Quinta María Cortez	**15** C4

DRINKING
Christine	(see 9)
El Faro Lighthouse Bar	(see 4)

ENTERTAINMENT
Plaza de Toros	**16** C3

SHOPPING
Alfarería Tlaquepaque	**17** D4
El Gato Gordo	**18** D4

TRANSPORT
Bus Station	**19** D2
Mario's Moto Rent	**20** D3

0 — 5 km
0 — 3 miles

Page in the Sun Bookshop-Café (Map pp454-5; ☎ 222-36-08; cnr Olas Altas & Diéguez) Buys and sells used English-language books, and serves great coffee.

EMERGENCY
Ambulance (☎ 222-15-33)
Fire (☎ 223-94-76)
Police (☎ 060, 223-25-00)

INTERNET ACCESS
PVC@fe.com (Map pp454-5; Olas Altas 250; per hr $3; ☯ 7am-1am) Wireless access, fast machines, good coffee and cheap Internet calls.
Storba's Caffe (Map pp454-5; per hr $2; ☯ 9am-10pm) Found upstairs, east of Plaza Principal, this café is fast, relaxed and central – but hot.
Vallart@Millenium (Map pp454-5; Madero 370; per hr $2; ☯ 9am-10:30pm) Fast but considerably cooler than Storba's Caffe.

INTERNET RESOURCES
Puerto Vallarta (www.puertovallarta.net) Sponsored by the visitors bureau and tourist board, this site provides a wealth of information on lodgings, activities and attractions.

LAUNDRY
There are many laundries around town, all of which are closed Sunday and charge less than $4 per load.
Lavandería Blanquita (Map pp454-5; Madero 407A)
Lavandería Elsa (Map pp454-5; Olas Altas 385)

MEDIA
Daily Vallarta Today (www.vallartatoday.com) is a better English-language newspaper than its competition, the weekly *PV Tribune*. Both are free. *Bay Vallarta* is a free monthly guide with useful culture and shopping listings.

MEDICAL SERVICES
Ameri-Med Urgent Care (Map p452; ☎ 226-20-80; Plaza Neptuno, Marina Vallarta) A modern American-style hospital charging American-style fees.
San Javier Marina Hospital (Map p452; ☎ 226-10-10; Av Ascencio 2760) Vallarta's best-equipped hospital.

MONEY
Although most businesses in Vallarta accept US dollars as readily as they accept pesos, their exchange rates suck. There are several banks around Plaza Principal; most of them have ATMs with rates analogous to those offered inside.

Vallarta has many *casas de cambio*; their rates differ and are slightly less favorable than the banks. Look for them on Insurgentes, Vallarta and the *malecón*.
American Express (Map pp454-5; ☎ 223-29-55; cnr Morelos & Abasolo)

POST
Main post office (Map pp454-5; Mina 188)

TELEPHONE & FAX
Pay phones (card only) are plentiful everywhere in town. Many Internet cafés offer long-distance service.
Telecomm (Map pp454-5; Hidalgo 582; ☯ 8am-7pm Mon-Fri, 9am-noon Sat & Sun) Offers fax as well as phone service.

TOURIST INFORMATION
Municipal tourist office (Map pp454-5; ☎ 223-25-00, ext 230; Juárez s/n; ☯ 8am-4pm Mon-Fri) Vallarta's busy but competent office, in the municipal building at the northeast corner of Plaza Principal, has free maps, multilingual tourist literature and bilingual staff.
State tourist office (Dirección de Turismo del Estado de Jalisco; Map p452; ☎ 221-26-76, 221-26-80; Plaza

---

BAHÍA DE BANDERAS

The Bahía de Banderas (Bay of Flags) is said to have been formed by an extinct volcano slowly sinking into the ocean. It now has a depth of some 1800m and is home to an impressive variety of marine life – almost every large marine animal is found here.

During the winter months humpback whales come here to mate. They leave their feeding grounds in Alaskan waters and show up in Mexico from around November to the end of March. Once arrived, they form courtship groups, mate, or bear the calves that were conceived the year before. By the end of March, the whales' attention turns to the long journey back to their feeding grounds up north.

With the humpbacks gone, the giant manta rays take their turn. During April you may see their acrobatic displays as they jump above the water's surface, flashing their 4m-wide wings in acrobatic displays that sometimes can be seen from boats or even from the shore.

CENTRAL PUERTO VALLARTA

INFORMATION
American Express.....................1 E2
Lavandería Blanquita................2 E6
Lavandería Elsa........................3 C7
Libros Libros Books Books.......4 E1
Main Post Office......................5 D3
Municipal Tourist Office...........6 D4
Page in the Sun Bookshop-Café..7 C7
PVC@fecom............................8 C7
Storba's Caffe..........................9 D4
Telecomm..............................10 E3
US Consulate..........................11 D4
Vallart@Millennium................12 E6

SIGHTS & ACTIVITIES
Bike Mex................................13 E5
Centro de Estudios Para
  Extranjeros..........................14 D5
Chico's Dive Shop...................15 E2
Cooperativa de Pescadores.....16 E1
Eco Ride................................17 E4
Los Arcos...............................18 D4
Museo del Cuale.....................19 C5
Ocean Quest..........................20 C6
Open Air Expeditions..............21 D5
Templo de Guadalupe.............22 D4

SLEEPING
Casa Andrea...........................23 C8
Casa de los Cuatro Vientos.....24 E3
Casa Kimberley.......................25 E5
Estancia San Carlos.................26 D6
Frankfurt Hotel.......................27 D7
Hacienda San Ángel................28 E4
Hotel Azteca..........................29 F6
Hotel Belmar..........................30 E6
Hotel Bernal...........................31 E6
Hotel Descanso del Sol............32 D8
Hotel Eloísa............................33 C6
Hotel Emperador.....................34 C8
Hotel Hortencia......................35 D6
Hotel Molino de Agua.............36 D6
Hotel Playa Los Arcos.............37 C7

Hotel Posada de Roger............38 D7
Hotel Posada del Pedregal.......39 D5
Hotel Posada Lily....................40 D7
Hotel Posada Río Cuale...........41 D6
Hotel Rosita...........................42 E1
Hotel Tropicana......................43 C8
Hotel Villa del Mar.................44 F6
Terraza Inn............................45 C8
Vallarta Sun Hotel..................46 C8

EATING
Archie's Wok..........................47 C8
Boca Bento............................48 C7
Café des Artistes.....................49 E2
Casa Naranjo..........................50 F6
Cenaduría Doña Raquel...........51 E2
El Palomar de los González.....52 E7
Esquina de los Caprichos........53 E4
Fajita Republic.......................54 C7
Gutiérrez Rizoc (GR)
  Supermarket.........................55 D6
Kaiser Maximilian...................56 C7
La Dolce Vita.........................57 E2
La Palapa...............................58 C8
La Piazzetta...........................59 C8
Las Palomas...........................60 D3
Las Tres Huastecas.................61 C8
Le Bistro Jazz Café.................62 E5
Mama Dolores' Diner..............63 C8
Mariscos Polo.........................64 E6
Mi Querencia.........................65 D3

No Name Café.......................66 D3
Oscar's Bar & Grill..................67 C5
Pancake House.......................68 D7
Planeta Vegetariano...............69 D4
Restaurant Gilmar...................70 E6
River Cafe.............................71 D5
Tacos de los Arcos..................72 D4
Trio.......................................73 D5

DRINKING
Café San Ángel.......................74 C8
Carlos O'Brian's......................75 E2
Club Roxy..............................76 D6
Kit Kat Klub...........................77 C8
La Barriga Cantina..................78 D6
La Bodeguita del Medio..........79 E1
La Noche...............................80 D6
Memories Café.......................81 D3
Sama Bar...............................82 C8

Parque
Hidalgo

Zona
Centro

To Airport (9km);
Bus Station (11km);
Tepic (176km)

Bahía de
Banderas

Seahorse
Statue

Malecón

Plaza
Principal

Banamex

0   400 m
0   0.2 miles

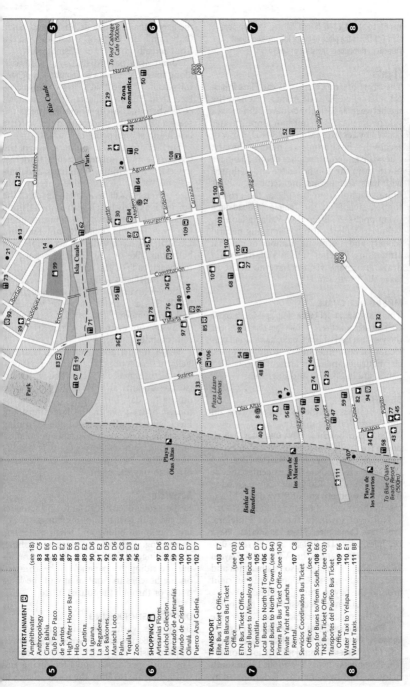

CENTRAL PACIFIC COAST

Marina, Local 144 & 146, Marina Vallarta; 9am-5pm Mon-Fri) This is the place to go for information about attractions throughout the state of Jalisco.

Sights

The heart of Zona Centro is the **Plaza Principal**, also called Plaza de Armas, just near the sea between Morelos and Juárez. On the sea side of the plaza is an outdoor amphitheater backed by **Los Arcos** (Map pp454–5), a row of arches that has become a symbol of the city. The wide *malecón* stretches about 10 blocks north from the amphitheater and is dotted with bars, restaurants, nightclubs and boutiques. Uphill from the plaza, the crown-topped steeple of the **Templo de Guadalupe** (Map pp454–5) is another Vallarta icon.

Puerto Vallarta also has amazing natural scenery and a growing number of cultural attractions. Beaches remain Vallarta's main draw, and many visitors have no desire to leave the warm sand.

MUSEO DEL CUALE

The tiny **Museo del Cuale** (Map pp454-5; Paseo Isla Cuale s/n; admission free; 10am-7pm Mon-Sat), near the western end of Isla Cuale, has a small collection of beautiful pottery, grinding stones, clay figurines and other ancient objects. Text panels are in Spanish and English.

BEACHES

Most beaches mentioned here feature on the Puerto Vallarta map (p452).

Only two beaches, **Playa Olas Altas**, which doesn't actually have 'high waves' (despite the name), and **Playa de los Muertos** (Beach of the Dead) are handy to the city center; they're both south of the Río Cuale. Gay men hang out at the southern end of Playa de los Muertos on the stretch of beach called **Blue Chairs**.

North of town, in the Zona Hotelera, are **Playa Camarones**, **Playa Las Glorias**, **Playa Los Tules**, **Playa Las Palmas** and **Playa de Oro**. Further north, at Marina Vallarta, is **Playa El Salado**. Nuevo Vallarta also has beaches and there are other, less developed beaches right around the bay to Punta de Mita.

South of town, accessible by minibuses plying the superbly scenic coastal Hwy 200, are **Playa Conchas Chinas**, **Playa Estacas**, **Playa Los Venados**, **Playa Punta Negra**, **Playa Garza Blanca** and **Playa Gemelas**. **Mismaloya**, the location for *The Night of the Iguana*, is about 12km south of town. The tiny scenic cove is dominated by

the gargantuan La Jolla de Mismaloya hotel. Only minibuses that say 'Mismaloya' on the front actually go as far as Mismaloya.

About 4km past Mismaloya, southwest along the coast, is **Boca de Tomatlán**, a peaceful seaside village that's less commercialized than Puerto Vallarta. It's in a small cove where the Río de Tomatlán meets the sea – a jungle-like place with quiet water, a beach and several small restaurants.

Further around the southern side of the bay are the more isolated beaches, from east to west, of Las Ánimas, Quimixto, Majahuitas and Yelapa, all accessible only by boat (see p467). **Playa de las Ánimas** (Beach of the Spirits) is a lovely beach with a small fishing village and some *palapa* restaurants offering fresh seafood. **Quimixto**, not far from Las Ánimas, has a waterfall accessible by a half-hour hike or you can hire a pony on the beach to take you up.

Playa Majahuitas is home to the secluded, rustic yet luxurious Majahuitas resort (see p460). It's a popular place for weddings and honeymoons and for folks trying to get away from their laptops, hair driers and cell (mobile) phones.

Yelapa, furthermost from town, is one of Vallarta's most popular cruise destinations. This picturesque cove is crowded with tourists, restaurants and parasailing operators during the day, but empties out when the tourist boats leave in the late afternoon. Electricity recently reached the charming village at Yelapa and the sizable population of foreign high-season residents is steadily increasing. There are several comfortable places to stay the night.

Activities

Restless souls need not go far to find activities like swimming with dolphins, bungee jumping, mountain biking and whale-watching. Snorkeling, scuba diving, deep-sea fishing, waterskiing, windsurfing, sailing, parasailing and riding the 'banana' can be arranged on the beaches in front of any of the large hotels or through the tourist office.

DIVING & SNORKELING

Below the warm, tranquil waters of the Bahía de Banderas is a world of stingrays, tropical fish and garishly colored corals. The most spectacular spots for diving and snorkeling are **Los Arcos**, the rocky islands in the bay just south of town (now a protected ecological zone), and the **Islas Marietas** at the entrance to the bay, surrounded by impressive reefs, tunnels, walls and underwater caves. Dolphins, whales and giant manta rays are often sighted between December and April.

Vallarta has several diving and snorkeling operators. Most dives include transport, gear and light meals. Water is clearest from May to November, with peak clarity in October and November. Most dive outfits also offer snorkeling trips, which usually means snorkelers tag along with divers.

Ocean Quest (Map pp454-5; ☎ 223-41-03; www.mexi coscuba.com; Cárdenas 230; snorkeling trips $25, 2-tank dive trips $65-115, PADI Open Water certification $280) is well regarded for its small-group excursions to both well- and lesser-known sites. English and German are spoken.

Vallarta Adventures (see p458) has 'gold palm' (PADI accredited) instructors and acclaimed service. Snorkeling/two-tank dive trips cost $25/99, and PADI Open Water certification is $370.

Chico's Dive Shop (Map pp454-5; ☎ 222-18-95; www chicos-diveshop.com; Paseo Díaz Ordaz 772; snorkeling/2-tank dive trips $25/79), the biggest outfit, usually offers hard-to-beat discounts; however, the shop is no longer PADI certified, and readers have written to caution that equipment is sometimes ill-maintained.

DEEP-SEA FISHING
Deep-sea fishing is popular all year, with a major international sailfishing tournament held every November. Prime catches are sailfish, marlin, tuna, red snapper and sea bass. Fishing trips can be arranged dockside at Marina Vallarta or at the cooperative on the *malecón*.

Cooperativa de Pescadores (Map pp454-5; ☎ 222-12-02; 1-8 person fishing charters from $90; ⏰ 7am-10pm Mon-Sat), with an office on the *malecón* adjacent to Hotel Rosita, acts as an agent for a long list of sportfishing boats. During the low season try your luck at fishing for a discount.

Fishing Puerto Vallarta (Map p452; ☎ 224-72-50; www.fishingpuertovallarta.4t.com; Marina Vallarta) offers the chance for up to four wanna-be fisherpeople to trawl from *The Carolina*, a 30ft sportfisher. Prices are $100 per person or $350 for the whole boat for up to four customers. Gear and hotel pickup is included.

WHALE-WATCHING & DOLPHIN ENCOUNTERS
A frequent, year-round visitor to Bahía de Banderas, the Pacific bottlenose dolphin is often seen leaping out of the water, or gliding along the bow of boats. Humpback whales also visit from late November to March to bear their calves.

Vallarta Adventures (see p458) offers close encounters with dolphins, ranging in price from $60 to $250.

Whale-watching trips operate from December to March, when humpback whales are in the bay mating, bearing young and caring for new calves. Open Air Expeditions (see Tours, p458) is a popular operator, with trips for $75; Vallarta Adventures also takes whale-watching trips, priced from $65.

HORSEBACK RIDING
Vallarta's jungly mountains are wonderful to explore from the privileged perspective of horseback. Most stables charge around $15 per hour, or $100 for a full-day excursion. For a short ride suitable for children, there are sometimes horses for rent around Playa Olas Altas, near the western end of Carranza.

Rancho El Charro (☎ 224-01-14; www.ranchoel charro.com; rides $47-100) is recommended for its healthy horses and scenic three- to eight-hour trots into the Sierra Madres. Several rides have been conceived for kids. Setting it apart from competitors are its multiday tours, including the tempting 'Overnight Lost in the Jungle Ride' ($350).

Rancho Palma Real (Map p452; ☎ 221-12-36; www.ranchopalmareal.com) is based in the village of Las Palmas. This outfit offers a couple of off-the-beaten-track routes and a popular excursion to El Salto, a lovely jungle waterfall.

GOLF & TENNIS
Vallarta's golfing credentials have been burnished in recent years with the opening of four new courses. Most acclaimed is the Jack Nicklaus–designed **Four Seasons Punta Mita** (Map pp454-5; ☎ 291-60-00; Four Seasons Resort Punta Mita; green fees/club rentals $260/60), where golfers are blissfully distracted from the challenging course by the sweeping ocean vistas. One hole, nicknamed 'Tail of the Whale,' is located on a natural island and requires the use of an amphibious golf cart.

CENTRAL PACIFIC COAST

Other courses:

Marina Vallarta Golf Club (Map p452; ☎ 221-00-73; Paseo de la Marina s/n; green fees $136) An exclusive 18-hole, par-74 course just north of Marina Vallarta.

Los Flamingos Golf Club (Map p452; ☎ 298-06-06; Hwy 200 s/n; green fees $95) Recently renovated, 13km north of town.

Most of the large luxury hotels have tennis courts and charge between $15 to $20 to smash the ball around. Call in advance to reserve a court.

Hotels welcoming nonguests for tennis:

NH Krystal Puerto Vallarta (Map p452; ☎ 224-02-02; Av Las Garzas s/n, Zona Hotelera)

Fiesta Americana (Map p452; ☎ 224-20-10; Paseo de las Palmas s/n, Zona Hotelera)

BUNGEE JUMPING

The good folks at the **Jump the Pacific** (Map p452; ☎ 228-06-70; www.vallarta-action.com; 🕙 10am-6pm) promise that if the cord breaks, your next bungee jump is free. From a platform jutting out over the sea cliffs it's a 40m plunge. It's 9km south of Puerto Vallarta on the road to Mismaloya.

WATER PARKS

Kids will enjoy **Splash Parque Acuático** (Map p452; ☎ 297-07-08; Carr Tepic Km 155; admission $9), which has 12 waterslides, a lazy river swimming pool and a daily dolphin show.

CRUISES

A host of daytime, sunset and evening cruises are available in Vallarta. The most popular ones are the cruises to Yelapa and Las Ánimas beaches; others go to the Islas Marietas, further out. Prices start at $45 for sunset cruises and beach trips; longer trips lasting four to six hours with meals and bottomless cocktails will set you back $80 to $100.

The **Marigalante** (☎ 223-03-09; www.marigalante .com.mx) is a reproduction Spanish galleon that does daytime cruises ($65) from 9am to 5pm and an evening cruise ($70) from 6pm to 11pm that culminates in a mock pirate attack on the *malecón*. It departs from the Terminal Maritima in Marina Vallarta, off Blvd Francisco Ascencio opposite Sam's Club. On Thursday **Diana Tours** (☎ 222-15-10) offers an all-day gay and lesbian cruise, with plenty of food, drink and snorkeling ($75). It leaves from Blue Chairs Beach Resort (see the boxed text, p464).

Courses

Courses at **Centro de Estudios Para Extranjeros** (CEPE; Map pp454-5; ☎ 223-20-82; www.cepe.udg.mx; Libertad 105-1) range from $93 for a week of basic tourist Spanish to $431 for a month of university credit courses. Private instruction costs $21 per hour. The center, associated with the Universidad de Guadalajara, provides lodging for $23 to $49 per night and also arranges homestays with local families. Two 'content courses' also are offered both in English and Spanish; one focuses on Mexican culture from an anthropological standpoint, the other focuses on modern Mexican history.

Tours

Several tour companies specialize in nature and outdoor tours. Choose between city, jungle, bicycle, horseback riding and archaeological tours.

Tour operators:

Eco Ride (Map pp454-5; ☎ 222-79-12; www.ecoride mex.com; Miramar 382; tours $45-175) Surrounded by the mountains, jungle and sea, Vallarta offers some truly thrilling mountain biking. This adventure-loving outfit offers guided one-day cycling tours suited for beginners and badasses alike. The most challenging is a 50km hair-raising expedition from El Tuito (a small town at 1100m) through Chacala and down to the beach in Yelapa. The views are stunning.

Vallarta Adventures (Map p452; ☎ 297-12-12; www.vallarta-adventures.com; Av Las Palmas 39, Marina Vallarta) Offers 'Canopy Adventures' (adult/child $77/55) and romantic dinner shows on a private beach ($82); these guys do it all with humor, enthusiasm and professionalism.

Open Air Expeditions (Map pp454-5; ☎ 222-33-10; www.vallartawhales.com; Guerrero 339) Offers bird-watching ($60 to $80), hiking ($60) and customized tours.

Festivals & Events

Semana Santa As with the rest of Mexico, Semana Santa is the busiest holiday of the year. Hotels fill up and hundreds (or thousands) of excess visitors camp out on the beaches and party.

Fiestas de Mayo This citywide fair with cultural and sporting events, concerts, carnival rides and art exhibits is held throughout May.

Sailfish tournament This major international tournament is held every November.

Gourmet food festival Puerto Vallarta's culinary community has hosted this mid-November festival since 1995.

Día de Santa Cecilia On November 22 the patron saint of mariachis is honored, with all the city's mariachis forming a musical procession to the Templo de Guadalupe in the

CENTRAL PACIFIC COAST

early evening. They come playing and singing, enter the church and sing homage to their saint, then go out into the plaza and continue to play.

Virgen de Guadalupe All of Mexico celebrates December 12 as the day of honor for the country's religious patron. In Puerto Vallarta the celebrations are more drawn out, with pilgrimages and processions to the cathedral day and night from November 30 until the big bash on December 12.

Sleeping

When it comes to accommodations you're spoiled for choice in Puerto Vallarta. Options include economical digs near the river, singular and stylish small inns and villas, party-happy beach hotels and luxurious mega-resorts.

The following prices are for the December to April high season; low-season rates can be as much as 20% to 50% less. For accommodations at peak times – Semana Santa or between Christmas and New Year – be prepared to spend more and be sure to book ahead. And remember, if you plan on staying a week or more, negotiate for a better rate; monthly rates can cut your rent by half.

BUDGET

Vallarta's cheapest lodgings are south of the Río Cuale, particularly along Madero. All rooms come with fan.

Hotel Hortencia (Map pp454–5; ☎ 222-24-84; www.hotelhortencia.com; Madero 336; s $23-35, d $28-40, tr $33-45, q $38-50) Budget digs of a most agreeable sort are found at this family-run hotel. Rooms are bright and welcoming with appealing tile work, quality furnishings and up-to-date bathrooms. In the small lobby you'll usually find most of the family sitting around waiting to welcome you.

Hotel Azteca (Map pp454–5; ☎ 222-27-50; Madero 473; s $27-32, d $32-37, tr/apt $37/47) This graceful old-timer offers decent rooms surrounding an intimate, shady, palm-potted courtyard. Street-facing rooms are lighter, but all offer good budget value. On the roof there are a few simple chairs and tables, affording tremendous views over the town and into the mountains.

Hotel Villa del Mar (Map pp454–5; ☎ 222-07-85; www.hvilladelmar.com; Madero 440; s $20-27, d $28-32, tr $33-37) This one-of-a-kind budget place, resembling a brick fortress, came into its own in the 1970s and hasn't changed

much since. The owners keep the hotel spick-and-span ('cleanness' it says on the business card) and the air is heavy with disinfectant. The cheapest rooms are tiny and dour with little light; you're much better off dropping the couple extra bucks for one with a terrace.

Hotel Bernal (Map pp454–5; ☎ 222-36-05; Madero 423; s/d $16/21) An old standby with dark, basic cleanish rooms around a courtyard.

MIDRANGE

Hotel Posada Lily (Map pp454–5; ☎ 222-00-32; Badillo 109; s $30-35, d $50-55) This amazingly priced option just off the beach offers 18 clean and pleasant rooms with fridge, TV and good light. The larger rooms have three beds – bring your friends! – and small balconies that overlook the street.

Hotel Belmar (Map pp454–5; ☎ 223-18-72; www.belmarvallarta.com; Insurgentes 161; s/d/tr $36/46/61 with air-con extra $6; ✷) The Belmar has long served budget-minded travelers with clean and comfy rooms that have few frills but plenty of personality. A bit small (but cozy), they have tiled floors, wee TVs and miniature bathrooms. Snag one with a balcony.

Hotel Posada del Pedregal (Map pp454–5; ☎ 222-06-04; A Rodríguez 267; s/d $40/50, tr $70-120) On a busy mercantile street this pleasant option has small, bright standard rooms and suites. All come with a fridge, tiled floors and attractive, modern bathrooms.

Hotel Emperador (Map pp454–5; ☎ 222-17-67; www.hotelemperadorpv.com; Amapas 114; d $55-80, ste $89-200; ✷ ▣ ☎) This contemporary beach hotel gives a lot of pizzazz for the peso with thoughtfully designed rooms and suites, many with incomparable views of the coast. Oceanfront rooms celebrate the sea with large balconies featuring dining tables and kitchenettes – so you can eat and prepare your food alfresco. Each room has a fridge, cable TV, in-room phones, a king-sized bed and a sleeper couch.

Terraza Inn (Map pp454–5; ☎ 223-54-31; www.terrazainn.com; Amapas 299; r $70-80) Nestled on terraces opposite Playa de los Muertos, this little gem is the perfect hideaway for couples craving romantic solitude. There are only 10 units – each is unique and attractive, with interesting architectural features like arched doorways, columns and brick ceilings with exposed timbers. Units each have a small kitchen.

Hotel Eloisa (Map pp454-5; ☎ 222-64-65; www.hotel eloisa.com; Cárdenas 179; s $64-83, d $76-90, tr $82-96, ste $148; ❄ ⓑ) With a great location near the beach, this recently renovated hotel is one of the best values in town. The pleasant standard rooms have rustic furniture, tiled floors and two double beds; some also feature views and furnished balconies. Up on the roof there's a small pool and gratifying views over the town and to the cathedral in the distance.

Vallarta Sun Hotel (Map pp454-5; ☎ 223-15-23; vallartasun@usa.net; Rodríguez 169; d $55-65; ⓟ ❄ ⓑ) This hotel's hillside location catches the ocean breezes, providing a measure of relief on scorching hot days. Each of the 21 spiffy and attractive units have mission-style ceilings, two beds, a desk, a fridge and hand-carved headboards. Six open up to the attractive pool; the brighter upstairs units have balconies and views out to sea.

Casa del Los Cuatro Vientos (Map pp454-5; ☎ 222-01-61; www.cuatrovientos.com; Matamoros 520; r/ste $60/69; ⓑ) The rooms are not large but are rather cozy with white brick walls, hand-painted trim and gleaming red-tiled floors. Quality furnishings add style and class. There's also a two-room suite with a large bedroom and two day beds. The rooftop bar is an attraction in itself, affording terrific views of the cathedral and the entire bay.

Hotel Posada Río Cuale (Map pp454-5; ☎ 222-04-50; riocuale@pvnet.com.mx; Serdán 242; d/tr $65/80; ❄ ⓑ) Well-situated and nicely appointed, this hotel offers good value. The grounds are leafy and pleasant, and the beach is only two blocks away. The rooms are tastefully decorated if a bit dark. The pool – a godsend in the summer heat – is centrally located and convenient to the bar.

Frankfurt Hotel (Map pp454-5; ☎ 222-34-03; www .ho telfrankfurt.com; Badillo 300; r/bungalows $30/41, apt $41-60) Set in a large, jungly garden, the Frankfurt is an urban tropical haven. The simple rooms are dated but immaculately kept, the bungalows stay cool on hot days and the apartments have kitchenettes and cable TV.

Also recommended:

Hotel Posada de Roger (Map pp454-5; ☎ 222-08-36; www.posadaroger.com; Badillo 237; s/d/tr/q $50/60/70/80; ❄) An agreeable, central hotel and travelers' hangout.

Estancia San Carlos (Map pp454-5; ☎ 222-54-84; Constitución 210; 2-/4-person apt $64/110; ⓟ ❄ ⓑ) The spacious and appealing apartments here provide exceptional value.

Hotel Rosita (Map pp454-5; ☎ 222-10-33; www.hotel rosita.com; Paseo Díaz Ordaz 901; d/tr $68/77; ❄ ⓑ) A vintage hotel with no-nonsense rooms.

TOP END

Puerto Vallarta's top-end options are mostly dominated by the large, luxurious chains. Many of the following are very special, small and stylish places and are a great alternative if you're looking for something intimate. Puerto Vallarta also has a good selection of good, large beach hotels that operate outside the auspices of the mega-chains – the cream of the crop include Hotel Tropicana, Hotel Playa Los Arcos and Buenaventura Hotel & Beach Club, all featured here.

Quinta Maria Cortez (Map p452; ☎ 221-53-17; www.quinta-maria.com; Calle Sagitario 132; ste $117-280; ❄ ⓑ) With its own distinct style (the proprietor calls it 'Mexiterranean'), this is perhaps the most atmospheric and sophisticated place to stay near Vallarta. Seven spacious and romantic suites, all of different sizes, are furnished with antiques and eclectic decor. Most come with kitchen, fireplace and sea views. Definitely reserve in advance.

Majahuitas (☎ 800-508-79-23; www.mexicobou tiquehotels.com/majahuitas; Playa Majahuitas; casitas $345) Peaceful, primitive and elegantly luxurious, this un-electrified, phoneless, romantic getaway is about as far from 'regular' life as you can get. There are only eight, open-air casitas on this secluded white-sand beach Playa Majahuitas is only reachable by a 20-minute boat ride from Boca de Tomatlán, which the resort will organize for you; reservations are essential.

Hacienda San Ángel (Map pp454-5; ☎ 222-26-92 www.haciendasananangel.com; Miramar 336; d incl breakfast $250-475; ⓟ ❄ ⓑ) Elicits 'oohs' and 'ahs from most guests, but for others the eye candy comes off as just a bit too sweet Enough with guitar-strumming angels and the soothing dripping fountains already Even the most jaded grump may eventually be won over by the thoughtful attentions of the staff and the culinary magic practiced in the oh-so-colonial kitchen. The nine suites are undeniably romantic and luxurious and breakfast is brought to your door each morning. Who could complain?

Casa Kimberley (Map pp454-5; ☎ 222-13-36; www .casa kimberley.com; Zaragoza 445; d incl full breakfast

---

THE AUTHOR'S CHOICE

Hotel Molino de Agua (Map pp454-5; ☎ 222-19-07; www.molinodeagua.com; Vallarta 130; s/d all-inclusive cabin $113/176, d/tr noninclusive cabin $101/113; ✗ ⌘) This lush property at the mouth of the Río Cuale offers a tranquil retreat right in the heart of town. The brick *cabañas* (cabins) are simple rustic-chic with no TVs to disturb your reverie; there are also rooms and popular suites with ocean views. Shady walkways lead past two splendid swimming pools and through abundant greenery. Two gigantic *hule de oro* (rubber trees) spread their limbs like outstretched arms, providing a shady embrace.

$110; ⌘) The two adjacent houses at Casa Kimberley, connected by a pink 'love bridge,' were where the famously tempestuous romance of Elizabeth Taylor and Richard Burton sizzled and burned. Burton bought Liz the first house as a birthday gift in 1962 and built the second mansion for himself. The three suites still retain the swanky allure of a cocktail-era love nest.

Casa Andrea (Map pp454-5; ☎ 222-12-13; www.casa-andrea.com; Rodríguez 174; 1-/2-bedroom apt per week $450/800; ✗ ⌘) This gorgeous retreat offers 10 beautifully decorated apartments on spacious grounds, with flowery garden patios and a striking pool. Each apartment is decorated with original paintings and native crafts, with king- or queen-sized beds and well-equipped modern kitchens. Children over the age of five are welcome.

Hotel Tropicana (Map pp454-5; ☎ 222-09-12; www.htropicanapv.com; Amapas 214; d $82-98, ste $132; ✗ ▯ ⌘) This venerable 160-room beach hotel is eminently romantic. The standard rooms are appealing with white brick walls, attractive carved headboards, hand-painted woodwork and rustic furniture.

Hotel Playa Los Arcos (Map pp454-5; ☎ 222-05-83, from the US 800-648-24-03; www.playalosarcos.com; Olas Altas 380; d $116-140, ste $166; ✗ ⌘) Rooms and suites are spacious and bright, with all the amenities that you would expect at this price level. Suites include fully equipped kitchens with dining tables. Kids stay free and an all-inclusive plan is available.

Buenaventura Hotel & Beach Club (Map p452; ☎ 226-70-00; www.hotelbuenaventura.com.mx; Av México 1301; s/d/tr $157/180/203; ✗ ▯ ⌘) This

tiny beach hotel offers appealing rooms and impressive hacienda-style architecture. The beach is not the biggest in town, but the waters are gentle and you can actually enjoy a measure of privacy. All-inclusive plans are available.

Eating

Foodies are pampered in Puerto Vallarta, and return visitors rate its cuisine scene as a prime attraction. A goodly number of noteworthy chefs from abroad have put down roots, offering competing menus of tremendous breadth and variety. But there's also a downside: the surplus of high quality and well-heeled tourists means that you'll be paying considerably more for your romantic dinner than in many other Mexican resorts. Fortunately, there a goodly number of economical, family-run eateries serving mouthwatering traditional Mexican fare, and the taco stands lining the streets of the Zona Romántica make for quick, delicious meals.

ISLA RÍO CUALE & SOUTH
Budget

Some of the tastiest and cheapest food in town comes from the taco stands along Madero in the early evening. Women sell delicious *tamales* and *flan* along Insurgentes at dusk.

Pancake House (Map pp454-5; ☎ 222-62-72; Badillo 289; mains $3-5; ☽ 8am-2pm) You may have to wait in line for the amazing array of pancakes and other breakfast goodies. Coffee fans should skip the free refills and buy themselves an espresso.

Las Tres Huastecas (Map pp454-5; ☎ 222-30-17; cnr Olas Altas & Rodríguez; mains $3-7; ☽ 7am-7pm) This is the place for delicious Mexican favorites in a homelike atmosphere, at local prices. The charming owner, a poet calling himself 'El Querreque,' recites verse as readily as he recites the house specialties.

Esquina de los Caprichos (Map pp454-5; ☎ 222-09-11; cnr Miramar & Iturbide; tapas under $4; ☽ noon-10pm Mon-Sat) This Spanish-Mexican hole-in-the-wall serves delicious garlic-heavy gazpacho, buttery grilled scallops and much more. It's a small, stark setting, but entertaining and popular.

Gutiérrez Rizoc (GR; Map pp454-5; cnr Constitución & Serdán; ☽ 6:30am-11pm) A nicely well-stocked supermarket.

THE AUTHOR'S CHOICE

Mama Dolores' Diner (Map pp454-5; ☎ 223-58-97; Olas Altas 534; mains $6-13; ☺ 9am-11pm Tue-Sun) This cheeky eatery is the only place in town to get good meatloaf or liver and onions (made just like they do on the New Jersey turnpike). On Sundays – turkey dinner night – the self-described 'saucy bitch' Mama Dolores herself comes in to splash the margaritas around.

Midrange

Boca Bento (Map pp454-5; ☎ 222-91-08; Badillo 180; mains $7-13; ☺ 6pm-11pm) Striking just the right balance with its 'Latina Asiatica cuisine,' this urbane newcomer has already earned fans for its *mu shu* duck *carnitas* (simmered in lard and served with a corn tortilla) with tomato-ginger salsa ($13).

Mariscos Polo (Map pp454-5; ☎ 222-03-64; Madero 362; mains $6-13; ☺ noon-10pm) This breezy, comfortable eatery serves seafood and salads in a warm, music-filled environment. Start with a smoked marlin taco ($1) and finish the job with a roasted shrimp skewer ($14) or octopus burrito ($6). Mmm!

Restaurant Gilmar (Map pp454-5; ☎ 222-39-23; Madero 418; mains $4-8; ☺ 8am-9pm Mon-Sat) Tasty Mexican dishes and seafood at reasonable prices.

Top End

Le Bistro Jazz Café (Map pp454-5; ☎ 222-02-83; Isla Río Cuale 16A; mains $10-30; ☺ 9am-midnight Mon-Sat) Overlooking the river, this classy spot is good for a martini but even better for its scrumptious cuisine and beautiful tropical scenery. The menu is replete with gourmet fare like mahimahi, shrimp Portuguese and 'lobster of desire.' For breakfast there are savory crepes and eggs Benedict.

River Cafe (Map pp454-5; ☎ 223-07-88; Isla Río Cuale 4; mains $10-22; ☺ 9am-midnight) Imaginative seafood dishes are a highlight at this well-regarded and delightfully situated restaurant. Try shrimp with pecans and orange sauce, or the yummy shellfish salad. There's live jazz in the evenings Thursday through Sunday.

Oscar's Bar & Grill (Map pp454-5; ☎ 223-07-89; Isla Rio Cuale 1; mains $10-21; ☺ 11am-11pm) Located on the peaceful seaward tip of Isla Cuale, this restaurant is a fine choice for a romantic meal. Enjoy dishes like vegetable crepes with corn and *poblano* peppers ($13) or super-fresh mahimahi fillet baked in basil and Parmesan ($21).

Red Cabbage Café (☎ 223-04-11; Rivera del Río 204A; mains $8-20; ☺ 5-10:30pm; ✗ ⚱) Though the atmosphere is casual, with fabulous eclectic and bohemian artwork, the food is serious *alta cocina* (gourmet) Mexican. Try the subtle *mole* or hearty vegetarian dishes. A pleasant 10-minute walk from the Zona Romántica, it's the only nonsmoking restaurant in town. Reservations recommended.

Archie's Wok (Map pp454-5; ☎ 222-04-11; Rodríguez 130; mains $9-18; ☺ 2-11pm Mon-Sat) This elegant, urbane restaurant has long showed Puerto Vallarta a thing or two about good eating. The menu changes but it's always Asian fusion, with savory fish in rich tropical sauces as the highlight. There's live music Thursday through Sunday.

Casa Naranjo (Map pp454-5; ☎ 222-35-18; Naranjo 263; mains $7-19; ☺ 6-11pm) This chic newcomer has an unabashed predilection for the color orange and a dining room that wraps around the exposed kitchen. On the menu is delicious, fussed-over fare like saffroned mussels, ginger-grilled scallops and invigorating cold soups.

La Palapa (Map pp454-5; ☎ 222-52-25; Púlpito 103; mains $7-48; ☺ 8am-1pm & 6-11pm) Elegant beach dining at its best. Tables are positioned to take full advantage of the sea views, making it a particularly marvelous spot for breakfast or sunset. Chilean sea bass with blonde miso and pickled ginger is just one of the delicacies on the menu.

Kaiser Maximillian (Map pp454-5; ☎ 222-50-58; Olas Altas 380B; mains $7-18; ☺ 8am-midnight Mon-Sat) Get your well-prepared Wiener schnitzel ($16) or fresh *röter rubensalat* (beet salad; $8) at this upscale Austrian restaurant. There's also good coffee, desserts, snacks and meals, all with an Austrian flavor.

La Piazzetta (Map pp454-5; ☎ 222-06-50; cnr Olas Altas & Gómez; mains $8-22; ☺ 4pm-midnight Mon-Sat) Good service, outdoor seating, decent pizza.

Fajita Republic (Map pp454-5; ☎ 222-31-31; cnr Badillo & Suárez; mains $9-18; ☺ 5pm-midnight) With pleasant open air dining on a leafy, atmospheric patio, this popular fajita factory grills up generous portions of shrimp, vegetables, steak and chicken with plenty of guacamole. Wash it all down with a pitcher of mango margarita.

NORTH OF THE RÍO CUALE
Budget
Cenaduría Doña Raquel (Map pp454-5; ☎ 222-30-25; Vicario 131; mains $3-5; ☼ 6-11:30pm Mon & Wed-Fri, 2-11pm Sat & Sun) You can smell the richness of the traditional Mexican basics served here from a block away. Friendly atmosphere and friendly prices.

Planeta Vegetariano (Map pp454-5; ☎ 222-30-73; Iturbide 270; buffet $3.50-6; ☼ 8am-10pm; **V**) Dreamy for vegetarians, serving up all-you-can-eat quality buffets at every meal. All around are wonderfully painted murals, and the hilly pedestrian street outside is a peaceful backdrop.

Tacos de los Arcos (Zaragoza 120; tacos $0.80; ☼ noon-midnight) This unpretentious, cozy eatery is in a class by itself. Simple but indulgent, with all the fixings you would expect.

Just north of the river, the Mercado de Artesanías (see p465) has simple stalls upstairs serving typical Mexican market foods.

Midrange
Mi Querencia (Map pp454-5; ☎ 222-20-30; Morelos 426; mains $6-18; ☼ 8am-2am) Seviche gets gussied up here with variations featuring coriander, pineapple, beet juice and oranges. Similar liberties are taken with the shrimp dishes.

La Dolce Vita (Map pp454-5; ☎ 222-38-52; Paseo Díaz Ordaz 674; mains $7-10; ☼ noon-2am) A cheerful, often crowded spot for wood-fired pizzas and people-watching. On Friday night there's handmade gnocchi.

No Name Café (Map pp454-5; ☎ 223-25-08; cnr Morelos & Mina; mains $5-20; ☼ 8am-1am) This restaurant and sports bar serves all-American favorites. It claims to serve the best ribs in Mexico: you be the judge. Phone for free delivery.

Top End
Trio (Map pp454-5; ☎ 222-42-28; Guerrero 264; mains $14-26; ☼ 6pm-midnight; ☒) The two European chefs at this elegant restaurant-bar-bistro put a lot of passion into the seasonal menu. Local and Mediterranean flavors blend beautifully in dishes like lamb ravioli, chili-roasted snapper or Lebanese salad. The rooftop bar area is choice for an after-dinner libation.

Las Palomas (Map pp454-5; ☎ 222-36-75; cnr Paseo Díaz Ordaz & Aldama; mains $9-28; ☼ 8am-11pm) This restaurant looks over the *malecón* from its comfortable perch, which makes it a popular place for people-watching. The menu includes seafood, chicken crepes and authentic Mexican specialties – plus the decor is smart and festive.

Café des Artistes (Map pp454-5; ☎ 222-32-28; Sánchez 740; mains $18-29; ☼ 6-11:30pm) This cosmopolitan restaurant has a romantic ambience to match its exquisite French cuisine. Local seafood is featured in many of the dishes, with adventurous meals like 'soft shell crab and beef tongue fantasy.' Reservations recommended.

El Palomar de los González (Map pp454-5; ☎ 222-07-95; Aguacate 425; mains $10-20) The superb view over the city and bay is a big draw at this hillside restaurant, especially at sunset. Jumbo shrimp and fillet steak are specialties. It's a steep climb up here, so get a taxi or work up an appetite.

Drinking
Unsurprisingly for a city where lounging around is one of the preferred activities, Vallarta has many choice spots for sipping a strong coffee or tipping a tipple. It's ridiculously easy to become inebriated in Puerto Vallarta, where two-for-one happy hours are as reliable as the sunset and the margarita glasses look like oversized snifters. Coffee shops open about 7am and close around midnight; most bars keep 'em coming well after midnight.

Café San Angel (Map pp454-5; ☎ 223-21-60; Olas Altas 449) Start your day in this artsy, relaxed café that has sidewalk tables filled with gringos sitting pretty, sipping their black coffee and nibbling on snacks and sweets.

La Barriga Cantina (Map pp454-5; Madero 259) Attracting gringos and locals, this cozy and friendly place has free pool and a jukebox.

La Bodeguita del Medio (Map pp454-5; ☎ 223-15-85; Paseo Díaz Ordaz 858) This graffiti-covered Cuban joint has live music, stiff *mojitos* and good views over the *malecón*.

El Faro Lighthouse Bar (Map p452; ☎ 221-05-41; Royal Pacific Yacht Club, Marina Vallarta; ☼ 5pm-2am) Not too many lighthouses serve cocktails, but this one sure does. Panoramic views of the bay in the moonlight are a surefire prelude to a kiss.

Other recommendations:

Memories Café (Map pp454-5; cnr Mina & Juárez; ☼ 7pm-midnight) Conversation is king at this down-to-earth, low-key spot.

Carlos O'Brian's (Map pp454-5; ☎ 222-14-44; Paseo Díaz Ordaz 786) A favorite drinking hole for rabble-rousing gringos.

GAY VALLARTA

Come on 'out' – the rainbow flag flies high over Puerto Vallarta and its formidable selection of gay bars, nightclubs, restaurants and hotels. The **Gay Guide Vallarta** (www.gayguidevallarta.com) booklet has tons of information and a helpful map for finding gay-friendly businesses. Useful websites include www.discoveryvallarta.com and www.doinitright.com.

Blue Chairs is the most popular, visible gay beach bar, with droves of gay couples enjoying the ubiquitous sun's rays and cool drinks. It's located at the south end of Playa de los Muertos.

CLUBS & NIGHTSPOTS

The following are just the tip of the iceberg.

Club Paco Paco (Map pp454-5; ☎ 222-18-99; www.pacopaco.com; Vallarta 278; cover $6) With a disco and cantina, this venerable institution is most famous for its transvestite revues, held at midnight and 3am Thursday to Sunday.

Los Balcones (Map pp454-5; ☎ 222-46-71; Juárez 182; cover $2-4, before 10pm free) One of the oldest gay haunts in town, with little upstairs balconies where hipsters like to be seen. Great cozy spaces and colorful walls accompany DJ'd music and nightly strippers.

Anthropology (Map pp454-5; Morelos 101; cover $6) A sizzling dance scene and a dark, intimate rooftop patio.

Palm (Map pp454-5; Olas Altas 508; cover $4, before 9pm free) Presents a different show every night amid spinning lights, snazzy colors and palm decor.

Depending on the alignment of the stars, the following gay bars are mostly mellow. **Kit Kat Klub** (Map pp454-5; ☎ 223-00-93; Púlpito 120) is an ultra-hip dinner-show spot with wicked martinis. **La Noche** (Map pp454-5; Cárdenas 257; ☒ 4pm-2am) is well loved for its convivial atmosphere & buff bartenders. **Sama Bar** (Map pp454-5; ☎ 223-31-82; Olas Altas 510; ☒ 5pm-2am) is a likable small place with big martinis.

RESORTS & INNS

Blue Chairs Beach Resort (Map p452; ☎ 222-50-40 www.bluechairs.com; Almendro 4; d $69-109, apt $79-129; ☒ ☒) Overlooking one of Mexico's most famous gay beaches, this resort is a good place to let it all hang out (although officially the beach has a 'no nudity' policy). There are bars and restaurants on the beach and a raucous nightspot with live entertainment on the roof. The breezy and attractive rooms have cable TV; apartments have kitchenettes.

Hotel Descanso del Sol (Map pp454-5; ☎ 222-52-29; www.descansodelsol.com; Suárez 583; s/d $90/110, ste $120-140; ☒ ☒) This hotel on the hill is a well-established enclave. Don't be surprised to find 20 men crammed into the hot tub at dusk. Standard rooms are chintzy, but the suites are much better with full kitchen and plenty of natural light. Some of the fixtures could use an update, but most guests don't quibble and spend most of their time on the roof enjoying the breathtaking panoramic views.

Paco's Paradise (Map pp454-5; ☎ 227-21-89; www.pacopaco.com; dm $30, ste $59-69) Accessible by boat only, this rustic (no electricity) getaway on 80,000 sq m of wilderness with a private beach is quite a deal. Groups leave from Club Paco Paco (see boxed text, above) at 11am.

Club Roxy (Map pp454-5; Vallarta 217) Live rock, blues and reggae classics in a gritty bar with a roadhouse feel.

Entertainment

Vallarta's main forms of nighttime entertainment revolve around dancing, drinking and dining. At night everyone and their brother strolls the *malecón*, choosing from a fantastic selection of restaurants, bars and hot nightspots. Entertainment is often presented in the amphitheater by the sea, opposite Plaza Principal. Softly lit Isla Cuale is a quiet haven for a romantic promenade in the early evening.

NIGHTCLUBS & DISCOS

Along the *malecón* are a bunch of places where teen and 20-something tourists get trashed and dance on tables. On a good night, they all stay open until 5am. You can see from the street which one has the most action. Cover charges are normally waived early in the week; on weekends they often include one or two drinks.

de Santos (Map pp454-5; ☎ 223-30-52; Morelos 771; weekend cover $10; ☻ Wed-Sun) Vallarta's choicest nightspot commands the most artful DJs and an open-air rooftop bar furnished with oversized beds. On the dance floor the music is frenetic, but there's also a mellow chill lounge.

Christine (Map p452; ☎ 224-69-90; Av Las Garzas s/n; cover $6) At the NH Krystal Puerto Vallarta (see p458), this flashy dance club is occasionally explosive, with cutting edge sound and lighting systems.

Also hit:

Hilo (Map pp454-5; ☎ 223-53-61; Paseo Díaz Ordaz 588; weekend cover $7-10) With epic statues of revolutionary heroes, it's a cool space well-designed for getting a groove on.

Zoo (Map pp454-5; ☎ 222-49-45; Paseo Díaz Ordaz 638; weekend cover $11) Good sound system, and cages in which to dance.

High After Hours Bar (Map pp454-5; Cárdenas 329; cover $10) Hipster haven featuring oxygen huffing and action 'til the sun comes to dance.'

Young locals drink and dance to loud Latin music at **La Cantina** (Map pp454-5; Morelos 700), or drink and do karaoke at **La Regadera** (Map pp454-5; Morelos 664).

BULLFIGHTS
Bullfights (admission $14-28) Held at 5pm on Wednesday from November to May, in the Plaza de Toros (Map p452) opposite the marina.

CINEMAS
Cine Bahía (Map pp454-5; ☎ 222-17-17; cnr Insurgentes & Madero; admission $3.80) Recent releases are often shown in English with Spanish subtitles.

FIESTAS MEXICANAS
These fun folkloric shows give tourists a crash course in not-very-contemporary Mexican culture.

La Iguana (Map pp454-5; ☎ 222-01-05; Cárdenas 311; admission $50; ☻ 7-11pm Thu & Sun) Said to be the original of this much-copied tourist entertainment, the deal here includes a Mexican buffet, open bar, live music, folkloric dances, mariachis, cowboy rope tricks, bloodless cockfights and a piñata.

Several of the big resort hotels also have Fiesta Mexicana nights, including the NH Krystal Puerto Vallarta (see p458). Admission is $48 and shows are at 7pm on Tuesday and Saturday.

MARIACHIS
Two places present regular mariachi music. One attracts tourists; the other is mainly for Mexicans.

Tequila's (Map pp454-5; ☎ 222-57-25; Galeana 104) This upstairs restaurant-bar features live mariachi music every night except Monday, starting around 7:30pm.

Mariachi Loco (Map pp454-5; ☎ 223-22-05; cnr Cárdenas & Vallarta; cover $3) Usually attracting a very enthusiastic all-Mexican crowd, this-restaurant-bar presents an entertaining (if slightly amateur) show of music, comedy and mariachi every night at 6:30pm and 10:30pm. It's a great bit of local color, but you'll need good Spanish to get the jokes.

Shopping
Vallarta is a haven for shoppers, with many shops and boutiques selling fashionable clothing, beachwear and crafts from all over Mexico. The following places have the good goods.

Mercado de Artesanías (Map pp454-5; ☎ 223-09-25; A Rodríguez 260) Selling everything from Taxco silver, sarapes (blankets with a head opening, worn as a cloak) and *huaraches* (woven leather sandals), to wool wall-hangings and blown glass.

Mundo de Cristal (Map pp454-5; ☎ 222-41-57; Insurgentes 333) The only glass factory in town has an amazing selection of hand-blown objects ranging from champagne flutes to large shimmering sculptures. Purchases are well-packed and they can be shipped internationally.

Puerco Azul Galería (Map pp454-5; ☎ 222-86-47; Constitución 325) A well-curated shop tempts with a treasure trove of movie posters, quirky original art, 'kitsch mexicana' and delightful curios.

Olinalá (Map pp454-5; ☎ 222-49-95; Cárdenas 274) This excellent gallery displays authentic Mexican dance masks, folk art, rural antiques, fine guitars and contemporary paintings.

El Gato Gordo (Map p452; ☎ 223-03-00; Av de México 1083) This rather small shop looks harmless enough, but it's chock full of *lucha libre* (Mexican wrestling) masks and Cuban cigars. These two products should not be used simultaneously.

Alfarería Tlaquepaque (Map p452; ☎ 223-21-21; Av de México 1100) This large showroom has been in business for decades, offering the best prices and selection of baked earthenware, blown glass and ceramics.

Artesanías Flores (Map pp454-5; ☎ 223-07-73; Cardenas 282) and **Huichol Collection** (Map pp454-5; ☎ 223-21-41; Morelos 490) sell Huichol beadwork, thread paintings and jewelry.

Getting There & Away

AIR

Gustavo Díaz Ordaz International Airport (Map p452) is 10km north of the city and is served by the following carriers:

Aeroméxico (☎ 224-27-77) Service to Los Angeles, San Diego, Guadalajara, La Paz, León, Mexico City, Morelia and Tijuana.

Alaska Airlines (☎ 221-13-50) Direct service to Los Angeles, San Francisco and Seattle.

America West (☎ 221-13-33) Direct service to Las Vegas, Los Angeles, Phoenix and San Diego.

American Airlines (☎ 221-17-99) Direct service to Austin, Chicago, Dallas, Mexico City and St Louis.

Continental (☎ 221-10-25) Direct service to Houston and Newark.

Frontier (from the US ☎ 800-432-13-59) Direct service to Denver and Kansas City.

Mexicana (☎ 224-89-00) Direct service to Chicago, Guadalajara, Los Angeles and Mexico City.

Ted (from the US ☎ 800-225-58-33) United's budget carrier offers direct service to Denver and San Francisco.

BUS

Vallarta's long-distance bus station (Map p452) is just off Hwy 200, about 10km north of the city center and 2km northwest of the airport.

Most intercity bus lines have offices (Map pp454–5) south of the Río Cuale. You can buy tickets from the offices without having to make a trip to the station. These include Elite, TNS and Estrella Blanca, on the corner of Badillo and Insurgentes; ETN, Primera Plus and Servicios Coordinados, at Cárdenas 268; and Transportes del Pacífico, at Insurgentes 282.

See the table below for daily departures from the main terminal:

CAR & MOTORCYCLE

Starting at about $60 per day, car rentals are pricey during the high season, but deep discounts are offered at other times. You'll do well to book online. For more information about renting cars in Mexico, see p1000.

Car rental agencies at the airport:

Avis (☎ 221-16-57)
Budget (☎ 221-17-30)

VALLARTA BUS SCHEDULE

Destination	Price	Duration	Frequency
Barra de Navidad	$17	3½hr	4 1st class
	$13	4hr	5 2nd class, or jump on a bus to Manzanillo to reach Barra de Navidad
Guadalajara	$32-39	5½hr	36 1st class
Manzanillo	$20	5hr	3 1st class
Mazatlán	$27-29	8hr	7 1st class, or take a bus to Tepic where buses depart frequently for Mazatlán.
Mexico City	$95	13hr	1 deluxe
(Terminal Norte)	$69-71	14hr	8 1st class
Rincón de Guayabitos	$6	1½hr	frequent 1st & 2nd class, buses to Rincón de Guayabitos also continue to Tepic
San Blas	$10	3½hr	1 2nd class 3pm, or take a bus to Tepic for transfer
San Patricio-Melaque	$13	3½hr	4 1st class
	$10	4hr	4 2nd class, or jump on a bus to Manzanillo to reach San Patricio-Melaque
Sayulita	$2	1hr	10 2nd class
Tepic	$12	3½hr	frequent 1st & 2nd class

Dollar (☎ 221-10-01)
Hertz (☎ 221-14-73)
National (☎ 221-12-26)

Mario's Moto Rent (Map p452; ☎ 229-81-42; Av Ascencio 998), opposite the Sheraton Buganvilias hotel, rents out trail bikes ($15 per hour) and scooters ($12 per hour).

Getting Around
TO/FROM THE AIRPORT
The cheapest way to get to/from the airport is on a local bus for $0.40. 'Aeropuerto,' 'Juntas' and 'Ixtapa' buses from town all stop right at the airport entrance; 'Centro' and 'Olas Altas' buses go into town from beside the airport entrance. A taxi from the city center costs around $6. From the airport to the city, taxis ask as much as $13, but shouldn't cost more than $8 to go to most parts of the city.

BICYCLE
For a two-wheeled buzz, **Bike Mex** (Map pp454-5; ☎ 223-16-80; Guerrero 361) and **Eco Ride** (see p458) rent out mountain bikes for guided or self-guided tours, from $25 per day.

BOAT
In addition to taxis on land, Vallarta also has water taxis to beautiful beaches on the southern side of the bay – beaches that are accessible only by boat.

Water taxis departing from the pier at Playa de los Muertos head south around the bay, making stops at Playa Las Ánimas (25 minutes), Quimixto (30 minutes) and Yelapa (45 minutes); the round-trip fare is $25 for any destination. Boats depart at 10am, 11am and 4pm, and return mid-afternoon (the 4pm boat from Puerto Vallarta returns in the morning).

A water taxi also goes to Yelapa from the beach just south of Hotel Rosita, on the northern end of the *malecón*, departing at 11:30am Monday to Saturday (one-way $14, 30 minutes).

Cheaper water taxis to the same places depart from Boca de Tomatlán, south of town, which is easily reached by local bus. Water taxis to Playa Las Ánimas (15 minutes), Quimixto (20 minutes) and Yelapa (30 minutes) depart from here hourly from 10am to 4pm; the one-way fare is $12 to any destination.

Private yachts and *lanchas* can be hired from the southern side of the Playa de los Muertos pier. They'll take you to any secluded beach around the bay; most have gear aboard for snorkeling and fishing. *Lanchas* can also be hired privately at Mismaloya and Boca de Tomatlán, but these are more expensive than from Puerto Vallarto.

BUS
Local buses that are marked 'Ixtapa' and 'Juntas' go to the bus station; 'Centro' and 'Olas Altas' buses run into town from beside the bus-station parking lot. A taxi between the center and the bus station costs $5 to $8.

Local buses operate every five minutes from 5am to 11pm on most routes, and cost $0.40. Plaza Lázaro Cárdenas at Playa Olas Altas is a major departure hub. Northbound local bus routes also stop in front of the Cine Bahía, on Insurgentes near the corner of Madero.

Northbound buses marked 'Hoteles,' 'Aeropuerto,' 'Ixtapa,' 'Pitillal' and 'Juntas' pass through the city heading north to the airport, the Zona Hotelera and Marina Vallarta; the 'Hoteles,' 'Pitillal' and 'Ixtapa' routes can take you to any of the large hotels north of the city.

Southbound 'Boca de Tomatlán' buses pass along the southern coastal highway through Mismaloya ($0.50, 20 minutes) to Boca de Tomatlán ($0.75, 30 minutes). They depart from Constitución near the corner of Badillo every 15 minutes from 6am to 11pm.

TAXI
Cab prices are regulated by zones; the cost for a ride is determined by how many zones you cross. A typical trip from downtown to the Zona Hotelera costs $4 to $7; the fare to Mismaloya is about $10. Always determine the price of the ride before you get in.

COSTALEGRE BEACHES
South of Puerto Vallarta, the stretch of Mexico's Pacific coast from Chamela to Barra de Navidad is blessed with many fine beaches. Tourism promoters and developers refer to this shoreline as the 'Costalegre' (Happy Coast) or the 'Mexican Riviera.'

Following are the beaches from north to south (with kilometer numbers measured from the junction of Hwys 80 and 200 just outside San Patricio-Melaque):

Playa Pérula (Km 76) A sheltered beach at the northern end of tranquil 11km-long Bahía de Chamela.

Playa Chamela (Km 72) Tourism is slowly creeping in.

Playa Negrito (Km 64) A pristine beach at the south end of Bahía de Chamela.

Playa Careyes & Playa Careyitos (Km 52) Endangered hawksbill sea turtles are making a comeback here, with the help of local activists.

Playa Tecuán (Km 33) A deserted white-sand beach 10km off the highway near an abandoned resort.

Playa Tenacatita (Km 30) On Bahía Tenacatita. Has crystal-clear snorkeling waters and a large mangrove lagoon with good bird-watching.

Playa Boca de Iguanas (Km 19) A wide-open 10km-long beach on Bahía Tenacatita.

Playa La Manzanilla (Km 13) A sheltered beach marking the southern end of public access to Bahía Tenacatita.

Playa Cuastecomates A pleasant beach 3km west of San Patricio-Melaque.

BAHÍA DE NAVIDAD

The tight arc of the Bahía de Navidad is practically ringed by deep, honey-colored sand with two resort towns at either end, waving amiably at each other. Situated 5km apart, Barra de Navidad and San Patricio-Melaque are siblings with distinct personalities. Barra is beloved for its attractive cobbled streets and aura of good living while San Patricio-Melaque, the scrappier of the two, draws budget-minded travelers seeking to get back to basics in a place that defies pretension.

San Patricio-Melaque

☎ 315 / pop 8000

Known by most as Melaque (may-*lah*-kay), this kick-back beach resort hasn't lost its old Mexico charm. Besides being a popular vacation destination for Mexican families and a low-key winter hangout for snowbirds (principally Canadians), the town is famous for its weeklong Fiesta de San Patricio (St Patrick's Day Festival) in March.

The crumbling ruins of the Casa Grande Hotel are an imposing reminder of the 1995 earthquake and the subsequent *maremotos* (tidal waves) that severely damaged the region.

ORIENTATION

Melaque is compact and walkable. Most hotels, restaurants and public services are concentrated on or near east–west Gómez Farías, which runs parallel to the beach, and north–south López Mateos, the main Hwy 200 exit. Barra de Navidad is 5km southeast of Melaque via Hwy 200 or 2.5km (about 30 to 45 minutes) by walking along the beach.

INFORMATION

Barra de Navidad's tourist office (see p471) has some basic information on Melaque.

Banamex (Gómez Farías s/n) Has an ATM and will change US and Canadian dollars; traveler's checks are changed from 9am to noon only.

Casa de Cambio Melaque (Gómez Farías s/n, Pasaje Comercial 11) Changes cash and traveler's checks.

Ciber@Net (Gómez Farías, Pasaje Comercial 27A; Internet access per hr $2; ☼ 9:30am-2:30pm & 4-8pm Mon-Sat)

El Navegante (Gómez Farías 48; Internet access per hr $2; ☼ 9am-2:30pm & 5-9pm Mon-Sat, 9am-2:30pm Sun)

Post office (Orozco) Located near Corona.

Telecomm (Morelos 53; ☼ 9am-2:30pm Mon-Fri) Offers the usual fax and phone services.

Total Laundry Service (Gómez Farías 26; per kg $1)

SIGHTS & ACTIVITIES

Simply relax and take it easy. The main activities are swimming, lazing on the beach, watching pelicans fish at sunrise and sunset, climbing to the *mirador* (lookout point) at the bay's west end, prowling the plaza and public market, or walking the beach to Barra de Navidad. A **tianguis** (indigenous people's market) is held every Wednesday starting around 8am; it's on Orozco two blocks east of the plaza.

The Only Tours (☎ 355-67-77; raystoursmelaque@ yahoo.com; Las Cabañas 26) runs popular snorkeling tours ($25) and tours to Colima ($50). For rent are mountain bikes ($6/10 per half-/full day), snorkeling gear and body boards (each $10 per day).

FESTIVALS & EVENTS

Fiesta de San Patricio This festival, honoring the town's patron saint, is Melaque's biggest annual celebration and takes place in March. A week of festivities – including all-day parties, rodeos, a carnival, music, dances and nightly fireworks – leads up to St Patrick's Day.

St Patrick's Day Held on March 17, this day is marked with a mass and the blessing of the fishing fleet. Take care when the *borrachos* (drunks) take over after dark.

SLEEPING

Rates vary greatly depending on the season; the following prices are for November

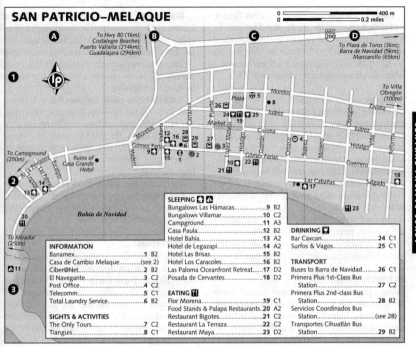

SAN PATRICIO–MELAQUE

through May. Discounts are common for longer stays.

Budget

Casa Paula (☎ 355-50-93; Vallarta 6; s/d $15/30) Staying here is like staying with the sweetest grandma ever. In this simple home there are four basic rooms with TVs and fridge around a courtyard. It's very quiet and a family atmosphere pervades.

Hotel Los Caracoles (☎ 355-73-08; www.loscaracoles.com.mx; Gómez Farías 26; s/d/bungalows $20/30/70) This fresh new hotel with 10 rooms and two bungalows is not on the beach but makes amends with clean, modern rooms with hand-painted headboards and tiled desks.

Bungalows Villamar (☎ 355-50-05; Hidalgo 1; s/d $20/28; 🐾) The Villamar has five spacious but worn garden bungalows, a pool and a beachfront terrace. It's popular with *norte americanos* (North Americans) because owner Roberto speaks English.

Hotel de Legazpi (☎ 355-53-97; hotel@delegazpi.com.mx; Las Palmas 3; d/tr $30/40, with kitchen $50; P 🐾) Right on the beach, the Legazpi has bright, if a bit worn, rooms. It's very popular for its ocean-view rooms; they cost the same as the other rooms but are hard to get.

Bungalows Las Hámacas (☎ 355-51-13; Gómez Farías 13; d/q $33/60; P 🐾) Ideal for larger groups, the beachfront Las Hamacas has chipping paint and worn but big rooms with full kitchens.

The Ejidal beachfront **campground** (campsites $2), at the west end of Av La Primavera, has no facilities but boasts a beautiful setting. Many of the nearby *enramadas* (*palapa* restaurants) charge a nominal fee for showers and bathroom usage.

Midrange

Hotel Bahía (☎ 355-68-94; Legazpi 5; r $30-35, bungalows $30-50; 🐾) Just half a block from the beach, this family-run place is one of Melaque's best deals. It's clean, very well maintained and has a communal open-air kitchen. Four of the 23 units have private kitchens.

Posada de Cervantes (☎ 355-65-74; posadadecervantes@hotmail.com; Salgado 132; bungalows $66-72; 🐾 🐾) This well-decorated, gay-welcoming inn has friendly management and charming sitting areas. The bungalows are a bit crammed, but some might call them cozy.

Hotel Las Brisas (☎ 355-51-08; Gómez Farías 9; s/d $33/45, bungalows $70-145;) The beachfront Las Brisas has one of the nicest pools in the neighborhood, outdoor communal cooking facilities, cheery staff and a small library. All rooms have fridge and TV.

Top-End

Las Paloma Oceanfront Retreat (☎ 355-53-45; www.lapalomamexico.com; Las Cabañas 13; studios incl breakfast $72-89; P) Original art abounds at this unique boutique resort that doubles as an art center. The singular, comfortable studios have kitchens and terraces with rewarding ocean views. Lush gardens, a 25m beachside swimming pool, a well-stocked library and Internet access make an extended stay here extremely tempting. Reservations are a must, particularly if you are interested in the drawing, painting or mask-making classes (held from November to April).

EATING & DRINKING

From 6pm to midnight, food stands serve inexpensive Mexican fare a block east of the plaza along Juárez. A row of pleasant *palapa* restaurants (mains $4 to $11) stretches along the beach at the west end of town.

Flor Morena (Juárez s/n; mains $1.50-3; 6-11pm Tue-Sun) You may have to wait to get a seat in this tiny, all-women-run place, but it's worth it. Everything is made fresh, there are plenty of vegetarian options and even the house specialty, shrimp *pozole*, costs less than $4.

Restaurant Maya (www.restaurantmaya.com; Obregón 1; mains $7-14; 6-11pm Wed-Sun & 10:30am-2pm Sun) The menu changes regularly but the quality at this Asian-fusion beachside hot spot is consistently excellent. Dinners include a range of gourmet salads, grilled meats and fish with exotic sauces, and there are appetizers like tequila lime prawns. Western favorites like eggs Benedict and rich omelettes with Brie rule the brunch menu.

Restaurant La Terraza (☎ 355-53-13; Guzmán 4; mains $2.50-5; 7am-10pm) This warm, family-run spot serves organic coffee and a full breakfast menu in the morning, with homemade bread, salads, salsa and traditional Mexican food for lunch and dinner. There's Internet access and a breezy 2nd-floor terrace, where on Friday nights there's a buffet ($12 to $15) and traditional dance performed by students from the local secondary school.

Restaurant Bigotes (☎ 355-69-34; López Mateos 2; mains $5-10; 8am-9pm) Seafood is the specialty at this pleasant beachfront *palapa;* try the *guachinango a la naranja* (red snapper à l'orange) or *camarones al cilantro* (cilantro shrimp). The two-for-one happy hour (2pm to 8pm) is popular.

Juguería María Luisa (cnr López Mateos & Corona; snacks $1-3) Whips up fresh fruit and vegetable juices, tortas (sandwiches) and burgers.

Surfos & Vagos (☎ 355-64-13; Juárez s/n; 8pm-2am) Rocking to an agreeable beat, this 2nd-floor, open *palapa* has a pool table and board games.

Bar Caxcan (cnr López Mateos & Juárez) The new kid in town thumps out techno beats, has a pool table and an extended happy hour and attracts mostly young men.

ENTERTAINMENT

During winter and spring, *corridas de toros* occasionally liven up the Plaza de Toros off Hwy 200 near the Barra turnoff. Watch for flyers promoting *charreadas* (Mexican rodeos), and keep an ear out for megaphone-equipped cars announcing *béisbol* (baseball) games and *fútbol* (soccer) matches.

GETTING THERE & AWAY

Air

For information on the nearest airport to Melaque, see, p474.

Bus

Melaque has three bus stations. Transportes Cihuatlán and Primera Plus/Servicios Coordinados are on opposite sides of Carranza at the corner of Gómez Farías. Both have 1st- and 2nd-class buses and ply similar routes for similar fares. The 1st-class Primera Plus bus station is a block east on Gómez Farías.

Buses trundling out of these stations:

Destination	Price	Duration	Frequency
Barra de Navidad	$0.30	10min	15min 6am-9pm, or take any southbound long-distance bus
Guadalajara	$23	5-7½hr	6 1st class
	$19	5-7½hr	10 2nd class
Manzanillo	$5	1-1½hr	10 1st class
	$4	1-1½hr	2nd class hourly 3am-11:30pm
Puerto Vallarta	$17	3½-5hr	2 1st class
	$14	3½-5hr	17 2nd class

Local buses for Villa Obregón and Barra de Navidad ($0.50, 15 to 20 minutes) stop near the plaza by the Paletería Michoacán every 15 minutes.

Taxi
A taxi between Melaque and Barra should cost no more than $5, or as little as $3, depending on how well *tu hablas espanglish*.

Barra de Navidad
☎ 315 / pop 4000
The charming town of Barra de Navidad (usually simply called Barra) is squeezed onto a sandbar between Bahía de Navidad and the Laguna de Navidad. Barra de Navidad first came to prominence in 1564 when its shipyards produced the galleons used by conquistador Miguel López de Legazpi and Father André de Urdaneta to deliver the Philippines to King Philip of Spain. By 1600, however, most of the conquests were being conducted from Acapulco, and Barra slipped into sleepy obscurity (a state from which it has yet to fully emerge).

ORIENTATION
Legazpi, the main drag, runs parallel to the beach. Veracruz, the town's other major artery and the highway feeder, runs parallel to Legazpi before merging with it at the southern end of town. This end of town terminates in a fingerlike sandbar. Buses drop passengers on Legazpi.

INFORMATION
Banamex (Veracruz s/n) This ATM is air-conditioned.
Beer Bob's Book Exchange (Tampico 8; ☺ noon-3pm Mon-Fri) You can exchange, but not buy, books here.
Casa de cambio (Veracruz 212)
Centro Virtu@l (Veracruz s/n; Internet access per hr $2; ☺ noon-9pm Mon-Fri, 10am-3pm Sat) Has a decent Internet connection.
Ciber@Money (Veracruz 212C; Internet access per hr $2.50; ☺ 9am-2pm & 4-7pm Mon-Fri, 9am-6:30pm Sat) Also has a decent Internet connection.
Mini-Market Hawaii (Legazpi at Sonora; ☺ noon-10pm) Head here for telephone and fax services.
Post office (cnr Sinaloa & Mazatlán)
Telecomm (Veracruz 212B; ☺ 9am-3pm Mon-Fri) Telephone and fax services.
Tourist office (☎ 355-83-83; www.costalegre.com; Jalisco 67; ☺ 9am-5pm Mon-Fri, 10am-6pm Sat & Sun) This regional office has information about more than just

Barra. It also has free maps and runs an information kiosk on the jetty during the high tourist season.
Vinos y Licores Barra de Navidad (Legazpi s/n; ☺ 8:30am-11pm) Money-changing facilities.

ACTIVITIES
Barra's steep and narrow beach is lovely to behold, but conditions can become too rough for swimming. The gentlest surf usually arrives in the mornings.

Surfboards, body boards, snorkeling gear kayaks, bicycles, cars and apartments can be rented from **Crazy Cactus** (☎ 355-60-99; Veracruz 165; ☺ 9:30am-6pm Mon-Sat). **Nauti-Mar Dive Shop** (☎ 355-57-91; Veracruz 204) rents out outfits for all manner of aquatic sports.

Boat Trips
Trips into the Laguna de Navidad are a Barra highlight. The boatmen's cooperative, **Sociedad Cooperativa de Servicios Turísticos** (Veracruz 40; ☺ 7am-9pm), offers a variety of boat excursions ranging from half-hour trips around the lagoon ($20 per boat) to all-day jungle trips to Tenacatita ($200 per boat). One popular tour heads across the lagoon to the village of Colimilla ($20, three hours). Prices (good for up to eight people) are posted at the open-air lagoonside office. The cooperative also offers fishing, snorkeling and diving trips.

For a short jaunt out on the water you could also catch a water taxi from a nearby dock and head over to the Grand Bay Hotel Wyndham Resort on Isla de Navidad or Colimilla ($2 round-trip; see p474).

Fishing
The waters near Barra are rife with marlin, swordfish, albacore, *dorado*, snapper and other more rarefied catches. Fishing trips be arranged at the boatman's cooperative for about $25 per hour, including gear. If a serious deep-sea fishing expedition is what you have in mind, pass on the *lanchas* and check out **Z Pesca** (☎ 355-60-99; Veracruz) or **Fantasía Pesca Deportiva** (☎ 355-68-24; Legazpi 213), both of which have better boats and equipment. A six-hour, all-inclusive (except beer) trip costs $180 to $250 depending on the size of the boat and number of fisherfolk.

Golf
Grand Bay Golf Course (☎ 355-50-50; Grand Bay Hotel Wyndham Resort, Isla Navidad; green fees 18/27 holes $216/240) is a celebrated 27-hole course with

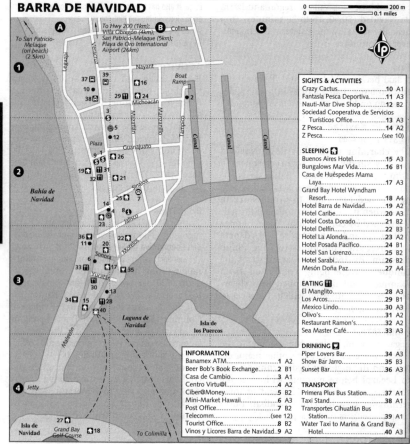

BARRA DE NAVIDAD

| | 0 — 200 m |
| | 0 — 0.1 miles |

To Hwy 200 (1km);
Villa Obregón (4km);
San Patricio-Melaque (5km);
Playa de Oro International
Airport (26km)

To San Patricio-
Melaque
(on beach)
(2.5km)

*Bahía de
Navidad*

*Laguna de
Navidad*

*Isla de
los Puercos*

Jetty

*Isla de
Navidad*   Grand Bay   Golf Course

To Colimilla

SIGHTS & ACTIVITIES
Crazy Cactus....................**10** A1
Fantasía Pesca Deportiva........**11** A3
Nauti-Mar Dive Shop............**12** B2
Sociedad Cooperativa de Servicios
Turísticos Office................**13** A3
Z Pesca.........................**14** A2
Z Pesca....................(see **10**)

SLEEPING
Buenos Aires Hotel..............**15** A3
Bungalows Mar Vida..............**16** B1
Casa de Huéspedes Mama
Laya............................**17** A3
Grand Bay Hotel Wyndham
Resort..........................**18** A4
Hotel Barra de Navidad..........**19** A2
Hotel Caribe....................**20** A3
Hotel Costa Dorado..............**21** B2
Hotel Delfín....................**22** B3
Hotel La Alondra................**23** A2
Hotel Posada Pacífico...........**24** B1
Hotel San Lorenzo...............**25** B2
Hotel Sarabi....................**26** B2
Mesón Doña Paz..................**27** A4

EATING
El Manglito.....................**28** A3
Los Arcos.......................**29** B1
Mexico Lindo....................**30** A3
Olivo's.........................**31** A2
Restaurant Ramon's..............**32** A2
Sea Master Café.................**33** A3

DRINKING
Piper Lovers Bar................**34** A3
Show Bar Jarro..................**35** B3
Sunset Bar......................**36** A3

TRANSPORT
Primera Plus Bus Station........**37** A1
Taxi Stand......................**38** A1
Transportes Cihuatlán Bus
Station.........................**39** A1
Water Taxi to Marina & Grand Bay
Hotel...........................**40** A3

INFORMATION
Banamex ATM.....................**1** A2
Beer Bob's Book Exchange........**2** B1
Casa de Cambio..................**3** A1
Centro Virtu@l..................**4** A2
Ciber@Money.....................**5** B2
Mini-Market Hawaii..............**6** A3
Post Office.....................**7** B2
Telecomm...................(see **12**)
Tourist Office..................**8** B2
Vinos y Licores Barra de Navidad.**9** A2

excellent vistas and greens carved into ocean dunes against a backdrop of mountains. Caddies and rental clubs are available.

FESTIVALS & EVENTS
Big-money international fishing tournaments are held annually for marlin, sailfish, tuna and *dorado*.

Torneo Internacional de Pesca This, the most important fishing tournament, is three days long and is held around the third week in January.

Torneo Internacional de Marlin This two-day event is held during late May or early June.

SLEEPING
Barra has fewer beachfront rooms than its neighbor Melaque. The prices listed here

are for the high season between November and May.

Budget
Hotel Caribe (☎ 355-59-52; Sonora 15; s $15-20, d $20-25) The popular Caribe is one of Barra's best budget deals. It has a rooftop terrace, hot water and 18 clean rooms, some of which are larger than others. Downstairs there's a pleasant garden offering respite on a hot afternoon. You'll be lucky to get a room here in winter.

Hotel Posada Pacífico (☎ 355-53-59; Mazatlán 136; s/d/bungalows $15/25/40; **P**) This friendly, comfortable posada (inn) has 25 large, clean rooms, plus four bungalows sleeping up to four people. Some English is spoken.

Casa de Huéspedes Mama Laya (☎ 355-50-88; Veracruz 69; r with/without bathroom $20/15) On the lagoon side of town, the Mama Laya has stark, worn rooms with TV. Expect to get to know the family that runs the place. Prices appear to be negotiable.

Hotel San Lorenzo (☎ /fax 355-51-39; Sinaloa 7; s/d $25/30) If all the other budget hotels in town are full, try the bright-orange San Lorenzo (the less-drab rooms are upstairs).

Midrange

Hotel Delfín (☎ 355-50-68; www.hoteldelfinmx .com; Morelos 23; d/t/ste $50/60/120; P 🖳 🛋) The Delfín is one of Barra's best hotels. It has large, pleasant rooms with shared balconies, a grassy pool area and an exercise room. Discounts are available for longer stays but repeat customers fill the place in winter.

Hotel Costa Dorado (☎ 355-64-10; Veracruz 174; s bungalows $40-50, d bungalows $60; P) This welcoming option offers 24 fastidious and whimsically tiled bungalows with diminutive TVs and good, firm mattresses. Grab an upstairs unit to benefit from the cross-breeze.

Bungalows Mar Vida (☎ 355-59-11; www.tomzap com/marvida.html; Mazatlán 168; apt $55; 🖾 🛋) The fine little Mar Vida has five newly remodeled studio apartments, all with satellite TV, cheerful tilework and hand-carved doors. Some English is spoken.

Hotel Barra de Navidad (☎ 355-51-22; www hotelbarradenavidad.com; Legazpi 250; s/d/tr/bungalows $62/72/78/144; 🖾 🛋) Providing Barra's best beach access, this glowingly white, modern beachside hotel harbors a shaded intimate courtyard and a small but inviting pool. The best rooms have ocean views and air-con.

Hotel La Alondra (☎ 355-83-73; www.alondraho el.com; Sinaloa 16; s $78-84, d $106-117, ste $182-264; P 🖾 🖳 🛋) This new five-story hotel tries to come off as a luxury hotel but falls short; the rooms have chintzy murals and balconies, but are otherwise generic. The best reason to pay the prices asked is for the commanding views on the upper floors.

Also recommended:

Buenos Aires Hotel (☎ 355-69-67; otelbuenosairesmx@yahoo.com.mx; Veracruz 209; s/d $50/60, ste $85-90; 🖾 🖾 🛋) Crisp and efficient with no children allowed.

Hotel Sarabi (☎ 355-64-10; www.hotelsarabi.com; Veracruz 196; bungalows $50-80; P 🖾) Clean and efficiently run. Ask about the 'third night free' promotion.

Top End

Getting away from it all is a matter of considerable luxury on Isla Navidad, a short water-taxi ride across the lagoon from Barra de Navidad.

Grand Bay Hotel Wyndham Resort (☎ 355-50-50; www.wyndham.com; Rinconada del Capitán s/n, Isla Navidad; d $350, ste $550-680; 🖾 🖳 🛋) This super-luxury resort is magnificent and very large. The same description applies to the rooms, which have marble floors, hand-carved furniture, and bathrooms that are big enough to herd sheep in. If the weather's not hot enough for you, spend some time in your suite's steam bath, or better yet at the pool's convenient swim-up bar. Justifying the hefty price tag are three grass tennis courts, golf packages, a 'kids' club' day-care center and big fluffy bathrobes.

Mesón Doña Paz (☎ 355-64-41; www.mesondona paz.com; Rinconada del Capitán s/n, Isla Navidad; d $350, ste $460-575; 🖾 🖳 🛋) For something really special, check into this gorgeous colonial-style lodge where every room has a balcony facing the limpid lagoon. The grounds are graced by a tranquil private bay, lookout point and lush landscaping. All-inclusive plans and golf packages are available. Be sure to ask about low season and promotional rates.

EATING

Several of Barra's many good restaurants are on the beachfront with beautiful sunset views, and others overlook the lagoon. Simple, inexpensive little indoor-outdoor places line Veracruz in the center of town. However, most are open only in the high season.

Sea Master Café (☎ 355-51-19; cnr Legazpi & Yucatán; mains $6-15; 🕑 lunch & dinner) With a very pleasant environment, perfect for tossing back cocktails, this place scores by taking liberties with seafood. For instance, a dish called '*piña* sea master' fills a pineapple with shrimp, peppers, mushrooms and a buttery Kahlua sauce. Who needs dessert?

Mexico Lindo (Legazpi 138; mains $4-14; 🕑 noon-10pm) With simple plastic tables under a corrugated tin roof, this place somehow manages to feel romantic and intimate at night. The menu features regional favorites like savory and sour tortilla soup, quesadillas, garlic fish tacos and shrimp *cevice*. A good selection of drinks and cocktails seals the deal.

El Manglito (☎ 355-85-90; Veracruz s/n; mains $7-10; ☻ 8am-7pm) An exuberantly decorated *palapa* overlooking the lagoon and a grand place to while away a hot afternoon watching the *lanchas* come and go. The service is slow but the seafood is so good that you won't mind.

Los Arcos (cnr Mazatlán & Michoacán; mains $3-5; ☻ 9am-11pm) One of the homiest places you'll eat at. Mom and Pop cooking is served to you in a tiny dining area. The menu is basic, with typical quesadillas and tacos.

Olivo's (cnr Legazpi & Guanajuato; mains $9-14) Diners are surrounded by artwork here, and can enjoy renowned Mediterranean food including baked lamb and pork fillets.

Restaurant Ramon's (☎ 355-64-35; Legazpi 260; mains $5-11; ☻ 7am-11pm) This casual and friendly *palapa* restaurant serves excellent fish tacos as well as other local and gringo favorites.

DRINKING
Sunset Bar (☎ 355-52-17; Jalisco 140; ☻ noon-2am) The waiter at this seaside saloon claims that 'the sunset' was named after the bar, and not the other way around. Humongous drink specials are served daily from 2pm to 10pm. A DJ spins nightly during the high season.

Piper Lovers Bar (☎ 355-67-47; www.piperlover.com; Legazpi 154A; ☻ 10am-2am) With its tough motorcycle-bar look and loud live music Wednesday through Saturday (from 9pm), this is the place to rock.

Show Bar Jarro (Veracruz; ☻ 9pm-4am) A down-to-earth, gay-friendly disco with pool tables and lagoon views, near Yucatán.

GETTING THERE & AROUND
Air
Barra de Navidad and Melaque are served by Playa de Oro International Airport (ZLO), 26km southeast of Barra on Hwy 200. The airport also serves Manzanillo. To get to town from the airport, take a taxi ($25, 30 minutes), or take a bus 15km to Cihuatlán and a cheaper taxi from there. For flight details, see p479.

Boat
Water taxis operate on demand 24 hours a day from the dock at the southern end of Veracruz, offering service to the Grand Bay Hotel Wyndham Resort ($1), the marina,

the golf course and Colimilla. Also see p471 for information on boat trips.

Bus
The long-distance buses stopping at San Patricio-Melaque (see p470) also stop at Barra De Navidad (15 minutes before or after). Transportes Cihuatlán's station is at Veracruz 228; Primera Plus and ETN operate from small terminals nearby, on the opposite side of Veracruz.

In addition to the long-distance buses, colorful local buses connect Barra and Melaque ($0.50, every 15 minutes, 6am to 9pm), stopping in Barra at the long-distance bus stations (buses stopping on the southbound side of the road loop round aLegazpi and back to Melaque).

Taxi
Catch taxis from the official **stand** (cnr Veracruz & Michoacán) to get the best price. A taxi to San Patricio-Melaque shouldn't cost above $5.

MANZANILLO
☎ 314 / pop 130,000
With a port that recently surpassed Veracruz to become the largest in Mexico, these are heady times for Manzanillo. Nowhere is the upbeat attitude more prevalent than downtown, where the waterfront was recently enhanced with a 3km boardwalk along the ocean and a capacious seaside *zócalo*. If you're after a dramatic setting for a stroll head to the boardwalk at dusk, when swarms of starlings do their best to blot out the sunset, and the giant Swordfish Memorial creates an imposing silhouette. Away from the center, miles of pristine and unpopulated beaches ring nearby Bahía de Santiago and Bahía de Manzanillo, and the lagoons surrounding town offer good bird-watching opportunities. Also, fans call Manzanillo the 'World Capital of Sailfish,' and each year fishing tournaments draw hopeful anglers from all around.

Orientation
Manzanillo extends 16km from northwest to southeast. The resort hotels and finest beaches begin at Playa Azul, across the bay from Playa San Pedrito, the closest beach to the center. Further around the bay is the Península de Santiago, a rocky outcrop holding Brisas Las Hadas resort and Playa La

Audiencia. Just west of the peninsula, Bahía de Santiago is lined with excellent beaches.

Central Manzanillo is bound by Bahía de Manzanillo to the north, the Pacific Ocean to the west and Laguna de Cuyutlán to the south. Av Morelos, the main drag, runs along the north edge of town center, beside the sea. At its east end it meets Av Niños Héroes, which leads to Hwy 200.

For information on getting to the city center from the airport and bus station, see p479.

Information

Several banks with ATMs are scattered around the city center.

Caseta Telefónica (Map p476; Av Morelos 144; ✆ 9am-10pm) Long-distance telephone and fax service. Public telephones are plentiful around the center.

HSBC (Map p476; Av México s/n) Currencies exchange.

Lavandería Lavimatic (Map p476; Madero; per kg $1.25; ✆ Mon-Sat) Within walking distance of the center, near Dominguez.

Members.com (Map p476; Juárez 116; Internet access per hr $2) Offers fast connections in a comfortable atmosphere.

Post office (Map p476; Galindo 30)

State tourism office (Map p475; ✆ 333-22-64; www .visitacolima.com.mx; Blvd Miguel de la Madrid 4960, Km 8.5; ✆ 9am-3pm & 5-7pm Mon-Thu, 9am-3pm Fri, 10am-2pm Sat) Dispenses information for Manzanillo and the state of Colima.

Tourist police (Map p476; Av 21 de Marzo; ✆ 332-10-04; Madero) Stationed behind the Presidencia Municipal.

Sights & Activities

MUSEO UNIVERSITARIO DE ARQUEOLOGÍA

The University of Colima's **archaeological museum** (Map p476; ✆ 332-22-56; cnr Niños Héroes & Glorieta San Pedrito; admission $1.50) presents interesting objects from ancient Colima state and rotating exhibits of contemporary Mexican art. At the time of research the museum was undergoing renovation and is scheduled to reopen in January 2007.

BEACHES

Playa San Pedrito (Map p476), 1km northeast of the *zócalo*, is the closest beach to town. The next closest stretch of sand, spacious **Playa Las Brisas** (Map p475), caters to a few hotels. **Playa**

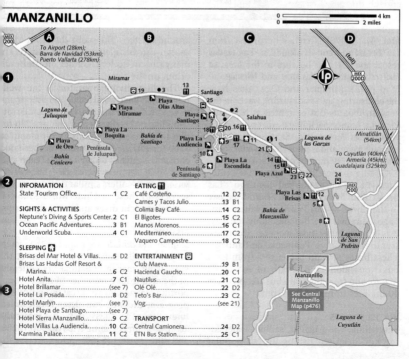

MANZANILLO

0 ——— 4 km
0 ——— 2 miles

To Airport (28km);
Barra de Navidad (53km);
Puerto Vallarta (278km)

Miramar

Laguna de Juluapan

Playa Miramar

Playa Olas Altas

Santiago

Playa Santiago

Salahua

Playa La Boquita

Bahía de Santiago

Playa de Oro

Península de Juluapan

Playa La Audiencia

Laguna de las Garzas

To Minatitlán (54km)

To Cuyutlán (40km);
Armería (45km);
Guadalajara (325km)

Bahía Cenicero

Playa La Escondida

Península de Santiago

Playa Azul

Playa Las Brisas

Bahía de Manzanillo

Laguna de San Pedrito

Manzanillo

See Central Manzanillo Map (p476)

Laguna de Cuyutlán

INFORMATION	
State Tourism Office	1 C2

SIGHTS & ACTIVITIES	
Neptune's Diving & Sports Center	2 C1
Ocean Pacific Adventures	3 B1
Underworld Scuba	4 C1

SLEEPING	
Brisas del Mar Hotel & Villas	5 D2
Brisas Las Hadas Golf Resort & Marina	6 C2
Hotel Anita	7 C1
Hotel Brillamar	(see 7)
Hotel La Posada	8 D2
Hotel Marlyn	(see 7)
Hotel Playa de Santiago	(see 7)
Hotel Sierra Manzanillo	9 C2
Hotel Villas La Audiencia	10 C2
Karmina Palace	11 C2

EATING	
Café Costeño	12 D2
Carnes y Tacos Julio	13 B1
Colima Bay Café	14 C2
El Bigotes	15 C2
Manos Morenos	16 C1
Mediterraneo	17 C2
Vaquero Campestre	18 C2

ENTERTAINMENT	
Club Maeva	19 B1
Hacienda Gaucho	20 C2
Nautilus	21 C2
Olé Olé	22 D2
Teto's Bar	23 C2
Vog	(see 21)

TRANSPORT	
Central Camionera	24 D2
ETN Bus Station	25 C1

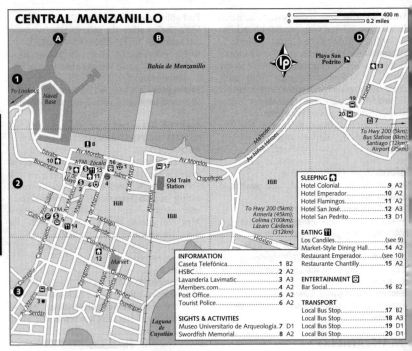

CENTRAL MANZANILLO

Bahía de Manzanillo

Playa San Pedrito

Naval Base

To Lookout

To Hwy 200 (5km);
Bus Station (8km);
Santiago (12km);
Airport (35km)

Old Train Station

To Hwy 200 (5km);
Armería (45km);
Colima (100km);
Lázaro Cárdenas
(312km)

Laguna de Cuyutlán

SLEEPING
Hotel Colonial...........................9 A2
Hotel Emperador.....................10 A2
Hotel Flamingos......................11 A2
Hotel San José.........................12 A3
Hotel San Pedrito....................13 D1

EATING
Los Candiles.........................(see 9)
Market-Style Dining Hall........14 A2
Restaurant Emperador..........(see 10)
Restaurante Chantilly.............15 A2

ENTERTAINMENT
Bar Social................................16 B2

TRANSPORT
Local Bus Stop........................17 B2
Local Bus Stop........................18 A3
Local Bus Stop........................19 D1
Local Bus Stop........................20 D1

INFORMATION
Caseta Telefónica.............................1 B2
HSBC..2 A2
Lavandería Lavimatic.........................3 A3
Members.com.....................................4 A2
Post Office...5 A2
Tourist Police.....................................6 A2

SIGHTS & ACTIVITIES
Museo Universitario de Arqueología..7 D1
Swordfish Memorial............................8 A2

Azul (Map p475) stretches northwest from Las Brisas and curves around to Las Hadas resort and the best beaches in the area: **La Audiencia**, **Santiago**, **Olas Altas** and **Miramar** (all Map p475). Miramar and Olas Altas have the best surfing and bodysurfing waves in the area; surfboards can be rented at Miramar. Playa La Audiencia, lining a quiet cove on the west side of Peninsula de Santiago, has more tranquil water and is popular for waterskiing and other noisy motorized water sports.

Getting to these beaches from the center is easy: local buses marked 'Santiago,' 'Las Brisas' and 'Miramar' head around the bay to the towns of San Pedrito, Salahua, Santiago, Miramar and beaches along the way. 'Las Hadas' buses take a more circuitous, scenic route down Peninsula de Santiago. These buses pick up passengers from local bus stops along the length of Av 21 de Marzo, and from the main bus station every 10 minutes from 6am to 11pm.

WATER SPORTS
Snorkeling, windsurfing, sailing, waterskiing and deep-sea fishing are all popular around the bay. The scuba diving in Manzanillo can be spectacular, and there are many sites to explore – either off the beach or out on the bay.

The best diving operator is the well-established **Underworld Scuba** (Map p475; ☎ 333 06-42; www.divemanzanillo.com; Hwy 200, Km 15). Its complete PADI dive center charges $80 for two-tank dives, including equipment, or $300 for PADI certification. Another good choice is **Neptune's Diving & Sports Center** (Map p475; ☎ 334-30-01; www.neptunesdiving.com; Hwy 200, Km 14.8), which offers similar dives, costs and services to those of Underworld Scuba. It also takes night dives and snorkeling trips.

FISHING
Sailfish and *dorado* are found in the water off Manzanillo during every season of the year, while marlin and tuna are generally in the area from November to March. Supporting Manzanillo's only catch-and-release program, the well-run **Ocean Pacific Adventures** (Map p475; ☎ 335-06-05; www.gomanzanillo .com/fishing) offers fishing trips on 26ft ($200) and 40ft cruisers ($260); prices are for the

whole boat and include gear, drinks and having your fish cooked up for dinner.

Festivals & Events

Fiestas de Mayo These fiestas celebrate celebrate the founding of Manzanillo in 1873. Festivities involve sporting competitions and other events over the first 10 days in May.

Fiesta de Nuestra Señora de Guadalupe Here, as elsewhere in Mexico, this festival is held from December 1 to 12 in honor of Mexico's revered manifestation of the Virgin Mary.

The biggest international sailfishing tournament is held here in November, with a smaller national tournament in February.

Sleeping

Central Manzanillo is safe, with the town's best cheap options within a block or two of the *zócalo*. There are more places in the somewhat shabby area a few blocks south of the city center. Around the bay, where the better beaches are located, hotels are more expensive; Playa Santiago, 30 minutes away by bus, is the exception, with one good budget option and a few well-priced midrange hotels.

BUDGET

Most budget options have worn but bearable rooms, with the exception of Hotel Colonial.

Hotel Colonial (Map p476; ☎ 332-10-80, 332-06-68; Bocanegra 100; s $25, d $28-32; **P** **※**) This atmospheric old hotel in the heart of downtown retains the character of a hacienda. Big rooms, tiled outdoor hallways and a thick colonial air make it the best deal in town. There's underground parking and a restaurant-bar on the premises.

Hotel San Pedrito (Map p476; ☎ 332-05-35; hotel sanpedrito@hotmail.com; Teniente Azueta 3; s/d $30/40; **P** **※** **❷**) This hotel sits next to Playa San Pedrito, the beach nearest to downtown. Old tiled rooms are generous in size, but worn and dank – see a few before deciding. From the *zócalo*, walk 15 leisurely minutes (just over 1km) east along the *malecón*, or catch a local bus and get off at the archaeology museum.

Hotel Emperador (Map p476; ☎ 332-23-74; Dávalos 69; s $15, d $18-20) Half a block from the *zócalo*, this simple but clean refuge has some top-floor rooms that are marginally brighter than the rest. The hotel's restaurant is good and is one of the cheapest in town.

Hotel Flamingos (Map p476; ☎ 332-10-37; Madero 72; s $14, d $17-20) On a quiet side street, this old cheapie offers 30 clean, basic rooms. Some can be musty; ask for one with two beds and an outside window.

Hotel San José (☎ 332-51-05; Cuauhtemoc 138; s/d/tr $15/25/35) This well-kept budget option near the market is a tad more pleasant than the cheapies near the waterfront.

Hotel Anita (Map p475; ☎ 333-01-61; r $32) This is the cheapest place on Playa Santiago, with endless remodeling efforts and 36 large, faded rooms.

MIDRANGE

Brisas del Mar Hotel & Villas (Map p475; ☎ 334-11-97; www.brisasdelmarmanzanillo.com; Playa Las Brisas; d/villas $60/100; **P** **※** **❷**) The beautiful, generous suites and villas at Brisas del Mar are all modern and colorfully decorated. They're beachside and within walking distance of some action. The pool is large enough for doing laps. All-inclusive plans are available.

Hotel Villas La Audiencia (Map p475; ☎ 333-08-61; Santiago Peninsula; r/villas from $76/92 **P** **※** **❷**) Although a bit far from Playa Audiencia (on the Santiago Peninsula), this moderately priced hotel is good value, especially for families. All the villas come with a kitchen and satellite TV.

The following hotels overlooking Playa Santiago are a winding 15-minute walk (or five-minute bus ride) from Santiago town, down the road leading off Hwy 200 past the ETN bus station. The hotels perch on a bluff overlooking the beach, and all have beachfront swimming pools.

Hotel Playa de Santiago (Map p475; ☎ 333-02-70; hoplasan@prodigy.net.mx; d/tr $61/80, ste $129-192; **❷**) Has a good family rate, with two children under 10 staying free; the private sea-view balconies are amazing.

Hotel Brillamar (Map p475; ☎ 334-11-88; r from $32, bungalows from $73-100; **※** **❷**) All breezy rooms come with TV, and bungalows have a kitchen.

Hotel Marlyn (Map p475; ☎ 333-01-07; d/ste from $54/73; **※** **❷**) Providing bang for the buck with pleasant rooms with TV and fan. The more expensive rooms have sea views and balconies.

TOP END

Most of Manzanillo's upmarket hotels are on or near the beaches outside the city center. Many sprawl along the beach side of the main road near Playa Azul. There are also plenty of all-inclusive resorts that are best booked ahead of time.

Hotel La Posada (Map p475; ☎ 333-18-99; www .hotel-la-posada.info; Cárdenas 201; s/d $58/78; P ☎) Right on the beach, this friendly, 'passionate pink' posada has spacious rooms with Mexican architectural touches. There's a breezy, well-appointed common area ideal for reading a book or chatting with the amiable staff.

Brisas Las Hadas Golf Resort & Marina (Map p475; ☎ 331-01-01; www.brisas.com.mx; Av Vistahermosa s/n, Playa Audiencia; incl breakfast r $292, ste $540-652; P ☒ ☒ ☐ ☎) Sitting like a Moroccan kingdom, it's so bright and white you'll need sunglasses when just walking around. Las Hadas has a choice of 234 spacious rooms and suites with marble floors, all-white furnishings and plentiful amenities; some even have private pools. Film buffs may know this is where the Bo Derek film *10* was made. There's also a golf course.

Also consider:

Hotel Sierra Manzanillo (Map p475; ☎ 333-20-00; Av de la Audiencia 1, Playa Audiencia; all-inclusive d $400, ste $458-482; P ☒ ☒ ☐ ☎) A white, sterile hotel beautifully situated above Playa Audiencia, with gorgeous ocean views.

Karmina Palace (Map p475; ☎ 334-13-00; www .karminapalace.com; Av Vista Hermosa 13, Playa Azul; d ste $425-449, all-inclusive q ste $994-1170; P ☒ ☒ ☐ ☎) Ideal for families, with a kids' club and several pools.

Eating

Several good down-to-earth options are on the *zócalo*, while chain and chainlike spots line Hwy 200 around the bay.

CENTRAL MANZANILLO

Restaurant Emperador (Map p476; ☎ 332-23-74; Hotel Emperador, Dávalos 69; mains $2-5) Good, cheap and simple, this intimate ground-floor restaurant is popular with locals and budget travelers. Highlights here are the set breakfasts and the meat-and-seafood *comida corrida*.

Restaurante Chantilly (Map p476; ☎ 332-01-94; Juárez 44; mains $3-10) This crowded cafeteria and *nievería* (ice-cream parlor) has reasonably priced meals and snacks, plus a generous *comida corrida*, genuine espresso and good ice cream.

Los Candiles (Map p476; ☎ 332-10-80; Hotel Colonial, Bocanegra 100; mains $4-11) This restaurant opens onto a pleasant patio, has a menu of

surf-and-turf fare, and a full bar with sports dominating the satellite TV.

A **market-style dining hall** (Map p476; cnr Madero & Cuauhtémoc; mains $2-5; 7am-6pm) has a number of inexpensive food stalls to choose from.

OUTSIDE THE CENTER

Many more restaurants are spread out around the bay all the way past the plaza in Santiago.

Café Costeño (Map p475; ☎ 333-94-60; Lázaro Cárdenas 1613, Playa Las Brisas; breakfasts $3-4.50; 9am-10:30pm Mon-Sat, 9am-1pm Sun) A good start to your day: French toast, hotcakes and omelettes are cheerfully served along with espresso and cappuccino. Sit in the shady garden out back.

El Bigotes (Map p475; ☎ 334-08-31; Hwy 200, Km 8.4; mains $9-22; 1pm-10pm) Popular for seafood, with dishes such as 'octopus drunken crazy' or 'snail garlic.' The beachside location is pretty fine, too.

Mediterraneo (Map p475; Hwy 200, Km 11; mains $6-12; 8am-11pm) Boasts generous salads, good crepes, pasta and several kinds of stuffed chicken breast. Try *tzatziki* for an appetizer while enjoying the golf course view.

Vaquero Campestre (Map p475; ☎ 334-14-48; Playa Audiencia; mains $8-15; 2-10:30pm Tue-Sat) Serves pitchers of margaritas and sangria to help lubricate the servings of grilled beef and seafood. *Palapa* roofs and a few animal heads and skins surround diners.

Manos Morenos (Map p475; ☎ 333-03-20; Carretera 200, Km 11; mains $6-13) At this *palapa* with a golf-course view, choose from fish with mango sauce or chicken with *huitlacoche* sauce. Or keep it simple with crepes or a generous salad.

Colima Bay Café (Map p475; ☎ 333-11-50; Carretera 200, Km 6.5, Playa Azul; mains $7-16; 2pm-1am) This super-fun Mexican restaurant keeps things lively, with professional service, DJ music is thumpin' and portions are more than generous.

Carnes y Tacos Julio (Map p475; ☎ 334-00-36; Carretera 200, Km 14.3; mains $4-11; 8am-midnight) Savory grilled meat is the specialty at this lively place, but breakfast, pasta and other tourist-friendly fare won't disappoint.

Entertainment

If you're in town on a Sunday evening, stop by the *zócalo*, where multiple generations come out to enjoy ice creams and the warm evening air. On the most atmospheric of nights a band belts out traditional music from the gazebo, and every night around sunset you can hear the cacophony of the resident *zanates'* (blackbirds) bombing squad – don't stand under any electrical wire for too long. And be sure to check out the *golondrinas* (swallows) perching on the wires later in the evening; it's eerily reminiscent of the Hitchcock classic *The Birds*.

Behind the doors of the **Bar Social** (Map p476; cnr Av 21 de Marzo & Juárez; ☿ noon-midnight Mon-Sat) is a world frozen in the past; congenial elderly bartenders dote on you as the jukebox plays scratchy decades-old singles.

Tourist nightlife starts in Playa Azul, with theme discos like **Vog** (Map p475; ☎ 333-18-75; Carretera 200, Km 9.2; cover women/men $10/15; ☿ Fri & Sat nights) and **Nautilus** (Map p475; ☎ 334-33-31; Carretera 200, Km 9.5; cover $15; ☿ Fri & Sat nights) and continues northwest around the bay. On the way back to Central Manzanillo, near Hotel Fiesta Mexicana, **Teto's Bar** (Map p475; ☎ 333-19-90; Carretera 200, Km 8.5) offers live music and dancing. **Olé Olé** (Map p475; Carretera 200, Km 7.5) is the place to dance to live salsa music.

Near Las Hadas resort in Santiago, **Hacienda Gaucho** (Map p475; ☎ 334-19-69; Playa Santiago) features dance music. On Playa Miramar, **Club Maeva** (Map p475; ☎ 335-05-96) houses Disco Boom Boom and the casual Solarium Bar (with a pool table); phone for reservations.

Getting There & Away

AIR

Playa de Oro International Airport lies between a long and secluded white sand beach and tropical groves of bananas and coconut, 35km northwest of Manzanillo's Zona Hotelera on Hwy 200.

Alaska Airlines (☎ 334-22-11; airport) Direct service to Los Angeles.

America West (from the US ☎ 800-235-92-92) Direct service from Phoenix.

Continental (from the US ☎ 800-231-08-56) Direct service to Houston.

Providing direct service to Mexico City:

Aero California (☎ 800-237-62-25)

Aeromexico (☎ 800-237-66-39)

Mexicana (☎ 800-531-79-21)

BUS

Manzanillo's new, airport-like, full-service Central Camionera (Map p475) is northeast of the center near Playa Las Brisas, just off Blvd Miguel de la Madrid (Hwy 200). It's an organized place with two tourist offices, phones, eateries and left-luggage facilities. Daily departures:

Destination	Price	Duration	Frequency
Armería	$3	45min	hourly 2nd class
Barra de Navidad	$6	1-1½hr	3 1st class
	$5	1-1½hr	10 2nd class
Colima	$6	1½-2hr	20 1st class
Guadalajara	$19-21	4½-8hr	frequent 1st class
	$14-18	4½-8hr	19 2nd class
Lázaro Cárdenas	$21	6hr	2 1st class
			2am & 6am
	$17	6hr	4 2nd class
Mexico City	$59-62	12hr	4 1st class
(Terminal Norte)	$50	4 2nd class	
Puerto Vallarta	$21	5-6½hr	4 1st class
	$18	5-6½hr	10 2nd class
San Patricio-	$6	1-1½hr	3 1st class
Melaque	$5	1-1½hr	10 2nd class

From its own terminal near Santiago at Carretera 200, Km 13.5, **ETN** (☎ 334-10-50) offers deluxe and 1st-class services to Barra de Navidad ($6, one to 1½ hours, three daily), Colima ($8, 1½ to two hours, seven daily) and Guadalajara ($28, five hours, seven daily). ETN also provides daily service to the airport in Guadalajara ($28).

Getting Around

There is no local or regional bus service to or from Playa de Oro airport. Most resorts have shuttle vans. **Transportes Turísticos Benito Juárez** (☎ 334-15-55) shuttles door-to-door to and from the airport. The fare is $28 for private service (one or two people) or $8 per person when three or more people share the ride. A taxi from the airport to Manzanillo's center or most resort hotels costs $25.

Local buses heading around the bay to San Pedrito, Salahua, Santiago, Miramar and beaches along the way depart every 10 minutes from 6am to 11pm from the corner of Madero and Domínguez, the corner of Juárez and Calle 21 de Marzo near the *zócalo*, and from the main bus station. Fares (pay the driver as you board) are $0.30 to $0.60, depending on how far you're -going.

Taxis are plentiful in Manzanillo. From the bus station buy a prepaid ticket for a colectivo taxi to ensure the best price. From the bus station, a cab fare is around $2 to the zócalo or Playa Azul, $6 to Playa Santiago and $9 to Playa Miramar.

CUYUTLÁN & EL PARAÍSO
☎ 313

The laid-back, black-sand-beach resort towns of Cuyutlán (population 1000) and El Paraíso (population 300) are popular with Mexicans but see very few norte americanos. Gentle waves and fun-in-the-sun activities, such as swimming, people-watching and boogie boarding, can be savored on or about the charcoal-colored sands. Cuyutlán has a better selection of hotels, but in El Paraíso the beach is less crowded and more tranquil.

Orientation & Information

Cuyutlán is at the southeastern end of Laguna de Cuyutlán, 40km southeast of Manzanillo and 12km west of Armería. Sleepy El Paraíso is 6km southeast of Cuyutlán along the coast, but 12km by road. Cuyutlán has a post office (El Paraíso does not), but neither town has a bank; for this you'll have to visit Armería. Both towns have public telephones and long-distance casetas (public telephone call stations) near their zócalos.

Sights & Activities

Cuyutlán is known for its **ola verde** (green wave), appearing just offshore in April and May. It's supposedly caused by little green phosphorescent critters, but it's the subject of much local debate. The **Centro Tortuguero** (☎ 328-86-76; admission $2; �---- 8:30am-5:30pm) is a beachside turtle sanctuary and environmental education center 4km toward Paraíso. **Lagoon trips** on the Palo Verde Estuary leave from the premises and cost $4.

Good **surfing** can be found 3km south of El Paraíso near Boca de Pascuale.

Sleeping & Eating

The area's beachfront accommodations are cheaper than at other coastal resorts. The high seasons here are Christmas and Semana Santa, when Cuyutlán's hotels are booked solid by Mexican families.

CUYUTLÁN

You can camp on the empty sands on either side of the hotels. Several of the beachfront enramadas rent out use of showers.

Hotel Morelos (☎ 326-40-13; Hidalgo 185; r with/without meals per person $25/13; ☒) Although rather old school, Hotel Morelos has 35 clean, spacious rooms (some remodeled – check a few), hot water and a decent, if somewhat greasy, restaurant. You'll find the hotel at the corner of Hidalgo and Veracruz.

Hotel María Victoria (☎ 326-40-04; Veracruz 10; per person $21; ℗ ☒) Located right on the beach, Cuyutlán's most luxurious hotel has a sea-view restaurant that serves fresh Mexican fare.

Hotel San Rafael (☎ 326-40-15; Veracruz 46; s/d $30/40; ☒) Next to the María Victoria, the remodeled San Rafael's most inviting rooms have sea views and share a large balcony.

EL PARAÍSO

None of the hotels in El Paraíso offer much more than crumbling, grubby cement cells for their guests.

Hotel Paraíso (☎ 322-10-32; r $29-35; ℗ ☒) This is the nicest place in town, with 60 decent rooms. It lies to the left of the T-intersection at the entrance to town.

Otherwise, you can camp on the beach or string up a hammock at one of El Paraíso's beachfront enramadas. All the enramadas serve basically the same food at similar prices; expect to spend $5 to $10 per person for a full, fresh meal.

Getting There & Away

Cuyutlán and Paraíso are connected to the world through Armería, a dusty but friendly little service center on Hwy 200, 46km southeast of Manzanillo and 55km southwest of Colima. From Armería a 12km paved road heads west past orchards and coconut plantations to Cuyutlán; a similar road runs 8km southwest from Armería to El Paraíso.

To reach either place by bus involves a transfer in Armería. Two bus lines – Sociedad Cooperativa de Autotransportes Colima Manzanillo and Autotransportes Nuevo Horizonte – have offices and stops just off Armería's main street. They both operate 2nd-class buses to Manzanillo every 15 minutes from 6am to 12am ($2.50, 45 minutes) and to Colima every half-hour from 5:45am to 10:30pm ($2.50, 45 minutes). Buses go every 20 minutes to Tecomán ($0.70, 15 minutes), where you can connect with buses heading southeast on Hwy 200 to Lázaro Cárdenas and elsewhere.

Buses to Cuyutlán and El Paraíso depart from Armería's market, one block north and one block east of the long-distance bus depots. To Cuyutlán ($0.75, 20 minutes), they depart every half-hour from 6am to 7:30pm. To El Paraíso ($0.65, 15 minutes), they go every 45 minutes.

No buses shuttle directly between Cuyutlán and El Paraíso. To go by bus, you must return to Armería and change buses again.

MICHOACÁN COAST

Highway 200 hugs the shoreline most of the way along the beautiful 250km coast of Michoacán, one of Mexico's most beautiful states. The route passes dozens of untouched beaches – some with wide expanses of golden sand, some tucked into tiny rocky coves, some at river mouths where quiet estuaries harbor multitudes of birds. Several have gentle lapping waves that are good for swimming, while others have big breakers suitable for surfing. Many of the beaches are uninhabited, but some have small communities. Mango, coconut, papaya and banana plantations line the highway, while the green peaks of the Sierra Madre del Sur form a lush backdrop inland.

Beaches

At the mouth of the Río Coahuayana on the Michoacán–Colima border, **Boca de Apiza** is a mangrove-lined beach with many competing seafood *enramadas*; turn off Hwy 200 at the town of Coahuayana. Kilometer markers begin counting down from Km 231 at the state border.

Twenty kilometers south, after the highway meets the coast, **San Juan de Alima** (Km 209) is popular with surfers and has many beachfront restaurants and several modern hotels.

A short distance down the coast, **Las Brisas** (Km 207) is another beachside community with places to stay. Still further along, **Playa La Ticla** (Km 183) is another surfing beach with beachfront *cabañas* for rent.

The next stop is **Faro de Bucerías** (Km 173), known for its clear, pale-blue waters, yellow sand and rocky islands. It's a good spot for camping, swimming and snorkeling, and the local Nahua community prepares fresh seafood.

Further along, white-sand **Playa Maruata** (Km 150) is certainly one of Michoacán's most beautiful beaches, with clear turquoise waters. This is the principal Mexican beach where black sea turtles lay their eggs; these and other species of sea turtles are set free here each year by conservation programs. Camping and discreet nude bathing are possible, and services include rustic *cabañas* and some *palapas* serving fresh seafood.

Further south, **Pichilinguillo** (Km 95) is in a small bay that's good for swimming. Further still are beautiful unsigned **Barra de Nexpa** (Km 56), popular with surfers; **Caleta de Campos** (Km 50), on a lovely little bay; **La Soledad** (Solitude), a very beautiful, tranquil little beach; and **Las Peñas**, another good surfing beach. **Playa Azul**, 24km northwest of Lázaro Cárdenas, is another laid-back beach community that is easy to visit and has surfable waves.

Barra de Nexpa

☎ 753 / pop 50

At Km 55.5, just north of Puente Nexpa bridge and 1km from the highway down a cobbled road, lies the small community of Nexpa. The salt-and-pepper bar of sand, and a good number of healthy waves (which build up and curl sharply in the mornings) are all that's necessary to bring in surfers from around the world. Rustic *cabañas*, good campsites and some decent restaurants add comfort to the mix, and the very laid-back feel completes the recipe for a peaceful stay.

Pablo's Palapa, near Chichos restaurant, repairs and rents out surfboards ($10 per day). There's a larger surf shop in the nearby service town of Caleta de Campos (see p482); a taxi will take you there for about $3.25.

SLEEPING & EATING

Rio Nexpa Rooms (☎ 753-531-52-55; www.surf-mexico.com/sites/nexpa; Caleta de Campos; r $30; P) This beautifully crafted southeast Asian–style *palapa*, about 200m inland along the river, has four comfortable rooms with three full-sized beds and a loft. There's a shared kitchen, a lagoonside garden area and a tranquil communal sitting room.

Gilberto's Cabañas (cabañas per person $10, camp/RV sites $3/9; P) Gilberto's offers a variety of *cabañas*, some more rustic than others, some with kitchen and most with hammocks. There's a communal kitchen and shower block for campers/RVs, and Gilberto offers taxi service to Caleta. Look for Gilberto's sign on the right side as you enter town.

Restaurant Chicho (cabañas $14-23, mains $3-10) has good food, good views and basic *cabañas* for rent. It's just south of the well-signed and always crowded **La Isla Restaurant** (r $11-$20, mains $3-12). Both are within eyeshot of the store at Gilberto's Cabañas. Gringos gather at La Isla in the morning for the serve-yourself coffee. There's also a casual book exchange and taxi service available.

Caleta de Campos
☎ 753 / pop 2000

A friendly little town on a bluff overlooking an azure bay, Caleta (Km 50) is a quiet place, but as it's a regional service center it has a pair of good, clean hotels and several friendly, satisfying places to eat. Caleta's paved main drag has all the essentials, including a *caseta*, late-night *taquerías* (taco stalls) and torta shops, a pharmacy and several grocery stores. Just off the main drag, near Hotel Yuritzi, is the area's best surf shop, **Surf y Espuma** (☎ 531-52-55; surfboard rental per day $9), which sells and rents out gear. The southern side of the bluff has perfect waves for novice surfers.

Hotel Yuritzi (☎ 531-53-53; www.hotelyuritzi.com; Corregidora 10; s $35-45, d $40-55, tr $45-60; P ✗ ☎) is modern, well maintained and comfortable, and is preferred by business travelers and families.

Hotel Los Arcos (☎ 531-50-38; s $25, d $30-35, with air-con & hot water $35; P ✗), toward the ocean at the end of the main drag, is a bit run-down, but the owners are friendly and the bird's-eye view of the Bahía de Bufadero's blowhole is stunning.

Hourly buses depart Caleta for Lázaro Cárdenas ($3.50, 1½ hours) from 5am to 7pm. A taxi between Caleta de Campos and Barra de Nexpa costs $3.50.

Playa Azul
☎ 753 / pop 3500

Playa Azul is a sleepy, dusty, little beach resort backed by lagoons that are fed by tributaries of the Río Balsas. It's usually quiet, with a negligible trickle of foreign travelers enjoying the long beach and surfable waves. A strong undertow, however, makes swimming touch and go; swimming is better (when it's not mosquito season) at Laguna Pichi, a couple of kilometers east along the beach, where boat trips take visitors to view the plants, birds and other animals that inhabit the surrounding mangrove forest.

You can string up a hammock at most of the beachfront *enramadas;* otherwise there are a couple of reasonable hotels, all with private bathrooms, in town.

Hotel María Teresa (☎ 536-00-05; Independencia 626; s $42-47, d $57-63; ✗ ☎) The 42 large and comfortable balconied rooms here are fresh and up-to-date. A poolside *palapa* restaurant-bar comes with an attractive patio area. Look for this place two blocks north of the plaza.

Hotel María Isabel (☎ 536-00-16; Madero s/n; d $25-40; P ✗ ☎) On the far (east) side of the plaza and a bit worn around the edges, this hotel has impeccably clean and very peaceful rooms.

Hotel Playa Azul (☎ 536-00-24/91; Carranza s/n; RV sites $15, r with/without air-con & TV $72/40; P ✗ ☎) The upmarket, 73-room Playa Azul has a small trailer park and enjoyable rooms around a garden courtyard with an inviting pool. The poolside Las Gaviotas restaurant/bar, open from 7:30am to 10:30pm, is a good bet for anything from pizza to *pozole* (mains range from $7 to $15).

Locals recommend two small family restaurants, Restaurant Galdy and Restaurant Familiar Martita, both on the market street near Madero, around the corner from Hotel Playa Azul. Both serve freshly squeezed juices and cheap good grub (such as the *comida corrida* for $3.25).

Combis run every 10 minutes from 5am to 9pm between Playa Azul and Lázaro Cárdenas ($1.25, 30 minutes, 24km). Taxis between Playa Azul and Lázaro Cárdenas cost around $10.

LÁZARO CÁRDENAS
☎ 753 / pop 78,000

As an industrial city, Lázaro has nothing of real interest for travelers – but because it's the terminus of several bus routes, travelers do pass through. Reasons to stop here include changing buses, stocking up on provisions, and heading 24km northwest to Playa Azul (see left). If you must spend the night here, you'll find several adequate hotels near the bus stations.

Sleeping & Eating
Hotel Reyna Pio (☎ 532-06-20; Corregidora 78; s/d $20/25; ✗) A good, friendly budget hotel

with clean, spacious rooms. It's located on the corner of Av 8 de Mayo, a block west of Av Lázaro Cárdenas and near the bus terminals.

Hotel Viña del Mar (☎ 532-04-15; Javier Mina 352; s/d $22/25; 🅿 🖭) Has a leafy, inviting courtyard with pool, but most rooms (all of which are darkish) are not around it. Still, they're good-sized and have TVs. It's half a block west of Av Lázaro Cárdenas.

Hotel Casablanca (☎ 537-34-80; Nicolás Bravo 475; s/d $36/48; 🅿 🖭 🖭 🖭) Caters to business travelers with TVs, pool (with Jacuzzi) and secure parking. The 56 modern rooms with balconies and wide windows overlook the city or inland mountains. Look for this high-rise a block east of Av Lázaro Cárdenas.

Many cheap restaurants cluster around the bus terminals. Locals recommend **Restaurant El Tejado** (Lázaro Cárdenas s/n; mains $4.50-10), between Corregidora and Javier Mina, for meats, seafood, six styles of frogs' legs and four pages of drinks. If you're tired of Mexican, **Restaurant Kame** (☎ 537-26-60; lunch $4.50), one block south of Estrella Blanca bus terminal, is an authentic Japanese eatery with a variety of delicious, multicourse set meals.

Getting There & Away

Lázaro has four bus terminals, all within a few blocks of each other. **Galeana** (☎ 532-02-62) and **Parhikuni** (☎ 532-30-06), with services northwest to Manzanillo and inland to Uruapan and Morelia, share a **terminal** (Lázaro Cárdenas 1810). Opposite, on the corner of Constitución de 1814, Autobuses de Jalisco, La Línea, Vía 2000 and Sur de Jalisco share another **terminal** (☎ 537-18-50; Lázaro Cárdenas 1791) and serve the same destinations as Galeana and Parhikuni, plus Colima, Guadalajara and Mexico City.

The **Estrella Blanca terminal** (☎ 532-11-71; Francisco Villa 65), two blocks west behind the Galeana terminal, is also home base for Cuauhtémoc and Elite. From here, buses head southeast to Zihuatanejo and Acapulco; up the coast to Manzanillo, Mazatlán and Tijuana; and inland to Uruapan, Morelia and Mexico City. The **Estrella de Oro terminal** (☎ 532-02-75; Corregidora 318) is one block southwest of Estrella Blanca, and serves Acapulco, Cuernavaca, Mexico City and Zihuatanejo.

Daily buses from Lázaro Cárdenas:

Destination	Price	Duration	Frequency
Acapulco	$19	6-7hr	12 1st-class Estrella Blanca
	$16	6-7hr	hourly 2nd-class Estrella Blanca
	$19	6-7hr	3 1st-class Estrella de Oro
	$15	6-7hr	11 2nd-class Estrella de Oro
Caleta de Campos	$4.50	1½hr	10 2nd-class Galeana
	$4.50	1½hr	4 2nd-class Sur de Jalisco
Colima	$17	4-6½hr	Same Autobuses de Jalisco buses as to Guadalajara
Guadalajara	$38	9-11hr	5 1st-class Autobuses de Jalisco
	$28	9-11hr	4 2nd-class Sur de Jalisco
Manzanillo	$26	6-7hr	2nd-class Autobuses de Jalisco at 2:30pm & 5:30pm
	$23	7hr	4 1st-class Elite
	$17.50	6-7hr	4 2nd-class Galeana
Mexico City	$44		2 1st-class Estrella de Oro
(Terminal Sur)	$45		5 1st-class Futura
	$45	12hr	5 1st-class Vía Plus
Morelia	$29	4-8hr	5 1st-class Futura
	$36	4-8hr	1 executive Parhikuni 'Plus'
	$30		14 2nd-class Parhikuni 'Plus'
Puerto Vallarta	$34	12hr	4 1st-class Elite
Uruapan	$12-17	3-6hr	Same buses as to Morelia
Zihuatanejo	$5-7	2-3hr	Same buses as to Acapulco

Combis to Playa Azul via La Mira ($1.25, 30 minutes, 24km) trawl Av Lázaro Cárdenas every 10 minutes from 5am to 9pm, stopping outside the Autobuses de Jalisco terminal, opposite Galeana. A taxi between Lázaro Cárdenas and Playa Azul costs $10 to $12.

TRONCONES

☎ 755 / pop 400

Not far northwest of Zihuatanejo (p489), Troncones' coastline has several kilometers of vacation homes, B&Bs and guest inns, the majority gringo-owned. It also has some amazing surfing, good swimming and snorkeling, and offers various terrestrial activities such as bird-watching and mountain biking. Though accommodations are moderately expensive, the place is addictively relaxed and friendly.

Orientation & Information

The village of Troncones is at the end of a 3km paved road from Hwy 200, and is about 100m from the beach – but most of what you'll be interested in is along the unpaved beachfront road. The dirt road starts at a T-intersection with the road from the highway and stretches along Playa Troncones in both directions: about 2km to the south (left) it ends, while north (right) from the T, it runs some 4km past Troncones Point to reach the calmer waters of Playa Manzanillo. The road continues a short way to the small village of Majahua, from which another dirt road (rough in the wet season) leads to Hwy 200 near Km 32.

The Inn at Manzanillo Bay (see opposite) provides Internet access at $1 for the first minute, and $0.20 for each additional minute. By the time you read this, wireless access (BYO laptop) should be available for a reasonable fee at the Tropic of Cancer Beach Club (see right). For good online prearrival information, check www.troncones.com.mx.

Activities
SURFING

Troncones and surrounds have several world-class surf spots. The beach breaks here can be excellent in summer, but the wave to chase is the left at **Troncones Point**. When it's small, the takeoff is right over the rocks (complete with sea urchins), but when it's big, it's beautiful and beefy and rolls halfway across the bay.

The surf shop at the Inn at Manzanillo Bay (see opposite) rents out an excellent selection of short- and longboards (from $18 per day) as well as boogie boards ($5 per half-day). It also offers surf lessons starting at $40, can buy and sell boards and arranges guided boat trips (from $100) to many of the best local surf spots. Troncosurfo, a couple of hundred meters inland from the T-intersection, also offers lessons, as well as board rentals and repairs.

OTHER ACTIVITIES

There's good **snorkeling** at Troncones Point off Playa Manzanillo, and you can rent equipment for $5 per half-day from the Inn at Manzanillo Bay (see opposite), which also rents out **mountain bikes** for about $18 per day; a good ride heads north along the beach as far as Saladita. **Costa Nativa Eco Tours** (☎ 044-755-556-36-16) leads various bicycle tours around the Troncones area for $20 per person (mountain bike and all equipment included). Other activities include **fishing**, **hiking**, **bird-watching** and **sea-turtle spotting**; many hoteliers can help arrange these activities.

Sleeping

Reservations are necessary almost everywhere in Troncones during the high season (November through April); several places also require multiple-night stays. Prices otherwise can be as much as 50% lower than those listed here, but be aware that many business owners aren't around in the low season, so places close down or are run by temporary staff. Two Troncones residents who between them manage several properties are Tina Morse at **Casa Ki** (☎ 553-28-15; casaki@yahoo.com), by the T-intersection, and Anita LaPointe at the **Tropic of Cancer Beach Club** (☎ 553-28-00; casacanela@yahoo.com), just south of Casa Ki. With some advance notice they can usually set you up with anything from a budget-priced room to a luxurious house.

BUDGET

The first listing here is not far south of the T-intersection; the second and third are a bit inland from the T.

Quinta d'Liz (☎ 553-29-14; www.playatroncones .com; d with breakfast $30) These six simple but stylish bungalows are just off the beach and come with fans and good beds, plus use of a communal kitchen. The combination of price, facilities, location and mellow management by the surfing owner make this one of the best deals in town.

Casa de la Amistad (d with fan/air-con $24/38, q with fan $34; ✦) This place has two basic upstairs rooms with air-con and a shared bath. The two downstairs fan rooms have an OK bath and good screens, and their floors are covered with seashells and coral. A hammock area and a big fridge for guests' use increase the appeal.

Miscelánea Jasmín (r with fan/air-con $24/47) Behind the in-town *abarrotes* (grocery) shop, this place has a few OK rooms, most with tinted windows. The fan rooms are nicer, overall; some share a large balcony.

MIDRANGE & TOP END
The following accommodations are spread out along the beachfront road. Going north from the T-intersection you reach first Casa Ki, then the Delfín Sonriente, Casas Gregorio, the Inn at Manzanillo Bay and Hacienda Edén. South from the T are Puesta del Sol and Casas Canela/Canelita.

Hacienda Edén (☎ 553-28-02; www.edenmex.com; bungalows $85-95, incl breakfast r $85-110, ste $110; P 🞨) On Playa Manzanillo, 4km north of the T-intersection, this tranquil beachfront gem has lovingly decorated bungalows, rooms and air-con suites, a gourmet restaurant and a full bar. Tropical hardwoods, Talavera tiles and other touches are used everywhere to great advantage. Screenage is first-rate, including over the otherwise roofless showers attached to the bungalows.

Casa Delfín Sonriente (☎ 553-28-03; in the US ☎ 831-688-65-78; www.casadelfinsonriente.com; r $65-119; 🞨 🞨) This striking Mediterranean-style seaside villa offers a variety of very well-furnished B&B accommodations. Some have air-con available (additional $15 per day), while others are nearly open-air, with hanging beds. All units have access to the gorgeous swimming pool, communal master kitchen and art supplies galore.

Casa Ki (☎ 553-28-15; www.casa-ki.com; 2-person bungalows $95-110, house $200) A charming retreat, Ki features a thoughtfully furnished main house sleeping up to six people (one-week minimum), and three colorful free-standing bungalows (three-night minimum stay, but breakfast included) with access to a communal kitchen. It's all set on a verdant beachside property.

Casas Gregorio (in the US ☎ 425-228-24-00; www.mexonline.com/gregorio.htm; bungalows $90-99, houses $188; 🞨) At the north end of Playa Troncones, Gregorio has two spacious two-bedroom, two-bathroom houses right at the beachside. Each has a fully equipped kitchen. The two bungalows are set back a bit and share a small kitchen; each will accommodate four people, with cleverly constructed, king-sized concrete 'bunk beds.'

Casas Canela & Canelita (☎ 553-28-00; www.tronconestropic.com/canela.html; r/house $40/125) Across the road from the beach, this two-building garden property is an affordable, comfortable option. Casa Canela, the house in front, sleeps six, and has a large kitchen and hammock-strewn front porch. Casa Canelita is a much more modest duplex with rooms that can be rented individually and that share a kitchen and terrace. All options require a three-night stay in the high season.

Inn at Manzanillo Bay (☎ 553-28-84; www.manzanillobay.com; Playa Manzanillo; bungalows $108; P 🞨 🞨) Almost 4km north of the main T-intersection, this inn has 10 well-appointed, thatched-roof bungalows with room safes, good mattresses, ceiling fans, mosquito nets and be-hammocked terraces. Other pluses are a popular restaurant, a full surf shop and easy access to the primo break at Troncones Point.

La Puesta del Sol (☎ 557-05-03, in the US ☎ 818-553-33-11; www.troncones.com.mx/puestadelsol; r $40-65, ste $95, penthouse $175) This attractive four-room, three-story *palapa* offers a simple 'surfers' room' right up to a superluxurious penthouse apartment.

Eating & Drinking
Be prepared to pay $2 per beer in most places.

Huachinango's (mains $8-10; 🞨 restaurant noon-10pm, bar till last person leaves, Wed-Mon) Just 100m south of the T-intersection, Huachinango's serves good seafood, pasta, shrimp and octopus, all with a heaping helping of ocean view. The specialty here is *huachinango sarandeado* (red snapper marinated in red salsa and then charcoal-grilled).

La Cocina del Sol (☎ 553-28-02; mains $4-9) The renowned chef here at Hacienda Edén's restaurant (see left), Christian, turns out some sublime dishes, wielding goat cheese, arugula and *jamón serrano* (cured Spanish-style ham) with equal dexterity. The kitchen is open for all meals (one dinner seating only, at 6:30pm – reservations recommended); on Sunday it puts on a rib barbecue.

Da Tiziano (☎ 559-28-63; mains $9-13; 🞨 5-10pm Wed-Mon) Folks in Troncones are excited about this authentically Italian place (run by authentic Italians), found a couple of hundred meters inland from the T-intersection. They give it high marks for its bruschetta, salads, and handmade pastas and pizzas baked in the wood-fired oven.

Inn at Manzanillo Bay (☎ 553-28-84; mains $7.50-13) At the Inn's (see p485) restaurant you can choose from Mexican dishes, American favorites (think cheeseburgers and hickory-smoked pork ribs) and such fusions as 'Thai-style' deep-fried shrimp tacos or a seared ahi tuna sandwich with wasabi mayonnaise.

Café Sol (breakfast $2.50-3.75, sandwiches $3.75-5.50; ☺ 8am-4pm Wed-Mon) The breakfasts come with a view at this two-story, open-air place run by the peripatetic chef from La Cocina del Sol. It's a short way north of the T-intersection and serves great egg dishes, homemade bread, smoothies, good espresso drinks and gelato, plus sandwiches; at night it morphs into a taco bar. Bonus: the 2nd floor is one of the few places in Troncones where you can get cell-phone reception.

Troncones and Majahua proper each have a few taco stands where you can eat well for under $3.25, as well as some beachfront *enramadas* where $12 goes a long way. Good beachfront restaurants include Costa Brava, north of the T-intersection and Doña Nica's Enramada, just south of the T-intersection. A few steps south of Doña Nica's is the **Tropic of Cancer** (mains $4-9; ☺ Wed-Mon), a popular restaurant-bar-beach club with swimming pool.

In Majahua Marta has an ideal bayside location and makes a *machaca* (fish cake, $4) like no other in all of Mexico – it's a must for adventurous eaters.

Getting There & Away

Driving from Ixtapa or Zihuatanejo, head northwest on Hwy 200 toward Lázaro Cárdenas. Just north of Km 30 you'll see the marked turnoff for Troncones; follow this winding paved road 3km west to the beach.

Second-class buses heading northwest toward Lázaro Cárdenas or La Unión from Zihuatanejo's long-distance terminals will drop you at the turnoff for Troncones ($2, 45 minutes) if you ask. You can also catch La Unión–bound buses from the stop a couple of blocks east of Zihuatanejo's market (see Map p490).

White *colectivo* vans and *minibuses* (2nd-class buses running short routes between towns) shuttle between Hwy 200 and

Troncones roughly every half-hour or so between 7am and 9am and from 2pm to 6pm ($1, about five minutes). In a pinch you would probably have no problems hitching in either direction.

A taxi from Ixtapa or the Zihuatanejo airport to Troncones costs around $57 to $64 and takes about 45 minutes, depending on where you're headed. It's cheaper to take a *colectivo* or even a cab from the airport to Zihuatanejo (see p498) and then catch a cab to Troncones: these can be bargained down to around $30.

IXTAPA

☎ 755 / pop 5000

Ixtapa (eeks-*tah*-pah), 245km northwest of Acapulco and next door to Zihuatanejo, is a glitzy, government-planned luxury resort with some fine beaches, a marina, golf courses, discos and several fairly expensive hotels.

Ixtapa was a coconut plantation and nearby Zihuatanejo a sleepy fishing village until 1970, when Fonatur – the Mexican government's tourism-development organization – decided that the Pacific coast needed a Cancún-like resort complex. Ixtapa was selected for its proximity to the US, average temperature of 27°C, tropical vegetation and lovely beaches. Fonatur bought up the coconut plantation, laid down infrastructure and rolled out the red carpet for hotel chains and real-estate developers.

Most of the services or stores you'll need in Ixtapa are found in the outdoor *centros comerciales* (shopping centers), all within walking distance of each other and easily reached from the main drag, Blvd Ixtapa.

Information

Telecomm (☺ 9am-3pm Mon-Fri) Found behind the tourist office.

Tourist office (Sefotur; ☎ 553-19-67; ☺ 8am-8:30pm Mon-Fri, 8am-3pm Sat) This state-run office is in Plaza Los Patios, opposite the Hotel Presidente Inter-Continental.

Tourist police (☎ 553-20-08; Centro Comercial La Puerta) Close to the tourist office.

The many unofficial sidewalk kiosks offering 'tourist information' are actually touting time-share schemes. Ixtapa has banks and *casas de cambio* where you can change US dollars and traveler's checks. The town

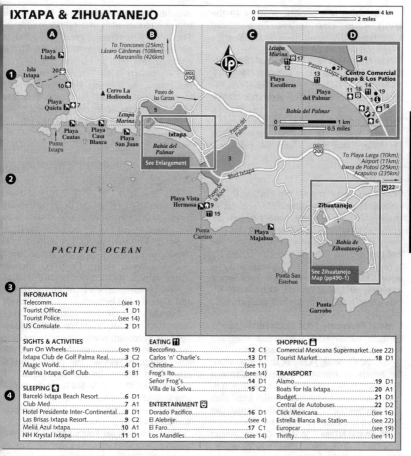

IXTAPA & ZIHUATANEJO

CENTRAL PACIFIC COAST

INFORMATION	
Telecomm	(see 1)
Tourist Office	1 D1
Tourist Police	(see 14)
US Consulate	2 D1

SIGHTS & ACTIVITIES	
Fun On Wheels	(see 19)
Ixtapa Club de Golf Palma Real	3 C2
Magic World	4 D1
Marina Ixtapa Golf Club	5 B1

SLEEPING	
Barceló Ixtapa Beach Resort	6 D1
Club Med	7 A1
Hotel Presidente Inter-Continental	8 D1
Las Brisas Ixtapa Resort	9 C2
Meliá Azul Ixtapa	10 A1
NH Krystal Ixtapa	11 D1

EATING 🍴	
Beccofino	12 C1
Carlos 'n' Charlie's	13 D1
Christine	(see 11)
Frog's Ito	(see 14)
Señor Frog's	14 D1
Villa de la Selva	15 C2

ENTERTAINMENT 🎭	
Dorado Pacífico	16 D1
El Alebrije	(see 4)
El Faro	17 C1
Los Mandiles	(see 14)

SHOPPING 🛍️	
Comercial Mexicana Supermarket	(see 22)
Tourist Market	18 D1

TRANSPORT	
Alamo	19 D1
Boats for Isla Ixtapa	20 A1
Budget	21 D1
Central de Autobuses	22 D2
Click Mexicana	(see 16)
Estrella Blanca Bus Station	(see 22)
Europcar	(see 19)
Thrifty	(see 11)

doesn't have a post office, but you can drop mail at big hotels.

Sights

BEACHES

Ixtapa's big hotels line **Playa del Palmar**, a long, broad stretch of white sand that's often overrun by parasail and jet-ski outfits. Be very careful if you swim here: the large waves crash straight down and there's a powerful undertow. The west end of this beach, just before the entrance to the lagoon, is locally called **Playa Escolleras** and is favored by surfers.

Further west, beyond the marina and Punta Ixtapa, are **Playa Quieta** and **Playa Linda**, both popular with locals. From Playa Linda's pier, frequent boats run to **Isla Ixtapa**, which is just offshore and has four beaches good for **snorkeling**; you can rent gear here for about $6 per day ($11.50 if you add a lifejacket). The island also has some seafood restaurants. The round-trip boat ride (five minutes each way, from 9am to 5pm) costs $3.

Activities

Bicycling is a breeze along a 15km *ciclopista* (bicycle path) that stretches from Playa Linda, north of Ixtapa, practically into Zihuatanejo. Mountain bikes can be rented in Ixtapa from **Fun on Wheels** (☎ 553-02-59; Centro Comercial Los Patios; ⏰ 9am-8pm) for $5/19 per hour/day.

Scuba diving is a popular pastime in the area's warm, clear waters. Both of the Zihuatanejo diving outfits (p493) take trips to several sites in the area.

The **Ixtapa Club de Golf Palma Real** (☎ 553-10-62) and the **Marina Ixtapa Golf Club** (☎ 553-14-10) both have 18-hole courses, tennis courts and swimming pools. The **yacht club** (☎ 553-11-31; Porto Ixtapa) is beside the Ixtapa Marina. **Horseback riding** is possible on Playa Linda.

Magic World (☎ 553-13-59; admission $7.50; ⏰ 10:30am-5:30pm) aquatic park has rides, waterslides, toboggans and other amusements.

Sleeping

Ixtapa's resorts are all top-end, with the cheapest running around $125 a night in the winter high season (January to Easter). Some resorts drop their rates by 25% or more at other times of year (outside of the holiday peaks). To get a better price, try arranging a package deal through a travel agent, including airfare from your home country, or check online. Otherwise, Zihuatanejo's accommodations are generally cheaper.

Hotel Presidente Inter-Continental (☎ 553-00-18, in the US 888-424-68-35; http://ixtapa.inter conti.com; Blvd Ixtapa s/n; d incl breakfast from $260; P ⊠ 🛉 🖳 🖭 🛉) One of the most popular hotels on the beach, the Presidente is 1st-class all the way, with a gym, sauna, tennis courts, five restaurants and a kids' club that teaches the little ones basic Spanish (on top of all the other activities).

NH Krystal Ixtapa (☎ 553-03-33; www.nh-hotels .com; Blvd Ixtapa s/n; d from $125; P ⊠ 🛉 🖭 🛉) Has some of the best-value rooms on the strip (all of them with ocean views), an excellent pool, one of the area's liveliest nightclubs and a highly regarded children's club, Krystalitos.

Barceló Ixtapa Beach Resort (☎ 555-20-00; www.barcelo.com; Blvd Ixtapa s/n; d all-inclusive from $232; P ⊠ 🛉 🖭 🛉) Another good family choice, the Barceló has especially fine pool and patio areas, as well as tennis courts and a gym. Its all-inclusive plan covers three meals, alcoholic beverages, gym use, tennis courts, room service and childcare.

Las Brisas Ixtapa Resort (☎ 553-21-21; www .brisas.com.mx; d from $197; P ⊠ 🛉 🖳 🖭 🛉) Enormous Brisas (423 rooms) sits alone on the small, lovely Playa Vista Hermosa, essentially laying claim to it. The main

structure's design is a bit dated, but gives all rooms a terrace with first-rate ocean views. The hotel also offers a great lobby bar, a plethora of pools and restaurants, a fitness center, a kids' club and tennis courts.

Two resorts a bit removed from central Ixtapa, do business almost exclusively through all-inclusive packages: **Club Med** (☎ 555-10-00; www.clubmed.com; Playa Quieta; d $246; ⏰ Nov 1-Sep 14), and **Meliá Azul Ixtapa** (☎ 550-00-00; www.solmelia.com; Playa Linda; d $249).

Eating

Ixtapa has plenty of restaurants in addition to those in the big hotels.

Villa de la Selva (☎ 553-03-62; Paseo de la Roca Lote D; mains $15-22; ⏰ 7pm-late) Reservations are a must at this elegant Italian-Mediterranean restaurant in the former home of Mexican president Luis Echeverría. The cliffside villa overlooks the ocean (sunsets are superb), near Las Brisas resort. Offerings include glazed salmon with couscous, duck breast, several pastas with and without shellfish, and a good wine list.

Beccofino (☎ 553-17-70; Veleros Lote 6, Ixtapa Marina Plaza; mains $16-23; ⏰ 9am-11pm) Indooroutdoor Beccofino enjoys a good reputation for delicious (if pricey) northern Italian cuisine, especially seafood and pastas. Several other good restaurants ring the marina.

Frog's Ito (☎ 553-22-82; Blvd Ixtapa s/n; sushi per piece $1.50-2.50, rolls $2-8.50) Opposite the Presidente Inter-Continental, this place serves sushi, noodle dishes and Asian salads.

Next door, **Señor Frog's** (☎ 553-22-82; Blvd Ixtapa s/n; mains $9-12.50) serves up zany antics along with familiar Mexican dishes, burgers and iguana. The same is true at **Carlos 'n' Charlie's** (☎ 553-00-85; Blvd Ixtapa s/n; mains $9-12.50).

Entertainment

All the big hotels have bars and nightclubs. Many also have discos; in the low season most of these charge less and open fewer nights.

Christine (☎ 553-04-56; Blvd Ixtapa s/n; admission up to $25) Christine has the sizzling sound and light systems you'd expect from one of the most popular discos in town.

El Alebrije (☎ 553-27-10; Paseo de las Garzas s/n; admission women/men $24/19) A fog machine, banks of computerized lights, pop, rock, house, salsa and merengue, open bar: what more do you want?

Carlos 'n' Charlie's (☎ 553-00-85; Blvd Ixtapa s/n) Things can get wild on this chain restaurant's dance floor right above the beach; on weekends it fills with hard-partying young tourists and locals.

Los Mandiles (Centro Comercial La Puerta) The upstairs bar-disco at this restaurant features a giant TV screen.

El Faro (☎ 553-10-27; Ixtapa Marina; ☺ 5pm-1am) Slow things down at this piano-bar, which is at the top of a 25m-high lighthouse – a great spot for watching the sunset.

Also deserving mention are the Sanca Bar at Barceló Ixtapa Beach Resort (opposite), where you can shake it to Latin music, and the excellent lobby bar at Las Brisas Resort (opposite).

Several of Ixtapa's big hotels hold evening 'Fiestas Mexicanas,' which typically include a Mexican buffet and open bar, entertainment (traditional dancing, mariachis and cockfighting demonstrations), door prizes and dancing; the total price is usually $35 to $42. The Barceló Ixtapa Beach Resort (opposite) holds fiestas year-round; in the high season several other hotels, including the **Dorado Pacífico** (☎ 553-20-25), also present fiestas. Reservations can be made directly or through travel agents.

Shopping
Tourist market (Blvd Ixtapa s/n; ☺ 9am-10pm) This market is packed with everything from tacky T-shirts to silver jewelry and hand-painted pottery. Shopping is much better in Zihuatanejo.

Getting There & Around
For information on getting to Zihuatanejo, the essential stop for getting to Ixtapa, see p497. Private *colectivo* vans provide transportation from the airport to Ixtapa for $9 per person, but not in the other direction. A taxi to the airport from Ixtapa costs $11 to $13.

There is no bus station within Ixtapa itself; the Central de Autobuses northwest of Zihuatanejo services both towns. Local Directo' and 'B Viejo' buses run frequently between Ixtapa and Zihuatanejo ($0.60), a 15-minute ride. They depart every 15 minutes from 5:30am to 11pm ($0.60). In Ixtapa, buses stop all along the main street, in front of all the hotels. In Zihuatanejo, buses depart from the corner of Juárez and Morelos. Buses marked 'Zihua-Ixtapa-Playa

Linda' continue through Ixtapa to Playa Linda, stopping near Playa Quieta on the way, and operate from 7am to 7pm.

Ixtapa has plenty of taxis. Always agree on the fare before climbing into the cab; between Zihuatanejo and Ixtapa it should be around $4. For prearranged service call **Radio Taxi UTAAZ** (☎ 554-33-11).

Ixtapa has several places that rent out motorbikes (at about $19 per hour, or $85 per day), including **Fun On Wheels** (☎ 553-02-59; ☺ 9am-8pm) in the Centro Comercial Los Patios. You usually need a driver's license and credit card; if you're not an experienced motorcyclist, Mexico is *not* the place to learn. See p497 for information on car rental.

ZIHUATANEJO
☎ 755 / pop 62,000
Like its sister city, Ixtapa, Zihuatanejo (see-wah-tah-*neh*-ho; also called Zihua) is quite touristy. Nevertheless, it retains an easygoing, coastal ambience and its setting on a beautiful bay (with several fine beaches) makes it a gratifying place to visit. Small-scale fishing is still an economic mainstay; if you stroll down by the pier early in the morning you can join the pelicans that greet successful fisherfolk and inspect the morning's catch. Needless to say, seafood is superb here.

Orientation
Though Zihua's suburbs are growing considerably, spreading around Bahía de Zihuatanejo and climbing the hills behind town, in the city's center everything is compressed within a few blocks. It's difficult to get lost; there are only a few streets and they're clearly marked. Ixtapa, 8km northwest, is easily reached by frequent local buses or by taxi. The airport is about 13km southeast of the city, and the long-distance bus terminals are about 2km northeast of town.

Information
EMERGENCY
Emergency (☎ 060; ☺ 24hr)
Hospital (☎ 554-36-50; Av Morelos) Near Mar Egeo.
Tourist police (☎ 554-23-55)

INTERNET ACCESS
Zihuatanejo is crawling with Internet cafés; the following places charge $1 per hour.
El Navegante Internet (Bravo 41)
Infinitum Internet (Bravo 12)

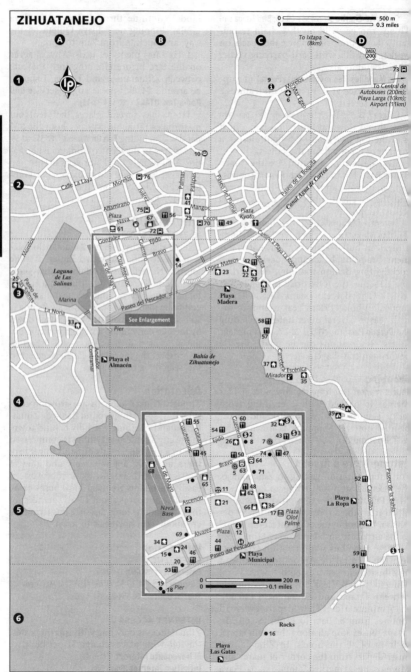

ZIHUATANEJO

To Ixtapa (8km)

To Central de Autobuses (200m); Playa Larga (10km); Airport (11km)

INFORMATION
América-Ixtamar Viajes...............**1** B5
Banamex.....................................**2** C4
Bancomer....................................**3** C4
Banorte......................................**4** C4
El Navegante Internet..................**5** B5
Hospital......................................**6** C1
Infinitum Internet........................**7** C4
Lavandería del Centro..................**8** C1
Municipal Tourist Office...............**9** C1
Post Office.................................**10** B2
Telecomm................................(see 10)
Telephone Casetas...................**11** C5
Tourist Kiosk (high season
only).....................................**12** C5
Tourist Office Branch...............**13** D5
Turismo Internacional del
Pacífico..............................**14** B3

SIGHTS & ACTIVITIES
Buceo Nautilus Divers...............**15** B5
Carlo Scuba..............................**16** C6
Museo Arqueológico de la Costa
Grande................................**17** C3
Sociedad Cooperativa José
Azueta.................................**18** B6
Sociedad de Servicios
Turísticos...........................(see 20)
Ticket Office for Boats to Playa Las
Gatas & Isla Ixtapa...............**19** B6
Whisky Water World..................**20** B6

SLEEPING
Angela's Hotel & Hostel............**21** C5
Bungalows Ley.........................**22** C3

Bungalows Pacíficos..................**23** C3
Casa de Huéspedes Elvira.........**24** B5
Hostal del Viajero....................**25** A3
Hotel Amueblados Valle...........**26** C4
Hotel Ávila..............................**27** C5
Hotel Brisas del Mar................**28** C3
Hotel Bugambilias....................**29** B2
Hotel Casa del Mar..................**30** D5
Hotel Palacios.........................**31** C3
Hotel Posada Michel.................**32** C3
Hotel Raúl Tres Marías.............**33** A3
Hotel Raúl Tres Marías Centro..**34** B5
Hotel Royal Sotavento.............**35** C4
Hotel Susy...............................**36** C5
La Casa Que Canta...................**37** C4
Posada Citlali..........................**38** C5
Trailer Park La Ropa.................**39** D4
Trailer Park Los Cabañas...........**40** D4
Zihua Inn Hotel........................**41** B2

EATING
Bad Bird Café..........................**42** C3
Banana's..................................**43** C4
Café Marina.............................**44** C5
Cafetería Nueva Zelanda...........**45** B4
Casa Elvira..............................**46** B5
Cenaduría Antelia....................**47** C4
Coconuts.................................**48** C5
Doña Licha..............................**49** C2
Il Paccolo................................**50** B5
La Gaviota...............................**51** D6
La Perla...................................**52** D5
La Sirena Gorda.......................**53** B6
Los Braseros............................**54** C4
Mariscos El Acacio...................**55** B4

Market....................................**56** B2
Puerta del Sol..........................**57** C3
Restaurant Kau-Kan.................**58** C3
Rossy's....................................**59** D5
Tamales y Atoles Any...............**60** C4

DRINKING
Café Zihuatanejo......................**61** B2
Jungle Bar...............................**62** C5

ENTERTAINMENT
Black Bull Rodeo......................**63** C5
Cine Paraíso..........................(see 1)
El Jumil................................(see 44)
Ventaneando...........................**64** C5

SHOPPING
Alberto's.................................**65** B5
Coco's Cabaña.........................**66** C5
Mercado Municipal de las
Artesanías...........................**67** B2
Mercado Turístico La Marina.....**68** B5
Pancho's...............................(see 1)

TRANSPORT
Aeroméxico.............................**69** B5
Buses to Petatlán, La Unión......**70** B2
Click Mexicana & Mexicana......**71** C5
Coacoyul Route Bus Stop (To Playa
Larga & Airport)...................**72** B2
Estrella de Oro Bus Station........**73** D1
Hertz......................................**74** C4
La Correa Route Bus Stop (To
Long-Distance Bus Stations)..**75** B2
Local Buses to Ixtapa...............**76** B2

LAUNDRY
Lavandería del Centro (554-97-91; Guerrero 17; per 3kg $4; 8am-8pm Mon-Sat, 10am-4pm Sun) Self-service is also available.

MEDICAL SERVICES
Dr Rogelio Grayeb (554-33-34, 044-755-551-33-35) provides medical assistance 24/7, speaks English and he makes house calls!

MONEY
Zihuatanejo has many banks and *casas de cambio* where you can change US dollars and traveler's checks.

Banks with ATMs:
Banamex (cnr Ejido & Guerrero)
Bancomer (cnr Juárez & Bravo; 8:30am-4pm Mon-Fri, 10am-2pm Sat)
Banorte (cnr Juárez & Ejido; 9am-4pm Mon-Fri, 10am-2pm Sat)

POST
Post office (8am-6pm Mon-Fri, 9am-1pm Sat) Located off Morelos, this post office is well signed, but still hard to find. Several other places in town also sell stamps.

TELEPHONE & FAX
Long-distance telephone and fax services are available at several *casetas*, including two on the corner of Galeana and Ascencio. Telmex card phones are all around town.
Telecomm (8am-6pm Mon-Fri, 9am-1pm Sat) Located within the post office (see left); has fax service.

TOURIST INFORMATION
Tourist kiosk (Álvarez s/n; 9am-8pm high season) Offers free information, maps and brochures in the heart of town.
Tourist office Municipal office (/fax 554-20-01; www.ixtapa-zihuatanejo.com; Zihuatanejo Pte s/n, Colonia La Deportiva; 8am-4pm Mon-Fri); Branch office (off Paseo de la Bahia; 8am-4pm Mon-Fri) The municipal office is found upstairs in the *ayuntamiento* (city hall), 2km northeast of the town center. Local buses between Ixtapa and Zihuatanejo stop out front. You'll find the branch office near the south end of Playa La Ropa.

TRAVEL AGENCIES
Various agencies provide travel services and arrange local tours.
América-Ixtamar Viajes (554-35-90; cnr Cuauhtémoc & Bravo)

Turismo Internacional del Pacífico (TIP; ☎ 554-75-10/11; cnr Juárez & Álvarez; ☺ 9am-2pm & 4-7pm Mon-Sat, 5-7pm Sun)

Dangers & Annoyances

A study published by the Mexican government's environmental agency, Profepa, cited 16 of the country's beaches as having unacceptably high levels of bacterial contamination. At the top of the list were Playas La Ropa, Las Gatas and Municipal, all on Bahía Zihuatanejo. This is the result of insufficiently treated sewage flowing into the bay. Ocean currents in winter keep the bay flushed out, but at other times of the year (particularly late summer and during periods of rain) – use discretion, and your nose), when deciding whether to swim.

Sights

MUSEO ARQUEOLÓGICO DE LA COSTA GRANDE

This small but recommended **archeology museum** (☎ 554-75-52; Plaza Olof Palme, Paseo del Pescador; admission $1; ☺ 10am-6pm Wed-Mon) houses exhibits on the history, archaeology and culture of the Guerrero coast, with Spanish captions; a free English-language brochure has translations.

BEACHES

Waves are gentle at all of Bahía de Zihuatanejo's beaches. If you want big ocean waves, head west toward Ixtapa.

Playa Municipal, in front of town, is the least appealing swimming beach on the bay. **Playa Madera** is a pleasant five-minute walk east from Playa Municipal along a concrete walkway (popular with young couples in the evening) around the rocky point.

Walk over the hill along the steep Carretera Escénica for another 15 to 20 minutes (less than 1km) from Playa Madera, past the *mirador*, and you'll reach the broad expanse of **Playa La Ropa**, bordered by palm trees and seafood restaurants. It's an enjoyable walk, with the road rising up onto cliffs that offer a fine view over the water. One of Zihua's most beautiful beaches, La Ropa is great for swimming, parasailing, waterskiing and sand-soccer. You can also rent sailboards and sailboats.

Opposite Zihuatanejo, **Playa Las Gatas** is a protected beach, crowded with sunbeds and restaurants. It's good for snorkeling (there's some coral) and as a swimming spot for children, but beware of sea urchins. Beach shacks and restaurants rent out snorkeling gear for around $6 per day.

Boats to Playa Las Gatas depart frequently from the Zihuatanejo pier, from 9am to 5pm. Buy tickets ($3 round-trip) at the booth at the foot of the pier; one-way tickets can be bought on board.

A boat goes to **Isla Ixtapa** (p487) from the Zihuatanejo pier, but only when there are eight or more passengers. It departs at 11am and leaves the island at around 4pm

---

WOULDN'T 'NO-CLOTHES BEACH' SELL BETTER?

Several place-names of the Zihuatanejo area have colorful stories behind them. 'Zihuatanejo' itself comes from the Nahuatl *Cihuatlán,* meaning 'place of women.' Depending whose version you believe, this derived from the fact that old Zihua was inhabited by a matriarchal society. Or that it was a ceremonial center which, like Isla Mujeres (p877) off the Yucatán Peninsula, was occupied solely by women. Or – least plausibly – that when the Spanish first arrived, the local menfolk stashed their women here and went off to hide. (Wouldn't it have a Spanish name, then?) In any case, the conquistadors added the diminutive suffix '-ejo,' supposedly to express their opinion of Zihua's insignificance. 'Ixtapa,' also from Nahuatl, means roughly 'covered in white,' and refers to the area's sands, or to the white guano left by seabirds on the rocky islands just offshore. Coulda been worse.

The names of beaches lining Bahía de Zihuatanejo also tell stories. Playa Madera (Wood Beach) was so dubbed after the timber that was once milled on its shore, loaded aboard ships and carried to various parts of the world; at one time there was also a shipyard here. Playa Las Gatas does not have a history involving pussycats; it's named for the gentle nurse sharks that once inhabited the waters, called 'gatas' because of their whiskers. And finally, the name of Playa La Ropa (Clothing Beach) commemorates the occasion when a Spanish galleon coming from the Philippines was wrecked and its cargo of fine silks washed ashore.

The cruise takes an hour each way ($10 round-trip).

About 10km south of Zihuatanejo, just before the airport, **Playa Larga** has big waves, beachfront restaurants and horseback riding. Nearby **Playa Manzanillo**, a secluded white-sand beach reachable by boat from Zihuatanejo, is said to offer the best snorkeling in the area. To reach Playa Larga, take a 'Coacoyul' combi ($0.60, 10 minutes) from Juárez opposite the market and get off at the turnoff to Playa Larga; another combi will take you from the turnoff to the beach.

Activities

SNORKELING & SCUBA DIVING

Snorkeling is good at Playa Las Gatas and even better at Playa Manzanillo, especially in the dry season when visibility is best. Marine life is abundant here due to a convergence of currents, and the visibility can be great – up to 35m. Migrating humpback whales pass through from December to February; manta rays can be seen all year, but you're most likely to spot them in summer, when the water is at its most clear, blue and warm. Snorkeling gear can be rented at Playa Las Gatas for around $6 per day.

Based in Playa Las Gatas, **Carlo Scuba** (☎ 554-60-03; www.carloscuba.com; Playa Las Gatas) offers a variety of PADI courses and will take you diving for $55/80 with one/two tanks.

Conveniently located in town, **Buceo Nautilus Divers** (☎ 554-91-91; www.nautilus-divers.com; Álvarez s/n; ⏰ 8am-4pm Mon-Sat) does all of the usual dives and also offers NAUI instruction and certification.

SPORTFISHING

Sportfishing is popular in Zihuatanejo. Sailfish are caught here year-round; seasonal fish include blue or black marlin (March to May), roosterfish (September to October), wahoo (October), mahimahi (November to December) and Spanish mackerel (December). Deep-sea fishing trips cost anywhere from $150 to $395, depending upon the size of the boat. Trips run up to seven hours and usually include equipment.

Two fishing outfits near Zihuatanejo's pier are **Sociedad Cooperativa José Azueta** (☎ 554-20-56; Muelle Municipal) and **Sociedad de Servicios Turísticos** (☎ 554-37-58; Paseo del Pescador 20). English is spoken at **Whisky Water World** (☎ 554-01-47; www.zihuatanejosportfishing.com; Paseo del Pescador 20).

Tours

Sailboats cruise local waters and can include snorkeling as part of the package. One is **Picante** (☎ 554-26-94, 554-82-70; www.picantecruises.com), a 23m catamaran based in Bahía de Zihuatanejo that offers a couple of different excursions. The 'Sail and Snorkel' trip ($68, 10am to 2:30pm) goes outside the bay for brief snorkeling (gear-rental $5) at Playa Manzanillo, about an hour's cruise away. The trip includes lunch, an open bar, flying from the spinnaker and a great party. The 2½-hour sunset cruise ($50, 5pm to 7:30pm) heads around the bay and out along the coast of Ixtapa. Reservations are required; private charters are also available.

Sleeping

Zihuatanejo has a good selection of reasonably priced places to stay. During the December to April high season many hotels fill up, so phone ahead to reserve a room; if you don't like what you get, you can always look for another room early the next day. The busiest times of year are Semana Santa and the week between Christmas and New Year; at these times you must reserve a room and be prepared to pony up extra pesos. Tourism is much slower and rates are often negotiable from mid-April to mid-December. Outside of peak seasons, many places will often offer 10% to 20% (negotiable) off rack rates for longer stays, if asked. The prices listed here are for the high season.

BUDGET

The budget hotels listed here are in central Zihuatanejo and have rooms with fans.

Angela's Hotel & Hostel (☎ 554-50-84; www.zihuatanejo.com.mx/angelas; Ascencio 10; dm/d $8.50/20; 🖥) Friendly, convenient and helpful, this hostel is hard to beat. Rooms are dark and crowded, but it's off a quiet street and offers a shared kitchen and Internet access ($1 per hour).

Casa de Huéspedes Elvira (☎ 554-20-61; Álvarez s/n; s $9.50, d $15-19) This decent cheapie offers eight rooms on two floors surrounding an open courtyard. Upstairs rooms are much better, with more light and privacy, but are accessible only via a rickety spiral staircase. Reservations are not taken.

Hostal del Viajero (Paseo de las Salinas 50; campsites/dm $3.75/7.50, r $9.50-11; ⊗) Just getting going at the time of research and a bit rough around the edges, this hostel showed potential. It has an agreeable garden, and other common spaces include a terrace with hammocks, a laundry area and a kitchen with drinking water. For $1.50 extra, guests can get a breakfast of fruit, bread and coffee. Shared bathrooms for the two three-bed dorms are nicer than the private ones.

Two very small, basic trailer parks run by friendly families allow camping (tent or car) just off Playa La Ropa.

Trailer Park Los Cabañas (☎ 554-47-18; campsite per person $6) Six clean spaces in the Cabañas family's backyard, with bath, showers, a laundry sink and electricity.

Trailer Park La Ropa (☎ 554-60-30; campsite per person $5) Half a block beyond Los Cabañas and with more spaces, La Ropa is certainly a bit funkier. It has shower and toilet facilities.

MIDRANGE
Central Zihuatanejo has several midrange lodgings that provide easy access to banks, restaurants and other services. Other possibilities include the Playa Madera area (a five-minute walk east from the center on quiet Eva S de López Mateos), Playa La Ropa (a bit further east) and the economical market area.

Hotel Amueblados Valle (☎ 554-20-84; luisavall@ prodigy.net.mx; Guerrero 33; 1-/2-bedroom apt $47/65) A great deal, especially for families or groups. A handful of large airy apartments come with full kitchens; some have balconies with partial mountain views. There's a wonderful sunny rooftop area; three-bedroom apartments are also available.

Hotel Raúl Tres Marías (☎ 554-21-91; r3marias noria@yahoo.com; La Noria 4; s/d $27/36) Across the lagoon footbridge, this economical, popular option comes with clean, spacious rooms. Its best features, however, are the large terraced patios that are dotted with chairs and hammocks and boast great views of the pier.

Hotel Royal Sotavento (☎ 554-20-32; www .beachresortsotavento.com; s/d incl breakfast from $58/71) Just above Playa La Ropa, at the northern end, the Sotavento is a well-maintained old favorite and has one of Zihuatanejo's most beautiful settings. Its white terraces are visible from all around the bay and offer incredible views; beds, bathrooms and screenage are all good, and the pool is large.

Bungalows Ley (☎ 554-45-63, 554-40-87; bunga lowsley@prodigy.net.mx; López Mateos s/n; 1-/2-bedroom bungalows $85/170; P ⊠) Well-kept and spacious, with unbeatable views and beach access, all only a short walk from the center. The bungalows are not fancy, but all have terraces, room safes and kitchens or kitchenettes (some are outdoors), and the biggest has a living room, dining room and two bathrooms. Great value.

Hotel Palacios (☎ /fax 554-20-55; hotelpalacios@ prodigy.net.mx; Adelita s/n; d $71-75; P ⊠ ⊒) Overlooking the east end of Playa Madera, agreeable Hotel Palacios is a family place with a swimming pool and beachfront terrace. Some rooms are on the smaller side, and not all have views, but they do all have good beds, bathrooms and screens.

Posada Citlali (☎ 554-20-43; Guerrero 4; s/d $33/43) This pleasant older posada features small rooms that are basic but well-kept, and have good ventilation and light. It has a dark, leafy central courtyard.

Hotel Raúl Tres Marías Centro (☎ 554-67-06; www.ixtapa-zihuatanejo.net/r3marias; Álvarez 52; r $64; P ⊠) Rooms at this spot are good and unpretentious, and many come with balcony. There's a popular downstairs restaurant, and in the high season breakfast is included.

Hotel Posada Michel (☎ 554-74-23; www.hotel michel-zihua.com; Ejido 14; s/d with fan $22/31, with air-con $27/36, tw with air-con $52; P ⊠) The small but quality rooms here have interesting creative touches in the bathrooms, though exterior doors and windows are on the flimsy side.

Zihua Inn Hotel (☎ 554-38-68; www.zihua-inn.com .mx; Palapas 119; r with fan/air-con $47/56; P ⊠ ⊒) Located near the market, the Zihua has four floors of light-filled, colorful, modern rooms, a decent pool with a children's section and a covered parking area.

Hotel Bugambilias (☎ 554-58-15; Mangos 28; s/d with fan $29/38, with air-con $38/47; P ⊠) The Boog has clean, bright decent-sized rooms next to the market, in a less-touristy but quite lively part of town. It's good value; balconied room 110 is the best of the lot.

Hotel Ávila (☎ 554-20-10; fax 554-20-10; Álvarez 8; r from $70; P ⊠) Fronting Playa Municipal, the Ávila has 27 spacious but forgettable rooms with cable TV – get one with a balcony overlooking the bay if you want something to remember.

Hotel Susy (☎ 554-23-39; cnr Guerrero & Álvarez; s/o $29/43; P ⊠) Just a block from Playa Municipal, this well-located place has some good-sized but unmemorable and even cheerless rooms – avoid the ground-floor ones, which are dark and musty.

TOP END

If you seek luxury and Ixtapa doesn't suit your taste, Playa La Ropa has a few stunning luxury hotels.

La Casa Que Canta (☎ 554-70-30, 800-710-93-45; www.lacasaquecanta.com; Carretera Escénica s/n; ste from $486; P ✖ ☐ ☎) Perched on the cliffs between Playas Madera and La Ropa, this award-winning luxury hotel uses gorgeous Mexican handicrafts, furniture and textiles to great effect throughout. All rooms have terraces, full sea views and amenities galore, including free minibar drinks and daily fresh fruit.

Hotel Brisas del Mar (☎ 554-21-42; www .hotelbrisasdelmar.com; López Mateos s/n; d from $175; ✖ ☐ ☎) This attractive red adobe-style hotel has a large swimming pool, a beachfront restaurant and a hilltop bar with fine views of the bay, as well as a spa with sauna and steam room and a small gym. All rooms have exquisite ocean-view terraces, safes, minibars and coffeemakers.

Bungalows Pacíficos (☎ /fax 554-21-12; bungpaci@ prodigy.net.mx; López Mateos s/n; bungalows $100) The six large bungalows here have ample (some are enormous) sea-view terraces with greenery, good bathrooms and fully equipped kitchens. The owner, a longtime Zihua resident, is a gracious and helpful hostess who speaks English, Spanish and German. Though maintenance is slipping a bit, clever construction maximizes breezes throughout all the rooms. From May to November the $70 rate makes Pacíficos a midrange option.

Hotel Casa del Mar (☎ 554-38-73; www.zihua-ca sadelmar.com; Caracolito s/n; r with fan/air-con $100/120; P ✖ ☎) This hideaway has garden and beachfront rooms, the latter with good air-con, all with OK beds and bathrooms. Crocodiles inhabit the mangrove-lined waterway bordering the property; the manager feeds them. Good thing the small pool is above ground.

Eating

Guerrero is famous for its *pozole*, found on most menus in town (especially on Thursday) and well worth a try.

Tiritas (raw fish slivers marinated with onion, green chili and vinegar, and served with soda crackers and spicy sauce) are Zihua's specialty, but you won't find them on many menus – look for them at carts near the bus stations, or request them at any beachfront *enramada*.

PASEO DEL PESCADOR

Seafood here is fresh and delicious; many popular (if touristy) fish restaurants run parallel to Playa Municipal. The following are the best options from west to east.

La Sirena Gorda (The Fat Mermaid; ☎ 554-26-87; Paseo del Pescador 90; mains $5-17; ☺ 8:30am-10:30pm Thu-Tue) Close to the pier, this place is a casual and popular open-air restaurant that's good for garlic shrimp, curry tuna and fish tacos, as well as burgers and traditional Mexican dishes.

Casa Elvira (☎ 554-20-61; Paseo del Pescador 8; mains $6-16; ☺ 1pm-10:30pm) This old hand turns out some tasty food like oysters Rockefeller, jumbo steamed shrimp and broiled octopus with garlic. Vegetarians will appreciate the soup, salad and spaghetti choices. Order the coconut custard for dessert.

Café Marina (☎ 554-24-62; Paseo Pescador; mains $5-12.50; ☺ 8am-9pm) This tiny chill place on the west side of the plaza bakes up some good pizzas, along with spaghettis and sandwiches. There's carrot cake and other goodies as well. Most tables are outside, taking advantage of the traffic-free area.

CENTRAL ZIHUATANEJO – INLAND

Many good inexpensive options lie a couple of blocks from the beach.

Doña Licha (☎ 554-39-33; Cocos 8; mains $5-8.50; ☺ 8am-6pm) Licha is known all along the coast for its down-home Mexican cooking, casual atmosphere and excellent prices. There are always several *comidas corridas* from which to choose including one delicious specialty, *pollo en cacahuete* (chicken in a peanut sauce); all come with rice, beans and handmade tortillas. Breakfasts are huge.

Tamales y Atoles Any (☎ 554-73-73; Guerrero 38; mains $5-8.50) This superfriendly place serves some of the most consciously traditional Mexican cuisine in town under its big *palapa* roof, and it's excellent. For something different, try the *caldo de mi patrón* (soup with chicken liver, feet and gizzard; literally translates to 'my boss's soup'), pineapple *tamales* or the squash blossoms with cheese; less-exotic dishes are easy to find on the bilingual menu. The several varieties of *atole* (a sweet, hot drink thickened with corn flour and flavored with chocolate, cinnamon or various fruits) are worth sampling as well.

Cenaduría Antelia (☎ 554-30-91; Bravo 14; meals under $3; ⏰ 9am-2:30pm & 6pm-midnight) Antelia's popular and friendly eatery has been dishing out tasty *antojitos mexicanos* (traditional Mexican snacks) and desserts since 1975. Tuck into a *tamal de chile verde* or a bursting bowl of daily *pozole*, and top it off with *calabaza con leche* (squash in milk) for dessert.

Cafetería Nueva Zelanda (☎ 554-23-40; Cuauhtémoc 23-30; mains $3-5) Step back in time at this spotless diner, where you can order a banana split or chocolate malt with your shrimp taco and chicken fajitas. Everything is available *para llevar* (to go), it's a great place for breakfast, and you can get a decent cappuccino anytime. There are entrances on both Cuauhtémoc and Galeana.

Los Braseros (☎ 554-87-36; Ejido 21; mains $3-10; ⏰ 9am-1am) This open-fronted eatery specializes in grilled and skewered meat and veggie combinations and is located in a festive, hangerlike space. Choose from 30 combinations, or go for seafood, chicken *mole*, crepes or a plateful of $0.40 tacos.

Mariscos El Acacio (Galeana 21; mains $4-12; ⏰ 11am-8pm Mon-Sat) A simple little seafood eatery offering authentic *tiritas*, shrimp cocktails and fried fish, among other tasty treats. Prices are unbeatable and the shady sidewalk tables are fine. It's open on Sundays in the high season.

Il Paccolo (☎ 559-08-38; Bravo 38; mains $6-10.50; ⏰ 4pm-midnight) Aching for Italian? This is the place to come. Order delicious pizzas, pastas, meats and seafood dishes, and consider the caramel crepe for dessert. The atmosphere is dark and low-key, and the bar is friendly.

Banana's (☎ 554-47-21; Bravo 9; mains $5-7; ⏰ 8am-4pm Mon-Sat, 8am-1pm Sun) This airy, small restaurant offers a pretty fair selection of Mexican dishes, Western breakfasts and tasty *licuados* (shakes made with milk, fruit and sugar; yogurt optional).

A hearty inexpensive breakfast or lunch is also available in the **market** (Juárez; ⏰ 7am-6pm), between Nava and González. The enormous Comercial Mexicana supermarket is behind the Central de Autobuses terminal.

AROUND THE BAY

La Casa Que Canta (☎ 554-70-30; Carretera Escénica s/n; mains $14-27; ⏰ 6:30-10:30pm) Both the views and food are fab at this intimate, multilevel, open-air restaurant inside the hotel. Dishes range from Asian fusion to Mexican specialties, and standards like lobster and rack of lamb. Reservations are required, as is 'casual elegant' attire.

Coconuts (☎ 554-79-80; Ramírez 1; mains $11-22; ⏰ noon-11pm) For a romantic dinner this upscale place is hard to beat. Fairy lights fill the outdoor courtyard, service is attentive and dishes include garlic snapper, leg of duck, *chiles rellenos* (stuffed chilies), vegetable tart and herb chicken.

Restaurant Kau-Kan (☎ 554-84-46; Carretera Escénica 7; mains $14-29; ⏰ 5pm-midnight) High on the cliffs, this renowned gourmet restaurant enjoys stellar views. Making a selection is exhausting when faced with choices like stingray in black butter sauce, marinated abalone or grilled lamb chops with couscous.

Bad Bird Café (López Mateos s/n; breakfast $3.75-5; ⏰ 8am-1pm Mon-Sat) Small and slightly discombobulated, the Bad Bird turns out very good breakfasts: waffles, egg dishes, fruit and homemade yogurt, complemented by good imported coffee and free Internet access. All profits go to support a local free clinic, and the namesake macaw is a real cutup.

Puerta del Sol (☎ 554-83-42; Carretera Escénica s/n; mains $7.50-18; ⏰ 5pm-midnight) Reservations are recommended in the high season at this romantic restaurant that hangs on the cliffs between Playas Madera and La Ropa. Spectacular bay and sunset views accompany the varied international menu, which features a lot of flambés. Ever seen a flaming saltimbocca?

On Playa La Ropa, **Rossy's** (☎ 554-40-04; mains $7-12; ⏰ 9am-9pm), **La Perla** (☎ 554-27-00; Caracolito; mains $7.50-15) and **La Gaviota** (☎ 554-38-16; mains $7.50-19; ⏰ noon-9pm) are all good seafood restaurants. Playa Las Gatas also has several restaurants offering fresh seafood.

Drinking

Jungle Bar (cnr Ascencio & Ramírez; ⏰ 7pm-2am) Bob your head to the kick-back bass pulsing at this streetside bar, which has gregarious, English-speaking staff and cheap drinks. It's a good place to meet locals and other travelers and to get the lowdown on town, though in the off-season its hours can be erratic.

Hotel Royal Sotavento (☎ 554-20-32; Playa La Ropa; ✹ 3-11pm, happy hour 6-8pm) Tucked into the hillside over Playa La Ropa, the Sotavento is a great spot to watch the sunset. Its relaxed bar affords a magnificent view over the whole bay.

Café Zihuatanejo (Cuauhtémoc 48; coffees under US$2; ✹ 8am-7pm Mon-Sat) This tiny place brews up espressos and cappuccinos made from locally grown organic coffee beans; it also sells whole beans by the kilo. To find it look for the potted palms and sidewalk tables.

Entertainment

For big-time nightlife, head to Ixtapa (see p488); Zihuatanejo is all about being mellow.

Black Bull Rodeo (☎ 554-11-29; cnr Bravo & Guerrero; ✹ from 9pm) Zihuatanejo's only real discotheque, this corner joint claims to have the best *norteño* band in town. There's also *cumbia*, merengue, salsa, electronica and reggae music on offer.

Ventaneando (☎ 554-39-30; Guerrero 24; ✹ 8pm-4am) Across the street from Black Bull Rodeo, this stuffy upstairs bar is a popular spot that attracts karaoke-loving crowds. It may not meet fire codes, however.

Cine Paraíso (☎ 554-23-18; Cuauhtémoc; admission $2.25) Shows two films nightly, usually in English with Spanish subtitles. It's found near Bravo.

Shopping

Zihua offers abundant Mexican handicrafts, including ceramics, *típica* (characteristic of the region) clothing, leatherwork, Taxco silver, wood carvings and masks from around the state of Guerrero.

El Jumil (☎ 554-61-91; Paseo del Pescador 9; ✹ 9am-2pm & 5-9pm Mon-Sat) This shop specializes in *guerrerense* masks. Guerrero is known for its variety of masks, and El Jumil stocks museum-quality examples. Many of these start at around $15, but there are also cheaper but delightful coconut-shell masks.

Coco's Cabaña (☎ 554-25-18; cnr Guerrero & Álvarez) Coco's stocks an impressive selection of handicrafts from all over Mexico.

Mercado Turístico La Marina (Calle 5 de Mayo; ✹ 8am-9pm) Has many stalls selling clothes, bags and knickknacks.

Mercado Municipal de las Artesanías (González; ✹ 9am-8pm) Similar to La Marina, but smaller. It's found near Juárez.

A few shops along Cuauhtémoc sell Taxco silver. **Alberto's** (☎ 554-21-61; Cuauhtémoc 12 & 15; ✹ 9am-10pm Mon-Sat, 10am-3pm Sun) and **Pancho's** (☎ 554-52-30; Cuauhtémoc 11; ✹ 9am-9pm Mon-Sat) have the best selection of quality pieces.

Getting There & Away

AIR

The **Ixtapa/Zihuatanejo international airport** (☎ 554-20-70) is 13km southeast of Zihuatanejo, a couple of kilometers off Hwy 200 heading toward Acapulco.

Carriers servicing the airport:

Aeroméxico Airport (☎ 554-22-37, 554-26-34); Zihuatanejo (☎ 554-20-18; Álvarez 34) Service to Mexico City, with many onward connections.

Alaska Airlines (☎ 554-84-57, 001-800-252-75-22) Service to Los Angeles and San Francisco.

American (☎ 800-904-60-00) Service to Dallas.

America West (☎ 800-235-92-92) Service to Phoenix and Las Vegas.

Continental (☎ 554-42-19) Service to Houston and Minneapolis.

Click Mexicana & Mexicana Airport (☎ 554-22-27); Zihuatanejo (☎ 554-22-08; Guerrero 22); Ixtapa (☎ 553-22-09; Dorado Pacífico, Blvd Ixtapa) Service to Mexico City.

Northwest (☎ 800-907-47-00) Service to Houston and Los Angeles.

BUS

Both long-distance bus terminals are on Hwy 200 about 2km northeast of the town center (toward the airport): the **Estrella Blanca terminal** (Central de Autobuses; ☎ 554-34-76/77) is a couple of hundred meters further from the center than the smaller **Estrella de Oro terminal** (☎ 554-21-75). See the boxed text on p76 for daily departures.

Manzanillo-bound buses continue to Puerto Vallarta ($50, 14 hours, 718km) and Mazatlán ($72, 24 hours, 1177km).

CAR & MOTORCYCLE

There are several car rental companies in Ixtapa and Zihuatanejo:

Alamo Airport (☎ 554-84-29); Ixtapa (☎ 553-02-06; Centro Comercial Los Patios)

Budget Airport (☎ 554-48-37); Ixtapa (☎ 553-03-97; Centro Comercial Ambiente, Blvd Ixtapa)

Europcar (☎ 553-10-32; Centro Comercial Los Patios, Ixtapa)

Hertz Airport (☎ 554-29-52); Zihuatanejo (☎ 554-22-55; Bravo 29)

Thrifty Airport (☎ 553-70-20); Ixtapa (☎ 553-30-19; NH Krystal Ixtapa, Blvd Ixtapa)

ZIHUATANEJO BUS SCHEDULE

Destination	Price	Duration	Frequency
Acapulco	$11.50	4hr	hourly 1st-class Estrella Blanca 5am-7:30pm
	$8.50	4hr	hourly 2nd-class Estrella Blanca
	$11.50	4hr	3 1st-class Estrella de Oro
	$8.50	4hr	13 2nd-class Estrella de Oro 5:30am-5pm
Lázaro Cárdenas	$6-8	1½hr	hourly 1st-class Estrella Blanca 5am-7:30pm
	$5	2hr	hourly 2nd-class Estrella Blanca 9am-10pm
	$4.50	2hr	11 2nd-class Estrella de Oro
Manzanillo	$30	8hr	3 1st-class Estrella Blanca at 10am, 10:50am, 8pm
Mexico City			
(Terminal Norte)	$42	9-10hr	2 1st-class Estrella Blanca at 6:45pm, 8pm
Mexico City	$50	8-9hr	1 deluxe Estrella Blanca 10:30pm
(Terminal Sur)	$42	8-9hr	5 1st-class Estrella Blanca
	$50	8-9hr	2 deluxe Estrella de Oro 10pm & 10:55pm
	$38	8-9hr	9 1st-class Estrella de Oro
Morelia	$32	5hr	6 deluxe Estrella de Oro
Puerto Escondido	$24	12hr	1 1st-class Estrella Blanca 7:20pm
Uruapan	$23	4hr	2 deluxe Estrella de Oro

If you're heading into the Michoacán highlands (to Uruapan or Pátzcuaro, for example) the scenic toll road Hwy 37D will save you hours (and cost you about $19 in tolls). Gas up before you leave town; there's a long Pemex-less stretch of road before Nueva Italia.

Getting Around
TO/FROM THE AIRPORT
The cheapest way to get to the airport is via a public 'Aeropuerto' *colectivo* ($0.65) departing from Juárez near González between 6:20am and 10pm. Private *colectivo* vans provide transportation from the airport to Ixtapa or Zihua ($9 per person), but they don't offer service to the airport. Taxis from Zihua to the airport cost $8.

BUS
For details on buses to Ixtapa, see p489.

The 'Correa' route goes to the Central de Autobuses from 5:30am to 9:30pm ($0.40, 10 minutes). Catch it on Juárez at the corner of Nava.

'Playa La Ropa' buses go south on Juárez and out to Playa La Ropa every half-hour from 7am to 8pm ($0.70).

'Coacoyul' *colectivos* heading toward Playa Larga depart from Juárez near the corner of González, every five minutes from 5am to 10pm ($0.60).

TAXI
Cabs are plentiful in Zihuatanejo. Always agree on the fare before getting in. Approximate sample fares (from central Zihua) include: $3.75 to Ixtapa, $2.50 to Playa La Ropa, $5 to Playa Larga and $1.50 to the Central de Autobuses. If you can't hail a taxi streetside, ring **Radio Taxi UTAAZ** (☎ 554-33-11).

SOUTH OF IXTAPA & ZIHUATANEJO
Barra de Potosí
☎ 755 / pop 400
A 40-minute drive southeast of Zihuatanejo, lovely Barra de Potosí has an endless fine-sand beach and a large lagoon brimming with bird life (bring repellent; it brims with other flying things, too). You can swim, take boat trips, rent a canoe and paddle around the estuary or go horseback riding or hiking on local trails. Seafood *enramadas* line the beach; the first, La Condesa, is one of the best. Try the *pescado a la talla* (broiled fish fillets) or *tiritas*, both local specialties, and don't pass up the savory handmade tortillas. Tendejón Lupita is a small grocery store at the edge of town as you enter.

During the low season (May to October), rates at the following places drop by between 20% and 40%.

Casa del Encanto (☎ 044-755-100-14-46; www .casadelencanto.com; d incl breakfast $80) is a knockout

B&B three blocks inland from Tendejón Lupita. Private yet open-air rooms blend interior with exterior to keep things as cool and relaxed as possible, aided by numerous hammocks and fountains. The six spacious rooms have good bathrooms and super-comfy beds. A separate bungalow (with full kitchen) holding up to four should be ready by the time you read this.

Bernie's Bed & Breakfast (☎ 044-755-556-63-33; www.zihuatanejo.net/playacalli; Playa Calli; d incl breakfast $110; ⊠) is a few kilometers toward Zihua from town. Bernie's four first-rate rooms are set back a bit in a well-constructed adobe building. The swimming pool is only a few steps from the beach, though. All rooms face the surf and have king-sized beds and ceiling fans. Bernie speaks excellent English, German, Spanish and French, and exudes a tranquility that settles over the place. Tips are included in the rates.

To reach the village from Zihuatanejo, head southeast on Hwy 200 toward Acapulco; turn off at the town of Los Achotes, 25km from Zihua, and drive another 9km. Any bus heading to Petatlán (they depart frequently from both of Zihua's main terminals, and from the stop a couple of blocks east of Zihua's market; see the map, p490) will drop you at the turnoff. Tell the driver you're going to Barra de Potosí; you'll be let off where you can catch a *camioneta* (pickup truck) going the rest of the way. The trip takes about an hour and a half, and the total cost is about $2.50 if you go by bus; a taxi from Zihua costs $35/45 one-way/round-trip (negotiable).

La Barrita
☎ 758 / pop 100
La Barrita (Km 187) is a shell-sized village on an attractive, rocky beach an hour southeast of Zihua (off Hwy 200). Not many tourists stop at this village, but surfers may want to check the beach breaks here and 3km north at **Loma Bonita**. Several restaurants have very basic rooms for rent, the best probably being those at **Restaurant Las Peñitas** (d/q $9.50/15). Second-class buses heading south from Zihua or north from Acapulco will drop you at La Barrita.

One of the more dramatic stretches of highway in Guerrero starts about 4km south of La Barrita; the road runs along clifftops above beaches and crashing surf.

Several roadside restaurants offer opportunities to enjoy the view.

PIE DE LA CUESTA
☎ 744 / pop 200
Ten kilometers northwest of Acapulco, Pie de la Cuesta is a narrow 2km strip of land bordered by a wide ocean beach, Playa Pie de la Cuesta, on one side and by the large, freshwater Laguna de Coyuca on the other (where Sylvester Stallone filmed *Rambo II*). It's quieter, more rustic, closer to nature and much more peaceful than neighboring Acapulco. The lagoon, three times as large as Bahía de Acapulco, contains a few islands, including Pájaros, a bird sanctuary.

Pie de la Cuesta is a great place to watch the sun set; it also has many oceanfront restaurants specializing in seafood, but there's no nightlife to speak of.

The one main road has two names: Av de la Fuerza Aérea Mexicana and Calzada Pie de la Cuesta. **Netxcom** (per hr $1; ⏲ 9am-10pm), on the main road, has a fast Internet connection and will let you plug in a laptop.

Activities
Swimming in the surf here can be dangerous due to a riptide and the shape of the waves; each year a number of people drown. The lagoon is better for swimming. Several clubs, including **Club de Ski Chuy** (☎ 460-11-04; Calzada Pie de la Cuesta 74), will take you waterskiing on the lagoon ($47 per hour). Wakeboarding is another possibility; try **Club Náutico Cadena Ski** (☎ 460-22-83; cadenax@yahoo.com; Calzada Pie de la Cuesta s/n). **Boat trips** on the lagoon give a glimpse of its attractions; at the time of research, Coyuca 2000 restaurant (see p501) was set to offer two-hour tours ($40 per person, including meal and drinks) looking at bird habitats, flora of the region, fishermen's homes and the like, finishing with a meal and drinks at the restaurant. Or head down to the boat launch along the southeast end of the lagoon and you'll be greeted by independent captains ready to take you for a tour. Finally, **horseback riding** on the beach runs around $15 an hour.

Sleeping
You can easily check out the 15 or so hotels that line the 2km stretch of road shown on the map.

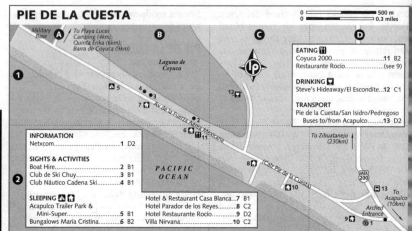

PIE DE LA CUESTA

0 ——— 500 m
0 ——— 0.3 miles

EATING 🍴
Coyuca 2000...............................**11** B2
Restaurante Rocío......................(see 9)

DRINKING 🍸
Steve's Hideaway/El Escondite...**12** C1

TRANSPORT
Pie de la Cuesta/San Isidro/Pedregoso
Buses to/from Acapulco.........**13** D2

INFORMATION
Netxcom.......................................**1** D2

SIGHTS & ACTIVITIES
Boat Hire......................................**2** B1
Club de Ski Chuy.........................**3** B1
Club Náutico Cadena Ski............**4** B1

SLEEPING 🏨
Acapulco Trailer Park &
Mini-Super...............................**5** B1
Bungalows María Cristina...........**6** B2

Hotel & Restaurant Casa Blanca...**7** B1
Hotel Parador de los Reyes.........**8** C2
Hotel Restaurante Rocío..............**9** D2
Villa Nirvana.............................**10** C2

Laguna de Coyuca

PACIFIC OCEAN

To Zihuatanejo
(230km)

To Acapulco
(10km)

Arched Entrance

BUDGET

Hotel Parador de los Reyes (☎ 460-01-31; fax 460-01-29; Av de la Fuerza Aérea Mexicana 305; s/d $9.50/15; P 🛏) This clean, economical choice is right beside the road and has a small courtyard swimming pool. It has 11 large, no-frills rooms.

Acapulco Trailer Park & Mini-Super (☎ 460-00-10; acatrailerpark@yahoo.com; Calz Pie de la Cuesta s/n; campsite per 1/2 people $15/19, RV sites $19-24; 🛏) Beachside with big spaces, clean facilities, friendly management and just enough shade, this is the nicest campground in the whole Acapulco area.

MIDRANGE

Quinta Erika (☎/fax 444-41-31; www.quintaerika.de.vu; Playa Luces; r incl breakfast $52; P 🛏) Six kilometers northeast of Pie de la Cuesta at Playa Luces, on 2 hectares of lagoonside land, this seven-room, quality lodging is one of the region's best places to relax for a few days. Rooms come with many amenities. The owner, who speaks German, Spanish and a little English, rents out kayaks and sailboats, and takes great pride in his place. Reservations are strongly suggested.

Villa Nirvana (☎ 460-16-31; www.lavillanirvana.com; rear Av de la Fuerza Aérea Mexicana 302; d $29-57, q $94, per additional person $9.50; P 🖥 🛏) Villa Nirvana's friendly American owners have thoughtfully landscaped and expanded this cheerful property. It has a variety of accommodations, some with ocean views, and all are comfortable and decorated with local

crafts. A beachside swimming pool, pleasant open-air restaurant (breakfast only) and bar, and complimentary (but limited, please) Internet access round out the good value.

Bungalows María Cristina (☎ 460-02-62; Av de la Fuerza Aérea Mexicana s/n; s/d/bungalows $24/29/71; P) Run by English-speaking Enrique and his friendly family, this is a clean, well-tended relaxing place with hammocks overlooking the beach. The large, four-to-five-person bungalows have kitchens and ocean-view balconies. A good budget choice. Rates double around Christmas and Easter.

Hotel & Restaurant Casa Blanca (☎ 460-03-24; casablanca@prodigy.net.mx; Av de la Fuerza Aérea Mexicana s/n; r $47; P 🍴 🛏) This well-tended beachfront place aspires to be a resort but doesn't quite pull it off. Happily, the restaurant retains a homelike atmosphere. Rates can go much higher in the latter part of December.

Hotel Restaurante Rocío (☎ 460-10-08; Av de la Fuerza Aérea Mexicana 9; s/d $24/38; P) The beds at this beachfront hotel-restaurant-bar are a bit springy and the place could use some sprucing up, but newer oceanside rooms cost the same as others.

Eating & Drinking

Restaurants here are known for fresh seafood. Plenty of open-air places front the beach, though some close early in the evening. Most of the hotels and guesthouses have restaurants, as do many of the waterskiing clubs. Food prices tend to be higher here than in Acapulco, so it may be worth bringing some groceries and getting a room with kitchen access.

Coyuca 2000 (☎ 460-56-09; Playa Pie de la Cuesta; mains $6-13, minimum purchase per person $7; ☑ 9am-2am Dec-Apr, 8am-10pm May-Nov) Pull up a chair on the sand, watch the waves and enjoy good fish *al mojo de ajo* (sautéed minced garlic) or in fajitas, plus other tasty seafood and meat dishes. Great mixed drinks enhance the casual atmosphere.

Restaurant Rocío (☎ 460-10-08; Av de la Fuerza Aérea Mexicana 9; mains $6-8.50) Serves a limited menu of a few seafood dishes and simple Mexican fare, such as quesadillas, under *palapas* on the beach.

Steve's Hideaway/El Escondite (☑ 9am-11pm) Esteban serves drinks, steaks and seafood at a bar on stilts over the water. You'll find it on the southeast side of the lagoon; the view over the water are great.

Getting There & Away

From Acapulco, catch a 'Pie de la Cuesta' bus on La Costera across the street from the Sanborns near the *zócalo*. Buses go every 15 minutes from 6am until around 8pm; the bumpy, roundabout ride costs $0.40 and takes 35 to 50 minutes if traffic isn't too bad. Buses marked 'Pie de la Cuesta – San Isidro' or 'Pie de la Cuesta – Pedregoso' stop on Hwy 200 near Pie de la Cuesta's arched entrance; those marked 'Pie de la Cuesta – Playa Luces' continue all the way along to Playa Luces, 6km further along toward Barra de Coyuca. *Colectivo* vans ($0.50) continue on from Barra de Coyuca back out to Hwy 200.

Colectivo taxis to Pie de la Cuesta operate 24 hours along La Costera and elsewhere in Acapulco's old town, and charge $1.25 for the half-hour, one-way trip. A taxi from Acapulco costs anywhere from $7 to $11 one-way (more after dark).

ACAPULCO

☎ 744 / pop 912,000

Acapulco's golden beaches, death-defying cliff divers, endless nightlife and towering resort hotels have been attracting more and more visitors in recent years, reversing a decline that began in the late 1970s. New touristic life is being breathed into the city, in part by American university students

who come to spend their spring break in a more welcoming and economical environment than Cancún.

Bustling Acapulco offers pockets of calm, from romantic cliffside bars and restaurants to the old town's charming shady *zócalo* and impressively sited 17th-century fort. The arc of beach that sweeps around many kilometers of Bahía de Acapulco can be a good place to relax – if you take the beach vendors in stride – but step off it and you'll find much of the city to be a bedlam of clogged traffic, crowded sidewalks and smoggy fumes (which at least make for a nice sunset).

From January to March the monthly normal high and low temperatures are 31°C and 21°C; from April to December the high is 32°C, with the low varying between 22°C and 24°C. Afternoon showers are common from June to September but rare the rest of the year.

History

The name 'Acapulco' is derived from ancient Nahuatl words meaning 'where the reeds stood' or 'place of giant reeds.' Archaeological finds show that when the Spanish discovered the Bahía de Acapulco in 1512, people had already been living in the area for some 2000 years.

The Spanish quickly established port and shipbuilding facilities in the substantial natural harbor, and in 1523 Cortés and two partners financed a road between Mexico City and Acapulco. This 'Camino de Asia' became the principal trade route between Mexico City and the Pacific; the 'Camino de Europa,' from Mexico City to Veracruz on the Gulf coast, completed the overland leg of the route between Asia and Spain.

Acapulco became the only port in the New World authorized to receive *naos* (Spanish trading galleons) from China and the Philippines. By the 17th century trade with Asia was flourishing, and English and Dutch privateers were busily looting ships and settlements along the Pacific coast. To fend off these pirates, the Fuerte de San Diego was built atop a low hill overlooking Bahía de Acapulco. It was not until the end of the 18th century that Spain permitted its American colonies to engage in free trade, ending the monopoly of the *naos*.

Upon gaining independence Mexico severed most of its trade links with Spain and

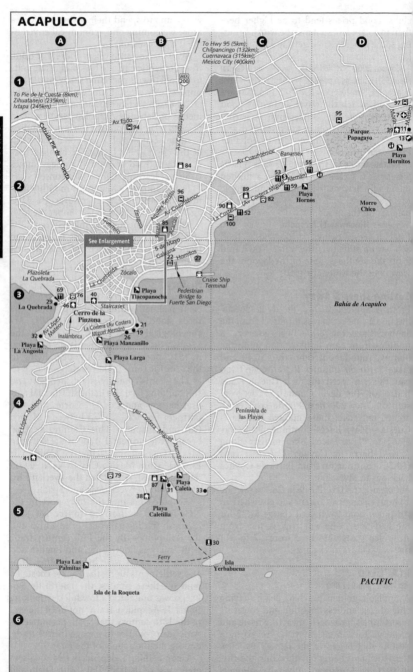

ACAPULCO

To Pie de la Cuesta (8km);
Zihuatanejo (235km);
Ixtapa (245km)

To Hwy 95 (5km);
Chilpancingo (132km);
Cuernavaca (315km);
Mexico City (400km)

MEX
200

Av Ejido
94

Av Cuauhtémoc

Av Constituyentes

95

Parque
Papagayo

97
7
39   11
13

Playa
Hornitos

Calzada Pie de la Cuesta

84

96

Aquiles Serdán

Zaragoza

Guerrero

Av Cuauhtémoc

Banamex

Av Cuauhtémoc

53   55
89
90   52
100
82
59

Playa
Hornos

La Costera (Av Costera Miguel Alemán)

Morro
Chico

See Enlargement

5 de Mayo
Galeana
22   Hornitos

La Quebrada

Zócalo

Playa
Tlacopanocha

Pedestrian
Bridge to
Fuerte San Diego

Cruise Ship
Terminal

Bahía de Acapulco

Plazoleta
La Quebrada

69
29   76
46   40

La Quebrada

Staircases

Cerro de la
Pinzona

La Costera (Av Costera
Miguel Alemán)

21
19
26

Playa Manzanillo

32

Playa
La Angosta

Inalámbrica

Av López Mateos

Playa Larga

La Costera (Av Costera Miguel Alemán)

Península de
las Playas

Av López Mateos

41

79

87
38   31

Playa
Caleta

33

Playa
Caletilla

30

Ferry

Isla
Yerbabuena

PACIFIC

Playa Las
Palmitas

Isla de la Roqueta

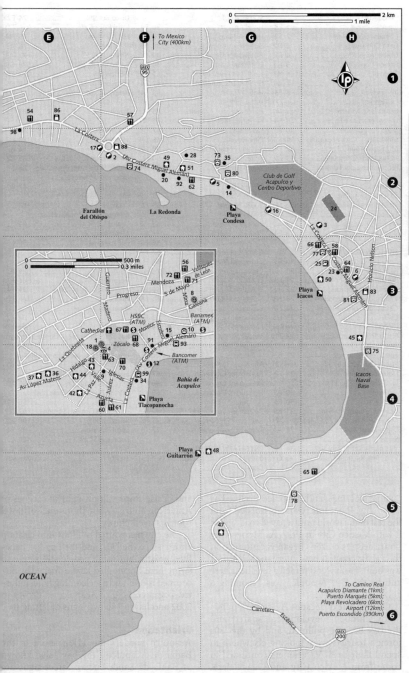

Spanish colonies, and Acapulco declined as a port city. It became relatively isolated from the rest of the world until a paved road linked it with Mexico City in 1927. As Mexico City flourished, its citizens began vacationing on the Pacific coast. A new international airport was built, Hollywood filmed a few flicks here and by the '50s Acapulco was becoming a glitzy jet-set resort.

Over the next decades Acapulco's population climbed, development soared and the bay became polluted, and by the '80s foreign tourists were looking elsewhere to spend their cash. Vacationers continued to come from Mexico City and Guadalajara, and cruise ships still brought in cargoes of American tourists, but thousands of hotel rooms stayed empty.

The city has poured millions into cleanup efforts since the '90s, and the bay has benefited greatly, but some people still refuse to swim there. Spring-breakers, attracted by discounted rooms and a welcoming hotel industry, began coming to Acapulco in droves in 2002 and haven't shown signs of letting up.

Orientation

Acapulco borders the 11km shore of the Bahía de Acapulco ('the bay,' also known as Bahía de Santa Lucía). Street signs are as scarce as safe crosswalks, and building numbers are erratic and often obscured or unused, but inquiring on the street will eventually lead you to your destination. As with most Spanish colonial cities, the cathedral and adjacent *zócalo* dominate the heart of the old central commercial district.

Old Acapulco (which promoters call 'Acapulco Náutico' which means 'Maritime Acapulco') comprises the western part of the city; Acapulco Dorado heads around the bay east from Playa Hornos; and Acapulco Diamante is a newer luxury resort area southeast of Acapulco proper, between the Bahía de Acapulco and the airport.

At the Bahía de Acapulco's west end, the Península de las Playas juts south and east from Old Acapulco. South of the peninsula is Isla de la Roqueta. From Playa Caleta on the south edge of the peninsula, Av López Mateos climbs west and then north to Playa La Angosta and La Quebrada before curling east back toward the city center.

Playa Caleta also marks the beginning of Acapulco's principal bayside avenue, Av Costera Miguel Alemán – often called 'La Costera' or 'Miguel Alemán' – which traverses the peninsula and then hugs the shoreline all the way around the bay to Playa Icacos and the naval base at the bay's eastern end. Most of Acapulco's hotels, restaurants, discos and points of interest are along or near La Costera. Just after the naval base, La Costera becomes Carretera Escénica, which rejoins the main branch of Hwy 200 after 9km, at the turnoff to Puerto Marqués. Hwy 200 then leads south past ritzy Playa Revolcadero and the airport (the latter is 23km from Acapulco).

Information

BOOKSTORES

For its size, Acapulco is woefully lacking in good bookstores.

La Tienda (Museo Histórico de Acapulco, Fuerte de San Diego, Hornitos s/n) Has the city's best Spanish-language academic section plus a limited selection in English.

Sanborns Playa Condesa (☎ 484-20-44; La Costera 3111); Old Acapulco (☎ 482-61-67; cnr Escudero & La Costera) The branch near the *zócalo* stocks a smaller selection than the branch near Playa Condesa.

EMERGENCY

Cruz Roja (Red Cross; ☎ 445-59-12) Provides ambulance service.

Locatel (☎ 481-11-00) Operated by Sefotur, this 24-hour hotline is for all types of emergencies.

Tourist police (☎ 440-70-22)

INTERNET ACCESS

It's impossible to walk more than a few blocks in Acapulco's major hotel districts without passing a cybercafé; most have quick connections and charge just under $1 per hour.

Big M@sternet (Hidalgo 6; ⏰ 9am-midnight; ❄) Family-run with air-con.

Internet (Galeana 13; ⏰ 10am-11pm) Fifteen computers and loud music.

Vig@net (Hidalgo 8; ⏰ 8am-midnight) Keeps more reliable hours than some.

LAUNDRY

Lavandería Azueta (Azueta 14A; wash & dry per kilo $1.25; ⏰ 9am-7pm Mon-Fri) Below Hotel Paola.

Lavandería Lavadín (☎ 482-28-90; cnr La Paz & Iglesias; wash & dry per kilo $1.25; ⏰ 8am-10pm Mon-Sat) There's a 3kg minimum.

MEDICAL SERVICES

Hospital Magallanes (☎ 485-61-94; Massieu 2) A well-established private hospital with English-speaking doctors and staff, offering a wide range of medical services.

MONEY

Omnipresent banks (many with ATMs) give the best exchange rates, and many will change US-dollar traveler's checks and euro banknotes. Conspicuous, ubiquitous *casas de cambio* pay a slightly lower rate, but are open longer hours and are less busy than banks; shop around, as rates vary. Banks and *casas de cambio* cluster around the *zócalo* and line La Costera. Hotels will also change money, but their rates are usually extortionate.

POST

Main post office (☎ 483-53-63; La Costera 125, Palacio Federal; ⏰ 8am-5:30pm Mon-Fri, 9am-1pm Sat)

TELEPHONE & FAX

You can make long-distance calls from the many Telmex card phones throughout the city, or from private *casetas* (with signs saying '*larga distancia*'). These abound near the *zócalo* and along La Costera.

Caseta Alameda Telephone and fax services, on the west side of the *zócalo*.

Telecomm (☎ 484-69-76; Main post office, La Costera 125, Palacio Federal) Fax, telephone and limited Internet services.

TOURIST INFORMATION

The following offices in the Centro de Convenciones all provide tourist information and assistance. The first and the third are in the yellow building out front.

Casa Consular (☎ /fax 481-25-33; La Costera 4455; ⏰ 9am-3pm Mon-Fri) Provides consular assistance to visitors of all nationalities.

Municipal tourist kiosk (⏰ 8:30am-10pm) City maintained; on the waterfront sidewalk across from the *zócalo*, mostly dispensing brochures.

Procuraduría del Turista (☎ /fax 484-45-83; La Costera 4455; ⏰ 8am-11pm) This government dispenser of visitor information will also try to resolve complaints, and problems with documents.

State tourist office (Sefotur; ☎ 484-24-23; sefotur@yahoo.com; La Costera 4455; ⏰ 9am-9pm Mon-Fri)

Dangers & Annoyances

A 2006 report ranked Acapulco fifth among Mexican cities for number of crimes committed per capita, which surpasses Mexico City. Smugglers use the Guerrero coast as a drop point for shipments of cocaine from Colombia, much of which then passes through Acapulco on its way to the United States. A significant portion is sold for use within the city itself, mostly in the form of crack. Violence between rival drug cartels has escalated greatly, and in late 2005 it may have spilled over into a touristed area when four city residents were killed in a hail of bullets in the parking lot of La Quebrada for reasons as yet unexplained. At least 15 people died in drug-related violence in early 2006, including four killed in a dramatic shootout between police and suspected traffickers on a downtown street a couple of kilometers inland from the beach.

All that said, to date at least, as far as physical harm goes, tourists who avoid Acapulco's inland neighborhoods probably have more to fear from the rough surf at Playa Revolcadero (which does claim lives), the raw sewage that flows into the bay following rains and the traffic on La Costera.

The Casa Consular receives many reports from visitors who have suffered thefts from their hotel rooms in the area around the *zócalo*. Secure your valuables!

Sights

Acapulco may not have a wealth of colonial architecture but it does have an interesting history, and a culture away from the beach. The history museum at the San Diego fort, the mask museum and the cliff divers are country highlights, not just city highlights.

FUERTE DE SAN DIEGO

This beautifully restored pentagonal fort was built in 1616 atop a hill just east of the *zócalo*. Its mission was to protect from marauding Dutch and English buccaneers the Spanish *naos* conducting trade between the Philippines and Mexico. It must have been effective because this trade route lasted until the early 19th century. Apparently the fort was also strong enough to forestall the takeover of the city for four months by independence leader José María Morelos y Pavón in 1812.

After a 1776 earthquake damaged most of Acapulco, the fort had to be rebuilt. It remains basically unchanged today, having been restored to top condition by the Instituto Nacional de Antropología e Historia (INAH). The panorama of Acapulco you get from the fort's surroundings is free and is, by itself, worth the trip.

The fort is now home to the **Museo Histórico de Acapulco** (☎ 482-38-28; admission $3.25; ⏰ 9:30am-6pm Tue-Sun), which has fascinating exhibits detailing the city's history, with Spanish and English captions. When skies are clear during the high season the museum puts on an evening **sound-&-light show** (⏰ 8pm Fri & Sat).

CASA DE LA MÁSCARA

This enchanting **mask museum** (admission by donation; ⏰ 10am-4pm Tue-Sun) is near the fort on the pedestrian portion of Morelos. It has an amazing collection of masks from around Mexico, including some by Afro-mestizos on the Costa Chica (p516), as well as masks from Cuba, Italy and Africa. A central room displays modern creations. The scant signage is in Spanish.

LA QUEBRADA CLAVADISTAS

The famous cliff divers of **La Quebrada** (the Ravine; adult/child under 9 $3/free; ⏰ shows 1pm, 7:30pm, 8:30pm, 9:30pm & 10:30pm) have been dazzling audiences since 1934, diving with fearless finesse from heights of 25m to 35m into the narrow ocean cove below. The last show usually features divers making the plunge holding torches. For a view from below the jump-off point, walk up Calle La

Quebrada from the *zócalo* or catch a cab (about $5); either way you climb down about 60 steps to the viewing platform. Be sure to tip the divers when they come through the crowd!

La Perla restaurant-bar (see p513) provides a great view of the divers from above, plus two drinks, for $18.

CENTRO DE CONVENCIONES
Acapulco's **convention center** (☎ 484-71-52, 484-70-98; La Costera 4455) is a huge complex with a permanent *galería de artesanías* (crafts gallery), temporary special exhibitions, a large plaza, theaters and concert halls. The grounds have reproductions of temples and statuary from archaeological sites throughout Mexico. Phone the center to ask about current offerings.

CENTRO CULTURAL ACAPULCO
Set around a garden alongside La Costera, this **cultural centre** (casa de la cultura; ☎ 484-23-90, for schedules ☎ 484-40-04; La Costera 4834; ☺ 9am-9pm) accommodates a groovy café–art gallery, a handicrafts shop, an open-air theater and an indoor auditorium.

BEACHES
Visiting Acapulco's beaches tops the list of must-dos for most visitors. The beaches heading east around the bay from the *zócalo* (**Playas Hornos**, **Hornitos**, **Condesa** and **Icacos**) are the most popular, though the west end of Hornos sometimes smells of fish. The high-rise hotel district begins on Playa Hornitos, on the east side of Parque Papagayo, and

heads east from there. City buses constantly ply La Costera, making it easy to get up and down the long arc of beaches.

Playas Caleta and **Caletilla** are two small, protected beaches blending into each other in a cove on the south side of Península de las Playas. They're both backed by a solid line of seafood *palapa* restaurants. The area is especially popular with families who have small children, as the water is very calm. All buses marked 'Caleta' heading down La Costera arrive here. The Mágico Mundo Marino aquarium (see p509) sits on an islet just offshore, forming the imaginary line between the two beaches; boats go regularly from the islet to Isla de la Roqueta.

Playa La Angosta is in a tiny, protected cove on the west side of the peninsula. From the *zócalo* it takes about 20 minutes to walk here. Or you can take any 'Caleta' bus and get off near Hotel Avenida, on La Costera, just one short block from the beach.

The beaches on **Bahía Puerto Marqués**, about 18km southeast of the *zócalo*, are very popular, and its calm waters are good for waterskiing and sailing. You get a magnificent view of Bahía de Acapulco as the Carretera Escénica climbs south out of the city. Frequent 'Puerto Marqués' buses run along La Costera every 10 minutes from 5am to 9pm.

Beyond the Puerto Marqués turnoff and before the airport, **Playa Revolcadero** is a long, straight beach that has seen a recent explosion in luxury tourism and residential development. Waves are large and surfing is popular here, especially in summer, but a

---

CHASING SUNSETS

All those beaches stretching around the Bahía de Acapulco, and not a single sunset – over the water, anyway. If you're aching to watch the sun sink slowly into the sea, you'll have to pick your spot carefully.

First off, think Old Acapulco. The only place where you can sit on the sand (within the city limits) and watch the sun set over the water is Playa La Angosta (see above), a sliver of a beach on the Península de las Playas. The bar at Hotel Los Flamingos (see p510), perched high on the peninsula's western cliffs, has an almost dizzying perspective of the event, always aided by hoisting a few to the fading sun. Plazoleta La Quebrada, near where the divers perform, is another great spot; the parking lot fills with people around sunset. One of the finest views of all is at the small Sinfonía del Mar (Symphony of the Sea), a stepped plaza built on the edge of the cliffs just south of La Quebrada. Its sole purpose is to give folks a magical view.

If you really feel like chasing the sunset, you should head over to Pie de la Cuesta (p499), about a half-hour's ride northwest of Acapulco. Its long, wide beach and hammock-clad restaurants are famous for spectacular sunsets.

strong undertow makes swimming dangerous; heed lifeguards' instructions. Horseback riding along the beach is popular.

ISLA DE LA ROQUETA

This island offers a popular (crowded) beach, and snorkeling and diving possibilities. You can rent snorkeling gear, kayaks and other water-sports equipment on the beach.

From Playas Caleta and Caletilla, boats make the eight-minute, one-way trip ($3 round-trip) every 20 minutes or so. The alternative is a glass-bottomed boat that makes a circuitous trip to the island ($5), departing from the same beaches but traveling via **La Virgen de los Mares** (the Virgin of the Seas), a submerged bronze statue of the Virgen of Guadalupe – visibility varies with water conditions. The trip takes about 45 minutes, depending on how many times floating vendors accost your boat. You can alight on the island and take a later boat back, but find out when the last boat leaves, usually around 5pm.

Activities

As one might expect, Acapulco's activities are largely beach based. There are nonbeach things to do, but generally everything is in the spirit of mega-vacation with once-in-a-lifetime adventure and/or adrenaline rush promised. For activities like scuba diving you should shop around and choose an outfit with which you're comfortable.

WATER SPORTS

Just about everything that can be done on or below the water is done in Acapulco. On the Bahía de Acapulco, waterskiing, boating, banana-boating and parasailing are all popular activities. To partake in any of these, walk along the Zona Dorada beaches and look for the (usually) orange kiosks. These charge about $7 for snorkeling gear, $23 for a five-minute parasailing flight, $29 for a jet-ski ride and $52 for one hour of waterskiing. The smaller Playas Caleta and Caletilla have sailboats, fishing boats, motorboats, pedal boats, canoes, snorkeling gear, inner tubes and water bicycles for rent.

Though Acapulco isn't really a scuba destination, there are some decent dive sites nearby. At least two outfitters offer quality services. **Acapulco Scuba Center** (☎ 482-94-74; www.acapulcoscuba.com; Paseo del Pescador 13 & 14) has PADI- and NAUI-certified instructors and offers several certification courses and guided day trips. All prices include a guide, gear, boat and refreshments, and range from $70 for a beginner dive to $350 for five-day PADI Open Water certification. A guided, two-tank dive for experienced divers costs $70.

Swiss Divers Association (SDA; ☎ 482-13-57; www.swissdivers.com; La Costera 100) is a first-rate shop at Hotel Caleta that also offers PADI and NAUI instruction – in Spanish, English and German – with dives and prices similar to those of Acapulco Scuba.

The best **snorkeling** is off small Playa Las Palmitas on Isla de la Roqueta (left). Unless you pony up for an organized snorkeling trip you'll need to scramble over rocks to reach it. You can rent gear on the Isla, or on Playas Caleta and Caletilla, which also have some decent spots. Both scuba operations mentioned here take half-day snorkeling trips for around $35 per person, including boat, guide, gear, food, drink and hotel transport.

Sportfishing is very popular in Acapulco and many companies offer six- to seven-hour fishing trips; book at least a day in advance and figure on a 6am or 7am departure time. Acapulco Scuba Center (see left) and **Fish-R-Us** (☎ 487-87-87, 482-82-82; www.fish-r-us.com; La Costera 100) both offer fishing trips starting at around $250 (for the entire eight-person boat, gear and bait). The captain can often combine individuals into a group large enough to cover the cost of the boat, for $70 to $80 per person

OTHER SPORTS

For tennis, try **Club de Golf Acapulco** (☎ 484-65-83; Costera Miguel Alemán s/n), **Club de Tenis Hyatt** (☎ 469-12-34; www.acapulco.hyatt.com; La Costera 1), **Villa Vera Racquet Club** (☎ 484-03-34; Lomas del Mar 35), **Hotel Panoramic** (☎ 481-01-32; Av Condesa 1) or Fairmont Acapulco Princess hotel (see p511).

Acapulco also has gyms, squash courts and other recreational facilities. The tourist office has information on sport.

The 50m-high bungee tower at **AJ Hackett Bungy** (☎ 484-75-29; La Costera 107; ☉ noon-midnight Mon-Thu, noon-2am Fri-Sun) is easy to spot on the Costera, and for $60 you can throw yourself (bungee included) from its platform – very exhilarating in the early morning.

CENTRAL PACIFIC COAST

CRUISES

Various boats and yachts offer cruises, most of which depart from around Playa Tlacopanocha or Playa Manzanillo near the *zócalo*. Cruises – from $12 for 1½ hours to over $25 for four hours – are available day and night. They range from glass-bottomed boats to multilevel craft (with blaring salsa music and open bars) to yachts offering quiet sunset cruises around the bay. A typical trip heads from Tlacopanocha around Península de las Playas to Isla de la Roqueta, passes by to see the cliff divers at La Quebrada, crosses over to Puerto Marqués and then returns around Bahía de Acapulco.

The **Victoria** (☎ 044-744-516-24-94), **Hawaiano** (☎ 482-21-99), **Fiesta** (☎ 482-20-55) and **Bonanza** (☎ 482-20-55) cruise operations are all popular; you can make reservations directly or through travel agencies and most hotels.

Acapulco for Children

Acapulco is very family friendly, with many fun options designed especially for children (but they're fun for adults, too).

PARQUE PAPAGAYO

This large **amusement park** (La Costera; admission free; ☺ 8am-8pm, rides operate 3-10pm), between Morín and El Cano, is full of tropical trees and easily accessed from Playas Hornos and Hornitos. Its attractions, for both kids and adults, include a go-kart track, a lake with paddleboats, a children's train, mechanical rides, a restaurant-bar, an aviary and animal enclosures with deer, rabbits, crocodiles and turtles. A 1.2km 'interior circuit' pathway is good for jogging. The park has entrances on all four sides.

CICI

The family water-sports park, **CICI** (☎ 484-19-60; La Costera 101; admission $9.50; ☺ 10am-6pm), is on the east side of Acapulco. Dolphins perform several shows daily, and humans occasionally give diving exhibitions. You can also enjoy an 80m-long water toboggan; a pool with artificial waves; the **Sky Coaster ride** (per person $15), which simulates the La Quebrada cliff-diving experience; and ascending 100m in a tethered balloon ($10 per person). Children who are two years and up pay full price, plus you'll need to rent a locker ($2). Also, if you use the toboggan you'll have to rent an inflatable ring ($2.50).

Any local bus marked 'CICI,' 'Base' or 'Puerto Marqués' will take you there.

MÁGICO MUNDO MARINO

This **aquarium** (☎ 483-12-15; adult/child 3-12 $3.75/2; ☺ 9am-6pm) stands on a small islet just off Playas Caleta and Caletilla. Highlights include a sea lion show, swimming pools, water toboggans and the feeding of crocodiles, turtles and piranhas.

Festivals & Events

Semana Santa Probably the busiest time of year for tourism in Acapulco. There's lots of action in the discos, on the beaches and all over town.

Festival Francés (French Festival) This festival, which began in 2004, is held in March and celebrates French food, cinema, music and literature.

Tianguis Turístico (www.tianguisturistico.com) Mexico's major annual tourism trade fair is held the second or third week in April.

Festivales de Acapulco Held for one week in May, featuring Mexican and international music at venues around town.

Acapulco Air Show Flight fans shouldn't miss this show, which takes place over three days around the beginning of November. Everything from biplanes to F-16s, plus wing-walking, parachute teams, precision aerobatics and high-speed fighter maneuvers over the bay and between the hotels. The USAF Thunderbirds team appeared at the show for the first time in 2005.

Virgen de Guadalupe The festival for Mexico's favorite figure is celebrated all night on December 11 and all the following day; it's marked by fireworks, folk dances and street processions accompanied by small marching bands. The processions converge at the cathedral in the *zócalo*, where children gather, dressed in costumes.

Sleeping

Acapulco has more than 30,000 hotel rooms. Rates vary widely by season; the high season is roughly from the middle of December until the end of Easter, with another flurry of activity during the July and August school holidays. At other times of year you can often bargain for a better rate, especially if you plan to stay a while. During Semana Santa or between Christmas and New Year's Day (at which times all bets are off on room prices) it's essential to book ahead. The prices listed here are for the high season.

BUDGET

Most of Acapulco's budget hotels are concentrated around the *zócalo* and on La Quebrada; the latter catches more breezes.

La Torre Eiffel (☎ 482-16-83; hoteltorreeiffel@ hotmail.com; Inalámbrica 110; s $11.50, d from $23; P ⚑) Perched on a hill above Plazoleta La Quebrada, the popular Eiffel has a small swimming pool, huge shared balconies and some spectacular sunset views. It's a bit out of the way, but the friendly, helpful management, good bathrooms and comfortable beds help make the climb worth it.

Hotel Angelita (☎ 483-57-34; La Quebrada 37; r per person $10) Clean, spacious rooms – each with at least one fan, hot-water bath and good screenage – are set back along a narrow, plant-filled courtyard. A paperback library augments the small TV room in front, where a friendly group of grandmotherly types sometimes gathers.

Hotel Asturias (☎ /fax 483-65-48; gerardomancera@ aol.com; La Quebrada 45; s/d $17/29, with air-con & TV $22/43; P ⚑ ⚑) This friendly, family-run hotel is clean and well-tended, with mostly pleasant rooms around a courtyard, cable TV in the lobby, a small swimming pool and a book exchange.

Hotel María Antonieta (☎ 482-50-24; Azueta 17; s/d $11.50/19) The 'Ma Antonieta' has 38 decent budget rooms with fan. They're very plain, but clean and good-sized, and guests have use of a communal kitchen.

Hotel Paola (☎ 482-62-43; Azueta 16; r per person $15) The positively pink Paola is clean and family run. Outside rooms have small private balconies, the interior rooms are quieter, and all are outfitted in pastels.

MIDRANGE

The majority of the high-rise hotels along La Costera tend to be expensive. But there are some good deals in older places around town. A few places offer rooms with fully equipped kitchens.

Hotel Boca Chica (☎ 483-67-41; www.bocachica hotel.com; Playa Caletilla; r from $60; P ⚑ ⚑) The family-run Boca Chica preserves the best elements of Acapulco's heyday as a resort town. Tucked into the rocks at the end of Playa Caletilla, it has a virtually private ocean cove for snorkeling, diving and boating. The comfortable rooms have views of Isla de la Roqueta, Playa Caletilla or the garden, and the seaside Marina Club Sushi & Oyster Bar (see boxed text, p513) is a real treat.

Hotel Etel Suites (☎ 482-22-40/41; etelsuites@terra .com.mx; Av La Pinzona 92; d/ste/apt from $45/57/99; P ⚑ ⚑ ⚑) High atop the hill overlooking Old Acapulco, the Etel is run by a delightful mother and daughter. The good-value, spotless suites and apartments all sleep at least three people, and most have expansive terraces with views of La Quebrada and the Pacific to one side and the bay to the other. Amenities include full kitchens, well-manicured gardens, a children's play area and a swimming pool.

Suites Selene (☎ 484-36-43; suitesselene@hotmail .com; Colón 175; d/q with kitchen $66/77, without kitchen $55/66; P ⚑ ⚑) One door from the sands of Playa Icacos, Selene is a great option, especially for long-stay self-caterers. Though a little worn, it has fine firm beds, good air-con (though only fans in the dining room/kitchens), good bathrooms, a nice deep pool and cable TV throughout.

Hotel Los Flamingos (☎ 482-06-90; www .flamingosacapulco.com; Av López Mateos s/n; r from $76; P ⚑ ⚑) Perched 135m over the ocean on the highest cliffs in Acapulco, this single-story classic boasts one of the finest sunset views in town, as well as a bar and restaurant. Rooms themselves are modest and comfortable, with great bathrooms and good screenage, and a long, shared lounging terrace. John Wayne, Johnny Weissmuller (best Tarzan ever!) and some of their Hollywood pals once owned the place.

Romano Palace Hotel (☎ 484-77-30, 800-090-15-00; www.romanopalace.com.mx; La Costera 130; r $71; P ⚑ ⚑) This 22-story hotel offers very good accommodations for the price: rooms have private balconies and floor-to-ceiling windows with great bayfront views (ask for a better upper-storey room). The faintly Asian decor is dated, but the marble bathrooms still look good. The Romano also has multiple restaurants and a beach club.

Hotel Misión (☎ 482-36-43; hotelmision@hotmail .com; Valle 12; r per person $19; P) Acapulco's oldest hotel certainly looks it from the outside, but step into the colonial compound's leafy, relaxing courtyard and things get nicer (one happy reader describes the Misión as 'a diamond in the rough'). Basic rooms feature colorful tiles, heavy Spanish-style furniture and comfortable beds in a variety of configurations. Some of the toilets lack seats.

Youth Hostel K3 (☎ 481-31-11; www.k3acapulco .com; La Costera 116; dm/r incl continental breakfast $20/57; ⚑ ⚑) It's shared bathrooms only here, and the rooms have almost a Japanese capsule-hotel feel. But dorms and private rooms have air-con, there's a shared kitchen and the terrace, bar and game room provide ample space for socializing. Most important – it's right across La Costera from the beach.

Hotel del Valle (☎ 485-83-36/88; cnr Morín & Espinoza; r with fan/air-con $57/71; P X R) On the east side of Parque Papagayo, near La Costera and popular Playa Hornitos, the del Valle has reasonably comfortable rooms, a small swimming pool and communal kitchens ($9.50 surcharge per day).

TOP END
The original high-rise zone begins at the eastern end of Parque Papagayo and curves east around the bay; new luxury hotels have been springing up on Playa Revolcadero, east of Puerto Marqués. Most of the establishments listed here offer at least a couple of rooms that are set up for disabled guests, and offer recreation programs for children (though these may be available only on weekends and during school vacations).

Off-season package rates and special promotions can be less than half the standard rack rates – ask reservation agents for special deals, or travel agents for air and lodging packages. Even during the high season, simply reserving through a hotel's website can sometimes save a lot off of walk-in rates. All prices given here are high-season rack rates.

Camino Real Acapulco Diamante (☎ /fax 435-10-10/20, in the US 800-722-64-66; www.caminoreal.com/acapulco/; Carretera Escénica, Km 14; r from $280; P X R) The Camino Real lies down a steep, gated 1km access road off the Carretera Escénica. It sits directly above its own small, rocky stretch of Playa Pichilingüe on the calm bay of Puerto Marqués. Each of the 157 luxuriously appointed rooms have a terrace or balcony looking out over the bay. This well-designed multilevel hotel has a spa, a gym, three shallow swimming pools and the usual multiplicity of bars and restaurants.

Fairmont Acapulco Princess (☎ 469-10-00, in the US 800-441-14-14; www.fairmont.com; Playa Revolcadero s/n; r from $300; P X R) This Aztec-themed place is BIG. Its core 'pyramid' has a towering, 15-story atrium lobby and is one of three huge structures that hold a total of 1015 guestrooms and suites. Almost 2 sq km of lushly landscaped grounds also contain a golf course, nine tennis courts, five swimming pools, two fitness centers

and a dozen bars and restaurants. Rooms come with varying views, but all have a high standard of comfort and lots of amenities.

Hyatt Regency Acapulco (☎ 469-12-34, in Mexico 800-005-00-00, in the US 800-233-12-34; www.acapulco.hyatt.com; La Costera 1; r from $175; P X R) The Hyatt is right on the beach and right in the middle of La Costera's action. Its 638 plush rooms and suites have marble bathrooms, and most have private balconies. Two inviting swimming pools, a passel of palm trees, a bevy of bars and restaurants (one serving kosher food from December to February) and an on-site synagogue round things out.

Park Royal (☎ 440-65-65; www.parkroyalhotels.com.mx; Costera Guitarrón 110; r all-inclusive per person from $200; P X R) The Park Royal's 218 rooms are spread out on several floors, but only about 40 of them have sea views. Most standards have two beds, a really big TV, great air-con and a bathroom done up in lovely subdued brown marble. A tram carries guests down to a large swimming pool sitting just above the hotel's relatively secluded stretch of beach, and a gym was going in at the time of research. Rack rates cover three meals a day and all the drinks you want.

Eating
OLD ACAPULCO
Emerging from the *zócalo*'s west side, Juárez has at least a dozen inexpensive, casual restaurants.

El Amigo Miguel (☎ 483-69-81; mains $4-8.50) Juárez 16 (☉ 10am-9pm); Juárez 31 (☉ 10am-9pm); La Costera s/n (☉ 11am-8pm) This chain features cheery, busy open-air restaurants with cheap and delicious seafood. Miguel has two restaurants opposite one another, on the same corner, with other branches around town.

Restaurant San Carlos (Juárez 5; mains $3-6) An open-air patio, good traditional Mexican fare and a $3 *comida corrida*. Want more? OK: the menu has an endless list of Mexican standards, including green and white *pozole*.

Restaurant Ricardo (Juárez 9; comidas corrida $3) Ricardo's is another good choice for cheap *comidas corridas* and tasty house specials like *camarones en ajo* (shrimp with garlic) or *pollo en salsa de cacahuete* (chicken in peanut sauce), all served under bright fluorescent light shining on white tile.

Restaurant Café Astoria (Plaza Álvarez, Edificio Pintos 4C; snacks $1.50-4, mains $3.75) This friendly café has indoor and outdoor tables in a shady, semiquiet spot just east of the cathedral. It serves some OK espresso drinks, including a massive $2 *capuchino tarro*.

El Nopalito (☎ 483-84-76; cnr La Paz & Ramírez; mains $3-3.50, comidas corrida $3; ☻ 7am-8pm) Reader-recommended, the 'Little Cactus' serves inexpensive and filling fish and meat dishes (*pozole* on Thursday, naturally) and a good *menú del día*.

Restaurant Charly (Carranza s/n; 4 tacos $2, mains $3.75-5) Just steps east of the *zócalo*, on the pedestrian alley of Carranza, economical Charly has shady sidewalk tables and offers up *barbacoa de chivo* (spiced goat meat surrounded by roasted maguey leaves and slow-cooked – in a pit, traditionally, but these days more often in a stovetop steamer) as both a main dish and in taco form.

Café Wadi (☎ 482-09-14; cnr Mina & Velásquez; coffee $1-2; ☻ 8am-8pm Mon-Sat) This is a great morning stop for good freshly roasted espresso drinks before you hit the nearby artisans' market.

Taquería Los Pioneros (☎ 482-23-45; cnr Mendoza & Mina; 5 tacos $2, mains $3.75-5; ☻ 9am-3am) The tacos are tiny but their various fillings are tasty, plus you can load up on accompaniments: jalapeños, pickled carrots, onions, cilantro etc. Food comes with plenty of open-air atmosphere, too, at the sweaty, busy, noisy intersection. Hang with locals and watch the elaborately painted buses go by (with luck you'll even spot the vomiting scene from *The Exorcist*).

For eat-in or takeout rotisserie-roasted chicken, head to the corner of Mina and Calle 5 de Mayo, where there are five places side by side, each serving up quarter/half/whole fowls for about $2/3.50/7.

LA COSTERA

Dozens of restaurants line La Costera as it heads east toward the high-rise hotels; most specialize in fresh seafood or flashy gimmicks. Many open-air beachfront restaurant/bars are opposite Romano Palace Hotel. Stroll along, browse the posted menu, and take your pick. Fast food chains litter La Costera, especially near the east end.

Fersato's (☎ 484-39-49; La Costera 44; mains $5.50-14) Opposite the Centro Cultural, this long-standing family establishment features top Mexican food served amid mock-hacienda decor. Taco varieties include *dorados* (lightly fried) and *de albañil* (literally 'bricklayer's tacos,' containing crispy fried pork skin, avocado, onion, tomato and chili).

Mariscos Pipo's (☎ 484-17-00; cnr La Costera & Nao Victoria; mains $7-19; ☻ 1-9pm) Pipo's has a varied menu that includes baby shark quesadillas, freshwater bass, grilled crawfish and scallop cocktail, all served in a large dining area with a simple, nautical theme.

El Gaucho (☎ 484-17-00; Hotel Presidente, La Costera 8; mains $7.50-22.50; ☻ 5pm-midnight) The Gaucho is upscale but not stuffy, and one of the top spots in town for a steak (though you pay dearly for it). All the meat is grilled in true Argentine style, and less-carnivorous or extravagant folk can choose from an assortment of pasta dishes. The short but decent wine list includes selections from Mexico, Chile, Spain and Argentina.

100% Natural (☎ 485-52-79; mains $4-7; Ⓥ 34 (La Costera 34); 112 (La Costera 112); 200 (La Costera 200; ☻ 24hr) This health-conscious chain has several branches along La Costera and elsewhere in town, all with a mellow ambience and good, friendly service. The food is consistently good, mostly vegetarian fare, including wholegrain breads and rolls and a large variety of fruit and veggie juice blends, *licuados* and shakes.

The huge air-conditioned Comercial Mexicana, Bodega Aurrera and Bodega Gigante combination supermarkets and big-box discount department stores are along La Costera between the *zócalo* and Parque Papagayo, among other places. Aside from fresh produce and all manner of groceries, you can find some pretty high-quality, ready-to-eat stuff in the bakery and deli departments.

THE AUTHOR'S CHOICE

Marina Club Sushi & Oyster Bar (☎ 482-78-79; Hotel Boca Chica, Playa Caletilla; nigirizushi per piece $1.50-3.50, sushi rolls $4.50-8, mains $6-16; ⏰ 1-10:30pm) Only ultrafresh seafood hits the plates at this intimate bayside spot. Live chocolate clams are flown in weekly from Baja, and the fish is limited to what's being caught locally at the moment. Have a drink under the high thatched roof and enjoy the view.

ELSEWHERE

Madeiras (☎ 446-56-36; Carretera Escénica 33; prix-fixe dinner $40; ⏰ 7-9:30pm Mon-Fri, 7-10:30pm Sat & Sun) Madeiras is a great spot for a romantic meal and has been in operation for more than 25 years. You construct four-course meals from the fairly wide menu of offerings that blend Old World favorites with Mexican flourishes, such as tournedos with Roquefort and *huitlacoche*, accompanied by a sauce made with *guajillo* chilies and Madeira. Decor is appealingly simple, but it can't compete with the spectacular views over Bahía de Acapulco from the terrace.

Restaurant La Perla (☎ 483-11-55; Hotel El Mirador, Plazoleta La Quebrada 74; dinner $33; ⏰ 7-11pm) First-rate views of the death-defying *clavadistas* (see La Quebrada Clavadistas, p506) almost justify the high price of a meal at this restaurant-bar; candlelit terraces and sea breezes are a bonus. The three-course menu is meat-heavy but includes several fish choices and a couple each of chicken and pasta dishes.

Entertainment

Acapulco's active nightlife probably out-does the beaches as the city's main attraction. Much of the entertainment revolves around discos-style nightclubs.

NIGHTCLUBS

Most clubs open around 10:30pm but don't get rolling until midnight or later. Cover charges vary seasonally and nightly; when they include an open bar you still usually need to tip your server. Dress codes prohibit shorts, sneakers and the like.

Palladium (☎ 446-54-90; Carretera Escénica s/n; cover incl open bar women/men $33/43) Hailed by many as the best disco in town, Palladium attracts a 20s-to-30s crowd with its fabulous views from giant windows. They also come for the hip-hop, house, trance, techno and other bass-heavy beats emanating from an ultraluxe sound system. Dress up, and expect to wait in line.

Baby'O (☎ 484-74-74; La Costera 22; cover $10-38) Very popular with the upscale crowd, Baby'O has a laser light show and Wednesday theme nights, and spins rock, pop, house and 'everything but electronica.' Drinks are not included in the cover charge.

Los Alebrijes (☎ 484-59-02; La Costera 3308; cover incl open bar women/men $26/36) This disco-concert hall bills itself as 'one of the largest and most spectacular discos in the world.' Less spectacular than big, it's usually packed with a young Mexican crowd. The music is a middle-of-the-road mix of mostly Latin rock and pop; open bar hours are 1am to 5am.

Disco Beach (☎ 484-82-30; La Costera s/n, Playa Condesa; cover incl open bar women/men $25/27; ⏰ Wed-Sat) This busy spot is in the line of beachfront restaurant-bars, right on Playa Condesa (the beach forms part of the dance floor). Dress policy is more relaxed here than at most other clubs, and the place draws a fairly young crowd. Music is house, disco, techno, hip-hop, '70s and '80s; women get in (and drink) for free on Wednesday; and the Friday foam parties can be wild. Check out Ibiza Lounge next door, too.

LIVE MUSIC & BARS

Most of the big hotels along La Costera have bars with entertainment, be it quiet piano music or live bands; head to the following for something different.

Nina's (☎ 484-24-00; La Costera 41; cover incl open bar $24; ⏰ 10pm-4am) Nina's is one of the best places in town for live *música tropical* (salsa, *cumbia*, cha-cha, merengue etc); it has a smokin' dance floor, variety acts and impersonators.

Salon Q (☎ 484-32-52, 481-01-14; La Costera 23; cover $11.50, with open bar $23; ⏰ 10:30pm-6am) This *'catedral de la salsa'* gives Nina's a run for its money, with first-rate salsa singers and bands, celebrity impersonators and a *Carnaval* atmosphere. Reservations are recommended; discounts for groups are available.

Tropicana (La Costera s/n, Playa Hornos; cover $4.50; ⏰ 10pm-4am) Like Nina's, Tropicana has a full spectrum of live *música tropical*, only without the bells and whistles.

Hotel Los Flamingos (☎ 482-06-90; López Mateos s/n) The one quiet spot in this rowdy bunch, the clifftop bar of Hotel Los Flamingos (see p510) has the hands-down best sunset-viewing/drinking spot in Acapulco. Not a car or hustler in sight, and you can sip *cocos locos* (cocktails made with rum, tequila, pineapple juice and coconut creme) to your heart's content.

New West (☎ 483-10-82; La Quebrada 81) This popular local bar has cheap beer, rodeo videos and a jukebox blaring *música ranchera* (Mexico's version of country music, covering a wide range of styles) and a smattering of US country-and-western hits. You *will* see cowboy hats and big belt buckles.

Hard Rock Cafe (☎ 484-00-47; La Costera 37; ◷ noon-2am) It's hard to miss the Hard Rock. Just northwest of CICI, this chain's Acapulco branch has live music from 10pm to 2am.

GAY VENUES
Acapulco has an active gay scene with several gay bars and clubs, mostly open from 10pm until about 4am. **Demas** (☎ 484-13-70; Piedra Picuda 17) is open only to men and has shows on Friday and Saturday; **Picante** (Piedra Picuda 16) is found behind Demas, with a minuscule dance floor, the occasional drag or stripper show, and a mostly male clientele; and **Relax** (☎ 484-04-21; Lomas del Mar 4; ◷ Thu-Sat) welcomes men and women.

DANCE, MUSIC & THEATER
The city's not all booze and boogying. The Centro de Convenciones (p507) presents plays, concerts (by the Acapulco Philharmonic, among others), dance and other performances, as does the Centro Cultural Acapulco (p507). Parque Papagayo (p509) sometimes hosts alfresco events.

SPORTS
Bullfights take place at the Plaza de Toros, southeast of La Quebrada and northwest of Playas Caleta and Caletilla, every Sunday at 5:30pm from January to March; for tickets, try your hotel, a travel agency or the **bullring box office** (☎ 482-11-81; Plaza de Toros; ◷ 10am-2pm). The 'Caleta' bus passes near the bullring.

Shopping
100% Mexico (☎ 486-28-45; www.100mexico.com; La Costera 24, Local 17; ◷ 10am-2pm & 4-10pm) For high-quality crafts from around Mexico, visit this government-run shop. You'll find tinwork, ceramics, textiles, paintings, glassware and much more.

Mercado de Artesanías (Parana) Bargaining is the rule at this 400-stall *mercado*, especially as the sellers often find soft touches among the many cruise-ship passengers. The market is located between Av Cuauhtémoc and Vicente de León and is Acapulco's main craft market. It's paved and pleasant, and an OK place to get better deals on everything that you see in the hotel shops – sarapes, hammocks, jewelry, huaraches, clothing and T-shirts.

Mercado Central (Diego H de Mendoza s/n) A truly local market, this sprawling indoor-outdoor bazaar has everything from *atole* to *zapatos* (shoes) – not to mention produce, hot food and souvenirs. Any eastbound 'Pie de la Cuesta' or 'Pedregoso' bus will drop you here; get off where the sidewalk turns to tarp-covered stalls.

Other handicraft markets include the Mercados de Artesanías Papagayo, Noa Noa, Dalia and La Diana, all on La Costera, and Mercado de Artesanías La Caletilla at the western end of Playa Caletilla.

Getting There & Away
Acapulco is accessible via Hwy 200 from the east and west, and by Hwy 95 and Hwy 95D from the north. It's 400km south of Mexico City and 235km southeast of Zihuatanejo.

AIR
Acapulco has a busy **airport** (☎ 466-94-34) with many international flights, most connecting through Mexico City or Guadalajara (both are short hops from Acapulco). All flights mentioned here are direct; some are seasonal.

Aeroméxico/Aerolitoral (☎ 485-16-25/00; La Costera 286) Service to Guadalajara, Mexico City and Tijuana.

America West (☎ 466-92-75; Airport) Service to Los Angeles and Phoenix.

American Airlines (☎ 481-01-61; La Costera 116, Plaza Condesa, Local 109) Service to Dallas and Chicago.

Aviacsa (☎ 466-92-09; Airport) Service regularly to Oaxaca, Mexico City and Tijuana.

Azteca (☎ 466-90-29; Airport) Service to Ciudad Juárez, Guadalajara and Tijuana.

Continental Airlines (☎ 466-90-46; Airport) Service to Houston, Minneapolis and Newark.

Mexicana & Click Mexicana (☎ 486-75-70; La Costera 1632, La Gran Plaza) Service to Mexico City.
Northwest (☎ 800-900-08-00; Airport) Service to Houston.

BUS

There are two major, 1st-class long-distance bus companies in Acapulco: Estrella de Oro and Estrella Blanca. The modern, air-conditioned **Estrella de Oro terminal** (☎ 800-900-01-05; Av Cuauhtémoc 1490), just east of Massieu, has free toilets, a Banamex ATM and a ticket machine that accepts bank debit cards (and luggage can also be left for $0.20 per hour, per piece). **Estrella Blanca** (☎ 469-20-80) has two 1st-class terminals: **Central Papagayo** (Av Cuauhtémoc 1605) just north of Parque Papagayo (left luggage $0.35 per hour, per piece), and **Central Ejido** (☎ 469-20-28/30; Av Ejido 47). The **Estrella Blanca 2nd-class terminal** (☎ 482-21-84; Av Cuauhtémoc 97) sells tickets for all buses, but only has departures to relatively nearby towns.

Estrella Blanca tickets are also sold a few agencies around town, including **Agencia de Viajes Zócalo** (☎ 482-49-76; La Costera 207, Local 2).

Both companies offer frequent services to Mexico City, with various levels of luxury; journey durations depend on whether they use the faster *autopista* (expressway; Hwy 95D) or the old federal Hwy 95.

CAR & MOTORCYCLE

Many car rental companies rent out 4WDs as well as cars; several have offices at the airport as well as in town, and some offer free delivery to you. Shop around to compare prices.

Rental companies in Acapulco:
Alamo (☎ 484-33-05, 466-94-44; La Costera 2148)
Avis (☎ 466-91-90; La Costera 97, Fiestamericana Hotel)
Budget (☎ 481-24-33, 466-90-03; La Costera 93, Local 2)
Hertz (☎ 485-89-47; La Costera 137)
Saad (☎ 484-34-45; www.acapulcorentacar.com; La Costera 28) Local rentals only.
Thrifty Airport (☎ 466-92-86); La Costera 139 (☎ 486-19-40)

ACAPULCO DAILY BUS SCHEDULE

Destination	Price	Duration	Frequency
Chilpancingo	$7	1¾hr	several 1st-class Estrella Blanca from Central Ejido
	$5.50	3hr	2nd-class Estrella Blanca every 30min 5am-7pm from 2nd-class terminal
	$7	1¾hr	frequent 1st-class Estrella de Oro
Cuernavaca	$24	4-5hr	3 1st-class Estrella Blanca from Central Papagayo
	$22	4-5hr	7 1st class
	$19	5hr	very frequent Estrella de Oro semi-directo
Iguala	$12.50	4hr	hourly 1st-class Estrella Blanca from Central Ejido
	$12.50	3hr	18 1st-class Estrella de Oro
	$11.50	3½hr	frequent Estrella de Oro semi-directo)
Mexico City	$43	6hr	1 deluxe Estrella Blanca from Central Papagayo
(Terminal Norte)	$29	6hr	several 1st-class Estrella Blanca from Central Papagayo
	$25	6hr	2 1st-class Estrella Blanca from Central Ejido
	$29	6hr	7 1st-class Estrella de Oro
Mexico City	$43	5hr	4 deluxe Estrella Blanca from Central Papagayo
(Terminal Sur)	$29	5hr	frequent 1st-class Estrella Blanca from Central Papagayo
	$29	5hr	8 1st-class Estrella Blanca from Central Ejido
	$29	5hr	frequent 1st-class Estrella de Oro
	$43	5hr	6 deluxe Estrella de Oro
Puerto Escondido	$22	7hr	5 1st-class Estrella Blanca from Central Ejido
	$18	9½hr	5 2nd-class Estrella Blanca from Central Ejido
Taxco	$15	4hr	3 1st-class Estrella Blanca from Central Ejido
	$15	4hr	2 1st-class Estrella de Oro
Zihuatanejo	$11.50	4-5hr	10 1st-class Estrella Blanca from Central Ejido
	$12.50	4-5hr	13 Estrella Blanca Primera Plus from Central Ejido
	$11.50	4-5hr	3 1st-class Estrella de Oro
	$8.50	4-5hr	12 2nd-class Estrella de Oro hourly 5am-5:30pm

CENTRAL PACIFIC COAST

Drivers heading inland on Hwy 95D need to have some cash handy. The tolls to Chilpancingo, about 130km north, total $25, including $6.50 just to get through the 'Maxi Túnel' beyond the edge of Acapulco. Though if you've been driving in the city, it may seem a small price to pay for being on the open road again.

Getting Around

TO/FROM THE AIRPORT

Acapulco's airport is 23km southeast of the zócalo, beyond the junction for Puerto Marqués. Arriving by air, you can buy a ticket for transportation into town from the colectivo desk at the end of the domestic terminal; it's about $7.50 per person for a lift to your hotel (a bit more if it's west of the zócalo).

Leaving Acapulco, phone **Móvil Aca** (☎ 462-10-95) 24 hours in advance to reserve transportation back to the airport; the cost varies depending on where your pickup is (from $15 to $19 per person or $28 to $38 for the whole vehicle holding up to five passengers). Taxis from the center to the airport cost around $17 to $22, depending on the amount of luggage.

CAR & MOTORCYCLE

If you can possibly avoid doing any driving in Acapulco, do. The streets are in poor shape and the anarchic traffic is often horridly snarled.

BUS

Acapulco has a good city bus system (especially good when you get an airbrushed beauty with a bumping sound system). Buses operate from 5am to 11pm and cost $0.50 with air-con, $0.40 without. From the zócalo area, the bus stop opposite Sanborns department store on La Costera, two blocks east of the zócalo, is a good place to catch buses – it's the beginning of several bus routes (including to Pie de la Cuesta) so you can usually get a seat. Taxi rides from any of the bus stations to La Costera and other points start at about $4.50.

There are several useful city routes:
Base–Caleta From the Icacos naval base at the southeast end of Acapulco, along La Costera, past the zócalo to Playa Caleta.
Base–Cine Río–Caleta From the Icacos naval base, cuts inland from La Costera on Av Wilfrido Massieu to Av Cuauhtémoc, heads down Av Cuauhtémoc through the

business district, turning back to La Costera just before reaching the zócalo, continuing west to Playa Caleta.
Puerto Marqués–Centro From opposite Sanborns, along La Costera to Puerto Marqués.
Zócalo–Playa Pie de la Cuesta From opposite Sanborns, to Pie de la Cuesta (see p499 for details).

TAXI

Hundreds of zippy blue-and-white VW cabs scurry around Acapulco like cockroaches, maneuvering with an audacity that borders on the comical. Drivers sometimes quote fares higher than the official ones, so ask locals the going rate (about $5) for your ride and agree on the fare with the cabby before you climb in.

COSTA CHICA

Guerrero's 'Small Coast,' extending southeast from Acapulco to the Oaxacan border, is much less traveled than its bigger brother to the northwest, though it has some spectacular beaches. Afro-mestizos (people of mixed African, indigenous and European descent) make up a large portion of the population. The region was a safe haven for Africans who escaped slavery, some from the interior, others (it's believed) from a slave ship that sank just off the coast.

On Hwy 200, 60km (about an hour's drive) east of Acapulco, **San Marcos** is an unremarkable town that is a marketplace for smaller communities in the area. The similar **Cruz Grande** is about 40km further east on Hwy 200. Both provide basic services including banks, gas stations and simple hotels. They're the only two towns of significant size before Cuajinicuilapa near the Oaxaca border.

A little over three hours' drive southeast of Acapulco, **Playa Ventura** (labeled Juan Álvarez on most maps) is a pristine beach with soft white and gold sands and clear water. A town (population 600) extends inland for about three blocks along a kilometer or so of the beach, offering a number of simple seafood restaurants and basic places to stay. To get here from Acapulco, first take a bus heading southeast on Hwy 200 from Acapulco to Copala ($6, 2½ hours, 120km) – buses depart from Estrella Blanca's 2nd-class terminal on Av Cuauhtémoc every half-hour from 3:30am to 7pm. From Copala, camionetas and microbuses depart for Playa Ventura about every half-hour

($1.50, 30 minutes, 13km) from just east of the bus stop.

The very same buses that depart from Acapulco for Copala also continue 13km east on Hwy 200 to **Marquelia** ($6.75, three hours). It's a market town with travelers' services, including several inexpensive hotels. The town offers access to an immense stretch of beach backed by coco palms – the beach follows the coastline's contours for many kilometers in either direction. From Marquelia's center you can take a *camioneta* (shared/private $0.50/2.75, 3km) to a section of the beach known as **Playa La Bocana**, where the Río Marquelia meets the sea and forms a lagoon. La Bocana has some *cabañas*, as well as *comedores* (small food stalls) with hammocks that diners can spend the night in. Another portion of the beach, **Playa Las Peñitas**, is reached by a 5km road heading seaward from the east end of Marquelia. Las Peñitas has two small hotels and some *cabañas* that also offer camping spaces.

About 200km southeast of Acapulco, **Cuajinicuilapa**, or Cuaji (*kwah*-hee, population 9000), is the nucleus of Afro-mestizo culture on the Costa Chica and is well worth a stop if you're at all interested in the mixed African-indigenous heritage that's unique to this region. The **Museo de las Culturas Afro-mestizas** (Museum of Afro-mestizo Cultures; ☎ 741-414-03-10; cnr Manuel Zárate & Cuauhtémoc; admission $0.50; ⏲ 10am-2pm & 4-7pm Tue-Sun) is a tribute to the history of African slaves in Mexico and, specifically, to local Afro-mestizo culture. Behind the museum are three examples of *casas redondas,* the round houses typical of West Africa that were built around Cuaji until as late as the 1960s. The museum is a block inland from the Banamex that's just west of the main plaza.

Buses for Cuaji ($11, five hours) depart Estrella Blanca's Central Ejido station in Acapulco hourly from 5am, and Estrella Blanca has several buses daily from Pinotepa Nacional ($2.75, 1½ hours) in Oaxaca state.

Also known as El Faro, **Punta Maldonado** is the last worthwhile beach before the Oaxaca border. The swimming is good and the surfing, on occasion, is excellent; the break is a reef/point favoring lefts. The village (population 1100) has some seafood restaurants on the beach and one small, unattractive hotel. To reach Punta Maldonado take a *camioneta* from Cuajinicuilapa ($2, 45 minutes);

they depart half-hourly from just off the main plaza, or you can take a taxi.

CHILPANCINGO
☎ 747 / pop 165,000 / elevation 1360m

Chilpancingo, capital of the state of Guerrero, is a university city and agricultural center. It lies on Hwys 95 and 95D, 130km north of Acapulco and 270km south of Mexico City. It's an administrative center and a rather nondescript place, located between the much more compelling destinations of Taxco and Acapulco.

The former **Palacio Municipal**, on the *zócalo,* has murals showing the city's important place in Mexico's history. In the spring of 1813, rebel leader José María Morelos y Pavón encircled Mexico City with his guerrilla army and demanded a congress in Chilpancingo. The congress issued a Declaration of Independence and began to lay down the principles of a new constitution. But Spanish troops eventually breached the circle around Mexico City, and Morelos was tried for treason and then executed.

Being a state capital, Chilpancingo has an **Inegi office** (☎ 472-88-04; Ramírez 18) selling government-produced topographical maps and city plans for locations in the state of Guerrero. For medical emergencies, call the **Cruz Roja** (Red Cross; ☎ 472-65-61).

Sleeping & Eating
The best eateries and lodgings are around the bus terminal and the *zócalo.*

Hotel El Presidente (☎ 472-97-31; cnr Calle 30 de Agosto & Insurgentes; s $29 d $33-38; **P**) The tidy, modern Presidente is only a block from the bus station and is visible from the highway and the bus terminal.

Del Parque Hotel (☎ 472-30-12; Colón 5; r $37) Just a block toward Acapulco from the *zócalo,* the modern Del Parque has clean, spacious, carpeted rooms done up in blue and white. Windows are double-glazed to minimize street noise, and the beds and bathrooms are very good. The ground floor contains the very popular Taco Rock restaurant, where you can get decent pizzas, sandwiches and breakfast for $3 to $6.

Hotel El Presidente has a popular mid-range restaurant-bar, and several other cheaper places are visible from the bus station. Just east (uphill) of the bus terminal, the lively public market's upstairs *fondas* (small eateries) are cheap places to fuel up – don't miss the pork specialties and *pozole* with *chicharrones* (fried pork skins) on Thursday.

Getting There & Away

Chilpancingo bus station is 1.5km away from the *zócalo*. It is served by the bus companies **Estrella Blanca** (☎ 472-06-34) and **Estrella de Oro** (☎ 472-21-30). Among the services offered are frequent buses to Acapulco ($7, 1½ hours), Iguala ($4.50, 1½ hours) and Mexico City ($18 to $23, 3½ hours), and at least two daily buses to Taxco ($9.50, three hours).

AROUND CHILPANCINGO
Chilapa

☎ 756 / pop 23,000 / elevation 1450m

Chilapa, one hour east of Chilpancingo by combi ($2.50), which leave from a small terminal on the south side of Chilpancingo's market (a block uphill from the main bus terminal), holds a traditional **market** every Sunday, starting very early in the morning. Market day has an almost pre-Hispanic feel; indigenous people pour out of the hills,

and all types of foodstuffs, handicrafts and animals are on display. Many vendors from this market cart their leftover wares to Acapulco on Monday. The towers of the city's 20th-century **cathedral** measure an impressive 47m high.

Olinalá

☎ 756 / pop 5200 / elevation 1350m

The remote and little-visited town of Olinalá is famous throughout Mexico for its beautiful lacquered boxes and other locally produced lacquered woodcraft. Linaloe, the fragrant wood traditionally used to make the boxes, grows in the area. It's in short supply these days, however, and is often substituted for by pine. The **Templo de San Francisco** is well worth a visit; its interior boasts much lacquered-wood ornamentation and a great mural of Heaven and Hell. You'll find simple hotels around the plaza and a few places to eat. Second-class buses from Chilpancingo to Tlapa will drop you at the crossroads for Olinalá (4½ hours); then catch a 3rd-class bus (one hour) to Olinalá.

Western Central Highlands

The Western Central Highlands hold some of Mexico's most memorable travel adventures. This region – which includes Guadalajara, Colima, Morelia, Pátzcuaro and Uruapan – isn't overly touristed or famous, making travel here very enjoyable. People are friendly, curious and helpful, especially in the smaller villages, and there's a certain sense of serenity and safety absent in the more touristy parts of the country. The weather is awesome and the region's geography spectacular, with endless verdant mountains, fertile valleys and rugged landscapes. These highlands are at the heart of Mexico, a relatively undiscovered part of the country and often a favorite for those lucky enough to glimpse them.

Despite its size, exciting Guadalajara – capital of Jalisco state – doesn't overwhelm; its pedestrian lanes, walkable streets and handy public transport make getting around easy. Morelia, Michoacán state's fine capital, offers stunning architecture and Santuario Mariposa Monarca, a butterfly sanctuary. Pátzcuaro, a captivating colonial town and the soul of Michoacán's indigenous Purépecha culture, is the epitome of Mexico's Día de Muertos celebration. Wonderful Uruapan and Colima are both near fascinating volcanoes: Paricutín, which rose from lush countryside almost overnight in 1943, the large snowy cones of Volcán Nevado de Colima, and bubbling Volcán de Fuego. This is a taste of the very best of Mexico.

WESTERN CENTRAL HIGHLANDS

TOP FIVE

- Taking in cosmopolitan **Guadalajara** (p521), a very Mexican city, and home of mariachi music, tequila, *charreadas* (Mexican rodeos) and the Mexican hat dance

- Exploring beautiful **Morelia** (p558), capital of Michoacán, which offers great architecture, fine food, a non-touristy atmosphere and a lively student population

- Visiting the **Santuario Mariposa Monarca** (Monarch Butterfly Sanctuary, p566), the fluttering winter resort for millions of migratory butterflies

- Relaxing in **Pátzcuaro** (p568), a gloriously peaceful and pretty highland town, and the soul of the Purépecha people

- Trekking up the snowy, extinct volcanic peak of **Volcán Nevado de Colima** (p557) or the still-smouldering **Volcán Paricutín** (p585)

- GUADALAJARA JANUARY DAILY HIGH: 24°C | 90°F
- GUADALAJARA JULY DAILY HIGH: 26°C | 79°F

History

The western central highlands were remote from the country's pre-Hispanic empires, though a fairly advanced agricultural village society flourished in parts of the region as early as 200 BC. In the 14th to 16th centuries AD, the Tarascos of northern Michoacán developed a major pre-Hispanic civilization, with its capital at Tzintzuntzan, near Pátzcuaro. The zenith of the Tarascan empire coincided with the Aztec empire, but the Tarascos always managed to fend off Aztec attacks. West of the Tarascos – and occasionally at war with them – was the Chimalhuacán confederation of four indigenous kingdoms, in parts of what are now Jalisco, Colima and Nayarit states. To the

north were Chichimecs, whom the Aztec regarded as barbarians.

Colima, the leading Chimalhuacán kingdom, was conquered by the Spanish in 1523. The whole region, however, was not brought under Spanish control until the 1529–3 campaigns of the notorious Nuño de Guzmán, who tortured, killed and enslaved indigenous people from Michoacán to Sinalo in his pursuit of riches, territory and glory. He was appointed governor of most of what he had conquered, until his misdeeds caught up with him, and he was sent back to Spain and imprisoned for life in 1538. These territories came to be called Nueva Galicia, and they retained some autonomy from the res of Nueva España until 1786.

A rebellion in Jalisco in 1540 set that rea aflame, in what is known as the Mixón War; it was ended the next year by an rmy led by the Spanish viceroy. Guadalara was established in its present location n 1542, after three earlier settlements were bandoned in the face of attacks by hostile ndigenous groups.

The region developed gradually, with anching and agriculture as mainstays, and uadalajara (always one of Mexico's bigest cities) became the 'capital of the west.' he church, with help from the enlightened ishop Vasco de Quiroga, fostered small inustries and handicraft traditions around e villages of Lago Pátzcuaro, in its effort to ase the poverty of the indigenous people.

In the 1920s, Michoacán and Jalisco were otbeds of the Cristero rebellion by Catholics gainst government antichurch policies. Láaro Cárdenas of Michoacán, as state goveror (1928–32) and then as Mexican president 1934–40), instituted reforms that did much) abate antigovernment sentiments.

Today both Jalisco and Michoacán hold nany of Mexico's natural resources – specially timber, mining, livestock, and griculture – and Jalisco has a notable omputer industry. Tourism also plays an nportant part of the region's economy. lowever, both states have seen large segents of their populations head to the US for ork. Michoacán, especially, has lost almost alf its population to emigration; money sent ome from this state approaches two billion ollars. But there are a few movements to ncourage local economies and stop this loss f people, mainly by developing agricultural r building projects, and by creating scholarips and entrepreneurs.

limate

he climate is pleasantly warm and dry ost of the year, with a distinct rainy seaon from June to September (when some 00mm of rain per month falls in most of e area). At lower altitudes, like the areas ear Uruapan and Colima, temperature and umidity rise, and tropical plants abound. higher-altitude places, such as Pátzcuaro, inter nights can get chilly.

etting There & Around

ll major cities in the western central ighlands (Guadalajara, Colima, Morelia,

Pátzcuaro and Uruapan) are well connected by buses from outside the region, as well as to each other. Guadalajara and Morelia have regular flights from many other cities in Mexico, as well as the United States.

GUADALAJARA

☎ 33 / pop 4 million / elevation 1540m

Second in size only to Mexico City, Guadalajara is nonetheless considered a more 'Mexican' city, and is a surprisingly manageable, safe and friendly metropolis. Many attractive pedestrian streets and plazas grace the city's Centro Histórico (Historic Center), offering passersby a plethora of gushing fountains, leafy shrubs, relaxing benches and interesting sculptures. The city's residents (nicknamed *tapatíos,* which also refers to anyone Jalisco-born) stroll around peacefully in this pleasant downtown area, lined with beautiful, elegant old buildings along with fashionable shops. And when they tire of the noise and congestion, nearby suburbs, like Zapopan, Tlaquepaque and Tonalá – formerly separate communities that have retained their small-town charm – become popular weekend jumps for visits or shopping trips.

Guadalajara's major contributions to the Mexican lifestyle include tequila, mariachi music, the broad-rimmed sombrero (hat), *charreadas* and the Mexican Hat Dance. It's also western Mexico's largest industrial center, and claims a healthy share of museums, galleries, historic buildings, festivals, nightlife and culture. As a traveler to this remarkable city, you'll find plenty of things to keep you busy and happy.

HISTORY

Guadalajara had a hard time getting started: it was established on its present site only after three settlements elsewhere had failed. In 1532, Nuño de Guzmán and a few dozen other Spanish families founded the first Guadalajara near Nochistlán (now in Zacatecas state), naming it after Guzmán's home city in Spain. Water was scarce, the land was hard to farm and – to top it all off – the indigenous people were hostile. Thus, in 1533, with their tails between their legs, the settlers moved to the pre-Hispanic village of Tonalá (today a suburb

GUADALAJARA

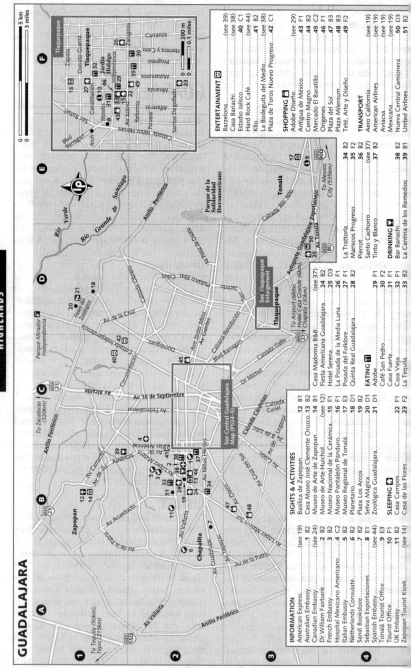

INFORMATION
American Express.	(see 19)
Australian Embassy.	1 B2
Canadian Embassy.	(see 24)
Dr William Fairbank.	2 B2
French Embassy.	3 B2
Hospital Mexicano Americano.	4 C2
Italian Embassy.	5 B2
Netherlands Consulate.	6 B2
Sandi Bookstore.	7 B2
Sebastian Exportaciones.	8 E1
Spanish Embassy.	9 E3
Tonalá Tourist Office.	10 F1
Tourist Office.	11 B2
UK Embassy.	12 B1
Zapopan Tourist Kiosk.	(see 14)

SIGHTS & ACTIVITIES
Basílica de Zapopan.	(see 19)
Casa Museo José Clemente Orozco.	13 B2
Museo de Arte de Zapopan.	14 B1
Museo de Arte Huichol.	(see 12)
Museo Nacional de la Cerámica.	15 F1
Museo Pantaleón Panduro.	16 F1
Museo Regional de Tonalá.	17 E3
Planetario.	18 D1
Plaza Los Arcos.	19 B2
Selva Mágica.	20 D1
Zoológica Guadalajara.	21 D1

SLEEPING
Casa Campos.	22 F1
Casa de las Flores.	23 F2
Casa Madonna B&B.	(see 37)
Fiesta Americana Guadalajara.	24 B2
Hotel Serena.	25 D3
La Posada de la Media Luna.	26 F1
Posada del Folklore.	27 F1
Quinta Real Guadalajara.	28 B2

EATING
Adobe.	29 F1
Café San Pedro.	30 F2
Casa Fuerte.	31 F1
Casa Vieja.	32 F1
La Tequila.	33 B2
La Trattoria.	34 B2
Mariscos Progreso.	35 F2
Pierrot.	(see 37)
Santo Cachorro.	36 F2
Tinto y Blanco.	37 B2

DRINKING
Bar Bariachi.	38 B2
La Cantina de los Remedios.	39 B1

ENTERTAINMENT
Barzelona.	(see 39)
Casa Bariachi.	(see 38)
Estadio Jalisco.	40 C1
Hard Rock Café.	(see 44)
Klio.	41 B2
La Bodeguita del Medio.	(see 38)
Plaza de Toros Nuevo Progreso.	42 C1

SHOPPING
Adobe Diseño.	(see 29)
Antigua de México.	43 F1
Centro Magno.	44 B2
Mercado El Baratillo.	45 C2
Orígenes.	46 F1
Plaza del Sol.	47 B3
Plaza Milenium.	48 B3
Teté, Arte y Diseño.	49 F2

TRANSPORT
Aero California.	(see 19)
American Airlines.	(see 19)
Aviacsa.	(see 19)
Mexicana.	(see 19)
Nueva Central Camionera.	50 D3
United Airlines.	51 B2

f Guadalajara). Guzmán disliked Tonalá, owever, and two years later had the settle- nent moved to Tlacotán, northeast of the nodern city. In 1541 this site was destroyed y a confederation of indigenous tribes led y the chief Tenamaxtli. The surviving olonists wearily picked a new site in the alley of Atemajac beside San Juan de Dios Creek, which ran where Calz Independ- ncia is today. The new Guadalajara was ounded on February 14, 1542, near where ne Teatro Degollado now stands.

Guadalajara finally prospered, and in 560 was declared the capital of Nueva alicia province. The city quickly grew into ne of colonial Mexico's most important opulation centers and was at the heart of rich agricultural region. It also became the tarting point for Spanish expeditions and issions to western and northern Nueva spaña – and to as far away as the Philip- ines. Miguel Hidalgo, a leader in the fight or Mexican independence, set up a revolu- onary government in Guadalajara in 1810, ut was defeated near the city in 1811, not ong before his capture and execution in hihuahua. The city was also the object f heavy fighting during the War of the eform (1858–61), and between Constitu- onalist and Villista armies in 1915.

By the late 19th century Guadalajara had vertaken Puebla as Mexico's second-biggest ty. Its population has mushroomed since WII, and now the city is a huge commer- al, industrial and cultural center, and the ommunications hub for a large region.

RIENTATION

uadalajara's large twin-towered cathedral, the heart of the city, is surrounded by ur lovely plazas. The plaza east of the athedral, Plaza de la Liberación, extends vo blocks to the Teatro Degollado, also a ty landmark. This whole area, along with few surrounding blocks, is known as the entro Histórico.

East of Teatro Degollado, the Plaza Tapatía edestrian precinct extends 500m to the In- ituto Cultural de Cabañas, another histori- lly significant building. Just south of Plaza apatía is Mercado San Juan de Dios, a huge ree-story market covering two city blocks.

Calz Independencia is a major north– uth central artery. From Mercado San an de Dios, it runs south to Parque Agua

Azul and the Antigua Central Camionera (Old Bus Terminal), still used by short- distance regional buses. Northward, it runs to the zoo and other attractions. Don't confuse Calz Independencia with Av Inde- pendencia, the east–west street one block north of the cathedral.

In the city center, north–south streets change names at Av Hidalgo, the street run- ning along the north side of the cathedral.

About 20 blocks west of the cathedral, the north–south Av Chapultepec is at the heart of Guadalajara's Zona Rosa, a smart area with modern offices and some fine restaurants. The long-distance bus termi- nal is the Nueva Central Camionera (New Bus Terminal), which is approximately 9km southeast of the city center past the suburb of Tlaquepaque.

INFORMATION
Bookstores

Stores with a good selection of books in English aren't common in Guadalajara.

Libros y Arte (Map pp524-5; ☎ 3617-8207; Cabañas; ☼ 10am-6pm Tue-Sat, 10am-3pm Sun) Located at the Instituto Cultural de Cabañas, this bookstore has mostly art and children's books in Spanish, along with a few titles in English.

Sanborns (Map pp524-5; ☎ 3613-6264; cnr Avs 16 de Septiembre & Juárez; ☼ 7:30am-midnight Sun-Wed, 7:30am-1am Thu-Sat) With magazines, maps and a few books in English. It's downstairs.

Sandi Bookstore (Map p522; ☎ 3121-4210; Av Tepeyac 718; ☼ 9:30am-7pm Mon-Fri, 9:30am-2pm Sat & Sun) About 1km west of Av López Mateos, Sandi offers an extensive travel section, including Lonely Planet guides. There's also plenty of maps and other books, all in English.

Cultural Centers

Alianza Francesa (Map pp524-5; ☎ 3825-5595; www .alianzafrancesa.org.mx/guadalajara; López Cotilla 1199; ☼ 9am-1pm & 4-8pm Mon-Fri, 9am-12pm Sat) Offers Francophiles classes, movies and a library – all French- oriented, of course.

Emergency

If you are a victim of crime you may first want to contact your embassy or consu- late (p975) and/or the State tourist office (p526).

Ambulance (☎ 065, 3616-9616)
General emergency (☎ 066, 080)
Fire (☎ 3619-5155)
Police (☎ 060, 3668-0800)

WESTERN CENTRAL HIGHLANDS

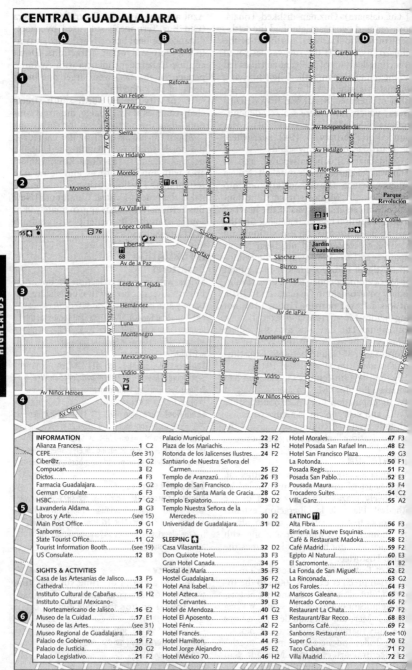

CENTRAL GUADALAJARA

WESTERN CENTRAL HIGHLANDS

DRINKING 🍸

La Fuente.....................................73 F2
La Maestranza...............................74 F2
Peña Cuicacalli.............................75 B4

ENTERTAINMENT 🎭

Angels Club..................................76 A2
Circus..77 F3
El Cubilete....................................78 F3
Ex-Convento del Carmen...............79 E2
La Prisciliana.................................80 F3
Lienzo Charros de Jalisco...............81 F6
Los Caudillos................................82 F3
Meridiano 60................................83 F3
Sexy's Bar....................................84 F3
Teatro Degollado..........................85 G2
Teatro Diana.................................86 F4

SHOPPING 🛍

El Charro.......................................87 G2
Mercado San Juan de Dios............88 H2

TRANSPORT

Aeroméxico...................................89 F2
Agencia de Viajes Hermes.............90 H2
Agencia de Viajes McCull..............91 G2
Antigua Central Camionera............92 G5
Bus 258 to Av López Mateos Sur....93 F1
Bus 275, TUR Bus to Zapopan........94 F2
Bus to Antigua Central Camionera &
　Parque Agua Azul........................95 G2
Buses to Nueva Camionera, Tonalá &
　Tlaquepaque...............................96 F2
Delta..97 A2
Horse Carriages............................98 F3
Par Vial Buses 400 & 500 to Zona
　Rosa...99 F1
Tequila Express Office..................100 F2
Trolley Bus 600 & Buses 60 & 62A to Zoo,
　Selva Mágica & Planetarium.......101 G2

Internet Access

Several Internet cafés in the city center charge about $1.50 per hour; connections are good.

Compucan (Map pp524-5; Medellín 46; 9am-8pm Mon-Sat)

Ciber@z (Map pp524-5; Paseo Degollado 134; 9am-11pm)

Dictos (Map pp524-5; Sánchez 163; 9am-9pm Mon-Sat)

Internet Resources

http://visita.jalisco.gob.mx Official website of Jalisco (in Spanish).

http://vive.guadalajara.gob.mx Official website of Guadalajara.

www.zapopan.gob.mx Official website of Zapopan (in Spanish).

www.tlaquepaque.gob.mx Official website of Tlaquepaque (in Spanish).

www.tonala.gob.mx Official website of Tonalá (in Spanish).

Laundry

Lavandería Aldama (Map pp524-5; ☎ 3617-6427; Aldama 125; 9am-6pm Mon-Sat) For clean duds, head southwest a few blocks from the city center to this laundry. Full service costs $4 per load; self-service is about $3. Note: it's in a gritty neighborhood.

Media

The Spanish-language *Público*, the city's most prominent daily newspaper, offers exhaustive entertainment listings on Friday. *Guadalajara Reporter* (www.guadalajarareporter.com) caters to expats living in the region, including Lago de Chapala and Puerto Vallarta. *Guadalajara Weekly* is a free, but not very informative, visitor newsletter, available at the tourist office and some hotels. Many of the newsstands in central Guadalajara sell English-language periodicals.

Medical Services

Dr William Fairbank (Map p522; ☎ 3616-4851; Justo Serra 2515-1; 9am-2pm & 4-6pm Mon-Fri) American doctor located 3km west of the city center.

Farmacia Guadalajara (Map pp524-5; ☎ 3613-7509; Moreno 170; 8am-10pm) Carries all sorts of first aid and sundry items, and can fill prescriptions. Many other branches in the city, some open 24 hours.

Hospital Mexico Americano (Map p522; ☎ 3641-3141; Colomos 2110) About 3km northwest of the city center; English-speaking medics available.

Money

Banks are plentiful in Guadalajara, and most have ATMs. **HSBC** (Map pp524-5; cnr Av Juarez & Molina; 8am-7pm Mon-Fri, 8am-3pm Sat) tends to keep the longest hours.

Many eager *casas de cambio* (money changers) on López Cotilla – in the few blocks east of Av 16 de Septiembre – offer competitive exchange rates, quicker service, longer hours and an altogether seedier atmosphere than you'll find in banks. Some require you to change a minimum of $100 and most will change traveler's checks. Shop around as their rates can vary.

American Express (Map p522; ☎ 3818-2319; Av Vallarta 2440; 9am-6pm Mon-Fri, 9am-1pm Sat) Located in the small Plaza Los Arcos shopping center, way west of the city center.

Post

Main post office (Map pp524-5; cnr Carranza & Av Independencia, 8am-7pm Mon-Fri, 9am-1pm Sat)

Telephone

There aren't many calling offices in Guadalajara; the cheapest way to dial home is to buy a Telmex phone card (look for the signs outside stores selling them) and then find a reasonably quiet public phone.

Toilets

It's not hard finding a legal place to pee in central Guadalajara. Interestingly enough it's the free toilets that are nicest; pay public toilets (usually $0.20) are pretty raunchy. Try the facilities at Sanborns (p523), fast-food outlets like McDonald's, and any government or public building with unrestricted entry (like the Palacio de Gobierno or the Ex-Convento del Carmen). Most markets have pay public toilets, and there are some bad ones in Plaza Tapatio (Map pp524–5) at the bottom of the stairs into the parking lot.

Tourist Information

State tourist office (Map pp524-5; ☎ 3668-1600, 800-362-22-00; Morelos 102 or Paseo Degollado 105; 9am-8pm Mon-Fri, 10am-2pm Sat & Sun) Enter from either Morelos or Paseo Degollado. English-speaking staff offer information on Guadalajara and the state of Jalisco. Also a good place for information on current happenings.

Tourist information booth (Map pp524-5; 9:30am-2:30pm & 5-7:30pm Mon-Fri, 10am-12:30pm Sat & Sun) In the Palacio de Gobierno, just inside the

WESTERN CENTRAL HIGHLANDS

entrance facing the Plaza de Armas. During cultural events and festivals other information booths pop up around the city center.

SIGHTS

Plaza de Armas & Palacio de Gobierno

The **Plaza de Armas** (Map pp524–5), on the south side of the cathedral, is a pleasant place to sit and imagine how the city was in colonial times. The roof of its fine central bandstand is attractively supported by bronze art nouveau ladies. Free concerts of Jaliscan music often take place here in the evening (see p541).

The impressive **palacio** (Map pp524–5; Av Corona btwn Morelos & Moreno; 🕙 9am-8pm), which currently houses state government offices, was finished in 1774. Its style mixes simple neoclassical features with riotous Churrigueresque decorations. The palacio's most interesting artistic feature, however, is the huge mural of Miguel Hidalgo looming over an interior stairway. An angry Hidalgo brandishes a torch in one fist while the masses struggle at his feet. This 1937 artwork is one of José Clemente Orozco's most famous masterpieces, and he uses it to address the pressing issues of his time: communism, fascism and religion. Another Orozco mural in the ex-Congreso (former Congress Hall) upstairs depicts Hidalgo, Benito Juárez and other figures important in Mexican history.

Cathedral

Guadalajara's twin-towered **cathedral** (Map pp524-5; Av 16 de Septiembre btwn Morelos & Av Hidalgo; 🕙 8am-8pm, closed during mass) is the city's main symbol and its most conspicuous landmark. Begun in 1558 and consecrated in 1618, it's almost as old as the city itself. Up close you can see that, a lot like the Palacio de Gobierno, the cathedral is an almost confusing stylistic hodgepodge. The exterior decorations, some of which were completed long after the consecration, are in Churrigueresque, baroque and neoclassical, among other styles. The towers date from 1848 and are much higher than the originals, which were destroyed in an earthquake in 1818. The interior includes Gothic vaults, Tuscany-style pillars and 11 richly decorated altars that were given to Guadalajara by King Fernando VII of Spain (1784–1833). The glass case nearest

the north entrance is an extremely popular reliquary, containing the hands and blood of the martyred Santa Inocencia. In the sacristy, which an attendant can open for you on request, is *La Asunción de la Virgen,* painted by Spanish artist Bartolomé Murillo in 1650.

Plaza de los Laureles & Palacio Municipal

Directly west of the cathedral, Plaza de los Laureles (Map pp524–5) is planted with laurel trees, hence the name. It's a good place to hang out and enjoy the great view of the cathedral. On its north side is the Palacio Municipal (City Hall; Map pp524–5), which was built between 1949 and 1952, but looks much older. Above its interior stairway is a somewhat frightening mural by Gabriel Flores, depicting the founding of Guadalajara.

Rotonda de los Jaliscenses Ilustres

The plaza on the north side of the cathedral is ringed by bronze sculptures of Jalisco's favorite characters (20 at last count), including writers, architects, revolutionaries, a composer and others. Some of them are buried beneath the Rotonda de los Jaliscenses Ilustres (Rotunda of Illustrious Jaliscans; Map pp524–5), the round pillared monument in the center of the plaza. Before the city establishment got egalitarian and added a woman to the mix, the rotunda was 'de los Hombres Ilustres.'

Museo Regional de Guadalajara

East of the Rotonda de los Jaliscenses Ilustres, this must-see **museum** (Map pp524-5; ☎ 3614-9957; Liceo 60; admission $3.25; 🕙 9am-5:30pm Tue-Sat, 9am-4:30pm Sun) has an eclectic collection covering the history and prehistory of western Mexico. Displays in the ground-floor natural history section include the skeleton of a woolly mammoth. The archaeological section has some well-preserved figurines, along with many fine artifacts of ceramic, silver, gold and other materials. Upstairs are galleries of colonial paintings, a history gallery covering the area since the Spanish conquest, and an ethnography section with displays about indigenous life in Jalisco. The museum building is the former seminary of San José, a late-17th-century baroque structure with two stories of arcades and several courtyards holding hidden delights, some of which can only be viewed from above; be sure to wander everywhere.

Plaza de la Liberación

East of the cathedral, Plaza de la Liberación (Map pp524–5) is a lively and impressive space, originally created by a 1980s urban renovation project, which involved the demolition of two whole blocks of colonial buildings (the redevelopment is still a source of controversy).

On the north side of the plaza, next to the Museo Regional, is the **Palacio Legislativo** (Map pp524–5), where the state congress meets, which is distinguished by massive stone columns in its interior courtyard. Across the street to the east is the **Palacio de Justicia** (State Courthouse; Map pp524–5), built in 1588 as part of the Convento de Santa María, Guadalajara's first nunnery. A 1965 mural by Guillermo Chávez, depicting Benito Juárez and other legendary Mexican lawmakers, graces the interior stairway.

Teatro Degollado

Home of the Guadalajara Philharmonic, the neoclassical **Teatro Degollado** (Map pp524–5; ☎ 3614-4773; Degollado; admission free; ☻ for viewing 12:30-2:30pm Mon-Fri) was begun in 1856, inaugurated 30 years later, and has been reconstructed several times since. Over the columns on its front is a frieze depicting Apollo and the Nine Muses. The five-tiered theater's interior is decorated with red velvet and gold, and is crowned by a Gerardo Suárez mural based on the fourth canto of Dante's *Divine Comedy*. The theater hosts frequent performances of music, dance and drama, and was renovated in 2005 – it now has a café.

Plaza Tapatía

Wide, lengthy, pedestrian **Plaza Tapatía** (Map pp524–5) sprawls to the east for more than 500m from behind Teatro Degollado, crossing over Calz Independencia at about its midpoint (but you can't really tell). It's a very pleasant extended plaza at the heart of Guadalajara, and offers both locals and tourists a break from the traffic-choked streets of the city center. There are plenty of opportunities for window-shopping, people-watching and snacking from street vendors. Street performers attract crowds,

and there's a small daily crafts market for browsing. When you hit the other end, at the Instituto Cultural de Cabañas, you can rest on one of several wonderfully whimsical bronze sculptures/benches – they make a great photo op, so bring your camera.

Instituto Cultural de Cabañas

This huge, neoclassical gem, at the east end of Plaza Tapatía, houses a school, cultural institute and **museum** (Map pp524-5; ☎ 3818-2800 ext 31014; Cabañas 8; admission $1, free Sun; ☻ 10am-6pm Tue-Sat, 10am-3pm Sun). It was built between 1805 and 1810 as the Hospicio Cabañas, an orphanage and home for invalids founded by Bishop Don Juan Cruz Ruiz de Cabañas. Designed by Spanish architect Manuel Tolsa and featuring 23 separate courtyards, the complex continued to serve mainly as an orphanage for over 150 years, often housing up to 450 children at a time. At one time or another it has also served as a nursing home, military barracks and jail. The complex was declared a Unesco World Heritage Site in 1997.

Between 1938 and 1939 José Clemente Orozco painted murals in the main chapel; these are the institute's main attraction and widely regarded as Orozco's finest work. Most notable is *El Hombre de Fuego* (Man of Fire) in the dome; it's been the subject of widely varying interpretations. Fifty-seven other frescoes cover the walls and ceiling of the chapel, which is furnished with benches on which you can lie back and look straight up.

The museum features a permanent exhibition of more than 100 Orozco drawings (mostly sketches for his on-site murals and paintings, plus temporary exhibition of painting, sculpture and engraving. The institute also hosts dance festivals, drama performances and concerts. Free tours in English and Spanish are available.

Plaza de los Mariachis

Plaza de los Mariachis, near the intersection of Av Javier Mina and Calz Independencia Sur, and just south of Mercado San Juan de Dois (Map pp524–5), is arguably the birthplace of mariachi music. It's more like a short pedestrian street than a plaza, but you can't miss the outdoor tables, where people sit, eat and drink while wandering mariachis offer their musical services – fo

bout $10 per song. These days the plaza is
bit run-down and the surrounding neigh-
orhood is grungy, so don't go wandering
oo far at night (though the plaza itself is
velier after dark).

olonial Churches

Central Guadalajara holds a dozen other
hurches, in addition to the ones already
mentioned, some quite impressive.

The **Santuario de Nuestra Señora del Carmen**
(Map pp524–5) – facing the small plaza on
he corner of Av Juárez and 8 de Julio –
s a lovely church, with lots of gold deco-
ation, old paintings and murals in the
ome. Closer to the city center, on the
orner of Loza and Av Hidalgo, is the or-
ate **Templo Nuestra Señora de las Mercedes**
(Map pp524–5), which was built in 1650;
nside are several fine large paintings, crys-
al chandeliers and lots of gold decora-
on. Six blocks further east is the fairly
nremarkable **Templo de Santa María de Gracia**
(Map pp524–5), which served as the city's
irst cathedral (1549–1618).

On the corner of Av 16 de Septiembre and
lanco, the **Templo de Aranzazú** (Map pp524–
), built from 1749 to 1752, has three or-
ate Churrigueresque golden altars. Beside
is the larger but less showy **Templo de San
rancisco** (Map pp524–5), built two centuries
arlier.

Museo de la Ciudad

History buffs will appreciate this **museum**
(Map pp524–5; ☎ 3658-3706; Av Independencia 684;
dmission $0.60, free Sun; ☉ 10am-5:30pm Tue-Sat,
0am-2:30pm Sun), an ex-convent, which today
ffers a well-displayed collection of artifacts
nd photos depicting Guadalajara's history
p until 1992. Exhibition rooms fringe two
ld courtyards, and the labels are in Span-
h. Cultural events are occasionally held
ere.

Universidad de Guadalajara & Templo Expiatorio

West of the city center, where Av Juárez
meets Av Federalismo, is shady **Parque Rev-
lución** (Map pp524–5). Three blocks fur-
her west at Av Juárez 975 is the **Paraninfo**
(Theater Hall), one of the main buildings
f the Universidad de Guadalajara (Map
p524–5). Inside, the stage backdrop and
ome feature large, powerful murals by

Orozco. In the back of the same building
is the **Museo de las Artes** (Map pp524–5; ☎ 3134-
1664; admission free; ☉ 10am-6pm Tue-Fri, 10am-4pm
Sat & Sun), which has temporary exhibits of
modern art and a good gift shop.

The next block south is the 1897 Gothic
Templo Expiatorio (Map pp524–5; ☉ 7am-11pm), accented by tall, fluted stone columns and
15m-high stained-glass windows. At 9am,
noon and 6pm, a door in the clock tower
opens and the 12 apostles march right out.

Casa-Museo José Clemente Orozco

During the 1940s, the great *tapatío* painter
and muralist, José Clemente Orozco (1883–
1949), lived and worked in this **house** (Map
p522; ☎ 3616-8329; Aurelio Aceves 29; admission free;
☉ 10am-6pm Tue-Sat, 10am-3pm Sun). There's currently only one of Orozco's murals on display, but the museum may acquire some of
his personal effects in the future. Until then
there are temporary exhibits.

Parque Agua Azul

About 20 blocks south of the city center,
Parque Agua Azul (Map pp524–5; Calz Independencia Sur;
adult/child $0.40/0.20; ☉ 10am-6pm Tue-Sun) is a large
verdant park offering pleasant relief from
the city hubbub. There are lots of benches
on which to rest, so bring a good book or
your sweetheart. The grassy and tree-filled
areas feature an orchid house, butterfly
house, aviary and children's playground.
The orchids are at their best in October,
November, April and May. Bus 60 (or any
marked 'Agua Azul') heading south on Calz
Independencia will drop you here from the
city center.

The **Casa de las Artesanías de Jalisco** (Map
pp524–5; ☎ 3619-4664; Calz Gallo 20; ☉ 10am-6pm Mon-Fri,
10am-5pm Sat, 10am-3pm Sun) is a large museum-
like store selling high-quality handicrafts
from all over Jalisco; look for pottery, glassware, jewelry, textiles, papier-mâché and
furniture. Prices are reasonable and there's
a small, free ceramics museum.

Zoológico Guadalajara, Selva Mágica & Planetario

The zoo, Selva Mágica children's amusement park and planetarium are near one
another on the northern outskirts of the
city. Trolleybus R600 and buses 60 and 62A
(marked 'Zoológico'), heading north on
Calz Independencia, drop you close by.

The **Zoológico Guadalajara** (Map p522; ☎ 3674-4488; www.zooguadalajara.com.mx; Paseo del Zoológico 600; adult/child $3.75/2; ⏰ 10am-5pm Wed-Sun) is a large, relatively pleasant zoo, with aviaries, a reptile house, a children's petting zoo and a train ride ($1.50 extra). Animals include lions, tigers and bears (oh my), as well as hippos, llamas and flamingos. The north end of the site provides a view of the Barranca de Oblatos, an impressive 670m-deep canyon. Stroller and wheelchair rentals are available.

Beside the zoo, off Calz Independencia Nte, is **Selva Mágica** (Map p522; ☎ 3674-1290; admission $3.50; ⏰ 10am-6pm Tue-Fri, 10am-8pm Sat & Sun), a children's amusement park with a dolphin-and-seal show, a trained-bird show and mechanical rides; the entry fee doesn't include ride packages, which cost $6 to $11.50.

If you exit the zoo via its main entrance (well east and south of its pedestrian entrance), you're about a 10-minute walk from the **planetarium** (Map p522; ☎ 3674-4106; Anillo Periférico 401; adult/child $0.60/0.30; ⏰ 10am-6pm Tue-Sun). It was being remodelled at research time, but should continue to have exhibits on astronomy and other science-related topics. There's also an excellent antique car museum – look for the 1928 Nash hearse and 1962 bug-sized BMW Isetta coupe 300. Planetarium shows (adult $1, child $0.50 extra) are held Tuesday to Friday at 11am and 1pm, and Saturday and Sunday at 1pm, 3pm and 5pm, but call ahead to confirm.

Zapopan

About 8km from the city center, on the northwestern edge of Guadalajara, the suburb of Zapopan (population 987,000) offers some interesting sights, including a large, well-tended plaza sporting a pretty copper-domed bandstand and lined with an inordinate number of shoe-shine stands. A **tourist kiosk** (⏰ Tue-Sun) can usually be found in front of the Museo de Arte de Zapopan along Paseo Tepitzintli, a pleasant pedestrian street (head straight out the basilica's front door).

The **Basílica de Zapopan** (Map p522), built in 1730, is home sweet home to Nuestra Señora de Zapopan, a tiny statue of the Virgin visited by pilgrims from near and far. The faithful will crawl up the basilica's aisle on their knees to pray for favors at her altar. Throughout the year the statue makes a tour of other churches in Jalisco, eventually reaching Guadalajara. On October 12, during the Fiestas de Octubre, the statue is taken from Guadalajara's cathedral and returned to Zapopan, amid much merrymaking; the occasion draws hundreds of thousands of pilgrims. The Virgin receives a new car each year for the procession, but the engine is never turned on (thus remaining 'virginal') – instead, the car is hauled along by ropes.

To the right of the basilica entrance, the small **Museo de Arte Huichol** (Map p522; ☎ 3636-4430; Plaza de las Américas; admission $0.50; ⏰ 9:30am-1:30pm & 3-6pm Mon-Sat, 10am-3pm Sun) sells Huichol handicrafts, and exhibits many colorful yarn paintings and other fine examples of Huichol arts and crafts. The worthwhile **Museo de Arte de Zapopan** (MAZ; Map p522; ☎ 3818-2575; www.mazmuseo.com; cnr Paseo Tepitzintli & Andador 23 de Enero; admission $2.25; ⏰ 10am-6pm Tue & Wed, Fri-Sun, 10am-10pm Thu) is one block east of Plaza de las Américas. It's a modern, well-curated museum, whose temporary exhibitions have included a small but fine selection of works by Diego Rivera and Frida Kahlo, and a whimsical showing of Anthony Browne prints that saw the top floor covered with turf, sticks, stones and sand.

Bus 275 Diagonal, and the turquoise TUR bus marked 'Zapopan,' heading north on Avs 16 de Septiembre or Alcalde, stop beside the basilica; the trip takes 20 minutes.

Tlaquepaque

Located 7km southeast of downtown Guadalajara, Tlaquepaque (tlah-keh-*pah*-keh; population 494,000) is an important center for arts production and contemporary design, offering some of Mexico's fanciest shopping. Look for wood carvings, sculpture, furniture, ceramics, jewelry, leather items and paintings. Quality is high, as are prices.

In the 19th century, Guadalajara's upper classes built substantial mansions here, which today house Tlaquepaque's most stylish restaurants, galleries and B&Bs. The suburb's darling plaza is graced with benches, flowers, monuments and a fountain. Pedestrian streets are popular with locals for long lunches, and help steer tourists into the fancy shops full of beautiful items from the area and all over Mexico. Restaurants are especially busy for Sunday lunch.

The **tourist office** (Map p522 ☎ 3562-7050 ext 2319; www.tlaquepaque.gob.mx; Morelos 88; ⏰ 9am-3pm Mon-Fri) is upstairs in the Casa del Artesano ьsk staff about two- to three-hour **walk-ьg tours** (donation) of the area, which include isits to local workshops and museums. hey're given in English or Spanish, but ьed to be reserved a few days in advance.

Spaced out along Independencia and гound El Parián (Tlaquepaque's famous ьariachi plaza) are a few tourist booths, ьpen daily more or less from 10am to 6pm, ьhich also dispense information.

The must-see **Museo Regional de la Cerámica** ьlap p522; ☎ 3635-5404; Independencia 237; admission ьe; ☒ 10am-6pm Tue-Sat, 10am-3pm Sun) sur-ьounds a shady courtyard, and has many ьell-displayed exhibits showing the differ-ьt types and styles of ceramic work and ьays made in Tlaquepaque and Michoacán. ьxplanations are in English and Spanish.

An excellent display of prize-winning ьeramics, from miniature figurines to huge ьrns, is housed at the **Museo Pantaleón Pan-ьuro** (Map p522 ☎ 3639-5646; Sánchez 191; admission ьe; ☒ 10am-6pm Tue-Sat, 10am-3pm Sun). Compe-ьtion winners from all over Mexico are well ьxhibited, and many come from Tonalá.

To get to Tlaquepaque, take bus 275 Di-ьзonal, 275B or 647 ($0.40). The turquoise ьUR bus marked 'Tonala' has air-con and ьmore comfortable ($0.80). All these buses ьave central Guadalajara from Av 16 de ьeptiembre between Cotilla and Madero; ьие trip takes about 20 minutes. As you near ьlaquepaque, watch for the brick arch and then a traffic circle. Get off at the next stop. Up the street a little, on the left, is Inde-pendencia, which will take you to the heart of Tlaquepaque.

Tonalá

This busy suburb (population 400,000) is about 13km southeast of downtown Guad-alajara. Unlike Tlaquepaque, there aren't many upscale art shops nestled in renovated mansions here, nor fancy pedestrian streets or elegant courtyard restaurants serving cutting-edge cuisine. What you will find, is a hodgepodge of stores and workshops selling much of the glassware and ceramics found in other parts of the country. Whole-sale buyers from all over the world come to shop here for bargain merchandise. The wide range of choices can be astounding.

On Thursday and Sunday, Tonalá be-comes a huge street market that covers doz-ens of streets and alleys, and takes hours to explore. Not only ceramics and glass are sold, you can also find many wood, metal, pottery, papier-mâché, straw and textile handicrafts, plus plenty of tasty treats to keep you going. Try to check out some factory stores, since the best crafts are often found at their source (the tourist office can help locate them, but you'll need to speak some Spanish). Be sure to examine all pieces very carefully, since many are seconds. There's also a fair load of junk, so be picky.

WESTERN CENTRAL HIGHLANDS

SHOPPING IN TLAQUEPAQUE

Tlaquepaque has some of Mexico's best shopping. Most of the larger stores focus on home decor, offering up plenty of ceramics, lighting fixtures and furniture. Many of the country's designers have set up shop here, and you can find some wonderfully creative pieces. If you need something transported, visit **Sebastian Exportaciones** (Map p522; ☎ 3124-6560; sebastianexp@prodigy.net.mx; Ejercito 45; ☒ 9am-2pm & 4-6pm Mon-Fri), which ships boxes (minimum 1 sq m) internationally.

At **Antigua de México** (Map p522; ☎ 3635-2402; Independencia 255; ☒ 10am-2pm & 3-7pm Mon-Fri, 10am-6pm Sat) gorgeous furniture showpieces, like great carved benches, are displayed in glorious courtyards. Designs are stunning – the best of Mexico. Pick up something for your mansion.

Origenes (Map p522; ☎ 3563-1041; Independencia 211; ☒ 10am-7pm Mon-Fri, 11am-7pm Sat, 11am-6pm Sun) is on a smaller scale than Antigua de México, but is still exceptional. It offers whimsical art, great pieces of lighting, old paintings and cowhide sofas. Heavenly hammocks are found in the courtyard.

Teté, Arte y Diseño (Map p522; ☎ 3635-7965; Juárez 173; ☒ 10am-7:30pm Mon-Sat) has lots of fun stuff for your house, including chandeliers galore, reproduction antique hardware and wonderful wood carvings.

Attached to its beautiful restaurant, **Adobe Diseño** (Map p522; ☎ 3639-8954; Independencia 195-A; ☒ 10am-7pm) is a large store offering metal sculpture, giant woven lighting fixtures, leather fur-niture and giant ceramic vases, among lots of other creative stuff.

The **Tonalá tourist office** (Map p522; ☎ 3284-3092; Tonaltecas 140; ☽ 9am-3pm Mon-Fri), on the main drag in the Casa de Artesanos, gives out maps and information. Ask staff about two- to three-hour **walking tours** (donation) of the area, which include visits to local artisan workshops. They're given in English or Spanish, but need to be reserved a couple of days in advance.

The **Museo Nacional de la Cerámica** (Map p522; ☎ 3284-3071 ext 1194; Constitución 104; admission free; ☽ 9am-5pm Mon-Fri, 9am-3pm Sat & Sun) houses an excellent and eclectic array of pots from all over Mexico, but they could be better labelled.

The **Museo Regional de Tonalá** (Map p522; ☎ 3683-2519; Ramón Corona 73; admission free; ☽ 9am-3pm Mon-Fri) is a small museum with a piddly collection of ceramics; the real reason you're here is to peek at the amazing carved wood and pottery masks, some decorated with real animal teeth and horsehair.

To get to Tonalá, take bus 275 Diagonal or 275D (both $0.40). The turquoise TUR bus marked 'Tonalá' has air-con and is more comfortable ($0.80). All these buses leave Guadalajara from Av 16 de Septiembre; the trip takes about 45 minutes. As you enter Tonalá, get off on the corner of Avs Tonalá and Tonaltecas, then walk three blocks north on Tonaltecas to the tourist office (in the Casa de Artesanos). From the Casa de Artesanos, it's three blocks east and two blocks north to the Plaza Principal.

COURSES

CEPE (Map pp524-5; ☎ 3616-4399; www.cepe.udg .mx; Universidad de Guadalajara, Apartado Postal 1-2130, Guadalajara, Jalisco 44100) The Universidad de Guadalajara's Centro de Estudios para Extranjeros (Foreign Student Studies Center; CEPE) offers several levels of intensive two- to five-week Spanish-language courses. Registration costs $100; five weeks' tuition of two to six hours per day is $322 to $965, and private lessons $22 per hour. Day trips and longer excursions to other parts of Mexico are available. Homestays or other lodging is also possible.

IMAC (Map pp524-5; ☎ 3613-1080; www.spanish -school.com.mx; Guerra 180) The Instituto Mexicano-Americano de Cultura (IMAC) offers one- to 52-week courses. You can choose to study from one to four hours per day, and weekly rates depend on how long you study. The registration fee is $50. Check its website for a complete listing of course prices, including homestays. Music and dance classes are also available, as are cultural excursions.

Instituto Cultural Mexicano-Norteamericano de Jalisco (Map pp524-5; ☎ 3825-5838; www.instituto cultural.com.mx; Av Díaz de León 300) This cultural institut teaches five levels of Spanish. Six weeks of instruction cos $450 (9am to noon Monday to Friday); one week costs $8 Cultural activities are offered twice a week, and homestay are available.

TOURS

Panoramex (Map pp524-5; ☎ 3810-5057; www.pan ramex.com.mx; Federalismo Sur 944) runs tours wit English-, French- and Spanish-speakin guides, leaving from Jardín San Francisco a 9.30am; book at the state tourist office. Tou include visits to Guadalajara's main sight ($12.50, five hours, Monday to Saturday to Chapala and Ajijic ($16, six hours, Tues day, Thursday and Sunday) and to the tow of Tequila, taking in the agave fields and tequila distillery ($19, 6½ hours, Monda Wednesday, Friday, Saturday, Sunday).

FESTIVALS & EVENTS

Major festivals celebrated in Guadalajar and its suburbs, include the following:

Feria de Tonalá An annual handicrafts fair in Tonalá, specializing in ceramics, is held the week before and the week after Semana Santa (which is the week before Easte and a couple of days after it).

Fiestas de Tlaquepaque Tlaquepaque's annual fiesta and handicrafts fair takes place mid-June to the first wee of July.

Fiesta Internacional del Mariachi (www.mariachi -jalisco.com.mx) In late August and early September mariachis come from everywhere to hear, play and celebrate the latest sounds.

Fiestas de Octubre (www.fiestasdeoctubre.com.mx) Beginning with a parade on the first Sunday in October, these fiestas last all month long and are Guadalajara's principal annual fair. Free entertainment takes place from noon to 10pm daily in the Benito Juárez auditorium at the fairgrounds (5km north of the city center), while elsewhere around the city are livestock shows, art and oth exhibitions,and sporting and cultural events. On October there's a procession from the cathedral to Zapopan (p530 **Feria Internacional del Libro** (www.fil.com.mx) This is one of the biggest book promotions in Latin America; held during the last week of November and first week of December.

SLEEPING

During holidays (Christmas and Easte you should reserve ahead, and expect to b quoted higher prices. Ask for discounts you're staying more than a few days.

Central Guadalajara

BUDGET

Hostal de María (Map pp524-5; ☎ 3614-6230; hostal demaria@prodigy.net.mx; Nueva Galicia 924; dm $15, s/d $30) Located in front of a tiny peaceful park, this new HI hostel offers clean and tidy dorms along with two small private rooms. It's intimate, has a pleasant patio in back with a communal kitchen, and even offers free continental breakfast.

Posada San Pablo (Map pp524-5; ☎ 3614-2811; http://sanpablo1.tripod.com; Madero 429; s/d/t $25/29/38, with shared bathroom $15/19/29; Ⓟ) A pleasant budget choice, complete with grassy back garden and sunny terrace. Upstairs rooms are better and more private, and some sport balconies. One single with bath goes for $16. Kitchen access available.

Hotel Posada San Rafael Inn (Map pp524-5; ☎ 3614-9146; http://sanrafael1.tripod.com; López Cotilla 619; s/d $25/29; Ⓟ 🖳) Most of the 11 rooms are old, dim and large here, with high ceilings. They're set around a nice, homey covered patio. It's a pretty basic set-up, and kitchen access is available.

Hostel Guadalajara (Map pp524-5; ☎ 3562-7520; www.hostelguadalajara.com; Maestranza 147; dm with/ without ISIC card $10.50/11.50; 🖳) This HI hostel offers basic tiled dorms, a simple kitchen and large common spaces. It's centrally located and pleasant enough, but the beds are springy and it can be noisy. Two private rooms are available for $33; both dorms and private rooms share common bathrooms.

Hotel Hamilton (Map pp524-5; ☎ 3614-6726; Madero 381; s & d $11.50, tw $18) Basic, not terribly clean, but very cheap and central. Rooms are bright for the most part, and come with open showers. TV is an extra $3.

Southeast of Mercado San Juan de Dios there's a cluster of budget hotels. This part of town is rough around the edges and thus more 'adventurous', but you can usually find a cheap room here when other places are full.

Hotel Azteca (Map pp524-5; ☎ 3617-7465; www.hotelazteca.com; Av Javier Mina 311; r from $29; Ⓟ) The most upscale choice in the area, offering a wide range of rooms. The best and brightest ones face the back (get a balcony), while inside rooms are dark; side rooms are both quiet and well lit. All have TV and fan, and there's a restaurant.

Hotel México 70 (Map pp524-5; ☎ 3617-9978; Av Javier Mina 230; s/d/tw $16/18/26) Bigger outside rooms with balconies have a wall of windows and are much better than the dark inside ones. Halls are bleak. Mexico hosted the World Cup in 1970; ask the receptionist why they've never won it.

Hotel Ana Isabel (Map pp524-5; ☎ 3617-7920; Av Javier Mina 164; s/d/tw $18/20/23) Three stories of small, dark but clean rooms are planted around a modest hallway patio strewn with fake plants. Bathrooms are tiny and cold, but there's hot coffee available all day.

Several cheap accommodation options are located around the Antigua Central Camionera (Old Bus Terminal), a busy area about 10 blocks south of the city center.

Posada Maura (Map pp524-5; ☎ 3619-7100; www.hostelworld.com/availability.php/pousadamaura-guadalajara-11689; Antonio Bravo 43; s/d $8.50/17, with shared bathroom $7/12.50) Just 10 good budget rooms are offered at this colorful, friendly place. It's basic, but has a bit of charm, and it's located in a non-touristy neighborhood.

Gran Hotel Canada (Map pp524-5; ☎ 3619-2092; fax 3619-2274; Dr Michel 218; s/d/tw $15/17/19) Rooms are good and comfortable enough, and come with TV, though bathrooms have open showers. If you're heading to the airport, the airport bus stops right outside the door of the hotel.

MIDRANGE

Hotel El Aposento (Map pp524-5; ☎ 3614-1612; Madero 545; s/d/ste $43/50/57; Ⓟ 😤) Rooms here are large and elegant, but could be better cleaned. Still, they're set around a lovely open courtyard filled with plants, a small fountain and tables (where you'll enjoy the complimentary breakfast). The suites upstairs are huge and offer plenty of privacy, while rooms toward the back are quieter.

Casa Vilasanta (Map pp524-5; ☎ 3124-1277; www.vilasanta.com; Rayón 170; dm $17, s/d $35) This colorful homestay-like posada is a good choice, offering 11 good rooms with bathroom and TV. Common areas are intimate, relaxing and dotted with pretty flowers, and there's kitchen use for guests. The rooftop terrace is cool. There's no sign; look for the bright blue building.

Posada Regis (Map pp524-5; ☎ 3614-8633; http://posadaregis.tripod.com; Av Corona 171; s/d/t $31/37/44) Even after a renovation and upping of prices, this funky old mansion still offers a decent deal. Rooms with TV are large, with high ceilings and original details, and there's a very spacious central common area. Downsides are noisy street-facing rooms and spotty plumbing.

Hotel Morales (Map pp524-5; ☎ 3658-5232; www .hotelmoralescom.mx; Av Corona 243; r from $74; P ✗ ✗ ⌨) A pretty fountain in the lobby greets you up front, though the windowless restaurant at the back is a bit stuffy. A recent remodel brightened things up at this old historic colonial hotel, whose past guests have included famous matadors, Mexican movie stars and even Pele.

Don Quixote Hotel (Map pp524-5; ☎ 3658-1299; fax 3614-2845; Héroes 91; s & d $45, tw $56; P) Good, cozy and comfortable rooms surround a covered patio with colonial overtones. There's an attached restaurant, and it's located near some of the city's popular night spots – a good drink or raunchy trannie show is just a short stagger away.

Hotel San Francisco Plaza (Map pp524-5; ☎ 3613-8954; www.sanfranciscohotel.com.mx; Degollado 267; s/d $44/47; P ✗) This hotel's covered, yet airy and plant- and fountain-filled courtyards, are surrounded by dark and simple – but spacious – rooms with tiny baths. Don't expect to be pampered by luxury, though there is a nice restaurant attached.

Hotel Francés (Map pp524-5; ☎ 3613-1190; www .hotelfrances.com, Maestranza 35; r from $60; P) The colonial Francés has been operating since 1610, but despite renovations rooms vary in comfort and sizes, and halls are a bit dark. Grab a balcony room if you can stand some street noise; otherwise the noise will be coming from the central arched stone courtyard, which is now a bar with daily live music.

La Rotonda (Map pp524-5; ☎ 3614-1017; www .hoteleselectos.com; Liceo 130; r from $50; P) Two stories of colorful rooms surround a bright colonial courtyard filled with tables. Some rooms are larger than others, and those facing inside aren't too bright – try to get one upstairs for more privacy and light. King-sized beds are available.

Hotel Jorge Alejandro (Map pp524-5; ☎ 3658-1051; Av Hidalgo 656; s/d $28/35; P) This former convent is popular with travelers and offers 20 pleasant rooms with TV, but baths are small and showers don't have curtains. Ask for a room at the back for more peace and quiet; stay three nights and win a 10% discount.

Hotel Fénix (Map pp524-5; ☎ 3614-5714; www .fenixguadalajara.com.mx; Av Corona 160; r from $74;

P ✗ ✗ ⌨) Big and popular, this multi-story hotel boasts a great central location, but despite a remodel the rooms aren't that modern or memorable. Snag a balcony room on one of the upper floors and the views might make a stay worthwhile.

Hotel Cervantes (Map pp524-5; ☎ 3613-6816; www .hotelcervantes.com.mx; Sánchez 442; s/d/tw $56/61/68; P ✗ ✗) A marble lobby and restaurant greet you up front, and while the 100 colorful rooms are modern and comfortable, they aren't luxurious. Amenities also include a couple of conference rooms and a 2nd-floor outdoor pool.

Hotel Serena (Map p522; ☎ 3600-0910; fax 3600-0015; Antigua Carretera Zapotlanejo 1500; r from $38; P ✗) Across the entrance from the Nueva Central Camionera (New Bus Terminal) and the only hotel nearby, this monster place offers hundreds of bad rooms that you can barely swing a cat in – unless you dish out for the suites ($58). Stay here only if you can't make it into the city center, a 20-minute bus ride away.

TOP END

Villa Ganz (Map pp524-5; ☎ 3120-1416; www.villa ganz.com; López Cotilla 1739; r from $230; P ⌨) The 10 gorgeously romantic (and all different) suites boast details like fireplaces, hammocks, brick ceilings, rustic wood furniture and fresh flowers on glass-top tables. Enjoy the elegant common spaces and lush, pretty garden. Continental breakfast is included and massage is available.

Trocadero Suites (Map pp524-5; ☎ 3120-1416; www.villaganz.com; López Cotilla 1188; studio $94, apt $120; P) Four one-bedroom apartments and three studios are wonderfully decked out to make you feel right at home. Apartments come with kitchenette, while studios have only fridge and hot beverage facilities. All have cable TV. Rates drop for long-term stays.

Casa Madonna B&B (Map p522; ☎ 3615-6554; www .casamadonna.com.mx; Lerdo de Tejada 2308; s $70, d $105-140; ✗) This intimate boutique hotel offers five simple, comfortable rooms and suites, along with cozy common areas both inside and out. Breakfast is included, and there's kitchen access. It's located a couple kilometers west of the city center.

Quinta Real Guadalajara (Map p522; ☎ 3669-0600; www.quintareal.com; Av México 2727; r from $352; P ✗ ✗ ⌨ ⌨) Guadalajara's most luxurious stay. Think suites with balcony, grand piano and Jacuzzi, antique furnishings and art, manicured grounds, stone arches and walls – and, of course, 1st-class service. Gather five friends and split the three-room presidential suite (only $1020).

Fiesta Americana Guadalajara (Map p522; ☎ 3818-1400; www.fiestamericana.com.mx; Aceves 225; from $208; P ⊠ 🕸 🖳) Way out along Av Lópéz Mateos Norte, this fine hotel offers almost 400 rooms on 22 stories, along with a complete range of services and amenities. Views are stunning from top floors, and a glass elevator adds elegance. Don't get a 'luxury' room – they aren't worth the extra cost. And don't pay the rack rate we list – call ahead and negotiate a better price.

Hotel de Mendoza (Map pp524-5; ☎ 3942-5151, 800-361-26-00; www.demendoza.com.mx; Carranza 16; from $105; P ⊠ 🕸 🖳 🕸) Originally built as a convent to the church next door, this refurbished hotel now offers 104 decent but unexceptional modern rooms (some split-level) with many amenities. It's a bit old world. Call the 800 number for special rates.

Hotel Casa Grande (☎ 3678-9000; www.casagrande.com.mx; r from $130; P ⊠ 🕸 🖳 🕸) Located about a 30-second walk from the airport's front doors, this business-oriented hotel has most of the amenities you could ask for – and rooms are decently comfortable. Halls are dark and impersonal, though. If you're flying out, you can blow your leftover pesos on a suite, which comes with Jacuzzi.

THE AUTHOR'S CHOICE

Casa de las Flores (Map p522; ☎ 3659-3186; www.casadelasflores.com; Santos Degollado 175; r $99-110; ⊠) On a typical local Mexican street, behind an unobtrusive door, lies one of Tlaquepaque's most intimate and relaxing stays. Just seven lovely, spacious rooms, all decorated with Mexican crafts, make guests feel right at home. The lush garden is a wonderful paradise with stone patios and a fountain, and is constantly buzzing with hummingbirds. Comfortable common areas make meeting other guests a pleasure, and your friendly hosts Stan Armington and José Gutiérrez tend to your every need. Gourmet breakfasts are served a few times per week – Stan used to work at Berkeley's Chez Panisse!

Tlaquepaque

Tlaquepaque, just 15 minutes away by bus from downtown Guadalajara, has some wonderful places to stay – especially B&Bs. It's a great choice if you prefer a more peaceful, smaller-city atmosphere, but still want to be close enough to the city's central tourist sights. Plus, Tlaquepaque's shopping options are great (see p530) – and you won't have to lug your purchases too far.

Casa Campos (Map p522; ☎ 3838-5296; www.hotelcasacampos.com; Miranda 30A; r from $80; 🕸) Six rooms and four suites all come simply and elegantly decorated here, but try to get an upstairs one as they're brighter. A relaxing courtyard is graced with caged parrots, and there's an attached restaurant and hip bar. Continental breakfast is included.

La Posada de la Media Luna (Map p522; ☎ 3635-6054; http://lamedialuna.tripod.com; Juárez 36; s/d $27/30) Just east of the El Parián plaza is this family-run place with 17 rooms around a sunny upstairs terrace. Rooms are all small, tidy and clean, and come with TV and breakfast.

Posada del Folklore (Map p522; ☎ 3838-2946; Prisciliano Sanchez 113; s & d $33) This intimate posada has just seven rooms lining a long open courtyard. Those in the back are quieter, as this place is also a small restaurant. All have high ceilings and adobe walls; some can be musty, so smell around a bit. There's a cool rooftop patio and Jacuzzi. Dorms may be available for US$$15 per person, but call first to see if they're set up.

EATING

With a couple of exceptions you won't find anything too fancy in the city center. Most eateries here serve up standard Mexican fare – no surprises. Guadalajara's best restaurants are scattered around the suburbs, so you'll have to make an extra effort to sample the city's finer cuisine (see Zona Rosa & Around, p537).

Centro Histórico & Around

All fancy hotels sport equally fancy restaurants. The ones at Hotel Francés and Hotel de Mendoza are magnificent old dining rooms. More adventurous stomachs can head to Mercado San Juan de Dios (Map pp524–5), home to scores of food stalls serving the cheapest eats in town. Smaller Mercado Corona (Map pp524–5), on the corner of Av Hidalgo and Santa Mónica, is similar. For picnic fodder there's a **Super G** (Map pp524-5; cnr Av Juárez & Martínez; 24hr) supermarket.

La Fonda de San Miguel (Map pp524-5; 3613-0809; Guerra 25; mains $9-15; 8:30am-midnight Tue-Sat, 8:30am-9pm Sun, 8:30am-6pm Mon) If you're looking for a romantic spot, try this place. It's set around a lush courtyard filled with hanging metal stars, colorful furniture and squawking parrots. The food (mostly meats and seafood) won't knock your socks off, but you're here for the atmosphere.

Café & Restaurant Madoka (Map pp524-5; 3613-0649; Martínez 76; mains $3-7) This classic, old-style hangout attracts mostly men, but is perfectly comfortable for women as well. It's popular for coffee, ice-cream and the *menú del día* ($4.50). Bring lots of conversation and check out the guys playing dominoes.

Restaurant La Chata (Map pp524-5; 3613-0588; Av Corona 126; mains $3.50-7.50) Quality food and large portions keep a legion of loyal patrons happy at this casual and efficient diner. The specialty is a *platillo jaliscense* (fried chicken with five sides); it also serves *pozole* (hominy soup), grilled meats and lots of breakfast choices.

Mariscos Galeana (Map pp524-5; 3124-3392; Galeana 154; mains $7-17; 8am-8pm Mon-Sat, 10am-7pm Sun) Seafood lovers in Guadalajara have been heading to this tasty, no-nonsense eatery since 1952. On the menu are ceviche tostadas, shrimp cocktails, fish soups, octopus salads and seafood platters. A special 'buffet' menu is available for $7.

Café Madrid (Map pp524-5; 3614-9504; Av Juárez 264; mains $2.50-5) A Guadalajara favorite for over 50 years, the Madrid sizzles up hamburgers, meat and Mexican dishes, along with good breakfast choices. Professional waiters in white coats offer brisk service, and the unfussy decor includes red booths.

Villa Madrid (Map pp524-5; 3613-4250; López Cotilla 553; mains $4.50-7; 11:30am-9pm Mon-Sat) This small, casual corner eatery is modern and bright, and popular for its quick yet healthy menu of sandwiches, salads, yogurt, *licuados* (a fruit-blended drink) and juices. There's live music on Saturday at 7pm.

Egipto Al Natural (Map pp524-5; 3613-6277; Sánchez 416; mains under $3.50; 11am-7pm Mon-Fri, 11am-6pm Sat; (V)) Vegetarians unite for soy burgers and more at this cheap and impersonal meat-free space near Villa Madrid. It closes early, so get those veggies down before dark.

Alta Fibra (Map pp524-5; 3424-1510; Sánchez 370B; mains under $3.50; 11am-7pm Mon-Fri, till 6pm Sat; (V)) Near to Egipto Al Natural and offering similar fare.

Los Faroles (Map pp524-5; 3658-6109; Av Corona 250; mains under $3.50; 7:30am-1am) You'll have a hard time finding quicker and cheaper food late at night than at this bright and open place. Tacos, quesadillas, *huaraches* (tortillas with layers of meat, cheese and veggies) and *tortas ahogadas* (sandwiches 'drowned' in sauce) are all on tap.

Sanborns Café (Map pp524-5; 3613-6283; Av Juárez 305; mains $5-9.50; 7am-1am Sun-Thu, 24h Fri & Sat) This casual café serves your typical Mexican dishes and almost looks like a branch of the US restaurant chain Denny's. Booths and serene music make it a popular standby, and it keeps long hours.

Sanborns Restaurant (Map pp524-5; 3603-1862; cnr Avs 16 de Septiembre & Juárez) For a fancier atmosphere than the café, but an identical menu and similar hours, head across the street to this place.

Taco Cabana (Map pp524-5; 3613-1539; Moreno 248; mains $3.50-6; 9am-11:30pm Mon-Thu, 9am-midnight Fri & Sat, noon-10:30pm Sun) With loud music and loud locals, this is a great casual place for cheap tacos and beer. There's also fancier grub, like seafood and grilled meat dishes. Free snacks arrive soon after your butt hits the seat. It's a very Mexican atmosphere, down to the soccer on TV.

La Rinconada (Map pp524-5; 3613-9925; Morelos 86; mains $4-9; noon-10pm) Located right smack in the middle of pedestrian Plaza Tapatía is this old, dark courtyard standby that's seen better days – but hangs in there, serving everything from tacos to pasta, to grilled shrimp to garlic mushrooms. The *menu ejecutivo* (set menu) includes soup, a main dish and drink ($5).

Plaza de las Nueve Esquinas

Half a dozen blocks south of the city center is this small and untouristy triangular block where several small streets intersect. It's a little neighborhood popular with eateries specializing in *birria*, a delicious meat stew.

Birriería las Nueve Esquinas (Map pp524-5; 3613-6260; Colón 384; mains $5.50-6.50; 8:30am-10pm Mon-Sat, 8:30am-7:30pm Sun) This friendly, homey restaurant serves up great food in an airy little dining room. The open kitchen has beautiful tiled surfaces, and out of it come

THE AUTHOR'S CHOICE

La Trattoria (Map p522; ☎ 3122-1817; Av Niños Héroes 3051; mains $6:50-10; ⏰ 1pm-midnight) This is one of Guadalajara's most popular eateries, and here's why: portions are large, prices are cheap, and the food is well prepared and delicious. It's Italian, so think *linguine e gamberi* (linguini with shrimp), *ravioli al gusto* (with spinach filling) and *scaloppine al limone* (beef medallions with lemon sauce). The antipasto bar ($6) is excellent, and a green salad comes with all mains. One thing for sure, you won't leave hungry. Reservations are crucial after 9pm, especially on weekends. To get here, take bus 51 A or B, or a taxi ($5).

ome very tasty *barbacoa de borrego* (tender aked lamb) and *birria de chivo* (goat stew). t serves Mexican breakfasts also.

ona Rosa & Around

Guadalajara's Zona Rosa is basically the few locks south of Av Chapultepec north and outh of Av Vallarta. It's home to some of he city's best cuisine. To get here, catch he westbound Par Vial 400 or 500 bus rom Avs Independencia and Alcalde. Taxis hould cost around $4.

El Sacromonte (Map pp524-5; ☎ 3825-5447; oreno 1398; mains $7-14; ⏰ 1:30pm-midnight Mon-Sat, 30-6pm Sun) One of the better restaurants n town, this festive eatery offers creative uisine in an airy courtyard setting. Tasty ishes include the eggplant tart, salmon ith panela cheese, and quesadillas with ose petals and strawberry aioli. Live music lls the air from Tuesday to Sunday.

Tinto y Blanco (Map p522; ☎ 3615-9535; Francisco avier Gamboa 235; mains $10-18; ⏰ 1:30pm-1:30am Mon- at) A limited menu of international dishes s cooked here, but it's enough. Choose rom salmon in pistachio sauce, duck breast ith fruit salad or tuna steak with ginger ver pasta. There's plenty of European and 1exican wines, by the glass or bottle, and ecor is elegant and intimate.

Restaurant Recco (Map pp524-5; ☎ 3825-0724; bertad 1981; mains $9-15; ⏰ 1pm-midnight Mon-Sat, 1-)m Sun) A menu of classy Italian dishes with Genovan influence are on offer at this very legant restaurant, located in an old man- on. Try house specialties, like the risotto

osso buco, chicken Kiev or steak tartare; there's plenty of great pasta dishes, too.

Santo Cachorro (Map p522; ☎ 3616-8472; Lerdo de Tejada 2379; mains $11-23; ⏰ 1pm-1am) This popular restaurant takes up a whole city block, and inside you'll find *palapa* dining pavilions amid the tropical gardens. Folks order dishes like steak fajitas, ribeye steak and tamarind shrimp, along with a wide selection of desserts. It even has its own gift shop.

La Tequila (Map p522; ☎ 3640-3440; Mexico 2916; mains $9-15; ⏰ 1pm-midnight Mon-Thu, 1pm-12:30am Fri & Sat, 1-6pm Sun) It's a bit far from the city center, and a little too trendy (in that touristy sort of way) for some, but the food sure looks good – try the coconut shrimp, lamb *barbacoa* or beef *molcajete* (types of meat stew). The real kicker, however, is the range of over 150 kinds of tequilas to try. Give this place a 'shot' – or two.

Pierrot (Map p522; ☎ 3630-2087; Justo Sierra 2355; mains $9-16; ⏰ 1:30pm-midnight Mon-Sat) Upscale French cuisine (with a little Mexican influence) is served in this pretty vine-covered building. Sample the escargots, veal scallope, saffron shrimp soup, or trout with almonds and butter. Say 'mais oui!' to the chocolate mousse and you'll soon be singing 'très bien!'

Tlaquepaque

Just southeast of the main plaza, El Parián is a block of restaurant-bars with plenty of tables crowding a pleasant inner courtyard. They're great for drinking and listening to live mariachi music, especially on weekends (when things are livelier). Waiters are eager, but don't plan on eating meals here – food quality is not a priority.

There are plenty of high-quality dining choices in the rest of town, however; just be aware that many close early.

Casa Fuerte (Map p522; ☎ 3639-6481; Independencia 224; mains $6-17; ⏰ 12:30-8pm) With tables set in a beautiful leafy patio, this long-popular restaurant serves up thoughtfully prepared versions of classic Mexican favorites. Try the *torta de elote colonial* (a corncake appetizer), the Oaxacan fillet with mole sauce, or the tamarind shrimp. Live music fills the air in the afternoon.

Adobe (Map p522; ☎ 3657-2792; Independencia 195; mains $13-19; ⏰ 12:30am-6:30pm Mon-Fri, 12:30-8pm Sat) Located behind the crafts and furniture showroom, this upscale yet relaxed restaurant serves tasty contemporary Mexican cuisine, like *pollo en nogada* (chicken with nut sauce) and *chili relleno de camarón* (chili stuffed with shrimp). The large salads are excellent.

Casa Vieja (Map p522; ☎ 3657-6250; Prieto 99; mains $7.50-10; ☻ 8am-10:30pm Mon-Thu, 8am-midnight Fri & Sat, 8am-10pm Sun) One of Tlaquepaque's best restaurants; worthy dishes include the tequila-marinated chicken, the shrimp-stuffed fish fillet, or the grilled steak with tamarind and chili sauces. Also try the *molcajete* (a kind of meat stew), and the cold coffee with kahlúa, pineapple juice, cream and tequila (!).

Mariscos Progreso (Map p522; ☎ 3639-6149; Progreso 80; mains $6-17; ☻ 11am-8pm) This pleasant outdoor courtyard restaurant focuses on seafood dishes, like ceviche tostadas, oyster cocktails, grilled shrimp and fish fillets, though a few meat dishes appear as well. There's plenty of tequilas to choose from, and service is good.

Café San Pedro (Map p522; ☎ 3639-0616; Juárez 85; coffees under $3; ☻ 9am-10:30pm) This hip and modern café sits under the arches across the street from El Parián, steaming up a tasty variety of cappuccinos, espressos and hot chocolates. Light meals and pastries are also available, and there are frozen concoctions and shady sidewalk seats for those hot days.

GAY GUADALAJARA

Guadalajara is one of the gayest cities in the country – some even call it 'The San Francisco of Mexico.' It's not nearly as open as SF, however, and discrimination (especially against transgender folks) definitely exists. The scene is opening up all the time, however, and if you're in the right spots things will seem pretty lively – though you'll still have to know where to look.

Guadalajara's so-called 'gay ghetto' radiates out a few blocks from the corner of Ocampo and Sánchez, in the city center, but Av Chapultepec's Zona Rosa (just west of the city center) is starting to see upscale establishments aimed at a gay clientele.

In June there are gay **pride marches** (www.marchadiversidadgdl.org) and the city even supports a **gay radio** (www.gdlgayradio.com). For general information check www.gaygdl.com. All websites are in Spanish.

To find the best of Guadalajara's gay scene, look no further than the following venues.

The wonderfully relaxed upstairs bar **La Prisciliana** (Map pp524-5; ☎ 3562-0725; Sánchez 394; ☻ 5pm-1:30am) offers intimacy in a fabulous old colonial building. Sometimes things get rowdy and there's a drag show, but usually you can just sit back and chat. The livelier downstairs pre-dance bar, Club Ye Ye, should be open by the time you read this.

Diagonally across from La Prisciliana, **Los Caudillos** (Map pp524-5; ☎ 3613-5445; cnr Sánchez 407; ☻ 5pm-3am Sun & Tue-Thu, 5pm-5am Wed, Fri & Sat) is a popular, loud and smoky two-storey disco, offering flashing lights, a few dance floors, and many lounges and bars. Both gay and straight dandies can be found carefully checking each other out here. Cover is $5 on Friday and Saturday.

Come after midnight, when the popular and relatively new **Circus** (Map pp524-5; ☎ 3616-0299; Galeana 277; ☻ 10pm-4am Mon & Thu, 10pm-5am Wed, 10pm-6am Fri & Sat) fills up tight with hot young gay things out to enjoy the intimate lounges, heart-shaped chairs and variety shows. It's in a historic building, and is also popular with lesbians; cover is $2.50

A glittery and upscale disco/restaurant/bar featuring modern lines, Latin techno sounds and go-go rounds, is found at **Angels Club** (Map pp524-5; ☎ 3615-2525; López Cotilla 1495B; ☻ 9:30pm-5am Wed-Sat, 6am-11am Sun). The mixed gay/straight clientele perch on dainty acrylic tables or lounge in the beanbag room. Security is heavy, so leave the Uzi at home. There are drag shows on Friday and Saturday at midnight; cover is $5.

Very plain and quirky, **Sexy's Bar** (Map pp524-5; ☎ 3658-0062; Degollado 273; ☻ 5pm-2am Mon-Thu, 6am-3am Fri-Sun) is known best for its trannie shows at 10:30pm nightly. However, there are also 10:30am shows from Friday to Sunday – a great way to wake up! Minimum consumption $3. On Saturday the back room becomes a small disco.

Link (Map pp524-5; ☎ 3677-7679; La Paz 2199; ☻ from 7pm Mon-Sat, from 5pm Sun) is a new and popular lounge bar located in a big old house in Zona Rosa. Most of the action takes place on the big white sofas on the front patio. It's tastefully decorated and caters to upscale yuppies who plan on heading over to the nearby Angels Club later in the evening.

DRINKING

The historic center has a few bars with snacks, drinks and sometimes live music.

La Maestranza (Map pp524-5; ☎ 3613-5878; Maestranza 179; ☺ 1pm-3am) Decked out in leather chairs and a vast array of bullfighting memorabilia, this upscale cantina attracts plenty of 20- and 30-somethings with its cheap beer (pitchers $10) and salty snacks. There's live rock music on Wednesday, and flamenco on Sunday.

La Fuente (Map pp524-5; Suárez 78; ☺ 8:30am-11pm Mon-Thu, 8:30am-midnight Fri & Sat) For a wonderfully local and slightly raunchy hangout, there's no beating La Fuente. Raucous live music starts in the afternoon – grab a drink and pretend to sing along. It's a mostly older male joint, though women frequent too. Come for the history and cultural experience – it's been going strong since 1921.

Hotel Francés (Map pp524-5; ☎ 3613-1190; Maestranza 35; ☺ noon-midnight) The dark marble courtyard bar at this hotel is a sedate and rather stuffy option, but it has an atmospheric old-world style. Live music includes piano, trios and mariachis (pity the poor hotel guests above). Happy hour runs from pm to 8pm.

Outside the historic center are some of the city's trendiest watering holes.

La Cantina de los Remedios (Map p522; ☎ 3817-410; Av de las Américas 1462; ☺ 1:30pm-2:30am Sun-Thu, 1:30pm-3:30am Fri & Sat) This popular restaurant-bar attracts the cool crowds with hip 'old' atmosphere and a happy hour that slams down two for one tequila shots. A live mariachi band plays Tuesday to Saturday at 2:30pm, and the upscale disco Barzelona is right next door.

Bar Bariachi (Map p522; ☎ 3616-9180; Av Vallarta 2808; ☺ 6pm-3am Mon-Sat) Crowded leather chairs and a dark atmosphere prevail at this intimate bar; head to the upstairs balcony tables for more air. There's live mariachi music and Ballet Folklórico on Friday and Saturday at 10pm. For the ladies (and men, when you think about it) – all the tequila you can drink for $5 (Tuesdays 6pm to 9pm).

ENTERTAINMENT

Guadalajara is in love with music of all kinds, and live performers can be heard any night of the week at one of the city's many venues (including restaurants). Discos and bars are plentiful, but ask around for the hottest current nightspots because – as we all know – style *will* be fickle.

For entertainment information stop by the tourist office and check out its weekly schedule of events; the bilingual staff will find something to suit your fancy. Also, buy the Friday edition of the daily newspaper *Público* – its entertainment insert, *Ocio*, includes a cultural-events calendar for the coming week, and is the place to get the scoop on restaurants, movies, exhibits and the club scene. *Occidental* and *Informador*. Spanish-language dailies also have entertainment listings, as does the weekly booklet *Ciento Uno*.

Popular venues hosting a range of drama, dance and music performances include the **Teatro Degollado** (Map pp524-5; ☎ 3613-1115) and the **Instituto Cultural de Cabañas** (Map pp524-5; ☎ 3668-1640), both downtown cultural centers, as well as the **Ex-Convento del Carmen** (Map pp524-5; ☎ 3030-1390; Av Juárez 638). The new kid on the block is **Teatro Diana** (Map pp524-5; ☎ 3818-3800 via Ticketmaster; www.teatrodiana.com; Av 16 de Septiembre 710), a brand new theater finished in 2005.

Ballet Folklórico

Ballet Folklórico de la Universidad de Guadalajara (☎ 3121-9664) The university's folkloric dance troupe stages grand performances at the **Teatro Degollado** (Map pp524-5; ☎ 3613-1115) a couple of times per week; check the tourist office for current schedules.

Casa Bariachi (Map p522 ☎ 3616-9900; Av Vallarta 2221; ☺ 1pm-3am Mon-Sat) This large, festive restaurant-bar seems an unlikely place for ballet of any sort, but it does put on shows at 2:30pm and 9:30pm daily – and they include mariachi performances, too. Bar Bariachi (left) has weekend shows.

Cinemas

Big shopping centers, like **Plaza del Sol** (Map p522; ☎ 3121-5750; Av López Mateos Sur), **Plaza Milenium** (Map p522; ☎ 3634-0509; Av López Mateos Sur) and **Centro Magno** (Map p522; ☎ 3630-1113; Av Vallarta 2425), have the best multiscreens, ideal for the latest US 'blow-it-up' flick. Several other cinemas, like the one at the **Ex-Convento del Carmen** (Map pp524-5; ☎ 3030-1390; Av Juárez 638), show international films and classics. Check *Ocio* (in the daily *Público*) or other local newspapers.

Alianza Francesa (Map pp524-5; ☎ 3825-5595; www.alianzafrancesa.org.mx/guadalajara; López Cotilla 1199) shows French films.

WESTERN CENTRAL HIGHLANDS

Mariachis

Pay your respects to the mariachi tradition in its home city. The Plaza de los Mariachis (p528), just east of the historic center, is a good place to sit and drink beer while being regaled by these passionate Mexican bands – though it's seen better days.

Way over in Tlaquepaque, the El Parián plaza (p537) has a courtyard mariachi gazebo surrounded by hundreds of tables; it's a great atmospheric place to catch some mariachis.

Casa Bariachi (Map p522; ☎ 3616-9900; Av Vallarta 2221; ☒ 1pm-3am Mon-Sat) This bright barn-like restaurant-bar has romantic lighting and leather chairs, along with piñatas and colorful *papel picado* (cutout paper) hanging from the ceiling. Big margaritas and lots of mariachis start the fun at 4pm and 11pm daily. It's about a 10-minute taxi ride west of the city center; nearby brother Bar Bariachi (p539), a few doors away, also plays mariachi music nightly.

Nightclubs

Guadalajara's slickest spots are outside the city center. Nightclubs here attract young, affluent locals who dress to impress. Wear your best threads, though if you act foreign you'll be labeled exotic and this will help you get past the sniffy bouncers. Ask clued-in hipsters about the current flavor-of-the-

month. For a hoot, check out the gay club (see the boxed text, p538) – hetros are welcome, and there are often raucous shows.

Klio (Map p522; ☎ 3630-2411; Av Américas 318; ☒ 10pm-5am Wed, Fri & Sat) One of the most chic discos in town. Inside are tight, dim spaces with loud electronica and house music playing. There's a $19 all-you-can-drink deal for men, and women drink for free before midnight ($15 for unlimited drinks afterwards). Friday nights are best here.

Barzelona (Map p522; ☎ 3817-6076; Av América 1462; ☒ 10pm-4am Wed, Fri & Sat) An exclusive club where you really need snappy dress. Inside, the multi-level, bowl-like setting offers nightly shows, including dancing girls on the bar. It's in a cluster of nightspots, so if you don't like it there are other nearby options. Cover for men is $7 on Friday and Saturday; on Wednesday it's $16, but includes some free drinks. Women always get in free.

Meridiano 60 (Map pp524-5; ☎ 3613-8489; Maestranza 223; ☒ 8pm-3am Wed, Thu & Sun, 8pm-4am Fri & Sat) This smallish downtown nightspot, sporting a jungly theme, attracts a young crowd. Live Brazilian, reggae and rock bands – all Mexican style – play on Saturday, while the rest of the week sees DJs spinning tunes. Check out the house cocktail, the *mamada* ($8) – a giant frothy cauldron of rum, beer, vodka, lemon

---

MARIACHIS

Not many images capture the heart and soul of Mexico better than a spirited group of proud-faced mariachis. Handsomely decked out in broad-rimmed sombreros and brightly matching *charro* suits, their traditional Mexican ballads entertain folks at crowded town plazas, festive wedding parties and noisily packed restaurants. Even doe-eyed sweethearts nuzzling on a park bench can get that special serenade.

Some historians contend that 'mariachi' is a corruption of the French word *mariage* (marriage) and that the name stems from the time of the French intervention (1861–67). Others say that the word arose from festivals honoring the Virgin Mary, and was probably derived from the name María with the Náhuatl diminutive '-chi' tacked on. It could also have come from the name of the stage upon which *jarabes* (folk dances) were performed. But whatever the root of its name, the music is known to have originated in Jalisco, in a region south of Guadalajara.

Back in the early 20th century, mariachi bands were made up of only stringed instruments – such as violins, guitars and a harp – and their repertoire was limited to traditional *tapatío* melodies. Today, however, most mariachi bands belt out their melodramatic tunes on three violins, two trumpets, a guitar, a *guitarrón* (deep-pitched bass) and a *vihuela* (high-pitched guitar). The exact number of violins, guitars and trumpets can vary quite a bit. Most of their broad repertoire of favorite Mexican ballads involve love, betrayal or machismo themes.

To check out some venues for this music, see above, or just keep an eye out for these roving jukeboxes on any Mexican street; if you're feeling sentimental they'll stop and play you a tune, but just make sure you agree on a price first.

juice and *jarabe* (sweet syrup). Cover is $6 on Saturday, $3 on Friday, for men only.

Other Live Music

State and municipal bands present free concerts of typical *música tapatía* in the Plaza de Armas at 6:30pm on most Tuesdays, Thursdays and Sundays, and on other days as well during holiday seasons (and especially for the Fiestas de Octubre, p532).

La Bodeguita del Medio (Map p522; ☎ 3630-1620; Av Vallarta 2320; ◷ 1:30pm-2:30am Mon-Sat, 1:30pm-1am Sun) Next door to Bar Bariachi is this pseudo-Cuban joint complete with graffiti decor. It's a restaurant upstairs (balcony tables are best) and bar downstairs. Live Cuban music plays from 2:30pm to 4:30pm, and 9:30pm to 2:30am, Monday to Saturday; no cover. There's Cuban dance lessons on Wednesday and Thursday from 6pm to 9pm. Check out the cigar display and sign stating: 'Life's too short to smoke cheap cigars.'

Instituto Cultural Mexicano-Norteamericano de Jalisco (Map pp524-5; ☎ 3825-5666; www.instituto cultural.com.mx; Díaz de León 300) Classical music concerts, opera and piano recitals are often hosted here.

Hard Rock Café (Map p522; ☎ 3616-4564; Av Vallarta 2425; ◷ 11am-2am) In the Centro Magno shopping center, this is your typical Hard Rock, with guitars on the walls and Tex-Mex burgers on the menu. Hidden inside, however, is a 1000-seat auditorium that has hosted several big-name international groups (check its schedule at www.tokinrecords.com, click on 'conciertos'). There's live rock music in the restaurant Wednesday to Sunday nights.

El Cubilete (Map pp524-5; ☎ 3616-4560; Río Seco 9; ◷ 10am-1am Mon-Wed, 10am-3am Fri & Sat, 10am-9pm Sun) Located a few blocks south of the city center, near Plaza de las Nueve Esquinas, is this bustling Cuban joint. Salsa, *cumbia* (a popular Colombian music genre with African origins), *trova* (troubadour-type folk music) and Cuban tunes (including *son*) get the action rolling from Wednesday to Saturday nights, and there is live acoustic guitar on Thursday. *Noche Cubana* is on the last Saturday of each month, highlighted with a Cuban band and cheap *mojitos*.

Sport

BULLFIGHTS & CHARREADAS

Plaza de Toros Nuevo Progreso (Map p522; ☎ 3637-9982; www.plazanuevoprogreso.com; north end of Calz Independencia; admission from $5) The bullfighting season is October to March, and the fights are held on select Sundays starting at 4:30pm. A couple of fights usually take place during the October fiestas; the rest of the schedule is sporadic. Check its website or the tourist office.

Lienzo Charros de Jalisco (Map pp524-5; ☎ 3619-0515; Dr Michel 572; admission $3-4) *Charreadas* are held at noon most Sundays in this ring behind Parque Agua Azul. *Charros* (cowboys) come from all over Jalisco and Mexico to wrestle down cows. *Escaramuzas* (cowgirls) perform daring sidesaddle displays, often showing more riding skill than the *charros!*

SOCCER

Fútbol is Guadalajara's favorite sport. The seasons are from August to December and from January to May or June. The city usually has at least three teams playing in the national top-level *primera división*: **Guadalajara** (Las Chivas; www.chivas.com.mx), the second most popular team in the country after América of Mexico City; **Atlas** (Los Zorros; www.atlas.com.mx); and **Universidad Autónoma de Guadalajara** (Los Tecos; www.tecos.com.mx).

The teams play at stadiums around the city, but **Estadio Jalisco** (Map p522; ☎ 3637-0563; Siete Colinas 1772; admission $3-8), the main venue (seating around 60,000), hosted World Cup matches in 1970 and 1986. Contact the stadium or tourist office for schedule information. Really big games cost a pocketful of pesos.

SHOPPING

Handicrafts from Jalisco, Michoacán and other Mexican states are available in Guadalajara's many markets. The Casa de las Artesanías de Jalisco, just outside Parque Agua Azul, has a good selection (see p529).

Tlaquepaque and Tonalá, two suburbs less than 15km from Guadalajara's center, are major producers of handicrafts and furniture (see p530 and p531 respectively).

Mercado San Juan de Dios (Map pp524-5; Mercado Libertad; cnr Av Javier Mina & Calz Independencia; ◷ 10am-9pm) This huge market has three floors of stalls offering everything from tools to tank tops to tortillas – and the salespeople are very eager to sell it all to you – bargain! The food court is good and cheap.

Mercado Corona (Map pp524-5; cnr Av Hidalgo & Santa Mónica; ◷ 9am-8pm) Near downtown is this block-long market, with cheap electronics, clothes, household items, knickknacks and food.

Mercado El Baratillo (Map p522; ☺ 8am-4pm Sun) This popular Sunday flea market stretches blocks in every direction on and around Av Javier Mina. It's blue-collar and grungy, but has great people-watching. To get there, take a Par Vial bus east along Av Hidalgo.

El Charro (Map pp524-5; ☎ 3614-7599; www.el-charro .net; Av Juárez 148; ☺ 9:30am-8:30pm Mon-Sat, 10:30am-4pm Sun) Buckles, boots, lariats, spurs, saddles and sombreros – no, this isn't a sex shop, though you *can* dress up like a Mexican cowboy, cowgirl or Mariachi. Several similar (and cheaper) shops are on Av Juárez to the east.

Guadalajara's richest citizens prefer to browse at the big shopping centers west of the city center, such as **Centro Magno** (Map p522; Av Vallarta 2425), 2km west of the city center; **Plaza del Sol** (Map p522; Av López Mateos Sur), 7km southwest of the city center; and **Plaza Milenium** (Map p522; Av López Mateos Sur), 7.5km southwest of the city center. All open approximately 10am to 9pm. To get to these malls, take bus 258 going west from San Felipe and Av Alcalde, or TUR 707 going west on Av Juárez.

GETTING THERE & AWAY
Air
Guadalajara's **Aeropuerto Internacional Miguel Hidalgo** (☎ 3688-5504) is 17km south of downtown, just off the highway to Chapala. Inside are ATMs, money-exchange, cafés, tequila shops and many car-rental booths. There's also a **tourist office** (☺ 8am-6pm).

A multitude of airlines offer direct flights to major cities in Mexico, the US and Canada. The following are some airlines serving Guadalajara:

Aero California (Map p522; ☎ 3616-2525; Av Vallarta 2440, Colonia Arcos Vallarta)

Aeroméxico (Map pp524-5; ☎ 800-021-40-10; Av Corona 196)

American Airlines (Map p522; ☎ 3616-4402, 800-904-60-00; Av Vallarta 2440, Colonia Arcos Vallarta)

Aviacsa (Map p522; ☎ 800-713-57-44; Av Vallarta 2440, Colonia Arcos Vallarta)

Delta (Map pp524-5; ☎ 3630-3530; López Cotilla 1701, Colonia Americana)

Mexicana (Map p522; ☎ 800-502-20-00; Av Vallarta 2440, Colonia Arcos Vallarta)

United Airlines (Map p522; ☎ 3813-4002; Mexico 3370, Plaza Bonita)

Bus
Guadalajara has two bus terminals. The long-distance bus terminal is the **Nueva Central Camionera** (New Bus Terminal; Map p522; ☎ 3600-0495), a large modern V-shaped terminal that is split into seven separate *módulos* (mini-terminals). Each *módulo* has ticket desks for a number of bus lines, plus restrooms, cafeterias and sometimes left-luggage services. The Nueva Central Camionera is 9km southeast of Guadalajara city center, past Tlaquepaque.

Buses travel to and from just about everywhere in western, central and northern Mexico. The same destination can be served by several companies in several different *módulos,* making price comparisons difficult and time-consuming, since the *módulos* are quite spread out. If you don't mind traveling in 1st class (and who doesn't?), you can check schedules and even buy your ticket in central Guadalajara. Try **Agencia de Viajes MaCull** (Map pp524-5; ☎ 3614-7014; López Cotilla 163; ☺ 9:30am-7pm Mon-Fri, 9:30am-2pm Sat) or **Agencia de Viajes Hermes** (Map pp524-5; ☎ 3617-3330; Calz Independencia Norte 254; ☺ 9:30am-3pm & 4pm-7:30pm Mon-Fri, 9:30am-3pm Sat). Both agencies sell only 1st-class bus tickets, which will cost exactly the same as at the Nueva Central Camionera.

Destinations include the following (departures are frequent):

Destination	Price	Duration
Barra de Navidad	$24	5½hr
Colima	$15	3hr
Guanajuato	$22	4hr
Manzanillo	$21	4hr
Mexico City (Terminal Norte)	$39	7-8hr
Morelia	$22	4hr
Pátzcuaro	$24	4½hr
Puerto Vallarta	$29	5hr
Querétaro	$29	5½hr
San Juan de los Lagos	$11.50	3hr
San Miguel de Allende	$33	5hr
Tepic	$17	3hr
Uruapan	$19	4½hr
Zacatecas	$24	5hr
Zamora	$11.50	2¼hr
Zapotlanejo	$2	30min

To take the deluxe option to some of these destinations – with inevitably higher fares – try **ETN** (Módulo 2); its waiting room is downright plush.

Guadalajara's other bus terminal is the **Antigua Central Camionera** (Old Bus Terminal; Map pp524-5; ☎ 3619-3312), which is about 1.5km south of the cathedral near Parque Agua Azul. From here 2nd-class buses serve destinations that lay roughly within 75km of Guadalajara. There are two sides to it: Sala A is for destinations to the east and northeast; Sala B is for destinations northwest, southwest and south. Some destinations, however, are served by both sides. There's a $0.05 charge to enter the terminal, which also offers a **left-luggage service** (⌚ 7.30am-8pm) in Sala B and some food stalls.

Destination	Price	Duration	Frequency
Ajijic	$3.50	1hr	half-hourly Autotransportes Guadalajara-Chapala from 6am to 9pm, departs Sala A
Chapala	$3.25	50min	half-hourly Autotransportes Guadalajara-Chapala from 6am to 9pm, departs Sala A
Ciudad Guzman	$8	3hr	frequent Sur de Jalisco, departs Sala B
San Juan Cosalá	$3.50	1¼hr	half-hourly Autotransportes Guadalajara-Chapala from 6am to 9pm, departs Sala A
Tequila	$3.50	1¾hr	hourly Tequila Plus from 6:30am to 8:30pm, departs Sala A Tala every 15min from 5:30am to 9:15pm, departs Sala B
Tapalpa	$6	3hr	frequent Sur de Jalisco, departs Sala B

Car

Guadalajara is 535km northwest of Mexico City and 344km east of Puerto Vallarta. Highways 15, 15D, 23, 54, 54D, 80, 80D and 90 all converge here, combining temporarily to form the Periférico, a ring road around the city.

Tolls and driving times to these destinations are as follows: Manzanillo ($24, three hours), Puerto Vallarta ($26, 3¾ hours) and Mexico City ($52, 5½ hours).

Guadalajara has many car rental agencies. Several of the large US companies are represented, but you may get a cheaper deal from a local company. Costs average $50 to $65 per day. Recommended agencies include the following:
Alamo (☎ 3613-5560)
Budget (☎ 3613-0027, 800-700-17-00)
Dollar (☎ 3826-7959, 3688-5659)
Hertz (☎ 3688-5633, 800-654-30-30)
National (☎ 3614-7994, 800-227-73-68)
Thrifty (☎ 3688-6318)

Train
The only train serving Guadalajara is the *Tequila Express* – a tourist excursion to the nearby town of Amatitán (see p546).

GETTING AROUND
To/From the Airport
The airport is 17km south of Guadalajara's center, just off the highway to Chapala. To get into town on public transport, walk outside the airport and head to the bus stop in front of Hotel Casa Grande, about 50m to the right. Take any bus marked 'Zapote' ($0.50) or 'Atasa' ($1) – both run every 15 minutes from about 5am to 10pm and take 40 minutes to the Antigua Central Camionera, from where there are many buses to the city center.

Taxis prices are $16 to the city center, $15 to the Nueva Central Camionera and $15 to Tlaquepaque. Buy fixed-price tickets inside the airport.

To get to the airport from Guadalajara's center, take bus 174 to the Antigua Central Camionera (the stop is in front of the Gran Hotel Canada) and then an 'Aeropuerto' bus (every 20 minutes, 6am to 9pm) from this stop. Taxis cost $16.

To/From the Bus Terminals
To reach the city center from the Nueva Central Camionera, take any bus marked 'Centro' ($0.40). You can also catch the more comfortable, turquoise-colored TUR bus ($0.80). These should be marked 'Zapopan' – don't take the ones marked 'Tonalá,' as these go away from Guadalajara's center. Taxis to the city center cost around $8, but you may have to bargain.

To get to the Nueva Central Camionera from the city center, take any bus marked 'Nueva Central' – these are frequent and leave from the corner of Av 16 de Septiembre and Madero.

To reach the city center from the Antigua Central Camionera, take any bus going north on Calz Independencia. To return to the Antigua Central Camionera from the city center, take bus 174 going south on Calz Independencia. Taxis cost $3.

Bus 616 ($0.40) runs between the two bus terminals.

Bus

Guadalajara has a comprehensive city bus system, but be ready for crowded, rough rides. On major routes, buses run every five minutes or so from 6am to 10pm daily, and cost $0.40. Many buses pass through the city center, so for an inner suburban destination you'll have a few stops to choose from. The routes diverge as they get further from the city center, and you'll need to know the bus number for the suburb you want. Some bus route numbers are followed by an additional letter indicating which circuitous route they will follow in the outer suburbs.

The TUR buses, which are painted a distinctive turquoise color, are a more comfortable alternative on some routes. They have air-con and plush seats ($0.80). If they roar past without stopping, they're full; this can happen several times in a row during rush hour – it can be enough to drive you completely crazy.

The tourist office has a list of the many bus routes in Guadalajara, and can help you get to your destination. Following are some common destinations, the buses that go there and a central stop where you can catch them.

Antigua Central Camionera Bus 174 going south on Calz Independencia.

Av López Mateos Sur Bus 258 at San Felipe and Av Alcalde, or TUR 707 going west on Av Juárez.

Nueva Central Camionera Bus 275B, 275 Diagonal or TUR marked 'Tonalá'; catch them all at Av 16 de Septiembre and Madero.

Parque Agua Azul Any bus marked 'Agua Azul' going south on Calz Independencia.

Planetarium, Zoo and Selva Mágica Bus 60 or 62A, or trolleybus R600 going north on Calz Independencia.

Tlaquepaque Bus 275B, 275 Diagonal or TUR marked 'Tlaquepaque' at Av 16 de Septiembre and Madero.

Tonalá Bus 275D, 275 Diagonal or TUR marked 'Tonalá' at Av 16 de Septiembre and Madero.

Zapopan Bus 275 or TUR marked 'Zapopan' going north on Avs 16 de Septiembre or Alcalde.

Zona Rosa Par Vial buses 400 and 500 at Avs (not Calz!) Independencia and Alcalde.

Horse Carriages

For that romantic touch, you can hire a horse carriage for $12 per half hour or $20 per hour. There's a carriage stand right at Jardín San Francisco and another in front of the Museo Regional de Guadalajara.

Metro

The subway system has two lines that cross the city. Stops are marked around town by a 'T' symbol. The subway is quick and comfortable enough, but doesn't serve many points of visitor interest. Línea 1 stretches north–south for 15km all the way from the Periférico Nte to the Periférico Sur. It runs more or less below Federalismo (seven blocks west of the city center) and Av Colón; catch it at Parque Revolución, on the corner of Av Juárez. Línea 2 runs east–west for 10km below Avs Juárez and Mina.

Taxi

Taxis are plentiful in the city center. All Guadalajara taxis have meters, but many taxi drivers would rather quote a flat fee for a trip. Generally it's cheaper to go by the meter – if you're quoted a flat fee and think it's inflated, feel free to bargain. Note that from 10pm to 6am a 'night meter' is used, and fares go up by 25%.

Typical day fares from the city center at the time of writing were $3 to the Antigua Central Camionera and Parque Agua Azul; $4 to Centro Magno; $7 to Zapopan; $6 to Tlaquepaque or the zoo; $7.50 to the Nueva Central Camionera or to Tonalá; and $15 to the airport. Settle the fare before you get into the taxi; there's no need to tip.

AROUND GUADALAJARA

There are plenty of distractions if you're looking to get away from the big city. San Juan de los Lagos, 150km northeast of Guadalajara, is a religious town with extensive markets, which makes a fun day trip. The liquor-producing town of Tequila, 50km to the northwest, needs no introduction. Lago de Chapala, 45km own south, offers pretty lake scenery and everal towns with a much slower pace nd distinctly different feel to Guadalaara. And further south and west, Jalisco's Zona de Montaña is home to several daring little mountain towns that are ideal for xploration and relaxation. So, when you re of Guadalajara's rattling urban vibes nd need a break, just hop on a bus and eady yourself for some more authentic Mexican' adventures.

AN JUAN DE LOS LAGOS

395 / pop 46,000 / elevation 1950m
Toward the northern finger of Jalisco state es San Juan de los Lagos, one of Mexico's nost important pilgrimage destinations nd a lively market city. On any given day ou can arrive at San Juan's beautiful rosecolored cathedral, and watch the faithful vork their way up the aisle on their knees, raying to the *virgencita* (virgin) for favors. t's a fascinating peek into the lives of beievers, but even atheists can enjoy San Juan. urrounding the cathedral are streets filled vith hundreds of busy market stalls where ou can browse for religious trinkets, virgin tatuettes, rosaries, jewelry, clothes, blanets, homewares and knick-knacks, along vith all sorts of sweets – coconut candy, amarind paste, *cajeta* (milk caramel), sugred nuts and *rompope* (a kind of eggnog). t's an interesting combination of faith nd capitalism.

Weekends are lively, but the city's busist periods are Christmas, Easter and the nonth of May, and during the Fiestas de a Virgen de la Candelaria (January 20 to ebruary 2) and Fiestas de la Virgen de la nmaculada Conceptión (December 1 to 8). he city has plenty of hotels, but they fill p at these times. For information there's **tourist office** (☎ 785-09-79; Segovia 10; 9amom Mon-Fri, 9am-5pm Sat, 9am-1pm Sun); it's located ne block behind the cathedral.

San Juan de los Lagos makes a long day rip from Guadalajara, but you really only eed a few hours here anyway. Frequent uses leave Guadalajara's Nueva Central Camionera ($11.50, three hours). Once ou get into town, head left for about aree blocks, go over the pedestrian bridge nd zig-zag around a couple of corners, ollowing the market stalls down to the athedral.

TEQUILA

☎ 374 / pop 25,000 / elevation 1219m
Don't expect tequila to be flowing down the streets of this modestly sized town, though the region is indeed surrounded by fields of blue agave, the cactus-like plant from which tequila is distilled. Tequila is located about 50km northwest of Guadalajara and has been home to the liquor of the same name since the 17th century. You can tour a couple of distilleries (yes, samples are given), hang out in the pleasant plaza and stroll along some atmospheric cobbled backstreets. And buy several bottles of tequila, of course.

If you come by bus, its last stop will probably be on Gorjón. Continue on foot away from the highway for about 10 minutes and you'll eventually arrive at the church; the plaza is beyond it. If you're in town from November 30 to December 12 you'll catch the Feria Nacional de Tequila (Tequila Fair), celebrated with *charreadas* (rodeos), parades and tequila exhibitions.

The biggest show in town is **Mundo Cuervo** (☎ 742-00-50; cnr Corona & José Cuervo; 10am-4pm Mon-Sat, 11am-1pm Sun), which produces José Cuervo tequila, and lots of it. Regular (hourly) tours take 1¼ hours and include tastings and a margarita. There are four kinds of tours to choose from, costing between $7.50 and $24. The distillery's beautiful complex is located across the street from the southwest corner of the plaza; you can't miss it.

The **Museo Nacional del Tequila** (☎ 742-24-10; Corona 34; adult/child under 11 $1.50/0.75; 10am-4pm Tue-Sun) is half a block south from the Cuervo complex. It's very well done, with photos, exhibits, tequila apparatus (including a huge vat), and good explanations (some in English) of the mechanics and history of the industry. There's also a display case with a collection of tequila bottles and shot glasses.

About 4½ blocks further south (the street, which changes names, bears slightly right) is the big, white **Perseverancia distillery** (☎ 742-02-43; Francisco Javier Sauza Mora 80; 11am-4pm Mon-Fri, 11am-noon Sun), producer of Sauza tequila. It's not as neatly set up for tourists as Cuervo – in other words, it's not quite as touristy – but is still impressive. Hourly tours cost $3.50.

If you can't stagger to the bus stop, check into the pretty **Hotel Posada del Agave** (☎ 742-07-74; Gorjon 83; s/d $18, tw $25), which has good budget rooms with TV and fan. For more comfort there's **Casa Dulce María Hotel** (☎ 742-32-40;

hotelcasadulcemaria@yahoo.com.mx; Abasolo 20; s/d $24, tw $43), a beautiful courtyard hotel with comfortable large rooms.

The fanciest way to get to the Tequila area is with the **Tequila Express** (in Guadalajara ☎ 33-3880-9099; www.tequilaexpress.com.mx; adult/child 6-11 $72/38). It departs Guadalajara's train station, located a couple blocks south of Parque Agua Azul, at 11am Saturday (occasionally on Sunday). The diesel loco heads to Amatitán, 39km from Guadalajara and home to the venerable Herradura distillery, which still employs traditional methods and apparatus. You'll get a tour of the distillery, a mariachi show, snacks, lunch and an open bar with *mucho* tequila. Book a few days ahead at Morelos 395, or call **Ticketmaster** (☎ 3818-3800).

Tequila Plus buses (Sala A, $3.50, 1¾ hour) leave Guadalajara's Antigua Central Camionera hourly on the half hour from 6:30am to 8:30pm. Tala buses (Sala B, $3.50, 1¾ hour) leave every 15 minutes from 5:30am to 9:15pm.

CHAPALA
☎ 376 / pop 20,000 / elevation 1550m

Lago de Chapala is Mexico's largest natural lake and lies serenely 45km south o Guadalajara. It's very picturesque, but th lake's levels have fluctuated wildly over th years. Guadalajara and Mexico City's wate needs take their toll, though over the las few years rainfall has been significant and i 2005 the lake's waters were back to norma Pollution is another issue, and fertilizer washed into the lake have nourished wate hyacinth, a decorative but fast-growin, invasive plant that clogs the lake's surface Lago de Chapala's problems, however haven't stopped escalating real estate price: supported by the legions of Western reti rees who live here. Indeed, the lake's near perfect climate and lovely countryside hav attracted what is probably the largest U and Canadian expat populations around.

One of the largest settlements on the lake Chapala took off as a resort after presiden

---

TEQUILA

Mexico's national drink has come a long way, baby. The Spanish conquistadores first cultivated the blue agave plant *(Agave tequilana weber)* as early as the mid-1550s, in the state of Jalisco. Tequila didn't become prominent until after independence, however, and its popularity didn't take off until the Mexican Revolution and the USA's prohibition years. Comfort during troubled times, indeed.

An agave plant is grown for at least eight years until its heart, called a *piña,* reaches the size of a beach ball (weighing up to 150kg), when it's harvested. It's then chopped, fed into ovens and cooked for up to three days. Afterwards the softened pulp is shredded and juiced, and the liquid is pumped into fermentation vats where it is usually mixed with yeast. In order to bear the 100% agave label, premium tequilas can legally add nothing else. Lesser tequilas, however, add sugar and sometimes flavoring and/or coloring agents. By law the mixture can contain no less than 51% agave if it is to be called tequila.

In the past tequila's growing popularity brought about a shortage of the slow-growing blue agave, but frantic planting has recently produced bumper crops that resulted in plummeting prices. To address this glut (and appease established farmers) the government will allow distillers to buy agave only from plots approved by the Tequila Regulatory Council.

The casual drinker need know only this: of the four varieties of tequila, which is best is a matter of personal taste. White or silver *(blanco* or *plata)* tequila is not aged, and no colors or flavors are added (though sugar may be) – it has a distinct agave flavor. The similar gold variety *(oro)* also is not aged, but color and flavor, usually caramel, are added. Tequila *reposado* (rested) has been aged from two to 11 months in oak barrels, and tends to taste sharp and peppery. Tequila *añejo* (aged) has the smoothest flavor and is aged at least one year in oak barrels.

In Mexico you can buy a decent bottle of tequila for $10, though for something better you'll need to spend $20 to $30. Above that you're getting into the exceptional and even sniffy range – yes, tequila has its own connoisseurs and snobs. And don't be looking for a 'special' worm *(gusano)* in each bottle. These are placed in *mezcal* (a cousin of tequila) bottles as a marketing ploy – and even if you buy some mezcal and drink up the little critter, it won't get you any higher (or hornier) than the liquor itself.

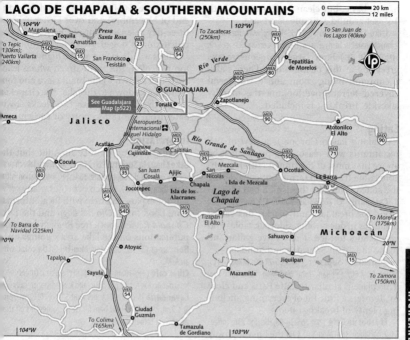

LAGO DE CHAPALA & SOUTHERN MOUNTAINS

orfirio Díaz vacationed here every year
rom 1904 to 1909. DH Lawrence wrote most
f *The Plumed Serpent* at Zaragoza 307, now
 beautiful villa (see right). Today Chapala
 a rather nondescript, modern and touristy
wn that gets busier when Guadalajarans
isit on weekends, but it also caters to its
ore permanent expat population.

Information

hapala has a **tourist office** (☎ 765-31-41; up-
airs at Madero 407; ☼ 9am-7pm Mon-Fri, 9am-1pm Sat
Sun), and **Libros de Chapala** (☎ 765-69-90; Madero
0; ☼ 9am-5pm Mon-Sat, 9am-2pm Sun), opposite
e plaza, has a few English novels, guide-
ooks and magazines.

Sights

t the foot of Av Madero, near the pier, is
 small park and a crafts market. Further
st, the expansive **Parque La Cristiania** (☼ 7am-
30pm) has a big swimming pool, tennis
urts, a playground and nice picnic lawns.
nter at Av Cristiania and Cotilla.

A small booth at the pier sells boat tickets
 Isla de los Alacranes (Scorpion Island), 6km

from Chapala, which has some restaurants
and souvenir stalls but isn't all that interesting. A round-trip, with 30 minutes on the
island, costs $24 per boatload; for one hour
it's $30. **Isla de Mezcala**, 15km from Chapala,
has the ruins of a fort and other buildings.
Mexican independence fighters heroically
held out there from 1812 to 1816, repulsing
several Spanish attempts to dislodge them
and finally winning a full pardon from their
enemies. A three-hour round-trip boat ride
(including wait) costs a whopping $112 for
up to eight people.

Sleeping

Quinta Quetzalcóatl (☎ 765-36-53; www.accommo
dationslakechapala.com; Zaragoza 307; r from $80; ℗
⚛) Behind the stone walls is an acre of lush
gardens, plus six unique and beautifully
decorated suites, each with their own private
patio. This is where DH Lawrence wrote
The Plumed Serpent in 1923. It's Aussie-
run and includes full breakfast. Reserve
ahead; adults only.

Hotel Las Palmitas (☎ 765-30-70; Juárez 531;
s/d/tw $18/21/26) This, the town's cheapest digs

has 15 basic, but clean budget rooms with TV, set around a simple courtyard.

Lake Chapala Inn (☎ 765-47-86; www.mexonline .com/chapalainn.htm; Paseo Ramon Corona 23; r $70; ▣ ☒ ▣ ▣) Four large, gorgeous rooms greet you at this pleasant inn. There's also a common living room and a wonderful covered terrace overlooking the marshy lakeside. Breakfast is included.

Eating

East along Paseo Corona is a slew of fish restaurants with reasonable prices. Just be aware that most of the finned critters probably come from fish farms, but considering the state of the lake this isn't a bad idea.

Café Paris (☎ 765-53-53; Madero 421; mains $3-7.50) Good for breakfast and snacks, this casual place has inside booths, sidewalk tables and an upstairs terrace. There's live guitar and piano music on Saturday and Sunday.

Restaurant Superior (☎ 765-21-80; Madero 415; mains $3-7.50; ☒ 8am-9pm Wed-Mon, 8am-5pm Tue) This place is similar to Café Paris and close by. It offers a little bit of everything, including plenty of breakfast items.

El Árbol de Café (☎ 765-39-08; Hidalgo 236; coffees $1-2; ☒ 8am-3pm Mon-Sat) On the busy highway to Ajijic is this small coffeeshop, with good lattes, mochas and cappuccinos. Snack on cakes, fruit and yogurt; the breakfast plate is under $3.

Getting There & Away

Autotransportes' Guadalajara–Chapala buses from Guadalajara's Antigua Central Camionera (Sala A) travel every half hour from 6am to 9pm ($3.25, 50 minutes). Once you get to Chapala's bus terminal, it's a 10-minute walk down Av Madero to the dry pier. There are long-distance services to Puerto Vallarta ($36) and Mexico City ($43), but to anywhere else you'll have to return to Guadalajara.

Buses connect Chapala and Ajijic every 20 minutes ($0.70, 15 minutes).

AJIJIC

☎ 376 / pop 15,000 / elevation 1550m

More endearing than nearby Chapala, Ajijic (ah-hee-*heek*) lies just 7km to the west, and is a comely little lakeshore town full of cobbled streets, touristy boutiques and galleries, and a few elegant restaurants. It's home to a sizable colony of Mexican, US and Canadian retirees and artists. It's fairly tranquil, except

for the nine-day Fiesta de San Andrés (at the end of November) and over Easter, when three-day re-enactment of Christ's trial and crucifixion is staged.

Buses will drop you on the highway at th top of Colón, the main street, which lead two blocks down to the main plaza and fou more blocks down to the lake. The chapel o the north side of the plaza, two blocks dowr dates from the 18th century or earlier.

Information

There's no tourist office in Ajijic, but th **Lake Chapala Society** (☎ 776-11-40; www.lakechapa society.org; 16 de Septiembre 16A; ☒ information offic 10am-2pm Mon-Sat), which provides many serv ices for expats, can help with local informa tion. Look for *El Ojo del Lago* and the *Lak Chapala Review*, both free English-languag publications on the lake area's goings on. **Bancomer** (☒ 8:30am-4pm Mon-Fri) On the plaza, wit an ATM. **Ciber café** (☒ 10am-8:30pm) On the plaza. Offers Internet access for $2 per hour, and long-distance calls. **Lavandería** (Morelos 24A; per load $3; ☒ 9:30am-2pm & 3-7pm Mon-Sat) Head here for clean clothes; it's off the northwest corner of the plaza.

Sleeping

Mis Amores (☎ 766-46-40; www.misamores.con Hidalgo 22B; r $65-75) Twelve beautiful, romanti rooms with TV and fridge are set aroun a small but lush tropical garden. All ar different from each other and very comfort able. There's a restaurant on the premise and breakfast is included.

La Nueva Posada (☎ 766-14-44; nuevaposada prodigy.net.mx; Donato Guerra 9; s/d from $68/78; ▣ ▣ This wonderful inn has large elegant room and villas with either terraces or balconie some boast lake views. The pool is tiny, bu surrounded by a patio full of plants, an there's a great grassy garden outside th good restaurant. Breakfast is included.

Ajijic Guesthouse B&B (☎ 766-21-49; www.aji guesthouse.com; Independencia 11; r $35-55; ▣) you're looking for intimacy, check out th four-room B&B. Rooms are nicely don and there are cozy common areas, incluc ing patios. The two cheapest rooms share bathroom. Bike and kayak use is free.

Laguna B&B (☎ 766-11-74; www.lagunamex.cor Zaragoza Ote 29; r $35; ▣) Just four comfortab rooms here, with tile floors and tradition decor. A nice common room and goo breakfast are included. Prices drop to $150 per week from April to September. Enter via the highway, and call ahead as the office closes at 3pm.

Hotel Estancia (☎ 766-07-17; hotelestanciaajijic@hotmail.com; Morelos 13; s/d $43/50) Enter via a flowery courtyard, surrounded by two floors of tasteful but simple rooms with TV. There's a cool rooftop terrace; prices drop 25% Sunday through Thursday.

Hotel Italo (☎ 766-22-21; marianabrandi60@hotmail.com; Guadalupe Victoria 8; s/d $24/31) Ajijic's cheapest rooms, clean and simple. The rooftop terrace has a nice view of the lake, and apartments are available for longer-term rentals.

Check out the following websites for more B&B options:

- www.lapalomabb.com
- www.losartistas.com
- www.swaninnajijic.com
- http://casafloresmexico.com

Eating & Drinking

Pedro's Gourmet (☎ 766-47-47; Ocampo 71; mains $7.50-10; ☽ noon-9pm Tue-Sat) Great food awaits in the pretty courtyard garden at this fine restaurant. Try the pan-fried red snapper with spicy salsa, or the Jamaican honey garlic chicken. There are also Asian dishes, like Pad Thai, curried spinach salad and miso soup. Prix-fixe is $10, and lunch specials are only $5.

Bruno's (☎ 766-16-74; Carretera Ote 20; mains $7-15; ☽ 12:30-3pm & 5:30-8pm) Ajijic's best meats (think sirloins, ribs and burgers) are served up at this very popular Canadian-run eatery. The creative stir-fries, pasta dishes and salads are also very good, but be prepared to rub elbows with other diners – it's a tight space.

Secret Garden Café (☎ 766-52-13; Hidalgo 8; mains under $4; ☽ 9am-6pm Mon, Tue, Thu & Fri, 9am-9pm Fri & Sat) Sit in the relaxing garden and enjoy treats like homemade soups, yogurt shakes, breakfast burritos, tasty hamburgers and organic coffees. The flan here is worth a trip to Ajijic alone.

60s in Paradise (☎ 766-47-21; Hidalgo 10; mains under $5; ☽ 11am-4pm Tue-Sat) American-run, so you know your homemade chili and Paradise burger are pretty authentic. French fries, Philly cheesesteak sandwiches, root beer floats, chocolate milkshakes and even strawberry sour cream pies can be had.

El Sabor de Oaxaca (☎ 766-44-68; Av Plaza del Sol 5; coffees under $3; ☽ 9am-9pm) Organic coffee beans from Oaxaca, Veracruz and Chiapas

are ground at this small and modern coffeeshop. The chocolate frappé is a refreshing sugar bomb on a hot day; decaf also available.

Tom's Bar (☎ 766-03-55; Constitución 32; ☽ 10am-midnight Sun-Thu, 10am-1am Fri & Sat) This Canadian-owned watering hole is an expat magnet, boasting sports on the tube and a courtyard in which to chat. Good bar food is available, and there's live piano music on Friday nights.

Getting There & Around

Autotransportes' Guadalajara–Chapala buses depart Guadalajara's Antigua Central Camionera (Sala A) every half hour from 6am to 9pm ($3.50, one hour). These buses drop you on the highway at Colón. Buses connect Chapala and Ajijic every 20 minutes ($0.70, 15 minutes).

Like to bike? Check out **Bicicletas Rayo** (☎ 766-53-46; Carretera Ote 11; ☽ 10:30am-8pm Mon-Sat). Bike rentals cost $2.50 per hour or $10 per day; you can cruise the 5km bike path that parallels the highway to Chapala.

SAN JUAN COSALÁ

☎ 387 / pop 3000 / elevation 1560m

At San Juan Cosalá, 10km west of Ajijic, there's a popular **thermal spa** (adult/child $10/5; ☽ 8:30am-7pm) in an attractive lakeside setting. The spa has seven swimming pools, plays loud music and attracts Mexican families on weekends. It's located between Hotels Balneario San Juan Cosalá and Villa Bordeaux; if you stay at either of these places entry to the spa is free.

Hotel Balneario San Juan Cosalá (☎ 761-02-22; www.hotelspacosala.com; La Paz 420; s/d $65/70; **P**) is a large complex with 34 basic and spacious, but rather cold rooms; some have lake views. It's good for families and groups. Next door, the more intimate **Hotel Villa Bordeaux** (☎ 761-04-94; s/d $65/75; **P**) offers 11 decent rooms and is for adults over 18; there's a nice grassy area and it's much more relaxing that its neighbor.

Autotransportes' Guadalajara–Chapala buses depart Sala A every half hour from 6am to 9pm for San Juan Cosalá ($3.50, 1¼ hours). Buses from Ajijic run every 20 minutes ($0.70, 15 minutes).

ZONA DE MONTAÑA

South of Lago de Chapala, the mountainous region of Jalisco – known as the

Zona de Montaña – has become a popular weekend getaway for Guadalajarans. They come, sometimes by the hordes, to enjoy the rural landscapes, endearing colonial villages, cooler temperatures and tasty local foods, like sweets, fruit preserves and dairy products.

Tapalpa

☎ 343 / pop 16,000 / elevation 2100m

Once a mining town, Tapalpa has now become a tourist magnet, but still maintains its sweet disposition and makes for a relaxing getaway. It perches daintily on the slopes of the Sierra Tapalpa, about 130km southwest of Guadalajara, and boasts two impressive churches, a darling plaza, cobbled streets, and delightfully rustic old buildings with balconies and red-tiled roofs. Good walking can be found in the surrounding area, which features pine forests, fishing streams and Las Piedrotas – some impressive rock formations in cow pastures 5km north of town. You can walk along a country road to these rocks, passing a funky old paper mill, hitch or take a taxi ($6). El Salto, a fine 105m-high waterfall, is about 13km south of town (taxi $12).

Don't miss the **Centro de Integración** (CITAC; ☎ 432-05-70; citac96@hotmail.com; Salto de Nogal 100; ☼ 9am-2pm & 3-7pm Mon-Thu, 9:30-4pm Fri), a school for special-needs youth, dedicated to teaching kids self-confidence along with computer and art skills. Wonderful recycled art is made from *papel malhecho*, a kind of papier-mâché. You can buy these creations at the school, or at its small stall in the Mercado de Artesano, on the plaza. To get to the school, head 200m down Calle Pastores (from Ignacio Lopez) and go right at the fork after about 100m.

There's a **tourist office** (☎ 432-06-50; ☼ 9am-3pm Mon-Fri, 10:30am-2:30pm Sat & Sun) on the plaza, and a Banorte bank with an unreliable ATM nearby; bring money from outside town, just in case.

Accommodation is available at a dozen hotels and guesthouses, though you should reserve on weekends and holidays (when prices can go up). The basic and musty, but acceptable **Hotel Tapalpa** (Matamoros 35; s/d $15/20), is the cheapest, and is right on the plaza. **Casa de Maty** (☎ 432-01-89; Matamoros 69; r Sun-Thu $56, Fri & Sat $75), almost next door, is the complete opposite, with luxurious

rooms and gardens. Another top-end stay is **Hostal Casona de Manzano** (☎ 432-11-41; www.hostallacasonademanzano.com; Madero 84; s/d Mon-Thu $47/67, Fri-Sun $56/75; P), sporting gorgeous courtyard rooms. In between, in both value and comfort, is the **Hotel Posada la Hacienda** (☎ 432-01-93; Quintero 120; s/d $22/30; P), right off the plaza, and **Las Margaritas** (☎ 432-07-99; 16 de Septiembre 81; r from $38), with well-decorated pleasant rooms and apartments.

Food is good here in Tapalpa. Sample tasty *tamales de acelga* (chard-filled *tamales*), sold at the cheap food stalls next to the church. Another scrumptious dish is *borrego al pastor* (grilled lamb), cooked up in the afternoon at **El Puente** (☎ 432-04-35; Hidalgo 324; ☼ Thu-Tue), a casual restaurant three blocks down from the church and just after the bridge. Other regional specialties include homemade sweets, *rompope* (eggnog), *ponche* (pomegranate wine) and *Barranca* (a tequila made from wild agave).

Hourly buses to Tapalpa leave from Guadalajara's Antigua Central Camionera ($6.50, 3½ hours). There are also buses to/from Cuidad Guzmán ($4.50, two hours). Buses in Tapalpa stop at the **Sur de Jalisco bus office** (Ignacio Lopez 10), a block down from the plaza.

Mazamitla

☎ 382 / pop 12,500 / elevation 2200m

Tranquil Mazamitla is south of Lago de Chapala and 132km by road from Guadalajara. This is a friendly, quiet and tidy mountain village, full of hilly cobbled streets, tiled roofs and whitewashed buildings. Everywhere in town you'll see small storefronts selling fruit preserves, cheeses, *rompope* and *cajeta* (milk caramel), and on Mondays there's a small lively **market** (☼ 8am-3pm) on Juárez. About 5km south of town is the leafy park **Los Cazos** (admission $1; ☼ 9am-5pm), which harbors the 30m waterfall El Salto. You can picnic or ride horses here; a taxi costs $5.

Mazamitla's **tourist office** (☎ 538-02-30; Porta Degollado 4; ☼ 9am-3pm Mon-Fri) is by the Asian-influenced church. There's a bank on the plaza. For Internet access try **Compudick** (Galeana 4; ☼ 10am-10pm) across from the food stalls.

There are a few sleeping options in town; prices rise during holidays. Right at the plaza **Posada Alpina** (☎ 538-01-04; posada_alpina@yahoo.com.mx; Reforma 8; s/d Mon-Thu $11.50/23, Fri-Sun $17/25) has nice patios and good, but small, rooms with TV (try for room 9).

WESTERN CENTRAL HIGHLANDS

Also close to the plaza is **Hotel Fiesta Mazamitla** (☎ 538-00-50; Reforma 2; s/d Mon-Thu $9.50/15, Fri-Sun $19/24), which has large, clean and comfortable rooms with TV. Unique **Hotel Cabañas Colina de los Ruiseñores** (☎ 044-33-3494-1210, in Guadalajara 3615-645; www.mazamitlahotelcabana.com.mx; Allende 50; s/d $15/29) is a wonderfully rustic place, offering comfortable tree house–like rooms and walkways with creative wood accents everywhere.

For eats, try **Posada Mazamitla** (☎ 538-06-8; Hidalgo 2; mains $3.50-5.50; 8:30am-6:30pm), a pleasant patio restaurant that on Sunday serves the town's landmark dish *El Bote* (a stew of meats, vegetables and *chiles serranos* in a base of pulque – a liquid fermented from the maguey plant). Another venerable restaurant is **La Troje** (☎ 538-00-70; Galeana 53; mains $7-10; 9am-7:30pm), at the edge of town, across from Pémex. It serves steak and seafood dishes, and is a great place for afternoon drinks. Mazamitla's cheapest food is served in stalls at the corner of Galeana and Allende between 8am and 10pm.

Frequent buses run daily from Guadalajara's Nueva Central Camionera ($7, three hours); they stop three blocks north of the plaza. From Colima there are seven buses daily ($9, 2¾ hours); these stop at the market, just a block west of the plaza. Other destinations include Zamora ($6), Morelia ($12.50) and Manzanillo ($14).

Ciudad Guzmán (Zapotlán el Grande)

☎ 341 / pop 89,000 / elevation 1500m

There isn't much for the tourist in busy Guzmán, but it's a pleasant-enough place to stop for the night. Guzmán is the closest large city to Volcán Nevado de Colima (p557); this lofty mountain is about 25km (as the vulture flies) southwest of Guzmán.

Guzmán's huge plaza is surrounded by arcades and boasts two churches: The Sagrado Corazón, a 17th-century church, and a more modern neoclassical cathedral. In its center is a stone gazebo with a homage to famous Mexican muralist José Clemente Orozco – called 'Man of Fire' – painted on its ceiling (the original is in Guadalajara; see p528). Indeed, Ciudad Guzmán is the birthtown of Orozco, and some of his original carbon illustrations and lithographs can be seen at the small **Museo Regional de las Culturas de Occidente** (Dr Ángel González 21; admission $2.25; 9:30am-5:30pm Tue-Sat).

The **tourist office** (☎ 413-53-13 ext 107; Lázaro Cárdenas 80; 8:30am-3pm Mon-Fri) is located upstairs in the yellow government building, two and a half blocks east of the plaza.

Need a bed? Try the good-value **Reforma Hotel** (☎ 412-44-54; Reforma 77; s/d/tw $11.50/23/24; P), half-way between the bus station and plaza. **Zapotlán Hotel & Villas** (☎ 412-00-40; http://mx.geocities.com/zapotlan_hotel_villas; Federico del Toro 61; r $22; P) has a nice lobby and great swimming pool, and it's right on the plaza. Rooms are noisy though. A good deal is **Tlayolan Hotel** (☎ 412-33-17; Javier Mina 35; s & d $16, tw $28), with small, clean and modern rooms; it's a few blocks southeast of the town center.

There are many restaurants around the plaza. Behind the cathedral is the market and the city's cheapest eats.

The bus terminal is about four blocks west of the plaza. Destinations include Guadalajara ($9, two hours), Colima ($7.50, one hour), Tapalpa ($4.50, two hours) and Mazamitla ($4.50, two hours). Buses to El Fresnito, the closest village to Volcán Nevado de Colima, run from the plaza ($1.50, 15 minutes).

INLAND COLIMA

The tiny state of Colima (5191 sq km) offers a widely varied landscape, from lofty volcanoes on its northern fringes to shallow lagoons near the Pacific coast. The climate is similarly diverse: cooler in the highlands and hot along the coast. This section deals with the inland area of the state; the narrow coastal plain is covered in the Central Pacific Coast chapter.

Colima, the semitropical state capital, is a relatively small but agreeable city, off the beaten tourist path. It's a must for visitors seeking a closer look at the two spectacular local volcanoes – the active, constantly steaming Volcán de Fuego (3820m), and the extinct, snowcapped Volcán Nevado de Colima (4240m). The latter can be reached relatively easily if you have a taste for adventure and a flexible budget, but access to the very active Volcán de Fuego is usually barred for safety reasons.

History

Pre-Hispanic Colima was remote from the major ancient cultures of Mexico. Seaborne contacts with more distant places might have been more important: legend says one king of Colima, Ix, had regular treasure-bearing visitors from China.

Colima produced some remarkable pottery, which has been found in over 250 sites, mainly tombs, dating from about 200 BC to AD 800. The pottery includes a variety of figures, often quite comical and expressive. Best known are the rotund figures of hairless dogs, known as Xoloitzcuintles (see the boxed text, p554).

Archaeologists believe the makers of the pottery lived in villages spread around the state. The type of grave in which much of it was found, the shaft tomb, occurs not only in the western Mexican states of Colima, Michoacán, Jalisco and Nayarit, but in Panama and South America as well.

When the Spanish reached Mexico, Colima led the Chimalhuacán indigenous confederation dominating Colima and parts of Jalisco and Nayarit. Two Spanish expeditions were defeated by the Colimans before Gonzalo de Sandoval, one of Cortés' lieutenants, conquered them in 1523. That year he founded the town of Colima, the third Spanish settlement in Nueva España, after Veracruz and Mexico City. In 1527 the town moved to its present site, from its original lowland location near Tecomán.

COLIMA

☎ 312 / pop 127,000 / elevation 550m

This fine capital city is a pleasant inland break for those traveling the coast. It's overshadowed by the actively puffing Volcán de Fuego – visible 30km to the north – which gives an edge to life here. A bigger concern, however, are earthquakes; the city has been hit by several major temblors over the centuries (the last in January 2003). Because of these devastating natural events Colima has few colonial buildings, despite having been the first Spanish city in western Mexico.

Despite these hazards, Colima remains an attractive (and growing) city graced by several lively plazas. It's only 45km from the coast, but is quite a bit cooler and less humid. There are a number of interesting things to do in the city, though some sights are eight or 10 blocks from the city center – so buff up your walking shoes. And once you've seen the city, some fine daytrips await the adventurous.

Orientation

Colima's Plaza Principal is the heart of the city. Portal Medellín is the row of arches on the north side, with Portal Morelos on the south side. Jardín Quintero lies behind the cathedral, while Jardín Núñez is three blocks further east. Street names change at Plaza Principal (also known as Jardín Libertad). Colima's long-distance bus terminal Terminal Foránea, is some 2km east of the city center, on the Guadalajara–Manzanillo road. There's also a local bus terminal, Terminal Rojos, for closer destinations, located 1.5km west of the city.

Information

You can change money at numerous banks and *casas de cambios* around the city center most banks have ATMs.

Centro Médico (☎ 312-40-45; Herrera 140; ⏰ 24hr)
Cl@Internet (Hidalgo 6; Internet per hr $2; ⏰ 9am-9pm)
Lavandería Amana (Domínguez 147-A; per load US3.50 ⏰ 8am-9pm Mon-Sat, 8am-3pm Sun)
Main post office (Madero 247; ⏰ 8am-5:30pm Mon-Fri)
Prestigio travel agency (☎ 313-10-11; Constitución 43b; ⏰ 9am-8pm Mon-Fri, 9am-5pm Sat, 9am-1pm Sun)
State tourist office (☎ 312-43-60; www.visitacolima com.mx; Palacio de Gobierno; ⏰ 8:30am-8pm Mon-Fri, 10am-2pm Sat) Open on Sunday during holidays.

Sights

AROUND PLAZA PRINCIPAL

The **cathedral**, or Santa Iglesia, on the east side of Plaza Principal (also known as Jardín Libertad) has been rebuilt several times since the Spanish first erected a cathedral here in 1527. The most recent reconstruction dates from just after the 1941 earthquake.

Next to the cathedral is the **Palacio de Gobierno**, built between 1884 and 1904. Local artist Jorge Chávez Carrillo painted the murals on the stairway to celebrate the 200th anniversary of the birth of independence hero Miguel Hidalgo, who was once parish priest of Colima. The murals depict Mexican history from the Spanish conquest to independence. There's also a **museum** (admission free; ⏰ 10am-6pm Tue-Sun) inside the palace with painting, currency and arms exhibits.

On the south side of the plaza Portal Morelos is a handsome colonnade shading outdoor tables. The **Museo Regional de Historia de Colima** (☎ 312-92-28; Portal Morelos 1; admission $3.25; ⏰ 9am-6pm Tue-Sat, 5-8pm Sun) display

COLIMA

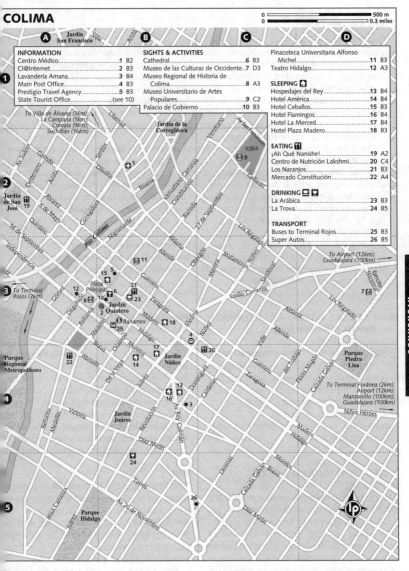

WESTERN CENTRAL HIGHLANDS

n excellent collection of ceramic vessels ad figurines (mostly people and adorable oloitzcuintle dogs) unearthed in Colima ate. There are also exhibits on the 19th- nd 20th-century history of the state, and an npressive reconstruction of a shaft tomb.

The **Teatro Hidalgo** (cnr Degollado & Independencia) as built in neoclassical style between 1871 and 1883 on a site originally donated to the city by Miguel Hidalgo. The theater was destroyed by the earthquakes of 1932 and 1941, and reconstruction was undertaken in 1942. At the time of writing the theater was again being repaired; during your tenure in town it may only be open for special events.

THE COLIMA DOG

One thing you will see while visiting a museum or souvenir shop in Colima, are the cute and curious dog statues called Xoloitzcuintles (sho-lo-itz-*kuint*-lehs). Though they were not confined only to this part of Mexico, so many of these shiny, red-clay figures have been uncovered by archaeologists in Colima state that they've become known as 'Colima dogs' to English speakers.

Xoloitzcuintle statues, produced from AD 200–900, were modeled after some of the first canines in pre-Hispanic Mexico. Often these figures are just standing on their four thick legs, but sometimes they're dancing joyfully with each other or sitting on their haunches smiling quizzically. It can be surprising how many poses and comical expressions the crafters of these figures have bestowed upon their short, pudgy subjects.

The Aztecs believed that Xoloitzcuintles helped human souls reach their final resting place in the afterworld, which explains why the statues (and the dogs themselves) have been found in tombs. Even their name confirms this – 'Xolotl' was the Aztec god who guided souls in the afterlife, and 'itzcuintle' is the Náhuatl word for dog. But even in life, Xoloitzcuintles were important to pre-Hispanic Mexicans. The dogs were believed to possess mystical curative powers and people often slept with them, hoping to be relieved of their ailments (and cold feet). This may be why they were also part of the ancient diet, a fact that would explain their charming rotundity and hairlessness.

Today the clay figures are prized by collectors, often fetching thousands of dollars each at auction. And Xoloitzcuintles still exist in the flesh as the purebred Mexican Hairless (Frida Kahlo kept them). It's now one of the oldest and rarest domesticated breeds in the world, so don't expect to see them on a menu anymore.

MUSEO DE LAS CULTURAS DE OCCIDENTE

The **Museum of Western Cultures** (☎ 313-06-08 ext 4; cnr Calz Galván & Ejército Nacional; admission $1.50; ⏰ 9am-7:30pm Tue-Sun) is about 1km east of the city center. It has exhibits of pre-Hispanic ceramic vessels, stone tools, weapons and musical instruments (including a conch blower) from Colima state. Most impressive are the human figures and Xoloitzcuintle dogs, but the wide variety of other figures includes mammals, reptiles, fish and birds.

MUSEO UNIVERSITARIO DE ARTES POPULARES

The must-see **University Museum of Popular Arts** (☎ 312-68-69; cnr Barreda & Gallardo; admission $1, free Sun; ⏰ 10am-2pm & 5-8pm Tue-Sat, 10am-1pm Sun) is about 1km north of Plaza Principal. On display are folk-art exhibits from Colima and other states, with a particularly grand collection of costumes and masks used in traditional Colima dances. Other impressive exhibits include textiles, basketry, painted gourds, instruments and miniature toy models.

Adjacent to the museum, the **Taller de Reproducciones** (⏰ mornings Mon-Sat) is a workshop making reproductions of ancient Coliman ceramic figures. Some of these figures may be on sale at the small museum shop.

PINACOTECA UNIVERSITARIA ALFONSO MICHEL

This beautiful **museum** (☎ 312-22-28; Cnr Guer & Constitución; admission $1; ⏰ 10am-2pm & 5-8pm Tu Sat, 10am-1pm Sun), in a 19th-century courtyar building, offers four halls filled with cor temporary art. Included are a permane collection of paintings by Colima's Alfons Michel, and works by other Mexican artist like José Clemente Orozco, David Alfar Siqueiros and Francisco Toledo. Temporai exhibitions by foreign artists also appear.

PARKS

The **Parque Regional Metropolitano**, on Dego lado a few blocks southwest of the city cente has a small sad zoo, a swimming pool ($1 snack kiosks and a forest with an artifici lake. Explore the forest paths on quadbik ($2.50 per 30 minutes), or cruise the lake b paddleboat ($2.50 per 30 minutes).

East of the city center on Calz Galvá **Parque Piedra Lisa** is named after its local famous Sliding Stone. Legend says that vis tors who slide on this stone will some da return to Colima, either to marry or to di

LA CAMPANA

This **archaeological site** (☎ 313-49-46; Av Te nológico s/n; admission $3; ⏰ 9am-5pm Tue-Sun) date rom as early as 1500 BC. Several low, pyramid-like structures have been excavated and restored, along with a small tomb that ou can look into, and a space that appears o be a ball court (very unusual in western Mexico). The structures seem to be oriented ue north toward Volcán de Fuego, which makes an impressive backdrop. It's about km north of Colima city and easily accesible by buses 7 and 22; taxis cost $3.

estivals & Events

he following festivals take place in or very ear Colima city:

iestas Charro Taurinas For two weeks in early February is celebration takes place in Villa de Álvarez, 5km north central Colima. There are parades accompanied by giant *ojigangos* puppets (caricatures of local figures). They start Colima's cathedral and go to Villa de Álvarez, where e celebrations continue with food, music, rodeos and ullfights.

eria de Todos los Santos The Colima state fair (late :tober and early November) includes agricultural and andicraft exhibitions, cultural events and carnival rides.

ía de la Virgen de Guadalupe From about ecember 1 to the actual feast day, on December 12, omen and children dress in costume to pay homage at e Virgin's altar in the cathedral. On Dec 11 *mañanitas* raditional songs) are sung.

leeping

otel Plaza Madero (☎ 330-28-95; Madero 165; s & d 88, tw $47; **P**) Strangely located inside a mall shopping mall, this hotel has colorul, pleasant rooms with cable TV. Get one acing the street (rooms 7 to 11); they come ith balcony and are brighter.

Hotel Ceballos (☎ 312-44-44; www.hotelceballos om; Portal Medellín 12; r from $77; **P**))n the north side of Plaza Principal, this ately five-star hotel has around 50 nicely emodeled rooms with high ceilings. Some ave French windows opening onto small alconies, but the least expensive rooms are nockingly small and dark – and not worth e price.

Hospedajes del Rey (☎ /fax 313-36-83; Av Rey olimán 125; s & d $31, tw $37; **P**) The good nodern rooms at this small hotel have cable V and fan, but those with two beds are a etter size. A $10 deposit is required; air-con osts more.

Hotel América (☎ 312-74-88; hamerica@hotelamerica om.mx; Morelos 162; s & d from $60, ste from $93; **P**) The suites here are nicest,

and overlook the hotel's lovely fountain patio. Standard rooms straddle maze-like outdoor halls and scream for a remodel – they're downright awful. There's a fancy restaurant, too.

Hotel La Merced (☎ 312-69-69; Hidalgo 188; s & d $21, tw $28; **P**) This old budget place is divided into two: the original back wing (with dark, colonial rooms), and the newer front area (those above the driveway are brightest). Rooms have TV and fan, and some are generously sized.

Hotel Flamingos (☎ 312-25-25; Av Rey Colimán 18; s & d $18, tw $21; **P**) A good budget choice. Rooms are bright and have solid beds, tiled floors, balconies and TVs, but those facing west bake in the afternoon sun. It was damaged in the big 2003 earthquake, so let's hope all has been restored properly!

Eating & Drinking

Many small restaurants around Plaza Principal offer good simple fare – just pick one that appeals. **Mercado Constitución** (7am-6pm Mon-Sat, 7am-2pm Sun), a couple of blocks south of Plaza Principal, has cheap food stalls serving juices, *pozole* and other lip-smackin' snacks.

¡Ah Qué Nanishe! (☎ 314-21-97; Calle 5 de Mayo 267; mains $3.75-7.50; 1pm-midnight Wed-Mon) The name of this restaurant means 'How delicious!' and the Oaxacan specialties here are good indeed. Order *moles* (thick spicy sauces), *chilis rellenos* (stuffed chilis) or *chapulines* (crunchy fried grasshoppers). On Sunday there's *barbacoa de borrego* (tender lamb).

Centro de Nutrición Lakshmi (☎ 312-64-33; Madero 265; meals under $3; 8am-9:30pm Mon-Sat, 10am-2pm & 6-9:30pm Sun) This natural-foods café serves healthy fare such as salads, veggie burgers, soy ceviche (!) and natural yogurt products. It caters more to take-out, but there are a few tables around a courtyard. There are also whole wheat breads, granola and herbal products for sale.

Los Naranjos (☎ 312-00-29; Barreda 34; mains $3-7) Saunter into this upscale spot and grab a seat in the nice patio out back. The menu offers a good general selection of tasty Mexican food and drink, with plenty of breakfast and coffee choices to help you wake up.

La Arábica (☎ 314-70-01; Barreda 4; coffees $1-2.50; 8am-2pm & 5:30-9:30pm Mon-Sat) Great espresso, cappuccinos, mochas and lattes are whipped up in this tiny space – it's mostly take-out, since there are just a few stools to perch on.

La Trova (☎ 314-11-59; Revolución 363; 🕑 7pm-2am Tue-Sun) Also a restaurant, this long-running 'bar bohemio' serves up live *trova* music at 9:30pm nightly. Tables are set up around a small intimate courtyard, and the atmosphere is laid-back and casual.

Getting There & Around

Colima's airport is near Cuauhtémoc, 12km northeast of the city center off the highway to Guadalajara (taxis $10). Both **Aeromar** (☎ 313-55-88) and **Aero California** (☎ 314-48-50) zoom to Mexico City daily; the latter also flies to Tijuana.

Colima has two bus terminals. The long-distance terminal is Terminal Foránea, 2km east of the city center at the junction of Av Niños Héroes and the city's eastern bypass. There's a **left-luggage facility** (🕑 6am-10pm). To reach Colima's center from this terminal, hop on a Ruta 4 or 5 bus (taxis $1.75). For the return trip catch the same buses on Calle 5 de Mayo or Zaragoza. Destinations with frequent departures include those in the following table:

Destination	Price	Duration
Ciudad Guzmán	$6	1-2hr
Guadalajara	$15	3hr
Manzanillo	$5	2hr
Mexico City (Terminal Norte)	$54	10hr

Colima's second bus terminal (serving local towns) is Terminal Rojos, about 1.5km west of Plaza Principal. Ruta 4 or 6 buses run to Colima's center from this terminal (taxis $1.50). To get back to this terminal, take any bus marked 'Rojos' going north on Morelos. Destinations from here include Comala ($0.60, 15 minutes, every 15 minutes), Manzanillo ($4.50, 1¾ hours, every half hour), Tecomán ($2.50, 45 minutes, every 20 minutes) and Armería ($2.75, 45 minutes, every half hour).

Taxi fares within town are $1 to $2. To rent a car to explore Colima's surrounding volcanoes and villages, try **Super Autos** (☎ 312-07-52; Av Rey Coliman 382); the cheapest ride will cost you around $50 per day (with 300km included).

AROUND COLIMA

Colima has some wonderful surroundin villages and scenic mountains to explore and much can be done on a daytrip and b public transport. For personalized tours con tact **Doug Vincent** (popote48980@yahoo.com), wh charges $50 per day (plus mileage/tolls).

Comala

☎ 312 / pop 9200 / elevation 600m

Nine kilometers north of Colima is this swee little town with great views of the nearb twin volcanoes, Fuego and Nevado. Comal has a leafy plaza with a fine white gazebe pretty flowering trees and a church sportin a mix of architectural styles. On sunny week ends both locals and tourists flock to th inviting *centros botaneros* (tapas bars), unde the arches along two sides of the plaza, fo afternoon drinks and snacks. They're ope from about noon to 6pm; try Fundador Res taurant (the sign says 'Don Camalón').

About a 30-minute walk from town i the excellent **Museo Alejandro Rangel Hidalg** (☎ 315-60-28; admission $2; 🕑 10am-2pm & 3:30-7p Tue-Fri, 10am-6pm Sat, Sun & holidays), in the Ex Hacienda Nogueras. Hidalgo (1923–2000 was a designer, painter and illustrator, an a fine collection of pre-Hispanic artifac (especially Xoloitzcuintle dogs), are no very nicely displayed in this museum. Loo for the sketch of Frida Kahlo. To get her walk 400m along Calle Degollado (left of th church); turn left at the T-intersection, g 1km, then turn right at the next T-intersectio and go another 1km. You can also take bus ($0.40, from behind the church) or taxi ($1.50).

Comala buses leave from Colima's Te minal Rojos ($0.60, 15 minutes, every 1 minutes). Buses back to Colima depart fro Comala's plaza.

Suchitlán

☎ 318 / pop 3850 / elevation 1200m

Small and hilly Suchitlán, 7km northeast (Comala, has rustic cobbled streets dotte with stray dogs and chickens. The village i famous for its animal masks and witche The masks are carved here and worn b dancers in the traditional *Danza de l Morenos*, which takes place here durin Semana Santa. This dance commemorate the legend that dancing animals enabled th Marys to rescue Christ's body, by distractin

AROUND COLIMA

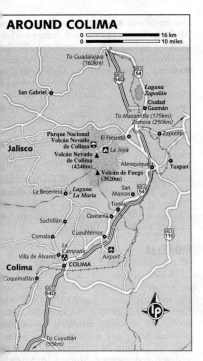

Four buses run daily from Colima's Terminal Rojos to La Becerrera ($1.25, one hour), but you'll have to walk the 1km to the lake.

Parque Nacional Volcán Nevado de Colima

This national park, straddling the border of Colima and Jalisco, includes two dramatic volcanoes: the still-active Volcán de Fuego and the inactive Volcán Nevado de Colima. Ciudad Guzmán (p551) is the closest city to the volcanoes, but Colima is a more pleasant base.

VOLCÁN DE FUEGO

Overlooking Colima from the north, 30km from the city as the vulture flies, is steaming Volcán de Fuego (3820m) – Mexico's most active volcano. It has erupted dozens of times in the past four centuries, with a big eruption about every 70 years. A major burp in 1913 spelled the end of one cycle of activity, then another began in the 1960s. The latest spurt of activity began in 1998, and has included pyroclastic flows, the growth of lava domes and significant eruptions. In June 2005 a large explosion sent ash 4.8km (three miles) into the sky, all the way to Colima. Current information about the volcano is posted on the website of the **Universidad de Colima** (www.ucol.mx/volcan in Spanish).

VOLCÁN NEVADO DE COLIMA

The higher and more northerly peak of Nevado de Colima (4240m) is accessible for most of the year. Remnants of a pine forest cover most of Nevado, and alpine desert appears at the highest altitudes. Wildlife frolicking in the area includes deer, wild boar, coyotes and even mountain lions.

The best months for climbing this volcano are the dry months of December through May. Keep in mind that temperatures from December to February can get down to 0°C. Snowfall is always possible on the upper slopes – *nevado* means 'snow covered.' The weather is very changeable, and the mountaintop attracts lightning strikes in stormy weather. The park's winter hours are 7am to 6pm (no cars up after 2pm). The summer rainy season is from July to September, when park hours are longer.

To access the volcano with your own car (rear-wheel drive cars are OK in the dry

he Roman guards. If you're interested in uying a mask, ask around for the homes f the mask makers.

Take a break at **Restaurant El Balcón de Don osé** (☎ 312-76-75; cnr Galeana & Azucena; mains $6.50- .50; ☷ 8:30am-6:30pm Tue-Sun), on the street into own. It has a good atmosphere and food, nd an airy dining room. On the plaza is **estaurant Portales Suchitlán** (☎ 395-44-52; tapas nder $5; ☷ 8:30am-6:30pm Tue-Sun), popular with ourists for its tapas and garden patio.

Buses to Suchitlán leave half-hourly from Colima's Terminal Rojos ($1, 45 minutes).

aguna La María

bout 13km past Suchitlán is the tiny *pueblo* f La Becerrera, and 1km up a side road is ovely green **Laguna La María** (☎ 312-320-88-91; dmission $0.75), a spring-fed lake surrounded y lush hills – it's a popular weekend fishig, boating and picnic spot. You can camp 1; showers available), or stay in one of the imple rooms with kitchen and TV ($29 o $65). There's also a restaurant, rowboat entals and a soccer field. Book ahead durng holiday times.

WESTERN CENTRAL
HIGHLANDS

winter season, if the road is good) you need to start early. Take highway 54D (the *cuota*, or toll road, $8.50) north from Colima for about 45 minutes and get off at the Tuxpan exit (or take the free highway 54 north about 1½ hours to Km 63). At the roundabout, follow the 'Guadalajara libre/Colima cuota' sign, cross over the white and yellow bridge and then follow the 'Guadalajara libre' sign. Parallel highway 54D for 10 minutes, then cross over it and head toward Ciudad Guzmán; just before you reach the town, turn left onto the El Grullo road. After 8.5km, on the left, you'll see the gravel road marked 'Nevado de Colima.' After winding almost 20km (45 minutes) you'll reach La Joya/Puerto Las Cruces (3500m), where you can sign in and pay the $0.50 entry fee (plus $1 per car). You can also camp here, and possibly stay in the basic *refugio* (there is a spring, but bring water just in case). Drive another 5km to the end of the road; the *micro-ondas* (radio antennae) are a 90-minute hike up. Getting to the very top (another 90 minutes) will require a good map and a compass (or GPS) – there are many trails and it's very easy to get lost. Going with a guide (see below) is recommended.

Driving up this volcano on the relatively good dirt road means that you'll be ascending to a high altitude very quickly. If you or anyone in your party feels lightheaded or dizzy, they may be suffering from *mal de montaña* (altitude sickness). That person should descend as quickly as possible, as this condition can be potentially fatal. For more on this health problem, see p1011.

Colima Magic (☎ 312-310-74-83 in Colima, www.colima magic.com) offers tours up the volcano (or to areas with good views of the volcanoes) with English-speaking guides. Tours cost $75 to $120, which includes transportation, food/ beverages and entry fees. The tourist office in Colima can also recommend guides.

INLAND MICHOACÁN

Some consider Michoacán to be Mexico's most beautiful state. Geographically it's certainly a visual treat, and home to part of the impressive Cordillera Neovolcánica – the volcanic range that gives the region both fertile soils and a striking mountainous landscape. Along a 200km stretch of

the *cordillera,* across the northern part o Michoacán, you can explore numerous fas cinating destinations: the spectacular Santu ario Mariposa Monarca (Monarch Butterfl Sanctuary), the handsome state capital o Morelia, the enchanting colonial town o Pátzcuaro, the very Mexican city of Uru apan (with its miniature tropical nationa park) and the famous Volcán Paricutín, short distance beyond Uruapan.

The name Michoacán is an Aztec wor meaning 'Place of the Masters of Fish. Northern Michoacán once had extensiv lakes, but most were drained for farmlan during the colonial period. Traditiona 'butterfly' nets are still used on Lago d Pátzcuaro, although today the main catch i tourists' pesos more than fish.

MORELIA

☎ 443 / pop 593,000 / elevation 1920m

Michoacan's glorious capital city has s many well-preserved colonial building that its center was declared a Unesco Worl Heritage Site in 1991. It's blessed with a go geous and imposing cathedral, an impor tant university and a lively cultural scene And yet, despite its picturesque building and active demeanor, Morelia isn't overl touristy. The few foreigners who do mak it here discover that this city is a good plac for an extended visit, especially to stud Spanish (see p562).

Morelia was one of the first Spanish cit ies in Nueva España, officially founded i 1541, although a Franciscan monastery ha been in the area since 1537. The first vice roy, Antonio de Mendoza, named it Val ladolid after the Spanish city of that name He encouraged families of Spanish nobilit to move here, and it became a very Spanish looking city, at least architecturally. B this time Nueva España had become th independent republic of Mexico, and i 1828 the city was been renamed Morelia i honor of local hero José María Morelos Pavón, a key figure in Mexico's independ ence movement.

Many of Morelia's downtown streets ar lined with colonial buildings, and it sti looks nearly as Spanish as it did before in dependence. City ordinances require tha all new construction in the city center b done in colonial style with arches, baroqu facades and walls of pink stone (the city

rademark characteristic). A good number
f streets remain fairly narrow, but unfortu-
ately they often get congested with traffic.

rientation
Morelia's extraordinary cathedral is the soul
f the city and a major landmark. East–west
treets change their names at the cathedral,
while north–south streets change names at
v Madero.

The elegant row of arched verandas fac-
ng the Plaza de Armas (or zócalo) is commonly called Portal Hidalgo; the arches on
basolo facing the west side of the plaza are
alled Portal Matamoros.

Morelia's bus terminal is about 4km
orthwest of the city center.

nformation
anks and ATMs are plentiful in the zócalo
rea, particularly on and near Av Madero.
merican Klean (Bravo 200; self-service load $3.75, full
rvice $7; ☻ 9am-7pm Mon-Sat, 8am-2pm Sun)
hatroom Cybercafé (Nigromante 132A; per hr $1.50;
☻ 9am-10pm Mon-Sat, noon-10pm Sun)
mergency (☎ 066)
ain post office (Av Madero Ote 369)
anborns (☎ 317-84-72; cnr Av Madero Pte & Zaragoza;
☻ 7:30am-midnight) English magazines, novels and maps.
ourist office (☎ 317-23-71; www.visitmorelia.com;
r Av Madero Pte & Nigromante; ☻ 9am-7pm)

ights
ATHEDRAL
Morelia's beautiful cathedral (glorious
hen it's lit up at night) dominates the zó-
alo and took more than a century to build
1640–1744). It hosts a combination of Herreresque, baroque and neoclassical styles: the
win 70m-high towers, for instance, have
lassical Herreresque bases, baroque mid-
ections and multicolumned neoclassical
ops. Inside, much of the baroque relief work
as replaced in the 19th century with more
alanced and calculated neoclassical pieces.
ortunately, one of the cathedral's interior
ighlights was preserved: a sculpture of the
eñor de la Sacristía made from dried corn
aste and topped with a gold crown from the
5th-century Spanish king Felipe II. Check
ut the large organ with 4600 pipes.

ALACIO DE GOBIERNO
he 17th-century **palacio** (Av Madero Oriente), ori-
nally a seminary and now state government

offices, has a simple baroque facade. Its most
interesting features, however, are the extensive and impressive murals inside, which depict the history of Morelia and Michoacán
state. These were commissioned in 1961, and
then brought to life by Mexican painter Alfredo Zalce; they're definitely worth a peek.

MUSEO REGIONAL MICHOACANO
Just off the zócalo, the **Michoacán Regional Museum** (☎ 312-04-07; Allende 305 & Abasolo; admission $3,
free Sun; ☻ 9am-7pm Tue-Sat, 9am-4pm Sun) is housed
in a late-18th-century baroque palace. The
museum displays a great variety of pre-
Hispanic artifacts, colonial art and relics,
and there are exhibits on the geology, flora
and fauna of the region. A highlight is the
mural by Alfredo Zalce, Cuauhtémoc y la
Historia, on the stairway. The right half of
the mural portrays people with a positive influence on Mexico, while the left half mostly
portrays those with a negative influence.

PALACIO DE JUSTICIA
Across from the regional museum is the Palacio de Justicia, built between 1682 and 1695
to serve as the city hall. Its facade is a chunky
and eclectic, but well-done mix of French and
baroque styles. The stairway in the courtyard
has a dramatic mural by Agustín Cárdenas
showing Morelos in action. A small two-
room **museum** (admission free; ☻ 10am-2pm & 5-8pm)
explains the history of Michoacán's justice
system through old photos and papers (look
for the grisly cadaver shots).

MUSEO DEL ESTADO
The **Michoacán State Museum** (☎ 313-06-29; Prieto
176; admission free; ☻ 9am-8pm Mon-Fri, 9am-2pm & 4-
7pm Sat & Sun) tells the story of Michoacán from
prehistoric times to the first contact between
the Tarascos and the Spanish. Downstairs
there's a wonderful collection of prehistoric
artifacts, from arrowheads to ceramic figures
to bone jewelry and a quartz skull. Upstairs
are documents detailing the Spanish conquest, the spread of religion, and the region's
agricultural and economic development.
Free cultural events often take place here.

MORELOS SITES
José María Morelos y Pavón, one of the
most important figures in Mexico's struggle
for independence from Spain, was born in
the house on the corner of Corregidora and

WESTERN CENTRAL HIGHLANDS

MORELIA

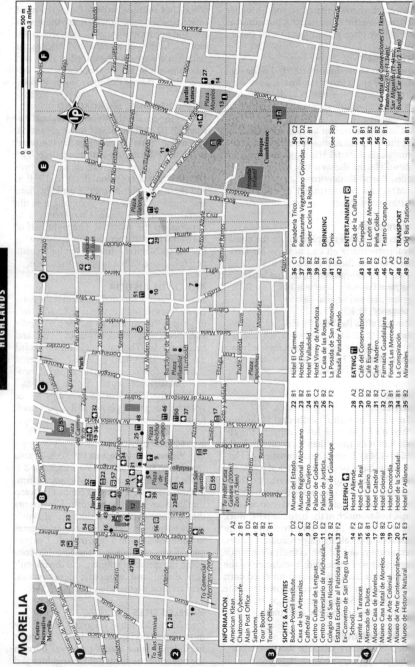

García Obeso, on September 30, 1765. Two centuries later the house (which dates from the 1650s) was declared a national monument and made into the **Museo Casa Natal de Morelos** (Morelos Birthplace Museum; ☎ 312-27-93; orregidora 113; admission free; 🕑 9am-8pm Mon-Fri, am-7pm Sat & Sun). The Morelos memorabilia consists mostly of old photos and documents; there's also a public library, audiorium and projection room. An eternal orch burns next to the projection room. Free international films and cultural events are occasionally held here.

In 1801 Morelos bought the Spanish-style house on the corner of Av Morelos and Soto y Saldaña. Today it's the **Museo Casa de Morelos** (Morelos House Museum; ☎ 313-26-51; Av Morelos Sur 323; admission $2.25, free Sun; 🕑 9am-7pm), with exhibits on Morelos' life and his role in the independence movement. There are also some nice period antiques, including liturgical items.

Morelos studied at the **Colegio de San Nicolás** (cnr Av Madero Pte & Nigromante), one block west of the zócalo. The Colegio later became the foundation for the Universidad Michoacana and is still used by the university. Upstairs, the Sala de Melchor Ocampo is a memorial room to another Mexican hero, reformer and governor of Michoacán. Preserved here is Ocampo's library, and a copy of the document he signed to donate his library to the college, just before being shot by firing squad on June 3, 1861 after his defeat by royalist forces.

PALACIO CLAVIJERO & MERCADO DE DULCES

From 1660 to 1767, the Palacio Clavijero was home to the Jesuit school of St Francis Xavier. After the Jesuits were expelled from Spanish dominions, the building served variously as a warehouse, prison and seat of the state legislature. In 1970 it was completely restored and renovated for use as state government offices. The majestic main patio has imposing colonnades and pink stonework.

Wander through the **Mercado de Dulces** (Sweets Market; 🕑 9am-10pm), on the western side of the palace, to sample the region's famous sweets (see the boxed text, p564). Some folksy Michoacán handicrafts and souvenirs are also sold here, but for high-quality handicrafts you'll do better at the Casa de las Artesanías (right).

MUSEO DE ARTE COLONIAL

South of Plaza del Carmen, this **museum** (☎ 313-92-60; Juárez 240; admission free; 🕑 9am-8pm Mon-Fri, 9am-7pm Sat & Sun) contains 18th-century religious paintings, lots of gruesome crucifixes, and an exhibit on how cornpaste figures are made. Look for the interesting ivory Christ with Asian features (which possibly arrived on a treasure ship from the Philippines) and the 'Poison Christ' made of mesquite and painted black – it was believed this figure could absorb poison from those stung or bitten by toxic animals.

CASA DE LAS ARTESANÍAS

The **House of Handicrafts** (☎ 312-12-48; Plaza Valladolid; 🕑 10am-8pm Mon-Sat, 10am-3pm Sun) occupies the Ex-Convento de San Francisco, and is attached to the Spanish renaissance-style Templo de San Francisco. Arts and handicrafts from all over Michoacán are displayed and sold here; they're expensive but are also some of the best you'll see anywhere in the state. Upstairs, small shops represent many of Michoacán's towns, with craftspeople demonstrating how the specialties of their area are made. You'll find guitars from Paracho, copperware from Santa Clara del Cobre, lacquerware, weaving, pottery and much more. The shops keep individual hours, which will vary from those listed here.

FUENTE LAS TARASCAS & EL ACUEDUCTO

At the east end of Madero Ote, the *fuente* (fountain) spouts from a tray of fruit supported by three bare-breasted Tarascan women. The original fountain here vanished mysteriously in 1940, and this replacement was installed in the 1960s. Adjacent Plaza Villalongín has another fine fountain.

El Acueducto (the Aqueduct) runs for several kilometers along Av Acueducto and makes a couple of bends around Plaza Villalongín. The aqueduct was built between 1785 and 1788 to meet the city's growing water needs. Its 253 arches make an impressive sight, especially at night when they are illuminated by floodlights.

PLAZA MORELOS & AROUND

Running roughly east from the Fuente Las Tarascas, the cobbled Calz Fray Antonio de San Miguel is a broad and elegant pedestrian promenade lined with fine old buildings. It leads about 500m to Plaza Morelos, an irregular but finely proportioned space surrounding the landmark **Estatua Ecuestre al Patriota Morelos**, a statue of Morelos on horseback trotting to battle. The Italian artist Giuseppe Ingillieri sculpted it between 1910 and 1913.

On the northeast edge of the plaza, the **Santuario de Guadalupe** is a delightfully overdone baroque church built from 1708 to 1716. The mauve-and-gold interior (including the psychedelic rotunda with yellow windows) dates from 1915, and will make you feel like you're inside a Fabergé egg. Beside the church, the **Ex-Convento de San Diego** was built in 1761 as a monastery and now houses the law school of the Universidad Michoacana.

The **Bosque Cuauhtémoc** is a large park with lots of trees, children's amusements and a couple of museums. Only modern art fans will appreciate the **Museo de Arte Contemporáneo** (☎ 312-54-04; Acueducto 18; admission free; ☻ 10am-8pm Mon-Fri, 10am-6pm Sat & Sun), a French-style 19th-century building housing changing exhibitions of contemporary art. The small **Museo de Historia Natural** (☎ 312-00-44; Ventura Puente 23; admission free; ☻ 9am-6pm), on the east side of the park, has displays of stuffed, dissected and skeletal animals, along with deformed human fetuses and freaky pickled animals. Bring a strong stomach.

CENTRO DE CONVENCIONES

This **convention center** (☎ 314-62-02; www.cecon expo.com.mx), about 1.5km south of the city center, holds several exposition buildings, including a theater (see p565). You can reach it on the Ruta Roja (red) combi heading east on Tapia or 20 de Noviembre.

Near the convention center is a **planetario** (planetarium; ☎ 314-24-65; admission $3.50), with 164 projectors simulating stars on a dome 20m in diameter (show times are 4:30pm and 6pm Monday to Friday, and 11pm, 1:30pm, 4:30pm and 6pm Saturday and Sunday). There's also an **Orquidario** (Orchid House; ☎ 314-62-29; admission $0.50; ☻ 9am-6pm Mon-Fri, 10:30am-3pm & 4-6pm Sat & Sun), which exhibits nearly 3000 species of wild and hybrid orchids. The best months for flowering are April, May and October, when there are vivid orchid expositions here.

PARQUE ZOOLÓGICO BENITO JUÁREZ

The **zoo** (☎ 314-04-88; Calz Juárez s/n; adult/child $1.75/1; ☻ 10am-5pm Mon-Fri, 10am-6pm Sat & Sun) is

3km south of the *zócalo*. It's generally a pleasant place, with most critters in naturalistic habitats, but the wolves and hyenas could use more space. Other animals include sea lions, giraffes, elephants, lots of birds, and reptiles. Gravel paths make it hard for strollers, but kids may enjoy the lake with rowboats for hire, a small train and playground.

The Ruta Guinda and Ruta Rosa combi or the Santa María bus (white with blue and-grey stripes), all heading south on Nigromante, will drop you off at the zoo entrance.

Courses

Few foreigners and plenty of culture make Morelia an exceptional place to learn Spanish. Ask for a discount if taking a course for more than two weeks.

Baden-Powell Institute (☎ 312-40-70; www .baden-powell.com; Antonio Alzate 565; private lessons per hr $14, group lessons per week $170) This small, well-run and affordable school offers courses in Spanish language, as well as Mexican politics, cooking, culture, guitar playing and salsa dancing. Homestays cost $22 per day, including meals.

Centro Cultural de Lenguas (☎ 312-05-89; www.ccl .com.mx; Av Madero Ote 560; group lessons per week $180, private lessons per week $280) This school offers Spanish-language classes running from two weeks, four hours daily (two on grammar, two on conversation). Homestays (per day $20 to $22, including meals) are available. A $100 deposit is required.

Centro Universitario de Michoacán (☎ 317-14-01; becky_alfaro@hotmail.com; Calz Fray Antonio de San Miguel 173; intensive courses per week $250) In a large colonial building, this school offers courses in Spanish language and Mexican culture. Classes run four hours daily in groups of five or fewer students. Homestays cost $20 per day, including meals.

Tours

For tours outside the city ask the tourist office for recommendations.

Leyendas de Morelia (☎ 312-02-34) An interesting 2½ hour night tour ($7) that covers some major sites in the city center, along with an underground crypt. Book via hotels or travel agencies.

Mex Mich Guías (☎ 390-47-34, 340-46-32; www .mmg.com.mx) Provides personalized tours and transport to many destinations in the area, including the Santuario Mariposa Monarca (per person $43).

Tranvía Kuanari (☎ 312-81-57) Offers three different loop tours of the city ($5.50 to $7) in imitation antique trolley cars, which depart from the tour booth in the Plaza de Armas.

estivals & Events

As well as the usual Mexican celebrations, Morelia's many annual festivals include the following:

eria de Morelia Morelia's biggest fair, running for three weeks in mid-May, hosts exhibits of handicrafts, agriculture and livestock, plus regional dances, bullfights and fiestas. May 18 is the city's founding date (1541) and is celebrated with a fireworks show.

eria de Órgano This international organ festival is held during the first two weeks of the Feria de Morelia.

umpleaños de Morelos Morelos' birthday is celebrated in September 30 with a parade and fireworks show.

estival Internacional de Cine de Morelia (www .moreliafilmfest.com) This major international shop window for Mexico's fecund film industry lasts for a week each October.

estival Internacional de Música (www.festival .orelia.com) The International Music Festival occurs for two weeks in mid-November and includes concerts, choirs and quartets. Each year a different country is highlighted.

ía de la Virgen de Guadalupe The Day of the Virgin of Guadalupe is celebrated on December 12 at the Templo e San Diego; in the preceding weeks typical Mexican roods are sold on the pedestrian street Calz Fray Antonio e San Miguel.

eria Navideña The Christmas Fair, with traditional Christmas items, foods and handicrafts from Michoacán, happens during the month of December.

leeping

As elsewhere, rates can rise about 20% during the holidays, especially December, January and for Día de Muertos (late October to early November).

UDGET

otel El Carmen (☎ 312-17-25; hotel_elcarmen@yahoo com.mx; Ruíz 63; s/d $19/26; P) Centrally located across from a park, this respectable hotel comes complete with 30 tasteful rooms and a pretty lobby. There are wood accents, and the whole ambience is comfortable and clean. For more light (and a balcony) get a room facing the front.

Hotel Casa Galeana (☎ 313-10-87; Galeana 507; s/d/ tw $19/27/30; P) Stay at this well-run posada for its small and dark, but quiet and neat, rooms with cable TV. It has a pastel theme and intimate tiled courtyard. It's a few blocks southwest of the city center.

Hostal Allende (☎ 312-22-46; Allende 843; dm $8.50, from $15) Private rooms at this pleasant hostel are dark, simple and clean, but the cheapest nes are pretty darn small. The sex-segregated

dorms hold four beds only. There's a tiny common kitchen, a wonderful courtyard with large bird cages and a blue-yellow color scheme. Show your HI or ISIC card and you'll receive a 10% discount.

Hotel Colonial (☎ 312-18-97; 20 de Noviembre 15; s/d from $12/15, tw $24) This 25-room colonial-style hotel offers large, somewhat charming rooms, with high beamed ceilings and old (maybe too old) touches. As always, interior rooms are dark and quiet, while exterior rooms (with balconies) are bright and noisy. Cable TV costs extra.

MIDRANGE

Hotel de la Soledad (☎ 312-18-88; www.hsoledad .com; Zaragoza 90; r from $78; P) For a gorgeous stay there's the Soledad, a well-located colonial hotel boasting beautiful courtyards and unique rooms of different sizes. Full-size carriages on the 2nd-floor hallways are reminders of when the building was a carriage house. The wonderfully old atmosphere will also take you back in time.

La Posada de San Antonio (☎ 312-37-19; www .moreliabedandbreakfast.com; Calz Fray Antonio de San Miguel 350; r $70) For something different in Morelia, try this intimate American-owned B&B. It's in a renovated adobe house, and offers just three simple rooms, a large common area and a nice garden out back. It's very quiet and peaceful.

Hotel Catedral (☎ 313-04-06; www.hotelcatedral morelia.com; Zaragoza 37; r $66; P) Within ringing distance of the cathedral, this attractive and historic colonial-style hotel comes with 45 modest rooms. Halls are wide and fringe a covered courtyard with ironwork details. For good views get a room with balcony.

Hotel Casino (☎ 313-13-28; www.hotelcasino.com .mx; Portal Hidalgo 229; r from $82; P ▣) Lying smack dab on the *zócalo* is this Best Western hotel, with 42 decent rooms. Those facing the street have balconies with views of the *zócalo*; the interior rooms overlook a nice covered courtyard with tables.

Posada Parador Amado (☎ 313-76-52; ely_mal donado@hotmail.com; Nervo 170; r $38; P) With an almost motel-like feel, this place has five apartment-style rooms with kitchen and dining areas. Some have two bedrooms, others are smaller; all come with cable TV.

Hotel Valladolid (☎ 312-00-27; Portal Hidalgo 245; r $65) The old-style rustic rooms at this large hotel don't quite mesh with the modern and almost futuristic halls (but *everyone's* a critic). Its location on the *zócalo* is excellent and can be best appreciated if you manage to snag a balcony.

Hotel Florida (☎ 312-18-19; www.unimedia.net .mx.hotelflorida.com; Av Morelos Sur 161; s/d $29/38) A conventional midrange choice is this non-pretentious hotel with a good location, and modern rooms sporting cable TV and sizeable baths. Ask for an outside room if you need sunlight.

Hotel Concordia (☎ 312-30-52; www.hotelconcordia morelia.com.mx; Gómez Farías 328; s/d $37/46; P 🖳) Located near the old bus station is this decent hotel, boasting a smart lobby and around 55 good-sized, comfortable and modern rooms with cable TV.

Hotel D'Atilanos (☎ 313-33-09; Corregidora 465; s/d/ tw $27/38/44) Fourteen large rooms with a bit of personality can be found at this colonial-style hotel, but ground-floor rooms are dark, most are average at best and fluorescent lighting doesn't improve things much. Ask for rooms 25 and 26; they come with balcony.

Hotel Calle Real (☎ 313-28-56, 800-451-5500; www .hjmorelia.com.mx; Av Madero Ote 766; r from $82; P 🖳 😣) Enter straight into a courtyard restaurant, which is a bit weird (reception's beyond the tables). Rooms are clean, quiet, neat, modern and, frankly, nothing special. It's a HoJo tho, and is located eight blocks east of center, near Bosque Cuauhtémoc.

TOP END

La Casa de las Rosas (☎ 312-45-45; www.lacasadela srosas.com; Prieto 125; ste $217-330; P 🖳) One of the most romantic (and expensive) stays in Michoacán. Four gorgeous suites offer almost-overdone touches, like gauzy curtains around stone bathtubs, gilded mirrors, period furniture and antique-looking rugs. Lush plantings make it a little paradise. Breakfast is included.

Hotel Villa Montaña (☎ 314-02-31; www.villamon tana.com.mx; Patzimba 201; r from $232; P 🗙 😣 🖳 🔔) Nestled 3km south of the city center is this hacienda-like luxury hotel, with spacious rooms boasting elegant furniture, fireplaces and private stone patios. Lush grounds host a heated swimming pool, tennis court, business center and spa. Views from the terrace bar are grand.

Hotel Virrey de Mendoza (☎ 312-06-33; www .hotelvirrey.com; Av Madero Pte 310; r $159, ste from $178; P 😣 🖳) Above the elegant lobby are

small but elegant rooms, furnished with an tiques and crystal chandeliers. They're a bi overpriced for what you get, but you'll b sleeping with the elite. Salma Hayek onc rested here – probably in the Virreynal suit ($327). Breakfast is included.

Eating

On the north side of the *zócalo*, under th arches of Portal Hidalgo, is a row of fanc restaurants and sidewalk cafés that are grea for people-watching.

Panadería Trico (☎ 313-42-32; 2nd fl, Valladoli 8; mains $3.50-5.50; ☺ 8am-9pm) A very popula place for its excellent food lineup, which in cludes soups, salads, sandwiches and lots o breakfast items. High-beamed ceilings an a stunning view of the cathedral are pluses Below is its popular bakery and deli.

Café Europa (☎ 317-07-20; Portal Galeana 14 mains $3-7.50) Sleek, chic and not for the meek this trendy, modern café serves mushroor crepes, caesar salads and baguette sand wiches, along with a great selection of tast coffees and smoothies.

San Miguelito (☎ 324-23-00; cnr Camelinas Beethoven; mains $7.50-17; ☺ 2-11pm Mon-Wed, 2pm midnight Thu-Sat, 2-5pm Sun) This eccentric res taurant, decorated with antiques and wack Mexican artifacts, is 1.5km south of the cit center. Food ranges from fish in banan leaves to pasta with cream sauce and all kind of steaks. There's plenty to drink as well.

Fonda Las Mercedes (☎ 312-61-13; Guzmán 4 mains $7.50-18; ☺ 1:30-midnight Mon-Sat, 1:30-6pm Su

---

SWEETS IN MORELIA

Dulces morelianos – delicious sweets made with ingredients like fruit, nuts, milk and sugar – are famous throughout the region. They're showcased at Morelia's Mercado de Dulces (p561). Some of the tastiest candies are the *ates* (fruit leathers), which are pro-duced from tamarind, guyaba and mango, and have chili, sugar and salt added. *Ob-leas* are little 'sandwiches', with a layer of *cajeta* (milk caramel) between thin wafers. Another local specialty – and probably the healthiest – is *gazpachos*, a snack made of chopped jicama, mango and pineapple or papaya, with cheese, chili, lime and salt sprinkled on top. Mix it up and dig in – it's delicious!

Cozy tables in an intimate stone courtyard, with potted palms and atmospheric lighting, adds up to romantic dining at this upscale spot. The menu offers dishes like trout Florentine, spaghetti with pesto, and T-bone steak.

Mirasoles (☎ 317-57-75; Av Madero Pte 549; mains $7.50-24; ☻ 1-11pm Mon-Sat, 1-6pm Sun) Authentic Michoacán cooking is on tap at this fancy restaurant, located in a beautiful historic building. Try the *churipu* (Purépecha chili soup with meat and vegetables), *chamarro* (pork leg in pulque) and *jahuácatas* (a traditional local *tamal*). There are over 100 wine selections (check out the wine cellar room).

Super Cocina La Rosa (cnr Tapia & Prieto; mains under $4; ☻ 8:30am-4:30pm) Food like your mom would make, if she'd been Mexican. An unpretentious family restaurant with filling *comida corrida* (set lunch) and a changing daily menu. Note the limited hours.

Café del Conservatorio (☎ 312-86-01; Tapia 363; mains $4.50-7.50; ☻ 9am-9:30pm Mon-Fri, 1:30-9:30pm Sat & Sun) With a lovely pedestrian setting next to a park, this relaxing outdoor café serves simple breakfasts, baguette sandwiches and plenty of coffees (along with a few cocktails).

La Conspiración (☎ 317-62-00; Av Morelos Nte 3; mains $7-19; ☻ 1pm-midnight Mon-Thu, 1pm-2am Fri & Sat) If you're casting about for seafood in Morelia, point your nose here. There's ceviche or seafood soup to start, then follow with garlic octopus, tacos with marlin and spaghetti with shrimp. It's an upscale place with good service.

Restaurante Vegetariano Govindas (☎ 313-3-68; Av Madero Ote 549; mains under $4; ☻ 10:30am-8:15pm) This small upstairs café serves cheap and healthy set meals that include soup, side, main, drink and dessert. Expect mains like burgers, salads and vegetarian versions of Mexican dishes.

Café Madero (☎ 312-25-58; Av Madero Ote 880) On the south side of Plaza Villalongín, this small but pleasant upstairs café does a good line in coffee, ice-cream and a few light breakfasts (and it offers Internet too).

Cheap food stalls with lots of tables can be found under the covered arches at **Plaza San Agustín** (cnr Abasolo & Corregidora; ☻ 1pm-11pm). Also check out the stalls at **Mercado San Juan** (Mercado Revolución; ☻ 9am-7pm).

The giant supermarket **Comercial Mexicana** (☻ 8am-10pm) is southwest of the city center

and east of the Bravo and Manuel Muñiz intersection (look for the pelican sign). For 24-hour convenience there's the ubiquitous **Farmacia Guadalajara** (cnr Av Morelos Sur & Valladolid), which sells snack food.

Drinking

Some fancy restaurants, such as Mirasoles and San Miguelito (opposite), have very nicely decked out bars, which make great places to relax with a beer or three.

Onix (☎ 317-82-90; Portal Hidalgo 261; ☻ 8am-1pm) Grab a *skorppio* (a drink highlighted with drowned scorpion) or a flavored martini, find a table back near the metal-and-stone waterfall, and enjoy the hip atmosphere at this trendy restaurant-bar. If you're hungry, there's crocodile on the menu.

El Revoltijo (☎ 312-66-28; Galeana 149; ☻ 1:30-11pm Sun-Wed, 1:30pm-1:30am Fri & Sat) Set in a large covered courtyard, this upscale watering hole offers a wonderfully airy atmosphere and trendy decor. Mixed drinks cost about $4.50, and include high-end liquors like Absolut, Chivas and Rémy Martin.

Entertainment

Being a university town as well as the capital of one of Mexico's most interesting states, Morelia has a lively cultural life. Stop by the tourist office or the **Casa de la Cultura** (☎ 313-12-68; Av Morelos Nte 485) for *Cartelera Cultural*, a free weekly listing of films and cultural events. Daily newspapers *El Sol de Morelia*, *La Voz de Michoacán* and *El Cambio de Michoacán* also publish current events.

For international films, dances, music and art exhibitions check what's up at the Museo Regional Michoacano, the Museo Casa Natal de Morelos and the Casa de la Cultura. The cathedral has occasional organ recitals (impressive in that space).

For theater experiences visit the **Teatro Ocampo** (☎ 312-37-34; cnr Ocampo & Prieto) or **Teatro Morelos** (☎ 314-62-02; www.ceconexpo.com.mx; cnr Camelinas & Ventura Puente), part of the Centro de Convenciones complex, 1.5km south of the city center. **Cinepolis** (☎ 312-12-88; cnr Gómez Farías & Tapia) screens movie blockbusters.

Peña Colibrí (☎ 312-22-61; Galeana 36; admission $2.50-5; ☻ 6pm-12:30am Mon-Thu, 6pm-2:30am Fri & Sat) For live music, this longstanding place offers a dark courtyard atmosphere, with Latin rhythms in the air. Snacks, dinner and drinks are available.

WESTERN CENTRAL HIGHLANDS

El León de Mecenas (☎ 314-74-18; Abasolo 325; admission $2.50-12.50; ☺ 6pm-2am Mon-Sat) You'll get everything here – blues, jazz, *trova*, flamenco, rock, Arabian and Mexican folk music. It has a good rustic ambience and also serves refreshments.

Getting There & Around
AIR
The **Francisco J Mújica Airport** (☎ 317-47-11) is 27km north of Morelia, on the Morelia–Zinapécuaro Hwy. There are no public buses, but taxis to the airport cost $15. Plenty of flights are available to cities in Mexico, and limited flights serve destinations elsewhere in North America.

Airlines servicing Morelia include the following:

AeroCuahonte (☎ 317-32-15) Located at the airport
Aeromar (☎ 324-67-77; Hotel Fiesta Inn, Pirindas 435)
Mexicana (☎ 313-94-30; Av Acueducto 60, Plaza Rebullones)

BUS & COMBI
Morelia's bus terminal is about 4km northwest of the city center. It's separated into three *módulos*, which correspond to 1st-, 2nd- and 3rd-class buses. To get into town from here take a Roja 1 combi (red) from under the pedestrian bridge, or catch a taxi ($2.50). Destinations with frequent departures include the following:

Destination	Price	Duration
Guadalajara	$22	4hr
Lázaro Cárdenas	$30	5hr
Mexico City (Terminal Norte)	$22	4¾hr
Mexico City (Terminal Poniente)	$22	4hr
Pátzcuaro	$3.50	1hr
Querétaro	$12	3-4hr
Uruapan	$10	2hr
Zamora	$9.50	2½hr
Zitácuaro	$8	3hr

Travel agencies in town have bus schedules and sell tickets (usually for 1st-class buses), which saves time and energy at the terminal.

Around town, small combis and buses operate from 6am until 10pm daily ($0.40). Combi routes are designated by the color of their stripe: Ruta Roja (red), Ruta Amarilla (yellow), Ruta Guinda (pink), Ruta Azul (blue), Ruta Verde (green), Ruta Cafe (brown) and so on. Ask at the tourist office for help with bus and combi routes.

TAXI
There are plenty of taxis around in the city center, and an average ride costs about $3, a little more to outer areas like the Centro de Convenciones.

CAR & MOTORCYCLE
To rent a car, call **Hertz** (☎ 313-53-28), at the airport, or **Budget** (☎ 315-99-42; Av Camelinas 2315).

SANTUARIO MARIPOSA MONARCA
In the easternmost part of Michoacán, straddling the border of México state, lies the 563 sq-km **Monarch Butterfly Sanctuary** (admission $3.50; ☺ 9am-6pm mid-Nov–Mar). Every autumn from late October to early November, millions of monarch butterflies arrive in these forested Mexican highlands for their winter hibernation, having flown from the Great Lakes region of the US and Canada, some 4500km away. At night and in the early morning the butterflies cluster together, covering whole *oyenal* (fir) trees and weighing down the branches. As the day warms up they begin to flutter around like gold and orange snowflakes, descending to the humid forest floor for the hottest part of the day. By midafternoon they might cover the ground completely, like a brilliant living carpet. An exceptionally good time to see them is on a warm, sunny afternoon in February (they don't fly as much in cloudy, cold weather).

In the warm spring temperatures of March the butterflies reach their sexual maturity and mate – abdomen to abdomen, with the males flying around carrying the females underneath. The exhausted males die shortly afterward, and the pregnant females fly north to Texas, Florida and other sites in the southeastern US. There they lay their eggs in milkweed bushes, then die themselves. The eggs hatch into caterpillars that feed on the milkweed, then make cocoons and emerge in late May as a new generation of butterflies. These young monarchs flutter to the Great Lakes region, where they themselves breed, so that by mid-August yet another generation is ready to start the long trip south to central Mexico. It takes from three to five generations of butterflies (living one to eight months each) to complete the entire round-trip journey from Canada to Mexico and back. This is one of the most complex migrations in the animal world, and exactly why they do it is still a mystery.

Monarch butterflies themselves are not in danger of extinction – there are other colonies in other parts of the world that are doing relatively well. The migratory behavior of this particular population is threatened, however. Milkweed, the plant upon which the monarchs depend, is considered by many to be a noxious weed and is being sprayed with insecticides. Habitat destruction is also a problem; the Santuario Mariposa Monarca is ecologically significant enough to have been decreed a Reserva de la Biosfera (giving it protected status), but illegal logging occurs in up to 60% of reserve lands. It's difficult to change traditions, as local farmers cut down the precious wood, plant corn and allow their livestock into butterfly territory. Some organizations are trying to change these patterns, offering local communities incentives to protect their forests. For more information check out the websites www.michoacanmonarchs.org and www.monarchwatch.org.

Visiting the Reserve

The reserve allows visitors from around mid-November through March, but exact opening dates vary year to year, depending on weather, temperatures and the butterflies' migration patterns. At the beginning or end of the season it's best to ask for information at the Morelia or Mexico City tourist offices before heading all the way out here. Also, some people do day trips or tours from Morelia (see p562) or Mexico City to see the butterflies, but this means up to eight hours of travel in one day. This method is not highly recommended.

Three of the reserve's five areas are open to visitors. They're a bit spread out, so you'll probably be visiting only one. Each has a different environment, though the butterflies are all the same.

El Campanario (better known as **El Rosario**, which is also the name of a nearby village) is the most popular sanctuary, and the easiest to reach via public transport from Angangueo (right). It also has the most commercial stands and has been most affected by illegal logging – you'll see more open space here. El Rosario is located about 12km up a good gravel road from the small, nondescript village of Ocampo. Getting to the butterflies requires a steep hike (or horse ride) of 3km to 4km. There are a couple of hotels in Ocampo, but the cute village of Angangueo (about a 45-minute drive away) is more interesting and has more services.

Sierra Chincua is 8km beyond Angangueo, way up in the mountains. This area has also been damaged by logging, but not as much as El Rosario. It's a less strenuous hike, so this sanctuary might be a better choice for those who want an easier walk. To get here from Angangueo take the 'Tlalpujahua' bus ($1) or a taxi ($5).

Cerro Pellón is the newest sanctuary open to the public, which means more intact forest and less tourism – for now. It's about a 40-minute drive southeast of Zitácuaro, the most convenient nearby city. There are a couple access points – Macheros and El Capulín – within 1.5km of each other, which can be reached by public transport from outside Zitácuaro's bus terminal (take a bus marked 'Aputzio', $0.80, which goes as far as the border to México state, then a taxi, $1 to $2). A taxi straight from Zitácuaro to the sanctuaries costs $12 to $15. The hike from the sanctuary entrances to the butterflies, much of it steep, takes up to two hours.

Most sanctuaries will have guides and horses ready to take you in case you don't want to hike. Expect to pay around $10 per horse, plus $10 for the guide. Note that the length of your hike/horseback ride will be shorter later in the season – the butterflies work their way down as the weather warms up. Parking your car can cost up to $2.50, depending on the sanctuary.

ANGANGUEO

☎ 715 / pop 5000 / elevation 2980m

In the past Angangueo has been the most popular base for butterfly-watchers, mostly

---

HIGH IS WHERE IT HAPPENS

Monarch butterflies like basking at altitude, so getting to them requires hiking (or horseback riding) up to 3000m. Hike slowly, take plenty of breaks (and water) and be aware of the symptoms of altitude sickness (see p1011).

because it's close to both the Sierra Chincua and the El Rosario sanctuaries. It's a scenic old mining town with winding streets and curious locals, and is spread out mostly along a single main drag (variously called Nacional and Morelos). Stop at the **tourist office** (☎ 156-00-44; ☷ 8am-8pm Nov-Apr), just downhill from the plaza.

Cheap sleeps include rickety **El Paso de la Monarca** (☎ 156-01-87; Nacional 20; r from $12.50), with claustrophobic rooms, and **Hotel Juárez** (☎ 156-00-23; Nacional 15; r $29), with basic rooms fringing a flowery garden. There's more comfort at the modern, pastel-colored **Hotel Margarita** (☎ 156-01-49; Morelos 83; r from $33) and nearby **Albergue Don Bruno** (☎ 156-00-26; Morelos 92; s/d from $56/69), which offers good upscale rooms (some with fireplace).

Restaurants in town include Los Geranios, at the Albergue Don Bruno, and Los Arcos, a cheap eatery near the plaza.

Frequent buses from Morelia go first to Zitácuaro ($8, three hours) before arriving in Angangueo ($1.50, 1¼ hours). From Mexico City's Terminal Poniente you can take Autobuses MTZ ($10.50, four hours, four daily) direct to Angangueo; there are many more buses that go through Zitácuaro, however.

To reach the El Rosario sanctuary from Angangueo, first take a bus to Ocampo ($1, 15 minutes, frequent), then another to El Rosario ($1.50, half hour, frequent), from the corner of Independencia and Ocampo. In season there are also *camionetas* (open-back trucks) that leave from the *auditorio* (auditorium) in Angangueo, or from outside hotels; these cost around $35 for around 10 people and take 45 bumpy minutes (via a back road) to reach the sanctuary.

ZITÁCUARO

☎ 715 / pop 79,000 / elevation 1940m

Zitácuaro is a small, busy city known for its baked bread and trout farms, and by itself doesn't have much for the tourist. It's a decent base for visiting the butterflies, however, and has a couple of minor tourist destinations nearby. The **Iglesia de San Pancho** (☷ 9am-2pm & 4-7pm) in the village of San Pancho (just south of Zitácuaro) is a restored 16th-century church with modern stained-glass windows; it was visited by Prince Charles in 2002, and highlighted in the movie *The Treasure of the Sierra*

Madre (which was actually filmed in the area). About 16km north of Zitácuaro lie the peaceful Matlazinca ruins of **Pirámides Los Al zati** (☷ 10am-5pm). Those who've visited othe ruins won't find the pyramids here overly impressive, but the views of surrounding countryside make for a nice picnic.

Most hotels in town are on the main drag, Av Revolución, and include the de cent and industrial **Hotel México** (☎ 153-28-11 Av Revolución Sur 22; r from $19; P), the bright and modern **Hotel California** (☎ 153-97-98; Av Revolu ción Nte 3; r from $33), and the clean and spaciou **Hotel América** (☎ 153-11-16; Av Revolución Sur 8; s/ $16/22). A couple of kilometers south of town is the region's best stay, **Rancho San Cayetano** (☎ 153-19-26; www.ranchosancayetano.com; Carreter a Huetamo Km 2.3; s/d incl service charge from $87/97 P ☷), which offers tasteful rooms, peace ful expansive grounds, and your graciou English- and French-speaking hosts Pabl and Lisette. Rustic suites are available, a are delicious gourmet meals (which cos extra). A taxi here is $3.

There are a few restaurants in town, in cluding **La Trucha Alegre** (☎ 153-98-09; Av Revolu ción Nte 2; mains $7-9). Try the house specialty trout, available cooked 10 different ways Rancho San Cayetano (see above) offers th area's best meals (breakfast/dinner $14/27 reserve one day in advance). Zitácuaro's bu terminal is 1km from the center. There ar frequent buses to and from Morelia ($8, thre hours) and Angangueo $1.50, 1¼ hours) along with many other destinations.

PÁTZCUARO

☎ 434 / pop 49,000 / elevation 2175m

The crown jewel of highland Michoacán and nestled in the heart of Purépecha coun try, is the lovely colonial city of Pátzcuaro Its center is filled with serene plazas, im pressive churches, pretty cobbled streets and tiled adobe buildings painted whit and reddish-brown. You couldn't ask for more beautiful place in which to explore o relax for a spell.

Central Pátzcuaro focuses on the fin Plaza Vasco de Quiroga (popularly know as Plaza Grande) and the smaller, busie Plaza Gertrudis Bocanegra (popularl known as Plaza Chica), with the local mar ket on its west side. The city center is fairl flat, but some streets climb steeply to th basilica just east of the plazas. It's a ver

valkable city, and most points of interest
re easily reached on foot.

Just 3km to the north lies scenic Lago de
Pátzcuaro, ringed by traditional Purépecha
villages and dotted with a few islands. One of
hese islands – Isla Janitzio – is Mexico's bigest magnet during early November's Día de
Muertos. At this time Mexicans from all over
he country descend here in hordes, though
plenty of tourists also come for Christmas,
New Year and Semana Santa. Make advance
reservations and bring warm clothes in
vinter – you're in the high country here.

History

Pátzcuaro was the capital of the Tarasco
people from about AD 1325 to 1400. After
he death of King Tariácuri, the Tarascan
tate became a three-part league, comprising Pátzcuaro, Tzintzuntzan and Ihuatzio.
The league repulsed Aztec attacks, but was
riendly to the Spanish, who first came to
he area in 1522. It was a bad idea: the Span-
sh returned in 1529 under Nuño de Guzmán, a conquistador of legendary cruelty.

Guzmán was so inhumane to the indig-
nous people that the Catholic Church and
he colonial government dispatched Bishop
Vasco de Quiroga, a respected judge and
leric from Mexico City, to clean up the mess
fter Guzmán was sent back to Spain to be
unished for his crimes. Quiroga, who ar-
ved in 1536, established a bishopric (based
nitially at Tzintzuntzan) and pioneered vil-
ge cooperatives based on the humanitarian
leas of Sir Thomas More's Utopia.

To avoid dependence on Spanish mining
ords and landowners, Quiroga successfully
ncouraged education and agricultural self-
ufficiency in the villages around Lago de
Pátzcuaro, with all villagers contributing
qually to the community. He also helped
ach village develop its own craft specialty.
The utopian communities declined after
is death in 1565, but the crafts traditions
ontinue to this day. Not surprisingly, Tata
Vascu, as the Tarascos called Quiroga, is
ighly venerated for his accomplishments.
You'll notice that streets, plazas, restaurants
nd hotels all over Michoacán are named
fter him.

Orientation

The lifeblood of central Pátzcuaro is its two
lazas. Ahumada heads north out of town,

toward the old Morelia–Uruapan Hwy 2km
away. Lago de Pátzcuaro is another 500m
further north from the highway.

The bus terminal lies on a ring road on
the southwest side of the city center, about
2km away.

Information

Several banks in the city center will change
your money; all have ATMs.

Consultorio Médicos del Centro (☎ 342-45-33;
Navarrete 44A; ⊗ 9am-2pm & 4-8pm Mon-Fri, 10am-
1pm Sat)

Icser Internet (Portal Morelos 64; per hr $1.25;
⊗ 9am-10pm)

Lavandería San Francisco (☎ 342-39-39; Terán 16;
per 3kg $4; ⊗ 9am-9pm Mon-Sat)

Meganet (Mendoza 8; per hr $1.25; ⊗ 9am-9.30pm)

Municipal tourist office (☎ 342-02-15; Portal
Hidalgo 1; ⊗ 10am-8pm)

Post office (Obregón 13; ⊗ 9am-4pm Mon-Fri, 9am-
1pm Sat)

State tourist office (☎ 342-12-14; Calle Buena Vista
7; ⊗ 10am-2pm & 5-7pm Mon-Fri, 10am-2pm Sat & Sun)

Sights

PLAZA VASCO DE QUIROGA
(PLAZA GRANDE)

Pátzcuaro's large, well-proportioned main
plaza is one of the loveliest in Mexico. A tall
statue of Vasco de Quiroga gazes serenely
down from the central fountain. The plaza is
ringed by trees and flanked by portales that
formed part of the facades of 17th-century
buildings. Once grand mansions, these
buildings are now mostly used as hotels, restaurants and shops. The sides of the plaza are
named (independently of the street names)
Portal Hidalgo (west side), Portal Aldama
(south side) and Portal Matamoros (east
side). The north side is Portal Allende east of
Iturbe, and Portal Morelos west of Iturbe.

PLAZA GERTRUDIS BOCANEGRA
(PLAZA CHICA)

Pátzcuaro's second main plaza is named
after a local heroine who was shot by firing
squad in 1818, for her support of the independence movement. Her statue adorns
the center of the plaza, and she looks like a
mighty tough woman.

The local market bustles away on the
west side of the plaza, where you can find
everything from fruit, vegetables and fresh
lake fish to herbal medicines, crafts and

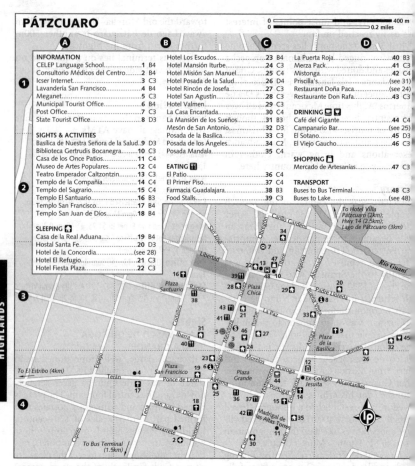

PÁTZCUARO

0 — 400 m
0 — 0.2 miles

WESTERN CENTRAL HIGHLANDS

To Hotel Villa
Pátzcuaro (2km);
Hwy 14 (2.5km);
Lago de Pátzcuaro (3km)

Río Guani

Plaza Santuario

Plaza Chica

Plaza de la Basílica

To El Estribo (4km)

Plaza San Francisco
Ponce de León

Plaza Grande

Ex-Colegio Jesuita

To Bus Terminal (1.5km)

---

clothing – including the region's distinctive striped shawls and sarapes. There's good cheap food, too.

On the north side of the plaza, the **Biblioteca Gertrudis Bocanegra** (☎ 342-54-41; cnr Padre Lloreda & Títere; 🕓 9am-7pm Mon-Fri, 10am-1pm Sat) occupies a 16th-century former San Agustín church. A large, colorful Juan O'Gorman mural covering the rear wall depicts the history of Michoacán from pre-Hispanic times to the 1910 revolution.

A small **Mercado de Artesanías** (🕓 8am-6pm) operates on the side street next to the library. The mostly wooden crafts sold here include grotesque masks, crucifixes, and carved forks and bowls. Quality is variable, but the prices are good.

On the west side of the library, the **Teatro Emperador Caltzontzin** was a convent until it was converted to a theater in 1936; it plays host to movies and cultural events.

BASÍLICA DE NUESTRA SEÑORA DE LA SALUD

This impressive church, built atop a preHispanic ceremonial site, was intended to be the centerpiece of Vasco de Quiroga's Michoacán community. The building wasn't completed until the 19th century and is only the central nave of the original design. Quiroga's tomb, the Mausoleo de Don Vasco, is just to the left inside the main west doors.

Behind the altar at the east end stands the much revered figure of the Virgin, Nuestra eñora de la Salud (Our Lady of Health). he image was made by Tarascos in the 16th entury, on Quiroga's request, from a corn-ob-and-honey paste called *tatzingue*. Soon fter people began to experience miraculous healings, and Quiroga had the words 'Salus nfirmorum' (Healer of the Sick) inscribed t the figure's feet. Ever since, pilgrims have ome from all over Mexico to ask this Virgin or a miracle. Many make their way on their nees across the plaza, into the church and long its nave. Walk up the stairs behind he image to see the many small tin repre-entations of hands, feet, legs and so on that ilgrims have offered to the Virgin.

MUSEO DE ARTES POPULARES

his excellent **folk art museum** (☎ 342-10-29; nr Enseñanza & Alcantarillas; admission $3; ⏰ 9am-7pm ue-Sat, 9am-4:30pm Sun) is housed in a spacious ld colonial building. On this site in 1540, Quiroga founded the original Colegio de San Nicolás, arguably the first university in the Americas. The institution was later moved to Valladolid (as Morelia was then called), and much of the present structure dates from the arly 18th century. In fact, the whole lot is uperimposed on pre-Hispanic stone struc-ures, some of which can be seen behind the nuseum courtyards. Look also for the taste-ul use of cows' knuckle bones as decorations etween the flagstones on the floor.

Permanent exhibitions include impressive ollections of ceremonial masks, religious rtifacts, gorgeous jewelry and stunning acquerware. There's also a room set up as typical Michoacán kitchen (note the large rick oven).

TEMPLO DE LA COMPAÑÍA & OTHER CHURCHES

uilt in the 16th century, the **Templo de la ompañía** (cnr Lerín & Alcantarillas), and the adja-ent plain white building, became a Jesuit raining college in the 17th century. The hurch is still in use and houses some relics rom Vasco de Quiroga. The college build-ng fell into ruin after the expulsion of the esuits. Restored in the early 1990s, it is now sed for community activities and often has ree temporary exhibits.

Pátzcuaro has several other old churches f interest, including **Templo del Sagrario** with delightfully creaky floors), **Templo an Juan de Dios** (home to dramatic drapes),

Templo San Francisco (sporting an interesting pink facade) and **Templo El Santuario** (prettier outside than in).

CASA DE LOS ONCE PATIOS

This **House of the 11 Courtyards** (Madrigal de las Altas Torres) is a fine rambling edifice built as a Do-minican convent in the 1740s. (Before that, the site held one of Mexico's first hospitals, founded by Vasco de Quiroga.) Today the house is a warren of small *artesanías* (handi-crafts, folk arts) shops, each specializing in a particular regional craft. Look for cop-perware from Santa Clara del Cobre, straw goods from Tzintzuntzan and musical in-struments from Paracho, as well as lacquer-ware, hand-painted ceramics and attractive textiles. It makes for a great wander.

In some shops you can see the artisans at work. Most shops are open from 10am to 7pm daily, with a lunch break in the afternoon.

EL ESTRIBO

A lookout point on a hill, El Estribo is 3.5km west of the city center, and offers a magnifi-cent view of the entire Lago de Pátzcuaro area. The cobbled, cypress-lined road up is popular with joggers – it takes up to an hour to walk to the viewing pavilion at the end. Take Ponce de León from the southwest cor-ner of Plaza Grande and follow the signs.

Courses

Centro de Lenguas y Ecoturismo de Pátzcuaro

(CELEP; ☎ 342-47-64; www.celep.com.mx; Navarrete 50; Two-week language course $290; language and culture program $450) One- and three-week programs are also available here. Courses involve four hours of classes Monday to Friday, and the cultural programs include activities Monday, Wednesday and Friday. Homestays (including meals) cost $20 per day.

Tours

Several tour guides operate around the Pátz-cuaro area.

Kevin Quigley and Arminda Flores (☎ 342-59-62, 344-08-80; tzipijo@ml.com.mx) Kevin is an American who does tours of the arts and crafts of the region (think shopping trips), while his Purépecha wife Arminda offers tours with a Purépecha-cultural focus. They charge $20 per hour for up to five people, and transport is provided.

Miguel Ángel Núñez (☎ 344-01-08; casadetierra@hotmail.com) English-speaking Miguel Ángel offers tours of the Pátzcuaro area and other destinations in

WESTERN CENTRAL HIGHLANDS

DIA DE MUERTOS WARNING

Pátzcuaro is usually a wonderfully serene little city, but when Día de Muertos rolls around it seems all of Mexico is trying to get in. If you plan on being here around the first two days of November, make sure you've made hotel reservations many months in advance. Be ready for crowds (watch your wallet) and bring a camera, as the markets are beautiful.

Isla Janitzio is witness to many colorful festivities, but its small cemetery is ground zero for many merrymakers and there will be crushing crowds. To escape them, visit the cemeteries in surrounding villages instead (try Ihuatzio, Tzurumútaro or Cucuchucho). Going after 3am is another strategy to avoid crowds (except on Janitzio, which is jam-packed all night long). Tzintzuntzan's cemetery is gorgeous, but it's gotten very popular in recent years.

Michoacán. Native culture, archaeology, colonial history, art and architecture are emphasized. Tour prices depend on the destination, but local tours cost $19 per person; transport is provided.

Rafaela Luft (☎ 342-19-47, 01-44-33-00-52-42; rluft@ ml.com.mx) Rafaela Luft, an art restorer, does three-hour walking tours of Pátzcuaro for $8 to $10 per person, depending on group size. Shorter Pátzcuaro walks are also available. Other destinations include Tzintzuntzan, Tupátaro, Morelia, Oponguio and Tingambato.

Festivals & Events

Pátzcuaro, and especially Isla Janitzio, are at the heart of Mexico's Day of the Dead celebrations (see the boxed text, p63), so heed the Día de Muertos warning (see boxed text, above). Many events, including parades, crafts markets, dancing, ceremonies, exhibitions and concerts, are held in Pátzcuaro and nearby villages on the days before and after Día de Muertos.

Other interesting events in Pátzcuaro include the following:

Pastorelas These dramatizations of the shepherds' journey to see the infant Jesus are staged in Plaza Grande around Christmas. *Pastorelas indígenas*, on the same theme but including mask dances, enact the struggle of angels against the devils that are trying to hinder the shepherds. These *pastorelas* are held in eight villages around Lago de Pátzcuaro, on different days between December 26 and February 2. Rodeos and other events accompany them.

Semana Santa Easter week is full of events in Pátzcuaro and the lakeside villages, including Palm Sunday processions Viacrucis processions on Good Friday morning, enacting Christ's journey to Calvary and the crucifixion itself; candlelit processions in silence on Good Friday evening; and, on Easter Sunday evening, a ceremonial burning of Judas in Plaza Grande. There are many local variations.

Nuestra Señora de la Salud On December 8, a colorfu procession to the basilica honors the Virgin of Health. Traditional dances are performed, including Los Reboceros Los Moros, Los Viejitos and Los Panaderos.

Sleeping

Pátzcuaro has some great accommodations During holidays and festivals, especially Dí de Muertos, secure reservations month ahead (or more, for the most popular places expect most hotels to put their prices up t and over 100% (and perhaps impose three day minimum stays). For an interesting sta in a lakeside village, see Ihuatzio (p576).

BUDGET

For one camping option see Hotel Vill Pátzcuaro (opposite).

Posada de los Ángeles (☎ 342-24-40; posac angeles@hotmail.com; Títere 16; s & d $26, tw $40) wonderful find, this friendly spot offers 1 excellent and comfortable rooms with cabl TV. There is a pleasant, flowery patio at th back, and a rooftop area with good view Second-floor rooms are brighter.

Hotel Posada de la Salud (☎ 342-00-58; posada de salud@hotmail.com; Serrato 9; s/d/tw $21/27/33) A gem c a family place, with 12 small but pretty room surrounding two courtyards (the one in th back is grassy and more private). Well run b two sisters, it's clean and great value.

Hotel de la Concordia (☎ 342-00-03; Portal Juáre 31; r w/shared bathroom $16-24, s & d $24, tw $45; P Well priced for its location, this atmos pheric hotel has attractive, high-ceilinge rooms around an open two-storey court yard with parking. The small upstairs res taurant faces Plaza Chica.

Hotel Valmen (☎ 342-11-61; Padre Lloreda 3 r from $16) One of Pátzcuaro's better budge choices, with 16 clean, simple and spaciou rooms (some brighter than others), an nice old tiled halls.

Hotel San Agustín (☎ 342-04-42; Portal Juárez 2 s/d $9.50/19) A dirt cheap option, but not bad one – and the location rocks. The ol building has some charm left; rooms wit outside windows are less depressing.

MIDRANGE

Mesón de San Antonio (☎ 342-25-01; www.mesonde
sanantonio.com; Serrato 33; s/d $33/41; 🖳) With just
seven rooms, surrounding a large old plant-
filled courtyard, this hacienda-like place has
a country feel. Rooms are huge, sparsely
decorated in a wonderfully rustic style, and
some have a fireplace. Beds are good, ceilings
are high and it's fairly quiet.

Posada Mandala (☎ 342-41-76; www.geocities.com
/mandala_mex; Lerín 14; r $24-38) Just four attractive
rooms are on offer at this small place. Two
downstairs rooms share a bathroom and are
cheaper, but the two charming upstairs rooms
(one composed of two separated spaces) have
a nice balcony and rooftop views.

Hotel Los Escudos (☎ 342-12-90; Portal Hidalgo 73;
s & d $60, tw $82; 🅿) This well-kept historical
hotel offers 32 gorgeous rooms, with antique
furnishings and pretty tiled bathrooms. Two
flowery courtyards provide peace. Some of
the larger rooms have lofts and fireplaces,
and the location's great. Prices drop dramatically in low season.

Hotel Rincón de Josefa (☎ 342-11-43; www.hotel
rincondejosefa.com.mx; Iturbe 29; s & d from $43, tw from
$70) Well located between the two plazas is
this pretty hotel. It's almost like a miniature
Italian village inside, with pastel colors,
brick arches, cute courtyards and plants all
around. Juliette balconies front the great
rooms, which come with tiled floors.

Hotel El Refugio (☎ 342-55-05; hotelcasadelrefugio@
hotmail.com; Mendoza 33; s & d $52, tw $70) A great
location adds to the appeal at this elegant
hotel, which comes complete with a fireplace
in the large covered courtyard. Comfortable
rooms are spacious, colorful and tastefully
done, and there's a bar downstairs.

Hotel Misión San Manuel (☎ 342-10-50; www.mision
sanmanuel.com; Portal Aldama 12; r from $52; 🅿 🖳)
Large rooms with high ceilings and attractive bathrooms surround two patios at this
former monastery. There's an atmospheric
old-world feel, plenty of tile and wood details, and a cute patio out the back.

Hostal Santa Fe (☎ 342-05-12; www.hostaldelvalle
.com; Lloreda 27; s/d $29/38; 🅿) Descend to the
Santa Fe's unusual but attractive lobby area –
it feels like a huge living room – and check
out the nicely decorated rooms, as some are
better than others (No 9 has a romantic terrace). There's a grassy garden at the back.

Hotel Fiesta Plaza (☎ 342-25-16; www.hotelfiesta
plaza.com; Plaza Gertrudis Bocanegra 24; r $83; 🅿) This
popular hotel boasts a spot-on location on
Plaza Chica, and a beautiful front colonial
courtyard with plenty of sitting areas. Most
of the 60 rooms come with cushy beds,
good lighting and pleasant bathrooms, but
a few aren't as nice (look around).

Hotel Villa Pátzcuaro (☎ 342-07-67; www.villa
patzcuaro.com; Av Lázaro Cárdenas 506; campsites per
person $6, trailer sites $15, r $40; 🐕) If you don't
want to stay in central Pátzcuaro there's a
peaceful choice, located 2km north of the
city center towards the lake. The wonderful rooms are rustic, comfortable and come
with fireplace, and there's also camping and
RV sites. Any bus to the lake will drop you
here; it's a block from the main road.

TOP END

Casa de la Real Aduana (☎ 342-02-65; www.lafoliamx
.com; Ponce de León 16; r $200-230) Pátzcuaro's finest
stay is at this 16th-century colonial house.
Five simple yet beautiful rooms come decorated with fine art and luxurious amenities,
and surround a glorious historical courtyard. Full breakfast is included; no children
allowed.

Posada de la Basílica (☎ 342-11-08; www.posadala
basilica.com; Arciga 6; r from $100; 🅿) For rustic lux-
ury there's this wonderful colonial hotel.
Twelve huge wood-floored rooms (some
with loft or fireplace) surround an open
courtyard with relaxing fountain and city-
to-lake views. Each has its own unique door-
knocker. There's a good restaurant as well.

La Casa Encantada (☎ 342-34-92; www.lacasaencan
tada.com; Dr Coss 15; r $89-130; 🖳) This wonder-
ful, US-run B&B offers 10 beautiful and
very comfortable rooms with artsy decor
and good amenities; two suites come with
kitchenette. There's a comfortable living
room and relaxing patios – it's like a little
paradise. Breakfast is gourmet.

Hotel Mansión Iturbe (☎ 342-03-68; www.mex
online.com/iturbe.htm; Portal Morelos 59; r $122; 🅿)
This posh hotel exudes colonial elegance,
with its high ceilings, polished wood floors
and antique furnishings. Modern amenities,
charming patios and a fabulous sitting room
are extra pluses. The 12 rooms vary, so ask
to see a couple. Breakfast is included.

La Mansión de los Sueños (☎ 342-57-08; www
.prismas.com.mx; Ibarra 15; r from $208) The 11 lux-
urious rooms are all different at this romantic courtyard hotel; some have fireplace,
lofts and even fantasy murals. All come

with cable TV, high ceilings and thick terry robes. Full breakfast and a welcome cocktail are included, and there's a good restaurant out the front.

Eating

Pátzcuaro has decent food, as long as you don't expect cutting-edge cuisine. Many restaurants serve *sopa Tarasca*, a rich tomato-based soup with cream, dried chili and bits of crisp tortilla. Another specialty is *corundas* – tamales with a little pork, bean and cream filling. You may also see *pescado blanco* (small 'white fish') sold as snacks near the pier – the taste is nothing special, however.

El Patio (☎ 342-04-40; Plaza Grande 19; mains $7-9; ☺ 8am-10pm) The limited menu at this popular eatery is not for vegetarians – it boasts mainly meats and seafood. The atmosphere is generally casual, but from Friday to Sunday there's live traditional music in the afternoons.

La Puerta Roja (☎ 342-58-59; Ibarra 18; mains $8-10.50; ☺ 1:30-10pm Tue-Sun) Located in an old house is this Spanish restaurant. Dishes include rabbit with pimientos, Andalucian pork, and shrimp with alcaparras. Tapas ($3.50 to $6.50) are also available, and there's coffee flan and crème Catalana for dessert.

Priscilla's (☎ 342-57-08; Ibarra 15; mains $7.50-14; ☺ 7:30am-10:30pm) Located at the posh La Casa de Los Sueños, this fancy place serves international dishes, like lasagna al prosciutto, fish-filled nopals and cheese fondue. Service is almost too attentive. There's courtyard dining on warm days, and live music plays on Saturday nights.

Restaurant Doña Paca (☎ 342-03-68; Portal Morelos 59; mains $6.50-10.50; ☺ 8:30am-10:30am & 2-8:30pm Mon-Sat, 8:30-10:30 & 2-6pm Sun) Attached to the Hotel Mansión Iturbe is this dark eatery. The menu is limited but still features dishes like *sopa Tarasca*, *chilis rellenos*, fish fillets and chicken fajitas. There's also a separate café with tables out on the sidewalk.

Mistonga (☎ 342-64-50; Dr Coss 4; mains $7.50-11; ☺ 1-10pm Tue-Sun) This enclosed courtyard restaurant serves Argentine specialties, like *milanesa* (a thin breaded steak), *churrasco* with *chimichurri* (steak marinated in a garlic, parsley and olive oil sauce) and garlic trout. There are a few pasta choices for vegetarians, plus *trova* music on weekends.

El Primer Piso (☎ 342-01-22; Plaza Grande 29; mains $7-11; ☺ 7am-10pm Mon & Wed-Sat, 7am-8pm Sun)

Once Pátzcuaro's premier restaurant, this upstairs place still serves reasonable food. Try the *chiles en nogada* (chilis in a sweet creamy white sauce) in season, or go for the fettucini with vodka or Hindu chicken with masala curry sauce.

Posada de la Basílica (☎ 342-11-08; Arciga 6; mains $5-11.50; ☺ 8am-10pm Thu-Tue, 8am-5pm Wed) The best thing at this upscale joint, located in the Posada de la Basílica, is the view from the picture windows, so come during daylight to see the lake. Order fish soup, garlic trout or one of the many meat dishes. Note: a 10% service charge is added to your bill.

Restaurante Don Rafa (☎ 342-04-98; Mendoza 30; mains $5-12; ☺ 8:30am-9pm) This narrow (and thus intimate) traditional restaurant has been going strong for decades. It's a standard for regional food, and offers a $5 *comida corrida* that includes soup (try the famous *sopa tarasca*), main dish (such as baked crepe) and dessert.

The market on Plaza Chica has inexpensive **food stalls** (☺ 8am-7pm) serving everything from fruit juices to tacos to tortas. For supermarket treats check out **Merza Pack** (Mendoza 24; ☺ 7am-9:45pm) or **Farmacia Guadalajara** (Ramos 22; ☺ 24hr).

Drinking

Pátzcuaro isn't a city for nightlife, but you can down a few at the airy sidewalk tables of **Campanario Bar** (Plaza Grande 14; ☺ 3-11pm), and there's also the loud, underground (literally) youth magnet **El Sótano** (Serrato 31; ☺ 6pm-1am Wed-Sun).

El Viejo Gaucho (☎ 342-03-68; Iturbe 10; admission $3; ☺ 6-11pm Tue-Sat) For something more cultural, good folk or *trova* music starts around 8pm at this restaurant/bar/live music venue.

Café del Gigante (Plaza Grande 41; coffees under $; ☺ 8:30am-10pm) Caffeine addicts can stop at this tiny café, where beans from Oaxaca, Uruapan and Veracruz bring on a good buzz.

Shopping

The Casa de los Once Patios is a good place to seek Michoacán crafts, but you can also try the main market and the Mercado de Artesanías, both next to Plaza Chica. On Friday mornings a ceramics market, with pottery from different villages, is held in Plaza San Francisco. There's also a small crafts market in front of the basilica every day.

Around the lake and in the Pátzcuaro area are several villages that make great destinations for shoppers. If you want some help, ring **Kevin Quigley** (☎ 342-59-62, 344-08-80; tzipijo@ml.com.mx), a friendly American based in Ihuatzio. He knows plenty about the area's crafts, and offers guided shopping trips for $20 per person (including transport).

Getting There & Around

Pátzcuaro's bus terminal is 1.5km southwest of the city center. It has a cafetería and left-luggage services.

To catch a bus heading to the center, walk outside the terminal, turn right (going past the fenced lot) and at the corner take any bus marked 'Centro' ($0.40). Taxis cost $2 (with a small surcharge after 11pm).

Buses back to the terminal (marked 'Central') leave from the northeast corner of Plaza Chica. Buses to the boat pier (marked 'Lago') also leave from near here. These buses run from about 6am to 10pm daily.

Common destinations that have frequent services include the following:

Destination	Price	Duration
Erongarícuaro	$0.90	35min
Guadalajara	$20	4½hr
Lázaro Cárdenas	$17	7hr
Mexico City (Terminal Poniente)	$25	5½hr
Mexico City (Terminal Norte)	$25	5½hr
Morelia	$3.25	1hr
Quiroga	$1	35min
Santa Clara del Cobre	$0.60	30min
Tzintzuntzan	$0.80	20min
Uruapan	$3.50	1hr
Irahuén	$1.25	50min

AROUND PÁTZCUARO
Lago de Pátzcuaro

Just 3km from central Pátzcuaro, this serene body of water is punctuated with a few small islands. Streams feeding the lake are being diverted, however, and pollution is also a serious problem. Still, it's a pleasant destination and is quite scenic as a whole.

To get to the *muelle* (dock), take a bus marked 'Lago' from Pátzcuaro's Plaza Chica. The touristy dock is lined with cheap fish eateries and souvenir shops. The ticket office is about 50m down, on the right side.

Isla Janitzio is a popular Mexican destination on weekends and holidays. It's heavily devoted to tourism, hosting dozens of knick-knack stands and fish restaurants. It's still well worth seeing, however, and has interesting pathways that eventually wind their way to the top, where a 40m-high **statue** (admission $0.60) of independence hero José María Morelos y Pavón stands. Inside the statue is a set of murals depicting Morelos' life. You can climb all the way up to his wrist for a panoramic view. There are no cars on the island.

The **Hotel Terhunukua** (☎ 342-04-38; r $19; 🖳) has small, modest rooms (some with views) and is 50m straight up from the dock.

Round-trip boat rides to Janitzio cost $3 and take 25 minutes each way; they leave when full (about every 30 minutes, quicker on weekends).

THE PURÉPECHA

About 125,000 Purépecha people call the greater Lago de Pázcuaro region home. You're likely to meet some in Pátzcuaro, though you'll get a better taste of their culture in the villages fringing the lake, which are almost purely indigenous.

The Purépecha are direct descendants of the Tarascos (or Tarascans), who gained prominence in the 14th century and established Tzintzuntzan as their capital (for information on their reconstructed ruins, see p577). They developed western Mexico's most advanced pre-Hispanic civilization with one hand, while continually repelling Aztec domination with another – quite a feat. The Tarascans might have originated from the more northerly, nomadic Chichimecs, but neither the modern Purépecha language nor the old Tarasco language has any established links to any other tongue. Distant connections with the Zuni (US Southwest) and Quechua (Peru) languages have been suggested, however.

The Tarascos were excellent craftspeople, and produced fine pottery, metalware and textiles. Many Purépecha villages still specialize in these crafts – a legacy of the enlightened bishop Vasco de Quiroga. The modern Purépecha also maintain one of the country's most vital religious traditions; the Día de Muertos (Day of the Dead) observances around Lago de Pátzcuaro are particularly famous.

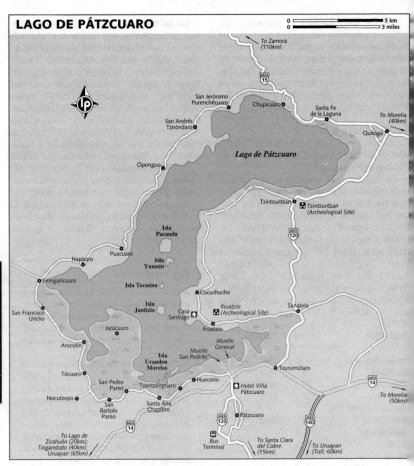

LAGO DE PÁTZCUARO

0 ——— 5 km
0 ——— 3 miles

To Zamora
(110km)

MEX 15

San Jerónimo
Purenchécuaro

Chupícuaro

Santa Fe
de la Laguna

To Morelia
(40km)

San Andrés
Tziróndaro

Quiroga

Oponguo

Lago de Pátzcuaro

Tzintzuntzan · Tzintzuntzan
(Archeological Site)

MEX 120

**Isla
Pacanda**

Napizaro

Puacuaro

**Isla
Yunuén**

Erongaricuaro

Isla Tecuéna

Cucuchucho

San Francisco
Uricho

**Isla
Janitzio**

Casa
Santiago

Ihuatzio
(Archeological Site)

Sanabría

Jarácuaro

Ihuatzio

Arocutín

Muelle
General

Muelle
San Pedrito

Tócuaro

**Isla
Uranden
Morelos**

Tzurumútaro

MEX 14

San Pedro
Pareo

Tzentzénguaro

Huecorio

Hotel Villa
Pátzcuaro

To Morelia
(50km)

Nocutzepo

San
Bartolo
Pareo

Santa Ana
Chapítiro

MEX 120

Pátzcuaro

MEX 14D

MEX 14

To Lago de
Zirahuén (20km);
Tingambato (40km);
Uruapan (65km)

Bus
Terminal

To Santa Clara
del Cobre
(15km)

To Uruapan
(Toll; 60km)

The small frijol-shaped **Isla Yunuén** is green, tranquil and has a strong Purépecha community. For overnight stays try **Cabañas de Yuñuen** (☎ 434-342-44-73; cabañas from $36). A handful of romantic and comfortable wood *cabañas* sleep up to 16 people; all come with TV and kitchenette.

Round-trip boat rides to Yunuén cost $14 for one to four people; try to hook up with others if you're by yourself. Boats leave when full, so you may have to wait around a bit.

Lakeside Villages

The villages surrounding Lago de Pátzcuaro make worthwhile and fun day trips. They can all be reached by local transport from Pátzcuaro's bus terminal. Or, to save time,

take a 'Lago' bus from Plaza Chica, and get off anywhere between the Posada de Don Vasco and Hwy 14; then wait by the road side for a bus heading to your village – this saves you from backtracking to the bus sta tion. Buses to Ihuatzio run directly from Plaza Chica.

Frequent combis run between the villages so you can visit several in one day. Trans port between Quiroga and Erongarícuaro i infrequent, however, so travel between the two may be quicker via Pátzcuaro.

IHUATZIO

Lying 14km from Pátzcuaro, Ihuatzio wa capital of the Tarascan league after Pátzcuar (but before Tzintzuntzan). Today it's just plain little village where everyone knows everyone else, until *you* walk into town.

The large, and partially restored **Ihuatzio archaeological site** (admission $2.25; ⏰ 10am-6pm) lies 1.1km up a cobbled road from the village's small plaza. These Tarascan ruins' main feature is an open ceremonial space, 200m long with two pyramid-like structures at its west end. Climbing the pyramids is forbidden, but you can walk to the top of the restored wall to their left (south) side for views. Two carved stone coyotes were found at the site; one is in the National Anthropology Museum in Mexico City, the other graces the bell tower of Ihuatzio's church.

For an interesting stay here, consider **Casa Santiago** (☎ 344-08-80; www.geocities.com/theother mexico; s/d with shared bathroom $45/60). It's located 1.5km west of Ihuatzio on the road to Cucuchucho, and run by a friendly US-Purépecha couple. It's best for folks who want to experience the countryside and a small local village. Five rooms and a suite ($90) are available.

ZINTZUNTZAN

The tiny town of Tzintzuntzan (tseen-*tsoon*-sahn) is about 15km north of Pátzcuaro. There's a pretty cemetery, along with some impressive buildings from both the pre-Hispanic Tarasco empire and the early Spanish missionary period. As you head into town you'll see ceramics, large stone carvings, straw goods (a local specialty) and other Michoacán *artesanías* for sale.

Tzintzuntzan is a Purépecha name meaning 'Place of Hummingbirds'. It was the capital of the Tarascan league at the time of invasions by the Aztecs in the late 15th century, and by the Spanish in the 1520s. The Purépecha chief came to peaceable terms with Cristóbal de Olid, leader of the first Spanish expedition in 1522. But this did not satisfy Nuño de Guzmán, who arrived in 1529 in his quest for gold, and had the chief burned alive. This barbaric act is depicted in the O'Gorman mural in Pátzcuaro's Biboteca Gertrudis Bocanegra.

Vasco de Quiroga established his first base here when he reached Michoacán in the mid-1530s, and Tzintzuntzan became the headquarters of the Franciscan monks who followed him. The town declined in importance after Quiroga shifted his base to Pátzcuaro in 1540.

On the lake side (west) of Av Cárdenas lies the **Ex-Convento de San Francisco**, a religious complex constructed partly with stones from the Tarascan site up the hill, which the Spanish demolished. Here Franciscan monks began the Spanish missionary effort in Michoacán in the 16th century. The olive trees in the churchyard are said to have been brought from Spain and planted by Vasco de Quiroga; they're believed to be the oldest olive trees in the Americas.

Straight ahead as you walk into the churchyard is the still-functioning **Templo de San Francisco**, built for the monks' own use. The old monastery's lovely cloister, to the left of the *templo,* includes a set of faded murals around the galleries of both floors, and Mudejar-patterned wooden ceiling ornamentation in each of the four ground-floor corners.

Toward the right rear corner of the complex stands the church built for the Purépechas, the **Templo de Nuestra Señora de la Salud**. This contains El Santo Entierro de Tzintzuntzan, a much-revered image of Christ. For most of the year it lies in a *caja de cristal* (glass coffin). On Good Friday, following an elaborate costumed passion play, the image is removed from its coffin and nailed to the large cross; being a Cristo de Goznes (hinged Christ), his arms can be extended and his legs crossed. After being taken down from the cross, the image is paraded through town until dark, when it is returned to the church. Penitents come from all over, some in chains or carrying crosses, some crawling on their knees. Thousands of candles are placed in the church for an all-night wake.

In the enclosed yard beside this church is the **Capilla Abierta de la Concepción**, an old open chapel (parts of it date to the 16th century).

Head out the monastery's front gate (where an art market runs on weekends), across the highway and up the hill; turn left when you reach the upper paved road and walk to the entrance (700m in all) of the **Tzintzuntzan archeological site** (Las Yácatas; $3.25; ⏰ 10am-5pm), an impressive group of five reconstructed round-based temples. Known as *yácatas,* they sit on a large terrace of carefully fitted stone blocks and are all that remain of the Tarascan empire. The hillside location offers great views of the town, lake and surrounding mountains; a small **museum** at the site's entrance is worth a peek as well.

WESTERN CENTRAL HIGHLANDS

QUIROGA

Quiroga is 7km northeast of Tzintzuntzan. Dating since pre-Hispanic times, the town is named after Vasco de Quiroga, who was responsible for many of its buildings and handicrafts. Now Quiroga has few original old buildings, but it's a great place to shop for *artesanías*. Every day there's a busy market, with hundreds of shops selling brightly painted wooden products, leatherwork, woolen sweaters, sarapes and much more.

On the first Sunday in July the **Fiesta de la Preciosa Sangre de Cristo** (Festival of the Precious Blood of Christ) is celebrated with a long torchlight procession. The procession is led by a group carrying an image of Christ crafted from a paste made of corncobs and honey.

ERONGARÍCUARO

A pretty 18km trip from Pátzcuaro, Erongarícuaro (or 'Eronga') is one of the oldest settlements on the lake. It's a peaceful village where you can stroll along streets lined with old Spanish-style houses, and then rest in the sweet little plaza. French artist André Breton (1896–1966) lived here for a time in the 1950s, visited occasionally by Diego Rivera and Frida Kahlo. Breton made the unusual wrought-iron cross in the forecourt of the church. The fine old seminary attached to the church has some very nice gardens out the back – look for the traditional Purépecha *troje* house.

Downhill from the plaza on Urueta Carrillo, **Muebles Finos Artesanales** (☎ 344-02-07; www .mfaeronga.com; ⊙ 9am-6pm Mon-Fri) is run by a US couple, and produces some amazingly beautiful and quirky hand-painted furniture. Custom orders are taken and tours are available.

On January 6, the **Fiesta de los Reyes Magos** (Festival of the Magic Kings) is celebrated with music and dance.

TÓCUARO

Some of Mexico's finest mask makers live in this sleepy town, 10km from Pátzcuaro. You wouldn't know it, though, as there are no traditional shopfronts – just a sign here and there. Behind closed doors many families are involved in the craft, but only a handful produce the highest-quality masks.

Tócuaro's best mask makers are **Juan Orta** (☎ 443-349-72-31; maskorta@hotline.com; ⊙ 10am-6pm) and his sons. To find them walk up

the street (Morelos) from the bus stop; after you pass Hidalgo, it's the first house on your left. Other mask makers within a block include **Felipe Horta Tera** (☎ 443-391-97-18; felipehorta2000@yahoo.com; ⊙ 9am-6pm) and **Gustavo Horta** (⊙ 443-373-73-59; ⊙ 8am-10pm).

One thing you won't find is a bargain – quality mask making is a recognized art and a fine mask takes up to a month or more to make. The best ones are wonderfully expressive, realistic and surrealistic but they'll cost hundreds of dollars.

Santa Clara del Cobre

☎ 434 / pop 12,300 / elevation 2180m

Santa Clara del Cobre, about 18km south of Pátzcuaro, was a copper-mining center from 1553 onward. Though the mines are closed, this nice little town still specializes in copperware, with dozens of workshops crafting objects from the ore. It's a fine town in which to wander around, and has a delightful plaza with an 18th-century church, whose forecourt pavement is decorated with slag from copper workshops.

One block north of the plaza is the small **Museo del Cobre** (☎ 343-02-54; Morelos 263; admission $0.20; ⊙ 10am-3pm & 5-7pm Tue-Sat, 10am-4pm Sun), which exhibits an impressive collection of copper bowls and other containers, but lacks any display labels. If you're here in August, ask about the 10-day-long **Feria del Cobre** (Copper Fair), held that month; exact dates vary.

Hotels in town include the **Oasis** (☎ 343-00-40; ade_zc@hotmail.com; Portal Hidalgo 14; s/d $15/23) and the **Real del Cobre** (☎ 343-02-05; Portal Hidalgo 19; s/d $16/26); both are good budget choices on the plaza. For fancier rooms try the **Camino Real** (☎ 343-02-81; Morelos Pte 213; r from $37; P) three blocks south of the plaza.

Buses from Pátzcuaro ($0.60, 30 minutes) leave every 15 minutes from 6am to 8:30pm.

Lago de Zirahuén

☎ 353 / pop (Zirahuén) 2300 / elevation 2240m

Smaller than Lago de Pátzcuaro, but much deeper and cleaner, this pretty blue lake lies about 22km southwest of Pátzcuaro. Right on its shoreline is the dusty but pleasant town of Zirahuén, a peaceful spot for camping and boating. It's a popular weekend destination for Mexicans, but you won't see many foreigners here.

Boat rides are the main touristy thing to do here. There are three docks: The *muelle general* (main dock; a block down from the main plaza), La Troje (at Las Cabañas de Zirahuén) and Los Cedritos (beyond the plaza about 400m). Various boats cost $30 to $75 for seven to 20 people; the number of passengers determines the final price. They're most likely to fill up on weekends.

You have several sleeping options. Resort-like **Las Cabañas de Zirahuén** (☎ 326-33-01; www.zirahuen.com; cabañas from $87) is lakeside and has the most upscale choices, while **Los Cedritos** (☎ 353-41-33; r from $39, campsites per person $4) is more like a fancy barracks, and offers grassy camping. Family-run **Casa Familiar** (☎ 353-41-17; r $33) has just three good modern rooms, and is right across from Las Cabañas de Zirahuén; look for the green facade.

Camping is free along the grassy lakeshore right before getting into town.

Three buses arrive daily from Pátzcuaro ($1.25, 50 minutes); there are hourly buses from nearby Santa Clara del Cobre ($1, 15 minutes).

URUAPAN
☎ 452 / pop 231,000 / elevation 1620m

When the Spanish monk, Fray Juan de San Miguel, arrived here in 1533, he was so impressed with the Río Cupatitzio and the lush vegetation surrounding it that he gave the area the Purépecha name Uruapan (oo-oo-*ah*-pahn), which roughly translates into 'Eternal Spring.' Fray Juan had a large market square, hospital and chapel built, and arranged streets in an orderly grid pattern that survives today.

Under Spanish rule, Uruapan quickly grew into a productive agricultural center, and today the region is renowned for high-quality *aguacates* (avocados), coffee, fruit and chocolate. The city bills itself as the 'Capital Mundial del Aguacate' (see boxed text, p581) and has an avocado fair in November. The town's craftspeople are famed for their handpainted cedar lacquerware, particularly trays and boxes.

Uruapan is a very traditional 'Mexican' city, retaining some colonial ambience. Its unusually long and narrow plaza buzzes with balloon vendors and families, and is a great place for people-watching. Attractive red-tile roofs top a few stucco buildings, and a lush hillside surrounds the city.

The splendid little national park, Parque Nacional Barranca del Cupatitzio, is just a 15-minute walk from city center. You should also visit the remarkable volcano Paricutín, 35km to the west.

Uruapan is 500m lower in altitude than Pátzcuaro, and is consequently much more humid and warm.

Orientation
Uruapan's heart is its long main plaza. Practically everything of interest to travelers is within walking distance of here.

Note that street names change often in Uruapan, both at the plaza and at various other points. The *portales* facing the plaza are named independently of the streets; Portal Degollado is the east side of the plaza, while Portal Carrillo and Portal Matamoros run along the south side. The north portal is Portal Mercado.

Information
Several banks (with ATMs), along with a few *cambios*, are near the central plaza.

Casa del Turista (☎ 524-06-67; www.uruapan.gob.mx; Carranza 20; ☼ 9am-7:30pm) The municipal tourist office.

Cyberhome (Independencia 10A; per hr $1; ☼ 9:30am-9pm)

Imperio PC (Madero 55; per hr $1; ☼ 9am-8pm Mon-Fri, 9am-5pm Sat)

Lavandería (☎ 523-26-69; cnr Carranza & Garcia; per kg $1.50; ☼ 9am-2pm & 4-8pm Mon-Sat)

Main post office (Ocaranza 22; ☼ 9am-3pm Mon-Fri, 9am-1pm Sat)

Secretaría de Turismo (☎ 524-71-99; Ayala 16; ☼ 8:30am-3pm & 4-7pm Mon-Fri, 9am-2pm & 4-7pm Sat, 10am-2pm Sun) The state tourist office.

Viajes Tzitzi (☎ 523-34-19; Ocampo 64; ☼ 9:30am-2pm & 4-7:30pm Mon-Fri, 9:30-2pm Sat) Next to Hotel Plaza Uruapan; sells ETN and Primera Plus bus tickets.

Sights
MUSEO DE LOS CUATRO PUEBLOS INDIOS
In the Huatápera, an old colonial building near the northeast corner of the central plaza, is this three-room **museum** (☎ 524-34-34; admission free; ☼ 9:30am-1:30pm & 3:30-6pm Tue-Sun). This courtyard edifice was one of the institutions established in the 1530s under the auspices of Vasco de Quiroga, and is reputedly the first hospital in the Americas. The decorations around the doors and windows were carved by Purépecha artisans in a Mudejar style. The museum showcases regional *artesanías*,

www.lonelyplanet.com

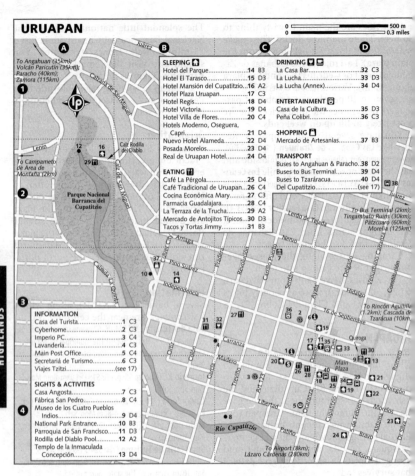

URUAPAN

To Anghuan (35km);
Volcán Paricutín (35km);
Paracho (40km);
Zamora (115km)

Calzada de San Miguel

Juárez

Lenin

Calz Rodilla
del Diablo

To Campameto
de Área de
Montaña (2km)

**Parque Nacional
Barranca del
Cupatitzio**

Calzada La Quinta

To Bus Terminal (2km);
Tingambato Ruins (30km);
Pátzcuaro (60km);
Morelia (125km)

Lerdo de Tejada

Nervo

Arriaga

Pino Suárez

Independencia

Culver Club

Piedra

Revolución

Carrillo Puerto

Serdán

Ayala

16 de Septiembre

Hidalgo

To Rincón Agulitlle
(1.2km); Cascada de
Tzaráacua (10km)

Madero

Ortiz

Carranza

Mádero

Treviño

Art 123

Libertad

Río Cupatitzio

Patiño

Quiroga

**Main
Plaza**

Obregón

Morelos

Bravo

Reforma

20 de Febrero

Cupatitzio

Aldama

Dr Silva

To Airport (8km);
Lázaro Cárdenas (280km)

like ceramics from Capula, lacquerware
from Quiroga and Purépecha pottery.

PARQUE NACIONAL BARRANCA DEL CUPATITZIO

This lovely tropical **park** (Independencia; adult/child
$1.25/0.50; 🕑 8am-6pm) is 1km west of the main
plaza. It follows the lushly vegetated banks of
the Río Cupatitzio from its source at the Rodilla del Diablo pool, near the park's north
end. Legend has it that the devil knelt here
and left the mark of his knee. Many cobbled
paths (nonwheelchair accessible) make for a
wonderful stroll over bridges and past waterfalls and fountains. There's even a trout farm
where you can 'fish', and a few restaurants
and snack stalls for refreshments.

FÁBRICA SAN PEDRO

This great old **textile factory** (☎ 524-06-7;
telaresuruapan@prodigy.com.mx; Treviño s/n; tours 9am-
6pm Mon-Sat) is a late-19th-century factor
now operated by Telares Uruapan. Hand
loomed and hand-dyed bedspreads, table
cloths and curtains, among other thing
are made here from pure cotton and woo
and they are available for sale. The origina
machines are over 100 years old and ar
still used – the place is essentially a work
ing museum of the industrial revolution
It is run by a fascinating couple from th
US who have lived in Uruapan for decade
Call ahead for a tour and see the entir
weaving process from cotton bale to fir
ished tablecloth.

WESTERN CENTRAL
HIGHLANDS

CASA ANGOSTA

Travelers seeking the unusual will appreciate this, the so-called **'world's narrowest house'** (☎ 524-30-19; Carrillo Puerto 50C; admission $1), a residence from 1985–2004. The one in Amsterdam is actually narrower, but this house is worth a curious peek. It's four stories high and 1.4m wide, and comes with two bedrooms, one bathroom and a tiny kitchen. Call Jorge Sepulveda after 8pm to make an appointment, or look for him at the small market a block south of the house – he sells pork there during the day (yup).

Festivals & Events

Semana Santa Palm Sunday is marked by a procession through the city streets. A major crafts competition takes place on this day, and two weeks after Palm Sunday a weeklong exhibition of Michoacán handicrafts fills the plaza.

Día de San Francisco St Francis, the patron saint of Uruapan, is honored with colorful festivities on October 4.

Festival de Coros y Danzas Around October 17 and 18 the Choir and Dance Festival is a contest of Purépecha dance and musical groups.

Festival del Cristo Rey On the last Sunday of October an evening procession parades an image of Christ along the town's winding streets, which are covered in murals made of flower petals or colored sawdust.

Feria del Aguacate The Avocado Fair is a big event for three weeks in November/December, and is celebrated with agricultural, industrial and handicraft exhibitions. Some years the record for the world's largest guacamole is attempted.

Sleeping

It's a good idea to reserve a room ahead of time for Día de Muertos (early November) and Semana Santa (March/April).

BUDGET

Campamento de Area de Montaña (☎ 523-23-09; Lenin s/n; camping per person $5, 3-room cabañas $140) In a 182-hectare nature reserve, about 4km west of the city center, is this cluster of buildings offering many sleeping arrangements (including pleasant grassy camping). Five rooms and a large dorm were being renovated at research time ($10 per person

WESTERN CENTRAL HIGHLANDS

HOLY GUACAMOLE! THE AMAZING AVOCADO

Explore the regions surrounding Uruapan and you may realize that avocados are big business here. Mexico is the world's largest producer of the fruit, with the majority grown in Michoacán state – especially around Uruapan. It's estimated that the region produces over one billion kilos of avocados annually, with only about 5% – including the best fruit – being exported. That's still a lot of guacamole crossing borders.

Avocados are thought to have originated in Mexico, Central America and the Andes region. The word 'avocado' comes from the Spanish 'aguacate,' which came from 'ahuacatl,' the Náhuatl word for testicle. The rich and sensuous fruit do indeed hang languidly in pairs, resembling a part of the male anatomy. The Aztecs even considered the fruit to have a special aphrodisiac quality, and would ban young women from strolling outdoors when avocados were being harvested.

Today there are over a hundred kinds of avocados. The Hass variety, however, is by far the most popular, accounting for about 80% of worldwide consumption. Commercial trees are produced by grafting (since production is faster and quality superior this way) rather than by seeding, and are currently being grown in a wide variety of temperate regions, such as California, South Africa, Spain, Israel, Brazil and, of course, Mexico. Mature avocado trees can produce up to 400 fruit annually and live for some 200 years.

The avocado is a wonderfully adaptable fruit, enjoyed all over the globe. It's cut into soups in Ecuador, puréed into drinks in the Philippines, mashed into sushi rolls in California and blended into ice-cream in Brazil. You can stuff it, batter it or cream it, all the while taking advantage of its high fiber, cholesterol-lowering abilities and anti-oxidant benefits. Just remember to use it in moderation, as a good-sized avocado can pack over 300 calories! And if you're lucky enough to have access to a tree, keep in mind that those rock-hard avocados don't start ripening until *after* you pick them.

Finally, if you're adventurous, or just unlucky enough to dislike the avocado's taste, try experimenting with mashed avocados in a facial (as a moisturizer) or rubbed into your hair (for shine). Or use them as a paste to treat itchy, red skin caused by eczema or dermatitis. What more could you ask from one of nature's most perfect fruits?

in each). Register at Parque Nacional Barrance del Cupatitzio; ask to see the 'oficina Area de Montaña' to enter without paying admittance. The reserve is best reached by taxi; tell the driver 'Calle Lenin frente a fraccionamiento Taximácuaro.'

Hotel del Parque (☎ 524-38-45; Independencia 124; s/d $22/26; **P**) Very handy to the national park, but 6.5 blocks west of the central plaza, is this pleasant budget choice – though front rooms attract traffic noise. The 14 plain rooms have cable TV, and are clean and spacious. There's also a rear patio area where you can wash small amounts of laundry.

Posada Morelos (☎ 523-23-02; Morelos 30; s/d with private bathroom $14/20, s/d with shared bathroom $6/10) A friendly place with small, basic but good rooms on two floors around a tiled outdoor courtyard. Get one upstairs for more privacy and light.

For hardcore peso-pinchers there are three well-located fleapit hotels at the east end of the plaza, with $10 (mostly bad) rooms: the **Moderno** (☎ 524-02-12) at No 4, the **Oseguera** (☎ 523-98-56) at No 2, and the **Capri** (☎ 524-21-86) at No 10.

MIDRANGE

Hotel Villa de Flores (☎ 524-28-00; Carranza 15; s/d $28/35) One of the better deals in town, this decent hotel has an excellent location and good rooms (most with cable TV) surrounding leafy outdoor patios. Some beds are saggy, however.

Hotel Regis (☎ 523-58-44; hotelregis@intermatsa .com.mx; Portal Carrillo 12; s/d $29/38; **P**) Located right smack on the plaza, this popular spot boasts a variety of decent rooms with pleasant decor and good beds. It's for early birds, though – the clean indoor patios are lined with dozens of songbirds in their cages.

Real de Uruapan Hotel (☎ 527-59-00; www.realde uruapan.com.mx; Bravo 110; r from $70, ste $89; **P** **Q**) Sixty-one fine and very comfortable rooms, some with balcony, complement the attractive stained-glass lobby. There's a good restaurant with views on the top floor. Suites come with more amenities and jets in the tub.

Hotel El Tarasco (☎ 524-15-00; contacto_hotelel tarasco@hotmail.com; Independencia 2; s/d $60/70; **P** **Q** **⊠**) Five floors of clean carpeted rooms, with semi-rustic decor and muted colors greet you at this upscale hotel. Nice mountain views are available, but the bathrooms need

a remodel. There's also a fancy restaurant and nice lobby, with a travel agency nearby.

Hotel Victoria (☎ 523-67-00; www.hotelvictoriaupn .com.mx; Cupatitzio 11; s/d $63/77; **P** **Q** **⊠** **☒**) An upmarket choice with presentable halls and comfortable, spacious rooms – those with a balcony are brighter. Try asking for a 20% discount to make this a more palatable deal.

Nuevo Hotel Alameda (☎ 523-41-00; hotelalameda@ vel.com; 5 de Febrero 11; s/d $30/38; **P** **⊠**) The lobby is bleak, but the rooms – complete with flowery bedspreads and basic bathrooms – are bearable enough, if a bit antiseptic. Some windows face an interior well, making for privacy but dim light.

TOP END

Hotel Mansión del Cupatitzio (☎ 523-21-00; www.man siondelcupatzio.com; Calz Rodilla del Diablo 20; s/c $107/129; **P** **☒** **Q** **☒**) A large, hacienda-style place, at the north end of Parque Naciona Barranca del Cupatitzio, and Uruapan's bes hotel. Elegant rooms are bright and comfortable, and the flowery gardens are lovely Many amenities stand at your fingertips, anc the restaurant overlooks the park's pools.

Hotel Plaza Uruapan (☎ 523-35-99; www.hote plazauruapan.com.mx; Ocampo 64; s/d from $64/80; **P** **Q** **☒**) The 120 rooms at this seven-storey hotel are good enough for its mostly busi ness clientele. Exterior rooms have balco nies and great views through large windows Beds are firm, and there's a gym with sauna Call for possible discounts.

Eating

Several places on the south side of the plaz serve decent breakfasts, economical *comi das corridas* and good à la carte meals fo dinner.

Tacos y Tortas Jimmy (cnr Carranza & Pradera mains under $3) If you won't eat tacos at stree stalls, try them at this tiny, friendly, fast industrial, four-table corner joint. They'r arguably the best in town, and come with a choice of salsas. It also serves tortas, but no much else – though this is enough.

La Terraza de la Trucha (☎ 524-86-98; Calz Rodil del Diablo 13; mains $6-8; ⏰ 9am-6pm; **P**) Shady open-air tables at this riverside restauran are very pleasant after a walk through th national park. It's opposite Hotel Mansió del Cupatitzio, at the park's northern exi The specialty is *trucha arco iris* (rainbov trout), and meat dishes are also on tap.

Café Tradicional de Uruapan (☎ 523-56-80; Carranza 5B; snacks & breakfast $3-6) Sip gourmet coffee and tea with Uruapan's elite in this dark womb of a café. It's elegantly decorated with a wood-carved interior, and also offers good breakfasts, snacks, burgers and pastries.

Cocina Económica Mary (☎ 519-48-69; Independencia 59; mains under $3; ⏲ 8am-5.30pm Mon-Sat) If you're looking for a cheap and delicious homemade meal, try this clean and popular family-style place. For $3 you get soup, a main course (think pork with squash, orange chicken or tongue with salsa) and a drink. Plan ahead; it closes early and isn't open on Sunday.

Rincón Aguililla (☎ 523-08-21; Chiapas 367; mains $7-11.50; ⏲ 11am-11pm; P) This popular large eatery serves mostly steaks, but there's also trout, fajitas and grilled rabbit on the menu. Grab a pitcher of fruit juice to down those free appetizers – you won't be going away hungry. It's located about 1km east of the plaza.

Café La Pérgola (☎ 523-50-87; Portal Carrillo 4; mains $3.75-8.50) This old place cooks up soups, salads, sandwiches and regional food. The atmosphere's a bit dark and the murals on the walls unusual, but it's still popular for its $5 *comida corrida* (soup, side, main dish, dessert and coffee or tea).

Mercado de Antojitos Típicos (⏲ 8am-11pm) Offers adventurous diners dozens of cheap food stalls (look for *pozole*) around a big square. Head one block north into the main market to find it.

Farmacia Guadalajara (Carranza 3) For 24-hour convenience.

Drinking & Entertainment

La Lucha (☎ 524-03-75; Ortiz 20; coffees $3; ⏲ 9am-9pm Mon-Sat) Service may be a bit brusque, but the coffee's good: try a double espresso, flavored cappuccino or hot chocolate. It's half a block from the plaza and has a good intimate atmosphere accented with solid wooden furniture. There's an annex at Portal Matamoros 16, on the plaza, with counter seating only.

La Casa Bar (☎ 524-36-11; Revolución 3; ⏲ 4-11:30pm) Offering lots of fancy coffees and cocktails (and even a few dinner options), this upscale joint caters to patrons who like it dark and moody. Its a good hangout for a beer and cigar (the latter on the menu); just grab a table by the balcony.

Peña Colibrí (☎ 519-01-94; Independencia 18; ⏲ 6pm-1am Mon-Thu, 6pm-3am Fri & Sat) There's good atmosphere at this colorful place; settle in under an arch or right in front of the small stage. Live music, such as *rumba flamenca, canto nuevo* or *trova cubana* (folkmusic fusions), plays daily from 10pm; cover charges depend on the day. There are plenty of drinks and a few snacks available.

Casa de la Cultura (☎ 524-76-13; Ortiz 1) Half a block north of the plaza, this place hosts exhibitions, occasional concerts and other events. Check with the tourist office to see what's cooking during your stay in town.

Shopping

Local crafts, such as lacquered trays and boxes, can be bought at the **Mercado de Artesanías** (⏲ 9am-6pm), opposite the entrance to Parque Nacional Barranca del Cupatitzio. The market, stretching more than 500m up Constitución from the main plaza to Calz Juárez, is also worth a browse. Fábrica San Pedro (see p580) is good for textiles.

Getting There & Around

Uruapan's bus terminal is 2km northeast of central Uruapan on the highway to Pátzcuaro and Morelia. It has a *caseta de teléfono* (public telephone call station), a cafeteria and a **left-luggage facility** (⏲ 7am-11pm). Frequent destinations include the following:

Destination	Price	Duration	Frequency
Angahuan	$1.50	1hr	Hourly
Colima	$22	6-8hr	More connections via Zamora or Guadalajara
Guadalajara	$15-24	4½hr	
Lázaro Cárdenas	$14	4hr	
Mexico City (Terminal Norte)	$30	7hr	
Mexico City (Terminal Poniente)	$30	5½hr	
Morelia	$9	2hr	
Paracho	$1.50	1hr	
Pátzcuaro	$3.50	1hr	
Tingambato	$1	30min	Same buses as those to Pátzcuaro or Morelia
Zamora	$8	2hr	

Local buses marked 'Centro' run from just outside the bus terminal to the plaza ($0.40). For taxis, buy a ticket inside the bus terminal ($1.75). For the return trip catch a 'Central Camionera' bus from the south side of the plaza.

The car-rental agency **Del Cupatitzio** (☎ 523-11-81; autorent@prodigy.net.mx) is located at the Hotel Plaza Uruapan (p582).

AROUND URUAPAN
Cascada de Tzaráracua

Ten kilometers south of downtown Uruapan is the popular 30m Tzaráracua **waterfall** (admission $0.75, cars $0.50 extra; ☯ 10am-6pm). To see it up close, however, you'll have to huff and puff down 557 sometimes slippery stone steps down into a small valley. Hiring one of the many horses in the touristy parking lot will cost $6 round-trip; the price is the same for the one-way trip back up.

There's a 20-minute hike upstream from Tzaráracua to the small but lovely Tzararacuita, a smaller cascade. Getting here is much more 'adventurous' and may require waterproof sandals, as the trail is less maintained and even hazardous at times. Still, you'll see few people. To get here, follow the steep muddy track beyond the Tzaráracua bridge, and after about 10 minutes turn right at the stone outcropping.

Hourly buses to Tzaráracua depart from in front of the Hotel Regis, on the south side of Uruapan's main plaza ($0.40). Taxis cost $6.

Tingambato

The **ruins** (admission $3; ☯ 9am-6pm) of this ceremonial site, which flourished from about AD 450 to 900, are near the village of the same name, about 30km from Uruapan on the road to Pátzcuaro. They show Teotihuacán influence and date from well before the Tarascan empire. Also known by its older name Tinganio, the compact and tidy complex includes a ball court (rare in western Mexico), an 8m-high stepped pyramid, and an underground tomb where a skeleton and 32 skulls were found. A small museum has photos of the excavation work and some pieces recovered from tombs.

Buses to Morelia leave from Uruapan's terminal every 20 minutes and stop in Tingambato ($1, 30 minutes). The ruins are 1.4km downhill on Calle Juárez, the first street on the right as you enter town.

Paracho

☎ 423 / pop 16,000 / elevation 2220m

Paracho, 40km north of Uruapan on Hwy 37, is a small Purépecha town famous for its high-quality, handmade stringed instruments. If you're in the market for a reasonably priced guitar, violin, cello or traditional Mexican *guitarrón*, this is the place to be. You can also attend free guitar concerts by first-rate musicians and watch some of the country's best luthiers at work. The liveliest time to come is during the annual **Feria Nacional de la Guitarra** (National Guitar Fair) in early August; it's a weeklong splurge of music, dance and exhibitions.

Don't miss the showcase **Expo Cuerdas** (☎ 525-03-70; 20 de Noviembre s/n; ☯ noon-5pm), in the Casa de la Cultura on the southeast corner of the main plaza. It has old and new guitars on display (classical, Hawaiian and steel-string), violins, *guitarrones* (a large mexican bass) and *vihuelas* (a small guitar). Some are made of exotic woods and have elaborate carvings and inlays. Guitars cost $150 to $850. Call for appointments outside its opening hours.

The other must-see, about two blocks southeast, is the **Centro para la Investigación y el Desarrollo de la Guitarra** (CIDEG; ☎ 525-01-90; www.cideg.org; cnr Nicolás Bravo & Hidalgo; admission free ☯ 9am-1pm & 3-6pm Mon-Fri, 9am-1pm Sat). It's a guitar museum, with good exhibits on the history of music and instrument-making. Among the displays are beautifully decorated guitars, including one with breasts along with a woman's mouth for the sound hole. Hmmm. CIDEG hosts free guitar concerts in its auditorium on the last Friday of every month.

Galeana Ruta Paraíso buses depart Uruapan's bus terminal every 15 minutes ($1.50, one hour) and stop along Calz Juárez on their way out of town (avoiding backtracking to the bus terminal). There's a stop at the corner of Venustiano Carranza, near the Juárez statue.

Zamora

☎ 351 / pop 125,000 / elevation 1560m

Zamora is about 115km northwest of Uruapan and 190km southeast of Guadalajara. It's a pleasant town in the center of a rich agricultural region known for its strawberries and potatoes. There are a few pedestrian areas around the lively plaza, which is the place to be on Sunday nights when live music plays in the bandstand. A large bustling market sells the city's famous and delicious *dulces* (sweets).

Founded in 1574, Zamora has an inordinate number of churches, including the large, neo-Gothic **Catedral Inconclusa** ('5 de Mayo Sur & Cazares Ote), started in 1898 and still not quite finished. Fifteen kilometers southeast of town at Tangancícuaro is the spring-fed and tree-shaded **Laguna de Camécuaro**, a lovely spot for drivers to stop and picnic.

For local information head to the **tourist office** (☎ 512-40-15; Morelos Sur 76; ⌚ 9am-2pm & 4-7pm Mon-Sat, 10am-2pm Sun). There are plenty of banks with ATMs around the plaza.

There are a few hotels in the town's center, which is just a short bus ($0.40) or taxi ($1.75) ride from the bus terminal. Try the good old rooms at **Posada Felix** (☎ 512-12-55; cnr Morelos & Corregidora; s/d/tw $19/24/28); don't confuse it with the overpriced Hotel Fenix across the street (which you should avoid unless you want a pool). For something fancier there's the quiet and good-value **Hotel Ana Isabel** (☎ 515-17-33; hanaisabel_01@hotmail.com; Guerrero 108 Pte; s/d $25/33; **P**) or the **Hotel Ram Val** (☎ 512-02-28; www.hotelramval.com.mx; Amado Nervo 40; s/d $29/37; **P** **✇**). Zamora's cheapest hotels are dumps.

The bus terminal has regular connections to Guadalajara ($11.50, 2¼ hours), Colima ($15, five hours), Uruapan ($7.50, two hours), Pátzcuaro ($6.50, two hours), Morelia ($8, 2½ hours) and Mexico City ($28, six hours).

VOLCÁN PARICUTÍN

On February 20, 1943, Dionisio Pulido, a Purépecha farmer, was ploughing his cornfield some 35km west of Uruapan when the ground began to shake and spurt steam, sparks and hot ash. The farmer tried at first to cover the moving earth, but when that proved futile, he fled. A volcano started to rise from the spot. Within a year it had risen 410m above the surrounding land, and its lava had engulfed the Purépecha villages of San Salvador Paricutín and San Juan Parangaricutiro. No one was hurt; the lava flow was gradual, giving the villagers plenty of time to evacuate.

The volcano continued to spit lava and increase in size until 1952. Today its large black cone stands mute, emitting gentle wisps of steam. Near the edge of the 20-sq-km lava field, the top of San Juan's church protrudes eerily from the sea of solidified, black lava. It's the only visible trace of the two buried villages.

An excursion to Paricutín from Uruapan, to see San Juan's church engulfed in a jumble of black boulders and/or to climb the volcanic cone, makes a fine day trip. At 2800m, the volcano is not memorably high – the much bigger Tancítaro towers to the south – but it's interesting and fairly easy to access. Getting to the church won't take all day, but if you want to climb Paricutín you should start early – try to get to Angahuan by 9am (earlier if you rely on public transport).

It's important to bring some food and water from Uruapan, as there's none on the route and there is only a limited selection available in Angahuan. You will also need good hiking shoes. One last thing to remember is that half of Angahuan's economy is dependent on the tourist dollar; think about this when dealing with guides.

As soon as you alight at Angahuan's bus stop, guides with horses will offer their services to the ruined church or volcano. Horses and a guide for two people should cost $48 to $65, depending on demand. To the volcano it's a 14km round-trip that takes about six hours – of which you'll spend four in the saddle – so your legs and butt will get sore. You'll have to climb up the last few hundred meters as the horses can't negotiate the steep scree.

If you'd rather walk to the volcano you'll need a guide, since the foot trail through the pine forest can be difficult to find. Expect to pay around $25 for a walking guide; the round-trip from Angahuan should take under eight hours. (Walking the horse trail is easier in terms of finding your way, but it's also longer and less interesting than the foot trail.) The walk up passes thickets of wildflowers, expanses of barren lava and sandy ash fields. It's not terribly difficult until the base of the volcano, but then you'll be huffing and puffing for about a half-hour until you reach the lip of the crater. The view from the top is wonderful, so enjoy it – especially since you've earned it!

ANGAHUAN

☎ 333 / pop (Angahuan) 3000 / elevation (Angahuan) 2693m

Angahuan, the nearest town to Volcán Paricutín, is a typical Purépecha town: wooden houses, dusty streets, more horses than cars and loudspeakers booming announcements in the Purépecha language. Greet locals with 'nar erandisti' (good morning) or 'nar chuscu' (good afternoon).

Sights

On the main plaza is the 16th-century **Iglesia de Santiago Apóstol**, with some fine carving around its door done by a Moorish stonemason who accompanied the early Spanish missionaries here.

The ruined **Templo San Juan Parangaricutiro** is a one-hour walk from where the bus lets you off on the highway – alternatively, hire horses and a guide ($20 to $30 for two people). Cross the highway and go down the street framed by the wire arch; after 10 minutes turn right at the main plaza, then after 200m go left at the fork (note the satellite dish). Keep on this road, which eventually leads out of town and to a dirt parking lot under the Centro Turístco de Angahuan (see right). The easy trail, flanked by barbed-wire fences, starts here.

Getting around the church site is surprisingly difficult, as the walls are filled with, and surrounded by, huge boulders of sharp black volcanic rock – be very careful. The missing tower was not a casualty of the volcano – it was never completed.

Sleeping

Cuartos Familiares (☎ 203-85-27; Camino al Paricutín s/n; s/d $15/24; **P**) There aren't many sleeping options in Angahuan, but this is a good one. Six rustic but pleasant rooms come with fireplace and bath. Look for the orange sign saying 'Cuartos Familiares' on the road to the ruined church, about 1km from the bus stop.

Centro Turístico de Angahuan (☎ 203-85-27; in Uruapan 523-39-34; angeles1946@hotmail.com; Camino al Paricutín s/n; campsites per person $3.75, dm $10.50, r $33; **P**) This 'tourist' complex has a variety of accommodation, a restaurant that sometimes shows a video about the eruption, and a lookout point with good views of the lava field, the protruding San Juan church tower and the volcano itself. Nonguests pay $0.75 to enter the complex, which might be worth it for the bathrooms.

Getting There & Away

Angahuan is 35km from Uruapan. Galeana 2nd-class buses leave the Uruapan bus terminal for Angahuan every 30 minutes from 5am to 7pm ($1.50, one hour). Alternatively, flag down a bus marked 'Los Reyes' on Calz Juárez (at Venustiano Carranza, near the Juárez statue) in Uruapan; this will save you backtracking to the bus terminal.

Buses return to Uruapan every 15 minutes until about 7pm, but a few may run much less frequently until 9pm. Double-check this information before getting stuck in Angahuan for the night.

WESTERN CENTRAL HIGHLANDS

Northern Central Highlands

Traversing the highlands the horizon seems to stretch forever, bending slightly at the edges, a faint reminder of the beloved globe on which we dwell. Here in the heart of Mexico it is this exposure to the elements, these sweeping rocky landscapes pasted with sharp light and the occasional colonial hamlet that are the only diversions from the windswept terrain.

Many have come over the years to find glory on the plateau. For the colonial Spanish it was for the enormous mineral wealth torn from the veins of their New World dominion. Glorious cathedrals and exquisite Old World mansions rose and fell on the backs of the conquered. Magnificent silver cities like Guanajuato and Zacatecas were among America's wealthiest, and evidence of the subtracted wealth is scattered across the region.

A visit to San Miguel de Allende, Querétaro or San Luis Potosí exhibits stunning blends of historic elegance and cosmopolitan panache. An air of revival finds ghost towns like Real de Catorce and Pozos nourished back to life, and a fusion of old and new inhabitants adds spice to the region's relics of the past. Modern artists and entrepreneurs replace miners, looking to tap this new vein of growth and hoping to extract fame and fortune from the fabled highlands.

The challenging environment has been a continual catalyst for change. An essential region of Mexico's storied past, this frontier spawned the synthesis of cultures and the independence of a new nation. Whichever area you choose to visit, you'll be enchanted by the culture's color and graceful blend of apparent opposites; a transcendent scene unconcerned with time.

TOP FIVE

- Taking in the superb museums, exquisite architecture and history in **Zacatecas** (p589), an elegant silver city
- Discovering the mystical mountains and fine Italian cuisine in **Real de Catorce** (p614), a reawakening ghost town
- Pampering yourself in expat posh **San Miguel de Allende** (p635), full of art, food and fiestas
- Meandering the crooked, cobbled alleyways of **Guanajuato** (p619), a boisterous student city with a very quixotic festival
- Winding along Hwy 120 in the **Sierra Gorda** (p656), a remote region of Unesco World Heritage sites

- LEÓN JANUARY DAILY HIGH: 18°C | 64°F
- LEÓN JULY DAILY HIGH: 24°C | 75°F

History

Up to the Spanish conquest, the northern central highlands were inhabited by fierce seminomadic tribes known to the Aztecs as Chichimecs. They resisted Spanish expansion longer than other Mexican peoples, but were ultimately pacified in the late 16th century. The wealth subsequently amassed by the Spanish was at the cost of many Chichimecs, who were used as slave labor in the mines.

This historically volatile region sparked the criollo vie for independence from Spain, which was conspired in Querétaro and San Miguel de Allende, and launched from Dolores Hidalgo in 1810 (see the boxed text, p633). A century later revolutionary Francisco Madero

released his Plan de San Luis Potosí, and the 1917 signing of Mexico's constitution in Querétaro cemented the region's leading role in Mexican political affairs.

Climate

Stretching northwest from Mexico City and comprising the southern part of the Altiplano Central (Central Plateau), the majority of the region is upland semidesert strewn with a wealth of cacti. The northern reaches boast higher elevations, drier and generally cooler weather, while the overall southern latitude offsets the plateau's altitude providing temperate valleys with rich oak-forested hills and chaparral. The highest mountains once contained rich pine

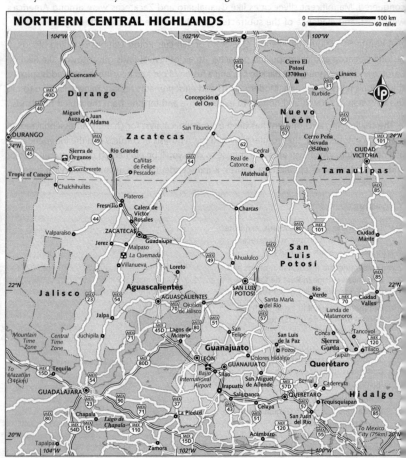

NORTHERN CENTRAL HIGHLANDS

forests of which only tiny pockets remain, except in the semitropical cloud forests of the Sierra Gorda to the east.

Parks & Reserves

The distinctive rock formations of the Sierra de Órganos (p600) create a land of fantastic towering sand castles petrified by time. Replicating organ pipes, among other shapes, this desert national park offers good camping and hidden hikes, and is often used as the location for Hollywood's Wild West.

The diverse ecological zones within the Reserva de la Biosfera Sierra Gorda (p656) host little-explored ecosystems that reward the considerable efforts required to reach them. Tucked into the cloud forests on the leeward side of the Sierra Oriental, even the most courageous can find a thrill. Waterfalls and caves abound and multi-day adventures are available.

Getting There & Around

Aeropuerto International del Bajío, halfway between León and Guanajuato, is the major hub for the region's southern cities. Other airports, all with direct US flights, include Aguascalientes, San Luis Potosí and Zacatecas. Buses constantly ply the toll roads between Mexico City, Guadalajara, Querétaro and San Luis Potosí. These larger hubs, including Zacatecas and Aguascalientes, also host connections to northern Mexico, the US border and beyond. Frequent local buses of all classes efficiently connect the major cities and all points in between.

ZACATECAS STATE

The state of Zacatecas (zak-a-*tek*-as) is one of Mexico's largest in area (73,252 sq km) but smallest in population (1.37 million). It's a dry, rugged, cactus-strewn expanse on the fringe of Mexico's northern semideserts, with large tracts almost blank on the map. The fact that it has any significant population is largely due to the abundance of *nopales* (paddle cactus; the most nutrient rich food of the region and an invaluable desert staple) and the mineral wealth the Spanish discovered here, mainly around the capital city Zacatecas. The climate is generally delightful – dry, clear and sunny, but not too hot.

ZACATECAS

☎ 492 / pop 119,000 / elevation 2445m

After traveling through a sea of rock and *nopal* it is hard to imagine stumbling upon this high desert gem. As the Spanish discovered, it is full of surprises. The most northern of Mexico's fabled silver cities, Zacatecas emanates an Old-World charm and boasts one of the countries most impressive cathedrals. A Unesco World Heritage site, sensitive restoration has returned the historic center to the architectural brilliance of its past. Getting through its exterior shell will reveal interiors fusing modern convenience and colonial style.

Ride an aerial cable car to the Cerro de la Bufa, an impressive rock outcrop, and take in the collage of church domes and rooftops in the meandering cityscape. Conversely, drop below the surface in a tour of the infamous Edén mine, and enjoy the underground vibrations of its disco. Whatever you do, the city's vitality will leave its mark, as this obscure destination never fails to draw in the savvy traveler.

History

Indigenous Zacatecos – one of the Chichimec tribes – mined local mineral deposits for centuries before the Spanish arrived; it's said that the silver rush here was started when a Chichimec gave a piece of the fabled metal to a conquistador. The Spaniards founded a settlement in 1548 and started mining operations that sent caravan after caravan of silver off to Mexico City. While some treasure-laden wagons were raided by hostile tribes, enough ore reached its destination to create fabulously wealthy silver barons in Zacatecas. Agriculture and ranching developed to serve the rapidly growing town.

By the early 18th century, the mines of Zacatecas were producing 20% of Nueva España's silver. At this time the city became an important base for missionaries spreading Catholicism as far north as the US states of Arizona and New Mexico.

In the 19th century, political instability diminished the flow of silver. Although silver production later improved under Porfirio Díaz, the revolution disrupted it. And it was here, in 1914, that Pancho Villa defeated a stronghold of 12,000 soldiers loyal to President Victoriano Huerta. After the revolution,

Zacatecas continued to thrive on silver. It remains a mining center to this day, with the 200-year-old El Bote mine still productive.

Orientation

The city center is in a valley between Cerro de la Bufa to the northeast and the smaller Cerro del Grillo to the northwest. Most attractions are within walking distance of the center. The two key streets are Av Hidalgo, running roughly north–south, with the cathedral toward its north end; and Av Juárez, running roughly east–west across the south end of Av Hidalgo. Av Hidalgo becomes Av González Ortega south of its intersection with Av Juárez.

Information

BOOKSTORES

Sanborns (cnr Avs Hidalgo & Allende) Best international periodicals and book selection.

INTERNET ACCESS

Most places charge around $1.50 per hour for Internet access.
Cybertech (Av Hidalgo 771)
Plaza Internet (east side of Jardín Independencia)

EMERGENCY

Ambulance, Fire, Police (☎ 066)

LAUNDRY

Lavandería El Indio Triste (Tolusa 826) Wash, dry and fold service $1.50 per kg.

MEDICAL SERVICES

IMSS hospital (☎ 924-27-34; cnr Avs Torreón & Doval)

MONEY

Banks in the center have ATMs, and change cash and traveler's checks.
San Luís Divisas (east side of Plaza Independencia) Changes US dollars.

POST OFFICE

Post office (☎ 922-01-96; Allende 111; 9am-4pm Mon-Fri, 9am-2pm Sat)

TELEPHONE

Telephone *casetas* are in the bus station, on Callejón de las Cuevas, off Av Hidalgo, and at the following locations.
Telecomm (cnr Avs Hidalgo & Juárez)
Voinet (Av Hidalgo s/n) Cheap, Internet-based long-distance phone calls.

TOURIST INFORMATION

State tourist office (☎ 924-05-52, 800-712-40-78; www.turismozacatecas.gob.mx; Av Hidalgo 403; 9am-8pm Mon-Sat, 10am-7pm Sun) Upstairs in an old colonial building. Helpful and has plenty of brochures (in Spanish). Some staff speak English.

Sights

Set amid dry, arid country, this historic city – particularly its Unesco World Heritage–listed central district – has much to detain you, from trips into an old silver mine to excellent museums and the ascent of la Bufa by *teleférico* (aerial cable car).

CATEDRAL

The pink-stone **cathedral** (admission free), on the south side of the Plaza de Armas is perhaps the ultimate expression of Mexican baroque. The cathedral was built between 1729 and 1752, just before baroque edged into its final Churrigueresque phase. And in this city of affluent silver barons, no expense was spared.

The highlight is the stupendous main facade. This wall of detailed yet harmonious carvings has been interpreted as a giant symbol of the tabernacle. A tiny figure of an angel holding a tabernacle can be seen at the middle of the design, the keystone atop the round central window. Above this, at the center of the third tier, is Christ, and above Christ is God. Other main statues include the 12 apostles, while a smaller Virgin figure is immediately above the doorway.

The south and north facades, though more simple, are also very fine. The central sculpture on the southern facade is of La Virgen de los Zacatecanos, the city's patroness. The north facade shows Christ crucified, attended by the Virgin Mary and St John.

PLAZA DE ARMAS

The plaza is the open space north of the cathedral. The **Palacio de Gobierno** on the plaza's east side was built in the 18th century for a colonial family. In the turret of its main staircase is a mural of the history of Zacatecas state, painted in 1970 by Antonio Rodríguez.

On the plaza's west side, the lovely white **Palacio de la Mala Noche**, which now houses state-government offices, was built in the late 18th century for a mine owner.

ZACATECAS

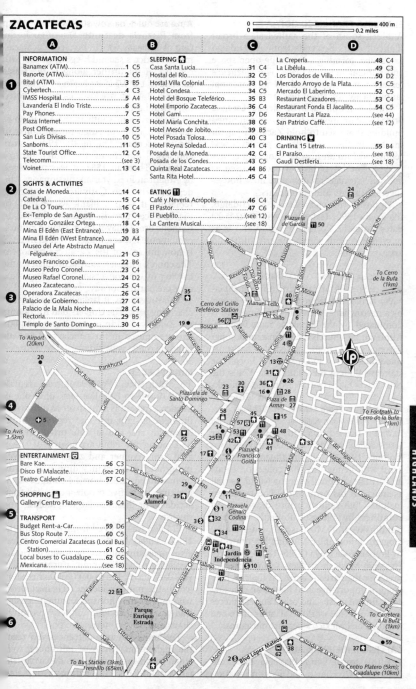

INFORMATION	
Banamex (ATM)	1 C5
Banorte (ATM)	2 C6
Bital (ATM)	3 B5
Cybertech	4 C3
IMSS Hospital	5 A4
Lavandería El Indio Triste	6 C3
Pay Phones	7 C5
Plaza Internet	8 C5
Post Office	9 C5
San Luís Divisas	10 C5
Sanborns	11 C5
State Tourist Office	12 C4
Telecomm	(see 3)
Voinet	13 C4

SIGHTS & ACTIVITIES	
Casa de Moneda	14 C4
Catedral	15 C4
De La O Tours	16 C4
Ex-Templo de San Agustín	17 C4
Mercado González Ortega	18 C4
Mina El Edén (East Entrance)	19 B3
Mina El Edén (West Entrance)	20 A4
Museo del Arte Abstracto Manuel Felguérez	21 C3
Museo Francisco Goita	22 B6
Museo Pedro Coronel	23 C4
Museo Rafael Coronel	24 D2
Museo Zacatecano	25 C4
Operadora Zacatecas	26 C4
Palacio de Gobierno	27 C4
Palacio de la Mala Noche	28 C4
Rectoría	29 B5
Templo de Santo Domingo	30 C4

SLEEPING	
Casa Santa Lucia	31 C4
Hostal del Río	32 C5
Hostal Villa Colonial	33 D4
Hotel Condesa	34 C5
Hotel del Bosque Teleférico	35 B3
Hotel Emporio Zacatecas	36 C4
Hotel Gami	37 D6
Hotel María Conchita	38 C6
Hotel Mesón de Jobito	39 B5
Hotel Posada Tolosa	40 C3
Hotel Reyna Soledad	41 C4
Posada de la Moneda	42 C4
Posada los Condes	43 C5
Quinta Real Zacatecas	44 B6
Santa Rita Hotel	45 C4

EATING	
Café y Nevería Acrópolis	46 C4
El Pastor	47 C6
El Pueblito	(see 12)
La Cantera Musical	(see 18)

La Crepería	48 C4
La Libélula	49 C3
Los Dorados de Villa	50 D2
Mercado Arroyo de la Plata	51 C5
Mercado El Laberinto	52 C5
Restaurant Cazadores	53 C4
Restaurant Fonda El Jacalito	54 C5
Restaurant La Plaza	(see 44)
San Patrizio Caffé	(see 12)

DRINKING	
Cantina 15 Letras	55 B4
El Paraíso	(see 18)
Gaudi Destilería	(see 18)

ENTERTAINMENT	
Bare Kae	56 C3
Disco El Malacate	(see 20)
Teatro Calderón	57 C4

SHOPPING	
Gallery Centro Platero	58 C4

TRANSPORT	
Budget Rent-a-Car	59 D6
Bus Stop Route 7	60 C5
Centro Comercial Zacatecas (Local Bus Station)	61 C6
Local buses to Guadalupe	62 C6
Mexicana	(see 18)

NORTHERN CENTRAL HIGHLANDS

PLAZUELA FRANCISCO GOITIA

A block south of the cathedral, a broad flight of stairs descends from Av Hidalgo to Tacuba, forming a charming open space and popular meeting place. The *plazuela*'s terraces are often used as an informal amphitheater by street performers.

North of the *plazuela*, the **Mercado González Ortega** is an impressive 1880s iron-columned building that used to hold Zacatecas' main market. In the 1980s the upper level was renovated into an upscale shopping center (p596). The lower level was once used as *bodegas* (storage rooms) and now houses several hip bars and restaurants.

Opposite the *plazuela* on Av Hidalgo, the lovely 1890s **Teatro Calderón** (☎ 922-81-20) dates from the Porfiriato period and is as busy as ever with plays, concerts, films and art exhibitions.

PLAZUELA DE SANTO DOMINGO

A block west of the cathedral, this small *plazuela* is reached from the Plaza de Armas by a narrow lane, Callejón de Veyna, and is dominated by the **Templo de Santo Domingo**. Although the church is done in a more sober baroque style than the cathedral, it has some fine gilded altars and a graceful horseshoe staircase. Built by the Jesuits in the 1740s, the church was taken over by Dominican monks when the Jesuits were expelled in 1767.

The **Museo Pedro Coronel** (☎ 922-80-21; Plaza de Santo Domingo s/n; admission $2; ⏰ 10am-4:30pm Fri-Wed) is housed in a 17th-century, former Jesuit college beside Santo Domingo. Pedro Coronel (1923–85) was an affluent Zacatecan artist who bequeathed his collection of art and artifacts from all over the world, as well as much of his own work. The collection includes 20th-century prints; drawings and paintings by Picasso, Rouault, Chagall, Kandinsky and Miró; some entertaining Hogarth lithographs; and fine ink drawings by Francisco de Goya (1746–1828). The pre-Hispanic Mexican artifacts seem chosen as much for their artistic appeal as their archaeological importance, and there's an amazing collection of masks and other ancient pieces from all over the world. It all adds up to one of provincial Mexico's best art museums.

CALLES DR HIERRO & AUZA

Leading south from Plazuela de Santo Domingo, Dr Hierro and its continuation Auza are quiet, narrow streets. About 100m from Plazuela de Santo Domingo is the **Casa de Moneda**, which housed Zacatecas' mint (Mexico's second biggest) in the 19th century. A bit further along is the **Museo Zacatecano** (☎ 922-65-80; Dr Hierro 301; admission $1.50; ⏰ 10am-5pm Wed-Mon), largely devoted to Huichol art.

Another 100m south is the **Ex-Templo de San Agustín**, built for Augustinian monks in the 17th century. During the 19th-century anticlerical movement, the church became a casino. Then, in 1882, it was purchased by American Presbyterian missionaries who destroyed its 'too Catholic' main facade, replacing it with a blank white wall. In the 20th century the church returned to Catholic use. Today it hosts art and cultural exhibitions. The adjoining former monastery is now the seat of the Zacatecas bishopric. The church's finest feature is the platensque carving of the conversion of St Augustine over the north doorway.

The street ends at **Jardín Juárez**, a tiny but charming park. The Universidad Autónoma de Zacatecas' administrative headquarters are housed in the neoclassical **Rectoría** building on its west side.

MINA EL EDÉN

The **Edén Mine** (☎ 922-30-02; tours adult/child $5.50/2.75; ⏰ every 15min 10am-6pm), once one of Mexico's richest, is a must-see as it provides dramatic insight into the region's source of wealth and the terrible price paid for it. Digging for fabulous hoards of silver, gold, iron, copper and zinc, the enslaved indigenous people, including many children, worked under horrific conditions. At one time up to five people a day died from accidents or diseases like tuberculosis and silicosis.

El Edén was worked from 1586 until the 1950s. Today the fourth of its seven levels is open to visitors. The lower levels are flooded. An elevator or miniature train takes you deep inside Cerro del Grillo, the hill in which the mine is located. Then guides who may or may not speak some English lead you along floodlit walkways past deep shafts and over subterranean pools.

The mine has two entrances. To reach the higher one (the east entrance), walk 100m southwest from Cerro de Grillo *teleférico* station; from this entrance, tours start

Colorful building at World Heritage site Tlacotalpan (p705)

JEFFREY BECOM

Alebrijes (carved animal toys), Oaxaca (p735)

LEE FOSTER

Hammocks for hire, Puerto Vallarta (p451)

ANTHONY PLUMMER

Boojum trees, Baja California (p266)

JOHN ELK III

Hand-woven baskets and belts, traditional handicrafts of the Tarahumara (p342)

Commemorations of Día de Muertos (p63)

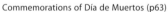

Birria, a goat meat dish, traditional in the Guadalajara area (p521)

with an elevator descent. To reach the west entrance from the town center, walk west along Av Juárez and stay on it after its name changes to Torreón at the Alameda. Turn right immediately after the IMSS hospital (bus 7 from the corner of Av Hidalgo goes up Av Juárez and past the hospital) and a short walk will bring you to the mine entrance where tours begin with a descent on the narrow-gauge railway.

For information about Disco El Malacate, the mine's nighttime alter ego, see p596.

TELEFÉRICO (AERIAL CABLE CAR)

Zacatecas' most exhilarating ride, and the easiest way to summit Cerro de la Bufa, is the Swiss-built **cable car** (☎ 922-01-70; adult/child/senior $3/2.50/2; ☽ 10am-4:30pm) that crosses high above the city from Cerro del Grillo. It's a short walk east from Mina El Edén (east entrance) to the *teleférico*'s Cerro del Grillo station. Alternatively, huff up the steep steps of Callejón de García Rojas, which lead straight to the *teleférico* from Genaro Codina. Cars depart every 15 minutes (except when it's raining or when winds exceed 60km/h), and the trip takes seven minutes.

CERRO DE LA BUFA

The most appealing of the many explanations for the name of the hill that dominates Zacatecas is that 'bufa' is an old Basque word for wineskin, which is certainly what the rocky formation looks like. The views from the top are superb, and there's an interesting group of monuments, a chapel and a museum up there.

The small **Museo de la Toma de Zacatecas** (☎ 922-80-66; admission $1.50; ☽ 10am-4:30pm Tue-Sun) commemorates the 1914 battle fought on the hill's slopes in which the revolutionary División del Norte, led by Pancho Villa and Felipe Ángeles, defeated President Victoriano Huerta's forces. This gave the revolutionaries control of Zacatecas, which was the gateway to Mexico City. The museum features descriptions of the battle and contemporary newspaper cuttings, all in Spanish.

La Capilla de la Virgen del Patrocinio, adjacent to the museum, is named after the patron saint of miners. Above the altar of this 18th-century chapel is an image of the Virgin said to be capable of healing the sick. Thousands of pilgrims flock here each year

around September 8, when the image is carried to the cathedral.

Just east of the museum stand three imposing equestrian **statues** of the victors of the battle of Zacatecas – Villa, Ángeles and Pánfilo Natera. A path behind the statues leads to La Bufa's rocky **summit**, where there are marvelous views on all sides. The hill is topped by a metal cross that is illuminated at night.

From the right of the statues, a path along the foot of the rocky hilltop leads to the **Mausoleum de los Hombres Blusters de Zacatecas**, with the tombs of Zacatecan heroes from 1841 to the present.

An exciting and convenient way to ascend la Bufa is by *teleférico* (see left). Alternatively, you can walk up by starting at Calle del Ángel from the cathedral's east end. To reach it by car, take Carretera a la Bufa, which begins at Av López Velarde beside the university library, a couple of kilometers east of the center. A taxi costs $4. All three routes end at the monuments, chapel and museum. Just above the *teleférico* station, the quaint, round building is a **meteorological observatory**.

You can return to town by the *teleférico* or by a footpath leading downhill from the statues.

MUSEO DE ARTE ABSTRACTO MANUEL FELGUÉREZ

This **art museum** (☎ 924-37-05; Ex Seminario de la Purisima Concepción; admission $2; ☽ 10am-4:30pm Wed-Mon) is a couple of blocks west of Tolosa, up some steep *callejones* (alleys). It specializes in abstract art, particularly the work of Zacatecan artist Manuel Felguérez, but also includes paintings, sculptures and installations by other artists. It's a varied and stunning collection. The building itself, originally a seminary, was later used as a prison, and has been renovated to create some remarkable exhibition spaces. There's also a popular café.

MUSEO RAFAEL CORONEL

The **Museo Rafael Coronel** (☎ 922-81-16; cnr Abasolo & Matamoros; adult/senior $2/1; ☽ 10am-5pm Thu-Tue), imaginatively housed in the ruins of the lovely 16th-century ex–Convento de San Francisco, houses Mexican folk art collected by the Zacatecan artist Rafael Coronel, brother of Pedro Coronel and son-in-law of Diego Rivera. The highlight is the astonishing, colorful display of over 2000 masks used in traditional dances and rituals. Also on display are pottery, puppets, instruments, pre-Hispanic objects and sketches by Rivera.

MUSEO FRANCISCO GOITIA

The **Museo Francisco Goitia** (☎ 922-02-11; Estrada 101; admission $2; ☺ 10am-4:30pm Tue-Sun) displays work by several 20th-century Zacatecan artists. Set in a fine former governor's mansion, above the pleasant Parque Enrique Estrada, it's well worth the short walk. Francisco Goitia (1882–1960) himself created some evocative paintings of indigenous people. There's also a striking Goitia self-portrait. Other artists represented include Pedro Coronel, Rafael Coronel and Manuel Felguérez.

Tours

A couple of agencies run city tours and excursions to nearby places of interest. Typical offerings include a four-hour city tour including the mine and the *teleférico* ($19); four-hour trips to Guadalupe ($15); and a six-hour excursion to the archaeological site of La Quemada and the town of Jerez ($18). The tourist office can recommend agencies, including:

De La O Tours (☎ 922-34-64; www.delaotours.com; Av Hidalgo 613)

Operadora Zacatecas (☎ 924-00-50; opzac@prodigy .net.mx; Av Hidalgo 630)

Festivals & Events

La Morisma Usually held on the last weekend in August. Features the most spectacular of many mock battles staged at Mexican fiestas commemorating the triumph of the Christians over the Muslims (Moors) in old Spain. Rival 'armies' parade through the streets in the mornings, then, accompanied by bands of musicians, enact two battle sequences between Lomas de Bracho and Cerro de la Bufa. One sequence portrays a conflict between Emperor Charlemagne and Almirante Balam, king of Alexandria. The other deals with a 16th-century Muslim rebellion.

Feria de Zacatecas Annual fair during the first three weeks in September. Renowned matadors fight famous local bulls; *charreadas* (rodeos), concerts, plays, film festivals, and agricultural and craft shows are staged. On September 8 the image of La Virgen del Patrocinio is carried to the cathedral from its chapel on Cerro de la Bufa.

Festival Internacional de Teatro de Calle In mid-October, drama takes to the streets in this vibrant week-long celebration of street theater.

Sleeping

Midrange and top-end hotels hike their rates during the high seasons of September's festivals, Christmas and Semana Santa (the week before Easter). At other times you may be able to get a discount on the prices listed here.

BUDGET

The cheapest central places don't have parking, but public lots charge about $1.50 per night. Cheapies further out on Blvd López Mateos suffer much street noise, but have parking, phones and cable TV. All places except the hostels have private bathrooms.

Hostal Villa Colonial (☎ /fax 922-19-80; hostalvilla colonial@hotmail.com; cnr Calle 1 de Mayo & Callejón Mono Prieto; dm/d $8.50/18; ▯) This lively, family-run HI-affiliate is *the* rendezvous point for shoestring travelers. Dorms have four beds, and a few new rooms have private bathroom. Amenities include kitchen, laundry, a cable TV/DVD lounge, bar, rooftop patio, book exchange and free bus-terminal pickup. Constantly evolving, the hostel will expand into a colonial building a block away. English and French are spoken and the hospitable owners often take guests out on the town.

Hostal del Río (☎ 924-00-35; Av Hidalgo 116; r $24) Often full, this 10-room hotel has a great location, some character and clean, comfortable rooms. Some rooms overlook the street, while the downstairs dwellings are dungeon-like.

Posada de los Condes (☎ 922-10-93; Av Juárez 107; s/d $23/28) This colonial building is three centuries old, but the late '60s remodel lacks the colonial-era charm. The carpeted rooms are bland but well kept, and few have exterior windows.

Other recommendations:

Hotel María Conchita (☎ 922-14-94; Blvd López Mateos 401; s/d $16/19; ℗) Top-floor rooms are worth the extra charge.

Hotel Gami (☎ 922-80-05; Blvd López Mateos 309; s/d $17/23; ℗) A bargain for those willing to share.

MIDRANGE

All these places have in-room phones and TVs.

Casa Santa Lucia (☎ 924-49-00; Av Hidalgo 717; low/high r from $70/102; ℗) This former bishop's residence straddles the mid- and upper-ranges, depending on the season, and is an easy stroll from the cathedral. It's small and appealing with a comfortable, rustic character.

Hotel Condesa (☎ 922-11-60; www.visitezacatecas .com; Av Juárez 102; s/d $37/42) Centrally located and recently renovated, the Condesa has 60 rooms around a covered courtyard. Nearly all have exterior windows and a few have balconies; those facing northeast have fine views of la Bufa.

Posada de la Moneda (☎ 922-08-81; posadadel moneda@hotmail.com; Av Hidalgo 413; s/d/ste $47/56/70) An imposing old building and a perfect location near the cathedral make this one of Zacatecas' most attractive three-star hotels. The spacious rooms are comfortable and nicely decorated, though they lack old-fashioned charm.

Hotel Reyna Soledad (☎ /fax 922-07-90; www.hos talreynasoledad.com.mx; Tacuba 170; r $71; P) Set in a converted 17th-century convent, there is a quiet colonial charm about this hotel. The rooms are ample and the rustic feel is nice for a location so central.

Hotel Posada Tolosa (☎ /fax 922-51-05; www.hotel posadatolosa.com; Juan de Tolosa 811; s/d $45/60; P ♿) A short walk up Hidalgo from the Plaza de Armas, the hotel is just below the *teleférico*. With pleasant rooms large enough to fit Juárez' army, there is ample space for the kinfolk; nanny optional.

TOP END

Hotel Mesón de Jobito (☎ /fax 924-17-22, 800-021-00-40; www.mesondejobito.com; Jardín Juárez 143; r/ste from $167/192; P ❌ ▯) Several restored buildings have been incorporated into this superb luxury hotel. The 53 finely decorated rooms, two excellent restaurants, bar and lobby are all rich with charm and historic character, and the service exemplifies attentiveness.

Quinta Real Zacatecas (☎ 922-91-04, 800-500-40-00; www.quintareal.com; Rayón 434; ste from $248; P ❌ ❌) The 49-room Quinta Real is one of Mexico's most fetching hotels, spectacularly situated around the country's oldest (now retired) bullring. The El Cubo aqueduct runs across the property and past the elegant restaurant (see p596). The least expensive rooms are spacious, comfortable master suites.

Santa Rita Hotel (☎ 925-41-41, 800-560-81-15; www.hotelsantarita.com; Av Hidalgo 507A; r/ste $172/242; P ❌ ▯) This new luxury hotel has a top location and mixes old and new styles well in its 35 suites. Sparing no detail, they incorporate all the modern touches in this superbly renovated colonial building. There is fine art throughout, showcasing Zacatecan artists and the town's cosmopolitan edge.

Other recommendations:

Hotel Emporio Zacatecas (☎ 925-65-00, 800-800-61-61; www.hotelesemporio.com; Av Hidalgo 703; r/ste $137/151; P ❌ ❌) Superb location, and the upstairs restaurant has a great view of the cathedral.

Hotel del Bosque Teleférico (☎ 922-07-45; www .hotelesdelbosque.com.mx; Paseo Díaz Ordaz s/n; ste from $92; P) Luxury suites with an excellent view plus full RV hookups ($14).

Eating

Many restaurants serve local specialties featuring ingredients like *nopal* and pumpkin seeds. Locally produced wine can be good and you might also like to try *aguamiel* (honey water), a nutritional drink derived from the maguey cactus. In the morning, look around Av Hidalgo for *burros* (donkeys) carrying pottery jugs of the beverage.

There are two central produce markets. Mercado El Laberinto's main entrance is on Av Juárez and budget eateries abound nearby. A bit to the southeast, Mercado Arroyo de la Plata is entered from the curved street Arroyo de la Plata.

AROUND AVENIDAS HIDALGO & JUÁREZ

It's a pleasure to walk these lively streets, comparing the many excellent eateries.

San Patrizio Caffé (☎ 922-43-99; Av Hidalgo 403C; drinks & snacks $1-2.50; ♾ 10am-10pm Mon-Sat, 5-10pm Sun) Below the tourist office, the nicest café in town boasts relaxing courtyard seating, light snacks, Illy espresso, fancy teas and an array of Italian sodas.

La Crepería (☎ 925-21-61; Tacuba 204; mains $5-11; ♾ 2-11pm Thu-Tue) Staying true to the French

> ### THE AUTHOR'S CHOICE
>
> **Los Dorados de Villa** (☎ 922-57-22; Pla-zuela de García 1314; mains $4-7; ♾ 3pm-1am) This place oozes Zacatecan historical tradition revolving around the infamous revolutionary Pancho Villa. Photos and news clippings adorn the walls creating a nostalgic ambiance of the era, but it is the exquisitely prepared regional cuisine that will linger in your travel memories…try the specialties, like *pozole verde* (hominy soup with pork and green salsa).

legacy, this fresh restaurant has delicious sweet and savory crepes. Enjoy light music and an upstairs view of the lively Calle Tacuba.

Café y Nevería Acrópolis (☎ 922-12-84; cnr Av Hidalgo & Plazuela Candelario Huizar; mains $4-8) Near the cathedral, this well-situated café is popular with locals and visitors for its excellent coffee, delicious cakes and light meals.

El Pueblito (☎ 924-38-18; Av Hidalgo 403D; mains $4-7; ☺ 1-11pm Wed-Mon) Located below the tourist office, El Pueblito offers Zacatecan specialties and tasty standard Mexican dishes. It has bright decor, entertainment and an enjoyable atmosphere.

La Libéula (☎ 925-22-11; Genaro Codina 752; mains $5-10; ☺ 2:30-8pm Mon, Wed & Thu, 2:30pm-1am Fri & Sat) An innovative restaurant-lounge fusing some Asian and Indian herbs with more traditional Zacatecan flavors. Try a range of tasty meat and veg dishes, and fresh local cheese. Also try the flavored tobacco from the hookah pipe to settle the stomach.

La Cantera Musical (☎ 922-88-28; Tacuba 2; mains $5-10) In the old storerooms below Mercado González Ortega, the Musical Quarry has classic and truly delicious Mexican food. It's a fun, if touristy, place with an open kitchen and live music most nights. Set breakfasts are under $5, and full meals, snacks and drinks are dispensed all day long.

Restaurant Cazadores (☎ 924-22-04; Callejón de la Caja 104; mains $6-12) 'Hunters' has a very meaty menu and is decorated with animal trophy heads. There is live music on weekends, but the main attraction is the location: upstairs overlooking lively Plazuela Goitia – request a window seat.

JARDÍN INDEPENDENCIA & AROUND

Restaurant La Plaza (☎ 922-91-04; Quinta Real Zacatecas, Rayón 434; mains $10-20) The Quinta Real's elegant dining room is especially memorable for its outlook to the aqueduct and bullring, as well as for its refined ambience and superb Continental cuisine. It's also a good choice for a formal breakfast or a cocktail in what used to be the bull-holding pen. Reservations recommended.

Restaurant Fonda El Jacalito (☎ 922-07-71; Av Juárez 18; mains $4-8; ☺ 8am-10:30pm) This bright, airy place is the best choice on Av Juárez, offering set breakfasts from $4, a good *comida corrida* (prix-fixe menu) and tasty versions of traditional favorites.

El Pastor (☎ 922-16-35; Independencia 214; mains $2-4; ☺ 8am-9pm) This friendly, family-run restaurant facing Jardín Independencia dishes out charcoal-roasted chicken, tortilla chips and salad. Pay a little more for chicken *mole* (stew) and rice.

Drinking

Cantina 15 Letras (☎ 922-01-78; Martires de Chicago 309) Stop for a drink at this smoky and crowded dive-bar classic, filled with bohemians, drunks and poets. Photos portray Zacatecas of old; there is art and occasional live music.

Gaudi Destilería (☎ 922-14-33; Mercado González Ortega Local 8; ☺ 10:30pm-3am) On street-level of the market's east side, this cave-like drinking den is popular with a stylish young crowd, especially on Thursday and Friday nights.

El Paraíso (☎ 922-61-64; cnr Hidalgo & Plazuela Goitia) This smart bar in the southwest corner of the Mercado González Ortega attracts a friendly, varied, mostly 30s clientele; it's busiest on Friday and Saturday.

Entertainment

Pick up a free copy of the monthly *Agenda Cultural* at the tourist office.

Disco El Malacate (☎ 922-30-02; Dovali s/n; cover $5; ☺ 9:30pm-2:30am Thu-Sat) Get down in a gallery of the Mina El Edén (p592) to a mix of Latin and US hits with a big mixed crowd of locals and tourists. The essential Zacatecas nightlife experience, it really gets going after midnight. Space is limited, so phone ahead to reserve a table – or risk getting left out of the shaft, so to speak.

Bare Kae (☎ 923-80-02; Grillo s/n; lounge ☺ 10am-10pm daily, bar/disco 10pm-3am Fri & Sat) El Malacate's polar opposite, this disco is at the other entrance to the mine, overlooking the city. The hippest dance spot for locals, the lounge is open daily without services, so bring a snack and enjoy the view.

Teatro Calderón (☎ 922-81-20; Av Hidalgo s/n; ☺ 10am-9pm) This top venue hosts a variety of cultural events including local and visiting theater, dance and music performances. Check with the State tourist office (p590) for current events.

Shopping

Zacatecas is known for silver, leather and colorful sarapes. Try along Arroyo de la Plata and in the indoor market off it. Upmarket Mercado González Ortega is the place to look for silver jewelry, local wines, leather *charrería* gear, sarapes and more.

The Zacatecas silversmith industry is being revived in a number of workshops at the **Centro Platero** (☎ 899-09-94; ☿ 9am-6pm Mon-Fri, 10am-3pm Sat), a few kilometers east of town at the 18th-century ex–Hacienda de Bernardez on the road to Guadalupe. Tour companies (see p594) can arrange visits, or you can make your own way there by taxi. If you just want to see the finished product, shop in their **gallery** (☎ 925-35-50; Villalpando 406; ☿ 10am-2pm & 4-8pm) in town.

Getting There & Away

AIR

Zacatecas' airport is 20km north of the city. Mexicana flies direct daily to/from Mexico City and Tijuana and weekly to/from Chicago and Los Angeles. Aero California flies from Zacatecas to Mexico City, Morelia and Tijuana.

Aero California (☎ 925-24-00; airport)
Mexicana (☎ 922-74-29; Av Hidalgo 408)

BUS

Zacatecas' main bus station is situated on the southwest edge of town, around 3km from the center. Many buses are *de paso* (which means that they stop here en route between other cities). The station has a luggage checkroom, a pharmacy and telephone *casetas*. The old bus station (the Centro Comercial Zacatecas) is found on Blvd López Mateos, but it has buses for only a few local destinations, such as Fresnillo and Villanueva (for Chicomostoc).

See the table below for daily departures, plus there are also frequent buses to Jerez and Torreón, and several a day to Chihuahua, Ciudad Juárez, Saltillo and Nuevo Laredo.

CAR & MOTORCYCLE

Prices begin from around $50 or $60 per day, with weeklong discount packages also available.

Avis (☎ 922-30-03; López Mateos 103) Has the best rates.
Budget Rent-a-Car (☎ 922-94-58; Blvd López Mateos 202) Across from Hotel Gami.

Getting Around

The cheapest way between the center and the airport is via **combi** (☎ 922-59-46; one-way $6). Taxis charge around $15.

Buses 7 and 8 provide a good tour of the center. Bus 8 from the bus station ($0.40)

ZACATECAS BUS SCHEDULE

Destination	Price	Duration	Frequency
Aguascalientes	$8	2hr	frequent 1st-class
	$7	2hr	hourly 2nd-class Estrella Blanca
Durango	$19	4½-6hr	13 1st-class Ómnibus de México & Transportes del Norte
	$15	4½-6hr	6 2nd-class Estrella Blanca
Fresnillo	$3	1-1½hr	hourly 1st-class Futura & Transportes del Norte
	$2.75	1-1½hr	hourly 2nd-class Estrella Blanca & Camiones de los Altos, from main bus station
Guadalajara	$23	4hr	hourly 1st-class Ómnibus de México, Chihuahuenses & Transportes del Norte
	$20	4hr	hourly 2nd-class Estrella Blanca & Rojo de los Altos daily
Guanajuato			take a León bus and change there for Guanajuato
León	$15	3hr	15 1st-class Ómnibus de México, Futura & Transportes del Norte
Mexico City			
(Terminal Norte)	$49	6-8hr	1 deluxe
	$40	6-8hr	16 1st-class Futura, Chihuahuenses & Ómnibus de México
Monterrey	$27	5hr	12 1st-class Transportes del Norte
	$23	5hr	10 2nd-class Estrella Blanca & Rojo de los Altos
Querétaro	$27	6hr	6 1st-class Futura, Chihuahuenses
	$25	7hr	2nd-class Estrella Blanca
San Luis Potosí	$10.50	3hr	8 1st-class Futura & Ómnibus de México
	$10	3hr	12 2nd-class Estrella Blanca

runs directly to the cathedral. Heading out of the center, they go south on Villalpando. Bus 7 runs from the bus station to the corner of Avs González Ortega and Juárez. Taxis from the bus station to the center cost around $3.

GUADALUPE
☎ 492 / pop 94,000
About 10km east of Zacatecas, Guadalupe boasts a historic former monastery, with one of Mexico's best colonial-art collections, and an impressive church that attracts pilgrims to honor the country's beloved virgin. Stroll around the quaint plaza whilst browsing in the antiques and handicrafts shops, all in between bites at a café or ice creamery.

The **Convento de Guadalupe** was established by Franciscan monks in the early 18th century as an apostolic college. It developed a strong academic tradition and was a base for missionary work in northern Nueva España until the 1850s. The convent now houses the **Museo Virreinal de Guadalupe** (☎ 923-23-86; Jardín Juárez s/n; admission $3, Sun free; 🕑 10am-4:30pm), with many paintings by Miguel Cabrera, Juan Correa, Antonio Torres and Cristóbal Villalpando. The art is almost entirely religious – expect lots of saints, angels and bloody crucifixions. The building itself has a wonderful medieval feel to it, and visitors can see part of the library and step into the choir on the church's upper floor, with its fine carved and painted chairs. From the choir area you can look down into the beautifully decorated 19th-century **Capilla de Nápoles**, which is located on the church's north side.

Beside the Museo Virreinal, the **Museo Regional de Historia** (☎ 923-20-89; admission $2; 🕑 10am-4:30pm Tue-Sun) has a good bookstore and gift shop, and a limited number of exhibits on the state's history.

The town holds a cultural festival at the end of September, and its annual fair during the first two weeks of December, focused on the **Día de la Virgen de Guadalupe** (December 12).

From Zacatecas, Transportes de Guadalupe buses run to Guadalupe every few minutes ($0.40, 20 minutes); catch one at the bus stop on Blvd López Mateos opposite the old bus station. Get off at a small plaza in the middle of Guadalupe where a 'Museo Convento' sign points to the right, along Madero. Walk 250m along Madero to Jardín Juárez, a sizable plaza. The museums are on the left

side of the plaza. To return to Zacatecas, catch the bus where you disembarked.

FRESNILLO & PLATEROS
☎ 493 / Fresnillo pop 105,000
Fresnillo is an unexciting town 58km north of Zacatecas, beside the highway to Durango and Torreón. The village of Plateros, 5km northeast, is home to the Santuario de Plateros, one of Mexico's most-visited shrines. If you're interested in Mexican Catholicism, you might find the shrine worth visiting. Otherwise, give both towns a miss.

Orientation
Fresnillo's bus station is on Ébano, 1km northeast of the town center on bus 3. Direct buses to Plateros depart Fresnillo's bus station hourly. If you need to go into Fresnillo for a meal or a room, you'll find it's a higgledy-piggledy place with three main plazas. The nicest of the three is Jardín Madero with the colonial church on its north side.

Santuario de Plateros
Pilgrims flock to this 18th-century church's altar to see *El Santo Niño de Atocha*, a quaint image of baby Jesus wearing a colonial pilgrim's feathered hat. A series of rooms is lined with thousands of *retablos* (ex-voto paintings) giving thanks to Santo Niño for all manner of miracles. Some go back to WWII, while others recall traffic accidents, muggings and medical operations. More recent ones include copies of school reports and academic records. The surrounding streets are lined with stalls selling gaudy religious artifacts – Santo Niño souvenirs especially.

Sleeping
There are a few hotels in Plateros for pilgrims planning to attend 6am Mass, but they aren't very restful. Fresnillo is a better overnight option.

Hotel Lirmar (☎ 932-45-98; Durango 400; s/d $15/20) Opposite Fresnillo's bus terminal, this is a fairly modern place with clean, comfortable rooms.

Hotel Maya (☎ 932-03-51; Ensaye 5; s/d $14/17) A block south of Av Juárez and a block west of Av Hidalgo in central Fresnillo, Hotel Maya has bright, fairly clean rooms with TV.

Hotel Casa Blanca (☎ 932-00-14; García Salinas 503; s/d $30/36) Three blocks east of Jardín Hidalgo, this place caters to business travelers.

NORTHERN CENTRAL HIGHLANDS

Getting There & Around

Fresnillo is well served by long-distance buses, though many are *de paso*. Frequent 1st-class buses serve Durango ($14, 3½ hours), Torreón ($21, five hours) and Zacatecas ($3, one hour); 2nd-class buses are even more frequent.

To Plateros, buy a ticket at the Parques Industriales counter in Fresnillo's bus station for a bi-hourly, 2nd-class bus ($0.75). Local bus 6 ($0.75) also goes to Plateros from Emiliano Zapata, 2½ blocks east of Jardín Madero.

JEREZ

☎ 494 / pop 38,000

A small country town 30km southwest of Zacatecas, Jerez has some fine 18th- and 19th-century buildings that testify to the wealth that silver brought to even the lesser towns of the Zacatecas region. Jerez holds a lively 10-day Easter fair starting on Good Friday, featuring *charreadas*, cockfights and other rip-snorting family fun.

Orientation & Information

Jardín Páez, the pleasant main plaza, has an old-fashioned gazebo and plenty of trees, birds and benches. The tourist office (☎ 945-68-24; Guanajuato 28) is two blocks north. **Efficient Inbox Cybercafé** (Salinas 2A), a block north, charges $1.50 per hour. Several banks (with ATMs) and card phones are around the plaza.

Sights

The 18th-century **Parroquia de la Inmaculada Concepción** and the 19th-century **Santuario de la Soledad** have fine stone carvings. Go one block south from Jardín Páez' southeast corner, then one block west for the shrine, or one block east for the church. Just past the shrine, on Jardín Hidalgo's north side, is the beautiful 19th-century **Teatro Hinojosa**.

Sleeping & Eating

There are a couple of good places to rest your head near the plaza, and several cheap eateries.

Posada Santa Cecilia (☎ 945-24-12; Constitución 4; s/d $21/24) Half a block north of the plaza's northeast corner, this place occupies an old but renovated building and offers modern comforts in appealing rooms.

Hotel Plaza (☎ 945-20-63; Plaza Principal Sur 8; s/d $9.50/14) This is the best of several cheapies

on the plaza, with small, bare, clean rooms with bathroom and TV (on request).

Leo Hotel (☎ 945-20-01; Calzada La Suave Patria s/n; r from $55; ℗ ☒) East of town on the road to Zacatecas, the modern Leo is the fanciest place around, with a heated pool, disco and a cinema next door.

Getting There & Around

The Jerez turnoff is near Malpaso, 29km south of Zacatecas on the Zacatecas–Guadalajara road. The Zacatecas–Jerez line runs 2nd-class buses from Zacatecas' bus station to Jerez ($2.75) every 30 minutes. There are also services by Ómnibus de México and Estrella Blanca/Rojo de los Altos. Jerez' bus station is on the east side of town, 1km from the center along Calz La Suave Patria. 'Centro-Central' buses ($0.35) run to/from the center. There are also several daily services to/from Fresnillo ($2.50).

CHICOMOSTOC

The impressive **ruins** (admission $3.25; ☸ 9am-5pm) of Chicomostoc stand on a hill overlooking a broad valley 45km south of Zacatecas, 2km east of the Zacatecas–Guadalajara road. Once thought to be the place where the Aztecs halted during their legendary wanderings toward the Valle de México, they're also known as **La Quemada**, from the charred remnants of their fiery destruction. The remote and scenic setting makes the ruins well worth the trip from Zacatecas.

The **site museum** (admission $0.75; ☸ 10am-4:30pm Tue-Sun) has fascinating archaeology exhibits and is architecturally designed to replicate the original ruins. Both the museum and the site have explanatory labels in English as well as Spanish.

Chicomostoc was inhabited between about AD 300 and 1200, and it probably peaked between 500 and 900 with as many as 15,000 people. From around AD 400 it was part of a regional trade network linked to Teotihuacán (see p195), but fortifications suggest that Chicomostoc later tried to dominate trade in this region.

Some of the ruins can be seen atop the hill to the left as you approach from the Zacatecas–Guadalajara road. Of the main structures, the nearest to the site entrance is the **Salón de las Columnas** (Hall of the Columns), probably a ceremonial hall. A bit further up the hill are a ball court, a steep offerings

NORTHERN CENTRAL HIGHLANDS

pyramid and an equally steep staircase leading toward the site's upper levels. From the upper levels of the main hill, a path leads westward to a spur hilltop with the remains of a cluster of buildings called **La Ciudadela** (the Citadel). A stone wall, probably built for defensive purposes late in Chicomostoc's history, spans the slopes to the north.

Getting There & Away

From Zacatecas' old bus station, board a 2nd-class bus for Villanueva ($2.75) and ask to be let off at *'las ruinas'*; you'll be deposited at the Restaurant Las Siete Cuevas. Walk 2km along the paved road going east to the site. Returning to Zacatecas, you may have to wait a while before a bus shows up – don't leave the ruins too late. Ómnibus de México and Rojo de los Altos have regular service from Zacatecas' 1st-class bus station to Villanueva and Guadalajara, and these may also stop at the La Quemada turnoff. You can also take an organized tour ($16) from Zacatecas (see p594).

SOMBRERETE

☎ 433 / pop 19,000

Looking like something from a western movie, Sombrerete is an archetypical old Mexican town, its timeworn buildings and traditional streets almost totally intact. The first settlements here were in the 1550s, and mines began extracting minerals that financed a rich legacy of churches, mansions and public buildings.

Opposite the cathedral, the **municipal tourist office** (☎ 935-14-38; Hidalgo s/n) doesn't see many tourists, but the staff can answer questions (in Spanish). Make reservations here if you are interested in guides or transport in the area, or in renting a **cabaña** ($46), with two bedrooms, bathroom and kitchen, in Parque Nacional Sierra de Órganos (see right). For detailed information on hiking and conservation, visit **La Casa de Usted** (☎ 935-01-81; Hidalgo 321) in Sombrerete and speak with Luis Martínez who has explored the Sierra for over 50 years. He named many of the famous formations and still leads trips on the full moon in October. Next door, the small **Museo Municipal** (Hidalgo 207; admission $0.75; ⏲ 8am-8pm Mon-Fri, 10am-3pm Sat & Sun) has folksy but well-displayed history exhibits.

Hotel Villa de Llerena (☎ 935-53-41; Hidalgo 338; s/d $14/19) is a comfortable, family-run option with a restaurant, in front of the Jardín Constitución.

Sombrerete's bus station is not far from the town center, and numerous buses stop here between Zacatecas and Durango. If you're driving, the main street is just south of Hwy 45.

PARQUE NACIONAL SIERRA DE ÓRGANOS

High on the western edge of Zacatecas state, the **Organ Range** (admission $2) is named for its distinctive rock formations, some of which resemble organ pipes – others reveal images limited only by the imagination. Many rock profiles have been named for Catholic imagery, like El Papa and Los Frailes. The clear sky and high desert scenery make an ideal backdrop for western movies: *The Cisco Kid*, *The Guns of San Sebastian* and *The Sons of Katie Elder* all filmed scenes here. The area was declared a national park in 2000. There's a small visitors center and seven cabañas (see left) for rent, a few picnic areas and campsites, but no other facilities and no year-round water source. The park is relatively small (2797 acres) and can be explored in a couple of days. Good day hikes are plentiful in adjacent valleys where you can spend an hour or stroll all day. Be sure to carry water, some food and wear a hat.

To get here, turn north off Hwy 45 at San Francisco de los Órganos, 20km west of Sombrerete, follow the road for 10km (the first 5km are paved) until you see rocky formations on your left, then take the next left to the park entrance.

AGUASCALIENTES STATE

The state of Aguascalientes (population 1.1 million) is one of Mexico's smallest. It was originally part of Zacatecas; according to local tradition, a kiss planted on the lips of dictator Santa Anna by the attractive wife of a prominent local politician brought about the creation of a separate Aguascalientes state.

Industry is concentrated in and around the capital city, also called Aguascalientes, but the rest of the state is primarily agricultural, growing corn, beans, chilies, fruit and grain on its fertile lands. The state's ranches produce beef cattle as well as bulls, which are sacrificed at bullfights countrywide.

AGUASCALIENTES

☎ 449 / pop 658,000 / elevation 1800m

Named for its hot springs, this prosperous industrial city has a few handsome colonial buildings in the well-planned central area. Aguascalientes also has several modern shopping malls and a very modern bullring. If you're interested in Mexican art, the museums devoted to José Guadalupe Posada and Saturnino Herrán justify a visit.

History

Before the Spanish arrived, a labyrinth of catacombs was built here; the first Spaniards called it La Ciudad Perforada (the perforated city). Archaeologists understand little of the tunnels, which are off-limits to visitors.

Conquistador Pedro de Alvarado arrived in 1522 but was driven back by the Chichimecs. A small garrison was founded here in 1575 to protect Zacatecas–Mexico City silver convoys. Eventually, as the Chichimecs were pacified, the region's hot springs sparked the growth of a town; a large tank beside the Ojo Caliente springs helped irrigate local farms that fed hungry mining districts nearby.

The city's industries began with processing agricultural products into textiles, wine, brandy, leather and preserved fruits, but now include a huge Nissan plant just south of town. Today, more than half of the state's population lives in the city.

Orientation

Aguascalientes is pancake-flat and easy to get around. The center of town is Plaza de la Patria, surrounded by some pleasant pedestrian streets. Shops, hotels, restaurants and some fine buildings are within a few blocks. Av Chávez/Calle 5 de Mayo is the main north–south artery; it passes through a tunnel beneath Plaza de la Patria. Av López Mateos, the main east–west artery, is a couple of blocks south of the plaza.

Information

BOOKSTORES

Casa Terán (☎ 994-10-09; Rivero y Gutiérrez 110; ☿ 9am-9pm Mon-Sat) Good bookstore and Mexican cultural center with a patio café.

INTERNET ACCESS

Most places charge around $1.50 an hour.
Internet ZU (Centro Parián)
Soltec (Juan de Montoro 114)

EMERGENCY

Police (☎ 970-09-28)

LAUNDRY

Lavandería (296 Carranza; per kg $2.25; ☿ 8am-2pm & 4-7pm Mon-Sat)

MEDICAL SERVICES

There are several pharmacies in the city centre that are open 24 hours.
Hospital Hidalgo (☎ 918-50-54, 915-31-42; Galeana 465)
Red Cross (☎ 915-20-55)

MONEY

Banks with ATMs are common around Plaza de la Patria and Expoplaza. *Casas de cambio* cluster on Hospitalidad, opposite the post office.
Money Tron (Juan de Montoro s/n; ☿ 9am-4pm Mon-Fri) Exchange house half a block east of the plaza with drive-through window.

POST OFFICE

Post office (☎ 915-21-18; Hospitalidad 108; ☿ 8am-6pm Mon-Fri, 9am-1pm Sat)

TELEPHONE

Card phones are numerous in the city center.
Telecomm (Galeana 102) Has personal *casetas*.

TOURIST INFORMATION

State tourist office (☎ 915-95-04, 800-949-49-49; www.aguascalientes.gob.mx; Palacio de Gobierno, Plaza de la Patria; ☎ 8am-8pm Tue-Fri, 10am-6pm Sat & Sun) Free city maps.

TRAVEL AGENCIES

Vania Turismo (☎ 918-76-16; Juan de Montoro 204)
Viajes Gomzo (☎ 915-41-24; Juan de Montoro 114)

Sights & Activities

PLAZA DE LA PATRIA

The well-restored 18th-century baroque **cathedral**, on the plaza's west side, is more magnificent inside than outside. Over the altar at the east end of the south aisle is a painting of the Virgin of Guadalupe by Miguel Cabrera. There are more works by Cabrera, colonial Mexico's finest artist, in the cathedral's *pinacoteca* (picture gallery); ask a priest to let you in.

Facing the cathedral's south side is **Teatro Morelos**, scene of the 1914 Convention of Aguascalientes, in which revolutionary factions led by Pancho Villa, Venustiano

AGUASCALIENTES

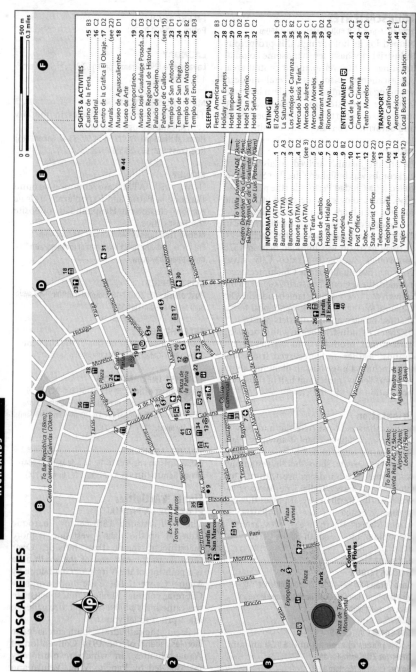

0   500 m
0   0.3 miles

SIGHTS & ACTIVITIES
Casino de la Feria.	**15** B3
Cathedral.	**16** C2
Centro de la Gráfica El Obraje.	**17** D2
Murals.	(see 22)
Museo de Aguascalientes.	**18** D1
Museo de Arte Contemporáneo.	**19** C2
Museo José Guadalupe Posada.	**20** D3
Museo Regional de Historia.	**21** C2
Palacio de Gobierno.	**22** C2
Palenque de Gallos.	(see 15)
Templo de San Antonio.	**23** D1
Templo de San Diego.	**24** C1
Templo de San Marcos.	**25** B2
Templo del Encino.	**26** D3

SLEEPING
Fiesta Americana.	**27** B3
Holiday Inn Express.	**28** C2
Hotel Imperial.	**29** D2
Hotel Maser.	**30** D2
Hotel San Antonio.	**31** D1
Hotel Señorial.	**32** C2

EATING
El Zodiac.	**33** C3
La Saturnina.	**34** A3
Los Antojos de Carranza.	**35** B2
Mercado Jesús Terán.	**36** D2
Mercado Juárez.	(see 3)
Casa Terán.	**37** C1
Mercado Morelos.	**38** D2
Restaurant Mitla.	**39** D2
Rincón Maya.	**40** D4

ENTERTAINMENT
Casa de la Cultura.	**41** C2
Cinemark Cinema.	**42** A3
Teatro Morelos.	**43** C2

TRANSPORT
Aero California.	(see 14)
Aeroméxico.	**44** E1
Local Buses to Bus Station.	**45** C2

INFORMATION
Banamex (ATM).	**1** C2
Bancomer (ATM).	**2** A3
Bancomer (ATM).	**3** B2
Banorte (ATM).	**4** D2
Banorte (ATM).	(see 3)
Casa Terán.	**5** C2
Casa de Cambio.	**6** D2
Hospital Hidalgo.	**7** B2
Internet ZU.	**8** C2
Lavandería.	**9** B2
Money Tron.	**10** C2
Post Office.	**11** C2
Soltec.	**12** C2
State Tourist Office.	(see 22)
Telecomm.	**13** C2
Telephone Caseta.	(see 12)
Vania Turismo.	**14** E1
Viajes Gomzo.	(see 12)

Carranza and Emiliano Zapata attempted unsuccessfully to mend their differences. Busts of these three, plus one of Álvaro Obregón, stand in the foyer, and there are a few exhibits upstairs.

On the plaza's south side, the red- and pink-stone **Palacio de Gobierno** is Aguascalientes' most noteworthy colonial building. Once the mansion of colonial baron Marqués de Guadalupe, it dates from 1665 and has a striking courtyard with a **mural** by the Chilean artist Osvaldo Barra. This depicts the 1914 convention, pointing out that some of its ideas were crystallized in Mexico's still-governing 1917 constitution – including the eight-hour workday. Barra, whose mentor was Diego Rivera, also painted the mural on the south wall, a compendium of the economic and historic forces that forged Aguascalientes (look for the depiction of the Mexico–USA border being drawn).

MUSEO JOSÉ GUADALUPE POSADA

The fascinating **Museo José Guadalupe Posada** (☎ 915-45-56; Jardín El Encino s/n; admission $1, Sun free; ☯ 11am-6pm Tue-Sun) is beside Jardín El Encino. Aguascalientes-native Posada (1852–1913) was in many ways the founder of modern Mexican art. His engravings and satirical cartoons during the Porfiriato dictatorship broadened the audience for art in Mexico, highlighted social problems and was a catalyst in the later mural phase influencing artists like Diego Rivera, José Clemente Orozco and Alfaro David Siqueiros. Posada's hallmark is the *calavera* (skull or skeleton), and many of his *calavera* engravings have been widely reproduced. Less well known are his engravings of current events for periodicals; the series on executions by firing squad conveys the violence of the revolutionary period. The museum has a large collection of Posada prints, each displayed alongside the original etched zinc plate so you can appreciate the demands of the printmaker's art. There's also a permanent exhibition of work by Posada's predecessor Manuel Manilla (1830–90), and temporary exhibitions of works by other Mexican artists.

TEMPLO DEL ENCINO

The **Templo del Encino** (Jardín El Encino; ☯ 11am-1pm & 5-7pm Mon-Fri), beside the Posada museum, contains a black statue of Jesus that some believe is growing. When it reaches an adjacent column, a worldwide calamity is anticipated. The huge *Way of the Cross* murals are also noteworthy. The shady plaza outside makes a nice picnic spot.

MUSEO DE AGUASCALIENTES

Another highly worthwhile stop is the handsome neoclassical **Museo de Aguascalientes** (☎ 915-90-43; Zaragoza 507; admission $1.25, Sun free; ☯ 11am-6pm Tue-Sun). The highlight is a permanent collection of work by the brilliant Mexican artist Saturnino Herrán (1887–1918) of Aguascalientes. Blending a graphic style reminiscent of art nouveau with Impressionistic touches of light and color, his portraits and illustrative work show great technical skill and sensitivity, and are some of the first to honestly depict the Mexican people. The very sensual sculpture *Malgretout* on the patio is a fiberglass copy of the marble original by Jesús Contreras.

TEMPLO DE SAN ANTONIO

Opposite the museum, **Templo de San Antonio** is a crazy quilt of architectural styles built around 1900 by self-taught architect Refugio Reyes. San Antonio's interior is highly ornate, with huge round paintings and intricate decoration highlighted in gold.

MUSEO REGIONAL DE HISTORIA

The **Museo Regional de Historia** (☎ 916-52-28; Av Carranza 118; admission $2.75, Sun free; ☯ 10am-7pm Tue-Sun) was designed by Refugio Reyes as a family home. It has several rooms of exhibits on Aguascalientes' history from the big bang to the *revolución*. It's only really worth checking out if you are a Mexican-history aficionado. There are a couple of nice cafés nearby on the same street.

CONTEMPORARY ARTISTS

The **Museo de Arte Contemporáneo** (☎ 915-79-53; cnr Morelos & Primo Verdad; admission $1, Sun free; ☯ 11am-6pm Tue-Sun), a modern museum displaying the work of Aguascalientes' artists, is well worth a look. Nearby, the **Centro de la Gráfica El Obraje** (☎ 994-00-74; Juan de Montoro 222; ☯ 10am-2pm & 4-8pm Mon-Fri), a workshop-studio-gallery for printmakers and graphic designers, hosts free bimonthly exhibitions.

EXPOPLAZA & AROUND

Half a kilometer west of Plaza de la Patria, via Av López Mateos or Nieto, Expoplaza is a modern shopping center with a **10-screen cinema** (tickets $4). On the mall's south side, the wide and somewhat soulless pedestrian promenade comes alive during the annual Feria de San Marcos (see below). At its west end, the mammoth **Plaza de Toros Monumental** is notable for its modern-colonial treatment of traditional bullring architecture.

On Expoplaza's east side, the pedestrian street Pani runs two blocks north to the 18th-century **Templo de San Marcos** and the shady **Jardín de San Marcos**. Heading east from there along the newly restored Av Carranza, there are a variety of hip new cafés and restaurants (opposite). The **Palenque de Gallos**, in the **Casino de la Feria** building on Pani, is the city's cockfighting arena. Near the northeast corner of Jardín de San Marcos, the **Ex–Plaza de Toros San Marcos**, the old bullring, is now a school for aspiring matadors.

HOT SPRINGS
It's no surprise that a town called Aguascalientes has geothermally heated springs. Relax and lose 200 years at the elegant **Baños Termales de Ojocaliente** (☎ 970-07-21; Tecnológico 102; private baths from $9; ☽ 7am-7pm). The restored 1808 architecture truly turns back the clock.

Nearby the **Centro Deportivo Ojo Caliente** (☎ 970-06-98; Carretera San Luis Potosí Km 1; admission $2.75; ☽ 7am-7pm), on the city's east edge, hosts large park-like grounds with modern facilities including tennis, volleyball and squash courts, and a restaurant. Camping is also available for $5. The communal pools have warmish water; the hot water is in **private pools** (from $4). Take bus 12 along Av López Mateos.

Tours
El Tranvía (adults/child $2.50/1.50), an imitation double-decker trolley car offers three different routes through the city, (three times daily, Tuesday to Sunday, between 10am and 6pm). Get tickets and information on walking tours from the state tourist office (p601).

Festivals & Events
Mexico's biggest annual state fair, **Feria de San Marcos**, centers on Expoplaza and routinely attracts a million visitors with exhibitions, bullfights, cockfights, rodeos, free concerts and an extravaganza of cultural events, including an international film festival. The fair starts in mid-April and lasts nearly a month. The big parade takes place on the saint's day, April 25.

During **Festival de las Calaveras**, from October 25 to November 4, Aguascalientes celebrates Día de los Muertos (Day of the Dead) with an emphasis on the symbolism of *calaveras* (skeletons), as depicted by local-artist Posada in the 19th century.

Sleeping
Prices skyrocket during the Feria de San Marcos and accommodations are completely booked for the fair's final weekend; residents run a lucrative home-stay service at this time. Ask around at the fair or tourist office if you're stuck.

BUDGET
Hotel Maser (☎ 915-35-62; yolandagm@prodigy.net.mx; Juan de Montoro 303; s/d $13/17; Ⓟ) The Maser has helpful management and 47 simple but clean rooms around a covered inner courtyard. The enclosed parking is free but a bit tight, and TV costs a couple of extra dollars.

Hotel San Antonio (☎ 915-93-41, 916-33-20; Zaragoza 305; s/d $16/21; Ⓟ) It's tough to beat this clean, courteous motel, especially if you are driving. The 24/7 drive-through reception window is strict about not admitting 'couples without luggage.' There's cable TV and the beds are firm, but the echoing engine noise from the enclosed courtyard parking lot can make it tough to sleep in.

Villa Juvenil INADE (☎ 970-08-63; cnr Avs Circunvalación Ote & Jaime Nunó; dm $4; Ⓟ Ⓡ) This youth hostel, 3km east of the center, is a cheap and somewhat sterile stay. There are clean separate-sex dormitories and an 11pm curfew. Take bus 20 from the bus station.

Overnight dry RV camping is possible at the Centro Deportivo Ojo Caliente (see left) if you pull in before the gate closes at 7pm.

MIDRANGE
Hotel Señorial (☎ 915-16-30/14-73; cnr Colón & Juan de Montoro; s/d $21/35) This friendly, 40-year-old, family-run hotel has 32 reasonable rooms with cable TV and phone. There's a variety of rooms, and if you like the daylight try for the ones with balconies.

Hotel Imperial (☎ 915-16-64; Calle 5 de Mayo 106; r from $30) The well-located Imperial is a fine-looking building outside, though the lobby and basic rooms are unimpressive. Modern and clean, the rooms have fans, TV and phone. Interior rooms are darker, quieter and cheaper than the exterior ones, some of which have balconies and plaza views.

TOP END

Holiday Inn Express (☎ 916-16-66, 800-009-99-00; hiexp@ags.acnet.net; Nieto 102; r/ste from $123/126; ⊠ ♨) The historic center's most comfortable option has 89 rooms with all the modern conveniences, and full facilities for business travelers. Discounts of 25% are available some weekends.

Fiesta Americana (☎ 918-60-10; www.fiestaamericana.com; Laureles s/n, Colonia Las Flores; r from $139; ℗ ⊠ ♨ ▢ ♨) This luxury chain hotel has 192 rooms and all the amenities, including a fitness center and inviting pool. Weekend rates start at around $90 for two and include brunch.

Quinta Real Aguascalientes (☎ 978-58-18; www.quintareal.com; Av Aguascalientes Sur 601; ste $175-220; ℗ ⊠ ♨ ▢ ♨) This is the slickest option of the luxurious resort-style hotels near the industrial zone on the outskirts of the city.

Eating

Four blocks north of the Plaza de la Patria, fresh produce is available in three markets: Mercado Juárez, Mercado Jesús Terán and Mercado Morelos. The pedestrian street Pani going south to Expoplaza has many bars and fast food options.

La Saturnina (☎ 994-04-49; Carranza 110; mains $3-5; ☽ 8:30am-10:30pm Tue-Sat, 8:30am-6pm Sun, 8:30am-1:30pm Mon) The name is in honor of the women Saturnino Herrán so beautifully painted. Set in an 18th-century former mansion, there are tales of tragic love, and the tormented ghost of the wealthy hacienda-owner's daughter. The ambiance takes you to a more romantic time, and the food is the tastiest and best priced in town.

Restaurant Mitla (☎ 916-61-57; Madero 220; mains $5-14) This large, clean and pleasant restaurant has been going since 1938. It's popular with locals and welcomes foreigners. There's a choice of good-value set breakfasts, four-course set lunches ($5) and a variety of well-prepared local specialties. It's a good place to linger over a coffee or drink.

Los Antojos de Carranza (☎ 953-23-31; Carranza 301; mains $4-8; ⊠) This is a smart place where you can get breakfast, big salads and very

well-prepared regional meat, poultry and fish dishes. It's also a good spot for a drink, and sometimes has live music or sports events on TV.

Rincon Maya (☎ 916-75-74; Abasolo 113; mains $5-10; ☽ 2pm-midnight Mon-Sat, 2-10:30pm Sun) Across the park from the Museo José Guadalupe Posada, this is your best option south of center. Delicious Yucatecan specialties like *cochinita pibil* (pit-style pork) and *sopa de lima* (lime soup).

El Zodiac (☎ 915-31-81; Galeana 113; mains $4-7; ☽ 8am-10:30pm) A variety of Mexican standards from seafood to brochetas, there is something for every sign. Try the mouthwatering *conejo adobado* (battered rabbit).

Entertainment

Pani, the pedestrian street between the Expoplaza and Jardín de San Marcos, is lively most evenings, with a good selection of bars and restaurants.

The trendy nightspots are out in the suburbs; **Centro Comercial Galerías** (☎ 912-66-12; Independencia 2351) is a shopping mall with several bars and discos, including the popular El Reloj, while the main drag for late-night discos is north of town on Av Colosio. Grab a cab for '80s' music at **República Bar** (☎ 914-56-15; Colosio 324; ☽ 10pm-3am Thu-Sat).

In a fine 17th-century building, the **Casa de la Cultura** (☎ 910-20-10; Carranza 101; ☽ 9am-2pm & 5-8pm Mon-Sat, gallery 9am-9pm daily) hosts art exhibitions, concerts, theater and dance events. The **Teatro Morelos** (☎ 915-19-41; Nieto 113 Plaza de la Patria) and the **Teatro de Aguascalientes** (☎ 978-54-14; cnr Chávez & Aguascalientes), south of the center, both stage a variety of cultural events. Free concerts, dance and theater are presented some Sunday lunchtimes in the courtyard of Museo José Guadalupe Posada (see p603).

Getting There & Away

AIR

Aéropuerto Jesús Terán (☎ 915-28-06) is 26km south of Aguascalientes off the road to Mexico City. Aeroméxico has daily direct flights to Guadalajara, Mexico City, Monterrey and Tijuana, plus direct flights to/from Los Angeles and New York. Aero California serves Guadalajara, Mexico City and Tijuana. Continental has daily flights to Houston and Los Angeles, and American flies daily to Dallas.

Airline offices include the following:

Aero California (☎ 918-76-16; Juan de Montoro 204)
Aeroméxico (☎ 442-14-80; Madero 474)

BUS

The bus station (Central Camionera) is 2km south of the center on Av Circunvalación Sur (aka Av Convención). It has a post office, card phones, a cafeteria and luggage storage.

Daily departures:

Destination	Price	Duration	Frequency
Guadalajara	$23	2½-4hr	4 deluxe ETN
	$18	2½-4hr	hourly 1st-class Primer Plus
	$16	2½-4hr	hourly Ómnibus de México & Futura
Guanajuato	$13	3hr	1 1st-class de paso Primera Plus 8pm
	$11	3hr	1 2nd-class Flecha Amarilla 6:45am, plus more-frequent services from León
León	$10	2hr	hourly 1st-class Primera Plus
	$7	2hr	2nd-class Flecha Amarilla half-hourly
Mexico City (Terminal Norte)	$47	6hr	6 deluxe ETN 1st-class daily
	$37	6hr	9 Primer Plus
	$35	6hr	hourly Futura & Ómnibus de México
	$30	6hr	5 2nd-class Flecha Amarilla
San Luis Potosí	$12	3hr	14 1st-class Futura
	$10	3hr	hourly 2nd-class Estrella Blanca
Zacatecas	$8.50	2hr	9 Transporte del Norte
	$8	2hr	13 1st-class Ómnibus de México & Futura
	$7	2hr	hourly 2nd-class Estrella Blanca

Plus there's frequent service to Ciudad Juárez, Monterrey, Morelia and Torreón, and two buses daily to San Miguel de Allende ($12).

Getting Around

Most places of interest are within easy walking distance of each other. Regular city buses ($0.40) run from 6am to 10:30pm;

red buses ($0.50) are more comfortable and follow the same routes.

Buses 3, 4 and 9 (marked 'Centro' or '5 de Mayo') run from the bus station to the city center. Get off at the first stop after the tunnel under Plaza de la Patria, on Calle 5 de Mayo or Rivero y Gutiérrez. From the city center to the bus station, take any 'Central' bus on Moctezuma opposite the cathedral's north side, or around the corner on Galeana.

Within town and to the bus station, the standard taxi fare is $2.75; to the airport it's about $15.

SAN LUIS POTOSÍ STATE

There are two major destinations of interest on the western expanse of the San Luis Potosí state: the historic capital city of San Luis Potosí and the ghost town Real de Catorce. A climatically diverse state, the majority of San Luis Potosí (poh-toh-see; population 2.4 million) is high and dry, with little rainfall. The exception is its eastern corner, which drops steeply to the tropical valleys near the Gulf coast.

Before the Spanish conquest, western San Luis Potosí was inhabited by warlike hunters and gatherers known as Guachichiles, the Aztec word for 'sparrows,' after their widespread custom of wearing only loincloths and, sometimes, pointed headdresses resembling sparrows' heads.

In the 18th century the area gained a reputation for maltreatment of indigenous people. This was partly because new clergy replaced the more compassionate Franciscans, who had tried to protect and educate indigenous people. Appalling labor conditions and discontent over expulsion of the Franciscans culminated in an uprising in 1767.

Today it's a fairly prosperous state. The northern silver mines are some of Mexico's richest, and gold, copper, lead and zinc are also extracted. Agriculture (corn, beans, wheat and cotton) and ranching are other major sources of wealth, as is industry, which is concentrated in the capital.

SAN LUIS POTOSÍ

☎ 444 / pop 678,000 / elevation 1860m

Once a major colonial city, the state capital has also been a center for mining, governments in exile, and a revolutionary hotbed. Now it's important as a regional capital and industrial center. Flat and laid out in an orderly grid, San Luis is less spectacular than colonial cities like Guanajuato and Zacatecas, but don't be deterred by the industrial outskirts: there is an abundance of pedestrian streets, open plazas and exquisite colonial buildings at its core. It is a university town, with an active nightlife and an air of cultural elegance, boasting an impressive colonial theater and numerous museums.

History

Founded in 1592, 20km west of the silver deposits in Cerro de San Pedro, San Luis is named Potosí after the immensely rich Bolivian silver town of that name, which the Spanish hoped it would rival.

The mines began to decline in the 1620s, but the city was well enough established as a ranching center to remain the major city of northeastern Mexico until overtaken by Monterrey at the start of the 20th century.

Known in the 19th century for its lavish houses and imported luxury goods, San Luis was twice the seat of President Benito Juárez' government during the 1860s' French intervention. In 1910 in San Luis, the dictatorial president Porfirio Díaz jailed Francisco Madero, his liberal opponent, during the presidential campaign. Freed after the election, Madero hatched his Plan de San Luis Potosí (a strategy to depose Díaz), announcing it in San Antonio, Texas in October 1910; he declared the election illegal, named Madero provisional president and designated November 20 as the day for Mexico to rise in revolt.

Orientation

Central San Luis stretches east from Alameda park (east) to Plaza de los Fundadores and Plaza San Francisco (west). This triangle has two more main plazas, Plaza del Carmen and the Plaza de Armas. Hotels and restaurants concentrate in the center, with cheaper lodgings near the old train station. An upscale commercial strip goes 3km west from Plaza de los Fundadores along Av Carranza.

Information

INTERNET ACCESS

Most places charge around $1 per hour.
Café Cibernetico (Av Carranza 416) Fast connections, good coffee.
Café Internet de la Paz (Guerrero 269)

LAUNDRY

Lavandería (Calle 5 de Mayo 870; 3kg $2.75)

EMERGENCY

Ambulance, Fire & Police (☎ 066)

MEDICAL SERVICES

Hospital Central (☎ 834-27-00, 834-27-01; Carranza 2395)
Red Cross (☎ 815-3635)

MONEY

Banks with ATMs are scattered around the Plaza de Armas and Plaza de los Fundadores. Several *casas de cambio* are along Morelos.
Banamex (cnr Obregón & Allende) Like other banks, changes cash and traveler's checks.

POST OFFICE

Post office (☎ 812-72-86; cnr Morelos & Ortega; ☽ 8am-2pm Mon-Fri)

TELEPHONE

There are many card phones in the center.
Telecomm (south side Plaza del Carmen)

TOURIST INFORMATION

Municipal tourist office (☎ 812-27-70; www.vive sanluispotosi.gob.mx; Palacio Municipal, east side of Plaza de Armas; ☎ 8am-8:30pm Mon-Fri, sometimes 8am-7:30pm Sat)
State tourist office (☎ 812-99-39, 800 343-38-87; www.descubresanluispotosi.com; Obregón 520; ☎ 8am-9pm Mon-Fri, 9am-2pm Sat) Has maps and brochures with lots of ideas for getting off the beaten track in San Luis Potosí state.

TRAVEL AGENCIES

2001 Viajes (☎ 812-29-53; Obregón 604)
Grey Line Turimex (☎ 814-17-56; Obregón 650)

Sights

PLAZA DE ARMAS & AROUND

Also known as Jardín Hidalgo, this plaza is the city's central square. It's fairly quiet as traffic is channeled away from it.

The three-nave baroque **cathedral**, built between 1660 and 1730, is on the plaza's east side. Originally it had just one tower; the northern tower was added in the 20th century. The marble apostles on the facade are replicas of statues in Rome's San Juan de Letrán basilica. The interior, remodeled in the 19th century, has a Gothic feel with sweeping arches carved in pink stone; the

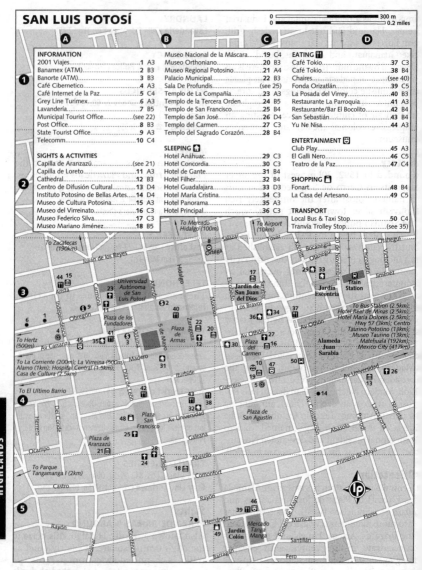

SAN LUIS POTOSÍ

INFORMATION
2001 Viajes..**1** A3
Banamex (ATM)....................................**2** B3
Banorte (ATM).....................................**3** B3
Café Cibernetico..................................**4** A3
Café Internet de la Paz.........................**5** C4
Grey Line Turimex................................**6** A3
Lavandería..**7** B5
Municipal Tourist Office..................(see 22)
Post Office...**8** B3
State Tourist Office...............................**9** A3
Telecomm..**10** C4

SIGHTS & ACTIVITIES
Capilla de Aranzazú..........................(see 21)
Capilla de Loreto...............................**11** A3
Cathedral...**12** B3
Centro de Difusión Cultural................**13** D4
Instituto Potosino de Bellas Artes......**14** D4
Museo de Cultura Potosina................**15** A3
Museo del Virreinato.........................**16** C3
Museo Federico Silva.........................**17** C3
Museo Mariano Jiménez....................**18** B5

Museo Nacional de la Máscara.........**19** C4
Museo Orthoniano.............................**20** B3
Museo Regional Potosino..................**21** A4
Palacio Municipal...............................**22** B3
Sala De Profundis..............................(see 25)
Templo de La Compañía.....................**23** A3
Templo de la Tercera Orden..............**24** B5
Templo de San Francisco...................**25** B4
Templo de San José............................**26** D4
Templo del Carmen...........................**27** C3
Templo del Sagrado Corazón.............**28** B4

SLEEPING
Hotel Anáhuac...................................**29** C3
Hotel Concordia.................................**30** C4
Hotel de Gante..................................**31** B4
Hotel Filher.......................................**32** B4
Hotel Guadalajara..............................**33** D3
Hotel María Cristina...........................**34** C3
Hotel Panorama.................................**35** A3
Hotel Principal...................................**36** C3

EATING
Café Tokio..**37** C3
Café Tokio..**38** B4
Chaires...(see 40)
Fonda Orizatlán.................................**39** C5
La Posada del Virrey..........................**40** B3
Restaurante La Parroquia...................**41** A4
Restaurante/Bar El Bocolito...............**42** B4
San Sebastián....................................**43** B4
Yu Ne Nisa..**44** A3

ENTERTAINMENT
Club Play...**45** A3
El Galli Nero......................................**46** C5
Teatro de la Paz................................**47** C4

SHOPPING
Fonart..**48** B4
La Casa del Artesano..........................**49** C5

TRANSPORT
Local Bus & Taxi Stop.........................**50** C4
Tranvía Trolley Stop...........................(see 35)

leaf motif on the arches is repeated in blue and gold on the ceiling.

Beside the cathedral, the 19th-century **Palacio Municipal** is a stocky building with powerful stone arches. Finished in 1838, it was the home of Bishop Ignacio Montes de Oca from 1892 to 1915. In the rear of the building's patio is a stone fountain carved

with the heads of three lions. The city's coat of arms in stained glass overlooks a double staircase.

Behind the cathedral, the **Museo Otho-niano** (☎ 812-74-12; Av Othón 225; admission $0.30; ☼ 10am-2pm & 4-6pm Tue-Sun) is the birthplace of a much celebrated Mexican poet, Manuel José Othón (1858–1906). The 19th-century home is furnished in period style and exhibits include some of Othón's manuscripts and personal effects.

The neoclassical **Palacio de Gobierno**, built between 1798 and 1816, lines the plaza's west side. Numerous important Mexicans have lodged here, but its most illustrious occupant was Benito Juárez – first in 1863 when he was fleeing from invading French forces, then in 1867 when he confirmed the death sentence on French puppet-emperor Maximilian. The palace is open during business hours; go left at the top of the stairs and ask a custodian to open the Salón de Juárez.

PLAZA DE LOS FUNDADORES & AROUND

The busy Plaza de los Fundadores (Founders' Plaza; aka Plaza Juárez) is where the city was born. On the north side is a large building housing offices of the Universidad Autónoma de San Luis Potosí. It was probably on this site that Diego de la Magdalena, a Franciscan friar, started a small settlement of Guachichiles around 1585. The building, which has a lovely courtyard, was constructed in 1653 as a Jesuit college.

To the west of these offices is the **Templo de la Compañía**, built by the Jesuits in 1675 with a baroque facade. A little further west is the **Capilla de Loreto**, a Jesuit chapel from 1700 with unusual twisted pillars.

Northwest of the plaza, the **Museo de Cultura Potosina** (☎ 812-18-33; Arista 340; adult/child $0.50/0.30; ☽ 10am-2pm & 4-6pm Tue-Fri, 10am-2pm Sat & Sun) has models and dioramas explaining the city's history, mainly for children.

PLAZA SAN FRANCISCO & AROUND

Dominated by its namesake church's bulk, this quiet square is one of the city's most fetching.

The interior of the 17th- and 18th-century **Templo de San Francisco** was remodeled in the 20th century, but the sacristy (the priest's dressing room), reached by a door to the right of the altar, is original and has a fine dome and carved pink stone. The **Sala De Profundis**, through the arch at the south end of the sacristy, has more paintings and a carved stone fountain. A beautiful crystal ship hangs from the main dome.

Along the street to the west of Templo de San Francisco, the **Museo Regional Potosino** ☎ 814-35-72; Galeana 450; admission $2.50, Sun free;

☽ 10am-7pm Tue-Sat, 10am-5pm Sun) was originally part of a Franciscan monastery founded in 1590. The ground floor has exhibits on pre-Hispanic Mexico, especially the indigenous people of the Huasteca. Upstairs is the lavish **Capilla de Aranzazú**, an elaborate private chapel for the monks constructed in the mid-18th century.

The small **Templo de la Tercera Orden** and **Templo del Sagrado Corazón**, both formerly part of the Franciscan monastery, stand together at the plaza's south end. Tercera Orden was finished in 1694 and restored in 1960. Sagrado Corazón dates from 1728–31.

A couple of blocks south and west of the plaza, the free **Museo Mariano Jiménez** (Museo de las Revoluciónes; ☎ 814-73-93; Calle 5 de Mayo 610; ☽ 10am-2pm & 4-6pm Tue-Fri, 9am-3pm Sat, 10am-2pm Sun) covers some of the most dramatic events in Mexican history. It has a rebellion theme and a good account of indigenous resistance to the Spanish conquest.

PLAZA DEL CARMEN

Plaza del Carmen is dominated by San Luis' most spectacular structure, the Churrigueresque **Templo del Carmen** (1749–64). On the vividly carved stone facade, hovering angels show the touch of indigenous artisans. The Camarín de la Virgen, with a splendid golden altar, is to the left of the main altar inside. The entrance and roof of this chapel are a riot of small plaster figures.

Beside the Templo de Carmen is the **Museo del Virreinato** (☎ 816-52-57; Villerías 155; admission $2; ☽ Tue-Fri 10am-7pm, 10am-5pm Sat & Sun), which has a large collection of paintings and artifacts from the Spanish vice-regency. Displaying the enormous wealth of the elite class, the museum holds little interest except for the enormous proliferation of keys.

Near the church, the neoclassical **Teatro de la Paz** (1889–94) contains a concert hall and exhibition gallery as well as a theater. Posters announce upcoming events.

The **Museo Nacional de la Máscara** (National Mask Museum; ☎ 812-30-25; Plaza del Carmen; admission $0.50; ☽ 10am-2pm & 5-7pm Tue-Fri, 10am-2pm Sat & Sun) is a distinguished 19th-century neoclassical building on the plaza's south side. Inside, 2000 ceremonial masks from all over Mexico are displayed with explanations of the dances and rituals in which they are used. Look for the *gigantes* (papier-mâché giants).

NORTHERN CENTRAL HIGHLANDS

PLAZA DE SAN JUAN DE DIOS

Transformed once again, the original 17th-century building on the north side of the Jardín de San Juan de Dios now houses the **Museo Federico Silva** (☎ 812-38-48; museofedericosilva@prodigy.net.mx; Obregón 80; admission $2; 10am-6pm Mon & Wed-Sat, 10am-2pm Sun). The building, once a hospital and later a school under *el porfiriato* (Porfiriato period), has been exquisitely transformed into a contemporary art museum. The building's previous neoclassical finish, was integrated well with the monolithic sculpture of Silva. There are also rotating exhibitions of internationally known contemporary sculptors and an excellent bookstore.

ALAMEDA & AROUND

The **Alameda Juan Sarabia** marks the eastern boundary of the downtown area. It used to be the vegetable garden of the monastery attached to the Templo del Carmen. Today it's a large, attractive park with shady paths.

Inside the **Templo de San José**, facing the Alameda's south side, lies the image of El Señor de los Trabajos, a Christ figure attracting pilgrims from near and far. Numerous *retablos* (altarpieces) around the statue testify to prayers answered in finding jobs, regaining health and passing exams.

The **Instituto Potosino de Bellas Artes** (☎ 822-12-06; cnr Av Universidad & Constitución; gallery 10am-1pm & 4-7:30pm Mon-Fri), a modern building in 'neo-indigenous' architectural style, hosts art exhibitions and performances. Two blocks east, the **Centro de Difusión Cultural** (☎ 812-43-33; cnr Av Universidad & Negrete; galleries 10am-2pm & 5-8pm Mon-Sat) is another interesting example of modern Mexican architecture, with a shape inspired by a spiral seashell. Inside, art galleries show changing contemporary exhibitions.

Just over the railway bridge east of the Alameda is the **Centro Taurino Potosino**, comprising the 7000-seat Plaza de Toros (bullring) and the **Museo Taurino** (☎ 822-15-01; cnr Universidad & Triana; noon-2:30pm & 5-8pm Mon-Sat, Sun bullfight days), a bullfighting museum displaying intricately decorated matador suits, historical posters, stuffed bulls' heads and more.

PARQUE TANGAMANGA I

This 3.3-sq-km **park** (Blvd Diagonal Sur), 2km southwest of the center, has a planetarium, outdoor theater, amusement park and acres of green open spaces. Inside the park, the **Museo de las Culturas Populares** (☎ 817-29-76; admission $0.25; 9am-4pm Tue-Sun) exhibits typical crafts and clothing from around the state, with some good pieces for sale. To get to the park, take a southbound 'Perimetral' bus, or bus 25 or 26, from the Alameda's west end.

Tours

The **Tranvía** (☎ 814-22-26), an imitation of an antique trolley, does a one-hour loop ($4) around the historic center, starting from Hotel Panorama (opposite). A few of the drivers speak English; ask when you purchase tickets.

Festivals & Events

Semana Santa Holy Week is celebrated with concerts, exhibitions and other activities; on Good Friday morning, Christ's passion is re-enacted in the barrio of San Juan de Guadalupe, followed by a silent procession through the city.

Festival Internacional de Danza This national festival of contemporary dance is held in the last two weeks of July.

Feria Nacional Potosina San Luis' National Fair, normally in the last two weeks of August, includes concerts, bullfights, rodeos, cockfights and agricultural shows.

Día de San Luis Rey de Francia On August 25 the city's patron saint, St Louis IX (king of France) is honored as the highlight of the Feria Nacional. Events include a large parade with floats and *gigantes*.

Sleeping

You'll enjoy San Luis more if you choose a hotel in the pedestrianized center, away from the traffic and among the attractive architecture.

BUDGET

Hotel de Gante (☎ 812-14-92/93; hotel_degante@hotmail.com; Calle 5 de Mayo 140; r $28-33) In the best location, Gante has spacious rooms along Madero with views overlooking the Plaza de Armas. They cost a bit more but are better than the interior rooms, which are stuffier and dark.

Hotel Principal (☎ 812-07-84; principal_hotelslp@hotmail.com; Sarabia 145; s/d $15/25) Three blocks east of the central plazas, the popular Principal has 18 reasonable rooms and a convenient location. It is far and away the best value in town.

NORTHERN CENTRAL HIGHLANDS

Other recommendations:

Hotel Guadalajara (☎ 812-46-12; Jiménez 253; s/d $26/33; Ⓟ) Facing a small plaza off a pedestrian street.

Hotel Anáhuac (☎ 812-65-05; Xóchitl 140; s/d $22/26; Ⓟ) Basic rooms are clean and comfortable.

MIDRANGE

Hotel Panorama (☎ 812-17-77, 800-480-01-00; www .hotelpanorama.com.mx; Av Carranza 315; r with/without air-con $72/61; Ⓟ ⓧ ▣ ⓡ) All 126 comfy rooms at this smart, service-oriented hotel opposite the Plaza de los Fundadores have floor-to-ceiling windows. Superior ones on the south side have private balconies overlooking the pool. A marble-clad lobby and piano bar make it popular with business travelers.

Hotel Filher (☎ 812-15-62; hotelfilher@hotmail .com; Av Universidad 375; s/d $37/41; Ⓟ) Just off the pedestrian street Zaragoza, this hotel has a historic feel and a grand staircase rising up from its interior courtyard. The rooms are clean and modern. Definitely try for a balcony overlooking Zaragoza.

Hotel María Cristina (☎ 812-94-08, 800-087-07-95; www.mariacristina.com.mx; Sarabia 110; s $49, d $61-69; Ⓟ ▣) A block northwest of the Alameda, the modern María Cristina caters to business travelers with a restaurant and bright carpeted rooms with cable TV, fan and phone. Some rooms have great city views.

Hotel Concordia (☎ 812-06-66, 800-711-13-18; concordia@prodigy.net.mx; cnr Avs Othón & Morelos; s/d $47/54; Ⓟ) The modernized Concordia occupies an old building and its 96 carpeted rooms all have cable TV and other amenities. Exterior rooms are nicer than interior ones.

TOP END

There are several upscale places that are east of the city fronting the highway near the bus station.

Hotel Real de Minas (☎ 449-84-00, 800-480-39-00; www.realdeminasdesanluis.com; Carretera 57 Km 426.6; r/ ste $110/120; Ⓟ ⓧ ▣ ⓡ) The best of the big hotels outside of the center has landscaped grounds, a 24-hour restaurant and 170 rooms with satellite TV. The chain offers heavily discounted promo rates (up to 50% off) when it's not full of conventioneers.

Hotel María Dolores (☎ 816-36-86, 800-480-16-00; Carretera 57 Km 1; s/d $82/91; Ⓟ ⓧ ⓡ) Opposite the bus station, this modern, motel-style place has a nightclub, bar, restaurant and 213 fully equipped rooms. Rack rates are often halved, making it a good deal.

Eating

One local specialty is *tacos potosinos* – tacos stuffed with chopped potato, carrots, lettuce and loads of *queso blanco* (white cheese), then smothered in *salsa roja* (red sauce). For the lowdown on SLP's upscale eateries, ask the tourist office for the booklet *Guía de Restaurantes*, which includes many interesting options outside the city center.

CITY CENTER

Fonda Orizatlán (☎ 814-67-86; Hernández 240; mains $5-9; Ⓨ 8am-11pm Mon-Thu, 8am-12:30am Fri & Sat, 8am-7pm Sun) Eight blocks south of the center, Fonda Orizatlán is locally renowned for its first-class Huasteca-style cuisine. Thursday, Friday and Saturday nights feature folkloric dances, and a buffet spread appears all day Sunday.

La Posada del Virrey (☎ 812-32-80; Jardín Hidalgo 3; mains $4-10) On Plaza de Armas' north side, the former home of Spanish viceroys dates from 1736. A social setting, some lunchtimes have live music playing in the attractive, covered courtyard. Breakfast specials are available as well as a set lunch and generous surf-and-turf meals, though most of the menu is unadventurous Mexican fare.

Chaires (☎ 811-32-91; Anáhuac 480; dishes $2-4) Next door on the Plaza de Armas is the best ice creamery and café. Indulge in their homemade ice cream and brownies while sipping coffee and surveying the local scene.

Restaurante La Parroquia (☎ 812-66-81; Av Carranza 303; mains $5-8) A popular place with *potosinos*, this restaurant has big windows looking onto Plaza de los Fundadores. It offers a four-course *comida corrida* and many à la carte dishes, including *cabrito* (kid) and *enchiladas potosinas*. A huge buffet spread appears at breakfast on Saturday and Sunday.

Yu Ne Nisa (☎ 814-36-31; Arista 350-60; mains $2.50 -5; ☎ 9:30am-6pm Mon-Sat, store until 8:30pm; Ⓥ) This small vegetarian restaurant and health-food shop offers healthy snacks – sandwiches, *gorditas* (fried tortilla topped with cheese) and soyburgers – plus mouth-watering smoothies. It also does a set lunch for $5.

Restaurante/Bar El Bocolito (☎ 812-76-94; Guerrero 2; mains $2.50-6.50) An interesting option with a friendly atmosphere is this restaurant facing charming Plaza San Francisco. It serves up huge platters of Huasteca-style food, with dishes like *mula india* (meat fried up with herbs and cheese). It also offers cheap breakfasts, tasty tacos and a $4 set lunch. It's a cooperative venture benefiting indigenous businesses, and features live music Thursday to Saturday from 9pm.

San Sebastián (☎ 814-69-20; Guerrero 555; mains $1-3; ☑ 7:30am-10pm) A central eatery with tasty breakfasts and traditional *antojitos* (tortilla-based snacks) for dirt cheap. The place is clean and to the point; also try the adequate buffet.

Café Tokio (☎ 814-61-89; cnr Zaragoza & Guerrero; mains $3-5; Original branch (☎ 812-58-99; Othón 415; ☒) A bright and sizable café with no trace of Japanese influence. Rather, it serves up Mexican and fast-food standards, and is popular for a cheap set lunch or late-night snack. The original branch faces the Alameda and is popular for ice cream or coffee after a stroll in the park.

AV CARRANZA
There's a growing selection of both hip and upscale restaurants west of the center along Av Carranza ('La Avenida').

La Corriente (☎ 812-93-04; Av Carranza 700; mains $5-10; ☑ 8am-midnight Mon-Sat, 8am-6pm Sun) One of the most attractive restaurants in town, La Corriente is found 400m west of Plaza de los Fundadores, at the start of the La Avenida strip. It specializes in regional and ranch-style food, which is presented either in an elegant dining room or a delightfully plant-filled courtyard. A good four-course set lunch ($5) is served Monday to Saturday and there is a live salsa band on the weekends from 10:30pm.

La Virreina (☎ 812-37-50; Av Carranza 830; mains $7-14; ☑ 1pm-midnight) A long-established gourmet favorite, the Virreina has a classic menu including both international and Mexican dishes, award-winning desserts and an excellent reputation.

Entertainment
San Luis has quite an active cultural scene. Ask in the tourist office about what's on and keep your eye out for posters. The free monthly *Guiarte* booklet and posters detail cultural attractions.

For a night of dancing, San Luis is steeped in Latin rhythms, but lacks more modern, cutting edge music. If you like salsa, then you are in luck. On the weekend grab your partner

and head to **El Galli Nero** (☎ 812-15-32; Hernández 210; cover $5; ☑ 10pm-2am) or La Corriente (left) to swing to live Caribbean music.

Within walking distance of the center on Av Carranza, it's hard to miss the lines behind the velvet rope outside **Club Play** (☎ 812-56-92; Carranza 333; ☑ 11pm-3am). Other popular discos, bars and music venues are found further west along Av Carranza and Himenez. Try **El Ultimo Barrio** (☎ 812-38-73; Jimenez 380A; cover $5; ☑ 9pm-3am) for live rock and pop covers.

The neoclassical, 1500-seat **Teatro de la Paz** (☎ 812-52-09; Villerias 2) presents a variety of local and visiting dance, theater and music ensembles most nights, and Sunday around noon. The **Orquesta Sinfónica** (☎ 814-36-01; tickets from $10) brings symphony to the theater in September and October. Concerts, theater, exhibitions and cultural events are also presented at places like the Teatro de la Ciudad, an open-air theater in Parque Tangamanga I, and the **Casa de la Cultura** (☎ 813-22-47; Carranza 1815), 2½km west of Plaza de los Fundadores.

Shopping
The main shopping district is between the Plaza de Armas and the Mercado Hidalgo. A few blocks further northeast is the larger, interesting Mercado República. Milky sweets are a local specialty and can be found in the markets and at shops along Av Carranza.

Fonart (☎ 812-39-98; Plaza San Francisco 6, ☑ 9am-2pm & 4-7pm Mon-Fri, 10am-5:30pm Sat) Like other shops in the government-run chain, this outlet has a good selection of quality handicrafts from all over Mexico.

La Casa del Artesano (☎ 814-89-90; Jardín Colon 23) For more local products try this shop full of *potosino* pottery, masks, woodwork and canework.

Getting There & Away
AIR
Aéropuerto Ponciano Arriaga (☎ 822-00-95) is 10km north of the city off Hwy 57. Aerolitoral offers direct service to/from Monterrey with connecting flights to San Antonio Texas and Mexico City. Aeromar serves Mexico City several times daily.

Airline offices:

Aerolitoral (☎ 822-22-29; airport)
Aeromar (☎ 817-79-36; Carranza 1030)

BUS

The **Terminal Terrestre Potosina** (TTP; ☎ 816-45-96; Carretera 57, 2½km east of the center, is a busy transport hub with deluxe, 1st-class and some 2nd-class bus services. Facilities available include card phones, a telephone *caseta*, 24-hour luggage storage and two cafés.

Daily departures:

Destination	Price	Duration	Frequency
Guadalajara	$31	5–6hr	10 deluxe ETN
	$21	5–6hr	12 1st-class Transportes del Norte
	$24	5–6hr	8 2nd-class Estrella Blanca
Guanajuato	$12.50	4hr	5 2nd-class Flecha Amarilla
Matehuala	$11.50	2½hr	hourly 1st-class Sendor
	$10	2½hr	hourly 2nd-class Estrella Blanca
Mexico City (Terminal Norte)	$36	5–6hr	12 deluxe ETN daily
	$29	5–6hr	frequent 1st-class Primera Plus & Ómnibus de México
	$24	5–6hr	8 2nd-class Flecha Amarilla
Monterrey	$45	7hr	2 deluxe ETN
	$34	7hr	hourly 1st-class Transporte del Norte & Futura
	$27	7hr	12 2nd-class Estrella Blanca
Querétaro	$18	2½–3½hr	3 deluxe ETN
	$14	3½hr	frequent 1st-class Primer Plus, Futura & Ómnibus de México
	$11	2½–3½hr	2nd-class Flecha Amarilla
San Miguel de Allende	$11	4hr	6 1st-class Flecha Amarilla
Tampico	$26	7–8hr	2 1st-class Oriente, Ómnibus de México or Futura
	$24	7–8hr	14 2nd-class Vencedor or Oriente
Zacatecas	$10.50	3hr	hourly 1st-class Ómnibus de México
	$10	3hr	2nd-class Estrella Blanca

Daily buses go to Aguascalientes, Ciudad Juárez, Ciudad Valles, Ciudad Victoria, Chihuahua, Dolores Hidalgo, León, Morelia, Nuevo Laredo, Saltillo and Torreón.

CAR & MOTORCYCLE

Car-rental prices range between $50 and $85 per day, and motorcycles are about $35. Vans and weeklong packages are also available.
Alamo(☎ 822-83-20; Av Carranza 1415)
Hertz (☎ 812-32-29; Obregón 670)

Getting Around

Taxis charge around $11 for the half-hour trip to/from the airport.

To reach the center from the bus station, exit, turn left, take the footbridge over the busy road, and take any 'Centro' bus. Bus 5, 'Central TTP,' is the most direct. A convenient place to get off is on the Alameda, outside the train station. A booth in the bus station sells taxi tickets ($3) to the center.

From the center to the bus station, take any 'Central TTP' bus southbound on Av Constitución from the Alameda's west side.

City buses run from 6:30am to 10:30pm. The basic *blanco* (white) buses cost $0.35; the better ones, in various colors, cost $0.40. For places along Av Carranza, catch a 'Morales' or 'Carranza' bus in front of the train station.

MATEHUALA

☎ 488 / pop 68,000 / elevation 1600m
The only town of any size on Hwy 57 between Saltillo and San Luis Potosí, Matehuala is an unremarkable but pleasant place high on the Altiplano Central. It was founded in the 17th century but has little left in the way of colonial charm. Most travelers just use it to get to Real de Catorce (see p614).

Hwy 57 bypasses the town to the east. There is a large parabolic 'arch of welcome' at each end of town – the arches are something of a Matehuala trademark. One wonders, did they come before or after the infamous fast-food chain?

Orientation & Information

Central Matehuala lies between two plazas: the shady Plaza de Armas and the bustling Placita del Rey 300m to the north, with its neo-Gothic–neoclassical cathedral. Cheaper hotels and the town's restaurants are in this area. Between the center and Hwy 57 is the shady Parque Vicente Guerrero.

NORTHERN CENTRAL HIGHLANDS

The bus station is found just west of the highway, 2km south of the center. To walk to the center, turn left out of the bus station and go straight along Av 5 de Mayo for 1½km, then turn left on Insurgentes for a few blocks to reach the Plaza de Armas.

The English-speaking **tourist office** (☎ 882-50-05; Carretera 57 Km 617), on the highway at Las Palmas Midway Inn, is a fount of information about San Luis Potosí state.

All essential services (ATMs, phones, Internet etc) are easily found around the main plazas.

Sleeping & Eating

Hotel María Esther (☎ 882-07-14; Madero 111; s/d $19/22; **P**) This family-run place has rooms facing the plant-filled second patio out back behind the restaurant. It's a block north and a block west of Placita del Rey.

Hotel Matehuala (☎ 882-06-80; cnr Bustamante & Hidalgo; s/d $21/24) Sleep in the most atmospheric place, with high ceilings and dark rooms, set around a large, covered courtyard. It's somewhat overpriced but convenient for buses to Real de Catorce, and they may give a discount. It's half a block north of the Plaza de Armas.

Hotel Álamo (☎ 882-00-17; Guerrero 116A; s/d $14/19) Located around a simple courtyard, the rooms are small, very clean and slightly brighter than Hotel Matehuala. Álamo is also convenient for buses to Real de Catorce.

Las Palmas Midway Inn (☎ 882-00-01/02; www .laspalmas.netfirms.com; Carretera 57 Km 617; s/d $66/75, RV sites $24; **P** 🅿 🖳 🐕 ♿) Out by the highway, this family-oriented place has nice rooms around landscaped gardens with a pool, mini-golf and a level trailer park with full hookups.

Restaurant Santa Fe (☎ 882-07-53; Morelos 709; mains $3-6.50) Facing shady Plaza de Armas, this long-standing local favorite is big, clean and has reasonable prices.

Restaurant Fontella (☎ 882-02-93; Morelos 618; mains $2.70-4.50) Located just north of the plaza Fontella does a solid, four-course *comida corrida* ($4) and has interesting regional dishes.

Getting There & Around

Frequent 1st- and 2nd-class buses head north and south, but Matehuala is mid-route so they may not have seats available.

Daily departures:

Destination	Price	Duration	Frequency
Mexico City			
(Terminal Norte)	$39	7½-8hr	8 1st-class direct
	$33	8hr	2 2nd-class *de paso*
Monterrey	$20	5hr	14 1st-class
	$16	5hr	4 2nd-class
Saltillo	$17	3hr	3 1st-class
	$15	3hr	frequent 2nd-class
San Luis Potosí	$11.50	2hr	hourly 1st-class
	$10	2 hr	hourly 2nd-class

Infrequent beige buses marked 'Centro' run from the bus station to the town center; buses marked 'Central' go the other way. Depending on your load, it can be quicker to walk. A taxi costs about $2.50.

TO/FROM REAL DE CATORCE

Sendor runs 1st-class buses from Matehuala's bus station to Real de Catorce ($4, two hours) at 8am, 10am, noon, 2pm and 6pm, with an extra departure at 6am on festival days; the bus can be caught in town about 15 minutes later on Guerrero, a little east of and across the street from Hotel Álamo on Méndez. Upon arrival in Matehuala, ask if you need to buy a ticket to Real in advance, and whether you can catch the bus in town the next day. If you buy a round-trip ticket, note the time stated for the return journey; readers have reported difficulty getting on a bus at a different time.

REAL DE CATORCE

☎ 488 / pop 1500 / elevation 2756m

This reawakening ghost town radiates magic. High on the fringes of the Sierra Madre Oriental, it was a wealthy silver-mining town of 40,000 people until early last century. Not long ago, it was nearly deserted, its cobblestone streets lined with crumbling buildings, its mint a ruin and a few hundred people eking out an existence from the annual influx of pilgrims, and old mine tailings.

Recently, Real has begun to attract trendier residents – well-to-do Mexicans and gringos looking for an unusual retreat. Artists have set up shop in restored old buildings, and filmmakers love the light in the surrounding hills. One day Real may become another Taxco or San Miguel de Allende, but thankfully it still has a ways to go.

You can visit Real de Catorce on a day-trip from Matehuala, but it's worth staying longer to explore the surrounding hills and soak up the unique atmosphere.

History

Real de Catorce translates as 'Royal of 14': the '14' probably comes from 14 Spanish soldiers killed here by indigenous resisters around 1700. The town was founded in the mid-18th century, and the church built between 1790 and 1817.

Real de Catorce reached its peak in the late 19th century when it was producing an estimated $3 million in silver a year, vying to surpass the famed Valenciana mine of Guanajuato. It had a bullring and shops selling European luxury goods. A number of opulent houses from this period still stand.

Just why Real became a ghost town within three decades is a bit of a mystery. Some locals claim that during the revolution (1910–20) *bandidos* hid out here and scared off other inhabitants. The state

---

HUICHOL VISIONS

The remote Sierra Madre Occidental, in and around the far north of Jalisco, is the home of the Huichol, one of Mexico's most distinctive and enduring indigenous groups. Fiercely independent people, they were one of the few indigenous groups not subjugated by the Aztecs. Traditionally, they lived by hunting deer and cultivating scattered fields of corn in the high valleys.

The arrival of the Spanish had little immediate effect on the Huichol, and it wasn't until the 17th century that the first Catholic missionaries reached the Huichol homelands. Rather than convert to Christianity, the Huichol incorporated various elements of Christian teachings into their traditional animist belief systems. In Huichol mythology, nature's elements assume a personal as well as a supernatural form. Gods become personalized as plants, totem animal species and natural objects, while their supernatural form is explored in religious rituals.

Every year the Huichol leave their isolated homeland and make a pilgrimage of some 400km across Mexico's central plateau to what is now northern San Luis Potosí state. In this harsh desert region, they seek out the *mezcal* cactus (*Lophophora williamsii*), often called peyote cactus. The rounded peyote 'buttons' contain a powerful hallucinogenic drug (whose chief element is mescaline) that is central to the Huichol's rituals and complex spiritual life. Most of the buttons are collected, dried and carried back to the tribal homelands, but a small piece is eaten on the spot, as a gesture to the plant. Small amounts of peyote help to ward off hunger, cold and fatigue, while larger amounts are taken on ritual occasions, such as the return from the annual pilgrimage. In particular, peyote is used by shamans whose visions inform them about when to plant and harvest corn, where to hunt deer or how to treat illnesses.

This hallucinogenic cactus has great cultural and spiritual significance, and its indiscriminate use by foreigners is regarded as offensive, even sacrilegious. There is also a concern that if too many peyote buttons are taken to meet tourist demands, the Huichol will have difficulty obtaining what they need for ceremonial purposes.

The Huichol have not generally intermarried with other indigenous groups or with the mestizo population, most retain their language and many still take part in the annual pilgrimages and peyote rituals. Development of a unique artistic style has brought new recognition to Huichol culture and provided many Huichol people with a source of income.

Traditionally, the main Huichol art forms were telling stories, making masks and detailed geometric embroidery. In the last few decades, the Huichol have been depicting their myths and visions graphically, using brightly colored beads or yarn pressed into a beeswax-covered substrate. Beadwork generally uses abstract patterns and is often done on wooden bowls, animal skulls or masks. The 'yarn pictures' are notable for their wealth of symbolism and surreal imagery.

Huichol artwork is sold in craft markets, shops and galleries in most big cities and tourist resorts. Prices are usually fixed, and the Huichol don't like to haggle. Huichol art is expensive compared with some souvenirs, but it takes a long time to produce, and each piece is unique. To see the best work, visit one of the specialist museums or shops in places like Zapopan (Guadalajara), Tepic, Puerto Vallarta or Zacatecas.

tourist guidebook explains, perhaps more plausibly, that the price of silver slumped after 1900.

Orientation

The bus from Matehuala drops you off after passing through the 2.3km Ogarrio tunnel. If you arrive in a car, leave it in the dusty parking area to the left of the market at the far end of the tunnel – local kids will promise to watch it all day for a few pesos. Or, they'll pester you to hire them as guides or to take you to a place to stay. Walk a few steps up from the parking lot to Lanzagorta, a stony street heading west through a row of shops, past the church to the center of town.

Information

Try surfing www.realdecatorce.net for a good overview of the town. Card phones are located around the plaza. There's no ATM here, so make sure you bring enough cash.

Artesanía Venado Azul (Constitución s/n) Charges $2 for dial-up Internet access.

Mesón de la Abundancia (☎ 887-50-44; Lanzagorta 11) A hotel that changes US dollars, traveler's checks and euros.

Sotano Real (Constitución s/n) Charges $2 for dial-up Internet access.

Super La Nueva Sorpresa (Lanzagorta 2; ⊙ 8am-8pm) Changes US dollars when they have pesos on hand, but don't count on it.

Telefone caseta (east side Plaza Hidalgo)

Tourist office (☎ 887-50-71; Presidencia Municipal, Constitución s/n; ⊙ 10am-4pm Mon-Fri, 10am-2pm Sat & Sun)

Sights & Activities

LA PARROQUIA

The charmingly timeworn *parroquia* (parish church), **Templo de la Purísima Concepción**, is an impressive neoclassical building. The attraction for thousands of Mexican pilgrims is the reputedly miraculous image of St Francis of Assisi on one of the side altars. A cult has grown up around the statue, whose help is sought in solving problems and cleansing sins.

Walk through the door to the left of the altar to find a roomful of *retablos*. These small pictures usually depict some life-threatening situation from which St Francis has rescued the victim, and they include a

REAL DE CATORCE

0 — 300 m
0 — 0.2 miles

INFORMATION	
Artesanía Venado Azul	1 B3
Card Phone	2 B2
Sotano Real	3 B2
Super la Nueva Sorpresa	4 B3
Telefone Caseta	5 B3
Tourist Office	6 B3

SIGHTS & ACTIVITIES	
Galería Vega M57	7 A2
Museo Parroquial	8 C3
Palenque de Gallos	9 A2
Plaza de Toros	10 A1
Taller de Platería	11 B3
Templo de la Purísima Concepción	12 B3

SLEEPING	
Corral de Conde II	13 B3
El Corral del Conde	14 B2
Hospedaje Familiar	15 B2
Hostal Alcazaba	16 A1
Hotel El Real	17 B3
Hotel El Real II	18 B2
Hotel Ruinas del Real	19 A2
Hotel San Juan	20 A2
Mesón de Abundancia	21 B3
Quinta La Puesta del Sol	22 A1
Rincón Magico	23 A1

EATING	
El Cactus Café	24 A2
El Tolentino	25 B2
Malambo	26 A3

DRINKING	
La Querencía	27 A2

SHOPPING	
Artesanal Wirikuta	28 B3
La Asociación Civil	29 B3

TRANSPORT	
4WDs to Estación Catorce	(see 31)
Bus Station	30 C3
Horses for Hire	31 A3
Jeeps to Estación Catorce	32 A3

brief description of the incident and some words of gratitude. Car accidents and medical operations are common themes. *Retablos* have become much sought after by collectors and are sometimes seen in antique shops. Many of those on sale have been stolen from churches – talk about bad karma.

Underneath the church, behind an old door on Lanzagorta, is the small **Museo Parroquial** (cnr Lanzagorta & Reyes; admission $0.25; ☺ infrequent Sundays), containing photos, documents and other miscellanea rescued from the crumbling town. Check out the representation of the popular ghost of *El Jerga*, an early miner, known to still make guest appearances.

Opposite the church's facade, **Casa de la Moneda**, the old mint, made coins for a few years in the 1860s. Current restoration is underway to restore this classic monument. There are tentative plans for a museum and cultural center, a café and various local craft shops.

Just up the street from the *parroquia* on Juárez there is a local silver workshop, **Taller de Platería**.

GALERÍA VEGA M57
Real's biggest **art gallery** (Zaragoza 3; ☺ 11am-4pm Sat, until 3pm Sun) hosts exhibitions of work in a variety of media in a restored colonial building. You might see a giant mobile in the courtyard, an installation in one of the spaces and displays of modern jewelry in another.

PALENQUE DE GALLOS & PLAZA DE TOROS
A block northwest of the plaza lies a monument to the town's heyday – **Palenque de Gallos** (Xicotencatl s/n; admission free; ☺ 9am-6pm), a cockfighting ring, built like a Roman amphitheater. It was restored in the 1970s and sometimes hosts theater or dance performances. Follow Zaragoza–Libertad north to the edge of the town where the restored bullring **Plaza de Toros** is used for soccer practice; the **Capilla** (☺ 8am-5pm) and *panteón* (cemetery) across the street are free and also worth a look.

HORSEBACK RIDING & HIKING
Numerous trails lead out into the stark and stunning countryside around Real. The most popular guided trail ride is the three-hour trip to **El Quemado**, the sacred

mountain of the Huichol. Here you'll find expansive views of the high-desert plateau and a small shrine to the sun god. Another good trip is to the **Pueblo Fantasmo** (Ghost Town). Guides, along with people with horses, congregate every morning around Plaza Hidalgo. Rates are around $5 an hour or a negotiable $50 for two people for a full day, including horses and a guide. Jeep trips and guided hiking trips can also be arranged. For best results, ask your hotel to suggest a guide.

If you prefer to hike by yourself, you can simply wander out from Real in almost any direction. But be prepared with water, a hat and strong footwear; it's unforgiving country.

Festivals & Events
Real is usually very quiet, but Semana Santa and Christmas are big events, and the **Fiesta de San Francisco** is huge. Between September 25 and October 12, 150,000 pilgrims come to pay homage to the figure of St Francis of Assisi in the town's church. Many of them just come for the day, by the busload to the Ogarrio tunnel, and from there on rickety horse-drawn carts. Thousands stay in the town too, filling every rentable room, and also sleeping rough in the plazas. The streets are lined with stalls selling religious souvenirs and food, while the town's trendy Italian restaurants close for a month. Tourists who desire the ghost-town experience should keep well away during this period. The **Festival del Desierto** cultural festival begins the second week in September and features folkloric music and dance performances in towns all around the region.

Sleeping
BUDGET
Several cheap *casas de huéspedes* (homes converted into simple guest lodgings) cater mainly to pilgrims; kids in the parking area can lead you to the more obscure ones. It can be very cold here in winter in the cheapest digs; bring a sleeping bag or request extra blankets.

Hospedaje Familiar (☎ 887-50-09; Constitución 21; s/d $10/14) As the name suggests, this household place has small, simple, clean rooms with private bathrooms. Recent additions and excellent views overlooking town from the terrace, make this place great value.

Hotel San Juan (cnr Constitución & Zaragoza; s/d $14/21) Located in an old building with innovative use of space, the quiet, family-run San Juan has small, rustic but clean rooms, some with a nice outlook over Plaza Hidalgo.

Rincón Magico (☎ 887-51-13; cnr Libertad & Zaragoza; s/d $33) This basic, *simpático* (friendly) spot has six apartments and is cheaper by the week. There is a bar and patio with expansive valley views.

MIDRANGE

Some very inviting upmarket accommodations await in old buildings, newly restored.

Hostal Alcazaba (☎ 887-50-75; vayssa31@hotmail.com; Libertad (Zaragoza 33); dm $15, r from $40, campsite $10; ℗) This midrange option is scenically situated (the name means 'well-protected high place') opposite the cemetery. There are three dorm-style spaces, and five cozy *casitas* (villas) with private bathroom, kitchen and panoramic views. The enormous property hosts excellent flora. Ask friendly owner Pedro about discounts for stays of longer than three nights.

Hotel Ruinas del Real (☎ 887-50-65/66; cnr Lerdo & Libertad; s/d $51/60, ste from $74) Real's best-known boutique hotel, in a wonderfully rebuilt stone building, is on the west side of town, a couple blocks uphill from Plaza Hidalgo. The rooms are colorful, spacious and well decorated. The really roomy Roberts and Hackman suites (as in Julia and Gene) have fireplaces, tubs and Jacuzzis.

THE AUTHOR'S CHOICE

Mesón de Abundancia (☎ 887-50-44; Lanzagorta 11; s/d $51/69, f $78-111) Step into this stone citadel and be transported to the once thriving days on this desert plateau. The original catalyst of commerce, this 19th-century bank building has been renovated and is now run as a hotel and restaurant by a Swiss-Mexican couple. All 12 rooms are large, quaint and decorated with local crafts. Three have balconies and great views. Rates rise $20 on weekends and holidays. There's an excellent restaurant and it's the only place in town that accepts credit cards.

Hotel El Real (☎ 887-50-58; www.hotelreal.com; Morelos 20; s/d $42/65; ▯) Another restored building houses this comfortable place with well-decorated but crowded bedrooms on three floors around an open courtyard. Some have views over the town and the hills. There's a good restaurant, and English, German and French are spoken.

Hotel El Real II (cnr Juaréz & Iturbide) Offers a similar style and price as the original, yet has slightly larger rooms, some with sweeping views.

El Corral del Conde (☎ 887-50-48; cnr Morelos & Constitución; r with TV from $36, ste $74) The original 11 spacious stone-walled rooms here are straight out of a medieval castle, though they're tastefully furnished and very comfortable.

El Corral del Conde II (cnr Morelos & Lanzagorta) This recently finished addition, just down the hill from the original, maintains the hotel's cozy colonial feel.

Quinta La Puesta del Sol (☎ 887-50-10; Libertad s/n; d $37; ℗) On the road to the bullring, this rambling modern hotel lacks Old-World charm but has a superb view down the valley. Amenities include satellite TV, covered parking and a restaurant.

Eating & Drinking

Food stalls around the plaza and along Lanzagorta serve standard Mexican snacks, while several restaurants compete (with each other and with the better hotels) to do the best Italian cuisine.

Mesón de Abundancia (☎ 887-50-44; Lanzagorta 11; mains $4-10) The bar and fireplace at the restaurant create a wonderful atmosphere and the Italian-Mexican meals are very good.

Hotel El Real (☎ 887-50-58; Morelos 20; mains $5-10; ☺ 8am-9pm) Serves good Italian, vegetarian and Mexican food.

El Cactus Café (☎ 887-50-56; Plaza Hidalgo; mains $3-7.50) On the plaza's west side, this cheery eatery is run by an Italian cook and his Mexican wife. You'll feel like you're eating in a friend's rustic kitchen while sharing family-style wooden tables and lingering over a glass of wine. It's nonsmoking, the bread and pasta are homemade and there are plenty of good Mexican and veggie options.

El Tolentino (☎ 887-50-92; Terán 7; mains $6-10; ☺ 6pm-midnight) Up the hill, behind the

Plaza Hidalgo, is this place – the newest addition to the string of nice restaurants in town. It serves international and Mexican specialties and the quaint atmosphere here is enhanced during weekends with the presence of live music.

Other recommendations:

Malambo (Lanzagorta 2; mains $5-10; ☽ noon-11pm Fri-Wed) Good pastries and more Italian on the south end of Plaza Hidalgo.

La Querencia (cnr Lerdo & Libertad) An atmospheric bar that combines a loungy feel with the rustic edge.

Shopping

As more of the itinerant artists who flock in during the high season to hawk their wares set up shop here permanently, the selection and quality of jewelry, silverwork and organic beauty products continues to improve. Check **Artesanal Wirikuta** (Lanzagorta s/n) for Hichol art or **La Asociación Civil** (☎ 887-50-42; Lanzagorta s/n; ☽ 10am-10pm) in front of Super La Nueva Sorpresa for excellent handmade clothes and handicrafts from all over the republic.

Getting There & Away

The main buses park on the east end of the tunnel. Mini connecting shuttles to the bus station drop off and pick up at the west end of the Ogarrio Tunnel in town. See p614 for bus schedules. Confirm the return bus schedule upon arrival.

If driving from Hwy 57 north of Matehuala, turn off toward Cedral, 20km west. After Cedral, you turn south to reach Catorce on what must be one of the world's longest cobblestone streets. It's a slow but spectacular zigzag drive up a steep mountainside. The Ogarrio tunnel ($2 per vehicle) is only wide enough for one vehicle; workers stationed at each end with telephones control traffic. You may have to wait a while for traffic in the opposite direction to pass. If it's really busy, you'll have to leave your car at the tunnel entrance and continue by pick-up or cart.

Vintage Jeep Willys leave Real around noon (and on demand), downhill from the plaza along Allende, for the rough but spectacular descent to the small hamlet of Estación de 14 ($3.25, one hour). From here, buses head to San Tiburcio, where there are connections for Saltillo and Zacatecas.

GUANAJUATO STATE

The taste of mineral riches found in Zacatecas caused Spanish prospectors to salivate at the potential prospects in these rocky highlands. Guanajuato (population 4.9 million), historically one of Mexico's wealthiest states, was soon tapped for silver, gold, iron, lead, zinc and tin. For two centuries the state produced enormous wealth, extracting up to 40% of the world's silver. Silver barons in Guanajuato city enjoyed opulent lives at the expense of indigenous people who worked the mines, first as slave labor and then as wage slaves.

Eventually the well-heeled criollo class of the Guanajuato and Querétaro states began to resent the dominance of Spanish-born colonists. After the occupation of much of Spain by Napoleon Bonaparte's troops in 1808 and subsequent political confusion in Mexico, provincial criollos began – while meeting as 'literary societies' – to draw up plans for rebellion (see boxed text, p633).

In addition to the quaint colonial towns of Guanajuato and San Miguel, Guanajuato state has several important industrial centers. It's also a fertile agricultural state – the strawberries that are grown around Irapuato are famous. And it's still an important source of silver, gold and fluorspar.

GUANAJUATO

☎ 473 / pop 78,000 / elevation 2017m

Gorgeous Guanajuato is crammed onto the steep slopes of a ravine, with narrow streets twisting around the hillsides and disappearing into a series of tunnels. This impossible topography was settled in 1559 because the silver and gold deposits that were found here were among the world's richest. Much of the fine architecture built from this wealth remains intact, making Guanajuato a living monument to a prosperous, turbulent past; the city was inscribed as a Unesco World Heritage site in 1988, keeping away traffic lights and neon signs.

But it's not only the past that resounds in Guanajuato's narrow cobbled streets. The University of Guanajuato, known for its arts programs, enrolls over 20,000 students, giving the city a youthful vibrancy and cultural life that are as interesting as the colonial architecture and exotic setting. The city's cultural year peaks in October with the Festival Internacional Cervantino (see p626).

History

One of the hemisphere's richest silver veins was uncovered in 1558 at La Valenciana mine and for 250 years the mine produced 20% of the world's silver. Colonial barons benefiting from this mineral treasure were infuriated when King Carlos III of Spain slashed their share of the wealth in 1765. The king's 1767 decree banishing the Jesuits from Spanish dominions further alienated both the wealthy barons and the poor miners, who held allegiance to the Jesuits.

This anger was focused in the War of Independence. In 1810 rebel leader Miguel Hidalgo set off the independence movement with his Grito de Independencia (Cry for Independence) in nearby Dolores (see the boxed text, p633). Guanajuato citizens joined the independence fighters and defeated the Spanish and loyalists, seizing the city in the rebellion's first military victory. When the Spaniards eventually retook the city they retaliated by conducting the infamous 'lottery of death,' in which names of Guanajuato citizens were drawn at random and the 'winners' were tortured and hanged.

Independence was eventually won, freeing the silver barons to amass further wealth. From this wealth arose many of the mansions, churches and theaters that make Guanajuato one of Mexico's most handsome cities.

In the late 1990s the state prospered under its PAN (National Action Party) governor, Vicente Fox Quesada, with Mexico's lowest unemployment rate and an export rate three times the national average. Fox was chosen as the PAN candidate for the 2000 presidential election, and his popularity sealed the victory.

Orientation

Guanajuato's center is quite compact, with a few major streets and lots of tiny *callejones*. It's ideal for walking, but tricky to drive around. The main street, running roughly east–west, is called Juárez from the Mercado Hidalgo to the basilica on Plaza de la Paz. East of the basilica, this street continues as a pedestrian street called Obregón to the Jardín de la Unión (the city's main plaza), then continues further east as Sopeña.

Roughly parallel to Juárez–Obregón is another long street, running from the Alhóndiga to the university, and bearing the names 28 de Septiembre, Pocitos and Lascuraín de Retana along the way. Hidalgo (aka Cantarranas) parallels Sopeña and is another important street. Once you know these streets you can't get lost – just walk downhill until you find one of them. You can, however, have a great time getting lost among the maze of crooked *callejones* winding up the hills from the center.

Traffic on these main arteries is one-way, traveling east to west. Vehicles (including public buses) going west to east must use the main underground roadway, Subterránea Padre Miguel Hidalgo, a one-way route along the dried-up Río Guanajuato riverbed. (The river was diverted after it flooded the city in 1905.) At least eight other tunnels have been constructed to cope with increasing traffic. The Tunel Noreste Ingeniero Ponciano Aguilar and Tunel Santa Fe, running one-way east to west, enable vehicles to bypass the city center altogether.

Surrounding central Guanajuato is the winding Carretera Panorámica, offering great views of the town and surrounding hills.

Information

EMERGENCY
Ambulance, Fire & Police (☎ 066)

INTERNET ACCESS
Quite a few places offer Internet access for around $1 an hour.
CyberCenter (Pasaje de los Arcos) Cramped, loud and smoky, but fast.
Internet Mexiquito (Independencia 6; ☺ 10am-10pm) A chill atmosphere with a nice coffee selection.

LAUNDRY
Lavandería Automática Internacional (Doblado 28; ☺ 10am-8pm Mon-Sat) Load of 3kg for $4.
Lavandería del Centro (Sopeña 26; ☺ 9am-8:30pm Mon-Fri, 9am-4pm Sat) Costs $2.50 per kg or $4.50 for up to 5kg.

MEDICAL SERVICES
Hospital General (☎ 733-15-73, 733-15-76; Carretera a Silao, Km 6.5)

MONEY
Banks along Av Juárez change cash and traveler's checks (but some only until 2pm), and

GUANAJUATO

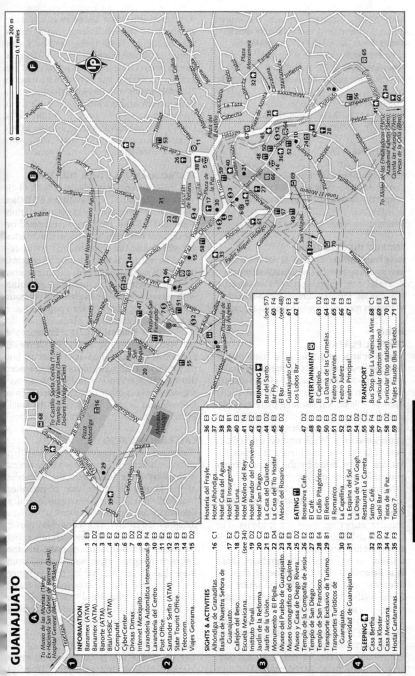

To Museo de las Momias (1km;
Ex-Hacienda San Gabriel de Barrera (2km);
Hospital General (6km); Dolores Hidalgo (52km)

200 m
0.1 miles

LP

INFORMATION
Banamex (ATM).....................**1**	E3
Banamex (ATM).....................**2**	D2
Banorte (ATM).....................**3**	D2
Bital/HSBC (ATM).................**4**	E2
Computel..............................**5**	E2
CyberCenter........................**6**	E3
Divisas Dimas......................**7**	E3
Internet Mexiquito..............**8**	D2
Lavandería Automática Internacional.**9**	F4
Lavandería del Centro.........**10**	E3
Post Office...........................**11**	E2
Santander Serfín (ATM)........**12**	E3
State Tourist Office.............**13**	E3
Telecomm...........................**14**	E3
Viajes Georama....................**15**	D2

SIGHTS & ACTIVITIES
Alhóndiga de Granaditas.....**16**	C1
Basílica de Nuestra Señora de	
Guanajuato.....................**17**	E2
Callejón del Beso................**18**	C3
Escuela Mexicana................(see 34)	
Instituto Tonali..................**19**	D2
Jardín de la Reforma............**20**	C3
Jardín de la Unión..............**21**	E3
Monumento a El Pípila........**22**	D4
Museo del Pueblo de Guanajuato.**23**	D2
Museo Iconográfico del Quijote.**24**	E3
Museo y Casa de Diego Rivera.**25**	D2
Templo de la Compañía de Jesús.**26**	E2
Templo de San Diego...........**27**	E3
Templo de San Francisco......**28**	E4
Transporte Exclusivo de Turismo.**29**	B1
Transportes Turísticos de	
Guanajuato.....................**30**	E2
Universidad de Guanajuato..**31**	E2

SLEEPING
Casa Bertha.........................**32**	F3
Casa Kloster........................**33**	D3
Casa Mexicana....................**34**	F4
Hostal Cantarranas.............**35**	F3
Hostería del Frayle..............**36**	E3
Hotel Alhóndiga..................**37**	C1
Hotel Casa de Agua.............**38**	B1
Hotel El Insurgente..............**39**	B1
Hotel Luna.........................**40**	E3
Hotel Molino del Rey...........**41**	F4
Hotel Parador del Convento..**42**	E2
La Casa del Quixote.............**43**	D2
La Casa de la Unión.............**44**	D2
La Casa del Tío Hostel.........**45**	D2
Mesón del Rosario..............**46**	D2

EATING
Bossanova Cafe...................**47**	D2
El Café................................**48**	E3
El Gallo Pitagórico..............**49**	E3
El Retiro.............................**50**	E3
Il Romano...........................**51**	D2
La Capellina.......................**52**	E3
La Esquina del Sol..............**53**	E2
La Oreja de Van Gogh.........**54**	D2
Restaurant La Carreta.........**55**	C2
Santo Café.........................**56**	F4
Sushi Bar...........................**57**	E3
Tasca de la Paz..................**58**	D2
Truco 7..............................**59**	E3

DRINKING
Bar del Santo.....................(see 57)	
Bar Fly..............................**60**	F4
El Bar................................(see 48)	
Guanajuato Grill.................**61**	E3
Los Lobos Bar....................**62**	E4

ENTERTAINMENT
El Capitolio........................**63**	D2
La Dama de las Camelias....**64**	E3
Teatro Cervantes...............**65**	F4
Teatro Juárez....................**66**	E3
Teatro Principal.................**67**	E3

TRANSPORT
Bus Stop for La Valencia Mine.**68**	C1
Funicular (bottom station)...**69**	F4
Funicular (top station)........**70**	D4
Viajes Frausto (Bus Tickets)..**71**	E3

To Castillo Santa Cecilia (1.5km);
Templo la Valenciana (3km);
Dolores Hidalgo (52km)

To Motel Las Embajadoras (1km;
Academia Falcón (3km);
Quinta Las Acacias (7km);
Presas de la Olla (8km)

have ATMs. Banorte, opposite the tourist office, is convenient and relatively quick.

Divisas Dimas (Juárez 33A; ⏱ 10am-8pm Mon-Sat) Convenient *casa de cambio* with decent rates.

Viajes Georama (☎ 732-51-01; Plaza de la Paz 34) American Express agent, doesn't exchange traveler's checks.

POST OFFICE
Post office (☎ 732-03-85; Ayuntamiento 25; ⏱ 9am-5pm Mon-Fri, 9am-1pm Sat)

TELEPHONE & FAX
Pasaje de los Arcos, an alley off the south side of Obregón near the tourist office, has card phones in reasonably quiet surroundings.

Computel (Ayuntamiento 25) Opposite post office, with fax and Internet.

Telecomm (cnr Sopeña & Rincón del Arte)

TOURIST INFORMATION
State tourist office (☎ 732-19-82, 800-714-10-86; www.guanajuato-travel.com, www.guanajuato.gob.mx; Plaza de la Paz 14; ⏱ 10am-2pm & 4-7:30pm Mon-Sat, 10am-2pm Sun) Friendly staff, mostly English-speaking, with free city maps and brochures (in Spanish and English).

Sights
CENTRAL PLAZAS
A wander around the beautiful main plazas, the bustling hubs of Guanajuato's social life, is a good introduction to Guanajuato's historic center. Starting from the east, pretty **Jardín de la Unión**, surrounded by restaurants and shaded by trees, is the social heart of the city. The elegant **Teatro Juárez** sits on its southeast corner. Walk west on Obregón to **Plaza de la Paz**, the small triangle beside the basilica, surrounded by the former homes of wealthy silver lords.

Meander west and south along the curving Av Juárez to **Plazuela de los Ángeles**, where the steps and ice-cream stands are popular gathering spots for students. The Callejón del Beso (see right) is just a few meters uphill from here.

Continue on Juárez to the handsome **Jardín de la Reforma**, behind the row of classical columns, and **Plaza San Roque**, where *entremeses* (theatrical sketches) are performed in the Cervantino festival (see p626). Nearby is the pleasant, shady **Plazuela de San Fernando**. These three linked spaces form a picturesque detour northwest of Av Juárez.

Further west on Av Juárez is the bustling area in front of Mercado Hidalgo.

A block north, **Plaza Alhóndiga** is a usually empty space with wide steps leading up to the Alhóndiga. From there, head back east along 28 de Septiembre (which changes names several times), past museums and the university, with a few twists and turns, to **Plaza del Baratillo** with its Florentine fountain. A right turn and a short block south from there will bring you back to Jardín de la Unión, where tourists and well-to-do locals congregate in the late afternoon, along with buskers, shoe shiners and snack vendors.

TEATRO JUÁREZ & OTHER THEATERS
The magnificent **Teatro Juárez** (☎ 732-01-83; Sopeña s/n; admission $2; ⏱ 9am-1:45pm & 5-7:45pm Tue-Sun when no performances are scheduled) was built between 1873 and 1903 and inaugurated by the dictator Porfirio Díaz, whose lavish tastes are reflected in the plush red and gold interior. The outside is festooned with columns, lampposts and statues; inside the impression is Moorish, with the bar and lobby gleaming with carved wood, stained glass and precious metals. The steps outside are a popular place to watch the scene on the plaza.

The **Teatro Principal** (☎ 732-15-23; Hidalgo s/n) and **Teatro Cervantes** (☎ 732-11-69; Plaza Allende s/n) are not as spectacular as Teatro Juárez, but they do host a full schedule of performances during the Cervantino festival, and less-regular shows at other times. Statues of Don Quixote and Sancho Panza grace the small Plaza Allende, in front of Teatro Cervantes.

CALLEJÓN DEL BESO
Narrowest of the many narrow alleys that climb the hills from Guanajuato's main streets is the **Alley of the Kiss**, where the balconies of the houses on either side of the alley practically touch. In a Guanajuato legend, a fine family once lived on this street, and their daughter fell in love with a common miner. They were forbidden to see each other, but the miner rented a room opposite, and the lovers exchanged furtive *besos* (kisses) from these balconies. Inevitably, the romance was discovered and the couple met a tragic end. From the Plazuela de los Ángeles on Av Juárez, walk about 40m up Callejón del Patrocinio to see the tiny alley on your left.

ALHÓNDIGA DE GRANADITAS
The site of the first major rebel victory in Mexico's War of Independence, **Alhóndiga**

de Granaditas (☎ 732-11-12; 28 de Septiembre; admission $3, Sun free, video camera $3; ☺ 10am-2pm & 4-6pm Tue-Sat, 10am-3pm Sun) is now a history and art museum.

The Alhóndiga was a massive grain-and-seed storehouse built between 1798 and 1808. In 1810 it became a fortress for Spanish troops and loyalist leaders. They barricaded themselves inside when 20,000 rebels led by Miguel Hidalgo attempted to take Guanajuato. It looked as if the outnumbered Spaniards would be able to hold out. Then, on September 28, 1810, a young miner named Juan José de los Reyes Martínez (aka El Pípila), under orders from Hidalgo, tied a stone slab to his back and, thus protected from Spanish bullets, set the gates ablaze. While the Spaniards choked on smoke, the rebels moved in and took the Alhóndiga, killing most of those inside. (El Pípila probably perished in the battle, but some versions of the story have it that he lived to a ripe old age.)

The Alhóndiga was used as a prison for a century, beginning in 1864, but it became a museum in 1967. There's also a fine art gallery. Don't miss Chávez Morado's dramatic murals of Guanajuato's history on the staircases.

MUSEO Y CASA DE DIEGO RIVERA

Diego Rivera's birthplace is now a **museum** (☎ 732-11-97; Pocitos 47; adult/student $1.50/0.50; ☺ 10am-6:30pm Tue-Sat, 10am-2:30pm Sun) honoring the painter. Rivera and a twin brother were born in the house in 1886 (his twin died at the age of two), and lived here until the family moved to Mexico City six years later.

In conservative Guanajuato, where Catholic attitudes prevail, the Marxist Rivera was *persona non grata* for years. The city now honors its once blacklisted son with a small collection of his work. The first floor contains the Rivera family's 19th-century antiques and fine furniture. The 2nd and 3rd floors have portraits of peasants and indigenous people, a nude of Frida Kahlo and some sketches of Rivera's memorable murals. There's a good gift-shop downstairs and the upper floors host temporary exhibitions of work by Mexican and international artists.

MUSEO ICONOGRÁFICO DEL QUIJOTE

The excellent and surprisingly interesting **museum** (☎ 732-33-76; Doblado 1; admission $2; ☺ 10am-6:30pm Tue-Sat, 10am-2:30pm Sun) fronts the tiny plaza in front of the Templo de San Francisco. Every exhibit relates to Don Quixote de la Mancha, the notorious Spanish literary hero. Enthusiasts find it fascinating to see the same subject depicted in so many different media by different artists in different styles. Paintings, statues, tapestries, even chess sets, clocks and postage stamps all feature the quixotic icon and his bumbling companion Sancho Panza.

UNIVERSIDAD DE GUANAJUATO

The **University of Guanajuato** (UGTO; ☎ 732-00-06 ext 8001; www.ugto.mx; Lascuraín de Retana 5), whose ramparts are visible above much of the city, is on Lascuraín de Retana one block up the hill from the basilica. It's considered one of Mexico's finest schools for music, theater, mine engineering and law. Some of the buildings originally housed a large Jesuit seminary, but the distinctive multistorey white-and-blue building with the crenellated pediment dates from the 1950s. The design was controversial at the time, but it's now recognized as a successful integration of a modern building into a historic cityscape.

MUSEO DEL PUEBLO DE GUANAJUATO

Located beside the university, this **art museum** (☎ 732-29-90; Pocitos 7; admission $1.50; ☺ 10am-6:30pm Tue-Sat, 10am-2:30pm Sun) has a collection ranging from colonial to modern times. The museum occupies the former mansion of the Marqueses de San Juan de Rayas, who owned the San Juan de Rayas mine. The private church upstairs in the courtyard contains a powerful mural by José Chávez Morado.

BASILICA & OTHER CHURCHES

The **Basílica de Nuestra Señora de Guanajuato** (Plaza de la Paz s/n; ☺ 8:30am-8pm), a block west of Jardín de la Unión, contains a jewel-covered image of the Virgin, patron of Guanajuato. The wooden statue was supposedly hidden from the Moors in a cave in Spain for 800 years. Felipe II of Spain gave it to Guanajuato in thanks for the wealth it provided to the crown. Also visit the small **Galería Mariana** (Plaza de la Paz s/n; ☺ 9am-2pm & 5pm-7pm; admission $1.50) to see other Catholic relics from the colonial period.

Other fine colonial churches include the **Templo de San Diego** (Jardín de la Union s/n;

8am-1pm & 5-8pm), opposite the Jardín de la Unión; the **Templo de San Francisco** (Doblado s/n; 8am-8pm); and the large **Templo de la Compañía de Jesús** (Lascuráin de Retana s/n; 8am-7:30pm), which was completed in 1747 for the Jesuit seminary whose buildings are now occupied by the University of Guanajuato.

FUNICULAR

This **incline railway** (Plaza Constancia s/n; one-way/round-trip $1/2; 8am-10pm Mon-Fri, 9am-10pm Sat, 10am-9pm Sun) inches up the slope behind the Teatro Juárez to a terminal and scenic bar near the El Pípila monument.

MONUMENTO A EL PÍPILA

The **monument** to El Pípila honors the hero who torched the Alhóndiga gates on September 28, 1810, enabling Hidalgo's forces to win the first victory of the independence movement. The statue shows El Pípila holding his torch high over the city. On the base is the inscription *'Aún hay otras Alhóndigas por incendiar'* (There are still other Alhóndigas to burn).

It's worth going up to the statue for the magnificent view over the city. Two routes from the center of town go up steep, picturesque lanes. One goes east on Sopeña from Jardín de la Unión, then turns right on Callejón del Calvario (you'll see the 'Al Pípila' sign). Another ascent, unmarked, goes uphill from the small plaza on Alonso. If the climb is too much for you, the 'Pípila-ISSSTE' bus heading west on Juárez will let you off right by the statue, or you can ride up in the funicular.

MUSEO DE LAS MOMIAS

The famous **Museum of the Mummies** (732-06-39; Camino a las Momias s/n; adult/child $5/2.75; 9am-6pm) at the *panteón* is a quintessential example of Mexico's obsession with death. Visitors from all over come to see scores of corpses disinterred from the public cemetery.

The first remains were dug up in 1865, when it was necessary to remove some bodies from the cemetery to make room for more. What the authorities uncovered were not skeletons but flesh mummified with grotesque forms and facial expressions. The mineral content of the soil and extremely dry atmosphere had combined to preserve the bodies in this unique way.

Today more than 100 mummies are on display in the museum, including the first mummy to be discovered, the 'smallest mummy in the world,' a pregnant mummy and plenty more. Since space is still tight in the cemetery, bodies continue to be exhumed if the relatives can't pay the upkeep fees. It takes only five or six years for a body to become mummified here, though only 1% or 2% of the bodies exhumed are 'display quality' specimens. The others are cremated.

The complex is on the western edge of town, a long walk or a 10-minute ride from Av Juárez on any 'Momias' bus.

MINA & TEMPLO LA VALENCIANA

For 250 years **La Valenciana mine** (732-05-70/80; admission $2; 8am-4pm), on a hill overlooking Guanajuato 5km north of the center, produced 20% of the world's silver, plus quantities of gold and other minerals. Shut down after the Mexican Revolution, the mine reopened in 1968 and is now run by a cooperative. It still yields silver, gold, nickel and lead, and you can see the ore being lifted out and miners descending the immense main shaft, 9m wide and 500m deep. Guides (ask for an English-speaker) will show you around the compound (they expect a tip), though you can't go inside the mine.

On the main road near the mine is the magnificent **Templo La Valenciana** (aka Iglesia de San Cayetano). One legend says that the Spaniard who started the mine promised San Cayetano that if it made him rich, he would build a church to honor the saint. Another says that the silver baron of La Valenciana, Conde de Rul, tried to atone for exploiting the miners by building the ultimate in Churrigueresque churches. Whatever the motive, ground was broken in 1765, and the church was completed in 1788. Templo La Valenciana's facade is spectacular, and its interior dazzles with ornate golden altars, filigree carvings and giant paintings.

Just downhill behind the church, the **Bocamina Valenciana** (732-05-70; adult/child $2/1; 10am-4pm) is another section of mineshaft that's open to visitors.

To get to La Valenciana, take a 'Cristo Rey' or 'Valenciana' bus (every 15 minutes) from the bus stop on Alhóndiga just north of 28 de Septiembre. Get off at Templo La Valenciana, then cross the road and follow the signs to the mine entrance.

Tomb of 7th-century King Pakal at the Templo de las Inscripciones (p836) in Palenque

Colectivo, the most common forms of transport (p1002)

Fruit-seller, Chiapas (p805)

Clavadista (cliff diver), Acapulco (p506)

EX-HACIENDA SAN GABRIEL DE BARRERA

Built at the end of the 17th century, this was the grand hacienda of Captain Gabriel de Barrera, whose family was descended from the first Conde de Rul of the famous La Valenciana mine. Opened as a museum in 1979, the **hacienda** (☎ 732-06-19; Camino Antiguo a Marfil Km 2.5; admission $2, camera $2, video $2.50; ☒ 10am-6pm) has been magnificently restored with period European furnishings.

The large grounds, originally devoted to processing ore from La Valenciana, were converted in 1945 to beautiful terraced gardens with pavilions, pools, fountains and footpaths – a lovely and tranquil retreat from the city.

The house and garden are 2.5km west of the city center. Take one of the frequent 'Marfil' buses heading west on Juárez and ask the driver to drop you at Hotel Misión Guanajuato.

Courses

Guanajuato is a university town and has an excellent atmosphere for studying Spanish. Group classes average around $6.50 per hour and private lessons average $14 an hour. Schools can arrange homestays with meals for $15 to $20 per day. Additional costs to ask about include registration

CRISTO REY: MEXICO'S GEOGRAPHIC HEART

Cristo Rey (Christ the King) is a 20m bronze statue of Jesus erected in 1950 on the summit of the Cerro de Cubilete, 15km west of Guanajuato on a side road off the road to Templo La Valenciana. It is said to be the exact geographical center of Mexico. For religious Mexicans there is a special significance in having Jesus at the heart of their country, and the statue is a popular attraction for Mexicans visiting Guanajuato.

Tour agencies offer 3½-hour trips to the statue (see right), but you can go on your own for $3.50 round-trip by an Autobuses Vasallo de Cristo bus from Guanajuato's bus station. Buses depart nine times between 6am and 6pm on weekdays, with additional buses on weekends and holidays. From the bus station it is possible to see the statue up on the hill in the distance. A taxi run is $12 each way.

and/or placement test fees, and costs for excursions and extracurricular activities.

Academia Falcón (☎ /fax 732-07-45; www.academia falcon.com; Paseo de la Presa 80) Well-established institute, 3km south of the centre, with two to five students per class. Registration is every Saturday morning.

Escuela Mexicana (☎ 732-50-05; www.escuelamexi cana.int.com.mx; Portrero 12) Small school with classes in Spanish (grammar, conversation, literature) and other topics from pre-Hispanic culture to dance, cooking and a new movie class. Homestay and on-site accommodation available.

Instituto Tonali (☎ 732-73-52; Juárez 4) Spanish classes at all levels, dance and cooking programs.

Universidad de Guanajuato (UGTO; ☎ 732-00-06 ext 8001; www.ugto.mx; Lascuráin de Retana 5) Summer Spanish courses, plus classes in Mexican and Latin American culture; sessions begin in early June and early July. Plus semester-long courses beginning in January and July.

Tours

Several agencies offer similar tours of Guanajuato's major sights (usually in Spanish). You can reach all the same places on local buses, but if your time is limited a tour may be useful.

Transporte Exclusivo de Turismo (☎ 732-59-68; cnr Av Juárez & Calle 5 de Mayo), in a kiosk, and **Transportes Turísticos de Guanajuato** (☎ 732-21-34; cnr Obregón & El Truco), below the front courtyard of the basilica, both offer Guanajuato colonial tours, which include the mummies, La Valenciana mine and church, and the Pípila monument and the Carretera Panorámica. Three-hour trips are $9.50 and depart up to three times daily. Longer tours go to Cristo Rey ($9.50) or make an eight-hour circuit through Dolores Hidalgo and San Miguel de Allende ($19). Five-hour night tours ($15) take in Guanajuato's views and nightspots, and the street parties called *callejoneadas* (see p629).

Festivals & Events

Baile de las Flores The Flower Dance takes place on the Thursday before Semana Santa. The next day, mines are open to the public for sightseeing and celebrations. Miners decorate altars to La Virgen de los Dolores, a manifestation of the Virgin Mary who looks after miners.

Fiestas de San Juan y Presa de la Olla The festivals of San Juan are celebrated at the Presa de la Olla park in late June. The 24th is the big bash for the saint's day itself, with dances, music, fireworks and picnics. Then on the first Monday in July, everyone comes back to the park for another big party celebrating the opening of the dam's floodgates.

Día de la Cueva Cave Day is a country fair held on July 31, when locals walk to a cave in the nearby hills, to honor San Ignacio de Loyola, and enjoy a festive picnic.

Fiesta de la Virgen de Guanajuato This festival, on August 9, commemorates the date when Felipe II gave the people of Guanajuato the jeweled wooden Virgin that now adorns the basilica.

Festival Internacional Cervantino (www.festivalcervantino.gob.mx) In the 1950s the arts festival was merely *entremeses* from Miguel Cervantes' work performed by students. It has grown to become one of Latin America's foremost arts extravaganzas. Music, dance and theater groups arrive from around the world, performing work that may have nothing to do with Cervantes. (A recent festival included Spanish ballet, German drama and Japanese percussion.) The festival lasts two to three weeks starting around the second week of October. Tickets range from $10 to $43. Tickets and hotels should be booked in advance. Advance tickets are available through the Ticketmaster website (www.ticketmaster.com.mx). In Guanajuato, buy tickets from the ticket office on the southeast side of Teatro Juárez (not in the theater ticket office).

Sleeping

The most classy in-town address is Jardín de la Unión, where several venerable hotels have rooms, bars and restaurants facing the lively but traffic-free plaza. Browse www .hotelesguanajuato.com for a thorough accommodations overview.

BUDGET

Casa Kloster (☎ 732-00-88; Alonso 32; dm/s/d with shared bathroom $9/11/19) The classic backpackers' choice is near all the action, a short block down an alley from the basilica. Birds and flowers grace the sunny courtyard, and well-tended rooms are clean and comfortable. Those facing the street can be noisy. Larger rooms cost slightly more. It's a relaxed, friendly place, but don't leave valuables lying around. Arrive early because it's often booked.

La Casa del Tío Hostel (☎ 733-97-28; www.lacasadeltiohostel.com; Cantarranas 47; dm/s/d $11/14/28; 🖳) This new hostel is clean and very centrally located. There is a pleasant common room with a kitchen and TV, a rooftop terrace and the friendly bilingual staff will help you get situated. The dorms on the 2nd floor are bright and airy overlooking the street, while the private rooms are darker and more secluded.

Casa Bertha (☎ /fax 732-13-16; casabertha92@hotmail.com; Tamboras 9; r per person with/without private bathroom from $14/12, apt per person from $19) This family-run *casa de huéspedes*, a few minutes east of the Jardín de la Unión, is a maze of 10 doubles and three family-size apartments, all with cable TV. It's a homelike, well-kept and central labyrinth, with modern bathrooms and a rooftop terrace with views over the town. Walk up the street beside the Teatro Principal to Plaza Mexiamora. Head straight uphill, take the first right, then turn left and follow the path to the door directly ahead.

Casa Mexicana (☎ 732-50-05; www.casamexicanaweb.com; Sóstenes Rocha 28; r per person with/without private bathroom from $14/10; 🖳) Smallish rooms surround a courtyard at this clean, friendly family-run place connected to the Escuela Mexicana language school (see p625). The bar next door is popular with language students and locals looking to practice their English.

Other recommendations:

Hostal Cantarranas (☎ 732-51-44; fax 732-17-08; Hidalgo 50; r $27-45) An old building with pleasant rooms (mostly apartments) and a sunny rooftop.

Hotel Alhóndiga (☎ 732-05-25; Insurgencia 49; s/d $19/23; 🅿) Family-run with clean, comfortable rooms, some with balconies.

MIDRANGE

Hotel San Diego (☎ 732-13-00; www.hotelerasandiego .com; Jardín de la Unión 1; r from $72) The four-store San Diego has 55 comfortable rooms and suites (for up to eight), a rooftop terrace and subterranean sports bar. Superior rooms with balconies cost the same as interior rooms.

Hotel Molino del Rey (☎ 732-22-23; mach1@avante .net; cnr Campanero & Belaunzaran; s/d $23/33) An easy stroll from the center, the 'King's Mill' is notable for its value and quiet, convenient location. Its 35 rooms are set around a pretty patio, though housekeeping standards are variable and some rooms are nicer than others. A small ground-floor restaurant serves tasty, inexpensive meals.

Mesón del Rosario (☎ /fax 732-32-84; Av Juárez 31; s $33-39, d $42-50) The building and entrance have a medieval feel that fits Guanajuato's ambiance. The rooms here are not medieval however, they are clean, comfortable and decent size with TV. The hotel is good value for their very central location, with higher rates on weekends.

Hotel El Insurgente (☎ 732-31-92; fax 732-69-8; Juárez 226; s/d $33/39) A very practical option

NORTHERN CENTRAL HIGHLANDS

just west of center, this place fills up its 85 rooms fast during festivals and holidays, when the price skyrockets. It generally is good value though, especially for the upper rooms with views of the city. There is a pleasant street-side restaurant with good inexpensive meals.

Motel de las Embajadoras (☎ 731-01-05; cnr Embajadoras & Paseo Madero; s/d $45/69; **P**) If you're driving and want to avoid the congested center, this motel has plenty of parking and is only five minutes uphill from the center on an 'Embajadoras' or 'Presa' bus. The restaurant-bar is elegant but inexpensive, and the lovely courtyard is full of plants, trees and birds. Clean, comfortable rooms have color TV and phone.

Hotel Parador del Convento (☎ 732-25-24; hpconv@prodigy.net.mx; Calz de Guadalupe 17; r from $48; **P**) A steep five-minute walk up behind the university, this one-time hostel has converted its simple carpeted rooms into comfortable private accommodations with cable TV.

TOP END

Some quaint old buildings in various parts of town have been restored as small boutique hotels. The road to La Valenciana has several posh places with lofty locations. Other upmarket places are in Marfil, a 15-minute drive or bus ride west of town.

Hotel Luna (☎ 732-97-25; www.hotelluna.com.mx; Jardín de la Unión 6; r from $89, exterior d from $104, ste from $129) Another handsome building facing the plaza, this 100-year-old hotel has been completely restored and modernized. Rooms combine contemporary facilities

---

THE AUTHOR'S CHOICE

Hotel Casa del Agua (☎ 734-19-74; Plaza de la Compañir 4; r from $81, ste $184) This completely remodeled colonial building has been finished with contemporary ambient touches matched with colonial elegance. The floor of the interior courtyard is a glass-covered pool which acts as a mirror reflecting a pleasant light throughout the interior. The 16 luxurious suites are simple, elegant and include all the modern conveniences, while maintain their colonial grace. Centrally located, there is hardly a better option for style in the heart of Guanajuato.

---

with old-style charm. Rates include breakfast, and you get a 10% discount if you pay by cash.

Quinta Las Acacias (☎ 731-15-17, in Mexico 800-710-89-38, in USA 888-497-41-29; www.quintalasacacias .com.mx; Paseo de la Presa 168; ste with breakfast $220-292; **P** **☒** **⌨** **☝**) This new nine-suite hideaway combines attentive service and intimate luxury in a former 19th-century, French-colonial summer residence. Caged parakeets warble in the patio, while sheets are turned down and a delightful plate of local cookies appears. Master suites are appointed with oversize beds and Talavera tiles; modern amenities include hydro-massage tubs and portable phones. Each suite is thoughtfully decorated with folk art from a different Mexican state. In the morning, you'll wake up to the waft of house-baked biscuits served with homemade jams.

La Casa del Quixote (☎ /fax 732-39-23; Pocitos 37; ste $112) This small eight-room retreat is built into a steep hillside overlooking town. The large, comfortable rooms are a real delight. All rooms have kitchenettes and living rooms, most have bathtubs and half have brilliant views.

Castillo Santa Cecilia (☎ 732-04-85, 800-012-08-58; www.hotelcastillosantacecilia.com; Camino a La Valenciana Km 1; r/ste $117/149; **P** **☝**) This large stone building looks like a castle, and the lobby, dining room and bars all aim for a medieval ambience. The rooms have all the modern amenities, and there are tennis courts, a good restaurant and wine bar.

Hostería del Frayle (☎ /fax 732-11-79; Sopeña 3; s/d $74/92; **P**) A block from the Jardín, this historic hotel – it was built in 1673 as the Casa de Moneda – has 37 attractive but dark rooms with high wood-beamed ceilings, satellite TV and other comforts. Service is friendly and the thick adobe walls keep things quiet.

Eating

For fresh produce and local sweets, the Mercado Hidalgo is a five-minute walk west of the main plaza on Juárez.

JARDÍN DE LA UNIÓN & AROUND

Truco 7 (☎ 732-83-74; El Truco 7; mains $2-6) This intimate, artsy café-restaurant-gallery attracts a loyal mixed crowd of students, travelers and teachers, with delicious food and a great atmosphere. Set lunches are inexpensive, and the breakfast and dinner choices are more imaginative than most places. Background music includes jazz, blues and classical.

La Capellina (☎ 732-72-24; Sopeña 3; mains $7-12; ☙ 2pm-midnight Thu-Sat, 1-6pm Sun, 2-11pm Tue & Wed) A pioneer in the fusion-cuisine trend in Guanajuato, this artsy restaurant comes up with some innovative dishes that are a fresh change from the Mexican and Italian standards. Try the Thai salad to start, followed by salmon in chili-tamarind sauce.

Santo Café (Puente de Campanero; mains $3-5; ☙ 8am-midnight) Stop by this alternative spot to check the latest university vibe. It serves good cheap international food and drinks overlooking a small pedestrian street, and there is local art on the walls and music of all styles. Live local bands play on weekends.

El Café (☎ 732-25-66; Sopeña 10; mains $3-7) This popular hangout is the place to socialize al fresco over cocktails or a light meal. There are more tables under umbrellas across the street, alongside Teatro Juárez.

La Esquina del Sol (☎ 732-18-73; Calle del Sol 10; mains $2-4; ☙ 9am-8pm Mon-Fri, 10am-8pm Sat; Ⓥ) A great range of quality veg food with an international flavor. Try their pitas, wholewheat sandwiches, pastas, soups and salads. They have a healthy *comida corrida* ($3.75) and the best selection of imported teas in town.

Sushi Bar (Alonso s/n; mains $3-8; ☙ 2-10:30pm Mon-Thu, 2-11:30pm Fri & Sat) Located inside Bar del Santo, this is not the greatest sushi and teppanyaki you'll ever taste, but it's a hip and admirable attempt and a good change from the usual Mexican fare.

El Retiro (☎ 732-06-22; Sopeña 12; mains $3-7) This lively traditional restaurant-bar attracts a regular crowd with a good *menú del día* (set menu) for $4 and live music Wednesday through Friday evenings from 9pm.

El Gallo Pitagórico (☎ 732-94-89; Constancia 10; mains $6-11) South of the Jardín, up the steep path behind Templo San Diego, this romantic restaurant is in a bright blue building with wonderful city views. The fine Italian cuisine includes assorted antipasti, rich minestrone and a range of pastas. It's well worth the walk. Service is good, the music is classical and most of the wines are imported.

The hotels on the west side of the Jardín de la Unión have good upscale restaurants

where you can enjoy the atmosphere of the plaza.

AV JUÁREZ & AROUND

Il Romanico (☎ 732-27-72; Av Juárez 24; mains $7-16; ☙ 8am-11pm Mon-Thu, 8am-midnight Fri & Sat, 8am-10pm Sun) A tastefully done Italian-style restaurant and bar. A café and gelato bar by day, this place does good Italian food in the evenings. An all-in-one type place you can get a fresh juice in the morning, crepes for lunch, and then go for pizza and hit the hip bar upstairs.

Tasca de La Paz (☎ 734-22-25; Plaza de la Paz 28; mains $5-9; ☙ 8:30am-11pm) This place opposite the basilica has outdoor tables on picturesque Plaza de la Paz for tapas, paella and other Spanish specialties. It's a bit pricey, but worth it for the authentic flavors and European ambience.

Restaurant La Carreta (☎ 732-43-58; Av Juárez 96; mains $2-4) Trust your nose: La Carreta does a good version of the standard *pollo al pastor* (grilled chicken) and *carne asada* (grilled beef), both served with large portions of rice and salad. The grill out front keeps it warm inside on cold days.

PLAZUELA SAN FERNANDO

This little plaza is home to an ever-changing slate of hip hangouts, and is a delightful place in the evening for a drink, a snack or a meal.

La Oreja de Van Gogh (☎ 732-69-03; Plazuela San Fernando 24; mains $3-7) 'Van Gogh's Ear' has Vincentish murals inside, congenial tables outside, cheap breakfast and a 5pm happy hour with cheap beer. The menu features burgers and your favorite Mexican dishes.

Bossanova Café (☎ 732-56-74; Plazuela San Fernando 24; mains $2-6) This hip French-Brazilian café has a quaint patio and intimate interior atmosphere. Be sure to sample their selection of excellent teas to help settle the stomach after one of their house-specialty crepes.

Entertainment

Every evening, the Jardín de la Unión comes alive with tourists and others crowding the outdoor tables, strolling, people-watching and listening to the street musicians. The state band and other groups give free concerts in the gazebo some evenings from 7pm.

NIGHTCLUBS & DISCOS

The plethora of drinking and dancing establishments in Guanajuato generally stay open from 9pm to 3am

Bar del Santo (Alonso s/n; 4pm-3am Mon-Sat) A nice mixed crowd, all locals know where to go to hear the newest cutting-edge local DJs and fusion, rock, funk and jazz bands.

Bar Fly (Sostenes Rocha 30) The place to go for reggae, ska, rock and electronic grooves and a very bohemian vibe. The bar is usually packed with local students and travelers.

Guanajuato Grill (732-02-85; Alonso 4; cover Thu $3, Fri & Sat $5) This casual disco and drink spot is frequented by affluent, energetic students who like loud dance music. It's packed after midnight on Friday and Saturday. On quieter nights they pull in the patrons with drink specials from 9pm to 10pm.

El Bar (732-56-66; Sopeña 10; cover Fri & Sat $3; 10pm-late Tue-Sat) Upstairs above El Café, this popular, friendly place swings to salsa music, attracting a mixed, but mostly young, crowd. Good dancers will feel right at home. Others can ask about Thursday evening salsa classes.

Los Lobos Bar (Doblado 2) This hard-rockin' dive next to the Corona distributor draws a golden-oldies crowd and sometimes features classic-rock cover bands.

El Capitolio (732-08-10; Plaza de la Paz 62; cover Fri & Sat $5; 9pm-3am Tue-Sat) Another disco blasting techno and dance music to big weekend crowds, Capitolio heavily promotes its karaoke and cheap-drink deals but manages a slightly more stylish ambience than the nearby Guanajuato Grill.

La Dama de las Camelias (732-75-87; Sopeña 32) For Latin sounds and a dose of dirty dancing in an artsy, gay-friendly atmosphere, check out La Dama, playing live and recorded salsa, flamenco, *danzón* (latin dance originally from Cuba), *son cubano* and Andean music.

CALLEJONEADAS

On Friday, Saturday and Sunday evenings, at around 8pm (or daily during festivals), *callejoneadas* (or *estudiantinas*) depart from in front of San Diego church on the Jardín de la Unión. The *callejoneada* tradition is said to have come from Spain. A group of professional singers and musicians, dressed in traditional costumes, starts up in front of the church, a crowd gathers, then the whole mob winds through the ancient alleyways of the city, playing and singing heartily. On special occasions they also take along a burro laden with wine; at other times wine is stashed midpoint on the route. Stories and jokes are told in between songs, though these are unintelligible unless you understand Spanish well. It's good fun and one of Guanajuato's most enjoyable traditions – even if it has become a bit touristy. There is no cost involved, except a small amount for the wine you drink. Tour companies and others try to sell you tickets for the *callejoneadas*, but you really don't need them!

PERFORMING ARTS

Guanajuato has three fine theaters, the 100-year-old **Teatro Juárez** (732-01-83; Sopeña s/n), **Teatro Principal** (732-15-23; Hidalgo s/n) and **Teatro Cervantes** (732-11-69; Plaza Allende s/n), none far from the Jardín de la Unión. Check their posters to see what's on. International films are screened in several locations, including the Teatro Principal, Teatro Cervantes and **Museo y Casa de Diego Rivera** (see p623).

The Viva la Magia program runs every weekend from March to September, with Guanajuato's theaters hosting a variety of music, dance and literary events on Thursday, Friday and Saturday evenings. The tourist office has details of what's on each week.

Getting There & Away

AIR

Guanajuato is served by the Aeropuerto Internacional del Bajío, which is about 30km west of Guanajuato, halfway between León and Silao. See p631 for detailed flight information.

BUS

Guanajuato's Central de Autobuses is way out on the southwest outskirts of town. It has a tourist office, card phones, restaurant and luggage checkroom. Deluxe and 1st-class bus tickets can be bought in town at **Viajes Frausto** (732-35-80; Obregón 10).

Daily departures:

Destination	Price	Duration	Frequency
Dolores Hidalgo	$4	1hr	2nd-class Flecha Amarilla every 20min 5:30am-10:20pm
Guadalajara	$26	4hr	6 deluxe ETN
	$22	4hr	9 1st-class Primera Plus
	$18	4hr	5 2nd-class Flecha Amarilla
León	$5	1hr	6 deluxe ETN
	$3.50	1hr	10 1st-class Primera Plus
	$3	1hr	2nd-class Flecha Amarilla or Flecha de Oro every 15min 5:30am-10:40pm
Mexico City (Terminal Norte)	$31	4½hr	9 deluxe ETN
	$25	4½hr	11 1st-class Primera Plus
	$23	4½hr	3 1st-class Futura or Ómnibus de México
San Luis Potosí	$12.50	4hr	2 1st-class Flecha Amarilla
San Miguel de Allende	$9	1½hr	2 deluxe ETN
	$7	1½hr	3 1st-class Primera Plus
	$5.50	1½hr	9 2nd-class Flecha Amarilla

There are also hourly 2nd-class Flecha Amarilla buses to Celaya, plus three to Querétaro. For Morelia, catch an Irapuato-bound bus and change there.

Getting Around

A taxi to Bajío International Airport will cost about $30. A cheaper option ($10) is a frequent bus to Silao, and a taxi from there.

'Central de Autobuses' buses run constantly between the bus station and city center up to midnight. From the center, you can catch them heading west on Juárez, or on the north side of the basilica. A taxi costs $3.50.

City buses ($0.35) run from 5am to 10pm. The tourist office is very helpful with bus information. Taxis are plentiful in the center and charge about $2 for short trips around town.

LEÓN

☎ 477 / pop 1.15 million / elevation 1854m

The industrial city of León, 56km west of Guanajuato, is a big bus-interchange point and a likable enough place if you need to stay overnight. From the 16th century it became the center of Mexico's ranching district, providing meat for the mining towns and processing hides into essential tack during the early mining days. León is still famous for its leather goods, though fashion footwear now outsells fancy saddles. The city's other products include steel, textiles and soap.

Orientation & Information

The heart of the city is the wide main Plaza de los Mártires del 2 de Enero (aka Plaza Principal), a well-groomed pedestrian space with the Palacio Municipal on its west side. The adjoining Plaza de los Fundadores and several nearby streets are also traffic-free and full of shoe shops, food vendors, cafés and restaurants.

A board in Plaza Principal shows a big map of the city center, and a nearby **tourist information booth** (10am-8pm Mon-Fri, noon-6pm Sat & Sun) has a free tourist map of the city. You could also try calling the **regional tourism office** (☎ 763-44-00/01, 800-716-53-66; www.leon-mexico.com; Lopez Mateo Ote 1511). Lively **La Monarca Internet Café & Bar** (Calle 5 de Mayo 103, 2nd fl; 9am-midnight) has balconies overlooking the plaza and decent connections for $1 per hour; to find the entrance in the evening, follow your nose and look for long lines approaching the woman selling *rico* (rich) tamales in the entryway. Other essentials like banks, ATMs and card phones are around the plazas.

Sights

Shopping and walking around León's historic heart are the main attractions; look for some fine architectural buildings like the neoclassical **Casa de Cultura** (☎ 714-43-01; www.leon.gob.aix/id), facing Plaza de los Fundadores, and the big, twin-towered, baroque **Catedral Basílica** (cnr Obregón & Hidalgo), a block northeast of the Casa de Cultura. The neoclassical 1869 **Teatro Doblado** (☎ 716-43-01; cnr Aldama & Moreno) still stages concerts, dance and drama. The **Museo de la Ciudad** (☎ 714-50-22; Aldama 134; admission $0.20; 9:30am-2:30pm & 5-7:30pm Tue-Fri, 9:30am-2:30pm Sat & Sun) exhibits contemporary work by local artists.

Festivals & Events

In January/February, the **Guanajuato State Fair** attracts millions of visitors with agricultural displays, music, dancing, carnival rides and bullfights. Hundreds of shoemakers display their wares in the **Centro de Exposiciones** (Conexpo; ☎ 771-25-00; cnr López Mateos & Francisco Villa) during the fair. Like Guanajuato, León also celebrates a Cervantino cultural festival, starting mid-October. If you happen to be in the area, the annual **Festival del Globo** hot-air balloon gathering in mid-December is worth craning your neck for.

Sleeping & Eating

The Centro Histórico has several hostelries at various standards. There are many cheap hotels near the bus station on Calle La Luz (walk to the right from the station's main exit – La Luz is the first cross-street).

Hotel Fundadores (☎ 716-17-27; fax 716-66-12; Ortiz de Domínguez 218; s/d $17/18) A block west of Plaza Principal, the two-star Fundadores offers clean, comfortable rooms with TV, phone and few frills.

Hotel Capri (☎ 714-11-90; Ortiz de Domínguez 117; s/d $27/35) The Capri has 50 quaint rooms with TV, fan and bathroom. The most comfortable of the three-star hotels in Centro, the location and price are excellent. Ask for an exterior room for additional light and a view.

Howard Johnson Hotel Condesa (☎ 788-39-29, 800-710-39-64; www.hjleon.com; Portal Bravo 14; r/ste $70/110; [P] [□]) On the main plaza's east side, this corporate favorite has comfortable rooms and frequent 50% discounts. The busy restaurant has pool tables, live music, outdoor tables and a very popular buffet lunch ($7.50).

Hotel Fiesta Americana (☎ 719-80-00; www.fiestaamericana.com.mx; López Mateos Ote 1102; r from $139; [P] [☒] [□]) This is the most luxurious of the several top-end hotels on López Mateos, the boulevard that runs east from the center and becomes Hwy 45 to the airport.

Restaurant Cadillac (☎ 716-84-07; Hidalgo 107; mains $3.50-7) On a pedestrian street north of the plazas, the Cadillac is decorated with Hollywood posters. The set lunch ($4) is good value, and it serves tasty American and Mexican favorites until late at night.

Panteón Taurino (☎ 713-49-69; Calz de los Héroes 408; mains $6-9). For something different, try this restaurant-bar-museum where you eat off the gravestones of ex-bullfighters. The walk is dark at night, so it's best to catch a cab.

Shopping

For quality shoes, browse the dozens of shops around the center, or the main leather district near the bus station. Just south of the bus station, Plaza del Zapato and **Plaza Piel** (cnr López Mateos & Hilario Medina) are shopping malls devoted entirely to footwear and leather goods. Ordinary-looking shops on La Luz and Hilario Medina can have extraordinary leather bargains.

Getting There & Away

AIR

Aeropuerto Internacional del Bajío is 20km southeast on the Mexico City road. Aerolitoral, Aeroméxico, American, Continental

NORTHERN CENTRAL
HIGHLANDS

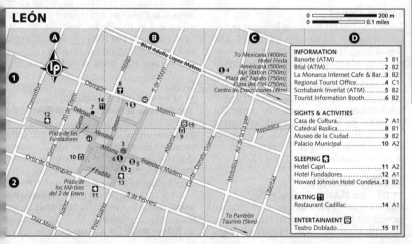

LEÓN

INFORMATION	
Banorte (ATM)	1 B1
Bital (ATM)	2 B2
La Monarca Internet Cafe & Bar	3 B2
Regional Tourist Office	4 C1
Scotiabank Inverlat (ATM)	5 B2
Tourist Information Booth	6 B2

SIGHTS & ACTIVITIES	
Casa de Cultura	7 A1
Catedral Basílica	8 B1
Museo de la Ciudad	9 B2
Palacio Municipal	10 A2

SLEEPING ⌂	
Hotel Capri	11 A2
Hotel Fundadores	12 A1
Howard Johnson Hotel Condesa	13 B2

EATING ⑪	
Restaurant Cadillac	14 A1

ENTERTAINMENT ◻	
Teatro Doblado	15 B1

and Mexicana offer direct flights to Acapulco, Guadalajara, Mexico City, Monterrey, Puerto Vallarta and Tijuana, plus a host of cities in the US.

Mexicana (☎ 714-95-00; López Matos 308) has an in-town office, but most other airline offices are at Bajío airport.

BUS

The **Central de Autobuses** (Blvd Hilario Medina s/n), just north of Blvd López Mateos 1½km east of the city center, has a cafeteria, left luggage, money exchange, Telecomm office and card phones. There are regular services to just about everywhere in northern and western Mexico.

Daily departures:

Destination	Price	Duration	Frequency
Guanajuato	$4	1hr	6 deluxe ETN
	$3.50	1hr	hourly 1st-class Primera Plus
	$3	1hr	2nd-class Flecha Amarilla every 15min
Mexico City			
(Terminal	$34	5hr	15 deluxe ETN
Norte)	$27	5hr	hourly 1st-class Primera Plus
	$23	5hr	2nd-class Herradura de Plata or Flecha Amarilla every 2hr
San Miguel	$13	2¼hr	2 deluxe ETN
de Allende	$10.50	2¼hr	2 1st-class Primera Plus

Getting Around

There's no bus service from Bajío airport to central León – a taxi costs about $14. The closest long-distance-bus station to the airport is in Silao; a taxi there from the airport will cost about $9.

From the bus station, turn left (south) and walk 150m to López Mateos, where 'Centro' buses ($0.40) go west to the city center. To return to the bus station, catch a 'Central' bus east along López Mateos, two blocks north of Plaza Principal. A taxi between the center and the bus station costs $3.

DOLORES HIDALGO

☎ 418 / pop 55,000 / elevation 1955m

Dolores is where the Mexican independence movement began in earnest. Here, at 5am on September 16, 1810, Miguel Hidalgo,

the parish priest, rang the bells to summon people to church earlier than usual and issued the Grito de Dolores, also known as the Grito de Independencia. His precise words have been lost to history but they boiled down to 'Long live Our Lady of Guadalupe! Death to bad government and the *gachupines*!' ('*Gachupines*' was a derisive term for the Spanish-born overlords who ruled Mexico.)

Hidalgo, Ignacio Allende and other conspirators had been alerted to the discovery of their plans to lead an uprising in Querétaro, so they decided to launch their rebellion immediately from Dolores.

Today, Hidalgo is Mexico's most revered hero, rivaled only by Benito Juárez in the number of civic monuments dedicated to him. Dolores was renamed in his honor in 1824. Visiting Dolores Hidalgo has acquired pilgrimage status for Mexicans, though it's not the most attractive town.

Orientation & Information

Everything of interest is within a couple of blocks of the Plaza Principal, which is a couple blocks north of the bus station.

The **tourist office** (☎ 182-11-64; ◷ 10am-6pm) is on the Plaza Principal's north side, in the Presidencia Municipal. The staff can answer, in Spanish, any questions about the town.

Cash and traveler's checks can be changed at several banks around the plaza (they all have ATMs). There are some *casas de cambio* too. **Puntonet.com** (Hidalgo s/n; ◷ 9am-8pm) has fast Internet connections for $0.75 an hour. Card phones are outside the tourist office and at the Flecha Amarilla bus station. There is a **post office** (☎ 182-08-07; cnr Puebla & Veracruz; ◷ 9am-2pm Mon-Sat) with Telcomm phones available in the same building.

Sights
PLAZA PRINCIPAL & AROUND

The **Parroquia de Nuestra Señora de Dolores**, the church where Hidalgo issued the Grito, is on the north side of the plaza. It has a fine 18th-century Churrigueresque facade. Some say that Hidalgo uttered his famous words from the pulpit, others claim that he spoke at the church door to the people gathered outside.

Adjacent to the church is the **Presidencia Municipal**, which has two colorful murals on the theme of independence. The plaza contains an **Hidalgo statue** (in Roman garb, on top of

MIGUEL HIDALGO: ¡VIVA MEXICO!

The balding head of the visionary priest Father Miguel Hidalgo y Costilla is familiar to anyone who's ogled Mexican statues or murals. A genuine rebel idealist, Hidalgo sacrificed his career and risked his life on September 16, 1810 when he launched the independence movement.

Born on May 8, 1753, son of a criollo hacienda manager in Guanajuato, he earned a bachelor's degree and, in 1778, was ordained a priest. He returned to teach at his alma mater and eventually became rector. But he was no orthodox cleric: Hidalgo questioned many Catholic traditions, read banned books, gambled, danced and had a mistress.

In 1800 he was brought before the Inquisition. Nothing was proven, but a few years later, in 1804, he found himself transferred as priest to the hick town of Dolores.

Hidalgo's years in Dolores show his growing interest in the economic and cultural welfare of the people. He started several new industries: silk was cultivated, olive groves were planted and vineyards established, all in defiance of the Spanish colonial authorities. Earthenware building products were the foundation of the ceramics industry that today produces fine glazed pots and tiles.

When Hidalgo met Ignacio Allende from San Miguel, they shared a criollo discontent with the Spanish stranglehold on Mexico. Hidalgo's standing among the mestizos and indigenous people of his parish was vital in broadening the base of the rebellion that followed.

Shortly after his Grito de Independencia, Hidalgo was formally excommunicated for 'heresy, apostasy and sedition.' He defended his call for Mexican independence and stated furthermore that the Spanish were not truly Catholic in any religious sense of the word but only for political purposes, specifically to rape, pillage and exploit Mexico. A few days later, on October 19, Hidalgo dictated his first edict calling for the abolition of slavery in Mexico.

Hidalgo led his growing forces from Dolores to San Miguel, Celaya and Guanajuato, north to Zacatecas, south almost to Mexico City and west to Guadalajara. But then, pushed northward, their numbers dwindled and on July 30, 1811, having been captured by the Spanish, Hidalgo was shot by a firing squad in Chihuahua. His head was returned to the city of Guanajuato, where it hung in a cage for 10 years on an outer corner of the Alhóndiga de Granaditas, along with the heads of independence leaders Allende, Aldama and Jiménez. Rather than intimidating the people, this lurid display kept the memory, the goal and the example of the heroic martyrs fresh in everyone's mind. After independence the cages were removed, and the skulls of the heroes are now in the Monumento a la Independencia in Mexico City.

a tall column) and a tree that, according to a plaque beneath it, was a sapling of the tree of the Noche Triste (Sad Night), under which Cortés is said to have wept when his men were driven out of Tenochtitlán in 1520.

The **Casa de Visitas**, on the plaza's west side, was the residence of Don Nicolás Fernández del Rincón and Don Ignacio Díaz de la Cortina, the two representatives of Spanish rule in Dolores. On September 16, 1810, they became the first two prisoners of the independence movement. Today, this is where Mexican presidents and other dignitaries stay when they come to Dolores for ceremonies.

MUSEO DE LA INDEPENDENCIA NACIONAL

The **National Independence Museum** (☎ 182-08-09; Zacatecas 6; adult/child Mon-Sat $1/free, Sun free; ◷ 9am-5pm) has few relics but plenty of information on the independence movement. It charts the appalling decline in Nueva España's in-

digenous population between 1519 (an estimated 25 million) and 1605 (1 million), and identifies 23 indigenous rebellions before 1800 as well as several criollo conspiracies in the years leading up to 1810. There are vivid paintings, quotations and details on the heroic last 10 months of Hidalgo's life.

MUSEO CASA DE HIDALGO

Miguel Hidalgo lived in this **house** (☎ 182-01-71; cnr Hidalgo & Morelos; adult/child Tue-Sat $2.50/free, Sun free; ◷ 10am-5:45pm Tue-Sat, 10am-4:45pm Sun) when he was Dolores' parish priest. It was here, in the early hours of September 16, 1810, that Hidalgo, Ignacio Allende and Juan de Aldama conspired to launch the uprising against colonial rule. It is now something of a national shrine. One large room is devoted to a collection of memorials to Hidalgo. Other rooms contain replicas of Hidalgo's furniture and independence-

DOLORES HIDALGO

INFORMATION
Banamex (ATM).....................1 D2
Bancomer (ATM)..................2 D1
Banorte (ATM).....................3 D2
HSBC (ATM).........................4 C1
Post Office..........................5 D2
Puntonet.com.....................6 C2
Telecomm........................(see 5)
Tourist Office......................7 D1

SIGHTS & ACTIVITIES
Casa de Visitas....................8 C1
Museo Casa de Hidalgo........9 C2
Museo de la Independencia
  Nacional.........................10 C1
Parroquia de Nuestra Señora
  de Dolores......................11 D1
Presidencia Municipal.......(see 7)
Statue of Hidalgo..............12 D1

SLEEPING
Hotel El Caudillo...............13 D1
Hotel Posada Hidalgo........14 C2

Posada Cocomacán............15 D1
Posada Dolores..................16 C1

EATING
Café La Taberna..............(see 22)
El Carruaje Restaurant.......17 D2
Fruti Yoghurt....................18 C2
Ice Cream Stand................19 D1
Ice Cream Stands..............20 D1
Restaurant El Delfín...........21 D2
Restaurant Plaza...............22 D2

SHOPPING
La Casa de las Artesanías....23 D2

TRANSPORT
Herradura de Plata & Pegasso
  Plus Bus Station.............24 C2
Primera Plus & Flecha Amarilla
  Bus Station....................25 C2

movement documents, including the order for Hidalgo's excommunication.

Festivals & Events

Dolores is the scene of major **Día de la Independencia** (16 September) celebrations, when the Mexican president often officiates. The **Fiestas Patrias** festivities start September 6 and the subsequent slate of cultural celebrations often doesn't end until November.

Sleeping

Most visitors stay here just long enough to see the church and museums, and enjoy an ice cream on the plaza.

Posada Cocomacán (☎ 182-60-86; www.posada cocomacan.com; Plaza Principal 4; s/d $31/41) The positively pink Cocomacán is the best place on the plaza. It has a good courtyard restaurant, rooftop-terrace bar and 38 clean rooms with TV, phones and good ventilation.

Hotel Posada Hidalgo (☎ /fax 182-04-77; hotelposa dahidalgo@hotmail.com; Hidalgo 15; s/d $32/37; P ⊡) This comfortable, modern hotel is conveniently located between the bus stations and the Plaza Principal. It's well managed and super-clean, though somewhat sterile. Rates include use of steam baths downstairs, which are also open to the public ($3.50).

Posada Dolores (☎ 182-06-42; Yucatán 8; s/d $15/21, without bathroom $6/11) This basic, friendly *casa de huéspedes* has the cheapest rooms in town, though they're pretty small. Pay a few pesos more for larger, renovated rooms with TV.

Hotel El Caudillo (☎ 182-01-98; cromero@prosat.net .mx; Querétaro 8; s/d $28/33; P) Opposite the east side of the church, El Caudillo has 32 carpeted rooms with cable TV. The rooms are clean, but a bit cramped. There is a nice restaurant-bar, and the on-site disco, Cesar's, goes off Thursday through Saturday.

Eating

Dolores is famous not only for its historical attractions but also for its ice cream. On the plaza's southwest and northeast corners you can get cones ($1.50) in a variety of unusual, fast-melting flavors including *mole, chicharrón* (fried pork skin), avocado, corn, cheese, honey, shrimp, whiskey, tequila and a dozen tropical-fruit flavors.

Fruti Yoghurt (Hidalgo s/n) This fruit stand is a fresh and healthy alternative. Also look for the delicious locally made *dulces* (sweets) at street stalls and in the markets.

El Carruaje Restaurant (☎ 182-04-74; Plaza Principal 8; mains $3-9) This huge place caters to day-tripping families with a $6 set lunch, live music at night and a big $8.50 weekend buffet.

Restaurant El Delfín (☎ 182-22-99; Veracruz 2; mains $4-8; ⏰ 9am-7pm) For surprisingly good seafood, check out this pleasant place one block east of the plaza. The fare here includes fish dishes, seafood soup and large shrimp servings.

Restaurant Plaza (☎ 182-02-59; Plaza Principal 17B; mains $4-10) A family place with good Mexican breakfasts, pasta, enchiladas and other *antojitos,* and a four-course set lunch ($6).

Café La Taberna (☎ 182-00-55; Plaza Principal 18; mains $1; ☿ noon-midnight Sun-Fri, 5pm-midnight Sat) This super-cheap café and bohemian hangout is the only alternative spot in sleepy Dolores. See young local artists displaying their talent.

Shopping

Ceramics, especially Talavera-ware (including tiles), have been the signature handicraft of Dolores ever since Padre Hidalgo founded the town's first ceramics workshop in the early 19th century. In the center, **La Casa de las Artesanías** (☎ 182-22-66; Plaza Princial 6) has the best variety, but if you've got wheels, stop by the ceramics workshops along the approach roads to Dolores for better prices. An increasing number of workshops make 'antique,' colonial-style furniture.

Getting There & Away

Nearly all buses to/from Dolores are 2nd-class. The Primera Plus/Flecha Amarilla station is on Hidalgo, 2½ blocks south of the plaza. Herradura de Plata/Pegasso Plus use a small station on Chiapas at Yucatán.

Daily departures:

Destination	Price	Duration	Frequency
Guanajuato	$3.75	1hr	2nd-class Flecha Amarilla every 20min 5:20am-9pm
Mexico City (Terminal Norte)	$22	5hr	1 1st-class Pegasso Plus noon
	$17.50	5hr	2nd-class Herradura de Plata or Flecha Amarilla every 40min 5:30am-9pm
San Miguel de Allende	$2.50	45min	2nd-class Flecha Amarilla every 30min 5:15am-9pm
	$2.50	45min	2nd-class Herradura de Plata every 20min

There are also regular 2nd-class connections to Querétaro ($6), León ($6.50) and San Luis Potosí ($8.50).

SAN MIGUEL DE ALLENDE

☎ 415 / pop 66,000 / elevation 1840m

Designated a national monument, San Miguel de Allende has all the panache of a cosmopolitan city and a history that precedes the name; it is true world charm with a facelift. The abundant presence of expatriate retirees has brought much urban renewal and cultural fusion, expanding art, music and dining venues, but don't expect an economic bohemian getaway. Once the draw of beatniks and creative types, art has been the overwhelming theme here since the '40s, with classic art institutions like Bellas Artes and the Instituto Allende adding an academic edge. San Miguel is internationally recognized for its magnificent light, colonial architecture and enchanting cobblestone streets, as well as for its art galleries and real-estate offices.

The town still maintains its quaint feel in the spring and fall when the foreigners fly north after winter and the busy summer Spanish lesson winds down, and when there are no festivals to celebrate in between. Undoubtedly the climate is one of its main attractions, cool and clear in winter, and warm and clear in summer, with occasional thunderstorms and heavy rain. Locals are especially fond of festivals, fireworks and parades, making the place even more colorful. It's easy for visitors to feel at home here; the shops, hotels, restaurants and bars are many and varied, and every other luxury is available.

History

The town, so the story goes, owes its founding to a few hot dogs. These hounds were dearly loved by a courageous barefooted Franciscan friar, Juan de San Miguel, who started a mission in 1542 near an often-dry river 5km from the present town. One day the dogs wandered off from the mission, and were later found reclining at the spring called El Chorro south of the present town. This site was so superior that the mission was moved.

San Miguel was then central Mexico's most northern Spanish settlement. Tarascan and Tlaxcalan allies of the Spanish were brought to help pacify the local Otomí and Chichimecs. San Miguel was barely surviving the fierce Chichimec resistance, until in 1555 a Spanish garrison was established to protect the new road from Mexico City to the silver center of Zacatecas. Spanish ranchers settled in the area, and it grew into a thriving commercial center known

NORTHERN CENTRAL HIGHLANDS

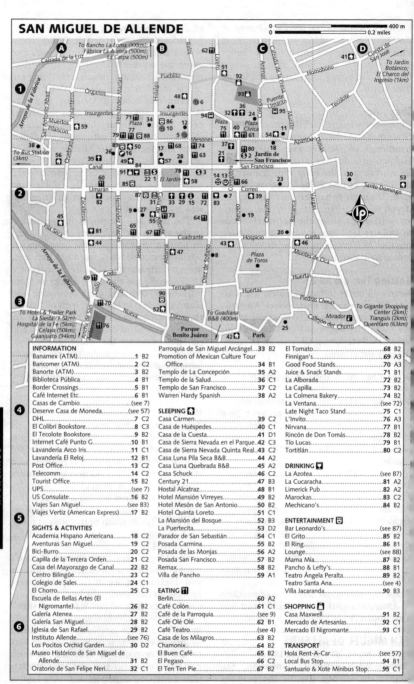

SAN MIGUEL DE ALLENDE

0 — 400 m
0 — 0.2 miles

INFORMATION
Banamex (ATM)...........................1 B2
Bancomer (ATM)........................2 C2
Banorte (ATM)...........................3 B2
Biblioteca Pública.......................4 B1
Border Crossings.........................5 B1
Café Internet Etc.........................6 B1
Casas de Cambio......................(see 7)
Deserve Casa de Moneda.........(see 57)
DHL...7 C2
El Colibrí Bookstore....................8 C3
El Tecolote Bookstore..................9 B2
Internet Café Punto G................10 B1
Lavandería Arco Iris..................11 C1
Lavandería El Reloj...................12 B1
Post Office................................13 C2
Telecomm................................14 C2
Tourist Office............................15 B2
UPS.......................................(see 7)
US Consulate............................16 B2
Viajes San Miguel...................(see 83)
Viajes Vertiz (American Express)...17 B2

SIGHTS & ACTIVITIES
Academia Hispano Americana....18 C2
Aventuras San Miguel...............19 C2
Bici-Burro................................20 C2
Capilla de la Tercera Orden.......21 C2
Casa del Mayorazgo de Canal...22 B2
Centro Bilingüe........................23 C2
Colegio de Sales......................24 C1
El Chorro.................................25 C3
Escuela de Bellas Artes (El
   Nigromante)..........................26 B2
Galería Atenea.........................27 B2
Galería San Miguel...................28 B2
Iglesia de San Rafael................29 B2
Instituto Allende...................(see 76)
Los Pocitos Orchid Garden........30 D2
Museo Histórico de San Miguel de
   Allende................................31 B2
Oratorio de San Felipe Neri.......32 C1

Parroquia de San Miguel Arcángel...33 B2
Promotion of Mexican Culture Tour
   Office...................................34 B1
Templo de La Concepción..........35 A2
Templo de la Salud...................36 C1
Templo de San Francisco...........37 C2
Warren Hardy Spanish...............38 A2

SLEEPING 🏠
Casa Carmen...........................39 C2
Casa de Huéspedes...................40 C1
Casa de la Cuesta....................41 D1
Casa de Sierra Nevada en el Parque...42 C3
Casa de Sierra Nevada Quinta Real...43 C2
Casa Luna Pila Seca B&B...........44 A2
Casa Luna Quebrada B&B..........45 A2
Casa Schuck............................46 C2
Century 21..............................47 B3
Hostal Alcatraz.........................48 B1
Hotel Mansión Virreyes.............49 B2
Hotel Mesón de San Antonio.....50 B2
Hotel Quinta Loreto...................51 C1
La Mansión del Bosque..............52 B3
La Puertecita............................53 D2
Parador de San Sebastián..........54 C1
Posada Carmina.......................55 B2
Posada de las Monjas................56 A2
Posada San Francisco................57 B2
Remax....................................58 B2
Villa de Pancho........................59 A1

EATING 🍴
Berlin.....................................60 A2
Café Colón..............................61 C1
Café de la Parroquia..............(see 9)
Café Olé Olé............................62 B1
Café Teatro..........................(see 4)
Casa de los Milagros.................63 B2
Chamonix...............................64 B2
El Buen Café............................65 B2
El Pegaso................................66 B2
El Ten Ten Pie..........................67 B2

El Tomato................................68 B2
Finnigan's................................69 A3
Good Food Stands....................70 A3
Juice & Snack Stands................71 B1
La Alborada.............................72 B2
La Capilla................................73 B2
La Colmena Bakery...................74 B2
La Ventana............................(see 72)
Late Night Taco Stand...............75 C1
L'Invito...................................76 A3
Nirvana..................................77 B1
Rincón de Don Tomás................78 B2
Tío Lucas................................79 B1
Tortitlán.................................80 B2

DRINKING 🍷
La Azotea............................(see 87)
La Cucaracha...........................81 A2
Limerick Pub............................82 A2
Marockas................................83 C2
Mechicano's............................84 B2

ENTERTAINMENT 🎭
Bar Leonardo's......................(see 87)
El Grito...................................85 B2
El Ring...................................86 B1
Lounge................................(see 88)
Mama Mía..............................87 B2
Pancho & Lefty's......................88 B1
Teatro Ángela Peralta................89 B2
Teatro Santa Ana..................(see 4)
Villa Jacaranda........................90 B3

SHOPPING 🛍️
Casa Maxwell..........................91 B2
Mercado de Artesanías.............92 C1
Mercado El Nigromante............93 C1

TRANSPORT
Hola Rent-A-Car...................(see 57)
Local Bus Stop.........................94 B1
Santuario & Xote Minibus Stop...95 C1

for its knives, textiles and horse tack. It also became home to some of Guanajuato's wealthy silver barons.

San Miguel's favorite son, Ignacio Allende, was born here in 1779. He became a fervent believer in the need for Mexican independence and was a leader of a Querétaro-based conspiracy that set December 8, 1810 as the date for an armed uprising (see boxed text, p633). After initial successes, Allende, Hidalgo and other rebel leaders were captured in 1811 in Chihuahua. Allende was summarily executed. When Mexico finally achieved independence in 1821 he was recognized as a martyr, and in 1826 the town was renamed San Miguel de Allende.

The Escuela de Bellas Artes was founded in 1938, and the town started to take on its current character when David Alfaro Siqueiros began mural-painting courses that attracted artists of every persuasion. The Instituto Allende opened in 1951, also attracting foreign students. Many were US citizens seeking to escape the conformity of post-WWII USA.

Orientation

The Plaza Principal, called El Jardín, is the town's focal point. The Gothic-like spires of the *parroquia* beside the Jardín can be seen from far and wide. The central area is small and straightforward, and most places of interest are within easy walking distance of the Jardín. Most streets change names at the Jardín. Canal/San Francisco on its north side, and Umarán/Correo on the south side, are the main streets.

Information

BOOKSTORES & LIBRARIES

Biblioteca Pública (☎ 152-02-93; Insurgentes 25; ☼ 10am-7pm Mon-Fri, 10am-2pm Sat) The public library functions as a cultural center with an emphasis on children's activities. Has an excellent collection of books in English and Spanish plus general reference books, novels and magazines. On-site Café Teatro is a great place for tea.

El Colibrí Bookstore (☎ 152-07-51; Diez de Sollano 30) Paperbacks, magazines and art books in English and Spanish.

El Tecolote Bookstore (☎ 152-73-95; Jesús 11; ☼ 10am-6pm Tue-Sat, 10am-2pm Sun) Many titles in English and Spanish.

EMERGENCY

Ambulance, Fire & Police (☎ 152-09-11)

Hospital de la Fe (☎ 152-25-45)

INTERNET ACCESS

Café Internet Etc (☎ 154-86-36; Reloj 37; ☼ 9:30am-6:30pm) English-speaking owner Juan Ortiz has a good bulletin-board of activities, good coffee, *comida corrida* ($5) and an excellent music exchange. Internet costs $1.50 per hour.

Internet Café Punto G (☎ 152-16-19; Hidalgo 23) High-speed Internet for $2 per hour and the best sushi in town.

INTERNET RESOURCES

Portal San Miguel (www.portalsanmiguel.com) A good overview of the town.

LAUNDRY

Laundromats charge around $4 to wash and dry up to 4kg.

Lavandería Arco Iris (☎ 152-53-86; Pasaje Allende, local N) Inside arcade off Mesones.

Lavandería El Reloj (☎ 152-38-43; Reloj 34A)

MEDICAL SERVICES

Hospital de la Fe (☎ 152-22-33, emergency 152-25-45; Libramiento a Dolores Hidalgo 43)

MEDIA

The weekly semi-bilingual (English/Spanish, but mostly English these days) newspaper, **Atención San Miguel** ($0.75) is full of local news, housing ads and yoga, Spanish, art and dance class schedules. You can buy it at the public library and elsewhere. The same sorts of things are advertised on notice boards in the Biblioteca Pública, on the Escuela de Bellas Artes and the language schools. Also look for other truly bilingual papers: the free *El Consejo* arts and culture tabloid, or the popular monthly *La Jerga*, advocating creative expression, humor and alternative perspectives. Concerning the arts, *El Petit Jornal* features prominent local artists and is the monthly source for upcoming exhibitions.

MONEY

There are several banks with ATMs in the couple of blocks east of the Jardín. There are also *casas de cambio* on Correro.

Deserve Casa de Moneda (☼ 9am-7pm Mon-Fri, 9am-5pm Sat) Exchange office inside Posada San Francisco.

POST

Border Crossings (☎ 152-24-97; www.bordercrossings ma.com; Mesones 57A; ☼ 9am-6pm Mon-Fri, 10am-3pm Sat) One of several places offering mail-forwarding, Internet access and phone-message services.

NORTHERN CENTRAL HIGHLANDS

Post office (cnr Correo & Corregidora) Mexpost express mail next door; DHL, FedEx and UPS all nearby on Correo.

TELEPHONE & FAX
Card phones are plentiful in the center, and there's a *caseta* at the bus station.
Telecomm (Correo 16) Telephone *caseta* two doors from post office.

TOURIST INFORMATION
Tourist office (☎ 152-09-00; www.turismosanmiguel .com.mx; Plaza Principal s/n; ☼ 10am-5pm Mon-Fri, 10am-2pm Sat & Sun) Adjacent to the Iglesia de San Rafael. Grab maps of the town and printed brochures in English and Spanish.

TRAVEL AGENCIES
Viajes San Miguel (☎ 152-25-37; www.viajessanmiguel .com; Diez de Sollano 4-Interior 3; ☼ 9am-7pm Mon-Fri, 10am-2pm Sat) Good deals including shuttle service.
Viajes Vertiz (☎ 152-18-56; www.viajesvertiz.com; Hidalgo 1A; ☼ 9am-2pm & 4-6:30pm Mon-Fri, 10am-2pm Sat) American Express agent; sells domestic and international air tickets.

Sights
PARROQUIA DE SAN MIGUEL ARCÁNGEL
The parish church's pink 'wedding cake' towers dominate the Jardín. These strange pinnacles were designed by indigenous stonemason Zeferino Gutiérrez in the late 19th century. He reputedly based the design on a postcard of a Belgian church, and instructed builders by scratching plans in the sand with a stick. The rest of the church dates from the late 17th century. In the chapel to the left of the main altar is the much-revered image of the *Cristo de la Conquista* (Christ of the Conquest), made in Pátzcuaro from cornstalks and orchid bulbs, probably in the 16th century. Irish visitors will be pleased to find a statue of St Patrick. The adjacent **Iglesia de San Rafael** was founded in 1742 and has undergone Gothic-inspired alterations.

MUSEO HISTÓRICO DE SAN MIGUEL DE ALLENDE
Near the *parroquia* is the house where Ignacio Allende was born, now the **history museum** (☎ 152-24-99; Cuna de Allende 1; admission $3; ☎ 9am-5pm Tue-Sun). Exhibits relate the interesting history of the San Miguel area, with special displays on Allende and the independence movement. A Latin inscription on the facade

reads *Hic natus ubique notus,* which means 'Here born, everywhere known.'

CASA DEL MAYORAZGO DE CANAL
This historic **house** (cnr Hidalgo & Canal), one of San Miguel's most imposing old residences, now houses Banamex offices. It's a handsome neoclassical structure with some late baroque touches. The original entrance is at Canal 4 and retains beautiful carved wooden doors.

TEMPLO DE SAN FRANCISCO
San Francisco church (cnr San Francisco & Juárez; admission free; ☼ 8am-9pm) has an elaborate late-18th-century Churrigueresque facade. An image of St Francis of Assisi is at the top. There's a free **museum** (☎ 152-09-47; ☼ 10am-2pm Mon-Fri) of religious paintings in the old convent beside the church.

CAPILLA DE LA TERCERA ORDEN
The **Chapel of the Third Order** (cnr San Francisco & Juárez; admission free; ☼ 8am-9pm) was built in the early 18th century and, like Templo de San Francisco, was part of a Franciscan monastery complex. The main facade shows St Francis and symbols of the Franciscan order.

ORATORIO DE SAN FELIPE NERI
This multi-towered and domed 18th-century **church** (Plaza Civica; ☼ 8am-9pm) is near the east end of Insurgentes. The pale-pink main facade is baroque with an indigenous influence. A passage to the right of this facade leads to the east wall, where a doorway holds the image of *Nuestra Señora de la Soledad* (Our Lady of Solitude). You can see into the cloister from this side of the church.

Inside the church are 33 oil paintings showing scenes from the life of San Felipe Nero, the 16th-century Florentine who founded the Oratorio Catholic order. In the east transept is a painting of the Virgin of Guadalupe by leading colonial-painter Miguel Cabrera. In the west transept is a lavishly decorated 1735 chapel, the **Santa Casa de Loreto**. It's a replica of a chapel in Loreto, Italy, legendary home of the Virgin Mary. If the chapel doors are open you can see tiles from Pueblo, Valencia and China on the floor and walls, and gilded cloth hangings. Behind the altar, the *camerán* (chapel behind the main church) has six elaborately gilded baroque altars. In one is a reclining wax figure of San Columbine; it contains the saint's bones.

TEMPLO DE LA SALUD

This **church** (Plaza Cívica; 8am-9pm), with a blue-and-yellow tiled dome and a big shell carved above its entrance, is just east of San Felipe Neri. The facade is early Churrigueresque. The church's paintings include one of San Javier by Miguel Cabrera. San Javier (St Francis Xavier, 1506–52) was a founding member of the Jesuits.

COLEGIO DE SALES

Once a college, founded in the mid-18th century by the San Felipe Nero order, **Colegio de Sales** (Plaza Cívica; 8am-6pm) has been renovated and regained its educational status as an extension of the University of León. It's adjacent to the **Templo de La Salud** (Plaza Cívica; 8am-9pm), which was once part of the same college. Many of the 1810 revolutionaries were educated here. Spaniards were locked up here when the rebels took San Miguel.

TEMPLO DE LA CONCEPCIÓN

The splendid **Church of the Conception** (cnr Zacateros & Canal; 8am-9pm) has a fine altar and several magnificent old oil paintings. Painted on the interior doorway are a number of wise sayings to give pause to those entering the sanctuary. The church was begun in the mid-18th century; its dome, added in the late 19th century by the versatile Zeferino Gutiérrez, was possibly inspired by pictures of Les Invalides in Paris.

ESCUELA DE BELLAS ARTES

The **School of Fine Arts** (Centro Cultural Nigromante; 152-02-89; Hernández Macías 75; admission free; 9am-8pm) is housed in the beautiful former monastery of La Concepción church, which was converted into a fine-arts school in 1938. It's officially named the Centro Cultural Ignacio Ramírez, after a leading 19th-century liberal thinker. His nickname is El Nigromante (The Sorcerer), and the center is also commonly called by this name.

INSTITUTO ALLENDE

This large 1736 **complex** (Ancha de San Antonio 20 & 22) has recently been divided between a school of higher education and an area focusing on Mexican culture and tourism.

Several patios, gardens and an old chapel divide the original home of the Conde Manuel de la Canal. Later it was used as a Carmelite convent, eventually becoming an art and language school in 1951. Above the entrance is a carving of the Virgin of Loreto, patroness of the Canal family.

MIRADOR & PARQUE BENITO JUÁREZ

One of the best views over the town and surrounding country is from the **mirador** (overlook) southeast of town. Take Callejón del Chorro, the track leading directly downhill from here, and turn left at the bottom, to reach **El Chorro**, the spring where San Miguel was founded. Today it gushes out of a fountain built in 1960, and there are still public washing tubs here. A path called Paseo del Chorro zigzags down the hill to the shady **Parque Benito Juárez**. Here generations of San Miguelenses have spent their leisure time among the abundant trees. Recently the park has undergone renovations including a new gazebo, enhanced pathways and an extensive playground, making the park more fit for family affairs.

JARDÍN BOTÁNICO EL CHARCO DEL INGENIO

The large Botanical Gardens (154-47-15; www.laneta.apc.org/charco/; off Antiguo Camino Real a Querétaro; admission $3; dawn-dusk), devoted mainly to cacti and other native plants of this semiarid region, is on the hilltop 1.5km northeast of town. It's a wildlife and bird sanctuary and a lovely place for a walk, particularly in the early morning or late afternoon, though women alone should steer clear of its more secluded parts. Pathways range along the slope above a reservoir and an impressive canyon where lies the namesake freshwater spring, the Charco del Ingenio (Pool of Ingenuity). Be sure to wander into the **Conservatory of Mexican Plants** (9am-4pm) inside the park, which houses a bewildering array of cacti and succulent species. See strange and endangered species from the Mexican landscape, host to the richest variety of cacti in the world.

The direct approach to the garden is to walk uphill from Mercado El Nigromante along Homobono and Cuesta de San José, then fork left up Montitlan past the Balcones housing development, from where signs point the way to the main entrance.

Alternatively, a 2km vehicle track leads north from the Gigante shopping center, 2.5km east of the center on the Querétaro road. Gigante can be reached on 'Gigante' buses from the bus stop on the east side of Jardín de San Francisco. A taxi to the gardens from the center costs about $2.50.

Closer to town, the **Los Pocitos Orchid Garden** (Santo Domingo 38; admission $1.50; ☺ 10am-2pm Tue-Sat) is home to 2000 plants covering 230 species. It's at its best in February, March and April.

GALLERIES

Galería San Miguel (☎ 152-04-54; Plaza Principal 14; ☺ 9am-2pm & 4-7pm Mon-Sat) and **Galería Atenea** (☎ 152-07-85; Jesús 2; ☺ 10am-2pm & 4-8pm Fri-Wed, noon-2pm Thu) are two of the best and most established commercial art galleries. For more contemporary art galleries and design studios of a variety of media, visit **Fábrica La Aurora** (☎ 152-13-12; Aurora s/n; ☺ 10am-6pm), a remodeled raw-cotton factory on the north end of town. In the parking lot is the lively circus tent **La Carpa** (p645). **Escuela de Bellas Artes** (p639) and **Instituto Allende** (p639) stage art exhibitions year-round. Other galleries advertise in the various local papers (see p637).

Activities

See Tours (right) for agencies that rent out bicycles and scooters and offer other enticing active options.

Posada de la Aldea opens its **swimming pool** (☎ 152-10-22; Ancha de San Antonio 15; admission $3.75) to nonguests most days, but it's more enjoyable to visit the *balnearios* (bathing spots) in the surrounding countryside (see p647).

Rancho La Loma (☎ 152-21-21; rancholaloma@ hotmail.com; Carretera Dolores Hidalgo s/n; per hr $30) rents horses and can arrange instruction and guides.

Courses

Several institutions offer Spanish courses, with group or private lessons, and optional classes in Mexican culture and history. There are also many courses in painting, sculpture, ceramics, music and dance. Most private lessons start around $14 an hour; group and long-term rates are much lower. Most courses are available year-round, except for a three-week break in December.

Academia Hispano Americana (☎ 152-03-49; www .ahaspeakspanish.com; Mesones 4) This place runs quality courses in the Spanish language and Latin American culture. The cultural courses are taught in elementary Spanish. One-on-one language classes, for any period you like, are also available. The school arranges homestays with Mexican families, with a private room and three meals per day, for around $23 per day.

Centro Bilingüe (☎ 152-54-00; www.geocities.com /centrobilingue; Correo 46) Offers Spanish instruction.

Escuela de Bellas Artes (☎ 152-02-89; Hernández Macías 75) Offers courses in art, dance, crafts and music. Most are given in Spanish and cost around $95 a month, plus materials. Registration is at the beginning of each month. Some classes are not held in July, and there are none in August.

Instituto Allende (☎ 152-01-90; www.instituto-allende .edu.mx; Ancha de San Antonio 22) Offers courses in fine arts, crafts and Spanish. Arts courses can be joined at any time and usually entail nine hours of attendance a week. Spanish courses begin every four weeks and range from conversational to total impact (maximum 12 students per class).

Warren Hardy Spanish (☎ 154-40-17, 152-47-28; www .warrenhardy.com; San Rafael 6) Offers Spanish instruction.

Tours

Aventuras San Miguel (☎ 152-64-06; aventurasma@ yahoo.com; Recreo 10; tours per day for groups of 3 or more $30; office ☺ 9am-2pm Mon-Sat) Rents scooters and conducts hiking, biking, camping and horseback-riding trips, as well as small group trips to many destinations in central Mexico.

Bici-Burro (☎ 152-15-26; www.bici-burro.com; Hospicio 1; trips $40-70) Conducts all-inclusive guided mountain-bike tours for groups of two or more. Popular trips include five- or six-hour excursions to Atotonilco or Pozos. It also rents bikes ($20 per day).

El Centro de Crecimiento Zamora (☎ 152-00-18) An English-language tour of the loveliest private homes and gardens in San Miguel begins at noon every Sunday from the Biblioteca Pública. Tickets go on sale at 11am. The cost is $16 for the two-hour tour, with three different houses visited weekly. Saturday tours of nearby ranches, haciendas and ruins are also offered, in aid of a disabled children's school.

Promotion of Mexican Culture (☎ 152-01-21, in USA 866-355-9655; www.pmexc.com; Hidalgo 18; walking tours $10-15, bus tours $55) This company conducts two-hour historical walking tours of central San Miguel, plus a variety of day tours by bus. Stop by their office in the Casa de Café for a brochure.

Festivals & Events

Since San Miguel is so well endowed with churches and patron saints (it has six), it also enjoys a multitude of festivals each month. You'll probably learn of some by word of mouth – or via firework bursts – while you're here.

Cristo de la Conquista The image of Christ in the *parroquia* is feted on the first Friday in March, with scores of dancers in elaborate pre-Hispanic costumes and plumed headdresses.

Semana Santa Two weekends before Easter, pilgrims carry an image of the Señor de la Columna (Lord of the Column) from Atotonilco, 11km north, to San Miguel's church of San Juan de Dios on Saturday night or Sunday morning. During Semana Santa, the many activities include the lavish Procesión del Santo Entierro on Good Friday and the burning or exploding of images of Judas on Easter Day.

Fiesta de la Santa Cruz This spring festival has its roots in the 16th century. It happens in the last week in May at Valle del Maíz, 2km from the center of town. Oxen are dressed in lime necklaces and painted tortillas, and their yokes festooned with flowers and fruit. A mock battle between 'Indians' and 'Federales' follows, with a wizard appearing to heal the 'wounded' and raise the 'dead.' Check for good live music as well.

Día de los Locos Mid-June features the day of the crazies, a colorful Carnavalesque parade through town toting all types of floats and people throwing out candy in costumes mostly of notorious characters.

Expresión in Corto Shared with the city of Guanajuato, this short-film festival in the first week of July is internationally recognized.

Chamber Music Festival The Escuela de Bellas Artes sponsors an annual festival of chamber music in the first two weeks of August.

Fiestas Patrias Two months of cultural programs kick off in mid-August; check with the tourist office for a full event schedule.

San Miguel Arcángel Celebrations honoring the town's chief patron saint are held around the third Saturday of September. There are cockfights, bullfights and *pamplonadas* (bull-running) in the streets. The party kicks off at 5am with an *alborada*, an artificial dawn created by thousands of fireworks around the cathedral. Traditional dancers from several states meet at Cruz del Cuarto, on the road to the train station wearing bells, feather headdresses, scarlet cloaks and masks, and walk in procession to the *parroquia* carrying flower offerings called *xuchiles*, some playing armadillo-shell lutes. Dances continue over a few days and include the Danza Guerrero in front of the *parroquia*, which represents the Spanish conquest of the Chichimecs.

Festival de Circo The first circus fest in Mexico, this celebration is held the second week in December at La Carpa (The Tent) just north of town.

San Miguel Music Festival This largely classical music festival presents an almost daily program with Mexican and international performers throughout the second half

BED & BREAKFAST, BOUTIQUE, BONANZA

If you like fantasy getaways in plush pockets of colonial grandeur mixed with world ethnic–themed rooms and garden adornments, then the converted mansions in San Miguel are your mecca. Recommendation is almost an obsolete task, as few of the options are sub-par, and the comparability between competing B&Bs is nil, the only alteration coming in the creativity of your room's theme name. There are several places that have targeted the Mexican artist and icon Frida Kahlo as their point of departure: blue walls and colonial furniture, with a spice of folkloric Mexican color so adored in her work. Other front-running themes are Asian Zen simplistic dens and Middle Eastern–inspired royal suites and, of course, the flavorful regional Mexican specials as well. Truly romantic, these retreats will engulf the senses and provide a luxurious way to enhance the light, color and already mystic ambience of colonial San Miguel.

of December. Most concerts are at the fine Teatro Ángela Peralta (see p645).

Sleeping

The better-value places are often full; reserve ahead if possible, especially during high seasons. Many hotels offer discounts to long-term guests. If you decide to stay a while, there are plenty of houses, apartments and rooms to rent (see p643).

BUDGET

Casa de Huéspedes (☎ 152-13-78; Mesones 27; s/d $14/23) This clean, pleasant upstairs hostelry has seven renovated rooms, two apartments and a rooftop terrace with good views. The two kitchenette units cost the same and you might negotiate a discount for a longer stay or at off-peak times.

Parador de San Sebastián (☎ 152-70-84; Mesones 7; r/tr $25/30; P) This central place is clean, quiet and quaint. Compare one of the newer, smallish rooms to one of the older ones around the courtyard with a fireplace before settling in.

Villa de Pancho (☎ 152-12-47; Quebrada 12; dm/s/d/ tr from $7.50/11/17/22) Jovial Pancho has a couple

NORTHERN CENTRAL HIGHLANDS

of rooms with shared bathrooms that rent for $70 per week or $275 per month. Same-day machine laundry service costs about $1 per kg. The restaurant serves tasty food and cheap beers.

Hostal Alcatraz (☎ 152-85-43; Reloj 54; dm from $10; 🖳) San Miguel's only HI-affiliated hostel is centrally located and appealing, with TV room and shared kitchen. Dorms are single-sex.

Trailer Park La Siesta (☎ 152-02-07; www.hotel lasiesta.com; Carretera Celaya 2km; RV sites $13; 🏊) This big grassy lot behind Hotel La Siesta is 2km south of town. It has 58 spaces with full hookups and showers, and shares the pool with the hotel, which charges $55 per night for basic doubles.

MIDRANGE

Casa Carmen (☎ 152-08-44; www.infosma.com/casa carmen; Correo 31; s/d $65/82) Centrally located in a charming colonial home, Natalie Moor-ing's B&B has 11 rooms with high-beamed ceilings, set around a pleasant courtyard with a fountain, flowers and orange trees. Rates include a delicious breakfast and lunch in the elegant dining room.

Posada Carmina (☎ 152-88-88; www.posada carmina.com; Cuna de Allende 7; s/d/ste from $62/78/91) Close to the Jardín, this former colonial mansion boasts large, attractive rooms, tiled bathrooms, phones and TV. There's a pleas-ant restaurant-bar in the leafy courtyard.

Posada de las Monjas (☎ 152-01-71; www.posada lasmonjas.com; Canal 37; s/d from $42/51; 🅿) This welcoming family-run monastery-turned-motel remains one of San Miguel's better values. The 65 carpeted rooms are comfortable and nicely decorated, and the bathrooms all have slate floors and hand-painted tiles. Rooms in the newer section out back are in better shape than those in the castle-like old section, and just as charming. Numerous terraces give lovely views over the valley. Restaurant, bar and laundry service are available, but readers warn against the breakfast. Rates are more for larger rooms and those with fireplaces.

Hotel Quinta Loreto (☎ 152-00-42; hqloreto@ cybermatsa.com.mx; Loreto 15; s/d $35/42; 🅿 🏊) This motel-style place is a long-time expat favorite. The 38 pleasant rooms, some with small private patio, are spread around large, leafy grounds. Many rooms are recently renovated, TV is available for an extra charge and the restaurant (open for breakfast and lunch) receives rave reviews. Stays of a week or longer net a 10% discount. Reservations recommended.

Guadiana B&B (☎ 152-49-48; www.hoteldeallende .com; Mesquite 11, Colonia Guadiana; s/d with breakfast $56/74) Ten rooms in a new Mediterranean-style home near the Guadiana Park, an easy 1km walk from the Jardín. A good value B&B offering a quiet stay.

Hotel Mesón de San Antonio (☎ 152-05-80; msan antonio@cibermatsa.com.mx; Mesones 80; r/ste $50/59; 🏊) Centrally located, this basic hotel has modern rooms around an attractive courtyard with a lawn and a small pool. Rates include breakfast and cable TV.

Hotel Mansión Virreyes (☎ 152-08-51; mansion virreyes@prodigy.net.mx; Canal 19; s/d/tr $54/63/102; 🅿) This colonial place half a block from the Jardín has 22 rooms (some renovated, some not) around two courtyards and a res-taurant-bar in the rear patio. There's a nice terrace and rates include breakfast.

La Mansión del Bosque (☎ 152-02-77; www.info sma.com/mansion; Aldama 65; s $47-65, d $68-102) Opposite Parque Benito Juárez, this long-running guesthouse has 23 unique rooms that haven't changed much since 1968. They are all comfortable and well-maintained, with decent furniture and original art. Rates are higher in winter and July/August, when the breakfast and dinner meal plan ($20) is mandatory. Reserve well in advance.

TOP END

Casa de Sierra Nevada Quinta Real (☎ 152-70-40, in Mexico 800-500-40-00, in USA & Canada 800-457-40-00; www .quintareal.com; Hospicio 35; r/ste from $200/300; 🅿 🏊) The most luxurious place in town has 33 units in five converted colonial mansions. It has a heated outdoor pool, day spa, two fine award-winning restaurants, views over the town, superbly appointed rooms and flawless service. Be sure to see its equally plush property, Casa de Sierra Nevada en el Parque, just east from Parque Benito Juárez.

Posada San Francisco (☎ 152-00-72; www.nafta connect.com/hsanfrancisco; Plaza Principal 2; r from $80 🅿 🗶 🖳) A classic hotel with a perfect location facing the Jardín. The newly re-modeled rooms provide a spacious colonial feel with double-paned glass to quiet the often-boisterous Jardín below. Valet park-ing costs $4 per day and there's a sidewalk café that's good for people-watching.

Casa de la Cuesta (☎ 154-43-24; www.casadela cuesta.com; Cuesta de San José 32; r $145) This highly ornate B&B and indigenous art gallery is perched on the hill just up from the town market. No detail was spared, from the entrance of sacred masks from different peoples in Mexico to the theme rooms. Try the bird room and wake up overlooking the whole town. Get a tour of the gallery, which supports indigenous artists in Mexico.

Casa Schuck (☎ /fax 152-06-57; www.casaschuck .com; Garita 3; r from $149) Just a couple of blocks up the hill from the Jardín, you can duck into this refuge of luxury. Each room is carefully crafted to a certain ambience, and the feeling ranges from quaint to royal. There are ample gardens and some fantastic views of town.

La Puertecita (☎ 152-50-11; www.lapuertecita.com; Santo Domingo 75; r from $176) This rambling property that meanders along the valley just above town offers seclusion in a forest setting. This retreat finds peace and quiet among the gurgling waters of the numerous fountains. The classical rooms range from simple to suite with full kitchens, spread along the hillside gardens. The restaurant is equally nice, and you can try out the waterslide if you get bored of all the quiet.

LONG-TERM ACCOMMODATIONS

Thinking of staying in San Miguel for more than a few weeks? Consider renting a house or apartment. Many lovely, fully furnished homes are only used for a few weeks a year, usually in winter, and are otherwise available for rent. Rates start at around $400 a month for a decent two-bedroom house. House-sitting is another possibility. Check the notice boards and tiers around town, scan the ads in the free

papers or contact one of the following local real-estate offices:

Century 21 (☎ 154-60-50; www.century21mexico.com; Aldama 10B)

Remax (☎ 152-73-63; www.realestate-sma.com; Portal Guadalupe 12)

Eating

San Miguel's eateries serve a startling variety of quality international cuisine. For thrifty travelers, there are plenty of more traditional options that cater to loyal crowds of local families.

BUDGET

Quality yet inexpensive places are still found in *centro*.

La Alborada (☎ 154-99-82; Diez de Sollano 11; dishes $2-4; ☽ 1-11pm Mon-Sat) Just around the corner from the Jardín you'll find this homelike alcove is a relaxing place to enjoy some good Mexican *antojitos*. Be sure to try the *pozole*, a rich soup made from chili *guajillo* with hominy complete with all the fixin's.

La Ventana (Diez de Sollano 11; dishes $1-3) This stroll-up café-window shares a nice patio with La Alborada. All caffeine combos and good pastries are found here with the added bonus of some of the finest organic roasts from Chiapas.

El Ten Ten Pie (☎ 152-71-89; Cuna de Allende 21; mains $3-6; ☽ 9am-midnight) This diminutive family-run hangout serves up home-style Mexican cooking with superb chili sauces. Try the inexpensive set lunch ($6.50), or *antojitos* like the tasty corn and squash tacos. Breakfast is great, the bar is full and there are always veggie options.

Tortitlán (☎ 152-33-76; Juárez 17; mains $2-5; ☽ 9am-7pm Mon-Sat, 10am-5pm Sun) Get yourself a heaping sandwich at this locally popular diner. Try to contain yourself while watching them grill up you order in the open kitchen – cruel, but great marketing – or phone for free delivery.

Café Colón (Mesones 25; set meals $2-3; ☽ 8am-5pm) This café is popular with locals for its cheap set breakfasts and lunches.

El Tomato (☎ 154-60-57; Mesones 62; mains $3-6; ☽ 9am-9pm Mon-Sat; Ⓥ) For something healthy, visit the Tomato, where light meals include pasta, whole-wheat sandwiches and salads, and feature fantastically fresh and tasty organic ingredients. There are also fresh-squeezed juices, and the set lunch ($6.50)

NORTHERN CENTRAL HIGHLANDS

is good value. The only drawback is that it isn't nonsmoking.

MIDRANGE
There are lively places facing the Jardín, where you pay a premium for the roaming musicians and ringside location, but don't be fooled: the best food is elsewhere.

Café de La Parroquia (☎ 152-31-61; Jesús 11; dishes $4-8; ☯ 8am-4pm Tue-Sat, 8am-2pm Sun) Enjoy the best breakfast in town in a tranquil courtyard setting. The food here is always good, so be sure to come back to La Brasserie (open from 5pm to 10pm, Tuesday to Saturday), its alter ego in the evening.

Chamonix (☎ 154-83-63; Diez de Sollano 17; dishes $6-11; ☯ 1-10pm Tue-Sat) Enjoy a nice meal in an inviting garden atmosphere. The menu mixes Mexican with French and Asian flavors. There is also a nice street-side lounge to have drinks after hours.

Café Olé Olé (☎ 152-08-96; Loreto 66; mains $5-10; ☯ 1-9pm) This friendly family-run café near the market is brightly decorated with bullfighting memorabilia. It's been eternally popular for its special: grilled chicken and beef fajitas.

Casa de los Milagros (☎ 152-00-97; Reloj 17; dishes $4-9; ☯ 1pm-midnight) This fresh place spins a taste of folkloric Mexico with bright painted colors, a courtyard and, of course, all kinds of Mexican *milagros* (miracles). Good value are the taco plates that come with ample portions and sides. There is a nice bar – a great place for margaritas and salsa dancing to the only Cuban group in town, on from 9pm on Wednesday, Friday and Saturday.

Finnigan's (☎ 152-02-57; Codo 7; mains $5-11; ☯ 10am-midnight Wed-Mon) This casual restaurant is set in a nice open courtyard that provides one of the best atmospheres in town. Enjoy a healthy blend of Mexican and Mediterranean food, while listening to some of the best live music in town including blues, latin, jazz, gypsy and samba.

Rincón de Don Tomás (☎ 152-37-80; Portal de Guadalupe 2; mains $6-11) The best restaurant on the Jardín has a solid menu of classic Mexican dishes like *chiles en nogada* (battered green chilies stuffed with meat and fruit) and *gorditas* using handmade tortillas.

El Buen Café (☎ 152-58-07; Jesús 23; mains $4-7; ☯ 9am-8pm Mon-Sat) Apart from the good coffee, this unpretentious place does healthy breakfasts, Mexican specialties and sweet home-baked goodies, each with an unexpected twist. Think ginger pancakes with homemade applesauce or thick oatmeal topped with blackberries and crème brûlée.

El Pegaso (☎ 152-13-51; Corregidora 6; mains $5-10; ☯ 8:30am-10pm Mon-Sat) A casual gringo favorite with good eggs Benedict, fresh bread and coffee. For lunch nosh on fancy sandwiches, and for dinner there's an intriguing mix of Mexican, Italian and Asian-inspired dishes, plus decadent desserts. Between bites, browse the intriguing assortment of dangling handicrafts.

TOP END
When money is no object, San Miguel is one of the country's best places to take a break from the lard and savor some fine cuisine.

Nirvana (☎ 150-00-67; Mesones 101; dishes $11-17; ☯ 8:30am-10pm Wed-Mon) Healthy and artistically done international fusion. Here you'll find a rich variety of tastes to suit even the most demanding palate, from watermelon *gazpacho* (spicy soup served cold) to venison in black-chili sauce.

Tío Lucas (☎ 152-49-96; Mesones 103; mains $8-13; ☯ noon-midnight) This US-style steakhouse is known for its beef and serves a good range of soups and salads; the Caesar is recommended. Happy hour runs from 6pm to 8pm weekdays and there's live blues or jazz nightly.

Berlin (☎ 152-94-32; Umarán 19; ☯ 1pm-1am) Stop in this cool, artsy spot for a tasty blend of German and Mexican food. The bar is very Euro and if you eavesdrop, you may get the scoop on where to find the next hip art opening.

L'Invito (☎ 152-73-33; Ancha de San Antonio 20; dishes $6-12; ☯ 1-11pm) Fresh and tasty Italian cuisine framed by a picture-perfect view of the *parroquia*, this pleasant restaurant on the grounds of the Instituto Allende is a promoter of 'slow food,' focusing on quality local and regional specialties.

La Capilla (☎ 152-06-98; Cuna de Allende 10; café $6-11, mains $15-20; ☯ 1-11pm Wed-Mon) The location – beneath the *parroquia* – is unique, and the atmosphere is magic at this elegant restaurant. While the menu offers 'tastes from Mexico and around the world,' the quality of food has slipped a bit in recent years as new and upcoming chefs battle their way into the decadent San Miguel scene. Downstairs the classy café-bar, an elegant place for drink, hosts live acoustic music.

SELF-CATERING & QUICK EATS

Snack carts on the Jardín offer cheap, tasty Mexican fare like *elotes* (steamed corn ears), hamburgers, hot dogs, fresh fruit salads and *tamales*. Reliable juice stands front the small plaza off Insurgentes, and the *taquería* on Mesones, just behind the San Francisco church, stays open late.

Downhill toward Instituto Allende, on the corner of Ancha San Antonio and tree-shaded Calle Nueva, several food stands alternate in the mornings and evenings, selling juice, *gorditas,* burritos, and tacos. They're very clean, the tastes are a treat and the experience is delightful.

La Colmena Bakery (Reloj 21; ☺ Mon-Sat) There are some excellent bakeries around town – don't miss this one.

Mercado El Nigromante (Colegio s/n) Has all the usual produce stands and market eateries only four blocks from the Jardín, but light years away from the gringo scene.

Drinking

La Azotea (☎ 152-82-75; Umarán 6) Above the restaurant Pueblo Viejo, this terrace is more of a lounge and tapas bar, with a smart, gay-friendly crowd and a less-touristy vibe.

Limerick Pub (☎ 154-86-42; Umarán 24) This traditional Irish pub has all the paraphernalia to fit the bill: a pool table, darts, classic tunes (mainly '80s), an Argentinian grill(?) and, of course, Guinness.

La Cucaracha (☎ 152-01-96; Zacateros 22) San Miguel's first bar, this fabled Beat dive is still rambling on. Stop in for cheap drinks and the occasional art opening, which brings in a live band. Women should bring a friend, for the crowd here is something of a mixed bag, where after hours all class lines are blurred. Everyone agrees the music is good. *Viva Mexico!*

Entertainment

LIVE MUSIC

Several restaurants double as drinking, dancing and entertainment venues. Most of the action is on Thursday, Friday and Saturday nights, but some places will have live music nightly.

Mama Mía (☎ 152-20-63; Umarán 8; cover $3-5; ☺ 8pm-2am) There are three separate areas for gigs, and weekends often see multiple bands performing. The main venue at this perennially popular place features live

rock/funk (Wednesday and Saturday). The restaurant patio attracts a more sophisticated crowd for live folk music, including South American music (Monday and Saturday), salsa (Friday and Saturday) and jazz (Sunday). Up front, Bar Leonardo's shows big-screen sports, and the terrace bar upstairs offers a fine view of the town. Serious nightlife gets going around 11pm.

Marockas (☎ 152-73-73; cnr Correo & Diez de Sollano) This rooftop café has live bands doing classic-rock covers from 10pm daily, and a 6pm to 9pm happy hour to get the students in early, but later on it's mostly an older crowd who appreciate the great views.

Mechicano's (☎ 152-02-16; Canal 16) This restaurant and bar is the culmination of San Miguel's night life. The Spanglish menu sums it up, and crowds eat up the highly kitsch theme. The open space allows for multiple bars with daily drink specials, and live jazz (Tuesday and Wednesday), salsa (Thursday) and rock on the weekends.

THEATER & CULTURAL EVENTS

For more formal entertainment, check out what's on in *Atención San Miguel.* The Escuela de Bellas Artes (p640) hosts a variety of cultural events, many in English; check its notice board for a current schedule.

Teatro Ángela Peralta (☎ 152-22-00; cnr Mesones & Hernández Macías) Built in 1910, this elegant venue often hosts local productions.

La Carpa (☎ 154-6981; Aurora s/n; ☺ 10am-2pm) Check with the monthly art review *El Petit Journal* and its affiliate La Carpa, a dynamic circus tent hosting alternative dance, gymnastic and aerobics classes, as well as monthly openings including live music, theater, art and circus acts.

CINEMA

Teatro Santa Ana (☎ 152-02-93; Reloj 50A; tickets $4) This small theater inside the library plays host to a good selection of independent and international films, both past and present, as well as an occasional local play.

Villa Jacaranda (☎ 152-10-15; Aldama 53; tickets $5.50) Projects recent releases of US movies on a big screen at 7:30pm daily. Entry includes a drink and popcorn.

The Biblioteca Pública (see p637) screens quality videos in the evening Tuesday to Saturday.

NORTHERN CENTRAL HIGHLANDS

NIGHTCLUBS & DISCOS

Pancho & Lefty's (☎ 152-19-58; Mesones 99; cover $3-5; ☺ 8pm-3am Wed, Fri & Sat) A young, affluent, hard-drinking crowd flocks here for live, loud rock, and blues covers. While upstairs the gay-friendly Lounge mixes DJ techno, disco, and chill-out.

El Ring (☎ 152-19-98; Hidalgo 25; cover $3-6; ☺ 10pm-3am Thu-Sat, nightly in high season) This flashy place is San Miguel's most popular club with young locals, blasting a mix of Latin, US and European dance music. On Wednesday it transforms into Club 27 and swings to salsa rhythms for a more refined crowd.

El Grito (☎ 152-00-48; Umarán 15; ☺ 10pm-3am) An oversized face shouts above the doorway of this upscale disco opposite Mama Mía.

Shopping

San Miguel has one of Mexico's biggest and best concentrations of craft shops, with folk art and handicrafts from all over the country. Local crafts include tinware, wrought iron, silver, brass, leather, glassware, pottery and textiles. Prices are not low, but quality is high and the range of goods is mind-boggling.

Casa Maxwell (☎ 152-02-47; Canal 14; ☺ 9am-2pm & 4-7pm Mon-Fri, 10am-2pm & 4-8pm Sat, 11am-3pm Sun) This rambling store offers a tremendous array of decorative and household goods. There are many, many more within a few blocks, especially on Canal, San Francisco and Zacateros.

The **Mercado de Artesanías** (Colegio s/n) is a collection of handicraft stalls in the alleyway between Colegio and Loreto; prices are lower than in San Miguel's smarter shops, but the quality varies. The **Mercado El Nigromante** (Colegio s/n) sells fruit, vegetables and assorted goods, mostly to the local community.

Be sure to hit the Tianguis (Tuesday market), the biggest weekly outdoor extravaganza beside the Gigante shopping center, 2.5km east of the center on the Querétaro road. Take a 'Gigante' or 'Placita' bus (10 minutes) from the Jardín's east side.

Getting There & Away

AIR

The nearest tarmac is Aeropuerto Internacional del Bajío, between León and Silao. There are direct flights to Acapulco, Guadalajara, Monterrey, Puerto Vallarta and Tijuana, plus a host of cities in the US. Most airlines have an office inside the airport.

Mexico City's airport is served by many more direct (usually cheaper) flights than Bajío, but the latter, around 1½ hours away by car, is more convenient for San Miguel.

BUS

The small Central de Autobuses is on Canal, 3km west of the center. ETN, Primera Plus and Pegasso Plus tickets can be bought in town at **PMC Tours** (☎ 152-01-21; Hidalgo 18).

Daily departures:

Destination	Price	Duration	Frequency
Celaya	$3	1¾hr	2nd-class Flecha Amarilla every 15min
Dolores Hidalgo	$2.50	1hr	2nd-class Flecha Amarilla or Herradura de Plata every 40min 6am-10pm
Guadalajara	$36	5hr	2 deluxe ETN
	$30	5½hr	6 1st-class Primera Plus
	$24	6hr	1 2nd-class Servicios Coordinados 7:50pm
Guanajuato	$10	1-1¼hr	2 deluxe ETN
	$7	1-1¼hr	4 1st-class Primera Plus
	$5.50	1-1½hr	2 1st-class Ómnibus de México
	$6.50	1-1½hr	10 2nd-class Flecha Amarilla
León	$12.50	2¼hr	2 deluxe ETN
	$12	2¼hr	1 1st-class Primera Plus
	$9	2¼hr	2 2nd-class Servicios Coordinados
Mexico City (Terminal Norte)	$23	3½-4hr	4 deluxe ETN
	$19	3½hr	2 1st-class Primera Plus & 2 1st-class Herradura de Plata
	$15.50	4hr	2nd-class Herradura de Plata semi-direct every 40min 7am-8pm
Querétaro	$7	1hr	3 deluxe ETN
	$4	1¼hr	2nd-class Flecha Amarilla or Herradura de Plata every 40min 7am-8pm

Other 1st-class buses serve Aguascalientes, Monterrey and San Luis Potosí. Americanos buses depart for Texas and Chicago at 5:30pm daily.

CAR & MOTORCYCLE

If you need a car for more than a few days, it may be worth going to Querétaro, or at least contacting rental agencies there. The only

San Miguel–based agency is **Hola Rent-a-Car** (☎ 152-01-98; www.holarentacar.com; Hotel San Francisco; ☼ 9am-2pm & 4-7pm), inside Posada San Francisco. Prices start around $60 per day for a manual-transmission compact Chevy. Reserve at least a week ahead, especially during the high season.

Getting Around
TO/FROM THE AIRPORT
A few agencies provide transport to/from Bajío, if there are enough passengers. Try **PMC Tours** (☎ 152-01-21), **Aventuras San Miguel** (☎ 152-64-06) or **Viajes Vertiz** (☎ 152-18-56). Alternatively, take a bus to Silao and get a taxi from there to the airport. For Mexico City airport, get a bus to Querétaro, and a bus direct to the airport from there.

Via bus from Bajío airport, you must make a connection in León. Taxis charge around $60 one-way.

TO/FROM THE CENTRE
Local buses ($0.35) run from 7am to 9pm daily. 'Central' buses run every few minutes between the bus station and the town center. Coming into town these go up Insurgentes, wind through the town a bit and terminate at Juárez in front of the Jardín de San Francisco. Heading out of the center, you can pick one up on Canal. A taxi between the center and the bus station costs around $2, as do most trips around town.

AROUND SAN MIGUEL DE ALLENDE
Hot Springs
Natural hot springs near San Miguel have been developed as *balnearios*, with swimming pools where you can soak in mineral waters amid pleasant surroundings. The *balnearios* are accessed via the highway north of San Miguel – take a Dolores Hidalgo bus from the San Miguel bus station, or a 'Santuario' minibus (half-hourly) from the bus stops on Puente de Umarán, off Colegio and opposite the Mercado El Nigromante. These buses will stop out front, or within walking or hitching distance, of all the main *balnearios*. Returning to town, hail a bus along the highway. Taxis (around $9 each way) are another option; you can ask the driver to return for you at an appointed time. Most places are crowded with local families on weekends but *muy tranquilo* (very peaceful) during the week.

The most popular *balneario* is **Taboada** (☎ 152-08-50; admission $4.50; ☼ 9am-6pm Wed-Mon), 8km north then 3¼km west down a signposted cobblestone road. It has a large lawn and three swimming pools: one Olympic-size with warm water, a smaller pool for children and a thermal spa that gets quite hot. A snack kiosk and a bar provide refreshments. Hourly 'Xote' minibuses, departing from Puente de Umarán, will get you within 1½km of Taboada. Jump off where the bus turns off the Taboada side road and walk the remaining 15 minutes to the hot springs.

Nearby, the family-oriented **Balneario Xote** (☎ 155-81-87; www.xoteparqueacuatico.com; adult/child $6/3; ☼ 9am-6pm) water park is 3½km off the highway down the same cobblestone road as Taboada. At the next turnoff beside the highway to Dolores Hidalgo is **Santa Verónica** (adult/child $3.75/3.25; ☼ 9am-6pm Sat-Thu).

Next up, **Escondido Place** (☎ 185-20-22; admission $7.50; ☼ 8am-5:30pm) has two warm outdoor pools and three connected indoor pools, each progressively hotter. The picturesque grounds have plenty of picnicking space, and there's a kiosk for drinks and snacks. It's 10km from San Miguel, 1km up a gravel road (a 15-minute walk) off the road to Dolores Hidalgo.

Just past Parador del Cortijo at Km 9.5, **La Gruta** (☎ 185-20-99; admission $6.50; ☼ 8am-5pm)

SANTUARIO DE ATOTONILCO

Turning west off the Dolores Hidalgo Hwy 11km north of San Miguel, and going 3km will bring you to the hamlet of Atotonilco, dominated by its sanctuary founded in 1740 as a spiritual retreat. Ignacio Allende married here in 1802. Eight years later he returned with Miguel Hidalgo and a band of independence rebels en route from Dolores to San Miguel to take the shrine's banner of the Virgin of Guadalupe as their flag.

A journey to Atotonilco is the goal of pilgrims and penitents from all over Mexico, and the starting point of an important and solemn procession two weekends before Easter, in which the image of the Señor de la Columna is carried to the church of San Juan de Dios in San Miguel. Inside, the sanctuary has six chapels and is vibrant with statues, folk murals and paintings. Restoration is ongoing. Traditional dances are held here on the third Sunday in July.

has three small pools where a thermal spring is channeled. The hottest is in a cave entered through a tunnel, with water gushing from the roof, lit by a single shaft of sunlight.

Pozos

☎ 412 / pop 2261 / elevation 2305m

Less than a hundred years ago, Mineral de Pozos was a flourishing silver- and copper-mining center of 50,000 people, but as the minerals played out the population dwindled leaving abandoned houses, mine workings and a large but unfinished church. Now visitors enjoy exploring the crumbling buildings and touring the surrounding area by horseback or mountain bike. You can also visit workshops that produce replicas of pre-Hispanic musical instruments like deerskin drums and rainmakers, which are used to accompany traditional dances in local fiestas.

Two inviting, aesthetically pleasing B&Bs-cum-galleries await side-by-side facing the sleepy main plaza. **Casa Mexicana Hotel** (☎ 293-00-14; www.casamexicanahotel.com; Jardín Principal 2; r from $80; **P**) is a 100-year-old hacienda, and was Pozos' first place to be converted to tourist lodging (and it was very well done). The unique, multilevel rooms – each with its own Picasso lithograph – are elegant and spacious. One has a tree growing inside. Also here is Café des Artistes. Like all great art, each plate attempts to balance and stimulate the senses, truly an artistic culinary experience. **Casa Montana** (☎ 293-00-32; www.casamonta nahotel.com; Jardín Principal 4A; r/ste $92/122) has had a total renovation that has turned this antique stone building into a comfortable B&B, restaurant and art gallery featuring haunting black-and-white photos by American Jack Spencer.

Posada de las Minas (☎ 293-02-13; www.posada delasminas.com; Doblado 1; r/apt $71/119) is an eloquently done refuge set in a restored 19th-century hacienda. Choose from unique rooms or apartments in a colonial setting. Meander the impressive cactus gardens surrounding the grounds, or have a drink at the bar and drift back to a slower time.

Pozos is 14km south of San Luis de la Paz, a detour east of Hwy 57. To get here by bus from San Miguel, go first to Dolores Hidalgo, then to San Luis de la Paz and then take a third bus to Pozos. By car it's about

45 minutes from San Miguel. Aventuras San Miguel runs day-trips to Pozos from San Miguel and Bici-Burro does it as a bike tour (see p640 for details).

QUERÉTARO STATE

Querétaro state (population 1.52 million) is primarily an agricultural and ranching state. Industry has developed around Querétaro city and San Juan del Río. The state also turns out opals, mercury, zinc and lead. Apart from Querétaro city, with its fine colonial architecture and storied history, there are other areas worth visiting, like the thermal springs of Tequisquiapan or the world's third-largest monolith, La Peña de Bernal. In the state's northeast corner, the rugged Sierra Gorda has little-visited archaeological sites and a dramatic road descending to old mission towns in a large biosphere reserve on the fringe of the Huasteca.

QUERÉTARO

☎ 442 / pop 612,000 / elevation 1762m

Exploring Querétaro's sprawling plazas, museums and clean pedestrian tributaries is a real pleasure. Not nearly as physically dramatic as its historical counterparts of Guanajuato or Zacatecas, this pleasantly organized city played a major role in Mexico's history, leading to its inscription as a Unesco World Heritage site in 1996. A growing sophistication makes for a lively evening stroll among the floodlit buildings of the colonial center.

History

The Otomí founded a settlement here in the 15th century that was soon absorbed by the Aztecs, then by Spaniards in 1531. Franciscan monks used it as a missionary base not only to Mexico but also to what is now southwestern USA. In the early 19th century, Querétaro became a center of intrigue among disaffected criollos plotting to free Mexico from Spanish rule. Conspirators including Miguel Hidalgo, met secretly at the house of doña Josefa Ortiz (La Corregidora), who was the wife of Querétaro's former *corregidor* (district administrator).

When the conspiracy was uncovered, the story goes, doña Josefa was locked in her house (now the Palacio de Gobierno) but managed to whisper through a keyhole to a co-conspirator, Ignacio Pérez, that their colleagues were in jeopardy, leading to Padre Hidalgo's call to arms (see the boxed text, p633).

In 1917 the Mexican constitution was drawn up by the Constitutionalist faction in Querétaro. The PNR (which later became the PRI, the Institutional Revolutionary Party) was organized in Querétaro in 1929, and it dominated Mexican politics for the rest of the 20th century.

Orientation

The historic center is fairly compact, with *andadores* (pedestrian streets) linking a number of lively plazas – which makes for pleasant strolling. The heart of things is Jardín Zenea, the main plaza, with Av Corregidora, the main downtown street, running along its east side. The Plaza de Armas (aka Plaza de la Independencia) is two blocks east, and the small Plaza de la Corregidora is a block north. The shady Alameda, a few blocks south, is popular for picnicking, jogging, strolling and relaxing in general. Madero/Calle 5 de Mayo is the boundary between north–south and east–west street addresses.

Information

There are card phones on Jardín Zenea, Plaza de Armas and elsewhere around the center. Handy no-name Internet places are at Libertad 32 and Carranza 9; both charge around $1 per hour. There are several banks with ATMs around Jardín Zenea. *Casas de cambio* are along Juárez and Colón.

Ambulance, Fire & Police (☎ 066)

Hospital Luis Martín (☎ 214-25-71; Zaragoza Pte 88)

Librería Cultural del Centro (☎ 224-24-61; cnr 16 de Septiembre & Corregidora; ⏰ 9am-8pm Mon-Fri, noon-5pm Sat) This central bookstore has a great selection of cultural titles as well as some books in English.

Post office (☎ 212-01-12; Arteaga 5; ⏰ 9am-5pm Mon-Fri)

Telecomm (Allende Nte 4) Has Internet and money-order services.

Tourist office (☎ 212-12-41, 238-50-67, 800-715-17-42; www.venaqueretaro.com; Pasteur Nte 4; ⏰ 9am-8pm) Has city maps and brochures.

Turismo Beverly (☎ 216-15-00; Tecnológico 118) The American Express agent, which also books airplane tickets.

Viajando por Mexico (☎ 212-34-52; Plaza Constitución) Information kiosk.

Sights

TEMPLO DE SAN FRANCISCO

This impressive **church** (cnr Av Corrigidora & Andadora 5 de Mayo; ⏰ 8-10am & 4-9pm) fronts Jardín Zenea. Pretty colored tiles on the dome were brought from Spain in 1540, around the time construction of the church began. Inside are some fine religious paintings from the 17th, 18th and 19th centuries.

MUSEO REGIONAL

The **Museo Regional** (☎ 212-20-31; cnr Av Corregidora & Jardín Zenea; admission $3; ⏰ 10am-7pm Tue-Sun) is beside Templo de San Francisco. The ground floor holds exhibits on pre-Hispanic Mexico, archaeological sites, Spanish occupation and the state's various indigenous groups.

Upstairs there are exhibits on Querétaro's role in the independence movement, post-independence history and many religious paintings. The table at which the Treaty of Guadalupe Hidalgo was signed in 1848, ending the Mexican–American War, is on display, as is the desk of the tribunal that sentenced Emperor Maximilian to death.

The museum is housed in part of what was once a huge monastery and seminary. Begun in 1540, the seminary became the seat of the Franciscan province of San Pedro y San Pablo de Michoacán by 1567. Building continued until at least 1727. The tower was the city's highest vantage point, and in the 1860s the monastery was used as a fort both by imperialists supporting Maximilian and by the forces who finally defeated him in 1867.

MUSEO DE ARTE DE QUERÉTARO

Adjacent to the Templo de San Agustín, **Querétaro's art museum** (☎ 212-23-57; Allende Sur 14; $2, Tue free; ⏰ 10am-6pm Tue-Sun) occupies a splendid baroque monastery built between 1731 and 1748. There are angels, gargoyles, statues and other ornamental details all over the building, particularly around the stunning courtyard.

The ground-floor display of 16th- and 17th-century European paintings traces interesting influences, from Flemish to Spanish to Mexican art. On the same floor you'll find 19th- and 20th-century Mexican paintings, a collection of paintings by 20th-century Querétaro artists and a hall for temporary exhibitions. The top floor has more art, from 16th-century mannerism to 18th-century baroque. There's a good bookstore and gift-shop.

MUSEO DE LA CIUDAD

Inside the ex-convent and old prison that held Maximilian, the 11-room **City Museum** (☎ 212-47-02; Guerrero Nte 27; admission $0.65, students free; ⏳ 11am-6:45pm Tue-Sun) has quite good alternating contemporary art exhibits. It's also worth checking out the **Museo de la Restauración de la Republica** (☎ 224-30-04; Guerrero Nte 23; admission free; ⏳ 9am-5pm) next door, as Querétaro's role in Mexico's history is quite interesting. Discover more about the period of French occupation and the eventual ousting of Emperor Maximilian.

TEATRO DE LA REPÚBLICA

This lovely old **theater** (☎ 212-03-39; cnr Juárez & Peralta; ⏳ 10am-2pm & 5-8pm Tue-Sun) was where a tribunal met in 1867 to decide the fate of Emperor Maximilian. Mexico's constitution was also signed here on January 31, 1917. The stage backdrop lists the names of its signatories and the states they represented. In 1929, politicians met in the theater to organize Mexico's ruling party, the PNR (now the PRI).

PALACIO DE GOBIERNO (CASA DE LA CORREGIDORA)

Doña Josefa Ortiz' home, where she informed Ignacio Pérez of the plans to arrest the independence conspirators, occupies the Plaza de Armas' north side. Today the building is the state-government building. The room where doña Josefa was imprisoned is upstairs, over the entrance – it's now the governor's conference room. The building can be visited during normal office hours, but there's not much to see.

CONVENTO DE LA SANTA CRUZ

Ten minutes' walk east of the center is one of the city's most interesting sights. The **monastery** (☎ 212-03-35; cnr Acuña & Independencia; donation requested; ⏳ 9am-2pm Tue-Fri, 9am-4:30pm Sat) was built between 1654 and about 1815 on the site of a battle in which a miraculous appearance of Santiago (St James) led the Otomí to surrender to the conquistadors and Christianity. Emperor Maximilian had his headquarters here while under siege in Querétaro from March to May 1867. After his surrender and subsequent death sentence, he was jailed here while awaiting the firing squad. Today it's used as a religious school.

A guide will provide insight into the Convento's history and artifacts, which include an ingenious water system and unique colonial ways of cooking and refrigeration. The guide will also relate several of the site's miracles, including the legendary growth of a tree from a walking stick stuck in the earth by a pious friar in 1697. The thorns of the tree form a cross. Tours are given in English or Spanish.

ACUEDUCTO & MIRADOR

Walk east along Independencia past Convento de la Santa Cruz, then fork right along Ejército Republicano, and you come to a **mirador** with a view of 'Los Arcos,' Querétaro's emblematic 1.28km **aqueduct**, with 74 towering arches built between 1726 and 1735. The aqueduct runs along the center of Av Zaragoza and still brings water to the city from 12km away.

Across the street from the mirador is the **Mausoleo de la Corregidora** (Ejercito Rupulicano s/n; ⏳ 8am-2pm & 4-7pm), the resting place of doña Josefa Ortiz and her husband, Miguel Domínguez de Alemán. Behind the tomb is a shrine with pictures and documents relating to doña Josefa's life.

OTHER CENTRAL SIGHTS

Plaza de la Corregidora is dominated by the **Monumento a la Corregidora** (cnr Corregidora & Andadora 16 de Septiembre), a 1910 statue of doña Josefa Ortiz bearing the flame of freedom.

A block west of Jardín Zenea is the **Fuente de Neptuno** (Neptune's Fountain; cnr Andador Madero & Allende), designed by noted Mexican neoclassical-architect Eduardo Tresguerras in 1797. Adjacent, the 17th-century **Templo de Santa Clara** (cnr Andador Madero & Allende; ⏳ 10am-6pm) has an ornate baroque interior. Two blocks west on Madero is the rather plain 18th-century **cathedral** (cnr Madero & Ocampo ⏳ 8am-2pm & 5-9pm). Hidalgo, which runs parallel to Madero two blocks north, is lined with many fine mansions.

At the intersection of Arteaga and Monte is the 18th-century **Templo de Santa Rosa de Viterbos** (⏳ 8am-2pm & 5-9pm), Querétaro's most splendid baroque church, with its pagoda-like bell tower, unusual exterior paintwork, curling buttresses, and lavishly gilded and marbled interior. The church also boasts what some say is the earliest four-sided clock in the New World.

Other notable colonial churches include the **Templo de San Antonio** (cnr Peralta & Corregidora Nte; ☒ 8am-2pm & 5-9pm) with two large pipe organs, elaborate crystal chandeliers and several oil paintings; and the **Templo de la Congregación** (cnr Pasteur Nte & 16 de Septiembre; ☒ 8am-2pm & 5-9pm) with beautiful stained-glass windows and a splendid pipe organ.

The **Casa de la Zacatecana** (☎ 224-07-58; Independencia 59; admission $2; ☒ 10am-6pm Tue-Sun) is a finely restored 17th-century home with its own murder mystery – look for the skeletons in the basement. The main attraction is the collection of 18th- and 19th-century furniture and decorations.

CERRO DE LAS CAMPANAS
A good 35-minute walk from the center, the **Cerro de las Campanas** (Hill of the Bells) was the site of Maximilian's execution. The emperor's family constructed a chapel here. Today the area is a park, with a statue of Benito Juárez, a café and the **Museo del Sitio (Siege) de Querétaro** (☎ 215-20-75; admission $0.10; ☒ 10am-2pm & 3:30-6pm). Hop on a west-bound 'Tecnológico' bus on Zaragoza at Alameda Hidalgo and get off at the Ciudad Universitaria.

Courses
Olé Spanish Language School (☎ 214-40-23; www.ole.edu.mx; Escobedo 32) offers a range of courses with homestay options and extracurricular programs. Prices start at $14 per hour, and weeklong courses range from moderate group classes for 15 hours from $142, to intensive 35 one-hour private classes for $365.

Tours
Guided tours of the city center on the Tranvía bus ($7.50) in English or Spanish, leave the tourist office hourly from 9am to 5pm depending on demand. Other tours are available at the information kiosk **Viajando por Mexico** (☎ 212-34-52; Plaza Constitución), including city tours ($6.50) and longer trips ($35) to regional attractions.

Festivals & Events
Querétaro's **Feria Internacional**, one of Mexico's biggest state fairs, happens in the first two weeks of December. While it focuses on livestock, it also covers industry, commerce, artistry and entertainment.

Sleeping
BUDGET
Jirafa Roja Hostel (☎ 212-48-25; www.jirafarojahostel.com; Calle 20 de Noviembre 72; dm from $11; ☐) A short walk from the historic center, the fun-loving Red Giraffe is Querétaro's only HI-affiliated hostel. The young owners, rooftop terrace and lively nightlife nearby all add up to a likely party. There's space for 20 in doubles, triples and quad rooms.

Hotel Posada Diamante (☎ 212-66-37; Allende Sur 45; s/d $22/28) Close to the center this newly finished posada is very clean and comfortable and only a short walk to the pedestrian plazas and the Alameda.

Mesón de Matamoros (☎ 214-03-75; Matamoros 10; s/d $23/25) Well-positioned on a lively little pedestrian street, this posada has 25 decent rooms around an enclosed courtyard, with several cafés and bistros nearby.

MIDRANGE
Hotel Hidalgo (☎ 212-00-81; www.hotelhidalgo.com.mx; Madero Pte 11; s/d $32/38; ℗) A few doors off the Jardín Zenea, the three-star Hidalgo was Querétaro's first hotel. Rooms vary greatly in size and appeal. The cheapest rooms are pokey, larger rooms with two beds cost more and the largest can hold up to seven people. They all have private bathrooms and some upper-floor rooms have small balconies.

Hotel Mesón de Obispado (☎ 224-24-64; Andador 16 de Septiembre 13; s/d $42/53) Located on one of Querétaro's liveliest pedestrian streets, you won't miss out on any action staying here. The bonus here is that the rooms are secluded from the noise and tucked back around an inside courtyard. The restaurant serves decent breakfast as well.

Hotel Plaza (☎ 212-11-38; Juárez Nte 23; s/d from $30/37) The respectable Plaza has 29 tidy, comfortable, charm-free rooms. Some have French doors and balconies facing the Jardín, offering plenty of light, air and noise for a few more pesos.

Posada Acueducto (☎ 224-12-89; Juárez Sur 64; s/d/tr $23/30/32) The 15 clean, remodeled rooms here are well kept and colorful, with fan and cable TV. The best rooms have private balconies. Children under 12 stay free.

Hotel Amberes (☎ 212-86-04; hamberes@prodigy.net.mx; Corregidora Sur 188; s/d/tr $42/46/70; ℗ ☒ ☐) Set in an older building this remodeled four-star hotel, opposite the Alameda Hidalgo,

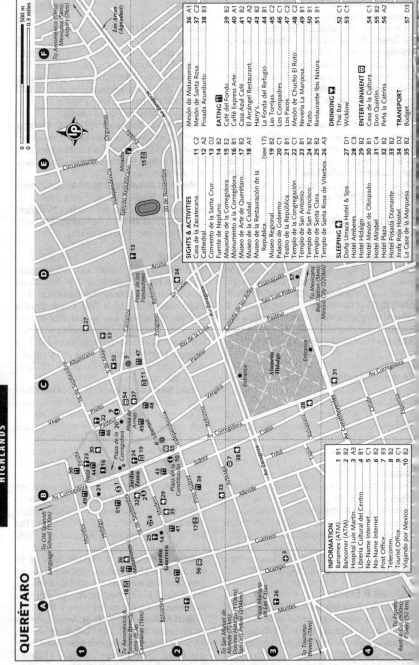

QUERÉTARO

INFORMATION

Banamex (ATM)................................	1 B1
Bancomer (ATM)...............................	2 B2
Hospital Luis Martín..........................	3 A3
Librería Cultural del Centro...............	4 B1
No-Name Internet.............................	5 C1
No-Name Internet.............................	6 B2
Post Office.......................................	7 B3
Telecomm...	8 B2
Tourist Office...................................	9 C1
Viajando por Mexico.........................	10 B2

SIGHTS & ACTIVITIES

Casa de la Zacatecana........................	11 C2
Cathedral...	12 A2
Convento de la Santa Cruz.................	13 D2
Fuente de Neptuno.............................	14 B2
Mausoleo de la Corregidora...............	15 E2
Monumento a la Corregidora..............	16 B1
Museo de Arte de Querétaro..............	17 B2
Museo de la Ciudad...........................	18 A1
Museo de la Restauración de la	
República..	(see 17)
Museo Regional..................................	19 B2
Palacio de Gobierno...........................	20 C1
Teatro de la República........................	21 B1
Templo de la Congregación................	22 C1
Templo de San Antonio......................	23 B1
Templo de San Francisco....................	24 B2
Templo de Santa Clara.......................	25 B2
Templo de Santa Rosa de Viterbos......	26 A3

SLEEPING

Doña Urraca Hotel & Spa....................	27 D1
Hotel Amberes...................................	28 C3
Hotel Hidalgo....................................	29 B2
Hotel Mesón de Obispado..................	30 B1
Hotel Mirabel....................................	31 C4
Hotel Plaza..	32 B2
Hotel Posada Diamante......................	33 B2
Jirafa Roja Hostel..............................	34 D2
La Casa de la Marquesa......................	35 B2

Mesón de Matamoros.........................	36 A1
Mesón de Santa Rosa.........................	37 C2
Posada Acueducto.............................	38 B3

EATING

Caffé del Fondo..................................	39 B2
Caffé Express Arte..............................	40 A1
Casa Azul Café...................................	41 B2
El Arcángel Restaurant.......................	42 A2
Harry's..	43 B2
La Fonda del Refugio..........................	44 B1
Las Torrijas..	45 C2
Los Compadres...................................	46 C1
Los Pacos..	47 C2
Mesón de Chucho El Roto..................	48 C1
Nevería La Mariposa...........................	49 B1
Pasto...	50 B1
Restaurante Ibis Natura......................	51 B1

DRINKING

Thai Bar...	52 C1
Wicklow..	53 C1

ENTERTAINMENT

Casa de la Cultura..............................	54 C1
Don Quintín......................................	55 B2
Peña la Catrina..................................	56 A2

TRANSPORT

Budget..	57 D3

is a business-traveler favorite. The smart rooms are carpeted, with air-con, cable TV and phone, and some of them also have park views

Hotel Mirabel (☎ 214-35-35, 800-401-39-00; www.hotelmirabel.com.mx; Av Constituyentes Ote 2; s/d/ste$65/85/96; P ✹ ☐) More demanding business travelers prefer the slicker Mirabel. The comfy, carpeted standard rooms (some with park views) have air-con and there's room service.

TOP END

La Casa de la Marquesa (☎ 212-00-92; www.lacasa delamarquesa.com; Madero 41; r/ste from $145/183; P ✹) For something extraordinary, try this magnificent 1756 baroque-Mudéjar mansion filled with lavish period furnishings, carved stonework, tiles and frescoes (some original). The 25 singular suites have names such as Alhambra and Maximiliano y Carlota, with style to match. Rates include continental breakfast and a welcome cocktail. Slightly less expensive rooms are in a separate building, Casa Azul, a couple of doors west on the corner of Madero and Allende. The Imperial Suite ($280) is unforgettable. Children under 12 are not admitted.

Doña Urraca Hotel & Spa (☎ 238-54-00, in Mexico 800-021-71-16, in USA 877-278-80-18; www.donaurraca .com.mx; Calle 5 de Mayo 117; r/ste from $193/237; P ✹ ☐ ✺) Ready for some pampering? Rates at this contemporary hideaway include two spa treatments. The 24 spacious, full-featured suites are lavished with fine touches like bathrobes and handmade herbal soaps. There's a gym, heated pool and outdoor Jacuzzi, and the restaurant's wine cellar morphs into a romantic, private dining room for two. Go on, spoil yourself!

Mesón de Santa Rosa (☎ 224-26-23; Pasteur Sur 17; r/ste from 119/168; P ✺) On the Plaza de Armas, Mesón de Santa Rosa is a finely restored 17th-century building built around three patios: one with a heated pool, one with a fountain and one with a restaurant. The 21 elegant, modern rooms are unique, and all come with a minibar and satellite TV.

Eating

Plaza de la Corregidora and Plaza de Armas are ringed by restaurants complete with outdoor tables and a vibrant evening

atmosphere. Most of them offer live music and post their menus out the front; have a stroll around and take your pick. The surrounding pedestrian streets also have many midrange restaurants and cafés catering to shoppers and workers.

AROUND PLAZA DE LA CORREGIDORA

Pasto (☎ 214-44-42; Peralta 19A; mains $7-14; ☯ noon-midnight) A cosmopolitan look for Querétaro, Pasto has an excellent fusion menu with dishes like shrimp fettuccini in squash-flower sauce or salmon-cilantro laksa. Top-off the gourmet meal with a tamarind mousse and a rooibos tea.

Los Compadres (☎ 212-98-86; Andador 16 de Septiembre 46; mains $2-4; ☯ 9am-10:30pm Tue-Sun) It would be embarrassing to go to Querétaro and not try their famous *gorditas*. They are famous throughout the country, but nobody does them like the originators. Stop in here for some of the most authentic local Mexican cuisine.

La Fonda del Refugio (☎ 212-07-55; Plaza de la Corregidora 26; mains $6-9; ☯ 1pm-2am) Like many of the established places on the plaza, this refuge has a pretty standard menu, with chicken dishes and steaks, and special nights for *pozole* and *parrillada* (barbecue). After 8pm Thursday to Saturday there's live music.

Nevería La Mariposa (☎ 212-11-66; Ángela Peralta 7; mains $1.50; ☯ 8am-9:30pm) Straight out of the '40s this Querétaro institution is known for its natural homemade ice cream and Mexican candies. Try flavors like *chabacano* and mango.

AROUND PLAZA DE ARMAS

Plaza de Armas has a handful of more upscale restaurants and cafés that have indoor and outdoor tables.

Los Pacos (☎ 224-22-65; Rio de la Loza 67; mains $5.50-11.50; ☯ 8am-10pm Mon-Fri, 10am-11:30pm Sat) Probably the best food you'll eat in Querétaro, the food here is the famous regional Oaxacan cuisine. All the *moles* one could ask for outside of Oaxaca. For a change of pace, go for the spicy yellow *mole* with beef or chicken.

Mesón de Chucho El Roto (☎ 212-42-95; Libertad 60; mains $5-10) The most popular place on the plaza boasts *alta cocina mexicana* (fancy Mexican food) and offers interesting variations on classic Mexican dishes and regional specialties like *tacos de flor y huit-lacoche* (squash-flower and corn-fungus tacos). There's a good wine list and you can linger over a drink.

Las Torrijas (☎ 214-52-98; Plaza de Armas 8; mains $4-8) Grab a friend and feast on the *molcajete* (stone grinder, piled with meat and veggies) for two. Filled with all types of surf and turf, you won't walk away unsatisfied, if you can walk away at all. Ringside plaza seats are also a bonus with daily classical guitar.

ELSEWHERE

Harry's (☎ 214-26-20; Hidalgo 12; Plaza Constitución s/n; mains $6-12; ☻ 8am-11pm Sun-Thu, 8am-1am Fri & Sat) You cannot beat the atmosphere of this New Orleans–style café. Sit out on the patio tables and have some jambalaya or blackened catfish and watch the crowds amble by. There is also a sophisticated bar for an early evening cocktail.

Casa Azul Café (☎ 212-00-92; cnr Madero & Allende; mains $4-9; ☻ 7am-5pm) La Casa de la Marquesa's attractive courtyard bistro boasts a gurgling fountain, fine food and a good upscale *comida corrida* ($10).

Café del Fondo (☎ 212-09-05; Pino Suárez 9; everything under $2.50; ☻ 8am-10pm) This relaxed, rambling alternative hangout is popular with chess-head punks and newspaper-reading elderstatesmen. You can get a set breakfast with eggs, *frijoles* (beans), bread roll, juice and house-roasted coffee, snacks or a four-course *comida corrida* with plenty of choices.

El Arcángel Restaurant (☎ 212-65-42; southwest cnr of Jardín Guerrero; mains $4.50-10; ☻ 8am-10pm) For a power breakfast or a slow-paced four-course set lunch ($8), join local businessfolk at this old-fashioned place with a pleasant patio.

Caffé Express Arte (☎ 182-24-01; Guerrero 2A; mains $3.50-6.50; ☻ 8am-midnight Mon-Sat) Enjoy a chai or espresso and a baguette in this nouveau French-café setting, located just south of the popular Museo de la Ciudad. In the open courtyard you'll find a smart crowd of locals tapped into the cultural beat.

Restaurante Ibis Natura (☎ 214-22-12; Juárez 47 Nte; mains $2-4; ☻ 8am-9:30pm **V**) Vegetarians and natural-food fans will enjoy the good-value *comida corrida* ($3.75) or the soyburgers with mushrooms and cheese.

Entertainment

Querétaro has cultural activities befitting a state capital and university city. Sit in the Plaza Principal any Sunday evening with local families enjoying concerts; the state band performs from 7pm to 9pm, sometimes with dancers. A *callejoneada* kicks off from the Plaza de Armas at 8pm Saturday in summer. The **Casa de la Cultura** (☎ 212-56-14; Calle 5 de Mayo 40) sponsors concerts, dance, theater and art events; stop by during office hours to pick up the monthly schedule.

Popular bars and clubs are popping up all over the historic center. Hip, international themes, such as the Irish pub **Wicklow** (☎ 307-60-63; Calle 5 de Mayo 86) and the electronic lounge **Thai Bar** (☎ 214-61-25; Calle 5 de Mayo 56), are evidence of the current cultural expansion and sophistication in Querétaro. Latin pop reigns as the music of choice at the trendy **Don Quintín** (☎ 214-51-12; Corregidora Sur 23) and a young and alternative crowd can find some great local live music at **Peña La Catrina** (☎ 183-09-50; Guerrero Sur 12A). Fashionable bars and nightclubs can also be found further out in the suburbs. Check the entertainment section of Friday's *Diario de Querétaro*, or ask the tourist office to suggest the latest hot and happening nightspots. There's a slew of bars, clubs and discos right the way along Av Constituyentes and Blvd Bernardo Quintana (get a taxi), the city's eastern and western ring roads.

Getting There & Away

AIR

The new **Aeropuerto Intercontinental** (☎ 419-235-2013), 8km northeast of the center, is a $10 taxi ride away. Aerocalifornia runs regular domestic flights to/from Mexico City, Guadalajara, Monterrey and Leon while Continental has flights to Los Angeles, San Antonio and Houston in the US.

In-town airline offices include **Aeroméxico** (☎ 229-00-91; Bernardo Quintana 4100, Col Alamos) and **Mexicana** (☎ 246-00-71; Bernardo Quintana 4100, Colonia Alamos).

BUS

Querétaro is a hub for buses in all directions; the modern Central Camionera is 5km southeast of the center. There's one building for deluxe and 1st-class (labeled A), one for 2nd-class (B) and another for local buses (C). Facilities include a café, telephone *casetas*, shops and luggage storage. Daily departures:

Destination	Price	Duration	Frequency
Guadalajara	$31	4½-5½hr	9 deluxe ETN
	$25	5hr	19 1st-class Primera Plus
	$23	4½-5½hr	frequent 2nd-class Flecha Amarilla & 10 Oriente
Guanajuato	$10.50	2½-3hr	3 1st-class Primera Plus
	$7.50	2½-3hr	4 2nd-class Flecha Amarilla, or catch frequent buses to Irapuato where buses frequently leave for Guanajuato
Mexico City (Terminal Norte)	$19	2½-3hr	deluxe ETN every 30min 5am-10pm
	$15	3½hr	1st-class Primera Plus every 20min 4:45am-11:30pm
	$14	3½/2hr	5 1st-class Ómnibus de México
	$12	4hr	2nd-class Flecha Amarilla, many direct
Mexico City (Terminal Poniente)	$12	4½hr	2nd-class Herradura de Plata every 40min
Mexico City Airport	$21	3½hr	21 1st-class Aeroplus
Morelia	$12	3-4hr	20 1st-class Primera Plus/ Servicios Coordinados
	$10	4½hr	10 2nd-class Flecha Amarilla
San Luis Potosí	$18	2½hr	2 deluxe ETN
	$14	2½hr	21 1st-class Primera Plus/ Servicios Coordinados
	$12	2¾hr	2nd-class Flecha Amarilla hourly
San Miguel de Allende	$7	1hr	4 deluxe ETN
	$4	1hr	2nd-class Herradura de Plata or Flecha Amarilla every 40min 6:20am-10pm
Tequisquiapan	$2.25	1hr	2nd-class Flecha Azul every 30min 7am-9pm

CAR & MOTORCYCLE
If you want a car to explore the Sierra Gorda, English-speaking **Express Rent-a-Car** (☎ 242-9028; www.queretaro-express.com; Hotel Real de Minas, Av Constituyentes Pte 124; per day/week from

$54/292) has competitive rates. **Budget** (☎ 213-44-98; Av Constituyentes Ote 73; per day/week from $55/328) is also worth checking.

Getting Around
Once you have reached the city center, you can easily visit most sights on foot. City buses ($0.50) run from 6am until 9pm or 10pm but can be infuriatingly slow. They leave from an open lot outside the bus station; turn right from the 2nd-class terminal, or left from the 1st-class side. Several routes go to the center including buses 8 and 19, which both go to the Alameda Hidalgo then up Ocampo. Newer Transmetro buses ($0.50) are quicker. For a taxi, get a ticket first from the bus station booth ($3 for up to four people).

For the bus station from the center, take city bus 19, 25 Zaragoza, 36 or any other saying 'Terminal de Autobuses' heading south on the east side of the Alameda Hidalgo.

TEQUISQUIAPAN
☎ 414 / pop 29,000 / elevation 1880m
This small town (teh-kees-kee-*ap*-an), 70km southeast of Querétaro, is a quaint weekend retreat from Mexico City or Querétaro. It used to be known for its thermal springs – Mexican presidents came here to ease their aches and tensions. Local industries now use most of the hot water, but there are still delightful cool-water pools, some set in pretty gardens at attractive hotels. It's a pleasure to simply stroll the streets lined with brilliant purple bougainvillea and colorful colonial buildings. Tequis is sometimes playfully abbreviated TX, pronounced '*teh*-kees'.

Orientation & Information
The bus station is a vacant lot southwest of town, a 10-minute walk along Niños Héroes from the center. The **tourist office** (☎ 273-02-95; www.tequis.info; east side Plaza Principal; 🕑 9am-7pm Mon-Fri, 10am-8pm Sat & Sun) has town maps and information on Querétaro state. On the plaza's southeast side, Bancomer has an ATM.

Sights & Activities
The Plaza Miguel Hidalgo is surrounded by *portales* (arcades), overlooked by the 19th-century neoclassical **La Parroquia de Santa María de la Asunción** (Plaza Miguel Hidalgo; 🕑 7am-8:30pm). The facade is somewhat plain by

NORTHERN CENTRAL HIGHLANDS

Mexican standards but the single clock tower brings a distinguished air to the plaza.

The **main market**, on Ezequiel Montes, and the **Mercado de Artesanías** (Crafts Market; 🕒 8am-7pm) on Carrizal, are a couple of blocks away through little lanes. The large, verdant **Parque La Pila** is a short distance past the Mercado de Artesanías along Ezequiel Montes.

Most hotel swimming pools are for guests only; an exception is Hotel Neptuno's **cool pool** (admission $4; 🕒 8am-6pm daily Apr-Oct, 8am-6pm Sat & Sun Nov-Mar). Other *balnearios* are just north of town along Hwy 120.

Look for migratory birds at the **Santuario de Aves Migratorios La Palapa** by the Centenario reservoir just south of town; it's on the right near the bus station if you approach Tequis from San Juan del Río. Other things you can do around Tequis. include horseback riding, tennis and golf (ask at the tourist office or your hotel).

Festivals & Events
Feria Internacional del Queso y del Vino (International Wine and Cheese Fair) From late May to early June; includes tastings, music and rodeo.
Fiestas Patrias Around Independence Day (September 16).

Sleeping & Eating
The best budget options are the posadas along Moctezuma. Demand is low Monday to Thursday, when you may be able to negotiate a discount. For a cheap meal, *fondas* (food stalls) cluster under awnings in the patio from 8am to 8pm, at the rear of the main market. Fancier restaurants around the plaza specialize in long lunches for large family groups.

Posada Tequisquiapan (☎ 273-00-10; Moctezuma 6; s/d $23/46; 🐕) This hotel has pretty gardens and a splendid grotto-like pool. Rooms are spacious and clean, with cable TV.

Hotel/Balneario Neptuno (☎ 273-02-24; hotel_neptune@hotmail.com; Juárez Oriente 5; s/d $37/47; 🐕) Two blocks east of Plaza Principal, the Neptuno has a big pool and lots of rooms, including larger family rooms.

Hotel La Plaza (☎ 273-00-56; www.tequisquiapan.com.mx/la_plaza; Juárez 10; r $38-63, ste $68-88; P 🐕) Facing the plaza, this hotel has a restaurant, sports bar and a choice of 15 rooms and suites of varying sizes.

Hotel El Relox (☎ 273-00-66; Morelos Pte 8; r from $103; P 🐕) This sprawling 110-room complex, 1½ blocks north of the plaza, is

set in extensive gardens with a restaurant, several pools, gym, tennis courts and private thermal pools (26°C to 38°C).

K'puchinos (☎ 273-10-46; Morelos 4; mains $4-9) With indoor and outdoor tables, this place on the plaza's west side is good for a set lunch ($7) or dinner. The menu is standard Mexican fare, with well-prepared mains, pastas, *antojitos*, a big coffee selection and live music on weekends.

Las Fuentes (☎ 273-41-34; Mateus 1; mains $8.50-15; 🕒 noon-8pm Mon-Thu, 11am-9pm Fri-Sun) Upstairs just off the plaza, this place serves generous portions and a good variety of *mariscos* (seafood) and *carnes* (meat), in a family-style atmosphere.

Getting There & Around
Tequis is 20km northeast on Hwy 120 from the larger town of San Juan del Río, which is on Hwy 57. A local bus ($0.40) from outside the bus station to the Mercado will let you off on Carrizal, a two-minute walk northeast of the Plaza Principal.

Buses to/from Tequis are all 2nd-class. Flecha Azul runs half hourly from 5:30am to 8pm to Querétaro ($2.75, one hour). Flecha Amarilla has connections to/from Mexico City's Terminal Norte ($11, three hours, two daily).

NORTHEAST QUERÉTARO STATE
Those heading to/from northeast Mexico, or with a hankering to get off the beaten track, might consider following Hwy 120 northeast from Tequisquiapan over the scenic Sierra Gorda to the lush Huasteca (see p661). It's possible to get to most places on the way by bus, but it's much easier with your own transport.

Highway 120
Heading north from Tequis, you pass the dusty town of Ezequiel Montes and then the winery **Cavas de Freixenet** (☎ 441-277-01-47; www.freixenetmexico.com.mx; tours 🕒 11am-3pm), where you can see wine being made by *método champenoise* during free 40-minute tours.

The next big town is Cadereyta, 38km from Tequis. On the east edge of town, signs point to the **Quinta Fernando Schmoll** (🕒 10am-5pm), a botanical garden with over 4400 varieties of cactus.

Continuing another 38km on Hwy 120, there's a turnoff going east to **San Joaquín**

QUINTESSENTIAL QUERÉTARO

The state of Querétaro has a nice blend of urban entertainment, colonial history and natural beauty. But somewhere between the capital cities, charming open plazas and the misty mountains of the Sierra Gorda is the Peña de Bernal. A kind of natural magnetic antennae, this rock spire has been drawing a crowd forever. The indigenous Otomí called the giant formation Má Hando, or 'in the middle of two,' and it held a sacred spiritual element. Later, upon naming the town, the Spanish took the Arabic word 'bernal,' which means 'a large rock outcrop isolated by a plain or the sea.' It must have seemed a refuge between two mountain ranges, or two plains perhaps, but regardless of the reason La Peña de Bernal has always stood out, and rightfully so, as it is the third-largest monolith in the world. Towering 288m (945ft) above the eastern flanks of the Sierra Gorda, it rises to a height of 2515m (8251ft) above sea level. A popular tourist attraction, the quaint town of Bernal draws its biggest crowds for the Vernal equinox when thousands of visitors dressed in white make the pilgrimage to take in the positive energy and the ridiculously good *gorditas*.

Follow the good, but very winding, road from the turnoff for 32km through the rugged mountains; stay on that road through San Joaquín, and continue a few steeply climbing kilometers to the little-visited archaeological site of **Ranas** (admission $2.50; ⏱ 9am-5pm), with well-built walls and circular steps incorporated into a steep hillside. There are ball courts and a small hilltop pyramid. Dating from as early as the 8th century, the site is appealing for its rugged forest setting. San Joaquín has basic lodgings and eateries.

JALPAN

Highway 120 winds up to a height of 2300m at **Pinal de Amoles** and makes several dramatic ups and downs (and 860 turns!) before reaching **Jalpan** at 760m. The attractive town centers on the **mission church**, constructed by Franciscan monks and their indigenous converts in the 1750s. The **Museo de la Sierra Gorda** (☎ 441-296-01-65; Fray Junípero Serra 1; adult/child $1/0.50; ⏱ 10am-3pm & 5-7pm) explores the region's pre-Hispanic cultures, and the mission-building period.

On the plaza opposite the church, **Hotel María del Carmen** (☎ 441-296-03-28; Independencia 8; s/d $27/32; P ⊠ ⊛) has clean, comfortable rooms, with air-con for $12 more.

On the plaza's west side, the attractive **Hotel Misión Jalpan** (☎ 441-296-02-55; www.hotel esmision.com.mx; Fray Junípero Serra s/n; r from $72; P ⊠ ⊛) has a good restaurant and all the comforts of home. Package deals including meals start at around $45 per person.

SIERRA GORDA MISSIONS

In the mid-18th century, Franciscans established four other beautiful missions in this remote region, inscribed as a Unesco World Heritage site in 2003. Their leader Fray Junípero Serra went on to found the California mission chain. The churches have been restored and are notable for their colorful facades carved with symbolic figures. Heading east from Jalpan on Hwy 120, there are missions at **Landa de Matamoros** (1760–68), **Tilaco** (1754–62), 10km south of the highway; and **Tancoyol** (1753–60), 20km north of the highway. The other mission is 35km north of Jalpan on Hwy 69 at **Concá** (1754–58).

RESERVA DE LA BIOSFERA SIERRA GORDA

Northwest of Jalpan, the 3830-sq-km **Sierra Gorda Biosphere Reserve** has a 240-sq-km core that covers a range of altitudes and is notable for the diversity of its ecological systems, from subtropical valleys to high deserts to coniferous forests. Contact **Promotur** (☎ 442-212-89-40; www.promoturqueretaro .com.mx; Independencia 77, Querétaro) for details about guided camping and hiking trips throughout the Sierra Gorda.

NORTHERN CENTRAL HIGHLANDS

Central Gulf Coast

Maybe it's the humid fecundity of the central Gulf coast that gives its inhabitants their slow, sultry smiles. Possibly it's the European influence that imbued them with reserved graciousness, and Afro-Caribbean culture that dissolved music into their veins. But whatever the subtle alchemy, the diverse residents of this region are as warmly welcoming as its lush landscape.

Shot through with rivers and waterfalls, this coastal crescent shelters Mexico's highest peak and one of its deepest karst pits. A diverse collection of remarkable architecture also competes to impress: the niched pyramids of El Tajín, evocative colonial edifices, and even surrealist stairways spiraling towards the sky. And the sounds of the Gulf coast are not limited to squawking birds gathering in the plazas at dusk, but are layered with *jarocho* guitars and bouncy marimbas, raucous laughter and cathedral bells.

Long after Hernán Cortés planted his boot on the sand of Veracruz, travelers are rediscovering this slice of Mexico. The rhythm of a journey here can be regulated to any pulse rate, from adrenaline-crazy to vacationing-lazy. For the former, opportunities range from summiting the icy Pico de Orizaba, to rafting rapids or diving wrecks in the Gulf. The latter may enjoy sprawling on a quiet beach, tasting local *huachinango a la veracruzana* or sipping margarita. Then there are the region's unburied treasures, like the immense Olmec heads in Xalapa's archaeological museum, or the myriad birdlife – from raptors to hummingbirds. Either way, you're sure to be seduced by the easygoing people and the warmth of their welcome.

TOP FIVE

- Time-traveling through Mexican civilizations at the **Museo de Antropología** (p682) in Xalapa, the region's most culture-rich and rewarding city
- Marveling at the mind behind the surrealist concrete pagodas and temples in beguiling **Xilitla** (p668)
- Sipping a cold one and puffing on a local *puro* under the **zócalo's portales** (p691) in Veracruz
- Taking in the extensive ruins of **El Tajín** (p676) and then gasping at the aerial aerobics performed by the Totonac *voladores*
- Exploring the beautiful lake district of **Los Tuxtlas** (p704) and its largely undiscovered coastline

- VERACRUZ JANUARY DAILY HIGH: 25.6°C | 78.1°F
- VERACRUZ JULY DAILY HIGH: 30.6°C | 87.1°F

History

OLMEC

The Olmecs, mesoamerica's earliest known civilization, built their first great center around 1200 BC at San Lorenzo, in southern Veracruz. It prospered until about 900 BC, when the city was apparently violently destroyed. Subsequently, La Venta in neighboring Tabasco served as the main Olmec center until around 400 BC, when it too seemingly met a violent end. Olmec culture lingered for several centuries at Tres Zapotes, as Veracruz gradually became subsumed by other influences.

CLASSIC VERACRUZ

After the Olmec decline, the Gulf coast centers of civilization moved west and north. El Pital, about 100km northwest of Veracruz port, flourished from about AD 100 to 600 and may have been home to more than 20,000 people.

The Classic period (AD 250–900) saw the emergence in central and northern Veracruz of several politically independent power centers sharing a religion and culture. Together they're known as the 'Classic Veracruz' civilization. Their hallmark is a unique style of carving, with curving and interwoven pairs of parallel lines. This style appears on three types of carved stone objects, all thought to be connected with the ritual ball game. They are the U-shaped *yugo,* representing a wooden or leather belt worn in the game; the long paddle-like *palma;* and the flat *hacha,* shaped somewhat like an ax head. The latter two, often carved in human or animal forms, are thought to represent items attached to the front of the belt. *Hachas* may also have been court-markers.

The most important Classic Veracruz center, El Tajín, was at its height over the period 600 to 900. Other main centers were Las Higueras, near Vega de Alatorre, close to the coast south of Nautla; and El Zapotal, near Ignacio de la Llave, south of Veracruz port. Classic Veracruz sites show Maya and Teotihuacán influences. These cultures exported cotton, rubber, cacao and vanilla to central Mexico, influencing developments in Teotihuacán, Cholula and elsewhere.

TOTONAC, HUASTEC, TOLTEC & AZTEC

By AD 1200, when El Tajín was abandoned, the Totonacs were establishing themselves from Tuxpan in the north to beyond Veracruz in the south. North of Tuxpan, the Huastec civilization, another web of small, probably independent states, flourished from 800 to 1200. The Huastecs were Mexico's chief cotton producers. As skilled stone carvers, they also built many ceremonial sites.

During this time, the warlike Toltecs, who dominated much of central Mexico in the early post-Classic age, moved into the Gulf coast area. They occupied the Huastec Castillo de Teayo between 900 and 1200. Toltec influence can also be seen at Zempoala, a Totonac site near Veracruz port. In the mid-15th century, the Aztecs subdued most of the Totonac and Huastec areas, exacting tributes of goods and sacrificial victims, and maintaining garrisons to control revolts.

COLONIAL ERA

When Cortés arrived on the scene in April 1519, he made Zempoala's Totonacs his first allies against the Aztecs by telling them to imprison five Aztec tribute collectors and vowing to protect them against reprisals. Cortés set up his first settlement, Villa Rica de la Vera Cruz (Rich Town of the True Cross), north of modern Veracruz port. Then he established a second settlement at La Antigua, where he scuttled his ships to prevent desertion before advancing to Tenochtitlán, the Aztec capital. In May 1520 he returned to Zempoala and defeated a rival Spanish expedition sent to arrest him.

All the Gulf coast was in Spanish hands by 1523. New diseases, particularly smallpox, decimated the indigenous population. Veracruz harbor became an essential trade and communications link with Spain, and was vital for anyone trying to rule Mexico, but the climate, tropical diseases and threat of pirate attacks inhibited the growth of coastal Spanish settlements.

19TH & 20TH CENTURIES

The population of Veracruz city actually shrank in the first half of the 19th century. In the second half, under dictator Porfirio Díaz, Mexico's first railway (1872) linked Veracruz to Mexico City, propelling the development of some industries.

In 1901 oil was discovered in the Tampico area, and by the 1920s the region was producing a quarter of the world's oil. Although

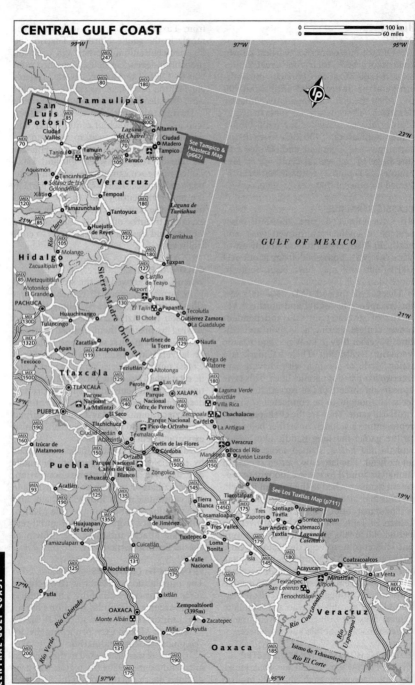

CENTRAL GULF COAST

that proportion eventually declined, new oil fields were found in southern Veracruz, and in the 1980s the Gulf coast still held well over half of Mexico's reserves and refining capacity. Oil continues to dominate the economy of the region today.

Climate

The central Gulf coast region is generally warm and humid, hotter along the coast, wetter in the foothills – it's the hottest and the wettest of all regions in the southeast. Two-thirds or more of the rain falls between June and September. Veracruz city receives about 1650mm of rain annually. From April to October it features temperatures well over 30°C, falling into the teens at night only from December to February. Tuxpan and Tampico, on the north coast, are a bit drier. Coatzacoalcos, in the southeast, gets more than 3m(!) of rain a year.

Parks & Reserves

Inland from the Gulf coast, two national parks have been established around volcanic cones. Parque National Pico de Orizaba (p703) protects Mexico's tallest mountain (5611m), a dormant volcano 25km northwest of Orizaba. Just north of here Parque Nacional Cofre de Perote (p687) encompasses another volcano, which is best accessed from the town of Perote, 50km west of Xalapa.

Dangers & Annoyances

Crime is not much of a problem in this region, but travelers should remain wary of petty theft in hotel rooms and pickpocketing in crowded market areas.

Mosquitos along the central Gulf coast carry dengue fever, especially in central and southeastern Veracruz. Baste yourself generously with mosquito repellent.

Getting There & Around

Veracruz port has a modern international airport, with flights from Mexico City, Monterrey, Reynosa and Villahermosa. Within the region, Tampico and Poza Rica are short hops from here. From the US, Continental has direct flights into Tampico and Veracruz from its Houston, Texas, hub.

Aerolitoral flies between Monterrey, Poza Rica, Reynosa and Veracruz, with connections to Villahermosa.

Frequent 1st-class buses go just about everywhere within the region and link the main cities here with Monterrey, Mexico City, Puebla and Oaxaca. The main company serving this area is ADO, with a superdeluxe fleet (UNO) and a deluxe fleet (ADO GL) as well as normal 1st-class buses. Greyhound buses run between the US and Mexico through their Mexican affiliates. Routes include Brownsville to Tampico.

The central Gulf coast region's highways are generally in great shape, but the ubiquitous *topes* (speedbumps) may get you down. If you don't expect to go speeding through the countryside, you'll be primed to enjoy the lush landscape as you bump on by.

TAMPICO & THE HUASTECA

Industrial, developed Tampico contrasts sharply with the verdant Huasteca, inland where the coastal plain meets the fringes of the Sierra Madre Oriental. Spread over the states of southern Tamaulipas, eastern San Luis Potosí, northern Veracruz and small corners of Querétaro and Hidalgo, the Huasteca is named after the Huastec people, who have lived here for about 3000 years.

Heading inland from the Huasteca, four steep, winding routes cross the sierra: Hwy 70, from Ciudad Valles to San Luis Potosí; Hwy 120, from Xilitla toward Querétaro; Hwy 85, from Tamazunchale to Ixmiquilpan (near which you can turn off toward Querétaro, Pachuca and Mexico City); and Hwy 105, from Huejutla to Pachuca and on to Mexico City via Hwy 85.

TAMPICO & CIUDAD MADERO
☎ 833

At the southern tip of Tamaulipas state, a few kilometers upstream from Río Pánuco's mouth, Tampico (population 316,000) is Mexico's busiest port – a tropical place where cantinas open late and the sweaty market always bustles. Mexican families flock to the beaches of Ciudad Madero (population 202,000) to the north, but foreigners will be more interested in Tampico's artfully redeveloped Plaza de la Libertad, surrounded by 19th-century, French-style buildings. Although prices are inflated by the oil business,

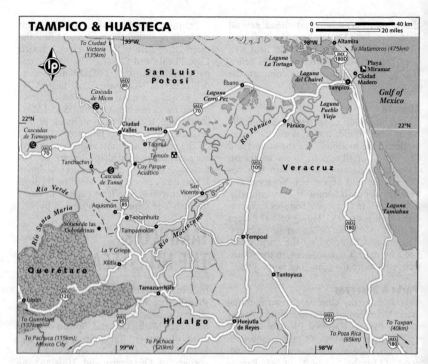

you don't have to hunt too hard for bargain accommodations and seafood.

History

In the 1530s a mission was established in Tampico to convert the Huastecs to Christianity. The town was destroyed by pirates in 1684 but was refounded in 1823 by families from Altamira, to the north. After the 1901 discovery of oil in the area, Tampico suddenly became the world's biggest oil port – rough, tough and booming. Although the city experienced its heyday in the 1920s, the oil and its profits were under foreign control until 1938, when the industry was nationalized by President Lázaro Cárdenas.

Mexico's 1970s and 1980s oil boom took place further down the coast, but the Tampico–Ciudad Madero area remains important. Pipelines and barge fleets bring oil from other Mexican fields to the area's refineries and harbor.

Orientation

Set near the mouth of the Río Pánuco, Tampico is ringed by extensive marshland,

several lakes (including Laguna del Chairel and Laguna del Carpintero) and numerous estuaries. Going south, the spectacular Puente Tampico (Tampico Bridge) crosses the Río Pánuco to Veracruz state.

Downtown Tampico centers on two attractive plazas: the *zócalo* (Plaza de Armas) and, to the southeast, the elegant Plaza de la Libertad. Hotels and restaurants of all grades are within a few blocks of these plazas.

South and east of Plaza de la Libertad is a run-down area containing the market, riverside docks, sleazy bars, and prostitutes and their clients. The unlit streets around the market and waterfront are best avoided after dark.

Addresses on east–west streets will usually have the suffix 'Ote' (Oriente; east) or 'Pte' (Poniente; west), while those on north–south streets are 'Nte' (Norte; north) or 'Sur' (south). The dividing point is the junction of Colón and Carranza, at the *zócalo's* northwest corner.

Heading northeast of central Tampico, it's 8km to Ciudad Madero, with Playa Miramar another 7km further away, on the Gulf of

Mexico. Northwest of Tampico, it's 17km to the heavily industrialized port of Altamira, the third town in this million-plus conurbation.

Information

EMERGENCIES
Ambulance, Fire & Police (☎ 066)

INTERNET ACCESS
Canarias Cybercafé (Carranza 214; per hr $1)

LEFT LUGGAGE
There are 24-hour left luggage lockers at the Tampico bus station.

MEDICAL SERVICES
Beneficencia Española, AC (☎ 213-23-63; Hidalgo 3909) There's quality medical care at this hospital.
Centro Médico de Tampico (☎ 214-03-60; Altamira 423 Pte)

MONEY
Numerous banks are scattered around the central plazas, all with 24-hour ATMs. If you have traveler's checks head to Bancomer on López de Lara.

POST
Post office (☎ 212-19-27; Madero 309)

TELEPHONES
Public telephones can be found in both plazas.

TOURIST INFORMATION
Tourist Office (☎ 229-27-65; dir.deseconomico @tampico.gob.mx; Av Ejército Mexicano; ☺ 9am-5:30pm Mon-Fri) Inconveniently located 3km northwest from the center, close to the junction with Hidalgo, but has helpful English-speaking staff and plenty of city and regional maps. There's also a desk at the airport.

Sights
Tampico does not have an excess of sights, but the two central squares boast some elegant buildings to admire, built in a style reminiscent of New Orleans with intricate wrought-iron balconies.

The revamped **Museo de la Cultura Huasteca** (Museum of Huastec Culture; ☎ 210-22-17; inside METRO, Espacio Cultural Metropolitano; admission free; ☺ 9:30am-5pm Tue-Sat) is in Tampico's modern cultural center. This complex also has two theaters and overlooks the Laguna del Carpintero. Well-organized displays feature exhibits on Huastec religion and culture, and the mesoamerican fertility cult, and there are some fine ceramics and artifacts. It's 2km from Tampico; take a 'Central Camionera' bus from Olmos and get off at the Parque Metropolitano stop. The center's a short walk away, over a pedestrian bridge.

Playa Miramar is about 15km from downtown Tampico. The 10km broad sandy beach is kept pretty clean, and the cobalt water is clear, if not crystalline. Simple restaurants here feature *mariscos* (seafood dishes) and margaritas, and each joint rents out shady *palapas* on its stretch of sand. On holidays and weekends the beach is crowded with families and thick with hawkers selling coconuts, cold beer and seashell souvenirs. At other times the stretch can be deserted. From central Tampico, take a 'Playa' bus ($0.50) or *colectivo* ($2) north on Alfaro.

Festivals & Events
Semana Santa (week preceding Easter Sunday) Activities at Playa Miramar include regattas, fishing and windsurfing competitions, sand-sculpture contests, music, dancing and bonfires. Warning: petty crime rises dramatically during this period, so take extra care.
Aniversario de la Repoblación de Tampico (April 12) Features a procession from Altamira that passes Tampico's *zócalo,* celebrating the city's refoundation in 1823.

Sleeping
All decent downtown places fill up quickly during holidays. Rates drop at quiet times and jump during Semana Santa.

BUDGET
Hotel Plaza (☎ 214-17-84; Madero 204 Ote; s/d $18/20; ☒) The best budget deal in town has friendly management and tidy rooms, most with bright bedspreads, and all with telephones and cable TV. There's a pizza place downstairs. Parking is available for about $3.75 a day at nearby Hotel Colonial.

Hotel Regis (☎ 212-02-90; fax 212-74-65; Madero 603 Ote; s/d $22/25; ☒) A secure place with friendly management, the Regis has very decent, bright, spotless rooms all with tiled floors, phones and cable TV. There's free coffee for guests, and a good economical restaurant downstairs.

MIDRANGE
Midrange hotels have air-con, hot water, cable TV and phones.

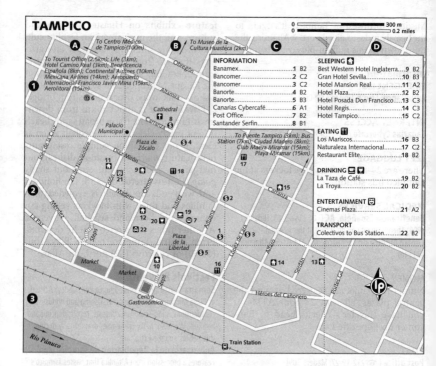

TAMPICO

Gran Hotel Sevilla (☎ 214-38-33, 800-570-39-11; www.granhotelsevilla.com.mx; Héroes del Cañonero 304 Pte; r $55-68; ✗ ✗) With a curved modern facade overlooking the Plaza de la Libertad, this hotel is both well located and excellent value. The well-appointed rooms have good-quality beds, stylish bathrooms and many enjoy great views. A free, if modest, continental breakfast is included.

Hotel Mansion Real (☎ 219-15-15; www.mansion real.com; Colón Sur 104; r $75; P ✗ 🖳) A classy hotel with an impressive lobby and very large, extremely comfortable rooms, each with two double beds, floor-to-ceiling windows, armchairs, a desk and a fridge/minibar.

Hotel Tampico (☎ 219-00-57; www.hoteltampico .com; Carranza 513 Ote; r $36; P ✗) A handsome building with a fine tiled lobby and plenty of character and period charm, even if the lady is showing her years. Rooms are old-fashioned but clean and a decent size.

Best Western Hotel Inglaterra (☎ 219-28-57, 800-715-71-23; www.hotelinglaterra.com; Díaz Mirón 116 Ote; r $57; P ✗ ✗ 🖳) Enjoys a terrific location on the corner of the *zócalo*, and though the very spacious rooms would benefit from

a little more love and attention to detail, they still represent fair value with huge windows and marble-floor bathrooms. Breakfast is included.

Hotel Posada Don Francisco (☎ /fax 219-28-35; Díaz Mirón 710 Ote; s/d $25/36; P ✗) The location is not great, but the hotel is secure. Rooms have colorful decor and carpets.

TOP END

Hotel Camino Real (☎ 229-35-35; www.caminoreal /tampico; Hidalgo 2000; s/d from $132/168; P ✗ ✗ 🖳 🖭 ⚥) Tampico's most luxurious hotel boasts a large pool, and well-presented, spacious rooms and bungalows facing a tropical garden. There's also a piano bar, restaurant and fitness room. It's 3km north of the center.

Club Maeva Miramar (☎ 230-02-02, 800-849-19-87, in the USA ☎ 888-739-01-13; www.maevamiramar .com.mx; Blvd Costero s/n, Playa Miramar; all-inclusive r $232; P ✗ ✗ 🖳 🖭 ⚥) Out by the beach, this large resort hotel has several pools and enormous rooms which come with all the comforts. All-inclusive prices cover all meals and beverages, live entertainment and access to a private strip of beach. Check the website for discounts and golfing package deals.

Eating

It's a breeze to get fresh seafood in Tampico, or try the local specialty – *carne asada a la tampiqueña*, steak marinated in garlic, oil and oregano and usually served with guacamole, strips of chili and corn chips.

Restaurant Elite (☎ 212-03-64; Díaz Mirón 211 Ote; mains $5-10.50) A spacious, formal restaurant with bustling waitresses and a long line-up of Mexican food served in generous portions, including excellent *carne asada a la tampiqueña*.

Los Mariscos (☎ 214-08-12; Héroes del Cañonero 409C Ote; fish dishes $8-12) Renowned for its seafood, this large, enjoyable place offers dozens of shrimp and fish choices, *caldos* (soup) and specials like *brocheta de filete a la poblana* ($9.50).

Naturaleza Internacional (☎ 212-49-79; Aduana 107 Nte; mains $3.50; ☻ 8am-8pm; Ⓥ) At the rear of a health-food store, this small air-conditioned place has a winsome breakfast buffet ($4) and dishes including *ensalada espinaca* ($3) and veggie *tamales*, as well as fresh juices and wholemeal breads.

For an inexpensive feed head to the Centro Gastronómico, just east of the market, where there are dozens of open-air stalls rustling up *mariscos*, tacos, tortas and breakfasts.

Drinking & Entertainment

La Taza de Café (☎ 219-04-20; Madero 303; ☻ 9:30am-9pm Mon-Sat) A tiny little café at the rear of a handicraft stall where you can sip an espresso and nibble on a *galleta* (cookie) or croissant.

La Troya (Hotel Posada del Rey, cnr Madero & Juárez) This bar-restaurant has balcony seats overlooking the plaza that catch the night breeze and make a great place for a cold margarita.

Life (☎ 217-44-60; Agua Dulce 506) A lounge bar 3km north of the center, just off Hidalgo, where the hipsters go to sip martinis.

Cinemas Plaza (☎ 214-24-39; Colón 100 Sur) Shows recent American films, subtitled in Spanish.

Getting There & Away

AIR

Aeropuerto Internacional Francisco Javier Mina is 15km north of downtown.

From Tampico, **Aerolitoral** (☎ 228-08-56; Airport) flies to Monterrey, Reynosa and

Veracruz, with connections to Villahermosa; **Mexicana** (☎ 228-36-62; Universidad 700-1) offers daily flights to Mexico City. **Continental** (☎ 800-900-50-00; Hidalgo 4503, Edificio Chairel Desp 205) operates flights between Tampico and Houston, Texas.

BUS

Tampico's modern bus station is 7km north of the center on Rosalio Bustamante. There are stores selling snacks, a call center, luggage storage ($0.50 per hour), but no restaurant – you will find taco stalls outside though.

First-class buses run to most major towns north of Mexico City and down the Gulf coast:

Destination	Price	Duration	Frequency
Ciudad Valles	$10	3hr	6 daily
Matamoros	$26	7hr	14 daily
Mexico City			
(Terminal Norte)	$32	10hr	16 daily
Monterrey	$36	7½hr	28 daily
Nuevo Laredo	$50	11hr	5 daily
Poza Rica	$16	5hr	hourly
San Luis Potosí	$27	8hr	7 daily
Tuxpan	$14	3½hr	hourly
Veracruz	$29	9½hr	18 daily

Deluxe and 2nd-class services also run to many of these destinations.

Long-distance 1st-class buses also go to Reynosa, Soto la Marina, Ciudad Victoria, Villahermosa and Xalapa. For Xilitla, Autonaves runs three daily 2nd-class buses, but it's often quickest to travel to Ciudad Valles on a 1st-class bus and get another connection there.

CAR & MOTORCYCLE

Hwy 180 north of Tampico is a good four-lane divided highway for about 80km, then it's a two-lane northeast to Aldama or northwest on Hwy 81 to Ciudad Victoria. Heading south from Tampico, Hwy 180 soars across the Puente Tampico and continues down to Tuxpan. It's an adequate two-lane road, but avoid driving it at night.

For car hire, these rental agencies are located at the airport:

Avis (☎ 228-05-85)
Budget (☎ 227-18-80)
Dollar (☎ 227-25-75)

Getting Around

Tampico's *colectivo* taxis are large, old US cars with destinations painted on the doors. They're inexpensive but slower than regular taxis, with frequent stops.

Transporte Terrestre (☎ 228-45-88) runs *colectivo* combis from the airport to anywhere in Tampico–Ciudad Madero for about $6 to $7, depending on distance.

Taxis from the bus station to the city center cost $3, *colectivos* are a little cheaper. From the city center to the bus station or METRO cultural center, take a 'Perimetral' or 'Perimetral-CC' *colectivo* ($0.50) from Olmos, a block south of the *zócalo*.

CIUDAD VALLES & AROUND

☎ 481 / pop 110,000 / elevation 71m

Ciudad Valles slumbers on the banks of the huge Río Valles. There are no sights here, but it's a good base for trips into the Huasteca. It's also a handy stop for motorists, close to the midpoint between Monterrey and Mexico City, at the intersection of Hwy 85 (the Pan-American) and Hwy 70 (running east–west from Tampico to San Luis Potosí).

Orientation & Information

Hwy 85, called Blvd México-Laredo in town, curves north–south through the city. To reach the main plaza, head six blocks west down Av Juárez or Av Hidalgo. Hwy 70 bypasses town on the south side.

The main bus station is 3km south of the center, off Hwy 85 (Carr Nacional México-Laredo). A good **tourist booth** (☺ 8am-3pm Mon-Sat) is on the west side of Hwy 85, about 250m north of the bus station. Between the plaza and Hwy 85, Juárez, the main drag, has the Internet café **C & A Computación** (Juárez 508) and banks including a Banamex (with ATM).

Sights & Activities

While Valles itself is pleasant enough it's the verdant countryside of the Huasteca and its azure rivers and plunging waterfalls that are this region's real appeal. They're most easily reached by car, but local buses can get you to most places…eventually.

Professionally organized rafting trips on the Río Tampaón, kayaking on the Río Micos, and rappel and camping trips are run by **Adventura Huasteca** (☎ 381-75-16; www .adventurahuasteca.com; Hotel Adventura Huasteca, Blvd México-Laredo 19 Nte).

TAMUÍN

The important Huastec ceremonial center of **Tamuín** (admission free; ☺ 7am-6pm) flourished from AD 700 to 1200. Today it's one of the few Huastec sites worth visiting, though it's nothing spectacular. The only cleared part of the large site is a plaza with platforms made of river stones. Look for a low bench with two conical altars, extending from a small platform in the middle of the plaza. The bench has the faded remains of some 1000-year-old frescoes believed to represent Quetzalcóatl, the feathered-serpent god.

Southwest of the main site are two un-restored pyramids on private property, and further southwest is Puente de Dios (God's Bridge), a notch in a ridgeline on the horizon. At the winter solstice, around December 21–22, you can stand on the main Tamuín platform and watch the sun set into the Puente de Dios, with the pair of pyramids exactly between them, all aligned with the Río Tampaón.

To get to the ruins, go to the town of Tamuín, 30km east of Ciudad Valles on Hwy 70. A kilometer or so east, turn south from the highway down a road marked 'Zona Arqueológica' and 'San Vicente.' Follow it roughly south for 5km to another 'Zona Arqueológica' sign, then head west 800m.

Frequent buses between Tampico and Ciudad Valles go through Tamuín. The Vencedor window in town sells tickets for local buses ($0.50) to the ruins; you'll have to walk the last 800m up the trail.

WATERFALLS & SWIMMING SPOTS

Many rivers flow eastwards from the well-watered slopes of the sierra, forming cascades, waterfalls and shady spots for cool swims. One of the nicest areas is around Tamasopo, 5km north of Hwy 70 and 55km west of Ciudad Valles. **Cascadas de Tamasopo** has good swimming and a beautiful natural arch.

The **Cascadas de Micos** are north of Hwy 70, a few kilometers west of Ciudad Valles. They're not so good for swimming, but rental canoes are available on weekends.

Another fun place to get wet is **Coy Parque Acuático** (☎ 382-41-59; Hwy Valles-Tamazunchale, Km 35; admission $5.50; ☺ 9am-6pm Sat & Sun). From April to August it's open daily. On Hwy 85 south of town, the park features waterslides and a swimming pool.

TANINUL
To reach this small village, head south off Hwy 70 between Ciudad Valles and Tamuín. The turnoff is marked by a sign for Hotel Taninul, a minor hot-springs resort. Next to the hotel, the small lovely **Museo Lariab** (☎ 382-00-00; admission $1; ☼ 9am-3pm Tue-Sun) has well-presented exhibits on the Huasteca, ancient and contemporary.

Sleeping
Most of the midrange and upmarket places are on Hwy 85.

Hotel Piña (☎ /fax 382-01-83; www.hotel-pina .com; Av Juárez 210; s/d $22/26, with air-con & TV $31/41; P ✶) This welcoming salmon-pink place has good-sized rooms, with wardrobes and bedside reading lights, that come with either ancient but powerful old fans or air-con. There's an excellent café downstairs.

Hotel Misión Ciudad Valles (☎ 382-00-66, 800-900-38-00; www.hotelesmision.com.mx; Blvd México-Laredo 15 Nte; r $48, superior class $62; P ✶ ☎) Bright, spacious but unexceptional rooms, some with slightly saggy beds, the Misión's trump cards are its verdant grounds dotted with animal topiary, and its magnificent palm-fringed pool.

Hotel Taninul (☎ 388-01-43; taninul@avantel.net; Hwy Valles-Tampico, Km 15; s/d $48/66; P ✶ ☎) Set in extensive grounds, this converted hacienda has a blissful, slightly sulfurous pool where you could easily lose a day wallowing in hot mineral water while watching squabbling parakeets. The accommodations are comfortable, though the air-con units' output can be a bit feeble. Located 15km east of Valles, it's a good option for travelers with their own vehicles.

Hotel Valles (☎ 382-00-50; hotelvalles@prodigy.net .mx; Blvd México-Laredo 36 Nte; r/ste $77/92, trailer sites $9.50; P ✶ ☎) The beautiful tropical gardens and large pool are the main draw here at this pleasant hotel, set off the highway 1km north of downtown Valles. There are different grades of rooms, but all are spacious, comfortable and well-appointed. The campground offers trailer sites with full hookups, and you'll find two fine restaurants.

These are some other alternatives; the first two are just along from the Misión:

Hotel San Fernando (☎ 382-22-80; www.prodigyweb .mx/hotelsanfernando; Blvd México-Laredo 17 Nte; s/d $42/49; P ✶ ☐) A well-run place with spacious rooms, ample parking and an in-house restaurant.

Hotel Adventura Huasteca (☎ 382-01-28; Blvd México-Laredo 19 Nte; s/d $39/42; P ✶) Warmly painted rooms with high ceilings, bright bedcovers, reading lights and dark-wood furniture.

Hotel Rex (☎ 382-00-11; Av Hidalgo 418; s/d $25/35; P ✶) A decent choice with 31 neat and tidy, if plain, rooms.

Hotel Condesa (☎ 382-00-15; Juárez 109; s/d $13/16) Venerable place with dark but cleanish, bargain-priced rooms.

Eating
La Troje (☎ 381-68-44; Blvd México-Laredo 26; dishes $3.25-6.50; ☕) This is an excellent choice for tasty Mexican food, and it also has a second branch at Hotel La Piña on Av Juárez 210. Both are very clean and efficiently run.

La Palapa (Hotel Valles, Blvd México-Laredo 36 Nte; mains $6-14; P) For somewhere more special, check out La Palapa, where they have a terrific *ensalada de palmito* and plenty of fish and meat dishes.

Sake (☎ 381-86-94; Blvd México-Laredo 48B; mains $6-11; ☼ 1-9pm Tue-Sun) This place offers Japanese and Chinese cuisine in stylish surrounds.

Getting There & Away
BUS
Just off Hwy 85, some 3km south of Juárez, the user-friendly bus terminal has a left-luggage room ($0.50 per hour) and a booth selling taxi tickets ($2 to the center). Many buses are *de paso* (buses that make many stops and are often late). Daily 1st-class buses depart from Ciudad Valles to several destinations:

Destination	Price	Duration	Frequency
Matamoros	$30	10hr	11 daily
Mexico City			
(Terminal Norte)	$32	10hr	9 daily
Monterrey	$29	8hr	19 daily
San Luis Potosí	$18	5hr	at least 1 hourly
Tampico	$10	3hr	6 daily

Second-class buses run more frequently and cost about 10% less; local routes have buses going to Pachuca, Ciudad Victoria, Tampico, Tamazunchale and Xilitla.

CAR & MOTORCYCLE
Hwy 70 west of Valles is spectacular as it climbs the Sierra Madre towards San Luis Potosí (262km) on the Altiplano Central.

It's a twisting road, and slow trucks will hold you up periodically. East to Tampico, Hwy 70 is in fairly good condition, and is straighter and faster. Going south, Hwy 85 heads to Tamazunchale and then southwest toward Mexico City. You can also continue east from Tamazunchale to Huejutla, circling the Huasteca back to Tampico, but this is a slow route over rough, if paved, roads.

AQUISMÓN & AROUND

☎ 482 / pop 1900 / elevation 137m

The mellow Huastec village of Aquismón – 45km south of Ciudad Valles and 5km up a side road west of Hwy 85 – nestles beneath a precipitous limestone ridge. It's a friendly place, and if you can, drop by to catch its colorful Saturday market or, even better, try to make it for a fiesta (see below).

Mexico's second-deepest pit, the astonishing **Sótano de las Golondrinas** (Pit of the Swallows; admission $1; ☺ dawn-dusk), is a 376m-deep, roughly cone-shaped cave 13km southwest of Aquismón. It's home to tens of thousands of swifts that emerge en masse just after sunrise and return at dusk – their beating wings sounding like a river running over rapids. The access road is rough, and suitable for 4WD vehicles only – local pick-up drivers charge about $20 for the round-trip, which takes an hour in each direction.

About 30km north of Aquismón (allow 1½ hours from Aquismón), the **Cascada de Tamul** plunges 105m into the pristine Río Santa María. Alternatively, you can reach the falls from Tanchachin, south of Hwy 70, by a 2½-hour river trip – this option is unavailable during flooding, when the falls can be up to 300m wide.

The bustling Huastec town of **Tancanhuitz**, called 'Ciudad Santos' on highway signs, is in a narrow, forested valley about 5km southeast of Aquismón, 3km east of Hwy 85. A busy **market** takes place here on Sundays, and pre-Hispanic Huastec remains can be seen near Tampamolón, a few kilometers east.

Tancanhuitz and Aquismón are the centers for the lively festivals of San Miguel Arcángel (September 28 and 29) and the Virgen de Guadalupe (December 12). Huastec dances performed include Las Varitas (Little Twigs) and Zacamsón (Small Music), which both imitate the movements

of wild creatures. In its full version, the Zacamsón dance has more than 75 parts, danced at different times of the day and night. At festivals, much drinking of aguardiente (sugarcane alcohol) accompanies the performances.

A short stroll from Aquismón's plaza, **Hotel La Mansión** (☎ 368-00-04; Carmona 16; r $14, with air-con $24; P ⊠) is a pleasant village inn with sparse tiled rooms with TV. The very simple but clean **Hotel San Cosme** (☎ 368-00-72; cnr Zaragoza & Av Juárez; s/d $10/14; P) is just off the plaza and has plain rooms with fans. Towels and soap are provided and there's hot water here.

For a good feed, head to Café Plaza, a very clean and well-run place on the square that serves good local food including enchiladas huastecas, tamales on Fridays and a mean cheesecake.

Buses from Ciudad Valles or Xilitla drop you at the crossroads of Hwy 85; colectivo taxis ($0.75) take you the last 4km to Aquismón.

XILITLA

☎ 489 / pop 5900 / elevation 1151m

Perched on a hilltop, surrounded on all sides by the sweeping slopes of the Sierra Madre Oriental, Xilitla (he-leet-la) is a gorgeous, historic little town. Virtually all visitors are here to explore the otherworldly beauty of Las Pozas, but the overgrown village of Xilitla has a temperate climate, ample colonial character and a charm of its own.

Orientation & Information

The central plaza occupies the highest part of the town, with streets falling away steeply on all sides. Virtually everything is within three or four blocks of this square, including the bus stop (there's no terminal) which is 200m to the southwest.

There's a Banorte (with ATM) on the plaza and several Internet cafés including **La Nave** (per hr $0.80), just west of the plaza which also offers discounted international calls. You'll find **Lavandería Secado** (Ocampo; wash & dry $3.50) behind Posada El Castillo.

The main day for the Xilitla coffee fair is August 27, but there are also Huapango dances and musical performances – characterized by intricate steps and falsetto singing – held in the week between August 25 and 30.

Sights

LAS POZAS

Xilitla's most famous attraction is **Las Pozas** (The Pools; admission $2; ☻ 9am-dusk) a bizarre-but-beautiful concatenation of concrete temples, pagodas, bridges, pavilions, sculptures and spiral stairways – built adjacent to an idyllic series of waterfalls. This surreal fantasy stands as a monument to the imagination of Edward James (see boxed text, below), the expertise of his site manager and friend Plutarco Gastelum, and the skill of the local workers who cast the elaborate constructions in the 1960s and 1970s. James originally intended many of the structures to be filled with tropical birds and boa constrictors, though this

dream was never realized and most of the buildings here lie in limbo, half-finished with the jungle encroaching on all sides and their exposed reinforcing rods rusting in the fecund forest air.

Los Pozas may be a magical place, a child's dream, but it's also a parent's nightmare: guardrails are nonexistent and one false step could lead to a nasty end. The lovely natural swimming pools make it a popular weekend picnic spot, but it can be nearly deserted during the week. The café here is open daily from 10am to 6pm.

Las Pozas is a 40-minute walk east of Xilitla, or alternatively, a 3km drive; *colectivos* ($2) leave frequently from the road behind the market.

EDWARD JAMES: AN ENGLISH ECCENTRIC

Rumored to be the illegitimate grandson of King Edward VII, Edward James was born in 1907 into a world of privilege and fabulous wealth – his family home was the 300-room West Dean country estate in Sussex, England. But James had an unhappy childhood (his father died when he was five while his mother never expressed any love for him) and he was schooled at Eton, which he hated.

After Oxford University, where his mode of transport was a Rolls Royce, James rejected the stiffness and conventions of the aristocracy and sought out the company of artists, poets and existentialists. His wealth allowed him the opportunity to become a generous patron: he bankrolled the publication of poems by John Betjeman, supported Dylan Thomas for a while and sponsored a ballet so his own wife could play the lead.

James entered a period of depression after the breakup of his marriage (his wife had wanted everything to do with his money and nothing to do with him) and moved from England to mainland Europe in the 1930s. He became absorbed in surrealist art, amassing the largest private collection in the world, collecting Picassos and becoming a patron of Magritte. He also commissioned work by Dalí who said to James 'Look, we move among a bunch of pseudo-realists, who…produce nothing but junk. So, they try to act like madmen to justify themselves. On the other hand, you who are real labor to act sane.'

In the late 1930s as war in Europe approached, James headed to America, bought a house in Hollywood and financially supported Rodia's Watts Towers. His thirst for adventure took him to New Mexico to visit DH Lawrence and Aldous Huxley, and into Mexico where he met Plutarco Gastelum who was to become his closest friend and building contractor of Las Pozas.

In 1945 he discovered Xilitla and was besotted by the exotic plants and birds of the forest. Initially he devoted himself to cultivating local orchids, declaring 'I wanted a Garden of Eden set up,' but when a freak snowfall destroyed his collection in 1962, he turned to a more enduring medium: concrete.

With the help of Plutarco Gastelum, he hired 40 local workers to craft giant, colored, concrete flowers beside his idyllic jungle stream. For the next 17 years, James and Gastelum created ever larger and stranger structures, many of which were never finished, at an estimated cost of $5 million.

James never considered himself an avant-gardist, saying 'If I'm a surrealist it's not because I was linked with the movement, it's because I was born one.' He died in 1984, making no provision to maintain his creation, which is already decomposing into another Mexican ruin. He gave away West Dean to a trust (www.westdean.org.uk) that now supports specialist conservation and restoration projects, visual and applied arts and a wide range of crafts from tapestry weaving to sculpture.

MUSEO DE EDWARD JAMES

Inside Posada El Castillo hotel this excellent **museum** (Ocampo 105; admission $3; ✆ 10am-6pm Tue-Sun) has been set up by the Gastelum family, who own the hotel and who fondly remember Edward James. The building itself has structural details strongly reminiscent of Las Pozas' architecture, including some soaring ornate concrete columns, while the original wood molds used to make the bamboo-inspired pillars are displayed. You'll also find some fine photographs chronicling the construction of Las Pozas and the life of James himself, as well as some of his poetry. The café here has tasty pastries and espresso coffee.

CONVENTO DE SAN AGUSTÍN

Brooding over the plaza, the austere former monastery **Convento de San Agustín** has a virtually unadorned facade. Built in 1557, its most intriguing feature is the row of tiny windows that line its upper north side – these mark the *celdas* (cells) of the resident monks. The only part of the complex that's open to the public is the single-naved chapel and small rear patio.

Sleeping

Hotel Guzmán (✆ 365-03-38; Corregidora 208; s/d $15/24, with air-con $24/29; P 🖳) Just off the plaza, this attractive stone building has three floors of excellent, well-kept, clean,

---

THE AUTHOR'S CHOICE

Posada El Castillo (✆ 365-00-38; www.jungle gossip.com; Ocampo 105; r/ste incl breakfast $40/95; 🖳) Displaying a good dose of Las Pozas' idiosyncratic style it's no surprise that this individualistic hotel was the family home of Edward James' friend and architect Plutarco Gastelum. Now run by Plutarco's family, it's one of Mexico's most enjoyable and welcoming guesthouses, where the spacious, stylishly decorated rooms have real character and have been furnished immaculately with antiques and some wonderful art. The suites 'Gran Vista' and 'Vista' offer the best views. Breakfast is served in the imposing dining room, which also contains an extensive library of videos and books. Outside there's a wonderful pool in a tropical garden.

---

comfortable rooms, many with lovely hand-carved wooden beds and polished wooden floorboards; many have lovely mountain views.

Hotel Ziyaquetzas (✆ 365-01-60; Hidalgo 110; s/d $18/21) Facing the plaza, this well-run place has some rustic character with spacious rooms that have chunky wooden beds and either plaza or hillside views.

Las Pozas (✆ 365-03-67; 2/4 people $29/46; P 🖳) *Cabañas* are scattered throughout the lower part of the estate. These rustic lodges, all with private bathrooms, certainly enjoy a unique location, though some of the interiors are a tad musty.

Eating

Look out for tasty local *acamaya* (freshwater crayfish) and *enchiladas huastecas*, which are served with *cecina* (thin strips of beef) on the side.

Restaurant Cayo's (✆ 365-00-44; Alvarado 117; dishes $3.50-8; ✆ 9am-9pm) Hearty Mexican food served in barnlike environs with ambience courtesy of a soap opera–tuned TV and a thunderous jukebox stuffed with romantic ballads.

La Flor de Café (✆ 365-03-76; Hidalgo 215; comida corrida $2; ✆ 6:30am-9pm) Run by a co-op of Nahua women, this little place offers local specialties including *zacahuiles* (huge *tamales*) as well as delicious seasonal *aguas frescas* (fruit blended with water and sweetener).

Also worth trying:

Taz Pizza (✆ 365-06-57; 3rd fl, Escobedo 116; pizzas $4-7)
Comedor Saris (Escobedo 220; breakfasts $2.75, antojítos $2-3.50)

Getting There & Away

Xilitla has regular connections on comfortable 2nd-class buses to Ciudad Valles ($4.50, 16 daily) and Tampico ($14, three daily). There are also buses to San Luis Potosí ($20, two daily). The southeast journey across northern Veracruz state towards Tuxpan by bus is very slow and involves at least three bus changes – at La Y Griega junction on Hwy 85 just east of Xilitla, Tamazunchale, and Huejutla – and it's actually quicker to travel via Valles and Tampico.

Hwy 120, heading west to Jalpan then southwest toward Querétaro, is an exciting route through the Sierra Gorda (see p656). Southeast of Xilitla, Hwy 85 veers through Tamazunchale before climbing steeply to

Ixmiquilpan (see p203), then continues to Pachuca. This is the most direct route from the Huasteca to Mexico City. It's a steep but scenic route over the Sierra Madre. Start early to avoid mist and fog.

HUEJUTLA DE REYES

☎ 789 / pop 38,500

Set in semitropical lowlands, Huejutla is a large market town with a wacky central plaza but no sights for travelers – though the big Sunday market, which attracts many Nahua people, is worth experiencing.

Several banks with 24-hour ATMs are clustered off the plaza around Morelos and Hidalgo. You'll find **Cafe Internet** (Juárez 14; per hr $1.25; ☺ 8:30am-9pm Mon-Sat) next to Hotel Rivieria.

Hotel Rivieria (☎ 896-30-20; Juárez 14), 500m from the 1st-class bus terminal, is a well-run place with small, spotlessly clean rooms with TV and fan. The more upmarket **Hotel Posada Huejutla** (☎ 896-03-03; Morelos 32; r $29; P ✗ ▣) has a gurgling fountain, pool and smart rooms with mod cons and patio seating.

Opposite Hotel Rivieria, **Los 3 Cebollas** (Juárez 21; snacks $3; mains $4.50-6.50) has *carnes a la plancha* and filling tortas and tacos.

SOUTH OF HUEJUTLA

Hwy 105 rolls through lush, hilly farmland near Tampico, but south of Huejutla it climbs into the lovely Sierra Madre Oriental. It's a tortuous, foggy road to Pachuca. On the way you'll pass old monasteries at **Molango** and **Zacualtipán**.

The highway then leaves the Sierra Madre and drops several hundred meters to scenic **Metzquititlán**, in the fertile Río Tulancingo Valley. The village of **Metztitlán**, 23km northwest up the valley, sports a fairly well preserved monastery. It was the center of an Otomí state that the Aztecs couldn't conquer.

NORTHERN VERACRUZ

The northern half of Veracruz, between the coast and southern fringes of the Sierra Madre Oriental, mainly consists of lush rolling pastureland. Teardrop-shaped Laguna de Tamiahua is the region's largest wetland, and offers fishing and birding, while the Gulf has some fine isolated (as

well as polluted) sandy beaches. The major archaeological attraction is El Tajín, usually reached from Papantla.

At the regular army checkpoints along this coast the soldiers are usually very respectful towards tourists.

TUXPAN

☎ 783 / pop 75,000

A steamy fishing town and minor oil port, Tuxpan (sometimes spelled Túxpam) is 300km north of Veracruz and 190km south of Tampico. Other than resting, refueling and crossing the broad Río Tuxpan to visit a curious little museum devoted to Cuban–Mexican friendship, there's little to do here. Playa Norte, the beach 12km to the east, is popular with vacationing Mexicans, though it's no idyllic seaside resort.

Orientation & Information

The narrow streets of the downtown area are on the north bank of the Río Tuxpan, six blocks upstream from the high bridge that spans the river. The riverfront road, Blvd Reyes Heroles, passes under the bridge and runs east to Playa Norte. A block inland from the riverfront is hotel-lined Av Juárez, with the Parque Reforma at its western end.

Tuxpan's **tourist office** (☎ 834-64-07; turismo tuxpam@yahoo.com.mx; grd fl, Palacio Municipal; ☺ 9am-7pm Mon-Fri, 10am-6pm Sat) has reasonable maps and tourist brochures. There are card phones in Parque Reforma, and banks with ATMs on Juárez. The post office is several blocks away, up on Mina, while you'll find several Internet cafés on Zapata.

Sights & Activities

Tuxpan is not over-endowed with sights. The one place that is definitely worth a visit is over on the river's south side. Though the exhibits are modest, the historical significance of the **Museo de la Amistad México-Cuba** (Mexican-Cuban Friendship Museum; Obregón s/n; donation requested; ☺ 8am-7pm) is compelling. Fidel Castro stayed in this suburban house, set in a lovely position overlooking the river, in 1956 while planning the Cuban revolution. On November 26 a private yacht overloaded with 82 revolutionaries set sail from here, taking seven days to reach Cuba (to find an ambush waiting).

There's a yellowing collection of maps, B&W photos and displays on José Martí

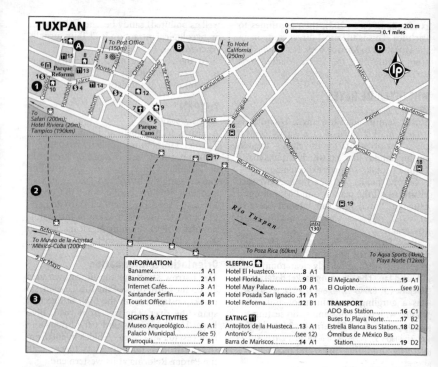

INFORMATION		
Banamex.....................**1** A1		
Bancomer...................**2** A1		
Internet Cafés..............**3** A1		
Santander Serfin...........**4** A1		
Tourist Office...............**5** B1		

SIGHTS & ACTIVITIES		
Museo Arqueológico........**6** A1		
Palacio Municipal............(see 5)		
Parroquia....................**7** B1		

SLEEPING		
Hotel El Huasteco............**8** A1		
Hotel Florida.................**9** B1		
Hotel May Palace............**10** A1		
Hotel Posada San Ignacio..**11** A1		
Hotel Reforma...............**12** B1		

EATING		
Antojitos de la Huasteca....**13** A1		
Antonio's......................(see 12)		
Barra de Mariscos............**14** A1		

El Mejicano....................**15** A1		
El Quijote.....................(see 9)		

TRANSPORT		
ADO Bus Station..............**16** C1		
Buses to Playa Norte.........**17** B2		
Estrella Blanca Bus Station..**18** D2		
Ómnibus de México Bus		
Station....................**19** D2		

and Che Guevara. To get there, take one of the small boats ($0.25) across the river, walk several blocks south to Obregón, then turn right – the museum is at the western end of Obregón.

The **Museo Arqueológico** (☎ 834-61-80; Parque Reforma) has been closed for years, but should eventually reopen sometime this century with artifacts including Totonac *caritas orientales* and Huastec religious statuary and necklaces.

Tuxpan's beach, **Playa Norte** is a wide strip stretching 20km north from Río Tuxpan's mouth, 12km east of town. Its beauty is diminished by a power station close by, but the water and sand are fairly clean and – holidays and weekends apart – it's usually almost empty. *Palapas* serve seafood and sell souvenirs. Local buses ($0.80, 25 minutes) marked 'Playa' leave every 20 minutes from the south side of Blvd Reyes Heroles and drop you at the south end of the beach.

Aqua Sports (☎ 837-02-59; Hwy Tuxpan-La Barra, Km 8.5; 2 dives $76), around 4km from downtown, is an established scuba-diving operation

that offers dives on nearby reefs or Isla de Lobos. Visibility is best between May and August. They can also arrange fishing trips, waterskiing and windsurfing.

Festivals & Events
A big **fishing tournament** brings hundreds of visitors to Tuxpan in late June or early July. Festivities for the **Assumption** (15 August) continue for a week with folk-dancing contests, bullfights and fireworks.

Sleeping
Hotels fill up quickly during holiday periods, but discounts may be available at other times. A few cheap hotels and campsites are available at Playa Norte.

BUDGET
Hotel Riviera (☎ 834-53-49; Blvd Reyes Heroles 17; s/d $29/34; P ☒) This renovated riverfront hotel is a good deal, with very generously sized, immaculately presented rooms with quality beds and furnishings. Accommodation in the front half of the hotel is more attractive; some rooms enjoy partial river views.

Hotel Posada San Ignacio (☎ 834-29-05; Ocampo 29; s/d $17/22) An extremely friendly, welcoming place in a quiet location, the bright cheery rooms, with ceiling fans and TV, surround a courtyard bursting with plants. They bleach the place down thoroughly every day.

Hotel El Huasteco (☎ 834-18-59; Morelos 41; s & d $22, tw $32; ✸) Look for the bunkeresque exterior. The rooms, though dark, are big, bare and clean, and set off mosaic-tiled corridors.

MIDRANGE
Midrange Tuxpan hotels come with cable TV, air-conditioning and phone.

Hotel Reforma (☎ 834-02-10; hotelreforma@prodigy .net.mx; Av Juárez 25; s/d $54/63; P ✕ ✸) A solid choice in the center of town, the elegant looking Reforma has attractive carpeted rooms with wooden furniture off a covered courtyard.

Or try these choices:

Hotel California (☎ 834-08-79; Arteaga 16; s/d with fan $20/31, with air-con $26/36; P ✸) Efficiently managed hotel with 40 comfortable, good-value rooms, all with TV.

Hotel May Palace (☎ 834-88-81; fax 834-88-82; Av Juárez 44; s/d $58/70; P ✕ ✸ ⬚) There's a roof deck with a pool, and though the rooms are looking dated, many have great river views.

Hotel Florida (☎ 834-02-22; fax 834-06-50; Juárez 23; s/d $40/50; P ✕ ✸) Has an art-deco lobby but the small rooms are more perfunctory, and some are showing their age.

Eating
The many *palapas* at Playa Norte are ideal for fresh fish or a shrimp cocktail (both $6) washed down with a cold beer.

El Mejicano (☎ 834-89-04; Morelos 49; buffet $4.50, mains $4-8.50; ☽ 8am-11pm Tue-Sat) A stylish, bustling place, decorated with sarape blankets and featuring an open kitchen that's very popular for breakfasts and lunch buffets.

Barra de Mariscos (☎ 834-46-01; Av Juárez 44; seafood $5-8) Enjoyable, atmospheric place where the chef-patron really cares about the freshness of his seafood; try the *pulpo con salsa de ajo* (octopus in garlic sauce) or *camarones a la plancha* (grilled shrimp).

Antojitos de la Huasteca (☎ 834-74-24; Parque Reforma; snacks $1-2, mains $4-7.50) Offers pavement seating facing the plaza and serves Mexican staples, breakfast options including *frutas con granola y yogurt* ($2.50), and the usual egg dishes.

Safari (☎ 834-10-70; Blvd Reyes Heroles 35; mains $9-13) Slightly contrived safari-themed restaurant on the riverfront with an air-conditioned interior. The cooking is quite creative, with plenty of salads – *congo* is prepared with spinach leaves, bacon and walnuts – as well as substantial seafood and meat dishes.

These air-conditioned hotel establishments are also good:

Antonio's (Hotel Reforma, Av Juárez 25; dishes $4-11)

El Quijote (Hotel Florida, Juárez 23; dishes $3.75-9)

Getting There & Around
Most 1st-class buses leaving Tuxpan are *de paso*, so book your seats in advance – you might have to take a 2nd-class bus to Poza Rica and a 1st-class line from there.

There are several bus terminals, but the ADO station (1st class and deluxe) on Rodríguez is the most convenient for the center. Ómnibus de México (ODM; 1st class) is under the bridge on the north side of the river. The modern Estrella Blanca terminal, two blocks east of the bridge on Alemán, runs mainly 2nd-class services, but also has a few 1st-class buses. Departures:

Destination	Price	Duration	Frequency
Matamoros	$42	11hr	2 ADO daily, also several UNO services
Mexico City (Terminal Norte)	$29	4hr	1 UNO daily
	$19	4hr	15 ADO daily
	$18	4hr	8 ODM daily
Papantla	$4	1¾hr	7 ADO daily
Poza Rica	$3	45 min	ADO at least hourly, 2nd-class every 30min
Tampico	$14	3½hr	26 ADO daily, 2nd-class every 30min
Veracruz	$17	5½hr	15 ADO daily
Villahermosa	$48	12hr	4 ADO daily
Xalapa	$17	5½hr	7 ADO daily

Covered launches ($0.30) ferry passengers across the river.

AROUND TUXPAN
Tamiahua, 43km north of Tuxpan by paved road, is at the southern end of Laguna de Tamiahua. It has a few seafood-shack restaurants, and you can rent boats for fishing

or trips out to the lagoon's barrier island. From Tuxpan take a 1st-class ODM bus ($1.50) or a more frequent 2nd-class bus.

Castillo de Teayo, 23km up a bumpy road west off Hwy 180 (the turnoff is 18km from Poza Rica), was one of the southernmost points of the Huastec civilization from about AD 800. Beside its main plaza is a steep, 13m-high restored pyramid topped by a small temple, built in Toltec style probably sometime between AD 900 and 1200.

Around the base of the pyramid are some stone sculptures which represent many different gods including a Mixcóatl deity linked with hunting, Quetzalcóatl, and Tlaloc, the 'goggle-eyed' rain god. Some of these are in Huastec style, while others are thought to be the work of Aztecs who controlled the area briefly before the Spanish conquest.

POZA RICA

☎ 782 / pop 175,000

The modern, bland oil city of Poza Rica is at the junction of highways 180 and 130. You might have to change buses here, but it's not worth staying the night.

If you do get stuck, the **Best Western Hotel Poza Rica** (☎ 822-01-12; fax 823-20-32; cnr Calles 2 Nte & 10 Ote; r/ste $67/88; P ⊠ ☒) is a good choice with well-equipped rooms and a café-restaurant.

The main Poza Rica bus station, on Puebla, east off Blvd Lázaro Cárdenas, has 2nd-class and some 1st-class buses. Most 1st-class buses leave from the adjoining ADO building, including the following departures:

Destination	Price	Duration	Frequency
Mexico City (Terminal Norte)	$15	5hr	hourly
Pachuca	$10	4hr	at least 2 daily
Papantla	$1.25	30min	20 daily
Tampico	$17	5hr	25 daily
Tuxpan	$3	45min	30 daily
Veracruz	$13	5hr	hourly

For El Tajín, take one of Transportes Papantla's frequent buses to Coyutla ($1) and ask to get off at the turnoff marked 'Desviación El Tajín,' about 30 minutes from Poza Rica; the ruins are a 500m stroll from the highway. Buses to El Chote, Agua Dulce or

San Andrés by Autotransportes Coatzintla and other 2nd-class companies also go past the Desviación El Tajín.

POZA RICA TO PACHUCA

The scenic 200km Poza Rica–Pachuca road, Hwy 130, is the direct approach to Mexico City from northern Veracruz. This winding, misty route climbs up to the Sierra Madre, across the semitropical north of Puebla state and into Hidalgo, passing through a region populated with many Nahua and Totonac indigenous people.

Huauchinango, roughly halfway between Poza Rica and Pachuca, is the center of a flower-growing area. You'll also find embroidered textiles in the busy Saturday market. A weeklong flower festival, known as the **feria**, includes traditional dances and reaches its peak on the third Friday in Lent.

Acaxochitlán, 25km west of Huauchinango, has a Sunday market; specialties include fruit wine and preserved fruit.

The traditional Nahua village of **Pahuatlán** is the source of many of the textiles from central Mexico: the tablecloths and clothes are woven with multicolored designs of animals and plants. Reach it by turning north off Hwy 130, about 10km past Acaxochitlán. About 30km from Hwy 130, a spectacular dirt road winds down to the village, which holds a sizable Sunday market. About half an hour's drive beyond Pahuatlán is **San Pablito**, an Otomí village where colorfully embroidered blouses abound.

Hwy 130 climbs steeply to Tulancingo, in the state of Hidalgo. See p203 for details on the rest of this route to Pachuca.

PAPANTLA

☎ 784 / pop 48,000 / elevation 196m

Spilling down over a hillside, Papantla is a manageably pleasant town, with an easy-going atmosphere and a delightful central plaza. It's the ideal jumping-off point for the nearby ruins of El Tajín and an important market town for the Totonacs, some of whom still wear traditional costume here: the men in loose white shirts and trousers, women in embroidered blouses and *quechquémitls* (traditional capes). The town is at the center of a vanilla-growing region – though unfortunately you're much more likely to notice the city's annoying traffic fumes than wafts of exotic scents.

Orientation & Information

Papantla lies just off Hwy 180, which runs southeast from Poza Rica. The center of town is uphill from the main road. From the *zócalo*, uphill (facing the cathedral) is south, and downhill is north.

The plaza is 1.5km south of the ADO bus station; turn left out of the terminal, then take the first right into Av Carranza, then left up Calle 20 de Noviembre, past the Transportes Papantla bus terminal and market to the *zócalo*. The ramshackle **tourist office** (☎ 842-00-26; 1st fl, Azueta 101; ☺ 9am-9pm Mon-Fri, 9am-3pm Sat & Sun) is just off the northwest corner of the *zócalo*.

You'll find two banks with ATMs on Enríquez just east of the *zócalo*, and **Tosan Internet** (Calle 5 de Mayo; per hr $1) opposite Hotel Tajín for fast connections. To get to the post office, take the street west of the church, then right on 16 de Septiembre. Walk four blocks, going left at the fork, and it's on your left.

Sights

Officially called Parque Téllez, the **zócalo** is terraced into the hillside below the **Iglesia de la Asunción**. Beneath this Franciscan cathedral, a 50m-long **mural** facing the square depicts Totonac and Veracruz history. A serpent stretches along the mural, bizarrely linking a pre-Hispanic stone carver, El Tajín's Pirámide de los Nichos and an oil rig.

At the top of the hill towers Papantla's **volador monument** (see p678 for information on *voladores* rites). This 1988 statue portrays a musician, eyes gazing to the heavens, playing his pipe as preparation for the four fliers to launch themselves into space. To reach the monument, take the street heading uphill from the southwest corner of the cathedral yard; at the end of the road, hang a left. Spanish inscriptions around its base give an explanation of the ritual. The area serves as lovers' lane on weekend nights.

On the edge of town on the road to El Tajín, the humble **Museo de Cultura Totonaca** Calle 16 de Septiembre; admission $1.75; ☺ 9am-6pm Mon-Sat) has exhibits on Totonac culture from pre-Hispanic times to the present. The Spanish-speaking Totonac guides give detailed explanations and can answer questions. White minibuses from Calle 16 de Septiembre can get you here for a couple of pesos.

Festivals & Events

The fantastic **feria de Corpus Christi**, in late May and early June, is the big annual event. As well as the bullfights, parades and *charreadas* that are usual in Mexico, Papantla celebrates its Totonac cultural heritage with spectacular indigenous dances. The main procession is on the first Sunday when *voladores* fly two or three times a day.

Papantla's other major celebration is the **Festival de Vainilla** (Vanilla Festival) on 18 June, featuring indigenous dancers, gastronomical delights sold in street stalls and vanilla products galore.

Sleeping

Papantla has a fairly poor selection of hotels. All of these places offer rooms with TVs and air-con.

Hotel Tajín (☎ 842-01-21; fax 842-10-62; Núñez 104; r $35-46; P ✖) This likeable hotel, with a distinctive pinkish facade, has character and enjoys a commanding position on the southeast corner of the plaza. The rooms are all well-kept, but vary quite a bit, many have nice Spanish-style tile-detailing, and some have balconies.

Hotel Provincia Express (☎ 842-16-45; hotprovi@prodigy.net.mx; Enríquez 103; s/d $35/44; ✖ ▢) Benefits from a fine plaza location, and though the rooms are clean and well-equipped, the decor is looking a bit tired.

Hotel Totonacapán (☎ 842-12-20; cnr Calle 20 de Noviembre & Olivo; s/d $29/33; ✖) About 400m downhill from the *zócalo*, this airy hotel has sparse – but large and comfy – rooms. The restaurant downstairs provides room service.

Hotel Pulido (☎ 842-10-79; Enríquez 205; s/d $15/21, with air-con $24/33; P ✖) A basic but acceptable place 250m east of the *zócalo*. The fan-only rooms are a fair budget deal.

Eating

Exotic offerings are nonexistent in provincially minded Papantla, but you will find fairly priced Mexican staples.

Plaza Pardo (☎ 842-00-59; 1st fl, Enríquez 105; mains $3.50-7) Park yourself on one of the balcony tables for a terrific view of the *zócalo* and tuck in to breakfast ($3 to $5) a sandwich or a substantial dish like *pollo al chiltepín*. Also good for a beer or an espresso.

La Hacienda (☎ 842-06-33; Reforma 100 Altos; most dishes $3-6) Offers a slightly cheaper menu and a different perspective of the *zócalo* than its rival the Pardo. There are the usual Mexican suspects, and good *mariscos* ($5.50 to $9).

Melo (☎ 842-39-90; Juárez 311; dishes $4-9) Enjoyable place between the ADO terminal and *zócalo* that scores for very filling breakfasts ($3), tortas and burgers ($1.50 to $3) and mains that include delicious *camarones con coco* (prawns cooked in coconut milk).

Restaurant Totonaca (Hotel Tajín, Núñez 104; mains $5-7.50) This semiformal hotel bar-restaurant has an extensive menu, with pasta at $2.50 and tasty *cecina* (meat) and chicken mains. There's also a short wine list, while the hilarious cocktail selection includes the have-to-try-it 'turbo muppet.'

Shopping

As Mexico's leading vanilla-growing center, Papantla offers quality vanilla extract, vanilla pods and *figuras* (pods woven into the shapes of flowers, insects or crucifixes). Try the regional vanilla liquor or vanilla-infused cigarettes. Mercado Hidalgo, at the northwest corner of the *zócalo*, has some pretty Totonac costumes, good baskets and vanilla souvenirs. Mercado Juárez, at the southwest corner opposite the cathedral, sells mainly food.

Getting There & Away

Few long-distance buses stop at Papantla's quaint station. Most are *de paso*, so book your bus out of town as soon as possible – you can also make reservations at **Ticket Bus** (☎ 842-12-30; Enríquez 111) just east of the plaza. If desperate, go to Poza Rica and get one of the more frequent buses from there. ADO is the only 1st-class line serving Papantla; slower 2nd-class Transportes Papantla (TP) leaves from a separate terminal.

Destination	Price	Duration	Frequency
Mexico City (Terminal Norte)	$16	5hr	7 daily
Poza Rica	$1	30min	about one ADO hourly & TP every 15min
Tampico	$16	5½hr	3 daily
Tuxpan	$4	1¾hr	7 daily
Veracruz	$12	4hr	8 daily
Xalapa	$14	4hr	11 daily

EL TAJÍN

Situated on a plain surrounded by low verdant hills 6km west of Papantla, the extensive ruins of El Tajín are the most impressive reminder of Classic Veracruz civilization. The name Tajín is Totonac for 'thunder,' 'lightning' or 'hurricane,' but though the Totonacs may have occupied the site later in its history, most of the structures here were built before that civilization became powerful.

El Tajín was first occupied about AD 100, but most of what's visible dates from the era AD 600 or 700. The years AD 600 to 900 saw its zenith as a town and ceremonial center. Around AD 1200 the site was abandoned, possibly after attacks by Chichimecs, and lay unknown to the Spaniards until about

---

PLAIN VANILLA

Vanilla is sexy. What's not seductive about the planet's only known edible orchid – an aphrodisiac, a spice second only to saffron as the most expensive in the world, a coveted pod once used to pay taxes to the Aztecs?

Now so commonplace that it connotes the bland and unoriginal, the sweetly fragrant yellow orchid known as *vanilla planifolia* was first cultivated by the Totonacs who believed that vanilla was a gift from the gods, and carefully guarded their methods of curing the pods. Mixed with cacao and other spices, vanilla is the historically overlooked but equally valued ingredient of *xocolatl*, the Aztec concoction that introduced chocolate to the rest of the world.

Still precious in value, real vanilla can take up to three years to cultivate and cure, and due to its expense and popularity, products from perfumes to ice cream incorporate synthetic vanilla flavor rather than the real thing.

But if you lust for the real thing, Papantla celebrates its Festival de Vainilla (Vanilla Festival), on 18 June. Local hotels can arrange visits to vanilla plantations; you'll catch the orchids blooming in April and May, and harvest time in early December. In the markets in town, you can pick up vanilla pods, extracts and liqueurs throughout the year.

1785, when an official found it while looking for illegal tobacco plantings.

Among El Tajín's special features are rows
of square niches on the sides of buildings,
numerous ball courts, and sculptures depicting human sacrifice connected with the
ball game. The archaeologist who did much
of the excavation here, José García Payón,
believed that El Tajín's niches and stone
mosaics symbolized day and night, light
and dark, and life and death in a universe
composed of dualities, though many are
skeptical of this interpretation. The ruins
were extensively reconstructed in 1991.

Orientation & Information

The **Tajín site** (admission $3.75, video camera $3;
🕑 8am-6pm) covers about 10 sq km, and you
need to walk a few kilometers to see it all.
There's little shade and it can get blazingly
hot, so an early start is recommended, along
with a water bottle and a hat. It'll take about
two hours to have a good look around the
site and museum. Most buildings and carvings here are labeled in English and Spanish, and some have information panels in
German and French as well.

Bordering the parking lot are stalls selling
food and handicrafts. The visitor center has
a restaurant, souvenir shops, a left-luggage
room, an information desk and a museum
with a model of the site. Those seeking more
information should look for the book *Tajín:
Mystery and Beauty,* by Leonardo Zaleta,
sometimes available (in several languages)
at the souvenir shops.

Two main parts of the site have been
cleared and restored: the lower area, containing the Pirámide de los Nichos (Pyramid of the Niches); and, uphill, a group of
buildings known as 'El Tajín Chico' (Little
Tajín). Most features of the site are known
by the labels used in a 1966 INAH survey, with many called simply 'Estructura'
(Structure) followed by a number or letter.

Plaza Menor

Beyond the Plaza del Arroyo, which is
flanked by pyramids on four sides and
could have been a marketplace, you come
to the **Plaza Menor** (Lesser Plaza), part of
El Tajín's main ceremonial center, with a
low platform in the middle. A statue on
the first level of Estructura 5, a pyramid
on the plaza's west side, represents either

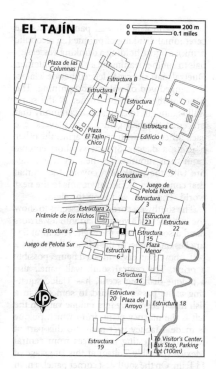

a thunder-and-rain god who was especially
important at El Tajín, or Mictlantecuhtli, a
death god. All of the structures around this
plaza were probably topped by small temples, and some were decorated with red or
blue paint – traces of which remain.

Juego de Pelota Sur

Some 17 ball courts have been found at El
Tajín. The **Juego de Pelota Sur** (Southern Ball
Court), between Estructuras 5 and 6, dates
from about 1150 and is the most famous of
the courts owing to the six relief carvings
on its walls depicting various aspects of the
ball-game ritual.

The panel on the northeast corner (on
the right as you enter the court from the
Plaza Menor) is the easiest to make out. At
its center, three ball-players wearing knee
pads are depicted carrying out a ritual
post-game sacrifice: one player is about to
plunge a knife into the chest of another,
whose arms are held by the third. A skeletal
death god on the left and a presiding figure
on the right look on. Another death god
hovers over the victim.

The central north wall panel depicts the ceremonial drinking of pulque (an alcoholic drink); a figure holding a drinking vessel signals to another leaning on a pulque container. Quetzalcóatl sits cross-legged beside Tláloc, the fanged god of water and lightning. The panel at the northwest corner of the same wall is thought to represent a ceremony that preceded the ball game. Two players face each other, one with crossed arms, the other holding a dagger. Speech symbols emerge from their mouths. To their right is a figure with the mask of a coyote, the animal that conducted sacrificial victims to the next world. The death god is on the right.

The southwest corner panel seems to show the initiation of a young man into a warriors band associated with the eagle. A central figure lies on a table; to the left, another holds a bell. Above is an eagle-masked figure, possibly a priest. The central south wall panel, also a pulque-drinking scene, has Tláloc squatting as he passes a gourd to someone in a fish mask, seemingly in a pulque vat. On the left is the maguey plant, from which pulque is made. Maguey isn't native to this part of Mexico, suggesting influences from central Mexico (possibly Toltec) at this late stage of El Tajín. On the southeast corner panel, a man offers spears or arrows to another, perhaps also in a eagle-warrior initiation ceremony.

Pirámide de los Nichos

El Tajín's most emblematic structure, the beautifully proportioned **Pyramid of the Niches** is just off the Plaza Menor. The six lower levels, each surrounded by rows of small square niches, climb to a height of 18m. The wide staircase on the east side was a late addition, built over some of the niches. Archaeologists believe that there were originally 365 niches, suggesting that the building may have been used as a kind of calendar. The insides of the niches were painted red and their frames blue. The only similar known building, probably of an earlier date, is a seven-level niched pyramid at Yohualichán near Cuetzalan, 50km southwest of El Tajín.

El Tajín Chico

The path north toward Plaza El Tajín Chico passes the **Juego de Pelota Norte** (Northern Ball Court), which is smaller and older than the southern court and also bears (fainter) carvings on its sides.

Many of the buildings of **El Tajín Chico** have geometric stone mosaic patterns known as 'Greco' (Greek); similar patterns are found in decorations at Mitla (Oaxaca), a later site. **Edificio I**, probably once a palace and covered by a protective *palapa* roof, has some terrific carvings, including representations of a razor-toothed reptilian figure. **Estructura C**, on the east side, with three levels and a staircase facing the plaza, was initially painted blue. **Estructura D**, behind Estructura B and off the plaza, has a large lozenge-design mosaic and a passage underneath.

Estructura A, on the plaza's north side, has a facade like a Maya roof comb, with a stairway leading up to a monumental doorway. This corbeled arch, its two sides jutting closer to each other until they are joined at the top by a single slab, is typical of Maya architecture, and its presence here is yet another oddity in the confusing jigsaw puzzle of pre-Hispanic cultures.

Northwest of Plaza El Tajín Chico is the unreconstructed **Plaza de las Columnas** (Plaza of the Columns), one of the site's most important structures. This area is fenced off with 'no access' signs. It originally housed an open patio, with adjoining buildings stretching over the hillside to cover an area of nearly 200m by 100m. Some spectacular reassembled columns, many showing wonderful carvings, are displayed in the site museum.

Voladores Performances

The Totonac *voladores* rite – traditionally carried out only once a year, but now performed almost daily for visitors – is a sort of slow-motion bungee jump from the top of a vertiginously tall pole. The rite begins with five men in elaborate textile costumes climbing to the top of the pole. Four of them sit on the edges of a small, square frame at the top, arrange their ropes and then rotate the frame to twist the ropes around the pole. The fifth man dances on the tiny platform above them while playing a *chirimía*, a small drum with a flute attached. When he stops playing, the others fall backward in unison. Arms outstretched, they revolve gracefully around the pole and descend to the ground, upside down, as their ropes unwind.

This ancient ceremony is packed with symbolic meanings. One interpretation is that it's a fertility rite and the fliers make invocations to the four corners of the universe before falling to the ground, bringing with them the sun and rain. It is also noted that each flier circles the pole 13 times, giving a total of 52 revolutions. The number 52 is not only the number of weeks in the modern year but also was an important number in pre-Hispanic Mexico, which had two calendars – one corresponding to the 365-day solar year, the other to a ritual year of 260 days. A day in one calendar coincided with a day in the other calendar every 52 solar years.

Totonacs carry out the *voladores* rite most days from a 30m-high steel pole beside the visitor center. Performances are usually around noon, 2pm and 4pm; before they start, a Totonac in traditional dress requests donations ($2) from the audience.

Getting There & Away

Frequent buses journey here from Poza Rica (see p674). From Papantla, buses marked 'Pirámides Tajín' leave from opposite the Pemex station at the lower end of Calle 20 de Noviembre. The site is 300m from the highway.

SOUTH OF PAPANTLA

Hwy 180 runs near the coast for most of the 230km from Papantla to Veracruz. Occasionally, strong currents can make for risky swimming here.

Tecolutla

☎ 766 / pop 3900

With a fine, gently shelving sandy beach and well-swept streets, this relaxed seaside resort is popular with middle-class Mexican families. Launches make trips up the Río Tecolutla just to the south and into the mangroves for fishing and wildlife watching. Prices for accommodations skyrocket during high season, quadrupling during Semana Santa. There's a bank with an ATM on the plaza.

Right on the beach, the **tortugario** (☎ 846-04-67; www.vidamilenaria.org.mx; donation required; ⏰ 9am-dusk) is a small conservation center run by Fernando Manzano Cervantes, known locally as 'papá tortuga,' who has been protecting and releasing green and Kemp's Ridley turtles here for the last 30 years. Visitors are welcome to look at the hatchlings, and also some iguanas.

You'll have your pick from dozens of hotels at most times of year. A couple of blocks from the plaza, the lime-green **Hotel Posada del Conquistador** (☎ /fax 846-02-81; cnr Obregón & Centenario; s/d $21/24; P ⓧ ⓡ) represents superb value for money, with spacious, spotless rooms and friendly management; the indoor pool is tiny though. For a beachfront location, **Hotel Oasis** (☎ 846-02-70; Agustín Lara 8; r $14-27; P), a 15-minute walk from the plaza, has attractive rooms, those upstairs catching the Gulf breeze through their bamboo screens; call for a free pick-up. The **Aqua Inn** (☎ 846-03-58; www.hotelaquainn.tripod.com; Aldama; s/d $43/62; P ⓧ ⓡ) is a sleek modern building with spacious renovated rooms and a rooftop pool.

You won't go hungry in Tecolutla, with inexpensive seafood everywhere. On the beach, all the *palapa* places sell cold beer, while seafood cocktail hawkers abound. There are numerous restaurants with very cheap set menus. Choose between **Merendero la Galera** (☎ 845-16-71; Obregón 17; set meals from $4) and **Mendo's** (Obregón 24; dishes $3-8), next door, for fresh fish or a *caldo de pescado*.

Tecolutla is 11km from Hwy 180 and the town of Gutiérrez Zamora. There are regular 2nd-class Transportes Papantla buses between Tecolutla and Papantla. Most 1st-class buses run from Gutiérrez Zamora, but there's an ADO office in Tecolutla a block from the beach, where you can book your ticket in advance; take a local bus ($0.70, 30 minutes) or taxi ($6) to get between the two.

Costa Esmeralda

The 20km Emerald Coast sports a smattering of hotels and trailer parks along a strip between Hwy 180 and the dark, sandy beach. It's a popular summer and holiday spot, but is deserted most of the year. At the north end of the coast, **La Guadalupe** is an OK stop. Further south, hotels get more upscale and expensive; near the village of Casitas, check out the sparkly **Hotel Playa Paraíso** (☎ 232-321-00-44; Hwy 180, Km 81; r $40; P ⓧ ⓡ), with a pool and attractive beach setting.

At the mouth of the Río Bobos, the small fishing town of **Nautla** dozes on the south side of a toll bridge. There's seafood at a couple of simple places near the brown beach.

Laguna Verde & Around

Mexico's sole nuclear power station is at **Laguna Verde**, about 80km north of Veracruz port on Hwy 180. The first unit began operating in 1989 and the second in 1996, but government plans for more reactors have been scrapped in the face of public protest. Reports by Greenpeace and a highly critical 2005 investigation by WANO (the World Association of Nuclear Operators) have highlighted numerous safety concerns.

Now just a fishing village 69km north of Veracruz, **Villa Rica** is the probable site of the first Spanish settlement in Mexico. Here you can explore traces of a fort and a church on the Cerro de la Cantera or bask on a lovely beach.

The nearby Totonac tombs of **Quiahuiztlán** (8am-dusk; admission $2) are beautifully situated on a hill overlooking the coast, with a terrific perspective of the huge incisor-shaped rocky outcrop known as the Peñon de Bernal. The site has two pyramids, more than 70 tombs (each resembling a small Talud-Tablero temple) and some fine, carved monuments including one that resembles a shark.

CENTRAL VERACRUZ

Hwy 180 echoes the curves of the coast, running past dark-sand beaches plotted with holiday homes and the ruins of Zempoala, to Cardel from where Hwy 140 branches west to Xalapa, the state capital. The countryside around Xalapa shelters appealing villages and dramatic river gorges that are increasingly popular for rafting expeditions. From Veracruz, Hwy 150D heads southwest to Córdoba, Fortín de las Flores and Orizaba, on the edge of the Sierra Madre.

CENTRAL COAST

North of the city of Veracruz lies the central coastal area, a popular vacation spot for beach-bound Mexican holidaymakers, and home to the Totonac ruins of Zempoala.

Zempoala
☎ 296 / pop 9500

The pre-Hispanic Totonac town of Zempoala (or 'Cempoala') holds a key place in the story of the Spanish conquest. Its ruins stand 42km north of Veracruz and 4km west of Hwy 180 in modern Zempoala. The turnoff is by a Pemex station 7km north of Cardel. *Voladores* performances (see p678)

are regularly held at the ruins, especially on holidays and on weekends, around 10am, noon and 2pm. Zempoala is most easily reached through Cardel – take a bus marked 'Zempoala' ($1) from the Cardel bus station, or a taxi ($6).

HISTORY
It's thought that Zempoala was first settled in pre-Classic times, but became a major Totonac center after about AD 1200. It fell subject to the Aztecs in the mid-15th century, when many of its buildings were given an Aztec-style makeover. The town boasted defensive walls, underground water and drainage pipes and, in May 1519 when the Spanish came, about 30,000 people. As Hernán Cortés, the Spanish colonist, approached the town, one of his scouts reported back that the buildings were made of silver – but it was only white plaster or paint shining in the sun.

Zempoala's portly chief, Chicomacatl, known to history as 'the fat cacique' from a description by Bernal Díaz del Castillo, struck an alliance with Cortés for protection against the Aztecs. But his hospitality didn't stop the Spanish from smashing his gods' statues and lecturing his people on the virtues of Christianity. Zempoalan workers went with the Spaniards when they set off for Tenochtitlán in 1519. The next year, it was at Zempoala that Cortés defeated the Pánfilo de Narváez expedition, which had been sent out by Cuba's governor to arrest him.

By the 17th century, Zempoala, devastated by disease, was reduced to just eight families. Eventually the town was abandoned. The present town dates from 1832.

ZEMPOALA RUINS
After you enter Zempoala, take a right turn where a sign says 'Bienvenidos a Cempoala.' The main **archaeological site** (admission $3; 9am-5:30pm) is at the end of this cobbled road.

The site is green and lovely, with palm trees and a mountain backdrop. Most of the buildings are faced with smooth, rounded, riverbed stones, but many were originally plastered and painted. A typical feature is battlement-like 'teeth' called *almenas*.

The **Templo Mayor** (Main Temple) is an 11m-high, 13-platform pyramid, originally plastered and painted. A wide staircase ascends to the remains of a three-room shrine on top (you're not allowed to climb it). In 1520 this was probably Pánfilo de Narváez' headquarters, which Cortés' men captured by setting fire to its thatched roof.

On first visiting Zempoala, the conquistador and his men lodged in **Las Chimeneas**. The hollow columns in front of the main structure were thought to be chimneys – hence the name. A temple probably topped the seven platforms here.

There are two main structures on the west side. One is known as the Gran Pirámide or **Templo del Sol**, with two stairways climbing its front side to three platforms on top, in typical Toltec-Aztec style. It faces east and was probably devoted to the sun god. To its north, the **Templo de la Luna** has a rectangular platform and ramps in front, and a round structure behind, similar to Aztec temples to the wind god Ehecatl.

East of Las Chimeneas beyond the irrigation channel, you'll see a building on your right called **Las Caritas** (Little Heads), named for niches that once held several small pottery heads. Three other structures formerly stood east of Las Caritas, in line with the rising sun. Another large wind-god temple, known as **Templo Dios del Aire**, is in the town itself – go back south on the site entrance road, cross the main road in town and then go around the corner to the right. The ancient temple, with its characteristic circular shape, is beside an intersection.

The small site **museum** has some interesting clay figurines, polychrome plates and obsidian flints.

Chachalacas
☎ 296 / pop 2000

Ten kilometers northeast of Cardel, this slightly scruffy-looking seaside 'resort' doesn't seem very appealing at first, but as soon as you get away from the central stretch there are miles of uncrowded grey sand beaches in both directions. If you follow the beach to the north for 2km there are some towering sand dunes. Most accommodations are geared to family groups, and at peak times they cost about $40 for a large room.

The well-run, family-owned **Hotel & Restaurant Yoli** (☎ 962-53-31; r $20, with air-con $29; P 🞕) by the bus stop is very pleasant with clean, spacious rooms. If it's full, try the second choice **Casa de Huespedes June** (☎ 962-56-11; r $19, with air-con $24) next door.

Chachalacas Hotel-Club (☎ 962-52-42, 800-508-96-36; chachalacas@prodigy.net.mx; r/ste $72/95; P 🞮 🞕 🞕) has luxurious rooms and on-site dining options. You're unlikely to find such a glut of wading pools elsewhere on the coast (they have 12!).

Places to eat are thick on the ground. Try the friendly **Restaurant de Colores** (set meals $4.50) for a good fresh-fish feed.

Cardel
☎ 296 / pop 18,500

Not an attractive town, Cardel (or José Cardel) is a transit point with little else to offer. The bus terminal, banks, restaurants and Internet cafés are scattered around the plaza. You'll find comfortable accommodations at **Bienvenido Hotel** (☎ 962-07-77; Cardel Sur 1; s/d $27/35; P 🞕).

From the Veracruz bus station, regular 1st-class ADO buses to Cardel cost $3; 2nd-class AU buses leave every 30 minutes and cost $2.75. The last bus back to Veracruz from Cardel is at 10:30pm.

La Antigua
☎ 296 / pop 900

Intriguing and dozy little La Antigua lies 2km east of the coastal Hwy 150, and 23km north of Veracruz. A Spanish settlement was established here near the mouth of Río Huitzilapan in 1525, after Villa Rica was abandoned, and it is said to be the place where conquistador Cortés scuttled his boats to banish any of his crews' thoughts of a return to Spain. The picturesque ruined building you see here is a 16th-century **custom house** (commonly called the 'Casa de Cortés'). The **Ermita del Rosario church**, probably dating from 1523, is one of the oldest found in the Americas, and the village also boasts an equally ancient-looking ceiba tree.

Accommodations (with mosquitoes!) are available at **Hotel La Malinche** (s/d $14/24; P 🞕), near the river. A few meters away is a row of seafood restaurants; head to the hospitable **Maravillas** (mains $4.50-6.50) for a filling meal of *robalito* or *mojarra* (fish). Boatmen offer trips from here (from $5 per person) along the Río Antigua and to some sand dunes. *Colectivo* taxis charge $0.50 from the village to the highway.

XALAPA

☎ 228 / pop 426,000 / elevation 1427m

Urbane, culturally vibrant Xalapa is the capital of Veracruz and unquestionably the most cosmopolitan city in the state. Sometimes spelled 'Jalapa' (but always pronounced 'ha-la-pa'), this civilized university city enjoys a temperate climate – misty, drizzly days are common and there's often a chill in the air in winter – and more bohemian bars and coffeehouses than you can shake a stick at.

The city's highlight is undoubtedly its superb anthropological museum, but its terraced parks and position among rolling hills give it a leafy, uncluttered appeal. And if the local authorities ever start a much-needed pedestrianization program to tackle Xalapa's terrible traffic woe, it really would be a delight.

You should allow a couple of days to get to know the city.

History

A pre-Hispanic town on this site became part of the Aztec empire around 1460, and Hernán Cortés and his men passed through in 1519. The Spanish town didn't take off until the annual trade fair of Spanish goods was first held here in 1720 (it ran until 1777). Today Xalapa is a commercial hub for the coffee and tobacco grown on the slopes, and the city is also well known for its flowers.

Orientation

The city center is on a hillside, with the plaza, Parque Juárez, more or less in the middle of things. Uphill is north. Xalapa's cathedral is on Enríquez, just east of the plaza. Many of the midrange hotels and restaurants are a little to the east, on Enríquez and Zaragoza. CAXA, the bus station, is 2km east of the city center, and the tremendous anthropology museum is 4km to the northwest.

Glossy tourist maps ($2) are available at the Palacio Municipal tourist information booth.

Information
BOOKSTORES

Libros y Arte Conaculta (☎ 840-87-43; Museo de Antropología, Av Xalapa s/n; ☯ 9am-5pm Tues-Sun) Offers a wide selection of books about art, architecture and history, including some English-language titles

EMERGENCIES

Ambulance, Fire & Police (☎ 066)

INTERNET ACCESS

Internet (Claviero 29; per hr $1)

Login (Gutiérrez Zamora 18; per hr $1) Has speedy connections.

INTERNET RESOURCES

Xalapa Tourist Network (www.xalapa.net)

LAUNDRY

Dani's (Barragán 22; wash & dry $3.50)

MEDIA

Performance A widely available free Spanish-language magazine devoted to the city's cultural scene.

MEDICAL SERVICES

Centro de Especialidades Médicas (☎ 814-46-24; Av Ruiz Cortines s/n; ☯ 8am-6pm) Hospital offering excellent medical care, located 5km west of the center.

MONEY

Banks with 24-hour ATMs are clustered along Enríquez–Gutiérrez Zamora.

HSBC (Gutiérrez Zamora 36; ☯ 9am-6pm Mon-Fri, 10am-2pm Sat) Offers quick exchange services.

POST

Post office (cnr Gutiérrez Zamora & Leño)

TELEPHONE & FAX

Telecomm (cnr Gutiérrez Zamora & Leño) Next to the post office. Offers discounted international phone and fax rates

TOURIST INFORMATION

Tourist Information Booth (☎ 842-12-00, ext 3025; Palacio Municipal; ☯ 9am-3pm & 4-7pm Mon-Fri) Under the arches of the Palacio Municipal, facing Parque Juárez.

Sights & Activities
MUSEO DE ANTROPOLOGÍA

Veracruz University's breathtaking **Museo de Antropología** (Museum of Anthropology; ☎ 815-09-20; Av Xalapa s/n; adult/child under 12yr $3.75/free; ☯ 9am-5pm Tue-Sun), devoted to the archaeology of the state, is one of Mexico's best museums. Its large collection includes seven huge Olmec heads (up to 3000 years old) and 29,000 other superb artifacts. The modernist museum building is architecturally stunning, allowing natural light to flood the exhibition space.

All exhibits are labeled in Spanish only, but you'll also find laminated English

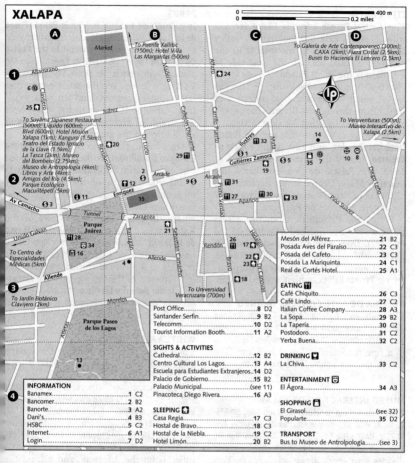

XALAPA

0 — 400 m
0 — 0.2 miles

To Puente Xallitic (150m); Hotel Villa Las Margaritas (500m)

To Galería de Arte Contemporáneo (300m); CAXA (2km); Plaza Cristal (2.5km); Buses to Hacienda El Lencero (2.5km)

To Suyama Japanese Restaurant (500m); Líquido (600m); Blvd Misión Xalapa (1km); Kangurú (1.5km); Teatro del Estado Ignacio de la Llave (1.5km); La Tasca (2km); Museo del Bombero (2.75km); Museo de Antropología (4km); Libros y Arte (4km); Amigos del Río (4.5km); Parque Ecológico Macuiltépetl (5km)

To Veraventuras (500m); Museo Interactivo de Xalapa (2.5km)

To Centro de Especialidades Médicas (5km)

To Jardín Botánico Clavijero (2km)

To Universidad Veracruzana (700m)

Parque Juárez

Parque Paseo de los Lagos

INFORMATION
Banamex	1 C2
Bancomer	2 B2
Banorte	3 A2
Dani's	4 B3
HSBC	5 C2
Internet	6 A1
Login	7 D2

Post Office	8 D2
Santander Serfin	9 B2
Telecomm	10 D2
Tourist Information Booth	11 A2

SIGHTS & ACTIVITIES
Cathedral	12 B2
Centro Cultural Los Lagos	13 A4
Escuela para Estudiantes Extranjeros	14 D2
Palacio de Gobierno	15 B2
Palacio Municipal	(see 11)
Pinacoteca Diego Rivera	16 A3

SLEEPING
Casa Regia	17 C3
Hostal de Bravo	18 C3
Hostal de la Niebla	19 C2
Hotel Limón	20 B2

Mesón del Alférez	21 B2
Posada Aves del Paraíso	22 C3
Posada del Cafeto	23 C3
Posada La Mariquinta	24 C1
Real de Cortés Hotel	25 A1

EATING
Café Chiquito	26 C3
Café Lindo	27 C2
Italian Coffee Company	28 A3
La Sopa	29 B2
La Tapería	30 C2
Postodoro	31 C2
Yerba Buena	32 C2

DRINKING
La Chiva	33 C2

ENTERTAINMENT
El Ágora	34 A3

SHOPPING
El Girasol	(see 32)
Popularte	35 D2

TRANSPORT
Bus to Museo de Antrolpología	(see 3)

information sheets in many rooms. Cameras are allowed, but you can't use a flash. Allow yourself a minimum of a couple of hours here, much more if you've a passion for meso-american culture. There's a small café on the upper floor, and an excellent bookstore.

The first spaces concentrate on the Olmec culture from southern Veracruz; the largest Olmec head here stands 2.7m high. Another San Lorenzo head is pocked with hundreds of small holes, thought to be deliberate mutilation at the time of San Lorenzo's fall. Sala 2 has the museum's most celebrated piece: a moving Olmec sculpture in green metamorphic stone, known as **El Señor de Las Limas** – a mournful-looking lord holding the body of a flaccid, perhaps lifeless, child in his arms.

There's an array of fine work associated with the ball game (see boxed text, p65): beautiful yokes used to protect the players' pelvises, and markers carved from volcanic stone. Other highlights include some murals from Las Higueras, and a collection of huge Classic-period pottery figures from El Zapotal. There are also codices that describe the first contact with Europeans.

The museum is set in spacious gardens on the west side of Av Xalapa, 4km north-west of the city center. To get there take a 'Tesorería-Centro-SEP' or 'Museo' bus ($0.50) from in front of the Banorte on Av Camacho. To return, take a bus marked 'Centro.' Buses can be infrequent or full, so a taxi may be worth the $1.50 fare.

CITY CENTER

The central **Parque Juárez** is like a terrace, with its south side overlooking the valley below and snowcapped mountains in the distance. Tucked beneath the west side of the plaza is the small **Pinacoteca Diego Rivera** (☎ 818-18-19; Herrera 5; admission free; ♡ 10am-6pm Tue-Sat), which houses a modest collection of works from throughout Rivera's life as well as some works by other Mexican artists.

On the plaza's north side are the **Palacio Municipal** arcades, and east is the **Palacio de Gobierno**, seat of the Veracruz state government. The Palacio de Gobierno has a fine mural by Mario Orozco Rivera depicting the history of justice; it's above the stairway near the eastern entrance on Enríquez.

Facing the Palacio de Gobierno across Enríquez is the unfinished **cathedral** (started in 1772), from where Revolución and Dr Lucio both lead up to the busy market zone. Further north, Dr Lucio crosses a deep valley via **Puente Xallitic**, a high, arched bridge.

GALERÍA DE ARTE CONTEMPORÁNEO

The state-run **Galería de Arte Contemporáneo** (Gallery of Contemporary Art; ☎ 818-04-12; Xalapeños Ilustres 135; admission $0.50; ♡ 10am-7pm Tue-Sun) is in a fine renovated colonial building 1km east of the city center, just past Arteaga. It shows worthwhile temporary exhibitions.

MUSEO INTERACTIVO DE XALAPA

This well-set up modern **museum** (MIX; ☎ 813-85-10; Av Vidal s/n; www.mix.mx; adult/child under 12yr $2.25/2, IMAX extra $4.25/3.75; ♡ 9am-5pm Mon-Fri, 10am-7pm Sat & Sun) is aimed at children and divides into seven areas: science, art, Veracruz culture, a young kids' zone, ecology, humans and communications. Displays utilize computers, video and electronics, and there are hands-on exhibits plus an IMAX theater. It's educational but also fun. The museum is in the southeast of town – take a Murillo Vidal bus ($0.50) or a taxi ($2).

MUSEO DEL BOMBERO

Devoted to firefighting, this **museum** (☎ 890-22-85; Ortíz 5; admission free; ♡ 9am-2pm & 4-8pm) has some fascinating exhibits, including an 1885 English horse-drawn fireman's carriage, a collection of helmets and plenty of information on the history of firefighting, from its origins in ancient Egypt to now. It's 3km north of Parque Juárez, just off Av Orizaba.

PARKS

Just south of Parque Juárez is **Parque Paseo de los Lagos**, winding 1km along either side of a lake. At its northern end is the **Centro Cultural Los Lagos** (☎ 812-12-99; Paseo los Lagos s/n; ccloslagos@yahoo.com.mx; admission $1; ♡ 9am-3pm & 6-9pm), a lovely, sophisticated escape that hosts courses, concerts and temporary cultural exhibits. If you're lucky, you'll hear the strains of orchestras practicing as you stroll through the grounds.

On a hill in the north of the city, **Parque Ecológico Macuiltépetl** is the thickly wooded cap of an extinct volcano; the turnoff is about 200m south of the anthropology museum. Paths popular with joggers and mountain-bikers spiral to the top, from where there are expansive views of the Xalapa area. At the summit, the small **Museo de la Fauna** (admission $1; ♡ 10am-5:30pm Tue-Fri) has some tethered eagles, snakes and other reptiles, and plenty of stuffed animals.

Southwest of the town center the attractive **Jardín Botánico Clavijero** (☎ 842-18-27; Antigua Carr a Coatepec, Km 2.5; admission free; ♡ 9am-5pm) has a fine collection of subtropical plants.

WHITEWATER RAFTING

There's exceptional rafting in the Xalapa region; contact these operators about trips on nearby rivers.

The established operator **Veraventuras** (☎ 818-95-79, 800-712-65-72; www.veraventuras.com.mx in Spanish; Santos Degollado 81 Int 8; half-day trips from $52) organizes trips ranging from half-day excursions on the Río Actopan to three-day expeditions on class IV rapids. The company's office is up the driveway, and behind the parking lot. Another good rafting operator is **Amigos del Río** (☎ 815-88-17; amigosdelrio@infose .net.mx; Chilpancingo 205; half-day trips from $47).

Rafting trips usually require a minimum of four to eight participants, so it's a good idea to contact the operators ahead of time. Weekend trips offer the best chance of joining up with other people.

Courses

The Universidad Veracruzana's **Escuela para Estudiantes Extranjeros** (School for Foreign Students; ☎ 817-86-87; www.uv.mx/eee; Gutiérrez Zamora 25 courses per hr from $20, per semester $215) offers short term programs in Spanish and Náhuatl languages, and Mexican culture. A homestay costs an additional $195 per week.

Tours

Roy Dudley (☎ 812-05-55; www.xalaparoy.com; 6hr tour per individual or couple $100) is an expat who has lived in Xalapa for over 30 years. He can customize trips in Xalapa and to neighboring villages like Xico.

Sleeping

Xalapa's accommodation options are excellent, offer good value, and many have real colonial-style character.

BUDGET

Hostal de la Niebla (☎ 817-21-74; www.delaniebla.com; Gutiérrez Zamora 24; dm/s $11/17; P 🖳) A modern Scandinavian-style hostel – very efficient, with two floors of six-person dorms and single rooms with bathrooms. There's access to lockers, a kitchen, a sun terrace and a café.

Posada Aves del Paraíso (☎ /fax 817-00-37; p _avesdelparaiso@hotmail.com; Dr Canovas 4; s/d $17/27) The spacious, tastefully decorated rooms with TV are named after various birds, and face a courtyard.

Also recommended:

Hostal de Bravo (☎ 818-90-38; Bravo 11; s/d $24/27) Family-run place with ten excellent-value, quiet, spacious and squeaky-clean rooms with quilts and TV.

Hotel Limón (☎ 817-22-04; fax 817-93-16; Revolución 8; s/d $10/11) Attractive hotel with a beautifully tiled lobby and en-suite rooms around a covered, somewhat echo-prone courtyard.

MIDRANGE

Mesón del Alférez (☎ 818-01-13; m_alferez@xal.mega red.net.mx; Sebastián Camacho 2; s/d/ste ind breakfast $42/49/57) For colonial ambience this wonderful inn simply can't be matched. The elegant rooms are spacious and atmospheric, boasting beamed ceilings as well as modern amenities. Rumbling background traffic

---

> **THE AUTHOR'S CHOICE**
>
> **Posada del Cafeto** (☎ /fax 817-00-23; Dr Canovas 8; s/d $31/38, apt from $55) The owners have really taken some trouble to create a homely atmosphere at this lovely, quiet, secure guesthouse. All the accommodations have real Mexican character, with high ceilings, wooden furniture and decorative local textiles. There's a delightful rear garden and a charming café where your complimentary breakfast is served.

---

noise is a drawback however. Breakfast is served in the sky-lit restaurant.

Real de Cortés Hotel (☎ 817-33-90; Clavijero 17; s/d $33/38; P 🖳) A renovated 19th-century town house with very good-value, well-kept, comfortable rooms, and dark-wood furniture around two patios.

Posada La Mariquinta (☎ 818-11-58; www.lamari quinta.xalapa.net; Alfaro 12; s/d from $37/46; P) A guesthouse in an 18th-century colonial residence, La Mariquinta offers rooms, suites and bungalows. Lodgings sit around a lovely garden at this centrally located but peaceful posada.

Other possibilities:

Casa Regia (☎ 812-05-91; fax 817-25-35; Hidalgo 12; s/d $31/35) Smart, if smallish, rooms all with wooden chests and bedside lights, in a friendly posada with an old-world feel.

Hotel Villa Las Margaritas (☎ 840-08-86, 800-719-43-67; www.villamargaritas.com in Spanish; Dr Lucio 186; s/d $50/58; P 🍴 🖳) This is the most central of the three Margarita hotels in the city, and has luxurious, if a tad chichi, rooms.

TOP END

Hotel Misión Xalapa (☎ 818-22-22, 800-260-26-00; misionxalapa@hotelesmision.com.mx; cnr Victoria & Busta-mante; r $92; P 🍴 🍴 🖳 🖳) This pink hilltop hotel in spacious grounds has a large outdoor pool, a restaurant serving Italian and Mexican cuisine, and a cafeteria. The large rooms offer all mod cons and some have fine views. It's 1km northwest of the parque.

Eating

Stylish cafés and restaurants abound in Xalapa, many offering plenty of healthy and vegetarian choices. One local specialty is *chiles rellenos* (stuffed peppers), while jalapeño chilies are from the region too.

Café Chiquito (☎ 812-11-22; Bravo 3; dishes $2.50-8) Defying its moniker, this large place with a bricked courtyard is popular with students for its healthy cuisine. Dishes include *burritas yucatecas* ($3.50) and fresh salads, or tuck into their daily buffet ($3). Local bands play here some nights.

Postodoro (☎ 841-20-00; www.postodero.com; Primo Verdad 11; pizzas from $4; ⏰ 12:30pm-12:30am Mon-Sat, 1:30-10:30pm Sun) Book ahead to dine at this large, stylish, atmospheric pizzeria, and try to reserve a table in the delightful covered patio. The good-value menu also takes in salads, saltimbocca ($7) and pasta including *ravioli arpino*, and there's a good wine list.

THE AUTHOR'S CHOICE

La Tapería (☎ 818-84-81; Aparicio s/n; tapas $1.50; ☺ 4:30pm-12:30am Tue-Sat) Intimate bodega-like Spanish-owned place, with excellent fresh *montaditos* (tapas), and dishes including *tortilla española* ($4) and *gambas al ajillo* (prawn fried in garlic). Also serves imported beers and excellent house wine by the glass ($2).

Café Lindo (☎ 817-35-15; Primo Verdad 21; dishes $1-6; ☺ 10am-11pm) Café Lindo dishes out sandwiches and snacks, espressos and carnivore-friendly main courses. This sociable place has live music most weekend nights.

Italian Coffee Company (☎ 812-12-44; Parque Juárez; snacks $3-5) Boasts a wonderful location on the edge of the plaza, with volcano views on clear days from the outdoor terrace. Offers *panini, bocadillos* and the full gamut of coffee combos.

Or try these:

La Sopa (☎ 817-80-69; Callejón Diamante 3A; meals $2.50; ☺ 11:30am-11pm) Busy bohemian place that has fine set meals, and live music on Friday and Saturday nights.

Yerba Buena (☎ 818-75-08; Illustres 22; dishes $2.75-4; Ⓥ) Tranquil, inexpensive vegetarian place with a daily set meal ($3), salads and good juices.

Suyâma Japanese Restaurant (☎ 841-31-55; Camacho 54A; 10-piece sushi rolls from $3; ☺ 2-11:30pm Mon-Sat, 2-6pm Sun) Upmarket place with a party fever in the air at weekends. There's a 100-peso minimum.

Drinking

The area south of Gutiérrez Zamora (Mata, Primo Verdad and Aparicio) is fertile drinking territory, where some of the restaurants listed offer live music. In this quarter, the tiny boho stronghold **La Chiva** (Mata 13; ☺ 2pm-2am Tue-Thu, noon-2am Fri-Sat) is highly popular for its alternative (electronica, hip-hop and rock *en español*) tunes. Further afield, **La Tasca** (☎ 814-11-82; Xicotencatl 76; ☺ 9pm-2am Wed-Sat), 2km west of the center is another student favorite, with live music and food.

Entertainment

El Ágora (☎ 818-57-30; Parque Juárez; ☺ 10am-10pm Tue-Sun, 9am-6pm Mon) is a busy arts center with a cinema, theater, gallery, bookstore and café.

The impressive state theater, **Teatro del Estado Ignacio de la Llave** (☎ 818-08-34; cnr Ignacio de la Llave & Camacho; ☺ from 8pm) hosts performances

by both the Orquesta Sinfónica de Xalapa and the Ballet Folklórico of the Universidad Veracruzana.

At the time of research the 'in' clubs were **Líquido** (Camacho 78; cover $3-5; ☺ 10pm-3am Thu-Sat) for house and Nortec tunes and **Blvd** (Camacho 93; cover $3-5; ☺ 10pm-3am Thu-Sat) directly opposite for Latin sounds. Both are 800m west of the Parque Juárez.

Shopping

Xalapa's hippie chicks hang out in Callejón Diamante, an alley lined with street vendors selling cheap jewelry and hammered tin mirrors.

Also check out **Popularte** (☎ 841-12-02; Gutiérrez Zamora 38) for local handicrafts, weavings and *jaranas* (small eight-stringed guitars) and **El Girasol** (☎ 841-41-98; Illustres 22) for silver, handmade cotton clothes and ceramics.

Getting There & Away

Xalapa is a transportation hub with excellent connections throughout the state and beyond.

BUS

Xalapa's modern, well-organized bus station, the **Central de Autobuses de Xalapa** (CAXA; ☎ 842-25-00; Calle 20 de Noviembre), is 2km east of the city center and has an ATM, cafés and a *caseta*. Deluxe service is offered by UNO, 1st-class service by ADO, and good 2nd-class services by AU.

Destination	Price	Duration	Frequency
Cardel	$3.50	1½hr	18 1st-class daily
	$3.25	1½hr	2nd-class every 20 min
Mexico City (TAPO)	$29	5¼hr	6 deluxe daily
	$17	5¼hr	28 1st-class daily
Mexico City (Terminal Norte)	$17	5¼hr	5 1st-class daily
Papantla	$14	4hr	10 1st-class daily
Puebla	$12	3¼hr	12 1st-class daily
	$8	3¼hr	14 2nd-class daily
Tampico	$29	10hr	2 1st-class daily
Veracruz	$6	2hr	1st-class every 20-30min 5am-11pm
	$5.50	2hr	18 2nd-class daily
Veracruz airport	$13	1¾hr	5 daily
Villahermosa	$28	8½hr	5 1st-class daily

Other places served by ADO include Acayucan, Campeche, Catemaco, Córdoba, Cancún, Fortín de las Flores, Mérida, Orizaba, Poza Rica, San Andrés Tuxtla, and Santiago Tuxtla. AU also goes to Salina Cruz.

CAR & MOTORCYCLE

For car rentals, try **Kanguro** (☎ 817-78-78; Camacho 1350; 24hr from $45). Hwy 140 to Puebla is narrow and winding until Perote; the Xalapa–Veracruz highway is very fast and smooth. Going to the northern Gulf coast, it's quickest to go to Cardel, then turn north on Hwy 180; the inland road via Tlapacoyan is scenic but slow.

Getting Around

For buses from CAXA to the city center, follow the signs to the taxi stand, then continue downhill to the big road, Av 20 de Noviembre. Turn right to the bus stop, from where any minibus or bus marked 'Centro' will pass within a block or two of Parque Juárez ($0.50). For a taxi to the city center, buy a ticket first in the bus station ($2.50), then walk down the ramp to the taxi stand. To return to the bus station, take a 'CAXA' bus east along Zaragoza.

AROUND XALAPA

The countryside around Xalapa has some dramatic landscapes with rivers, gorges and waterfalls, and some appealing old towns lie nearby.

Hacienda El Lencero

About 12km from Xalapa on the Veracruz highway, a signposted road branches off to the right for a few kilometers to the highly impressive **Museo Ex-Hacienda El Lencero** (Hwy Xalapa-Veracruz, Km 10; admission $2, free Tue; 🕙 10am-5pm Tue-Fri). Well worth a visit, this grand former estate was once one of the first inns between Mexico City and Veracruz. The dictator General Antonio López de Santa Anna owned the property from 1842 to the mid-1850s; the hacienda, chapel and other buildings date mostly from this period. The superbly restored house is furnished with antiques, and the gardens and lake are delightful. Don't miss the *higuera monumental* (a huge fig tree said to be 500 years old).

From Xalapa, catch one of the regular 'Banderia' buses ($2) from outside the Plaza Cristal shopping center.

El Carrizal

South of the Veracruz road, 44km from Xalapa, the balmy El Carrizal hot springs feed several sulfurous pools. The **spa-resort** (☎ 228-818-97-79; bungalows $42) also houses a good restaurant with fresh seafood and crayfish and a *temascal* (steam bath). Whitewater-rafting trips can also be organized here.

Coatepec & Xico

Coatepec (population 48,500), a charming colonial town 15km south of Xalapa, is known for its coffee and orchids. The **María Cristina orchid garden**, on the main square, is open daily. Xico (population 15,000) is a pretty colonial village, 8km south of Coatepec. From Xico it's a pleasant 2km walk to the plunging 40m **Texolo waterfall**.

Buses go about every 15 minutes to Coatepec or Xico from Av Allende, about 1km west of central Xalapa ($1).

Parque Nacional Cofre de Perote

The 4274m-high Cofre de Perote volcano is southwest of Xalapa, but often obscured by mist. From the town of Perote, 50km west of Xalapa on Hwy 140, Calle Allende continues southwest to become a dirt road that climbs 1900m in 24km, finishing just below the summit. There's no public transportation here.

Valle Alegre

To reach this 'Happy Valley' **ecological reserve** (admission $3.50; 🕙 9am-6pm) take the highway toward Puebla and turn south after 15km, just west of Las Vigas. Follow the side road through El Llanillo to Tembladeras, where you'll find **Valle Alegre Hostel** (☎ 228-812-20-54; www.vallealegre.com.mx; dm $13, cabañas $98). Hiking, biking (per hour $4.50), rappel ($19) and wildlife-watching trips are offered. There's a good **restaurant** (🕙 9am-9pm Sat & Sun only) here. AU buses ($3) leave daily from Xalapa's CAXA.

VERACRUZ

☎ 229 / pop 569,000

O heroic town! Festive, frenetic Veracruz revels in peripatetic mariachis, pleasingly aesthetic colonial buildings and a kinetic fervor that starts in its *zócalo* and pervades its denizens (called *jarochos*). Bands flock to town during Carnaval, which stands as Mexico's biggest and wildest. Land and seashore offer you chances to cruise past historical attractions, to booze and party with locals or merely to snooze in a shaded plaza. In Veracruz, tropical hedonism is the norm.

Though tourists may take the city by storm, it retains an almost small-town charm – warm, vivacious and vibrant.

History

The coast here was occupied by Totonacs, with influences from Toltec and Aztec civilizations. This mix of pre-Hispanic cultures can be seen at Zempoala, 42km to the north. After the Spanish conquest, Veracruz provided Mexico's main gateway to the outside world for 400 years. Invaders and pirates, incoming and exiled rulers, settlers, silver and slaves – all came and went to make the city a linchpin in Mexico's history.

SPANISH CONQUEST & PIRATE RAIDS

Hernán Cortés made his first landing here at an island 2km offshore, which he named 'Isla Sacrificios' because of the remains of human sacrifices he found there. He anchored off another island, San Juan de Ulúa, on Good Friday (April 21), 1519, where he made his first contact with Moctezuma's envoys. Cortés founded the first Spanish settlement at Villa Rica, 69km north, but this was later moved to La Antigua, and finally to the present site of Veracruz in 1598.

Veracruz became the Spaniards' most important anchorage, and until 1760 it was the only port allowed to handle trade with Spain. Tent cities blossomed for trade fairs when the fleet from Spain made its annual arrival, but because of seaborne raids and tropical diseases (malaria and yellow fever were rampant) Veracruz never became one of Mexico's biggest cities.

In 1567 nine English ships under the command of John Hawkins sailed into Veracruz harbor, with the intention of selling slaves in defiance of the Spanish trade monopoly. They were trapped by a Spanish fleet, and only two of the ships escaped. One of them, however, carried Francis Drake, who went on to harass the Spanish in a long career as a sort of licensed pirate. The most vicious pirate attack of all occurred in 1683, when the Frenchman Laurent de Gaff, with 600 men, held the

5000 inhabitants of Veracruz captive in the town church with little food or water. De Gaff's men killed anyone who tried to escape, piled the Plaza de Armas with loot, got drunk, raped many of the women and threatened to blow up the church unless the people revealed their secret stashes. They left a few days later, much richer.

19TH & 20TH CENTURIES

In 1838 General Antonio López de Santa Anna, who had been routed in Texas two years earlier, fled Veracruz in his underwear under bombardment from a French fleet in the 'Pastry War' (the French were pressing various claims against Mexico, including that of a French pastry cook whose restaurant had been wrecked by unruly Mexican officers). But the general responded heroically, expelling the invaders and losing his left leg in the process.

When the 10,000-strong army of Winfield Scott attacked Veracruz in 1847 during the Mexican-American War, more than 1000 Mexicans were killed in a weeklong bombardment before the city surrendered.

In 1859, during Mexico's internal Reform War, Benito Juárez' Veracruz-based liberal government promulgated the reform laws that nationalized church property, and put education into secular hands. In 1861 when Juárez, having won the war, announced that Mexico couldn't pay its foreign debts, a joint French-Spanish-British force occupied Veracruz. The British and Spanish planned only to take over the customhouse and recover what Mexico owed them, but Napoleon III intended to conquer Mexico. Realizing this, the Brits and Spaniards went home, while the French marched inland to begin their five-year intervention.

Napoleon III's reign came to an end, however, and Veracruz again began to flower. Mexico's first railway was built between Veracruz and Mexico City in 1872 and, under the dictatorship of Porfirio Díaz, investment poured into the city.

In 1914, during the civil war that followed Díaz' departure in the 1910–11 revolution, US troops occupied Veracruz to stop a delivery of German arms to the conservative dictator Victoriano Huerta. The Mexican casualties caused by the intervention alienated even Huerta's opponents. Later in the civil war, Veracruz was, for a while

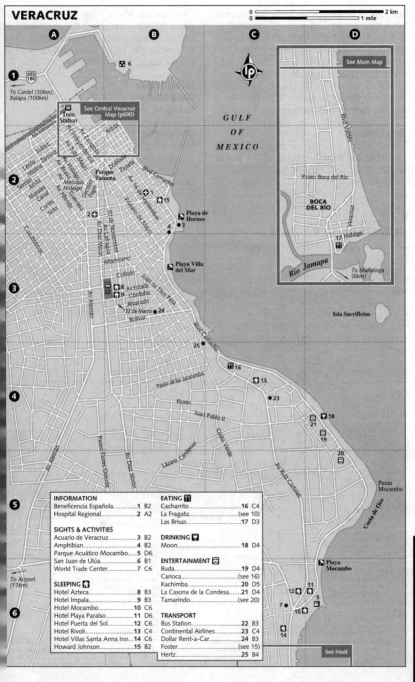

VERACRUZ

0 _____ 2 km
0 _____ 1 mile

GULF
OF
MEXICO

To Cardel (30km);
Xalapa (100km)

See Main Map

Paseo Boca del Río

BOCA DEL RÍO

Río Jamapa

To Mandinga (8km)

Train Station

See Central Veracruz Map (p690)

Parque Zamora

Playa de Hornos

Playa Villa del Mar

Isla Sacrificios

Paseo de las Jacarandas

Punta Mocambo

To Airport (11km)

Playa Mocambo

Costa de Oro

INFORMATION

| Beneficencia Española | **1** B2 |
| Hospital Regional | **2** A2 |

SIGHTS & ACTIVITIES

Acuario de Veracruz	**3** B2
Amphibian	**4** B2
Parque Acuático Mocambo	**5** D6
San Juan de Ulúa	**6** B1
World Trade Center	**7** C6

SLEEPING

Hotel Azteca	**8** B3
Hotel Impala	**9** B3
Hotel Mocambo	**10** C6
Hotel Playa Paraíso	**11** D6
Hotel Puerta del Sol	**12** C6
Hotel Rivoli	**13** C4
Hotel Villas Santa Anna Inn	**14** C6
Howard Johnson	**15** B2

EATING

Cacharrito	**16** C4
La Fragata	(see 10)
Las Brisas	**17** D3

DRINKING

| Moon | **18** D4 |

ENTERTAINMENT

Buda	**19** D4
Carioca	(see 16)
Kachimba	**20** D5
La Casona de la Condesa	**21** D4
Tamarindo	(see 20)

TRANSPORT

Bus Station	**22** B3
Continental Airlines	**23** C4
Dollar Rent-a-Car	**24** B3
Foster	(see 15)
Hertz	**25** B4

See Inset

the capital of the reformist Constitutionalist faction led by Venustiano Carranza.

Today, Veracruz is Mexico's most important deep-water port – handling around 70% of exports to the Americas and Europe – and a key center for the manufacturing and petrochemical industries. Tourism, particularly from the domestic sector is another large income earner, and peaks during Carnaval

Orientation

Center of the action is the *zócalo*, site of the cathedral and Palacio Municipal. The harbor is 250m east, with the San Juan de Ulúa fort on its far side. Blvd Camacho (El Boulevard) follows the coast to the south, past naval and commercial anchorages and some not-so-

clean beaches. About 700m south of the *zócalo* along Av Independencia is the green space of Parque Zamora, with Mercado Hidalgo just to its west. The bus terminal is 2km south of Parque Zamora along Díaz Mirón.

Information

EMERGENCIES
Ambulance, Fire & Police (☎ 066)

INTERNET ACCESS
Internet (Map p690; Lerdo 20A; per hr $1.50; ⏰ 8:30am-9pm). Also offers discounted phone calls.

LAUNDRY
Lavandería Mar y Sol (Map p690; Av Madero 16; wash & dry $3; ⏰ 8am-6:30pm Mon-Sat)

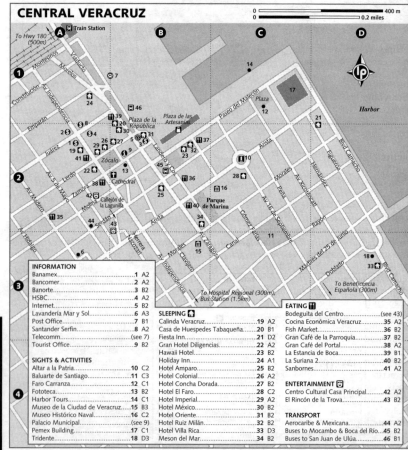

CENTRAL VERACRUZ

0 —————— 400 m
0 —————— 0.2 miles

INFORMATION	
Banamex	**1** A2
Bancomer	**2** A2
Banorte	**3** B2
HSBC	**4** A2
Internet	**5** B2
Lavandería Mar y Sol	**6** A3
Post Office	**7** B1
Santander Serfin	**8** A2
Telecomm	(see 9)
Tourist Office	**9** B2

SIGHTS & ACTIVITIES	
Altar a la Patria	**10** C2
Baluarte de Santiago	**11** C3
Faro Carranza	**12** C1
Fototeca	**13** B2
Harbor Tours	**14** C1
Museo de la Ciudad de Veracruz	**15** B3
Museo Histórico Naval	**16** C2
Palacio Municipal	(see 9)
Pemex Building	**17** C1
Tridente	**18** D3

SLEEPING	
Calinda Veracruz	**19** A2
Casa de Huespedes Tabaqueña	**20** B1
Fiesta Inn	**21** D2
Gran Hotel Diligencias	**22** A2
Hawaii Hotel	**23** B2
Holiday Inn	**24** A1
Hotel Amparo	**25** B2
Hotel Colonial	**26** A2
Hotel Concha Dorada	**27** B2
Hotel El Faro	**28** C2
Hotel Imperial	**29** A2
Hotel México	**30** B2
Hotel Oriente	**31** B2
Hotel Ruiz Milán	**32** B2
Hotel Villa Rica	**33** D3
Meson del Mar	**34** B2

EATING	
Bodeguita del Centro	(see 43)
Cocina Económica Veracruz	**35** A2
Fish Market	**36** B2
Gran Café de la Parroquia	**37** B2
Gran Café del Portal	**38** A2
La Estancia de Boca	**39** B1
La Suriana 2	**40** B2
Sanborns	**41** A2

ENTERTAINMENT	
Centro Cultural Casa Principal	**42** A2
El Rincón de la Trova	**43** B2

TRANSPORT	
Aerocaribe & Mexicana	**44** A2
Buses to Mocambo & Boca del Río	**45** A2
Buses to San Juan de Ulúa	**46** B1

LEFT LUGGAGE
There's a 24-hour facility in the 2nd-class bus station.

MEDICAL SERVICES
Beneficencia Española (Map p689; ☎ 932-00-21; Av 16 de Septiembre 955) Hospital offering general medical services.
Hospital Regional (Map p689; ☎ 937-55-00; Av Diaz Mirón 165)

MONEY
There's a cluster of banks on the corner that's a block north of the *zócalo*, all with ATMs.

POST
Post office (Map p690; Plaza de la República 213) A five-minute walk north of the *zócalo*.

TELEPHONE
Card phones proliferate around the *zócalo*.
Internet (Map p690; Lerdo 20A). Calls per minute to the US and Canada cost $0.30, to the EU cost $0.50.

TOURIST INFORMATION
Tourist office (Map p690; ☎ 989-88-17; www.veracruz turismo.com.mx; Palacio Municipal; ❂ 8am-8pm Mon-Fri, 10am-6pm Sat & Sun) Has helpful (mostly English-speaking) staff and plenty of maps, coupon books and brochures.

Sights & Activities

ZÓCALO
Veracruz' *zócalo* (Map p690) – also called the Plaza de Armas, Plaza Lerdo and Plaza de la Constitución – is the city's hub for *jarochos* and visitors alike. It's a handsome public space, framed on three sides by *portales* (arcades), the 17th-century **Palacio Municipal** and an 18th-century **cathedral**. The level of activity accelerates with the day, from breakfast under the arches, through a leisurely lunch, to afternoon entertainment on an outdoor stage. In the evening, as the sweat cools off Veracruz bodies, the *zócalo* becomes a swirling, multifaceted party, with cool drinks and competing street entertainers (see p696).

HARBOR & MALECÓN
Veracruz' harbor is still busy, though oil ports such as Tampico and Coatzacoalcos now handle greater tonnages. The Paseo del Malecón (also called Insurgentes) is a pleasant **waterfront walk**, starting with the Plaza de las Artesanías which has stalls selling a kaleidoscopic selection of tacky souvenirs.

Stroll out along the *malecón* and view the ships, cranes and ancient fortress across the water, or take a sightseeing boat trip (see p693) for a closer look. At the corner of Blvd Camacho are monuments to the city's defenders against the Americans in 1914 and to all sailors who gave their lives to the sea. The high-rise **Pemex building** (Map p690;) here is an early example of modern Mexican architecture; built in 1940, it now houses Pemex offices and has some interesting murals.

Two blocks inland from the *malecón* is the 1998 **Altar a la Patria** (Map p690;), a solemn obelisk beneath which are buried the remains of those who defended Veracruz during its numerous conflicts.

FOTOTECA
On the southeast side of the *zócalo* this superb **arts center** (Map p690; ☎ 932-87-67; www .fototecadeveracruz.org in Spanish; Callejón El Portal de Miranda 9; ❂ 10am-7pm Tue-Sun) has rotating photographic and video exhibitions, from cutting-edge urban images to beautifully composed portraits. It's spread over three floors of a restored colonial building, and has a good bookstore on the ground floor.

FARO CARRANZA
Facing the waterfront on the *malecón*, the cream-colored **Faro Carranza** (Map p690) holds a lighthouse and navy offices. The Mexican navy goes through an elaborate parade in front of the building on Monday mornings. Venustiano Carranza lived here during the revolution, in 1914 and 1915, and it was here that the 1917 Mexican Constitution was drafted. A large statue of Carranza stands in front, while the pond at his feet is home to numerous terrapins. Exhibits on Carranza and his political struggles are in the Museo Histórico Naval.

SAN JUAN DE ULÚA
This **fortress** (Map p689; ☎ 938-51-51; admission $3.50; ❂ 9am-4:30pm Tue-Sun) protecting Veracruz harbor was originally an island, but it's now connected to the mainland by a causeway. In 1518 the Spaniard Juan de Grijalva landed here during an exploratory voyage from Cuba. The next year Cortés also arrived here, and it subsequently became the main entry point for Spanish newcomers to Mexico. The Franciscan chapel is thought

to have been built in 1524 and the first fortifications in the 1530s, but most of what can be seen now was built progressively between 1552 and 1779.

The central part of the fortress, Fuerte San José, has also been a prison, most notoriously during the Porfirio Díaz regime. Many inmates died of yellow fever or tuberculosis.

Today San Juan de Ulúa is an empty ruin of passageways, battlements, bridges and stairways. Guided tours are available in Spanish and, sometimes, English. To get there, take a 'San Juan de Ulúa' bus ($0.50) from the east side of Plaza de la República. The last bus back to town leaves at 6pm.

BALUARTE DE SANTIAGO

Until 1880 Veracruz was a walled city, surrounded by mighty medieval defenses that incorporated nine bastions. The only surviving fort is the **Baluarte de Santiago** (Map p690; ☎ 931-10-59; Canal s/n; admission $3.50; ❂ 10am-4:30pm Tue-Sun), built in 1526 beside a canal at what was then the waterfront. Inside is a small exhibit of pre-Hispanic gold jewelry known as 'Las Joyas del Pescador' (The Fisherman's Jewels). The name refers to some fabulous gold artifacts discovered by a fisherman in Veracruz harbor in 1976, but most pieces on display here come from other sources. The price covers admission to the fort interior, but you can walk around the outside battlements anytime for free.

ACUARIO DE VERACRUZ

Veracruz' **aquarium** (Map p689; ☎ 931-10-20; www .acuariodeveracruz.com; Blvd Camacho s/n; adult/child $6/3, Tiburonería $29/15; ❂ 10am-7pm) is inside the Plaza Acuario shopping mall at Playa de Hornos, about 2km south of the city center. There's a large donut-shaped tank filled with sharks, rays and turtles that glide and duck 'n' dive around visitors. Other tanks house freshwater and saltwater fish, reptiles and amphibians, river otters and even manatees. But for a really dramatic close encounter climb into the Tiburonería – a transparent perspex safety cage that is lowered into a pool of feeding sharks!

MUSEUMS

The **Museo de la Ciudad de Veracruz** (Veracruz City Museum; Map p690; ☎ 931-84-10; Av Zaragoza 39; admission $2.75; ❂ 10am-6pm Tue-Sun) is a good place

to gain an overview of the city's history, with fine paintings, drawings and displays. The city's complex ethnic make-up is explained – its indigenous American origins, the influx of African slaves, through to modern-day immigration from Syria and Lebanon.

Occupying a former school for naval officers, the **Museo Histórico Naval** (Map p690; ☎ 931-40-78; Arista 418; admission free; ❂ 9am-5pm Tue-Sun) covers Mexico's maritime heritage and naval history. Along with rooms full of weapons and model ships, the museum holds well-presented exhibits on the US attacks on Veracruz in 1847 and 1914, and on revolutionary hero Venustiano Carranza. Information is in Spanish only.

BEACHES & LAGOONS

In general, the further south you go, the cleaner the beaches get. Hence, few people venture into the water at Playa de Hornos, just south of the city center, or at Playa Villa del Mar, a little further away. The beaches are more acceptable south of the city at **Costa de Oro** and at **Playa Mocambo**. If you don't want to risk the sea water, there's an Olympic-sized (50m) pool at the **Parque Acuático Mocambo** (Map p689; ❂ 10am-6pm; admission $5) just in front of the Hotel Mocambo, which also has a café and sunloungers.

Some 11km south of the *zócalo*, the **Boca del Río** (Mouth of the River) area has plenty of popular seafood restaurants. Over the bridge, the coastal road continues to **Mandinga**, where you can hire a boat to explore the lagoons, and the fishing village of **Antón Lizardo**, where you can relax in the sun with a drink or an ice cream. For details on getting yourself there, see p697.

DIVING & SNORKELING

The beaches near Veracruz may not be inviting, but there is good diving – including at least one accessible wreck – on the reefs near the offshore islands. Part of the area has been designated an underwater natural park. **Tridente** (Map p690; ☎ 931-79-24; tridente _ver@hotmail.com; Blvd Camacho 165A; 2 dives $82), a PADI dive school, arranges dive and snorkel excursions from Veracruz and Antón Lizardo. Scuba trips normally require a minimum of two people, and include a guide and equipment. Guides speak English, Spanish, French and even a little Russian.

Amphibian (Map p689; ☎ 931-09-97; Lerdo 117; www .amphibian.com.mx) is another outfit offering activity-based tours; in addition to diving and snorkeling trips, they also run caving, rafting (from $52), trekking, rock-climbing (from $120) and kayaking trips.

Tours

Boats from the *malecón* offer hour-long **harbor tours** (Map p690; per person $5; ☿ 7am-7pm). They leave when they're full, about every 30 minutes, so be prepared for a wait – particularly in the slow season.

Festivals & Events

Carnaval (February or March) Veracruz erupts into a nine-day party before Ash Wednesday each year with flamboyant parades winding through the city daily, beginning with one devoted to the 'burning of bad humor' and ending with the 'funeral of Juan Carnaval.' Chuck in fireworks, dances, salsa and samba music, handicrafts, folklore shows and children's parades and it adds up to one of Mexico's greatest fiestas. See the tourist office for a program of events.

Festival Internacional Afrocaribeño (last two weeks of July) This festival of Afro-Caribbean culture features academic and business forums and a trade show, but the main attractions are the dance and music performances (many of them free), film screenings and art expositions, with many nations from the Caribbean and Latin America participating.

Sleeping

Hotel prices, except at the budget level, vary according to demand in Veracruz, and can shift from day to day at busy times of the year. The prices quoted here are high season (mid-July to mid-September) rates. Note that many midrange and luxury hotels bump up their rates by an additional 15% during Carnaval, Easter, Christmas and New year. Book your accommodation in advance during these busy times.

Low season rates are typically 25% cheaper than the rates we have quoted. Because hotel rates are so flexible in Veracruz, discounts and special package offers are very common. You'll often get a discount if you ask for one.

It's convenient and fun to stay on or near the *zócalo*, while many more expensive resort hotels are around Mocambo beach.

BUDGET

Most budget places are near the bus station or around the fringes of the *zócalo*. Count on hot water, but check for adequate ventilation and a working fan at these hotels.

Hotel Amparo (Map p690; ☎ 932-27-38; Serdán 482; s/d $14/17; **P**) The best budget deal in town, this secure, well-managed place a few blocks south of the *zócalo* has cheery, tiled communal areas and spick-and-span rooms with fans and small desks.

Hotel Impala (Map p689; ☎ 937-01-69; fax 935-12-57; Orizaba 650; s/d $25/30; **P** ⊠) Your peso packs some punch at the Impala, near the bus station: comfy rooms smell fresh and come with air-con, cable TV and phones.

Hotel Villa Rica (Map p690; ☎ 932-48-54; Blvd Camacho 165; s/d $18/27) A welcoming place near the sea with small, tidy and breezy rooms, with tiny tiled balconies and communal sitting areas.

Also worth considering:

Hotel Azteca (Map p689; ☎ /fax 937-42-41; Calle 22 de Marzo 218; r $20; ⊠) Close to the bus station, the friendly Azteca is a good deal with clean, quiet rooms with phone and TV, and a small courtyard.

Hotel México (Map p690; ☎ 931-57-44; Morelos 343; s/d $15/19, with air-con $24/29; ⊠) Has a good location near the *zócalo*, but the garishly painted rooms with TV are nothing special.

Casa de Huespedes Tabaqueña (Map p690; Morelos 325; s $10) Very basic rooms, all with fans and bathrooms, but some without windows. Dirt cheap and very central.

MIDRANGE

All midrange options have air-con and TV. The following places are in the *zócalo* and *malecón* area.

Calinda Veracruz (Map p690; ☎ 931-22-33, 800-900-00-00; www.hotelescalinda.com.mx; cnr Av Independencia & Lerdo; r $83; ⊠) Elegant hotel that enjoys a first-rate location, and some of the comfortable, if small, rooms here have oblique views of the *zócalo*. There's a lovely 1st-floor pool and sun deck.

Hotel Colonial (Map p690; ☎ 932-01-93; www.hcolonial.com.mx; Lerdo 117; s $48-59, d $55-68; **P** ⊠ ▢ ▨) If you can get past the weird tunnel-like lobby and indifferent staff, the perfect location and well-appointed, smallish rooms are quite appealing. The indoor pool is tiny.

Hotel Ruiz Milán (Map p690; ☎ 932-37-77, 800-221-42-60; ventas@ruizmilan.com.mx; cnr Paseo del Malecón & Farías; s/d from $63/79; **P** ⊠ ▨) A fine waterfront location and plush, colorful rooms with all the trimmings including polar air-con. Be sure to get a balcony room with a view of the harbor.

Hotel Oriente (Map p690; ☎ /fax 931-24-90; Lerdo 20; s/d/tw $43/49/57; **P** **☒**) Well-run place with friendly staff where the rooms are a little old-fashioned, but have phones and wooden furniture. There's a restaurant downstairs.

Hotel Concha Dorada (Map p690; ☎ 931-29-96, 800-712-53-42; conchadorada@yahoo.com.mx; Lerdo 77; r with fan $30, with air-con $46; **☒**) Has a very modest little lobby, but the fan-cooled rooms with TV and phone offer fair value considering the location. Some have *zócalo*-facing balconies.

Hotel Rivoli (Map p689; ☎ 923-22-90; www.hotel rivoli.com; Av Ruíz Cortines 486; $73/85; **P** **☒** **☒** **▣** **☒**) Sleek modern hotel, with a minimalist lobby, complete with giant boulders and modish lighting and a hip little bar zone. Many of the Rivoli's stylish rooms have ocean views and marble-floor shower rooms. It's 150m from the beach and 5km south of the *zócalo*.

Hotel Villas Santa Ana Inn (Map p689; ☎ /fax 922-47-57; Suárez 1314; s/d $36/45, bungalows from $64; **P** **☒** **▣** **⚤**) A short walk from Playa Mocambo, this inn is ideal for families, with a garden, pool and 20 spacious suites decorated with Diego Rivera prints. The hotel faces the inland side of the Blvd Valdés; look for the easily missed first street on the right, a couple of hundred meters south of the roundabout by Hotel Mocambo.

Howard Johnson (Map p689; ☎ 931-00-11; Blvd Camacho 1263; s/d $58/76; **P** **☒** **▣**) About 2.5km south of the *zócalo*, close to the aquarium and Playa Villas del Mar, this hotel has large rooms, many with floor-to-ceiling windows offering uninterrupted sea views.

Also worth considering:

Hotel el Faro (Map p690; ☎ 931-65-38; www.hotelel faro.com.mx; Av 16 de Septiembre 223; s/d $29/36; **☒**)

THE AUTHOR'S CHOICE

Meson del Mar (Map p690; ☎ 932-50-43, 800-581-55-55; www.mesondelmar.com.mx; Morales 543; s & d/ste $51/60; **☒** **▣**) A wonderfully atmospheric 18th-century mansion that's been converted to a guesthouse by its ever-helpful, English-speaking Mexican owner, with no expense spared. All rooms have beamed roofs and stylish tiled bathrooms, and many have an additional mezzanine level with an extra double bed. There's a great little ground-floor café, free Internet access, and special discounts for backpackers.

Quiet hotel with pleasant, plain, smallish rooms all with phones and cable TV. There's an Internet café and snack bar off the lobby.

Hawaii Hotel (Map p690; ☎ 938-00-88; hawaii@infosel .net.mx; Paseo del Malecón 458; s/d $49/54; **P** **☒** **▣**) Boasts a gleaming-white marble lobby and spacious, cool rooms, many with marvelous views of the *malecón* and industrial cranes.

Hotel Imperial (Map p690; ☎ 931-45-08, 800-522-01-11; imperialver@prodigy.net.mx; Lerdo 153; s/d $36/45; **☒**) Its faded, once-classic lobby and vintage elevator are a reminder of more halcyon days, but the rooms here are now showing their years.

TOP END

Features of these higher-end city-center hotels include business centers, conference rooms, upscale restaurants and gyms.

Holiday Inn (Map p690; ☎ 932-45-50; hichvera@ prodigy.net.mx; Morelos 225; r/ste $86/105; **P** **☒** **▣**) Two blocks from the *zócalo*, this very stylish hotel occupies a former convent from the colonial era, and has a small trapezoidal pool. The rooms have real character with exposed wood beams, beautiful ceramic sinks, painted details and wooden furniture, while the suites are enormous.

Gran Hotel Diligencias (Map p690; ☎ 923-02-80, 800-505-55-95; www.granhoteldiligencias.com; Av Independencia 1115; r $105; **P** **☒** **☒** **▣**) Superbly renovated landmark hotel, in converted colonial premises, directly opposite the *zócalo*. The huge rooms are seriously swanky, if slightly chintzy, many with terrific views and all with modish bathrooms with tubs.

Fiesta Inn (Map p690; ☎ 923-15-00; www.fiestainn .com; Figueroa 68; r/ste $169/182; **P** **☒** **☒** **▣**) Harborside hotel with a gorgeous pool bordered with palms, and huge suite-style rooms, all with marble floors and bathtubs and some with stunning views of the *malecón*. Junior suites have kitchenettes with mini-fridges and coffeemakers.

Hotel Mocambo (Map p689; ☎ 922-02-00, 800-290-01-00; www.hotelmocambo.com.mx; Blvd Ruiz Cortines 4000; r/ste $109/133; **P** **☒** **▣**) Sitting pretty on a hilltop just behind the beach, this stylish, if aging, Italianate resort still retains a classy demeanor: its all-encompassing nautical theme comes complete with steering-wheel window frames. The rooms are spacious, but surprisingly simply furnished and with ocean – or at worst, horizon – views. Amenities include three sizable pools (two indoors), tennis courts and an incredible restaurant.

The following luxury resorts around Playa Mocambo boast pools, gardens and private beaches:

Hotel Playa Paraíso (Map p689; ☎ 923-07-00, 800-715-48-18; www.playaparaiso.com.mx; Blvd Ruiz Cortines 3500; r $87; P ⊠ ⊠ ⊡ ⊠) A little sparkle has worn off over the years, but the Playa Paraíso still possesses a relaxed elegance and offers spacious rooms and a restaurant with sweeping views.

Hotel Puerta del Sol (Map p689; ☎ 989-05-04, 800-110-01-23; www.hotelpuertadelsolveracruz.com; Av Ruiz Cortines 3495; r $105; P ⊠ ⊠ ⊡ ⊠) Upmarket colossus with terrific views from its luxurious rooms, a beach club, and in-house shopping mall.

Eating

Food in Veracruz is nothing short of wonderful. Veracruzana sauce, found on fish all over Mexico, is made from onions, garlic, tomatoes, olives, green peppers and spices. International cuisine is available – but with so much flavorsome Mexican fare around, why bother?

ZÓCALO AREA

The cafés under the *portales* are as much for drinks and atmosphere as for food, particularly at night when music is the draw. Menus are very similar here, so saunter by and find one that appeals to you. The best location for an inexpensive lunch is Callejón de la Lagunilla, 200m southwest of the *zócalo*, which has several excellent budget eateries.

Sanborns (Map p690; ☎ 931-00-91; Av Independencia 1069; mains $5-12) This ever-busy restaurant has a terrace facing the *zócalo* as well as a large air-conditioned interior and a long menu of international and Mexican dishes. It's a relaxed place to take stock of the city at breakfast time, or later for a *comida corrida* ($7.50).

Bodeguita del Centro (Map p690; ☎ 932-22-82; Callejón de la Lagunilla 77; comida corrida $2.50; ⏱ 1:30-6pm Mon-Sat) Simple family-run place with a tiled interior where all set meals come with rice, beans, home-brewed salsa, and a sweet. If it's full try the Pink Panther a few doors down.

La Estancia de Boca (Map p690; ☎ 932-32-75; cnr Morelos & Juárez; mains $5-10.50; ⏱ 11am-10pm) Enjoyable, upscale place where you can try authentic regional specialties like *molcajete* ($7) – a pre-Hispanic dish with tomatoes, garlic, onion and nopal.

Gran Café del Portal (Map p690; ☎ 931-27-59; cnr Av Independencia & Zamora; meals $3-9; ⏱ 7am-midnight) This is cavernous, convivial café is a mariachi magnet. It has a pavement terrace and a menu of international faves and regional classics including steak *tampiqueño*.

Cocina Económica Veracruz (Map p690; ☎ 31-00-80; cnr Zamora & Av Madero; comida corrida $2.25; ⏱ 11am-8pm) Two blocks southwest of the *zócalo*, this place is aimed at locals, not tourists. It serves cheap, basic, wholesome Mexican food at unbeatable prices.

HARBOR

Gran Café de la Parroquia (Map p690; ☎ 932-25-84; Farías 34; meals $3.50-11; ⏱ 6am-midnight) This busy restaurant-coffeehouse faces the harbor and buzzes from daylight until midnight. Pull up a pew and sip a coffee – customers request refills by clinking spoons on glasses – or gorge yourself on dishes like *rueda de pescado a la parrilla* (grilled fish; $11).

La Suriana 2 (Map p690; ☎ 931-70-99; Av Zaragoza 286; dishes $2.50-8; ⏱ 11am-7pm) La Suriana has a noisy location but a friendly family feel with excellent seafood at budget prices – come here for a fine *caldo de camarón* (prawn soup) or *pulpo veracruzano* (calamari).

The top floor of the municipal **fish market** (Map p690; Landero & Cos; ⏱ 9am-6:30pm) is rammed until early evening with *comedores* doing bargain fish fillets and *shrimp al mojo de ajo*. Not for the faint of stomach, the market is heavy on atmosphere and fishy aromas.

DOWN THE COAST

The majority of upmarket restaurants are along the seafront, between the aquarium

---

THE AUTHOR'S CHOICE

La Fragata (Map p689; ☎ 922-02-00 ext 126; Hotel Mocambo, Blvd Ruiz Cortines 4000; mains $6-14; ⏱ 2-11pm) A unique experience, this hotel restaurant is the most atmospheric place to eat in Veracruz. The dining room – complete with mahogany floorboards and a high, timbered roof – takes on a nautical theme, complete with a ship's wheel and other seafaring paraphernalia. Sip your wine from pewter goblets while feasting on cuisine like *arroz a la tumbada* (seafood and rice) or the house-special *brocheta de pescado* (fish kebabs; $14).

CENTRAL GULF COAST

and the village of Boca del Río, 10km south of the center, which is packed with lunching Mexican families on Sundays, munching *pescado zarandeado* (a Mexican fish dish). These places are listed in the order that you come to them, heading south of the *zócalo*.

Cacharrito (Map p689; ☎ 935-92-46; Blvd Ruiz Cortines 15; mains $5-22) Classy, formal Argentine restaurant 5km south of the *zócalo* that has to be the best place to eat meat in town. *Parrilladas* (barbequed meat; $17 to $37) are the house specialty but you'll also find pastas ($4.50 to $10) and salads.

Las Brisas (Map p689; ☎ 986-21-71; Zamora 310, Boca del Río; dishes $3-9) A popular choice for fresh seafood in Boca del Río, though there are several more worthwhile alternatives along the riverside.

Mandinga, about 8km further down the coast from Boca del Río, is also known for its seafood (especially *langostinos bicolores*) and has a clutch of small restaurants.

Drinking & Entertainment

The area around the *zócalo* is surprisingly bereft of decent bars, but overloaded with scruffy, hard-drinking cantinas, some of which are pretty sleazy. For a beer or a coffee with a view, head to the *zócalo portales* or the *malecón*. Most of the city's hip bars are well south of the center – cruise the coast road along Costa de Oro and you'll pass several. The city's beautiful people hang out at places like **Moon** (Blvd Camacho 600; 1pm-5am Tue-Sun), which has a wonderful outdoor ocean-facing deck, a sushi bar, DJs and lounge-style leather seating.

For a ringside-seat view of Veracruz' prime-time variety show, grab a café seat under the *zócalo portales*. It's an undeniably touristy but enjoyable experience, as pencil-wielding caricaturists and textile-hawking indigenous *campesinos* compete for your pesos while wandering mariachis, marimba bands and one-man-band musical freak shows vie to be heard. On weekends, visiting bands and dancers often set up on a temporary stage. Sometimes you'll find whole groups of revelers going wild; other times it's all staid tourists sitting at their tables waiting for something to happen.

If you hanker for something more sedate, ask the tourist office for information on concerts and cultural events. **Centro Cultural Casa Principal** (Map p690; ☎ 932-69-31; Molina 315;

admission $1; ☻ 10am-6pm Tue-Sun) hosts art exhibitions and cultural events.

LIVE MUSIC

La Casona de la Condesa (Map p689; ☎ 130-12-82; Blvd Camacho 2015; cover $3, Sat $4.50; ☻ 10pm-5am Tue-Sun) Those looking for a less teenybopper-oriented evening than is offered by the city's nightclubs might try La Casona, which offers great mixed drinks and solid live music every night it's open.

El Rincón de la Trova (Map p690; ☎ 918-54-25; Callejón de la Lagunilla 59) About to re-open after a stylish refurbishment at the time of research. The owners plan to showcase live music (Thursday through Saturday from 8pm to 3am).

NIGHTCLUBS

Most of the action is spread out along the coast road Blvd Camacho between Playa de Horno south to Playa Mocambo. Cover charges range between $3 and $10 (which usually includes a free drink); Friday and Saturday nights are more expensive. Don't even think about arriving before midnight unless you like strutting your stuff on your own. During holiday times, the entire area becomes an outdoor party, with bars and snack stalls along Blvd Camacho, live loud music, and dancing in the streets. These are some of the most popular spots:

Buda (Map p689; ☎ 922-45-59; Blvd Camacho 69) Cutting-edge club where the city's house-and techno-loving hipsters gather to groove and schmooze.

Carioca (Map p689; ☎ 935-15-95; Hotel Lois, Blvd Ruiz Cortines 10) Know your pasos beforehand at this hip salsa club.

Tamarindo (Map p689; ☎ 100-37-76; cnr Blvd Camacho & Militar; ☻ 9pm-3am Wed-Sat) Retro-style club that plays hits from the '60s, '70s and '80s.

Kachimba (Map p689; ☎ 927-19-80; www.kachimba.com; cnr Blvd Camacho & Militar; cover $8; ☻ from 8pm) Call ahead for reservations at this venue with live Cuban shows and salsa music.

Getting There & Away

AIR

Frequent flights between Veracruz and Mexico City are offered by Mexicana and Aeroméxico; the latter also flies to/from Tampico and Villahermosa, and Mexicana flies to Tampico and to Cancún via Mérida. Aerocaribe has direct flights to Minatitlán, with onward connections to Cancún and other destinations. Direct flights from Houston are offered by Continental.

Aerocaribe & Mexicana (Map p690; ☎ 932-22-42, 800-502-20-00; fax 932-86-99; cnr Serdán & Av 5 de Mayo)

Continental airlines (Map p689; ☎ 922-60-08; Blvd Ruiz Cortines 1600)

BUS

Veracruz is a major hub, with good services up and down the coast and inland along the Córdoba–Puebla–Mexico City corridor. Buses to and from Mexico City can be heavily booked at holiday times.

The bus station is about 3km south of the zócalo. The 1st-class/deluxe area fronts Av Díaz Mirón on the corner with Xalapa, and has ATMs. Though modern, it's quite inconvenient for users. The waiting area has phones and a snack bar, but you won't be allowed in if you don't have a ticket. Note the left-luggage room closes at night, and the only alternative is to buy a token for an overpriced locker. Behind the 1st-class station, the 2nd-class side is entered from Av Lafragua. There's a 24-hour luggage room here. Daily departures include the following:

Destination	Price	Duration	Frequency
Acayucan	$14	3½hr	14 1st-class & frequent 2nd-class
Catemaco	$7.50	3½hr	9 1st-class & 11 2nd-class
Córdoba	$6.50	1¾hr	30 1st-class & hourly 2nd-class
Mexico City (TAPO)	$24	5½hr	18 1st-class & regular 2nd-class
Oaxaca	$28	7hr	3 1st-class & 1 2nd-class direct
Orizaba	$8	2½hr	28 1st-class & at least 10 2nd-class directs
Papantla	$12	4½hr	7 1st-class & hourly 2nd-class
Puebla	$15	3½hr	7 1st-class & at least 4 2nd-class directs
San Andrés Tuxtla	$7	3hr	10 1st-class & frequent 2nd-class
Santiago Tuxtla	$6.50	2½hr	14 1st-class & frequent 2nd-class
Tampico	$29	9½hr	18 1st-class
Tuxpan	$16	5½hr	15 1st-class
Villahermosa	$26	7½hr	13 1st-class
Xalapa	$6	2hr	1st-class every 20-30min 6am-midnight & hourly 2nd-class

Buses leaving Veracruz also go to Campeche, Cancún, Chetumal, Matamoros, Mérida, Nuevo Laredo and Salina Cruz.

CAR & MOTORCYCLE

Many car-rental agencies have desks at the Veracruz airport. There are also some larger agencies scattered around town. Rates start at $45 per day for a small sedan or from $62 for a jeep-style vehicle.

Dollar (Map p689; ☎ 935-88-08; fax 935-88-07; Bolivar 501B)

Foster (Map p689; ☎ 932-50-50; yindaguirre@hotmail .com; Blvd Camacho 1291)

Hertz (Map p689; ☎ 937-47-88; Hotel Costa Verde, Blvd Camacho 3797)

Getting Around

Veracruz airport (☎ 934-70-00) is 11km southwest of town near Hwy 140. It's small, modern and well organized, and has a café, restaurant and a newsagents selling Time and the Economist. There's no bus service to or from town; taxis cost $12.

To get into the city center from in front of the 1st-class bus station, take a bus marked 'Díaz Mirón y Madero' ($0.50). It will head to Parque Zamora then up Madero. For the zócalo, get off on the corner of Madero and Lerdo and turn right. Returning to the bus stations, pick up the same bus going south on Av 5 de Mayo. Booths in the 1st- and 2nd-class stations sell taxi tickets (to the zócalo area costs $2.75).

Buses marked 'Mocambo–Boca del Río' ($1 to Boca del Río) leave regularly from the corner of Zaragoza and Serdán, near the zócalo; they go via Parque Zamora then down Blvd Camacho to Playa Mocambo (20 minutes) and on to Boca del Río (30 minutes).

AU buses to Antón Lizardo stop at Boca del Río and Mandinga. They leave from the 2nd-class station every 20 minutes until 9pm; the last one back to town is about 9:30pm.

From the malecón, **open-top buses** (www.turi bus.com.mx; children/adults $4/8) make a 50-minute circuit of the city's attractions, traveling along the coast as far as Boca del Río. You can hop-on, hop-off anywhere en route.

CÓRDOBA & FORTÍN DE LAS FLORES
☎ 271

Córdoba (population 135,000, elevation 924m) lacks big-ticket natural or cultural attractions, but this proud colonial town does have an enjoyable atmosphere and agreeably temperate climate. About 125km west of Veracruz, the city lies in the foothills of Mexico's central mountains, surrounded by enticing, fertile countryside.

In 1618, 30 Spanish families founded Córdoba in order to stop escaped African slaves from attacking travelers between Mexico City and the coast; consequently, the town is known as 'La Ciudad de los Treinta Caballeros' (City of the 30 Knights). Today it's a commercial and processing center for produce such as sugarcane, tobacco and coffee from the nearby hillsides, and fruit from the lowlands.

Just west of Córdoba, Fortín de las Flores (population 21,000, elevation 970m) is a cut flower-cultivation center, with plenty of color evident around town in its nurseries and private gardens. Peaceful Fortín is popular as a weekend retreat for the Mexico City middle class, but there's little for most travelers here.

Orientation

Córdoba's central Plaza de Armas sports fine 18th-century *portales* on three sides, with a row of busy cafés under the arches on the northeast. The city streets have numbers, not names. Avs 2, 4, 6 etc are northeast of the plaza; Avs 3, 5, 7 etc are southwest of the plaza. The Calles are at right angles to the Avenidas, with Calles 2, 4, 6 etc northwest of the plaza and the odd-numbered Calles to the southeast.

Fortín's big, open plaza, the Parque Principal, shelters the Palacio Municipal in the middle and a cathedral on the south side. It's 7km from central Córdoba, but the towns have grown into each other along Hwy 150.

Information

Banks around the Plaza de Armas have 24-hour ATMs and change traveler's checks.

All Clean (Av 5 No 624) Laundry here costs $3 for 3kg washed and dried.

eWorld Ciber Café (Calle 4 No115; Internet access per hr $1)

Post office (Av 3 s/n) Just northwest of the plaza.

Sanatorio Covadonga (☎ 714-55-20; www.sanatorio covadonga.com.mx in Spanish; Av 7 No 1610; ⊗ 24hr) Provides urgent medical care at all hours.

Tourist office (☎ 717-17-00 ext 1778; turismo@mpio cordoba.gob.mx; Palacio Municipal; ⊗ 8:30am-7pm) On the northwest side of the plaza. Helpful staff offer

maps, information and a monthly schedule of activities. Volunteers sometimes give tourists free tours of the sights (in Spanish).

Sights & Activities

The **Ex-Hotel Zevallos**, built in 1687, is not a hotel but the former home of the *condes* (counts) of Zevallos. It's on the northeast side of Córdoba's Plaza de Armas, behind the *portales*. Plaques in the courtyard record that Juan O'Donojú and Agustín de Iturbide met here after Mass on August 24, 1821, and agreed on terms for Mexico's independence. O'Donojú (the new Spanish viceroy) and Iturbide (leader of the anti-imperial forces) concluded it was useless for Spain to try to cling to its colony. They also concurred that a Mexican, not a European, should be head of state – Iturbide went on to a brief reign as Emperor Agustín I. The building is now notable mainly for its café-restaurants.

At the southeast end of Plaza de Armas is the imposing baroque **Catedral de la Inmaculada Concepción** which dates from 1688. It has an elaborate facade flanked by twin bell-towers, and a gaudy interior complete with lashings of gold leaf and marble floors.

Half a block southwest of the plaza, the **Museo de Antropología** (Calle 3 s/n; admission free; ⊗ 9am-2pm & 4-8pm) has a modest but interesting collection of artifacts. There's a fine, sun-shaped, Aztec ball-court marker, some select Olmec figurines and a replica of the magnificent statue of El Señor de Las Limas that resides in Xalapa's Museo de Antropología. Also here is a *pebetero*, one of the huge flaming torches used during the 1968 Mexican Olympics.

Faraventuras runs trips to waterfalls, caves, underground rivers and other natural attractions in the area. Climbs up Pico de Orizaba, for a group of six people, will cost you around $65 per person per day with guide, equipment and food. Contact the company at its head office in the **Xochitl travel agency** (☎ 713-16-95; http://communities .msn.com.mx/faraventuras in Spanish; Av 3 Pte No 113) in Fortín de las Flores – just a couple of blocks from the plaza.

Festivals & Events

On the evening of **Good Friday**, Córdoba marks Jesus' crucifixion with a procession of silence, in which thousands of residents

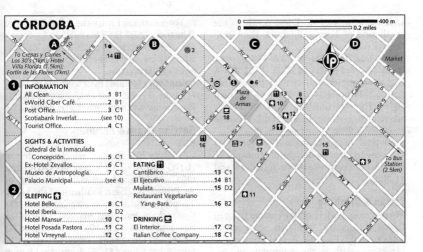

walk through the streets behind an altar of the Virgin. Everyone holds a lit candle, no one utters a word, and the church bells are eerily quiet.

April, May and June are the best months to see flowers blooming; Fortín's annual **flower festival** runs for a week in late April or early May.

Sleeping

Córdoba accommodation options are not extensive, but they are fair value.

CÓRDOBA

Hotel Posada Pastora (☎ 712-88-82; Calle 5 No 517; s/d $21/24, with air-con $27/29; P ⚥) It's quite unprepossessing from the outside but this renovated place with friendly management has excellent-value, spotless rooms with stylish details: huge king-size beds with modish wooden headboards, and attractive wardrobes and tables.

Hotel Mansur (☎ 712-60-00; fax 712-69-89; Av 1 No 301; s/d/tw $34/37/40; P ⚥) The lobby, with country manor–style wood paneling and easy armchairs, sets a welcoming tone. Though the fair-sized rooms can't match the lobby for period character, all have cable TV and phones, and some have spacious common balconies that overlook the plaza.

Hotel Iberia (☎ 712-13-01; hoteliberiacordoba@hotmail.com; Av 2 No 919; s/d with fan $15/18, with air-con $20/22; P ⚥ ⚥) A great budget deal, this place has three floors of small, modern rooms with arched brick window frames,

cable TV and wardrobes. There's a courtyard in the center.

Hotel Bello (☎ 712-81-22; cnr Av 2 & Calle 5; s/d $36/41; P ⚥ ⚥) This rather soulless, modern, concrete block actually is good value, with well-maintained rooms that even have a little sparkle, quality beds and furnishings, multi-channeled TV and spacious bathrooms. There's a restaurant and free Internet access.

Hotel Virreynal (☎ 712-23-77; fax 712-03-95; Av 1 No 309; s/d $27/30; ⚥) The vibrant tiled stairways and lobby exude colonial charm, but the Virreynal's functional rooms are much more plain Jane than Spanish princess – those facing the street have terrific views of the cathedral, but can be a bit noisy.

Hotel Villa Florida (☎ 716-33-33; www.villaflorida.com.mx; Av 1 No 3002; r/ste $62/118; P ⚥ ⚥) Córdoba's most upmarket option has a big pool, restaurant and lovely gardens with a fountain. Here's the rub: it's 1.5km northwest of the center.

FORTÍN DE LAS FLORES

Hotel Posada Loma (☎ 713-06-58; www.hotelposadaloma.com; Blvd Córdoba-Fortín Km 333; s/d $55/59, bungalows from $80; P ⚥ ⚥) This small, delightful hotel has a peaceful parklike setting: gardens and terraces, birds and orchids, and a great pool. The airy accommodations are great, with air-con and fireplaces for the winter nights, while the bungalows all have kitchenettes. Breakfast in the restaurant, which offers a spectacular view of Pico de

Orizaba, is unbeatable. Loma is just off the south side of Hwy 150, about 1km from central Fortín.

Gran Hotel El Pueblito (☎ 713-00-33; hotelpueblito @hotmail.com; Av 2 Ote 505; s/d $28/35; P ⚡ ❄) A slightly humbler option than the Posada Loma, this hotel is charming in its own right. The spacious, comfortable rooms are named, not numbered, and laid out to resemble a little village. A gem of a swimming pool, tennis courts and bougainvillea combine to create a delightful atmosphere. Look for the entrance between Calles 9 and 11 Nte.

Eating & Drinking

There's more variety on the cuisine front in Córdoba compared to Fortín. The *portales* cafés near the Plaza de Armas are popular places to eat throughout the day, though the constant stream of street hawkers plying the tables can get a bit wearisome. For fine seafood, try the restaurants on Calle 15 between Avs 5 and 7, where fish dishes and seafood cocktails go for around $6.

Mulata (☎ 717-66-63; Av 1 No 721; mains $4-14) A contemporary, stylish restaurant with a sky-lit dining area, voguish seating and an ambitious, European-influenced menu with starters like *jamón serrano con espárragos* (cured ham and asparagus) and mains including *pescado al pibil* (fish cooked in a pit). It's also open for breakfast.

El Ejecutivo (☎ 712-86-93; Av 5 No 61; mains $1.75-6) Family-run *comedor*, with walls bedecked in cheery sarapes, that serves up Mexican staples and great tortas – try a *pierna con manchego* (ham with cheese).

Restaurant Vegetariano Yang-Bara (☎ 712-69-34; Av 5 No 100; veggie comida corrida $2; 🕙 9am-7pm Mon-Sat; V) A humble veggie oasis, Yang-Bara offers inexpensive snacks, yummy juices and a cheap, healthy *comida corrida*.

Crepas y Carnes Los 30's (☎ 712-33-79; Av 9 No 2004; crêpes $2.50-5.50; 🕙 1pm-midnight) Mouthwatering sweet and savory crêpes, and next door they serve Sicilian pizza ($5 to $6) and other Italian specialties. It's quite a hike from the plaza, at the corner of Calle 20.

Cantábrica (Calle 3 No 9; mains $7-13; 🕙 noon-10pm) Formal, upmarket air-conditioned restaurant that's a good choice for paella or *tortilla española*. It also has a very popular lunch buffet (2pm to 6pm, $7 to $11).

For a caffeine hit try the following cafés:

El Interior (☎ 727-17-17; Av 3 No 318, Int 2; coffee $1.25; 🕙 9am-9pm Mon-Sat, 10am-8pm Sun) In a shady arcade, this café and gift shop has luscious desserts and makes a decent cappuccino.

Italian Coffee Company (Plaza Jardín, cnr Calle 1 & Av 3; coffee $1.25-2.25) Inside a small shopping mall, this Starbucks-style place offers plenty of coffee combos.

Getting There & Around

BUS

Córdoba's bus station, which has deluxe (UNO and ADO GL), 1st-class (ADO and OCC) and 2nd-class (AU) services, is at Av Privada 4, 2.5km southeast of the plaza. To get to the town center from the station, take a local bus marked 'Centro' or buy a taxi ticket ($1.50). To Fortín de las Flores and Orizaba, it's more convenient to take a local bus ($1.25) from Av 11 than to go out to the Córdoba bus station. As always, 2nd-class buses run more often to midrange destinations, take longer and cost 10% less than the corresponding 1st-class service. Long-distance deluxe and 1st-class buses from Córdoba include the following departures:

Destination	Price	Duration	Frequency
Mexico City (TAPO)	$19	4½hr	30 daily
Oaxaca	$21	6hr	2 daily
Puebla	$11	3hr	at least 12 daily
Veracruz	$6.50	1¾hr	at least 1 hourly
Veracruz airport	$13	1¾hr	6 daily
Xalapa	$9	3½hr	16 daily

In Fortín, local buses arrive and depart from Calle 1 Sur, on the west side of the plaza. The ADO depot on the corner of Av 2 and Calle 6 has mainly *de paso* services to Mexico City, Veracruz, Puebla and Xalapa. UNO has two deluxe buses daily to Mexico City; ADO GL has one. Prices are about the same as those from Córdoba.

CAR & MOTORCYCLE

Córdoba, Fortín de las Flores and Orizaba are linked by toll Hwy 150D, the route that most buses take, and by the much slower Hwy 150. A scenic back road goes through the hills from Fortín, via Huatusco, to Xalapa.

ORIZABA

☎ 272 / pop 122,000 / elevation 1219m

Orizaba, 16km west of Córdoba, mainly attracts visitors intent on tackling the nearby Pico de Orizaba, one of Mexico's most spectacular volcanoes and its highest peak. But the city itself, founded by the Spanish to guard the Veracruz–Mexico City road, has an easy-going appeal, and at times seems more an overgrown highland village than a small city. A few fine architectural attractions and church domes survived the 1973 earthquake, and there's an excellent art museum.

An industrial center in the late 19th century, its factories were early centers of the unrest that led to the unseating of dictator Porfirio Díaz. Today it has a big brewery and cement, textile and chemical industries.

Orientation

The central plaza is Parque Castillo, with the irregularly shaped Parroquia de San Miguel on its north side. Madero, a busy street bordering the plaza's west side, divides Avenidas into Oriente (Ote; east) and Poniente (Pte; west). Av Colón, on the south side, is the boundary between the Norte and Sur Calles. All of the other streets have numbers rather than names. Av Pte 7–Av Ote 6, three blocks south of the plaza, is the main east–west artery.

Information

Two banks with ATMs are on Av Ote 2, a block south of the plaza.

Cruz Roja (☎ 725-05-50; Av Colón Ote 253; consultation fee $2.50; ☽ 24hr) Provides medical care.

Post office (Av Ote 2)

Sitiworld (Av Ote 2 No 119; per hr $1) Internet access.

Tourist office (☎ 728-91-36; www.orizaba.gob.mx/turismo .htm; Palacio de Hierro; ☽ 8am-3pm & 4-8pm Mon-Fri, noon-8pm Sat, noon-4pm Sun) Has enthusiastic staff and plenty of brochures, though not much practical information.

Sights

The Parque Castillo has an imposing parish church, the **Parroquia de San Miguel**, on its north side, which is mainly 17th century in style, with several towers and some Puebla-type tiles. Opposite the west flank of the church is the city's most arresting structure: the **Palacio de Hierro** (see boxed text, p702).

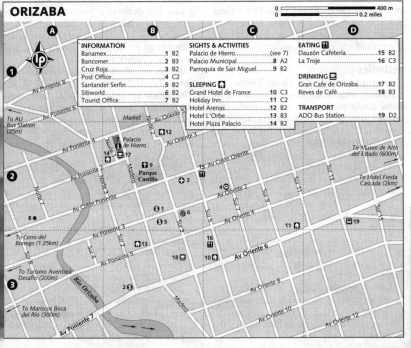

ORIZABA

0	400 m
0	0.2 miles

INFORMATION
Banamex.....................................1 B2
Bancomer...................................2 B3
Cruz Roja....................................3 B2
Post Office..................................4 C2
Santander Serfin.......................5 B2
Sitiworld.....................................6 B2
Tourist Office.............................7 B2

SIGHTS & ACTIVITIES
Palacio de Hierro...................(see 7)
Palacio Municipal.....................8 A2
Parroquia de San Miguel.........9 B2

SLEEPING 🛏
Grand Hotel de France.........10 C3
Holiday Inn..............................11 C2
Hotel Arenas...........................12 B2
Hotel L'Orbe............................13 B3
Hotel Plaza Palacio.................14 B2

EATING 🍴
Dauzón Cafetería...................15 B2
La Troje....................................16 C3

DRINKING 🍷
Gran Cafe de Orizaba............17 B2
Reves de Café.........................18 B3

TRANSPORT
ADO Bus Station.....................19 D2

To AU Bus Station (25km)
To Cerro del Borrego (1.25km)
To Turismo Aventura Desafío (200m)
To Mariscos Boca del Río (300m)
To Museo de Arte del Estado (600m)
To Hotel Fiesta Cascada (2km)

Av Poniente 8
Av Poniente 6
Market
Av Oriente 1
Av Oriente 3
Av Poniente 4
Palacio de Hierro
Av Oriente 3
Parque Castillo
Av Colón Oriente
Av Oriente 2
Av Poniente 3
Av Oriente 4
Av Poniente 5
Av Oriente 6
Av Colón Poniente
Av Oriente 8
Av Oriente 10
Av Oriente 12
Av Poniente 7
Río Orizaba
Madero
Norte 2
Sur 2
Sur 3

THE IRON PALACE

Orizaba's most remarkable structure is its monumental **Palacio de Hierro** (Iron Palace), off the northwest corner of the plaza, which covers an entire city block. This art nouveau–style landmark, built entirely from cast iron and steel, actually began life as the Belgian pavilion at the Paris International Exhibition in the late 19th century.

It was designed by Frenchman Alexandre Gustave Eiffel, a master of metallurgy who not only gives his name to the Eiffel Tower in Paris, but who also engineered the Statue of Liberty's iron framework and the Panama Canal's system of locks.

Orizaba's mayor, Don Julio Vélez, eager to acquire an impressive European-style Palacio Municipal for his town, bought the prefabricated building for $13,800 in 1892. Piece by piece the pavilion was dismantled and shipped to Mexico in three separate steamboats. Over 3000 containers filled with panels, columns and rivets were dispatched by rail, and reassembled in Orizaba.

Today the building, surrounded by elegant verandas on all sides and with a tiered central clocktower, is gleaming again after a recent renovation. It's now home to municipal offices including the tourist office, a library, a minuscule beer museum and a stylish café.

MUSEO DE ARTE DEL ESTADO

Orizaba's wonderful **State Art Museum** (☎ 724-32-00; cnr Av Ote 4 & Calle Sur 25; admission $1.25; ☺ 10am-5pm Tue-Sun) is housed in a gorgeously restored colonial building dating from 1776, which has been at various times a church, a hospital and a military base. The museum is divided into rooms that include one of Mexico's most important permanent Diego Rivera collections; there are also contemporary works by regional artists; and paintings of Veracruz through the eyes of travelers.

Activities

The canyon beside the Hotel Fiesta Cascada features a beautiful waterfall emerging from dense forest, and offers spectacular **hiking** possibilities. A forest-flanked trail begins a few meters west of the hotel and then descends to the canyon floor, where it forks. To the left, the trail follows the river for several kilometers. To the right, it crosses a footbridge beside the waterfall and a small power station, before reaching a rough road that winds northwest into the mountains, passing through forest and farmland.

Looming over the Alameda park, west of town, the **Cerro del Borrego** offers brilliant views if you get to the top very early, before the mist rolls in.

Turismo Aventura Desafío (☎ 725-06-96; Av Pte 3 No 586) arranges various adventure activities in nearby hills, mountains and canyons, including climbs part way up Pico de Orizaba from $175 per person.

Sleeping

Hotel Arenas (☎ /fax 725-23-61; Av Nte 2 No 169; s/d $12/17) Very agreeable, friendly little hotel with rooms around a lush garden filled with orange and pine trees. Its clean rooms come with cable TV and there's a small café too.

Grand Hotel de France (☎ 725-23-11; www.hotel defrance.com.mx; Av Ote 6 No 186; s/d/ste $27/35/51; P ☒) Your peso goes a long way in this pleasingly decorated hotel where attractive, pastel-shaded rooms have wardrobes, phones and TV – though some do suffer a degree of traffic noise. There's a bar and restaurant here too.

Holiday Inn (☎ 724-00-77; holidayinnorizaba@hotmail .com; Av Ote 6 No 464; r/ste $65/85; P ☒ ☒ ☐ ☒) The newly renovated Holiday Inn offers surprisingly homey, good-value rooms, with stylish curtains, safes, attractive wood furniture and socket connections for laptops. The pool is tiny (but it is heated) and there's a gym.

Hotel L'Orbe (☎ 725-50-33; fax 725-53-44; Av Pte 5 No 33; s/d/ste $28/33/51; P ☐) The extremely generously sized rooms – with comfortable beds and chairs and some with fine volcano views – are the main attraction here, and though fans are provided, there's no air-conditioning. There's a restaurant-bar.

Hotel Plaza Palacio (☎ 725-99-33; Av Pte 2 No 2; s/d $22/28; P) Large place with many functional, carpeted rooms with fans and TV.

Hotel Fiesta Cascada (☎ 724-15-96; fax 724-55-99; Hwy Puebla-Córdoba Km 275; s/d $41/46, bungalows from $44; P ☒ ☒) The Cascada sits above a gorgeous canyon and has a pool, gardens and a private patch of rain forest. Charming, spacious rooms with minibar, TV and phone come at a terrific price. It is 2km east of the center.

Eating & Drinking

In sedate Orizaba, many of the moderately priced restaurants close early.

Gran Cafe de Orizaba (☎ 724-44-75; cnr Av Pte 2 & Madero; snacks $2.75-4) Sitting pretty inside the Palacio de Hierro, this stately café is by far Orizaba's most evocative place for a snack or a drink. Sip gourmet organic coffee (from Zimbabwe, Sumatra or Ethiopia) or tea (Darjeeling or Yunnan) on the veranda or tuck into a tostada, crêpe or baguette inside the beautiful interior, with its polished wood floors, elegant seating and pictures of old Orizaba.

La Troje (☎ 725-08-05; Sur 5 No 225; comida corrida $4.50, mains $5-12) With wood paneling and exposed brick walls, La Troje offers stylish setting for all things Mexican, including a five-course *comida corrida*.

Mariscos Boca del Río (Av Pte 7 s/n; seafood $5-7; ⏰ noon-8pm Tue-Sun) It may look humble, but this is the best seafood restaurant in town, with big portions of economical shrimp, fish and squid dishes. An imposter restaurant of the same name lies north of the plaza.

Dauzón Cafetería (☎ 726-36-19; cnr Sur 5 & Av Colón; snacks $3, mains $2.50-6; ⏰ 8am-9pm Mon-Thu, 8am-10pm Fri-Sun; **V**) The insipid color scheme isn't that inviting, but step in for an extensive selection of (mainly) vegetarian options, including soy chorizo and bacon-esque baguettes.

Reves de Cafe (☎ 725-47-35; Sur 3 No 225; coffee $1.25; ⏰ 10am-10pm Mon-Sat, 5-10pm Sun) Fashionable with Orizaba's bright young things, this courtyard café has flavorsome cakes and excellent coffee.

For a cheap feed, head to the plaza for tacos and snacks.

Getting There & Around

Local buses from Fortín and Córdoba stop four blocks north and six blocks east of the town center, around Ote 9 and Nte 14. The AU (2nd-class) bus station is at Zaragoza Pte 425, northwest of the center. To reach the city center from here, turn left outside the depot, cross the bridge, take the first fork right and head for the church domes.

The modern 1st-class bus station is on the corner of Ote 6 and Sur 13, and has

ATMs and handles all ADO, ADO GL and deluxe UNO services.

Destination	Price	Duration	Frequency
Córdoba	$1.50	30min	29 1st-class daily
Mexico City (Terminal Norte)	$17	4hr	7 1st-class daily & frequent AU
Mexico City (TAPO)	$17	4hr	15 1st-class daily & frequent AU
Oaxaca	$20	5hr	3 1st-class daily
Puebla	$10.50	2½hr	14 1st-class daily & frequent AU
Veracruz	$8	2¼hr	27 1st-class daily & frequent AU
Xalapa	$11	4hr	13 1st-class daily

There are also 1st-class services to Tehuacán, Tampico and Villahermosa.

Toll Hwy 150D, which bypasses central Orizaba, goes east to Córdoba and west, via a spectacular ascent, to Puebla (160km). Toll-free Hwy 150 runs east to Córdoba and Veracruz (150km) and southwest to Tehuacán, 65km away over the hair-raising Cumbres de Acultzingo.

AROUND ORIZABA
Pico de Orizaba

Mexico's tallest mountain (5611m), called 'Citlaltépetl' (Star Mountain) in the Náhuatl language, is 25km northwest of Orizaba. This dormant volcano has a small crater and a three-month snowcap. From the summit, in good weather, one can see Popocatépetl, Iztaccíhuatl and La Malinche to the west and the Gulf of Mexico 96km to the east. The only higher peaks in North America are Mt McKinley in Alaska and Mt Logan in Canada.

The most common route up Orizaba is from the north, using as a base the small town of **Tlachichuca** (2600m), which has plenty of stores selling supplies and bottled water. Tlachichuca can be reached by white minibuses departing from the bus terminal in Ciudad Serdán ($1, one hour). Serdán, in turn, can be reached from Puebla ($3, two hours) or Orizaba ($3.75, two hours). Infrequent AU buses also run directly between Tlachichuca and Puebla ($4, four hours).

Unless you have navigation skills and a good map, and your group has some experience of snow and ice-climbing techniques, you should not attempt this climb without a guide. Remember to allow several days for acclimatization beforehand. From Tlachichuca, take a taxi to Villa Hidalgo at 3400m ($18, 15km), then either walk or continue by vehicle 10km further to the mountain hut (*refugio* or *albergue*) called 'Piedra Grande,' at 4200m. This walk will help with acclimatization, though it's also possible to charter a 4WD all the way to Piedra Grande for around $48. The *refugio* is big but basic, and you'll need to bring a sleeping mat, sleeping bag, stove and cooking gear. Some climbers have reported mice here, so keep your food containers covered.

Most climbers start at around 2am for the final climb and try to reach the summit around sunrise or shortly after, before mist and cloud envelop the mountain. The climb is moderately steep over snow that's usually hard. It's not technically difficult (though classified as 'extreme' by international standards), but crampons are essential, as are ropes and ice axes for safety. Allow five to 10 hours for the ascent, depending on the conditions and your abilities, and another three hours to return to the *refugio*. You can arrange to be picked up by 4WD at Piedra Grande after returning from the climb.

Experienced climbers doing the northern route can make all the necessary arrangements in Tlachichuca, but get maps well in advance. The 1:50,000 Inegi map is supposed to be the best, but it can be hard to obtain. Some specialist books on climbing in Mexico have adequate maps, including *Mexico's Volcanoes*, by RJ Secor. The best climbing period is October to March, with the most popular time being December and January.

In Tlachichuca, the Reyes family runs **Servimont** (☎ 245-451-50-09; www.servimont.com .mx; Ortega 1A), a climber-owned outfit that offers a wide range of trips up the mountain. Basic accommodations ($15 per person) and good meals are available in a charming, former soap factory that also serves as the company office. Servimont also acts as a Red Cross rescue facility and has an excellent reputation for safety. It's the longest-running operation in the area by far. Make reservations four months in advance. Three-day trips, including a guide and equipment, start at $350 per person for a group of four or more.

Other guides also operate in Tlachichuca and you can book them in Orizaba and elsewhere. They may offer lower rates than Servimont, but a few have been known to cut corners when it comes to safety.

You can also hole up in Tlachichuca at the friendly and commodious **Hotel Gerar** (☎ 245-451-50-75; hotel_gerar@hotmail.com; Av 20 de Noviembre 200; s/d $6/12; P) or the equally hospitable **Hostal Limón** (☎ 245-451-50-82; cancholashouse@yahoo.com .mx; Av 3 Pte 3; s/d $17/23; P). Staff can help with arranging guides and providing information at both these places. On the plaza, **La Casa Blanca** (mains $3.50-6) serves up the usual Mexican culinary suspects and righteous steaks.

An alternative and less-used route is from the south, via the villages of **Atzitzintla** and **Texmalaquilla** and a *refugio* at 4750m. Only very proficient climbers should attempt this route, with the services of an experienced local guide. The route has claimed several lives in the last few years due to summer droughts which have reduced the snow coating and made the Jamapa Glacier extremely hazardous to navigate. Local rescue teams only have very rudimentary rescue and safety equipment.

Zongolica

A road leads 38km south from Orizaba to the mountain village of Zongolica, where isolated indigenous groups have unique styles of weaving. Buses leave Orizaba from Ote 3 between Nte 12 and Nte 14 every half-hour.

SOUTHEAST VERACRUZ

Southeast of Veracruz port is a flat, hot, wet coastal plain, crossed by rivers and sheltering the serene port town of Tlacotalpan. South and southeast of Tlacotalpan is a hilly, green and fertile region known as Los Tuxtlas (*tooks*-tlahs), home to myriad lakes and waterfalls, as well as an agreeable climate. Catemaco, a small lakeside resort, draws plenty of Mexican vacationers, while the sparkling coastline just north of there harbors some terrific beaches.

Los Tuxtlas is the western fringe of the ancient Olmec heartland, and Olmec artifacts can be observed at Santiago Tuxtla, Tres Zapotes and San Lorenzo. The basalt for the huge Olmec heads was quarried from Cerro Cintepec in the east of the Sierra de los Tuxtlas and then moved, probably by roller and raft, to San Lorenzo, 60km to the south.

The southeastern end of Veracruz state, bordering Tabasco and Chiapas, is home to oil metropolises such as Minatitlán and Coatzacoalcos, neither of which holds any attractions for visitors other than the fun of pronouncing their names.

TLACOTALPAN

☎ 288 / pop 9000 / elevation 10m

A tranquil, charming old town on the north bank of the wide Río Papaloapan, Tlacotalpan was a major port in the 19th century. Having preserved its broad plazas, colorful houses and cobbled streets, it received Unesco World Heritage status in 1998.

Information

There is a Scotiabank ATM next door to Posada Doña Lala.

Internet Café (Alegre s/n) A block south from the *zócalo*.

Post office (8am-4pm Mon-Fri) Around the corner from the tourist office.

Tourist office (Palacio Municipal; 9am-3pm Mon-Fri) Under the green and red *portales* facing Plaza Hidalgo. The office has helpful town maps.

Sights

Enjoy idiosyncratically narrated tours of Tlacotalpan's mini-museums, starting with **Museo Salvador Ferrando** (Calle Alegre 6; admission $1; 10:30am-5pm Tue-Sun), displaying assorted artifacts from the town's colonial history. Move on to **Casa Museo Agustín Lara** (Beltrán 6; admission $1; 10am-5pm Mon-Sat), featuring memorabilia of *tlacotalpeño* Agustín Lara (1900–70), a legendary and prolific musician, composer and Casanova. Locals may point you down the road to the **Mini-Zoológico Museo** (Carranza 25; donation $1; 10am-5pm Mon-Sat), the home of Don Pío Barrán, who keeps several crocodiles and a range of artifacts, including a locally excavated mastodon tooth and a sword that supposedly belonged to Porfirio Díaz.

Move on to the pink **Casa de la Cultura Agustín Lara** (884-22-02; Carranza 43; 9am-5pm), where art exhibits, folkloric dance rehearsals and *jarocho* music lessons are free for visitors to observe; the gallery upstairs may exact an admission fee.

Festivals & Events

In late January and early February, Tlacotalpan's lively **Candelaria** festival features bull-running in the streets and an image of the Virgin floating down the river followed by a flotilla of small boats.

Sleeping & Eating

Prices triple or quadruple during the Candelaria holiday.

Hotel Posada Doña Lala (884-25-80; fax 884-25-81; Av Carranza 11; r $24, with air-con $34; P 🛏 🖭) Near the river, the Doña Lala has the most personality of Tlaco's hotels, adorned with imaginative paintings and providing spotless, spacious rooms.

Hotel Reforma (884-20-22; Av Carranza 2; s/d $19/29 with air-con $24/38; P 🛏) Right off Plaza Zaragoza, this friendly hotel is clean, cool and sunny. All rooms have cable TV.

Hotel Tlacotalpan (884-20-63; hoteltlacotalpan@tlaco.com.mx; Beltrán 35; s & d $34, tw $42; P 🛏 🖭) Two blocks from the bus station, this low-key place has blue *portales*, and rooms surrounding a simple courtyard.

Hotel Candelaria (884-31-20; Beltrán 66; r incl full board $95; 🛏) The modern Hotel Candelaria is geared to holidaying Mexican families. Front rooms have tiny balconies over the street.

For good eats, try **Restaurante Doña Lala** (884-25-80; Av Carranza 11) or one of the terrific open-air eateries selling fresh seafood on the riverfront. In the center of town, a couple of lovely cafés face Plaza Hidalgo and the *zócalo*.

Shopping

Around the plazas are *artesanías* shops selling local handicrafts such as crocheted lace, and tiny chairs made from wood and leather.

Getting There & Around

Hwy 175 runs from Tlacotalpan up the Papaloapan valley to Tuxtepec, then twists and turns over the mountains to Oaxaca (320km). ADO offers service to Mexico City, Puebla, Xalapa and Veracruz, while Cuenca and Transportes Los Tuxtlas (TLT) buses cover local routes.

SANTIAGO TUXTLA

☎ 294 / pop 16,000 / elevation 180m

Pretty Santiago, founded in 1525, is a very tranquil valley town set in the rolling green foothills of the volcanic Sierra de los Tuxtlas. It has a rustic charm of its own, with a lovely leafy plaza and largely traffic-free streets. Visitors pass through here en route to see the Olmec artifacts at Tres Zapotes, 23km away.

All buses arrive and depart within a few meters of the junction of Calle Morelos and the highway. To get to the center, continue down Morelos, then turn right into Ayuntamiento which leads to the zócalo, a few blocks away. The post office is on the zócalo, as are two banks (both with ATMs), while Linx Internet is at Ayuntamiento 99.

The **Olmec head** in the zócalo is known as the 'Cobata head,' after the estate (west of Santiago) where it was found. Thought to be a very late or even post-Olmec production, it's the biggest known Olmec head, weighing in at 40 tonnes, and unique in that its eyes are closed.

The interesting **Museo Tuxteco** (☎ 947-10-76; adult/seniors & child under 13yr $3/free; ⏰ 9am-6pm Mon-Sat, 9am-4pm Sun & holidays), on the plaza, exhibits Olmec stone carvings, including another colossal head (this one from Nestepec west of Santiago), a monkey-faced *hacha* (ax) with obsidian eyes, and a copy of Monument F, or 'El Negro,' from Tres Zapotes, which is an altar or throne with a human form carved into it. Numerous other artifacts are also on display here.

Santiago celebrates the festivals of **San Juan** (June 24) and **Santiago Apóstol** (St James; July 25) with processions and dances including the Liseres, in which the participants wear jaguar costumes. The dance costumes also come out the week before Christmas.

The guesthouse **Hotel Morelos** (☎ 947-04-74; Obregón 12; s/d/tw $11/16/18) is easy to miss, because it's a family home – the entrance is almost opposite the Transportes Los Tuxtlas bus station, a block south of Ayuntamiento. You'll find smallish, neat rooms, some brighter than others, all with cable TVs, fans and private hot-water bathrooms.

Representing the only other deal in town, the good-value **Hotel Castellanos** (☎ 947-02-00; fax 947-04-00; cnr Calle 5 de Mayo & Comonfort; s/d $23/25; P 🛇 🛋) is a very quirky hotel in a circular building on the north side of the zócalo. There are amazing views from the top floor (particularly from rooms 605 and 604) and all cheery accommodations have wood paneling, marble sinks, cable TVs and big wardrobes. Staff are very affable, and there's a fair-sized pool and good restaurant with

main dishes from $4. On the zócalo, **Restaurant La Joya** (☎ 947-01-77; mains $2.75-6) is not fancy, but is fair value with snacks, fresh fish and good coffee.

All local and regional buses, and *colectivo* taxis to San Andrés (every 15 minutes), stop at the junction of Morales and the highway. There's a tiny ADO office on the highway itself while the Transportes Los Tuxtlas and AU stops are just down Morelos.

From Santiago, ADO has 10 *de paso* buses a day going west to Veracruz ($7, 2½ hours) via Alvarado, five a day going east to Coatzacoalcos ($7.50, 2½ hours) via Catemaco ($1.75, one hour), and five a day to Acayucan ($5, two hours). There are also very frequent 2nd-class buses to San Andrés Tuxtla, Catemaco and Veracruz, and regular services to Acayucan and Tlacotalpan.

TRES ZAPOTES
☎ 294 / pop 3600

The important late-Olmec center of Tres Zapotes is now just a series of mounds in maize fields, but there are many interesting finds displayed at the museum in the village of Tres Zapotes, 23km west of Santiago Tuxtla.

Tres Zapotes was occupied for over 2000 years, from around 1200 BC to AD 1000. It was probably first inhabited while the great Olmec center of La Venta (Tabasco) still flourished. After the destruction of La Venta (about 400 BC), the city carried on in what archaeologists regard as an 'epi-Olmec' phase – a period when the spark had gone out of Olmec culture, and other civilizations, notably Izapa and Maya, were coming to the fore. Most of the finds are from this later period.

At Tres Zapotes in 1939, Matthew Stirling, the first great Olmec excavator, unearthed part of an interesting chunk of basalt. One side was carved with an epi-Olmec 'werejaguar,' the other with a series of bars and dots that dated the piece to September 3, 32 BC, which confirmed that the Olmecs had developed a very early writing system – though even earlier dates have subsequently been discovered. In 1969 a farmer came across the rest of the stone, now called Stela C, which bore the missing part of Stirling's date.

At the **Museo de Tres Zapotes** (admission $2.50; ⏰ 8am-6pm), the objects are arranged on a disappointingly small cross-shaped platform. On the far side is the 1.5m Tres Zapotes head, dating from about 100 BC, which was the first Olmec head to be discovered in modern times; it was found by a hacienda worker in 1862. Opposite the head is Stela A, the biggest piece, with three human figures in the mouth of a jaguar. This originally stood on its end. To the right of Stela A are two pieces. One is a sculpture of what may have been a captive with hands tied behind his or her back. The other piece has a toad carved on one side and a skull on the other.

Beyond Stela A is an altar or throne carved with the upturned face of a woman, and beyond that, in the corner, is the less interesting part of the famous Stela C. (The part with the date is in the Museo Nacional de Antropología, but a photo of it is on the wall here.) The museum attendant is happy to answer questions in Spanish or give a tour (be nice and tip him $0.50 or so).

The road to Tres Zapotes goes southwest from Santiago Tuxtla; a 'Zona Arqueológica' sign points the way from Hwy 180. Eight kilometers down this road, you fork right onto a newly paved stretch for the last 15km to Tres Zapotes village. It comes out at a T-junction next to the Sitio Olmeca taxi stand. From here you walk to the left, then turn left again to reach the museum.

To get to Tres Zapotes, take a green-and-white taxi ($1.75/10 for colectivo/private) from Santiago Tuxtla. They leave from the Sitio Puente Real, on the far side of the pedestrian bridge at the foot of Zaragoza, the street going downhill beside the Santiago Tuxtla museum. Infrequent TLT buses ($1.25) also make the trip.

SAN ANDRÉS TUXTLA

☎ 294 / pop 56,000 / elevation 300m

The lively large town of San Andrés is in the center of Los Tuxtlas, and is Mexico's cigar capital. That said, its appeal – other than as a puro-producing center – is pretty limited, as it's a fairly mundane provincial place. However the surrounding countryside – a rolling evergreen landscape replete with maize and sugarcane fields, bananas and bean crops – is scenic, and there are waterfalls and the dormant Volcán San Martín (1748m) to explore.

Orientation & Information

The main bus station is on Juárez, 1km northwest of the plaza. The cathedral is on the plaza's north side, the Palacio Municipal on the west side and a Banamex (with ATM) on the south side. The market is three blocks west.

The post office is on Lafragua; head down Calle 20 de Noviembre directly across the plaza from the Palacio Municipal and follow it around to the left. Heading southeast of the plaza along Madero, which is thick with restaurants, you'll find the cybercafé **Pl@ynet** (cnr Carranza & Madero; per hr $1) after 250m.

Sights

Watch and inhale as the puros are speedily rolled by hand at the **Santa Clara cigar factory** (☎ 947-99-00; ventas@tabasa.com; Blvd 5 de Febrero 10; admission free; ☺ 8am-5pm Mon-Fri, 8am-noon Sat), on the highway a block or so from the bus station. Cigars in assorted shapes and sizes, including the monstrous Magnum, are available for purchase at factory prices, and the 50 torcedores employed here (who together roll out 10,000 puros a day) are happy to demonstrate their technique.

Twelve kilometers from San Andrés, a 242-step staircase leads down to the **Salto de Eyipantla** (admission $0.50), a 50m-high, 40m-wide waterfall. Follow Hwy 180 east for 4km to Sihuapan, then turn right down a dirt road to Eyipantla. Frequent TLT buses ($1) make the trip, leaving from the corner of Cabada and Calle 5 de Mayo, near the market.

The **Laguna Encantada** (Enchanted Lagoon) occupies a small volcanic crater 3km northeast of San Andrés. A dirt road goes there but no buses do; travelers and locals report muggings in the area.

At **Cerro del Gallo** near Matacapan, just east of Sihuapan, is a pyramid in Teotihuacán style, dating from AD 300 to 600. It may have been on the route to Kaminaljuyú in Guatemala, a major Teotihuacán outpost.

Sleeping

San Andrés has some good-value budget and midrange places, though nothing in the luxury bracket. All the following places (except the first) are within a block or two of the zócalo.

Hotel Posada San Martín (☎ 942-10-36; Juárez 304; s & d $28, tw $35; P ✖ ☎) Midway between the bus station and the *zócalo*, this hacienda-style posada is a fabulous deal, with a pool, a peaceful garden, and pretty details like yellow-and-blue sinks in the comfy rooms.

Hotel Isabel (☎ /fax 942-16-17; Madero 13; s/d $19/25, with air-con $27/33; **P** **⊠**) A hospitable good-value place with spacious, very well-kept, if plain, rooms with cable TV; most enjoy plenty of natural light.

Hotel Posada San José (☎ 942-10-10; Domínguez 10; s/d $15/18, with air-con $22/30; **P** **⊠**) Cheap, convenient place with large, though un-remarkable, rooms around a lobby sitting area. It's 200m northeast of the plaza.

Hotel de los Pérez (☎ 942-07-77; www.hoteldelosperez.com; Rascón 2; s/d $26/35; **P** **⊠**) Sparse rooms with comfortable beds and writing desks, though the air-con fittings are ancient. It's just west of the plaza.

Eating

Refugio La Casona (☎ 942-07-35; Madero 18; dishes $2-7; ⊗ 7am-2am) This surprisingly trendy bar-restaurant is housed in a lovely colonial building with a peaceful, leafy rear garden. It serves great breakfasts, a bargain set lunch ($3), and a variety of Mexican dishes. There's also live bohemian music (from 9pm) most nights.

Restaurant & Cafetería del Centro (Rascón; dishes $4-5; ⊗ 7am-midnight) Beneath the Hotel de los Pérez, this restaurant is good for American-style breakfasts, snacks and set meals; they whip up a mean burger.

Restaurant Winni's (☎ 942-01-10; Madero 10; dishes $3-6.50) Cheap, unpretentious place that offers egg dishes, *antojitos*, substantial mains, pizza and cakes of all colors.

Café Toxtlán (Madero 170; ⊗ 8am-2pm & 4-11pm Mon-Sat) Friendly, stylish café that's ideal for a cuppa joe and a *panini*.

Getting There & Away

San Andrés is the transport center for Los Tuxtlas, with fairly good bus services in every direction – 1st-class with ADO and 2nd-class with AU. Rickety but regular TLT buses are often the quickest way of getting to local destinations; they leave from a block north of the market, and skirt the north side of town on Calle 5 de Febrero (Hwy 180). *Colectivo* taxis (about every 15 minutes) to Catemaco and Santiago also leave from the market – they're speedier than the bus but cost a fraction more.

Destination	Price	Duration	Frequency
Acayucan	$5	2¼hr	9 1st-class daily & TLT every 20min
Campeche	$36	12½hr	2 1st-class daily
Catemaco	$0.80	25 min	14 1st-class daily & TLT every 15min
Mérida	$44	15hr	1 1st-class at 9.15pm daily
Mexico City (TAPO)	$31	9hr	8 1st-class daily
Puebla	$22	7hr	4 1st-class daily
Santiago Tuxtla	$0.80	25min	regular 2nd-class daily & TLT every 10min
Veracruz	$7	3hr	12 1st-class daily & TLT every 10min
Villahermosa	$16	6hr	7 1st-class daily
Xalapa	$12.50	5hr	10 1st-class daily

CATEMACO

☎ 294 / pop 25,000 / elevation 340m

This pretty town on the western shore of beautiful Laguna Catemaco makes its living mainly from fishing, and from Mexican families who flood in during July and August and for Christmas, New Year and Semana Santa. Sadly, as one of the state's few real tourist places, hawkers can be a bit of a hassle. The town also has a reputation as a center of sorcery and witchcraft (see boxed text, p710).

Orientation & Information

Catemaco slopes gently down to the lake. A **tourist office** (Map p709; ☎ 943-00-16; Municipalidad; ⊗ 9am-3pm & 6-9pm Mon-Fri) on the north side of the *zócalo* offers limited practical information, but staff can give you a map of the town and the surrounding region. The **post office** (Map p709; Cuauhtémoc s/n) is four blocks west of the central plaza.

Bancomer (Map p709; Boettinger), with an ATM, changes cash but not traveler's checks – try Hotel Los Arcos, which sometimes changes American Express traveler's checks at poor rates. On the west side of the *zócalo*, **@ctual's Internet** (Map p709; Boettinger s/n; per hr $1) has flat-screen monitors and a super-fast connection.

Sights

Ringed by volcanic hills, **Laguna Catemaco** is roughly oval and 16km long. East of town are a few gray-sand beaches where you can swim in murky water.

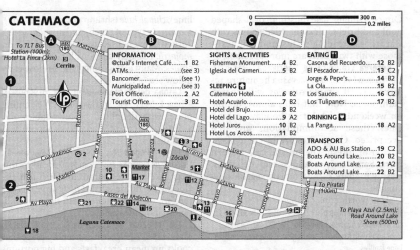

CATEMACO

To TLT Bus Station (100m); Hotel La Finca (2km)

0   300 m
0   0.2 miles

INFORMATION
@ctual's Internet Café.......**1** B2
ATMs..................................(see 3)
Bancomer..........................(see 1)
Municipalidad..................(see 3)
Post Office........................**2** A2
Tourist Office....................**3** B2

SIGHTS & ACTIVITIES
Fisherman Monument........**4** B2
Iglesia del Carmen............**5** B2

SLEEPING
Catemaco Hotel.................**6** B2
Hotel Acuario....................**7** B2
Hotel del Brujo..................**8** B2
Hotel del Lago..................**9** A2
Hotel Juros.......................**10** B2
Hotel Los Arcos................**11** B2

EATING
Casona del Recuerdo.......**12** B2
El Pescador......................**13** C2
Jorge & Pepe's.................**14** B2
La Ola..............................**15** B2
Los Sauces.......................**16** C2
Los Tulipanes...................**17** B2

DRINKING
La Panga..........................**18** A2

TRANSPORT
ADO & AU Bus Station....**19** C2
Boats Around Lake...........**20** B2
Boats Around Lake...........**21** A2
Boats Around Lake...........**22** B2

To Piratas (100m)
To Playa Azul (2.5km); Road Around Lake Shore (500m)

Laguna Catemaco

The lake contains several islands. On the largest, Isla Tenaspi, Olmec sculptures have been discovered. **Isla de los Monos** (Monkey Island; Map p711), also called Isla de los Changos, holds about 60 red-cheeked *Macaca arctoides* monkeys, originally from Thailand. They belong to the University of Veracruz, which acquired them for research. Despite pleas for the animals to be left alone, boat operators bring food so tourists can get close-up photos.

On the northeast shore of the lake, the vaguely New Age **Reserva Ecológica de Nanciyaga** (Map p711; ☎ 943-01-99; www.nanciyaga.com; Hwy Catemaco-Coyame, Km 7; admission $2.75; 9am-2pm & 4-6pm) preserves a small patch of rain forest. A guided walk in Spanish includes the chance to have a spa experience with mineral mud, or the guilty-minded might be tempted by a shamanic-style 'spiritual cleansing.' Replicas of Olmec ruins are scattered around the site. It's all well laid-out but a bit contrived – indeed, *Medicine Man*, a Sean Connery film, was shot here. Call ahead to reserve a **temascal** (sweat lodge; per person $25; 8pm Sat). The reserve can be reached by *pirata* (pickup truck, $0.80) or by boat.

Boats moored along the lakeside offer trips around the islands and across to the ecological reserve at Nanciyaga – a group of six costs $45, or it's $6 per person.

Sleeping

Prices fluctuate according to demand in places above the budget category, so bargain hard for a good deal and beware steep price hikes on high-season weekends, holidays and the March witch-doctor convention.

BUDGET

Hotel Acuario (Map p709; ☎ 943-04-18; cnr Boettinger & Carranza; s/d $19/24; P) A well-kept place with small, plain quarters with fans; some are extremely en suite – the bathroom is smack bang in the middle of the room!

Hotel del Brujo (Map p709; ☎ 943-12-05; Malecón s/n; s/d/tw $19/27/37; P) A secure family-owned place right on the lakeshore with spacious if sparsely furnished rooms, most with air-con and many with magnificent, lake-facing balconies.

MIDRANGE & TOP-END

Hotel Los Arcos (Map p709; ☎ 943-00-03; www.arcos hotel.com.mx; Madero 7; s/d from $38; P) The well-managed Los Arcos has helpful staff, a small swimming pool (and one for kids too) and light, airy, comfortable rooms with hand-painted headboards and access to pleasant plant-filled sitting areas.

Hotel La Finca (Map p711; ☎ 943-03-22, 800-523-46-22; www.lafinca.com.mx; Hwy 180, Km 147; r from $71; P) In leafy gardens 2km west of town, this sleek, modern hotel has attractive rooms, most with large balconies and lake views. There's a pool with slides and a hot tub. It's excellent value, except on Saturday nights and during the peak season when prices rise about 40%.

Catemaco Hotel (Map p709; ☎ 943-02-03; hcatemaco @yahoo.com.mx; Carranza 8; s/d from $31/35; P)

Offers a huge, heat-busting, oval-shaped pool and bright, pleasant, tiled rooms with wardrobes, reading lights and phones – those with twin beds are more spacious.

Reserva Ecológica de Nanciyaga (Map p711; cabañas from $44-55, camp sites $3) The nature reserve has 10 simple *cabañas* with shared bathrooms. Note that rates almost double on weekends and during holiday periods, when these accommodations are well overpriced. Camp sites are in an adjacent stretch of forest. The on-site café is open from 8am to 5pm and serves delicious, freshly prepared – and mostly vegetarian – cuisine.

Also worth considering:

Hotel del Lago (Map p709; ☎ 943-01-60; fax 943-04-31; cnr Av Playa & Abasolo; r from $36; P ⊠ ⊛) A lakefront hotel with functional rooms geared to accommodating large families.

Hotel Playa Azul (Map p711; ☎ 943-00-01; www.playa azulcatemaco.com; r $72, bungalows from $96, trailer sites $11; P ⊠ ⊛) Situated 2.5km east of town by the lake, this hotel adjoins a patch of rain forest and has a huge pool.

Hotel Juros (Map p709; ☎ 943-00-84; Av Playa 14; s/d $27/39, r with air-con $47; P ⊠ ⊛) The rooftop pool is this place's trump card, while the rooms are a bit overpriced – bargain for a better deal.

Eating & Drinking

The lake provides the specialties here: *tegogolo* (a snail reputed to be an aphrodisiac and best eaten in a sauce of chili, tomato, onion and

lime), *chipalchole* (shrimp or crab-claw soup), *mojarra* (a type of perch) and *anguilas* (eels). *Tachogobi* is a hot sauce sometimes served on *mojarra;* eels may come with raisins and hot chilies. Many eating spots tend to close early in low season.

Casona del Recuerdo (Map p709; ☎ 943-08-13; Aldama 4; dishes $4-8; ⊙ 11am-10pm) Welcoming place, with delightful balcony tables and a flirtatious parrot, that serves superb seafood dishes.

Jorge & Pepe's (Map p709; ☎ 943-12-99; Paseo del Malecón s/n; dishes $3-7; ⊙ 9am-9pm) Head to this large lakefront restaurant for fresh fish, including the house-special *filete de pez Jorge's* ($6.50), which is cooked with tomato, chili, onion and pineapple.

Los Tulipanes (Map p709; cnr Av Playa & Mantilla; dishes $2.75-5) Inexpensive, friendly place that cooks up mean breakfasts and big portions of Mexican food and fish.

La Ola (Map p709; ☎ 943-00-10; Paseo del Malecón s/n; dishes $3-8; ⊙ 9am-9pm) Vast waterfront restaurant serving fish, *marsicos* and meat, though few tables actually have a view of the lake.

El Pescador (Map p709; Paseo del Malecón s/n; dishes $3.50-8; ⊙ 11:30am-10:30pm) and **Los Sauces** (Map p709; Paseo del Malecón s/n; dishes $3-8; ⊙ noon-10pm) are two other lakeside spots that are popular for a bite and a beer. Cruise by the *palapa*-roofed **La Panga** (Map p709; Paseo de Malecón s/n; ⊙ 8am-midnight) bar, which juts out into the lake, for cocktails.

THE WITCHING HOUR

On the first Friday in March each year, hundreds of *brujos* (shamans), witches and healers from all over Mexico descend on Catemaco to perform a mass cleansing ceremony on Cerro Mono Blanco (White Monkey Hill), just north of the town. The event is designed to rid them of the previous years' negative energies, presumably accumulated after performing too many dubious dark arts, though the whole occasion has become more commercial than supernatural in recent years. Floods of Mexicans also head into town at this time to grab a shamanic consultation and eat, drink and be merry in a bizarre mix of otherworldly fervor and hedonistic indulgence.

The hours just after the event are regarded as especially auspicious, as it's believed that the *brujos* are at their most powerful just after this mass purification. All manner of practices are offered, from *limpias* (cleansings) and tarot readings to black magic ceremonies of serious intent (and cost). Though the commercial nature of the event is pretty rampant, witchcraft traditions in this part of Veracruz do go back centuries – mixing ancient indigenous beliefs, Spanish medieval traditions and voodoo practices from West Africa. In 2003 a state legislator attempted to ban the convention under the premise that it ran contrary to Roman Catholic doctrines, but the move proved unpopular and was quashed – many Mexicans may consider themselves devout Catholics but like to use the services of a *cuandero* (healer) or shaman. Many of these *brujos* multi-task as medicine men (using both traditional herbs and, often surreptitiously, mixing potions with modern pharmaceuticals), shrinks and black magicians (casting evil spells on enemies of their clients).

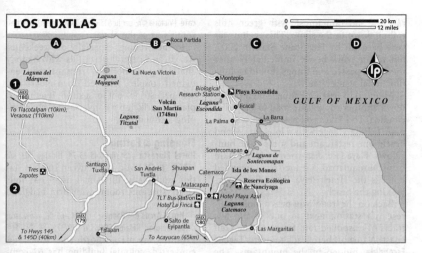

LOS TUXTLAS

0 — 20 km
0 — 12 miles

Laguna del Márquez

MEX 180
To Tlacotalpan (10km);
Veracruz (110km)

Laguna Majagual

La Nueva Victoria

Roca Partida

Montepio

Biological Research Station

Volcán San Martín (1748m) ▲

Laguna Titzatal

Laguna Escondida

Playa Escondida

Jicacal

La Palma

La Barra

GULF OF MEXICO

Tres Zapotes

Santiago Tuxtla

San Andrés Tuxtla

Sihuapan

Matacapan

TLT Bus Station

Hotel La Finca

MEX 179

Talapan

Salto de Eyipantla

To Hwys 145 & 145D (40km)

To Acayucan (65km)

Sontecomapan

Laguna de Sontecomapan

Isla de los Monos

Catemaco

Reserva Ecológica de Nanciyaga

Hotel Playa Azul

Laguna Catemaco

MEX 180

Las Margaritas

Getting There & Away

Long-distance buses serving Catemaco are not that regular at all, so consider traveling via San Andrés Tuxtla (12km to the west on Hwy 180) or Acayucan (80km to the south) instead. ADO and AU buses operate from a delightful little terminal by the lakeside in the east of town. Local 2nd-class buses run from the TLT bus stop, which is 700m west of the plaza by the junction with the highway. *Colectivo* taxis arrive and depart from El Cerrito, a small hill about 400m to the west of the plaza on Carranza.

First-class bus services include the following:

Destination	Price	Duration	Frequency
Acayucan	$3.75	1½hr	4 daily
Córdoba	$13	5hr	5 daily
Mexico City (TAPO)	$30	12hr	8 daily
Puebla	$23	6hr	2 daily
Santiago Tuxtla	$1.75	1hr	10 daily
Veracruz	$7.50	3½hr	12 daily
Xalapa	$13	5½hr	4 daily

To explore the villages and country east of the lake, where the mountain Santa Marta stands out, take a *pirata* (pickup truck) heading towards Las Margaritas (around $2). They leave about every hour or two from a corner five blocks north of the ADO station.

AROUND CATEMACO

About 4km northeast of Catemaco, the road forks. The section to the right follows the east side of the lake past the Reserva Ecológica Nanciyaga to Coyame and Las Margaritas; the road to the left is sealed and scenic as it goes over the hills toward the coast. At **Sontecomapan**, 15km from Catemaco, you can turn right (east) off the main road and go down to the lagoon side, where there are a few restaurants; stroll to the left for 100m to find the idyllic **Pozo de los Enanos** (Well of the Dwarves) swimming hole. Several **ejidos** (communal villages; ☎ 295-661-61-70) near here, including Sontecomapan, form an ecotourism network and can organize trips to local sights, including waterfalls and archaeological sites. They also provide accommodations and meals for travelers; call ahead to make arrangements.

From the *ejidos*, you can rent boats for excursions into the mangroves around Laguna de Sontecomapan. It's 20 minutes by boat to the mouth of the lagoon, where there's a beach near the fishing village of **La Barra**. There, you can stay at the lovely, peaceful **Los Amigos** (☎ 294-943-01-01; www.losamigos.com.mx; cabañas $35; P) where the *cabañas* have spectacular views of the bay, and the owners offer good regional cuisine and rent out snorkels and kayaks. La Barra can also be reached by a side road from La Palma, 8km north of Sontecomapan.

The road is rough after Sontecomapan, but the countryside is lovely – mainly cattle ranches and rain forest, with green hills rolling down to the shore. This region was very hard hit by Hurricane Stan in 2005, but work began immediately after the storm passed and things should be fully functional again by now.

About 5km past La Palma, a sign points down another rough side road to Playa Escondida. This takes you past **Jicacal**, a small, poor fishing village with a long, gray-sand beach, one restaurant and some basic bungalows. **Playa Escondida** itself is about 4km from the main road. A reader-recommended hotel is the Hotel Playa Escondida, overlooking the beach.

Back on the 'road' you pass a biological-research station next to one of the few tracts of unspoiled rain forest on the Gulf coast. A turnoff here leads to pretty **Laguna Escondida**, hidden in the mountains. The end of the road is at **Montepío**, where there's a picturesque beach at the river mouth, with some places to eat and **Posada San José** (☎ 294-942-10-10; s/d \$14/16, with air-con \$22/27; P ☒), a reasonably comfortable place to sleep.

Public transportation to Sontecomapan and beyond is by *piratas*. These leave Catemaco every half hour or so (when they're full) from 6am to 3pm, going from the corner of Revolución and the Playa Azul road (from the northeast corner of the plaza – walk five blocks east and six blocks north, and look for vehicles congregating). The full 39km trip to Montepío, with its numerous stops, takes about two hours and costs \$3.

ACAYUCAN

☎ 924 / pop 47,000

Acayucan is a hot, unremarkable, busy town at the junction of Hwy 180 (between Veracruz and Villahermosa) and Hwy 185 (which goes south across the Isthmus of Tehuantepec to the Pacific coast). There's no reason at all to stay here, but if you do get stuck there are facilities for travelers.

The bus station is on the east side of town. To reach the central plaza, walk uphill through the market to Av Hidalgo, turn left and walk six blocks. The plaza has a modern church on the east side and the town hall on the west. Several banks alongside the plaza have ATMs and also change traveler's checks. There is a generic **Internet**

café (Victoria s/n; per hr \$1; ☯ 8:30am-10pm) on the south side of the plaza.

In the evening, especially on weekends, Acayucan's central plaza fills with happily chattering schoolkids, romantically entwined couples, wizened town elders and solo pedestrians out for a stroll. It's the best place to strike up a conversation while sipping a cool drink.

Sleeping & Eating

Hotel Floresta (☎ /fax 245-13-74; Hidalgo 503; s/d \$17/22; P ☒) Midway between the bus station and plaza, this small hotel has fine, clean, spacious rooms with firm beds and desks.

Hotel Arcos del Parque (☎ 245-65-06; www.arcos delparque.com; Hidalgo 804; s/d \$29/37; P ☒ ☒) Fronting the plaza's north side, this large, converted, colonial building has 62 comfortable rooms and a nice pool. Its two affiliated restaurants have good *antojitos* and meals (\$3 to \$12).

Hotel Kinaku (☎ /fax 245-04-10; Ocampo Sur 7; s/d/ste \$42/49/64; P ☒ ☒) Acayucan's most expensive hotel, which is located in a large modern block, is not brilliant value for money, but the upper-floor rooms do have sweeping views. There's a formal restaurant here, with mains priced between \$5 and \$11.

Los Esteros (☎ 245-15-56; Aleman 2; dishes \$5.50-9.50) Just off Hidalgo, between the bus station and plaza, this smart, friendly, air-conditioned restaurant has satisfying meat dishes including steaks and *costillas a la cantonesa* (\$10).

Los Tucanes Cafetería (snacks \$3-6; ☯ 24hr) On the north end of the pedestrian alley a block west of the plaza, this popular cafeteria has good-value meals.

Getting There & Away

Most 1st-class buses (ADO and OCC) are *de paso*, but the computerized reservation systems indicate if seats are available. UNO and ADO GL run a few deluxe services, while AU and Sur provide quite good 2nd-class service. All these companies operate from the same terminal on the lower side of the market. TLT provides very rough, slightly cheaper services to the Tuxtlas from the edge of the market. Travel times given below are by direct buses where available.

Destination	Price	Duration	Frequency
Catemaco	$3.75	1½hr	3 1st-class daily & frequent 2nd-class
Mexico City (TAPO)	$33	7hr	7 1st-class daily
Santiago Tuxtla	$3.25	2¼hr	hourly 2nd-class
Tuxtla Gutiérrez	$19	8hr	7 1st-class daily
Veracruz	$14	3½hr	14 1st-class daily
Villahermosa	$11.50	3½hr	13 1st-class daily

Buses also run to Santiago Tuxtla, Tapachula and Juchitán. The toll highway, 145D, passes south of town. Heading east, it's signposted to Minatitlán; heading west, toward Córdoba or Veracruz, it's marked to 'Isla' (referring to the inland town of Isla, not to any island). The tolls are expensive, costing more than $30 to get to Córdoba.

Local buses run between the terminal and city center ($0.50); a taxi costs $1.50.

SAN LORENZO

Near the small town of Tenochtitlán, 35km southeast of Acayucan, San Lorenzo was the first of the two great Olmec ceremonial centers. It had its heyday from about 1200 to 900 BC.

Ten Olmec heads, stone thrones and numerous smaller artifacts have been found here, but most of the finds are in museums elsewhere. Black obsidian tools were imported from Guatemala or the Mexican highlands, and basalt rock for the heads was brought in from the Tuxtlas. Such wide contacts, and the organization involved in building the site, demonstrate how powerful the rulers of San Lorenzo were.

The main structure was a platform about 50m high, 1.25km long and 700m wide, but now the San Lorenzo site is nothing more than a low hill. The **'museum'** (admission free; ☻ 8am-5pm) here is just two disappointingly tiny rooms of stone artifacts and a single large head.

Another site, **El Azazul**, about 7km further south, has some remarkably well-carved, kneeling stone figures said to be over 1000 years old. Locals here will show you around for a few pesos.

Unless you're totally into archaeology it's not worth visiting these sites by public transportation. From Acayucan take a bus to Texistepec (south of the Minatitlán road), then another bus to Tenochtitlán, followed by a local bus or taxi to the *zona arqueológica* south of town. The entire trip costs about $7 and takes about three centuries – OK, 2½ hours, but who's counting by now?

The Azazul site is virtually inaccessible by public transportation, but a taxi driver might consent to take you for about $2.50. If you're driving, head 7km past the San Lorenzo museum and look for a road branching left and a hut on the right. Exploring these sites is much less traumatic with your own wheels.

Oaxaca State

Rugged, southern Oaxaca (wah-*hah*-kah) is a world away from central Mexico. Separated by a barrier of sparsely populated mountains, it has always pursued its own destiny – though the insulating effect of the mountains has recently been reduced by the spectacular Hwy 135D.

Oaxaca enjoys a slower, sunnier existence than that of its northern neighbors and has a magical quality influenced by its dry, rocky landscape, bright southern light and large indigenous population. The last is the driving force behind the state's fine handicrafts and booming art scene, and the main inspiration for Oaxaca's amazing output of creative cuisine.

Oaxaca city lies at the junction of the three Valles Centrales, with their village markets and ruins of pre-Hispanic towns, such as Monte Albán, Mitla and Yagul. Mexico's newest tourist resort is still growing on Oaxaca's magnificent Bahías de Huatulco coast, but travelers enjoy a more relaxed scene at older spots like Puerto Escondido, Puerto Ángel and Zipolite.

The dramatic backcountry of the region is increasingly accessible thanks to an exciting new wave of active-tourism ventures based in Oaxaca city.

The western two-thirds of the state are rugged and mountainous, while the eastern third lies on the hot, low-lying Istmo de Tehuantepec. Oaxaca also has a thin plain along the Pacific coast and a low-lying north-central region bordering Veracruz state. This combination of temperate and tropical zones and several mountain ranges gives Oaxaca spectacularly varied landscapes, and a greater biodiversity than any other Mexican state.

TOP FIVE

- Feasting your eyes and your stomach on the incomparable artistic and culinary delights of colonial **Oaxaca city** (p717)

- Exploring the superb hilltop ruins and tombs of **Monte Albán** (p739), the ancient Zapotec capital

- Hiking through the cool highland forests of the **Sierra Norte** (p746)

- Watching world-class surfers get tubular in mellow **Puerto Escondido** (p754)

- Chilling on the beach down at **San Agustinillo** (p773) and other great tropical sands nearby

- OAXACA CITY JANUARY DAILY HIGH: 25°C | 77°F
- OAXACA CITY JULY DAILY HIGH: 28°C | 82°F

OAXACA STATE

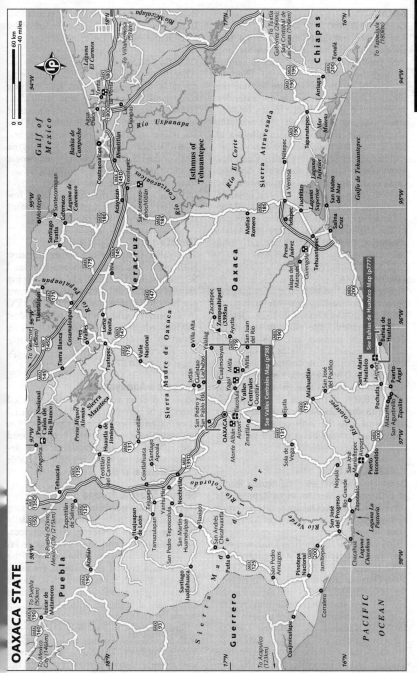

See Valles Centrales Map (p738)

See Bahías de Huatulco Map (p777)

History

ZAPOTECS & MIXTECS

The Valles Centrales (Central Valleys) have always been the hub of Oaxacan life, and their pre-Hispanic cultures reached heights rivaling those of central Mexico. The hilltop city of Monte Albán here became the center of the Zapotec culture, and extended its control over much of Oaxaca by conquest, peaking between AD 300 and 700. Monte Albán declined suddenly; by about 750 it was deserted, as were many other Zapotec settlements in the Valles Centrales. From about 1200, the surviving Zapotecs came under the growing dominance of the Mixtecs from Oaxaca's northwest uplands, renowned potters and metalsmiths. Mixtec and Zapotec cultures became entangled in the Valles Centrales before the Aztecs conquered them in the 15th and early 16th centuries.

COLONIAL ERA

The Spaniards had to send at least four expeditions before they felt safe enough to found the city of Oaxaca in 1529. Hernán Cortés donated large parts of the Valles Centrales to himself and was officially named Marqués del Valle de Oaxaca. The indigenous population dropped in number disastrously. The population of the Mixteca region in the west is thought to have fallen from 700,000 at the time of the Spanish arrival to about 25,000 by 1700. Rebellions continued into the 20th century, but the indigenous peoples never united to form a serious threat.

JUÁREZ & DÍAZ

Benito Juárez, the great reforming leader of 19th-century Mexico, was a Zapotec. He served two terms as Oaxaca's state governor before being elected president of Mexico in 1861 (see p753).

Juárez appointed Porfirio Díaz, son of a Oaxaca horse trainer, as state governor in 1862. Juárez died in 1872, and from 1877 to 1910 Díaz controlled Mexico with an iron fist, bringing the country into the industrial age but also fostering corruption, repression and, eventually, the revolution in 1910. In Valle Nacional in northern Oaxaca, tobacco planters set up virtual slave plantations – most of the 15,000 plantation workers had to be replaced annually after dying from disease, beatings or starvation. Indigenous lands were commandeered by foreign and mestizo coffee planters.

OAXACA TODAY

After the revolution, about 300 *ejidos* (communal landholdings) were set up, returning some land to the people who worked it. However, land ownership remains a source of conflict today. With little industry, Oaxaca is one of Mexico's poorest states, and many Oaxacans leave home to work in the cities or the US. The situation is made worse in some areas, notably the Mixteca, by deforestation and erosion. Tourism thrives in Oaxaca city, nearby villages and a few places on the coast, but underdevelopment still prevails in the backcountry.

Climate

The Valles Centrales are warm and dry, with most rain falling between June and September. On the coast and in low-lying areas it's hotter and a bit wetter. The average high in Oaxaca city ranges from 25°C in December and January (the coldest months, when lows average about 8°) to about 30° in March through May, the hottest months. The rest of the year, average highs are about 27°.

Dangers & Annoyances

Buses and other vehicles traveling isolated stretches of highway, including the coastal Hwy 200 and Hwy 175 from Oaxaca city to Pochutla, have occasionally been stopped and robbed. Though incidents have decreased in recent years, it's still advisable not to travel at night.

Getting There & Around

Oaxaca city has good bus links with Mexico City and Puebla to the north, and a few daily services to/from Veracruz, Villahermosa, Tuxtla Gutiérrez and San Cristóbal de las Casas. Services between the city and the state's main coastal destinations are fairly frequent, though mostly 2nd class. Plenty of buses (again, mostly 2nd class) also travel along coastal Hwy 200 into Oaxaca from Acapulco and Chiapas.

Several daily flights link Oaxaca city with Mexico City. Further flights go east to Tuxtla Gutiérrez, Tapachula, Villahermosa and beyond. Small planes hop over the mountains between Oaxaca city and the coastal resorts Puerto Escondido and Bahías de Huatulco, which you can also reach direct from Mexico City.

OAXACA CITY

☎ 951 / pop 263,000 / elevation 1550m

The state's capital and only large city has a colonial heart of narrow, straight streets, liberally sprinkled with fine, old stone buildings. Oaxaca is relaxed but stimulating; remote but cosmopolitan. Its dry mountain heat, manageable scale, old buildings, broad shady plazas and leisurely cafés help slow the pace of life. At the same time, diverse Oaxacan, Mexican and international influences create a spark of excitement. The city has some first-class museums and galleries, arguably the best handicrafts shopping in Mexico, and vivacious cultural, restaurant, bar and music scenes. It's a capital of the modern Mexican art world and an increasingly popular location for Spanish-language courses or for simply hanging out.

Head first for the *zócalo* (main plaza) and taste the atmosphere. Then ramble and see what markets, crafts, galleries, cafés, bars and festivities you run across. Allow time, if you can, for more than one trip out to the many fascinating places in the Valles Centrales and outlying mountain areas. Oaxaca is a jumping-off point for great hiking, biking, bird-watching, climbing and other activities.

HISTORY

The Aztec settlement here was called Huax-yácac (meaning 'In the Nose of the Squash'), from which the word 'Oaxaca' is derived. The Spanish laid out a new town around the existing *zócalo* in 1529. It quickly became the most important place in southern Mexico.

In the eighteenth-century, Oaxaca city grew rich from exports of cochineal (a red dye made from tiny insects living on the prickly-pear cactus) and from the weaving of textiles. By 1796 it was probably the third-biggest city in Nueva España, with about 20,000 people (including 600 clergy) and 800 cotton looms.

In 1854 an earthquake destroyed much of Oaxaca city. It was decades later, under the presidency of Porfirio Díaz, before Oaxaca began to grow again; in the 1890s its population exceeded 30,000. Then in 1931 another earthquake left 70% of the city uninhabitable.

Oaxaca's major expansion has come in the past 25 years, with tourism, new industries and rural poverty all encouraging migration from the countryside. The population of the city proper has almost doubled in this time, and together with formerly separate villages and towns it now forms a conurbation of perhaps 450,000 people.

ORIENTATION

Oaxaca centers on the *zócalo* and the adjoining Alameda de León plaza in front of the cathedral. Calle Alcalá, running north from the cathedral to the Iglesia de Santo Domingo (a universally known landmark), is open for pedestrians only for three blocks.

The road from Mexico City and Puebla traverses the northern part of Oaxaca as Calz Niños Héroes de Chapultepec. The 1st-class bus station is situated on this road, 1.75km northeast of the *zócalo*. The 2nd-class bus station is almost 1km west of the center, near the main market, the Central de Abastos. Oaxaca airport is 6km south of the city, 500m off Hwy 175. See p737 for details on getting to/from the city center.

The blocks north of the *zócalo* are smarter, cleaner and less traffic-infested than those to the south. The commercial area occupies the blocks southwest of the *zócalo*.

Maps

Inegi (☎ 512-48-00; cnr Zapata & Escuela Naval Militar, Colonia Reforma; ⊕ 8:30am-8:30pm Mon-Fri), on a northern extension of Netzahualcóyotl, sells a great range of topographical maps covering Oaxaca; you can also consult maps and census statistics for free.

INFORMATION
Bookstores

Amate (Map pp720-1; ☎ 516-69-60; www.amatebooks; Plaza Alcalá, Alcalá 307-2; ⊕ 10:30am-2:30pm & 3:30-7:30pm Mon-Sat) Probably the best English-language bookstore in all Mexico, stocking almost every Mexico-related title (in print) in English.
Librería Universitaria (LU; Map pp720-1; ☎ 516-42-43; Guerrero 108; ⊕ 9:30am-2pm & 4:30-8pm Mon-Sat) Located just off the *zócalo*, long-standing LU sells some English-language books about Oaxaca and Mexico, as well as maps and secondhand paperbacks.

OAXACA STATE

OAXACA CITY

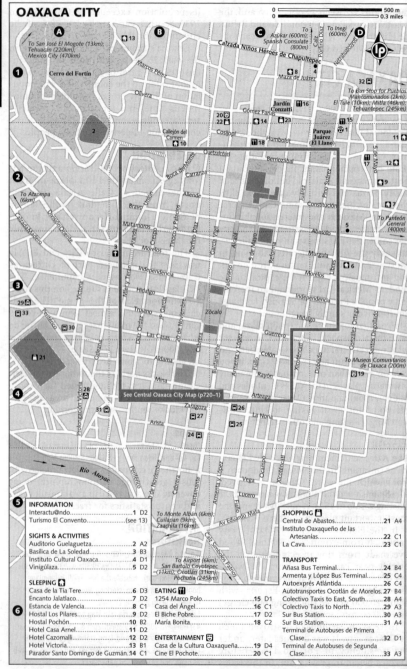

Proveedora Escolar (Map pp720-1; ☎ 516-04-89; Independencia 1001; ☺ 9am-8pm Mon-Sat) Has a great upstairs section devoted to history, literature, archaeology and anthropology. Titles are mostly in Spanish.

Emergency
Ambulance, Fire & Police (☎ 066)
Ceprotur (Centro de Protección al Turista; Map pp720-1; ☎ 514-21-55; Murguía 206; ☺ 8am-9pm) Ceprotur exists to help tourists with any legal problems, complaints, lost documents and the like. Though located in the state tourist office at the time of research, they had plans to move.

Internet Access
They're everywhere!
C@fe Internet (Map pp720-1; Valdivieso 120; per hr $1; ☺ 8am-11pm) One block from the *zócalo*.
dspot (Map pp720-1; García Vigil 512D; per hr wireless/wired $0.60/0.90; ☺ 9am-10pm) Behind La Biznaga restaurant; excellent connections.
Fray-Net (Map pp720-1; Murguía 309A; per hr $0.50; ☺ 9am-8:30pm Mon-Sat)
Inter@ctive Internet (Map pp720-1; Alcalá 503; per hr $0.60; ☺ 8:30am-10pm) Good connections.

Laundry
Same-day wash-and-dry service is available at several laundries. All charge $4.50 to $5 for a 3.5kg (7.7lb) load; most will charge fractions for smaller loads. Many hotels offer laundry service as well.
Lava-Max (Map pp720-1; ☎ 545-87-46; cnr Bravo & Tinoco y Palacios; ☺ 8am-8:30pm Mon-Sat) Has a few self-service machines as well as the full-service option.
Lavandería Antequera (Map pp720-1; ☎ 516-56-94; Murguía 408; ☺ 9am-8pm Mon-Fri, 9am-6pm Sat) Also does dry cleaning, and offers free delivery to hotels in the area.

Libraries
Biblioteca Circulante de Oaxaca (Oaxaca Lending Library; Map pp720-1; ☎ 518-70-77; Pino Suárez 519; ☺ 10am-2pm & 4-7pm Mon-Fri, 10am-1pm Sat) Sizable collection of books and magazines on Oaxaca and Mexico in English and Spanish; two-month visitor membership ($20 plus $29 deposit) allows you to borrow books. Also offers wireless Internet access.
Instituto de Artes Gráficas de Oaxaca (Map pp720-1; ☎ 516-69-80; Alcalá 507; ☺ 9:30am-8pm) The excellent library here covers art, architecture, literature, botany, ecology and history. For more on the institute itself, see p724.

Media
Go-Oaxaca (www.go-oaxaca.com) Free bilingual English and Spanish) paper that is published monthly.

Available at various places around town. It contains a lot of interesting articles, useful practical information for tourists, as well as details about cultural events and small advertisements.
Notice boards (Map pp720-1; Plaza Gonzalo Lucero, Calle 5 de Mayo 412) Check these for ads for rental apartments, classes in everything from Spanish to yoga, and other interesting stuff. You'll also find useful notice boards in the language schools.
Oaxaca Times (www.oaxacatimes.com) Available at various places around town. Similar to *Go-Oaxaca* but in English only.

Medical Services
Clínica Hospital Carmen (Map pp720-1; ☎ 516-26-12; Abasolo 215; ☺ 24hr) One of the town's best private hospitals, with emergency facilities and English-speaking doctors.

Money
There are plenty of ATMs around the center, and several *casas de cambio* (exchange houses) and banks will change US-dollar cash and traveler's checks.
Banamex (Map pp720-1; ☎ 514-57-47; Valdivieso 116; ☺ 11am-6pm Mon-Fri)
Consultoria Internacional (Map pp720-1; ☎ 514-91-92; Armenta y López 203C; ☺ 8:30am-7pm Mon-Fri, 9am-2pm Sat) Changes cash euros, yen, pounds sterling, Canadian dollars and Swiss francs.
HSBC (Map pp720-1; ☎ 516-19-67; cnr Armenta y López & Guerrero; ☺ 8am-7pm Mon-Sat)

Post
Main post office (Map pp720-1; Alameda de León; ☺ 8am-7pm Mon-Fri, 9am-1pm Sat)

Telephone & Fax
Telmex card phones are available around the *zócalo* and elsewhere. Many call offices are scattered around town.
ATSI (Map pp720-1; Calle 20 de Noviembre 402) Cheaper than pay phones for national long-distance calls and calls to Europe; offers fax service as well.
dspot (Map pp720-1; García Vigil 512D; ☺ 9am-10pm) Behind La Biznaga restaurant; offers probably the cheapest foreign calls in town, via the Internet.
Interactu@ndo (Map p718; Pino Suárez 804) Calls cost around $0.40 per minute to the US, and $0.80 to the rest of world.

Toilets
Clean facilities (Map pp720-1) under the bandstand in the middle of the *zócalo* cost $0.20.

CENTRAL OAXACA CITY

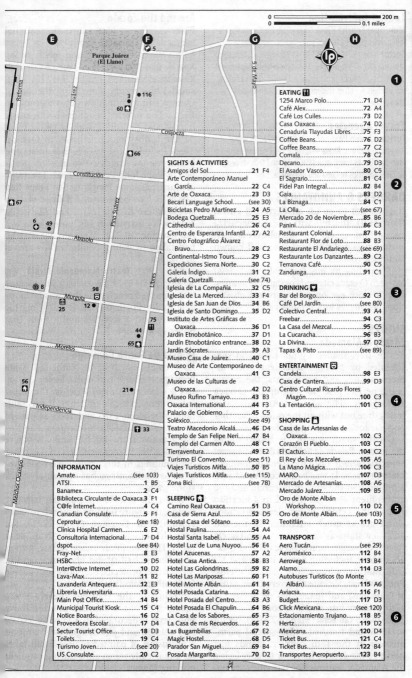

Tourist Information

Municipal Tourist Kiosk (Map p718; cnr García Vigil & Independencia; ☺ 10am-7pm)

Sectur (Map pp720-1; ☎ 576-48-28; www.aoaxaca.com; Murguía 206; ☺ 8am-8pm) This state tourism department usually has someone in attendance who can speak English, but workers are often student volunteers with limited knowledge.

Travel Agencies

Turismo Joven (Map pp720-1; ☎ 514-22-20; www .turismojoven.com; Alcalá 407, Local 19; ☺ 9am-7pm Mon-Sat) Books tours, issues ISIC cards and sells student air fares and trips to Cuba and elsewhere.

DANGERS & ANNOYANCES

It's best not to go up on Cerro del Fortín (Fort Hill), the hill with the Guelaguetza auditorium, except for special events such as the Guelaguetza festival. It's a well-known haunt for robbers.

If traveling by bus (especially 2nd-class) between Oaxaca city and coastal destinations, keep a close eye on your personal possessions, as thieves lurk on buses and beaches.

SIGHTS
Zócalo & Alameda

Traffic-free, shaded by tall trees and surrounded by *portales* (arcades) with numerous cafés and restaurants, the *zócalo* is the perfect place to soak up the Oaxaca atmosphere. The adjacent Alameda, also traffic-free but without the cafés, is another popular local gathering place.

On the south side of the *zócalo* stands the former **Palacio de Gobierno** (State Government Palace; Map pp720-1), once the scene of frequent mass protests. It was being converted into a museum at the time of research, and the government seat had moved to a location east of the center, where demonstrations won't get as much attention. In the old *palacio* a stairway mural by Arturo García Bustos depicts famous Oaxacans and Oaxaca history, including Benito Juárez and his wife, Margarita Maza, José María Morelos, Porfirio Díaz, Vicente Guerrero (being shot at Cuilapan) and Juana Inés de la Cruz, a 17th-century nun and love poet.

Oaxaca's **cathedral** (Map pp720-1), begun in 1553 and finished (after several earthquakes) in the 18th century, stands just north of the *zócalo*. Its main facade, facing the Alameda, features fine baroque carving.

Around the Zócalo

Fine, carved facades adorn the colonial **Iglesia de La Compañía** (Map pp720-1; cnr Trujano & Flores Magón; admission free) and **Iglesia de San Juan de Dios** (Map pp720-1; cnr Aldama & Calle 20 de Noviembre; admission free). The latter is a beautiful small 17th-century church, on the site of Oaxaca's first church (which was built in 1526). The interior is adorned with many murals and paintings, with large canvases on the history of Christianity in Oaxaca. These include the story of Juan Bautista and Jacinto de los Ángeles, two martyrs beatified by Pope John Paul II in 2002. The 18th-century baroque **Templo de San Felipe Neri** (Map pp720-1; cnr Independencia & JP García; admission free) is where Benito Juárez and Margarita Maza were married in 1843; Margarita was the daughter of Don Antonio Maza, who had taken in young Benito on his arrival in Oaxaca.

The 1903 **Teatro Macedonio Alcalá** (Map pp720-1; ☎ 514-69-89; Independencia 900; admission free) is in the French style that was fashionable under Porfirio Díaz. It has a marble stairway and a five-tier auditorium that holds 1300 people.

Iglesia de Santo Domingo

Four blocks north of the cathedral, **Santo Domingo** (Map pp720-1; cnr Alcalá & Gurrión; ☺ 7am-1pm & 4-8pm except during Mass) is the most splendid of Oaxaca's churches. It was built mainly between 1570 and 1608 as part of the city's Dominican monastery. The finest artisans from Puebla and elsewhere helped with its construction. Like other big buildings in this earthquake-prone region, Santo Domingo has immensely thick stone walls.

Amid the fine carving on the baroque facade, the figure holding a church is Santo Domingo de Guzmán (1172–1221), the Spanish monk who founded the Dominican order. The Dominicans observed strict vows of poverty, chastity and obedience, and in Mexico they protected the indigenous people from other colonists' excesses.

Excluding the transept, nearly every square inch of the church's interior above floor level is decorated in 3-D relief: elaborate colored and gilt designs swirl around a profusion of painted figures. It all takes on a magically warm glow during candlelit evening Masses.

Museo de las Culturas de Oaxaca

The beautiful monastery buildings adjoining the Iglesia de Santo Domingo house the don't-miss **Museo de las Culturas de Oaxaca** (Museum of Oaxacan Cultures; Map pp720-1; ☎ 516-29-91; cnr Alcalá & Gurrión; admission $3.75, over 60yr & under 13yr free; ☧ 10am-7pm Tue-Sun), which takes you right through the history and cultures of Oaxaca state up to the present day. Explanatory material is in Spanish, but you can rent good audio guides in English for $5 ($4 for Spanish).

A gorgeous stone cloister serves as an antechamber to the museum proper. The museum emphasizes the direct lineage between Oaxaca's pre-Hispanic and contemporary indigenous cultures, illustrating continuity in such areas as crafts, medicine, food, drink and music. Exhibits feature plenty of archaeological relics, colonial art, furniture, machinery and household items from every era of the state's existence.

The greatest highlight is the Mixtec treasure from Tumba 7 at Monte Albán. This treasure dates from the 14th century, when Mixtecs reused an old Zapotec tomb to bury one of their kings and his sacrificed servants. With the bodies they placed a hoard of beautifully worked silver, turquoise, coral, jade, amber, jet, pearls, finely carved bone, crystal goblets, a skull covered in turquoise, and gold (a lot of gold). The treasure was discovered in 1932 by Alfonso Caso.

Museo Rufino Tamayo

This excellent **pre-Hispanic art museum** (Map pp720-1; ☎ 516-47-50; Morelos 503; admission $3; ☧ 10am-2pm & 4-7pm Mon-Sat, 10am-3pm Sun) was donated to Oaxaca by its most famous artist, the Zapotec Rufino Tamayo (1899–1991). The collection, housed in a fine 17th-century building, focuses on the aesthetic qualities of pre-Hispanic artifacts and traces artistic developments in preconquest times. It has some beautiful pieces and is strong on the Preclassic era and on lesser-known civilizations such as those of Veracruz and western Mexico.

Museo de Arte Contemporáneo de Oaxaca

Occupying a handsome colonial house that was built around 1700, the **Museo de Arte Contemporáneo de Oaxaca** (MACO; ☎ 514-22-28; Alcalá 202; admission $1; ☧ 10:30am-8pm Wed-Mon) exhibits contemporary art from Oaxaca, Mexico and around the world. Sometimes works by leading Oaxacan artists such as Rufino Tamayo, Francisco Toledo or Rodolfo Morales are on show.

OAXACAN ART: THE NEW WAVE Neil Pyatt

Following the death of Rufino Tamayo in 1991, the chain of command in Oaxacan art was again upset in 2000 with the sad death of Rodolfo Morales from Ocotlán, a tireless portrayer of Oaxacan life and feeling. You can recognize most Morales paintings by their trademark childlike angel figures. The Oaxacan maestros who remain are Francisco Toledo, Luis Zárate and Sergio Hernández, who share a certain stereotypical imagery that is now being rejected by the most innovative of young Oaxacan painters who strive for new styles and new directions.

Advanced commercially as well as artistically, young Oaxacans such as Demián Flores, Guillermo Olguín, Soid Pastrana and Luis Enrique Hampshire have spent lengthy periods of study abroad, which has helped to create international markets for their work. Their styles combine modern thought with ancient forms of illustration, and they differ as much from each other as from their supposedly higher-ranking predecessors.

Opening nights, preview showings, seminars and workshops occur regularly in Oaxaca and are well publicized. They provide the best way to keep up with the local, national and even international art scenes. The Oaxacan nightlife and artistic communities are inextricably intertwined due to the size of the city and its self-styled role as a spiritual home to the strong hedonistic side of the Mexican personality. This relationship continues to inspire the exceptionally creative resident population. In practical terms, this means most bar-owners offer flyer and poster space to such events and will probably count at least one resident artist, writer or other knowledgeable party among their staff or regular clientele.

Neil Pyatt is a Oaxaca-based freelance writer who puts a psychology and anthropology background to use dissecting Mexican culture, in both English and Spanish, for a number of publications.

Basílica de la Soledad

The image of Oaxaca's patron saint – the Virgen de la Soledad (Virgin of Solitude) – resides in the 17th-century **Basílica de la Soledad** (Map p718; Independencia), 3½ blocks west of the Alameda. The church, with a richly carved baroque facade, stands where the image is said to have miraculously appeared in a donkey's pack in 1543. The virgin was later adorned with enormous worldly riches – but lost her 2kg gold crown, a huge pearl and several hundred diamonds to thieves in the 1990s. The shady plaza **Jardín Sócrates** (Map pp720-1), east of the basilica, is full of *neverías* (sorbet stands) and makes a pleasant place in which to relax and observe Oaxacan life.

Galleries

At the forefront of contemporary Mexican art, Oaxaca attracts artists, art dealers and art buyers from far and wide. Some of the best Mexican art and photography is on show in the city's burgeoning number of commercial galleries (admission to all of them is free), and the **Museo de Arte Contemporáneo de Oaxaca** (see p723) is another place where you'll often see first-rate contemporary art.

Arte Contemporáneo Manuel García (Map pp720-1; ☎ 514-10-93; www.galeriamanuelgarcia.com; Portal Juárez 110; ⏲ 11am-2pm & 4:30-8pm Mon-Sat) Delightfully avant-garde stuff, beautifully rendered in various mediums by Mexican and international artists.

Arte de Oaxaca (Map pp720-1; ☎ 514-15-32; www.artedeoaxaca.com in Spanish; Murguía 105; ⏲ 11am-3pm & 5-8pm Mon-Sat) Part of the Fundación Cultural Rodolfo Morales (see p748), this sophisticated gallery provides a beautiful setting in which to enjoy art. It includes a room devoted to Morales' work.

Bodega Quetzalli (Map pp720-1; ☎ 514-62-68; Murguía 400; ⏲ 10am-2pm & 5-8pm Mon-Sat) Sister space to Galería Quetzalli, leaning slightly more to the avant-garde. The very large, open space features roughly one artist per month.

Centro Fotográfico Álvarez Bravo (Map pp720-1; cnr Bravo & García Vigil) Good photo-exhibition center and a library of photography books in a space that was very nicely rehabilitated in 2005.

Galería Índigo (Map pp720-1; ☎ 514-38-89; Allende 104; ⏲ 11am-3pm & 4:30-8:30pm Mon-Sat) Classy gallery with eclectic stock of painting, weaving and sculpture, from traditional to contemporary.

Galería Quetzalli (Map pp720-1; ☎ 514-00-30; Constitución 104; ⏲ 10am-2pm & 5-8pm Mon-Sat) Oaxaca's leading serious gallery, free of 'folklorism.' It handles the biggest names in Oaxacan art including Francisco Toledo and Sergio Hernández.

La Mano Mágica (Map pp720-1; ☎ 516-42-75; www.lamanomagica.com; Alcalá 203; ⏲ 10:30am-3pm & 4-8pm Mon-Sat) Chiefly a classy crafts store, 'The Magic Hand' also has some art, including prints by the likes of Tamayo and Toledo. See also p735.

Calle Alcalá

Pedestrian-only for three blocks, and with many of its colonial-era stone buildings cleaned up and restored, **Calle Alcalá** (Map pp720-1) makes a good route from the city center north to Iglesia de Santo Domingo.

Jardín Etnobotánico

In former monastic grounds behind the Iglesia de Santo Domingo, the **Jardín Etnobotánico** (Ethnobotanical Garden; Map pp720-1; ☎ 516-79-15; cnr Constitución & Reforma; admission free) features plants from around the state, including a staggering variety of cacti. Though it has only been growing since the mid-1990s, it's already a fascinating demonstration of Oaxaca's biodiversity. Visits are by guided tour only (tours in English at 11am Saturday, and in Spanish between 10am and 5pm Tuesday to Saturday). At the time of research, group sizes were limited, with participants required to sign up a few days beforehand.

Instituto de Artes Gráficas de Oaxaca

Almost opposite Santo Domingo, in a beautiful colonial house donated by artist Francisco Toledo, the **Instituto de Artes Gráficas de Oaxaca** (Oaxaca Graphic Arts Institute, IAGO; Map pp720-1; ☎ 516-69-80; Alcalá 507; admission free; ⏲ 9:30am-8pm) offers changing exhibitions of graphic art as well as a superb arts library.

Museo Casa de Juárez

The house where Benito Juárez found work as a boy with bookbinder Antonio Salanueva is now the interesting little **Museo Casa de Juárez** (Juárez House Museum; Map pp720-1; ☎ 516-18-60; García Vigil 609; admission $2.75; ⏲ 10am-7pm Tue-Sun), showing how simply the middle-class of early-19th-century Oaxaca lived. The binding workshop is preserved, along with pictures and other memorabilia of Juárez.

ACTIVITIES

Several well-established outfits with an ecological and/or community ethic will send you hiking or biking in the mountains or valleys; spotting rare birds; or lending a hand to help the city's impoverished street children. For bird-watching, **Turismo de Aventura Teotitlán** in Teotitlán del Valle (see p742) is also recommended.

Bicicletas Pedro Martínez (Map pp720-1; ☎ /fax 514-59-35; www.bicicletaspedromartinez.com; Aldama 418; ☼ 9am-7pm Mon-Sat), run by an amiable mountain-biking champion, offers a variety of rides, including four-hour jaunts to the northern fringe of the city ($43) and two-day, all-inclusive bike-and-hike trips in the Santiago Apoala area (see p751) for $188. Pedro also takes four-day Oaxaca–Puerto Escondido expeditions for around $425. Most trips have a two-person minimum and on several rides there are discounts for five or more people. Keen bikers of all levels enjoy Pedro's trips. He rents out bikes, too (see p737).

Centro de Esperanza Infantil (Oaxaca Street Children; Map pp720-1; ☎ 501-10-69; www.oaxacastreetchildren .org; Crespo 308; ☼ 9am-7pm Mon-Fri, 10am-3pm Sat) is a center for street children. It sponsors and cares for kids who are homeless or who have to support their deeply impoverished families by shining shoes or selling chewing gum. Many are from the Triqui ethnic group and have fled political violence in western Oaxaca. The center has a dining room, a library, computers, classrooms and a kindergarten. The staff does a great job and welcomes donations, sponsors, and volunteers to help with meals, the on-site medical center and activities such as art, English and computer classes.

Expediciones Sierra Norte (Map pp720-1; ☎ 514-82-71; www.sierranorte.org.mx in Spanish; Bravo 210; ☼ 9am-3pm & 4-7pm Mon-Fri, 9am-2pm Sat) is a very well-run rural community organization that offers walking, mountain biking and accommodations in the beautiful Sierra Norte, northeast of the city.

Tierraventura (Map pp720-1; ☎ 501-13-63; www .tierraventura.com; Abasolo 217; ☼ 10am-3pm Mon-Sat), run by a multilingual Swiss and German couple, is friendly and very well organized. It takes groups of up to six people on trips in the Valles Centrales, Sierra Norte, Mixteca, Pacific coast and elsewhere in Oaxaca state. Some fairly remote destinations are included, and there's a focus on hiking, nature, crafts, meeting locals, and traditional medicine, wherever possible working with local-community tourism projects. On most

trips prices range between $57 and $89 per person per day.

Zona Bici (Map pp720-1; ☎ 516-09-53; García Vigil 406, int 1; ☼ 10:30am-8:30pm Mon-Sat) takes easy to moderate four-hour mountain-biking trips in the Valles Centrales for around $33 per person (minimum two people). The Italian owner will set a more strenuous pace if you want. He rents out bikes, too (see p737).

COURSES
Language

Oaxaca has several popular and well-established language schools, and new ones are popping up all the time. All schools offer group instruction at a variety of levels from Monday to Friday, and most emphasize the spoken language. Most can also provide individual classes and a range of special subjects and packages. Textbooks and other materials are an additional cost at some schools: ask about this before signing up.

Many schools also offer extra activities such as dance, weaving or cooking classes, movies, tours and *intercambios* (meetings with local people for Spanish and English conversation). They can also arrange accommodations for you in hotels, in self-catered places or with families. For family accommodation, where you will normally have your own room, the costs vary; some families charge $15 a day with breakfast, $18 for two meals or $20 for three.

Amigos del Sol (Map pp720-1; ☎ 514-34-84; www .oaxacanews.com/amigosdelsol.htm; Libres 109; 15hr per week $90) This is a small school, popular with travelers. It has a maximum class size of five people. Start any Monday through Friday (go to the school at 8:45am). There's no minimum duration and no charge for registration or textbooks.

Becari Language School (Map pp720-1; ☎ 514-60-76; www.becari.com.mx; Bravo 210; 15/20/30hr per week $105/140/210) A medium-sized school with maximum class size of five people. Start any Monday morning. There's a $70 registration fee.

Instituto Cultural Oaxaca (Map p718; ☎ 515-34-04; www.instculturaloax.com.mx; Juárez 909; per 4-week total-immersion course $450) The Instituto Cultural's popular seven-hour-a-day program includes *intercambios* and workshops in arts, crafts and culture; many classes are held in the school's spacious gardens and terraces. It's possible to enrol for less than the full four weeks. There's a $50 registration fee.

Oaxaca International (OI; Map pp720-1; ☎ 514-72-24; www.oaxacainternational.com; Libres 207; 15/20/30hr per week $80/113/175) Several readers have praised OI,

OAXACA STATE

which includes a wide range of workshops with its lessons – from cooking to crafts to dance. Its offerings are tailored to student interest. Special programs for professionals are offered.

Soléxico (Map pp720-1; ☎/fax 516-56-80; www.solexico .com; Abasolo 217; 15/25hr per week for 1st 2 weeks $114/167, rates decrease thereafter) A professionally run school with branches in Playa del Carmen and Puerto Vallarta, enabling students to split their time between the locations. Soléxico has a refined 12-level system and you'll be taught at the appropriate one even if you are the only person at that level. Fees include cooking and salsa classes, movies and social gatherings and *intercambios* but not textbooks. Start any Monday. Soléxico offers the chance of volunteer work in local social projects.

Vinigúlaza (Map p718; ☎ 513-27-63; www.vinigulaza .com; Abasolo 503; 15/20hr per week $83/110) The maximum class size at this competitively priced school is six people. Classes are conversation-based. Start any Monday.

Private tutors are not hard to find; check notice boards (see p719) or ask at the schools.

Cooking

Several Oaxacan cooks regularly impart their secrets to those wanting to re-create special flavors back home. The following well-received classes are (or can be) held in English, and include market visits to buy ingredients.

La Casa de los Sabores (Map pp720-1; ☎ 516-57-04; www.lasbugambilias.com; Libres 205; 4hr class per person $60) Pilar Cabrera, owner of La Olla restaurant, gives classes from 9:30am to 2pm on Wednesday and Friday at her guesthouse in central Oaxaca (see p729). Participants prepare and eat a five-course meal, usually including some vegetarian dishes. The price is reduced if you attend more than one class, or if more than 10 people attend.

La Casa de mis Recuerdos (Map pp720-1; ☎ 515-56-45; www.misrecuerdos.net; Pino Suárez 508; classes from $65) Nora Gutiérrez, from a family of celebrated Oaxacan cooks, conducts classes for groups of up to 10 people at her family's charming B&B (see p729). You prepare a Oaxacan lunch, then sit down to eat it. Price depends on the number of participants and what they want to cook. Vegetarian classes are available.

Seasons of My Heart (☎ 518-77-26; www.seasonsof myheart.com; per 1-day class $75, per 1-week course incl hotel & meals $1695) This cooking school at a ranch in the Valle de Etla is run by American chef and Oaxacan food expert Susana Trilling. It offers classes in Mexican and Oaxacan cooking, from one-day group sessions (most Wednesdays) to three-day and weeklong courses, plus culinary tours around Oaxaca state.

TOURS

If you're short on time, a guided trip can save hassles and be lots of fun. A typical four-hour group trip to El Tule and Mitla, or to Arrazola, Cuilapan and Zaachila, costs around $18 per person, as do trips to Monte Albán. Longer trips – for example to Teotitlán del Valle, Yagul and a *mezcal* (a liquor made from maguey) distillery – are around $26 to $30. Admission fees and meals are extra. Many hotels will book these tours, as will the following agencies.

Continental-Istmo Tours (Map pp720-1; ☎ 516-96-25; Alcalá 201)

Turismo El Convento (www.oaxacaexperts.com) Camino Real Oaxaca (Map pp720-1; ☎ 516-18-06; Calle 5 de Mayo 300); Hotel Victoria (Map p718; ☎ 513-31-88; Lomas del Fortín 1)

Viajes Turísticos Mitla Hotel Rivera del Ángel (Map pp720-1; ☎ 516-61-75; Mina 518); Hostal Santa Rosa (Map pp720-1; ☎ 514-78-00; Trujano 201)

FESTIVALS & EVENTS

All major national festivals are celebrated here, and Oaxaca has some unique fiestas of its own, the biggest and most spectacular being the **Guelaguetza** (www.aoaxaca.com/guela guetza). It's held from 10am to 1pm on the first two Mondays after July 16. This brilliant feast of Oaxacan folk dance takes place in the open-air Auditorio Guelaguetza (Map p718) on Cerro del Fortín. Thousands of people flock into Oaxaca, turning the city into a feast of celebration and regional culture (and a rich hunting ground for visiting pickpockets, so stay alert).

On the appointed Mondays, known as Los Lunes del Cerro (Mondays on the Hill), magnificently costumed dancers from the seven regions of Oaxaca state perform a succession of dignified, lively or comical traditional dances, tossing offerings of produce to the crowd as they finish. The excitement climaxes with the incredibly colorful pineapple dance by women of the Papaloapan region, and the stately, prancing Zapotec Danza de las Plumas (Feather Dance), which re-enacts, symbolically, the Spanish conquest.

Seats in the amphitheater (which holds perhaps 10,000 people) are divided into four areas called *palcos*. For Palcos A and B, the two nearest the stage, tickets (around $38) go on sale online about three months beforehand. Nearer festival time they're also available at outlets in the city, typically from Teatro Macedonio Alcalá (see p722). Tickets guarantee a seat, but you should arrive before 8am if you want one of the better ones. The two much bigger rear *palcos*, C and D, are free and fill up early – if you get in by 8am you'll get a seat, but by 10am you'll be lucky to get even standing room. Wherever you sit, you'll be in the open air, with no shelter – for hours – so equip yourself accordingly.

A number of towns and villages around Oaxaca city now stage their own smaller Guelaguetzas on or near the same dates as the big one. They can make a refreshing change from the hubbub and crowds of Oaxaca. Tlacochahuaya village has a particularly attractive site on a hillside overlooking the village.

Many other events have grown up around the Guelaguetza. Highlights include the **Desfile de Delegaciones** (on Saturday afternoons preceding Guelaguetza Mondays), a parade of the regional delegations through the city center; and the **Bani Stui Gulal** (on Sunday evenings preceding Guelaguetza Mondays), a vibrant show of music, fireworks and dance telling the history of the Guelaguetza, held in the Plaza de la Danza by the Basílica de la Soledad. There's also a *mezcal* fair, and lots of concerts, exhibitions and sports events. Programs are widely available.

The origins of the Guelaguetza lie in pre-Hispanic rites that honor maize and wind gods. After the Spanish conquest, the indigenous festivities became fused with Christian celebrations for the Virgen del Carmen (July 16). Celebrations in something like their present form began in 1932, and the purpose-built amphitheater was opened in 1974. 'Guelaguetza' is a Zapotec word meaning 'cooperation' or 'exchange of gifts,' referring to the tradition of people helping each other out at such times as weddings, births and deaths.

There are many other festivals throughout the year.

Fiesta de la Virgen del Carmen About a week or more before July 16, the streets around the Templo del Carmen Alto on García Vigil become a fairground, and the nights are lit by processions and fireworks.

Blessing of Animals Pets are dressed up and taken to the Iglesia de La Merced (Map pp720–1), on Independencia, at about 5pm on August 31.

Día de Muertos (Day of the Dead) Held on November 2, the Día de Muertos is a big happening here, with associated events starting several days in advance. These include music and dance at the main cemetery, the Panteón General (Map p718), on Calz del Panteón about 1.25km east of the *zócalo*. Some guesthouses and agencies arrange guided tours and excursions to village events.

Posadas Nine nighttime neighborhood processions symbolizing Mary and Joseph's journey to Bethlehem take place between December 16 and 24.

Día de la Virgen de la Soledad Processions and traditional dances, including the Danza de las Plumas, take place at the Basílica de la Soledad (Map p718) on December 18.

Noche de los Rábanos (Night of the Radishes) On December 23 amazing figures carved from radishes are displayed in the *zócalo*.

Calendas (December 24) These Christmas-Eve processions from churches converge on the *zócalo* at about 10pm on December 24, bringing music, floats and fireworks.

SLEEPING

Prices given here are for Oaxaca's high seasons, generally mid-December to mid-January, a week each side of Easter and Día de Muertos, and from mid-July to mid-August (dates vary from one establishment to another). Outside of these periods many places drop their prices by between 15% and 30%. Those in the hardcore budget bracket tend to hold prices steady throughout the year.

THE AUTHOR'S CHOICE

Camino Real Oaxaca (Map pp720–1; ☎ 501-61-00, in US & Canada ☎ 800-722-6466; www.caminoreal.com/oaxaca; Calle 5 de Mayo 300; r $328-412; Ⓟ Ⓧ Ⓧ Ⓡ) Built in the 16th century as a convent, the majestic Camino Real served time as a prison, and was converted into a hotel in the 1970s. The old chapel is a banquet hall; one of the five attractive courtyards contains an enticing swimming pool; and the bar is lined with books on otherworldly devotion. Beautiful thick stone walls help keep the place cool and add to the considerable atmosphere. The 91 rooms are well decorated in colonial styles, and have marble sinks, safes and good bathrooms. The building has been designated a national treasure by the Mexican government and an historic monument by Unesco.

OAXACA STATE

Budget

Oaxaca has more backpacker hostels than any other city in Mexico, and many budget hotels as well. Hostels in the following listings all have shared bathrooms and, unless stated, kitchens where you can cook up your own meals.

Hostal Paulina (Map pp720-1; ☎ 516-20-05; www .paulinahostel.com; Trujano 321; dm/s/d/tr/q all incl breakfast $12/27/29/43/57) Impeccably clean and efficiently run, this splendid 92-bed hostel provides bunk dorms for up to 11 people, and rooms with one double bed and one pair of bunks, all with lockers. There's a 4% discount if you have an HI or ISIC card. A neat, green little interior garden and a roof terrace add to the appeal. There are no cooking facilities, but there should have free Internet by the time you read this.

Hostel Luz de Luna Nuyoo (Map pp720-1; ☎ 516-95-76; mayoraljchotmail.com; Juárez 101; dm $7, hammock or tent per person $5) Readers continue to praise this friendly, medium-sized hostel run by a pair of Oaxacan musician brothers. Separate bunk rooms for women, men and couples (eight beds each) open on to a wide patio; you can hang a hammock or stay in the rooftop *cabaña*. A few self-contented dogs add to the tranquil atmosphere, and there's a good shared kitchen.

Hostal Pochón (Map p718; ☎ 516-13-22; www.hostal pochon.com; Callejón del Carmen 102; dm $7, d/tw $16/22; 🖳) This hostel gets high marks from readers. It has six four-bed dorms and a couple of private rooms, a full kitchen, good common areas and no curfew, and offers bike rental, luggage storage, cheap phone calls and free Internet access. Beds are comfortable and the common areas brightly painted.

Posada Margarita (Map pp720-1; ☎ 516-28-02; Plaza de las Vírgenes, Plazuela Labastida 115; s/d $15/17, with private bathroom s $24/29) The Margarita's nine very plain but clean rooms are good value, just a stone's throw from the cafés and restaurants of Calle Alcalá.

Hotel Posada El Chapulín (Map pp720-1; ☎ 516-16-46; hotelchapulin@hotmail.com; Aldama 317; s/d/tr/q $24/27/29/38; 🖳) A good, eight-room family-run hotel, perennially full of international backpackers, with roof terrace, TV and fans in rooms. The hotel is opening an overflow facility in nearby Zaachila where staff will take guests by van.

There are plenty of other budget places:
Hostal Santa Isabel (Map pp720-1; ☎ 514-28-65,

516-74-98; hostalsantaisabeloax@hotmail.com; Mier y Terán 103; dm $6, d $7.50-9.50, incl breakfast; 🖳) A relaxed, friendly hostel with room for about 40 people in bunk dorms (one for women only) and varied bedrooms, all surrounding two patios with plants. It has lockers, and bicycles to rent at $0.50 per hour.

Magic Hostel (Map pp720-1; ☎ 516-76-67; www .magichostel.com.mx; Fiallo 305; dm $7, s/d $7.50/15; 🖳) Oaxaca's social, party-scene hostel with plentiful sitting areas and rooftop honor bar (open 8pm to 11pm) and lounge, but little care wasted on the rooms. Variously sized dorms (women-only and mixed) and private rooms accommodate about 40 people in all.

Midrange

Oaxaca boasts some delightful hotels and B&Bs, many of them in colonial or colonial-style buildings.

Las Bugambilias (Map pp720-1; ☎ /fax 516-11-65, in US ☎ 321-249-9422; www.lasbugambilias.com; Reforma 402; s $70-85, d $75-100, incl breakfast; ✂ ⊠ 🖳) This delightful B&B has nine rooms decorated with inspired combinations of folk and contemporary art. Some have air-con and/or a balcony; all have tiled bathrooms and fans. A big treat here is the gourmet two-course Oaxacan breakfast. Further attractions include a high-speed Internet connection, cheap international phone calls and an inviting roof terrace with fantastic views.

Hostal Casa del Sótano (Map pp720-1; ☎ /fax 516-24-94; www.hoteldelsotano.net; Tinoco y Palacios 414; r $71-92; 🖳) This small, modern, quality hotel is very well done up in colonial style. The good-sized rooms are arranged along two elegant patios with fountains, little water gardens and pools, and have solid wooden furnishings, cable TV, phone and fan. Some have balconies. The Sótano also has a restaurant and a high terrace with amazing views.

Hotel Las Golondrinas (Map pp720-1; ☎ 514-32-98; lasgolon@prodigy.net.mx; Tinoco y Palacios 411; s/d/tr $39/43/52; ⊠ 🖳) Lovingly tended by friendly owners and staff, this fine small hotel has about 30 rooms that open out onto three beautiful, leafy labyrinthine patios. It's often full, so you should try to book ahead. None of the rooms is huge but all are tastefully decorated and immaculately clean. Good breakfasts (not included in room rates) are served in one of the patios. Very good value!

Hotel Posada Catarina (Map pp720-1; ☎ 516-42-70; Aldama 325; s $34, d $43-58; 🖳) Posada Catarina is on a busy street southwest of the *zócalo*, but inside it's spacious and elegant with lush garden patios and a dramatic rooftop terrace. Rooms are clean and comfortable, if poorly ventilated. Readers love it.

Hotel Las Mariposas (Map pp720-1; ☎ 515-58-54; www.lasmariposas.com.mx; Pino Suárez 517; s/d $35/40, apt s/d $40/45, all incl breakfast; 🖳) Las Mariposas offers six studio apartments (with small kitchens) and seven rooms. All are large, spotlessly clean and simply but prettily decorated. It's a tranquil, friendly and very secure place. Free wireless Internet access, a library, a kitchen guestss use, luggage storage and a good breakfast are among the many extras that make this a great deal.

Hotel Posada del Centro (Map pp720-1; ☎ /fax 516-18-74; www.mexonline.com/posada.htm; Independencia 403; s/d $24/29, with private bathroom $46/50; 🅿) Attractive, centrally situated Posada del Centro has two large, verdant patios where breakfast is available. The 22 rooms have fans and pleasing Oaxacan artisan-work; there's an ample roof terrace; and staff are young, bright and helpful.

Hotel Azucenas (Map pp720-1; ☎ 514-79-18, 800-717-25-40, in US & Canada ☎ 800-882-6089; www.hotel azucenas.com; Aranda 203; s/d $47/52) The Azucenas is a small, welcoming, Canadian-owned hotel in a beautifully restored colonial house. There are 10 cool, white, tile-floored rooms, and a delicious buffet breakfast ($3.75) is served on the attractive roof terrace. Streetside rooms may get early-morning noise.

Hotel Cazomalli (Map p718; ☎ 513-86-05; www .hotelcazomalli.com; El Salto 104; d/tr/q $61/66/80; 🖳) The welcoming, family-run Cazomalli, decked with tasteful Oaxacan artwork, is five minutes' walk from the 1st-class bus station, in quiet Colonia Jalatlaco. The 18 rooms all have safe, fan and hair dryer, and the roof terrace has lovely views. Breakfast is available.

La Casa de los Sabores (Map pp720-1; ☎ 516-57-04; www.lasbugambilias.com; Libres 205; s/d incl breakfast $59/72; 🗶 🖳) Sabores offers five individually decorated, high-ceilinged rooms with ultra-comfortable beds. Four of the rooms are around the quiet patio in which owner Pilar Cabrera gives her twice-weekly cooking classes (see p726). The breakfasts are large and gourmet, and the service attentive. A roof terrace provides a change of scene, and is the venue for the fifth room.

Hotel Casa Arnel (Map p718; ☎ 515-28-56; www .casaarnel.com.mx; Aldama 404, Colonia Jalatlaco; s/d $12.50/25, with private bathroom from $40/50; 🖳) Family-run Casa Arnel is five minutes' walk from the 1st-class bus station (head to the right on Calz Niños Héroes, turn immediately right on Calle 5 de Mayo and watch for the signs). The clean, smallish rooms surround a big, leafy courtyard. The common areas, including hammock spots and a sundeck, have some great views. Arnel offers many travelers' services, including car rental.

Casa de la Tía Tere (Map p718; ☎ 501-18-45, fax 501-18-88; www.mexonline.com/tiatere.htm; Murguía 612; r incl continental breakfast $71-92; 🅿 🖳 🔊) Tere has 12 large, uncluttered rooms with tiled floors, most around a vine-draped patio, some with balconies, all with good showers. There's a small gym, and this is one of few accommodations in central Oaxaca with a swimming pool. Tere also offers a large, clean kitchen and dining room for guests, laundry service and low-cost phone calls, plus free coffee and Internet.

Parador Santo Domingo de Guzmán (Map p718; ☎ /fax 514-21-71; www.paradorstodomingo.com.mx; Alcalá 804; d/tr/q $78/85/91, per week $469/496/524; 🅿 🔊) This unprettified apartment hotel, 1½ blocks north of the Jardín Etnobotánico, offers spacious, bright well-appointed apartments. Each has two queen beds, a sitting room, bathroom, cable TV, safe, fan and well-equipped kitchen. There's hotel-style room service with clean sheets daily.

Hotel Monte Albán (Map pp720-1; ☎ /fax 516-27-77; hotelmontealban@prodigy.net.mx; Alameda de León 1; s interior/exterior $43/52, d $52/57) In a grand old high-ceilinged building smack on the Alameda de León, the Monte Albán is an atmospheric place all in all, though the fluorescent lighting and somewhat threadbare rooms diminish the romance. The cheaper, interior rooms are no great shakes, but the exterior rooms are large and have balconies or views of the cathedral. The hotel restaurant serves three meals and has nightly Guelaguetza shows (see p734).

Numerous rental apartments and houses are available. Check notice boards, the *Go-Oaxaca* and *Oaxaca Times* papers (including their online editions) and the Spanish-language paper *Noticias*.

Top End

Top-end accommodations range from a converted convent to modern resort hotels.

La Casa de mis Recuerdos (Map pp720-1; ☎ 515-56-45; www.misrecuerdos.net; Pino Suárez 508; s $53-66, d $83-96, all incl breakfast; 🗶) A marvelous decorative aesthetic prevails throughout this guesthouse. Old-style tiles, mirrors, *milagros* (ex-votos), masks, tinwork and all sorts of other Mexican crafts adorn the walls and halls. The best rooms overlook a fragrant central garden; two have air-con and two have a shared bathroom. The large breakfast is served in the beautiful dining room. Streetside room windows are double-glazed, but may still get some noise. There's a minimum stay of three nights.

Hostal Los Pilares (Map p718; ☎ 518-70-00; www .lospilareshostal.com; Curtidurías 721, Colonia Jalatlaco; s/d/tr $85/113/131; 🖳 🐾) Opened in mid-2005, Pilares is a very well-equipped, faux-colonial-style hotel. Rooms have plasma TVs (with Sky satellite reception), minibars, good-quality beds and attractive furniture. The hotel has garden-terrace dining, a bar, a pool and a Jacuzzi.

Casa de Sierra Azul (Map pp720–1; ☎ 514-84-12; www.mexonline.com/sierrazul.htm; Hidalgo 1002; r $117-139) The Sierra Azul is a 200-year-old house converted into a beautiful small hotel, centered on a broad courtyard with a fountain and stone pillars. The 14 good-sized, tasteful rooms have high ceilings, old-fashioned furnishings and clean tiled bathrooms.

Hostal Casa Antica (Map pp720–1; ☎ 516-26-73; www.hotelcasantica.com; Morelos 601; r $97-121; 🐾 🖳 🐾) The remodel and furnishings of this 200-year-old former convent sometimes work, and sometimes don't. It's a comfortable enough place, with lots of exposed stone/brick in rooms, most of which have safes.

Parador San Miguel (Map pp720–1; ☎ 514-93-31; www.mexonline.com/paradorsanmiguel.htm; Independencia 503; r $121-131; 🐾) One of Oaxaca's new wave of good modern hotels decorated in traditional style, Parador San Miguel has 23 sizable rooms with orange and green hues and pleasing wrought-iron and wooden touches. Each has a phone, safe, TV and either one king-sized or two double beds. Also here is the excellent Restaurante El Andariego (see opposite).

Hotel Victoria (Map p718; ☎ 515-26-33; www.hotel victoriaoax.com.mx; Lomas del Fortín 1; r $143, villa $175, junior ste $241; 🅿 🐾 🐾 🖳 🐾) The Victoria stands on the lower slopes of Cerro del Fortín, surrounded by big gardens and with tennis courts and an Olympic-sized pool. Many of the 149 large, comfortable, bright rooms and suites have fine views over the city. The restaurant, overlooking the gardens,

is excellent, with pasta, meat and fish mains from $5.50 to $11. The hotel runs a free shuttle to/from the city center several times daily; a taxi is $2.50 to $3.

A pair of beautifully decorated houses – **Encanto Jalatlaco** (Map p718; Niños Héroes 115) and **Estancia de Valencia** (Map p718; Maza de Juárez 207) – have a total of seven unique spaces, available through La Casa de Mis Recuerdos (see p729). The houses brim with artwork, textiles, *artesanías* (handicrafts) and charming furniture, and many amenities, including fresh flowers, a fridge and coffeemaker (with coffee). Rooms at both range from $100 to $120. Encanto Jalatlaco has a free-standing bungalow among its four accommodations, while Estancia de Valencia is a superbly remodeled old house with three bedrooms, two terraces, a patio and fountain.

EATING

The menus at many of the Oaxaca's restaurants, especially the higher-end places, have good English descriptions of the dishes.

Around the Zócalo

All the cafés and restaurants beneath the *zócalo* arches are great spots for watching Oaxaca life, but quality and service vary.

Terranova Café (Map pp720–1; ☎ 514-05-33; Portal Juárez 116; mains $4.50-7.50) Terranova serves good breakfasts until 1pm (with a $9 unlimited

---

THE AUTHOR'S CHOICE

Restaurante Los Danzantes (Map pp720–1; ☎ 501-11-84; Alcalá 403; mains $11-15; ⏰ 1:30-11:30pm) Innovative Mexican food and a dramatic architect-designed setting make Los Danzantes one of the most exciting places to eat in Oaxaca. The formerly derelict colonial patio now sports high patterned walls of adobe brick, tall wooden columns and cool pools of water in an impeccably contemporary configuration, half open to the sky. Efficient and welcoming young staff serve up a small but first-class selection of food: you could start with a delicious salad or a *sopa de nopales con camarón* (prawn and prickly pear cactus soup) and follow it with pork ribs in plum sauce. Wine selections and desserts are very good, and the restaurant has its own lines of cigars and *mezcal* (a liquor made from maguey).

buffet on Sunday), and a variety of mostly Oaxacan and Mexican standards for lunch and dinner. Children's plates are also on offer.

El Asador Vasco (Map pp720-1; ☎ 514-47-55; Portal de Flores 10A; mains $8-15; ☺ 1pm-11:30pm) Upstairs at the southwest corner of the *zócalo*, the Asador Vasco serves up good Oaxacan, Spanish and international food. It's strong on meat and seafood. For a table overlooking the plaza on a warm evening, book earlier in the day.

Mercado 20 de Noviembre (Map pp720-1; btwn Cabrera & Calle 20 de Noviembre; mains $1.75-3) Cheap *oaxaqueño* meals can be had in this market south of the *zócalo*. Most of the many *comedores* (small eateries within a market) here serve up local specialties such as chicken in *mole negro* (cooked in a very dark sauce of chilies, fruits, nuts, spices and chocolate). Pick a *comedore* that's busy – they're worth the wait. Many stay open until early evening, but their food is freshest earlier in the day.

El Sagrario (Map pp720-1; ☎ 514-03-03; Valdivieso 120; mains $3.75-12) This popular and reliable spot half a block north of the *zócalo* serves Mexican, Italian, steaks and burgers on three floors.

West of the Zócalo

Café Alex (Map pp720-1; ☎ 514-07-15; Díaz Ordaz 218; mains $3.25-4.50; ☺ 7am-10pm Mon-Sat, 7am-1pm Sun) Airy, full of people, clean and comfortable – Alex is a great place to fill up on good cheap food. Breakfast combinations are only part of the larger menu of traditional Oaxacan dishes.

Restaurante El Andariego (Map pp720-1; ☎ 514-93-31; Independencia 503; menú del día $5.50, mains $4.50-7.50) This bright restaurant at the front of the Parador San Miguel hotel is especially popular for its economical four-course set lunches.

Restaurant Colonial (Map pp720-1; ☎ 516-51-93; Calle 20 de Noviembre 112; lunch $3.50; ☺ 8am-5:30pm Mon-Sat) The Colonial's 10 or so tables fill up with locals for the good-value four-course *comida corrida* (set-price lunch), which includes soup, rice, a main course such as *pollo a la naranja* (chicken *à l'orange*), dessert and *agua de fruta* (fruit water).

Fidel Pan Integral (Map pp720-1; Calle 20 de Noviembre 211; baked goods $0.30-0.50; ☺ 9am-9:30pm Mon-Sat) Fidel is a brown bread–lover's dream, serving

---

> ### CHOCOLATE THE OAXACA WAY
>
> Chocolate is a Oaxacan favorite. A bowl of steaming hot chocolate to drink, with porous sweet bread to dunk, is the perfect warmer when winter sets in 1500m above sea level. The mix, to which hot milk or water is added, typically contains cinnamon, almonds and sugar as well as ground-up cocoa beans. The area around the south end of Oaxaca's Mercado 20 de Noviembre has several shops specializing in this time-honored treat – and not just chocolate for drinking but also chocolate for *moles* (dishes with chili-based sauces), hard chocolate for eating, and more. You can sample chocolate with or without cinnamon; light or dark chocolate with varying quantities of sugar; and many other varieties at any of these places. And most of them have vats where you can watch the mixing.

wholegrain cookies, *pandulces* (sweet breads) and even croissants.

North of the Zócalo

Casa Oaxaca (Map pp720-1; ☎ 516-88-89; Constitución 104A; mains $6-15; ☺ 1pm-11pm Mon-Sat) Oaxacan fusion at its best. The chef here works magic combining ingredients and flavors: witness the chayote and banana puree, or the 'cannelloni' with thinly sliced jicama in place of pasta tubes, surrounding a filling of grasshoppers and *huitlacoche* (a black fungus that grows on young corn). Presentation is outstanding, and all is enhanced by the courtyard setting and a good selection of wines. The only negative is that waiters sometimes do a hard sell on food and wine.

La Olla (Map pp720-1; ☎ 516-66-68; Reforma 402; dishes $2.50-9, menú del día $7.50; ☺ 8am-10pm Tue-Sat, 9am-10pm Sun; Ⓥ) This excellent restaurant is run by Pilar Cabrera, who teaches cooking classes (p726) and manages La Casa de Los Sabores (p729). It produces marvelous Oaxacan specialties, good wholegrain tortas, juices, and salads made with organic lettuce. There are plenty of vegetarian choices, and fine breakfasts ($2.50 to $4.50), and the *menú del día* lunch special is a multicourse gourmet treat.

La Biznaga (Map pp720-1; ☎ 516-80-00; García Vigil 512; mains $7-9.50; ☺ 1-10pm Mon-Sat, 2-8pm Sun)

Cutting-edge La Biznaga is the work of two brothers from the Distrito Federal. The courtyard is ringed with slick art; an eclectic music mix plays; and someone will take your order, eventually (for best results, sit close to the full bar). People rave about the mestizo-cuisine dishes here (including great salads made with organic produce), and fish, fowl and meats are cleverly prepared and presented.

Zandunga (Map pp720-1; ☎ 044-951-156-27-02; cnr García Vigil & Carranza; mains $5.50-6; ⏰ 2-11pm Mon-Sat) Give *istmeño* cooking a preview here before you head off to Tehuantepec. The *cochito horneado* (baked pork) goes down easy, as do the *tamales de cambray* (beef and chicken stuffed in a banana leaf) and other dishes. The corner location's warm decor includes A-grade artwork on the walls and low light, and service is friendly and low-key.

Café Los Cuiles (Map pp720-1; ☎ 514-82-59; Plaza de las Vírgenes, Plazuela Labastida 115-1; breakfast $2.50-3.50, salads, soups & snacks $1.50-3; ⏰ 8am-10pm) Los Cuiles is an excellent spot for breakfast, for outstanding organically grown, fair-traded coffee or for light eats at any time of day, with a handy central location and spacious lounge-gallery feel. Sit inside and make use of the wi-fi Internet access, or enjoy the courtyard and its fountain.

María Bonita (Map p718; ☎ 516-72-33; cnr Alcalá & Humboldt; breakfast $3-5, mains $5.50-9; ⏰ 8:30am-9pm Tue-Sat, 8:30am-5pm Sun) Readers love the economical and tasty variety of traditional Oaxacan food here. Precede your *mole* with one of a good range of appetizers ($3 to $5.50) and soups, such as the *sopa Xóchitl* (squash, squash blossom and sweet corn). The old building is on a noisy traffic corner, but the tasteful art on the walls and relaxed, unhurried service make it all OK.

Gaia (Map pp720-1; ☎ 516-70-79; Plaza de las Vírgenes, Plazuela Labastida 115-3; breakfast $3.75-6, smoothies $2.75, salads $3; Ⓥ) Behind Café Los Cuiles, and sharing courtyard space with it, Gaia is a mellow café–juice bar serving many veggie choices. Choose from breakfast combinations, *panini*, omelettes, frittatas, excellent organic salads, pastas, and good cold veggie soups with yogurt. There's also a wide range of healthy and delicious juice blends, *licuados* (milk shakes made with milk, fruits, yogurt and honey) and smoothies.

1254 Marco Polo Pino Suárez (Map p718; ☎ 513-43-08; Pino Suárez 806; breakfast $2.50-3, mains $5-9.50; ⏰ 8am-6pm Wed-Mon) Calle 5 de Mayo (Map pp720-1; ☎ 514-43-60; Calle 5 de Mayo 103; breakfast $2.50-3, mains $5-9.50; ⏰ 8am-10:30pm Mon-Sat) With a popular spot opposite El Llano park, the Pino Suárez branch of Marco Polo has a large garden dining area, attentive waiters and great food. The large breakfasts come with bottomless cups of coffee; from noon until closing, *antojitos* (tortilla-based snacks like tacos), ceviches and oven-baked seafood are the main draws. The downtown branch has the same excellent menu and good service.

Decano (Map pp720-1; Calle 5 de Mayo 210; dishes $3-4.50) Decano's simple, economical food choices, good music mix and relaxed atmosphere make it a good spot to enjoy everything from breakfast to a good *menú del día*, tasty light eats or drinks with friends.

Coffee Beans García Vigil (Map pp720-1; ☎ 501-01-40; García Vigil 409E; breakfast & mains $3-6; ⏰ 8am-midnight Sun-Thu, 8am-2am Fri & Sat) Calle 5 de Mayo (Map pp720-1; Calle 5 de Mayo 500C; coffee $1.25-2; ⏰ 8am-midnight) They roast and brew some of the best coffee in town here; it's strong, tasty and available in several forms, including a good variety of espresso drinks. The García Vigil branch also offers a large assortment of breakfasts, crepes, sandwiches and teas, and a pool table, full bar and live music on Friday and Saturday. The smaller, easier-going branch on Calle de Mayo serves great coffee and tea, as well as some good desserts, cookies and the like in its upstairs-downstairs location.

Comala (Map pp720-1; García Vigil 406; sandwiches $3-5; ⏰ 9am-11pm Mon-Sat) Comala's sandwiches are made with excellent bread (rolls or ciabatta) and contain ingredients like prosciutto, olives and mozzarella. The *hamburguesa de res* ($5) is a big, juicy, filling burger, which probably won't leave you with any room for the salads and soups.

El Biche Pobre (Map p718; ☎ 513-46-36; cnr Calz de la República & Hidalgo; mains $3-6.50; ⏰ 8am-9pm Wed-Mon) El Biche Pobre, 1.5km northeast of the *zócalo*, is an informal place serving a range of Oaxacan food at about a dozen tables – some tables are long enough to stage lunch for a whole extended Mexican family. For an introduction to local cuisine you can't beat the $6.50 *botana surtida*, a dozen assorted little items that add up to a tasty meal.

Restaurant Flor de Loto (Map pp720-1; ☎ 514-39-44; Morelos 509; mains $3.25-5; Ⓥ) Flor de Loto takes a pretty good stab at pleasing a range of palates, from vegan to carnivore. The chicken brochette ($4.50) is a large and very tasty choice. Vegetarian options include spinach burgers, soy burgers and *vegetales al gratín* (vegetables with melted cheese). The *comida corrida* ($4.50) is a real meal.

Cenaduría Tlayudas Libres (Map pp720-1; Libres 212; tlayudas around $3; ☯ 9pm-4:30am) Drivers double-park along the entire block to eat here. The *tlayudas* are large, light, crisp, hot tortillas folded over frijoles, *quesillo* (a stringy goat's cheese from Oaxaca) and your choice of salsa. They make a filling, tasty meal, but half the fun is taking in the great local, late-night scene as motherly cooks fan the streetside charcoal grills, raising showers of sparks. Sit on benches around the range or at tables in the adjacent building.

Panini (Map pp720-1; ☎ 501-20-36; Matamoros 200A; panini & cakes $3.50-3.75; ☯ 9am-9pm Mon-Sat; Ⓥ) This is a great little place to drop into for a fine ciabatta torta – with vegetarian varieties available – as well as salad, sweet crepe, carrot cake or walnut strudel.

Casa del Ángel (Map p718; ☎ 518-71-67; Dalevuelta 200; breakfast $3.25, sandwiches $2-2.50, dishes $2.50; ☯ 8:30am-6pm; Ⓥ) This small, quiet courtyard café adjoins a yoga studio and health-food store three blocks north of the ethnobotanical gardens. It serves salads, soy burgers, chai and delectable sandwiches on homemade whole-wheat bread (but steer clear of the espresso).

DRINKING

Tapas & Pisto (Map pp720-1; ☎ 514-40-93; Alcalá 403; 5pm-2am Tue-Sun) Upstairs from Los Danzantes restaurant and in keeping with its ultra-sensual theme, T&P has a black light in the bar, and a rooftop terrace with fabulous views, well removed from the bar itself.

Café Del Jardín (Map pp720-1; Portal de Flores 10) The Jardín, meeting place of local journalists and scribes, has a peerless position beneath the arches at the southwest corner of the *zócalo*. It's a fine spot for a beer.

Freebar (Map pp720-1; Matamoros 100C; ☯ 9pm-2am Tue-Sun) Freebar hosts a young and vibrant crowd that doesn't mind being rammed together to soak up beer and the atmosphere. Nicknamed *la pecera* (the goldfish bowl) with good reason.

Bar del Borgo (Map pp720-1; Matamoros 100B; ☯ 10am-1am) A very small but neatly arranged,

semisubterranean space, the Borgo offers some unique street views and a jazzy, arty atmosphere. Check it out!

La Divina (Map pp720-1; ☎ 582-05-08; Gurrión 104; ☯ 5pm-1am Tue-Sun) Loud, busy La Divina, across the street from Iglesia de Santo Domingo, has a disco-esque interior, and music from Spanish-language rock to house to English pop. A mixed-nationality crowd generates a warm atmosphere that spills out into the street (if you're lucky). Drinks start at around $2.

La Casa del Mezcal (Map pp720-1; Flores Magón 209; ☯ 10am-1am) Open since 1935, this is one of Oaxaca's oldest bars, 1½ blocks south of the *zócalo*. It's a cantina, but a safe one. One room has a large stand-up bar and shelves full of *mezcal* ($2 to $3 a shot); the other room has tables where *botanas* (snacks) are served. Most, but not all, patrons are men.

La Cucaracha (Map pp720-1; ☎ 501-16-36; Porfirio Díaz 301A; ☯ 7pm-2am Mon-Sat) A good place to make acquaintances with some classic Mexican beverages – this specialist bar stocks 40 varieties of *mezcal*, including fruit-flavored and some from jugs full of scorpions. A six-flavor sampler runs $9.50, while shots are $2 and $4. Various tequilas are also on offer. Everyone's welcome here, food is available, and on Friday and Saturday a small disco operates in one corner, and live Latin music (*trova* – troubadour-type folk music; *bolero*; and *rancheras* – Mexico's urban 'country music') in another.

Two other places worth a mention are **La Biznaga** (Map pp720-1; ☎ 516-80-00; García Vigil 512; mains $7-9.50; ☯ 1-10pm Mon-Sat, 2-8pm Sun) and **Colectivo Central** (Map pp720-1; ☎ 514-20-42; Hidalgo 302; ☯ 10pm-2am Wed-Sat). Central was closed due to licensing problems at the time of research. Should it reopen (it's happened before) you'll likely find a 20- and 30-something creative crowd in a good-looking bar with nightclub leanings, owned and regularly re-designed by one of Oaxaca's innovative painters, Guillermo Olguín. The Central hosts rarely seen live music acts and independent films, and uses its wall space as an alternative gallery for celebrated and unheard-of artists.

ENTERTAINMENT

Thanks to its student and tourist populations, Oaxaca has a bright entertainment and cultural scene.

Cinemas

Cine El Pochote (Map p718; ☎ 514-11-94, 516-69-80; García Vigil 817; admission free, donations accepted; ☺ screenings 6pm & 8pm Tue-Sun) El Pochote shows independent, art-house and classic Mexican and international movies (the latter in their original languages with Spanish subtitles). There's usually a different theme each month. It's a little tricky to find; you need to duck under the old aqueduct into Parque El Pochote, itself designed by the prolific Francisco Toledo.

Cultural Centers

The **Centro Cultural Ricardo Flores Magón** (Map pp720-1; ☎ 514-62-93; Alcalá 302) and the **Casa de la Cultura Oaxaqueña** (Map pp720-1; ☎ 516-24-83; Ortega 403) both stage varied musical, dancing, theatrical and artistic events several evenings a week, and on a few mornings. These are largely nontouristic events and many of them are free; drop by to see the programs.

Guelaguetza Shows

If you're not lucky enough to be in Oaxaca for the Guelaguetza itself (see p726), it's well worth attending one of the regular imitations.

Camino Real Oaxaca (Map pp720-1; ☎ 516-06-11; Calle 5 de Mayo 300; admission incl buffet dinner $30; ☺ 7pm Fri) The classy Camino Real hotel stages a highly colorful three-hour Guelaguetza show in what used to be a convent chapel. Extra shows are held on Monday and Wednesday in the high season.

Casa de Cantera (Map pp720-1; ☎ 514-75-85; Murguía 102; admission $14; ☺ 8:30pm) A lively mini-Guelaguetza is staged here nightly, in colorful costume with live music. To make a reservation, phone or stop by during the afternoon. Food and drinks are available.

Hotel Monte Albán (Map pp720-1; ☎ 516-27-77; Alameda de León 1; admission $8; ☺ 8:30pm) This hotel presents a 1½-hour version nightly, to live music in the high season and to recorded music at other times.

Live Music

Candela (Map pp720-1; ☎ 514-20-10; Murguía 413; admission $2-3 Tue & Wed, $5 Thu-Sat; ☺ 1pm-2am Tue-Sat) Candela's writhing salsa band and beautiful colonial-house setting have kept it at the top of the Oaxaca nightlife lists for over a decade. Arrive fairly early (9:30pm

to 10:30pm) to get a good table, and either learn to dance (free lessons from 9pm to 10pm) or learn to watch. Candela is a restaurant, too, with a good lunchtime *menú del día* ($4). Tuesday and Wednesday are mellow *trova* nights, but salsa, merengue and *cumbia* (a Colombian dance style) take over Thursday through Saturday.

La Tentación (Map pp720-1; ☎ 514-95-21; Matamoros 101; admission $4; ☺ 9pm-2am Tue-Sun) Some locals think it's a bit of a dump, but foreigners and residents alike have a great time when this erratic venue gets up a good head of steam. This is most likely to happen on Friday and Saturday, when you can move to live salsa, merengue and *cumbia*. The weeknights with a DJ tend to be lame.

Other places with regular live music include **La Cucaracha** (see p733) and **Azúkar** (☎ 513-11-70; cnr Porfirio Díaz & Escuela Naval Militar; ☺ Thu-Sat). Azúkar is about six blocks north of Calz Niños Héroes de Chapultepec in Colonia Reforma. It alternates between live salsa and other *música tropical* (Mexican dance music originating from the Caribbean and South America) and DJs spinning house, techno and electronica. If it doesn't suit your fancy, head to the *banda* (Mexican big-band music) club next door for a dose of quintessentially Mexican music.

Free concerts in the *zócalo* are given by the state marimba (wooden xylophone) ensemble or state band several evenings each week at 7pm, and at 12:30pm on Wednesday and Sunday.

SHOPPING

The state of Oaxaca has the richest, most inventive folk-art scene in Mexico, and the city is its chief marketplace. You'll find the highest-quality crafts mostly in the smart stores on and near Alcalá, Calle 5 de Mayo and García Vigil, but prices are lower in the markets. You may not pay more for crafts purchased in the city (rather than in the villages where most of them are made) but a lot of your money may be going to intermediaries. Some artisans have grouped together to market their own products directly (see Craft Shops, opposite).

Oaxacan artisans' techniques remain pretty traditional – back-strap and pedal looms, hand-turning of pottery – but new products frequently appear in response to the big demand for Oaxacan crafts. The colorful wooden fantasy animals known as *alebrijes* were developed less than 20 years ago from toys that Oaxacans had been carving for their children for centuries.

Special crafts to look out for include the distinctive black pottery from San Bartolo Coyotepec; blankets, rugs and tapestries from Teotitlán del Valle; *huipiles* (women's sleeveless tunics) and other indigenous clothing from anywhere in the state; the creative pottery figures made by the Aguilar sisters and other residents of Ocotlán; and stamped and colored tin from Oaxaca city itself. Jewelry is also made and sold here – you'll find pieces using gold, silver or precious stones, but prices are a bit higher than in Mexico City or Taxco. Many shops can mail things home for you.

Rugs or blankets with muted colors are less likely to have been made with synthetic dyes than some of the more garish offerings. There are various ways to assess the quality of a woven rug:

- gently tug at the fibers to see how tightly it's woven;
- rub your fingers or palm on it for about 15 seconds – if balls appear, the quality is poor;
- crumple it up a bit, then spread it on the floor – the creases will disappear from good rugs.

Just as fascinating, in its way, as the fancy craft stores is Oaxaca's commercial area stretching over several blocks southwest of the *zócalo*. Oaxacans flock here, and to the big Central de Abastos market, for all their everyday needs.

Markets

Mercado de Artesanías (Crafts Market; Map pp720-1; cnr JP García & Zaragoza) This sizable indoor crafts market is strong on pottery, rugs and textiles. As you walk through you're likely to see many of the vendors passing the time by plying their crafts, such as weaving or embroidering.

Central de Abastos (Supplies Center; Map p718; Periférico) The enormous main market is a hive of activity every day, with Saturday the biggest day. If you look long enough, you can find almost anything here. Each type of product has a section to itself, and you can easily get lost in the profusion of household goods, CDs and *artesanías*,

and the overwhelming quantities of fruit, vegetables, sugarcane, maize and other produce that's grown from the coast to the mountaintops.

Mercado Juárez (Map pp720-1; btwn Flores Magón & Calle 20 de Noviembre) This indoor market, a block southwest of the *zócalo*, concentrates on food (more expensive than the Central de Abastos) but also has flowers and some crafts, especially leatherwork.

Mercado 20 de Noviembre (Map pp720-1; btwn Cabrera & Calle 20 de Noviembre) A block south of the Mercado Juárez, Calle 20 de Noviembre is mainly occupied by *comedores* but has a few inexpensive craft stalls on its west side.

Craft Shops

MARO (Map pp720-1; ☎ 516-06-70; Calle 5 de Mayo 204; ✹ 9am-8pm) This is a sprawling store with a big range of good work at good prices, all made by the hundreds of members of the MARO women artisans' cooperative around Oaxaca state. Whether you buy a stamped tin mirror or a woven-to-order rug, you know your money is going direct to the makers.

La Mano Mágica (Map pp720-1; ☎ 516-42-75; www.lamanomagica.com; Alcalá 203; ✹ 10:30am-3pm & 4-8pm Mon-Sat) You'll find some wonderfully original and sophisticated craft products at this shop, including work by one of its owners, the Teotitlán del Valle master weaver Arnulfo Mendoza. Some Mendoza pieces go for thousands of dollars, and when you see them you'll understand why.

Instituto Oaxaqueño de las Artesanías (IAO; Map p718; ☎ 514-40-30; www.oaxaca.gob.mx/ioa; García Vigil 809; ✹ 9am-8pm Mon-Fri, 10am-5pm Sat, 10am-1pm Sun) Government-run IAO offers a large variety of beautiful craft items, including some gorgeous textiles. Walk atop the aqueduct to reach the entrance.

Casa de las Artesanías de Oaxaca (Map pp720-1; ☎ 516-50-62; Matamoros 105; ✹ 9am-9pm Mon-Sat, 10am-6pm Sun) This store sells the work of 80 family workshops and craft organizations from around Oaxaca state. Its patio is surrounded by several rooms that are full of varied crafts.

Oro de Monte Albán (Map pp720-1; ☎ 516-45-28, www.orodemontealban.com) Plaza Alcalá (Alcalá 307); Casa Vieja (Alcalá 403); Alcalá 503 (Alcalá 503); Taller (workshop; Gurrión C) This firm's goldsmiths produce high-class jewelry in gold, silver and semiprecious stones, including copies of pre-Hispanic jewelry and pieces inspired

TIRED OF TEQUILA?

Central Oaxaca state – especially around Santiago Matatlán and the Albarradas group of villages, south and east of Mitla – produces probably the best *mezcal* in Mexico (and therefore the world). Just like its cousin tequila, *mezcal* is made from the maguey plant and is usually better when *reposado* or *añejo* (aged). There are also some delicious *crema* varieties with fruit or other flavors.

Several Oaxaca shops southwest of the *zócalo* specialize in *mezcal*. Try **El Rey de los Mezcales** (Map pp720-1; Las Casas 509) or look along Aldama, JP García or Trujano. Around $11 will buy you a decent bottle, but some $4 *mezcals* are also fine. Some bottles made from wild agave cost up to $40. For some export-quality *mezcals* from Santiago Matatlán (up to $55), head to **La Cava** (Map p718; ☎ 515-23-35; Gómez Farías 212B; ☯ 10am-3pm & 5-8pm Mon-Sat), north of the center. It has a good selection of wines, too.

by colonial-era designs. The workshop tour (in Spanish) is very interesting and includes a demonstration of lost-wax casting.

Corazón El Pueblo (Map pp720-1; ☎ 516-69-60; Alcalá 307; ☯ 10:30am-2:30pm & 3:30-7:30pm Mon-Sat) Folk art from surrounding villages.

Teotitlán (Map pp720-1; cnr Gurrión & Alcalá) Has blankets and rugs.

GETTING THERE & AWAY
Air
Direct flights to/from Mexico City (one hour) are operated by Mexicana at least four times daily and Aviacsa once, while Azteca flies once a day except Thursday. Continental has daily flights to/from Houston, Texas. Aviacsa also flies daily to Acapulco, Tijuana and Hermosillo, and Aeroméxico flies to Tijuana and Tuxtla Gutiérrez.

Click Mexicana has one daily flight to/from Tuxtla Gutiérrez, continuing to/from Villahermosa, Mérida, Cancún and Havana. Aviacsa has daily nonstop flights to/from Tijuana and Hermosillo.

For the spectacular half-hour hop over the Sierra Madre del Sur to Puerto Escondido and Bahías de Huatulco on the Oaxaca coast, Aero Tucán (with a 13-seat Cessna) flies daily to/from both destinations, with

fares to either around $100 one way, as well as to Puebla on Friday and Sunday, and Tuxtla Gutiérrez on Monday, Wednesday and Friday. Aerovega flies a seven-seater daily to/from Puerto Escondido ($90 one way) and Bahías de Huatulco ($100).

AIRLINE OFFICES
Aeroméxico (Map pp720-1; ☎ 516-10-66; Hidalgo 513; ☯ 9am-7pm Mon-Fri, 9am-5:30pm Sat)
Aero Tucán (Map pp720-1; ☎ 501-05-30; Alcalá 201, Interior 204)
Aerovega (Map pp720-1; ☎ 516-49-82; aerovega@prodigy.net.mx; Alameda de León 1; ☯ 9am-8pm Mon-Fri, 9am-5pm Sat)
Aviacsa Centro (Map pp720-1; ☎ 513-72-14; Pino Suárez 604); Airport (☎ 511-50-39)
Azteca (☎ 01-800-229-83-22; airport)
Mexicana & Click Mexicana Centro (Map pp720-1; ☎ 516-73-52; Fiallo 102); Airport (☎ 511-52-29)

Bus
The **Terminal de Autobuses de Primera Clase** (1st-class bus station; Map p718; ☎ 515-12-48; Calz Niños Héroes de Chapultepec 1036) is 2km northeast of the *zócalo*. Also known as the Terminal ADO, it's used by UNO (deluxe service), and ADO GL (executive), ADO, OCC (Ómnibus Cristóbal Colón; 1st class) and Sur, AU and Cuenca (*económico*). The **Terminal de Autobuses de Segunda Clase** (2nd-class bus station; Map p718; Las Casas) is 1km west of the *zócalo*; the main long-distance companies using it are **Estrella del Valle/Oaxaca Pacífico** (EV/OP; ☎ 516-54-29), **Fletes y Pasajes** (Fypsa; ☎ 516-22-70) and **Transportes Oaxaca-Istmo** (TOI; ☎ 516-36-64). Unless otherwise noted, buses mentioned in this section use one of these two main stations.

It's advisable to buy your ticket a day or two in advance for some of the less-frequent services, including buses to San Cristóbal de Las Casas and the better services to the coast. **Ticket Bus** (Map pp720-1; ☯ 8am-10pm Mon-Sat, 8am-9pm Sun; 20 de Noviembre ☎ 514-66-55; Calle 20 de Noviembre 103D; Valdivieso ☎ 516-38-20; Valdivieso 2A), in the city center, sells tickets for trips with UNO, ADO and ADO GL, OCC, Sur and AU throughout Mexico.

For the Oaxaca coast, as always, it's safest to travel in daylight, and you won't miss the amazing views (or get as motion-sick). Mind your wallet and carry-on luggage, as thieves work these routes. **Autoexprés Atlántida** (Map p718; ☎ 514-70-77; La Noria 101) runs 14-seat air-conditioned vans nine times daily by the spectacular Hwy 175 to Pochutla ($11.50, 6½ hours), the jumping-off point for Puerto Ángel, Zipolite, Mazunte and other nearby beaches. Also by Hwy 175, EV/OP runs 2nd-class *directos* (buses that make very few stops) at 9:45am, 2:45pm and 10:30pm to Pochutla (by day/night $8.50/9, six hours) and Puerto Escondido ($10/10.50, seven hours) from the 2nd-class terminal; the first two stop fifteen minutes later at the **Armenta y López terminal** (Map pp720-1; ☎ 501-02-88; Armenta y López 721), 500m south of the *zócalo*. From the 2nd-class bus station, EV/OP runs 10 *ordinarios* (buses that stop whenever passengers want to get on or off) to Pochutla ($7.50, seven hours) and Puerto Escondido ($8.50, 8½ hours), one bus to Santa Cruz Huatulco ($10.50, 7½ hours) at 10pm and a *directo* to Puerto Ángel ($7, seven hours).

OCC and ADO GL run a total of six buses daily by the longer but less-winding Salina Cruz route to Bahías de Huatulco ($19 to $25, eight hours). Five continue to Pochutla ($21, nine hours) and Puerto Escondido ($21, 10 hours). **Estrella Roja Sur** (☎ 516-06-94) runs six or seven buses daily to Puerto Escondido ($9.50, 6½ to seven hours) by the more direct but poorly paved Hwy 131.

Other daily bus departures from Oaxaca:

Destination	Price	Duration	Frequency
Mexico City	$32-42	6hr	47 from 1st-class terminal
(most to TAPO)	$19	6hr	3 Fypsa
Puebla	$25-29	4½hr	12 from 1st-class terminal
San Cristóbal de Las Casas	$32-38	12hr	3 from 1st-class terminal
Tapachula	$28-32	10hr	2 from 1st-class terminal
Tehuantepec	$12	4½hr	16 from 1st-class terminal
	$11	4½hr	7 Sur
	$7.50	5½hr	13 TOI
Tuxtla Gutiérrez	$27-32	10hr	4 from 1st-class terminal
	$16	10hr	5 Fypsa & TOI
Veracruz	$30-35	6hr	4 from 1st-class terminal
Villahermosa	$41	12hr	3 from 1st-class terminal

Car & Motorcycle

Hwy 135D branches south off the Mexico City–Veracruz highway (150D) east of Puebla for a spectacular traverse of Oaxaca's northern mountains en route to Oaxaca city. Tolls from Mexico City to Oaxaca on highways 150D and 135D total $30 (from Puebla, $19); the trip takes five to six hours. For some reason the 135D is also numbered 131D in some stretches. The main toll-free alternative, via Huajuapan de León on Hwy 190, takes several hours longer.

Car-rental prices can start as low as $35 a day, including tax and insurance, for an old-style VW Beetle without air-con, but you might prefer to pay a little more for something more comfortable. Rental car agencies in Oaxaca:

Alamo Centro (Map pp720-1; ☎ 514-85-34; Calle 5 de Mayo 203); Airport (☎ 511-62-20)

Budget (Map pp720-1; ☎ 516-44-45; Calle 5 de Mayo 315A); Airport (☎ 511-52-52)

Hertz Centro (Map pp720-1; ☎ 516-24-34; Plaza de las Vírgenes, Plazuela Labastida 115); Airport (☎ 511-54-78)

GETTING AROUND
To/From the Airport

Transporte Terrestre combis from the airport will take you to anywhere in the city center for $2.75. Catching a cab outside the terminal should cost between $9.50 and $11.50, depending on your destination. If you want to avoid possible hassles, a ticket taxi desk at the south end of the terminal charges $12.

You can book a combi seat from the city to the airport a day or more ahead at **Transportes Aeropuerto** (Map pp720-1; ☎ 514-43-50; Alameda de León 1G; ⏰ 9am-2pm & 5-8pm Mon-Sat).

Bicycle

Two full-service shops rent out good mountain bikes: **Bicicletas Pedro Martínez** (Map pp720-1; ☎ 514-59-35; Aldama 418; per day $11.50) and **Zona Bici** (Map pp720-1; ☎ 516-09-53; García Vigil 406; per day $12, per hr $2.50). Rentals at both include helmet, lock and tools, and both offer bike tours (see Activities, p724). They also sell new and used bikes and equipment.

Car & Motorcycle

There are several guarded parking lots in the city center. **Estacionamiento Trujano** (Map pp720-1; Trujano 219; ⏰ 6am-11pm) charges $2.75 for an overnight stay (8pm to 8am) and $0.80 per hour from 8am to 8pm.

Bus

Most points of importance in the city are within walking distance of each other, but you may want to use city buses ($0.30) to and from the bus stations.

From the 1st-class bus station a westbound 'Juárez' bus will take you down Juárez and Melchor Ocampo, three blocks east of the *zócalo*; a 'Tinoco y Palacios' bus will take you down Tinoco y Palacios and JP García, two blocks west of the *zócalo*. To return to the bus station, take an 'ADO' bus north up Xicoténcatl or Pino Suárez, four blocks east of the *zócalo*, or up Díaz Ordaz or Crespo, three blocks west of the *zócalo*.

Buses between the 2nd-class bus station and the center crawl along congested streets – it's almost as quick to walk. 'Centro' buses head toward the center along Trujano, then turn north up Díaz Ordaz. To the 2nd-class bus station, 'Central' buses go south on Tinoco y Palacios, then west on Las Casas.

Taxi

A taxi anywhere within the central area, including the bus stations, costs $3.50 to $4.

VALLES CENTRALES

Three valleys radiate from the city of Oaxaca: the Valle de Tlacolula, stretching 50km east; the Valle de Etla, reaching about 40km north; and the Valle de Zimatlán, stretching about 100km south. In these Valles Centrales (Central Valleys), all within day-trip distance of Oaxaca city, you'll find much to fascinate – craft-making villages, preHispanic ruins and busy country markets. The people are mostly Zapotec.

Getting There & Away

Most of the places in the Valle de Tlacolula, east of Oaxaca, are within walking distance of the Oaxaca–Mitla road, Hwy 190. Transportes Oaxaca-Istmo's buses to Mitla, every few minutes from Gate 9 of Oaxaca's 2nd-class bus station, will drop you anywhere along this road. There are further services to some specific towns and villages. South from Oaxaca, Hwy 175 goes through San Bartolo Coyotepec, Ocotlán and Ejutla. Separate roads go to Monte Albán, Cuilapan and

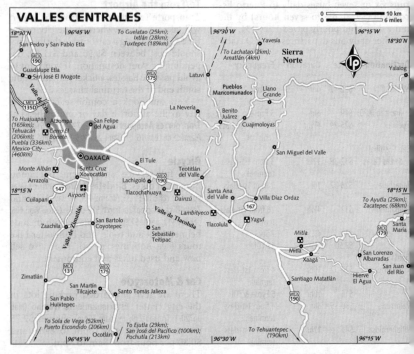

MARKET DAYS

Markets in the towns of the Valles Centrales offer all manner of foodstuffs and produce, as well as handicrafts, cookware, recorded music and sundries of all sorts, many of which are cheap imports these days. The scene is not to be missed; markets draw buyers and sellers from near and far, and bombard the senses with colors, sounds and smells.

At markets with plastic tarps set up for shade, taller visitors will find themselves constantly ducking under guy ropes, iron bars and hanging merchandise, but it's a small price to pay to see the continuation of a ritual that has been taking place for many hundreds, if not thousands, of years.

Markets are at their busiest in the morning and most of them start to wind down in the early afternoon. The region's main markets:

Sunday Tlacolula
Tuesday Atzompa
Wednesday San Pedro y San Pablo Etla
Thursday Zaachila and Ejutla
Friday Ocotlán, Santo Tomás Jalieza and San Bartolo Coyotepec
Saturday Mitla

Zaachila. Further details on bus services are given under the individual sites and villages.

An alternative to traveling by bus, costing twice as much (but still cheap!), is to take a *colectivo* (a minibus or car that picks up and drops off passengers along a predetermined route) taxi. These run to places north of Oaxaca (such as Atzompa and San José El Mogote) from Trujano on the north side of the 2nd-class bus station; and to places to the east, south and southwest (including El Tule, Teotitlán del Valle, San Bartolo Coyotepec, Ocotlán, Arrazola, Cuilapan and Zaachila) from Prolongación Victoria just southeast of the Central de Abastos market. They leave when they're full (five or six people).

MONTE ALBÁN
☎ 951

The ancient Zapotec capital of **Monte Albán** (☎ 516-12-15; admission $3.75; ☣ 8am-6pm) stands on a flattened hilltop 400m above the valley floor, just a few kilometers west of Oaxaca. It's one of the most impressive ancient sites to be found in Mexico, and it has the most spectacular 360-degree views. Its name, Monte Albán (mohn-teh ahl-*bahn*) means White Mountain.

At the entrance to the site are a very good museum (with sculpture, pottery and other artifacts from the site, including several skulls and a re-created burial; explanations in Spanish only), a café, a bookstore and a branch of the jewelry store Oro de Monte Albán. Official guides offer their services outside the ticket office for tours in Spanish, English, French and Italian (around $20 for a small group). Portions of the site are wheelchair-accessible, via a lift and special walkways. A good scale model of the site, with a handy north point, lies just past the entrance turnstiles.

History

Monte Albán was first occupied around 500 BC, probably by Zapotecs. It likely had early cultural connections with the Olmecs to the northeast.

Archaeologists divide Monte Albán's history into five phases. The years up to about 200 BC (phase Monte Albán I) saw the leveling of the hilltop, the building of temples and probably palaces, and the growth of a town of 10,000 or more people on the hillsides. Hieroglyphs and dates in a dot-and-bar system carved during this era may well mean that the elite of Monte Albán were the first people to use writing, and a written calendar, in Mexico. Between 200 BC and about AD 300 (Monte Albán II) the city came to dominate more and more of Oaxaca. Buildings of this period were typically made of huge stone blocks and had steep walls.

The city was at its peak from about 300 to 700 (Monte Albán III), when the main and surrounding hills were terraced for dwellings, and the population reached about 25,000. Most of what we see now dates from this time. Monte Albán was the center of a highly organized, priest-dominated society, controlling the extensively irrigated Valles Centrales, which held at least 200 other settlements and ceremonial centers. Many Monte Albán buildings were plastered and painted red, and *talud-tablero* (stepped building style with alternating vertical and sloping sections) architecture indicates influence from Teotihuacán. Nearly 170 underground tombs from this period have been found, some of them elaborate and decorated with

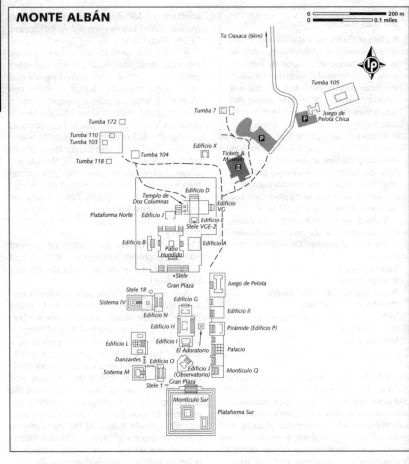

MONTE ALBÁN

0 — 200 m
0 — 0.1 miles

To Oaxaca (6km)

Tumba 105

Tumba 7

Juego de
Pelota Chica

Tumba 172

Tumba 110
Tumba 103

Edificio X

Tickets &
Museum

Tumba 104

Tumba 118

Edificio D

Templo de
Dos Columnas

Edificio
VG

Plataforma Norte

Edificio J

Edificio E

Stele VGE-2

Edificio B

Patio
Hundido

Edificio A

Stele

Gran Plaza

Juego de Pelota

Stele 18

Edificio G

Sistema IV

Edificio N

Edificio II

Edificio H

Pirámide (Edificio P)

Edificio L

Edificio I

El Adoratorio

Palacio

Danzantes

Edificio O

Sistema M

Edificio J
(Observatorio)

Monticulo Q

Stele 1

Gran Plaza

Monticulo Sur

Plataforma Sur

frescoes. Skulls that have had holes drilled, cut or scraped into them have been found in more than 20 burials here – thought to be evidence of medical treatments unique in ancient Mexico.

Between about 700 and 950 (Monte Albán IV), the place was abandoned and fell into ruin. Monte Albán V (950–1521) saw minimal activity, except that Mixtecs arriving from northwestern Oaxaca reused old tombs here to bury their own dignitaries.

Sights
GRAN PLAZA

The **Gran Plaza**, about 300m long and 200m wide, was the center of Monte Albán. Its visible structures are mostly from the

peak Monte Albán III period. Some were temples, others residential. The following description takes you clockwise around the plaza. Many of the structures in and around the plaza are cordoned off to prevent damage by too many visitors' feet.

The stone terraces of the deep, I-shaped **Juego de Pelota** (Ball Court), constructed about 100 BC, were probably part of the playing area, not stands for spectators. The **Pirámide** (Edificio P) was topped by a small pillared temple and was probably an observatory of some sort. At the bottom of its staircase a very low tunnel leads into a tomb. The **Palacio** (Palace) bears atop it a patio surrounded by the remains of typical Monte Albán III residential rooms.

The big **Plataforma Sur** (South Platform), with its wide staircase, is still good for a panorama of the plaza and the surrounding mountains, and has some carvings at the corner of its eastern base. **Edificio J**, an arrowhead-shaped building constructed about 100 BC and riddled with tunnels and staircases (unfortunately you can't go inside), stands at an angle of 45 degrees to the other Gran Plaza structures and was an observatory. Figures and hieroglyphs carved on its walls record Monte Albán's military conquests of other towns.

Edificio O, at the front of **Sistema M** (a patio-temple-altar complex from the Monte Albán III phase), was added to an earlier structure in an apparent attempt to conceal the plaza's lack of symmetry. (The rock mounds supporting the Plataforma Sur and Plataforma Norte are not directly opposite each other.)

Edificio L is an amalgam of the Monte Albán I building that contained the famous Danzante carvings and a later structure built over it. The **Danzantes** (Dancers), some of which are seen around the lower part of the building, are thought to depict leaders of conquered neighboring people. Carved between 500 and 100 BC, they generally have open mouths (sometimes downturned in Olmec style) and closed eyes. Some have blood flowing from where their genitals have been cut off. Hieroglyphs accompanying them are the earliest known examples of true writing in Mexico.

Sistema IV, the twin to Sistema M, combines typical Monte Albán II construction with overlays from Monte Albán III and IV.

PLATAFORMA NORTE

The **North Platform**, over a rock outcrop, is almost as big as the Gran Plaza, and offers the best views, overall. It was rebuilt several times over the centuries. Chambers on either side of the main staircase contained tombs, and columns at the top of the stairs supported the roof of a hall. On top of the platform is a ceremonial complex built between AD 500 and 800; points of interest here include the **Patio Hundido** (Sunken Patio), with an altar at its center, **Edificios D, VG** and **E** (which were topped with adobe temples) and the **Templo de Dos Columnas**. **Stele VGE-2**, on the southern side of Edificio E, shows members of Monte Albán's ruling class of around AD 800 – four women and a fifth figure represented by a jaguar.

TOMBS

To help preserve them, most of Monte Albán's ancient tombs are usually closed to visitors. But if you're lucky you may be able to peer into one of the following.

Tumba 104

Tomb 104, behind Plataforma Norte, dates from AD 500 to 700. Above its underground entrance is an urn in the form of Pitao Cozobi, the Zapotec maize god, wearing a mask of Cocijo, the rain god (whose forked tongue represents lightning). The walls are covered with colorful Teotihuacán-style frescoes. The figure on the left wall is probably the Zapotec flayed god and god of spring, Xipe Tótec; on the right wall, wearing a big snake-and-feather headdress, is Pitao Cozobi again.

Tumba 7

This tomb, just off the main parking lot, was built around AD 800, beneath a dwelling. In the 14th or 15th century it was reused by Mixtecs to bury a dignitary, two sacrificed servants – and one of the richest ancient treasure hoards in the Americas – the famed Mixtec treasure, now in the Museo de las Culturas de Oaxaca (p723).

Tumba 105

Tomb 105, behind the Juego de Pelota Chica (Small Ball Court), features decaying Teotihuacán-influenced murals of a procession of figures. The figures may represent nine gods of death (or gods of night) and their female consorts. It lies beneath one of Monte Albán's biggest palace-residences, built between AD 500 and 800.

Getting There & Away

Autobuses Turísticos (Map pp720-1; ☎ 516-53-27) runs buses to the site from Hotel Rivera del Ángel, at Mina 518 in Oaxaca, a 10- to 15-minute walk six blocks southwest of the zócalo. The buses leave every hour from 8:30am to 3:30pm (details of the schedule change from time to time). The ride up takes 20 minutes. The $3 fare includes a return trip at a designated time, giving you about two hours at the site. If you want to stay longer, you must hope for a spare place on a later return bus and pay a further $1.50. The last bus back leaves Monte Albán at 6pm.

A taxi from Oaxaca to Monte Albán costs about $8, and althought there are usually taxis at Monte Albán waiting to bring you back to Oaxaca, you may have to pay more for the return journey. Walking up from the city center takes about 1½ hours.

EL TULE
pop 6800 / elevation 1550m
The village of El Tule, 10km east of Oaxaca along Hwy 190, draws crowds of visitors for one very good reason: **El Árbol del Tule** (The Tree of El Tule; admission $0.30; 🕘 9am-5pm), which is claimed (incorrectly) to be the largest single biomass in the world. This vast *ahuehuete* (a type of cypress), 58m around and 42m high, dwarfs the 17th-century village church in whose churchyard it towers. Its age is equally impressive: the tree is officially reckoned to be between 2000 and 3000 years old.

Long revered by Oaxacans, the Árbol del Tule is under threat from nearby industries and housing that tap its water sources. Local campaigners are trying to win Unesco World Heritage status for the tree. They argue that the only long-term solution is integral protection of the 110-sq-km basin that supplies the tree's water, including reforestation in the mountains above and the creation of a large green zone in the valley.

Autotransportes Valle del Norte buses go to El Tule (from $0.45, every 10 minutes) from the 2nd-class bus station in Oaxaca.

DAINZÚ
Twenty-one kilometers from Oaxaca along the Mitla road, a track leads 1km south to the small but interesting **ruins of Dainzú** (admission $2.25; 🕘 8am-5pm).

To the left as you approach you'll find the pyramidlike Edificio A, 50m long and 8m high, built about 300 BC. Along its bottom wall were some 50 bas-reliefs of feline figures, masks and heads, mostly related to the ball game; they're now gathered under a corrugated metal roof. Among the ruins below Edificio A are a partly restored ball court from about AD 1000 and a sunken tomb (inside Edificio B) whose entrance is carved with a representation of a crouching jaguar. In the scrub at the top of the hill behind

the site are more rock carvings similar to those of Edificio A, but you'll need a guide to find them (ask the caretaker).

TEOTITLÁN DEL VALLE
☎ 951 / pop 4600 / elevation 1700m
This famous weaving village is 4km north of Hwy 190, about 25km from Oaxaca. Blankets, rugs and sarapes (blankets with an opening for the head, worn as a cloak) wave at you from houses and showrooms along the road into the village (which becomes Av Juárez as it approaches the center), and signs point to the central **Mercado de Artesanías**, where yet more are on sale. The variety of designs is enormous – from Zapotec gods and Mitla-style geometric patterns to imitations of paintings by Rivera, Picasso and Escher.

The weaving tradition here goes back to pre-Hispanic times: Teotitlán had to pay tributes of cloth to the Aztecs. Quality is still high, and traditional dyes made from cochineal, indigo and moss have been revived. Many shops have weavers who work and are happy to demonstrate how they obtain natural dyes. Teotitlán's most celebrated weaver, Arnulfo Mendoza (born 1954), works in a large house–guest retreat overlooking the north end of the village. You can see fine examples of his work in Oaxaca at La Mano Mágica (p724).

The village itself is very tranquil and tidy. Facing the Mercado de Artesanías on the central plaza is the **Museo Comunitario Balaa Xtee Guech Gulal** (☎ 524-44-63; admission $1; 🕘 10am-6pm Tue-Sun), a community museum with local archaeological finds and displays on local crafts and traditions (in English as well as Spanish and Zapotec). From the plaza, steps rise to a fine broad churchyard with the handsome 17th-century **Templo de la Virgen de la Natividad** in one corner. The whole thing was built atop a Zapotec ceremonial site, many of whose carved stones can be seen in the church walls; look especially in the inner patio.

Turismo de Aventura Teotitlán (☎ 524-43-71; roque_antonio740@hotmail.com; Av Juárez 59), across from Restaurante Tlamanalli, offers birdwatching, mountain-biking or hiking trips and village tours, mostly with English-speaking guides, for $30 to $55. Roque Antonio Santiago's birding trips get good reports; he takes clients to the coastal lagoons and elsewhere.

Calle 2 de Abril No 12 (☎ 524-41-64; Calle 2 de Abril 12; d incl breakfast $43, r for up to 5 people $52), a house belonging to friendly, English-speaking Elena González, has weaving looms in the courtyard and three bright, clean and modern upstairs rooms, each with private bathroom and hot water.

Arnulfo and Mary Jane Mendoza's serene retreat, **Casa Sagrada** (☎ 516-42-75; www.casasagrada.com; s/d 2-night minimum incl breakfast & dinner $110/190), is geared largely toward groups, but individuals are welcome. The 12 lovely rooms are decorated with vintage *artesanía*, giving you a taste of old Mexico. The property has panoramic views over the village and valley, a large yoga studio, and horses wandering about. Activities on offer (some of which require advance planning) include riding, hiking, biking, birding expeditions and cooking classes.

Traditional Oaxacan dishes at **Restaurante Tlamanalli** (☎ 524-40-06; Av Juárez 39; mains $6.50-16; ☏ 1-4pm Tue-Sun) are so well prepared that some locals point to them as serving the best restaurant fare in the states. Exhibits on weaving add to the interest. Note that Teotitlán has two Juárez 39s; this one is lower down, in the town proper.

Autotransportes Valle del Norte buses run to Teotitlán ($0.70, 50 minutes, hourly 7am to 9pm Monday to Saturday) from Gate 29 at Oaxaca's 2nd-class bus station; the last bus back to Oaxaca from the village leaves about 7pm. Alternatively, get any Mitla- or Tlacolula-bound bus to the signposted Teotitlán turnoff on Hwy 190 ($0.70), then a *colectivo* taxi ($0.40) to the village.

LAMBITYECO

This small **archaeological site** (admission $2.25; ☏ 8am-5pm) is on the south side of the Mitla road, 29km from Oaxaca. Between AD 600 and 800, Lambityeco became a sizable Zapotec center of about 3000 people. Its interest today lies in two patios containing striking sculptures, which unfortunately can only be viewed at a distance from atop a mound above them. In the first patio are two carved stone friezes, each showing a bearded man holding a bone (a symbol of hereditary rights) and a woman with a Zapotec hairstyle (one couple is Mr Four Human Face and Mrs 10 Monkey). Both these couples, plus a third in stucco on a tomb in the patio, are thought to have occupied the building around the patio and to have ruled Lambityeco in the 7th century. The second patio has two heads of the rain god Cocijo. On one, a big headdress spreading above Cocijo's stern face forms the face of a jaguar. Transportes Oaxaca-Istmo's buses to the Mitla road, every few minutes from Gate 9 of Oaxaca's 2nd-class bus station, will drop you anywhere along this road.

OAXACA'S COMMUNITY MUSEUMS

Oaxaca state is in the forefront of Mexico's admirable community-museums movement. Of the more than 100 villages around the country that have set up these small museums to foster their unique cultures and keep their archaeological and cultural treasures 'at home,' 17 are scattered around Oaxaca.

Unión de Museos Comunitarios de Oaxaca (☎ 951-516-39-13; Colón 1016, Oaxaca) in Oaxaca city has full information on these small but often fascinating museums. The office also offers organized group trips to various museum villages, including **San José El Mogote** (p750; $23), **Santa Ana del Valle** (p744; $29) and **San Martín Huamelulpan** (p752; $61). The prices here are per person for groups of five; they drop significantly for groups of 10. The excursions include traditional local meals and visits to local artisans or healers, archaeological sites and so on. The trip to San Martín Huamelulpan includes four meals and a night's lodging, as well as a demonstration of traditional medicine practices and – usually – a *temazcal* (traditional sweat lodge). If you're up for an off-the-beaten-track adventure, consider visiting the museums at Natividad in the Sierra Norte, with a re-creation of an old gold mine; Cerro Marín near Valle Nacional, which tells the story of the villagers' struggle for rights to use their local spring; or San Miguel Tequistepec near Coixtlahuaca, with fascinating pre-Hispanic material in the restored 16th-century house of a *cacique* (regional warlord or political strongman). Simple accommodations are available at or near several of these outlying villages.

TLACOLULA

pop 11,000 / elevation 1650m

This town, 31km from Oaxaca, holds one of the Valles Centrales' major **markets** every Sunday, with the area around the church becoming a packed throng. Crafts, foods and plenty of everyday goods are on sale. It's a treat for lovers of market atmosphere. Even on nonmarket days you can see women in colorful traditional dress, and the meat market in front of the church is often in full swing, its vendors constantly whisking flies off their products.

The interior of domed 16th-century **Capilla del Santo Cristo** is a riot of golden, indigenous-influenced decoration comparable with the Capilla del Rosario in the Iglesia de Santo Domingo, Oaxaca city. Among the ceiling ornamentation are plaster martyrs who stand holding their severed heads in their hands. The church was one of several founded in Oaxaca by Dominican monks.

Transportes Oaxaca-Istmo and Fletes y Pasajes buses run to Tlacolula from Oaxaca's 2nd-class bus station ($1, one hour, every few minutes).

SANTA ANA DEL VALLE

☎ 951 / pop 2250 / elevation 1700m

Santa Ana, 4km north of Tlacolula, is another village with a time-honored textile tradition. Today it produces woolen blankets, sarapes and bags. Natural dyes have been revived, and traditional designs – flowers, birds, geometric patterns – are still in use. On the central plaza is the richly decorated 17th-century **Templo de Santa Ana** (🕑 irregular hrs) and the **Museo Comunitario Shan-Dany** (☎ 562-17-05; admission $1; 🕑 10am-2pm & 3-6pm), a community museum with exhibits on local textiles, archaeology and history (the Mexican Revolution dominates) and the Zapotec Danza de las Plumas. It has some fine pre-Hispanic ceramic pieces. Nearby is a small **Mercado de Artesanías** with local textiles. There are a few textile workshops that you can visit, but you need to ask around.

Buses and minibuses run frequently from Tlacolula to Santa Ana until about 7pm (8pm on Saturday and Sunday).

YAGUL

The **Yagul ruins** (admission $3; 🕑 8am-6pm) are finely sited on a cactus-covered hill, 1.5km to the north of the Oaxaca–Mitla road.

Unless you have a vehicle you'll have to walk the 1.5km – but the ruins' setting makes the effort well worthwhile. The signposted turnoff is 34km from Oaxaca.

Yagul was a leading Valles Centrales settlement after the decline of Monte Albán. Most of what's visible was built after AD 750.

Patio 4, down to the left as you reach the main part of the site from the entrance, was surrounded by four temples. On its east side is a carved-stone animal, probably a jaguar. Next to the central platform is the entrance to one of several underground **Tumbas Triples** (Triple Tombs).

The beautiful **Juego de Pelota** (Ball Court) is the second-biggest in Mesoamerica (after one at Chichén Itzá – see p942). To its west, on the edge of the hill, is **Patio 1**, with the narrow **Sala de Consejo** (Council Hall) along its north side.

The labyrinthine **Palacio de los Seis Patios** (Palace of the Six Patios) was probably the leader's residence. Its walls were plastered and painted red.

It's well worth climbing the **Fortaleza** (Fortress), the huge rock that towers above the ruins. The path passes **Tumba 28**, made of cut stone. Several overgrown ruins perch atop the Fortress – and the views are marvelous.

MITLA

☎ 951 / pop 7500 / elevation 1700m

The stone 'mosaics' of ancient Mitla, 46km southeast of Oaxaca, are unique in Mexico. Today they are surrounded by a modern Zapotec town.

Orientation

If you tell the bus conductor from Oaxaca that you're heading for *las ruinas*, you should be dropped at a Y junction (*la cuchilla*). From here it's about 1.5km to the ruins' ticket office: go north along Av Morelos, and continue through the plaza toward the three-domed Iglesia de San Pablo. The ticket office is behind this church.

Ruins

The **ruins** (☎ 568-03-16; admission Grupo del Norte & Grupo de las Columnas $3; 🕑 9am-5pm) date mostly from the last two or three centuries before the Spanish conquest. This was when Mitla was probably the most important of Zapotec religious centers, dominated by high priests who performed (literally) heart-wrenching human sacrifices. Evidence points to a short period of Mixtec domination here in the 14th century, followed by a Zapotec reassertion before the Aztecs arrived in 1494. Somewhere beneath the town may be a great undiscovered tomb of Zapotec kings; 17th-century monk Francisco de Burgoa wrote that Spanish priests found it but sealed it up. It's thought that each group of buildings we see at Mitla was reserved for specific occupants – one for the high priest, one for lesser priests, one for the king and so forth.

The **Grupo de las Columnas** (Group of the Columns), the major group of buildings, is just south of the Iglesia de San Pablo. It had two main patios, each lined on three sides by long rooms. Along the north side of the Patio Norte is the **Salón de las Columnas** (Hall of the Columns), 38m long with six massive columns and unusual, very big one-piece lintels over doorways. At one end of this hall, a passage (still bearing traces of its original plaster and red paint) leads into **El Palacio**, which holds some of Mitla's best stonework 'mosaics.' Each little piece of stone was cut to fit the design, then set in mortar on the walls and painted. The 14 different geometric designs at Mitla are thought to symbolize the sky and earth, a feathered serpent and other important beings. Many Mitla buildings were also adorned with painted friezes. You can see most of them in one place by looking at the outside northwest corners of the Columns Group.

The Patio Sur holds two underground tombs, unapproachable at the time of research. The **Grupo del Norte** (North Group) is similar to the Grupo de las Columnas but not as well preserved. The Spaniards built Mitla's church over one of the group's patios in 1590. The **Grupo del Arroyo** (Stream Group), which you pass on the way in from town, is the most substantial of the other groups. Remains of forts, tombs and other structures are scattered for many kilometers around.

Sleeping & Eating

Hotel La Zapoteca (☎ 568-00-26; Calle 5 de Febrero 12; d/tr/q $19/24/33) En route to the ruins' entrance, only a few hundred meters away, is this modest, reasonably clean hotel, with uncomfortable overstuffed pillows, occasional plumbing problems and a restaurant.

Hotel Don Cenobio (☎ 568-03-30; www.hoteldon cenobio.com; Av Juárez 3; r $61-80; P ♠) Set on

the central plaza, this is the town's classiest hotel. Rooms were still being added to the hotel at the time of research, but the functioning ones were comfortable and fan-cooled, with good bathrooms.

Restaurante Don Cenobio (☎ 568-03-30; www .hoteldoncenobio.com; Av Juárez 3; mains $5-7.50; ♡ restaurant 10am-6pm Wed-Mon) The classiest restaurant in town is part of the classiest hotel. It serves mainly Oaxacan and Mexican fare near a green courtyard swings and a slide for the kids.

Restaurant Doña Chica (Av Morelos 41; mains $3.75-5; ♡ 10am-9pm) This homey, simple restaurant is less than 100m from *la cuchilla* on the street leading to the center and ruins. It serves straightforward and delicious Oaxacan dishes such as *moles*, enchiladas and *tasajos* (very thin cuts of meat rubbed with chili paste). Good *antojitos*, soups and salads cost around $2.50.

Shopping

Mitla's streets are sprinkled with shops selling local *mezcal* (see the boxed text, p736). Many of them will invite you to taste a couple of varieties. Many other shops, and the large **Mercado de Artesanías** near the ruins, sell local textiles. Some of the tablecloths are attractive buys.

Getting There & Around

Transportes Oaxaca-Istmo buses to Mitla ($1.50, 1¼ hours, every few minutes from 5am to 7pm) leave from Gate 9 of Oaxaca's 2nd-class bus station, and Fypsa has buses every 10 minutes between 6am and 9pm ($1.25). The last bus back to Oaxaca leaves Mitla at about 8:30pm. A taxi from *la cuchilla* to the ruins costs $2, as do *colectivo* taxis (per person) from Oaxaca to Mitla.

HIERVE EL AGUA
elevation 1800m

A new leg of highway goes eastward past Mitla a few kilometers to the turnoff for **Hierve El Agua** (The Water Boils; admission $1.50; ♡ 9am-6pm). As at Pamukkale, in Turkey, mineral springs here run into bathing pools with a striking cliff-top location and expansive panoramas. The cool, mineral-laden water doesn't really boil, but bubbles out of the ground, depositing its load over the steep hillside to create formations that look like huge frozen waterfalls. Altogether it makes for a unique bathing experience. The waters here were used for irrigation as long ago as 1300 BC; you can see small channels carved in the rock.

Hierve El Agua is a popular destination for *oaxaqueños* on their days off. But check before you come that it's open: in recent years the site has, at times, been closed owing to an ownership dispute between local villages. Above the pools and cliffs are a number of **comedores** (antojitos $2-3), and half a dozen **cabañas** (cabins; per person $7) that provide accommodations in simple rooms.

The area is dotted with maguey fields: San Lorenzo Albarradas, nearby San Juan del Río and the other 'Albarradas' villages produce some of Oaxaca's finest *mezcal*.

Viajes Turísticos Mitla in Oaxaca (see Tours, p726) runs trips to Hierve El Agua, giving you three hours at the waters ($18 return). The same company and other agencies in Oaxaca also offer day trips combining Hierve El Agua with Mitla and Teotitlán for $25 to $30 per person.

A Fypsa bus leaves Oaxaca's 2nd-class bus station for Hierve El Agua ($3, two hours) at 8am daily, passing through Mitla at about 9:15am. *Camionetas* (pickup trucks), which are infrequent except on Saturday and Sunday, run from the street outside Mitla bus station to Hierve El Agua ($2.50, one hour) whenever they have six or seven people. On busy days there's also a bus from Mitla to Hierve El Agua ($2.50) at noon. By car, take the exit (signed Hierve el Agua) from the highway that bypasses Mitla to the south, to tiny Xaagá, from which a new, unpaved and very scenic (if steep in parts) road leads 13km to the site.

PUEBLOS MANCOMUNADOS

The Pueblos Mancomunados (Commonwealth of Villages) comprises eight small, remote Zapotec villages in the thickly forested highlands of the Sierra Norte, highlands that form the northern boundary of the Valle de Tlacolula. For centuries, in a unique form of cooperation, the villages have pooled the natural resources of their 290-sq-km territory, which include extensive pine and oak forests, sharing the profits from forestry and other enterprises among all their families. In an effort to provide extra local income, stem a modern population decline and maintain sustainable uses

of their forests, the villages have set up an excellent ecotourism program, **Expediciones Sierra Norte** (Map pp720-1; ☎ 951-514-82-71; www.sierranorte.org.mx in Spanish; Bravo 210, Oaxaca; ☺ 9am-3pm & 4-7pm Mon-Fri, 9am-2pm Sat). The program offers simple but good and comfortable lodgings, and walking and mountain biking along more than 100km of scenic tracks and trails. It's a great way to experience this unique region of Oaxaca, which is completely different from the dry Valles Centrales or the tropical Pacific coast. Elevations range from 2200m to over 3200m, and the landscapes with their canyons, caves, crags, waterfalls and panoramic lookouts are spectacular. The area's natural diversity is amazing: over 400 bird species, 350 butterflies, all six Mexican wildcats (including the jaguar) and nearly 4000 plants have been recorded in the Sierra Norte. The variety of wildflowers here is astonishing, too. One highlight walk is the beautiful Latuvi-Lachatao canyon trail, which follows a pre-Hispanic track that connected Oaxaca's Valles Centrales with the Gulf of Mexico and passes through cloud forests festooned with bromeliads and hanging mosses. The villages themselves are mostly poor, simple and well cared for.

The trained local guides will almost certainly only speak Zapotec and Spanish but are knowledgeable about the plants, wildlife and ecology of these sierras. You can go without a guide, but if you do, be ready to get lost because trail marking is less than perfect. For accommodations and meals, each village has plain but comfortable *cabañas* (mostly with shared bathrooms with hot showers, and some with fireplaces), a designated camping ground, and at least one *comedor* serving cheap, good local meals.

Your best option is to contact Expediciones Sierra Norte's office in Oaxaca, which has full information on trails, tracks, accommodations and how to prepare, and takes bookings for both guided and independent trips. The office also sells a very useful guide with map for $5. Be ready for much cooler temperatures: in the Sierra Norte's higher, southern villages it can be freezing in winter. The rainiest season is from late May to September, but there's little rain from January to April.

Prices for visiting the Pueblos Mancomunados: guide for up to five people per day

$11.50; *cabaña* accommodation per person per night $12.50; camping per person $3.75 (bring your own tent); bicycle rental (only in Benito Juárez and Cuajimoloyas) per day $15; *huentzee* (contribution to maintenance costs) per visit $5. Fully organized trips including meals, accommodations, transportation and an English-speaking guide, for two days, costs $141, on foot or on bike. Some adventure travel agencies, such as Tierraventura in Oaxaca (see p725), can take you to the Pueblos Mancomunados: this costs more but they take the work out of the planning, preparation and transportation.

The most common starting villages are Cuajimoloyas (elevation 3180m) and Llano Grande (2900m), both with regular bus service, and Benito Juárez (2750m), with less-frequent bus service. All are at the higher, southern end of the Sierra Norte, so that walks or rides starting here will be more downhill than up. A good place to end up is at Amatlán in the north, where the comfortable cabins have fireplaces. Nearby Lachatao is almost a ghost village but has a huge 17th-century church, a fruit of the riches produced by nearby colonial gold mines.

It's also possible to base yourself in one village and take local walks or rides from there, with or without guides. Some superb lookout points are accessible from the southern villages, such as the 3000m El Mirador, a 2.5km walk from Benito Juárez, or the 3280m-high Yaa-Cuetzi lookout, 1km from Cuajimoloyas. From Yaa-Cuetzi in clear weather you can see such distant mountains as Pico de Orizaba and Zempoaltépetl. Within a couple of hours' walk of Llano Grande you can reach Piedra Larga, a rocky crag with superb views, or the Cueva Iglesia, a cave and canyon hidden in the mountain forests.

Extra accommodations in Benito Juárez include a state government–run self-catering **tourist yú'u** (dm $12.50, d $38, 4-bed cabaña per person $12.50). You can reserve accommodation and guides through the village's helpful **ecotourism office** (☎ 954-545-99-94), and places in the *yú'u* (a Zapotec word meaning 'house') can also be booked through the tourist offices in Oaxaca.

Cuajimoloyas has extra accommodations in the form of the Hostal Yacuetzi, with five rooms sharing one bathroom. You can reserve accommodations and guides through

Cuajimoloyas' **ecotourism office** (☎ 951-524-50-24; Av Oaxaca 15). To reserve accommodations and guides at Llano Grande, contact the village's Comité de Ecoturismo (☎ 01-200-125-75-41 through 43) via *casetas telefónicas* (public telephone call stations).

Getting There & Away

Cuajimoloyas and Llano Grande have the best bus links with Oaxaca: five daily buses (to Cuajimoloyas $2.25, two hours; to Llano Grande $2.50, 2½ hours) from the 2nd-class bus station with **Flecha del Zempoaltépetl** (☎ 951-516-63-42). For Benito Juárez ($2.75, two hours) and Latuvi ($2.50, three hours), Transportes Ya'a-Yana buses leave from Calle Niño Perdido 306, Colonia Ixcotel, Oaxaca, at 4pm (5pm during the daylight saving period) Monday, Tuesday, Friday and Saturday. The stop is next to a Pemex gas station on Hwy 190, a couple of kilometers east of the 1st-class bus station; a taxi is the easiest way there from the city center. Returning to Oaxaca, the buses leave Latuvi at 4am and Benito Juárez at 5am on the same days. Another way to reach Benito Juárez is to take a Cuajimoloyas-bound bus to the Benito Juárez turnoff *(desviación de Benito Juárez)*, 1¾ hours from Oaxaca, then walk 3.5km west along the unpaved road to the village.

Transportes Ya'a-Yana also runs buses from the same stop in Oaxaca at 4pm daily to Amatlán ($2.50, 2¼ hours) and Lachatao ($3, 2½ hours). Returning to Oaxaca, the buses leave Lachatao at 5am and Amatlán at 5:15am.

Unlike Oaxaca, the Pueblos Mancomunados does not observe daylight saving time – so triple-check all bus departure times for your return trip!

SAN BARTOLO COYOTEPEC

☎ 951 / pop 3000 / elevation 1550m

All the polished, black, surprisingly light pottery, called *barro negro*, that you find around Oaxaca (in hundreds of shapes and forms – candlesticks, jugs and vases, decorative animal and bird figures) comes from San Bartolo Coyotepec, a small village with a colorfully painted church, 11km south of the Oaxaca. To head to the pottery's source, look for the signs to the **Alfarería Doña Rosa** (☎ 551-00-11; www.go-oaxaca.com/dona_rosa.htm; Juárez 24; ⏱ 9am-7pm), a short walk east off the highway. Several village families make and sell the *barro negro*, but it was Rosa Real Mateo (1900–80) who invented the method of burnishing it with quartz stones for the distinctive shine. Her family *alfarería* (potter's workshop) is the biggest in the village, and demonstrations of the process are given whenever a tour bus rolls in (several times a day). The pieces are hand-molded by an age-old technique that uses two saucers functioning as a rudimentary potter's wheel. Then they are fired in pit kilns; they turn black because of the iron oxide in the local clay and because smoke is trapped in the kiln.

The town has an excellent new state-sponsored museum, the **Museo Estatal de Arte Popular de Oaxaca** (admission $2; ☺ 10am-6pm Tue-Sun), on the south side of the plaza, across the highway from the church. It features folk art from around the state, including ceramics, baskets, knives, wood sculptures, rugs, tinwork and more. The museum itself is very modern and rather nicely done. Changing exhibitions spotlight various towns, and the stuff upstairs is for sale at good fixed prices.

Buses from Oaxaca to San Bartolo ($0.50, 20 minutes) go every few minutes from the terminal at Armenta y López 721, 500m south of the Oaxaca *zócalo*.

SAN MARTÍN TILCAJETE & SANTO TOMÁS JALIEZA

The village of San Martín Tilcajete (population 1800), 1km west of Hwy 175, 24km south of Oaxaca, is the source of many of the bright copal-wood *alebrijes* (animal figures) seen in Oaxaca. You can see and buy them in makers' houses, many of which have 'Artesanías de Madera' (Wooden Handicrafts) signs outside.

The women of Santo Tomás Jalieza (population 1000), on the east side of Hwy 175, 2km south of the San Martín Tilcajete turnoff, weave high-quality textiles on backstrap looms; there is often fine detail work on their *fajas* (cotton waist-sashes), with pretty animal or plant designs. There's a permanent **Mercado de Artesanías** in the village square, selling tablecloths, table mats and embroidered dresses as well as more traditional weavings. It opens daily but is busiest on Friday to coincide with the Ocotlán market. *Colectivo* taxis run from Ocotlán.

OCOTLÁN
pop 13,000 / elevation 1500m

The sprawling Friday market in and around the central plaza of Ocotlán, 31km south of Oaxaca, dates back to pre-Hispanic times and is one of the biggest in the Valles Centrales. Ocotlán's most renowned artisans are the four Aguilar sisters and their families, who create whimsical, colorful pottery figures of women with all sorts of unusual motifs. The Aguilars' houses are together on the west side of the highway as you come into Ocotlán from the north – spot them by the pottery women on the wall. Most renowned are the family of **Guillermina Aguilar** (Prolongación de Morelos 430), who turn out, among other things, miniature re-creations of Frida Kahlo works (for more on Kahlo, see boxed text, p145).

Ocotlán was the hometown of artist Rodolfo Morales (1925–2001), who turned his international success to Ocotlán's benefit by setting up the **Fundación Cultural Rodolfo Morales** (Morelos 108). He did this to promote the arts, heritage and social welfare of Oaxaca's Valles Centrales.

Morales and the foundation renovated the handsome 16th-century church overlooking the main plaza, the **Templo de Santo Domingo**, which now sports beautiful, colorful paintwork inside and out. It has also turned the adjoining **Ex-Convento de Santo Domingo** (admission $2.25; ☺ 9am-6pm), previously a dilapidated jail, into a first-class museum of popular and religious art, including several of Morales' own canvases and a room of folk art dominated by the Aguilar sisters. Morales' ashes are interred here, too.

Estrella del Valle/Oaxaca Pacífico runs buses to Ocotlán ($1.25, 45 minutes, every few minutes from 5am to 9:30pm) from the terminal at Armenta y López 721 in Oaxaca. Autotransportes Ocotlán de Morelos operates a similar service from 6am to 9pm from its terminal on Cabrera.

SAN JOSÉ DEL PACÍFICO
☎ 951 / pop 500 / elevation 2750m

The small mountain village of San José del Pacífico, 102km south of Ocotlán (about 50 minutes past Miahuatlán), is just outside the Valles Centrales on Hwy 175 heading toward Pochutla and the coast. The scenery is spectacular and it's a good base for walks through the cool mountain pine forests to waterfalls. The San José area is also famed for its magic mushrooms.

The best place to stay is **Cabañas y Restaurante Puesta del Sol** (☎ 510-75-70; www.sanjosedelpacifico.com; r $29, cabañas per 2/5 people $38/47; P ꦽ), beside Hwy 175, 1km north of the village. It offers superb views and beautiful wooden rooms and *cabañas* set in spacious hillside grounds, all with hot showers. The *cabañas* have fireplaces, too. The tap water is from a spring and is drinkable. A decent restaurant serves *antojitos* and omelettes for around $2.50 and meat dishes for around $4. Cheaper, basic rooms are available in the village itself (look for signs).

All Hwy 175 buses between Oaxaca and Pochutla stop at San José, as do Autoexprés Atlántida's vans ($6 from Oaxaca).

ARRAZOLA
pop 1000

Below the west side of Monte Albán and about 4km off the Cuilapan road, Arrazola produces many of the colorful copal *alebrijes* that are sold in Oaxaca. You can see and buy them in artisans' homes.

CUILAPAN
pop 11,000 / elevation 1570m

Cuilapan (sometimes spelled Cuilápam), 9km southwest of Oaxaca, is one of the few Mixtec villages in the Valles Centrales. It's the site of a beautiful, historic Dominican monastery, the **Ex-Convento Dominicano** (admission to cloister $2.25; ☺ 9am-6pm), whose pale stone seems almost to grow out of the land.

In 1831, Mexican independence hero Vicente Guerrero was executed at the monastery by soldiers supporting the rebel conservative Anastasio Bustamante, who had just deposed the liberal Guerrero from the Mexican presidency. Guerrero had fled by ship from Acapulco, but the ship's captain put in at Huatulco and betrayed him to the rebels. Guerrero was transported to Cuilapan to die.

From the monastery entrance you reach a long, low, unfinished church that has stood roofless since work on it stopped in 1560. Its enormous, broken-off arches, impressive stonework and minute detailing are more staid and European than those of other monasteries in the area, but are quite dignified.

Beyond is the church that succeeded it, which contains the tomb of Juana Donají

(daughter of Cocijo-eza, the last Zapotec king of Zaachila). It's only open for Mass, around 7am to 8am and 5pm to 6pm most days. Around the church's right-hand end is a two-storey renaissance-style cloister; some rooms have faded 16th- and 17th-century murals. A painting of Guerrero hangs in the small room where he was held, and outside stands a monument on the spot where he was shot.

Añasa (Bustamante 604), six blocks south of Oaxaca's *zócalo*, runs buses to Cuilapan ($0.40, 20 minutes, every 15 minutes from 5:30am to 9pm).

ZAACHILA
☎ 951 / pop 12,000 / elevation 1520m

This part-Mixtec, part-Zapotec village, about 6km beyond Cuilapan and 4km west of Coyotepec, has a large, busy Thursday market. Zaachila was one of the only Mixtec-Zapotec city states remaining when the Spanish arrived. Its last Zapotec king, Cocijo-eza, converted to Christianity, taking the name Juan Cortés. He died in 1523.

Behind the village church, which overlooks the main plaza, a sign indicates the entrance to the **Zona Arqueológica** (Archaeological Zone; admission $2.25; ☺ 9am-6pm), a small assortment of mounds where you can enter two small tombs used by the ancient Mixtecs. Both are in the same mound, near the ticket office. Tumba No 1 retains sculptures of owls, a turtle-man figure and various long-nosed skull-like masks. Tumba No 2 has no decoration but in it was found a Mixtec treasure hoard comparable with that of Tumba 7 at Monte Albán – and now in the Museo Nacional de Antropología (p138) in Mexico City. When Mexican archaeologists tried to excavate these tombs in the 1940s and 1950s, they were run off by irate Zaachilans. The tombs were finally excavated under armed guard in 1962. You can see photos of some of the objects that were carted off to the national anthropology museum.

The **Restaurante Típico La Capilla** (☎ 528-61-15; Carretera Oaxaca-Zaachila, Km 14; mains $4.50-9.50; ☺ 7am-7pm) may look like a tourist trap, but it serves top-quality Oaxacan *antojitos* and mains, including a superb *mole negro*, heavenly cheese, and rich *barbacoa de chivo* (goat meat surrounded by roasted maguey leaves and slow-cooked – in a pit, traditionally, but these days more often in a stovetop steamer). A small **bestiary**, plus swings and slides, keeps the kids happy. The complex is next to a water tower, 1km west of Zaachila center on the old Cuilapan road; it gets packed with Oaxacans on Sundays.

Añasa buses to Cuilapan (see p749) continue to Zaachila ($0.40, 25 minutes from Oaxaca). It also has a direct service (20 minutes) via the 'new' road that heads straight south from Oaxaca, bypassing Cuilapan, for the same price.

ATZOMPA

pop 14,000 / elevation 1600m

Atzompa, 6km northwest of Oaxaca, is one of the leading pottery-making villages in the Valles Centrales. A lot of its very attractive, colorful work is sold at excellent prices in the **Mercado de Artesanías** (Crafts Market; Av Libertad 303) on the main street entering the village from Oaxaca. The restaurant at this market is good for a moderately priced snack or lunch.

From the church up in the village center, a 2.5km road (mostly dirt) leads south up **Cerro El Bonete**. The road ends a few minutes' walk from the top of the hill, which is dotted with unrestored pre-Hispanic ruins.

Choferes del Sur, at Gate 39 of Oaxaca's 2nd-class bus station, runs buses every 10 minutes to Atzompa ($0.30, 30-45 minutes). If driving yourself, follow Calz Madero northwest out of Oaxaca, turn left along Masseu (signposted 'Monte Albán') at a big intersection on the fringe of town, then go right at traffic signals after 1.5km.

SAN JOSÉ EL MOGOTE

Fourteen kilometers northwest of central Oaxaca on Hwy 190, a westward turnoff signposted to Nazareno (just opposite the turnoff to the Academia Estatal de Policía) leads 1.5km to the tiny village of San José El Mogote. Long ago, before Monte Albán became important, Mogote was the major settlement in Oaxaca. It was at its peak between 650 and 500 BC, and flourished again between 100 BC and AD 150, with a main plaza that was almost as big as Monte Albán's. The major surviving structures (partly restored) are a ball court and a sizable pyramid mound on the village periphery.

The interesting community museum, the **Museo Comunitario Ex-Hacienda El Cacique**

(admission $1; ☻ 9am-1pm & 3-5pm), is in the former landowner's hacienda in the village center. If you find it closed, look for its *encargado* (keeper) two houses behind the primary school. To climb to the top of the ruins, detour to your left on the way to the *encargado's* house. A museum highlight is 'El Diablo Enchilado' (the Chilied Devil), a pre-Hispanic brazier in the form of a bright red grimacing face. The museum also has interesting material on the villagers' 20th-century struggle for land ownership.

Colectivo taxi is the simplest way to get to Mogote. Catch one from the Valles Centrales on Trujano, on the north side of the 2nd-class bus station.

WESTERN OAXACA

The rugged, mountainous west of Oaxaca state (and adjoining bits of Puebla and Guerrero states) is known as the Mixteca, for its Mixtec indigenous inhabitants. It was from here in about the 12th century that Mixtec dominance began to spread to the Valles Centrales. The Mixtecs were famed workers of gold and precious stones, and it's said that Aztec emperor Moctezuma would only eat off fine Mixteca-Puebla ceramics.

Today you will see that much of the region is overfarmed, eroded and deforested, and that politics and business are dominated by mestizos. Many Mixtecs have to emigrate for work. Foreign visitors are not at all frequent here, although some guided trips are available from Oaxaca with Tierraventura (see p725).

Sleeping

You can visit the Mixteca in a long day trip from Oaxaca, but basic hotels or *casas de huéspedes* (homes converted into simple guest lodgings) are available for visitors in Nochixtlán, Coixtlahuaca, Tamazulapan, San Pedro Teposcolula and Putla, while Tlaxiaco and Huajuapan de León have better lodgings. In Huajuapan, a good, inexpensive choice is **Hotel Colón** (☎ 953-532-08-17; Colón 10; s/d $19/24; P), a motel-style place with a courtyard surrounded by two floors of rooms. It's clean, green and friendly, and rooms have TV and fan.

Getting There & Away

Buses run from Mexico City's TAPO to several Mixteca towns. Santiago Apoala has a bus service three days a week to/from Nochixtlán. You can also reach Apoala by taxi or *camioneta* from Nochixtlán. Several buses a day head south from Tlaxiaco to Pinotepa Nacional (seven hours).

Other bus daily departures from Oaxaca:

Route	Price	Duration	Frequency
Coixtlahuaca	$6		6 Fypsa
Huajuapan de León	$3.75	3½hr	2nd-class Sur every 30min 5:30am-9pm
Nochixtlán	$7	1¼hr	8 1st-class ADO
	$2	1½hr	2nd-class Sur every 30min 5:30am-9pm, continues to Yanhuitlán
Tejupan	$3	2¼hr	2nd-class Sur every 30min 5:30am-9pm
Teposcolula	$2.50	2½hr	2nd-class Sur hourly from 6:30am-7:30pm
Tlaxiaco	$3	3hr	2nd-class Sur hourly from 6:30am-7:30pm

SANTIAGO APOALA

☎ 555 / pop 200

This small village, 2000m above sea level in a stunning green valley flanked by cliffs, is 40km north of Nochixtlán and is a great place to get off the beaten track.

The journey from Nochixtlán, via unpaved roads, can take up to two hours. The scenery around Apoala is spectacular, with the 60m waterfall Cascada Cola de la Serpiente and the 400m-deep Cañón Morelos among the highlights. Several Oaxaca active-tourism agencies (p724) run trips here, typically of two days, with a three-hour walk through the canyon to the village on the first day, and a walk to the waterfall (where you can usually have a swim) the next day.

You can also do it independently: the village's **Comité de Turismo** (Tourism Committee; ☎ 151-91-54) has a reasonably comfortable three-room **Parador Turístico** (s/d $8.50/17, 4-/8-person tents $11.50/23). Reserve direct or book through **Sectur** (☎ 576-48-28; www.aoaxaca.com; Murguía 206; ☒ 8am-8pm) in Oaxaca. Meals at the parador cost $3 each (phone ahead to check availability, but take a few supplies just in case), mountain-bike rental is $2.50/9.50 per hour/day, and each group of up to five people has to pay a $5 access charge. Comité

de Turismo can also arrange accommodations and meals in private homes at prices similar to the parador's.

YANHUITLÁN, COIXTLAHUACA & SAN PEDRO TEPOSCOLULA

Among colonial Mexico's finest architectural treasures are the beautiful 16th-century **Dominican monasteries** (☒ 10am-5pm) of the three Mixteca villages Yanhuitlán (population 839), Coixtlahuaca (population 971) and San Pedro Teposcolula (population 1318). Their restrained stonework fuses medieval, plateresque, renaissance and indigenous styles, and all three have ornate interior decoration, including enormous gilt wooden *retablos* (altarpieces). The **Yanhuitlán monastery** (admission $1) and **Coixtlahuaca monastery** (admission free) were undergoing restoration work at the time of research, most notably of their main altarpieces.

Coixtlahuaca's monastery is perhaps the most interesting of the group. Its pure renaissance facade and the arches of its graceful, ruined *capilla abierta* (open chapel, used in early Mexican monasteries for preaching to crowds of indigenous people) both bear Mixtec religious symbols, most notably serpents and eagles. You can climb to the 2nd floor and roof for views of the rocky landscape. Coixtlahuaca is a few kilometers east of the Coixtlahuaca tollbooth on 135D, about 30km north of Nochixtlán.

The towering monastery at Yanhuitlán, built atop an important Mixtec religious site, looms beside Hwy 190, 14km northwest of Nochixtlán. The church contains valuable works of art, and a fine Mudejar ceiling is suspended beneath the choir loft, which has an impressive pipe organ.

About 20km southwest of Yanhuitlán, on Hwy 125, is the relaxed, friendly town of San Pedro Teposcolula (not to be confused with San Juan Teposcolula, which is closer to Yanhuitlán). Extensive restorations on its **monastery** (admission free) were recently completed: the stately *capilla abierta* has several finely carved arches, and the adjoining church is fully outfitted and functioning. Buildings around the town plaza are painted a lively red and white, and you'll find good accommodation in the clean, tiled rooms of **Hotel Juvi** (☎ 953-518-20-64; s/d/tr $12.50/16/18; P), just across Hwy 125 from the monastery.

SAN MARTÍN HUAMELULPAN

☎ 951 / pop 130 / elevation 2235m

The turnoff for San Martín is 22km south of San Pedro Teposcolula, and the village itself lies 1km off Hwy 125. The friendly, tranquil community and its piney surrounds are home to practitioners of traditional medicine renowned for their powers. Its **Museo Comunitario Hitalulu** (☎ 510-49-49; Plaza Cívica; admission $1; ⏱ 10am-5pm Tue-Sun) has one wing focusing on the healers and the plants they use. The other wing holds some excellent artifacts from the archaeological site that's spread across the hills above town. Explanations are all in Spanish.

Only 200m or so behind the museum are the ruins of a major Mixtec ceremonial center, much of it as yet unexcavated. Walk away from the highway and past the church to reach the large restored section, built on several levels and including a ball court, an altar, and a temple whose lower chambers are thought to have been a holding cell for sacrificial victims. When walking here from the museum, pass the church keeping it to your left. As you do so, note the carved figures of skulls that were taken from the site and incorporated into the church's arch and side wall; they are from various stages of the Mixtec culture.

The community has built a modest minihotel that will accommodate up to 28 people, with cooking facilities, a fridge and four small *temazcales* in which guests can experience a traditional steambath. Rates start at $2.75. Contact the Unión de Museos Comunitarios office in Oaxaca (see the boxed text, p743) to arrange lodging.

SOUTH FROM TLAXIACO

About 18km south of Huamelulpan on Hwy 125 lies Tlaxiaco (population 14,000), which has an interesting Saturday **market** on and around the main plaza. Also on the plaza is **Hotel del Portal** (☎ 953-552-01-54; Plaza de la Constitución 2; r $20-25; P), with clean, quiet rooms out the back and a good, moderately priced restaurant in an atmospheric old courtyard in the front.

South of Tlaxiaco, Hwy 125 winds through the remote Sierra Madre del Sur to Pinotepa Nacional, on coastal Hwy 200. The route's major town is Putla, 95km from Tlaxiaco. Just before Putla is San Andrés Chicahuaxtla, in the small territory of the indigenous Triquis. The Amuzgo people of San Pedro Amuzgos, 73km south of Putla, are known for their fine *huipiles*.

NORTHERN OAXACA

Highway 175, scenic but rough in parts, crosses Oaxaca's northern sierras to Tuxtepec (population 92,000), the main town in the low-lying Papaloapan region of far northern Oaxaca. In culture and geography, the region is akin to neighboring Veracruz. In the Sierra Mazateca west of Tuxtepec is Huautla de Jiménez, where – according to legend – the likes of Bob Dylan, the Beatles, Timothy Leary and Albert Hoffman (the inventor of LSD) used to go to trip on the local *hongos* (hallucinogenic mushrooms). They did this under the guidance of María Sabina, Huautla's famed *curandera* (medicine woman) – María Sabina died in 1985,

---

PEOPLES OF OAXACA

Oaxaca is home to 15 indigenous groups, each with its own language, customs and colorful traditional costume (though most of their members also speak Spanish and many wear mainstream clothing). These groups account for about a third of the state's population of 3.6 million, and form a strong presence throughout the region.

Oaxaca's approximately 500,000 Zapotecs live mainly in and around the Valles Centrales and on the Isthmus of Tehuantepec. Isthmus Zapotecs have resisted pressure to assimilate for centuries. About 500,000 Mixtecs are spread around the mountainous borders of Oaxaca, Guerrero and Puebla states, with more than two-thirds of them in Oaxaca. The state's other large indigenous groups include 160,000 or so Mazatecs in the far north, 100,000 Mixes in the highlands northeast of the Valles Centrales, and 100,000 Chinantecs around Valle Nacional in the north.

In Oaxaca city you may well see Triquis, from western Oaxaca; the women wear bright red *huipiles* (sleeveless tunics). The Triquis are only about 15,000 strong and have a long history of violent conflict with mestizos and Mixtecs over land rights.

out others follow in her footsteps and small numbers of foreigners still make their way to Huautla. Fresh mushrooms appear in the rainy season from June to August. Locals disapprove of mushroom-taking just for thrills.

GUELATAO & IXTLÁN

☎ 951

On Hwy 175, 60km from Oaxaca, Guelatao village was the birthplace of Benito Juárez. By the pretty lake at the center of the village is a statue of the boy Benito as a shepherd. Among the adjacent municipal buildings are two statues of Juárez and a small exposi-tion, the **Sala Homenaje a Juárez** (admission free; ☺ 9am-4pm Wed-Sun).

Benito Juárez (1806–72) was one of Mex-ico's most revered national heroes. He was born in the mountain village of Guelatao, and his Zapotec parents died when he was three. At the age of 12, knowing only a few words of Spanish, he walked to Oaxaca and found work at the house of Antonio Salanueva, a bookbinder. Salanueva saw the boy's potential and decided to help pay for an education Juárez otherwise might not have received.

Juárez trained for the priesthood but abandoned it to work as a lawyer for poor vil-lagers. He became a member of the Oaxaca city council and then of the Oaxaca state government. As state governor from 1848 to 1852, he opened schools and cut bureaucracy. The conservative national government exiled him in 1853, but he re-turned to Mexico in the 1855 Revolution of Ayutla that ousted General Santa Anna. Juárez became justice minister in Mexico's new liberal government. His Ley Juárez (Juárez Law), which transferred the trials of soldiers and priests charged with civil crimes to ordinary civil courts, was the first of the Reform laws, which sought to break the power of the Catholic Church. These laws provoked the War of the Reform of 1858 to 1861, in which the liberals eventu-ally defeated the conservatives.

Juárez was elected Mexico's president in 1861 but had only been in office a few months when France, supported by con-servatives and clergy, invaded Mexico and forced him into exile again. In 1867, with US support, Juárez ousted the French and their puppet emperor, Maximilian.

One of Juárez' main political achieve-ments was to make primary education free and compulsory. He died in 1872, a year after being elected to his fourth presiden-tial term. Today countless statues, streets, schools and plazas preserve his name and memory, and his sage maxim 'El respeto al derecho ajeno es la paz' ('Respect for the rights of others is peace') is widely quoted.

In the small town of Ixtlán, 3km beyond Guelatao on Hwy 175, is the baroque **Tem-plo de Santo Tomás**, where baby Benito was baptized. Note this church's finely carved west facade. On Ixtlán's plaza you'll also find a community ecotourism venture, **Shiaa-Rua-Via** (☎ /fax 553-60-75; http://oaxaca.host .sk in Spanish), which offers cabaña accommo-dation, guided hikes and mountain biking. The services are similar to those offered by Expediciones Sierra Norte (see p746) in the nearby Sierra Norte country of the Pueblos Mancomunados.

Around seven daily buses depart Oaxaca's 1st-class station for Guelatao ($3, 1½ hours) and Ixtlán ($3.25, 1¾ hours). For $1 less, the bus companies **Benito Juárez** (☎ 951-516-57-76) and **Flecha del Zempoaltépetl** (☎ 951-516-63-42) run 10 daily buses from Oaxaca's 2nd-class bus station

OAXACA COAST

A laid-back spell on the beautiful Oaxaca coast is the perfect complement to the inland attractions of Oaxaca city and the Valles Centrales. The trip down Hwy 175 from Oaxaca is spectacular: south of Mia-huatlán you climb into pine forests, then descend into ever lusher and hotter tropical forest.

The once-remote fishing villages and former coffee ports of Puerto Escondido and Puerto Ángel are now informal tourist resorts. Puerto Escondido has famous surf and a lively travelers' scene, while Puerto Ángel is the hub for a series of wonderful beaches with limitless low-cost accommo-dations – among them the fabled Zipolite and its increasingly popular neighbor, Ma-zunte. To the east, a bigger tourist resort has been developed on the scenic Bahías de Huatulco.

West of Puerto Escondido, nature-lovers can visit the lagoons of San José Manialtepec

OAXACA STATE

and Chacahua (teeming with bird life), and hang at Chacahua village.

The coast of Oaxaca is hotter and much more humid than the state's highlands. Most of the year's rain falls between June and September, turning everything green. From October the landscape starts to dry out, and by March many of the trees are leafless. May is the hottest month.

Note that, with variations, the high tourism seasons on this coast are from January to Easter and for most of July and August; the room rates we list are for these high periods. Many places drop rates by 25% or more in other seasons, and raise them by at least as much for the peak periods around Christmas and Easter (a week or more on either side).

The Oaxaca coast is an impoverished region apart from its few tourism spots. Though incidents have decreased in recent years, there have been cases of highway robbery along Hwy 200 from Pochutla northwest to Acapulco. Much of coastal Oaxaca is cattle country, and the numbers of cows (as well as *burros* – donkeys – and horses) wandering loose on the highway give new meaning to the term 'free range.' Robbery and roadkill both ramp up at night, so try to do your traveling in the daytime.

PUERTO ESCONDIDO

☎ 954 / pop 20,000

Known to surfers since before paved roads reached this part of Oaxaca, Puerto Escondido (Hidden Port) remains relaxed and inexpensive with a great travelers' scene. It has several beaches, a broad range of accommodations, some excellent restaurants, plenty of cafés and a spot of nightlife. Several interesting ecotourist destinations are close by.

Any hint of breeze is a blessing in Puerto, and you're more likely to get a breeze up the hill than down at sea level.

Orientation

The town rises above the small, south-facing Bahía Principal. Highway 200, here called the Carretera Costera, runs across the hill halfway up, dividing the upper town – where buses arrive and most of the locals live and work – from the lower, tourism-dominated part. The heart of the lower town is referred to by all as El Adoquín.

This is the pedestrianized (from 5pm unti late) section of Av Pérez Gasga (*adoquín i* Spanish for paving stone). The west end o Av Pérez Gasga winds up the slope to mee Hwy 200 at an intersection with traffic sig nals, an intersection known as El Crucero.

Bahía Principal curves around at its eas end to the long Playa Zicatela, the hub o the surf scene, with loads of places to stay and eat. About 1km west of El Crucero the area above Playa Carrizalillo has a few places to stay, restaurants and services.

The airport is 4km west of the center or the north side of Hwy 200, and the mair bus terminal (Central Camionera) is in the upper part of town between Calles 3 and < Pte, north of Calle 10 Norte (see Gettin; Around, p762, for more information).

Information

BOOKSTORES

PJ's Book Bodega (☎ 541-00-36-56; Calle del Morro s/n, Zicatela) A large collection of new and used books in English, Spanish and other languages.

EMERGENCY

Tourist Police (☎ 582-34-39; Av Pérez Gasga s/n; 24hr Assistance in English or Spanish.

INTERNET ACCESS

Cofee Net (Calle del Morro 310, Zicatela; per hr $1.50; ☉ 24hr) Located in the Hotel Surf Olas Altas; free coffee.
Copacabana (Av Pérez Gasga 705; per hr $1)
Internet Acuario (Calle del Morro s/n, Zicatela; per hr $1.50) Found in the Hotel Acuario building.

LAUNDRY

Lava-Max (☎ 540-16-17; Av Pérez Gasga 405A; ☉ 8am 8pm) Self-serve wash up to 3.5kg of clothes for $1.30 (plus $0.70 for detergent and $1.25 for dryer); complete wash an dry service costs $1.20 per kg.

MEDIA

The free monthly paper *El Sol de la Costa* (www .elsoldelacosta.com), in Spanish and Eng lish, is full of information about what's or and what to do.

MEDICAL SERVICES

IMSS clinic (☎ 582-01-42; Calle 2 Pte s/n)

MONEY

Many hotels give a fair rate for dollars. Th town's *casas de cambio* open longer hour than the banks, and most change US-dolla

PUERTO ESCONDIDO

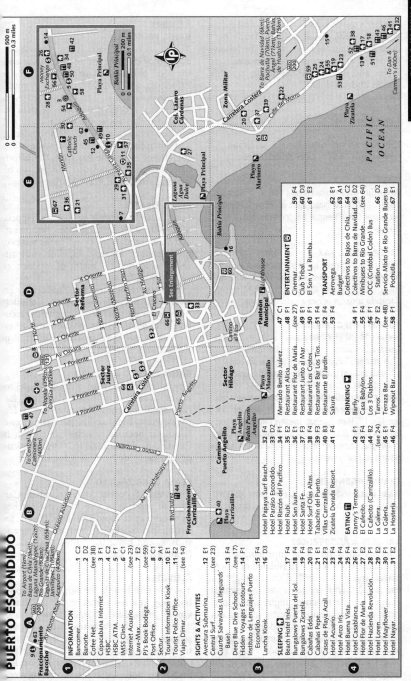

INFORMATION
Bancomer............................	1 C2
Banorte.............................	2 D2
Coffee Net..........................	(see 38)
Copacabana Internet...............	3 F1
HSBC................................	4 C2
HSBC ATM...........................	5 F1
IMSS Clinic.........................	6 C1
Internet Acuario....................	(see 23)
Lava-Max...........................	7 E2
PJ's Book Bodega...................	(see 59)
Post Office.........................	8 C1
Sectur..............................	9 A1
Tourist Information Kiosk...........	10 E1
Tourist Police Office...............	11 E1
Viajes Dimar........................	(see 14)

SIGHTS & ACTIVITIES
Aventura Submarina................	12 E1
Central Surf........................	(see 23)
Cuartel Salvavidas (Lifeguards' Base).............................	13 F1
Deep Blue Dive School.............	(see 17)
Hidden Voyages Ecotours..........	14 F1
Instituto de Lenguajes Puerto Escondido........................	15 F4
Lancha Kiosk.......................	16 D3

SLEEPING
Beach Hotel Inés...................	17 F4
Bungalows Puerta del Sol..........	18 F4
Bungalows Zicatela.................	19 F4
Cabañas Edda.......................	20 F3
Cabañas Pepe.......................	21 F3
Casas de Playa Acali...............	22 F3
Hotel Acuario......................	23 F4
Hotel Arco Iris.....................	24 F4
Hotel Buena Vista..................	25 F4
Hotel Casablanca...................	26 F1
Hotel Flor de María................	27 F2
Hotel Hacienda Revolución.........	28 F1
Hotel Loren........................	29 E2
Hotel Mayflower....................	30 F1
Hotel Nayar........................	31 E2
Hotel Papaya Surf Beach...........	32 F4
Hotel Paraíso Escondido...........	33 D2
Hotel Rincón del Pacífico..........	34 F1
Hotel Rubí.........................	35 E2
Hotel San Juan.....................	36 E1
Hotel Santa Fe.....................	37 F3
Hotel Surf Olas Altas..............	38 F4
Tabachín del Puerto................	39 F3
Villas Carrizalillo..................	40 B3
Zicatela Dorada Resort.............	41 F4

EATING
Danny's Terrace....................	42 F1
El Cafecito.........................	43 F4
El Cafecito (Carrizalillo)..........	44 B2
La Galera...........................	45 E2
La Galería..........................	(see 24)
La Hostería........................	46 F4
Mercado Benito Juárez.............	47 C1
Restaurant Alicia..................	48 C1
Restaurant Flor de María..........	(see 27)
Restaurant Junto al Mar...........	49 F1
Restaurant Los Crotos.............	50 F1
Restaurante Bar Los Tíos...........	51 F4
Restaurante El Jardín..............	52 F4
Sakura.............................	53 F4

DRINKING
Barfly..............................	54 F1
Casa Babylon.......................	55 F4
Los 3 Diablos.......................	56 F1
Tarros.............................	57 E2
Terraza Bar........................	(see 48)
Wipeout Bar........................	58 F1

ENTERTAINMENT
Cinemar............................	59 F4
Club Tribal.........................	60 D3
El Son y La Rumba..................	61 E3

TRANSPORT
Aerovega...........................	62 E1
Budget.............................	63 A1
Colectivos to Bajos de Chila.......	64 C2
Colectivos to Barra de Navidad.....	65 D2
Minibuses to Río Grande...........	(see 64)
OCC (Cristóbal Colón) Bus Station...........................	66 D2
Servicio Mixto de Río Grande Buses to Pochutla........................	67 E1

traveler's checks, cash US dollars and euros. A handy **HSBC ATM** (El Adoquín) stands next door to Restaurant Los Crotos. The following banks in the upper part of town all have ATMs and will change US-dollar traveler's checks and US dollars.

Bancomer (cnr Calles 3 Pte & 2 Norte; ⊙ 9am-2pm Mon-Sat)

Banorte (Av Hidalgo 4; ⊙ 9am-4pm Mon-Fri, 10am-4pm Sat)

HSBC (Calle 1 Norte; ⊙ 8am-7pm Mon-Sat) Located between Calles 2 & 3 Pte, it also changes cash euros.

POST

Post office (cnr Av Oaxaca & Calle 7 Norte; ⊙ 8am-3pm Mon-Fri) A 20- to 30-minute uphill walk from El Adoquín, but you can take a 'Mercado' bus or *colectivo* taxi up Av Oaxaca.

TELEPHONE & FAX

You'll find Telmex card phones and a couple of telephone *casetas* on the Adoquín, and more card phones along Calle del Morro on Zicatela and in other parts of town.

TOURIST INFORMATION

Sectur (☎ 582-01-75; www.aoaxaca.com; cnr Carretera Costera & Blvd Juárez; ⊙ 9am-2pm & 4-7pm Mon-Fri, 10am-2pm Sat) This state tourist office (the sign probably still reads Sedetur) is about 2.5km west of the center on the road to the airport.

Tourist information kiosk (ginainpuerto@yahoo.com; cnr Av Pérez Gasga & Marina Nacional; ⊙ 9am-2pm & 4-6pm Mon-Fri, 10am-2pm Sat) This very helpful place is at the west end of El Adoquín. Gina Machorro, the energetic, multilingual information officer usually found here, happily answers your every question.

TRAVEL AGENCIES

Viajes Dimar (☎ 582-15-51; Av Pérez Gasga 905B) You can buy air tickets here, as well as book rental cars and excursions.

Dangers & Annoyances

Puerto's safety record is improving, but to minimize any risks, avoid isolated or empty places, and stick to well-lit areas at night (or use taxis). Some residents say the greatest danger on the beach at night is the local cops: drinking, peeing or even making out beachside can invite a shakedown.

Beware of thieves on buses when going to or from Acapulco or Oaxaca, and be sure to get a ticket for any bags placed in the baggage hold.

Beaches

BAHÍA PRINCIPAL

The main town beach is long enough to accommodate restaurants at its west end, the local fishing fleet in its center (Playa Principal), and sun worshipers and young body-boarders at its east end (called Playa Marinero). Occasional flocks of pelicans wing in inches above the waves. Boats bob on the swell, and a few hawkers wander up and down the beach. The smelly water that sometimes enters the bay from the inaptly named Laguna Agua Dulce will put you off dipping away from Playa Marinero.

PLAYA ZICATELA

Long, straight Zicatela is Puerto's happening beach, with enticing cafés, restaurants and accommodations as well as the waves of the legendary 'Mexican Pipeline,' just off shore, which test the mettle of experienced surfers from far and wide.

Nonsurfers beware: the Zicatela waters have a lethal undertow and are definitely not safe for the boardless. Lifeguards rescue several careless people most months (their base, the Cuartel Salvavidas, is in front of Restaurante El Jardín).

BAHÍA PUERTO ANGELITO

The sheltered bay of Puerto Angelito, about 1km west of Bahía Principal, has two small beaches separated by a few rocks. Playa Manzanillo, the eastern one, is quieter because vehicles can't reach it. Puerto Angelito is a 20- to 30-minute walk or a $2 taxi ride from El Adoquín.

PLAYA CARRIZALILLO

Just west of Puerto Angelito, small Carrizalillo beach is in a rockier cove reached by a stairway of about 170 steps. It's OK for swimming, snorkeling, body-boarding and surfing, and has a bar with a few *palapas* (thatched-roof shelters).

Activities

You can rent boards for surfing and body-boarding in a few places on Playa Zicatela. One is **Central Surf** (☎ 582-22-85; www.centralsurfshop.com; Calle del Morro s/n; short board or body-board & fins per hr/day $3.75/9.50, long board per hr/day $3.75/14), in the Hotel Acuario building. Central Surf also offers surfing lessons (in English or Spanish) for $29 per hour. Other places offering rent-

and lessons, for about the same prices as at Central Surf, include **PJ's Book Bodega** (☎ 541-00-36-56; Calle del Morro s/n, Zicatela), which also buys and sells boards, and the **Instituto de Lenguajes** (☎ 582-20-55; Carretera Costera, Zicatela).

Lanchas (fast, open, outboard boats) from the west end of Bahía Principal will take groups of four people out for about an hour's **turtle-spotting** (and, in winter, sometimes dolphin-spotting) for around $30, with a drop-off at Puerto Angelito or Playa Carrizalillo afterwards.

Local marlin and sailfish anglers will take two to four people **fishing** with them for three hours for $84. Ask at the *lancha* kiosk at the west end of Bahía Principal. The price includes cooking some of the catch for you at one of the town's seafood restaurants.

Diving is another possibility. PADI-certified **Aventura Submarina** (☎ 582-23-53; asubmarina@hotmail.com; Av Pérez Gasga 601A; 1-/2-tank dive trips per person $38/57, Discover Scuba Diving course $71, 4-day Open Water certification course $328) teaches diving courses and leads dive trips for all levels of experience. **Deep Blue Dive School** (☎ 582-07-92; lorenzo2escondido.com; Calle del Morro s/n, Zicatela; 1-/2-tank dive trips per person $40/60, minimum 2 people), in Beach Hotel Inés, also offers a variety of trips, as well as PADI courses and certificates.

Horseback riding on Playa Zicatela looks fab. Ask the guys on the beach or arrange your rides through Beach Hotel Inés (p758).

Courses

Instituto de Lenguajes Puerto Escondido (☎ 582-20-55; www.puertoschool.com; Carretera Costera, Zicatela; per 1/2 people per hr $10/16) offers good language courses by native Spanish speakers, plus surfing, cooking and salsa lessons. The breezy hilltop site has great views of the Pipeline's main peak. The American-run Instituto will arrange homestays starting at $135 per week (for food and housing) and can place students in community-service programs.

Festivals & Events

Semana Santa (the week before Easter and a couple of days after it) is a big week for local partying; a local **surf carnival** is held at this time. At least two international surf contests are held on Zicatela each year: the **International Surfboard Contest** in August, and the **International Surfing Tournament** in mid-November. National surfing championships happen on the last weekend of November.

November is a big month in other ways, too: the **Festival Costeña de la Danza** (a fiesta of Oaxaca coastal dance), a **sailfishing contest** and **art exhibitions** all take place over the second and/or third weekends of the month.

Sleeping

The two main accommodation zones are the central Av Pérez Gasga area and the surf beach of Playa Zicatela. In the peak seasons the most popular places will probably be full, especially on Zicatela. Your best chance of getting into a place you like, if you haven't booked ahead, is to ask early in the day, at about 9am or 10am. In the low season many places drop prices drastically from those that we list, and some offer discounts for longer stays.

Several apartments and houses are available for short- and long-term stays. Apartments start at $400/800 per month in the low/high season; houses overlooking the beach start at around $1500. Ask at the tourist information kiosk on Av Pérez Gasga.

BUDGET

Playa Zicatela is about the only beach with decent budget accommodations, and the supply is limited. There are a number of budget spots in the area around Av Pérez Gasga.

Dan & Carmen's (☎ 582-27-60; www.casadanycarmen.com; Jacaranda 14, Colonia Santa María; cabañas $19, r with garden view/sea view/big sea view $26/33/38; Ⓟ Ⓢ) This excellent place offers 13 self-contained units with fully equipped kitchens and attractive Talavera-tiled bathrooms (Talavera tiles are colorful, hand-painted tiles designed with Asian, Spanish-Arabic and Mexican indigenous influences). Units vary in size from small, one-/two-person *cabañas* to larger, three-/four-person family rooms, with terrace and views. There's a terrific extra-long lap pool. Reservations are essential. It's up the paved road just south of Hotel Papaya Surf Beach, then right across a small bridge.

Hotel Papaya Surf Beach (☎ 582-11-68; www.papayasurf.com; Calle del Morro s/n; d with fan/air-con US28/$36; Ⓧ Ⓢ) Italian-run Papaya has at least 19 rooms with good bathrooms and mosquito screens. Upstairs rooms have shared balconies with hammocks. A restaurant-bar, rooftop *palapa* and pool round out the scene; the combination of beachfront location and facilities make the place good value.

Hotel Buena Vista (☎ /fax 582-14-74; www.prodigy web.net.mx/buenavista101; Calle del Morro s/n; d/tr $24/33, with kitchen $29/38) Another good value is the well-built Buena Vista, set above Playa Zicatela and reached by a steep flight of steps from Calle del Morro. Its good-sized, spotless rooms all have one double bed and one single, mosquito screens or nets, and hot-water bathroom. Many have breezy balconies, some with great views.

Cabañas Edda (☎ 582-23-22; Carretera Costera s/n; s/d cabañas $4/8, with private bathroom $6/12, campsites per person $3) Though it's not really a beach place, Edda's extensive grounds and basic lodgings above Zicatela are well kept, and all guests can use the common kitchen and laundry facilities. All rooms have screens or nets, and ceiling or floor fans; many of the private-bathroom *cabañas* have tiled floors. Some units are rather close to the highway.

Hotel Rubi (☎ 582-36-84; www.eladokin.com/ hoteles/hotelrubi; Av Pérez Gasga 309; d/tr/q $19/27/34; P ☒ ☒) Opened in 2003, the Rubi is one of the only hotels in the budget category that offers air-con. All rooms have two double beds and OK bathrooms. None have a sea view, but the small pool and proximity to the bay make it an attractive package.

Hotel Loren (☎ 582-00-57; fax 582-05-91; Av Pérez Gasga 507; d/tr/q with fan $24/33/43, with air-con $33/43/52; P ☒ ☒) A minute uphill from El Adoquín, this friendly, sky-blue-and-lobster-colored hotel has bare, dimly lit but spacious rooms. All have two or three (somewhat springy) double beds, cable TV and balconies; some catch a sea view. It's a good place for the price.

Cabañas Pepe (☎ 582-20-37; Merklin 101; d $18-30) Not far below El Crucero, friendly, family-run Pepe's is geared to backpackers and offers 12 simple, well-maintained rooms with two good double beds, fans, nets and hot-water bathrooms. Five have superb views and a shared balcony; the others have hammocks slung outside for relaxing in the shade.

Hotel Mayflower (☎ 582-03-67; minnemay7@hot mail.com; Andador Libertad s/n; dm/s/d/tr $7.50/21/26/30) The attractive, popular Mayflower, beside the steps leading down to El Adoquín from the east end of Merklin, has five fan-cooled dorms (the largest has seven beds; none have bunk beds) with room for more than 40 people. Rates include filtered water and the use of a kitchen with fridge and microwave. The 16 pleasing private rooms have

fans and bathrooms. There are semi-open sitting areas, a billiard table, board games, a safety box and luggage storage facilities. An HI card gets you a 10% discount.

MIDRANGE

There's plenty of choice near the beaches. Zicatela is sublime but it can get hectic in high seasons. There's also a good range of places around Av Pérez Gasga.

Beach Hotel Inés (☎ /fax 582-07-92; www.hotelines .com; Calle del Morro s/n; r $18-75; P ☒ ☒ ☒) German-run Inés has a wide range of bright, cheerful *cabañas*, rooms, bungalows and suites. All have safes, good mosquito screens and fans; most have wireless Internet access, some come with kitchens and some come with air-con. Lovely art and *artesanía* abound, and other pluses include a sauna, sundeck and spa, and a relaxed, shaded pool area with a café serving good food. You can arrange horseback riding and scuba here as well.

Hotel Flor de María (☎ 582-05-36; www.mexonline .com/flordemaria.htm; 1a Entrada a Playa Marinero; d $48-55, per additional person $10; ☒ ☒) A friendly Canadian couple runs this hotel on a lane behind Playa Marinero. The 24 ample rooms are around a columned patio; all have two double beds, safes, large, good bathrooms and well-rendered painted murals and door panels. Two rooms have sea views. Extras include a rooftop pool and bar with fabulous views, and a good international restaurant.

Hotel Arco Iris (☎ /fax 582-04-32; www.oaxaca-mio .com/arcoiris.htm; Calle del Morro s/n; d/tr/q from $57/61/66; P ☒) The attractive, colonial-style Arco Iris has 32 big, clean rooms with balconies or terraces, most looking straight out to the surf, plus a large pool and a good upstairs restaurant-bar open to the breeze. All rooms have two double beds and ceiling fans, and some have a kitchen. You can also park a camper in the sizable grounds.

Tabachín del Puerto (☎ 582-11-79; www.tabachin .com.mx; Zicatela; d incl breakfast $65-85, per additional person $15, child under 12yr free; P ☒) Tabachín's gracious and erudite owner offers six studio-rooms of varying sizes (including enormous), in varying states of maintenance. All have kitchen, TV and phone; most have balcony access, and some have sea views. The good breakfasts, which include vegetarian choices and organically grown coffee and fruits from the owner's farm in Nopala, draw nonguests as well and are always lively occasions. You'll find Tabachín at the end of a short lane behind Hotel Santa Fe.

Hotel Acuario (☎ 582-03-57; fax 582-10-27; Calle del Morro s/n; r $70-120; P 🅧 🖵 🅡) The 30 or so accommodations here range from cramped rooms to wooden *cabañas* to spacious upstairs rooms with terrace and beach view. The more substantial bungalows have the most appealing interiors and have kitchens. Acuario's complex includes a surf shop, Internet café and an inviting pool area. Prices drop by half out of season.

Bungalows Zicatela (☎ /fax 582-07-98; www.bungalowszicatela.com.mx; Calle del Morro s/n; s/d $19/38, bungalows with fan $47, with air-con & view $66; 🅧 🅡) The straightforward Zicatela has a sociable pool and restaurant and all of its 40-odd accommodations are a good size, solidly built and with mosquito-netted windows. Though squeezed a little tightly together, they have good beds and bathrooms, and most bungalows have kitchens.

Bungalows Puerta del Sol (☎ 582-29-22; Calle del Morro s/n, Zicatela; r $49; 🅡) This place has a small pool, a communal kitchen and 16 spacious, solidly built rooms with fan, balcony and hammock (some rooms have two double beds).

Casas de Playa Acali (☎ 582-07-54; arnulfodiaz59@hotmail.com; Calle del Morro s/n; cabañas $37, bungalows $50, r $68; 🅧 🅡) Acali's fenced property holds a fair bit of greenery. The varnished-wood *cabañas* are rustic but ample, each with one double and one single bed. The bungalows have decent bathrooms, screens and beds (two doubles in each), as well as kitchens. The more expensive rooms climb up the hillside in blocks, and have air-con, large upstairs kitchens and decks on which to relax.

Hotel Hacienda Revolución (☎ /fax 582-18-18; www.haciendarevolucion.com; Andador Revolución 21; d/tr/q room $33/38/43, d/tr casita $43/47) On a flight of steps leading up from El Adoquín, this Revolution-themed place has 11 attractive and spacious rooms around a garden-courtyard with a beautiful central fountain. Rooms have colorful paintwork and Talavera-tiled hot-water bathrooms; most have a patio and hammock. Casitas are set apart under a shared roof and are even nicer than rooms; each has a hammock on the patio. A

restaurant in the shady area below opens from December to March.

Hotel Nayar (☎ 582-01-13; fax 582-03-19; www.oaxaca-mio.com/hotelnayar.htm; Av Pérez Gasga 407; s/d with air-con $41/47; P 🅧 🅡) The Nayar was built in a '60s-modern style that looks much better once you get inside. Its 41 rooms have good beds, OK bathrooms with hot water, and small balconies. Fifteen rooms have sea views, and the view from the terrace is excellent. The pool is in a big garden by the entrance.

Hotel San Juan (☎ 582-05-18; www.hotelsanjuan.cjb.net; Merklin 503; d from $27, r with air-con $45; P 🅧 🅡) The friendly San Juan, just below El Crucero, has 31 good, straightforward rooms. All have hot water, mosquito screens, cable TV and a security box; some have terraces and excellent views. The hotel also boasts a pool and a rooftop sitting area.

Hotel Rincón del Pacífico (☎ 582-00-56; www.rincondelpacifico.com.mx; El Adoquín 900; s/d/tr/q with fan $30/38/45/54, with air-con $53/66/79/94; 🅧) This hotel has 30 spacious, big-windowed rooms (half with air-con, some with sea views) with good beds and hot-water bathrooms around a palm-filled courtyard. The staff are helpful and the hotel has a beachside café-restaurant.

Hotel Casablanca (☎ 582-01-68; www.ptohcasablanca.com; El Adoquín 905; s/d/tr/q $33/47/57/66; 🅡) The friendly Casablanca is right at the heart of things on the inland side of El Adoquín, and it fills up quickly with guests. It has a small pool and 21 large, clean tile-floored rooms with fan. Some have fridges; the best are streetside with balconies.

Zicatela Dorada Resort (☎ /fax 582-37-27; www.zicatela.mx.gs; Calle del Morro s/n; r with fan $55, with air-con $71; P 🅧 🅡) Still being decorated at the time of research, the semi-Mediterranean-style Zicatela Dorada features 60 rooms with hot water and cable TV. The rooms are set around a courtyard with swimming pool, bar and restaurant. Most have two double beds; the upper ones have small balconies and air-con.

TOP END

Hotel Santa Fe (☎ /fax 582-01-70; in the US ☎ 888-649-6407; www.hotelsantafe.com.mx; cnr Blvd Zicatela & Calle del Morro; r $120, bungalows $130, junior ste $155, master ste $260; P 🅧 🖵 🅡) The well-landscaped, neocolonial Santa Fe has more than 60 well-designed rooms set around pools and small terraces. Rooms vary in size and view, but they all have air-con and room safes. Also available are appealing bungalows with kitchens, and two impressive master suites furnished with colonial antiques and fabulous modern art. The views are spectacular from the suites and their wraparound terraces.

Villas Carrizalillo (☎ 582-17-35; www.villas carrizalillo.com; Av Carrizalillo 125, Carrizalillo; apt $80-125) Sublimely perched on the cliffs above the small Bahía Carrizalillo, Villas Carrizalillo has apartments for two to six people, with fully equipped kitchens and private terraces. Some have stunning sea views. A path goes directly down to Playa Carrizalillo.

Hotel Surf Olas Altas (☎ 582-23-15; ☎ /fax 582-00-94; www.surfolasaltas.com.mx; Calle del Morro 310, Zicatela; d/tr/q $117/131/145; P ⁂ ▢ ▣) This modern, three-storey 61-room hotel has less character than some of the smaller places, but the rooms are spotless and ample, and set well back from the street. Most have two double beds, room safe, air-con and satellite TV. Some rooms catch a sea view and some look over the pool, but some do neither.

Hotel Paraíso Escondido (☎ 582-04-44; Unión 10; d $99, tr & q $141; ⁂ ▢ ▣) The rambling neo-colonial Paraíso is decorated with tiles, pottery, stained glass and stone sculpture. Its 20 clean fair-sized rooms have good baths, old-fashioned red-tiled floors and small terraces. The hotel also has a library and an attractive restaurant/bar/pool area.

Eating

Puerto Escondido has some excellent eateries, a large proportion of them Italian thanks to the tide of Italian travelers drawn here by the movie *Puerto Escondido*. Most of the eateries are at least partly open-air. You'll eat some of the freshest fish and seafood you've ever had. Tofu products, and a mind-boggling range of fruit and vegetable juices – and milk and yogurt combos – make this a vegetarian's paradise.

UPPER TOWN
Mercado Benito Juárez (cnr Calles 8 Norte & 3 Pte; fish plates $4, veg plates $3) Several clean stalls in the market prepare good fare, and the sights and smells of the produce section also make it worth a wander, even if you're not hungry.

PLAYA ZICATELA
Sakura (Calle del Morro s/n; mains $3.75-15, sushi per pair $2.50-3.75, rolls $3.50-5, noodle dishes $3.75-7.50) Eating raw fish with your toes in the sand (or on cement, if you prefer), watching the Pipeline's curl…does it get any better than this? The Japanese chefs put out some excellent, tight, super-fresh *nigirizushi* (hand-pressed sushi) or you can choose from tempura, tofu and teriyaki dishes, curries and spring rolls.

La Hostería (☎ 582-00-05; Calle del Morro s/n; mains $3-9; ◷ 8am-12:30am; V) The Hostería is a labor of love, from its gleaming, super-pro kitchen (with computerized, wood-fired pizza oven) down to the excellent Talavera-tiled bathrooms. A broad selection of delicious Italian, Mexican and international dishes – including many veggie selections – is paired with a great wine list, and the espresso is one of the best in town.

Restaurant Flor de María (☎ 582-05-36; 1a Entrada a Playa Marinero; mains $3.75-11.50, breakfast $2.50-3; V) Inside the hotel of the same name, this restaurant has a dinner menu that changes daily depending on what's fresh, and includes fish, grilled meats and Italian dishes. There's always a vegetarian option.

Restaurante El Jardín (☎ 582-23-15; Calle del Morro s/n; dishes $3.50-7; ◷ 8am-11pm; V) This *palapa* restaurant in front of the Hotel Surf Olas Altas serves very good vegetarian dishes, including *gado-gado* (vegetables with peanut sauce), tempeh dishes, hummus, many salad varieties, and tofu offerings. The menu also includes some seafood dishes and an extensive beverage and juice list.

El Cafecito (☎ 582-05-16; Calle del Morro s/n; breakfast $2.50-3.75, lunch & dinner mains $2.75-6.50) The cinnamon rolls alone are worth a visit, but the Cafecito also serves good breakfasts, whole-wheat tortas, espressos and excellent, inexpensive pastries, croissants and cakes. However, the service was a little sullen last time. A second El Cafecito at Carrizalillo on Blvd Juárez features the same great food and the same service.

Restaurante Bar Los Tíos (Calle del Morro s/n; mains $3-5.50; ◷ 9am-10pm Wed-Mon) Right on the beach rather than across from it, the 'uncles' serve great *licuados* and several fresh fruit juices to go with their tasty egg dishes, *antojitos*, burgers, salads and seafood. It's wonderfully relaxed and very popular with locals.

Hotel Santa Fe (☎ 582-01-70; cnr Blvd Zicatela & Calle del Morro; pasta dishes $6.50-9, seafood dishes $13-17, veg & vegan dishes $5-6.50; **Ⓥ**) The airy and romantically sited restaurant at this hotel looks down on the west end of the Pipeline. Sink into a comfy leather chair and choose from the list of inspired vegetarian and vegan meals. Seafood choices are average, but service is excellent.

La Galera (☎ 582-04-32; Hotel Arco Iris, Calle del Morro s/n; menú del día $5.75, mains $4-9.50) This restaurant has a good, open-air upstairs setting, and tasty mixed Mexican and international fare. Main dishes focus on fish and meat but the *menú del día* is usually a three-course (plus drink) vegetarian meal.

Zicatela also has two or three small stores selling snacks, drinks and some of the various sundries travelers find useful.

AV PÉREZ GASGA

La Galería (☎ 582-20-39; mains $4.50-11.25) At the west end of El Adoquín, La Galería is one of Puerto's more agreeable Italian spots, with art on the walls and good fare on the tables. The pasta dishes and pizza are original and tasty, and the jumbo mixed green salad is a real treat. You can breakfast here too.

Restaurant Junto al Mar (JaM; ☎ 582-12-72; mains $5.75-13) On the bay side of El Adoquín, the JaM has a terrace overlooking the beach. Attentive waitstaff serve up excellent fresh seafood; the squid dishes and the fish fillet *a la veracruzana* (tomato, onion and pepper sauce) get the thumbs up.

Restaurant Los Crotos (☎ 582-00-25; mains $6-11.25; ☼ 7am-11pm) With romantic night lighting and an attractive setting almost on the sands of Playa Principal, and a good selection of seafood rounding out its menu, Los Crotos is an appealing choice.

Danny's Terrace (☎ 582-02-57; El Adoquín; mains $6-8.50) Reader-recommended Danny's is beachside at Hotel Rincón del Pacífico. In addition to the usual seafood, chicken and meat dishes, they serve up…vichyssoise! A decent selection of desserts and wines ties up the package.

Restaurant Alicia (El Adoquín; dishes $3-8.50) Economical little Alicia offers multiple spaghetti variations, seafood cocktails and good fish dishes. Breakfasts and beer are cheap, too; why not try them together?

Drinking

Casa Babylon (Calle del Morro s/n, Zicatela; ☼ 10am-late) This cool little travelers' bar has board games and a big selection of secondhand books to sell or exchange. The owner prides herself on her specialty cocktails: *mojitos* and *caipirinhas*.

Barfly (El Adoquín) The second-storey balcony, drink mixes and music draw a lively crowd most nights.

Rival drinking dens with loud music on the Adoquín include Terraza Bar, Wipeout Bar and Los 3 Diablos. **Tarros** (Marina Nacional), around the corner, is in the same league. Most of these hold two-for-one happy hours from 9pm to 10pm, but don't expect much action before 11pm.

A few bars and restaurants overlooking the sea, including Danny's Terrace (see left) off the Adoquín and the bar at Hotel Arco Iris (p758) in Zicatela, have happy hours from about 5pm to 7pm to help you enjoy Puerto's spectacular sunsets.

Entertainment

El Son y La Rumba (☎ 582-10-30; Calle del Morro s/n, Marinero; ☼ 7pm-late Tue-Sun) Tucked against the rocks at the Zicatela end of Playa Marinero, this friendly place usually features the acoustic guitar and vocals of Mayca, who performed the music for the film *Puerto Escondido*. She performs mostly bolero, Mexican *son* (guitars plus harp or violin with witty, frequently improvised lyrics) and *trova*. Guest artists playing a wide variety of music also pass through.

Club Tribal (Marina Nacional; admission $5; ☼ 10pm-4am Fri low season, 10pm-4am Fri & Sat high season) One of a cluster of discos a block or so southwest of the Adoquín.

La Hostería (Calle del Morro s/n) The Hostería restaurant shows the 1993 Italian travel-and-crime movie *Puerto Escondido* at 6pm nightly. This film (directed by Gabriele Salvatores, who also did *Mediterraneo*) has attracted thousands of Italians and others to Puerto and is worth seeing, even if it makes the town seem more remote than it really is.

Cinemar (Calle del Morro s/n; admission with popcorn & drink $4.25; ☼ films shown 5pm, 7pm & 9pm) Air-conditioned Cinemar, sharing the building with PJ's Book Bodega, shows films ranging from classics to latest general releases, in Spanish and English.

Shopping

The Adoquín is great for browsing and wandering around through shops and stalls, which sell fashions from surf designers and from Bali. New Age and silver jewelry, souvenirs, and classy crafts that are works of art can also be hunted down here.

Getting There & Away

AIR

Aero Tucán (☎ 582-17-25; Puerto Escondido airport) and **Aerovega** (☎ 582-01-51; Av Pérez Gasga 113) fly to/from Oaxaca – see Getting There & Away, p736 for details. **Click Mexicana** (☎ 01-800-122-54-25) flies nonstop to and from Mexico City twice daily. **Continental Express** (☎ 800-900-50-00) flies from Houston to Bahías de Huatulco between one and four times a week in winter, and from there it's an easy bus ride to Puerto Escondido.

BUS

All long-distance lines use the main bus terminal, except **OCC** (☎ 582-10-73), which at the time of research was breaking ground on a new facility on the Carretera Costera just west of Av Oaxaca (its old one is on Calle 1 Norte east of 1 Oriente). The main bus terminal (officially called the Central Turística de Autobuses, but generally known as the Central Camionera) is in the upper part of town between 3 and 4 Poniente, north of 10 Norte. Bus companies include **Estrella Blanca** (EB; ☎ 582-00-86), Estrella del Valle/Oaxaca Pacífico (EV/OP) and **Estrella Roja Sur** (ERS; ☎ 582-38-99). OCC, and a couple of Estrella Blanca buses to Mexico City, have the only true 1st-class bus services.

There are frequent daily departure to Oaxaca. It's advisable to book in advance for all OCC buses and for the better services to Oaxaca.

Route	Price	Duration	Frequency
Via Hwys 200 & 175	ordinario/directo $8/8.50-9.50	6½-7½hr	14 EV/OP daily
Via Hwy 131 *	$9.50	6-8hr	5 ERS daily
Via Hwys 200 & 190 **	$20	10-11hr	3 OCC daily

* (This is a shorter route on poor roads)
** (The longest but smoothest route)

There are several departures to other destinations:

Destination	Price	Duration	Frequency
Acapulco	$22	8hr	3 semi-directo EB daily
	$18	9½hr	9 ordinario EB daily
Bahías de Huatulco	$6	2½hr	11 OCC daily
	$6.50	2½hr	8 EB daily
Cuajiniculapa	$8.50-10.50	3½hr	12 buses daily
Juchitán	$15	6hr	OCC
Mexico City	$48	18hr	1 OCC per day
	$42	13hr	EB
Pochutla	$3.50	1½hr	7 OCC daily
	$4	1½hr	8 EB daily
	$2.25	1½hr	Servicio Mixto de Río Grande buses from El Crucero every 20min 5am-7pm
San Cristóbal de las Casas	$31	14hr	2 OCC per night
Salina Cruz	$9 to $12.50	5hr	EB
Tehuantepec	$14	5½hr	OCC
Tuxtla Gutiérrez	$28	12hr	2 OCC per night

Warning: keep a particularly close eye on your belongings when going to or from Acapulco or Oaxaca, and be sure to get a ticket for any bags placed in the baggage hold.

CAR & MOTORCYCLE

Budget (☎ 582-03-12; Blvd Juárez), opposite the tourist office, charges walk-ins $90 a day for its cheapest cars, including unlimited kilometers and insurance.

Getting Around

A taxi from the **airport** (☎ 582-04-92) costs around $3.50 – if you can find one that is (try looking on the main road outside the airport). Otherwise, *colectivo* combis ($4 per person) will drop you anywhere in town. Taxis from the bus station to most places in town should cost you no more than $3.

If you don't want to walk between the central Av Pérez Gasga/Bahía Principal area and the outlying beaches, taxis are the only available transportation – they wait at each end of El Adoquín. The standard fare to Playa Zicatela is $2.

AROUND PUERTO ESCONDIDO
Laguna Manialtepec

This lagoon, 6km long, begins 14km west of Puerto Escondido along Hwy 200. It's home to ibis, roseate spoonbills, parrots and pelicans, and to several species of hawk, falcon, osprey, egret, heron, kingfisher and iguana. The best months for observing birds are December to March, and they're best seen in the early morning. The lagoon is mainly surrounded by mangroves, but tropical flowers and palms accent the ocean side.

Several restaurants along the lagoon's north shore (just off Hwy 200) run boat trips. Some of them also have *colectivo* service geared more toward locals who just want to get to the other end of the lagoon. To reach these places from Puerto Escondido, take a Río Grande–bound minibus from Calle 2 Norte just east of the Carretera Costera, in the upper part of town, leaving every half-hour from 6am to 7pm ($0.90).

Las Hamacas (☎ 954-588-85-52; 2½hr trip for up to 5 people $56; ☺ 9am-8pm), at the eastern end of the lake, is a Spanish-Mexican operation renting out single- and double-seat kayaks for $5 per hour. Boat tours (one to five passengers) start at $43. The food's good, too, and you can go water-skiing for $56 an hour. **Restaurant Isla del Gallo** (2hr trip for up to 6 people $56, colectivo service 8am-5pm in peak tourism periods per person $7), halfway along the lake, offers shaded boat trips, and the boatmen know their birds. Good grilled fish and seafood are available at the restaurant for $6 to $9.50.

Restaurán Puesta del Sol (☺ 954-588-38-67; Km 24; 2½hr trip for up to 5 people $47, colectivo service per person $7.50-9.50), toward the west end of the lake, is another recommended embarkation point. One- or two-person kayaks are $5 per hour; fish and shrimp dishes cost $6 to $7.50.

Several early-morning or sunset tours (from four to five hours including road time) can be booked from Puerto Escondido. Not all of them include English-speaking guides.

Hidden Voyages Ecotours (☎ 954-582-15-51; www.wincom.net/~pelewing; Viajes Dimar, Av Pérez Gasga 905B; tours for 4-10 people Dec 1-Apr 1 per person $37-40) offers highly recommended trips; morning tours are led by a knowledgeable Canadian ornithologist. **Lalo's Ecotours** (☎ 954-588-91-64; www.lalo-ecotours.com; Las Negras Mixtepec; tours per person $29) is run by a lagoon local who has

worked as a boatman for Hidden Voyages and knows his birds. Tours are year-round. Lalo speaks some English and also rents out kayaks, leads nature hikes and offers nighttime visits to the lagoon when it contains phosphorescent plankton, a magnificent occasional occurrence. He will arrange transport from Puerto Escondido, or you can seek him out in the village toward the lagoon's western edge.

At the time of research, a new hotel-bar-restaurant, **Doña Marina** (☎ 954-588-36-50) was being built just west of the Restaurán Puesta del Sol, with a small swimming pool and sailboats renting at $19 per hour.

Bajos de Chila

The Mixtec ball game of *pelota mixteca* is a five-a-side team sport descended from a pre-Hispanic ritual ball game. It's played at 3pm every Saturday (5pm if the weather is hot) in the village of Bajos de Chila, 10km west of Puerto Escondido along Hwy 200. This is a living relic of Mexico's ancient culture, played for the enjoyment of the participants. The field, called the *patio* or *pasador,* is easy to find in the village. *Colectivos* leave Puerto Escondido's bus station every 30 minutes, stopping at Calle 2 Norte just east of the Carretera Costera on their way to Bajos de Chila ($0.50, 15 minutes). For more on the ball game, see boxed text, p65.

Barra de Navidad

The Palmazola and Los Naranjos coastal lagoons, near this village just off Hwy 200, 6km southeast of Puerto Escondido, offer another chance to get close to the abundant bird life of the Oaxaca coast – and to the local crocodile population. Villagers have formed a society to protect the lagoons and offer guided visits ($15 per person) lasting about 1¼ hours. The tours include a half-hour boat ride, and are best in the early morning or late afternoon. Unaccompanied visits are not permitted. Barra de Navidad is a short walk south from Hwy 200 on the east side of the Río Colotepec bridge; catch a 'La Barra' *colectivo* from the highway west of Av Oaxaca in Puerto.

Other Destinations

The mainly Mixtec town of **Jamiltepec**, 105km west of Puerto Escondido on Hwy 200, holds a colorful Sunday market with many people in traditional clothing.

The town of **Nopala**, about 35km northwest of Puerto Escondido off Hwy 131, is set in the foothills of the Sierra Madre del Sur in the indigenous Chatino region. You can visit organic-coffee plantations and see ancient steles, and witness a display of local archaeology and Chatino culture in the Palacio Municipal (town hall). In winter, the owner of Tabachín del Puerto (p758) opens the pleasant Posada Nopala here.

LAGUNAS DE CHACAHUA

Heading west from Puerto Escondido toward Acapulco, Hwy 200 alternately climbs hills and descends into river valleys, many of which contain coco-palm plantations. The road wends near a coast studded with lagoons, pristine beaches and prolific bird and plant life. Settlements in this region contain many descendants of African slaves who escaped from the Spanish.

The area around the coastal lagoons of Chacahua and La Pastoría forms the beautiful **Parque Nacional Lagunas de Chacahua**, which attracts migratory birds from Alaska and Canada in winter. Mangrove-fringed islands harbor roseate spoonbills, ibis, cormorants, wood storks, herons and egrets, as well as mahogany trees, crocodiles and turtles. El Corral, a mangrove-lined waterway filled with countless birds in winter, connects the two lagoons.

Zapotalito

Sixty kilometers from Puerto Escondido, a 5km road leads south from Hwy 200 to Zapotalito, a small fishing village at the eastern end of La Pastoría lagoon. A few simple restaurants flank the lagoon. A cooperative here runs four-hour *lancha* tours of the lagoons, costing $75 for a boat carrying up to 10 people. The trips visit islands, channels to the ocean and the fishing village of Chacahua, at the western end of the park. For details on getting to Chacahua from Zapotalito, see Getting There & Away (right).

Chacahua

Chacahua village straddles the channel that connects the west end of Chacahua lagoon to the ocean. The ocean side of the village, fronting a wonderful beach, is a perfect place to bliss out. The waves here (a right-hand

point break) can be good for surfers, including beginners, but there are some strong currents; check where it's safe to swim. The inland half of the village contains a **crocodile-breeding center** (admission free) with a rather sorry collection of about 320 creatures kept for protection and reproduction. They range from 15cm to 3.5m in length; Chacahua's wild croc population (not human-eating) has been decimated by hunting.

Tours

Among the Puerto Escondido agencies offering good day trips is **Hidden Voyages Eco-tours** (☎ 954-582-15-51; www.wincom.net/~pelewing; Viajes Dimar, Av Pérez Gasga 905B; per person $52, minimum 6 people) Tours are run Thursday only from December to March.

Sleeping & Eating

Restaurante Siete Mares (cabañas d $19; mains $5.50-7.50) At the west end of the beach, Siete Mares prepares phenomenal fish and seafood meals. It has some of Chacahua's better *cabañas*, 300m away along the beach, with two beds, fans, nets and clean bathrooms. The señora here will lock up your valuables.

Cabañas Los Almendros (r & cabañas $12-31) The waters of the lagoon lap against this place, just two minutes' walk from the beach. It's run by a friendly young couple, and although it's not luxury, it's fine. There are three *cabañas* and a couple of other rooms – the upstairs *cabaña* is the pick of the bunch. The shared bathroom is acceptable.

Several places along the beach at Chacahua village offer basic *cabañas*. You can sleep in a hammock or camp for free if you eat at a particular establishment. However, this sleeping arrangement is not exactly secure, and some readers have complained of theft.

Getting There & Away

From Puerto Escondido you first have to get to the town of Río Grande, 50km west on Hwy 200. Río Grande–bound minibuses ($1.50, one hour) leave Calle 2 Norte just east of the Carretera Costera, in the upper part of Puerto Escondido, about every half-hour. All Estrella Blanca buses between Puerto Escondido and Acapulco stop at Río Grande too. From the minibus stop in Río Grande, cross the dirt road and get a *colectivo* taxi ($1) to Zapotalito, 14km southwest.

The simplest one-way route from Zapotalito to Chacahua village is by a combination of shared *lancha regular* and *camioneta*, for $3. This route is adventurous but misses out on the delights of the Lagunas de Chacahua. You travel half an hour across the lagoon from Zapotalito to meet with a *camioneta* that makes the half-hour trip along the spit to Chacahua. *Lanchas* leave Zapotalito every two hours from 7:20am to 5:20pm (schedule subject to change); the last return is at 5pm. The *lancha* departure point is 300m further along the main road beyond the tours departure point.

Shared *directo* boats to Chacahua village (per person $5, 45 minutes, 25km), which take you the full length of the lagoons, also leave from 300m beyond the tours departure point. They have no schedule, however, and only leave when $50 worth of fares are aboard, so you may have a long wait. You should be able to return to Zapotalito by direct boat but you need to allow for waiting time. If this fails, take the last afternoon *camioneta/lancha regular* service. Check its departure time before you settle in for the day!

Chacahua village is linked to San José del Progreso, 29km north on Hwy 200, by a sandy track that is impassable in the wet season. A very few *camionetas* travel this route daily ($2.75) when possible.

PINOTEPA NACIONAL
☎ 954 / pop 23,000

This is the biggest town between Puerto Escondido (140km east) and Acapulco (260km west). To the southwest there's a fine beach, **Playa Corralero**, near the mouth of Laguna Corralero (from 'Pino' go about 25km west on Hwy 200, then some 15km southeast). You can sleep in a hammock at one of Corralero village's *comedores*; 10 *camionetas* run there daily from Pinotepa ($1.75, one hour). Pinotepa is a good base for exploring the surrounding area's small towns and villages, famous for crafts such as wooden masks and traditional, colorful embroidered garments.

Hotel Las Gaviotas (☎ 543-24-02; Carretera a Acapulco s/n; s/d $14/17, with air-con $19/24; P ☒), a semimodern hotel about 600m east of the bus station, has decent rooms with good bathrooms and OK beds. **Hotel Carmona** (☎ 543-23-22; Porfirio Díaz 401; s/d $17/24, with air-con

$25/34; ☒ ☒), on the main road about 500m west of the main plaza, is clean, well run and fairly quiet. Rooms have hot-water bathroom and TV.

Pino's bus terminal is about 2km west of the central plaza. All Estrella Blanca buses between Puerto Escondido and Acapulco stop here. It's three hours to Puerto Escondido (1st class/*ordinario* $7.50/6.50) and five to 6½ hours to Acapulco (1st class/*ordinario* $13/12). First-class OCC buses and 2nd-class Fypsa buses travel north on Hwy 125 through the Mixteca, some reaching Oaxaca (1st class $20, 10 hours) that way. Estrella Roja has two buses nightly to Oaxaca via Hwy 131 ($14, nine to 10 hours).

POCHUTLA
☎ 958 / pop 13,000

This bustling, sweaty market town is the starting point for transportation to the nearby beach spots of Puerto Ángel, Zipolite, San Agustinillo and Mazunte. Of all these towns, Pochutla is the only one with banks.

Orientation

Hwy 175 from Oaxaca runs through Pochutla as Cárdenas, the narrow north–south (uphill–downhill, for the cardinally challenged) main street, and meets coastal Hwy 200 about 1.5km south of town. Everything described in this section is on Cárdenas, with the approximate midpoint (and point of reference) for sites being Hotel Izala. The long-distance bus stations cluster around 300m to 400m downhill from the Izala.

Information

HSBC (1½ blocks uphill; ☒ 8am-7pm Mon-Fri, 8am-3pm Sat) Changes traveler's checks and US dollars; also has an ATM and provides over-the-counter Visa-card cash advances (take your passport).

Post office (Cárdenas; ☒ 8am-3pm Mon-Fri) About 150m downhill.

Scotiabank Inverlat Has an ATM.

Telnet (Cárdenas 94; Internet per hr $1; ☒ 8am-10pm Mon-Sat) Opposite the EV/OP bus terminal; has fast connections plus long-distance telephone service.

Sleeping & Eating

Hotel Costa del Sol (☎ /fax 584-03-18; Cárdenas 47; s & d/tw with fan $20/22, with air-con $24/29; P ☒) Probably Pochutla's best central hotel. It's 1½ blocks uphill from the Izala, and has a few artistic touches and some greenery. Rooms have good bathrooms, erratic hot water, and cable TV.

Hotel Izala (☎ 584-01-15; Cárdenas 59; s/d with fan $15/24, with air-con $24/33; **P** ✗) The Izala offers plain, clean rooms, with cable TV, on two levels around a leafy courtyard.

Hotel Santa Cruz (☎ /fax 584-01-16; Cárdenas s/n; s/d with shared bathroom & fan $10/12, with private bathroom $12/15, with private bathroom & air-con $20/25; ✗) The Santa Cruz has simple, good-sized, adequate rooms. It's situated about 150m north of the main cluster of bus stations. Some private bathrooms lack toilet seats; the air-con is good in those rooms that have it.

Restaurant y Marisquería Los Ángeles (Cárdenas s/n; mains $4-9; ⏰ 10am-9pm Mon-Sat) This breezy little upstairs place – found downhill from the Colón bus station – serves some seafood dishes, including a good *coctel de pulpo* (octopus cocktail). The menu is rounded out by Mexican standards and hamburgers for the less adventurous.

Getting There & Away

The three main bus stations – in downhill order on the lower end of Cárdenas – are Estrella del Valle/Oaxaca Pacífico (EV/OP,

2nd class) on the left side of the street, OCC (1st class)/Sur on the right side and Estrella Blanca (EB, 2nd class), also on the right side.

OAXACA

Oaxaca is 245km away by Hwy 175 (six to seven hours) or 450km by the straighter Hwys 200 and 190 (eight to nine hours, via Salina Cruz). At the time of research OCC had three daily buses going by the Salina Cruz route ($20) – but remember that schedules and routings are always changeable. EV/OP runs three *directo* ($9, six hours) and 13 *ordinario* ($7, seven hours) buses via the winding Hwy 175. **Autoexprés Atlántida** (☎ 584-01-16; Hotel Santa Cruz, Cárdenas s/n) runs nine daily air-conditioned vans, taking up to 14 people, by Hwy 175 ($12, 6½ hours) between 4am and 11pm. You can reserve by phone and pay one hour beforehand if you wish. Two other companies – Eclipse 7 (across the street from Atlántida) and Delfines (just uphill from Atlántida) offer similar service. Helpfully, drivers will usually agree to stop when you need a bathroom break, or want to take photos (or vomit, as some people tend to do on this route).

LOCAL TRANSPORT

Transportation services to the nearby coast change frequently. When things are going well, frequent *camionetas* (pickup tricks) and *colectivo* (shared) taxis run from Pochutla to Puerto Ángel, Zipolite, San Agustinillo and Mazunte between 7am and 7pm. They usually pick up passengers in Pochutla in front of Mueblería García, a furniture store about five doors uphill from Hotel Santa Cruz, on the same side of Cárdenas. At the time of writing, *camioneta* service through Puerto Ángel was irregular, but frequent *colectivo* taxis were running to Puerto Ángel ($0.70, 20 minutes, 13km), Zipolite ($1.50, 30 minutes), San Agustinillo ($2, 40 minutes) and Mazunte ($2, 45 minutes). Some *camionetas* and *colectivos* go via San Antonio on Hwy 200 northwest of Mazunte (not via Puerto Ángel) and thus are quicker than the *colectivo* taxis for Mazunte and San Agustinillo, though longer for Zipolite.

If you can catch one, *camionetas* between Pochutla and the beach towns cost about $0.50 to Puerto Ángel and $0.80 to Zipolite and Mazunte, and are a fun way to travel. Private cabs during the day should cost around $6 to Puerto Ángel, $9 to Zipolite and $11 to San Agustinillo or Mazunte, but you may have to negotiate hard to even get close to these prices; at night they charge more.

Taxis have the name of their home base written on their sides. Those from San José Pochutla are allowed to charge for *servicio especial* (private service) from Pochutla and along the coast, and they will often try to overcharge, so avoid them, if possible. Instead, go for the *colectivo* taxis (based in Mazunte, Puerto Ángel, Zipolite and so forth), which are painted two-tone, either dark red and white, or cream and blue. Any time you have to take an *especial* (at night, for example), try your hardest to bargain. Most services will happily stop virtually anywhere to pick you up or drop you off.

OTHER DESTINATIONS
Bus departures:

Destination	Price	Duration	Frequency
Acapulco	$27	8-9hr	7 EB semi-directo daily
Bahías de Huatulco	$2.25	1hr	8 OCC daily
	$2.25	1hr	5 EB daily
	$1.50	1hr	Sur every 40min
	$1.25	1hr	Transportes Rápidos de Pochutla every 15min 5:30am-8pm from terminal just uphill from EV/OP)
Juchitán	$12	5hr	5 OCC daily
Mexico City	$50	15-16hr	1 OCC daily 7:20pm
	$45	14-15hr	2 EB daily
Pinotepa Nacional	$12	4hr	7 EB daily
	$4	1hr	7 EB semi-directo daily
	$2.50	1½hr	Sur hourly 7:30am-7:30pm
Puerto Escondido	$3.75	1½hr	5 OCC daily
	$4	1hr	7 EB semi-directo daily
	$2.50	1½hr	Sur hourly 7:30am-7:30pm
San Cristóbal de Las Casas	$30	12hr	2 OCC daily at 7:45pm & 10:45pm
Tehuantepec	$11	4½hr	5 OCC daily
Tuxtla Gutiérrez	$25	10hr	2 OCC daily at 7:45pm & 10:45pm
Zihuatanejo	$38	12hr	7 EB daily

PUERTO ÁNGEL
☎ 958 / pop 3000

Thirteen kilometers south of Pochutla, the small fishing town, naval base and travelers' hangout of Puerto Ángel (pwer-toh *ahn*-hel) straggles around a picturesque bay between two rocky headlands. Many travelers prefer to stay out on the beaches a few kilometers west at Zipolite, San Agustinillo or Mazunte, but the marginally more urban Puerto Ángel is a good base too. It offers its own little beaches, some good places to stay and eat, and easy transportation to/from Zipolite.

Orientation
The road from Pochutla emerges at the east end of the small Bahía de Puerto Ángel. The road winds around the back of the bay, over an often-dry *arroyo* (stream) and up a hill. It then forks – right to Zipolite and Mazunte, left down to Playa del Panteón.

It's called Blvd Uribe through most of town, though after it crosses the *arroyo* it's also referred to as Carretera a Zipolite.

Information
The nearest banks are in Pochutla, but several accommodations and restaurants will change cash or traveler's checks at their own rates.

Caseta Telefónica Lila (Blvd Uribe) Has Internet, phone and fax services.

Farmacia El Ángel (☎ 584-30-58; Vasconcelos) Dr Constancio Aparicio's practice is here, from 9am to 2pm and 4pm to 8pm Monday to Saturday.

G@l@p@gos (Blvd Uribe s/n; Internet per hr $1.50) You can also make phone calls here.

Gel@net (Vasconcelos 3; Internet per hr $1.50; ☣ 9am-10pm) Has telephone, fax and Internet services.

Post office (Av Principal; ☣ 9am-2pm Mon-Fri) At the east end of town.

Tourist office (Blvd Uribe; ☣ 9am-4pm & 5:30-8pm Mon-Fri) In a *palapa*-roofed building at the entrance to the pier; useful for transportation details.

Beaches
Playa del Panteón, on the west side of Bahía de Puerto Ángel, is shallow and calm and its waters are cleaner than those near the pier across the bay.

About 500m up the road toward Pochutla, a sign points along a path to **Playa Estacahuite**, 700m away. The three tiny, sandy bays here are all good for snorkeling, but watch out for jellyfish. A couple of shack restaurants serve good, reasonably priced seafood or spaghetti, and often have snorkels to rent.

The coast northeast of Estacahuite is dotted with more good beaches, none of them very busy. A good one is **Playa La Boquilla**, on a small bay about 5km out, the site of Bahía de la Luna accommodations and restaurant (see p769). You can get here (when it's dry) by a 3.5km road from a turnoff 4km out of Puerto Ángel on the road toward Pochutla. A taxi from Puerto Ángel costs $4.50 each way, but it's more fun to go by boat – you can ask a fisherman to take a few people from Playa del Panteón or from the pier for the 10 minute trip across the bay for around $11 per person, including a return trip at an agreed time.

Activities
Snorkeling and **fishing** are popular and you can also go **diving**. The drops and canyons out to sea from Puerto Ángel are suitable

PUERTO ÁNGEL

```
0          200 m
0          0.1 miles
```

INFORMATION
Caseta Telefónica Lila...1 B2
Farmacia El Ángel.........2 C2
G@l@p@gos.................3 B2
Gel@net.....................4 C3
Post Office..................5 D3
Tourist Office..............6 C3

SIGHTS & ACTIVITIES
Azul Profundo..............7 A2
Byron Luna..................8 A3

SLEEPING
Casa Arnel....................9 B2
Casa de Huéspedes Gundi
y Tomás.....................10 B2

El Almendro....................11 C2
Hotel Cordelia's.............12 A2
Hotel Puesta del Sol........13 A2
Hotel Soraya..................14 C3
La Buena Vista................15 B1
La Posada Cañón Devata..16 A2

Penelope's......................17 A2
Villa Serena Florencia..18 C2

EATING
Beto's............................19 A2
Other Beach
   Restaurants...........(see 20)
Restaurante Susy........20 A3

TRANSPORT
Buses to Oaxaca........21 C3
Taxi Stand..................22 C3

To Zipolite (2.5km);
Mazunte (5km);
Puerto Escondido (71km)

To Playa Estacahuite (700m);
Playa La Boquilla,
Bahía de la Luna (7.5km);
Pochutla (13km);

Naval Base •

Blvd Uribe

Arroyo

Azueta

Calle del Tajo

Vasconcelos

Av Principal

Panteón

Playa del
Panteón

Playa
Principal

Beach
Restaurants

Bahía de Puerto Ángel

Pier

La Playita

---

for very deep dives; there's also a dive to an 1870 shipwreck.

Many café-restaurants on Playa del Panteón rent out snorkeling gear (per hour/ day $2.75/6.75). **Byron Luna** (☎ 584-31-15; 3hr trips for 4-5 people $57) offers snorkeling and fishing trips to four beaches. Byron is great fun and enjoys spotting dolphins, orcas and turtles. Look for him at his home next to Restaurant Susy (p770). **Azul Profundo** (☎ 584-31-09; azul _profundomx@hotmail.com; Playa del Panteón; 4hr snorkeling trips per person $9.50, fishing trips per person per hr $31, diving $38), run by friendly Chepe, offers snorkeling, fishing and diving at all levels. Also on offer is a five-day SSI certification course for $337. Ask at Hotel Cordelia's (opposite) if you can't find him on the beach.

Sleeping

Places with an elevated location are more likely to catch any breeze. Note that some places suffer from a water shortage.

BUDGET

La Posada Cañón Devata (☎ 584-31-37; www.posada pacifico.com; s/d with fan $29/33, 2-person bungalows

$66, per additional adult $19, all incl breakfast; ✆ closed Jun; **P**) On a woodsy hillside behind Playa del Panteón (off Sáenz de Barandas), the friendly Cañón Devata has a variety of attractive accommodations scattered about its sprawling property. It's run by the artistic and ecologically minded López family, and is a good place for those seeking a quiet retreat. Yoga courses are on offer, and the super-clean restaurant prepares fine food (see opposite).

Hotel Puesta del Sol (☎/fax 584-30-96; www .puertoangel.net; Blvd Uribe s/n; s $11.50, d $15-18, d with private bathroom $25-32; ✆) The friendly German/Mexican-owned Puesta del Sol offers sizable, clean rooms with fans and screens. Some sleep up to six people. The more expensive ones have their own terraces and hot-water bathroom. The sitting room has a small library and satellite TV. Hammocks on a breezy terrace invite relaxation, and breakfast is available.

Penelope's (☎ 584-30-73; Cerrada de la Luna s/n; r $14-24, with private bathroom $29, all incl continental breakfast) Penelope's, with just four rooms, is set in a quiet, leafy neighborhood high above

Playa del Panteón. It's just off the Zipolite road, clearly signposted a couple of hundred meters beyond the fork to Playa del Panteón. The rooms are clean, with good beds and screens, decent bathrooms and ceiling fans. An attractive terrace restaurant serves economical meals, and hammocks provide lounging opportunities. The new management may start offering yoga classes.

Casa de Huéspedes Gundi y Tomás (☎ 584-30-68; www.puertoangel-hotel.com; r with/without bathroom $29/24) This tranquil guesthouse off Blvd Uribe has a variety of brightly decorated, basic rooms, all with fans, mosquito nets and/or screens, and some offbeat artistic touches. Good food is available, including homemade bread, mainly vegetarian snacks, fruit drinks and a nightly $6.50 *menú*. The main dining area and one clutch of rooms have outstanding views. Gundi, the friendly German owner, speaks good English and Spanish and provides a safe for valuables; a book exchange; bus and plane tickets; and an exchange service for cash or traveler's checks.

El Almendro (☎ 584-30-68; www.puertoangel-hotel .com; r $29, bungalow $57) Set in a shady garden up a little lane off Blvd Uribe, El Almendro has six clean, brightly painted, basic rooms with OK beds and bathrooms, plus a bungalow for up to six people. From November to April the 6pm to 7pm happy hour is followed by a barbecue dinner ($7) of marinated meats or fish, salad from the salad bar and baked potatoes.

Hotel Cordelia's (☎ 584-31-09; Playa del Panteón; d with/without ocean view $33/19, tr $38/57; P ⊠) Cordelia's is a newer hotel right in the middle of this lovely beach. Run by the same family as the Azul Profundo dive shop, it has at least eight mosquito-screened rooms, four of which are spacious with good-sized Talavera-tiled bathrooms, and terraces overlooking the sea. Construction was ongoing at the time of research, and Cordelia was about to install air-con and hot water in all rooms.

Casa Arnel (☎/fax 584-30-51; arnelpto.angel@huatulco.net.mx; Azueta 666; s/d $24/29; 🖳) Casa Arnel, up the lane past the market, has five clean, ample tile-floored rooms with fans, and OK beds and bathrooms. *Refrescos* (soft drinks), coffee and tea are available, and there's an upstairs hammock area, a small library and a place to wash and dry clothes.

MIDRANGE

La Buena Vista (☎/fax 584-31-04; www.labuenavista .com; La Buena Compañía s/n; d $35-48, per additional person $6; ⊠) The 19 big rooms and five excellent mud-brick bungalows on this verdant property are kept scrupulously clean. All have fans, mosquito screens, comfortable beds, and private bathrooms with pretty Talavera tiles. Many have breezy balconies with hammocks, and some have excellent views. Wood, stone and brick are cleverly used throughout. There's a good restaurant on an expansive terrace, and a gorgeous pool area.

Bahía de la Luna (☎ 589-40-20; www.bahiadela luna.com; Playa La Boquilla; s/d/tr from $61/72/111, 4-person house $205, each additional person $11; P) This tropical hideaway out at gorgeous Playa La Boquilla has attractive adobe bungalows set on a tree-filled hillside overlooking the beach. Two two-bedroom bungalows can hold up to five people, and a house holds up to eight. It also has a good beachside restaurant-café with moderate prices, and offers snorkeling gear, sea kayaks, and yoga and meditation instruction.

Villa Serena Florencia (☎/fax 584-30-44; villa serenaoax@hotmail.com; Blvd Uribe s/n; s/d/tr $24/33/38, air-con extra $3) The well-established Florencia has 13 agreeable, smallish rooms with fans and screens. It also offers a shady sitting area and a good Italian restaurant.

Hotel Soraya (☎ 584-30-09; Vasconcelos s/n; d with fan $29-38, tr with fan $33-43, q with fan $38-47; d/tr/q with air-con $47/52/57; P ⊠) Overlooking the bay, the Soraya has 32 clean, tiled-floor rooms with fairly good beds and good bathrooms. All have balconies and some have very good views.

Eating

La Buena Vista (☎/fax 584-31-04; La Buena Compañía s/n; breakfast $2.50-4, dinner mains $5-8; ⏲ Mon-Sat) Be sure to pre-book dinner outside of the high seasons! On an airy terrace overlooking the bay, the restaurant of La Buena Vista offers well-prepared Mexican and Italian fare, from hotcakes to *chiles rellenos* (stuffed chilies) with a *quesillo* filling.

La Posada Cañón Devata (☎ 584-31-37; breakfast $3-4, dinner $15; ⏲ breakfast 8:30am-noon, dinner from 7:30pm; Ⓥ) Outsiders are welcome here. The restaurant is at the hotel of the same name, off Sáenz de Barandas. A good three-course dinner is served at long tables in a lovely palm-roofed, open-sided dining room. Fare comprises whole-food vegetarian and fish dishes. Book early in the day.

Villa Serena Florencia (☎ 584-30-44; Blvd Uribe s/n; dishes $3-7) This Italian restaurant, part of its eponymous hotel and a reliable standby, turns out good pasta and Mexican dishes, salads and pizzas, all at very good prices. Breakfasts (served in the high season only) are good value.

Beto's (Carretera a Zipolite s/n; dishes $3-5; ☷ 4pm-midnight) On the uphill stretch of Blvd Uribe, Beto's is a relaxed, economical, friendly and clean little place with a large terrace. Meals include fish fillets ($3.75), ceviche ($3), and chicken and beef dishes ($4.25 to $5).

The restaurants on Playa del Panteón offer fish and seafood for $5 to $11, plus cheaper fare such as *entomatadas* (variation of enchiladas) and eggs. Be careful about the freshness of seafood in the low season. The setting is very pretty after dark. **Restaurante Susy** (☎ 584-30-19) is one of the better beachside establishments.

You'll also find several economical places to eat on the main town beach, though none of these is very well frequented.

Getting There & Away
See boxed text, p766 for details of transportation from Pochutla. An EV/OP bus to Oaxaca ($7.50, seven hours) departs at 10pm nightly from near the foot of Vasoncelos. A taxi to or from Zipolite costs $0.50 by *colectivo*, or $3 for the whole cab ($5 after dark and even more after 10pm or 11pm). You can find cabs on Blvd Uribe; there's a stand at the foot of Vasconcelos.

A taxi to Huatulco airport costs $35; to Puerto Escondido airport it's $45.

ZIPOLITE
☎ 958 / pop 1200
The beautiful 1.5km stretch of pale sand called Zipolite, beginning about 2.5km west of Puerto Ángel, is fabled as southern Mexico's perfect budget chill-out spot.

Inexpensive places to stay and eat line nearly the whole beach, many still reassuringly ramshackle and wooden. Some have conical thatched roofs.

Zipolite is a great place to take it easy, with a magical combination of pounding sea and sun, open-air sleeping, eating and drinking, unique scenery and the travelers' scene. It's the kind of place where you may find yourself postponing departure over and over again. The cluster of larger establishments toward the beach's west end is, for many, the hub of Zipolite, but there's plenty of room elsewhere if you want to really kick back.

Total nudity is more common at the western end of the beach.

Orientation
The eastern end of Zipolite (nearest Puerto Ángel) is called Colonia Playa del Amor, the middle part is Centro, and the area toward the western end (divided from Centro by a narrow lagoon and creek) is Colonia Roca Blanca. The few streets behind the beach are mostly nameless; Av Roca Blanca, a block back from the beach in Colonia Roca Blanca, is the most prominent and is more commonly known as the Adoquín, for its paving blocks.

Information
The nearest banks are in Pochutla, but some accommodations may accept US dollars or euros. A combination surf shop and money exchange lies at the west end of the Adoquín.

ADSL Infinitum (Av Roca Blanca; Internet per hr $1.50; ☷ 9am-9pm) Has Internet and long-distance phone services.

Caseta Oceana (Av Roca Blanca) Has long-distance phone service.

Lavandería Paty (Av Roca Blanca; same-day laundry service per kg $1.25; ☷ 8am-5pm Mon-Sat) On the main road east of Casa de Huéspedes Lyoban.

Dangers & Annoyances
Beware: the Zipolite surf is deadly. It's fraught with riptides, changing currents and a strong undertow. Locals don't swim here, and going in deeper than your knees can be risking your life. Local voluntary *salvavidas* (lifeguards) have rescued many, but they don't maintain a permanent watch, and people drown here yearly. The shore break is one only experienced surfers should attempt.

Theft can be a problem, and it's not advisable to walk along the Puerto Ángel–Zipolite road or the beach after dark.

Sleeping
Most accommodations are right on the beach, where nearly every business rents out small rooms, *cabañas* or hammocks.

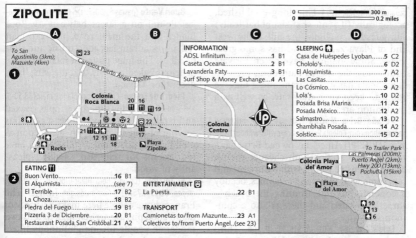

ZIPOLITE

0 — 300 m
0 — 0.2 miles

To San
Agustinillo (3km);
Mazunte (4km)

Carretera Puerto Ángel–Zipolite

Colonia
Roca Blanca

Av Roca Blanca

Rocks

Playa
Zipolite

Colonia
Centro

To Trailer Park
Las Palmeras (200m);
Puerto Ángel (2km);
Hwy 200 (13km);
Pochutla (15km)

Colonia Playa
del Amor

Playa
del Amor

INFORMATION
ADSL Infinitum.....................1 B1
Caseta Oceana.....................2 B1
Lavandería Paty...................3 B1
Surf Shop & Money Exchange...4 A1

SLEEPING
Casa de Huéspedes Lyoban......5 C2
Chololo's.............................6 D2
El Alquimista........................7 A2
Las Casitas...........................8 A1
Lo Cósmico...........................9 A2
Lola's.................................10 D2
Posada Brisa Marina..............11 A2
Posada México.....................12 A2
Salmastro............................13 D2
Shambhala Posada................14 A2
Solstice...............................15 D2

EATING
Buon Vento.........................16 B1
El Alquimista.....................(see 7)
El Terrible...........................17 B2
La Choza.............................18 B2
Piedra del Fuego...................19 B1
Pizzería 3 de Diciembre..........20 B1
Restaurant Posada San Cristóbal.21 A2

ENTERTAINMENT
La Puesta............................22 B1

TRANSPORT
Camionetas to/from Mazunte.....23 A1
Colectivos to/from Puerto Ángel..(see 23)

Unless otherwise stated, rooms here have shared bathrooms, and beds have mosquito nets. Rates are for the high season (roughly mid-November to mid-April, as well as August for many places).

Posada México (☎ 584-31-94; www.posadamexico .com; Av Roca Blanca; r $15-2) Opened in 2004, the latest arrival on the Zipolite beachfront injects some welcome freshness. All rooms have safes and good beds, and pleasing Italian-sensibility touches are everywhere, including in the common bathrooms. A chef from the Cinqueterre will serve up meals in the restaurant (open December to April only).

El Alquimista (www.el-alquimista.com; bungalows $50) Attached to one of Zipolite's best restaurants (see p772), this place has eight fine bungalows on the beach at the west end of Playa Zipolite, each with homespun textiles, fan, bathroom and hammocked porch. They're often full.

Las Casitas (☎ 585-72-63; www.las-casitas.net; s bungalows $17, d bungalows $24-43, tr bungalows $29-38) Set back from the west end of Playa Zipolite on a hill, six of the seven tasteful, semi–open air bungalows here have private bathrooms and kitchens. Most have good views as well, at least in the dry, leafless season, and some have swinging beds. Meals in the beautifully sited restaurant cost from $20.

Lo Cósmico (www.locosmico.com; hammocks $5, d cabañas $10-25, per additional person $5) Very relaxed Lo Cósmico has conical-roofed *cabañas* dotted around a tall rock outcrop. Each has a

double bed, hammock and fan; the cheaper ones are a bit enclosed while the pricier ones have two floors and views. The hammock area is on a cliff top overlooking the beach, and has lockers, while a security box is available to *cabaña* guests. Some private bathrooms are going in to supplement the mediocre common ones, and there's a good on-site restaurant. You'll find Lo Cósmico at the west end of Playa Zipolite.

Solstice (www.solstice-mexico.com; Colonia Playa del Amor; dm $11, studios $27-32, bungalows $39) This excellent, friendly, Dutch-owned retreat, set back from the beach, specializes in yoga courses. Thatched bungalows, studios and dorm accommodations, all fan-cooled, are set around a central space; decor is bright and homey. Bathrooms have a barrel and bucket in lieu of showers. The yoga room is large and inviting, with a full inventory of props. Book ahead, as group retreats fill up the place.

Casa de Huéspedes Lyoban (☎ 584-31-77; www .lyoban.com.mx; Colonia Playa del Amor; hammocks $6, s/d/tr $13/16/21) Relaxed, friendly Lyoban has basic, clean rooms: the beds are comfy, but the walls don't reach the ceiling. Common areas include a sociable bar-restaurant space with board games; ping-pong, foosball and pool tables; a small library and an upstairs deck for lounging. The hammock price includes a blanket, a sturdy locker and shower usage.

Shambhala Posada (Casa Gloria; www.advantagemex ico.com/shambhala; hammocks $4, dm $6, s $7-8, d $8-9, cabañas from $25; (**P**)) This long-established, ecologically (if somewhat shambhal-ically) run guesthouse climbs the hill at the west end of Playa Zipolite, and has some great views. Some lodgings have decent private bathrooms; the shared bathrooms are OK. Shambhala has a restaurant and a luggage room to keep your stuff safe, as well as a meditation area.

Posada Brisa Marina (☎ 584-31-93; brisamari naca@yahoo.com; Colonia Roca Blanca; r with/without bathroom $30/15; (**P**)) American-owned Brisa has a rear wooden section with cheaper rooms. More-expensive rooms with bathroom and fan, some with views and balconies, occupy a concrete building fronting the beach – these have safes, and there is also a common safe.

Lola's (☎ 584-32-01; s/d $15/30; **P** 🖵) Third from the east end of Playa del Amor, Lola's has 25 reasonable rooms on two levels of a brick building. They come with good beds, tiled floors, OK private bathrooms, fans and mosquito screens.

Chololo's (☎ 584-31-59; r with/without bathroom $25/20; **P**) With five simple rooms at the easternmost spot on Playa del Amor, this very friendly place also serves good Mexican and Italian food.

Salmastro (☎ 584-31-61; r $12-32; **P**) Also at the east end of Playa del Amor, Salmastro's eight basic rooms (some upstairs, and some with sea views) have good beds and thatched roofs.

Trailer Park Las Palmeras (Fernando's Camp Ground, Carretera Puerto Ángel-Zipolite; camp site $2 plus per person $2; **P**) This small park, beside the road from Puerto Ángel as you enter Zipolite, has a grassy plot edged with trees. Rates include showers and toilets, water for washing and 24-hour caretaking.

Eating

Eating and drinking in the open air a few steps from the surf is an inimitable Zipolite experience. Most accommodations have a restaurant of some kind, and some good independent places serve food as well.

El Alquimista (mains $3.50-9.50; 🕓 3pm-midnight) One of Zipolite's classiest restaurants, the Alchemist is delightfully sited in a sandy cove at the west end of Playa Zipolite. Its very wide-ranging fare runs from falafel tortas to good meat and chicken dishes, complemented by a full bar and good espresso.

Buon Vento (pastas $3.50-5; 🕓 6pm-midnight Thu-Tue) Found on a street between Av Roca Blanca and the main road, this excellent Italian restaurant has good music and subtle vibes. The huge pasta list includes some delicious baked options, and the wine list is decent for Mexico.

Piedra de Fuego (Colonia Roca Blanca; mains $3.50-5; 🕓 3pm-11pm) At this superbly simple, relaxed and family-run place, you'll get a generous serving of fish fillet or prawns, accompanied by rice, salad and tortillas. They have four rooms for rent also, smelling pleasantly of wood.

El Terrible (Colonia Roca Blanca; pizzas $5.50-7.25, crepes $2.25-4.75; 🕓 6am-midnight Fri-Wed) The Francophone couple here make a variety of damn good pizzas, large enough to feed two moderate people or one gluttonous travel writer. Fresh anchovies, anyone? Sweet and savory crepes are also served.

Lo Cósmico (dishes $3-5; 🕓 8pm-4pm; **V**) Mellow out on the rocks above the beach at this open-air restaurant. Found at the west end of Playa Zipolite, and attached to the accommodations of the same name, Cósmico provides good food from an impeccably clean kitchen – especially tasty are the crepes (sweet and savory) and salads.

Pizzería 3 de Diciembre (Colonia Roca Blanca; prices $3.75-6; 🕓 7pm-2am Wed-Sun) The 3 de Diciembre serves not only excellent pizzas but also good pastry pies with fillings such as cauliflower-and-parmesan or baked spinach. It's great for late-night munchies.

La Choza (☎ 584-31-90; Colonia Roca Blanca; mains $5-8) La Choza's beachside restaurant has a wide-ranging menu including many Mexican favorites (most done well), with generous servings.

Restaurant Posada San Cristóbal (☎ 584-31-91; Colonia Roca Blanca; mains $3.50-11.50) St Chris' wide variety of food runs from several breakfast items to *antojitos*, salads, whole fish, prawns, octopus and chicken.

Drinking & Entertainment

Zipolite's beachfront restaurant-bars have unbeatable locations for drinks around sunset and after dark. Those toward the west end of the beach are generally the most popular – especially **El Alquimista** (left), which plays cool music and serves cocktails as well as the usual beer, *mezcal* and so forth. The swing seats at the bar can get tricky after you've had a few. The open-air *discoteca* La Puesta (Colonia Roca Blanca; 9pm-late Tue-Sat) provides slightly more-active nightlife than the bars, cranking out tunes into the wee hours. Nothing much happens before midnight.

Getting There & Away

See boxed text, p766 for details on transportation from Pochutla and Puerto Ángel. The *camionetas* between Pochutla via Mazunte and San Agustinillo terminate on the main road at the far west end of Zipolite (about 2km from the east end of the beach). *Colectivo* taxis from Puerto Ángel will go to the same spot too, but pass along the length of Av Roca Blanca en route, so are a better bet if you're heading for the east end of the beach.

After dark, a non-*colectivo* taxi is your only option for getting to Puerto Ángel or San Agustinillo (about $5 from 6pm until about 10pm, more after that).

SAN AGUSTINILLO

958 / pop 250

Long, straight and nearly empty Playa Aragón stretches west from the headland at the west end of Zipolite to the growing village of San Agustinillo. Footpaths behind Shambhala Posada cross the headland from Zipolite; by the main coast road, it's a 4km drive. Most tourist facilities are right on or just off the main road.

San Agustinillo's small curved bay has waves that are perfect for **boogie-boarding** and often good for **body-surfing**. The **swimming** is very good as well, but stay away from the rocks. Several relaxed little places to stay and a line of open-air beach *comedores* round out the picture. San Agustinillo has much more of a family atmosphere than its sometimes hedonistic neighbors of Zipolite and Mazunte, and has generally higher standards of sanitation. You can rent surfboards and boogie-boards at México Lindo y qué Rico! (right) for $5 and $3 per hour respectively; snorkeling gear costs $2 per hour ($4 per day). Staff also will hook you up with surfing lessons, snorkeling trips, guided hikes, coffee finca tours and other activities. Palapa Olas Altas (p774) offers 1½-hour *lancha* trips for $15 per person for turtle-viewing (and occasionally dolphin-viewing). Internet access at Hotel Malex (p774), on the east side of town, is $1.50 per hour.

The coast between Zipolite and Puerto Escondido is a major sea-turtle nesting ground. Until hunting and killing sea turtles was banned in Mexico in 1990, San Agustinillo was the site of a slaughterhouse where some 50,000 turtles were killed per year for their meat and shells.

Sleeping & Eating

As with most places along the coast, unscreened rooms (and sometimes screened rooms) come with mosquito nets over the beds. Three places – Rancho Cerro Largo, Hotel Malex and Rancho Hamacas – have stunning positions atop the steep slope backing Playa Aragón (between Zipolite and San Agustinillo). They can be reached by drivable tracks from the road or by paths up from the beach.

Un Sueño (www.unsueno.com; d/tr/q $55/70/90; P) Sueño, at the east end of Playa San Agustinillo, boasts four large, freestanding beachfront *cabañas*. Each has its own terrace with hammock, table and chairs, and artistic touches throughout, especially in the bathrooms. Fans augment the breeze coming through slatted-shutter windows. More *cabañas* were being built at the time of research.

Rancho Cerro Largo (RCL; ranchocerrolargomx@yahoo .com.mx; Playa Aragón; s $45-75, d $45-85, per additional person $20, all incl breakfast & dinner; P) The RCL offers a variety of excellent accommodation in some half-dozen fan-cooled *cabañas* (individual and shared, some with private bathrooms and some with tiny fridges). The beds and meals are top-notch, and the views from the shared toilets are superb.

México Lindo y qué Rico! (fafinyleila@latinmail.com; r $30; closed October) Fourth along from the west end of Playa San Agustinillo, México Lindo's seven large rooms feature slatted windows, fans, and some bright touches like tiled bathrooms. Especially good are the breezy upstairs pair of rooms under the tall *palapa* roof. The young, friendly owners serve good food (mains $4 to $7), including pizzas from a brick oven.

Paraíso del Pescador (from US or Canada 705-266-7771; www.paraiso-del-pescador.com; d/q $35/50; P) Uphill from the road, and in the center of town, Pescador's spacious, modern rooms all have tiled floors and good bathrooms, beds, air-con and screens, and come complete with delicious views. The

Canadian co-owner does sportfishing trips, and you can get decent coffee in the friendly restaurant.

Casamar (☎ 589-24-01; http://home1.stofanet .dk/casamar; r $35/45, ste $65) Casamar has two serviceable downstairs rooms with good hot-water bathrooms and two springy double beds each. The star here is the upstairs suite, with its large salon, ample balcony with shady hammock area, and kitchen (fridge and microwave). Beachside there's a small garden area with soaking pool. You'll find Casamar at the west end of Playa San Agustinillo.

Rancho Hamacas (☎ 589-85-48; hamacasilva@hot mail.com; Playa Aragón; cabañas with/without kitchen $25/20; Ⓟ) Further west on the hilltop from Rancho Cerro Largo, Rancho Hamacas has six *cabañas* with double beds. Half have fridges and gas burners. The owners make and sell beautiful, strong hammocks (around $60 to $170, depending on size), and serve food at their restaurant from December to March.

Palapa Olas Altas (hammocks/campsite per person $4/5, r with/without bathroom $30/15) Olas Altas has 16 palatable fan rooms, one with sea views, at the west end Playa San Agustinillo. The beachside restaurant serves decent food (mains $5 to $7) of the seafood and tortilla variety.

Palapa de Evelia (breakfast $2.50-3.50, mains $6-7.50; ☾ 8am-5pm) Third along from the west end of Playa San Agustinillo, Evelia serves some of the best food on the beach, with straightforward but well-prepared fish and seafood, and great guacamole.

Hotel Malex (589-81-95; malex_hotelweb@hotmail .com; r with/without kitchenette $45/35) The Malex, which opened in 2004 on the east side San Agustinillo, is unprepossessing from outside. Inside, its four upstairs tiled-floor rooms are done in cheerful white and blue, with close-up sea views, good bathrooms, beds and wall fans, and well-screened windows. The one kitchenette is fully supplied with a small fridge and five-burner gas stove.

Getting There & Away

See boxed text, p766 for information about transportation from Pochutla. *Colectivo* taxis to or from Zipolite or Mazunte cost $0.50, and *camionetas* between Roca Blanca (Zipolite) and Mazunte run $0.30. The journey is only about 15 minutes long.

MAZUNTE
☎ 958 / pop 450

A kilometer west of San Agustinillo, Mazunte has a fine, curving, sandy beach, an interesting turtle research center, and a variety of places to places to stay and eat (many of them inexpensive and right on the sand). It's well known as a travelers' hangout and in recent years has seen an increase in foreign residents, attracted either by the area's beauty or, as one put it, the 'old-time hippie vibe.' After 1990, when the turtle industry was banned, several attempts at replacing Mazunte's former mainstay were made. Among those that stuck are the research center, a natural cosmetics factory and tourism.

Orientation & Information

The paved road running west from Zipolite to Hwy 200 passes through the middle of Mazunte. Three sandy lanes run about 500m from the road to the beach. The western lane is called Camino al Rinconcito, because the west end of the beach is known as El Rinconcito, while the middle lane is Camino a la Barrita. The eastern lane shall remain nameless. Mazunet, on Camino al Rinconcito near the main road, offers Internet access for $1.50 per hour.

Sights & Activities

The popular **Centro Mexicano de la Tortuga** (Mexican Turtle Center, Museo de la Tortuga; ☎ 584-30-55; cmt_mazunte@hotmail.com; admission $1.50; ☾ 10am-4:30pm Wed-Sat, 10am-2:30pm Sun) is a turtle aquarium and research center containing specimens of all seven of Mexico's marine turtle species. They're on view in fairly large tanks – it's enthralling to get a close-up view of these creatures, some of which are BIG! Visits are guided (in Spanish) and start every 10 to 15 minutes.

Mazunte's natural cosmetics workshop-store, **Cosméticos Naturales** (☾ 9am-4pm Mon-Sat, 9am-2pm Sun), is on the Pacific side of the main road toward the west end of the village. A small cooperative making shampoo and cosmetics from natural sources (like maize, coconut, avocado and sesame seeds), it also sells organic coffee, peanut butter and natural mosquito repellents, and rents rooms that are clean, good value and share bathrooms.

Aromatherapy massage is available at Cabañas Balamjuyuc (see opposite) – a full-body massage costs $22 per hour.

PUNTA COMETA

This rocky cape, jutting out from the west end of Mazunte beach, is the southernmost point in the state of Oaxaca and a fabulous place to be at sunset, with great long-distance views in both directions along the coast. You can walk here in 30 minutes, over the rocks from the end of Mazunte beach, or start up the path that leads from the beach to Cabañas Balamjuyuc and make the first left.

PLAYA VENTANILLA

Some 2.5km along the road west from Mazunte a sign points left to Playa Ventanilla, 1.2km down a dirt track. The settlement here includes a handful of simple homes, a couple of *comedores* and the *palapa* of **Servicios Ecoturísticos La Ventanilla** (☎ 589-92-77; laventanillamx@yahoo.com.mx; 1½hr lagoon tours adult/child $5/2.50, under 6yr free; tours 8:30am-5pm). It's a local cooperative providing interesting 10-passenger canoe trips on a mangrove-fringed lagoon, the Estero de la Ventanilla, 400m along the beach. You'll see river crocodiles (there are about 380 in the lagoon), lots of water birds (most prolific from April to July) and, in an enclosure on an island in the lagoon, a few white-tailed deer. For the best fauna-spotting, make your trip in the early morning. Servicios Ecoturísticos also offers three-hour horseback rides ($20; by reservation only) to another lagoon further west.

Frequent *camionetas* pass the turnoff, leaving you with the 1.2km walk. A taxi from Mazunte costs upwards of $3.

Sleeping

Most places along Playa Mazunte (including restaurants) have basic rooms or *cabañas*, hammocks to rent and often tent space. Bathrooms are shared unless otherwise stated. Security can be a problem here. Alta Mira and Cabañas Balamjuyuc are perched next to each other on a hilltop above the west end of the beach, with some superb views. Their entrances are about 400m along a road that leads uphill from Camino al Rinconcito, and they're also reachable by steps up from the beach (it can be a hot climb).

Cabañas Ziga (☎ 583-92-95; d with/without bath-room $38/20;) Friendly Ziga is near the end of the easternmost access road, on a breezy Playa Mazunte–side promontory that gives up some marvelous views for a very short climb. It has a good restaurant, a little flower garden and 17 fan rooms, all with good mosquito nets. Those with private bathrooms have tiled floors and good beds, as well as hammocks and terraces. Some of the best views are from the shared-bathroom quarters, which are in a wooden section at the front of the hotel.

Posada Arigalan (www.arigalan.com; d $50-65, tr $65; ⊠) Up a steep dirt track (above east end of Playa Mazunte) from the main road, between Mazunte and San Agustinillo, Arigalan has commanding views of the Pacific and Punta Cometa; lovely landscaping; and nine simply but tastefully furnished rooms with air-con. Its restaurant is open mid-November to mid-January (room rates outside this time are 30% lower). A trail from the beach provides access as well.

Alta Mira (☎ /fax 584-31-04; www.labuenavista.com/alta_mira; Camino a Punta Cometa; d $35-40;) The Alta Mira is run by the people from La Buena Vista (p769) at Puerto Ángel, and its 10 electricity-free rooms are among Mazunte's classiest and comfiest. They all come with beautiful Talavera-tiled bathrooms, mosquito nets and terraces with hammocks, and they're strung beside steps leading down the hillside – most catch some breeze and excellent views. The restaurant serves breakfast and dinner, and there's a safety deposit box.

Cabañas Balamjuyuc (www.balamjuyuc.com; Camino a Punta Cometa; hammocks $4.50, tents s/d $7/11.50, s $11, d $16-40, per additional person $5;) This quiet, tree-covered property has about seven *cabaña* rooms, some of which are large and airy with good sea views. The shared showers are prettily tiled, and for true budget travelers there's a *palapa* with hammocks and tents (with mattresses). A safety box is available for storing valuables. The restaurant serves breakfast for $2.50 to $3 and mains cost from $2 to $7 (vegetarians are catered for).

Palapa El Pescador (campsite per person $5, r $15) This popular restaurant (p776) in the middle of Playa Mazunte has a small tent/hammock area on the sand and good, clean upstairs rooms with power.

Restaurante Tania (☎ 583-95-94; d $20) Near the end of 2005 Tania completed a few simple rooms on the hill about 600m from the beach, above its restaurant (see right). They're solid if not cheerful, with ceiling fans and a removed sea view.

La Nueva Luna (Camino a La Barrita; r per person $7.50) Off the beach a couple of hundred meters, the Luna is an exception among low-end Mazunte lodgings in that it has plenty of good (shared) bathrooms, as well as a shared kitchen. The three rooms are adjacent to a bar that was about to open at the time of research (we're not certain how well the two areas will coexist).

El Agujón (elagujonmazunte@yahoo.com.mx; Camino al Rinconcito; s/d cabaña $6.50/11; **P**) Friendly El Agujón has 10 small, very rustic, clean *cabañas* on the hillside just above its restaurant (below).

Estrella Fugaz (☎ 583-92-97; estrellafugazmazunte@hotmail.com; Camino al Rinconcito; r per person $15-20) The nine rooms here tend toward the gloomy and some are a bit odorous, but all have fans and mosquito nets and sleep up to four people. The restaurant upstairs has a good selection of Mexican and international dishes (mains $3.50 to $7), as well as vegetable/fruit drinks and coffees.

Palapa Yuri (hammocks per person $5; tr with shared bathroom $15, d with private bathroom $29) Yuri's adequate rooms are plain but clean, and have fans. Those with shared bathroom have OK views; a thatched roof blocks the view from those with private bathroom. There's also a safety deposit box. You'll find Yuri near the east end Playa Mazunte.

Palapa Omar (hammocks & campsite per person $2.50, r per person $10) Omar is beside the end of the middle lane, Camino a la Barrita, heading to Playa Mazunte. The eight rooms in brick buildings have mosquito nets, fans and one or two double beds.

Eating

Most places to stay are also places to eat, or vice versa.

Palapa El Pescador (dishes $2.50-7) One of the best and most popular places, with fish, seafood and lighter eats such as quesadillas, tacos, fruit salad, eggs and tortas. It's on Playa Mazunte, east of the lagoon.

El Agujón (Camino al Rinconcito; dishes $2.25-7) Another good restaurant, with a wide range from large and excellent French-bread tortas to crepes, fish and, in the evening, pizzas.

Restaurante Bar Bella Vista (fish fillets $4.50, spaghetti $3.50) Attached to Cabañas Ziga (at the

east end of Playa Mazunte) and, with its elevated position, it catches a breeze.

La Dolce Vita (mains $5-8; ☾ closed October) This Italian restaurant, on the main road (east of Cosméticos Naturales) is well known for its excellent food.

La Empanada (sushi $3-4, rice dishes $1-5; ☾ from 5pm low season, 9am-late high season) Choose from a Mexican-Asian mix of delectable items including vegetable and fish sushi, all lovingly prepared. La Empanada is on the main road, on the western edge of town.

Restaurante Tania (comida corrida $3.50, fish fillets $4.50-5, veg dishes $2-3) Tania scores high for both good-value food and hospitality. It is on the main road, on the west edge of town.

Entertainment

La Nueva Luna (Camino a La Barrita; ☾ 6pm-late, closed October) Adjacent to the lodgings of the same name (see left), this bar was nearly ready to open at the time of research. It has a ping-pong table and a pleasant ambience. The Argentine operator hopes to have live music from December to April, and to serve mixed drinks made with natural fruit juices.

Getting There & Away

See boxed text, p766 for information about transportation from Pochutla. *Camionetas* run between Mazunte and San Agustinillo or Zipolite ($0.40, 10 minutes).

BAHÍAS DE HUATULCO

☎ 958 / pop 18,000

Mexico's newest big coastal resort lies along a series of beautiful sandy bays, the Bahías de Huatulco (wah-*tool*-koh), 50km east of Pochutla. This stretch of coast had just one small fishing village until the 1980s. The Mexican government has trodden more gently here than at other resort projects: pockets of development are separated by tracts of unspoiled shoreline, the maximum building height is six stories, and water-processing plants assure no sewage goes into the sea. Lower than expected occupancy rates have slowed development, and, for now, Huatulco is still a relatively uncrowded resort, with a succession of scenic beaches lapped by beautiful water and backed by forest. You can be active here – agencies offer all sorts of pursuits, from rafting and horseback riding to diving and kayaking – but Huatulco is not a place to stay long on a tight budget.

BAHÍAS DE HUATULCO

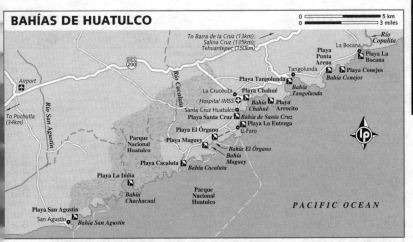

The Parque Nacional Huatulco, declared in 1998, protects 119 sq km of land, sea and shoreline west of Santa Cruz Huatulco. Balancing this, a cruise-ship pier has gone in at Bahía de Santa Cruz, and between October and May an average of two ships a week dock here.

Orientation

A divided road leads about 5km down from Hwy 200 to La Crucecita, the service town for the resort. La Crucecita has the bus stations, market, most shops and virtually the only cheap accommodations. One kilometer south, on Bahía de Santa Cruz, is Santa Cruz Huatulco (often just called Santa Cruz), with pretty plush hotels and a harbor. The other developments are at Bahía Chahué, 1km east of Santa Cruz, with mainly midrange hotels; Tangolunda, 4km further east with most of the luxury hotels; and El Faro, near Playa La Entrega, 2.5km south of Santa Cruz.

The Huatulco bays are strung along the coast about 10km in each direction from Santa Cruz. From west to east, the main ones are San Agustín, Chachacual, Cacaluta, Maguey, El Órgano, Santa Cruz, Chahué, Tangolunda and Conejos.

The airport is 400m north of Hwy 200, 12km west of the turnoff to La Crucecita.

Information

EMERGENCY

Dr Andrés González Ayvar (☎ 587-06-00, 044-958-587-60-65) Provides 24-hour medical assistance.

INTERNET ACCESS

The two La Crucecita facilities listed here have swift connections and allow laptops to jack in for the same price ($1 per hour).
El Telefonito (Map p778; Flamboyán 208; ☯ 24hr)
Surf Conejo (Map p778; Guamuchil 208)

LAUNDRY

Lavado Express (Map p778; ☎ 587-27-37; Av Bugambilia 402, La Crucecita; ☯ 9am-9pm Mon-Sat, 10am-3pm Sun) Washes and dries 3kg for $4.50. Ask for it *sin suavizante* to avoid the perfumey fabric softener.

MEDICAL SERVICES

The big hotels have English-speaking doctors on call.
Hospital IMSS (Map p777; ☎ 587-11-84; Blvd Chahué) Halfway between La Crucecita and Bahía Chahué; some doctors speak English.

MONEY

La Crucecita has several ATMs and banks:
Banamex (Map p778; cnr Carrizal & Guamuchil) You'll find the bank's ATM here.
HSBC (Map p778; cnr Av Bugambilia & Sabalí; ☯ 9am-7pm Mon-Sat) Changes cash and traveler's checks and has two ATMs, with another in Hotel Plaza Conejo.

There are further facilities in Santa Cruz Huatulco and Tangolunda:
Banamex (Map p780; Blvd Santa Cruz, Santa Cruz) Changes cash and traveler's checks and has an ATM.
Bancomer (Map p780; Blvd Santa Cruz, Santa Cruz)
HSBC (Blvd Juárez, Tangolunda) You'll find an ATM here, in front of Hotel Gala.

LA CRUCECITA

INFORMATION
Bahías Plus...........................1 B3
Banamex (ATM)....................2 B3
El Telefonito.........................3 B4
HSBC....................................4 A2
HSBC (ATM)...................(see 18)
Lavado Express.....................5 B4
Post Office............................6 C3
Surf Conejo....................(see 18)
Tourist Information Kiosk.......7 B3
Tourist Office........................8 B4

SIGHTS & ACTIVITIES
Centro de Buceo Sotavento.....9 B4
Park Entrance......................10 C3
Park Entrance......................11 B2
Parroquia de Nuestra Señora
de Guadalupe....................12 A3
Turismo Conejo...............(see 18)

SLEEPING
Hotel Arrecife.....................13 A4
Hotel Busanvi I...................14 B3
Hotel Flamboyant................15 A3
Hotel Jaroje.......................16 B4
Hotel María Mixteca............17 B3
Hotel Plaza Conejo..............18 B3
Hotel Suites Begonias..........19 B4
Misión de los Arcos.............20 A3
Posada Michelle..................21 A2

EATING
Comedores.........................22 B3
Don Wilo...........................23 B3
El Patio.............................24 B3
Paletería Zamora................25 B3
Restaurant La Crucecita.......26 B4
Restaurant-Bar Oasis...........27 B3
Terra-Cotta........................28 A3
Tostado's Grill...............(see 3)

DRINKING
La Crema...........................29 B3

ENTERTAINMENT
Cinemas Huatulco...............30 B3
La Peña.............................31 B3

TRANSPORT
Budget..............................32 A3
Bus Stop...........................33 B3
Colectivo Taxi & Microbus
Stop...............................34 B3
Estrella Blanca Bus Station...35 A2
OCC & Sur Bus Station.........36 A2
Transportes Rápidos de Pochutla
Bus Stop.........................37 A1

POST

Post office (Map p778; Blvd Chahué, La Crucecita) Three hundred meters east of Plaza Principal.

TOURIST INFORMATION

Tourist information kiosk (Map p778; Plaza Principal, La Crucecita; 9am-2pm & 4-7pm Mon-Fri, 9am-1pm Sat, closed in off-season)

Tourist office (Map p778; 587-18-71; turismohuatulco@hotmail.com; cnr Av Bugambilia & Ceiba, La Crucecita; 9am-5pm Mon-Fri, 9am-1pm Sat, closed in off-season) Upstairs in the Casa de la Cultura.

Parque Nacional Huatulco (Map p780; 587-08-49; Santa Cruz; 9am-noon, 2-6pm Mon-Fri) Upstairs at the port.

State tourist office (581-01-77; sedetur@oaxaca .gob.mx; Blvd Juárez s/n; 8am-4pm Mon-Fri, 9am-2pm Sat) In Tangolunda, on the left as you arrive from the west.

TRAVEL AGENCIES

Bahías Plus (Map p778; 587-02-16; Carrizal 704, upstairs, La Crucecita) Can help with air tickets; also books rafting tours, coffee finca visits and so forth.

Sights & Activities

La Crucecita's modern church, the **Parroquia de Nuestra Señora de Guadalupe** (Plaza Principal; admission free), has an impressively large image of the Virgin painted on its ceiling. The rest of the area's attractions are on the water, at the beaches or in jungle hinterland. You can sail, snorkel, dive, kayak, surf, fish, raft, canoe, walk in the jungle, watch birds, ride horses, rappel, canyon, cycle, visit a coffee plantation and waterfalls and more. Most outings cost $23 to $33. Bahías Plus travel agency (see opposite), **Turismo Conejo** (Map p778; ☎ 587-00-09; turismoconejo@hotmail.com; Hotel Plaza Conejo, Guamuchil 208, La Crucecita) and several hotels will book many of the activities listed here.

BEACHES

Huatulco's beaches are sandy with clear waters (though boats and jet skis leave an oily film here and there). Like the rest of Mexico, all beaches are under federal control, and anyone can use them – even when hotels appear to treat them as private property. Some have coral offshore and excellent snorkeling, though visibility can be poor in the rainy season.

Lanchas will whisk you out to most of the beaches from Santa Cruz Huatulco harbor any time between 8am and 5pm or 6pm, and they'll return to collect you by dusk. Taxis can get you to most beaches for less money, but a boat ride is more fun. Hire and board the lanchas beside the harbor (Map p780). Round-trip rates for up to 10 people: Playa La Entrega ($18), Bahía Maguey and Bahía El Órgano ($46) and Playa La India ($73). Another possibility for a fun day is a 6½-hour, **seven-bay boat cruise** (per person $20; ⏱ 11am-5:30pm) with an open bar. A *lancha* will make the same excursion (less the booze) for $120 for up to 10 people.

At Santa Cruz Huatulco, the small, accessible **Playa Santa Cruz** is rather pretty, though its looks are somewhat marred by the cruise-ship pier. **Playa La Entrega** lies toward the outer edge of Bahía de Santa Cruz, a five-minute *lancha* trip or 2.5km by paved road from Santa Cruz. The 300m-long beach, backed by a line of seafood *palapas*, can get crowded, but it has calm water and good snorkeling in a large area from which boats are cordoned off. 'La Entrega' means 'The Handover': here in 1831, Mexican independence hero Vicente Guerrero was betrayed to his enemies by a Genoese sea captain. Guerrero was taken to Cuilapan near Oaxaca and shot.

Some of the western bays are accessible by road; at times groups of young men congregate in the bays' parking lots, offering to 'watch your car,' and touting for the beach restaurants. A 1.5km paved road diverges to **Bahía Maguey** from the road to La Entrega, about half a kilometer out of Santa Cruz. Maguey's fine 400m beach curves around a calm bay between forested headlands. It

has a line of seafood *palapas*. There's good snorkeling around the rocks at the left (east) side of the bay. **Bahía El Órgano**, just east of Maguey, has a 250m beach. You can reach it by a narrow 10-minute footpath that heads into the trees halfway along the Santa Cruz–Maguey road. El Órgano has calm waters that are good for snorkeling, but it lacks *comedores*.

The beach at **Bahía Cacaluta** is about 1km long and protected by an island, though there can be undertow. Snorkeling is best around the island. Behind the beach is a lagoon with bird life. The road to Cacaluta (which branches off just above the parking lot for Maguey) is paved except for the last 1.5km, but it can be a long, hot walk, and there are no services at the beach itself. You wouldn't want to leave a car at pavement's end, either, as it's quite isolated. A more pleasant way to get there is to take one of the *lanchas* from Santa Cruz Huatulco harbor. Cacaluta has a research station for the study of turtles and sea snails.

Bahía Chachacual, inaccessible by land, has a headland at each end and two beaches. The easterly **Playa La India** is one of Huatulco's most beautiful beaches and is one of the area's best places for snorkeling.

If you head 1.7km west of the airport to a crossroads on Hwy 200, then 13km down a dirt road, you'll find **Bahía San Agustín**. After 9km the road fords a river. The beach is long and sandy, with a long line of *palapa comedores*, some with hammocks for rent overnight. It's popular with Mexicans on weekends and holidays, but quiet at other times. Usually the waters are calm and the snorkeling is good (some of the *comedores* rent out equipment).

A paved road runs to the eastern bays from La Crucecita and Santa Cruz, continuing eventually to Hwy 200. **Bahía Chahué** has a good beach and a new marina at its east end. Further east, **Bahía Tangolunda** is the site of the major top-end hotel developments to date. The sea is sometimes rough here. Be wary of currents and be sure to heed the colored-flag safety system. Tangolunda has an 18-hole **golf course**, too. Three kilometers further east is the long sweep of **Playa Punta Arena**, on Bahía Conejos. Around a headland at the east end of Bahía Conejos is the more sheltered **Playa Conejos**, unreachable by road.

OAXACA STATE

SANTA CRUZ HUATULCO

INFORMATION
Banamex............................1 B2
Bancomer............................2 B2
Parque Nacional Huatulco Office..3 D2

SIGHTS & ACTIVITIES
Hurricane Divers........................4 C3
Snorkel Hire.........................(see 14)

SLEEPING
Hotel Castillo Huatulco...............5 C1
Hotel Marina Resort...................6 D2
Hotel Sol y Mar........................7 B3

EATING
Café Huatulco..........................8 C2
Jardín del Arte........................9 B3
Restaurant Ve El Mar.................10 D3

SHOPPING
Mercado de Artesanías.............11 C2

TRANSPORT
Aero Tucán............................12 C1
Colectivo Taxi & Microbus Stop...13 C2
Lancha Tickets & Embarkation...14 C2
Private Taxi Stand...................15 C2

To Chahué Hotels (600m);
Bahía Chahué (600m);
Plaza Chahué (800m);
La Crucecita (1km);
Tangolunda (3km)

To Playa La
Entrega (2.5km);
Bahía Maguey (5km)

PARQUE ECOLÓGICO RUFINO TAMAYO

This park (Map p778) on the edge of La Crucecita is composed mainly of natural vegetation, with some paved paths and tile-roofed shelters with benches.

SNORKELING & DIVING

You can rent **snorkeling gear** beside the *lancha* kiosk at Santa Cruz harbor for about $5.75 a day, and at Playa Maguey for $5.50 a day. Tour guides will take you snorkeling for $20 to $45, or you can arrange a trip with one of the dive outfits listed here.

Huatulco has around 13 dive sites, with a wide variety of fish and corals, as well as dolphins and sea turtles. At least two companies will take you diving and offer instruction from beginners' sessions through to full certification courses:

Centro de Buceo Sotavento (scubasota@hotmail.com; www.tomzap.com/sotavento.html) La Crucecita (Map p778; ☎ 587-21-66; Plaza Oaxaca, Local 18 Interior, Flamboyán); Tangolunda (☎ 581-00-51; Plaza Las Conchas, Local 12) This excellent local company offers a range of options from a four-hour introduction ($65) to full certification (five days; $320) or specialty night dives ($65); it also takes

two-hour fishing trips for one to six people ($45 to $80, depending on the vessel), as well as snorkeling trips for $15 per person.

Hurricane Divers (Map p780; ☎ 587-11-07; www .hurricanedivers.com; Playa Santa Cruz, Santa Cruz) The professional international crew here speak English, Spanish, Dutch and German, and offer a variety of courses and dives. One-tank dives are $50; PADI programs (with ocean dive) start at $95. The staff take half-day and full-day snorkeling trips as well ($50/100).

RAFTING

The Copalita and Zimatán Rivers near Bahías de Huatulco have waters ranging from Class 1 to Class 4/5, in rafting terms. They're at their biggest between July and November. Turismo Conejo (see p779) books rafting and kayaking trips for $61 to $66 per person, or you could contact **Pablo Nárvaez** (☎ 585-03-03; pablo_rafting@yahoo.com).

HORSEBACK RIDING

Rancho Caballo de Mar (☎ 587-03-66) takes 3½-hour beach and forest rides for $47 (reservations are necessary, but riding experience isn't). English and French are spoken.

Sleeping

All midrange and top-end rooms listed here are air-conditioned. Rates quoted in those categories are for the high seasons (roughly December to April and July to mid-August). Peak periods around Christmas and Easter see considerably higher rates. Budget hotels maintain their prices year-round, with the exception of holiday peak periods (when their rates roughly double).

BUDGET

Hotel Arrecife (Map p778; ☎ 587-17-07; hotel arrecife@ hotmail.com; Colorín 510, La Crucecita; s with fan $26-32, d with fan $30-35, d with air-con $39; P ✷ ▢ ▣) In a quiet, leafy neighborhood, the Arrecife has a small pool and a good little restaurant. Of the 24 rooms, the best are sizable, with two double beds, air-con (some old units) and balcony; others are small and open straight onto the street.

Hotel Busanvi I (Map p778; ☎ 587-00-56; Carrizal 601, La Crucecita; s/d with air-con $14/28; ✷) The plain, large-ish rooms here are a deal. Comfy beds, modern air-con and a small common area are all good, and the showers are excellent. Six of the rooms have balconies, and prices stay low year-round.

Posada Michelle (Map p778; ☎ 587-05-35; Gardenia 8, La Crucecita; d $29, tr & q $47; ✷) The Michelle is next to the Estrella Blanca bus station and can be noisy until 9pm. Beds are springy and bathrooms poor, but the dozen or so rooms are brightly decorated and have decent air-con and cable TV. A little sitting area with hammocks adds some appeal as well.

Hotel Sol y Mar (Map p780; ☎ 587-16-61; Mitla s/n, Santa Cruz Huatulco; r $30) This small hotel, with good-sized rooms that have fans and decent bathrooms, was still coming together at the time of research. Prices may rise as hot water and air-con are installed.

MIDRANGE

Santa Cruz' and Bahía Chahué's midrange options are generally more luxurious than those in La Crucecita.

Hotel Jaroje (Map p778; ☎ /fax 583-48-01; jaroje .tripod.com.mx; Av Bugambilia 304, La Crucecita; s/d incl continental breakfast $29/38; ✷ ▢) Bright, fresh, three-storey Jaroje has good-sized, pleasantly decorated rooms with air-con, cable TV and fine bathrooms. Prices include 15 minutes of email-checking.

Hotel María Mixteca (Map p778; ☎ 587-23-36; fax 587-23-38; www.travelbymexico.com/oaxa/mariamixteca; Guamuchil 204, La Crucecita; s/d/tr $50/55/60; ✷ ▢) Small and good value, the María Mixteca opened in 2004. It has 14 modern, very well-equipped rooms on two upper floors, with super-comfy beds, great bathrooms, and room safes.

Misión de los Arcos (Map p778; ☎ 587-01-65; www .misiondelosarcos.com; Gardenia 902, La Crucecita; r/ste $57/61; P ✷ ▢) This 13-room American-owned hotel is embellished by a touch of interior greenery. It has big, bright comfortable rooms (all decorated in simple white and beige), a gym and a good restaurant.

Hotel Suites Begonias (Map p778; ☎ 587-03-90; getosa@prodigy.net.mx; Av Bugambilia 503, La Crucecita; d/ tr $57/66) Most of the lodgings here are comfortable two-room suites with two double beds and attractive bathrooms.

Hotel Posada Edén Costa (☎ 587-24-80; www .edencosta.com; Calle Zapoteco s/n, Bahía Chahué; r $77, ste with salon & kitchen $137; P ✷ ▣) Swiss- and Laotian-owned Edén Costa, a block inland from Blvd Juárez, has quiet rooms with nice touches. Most overlook the small pool. The attached restaurant, L'échalote (p783), is a big bonus.

Hotel Flamboyant (Map p778; ☎ 587-01-13; flam boyhuatulco@prodigy.net.mx; Plaza Principal, La Crucecita; r incl breakfast $89; P ✷) This pink hotel has a pleasant courtyard, an attractive pool, its own restaurant and 70 rooms. Decor is Oaxacan folksy.

Hotel Plaza Conejo (Map p778; ☎ 587-00-09; turismo conejo@hotmail.com; Guamuchil 208, La Crucecita; s $29, d from $47; ✷ ▢) This friendly hotel has 10 tidy, bright, clean rooms off an interior patio. Air-con is good; bathrooms so-so.

TOP END

Air/lodging packages are your best bet for a good-value holiday in a top-end Huatulco hotel. Another way to save is to look for promotions on hotel websites; you can often find prices well below the rack rates that we've provided here.

Quinta Real (☎ 581-04-28; www.quintareal.com; Paseo Juárez 2, Tangolunda; ste from $346; P ✕ ✷ ▢ ▣) The utterly gorgeous Quinta Real has a hilltop position at the west end of Tangolunda. Its 27 suites each have a Jacuzzi and an ocean view; some have fountain-fed private pools that seem to spill down the hillside to the beach and main swimming-pool area.

Casa del Mar (☎ 581-02-03; Balcones de Tangolunda 13, Tangolunda; ste from $120; P ✕ ⬛ ⬛) Elegant and sensationally sited Casa del Mar, east of Tangolunda's main hotel cluster, has 25 well-appointed suites with great views, and a beautiful pool and restaurant. Reservations recommended.

Las Brisas (☎ 583-02-00; www.brisas.com.mx; Bahía de Tangolunda Lote 1, Tangolunda; r from $188, ste from $204; P ✕ ✕ ⬛ ⬛ 👶) Sprawling across more than 22 hectares, with its own four beaches, this former Club Med boasts 484 rooms, most with ocean views. It also offers 12 tennis courts; volleyball, squash and basketball courts; a children's club (babysitting available); and a full range of aquatic activities.

Camino Real Zaashila (☎ 581-04-60; www.camino real.com/zaashila; Blvd Juárez 5, Tangolunda; r incl breakfast from $205; P ✕ ✕ ⬛ ⬛) Located toward the east end of Tangolunda, this tranquil, attractive, Mediterranean-style property has a big pool in lovely gardens. There are 120 rooms, of which 41 come with their own small pool, and of course, a higher price!

Hotel Marina Resort (Map p780; ☎ 587-09-63; www .hotelmarinaresort.com; Tehuantepec 112, Santa Cruz; r/ste incl buffet breakfast $142/177; ✕ ⬛) This 50-room resort, on the east side of Santa Cruz harbor, has three pools, a nearby *temazcal* and beach club, and lots of pastel green. Rooms have balconies, while suites have kitchenettes and private terraces with marina views.

Hotel Castillo Huatulco (Map p780; ☎ 587-01-44; www.boyce.com.mx; Blvd Santa Cruz 303, Santa Cruz; r $153; P ✕ ⬛) Colonial-style Castillo Huatulco has an attractive pool, a restaurant and 112 good-sized, brightly decorated rooms, with safes. Transportation to the Castillo's beach club on Bahía Chahué is free. The hotel also offers packages that provide a third night for free.

Eating

LA CRUCECITA

Restaurant-Bar Oasis (Map p778; ☎ 587-13-00; Flamboyán 211, Plaza Principal; mains $5.50-11.50) The Oasis has good, moderately priced fare, including tortas, fish fillets, steaks, Oaxacan specialties, sushi and other Japanese food. It's a popular breakfast spot but the execrable pop music can be hard to take in the morning.

Tostado's Grill (Map p778; ☎ 587-02-19; Flamboyán 306; mains $5.50-12) Much of the menu features Italian food, but you can also order a mean

spinach salad with bacon. It's found in front of Hotel Posada del Parque.

Don Wilo (Map p778; ☎ 587-06-23; Guanacastle, Plaza Principal; mains $5-15; ⏱ closed Tue) The Don's Oaxacan dishes, including *tamales* and *tlay-udas*, are very popular. He also serves fish, steaks and pizza.

Restaurant La Crucecita (Map p778; ☎ 587-09-06; cnr Av Bugambilia & Chacah; mains $5-9; ⏱ 7am-11pm) This inexpensive spot is a block from the plaza. Its *sincronizadas a la mexicana* (fried ham-and-cheese tortillas; $4) make a good *antojito*. Tasty *licuados* ($2) with yogurt or milk are a specialty. Early in the day, watch the chef prepare serious quantities of *salsa roja*.

El Patio (Map p778; ☎ 587-02-11; Flamboyán 214; breakfast $3.50-5.50, mains $5.50-9) A appealing garden patio with tables out the back welcomes you here. The breakfasts are good deals; the rest of the day you're offered the usual range of fish, seafood, chicken dishes and Oaxacan specialties, as well as a full selection of alcoholic drinks.

Terra-Cotta (Map p778; ☎ 587-12-28; cnr Gardenia & Tamarindo; breakfast $3-4.50, sandwiches $6.50; ⏱ 8am-11:30pm) Soothing air-con and a garden view complement the good food at popular, American-run Terra-Cotta. Egg dishes, waffles, baguettes, fine espresso and ice cream go down easy, as do the several Mexican dishes on the menu.

Paletería Zamora (Map p778; cnr Flamboyán & Av Bugambilia) Don't let the name fool you; in addition to the wide variety of Popsicles and ice cream, Zamora blends up a full range of fresh fruit drinks, *licuados* and *aguas frescas* ('cool waters' – fruit blended with water and sweetener).

Comedores (Map p778; Mercado, cnr Av Bugambilia & Guanacastle; fish or shrimp platters $5.50-6.50) The very clean *comedores* at the market serve up good food, including *enfrijoladas* (tortillas smothered in beans, with a sprinkling of cheese) or *entomatadas* for $3.25.

SANTA CRUZ HUATULCO

Restaurant Ve El Mar (Map p780; ☎ 587-03-64; Playa Santa Cruz; mains $8.50-10; ⏱ 8am-10pm) Food at the eateries on Playa Santa Cruz is mostly average, but this place at the east end is an exception. The seafood is fine, and the *salsas picantes* (hot sauces) and margaritas potent. Try a whole fish, an octopus or shrimp dish or, if you have $24 to spare, lobster.

Jardín del Arte (Map p780; ☎ 587-00-55; Hotel Marlin, Mitla 28; mains $6-13) This restaurant features international cuisine with a French touch, and homemade bread. You can enjoy crepes, fish dishes and the occasional *codorniz* (quail), or a sociable breakfast on the terrace.

Café Huatulco (Map p780; ☎ 587-12-28; Plaza Santa Cruz; breakfast $4.50-6, coffee $1.50-3.50, cake $3; ☯ 8am-10:30pm) Mid-plaza near the harbor, Huatulco serves good Pluma coffee in many different ways – the *capuchino paraíso* (cold cappuccino with a dollop of ice cream) is well worth a try.

BAHÍA CHAHUÉ & TANGOLUNDA

L'échalote (☎ 587-24-80; Calle Zapoteco s/n, Bahía Chahué; mains $7.50-14, desserts $4-7; ☯ 2-11pm Tue-Sun) This *palapa*-roofed restaurant is attached to the Hotel Posada Edén Costa (p781) in Chahué. The Swiss-French chef prepares French, Thai, Vietnamese, Oaxacan and other dishes. The Thai salad with prawns and bean sprouts is delicious. Quiche Lorraine, *nem* (spring rolls) and the chicken-liver salad are quite good, and the desserts aren't too shabby, either.

Casa del Mar (☎ 581-02-03; Balcones de Tangolunda 13, Tangolunda; starters $4-8, mains $7-13.50) A great view and romantic setting make it worth the trouble to get here. Try the *tamal de pescado* (steamed corn dough stuffed with fish). Flambéed bananas to finish? Why not?

Tangolunda's big hotels offer a choice of expensive bars, coffee shops and restaurants.

BEACHES

There are decent seafood *palapas* at Playas La Entrega, Maguey, San Agustín and La Bocana. A whole grilled *huachinango* (red snapper) costs $6 to $9.

Drinking & Entertainment

La Crema (Map p778; ☎ 587-07-02; cnr Flamboyán & Carrizal, La Crucecita; ☯ 7pm-3am) This dark, moody bar has a good music mix and delicious wood-oven pizza.

La Peña (Map p778; Carrizal s/n, La Crucecita; ☯ 7pm-3am) Head across the street from La Crema for a great Latin party vibe, with good live music, Cuban-style, from Tuesday to Saturday.

La Papaya (Blvd Juárez, Bahía Chahué; ☎ 583-94-11; cover $11; ☯ 11pm-5am Thu-Sat) This long-standing disco above Plaza del Mezcal appeals to the 18-to-25 age group.

Noches Oaxaqueñas (☎ 581-00-01; Blvd Juárez s/n, Tangolunda; admission $10; ☯ 8:30pm Tue, Thu & Sat off-season, 8:30pm daily high season) Catch a Guelaguetza regional dance show here – drinks and/or dinner ($7 to $17) are extra. It's located by the Tangolunda traffic circle.

Cinema Huatulco (Map p778; Guamuchil s/n) This cinema is in La Crucecita's Plaza Madero, a shopping mall at the corner of Guamuchil and Carrizal. It shows a blend of Hollywood and Mexican films.

Shopping

Mercado de Artesanías (Map p780), Santa Cruz' market, has a wide range of beach gear and handicrafts, including some good jewelry and textiles. However, with the cruise ships arriving constantly you're not likely to find many bargains.

Getting There & Away

AIR

Mexicana and its subsidiary Click Mexicana offer three to five flights daily to/from Mexico City. Aero Tucán (with a 13-seat Cessna) flies daily to/from Oaxaca, as does Aerovega, with a seven-seater. **Continental Express** (☎ 800-900-50-00) flies from Houston from one to four times a week in winter, and cheap charters from Canada, the US and the UK are sometimes available.

Airline offices:

Aero Tucán (Map p780 ☎ 587-24-27; Zona Comercial, Hotel Castillo Huatulco, Santa Cruz)

Mexicana & Click Mexicana Bahía Chahué (☎ 587-02-23; Plaza Chahué, Blvd Juárez, Local 3); Airport (☎ 581-90-08)

BUS

The main bus stations are located on Gardenia in La Crucecita. Some buses coming to Huatulco are marked 'Santa Cruz Huatulco,' but they still terminate in La Crucecita. Make sure your bus is not headed to Santa María Huatulco, which is a long way inland.

First-class **OCC** (Map p778; ☎ 587-02-61; cnr Gardenia & Ocotillo) is four blocks from the plaza. Most of its buses are *de paso* (buses that started their journeys somewhere else but are stopping to let off and take on passengers). Sur buses pull up here, too. **Estrella Blanca** (EB; Map p778; ☎ 587-03-90; cnr Gardenia & Palma Real) has 1st-class services that are quick and fairly comfortable, and *ordinario* buses that are typical *ordinario*.

Destination	Price	Duration	Frequency
Acapulco	$28	10hr	7 Estrella Blanca daily
Juchitán	$9	4hr	OCC
Mexico City	$43-50	15hr	OCC & EB
Oaxaca	$19	8hr via	3 OCC daily
		Salina Cruz	
Pochutla	$2.25	1hr	6 OCC daily
	$2.50	1hr	7 Estrella Blanca daily
	$1.25		every 15min 6am-8pm Transportes Rápidos de Pochutla, from Blvd Chahué opposite the north end of Av Bugambilia in La Crucecita
Puerto	$6	2½hr	6 OCC daily
Escondido	$3	2½hr	12 Sur daily
	$6.50	2½hr	7 Estrella Blanca daily
San Cristóbal	$27	13hr	OCC
de Las Casas			
Tapachula		10hr	OCC
Tehuantepec	$8	3½hr	8 OCC daily
	$7	3½hr	2 Sur daily
Tuxtla	$22	10hr	OCC
Gutiérrez			
Zihuatanejo	$43	14hr	1 EB daily

CAR

Car-rental agencies:

Budget (Map p778; ☎ 587-00-10; cnr Ocotillo & Jazmín, La Crucecita)

Hertz (☎ 581-90-92; airport)

Getting Around
TO/FROM THE AIRPORT

Transportación Terrestre (☎ 581-90-14) provides *colectivo* combis for $8 per person from the airport to La Crucecita, Santa Cruz or Bahía Chahué and for $9 to Tangolunda. Get tickets at the company's airport kiosk. For a whole cab at a reasonable price, walk just outside the airport gate, where you can pick up one for about $13 to La Crucecita, Santa Cruz or Tangolunda, or $14 to Pochutla. Even cheaper, walk 400m down to Hwy 200 and catch a minibus for $0.70 to La Crucecita or $1.50 to Pochutla. Those buses heading to La Crucecita may be marked 'Santa Cruz' or 'Bahías Huatulco' or something similar.

BUS & COLECTIVO

Colectivo taxis and minibuses provide transportation between La Crucecita, Santa Cruz Huatulco and Tangolunda. In La Crucecita

catch them just east of the corner of Guamuchil and Carrizal, one block from the Plaza Principal. In Santa Cruz they stop by the harbor, and in Tangolunda at the traffic circle outside Hotel Gala. Fares are the same in either: from La Crucecita to Santa Cruz it's $0.30, and to Tangolunda it's $0.50.

TAXI

Official taxi rates are posted on the east side of the Plaza Principal in La Crucecita, from where you pay around $1.50 to Santa Cruz, $2.50 to Tangolunda, $4.50 to Bahía Maguey and $9.50 to the airport. By the hour, cabs cost $15. There is a taxi stand on the east side of the main plaza.

AROUND BAHÍAS DE HUATULCO
Barra de la Cruz
☎ 958 / pop 700

This tranquil fishing village is reached via a 1.5km road that heads coastward from Hwy 200 about 20km east of Santa Cruz Huatulco. At the mouth of the Río Zimatán, Barra is known for its great surf; the right-hand point break gets up to a double overhead. A lack of undertow also makes for good swimming. Barra's beach has showers, toilets and a *comedor* offering food, drinks, plenty of hammocks and shade. The municipality charges $1 per person to pass along the road to the beach, and imposes a 7:30pm curfew; after sunset it's 'hasta la vista, baby.'

You can rent surfboards outside the toll gate for $9.50 per day. Villagers rent rooms in their houses for about $5 a night, but conditions are rustic. Go upscale and stay at **Barradise** (☎ 585-03-03; pablo_rafting@yahoo.com; r $14-19), in two fan-cooled rooms above the surf shop. It's ably run by the Pablo Nárvaez, who, in addition to surf guiding, can also take you rafting, mountain biking and birding, and has the certificates to prove it.

Taxis from La Crucecita to Barra cost about $9.50, or $15 all the way to the beach. Eastbound 2nd-class buses will drop you at the turnoff on Hwy 200; the total distance from there to the beach is just under 4km.

Highway 200 provides almost no views of the Pacific from Huatulco to the east, until you begin to approach Salina Cruz – then it's mostly tantalizing glimpses of sea and beaches with enormous dunes piled against rocks, testament to the force of the winds that blow across the isthmus.

ISTHMUS OF TEHUANTEPEC

Eastern Oaxaca is the southern half of the 200km-wide Isthmus of Tehuantepec (teh-wahn-teh-*pek*), Mexico's narrowest point. Dramatic mountains are seldom out of view, but this is hot, flat country. Zapotec culture is strong here, and foreign visitors few. Stay and you'll encounter lively, friendly people, and may even get an impromptu tour from schoolkids curious to see a foreign face.

A fast toll highway from Oaxaca to the coast is being built, and may bring changes. Its final leg already skirts the unattractive oil refinery city of Salina Cruz. About 15km northeast of Juchitán, near La Ventosa (where Hwy 185 to Acayucan diverges from Hwy 190 to Chiapas), strong north winds blow, sometimes toppling high vehicles.

History & People

In 1496 the isthmus Zapotecs repulsed the Aztecs from the fortress of Guiengola, near Tehuantepec, and the isthmus never became part of the Aztec empire. Later there was strong resistance to the Spanish here, and an independent spirit pervades the region to this day.

Isthmus women are open and confident, and take a leading role in business and government. Many older women still wear embroidered *huipiles* and big printed skirts. For the numerous *velas* (fiestas), Tehuantepec and Juchitán women display velvet or sateen *huipiles*, gold and silver jewelry (a sign of wealth), skirts embroidered with fantastically colorful silk flowers, and odd headgear. Many isthmus fiestas feature the *tirada de frutas*, in which women climb on roofs and throw fruit on the men below!

TEHUANTEPEC

☎ 971 / pop 38,000

Tehuantepec is a friendly town, 245km from Oaxaca city, often with a fiesta going on in one of its *barrios*.

Orientation

The Oaxaca–Tuxtla Gutiérrez highway (190) meets Hwy 185 from Salina Cruz about 1km west of Tehuantepec. The combined high-

ways then skirt the west edge of the town center and turn east to form the northern edge of town. Tehuantepec's bus stations – collectively known as La Terminal – cluster here, south of the highway (1.5km northeast of the town center via the highway – but considerably closer in a straight line). To walk to the plaza from La Terminal, follow Av Héroes until it ends at a T-junction, then turn right along Guerrero for four blocks to another T-junction. Then go one block left along Hidalgo – the Palacio Municipal stands on the south side of the plaza.

Information

Bancomer and Banorte banks, on Calle 5 de Mayo a few steps west of the Palacio Municipal, both have ATMs; Banorte changes US dollars.

Café Internet La Frontera (Calle 5 de Mayo; Internet per hr $1; ⏰ 9am-9pm) Located next door to Banorte, this is one of several Internet places in town.

Cruz Roja (Red Cross; ☎ 715-02015) Call in a medical emergency.

Santander Serfin (Calle 22 de Mayo; ⏰ 9am-4pm Mon-Sat) North side of the plaza; will change traveler's checks and cash US dollars.

Sights

EX-CONVENTO REY COSIJOPÍ

This former Dominican monastery, north and west of the plaza on a short street off Guerrero, is Tehuantepec's **Casa de la Cultura** (Callejón Rey Cosijopí; admission free; ⏰ 9am-2pm & 5-8pm Mon-Fri, 9am-2pm Sat). It bears traces of old religious frescoes and has modest but interesting exhibits of traditional dress, archaeological finds, historical photos and the like. King Cosijopí, the local Zapotec leader at the time, provided the funds for its construction in the 16th century, at the urging of Hernán Cortés.

GUIENGOLA

The hillside **Zapotec stronghold** of Guiengola, where King Cosijoeza rebuffed the Aztecs, is north of Hwy 190 from a turnoff 11km out of Tehuantepec. A sign at Puente Las Tejas (Tejas Bridge; there was a military checkpoint here at the time of research) just past the Km 240 marker points to 'Ruinas Guiengola.' A guide (recommended) may be waiting here or nearer to the site. The unpaved 7km road in is passable in dry weather, though the last kilometer or so (heading uphill) requires a high-clearance vehicle. The road ends at a signed trailhead, and about an hour's sweaty walk uphill gets you to the remains of two pyramids, a ball court, a 64-room complex and a thick defensive wall. You'll also see interesting limestone formations and some fine views over the isthmus.

Non-drivers should catch a bus to Jalapa del Marqués from La Terminal. From Las Tejas it's about a 2½-hour walk. Take plenty of water, and start early – 6am or earlier – to take advantage of the morning cool.

MARKET
Tehuantepec's dim, almost medieval, indoor market is open daily on the west side of the plaza. It spills out into the surrounding streets, where flowers are often for sale.

Sleeping
Hotel Donají (☎ 715-00-64; hoteldonaji@hotmail.com; Juárez 10; s/d/tr/q with fan $16/23/31/38, with air-con $23/30/40/43; P 🅿 🛂) Bright Donají, two blocks south of the east side of the central plaza, has clean rooms with TV on two upper floors around a shady, colorful patio. Bonuses include a small gym and pool.

Guiexhoba (☎ 715-17-10; guiexhoba@prodigy.net .mx; Carretera Panamericana Km 250.5; s/d/tr $40/50/60; P 🅿 🛂) This motel is at the junction of Hwys 185 and 190, a kilometer southwest of the center. Rooms are large, as is the covered swimming pool, but those on the Hwy 190 side can be noisy – although the air-con may drown that out. The restaurant is pricey, but serves big salads and good espresso.

Hotel Oasis (☎ 715-00-08; Ocampo 8; r with fan $15-18, with air-con $25; P) This budget hotel is a block south of the plaza, with 26 basic rooms and warm showers.

Eating
Bar Restaurante Scarú (☎ 715-06-46; Callejón Leona Vicario 4; dishes $4-11) Two blocks east and 50m north of Hotel Donají, friendly Scarú occupies an 18th-century house with a courtyard and colorful modern murals of Tehuantepec life. Sit beneath a fan, quaff a *limonada* and sample one of the many varied dishes on offer. On weekends old-timers plunk out marimba tunes.

The market has the usual eateries, and at night the entire east sidewalk of the plaza is lined with plastic tables and chairs beside carts serving cheap tacos and other delights.

Getting There & Away
At La Terminal, OCC and ADO (both 1st class) and Sur and AU (both 2nd class) share one building. Some 1st-class buses are *de paso*. Transportes Oaxaca-Istmo (TOI, 2nd class) is next door, nearer to the highway.

Buses to Juchitán ($1.50, 30 minutes) depart across the street from OCC at least every half-hour during daylight. Other services:

Destination	Price	Duration	Frequency
Acayucan	$11	4½hr	6 1st-class ADO daily
Bahías	$8	3½hr	3 1st class daily
de Huatulco	$6.50	3½hr	2 Sur 2nd class daily
Mexico City			
(TAPO)	$46-54	11½hr	6 1st-class & deluxe daily
	$41	13hr	3 2nd-class AU daily
Oaxaca	$12	4½hr	15 1st class daily
	$11	4½hr	7 Sur 2nd-class daily
	$7.50	5½hr	13 TOI daily
Pochutla	$10	4½hr	3 1st-class OCC daily
Puerto	$14	6½ hr	3 1st-class OCC daily
Escondido			
Tapachula	$23	6½hr	2 1st-class OCC daily
Tuxtla	$14	5½hr	3 1st class daily
Gutiérrez	$9	5½hr	5 TOI daily
San Cristóbal			Take bus to Tuxtla
de Las Casas			Gutiérrez and catch connecting bus
Villahermosa	$23	7½hr	3 1st-class ADO daily

Getting Around
Taxis between La Terminal and the plaza cost about $1.75. A local variation on the Mexican theme of three-wheeled transportation is the *motocarro*, where passengers sit (or stand, to better catch the breeze) on a platform behind the driver. The sight of colorfully garbed women riding tall will linger in your memory. *Motocarros* congregate by the railway track west of the market.

JUCHITÁN
☎ 971 / pop 68,000
Istmeño culture is strong in this friendly town, which is visited by few gringos.

Orientation & Information
Prolongación 16 de Septiembre leads into Juchitán from a busy intersection (with traffic signals) on Hwy 190, on the north edge of town. The main bus terminal is 100m toward town from there. The street

curves left, then right, then divides into 5 de Septiembre (right fork) and 16 de Septiembre (left), before emerging as opposite sides of the central plaza, Jardín Juárez, after seven blocks. The Palacio Municipal is the Jardín's eastern boundary.

The Jardín has banks with ATMs; in the southwest corner, **Scotiabank** (9am-5pm Mon-Fri) changes traveler's checks and cashes US dollars. Internet places abound, particularly on Prolongación 16 de Septiembre. Most charge $1 an hour; try **La-Net@.com** (noon-midnight), opposite Hotel López Lena Palace. Head to **Hospital Fuentes** (711-14-41; Efraín R Gómez s/n) in a medical emergency.

Sights

Jardín Juárez is a lively central square. In a market on the east side, and spilling into the streets, you'll find traditional Isthmus women's costumes, and maybe iguana on the menus of the *comedores*.

Juchitán's **Lidxi Guendabiaani** (Casa de la Cultura; Belisario Domínguez; admission free; 10am-3pm & 5-8pm Mon-Fri, 10am-2pm Sat) is a block south and west of Jardín Juárez. It has interesting archaeological and art collections, with works by 20th-century Mexican artists including Rufino Tamayo and the prolific *juchiteco* Francisco Toledo. It's by the church, around a big patio that buzzes with children.

Sleeping & Eating

Hotel López Lena Palace (711-13-88; Prolongación 16 de Septiembre 70; s & d $24-31, tw $42; P) Look for the mock Arabic exterior about halfway between the bus station and town center. The Lena has OK rooms with comfy beds; the best value are the cheerful but windowless 'minis,' with excellent air-con and showers. Attached Restaurant El Califa (mains $3 to $13) offers some excellent dishes, including fresh salads and stuffed fish, but the breakfasts leave something to be desired.

Hotel Santo Domingo del Sur (711-10-50; sto@prodigy.net.mx; Carretera Juchitán-Tehuantepec; s/d/ r with air-con $36/48/59; P) By the Hwy 190 crossroads, popular Santo Domingo has decent rooms (some have poor bathrooms), a large pool surrounded by a garden, and a good restaurant (meals $3 to $14).

Casagrande Restaurant (711-34-60; mains 4.50-14) The flashest eatery in town, with a pleasant covered courtyard, ceiling fans and tall plants. All meals, from regional dishes

to seafood, have 15% tax added. It's located on the south side of Jardín Juárez; the Casagrande cinema sign makes it easier to find.

Café Santa Fe (711-15-45; Cruce de Carretera Transístmica; dishes $4-8; 24hr) For cool air and good food, try this place, handily wedged between the main bus stations and the highway. White-coated waiters briskly serve excellent breakfasts and good espresso.

Getting There & Away

OCC and ADO (1st class) and Sur and AU (2nd class) use the bus terminal on Prolongación 16 de Septiembre; they're housed in separate structures. Frequent 2nd-class Istmeño buses to Tehuantepec ($1.25, 30 minutes) and Salina Cruz ($2, one hour) stop at the next corner south on Prolongación 16 de Septiembre during daylight. Fypsa's terminal (2nd class) is separated from the main one by a Pemex station and Café Santa Fe.

Some buses are *de paso* and leave in the middle of the night; others originate in Salina Cruz and stop at Juchitán not long after.

Destination	Price	Duration	Frequency
Acayucan	$9	4hr	frequent Sur buses
Bahías de Huatulco	$9	4hr	5 1st-class buses
Huatulco	$8	4hr	hourly Sur buses 3am-5pm
Mexico City (TAPO)	$42-67	12hr	11 1st-class, deluxe & 2nd-class buses
Oaxaca	$9-17	5-6hr	20 1st-class buses daily, 6 Sur buses & Fypsa hourly
Pochutla	$12	5hr	5 1st-class buses
Puebla	$35-67	10hr	1st-class or deluxe buses
Puerto Escondido	$16	7hr	5 1st-class buses
San Cristóbal de Las Casas	$18	9hr	3 1st-class buses
Tapachula	$22	6hr	2 1st-class buses
Tuxtla Gutiérrez	$8-14	5hr	frequent OCC & Fypsa
Villahermosa	$23	7hr	7 ADO buses
Veracruz	$29	8hr	1st-class or deluxe buses

Getting Around

'Terminal-Centro' buses run between the bus station and Jardín Juárez. A taxi costs $1.50.

Tabasco & Chiapas

These neighbor states could hardly stand in clearer contrast. Smaller Tabasco – on the main route between central Mexico and the Yucatán Peninsula – is less varied than Chiapas. A largely flat, steamy, well-watered lowland, it has fewer visitors, but those who do drop in discover a place with fascinating pre-Hispanic heritage from the Olmec and Maya civilizations, a relaxed tropical lifestyle, an increasingly entertaining capital city in Villahermosa, and a unique environment of enormous rivers, endless wetlands and good Gulf of Mexico beaches.

Chiapas is a green jewel tucked into Mexico's southernmost corner – its hot emerald jungles sparkling with beautiful Maya ruins and waterfalls, its cool, mist-wrapped highlands the redoubt of the most traditionalist and unreconstructed of contemporary Maya peoples. Here, the Maya bequeathed us the stunning architecture of jungle-shrouded Palenque, Yaxchilán, Bonampak and Toniná. Their descendants give Chiapas a uniquely colorful indigenous identity, and since 1994 have led the battle for indigenous rights under the Zapatista banner. At its heart sits the tranquil highland town of San Cristóbal de Las Casas, rich in colonial architecture and surrounded by almost medieval Maya villages, but buzzing with a 21st-century international cultural scene too. North from San Cristóbal you descend through pine forests to the turquoise Agua Azul waterfalls, and the temples of Toniná and Palenque. Eastward lies the steamy Lacandón Jungle, Mexico's largest rainforest, home to a huge animal and plant diversity and countless jungle rivers and lakes. The humid Pacific coastal region, El Soconusco, has lagoons and mangroves to explore and, for time out, there's the sleepy beach town of Puerto Arista.

TOP FIVE

- Exploring the exquisite temples, tombs and palaces at the incomparable Maya site of **Palenque** (p833)

- Enjoying the unique blend of indigenous and international cultures in the tranquil highland town of **San Cristóbal de Las Casas** (p812)

- Buzzing along the jungle-clad Usumacinta River to the remote ruins of **Yaxchilán** (p847)

- Watching the sun set into the Pacific from the sands of **Puerto Arista** (p857)

- Admiring the mysterious art of the ancient Olmecs at **Villahermosa** (p792) and **La Venta** (p802)

★ La Venta
★ Villahermosa
Palenque ★
San Cristóbal de Las Casas ★
Yaxchilán ★
★ Puerto Arista

■ VILLAHERMOSA JANUARY DAILY HIGH: 25°C | 76°F

■ VILLAHERMOSA JULY DAILY HIGH: 30°C | 86°F

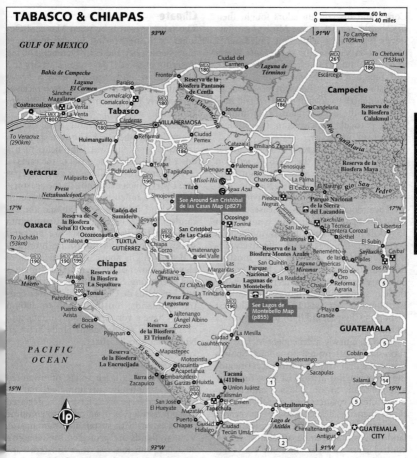

TABASCO & CHIAPAS

History

Tabasco and Chiapas have hosted as rich a procession of cultures as anywhere in Mexico. It was at La Venta in western Tabasco that mesoamerica's 'mother culture,' the Olmec, reached its greatest heights of development between about 800 and 400 BC, after first emerging in San Lorenzo, Veracruz. Olmec religion, art, astronomy and architecture deeply influenced all Mexico's later civilizations.

Low-lying, jungle-covered eastern Chiapas gave rise to some of the most splendid and powerful city-states of another great civilization, the Maya, during the Classic period (approximately AD 250–900), places such as Palenque, Yaxchilán and Toniná.

Dozens of lesser Maya powers – including Bonampak, Comalcalco and Chinkultic – prospered in eastern Chiapas and Tabasco during this time, as Maya culture reached its peak of artistic and intellectual achievement. The ancestors of many of the distinctive indigenous groups of highland Chiapas today appear to have migrated to that region from the lowlands after the Classic Maya collapse around AD 900.

Pre-Hispanic Tabasco was the prosperous nexus of a far-reaching trade network extending round the Yucatán coast as far as Honduras, up the rivers to the jungles and mountains of Guatemala, and westward to highland central Mexico. And it was near Frontera, Tabasco, in 1519 that Hernán

Cortés and his conquistadors fought their first battle against native Mexicans, afterwards founding a settlement called Santa María de la Victoria. In 1641, Santa María was moved inland to escape pirate attacks, and renamed Villahermosa de San Juan Bautista. However, Tabasco remained an impoverished backwater until recent decades; now the development of its mineral riches, particularly petroleum, has brought widespread prosperity.

Central Chiapas was brought under Spanish control by the 1528 expedition of Diego de Mazariegos, and outlying areas were subdued in the 1530s and '40s, though Spain never gained full control of the Lacandón Jungle. New diseases arrived with the Spaniards, and an epidemic in 1544 killed about half Chiapas' indigenous population. Chiapas was ineffectively administered from Guatemala for most of the colonial era, with little check on the colonists' excesses against its native people, though some church figures, particularly Bartolomé de Las Casas (1474–1566), the first bishop of Chiapas, did fight for indigenous rights.

In 1822, a newly independent Mexico unsuccessfully attempted to annex Spain's former Central American provinces (including Chiapas). But in 1824 Chiapas opted by a referendum to join Mexico rather than the United Provinces of Central America. From then on, a succession of governors appointed by Mexico City, along with local landowners, maintained an almost feudal control over Chiapas. Periodic uprisings bore witness to bad government, but the world took little notice until January 1, 1994, when the Zapatista rebels suddenly and briefly occupied San Cristóbal de Las Casas and nearby towns by military force. The rebel movement, with a firm and committed support base among disenchanted indigenous settlers in eastern Chiapas, quickly retreated to remote jungle bases to campaign for democratic change and indigenous rights. More than a decade later, the Zapatistas have failed to win any significant concessions at national level (see the boxed text, p828), although increased government funding steered toward Chiapas did result in noticeable improvements in the state's infrastructure, development of tourist facilities and a growing urban middle class.

Climate

The rainy season is between May and October, with the heaviest rainfall mostly in June, September and early October. During the rainy season the days often start dry and fairly bright, and there's usually a heavy downfall in the afternoon. Tabasco receives particularly heavy rainfall (about 1500mm annually).

Between November and April, warm sunny days are the norm. The hottest months are April and May, when the fields turn a dusty brown before the onset of the rains.

Temperatures in Tabasco and Chiapas don't vary much according to the season – altitude is a much more influential factor. All lowland areas (most of Tabasco, the Lacandón Jungle, Palenque, the Usumacinta area and the Pacific coast) are hot and sticky all year, with punishing humidity and daily highs above 30°C. In the more elevated center of the region, the climate is less enervating. San Cristóbal de Las Casas and Los Altos de Chiapas – the state's central highlands, mostly 2000m to 3000m high – have a very temperate climate, and evenings can get decidedly chilly between November and February.

Parks & Reserves

The region has large tracts of untamed (if not completely untrammeled) nature, and several large areas have been declared biosphere reserves in an effort to combine conservation with sustainable human use. Vital wetlands are protected by Tabasco's 30,300-sq-km Reserva de la Biosfera Pantanos de Centla (p804) and the Reserva de la Biosfera La Encrucijada (1449 sq km; p858) in Chiapas. The Reserva de la Biosfera Montes Azules (3312 sq km; p831 and p849) and the Reserva de la Biosfera Lacan-tun (619 sq km; see the boxed text, p849) in eastern Chiapas battle to preserve what's left of the Lacandón Jungle, while the Reserva de la Biosfera El Triunfo (1192 sq km; p856), in the Sierra Madre de Chiapas, includes rare cloud forests and other mountain forests. Montes Azules and El Triunfo are on the Unesco as well as the Mexican biosphere reserve list. There are also three national parks in the region: Cañón del Sumidero (218 sq km; p812), Lagos de Montebello (60 sq km; p855) and Palenque (17 sq km; p835).

Language

While Spanish is the first tongue of the majority of the population, and the *lingua franca* of most others, Chiapas, with its high indigenous population, is also home to at least eight non-Spanish tongues, mostly mutually unintelligible branches of the Maya language family. Language is a key ethnic identifier for indigenous people. Around two-thirds of speakers of indigenous languages also speak Spanish, though the level is lower in remoter places and among women and the elderly.

The two most widely spoken indigenous languages, each with perhaps 400,000 speakers, are Tzeltal and Tzotzil. Tzeltal is to some extent used instead of Spanish as a *lingua franca* between different groups. The other most important Chiapas indigenous languages are Chol, with around 200,000 speakers, and Tojolabal and Zoque, each with about 50,000. See the boxed text, p825, for more on Chiapas' indigenous peoples.

Tabasco's population is mainly mestizo and the one sizable indigenous group is the Chontales, around 50,000 strong, who speak another language of the Maya group.

Dangers & Annoyances

Though there had been no notable Zapatista-related incidents affecting travelers for some time up to the time of writing, you should always keep an ear to the ground if you plan to travel off the main roads in the Chiapas highlands, the Ocosingo area and far eastern Chiapas. Tensions can rise at any time in these areas, and Zapatistas have carried out occasional anti-tourism activities, including the brief kidnapping of kayakers in the Lacandón Jungle and the seizure of a guest ranch near Ocosingo – both a few years ago. Unknown outsiders might also be at risk in these areas because of local political or religious conflicts. Take local advice about where to avoid going.

Make sure your tourist card and passport are in order, and if your visit extends beyond plain tourism (volunteer work or human-rights observation, for instance), ask in advance at a Mexican consulate or embassy about visa requirements.

In the towns and along the main roads, politically related dangers are minimal. There are regular army checkpoints on some routes, particularly the Carretera

Fronteriza along the Guatemalan border from Palenque to the Lagos de Montebello. These checkpoints generally increase security for travelers. The far east of Chiapas, through which the Carretera Fronteriza passes, is an area where illegal drugs and migrants are smuggled into Mexico, and the area thus has a dangerous reputation. It's best to be off the Carretera Fronteriza before dark. For similar reasons the border crossings with Guatemala near Tapachula are places you should aim to get through early in the day.

Highway holdups targeting tourist-carrying vehicles are a danger on Hwy 199 between Ocosingo and Palenque, especially within about 20km either side of the Agua Azul turnoff. Vans, buses and cars have all been stopped and robbed, sometimes at gunpoint, on this stretch. Travel by day, preferably early, to minimize risks here.

Indigenous villages are often extremely close-knit, and their people can be suspicious of outsiders and particularly sensitive about having their photos taken. In some villages cameras are, at best, tolerated – and sometimes not even that. Photography is banned in the church and during rituals at San Juan Chamula, and in the church and churchyard at Zinacantán. You may put yourself in physical danger by taking photos without permission. If in any doubt at all, ask first.

Having said all this, unpleasant incidents of any kind affecting travelers are extremely rare, and you're unlikely to have anything other than a trouble-free time in Chiapas or Tabasco.

Getting There & Around

A new toll *autopista* (expressway) between Coatzacoalcos (Veracruz state) and Ocozocoautla (Chiapas) has reduced the average driving time from Mexico City to Tuxtla Gutiérrez (the Chiapas state capital) from 14 to 10 hours. Another new *autopista*, between Ocozocoautla and Arriaga on Chiapas' coastal plain, was due to open in 2006, and the existing Coatzacoalcos–Villahermosa *autopista* is being extended east across Tabasco towards the Yucatán Peninsula.

The Pan-American Hwy (190) passes through Tuxtla Gutiérrez and San Cristóbal de Las Casas to enter Guatemala at Ciudad Cuauhtémoc/La Mesilla (p856), 84km from

Huehuetenango, Guatemala. The other main route to Guatemala is Hwy 200 along Chiapas' coastal plain, leading to two border crossings near the city of Tapachula (p862). It's also possible to cross direct into Guatemala's northern Petén region, using boat services on the Río Usumacinta (Frontera Corozal to Bethel; p846) or Río San Pedro (El Ceibo to El Naranjo; p805).

The airports at Villahermosa (p798) and Tuxtla Gutiérrez (p810) both have direct daily flights to and from Mexico City, Mérida, Cancún and Oaxaca, as well as between each other. Villahermosa also has direct flights to/from Houston, Texas. Tapachula (p861) has daily flights to/from Mexico City.

There are plenty of swift daily bus links between Mexico City and the region's major cities: Villahermosa (10 to 12 hours from the capital), Tuxtla Gutiérrez (12 hours), San Cristóbal de Las Casas (14 hours) and Tapachula (18 hours) – plus a few to Palenque and Comitán. Bus links to the Yucatán Peninsula are plentiful from Villahermosa, but there's only a few daily from Tuxtla Gutiérrez, San Cristóbal de Las Casas or Palenque. A few daily buses run between Oaxaca and Villahermosa, Tuxtla Gutiérrez, San Cristóbal and Palenque, and between Puerto Escondido, Tuxtla and San Cristóbal.

Bus links within the region are fairly good, and minibuses, Suburban-type vans and colectivo taxis offer a speedier alternative on some major routes (including Tuxtla Gutiérrez and Comitán to San Cristóbal).

TABASCO

They say that Tabasco has more water than land, and looking at all the lagoons, rivers and wetlands on the map you can certainly believe that's true, at least during the rainy season. It's always hot and sweaty here, marginally less so when you catch a breeze along the Gulf of Mexico or if you venture into the southern hills. Few travelers linger in Tabasco longer than it takes to see the outstanding Olmec stone sculpture in Villahermosa's Parque-Museo La Venta. But this is actually a very rewarding slice of the real Mexico, with few other tourists, some intriguing pre-Hispanic sites (both the Olmecs and the Maya flourished here), a large and lively capital city, a beautiful natural environment and a relaxed populace with an insatiable love for música tropical. Thanks to onshore and offshore oil exploitation by Mexico's state oil company, Pemex, Tabasco has emerged from poverty to become one of Mexico's more prosperous states.

VILLAHERMOSA
☎ 993 / pop 673,000
This sprawling, flat, hot and humid city, with over a quarter of Tabasco's population, has never the 'beautiful town' that its name implies, but it is at last taking advantage of its position on the winding Río Grijalva, with a welcome riverside leisure development a couple of blocks from the pedestrianized city center. Villahermosa's main visitor attraction is the open-air Parque-Museo La Venta, a combined Olmec archaeological museum and zoo in an attractive lakeside park. There's also a regional anthropology museum and an improving cultural and entertainment scene that may tempt you to hang around longer than a single day or night.

Oil money has pumped modernity and commerce into some of the outer districts, where you'll find glitzy malls, imposing public buildings and luxury hotels.

Orientation
In this sprawling city you'll find yourself walking some distances in the sticky heat, and occasionally hopping on a minibus (combi) or taking a taxi. The central area, known as the Zona Luz, extends north–south from Parque Juárez to the Plaza de Armas, and east–west from the Río Grijalva to roughly Calle 5 de Mayo. The main bus stations are between 750m and 1km to its north.

Parque-Museo La Venta lies 2km northwest of the Zona Luz, beside Av Ruíz Cortines, the main east–west highway crossing the city. West of Parque-Museo La Venta is the Tabasco 2000 district of modern commercial and government buildings.

Information
INTERNET ACCESS
Cybercafés are plentiful. Rates are $0.75 to $1 per hour.
Milenium (Map p794; Sáenz 130; ✆ 8am-10pm Mon-Sat, 9am-5pm Sun)
Multiservicios (Map p794; Aldama 621C; ✆ 8am-9pm Mon-Sat, 9am-5pm Sun)

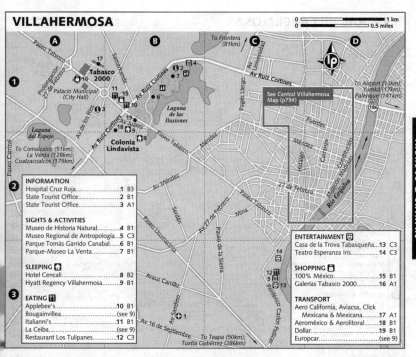

VILLAHERMOSA

INFORMATION
Hospital Cruz Roja..................1	B3
State Tourist Office.................2	B1
State Tourist Office.................3	A1

SIGHTS & ACTIVITIES
Museo de Historia Natural............4	B1
Museo Regional de Antropología....5	C3
Parque Tomás Garrido Canabal......6	B1
Parque-Museo La Venta..............7	B1

SLEEPING
Hotel Cencali........................8	B2
Hyatt Regency Villahermosa........9	B1

EATING
Applebee's.........................10	B1
Bougainvillea....................(see 9)	
Italianni's........................11	B1
La Ceiba..........................(see 9)	
Restaurant Los Tulipanes..........12	C3

ENTERTAINMENT
Casa de la Trova Tabasqueña...13	C3
Teatro Esperanza Iris...............14	C3

SHOPPING
100% México.........................15	B1
Galerías Tabasco 2000.............16	A1

TRANSPORT
Aero California, Aviacsa, Click	
Mexicana & Mexicana.........17	A1
Aeroméxico & Aerolitoral.........18	B1
Dollar..............................19	B1
Europcar..........................(see 9)	

LAUNDRY

Lavandería Top Klean (Map p794; ☎ 312-28-56; Madero 303A; next-day/same-day service per kg $1.75/2.50; ❍ 8:30am-8pm Mon-Sat)

MEDICAL SERVICES

Hospital Cruz Roja (Map p793; ☎ 315-55-55; Av Sandino s/n) A short ride southwest of the Zona Luz.
Unidad Médica Guerrero (Map p794; ☎ 314-56-97/98; Calle 5 de Mayo 444; ❍ 24hr) Emergency service.

MONEY

Most banks have ATMs and exchange currency.
Bancomer (Map p794; cnr Zaragoza & Juárez; ❍ 8:30am-3pm Mon-Fri, 10am-4pm Sat)
Santander Serfin (Map p794; Madero 584; ❍ 9am-4pm Mon-Fri)

POST

Main post office (Map p794; Sáenz 131; ❍ 9am-3pm Mon-Fri, 9am-1pm Sat)

TOURIST INFORMATION

State tourist office (☎ 800-216-08-42; www.visite tabasco.com, www.etabasco.gob.mx/turismo; Parque-

Museo La Venta Map p793; ☎ 314-16-42; ❍ 8am-4pm Tue-Sun; Tabasco 2000 Map p793; ☎ 316-36-33; Av de los Ríos s/n; ❍ 8am-4pm Mon-Fri, 8am-1pm Sat) The Tabasco 2000 office is the main one: to get there from the Zona Luz, take a 'Fracc Carrizal' combi ($0.50) from Madero, just north of Parque Juárez, get off at the big traffic circle surrounded by banks after you cross Av Ruíz Cortines, and walk one block to the left along Av de los Ríos. Staff are helpful and have a glut of glossy material.

Sights

Apart from Parque-Museo La Venta, the pedestrianized Zona Luz is an enjoyable place to explore, and its busy lanes – full of hawkers' stalls and salsa-blaring clothes stores and dotted with cafés and galleries – buzz with tropical atmosphere.

PARQUE-MUSEO LA VENTA

The fascinating outdoor **Parque-Museo La Venta** (Map p793; ☎ 314-16-52; Av Ruíz Cortines; admission $3.75; ❍ 8am-5pm, last admission 4pm, zoo closed Mon; ♿) was created in 1958, when petroleum exploration threatened the highly important ancient Olmec settlement of La Venta in western Tabasco (p802). Archaeologists moved the

TABASCO & CHIAPAS

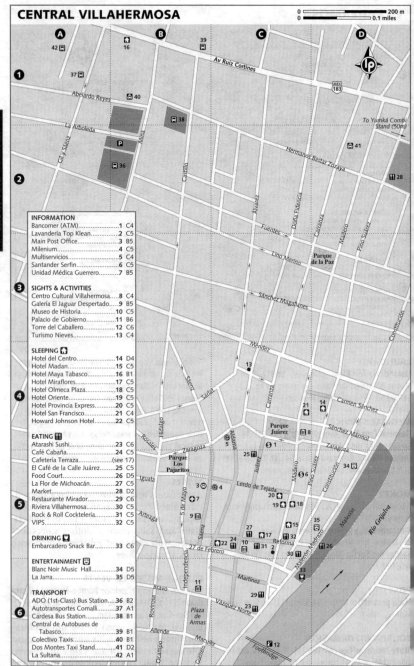

CENTRAL VILLAHERMOSA

0   200 m
0   0.1 miles

INFORMATION
Bancomer (ATM)...........................**1** C4
Lavandería Top Klean..................**2** C5
Main Post Office..........................**3** B5
Milenium......................................**4** C5
Multiservicios.............................**5** C4
Santander Serfin.........................**6** C5
Unidad Médica Guerrero............**7** B5

SIGHTS & ACTIVITIES
Centro Cultural Villahermosa.....**8** C4
Galería El Jaguar Despertado......**9** B5
Museo de Historia......................**10** C5
Palacio de Gobierno...................**11** B6
Torre del Caballero....................**12** C6
Turismo Nieves..........................**13** C4

SLEEPING
Hotel del Centro.........................**14** D4
Hotel Madan...............................**15** C5
Hotel Maya Tabasco...................**16** B1
Hotel Miraflores.........................**17** C5
Hotel Olmeca Plaza....................**18** C5
Hotel Oriente..............................**19** C5
Hotel Provincia Express..............**20** C5
Hotel San Francisco....................**21** C4
Howard Johnson Hotel...............**22** C5

EATING
Atarashi Sushi.............................**23** C6
Café Cabaña...............................**24** C5
Cafetería Terraza..................(see **17**)
El Café de la Calle Juárez...........**25** C5
Food Court..................................**26** D5
La Flor de Michoacán..................**27** C5
Market..**28** D2
Restaurante Mirador...................**29** C6
Riviera Villahermosa...................**30** C5
Rock & Roll Cocktelería..............**31** C5
VIPS..**32** C5

DRINKING
Embarcadero Snack Bar..............**33** C6

ENTERTAINMENT
Blanc Noir Music Hall.................**34** D5
La Jarra......................................**35** D5

TRANSPORT
ADO (1st-Class) Bus Station.......**36** B2
Autotransportes Comalli.............**37** A1
Cardesa Bus Station...................**38** B1
Central de Autobuses de
   Tabasco..................................**39** B1
Colectivo Taxis...........................**40** B1
Dos Montes Taxi Stand...............**41** D2
La Sultana...................................**42** A1

site's most significant finds, including three colossal stone heads, to Villahermosa.

Plan two to three hours for your visit, and take mosquito repellent (the park is set in humid tropical woodland). Snack stands and a little cafeteria provide sustenance. Inside, you come to the **zoo** first. This is devoted to animals from Tabasco and nearby regions: cats include jaguars, ocelots and jaguarundi, and there are white-tailed deer, spider monkeys, crocodiles, boa constrictors, peccaries and plenty of colorful birds, including scarlet macaws and keel-billed toucans.

There's an informative display in English and Spanish (like most information here) on Olmec archaeology as you pass through to the **sculpture trail**, whose start is marked by a giant *ceiba* (the sacred tree of the Olmec and Maya). This 1km walk is lined with finds from La Venta. Among the most impressive, in the order you come to them, are Stele 3, which depicts a bearded man with a headdress; Altar 5, depicting a figure carrying a child; Monument 77, 'El Gobernante,' a very sour-looking seated ruler; the monkey-faced Monument 56; Monument 1, the colossal head of a helmet-wearing warrior; and Stele 1, showing a young goddess (a rare Olmec representation of anything female). Animals that pose no danger, such as coatis, squirrels and black agoutis, roam freely around the park.

After dark, a **sound-and-light show** (admission $9.50; 8pm & 9pm) takes you around 13 of the most interesting archaeological items, with video sequences and passages of poetry by Carlos Pellicer Cámara (1897–1977), the Tabascan scholar and poet responsible for salvaging the artifacts of La Venta. If you have enough Spanish, it's an atmospheric experience.

Next to the park entrance, the **Museo de Historia Natural** (Map p793; 314-21-75; admision $1.50; 9am-5pm Tue-Sun) has quite well set-out displays on dinosaurs, space, early humanity and Tabascan ecosystems (all in Spanish).

Parque-Museo La Venta is 3km from the Zona Luz. A 'Fracc Carrizal' combi from Madero, just north of Parque Juárez in the Zona Luz, will drop you on Paseo Tabasco just short of Av Ruíz Cortines; then walk 1km northeast across Parque Tomás Garrido Canabal and along the Malecón de las Ilusiones, a lakeside path, to the entrance.

MUSEO REGIONAL DE ANTROPOLOGÍA

The **Regional Anthropology Museum** (Map p793; 312-63-44; Periférico Carlos Pellicer; admission $2.50; 9am-5pm Tue-Sun) is a little dilapidated and poorly labeled (in Spanish only), but still holds some interesting exhibits. It's best to begin on the upper level, which outlines mesoamerica's many civilizations with the aid of a pretty good sculpture collection. After you've brushed up on the broad picture, the middle floor concentrates on Olmec and Maya cultures in Tabasco, with second-grade sculptures from La Venta, and Classic Maya urns from Tapijulapa and Tacotalpa. Finally, on the ground floor is one of the smaller Olmec heads from La Venta and some large Classic Maya steles from Reforma and Tortuguero.

The museum is 1km south of the Zona Luz. You can walk (about 20 minutes), or catch a 'CICOM' combi or microbus heading south on Constitución.

MUSEO DE HISTORIA

The **History Museum** (Map p794; 314-21-72; Juárez 402; admission free; 9am-8pm Tue-Sun) is housed in a striking 19th-century building known as La Casa de los Azulejos (House of Tiles). The exhibits on Tabasco history are very sparse, but the Spanish *azulejos* themselves, which cover the facade and most of the interior, are gorgeous.

GALLERIES

Central Villahermosa has several art and photo galleries, staging varied exhibits of Tabascan and other Mexican work, with free admission. **Galería El Jaguar Despertado** (Map p794; 314-12-44; Sáenz 117; 9am-9pm Mon-Sat, 10am-3pm Sun), the modernist concrete-and-glass **Centro Cultural Villahermosa** (Map p794; 314-54-73; cnr Madero & Zaragoza; 10am-7pm Tue-Sun) and the gallery in the **Palacio de Gobierno** (Map p794; Independencia 2; 10am-2pm & 5-8pm) have some of the best shows.

TORRE DEL CABALLERO

This **lookout tower** (Map p794; admission free; 8am-6pm), on a footbridge over the Río Grijalva, affords good panoramas over the city and river.

TABASCO 2000

The Tabasco 2000 complex (Map p793), with its modern government buildings, convention center, fountains, restaurants and Galerías Tabasco 2000 shopping mall, is a testimony to the prosperity oil has brought to Villahermosa. It's convenient to come here for a browse and a bite after visiting the Parque-Museo La Venta, or take a 'Fracc Carrizal' combi from Madero just north of Parque Juárez.

Tours

Turismo Nieves (Map p794; ☎ 314-18-88; reservaya@ turismonieves.com.mx; Sarlat 202; ☺ 8am-8pm Mon-Sat) offers a range of comprehensive tours around Tabasco, including an eight-hour 'Ruta del Cacao' day trip northwest of Villahermosa ($89 per person, minimum two people), which packs in a turtle farm, two cacao haciendas, Comalcalco ruins and a boat trip on Laguna Mecoacán.

Sleeping

As an oil town, Villahermosa is well supplied with comfortable midrange and top-end hotels with good amenities, some of which offer heavily discounted weekend rates. Inviting budget options are scarcer. Air-conditioning is standard in the midrange and top-end places.

BUDGET

Hotel Oriente (Map p794; ☎ 312-01-21; fax 312-11-01; Madero 425; s/d/tr with fan $18/25/31, with air-con $27/33/42; ☒) The Oriente is a well-run downtown hotel where the comfortable rooms are kept spick-and-span, and the bathrooms even have a little sparkle. All rooms have TV.

Hotel San Francisco (Map p794; ☎ 312-31-98; Madero 604; s/d/tr/q $20/26/32/36; ☒) The lobby is gloomy, but the rooms are decent enough, and all come with air-con and TV. There's an elevator to the upper floors.

Hotel del Centro (Map p794; ☎ 312-25-65; gbrondo@ prodigy.net.mx; Pino Suárez 209; r $19-24, tr/q $28/33; ☒) A slightly shambolic, but acceptable, basic budget hotel, where all the rooms have TV and fan.

MIDRANGE

Hotel Madan (Map p794; ☎ 314-05-24, 800-543-47-77; www.bestwestern.com; Madero 408; r $50; ☒ ☒) Representing excellent value for money, the Best Western Madan has 40 bright, spacious rooms with nice wooden furniture, coffeemakers and attractive bathrooms; the

king-size beds are ample enough for a sumo wrestler. The in-house restaurant and bar are good too.

Hotel Maya Tabasco (Map p794; ☎ 312-11-11, 800-237-77-00; www.bestwestern.com; Av Ruíz Cortines 907; r $81; ☒ ☒ ☒) One kilometer north of the Zona Luz, this business-orientated Best Western hotel has good-sized, well-equipped, modern rooms, most with bathtub. Add the attractive gardens, large pool, good restaurant, two bars with evening entertainment, ATM and free transportation to the airport and Parque-Museo La Venta, and it's a pretty good package. Rates fall to $67 at weekends.

Hotel Miraflores (Map p794; ☎ 358-04-70, 800-234-02-29; www.miraflores.com.mx; Reforma 304; s/d/tr/ste $53/57/65/71; ☒ ☒ ☒) Set on a traffic-free street, the Miraflores provides large, bright rooms with ample bathrooms, telephones, cable TV, tile floors and in some cases balconies. Downstairs is a café, a restaurant and two bars. Not a bad deal.

Howard Johnson Hotel (Map p794; ☎ 314-46-45, 800-780-72-72; www.howardjohnson.ws; Aldama 404; s/d $52/59, r Fri-Sun $47; ☒ ☒ ☒) The Howard Johnson is comfortable and in the heart of town, but some rooms suffer a degree of traffic noise – ask for one overlooking the pedestrian streets Aldama or Reforma.

Hotel Cencali (Map p793; ☎ 315-19-99, 800-112-50-00; www.cencali.com.mx; Av Juárez, Colonia Lindavista; r $82; ☒ ☒ ☒ ☒ ☒) The Cencali boasts an excellent quiet location not far from Parque-Museo La Venta, and 160 good-size rooms with balconies, bathtubs and in many cases, views of the Laguna de las Ilusiones. There's a great swimming pool in tropical gardens beside the lake. The rate comes down to $66 some weekends.

Hotel Provincia Express (Map p794; ☎ 314-53-76; villaop@prodigy.net.mx; Lerdo de Tejada 303; r $44; ☒ ☒ ☒) The 48 rooms vary between drab and bright, but all have decent-quality beds, reading lights, cable TV and private bathroom.

TOP END

Hyatt Regency Villahermosa (Map p793; ☎ 310-12-34; www.villahermosa.regency.hyatt.com; Av Juárez 106, Colonia Lindavista; r $196, Fri-Sun $98; ☒ ☒ ☒ ☒ ☒) Villahermosa's smartest hotel has amenities that include a large swimming pool, a smaller kids' pool, tennis courts, two restaurants, two bars and one restaurant-bar. All 207 bright luxuriously appointed rooms and suites come with modem connections and glass-walled hydromassage showers. And the weekend rates put it within reach of some nonexpense-account budgets!

Hotel Olmeca Plaza (Map p794; ☎ 358-01-02, 800-201-09-09; www.hotelolmecaplaza.com; Madero 418; r $112, Fri-Sun $65; P ⊠ ⊠ ⊠) The classiest downtown hotel recently added an open-air pool and well-equipped gym. Rooms are modern and comfortable, with writing desks and good large bathrooms, and there's a quality restaurant on-site.

Eating

Villahermosa's eclectic collection of hotel restaurants, chain restaurants and seafood/Tabascan/Japanese/Italian specialists will keep you happy for the duration of your stay.

ZONA LUZ & MALECÓN

Hotel Madan (Map p794; ☎ 314-05-24; Madero 408; breakfast $2.50-4.50, mains $5-7) It's nothing glamorous, but this is a very reliable and popular hotel restaurant, with mainly Mexican dishes and efficient, friendly service.

Atarashi Sushi (Map p794; ☎ 314-70-26; Vázquez Norte 203; mains $5-15; ☼ noon-midnight; ☒) Air-conditioned Atarashi presents a tasty Mexican angle on Japanese food, offering all sorts of tantalizing – and satisfying – seafood, meat, vegetable and sauce combinations.

Riviera Villahermosa (Map p794; ☎ 312-44-68; Constitución 104; mains $7.50-17; ☼ 2pm-2am Mon-Sat, 2-7pm Sun; ☒) The Euro-Mex menu is pretty good, and the air-conditioned 4th-floor setting with floor-to-ceiling windows overlooking the river is spectacular. Steaks, seafood and pasta are all good here.

Food Court (Map p794; Malecón Madrazo; mains $5-10; ☼ 10am-11pm) This open-air eating and drinking area on the deck beside the river has the greatest location in town. Several of the city's best eateries have branches here.

Restaurante Mirador (Map p794; ☎ 314-34-95; Madero 105; mains $7-12; ☼ noon-9:30pm Mon-Sat, noon-7pm Sun; ☒) A smart, air-conditioned, upstairs restaurant, specializing in fish and seafood.

Rock & Roll Coctelería (Map p794; ☎ 312-05-93; Reforma 307; seafood cocktails $6.50-8; ☼ 9am-11pm) A maelstrom of heat, swirling fans, a thumping jukebox and garrulous punters. Everyone's here for the *cocteles* (fish or seafood,

tomato sauce, lettuce, onions and a lemon squeeze) and the cheap beer.

The Juárez pedestrian mall has several cafés with indoor and outdoor tables, good for breakfast or a drink or snack (you may be serenaded by a marimba team). Good bets are **Café Cabaña** (Map p794; ☎ 314-44-94; Juárez s/n; ☼ 7:30am-10pm Mon-Sat, 8:30am-9pm Sun) and **El Café de la Calle Juárez** (Map p794; ☎ 312-34-54; Juárez 513; ☼ 8am-11pm), both with breakfasts for between $2.50 and $5, and coffees at $1 to $2.

Also recommended are the following:

Hotel Olmeca Plaza (Map p794; ☎ 358-01-02; Madero 418; mains $7-12.50) A quality hotel restaurant with good service.

Cafetería Terraza (Map p794; ☎ 358-04-70; Hotel Miraflores, Reforma 304; mains $7-9.50; ☼ 7.30am-10pm) A reliable hotel café-restaurant, with filling portions of well-priced Mexican staples.

La Flor de Michoacán (Map p794; Juárez s/n; items $0.60-2; ☼ 8am-9pm) Delicious fresh juices, *licuados* (smoothies), frozen yogurt and fruit cocktails.

VIPS (Map p794; ☎ 314-39-71; Madero 402; mains $6-10) This chain restaurant, popular with families, offers a menu of Mexican and international food in very clean surroundings.

Market (Map p794; Hermanos Bastar Zozaya s/n; ☼ 5am-7pm) Fresh vegetables, chilies, fish, meat and big dollops of local atmosphere.

OTHER AREAS

Hyatt Regency Villahermosa (Map p793; ☎ 310-12-34; Av Juárez 106, Colonia Lindavista) The top hotel in town has two of the best restaurants, both serving a big choice of Mexican and international dishes: the Bougainvillea (mains $8 to $14, open noon to 3pm and 6.30pm to 10pm), with live jazz in the evenings, and La Ceiba (sandwiches and salads $5 to $7, mains $13 to $18, open 6am to noon and 1pm to midnight), which also serves some buffet meals.

Italianni's (Map p793; ☎ 317-72-57; Prolongación Paseo Tabasco 1404; mains $7-14; ☼ 1-11pm Mon-Wed, 1pm-1am Thu-Sat, 1-10pm Sun) This quality Italian restaurant serves well-prepared pasta, pizzas, salads, chicken and steaks, and plenty of Italian wine, amid classic check tablecloths and even Mediterranean-style window shutters.

Restaurant Los Tulipanes (Map p793; ☎ 312-92-09; Periférico Carlos Pellicer 511; mains $7.50-17; ☼ 8am-10pm Mon-Sat, 11am-6pm Sun) Overlooking the Río Grijalva, near the Museo Regional de Antropología, Los Tulipanes is the best place in town for Tabasco specialties including seafood-filled corn tortillas, and

TABASCO & CHIAPAS

empanadas of *pejelagarto*, the tasty fresh-water 'lizard fish' that is a symbol of Tabasco. It also serves steaks, chicken, *róbalo* (snook) and other fish – and on Sundays a Tabascan buffet ($14) that's the perfect opportunity to gorge yourself silly.

Applebee's (Map p793; ☎ 317-70-30; cnr Av Ruíz Cortines & Paseo Tabasco; mains $9.50-15;) A clean, air-conditioned, grill, burger and salad restaurant not far from Parque-Museo La Venta – with chocolate-chip cheesecake too!

Drinking

A cluster of bars with and without music is strung along the riverside Malecón Madrazo, and some hotels have good bars too.

For cooling beers, the Malecón's **Food Court** (Map p794; Malecón Madrazo; 10am-11pm) and **Embarcadero Snack Bar** (Map p794; ☎ 314-46-44; Malecón Madrazo Kiosco 1; snacks $1.50-5; 10am-3am) are fine, breezy, open-air spots. The Embarcadero also provides rock music, big-screen TV and good snacks.

Entertainment

To find out what's on in the way of performances, check the website of **Tabasco's culture and sports department** (www.secured .gob.mx), or pick up the free monthly guide *Enterarte*.

La Jarra (Map p794; ☎ 312-15-24; Malecón Madrazo 607; admission $3; 8pm-3am Thu-Sat) Bands play rock, hip-hop and reggae covers at this upstairs bar on the inland side of Malecón.

Blanc Noir Music Hall (Map p794; ☎ 314-51-76; www.blancnoir.com.mx; Malecón Madrazo 645; admission $3; 8am-3pm Tue-Sat) A two-level club with big windows facing the river, Blanc Noir often has local bands playing after 10pm Thursday to Saturday (the $3 admission to see bands includes one beer).

Riviera Villahermosa (Map p794; ☎ 312-44-68; Constitución 104; admission free; 8pm-4am Thu-Sat, 2-7pm Sun) A trendy 5th-floor electro-pop bar with great views.

Casa de la Trova Tabasqueña (Map p793; ☎ 314-21-22; Av Carlos Pellicer Cámara s/n; admission free) *Trova* artists play once or twice most weeks, usually at 8pm Wednesday, Thursday or Friday, at this café-style venue next to the Museo Regional de Antropología.

Teatro Esperanza Iris (Map p793; ☎ 314-42-10; Av Carlos Pellicer Cámara s/n; admission up to $3) Villahermosa's main theater often stages folkloric dance, theater, cinema and music.

Shopping

You might find something you like among the Tabascan baskets, wickerwork, hats, gourds and pottery at **Artesanías de Tabasco** (☎ 316-28-22) in the **Galerías Tabasco 2000 mall** (Map p793; 10:30am-8:30pm Sun-Fri, 10:30am-9pm Sat). Galerías Tabasco 2000 has fashion, jewelry, shoe and music stores, coffee bars and places to eat – all in air-con comfort. **100% Mexico** (Map p793; cnr Av Ruíz Cortines & Paseo Tabasco; noon-8pm) sells quality crafts from all over Mexico.

Getting There & Away

AIR

Villahermosa's **Aeropuerto Rovirosa** (☎ 356-01-57) is 13km east of the center, off Hwy 186. Nonstop or one-stop direct flights to/from Villahermosa include the following:

Cancún Click Mexicana, daily.
Houston, Texas Continental, daily except Saturday.
Mérida Aviacsa and Click Mexicana, both daily.
Mexico City Aero California, Aeroméxico, Aviacsa and Mexicana; total eight or more daily.
Monterrey Aerolitoral and Aviacsa; total two or three daily.
Oaxaca Click Mexicana, daily.
Tuxtla Gutiérrez Click Mexicana, daily.
Veracruz Aerolitoral, one or two daily.

AIRLINE OFFICES

Aero California (Map p793; ☎ 316-80-00; Local 4, Plaza D'Atocha Mall, Tabasco 2000)
Aeroméxico & Aerolitoral (Map p793; ☎ 315-27-77; cnr Av Ruíz Cortines & Sagitario)
Aviacsa (Map p793; ☎ 316-57-00; Local 8, Plaza D'Atocha Mall, Tabasco 2000)
Continental Airlines (☎ 356-02-67; Aeropuerto Rovirosa)
Mexicana & Click Mexicana (Map p793; ☎ 316-31-33; Locales 5 & 6, Plaza D'Atocha Mall, Tabasco 2000)

BUS & COLECTIVO TAXI

The 1st-class **ADO bus station** (Map p794; ☎ 312-84-22; Mina 297) is 750m north of the Zona Luz. It has a **luggage room** (bag per hr $0.40-1.25; 7am-11pm) and cafés. Deluxe and 1st-class UNO, ADO and OCC buses run from here, as well as a few 2nd-class services, but many are *de paso* (buses which have started their journeys elsewhere, but are stopping to let off and take on passengers), so buy your onward ticket in advance if possible. It's possible to do this at the Ticket Bus *cajero automático* (ticket machine) on Madero between the Madan and Olmeca Plaza hotels.

Departures from the ADO terminal (most in the evening) include the following:

Destination	Price	Duration	Frequency
Campeche	$20-27	6-7hr	20 daily
Cancún	$46-81	12-14hr	21 daily
Mérida	$27-54	8-10hr	20 daily
Mexico City (TAPO)	$50-82	10-12hr	29 daily
Oaxaca	$37	12hr	3 daily
Palenque	$5-6.50	2½hr	12 daily
San Cristóbal de Las Casas	$16-24	7-8hr	3 daily
Tenosique	$10	3-3½hr	12 daily
Tuxtla Gutiérrez	$17-19	5-9½hr	11 daily
Veracruz	$27-43	6-7½hr	18 daily

Transportation to most destinations within Tabasco goes from other terminals north of the ADO. The 2nd-class **Cardesa bus station** (Map p794; ☎ 314-30-79; cnr Bastar Zozaya & Castillo) has the following services:

Destination	Price	Duration	Frequency
Comalcalco	$2.50	1½hr	vans every 30min 5am-9pm
Frontera	$2.75	1½hr	hourly buses 5am-9pm
Palenque	$4.50	2½hr	8 buses daily
Paraíso	$2.75	2hr	18 buses daily

The main 2nd-class bus station is the **Central de Autobuses de Tabasco** (Map p794; ☎ 312-41-84; cnr Av Ruíz Cortines & Castillo) on the north side of Av Ruíz Cortines. Departures include the following:

Destination	Price	Duration	Frequency
Comalcalco	$2.25	1½hr	every 30-60min 5am-9pm
Frontera	$2	1½hr	every 30min 4:30am-9pm
Jonuta	$5	2½hr	5 daily
La Venta	$5	2hr	every 30min 4:30am-11pm
Paraíso	$2.75	2hr	every 30-60min 5am-9pm
Tenosique	$7	3½hr	11 daily

For Teapa, **La Sultana** (Map p794; ☎ 314-48-82; Av Ruíz Cortines 917) runs comfortable 2nd-class buses ($2.75, one hour) every 30 minutes, 5am to 10:30pm. Further vans for Comalcalco ($2.50, one hour) are operated by **Autotransportes Comalli** (Map p794; ☎ 504-74-78; Gil y Sáenz) every 20 minutes, 5:30am to 10pm.

Colectivo taxis to Paraíso ($4.50, 1½ hours) and Frontera ($4, 1¼ hours) go from a yard on Reyes (Map p794), north of the ADO bus station.

CAR & MOTORCYCLE
Most rental companies have desks at the airport.

Dollar (Map p793; ☎ 315-80-88; Torre Empresarial, Paseo Tabasco 1203)

Europcar (Map p793; ☎ 352-45-10; Hyatt Regency Villahermosa, Av Juárez 106, Colonia Lindavista)

Getting Around
A taxi from the airport to the city costs around $18 ($15 from the city to the airport) and takes about 25 minutes. Alternatively, go to the road outside the airport parking lot and pick up a *colectivo* taxi for $1.25 per person. These terminate at the **Dos Montes taxi stand** (Map p794; Carranza), about 1km north of the Zona Luz. You can catch them at the same stop to return to the airport.

Any taxi ride within the area between Av Ruíz Cortines, the Río Grijalva and Paseo Usumacinta costs $1.50. Combi rides within the same area are $0.50. From the ADO bus station to the Zona Luz, it's easiest to take a taxi, because you have to walk about halfway to the Zona Luz to reach a combi route. From the Zona Luz to the ADO, take a 'Chedraui,' 'ADO' or 'Cardesa' combi north on Malecón Madrazo.

AROUND VILLAHERMOSA
Yumká
This **Tabascan safari park** (☎ 356-01-07; www.yumka.org; Ranchería Las Barrancas; over/under-11 $5/2.50, lake extra $2; ⊙ 9am-5pm; ⑆), 17km east of Villahermosa (4km past the airport), is hardly a Kenyan game drive, but the space and greenery do offer a break from the city. Yumká is divided into jungle, savanna and lake zones, representing Tabasco's three main ecosystems. Visits take the form of guided tours of the three areas (30 minutes each). In the jungle zone you see regional Mexican species such as howler monkeys, jaguars, scarlet macaws and toucans. The savanna, viewed from a tractor-pulled trolley, has an African section with elephants, giraffes, zebras and

hippos, and an Asian section with axis deer, antelope, buffalo and gaur (the largest ox in the world). You tour the lake by boat and should see plenty of birds, including herons and pelicans.

Combis to Yumká ($0.90, 40 minutes) go every 15 to 20 minutes from 9am from Amado Nervo, beside Villahermosa market. The last one back leaves Yumká at 5pm.

WESTERN TABASCO
Comalcalco

☎ 933 / pop 41,000

Comalcalco, 51km northwest of Villa-hermosa, is typical of the medium-sized towns of western Tabasco – hot, bustling, quite prosperous and spread around a broad, open central plaza (Parque Juárez).

What make it especially worth visiting are the impressive ruins of **ancient Comalcalco** (admission $3.25; ☉ 10am-4pm), 3.5km north. This Maya site is unique because many of its buildings are constructed of bricks and/or mortar made from oyster shells. Comalcalco was at its peak between AD 600 and 1000, when ruled by the Chontals. It remained an important center of commerce for several more centuries, trading in a cornucopia of pre-Hispanic luxury goods: cacao, salt, feathers, deer and jaguar skins, wax, honey, turtle shells, tobacco, chilies, manta-ray spines, cotton, polychrome ceramics, copal, jade and greenstone *hachas* (flat, carved-stone objects associated with the ritual ball game).

The museum at the entrance has a fine array of sculptures and engravings of human heads, deities, glyphs and animals such crocodiles and pelicans.

The site's buildings have information panels in Spanish and English. The first you reach is the great brick-built, tiered pyramid, Templo 1. At its base are remains of large stucco sculptures, including the feet of a giant winged toad. Further temples line Plaza Norte, in front of Templo I. In the far (southeast) corner of the site rises the Gran Acrópolis, with views from its summit over a canopy of palms to the Gulf of Mexico. The Acrópolis is fronted by Templo V, a burial pyramid that was once decorated on all sides with stucco sculptures of people, reptiles, birds and aquatic life. At Templo V's western foot is Templo IX, with a tomb lined by nine stucco sculptures showing

a Comalcalco lord with his priests and courtiers. Above Templo V is the crumbling profile of El Palacio, with its parallel 80m-long corbel-arched galleries, probably once Comalcalco's royal residence.

The site is 1km (signposted) off the Comalcalco–Paraíso road. Vans to the turnoff ($0.50) stop outside Comalcalco's ADO terminal (see below). A taxi to the site costs around $2.

Hacienda La Luz (☎ 334-11-26; Blvd Rovirosa; 1hr tour per person $3.50; ☉ 10am-5pm), one of several local plantations making chocolate from home-grown cacao, is just 300m from Comalcalco's central Parque Juárez: walk 250m west along Calle Bosada to its end at Blvd Rovirosa, turn right and you'll see the hacienda's white gate-posts across the road. The tour (minimum two people) takes you round the beautiful house, gardens and cacao plantation, and shows traditional methods of turning cacao beans into chocolate.

SLEEPING & EATING

Hotel Copacabana (☎ 334-19-33; www.hotelcopa cabana.com.mx; cnr Juárez & Serdán; s/d $49/58; P ☒ ⬛) The best hotel in town, the Copa cabana has large, very clean, pink rooms with quality air-conditioning. Staff are professional. The restaurant (mains $7 to $15) here is one of Comalcalco's best, with well-prepared seafood and meat dishes.

Hotel Santander (☎ 334-44-58; Escobedo 103; s/d $28/30; P ☒) The Santander, just off the main street (Juárez), offers clean, tile-floored, air-conditioned rooms, free morning coffee and a neat little café.

Bariloche (☎ 334-63-73; 5 de Mayo 109; mains $7-13; ☉ 8am-2am; ☒) A fine variety of local and other dishes is on offer at this air-conditioned, art-print–hung restaurant on the plaza, and there's live tropical music from 8pm Wednesday to Saturday. Try the prawns with tequila and *chipotle* mayonnaise for starters.

GETTING THERE & AWAY

Comalcalco's **ADO terminal** (☎ 334-00-07; cnr López Mateos & Monserrat) by the clock tower (El Reloj) is on the main road, 300m east of the center. It has 1st- and 2nd-class buses to Villahermosa ($3.50, 1½ hours, seven daily), Paraíso ($1.25, 20 minutes, 25 daily), Frontera ($5.50, 2½ hours, two daily) and more distant destinations.

MIDDLEMEN OF MESOAMERICA

Pre-Hispanic Tabasco was a key commercial crossroads, thanks to the natural riches of its fertile territory, and its location at the nexus of water trade routes from the Maya area with land routes from central Mexico. The rivers that feed into Tabasco's wetlands and lagoons were key routes for reaching far into Chiapas and Guatemala, while coastal traders plied their canoes all the way round the Yucatán coast as far as Honduras. These lucrative and far-reaching commercial activities seem to have been concentrated in the hands of a group called the Putún, who appear to have combined Maya cultural elements with influences from the civilizations of central Mexico, including the Toltecs and Aztecs. Cacaxtla, near Puebla in central Mexico (see p209), is considered a Putún site, and the Itzá people who founded the great city of Chichén Itzá on the Yucatán Peninsula in the 10th century may also have been Putún. With their large ocean-going canoes, the Putún established trading colonies at Isla Cerritos and Cozumel, off the Yucatán Peninsula, and even at the mouth of Río Dulce on the Caribbean coast of Guatemala. It was likely one of their canoes that Columbus encountered off Honduras in 1502: the craft was reported as being as long as a Spanish galley, with a cabin, two dozen crew and a large cargo that included cacao, copper bells and axes, cotton clothing and wooden swords with obsidian blades.

Paraíso & Around

☎ 933 / pop (Paraíso) 24,000

Twenty kilometers north of Comalcalco, Paraíso is doing very nicely from the economic spin-offs of Pemex oil installations on the nearby coast at Dos Bocas, and is something of a recreation center for western Tabasco. Wide, sandy beaches front the warm, clean waters of the Gulf of Mexico north of town: Playa Varadero (7.5km from town), Playa El Paraíso (9km) and Balneario Palmar (10.5km) all have simple beach restaurants but only El Paraíso (where parking costs $7) normally has midweek service.

At Puerto Ceiba, 6km northeast of Paraíso, the **Parador Turístico Puerto Ceiba** (☎ 333-22-57; 5 de Febrero s/n; mains $7-8; ☯ noon-7pm or later) is an enjoyable waterfront restaurant where you can take **boat rides** (up to 14 people $28; 1¼hr; ☯ 10am-6pm) along the palm-lined Río Seco and into Laguna Mecoacán, with its mangroves and bird life. It's also possible to rent kayaks here. Follow the Puente del Bellote bridge over the lagoon's mouth and you'll reach several more restaurants serving fresh seafood. The first, popular **Restaurant La Posta** (☎ 335-40-92; mains $6.50-8; ☯ noon-7pm or later), serves seafood on a deck right over Laguna Mecoacán, and offers more boat rides ($9.50 for 20 minutes on the *laguna*, and other trips up to $66, for up to eight people). The road continues, through several villages and over many, many *topes* (speed bumps), to Frontera, 75km east.

Westward from Paraíso, a wonderful road makes its way along the **Barra de Tupilco**, a palm-covered sandspit strung between the Gulf of Mexico and a succession of lagoons, all the way to scruffy Sánchez Magallanes, 80km from Paraíso. The spectacular trip passes an endless succession of palm-lined, sandy beaches, with ospreys, pelicans and frigate birds cruising overhead. Where stretches of road have been washed away by the sea, vehicles have to detour through the property of enterprising locals who charge unofficial tolls adding up to about $5.

SLEEPING & EATING

Hotel Solimar (☎ 333-28-72; Ocampo 114; s/d $48/56; P ☒ ▢) Half a block north of Paraíso's plaza, the Solimar has comfortable, pretty, air-conditioned rooms with alpine prints to help you feel cooler, and also one of the best eateries in town, the spick-and-span Restaurant Costa Carey (mains $5 to $11).

Hotel Sabina (☎ 333-24-83; Ocampo 115; r with fan $24, with air-con $30-38; P ☒) A cheaper hotel on the plaza; avoid the dank ground-floor singles.

GETTING THERE & AROUND

Paraíso's **ADO terminal** (☎ 333-02-35; Av Romero Zurita), 1.5km south of the center, has 2nd-class buses to Comalcalco ($1.25, 20 minutes, three or four hourly) and Villahermosa ($2.75, two hours, every half-hour) and two 1st-class buses to Frontera ($4, two hours).

A taxi to Puerto Ceiba or any of Paraíso's beaches costs $2 to $3. From Paraíso's 2nd-class bus station, **Central Camionera** (Serdán s/n), eight blocks north of the central plaza then four blocks east, Transportes Pancho Villa (TPV) runs four daily buses along the Barra de Tupilco to Sánchez Magallanes ($5, two hours). TPV also runs buses from Sánchez Magallanes to La Venta.

La Venta
☎ 923 / pop 9500

Most of the monuments from La Venta are at Villahermosa's Parque-Museo La Venta (p793), but this ancient Olmec ceremonial center still has the fascination of being the largest and most important 'capital' of Mexico's mother culture. The **site** (admission $2.75; ☧ 8am-4pm) is at the small town of La Venta, 128km west of Villahermosa. La Venta flourished between about 800 and 400 BC, on a natural plateau rising about 20m above an area of fertile, seasonally flooded lowlands. Matthew Stirling is credited with discovering, in the early 1940s, four huge Olmec heads sculpted from basalt, the largest more than 2m high. A lot of other fascinating sculpture has been found here too. It's thought that the Olmecs brought the stone for their monuments from hills 100km east and west, using systems of sledges and river rafts.

The museum at the site entrance holds three badly weathered Olmec heads, recovered since the founding of Parque-Museo La Venta in 1958, plus replicas of some of the finest La Venta sculptures that are no longer here. Further replicas are arranged decoratively around the site itself. The heart of the site is the 30m-high Edificio C-1, a rounded pyramid constructed out of clay and sand. Ceremonial areas and more structures stretch to the north and south of this, today mostly defined by low mounds and cleared vegetation. Those to the south stretch far into the jungle area beyond the plaza of Complejo B. At the north end of the site, Complejo A was once an important ceremonial area and many sculptures and rich offerings were found here in the 1940s and '50s – before oil exploitation modified the area.

La Venta town is 4km north of Hwy 180. The **ADO terminal** (☎ 232-03-97; Juárez 37), on the main street, has services to Villahermosa ($5, two hours) every 30 minutes, 7am to 11pm. The archaeological site is 800m north from the bus station.

Malpasito
pop 400 / elevation 200m

Up in Tabasco's beautiful and mountainous far southwestern corner, tiny Malpasito is the site of mysterious ancient Zoque ruins, and one of several *ejidos* (communal landholdings) in this district with ecotouristic activities promoted under the name Agua Selva. Malpasito is just 1km west of the Caseta Malpasito tollbooth and intersection on the recently built Coatzacoalcos–Ocozocoautla autopista.

Malpasito's **ruins** (admission $2.50; ☧ 10am-5pm) are 600m (signposted) above the village. Apart from the beautiful setting, what's remarkable about this little-visited site dating from AD 700–900, is its petroglyphs (rock carvings). Over 100 petroglyphs showing birds, deer, monkeys, people, and temples with stairways are scattered around the Malpasito area, of which about 10 are at the archaeological site.

The site is arranged in a series of stepped platforms on the forested hillside. On the main plaza level is a ball court and a steam bath, which was probably used for pre-game purification rituals. Steps lead up to the Patio Sur, which was the main ceremonial area, dominated by the stepped Structure 13 on its top side. A small path leading half-right from the top of these steps leads to petroglyph groups after 100m and 150m. Past the second group, the path goes through the site's perimeter fence after 30m, and turns sharp right 80m later. After another 200m (downhill), a barely visible side path leads 40m through trees to the large, flat Petroglyph 112, unmarked and partly moss-covered, but with unmistakable temple and stairway carvings. Back on the main path, 100m past the Petroglyph 112 turning, you reach a forest waterfall with an inviting swimming hole at its foot.

More petroglyphs and swimming holes are to be found in Malpasito's **Parque Eco-Arqueológico** (admission $9.50; ☧ 8am-5pm), also just above the village, a beautiful slice of jungle, rivers and waterfalls with a rich variety of flora. The admission charge includes a guided walk of about two hours, and you can also abseil down a waterfall ($14) or ride a 160m zip line ($5).

Malpasito's **Albergue** (in Mexico City ☎ 55-5151-5229; cabaña per person $9.50; meals $4-7) provides meals and simple but well looked-after wooden cabins with private cold-water bathroom, concrete floors and tile roofs. Here you can hire guides ($14 per day) for day walks up some of the dramatic-looking nearby hills.

TRT buses from Villahermosa's 2nd-class bus station (see p798) heading to Tuxtla Gutiérrez by the old Hwy 187, will drop you at the Malpasito turnoff ($6, three hours, six daily), from which it's 5km west to the village, crossing over the autopista en route. Second-class buses from Tuxtla Gutiérrez' Rápidos del Sur terminal (see p810) will drop you at the Caseta Malpasito ($5, two hours, eight daily), on the autopista just 1km from Malpasito.

SOUTHERN TABASCO

Teapa

☎ 932 / pop 26,000 / elevation 50m

This bustling town, 50km south of Villahermosa, is a good base for exploring southern Tabasco's natural attractions.

At the **Grutas del Coconá** (☎ 322-05-45; admission $2; 🕑 10am-5pm), 4km northeast of the center, a well-made concrete path leads 500m into a subtly lit cavern, with pools, bats, plenty of stalactites and stalagmites, and a small museum contains pre-Hispanic ritual items found in the cave. Combis marked 'Mercado Eureka Coca Florida' ($0.50, 10 minutes) will take you there every few minutes from Bastar beside Teapa's central church (and are not part of an international cocaine-trafficking route).

The **Balneario Río Puyacatengo** is a collection of popular riverside restaurants and bathing spots, 3km from town on the Tacotalpa road ($1.50 by taxi).

SLEEPING & EATING

Hotel Quintero (☎ 322-13-95; Bastar 108; s/d/tr $24/ 27/29; 🌣) This central hotel provides reasonably sized, clean, air-conditioned rooms, around a rather antiseptic concrete courtyard.

Hacienda Los Azufres (☎ 327-58-06; Carretera Teapa-Pichucalco Km 5.5; r $38, f $54, with private thermal bath $59; P 🌣 🌊) This hotel-cum-thermal-spa is in the countryside, 8km west of central Teapa, on Hwy 195 to Tuxtla Gutiérrez. Public admission to the large, open-air, sulfurous swimming pools is $3. The rooms are reasonably attractive, with cheery tiling, and some have their own little thermal

bathroom open to the sky. Relaxation and exfoliant massages are also available, for around $30.

La Galería (☎ 322-18-37; Méndez 157; 2-person pizzas $5-7.50; 🕑 6-11pm) Try juicy pizzas amid a dizzying array of kitsch murals and photographs of local beauty queens. No alcohol is served but there's a good selection of other thirst-quenchers.

GETTING THERE & AWAY

The **OCC terminal** (☎ 232-23-11; Méndez 218) is 300m from the plaza, along the main street. Buses leave for Tuxtla Gutiérrez ($12, four hours) twice daily. **La Sultana** (☎ 322-19-23; Damián Pizá 17), near the market and 600m from the plaza, runs comfortable 2nd-class buses to Villahermosa ($2.75, one hour) every 30 minutes, 4am to 9:30pm.

Tapijulapa

☎ 932 / pop 2700 / elevation 200m

This pretty riverside village of red tile–roofed white houses, presided over by a 17th-century church, sits among the lushly forested hills of far southern Tabasco, 36km from Teapa. Several shops sell local wicker and wood crafts.

The beautiful jungle park **Villa Luz** (admission free; 🕑 8am-5pm) is a five-minute boat ride (per person one-way/round-trip $1.50/2.50) along the Río Oxolotán from the village's *embarcadero* (boat landing) – you may have to get local boys to whistle a boat up for you. From the landing, it's a 1km walk to the park's Casa Museo, the former country villa of Tomás Garrido Canabal, the rabidly anticlerical governor of Tabasco in the 1920s and '30s (he demolished Villahermosa's 18th-century baroque cathedral, banned alcohol and gave women the vote). From here other paths lead 600m to the *cascadas* (beautiful waterfalls tumbling into a river, with pools for a refreshing dip) and 900m to the Cueva de las Sardinas Ciegas (Cave of the Blind Sardines), named for the sightless fish that inhabit the sulfurous river inside the cave. You're only permitted to go a few steps down into the cave because of the strong odors. You need about two hours to walk the 5km required to see the waterfalls, house and cave.

Kolem-Jaa' (in Villahermosa ☎ 993-314-31-92; www .kolemjaa.com; day package $22-49, 2-day/1-night package $103; P 🚶) is a jungle eco/adventure tourism center, adjacent to Villa Luz and 6km by road from Tapijulapa. The excitements include commando trails, zip lines across a river and through the jungle canopy, and horseback and mountain-bike riding. Accommodations are in comfortable duplex cabins.

On Tapijulapa's central plaza, **Restaurant Mariquito** (☎ 322-40-07; Parque Carlos Pellicer; dishes around $4; ⏲ 7am-8:30pm) cooks up local specialties, such as *mone de pollo* (chicken steamed with *hierba santa*) and *caldo de shote* (a stew made with a type of river mollusk).

To reach Tapijulapa by bus from Teapa, first take a bus to Tacotalpa ($0.80, 30 minutes, every 30 minutes 6am to 8pm) from Teapa's OCC terminal. Buses to Tapijulapa ($0.80, 45 minutes, hourly until 6pm) leave from Tacotalpa's Mercado Faustino Méndez Jiménez, across the street from the stop where buses from Teapa arrive. The last bus back leaves Tapijulapa at 7pm.

EASTERN TABASCO
Frontera
☎ 913 / pop 23,000

This somewhat rough-and-ready fishing port and oil town sits on the east bank of the vast Río Grijalva, 81km northeast of Villahermosa. The river here, just 8km from its mouth on the Gulf of Mexico, is in fact a combination of the Grijalva and the Usumacinta, Mexico's most voluminous river, whose main branch joins the Grijalva 15km upstream. Between them, these two rivers drain most of Tabasco and Chiapas and about half of Guatemala. Frontera unfortunately fails to make anything of its stunning location, with no public access to the riverfront anywhere near the town center, but you get a great sense of the river's might from the more-than-1km-long bridge that carries Hwy 180 over it 4km south of town. In 1519 the Spanish conquistadors under Cortés scored their first military victory near here, defeating the local inhabitants somewhere among the nearby marshes in what's become known as the Battle of Centla. The locals fled in terror from the mounted Spaniards, thinking horse and rider to be one single mighty beast. Afterwards the natives made Cortés a gift of 20 women, one of whom, Doña Marina or La Malinche, became his indispensable interpreter, and lover. In the 20th century, Frontera was probably the setting for Graham Greene's novel *The Power and the Glory*. The main reason to stop here today is to visit the Reserva de la Biosfera Pantanos de Centla (below).

The newly modernized **Hotel Marmor Plaza** (☎ 332-00-01; Juárez 202; s/d/tr $36/40/47; P ⬚), on Frontera's central plaza, is quite a find: beautiful, good-sized, sparkling-clean rooms come with spot lighting, silent air-conditioning and gleaming bathrooms. **Hospedaje Star** (☎ 332-50-67; Obregón 506; r $28-33; ⬚), just round the corner, is an acceptable alternative, with good big rooms holding up to four.

For eating, the bright, air-conditioned **Café del Puerto** (cnr Madero & Aldama; breakfasts, salads & antojitos $2-6; ⏲ 8:30am-midnight; ⬚), on the plaza, has the best ambience, and well-prepared food.

From the **ADO terminal** (☎ 332-11-49; Zaragoza 609), six blocks from the plaza, 1st-class buses leave for Villahermosa ($3.75, 1½ hours, 25 daily), Paraíso ($4, two hours, two daily) and Campeche ($14 to $16, 4½ hours, three daily).

Reserva de la Biosfera Pantanos de Centla

This 3030-sq-km biosphere reserve protects a good part of the wetlands around the lower reaches of two of Mexico's biggest rivers, the Usumacinta and the Grijalva. These lakes, marshes, rivers, mangroves, savannas and forests are an irreplaceable sanctuary for countless creatures, including the West Indian manatee and Morelet's crocodile (both endangered), six kinds of tortoise, tapir, ocelots, jaguars, howler monkeys, 60 fish species including the *pejelagarto*, and 230 bird species – not to mention 15,000 people scattered in 90 small waterside villages.

A paved, and in parts rough road follows the broad winding Río Usumacinta, right across the reserve from the Grijalva bridge near Frontera, eventually reaching the town of Jonuta (from which other roads lead to the major east–west Hwy 186). Ten kilometers along this road, **Punta Manglar** (in Villahermosa ☎ 993-315-44-91; Hwy Frontera-Jonuta, Km 10; ⏲ 9am-5pm) is an embarkation point for boat-and-foot excursions into the mangroves (one to 1½ hours, $94 for up to 10 people), on which you should see crocodiles, iguanas, birds and, with luck, howler monkeys. If there are just a couple of you they'll probably take you for half-price.

The reserve's visitors center, the **Centro de Interpretación Uyotot-Ja** (☎ 993-313-93-62; Carretera Frontera-Jonuta Km 12.5; admission by donation; ❂ 9am-5pm Tue-Sun), is a further 2.5km along the road. Here, a 20m-high observation tower overlooks the awesome confluence of the Grijalva, the Usumacinta and a third large river, the San Pedrito – a spot known as Tres Brazos (Three Arms). Guides lead you round a nature trail and displays on the wetlands, and boat trips (two hours, up to 10 people $141) are available – March to May is the best birding season. Next door, **El Negro Chon** (☎ 913-331-31-99; mains $4-7.50; ❂ 9am-6pm Tue-Sun) serves tasty fish and prawn dishes under a *palapa* (thatched roof) that catches delicious breezes off the river.

Gray combis and *colectivo* taxis from Calle Madero in Frontera (combis half a block south of the plaza, and *colectivos* 1½ blocks south of the plaza) charge $1 for the 15-minute trip to Punta Manglar or Uyotot-Ja. Some continue to Jonuta ($5, three hours), where buses leave for Villahermosa, Palenque and other destinations.

Tenosique
☎ 934 / pop 32,000
On the voluminous Río Usumacinta, amid farmland in far southeastern Tabasco, Tenosique is, for travelers, primarily a halt on a route into Guatemala. From the small border town of El Ceibo, 60km southeast of Tenosique, boats head along the Río San Pedro to El Naranjo, Guatemala, where you can catch onward transportation to Flores. A new road between El Ceibo and El Naranjo might be open by the time you get there.

The mighty Usumacinta issues from jungle-clad hills at **Boca del Cerro**, 8km southwest of Tenosique on Hwy 203. *Lancha* (fast, open, outboard boat) operators, at the *embarcadero* on the west side of the bridge, charge around $40 per boat for a 1½-hour trip up the river to the start of the rapids-strewn San José canyon and back.

SLEEPING & EATING
Hotel La Casona (☎ 342-11-51; Calle 27 No 8; s/d $17/21; Ⓟ ❂) Friendly La Casona, two blocks off the main street (Calle 26, also called Blvd Pino Suárez), has just nine rooms on two floors around a pretty courtyard adorned with lovable ceramic frogs. Rooms have cable TV, air-con, fan and pretty tiled bathrooms.

Hotel Hacienda Tabasqueña (☎ 342-27-31; Calle 26 No 512; s/d with fan $14/18, with air-con $21/27; ❂) On the main street, this is larger and less cared for than La Casona but still acceptable. It has a small restaurant.

Restaurant Los Tulipanes (☎ 342-17-45; cnr Calles 27 & 22; mains $3.75-7.50; ❂ 7am-5pm) The best place to eat, one block off the main street, spreads under a large palm-thatch roof, with live marimba music from 2pm. A good range of fish, steaks and seafood is served.

GETTING THERE & AROUND
The **ADO bus station** (☎ 342-14-41; Prolongación Calle 20 s/n) is on the southwest edge of town, about 2.5km from the center. Seventeen daily 1st- and 2nd-class services go to Emiliano Zapata ($2.25 to $3, one hour) and Villahermosa ($7 to $10, three to 3½ hours). If you're heading for the Yucatán Peninsula, it's usually quickest to get a bus to Emiliano Zapata and change there. Buses ($0.50) and *colectivo* taxis ($1.50) run from the bus station to the center.

To Guatemala
Buses to the border at El Ceibo ($3, one hour, hourly 6am to 5pm) leave from the corner of Calles 16 and 45, beside the market two blocks off the main Calle 26. From the border, pickups ($1 to $2, 10 minutes) take passengers to the *embarcadero* for frequent *lanchas* up the Río San Pedro to El Naranjo (per person $3, 30 minutes) until around 5pm. El Naranjo has money-changers, a bank and places to stay, and minibuses and buses ($3.25, two to three hours) leave for Flores at least hourly until about 6pm. You can get from Tenosique to Flores in around six hours total.

CHIAPAS

Chiapas is Mexico's most enigmatic state. It's a fascinating, exciting place to visit, with wildly beautiful landscapes, rich and mysterious indigenous cultures, the colonial charm of San Cristóbal de Las Casas, an array of exotic Maya ruins and an ever-improving tourism infrastructure.

There are major banana- and coffee-growing regions in the fertile Soconusco, and large swaths of ranchland scattered around the state. Chiapas is also blessed with oil and gas resources, and generates more than half of Mexico's hydroelectric power. The cities and towns are home to a growing middle class. Yet despite this wealth, the people of rural Chiapas, especially the indigenous people, are among the poorest in the country. Indigenous people's average income in Chiapas is only one-third of other people's income, over one-third of indigenous homes have no running water or electricity, and illiteracy in Chiapas is the highest in Mexico. These inequities helped spark the state's Zapatista revolutionary movement, and it's still impossible not to notice them as you travel round Chiapas.

TUXTLA GUTIÉRREZ
☎ 961 / pop 481,000 / elevation 530m
Chiapas' state capital is a lively, fairly modern city, but not even its best friends would call it charming. Insignificant until it became the capital in 1892, Tuxtla Gutiérrez sprawls across a valley toward the western end of Chiapas' hot and humid central depression, and its crowds, bustle and traffic are an anomaly in this predominantly rural state. The chief attractions around here are the zoo (one of Mexico's best), and the jungle-clad, 800m-deep Cañón del Sumidero (p812), just outside Tuxtla.

Orientation
The city center is Plaza Cívica, with the always-busy main east–west street, Av Central, running across its south side. West of the center, Av Central becomes Blvd Dr Belisario Domínguez; many of the Tuxtla's best hotels and restaurants are strung along this road. Eastward, Av Central changes names to Blvd Ángel Albino Corzo.

MAPS
Inegi (☎ 613-17-83; 6a Av Sur Pte 670, Barrio San Pascualito; ✆ 8:30am-4:30pm Mon-Fri), southwest of the center, sells 1:25,000 and 1:50,000 topographic maps of many parts of Chiapas and other Mexican states.

Information
INTERNET ACCESS
Cyber Comic's (Av Central Pte 457-2; per hr $0.60; ✆ 9am-11pm)
El Chi@p@neco (4a Calle Ote Sur 115; per hr $0.50; ✆ 8:30am-11pm Mon-Sat, 10am-10pm Sun)

LAUNDRY
Lavandería Zaac (2a Av Pte Ote 440; per 3kg $3; ✆ 8am-2pm & 4:30-8pm Mon-Fri, 9am-4pm Sat)

MONEY
Many banks exchange currency and have ATMs.
Bancomer (Av Central Pte 314; ✆ 8:30am-4pm Mon-Fri)
HSBC (Calle Central Nte 137; ✆ 8am-6pm Mon-Sat)

POST
Post office (1a Av Nte Ote; ✆ 8:30am-4pm Mon-Fri, 8:30am-1pm Sat)

TOURIST INFORMATION
Municipal Tourist Office (☎ 614-83-83 ext 111; Edificio Valanci, Av Central Pte 554; ✆ 8am-4pm Mon-Fri, until 2pm Sat)
Secretaría de Turismo (☎ 602-51-27, 800-280-35-00; www.turismochiapas.gob.mx; Blvd Belisario Domínguez 950; ✆ 8am-8pm Mon-Fri, 9am-3pm Sat & Sun) Chiapas' state tourism department has excellent maps and booklets to give out. English- and French-speakers are available on its toll-free phone number. The office is in a building marked Secretaría de Desarrollo Económico, 1.6km west of Plaza Cívica.

Sights
The heart of the city, around the Plaza Cívica, is the liveliest area during the daytime, though the main attractions are scattered around the suburbs.

PLAZA CÍVICA
Tuxtla's broad and lively main plaza occupies two blocks, and is flanked by an untidy array of concrete civic and commercial structures. At its southern end, across Av Central, is the whitewashed modern **Catedral de San Marcos**. The cathedral's clock tower tinkles out a tune on the hour to accompany a kitsch merry-go-round of apostles' images that emerges from its upper levels.

ZOOLÓGICO MIGUEL ÁLVAREZ DEL TORO
Chiapas, with its huge range of natural environments, has the highest concentration of animal species in North America – including several varieties of big cat, 1200 butterfly species and over 600 birds. About 180 of these species, many of them in danger of extinction, are to be found in relatively spacious enclosures at Tuxtla's excellent **zoo** (☎ 614-47-65; Calz Cerro Hueco s/n; admission $2; ✆ 8:30am-5pm Tue-Sun; ♿).

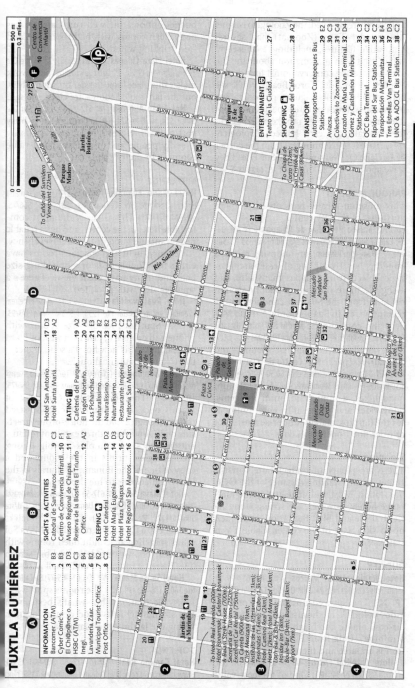

TUXTLA GUTIÉRREZ

INFORMATION
Bancomer (ATM)	1 B3
Cyber Comic's	2 B3
El Chiapanec o	3 D3
HSBC (ATM)	4 C3
Inegi	5 B4
Lavandería Zaac	6 B2
Municipal Tourist Office	7 B2
Post Office	8 C3

SIGHTS & ACTIVITIES
Catedral de San Marcos	9 B3
Centro de Convivencia Infantil	10 F1
Museo Regional de Chiapas	11 F1
Reserva de la Biosfera El Triunfo Office	12 A2

SLEEPING 🛏
Hotel Catedral	13 D2
Hotel María Eugenia	14 D3
Hotel Plaza Chiapas	15 C2
Hotel Regional San Marcos	16 C3
Hotel San Antonio	17 D3
Hotel Santa María	18 A2

EATING 🍴
Cafetería del Parque	19 A2
El Fogón Norteño	20 A2
Las Pichanchas	21 E3
Naturalíssimo	22 B2
Naturalíssimo	23 B2
Restaurante Imperial	24 D3
Trattoria San Marco	25 C2
	26 C3

ENTERTAINMENT 🎭
Teatro de la Ciudad	27 F1

SHOPPING 🛍
La Boutique del Café	28 A2

TRANSPORT
Autotransportes Cuxtepeques Bus Station	29 E2
Aviacsa	30 C3
Colectivos to Zoomat	31 C4
Corazón de María Van Terminal	32 D4
Gómez y Castellanos Minibus Station	33 C3
OCC Bus Terminal	34 C2
Rápidos del Sur Bus Station	35 C2
Transportación Mactumatza	36 E4
Tres Estrellas Van Terminal	37 D3
UNO & ADO GL Bus Station	38 C2

TABASCO & CHIAPAS

Recently remodeled, the Zoológico Miguel Álvarez del Toro (Zoomat) has several innovative features, including a 'museum' about itself with information about the life of its pioneering conservationist founder Dr Miguel Álvarez del Toro. Beasts you'll see here include ocelots, jaguars, pumas, tapirs, red macaws, toucans, three species of crocodile, snakes and spider monkeys. To get to the zoo take a 'Cerro Hueco, Zoológico' *colectivo* ($0.50, 20 minutes) from the corner of 1a Calle Ote Sur and 7a Av Sur Ote. They leave about every 20 minutes. A taxi is $3.

PARQUE MADERO

This museum-theater-park area is 1.25km northeast of the city center.

The **Museo Regional de Chiapas** (☎ 612-04-59; Calz de los Hombres Ilustres s/n; admission $3.25, Sun free; ☯ 9am-4pm Tue-Sun), an imposing modern building, has a sampling of lesser archaeological pieces from Chiapas' many sites, and a slightly more interesting history section running from the Spanish conquest to the revolution, all in Spanish only. Parque Madero also contains the **Jardín Botánico** (Botanic Garden; admission free; ☯ 9am-4pm Tue-Sun) – a nice bit of woodland with minimal labeling – and a children's park, the **Centro de Convivencia Infantil** (admission free, rides each $0.50-1.25; ☯ 9am-8:30pm Tue-Fri, until 9:30pm Sat & Sun; ♿), with mini quad bikes, a mini train, mini dodgems, pony rides and other mini entertainment for the (approximately) under-sevens. A lot of rides don't open weekdays.

Sleeping

There are plenty of budget hotels in the center, within walking distance of the OCC bus station. Most midrange luxury and midrange hotels, however, are strung along Av Central Pte and Blvd Belisario Domínguez, up to 4km west of the center. Cable TV is standard.

BUDGET

Hotel Regional San Marcos (☎ /fax 613-19-40; sanmarcos@chiapas.net; 2a Calle Ote Sur 176; s/d $30/34; P ⊠) The spruced-up San Marcos provides colorful, medium-sized rooms with air-con, phone and bright yellow trim, just a minute's walk from Plaza Cívica. Reception is amiable and there's a restaurant.

Hotel Catedral (☎ 613-08-24; 1a Av Nte Ote 367; s/d/tr/q $20/25/29/34; P) One of the best-value

budget options, the well-run Catedral has neat, clean rooms with bathroom, fan and free drinking water.

Hotel Plaza Chiapas (☎ 613-83-65; 2a Av Nte Ote 299; s/d/tr $16/19/28) Bright exterior paintwork makes this place look classier than it really is, but the fan-cooled rooms are clean enough.

Hotel San Antonio (☎ 612-27-13; 2a Av Sur Ote 540; r $14, tw & tr $24; P) Though in a busy part of town, Hotel San Antonio is run by friendly people and has clean, good-value rooms with pretty prints.

MIDRANGE

Hotel María Eugenia (☎ 613-37-67; www.mariaeugenia.com.mx; Av Central Ote 507; s/d $66/75; P ⊠ ☐ ☎) This is easily the most comfortable hotel in the center, and has a reliable restaurant and good in-house travel agency. All 83 airy, light and spacious rooms have either two double beds or a huge king-size bed, and many have great views. There's a small garden with pool, too.

Hotel Real Avenida (☎ 612-23-47; www.hotelrealavenida.com; Av Central Pte 1230; r $55-65, tr/q $73/93; P ⊠) Spotless medium-size rooms with phone and cable TV, just 1km west of Plaza Cívica, make this new hotel a solid choice – there's no restaurant though.

Hotel Bonampak (☎ 602-59-16/21; hotbonam@prodigy.net.mx; Blvd Belisario Domínguez 180; s/d $66/75; P ⊠ ☎) The Bonampak, 1.6km west of Plaza Cívica, has comfortable, good-sized rooms, though avoid the noise-prone streetside ones. A pool and three excellent restaurants in the same complex are big pluses; archaeological prints in the rooms and a copy of one of the Bonampak murals in the lobby add a spark to the decor.

Hotel Maya Sol (☎ 617-50-60; www.hotelmayasol-chiapas.com; Blvd Belisario Domínguez 1380; s/d/ste $66/75/112; P ⊠ ☐ ☎) Three kilometers west of Plaza Cívica, the remodeled Maya Sol offers sparkling air-conditioned rooms with large mirrors, writing desks and big-screen TV. There's a restaurant and small pool.

Hotel Santa María (☎ /fax 614-65-77; 8a Calle Pte Nte 160; r $38-42; P ⊠) The rooms sport a few folksy decorations, but what's best about this small hotel is its good central location facing the Jardín de la Marimba.

TOP END

Hotel Camino Real (☎ 617-77-77, 800-901-23-00; www.caminoreal.com; Blvd Belisario Domínguez 1195; r incl breakfast $117; (P X X L R) The huge, five-star Camino Real rises like some contemporary castle of the hospitality industry, 3km west of Plaza Cívica. The spectacular interior features a pool and waterfall in a large, verdant atrium-courtyard, full of free-flying tropical birds. Commodious rooms come with green marble bathrooms, all mod cons and wheelchair access. Other amenities include a spa and tennis courts.

Holiday Inn (☎ 617-10-00, 800-009-99-00; www .holiday-inn.com/tuxtla; Blvd Belisario Domínguez Km 1081; r $120; (P X L R) This hotel, in an attractive, modern Arabic style, is 4km west of the center. The rooms are business-class, with marble floors, coffeemakers and other mod cons, and the hotel has a business center, huge pool and an Italian restaurant. On Friday, Saturday and Sunday, or if you stay two nights, the rate drops to $93.

Eating

Tuxtla is strong on meaty grill houses, but also caters to plenty of other palates, including vegetarian ones.

Cafetería Bonampak (☎ 602-59-33; Hotel Bonampak,Blvd Belisario Domínguez 180; mains $5-7.50; X) For a satisfying meal at any time of day you can't beat this air-conditioned hotel restaurant, with its bright ambience and good service. The long menu runs from prawn cocktails and *antojitos* (corn- and tortilla-based snacks) to beef, chicken and some yummy cakes and desserts.

Balam Steak House (☎ 602-59-33; Hotel Bonampak, Blvd Belisario Domínguez 180; mains $8.50-18; X 1-11pm) Next door to Cafetería Bonampak, the equally popular and well-run Balam serves done-to-a-turn steaks and mixed grills, in spacious surrounds with full-wall windows and lots of greenery.

El Fogón Norteño (☎ 612-95-01; cnr 1a Av Nte Pte & 9a Calle Pte Nte; mains $3.75-6) A bustling grill house overlooking the Jardín de la Marimba (see right), with well-prepared meat dishes at excellent prices. Most come with tasty *frijoles charros* (beans cooked with bacon or other pork products).

Naturalíssimo (breakfast $3-4.50, antojitos $2.50-3.75, lunch $5.50; V ; 6a Calle Pte Nte 124 ☎ 613-53-43; X 7am-10:30pm Mon-Sat, 8am-10:30pm Sun; Av Central Pte 648 ☎ 613-36-16; X 10am-10pm Mon-Sat, 1-10pm Sun; Av Central Ote 523 ☎ 613-96-48; X 7am-10:30pm Mon-Sat, 8am-10:30pm Sun) Cheery, vegetarian Naturalíssimo offers healthy breakfasts, whole-wheat bread, *tortas* and *chilaquiles* (fried tortilla strips with chili sauce and sometimes meat and eggs), wonderful thirst-quenching fruit juices and *licuados*, multi-flavored yogurt and ice cream and, at the 6a Calle Pte Nte branch, a tasty three-course lunch.

Las Pichanchas (☎ 612-53-51; www.laspichanchas .com.mx; Av Central Ote 837; mains $4.50-7.50; X noon-midnight; ♿) This courtyard restaurant specializes in Chiapas food with live marimba music and, from 9pm to 10pm every night, a show of colorful traditional Chiapas dances that whips up quite a party atmosphere. Try the tasty *tamales* (cornmeal dough wrapped with meat or veggies and steamed), or *pechuga jacuané* (chicken breast stuffed with beans in a *hierba santa* sauce), and leave room for *chimbos*, a dessert made from egg yolks and cinnamon.

La Carreta (☎ 602-54-33; Blvd Belisario Domínguez 703; mains $7-18; X 1pm-midnight) A hugely popular, two-level, plant-draped grill house 1.75km west of the Plaza Cívica, with a festive atmosphere despite live music of the *My Way* genre.

Trattoria San Marco (☎ 612-69-74; Calle Ote Sur, Local 5; small/medium pizza $4.50/7) San Marco has a prime, traffic-free location just behind the cathedral. Snack on a sub, baguette or salad, or delve into the extensive pizza menu. It also serves *papas al horno* (potatoes with filling) and good savory crepes.

Cafetería del Parque (☎ 612-6000; 8a Calle Pte Sur 113; antojitos $3-4, mains $5-7; X 8am-10:30pm; X) This is one of the better eateries around the Jardín de la Marimba and, with its air-conditioning reinforced by Arctic-blue decor, definitely your place if you need to cool off.

Restaurante Imperial (☎ 612-06-48; Calle Central Nte 263; mains $2.50-3.50, comida corrida $3.50) This busy, efficient place beside Plaza Cívica offers a wholesome two-course *comida corrida* (set lunch) with plenty of choice. There's a full breakfast menu too, and good drinking chocolate.

Entertainment

Jardín de la Marimba, a leafy plaza eight blocks west of Plaza Cívica, is fun in the evening, especially at weekends. Popular free marimba concerts are held nightly from 6:30pm to 9:30pm, often with people dancing around the central bandstand. Several places to eat and drink surround the plaza.

TABASCO & CHIAPAS

Teatro de la Ciudad (☎ 613-13-49; Calz de los Hombres Ilustres, Parque Madero) The City Theater stages everything from opera and folkloric dance to film seasons.

CLUBS

Clubbers head for the 'Zona Dorada', 2km to 4km west of the center along Blvd Belisario Domínguez. These places start to fill up around 11:30pm on Friday and Saturday, and party till 4am or 5am. They all charge $2 to $3 at these times and have pretty easygoing door policies.

Tesomatas (☎ 602-68-62; Blvd Belisario Domínguez 2138; ☽ from 9pm Tue-Sun) This is a bit glitzy, but still relaxed, often with live reggae. It's about 2.5km from Plaza Cívica.

Boule-Bar (☎ 617-10-00; Holiday Inn, Blvd Belisario Domínguez Km 1081; ☽ 9pm-3am Wed-Sat) The slickest spot around, with live salsa starting around midnight; it's 4km from Plaza Cívica.

Loch Bar (☎ 615-14-28; Callejón Emiliano Zapata 207; ☽ from 9pm Tue-Sun) If you fancy dancing to '70s and '80s tracks, try this place, down a lane beside Hotel Maya Sol, 3km from Plaza Cívica.

Baby (☎ 615-91-20; Callejón Emiliano Zapata 207; ☽ from 9pm Thu-Sat) Tuxtla's headquarters of *grupera* music, or 'Tux-Mex' as they call it here – it's next door to Loch Bar.

Cubo (☎ 121-43-50; Blvd Belisario Domínguez 2535; ☽ from 9pm Tue-Sat) Techno's the beat here, in a glass-walled upstairs space with long-distance views – 3km from Plaza Cívica.

Shopping

Instituto de las Artesanías (☎ 611-09-50; Blvd Belisario Domínguez 2035; ☽ 10am-8pm Mon-Sat, until 3pm Sun) The Chiapas Crafts Institute, 2km west of Plaza Cívica, sells a great range of the state's *artesanías* (handicrafts), from Amatenango 'tigers' and funky Cintalapa ceramic suns to colorful highland textiles.

La Boutique del Café (cnr 8a Calle Pte Nte & 1a Av Nte Pte; ☽ 10am-9pm Tue-Fri, 4-9pm Sat-Mon) The biggest range of Chiapas coffees you'll ever find in one place. Can't decide? It's hard to beat the flavor of organic Café Mam, produced by an indigenous cooperative in the remote Motozintla area – around $6 per kilogram.

Getting There & Away
AIR

Tuxtla's **Aeropuerto Francisco Sarabia** (☎ 671-53-11; Carretera Escuela de Veterinaria Km 1.5), also called

Aeropuerto Terán, is 8km southwest of the city center. A taxi costs $5 to $6.

Click Mexicana (☎ 602-57-71; Blvd Belisario Domínguez 1748) flies direct to Mexico City five times daily, and to Oaxaca, Villahermosa, Mérida and Cancún once daily. **Aviacsa** (☎ 800-006-22-00; Av Central Pte 160) has four daily flights to Mexico City and one to Tapachula.

BUS, COLECTIVO & VAN

The main terminal of **OCC** (☎ 612-51-22; 2a Av Nte Pte 268) is just two blocks west of Plaza Cívica. Second-class **Rápidos del Sur** (☎ 612-51-22; 2a Av Nte Pte 268) is next door, and the deluxe ADO GL and **UNO** (☎ 612-16-39) have their terminal across the street. Daily departures from these terminals include the following:

Destination	Price	Duration	Frequency
Cancún	$55-65	20hr	1 deluxe & 2 1st-class
Comitán	$7.50	3½hr	2 deluxe & 19 1st-class
Mérida	$41-49	15hr	1 deluxe & 1 1st-class
Mexico City (Most go to TAPO)	$59-85	12-15hr	7 deluxe & 10 1st-class
Oaxaca	$26-31	10hr	1 deluxe & 3 1st-class
Palenque	$12.50-16	7hr	2 deluxe & 6 1st-class
Puerto Escondido	$27	9½-13hr	2 1st-class
San Cristóbal de Las Casas	$3-4.50	2hr	9 deluxe & 35 1st-class
Tapachula	$14-34	6-7hr via Tonalá or 9½hr via Comitán	7 deluxe, 18 1st-class & 27 2nd-class
Tonalá	$6-10	3hr	3 deluxe, 12 1st-class & 27 2nd-class
Villahermosa	$10-19	4½-9hr	2 deluxe, 7 1st-class & 4 2nd-class

For San Cristóbal de Las Casas there are quicker alternatives, taking 1½ hours or less. Vans of **Corazón de María** (☎ 612-54-21; 3a Av Sur Ote 422) and **Tres Estrellas** (☎ 678-68-62; 2a Av Sur Ote 521) cost $3.50 and leave every 20 to 30 minutes from around 5am to 10pm; *colectivo* taxis of **Transportación Mactumatza** (☎ 613-71-79; 3a Av Sur Ote 847) run round the clock for $4.

CAR & MOTORCYCLE

Rental companies in Tuxtla include the following:

Budget (☎ 615-13-82; Blvd Belisario Domínguez 2510)

Excellent (☎ 602-57-21; Local 9, Plaza Bonampak, Blvd Belisario Domínguez 302)

Hertz (☎ 615-53-48; Hotel Camino Real, Blvd Belisario Domínguez 1195)

Getting Around

All *colectivos* ($0.40) on Blvd Belisario Domínguez-Av Central-Blvd Albino Corzo run at least as far as the Hotel Bonampak and state tourist office in the west, and 11a Calle Ote in the east. Stops are marked by '*parada*' signs. Taxis within the city cost $2 ($2.50 after dark).

AROUND TUXTLA GUTIÉRREZ
Chiapa de Corzo

☎ 961 / pop 32,000 / elevation 450m

Chiapa de Corzo is an attractive colonial town with an easygoing, provincial air. Set on the north bank of the broad Río Grijalva, it's 12km east of Tuxtla Gutiérrez, and is the main starting point for trips into the Cañón del Sumidero (p812).

HISTORY

Chiapa de Corzo has been occupied almost continuously since about 1500 BC, which makes it important to archaeologists, though its pre-Hispanic remains are of little interest to the nonspecialist.

Before the Spaniards arrived, the warlike Chiapa tribe had their capital, Nandalumí, a couple of kilometers downstream from here, on the opposite bank of the Grijalva. When Diego de Mazariegos invaded the area in 1528, the Chiapa apparently hurled themselves by the hundreds to their death in the canyon rather than surrender.

Mazariegos founded a settlement called Chiapa de Los Indios here, but quickly shifted his base to San Cristóbal de Las Casas, where he found the climate and natives more manageable.

ORIENTATION & INFORMATION

Buses from Tuxtla stop on the north side of central Plaza Ángel Albino Corzo, or just past it on Av 21 de Octubre. The *embarcadero* for Cañón del Sumidero boat trips is two blocks south of the plaza down 5 de Febrero.

BBVA Bancomer (☎ 616-06-53; Plaza Ángel Albino Corzo 5; ☑ 8:30am-4pm Mon-Fri) On the east side of the plaza, it has an ATM.

Tourist office (5 de Febrero 11; ☑ 9am-3pm Mon-Sat) Just off the southwest corner of the plaza.

SIGHTS

Impressive arcades frame three sides of the plaza. **La Pila**, a handsome colonial brick fountain completed in 1562 in Mudejar-Gothic style, and said to resemble the Spanish crown, stands toward the southeast corner.

The large **Templo de Santo Domingo de Guzmán**, one block south of the plaza, was built in the late 16th century by the Dominican order. Its adjoining convent is now the **Centro Cultural** (☎ 616-00-55; Mexicanidad Chiapaneca 10; admission free; ☑ 10am-5pm Tue-Sun), home to an exposition of the wood and lino prints of talented Chiapa-born Franco Lázaro Gómez (1922–49) as well as the **Museo de la Laca**, dedicated to the local craft specialty: lacquered gourds. The museum holds pieces dating back to 1606 and samples of lacquerwork from other centers in Mexico, China, Japan and Thailand.

FESTIVALS & EVENTS

Fiesta de Enero (January 9 to 21) is one of Mexico's liveliest and most extraordinary festivals, including nightly dances involving cross-dressing young men, known as Las Chuntá. Women don the highly colorful, beautifully embroidered *chiapaneca* dress, and blond-wigged, mask-toting *Parachicos* (impersonating conquistadors) parade on January 15, 17 and 20. A canoe battle and fireworks extravaganza follows on the final evening.

SLEEPING

Hotel Los Ángeles (☎ 616-00-48; www.losangeles chiapas.com; Grajales 2; r with fan/air-con $21/26; P 🗙) This hotel at the southeast corner of the plaza has spotless rooms with hot-water bathroom, cable TV and fan. Upstairs rooms lack air-con, but are bigger and catch more breeze.

Hotel La Ceiba (☎ 616-07-73; www.hlaceiba.com; Av Domingo Ruíz 300; s/d $54/60; P 🗙 🞋) La Ceiba has an inviting pool, extensive gardens and 91 simple but well-kept air-conditioned rooms with cable TV. It's two blocks west of the plaza.

EATING

Restaurant Los Corredores (☎ 616-07-60; www.los corredores.com.mx; Madero 35; mains $5-8) Facing the southwest corner of the plaza, Los Corredores does a bit of everything: good breakfasts, reasonably priced fish plates and a few local specialties including *pepita con tasajo* (beef with a spicy pumpkin-seed sauce).

Restaurante Italiano Valle d'Aosta (☎ 616-12-43; 5 de Febrero 211; mains $5.50-8.50; ☺ 1pm-midnight Mon-Sat, 1-10pm Sun) No mean Italian restaurant this, with an Italian-trained chef, on the street leading down to the *embarcadero*. Pizzas and pasta are prepared on the spot.

Restaurant Jardines de Chiapa (☎ 616-01-98; Madero 395; mains $3.50-7; ☺ 9am-6:30pm) One block along Madero from Los Corredores, this large place is set around a garden patio. The long menu includes tasty *cochinito al horno* (oven-baked pork).

The eight restaurants by the *embarcadero* have near-identical, and equally overpriced, menus. The river views are nice though.

GETTING THERE & AWAY

Microbuses from Tuxtla Gutiérrez to Chiapa de Corzo ($0.90, 20 minutes) are run by **Gómez y Castellanos** (☎ 613-31-80; 3a Calle Ote Sur 380), every few minutes from 5am to 10pm.

Buses to and from San Cristóbal de Las Casas stop at a gas station on Hwy 190, on the northeast edge of Chiapa de Corzo. Microbuses ($0.40) run between here and the top end of Chiapa's plaza; a taxi is $1.50.

Cañón del Sumidero

The Sumidero Canyon is a spectacular fissure in the earth, found east of Tuxtla Gutiérrez. In 1981 the Chicoasén hydroelectric dam was completed at its northern end, damming the Río Grijalva which flows through the canyon, and creating a 25km-long reservoir.

The canyon can be viewed from above at five *miradores* (lookout points); bus tours to these ($6, 3½ hours) leave Tuxtla's cathedral at 9am and 1pm daily (except Monday) if a minimum of five people show up. The departure point for this trip may change, so check with a tourist office. Most people however choose to see the canyon from below, using one of the fast **lancha** (return trip $9; ☺ 8am-4pm) that speed between the canyon's towering rock walls. This is about a two-hour return trip, starting at either Chiapa de Corzo or the Embarcadero Cahuaré, 5km north of Chiapa along the road to Tuxtla. You'll rarely have to wait more than half an hour for a boat to fill up. Bring a drink, something to shield you from the sun and, if the weather is not hot, a layer or two of warm clothing.

It's about 35km from Chiapa de Corzo to the dam. Soon after you pass under Hwy 190, the canyon walls tower an amazing 800m above you. Along the way you'll see a variety of birds – herons, cormorants, vultures, kingfishers – plus probably a crocodile or two. The boat operators will point out a few odd formations of rock and vegetation, including one cliff face covered in thick hanging moss, resembling a giant Christmas tree. Hopefully your *lancha* won't have to plow through a Sargasso Sea of floating plastic garbage, as has sometimes happened when wet-season rains wash trash from Tuxtla Gutiérrez into the Grijalva.

Soon after the 'Christmas tree,' 40 minutes from Chiapa de Corzo, is the **Parque Ecoturístico Cañón del Sumidero** (☎ 961-600-66-54; www.sumidero.com; admission incl food & drinks $27, 6-12-year-olds $20; ☺ 10am-4:30pm; ⓓ). This adventure park, occupying a jungle-clad bank of the canyon, offers a range of fun activities, at a price. The large, scenic swimming pool, aviary, crocodile pool, mini-zoo and jungle trails are included in the admission, but you have to pay between $3.50 and $10 each for abseiling, mountain biking, kayaking and zip-lining, plus $11.50 for the return trip in the park's *lanchas* from Chiapa de Corzo or Cahuaré.

SAN CRISTÓBAL DE LAS CASAS
☎ 967 / pop 129,000 / elevation 2160m

The journey from Tuxtla Gutiérrez to the beautiful colonial town of San Cristóbal (cris-*toh*-bal) is only 80km, but it lifts you into a different world. From the steamy lowlands you seem to climb endlessly through the clouds before descending into the temperate, pine-clad Valle de Jovel, where San Cristóbal lies.

The remote Chiapas highlands were a refuge for ancient Maya after the collapse of lowland Maya civilization more than 1000 years ago. Even under Spanish rule the area remained a world apart, ostensibly governed from Guatemala City but in reality left pretty much to its own devices (or rather, those of its colonial masters). Today San Cristóbal is at the heart of one of the most deeply rooted indigenous areas in Mexico, surrounded by dozens of Tzotzil and Tzeltal villages where age-old customs coexist with elements of modernity.

The town has been a favorite travelers' haunt for decades, and it's easy to see why.

It's a pleasure to explore San Cristóbal's cobbled streets and markets, soaking up the unique ambience and the wonderfully clear highland light. Some special creative energy here attracts an ever-changing community of artsy, socially aware Mexicans and foreigners. The city is a gathering place for sympathizers (and some opponents) of the Zapatista rebels, and a base for organizations working with Chiapas' indigenous people. San Cristóbal also has a terrific selection of accommodations, and a cosmopolitan array of cafés, bars and restaurants.

History

Diego de Mazariegos founded San Cristóbal as the Spanish regional base in 1528. Its Spanish citizens made fortunes from wheat, while the indigenous people lost their lands and suffered diseases, taxes and forced labor. The church afforded some protection against colonist excesses. Dominican monks reached Chiapas in 1545, and made San Cristóbal their main base. The town is now named after one of them, Bartolomé de Las Casas, who was appointed bishop of Chiapas and became the most prominent Spanish defender of indigenous people in colonial times. In modern times Bishop Samuel Ruiz, who retired in 1999 after a long tenure, followed in Las Casas' footsteps, defending the oppressed indigenous people and earning the hostility of the Chiapas establishment.

San Cristóbal was the Chiapas state capital from 1824 to 1892, but remained relatively isolated until the 1970s, when tourism began to influence its economy. Recent decades have seen an influx of indigenous villagers into the 'Cinturón de Miseria' (Belt of Misery), a series of impoverished, violence-ridden, makeshift colonies around San Cristóbal's Periférico (ring road). Many of these people are here because they have been expelled from Chamula and other communities as a result of internal politico-religious conflicts. Most of the craft sellers around Santo Domingo church and the underage hawkers around town come from the Cinturón de Miseria.

San Cristóbal was catapulted into the international limelight on January 1, 1994, when the Zapatista rebels selected it as one of four places in which to launch their revolution, seizing and sacking government offices in the town before being driven out within a few days by the Mexican army. Political and social tensions remain, but San Cristóbal's future as a magnet for travelers looks secure, with a burgeoning tourist sector and cultural scene, a booming property market and a growing middle class.

Orientation

San Cristóbal is easy to walk around, with straight streets rambling up and down several gentle hills. The Pan-American Hwy (Hwy 190, Blvd Juan Sabines, 'El Bulevar') runs through the southern part of town. Nearly all transportation terminals are on, or just off, the Pan-American. From the OCC bus terminal here, it's six blocks north up Insurgentes to the central square, Plaza 31 de Marzo. Calle Real de Guadalupe, heading east from the plaza, has a concentration of places to stay and eat, and some crafts shops. A long pedestrian mall, the Andador Turístico (or Andador Eclesiástico), runs up Avs Hidalgo and 20 de Noviembre from the Arco de El Carmen in the south to the Templo de Santo Domingo in the north, crossing Plaza 31 de Marzo en route.

Information

BOOKSTORES

La Pared (☎ /fax 678-63-67; lapared9@yahoo.com; Hidalgo 2; ☽ 10am-2pm & 4-8pm Tue-Sat, noon-2pm & 4-8pm Sun) Stocks a great choice of new and used books in English, including Lonely Planet guides. It's run by a friendly American, Dana Burton, who also trades used books.
Librería Chilam Balam (☎ 678-04-86; Utrilla 33; ☽ 9am-8pm)
Libros Soluna (☎ 678-68-05; Real de Guadalupe 13B; ☽ 9am-8pm)

INTERNET ACCESS

San Cristóbal has dozens of inexpensive cybercafés.
Centro Cultural El Puente (Real de Guadalupe 55; per hr $0.60; ☽ closed Sun) Has a CD burner (per hr $1.50) and scanner too.
Los Faroles (Real de Guadalupe 31; per hr $0.60)
Otisa (Real de Guadalupe 3A; per hr $0.50)
Sayvar Internet (Hidalgo 12A; per hr $0.70) Has webcams and headphones.

LAUNDRY

Lavandería (Real de Guadalupe 70A; per 5kg $3.75; ☽ 8am-8pm)

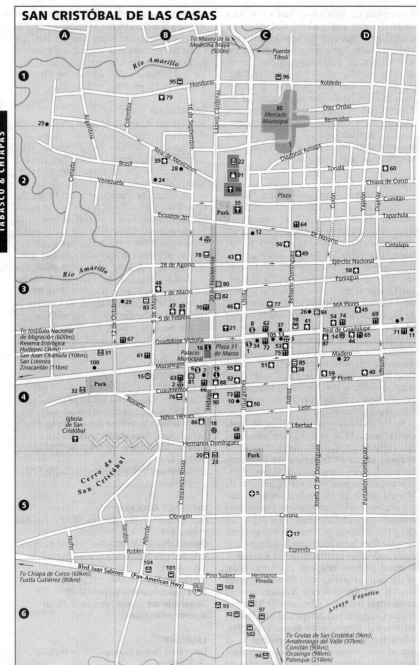

SAN CRISTÓBAL DE LAS CASAS

To Museo de la
Medicina Maya
(500m)

Puente
Tíboli

Río Amarillo

Honduras

Robledo

Díaz Ordaz

Bermudas

Mercado
Municipal

Diagonal Arriaga

Tonalá

Chiapa de Corzo

Real de Mexicanos

Comitán

Tapachula

Brasil

Plaza

Venezuela

Escuadrón 201

Park

Dr Navarro

Cintalapa

Río Amarillo

28 de Agosto

Ejército Nacional

Paniaguá

1 de Marzo

MA Flores

5 de Febrero

To Instituto Nacional
de Migración (600m);
Reserva Ecológica
Huitepec (3km);
San Juan Chamula (10km);
San Lorenzo
Zinacantán (11km)

Real de Guadalupe

Guadalupe Victoria

Palacio
Municipal

Plaza 31
de Marzo

Madero

Mazariegos

Park

Rossete

Cuauhtémoc

Iglesia
de San
Cristóbal

Niños Héroes

Hermanos Domínguez

Park

Cerro de
San Cristóbal

Corzo

Obregón

Corona

Esponda

Blvd Juan Sabines (Pan-American Hwy)

To Chiapa de Corzo (68km);
Tuxtla Gutiérrez (80km)

Pino Suárez

Hermanos
Pineda

MEX
190

Arroyo Fogótico

To Grutas de San Cristóbal (9km);
Amatenango del Valle (37km);
Comitán (90km);
Ocosingo (98km);
Palenque (218km)

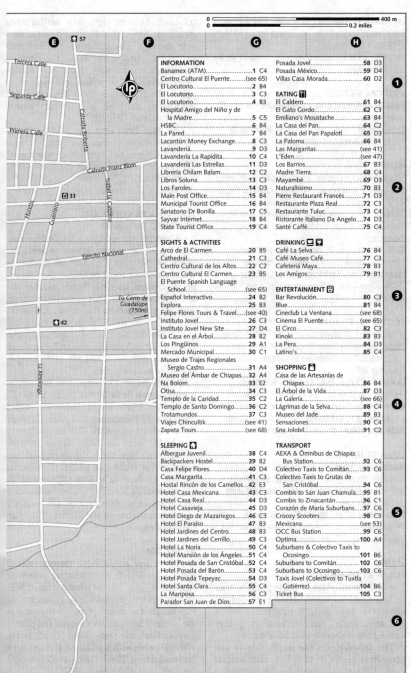

0 — 400 m
0 — 0.2 miles

INFORMATION
Banamex (ATM)................................**1** C4
Centro Cultural El Puente.........(see 65)
El Locutorio....................................**2** B4
El Locutorio....................................**3** B4
El Locutorio....................................**4** B3
Hospital Amigo del Niño y de
la Madre.......................................**5** C5
HSBC..**6** B4
La Pared...**7** B4
Lacantún Money Exchange............**8** C3
Lavandería......................................**9** D3
Lavandería La Rapidita..................**10** C4
Lavandería Las Estrellas................**11** D3
Librería Chilam Balam...................**12** C2
Libros Soluna................................**13** C3
Los Faroles....................................**14** D3
Main Post Office............................**15** B4
Municipal Tourist Office................**16** B4
Sanatorio Dr Bonilla.....................**17** C5
Sayvar Internet..............................**18** B4
State Tourist Office.......................**19** C4

SIGHTS & ACTIVITIES
Arco de El Carmen........................**20** B5
Cathedral......................................**21** C3
Centro Cultural de los Altos.........**22** C2
Centro Cultural El Carmen............**23** B5
El Puente Spanish Language
School.....................................(see 65)
Español Interactivo.......................**24** B2
Explora...**25** B3
Felipe Flores Tours & Travel.....(see 40)
Instituto Jovel...............................**26** C3
Instituto Jovel New Site................**27** D4
La Casa en el Árbol.......................**28** B2
Los Pingüinos...............................**29** A1
Mercado Municipal.......................**30** C1
Museo de Trajes Regionales
Sergio Castro...............................**31** A4
Museo del Ámbar de Chiapas.......**32** A4
Na Bolom.....................................**33** E2
Otisa..**34** C3
Templo de la Caridad....................**35** C2
Templo de Santo Domingo...........**36** C2
Trotamundos................................**37** C3
Viajes Chincultik......................(see 41)
Zapata Tours...........................(see 68)

SLEEPING
Albergue Juvenil...........................**38** C4
Backpackers Hostel.......................**39** B2
Casa Felipe Flores.........................**40** D4
Casa Margarita..............................**41** C3
Hostal Rincón de los Camellos......**42** E3
Hotel Casa Mexicana.....................**43** B3
Hotel Casa Real.............................**44** D3
Hotel Casavieja.............................**45** D3
Hotel Diego de Mazariegos...........**46** C3
Hotel El Paraíso............................**47** B3
Hotel Jardines del Centro..............**48** B3
Hotel Jardines del Cerrillo............**49** C3
Hotel La Noria..............................**50** C4
Hotel Mansión de los Ángeles.......**51** C4
Hotel Posada de San Cristóbal......**52** C4
Hotel Posada del Barón.................**53** C4
Hotel Posada Tepeyac...................**54** D3
Hotel Santa Clara..........................**55** C4
La Mariposa..................................**56** C3
Parador San Juan de Dios..............**57** E1

Posada Jovel.................................**58** D3
Posada México..............................**59** D4
Villas Casa Morada........................**60** D2

EATING
El Caldero.....................................**61** B4
El Gato Gordo...............................**62** C3
Emiliano's Moustache....................**63** B4
La Casa del Pan............................**64** C2
La Casa del Pan Papalotl...............**65** D3
La Paloma......................................**66** B4
Las Margaritas..........................(see 41)
L'Eden......................................(see 47)
Los Barrios...................................**67** B3
Madre Tierra................................**68** C4
Mayambé......................................**69** D3
Naturalíssimo...............................**70** B3
Pierre Restaurant Francés..............**71** D3
Restaurante Plaza Real..................**72** C3
Restaurante Tuluc.........................**73** C4
Ristorante Italiano Da Angelo.......**74** D3
Santé Caffé...................................**75** C4

DRINKING
Café La Selva................................**76** B4
Café Museo Café...........................**77** C3
Cafeteriá Maya.............................**78** B3
Los Amigos...................................**79** B1

ENTERTAINMENT
Bar Revolución..............................**80** C3
Blue..**81** B4
Cineclub La Ventana.................(see 68)
Cinema El Puente......................(see 65)
El Circo...**82** C3
Kinoki...**83** B3
La Pera...**84** D3
Latino's...**85** C4

SHOPPING
Casa de las Artesanías de
Chiapas.....................................**86** B4
El Árbol de la Vida........................**87** D3
La Galería.................................(see 66)
Lágrimas de la Selva.....................**88** C4
Museo del Jade............................**89** B3
Sensaciones..................................**90** C4
Sna Jolobil...................................**91** C2

TRANSPORT
AEXA & Ómnibus de Chiapas
Bus Station................................**92** C6
Colectivo Taxis to Comitán...........**93** C6
Colectivo Taxis to Grutas de
San Cristóbal.............................**94** C6
Combis to San Juan Chamula........**95** B1
Combis to Zinacantán...................**96** C1
Corazón de María Suburbans.........**97** C6
Croozy Scooters............................**98** C3
Mexicana.................................(see 53)
OCC Bus Station...........................**99** C6
Optima.......................................**100** A4
Suburbans & Colectivo Taxis to
Ocosingo.................................**101** B6
Suburbans to Comitán.................**102** C6
Suburbans to Ocosingo...............**103** C6
Taxis Jovel (Colectivos to Tuxtla
Gutiérrez)................................**104** B6
Ticket Bus..................................**105** C3

Lavandería La Rapidita (☎ 678-80-59; Insurgentes 9; self-service per 5kg $2.50; service wash per 3kg $4.50; ⏱ 8:30am-8pm Mon-Sat)

Lavandería Las Estrellas (Real de Guadalupe 75; per kg $1; ⏱ 6am-9pm)

MEDICAL SERVICES

Hospital Amigo del Niño y de la Madre (☎ 678-07-70; Insurgentes) General hospital with emergency facilities.

Sanatorio Dr Bonilla (☎ 678-07-93; Juárez 60) Dr Renato Zárate here is an English-speaking doctor.

MONEY

Most banks require a photocopy of your passport if you want to change cash or traveler's checks.

Banamex (Plaza 31 de Marzo; ⏱ 9am-4pm Mon-Fri, 10am-2pm Sat) Has an ATM and a dedicated exchange counter.

HSBC (Mazariegos 6; ⏱ 8am-7pm Mon-Sat, 10am-2:30pm Sun) Also has an ATM and is open the longest hours.

Lacantún Money Exchange (Real de Guadalupe 12A; ⏱ 9am-2pm & 4-8pm) Open outside bank hours but rates are worse.

POST & TELEPHONE

El Locutorio (☎ 631-60-63; Rosas 7C; ⏱ 8am-10pm) Offering inexpensive international calls, there are also branches at Belisario Domínguez 6A and Calle 20 de Noviembre 20A.

La Pared (☎ /fax 678-63-67; lapared9@yahoo.com; Hidalgo 2; ⏱ 10am-2pm & 4-8pm Tue-Sat, noon-2pm & 4-8pm Sun) The cheapest international calls in town: $0.15 a minute to the US and Canada, $0.20 to Western Europe.

Main post office (☎ 678-07-65; Allende 3)

TOURIST INFORMATION

Municipal tourist office (☎ 678-06-65; Palacio Municipal, Plaza 31 de Marzo; ⏱ 8am-8pm Mon-Fri, 9am-8pm Sat & Sun) Staff are generally helpful and knowledgeable about the San Cristóbal area.

State tourist office (☎ 678-65-70; Hidalgo 1B; ⏱ 8am-9pm Mon-Fri, 9am-8pm Sat, 9am-2pm Sun) Has English-speaking staff and plenty of leaflets.

Sights

PLAZA 31 DE MARZO

The leafy main plaza is a fine place to take in San Cristóbal's unhurried highland atmosphere. Shoe shiners, newspaper sellers and *ambulantes* (itinerant vendors) gather around the elaborate iron bandstand.

The **cathedral**, on the north side of the plaza, was begun in 1528 but, after several natural disasters, wasn't finally completed

till 1815. Sure enough, new earthquakes struck in 1816 and 1847, causing considerable damage. The cathedral was restored in 1920–22 and in the 1990s the detailed stonework on the west facade was attractively picked out in yellow, red and white paint. The gold-leaf interior has five gilded altarpieces featuring 18th-century paintings by Miguel Cabrera.

The **Hotel Santa Clara** (see p819), on the plaza's southeast corner, was built by Diego de Mazariegos, the Spanish conqueror of Chiapas. His coat of arms is engraved above the main portal. The house is a rare secular example of plateresque style in Mexico.

TEMPLO & EX-CONVENTO DE SANTO DOMINGO

North of the center, along 20 de Noviembre, the 16th-century **Templo de Santo Domingo** (admission free; ⏱ 6:30am-2pm & 4-8pm) is San Cristóbal's most beautiful church, especially when its pink facade catches the late-afternoon sun. This baroque frontage, with its outstanding filigree stucco work, was added in the 17th century and includes the double-headed Hapsburg eagle, symbol of the Spanish monarchy in those days. The interior is lavishly gilded, especially the ornate pulpit.

Around Santo Domingo and the neighboring **Templo de La Caridad** (built in 1712), Chamulan women and bohemian types from around Mexico conduct a colorful daily **crafts market** (see p823). The ex-monastery attached to Santo Domingo contains two interesting exhibits: one is the weavers' showroom of **Sna Jolobil** (see p823); the other is the **Centro Cultural de los Altos** (☎ 678-16-09; Calz Lázaro Cárdenas s/n; admission $3.25, free Sun & holidays; ⏱ 9am-6pm Tue-Sun) with a reasonable Spanish-language museum on the history of the San Cristóbal region.

NA BOLOM

A visit to this atmospheric **museum-research center** (☎ 678-14-18; www.nabolom.org; Guerrero 33; view house only $3.25, 1½hr tour in English or Spanish $4.25; ⏱ 10am-5pm, tours 11:30am & 4:30pm) is a fascinating experience. For many years Na Bolom was the home of Swiss anthropologist and photographer Gertrude Duby-Blom (Trudy Blom; 1901–93) who, with her Danish archaeologist husband Frans Blom (1893–1963), bought the 19th-century house in 1950.

While Frans explored and surveyed ancient Maya sites all over Chiapas (including Palenque, Toniná and Chinkultic), Trudy studied, photographed and fought to protect the scattered Lacandón people of eastern Chiapas and their jungle environment (see p845 and the boxed text, p825). Since Trudy's death, Na Bolom has continued the thrust of the Bloms' work, with the house operating as a museum and research center for the study and support of Chiapas' indigenous cultures and natural environment, and as a center for community and environmental programs in indigenous areas. The library of more than 9000 books and documents here is a major resource on the Maya.

Na Bolom means 'Jaguar House' in the Tzotzil language (as well as being a play on its former owners' name). It's full of photographs, archaeological and anthropological relics and books (see p813). The house tour provides a revealing insight into the lives of the Bloms and the Chiapas of half a century and more ago – though the picture presented of the Lacandones does dwell more on their past than their present.

Na Bolom also offers guest rooms (see p820) and meals (see p822), and accepts volunteers for work on some of its programs.

MERCADO MUNICIPAL
For a strong taste of the region's indigenous character, visit San Cristóbal's busy municipal **market** (☉ approx 7am-5pm), eight blocks north of the main plaza between Utrilla and Belisario Domínguez. It's quite an assault on the senses, as vendors peer from behind pyramids of tomatoes and mangoes, and you'll find dozens of varieties of chilies, as well as bloody butchers' stalls and fly-plagued dried-shrimp stands. Stay alert: tourists have had pockets picked and bags snatched in the market's narrow alleys.

MUSEO DE LA MEDICINA MAYA
The award-winning **Maya Medicine Museum** (☎ 678-54-38; www.medicinamaya.org; Av Salomón González Blanco 10; admission $2; ☉ 10am-6pm Tue-Fri, 10am-4pm Sat & Sun) does a great introductory job of explaining the system of traditional medicine used by many indigenous people in the Chiapas highlands. Traditional Maya medicine is a matter of praying to the spirit of the earth, listening to the voice of the

blood and expelling bad spirits from the soul, with the aid of candles, bones, pine needles, herbs and the occasional chicken sacrifice. This museum, on the northern edge of town, is run by Omiech, a group of 600 indigenous healers, midwives, herbalists and prayer specialists. Tableaux of (among other things) a ritual scene inside a church and a midwife assisting at a birth, and a video about the work of traditional midwives, help to bring it all alive. Explanatory material is available in English, Spanish, French and German. Also on the site is a medicinal plant garden, a herbal pharmacy and a *casa de curación*, where treatments are carried out.

MUSEO DE TRAJES REGIONALES SERGIO CASTRO
The privately run **Museum of Regional Costumes** (☎ 678-42-89; Guadalupe Victoria 38; admission by donation) can only be visited by appointment, best made by telephone the afternoon or morning before you want to visit. It's a fascinating collection of indigenous costumes, musical instruments and assorted curios belonging to Sergio Castro – a Mother Teresa-type figure, but male and Mexican – who can guide you round in several languages, including English, French and Italian. Your donation goes toward supporting Maya communities in Chiapas. The best time for visits (when Sergio is most likely to be available) is 5pm to 7pm.

CAFÉ MUSEO CAFÉ
This combined café and **coffee museum** (☎ 678-78-76; MA Flores 10; admission $1; ☉ 9am-9:30pm) is a venture of Coopcafé, a grouping of 17,000 small-scale, mainly indigenous, Chiapas coffee growers. The museum covers the history of coffee and its cultivation in Chiapas, from highly exploitative beginnings to the community-based indigenous coffee production that's increasingly well marketed today. The information is translated into English and you can taste some of that flavorful organic coffee in the café, where good snacks and breakfasts ($2 to $4.50) are served too.

MUSEO DEL ÁMBAR DE CHIAPAS
Chiapas amber – fossilized pine resin, around 30 million years old – is known for its clarity and diverse colors. Most is mined around Simojovel, north of San Cristóbal. The **Chiapas**

Amber Museum (www.museodelambar.com.mx; Plazuela de la Merced; admission $2; ✆ 10am-2pm & 4-7pm Tue-Sun) explains all things amber (with information sheets in English and other languages) and displays and sells some exquisitely carved items and insect-embedded pieces.

ARCO, TEMPLO & CENTRO CULTURAL DEL CARMEN

The **Arco de El Carmen**, at the southern end of the Andador Turístico on Hidalgo, dates from the late 17th century and was once the city's gateway. The ex-convent just east is a wonderful colonial building, with a large peaceful garden. It's now the **Centro Cultural El Carmen** (Hermanos Domínguez s/n; admission free; ✆ 9am-6pm Tue-Sun), hosting art and photography exhibitions and the odd musical event.

Courses

Several language schools offer instruction in Spanish, with flexibility to meet most level and schedule requirements. Weekly rates given below are for three hours' tuition five days a week, and seven nights' family accommodations with three meals a day. Many variations are available.

El Puente Spanish Language School (✆ 678-37-23; centroelpuente@prodigy.net.mx; Real de Guadalupe 55; individual/group per week $220/182) Housed in the Centro Cultural El Puente, which also has a vegetarian café, Internet café, cinema, gallery and alternative therapy center. Classes are offered for any period from one day.

Español Interactivo (✆ /fax 631-55-25; www.study spanishinchiapas.com; 5 de Mayo 67; small-group per week $203, individual classes-only per hr $11) This recently founded branch of a successful Oaxaca school offers optional cooking and dance classes and field trips, as well as language learning. Start any Monday for a minimum of one week.

Instituto Jovel (✆ /fax 678-40-69; www.institutojovel.com; MA Flores 21; individual/group per week $240/185, classes-only individual/group per hr $11/8) Instituto Jovel is professional and friendly, and has a top-class reputation among students. Most tuition is one-to-one. A $40 registration fee is required as well as the fees. Instituto Jovel has plans to move to Madero 45.

La Casa en el Árbol (✆ 674-52-72; www.lacasaenelarbol.org; Real de Mexicanos 10; individual tuition per hr $7.50, 7 days family accommodations $100) The 'Tree House' is an enthusiastic, socially committed, European-run school that teaches Tzeltal and Tzotzil as well as Spanish, and offers classes in English, French and Italian to locals. It offers lots of out-of-school activities and is also a base for volunteer programs.

Tours

Many agencies in San Cristóbal offer a variety of tours, often with guides who speak English, French or Italian (for tours of indigenous villages around San Cristóbal, see p825). Following are typical day-trip prices per person (usually with a minimum of four people):

Chiapa de Corzo & Cañón del Sumidero ($20, 6-7 hours)

Lagos de Montebello, Grutas de San Cristóbal, El Chiflón waterfalls ($25-30, 9-10 hours)

Palenque, Agua Azul, Misol-Ha ($28-33, 14 hours)

Recommended tour agencies (most open approximately 8am to 9pm) include the following:

Felipe Flores Tours & Travel (✆ /fax 678-39-96; www.felipeflores.com; Casa Felipe Flores, JF Flores 36)

Otisa (✆ 678-19-33; www.otisatravel.com; Real de Guadalupe 3C)

Trotamundos (✆ /fax 678-70-21; Real de Guadalupe 26C)

Viajes Chincultik (✆ 678-09-57; agchincultik@prodigy.net.mx; Casa Margarita, Real de Guadalupe 34)

Zapata Tours (✆ /fax 674-51-52; www.zapatatours.com; Insurgentes 19) Above Restaurant Madre Tierra.

The following agencies specialize in more active trips:

Explora (✆ 678-42-95; www.ecochiapas.com; 1 de Marzo 30; ✆ 9am-2pm & 4:30-8pm Mon-Sat) Adventure trips in and around the Lacandón Jungle (for five days $330, minimum four people) including river kayaking and rafting, nights in remote ecolodges and visits to Maya ruins; also, between July and October, raft/kayak expeditions in the remote and spectacular La Venta canyon in northwestern Chiapas.

Los Pingüinos (✆ 678-02-02; Ecuador 4B; www.bike mexico.com/pinguinos) Bicycle tours from half a day to two weeks (see also p824 and p826).

Festivals & Events

Semana Santa The crucifixion is acted out on Good Friday in the Barrio de Mexicanos in the northwest of town.

Feria de la Primavera y de la Paz (Spring and Peace Fair) Easter Sunday is the start of the week-long town fair, with parades, musical events, bullfights and so on.

Festival Cervantino Barroco In late October and early November, this is a lively cultural program with music, dance and theater.

Sleeping

San Cristóbal has a glut of budget-priced accommodations, but also a number of appealing and atmospheric midrange hotels often set in colonial or 19th-century mansions, and a smattering of top-end luxury. The high seasons here are during Semana Santa and the following week, the months of July and August, plus the Día de Muertos and Christmas–New Year's holidays.

BUDGET

Casa Margarita (☎ 678-09-57; agchincultik@prodigy.net.mx; Real de Guadalupe 34; s/d/tr/q $24/28/33/42; ⬚) This popular and well-run travelers' haunt offers tastefully presented, impeccably clean rooms, and a pretty courtyard at the center of things. Rates can go down by $5 to $10 off-season or if you don't want TV. There's free Internet and an in-house travel agency.

Posada México (☎ 678-00-14; posadamexico@hotmail.com; Josefa Ortiz de Domínguez 12; dm $6, s/d with shared bathroom $12.50/15, with private bathroom $14/19, all incl cooked breakfast; ⬚) This HI hostel is run by friendly young folk and has pretty gardens, good bright rooms and dorms (one for women only), a kitchen and free Internet, plus terraces, patios and lounges to relax in. You're asked to maintain quiet after 10pm. HI cards bring a $2 discount per room ($1 in dorms).

Posada Jovel (☎ 678-17-34; www.mundochiapas.com/hotelposadajovel; Paniagua 28; s/d without bathroom $10.50/16, with bathroom $19/26, 'hotel' r $36-39; ⊠ ⬚) Most rooms in the original 'posada' building have stripped wooden floors, bedside lights and highland blankets, while those in the 'hotel' section across the street, surrounding a pretty garden, are larger and brightly decorated, with cable TV.

Hostal Rincón de los Camellos (loscamellos@hotmail.com; Real de Guadalupe 110; dm $5, s/d/tr/q with shared bathroom $7.50/13.50/19/23, with private bathroom $10.50/17/23/28) 'Camels' Corner' is a clean, tranquil little spot run by welcoming French folk. The rooms, each colorfully and carefully decorated in a different country or continent theme, are set round two patios, and there's a grassy little garden at the back, plus a handwashing sink and free coffee.

Albergue Juvenil (Youth Hostel; ☎ 678-76-55; youth@sancristobal.com.mx; Juárez 2; dm $4.50-5, r $10.50; ⊠) This popular hostel offers solid bunk beds in clean four- to eight-person dorms, and private rooms for one or two. The communal bathrooms are spotless, and there's a kitchen and communal TV area.

Backpackers Hostel (☎ 674-05-25; www.mundomaya.com.mx; Real de Mexicanos 16; camping per person

$2.75, dm $5-6, s/d with shared bathroom $9.50/15, with private bathroom $14/19, all incl breakfast; ⬚) Backpackers is a friendly, sociable and well-run hostel with good dorm rooms (one for women only), a guest kitchen and a grassy garden. There's 10% off for HI cardholders.

Hotel Posada Tepeyac (☎ 678-01-18; Real de Guadalupe 40; s $8.50-18, d $11.50-26) A neat small hotel in the heart of the Real de Guadalupe travelers' scene. The 36 clean rooms, around a couple of pretty little patios, sport hard-to-ignore color schemes from blue-and-pink to yellow-and-orange.

Also recommended are the following:

Hotel Posada del Barón (☎ /fax 678-08-81; hotelbaron@hotmail.com; Belisario Domínguez 2; s/d/tr/q $17/20/25/29) Straightforward, good-value rooms along a wood-pillared patio.

Hotel Casa Real (☎ 678-13-03, 674-69-91; Real de Guadalupe 51; s/d with shared bathrooms $7/13.50) A quiet, amicable place, particularly popular among women travelers, with small clean rooms and two pretty little patios.

La Mariposa (☎ 674-58-59; Belisario Domínguez 28; dm $6, s/d $7/13.50) A friendly, informal, little Italian-run hostel.

MIDRANGE

Hotel Casavieja (☎ /fax 678-68-68; www.casavieja.com.mx; MA Flores 27; r/tr $70/75) The Casavieja is set in a beautifully renovated 18th-century house, with lots of wooden pillars, balustrades and old-world atmosphere, yet also modern comforts. The large comfortable rooms, arranged around flowery courtyards, all have two double beds, cable TV and phone. Service is attentive and friendly, and a neat restaurant serves traditional Mexican dishes. Rates come down by about $20 per room outside the high seasons.

Hotel Santa Clara (☎ 678-11-40; www.hotelescoloniales.com; Insurgentes 1; s/d/tr/q $47/61/70/80; ⬚) The Santa Clara, on the main plaza, has a number of sizable rooms, though they vary in quality so ask to look before you check in. Wooden bedsteads, pretty tiling, plus antique art and sculpture maintain an apt old-fashioned air in this historic building (see p816). There's a restaurant, a bar-lounge, a courtyard with caged red macaws and another with a swimming pool. Off-season, two people can often get a room for $47 with breakfast.

Hotel Posada de San Cristóbal (☎ 678-68-81; Insurgentes 3; s/d/tr $30/36/40; Ⓟ) Just a block off the plaza, this good-value small hotel has 10 large airy rooms, with plenty of colonial style, around a restaurant courtyard, and smaller newer rooms at the rear. All are attractively furnished, with cable TV.

Hotel El Paraíso (☎ 678-00-85; www.hotelposada paraiso.com; 5 de Febrero 19; s/d/tr $39/53/66) Colonial-style El Paraíso has a bright wood-pillared patio and courtyard garden, and lots of character. The high-ceilinged rooms are not huge, and some have limited natural light, but several are bi-level with an extra bed upstairs. The in-house restaurant, L'Eden, is excellent (see opposite).

Na Bolom (☎ 678-14-18; www.nabolom.org; Guerrero 33; s/d/tr/q incl breakfast $60/76/85/100; 🖳) This famous museum/research institute (p816), about 1km from the plaza, has 17 stylish guest rooms, 12 in the main house and five in the gardens, all loaded with character and all but one with log fires. Meals are served in the house's stately dining room. Room rates include a house tour and wireless Internet.

Hotel La Noria (☎ 678-68-98; www.hotel-lanoria .com; Insurgentes 18A; r $47, tr $56; 🅿 🖳) La Noria has 30 comfortable, brightly decorated, spotlessly clean rooms, with attractive tiled bathrooms, phone and cable TV. Rates drop by $10 to $20 outside high season.

Hotel Mansión de los Ángeles (☎ 678-11-73; hotelangeles@prodigy.net.com; Madero 17; s/d/tr/q $52/56/61/66; 🅿) This centrally situated 17th-century house has 20 good carpeted rooms around two patios. Rooms upstairs are bigger, with two double beds. One patio contains a wood-and-glass-roofed restaurant.

Hotel Jardines del Cerrillo (☎ /fax 678-12-83; www.hotelesjardines.com; Belisario Domínguez 27; r $36-37, with 2 d beds $50; 🅿) Friendly El Cerrillo has a flowery, glass-covered courtyard and a variety of good-sized, prettily painted, carpeted rooms with cable TV and phone.

Hotel Jardines del Centro (☎ /fax 678-81-39; www .hotelesjardines.com; 1 de Marzo 29; r $40, tr or q from $50; 🅿) Some of the brightly painted rooms here surround a very pretty garden patio; others are on three floors around a second courtyard where cars can be parked.

Hotel Diego de Mazariegos (☎ 678-08-33; www .diegodemazariegos.com; 5 de Febrero 1; r/tr/q $80/88/93; 🅿) This classy, long-established hotel occupies two 18th-century mansions built around beautiful, wide courtyards. The 76 rooms are large, and decked out with traditional fabrics and fittings, but also have modern comforts including cable TV. Some have fireplaces ($1.25 per load of wood). The hotel has a lively tequila-and-mariachi-theme bar.

TOP END

Parador San Juan de Dios (☎ /fax 678-11-67; www .sanjuandios.com; Calz Roberta 16; ste $165; 🅿) A stunning boutique hotel on the northern edge of town, the Parador San Juan de Dios offers voluminous and luxurious suites furnished with fascinating antique and modern art and artisanry (much of which is for sale). The hotel occupies the former Rancho Harvard, which dates from the 17th century and has lodged many anthropologists and archaeologists. It has beautiful gardens, vast lawns and a top-class restaurant with an inventive, expensive Chiapas/Mediterranean menu. Off-season deals can reduce rates to $94 for two, including breakfast.

Hotel Casa Mexicana (☎ 678-06-98; www.hotelcasa mexicana.com; 28 de Agosto 1; s/d/tr $80/89/102, ste $140-168; 🅿 🖳) A gallery as well as hotel of colonial charm, the stylish and inviting Casa Mexicana displays modern art alongside traditional fabrics and solid wood pillars and furnishings. The main patio is filled with a lush tropical garden, the 55 attractive rooms are equipped with cable TV, and there's a restaurant, bar and sauna.

Villas Casa Morada (☎ 678-44-40; www.geocities .com/lacasamorada; Dugelay 45; studio/villa $40/85; 🖳) These are tasteful, modern apartments with kitchen, phone, cable TV, fireplaces and chamber-maid service.

Eating

The travel and tourism scene has yielded a huge variety of cuisine in San Cristóbal's increasingly sophisticated and professional restaurants. It's possible to find most kinds

---

THE AUTHOR'S CHOICE

Mayambé (☎ 674-62-78; Real de Guadalupe 66; mains $3.75-6.50; ☯ 9:30am-11pm or later; **V**) This superb courtyard restaurant boasts a wonderful Asian, Middle Eastern and Mediterranean menu, including plenty of vegetarian options. Tuck into delicious Indian and Thai curries, Greek and Lebanese treats including great hummus and falafel, and to-die-for lassis and juices. There's mellow live music some evenings, and a fireplace to warm things up on those cool highland nights.

---

of global food here, and there's plenty of choice for vegetarians.

REAL DE GUADALUPE AREA

El Gato Gordo (☎ 678-83-13; Real de Guadalupe 20; mains $2.50-4.50; ☯ 1-11pm Wed-Mon; **V**) Gato Gordo attracts travelers in droves for its excellent, well-prepared food at terrific prices. There's an unbeatable set lunch ($2.50) and excellent pasta, crepes, Mexican snacks and meat dishes, plus a great choice of drinks.

Ristorante Italiano Da Angelo (Real de Guadalupe 40; mains $4.50-7.50; ☯ 2-11pm Wed-Sun, 6:30-11pm Mon & Tue; **V**) Good Italian food and warm Italian atmosphere are a surefire hit. Pizzas are constructed at a counter in the dining area, overlooked by the obligatory pix of the old country. Plenty of pasta, meat dishes and wine are on offer too.

La Casa del Pan Papalotl (☎ 678-37-23; Centro Cultural El Puente, Real de Guadalupe 55; ☯ 9am-10pm; **V**) This excellent courtyard vegetarian restaurant does a particularly good buffet lunch, costing from $3.50 to $6, depending how many courses you have.

Pierre Restaurant Francés (☎ 678-72-11; Real de Guadalupe 73; mains $5-15; ☯ 1:30-10:30pm) A super French restaurant whose perfectionist owner even makes his own pasta, butter, cheese and bread. Sunday is the best buy at $9.50 for a four-course lunch.

Las Margaritas (☎ 678-09-57; Real de Guadalupe 34A; mains $4.50-10) The restaurant at Casa Margarita has fairly generous portions and efficient service, though prices are a touch high. Live music some nights usually gets people dancing.

Restaurante Plaza Real (☎ 678-09-92; Real de Guadalupe 5; mains $4.50-9.50; ☯ 7am-11pm; **V**) The

well-prepared meat, poultry and vegetarian dishes at this classy eatery have international appeal, but also authentic Mexican flavor. It's set in the tranquil, wood-pillared courtyard of what was once Chiapas' state congress building, surrounded by upmarket craft and jewelry shops.

Santé Caffé (Madero 22; light meals $2.50-5; ☯ 9am-midnight or 1am; **V**) With a mod design and cool jazz soundtracks that you might find in a New York lounge, Santé has something different on the menu too. It's a tough choice between avocado and goat-cheese mousse, sushi rolls, crepes, creative salads and platters of cheese or cold meats.

PLAZA 31 DE MARZO & WEST

L'Eden (☎ 678-00-85; Hotel El Paraíso, 5 de Febrero 19; mains $4.50-11.50; ☯ 7am-noon & 1-11pm) This quality restaurant's tempting European and Mexican menu includes *sopa azteca* and succulent meat dishes. There's a lengthy wine list too, including French and Spanish vintages.

El Caldero (5 de Mayo 4; soups $3.50; ☯ 1-10pm Thu-Tue) Simple, friendly little El Caldero specializes in delicious, filling Mexican soups – *pozole* (shredded pork in broth), *mondongo* (tripe), *caldo* (broth) – with avocados, tortillas and various salsas. Great for an authentic and inexpensive local meal.

Los Barrios (☎ 678-19-10; Guadalupe Victoria 25; mains $6-9.50; ☯ 1-10pm) This newcomer serves up innovative and tasty Mexican fare – try the breaded prawns in coconut-and-tamarind sauce, or banana-stuffed chicken breast in spicy *adobo* (chili) sauce, or one of the imaginative salads.

SOUTH OF PLAZA 31 DE MARZO

Madre Tierra (☎ 678-42-97; Insurgentes 19; mains $2.50-5; ☯ 8am-10pm; **V**) Madre Tierra has a tranquil patio and atmospheric dining room for an eclectic, appetizing and mainly vegetarian menu: wholesome soups, lasagne, quiches, great sandwiches, salads and jacket potatoes. Breakfasts here ($2.50 to $3.50) are superb too.

Restaurante Tuluc (☎ 678-20-90; Insurgentes 5; breakfasts $2.75-3.75, mains $4-7; ☯ 7am-10pm) Tuluc, one and a half blocks from the plaza, consistently serves up a big variety of good, mainly Mexican food at reasonable prices.

La Paloma (☎ 678-15-47; Hidalgo 3; mains $4-11; ☯ 9am-11:45pm) An elegant, spacious restaurant

TABASCO & CHIAPAS

with a glass atrium roof and greenery that includes bamboo and banana trees. The menu is creative and varied, with tasty pasta, beef, chicken and fish dishes.

Emiliano's Moustache (☎ 678-72-46; Rosas 7; breakfasts & snacks $1.75-5, mains $2.75-6; ☽ 8am-1am) This large, enjoyable place specializes in tacos filled with combinations of meat, vegetable or cheese. The meat *filetes* are also excellent, and vegetarian possibilities exist too (including veggie tacos).

NORTH OF PLAZA 31 DE MARZO

La Casa del Pan (☎ 678-58-95; Dr Navarro 10; snacks & mains $2.75-5.50; ☽ 8am-10pm Tue-Sun; Ⓥ) This relaxed restaurant-bakery emphasizes local organic ingredients, offering great breakfasts and lots of vegetarian fare through the day: whole-wheat sandwiches, salads, *hojaldres* (vegetable strudels) and pizzas.

Naturalíssimo (☎ 678-99-98; 20 de Noviembre 4; snacks & mains $2.50-3.75; ☽ 7am-8pm; ✗ Ⓥ) A health-food store-cum-restaurant in a courtyard with a splashing fountain, Naturalíssimo serves good breakfasts, snacks and set meals, and lush *licuados* and juices.

Na Bolom (☎ 678-14-18; Guerrero 33; dinner $10.50) For unique ambience, reserve for dinner (7pm) with the assembled company at Na Bolom (p816). Everyone sits at one long wooden table in the Bloms' old dining room. Vegetables are organically grown in the garden.

Drinking
COFFEE

Many San Cristóbal cafés advertise 'organic,' 'indigenous,' 'cooperative' or at least 'ecological' Chiapas coffee. Following are three courtyard places that do genuinely serve and promote organic, indigenous-grown (and tasty) coffee:

Café La Selva (☎ 678-72-43; Rosas 9; ☽ 9am-11:30pm)

Café Museo Café (☎ 678-78-76; MA Flores 10; ☽ 9am-9:30pm)

Cafetería Maya (☎ 678-91-46; 20 de Noviembre 12C; ☽ 8am-10pm) Has a permanent photo exhibition on the Zapatista movement.

BARS

Any night of the week except Sunday you can hear at least five live bands within a couple of blocks of the plaza, in venues where Mexicans and foreigners mingle easily. The music is as eclectic as the musicians –

reggae, ska, rock (*en español* and *en inglés*), hip-hop, tropical, Cuban, Mexican *son*. Atmosphere in nearly all these places is reassuringly relaxed and informal – no heavy bouncers or face control.

Los Amigos (Honduras 4; ☽ 9am-8pm) A popular but spacious and unraucous cantina, Los Amigos is close to the Chamula van terminal. From 2pm to 5pm it offers two beers for $2.50, with large tasty *botanas* (free snacks) – can be a lot of fun. Women are welcome.

Entertainment
CLUBS & LIVE MUSIC

Bar Revolución (1 de Marzo 11; ☽ noon-11:30pm Mon-Sat) There's a great atmosphere here, with two nightly bands and travelers and locals doing their best to converse and listen to the music simultaneously.

El Circo (☎ 678-56-63; 20 de Noviembre 7; admission after midnight $1; ☽ 8pm-3am Mon-Sat) A slightly hipper venue across the street from the Revolución. A reggae/rock band normally plays in the front bar, while the larger electro/pop dance room in the back opens Thursday to Saturday. Both are usually packed.

Madre Tierra (☎ 678-42-97; Insurgentes 19; ☽ 8am-3pm) The third stop on San Cristóbal's most trodden nocturnal 'Ruta Maya,' the Madre Tierra's smoky Bar Upstairs presents live reggae and Cuban *son* on alternate nights.

Blue (☎ 678-22-00; Rosas 2; admission after 11pm Thu-Sat around $2; ☽ 8pm-3am Mon-Wed, 9pm-4am or 5am Thu-Sat) Also very popular, Blue rocks on a little later than the foregoing places and feels the need to employ a couple of (fairly friendly) bouncers. A reggae/ska band was resident at research time. There's billiards in one room.

Latino's (☎ 678-99-27; Madero 23; admission Thu-Sat $1.50; ☽ 8pm-3am Mon-Sat) A bright restaurant-cum-dance spot where the city's *salseros* gather to groove. A salsa/merengue/cumbia band plays Thursday to Saturday.

La Pera (☎ 678-12-09; MA Flores 23; ☽ 1-11pm) An artsy but relaxed café-gallery-bar, not too sceney, La Pera often stages live music late in the week. It could be blues, jazz, *trova* or something completely different.

CINEMA

San Cristóbal is a fine place to immerse yourself in Mexican- and Latin American-theme cinema, political documentaries and art-house movies. The following places show two films a day (usually at 6pm and 8pm), charging $2 per movie:

Cineclub La Ventana (☎ 678-42-97; Madre Tierra, Insurgentes 19) Three screenings Friday to Sunday.

Cinema El Puente (☎ 678-37-23; Centro Cultural El Puente, Guadalupe 55) Closed Sunday.

Kinoki (1 de Marzo 22)

Shopping

The outstanding indigenous *artesanías* of the Chiapas highlands are textiles such as *huipiles* (sleeveless tunics), blouses and blankets; Tzotzil weavers are some of the most skilled and inventive in Mexico. Another Chiapas specialty is amber, sold in numerous shops alongside silver, turquoise, jade, red coral and lapis-lazuli in a range of well-made, attractive jewelry. When buying amber, beware of plastic imitations: the real thing is never cold and never heavy, and when rubbed should produce static electricity and a resiny smell.

The thickest clusters of craft shops are on Real de Guadalupe and the Andador Turístico. But there's also a big range of goods at good prices at the busy daily crafts market around Santo Domingo and La Caridad churches, including local and Guatemalan textiles, woolen rugs and blankets, leather bags and belts, Zapatista dolls, hippie jewelry, *animalitos* (little pottery animal figures) from Amatenango del Valle and more.

Sna Jolobil (☎ 678-26-46; Calz Lázaro Cárdenas s/n; ⊗ 9am-2pm & 4-6pm Mon-Sat) Next to Santo Domingo, Sna Jolobil shows and sells some of the very best *huipiles*, blouses, skirts, rugs and other woven items, with prices ranging from a few dollars for small items to over $1000 for the best *huipiles* (the fruit of many months' work). Sna Jolobil is a cooperative of 800 indigenous women weavers from the Chiapas highlands, founded in the 1970s to foster the important indigenous art of backstrap-loom weaving. It has revived many half-forgotten techniques and designs.

Casa de Las Artesanías de Chiapas (☎ 678-11-80; cnr Niños Héroes & Hidalgo; ⊗ 10am-9pm Mon-Sat, 10am-3pm Sun) This also sells a good range of Chiapas crafts.

Museo del Jade (☎ 678-25-57; 16 de Septiembre 16) Has particularly classy jewelry, with pre-Hispanic reproductions carved in jade and other materials, and also contains a museum

section (admission $2.75, open noon to 8pm Monday to Saturday, until 6pm Sunday) with replicas of ancient Olmec pieces and a full-size replica of Pakal's tomb at Palenque.

You'll also find great jewelry at pretty fair prices at the following places:

El Árbol de La Vida (☎ 678-50-50; Real de Guadalupe 27)

La Galería (☎ 678-15-47; Hidalgo 3) Also with textiles, Huichol art and pre-Hispanic reproductions.

Lágrimas de la Selva (Hidalgo 1C)

Sensaciones (☎ 631-55-80; Hidalgo 4A)

Getting There & Away

Instituto Nacional de Migración (☎ 678-65-94; Diagonal El Centenario 30) is on a corner with the Pan-American Hwy, 1.2km west of the OCC bus station.

From Tuxtla Gutiérrez you'll either travel here via serpentine Hwy 190, or by a fast new toll highway that when fully open will reduce the 80km trip from two hours to little more than one. At the time of writing only the more westerly half of the new highway was open – owing to a protracted legal dispute over an uncompleted bridge – and large vehicles such as full-size buses and trucks were unable to use it at all. Smaller vehicles including cars and vans can use the completed part for a toll of $1.50.

See p791 for a warning about Hwy 199 from San Cristóbal to Palenque.

AIR

San Cristóbal's airport, about 15km from town on the Palenque road, has no regular passenger flights. **Mexicana** (☎ 678-93-09; Belisario Domínguez 2B) sells flights from Tuxtla Gutiérrez.

BUS, COLECTIVO & VAN

There are around a dozen terminals, mostly on or just off the Pan-American Hwy. Most important is the 1st-class terminal of **OCC** (☎ 678-02-91; cnr Pan-American Hwy & Insurgentes), also used by ADO and UNO 1st-class and deluxe buses, and 2nd-class Transportes Dr Rodulfo Figueroa (TRF). Tickets for all these lines are sold at **Ticket Bus** (☎ 678-85-03; Real de Guadalupe 5A; ⊗ 9am-2pm & 4-7pm Mon-Sat, 9am-4pm Sun) in the center of town.

Avisa (2nd-class) is 150m west of OCC along the highway; 1st-class **AEXA** (☎ 678-61-78) and 2nd-class Ómnibus de Chiapas share a terminal on the south side of the highway; and various Suburban-type vans and *colectivo* taxi services have depots on the highway in the same area. Daily departures are listed in the box below:

For Guatemala, several agencies, including Viajes Chincultik and Otisa (see p818), offer daily van service to Huehuetenango (around $35, five hours), Quetzaltenango ($40, eight hours), Panajachel ($50, 10 hours) and Antigua ($60, 12 hours).

CAR

Optima (☎ 674-54-09; optimacar1@hotmail.com; Mazariegos 39) rents VW Beetles for $52 per day, including unlimited kilometers, insurance and taxes. It will often give large discounts for payment in cash, and has more expensive cars, too.

Getting Around

Combis go up Rosas from the Pan-American Hwy to the town center. Taxis cost $1.75 within the town ($2.25 after 11pm).

Friendly **Los Pingüinos** (8am-8pm ☎ 678-02-02; Ecuador 4B; www.bikemexico.com/pinguinos; bike hire 3/4/5/9/24 hrs $7.50/9.50/10.50/11.50/14; office ☻ 10am-2:30pm & 3:30-7pm Mon-Sat) rents decent-quality mountain bikes with lock and

maps. You need to deposit your passport or credit card. It can advise on good and safe routes.

Also-friendly, **Croozy Scooters** (☎ 631-43-29; www.prodigyweb.net.mx/croozyscooters; Belisario Domínguez 7; scooter hire 1/5/9/24 hrs $7/19/24/33; ☻ 9am-7pm), run by a pair of young Australians, rents well-maintained 90cc scooters. The price includes insurance, maps and helmets; deposit your passport.

AROUND SAN CRISTÓBAL

The inhabitants of the beautiful Chiapas highlands are descended from the ancient Maya and maintain some unique customs, costumes and beliefs (see the boxed text, opposite).

Markets and festivals often give the most interesting insight into indigenous life, and there are plenty of them. Weekly **markets** at the villages are nearly always on Sunday. Proceedings start as early as dawn, and wind down by lunchtime. Occasions like **Carnaval** (late February/early March), for which Chamula is particularly famous, **Semana Santa**, and **Día de Muertos** (November 2) are celebrated almost everywhere.

SAN CRISTÓBAL DE LAS CASAS BUS SCHEDULE

Destination	Price	Duration	Frequency
Campeche	$27-33	11hr	2 from OCC terminal
Cancún	$51-60	16-18hr	4 from OCC
Chiapa de Corzo	$2	1¼hr	Avisa every 30min 5am-8pm
Ciudad Cuauhtémoc (Guatemalan border)	$8.50	3½hr	5 from OCC)
Comitán	$2.50-3.50	1¾hr	12 from OCC, Avisa every 30min 5am-8pm & other buses, vans and *colectivo* taxis leave from the south side of the Pan-American Hwy
Mérida	$38-44	13hr	2 from OCC
Mexico City (TAPO)	$63-94	14hr	8 from OCC
Oaxaca	$29-35	12-18hr	3 from OCC
Ocosingo	$2.75-3.75	2¼hr	13 from OCC, 4 AEXA & *colectivo* taxis and vans leave every few minutes 3am-9pm from the north side of the Pan-American Hwy
Palenque	$7-11	5hr	11 from OCC & 4 AEXA
Pochutla	$28	10-14hr	2 from OCC
Puerto Escondido	$31	11-15hr	2 from OCC
Tuxtla Gutiérrez	$2.50-4.50	1¼-1¾hr	20 from OCC, 4 AEXA, Ómnibus de Chiapas every 20min 6am-6pm, Avisa every 30min 5am-8pm, Taxis Jovel *colectivos* operate 24-hours and Corazón de María vans leave 4am-9pm
Villahermosa	$16-24	7-8hr	3 from OCC

INDIGENOUS PEOPLES OF CHIAPAS

Of the 4.2 million people of Chiapas, around 1.25 million are indigenous (mostly from Maya groups). This high indigenous presence and the cultural variety it entails are among the most fascinating aspects of the state. Each of the eight principal indigenous peoples of Chiapas has its own language, beliefs and customs.

The indigenous people who travelers are most likely to encounter are the Tzotziles, who mainly live in a highland area centered on San Cristóbal de Las Casas (about 50km from east to west, and 100km from north to south), and the Tzeltales, chiefly found in the region between San Cristóbal and the Lacandón Jungle. Each of these groups is about 400,000 strong. Their traditional religious life is nominally Catholic, but involves some distinctly pre-Hispanic elements and goes hand in hand with some unusual forms of social organization, such as the annual rotation of the honored but expensive community leadership positions known as *cargos*. Most of the people live in the hills outside the villages, which are primarily market and ceremonial centers.

Tzotzil and Tzeltal clothing is among the most varied, colorful and elaborately worked in Mexico. It not only identifies wearers' villages but also marks them as inheritors of ancient Maya traditions. Many of the seemingly abstract designs on these costumes are in fact stylized snakes, frogs, butterflies, birds, saints and other beings. Some motifs have religious-magical functions: scorpions, for example, can be a symbolic request for rain, since they are believed to attract lightning.

The Lacandones, long the most mysterious of Chiapas indigenous groups because they dwelt deep in the Lacandón Jungle and largely avoided contact with the outside world until the 1950s, now number 800 or so and live in three main settlements in that same region. Low-key tourism is quite developed in the largest village, Lacanjá Chansayab (see p845). You may encounter Lacandones at Palenque, where they sell bows, arrows and other crafts, and are readily recognizable in their white tunics and with their long black hair cut in a fringe. Most Lacandones have now abandoned their traditional animist religion in favor of Presbyterian or evangelical forms of Christianity.

Other Chiapas indigenous peoples include about 200,000 Choles, mainly in the north of the state, some 50,000 Zoques in the northwest, and the 50,000 Tojolabales, mainly in the eastern municipality of Las Margaritas.

Today, long-standing indigenous ways of life are being challenged both by evangelical Christianity – opposed to many traditional animist-Catholic practices – and by the Zapatista movement, which rejects the cargo system and is raising the rights and profile of women. The Zapatista revolution was in large measure a response to the plight of indigenous peoples, who are treated as second-class citizens in economic and political terms, and who live, on the whole, on the least productive land in the state. Many highland indigenous people have emigrated to the Lacandón Jungle to clear new land, or to the cities in search of work. But despite their problems, indigenous identities and self-respect survive. Indigenous people may be suspicious of outsiders, and may resent interference in their religious observances or other aspects of life, but if treated with due respect they are likely to respond in kind.

During Carnaval, groups of minstrels stroll the roads in tall, pointed hats with long, colored tassels, strumming guitars and chanting. Much *posh*, an alcoholic drink made from sugarcane, is drunk.

It's particularly important to be respectful of local customs in this part of Mexico (see p791). While walking or riding by horse or bicycle by day along the main roads to Chamula and Zinacantán should not be risky, however it's not wise to wander into unfrequented areas or down isolated tracks.

Tours

Exploring the region with a good guide can open up doors and give you a feel for indigenous life and customs you could never gain alone. Many San Cristóbal agencies (see p818) offer four- or five-hour trips to local villages, usually San Juan Chamula and Zinacantán.

Alex & Raúl (☎ 967-678-37-41; alexraultours@yahoo .com.mx; per person $12.50) Enjoyable and informative English or Spanish minibus tours; Alex, Raúl and/or a colleague wait by San Cristóbal's cathedral at 9:30am daily. Trips to Tenejapa (Thursday and Sunday), San Andrés

Larraínzar or Amatenango del Valle ($14) can also be arranged for a minimum of four people.

Mercedes Tour (☎ 967-674-03-76; alexvald@yahoo .com; 5-6hr trips per person $12.50) The Mercedes Tour, led for years by Mercedes Hernández Gómez, a fluent English-speaker who grew up in Zinacantán, is now usually led by colleagues as Mercedes has moved on to other interests, including Buddhism. It's still an informative and entertaining trip (in English only), again dwelling on local Maya cosmology and religion. Look for someone twirling a colorful umbrella just before 9am daily near the kiosk in San Cristóbal's main plaza.

Viajes Chincultik (☎ 967-678-09-57; agchincultik@ prodigy.net.com; Casa Margarita, Real de Guadalupe 34; per person $14) Informative Chamula and Zinacantán trips in English, Italian and French, with an emphasis on history, shamanism and Maya cosmology.

BICYCLE & SCOOTER TOURS

Croozy Scooters (See also p824) Does free tours to Chamula and Zinacantán some days of the week, if you take its nine-hour (9am to 6pm) scooter rental option.

Los Pingüinos (☎ 8am-8pm 678-02-02; www.bike mexico.com/pinguinos; Ecuador 4B, San Cristóbal; ☯ office 10am-2:30pm & 3:30-7pm Mon-Sat) The friendly English-, German- and Spanish- speaking folk at Los Pingüinos operate guided half-day mountain-bike tours of 20km to 25km, costing $25 to $27 per person. Most trips are to little-visited scenic country areas east of San Cristóbal, passing through cloud forests; one route crosses a limestone bridge. Reserve one day or more ahead. They also offer longer tours (up to several days) around the Chiapas highlands and beyond.

HORSEBACK RIDING

Almost any travel agency or place to stay in San Cristóbal can arrange a four- or five-hour guided ride to San Juan Chamula for $9 to $12. Ask around for current recommendations. Don't take anything too valuable with you: riders have on occasion been robbed en route.

Getting There & Away

Transportation to most villages goes from points around the Mercado Municipal in San Cristóbal. Some services finish by lunchtime. Combis to San Juan Chamula ($0.70) leave from Calle Honduras frequently from 4am to about 6pm; for Zinacantán, combis and *colectivo* taxis (both $1) go at least hourly, 5am to 7pm, from a yard off Robledo.

Reserva Ecológica Huitepec

The entrance to **Huitepec Ecological Reserve** (self-guided visits $1.50; ☯ 9am-3pm Tue-Sun) is about 3.5km from San Cristóbal, on the road to San Juan Chamula. Set on the slopes of Cerro Huitepec (2750m), an extinct volcano, the reserve rises from evergreen oak woods to cloud forest rich with bromeliads, ferns and orchids. Huitepec's self-guided trail starts at the entrance and not only takes you into rare cloud forest but also gives you the chance to see some 100 bird species and to enjoy superb long-distance views. The trail is 2.5km, with a total ascent of 250m, and most people spend around two to 2½ hours on it.

San Juan Chamula

pop 3100 / elevation 2200m

The Chamulans are a fiercely independent Tzotzil group, about 80,000 strong. Their main village, San Juan Chamula, 10km northwest of San Cristóbal, is the center for some unique religious practices – although conflicts between adherents of traditional Chamulan Catholicism and converts to evangelical, Pentecostal and other branches of Christianity have resulted in the expulsion of many thousands of Chamulans from their villages in the past couple of decades. Here, as at other places in Mexico and Central America, rejection of Catholicism was also in part a political rejection of the longstanding supremacy of the Catholic mestizo majority. In San Juan Chamula, evangelism is associated with the Zapatista movement. Most of the exiles now inhabit the shantytowns around San Cristóbal.

Chamulan men wear loose homespun tunics of white wool (sometimes, in cool weather, thicker black wool), but *cargo-holders* – those with important religious and ceremonial duties – wear a sleeveless black tunic and a white scarf on the head. Chamulan women wear fairly plain white or blue blouses and/or shawls and woolen skirts.

Outsiders are free to visit San Juan Chamula, but a big sign at the entrance to the village strictly forbids photography in the village church or at rituals. Nearby, around the shell of an older church, is the village **graveyard**, with black crosses for people who died old, white for the young, and blue for others. There's a small village museum, **Ora Ton** (admission by donation; ☯ 9am-5pm) near this old church.

Starting at dawn on Sunday, people from the hills stream into the village for the

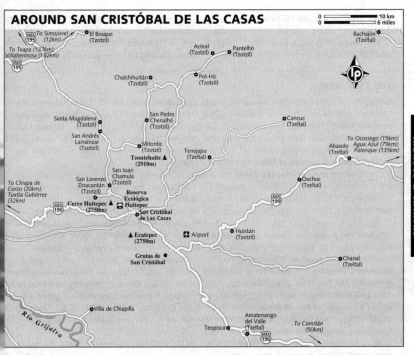

AROUND SAN CRISTÓBAL DE LAS CASAS

0 .... 10 km
0 .... 6 miles

To Simojovel (12km) — MEX 195
El Bosque (Tzotzil)

To Teapa (137km); Villahermosa (182km) — MEX 195

Acteal (Tzotzil) • Pantelhó (Tzotzil)

Bachajón (Tzeltal)

Chalchihuitán (Tzotzil)

Pol-Hó (Tzotzil)

Santa Magdalena (Tzotzil)

San Pedro Chenalhó (Tzotzil)

Cancuc (Tzeltal)

San Andrés Larraínzar (Tzotzil)

Mitontic (Tzotzil)

Tenejapa (Tzeltal)

Tzontehuitz ▲ (2910m)

San Juan Chamula (Tzotzil)

San Lorenzo Zinacantán (Tzotzil)

To Ocosingo (15km); Agua Azul (79km); Palenque (135km)

Abasolo (Tzeltal)

To Chiapa de Corzo (20km); Tuxtla Gutiérrez (32km) — MEX 190

Cerro Huitepec ▲ (2750m)

Reserva Ecológica Huitepec

Oxchuc (Tzeltal)

MEX 199

San Cristóbal de Las Casas

▲ Ecatepec (2750m)

✈ Airport

Huixtán (Tzotzil)

Grutas de San Cristóbal

Chanal (Tzeltal)

Río Grijalva

Villa de Chiapilla

Amatenango del Valle (Tzeltal)

To Comitán (50km)

Teopisca • — MEX 190

weekly **market** and to visit the main church. Busloads of tourists also stream in, so you might prefer to come another day (though avoid Wednesday, when the church is often all but deserted due to local superstitions). Local crafts (mainly textiles) are sold every day for the passing tourist trade.

The **Templo de San Juan**, Chamula's main church, white with a very colorfully painted door arch, stands beside the main plaza. A sign tells visitors to obtain tickets ($1.50) at the **tourist office** (🕑 9am-6pm), beside the plaza, before entering the church. Inside, hundreds of flickering candles, clouds of incense, and worshipers kneeling with their faces to the pine-needle-carpeted floor make a powerful impression. Chanting *curanderos* (literally 'curers'; medicine men or women) may be rubbing patients' bodies with eggs or bones. Images of saints are surrounded with mirrors and dressed in holy garments. Chamulans revere San Juan Bautista (St John the Baptist) above Christ, and his image occupies a more important place in the church.

Christian festivals are interwoven with older ones here: the important **Carnaval** cele-

brations also mark the five 'lost' days of the ancient Long Count calendar, which divided time into 20-day periods (18 of these make 360 days, leaving five to complete a year). Other festivals include ceremonies for San Juan Bautista (with up to 20,000 people gathering to dance and drink on June 24) and the annual change of cargos (December 30 to January 1).

San Lorenzo Zinacantán

pop 3700 / elevation 2558m

The orderly village of San Lorenzo Zinacantán, about 11km northwest of San Cristóbal, is the main village of the Zinacantán municipality (population 45,000). Zinacantán people, like Chamulans, are Tzotzil. The men wear distinctive pink tunics embroidered with flower motifs and may sport flat, round, ribboned palm hats. Women wear pink or purple shawls over richly embroidered blouses.

A small **market** is held on Sundays until noon, and during fiesta times. The most important celebrations are for La Virgen de La Candelaria (August 7–11) and San Sebastián (January 19–22).

Zinacantecos are great flower growers and have a particular love for the geranium, which – along with pine branches – is offered in rituals for a wide range of benefits.

The huge central **Iglesia de San Lorenzo** (admission $1.50) was rebuilt following a fire in 1975. Photography is banned in the church and churchyard. The small thatched-roofed

THE ZAPATISTAS

On the day of Nafta's initiation (January 1, 1994), a previously unknown leftist guerrilla army, the Ejército Zapatista de Liberación Nacional (EZLN, Zapatista National Liberation Army), emerged from the forests to occupy San Cristóbal de Las Casas and other towns in Chiapas. Linking anti-globalization rhetoric with Mexican revolutionary slogans their declared goal was to overturn a wealthy local oligarchy's centuries-old hold on land, resources and power and to improve the wretched living standards of Mexico's indigenous people.

The Mexican army evicted the Zapatistas in days, with about 150 people (mostly Zapatistas) killed in the fighting, and the rebels retreated to hideouts on the fringes of the Lacandón Jungle to wage a propaganda war, mainly fought via the Internet. The Zapatistas' balaclava-clad, pipe-puffing Subcomandante Marcos (actually a former university professor named Rafael Guillén) rapidly became a cult figure. High-profile conventions against neoliberalism were held and international supporters flocked to Zapatista headquarters at La Realidad, 80km southeast of Comitán. Zapatista-aligned peasants took over hundreds of farms and ranches in Chiapas.

Zapatista and Mexican government negotiators agreed to a set of accords on indigenous rights and autonomy at San Andrés Larraínzar, north of San Cristóbal, in 1996. However, the governing PRI (Institutional Revolutionary Party) never ratified these agreements, and through 1997 and 1998, tension and killings escalated in Chiapas. A PRI-linked paramilitary group massacred 45 people in the village of Acteal, north of San Cristóbal, in 1997. By 1999, an estimated 21,000 villagers had fled their homes after the Mexican army, aided and abetted by paramilitaries, launched a campaign of intimidation.

After Vicente Fox was elected Mexico's president in 2000, two attempts to make the necessary constitutional changes failed, as Congress watered down drafts based closely on the San Andrés accords. The Zapatistas refused to participate in further talks, concentrating instead on consolidating their revolution and their autonomy in the villages of highland and eastern Chiapas, where their support lay. In 2003 they established five regional 'Juntas de Buen Gobierno' (Committees of Good Government), in villages where they also started to set up schools and clinics. Parts of the Chiapas countryside remain tense, and occasional incidents have propelled the unresolved conflict onto the international news agenda – such as the Zapatista seizure of the American-owned Rancho Esmeralda near Ocosingo in 2003. The Zapatistas have also loudly denounced the concept of ecotourism.

By 2005 Zapatista political influence was slight outside their own enclaves, and many former supporters were disillusioned with the EZLN's intransigent stance. Then suddenly, after four years of silence, Marcos announced a new Zapatista political struggle for all Mexico's exploited and marginalized people, not just the indigenous. In the 'Sixth Declaration of the Lacandón Jungle,' Marcos rejected all cooperation or dialog with mainstream political parties, launching instead La Otra Campaña (The Other Campaign), a movement to run parallel to, but distinct from, Mexico's 2006 presidential election campaign. On January 1, 2006, Marcos, now styling himself Subdelegado Zero, set off by motorcycle from the jungle village of La Garrucha at the head of a six-month Zapatista tour of all Mexico's states. The aim was to forge a new leftist political front by making contact with other groups around the country, to develop a new methodology of 'liberation from below' and a new civilian, peaceful, anticapitalist approach to politics.

If it sounds hopelessly vague and idealistic, the Zapatista leadership has pointed out: 'For 500 years the authorities have refused to listen to us. We have time on our side.' You can find out how La Otra Campaña is coming along at the Zapatista website, www.ezln.org.mx. Further background on the Zapatistas is available in *The Zapatista Reader*, an anthology of words by writers from Octavio Paz and Gabriel García Márquez to Marcos himself, and at websites such as **Global Exchange** (www.globalexchange.org), **SiPaz** (www.sipaz.org) and **IMC** (chiapas.mediosindependientes.org).

Museo Jsotz' Levetik (admission by donation; ⏲ 9am-5pm), three blocks below the central basketball court, covers local culture and has some fine textiles and musical instruments.

Grutas de San Cristóbal

The entrance to this long **cavern** (admission $1.50; ⏲ 9am-5pm) is among pine woods 9km southeast of San Cristóbal, a five-minute walk south of the Pan-American Hwy. The first 350m or so of the cave has a concrete walkway and is lit. The army took control of the land around the caves in 2003, though visitors are still welcome.

To get there take a Teopisca-bound *colectivo* taxi from the Pan-American Hwy, about 150m southeast of the OCC bus station in San Cristóbal, and ask for 'Las Grutas' ($1.50).

Amatenango del Valle

pop 3400 / elevation 1869m

The women of this Tzeltal village by the Pan-American Hwy, 37km southeast of San Cristóbal, are renowned potters. Pottery here is still fired by a pre-Hispanic method, building a wood fire around the pieces rather than putting them in a kiln. Amatenango children find a ready tourist market with *animalitos* – little pottery animal figures that are inexpensive but fragile. If you visit the village, expect to be surrounded within minutes by young *animalito*-sellers.

From San Cristóbal, take a Comitán-bound bus or combi.

OCOSINGO

☎ 919 / pop 29,000 / elevation 900m

Around the halfway mark of the 220km journey from San Cristóbal to Palenque, set in a broad temperate valley midway between the cool misty highlands and the steamy lowland jungle, is the bustling town of Ocosingo, a market hub for a large area. Ocosingo is just a few kilometers from the impressive Maya ruins of Toniná, and is a jumping-off point for beautiful Laguna Miramar.

The market area along Av 2 Sur Ote, three to five blocks east (downhill) from the central plaza, is the busiest part of town. The **Tianguis Campesino** (Peasants' Market; cnr Av 2 Sur Ote & Calle 5 Sur Ote; ⏲ 6am-5pm) is for the area's small-scale food producers to sell their goods direct; officially only women

are allowed to trade here, and it's a colorful sight, with many of the traders in traditional dress.

The valleys known as Las Cañadas de Ocosingo, between Ocosingo and the Reserva de la Biosfera Montes Azules to the east, form one of the strongest bastions of support for the Zapatistas, and Ocosingo saw the bloodiest fighting during the 1994 rebellion, with about 50 rebels killed here by the Mexican army. The town has been calm since, but the Zapatistas have consolidated their support in the region despite the presence of a large Mexican army garrison near Toniná ruins, and have seized a number of ranches in recent years. One (seized in 2003) was the American-owned nut farm-cum-guest ranch, Rancho Esmeralda, near Toniná. Its owners have since set up an excellent guesthouse in Ocosingo (see below).

Orientation & Information

Ocosingo spreads east (downhill) from Hwy 199. Av Central runs down from the main road to the broad central plaza, overlooked from its east end by the Templo de San Jacinto. Hotels, restaurants and services are along Calle Central Nte, running off the north side of the plaza, and elsewhere close by.

Santander Serfin (Central Nte 10; ⏲ 9am-4pm Mon-Fri) and **Banamex** (Av Central; ⏲ 9am-2:30pm Mon-Fri) on the plaza both exchange currency and have ATMs. Two cybercafés on Calle Central Nte charge $0.80 per hour.

Sleeping

Hospedaje Esmeralda (☎ 673-00-14; www.ranchoesmeralda.net; Central Nte 14; s/d/tr/q with shared bathroom $13.50/22/26/32; Ⓟ) Set up by the owners of the Rancho Esmeralda, this welcoming, helpful and small guesthouse has five attractive rooms, all with bright indigenous bedcovers, fans and a folder of useful information about the area. A snug bar area with good music adjoins the restaurant (p830). Enjoyable horse-riding excursions ($19, about two hours) in the countryside outside Ocosingo are offered. One room, with private bathroom, costs a couple of dollars extra.

Hotel Margarita (☎ 673-12-15; hotelmargarita@prodigy.net.mx; Central Nte 19; s/d/tr/q $21/25/27/33; Ⓟ)
Next to Hospedaje Esmeralda, the friendly,

TABASCO & CHIAPAS

recently renovated Margarita has clean and comfortable rooms, all with TV, fan, two big double beds and large framed posters of Chiapas attractions.

Hotel Central (☎ 673-00-24; Av Central 5; s/d/tr $15/19/21; ℗) This neat little hotel has a prime location on the north side of the main plaza, and simple, spotless rooms with fan, bathroom and cable TV.

Eating

Las Delicias (☎ 673-00-24; Av Central 5; mains $5-7.50) Set on Hotel Central's veranda, overlooking the plaza, this reliable restaurant has big portions and good breakfasts ($2.75 to $5.50).

Restaurant Esmeralda (☎ 673-00-14; Hospedaje Esmeralda, Central Nte 14; mains $5-7) Excellent home-style international and Mexican fare is served here, including healthy buffet breakfasts ($3.75) and dinner favorites like chicken curry and pork fajitas.

Restaurant El Campanario (☎ 673-02-51; Av Central Ote 2; mains $3.75-7; ⏰ 7am-10:30pm) A few doors east of Las Delicias, El Campanario makes an effort with bright tablecloths and a trilingual menu (Spanish, English, French), serving a typical Chiapas tourist menu of meat, egg and seafood.

Fábrica de Quesos Santa Rosa (☎ 673-00-09; 1 Ote Nte 11) Ocosingo is known for its *queso amarillo* (yellow cheese). There are six main types, including *'de bola,'* which comes in 1kg balls ($5.50) with an edible wax coating and a crumbly, whole-fat center.

Getting There & Away

Servicios Aéreos San Cristóbal (☎ 967-673-01-88, mobile 919-675-57-98; sasc_ocosingo@hotmail.com) does small-plane charters from Ocosingo's airstrip, 3km out of town toward Toniná. Destinations include San Quintín near Laguna Miramar (opposite) for $470 round-trip (up to four passengers), and day trips to Bonampak and Yaxchilán ($620 round-trip).

Road travelers should try to be off the Ocosingo–Palenque road before late afternoon. The section in the vicinity of Agua Azul is notorious for highway robberies at night or in the late afternoon.

Ocosingo's OCC bus terminal (1st-class and deluxe) is on Hwy 199, 600m west of the plaza; AEXA (1st-class) stops at Zugey restaurant across the road. Daily departures are listed in the box below.

Buses from the OCC terminal also go to Campeche, Cancún, Mérida and Villahermosa.

TONINÁ

The towering ceremonial core of **Toniná** (☎ 919-673-12-24; admission $3.25; ⏰ 8am-5pm), overlooking a pastoral valley 14km east of Ocosingo, comprises one of the Maya world's most imposing temple complexes. This was the city that brought mighty Palenque to its knees, and Toniná's fascinating history (see the boxed text, opposite) is well explained in the neat site museum.

The path from the entrance and museum crosses a stream and climbs to the broad, flat Gran Plaza. At the south end of the Gran Plaza is the **Templo de la Guerra Cósmica** (Temple of Cosmic War), with five altars in front of it. Off one side of the plaza is a **ball court**, inaugurated around AD 780 under the rule of the female regent Smoking Mirror. A decapitation altar stands cheerfully beside it.

To the north rises the ceremonial core of Toniná, a hillside terraced into a number of platforms, rising 80m above the Gran Plaza. At the right-hand end of the steps, rising from the first to the second platform, is the entry to a **ritual labyrinth** of passages.

Higher up on the right-hand side is the **Palacio de las Grecas y de la Guerra** (Palace of the Grecas and War). The *grecas* are a band of geometrical decoration forming a zigzag

---

OCOSINGO BUS SCHEDULE

Destination	Price	Duration	Frequency
Palenque	$3.75-7.50	2¼hr	10 from OCC, 4 AEXA & vans leave about every 30 minutes from Hwy 199, 800m north of the OCC terminal
San Cristóbal de Las Casas	$2.75-3.75	2¼hr	8 from OCC, 4 AEXA & vans and *colectivo* taxis leave every 20-30min from a yard just up the road from OCC
Tuxtla Gutiérrez	$6-9.50	4hr	8 from OCC

PLACE OF THE CELESTIAL CAPTIVES

The prelude to Toniná's heyday was the inauguration of the Snake Skull-Jaguar Claw dynasty in AD 688. The new rulers, ambitious and military-minded, contested control of the region with Palenque, constantly harassing their rival state from around AD 690. The Palenque ruler K'an Joy Chitam II was captured by Toniná in 711 and probably had his head lopped off here.

Toniná became known as the Place of the Celestial Captives, for in some of its chambers were held the captured rulers of Palenque and other Maya cities, destined either to be ransomed for large sums or to be decapitated. A recurring image in Toniná sculpture is that of captives before decapitation, thrown to the ground with their hands tied.

Toniná enjoyed a final flowering under a king known as Ruler 8, who styled himself 'He of Many Captives.' Around AD 900 the city was rebuilt in a simpler, austere style. But Jaguar Serpent, in 903, was the last ruler of whom any record has been found. Classic Maya civilization was ending here, as elsewhere, and Toniná has the distinction of having the latest of all recorded Long Count dates, AD 909.

X-shape, possibly representing Quetzal-cóatl. To its right is a rambling series of chambers, passages and stairways, believed to have been Toniná's administrative headquarters.

Higher again is Toniná's most remarkable sculpture, the **Mural de las Cuatro Eras** (Mural of the Four Eras). Created between AD 790 and 840, this stucco relief of four panels – the first, from the left end, has been lost – represents the four suns, or four eras of human history. The people of Toniná believed themselves to be living in the fourth sun – that of winter, mirrors, the direction north and the end of human life. At the center of each panel is the upside-down head of a decapitated prisoner. Blood spurting from the prisoner's neck forms a ring of feathers and, at the same time, a sun. In one panel, a dancing skeleton holds a decapitated head. To the left of the head is a lord of the underworld, resembling an enormous rodent.

Up the next steps is the seventh level, with remains of four temples. Behind the second temple from the left, steps descend into the very narrow **Tumba de Treinta Metros** (Thirty-Meter Tomb), which is definitely not for the claustrophobic or obese!

Above here is the acropolis, the abode of Toniná's rulers and site of its eight most important temples – four on each of two levels. The right-hand temple on the lower level, the **Templo del Monstruo de la Tierra** (Temple of the Earth Monster), has Toniná's best-preserved roof comb, built around AD 713.

On the topmost level, the tallest temple, the **Templo del Espejo Humeante** (Temple of

the Smoking Mirror), was built by Zots-Choj, who took the throne in AD 842. In that era of the fourth sun and the direction north, Zots-Choj had to raise this, Toniná's northernmost temple, highest of all, which necessitated a large, artificial northeast extension of the hill.

Getting There & Away

Combis to Toniná ($1) leave from opposite the Tianguis Campesino in Ocosingo every 45 minutes from early morning onward. The last one returns around 5pm.

LAGUNA MIRAMAR
elevation 400m

Ringed by rainforest, pristine Laguna Miramar, 140km southeast of Ocosingo in the **Reserva de la Biosfera Montes Azules** (Montes Azules Biosphere Reserve), is one of Mexico's most remote and exquisite lakes. Frequently echoing with the roars of howler monkeys, the 16-sq-km lake has a beautiful temperature all year and is virtually unpolluted. The lake is accessible thanks to a successful ecotourism project in the village of **Emiliano Zapata**, near its western shore. *Ejido* life in Emiliano Zapata, a poor but well-ordered Maya community, is fascinating too. This spread-out settlement of huts and a few concrete communal buildings sits on a gentle slope running down to the Río Perlas – a beautiful bathing place. It's forbidden to bring alcohol or drugs into the village.

Miramar is not the easiest of places to get to. Try to visit outside the late-August to late-October rainy period, when land access can be more difficult and foot trails muddy.

When you reach Emiliano Zapata, ask for the Presidente de Turismo. Through him you must arrange and pay for the services you need – a guide costs $9.50 per day, the overnight fee is $2.75, and rental of a *cayuco* (traditional canoe for two or three people) for exploring the lake is $9.50.

The 7km walk from Emiliano Zapata to the lake, through *milpas* (cornfields) and forest that includes *caoba* (mahogany) and the *matapalo* (strangler fig) trees, takes about 1½ hours. At the lake, you may hear jaguars at night. Other wildlife includes spider monkeys, tapirs, macaws and toucans; butterflies are prolific. Locals fish for *mojarra* (perch) in the lake, and will assure you that its few crocodiles are not dangerous. It takes about 45 minutes to canoe across to Isla Lacan-Tun, an island rich in the overgrown, ruined remains of a pre-Hispanic settlement. The Chol-Lacantún Maya people here remained unconquered by the Spanish until the 1580s. At the time of writing it was unfortunately not possible to visit the island, as it is looked after by another village, but this situation may change.

Sleeping & Eating

At the lakeshore, you can camp or sling a hammock under a *palapa* shelter for $5 per person. A small, basic guesthouse next to the Río Perlas in Emiliano Zapata, **Posada Zapata** (in Mexico City ☎ 55-5150-5618; per person $5) has six rooms, no sheets, shared showers and lockers. Meals (around $3 each) are available in villagers' homes (order in advance), or you can eat at the basic *comedores* in the neighboring village of San Quintín, which has a large Mexican army garrison.

Getting There & Away

Some agencies in San Cristóbal de Las Casas run three- or four-day trips to Miramar from San Cristóbal, with prices starting around $300 per person (see p818). You can also get there yourself from Ocosingo, either in a tiny Cessna plane with Servicios Aéreos San Cristóbal (see p830), or by passenger-carrying truck along 138km of rough road ($7, six hours or more). The trucks (known as *tres toneladas,* three-tonners) leave around 9am, 10:30am and 12:30pm from just south of Ocosingo's Tianguis Campesino; the route runs through the area known as Las Cañadas de Ocosingo, a Zapatista stronghold. Your

documents may be checked at Mexican army or Zapatista village checkpoints; keep your passport and tourist card handy.

By truck or plane you'll arrive in San Quintín, Emiliano Zapata's neighboring village (which is anti-Zapatista and has a large army garrison). A track opposite a military complex beside San Quintín's airstrip leads to the middle of *ejido* Emiliano Zapata, about a 15- to 20-minute walk. Trucks head back from San Quintín to Ocosingo at approximately 3am, 6am and 10:30am.

AGUA AZUL & MISOL-HA

These spectacular water attractions – the thundering cascades of Agua Azul and the 35m jungle waterfall of Misol-Ha – are both short detours off the Ocosingo-Palenque road. (Note that during the rainy season, they lose part of their beauty as the water gets murky, though the power of the waterfalls is magnified.)

Both are most easily visited on an organized day tour from Palenque, though it's possible, if probably not cheaper, to go independently too. There are accommodations at Misol-Ha.

Warning: this area is unfortunately the scene of repeated robberies and attempted robberies of tourists. The Misol-Ha access road and areas away from the most visited sections of the Agua Azul falls have been the scene of robberies, sometimes armed. In addition, robbery on Hwy 199 within about 20km either side of the Agua Azul turnoff can almost be described as common. To minimize the risks, don't walk the access roads, stick to the main paved trail at Agua Azul, and don't be on Hwy 199 in the Agua Azul vicinity after midafternoon.

Agua Azul

The turnoff for these waterfalls is halfway between Ocosingo and Palenque, some 60km from each. Agua Azul is a breathtaking sight, with its powerful and dazzling white waterfalls thundering into turquoise (most of the year) pools surrounded by verdant jungle. On holidays and weekends the place is thronged; at other times you'll have few companions.

The temptation to swim is great, but take extreme care. The current is deceptively fast, the power of the falls obvious, and there are many submerged hazards like rocks and dead trees. Ignore the sign that says, in English, 'Dangerous Not To Swim' – a fatally unpunctuated translation of '*Peligro – No Nadar*'! People do drown here.

A paved road leads 4.5km down to Agua Azul from Hwy 199, passing through the territory of one *ejido* into a second, whose territory includes the falls. You will probably have to pay $1 per person to enter each *ejido*. A well-made stone and concrete path with steps runs 700m up beside the falls from the parking area, lined by **comedores** (mains $3-6) and souvenir stalls.

Misol-Ha

Just 20km south of Palenque, spectacular Misol-Ha cascades 35m into a wonderful wide pool surrounded by lush tropical vegetation. It's a sublime place for a dip when the fall is not excessively pumped up by wet-season rains. A path behind the main fall leads into a cave, which gives a great close-up experience of the power of the fall. **Misol-Ha** (admission $1) is 1.5km off Hwy 199 and the turn is signposted.

Centro Turístico Ejidal Cascada de Misol-Ha (☎ 214-257-01-48, in Mexico City ☎ 55-5329-0995 ext 7006; www.misol-ha.com; d/tr/q $27/38/49; P) has great wooden cabins among the trees near the fall, with bathrooms and mosquito netting, plus a good open-air **restaurant** (mains $3.50-7; ☯ 7am-6pm).

Getting There & Away

Most Palenque travel agencies (see p839) offer daily trips to Misol-Ha and Agua Azul. Trips cost $11.50 to $13, including admission fees, and last six or seven hours, spending 30 to 60 minutes at Misol-Ha and two to three hours at Agua Azul.

To visit the sites independently from Palenque, hire a taxi (around $25 to Misol-Ha with a one-hour wait, or $55 to Agua Azul with a two-hour wait); or, for Agua Azul, take an Ocosingo-bound AEXA bus, or van from 4a or 5a Pte Sur, as far as the Agua Azul *crucero* (turnoff) for $2 to $2.50. *Camionetas* (pickup trucks) at the turnoff charge $1 for the run down to Agua Azul.

PALENQUE

☎ 916 / pop 37,000 / elevation 80m

The ancient Maya city of Palenque, with its exquisite architecture in a superb jungle setting, is one of the marvels of Mexico.

Modern Palenque town, a few kilometers to the east, is a sweaty, humdrum place with limited attraction except as a jumping-off point for the ruins. Many prefer to base themselves at one of the forest hideouts along the road between the town and the ruins, including the funky travelers' hangout El Panchán.

History

The name Palenque (Palisade) is Spanish and has no relation to the city's ancient name, which may have been Lakamha (Big Water). Palenque was first occupied around 100 BC, and flourished from around AD 630 to around 740. The city rose to prominence under the ruler Pakal, who reigned from AD 615 to 683. Archaeologists have determined that Pakal is represented by hieroglyphics of sun and shield, and he is also referred to as Sun Shield (Escudo Solar). He lived to the then-incredible age of 80.

During Pakal's reign, many plazas and buildings, including the superlative Templo de las Inscripciones (Pakal's own mausoleum), were constructed in Palenque. The structures were characterized by mansard roofs and very fine stucco bas-reliefs.

Pakal's son Kan B'alam II (684–702), who is represented in hieroglyphics by the jaguar and the serpent (and also called Jaguar Serpent II), continued Palenque's expansion and artistic development. He presided over the construction of the Grupo de las Cruces temples, placing sizable narrative stone steles within each.

During Kan B'alam II's reign, Palenque extended its zone of control to the Usumacinta river, but was challenged by the rival Maya city of Toniná, 65km south. Kan B'alam's brother and successor, K'an Joy Chitam II (Precious Peccary), was captured by forces from Toniná in 711, and probably executed there. Palenque enjoyed a resurgence between 722 and 736, however, under Ahkal Mo' Nahb' III (Turtle Macaw Lake), who added many substantial buildings.

After AD 900, Palenque was largely abandoned. In an area that receives the heaviest rainfall in Mexico, the ruins were soon overgrown, and the city remained unknown to the Western world until 1746, when Maya hunters revealed the existence of a jungle palace to a Spanish priest named Antonio de Solís. Later explorers claimed Palenque

PALENQUE

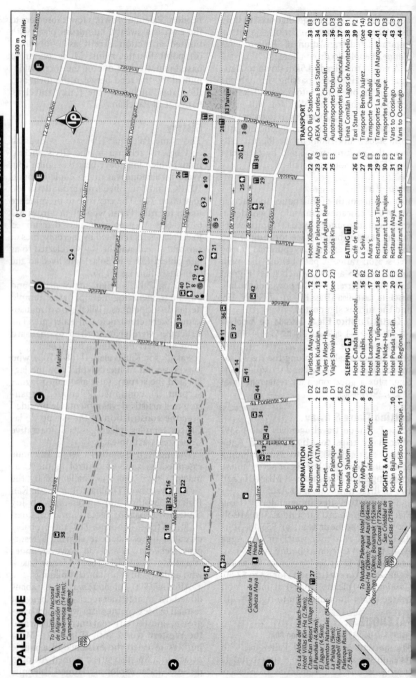

INFORMATION
Banamex (ATM)...................................**1** D2
Bancomer (ATM).................................**2** E2
Cibernet..**3** E3
Clínica Palenque...............................**4** D1
Internet Online..................................**5** E2
Posada Shalom...................................**6** D2
Post Office..**7** F2
Red M@ya...**8** D2
Tourist Information Office..................**9** E2

SIGHTS & ACTIVITIES
Kichan Bajlum.................................**10** E2
Servicio Turístico de Palenque........**11** D3
Turística Maya Chiapas....................**12** D2
Viajes Kukulcán...............................**13** C3
Viajes Misol-Ha................................**14** C3
Viajes Shivalva.........................(see 22)

SLEEPING
Hotel Cañada Internacional.............**15** A2
Hotel Chablis...................................**16** B2
Hotel Lacandonia............................**17** D2
Hotel Maya Tulipanes......................**18** B2
Hotel Nikte-Ha.................................**19** D2
Hotel Posada Tucán.........................**20** E3
Hotel Regional................................**21** D3

| Hotel Xibalba...................................**22** B2 |
| Maya Palenque Hotel.......................**23** A3 |
| Posada Aguila Real...........................**24** C3 |
| Posada Kin.......................................**25** E3 |

EATING
Café de Yara....................................**26** E2
La Selva...**27** A3
Mara's..**28** D2
Restaurant Las Tinajas......................**29** E3
Restaurant Las Tinajas......................**30** E3
Restaurant Maya...............................**31** F2
Restaurant Maya Cañada..................**32** B2

TRANSPORT
ADO Bus Station...............................**33** B3
AEXA & Cardesa Bus Station.............**34** C3
Autotransporte Chamoán...................**35** D2
Autotransportes Otolum....................**36** D3
Autotransportes Río Chancalá...........**37** D3
Línea Comitán Lagos de Montebello..**38** B1
Taxi Stand..**39** F2
Transporte Benito Juárez...........(see 14)
Transporte Chambalú.......................**40** D2
Transportes La Jungla del Marquez....**41** C3
Transportes Palenque.......................**42** D3
Vans to Ocosingo.............................**43** F2
Vans to Ocosingo.............................**44** C3

was capital of an Atlantis-like civilization. The eccentric Count de Waldeck, who in his 60s lived atop one of the pyramids for two years (1831–33), even published a book with fanciful neoclassical drawings that made the city resemble a great Mediterranean civilization.

It was not until 1837, when John L Stephens, an amateur archaeology enthusiast from New York, reached Palenque with artist Frederick Catherwood, that the site was insightfully investigated. And another century passed before Alberto Ruz Lhuillier, the tireless Mexican archaeologist, uncovered Pakal's hidden crypt in 1952. Today it continues to yield fascinating and beautiful secrets – most recently, a succession of sculptures and frescoes in the Acrópolis del Sur area, which have vastly expanded our knowledge of Palenque's history.

Frans Blom, the mid-20th-century investigator, remarked: 'The first visit to Palenque is immensely impressive. When one has lived there for some time this ruined city becomes an obsession.' It's not hard to understand why.

Orientation

Hwy 199 meets Palenque's main street, Av Juárez, at the Glorieta de la Cabeza Maya, an intersection with a large statue of a Maya chieftain's head, at the west end of the town. From here Juárez heads 1km east to the central square, El Parque. The main bus stations are on Juárez just east of the Maya head statue.

A few hundred meters south from the Maya head, the paved road to the Palenque ruins, 7.5km away, diverges west off Hwy 199. This road passes the site museum after about 6.5km, then winds on about 1km further to the main entrance to the ruins.

Accommodations are scattered around the central part of town and along the road to the ruins. The commercial heart of town, where you hardly ever see another tourist, is north of the center along Velasco Suárez.

Information

INTERNET ACCESS

There are over a dozen cybercafés. Most charge around $0.80 per hour.

Cibernet (Independencia; ☼ 8am-11pm)
El Panchán (Carretera Palenque-Ruinas Km 4.5; per hr $1.50; ☼ 10am-11pm)

Internet Online (Juárez s/n; ☼ 7am-10:30pm)
Red M@ya (Juárez 133; ☼ 9am-10pm)

LAUNDRY

Several town-center hotels offer same-day public laundry service.

Hotel Nikte-Ha (☎ 345-05-97; Juárez 133; per kg $1.50)
Posada Shalom (☎ 345-09-44; Juárez 156; per kg $2)

MEDICAL SERVICES

Clínica Palenque (☎ 345-02-73; Velasco Suárez 33; ☼ 9:30am-1:30pm & 5-8pm) Dr Alfonso Martínez speaks English.

MONEY

Outside banking hours, try travel agents if you don't have a card for the ATMs at the banks on Juárez.

Banamex (Juárez 62; ☼ 8am-4pm Mon-Fri, 10am-2pm Sat)
Bancomer (Juárez 96; ☼ 8am-4pm Mon-Fri, 10am-3pm Sat)

POST & TELEPHONE

Several agencies along Juárez offer cut-rate international calls.

Post office (Independencia s/n; ☼ 9am-6pm Mon-Fri)

TOURIST INFORMATION

Tourist information office (cnr Juárez & Abasolo; ☼ 9am-9pm Mon-Sat, 9am-1pm Sun) Has reliable town and transportation information and a few maps.

Palenque Ruins

Ancient **Palenque** (admission $3.75; ☼ 8am-5pm, last entry 4:30pm) stands at the precise point where the first hills rise out of the Gulf Coast plain, and the dense jungle covering these hills forms an evocative backdrop to Palenque's exquisite Maya architecture. Hundreds of ruined buildings are spread over 15 sq km, but only a fairly compact central area has been excavated. Everything you see here was built without metal tools, pack animals or the wheel.

As you explore the ruins, try to picture the gray stone edifices as they would have been at the peak of Palenque's power: painted blood-red with elaborate blue and yellow stucco details. The forest around these temples is still home to howler monkeys (which you may well hear and even see), toucans and ocelots. The ruins and surrounding forests form a national park, the Parque Nacional Palenque, for which you must pay a separate $1 admission fee at Km 4.5 on the road to the ruins.

About 1400 people visit Palenque on an average day, and this rises to 6000 or 7000 in the summer holiday season. Opening time is a good time to visit, when it's cooler and not too crowded, and morning mist may still be wrapping the temples in a picturesque haze.

Bring sunscreen with you. Refreshments, hats and souvenirs are available outside the main entrance, and there are cafés there and at the museum.

Official site **guides** (2hr tour for up to 7 people in English/Spanish/French/Italian $52/42/56/56) are available by the entrance. A Maya guide association, **Guías e Interpretes Mayas** (☎ 341-76-88), also has a desk here and offers informative two-hour tours in Spanish, English or Italian at the same prices. Fascinating and entertaining in-depth tours of around five hours (usually $100 for groups of five to 10) are given by **Maya Exploration Center** (www .mayaexploration.org), a group of archaeologists who work on Maya sciences such as astronomy and math, and map unexplored ruins. Email them from the website or ask for Alonso Méndez at El Panchán (p839). Their website is packed with interest for Palenque fans – as is another Palenque archaeologists' site, the **Group of the Cross Project** (www.mesoweb.com/palenque).

Most visitors take a combi or taxi to the ruins' main (upper) entrance, see the major structures and then walk downhill to the museum, visiting minor ruins along the way. Note that it's not permitted to exit the site this way before 9am or after 4pm.

Transportes Chambalú (☎ 345-04-66; Allende s/n) and **Transportes Palenque** (☎ 345-24-30; cnr Allende & 20 de Noviembre) run combis to the ruins about every 15 minutes from 6am to 6pm daily ($1 each way). They will pick you up or drop you anywhere along the town-to-ruins road.

Note that the mushrooms sold by locals along the road to the ruins from about May to November aren't for your salad, they are a potent hallucinogenic.

TEMPLO DE LAS INSCRIPCIONES GROUP

As you walk in from the entrance, passing to the south of the overgrown Templo XI, the vegetation suddenly peels away to reveal most of Palenque's most magnificent buildings in one sublime vista. A line of temples rises in front of the jungle on your right, culminating in the Templo de las Inscripciones about 100m ahead; El Palacio, with its trademark tower, stands to the left of the Templo de las Inscripciones; and the Grupo de las Cruces rises in the distance beneath a thick jungle backdrop.

The first temple on your right is Templo XII, called the **Templo de La Calavera** (Temple of the Skull) for the relief sculpture of a rabbit or deer skull at the foot of one of its pillars. The second temple has little interest. Third is **Templo XIII**, containing a tomb of a female dignitary, whose remains were found colored red as a result of treatment with cinnabar, when unearthed in 1994. You can enter this Tumba de la Reina Roja (Tomb of the Red Queen) to see her sarcophagus. With the skeleton were found a malachite mask and about 1000 pieces of jade. Some speculate, from resemblances to Pakal's tomb next door, that the 'queen' buried here was his wife.

The **Templo de las Inscripciones** (Temple of the Inscriptions), perhaps the most celebrated burial monument in the Americas, is the tallest and most stately of Palenque's buildings. Constructed on eight levels, the Templo de las Inscripciones has a central front staircase rising 25m to a series of small rooms. The tall roof comb that once crowned it is long gone, but between the front doorways are stucco panels with reliefs of noble figures. On the interior rear wall are three panels with the long Maya inscription, recounting the history of Palenque and this building, for which Mexican archaeologist Alberto Ruz Lhuillier named the temple. From the top, interior stairs lead down into the tomb of Pakal (now closed to visitors indefinitely, to avoid further damage to its murals from the humidity inevitably exuded by visitors). Pakal's jewel-bedecked skeleton and jade mosaic death mask were removed from the tomb to Mexico City, and the tomb was re-created in the Museo Nacional de Antropología. The priceless death mask was stolen in 1985, but the carved stone sarcophagus lid remains here – you can see a replica in the site museum (see p839).

The tomb of Ruz Lhuillier, who discovered Pakal's tomb in 1952, lies under the trees in front of Templo XIII.

PALENQUE RUINS

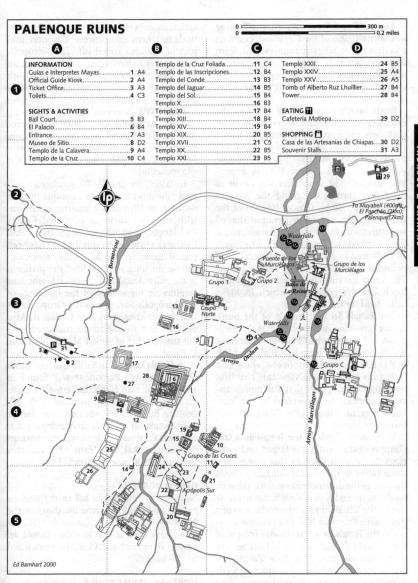

0   300 m
0   0.2 miles

INFORMATION	
Guías e Interpretes Mayas	**1** A4
Official Guide Kiosk	**2** A4
Ticket Office	**3** A3
Toilets	**4** C3

SIGHTS & ACTIVITIES	
Ball Court	**5** B3
El Palacio	**6** B4
Entrance	**7** A3
Museo de Sitio	**8** D2
Templo de la Calavera	**9** A4
Templo de la Cruz	**10** C4

Templo de la Cruz Foliada	**11** C4
Templo de las Inscripciones	**12** B4
Templo del Conde	**13** B3
Templo del Jaguar	**14** B5
Templo del Sol	**15** B4
Templo X	**16** B3
Templo XI	**17** B3
Templo XIII	**18** B4
Templo XIV	**19** B4
Templo XIX	**20** B5
Templo XX	**21** C5
Templo XXI	**22** B5
Templo XXI	**23** B5

Templo XXII	**24** B5
Templo XXIV	**25** A4
Templo XXV	**26** A5
Tomb of Alberto Ruz Lhuillier	**27** B4
Tower	**28** B4

EATING	
Cafetería Motiepa	**29** D2

SHOPPING	
Casa de las Artesanías de Chiapas	**30** D2
Souvenir Stalls	**31** A3

Ed Barnhart 2000

TABASCO & CHIAPAS

To Mayabell (400m);
El Panchán (7km);
Palenque (7km)

Waterfalls

Puente de los
Murciélagos

Grupo de los
Murciélagos

Grupo 1   Grupo 2

Baño de
La Reina

Grupo
Norte

Waterfalls

Grupo C

Templo de la Cruz

Grupo
de las Cruces

Acrópolis Sur

Arroyo Bernasconi

Arroyo Otolum

Arroyo Murciélagos

EL PALACIO

Diagonally opposite the Templo de las Inscripciones is the **Palace**, a large structure divided into four main courtyards, with a maze of corridors and rooms. Built and modified piecemeal over 400 years from the 5th century on, it probably really was the residence of Palenque's rulers. Its tower, built in the 8th century by Ahkal Mo' Nahb' III and restored in 1955, has remnants of fine stucco reliefs on the walls, but you're not allowed to climb up inside it. Archaeologists believe the tower was constructed so that Maya royalty and priests could observe the sun falling directly into the Templo de las Inscripciones during the winter solstice.

The northeastern courtyard, the **Patio de los Cautivos** (Patio of the Captives), contains a collection of relief sculptures that seem disproportionately large for their setting; it's conjectured that they represent conquered rulers and were brought from elsewhere.

In the southern part of the complex, the extensive subterranean bathrooms included six toilets and a couple of sweat baths.

GRUPO DE LAS CRUCES

Pakal's son, Kan B'alam II, was a prolific builder, and soon after the death of his father started designing the temples of the Grupo de las Cruces (Group of the Crosses). All three main pyramid-shaped structures surround a plaza southeast of the Templo de las Inscripciones. They were all dedicated in AD 692 as a spiritual focal point for Palenque's triad of patron deities. The 'cross' carvings in some buildings here symbolize the ceiba tree, which in Maya belief held up the universe.

The **Templo del Sol** (Temple of the Sun), on the west side of the plaza, has the best-preserved roof comb at Palenque. Carvings inside, commemorating Kan B'alam's birth in AD 635 and accession in 684, show him facing his father. Some view this beautiful building as sure proof that Palenque's ancient architects were inspired by the local hallucinogenic mushrooms. Make up your own mind!

Steep steps climb to the **Templo de la Cruz** (Temple of the Cross), the largest and most elegantly proportioned in this group. The stone tablet in the central sanctuary shows the lord of the underworld smoking tobacco on the right, and Kan B'alam in full royal attire on the left. Behind is a reproduction of a panel depicting Kan B'alam's accession.

On the **Templo de la Cruz Foliada** (Temple of the Foliated Cross), the corbel arches are fully exposed, revealing how Palenque's architects designed these buildings. A well-preserved inscribed tablet shows a king (probably Pakal) with a sun shield emblazoned on his chest, corn growing from his shoulder blades, and the sacred quetzal bird on his head.

ACRÓPOLIS SUR

In the jungle south of the Grupo de las Cruces is the **Southern Acropolis**, where archaeologists have recovered some terrific finds in recent excavations. You may find part of the area roped off. The Acrópolis Sur appears to have been constructed as an extension of the Grupo de las Cruces, with both groups set around what was probably a single long open space.

Templo XVII, between the Cruces group and the Acrópolis Sur, contains a reproduction carved panel depicting Kan B'alam, standing with a spear, with a bound captive kneeling before him (the original is in the site museum).

In 1999, in **Templo XIX**, archaeologists made the most important Palenque find for decades: an 8th-century limestone platform with stunning carvings of seated figures and lengthy hieroglyphic texts that detail Palenque's origins. A reproduction has been placed inside Templo XIX – the central figure on the long south side of the platform is the ruler Ahkal Mo' Nahb' III, who was responsible for several of the buildings of the Acrópolis Sur, just as the Grupo de las Cruces was created by Kan B'alam II. Also on view is a wonderful reproduction of a tall stucco relief of Ahkal Mo' Nahb''s son, U Pakal.

In **Templo XX**, built in 540, a frescoed tomb of an unknown personage was found in 1999. Ahkal Mo' Nahb' undertook a complete remodeling of this pyramid in the 8th century, but his work was never completed.

In **Templo XXI** in 2002, archaeologists discovered a throne with very fine carvings depicting Ahkal Mo' Nahb', his ancestor the great Pakal, and his son U Pakal.

GRUPO NORTE

North of El Palacio is a **ball court** (juego de pelota) and the handsome buildings of the Northern Group. Crazy Count de Waldeck (see p835) lived in the so-called **Templo del Conde** (Temple of the Count), constructed in AD 647.

NORTHEASTERN GROUPS

East of the Grupo Norte, the main path crosses Arroyo Otolum. Some 70m beyond the stream, a right fork will take you to **Grupo C**, a set of jungle-covered buildings and plazas, thought to have been lived in from about AD 750 to 800.

If you stay on the main path, you'll descend steep steps to a group of low, elongated buildings, probably occupied residentially around AD 770 to 850. The path goes alongside the Arroyo Otolum, which here tumbles down a series of small falls forming natural bathing pools known as the **Baño de la Reina** (Queen's Bath). Unfortunately it's not permitted to bathe here.

The path continues to another residential quarter, the **Grupo de Los Murciélagos** (Bat Group), then crosses the **Puente de los Murciélagos**, a footbridge across Arroyo Otolum.

Across the bridge and a bit further downstream, a path goes west to **Grupos 1 and 2**, a short walk uphill. These ruins, only partly uncovered, are in a beautiful jungle setting. The main path continues downriver to the road, where the museum is a short distance along to the right.

MUSEO DE SITIO

Palenque's **Site Museum** (☎ 348-93-31; Carretera Palenque-Ruinas Km 7; admission free; ☒ 9am-4:30pm Tue-Sun) does a wonderful job of displaying finds from the site and interpreting, in English and Spanish, Palenque's history. It includes a copy of the lid of Pakal's sarcophagus (depicting his rebirth as the maize god, encircled by serpents, mythical monsters and glyphs recounting his reign) and recent finds from Templo XXI. Next door is the Cafetería Motiepa (p842) and the **Casa de la Artesanías de Chiapas** (☎ 348-93-31; ☒ 9am-5pm Tue-Sun), a well-stocked handicraft shop.

El Panchán

Just off the road to the ruins, **El Panchán** (www.elpanchan.com; Carretera Palenque-Ruinas Km 4.5) is a legendary travelers' hangout, set in a patch of dense rainforest – the epicenter of Palenque's alternative scene and home to a bohemian bunch of Mexican and foreign residents and wanderers, including a number of archaeologists and anthropologists. Once ranchland, the area has been reforested by the remarkable Morales family, some of whom are among the leading archaeological experts on Palenque. El Panchán has several (fairly rustic) places to stay (see p840), a couple of restaurants, a set of sinuous streams rippling their way through every part of the property, nightly entertainment, a meditation temple, a *temazcal* (pre-Hispanic steam bath) and a constant stream of interesting visitors from all over the world. **Maya Exploration Center** (www.mayaexploration.org) provides lectures, slide

shows and documentary films (admission around $3) at weekends in the main tourism seasons.

Tours

Numerous travel agencies in Palenque offer transportation packages to Agua Azul and Misol-Ha (see p832), to Bonampak, Yaxchilán and Lacanjá (see p843), and to Flores, Guatemala (p843). They include the following, most open from around 8am to 9pm daily:

Kichan Bajlum (☎ 345-24-52; www.kichanbajlum.com; Juárez s/n)

Servicio Turístico de Palenque (☎ 345-13-40; www.stpalenque.com; cnr Juárez & 5 de Mayo)

Transportes Chambalú (☎ 345-04-66; Allende s/n)

Turística Maya Chiapas (☎ 345-07-98; www.tmaya chiapas.com.mx; Juárez 123)

Viajes Kukulcan (☎ 345-15-06; www.kukulcantravel .com; Juárez s/n)

Viajes Misol-Ha (☎ 345-16-14; www.palenquemx.com /viajesmisolha; Juárez 148)

Viajes Shivalva (☎ 345-04-11; www.palenquemx.com /shivalva; Merle Green 9, La Cañada)

Sleeping

The first choice to make is whether you want to stay in or out of Palenque town. Most out-of-town places, including El Panchán, are along the road to the ruins. Palenque town is not particularly attractive, but if you stay here you'll have plenty of restaurants, banks, cybercafés and travel agents close by. Budget accommodations predominate both in and out of town, but many of the better budget places are midrange in quality.

Prices given here are for the high season, which is normally mid-July to mid-August, mid-December to early January, and Semana Santa. Rates can fall by up to 35% at other times, especially in the midrange and top end.

IN TOWN
Budget

Hotel Lacandonia (☎ 345-00-57; Allende s/n; s/d $28/33; ℗ ☒ ☒) An excellent-value modern hotel in the center of town, whose tasteful, light, airy accommodations all have stylish furnishings including wrought-iron beds, reading lights and cable TV.

Hotel Posada Tucán (☎ 345-18-59; merisuiri@ hotmail.com; 5 de Mayo 3; s/d/tr/q with fan $14/17/24/28, r/tr/q with air-con $24/28/33; ☒) Posada Tucán has a breezy upstairs location and attractive, clean, fair-sized rooms boasting TV and nicely tiled bathrooms.

Posada Águila Real (☎ 345-00-04; 20 de Noviembre s/d; r $28, tr & q $38; 🔀) Seventeen spotless, well-kept, blue-and-yellow rooms are arranged on three floors around an open-air patio here. The new rooms on the upper floors are the best, but all have good-quality beds, air-con and TV. There's a small café-restaurant too.

Hotel Regional (☎ /fax 345-01-83; Juárez 119; s/d/ tr/q $17/19/28/38, tr/q with air-con $38/47; 🔀) Something slightly different from the run of the Av Juárez mill: bright paintwork and extremely bright murals enliven the rooms here, on two floors around a courtyard with a turtle pond. The bathrooms are tiny.

Hotel Nikte-Ha (☎ 345-05-97; Juárez 133; r $33; 🔀) One of several unimaginative places along Juárez, the Nikte-Ha has 12 clean, modern rooms with decent beds, tiled floors, air-con and TV. Most look onto an interior well, but are fairly bright.

Posada Kin (☎ 345-17-14; Abasolo 1; r $19-21, tr/q $24/26) An adequate posada with four floors of clean, light rooms with fans, around a central patio. Checkout time is 10am.

Midrange

These hotels are in the leafy La Cañada area at the west end of town.

Hotel Xibalba (☎ 345-04-11; www.palenquemx .com/shivalva; Merle Green 9; r $52, tr/q $56/61; 🅿 🔀 🖥) The Xibalba enjoys a quiet location and has 15 attractive rooms in two buildings (the main one in imitation of the ancient Maya corbel roof style). All rooms have air-con, cable TV and good spotless bathrooms, and the bigger ones boast two double beds and bathtubs. The hotel has its own restaurant and travel agency.

Hotel Chablis (☎ 345-08-70; fax 345-03-65; Merle Green 7; r $56, tr/q $61/66; 🅿 🔀) Opposite the Xibalba, this small hotel offers well-presented, spacious rooms, all with two double beds, air-con and balcony.

Hotel Cañada Internacional (☎ 345-20-94; palen quemike@yahoo.com.mx; Juárez 1; r/tr/q $66/70/75; 🅿 🔀 🖥) The Cañada Internacional has a small pool and large, comfortable rooms on four storeys, all with bright textiles, air-con and two double beds. It's a bit soulless, though.

Top End

Maya Palenque Hotel (☎ 345-07-80; www.bestwest ern.com; cnr Juárez & Merle Green; r/ste $102/121; 🅿 🔀 🖥 🖳) The Maya Palenque, a Best Western hotel, has good-sized air-conditioned rooms, all with two double beds, cable TV, phone and balcony, enjoying plenty of natural light. A big plus is the big pool in leafy gardens.

Hotel Maya Tulipanes (☎ 345-02-01; www.maya tulipanes.com.mx; Cañada 6; r $92, tr/q $100/108; 🅿 🔀 🖥 🖳) Another plush La Cañada tourist hotel, this has large, comfortable, air-conditioned rooms with two wrought-iron double beds and a tropical touch to the decor. It's neatly designed around a central garden with a small pool and restaurant.

OUTSIDE TOWN

There are also some wonderful places along the road to the ruins. Many of these are in El Panchán, a cluster of budget accommodations and eateries and a general alternative hangout scattered around a beautiful patch of jungle just off the road to the ruins, at Carretera Palenque-Ruinas Km 4.5 (p839). Here – and at Elementos Naturales and Mayabell, further towards the ruins – you can sleep amid the sounds and sensations of the forest. Combis between town and ruins (see p835) will drop and pick you up anywhere along this road.

Budget

Margarita & Ed Cabañas (☎ 341-00-63, mobile 916-100-78-14; edcabanas@yahoo.com; El Panchán; cabañas s & d $14-15, r with fan $14-24, with air-con $28; 🅿 🔀) Margarita and Ed, a welcoming Mexican-US couple, defy the odds and maintain scrupulously clean rooms with private bathroom in the middle of the Panchán jungle. The rustic screened *cabañas* are well kept, too, and come with reading lights and private bathrooms. There's free drinking water for all. Some rooms are big enough for five (at extra cost).

Mayabell (☎ 345-14-64, mobile 916-348-42-71; www .mayabell.com.mx; Carretera Palenque-Ruinas Km 6; hammock shelter or camping per person $2.75, hammock to rent $1.50, small vehicle without hookups $2, vehicle site with hookups $14, cabaña s $14-19, d $19-23, s/d r with fan $33/38, with air-con $47/52; 🅿 🔀 🖳) This spacious grassy campground is just 400m from the site museum and has a plethora of sleeping options, a large heat-busting pool and an enjoyable restaurant (p842). Happy campers and hammock-heads share clean toilet and shower blocks. Rooms with air-con are very homey and comfortable; those with fan are basic. The *temazcal* is $7.50 per person (up to eight people).

El Jaguar (☎ 348-05-20; elpanchan@yahoo.com; Carretera Palenque-Ruinas Km 4.5; hammock space $2, cabaña with shared bathroom s/d $7.50/9.50, with private bathroom s/d/tr $12.50/14/17; **P**) Just across the road from El Panchán, and under the same ownership as Chato's Cabañas, El Jaguar has more open grounds but the same creek running through it. Neat, clean cabins of wood, plaster and thatch have private bathrooms; simpler ones with mosquito-net windows share bathrooms.

Chato's Cabañas (☎ 348-05-20; elpanchan@yahoo.com; El Panchán; cabaña with shared bathroom s/d $7.50/9.50, s/d/tr with private bathroom $12.50/14/17; **P**) Chato's 40 wood and concrete cabins, dotted around the Panchán jungle, vary a little in design, but all have screened windows and fans, and some have nice little porches. Some are a bit dilapidated but still waterproof.

Elementos Naturales (enpalenque@hotmail.com; Carretera Palenque-Ruinas Km 5; hammock space $2, camping per person incl breakfast $5, dm incl breakfast $7.50, d cabaña incl breakfast $17; **P**) It's about 600m on from El Panchán to this calm spot with *cabañas* and *palapa* shelters set around extensive grassy gardens. The *cabañas* (for up to five) and dorms (eight bunks each) have fan, mosquito screens, electric light and their own clean bathrooms. There's also a restaurant, grocery shop and even a small football field here.

Rakshita's (mobile ☎ 916-100-69-08; www.rakshita.com; El Panchán; hammock space $2, dm or rented hammock $5, s/d cabaña $9.50/14) Rakshita's has a cozy four-person dorm with lockers and shared bathroom, a *palapa* for hammocks, and simple *cabañas* with private bathroom, fans and mosquito-netted windows. There's a meditation, tai chi and yoga center here.

Jungle Palace (☎ 348-05-20; elpanchan@yahoo.com; El Panchán; s/d cabaña with shared bathroom $7.50/9.50) Offers rudimentary screened cabins, some of which back onto a stream. Hammock-slingers pay just $2 a night and lockers are $1 or $1.50 per day.

Midrange

La Aldea del Halach-Uinic (☎ 345-16-93; laaldeapalenque.com; Carretera Palenque-Ruinas Km 2.7; cabaña per person $12, air-con cabaña $75; **P** ⊠ ⊠) Some 3km from town, the Halach-Uinic has over 40 *palapa*-roofed *cabañas* in spacious gardens. The air-conditioned accommodations are large and bright, with their own bathrooms and terraces, and have been attractively decorated using stone, rock and tree branches. The cheaper *cabañas*, with clean shared bathrooms, are smaller but also fine, with mosquito-screens and nets, indigenous-style blankets and hammocks on a little porch. There's a small pool and a restaurant.

Hotel Villas Kin-Ha (☎ 345-05-33; www.villaskinha.com; Carretera Palenque-Ruinas Km 2.7; r $62-82; **P** ⊠ ⊠) The Kin-Ha has over 90 rooms and bungalows set around its pretty gardens, but doesn't seem crowded. Most accommodations are palm-thatched and wood-beamed, and all are air-conditioned. The grounds hold two good pools, an open-sided *palapa* restaurant and an auditorium (see p842).

Top End

Chan-Kah Resort Village (☎ 345-11-00; www.chan-kah.com.mx; Carretera Palenque-Ruinas Km 3; r/ste $117/307; **P** ⊠ ⊠) This quality resort on the road to the ruins, 3.5km from town, has handsome, well-spaced wood-and-stone cottages with generous bathrooms, ceiling fans, terrace and air-con. But the real draws are the stupendous Edenesque 70m stone-lined swimming pool and lush jungle gardens. There's a good open-air restaurant, bar and games room too. It's rarely busy, except when tour groups block-book the place.

Nututun Palenque Hotel (☎ 345-01-00; www.nututun.com; Carretera Palenque-Ocosingo Km 3.5; r $108-118; **P** ⊠ ⊠) The Nututun, 3.5km south of town on the road toward San Cristóbal, has spacious, comfortable, air-conditioned rooms in large and exuberant tropical gardens. As well as a good pool in the gardens, there's a wonderful bathing spot (free for guests, $2 for others) in the Río Chacamax, which flows through the hotel property. The hotel restaurant is ordinary, however.

Eating

Palenque is definitely not the gastronomic capital of Mexico, but there's an improving dining scene and prices are fair.

Restaurant Las Tinajas (cnr 20 de Noviembre & Abasolo; mains $4-9; ☯ 7:30am-10pm) Gargantuan portions and excellent home-style cooking make Las Tinajas a perennial travelers' favorite. Both branches, one either side of the same intersection, have exactly the same menu and equally good cooking, but the newer – more westerly one – is considerably airier. *Camarones al guajillo* (prawns with a not-too-hot type of chili) and *robalo a la veracruzana* (snook in a tomato/olives/onion sauce) are both delicious.

Don Mucho's (☎ 348-05-20; El Panchán; snacks $1.50-3.50, mains $3.50-8.50) Ever-popular Don Mucho's provides great-value meals in a jungly El Panchán setting, with a slightly magical candle-lit atmosphere at night. Busy waiters bring pasta, fish, meat, plenty of *antojitos,* and pizzas (cooked in a purpose-built Italian-designed wood-fired oven) that are some of the finest this side of Naples. And there's live music around 8pm or 9pm, plus fire dancing most nights!

Restaurant Maya Cañada (☎ 345-02-16; Merle Green s/n; mains $5.50-13) This relatively upmarket and professionally run restaurant in the leafy La Cañada area serves fine steaks and terrific seafood kebabs. It's open to the air and has a cool upstairs terrace.

La Selva (☎ 345-03-63; Hwy 199; mains $5-15; ☯ 1-11pm) Palenque's most upmarket restaurant, 200m south of the Maya head intersection, serves up well-prepared steaks, seafood, salads and *antojitos* under a big *palapa* roof, with jungle-themed stained-glass panels brightening one wall.

Restaurant Maya (☎ 345-00-42; cnr Independencia & Hidalgo; mains $5-9; ☯ 7am-11pm) This long-established, neat and clean place facing El Parque, serves up a good range of meat, fish and *antojitos,* and decent breakfasts, under whirring fans.

Café de Yara (☎ 345-02-69; Hidalgo 66; snacks & breakfasts $2.50-4.50, mains $4.50-8; ☯ 7am-11pm) An efficient and modern café, good for breakfasts, spaghetti and salads, the Yara also serves fine organic Chiapas coffee in espresso, cappuccino, latte and other forms.

Mara's (☎ 345-25-78; Juárez 1; mains $5.50-8.50; ☯ 7am-11pm) Mara's is out of exactly the same mold as nearby Restaurant Maya – just with a touch less order and care. Amuse yourself with the menu translations, such as 'shrimp food tuffs bigger' for large prawn cocktail.

Rakshita's (El Panchán; items $2-3; ☒ Ⓥ) Vegetarian Rakshita's, beside a tinkling Panchán stream, offers tasty light meals from

French toast and quesadillas to omelettes and salads.

Cafetería Motiepa (Carretera Palenque-Ruinas Km 6; snacks $2-4; ☯ 9am-4pm) Next to the site museum near the ruins, this is a good stop for a snack or drink.

Mayabell (☎ 345-14-64; Carretera Palenque-Ruinas Km 6; mains $5-9) The open-sided restaurant at Mayabell campground serves up a good range of good *antojitos* and meat and fish dishes.

Entertainment

Drinks in restaurants are about as lively as it gets in town, but a couple of spots out on the road to the ruins offer a bit of diversion. At Panchán, also keep an eye open for the stunning music, dance and multimedia shows of Teatro en la Selva, staged about once a month.

La Palapa (for information ☎ 345-04-21; Carretera Palenque-Ruinas Km 5; ☯ until 3am) Locals from town, as well as travelers, head to this 'jungle lounge.' Reggae, psycho, salsa and electronica play in a large *palapa* with tables, chairs, dance space and even sofas. Food's available too.

Mayan Theater (☎ 345-05-33; reservaciones@villas-kinha.com; Hotel Villas Kin-Ha, Carretera Palenque-Ruinas Km 2.7; admission $11.50) A theatrical show based on ancient Palenque is staged in the Kin-Ha's auditorium (constructed around a sacred ceiba tree) if a minimum 12 people reserve. Times vary.

Getting There & Away

Palenque's airport, 3km north of town along Hwy 199, has been closed to regular passenger flights for several years.

The **Instituto Nacional de Migración** (☎ 345-07-95; 6km north of town on Hwy 199; ☯ 8am-4pm) can be reached by 'Playas' combis that run here from the Autotransportes Otolum terminal on Allende ($0.90).

See p791 for a warning about Hwy 199 between Palenque and San Cristóbal. There are also occasional reports of theft on board buses to and from Mérida, especially at night.

The main bus terminal is that of **ADO** (☎ 345-13-44; Juárez s/n), with deluxe and 1st-class services; it's also used by OCC (1st-class) and TRS (2nd-class). **AEXA** (☎ 345-26-30; Juárez 159), with 1st-class buses, and Cardesa (2nd-class), are 1½ blocks east. Vans to

Ocosingo wait on 4 and 5 Pte Sur, near the bus stations, and leave when full. **Transportes Palenque** (☎ 345-24-30; cnr Allende & 20 de Noviembre) and **Autotransportes Río Chancalá** (☎ 341-33-56; Calle 5 de Mayo 120) run vans to Tenosique.

It's a good idea to buy your outward bus ticket a day in advance. Daily departures include the following:

Destination	Price	Duration	Frequency
Campeche	$18-25	5½-7hr	4 from ADO
Cancún	$41-48	13-14hr	5 from ADO
Mérida	$27-30	8hr	4 from ADO
Mexico City	$56	13hr	3 from ADO
Oaxaca	$42	14½hr	1 from ADO
Ocosingo	$3.75-7.50	2½hr	9 from ADO, 6 AEXA & vans leave about every 30min
San Cristóbal de Las Casas	$7-11	5¼hr	8 from ADO & 6 AEXA
Tenosique	$4-5	2hr	Transportes Palenque vans hourly 5am-7pm
Tulum	$36-41	11hr	4 from ADO
Tuxtla Gutiérrez	$10-16	7hr	8 from ADO & 6 AEXA
Villahermosa	$4.50-7	2hr	17 from ADO & 10 AEXA

For information on transportation along the Carretera Fronteriza (for Lacanjá Chansayab, Bonampak, Yaxchilán, Guatemala and other destinations), see p844.

Getting Around

Taxis wait at the northeast corner of El Parque and at the ADO bus station; they charge $3.75 to El Panchán or Mayabell, and $5 to the ruins.

BONAMPAK, YAXCHILÁN & THE CARRETERA FRONTERIZA

The ancient Maya cities of Bonampak and Yaxchilán, southeast of Palenque, are easily accessible thanks to the Carretera Fronteriza, a paved road running parallel to the Mexico–Guatemala border, all the way from Palenque to the Lagos de Montebello, around the fringe of the Lacandón Jungle. Bonampak, famous for its frescoes, is 148km by road from Palenque; the bigger and more important Yaxchilán, with a peerless jungle setting beside the broad and

swift Río Usumacinta, is 173km by road, then about 22km by boat.

The Carretera Fronteriza also gives access to the Lacandón village of Lacanjá Chansayab (p845), and its several surrounding attractions, and to the excellent ecolodge Las Guacamayas in Reforma Agraria (p849). In addition it's the main route from Chiapas to Guatemala's northern Petén region (home of several major Maya sites including mighty Tikal), via the town of Frontera Corozal.

Dangers & Annoyances

Drug trafficking and illegal migration are facts of life in this border region, and the Carretera Fronteriza more or less encircles the main area of Zapatista rebel activity and support, so you'll encounter numerous military checkpoints along the road. You shouldn't have anything to fear from these checks. For your own security, it's best to be off the Carretera Fronteriza before dusk – especially the most isolated section in the far southeast, between Benemérito de las Américas and the Chajul turnoff.

This part of Mexico tends to ignore daylight saving time, so triple-check all transportation schedules! And don't forget insect repellent.

Tours

It's perfectly possible to visit this area independently, and to travel through to Guatemala likewise, but there are also tour options. Many Palenque travel agencies (see p839) run day tours to Bonampak and Yaxchilán for around $60 per person, usually including entry fees, two meals and transportation in an air-conditioned van. There's also a two-day version for around $105, with an overnight stay at Lacanjá Chansayab (often referred to as the 'Ecological Reserve' in the publicity). Most of the same agencies offer transportation packages from Palenque to Flores, Guatemala – usually via an air-conditioned van to Frontera Corozal, river launch up the Usumacinta to Bethel in Guatemala, and public bus on to Flores – 10 or 11 hours altogether, for around $42. Two-day packages to Flores, visiting Bonampak and Yaxchilán en route, are around $115.

Check carefully the details of these offers: how many meals, what transportation, and so on.

TABASCO & CHIAPAS

Getting There & Away

From Palenque, **Autotransporte Chamoán** (Hidalgo s/n) runs vans to Frontera Corozal ($6, 2½ to three hours, 12 times daily). **Transporte Benito Juárez** (☎ 916-345-28-08; cnr Juárez & 20 de Noviembre) runs combis to Benemérito ($6, 3½ hours, every 30 minutes from 4am to 5:30pm). **Autotransportes Río Chancalá** (☎ 916-341-33-56; 5 de Mayo 120), running to Benemérito hourly from 4am to noon, charges $1 less, but terminates at the north edge of Benemérito.

Línea Comitán Lagos de Montebello (☎ 916-345-12-60; Velasco Suárez s/n), two blocks west of Palenque market, runs vans to Benemérito ($6) seven times daily (5:45am to 2:45pm), with the first four services (5:45am, 7:15am, 8:45am and 10:15am) continuing round the Carretera Fronteriza to the Lagos de Montebello ($14, seven hours to Tziscao) and Comitán ($17, eight hours).

All these services stop at San Javier ($3.50 to $4.50, two hours), the turnoff for Lacanjá Chansayab and Bonampak, 140km from Palenque; and at Crucero Corozal ($4 to $5, 2½ hours), the intersection for Frontera Corozal.

Drivers should note: there are no gas stations on the Carretera Fronteriza, but plenty of entrepreneurial locals sell gasoline from large plastic containers. Watch for '*Se vende gasolina*' signs.

Bonampak

Bonampak's setting in dense jungle hid it from the outside world until 1946. Stories of how it was revealed are full of mystery and innuendo, but it seems that Charles Frey, a young WWII conscientious objector from the US, and John Bourne, heir to the Singer sewing machine fortune, were the first outsiders to visit the site when Chan Bor, a Lacandón, took them there in February 1946. Later in 1946 an American photographer, Giles Healey, was also led to the site by Chan Bor and found the Templo de las Pinturas with its famous murals.

The site of **Bonampak** (admission $3; ☉ 8am-4:45pm) spreads over 2.4 sq km, but all the main ruins stand around the rectangular Gran Plaza. Never a major city, Bonampak spent most of the Classic period under Yaxchilán's sphere of influence. The most impressive surviving monuments were built under Chan Muwan II, a nephew of the Yaxchilán's Itzamnaaj B'alam II, who acceded to Bonampak's throne in AD 776. The 6m-high **Stele 1** in the Gran Plaza depicts Chan Muwan holding a ceremonial staff at the height of his reign. He also features in **Stele 2** and **Stele 3** on the Acrópolis, which rises from the south end of the plaza.

However, it's the astonishing frescoes inside the modest-looking **Templo de las Pinturas** (Edificio 1) that have given Bonampak its fame – and its name, which means 'Painted Walls' in Yucatecan Maya.

Diagrams outside the temple help interpret these murals, which are the finest known from pre-Hispanic America, but which have weathered badly since their discovery. (Early visitors even chucked kerosene over the walls in an attempt to bring out the colors.) Room 1, on the left as you face the temple, shows the consecration of Chan Muwan II's infant son, who is seen held in arms toward the top of the right end of the room's south wall (facing you as you enter). Witnessing the ceremony are 14 jade-toting noblemen. The central Room 2 shows tumultuous battle scenes on its east and south walls and vault, while on the north wall Chan Muwan II, in jaguar-skin battle dress, presides over the torture (by fingernail removal) and sacrifice of prisoners. A severed head lies below him, beside the foot of a sprawling captive. Room 3 shows a celebratory dance on the Acrópolis steps by lords wearing huge headdresses, and on its east wall three white-robed women puncture their tongues in a ritual bloodletting. The sacrifices, the bloodletting and the dance may all have been part of the ceremonies surrounding the new heir.

In reality, the infant prince probably never got to rule Bonampak; the place was abandoned before the murals were finished, as Classic Maya civilization evaporated.

The Bonampak site abuts the Reserva de la Biosfera Montes Azules, and is rich in wildlife. *Refrescos* (refreshments) and snacks are sold at the entrance to the Monumento Natural Bonampak protected zone, 8km before the ruins, and by the archaeological site entrance.

GETTING THERE & AWAY

Bonampak is 12km from San Javier on the Carretera Fronteriza. The first 3km, to the Lacanjá Chansayab turnoff, is paved, and the rest is good gravel/dirt road through the

BONAMPAK   0 ⌒ 50 m

To Site Entrance
(500m)

Edificio 15   Edificio 16

Gran Plaza

Stele 1

Edificio 1
(Templo de
las Pinturas)

Stele 3   Edificio 17

Stele 2

Edificio 3

Edificio
2

forest. Taxis will take you from San Javier or the Lacanjá turnoff to the ruins and back for $5 per person, including waiting time. Private vehicles cannot pass the Monumento Natural Bonampak entrance, 1km past the Lacanjá turnoff, but you can rent bicycles there for $5 for three hours, or take a combi to the ruins for $7 round-trip.

Lacanjá Chansayab

pop 600 / elevation 320m

Lacanjá Chansayab, the largest Lacandón Maya village, is 6km from San Javier on the Carretera Fronteriza, and 12km from Bonampak. Its family compounds are scattered around a wide area, many of them with creeks or even the Río Lacanjá flowing past their grassy grounds. Low-key tourism is now an important income-earner and many families run 'campamentos' with rooms, camping and hammock space. As you approach the village you'll cross the Río Lacanjá on a bridge, from which it's about 700m to a central intersection where tracks go left (south), right (north) and straight on (west).

The *campamentos* all offer guided walks through the surrounding forests to the 8m-high, 30m-wide **Cascada Ya Toch Kusam** waterfall, the little-explored ancient Maya **Lacanjá ruins**, and the 2.5km-long **Laguna Lacanjá**. The waterfall can actually be reached by a self-guiding trail, the 2.5km **Sendero Ya Toch Kusam** (admission $3.50), which starts 200m west of the central intersection. To continue from the fall to the ruins (a further 2km or so) you

do need a guide. A typical three-hour guided walk to the fall and ruins costs $20 per group, plus the admission fee for the trail.

Staying at Lacanjá is an interesting experience, and the Lacandón people are amiable and welcoming, though don't expect to find much evidence of their old way of life: the villagers here are now predominantly Presbyterian and attuned to the modern world, and only a few wear the traditional long white Lacandón tunic. Some have developed their traditional crafts into commercial *artesanías*, and you may want to budget some pesos for the pottery, wood carvings, seed necklaces, arrows and drums that they sell.

SLEEPING & EATING

The *campamentos* mentioned here are just a selection from several in existence.

Campamento Río Lacanja (www.ecochiapas.com/la canja; bunk $9.50, d $24, Ya'ax Can r/tr/q $38/45/52; P) These accommodations 2km south of the central intersection are among the best, though they're also among the priciest. Rustic semi-open-air wood-frame cabins with mosquito nets stand close to the jungle-shrouded Río Lacanjá, open to the sounds and sights of the forest and river, while a separate group of large rooms with fans, two solid wooden double beds, tile floors and hot-water bathroom is called Cabañas Ya'ax Can. There's also a restaurant here serving all meals ($3.50 to $5). As well as guided walks, rafting trips on the Río Lacanjá – which has waterfalls up to 2.5m high but no rapids – are offered for a minimum of four people: a half-day outing including Lacanjá ruins and Cascada Ya Toch Kusam (both reached on foot from the river) costs $52 per person; an overnight rafting and camping trip also visiting Bonampak ruins is $80 per person. Rafting trips and tours taking in Campamento Río Lacanjá can be reserved through **Explora** (☎ 967-678-42-95; www.ecochiapas .com; 1 de Marzo 30; ☷ 9am-2pm & 4:30-8pm Mon-Sat) in San Cristóbal de Las Casas.

Campamento Vicente Paniagua (r with shared bathroom per person $5, s/d/tr/q with private bathroom $9.50/19/28/38; meals $4-5; P) This friendly *campamento* in nice riverside gardens, 600m west from the central intersection, has a small block of large clean rooms with private bathrooms, plus cheaper, more basic, small wooden rooms.

Campamento Chambor Kin (camping per person $2.50, r with shared bathroom per person $5, s/d/tr/q with private bathroom $9.50/19/28/38; meals $3-4; **P**) Just north of the central intersection, Chambor Kin has similar accommodations to Vicente Paniagua, in another pretty creekside garden setting.

Camping Margarito (camping per person $2, d/q with shared bathroom $14/19, s/d/tr/q with private bathroom $14/24/33/47; **P**) These lodgings, run by a friendly Lacandón family, are at the fork where the Lacanjá and Bonampak roads diverge, 3km from San Javier. You can choose between large, clean rooms with two double beds and private bathroom, and smaller rooms with shared bathrooms, or camp on the grassy lawn area. Meals are available too.

GETTING THERE & AWAY

A taxi to Lacanjá Chansayab from San Javier costs $5, or $1.50 per person on a *colectivo* basis.

Frontera Corozal

pop 5300 / elevation 200m

This riverside frontier town (formerly called Frontera Echeverría) is an indispensable stepping-stone to the beautiful ruins of Yaxchilán, and is on the main route between Chiapas and Guatemala's Petén region. Inhabited mainly by Chol Maya, who settled here in the 1970s, Frontera Corozal is 16km by paved road from Crucero Corozal junction on the Carretera Fronteriza. The broad Río Usumacinta, flowing swiftly between jungle-covered banks, forms the Mexico–Guatemala border here.

Long, fast, outboard-powered *lanchas* come and go from the river *embarcadero*. Almost everything you'll need is on the paved street leading back from the river here – including the **immigration office** (7am-6pm), 400m from the *embarcadero,* where you should hand in/obtain a tourist card if you're leaving for/arriving from Guatemala.

The neat and modern **Museo de la Cuenca del Usumacinta** (Museum of the Usumacinta Basin; admission free; 8am-6pm), opposite the immigration office, has good examples of Chol Maya dress, and some information in Spanish on the area's post-conquest history, but pride of place goes to two fine and intricately carved steles retrieved from the nearby site of Dos Caobas.

SLEEPING & EATING

Escudo Jaguar (201-250-80-57; mx.geocities.com /hotel_escudojaguar; camping per person $6; cabaña with shared bathroom d/tr $14/22, cabaña with 1/2/3 d beds $31/47/62; **P**) Professionally run by a local Chol organization, Escudo Jaguar overlooks the river 300m from the *embarcadero*. Its solidly built, pink, thatched *cabañas* are all kept spotless, and come equipped with fans and mosquito nets. The best are very spacious and have hot showers and terraces strung with hammocks. Room prices dip by up to 30% outside the high seasons. There's also a good restaurant (mains $5 to $6.50, breakfasts $4 to $5.50, open 7am to 8pm) serving straightforward, well-prepared Mexican dishes.

Tsol K'in Nueva Alianza (in Mexico City 55-5329-0995 ext 8061; www.ecoturlacandona.com; ctnuevaalianza@ hotmail.com; s/d with shared bathroom $7.50/15, f $61-84; **P**) Friendly, Chol-run Nueva Alianza, among trees 150m along a side road from the museum, provides well-built family rooms with fans, bathrooms and good wooden furniture. The budget rooms are small and plain, with wooden walls that don't reach the ceiling, but are well kept. There's also another good restaurant (mains $3.50 to $5.50, breakfasts $2 to $3.50, open 7am to 8pm).

GETTING THERE & AWAY

If you can't get a bus or combi direct to Frontera Corozal, get one to Crucero Corozal, 16km southeast of San Javier on the Carretera Fronteriza, where taxis ($2.50 per person *colectivo,* $7 otherwise) and occasional vans ($2) run to Frontera Corozal.

Autotransporte Chamoán vans run from Frontera Corozal *embarcadero* to Palenque ($6, 2½ to three hours) around 10 times daily, with the last departure at 3pm.

Lanchas leave for Bethel (40 minutes upstream) on the Guatemalan bank of the Usumacinta, and for La Técnica, directly opposite Frontera Corozal. Four **lancha organizations** (boat to Bethel for 3/4/7/10 people $33/42/52/66) have desks in a thatched building near the *embarcadero,* and all charge the same prices. Information in Frontera Corozal is unreliable on onward buses within Guatemala from Bethel to Flores ($4, four hours), but there are normally departures around 5am, 11am or noon, 2pm and 4pm, Guatemalan time – the same as Frontera Corozal time unless daylight saving is in force in

Frontera Corozal (Guatemala never applies daylight saving). *Lanchas* to La Técnica go on a *colectivo* basis, with fares negotiable (under $1 per person if you're lucky). Buses from La Técnica to Flores ($5, five hours) leave around 4am and 10am or 11am, stopping for immigration in Bethel. The *lanchas* can carry bicycles and even motorcycles.

Yaxchilán

Jungle-shrouded **Yaxchilán** (admission $3.75; ☺ 8am-4:45pm, last entry 4:15pm) has a terrific setting above a horseshoe loop in the Usumacinta. The control this location gave it over river commerce, and a series of successful alliances and conquests, made Yaxchilán one of the most important Classic Maya cities in the Usumacinta region. Archaeologically, Yaxchilán is famed for its ornamented facades and roof combs, and its impressive stone lintels carved with conquest and ceremonial scenes. A flashlight is a help in exploring some parts of the site.

Another feature of these ruins are the howler monkeys that come to feed in some of the tall trees here. You'll almost certainly hear their roars, and you stand a good chance of seeing some. Spider monkeys, and occasionally red macaws, are also sometimes sighted here.

Yaxchilán peaked in power and splendor between AD 681 and 800 under the rulers Itzamnaaj B'alam II (Shield Jaguar II, 681–742), Pájaro Jaguar IV (Bird Jaguar IV, 752–68) and Itzamnaaj B'alam III (Shield Jaguar III, 769–800). The city was abandoned around AD 810. Inscriptions here tell more about its 'Jaguar' dynasty than is known of almost any other Maya ruling clan. The shield-and-jaguar symbol appears on many Yaxchilán buildings and steles; Pájaro Jaguar IV's hieroglyph is a small jungle cat with feathers on its back and a bird superimposed on its head.

At the site, *refrescos* are sold at a shack near the river landing. Most of the main monuments have information boards in three languages, including English.

As you walk toward the ruins, a signed path to the right leads up to the **Pequeña Acrópolis**, a group of ruins on a small hilltop – you can visit this later. Staying on the main path, you soon reach the mazy passages of **El Laberinto** (Edificio 19), built between AD 742 and 752, during the interregnum

between Itzamnaaj B'alam II and Pájaro Jaguar IV. Dozens of bats shelter under the structure's roof today. From this complicated two-level building you emerge at the northwest end of the extensive **Gran Plaza**.

Though it's hard to imagine anyone here ever wanting to be hotter than they already were, **Edificio 17** was apparently a sweat house. About halfway along the plaza, **Stele 1**, flanked by weathered sculptures of a crocodile and a jaguar, shows Pájaro Jaguar IV in a ceremony that took place in 761. **Edificio 20**, from the time of Itzamnaaj B'alam III, was the last significant structure built at Yaxchilán; its lintels are now in Mexico City. **Stele 11**, at the northeast corner of the Gran Plaza, was originally found in front of Edificio 40. The bigger of the two figures visible on it is Pájaro Jaguar IV.

An imposing stairway climbs from Stele 1 to **Edificio 33**, the best-preserved temple at Yaxchilán, with about half of its roof comb intact. The final step in front of the building is carved with ball-game scenes, and splendid relief carvings embellish the undersides of the lintels. Inside is a statue of Pájaro Jaguar IV, minus his head, which he lost to treasure-seeking 19th-century timber cutters.

From the clearing behind Edificio 33, a path leads into the trees. About 20m along this, fork left uphill; go left at another fork after about 80m, and in some 10 minutes, mostly going uphill, you'll reach three buildings on a hilltop: **Edificio 39**, **Edificio 40** and **Edificio 41**. Climb to the top of Edificio 41 for great views across the top of the jungle to the distant mountains of Guatemala.

GETTING THERE & AWAY

River launches take 40 minutes running downstream from Frontera Corozal, and one hour to return. Four *lancha* outfits, with desks in a thatched building near the Frontera Corozal *embarcadero*, all charge the same prices for **trips** (return journey with 2½ hours at the ruins for 3/4/7/10 people $56/66/84/113). *Lanchas* normally leave frequently until 1:30pm or so, and it's often possible to hook up with other travelers or a tour group to share costs.

Benemérito de las Américas
pop 6500 / elevation 200m

South of Frontera Corozal you soon enter the far eastern corner of Chiapas known as Marqués de Comillas (for its Spanish

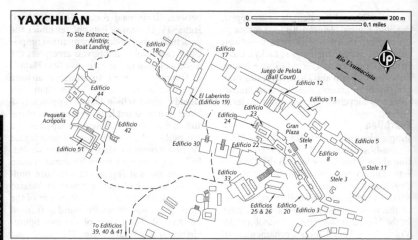

YAXCHILÁN

former landowner). After oil explorers opened tracks into this jungle region in the 1970s, land-hungry settlers poured in from all over Mexico. Ranching and logging have made some settlers rich, while others profit from smuggling drugs or immigrants. Note that for your own security, it's best to be off the Carretera Fronteriza before dusk – especially the most isolated section in the far southeast, between Benemérito de las Américas and the Chajul turnoff.

Benemérito de las Américas is the region's main town. Sat on the west bank of the Río Salinas – an Usumacinta tributary that forms the Mexico–Guatemala border here – it's a bit forlorn, with an almost 'Wild West' atmosphere and no attractions except as a staging post (a possible route into northern Guatemala starts here). The main street is a 1.5km-long stretch of the Carretera Fronteriza. **Hotel de Las Américas** (s/d $19/24, d with air-con $30; **P** 🛜), on the highway at the south end of town, is an unfinished but already dilapidated hotel, whose fairly clean rooms at least have fans and bathrooms with hot water. For security, check that the windows close properly. The best food is at the log-cabin **Restaurant Viejo Oeste** (mains $3.75-9.50; 🕑 9am-9pm), on the highway in the middle of town.

GETTING THERE & AWAY

Transporte Benito Juárez, on the highway toward the north end of town, runs combis to Palenque ($6, three to 3½ hours) every 30 minutes from 4am to 5:30pm, stopping at Crucero Corozal ($2, 45 minutes) and San Javier ($2.50, one hour) en route. Línea Comitán Lagos de Montebello, on the highway toward the south end of town, runs seven vans to Palenque ($6, three to 3½ hours) between 4am and 3:15pm, and nine along the Carretera Fronteriza and Pan-American Highway to Comitán ($11, five hours) between 4:15am and 2pm.

At Benemérito's river *embarcadero* (1km off the main street), you can hire a *lancha* for $150 to $200 (negotiable) to take you three or four hours up the Río Salinas and Río de la Pasión to Sayaxché (Guatemala), a base for visiting the interesting Maya ruins of Ceibal, Aguateca and Dos Pilas. On the way, you have the opportunity to stop and see more ruins at Pipiles and Altar de los Sacrificios.

An alternative is to take a *lancha* a short distance downriver to Laureles, on the Guatemalan side (*colectivo* $2, *especial* $15). Buses leave Laureles at around 3am, 4am and 5am for El Subín ($2.75, 2½ hours), a junction on the Flores–Sayaxché road with plenty of minibuses and buses to both towns.

Benemérito has no immigration post; you must pick up or hand in Mexican tourist cards at Frontera Corozal.

Benemérito de las Américas to Lagos de Montebello

Below Benemérito, the Carretera Fronteriza heads 60km south before turning west. Deforestation gradually gives way to more intact forest, with the road crossing several rivers, but you still pass numerous villages founded in recent decades, some of them settled by Guatemalan refugees. West of Ixcán you climb more than 1000m up to the cooler, pine-forested highlands around the Lagos de Montebello.

REFORMA AGRARIA

The reason to come to this small village off the highway, 49km southwest of Benemérito,

is the beautiful ecolodge **Las Guacamayas** (☎ / fax 201-250-80-04, in Mexico City ☎ 55-5151-1869; Ejido Reforma Agraria; camping per person $2.50, dm $7, s/d/tr/q cabaña $28/42/47/52, meals each $5; P), which is the heart of an impressive community program to protect the local population of scarlet macaws. This spectacular and endangered member of the parrot family once ranged as far north as Veracruz, but its only Mexican home today is far eastern Chiapas. Numbers

---

THE LACANDÓN JUNGLE & THE USUMACINTA RIVER

The Selva Lacandona (Lacandón Jungle), in eastern Chiapas, occupies just one quarter of 1% of Mexico. Yet it contains more than 4300 plant species, about 17% of the Mexican total; 450 types of butterfly, 42% of the national total; at least 340 birds, 32% of the total; and 163 mammals, 30% of the Mexican total. Among these are such emblematic creatures as the jaguar, red macaw, white turtle, tapir and harpy eagle.

This great fund of natural resources and genetic diversity is the southwest end of the Selva Maya, a 30,000-sq-km corridor of tropical rainforest stretching from Chiapas across northern Guatemala into Belize and the southern Yucatán. But the Lacandón Jungle is shrinking fast, under pressure from ranchers, loggers, oil prospectors, and settlers desperate for land. From around 15,000 sq km in the 1950s, an estimated 3000 to 4500 sq km of jungle remains today. Most of what's left is in the Reserva de la Biosfera Montes Azules and the neighboring Reserva de la Biosfera Lacan-tun.

Waves of land-hungry settlers deforested the northern third of the Lacandón Jungle by about 1960. Also badly deforested are the far eastern Marqués de Comillas area (settled since the 1970s) and Las Cañadas, between Ocosingo and Montes Azules. Struggling Las Cañadas settlers have always provided some of the Zapatista rebels' strongest support.

The Montes Azules reserve has itself become something of a battleground between environmental groups and settlers in recent years. According to Conservation International (CI), at least 10 new communities have been established illegally inside the reserve since 2000. Some have since been relocated. Many of the communities within the reserve back the Zapatistas, whose supporters argue that the settlers are using the forests in sustainable ways, and claim that CI seeks to exploit the forests for the benefit of the Mexican biotechnology giant Grupo Pulsar.

Intimately intertwined with the wellbeing of the Lacandón Jungle is that of the Río Usumacinta, the largest river between Venezuela and the US, which discharges an estimated 105 billion cubic meters of fresh water into the Gulf of Mexico in Tabasco each year. The Usumacinta forms the Mexico–Guatemala border along the eastern fringe of the Lacandón Jungle and, with its tributaries, drains not only all the Lacandón Jungle but a large part of the rest of Chiapas, and about half of Guatemala. Like the jungle around it, the river is an inestimable ecological and genetic treasure. *Lacantunia enigmatica*, a species of catfish discovered in Usumacinta tributaries in 2005, represents only the second new fish family revealed to science since 1938.

The Usumacinta basin, including the Lacandón Jungle, has long supported human life too, and during the Classic Maya period important cities such as Yaxchilán and Piedras Negras (Guatemala) flourished on the river's banks.

Governmental proposals to build a large hydroelectric dam on the Usumacinta resurface every few years, sending environmentalists, archaeologists and others scurrying noisily to the barricades. The most recent plan, made by President Fox in 2001 for a dam at Boca del Cerro near Tenosique, was shelved, but talk of a new scheme is never far beneath the surface. Many of those who are concerned for the Usumacinta basin argue that a joint Mexican-Guatemalan protection plan is the best answer – something yet to approach reality. To find out more about this vital river and the challenges it faces, visit **goMaya** (www.gomaya.com) or read Christopher Shaw's marvelous *Sacred Monkey River*.

at Reforma Agraria have doubled to around 40 pairs since 1991, when the 14.5-sq-km macaw reserve was founded. The birds move in and out of the reserve in seasonal pursuit of food; the best months for observing them are December to June, when they are nesting.

The very friendly and welcoming lodge is right on the bank of the broad Río Lacantún, one of the Usumacinta's major tributaries, with the Reserva de la Biosfera Montes Azules on the opposite bank. Large, comfortable, thatch-roofed *cabañas*, with full mosquito screens, verandas and ample bathrooms with hot showers, are spread around the extensive grounds, linked by wooden walkways. The lodge has a good restaurant overlooking the river, serving straightforward but satisfying Mexican meals.

Two-hour guided macaw-spotting walks cost $14 – they're best in the early morning or at dusk. The reserve also keeps half a dozen macaws in an enclosure so that you can get a close-up look. Boat trips into the Montes Azules reserve cost $66/94 for two/three hours – you should spot crocodiles and howler monkeys, and with luck toucans and white-tailed deer.

Getting There & Away

The road to Reforma Agraria turns west off the Carretera Fronteriza 8km south of Benemérito. It's paved as far as Pico de Oro (25km from the highway), then unpaved for 16km. Beyond Reforma Agraria the road continues unpaved for 33km to rejoin the Carretera Fronteriza 5km south of Chajul. It's normally perfectly passable in an ordinary saloon car, but in the rainy season you should ask ahead about its condition. From Palenque, **Transportes La Jungla del Marquez** (20 de Noviembre s/n) runs combis to Pico de Oro ($9, four hours), leaving about every two hours from 8am to 2pm, and passing through Benemérito approximately three hours later. Occasional *camionetas* also run from Benemérito to Pico de Oro ($2.50, 40 minutes). *Camionetas* run from Pico de Oro to Reforma Agraria ($1.50, one hour), and vice versa, about hourly from 6am or 7am till early afternoon. A taxi from Benemérito to Reforma Agraria costs around $30. From Comitán, around eight vans a day run to Reforma Agraria ($9, 4½ hours), passing through the Lagos de Montebello en route (see p853 for further details).

LAS NUBES

If you're driving, a detour to these beautiful and dramatic waterfalls and rapids on the turquoise Río Santo Domingo is well worth your time. Las Nubes is 12km off the Carretera Fronteriza from a turning signed 'Centro Turístico Las Nubes,' 55km from Tziscao. Some of the river pools are great swimming spots, and rustic cabins are available if you don't want to leave in a hurry.

COMITÁN

☎ 963 / pop 80,000 / elevation 1560m

Comitán is an orderly and fairly prosperous town with some colonial character, set on a high plain 90km southeast of San Cristóbal. Many travelers bypass Comitán on their way to Guatemala, but it's a very agreeable place to spend a few days, with some good places to stay and eat, a few interesting little museums, and several natural and archaeological attractions less than an hour away in the surrounding big-sky countryside.

The first Spanish settlement here, San Cristóbal de los Llanos, was founded in 1527.

Orientation & Information

Comitán is set on hilly terrain, with a beautiful broad main plaza. Hwy 190 (the Pan-American), here named Blvd Dr Belisario Domínguez and often just called 'El Bulevar,' passes through the west of town.

Banorte (1a Calle Sur Pte 5; ☽ 9am-4pm Mon-Fri, 10am-2pm Sat) Currency exchange and ATM.

Cyber@dicts (Local 13B, Pasaje Morales; Internet per hr $0.50; ☽ 9am-10pm)

Post office (Av Central Sur 45; ☽ Mon-Fri 9am-3pm)

Tourist office (☎ 632-40-47; Calle Central Ote 6; ☽ 8am-4pm Mon-Fri, 8am-2pm Sat) On the north side of the plaza, with helpful, fairly well-informed staff.

Sights

Just south of the main plaza is the **Casa Museo Dr Belisario Domínguez** (☎ 632-13-00; Av Central Sur 35; admission $0.50; ☽ 10am-6:45pm Tue-Sat, 9am-12:45pm Sun), the family home of Comitán's biggest hero (see boxed text, opposite) and the site of his medical practice. It provides (in Spanish) fascinating insights into the state of medicine and the life of the professional classes in early-20th-century Chiapas (with a reconstruction of the on-site pharmacy), as well as the heroic tale of Domínguez' political career, ending in his assassination.

MARTYR FOR FREE SPEECH

Comitán is officially called Comitán de Domínguez, and avenues and boulevards all over Chiapas are named for Belisario Domínguez. This *comiteco* was a true local hero who devoted his life to helping others and died for speaking the truth.

Belisario Domínguez (1863–1913) was a local doctor who, after training in Paris, set up a state-of-the-art practice in Comitán and held free consultations for the poor three days a week. Appointed mayor of Comitán in 1911, he introduced a street-cleaning service and a drinkable water supply, and improved schools and hospitals. Comitán still has some of the cleanest streets and best medical facilities in Mexico today.

In 1912, during the turbulent years of the Mexican Revolution, Domínguez was elected a national senator. When president Francisco Madero was deposed, executed and replaced by his turncoat general Victoriano de la Huerta, Domínguez prepared a discourse for congress calling for the overthrow of Huerta, vilifying him as 'a bloody, ferocious soldier who murders without hesitation or scruple anyone who gets in his way,' who had 'gained power by betrayal' and whose first act as president was 'the cowardly murder of the president and vice-president who had been legally anointed by popular vote.' Domínguez was barred from presenting his discourse in congress, but he distributed it in printed form around Mexico City; upon which Huerta had him arrested, taken to Coyoacán cemetery, and murdered. The uproar this provoked led Huerta to dissolve congress and arrest 90 of its members, which only fomented further opposition to his rule, and Huerta was finally forced to resign in 1914.

Today, a statue of Belisario Domínguez, inscribed with words from his famed discourse, stands outside the senate building in Mexico City, and since 1954 the highest accolade bestowed by Mexico's government has been the Belisario Domínguez Medal of Honor, awarded annually to an eminent Mexican with a distinguished lifetime career who has contributed most 'toward the welfare of mankind and the nation.'

One block further down this street is a neat little modern art museum, the **Museo de Arte Hermila Domínguez de Castellanos** (☎ 632-20-82; Av Central Sur 51; admission $0.50; ﹆ 9am-6pm Mon-Sat), with work by prominent Mexican artists, including José Luis Cuevas and Arnulfo Mendoza, as well as good temporary shows.

The **Museo Arqueológico de Comitán** (☎ 632-57-60; 1a Calle Sur Ote; admission free; ﹆ 9am-6pm Tue-Sun), just east of the plaza, displays artifacts from the area's many archaeological sites. The misshapen pre-Hispanic skulls on display – deliberately 'beautified' by squeezing infants' heads between boards – make you wonder what kind of thoughts would have taken shape inside such distorted brains.

On the plaza itself, the **Iglesia de Santo Domingo** (﹆ 10am-7pm) dates back to the 16th and 17th centuries, and sports unusual and handsome blind arcading on its tower. Its former monastic buildings next door are now the **Centro Cultural Rosario Castellanos** (admission free; ﹆ 9am-8pm Mon-Fri, 10am-5pm Sat & Sun) with a pretty wood-pillared patio featuring a mural on local history.

Tours

Agencia de Viajes Tenam (☎ 632-16-54; Pasaje Morales 8A) does tours to Tenam Puente, Lagos de Montebello and either the Chinkultic ruins or El Chiflón waterfalls, for $75 for up to six people.

Festivals & Events

Festival Internacional Rosario Castellanos is a week-long fiesta in early July, with free admission for many events.

Sleeping

There are some very good-value accommodations here.

BUDGET

Hotel del Virrey (☎ 632-18-11; hotel_delvirrey@hotmail.com; Av Central Nte 13; s/d/tr/q $28/32/36/40; ℗ 🖵) The friendly Virrey, in a 19th-century house, has characterful, artfully kitted-out rooms of varying sizes around a pretty courtyard. All have cable TV and spotless tiled bathrooms, and some upstairs enjoy a nice view of nearby El Calvario church.

Pensión Delfín (☎ 632-00-13; Av Central Sur 21; s/d/tr/q $19/25/33/38; ℗) The Delfín, on the west side

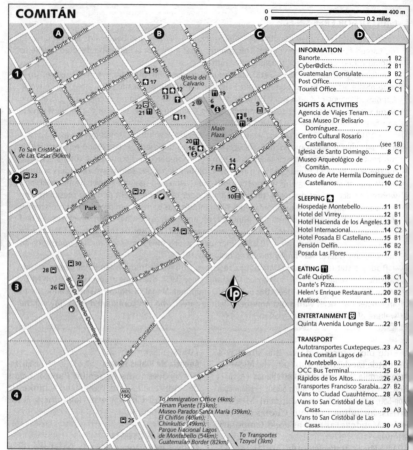

of the main plaza with a plant-filled patio, has well-kept, decent-sized rooms, some with wood paneling and all with cable TV.

Hotel Internacional (☎ 632-01-10; Av Central Sur 16; r $34; P) This downtown hotel is good value considering its comfort levels and stylish decor. All rooms have two double beds, TV and attractive bathrooms, but try to avoid those at the north end of the building, adjacent to a disco.

Posada Las Flores (☎ 632-33-34; 1a Av Pte Nte 17; s/d with shared bathroom $7.50/11.50, with private bathroom $14/16) Clean rooms with hot water and wood ceilings surround a pretty patio here.

Hospedaje Montebello (☎ 632-35-72; f_montebello@prodigy.net.mx; 1a Calle Nte Pte 10; s/d with shared bathroom $6/11.50, s with private bathroom $7-10.50,

d $13.50-17) A welcoming cheapie with large, tiled and clean rooms around a courtyard. Nos 10 to 12 are among the best rooms.

MIDRANGE

Hotel Posada El Castellano (☎ 632-33-47; www.posadaelcastellano.com.mx; 3a Calle Nte Pte 12; s/d/tr/q $32/36/40/43; P 🖳) This excellent hotel is colonial in style but modern in build and amenities. Comfy rooms, equipped with fan, cable TV and solid wood furniture, are on two floors around wood-pillared patios. Staff are amiable and there's a nice restaurant.

TOP END

Hotel Hacienda de los Ángeles (☎ 632-00-74; www.haciendadelosangeles.com; 2a Calle Nte Pte 6; r $66-84, ste

$113-141; (P) (X) (R)) Comitán's single luxury hotel, new in 2004, provides professional service and spacious accommodations with sober, classical-style decor. All rooms have at least two double beds or one king-size bed, air-con, cable TV, bathtub and quality furnishings, and most have hydro-massage. There's even a good pool with its own bar.

Eating

Café Quiptic (632-06-24; 1a Av Ote Sur s/n; breakfast $3.50-6.50, mains $5-6.50; 8am-11pm) At the southeast corner of the plaza, the Quiptic is set under an impressive stone colonnade and run by indigenous coffee growers. It serves tasty and filling breakfasts, plus superb organic coffee, salads, *antojitos*, meat dishes and desserts.

Matisse (632-71-52; 1a Av Pte Nte 16; mains $7-9.50; 2-11pm Tue-Sat, 2-5pm Sun) This stylish and popular Matisse serves inventive food in warm, wood-pillared surroundings. Start with a carpaccio or the excellent *fusiole* salad (spinach with nuts, bacon, avocado and balsamic oil), and follow it up with a beef *filete* or a creative pasta dish like rigatoni Venecia (with prawns, squid and a basil-and-wine sauce). There's plenty of wine and cocktails too, and a neat patio for alfresco dining when the temperature's right.

Dante's Pizza (632-03-09; 1a Av Ote Nte 8; pizzas 1-person $5-6, 2-person $8-9; 9am-11pm) Satisfying pizzas in a spacious upstairs locale where you can also go online for $1 per hour. Pasta, empanadas and *quesos fundidos* (melted cheese) are served here too, at lower prices.

Helen's Enrique Restaurant (632-17-30; Av Central Sur 19; mains $4.50-7; 8am-11:30pm) This long-running eatery, with a terrace overlooking the plaza, is OK for chicken and meat dishes, breakfasts and *antojitos* – or just for an evening beer.

Entertainment

Quinta Avenida Lounge Bar (1a Av Pte Nte 20; admission free-$3; 8pm-approx 3am Thu-Sat) High, stainless-steel tables and chairs don't permit much lounging, but this place fills up for live music and dancing from 11pm – at last check it was rock on Thursdays, *banda* on Saturdays.

Getting There & Around

Comitán's **OCC bus terminal** (632-0980; Blvd Dr Belisario Domínguez Sur 43) is on the Pan-American Hwy. Destinations served from here include the following:

Destination	Price	Duration	Frequency
Ciudad Cuauhtémoc	$4.50	1¾hr	5 daily
San Cristóbal de Las Casas	$2.50-4	1¾hr	16 daily
Tapachula (via Motozintla)	$12.50	5½hr	8 daily
Tuxtla Gutiérrez	$6-7.50	3½hr	16 daily

OCC also serves Oaxaca, Mexico City, Palenque, Villahermosa, Playa del Carmen and Cancún.

'Centro' combis and microbuses, across the road from the OCC terminal, take you to the main plaza for $0.40; a taxi is $1.50.

You can also reach San Cristóbal by Suburban vans ($2.75) and *colectivo* taxis ($3.50) from **Rápidos de los Altos** (Blvd Dr Belisario Domínguez Sur btwn 1a & 2a Calle Sur Pte). Further vans to San Cristóbal leave from two other stops across the road; vans for Ciudad Cuauhtémoc ($2.50, every 20 to 30 minutes, 5am to 4pm) leave from a stop just north of Rápidos de los Altos.

Vans to the Lagos de Montebello and along the Carretera Fronteriza are run by **Línea Comitán Lagos de Montebello** (632-08-75; 2a Av Pte Sur 23). There are departures to Laguna Bosque Azul ($2.50, one hour) and Tziscao ($2.50, 1¼ hours) every 20 to 30 minutes from 3am to 6pm; to Reforma Agraria ($9, 4½ hours) at 3am, 8:55am and 11:30am; to Benemérito de las Américas ($11, five hours) eight times daily, 4am to 2:30pm; and to Palenque ($17, eight hours) five times daily, 4am to 10am. **Transportes Tzoyol** (632-77-39; 4a Av Pte Sur 1039) runs further vans to Reforma Agraria, five times daily, 3am to 12:45pm, as well as to Amatitlán ($5, three hours) six times a day between 4am and 2pm.

There is an **immigration office** (632-22-00; Carretera Panamericana; 8am-3pm Mon-Fri) on the Pan-American Hwy just past the turning for Tzimol, 5km south of the town center.

AROUND COMITÁN
El Chiflón

These mighty waterfalls tumble off the edge of an escarpment 41km southwest of Comitán. For an up-close experience of sheer awesome power, El Chiflón is hard to beat. The local *ejido*, **San Cristobalito La Cascada** (☎ 963-703-65-84; admission $1; ☼ 7am-5:30pm), has set up a number of attractive amenities on the approach to the falls, including comfortable, well-built *cabañas* (d $28, q $38-42), all with bathroom and mosquito nets, and the good open-air **Restaurant La Ceiba** (light meals $2.50-3.75, mains $5-7; ☼ 7am-6pm). A 1km approach road heads up from Hwy 226 to the parking area, from which a well-made path leads 1.3km up alongside the forest-lined Río San Vicente (which has good swimming spots) to a series of increasingly dramatic and picturesque waterfalls. Finally you reach the 70m Velo de Novia fall: prepare to be drenched by flying spray.

From Comitán, **Autotransportes Cuxtepeques** (Blvd Dr Belisario Domínguez Sur btwn 1a & 2a Calle Nte Pte) runs vans and buses to the El Chiflón turnoff on Hwy 226 ($2, 45 minutes), about every 30 minutes, 5am to 4pm. If you're driving, take the Tzimol turning off the Pan-American Hwy, 5km south of central Comitán.

Tenam Puente

These **Maya ruins** (admission free; ☼ 9am-4pm) feature three ball courts, a 20m tiered pyramid and other structures rising from a terraced, wooded hillside. Like Chinkultic (see right) Tenam Puente was one of a set of fringe Classic Maya settlements in this part of Chiapas that – unlike more famed lowland sites such as Palenque and Yaxchilán – seem to have survived in the Postclassic period, possibly as long as AD 1200. It has a pleasant rural setting and good long-distance views.

A 5km-long paved road leads west to the site from Hwy 190, 9km south of Comitán. **Transportes Francisco Sarabia** (3a Av Pte Sur 8, Comitán) runs combis every 45 minutes, 7am to 6pm, to the site ($1.25) or to the village of Francisco Sarabia, 2km before Tenam Puente. The last bus from the ruins returns at 4pm. A taxi costs $12 return with an hour at the ruins.

Museo Parador Santa María

This beautiful **hotel-cum-museum** (☎ /fax 963-632-51-16; www.paradorsantamaria.com.mx; Carretera La Trinitaria-Lagos de Montebello Km 22; r $113; Ⓟ), 1.5km off the road to the Lagos de Montebello, is the most luxurious and atmospheric place to stay in the Comitán area. The restored 19th-century hacienda is decorated throughout with period furniture and art; some of the eight rooms have tiled bathtubs and fire-

places, and all look over expansive grassy lawns to the countryside beyond. The chapel here is a **religious art museum** (admission $2; ☼ 9am-6pm), open to all, with an interesting array of colonial-era work from Europe and the Philippines as well as Mexico and Guatemala. Look for the haunting 17th-century ivory saint's head from the Philippines, and the child Jesus attributed to the Spanish baroque genius Juan Martínez Montañés. There's also an excellent **restaurant** (mains $8.50-12.50; ☼ 8am-7pm), serving Chiapas and international dishes with some organic ingredients grown on-site. Look for the sign 22km from La Trinitaria on the Montebello road.

Chinkultic

These dramatically sited **ruins** (admission $2.75; ☼ 10am-4pm) lie 2km north of the road to the Lagos de Montebello, 48km from Comitán. The access road is paved.

Chinkultic was a minor Maya power during the late Classic period and, like Tenam Puente, may have survived into Postclassic times. Of 200 mounds scattered over a wide area, only a few have been cleared, but the site is worth a visit.

The ruins are in two groups. From the entrance, first take the path to the left, which curves around to the right below one of Chinkultic's biggest structures, E23, still covered in thick vegetation. The path reaches a grassy plaza with several weathered steles, some carved with human figures, and a long ball court on the right.

Return to the entrance, from which another path heads to the **Plaza Hundida** (Sunken Plaza), crosses a stream, then climbs steeply up to the **Acrópolis**, a partly restored temple atop a rocky escarpment, with remarkable views over the surrounding lakes and forests and down into a cenote 50m below – into which the Maya used to toss offerings of pottery, beads, bones and obsidian knives.

El Pino Feliz (☎ 963-102-10-89; Carretera La Trinitaria-Lagos de Montebello; r per person $5; Ⓟ), the roadside 'Happy Pine,' is by the highway just over 1km east of the Chinkultic turnoff. It has simple wood cabins with up to three double beds, and reliable hot water in the shared bathrooms. It also provides excellent meals (main dishes $2 to $3). The Albores family here make you feel part of the family, and can arrange walking or biking guides.

Lagos de Montebello

The temperate forest along the Guatemalan border east of Chinkultic is dotted with over 50 small lakes of varied hues, known as the Lagos (or Lagunas) de Montebello. The area is very picturesque, refreshing and peaceful. The paved road to Montebello turns east off Hwy 190 just north of La Trinitaria, 16km south of Comitán. It passes Chinkultic after 32km, and enters the Parque Nacional Lagunas de Montebello 5km beyond. A further 800m along is a ticket booth, where you must pay a $1 park admission fee. Here the road forks – north to the Lagunas de Colores (2km to 3km) and east to the village of Tziscao (9km), beyond which it becomes the Carretera Fronteriza, continuing east to Ixcán and ultimately Palenque (see p843).

SIGHTS & ACTIVITIES

From the park ticket booth, the northward road leads to the **Lagunas de Colores**, five lakes whose vivid hues range from turquoise to deep green: **Laguna Agua Tinta**, **Laguna Esmeralda**, **Laguna Encantada**, **Laguna Ensueño** and, the biggest, **Laguna Bosque Azul**, on the left where the paved road ends. There's a nice walk from here to the **Grutas San Rafael del Arco**, a group of caves. Follow the track ahead from the parking lot, turn left after 500m at the 'Gruta San Rafael del Arco' sign, then follow the path, mostly downhill, for 500m to 600m to a 'Grutas' sign. To the left here, a river rushes through a natural rock arch. To the right, the path forks after 60m. The left branch leads 100m to a riverside cave downstream from the rock arch; the right branch leads 40m to a more extensive cave that turns out to be the bottom of a sinkhole. Boys at the Laguna Bosque Azul parking lot will offer to take you on small horses to the caves for $5, or to **Dos Cenotes**, a pair of sinkholes in the forest, or the Laguna de Montebello (about one hour away).

Along the eastward road from the park ticket booth, after 3km a track leads 200m north to the **Laguna de Montebello**, one of the area's larger lakes, with a flat open area along its shore, and more boys offering horseback rides to Dos Cenotes (\$10, one hour return). Three kilometers further along the Tziscao road, another track leads left to the **Cinco Lagunas** (Five Lakes). Only four are visible from the road, but the second, **La Cañada**, on the right after about 1.5km, is one of the most beautiful Montebello lakes, nearly cut in half by two rocky outcrops.

One kilometer nearer to Tziscao, another track leads 1km north to cobalt-blue **Laguna Pojoj**, with an island in the middle. **Laguna Tziscao**, on the Guatemalan border, comes into view 1km past the Pojoj turnoff. The turning into Tziscao village, a pretty and spread-out place stretching down to the lakeside, is a little further again. Quetzal birds inhabit the border forests near here and you should be able to find a local guide who'll take you to where they may be seen.

SLEEPING & EATING

Hotel Tziscao (☎ 963-633-52-44; camping per person $2.50, r or cabaña per person $11.50; restaurant dishes $2.50-3.50; **P**) By the lake in Tziscao village, 2km from the highway turnoff, this basic but well-kept place has extensive, grassy grounds that include a sandy beach with terrific views across the lake to the foothills of the Cuchumatanes in Guatemala. You can rent two-person kayaks for $5 per hour, or bicycles for $2 per hour. There are rooms in the main building, but some of the good wooden *cabañas* have an ideal position, almost on the waterside. All accommodations have private bathroom.

Cabañas de Doña Josefa (☎ 963-632-59-71; cabaña $14; **P**) These rustic, two-storey *cabañas* are on the northwest side of Laguna Bosque Azul, 1km along a drivable track from the lake's main parking lot. Some have private toilet, but the only washing facility is the lake. Meals are usually available at weekends and holidays.

Beside the Laguna Bosque Azul parking lot, several basic **comedores** (dishes $2-3; ☺ approx 9am-4pm) serve drinks and simple plates of *carne asada* (roasted meat) or quesadillas.

GETTING THERE & AWAY

You can make a day trip to Chinkultic and the lakes from Comitán (see p851) or San Cristóbal de Las Casas (p818) by public transportation or on a tour. See p853 for details of the public services from Comitán; these go all the way to Laguna Bosque Azul and Tziscao, and will drop you at the turnoffs for Museo Parador Santa María, Chinkultic, and the other lakes mentioned above.

The last vehicles back to Comitán leave Tziscao around 5pm, and Laguna Bosque Azul around 5:30pm.

CIUDAD CUAUHTÉMOC

pop 2200

Cuauhtémoc 'City' amounts to little more than a few houses and a *comedor* or two, but it's the last and first place in Mexico on the Pan-American Hwy (190). Comitán is 83km north, and the Guatemalan border post is 4km south at La Mesilla. Taxis ($0.50 *colectivo*, $2.50 private) ferry people between the two sides. There are banks and money-changers on both sides of the border.

Frequent vans, combis and buses run to and from Comitán ($2.50 to $4.50,

1¾ hours), about every 20 to 30 minutes, 5am to 5pm. A few OCC buses run to San Cristóbal de Las Casas ($8.50, 3½ hours) and beyond between 12:30pm and 9:30pm, but it's usually quicker to get to Comitán and pick up onward transportation there.

From La Mesilla, buses leave for Huehuetenango ($1.50, two hours) and Quetzaltenango ($4, 3½ hours) at least 20 times a day between 6am and 6pm.

RESERVA DE LA BIOSFERA EL TRIUNFO

The luxuriant cloud forests, high in the remote El Triunfo Biosphere Reserve in the Sierra Madre de Chiapas, are a bird-lover's paradise and a remarkable world of trees and shrubs festooned with epiphytes, ferns, bromeliads, mosses and vines. The cool cloud forest is formed by moist air rising from the hot, humid lowlands to form clouds and rain on the uplands.

The Sierra Madre de Chiapas is home to over 300 bird species, of which more than 30 are nonexistent or rare elsewhere in Mexico. This is the one place in the country where chances are good of seeing the resplendent quetzal. Also here are the extremely rare horned guan (big as a turkey, but dwelling high in the trees), the azure-rumped tanager, black guan and blue-tailed and wine-throated hummingbirds. Visitors see hundreds of butterfly species and, often, jaguar and tapir tracks.

Visits are controlled. Most visitors go in the driest months, January to May; avoid the wettest months, September and October. To make arrangements, contact – at least a month in advance, preferably more – **Claudia Virgen, Coordinador del Programa de Visitas Guiadas, Ecoturismo, Reserva de la Biosfera El Triunfo** (☎ 961-612-13-94; ecotriunfo@prodigy.net.mx; Av Central Pte 847 Interior 3, Tuxtla Gutiérrez, Chiapas 29000). A normal visit – $440 per person (minimum two) – starts with one night in a hotel in the nearest town, Jaltenango (also called Ángel Albino Corzo), followed by four nights at the basic Campamento El Triunfo, 1850m high in the reserve. The price includes guides who are expert bird-spotters, transportation between Jaltenango and the coffee-growing village of Finca Prusia, and mules to carry your baggage on the 14km hike between Finca Prusia and Campamento El Triunfo (three to four hours uphill on the way in). **Autotransportes Cuxtepeques** (☎ 961-613-39-71; cnr 10a Calle Ote Nte &

3a Av Nte Ote, Tuxtla Gutiérrez) runs around 15 buses daily to Jaltenango ($7, four hours).

EL SOCONUSCO

Chiapas' fertile coastal plain, 15km to 35km wide, is called the Soconusco. It's hot and humid year-round, with serious rainfall from mid-May to mid-October. The lushly vegetated Sierra Madre de Chiapas, rising steeply from the plain, provides an excellent environment for coffee, bananas and other crops. In the 15th century this was the Aztecs' most distant province, called Xoconochco (from which Soconusco is derived).

Tonalá

☎ 966 / pop 33,000

This sweaty, bustling town on Hwy 200 is the jumping-off point for Puerto Arista. There's a helpful **tourist office** (☎ 663-27-87; cnr Hidalgo & 5 de Mayo; ☺ 8am-4pm Mon-Fri) on the main street (Hidalgo), two blocks east of the central plaza. You can check your email across the street at **El Ratón Vaquero** (Hidalgo s/n; Internet per hr $0.70; ☺ 8am-10pm Mon-Sat, 8am-3pm Sun) and change money or use the ATM at **Banamex** (Hidalgo 137; ☺ 8am-6pm Mon-Fri, 10am-2pm Sat), a block nearer the plaza.

Hotel Tonalá (☎ 663-04-80; Hidalgo 172; r with fan $19-23, with air-con $24-26; [P] [☒]), about halfway between the plaza and the OCC bus station, this is a fair budget choice if you need a room. Rooms are past their first flush of youth, but all have bathrooms and they're kept clean. **Hotel Grajandra** (☎ 663-01-44; Hidalgo 204; s/d with fan $24/28, with air-con $38/347; [P] [☒]) is a friendly place next to the OCC bus terminal, with bright, large rooms.

The **OCC bus terminal** (☎ 633-05-40; Hidalgo s/n), with deluxe and 1st-class buses, is 600m west of the central plaza. **Rápidos del Sur** (RS; ☎ 663-05-29; Hidalgo s/n), with 2nd-class buses, is 250m east of the plaza.

Destination	Price	Duration	Frequency
Tapachula	$7.50-14	3hr	21 from OCC & 35 RS
Tuxtla Gutiérrez	$6-10	3hr	16 from OCC & 35 RS

Most Tapachula buses stop at Escuintla ($5.50 to $7, 2½ hours). OCC also runs buses to Mexico City, Oaxaca and Puerto Escondido. For Puerto Arista, a 20-minute ride away, colectivo taxis ($1.25) run from Matamoros, one block downhill on 5 de Mayo from the tourist office, and combis ($1) leave from Juárez, one block further downhill, both until 7pm. A taxi is $7.50 (you might be asked for $9.50 at night).

Puerto Arista

☎ 994 / pop 1000

Most of the time Puerto Arista, 18km southwest of Tonalá, is an ultra-sleepy little fishing and part-time tourist town where the most action you'll see is a piglet breaking into a trot because a dog has gathered the energy to bark at it. You get through a lot of drinks while you watch the Pacific waves roll up and down the infinite expanse of gently sloping sands that is Puerto Arista's beach. The torpor is disturbed at weekends, and shattered during Semana Santa, August and the Christmas–New Year's holidays, when holidaying chiapanecos roll in from the towns and cities inland. A smattering of international travelers can usually be found hanging out here at most times of year.

PA's single, potholed, street is little more than a scruffy strip of palm-shack restaurants and salt-bitten concrete hotels, but the ultra-relaxed ambience soon starts to grow on you. The endless beach and ocean are wonderfully clean here, and you may never swim in warmer seas, but take care where you go in – riptides (known as canales) can sweep you a long way out in a short time.

The only real street, called (seemingly interchangeably) Av Matamoros, Blvd Zapotal or Blvd González Blanco, parallels the beach, one block inland. The road from Tonalá hits it at a T-junction by a lighthouse, the midpoint of town. Public transportation terminates here, although colectivo taxis will take you to your door for an extra $1.

The nearest ATMs and cybercafés are in Tonalá (left).

SIGHTS & ACTIVITIES

The **Campamento Tortuguero** (Turtle Camp; ☎ 961-658-89-19; admission free; ☺ 7am-6pm), 2.5km northwest along the single street from the lighthouse, collects thousands of newly-laid sea turtle eggs from 40km of beach during the July-to-September nesting season, incubates them and releases the hatchlings when they hatch seven weeks later. Visitors are welcome and can help release the hatchlings. At the camp, run by Chiapas' state ecology institute, you'll also see injured turtles recuperating in tanks, and caimans bred for release in Reserva de la Biosfera La Encrucijada (right).

About 300m behind the eastern beach, **Estero Prieto** is a treacle-colored mangrove estuary. Rare boat-billed herons and other water birds are common here, and there are caimans, freshwater turtles and a few iguanas. You can kayak here; ask at **José's** (☎ 600-90-48; rrounding85@hotmail.com).

SLEEPING & EATING
There are plenty of places in both directions from the lighthouse. The more expensive ones often drop their prices outside the high seasons of Semana Santa, July–August and Christmas–New Year's.

José's Camping Cabañas (☎ 600-90-48; rrounding 85@hotmail.com; camping per person $2.75, s/d/tr with shared bathroom $9.50/13/16, d/tr/q with private bathroom $19/24/29; P 🕸) Run by a Canadian who's been living here for three decades, this is a welcoming place to stay and relax. It has a small pool and the simple but impeccably kept brick-and-thatch *cabañas* – all with mosquito screens, fan and shaded sitting areas – are dotted about an extensive coconut and citrus grove. José enjoys socializing with his guests and creates delicious home-cooked meals, from rice 'n' beans ($2.75) to fish or prawn dishes (around $8). Kayak rentals for the bird-rich estuary to the rear are $2.75 per person for one to 1½ hours. To find José's, follow the main street southeast from the lighthouse for 800m, then turn left (inland) by Hotel Lucero.

Hotel Lucero (☎ 600-90-42; Matamoros 800; r $42, q $61-70; P 🕸 🕸) The Lucero, 800m southeast of the lighthouse, doesn't front the beach, but does have comfortable, pastel-shaded, air-conditioned rooms with up to three double beds. And its big double pool and open-air Restaurant Flamingos (mains $6.50 to $8.50, open 8am to 5pm, dinner also in high season), across the street, *do* front the beach.

Hotel Arista Bugambilias (☎ 600-90-44; r/ste $75/118; P 🕸 🕸) About 400m northwest of the lighthouse, the Bugambilias has an enticing pool, plus restaurant and bar, in beachfront gardens. The rooms have air-con and TV and are good-sized but plain.

The following are also OK:

Agua Marina (☎ 600-90-18; s/d/tr/q with fan $14/19/ 24/28, with air-con $19/24/33/38; 🕸) Has 24 clean rooms of varied size and appeal, 400m northwest of the lighthouse.

Hotel Lizeth (☎ 600-90-38; r/tr with fan $33/47, with air-con $38/56; P 🕸) A plain, clean, three-storey place just northwest of the lighthouse.

Cabañas Amazonia (☎ 600-90-50; cabaña $9.50-14, meals $2-5; P 🕸) Next to José's, has less pristine cabañas with small built-in bathrooms, in extensive grounds.

Choosing between the many, very similar beachfront *palapa* eateries is a matter of personal fancy. Those with most customers are likely to be the best. Fish and prawn dishes cost $5 to $7; eggs, chicken and *bistec* are $2.50 to $3.50. *Robalo* (snook) is the quality fish here; *huachinango* (snapper), *mojarra* (bass or perch) and *pargo* (sea perch) are pretty good too.

Reserva de la Biosfera La Encrucijada
This large biosphere reserve protects a 1448-sq-km strip of coastal lagoons, sandbars, wetlands, seasonally flooded tropical forest and the country's tallest mangroves (some above 30m). This ecosystem is a vital wintering and breeding ground for migratory birds and harbors one of Mexico's biggest populations of jaguars, plus spider monkeys, turtles, crocodiles, caimans, boa constrictors, fishing eagles and lots of waterfowl – many in danger of extinction.

A ride in a *lancha* through the reserve takes you between towering mangroves and past palm-thatched lagoonside villages. Birding is good any time of year, but best during the November–March nesting season. *Lanchas* also serve Barra de Zacapulco, a small settlement on a sandbar between ocean and lagoon, with a handful of *palapa comedores* and a sea-turtle breeding center nearby.

The nearest town is Acapetahua, 6km southwest of Escuintla. **Hotel El Carmen** (☎ 918-647-00-62; Av Central s/n, Acapetahua; r $12; 🕸) has clean, gaily painted rooms with bathroom, air-con and TV. At the Barra de Zacapulco *comedores* you can camp or sling a hammock for $2 per person; some have *cabañas* (r $9.50-14) too. A big plate of fresh prawns with salad and tortillas costs around $5.

To get to La Encrucijada, take a bus along Hwy 200 to Escuintla, then a *colectivo* taxi to Acapetahua ($0.50, 10 minutes). Beside the railway in Acapetahua, get a combi or bus 18km to Embarcadero Las Garzas ($1, 20 minutes). These run about every 30 minutes till 4pm.

From Embarcadero Las Garzas, a *colectivo lancha* ($2.50) to Barra de Zacapulco takes 25 minutes. The last *lancha* back from Barra de Zacapulco may be as early as 3:30pm, and the last combi from Embarcadero Las Garzas to Acapetahua goes about 5pm. Two- to three-hour private *lancha* tours from Embarcadero Las Garzas officially cost $113 for up to 10 people, but you can try bargaining.

TAPACHULA

☎ 962 / pop 198,000 / elevation 100m

Mexico's bustling southernmost city is hot, humid and busy year-round. A commercial center, not only for the Soconusco but also for cross-border trade with Guatemala, it's short on tourist attractions, but combines tropical vivacity with an element of urban sophistication. Most travelers simply pass through here on the way to or from Guatemala, but the surrounding area, dominated by the towering 4110m cone of Volcán Tacaná, is well worth investigating.

The city's heart is the large, lively Parque Hidalgo, with vistas of Tacaná to the north on clear days.

Information

HSBC (cnr 2a Nte & 1a Pte; ◷ 8am-7pm Mon-Sat) Money exchange and ATM.

Infinitum (5a Pte 16; Internet per hr $0.70; ◷ 9am-9pm)

Instituto Nacional de Migración (☎ 625-03-94; Vialidad 435, Fraccionamiento Las Vegas; ◷ 9am-3pm & 6pm-2am) Immigration office.

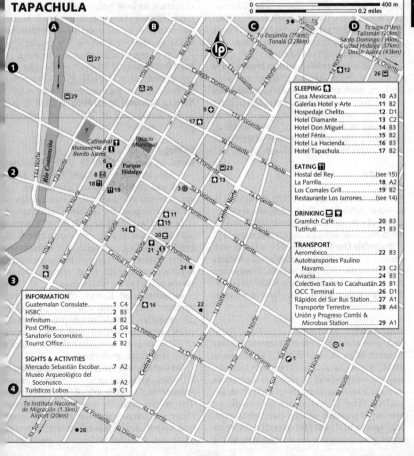

TAPACHULA

SLEEPING 🛏
Casa Mexicana....................10 A3
Galerías Hotel y Arte............11 B2
Hospedaje Chelito................12 D1
Hotel Diamante....................13 C2
Hotel Don Miguel................14 B3
Hotel Fénix........................15 B3
Hotel La Hacienda................16 B3
Hotel Tapachula..................17 B2

EATING 🍴
Hostal del Rey....................(see 15)
La Parrilla..........................18 A2
Los Comales Grill.................19 B2
Restaurante Los Jarrones........(see 14)

DRINKING 🍷
Gramlich Café......................20 B3
Tutifruti............................21 B3

TRANSPORT
Aeroméxico........................22 B3
Autotransportes Paulino
 Navarro..........................23 C2
Aviacsa............................24 B3
Colectivo Taxis to Cacahuatán..25 B1
OCC Terminal......................26 D1
Rápidos del Sur Bus Station.....27 A1
Transporte Terrestre.............28 A4
Unión y Progreso Combi &
 Microbus Station................29 A1

INFORMATION
Guatemalan Consulate............1 C4
HSBC................................2 B3
Infinitum............................3 B2
Post Office.........................4 D4
Sanatorio Soconusco..............5 C1
Tourist Office......................6 B2

SIGHTS & ACTIVITIES
Mercado Sebastián Escobar......7 A2
Museo Arqueológico del
 Soconusco........................8 A2
Turísticos Lobos...................9 C1

Post office (1a Ote s/n)

Sanatorio Soconusco (☎ 626-50-74, 4a Nte 68) A clinic with 24-hour emergency service.

Tourist office (☎ 626-18-84 ext 116; 8a Nte s/n; ☺ 8:30am-8pm Mon-Sat) Helpful folk, located on the west side of the plaza.

Sights

The modernized, well-displayed **Museo Arqueológico del Soconusco** (☎ 626-41-73; 8a Nte 20; admission $2.50; ☺ 9am-6pm Tue-Sun) faces Parque Hidalgo. Steles and ceramics from Izapa (see opposite) are prominent – on the steles, the top fringe represents the sky and gods, the middle depicts earthly life, and the bottom fringe shows the underworld. There are also 5000-year-old early stone heads and figurines from the coastal marshes, a collection of pre-Hispanic musical instruments (drums, conch trumpets, scrapers made from human bones…), and other items displaying Olmec, Teotihuacán, Maya and Aztec influences. Explanatory material is in Spanish only.

Tapachula's **Mercado Sebastián Escobar** (cnr 5a Pte & 12a Nte; ☺ 7am-7pm) is a good spot to soak up local atmosphere – a dark, multi-level warren where locals come for many of their everyday needs, including ax-clutching statuettes of Death ($20 to $200) to bring luck and protection to devotees of the Santa Muerte cult (see the boxed text, p151).

Sleeping

BUDGET

Hotel Diamante (☎ 628-65-81; 7a Pte 43; s with fan $16-22, with air-con $24-29, d with fan $22-27, with air-con $32-37; P ✕) A good-value hotel with modern air-conditioning, clean rooms and cable TV.

Hospedaje Chelito (☎ 626-24-28; 1a Nte 107; s/d/tr with fan $15/18/21, r/tr with air-con $25/27; ✕) A short walk from the OCC bus station, Chelito has medium-sized clean rooms with cable TV. There's no hot water, but there is an economical café.

MIDRANGE

Casa Mexicana (☎ 626-66-05; casamexicanaposada@ yahoo.com; 8a Sur 19; s/d $47/57; ✕) Open since 2004, Casa Mexicana combines plants, creative color schemes, antiques and art to achieve a tasteful, cozy effect unique in Tapachula. The 10 rooms are on two floors around a tropical garden-patio that even manages to find space for a small pool. With a welcoming English-speaking owner and a

small bar and restaurant serving good home-made meals, this is a choice place to stay.

Galerías Hotel y Arte (☎ 642-75-90; 4a Nte 21; s $34, d $40-42, tr/q $48/54; P ✕ ⌨) Galerías is an excellent small hotel with large, comfortable air-conditioned rooms, all with modem access, art prints and attractive bathrooms.

Hotel Tapachula (☎ 626-60-60; www.hoteltapachula.com; 9a Pte 17; s/d $62/72, ste $80-93; P ✕ ⌨) This glass-fronted luxury hotel is the poshest address in town. Large, stylish, marble-floored rooms, some with volcano views, come with either king- or queen-size beds or two doubles. There's a good restaurant, a small pool and an elevator.

Hotel Fénix (☎ 628-96-00; www.fenix.com.mx; 4a Nte 19; s/d with fan $19/23, with air-con $32/40, with air-con & TV $39/49; P ✕) The Fénix has a selection of rooms, so look before you sleep. The remodeled ones at the rear are generally better. Some fan rooms are good-sized while some of the more expensive ones are smaller.

Also recommended are the following:

Hotel Don Miguel (☎ 626-11-43; www.hoteldon miguel.com.mx; s/d/ste $47/59/72; P ✕) With bright, air-conditioned rooms and a good restaurant, but no lift.

Hotel La Hacienda (☎ 626-61-00; fax 625-20-61; 2a Sur 14; s/d/tr $30/36/45; P ✕) A modern, comfortable place in colonial style.

Eating

Hostal del Rey (☎ 625-07-55; 4a Nte 17; breakfasts $4-5, mains $5.50-9; ☺ 7am-11pm) Prettily decorated and staffed by bow-tied waiters, the spacious, air-conditioned Hostal del Rey is particularly good for leisurely breakfasts.

La Parrilla (☎ 626-40-62; 8a Norte 14; antojitos $1.75-6.50, mains $5-8.50; ☺ 7:30am-12:30am) A bright, bustling and efficient downtown eatery, with a wide-ranging menu including *supertacos* (generous meat, veg and cheese combos) and great fruit salads.

Restaurante Los Jarrones (☎ 626-11-43; Hotel Don Miguel, 1a Pte 18; mains $8.50-14; ✕) Perennially popular, Los Jarrones provides welcome air-conditioning and a big choice of Mexican and international fare. There's often live music at dinner.

Los Comales Grill (☎ 626-24-05; 8a Nte 4; mains $5-8; ☺ 24hr) Open-air Los Comales has a prime location on the south side of Parque Hidalgo. The menu includes good *caldo tlalpeño* (hearty chicken, vegetable and chili soup) and decent steaks. There's marimba music Thursday, Saturday and Sunday evenings.

Drinking

Gramlich Café (1a Pte 9; coffees & snacks $1-2.50; ⊗ 8:30am-9:30pm Mon-Fri, 9am-9:30pm Sat, 2-10pm Sun) Tapachula is blessed with several air-conditioned coffee houses; this is one of the nicest and neatest.

Tutifruti (☎ 626-67-50; 1a Pte 14A; juices & licuados $1.75; ⊗ 9am-9pm) Slake your tropical thirst with great big combination fruit juices and *licuados*.

Getting There & Away

AIR

Aviacsa (☎ 625-40-30; Central Nte 18) flies to/from Mexico City twice daily, and **Aeroméxico** (☎ 626-39-21; Central Ote 4) once daily. Tapachula's **airport** (☎ 626-41-89; Carretera Tapachula-Puerto Madero Km 18.5) is 20km southwest of the city. **Transporte Terrestre** (☎ 625-12-87; 2a Sur 68), with a booth in the arrivals hall, charges $7 per person from the airport to any hotel in the center, and $5 from hotels to the airport.

BUS

Deluxe and 1st-class buses go from the **OCC terminal** (☎ 626-28-81; 17a Ote s/n), 1km north-east of Parque Hidalgo. The main 2nd-class services are by **Rápidos del Sur** (RS; 9a Pte 62). Daily departures include the following:

Destination	Price	Duration	Frequency
Comitán			
(via Motozintla)	$12.50	6hr	6 from OCC
Escuintla	$2-4	1hr	7 from OCC & 31 RS
Mexico City	$68-94	18hr	12 from OCC
Oaxaca	$30-35	12hr	2 from OCC
San Cristóbal			
de Las Casas			
(via Motozintla)	$16	7hr	6 from OCC
Tonalá	$7.50-14	3hr	12 from OCC & 31 RS
Tuxtla Gutiérrez	$14-34	7hr	16 from OCC & 31 RS

Other buses from the OCC station go to Palenque, Puerto Escondido and Villahermosa. There are also five daily buses from here to Guatemala City (six hours): **Trans Galgos Inter** (www.transgalgosinter.com.gt) at 6am, 10am and 3pm ($22), **Línea Dorada** (www.tikalmayanworld.com) at 6:30am ($14) and **Tica Bus** (www.ticabus.com) at 7am ($14).

Galgos also runs two daily buses to San Salvador, El Salvador ($28, nine hours) via Escuintla in Guatemala. The Tica Bus service continues all the way to Panama City, with several overnight stops en route.

For destinations in western Guatemala, including Quetzaltenango, it's best to get a bus from the border (see p862).

Getting Around

Taxis within the central area (including to the OCC terminal) cost $1.50 ($2 at night).

AROUND TAPACHULA

Izapa

The pre-Hispanic ruins at Izapa are important to archaeologists, and of real interest to archaeology buffs. Izapa flourished from approximately 200 BC to AD 200, and its carving style (mostly seen on tall slabs known as steles, fronted by round altars) shows descendants of Olmec deities, with their upper lips unnaturally lengthened. Some Maya monuments in Guatemala are similar, and Izapa is considered an important 'bridge' between the Olmecs and the Maya. Izapa had 91 known stele-and-altar pairings, and you can see some well-preserved examples in the Tapachula museum (opposite).

Izapa is around 11km east of Tapachula on the Talismán road. There are three groups of **ruins** (per site $0.50; ⊗ 8am-2pm), each looked after by a caretaking family. The northern group is on the left of the road if you're going from Tapachula – watch out for the low pyramid mounds; you'll also see a ball court and several carved steles and altars. For the other groups, go back 700m toward Tapachula and take a signposted dirt road to the left. You'll pass houses with 2000-year-old sculptures lying in their gardens. After 800m you'll reach a fork with signs to Izapa Grupo A and Izapa Grupo B, each about 250m further on. Grupo A has 10 very weathered stele-and-altar pairings around a field. Grupo B is a couple of grass-covered mounds and more stone sculptures, including three curious ball-on-pillar affairs.

To get there from Tapachula take a combi or microbus ($1) of **Unión y Progreso** (☎ 962-626-33-79; 5a Pte 53).

Santo Domingo, Unión Juárez & Volcán Tacaná

☎ 962

Volcán Tacaná's dormant cone towers over the countryside north of Tapachula. Even if you're not interested in climbing to its summit, two villages make an attractive trip, their cooler climate offering welcome relief from the Tapachula steam bath.

Santo Domingo (population 3700) lies 34km northeast of Tapachula, amid coffee plantations. The imposing three-storey wooden 1920s *casa grande* of the German immigrants who formerly owned the coffee plantation here, has been restored as the **Centro Turístico Santo Domingo** (☎ 629-12-75; admission free; mains $4.50-7; ⊙ 9am-6pm), with a restaurant, small coffee museum and well-tended tropical garden.

Nine kilometers beyond Santo Domingo, **Unión Juárez** (population 2600, elevation 1300m) is the starting point for ascents of Tacaná and other, less demanding walks. Tapachula folk like to come up here on weekends and holidays to cool off and feast on *parrillada,* a cholesterol-challenging plate of grilled meat and a few vegetables.

The best months to climb Tacaná are late November to March. There are two routes up the mountain from Unión Juárez. Neither requires any technical climbing, but you need to allow two or three days for either, preferably plus time to acclimatize. Be prepared for extreme cold at the top. The less steep route is via Chiquihuites, 12km from Unión Juárez and reachable by vehicle. From there it's a three-hour walk to Papales, where you can sleep in huts for a donation of a dollar or two. From Papales to the summit is about a five-hour ascent. The other route is via Talquián (about two hours' walk from Unión Juárez) and Trigales (five hours from Talquián). It's about a six-hour climb from Trigales to the summit. The two routes meet a couple of hours below the summit, and on both you have access to huts for free shelter.

Combis from Unión Juárez will carry you to the small town of Córdoba, about halfway to Talquián, also passing the turnoff for Chiquihuites (about 1½ hours' walk away). It's a good idea to get a guide for Tacaná in Unión Juárez. Ask for the Valera brothers at **Hotel Colonial Campestre** (☎ 647-20-00), or Humberto Ríos at **Café Montaña** (☎ 647-22-56). Expect to pay somewhere between $40 and $90 for most ascents.

Another place to head for in the area is **Pico del Loro**, a parrot's beak–shaped over-hanging rock that offers fine panoramas. The rock is 5km up a drivable track that leaves the Santo Domingo–Unión Juárez road about halfway between the two villages. Or ask directions to **La Ventana** (The Window), a lookout point over the valley of the Río Suchiate (the international border), or the **Cascadas Muxbal**, each about one hour's walk from Unión Juárez.

SLEEPING & EATING
Hotel Colonial Campestre (☎ 647-20-15; s/d $23/26, mains $4-6.50) This hotel, one and a half blocks below Unión Juárez' plaza, has spacious rooms with bathroom and TV, good views, and a restaurant (parrillada for two $13).

Hotel Aljoad (☎ 647-21-06; s/d $12/23) Just north of Unión Juárez' plaza, Hotel Aljoad has clean, tidy rooms around a large patio, all with hot-water bathrooms. Inexpensive meals are available.

There are plenty of *comedores* and restaurants around Unión Juárez' plaza.

GETTING THERE & AWAY
From Tapachula, first take a *colectivo* taxi ($1.50, 30 minutes) from 10a Norte, between 9a and 11a Pte, to Cacahoatán – 20km north. From where these terminate in Cacahoatán, Transportes Tacaná combis head on to Santo Domingo ($0.80, 30 minutes) and Unión Juárez ($1, 45 minutes).

Coffee Fincas
The hills north of Tapachula are home to numerous coffee *fincas* (ranches), many of them set up by German immigrants around 100 years ago, and some now welcoming visitors with tours, restaurants and other facilities. **Turísticos Lobos** (☎ 962-118-18-10; 17a Ote 12, Tapachula) does seven-hour coffee-plantation tours for $50 per person.

Border Towns
It's 20km from Tapachula to the international border at Talismán, opposite El Carmen in Guatemala. The border crossing between Ciudad Hidalgo – 37km from Tapachula, opposite Ciudad Tecún Umán in Guatemala – is busier, more chaotic and possibly less safe. There have been robberies and shootings in both border areas, including robberies of tourists in Ciudad Tecún Umán. Both border points have money-changing facilities and are open 24 hours –

though you should get through by early afternoon for greater security and to ensure onward transportation.

GETTING THERE & AWAY
Combis of **Autotransportes Paulino Navarro** (☎ 962-626-11-52; 7a Pte 5, Tapachula) head to Ciudad Hidalgo ($1.25, 30 minutes) every 10 minutes, 5:30am to 8:30pm. Buses of **Rápidos del Sur** (9a Pte 62, Tapachula) cover the same route ($1.25), leaving every 20 minutes, 5am to 6pm.

Combis of **Unión y Progreso** (☎ 962-626-33-79; 5a Pte 53) leave for Talismán every few minutes, 5am to 10pm ($1). A taxi from Tapachula to Talismán takes 20 minutes and costs around $8.

You can also catch combis to either border from the street outside the OCC bus station in Tapachula.

Frequent buses leave Ciudad Tecún Umán until about 6pm for Guatemala City ($6, six hours) by the Pacific slope route, through Retalhuleu and Escuintla. Buses to Quetzaltenango ($2.50, 3½ hours) depart up to about 2pm.

The majority of buses from El Carmen, including around 20 a day to Guatemala City ($6.50, seven hours), go via Ciudad Tecún Umán, and then head along the Pacific slope route. For Quetzaltenango, you can either take one of these and change at Coatepeque or Retalhuleu, or alternatively get a *colectivo* taxi to Malacatán, on a more direct road to Quetzaltenango via San Marcos, and then look for onward transportation there.

If you're heading for Lake Atitlán or Chichicastenango, you need to get to Quetzaltenango first.

Drivers: the processing point for vehicle import permits, whether you're entering or leaving Mexico by these borders, is north of Tapachula on Hwy 200, at Carretera Tapachula-Huixtla Km 8.

TABASCO & CHIAPAS

Yucatán Peninsula

Around 80% of all flights to Mexico go via Cancún. At any hour, on any day in Cancún airport, the newly arrived await their bags and anticipate the journey that beckons. Some come to explore deep jungle, others deep sea; some are on yoga retreats, others honeymoons; some plan to study Maya cosmology, others Maya cuisine; some will work on their Spanish, others their tans. Whatever led them here, their hopes should be met...and surpassed.

The Yucatán Peninsula's allure is endless, with its natural beauty the universal attraction. Warm, turquoise water and powdery sand hem the Caribbean coast. Offshore, underwater reef gardens thrive with vibrant coral and tropical fish. Inland, vast nature reserves protect populations of rare mammals, reptiles, birds and plants, and crystalline-blue cenotes (limestone sinkholes/caverns filled with water) accent the land. The architectural masterpieces of powerful Maya civilizations past are another draw to this unique peninsula. Towering pyramids and monuments rise from the forest, often jungle-strangled but intact and inviting exploration.

The greatest appeal of the Yucatán Peninsula for many, is its deep cultural heritage. Socially and geographically isolated from the rest of Mexico for centuries (national roads didn't reach the peninsula until the 1960s), the residents of the Yucatán preserved a unique identity. Most people living on the peninsula today are direct descendants of the great empire builders of the past, and many practice some of their ancestors' customs, be it in language, cuisine, dress or religion. Natives of the peninsula are known for their relaxed, dignified and giving character, and you'll find that your hosts generously return any warmth you extend.

TOP FIVE

- Relaxing into the sweet, slow rhythm of village life in **Mahahual** (p909)
- Trekking deep into the mysterious world of Maya temples and wild jungle in **Reserva de la Biosfera Calakmul** (p962)
- Reveling in the abundant, thriving daily arts and cultural offerings of **Mérida** (p917)
- Exploring magical **Chichén Itzá** (p940) before the crowds and heat arrive; climbing through dense morning fog to the clear sky atop towering pyramid El Castillo
- Indulging in the hedonistic pleasures of **Playa del Carmen** (p892): sun basking, sea bathing, beach-clubbing, taco tasting, fine dining, cerveza sipping, 'til-dawn dancing...

YUCATÁN PENINSULA

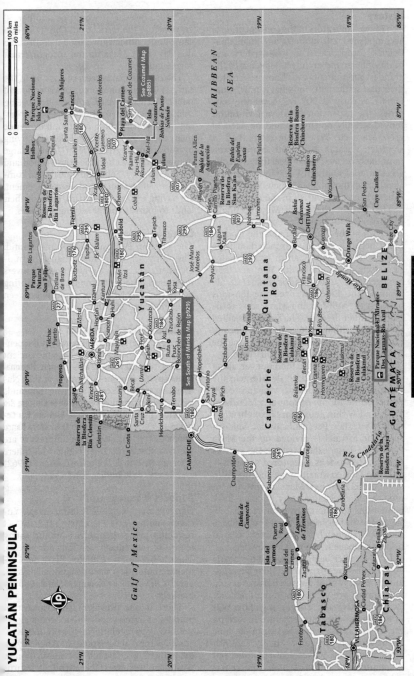

History

The Maya – inventors of the concept of zero; accomplished astronomers and mathematicians; sophisticated artists, writers and philosophers; and architects of some of the grandest monuments ever known – created their first settlements in (what is now) Guatemala as early as 900 BC. Over the centuries, the expansion of Maya civilization moved steadily northward and by AD 550 great Maya city-states were established in southern Yucatán. In the 9th century, and most likely because of political upheaval, the great cities of southern Yucatán were slowly abandoned, though by 850 new Maya civilizations began to flourish in the north.

The last of the great Maya capitals, Mayapán (p930), started to collapse around 1440, when the Xiú Maya and the Cocom Maya began a violent, protracted struggle for power. In 1540, Spanish conquistador Francisco de Montejo the Younger (son of legendary conquistador Francisco de Montejo the Elder) utilized the tensions between the still-feuding Maya sects to finally conquer the area. The Spaniards allied themselves with the Xiú against the Cocom, finally defeating the Cocom and gaining the Xiú as reluctant converts to Christianity.

Francisco de Montejo the Younger, along with his father, Francisco de Montejo the Elder, and cousin (named…you guessed it, Francisco de Montejo) founded Mérida in 1542, and within four years brought most of the Yucatán Peninsula under Spanish rule. The Spaniards divided up the Maya lands into large estates where the natives were put to work as indentured servants.

When Mexico won its independence from Spain in 1821, the new Mexican government used the Yucatecan territory to create huge plantations for the cultivation of tobacco, sugarcane and *henequén* (agave rope fiber). The Maya, though legally free, were enslaved in debt peonage to the rich landowners.

In 1847, after being oppressed for nearly 300 years by the Spanish and their descendants, the Maya rose up in a massive revolt, massacring whole towns full of *ladinos* (whites). This was the beginning of the War of the Castes, the most organized rebellion the Americas had witnessed since the time of the Spanish Conquest. Finally, in 1901, after more than 50 years of sporadic, but often intense violence, a tentative peace was reached; however, it would be another 30 years before the territory of Quintana Roo came under official government control. To this day some Maya do not recognize that sovereignty.

The commercial success of Cancún in the early 1970s led to hundreds of kilometers of public beach along the Caribbean coast being sold off to commercial developers, displacing many small fishing communities. While many indigenous people still eke out a living by subsistence agriculture or fishing, large numbers now work in the construction and service industry. Some individuals and communities, often with outside encouragement, are having a go at ecotourism, opening their lands to tourists and/or serving as guides.

Climate

The Yucatán Peninsula is hot and humid. The rainy season is mid-August to mid-October, when there's afternoon showers most days. The best time to visit is during the dryer, slightly cooler months between November and March.

National Parks & Reserves

There are several national parks on the peninsula, some scarcely larger than the ancient Maya cities they contain – **Parque Nacional Tulum** (p900) is a good example of this. National biosphere reserves covering thousands of hectares surround **Reserva de la Biosfera Río Lagartos** (p950), **Reserva de la Biosfera Ría Celestún** (p938) and **Reserva de la Biosfera Banco Chinchorro** (p910). Even more impressive are the two vast Unesco-designated biosphere reserves: **Reserva de la Biosfera Calakmul** (p962) and **Reserva de la Biosfera Sian Ka'an** (p906).

Dangers & Annoyances

Dangers are few. Violent crime in the Yucatán Peninsula is extremely rare; in fact residents pride themselves on the safety record of their neighborhoods and streets. Theft in big cities – Cancún, Playa del Carmen and Mérida – does occasionally occur, usually in very crowded areas, such as busy markets.

There is one prevalent annoyance that borders on crime, and which occurs at gas stations – particularly in heavily touristed areas on the Caribbean coast. After paying for gas with a single bill or combination of peso denominations, the attendant returns claiming you didn't pay enough and you owe more. They are counting on you being unfamiliar with the local currency and flustered by the situation – which most travelers are – and obediently handing over more cash – which most travelers do. The best way to prevent this scam is to hold up individual bills and announce their denomination (eg 'one hundred pesos') as you pay, showing you are aware of the amount you are giving. Say it in English, Spanish, Pig Latin…the universal message of 'I won't be suckered' will be understood.

Getting There & Away

The majority of flights into the peninsula arrive at Aeropuerto International de Cancún, and virtually all flights into Cancún from the rest of the world pass through the US or Mexico City. The region's other four international airports are at Cozumel, Chetumal, Mérida and Campeche, with only Cozumel and Mérida receiving direct flights from the US and Canada.

Getting Around

Before the late 1960s there was little infrastructure in the Yucatán Peninsula, which means that most of the main roads and highways are relatively new, and the construction and expansion of highways, roads and thoroughfares (mostly to facilitate tourism) continues. Except in the downtown areas of Cancún and Mérida, car travel in the Yucatán is convenient and easy.

The bus system in the peninsula is reliable and inexpensive. First- and 2nd-class buses will carry you safely and comfortably between all major cities and towns, and most sites in between. Buses run from the peninsula's major cities (Campeche, Cancún, Chetumal and Mérida) to most other parts of Mexico as well.

QUINTANA ROO

The state of Quintana Roo, Mexico's only Caribbean real estate, stretches north from the border with Belize to the extreme northeastern tip of the Yucatán Peninsula. Its barrier reef – the world's second largest – runs almost this entire distance, ending at Isla Mujeres. This and the other reefs along the coast, all bathed in crystal-clear Carib-

bean waters teeming with tropical fish, provide a profusion of excellent diving and snorkeling sites, ranked among the world's best. Quintana Roo is also home to several impressive Maya ruins and to resorts of every size and flavor.

Owing in part to its geographic isolation and the effects of the War of the Castes, the region did not have an official name until 1902, when it was given the status of territory and named after Andrés Quintana Roo, the poet-warrior-statesman who presided over the drafting of Mexico's constitution. In 1974, largely as a result of the development of Cancún, the territory achieved statehood.

In more recent history, Quintana Roo gained notoriety when Wilma, one of the strongest hurricanes on record, hit the northeast corner of the state with obliterating force (winds over 240km per hour) and excruciating duration (72 hours). After the devastating cyclone finally passed it appeared that it would be years before the worst-hit areas – Cancún, Isla Holbox, Isla Mujeres, Cozumel and Puerto Morelos – would recover. That was in late October 2005. By spring of 2006 these most-effected regions were already standing again, shaken but tall, and clearly on the road to recovery. Though it will be a long, long time before this traumatic event ceases to haunt those who endured it, visitors – whether returning or new – will most likely view this region as the environmental and cultural jewel it has always been.

CANCÚN

☎ 998 / pop 577,000

In the 1970s Mexico's tourism planners decided to take a gamble: they set out to duplicate the tourist sensation of Acapulco by designing a brand-new, world-class resort…from scratch. As the story goes, the planners entered the necessary variables – beach, sun, sea, open building space – into their computer. The machine processed the data and calculated the definitive plot points for paradise: Cancún, a deserted spit of sugary sand just offshore from the tiny fishing village of Puerto Juárez on the Yucatán Peninsula's pristine Caribbean coast. With the location set, the colossal project proceeded, with vast sums poured into landscaping, infrastructure and devel-

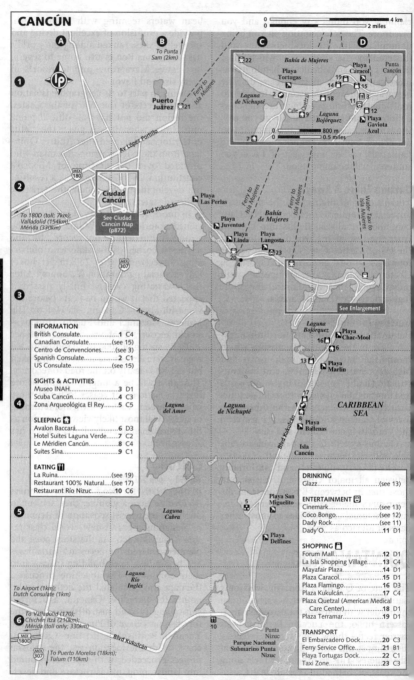

CANCÚN

0   4 km
0   2 miles

YUCATÁN PENINSULA

INFORMATION
British Consulate.....................**1** C4
Canadian Consulate............(see **15**)
Centro de Convenciones........(see **3**)
Spanish Consulate.................**2** C1
US Consulate........................(see **15**)

SIGHTS & ACTIVITIES
Museo INAH..........................**3** D1
Scuba Cancún........................**4** C3
Zona Arqueológica El Rey......**5** C5

SLEEPING
Avalon Baccará......................**6** D3
Hotel Suites Laguna Verde......**7** C2
Le Méridien Cancún...............**8** C4
Suites Sina............................**9** C1

EATING
La Ruina................................(see **19**)
Restaurant 100% Natural.....(see **17**)
Restaurant Río Nizuc.............**10** C6

DRINKING
Glazz...................................(see **13**)

ENTERTAINMENT
Cinemark.............................(see **13**)
Coco Bongo..........................(see **12**)
Dady Rock............................(see **11**)
Dady'O................................**11** D1

SHOPPING
Forum Mall............................**12** D1
La Isla Shopping Village.........**13** C4
Mayafair Plaza.......................**14** D1
Plaza Caracol.........................**15** D1
Plaza Flamingo.......................**16** D3
Plaza Kukulcán.......................**17** C4
Plaza Quetzal (American Medical
  Care Center).....................**18** D1
Plaza Terramar.......................**19** D1

TRANSPORT
El Embarcadero Dock.............**20** C3
Ferry Service Office................**21** B1
Playa Tortugas Dock..............**22** C1
Taxi Zone.............................**23** C3

opment, yielding straight and well-paved roads, potable tap water and palatial resorts strung along great swaths of white beaches. Soon the pace of hotel construction could barely keep up with the demand for rooms, and the tourist success of Cancún quickly surpassed that of Acapulco and that of the developers' most ambitious dreams.

Most visitors to the insular world of Cancún's beach resorts don't venture much past their hotels, but the real Cancún – not the Hollywood movie, the genuine place – can be found easily just minutes away from the hotel zone. Downtown Cancún has all the energy, bustle and sophistication of any modern city. It also has comfortable accommodations, shady parks, quiet neighborhoods and excellent restaurants. Best of all, it makes for a convenient base from which to explore the rest of the region.

Orientation

Cancún is actually made up of two very distinct areas: the downtown area, Ciudad Cancún, and the hotel zone, Zona Hotelera. On the mainland lies Ciudad Cancún. The area of interest to tourists is referred to as *el centro* (downtown). The main north–south thoroughfare is Av Tulum, a 1km-long tree-shaded boulevard lined with banks, shopping centers and restaurants. There are also quite a few nice, small hotels in the downtown area, many with swimming pools. Though not near the water, the beach is just a taxi or bus ride away from downtown accommodations.

The sandy spit of an island, Isla Cancún, is usually referred to as the Zona Hotelera (*so*-na oh-te-*le*-ra). Blvd Kukulcán, a four-lane divided avenue, leaves Ciudad Cancún and goes eastward out on the island several kilometers, passing condominium developments, several hotels and shopping complexes, to Punta Cancún (Cancún Point) and the Centro de Convenciones (Convention Center).

From Punta Cancún, the boulevard heads south for 13km – flanked on both sides for much of the way by mammoth hotels, shopping centers, dance clubs, and many restaurants and bars – to Punta Nizuc (Nizuc Point), where it turns westward and rejoins the mainland. From there, the boulevard cuts through light tropical forest for a few

more kilometers to its southern terminus at Cancún's international airport.

Few of the buildings in the Zona Hotelera have numbered addresses. Instead, because the vast majority of them are on Blvd Kukulcán, their location is described in relation to their distance from Km 0 – the boulevard's northern terminus in Ciudad Cancún, identified with a roadside 'Km 0' marker. Each kilometer is similarly marked.

Information
BOOKSTORES
Fama (Map p872; ☎ 884-56-86; Av Tulum 27) With a good selection of domestic and international newspapers and magazines. Also a variety of international books, plus Mexican road maps and atlases.

EMERGENCY
Cruz Roja (Red Cross; ☎ 884-16-16)
Fire (☎ 060)
Police (☎ 060)

INTERNET ACCESS
There is a string of Internet cafés across the street and around the corner from the bus station on Av Uxmal (Map p872).

LAUNDRY
Lava y Seca (Map p872; Crisantemos 20; per 3kg $4)

LEFT LUGGAGE
There are **baggage lockers** (per 24hr $5) at Cancún's international airport, just outside customs at the international arrival area. There is also **luggage storage** (per hr $0.50) upstairs at the bus terminal.

MEDICAL SERVICES
Hospital Americano (Map p872; ☎ 884-61-33; Viento 15; ◷ 24hr) This medical center, off Av Tulum, offers 24-hour emergency service and has English-speaking staff.

MONEY
There are several banks with ATMs on Av Tulum, between Avs Cobá and Uxmal.

POST
Main post office (Map p872; cnr Avs Sunyaxchén & Xel-Ha)

TOURIST INFORMATION
Cancún Convention & Visitors Bureau (Map p872; ☎ 884-65-31; Av Cobá; ◷ 9am-2pm & 4-7pm Mon-Fri) Near Av Tulum, this office has friendly English-speaking staff and dispenses plenty of fliers, maps and information.

State Tourism Office (Map p872; ☎ 884-80-73; Pecari 23; ☺ 9am-9pm Mon-Fri) A good resource for tourist information on Cancún as well as the entire state of Quintana Roo. It's located off Av Tulum near Av Cobá.

TRAVEL AGENCIES
Nómadas (Map p872; ☎ 892-23-20; www.nomadas travel.com; Av Cobá 5) Operates from the lobby of Soberanis Hostel. It specializes in inexpensive flights and tours, including special deals to Cuba. Travel insurance and International Student Identification Cards (ISIC) are also available.

Dangers & Annoyances
Cancún has a reputation for being safe, and the Zona Hotelera is particularly well policed and secure; however, it is always best not to leave valuables unattended in your hotel room or beside your beach towel.

Vehicular traffic on Blvd Kukulcán, particularly as it passes between the malls, bars and discotheques at Punta Cancún, is a serious concern. Drivers (often drunk) hit pedestrians (often drunk) on a frighteningly regular basis along this stretch.

Sights & Activities
ZONA ARQUEOLÓGICA EL REY
In the **Zona Arqueológica El Rey** (Map p868; Blvd Kukulcán; admission $3; ☺ 8am-5pm), the Maya ruin on the west side of Blvd Kukulcá between Kms 17 and 18, a simple temple and several ceremonial platforms make up this small but very accessible archaeological site. Kids find these ruins particularly appealing because they are compact and easy to explore, and the local iguana population will readily eat out of bread-bearing little hands. Though unnatural, the practice isn't harmful to the lizards, and children seem thrilled by the interaction.

MUSEO INAH
The **archaeological museum** (Map p868; ☎ 883-03-05; admission $3.50; ☺ 9am-8pm Tue-Fri, 10am-7pm Sat & Sun), operated by the National Institute of Anthropology and History (INAH), is on the south side of the Centro de Convenciones in the Zona Hotelera. Most of the items – including jewelry, masks and intentionally deformed skulls – are from the postclassic period (AD 1200–1500). Also here are part of a classic-period hieroglyphic staircase (inscribed with dates from the 6th century) and the stucco head that gave the local archaeological zone its name of El Rey (the King).

Most of the informative signs are in Spanish only, but at the ticket counter you can get a fractured-English information sheet detailing the contents of the museum's 47 showcases.

BEACHES
Under Mexican law, you have the right to walk and swim on every beach in the country, except those within military compounds. In practice, it is difficult to approach many stretches of beach without walking through the lobby of a hotel, particularly in the Zona Hotelera. However, unless you look suspicious or you look like a local (the hotels tend to discriminate against locals, particularly the Maya), you'll usually be able to cross the lobby unnoticed and proceed to the beach.

Starting from Ciudad Cancún in the northwest, all of Isla Cancún's beaches are on the left-hand side of the road (the lagoon is on your right; all appear on Map p868). The first beaches are **Playa Las Perlas**, **Playa Juventud**, **Playa Linda**, **Playa Langosta**, **Playa Tortugas** and **Playa Caracol**; after rounding Punta Cancún, the beaches to the south are **Playa Gaviota Azul**, **Playa Chac-Mool**, **Playa Marlin**, the long stretch of **Playa Ballenas** and finally, at Km 17, **Playa Delfines**.

Delfines is about the only beach with a public parking lot; unfortunately, its sand

---

WARNING

Cancún's ambulance crews respond to as many as a dozen near-drownings per week. The most dangerous beaches seem to be Playa Delfines and Playa Chac-Mool.

As experienced swimmers know, a beach fronting on open sea can be deadly dangerous, and Cancún's eastern beaches are no exception. Though the surf is usually gentle, undertows can be powerful, and sudden storms (called *nortes*) can blacken the sky and sweep in at any time without warning. The local authorities have devised a system of colored pennants to warn beachgoers of potential dangers. Look for the following pennants on the beaches before you swim:

Blue Normal, safe conditions.

Yellow Use caution, changeable conditions.

Red Unsafe conditions; use a swimming pool instead.

---

is coarser and darker than the exquisite fine sand of the more northerly beaches.

WATER SPORTS

For decent **snorkeling**, you need to travel to one of the nearby reefs. Resort hotels, travel agencies and various tour operators in the area can book you on day-cruise boats that take snorkelers to the barrier reef, as well as to other good sites within 100km of Cancún. To see the sparse aquatic life off Cancún's beaches, you can rent snorkeling equipment for about $10 a day from most luxury hotels.

For diving, try **Scuba Cancún** (Map p868; ☎ 849-75-08; www.scubacancun.com.mx; Blvd Kukulcán Km 5), a family-owned, PADI-certified operation with many years of experience. The bilingual staff are safety orientated and environmentally aware, and offer a variety of dive options (including cenote and night dives), as well as snorkeling and fishing trips, all at reasonable prices.

Deep-sea fishing excursions ($120 per four hours) can be booked through a travel agent or one of the large hotels. Most of the major resorts rent **kayaks** ($15 per day) and the usual water toys; a few make them available to guests free.

Cancún for Children

Usually thought of as an exclusively adult playground, Cancún actually has a lot to offer kids – mainly the sand, sun and surf. The beach here is endless, and the water in many places is calm and shallow enough for even young children to be introduced to **snorkeling**.

Young explorers will find **Zona Arqueológica El Rey** (opposite) appealing, as much for the easy-to-climb ancient structures as for the easy-to-observe local lizard population there. For specific kid-friendly venues, try one of the eco-parks, **Xcaret** (p897) or **Xel-Há** (p898), south of Cancún. You may not enjoy the parks' contrived eco-theme, but kids seem to love it. Most hotels offer tours to these spots, or you can easily reach them by bus or car.

Tours

Ecocolors (Map p872; ☎ 884-37-67; www.ecotravel mexico.com; Calle Camarón 32) This highly eco-ethical outfit offers a range of aquatic and jungle trips, ranging from one-day excursions to two-week explorations.

Nómadas (Map p872; ☎ 892-23-20; www.nomadas travel.com; Av Cobá 5) Operates from the lobby of Soberanis Hostel, offering professional easygoing group tours at reasonable rates.

Sleeping

As in other popular Yucatán Peninsula destinations, the rates of most Cancún hotels change with the tourist seasons. Broadly, Cancún's high season is from mid-December through March. All prices quoted here are for high season unless otherwise specified; low-season rates can be significantly lower.

DOWNTOWN
Hostels

Downtown Cancún has an abundance of quality hostels, with new ones opening all the time. Some double rooms in hostels match the comfort of a hotel room for half the price.

Soberanis Hostal (Map p872; ☎ 884-45-64, 800-101-01-01; www.soberanis.com.mx; Av Cobá 5; dm $12, d $40; ✍ 🖳) Primarily a hotel, with one four-bed dorm room available, the Soberanis offers good value. All rooms have comfortable beds, tiled floors and cable TV. Continental breakfast is included. Internet facilities, a phone center, activity room, tour agency, cafeteria and bar are also on-site.

Hostal Haina (Map p872; ☎ 898-20-81; www.haina hostal.com; Orquideas 13; dm $11, d $33; ✍ 🖳) This small and quiet inn-like hostel is an excellent option. There's no boarding-house lineup of beds, the three dorm rooms sleep no more than six apiece, and the private doubles rival the comfort of most hotel rooms. There's a well-equipped kitchen and continental breakfast is included.

Hostel Chacmool (Map p872; ☎ 887-58-73; Gladiolas 18; www.chacmool.com.mx; dm $12, d $30; ✍ 🖳 🅿) On the corner across from Parque de las Palapas, this attractive amenity-filled hostel has dorm rooms and fairly spacious private doubles – all with air con. The adjoining sidewalk café serves healthy snacks and salads, and the upstairs balcony is a lively meeting spot. Breakfast is included.

Mexico Hostels (Map p872; ☎ 887-01-91; www.mexi cohostels.com; Palmera 30; dm $10, d $30; ✍ 🖳) Welcoming, homelike, quiet and clean. This is a quality hostel for travelers of all ages. A fully equipped communal kitchen, book exchange, Internet access and laundry

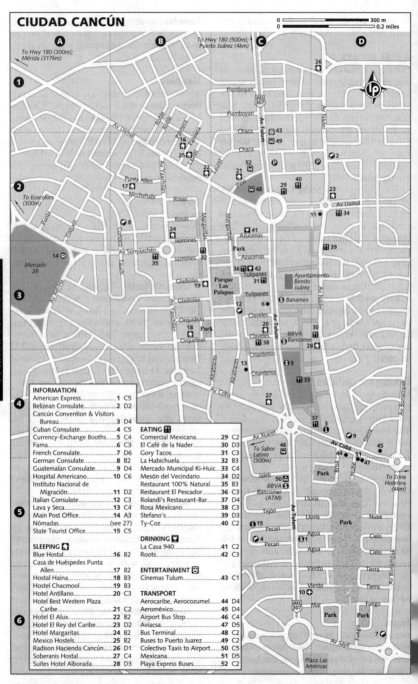

CIUDAD CANCÚN

THE AUTHOR'S CHOICE

Hotel El Rey del Caribe (Map p868; ☎ 884-20-28; www.reycaribe.com; cnr Avs Uxmal & Náder; d $60; 🅿 ✕ 🕸 🔁) Do yourself and the environment a favor, and stay at this oasis of calm in the heart of the city. El Rey is a true eco-tel that composts, uses solar collectors and cisterns, gardens with grey water, and even has a few composting toilets. The 25 suites have fully equipped kitchenettes, good showers, comfy beds, cable TV and phones. There's a lush courtyard, lovely small pool and off-street parking. The shoes-off garden café serves healthy fruit-filled breakfasts and organic coffee. Massage, mud baths, reiki and early morning tai-chi sessions are also available.

---

facilities are available. Continental breakfast is included.

Blue Hostal (Map p872; ☎ 892-46-73; www.blue hostal.com; Palmera No 1-3; dm $10, d $30; 🕸 🖳) Some hostels have rooftop bars…this rooftop bar has a hostel. Its chic and urban, catering to the young and nocturnal. It's located directly across (and at the opposite end of the cozy spectrum) from Mexico Hostels.

Hotels

Radisson Hacienda Cancún (Map p872; ☎ 881-65-00; www.radisson.cancun.com.mx; Av Náder 1; r from $95; 🅿 🕸 🖳 🔁) The Radisson offers all the amenities of the more expensive hotels in the Zona Hotelera, with one exception: beachfront property. To make up for this, the hotel offers its guests free access and shuttle service to the Avalon Bay Beach Club. There is a large pool in the lush patio area, as well as bar and restaurant.

Hotel Best Western Plaza Caribe (Map p872; ☎ 884-13-77, in the US 800-780-7234; www.hotelplazacar ibe.com; Pinol; d $100; 🕸 🔁) Directly across from the bus terminal, this franchise hotel offers 140 comfortable rooms with all the amenities, including pool, bar and restaurant.

Suites Hotel Alborada (Map p872; ☎ 884-15-84; www.suitesalborada.com; Av Náder 5; d $70; 🕸) In a quiet downtown neighborhood, these standard, comfy one and two-room suites have small kitchenettes, phones and cable TV. A pleasant sidewalk restaurant sits next door.

Hotel Antillano (Map p872; ☎ 884-11-32; www.hotel antillano.com; Claveles 1; d $65; 🕸 🔁) Five blocks

south of the bus terminal, just off Av Tulum, this pleasant hotel has a pool and 48 light and airy guestrooms, with comfortable beds, telephones and cable TV.

Hotel Margaritas (Map p872; ☎ 884-93-33; cnr Avs Yaxchilán & Jazmines; d $85; 🕸 🔁) This cheerful, friendly hotel has 100 bright, clean guestrooms, all with phones and cable TV. There is a sunny pool patio and a good restaurant-bar.

Hotel El Alux (Map p872; ☎ 884-66-13; Av Uxmal 21; s/d $28/37; 🕸) The Alux has 35 spacious (though slightly dark) rooms, each with hot shower, phone and TV.

Casa de Huéspedes Punta Allen (Map p872; ☎ 884-02-25; Punta Allen 8; d $33-37; 🕸) From Av Uxmal, walk south along Av Yaxchilán and take the first right, Punta Allen, to find this friendly family-run guesthouse. The ample rooms are worn, but clean, and come with private bathroom.

ZONA HOTELERA

The Zona Hotelera is full of palatial resorts, most of them all-inclusive. Here 'midrange' is a relative term and 'budget' nonexistent.

Avalon Baccará (Map p868; ☎ 883-20-77; www.ava lonvacations.com; Blvd Kulkulcán Km 11.5; r from $200; 🅿 🕸 🖳 🔁) The 27-room Baccará is considered a boutique hotel by Cancún standards, and it is – relatively speaking – the most intimate choice on the beach. The rooms are richly appointed with Mexican furnishings, art and textiles, and each has a kitchenette, living room, dining area and balcony with Jacuzzi. The highlight is the artistically designed pool area next to the beach…and, of course, the beach itself.

Le Méridien Cancún (Map p868; ☎ 881-22-00, in the US 800-543-4300; www.lemeridien.com; Blvd Kukulcán Km 14; r from $365; 🅿 🕸 🖳 🔁) This is one of the classiest hotels in Cancún, and is smaller (relatively) than the other cruise ship–sized resorts in the Zona Hotelera. Each room is warm and elegant, and features huge marble-tiled baths. The on-site European spa offers an array of exotic treatments. If the pool, beach and tennis courts aren't enough, you can go windsurfing, scuba diving or horseback riding.

Hotel Suites Laguna Verde (Map p868; ☎ 883-34-14; www.hotel-ste-laguna-verde-cancun.world-hotel-network.com; Paseo Pok-Ta-Pok Km 1; d $90; 🅿 🕸 🔁) The spacious, clean and comfortable rooms here are equipped with kitchenettes, dining tables and a couch. There's also a nice pool and a good restaurant. Though the hotel is not on the beach, guests have access to the nearby Fat Tuesday beach club.

Suites Sina (Map p868; ☎ 883-10-17; www.cancun sinasuites.com.mx; Calle Quetzal 33; ste from $100) Each of the 33 spacious suites has a kitchen, two baths, two double beds, a separate living room (with a sofa bed) and satellite TV. Other amenities include a pool, bar and restaurant.

Eating

Cancún has a variety of good cafés and restaurants. Downtown establishments are more economical and offer more local flavor – ambiance and cuisine-wise. Restaurants in the Zona Hotelera tend to be super-sized and overpriced.

CAFÉS

Ty-Coz (Map p872; ☎ 884-60-60; Av Tulum; sandwiches $3-4; ☺ Mon-Sat) This tidy café, popular with the local lunch crowd, is in a small shopping center across from the bus terminal, behind the Comercial Mexicana supermarket. Its specialties are tasty stuffed baguettes and filled croissants. The espresso drinks are good, too.

El Cafe de la Nader (Map p872; ☎ 884-15-84; Av Náder 5; mains $7-9) This shaded-street sidewalk café is a popular local meeting spot. Enjoy a traditional breakfast, or a light lunch or dinner (sandwiches, soups, salads), and very friendly service.

Mesón de Vecindario (Map p872; ☎ 884-89-00; Av Uxmal 23; mains $7-9) This inviting and relaxed chalet-esque spot specializes in fondue of all sorts, as well as salads and pasta dishes.

RESTAURANTS

Stefano's (Map p872; ☎ 887-99-64; Av Náder 60; mains $7-15) Set snugly back from the street, this fabulously inventive restaurant – primarily Italian with a dash of Mexican *sabor* (flavor) – serves creations like *rigatoni* in tequila sauce. The pasta is homemade and the pizza is right out of the oven. It has a long wine list and daily lunch specials are available.

La Habichuela (Map p872; ☎ 884-31-58; Margaritas 25; mains $12-30) La Habichuela's dimly lit courtyard is full of romantic ambience. The house specialty, *habichuela* (string-bean soup), is excellent, as is the shrimp in tequila sauce. Save room for a taste of Xtabentun (Maya anise and honey liqueur).

Rosa Mexicano (Map p872; ☎ 884-63-13; Claveles 4; mains from $10) A long-standing favorite, this is the place to go for unusual Mexican dishes in a pleasant hacienda atmosphere. Try the squid sautéed with three chilies, or the shrimp in a *pipián* sauce (made of ground pumpkin seeds and spices).

La Ruina (Map p868; Plaza Terramar; mains $6.25) This place faces Blvd Kukulcán, near Km 8.5. The highlights are the delicious traditionally Mexican meals.

Restaurant Río Nizuc (Map p868; mains $5-8) At the end of a short, nameless road near Blvd Kukulcán Km 22, this outdoor restaurant, which is flanked by mangroves, is a nice place to settle in a chair under a *palapa* (thatched-roof shelter) and watch convoys of snorkelers pass by. Fresh octopus, conch and fish are served in various ways.

Rolandi's Restaurant-Bar (Map p872; ☎ 883-25-27; Av Cobá 12; mains $7-10) This attractive Italian eatery, between Avs Tulum and Náder just off the southern roundabout, serves elaborate pizzas and pasta dishes.

Gory Tacos (Map p872; Tulipanes 26; mains $4-8) Don't let the name spoil your appetite; this *taquería* serves excellent tacos, burgers and veggie meals.

Restaurant El Pescador (Map p872; ☎ 884-26-73; Tulipanes 28; mains $7-12) Many locals insist this place offers the best seafood in town. It's definitely popular, and you will most likely have to wait for a table. Traditional Mexican dishes are also served, and are considerably less expensive than the seafood fare.

QUICK EATS

Restaurant 100% Natural Ciudad Cancún (Map p872; ☎ 884-36-17; Av Sunyaxchén; mains $4-10); Cancún (Map p868; ☎ 885-29-04; Plaza Kukulcán, Blvd Kukulcán Km 13; mains $4-10) These branches are part of the health-food restaurant chain serving fresh and frothy blended juice – a wide selection of yogurt-fruit-vegetable combinations – and pasta, fish and chicken dishes.

Comercial Mexicana (Map p868; cnr Avs Tulum & Uxmal) This centrally located supermarket has a good selection of produce, meat, cheese and bread. There is also an ATM on the premises.

Drinking

Roots (Map p872; ☎ 884-24-37; Tulipanes 26; ☺ Mon-Sat) This relaxed venue is a great place to have a drink and enjoy live music – usually jazz.

La Casa 940 (Map p872;; cnr Margaritas & Azucenas) A funky, laidback rasta club featuring live reggae on weekends.

Glazz (Map p868; ☎ 883-18-81; La Isla Shopping Village) This sleek and hip lounge specializes in cocktails.

Entertainment

CINEMAS

In general, Hollywood movies are shown in English with Spanish subtitles; however, English-language children's movies are usually dubbed in Spanish. Tickets cost about $5 for children and adults.

Cinemas Tulum (Map p872; ☎ 884-34-51; Av Tulum 10) This theater shows Hollywood movies in English with Spanish subtitles, as well as foreign films and current Mexican releases.

Cinemark (Map p868; ☎ 883-56-03; La Isla Shopping Village) This cineplex shows only English-language, first-run Hollywood hits.

NIGHTCLUBS

Much of the Zona Hotelera's nightlife is aimed toward a young crowd, and is loud and booze-oriented. Most of the dance clubs charge around $15 cover. Some don't open their doors before 10pm, and most don't close before dawn.

Coco Bongo (Map p868; ☎ 883-50-61; Forum Mall, Blvd Kukulcán Km 9) A favorite with spring breakers, this is often a featured venue for MTV spring-break coverage. The party starts early with live entertainment (celebrity impersonators, clowns, dancers) and continues all night with live music and dancing – on the floor, on the stage, on the tables, on the bar…

Dady'O (Map p868; ☎ 800-234-97-97; Blvd Kukulcán Km 9) Opposite the Forum Mall, the setting is a five-level black-walled faux cave, with a two-level dance floor and zillions of laser beams and strobes.

Dady Rock (Map p868; Blvd Kukulcán Km 9) This steamy rock 'n' roll club with live music is next door to Dady'O. It attracts a slightly older, though no less subdued, crowd than its neighbor.

Sabor Latino (☎ 892-19-16; cnr Avs Xcaret & Tankah) An ever-lively salsa club featuring live music and all-night dancing.

Shopping

Many of the malls in the Zona Hotelera are as massive and ornate as the neighboring hotels. Following are the principal players

among the major shopping malls along Blvd Kukulcán, between approximately Km 8 and Km 13 (all appear on Map p868):

Plaza Caracol (☎ 883-29-61; Blvd Kukulcán Km 8.5)

Mayfair Plaza (☎ 883-05-71; Blvd Kukulcán Km 8.5)

Forum Mall (☎ 883-44-25; Blvd Kukulcán Km 9.5)

Plaza Flamingo (☎ 883-29-45; Blvd Kukulcán Km 11.5)

La Isla Shopping Village (☎ 883-50-25; Blvd Kukulcán Km 12.5)

Plaza Kukulcan (☎ 885-22-00; Blvd Kukulcán Km 13).

Along with the usual mall stores (The Gap, Guess, Hugo Boss), there are a myriad of super-chic boutiques selling everything from Colombian emeralds to Cuban cigars in these places, all at exorbitant prices. Still, window-shopping in these chi-chi malls costs the same here as anywhere else, and is a lot more fun – there's just so much not to buy.

Bargain hunting doesn't get much better downtown. For last-minute purchases before flying out of Cancún, try the **Mercado Municipal Ki-Huic** (Map p872; Av Tulum), north of Av Cobá, a warren of stalls and shops carrying a wide variety of souvenirs and handicrafts. It's a 100% tourist trap, so even hard bargaining may not yield the required results.

Getting There & Away

AIR

About 8km south of the city center, **Aeropuerto International de Cancún** (Cancún international airport; ☎ 886-00-49) is the busiest in southeast Mexico. The following airlines service Cancún:

AeroCaribe (Map p872; ☎ 884-20-00; Plaza América, Av Cobá 5)

Aeroméxico (Map p872; ☎ 287-18-60; Av Cobá 80)

Alaska Airlines (☎ 886-08-03) Located at the airport.

American Airlines (☎ 886-01-63, 800-904-60-00) Located at the airport.

Aviacsa (Map p872; ☎ 887-42-11; Av Cobá 37)

Continental (☎ 886-00-40, 800-900-50-00) Located at the airport.

Delta (☎ 886-03-67) Located at the airport.

Mexicana (Map p872; ☎ 886-00-68, 800-502-20-00; Av Tulum 269)

Northwest (☎ 886-00-44) Located at the airport.

BOAT

Puerto Juárez, the port for passenger ferries to Isla Mujeres, is about 4km north of the city. Punta Sam, for slower car ferries to Isla Mujeres, is about 8km north of the center. In the Zona Hotelera, a ferry shuttle service to

Isla Mujeres is available daily at both **El Embarcadero** (Playa Linda, Blvd Kukulcaán Km 4) and Playa Tortugas near **Fat Tuesday's** (Blvd Kukulcaán, Km 6.35). See the Isla Mujeres section (p881) for extra transport info to and from Cancún.

BUS

The **bus terminal** (Map p872; cnr Avs Uxmal & Tulum) occupies the wedge formed where Avs Uxmal and Tulum meet. Services are available in 2nd and 1st class, and in several luxury options. Across from the bus terminal, a few doors from Av Tulum, is the ticket office and mini-terminal of **Playa Express** (Map p872; Pino). It runs shuttle buses down the Caribbean coast to Tulum and Felipe Carrillo Puerto about every 30 minutes until early evening, stopping at big towns and points of interest en route.

Following are some of the major routes serviced daily:

CAR & MOTORCYCLE

Car-rental agencies in Cancún include the following:

Alamo (☎ 886-01-79; www.goalamo.com)
Avis (☎ 886-02-22; www.avis.com)
Budget (☎ 886-00-26; www.drivebudget.com)
Dollar (☎ 886-01-79; www.dollar.com)
Hertz (☎ 886-01-50; www.hertz.com.mx)
Thrifty (☎ 886-03-93; www.thrifty.com)

All have counters at the airport. You usually receive better rates if you reserve ahead.

Getting Around
TO/FROM THE AIRPORT

If you don't want to pay $40 for a taxi ride into town, there are a few options. Comfortable shared vans charging $10 leave from the curb in front of the international terminal about every 15 minutes, heading for the Zona Hotelera via Punta Nizuc. They head into town after the island, but it can take up to 45 minutes to get downtown. If volume allows, however, they will separate passengers into downtown and Zona groups. To get downtown more directly and cheaply, exit the terminal and pass the parking lot to a smaller dirt lot between the Budget and Executive car-rental agencies, where there is a ticket booth for buses ($5) that leave the lot every 20 minutes or so between 5:30am and midnight. They travel up Av Tulum, one of their most central stops being across from the Chedraui supermarket on Av Cobá (confirm your stop with the driver, as there are two Chedrauis in town). At the time of research there were plans for a bus service between the airport and the bus terminal ($1.50).

If you follow the access road out of the airport and past the traffic-monitoring booth

---

CANCÚN BUS SCHEDULE

Destination	Price	Duration	Frequency
Chetumal	$16	5½hr	frequent buses
Chichén Itzá	$8	4hr	hourly buses from 5am to 9pm
Felipe Carrillo	$11	4hr	8 Riviera buses
Puerto	$9	4hr	hourly 2nd-class Mayab buses
Mérida	$22	4hr	15 deluxe & 1st-class UNO, ADO GL & Super Expresso buses
	$16	4hr	hourly 2nd-class Oriente buses from 5am to 4pm
Mexico City	$80	24hr	1 1st-class ADO buses
(TAPO)	$88	24hr	2 deluxe ADO GL buses
Mexico City			
(Terminal Norte)	$80	24hr	1 1st-class ADO bus
Playa del Carmen	$4	70min	1st-class Riviera buses every 15min 5am to midnight
	$3	70min	frequent 2nd-class buses
Puerto Morelos	$2	40min	Playa Express bus every 30mins until 4:30pm, and numerous other services
Ticul	$17	6hr	6 2nd-class Mayab buses
Tizimín	$7	3-4hr	9 2nd-class Noreste & Mayab buses
Tulum	$6	2-2½hr	7 1st-class Riviera, and numerous other services
Valladolid	$10	2hr	frequent 1st-class ADO buses
	$8	2hr	2nd-class Oriente buses
Villahermosa	$48	12hr	11 1st-class buses

(a total of about 300m), you can often flag down a taxi leaving the airport empty that will take you downtown for about $5 to $7.

To get to the airport you can catch the airport bus on Av Tulum, just south of Av Cobá outside the Es 3 Café, or a *colectivo* (minibus or car that picks up and drops off passengers on a predetermined route) from the stand in the parking area a few doors south; they leave when full. *Colectivos* run from 6am to 9pm and cost $3 per person. The official rate for private taxis from town is $15.

Riviera runs buses to/from Playa del Carmen ($7.25, 45 minutes to one hour, 11 express 1st-class buses between 7am and 7:30pm). Tickets are sold at a counter in the international terminal of the airport.

BUS

To reach the Zona Hotelera from downtown, catch any bus with 'R1,' 'Hoteles' or 'Zona Hotelera' displayed on the windshield as it travels south along Av Tulum or east along Av Cobá. The fare each way is $0.60.

To reach Puerto Juárez and the Isla Mujeres ferries, catch a Ruta 13 ($0.40, 'Pto Juárez' or 'Punta Sam') bus at the stop in front of Cinemas Tulum (next to McDonald's) on Av Tulum, north of Av Uxmal.

TAXI

Cancún's taxis do not have meters. There is a sign listing official fares on the northeast outside wall of the bus terminal; if you can't refer to it you'll probably have to haggle. From downtown to Punta Cancún is $8, to Puerto Juárez $3.

ISLA MUJERES

☎ 998 / pop 13,000

Isla Mujeres (Island of Women) has a reputation as a backpackers' Cancún – a quieter island where many of the same amenities and attractions cost a lot less. Isla Mujeres offers popular sunbathing beaches and plenty of diving and snorkeling sites. The island's chief attributes are a relaxed tropical social life and waters that are brilliant blue and bathtub warm.

History

Although many locals believe Isla Mujeres got its name because Spanish buccaneers kept their lovers there while they plundered galleons and pillaged ports, a less

romantic, but still intriguing, explanation is probably more accurate. In 1517, Francisco Hernández de Córdoba sailed from Cuba to procure slaves for the mines there. His expedition came upon Isla Mujeres, and in the course of searching it the conquistadors located a stone temple containing clay figurines of Maya goddesses. Córdoba named the island after the icons.

Today some archaeologists believe that the island was a stopover for the Maya en route to worship their goddess of fertility, Ixchel, on the island of Cozumel. The clay idols are thought to represent the goddess.

Orientation

The island is 8km long, between 300m and 800m wide, and 11km off the coast. The town of Isla Mujeres is at the island's northern tip, and the ruins of the Maya temple are at the southern tip; the two are linked by Av Rueda Medina, a loop road that hugs the coast. Between Isla Mujeres and the ruins are a handful of small fishing villages, several saltwater lakes, a string of westward-facing beaches, a large lagoon and a small airport.

ISLA MUJERES

0 — 1 km
0 — 0.5 miles

Punta Norte

See Isla Mujeres
(Town) Map (p878)

Car ferry to
Punta Sam

Ferry to Puerto
Juárez

Airstrip

CARIBBEAN
SEA

Ferries to Cancún's Zona Hotelera

Laguna
Makax

Bahía de
Mujeres

Carr Sac Bajo

Av Rueda Medina

Salina
Grande

Tortugranja
(Turtle Farm)

Playa Pescador

Playa
Lancheros

Arrecife
Manchones

Playa
Indios

Hotel Garrafón de Castilla

Casa de
los Sueños

Playa Garrafón

Casa O's

Lighthouse

Punta
Sur

Mayan Ruins

The best snorkeling sites and some of the best swimming beaches are on the island's southwest shore; the eastern shore is washed by the open sea, and the surf there is dangerous. The ferry docks, the town and the most popular sand beach (Playa Norte) are at the northern tip of the island.

Information

Beat (Map p878; Guerrero between Madero & Morelos; per hr $1.50) Offers fast Internet connections.

Cafe Internet Adrian's (Map p878; Morelos; per hr $1.20) has decent machines, and inexpensive phone service to the US and Canada (per min 3 pesos).

HSBC (Map p878; Av Rueda Medina) Across from the ferry dock; has an ATM.

Laundry Express (Map p878; cnr Avs Guerrero & Madero; per 3kg $3)

Lavandería Automática Tim Phó (Map p878; Juárez at Abasolo; 3kg load $3)

Medical center (Map p878; Guerrero)

Police (☎ 066)

Post office (Map p878; Guerrero)

Tourist information office (Map p878; ☎ 877-07-67; Av Rueda Medina; 🕙 8am-8pm Mon-Fri, 9am-2pm Sat & Sun)

Sights & Activities
TORTUGRANJA (TURTLE FARM)

Three species of sea turtle lay eggs in the sand along the island's calm western shore. Although they are endangered, sea turtles are still killed throughout Latin America for

ISLA MUJERES (TOWN)

Playa Secreto
Playa Norte
CARIBBEAN SEA
Playa Pancholo
Mercado Municipal
Cemetery
Plaza Isla Mujeres
Lighthouse
Bahía de Mujeres
Plaza
Iglesia de la Inmaculada Concepción

To Punta Sam (6km); Puerto Juárez (10km)
To Zona Hotelera (13km); Cancún (13km)
To Tortugranja (Turtle Farm) (5km); Southern Beaches (5km); La Casa de los Sueños (7km)

their eggs and meat, both of which are considered a delicacy. In the 1980s efforts by a local fisherman led to the founding of the **Isla Mujeres Tortugranja** (Map p877; ☎ 877-05-95; Hwy Sac Bajo, Km 5; admission $2; ☺ 9am-5pm), which protects the turtles' breeding grounds and places wire cages around their eggs to protect against predators. Hatchlings live in three large pools for up to a year, at which time they are tagged for monitoring and released. Because most turtles in the wild die within their first few months, the practice of guarding them until they are a year old greatly increases their chances of survival. Moreover, the turtles that leave this protected beach return each year, which means their offspring receive the same protection. The main draw here is several hundred sea turtles, ranging in weight from 150g to more than 300kg. The farm also has a small but good-quality aquarium, displays on marine life and a gift shop. Tours are available in Spanish and English. The facility is easily reached by taxi (about $3 from town). If you're driving, biking or walking, bear right at the unsigned 'Y' south of town.

MAYA RUINS
At the south end of the island lie the severely worn remains of the **temple** (Map p877) dedicated chiefly to Ixchel, Maya goddess of the moon and fertility. This is the temple that Francisco Hernández de Córdoba's expedition came upon in 1517. The conquistadors found various clay female figures here; whether they were all likenesses of Ixchel or instead represented several goddesses is unclear. In 1988, Hurricane Gilbert nearly completely destroyed the ruins. Except for a still-distinguishable stairway and scattered remnants of stone buildings, there's little left to see other than the sea (a fine view) and, in the distance, Cancún. The ruins are beyond the lighthouse, just past Playa Garrafón. From town, a taxi costs about $5.

BEACHES
Walk west along Calles Hidalgo or Guerrero to reach the town's principal beach, **Playa Norte** (Map p878), sometimes called Playa Los Cocos or Cocoteros. The slope of the beach is gradual, and the transparent and calm waters are only chest-high even far from shore. Playa Norte is well supplied with bars and restaurants, and can be crowded at times.

About 5km south of town is **Playa Lancheros** (Map p877), the southernmost point served by local buses. The beach is less attractive than Playa Norte, but it sometimes has free musical festivities on Sunday. A taxi ride to Lancheros is $2 from town.

Another 1.5km south of Lancheros is **Playa Garrafón** (Map p877), with translucent water, colorful fish and little sand. Unfortunately the reef here has been heavily damaged by hurricanes and careless visitors. The water can be very choppy, sweeping you into jagged areas, so it's best to stay near shore. Avoid the overhyped Parque Natural and visit instead the **Hotel Garrafón de Castilla** (Map p877; ☎ 877-01-07; Hwy Punta Sur Km 6; admission $2; ☺ 9am-5pm), which offers chairs, umbrellas, showers and baths with the entrance fee. Snorkeling gear is $6 extra. It has a roped-off swimming area, as well as a restaurant and snack bar. Locker and towel rentals are also available. Taxis from town cost about $4.

DIVING & SNORKELING
Within a short boat ride of the island are a handful of lovely reef dives, such as Barracuda, La Bandera, El Jigueo and Manchones. A popular nonreef dive is to a cargo ship resting in 30m of water 90 minutes by boat northeast of Isla Mujeres. Known as **Ultrafreeze** (El Frío) because of the unusually cool water found there, the site contains the intact hull of a 60m-long cargo ship.

At all the reputable dive centers you need to show your certification card, and you will be expected to have your own gear, though any piece of scuba equipment is usually available for rent. One reliable shop is **Coral Scuba Dive Center** (Map p878; ☎ 877-07-63; www .coralscubadivecenter.com; Matamoros & Av Rueda Medina), which offers dives for $30 to $100, and snorkeling for $15. Another reliable place is friendly **Sea Hawk Divers** (Map p878; ☎ 877-02-96; abarran@prodigy.net.mx; Carlos Lazo), with dives for $45 to $55 and snorkeling for $20.

Sleeping
Each hotel seems to have a different high season; prices here are for mid-December through March, when you can expect many places to be booked solid by noon (earlier during Easter week). Some places offer substantially lower rates in low-season periods.

BUDGET

Poc-Na Hostel (Map p878; ☎ 877-00-90; www.pocna .com; cnr Matamoros & Carlos Lazo; campsites per person $6.50, dm $12, d $26-36; ✖ ☐) On 100m of beach-front property, this is the Club Med of hostels. There is a beach restaurant-bar, airy *palapa*-roofed communal space, plus a billiard and game room. There's live music every Saturday night and spontaneous festivities other days. Breakfast is included.

Urban Hostel (Map p878; ☎ 879-93-42; cnr Matamoros & Hidalgo; dm $9, d $20; ☐) Kickback but not quiet, this place is in the middle of whatever action there is in town; in fact, the rooftop bar often *is* the action in town. Expect to have fun, but not a long night's sleep. There's a communal kitchen and a generous breakfast is included.

Hotel Marcianito (Map p878; ☎ 877-01-11; Abasolo 10; d $35) The 'Little Martian' is a neat, tidy hotel offering 13 comfortably furnished, fan-cooled rooms.

MIDRANGE

Casa Maya (Map p878; ☎ 877-00-45; www.kasamaya .com.mx; Calle Zazil-Ha 129; d from $65; ✖) Primely located on gentle Playa Secreto, this cheerful (and a smidge kitschy) place has rooms and *cabañas* (cabins) of different sizes and configurations. There's a lounge and two kitchens for guests' use. Continental breakfast is included.

Posada del Mar (Map p878; ☎ 877-00-44; Av Rueda Medina 15; d $60-85; ✖ ♨) This big hotel was one of the island's first. It's simple, quiet and comfortable, and just a block from the beach. The rooms are spacious and clean, and those in the main building have sea views. There's also a very attractive garden pool area.

Elements of the Island (Map p878; ☎ 103-25-86; Av Juárez 64; d $80; ✖) Run by a friendly, health-conscious Austrian-Peruvian couple, this quiet neighborhood inn has three modern, tastefully tranquil rooms in a small garden setting. The contemporary café serves organic coffee, light veggie meals and snacks. A rooftop yoga class is available in the morning.

Hotel Mesón del Bucanero (Map p878; ☎ 877-02-10; www.bucaneros.com; Hidalgo; d from $50; ✖) The tasteful modern rooms here (most with air-con) all have TV, balcony, bath and fridge. The central locale is convenient but sometimes noisy. There's a popular street-side restaurant, too.

Hotel Roca Mar (Map p878; ☎ 877-01-01; Av Bravo; d from $45; ♨) You could get seasick in an oceanside room here; the surf is dramatically close. All rooms are simple and slightly worn, but clean. Streetside rooms are a decent deal; you pay considerably more for a wave-breaking view.

Hotel Francis Arlene (Map p878; ☎ 877-03-10; Guerrero 7; r with fan/air-con $45/50; ✖) This home-like hotel offers good-sized, comfortable rooms with fan and fridge. Most have a king-sized bed or two doubles, and all have balconies, many with sea views.

TOP END

Hotel Secreto (Map p878; ☎ 877-10-39; www.hotel secreto.com; Punta Norte; d from $200; ✖ ♨) Situated on a secluded cove, this is the most serene retreat on the north end of the island. Rooms are cream-hued and soothing, with big luscious beds and lots of air and light. If you tire of the beautiful beach (which you won't), there's the beautiful pool.

Hotel Na Balam (Map p878; ☎ 877-02-79; www .nabalam.com; Zazil-Ha; r from $170; ☐ ♨) Earthy and elegant, this tropical retreat fronts a pristine section of Playa Norte near the northern tip of the island. Most of the white, crisp, airy rooms face the beach, while a few thatched units surround the pool. The hotel's Zazil-Ha Restaurant is reputable for artisan cuisine and low-lit ambiance. The *palapa* bar makes for excellent sunset-watching. Complimentary morning yoga is offered Monday, Wednesday and Friday.

Casa de los Sueños (Map p877; ☎ 877-06-51; www .casadelossuenosresort.com; Carretera El Garrafón; d from $250; ✖ ♨) A secluded and romantic boutique B&B, nestled away on the south end of the island atop a bluff overlooking Bahía de Mujeres. The sleek modern Mexican architecture nears sublimity with the cliff-side pool that appears to merge seamlessly with the sea. Breakfast is included. Yoga and full spa services are offered at the chic Spa Zenter.

Eating

Mañana (Map p878; ☎ 877-04-30; cnr Matamoros & Guerrero; sandwiches $2-5) Bright and friendly, this is a hang-out-as-long-as-you-like kind of place. The menu features creative baguette sandwiches, including some savory breakfast ones. There's a selection of Middle Eastern dishes and lots of veggie options, plus good juices and coffee. The bookshelves are well stocked with titles to buy or trade.

Le Bistro Français (Map p878; Matamoros; mains $5-10) This place fills up fast for breakfast (due only in part to free coffee refills). The main draw is the unique French-Mex fusion of flavors the chefs combine. It's popular for lunch and dinner too.

Comono (Map p878; Hidalgo; mains $4-10) This stylish tapas bar might look more at home on Quinta Ave in Playa, but with its delicious fare it's a welcome addition anywhere. Enjoy organic salads, scrumptious breaded fried cheese, Middle Eastern/Israeli specialties and fresh seafood. There's also a lounge bar on roof.

Picus (Map p878; Av Rueda Medina; mains $6-15) Just north of the ferry dock, this on-the-beach spot serves excellent fresh-caught seafood, including fish filet, shrimp cocktails and ceviche.

Pizza Rolandi (Map p878; Hidalgo; mains $5-10, pizzas $6-10) The popular Rolandi is best loved for its wood-fired pizza and calzone. The menu also includes pasta, salads and fresh fish.

La Lomita (Map p878; Juárez; mains $4-6) 'The Little Hill' serves good, inexpensive Mexican food, specializing in seafood and chicken dishes.

Los Aluxes Coffee House (Map p878; Matamoros; sandwiches $4-5) This small and friendly café serves bagels with cream cheese, croissants, muffins, sandwiches and very good espresso drinks…iced if you like.

Gózalo (Map p878; Juárez; sandwiches & salads $2-5; ☑ 10:30am-6pm) Offering an array of organic salads and fresh sandwiches to go, this is the place to stop before heading out for the day, or coming in for the evening.

Drinking & Entertainment

La Peña (Map p878; Guerrero) Off the north side of the plaza, this very attractive English-run bar has a relaxed atmosphere, live music and a welcome sea breeze.

Fayne's (Map p878; Hidalgo) Fayne's features live reggae, salsa and lots of dancing. There's tasty Caribbean fare if you work up an appetite.

Om (Map p878; Matamoros) Vibey Middle Eastern–feel lounge with mellow techno, jazz and Latin sounds. There's a unique draft-beer-at-your-table setup, an extensive wine list and array of teas.

Monkey Business (Map p878; Guerrero) A hip, fun, dance-all-night club.

Casa O's (Map p877; Careterra El Garrafón; ☑ 1pm-11pm) Near the south end of the island, refined and inviting, this bluff-top, open-air restaurant-bar is the spot to enjoy a flawless view and cool drink.

Getting There & Away

There are four main points of embarkation to reach Isla Mujeres. The following descriptions start from the northernmost port and progress southeast. To reach Puerto Juárez or Punta Sam from downtown Cancún, catch a northbound bus on Av Tulum ($0.40) displaying signs with those destinations.

PUNTA SAM

Punta Sam, about 8km north of central Cancún, provides the only vehicle-carrying service to Isla Mujeres. The car ferries, which also carry passengers, take about an hour to reach the island. Departure times are 8am, 11am, 2:45pm, 5:30pm and 8:15pm from Punta Sam; from Isla Mujeres they are 6:30am, 9:30am, 12:45pm, 4:15pm and 7:15pm. Walk-ons and vehicle passengers pay $1.50; cars cost $20, vans $25, motorcycles $8 and bicycles $6. If you're taking a car in high season, get in line an hour or so before departure time. Tickets go on sale just before the ferry begins loading.

PUERTO JUÁREZ

About 4km north of central Cancún is Puerto Juárez, from where express boats head to Isla Mujeres every 30 minutes from 6am to 8pm ($4 one way, 25 minutes), with a final departure at 9pm. Slower boats ($2 one way, 45 minutes) run roughly every hour from 5am to 5:30pm.

EL EMBARCADERO

The shuttle departs from the El Embarcadero dock at Playa Linda in the Zona Hotelera approximately five times daily between 9:30am and 4:15pm, returning from Isla Mujeres at 12:30pm, 3:30pm and 5:15pm. The round-trip fare is $15 and includes soft drinks. Show up at the terminal at least 20 minutes before departure so you'll have time to buy your ticket and get a good seat on the boat. It's the beige building between the Costa Real Hotel and the channel, on the mainland side of the bridge (Blvd Kukulcán Km 4).

PLAYA TORTUGAS

The shuttle departs Cancún's Zona Hotelera from the dock near Fat Tuesday's on Playa Tortugas (Km 6.35). Check the schedule for departure and return times. The one-way fare is $10 (40 minutes).

Getting Around

BICYCLE

Cycling is an excellent way to get around the island. A number of shops rent bicycles for about $2/7 per hour/day; most will ask for a deposit of about $10.

BUS & TAXI

By local (and infrequent) bus from the market or dock, you can get within 1.5km of Playa Garrafón (the terminus is Playa Lancheros). Unless you're pinching pennies though, you'd better off taking a taxi anyway – the most expensive one-way trip on the island is under $5. Taxi rates are set by the municipal government and are posted at the taxi stand just south of the ferry dock.

SCOOTER & GOLF CART

If you rent a scooter or 50cc Honda 'moped,' shop around, compare prices and look for places with new or newer machines in good condition, with full gas tanks, requesting reasonable deposits. The cost per hour is usually $8, with a two-hour minimum, or $28 all day. Shops away from the busiest streets tend to have better prices, but not necessarily better equipment.

Many people find golf carts a good way to get around the island, and lots of them can be seen tooling down the roads; the average cost is $12 per hour or $35 per day. **Ppe's Moto Rent** (Map p878; ☎ 877-00-19; Hidalgo) is a good rental place for scooters and golf carts.

PARQUE NACIONAL ISLA CONTOY

From Isla Mujeres it's possible to take an excursion by boat to tiny, uninhabited Isla Contoy, a national park and bird sanctuary 25km north. Its dense foliage is home to more than 100 species, including brown pelicans, olive cormorants, wild turkey, brown boobies and red-pouched frigates, and it's subject to frequent visits by red flamingos, snowy egrets and white herons.

There is good snorkeling both en route to and just off Contoy, which sees about 1500 visitors a month. Bring mosquito repellent.

ISLA HOLBOX

☎ 984 / pop 1700

Isla Holbox (hol-*bosh*) is a pristine beach site not yet swamped by foreigners, though guesthouses and hotels (mostly Italian and Majorcan) are going up rapidly. The island is 25km long and 3km wide, with seemingly endless beaches, tranquil waters and a galaxy of shells in various shapes and colors.

Part of the Yum Balam Reserve, the island is home to an array of protected flora and fauna species. From April to October, over 400,000 flamingos visit the island. Dolphins are a common site year-round, and during summer enormous, gentle whale-sharks swim past. The only wildlife you won't enjoy encountering are the mosquitoes. Bring repellent and be prepared to stay inside for a couple of hours each evening.

After Hurricane Wilma hit the Yucatán Peninsula in October 2005, media attention focused on well-known, heavily touristed areas, like Cancún and Cozumel. Overlooked, and sometimes flatly ignored, were lesser-known locales: Isla Holbox was one of these. Although it was barely publicized inter-nationally, or even nationally, this small island community suffered severely from the storm. With little government assistance or relief aid, Holbox has had a harder, slower time rebounding than other more touristed areas. But steady regeneration continues and, with any luck, by the time you read this there will be little trace of Wilma's impact left on either the land or minds of the people.

The town of Holbox has sandy streets and few vehicles. Everything is within walking distance of the central plaza (el Parque), and locals will happily give directions. There are no banks on the island and few places accept credit cards, so bring ample cash.

Sleeping

From budget to top end, Holbox offers a variety of accommodations. Rates listed are for high season.

Note: some of the hotels pay taxi drivers to bring guests to them; don't let a driver's suggestion on where to stay sway you.

BUDGET

Posada Los Arcos (☎ 875-20-43; Juárez; d with fan air-con $20/23; ✴) The best budget option in town, with good-sized bright rooms surrounding a central courtyard.

Posada d'Ingrid (☎ 875-20-70; d with fan/air-con $25/35; 🛇) A friendly place one block west and one block north of the central plaza. All rooms have hot water and TV.

MIDRANGE & TOP END
All of the following accommodations are on the beach and all are fan-cooled.

Hotelito Casa Las Tortugas (☎ 875-21-19; www .holboxcasalastortugas.com; d $45) Nestled between palms and flourishing bougainvillea, these lovely *palapa* units are bright, airy and clean, with comfy beds and tiled bathrooms. Some units have kitchenettes. There is a small café where the hospitable hosts serve breakfast, and a great shared common space – a sort of lookout hut – on the upstairs balcony with expansive sea views.

Posada Mawimbi (☎ 875-20-03; www.mawimbi .com.mx; d $45) Next door to Las Tortugas, the Mawimbi shares much of the same charms as its neighbor, though the units are a little darker. Each room has a balcony, comfortable beds and a hammock, and a few have kitchenettes. During summer months, staff at Mawimbi guide whale-shark watching expeditions. They also organize dive trips – for expert divers only.

Resort Xaloc (☎ 875-21-60; www.holbox-xalocresort com; d $120; 🛇) This intimate eco-resort is comprised of 18 individual palm-roofed *cabañas*. Each is rustic and romantic, with tile floors, wood-beamed ceilings, spacious bathrooms and big comfy beds, and all have porches with hammocks. There are two swimming pools, a restaurant and bar, plus a small library and games room. Breakfast is included.

Villas Chimay (☎ 875-22-20; www.holbox.info/; d $75) This Swiss-owned eco-getaway is 1km west of town, on a secluded section of beach. There are seven cheery *palapa*-topped bungalows and a good restaurant-bar. The extremely eco-conscious and knowledgeable staff organize walking tours and kayaking trips.

Villas Delfines (☎ 884-86-06; www.holbox.com; d $100) This charming place is an eco-tel that composts waste, catches rainwater and uses solar power. Its large beach bungalows are built on stilts, fully screened and fan-cooled. Meal plans are also available.

Eating & Drinking
The specialty on the island is, of course, seafood. The restaurants in the beach hotels tend to be good but pricey; an exception is the restaurant at **Hotel Faro Viejo** (meals $5-10), which has a good menu and a prime right-on-the-beach location.

Pizzería Edelyn (Central Plaza; pizza $4.50-15, mains $4-8) This popular pizzeria serves pizza and a range of tasty seafood dishes.

La Peña Colibrí (Central Plaza; meals $3-5) This cozy spot serves Mexican dishes with an international flair. Most weekends there is low-key live musical entertainment, often a flamenco dancer and an accompanying guitarist.

Jugos Y Licuados La Isla (Central Plaza; snacks $1.50-3) Next door to La Peña Colibrí (and owned by the same people), this little juice bar/café serves generous portions of fruit salad and freshly blended fruit drinks. It's also a good place for a strong cup of coffee.

Getting There & Away
There's a launch that ferries passengers ($3.50, 25 minutes, several times daily from 5am to 6pm winter and 6am to 7pm summer) to Holbox from the port village of Chiquilá. It is usually timed to meet arriving and departing buses. Three 2nd-class buses (two Mayab, one Noreste) leave Cancún daily for Chiquilá ($6, 3½ hours, around 8am, 12:30pm and 1:45pm). There are also Oriente buses that travel daily from Valladolid ($6, 2½ hours, 1:30pm). Another way to go is to take a 2nd-class bus traveling between Mérida and Cancún to El Ideal, on Hwy 180 about 73km south of Chiquilá. From there you can take a taxi (about $20) or catch one of the Chiquilá-bound buses coming from Cancún, which pass through El Ideal daily around 10:30am and 3:30pm. Schedules are subject to change; verify ahead of time.

If you're driving, you can either park your car in Chiquilá ($3 per day) or try to catch the infrequent car ferry to Holbox. It doesn't run on a daily schedule, and you'll really have no use for a car once you arrive.

PUERTO MORELOS
☎ 998 / pop 3000
Puerto Morelos, 33km south of Cancún, is a quiet fishing village known principally for its car ferry to Cozumel and its laidback culture. It has some good hotels, and travelers who spend the night here find it refreshingly free of tourists. Scuba divers come to explore the splendid stretch of barrier reef 600m offshore, reachable by boat.

Two kilometers south of the turnoff for Puerto Morelos is the **Jardín Botánico Dr Alfredo Barrera** (admission $7; 🕑 9am-5pm Mon-Sat), with 3km of trails through several native habitats flourishing with orchids, bromeliads and other flora.

Information

This small town centers around the main plaza. An HSBC ATM is located at the northeast corner of the plaza. Diagonally across the plaza from the bank you will find Computips, an air-conditioned Internet center. Also on the plaza is the fabulous **Alma Libre bookstore** (☎ 871-07-13; 🕑 Tue-Sun), with hundreds of new and used titles in a variety of languages (mostly English) on myriad topics. The friendly Canadian owners are a fount of info and tips for visitors.

Sleeping & Eating

Rancho Sak Ol (☎ 871-01-81; www.ranchosakol.com; d downstairs/upstairs $70/80; P 🐕) Formerly Rancho Libertad, this mellow B&B located 1km south of the main plaza, just beyond the ferry terminal, has 15 charming guestrooms in one- and two-storey thatched bungalows, some with air-con. There's a pleasant beach, and rates include breakfast and the use of bikes and snorkel gear.

Posada Amor (☎ 871-00-33; d from $45) One hundred meters southwest of the plaza, the Amor has been in operation for many years. The pleasant rooms are fan-cooled. It has a shady back area with tables, chairs and an abundance of plants. The restaurant serves good home-cooked meals ($5 to $10).

La Nueva Luna (☎ 871-05-13; Av Rojo Gómez; mains $4-7; 🕑 Wed-Mon) This is the place to go for hearty sandwiches and healthy faux-meat veggie dishes, like soy burgers, soy ham, soy hotdogs (and soy forth). This is also a good place to find out about yoga classes and spiritual retreats offered in and around town.

Mama's Bakery (☎ 845-68-10; dishes $3-6) Mama's is a couple of blocks north of La Nueva Luna. In addition to a variety of gourmet breads it serves brownies, cakes and coffee, plus good breakfasts and fruit-juice blends.

John Gray's Kitchen (☎ 871-06-55; Av Niños Héroes; mains $9-12; 🕑 6-10pm Mon-Sat) John cooks up some really delicious dinners. The eclectic menu changes frequently and may include anything from Thai chicken curry to pork chops.

Getting There & Away

Playa Express and Riviera buses traveling between Cancún and Playa del Carmen drop you by the side of Hwy 307. Some Mayab buses enter town.

The plaza is 2km from the highway. Taxis are usually waiting by the turnoff to shuttle people into town, and there's usually a taxi or two near the plaza to shuttle people back over to the highway. The official local rate is $2 each way, for as many people as you can stuff in.

The **Transbordador** (Vehicle Ferry; ☎ 871-06-14, in Cozumel 987-872-09-50; per person/car with driver $6/80) leaves Puerto Morelos for Cozumel most days at 5am, with an additional departure on Sunday and Monday at 2pm. On other days a second departure occurs sometime between 10am and 4pm. All times are subject to change according to season or the weather; during high seas the ferry won't leave at all. Unless you plan to stay awhile on Cozumel, it's really not worth shipping your vehicle. You must get in line at least two hours before departure and hope there's enough space. The voyage takes anywhere from 2½ to four hours. Departure from Cozumel is from the dock in front of the Hotel Sol Caribe, south of town along the shore road.

COZUMEL

☎ 987 / pop 70,000

Cozumel, 71km south of Cancún, is a teardrop-shaped coral island ringed by crystalline waters. It is Mexico's only Caribbean island and, measuring 53km by 14km, it is also the country's largest. Called Ah-Cuzamil-Peten (Island of Swallows) by its earliest inhabitants, Cozumel has been a favorite destination for divers since 1961, when a Jacques Cousteau documentary about its glorious reefs first appeared on TV. Today, no fewer than 100 world-class dive sites have been identified within 5km of Cozumel, and no less than a dozen of them are shallow enough for snorkeling.

History

Maya settlement here dates from AD 300. During the postclassic period Cozumel flourished as a trade center and, more importantly, a ceremonial site. Every May, woman on the Yucatán Peninsula and beyond was expected to make at least one

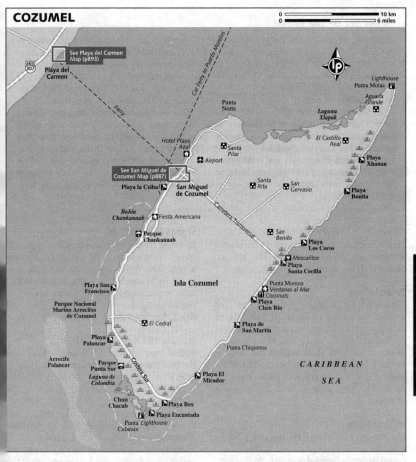

COZUMEL

0 — 10 km
0 — 6 miles

Playa del Carmen
See Playa del Carmen Map (p893)
MEX 307
Car Ferry to Puerto Morelos
Ferry
Punta Norte
Lighthouse Punta Molas
Aguada Grande
Laguna Xlapak
Hotel Playa Azul
Santa Pilar
Airport
El Castillo Real
Playa Xhanan
See San Miguel de Cozumel Map (p887)
Playa la Ceiba
San Miguel de Cozumel
Santa Rita
San Gervasio
Playa Bonita
Bahía Chankanaab
Fiesta Americana
Carretera Transversal
Parque Chankanaab
San Benito
Playa Los Cocos
Mezcalitos
Playa Santa Cecilia
Playa San Francisco
Isla Cozumel
Punta Morena
Ventanas al Mar
Coconuts
Playa Chen Río
Parque Nacional Marino Arrecifes de Cozumel
El Cedral
Playa de San Martín
Punta Chiqueros
Playa Palancar
Costera Sur
CARIBBEAN SEA
Arrecife Palancar
Parque Punta Sur
Laguna de Colombia
Playa El Mirador
Chun Chacab
Playa Box
Playa Encantada
Punta Celarain
Lighthouse

YUCATÁN PENINSULA

See Playa del Carmen Map (p893)
See San Miguel de Cozumel Map (p887)

pilgrimage here, to pay tribute to Ixchel – the goddess of fertility and the moon – at a temple erected in her honor at San Gervasio, near the center of the island.

At first Spanish contact with Cozumel (in 1518 by Juan de Grijalva and his men), there were at least 32 Maya building groups on the island. According to Spanish chronicler Diego de Landa, Cortés sacked one of the Maya centers a year later. He left the others intact, apparently satisfied with converting the island's population to Christianity. Smallpox introduced by the Spanish wiped out half of the 8000 Maya. Of the survivors, only about 200 escaped genocidal attacks by conquistadors in the late 1540s.

The island remained virtually deserted into the late 17th century, its coves providing sanctuary for several notorious pirates, including Jean Lafitte and Henry Morgan. In 1848 Maya fleeing the War of the Castes began to resettle Cozumel. At the beginning of the 20th century the island's mostly mestizo population grew, thanks to the craze for chewing gum. Cozumel was a port of call on the *chicle* export route, and locals harvested chicle on the island. After the demise of *chicle*, Cozumel's economy remained strong owing to the construction of a US air base during WWII.

When the US military departed, the island fell into an economic slump, and many of its people moved away. Those who stayed

---

IN THE EYE OF THE STORM

In October 2005 Hurricane Wilma hovered over the island for 72 interminable hours, leaving in her path what seemed an irreparable measure of destruction. With the intrepid determination of a close-knit community and an infusion of government funds, however, within months most of the island's homes were repaired, many hotels, restaurants and shops were back in business, and even ferry and cruise ships were arriving on regular schedules. That said, the scars of the cyclone are still visible on parts of the coast, and reconstruction efforts continue in many areas.

As for the natural environment, Wilma leveled much of the jungle vegetation, but, like the island's other inhabitants, within weeks it began to rebound. Wilma did damage parts of the reef – parts that won't regenerate for decades to come – but she also revealed new, previously obscured dive sites that divers are just beginning to discover and explore. Diving and snorkeling here is altered, but no less spectacular than ever. And as for the shoreline, well that's where Wilma is begrudgingly afforded modicum of forgiveness, if not thanks: the hurricane delivered kilometers of new white sand to the east coast beaches, making them wider and more stunning than ever.

---

fished for a living until 1961, when Cousteau's documentary broadcast Cozumel's glorious sea life to the world. The tourists began arriving almost overnight.

Orientation

It's very easy to make your way on foot around the island's only town, San Miguel de Cozumel. The waterfront boulevard is Av Rafael Melgar, and along Melgar, south of the main ferry dock (called the 'Muelle Fiscal'), is a narrow sand beach. The main plaza, Plaza Mayor, is just opposite the ferry dock. The airport is around 2.2km north of town.

Information

For currency exchange, try any of the banks near the main plaza. All have ATMs.

Centro Médico de Cozumel (Map p887; ☎ 872-35-45; cnr Calle 1 Sur & Av 50 Nte) Come here for medical assistance or in case of emergency.

Crew Office (Map p887; Av 5 No 201; per hr $1) Offers Internet access.

Fama (Map p887; Av 5 Nte) This bookstore carries books and periodicals in English and Spanish, as well as some CDs.

Lavandería Siempre Limpio (Map p887; Av 25; per kg $1)

Police (☎ 060)

Post office (Map p887; Calle 7 Sur)

Tourist Information Booth (Map p887; ☖ 8am-4pm Mon-Sat) Located at the ferry dock.

Tourist Information Office (Map p887; ☎ 872-75-63; Plaza Mayor; ☖ 9am-3pm Mon-Fri)

Tourist Police Kiosk (Map p887; Plaza Mayor; ☖ 9am-11:30pm) The police are helpful with information and directions.

Sights & Activities

In order to see most of the island you will have to rent a bicycle, moped or car, or take a taxi. The following route will take you south from San Miguel, then counterclockwise around the island. There are some places along the way to stop for food and drink, but it's a good idea to bring water.

MUSEO DE LA ISLA DE COZUMEL

Before you explore the island, check out the fine **Museo de la Isla de Cozumel** (Map p887; Av Rafael Melgar; admission $3; ☖ 9am-6pm). Exhibits present a clear and detailed picture of the island's flora, fauna, geography, geology and ancient Maya history. Thoughtful and detailed signs in English and Spanish accompany the exhibits. It's a good place to learn about coral before hitting the water, and it's one not to miss before you leave the island. Hours may vary seasonally.

PARQUE CHANKANAAB

On the bay of the same name, **Parque Chankanaab** (Map p885; admission $10; ☖ 6am-6pm) is a very popular snorkeling spot, though there's not a lot to see in the water beyond brightly colored fish. The beach is a beauty though, and 50m inland is a limestone lagoon surrounded by iguanas and inhabited by turtles. You're not allowed to swim or snorkel there, but it's picturesque nevertheless.

At the time of research, Parque Chankanaab was closed due to damage from Hurricane Wilma, but had plans to quickly reopen.

SAN MIGUEL DE COZUMEL

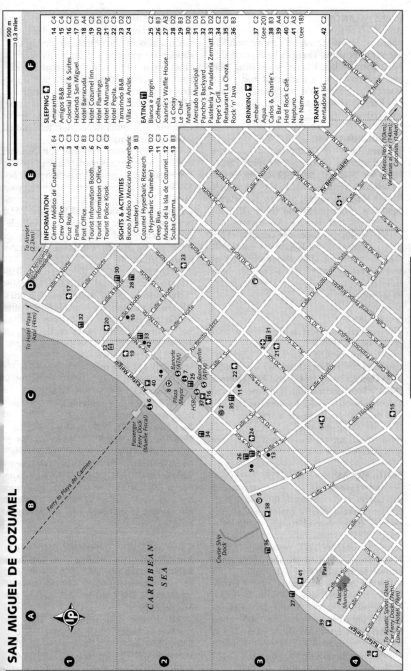

500 m
0.3 miles

INFORMATION
Centro Médico de Cozumel	1 E4
Crew Office	2 C3
Cruz Roja	3 C3
Fama	4 C2
Post Office	5 B3
Tourist Information Booth	6 C2
Tourist Information Office	7 C2
Tourist Police Kiosk	8 C2

SIGHTS & ACTIVITIES
Buceo Médico Mexicano (Hyperbaric Chamber)	9 B3
Cozumel Hyperbaric Research (Hyperbaric Chamber)	10 D2
Deep Blue	11 C3
Museo de la Isla de Cozumel	12 C1
Scuba Gamma	13 B3

SLEEPING
Amaranto	14 C4
Amigos B&B	15 C4
Colonial Hotel & Suites	16 C2
Hacienda San Miguel	17 D1
Hotel Barracuda	18 A4
Hotel Cozumel Inn	19 C2
Hotel Flamingo	20 D1
Hotel Marruang	21 C2
Hotel Pepita	22 C3
Tamarindo B&B	23 D2
Villas Las Andas	24 C3

EATING
Bianca e Jorgini	25 C2
Coffeelia	26 B3
Jeannie's Waffle House	27 A3
La Cocay	28 D2
Le Chef	29 B3
Manafí	30 D2
Mercado Municipal	31 D3
Pancho's Backyard	32 D1
Pastelería y Panadería Zermatt	33 D2
Pepe's Grill	34 C3
Restaurant La Choza	35 C3
Rock 'n' Java	36 B3

DRINKING
Ambar	37 C2
Aqua	(see 20)
Carlos & Charlie's	38 B3
Fu Bar	39 A4
Hard Rock Café	40 C2
Neptuno	41 A3
No Name	(see 18)

TRANSPORT
Rentadora Isis	42 C2

CARIBBEAN SEA

Ferry to Playa del Carmen

To Airport (2.2km);

To Hotel Playa Azul (4km);

Passenger Ferry Dock (Muelle Fiscal)

Plaza Mayor

Cruise Ship Dock

Park

Palacio Municipal

To Acuatic Sports (2km); Car Ferry Docks (7km); Luxury Hotels (7km)

To Mezcalitos (10km); Ventanas al Mar (14km); Coconuts (14km)

YUCATÁN PENINSULA

PLAYA PALANCAR

About 17km south of town, Palancar (Map p885) is one of the island's nicest publicly accessible beaches. There's a beach club that rents hydro bikes, kayaks, snorkeling gear and sailboats, plus a restaurant and a dive operation. Nearby **Arrecife Palancar** (Palancar Reef) has some very good diving and snorkeling spots.

PARQUE PUNTA SUR

The southern tip of the island has been turned into the overpriced eco-park **Parque Punta Sur** (Map p885; ☎ 872-09-14; admission $10; ⊕ 9am-5pm). Visitors board an open vehicle for the 3km ride to visit picturesque **Celarain lighthouse** (Map p885) and the small nautical museum at its base. Another vehicle carries visitors to **Laguna de Colombia** (Map p885), part of a three-lagoon system that is the habitat of crocodiles and many resident and migratory waterfowl. A pontoon-boat ride on the lagoon ($3) gives you a chance to see more birds.

EAST COAST

The eastern shoreline is the wildest part of the island, and it comes highly recommended for beautiful seascapes. Unfortunately, except at **Punta Chiqueros** (Map p885), **Playa Chen Río** (Map p885) and **Punta Morena** (Map p885), swimming is dangerous on Cozumel's east coast, because of riptides and undertows. There are a few small restaurants along the road which serve seafood; most are expensive, but they have great views of the sea.

PUNTA MOLAS

Beyond where the east-coast highway meets the Carretera Transversal, intrepid travelers may take a poorly maintained, infrequently traveled road toward **Punta Molas** (Map p885), the island's northeast point, accessible only by 4WD or on foot. About 17km down the road are the Maya ruins known as **El Castillo Real** (Map p885), and a few kilometers further is **Aguada Grande** (Map p885). Both sites are quite far gone, their significance lost to time. In the vicinity of Punta Molas are some fairly good **beaches** and a few more minor ruins. If you head down this road be aware of the risk: if your vehicle breaks down, you can't count on flagging another motorist for help.

DIVING & SNORKELING

Cozumel is one of the most popular diving destinations in the world. Its diving conditions are unsurpassed for many reasons, chief among them is the fantastic year-round visibility (50m and greater) and jaw-droppingly awesome variety of marine life. Many of the dive sites are within the protected Parque Nacional Marino Arrecifes de Cozumel (Cozumel Reefs Marine National Park), declared in 1996.

There are scores of dive centers on Cozumel and dozens more in Playa del Carmen (p892). Prices vary, but in general expect to pay about $70 for a two-tank dive (less if you bring your own BCD and regulator), $60 for an introductory 'resort' course, and $350 for PADI open water–diver certification. Multiple-dive packages and discounts for groups, or those paying in cash, can bring these rates down significantly.

There are dozens of dive shops and instructors in Cozumel. The following list includes some of the most reputable ones. All are in central San Miguel. Some offer snorkeling and deep-sea fishing trips, as well as dives and diving instruction.

Acuatic Sports (☎ 872-06-40; www.scubacozumel.com; cnr Av 15 Sur & Calle 21 Sur) Personable owner, Sergio Sandoval, has been diving professionally for more than 30 years (he dove with Jacque Cousteau back in the day). Sandoval is an expert guide and instructor; he is also a talented underwater photographer who is willing to share his techniques with interested divers.

Deep Blue (Map p887; ☎ 872-56-53; www.deepblue cozumel.com; cnr Av 10 Sur & Salas) This operation has good gear and fast boats. Among others, it offers trips to Arrecife Cantarell when the eagle rays are congregating.

Scuba Gamma (Map p887; ☎ 878-42-57; www.scubagam ma.com; Calle 5 Sur) New squid on the block, Scuba Gamma is a small French outfit run by dedicated professionals who specialize in small group dives and personalized instruction.

There are several hyperbaric chambers in San Miguel. Two reliable ones are **Buceo Médico Mexicano** (Map p887; ☎ 872-14-30; Calle 5 Sur) and **Cozumel Hyperbaric Research** (Map p887; ☎ 872-01-030; Calle 6 Nte) in the Médica San Miguel clinic.

All of the best snorkeling sites are reached by boat. A half-day tour will cost $30 to $50, but you'll do some world-class snorkeling. For an impressive, but less dramatic, snorkeling experience you can walk

---

RESPONSIBLE DIVING

Please consider the following tips when diving, and help preserve the ecology and beauty of reefs:

■ Never use anchors on the reef, and take care not to ground boats on coral.

■ Avoid touching or standing on living marine organisms, or dragging equipment across the reef. Polyps can be damaged by even the gentlest contact. If you must hold on to the reef, only touch exposed rock or dead coral.

■ Be conscious of your fins. Even without contact, the surge from fin strokes near the reef can damage delicate organisms. Take care not to kick up clouds of sand, which can smother organisms.

■ Practice and maintain proper buoyancy control. Major damage can be done by divers descending too fast and colliding with the reef.

■ Take great care in underwater caves. Spend as little time within them as possible, as your air bubbles may be caught within the roof and thereby leave organisms high and dry. Take turns to inspect the interior of a small cave.

■ Resist the temptation to collect or buy corals or shells, or to loot marine archaeological sites (mainly shipwrecks).

■ Ensure that you take home all your rubbish and any litter you may find as well. Plastics in particular are a serious threat to marine life.

■ Do not feed fish.

■ Minimize your disturbance of marine animals. *Never* ride on the backs of turtles.

For important diver safety information, please refer to the boxed text Safety Guidelines for Diving (p968).

---

into the gentle surf at Playa La Ceiba, Bahía Chankanaab, Playa San Francisco and elsewhere.

Sleeping

Prices listed in all categories are winter rates (the high season from January to April) and may be much lower at other times of year.

BUDGET

Hotel Pepita (Map p887; ☎ 872-00-98; Av 15 Sur; d $30; ☒) This is a friendly place, with well-maintained rooms grouped around a garden. All have two double beds and fridges, and there's free morning coffee.

Hotel Cozumel Inn (Map p887; ☎ 872-03-14; Calle 4 Nte; d with fan/air-con $30/37; ☒ ☒) This hotel has 30 decent rooms and a small swimming pool. The well-maintained and pleasant rooms all have comfortable beds and hot showers.

Hotel Marruang (Map p887; ☎ 872-16-78; Calle Dr Adolfo Rosado Salas 440; r $28) This hotel, entered via a passageway across from the municipal market, is simple and clean, with well-screened fan-cooled rooms.

MIDRANGE

Tamarindo B&B (Map p887; ☎ 872-61-90; www.tamarindoamaranto.com; Calle 4 Nte 421; d from $42; ☒) Owned and operated by an extremely hospitable Mexican-French couple Jorge and Eliane, this beautifully designed B&B has five guest rooms, each tastefully decorated with Mexican folk art and pleasing small touches. All rooms have cable TV and an ample tiled bathroom; a couple have air-con. A generous full breakfast is included.

Amaranto (Map p887; ☎ 872-32-19; www.tamarindoamaranto.com; Calle 5 Sur; d $55) Designed and run by the personable couple who own the Tamarindo, the Amaranto is another excellent choice. Unlike its counterpart, this is not a B&B, but the self-contained units each have a small kitchenette (no stove, microwave only). The rustic top-floor tower suite is an especially cozy roost.

Amigo's B&B (Map p887; ☎ 872-38-68; www.bacalar.net; Calle 7 Sur; d $65; ☒ ☒) The three colorful, well-appointed, cottage-style rooms here are worth the hike from town. All have kitchenettes, there's a huge garden with fruit trees and a nice big pool. Breakfast is included.

Villas Las Anclas (Map p887; ☎ 872-61-03; www.las anclas.com; Av 5 Sur; d $80; ☒) These are very attractive, two-storey suites with kitchenettes clustered around a tropical garden. A complimentary breakfast is served in your suite.

Hotel Flamingo (Map p887; ☎ 872-12-64; www .hotelflamingo.com; Calle 6 Nte; d $60; ☒) A centrally located mid-sized hotel with a surprisingly homelike feel. The spacious rooms surround a shady courtyard, and there's a relaxing sun deck on the roof. Otherwise quiet, the lobby bar is the scene of lively weekend festivities; the best strategy to deal with the rise in decibels is to join the party.

Hotel Barracuda (Map p887; ☎ 872-00-02; Av Rafael Melgar 628; d $75; ☒ ☐) On the beach, five blocks south of downtown, the Barracuda is a good spot for divers, snorkelers or anyone who wants to enjoy the water. There's a pier, diveshop, rinse tank and gear storage. Most rooms have sea views; all have a small fridge. There's an inviting pool and very good seaside restaurant.

Hacienda San Miguel (Map p887; ☎ 872-19-86; www.haciendasanmiguel.com; Calle 10 Nte; r $70; ☒) Built and furnished to resemble an old hacienda, this hotel seems a little out of place in its island habitat, but has a lot of charm nonetheless. All rooms surround a parklike courtyard, and all have fully equipped kitchenettes. Niceties include bathrobes, and a continental breakfast is served in your room.

Colonial Hotel & Suites (Map p887; ☎ 872-90-90; www.suitescolonial.com; Av 5 Sur; r $70) The Colonial is down a passageway off Av 5 Sur, near Calle Dr Adolfo Rosado Salas. It has studios and nice, spacious, one-bedroom suites (some sleep four people) with kitchenettes. All rooms have cable TV and a fridge, and breakfast is included.

For off-the-beaten-path rentals of a week or longer, contact **Cozumel Concierge** (☎ 878-43-23; www.cozumelconcierge.com).

TOP END

Hotel Playa Azul (Map p885; ☎ 872-01-99; www.playa -azul.com; Carretera a San Juan Km 4; d from $145; P ☒ ☎) On its own pretty stretch of beach, this hotel north of town offers spacious and comfortable rooms; all of them have balconies with sea views. The hotel has a bar, restaurant and gorgeous pool.

Ventanas al Mar (Map p885; ☎ 111-09-96; www.coz umel-hotels.net/ventanas-al-mar; Carretera Costera Km 43.5; d from $90; ☒) Fronting a vast expanse of white

---

---

beach, this is the only hotel on the unspoilt east side of the island. The surf is wild here, and not swimmable, but the views are spectacular. The hotel offers simple but very big sea-facing rooms, each with a small kitchenette. There's a sweet enclosed communal area where breakfast (included) is served.

Fiesta Americana (Map p885; ☎ 872-26-22, in the US 800-343-7821; www.fiestamericana.com; Hwy a Chankanaab, Km 7.5; r from $125; P ☒ ☎) This dive resort has plenty of gardens, a spectacular swimming pool, 172 mostly ocean view–blessed rooms (with balconies, safes and full minibars) and 56 'Tropical Casitas' behind the main building.

Eating

BUDGET

Cheapest of all, and with tasty food, are the little market *loncherías* (snack stalls) next to the **Mercado Municipal** (Map p887; Calle Dr Adolfo Rosado Salas). All offer soup and a main course for about $3, with a large selection of dishes available; ask about cheap *comidas corridas* (prix-fixe options) not listed on the menu.

Coffeelia (Map p887; Calle 5 Sur; breakfast $3-5) There's very friendly service, a great laidback ambience and seating inside or outside on the shaded patio here. The menu includes quiches, salads, vegetarian dishes and premium organic coffee.

Pastelería y Panadería Zermatt (Map p887; cnr Av 5 Nte & Calle 4 Nte; meals $0.50-2) Try this place for delicious baked goods, including whole-wheat breads. It also serves excellent espresso drinks.

MIDRANGE

Rock'n Java (Map p887; ☎ 872-44-05; Av Rafael Melgar 602; mains $4-8) A relaxed and inviting seaside café. The menu brims with healthy – mostly vegetarian – choices, including big salads and tasty garden burgers. Internet access is available (per hour $1), and there's a selection of books to buy or exchange.

Bianca e Jorgini (Map p887; ☎ 872-01-97; Calle 1 Sur; mains $5-10) The menu boasts an eclectic mix of Euro-Mexican here, with a selection of seafood dishes, too. The plaza-side locale is pleasant, and the Corona cheap and cold.

Restaurant La Choza (Map p887; ☎ 872-09-58; cnr Calle Dr Adolfo Rosado Salas & Av 10 Sur; mains $8-12) An excellent and popular restaurant, specializing in authentic regional cuisine. All mains include soup.

Jeannie's Waffle House (Map p887; ☎ 872-60-95; Av Rafael Melgar & Calle 11 Sur; breakfast $3-7, sandwiches $5-6) The sea views are great from the outdoor courtyard here. Jeannie's serves waffles (of course), hash browns, egg dishes, sandwiches and other light fare.

Le Chef (Map p887; cnr Av 5 & Calle 5 Sur; mains $5-10; ☾ lunch & dinner) A cheerful corner café, adjacent to a very popular culinary shop, Le Chef specializes in light dishes – many veggie – like homemade pasta, soups and salads.

Coconuts (Map p885; Carretera Costera Km 43; mains $6-10) On a bluff on the east side of the island overlooking the sea, Coconuts' setting is beautiful and the mood easygoing. There's a satisfying casual beach menu – seafood, burgers and fries, and (very good) guacamole.

TOP END

La Cocay (Map p887; ☎ 872-44-07; Calle 8 Nte No 208; mains $17-25) Set in a home on a quiet street, La Cocay is stylishly intimate. The menu features primarily Mediterranean cuisine, with an emphasis on light pasta dishes and the freshest seafood. Menus change regularly, but the high quality is consistent.

Pancho's Backyard (Map p887; ☎ 872-21-41; cnr Av Rafael Melgar & Calle 8 Nte; mains $10-22) This atmospheric restaurant is set in an intimate and handsomely decorated inner courtyard. The food (mostly seafood) is as good as the ambience.

Manatí (Map p887; cnr Calle 8 Nte & Av 10 Nte; mains $8-18) This nice New Age restaurant serves inventive cuisine. There's usually one veggie dish on the menu, as well as pasta, chicken and fish dishes, plus espresso drinks.

Pepe's Grill (Map p887; Av Rafael Melgar; mains $20-25) This is traditionally considered Cozumel's finest restaurant, and the prices reflect this reputation. It's mostly meat (steaks and prime rib).

Drinking & Entertainment

Ambar (Map p887; Av 5 Sur; ☾ Thu-Tue) The lovely garden area of this chic bar is a romantic spot to enjoy a drink, with live music on Saturday.

Aqua (Map p887; Hotel Flamingo, Calle 6 Nte) A relaxed, friendly place to have a drink any day or night of the week…and a dance on weekend evenings. There's usually live music on Friday, and an excellent salsa band on Saturday.

Fu Bar (Map p887; Av Rafael Melgar) A stylish new bar with a mellow vibe and rooftop lounge.

Carlos & Charlie's (Map p887; Av Rafael Melgar) Near the cruise ship dock, by day this huge bar swarms with cruiseshipsters, by night it rocks with partying locals.

Hard Rock Café (Map p887; Av Rafael Melgar) Across from the passenger ferry dock, the popular Hard Rock has live music most nights of the week.

Neptuno (Map p887; cnr Av Rafael Melgar & Calle 11 Sur; ☾ Thu-Sat) Even when it's crowded there's still lots of room to dance in this enormous club.

No Name (Map p887; Av Rafael Melgar) Originally designed for cruise ship crewmembers, as a refuge from 'cones' (a term they use for passengers who block passageways like obstacle cones), this pleasant pool patio and oceanfront restaurant-bar adjacent to the Hotel Barracuda is a nice spot for a dip and/or sip.

Mescalitos (Map p885; junction of Carreteras Transversal & Costera) On the east side of the island, this relaxed beach hangout is a good spot to stop and have a snack, drink a beer, swing in a hammock or soak up the beauty of the Caribbean view.

Getting There & Away

AIR

Small, convenient Cozumel International Airport is just a short distance (about 3km) from downtown San Miguel. There are some direct flights from the US, but European flights are usually routed via the US or Mexico City. **Continental** (in the US ☎ 800-231-0856; www.continental.com) has direct flights from Newark and Houston. **Mexicana** (☎ 872-02-63) flies direct to Mexico City on Saturday and Sunday.

Aerocozumel (☎ 872-09-28), with offices at the airport, flies a few times daily between Cancún and Cozumel.

BOAT
Passenger ferries run from Playa del Carmen (p896), and vehicle ferries run from Puerto Morelos (p884). See those sections for more details.

Getting Around
TO/FROM THE AIRPORT
The airport is about 2km north of town. You can take a van from the airport into town for about $7 (slightly more to the hotels south of town), but you'll have to take a taxi ($5 from town, $10 to $20 from southern hotels) to return to the airport.

BICYCLE
Cycling can be a great way to get to Bahía Chankanaab and other spots on this flat island. Bicycles typically rent for $7 to $12 for 24 hours.

CAR & MOTORCYCLE
Rates for rental cars are usually $40 (for a beat-up VW Beetle) to $60 per day, all-inclusive, though you'll pay more during late December and January. There are plenty of agencies around the main plaza. **Rentadora Isis** (Map p887; ☎ 872-33-67; Av 5 Nte 181) rents cars, bicycles and scooters.

Note that some agencies will deduct tire damage from your deposit, even if tires are old and worn. Be particularly careful about this if you're renting a 4WD for use on unpaved roads; straighten out the details before you sign.

There's a gas station on Av Benito Juárez, five blocks east of the main plaza.

Mopeds are one way to tour the island on your own, and rental opportunities abound. The standard price is $35 to $40 a day ($25 to $30 in the low season), with gas, insurance and tax included.

To rent, you must have a valid driver's license, and you must leave a credit-card slip or put down a deposit (usually $100). There is a helmet law, and it is enforced the fine for not wearing one is $25), although

most moped-rental agents won't mention it. Before you sign a rental agreement, be sure to request a helmet. Keep in mind that you're not the only one unfamiliar with the road here, and some of your fellow travelers may be hitting the bottle. Drive carefully.

TAXI
Fares in and around town are about $3 per ride; luggage may cost extra. Taxi service between town and the airport costs about $15. There is no bus service anywhere on the island.

PLAYA DEL CARMEN
☎ 984 / pop 60,000
In years past, travelers only passed through Playa del Carmen to catch the Cozumel-bound ferry, and few lingered long in the sleepy town. As Cancún's popularity grew over the years, however, the number of travelers roaming this part of the Yucatán Peninsula increased proportionately, as did the number of hotels and restaurants serving them. Today, Playa del Carmen is not only the fastest growing city in all of Mexico…but in all the *world*. But guess what? You'd never know it. One of Playa's main allures is that it retains much of the laidback fishing village ethos that drew so many here in the first place.

What's to do in Playa? Other than ice fishing, you can do pretty much anything. Swim. Dive. Snorkel. Shop. Sail. Bike. Dance. Drink. Eat. Be merry. Drink some more. Comb the beach. Worship the sun. Lounge in the shade. Read a guidebook. Yawn.

Orientation
Playa is laid out on an easy grid, with odd-numbered *avenidas* (avenues) numbering in jumps of five from east to west (with 1 Av paralleling the beach), and *calles* (streets) increasing by twos south to north. Most hotels, restaurants, bars and shops are concentrated on or around Quinta Av (5th Av) Much of Quinta Av is for pedestrians only and it is this section that is most lively – day and night.

Information
There are many banks with ATMs around town.
Centro de Salud (☎ 873-03-14; 15 Av) For medical service
Fire & Police (☎ 060)

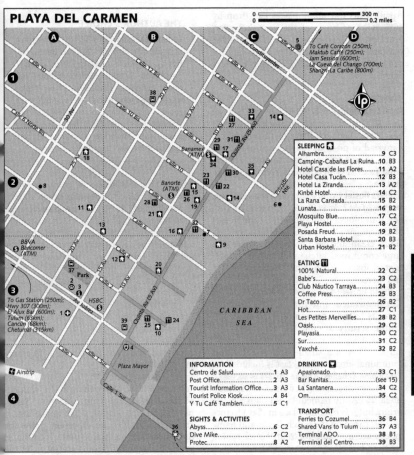

PLAYA DEL CARMEN

To Café Corazón (250m);
Maktub Caffé (250m);
Jam Session (600m);
La Cueva del Chango (700m);
Shangri-La Caribe (800m)

CARIBBEAN SEA

To Gas Station (250m);
Hwy 307 (300m);
El Alux Bar (600m);
Tulum (63km);
Cancún (68km);
Chetumal (315km)

Plaza Mayor

Airstrip

SLEEPING 🏠
Alhambra.....................................9 C3
Camping-Cabañas La Ruina..10 B3
Hotel Casa de las Flores........11 A2
Hotel Casa Tucán...................12 B3
Hotel La Ziranda....................13 A2
Kinbé Hotel............................14 C2
La Rana Cansada...................15 B2
Lunata...................................16 B2
Mosquito Blue........................17 C2
Playa Hostel..........................18 A2
Posada Freud.........................19 B2
Santa Barbara Hotel..............20 B3
Urban Hostel.........................21 B2

EATING 🍴
100% Natural..........................22 C2
Babe's....................................23 C2
Club Náutico Tarraya.............24 B3
Coffee Press...........................25 B2
Dr Taco.................................26 B2
Hot..27 C1
Les Petites Merveilles.............28 B2
Oasis.....................................29 C2
Playasia.................................30 C2
Sur..31 C2
Yaxché...................................32 B2

DRINKING 🍷
Apasionado............................33 C1
Bar Ranitas.......................(see 15)
La Santanera.........................34 C2
Om.......................................35 C2

INFORMATION
Centro de Salud........................1 A3
Post Office................................2 A3
Tourist Information Office........3 A3
Tourist Police Kiosk..................4 B4
Y Tu Café Tamblen...................5 C1

SIGHTS & ACTIVITIES
Abyss.......................................6 C2
Dive Mike.................................7 C2
Protec......................................8 A2

TRANSPORT
Ferries to Cozumel...................36 B4
Shared Vans to Tulum 37 A3
Terminal ADO.........................38 B1
Terminal del Centro................39 B3

YUCATÁN PENINSULA

Post office (cnr 15 Av & Av Juárez)

Tourist Information Office (☎ 873-28-04; cnr Av Juárez & 15 Av; 🕑 9am-9pm Mon-Sat, 9am-5pm Sun)

Tourist Police Kiosk (☎ 873-02-91; Main Plaza)

Y Tu Café También (cnr Calle 20 & Quinta Av; Internet per hr $1.50) Offers air-con, new machines and wi-fi.

Sights & Activities

DIVING & SNORKELING

Playa is one of the best places on the coast to dive and snorkel. If you like, you can grab a snorkel and mask and dive in right from the beach. However, the most spectacular underwater sites are at the offshore reefs. Additionally Playa is a popular jump-off spot for exploring the many mysterious underwater caves and cenotes in the region.

The following are all premium outfits that offer instruction, certification courses, and scuba and snorkeling trips – including some night excursions – to the reefs and outlying caverns:

Abyss (☎ 873-21-64; www.abyssdiveshop.com; Calle 12) Located at the beach.

Dive Mike (☎ 803-12-28; www.divemike.com; Calle 8) Located between Quinta Av and the beach.

Protec (☎ 803-11-68; www.protecdiving.com; Calle 4)

Sleeping

Room prices in Playa – more so than anywhere else in the peninsula – are highly volatile and subject to change depending on how busy things are. The room prices listed are for the busy winter season (January to

April). Prices at many places can drop by 40% at other times of the year, however; hotel prices during the apex of the tourist season – approximately Dec 20 to Jan 5 – can jump as high as 40% above the prices listed.

BUDGET

Hotel Casa Tucán (☎ 873-02-83; Calle 4; d $25-30, apt $60; 🏊) Just a couple of blocks from the beach, this laidback Playa institution offers a myriad of no-frills lodging options, from single rooms to small apartments. There's a big (and very deep) pool, rooftop lounge and bar.

Playa Hostel (☎ 879-39-28; www.hostelworld.com; cnr 25 Av & Calle 8; dm $9.50, d $20) On a quiet corner, four blocks from the action (and noise) of Quinta Av, this hostel is unusually spacious, clean and well managed. There is a large communal kitchen and a big, comfy, central space with couches, hammocks, TV and stereo.

Urban Hostel (☎ 879-93-42; 10 Av; dm $10, d $25; 🖥) Renovated and drastically improved from its last incarnation, the Urban is still a little scruffy around the edges, but the relaxed, friendly vibe compensates for its quirks. There's a small rooftop patio and communal kitchen. Breakfast is included.

Camping-Cabañas La Ruina (☎ 873-04-05; Calle 2; tents & hammocks per person $6, d $18-25, with bathroom $30-38; 🏊) Aptly named, La Ruina is a bit of a ruin, but it is the only place in Playa to (officially) camp on the beach. Tents and hammocks are available for rent. Hotel rooms are tired but clean.

MIDRANGE

Alhambra (☎ 873-07-35; www.alhambra-hotel.net; Calle 8; d from $85; 🏊) This Casablanca-esque beachfront retreat seeks to soothe. The relaxed setting features crisp white, airy rooms; massage; professional yoga classes; sincerely welcoming staff; and, of course, the stress-zapping backdrop of plush sand and blue sea. There's a very good bar-restaurant (with healthy veggie choices) on the premises, too.

Hotel Casa de las Flores (☎ 873-28-98; www.hotel casadelasflores.com; 20 Av; d from $65; 🏊 🖥) This handsomely refurbished colonial-style home is an excellent choice. It's conveniently located in walking distance to Quinta Av and the beach but far enough away to be private and quiet. Lounge by the lovely pool

THE AUTHOR'S CHOICE

La Rana Cansada (☎ 873-03-89; www.ranacan sada.com; Calle 10; d $65; 🏊) Just off Quinta, but a quiet world away, La Rana Cansada's personable Swedish owners combine native Scandinavian sensibility with local color to create a mood of cultured warmth. Each room is distinct; ask to see a few. The upstairs chalet-esque unit ($150) is a uniquely sweet suite. There's a communal kitchen, and cozy Bar Ranitas adjoins.

and/or take advantage of complimentary passes to a choice of popular beach clubs.

Posada Freud (☎ 873-06-01; www.posadafreud.com; Quinta Av; d from $50; 🏊) Rich with character and whimsy, this place is an original charmer and would be a must-stay if it weren't for the neighbors. Loud music at the hotel bar next door can go on until 2am…on the other hand, there's a lively bar next door open until 2am!

Kinbé Hotel (☎ 873-04-41; www.kinbe.com; Calle 10; d from $60; 🏊) Near 1 Av, the inviting rooms in this contemporary hotel are full of artistic atmosphere. There's a lush tropical garden, a courtyard, and a rooftop terrace with amazing panoramic views.

Santa Barbara Hotel (☎ 873-12-27; www.hsbplaya .com; Quinta Av; d $80; 🏊) With earthy finishings – adobe tile, wood trim, Talavera inlay, natural fabrics – rooms are appealing, if cramped. Doubles are especially petite for the price. The central Quinta location is prime though, and rooms are set from the street so they're fairly quiet.

Hotel La Ziranda (☎ 873-39-29; www.hotellaziranda .com; Calle 4; d $45) A great deal. Housed in two attractive buildings, Ziranda has 15 simple and comfortable rooms with terraces or patios. Lush manicured grounds surround the property.

TOP END

Shangri-La Caribe (☎ 873-12-45; www.shangrilacaribe .net; Calle 38; d $175-325; 🏊 🖥 🏊) As the town has encroached north, Shangri-La is no longer an entirely sequestered oasis, but it remains a sheltered gem for sure, and its wide sweep of sugar-sand beach is generally trafficked only by guests. There are dozens of *cabañas*, but you wouldn't know it; the grounds are extensive enough that most feel private. Full breakfast *and* dinner is included.

Acanto (☎ 873-12-52; www.acantohotels.com; Calle 16; d $140; 🌀 🅿 💻 🐾) Designed in the current fashionable Playa style of East-meets-Far East (Moorish accents, Buddha images, Persian rugs, futons), this boutiquelike upscale hotel does trendy with class. The seven studio suites have full kitchens, private patios and a separate sleeping space with romantic gossamer-curtained beds. It's half a block from the beach.

Mosquito Blue (☎ 873-12-45; www.mosquitoblue .com; Quinta Av; d $140; 🌀 💻 🐾) One of the first hotels in Playa designed to conjure Mediterranean oasisness. Rooms are furnished in mahogany with puffy-pillowed sofas and sumptuous beds. There are two cloistered interior courtyards with pools, a bar and restaurant. It has wi-fi and laptops are available for loan.

Lunata (☎ 873-08-84; www.lunata.com; Quinta Av; d from $110; 🌀) Lunata strikes a balance between the heart of Quinta and the center of calm. The stylistic aim is hacienda-urbane, but the earthen walls, wood beams and low mellow light evoke a near-monastic mood. The tasteful rooms have genuine Mexican *sabor*.

Eating

Eating options in Playa del Carmen are bountiful. You could spend days just tasting your way around the block. And in that same block you'd probably find something to satisfy every budget and craving. Listed are some tried and trues, culled from blocks of experience.

CAFÉS
Café Corazón (☎ 803-27-72; Quinta Av; mains $5-9) A sophisticated yet cozy hangout, serving rich coffee and espresso – possibly the best in town.

Coffee Press (Calle 2; breakfast $3-4, lunch $4) Near Quinta Av, this is another place for a caffeine fix, with a selection of gourmet coffees and teas. The breakfasts are really good – not heavy but filling – and there's light lunch fare in the afternoon.

100% Natural (cnr Quinta Av & Calle 10; mains $4-9) Yes, it's a franchise, but the trademark fruit and vegetable juice blends, salads, chicken dishes and other healthy foods are delicious and filling. The green courtyard is inviting, and the service is excellent.

RESTAURANTS
Oasis (Calle 12; mains $5-12) Attractive and unpretentious, Oasis serves some of the best seafood on the coast – Caribbean or otherwise. Really. It's *so* good. The *ceviche mixto* (mixed seafood 'cooked' in lime juice) is the freshest, chunkiest, limeiest around, and the seafood tacos – especially the fish ones – are scrumptious! Oh, and as for the *caldo de mariscos* (seafood soup)…yum! It offers excellent service too.

Babe's (Calle 10; mains $5-10) This Asian fusion spot serves very good Thai food, including perfectly spiced, home-style *tom ka gai* (chicken and coconut-milk soup) brimming with veggies. The Vietnamese salad (with shrimp and mango) is delicious. Any choice will satisfy. Half orders are available too. There is a second location on Quinta Av.

Maktub Caffé (☎ 803-38-86; Quinta Av; mains $5-9) Enjoy tastily prepared Middle Eastern favorites – such as tabouleh, *baba ganoush*, hummus – served in a small, Marrakesh-hip, sit-on-the-floor setting. Excellent lunch deals ($3 to $5) are also available.

Sur (☎ 803-32-85; Quinta Av; lunch $8-15, dinner $10-25) Relaxed and refined, this breezy, white stucco open-air Argentinean restaurant serves fresh grilled meat and seafood, light pasta dishes, salads and pizza, and has an extensive wine list.

Yaxché (☎ 873-25-02; Calle 8; mains $10-25) Yaxché is a Playa institution and one of the most celebrated restaurants in town – many argue the best. The best Yucatecan restaurant? Agreed. Dishes are authentic and nicely seasoned.

THE AUTHOR'S CHOICE
La Cueva del Chango (☎ 876-25-37; Calle 38; mains $5-12) The earthy, wood and stone 'Monkey Cave' hides inconspicuously in a flourish of thick wild greenery. Harmonious design and unpretentious artistry make this a deeply appealing place. During the day, La Cueva is popular for breakfasts (eggs, fruit, homemade granola) and lunches (organic salads and sandwiches). Nightfall and candlelight transform La Cueva into an intimate venue serving delicious creations, like salad of *nopales* (cactus) and *chili rellenos* (stuffed peppers) filled with shrimp and squash. The wine list is 100% Mexican. It's located between Quinta Av and the beach.

Playasia (☎ 873-00-83; Quinta Av; mains $10-30) The Japanese chef uses the freshest-grade sashimi to make arguably the best sushi in town. Other treats include a delectable, buttery smooth conch salad. Set around a soothing pool, tables are each individually sheltered and fitted with a mood-setting candlelit lantern.

Club Náutico Tarraya (Calle 2; mains $4-7) Dating back to the 1960s, this beachfront joint is a Playa classic, and it continues to offer decent food at decent prices.

QUICK EATS

Dr Taco (10 Av; mains $3-7) Taco prescriptions filled here. Dr Carlo, a physician, and his wife Cecilia run this hip hole-in-the-wall serving shrimp burgers, stuffed peppers, veggie treats and, of course, tacos.

Hot (☎ 876-43-70; Calle 14; breakfast $4) This is the place for fresh-from-the-oven scrumptiousness, such as banana bread, muffins and Kahlua brownies. The coffee is strong and the breakfast egg dishes – especially the chili cheese omelettes – are extremely tasty too.

Les Petites Merveilles (☎ 877-12-42; Calle 8; mains $1-3) Buttery croissants, fresh bread and desserts. A French patisserie with universal mmm.

Drinking & Entertainment

Jam Session (☎ 803-49-15; Quinta Av) This musician-run club at the south end of Quinta Av, near Calle 40, has the best-quality live music in town, from jazz to reggae, blues and rock.

Apasionado (☎ 803-11-00; Quinta Av) This *palapa*-roofed venue glows with candlelight and good vibes. There's live Latin jazz nightly.

Om (Calle 12) Sheik-chic: sheer curtains, big pillows, huge candles and mystic lounge beats.

La Santanera (Calle 14) Join a super stylish DJ-spun party until dawn.

Bar Ranitas (Calle 10 btwn Avs Quinta & 10) A snug, inviting neighborhood bar.

El Alux (☎ 803-07-13; Av Juárez; ☺ 7pm-2amTue-Sun) Located two blocks west of Hwy 307, this unique bar occupies a real cave – replete with stalactites, stalagmites and natural freshwater pools. Candlelight adds to the subterranean mood…and detracts from oxygen supplies! A shot or two and you're floating on (thin) air.

Getting There & Away

BOAT

Ferries to Cozumel run nearly every hour, on the hour, from 6am to 11pm daily ($8 one way). The open-air boat takes between 45 minutes and an hour, while the air-conditioned catamaran, which leaves from the opposite side of the pier, takes closer to half an hour (it's the same ticket, same price, just less frequent).

BUS

Playa has two bus terminals. **Terminal del Centro** (cnr Quinta Av & Av Juárez) is the older bus terminal – receiving all 2nd-class buses – and is opposite the main plaza. All the Riviera buses leave from Terminal del Centro; buses to Cancún and its airport have a separate ticket counter, on the Av Juárez side. The 1st-class **Terminal ADO** (20 Av nr Calle 12) is several blocks to the north. A taxi to the main plaza from Terminal ADO will cost about $1.25. Buses travel daily from Play del Carmen to the following locations:

Destination	Price	Duration	Frequency
Cancún	$4	1hr	Riviera buses every 10min
Cancún international airport	$7	45min-1hr	9 direct Riviera buses between 7am & 7:30pm
Chetumal	$15	5-5½hr	12 Riviera buses
	$14	5-5½hr	11 2nd-class Mayab buses
Chichén Itzá	$16	3½hr	1 Riviera bus at 7:30am
Cobá	$4.50	1½hr	1 Riviera bus at 7:30am
Mérida	$20	5-8hr	9 1st-class Super Expresso buses
Palenque	$33-40	10hr	3 1st-class buses
San Cristóbal de Las Casas	$40-50	16hr	3 1st-class buses
Tulum	$3	1hr	frequent Riviera & Mayab buses
Valladolid	$6.25-11	2½-3½hr	frequent Riviera & Mayab buses

CAR & MOTORCYCLE

Sixty-eight kilometers south of Cancún just off Hwy 307, Playa del Carmen is an easy and direct drive from Cancún. Other points south along the well-paved Hwy 307 (including Tulum, 63km) are also easily reached from Playa by car.

COLECTIVOS

Shared vans head south to Tulum ($2, 45 minutes) from Calle 2 near 20 Av, about every 15 minutes from 5am to 10pm daily.

PLAYA DEL CARMEN TO TULUM

Xcaret

Once a precious spot open to all, **Xcaret** (☎ 984-871-52-00; admission adult/child $50/25; ☻ 8:30am-10pm), pronounced 'shkar-*et*,' about 10km south of Playa del Carmen, is now a heavily Disneyfied 'ecopark.' There are still Maya ruins and a beautiful inlet on the site, but much of the rest has been created or altered using dynamite, jackhammers and other terra-forming techniques. The park offers a cenote and 'underground river' for swimming, a restaurant, an evening show of 'ancient Maya ceremonies' worthy of Las Vegas, a butterfly pavilion, a botanical garden and nursery, orchid and mushroom farms, and a wild-bird breeding area.

Paamul

Paamul, 87km south of Cancún, is a de facto private beach on a sheltered bay. Like many other spots along the Caribbean coast, it has signs prohibiting entry to nonguests, but people still go (parking is limited).

The attractions are the beach and the great diving. The sandy beach is fringed with palms, but there are many small rocks, shells and spiked sea urchins in the shallows offshore, so take appropriate measures. The large RV park here is a favorite with snow-birds; the 'BC' license plates you'll see are from British Columbia, not Baja California. There is also an attractive alabaster sand beach about 2km north.

Giant sea turtles come ashore here at night in July and August to lay their eggs. If you run across one during an evening stroll along the beach, keep a good distance away and don't shine a flashlight at it, as that will scare it off. Do your part to contribute to the survival of the turtles, which are endangered; let them lay their eggs in peace.

Cabañas Paamul (☎ 984-875-10-51; www.paamul .com.mx; campsites $10 per person, RV sites $20, d cabaña $70; **P** **⌘**) Most of the RV sites are occupied most, if not all, of the year. For the rest of us, there are 10 spacious beachfront *cabañas*, a couple of (not as attractive) hotel rooms, and campsites with shared bathroom facilities.

There's an on-site restaurant serving Mexican standards.

Xpu-Há

Pronounced 'shpoo-*ha*,' this beach area, about 95km south of Cancún, extends for several kilometers. It's reached by numbered access roads (most of them private).

At the end of X-4 (Xpu-Há access road 4), the very laid-back **Hotel Villas del Caribe** (☎ 984-873-21-94; www.xpuhahotel.com; r from $55) sits on a lovely stretch of beach. All rooms have a terrace or balcony and are clean and quiet. The personable owners offer massage, yoga and meditation classes. The on-site **Café del Mar** (☻ Tues-Sun) serves excellent food, with many veggie options.

Most other accommodations on the beach are all-inclusive resorts, including **Copacabana** (☎ 984-875-18-00; www.hotelcopacabana.com; d$100) and the wheelchair-accessible **Xpu-Ha Palace** (☎ 984-875-10-10; www.palaceresorts.com; $125).

Akumal

Famous for its beautiful beach, Akumal (Place of the Turtles) does indeed see some sea turtles come ashore to lay their eggs in the summer, although fewer and fewer arrive each year thanks to resort development. Akumal is one of the Yucatán Peninsula's oldest resort areas, and consists primarily of pricey hotels and condominiums on nearly 5km of wide beach, bordering four consecutive bays.

Although an increasing population is taking a heavy toll on the reefs that parallel Akumal, diving remains the area's primary attraction. Dive trips and deep-sea fishing excursions are offered by **Akumal Dive Shop** (☎ 984-875-90-32; www.akumal.com). A one-tank dive costs $45, two-tank $60. Deep-sea fishing trips cost $120 per person for a two-hour excursion. Located in the center of town, the very active environmental NGO **Centro Ecológico Akumal** (☎ 984-875-90-95; www.ceakumal .org) offers night turtle tours ($10) from May to September. This organization is always looking for competent and committed volunteers; if interested enquire on-site or online.

The hotel and restaurant **Que Onda** (☎ 984-875-91-01; www.queondaakumal.com; r from $75) is set amid an expanse of greenery in a fairly residential area, only 50m from Laguna Yal-kú. The six fan-cooled rooms have tiled floors and good beds; upstairs rooms have

YUCATÁN PENINSULA

balconies. There is a lovely pool, free Internet access, bicycles and snorkeling equipment. The restaurant serves delicious homemade pasta.

On the beach, **Villa Las Brisas** (☎ 984-876-21-10; www.aventuras-akumal.com; r from $65) is an attractive, modern place with condos and a studio apartment – all under one roof. The friendly owners speak English, Spanish, German, Italian and some Portuguese. The turnoff to get here is 2.5km south of the turnoff for Playa Akumal.

Just outside the entrance of Akumal is a minimarket that stocks a good selection of inexpensive food. Super homelike and inviting **Turtle Bay Café** (meals $5-10), just inside the entrance, serves excellent breakfasts and fresh homemade baked goods. It's open for lunch too, and sometimes dinner.

Xel-Há

About 45km south of Playa del Carmen is this, a once-pristine natural lagoon brimming with iridescent tropical fish. **Xel-Há** (☎ 984-875-60-00; admission adult/child $25/13; �
9am-6pm), pronounced 'shell-ha,' is now a private park with landscaped grounds, developed cenotes, caves, nature paths, several restaurants-bars and more. It's very touristy, but the lagoon is still beautiful and still home to many tropical fish.

Most buses traveling between Playa and Tulum will drop you at Xel-Há.

If driving, you will see very visible signs for the park posted along Hwy 307; the entrance to the park is right off the highway.

Bahías de Punto Solimán

These two protected bays are one of the best-kept secrets on the coast. Located 123km south of Cancún, and 11km north of Tulum (turn off Hwy 307 at the big white signed exit reading 'Oscar y Lalo'), this area offers good wildlife watching, kayaking, excellent snorkeling, and long white swathes of palm-shaded beach. On the north bay sits **Oscar y Lalo** (☎ 984-804-69-73; mains $10-25), a spacious restaurant overlooking the water. The food is very good and comes in heaped portions. The owners also rent kayaks.

On the south bay (also known as Bahía de San Francisco) private homes – many very luxurious – line the road. Most of them rent for the week at well over $1000. There are a

couple – though still not cheap – exceptions to this rule. Note, however, there is a three-night minimum stay at both of the following options.

At **Casa Nah Uxibal** (www.nahuxibal.com; apt $135-275) the main villa, a *palapa*-roofed retreat, is adorned with rich wood, earthy tile and stone, and boasts a spectacular 35ft-high ceiling. The four other units on the extensive beachfront property include two lovely light and airy studios, with beautifully tiled kitchen and bathroom. Most special of all though, are the two private and beautifully appointed casitas nestled amid lush greenery *right* on the white beach.

Casa del Corazón (www.locogringo.com; per night from $150) rents three cozy, artistically furnished, fully-equipped beach bungalows, all set amid palms and shady vegetation just steps from the beach.

Cenotes

On the west side of the highway south of Paamul are several cenotes you can visit (and usually swim in) for a price. A few kilometers south of Akumal is the turnoff for Cenote Dos Ojos, which provides access to the **Nohoch Nah Chich cave system**, the largest underwater cave system in the world. You can take guided snorkel and dive tours of some amazing underwater caverns here, floating past illuminated stalactites and stalagmites in an eerie wonderland.

Hidden Worlds (☎ 984-877-85-35; www.hiddenworlds .com.mx) is an American-run outfit offering three-hour snorkeling tours for $40, and one- or two-tank dive tours for $50 or $80 respectively. The snorkeling price includes flashlights, wet suit, equipment and transportation to the cenotes on a unique 'jungle mobile.' The drive through the jungle is a unique experience in itself, and the guides are very knowledgeable and informative. The diving tours are at 9am, 11am and 1pm daily; equipment rental costs extra. You don't need to make a reservation, but it never hurts to call.

These are cavern (as opposed to cave) dives, and require only standard open-water certification. However, don't try doing it on your own. Cavern diving without an experienced guide (preferably one with cave certification) can be just as deadly as cave diving.

TULUM

☎ 984 / pop 8000

Some 130km south of Cancún, Tulum's main attractions are at the waterfront, including Maya ruins, powdery beaches and a profusion of *cabañas*. The area's foreign population has been steadily increasing as new hotels and restaurants open in town and at the beach.

Orientation

Traveling southbound toward Tulum, the first thing you reach is Tulum Crucero, the junction of Hwy 307 and the old access road to the ruins. The new access road is 400m further south, and leads another 600m to the Tulum ruins. Another 1.5km south on the highway brings you to the

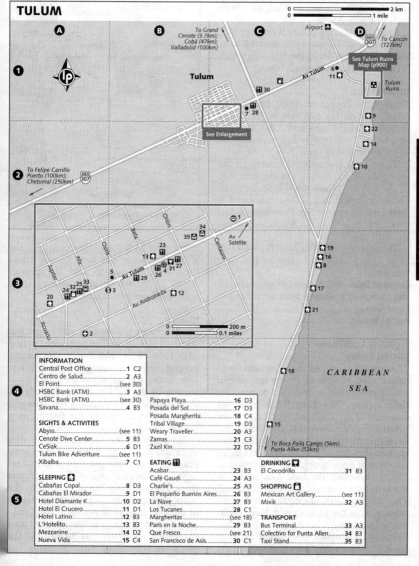

TULUM

Tulum

To Grand Cenote (3.7km); Cobá (47km); Valladolid (100km)

Airport

To Cancún (127km)

See Tulum Ruins Map (p900)

Tulum Ruins

To Felipe Carrillo Puerto (100km); Chetumal (250km)

Av Satelite

YUCATÁN PENINSULA

CARIBBEAN SEA

To Boca Paila Camps (5km); Punta Allen (52km)

INFORMATION	
Central Post Office	**1** C2
Centro de Salud	**2** A3
El Point	(see 30)
HSBC Bank (ATM)	**3** A3
HSBC Bank (ATM)	(see 30)
Savana	**4** B3

SIGHTS & ACTIVITIES	
Abyss	(see 11)
Cenote Dive Center	**5** B3
CeSiak	**6** D1
Tulum Bike Adventure	(see 11)
Xibalba	**7** C1

SLEEPING	
Cabañas Copal	**8** D3
Cabañas El Mirador	**9** D1
Hotel Diamante K	**10** D2
Hotel El Crucero	**11** D1
Hotel Latino	**12** B3
L'Hotelito	**13** B3
Mezzanine	**14** D2
Nueva Vida	**15** C4

Papaya Playa	**16** D3
Posada del Sol	**17** D3
Posada Margherita	**18** C4
Tribal Village	**19** D3
Weary Traveller	**20** A3
Zamas	**21** C3
Zazil Kin	**22** D2

EATING	
Acabar	**23** B3
Café Gaudí	**24** A3
Charlie's	**25** A3
El Pequeño Buenos Aires	**26** B3
La Nave	**27** B3
Los Tucanes	**28** C1
Margheritas	(see 18)
Paris en la Noche	**29** B3
Que Fresco	(see 21)
San Francisco de Asís	**30** C1

DRINKING	
El Cocodrillo	**31** B3

SHOPPING	
Mexican Art Gallery	(see 11)
Mixik	**32** A3

TRANSPORT	
Bus Terminal	**33** A3
Colectivo for Punta Allen	**34** B3
Taxi Stand	**35** B3

Cobá junction, where there is a gas station and the San Francisco de Asís supermarket; turning right (west) at this junction takes you to Cobá. The road to the left (east) leads about 3km to the north–south road servicing Tulum's Zona Hotelera, the string of beachfront lodgings extending 10km south from the ruins. This road eventually enters the Reserva de la Biosfera Sian Ka'an (p906), continuing some 50km past Boca Paila to Punta Allen.

South of the Cobá junction on Hwy 307, is the town of Tulum itself, referred to as Tulum Pueblo; it flanks the highway, which is called Av Tulum through town.

Information

There are a couple of HSBC banks with ATMs, one on the east side of Av Tulum (between Calles Osiris and Alfa), and one next to San Francisco de Asís supermarket, at the north end of town.

There are a few Internet centers on the west side of Av Tulum. On the east side of Av Tulum, **Savana** (per hr $1.50), between Calles Orion and Beta, is air-conditioned. **El Point** (per hr $2), next to San Francisco de Asís supermarket, is also air-conditioned and has excellent machines.

The central post office is on the west side of Av Tulum, between Av Satelite and Calle Centauro.

Centro de Salud (☎ 871-20-50; Calle Andrómeda) This clinic has professional, affordable health care, and some English-speaking staff.

Police (☎ 060)

Sights & Activities

TULUM RUINS

Though well preserved, the **Tulum Ruins** (Parque Nacional Tulum; admission $4; ⏰ 7am-5pm) would hardly merit rave reviews if it weren't for their setting. The grayish-tan buildings dominate a palm-fringed beach lapped by turquoise waters. Even on dark and stormy days, the majestic cliff-top ruins overlooking vast stretches of pristine beach are fit for the cover of a guidebook. Just don't come to Tulum expecting anything comparable to the architecture at Chichén Itzá or Uxmal. The buildings here, decidedly Toltec in influence, were the product of a Maya civilization in decline.

Tulum is a prime destination for tour buses. To best enjoy the ruins, visit them

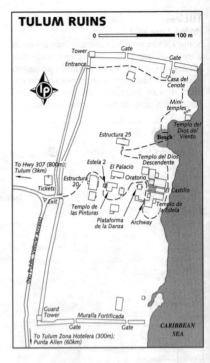

either early in the morning or late in the afternoon, when the tour groups aren't there. Parking costs $3, and the optional shuttle to the site (about a seven-minute walk) is $2 per round-trip.

History

Most archaeologists believe that Tulum was occupied during the late postclassic period (AD 1200–1521), and that it was an important port town during its heyday. When Juan de Grijalva sailed past in 1518, he was amazed by the sight of this walled city, its buildings painted a gleaming red, blue and yellow, and a ceremonial fire flaming atop its seaside watchtower.

The ramparts that surround three sides of Tulum (the fourth side being the Caribbean Sea) leave little question as to its strategic function as a fortress. Several meters thick and standing 3m to 5m high, the walls protected the city during a period of considerable strife between Maya city-states. Not all of Tulum was situated within the walls; the vast majority of the city's residents lived outside them. The civic-ceremonial buildings and palaces likely housed Tulum's ruling class.

The city was abandoned about 75 years after the Spanish conquest. It was one of the last ancient cities to be abandoned; most others had been given back to nature long before the arrival of the Spanish. Maya pilgrims continued to visit over the years, and Maya refugees from the War of the Castes took shelter there from time to time.

The name 'Tulum' is Maya for 'wall,' though that was not how its residents knew it. They called it Zama, or 'Dawn.' 'Tulum' was apparently applied by explorers during the early 20th century.

The Site

The two-storey **Templo de las Pinturas** was constructed in several stages around AD 1400–1450. Its decoration was among the most elaborate at Tulum, and included relief masks and colored murals on an inner wall. The murals have been partially restored, but are nearly impossible to make out. This monument might have been the last built by the Maya before the Spanish conquest, and with its columns, carvings, two-storey construction and the stela out front, it's probably the most interesting structure at the site.

Overlooking the Caribbean is Tulum's tallest building, a watchtower appropriately named **El Castillo** (the Castle) by the Spaniards. Note the Toltec-style serpent columns at the temple's entrance, echoing those at Chichén Itzá.

The **Templo del Dios Descendente** (Temple of the Descending God) is named for the relief figure above the door – a diving figure, partly human, that may be related to the Maya's reverence for bees. This figure appears at several other east-coast sites and at Cobá.

The restored **Templo de la Estela** (Temple of the Stela) is also known as the Temple of the Initial Series. Stela 1, now in the British Museum, was found here. The stela was inscribed with the Maya date corresponding to AD 564 (the 'initial series' of Maya hieroglyphs in an inscription gives its date). At first this confused archaeologists, who believed Tulum had been settled several hundred years later than this date. It's now believed that Stela 1 was brought to Tulum from Tankah, 4km to the north, a settlement dating from the classic period.

El Palacio (the Palace) features a beautiful stucco carving of a diving god over its main doorway.

The **Templo del Dios del Viento** (Temple of the Wind God) provides the best views of El Castillo juxtaposed with the sea below. It's a great place for snapping photos.

DIVING & SNORKELING

Diving and snorkeling are big draws here. The lure is not only the fabulous ocean reefs but also the multiple mysterious underwater caves and cenotes which are concentrated in this area. The following are all safe and professional outfits that offer instruction, certification courses, and scuba and snorkeling trips to the reefs and nearby caverns:

Abyss (☎ 871-26-08; www.abyssdiveshop.com; Hotel El Crucero, Tulum Crucero) Located in Hotel El Crucero, Abyss specialize in ocean dives (two tank $60) and offer cenote dives (two tank $100).

Cenote Dive Center (☎ 871-22-32; www.cenotedive .com; cnr Av Tulum & Calle Osiris) Specializes in guided cavern dives ($125) and cenote dives ($90), as well as cenote snorkeling trips ($35).

Xibalba (☎ 807-45-79; www.xibalbadivecenter.com; Av Tulum) Owned and operated by extremely skilled and experienced cave divers. They offer guided cenote dives ($110), as well as a series of cave-diving certification courses. They also offer expert open-water instruction and dives.

Tours

CESiaK (Centro Ecológico Sian Ka'an; ☎ 871-24-99; www .cesiak.org; Tulum Crucero) Adjacent to hotel El Crucero, CESiaK is an outstanding environmental organization committed to promoting sustainable travel through conservation and education. It offers guided tours to Reserva de la Biosfera Sian Ka'an (p906), including all-day excursions (per person, lunch included, $80) and sunset bird-watching trips (per person $70).

Tulum Bike Adventure (☎ 871-26-10; Hotel El Crucero, Tulum Crucero) Located in Hotel El Crucero, offering bike tours to local cenotes ($40) and the Reserva de la Biosfera Sian Ka'an (p906; $60), and even overnight excursions to Punta Allen ($120).

Sleeping

Hotels in town and near the ruins are the logical place to stay if you're just passing through or only want to visit the ruins. If it is the beach you're after, the Zona Hotelera is a better choice. The following listings give high-season lodging rates. Low-season rates can be reduced by as much as 50%.

TULUM PUEBLO

Hotel El Crucero (☎ 871-26-10; www.el-crucero.com; Tulum Crucero; dm $7.50, d $35, theme r $50; P ☒ ☐) North of town, a limestone's throw away from the ruins, El Crucero features three dorm rooms, five nicely appointed double rooms and four large, kind of silly, but comfortable theme rooms, featuring whimsical murals. An excellent restaurant-bar is on-site, as is a professional dive shop and art gallery. Bike rentals are available, and the beach is just a long walk/short bike ride away.

Hotel Latino (☎ 871-26-74; Av Andrómeda; dm/d $16/60; ☒) Cool, crisp, whitewashed and minimalist, this hotel longs to be on a hip beach somewhere. The rooms (including the attractive dorm room) are all spotless and comfortable, with great mattresses.

Weary Traveler (☎ 871-23-90; www.intulum.com; Av Tulum; dm $10, d $20; ☐) The popular Weary is 100m south of the bus terminal. The small dorm rooms have two bunk beds, a fan and bathroom with shower. There is a relaxing, shaded courtyard with a bar and communal kitchen. Shuttle service is provided to and from the beach at no cost. Free Salsa lessons are also available, as well as a big breakfast daily.

L'Hotelito (☎ 871-20-61; Av Tulum; d with fan/aircon $55/65; ☒) Three blocks north of the bus terminal, this nice Italian-run place has clean, quiet rooms. Those upstairs have good ventilation, those downstairs have air-con. There's a good restaurant, too.

ZONA HOTELERA

Along the coastal road leading to Punta Allen, which begins less than 1km south of the ruins, is a string of *cabaña* hotels. A few cater primarily to backpackers and campers, and most have simple restaurants. The primitive *cabañas* can be unsecure; never leave valuables unattended in a *cabaña*.

The following places are ordered north to south. As a rule, the further south you travel along the beachfront road, the more expensive accommodations become. There are over 60 hotels along this stretch of beach, we've listed our recommended choices.

Cabañas El Mirador (☎ 879-60-19; cabañas with hammock/bed $10/25) Closest to the ruins, this place has 28 cabins (half with sand floors), most with beds, some with hammocks. The beach is wide here, and there's a decent restaurant with excellent views.

Zazil Kin (☎ 871-24-17; d $20, with bathroom $25-40) Zazil Kin is the most popular inexpensive place on the beach. It's clean, secure and always lively. There's a good dive center, basketball court, ever- happening restaurant-bar and a nice stretch of beach.

Mezzanine (☎ 804-14-52; www.mezzanine.com.mx; d $200) A seductive boutique hotel set on a low bluff overlooking the sea. There are only four rooms – all doubles and all romantically sleek. There's an excellent Thai-fusion restaurant and an otherwise mellow bar that turns into a party-scene extraordinaire on Friday night.

Hotel Diamante K (☎ 871-23-76; www.diamantek .com; r $30-60, with bathroom $60-200) This ecotel's lovely *cabañas* have suspended beds and a table for candles (the solar-generated electricity goes off at 11:30pm). It has a small beach, and a fine bar and vegetarian restaurant. It's often full even in the low season.

Tribal Village (☎ 804-25-13; www.tribalvillage tulum.com; campsites $5, d from $30) Funky, friendly and clean, Tribal Village is all chill and good vibes. *Cabañas* come in different sizes and configurations; all comfortable and safe. There's plenty of camping, and a very good café specializing in tasty fusion fare.

Papaya Playa (☎ 804-64-44; www.papayaplaya.com; d from $40) Recently reinvented and updated, the Papaya is an attractive option. There is a choice of *cabañas* with shared (very clean) bathroom; or tasteful villas, featuring a bedroom and private bathroom. The restaurant-bar is popular and open until late. Choose your room accordingly.

Cabañas Copal (toll free US or Canada ☎ 877-532-67-37; www.cabanascopal.com; d $35, with bathroom from $65; ☐) The *cabañas* here are lovely and overlook a clothing-optional stretch of beach. Amenities include a holistic spa, *temascal*, flotation chamber, yoga classes, restaurant-bar and Internet café.

Posada del Sol (☎ 871-23-76; d from $50) This place is run by artists, and it shows. The rooms are showpieces in themselves. Nothing fancy, just a fine, earthy, aesthetic that is *so* appealing. The property flanks both sides of the road, with rooms on the west side (furthest from the beach) being less expensive. There's a nice folk art shop on-site.

Zamas (☎ 415-387-98-06; www.zamas.com; d $80-150) Zamas' romantic *cabañas* all have terraces with two hammocks, 24-hour electricity, purified drinking water, big private bathrooms and two comfy beds with mosquito nets. The lovely and regionally acclaimed restaurant, Que Fresco, overlooks the rocks, sea and beach.

Posada Margherita (☎ 100-37-80; www.posadamargherita.com; d $70-140) The six rooms at this eco-friendly hotel are tiled and bright, with verandas or balconies. The beach here is particularly wide and lovely. Some of the rooms, and all of the grounds, are wheelchair accessible. There's a very good dive shop, which also offers scuba diving for those with limited mobility. The Italian restaurant is one of the – if not *the* – best around.

Nueva Vida (☎ 877-20-92; www.tulumnv.com; d $110-260) This eco-retreat is secluded and tranquil, and fronts a vast, sugary beach. The seven rustic *cabañas* are spread out in the jungle back from the shore, and elevated on stilts so as not to disturb the dunes. The 24-hour electricity is completely solar or wind generated. There's a nice family-run restaurant. Breakfast is included.

Boca Paila Camps (☎ 871-24-99; www.cesiak.org; d $65) On the Tulum–Punta Allen road, 4km from the entrance of the Reserva de la Biosfera Sian Ka'an and nestled amid lush jungle, this lovely eco-oasis, run by the Tulum-based ecology group CESiaK (p901), has 15 elevated, low environmental–impact (solar power, compost toilets) *palapa* units, and an excellent on-site restaurant. The staff – all committed conservationists – offer in-depth educational tours of the surrounding reserve.

Eating & Drinking

Acabar (Av Tulum; mains $5-10) Natural wood, earthy hues, candlelight – all fused with a hint of zen – this relaxed, spacious split-level restaurant-bar is the classiest act in town. The menu features a delicious blend of international styles.

Margheritas (Margheritas, Zona Hotelera; mains $8-25) This atmospheric, sand-floor Italian restaurant lives up to its rep, offering some of the finest cuisine around. All the pasta is homemade (a rarity) and the sauces are subtle and savory.

Mezzanine (Mezzanine, Zona Hotelera; mains $7-25) The inventive chef at this ultra stylish Thai-fusion restaurant-lounge creates unforgettable specialties (try the *tom kha gai*). On Friday nights, DJs invent an equally memorable and tasty groove.

La Nave (Av Tulum, btwn Calles Orion & Beta; mains $5-9; ◷ Mon-Sat) If you come here for breakfast, you'll be tempted to come back for lunch and dinner. From the fresh-baked bread to the wood-fired pizza and the ceviche – it's all fresh and satisfying.

Que Fresco (Zamas, Zona Hotelera; mains $5-15) An Italian-leaning spot serving tasty meals all day, with the big breakfasts a particular treat.

Charlie's (Av Tulum; mains $5-10) A tourist magnet at first glance, Charlie's is actually an authentic family-owned restaurant, delivering excellent Mexican fare, including delicious *chili rellenos* filled with cheese mousse and pecans. The black beans are unusually good and the salsa pure garlicky joy.

El Pequeño Buenos Aires (Av Tulum; mains $5-17) An authentic Argentine barbeque joint, serving generous portions of steak, chicken and seafood. The chicken brochettes are particularly juicy and the *empanadas* (filled puff-pastry) – especially the spinach and cheese – are full of flavor. It offers good service, and there's a nice wine selection.

Paris en la Noche (Av Tulum; mains $5-10) The French owner takes crepes very seriously here, and it's a good thing…they're seriously good. Start with spinach and goat's cheese and work your way toward a sweet chocolate finish.

Los Tucanes (Av Tulum; meals $4-7) This bright and airy, family-run spot serves good traditional Yucatecan fare.

Café Gaudi (Av Tulum; mains $3-7) A snug little café, serving very good coffee and espresso, as well as satisfying light fare like sandwiches and salad.

El Cocdrillo (Av Tulum; drinks $2-5) A low-key live music venue, featuring anything from rasta to rock and folk.

San Francisco de Asís (Av Tulum) This large, well-stocked supermarket is at the very north end of town, at the junction of Av Tulum and the road to Cobá. If you are heading to the beach, it's a good idea to stop here first and stock up on food and supplies.

Shopping

Mexican Art Gallery (☎ 745-89-79; Hotel El Crucero, Tulum Crucero; ◷ 9am-2pm Mon-Sat) This gallery, adjacent to the Hotel El Crucero, features the original works (paintings and murals) of owner Enrique Díaz, whose work is original, often political and consistently compelling.

YUCATÁN PENINSULA

Mixtic (☎ 871-21-36; Av Tulum; ☺ Mon-Sat) Stocks fine-quality Mexican folk art, crafts and jewelry from all over the country.

Getting There & Around

You can walk from Tulum Crucero to the ruins (800m). The *cabañas* begin about 600m south of the ruins and can be reached by taxi from Tulum Pueblo; fares are fixed and reasonable: to the ruins costs $4, to most of the *cabañas* $6.

The **bus terminal** (Av Tulum) is toward the southern end of town. When leaving Tulum, you can also wait at Tulum Crucero for a Playa Express or regular intercity bus. There are many buses daily from Tulum to the following locales:

Destination	Price	Duration
Cancún	$5-6	2hr
Chetumal	$9-11	3½-4hr
Chichén Itzá	$7.25	3hr
Cobá	$3	45min
Felipe Carrillo Puerto	$4-5	1¾hr
Mérida	$14	7hr
Playa del Carmen	$3	1hr
Valladolid	$4-5	2hr

GRAND CENOTE

About 3.7km west of Tulum on the road to Cobá is Grand Cenote, a worthwhile stop on your way between Tulum and the Cobá ruins, especially if it's a hot day. You can **snorkel** ($5) among small fish in the caverns here, if you bring your own gear.

COBÁ

☎ 984 / pop 300

You'll dodge potholes and butterflies for much of the 42km ride from Tulum here, but once you arrive you'll be glad you came. Among the largest of Maya cities, Cobá offers the chance to explore mostly unrestored antiquities set deep in tropical jungle. Though Cobá receives many visitors, it's so expansive that a feeling of real solitude pervades the site, and the long shaded paths leading from one set of buildings to the next can feel like a private passageway back through time.

History

Cobá was settled much earlier than Chichén Itzá or Tulum, and construction reached its peak between AD 800 and 1100. Archaeologists believe that this city once covered 50 sq km and held a population of 40,000 Maya.

Cobá's architecture is a mystery; its towering pyramids and stelae resemble the architecture of Tikal, which is several hundred kilometers away, rather than the much nearer sites of Chichén Itzá and the northern Yucatán Peninsula.

Some archaeologists theorize that an alliance with Tikal was made through marriage, to facilitate trade between the Guatemalan and Yucatecan Maya. Stelae appear to depict female rulers from Tikal holding ceremonial bars and flaunting their power by standing on captives. These Tikal royal females, when married to Cobá's royalty, may have brought architects and artisans with them.

Archaeologists are also baffled by the extensive network of *sacbés* (stone-paved avenues) in this region, with Cobá as the hub. The longest runs nearly 100km, from the base of Cobá's great pyramid Nohoch Mul to the Maya settlement of Yaxuna. In all, some 40 *sacbés* passed through Cobá, parts of the huge astronomical 'time machine' that was evident in every Maya city.

The first excavation was by the Austrian archaeologist Teobert Maler in 1891. There was little subsequent investigation until 1926, when the Carnegie Institute financed the first of two expeditions led by Sir J Eric S Thompson and Harry Pollock. After their 1930 expedition, not much happened until 1973, when the Mexican government began to finance excavation. Archaeologists now estimate that Cobá contains some 6500 structures, of which just a few have been excavated and restored, though work is ongoing.

Orientation

The small village of Cobá, 2.5km west of the Tulum–Nuevo Xcan road, has some small cheap hotels and several basic low-cost restaurants. At the lake, turn left for the ruins and right for the upscale Villas Arqueológicas Cobá hotel.

Information

The **Cobá ruins** (admission $4; ☺ 7am-6pm) has a parking lot charging $1.50 per passenger car.

Be prepared to walk several kilometers on paths, depending on how much you want to

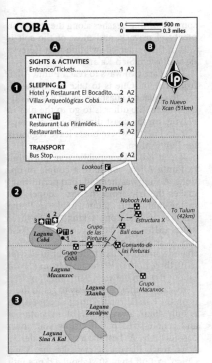

COBÁ

	0 500 m
	0 0.3 miles

SIGHTS & ACTIVITIES
Entrance/Tickets...........................1 A2

SLEEPING
Hotel y Restaurant El Bocadito....2 A2
Villas Arqueológicas Cobá............3 A2

EATING
Restaurant Las Pirámides..............4 A2
Restaurants....................................5 A2

TRANSPORT
Bus Stop...6 A2

see. Bring insect repellent and water; the shop next to the ticket booth sells both. Avoid the midday heat if possible. Most people spend around two hours at the site.

A short distance inside, at the Grupo Cobá, are bicycles available for rent (per day $2.50). These are useful if you really want to get around the further reaches, and the breeze they create is cooling.

You may want to buy a book about Cobá before visiting the site – on-site signage and maps are minimal and cryptic. Guides near the entrance size you up and charge whatever they think you're worth, anywhere from $8 to over $65, depending on the length of the tour. Tours can be worth it, as guides are knowledgeable about the latest restoration work. The Nohoch Mul pyramid is the only structure the public is allowed to climb.

Sights
GRUPO COBÁ
Walking just under 100m along the main path from the entrance and turning right, brings you to the **Templo de las Iglesias**

(Temple of the Churches), the most prominent structure in the Cobá Group. It's an enormous pyramid, with views from the top taking in the Nohoch Mul pyramid and surrounding lakes, but climbing it is forbidden.

Back on the main path and 30m further along, you pass through the **juego de pelota**, a well-restored ball court.

GRUPO MACANXOC
About 500m beyond the *juego de pelota*, the path forks. Going straight gets you to the **Grupo Macanxoc**, a group of stelae that bore reliefs of royal women who are thought to have come from Tikal. They are badly eroded, and it's a 1km walk, but the flora along the way is interesting.

CONJUNTO DE LAS PINTURAS
Though it's signed to the left at the fork, if you're on foot you can reach the **Conjunto de las Pinturas** (Group of Paintings) by heading toward the Grupo Macanxoc a very short distance and turning left. The temple here bears traces of glyphs and frescoes above its door, and remnants of richly colored plaster inside.

You approach the temple from the southeast. Leave by the trail at the northwest (opposite the temple steps) to see several stelae. The first of these is 20m along, beneath a *palapa*. Here a regal figure stands over two others, one of them kneeling with his hands bound behind him. Sacrificial captives lie beneath the feet of a ruler at the base. Continue along the path past another badly weathered stela and a small temple to rejoin the Nohoch Mul path and turn right.

NOHOCH MUL
A walk of 800m more brings you to **Nohoch Mul** (Big Mound), also known as the Great Pyramid, built on a natural hill. Along the way is another ball court – at the north end of which lie weathered stelae – and the track then bends between piles of stones (a ruined temple) before passing Templo 10 and Stele 20. The exquisitely carved stela bears a picture of a ruler standing imperiously over two captives. Eighty meters beyond stands the Great Pyramid.

At 42m high, the Great Pyramid is the tallest Maya structure on the Yucatán Peninsula. There are two diving gods carved over

YUCATÁN PENINSULA

the doorway of the temple at the top (built in the postclassic period, AD 1100–1450), similar to the sculptures at Tulum. The view is spectacular!

Sleeping & Eating

There's no organized campground, but you can try finding a place along the shore of the lake, which is inhabited by crocodiles (local children can show you a safe swimming spot).

Hotel y Restaurant El Bocadito (☎ 985-852-00-52; r $20) The hotel has very simple, fan-cooled rooms with private bathroom. The restaurant is very well run and serves a great *menú* (set meal) for about $5. You can also store luggage here while you visit the ruins. The bus terminal is also located here.

Villas Arqueológicas Cobá (☎ 998-858-15-27, in the US 800-258-2633; d $70) This Club Med hotel next to the lake has a swimming pool and a mediocre restaurant to complement its rooms. It's a nice place to relax and is the best value among the Villas Arqueológicas on the Yucatán Peninsula.

Restaurant Las Pirámides (mains $5-11) A few doors down from the Club Med, this restaurant has good lake views and friendly service.

There are several small restaurants by the site parking lot, including Restaurant El Faisán and Restaurant El Caracol, both of which serve inexpensive meals ($4 to $6).

Getting There & Away

Hotel y Restaurant El Bocadito (☎ 985-852-00-52) also serves as Cobá's bus terminal and *colectivo* taxi terminus.

There are six to eight buses daily between Tulum and Cobá ($3, 45 minutes). Six of these also serve Playa del Carmen ($4.50, 1½ hours). A combi (minibus) between Cobá and Tulum charges $5 per person. There is also bus service to Valladolid ($2.50, one hour), Chichén Itzá ($5, 1½ hours) and Mérida ($11, 3½ hours).

The 31km road from Cobá to Chemax is arrow straight and in good shape. If you're driving to Valladolid or Chichén Itzá, this is the way to go.

TULUM TO PUNTA ALLEN

Punta Allen is at the end of a narrow stretch of land that reaches south nearly 40km from its start just below Tulum. There are some charming beaches along the way, with plenty of privacy, and most of the spit is within the protected, wildlife-rich Reserva de la Biosfera Sian Ka'an.

There are two ways to reach Punta Allen from Tulum. One is to take the unpaved, muffler-busting coastal road that goes directly there; the other is to go to the pier in Playón, on the coast directly east of Felipe Carillo Puerto, where boats leave regularly for Punta Allen.

If you are taking public transportation to Punta Allen, you have a couple of options. A van (weather and road permitting) makes the trip from the taxi cooperative in the middle of Tulum Pueblo to Punta Allen at around 2pm, taking two to three hours ($15). Alternatively, you can take a bus to Felipe Carrillo Puerto and then a shared van from there to the pier in Playón ($10, three hours). Water taxis from Playón (about $4) run between 9am and 5pm.

By car, the most direct way to get to there is on the coastal road. Though Punta Allen is only 40km away from Tulum, potholes and cenote-sized puddles slow you down considerably. At best it's a rattling ride.

To reach Playón by car take the 'Vigía Chico' exit off Hwy 307 (about 42km south of Tulum) and drive another 42km (on an unpaved road, about two hours) to the boat landing.

Reserva de la Biosfera Sian Ka'an

Over 5000 sq km of tropical jungle, marsh, mangroves and islands on Quintana Roo's coast have been set aside by the Mexican government as a large biosphere reserve. In 1987, the UN appointed it a World Heritage Site – an irreplaceable natural treasure.

Sian Ka'an (Where the Sky Begins) is home to howler monkeys, anteaters, foxes, ocelots, pumas, crocodiles, eagles, raccoons, tapirs, *javelinas* (peccaries), giant land crabs, jaguars and hundreds of bird species, including *chocolateras* (roseate spoonbills) and some flamingos. There are no hiking trails through the reserve; it's best explored with a professional guide. Tour operators based in Tulum are your best option (for details, see p901).

Punta Allen

Punta Allen is a mellow little paradise, surrounded by protected jungle and flanked by the calm waters of Asuncion Bay and the turquoise sea. The thriving reef 400m from shore offers snorkelers and divers wondrous sights. And birders will be captivated by the abundance and variety of avian life.

The area is also famous for its bonefishing, which attracts many people far and wide. Some of the guides listed here, as well as cooperatives in town, offer fishing trips for about $200, including lunch. Some places, such as the Cuzan Guest House or Ascension Bay Beach Club (see, below) offer all-inclusive week-long packages, with accommodations, boats, guides and meals for around $2400 a week.

Four Punta Allen locals with training in English, Maya history, natural history and bird-watching offer nature and snorkeling tours for about $125 per group: **Baltazar Madera** (☎ 984-871-20-01); **Marcos Nery** (☎ 984-871-24-24); and **Chary Salazar** (enquire directly at Chary's Restaurant). The latter two are experts on endemic and migratory bird species, and Chary also leads interactive cultural community tours. For exploration of nearby jungle ruins or an in-depth tour to the archaeological site of Muyil, contact Maya historian and guide **Tomás Trulzsch** (☎ 984-806-74-90).

SLEEPING & EATING

Cuzan Guest House (☎ 983-834-03-58; www.flyfish .mx.com; d $40-80) The Crusoe-esque beach *cabañas* here are equipped with all necessary comforts: 24-hour solar electricity, private bathrooms with hot showers, good beds and fans. Open for breakfast, lunch and dinner, the guesthouse's restaurant-bar is the most popular in town.

Serenidad Shardon (☎ 984-876-18-27; www .shardon.com; camp sites $15, cabañas $30-40, beach house $60) There are accommodations for everyone on this wide beachfront property – tents, dorm beds, *cabañas*, beach houses and a lovely white beach for all to share. Easygoing owners, Shon and Niki, are happy to arrange tours, yoga classes, massage or just to leave you be.

Ascension Bay Beach Club (☎ 800-819-0750; www .ascensionbay.com; d $90) Primarily a fishing club specializing in package deals, the ABBC will on occasion rent its pleasant beachfront *cabañas* to walk-in visitors.

Posada Sirena (☎ 984-877-85-21; www.casasirena .com; d $30-50) At the north end of town, 100m

from the beach, these spacious, fully and funkily furnished *cabañas* have kitchens, electricity and hot-water showers. It's a very good deal.

Chary's Restaurant (mains $8) Depending on demand, this friendly open-air spot is open for three tasty meals a day.

FELIPE CARRILLO PUERTO

☎ 983 / pop 23,000

Now named for a progressive governor of Yucatán, this crossroads town 95km south of Tulum was once known as Chan Santa Cruz, the rebel headquarters during the War of the Castes.

Carrillo Puerto offers the visitor little in the way of attractions, but it's a transit hub and the first town of consequence if you're arriving from the Mérida/Ticul/Uxmal area. There's a gas station on the highway and inexpensive air-conditioned accommodations.

History

By the spring of 1849, the Maya faced what appeared to be certain victory in the War of the Castes. Confident with their success and eager to get back to their lands to begin that year's planting, many put down their arms and returned home. The *ladinos* (person of mixed ancestry; usually indigenous and Spanish; ie most Mexicans) seized this reprieve to fortify their forces with new troops and weapons from Mexico City. By that summer the reinforced *ladino* army began to prevail, taking brutal revenge on Maya communities throughout the north. Many Maya began to flee to the peninsula's southeast coast, seeking refuge in the relatively uninhabited region. Living in the jungle, the refugees banded together under the charismatic leadership of José María Barrera.

In 1850, Barrera and a group of his followers announced they had found a 'talking cross' erected by a cenote (cenotes were often considered shrines) in the woods. The cross told the Maya that they were the chosen people, and exhorted them to continue the struggle against the whites, assuring them victory if they did so. The Cruzob (followers of the cross) soon founded their own town: Chan Santa Cruz (Small Holy Cross) – which is today Felipe Carillo Puerto.

The oracular cross guided the Cruzob triumphantly in battle for years. In 1857 they conquered the fortress at Bacalar and claimed for themselves all territory from Tulum to the Belizean border. From 1901 to 1915, Mexican troops occupied Chan Santa Cruz, sending the Maya back into the jungle where they artfully and successfully engaged in guerrilla warfare. By 1915 the Mexicans retreated and the Chan Santa Cruz Maya reclaimed their city. In the 1920s a boom in the chicle market brought prosperity to the region, and heightened Mexico City's interest in the territory. After years of negotiation the Chan Santa Cruz Maya finally signed a peace treaty with Mexico and, in 1930, came under Mexican rule.

Though the Cruzob no longer officially govern the region, many Maya continue to worship the talking cross. Many followers of the cult remain in or around Chan Santa Cruz, where they revere the cross to this day. While in town you may see followers of the cross visiting the Santuario de la Cruz Parlante, the cenote where the cross was kept – especially if you visit on May 3, the day of the Holy Cross.

Sights

The **Santuario de la Cruz Parlante** (Sanctuary of the Talking Cross) is five blocks west of the gas station on Hwy 307. Because of its sacred importance, some townspeople don't readily welcome strangers into the sanctuary, especially those with cameras. The **Casa de Cultura** on the plaza has art exhibitions, workshops and the occasional exhibit on the War of the Castes. Be sure to check the mural outside.

Sleeping & Eating

Hotel Esquivel (☎ 834-03-44; Calle 65 No 746; d $30-45; ✷) The Esquivel is around the corner from

the plaza and bus terminal. The clean rooms are all very comfortable and have TVs.

El Faisán y El Venado (☎ 834-07-02; Av Juárez 7812; d $30; ✷) The 30 rooms here feature private bathroom, firm mattresses, TV and ceiling fans. The adjoining restaurant (meals $3 to $5) has very good, reasonably priced food.

Restaurant 24 Horas (Av Juárez; mains $3.50-5) This friendly restaurant is a few dozen meters south, with food a bit cheaper than El Faisán's.

Getting There & Away

Most buses serving Carrillo Puerto are *de paso* ('in passing'; they don't originate there). The following destinations are serviced daily:

Destination	Price	Duration	Frequency
Cancún	$11	3½-4hr	9 1st-class buses
	$9	3½-4hr	hourly 2nd-class buses
Chetumal	$7.25	2-3hr	4 1st-class buses
	$6	2-3hr	14 2nd-class buses
Mérida	$12	5½hr	11 2nd-class buses
Playa del Carmen	$7.50	2½hr	9 1st-class buses
	$6.25	2½hr	hourly 2nd-class buses
Ticul	$9	4½hr	11 2nd-class buses, change at Ticul or at Muna for Uxmal
Tulum	$4.75	1¾hr	9 1st-class buses
	$3.75	1¾hr	hourly 2nd-class buses

COSTA MAYA

The coast south of the Reserva de la Biosfera Sian Ka'an to the small fishing village of Xcalak (shka-*lak*), is often referred to as the Costa Maya. Development of the area has been in fits and starts: Xcalak is now

---

NO SMALL WONDER

The Irish have leprechauns, Scandinavians have elves and Snow White has her dwarfs. In Maya mythology the equivalent big-spirited, small-bodied inhabitants of the forest are called *aluxes* (a-*loosh*-es). These very clever, often mischievous little people are said to live in caves, and make themselves seen only occasionally and usually to small children.

Aluxes hold an important position in Maya legend and are believed to have the ability to travel between the human world and that of the spirits. They're attributed with the power to both assist those who believe in them, and wreak havoc on those who don't, and the Maya traditionally demonstrated their confidence in the *aluxes* by making offerings to the magical beings. Some farmers today – as their ancestors have for generations – leave gifts of food and drink to the *aluxes* in gratitude for their help in aiding crops and bringing good luck to a family or community.

linked to Hwy 307 by a paved road, and the town of Mahahual to the north has a cruise-ship pier. Realtors' advertisements and 'Land for Sale' signs are abundant on the coastal road, but Mahahual and Xcalak remain for the moment relatively primitive parts of Mexico. There are very few services, and most residents have electricity only a few hours a day…if at all.

Mahahual

☎ 983 / pop 8000

Most days Mahahual's sandy beachfront main street bustles with crowds of trinket buyers and beach-bar hoppers, but by late afternoon the tide of cruise-ship tourists recedes back to sea, and this quiet town regains its mellow composure. Over the past few years Mahahual has faced increasing pressure by developers and tourist operations. Newer, bigger resorts are being constructed north of town, and cruise ships arrive in greater numbers more frequently. The town's anti-development and environmental activists struggle tirelessly (often successfully) to slow this trend, and for the time being Mahahual remains one of the most appealing enclaves on the coast.

With the barrier reef only a couple of hundred meters from shore, and spectacular Reserva de la Biosfera Banco Chinchorro (the largest atoll in the Caribbean; p910) just 40km off the coast, you will enjoy some of the best diving and snorkeling in the Caribbean here. **Dreamtime Dive Resort** (☎ 834-58-18; www.dreamtimediving.com; Km 2.5) offers a variety of diving and snorkeling classes and excursions, including trips to Chinchorro. The only not-so-dreamy aspect of this outfit is that it caters principally to large groups of cruise-ship passengers. For equally professional, but more intimate small group ventures, contact the very personable and extremely sea-savvy **Joaquin (Huacho) Corrales Solís** (☎ 999-125-91-91; brumars@hotmail.com; Km 9).

Note: there are no banks in Mahahual and few places take credit cards.

From Hwy 307, take the signed turnoff for Mahahual. The turnoff is 68km south of Felipe Carrillo Puerto (1km south of Limones) and 46km north of Bacalar.

SLEEPING & EATING

The following establishments are divided into two groups: those in town and those south of town fronting the beach on a portion of the bay locally known as Bahía Bermejo (Bermejo Bay). Many visitors prefer to be close to the cozy heart of town, with its restaurants, busy beach life and emerging night scene, but travelers seeking away-from-it-all tranquility will want to stay at one of the beachside *cabañas* of Bahía Bermejo.

Town

Luna de Plata Hotel & Restaurant (Km 2; d $40) Located toward the quieter south end of town, the four fan-cooled guest rooms here are smallish but cheery. The savory aromas that waft through your window are from the adjacent restaurant (mains $7 to $15; open Monday to Saturday lunch and dinner), which serves tasty pizza, pasta and seafood.

La Posada de Los 40 Cañones (☎ 834-58-03; www.los40canones.com; d fan/air con $55/65; ✷) If you're craving a cool night's sleep, the modern, centrally located 40 Cañones is the place to be; it's the only hotel in town with air-con.

Las Cabañas del Doctor (☎ 832-21-02; campsite $2.50 per person, d $25) The Doctor is good for an ailing wallet. The tidy grounds have several rows of closely grouped *cabañas*. Campsites are somewhat spacious, and the shared bathrooms very clean.

Casa del Mar (Km 2; mains $3-7; ☽ breakfast & lunch) A small, friendly beachside café serving espresso, fresh baked goods, sandwiches, veggie dishes and shrimp tacos. At the time of research, the owner also planned to open a promising new spot, Mango Café, at the north end of town.

Cat's Meow (mains $7-10; ☽ lunch & dinner) The cheerful yellow wooden house at north corner of town. Wildly popular with cruise-ship patrons, by day this sidewalk bakery and restaurant overflows with nacho-eating Corona drinkers. By evening, though, crowds ebb. Seafood and chicken are specialties but the main draw is the dessert menu, which features *seven* types of homemade cheesecake.

For fresh rotisserie chicken, try Las Brasas Pollo Asado at the south end of town. For groceries, Mini Super Don Chepe in the center of town has the best prices.

Bahía Bermejo

The following places are found along the beach road (Carretera Mahahual–Xcalak) south of town, and are ordered according to their location (north to south), *not* by preference.

Maya Luna (☎ 836-09-05; www.hotelmayaluna.com; Km 5.2; d $80, kids 6 & under free) Likeable Dutch innkeepers Jan and Carolien have created a tranquil oasis here, consisting of four artistically designed beachfront units, each with a private rooftop sea-view terrace ideal for sun-worshipping or moon-bathing. The stylish but simple beachside restaurant-bar (mains $8 to $12; open breakfast, lunch and dinner Tuesday to Sunday) serves inventive dishes (many veggie), like stuffed papaya or fish with mango sauce. Hotel guests enjoy complimentary breakfast.

Balamku Inn (☎ 838-00-83; www.balamku.com; Km 5.7; d $70-75; 🖳) On a particularly clean stretch of palm-dotted beach, these gorgeous, breezy, curved-walled, high-ceilinged *cabañas* all enjoy spectacular ocean views. The welcoming hosts, Carol and Alan, are as eco-friendly as they are people-friendly, using 100% green technologies (solar/wind power, rainwater collection and waste composting). Wi-fi access is available, and a full and scrumptious homemade breakfast is included.

Siyaj-k'in (www.dondenaceelsol.com; Km 5.8; campsite $5, d $35) Next door to – but a far cry from – classy Balamku, this friendly family-run site offers beachside camping and four individual units (two rugged bamboo-sided *cabañas* and two plain upstairs ocean-facing rooms), each with 24-hour electricity and hot showers.

Travel'in (Km 6; campsites $3.50, d $20) Owned and lovingly run by Dutch native Justa, this small, basic campground and inn (just three rooms, all shared bathroom) is an inviting backpacker's retreat. The main attraction, besides the relaxed environment, is the earthy and intimate restaurant-bar (mains $3 to $10; open breakfast, lunch and dinner Monday to Saturday), which serves delicious homemade baked goods, including bread, pizza and pita. There's an array of healthy sandwiches and pizzas to choose from, as well as daily house specials.

Kohun Beach (http://kohunbeach.o-f.com; Km 7; units $40) The three cozy *palapa* units are tucked under the palms just footsteps from the beach; each has tiled floors, hot-water showers, 24-hour electricity and big, comfortable wood-framed beds. A generous continental breakfast is included. This is a very good deal.

Margarita del Sol (www.margaritadelsol.com; Km 7; d $85) A good family option. The modern self-contained beachside studios comfortably sleep four people. Each has a dining area and small, well-equipped kitchenette. Other amenities include TV and wi-fi. Kayaks and bikes are free for guest use.

Kabah-Na (http://kabahna.com; Km 8.6; d without/ with bathroom $30/35) Laidback Kabah-Na enjoys a secluded end-of-the-road feel. Three of the five artistically earthy *cabañas* have private tiled bathrooms – none has electricity, but candles and starlight enhance the rustic mood. Breakfast is included, and depending on demand, the on-site restaurant-café will open for lunch and dinner too.

Xcalak
☎ 983 / pop 3000

Xcalak's appeal lies in its quiet atmosphere, Caribbean-style wooden homes, swaying palms and pretty beaches. Another draw here (as in Mahahual) is the possibility of exploring **Reserva de la Biosfera Banco Chinchorro**, the largest coral atoll in the Northern Hemisphere, 40km northeast. So many vessels have collided with the ring of islands that parts of it resemble a ship graveyard. However, divers with dreams of exploring sunken ships will be disappointed; the wreck remains are not very deep down and can be easily viewed with mask and snorkel. Not as novel as the atoll, but spectacular as always, is the much closer barrier reef, which provides an abundance of diving and snorkeling opportunities.

Please note: like other remote villages in the area, there are no banks here and few places accept credit cards.

Xcalak to Chinchorro (XTC) Dive Center (☎ 831-04-61; www.xcalak.com.mx), an extremely professional outfit about 300m north of town on the coast road, offers dive and snorkel trips to the wondrous barrier reef just offshore, and it is the only group in Xcalak with official permission to lead trips to Banco Chinchorro.

SLEEPING & EATING
Maya Village (campsite $6, d $15) The only budget option here, though not always open, is located just over the bridge on the north side of town. There are a few campsites and three very basic, sand-floor *cabañas*. The beach bar is funky and fun, and home to

(when open) popular Friday- and Saturday-night barbecues.

The following places are among a handful on the old coastal road, leading north from town (most run by Americans or Canadians) and are listed according to their location (south–north), *not* by preference. All listed have ceiling fans, 24-hour electricity (from solar or wind with generator backup), hot-water bathrooms, bikes, snorkels and/or sea kayaks for guests' use. And, most importantly, they all front lovely white beaches with docks from which to swim or snorkel. Rates given are higher winter prices.

Hotel Tierra Maya (☎ 831-04-04; in the US 800-216-1902; www.tierramaya.net; d $96-108; ❄) A modern beachfront hotel 2km north of town, featuring seven tastefully appointed rooms with private sea-facing balconies. Air-con (in some rooms) is $15 extra per night. Fresh and tasty homemade meals can be enjoyed at the charming on-site Mayan Grill Restaurant (mains $8 to $15; open breakfast and dinner). A light buffet breakfast is included.

Costa de Cocos (☎ 831-01-10; www.costadecocos.com; d $90; 🖵) Fabulously popular with fly fishermen, this mellow resort with its close-to-town location, pristine beach and home-like *cabañas*, makes a sweet getaway spot for non-fishing enthusiasts too. There is also an on-site dive shop offering professional excursions and instruction for those who want to scuba or snorkel. The restaurant-bar (mains $7 to $15; open 7:30am to 10pm) is a popular hangout that serves fresh gooey pizza and catch-of-the-day fare. Guests enjoy a generous buffet breakfast and free Internet access.

Casa Carolina (☎ 839-19-58; www.casacarolina.net; d $100) Intimate Casa Carolina has four attractive guestrooms, each with a large private sea-view balcony. Rooms are equipped with small kitchenettes, and the handsome bathrooms try to out-tile each other with Talavera inlay. All levels of scuba instruction (NAUI) are offered here, as well as recreational dives on the barrier reef. Homemade breakfast is included.

Playa Sonrisa (☎ 839-46-63; www.playasonrisa.com; d $100) 'All you need is your smile' is the motto at this clothing-optional resort, and many guests wear little else. The beach is lovely and the long pier is perfect for swimming and/or (all over) sunning. Guest rooms are bright and comfy, and the cozy,

for-guests-only restaurant-bar serves generous continental breakfast (included) and delicious dinners – most nights.

Sand Wood Villas (☎ 839-54-28; www.sandwood.com; r from $130) Simple, but cheery and very spacious, the three beachfront villas each have two bedrooms, two baths, a living room, and a fully equipped kitchen plus private balcony. Great for families or groups.

Sin Duda (☎ 831-00-06; www.sindudavillas.com; d from $87) Eight kilometers from town, nestled in lush greenery between the turquoise sea and blue lagoon, this remote beachfront spot is restful *sin duda* ('without doubt'). The owners architecturally designed the creative complex of rooms, and all accommodations are appointed with folk art and flair. The four resident corgis make lousy watchdogs, but cozy foot warmers. Breakfast is included.

Leaky Palapa (mains $8-15; ✆ dinner Fri-Mon) Don't be fooled by the humble premises or modest prices, Canadian chefs Linda and Maria practice culinary alchemy out of this funky beach hut.

Of the other eateries in town, **Lonchería Silvia** (meals $4-7; ✆ lunch & dinner) is the most likely to be open, and it serves good fish dinners. **Restaurant Bar Xcalak Caribe** (mains $7-15; ✆ lunch & dinner), one block south of the wharf and just across the street from the beach, serves very good fried fish, ceviche and cold beer. Grocery trucks service the coast road most days, and there are several small, so-so stocked markets in town.

GETTING THERE & AROUND
From Hwy 307, a few kilometers before Mahahual, turn right (south) and follow the signs to Xcalak (another 60km).

Sociedad Cooperativa del Caribe buses depart Chetumal's main bus terminal daily for Xcalak ($5.50, 200km, five hours, 5:40am and 3:15pm). From Felipe Carrillo Puerto, catch a bus to Limones, from where buses to Xcalak ($4.25) depart at around 6:30am and 4:30pm. Buses depart Xcalak for Chetumal at 5am and 2:30pm, and leave for Limones at around 8:30am and 6:30pm.

LAGUNA BACALAR
A large, clear, turquoise freshwater lake with a bottom of gleaming white sand, Laguna Bacalar comes as a surprise in this region of tortured limestone and scrubby jungle.

The small, sleepy town of Bacalar, just east of the highway, 125km south of Felipe Carrillo Puerto, is the only settlement of any size on the lake. It's noted mostly for its old Spanish fortress and its popular *balnearios* (bathing places).

The fortress, **Fuerte San Felipe Bacalar** (admission $2; 🕑 9am-8pm Tue-Sun), was built above the lagoon to protect citizens from raids by pirates and Indians. It served as an important outpost for the whites in the War of the Castes. In 1859 it was seized by Maya rebels, who held the fort until Quintana Roo was finally conquered by Mexican troops in 1901. Today, with formidable cannons still on its ramparts, the fortress remains an imposing sight. It houses a **museum** exhibiting colonial armaments and uniforms from the 17th and 18th centuries.

Costera Bacalar & Cenote Azul

The road that winds south for several kilometers along the lakeshore from Bacalar town to Cenote Azul, is called the Costera Bacalar (also known as Calle 1). It passes a few lodging and camping places along the way. Cenote Azul is a 90m-deep natural pool on the southwest shore of Laguna Bacalar, almost at the end of the end of the road and just 200m east of Hwy 307.

Sleeping & Eating

Casita Carolina (☎ 983-834-23-34; www.casitacarolina .com; campsites per person $4.50; d $25-45) This delightful place is about two blocks south of the fort. It has an expansive lawn leading down to the lake, five fan-cooled rooms and a deluxe *palapa*. Guests may rent kayaks ($4.50 per day). Camping is limited to two campsites.

Amigos B&B Laguna Bacalar (☎ 987-872-38-68; www.bacalar.net; d $45-55; 🖳) Brought to you by the same hospitable family who run Amigos B&B in Cozumel, this ideally located lakefront property (about 500m south of the fort) has three spacious guest rooms and a comfy shared common area. Breakfast is included.

Hotelito Paraíso (☎ 983-834-27-87; Calle 14; campsites per person $4.50, d $30) A little scruffy and worn, but comfortable enough, the six rooms here all have private bathrooms and small equipped kitchens. Camping is available on the lawn near the water, and campers have access to shared bathroom facilities. It's near Blvd Costero.

Hostel Ximba Li (☎ 983-834-25-16; Av 3; dm $7) This simple new hostel is located a couple of blocks from the lake at Calle 30, and is a short walk from town. Breakfast is included.

Of the few places to eat right in town, Orizaba's at the northwest corner of the plaza is a good choice. Serving consistently good Yucatecan meals, the lake view restaurant at the quaintly kitsch **Hotel Laguna** (☎ 983-834-22-06) is popular. The restaurant at Balneario Ejidal serves fresh ceviche and good grilled fish.

Getting There & Away

Coming from the north by bus, ask the driver to drop you in Bacalar town, at the Hotel Laguna or at Cenote Azul (as you wish); check before you buy your ticket to see if the driver will stop.

Departures from Chetumal's minibus terminal on Av Primo de Verdad to the town of Bacalar leave about once an hour from 5am to 9pm ($1.75, 45 minutes); some northbound buses departing from the bus terminal will also drop you near the town of Bacalar ($1.50).

If you are driving, take Hwy 307 north for 25km, and exit at the turnoff marked Cenote Azul and Costera Bacalar.

CHETUMAL

☎ 983 / pop 150,000

Before the Spanish conquest, Chetumal was an important Maya port for shipping gold, feathers, cacao and copper to the northern Yucatán Peninsula. After the conquest the town was not actually settled until 1898. It was founded in order to put a stop to the illegal trade in arms and lumber carried on by the descendants of the War of the Castes rebels. Dubbed Payo Obispo, the town changed its name to Chetumal in 1936. In 1955 it was virtually obliterated by Hurricane Janet.

The rebuilt city is laid out on a grand plan with a grid of wide boulevards along which traffic speeds (be careful at stop signs).

Chetumal is the gateway to Belize. With the peso so low against the neighboring currency, Belizean shoppers frequently come to Chetumal.

Orientation

Despite Chetumal's sprawling layout, the city center is easily manageable on foot, and

YUCATÁN PENINSULA

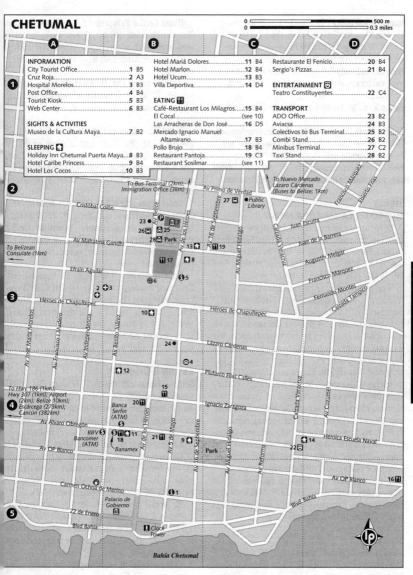

CHETUMAL

INFORMATION
City Tourist Office..................1 B5
Cruz Roja.............................2 A3
Hospital Morelos...................3 B3
Post Office...........................4 B4
Tourist Kiosk........................5 B3
Web Center..........................6 B3

SIGHTS & ACTIVITIES
Museo de la Cultura Maya.......7 B2

SLEEPING
Holiday Inn Chetumal Puerta Maya..8 B3
Hotel Caribe Princess..............9 B4
Hotel Los Cocos....................10 B3

Hotel Mariá Dolores...............11 B4
Hotel Marlon........................12 B4
Hotel Ucum.........................13 B3
Villa Deportiva......................14 D4

EATING
Café-Restaurant Los Milagros......15 B4
El Cocal...........................(see 10)
Las Arracheras de Don José.....16 D5
Mercado Ignacio Manuel
    Altamirano......................17 B3
Pollo Brujo..........................18 B4
Restaurant Pantoja................19 C3
Restaurant Sosilmar...........(see 11)

Restaurante El Fenicio............20 B4
Sergio's Pizzas......................21 B4

ENTERTAINMENT
Teatro Constituyentes.............22 C4

TRANSPORT
ADO Office..........................23 B4
Aviacsa..............................24 B3
Colectivos to Bus Terminal.......25 B2
Combi Stand........................26 B2
Minibus Terminal..................27 C2
Taxi Stand...........................28 B2

---

t contains several hotels and restaurants. This is a big, but very lightly touristed city.

Information

There is an ATM at the bus terminal, and banks with ATMs are scattered about town, with a cluster of them on Av Obregon near Av Benito Juárez.

City tourist office (☎ 835-05-00; cnr Avs 5 de Mayo & Carmen Ochoa; ⏱ 8:30am-4:30pm Mon-Fri) Provides helpful information, including details about attractions in neighboring Belize.

Cruz Roja (Red Cross; ☎ 832-05-71; cnr Avs Independencia & Heroes de Chapultapec)

Hospital Morelos (☎ 832-45-95) Northeast of Cruz Roja in the same block.

Immigration office (☎ 832-63-53; Av de los Héroes; ⏱ 9am-11pm Mon-Fri) On the left, about four blocks north of Av Insurgentes (and the bus terminal). You can get tourist-card extensions here.

Novedades Laudy (left-luggage service per hr $0.50; ⏱ 24hr) Located at the bus terminal, this place safely stores bags.

Post office (☎ 832-00-57; cnr Plutarco Elías Calles & Av 5 de Mayo)

Tourist kiosk (⏱ 9am-8:30pm Mon-Fri, 9am-3pm Sat) This is a smaller kiosk at the corner of Efraín Aquilar and Av de los Heroes.

Web Center (Efraín Aguilar; per hr $1) One of several Internet cafés across from the Mercado Ignacio Manuel Altamirano.

Sights
MUSEO DE LA CULTURA MAYA
A bold showpiece designed to draw visitors from as far away as Cancún, the **Museo de la Cultura Maya** (☎ 823-68-38; Av de los Héroes; admission $5.50; ⏱ 9am-7pm Tue-Thu & Sun, 9am-8pm Fri & Sat) is the city's claim to cultural fame.

The museum is organized into three levels, mirroring Maya cosmology. The main floor represents this world, the upper floor the heavens and the lower floor the underworld. Though the museum is short on artifacts, the various exhibits cover all of the lands of the Maya, and seek to explain their thoughts, beliefs and way of life. There are beautiful scale models of the great Maya buildings as they may have appeared, replicas of stelae from Copán, Honduras, reproductions of the murals found in Room 1 at Bonampak, Chiapas (p844) and artifacts from sites around Quintana Roo. Ingenious interactive mechanical and computer displays illustrate the Mayas' complex numerical and calendar systems.

The museum's courtyard has salons for temporary exhibits of modern Mexican artists (such as Rufino Tamayo) and paintings reproducing Maya frescoes.

Sleeping
Holiday Inn Chetumal Puerta Maya (☎ 835-04-00; Av de los Héroes 171; d $110; 🅿 🖧 🖵) The nicest option in town, its comfortable rooms overlook a small courtyard with a swimming pool set amid tropical gardens. There's a pleasant on-site restaurant-bar.

Hotel Los Cocos (☎ 832-05-44; cnr Av de los Héroes & Calle Héroes de Chapultepec; d with air-con & TV $68; 🅿 🖧 🖵) This hotel has comfortable rooms with fridges, a guarded parking lot and a nice swimming pool.

Hotel Caribe Princess (☎ 832-09-00; Av Álvaro Obregón 168; d $40; 🅿 🖧) This quiet hotel is well run and nicely appointed. All rooms have phone and TV, and there's off-street parking.

Hotel Marlon (☎ 832-94-11; Av Benito Juárez; d $45; 🅿 🖧 🖵) A friendly, clean, modernish hotel. Comforts include TV, a pool, restaurant and bar.

Hotel María Dolores (☎ 832-05-08; Av Álvaro Obregón 206; d $20; 🅿) This hotel, west of Av de los Héroes, is the best for the price. Beds are a bit saggy, but some of the fan-cooled rooms are spacious, and there's off-street parking.

Hotel Ucum (☎ 832-07-11, 832-61-86; Av Mahatma Gandhi 167; d with fan/air-con $20/25; 🅿 🖧 🖵) Hotel Ucum has lots of simple rooms around a central courtyard/parking area. There's a small pool, and the hotel restaurant is inexpensive and good.

Villa Deportiva (☎ 832-05-25; Heroica Escuela Naval; campsites per person $2, dm $4) Off Calz Veracruz, just past the eastern end of Av Álvaro Obregón, this hostel is the cheapest place in town. It has single-sex dorms (four bunks to a room) and serves three meals a day, each for under $3.

Eating & Drinking
Sergio's Pizzas (☎ 832-08-82; Av Álvaro Obregón 182; pizza $4-18, mains $5-15) This air-conditioned pub and pizzeria serves pizza, of course, plus Mexican dishes. There's frosty beer and an extensive wine list. It's open for breakfast too.

Las Arracheras de Don José (cnr Blvd de la Bahía & Av OP Blanco; mains $5-10) A refreshing breezy bay-facing favorite. You can order tacos galore, plus fajitas and other Mexican dishes. A rainbow of salsas compliments every dish.

El Cocal (☎ 832-05-44; Hotel los Cocos, cnr Av de los Héroes & Calle Héroes de Chapultepec; mains $5-15; ⏱ 8am-10pm Sun-Thu, 8am-1am Fri & Sat) This popular social hub is an attractive terraced spot, specializing in regional cuisine.

Café-Restaurant Los Milagros (Calle Ignacio Zaragoza; breakfast $3-4, mains $4-5) This place serves espresso and meals indoors and out. It's a favorite with Chetumal's student set.

Restaurante El Fenicio (cnr Avs de los Héroes & Zaragoza; mains $4-11; ⏱ 24hr) Never closed and always busy, El Fenicio serves Yucatecan and Mexican fare, including a tasty build-it-yourself taco plate and around-the-clock breakfast.

Restaurant Sosilmar (Hotel María Dolores, Av Álvaro Obregón 206; mains $4-6) A bright and simple restaurant serving big platters of fish or meat.

Pollo Brujo (Av Álvaro Obregón; chicken $4) This restaurant is west of the Sosilmar. You can buy a juicy roasted chicken and dine in the air-conditioned salon.

Restaurant Pantoja (cnr Avs Mahatma Gandhi & 16 de Septiembre; mains $3-5) The Pantoja is a family-run restaurant that opens early for breakfast and later provides enchiladas and other main dishes.

Mercado Ignacio Manuel Altamirano (meals $2.50-3.50) Across from the Holiday Inn, the market has small, simple eateries serving set meals.

Getting There & Away
AIR
Chetumal's small airport is 2km northwest of the city center along Av Álvaro Obregón.

Aviacsa (☎ 832-77-65, airport 832-77-87; Av 5 de Mayo) flies daily to Mexico City.

For flights to Belize City (and on to Tikal) or to Belize's cayes, cross the border into Belize and fly from Corozal.

BUS
The bus terminal is about 2km north of the city center near the intersection of Avs Insurgentes and Belice. ADO, Sur, Cristóbal Colón, Omnitur del Caribe, Maya de Oro, Mayab and Novelo's, among other bus companies, provide service. The terminal has lockers, a bus information kiosk, an ATM, post office, international phone and fax services, an exchange counter, cafeteria and shops. East of the bus terminal is a huge San Francisco de Asís department store.

You can also buy ADO tickets and get information about most bus services at the

YUCATÁN PENINSULA

CHETUMAL BUS SCHEDULE

Destination	Price	Duration	Frequency
Bacalar	$1.50	45min	hourly minibuses
	$1.75	45min	frequent Mayab buses from the minibus terminal
Belize City (Belize)	$8	3-4hr	20 1st-class buses
	$6	3-4hr	20 2nd-class buses; Novelo's and Northern buses depart from Nuevo Mercado between 4:30am and 6pm, some depart from the bus terminal 15 minutes later.
Campeche	$20	6½-9hr	1 1st-class ADO bus at noon
	$16	6½-9hr	2 2nd-class buses
Cancún	$18	5½hr	frequent 1st-class buses
	$16	5½hr	frequent 2nd-class buses
Corozal (Belize)	$2	1hr with border formalities	2nd-class buses
Escárcega	$11-13	6hr	9 buses between 4:15am & 10:30pm
Felipe Carrillo Puerto	$6-7	2-3hr	frequent buses
Flores (Guatemala)	$38	8hr	5 1st-class Servicio San Juan & Mundo Maya buses between 6:20am & 2:30pm
Mahahual	$4	4hr	4 2nd-class buses at 4am, 6am, 10:55am & 3:15pm
Mérida	$19	6-8hr	8 deluxe Omnitur del Caribe & Super Expresso buses
	$16	6-8hr	3 2nd-class Mayab buses
Orange Walk (Belize)	$4	2¼hr	frequent 1st-class buses
	$3	2¼hr	frequent 2nd-class buses) See Belize City schedule.
Playa del Carmen	$12-15	4½-6hr	frequent buses
Ticul	$15	6hr	6 buses
Tulum	$12	3½-4hr	frequent buses
Valladolid	$12	6hr	2 2nd-class buses
Veracruz	$49	16hr	2 1st-class buses
Villahermosa	$26	7-9hr	5 buses
Xcalak	$5.50	5hr	2 2nd-class buses at 5:40am & 3:15pm
Xpujil	$4.75-5.75	2-3hr	9 buses

ADO office (Av Belice), just west of the Museo de la Cultura Maya.

Many local buses, and those bound for Belize, begin their runs from the **Nuevo Mercado Lázaro Cárdenas** (Calz Veracruz) at Confederación Nacional Campesina (also called Segundo Circuito), about 10 blocks north of Av Primo de Verdad. From this market, some Belize-bound buses continue to the bus terminal and depart from there 15 minutes later. Tickets can be purchased at the market, on board the buses or at the bus terminal.

The **minibus terminal** (cnr Avs Primo de Verdad & Miguel Hidalgo) has services to Bacalar and nearby destinations. Daily departures listed are from the bus terminal unless otherwise noted.

Getting Around

Taxis from the stand at the bus terminal charge $2 to the city center (agree on the price before getting in; some will try to charge per person). You can try to avoid haggles by walking out of the terminal to the main road (Av Insurgentes), turning left (east) and walking a little over a block to the traffic circle at Av de los Héroes to hail a taxi. From here you can also catch the cheapest ride to the city center ($0.40), in an eastbound ('Santa María' or 'Calderitas') combi. The route will be circuitous. To reach the bus terminal from the city center, head for the **combi & taxi stands** (Av Belice) behind the Museo de la Cultura Maya. By combi ask to be dropped off at the *glorieta* (traffic circle) at Av Insurgentes. Head left (west) to reach the bus terminal.

KOHUNLICH

The archaeological site of **Kohunlich** (admission $4; ☽ 8am-5pm) is being aggressively excavated, though most of its nearly 200 mounds are still covered in vegetation. The surrounding jungle is thick, but the archaeological site itself has been cleared selectively and is now a delightful forest park.

These ruins, dating from the late preclassic (AD 100–200) and the early classic (AD 250–600) periods, are famous for the great **Templo de los Mascarones** (Temple of the Masks), a pyramid-like structure with a central stairway flanked by huge, 3m-high stucco masks of the sun god. The thick lips and prominent features are reminiscent of Olmec sculpture. Of the eight original masks, only two are relatively intact following the ravages of archaeology looters.

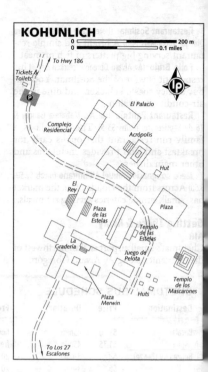

A few hundred meters southwest of Plaza Merwin are the **Los 27 Escalones** (27 Steps), the remains of a once-extensive residential area, with photogenic trees growing out of the steps themselves.

The hydraulic engineering at the site was a great achievement; 90,000 of the site's 210,000 sq meters were cut to channel rainwater into Kohunlich's once-enormous reservoir.

Getting There & Away

There is no public transportation running directly to Kohunlich. To visit the ruins without your own vehicle, you need to start early, taking a bus to the village of Francisco Villa near the turnoff to the ruins, then either hitching or walking the 8.5km to the site.

Better still, take a taxi from Chetumal to the ruins and have the driver wait for you. A round-trip taxi fare, including the wait, will cost about $60 per party. Another means is to travel to Xpujil and book a tour from there.

To return by bus to Chetumal or head west to Xpujil or Escárcega, you must hope to flag down a bus on the highway; not all buses will stop.

YUCATÁN STATE

Yucatán State has always been the most culturally rich region of the peninsula. It's here that Maya and Spanish civilizations collided centuries ago, and where the combination (both disparate and harmonious) of those mighty legacies thrives today. The state is home to the old Maya empires of Chichén Itzá and Uxmal as well as the Colonial urban gems of Izamal, Valladolid and Mérida, the state's grand capital. Outside the cities, haciendas (plantation estates of centuries past) make appealing destinations, as many are being resurrected to their former grandeur, and reinvented as (often affordable) hotels and retreats. The region is rife with explorable caves and swimmable freshwater pools, and bird enthusiasts will enjoy the small coastal communities of Celestún and Rio Largartos, where populations of wild, fiery flamingos outnumber the towns' resident humans.

MÉRIDA

☎ 999 / pop 720,000

Mérida, once the grand Maya city of T'hó, has been the dominant metropolitan center in the Yucatán region since the Spanish Conquest. Today the capital of the state of Yucatán is a vital and prosperous city, whose deep intellectual and artistic roots have nurtured its emergence into an internationally recognized center for the arts and culture.

All week long engaging events take place here, be it folkloric dances, poetry readings, concerts, theatrical performances, gallery openings, indie film festivals. And the scene becomes even more vibrant on weekends, when the city center is blocked to all but pedestrians. At this time the colonial heart of the city comes alive with art, music and dance.

History

Francisco de Montejo the Younger founded a Spanish colony at Campeche, about 160km to the south, in 1540. From here he was able to take advantage of political dissension among the Maya, conquering T'hó (now Mérida) in 1542. By the end of the decade, Yucatán was mostly under Spanish colonial rule.

When Montejo's conquistadors entered the defeated T'hó, they found a major Maya settlement of lime-mortared stone that reminded them of Roman architectural legacies in Mérida, Spain. They promptly renamed the city and proceeded to build it into the regional colonial capital, dismantling the Maya structures, and using the materials to construct a cathedral and other stately buildings. Mérida took its colonial orders directly from Spain, not from Mexico City, and Yucatán has had a distinct cultural and political identity ever since.

During the War of the Castes only Mérida and Campeche were able to resist the rebel forces. Near surrender, the ruling class in Mérida was saved by reinforcements sent from central Mexico in exchange for Mérida's agreement to take orders from Mexico City. Although Yucatán is part of Mexico, there is still a strong feeling in Mérida and other parts of the state that locals stand a breed apart.

Mérida now is the peninsula's center of commerce, a bustling city that has benefited greatly from the *maquiladoras* (assembly-plant operations) that opened in the 1980s and '90s, and tourism, which also picked up, (and steadily advanced) during that time.

Orientation

Many services that most visitors want are within five blocks of the Plaza Grande. Odd-numbered streets run east–west, and their numbers increase by twos going from north to south (for example, Calle 61 is a block north of Calle 63); even-numbered streets run north–south, and increase by twos from east to west. The two principal north–south running streets downtown are Calle 62 and its parallel, Calle 60. Calle 60 followed to its northern end runs into Paseo Montejo.

Information
BOOKSTORES

Librería Dante (☎ 928-26-11; Plaza Grande) There's a convenient branch next to La Via Olimpio, and a smaller branch on the corner of Calles 58 and 60. Librería Dante sells paperbacks in English, including some guidebooks. It also has an extensive selection on art and archaeology. Look for John L Stephen's fascinating account *Incidents of Travel in Yucatán*. First published in 1843, it is now out of print but editions can sometimes be found here.

EMERGENCY

Cruz Roja (Red Cross; ☎ 924-98-13)
Emergency (☎ 066; ☾ 24hr)
Fire (☎ 924-92-42)
Police (☎ 930-32-00)
Tourist Police (☎ 925-25-55, ext 260)

YUCATÁN PENINSULA

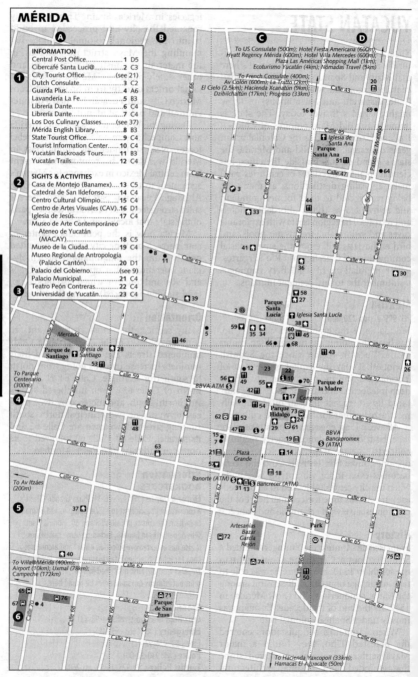

MÉRIDA

INFORMATION
Central Post Office.................... 1 D5
Cibercafé Santa Luci@.............. 2 C3
City Tourist Office..................(see 21)
Dutch Consulate...................... 3 C2
Guarda Plus............................. 4 A6
Lavandería La Fe...................... 5 B3
Librería Dante......................... 6 C4
Librería Dante......................... 7 C4
Los Dos Culinary Classes........(see 37)
Mérida English Library.............. 8 B3
State Tourist Office.................. 9 C4
Tourist Information Center...... 10 C4
Yucatán Backroads Tours........ 11 B3
Yucatán Trails........................ 12 C4

SIGHTS & ACTIVITIES
Casa de Montejo (Banamex).... 13 C5
Catedral de San Ildefonso...... 14 C4
Centro Cultural Olimpio.......... 15 C4
Centro de Artes Visuales (CAV).16 D1
Iglesia de Jesús...................... 17 C4
Museo de Arte Contemporáneo
  Ateneo de Yucatán
  (MACAY)............................. 18 C5
Museo de la Ciudad................ 19 C4
Museo Regional de Antropología
  (Palacio Cantón)................. 20 D1
Palacio del Gobierno............(see 9)
Palacio Municipal.................... 21 C4
Teatro Peón Contreras............ 22 C4
Universidad de Yucatán.......... 23 C4

To US Consulate (500m); Hotel Fiesta Americana (600m);
Hyatt Regency Mérida (600m); Hotel Villa Mercedes (600m);
Plaza Las Américas Shopping Mall (1km);
Ecoturismo Yucatán (4km); Nómadas Travel (5km)

To French Consulate (400m);
Av Colón (600m); La Tratto (2km);
El Cielo (2.5km); Hacienda Xcanatún (9km);
Dzibilchaltún (17km); Progreso (33km)

Parque Santa Ana

Iglesia de Santa Ana

Parque Santa Lucía

Iglesia Santa Lucía

Parque de la Madre

Parque Hidalgo

Parque de Santiago

Iglesia de Santiago

Mercado

To Parque Centenario (300m)

BBVA ATM

Parque de la Madre

Congreso

BBVA Bancapromex (ATM)

Plaza Grande

Banorte (ATM)   Bancrecer (ATM)

To Av Itzáes (200m)

Artesanías Bazar García Rejón

Park

To Villa Mérida (400m);
Airport (10km); Uxmal (78km);
Campeche (172km)

Parque de San Juan

To Hacienda Yaxcopoil (33km);
Hamacas El Aguacate (50m)

Calle 66
Calle 64
Calle 62
Calle 60
Calle 58
Calle 56
Calle 54
Calle 55A
Paseo de Montejo

Calle 43
Calle 45
Calle 47
Calle 47A
Calle 49
Calle 51
Calle 53
Calle 55
Calle 57
Calle 59
Calle 61
Calle 63
Calle 65
Calle 67
Calle 69
Calle 71

Calle 72
Calle 70
Calle 68
Calle 66
Calle 64
Calle 65A

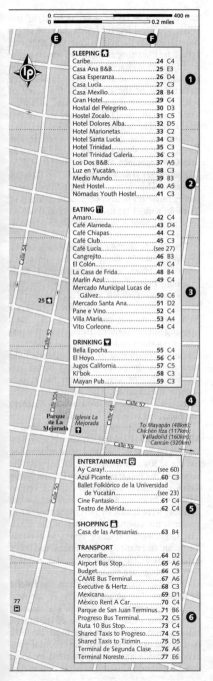

SLEEPING
Caribe...................................24 C4
Casa Ana B&B.......................25 E3
Casa Esperanza....................26 D4
Casa Lucía............................27 C3
Casa Mexilio.........................28 B4
Gran Hotel...........................29 C4
Hostal del Pelegrino.............30 D3
Hostal Zocalo.......................31 C5
Hotel Dolores Alba...............32 D5
Hotel Marionetas..................33 C2
Hotel Santa Lucía.................34 C3
Hotel Trinidad......................35 C3
Hotel Trinidad Galería...........36 C3
Los Dos B&B.........................37 A5
Luz en Yucatán....................38 C3
Medio Mundo.......................39 B3
Nest Hostel..........................40 A5
Nómadas Youth Hostel..........41 C3

EATING
Amaro..................................42 C4
Café Alameda.......................43 D4
Café Chiapas........................44 C2
Café Club..............................45 C3
Café Lucía.........................(see 27)
Cangrejito............................46 B3
El Colón...............................47 C4
La Casa de Frida...................48 B4
Marlín Azul...........................49 C4
Mercado Municipal Lucas de
    Gálvez.............................50 C6
Mercado Santa Ana...............51 D2
Pane e Vino..........................52 C4
Villa María............................53 A4
Vito Corleone.......................54 C4

DRINKING
Bella Epoca.........................55 C4
El Hoyo...............................56 C4
Jugos California....................57 C5
Ki'bok.................................58 C3
Mayan Pub...........................59 C3

ENTERTAINMENT
Ay Caray!.........................(see 60)
Azul Picante........................60 C3
Ballet Folklórico de la Universidad
    de Yucatán...................(see 23)
Cine Fantasio.......................61 C4
Teatro de Mérida..................62 C4

SHOPPING
Casa de las Artesanías..........63 B4

TRANSPORT
Aerocaribe...........................64 D2
Airport Bus Stop...................65 A6
Budget.................................66 C3
CAME Bus Terminal...............67 A6
Executive & Hertz.................68 C3
Mexicana.............................69 D1
México Rent A Car................70 C4
Parque de San Juan Terminus..71 B6
Progreso Bus Terminal...........72 C5
Ruta 10 Bus Stop..................73 C4
Shared Taxis to Progreso.......74 C5
Shared Taxis to Tizimín..........75 D5
Terminal de Segunda Clase....76 A6
Terminal Noreste...................77 E6

Parque de La Mejorada
Iglesia La Mejorada

To Mayapán (48km);
Chichén Itza (117km);
Valladolid (160km);
Cancún (320km)

INTERNET ACCESS

Internet cafés abound. For convenient hours, air-conditioning and free coffee try **Cibercafé Santa Lucí@** (cnr Calles 62 & 55; per hr $1; 8am-1am).

INTERNET RESOURCES

Yuncatan Living (www.yucatanliving.com) Although very much oriented toward the local expat community, this website contains regional insights useful to travelers.

Yucantan Today (www.yucatantoday.com) The online version of the weekly *Yucatan Today*, an excellent source for current events and local business listings.

LAUNDRY

Lavandería La Fe (Calle 64 No 470; per 3kg $4)

LEFT LUGGAGE

Guarda Plus (Calle 70; per bag per hr $0.50; 6am-10pm) Located across from CAME bus terminal.

LIBRARIES

Mérida English Library (924-84-01; www.merida englishlibrary.com; Calle 53 No 524) A great resource. Feel free to borrow a book or two.

MEDICAL SERVICES

Clínica de Mérida (925-41-00; Av Itzaés No 242) Private clinic with English-speaking medical staff.

MONEY

You'll find banks and ATMs throughout the city, with many near Plaza Grande.

POST

Central Post Office (cnr Calles 65 & 56)

TOURIST INFORMATION

City Tourist Office (928-20-20; Plaza Grande, Calle 62; 8am-8pm)

State Tourist Office (930-31-03; Plaza Grande, Calle 61; 8am-9pm)

Tourist Information Center (924-92-90; cnr Calles 60 & 57A; 8am-8pm)

TRAVEL AGENCIES

Nómadas Travel (948-11-87; www.nomadastravel .com; Calle 62 No 433) Student discount tickets are available here, as well as International Student Identity Cards (ISIC), and low fares to Cuba.

Yucatán Trails (928-25-82; Calle 62 No 482) The friendly Canadian owner, Denis Lafoy, takes care of national and international flight arrangements, as well as local excursions and packages.

Dangers & Annoyances

Guard against pickpockets and bag-snatchers in the market district.

It is likely that individuals claiming to be official tour guides will approach you on the street and offer to show you the sights. Legitimate state and city guides do not solicit on the street and these are considered by the tourism office to be 'pirates.'

At night, in the city center or along the Paseo de Montejo, single women are safe; but, please note that the area around the CAME bus terminal at night can be dangerous.

Most corners have traffic lights *and* traffic cops, one signaling you to go and the other to stop. Drivers are impatient, streets narrow, and buses merciless.

Sights

PLAZA GRANDE

The Plaza Grande has been the city's hub since Maya times. A large but intimate square, it's the logical place to start a tour of Mérida. Also known as 'El Centro' (center of town) or the Plaza Principal, the Plaza Grande was the religious and social center of the ancient Maya city T'hó. Under the Spanish it was the Plaza de Armas (Parade Ground), laid out by Francisco de Montejo the Younger. The plaza is surrounded by some of the city's most impressive and harmonious colonial buildings, and its well tended laurel trees provide welcome shade. On Sunday, hundreds of *meridanos* take their *paseo* (stroll) here.

On the plaza's east side, on the former site of a Maya temple, is one of Mexico's oldest churches **Catedral de San Ildefonso** (Calle 61; 6am-noon & 4-7pm). Construction of the church began in 1561, but it wasn't completed until 1598. Hundreds of Maya workers labored to build this stark church, often using stones from their ancestors' destroyed temple. The crucifix behind the altar is **Cristo de la Unidad** (Christ of Unity), a symbol of reconciliation between Spanish and Maya descendents. Right, over the south door, is a painting of Tutul Xiú, *cacique* of Maní, paying respect to his ally Francisco de Montejo the Younger at T'hó (de Montejo and Xiú jointly defeated the Cocom; Tutul Xiú converted to Christianity and his descendants still live in Mérida).

In the small chapel to the left of the altar is a replica (the original was destroyed during the Mexican Revolution) of Mérida's most famous religious artifact, a statue called **Cristo de las Ampollas** (Christ of the Blisters). Local legend holds that the original statue was carved from a tree that was struck by lightning and burned for an entire night without charring. It is also said to be the only object to have survived the fiery destruction of the church in the town of Ichmul (though it was blackened and blistered from the heat). The statue was moved to the Mérida cathedral in 1645.

South of the cathedral, housed in the former archbishop's palace, is the **Museo de Arte Contemporáneo Ateneo de Yucatán** (MACAY; Calle 60; 928-31-91; admission $2.50; 10am-6pm Wed-Mon). This attractive light-filled, two-storey museum holds permanent exhibits of Yucatán's most famous painters and sculptors, plus impressive exhibits from contemporary Mexican artists.

The **Casa de Montejo** (Palacio de Montejo; Calle 63; 9am-5pm Mon-Fri, 9am-2pm Sat), on the south side of the Plaza Grande, dates from 1549. It originally housed soldiers, but was converted into a mansion, which served members of the Montejo family until 1970. Now it shelters a bank, and you can enter during the bank's opening hours. At other times, content yourself with a close look at the facade, where triumphant conquistadors with halberds hold their feet on the necks of generic barbarians (supposedly not Maya, though the association is inescapable). Also gazing across the plaza from the facade are busts of Montejo the Elder, his wife and his daughter.

Across the square from the cathedral is Mérida's **Palacio Municipal** (City Hall; Calle 62; 9am-5pm, Mon-Fri), built in 1542 and twice refurbished (in the 1730s and the 1850s). Occupying the corner of the plaza, is the **Centro Cultural Olimpo** (Calle 61), Mérida's municipal cultural center. Attempts to create a modern exterior for the building were halted by government order to preserve the colonial character of the plaza. The ultramodern interior serves as a venue for music and dance performances, and other exhibitions. Schedules for these, and frequent film showings, are posted outside.

On the north side of the plaza, the **Palacio de Gobierno** (Calle 61; admission free; 8am-9pm) houses the state of Yucatán's executive government offices (and one of its tourist information offices). It was built in 1892 on the site of the palace of the colonial governors. Inside are murals painted by local artist Fernando Castro Pacheco; completed in 1978, they were 25 years in the making and portray a symbolic history of the Maya and their interaction with the Spaniards.

CALLE 60
A block north of Plaza Grande, beyond shady Parque Hidalgo, rises the 17th-century **Iglesia de Jesús**, also called Iglesia de la Tercera Orden. Built by the Jesuits in 1618, this is the sole surviving edifice from a complex of buildings that once filled the entire city block. This church was built from the stones of an old Maya temple that occupied the same site. The Spaniards systematically destroyed any carved surfaces on stones used for building, but a few traces survived. Look closely at the west wall facing Parque Hidalgo, and you can see two stones still with Maya marks.

North of the church is the lavish **Teatro Peón Contreras** (cnr Calles 60 & 57), built between 1900 and 1908, during Mérida's *henequén* heyday. Inside the influence of the Italian architects who designed this theatre is clear. The main staircase is made of pure Carrara marble, and frescoes by Italian artists adorn the dome. Outside of performance hours, the guard may let you in to see the theater.

Across Calle 60 from the theater is the main building of the **Universidad de Yucatán**. Though the Jesuits had provided education to Yucatán's youth for centuries, the modern university was established in the 19th century by Governor Felipe Carrillo Puerto and General Manuel Cepeda Peraza.

A block north of the university is pretty **Parque Santa Lucía** (Calles 60 & 55). When Mérida was smaller, this was where travelers would get on or off the stagecoaches that linked towns and villages with the provincial capital. The **Bazar de Artesanías**, local handicrafts market, is held here at 11am on Sunday.

PASEO DE MONTEJO
The Paseo de Montejo was an attempt by Mérida's 19th-century city planners to create a wide boulevard, akin to the Paseo de la Reforma in Mexico City or the Champs Élysées in Paris. Though more modest than its predecessors, it is a beautiful wide swath of green in an otherwise urban setting.

Europe's architectural and social influence can be seen along the *paseo* in the fine mansions built by wealthy families around the end of the 19th century. The greatest concentrations of surviving mansions are north of Calle 37 – three blocks north of the Museo Regional de Antropología (below).

MUSEO DE LA CIUDAD
The **City Museum** (Calle 61; admission free; ⊙ 10am-2pm & 4-8pm Tue-Fri, 10am-2pm Sat & Sun) Small but worthwhile, with artifacts, exhibits, and good photos of the city and region. Signs in English explain subjects, such as Maya traditions, history and the process of *henequén* production.

MUSEO REGIONAL DE ANTROPOLOGÍA
The Palacio Cantón holds the **Museo Regional de Antropología** (cnr Paseo de Montejo & Calle 43; admission $3.50; ⊙ 8am-8pm Tue-Sat, 8am-2pm Sun). Construction of the mansion took from 1909 to 1911; its owner, General Francisco Cantón Rosado (1833–1917), died just six years later. Its splendor and pretension make it an apt symbol of the grand aspirations of Mérida's elite during the last years of the Porfiriato, the period from 1877 to 1911 when Porfirio Díaz had despotic sway over Mexico.

CENTRO DE ARTES VISTUALES
Just north of Parque Santa Ana, this new **gallery** (☎ 928-00-90; Calle 60; admission free; ⊙ 11am-8pm) features exhibits by regional and national artists. Workshops and classes are also offered (Spanish only).

Mérida for Children
Children's Story Hour Held at 10am on Saturday at the Mérida English Library (p919). Readings by the Story Lady (in English) appeal to four- to nine-year-olds.
Mérida en Domingo A super kid-friendly event (p926) that takes place every Sunday downtown.
Parque Centenario About 12 blocks west of the Plaza Grande is this large, verdant park. You'll embrace the shade and kids will enjoy the (slightly rickety) playgrounds. The park's Zoo (admission free; open 8am to 5pm Tuesday to Sunday) houses native monkeys, birds and reptiles.

Courses
Centro de Idiomas del Sureste (CIS; ☎ 926-11-55; www.cisyucatan.com.mx; Calle 14 No 6) This long-established Spanish-language school has three locations citywide. Courses begin every Monday year-round and run for a minimum of two weeks. Two-weeks' tuition costs $370; housing is available, per week from $135.
Georgia Charuhas (☎ 923-25-23; www.georgiacharuhas.com) Thirty-year resident of Mérida, acclaimed local artist and teacher, Georgia Charuha, specializes in drawing, painting and collage. Students of all levels welcome. A three-hour class costs $50.

Los Dos Culinary Classes (☎ 928-11-16; www.los-dos .com; Calle 68 No 517) Celebrated Chef, David Sterling, conducts classes in Yucatecan cuisine from his spectacular kitchen. One- to three-day courses cost $100 per day. Accommodations at Los Dos B&B (spectacular home of spectacular kitchen) are also available; see Sleeping (p924).

Tours

CITY TOURS

City Tourist Office (☎ 928-20-20; Plaza Grande, Calle 60) The City Tourist Office, housed in the Palacio Municipal, offers free daily one-hour guided walking tours of the historic center. Tours depart from the Palacio Municipal at 9:30am Monday to Saturday.

Mérida City Tours (☎ 927-61-19) This two-hour bilingual tour is conducted from an open-air bus that passes by Mérida's most popular points of interest. Tours are at 10am, 1pm, 4pm, 7pm Monday to Saturday, and 10am and 1pm on Sunday. Adults pay $7, kids aged six to 10 $4.

Mérida House & Garden Tour (☎ 924-84-01) Local designer, Keith Heitke, leads two-hour walking tours around the city center with visits to a few select showcase colonial homes. Tours depart from the Mérida English Library (p919) Wednesday mornings at 9am and cost $20.

REGIONAL TOURS

Mérida is an excellent base from which to take off on numerous regional adventures. From one-day excursions to multiday journeys, the following list is a great starting point.

Ecoturismo Yucatán (☎ 920-27-72; www.ecoyuc.com; Calle 3 No 235) This reputable outfit is passionate about sharing and protecting the state's natural treasures. Trips focus on archaeology, birding, natural history, biking and kayaking. One-day excursions are $50, 10-day jungle tours $1400.

Iluminado Tours (☎ 923-34-55; www.iluminado-tours .com) Canadian Trudy Woodcock's specialized tours emphasize the inner trek as well as the external journey. Art, spirituality and Maya mysticism are central themes. Iluminado can arrange anything from customized day trips ($75) to seven or 10-day excursions (approximately $1300 to $1500).

Nómadas Youth Hostel (☎ 924-52-23; www.nomadas travel.com; Calle 62 No 433) Nómadas offers low prices (about $30) for a variety of tours, including a Celestún Flamingo tour, Chichén Itzá, Uxmal and Calakmul. Groups meet at the hostel for a shared breakfast (included) before departing.

Yucatán Backroads Tours (☎ 924-01-17; www.yucatan backroads.com; Calle 53 No 508) Native Yucatecan, Ivan de Léon, specializes in intensive one-day excursions (approx $100 per person). The off-the-beaten-path itineraries include stops at remote *pueblos*, haciendas and hidden nature spots.

Festivals & Events

Festival Internacional de los Artes Held in January, this annual celebration, inaugurated in 2005, taps into Mérida's rich artistic reserves and showcases international talent. For approximately three weeks, venues throughout the city center feature art exhibits, literary readings, film, theater debuts and a range of musical offerings.

Carnaval (www.merida.gob.mx/carnaval) In February or March, prior to Lent, Carnival in Mérida is celebrated with greater vigor than anywhere else on the peninsula. Festivities include music, parades, colorful costumes and dancing.

Kihuic At the end of February or beginning of March, this is a colorful market that fills the Plaza Grande with artisans who come from all over Mexico to display their crafts.

Cristo de las Ampollas From late September through mid-October, *gremios* (guilds or unions) venerate the Cristo de las Ampollas (Christ of the Blisters) with daily folkloric processions (11am to 1pm) at the cathedral in Plaza Grande.

Día de los Muertos and Exposición de Altares On November 1 every year, the Maya honor the spirits of their ancestors with altars and offerings. Representatives from outlying regions come annually to Mérida and erect elaborate altars in the Plaza Grande.

Toh Yucatán Bird Festival Sponsored by Ecoturismo Yucatán (see Regional Tours, left), this four-day event in December attracts flocks of birders who come to participate in talks, workshops and, of course, bird-watching field trips.

Sleeping

From hostels to haciendas, there's an abundance of quality accommodations in Mérida. So many, in fact, it's hard to limit the list. Prices fluctuate between low and high season (mid-December to April), but not wildly like on the Caribbean coast. High-season rates are given here.

BUDGET

Hotel Trinidad (☎ 923-20-33; www.hoteltrinidad.com; Calle 62 No 464; d from $32; ☒) Den-like and cozy the rooms here (with original contemporary artwork) surround two leafy courtyards Communal space includes a pub, billiard room, rooftop patio with Jacuzzi, and a well-equipped kitchen. Guests can use the small pool at Hotel Trinidad Galería. Continenta breakfast is included, and there's wi-fi, too.

Hotel Trinidad Galería (☎ 923-24-63; Calle 60 N 456; s/d $22/25; ☒) Run by artist/owner Manolc Rivera, this hotel is downright silly. Once ar appliance showroom, this place went from electric to eclectic. Tangled in a labyrintl of vegetation, original paintings, sculptures dolls, toys and inflatable superheros fill ever wall, nook and cranny. Rooms vary in size check a few. There's a small shaded pool.

Hostal del Peregrino (☎ 924-54-91; www .hostaldelperegrino.com; Calle 51 No 488; dm $12, d $30) A lovingly renovated colonial on a quiet street north of the city center. Earthy, homelike and tasteful, the Peregrino gives you B&B comfort at hostel prices, with breakfast included. There's also an attractive terrace bar and easy street parking.

Nómadas Youth Hostel (☎ 924-52-23; www .nomadastravel.com; Calle 62 No 433; hammock or tent $5, dm $7, d $15; 🖳) A Mérida institution, this backpacker favorite is spacious, clean and extremely well run. There's a fully equipped communal kitchen and hand-laundry facilities. Continental breakfast is included. Nómadas also has a lively nightlife: on Tuesday and Friday guests enjoy live *Trova* (folk music), and free salsa dance classes occur during the rest of the week.

Hostel Zocolo (☎ 930-95-62; hostel_zocolo@yahoo .com; cnr Calles 63 & 62; dm $9, d $18; 🖳) Housed in a grand historic building on Plaza Grande, the Zocolo is a class act: architecturally awesome, clean, professionally run, with excellent beds, spacious doubles, inviting shared spaces and a fully equipped communal kitchen. Continental breakfast is included.

Nest Hostel (☎ 928-83-65; www.nesthostel.com; Calle 57 No 547-B; dm $9, d $18; 🖳) The lively and cheery Nest attracts mostly social fledglings. It has a sunny patio with a tiny pool, and a comfy TV room. A small breakfast is included.

MIDRANGE

Luz en Yucatán (☎ 924-00-35; www.luzenyucatan.com; Calle 55 No 499; r $40-70; 🐾 🖳) Two beers on arrival is the delightfully eccentric owner's policy. Madeline – usually with parrot, Godzilla, perched on her shoulder – will make you feel immediately at home. Each of the seven rooms that surround the courtyard and small pool is an original work, dedicated to comfort and coziness; all are equipped with cable TV, and most with a small kitchenette. Special services available upon request include massage, pedicures, yoga and Spanish lessons.

Medio Mundo (☎ 924-54-72; www.hotelmediomundo .com; Calle 55 No 533; r with fan $45-55, with fan & air-con $60-65; 🐾 🖳) This urban oasis exudes peace and tranquility. The owners and gracious hosts, Nicole and Nelson, have transformed a once-dilapidated home into a virtual *Architectural Digest* centerfold. The colors – from the paint on the walls to the flowers in the courtyard – are orchestrated to evoke just the right mood, and every detail (including the quiet air-con and not-too-soft, not-too-hard beds) has

been attended to. What this hotel doesn't have is distractions: no phone, no TV, no noise. Healthy breakfasts ($8) and organic coffee are served at the poolside patio.

Casa Esperanza (☎ 923-47-11; www.casaesperanza .com; Calle 54 No 476; r from $70; 🐾 🖳) The expansive peaceful grounds and garden invoke an almost monastic feel here. Tasteful art (carvings, tile, sculpture, painting) adorn corners and walls; many of the pieces are religious artifacts, enhancing the sanctuary-like mood. There are three rooms, all lovely, with the deluxe courtyard suite the nicest ($90). Gourmet breakfast is included. Pets welcome.

Hotel Marionetas (☎ 928-33-77; www.hotelmarion etas.com; Calle 49 No 516; d $85; 🐾 🖳 🖳) A very pretty boutique inn north of the city center. The eight high-ceilinged rooms are impeccably decorated with upscale style, and the manicured grounds, with fountain and pool, are brochure perfect. The café is for guests only and offers snacks and espresso. A generous continental breakfast is included.

Casa Mexilio (☎ 928-25-05, in the US ☎ 800-538-68-02; www.casamexilio.com; Calle 68 No 495; r $85; 🐾 🖳 🖳) A cool grotto of calm. Each of the eight spacious rooms exudes stylish Mexican earthiness and all are set among an exuberance of shady vegetation. The lush courtyard with pool and Jacuzzi is the perfect antidote to Mérida's hot, busy streets.

Caribe (☎ 924-90-22; Calle 59 No 500; d $50; 🅿 🐾 🖳) On Parque Hidalgo, the classic Caribe was first erected as a convent in 1650. The deluxe suites are lovely, but the quaint standard rooms seem a bit tired in comparison. There's a rooftop pool with great views, and a parkside café.

Gran Hotel (☎ 924-77-30; Calle 60 No 496; d $55; 🅿 🖳) Fidel Castro chose to stay here when he was in town. The classic Gran Hotel was built in 1901 and retains many original decorative flourishes. The 28 rooms have period furnishings, and the most charming overlook Parque Hidalgo.

Hotel Santa Lucía (☎ 928-26-72; www.hotelsanta lucia.com.mx; Calle 55 No 508; d $40; 🐾 🖳) This pink colonial hotel across the street from Parque Santa Lucía is a favorite among travelers. It has a small pool, and all 51 rooms are clean and have TV and telephone.

Hotel Dolores Alba (☎ 928-56-50, 800-849-50-60; www.doloresalba.com; Calle 63; d $40; 🅿 🐾 🖳) The quiet, friendly Dolores Alba offers excellent value. Rooms are set around two very large courtyards; all those in the new, modern wing are quite spacious and face the pool. The only drawback is the hotel's relative distance from the city center.

Casa Ana B&B (☎ 924-00-05; www.casaana.com; Calle 52 No 469; d $30-45; 🔀) Friendly Casa Ana offers four very pleasant, courtyard-facing rooms in a quiet neighborhood residence. Breakfast is included. Air-con costs $10 extra.

TOP END

Hacienda Xcanatún (☎ 941-02-13, 888-883-36-33; www.xcanatun.com; Km 12 Carretera Mérida-Progreso; ste from $300; P 🔀 🖳 🏊) About 20 minutes north of town, this hotel offers accommodations in a fairly quiet and remote setting. It's in the village of Xcanatún, so it's not as secluded as some hacienda resorts, but at the same time it is in convenient proximity to Mérida. The 18 luxury suites are set amid a garden of prolific color and charm, and each has its own patio with Jacuzzi. The romantic on-site restaurant, Casa de Piedra (opposite), is one of the best around.

Los Dos B&B (☎ 928-11-16; www.los-dos.com; Calle 68 No 517; d $125; 🔀 🏊) The two rooms here are often reserved for culinary school students (see p922), but if one is available, and you seek sumptuous elegance, book it. The owners, David and Keith, have artistically refurbished this 19th-century colonial to its original glory – if not beyond. Breakfast is prepared by Chef David himself.

Villa @ Mérida (☎ 928-84-66, 888-737-2124; www .thevillasgroup.com; Calle 59 No 615A; ste from $300; P 🔀 🖳 🏊) Style-wise, this stately villa is in keeping with the current hacienda trend, but it offers rugged rural-chic right in the city. The seven high-ceilinged, fluffy-bedded rooms are honeymoon perfect. The grounds are extensive and green, and shelter a pretty, secluded pool.

Casa Lucía (☎ 928-07-40; www.hotelcasalucia.com .mx; Calle 60 No 474A; r from $140; P 🔀 🏊) Nestled behind its popular restaurant, Café Lucía (see opposite), this boutique hotel offers small-scale grandeur in the heart of Mérida. The rosebush-lined garden holds a big patio with a pool and gurgling fountain – all lovely by day, magic by night. The suites are decked out in fine period pieces and original art, but are equally fitted with modern comforts.

For more conventional luxury, the following hotels form a grand trio north of the city center on Av Colón.

Hotel Fiesta Americana Mérida (☎ 942-11-11, in the US 800-343-78-21; www.fiestaamericana.com; Calle 56A No 451 at Av Colón; r from $150; P 🔀 🖳 🏊) An enormous, modern neocolonial hotel, housing a complex of businesses, chic shops and restaurants.

Hotel Villa Mercedes (☎ 924-90-00; www.hotel villamercedes.com.mx; Av Colón 500 at Calle 60; r from $110; P 🔀 🖳 🏊) A refurbished art-nouveau mansion, smaller (84 rooms) and more intimate (as mansions go) than its counterparts.

Hyatt Regency Mérida (☎ 942-02-02; www.hyatt .com; Av Colón 344; r from $160; P 🔀 🖳 🏊) The 17-storey Hyatt has basic necessities, like tennis courts, gym, spa and a giant rooftop pool.

Eating

Eateries in Mérida come in every size and flavor – Arab, Asian, European, Mexican, Yucatecan, or a fusion of any or all.

CAFÉS

Café Club (☎ 923-15-92; Calle 55 No 496; breakfast $4-6; ⏰ 7am-5pm Mon-Sat) With strong coffee and generous servings, this very friendly mostly veggie café, is a happy place to start the day. And if you like it, come back for its good set lunch specials ($4). Internet access is also available for $1 per hour.

Amaro (☎ 928-24-52; Calle 59; mains $6-10) Chilled hangout by day, romantic candlelit spot by night. Veggie-centric Amaro has a creative selection of healthy salads, soups, crepes and pizza. First-rate acoustic music is performed Wednesday to Sunday.

Café Alameda (☎ 928-36-35; Calle 58 No 474; mains $5; ⏰ 8am-5pm Mon, Wed-Sat) Enjoy excellent authentic Middle Eastern veggie favorites, including baba ganoush, humus and tabouleh. Chewy tough but surprisingly savory, the meat brochetas (shish kabobs) are a treat.

Café Chiapas (☎ 928-28-64; Calle 60 No 440A; ⏰ Mon-Sat) A small corner place with very good coffee and espresso – including iced drinks. Ground coffee is available too.

RESTAURANTS

La Casa de Frida (☎ 928-23-11; Calle 61 No 526; mains $8-15; ⏰ 6-11pm Tue-Sat) Fusing Mexican, French and Yucatecan influences, the mains are deliciously innovative here. And though the menu is serious, the mood is playful. Delicate hanging lanterns offset the candy pink walls, all of which are adorned with Kahlo's image and prints.

Café Lucia (☎ 928-07-40; Calle 60 No 474; mains $8-15) This quiet, chic gallery-restaurant features a tasteful display of works by local and international artists. If you'd prefer to eat outside, there is romantic seating across the street in Parque Santa Lucia, where local musicians play table-side *Trova*. The menu features very good seafood, steak and pasta, and the service is excellent.

Casa de Piedra (☎ 941-02-13; Carretera Mérida, Km 12-Progreso; mains $15-25) Famed restaurant of the luxurious Hacienda Xcanatún (see opposite) specializing in French-Yucatecan cuisine. Many consider this the best food in the region; it is very good, but it's the garden setting that's superlative – pure candlelit charm.

La Tratto (☎ 927-04-34; Prolongación Montejo 479A; mains $10-20; ☺ 7pm-2am) Upscale and trendy, La Tratto's sidewalk tables are ever-brimming with stylish *meridanos*. Prices are high, but so is the service and quality – mains are *very* good. Score excellent two-for-one deals on Monday (steak) and Wednesday (pasta).

Villa María (☎ 923-33-57; Calle 59 No 553; mains $15-25) The ambiance of this fabulous colonial mansion is reason enough for a visit, but its Viennese chef tops the experience with his menu of international delicacies. Critics claim inconsistency. Enthusiasts say take a chance!

Pane e Vino (☎ 928-62-28; Calle 62; mains $7-9; ☺ Tue-Sun) With wood accents, low light and warm appeal, this Italian restaurant serves generous portions of standard pizza and pasta dishes, with veggie options too.

Marlín Azul (Calle 62 No 488; mains $5; ☺ 10am-5pm) Frequented by locals, but rarely tourists, this small, blue hole-in-the-wall serves fine fresh seafood. The *ceviche mixto* is arguably the best choice on the menu.

Cangrejito (☎ 928-27-81; Calle 57 No 523; tacos $1; ☺ 10am-5pm) Pope John Paul II chose to eat at this humble establishment during his visit in 1984. Blessed by the 'holy sea,' the veteran chefs assemble a tasty variety of fresh seafood (crab, fish, shrimp) tacos. Try a sampling.

QUICK EATS

Vito Corleone (☎ 923-68-46; Calle 59 No 508; pizza $3-7) Look for the rickety bike hanging from the ceiling over the broad open entrance. This funky pizzeria serves up atmosphere and good wood-fired pizza. The toppings are a bit pre-packagey, but the crust is oven fresh.

Mercado Municipal Lucas de Gálvez (cnr Calles 56 & 56A; snacks $3) The bustling market is full of small eateries. Upstairs joints have tables, chairs and varied menus. Downstairs at the north end are *taquerías* (taco stalls), while near the south end are *coctelerías* (cocktail bars) serving seafood cocktails.

Mercado Santa Ana (cnr Calles 60 & 47; snacks $3) Next to Santa Ana Park, this neighborhood open-air market is a calmer alternative to the main market. The short string of food stalls serves excellent tacos and snacks.

El Colón (Plaza Mayor; Calle 61) On the north end of the plaza, serving refreshing sorbets and ice cream in a variety of local fruit flavors.

Jugos California (Plaza Mayor; cnr Calles 63A & 58) Every local fruit is juiced here (mango, pitaya, mamey, papaya). Create a thirst-quencher.

Drinking

Bella Epocha (Calle 60 No 495) This elegant restaurant excels more at ambiance than cuisine. Forget the sit-down extravagance and enjoy the vintage romance with a drink on one of the balconies. Order a side of *panuchos* (small, open tortilla topped with meat, cheese or veggies). Perfect.

El Hoyo (Calle 62 No 487) This chilled, kickback café-bar serves beer, wine and…waffles!

Ki'bok (☎ 928-55-11; Calle 60) This labyrinthine bar-restaurant offers a menu of nooks, patios and balconies where you can sip drinks. There are good daily happy-hour specials.

Amaro (☎ 928-24-52; Calle 59) Have a drink and enjoy professional – and often extremely talented (check out Angélica Balado if she's around) – *Trova* musicians perform on Wednesday to Sunday evenings.

Entertainment

CULTURAL EVENTS

Mérida's cultural life is thriving, with different musical or theatrical performances going on every day. Check the schedule of current events with a copy of *Yucatán Today* (available at tourist offices and most hotels, or online at www.yucatantoday.com).

Ballet Folklórico de la Universidad de Yucatán (University of Yucatán; cnr Calles 60 & 57; adult $2) Every Friday night at 9pm, the university's folk dance troupe puts on an impressive and authentic performance of regional dances.

Centro Cultural Olimpio (☎ 928-20-20; Plaza Grande) There's something interesting – from films to concerts to art installations – scheduled nearly every night of the week here. Admission varies, but should cost above about $5.

Teatro Peón Contreras (cnr Calles 60 & 57) This grand theater features international, Mexican, and local dance and musical performances most nights of the week. (Check with the theater for a current schedule of events; tickets are rarely over $8). The very impressive Mérida symphony generally performs here on Friday at 9pm and Sunday at noon.

Mérida en Domingo (Plaza Grande; ☯ 9am-9pm) 'Mérida on Sunday' is a lively fair that takes place every weekend. The main plaza and Calle 60 – from the plaza to Parque Santa Lucia – are closed to traffic. Food and drink stands are set up, art activity booths are available for kids, and there's a small flea market and book exchange. From 11am bands – jazz, folk, classical – play in front of the Palacio del Gobierno. Around 7pm in Parque Hidalgo, live salsa music and dancing begins.

Noche Mexicana (☯ 9am-9pm) A free outdoor traditional Mexican music and dance performance that takes place on Saturday in a small park, near Paseo de Montejo.

NIGHTCLUBS
Azul Picante (Calle 60) This club features live Latin pop and salsa.

Ay Caray! (Calle 60) A popular-with-locals bar that features live (and loud) music – usually rock – most nights.

El Cielo (Prolongación de Montejo at Calle 25) The rich kids' flavor-of-the-month, a super-chic club spinning house, rock and reggae.

Mambo Café (☎ 987-75-33; Plaza Las Américas Shopping Mall) The always-crowded Mambo, approximately 1km north of the city center, has live salsa bands on Friday and Saturday.

CINEMAS
Mérida has several cinemas, most of which show first-run Hollywood fare in English, with subtitles.

Cine Fantasio (Parque Hidalgo) Screens international and art films.

Cinepolis (Plaza Las Américas Shopping Mall) A big modern cineplex showing first-run Hollywood flicks, almost all in English with subtitles.

Teatro Mérida (Calle 62) The main indie cinema, the venue for art-house films and film festivals.

Shopping
Mérida is a fine place for buying Yucatecan handicrafts. Purchases to consider include traditional Maya clothing, such as the colorful embroidered *huipiles* (women's

tunics), panama hats woven from palm fibers and, of course, the wonderfully comfortable Yucatecan hammocks.

Mercado Municipal Lucas de Gálvez (cnr Calles 56 & 56A) Southeast of the Plaza Grande is Mérida's main market. The surrounding streets are part of the large market district and are lined with shops selling pretty much everything.

HANDICRAFTS
Casa de las Artesanías (Calle 63; ☯ 9am-8pm Mon-Sat, 10am-2pm Sun) A government-supported market for local artisans selling earthenware, textiles, wicker baskets, sandals, wind chimes, ceramic dolls, vases, purses and pouches, figurines of Maya deities and bottles of locally made liqueurs. It is also one of the only places where you can find genuine filigree jewelry. Prices are fixed and mostly reasonable.

PANAMA HATS
Locally made panama hats are woven from *jipijapa* palm leaves in caves, where humid conditions keep the fibers pliable. Once exposed to the relatively dry air outside, the panama hat is surprisingly resilient to crushing. The best-quality hats have a fine, close weave of slender fibers; the coarser the weave, the lower the price should be. Prices range from a few dollars for a basic hat, to $80 or more for top quality one. They can be found at the Casa de las Artesanías and elsewhere.

HAMMOCKS
'The Yucatán hammock is an honest hammock and does not play dirty tricks in the middle of the night,' wrote travel writer Michel Peissel in 1964. A well-made hammock is not only a fine alternative to a mattress; it is a fine work of art. Mérida is one of the best places to buy a Yucatecan hammock, but only if you know where to shop. Street vendors and many small shops sell tacky, uncomfortable, made-for-tourists renditions. The best place in town to shop for a quality hammock is at the reputable **Hamacas El Aguacate** (☎ 928-64-69; cnr Calles 58 & 73). If you want to venture out of town, you can go to the nearby village of Tixcocob (buses run from the Progreso bus terminal) and watch hammock makers at work. It is also a good place to find a well-crafted hammock at a fair price (between $15 and $25 for smaller hammocks, and up to $50 for a large one).

Getting There & Away

AIR
Mérida's modern airport is a 10km, 20-minute ride southwest of the Plaza Grande, off Hwy 180 (Av de los Itzáes). It has car-rental desks, an ATM and a currency exchange booth, and a tourist office where staff can help with hotel reservations.

Most international flights to Mérida are connections through Mexico City or Cancún. Nonstop international services are provided by Aeroméxico (Los Angeles and Miami) and Continental (Houston). Scheduled domestic flights are operated mostly by smaller regional airlines, with a few flights by Aeroméxico and Mexicana.

The following airlines service Mérida:

Aerocaribe (☎ 928-67-90; www.aerocaribe.com; Paseo de Montejo 500B)

Aeroméxico (☎ 920-12-60; www.aeromexico.com; Hotel Fiesta Americana, Calle 56A No 451 at Av Colón)

Aviacsa (☎ 925-68-90; www.aviasca.com.mx; Hotel Fiesta Americana, Calle 56A No 451 at Av Colón) Also with a desk at the airport (☎ 946-18-50).

Continental Airlines (☎ 800-900-50-00; www.continental.com) Located at the airport.

Mexicana (☎ 924-69-10; www.mexicana.com.mx; Paseo de Montejo 493)

BUS
Mérida is the bus transportation hub of the Yucatán Peninsula. Take care with your gear on night buses and those serving popular tourist destinations (especially 2nd-class buses). Note that there have been many reports of theft on the night runs to Chiapas.

Hotel Fiesta Americana (Calle 56A No 451 at Av Colón) has a small 1st-class bus terminal on the west side of the hotel complex, aimed at guests staying at the luxury hotels on Av Colón, far from the city center. Don't arrive here by bus unless you'll be staying at the Fiesta, Villa Mercedes or Hyatt hotels. From here ADO GL and Super Expresso have services between Mérida and Cancún, Campeche, Chetumal and Playa del Carmen.

Parque de San Juan (Calle 69) is the terminus for shared taxis, vans and Volkswagen combis going to Dzibilchaltún Ruinas, Muna, Oxkutzcab, Petó, Sacalum, Tekax and Ticul.

Progreso (Calle 62 No 524) is a separate bus terminal for Progreso-bound buses.

CAME bus terminal (☎ 924-83-91; Calle 70) is Mérida's main bus terminal, seven blocks southwest of Plaza Grande. Come here for (mostly 1st-class) buses to points around the Yucatán Peninsula and well beyond (eg Campeche, Cancún, Mexico City, Palenque, San Cristóbal de Las Casas and Villahermosa). Bus lines include the economical ADO and Altos (air-con, a few stops, no bathroom), and the deluxe lines ADO GL, Maya de Oro, Super Expresso and UNO (air-con, nonstop, with bathrooms).

Terminal de Segunda Clase (Calle 69) is around the corner from CAME bus terminal. From here ATS, Mayab, Omnitur del Caribe, Oriente, Sur, TRP and TRT run mostly 2nd-class buses to points in the state and around the peninsula.

Terminal Noreste (Calle 67) is the Noreste bus line's terminal; LUS uses it as well. Buses run from here to many small towns in the northeast, including Tizimín and Río Lagartos, and there's frequent service to Cancún and points along the way, and small towns south and west of Mérida, including Celestún, Ticul and Oxkutzcab.

Following are the major routes serviced daily from Mérida:

CAR & MOTORCYCLE
The optimal way to tour the many archaeological sites south of Mérida is by car. However, getting around town is definitely better done on foot or with public transportation, so hold off renting a car until you've gotten well oriented.

México Rent A Car (☎ 923-36-37; Calle 57A) offers rates the big-name agencies can't touch, especially if you're paying cash. It's sometimes possible to get a VW Beetle for as little as $25 a day, and long-term rentals can reduce prices even more.

Several other agencies have branches at the airport, as well as on Calle 60 between Calles 55 and 57, including **Budget** (☎ 928-66-59), **Executive** (☎ 923-37-32) and **Hertz** (☎ 924-28-34).

Getting Around

TO/FROM THE AIRPORT
Bus No 79 ('Aviación') travels between the airport and city center every 15 to 30 minutes until 9pm, with occasional service until 11pm. The best place to catch the return bus ($0.70) is on Calle 70 just south of Calle 69, near the corner of the CAME bus terminal.

Transporte Terrestre (☎ 946-15-29) provides speedy service between the airport and the

YUCATÁN PENINSULA

MÉRIDA BUS SCHEDULE

Destination	Price	Duration	Frequency
Campeche	$8	2½-3½hr	frequent ADO 1st-class buses
(short route via Bécal)	$7	2½-3½hr	ATS 2nd-class buses every 30min until 7pm
Campeche	$7.50	4hr	5 Sur 2nd-class buses btwn 6am-5pm
(long route via Uxmal)			
Cancún	$22	4hr	20 Super Expresso buses
	$16	14hr	6 Oriente 2nd-class buses
Celestún	$4	2hr	15 2nd-class
Chetumal	$19	6-8hr	8 deluxe Omnitur del Caribe & Super Expresso buses
	$16	6-8hr	3 Mayab 2nd-class buses
Chichén Itzá	$4.50-6.25	2-2½hr	3 Super Expresso & 16 Oriente 2nd-class buses, but some Cancún-bound buses stop at Chichén Itzá during the day, and at night in nearby Pisté.
Cobá	$11	3½hr	1 deluxe Super Expresso at 1pm
	$8	3½hr	1 Oriente bus at 5:15am
Escárcega	$14	5½hr	1 Altos 1st-class buses
	$16	5½hr	5 ADO 1st-class buses
	$13	5½hr	many Sur 2nd-class buses
Felipe Carrillo Puerto	$12	5½hr	7 Mayab 2nd-class buses
	$13	5½hr	5 TRP 2nd-class buses
Izamal	$3	1½hr	frequent Oriente 2nd-class buses
Mayapán Ruinas	$2	2hr	15 LUS 2nd-class buses, from Terminal Noreste
Mexico City (TAPO)	$75	20hr	4 ADO 1st-class buses between 10am-9:15pm
Mexico City (Terminal Norte)	$77	19hr	1 ADO 1st-class bus at 12:05pm
Palenque	$29	8-9hr	1 deluxe Maya de Oro bus
	$26	8-9hr	3 ADO 1st-class buses
	$24	8-9hr	1 Altos bus
Playa del Carmen	$20	5-7hr	10 deluxe Super Expresso buses
Progreso	$1.25	1hr	every 20min from 8am-9pm, from the Progreso bus terminal. For the same ticket price, shared taxis or vans (some with air-con) take off from a parking lot at Calle 60 between Calles 65 and 67.
Río Lagartos	$6-8	3-4hr	3 Noreste 1st- & 2nd-class buses from 9am
Ticul	$3.50	2hr	frequent 2nd-class Mayab buses. For $2.75 there are also frequent minibuses (combis and vans) from Parque de San Juan.
Tizimín	$8	2½-4hr	several 1st-class Noreste buses
	$7	2½-4hr	several 2nd-class Noreste buses
Tulum	$13	4hr	3 deluxe Super Expresso buses via Cobá at 6:30am, 11am & 1pm
Tuxtla Gutiérrez	$45	13-16hr	1 deluxe Maya de Oro bus at 9:30pm
	$37	13-16hr	1 Altos bus at 7:15pm; you can change at Palenque or Villahermosa
Uxmal	$6	1½hr	1 ATS
Valladolid	$8	2½-3½hr	frequent buses, including deluxe Super Expresso
	$6	2½-3½hr	frequent 2nd-class Oriente and ATS buses
Villahermosa	$30	8-9hr	10 ADO 1st-class buses
	$50	8-9hr	2 superdeluxe UNO buses at 9:30pm and 11pm
	$48	8-9hr	1 ADO GL bus at 5:30pm

city center, charging $11 per carload (same price for hotel pick-up). A taxi from the city center to the airport should cost you about $9.

BUS

City buses are cheap at $0.50. To travel between the Plaza Grande and the neighborhoods to the north along Paseo de Montejo, catch the Ruta 10 at the corner of Calles 58 and 59, half a block east of the Parque Hidalgo. Alternatively, catch a 'Tecnológico,' 'Hyatt' or 'Montejo' bus on Calle 60 and get off at Av Colón. To return to the city center you can catch any bus heading south on Paseo de Montejo with a 'Centro' sign.

TAXI

Taxis in Mérida are not metered. Rates are fixed, with a $3.50 minimum fare, which will get you from the bus terminals to all downtown hotels. Most rides within city limits do not exceed $6. Taxi stands can be found at most of the *barrio* (neighborhood of a town or city) parks, or call **Taximetro** (☎ 928-54-27); service is available 24 hours (dispatch fees are an extra $1 to $2).

SOUTH OF MÉRIDA
Hacienda Yaxcopoil

This is a vast estate that once grew and processed *henequén*; its numerous French Renaissance-style buildings have now been restored and turned into a museum of the

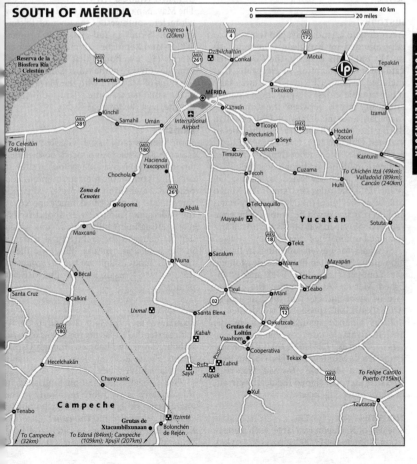

SOUTH OF MÉRIDA

17th century. **Hacienda Yaxcopoil** (☎ 999-900-11-93; www.yaxcopoil.com; admission $5, kids free; ☺ 8am-6pm Mon-Sat, 9am-1pm Sun) is on the west side of Hwy 261, 33km southwest of central Mérida. If you want to extend your visit, there is a guesthouse ($60 for two people, $10 for each additional guest). It's best to book ahead.

Mayapán

The **Mayapán ruins** (Ruinas de Mayapán; admission $3; ☺ 8am-5pm) are some 50km southeast of Mérida, on Yucatán state Hwy 18. Though far less impressive than many Maya sites, Mayapán is historically significant. Its main attractions are clustered in a compact core, and visitors often have the place to themselves.

HISTORY

According to legend, Mayapán was supposedly founded by Kukulcán (Quetzalcóatl) in AD 1007. His dynasty, the Cocom, organized a confederation of city-states that included Uxmal, Chichén Itzá and many other notable cities. Despite their alliance, animosity arose between the Cocom of Mayapán and the Itzáes of Chichén Itzá during the late 12th century, and the Cocom stormed Chichén Itzá, forcing the Itzá rulers into exile. The Cocom dynasty emerged supreme in all of northern Yucatán.

Cocom supremacy lasted for almost 250 years, until the ruler of Uxmal, Ah Xupán Xiú, led a rebellion of the oppressed city-states and overthrew Cocom hegemony. The great capital of Mayapán was utterly destroyed and remained uninhabited ever after.

Struggles for power continued in the region until 1542, when Francisco de Montejo the Younger conquered T'hó and established Mérida. At that point the current lord of Maní and ruler of the Xiú people, Ah Kukum Xiú, proposed to Montejo a military alliance against the Cocom, his ancient rivals. Montejo accepted, and Xiú was baptized as a Christian, taking the name Francisco de Montejo Xiú. The Cocom were defeated and – too late – the Xiú rulers realized that they had signed the death warrant of Maya independence.

THE SITE

The city of Mayapán was large, with a population estimated at 12,000; it covered 4 sq km,

all surrounded by a great defensive wall. In the early 1950s and early '60s, archaeologists mapped over 3500 buildings, 20 cenotes and traces of the city wall. The late postclassic workmanship is inferior to that of the great age of Maya art.

Among the structures that have been restored is the **Castillo de Kukulcán**, a climbable pyramid with fresco fragments around its base and, at its rear side, friezes depicting decapitated warriors. The **Templo Redondo** (Round Temple) is vaguely reminiscent of El Caracol at Chichén Itzá. Close by is Itzmal Chen, a cenote that was a major Maya religious sanctuary. Excavation and restoration continue at the site.

GETTING THERE & AWAY

The Mayapán ruins are just off Hwy 18, a few kilometers southwest of the town of Telchaquillo. LUS runs 15 2nd-class buses between 5:30am and 8pm from Terminal Noreste in Mérida ($2, two hours) that will let you off near the entrance of the ruins. Don't confuse the ruins of Mayapán with the Maya village of the same name, some 40km southeast of the site, past the town of Teabo.

Uxmal

Some visitors rank **Uxmal** (admission $9 Mon-Sat, $4 Sun; ☺ 8am-5pm), pronounced 'oosh-*mahl*,' among the top Maya archaeological sites. It certainly is one of the most harmonious and peaceful. Fascinating, well-preserved structures made of pink-hued limestone cover the wide area. Adding to its appeal is Uxmal's setting in the hilly Puuc region, which lent its name to the architectural patterns in this area. *Puuc* means 'hills,' and these, rising to about 100m, are the only ones in the northwest region of the otherwise flat peninsula.

HISTORY

Uxmal was an important city and its dominance extended to the nearby towns of Sayil, Kabah, Xlapak and Labná. Although Uxmal means 'Thrice Built' in Maya, it was actually constructed five times.

That a sizable population flourished in this dry area is yet more testimony to the engineering skills of the Maya, who built a series of reservoirs and *chultunes* (cisterns) lined with lime mortar to catch and hold water during the dry season. First settled

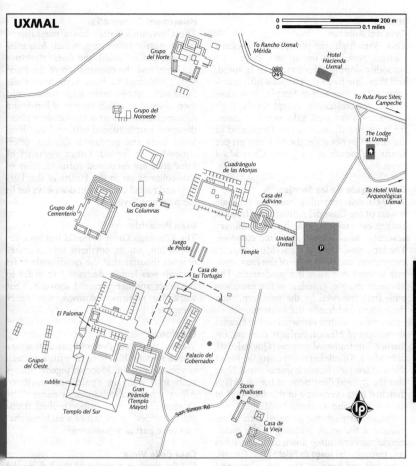

UXMAL

in about AD 600, Uxmal was influenced by highland Mexico in its architecture, most likely through contact fostered by trade. This influence is reflected in the town's serpent imagery, phallic symbols and columns. The well-proportioned Puuc architecture, with its intricate, geometric mosaics sweeping across the upper parts of elongated facades, was also strongly influenced by the slightly earlier Río Bec and Chenes styles.

The scarcity of water in the region meant that Chac-Mool, the rain god or sky serpent, was supreme in importance. His image is ubiquitous at the site in the form of stucco masks protruding from facades and cornices. There is much speculation as to why Uxmal was abandoned in about

900; drought conditions may have reached such proportions that the inhabitants had to relocate.

Rediscovered by archaeologists in the 19th century, Uxmal was first excavated in 1929 by Fr`ans Blom. Although much has been restored, much has yet to be discovered.

INFORMATION

The price of admission, if you retain the wristband ticket, includes a 45-minute **sound-and-light show** (8pm in summer, 7pm in winter). It's in Spanish, but translation devices are available ($3). The cost of the show only is $4, applicable toward the next day's site admission.

Parking costs $1 per car.

SIGHTS
Casa del Adivino
This 39m-high temple (the Magician's House), was built on an oval base. The smoothly sloping sides have been restored, and they date from the temple's fifth incarnation. The four earlier temples were covered in the rebuilding, except for the high doorway on the west side, which remains from the fourth incarnation. Decorated in elaborate Chenes style, the doorway proper forms the mouth of a gigantic Chac-Mool mask.

Cuadrángulo de las Monjas
The 74-room, sprawling Nuns' Quadrangle is west of the Casa del Adivino. Archaeologists guess variously that it was a military academy, royal school or palace complex. The long-nosed face of Chac-Mool appears everywhere on the facades of the four separate temples that form the quadrangle. The northern temple, grandest of the four, was built first, followed by the southern, then the eastern and finally the western.

Several decorative elements on the facades show signs of Mexica, perhaps Totonac, influence. The feathered-serpent (Quetzalcóatl, or in Maya, Kukulcán) motif along the top of the west temple's facade is one of these. Note also the stylized depictions of the *na* (Maya thatched hut) over some of the doorways in the northern and southern buildings.

Passing through the corbeled arch in the middle of the south building of the quadrangle and continuing down the slope, takes you through the **Juego de Pelota** (Ball Court). Turn left and head up the steep slope and stairs to the large terrace.

Casa de las Tortugas
To the right at the top of the stairs is the House of the Turtles, which takes its name from the turtles carved on the cornice. The Maya associated turtles with the rain god, Chac-Mool. According to Maya myth, when the people suffered from drought so did the turtles, and both prayed to Chac-Mool to send rain.

The frieze of short columns, or 'rolled mats,' that runs around the temple below the turtles is characteristic of the Puuc style. On the west side of the building a vault has collapsed, affording a good view of the corbeled arch that supported it.

Palacio del Gobernador
The Governor's Palace has a magnificent facade nearly 100m long, which Mayanist Michael D Coe called 'the finest structure at Uxmal and the culmination of the Puuc style'. Buildings in Puuc style have walls filled with rubble, faced with cement and then covered in a thin veneer of limestone squares; the lower part of the facade is plain, the upper part festooned with stylized Chac-Mool faces and geometric designs, often lattice-like or fretted. Other elements of Puuc style are decorated cornices, rows of half-columns (as in the House of the Turtles) and round columns in doorways (as in the palace at Sayil).

Gran Pirámide
The 32m-high Great Pyramid has been restored only on its northern side. Archaeologists theorize that the quadrangle at its summit was largely destroyed in order to construct another pyramid above it. That work, for reasons unknown, was never completed.

El Palomar
West of the Great Pyramid sits a structure whose roofcomb is latticed with a pattern reminiscent of the Moorish pigeon houses built into walls in Spain and northern Africa – hence the building's name, 'The Dovecote'. The nine honeycombed triangular 'belfries' sit on top of a building that was once part of a quadrangle.

Casa de la Vieja
Off the southeast corner of the Palacio del Gobernador is a small complex, largely rubble, known as the Casa de la Vieja (Old Woman's House). In front of it is a small *palapa* sheltering several large phalluses carved from stone.

SLEEPING & EATING
There is no town at Uxmal – only the archaeological site and several nearby hotels. Attractive lodging options are also available 16km south, in the quaint town of Santa Elena (opposite).

Rancho Uxmal (☎ 997-972-62-54; d $30; P ☒) This friendly hotel, located 2km north of the entrance to the ruins, has 23 basic, serviceable guestrooms, a swimming pool and a nice shaded restaurant.

Hotel Villas Arqueológicas Uxmal (☎ 997-976-20-20, in the US ☎ 800-258-2633, in France ☎ 801-80-28-03; www.clubmed.com; d $70; P 🏊 🍴) Located near the entrance to the ruins, this attractive Club Med–run hotel has a swimming pool, tennis courts and pleasant restaurant.

Lodge at Uxmal (☎ 997-976-21-02, in the US ☎ 800-235-4079; www.mayaland.com; d from $150; P 🏊 🍴) Mayaland Resorts' lodge, just opposite the entrance to the archaeological site, is Uxmal's most luxurious hotel. There are two pools and a restaurant-bar.

Hacienda Uxmal (☎ 997-976-20-12, in the US ☎ 800-235-4079; www.mayaland.com; d $185; P 🏊 🍴) This is another Mayaland Resort, 500m from the ruins and across the highway. It originally housed the archaeologists who explored and restored Uxmal. Wide, tiled verandas, high ceilings, lush gardens, a pretty swimming pool and tennis courts make this a very comfortable place to stay.

GETTING THERE & AWAY

Uxmal is 78km (1½ hours) from Mérida. The inland route between Mérida and Campeche passes Uxmal, and most buses coming from either city will drop you here. When you want to leave though, passing buses may be full (especially on Saturday and Monday).

ATS buses depart Mérida's Terminal de Segunda Clase at 8am daily, on a whirlwind excursion ($10) to the Ruta Puuc sites, Kabah and Uxmal, heading back from Uxmal's parking lot at 2:30pm. This 'tour' is transportation only, and the time spent at each site is enough to get only a nodding acquaintance.

Organized tours of Uxmal and other sites can be booked in Mérida (p922).

If you're going from Uxmal to Ticul, first take a northbound bus to Muna ($0.50, 20 minutes), from where you can catch one of the frequent buses to Ticul ($1, 30 minutes).

Santa Elena

Located 16km east of Uxmal and 7km north of Kabah, the sweet town of Santa Elena makes an excellent base from which to explore the many nearby archaeological sites of the Ruta Puuc (including Kabah, Sayil, Xlapak and Labná, and the Grutas de Loltún).

For lodging, the following two places are both special havens.

At **Bungalows Sacbé** (☎ 985-858-12-81; www.sacbebungalows.com.mx; Hwy 261; d $22-28), 1km south of town, the combination of Eden-like surroundings and the hosts' gentle nature makes it a sanctuary of palpable peace. There are eight very simple, clean and comfortable cabins, all with private bathroom and fans, set amid a botanical garden thriving with plant and bird life. The Mexican-French hosts, Edgar and Annette (both speak excellent English), can provide detailed information of the surrounding natural environment, local towns and archeological sites. A good breakfast is available ($4).

Situated on the southeastern edge of Santa Elena, the lovely B&B **Flycatcher Inn** (www.flycatcherinn.com; d $40-70, cottage $60) offers four sophisticated, artistically designed and decorated rooms, and one private cottage. The lush grounds are serene and the friendly owners, Kristine and Santiago (she American, he Yucatecan), offer a wealth of helpful visitor info and tips. Tropical breakfast is included.

There are two good eateries in town serving Yucatecan dishes: **El Chac-Mool** (☎ 997-971-0191; Calle 18 No 211; mains $5-7; ◷ 8am-8pm), and just off the main plaza, **La Central** (mains $5-7; ◷ noon-8pm).

Kabah

After Uxmal, Kabah (AD 750–950) was the most important city in the region. The **ruins** (admission $3; ◷ 8am-5pm) straddle Hwy 261. The guard shack-cum-souvenir shop (selling snacks and cold drinks) and the bulk of the restored ruins are on the east side of the highway.

The facade of **El Palacio de los Mascarones** (Palace of Masks) is an amazing sight, covered in nearly 300 masks of Chac-Mool, the rain god or sky serpent. Most of their huge curling noses are broken off; the best intact beak is at the building's south end. These curled up noses may have given the palace its modern Maya name, Codz Poop (Rolled Mat).

Once you're up to your ears in noses, head around back to check out the two restored **atlantes** (an atlas – plural 'atlantes' – is a male figure used as a supporting column). These are especially interesting as they're among the very few 3-D human figures you'll see at a Maya site. One is headless

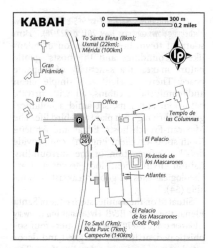

KABAH

To Santa Elena (8km);
Uxmal (22km);
Mérida (100km)

Gran
Pirámide

El Arco

Office

Templo de
las Columnas

El Palacio

Pirámide de
los Mascarones

Atlantes

El Palacio
de los Mascarones
(Codz Pop)

To Sayil (7km);
Ruta Puuc (7km);
Campeche (140km)

0 — 300 m
0 — 0.2 miles

and the other wears a jaguar mask atop his head. A third atlas stands by the office near the entrance.

From here be sure to check out **El Palacio** (The Palace), with its groups of decorative *columnillas* (little columns) on the upper part of the facade; these are a distinctive characteristic of Puuc architectural style. A couple of hundred meters through the jungle from here is **Templo de las Columnas**. This building has more rows of impressive decorative columns.

Across the highway from El Palacio, a path leads to the **Gran Pirámide** (Great Pyramid). And from the Great Pyramid the path ends at the impressive, restored **monumental arch**. It's said that the *sacbé* (cobbled and elevated ceremonial road) leading from here goes through the jungle all the way to Uxmal, terminating at a smaller arch; in the other direction it goes to Labná. Once, much of the Yucatán Peninsula was connected by these marvelous 'white roads' of rough limestone.

Kabah is 100km from Mérida, a ride of about two hours (see p933). Buses will usually make flag stops at the entrance to the ruins.

Ruta Puuc

Just 5km south of Kabah on Hwy 261, a road branches off to the east and winds past the ruins of Sayil, Xlapak and Labná, ending at the Grutas de Loltún. This is the Ruta Puuc, and its sites offer some marvel-

ous architectural detail and a deeper acquaintance with the Puuc Maya civilization, which flourished between about AD 750 and 950.

The most convenient way to visit the Ruta Puuc sites is by car; however, there is a reliable bus service that tours the route daily as well (see p936).

SAYIL

The ruins of **Sayil** (admission $3; ☉ 8am-5pm) are 4.5km from the junction of the Ruta Puuc with Hwy 261.

Sayil is best known for **El Palacio**, the huge three-tiered building with a facade some 85m long, reminiscent of the Minoan palace on Crete. The distinctive columns of Puuc architecture are used here over and over – as supports for the lintels, as decoration between doorways and as a frieze above them – alternating with huge stylized Chac-Mool masks and 'descending gods.'

Taking the path south from the palace for about 400m and bearing left, you come to the temple **El Mirador**, whose roosterlike roof-comb was once painted bright red. About 100m beyond El Mirador, beneath a protective *palapa*, is a stela bearing the relief of a fertility god with an enormous phallus.

LABNÁ

This is the site not to miss. Archaeologists believe that, at one point in the 9th century, some 3000 Maya lived at **Labná** (admission $3; ☉ 8am-5pm). To support such numbers in these arid hills, water was collected in *chultunes*. At Labná's peak there were some 60 *chultunes* in and around the city; several are still visible.

El Palacio, the first building you come to at Labná, is one of the longest in the Puuc region, and much of its interesting decorative carving is in good shape. On the west corner of the main structure's facade, is a serpent's head with a human face peering out from between its jaws, the symbol of the planet Venus. Toward the hill from this is an impressive Chac-Mool mask, and nearby is the lower half of a human figure (possibly a ballplayer) in loincloth and leggings.

The lower level has several more well-preserved Chac-Mool masks, and the upper level contains a large *chultún* that still holds water. The view from there, of the site and the hills beyond, is impressive.

YUCATÁN PENINSULA

From the palace a limestone-paved *sacbé* (ceremonial road) leads to **El Arco Labná**, which is best known for its magnificent arch, once part of a building that separated two courtyards. The corbeled structure, 3m wide and 6m high, is well preserved, and the reliefs decorating its upper facade are exuberantly Puuc in style.

Standing on the opposite side of the arch and separated from it by the *sacbé* is a pyramid known as **El Mirador**, topped by a temple. The pyramid itself is largely stone rubble. The temple, with its 5m-high roofcomb, is well positioned to be a lookout, hence its name.

GRUTAS DE LOLTÚN

Fifteen kilometers northeast of Labná, a sign points out the left turn to the Grutas de Loltún, 5km further northeast. The road passes through lush orchards and some banana and palm groves, a refreshing sight in this dry region.

The **Loltún Caverns** (admission $5; ⏰ 9am-5pm) is the largest, most interesting cave system on the Yucatán Peninsula, and a treasure trove of data for archaeologists. Carbon dating of artifacts found here reveals that humans used the caves 2500 years ago. Chest-high murals of hands, faces, animals and geometric motifs were apparent as recently as 20 years ago, but so many people have touched them that barely a trace remains. Now, visitors to the illuminated caves see mostly natural limestone formations, some of which are quite lovely.

To explore the labyrinth, you must take a scheduled guided tour at 9:30am, 11am, 12:30pm, 2pm, 3pm or 4pm. The service of the guides is included in the admission price, but since they receive little of that, an additional tip ($2 to $5 per person) is appreciated.

GETTING THERE & AWAY

Buses run frequently between Mérida and Oxkutzcab (pronounced 'osh-kootz-kahb') via Ticul. Loltún is 7km southwest of Oxkutzcab, and there is usually some transportation along the road. A taxi from Oxkutzcab may charge $7 or so, one way.

If you're driving from Loltún to Labná, turn right out of the Loltún parking lot and take the next road on the right, which passes Restaurant El Guerrero's driveway (do not take the road marked for Xul). After 5km turn right at the T-intersection to join the Ruta Puuc west.

Ticul

☎ 997 / pop 27,000

Ticul, 30km east of Uxmal and 14km northwest of Oxkutzcab, is the largest town in this ruin-rich region. It has decent hotels and restaurants, and good transportation. Although there is no public transportation to the Ruta Puuc from Ticul, it is possible to stay the night here and take an early morning bus to Muna, arriving there in time to catch a tour bus to the Ruta Puuc ruins. Ticul is also a center for fine *huipil* weaving, and ceramics made here from the local red clay are renowned throughout the Yucatán Peninsula.

Because of the number of Maya ruins in the vicinity from which to steal building blocks, and the number of Maya in the area needing conversion to Christianity, Franciscan friars built many churches in the region that is now southern Yucatán state. Among them is Ticul's **Iglesia de San Antonio de Padua**, construction of which dates from the late 16th century. Although looted on several occasions, the church has some original touches, among them the stone statues of friars in primitive style flanking the side entrances, and a Black Christ altarpiece ringed by crude medallions.

Saturday mornings in Ticul are picturesque: Calle 23 in the vicinity of the market is closed to motorized traffic, and the street

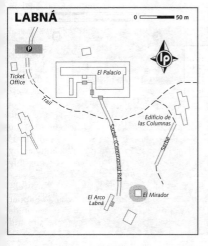

LABNÁ

0 ——— 50 m

P

Ticket Office

Trail

El Palacio

Edificio de las Columnas

Sacbé (Ceremonial Rd)

Sacbé

El Arco Labná

El Mirador

YUCATÁN PENINSULA

fills with three-wheeled cycles transporting shoppers between the market and their homes.

ORIENTATION & INFORMATION

Ticul's main street is Calle 23, sometimes called the Calle Principal, going from the highway northeast past the market to the main plaza, or 'Plaza Mayor'. Ticul's main street is Calle 23, sometimes called the Calle Principal, going from the highway northeast past the market to the main plaza. A post office faces the plaza, as do banks with ATMs and an Internet café; the bus terminal is less than 100m away. Diagonally opposite Plaza Mayor is the recently built Plaza de la Cultura, which is all cement and stone, but is nevertheless an agreeable place to take the evening breeze, enjoy the view of the church and greet passing townspeople.

SLEEPING

Hotel Plaza (☎ 972-04-84; www.hotelplazayucatan.com; cnr Calles 23 & 26; r with fan/air-con $30/35; P ❄) This is considered the nicest hotel in town. Rooms are very comfortable, and a large mango tree shades the courtyard restaurant.

Hotel San Antonio (☎ 927-19-83; cnr Calles 25A & 26; s/d $25/32; P ❄) The rooms in this newish hotel have comfortable beds, good air-con, TV and telephone. The restaurant is decent too.

Hotel Sierra Sosa (☎ 972-00-08; Calle 26 No 199A; s/d with fan $15/20, with air-con $19/22; ❄) This clean and friendly hotel is just northwest

of the plaza. Rooms in the back tend to be a little dark.

EATING

Restaurant Los Almendros (☎ 972-00-21; Carretera a Chetumal; mains $5-12) Near the southern entrance of town, the original Almendros (now with fancier branches in Mérida and Cancún) specializes in hearty Yucatecan food. The original chefs at this restaurant are credited with having invented the Yucatecan specialty *poc-chuc* (pork with tomatoes and onions in a sour-orange sauce). Whether they invented it or not, they have certainly perfected the recipe.

Restaurant Plaza (☎ 972-04-84; Hotel Plaza, cnr Calles 23 & 26) A friendly, open-air café in the Hotel Plaza serving Yucatecan fare. Makes a cheery breakfast stop.

Pizzería La Gondola (☎ 972-01-12; cnr Calles 23 & 26A; pizza $5-10; ❤ 9am-11pm) Serving good pizza and standard pasta dishes, this is the only place open late.

Restaurant El Colorín (Calle 26 No 199B; set meals $4) For a tasty homemade meal, try this cheap restaurant, half a block northwest of the plaza.

El Mercado (Calle 28A) Ticul's lively market provides all the ingredients for picnics and snacks. It also has lots of wonderful eateries.

GETTING THERE & AWAY

Ticul's **bus terminal** (Calle 24) is behind the massive church. Mayab runs frequent 2nd-class buses between Mérida and Ticul ($3.50, two

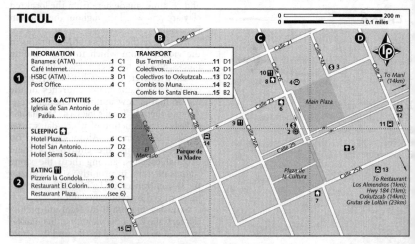

TICUL

0 — 200 m
0 — 0.1 miles

INFORMATION	
Banamex (ATM)	1 C1
Café Internet	2 C2
HSBC (ATM)	3 D1
Post Office	4 C1

SIGHTS & ACTIVITIES	
Iglesia de San Antonio de Padua	5 D2

SLEEPING	
Hotel Plaza	6 C1
Hotel San Antonio	7 D2
Hotel Sierra Sosa	8 C1

EATING	
Pizzería la Gondola	9 C1
Restaurant El Colorín	10 C1
Restaurant Plaza	(see 6)

TRANSPORT	
Bus Terminal	11 D1
Colectivos	12 D1
Colectivos to Oxkutzcab	13 D2
Combis to Muna	14 B2
Combis to Santa Elena	15 B2

El Mercado
Parque de la Madre
Main Plaza
Plaza de la Cultura

To Maní (14km)
To Restaurant Los Almendros (1km); Hwy 184 (1km); Oxkutzcab (14km); Grutas de Loltún (23km)

hours) from 4:30am to 9:45pm. There are 11 buses to Felipe Carrillo Puerto ($9, 4½ hours), frequent buses to Oxkutzcab ($0.70, 20 minutes), in addition to five daily to Chetumal ($13, 6½ hours). There are also seven Mayab buses to Cancún daily ($17, six hours), three of which also serve Tulum ($12, eight hours) and Playa del Carmen ($15, seven hours). Super Expresso has a less-frequent 1st-class service to some of these destinations.

Colectivos depart from the intersection of Calles 24 and 25 between 5am and 7pm, and head directly to Mérida's Parque de San Juan ($1, 1½ hours). *Colectivos* for Oxkutzcab ($0.80, 30 minutes) leave from Calle 25A on the south side of the church between 7am and 8:30pm.

Combis going to Santa Elena ($0.80, 20 minutes), the village between Uxmal and Kabah, depart from Calle 30 just south of Calle 25, between 6:15am and 7:45pm. They take Hwy 02 and drop you off to catch another bus northwest to Uxmal (15km) or south to Kabah (3.5km). You can also take a combi or bus to Muna on Hwy 261 and another south to Uxmal (16km).

Ruta Puuc–bound travelers can catch one of the early-morning buses from Ticul to Muna and pick up the ATS tour bus ($5) for Labná, Sayil, Xlapak, Kabah and Uxmal at 9am on its way from Mérida. It returns to Muna at 3pm. Any of the buses leaving Ticul between 6am and 8am for Muna ($1) will get you there in time to catch the Ruta Puuc bus (all 2nd-class Mérida-bound buses stop in Muna). Combis for Muna ($1) leave from the southeast corner of Calle 23 at the corner of Calle 28.

Those headed east to Quintana Roo and the Caribbean coast by car can take Hwy 184, which runs from Ticul all the way to Felipe Carrillo Puerto (210km).

DZIBILCHALTÚN

Lying about 17km due north of central Mérida, **Dzibilchaltún** (Place of Inscribed Flat Stones; admission $6; ✆ 8am-5pm) was the longest continuously utilized Maya administrative and ceremonial city, serving the Maya from around 1500 BC until the European conquest in the 1540s. At the height of its greatness, Dzibilchaltún covered 15 sq km. Some 00 structures were mapped by archaeologists in the 1960s; few of these have been excavated and restored

The **Templo de las Siete Muñecas** (Temple of the Seven Dolls), which got its name from seven grotesque dolls discovered here during excavations, is a 1km walk from the central plaza. It would be most unimpressive, but for its precise astronomical orientation: the rising and setting sun of the equinoxes 'lights up' the temple's windows and doors, making them blaze like beacons, signaling the year's important turning points.

The **Cenote Xlacah**, now a public swimming hole, is more than 40m deep. In 1958 a National Geographic Society diving expedition recovered more than 30,000 Maya artifacts, many of ritual significance, from the cenote. The most interesting of these are now on display in the site's museum. South of the cenote is **Estructura 44**, which at 130m is one of the longest Maya structures in existence.

Parking costs $1. Minibuses and *colectivo* taxis depart frequently from Mérida's Parque de San Juan, on Calle 69 between Calles 62 and 64, for the village of Dzibilchaltún Ruinas ($0.80, 30 minutes), only a little over 1km from the museum.

PROGRESO
☎ 969 / pop 55,000
If Mérida's heat has you dying for a quick beach fix, or you want to see the longest *muelle* (wharf; 7km) in Mexico, head to Progreso (also known as Puerto Progreso). Otherwise there's not a lot here to warrant more than a short stay. As with other Gulf beaches, the water is murky, though the beach is actually quite nice – well-groomed and long – and the white sand is enjoyable until the afternoon, when whipping winds start to fling it in your eyes. None of this deters *meridanos* from coming in droves on weekends, especially in summer.

Progreso's street grid confusingly employs two different numbering systems, 50 numbers apart. The city center's streets are numbered in the 60s (10s), 70s (20s) and 80s (30s). This text uses the high numbers. Even-numbered streets run east–west and decrease by twos eastward; odd ones decrease by twos northward. The bus terminal is west of Calle 82, a block north (toward the water) of the main plaza. It's six short blocks from the plaza on Calle 80 to the waterfront Malecón (Calle 69) and *muelle*; along the way are a few banks with ATMs.

Sleeping & Eating

Casa Quixote (☎ 935-29-09; www.casaquixote.com; Calle 23; r $40-80; P ❋ ❧) Once an aristocrat's summer home, this elegant yellow house, half a block from the beach, is now a pleasant B&B. The Texan owners cook up healthy breakfasts (included in the rates) and invite you – and nonguests – to their Saturday-night barbeque.

Casa Isidora (☎ 935-45-95; www.casaisidora.com; Calle 21; r $35-45; P ❋ ❧) A grand old home converted into a very sweet inn with ample high-ceilinged guest rooms. There's a garden and pool. Breakfast is included.

Hotel Real del Mar (☎ 935-07-98; cnr Malecón & Calle 70; d with fan/air-con $30/45; ❋) This place features 13 worn but comfortable rooms, with various configurations of beds and views. Wheelchair-accessible rooms are available.

Restaurant Los Pelícanos (mains $5-15) Part of the Hotel Real del Mar, this restaurant has a *palapa*-topped terrace, sea views and a good menu with moderate prices. The grilled fish main dishes are especially generous.

Le Saint Bonnet (☎ 935-22-99; cnr Malecón & Calle 78; mains $5-8) This is where locals go for seafood. The fish is fresh and inexpensive.

Restaurant El Cordobes (Calle 80 & 81; mains $4-8) On the plaza, this restaurant is housed in a 100-year-old building with lots of character. The food is decidedly Yucatecan and decidedly good.

Getting There & Away

Progreso is 33km due north of Mérida, along a fast four-lane highway that's basically a continuation of the Paseo de Montejo. If you're driving, head north on the Paseo and follow signs for Progreso. Buses to and from Mérida arrive at the **bus terminal** (Calle 79). For bus departures from Mérida, see p927.

CELESTÚN

☎ 988 / pop 6200

Celestún is in the midst of a wildlife sanctuary abounding in resident and migratory waterfowl – flamingos the star attraction. And, because it's sheltered by the peninsula's southward curve, there's an abundance of marine life. Celestún makes a good beach-and-bird day trip from Mérida, and it's also a great place to kick back and do nothing for a few days. Fishing boats dot the white-sand that stretches to the north for kilometers, a fine place to watch the sun set into the sea.

Calle 11 is the road into town (due west from Mérida) ending at Calle 12, the dirt road paralleling the beach along which lie most of the restaurants and hotels.

Flamingo Tours

The Reserva de la Biosfera Ría Celestún's 591 sq km are home to a huge variety of animal life, including a large flamingo colony.

Given the winds, the best time to see birds is in the morning, though from 4pm onward they tend to concentrate in one area after the day's feeding, which can also make for good viewing. There are two places to hire a boat for bird-watching: from the bridge on the highway into town (about 1.5km from the beach) and from the beach itself.

The best months to see the flamingos are from March to September. Tours from the beach last 2½ to three hours and begin with a ride south along the coast for several kilometers, during which you can expect to see egrets, herons, cormorants, sandpipers and many other species of bird. The boat then turns into the mouth of the *ría* (estuary) and passes through a 'petrified forest,' where tall coastal trees once belonging to a freshwater ecosystem were killed by saltwater intrusion long ago, but remain standing, hard as rock.

Continuing up the *ría* takes you under the highway bridge where the other tours begin, and beyond which are the flamingos. Depending on the tide, the hour and the season, you may see hundreds or thousands of the colorful birds. Don't encourage your captain to approach them too closely; a startled flock taking wing can result in injuries and deaths (for the birds). In addition to taking you to the flamingos, the captain will wend through a 200m-long mangrove tunnel and go to one or both (as time and inclination allow) of the freshwater cenotes welling into the saltwater of the estuary where you can take a refreshing dip.

The asking price for this type of tour is $120 per boatload (up to six passengers). Boats depart from several beachside spots including from outside Restaurant Celestún at the foot of Calle 11. The restaurant's beachfront *palapa* is a pleasant place to wait for a group to accumulate.

Tours from the bridge, where there is parking lot, ticket booth and a place to wait for fellow passengers, are cheaper. For $6 per boat (again, up to six passengers) plus

$2 per passenger, you get the latter part of the tour described earlier: flamingos, mangrove tunnel and spring. It's also possible to tour from the bridge south to the 'petrified forest' and back (also $40), or to combine the two (each lasts about 1¼ hours).

With either operation, bridge or beach, your captain may or may not speak English. English-speaking guides can be hired at the bridge; this may reduce the maximum possible number of passengers. Bring snacks, water and sunscreen for the longer tours, and cash for any of them. There is no bank in town, and tour operators don't accept credit cards or traveler's checks.

Mérida's **Nómadas Youth Hostel** (☎ 999-924-52-23; www.nomadastravel.com; Calle 62 No 433, Mérida) books day trips to see the flamingos for around $30, leaving Mérida at 9am and returning at 5pm. They include transportation, guide, a boat tour and lunch. For details, see p922.

Sleeping

Except for the first option, Celestún's hotels are all on Calle 12, within a short walk of one another. Try to book ahead if you want a sea view, especially on weekends.

Eco-Paraíso Xixim (☎ 916-21-00; www.ecoparaiso com; d $200; ⓟ ⓡ) This remote eco-resort is at the end of a dirt road, 9km north of Celestún. Fifteen individual, lovely *palapas* are nestled between miniature coconut palms along a private 5km stretch of virgin beach. It could be considered just another luxury point, but its eco-centric policies set it apart. All gray and black water is recycled, and most of the energy is derived from solar panels. The surrounding natural environment is protected and respected, which allows turtles to safely breed here. Amenities include a very good restaurant, bar, pool, and guided ecotours. Check the website for less expensive, all-inclusive packages.

Eco Hotel Flamingos Playa (in Mérida ☎ 999-29-57-08; Calle 12; d $44; ⓧ ⓛ ⓡ) About three blocks north of Calle 11, the newish Flamingos has decent rooms with air-con, fan, TV and purified water. There's a small beachside pool, a restaurant-bar and Internet facilities.

Ria Celestún Hostel (☎ 916-21-70; www.homecasa et; cnr Calles 12 & 13; dm $7, d $15) Having started out with so much promise, this hostel has once slipped. With hope it will clean up

its act (literally) and get back to its former level of hygiene and comfort. There's a full kitchen and a nice communal area, with books, games and a TV. Internet access is available, as are bike rentals. Marcos, the friendly owner and a native of Celestún, can arrange inexpensive tours of the area.

Hotel María del Carmen (☎ 916-21-70; Calle 12; d with fan/air-con $26/31; ⓧ) South of Calle 11, this hotel has 14 clean, standard beachfront rooms. Those on the upper floors have balconies facing the sea.

Eating & Drinking

Celestún's specialties are crab, octopus and, of course, fresh fish. Service and decor vary from restaurant to restaurant, but the menus and prices are all very similar. Many restaurants have outdoor seating on the beach.

El Lobo (breakfast & mains $4-7) This Dutch-owned establishment on the southwest edge of the plaza is a great breakfast spot, with good espresso drinks. Later in the day you can come back for pizza or pasta.

La Playita (mains $5-7) On the beach, just past the foot of Calle 11, this friendly restaurant offers large portions of fresh seafood.

Restaurante Chivirico (cnr Calles 11 & 12; mains $5-7) Come here for good food and a good laugh. English translations on the menu include 'fish to I wet of garlic' (*pescado en mojo de ajo…*fish in garlic sauce), which is very good. So is the crab salad.

Getting There & Away

Buses from Mérida head for Celestún ($4, two hours) 15 times daily between 5am and 8pm from the Terminal Noreste. The route terminates at Celestún's plaza, a block inland from Calle 12. Returning to Mérida, buses run from 5am to 8pm daily.

By car from Mérida, the best route to Celestún is via the road out of Umán.

IZAMAL

☎ 988 / pop 14,500

In ancient times, Izamal was a center for the worship of the supreme Maya god, Itzamná, and the sun god, Kinich-Kakmó. A dozen temple pyramids were devoted to these or other gods. It was probably these bold expressions of Maya religiosity that provoked the Spaniards to build the enormous Franciscan monastery that stands today at the heart of this town.

Just under 70km east of Mérida, Izamal is a quiet, colonial gem of a town, nicknamed La Ciudad Amarilla (the Yellow City) for the yellow paint that brightens the walls of practically every building. It is easily explored on foot and makes a great day trip from Mérida.

Sights

When the Spaniards conquered Izamal, they destroyed the major Maya temple, the Ppapp-Hol-Chac pyramid, and in 1533 began to build from its stones one of the first monasteries in the New World. Work on **Convento de San Antonio de Padua** (admission free; ◷ 6am-8pm) was finished in 1561. Under the monastery's arcades, look for building stones with an unmistakable mazelike design; these were clearly taken from the earlier Maya temple.

The monastery's principal church is the **Santuario de la Virgen de Izamal**. Here the **Atrium**, a huge arcaded courtyard, is where the **fiesta of the Virgin of Izamal** takes place each August 15; and where a dramatic sound-and-light show ($4) is presented at 8:30pm on Tuesday, Thursday, Friday and Saturday nights.

Three of the town's original 12 Maya **pyramids** have been partially restored so far. The largest is the enormous **Kinich-Kakmó** (free admission; ◷ 8am-5pm), three blocks north of the monastery.

Sleeping & Eating

Macanché B&B (☎ 954-02-87; www.macanche.com; Calle 22 No 305; d $30-65; ⚇ ⛱) About three long blocks east of the monastery, this charming B&B, run by welcoming hosts Emily and Alfred, has a cluster of cottages in a jungle setting, with 13 pretty rooms, many with kitchenettes. There's a unique rock-bottom pool as well as a *temascal* steam bath. Services include yoga classes and professional massage. A big complimentary breakfast is also offered.

Hotel Canto (d $17) Directly in front of the monastery, the Canto's location and price are the only things recommending it. The rooms, though tidy and colorful, are pretty musty.

Kinich (☎ 954-04-89; Calle 27; mains $5-10) Located next to the Kinich-Kakmó archeological site, this very friendly restaurant serves excellent traditional Yucatecan dishes in a pretty garden-side setting.

El Toro (Calle 33 No 303; mains $3-7; ◷ Tue-Sun) A cheery place located near the main plaza, serving Yucatecan food in a friendly setting.

If you have a car you may want to explore the small town of Sudzal, 8km south of Izamal. The main draw here, aside from its inherent Maya charm, is the following hacienda.

Hacienda San Antonio Chalanté (☎ 999-109-40-92; www.haciendachalante.com; r from $40-70) Unlike the fussy opulence of so many restored haciendas, this 700-acre spread is still partly a working ranch and offers authentic rugged *rancho* appeal. The 10 rooms come in an assortment of sizes and styles – all very attractive. If you like, owner and accomplished equestrian, Diane, can give you a horseback tour of the estate.

Tacos al Fagon (mains $3-5) The best (and pretty much only) eatery in Sudzal is run by the same folks as Hacienda San Antonio Chalanté and serves tasty BBQ.

Getting There & Away

Oriente operates frequent buses between Mérida and Izamal ($3, 1½ hrs) from the 2nd-class terminal. There are buses from Valladolid ($3, two hours) as well. Coming from Chichén Itzá you must change buses at Hóctun. Izamal's bus terminal is just one block west of the monastery.

Other services from Izamal include buses to Tizimín ($5, 2½ hrs) and Cancún ($9 six hours).

Driving by car from the west, turn north at Hóctun to reach Izamal; from the east turn north at Kantunil.

CHICHÉN ITZÁ

The most famous and best restored of the Yucatán Peninsula's Maya sites, Chichén Itzá will awe even the most jaded visitor. Many mysteries of the Maya astronomical calendar are made clear when one understands the design of the 'time temples' here. Other than a few minor passageways, El Castillo is now the only structure at the site you're allowed to climb or enter.

At the vernal and autumnal equinoxes (March 20–21 and September 21–22), the morning and afternoon sun produces light-and-shadow illusion of the serpent ascending or descending the side of El Castillo's staircase. Chichén is mobbed on these dates, however, making it difficult to get close enough to see. The illusion is almost as good in the week preceding and following each equinox, and is re-created nightly in the sound-and-light show year-round.

History

Most archaeologists agree that the first major settlement at Chichén Itzá, during the late classic period, was pure Maya. In about the 9th century the city was largely abandoned, for reasons unknown. It was resettled around the late 10th century, and Mayanists believe that shortly thereafter it was invaded by the Toltecs, who had migrated from their central highlands capital of Tula, north of Mexico City. Toltec culture was fused with that of the Maya, incorporating the cult of Quetzalcóatl (Kukulcán, in Maya). Throughout the city, you will see images of both Chac-Mool, the Maya rain god, and Quetzalcóatl, the plumed serpent.

The substantial fusion of highland central Mexican and Puuc architectural styles makes Chichén unique among the Yucatán Peninsula's ruins. The fabulous El Castillo and the Plataforma de Venus are outstanding architectural works, built during the height of Toltec cultural input.

The warlike Toltecs contributed more than their architectural skills to the Maya. They elevated human sacrifice to a near obsession, and there are numerous carvings of the bloody ritual in Chichén demonstrating this. After a Maya leader moved his political capital to Mayapán, while keeping Chichén as his religious capital, Chichén Itzá fell into decline. Why it was subsequently abandoned in the 14th century is a mystery, but the once-great city remained the site of Maya pilgrimages for many years.

Orientation

Most of Chichén's lodgings, restaurants and services are ranged along 1km of highway in the village of Pisté, to the western side of the ruins. It's 1.5km from the ruins' main entrance to the first hotel (Pirámide Inn) in Pisté. Hwy 180 is known as Calle 15A as it crosses through Pisté.

Information

The main entrance to **Chichén Itzá** (Mouth of the Well of the Itzáes; admission Mon-Sat $9, Sun $4; 🕑 8am-6pm summer, 8am-5:30pm winter) is the western one, with a large parking lot (parking $1) and a big, modern entrance building, the **Unidad de Servicios** (🕑 8am-10pm). The Unidad has a small but worthwhile **museum** (🕑 8am-5pm), with sculptures, reliefs, artifacts, and explanations of these in Spanish, English and French.

The Auditorio Chilam Balam, next to the museum, sometimes has video screenings about Chichén and other Mexican sites. (The picture quality is awful, but the air-con is great.) Facilities include two bookstores with an assortment of guides and maps, a currency-exchange desk and, around the corner from the ticket desk, a free *guardería de equipaje* (left-luggage facility) where you can leave your belongings while you explore the site.

The 45-minute **sound-and-light show** is performed beneath El Castillo (below). If you don't have a ruins ticket the cost is $3, which is applicable toward the admission price for the following day. Performances are held at 8pm in summer and 7pm in winter.

Visiting the Ruins

EL CASTILLO

As you approach from the turnstiles at the Unidad de Servicios into the archaeological zone, **El Castillo** (also called the Pyramid of Kukulcán) rises before you in all its grandeur. The first temple here was pre-Toltec, built around AD 800, but the present 25m-high structure, built over the old one, has the plumed serpent sculpted along the stairways and Toltec warriors represented in the doorway carvings at the top of the temple.

The pyramid is actually the Maya calendar formed in stone. Each of El Castillo's nine levels is divided in two by a staircase, making 18 separate terraces that commemorate the 18 20-day months of the Vague Year. The four stairways have 91 steps each; add the top platform and the total is 365, the number of days in the year. On each facade of the pyramid are 52 flat panels, which are reminders of the 52 years in the Calendar Round.

To top it off, during the spring and autumn equinoxes, light and shadow form a series of triangles on the side of the north staircase that mimic the creep of a serpent (note the carved serpent's heads flanking the bottom of the staircase). The serpent ascends in March and descends in September.

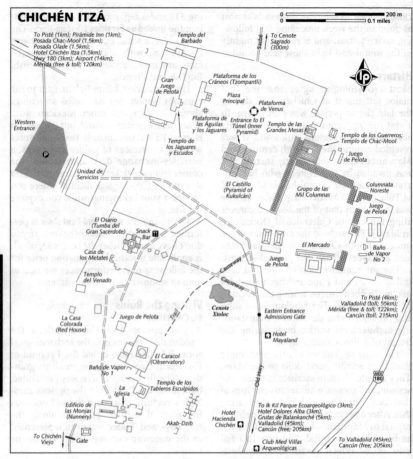

CHICHÉN ITZÁ

0 _____ 200 m
0 _____ 0.1 miles

To Pisté (1km); Pirámide Inn (1km);
Posada Chac-Mool (1.5km);
Posada Olade (1.5km);
Hotel Chichén Itza (1.5km);
Hwy 180 (3km); Airport (14km);
Mérida (free & toll); 120km)

Templo del Barbado

Gran Juego de Pelota

Templo del Barbado

Plataforma de los Cráneos (Tzompantli)

Plaza Principal

Plataforma de Venus

To Cenote Sagrado (300m)

Plataforma de las Águilas y los Jaguares

Entrance to El Túnel (Inner Pyramid)

Templo de las Grandes Mesas

Western Entrance

Templo de los Jaguares y Escudos

El Castillo (Pyramid of Kukulcán)

Grupo de las Mil Columnas

Templo de los Guerreros; Templo de Chac-Mool

Juego de Pelota

Columnata Noreste

Juego de Pelota

Unidad de Servicios

El Osario (Tumba del Gran Sacerdote)

Snack Bar

Casa de los Metates

El Mercado

Baño de Vapor No 2

Juego de Pelota

Templo del Venado

Causeway

Causeway

To Pisté (4km);
Valladolid (toll; 55km);
Mérida (free & toll; 122km);
Cancún (toll; 215km)

La Casa Colorada (Red House)

Juego de Pelota

Trail

Cenote Xtoloc

Eastern Entrance Admissions Gate

Hotel Mayaland

El Caracol (Observatory)

Baño de Vapor No 1

La Iglesia

Templo de los Tableros Esculpidos

Edificio de las Monjas (Nunnery)

Akab-Dzib

To Ik Kil Parque Ecoarqeológico (3km);
Hotel Dolores Alba (3km);
Grutas de Balankanché (5km);
Valladolid (45km);
Cancún (free; 205km)

To Chichén Viejo

Gate

Hotel Hacienda Chichén

Old Hwy

MEX 180

Club Med Villas Arqueológicas

To Valladolid (45km);
Cancún (free; 205km)

The older pyramid, inside El Castillo, boasts a red jaguar throne with inlaid eyes and spots of jade, and it also holds a Chac-Mool figure. The entrance to **El Túnel** (11am-3pm & 4-4:45pm), the passage up to the throne, is at the base of El Castillo's north side.

GRAN JUEGO DE PELOTA

The great ball court, the largest and most impressive in Mexico, is only one of the city's eight courts, indicative of the importance of the games held here. The court is flanked by temples at either end and bounded by towering parallel walls with stone rings cemented up high.

There is evidence that the ball game may have changed over the years. Some carvings show players with padding on their elbows and knees, and it is thought that they played a soccerlike game with a hard rubber ball, the use of hands forbidden. Other carvings show players wielding bats; it appears that if a player hit the ball through one of the stone hoops, his team was declared the winner. It may be that during the Toltec period the losing captain, and perhaps his teammates as well, were sacrificed. Along the walls of the ball court are stone reliefs, including scenes of players being decapitated.

The court's acoustics are amazing – a conversation at one end can be heard 135m away at the other, and a clap produces multiple loud echoes.

TEMPLO DEL BARBADO & TEMPLO DE LOS JAGUARES Y ESCUDOS

The structure at the northern end of the ball court, called the **Temple of the Bearded Man** after a carving inside of it, has some finely sculpted pillars and reliefs of flowers, birds and trees. The **Temple of the Jaguars and Shields**, built atop the southeast corner of the ball court's wall, has some columns with carved rattlesnakes and tablets with etched jaguars. Inside are faded mural fragments depicting a battle.

PLATAFORMA DE LOS CRÁNEOS

The **Platform of Skulls** ('*tzompantli*' in Náhuatl) is between the Templo de los Jaguares and El Castillo. You can't mistake it, because the T-shaped platform is festooned with carved skulls and eagles tearing open the chests of men to eat their hearts. In ancient days this platform held the heads of sacrificial victims.

PLATAFORMA DE LAS ÁGUILAS Y LOS JAGUARES

Adjacent to the *tzompantli*, the carvings on the **Platform of the Eagles and Jaguars** depicts those animals gruesomely grabbing human hearts in their claws. It is thought that this platform was part of a temple dedicated to the military legions responsible for capturing sacrificial victims.

CENOTE SAGRADO

A 300m rough stone road runs north (a five-minute walk) to the huge sunken well that gave this city its name. The **Sacred Cenote** is an awesome natural well, some 60m in diameter and 35m deep. The walls between the summit and the water's surface are ensnared in tangled vines and other vegetation.

GRUPO DE LAS MIL COLUMNAS

Comprising the **Templo de los Guerreros** (Temple of the Warriors), **Templo de Chac-Mool** (Temple of Chac-Mool) and **Baño de Vapor** (Sweat House or Steam Bath), this group, behind El Castillo, takes its name (Group of the Thousand Columns) from the forest of pillars stretching south and east.

EL OSARIO

The Ossuary, otherwise known as the Bonehouse or the **Tumba del Gran Sacerdote** (High Priest's Grave), is a ruined pyramid south-

west of El Castillo. As with most of the buildings in this southern section, the architecture is more Puuc than Toltec. It's notable for the serpent heads at the base of its staircases.

EL CARACOL

Called **El Caracol** (the Snail) by the Spaniards, for its interior spiral staircase, this observatory is one of the most fascinating and important of all the Chichén Itzá buildings. Its circular design resembles some central highlands structures, although, surprisingly, not those of Toltec Tula. In a fusion of architectural styles and religious imagery, there are Maya Chac-Mool raingod masks over four external doors facing the cardinal directions. The windows in the observatory's dome are aligned with the appearance of certain stars at specific dates. From the dome the priests decreed the times for rituals, celebrations, cornplanting and harvests.

EDIFICIO DE LAS MONJAS & LA IGLESIA

Thought by archaeologists to have been a palace for Maya royalty, the so-called **Edificio de las Monjas** (Nunnery), with its myriad rooms, resembled a European convent to the conquistadors, hence their name for the building. The building's dimensions are imposing: its base is 60m long, 30m wide and 20m high. The construction is Maya rather than Toltec, although a Toltec sacrificial stone stands in front of the building. A smaller adjoining building to the east, known as **La Iglesia** (the Church), is covered almost entirely with carvings.

AKAB-DZIB

On the path east of the Nunnery, the Puuc-style **Akab-Dzib** is thought by some archaeologists to be the most ancient structure excavated here. The central chambers date from the 2nd century. The name means 'Obscure Writing' in Maya and refers to the south-side annex door, whose lintel depicts a priest with a vase etched with hieroglyphics that have never been translated.

GRUTAS DE BALANKANCHÉ

In 1959, a guide to the Chichén ruins was exploring a cave on his day off when he came upon a narrow passageway. He followed the passageway for 300m, meandering through a series of caverns. In each, perched on mounds amid scores of glistening stalactites, were hundreds of ceremonial treasures the Maya had placed there 800 years earlier: ritual metates and *manos* (grinding stones), incense burners and pots. In the years following the discovery, the ancient ceremonial objects were removed and studied. Supposedly all the objects here are the originals, returned and placed exactly where they were found.

The **Grutas de Balankanché** (adult/child $5/free; ✆ 9am-5pm) are located 5km east of the ruins of Chichén Itzá, on the highway to Cancún. Compulsory 40-minute tours (minimum six people) are accompanied by poorly recorded narrations: English (11am, 1pm and 3pm); Spanish (9am, noon, 2pm and 4pm); and French (10am).

IK KIL PARQUE ECOARQUEOLÓGICO

A little over 3km east of the eastern entrance to the ruins is **Ik Kil Parque Ecoarqueológico** (✆ 985-851-00-00; adult/child $4/2; ✆ 9am-5pm), whose cenote has been developed into a divine swimming spot. Small cascades of water plunge from the high limestone roof, which is ringed by greenery. A good buffet lunch costs an extra $6. Get your swim in by no later than 1pm to beat the tour groups.

Sleeping

BUDGET

Pirámide Inn (✆ 985-851-01-15; www.piramideinn.com; Calle 15A No 30; campsites per person $4, d from $35 P ✖ ✆) This hotel on the west side of Pisté is the most attractive bargain in town. Campers may pitch a tent or hang a hammock under a shaded *palapa*; they also have use of clean, shared bathrooms and showers. The hotel rooms are ample and clean. The good restaurant offers lots of veggie options.

Posada Olalde (✆ 985-851-00-86; Calle 6; s/d $15/20) Two blocks south of the highway by Artesanías Guayacán, this is the best of Pisté's several small pensions, offering seven clean, quiet and attractive rooms. There are four rustic bungalows on the premises as well, and the friendly manager speaks good English.

Posada Chac-Mool (✆ 985-851-02-70; Calle 15A; d $37; ✖) Just east of the Hotel Chichén Itzá, on the opposite (south) side of the highway in Pisté, the Chac-Mool has basic doubles.

MIDRANGE

Club Med Villas Arqueológicas (✆ 985-851-00-34; in the US 800-258-2633, in France 801 802 803; www.clubmed .com; d $85; P ✖ ✆) This is the only midrange-priced hotel next to the ruins, and is only 300m from the east entrance. It is an exact clone of the Club Med villas at Cobá and Uxmal, except that the beds are larger and the rooms smaller. The grounds are lush, and there's a relaxing poolside bar and good restaurant.

Hotel Dolores Alba (✆ 985-858-15-55; www.do loresalba.com; Hwy 180 Km 122; d $44; P ✖ ✆) This hotel is across the highway from Cenote Ik Kil, just over 3km east of the eastern entrance to the ruins, and 2km west of the Grutas de Balankanché. Its 40 rooms are simple but pleasingly decorated and face two inviting swimming pools. There's a restaurant, and staff will transport you to (but not from) the Chichén ruins.

Hotel Chichén Itzá (✆ 985-851-00-22; www.maya land.com; Calle 15A No 45; d $40-60; P ✖ ✆) On the west side of Pisté, this place has 42 pleasant rooms with tile floors and old-style brick-tile ceilings. Rooms in the upper range face the pool and nicely landscaped grounds. Breakfast is included.

TOP END

Hotel Mayaland (✆ 998-887-24-50, in the US 800-235-4079; www.mayaland.com; d $150, bungalows from $200; P ✖ ✆) Less than 100m from the ruins' main entrance, this hotel was built around 1923 and is the most gracious in Chichén's vicinity, with multiple pools and restaurants, and vast green grounds.

Hotel Hacienda Chichén (in Mérida ✆ 999-924-21-50, in the US 800-624-8451; www.haciendachichen.com; d from $140; P ✖ ✆) About 200m further from Hotel Mayaland, this is an elegant converted colonial estate that dates from the 16th century. It was here that the archaeologists who excavated Chichén during the 1920s lived. Their bungalows have been refurbished, new ones have been built and a swimming pool has been added.

Eating

The highway through Pisté is lined with more than 20 small restaurants. The cheapest are the market eateries on the main plaza opposite the huge tree. The others are arranged along the highway from the town square to the Pirámide Inn. Any of the *pollo asado* (roast chicken) joints along the way consistently deliver juicy finger-lickin' flavor.

Restaurant Hacienda Xaybe'h (buffet lunch & dinner $10-15) Set back from the highway opposite the Hotel Chichén Itzá, this big restaurant has decent food. Diners can use its swimming pool for free.

El Carrousel (mains $4-6) On Calle 15 near Pisté's main plaza, this is a popular local restaurant specializing in Yucatecan dishes, such as *sopa de lima* (lime soup) and *pollo pibil* (chicken wrapped in banana leaves).

Restaurant y Cocina Económica Chichén Itzá (mains $3-5) Also on Calle 15 near Pisté's main plaza, this simple place serves good sandwiches, omelets and enchiladas.

Getting There & Away

A modern airport lies about 14km east of Pisté. At the time of research it was yet to receive anything other than local charter flights.

When all goes well, Oriente's 2nd-class buses pass daily through Pisté bound for Mérida ($4.50, 2½ hours, hourly between 7:30am and 9:30pm). Oriente buses go to and from Valladolid ($1.50, 50 minutes, hourly between 7:30am and 8:30pm) and Cancún ($8, four hours, hourly between 7:30am and 8:30pm). A bus travels once daily at 1.30am to and from Chiquilá ($7, four hours to reach Isla Holbox).

First-class bus departures include the following:

Destination	Price	Duration	Frequency
Cancún	$12	2½hr	once daily at 4:30pm
Cobá	$5	1½hr	twice daily at 8am and 4:30pm
Mérida	$6.25	1¾hr	twice daily at 2:30pm and 5pm)
Playa del Carmen	$15	3½hr	twice daily at 8am and 4:30pm
Tulum	$7.50	2½hr	twice daily at 8am and 4:30pm

Shared vans to Valladolid (40 minutes, $1.75) pass through town regularly.

Getting Around

Buses passing through Pisté stop near the east and west sides of town; during Chichén Itzá's opening hours they also stop at the ruins (check with the driver), and they will take passengers from town for about $0.60 when there's room. For a bit more, 2nd-class buses will also take you to the Hotel Dolores Alba/Cenote Ik Kil and the Grutas de Balankanché (be sure to specify your destination when buying your ticket).

There is a taxi stand near the west end of town; the asking price to the ruins is $2.75. There are sometimes taxis at Chichén's parking lot, but make advance arrangements if you want to be sure of a ride.

VALLADOLID

☎ 985 / pop 40,000

Valladolid is a relatively small and affordable place, which is manageable to get around. It has an easy pace of life, many handsome colonial buildings, and several fine hotels and restaurants. It's a perfect place to stop and spend a day or three getting to know the real Yucatán, and it makes a good base from which to visit the surrounding area, including Chichén Itzá.

History

Valladolid was once the Maya ceremonial center of Zací (pronounced 'sah-*kee*'). The initial attempt at conquest in 1543 by Francisco de Montejo, nephew of Montejo the Elder, was thwarted by fierce Maya resistance, but the Elder's son, Montejo the Younger, ultimately took the town. The Spanish laid out a new city on the classic colonial plan.

During much of the colonial era, Valladolid's physical isolation from Mérida kept it relatively autonomous from royal rule. The Maya of the area suffered brutal exploitation, which continued after Mexican independence. Barred from entering many areas of the city, the Maya made Valladolid their first point of attack in 1847 when the War of the Castes began. After a two-month siege the city's defenders were finally overcome. Many fled to the safety of Mérida; the rest were slaughtered.

Today Valladolid is a prosperous seat of agricultural commerce, with some light industry thrown in. Most *vallisetanos* speak Spanish with a soft and clear Maya accent.

Orientation

The old highway passes through the city center, though all signs urge motorists toward

VALLADOLID

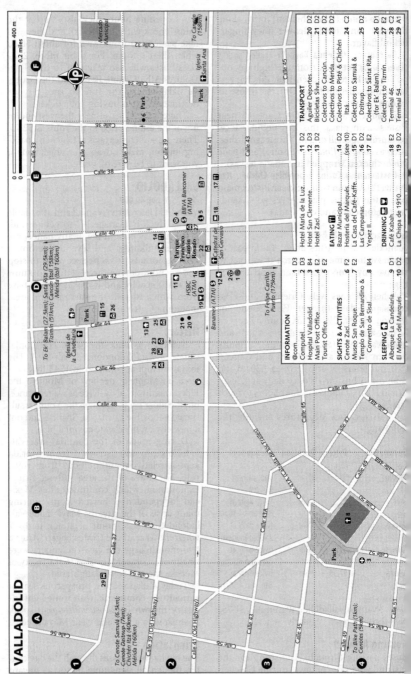

INFORMATION
@com..1	D3
Computel....................................2	D3
Hospital Valladolid.......................3	B4
Main Post Office..........................4	E2
Tourist Office..............................5	E2

SIGHTS & ACTIVITIES
Cenote Zací.................................6	F2
Museo San Roque........................7	E2
Templo de San Bernardino &	
Convento de Sisal......................8	B4

SLEEPING
Albergue La Candelaria................9	D1
El Mesón del Marqués................10	D2

Hotel María de la Luz................11	D2
Hotel San Clemente..................12	D3
Hotel Zací..............................13	D2

EATING
Bazar Municipal.......................14	D2
Hostería del Marqués...........(see 10)	
La Casa del Café-Kaffe.............15	D1
Las Campanas..........................16	D2
Yepez II.................................17	E2

DRINKING
Café Kabah.............................18	E2
La Chispa de 1910....................19	D2

TRANSPORT
Aguilar Deportes.......................20	D2
Bicicletas Silva.........................21	D2
Colectivos to Cancún.................22	D2
Colectivos to Mérida.................23	D2
Colectivos to Pisté & Chichén	
Itzá....................................24	C2
Colectivos to Samulá &	
Dzitnup..............................25	D2
Colectivos to Santa Rita	
(for Ek' Balam)....................26	D1
Colectivos to Tizmín.................27	E2
Terminal 46............................28	C2
Terminal 54............................29	A1

the toll road north of the city. To follow the old highway eastbound, take Calle 41; westbound, take Calle 39. Most hotels are on the main plaza, called Parque Francisco Cantón Rosado, or within a block or two of it.

Information

Various banks, most with ATMs, are near the city center of town. Most Internet places charge about $1.50 per hour. The main post office is located on the east side of the plaza.

@.com (Calle 42; per hr $1.50) Offers reliable Internet access.

Hospital Valladolid (☎ 856-28-83; cnr Calles 49 & 52; ☽ 24hr) Near the Convento de Sisal, the hospital handles emergencies.

Tourist office (☎ 856-18-65; cnr Calles 40 & 41; ☽ 9am-8pm) On the northeast corner of the plaza, it has maps and information.

Sights & Activities

TEMPLO DE SAN BERNARDINO & CONVENTO DE SISAL

The **Church of San Bernardino de Siena** and the **Convent of Sisal**, just under 1km southwest of the plaza at the end of Calle 41A, are said to be the oldest Christian structures in Yucatán. They were constructed in 1552 to serve the dual functions of fortress and church.

If the convent is open, you can go inside. Apart from the likeness of the Virgin of Guadalupe on the altar, the church is relatively bare, having been stripped of its decorations during the uprisings of 1847 and 1910.

MUSEO SAN ROQUE

Less than a block east of the plaza, the church turned museum **Museo San Roque** (Calle 41; admission by donation; ☽ 9am-9pm) is modest but very nicely done. Models and exhibits relate the history of the city and the region, and other displays focus on various aspects of traditional Maya life, including religious offerings and ceremonies, masks and instruments, medicines, handicrafts and food.

CENOTES

Among the region's several underground cenotes is **Cenote Zací** (Calle 36; admission $0.50; ☽ 8am-5pm), set in a park that also holds traditional stone-walled thatched houses and a small zoo. People swim in Zací, though being mostly open it has some dust and algae.

A bit more enticing, but less accessible, is **Cenote Dzitnup** (Xkekén; admission $2; ☽ 7am-6pm), 7km west of the plaza. It's artificially lit and very swimmable, and a massive limestone formation dripping with stalactites hangs from its ceiling. Across the road and a couple hundred meters closer to town is **Cenote Samulá** (admission $1), a lovely cavern pool with *álamo* (poplar) roots stretching down many meters from the middle of the ceiling to drink from it.

Pedaling a rented bicycle to the cenotes takes about 20 minutes from the city center, from where you should take all-colonial Calle 41A (Calz de los Frailes), then turn left onto the *ciclopista* (bike path) paralleling the road to Mérida. Turn left again at the sign for Dzitnup; Samulá will be off this road to the right, and Dzitnup a little further on the left.

Taxis from Valladolid's main plaza charge $7 for the round-trip excursion to Dzitnup and Samulá, with an hour's wait (this is the locals' price; your rate may vary). You can also hop aboard a westbound bus; ask the driver to let you off at the Dzitnup turnoff (2km from the site); or catch a *colectivo* taxi ($1) on the corner of Calles 39 and 44.

Sleeping

El Mesón del Marqués (☎ 856-20-73; Calle 39 No 203; d $50; ☒ ☒) On the north side of the plaza, this has long been considered the best hotel in town. It has two colonial courtyards, a pool, a good restaurant, and guestrooms with air-con, ceiling fans and cable TV.

Hotel María de la luz (☎ 856-20-71; www.maria delaluzhotel.com; Calle 42 No 193; d $35; ☒ ☒) This is the best value in town. At the northwest corner of the plaza, this colonial house has comfortable rooms with TV. The pool is especially nice.

Hotel San Clemente (☎ 856-22-08; www.hotelsan clemente.com.mx; Calle 42 No 206; d $35; ☒ ☒) Located on the corner of the plaza, across from the cathedral, the San Clemente has a nice pool and 64 rooms decorated in mock-colonial style, each with cable TV.

Hotel Zací (☎ 856-21-67; Calle 44 No 191; d with fan/air-con $30/35; ☒) This well-kept hotel has 48 rooms with TV, decorated nearly identically to San Clemente's (or vice versa), all situated around a quiet courtyard with a bar.

Alberque La Candelaria (☎ 856-22-67, 800-800-26-25; Calle 35 No 201F; dm $8, d $20) This HI affiliate

DEEP MYSTERY

In a cataclysmic collision 65 million years ago, a huge meteor struck the area that is now the Yucatán Peninsula, leaving a 284km-wide crater on the land's surface. Millions of years later, cracks formed just below the limestone surface of the crater's perimeter and rainwater began filling the cavities that these fissures created. Eventually the domed surface layer around the underground chambers began to erode and crumble, revealing the intricate vascular system of underground rivers and cenotes that lay beneath.

According to Maya cosmology there are three levels of existence: heaven (which itself has several strata), earth and the nine-tiered underworld, Xibalba. The Maya viewed cenotes as entranceways into the afterworlds, and they believed that anyone who was sacrificed to the cenotes as an offering to the gods would avoid Xibalba and go directly to heaven. (Direct access to heaven was also given to women who died in childbirth and soldiers killed in battle.)

In 2002, the National Institute of Anthropology and History (INAH) in Mexico City began a six-year study of some of the Yucatán's nearly 3000 cenotes. The marine anthropologists are finding that not only subjects of sacrifice (usually virgins or captured enemy warriors) were thrown into the cenotes' depths but that, as a send off to the other worlds, many dead – from the regal in full funerary finery to commoners – were also deposited in the watery graves.

Today as many as 10,000 people a year visit the region's cenotes to swim, snorkel and dive. Anthropologists hope that so much activity in the cenotes won't disturb the evidence that may lay many meters below the water's crystalline surface.

is in a classic old house on the north side of the park, across from Iglesia de la Candelaria. It's an extremely attractive, well-run hostel, with full kitchen, self-service laundry, a common area with cable TV, Internet access and a serene back area. The owners provide loads of information about the area and arrange tours.

Eating

Hostería del Marqués (☎ 856-20-73; Calle 39 No 203; mains $4-6) The best restaurant in town is in the hotel El Mesón del Marqués. It serves delicious food in the beautiful and tranquil courtyard. Try the Yucatecan sampler dish for a taste of a variety of regional specialties.

Las Campanas (cnr Calles 41 & 42; mains $5-10) A pleasant corner spot across from the plaza, serving generous portions of Yucatecan fare. It has live acoustic music performances most nights.

Yepez II (Calles 41 No 148; mains $5-10) Airy and spacious with garden patio seating, Yepez serves good traditional Mexican (not Yucatecan) dishes. There's live music on weekends.

La Casa del Café-Kaffé (☎ 856-28-79; Calle 44; mains $2-4) Serves excellent espresso and good breakfasts, plus light lunch and dinner fare.

Hotel María de la Luz (Calle 42 No 193; mains $4-6) This hotel has breezy tables overlooking the plaza. It serves a tasty and bountiful breakfast, and very good seafood mains for lunch and dinner.

Bazar Municipal (cnr Calles 39 & 40; set meals $2-3) This is a collection of market-style cookshops at the plaza's northeast corner, popular for their big, cheap breakfasts. At lunch and dinner there are *comidas corridas* (set meals) – check the price before you order.

Drinking & Entertainment

On Sunday from 8pm to 9pm the municipal band or other local groups perform live music in the main plaza.

Café Kabah (cnr Calles 40 & 41) A spacious homelike upstairs spot overlooking the plaza. The specialty is espresso drinks, caffeinated in the morning…caffeinated *and* spiked at night. The drinks – enhanced or otherwise – are all very good but *sweet*. Ask for '*poca azúcar*'.

La Chispa de 1910 (☎ 856-26-68; Calle 41 No 201; 6pm-1am Mon-Thu, 5pm-3am Fri-Sun) Located a half-block from the main plaza, La Chispa is a lively bar and restaurant popular with young locals.

Shopping

Yalat (cnr Calles 39 & 40) On the northeast corner of the main plaza, this gallery-like shop sells genuine and fine-quality popular Mexican art and clothing.

Getting There & Around

BICYCLE

A few places rent bikes in the city center. Check out **Bicicletas Silva** (Calle 44) and neighboring **Aguilar Deportes** (Calle 44), which both offer bikes for $1 per hour.

BUS

Valladolid has two bus terminals: the convenient **Terminal 46** (cnr Calles 39 & 46), two blocks from the plaza, and **Terminal 54** (cnr Calles 37 & 54), five blocks further northwest. All buses going through Valladolid stop at both terminals. Many 1st-class buses running between Cancún and Mérida don't go into the city center at all, but drop passengers near the toll road's off-ramp. Free shuttles then take passengers into Valladolid.

The principal services are Oriente, Mayab and Expresso (2nd class), and ADO and Super Expresso (1st class). Following are the major routes' daily services from Valladolid:

Destination	Price	Duration	Frequency
Cancún	$8-10	2-3hr	frequent buses from 8:30am-9:30pm
Chetumal	$12	6hr	5 Mayab 2nd-class buses
Chichén Itzá/Pisté	$1.50	45min	17 Oriente Mérida-bound buses from 7:30am-6pm, stopping near the ruins during the day
Chiquilá	$6	2½hr	2nd-class bus at 1:30am
Cobá	$4	1hr	3 1st-class buses
	$2.50	1hr	3 2nd-class buses
Izamal	$3	2hr	3 2nd-class buses
Mérida	$6-8	2-3hr	frequent buses
Playa del Carmen	$11	3-3½hr	3 1st-class buses
	$6.25	3-3½hr	5 2nd-class buses
Tizimín	$2	1hr	12 buses
Tulum	$5	2hr	3 1st-class buses
	$4.50	2hr	3 2nd-class buses

COLECTIVOS

Often faster, more reliable and more comfortable than buses are *colectivos*. Direct services to Mérida ($5, two hours) depart from Calle 39 just east of Calle 46; Cancún *colectivos* ($6, two hours) depart from in front of the cathedral – confirm that the route is nonstop. *Colectivos* for Pisté and Chichén Itzá ($1.75, 40 minutes) leave from Calle 46, north of Calle 39, and for Tizimín ($1.75, 40 minutes) from the east side of the plaza at Calle 40.

It's possible to catch a *colectivo* from Calle 44 for the village of Santa Rita ($1), a 2km walk from Ek' Balam. A round-trip taxi ride from Valladolid with an hour's wait at the ruins will cost around $20. **Alberque La Candelaria** (☎ 856-22-67, 800-800-26-25; Calle 35 No 201F) can arrange tours (for more details, see p947).

EK' BALAM

Vegetation still covers much of the ruins of **Ek' Balam** (admission $3; 🕐 8am-5pm), but excavations and restoration continue to reveal stunning finds. As you enter, beyond the impressive freestanding arch are identical temples, **Las Gemelas** (the twins), beyond which is a long **ball court**.

Most impressive is the **Acropolís** – a massive, towering pyramid. At its base are stucco skulls, and to its right side are unusual winged human figures. Three-quarters up the pyramid, and protected by an archeologist-erected thatched *palapa*, is the phenomenal **El Trono** (The Throne), a huge jaguar mouth entrance with 360-degree dentition; this is presumed to be the entrance to the tomb of King Ukit-Kan-Lek-Tok, the powerful ninth-century ruler. The top of the Acropolís offers spectacular views of the site, and the jungle beyond, whose canopy hides treasures yet unearthed.

The turnoff for this fascinating archaeological site is due north of Valladolid, 17km along the road to Tizimín. Ek' Balam is another 10.5km east.

If you can, stay a couple of days. In the nearby town of Ek-Balam you'll find unique lodging at the enchanted eco-oasis **Genesis Ek-Balam** (☎ 985-858-93-75; www.genesisretreat.com; d $45). Canadian and passionate environmentalist, Lee Christie, built and runs this low-impact jungle-garden retreat. The eight artistically whimsical and comfortable units are set amid the exuberant foliage. There's a small cenote pond, rock garden, organic vegetable patch and lovely limestone pool. The casual on-site restaurant serves creative concoctions, many of which contain

YUCATÁN PENINSULA

the traditional Maya medicinal leaf *chaya* (a bit like spinach). Other treats include chili-chocolate cookies (yum!) and avocado ice-cream.

TIZIMÍN

☎ 986 / pop 42,000

Travelers bound for Río Lagartos change buses in Tizimín, a ranching center. There is little to warrant an overnight stay, but the tree-filled Parque Principal is pleasant, particularly at sundown.

Banks on the southwest side of Parque Principal have ATMs.

Two impressive colonial structures – **Parroquia Los Santos Reyes de Tizimín** (Church of the Three Wise Kings) and its former **Franciscan monastery** (the ex-*convento*) – are worth a look.

Hotel 49 (Calle 49 No 373A; d fan/air-con $18/26; ❌ P) has clean, comfortable rooms, and secure parking.

The restaurant **Tres Reyes** (☎ 863-21-06; cnr Calles 52 & 53; mains $6-10) on the main square is a pleasant surprise. The ranch-style food is very good, as is the friendly service. The **market** (☼ 8am-8pm), two blocks north of the church, has the usual inexpensive and tasty eateries.

Oriente (shared with Mayab, both 2nd-class buses only) and Noreste (1st- and 2nd-class buses) share a terminal on Calle 47 between Calles 46 and 48. Noreste's 1st- and 2nd-class bus terminal is around the corner on Calle 46. Departures to the following destinations travel daily from Tizimín:

Destination	Price	Duration	Frequency
Cancún	$7-8	3-3½hr	Mayab & Noreste buses between 3am & 8pm
Izamal	$5	2½hr	3 Oriente bus at 5:15am, 11:20am & 4pm
Mérida	$8	2¼hr	10 1st-class Noreste buses between 4:30am-6:30pm
Río Lagartos	$1	1hr	8 Noreste buses between 6am-7:45pm
San Felipe	$2	1½hr	Catch one of the buses going to Río Lagartos that continues to San Felipe
Valladolid	$2	1hr	7 Oriente buses between 5:30am-7pm

RÍO LAGARTOS

☎ 986 / pop 220

The largest and most spectacular flamingo colony in Mexico warrants a trip to this fishing village – 103km north of Valladolid, 52km north of Tizimín and lying within the Reserva de la Biosfera Ría Lagartos. The mangrove-lined estuary is also home to snowy egrets, red egrets, tiger herons, snowy white ibis, hundreds of other bird species and a small number of the crocodiles that gave the town its name (Alligator River).

The Maya knew the place as Holkobén and used it as a rest stop on their way to the nearby lagoons (Las Coloradas), from which they extracted salt. (Salt continues to be extracted, on a much vaster scale now.) Spanish explorers mistook the inlet for a river and the crocs for alligators, and the rest is history…

Flamingo Tours

The brilliant orange-red birds can turn the horizon fiery when they take wing. You can generally get to within 100m of flamingos before they walk or fly away. Depending on your luck, you'll see either hundreds or thousands of them.

The four primary haunts, in increasing distance from town, are Punta Garza, Yoluk, Necopal and Nahochín (all flamingo feeding spots named for nearby mangrove patches). Prices vary with boat, group size (maximum five) and destination. The lowest you can expect to pay is around $45; a full boat to Nahochín runs to as much as $65.

The best tours are given by the licensed guides operating from **Restaurante-Bar Isla Contoy** (☎ 862-00-00; Calle 19) at the waterfront. They offer extensive day tours as well as night excursions. Crocodiles are a common nocturnal sight, and from May through September sea turtles are easily spotted.

Alternatively, you can negotiate with one of the eager men in the waterfront kiosks near the entrance to town. They speak English and will connect you with a captain (who usually doesn't speak English).

Sleeping & Eating

Most residents aren't sure of the town's street names, and signs are few. The road into town is north–south Calle 10, which ends at the waterfront Calle 13.

Posada Leyli (☎ 862-01-06; cnr Calles 14 & 11; d with bathroom $18) Two blocks south of Calle 10, this place has six *very* basic, fan-cooled rooms. *La encargada* (the manager) sometimes needs to be sought out; ask a neighbor or at the waterfront kiosks.

Hotel Villas de Pescadores (☎ 862-00-20; Calle 14; d $33) This hotel is two blocks north of the Leyli, near the water's edge, and offers nine very clean rooms, each with good cross-ventilation (all face the estuary) and views. The owner rents bicycles and canoes, and, if asked, is happy to share his wealth of regional knowledge.

Restaurante-Bar Isla Contoy (Calle 19; mains $4-6) This popular spot at the waterfront serves generous helpings of fresh fish – the shrimp-stuffed fillet is especially good. Isla Contoy is also a good place to meet other travelers and form groups for the flamingo boat tours.

Getting There & Away
Several buses run between Tizimín ($1, one hour), Mérida ($6 to $8, three to four hours) and Cancún ($7, three to four hours). There are buses to San Felipe ($1, 20 minutes) several times a day.

SAN FELIPE
This seldom-visited fishing village, 12km west of Río Lagartos, makes a nice day trip or overnight stay. Birding and the beach are the main attractions, both of which are just across the estuary at Punta Holohit.

To get to the friendly, clean and cleverly constructed **Hotel San Felipe de Jesús** (☎ 986-862-20-27; sanfelip@prodigy.net.mx; r $25-35), turn left at the water and proceed 100m. Six of the 18 rooms are large and have private balconies and water views. The restaurant offers tasty seafood.

Six buses a day travel from Tizimín through Rio Largatos and continue to San Felipe ($2, 1½ hours). You can also catch a bus directly to San Felipe from Río Lagartos ($1, 20 minutes).

CAMPECHE STATE

Campeche is the first of the Yucatán Peninsula's three states that travelers hit when coming overland from other parts of Mexico. It isn't as heavily explored as the other states, but it's slowly emerging as one of

Mexico's top destinations – as rapid excavation, restoration and reconstruction work continues at many archaeological sites throughout the state. Today visitors can enjoy the spectacular but still uncrowded Maya ruins of Edzná (p958), Calakmul (p962), and Chicanná (p962); the impressive walled city of Campeche (p954), with its colonial fortifications, architecture and storybook-like history of pirates and war; and the Reserva de la Biosfera Calakmul (p962), Mexico's largest biosphere jungle reserve, rife and thriving with exotic plant and wildlife.

CAMPECHE
☎ 981 / pop 275,000
A relaxed scene plays out each sunset along Campeche's broad *malecón* (waterfront boulevard): joggers jog, kids squeal, coiffed Spaniels walk their well-groomed owners, couples cuddle, thinkers think. And, as habitual as this ritual is, heads still turn and mouths drop when the sun performs her own daily rite: setting the sky ablaze in slow-burning color before slipping back to sea.

Whether at the water's edge or in the city center, Campeche is just so...pretty. In a huge campaign to resurrect the center to its colonial glory, millions of pesos and tons of labor have gone into gussying up the heart of the city (now a Unesco World Heritage Site). Parks are manicured, monuments gleam, the cobbled stone streets are always swept clean, and every building and home has been newly painted in bright pastel hues and white, white trim...like frosted petit fours they stand row after row.

Campechanos exude a dignified calm and express a humble pride toward their city. Their economy has never depended on tourism and you'll find that most residents are indifferent to your presence. If you're tired of hawkers and timeshare hustlers, you've found safe refuge here.

History
Campeche was once a Maya trading village called Ah Kin Pech (Lord Sun Tick) and was ruled by its fearless leader, Moch-Cuouh. The first Europeans – a Spanish expedition – landed on the shores of Ah Kin Pech in 1517. Moch-Cuouh granted the parched sailors water, but warned them not to stay. Feeling quite invincible and in no hurry to move

YUCATÁN PENINSULA

YUCATÁN PENINSULA

CAMPECHE

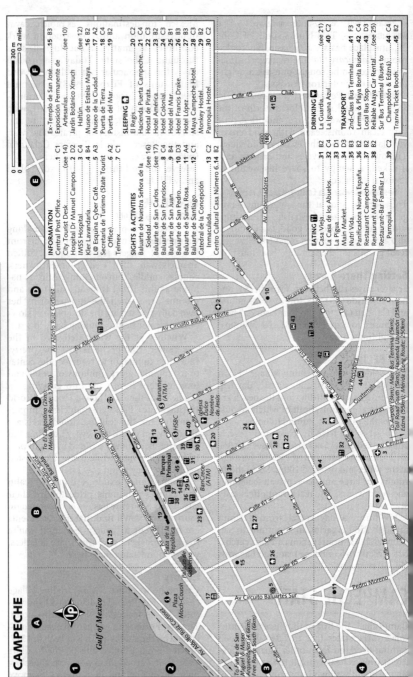

Gulf of Mexico

0 — 300 m
0 — 0.2 miles

on, the Spaniards ignored Moch-Cuouh's demand. Infuriated by the Spaniards' defiance, Moch-Cuouh and his men attacked the Spanish ship, murdering everyone aboard. Over the next two decades more Spanish galleons arrived, this time with the express purpose of conquering Moch-Cuouh's kingdom, but all of them met with the same fate as that first fateful crew.

It wasn't until 1540, after Moch-Cuouh's death, that the Conquistadors – led by Francisco de Montejo the Younger – gained enough control over the region to establish a surviving settlement. They named it Villa de San Francisco de Campeche.

The small city soon flourished and became the major port of the Yucatán Peninsula. Locally grown timber and dyewoods were major exports to Europe. Gold and silver, mined in other regions, were also brought to Campeche for export. This wealth did not escape the notice of pirates, who started arriving only six years after the town was founded. For two centuries the violent buccaneers terrorized Campeche. They robbed citizens, raped women and burned buildings. In the most gruesome assault, in early 1663, various pirate hordes set aside their rivalries to converge as a single flotilla upon the city, where they massacred scores of *campechanos*.

This tragedy finally spurred the Spanish monarchy to take preventive action, but it was not until five years later, in 1668, that work on constructing the 3.5m-thick protective ramparts began. After 18 years of building, a 2.5km hexagon incorporating eight strategically placed *baluartes* (bulwarks) surrounded the city. A segment of the ramparts extended out to sea so that ships literally had to sail into a fortress, easily defended, to gain access to the city.

Today the local economy is largely driven by shrimping and offshore petroleum extraction, and the prosperity brought by these activities has helped fund the city center's renovation.

Orientation

Though the bastions still stand, the city walls themselves have been mostly razed and replaced. Today Av Circuito Baluartes rings the city center, just as the walls once did. Many of the streets making up the circuit are paved with stone taken from the demolished wall.

A multilane boulevard, with both bicycle and pedestrian paths on its seaward side, extends over several kilometers in either direction along Campeche's shoreline, changing names a few times as it goes. The stretch closest to the city center is named Av Adolfo Ruiz Cortínez, although it is commonly referred to as *el malecón* (the seafront drive).

Information

EMERGENCY
Cruz Roja (Red Cross; ☎ 065)
Fire (☎ 060)
Police (☎ 816-36-35)

INTERNET ACCESS
L@ Esquina Cyber Cafe (cnr Calle 12 & Av Circuito Baluartes Sur; per hr $1.50)

LAUNDRY
Kler Lavandería (cnr Calles 61 & 16; per kg $1) Wash, dry and fold, with a minimum 3kg load.

MEDICAL SERVICES
Hospitalj Campos (☎ 811-11-42; Av Circuito Baluartes Nte, btwn Calles 14 & 16)
IMSS Hospital (☎ 816-52-02; cnr Av Circuito Baluartes Este & Av Central)

MONEY
Banks with ATMs can be found near Parque Principal.

PHONE
Telmex office (Calle 8)

POST
Central post office (☎ 816-21-34; cnr Av 16 de Septiembre & Calle 53)

TOURIST INFORMATION
City tourist desk (Calle 57 No 6; ◷ 9am-3:30pm & 6-9pm Mon-Fri) Northwest of the Centro Cultural Casa Número 6.
Secretaría de Turismo (☎ 816-67-67; Plaza Moch-Couoh; ◷ 9am-3pm & 6-9pm) Off Av Adolfo Ruiz Cortínez, this office has good maps of the city and dispenses tourist magazines with information about what's going on around town and in the state.

Sights

Most of Campeche's historic sites are contained in the old city, within the city walls, and are easily accessible on foot.

OLD CITY CENTER

The **Baluarte de Nuestra Señora de la Soledad** (cnr Calles 8 & 57) holds the **Museo de Estelas Maya** (admission $2.50; ☺ 8am-7:30pm Tue-Sun). Many of the Maya artifacts here are badly weathered, but the precise line-drawing next to each stone shows what the designs once looked like. You can take in the vista from the roof here as well.

Parque Principal, Campeche's main plaza, is the center of the city and a pleasant place where locals go to sit and think, chat, smooch, plot, snooze, have their shoes shined, or stroll and cool off after the heat of the day. Come for the concerts held here on Sunday evening.

Construction of the grand **Catedral de la Concepción Inmaculada** (Parque Prinicpal), on the northeast side of the main plaza, began in 1650, but wasn't finished until two centuries later in 1850. Inside, the black-and-white marble floor is especially dramatic, as is the carved ebony Holy Sepulcher decorated with a flock of stamped silver angels.

The 18th-century **Centro Cultural Casa Número 6** (Calle 57; admission free; ☺ 9am-9pm), on the southwest side of Parque Principal, is furnished with lovely period pieces; once inside it's easy (and fun) to imagine how the city's high society lived back then. It also contains several computer-interactive exhibits, providing information about the main tourist attractions in the city and state of Campeche. Free (Spanish only) guided tours of the building are also available.

The **Baluarte de Santiago** (cnr Calle 8 & Av Circuito Baluartes Norte; admission free; ☺ 9am-3pm & 5-8pm Mon-Fri, 9am-1pm & 4-8pm Sat, 9am-1pm Sun) houses a minuscule yet lovely tropical garden, the **Jardín Botánico Xmuch Haltún**, with 250 species of tropical plants set around a courtyard of fountains.

The **Baluarte de San Pedro** (admission free; ☺ 9am-3pm & 5-9pm) is in the middle of a complex traffic intersection at the beginning of Av Gobernadores. Within the bulwark is the **Exposición Permanente de Artesanías**, a regional crafts sales center.

Puerta de Tierra (Calle 59; admission free; ☺ 8am-9pm) is a great stone fortress, built in 1732. It remains virtually intact and even the massive wooden door is original. There is an interesting little museum with an early 18th-century five-ton cannon in the entrance. Inside, portraits of pirates don the walls.

Baluarte de San Carlos (Calle 8; admission free; ☺ 9am-2pm Mon, 8am-8pm Tue-Sat, 8am-2pm Sun) contains the modest **Museo de la Ciudad** (City Museum). There's a good scale model of the old city, historical photos, specimens of dyewood and the like. You can visit the dungeon, or escape to the roof for a breathtaking view of the sea.

The **Ex-Templo de San José** (cnr Calles 10 & 63) is an absolute visual delight. The Jesuits built this baroque church in 1756. Its block-long facade is covered in striking blue and yellow Talavera tiles, and one spire is topped by a lighthouse replete with weather vane.

FUERTE DE SAN MIGUEL & MUSEO ARQUEOLÓGICO

Four kilometers southwest of Plaza Moch-Couoh, a road turns left off the *malecón*, and climbs for about 600m to **Fuerte de San Miguel** (admission $2.50; ☺ 9am-7pm Tue-Sat, 9am-noon Sun). This colonial fortress is now home to an excellent **archaeological museum**, where you can see objects found at the ancient Maya sites of Calakmul, Edzná and Jaina, an island north of the city once used as a burial site for Maya aristocracy.

Among the objects on display are stunning pieces of jade jewelry and exquisite vases, masks and plates. The star attractions are the jade burial masks from Calakmul. Also displayed are stelae, weapons, arrowheads, seashell necklaces and clay figurines.

The fort is itself a thing of beauty. In mint condition, it's compact and comes equipped with a dry moat and working drawbridge, and it's topped with several cannons. The views from here are fabulous.

For $0.50, 'Lerma' or 'Playa Bonita' buses depart from the market and travel counterclockwise most of the way around the *circuito* before heading down the *malecón*. Tell the driver you're going to the Fuerte de San Miguel. The turnoff for the fort, Av Escénica, is across from the old San Luis artillery battery. To avoid the strenuous walk from the coastal road up the hill (about 600m), you can take a taxi or the *tranvía* (trolley) – see Tours (opposite).

Festivals & Events

There's no cost to attend either of the following festive performances:

Folk music and dancing From September to May the Secretaría de Turismo sponsors free performances, which take place at 7pm Saturday (weather permitting) at Plaza de la República; and 8:30pm Thursday at the Centro Cultural Casa Número 6.

Parque Principal On Wednesday through Sunday nights, there is always something going on at the Parque Principal, be it jazz, rock, marimba groups or the Banda del Estado (State Band).

Tours

Three different tours by motorized *tranvía* depart daily from Parque Principal; buy tickets from the Tranvía ticket booth. Hourly between 9am and 9pm, the 'Tranvía de la Ciudad' (45min, $8) heads off on a tour of the principal neighborhoods of the historic city center. On the same schedule, 'El Guapo' goes to the Fuerte de San Miguel and its twin on the north side of the city, the Fuerte de San José, which contains a modest maritime museum. You don't get enough time to take in the archaeological museum; if that's your goal, just use the *tranvía* to get there, then walk down the hill. The third tour departs at 9am and 5pm to the Fuerte de San José.

Recommended tour agencies include the following:

Monkey Hostel (☎ 811-65-00; cnr Calles 10 & 57; tours $15-35) Offers shuttle service to Maya sites Edzná and Kin-Há; Calakmul, Becán, Chicanná and Xpuhil; and the Ruta Puuc sites.

Servicios Turísticos Xtampak (☎ 812-64-85; xtampak@elfoco.com; Calle 57) This company offers archaeological tours ($30) to Edzná, Calakmul and the various sites around Xpujil in eastern Campeche, among other places.

Sleeping

BUDGET

Hostal de Pirata (☎ 811-17-57; Calle 59 No 47; dm/d $8/20; 🖳) Native *campechano* and architect owner, Eric (aka '*el arcitecto*') is a history buff and collector extraordinaire. The cannon, the bottles, the coins…authentic treasures all. Past the curious reception-cum-museum, you step into a warm family-feel establishment. Staff are very friendly and the courtyard café-bar is a welcoming hangout. The rooms and bathrooms are hyper-clean, and there's a kitchen/laundry/kickback patio on the roof.

Parroquia Hostel (☎ 816-25-30; www.hostalparroquia.com; Calle 55 No 8; dm/d $10/20; 🖳) The wide-open, street-side reception area fronts a surprisingly calm abbeylike cloister of rooms here. Dark wood accents, warm-hued tiles

and arched windows contribute to an intimate inn atmosphere. There's a grassy back patio, shared open-air kitchen, pub-like bar and new laundry facility.

Hotel Colonial (☎ 816-22-22; Calle 14 No 122; r $24, with air-con $33; 😵) Antique, quirky and charming…and that's just the staff. Housed in what was once the mansion of doña Gertrudis Eulalia Torostieta y Zagasti, former Spanish governor of Tabasco and Yucatán, this hotel's rep rests mainly on its laurels. It's lofty past is now tempered by a hint of must and thick coats of bright pastel paint. The period plumbing looks intimidating (there's not much room to rest *your* laurels), but functions with gusto.

Monkey Hostel (☎ 811-65-00; www.hostalcampeche.com; cnr Calles 10 & 57; dm $8, d $18; 🖳) The rooftop terrace of this grand old building, overlooking Parque Principal, offers idyllic views of the park and cathedral; however, the inner vista is not quite as alluring. With a someone-left-the-kids-home-alone ambiance, the Monkey is chilled but disheveled. Kitchen and laundry facilities are available, as well as a book exchange. Continental breakfast is included.

MIDRANGE

Hotel América (☎ 816-45-88; Calle 10 No 252; d $35, with air-con $42; 🅿 😵 🖳) Worn grace characterizes this converted stately colonial home. Each sparingly furnished, but spacious and high-ceilinged room, has shiny original black-and-white tile floors and two double beds. The rooms with balconies are most appealing but most noisy. A small breakfast is included. Free Internet access is available at the (get in line) front-desk computer.

El Regis (☎ 816-31-75; Calle 12 No 148; d $33; 😵) A poor hombre's Hotel América. Tired but homelike, El Regis has the same checkerboard floor and tall-walled old elegance of its counterpart, only it's less polished and tended, and more laidback. All seven big bright rooms have non-cable TV and a choice of beds: springy or swayback.

Hotel Francis Drake (☎ 811-56-26; www.hotelfrancisdrake.com; Calle 12 No 207; d $60; 🅿 😵 🖳) The Francis Drake makes a sincere attempt at upscale comfort. it has the comfort part down, but the elegance is quaintly forced. Though uniform, the 24 rooms are clean and spacious, and include amenities like minibar, desk and Internet connection.

Hotel López (☎ 816-33-44; Calle 12 No 189; d $45; P ☒ ☐) A remodel of the three-storey López left both the hotel's rooms and its character slightly sterilized. Each of the spotless, modern, nondescript but comfortable rooms has satellite TV and wi-fi. A small espresso bar adjoins the lobby.

Maya Campeche Hotel (☎ 816-80-53; www.maya campechehotel.com.mx; Calle 57 No 40; d $45; ☒ ☐) Think orange. This simple and modest new hotel in the colonial center has 15 orange (wall trim, floor tiles, bedspreads) rooms. They're all a little cramped and uninspired (except for the color!) but perfectly comfortable and very clean, and each features satellite TV and wi-fi.

TOP END

Hacienda Puerta Campeche (☎ 816-75-35; www .haciendasmexico.com; Calle 59 No 71; r from $275, kids 11 & under free; P ☒ ☐ ☒) For an authentic countryside rambling estate hacienda experience, you'll have to head out of town. To indulge in intimate hacienda-style rustic sumptuousness stay here. Hacienda Puerta Campeche is part of the luxury chain that includes Hacienda Uayamón, but is the only one in the series with an urban address. Step out the front door and you're in one of the most picturesque corners of the city. Step inside and you're in a soothing world apart…where a pale turquoise pool meanders into earth-toned rooms and siesta-inducing hammocks sway in wait.

Hacienda Uayamón (☎ 829-75-27; www.haciendas mexico.com; Carretera Uayamón-China-Edzná Km 20; r from $250, kids 11 & under free; P ☒ ☐ ☒) The city center is only 35km away and myriad sightseeing expeditions can be arranged from here, but once you've arrived you'll likely feel your wanderlust fade. The sprawling grounds and grand buildings (some dating back to the 1700s) are impressive, and the 12 individual detached villas embody a mix of old-world grandeur and modern grace. There's an excellent – mostly organic – restaurant, spa with unique pool (housed between the remaining walls of a dilapidated ballroom), horseback riding and mountain biking.

Hotel Del Mar (☎ 811-91-91; www.delmarhotel .com.mx; Av Adolfo Ruiz Cortínez 51; d with city/sea view $90/110; P ☒ ☒) Once a top contender, the Del Mar can no longer compete with the hacienda crowd. It does have what the others don't though: fabulous ocean views. And the dated but spacious rooms are equipped with creature comforts (like satellite TV, wi-fi and phone). There are two restaurants, a café, bar, computer facilities, a gym and a big sun-drenched pool.

Eating

Most restaurants are in the city center, a close walk from any downtown hotel (with the exception of the first listing).

RESTAURANTS

El Langostino (☎ 815-40-56; Calle 10-B; mains $7-15; ☒ lunch & dinner) This bustling family seafood restaurant, north of the city center, is out of the way but worth the trip. The seafood pasta dishes, *caldo de mariscos* (seafood soup), fish filets, ceviche…everything is so good. If you order a beer first you may never get around to ordering anything else; the yummy seafood *botanas* (appetizers) that accompany drinks are so generous, they're a meal in themselves. The most direct – not the shortest, but the simplest – way to get to El Langostino is to follow the *malecón* north for about 1.5km. (The name of the seafront avenue changes from Av Adolfo Ruiz Cortínez to Av Pedro Saínz, but that's unimportant, just stay along the water.) Turn right on the street (Calle 10-B) directly across from the huge pier. Go up two blocks and the restaurant is on the right. There's a yellow and red sign.

La Pigua (☎ 811-33-65; Av Alemán 179A; mains $7-13; ☒ noon-6pm) The bright blue entrance leads you into this pretty little restaurant, considered by locals to be the finest in Campeche. The seafood menu is extensive, and every item fresh and seasoned with regional flair. The *arroz con pulpo* (rice with squid) is particularly good.

La Casa de los Abuelos (Calle 61; mains $5-12; ☒ 10am-10pm) The mood fits the name (The Grandparents' House). This is a comforting place, and it's hard not to come back again and again. The fare is savory Yucatecan, just like your *abuela* (granny) used to make.

Casa Vieja (☎ 811-13-11; Calle 10 No 319; main $8-15) The creative fusion Cuban-Yucatecan fare is a good reason to come here, the collection of contemporary art on the walls is another, but the best reason to eat at Casa Vieja is the big breezy terrace overlooking the plaza.

Restaurant Marganzo (☎ 811-38-98; Calle 8; breakfast $4-7, mains $7-15) This popular restaurant faces the Baluarte de Nuestra Señora. It serves good breakfasts and juices (carrot and beet among them), plus espresso drinks. Lunch and dinner feature an extensive seafood menu. The atmosphere in the evening is fairly formal.

Restaurant-Bar Familiar La Parroquia (Calle 55 No 8; breakfast $4.50-5, mains $5-7; ⏲ 24hr) La Parroquia is the complete family restaurant-café hangout. Substantial and tasty breakfasts are served in the morning; traditional and regional dishes are offered during the rest of the day and through the night. You can even drop in for a taco 5am.

Restaurant Campeche (☎ 816-21-28; Calle 57; mains $5-9; ⏲ 6:30am-midnight) On the Parque Principal, this brightly lit place is housed in the building where Justo Sierra, founder of Mexico's national university, was born. The on-square location and convenient hours are this restaurant's most appetizing features. The menu offers a wide selection of promising choices, but delivers pretty lackluster fare.

QUICK EATS

Nutri Vida (Calle 12 No 167; mains $4; ⏲ Mon-Sat) Nutri Vida is a health-food store, which also serves healthy vegetarian treats, such as *aguas* (fruit juices), fresh salads and soy burgers.

Panificadora Nueva España (☎ 816-28-87; cnr Calles 10 & 59; ⏲ 6:30am-9:30pm) This bakery has an assortment of just-out-of-the-oven goods; especially yummy is the *pan dulce* (sweet bread). The nonbaked items – the enticing little chocolate doodads and such in the front case – are not as good.

El Mercado (Main Market; Av Circuito Baluartes Este; ⏲ 8am-5pm) Occupying two city blocks just east of the city center outside the wall is the main market, where you can find fresh produce, and lots of food stands selling treats like fresh fish tacos ($2 to $4).

Drinking

A pleasant spot to enjoy a drink is on the lush patio at **La Iguana Azul** (Calle 55), opposite La Parroquia, or at the bar at **Casa Vieja** (☎ 811-13-11; Calle 10 No 319) above the plaza. The most refined venue in town is **La Guardia** (☎ 816-75-35; Calle 59 No 71), the bar in Hacienda Puerta Campeche (opposite).

Getting There & Away

AIR

The tiny airport is at the end of Av López Portillo (reached by Av Central), which is 3.5km southeast of Plaza Moch-Couoh. **Aeroméxico** (☎ 816-66-56) flies to Mexico City twice daily.

BUS

Campeche's **main bus terminal** (ADO; cnr Avs Patricio Trueba & Casa de la Justicia) is about 20 blocks south of Av Circuito Baluartes Este (note that Av Patricio Trueba is also known as Av Central). At the time of research the **2nd-class bus terminal** (cnr Avs Gobernadores & Chile) was 1.7km east of Plaza Moch-Cuouh – about 1.5km from most hotels. Note that this bus terminal may move to the same location as the main bus terminal.

Though most of its buses leave from the main bus terminal, **Sur** (Av República) has a terminal for buses to Champotón across from the Alameda (south of the market). Rural buses for Edzná and other parts depart from here as well.

There have been reports of theft on night buses, especially to Chiapas; keep a close eye on your bags.

For daily buses from Campeche, see the box on the following page.

CAR & MOTORCYCLE

Reliable Maya Car Rental (☎ 811-91-91; www .delmarhotel.com.mx; Hotel del Mar, Av Adolfo Ruiz Cortínez 51) rents compact cars for $60 per day. Around the corner, **Rentamar** (☎ 811-64-61; Calle 59; ⏲ 9am-7pm) rents cars ($50 per day), motorcycles ($27 per day) and bikes ($12 per day)

Whether you're heading for Edzná, the long route (Hwy 261) to Mérida, or the *via cuota* (toll road) going south, take Av Central and follow signs for the airport and Edzná. For the free slow route south (Hwy 180), you can just head down the *malecón*.

For the non-toll, short route to Mérida, head north on the *malecón*; it curves right eventually and hits the highway at a Pemex gas station.

Getting Around

Local buses all originate at the market. Most charge $0.35 and go at least partway around the Av Circuito Baluartes counterclockwise before heading to their final destinations.

CAMPECHE BUS SCHEDULE

Destination	Price	Duration	Frequency
Bolonchén de Rejón	$5	3-4hr	4 buses
Cancún	$27	6hr	two direct 1st-class buses
	$22	7hr	1 2nd-class bus via Mérida
Chetumal	$27	9hr	1 1st-class bus at noon
	$17	9hr	2 2nd-class buses at 8:15am & 10pm
Edzná	$2	1½hr	6am & 10am then hourly until 6pm, from the Sur bus terminal
Escárcega	$8	2½hr	5 1st-class buses
	$6	2½hr	frequent 2nd-class buses daily
Hopelchén	$3.50	2hr	several 2nd-class buses
Mérida	$8	2½-3hr	hourly 1st-class buses via Bécal
	$7	2½-3hr	2nd-class buses every 30min until 7pm, via Bécal
Mérida	$7.50	4hr	5 2nd-class buses between 6am-5pm via Uxmal
Mexico City			
(TAPO)	$65-78	18hr	4 1st-class buses & 1 deluxe bus
Palenque	$23	5hr	1 deluxe bus at midnight
San Cristóbal de Las Casas	$33	14hr	1 deluxe bus at midnight
Villahermosa	$24	6hr	8 1st-class buses
Xpujil	$15	6-8hr	1 1st-class bus at noon
	$12	6-8hr	4 2nd-class buses, incl one via Hopelchén

Ask a local where along the *circuito* you can catch the bus you want.

Taxis have set prices for destinations on a sign posted in the back seat, but agree on a price with the driver before you get in; by the hour prices are $7.75. The fare between the main bus terminal and the city center is around $2.50. Between the airport and the city center should cost $7. *Colectivo* taxis from the airport charge about $3 per person.

AROUND CAMPECHE
Edzná

The closest major ruins to Campeche are about 53km to the southeast. **Edzná** (admission $3; ⏰ 8am-5pm) covered more than 17 sq km and was inhabited from approximately 600 BC to the 15th century AD. Most of the visible carvings date from AD 550–810. Though it's a long way from such Puuc Hills' sites as Uxmal and Kabah, some of the architecture here has elements of the Puuc style. What led to Edzná's decline and gradual abandonment remains a mystery.

Beyond the entrance is a *palapa* protecting carvings and stelae from the elements. A path from here leads about 400m through vegetation to the zone's big draw, the **Plaza Principal** (follow the signs for the Gran Acrópolis), which is 160m long, 100m wide and surrounded by temples. On your right as you enter from the north is the **Nohochná** (Big House), a massive, elongated structure that was topped by four long halls likely used for administrative tasks, such as the collection of tributes and the dispensation of justice. The built-in benches facing the main plaza were designed for spectators to view theatrical and ritual events.

Across the plaza is the **Gran Acrópolis**, a raised platform holding several structures, including Edzná's major temple, the 31m-high **Edificio de los Cinco Pisos** (Five-Story Building). It rises five levels from its vast base to the roofcomb and contains many vaulted rooms. A great central staircase of 65 steps goes right to the top. Some of the weathered carvings of masks, serpents and jaguars' heads that formerly adorned each level are now in the *palapa* near the ticket office.

The current structure is the last of four remodels, and was done primarily in the Puuc architectural style. Scholars generally agree that this temple is a hybrid of a pyramid and a palace. The impressive roofcomb is a clear reference to the sacred buildings at Tikal in Guatemala.

In the Pequeña Acrópolis, to the south of the main plaza, is the *palapa*-protected

Templo de Mascarones (Temple of Masks), which features carved portrayals of the sun god, Kinich-Ahau. The central motif is the head of a Maya man whose face has been modified to give him the appearance of a jaguar.

From Campeche, buses leave from outside the Sur Champotón terminal at 7am, 8am, 9am and 10am ($2, 55km, 1½ hours). The last bus returning to Campeche passes near the site at about 3pm.

Coming from the north and east, get off at San Antonio Cayal and catch a bus 20km south to Edzná. If you're headed north when leaving Edzná, you'll have to depend on the occasional bus to get you to San Antonio Cayal, where you can catch a Ruta Chenes (Chenes Route) bus north to Hopelchén, Bolonchén de Rejón and ultimately Uxmal.

Coming by car from Campeche, take Av Central out of town and follow the signs to the airport and Edzná. If you drove to Edzná from the north and are headed to Campeche city, don't retrace your route to San Antonio Cayal; just bear left shortly after leaving the parking lot and follow the signs westward.

Tours (p955) of Edzná from Campeche start at about $30 per person.

Bolonchén de Rejón & Xtacumbilxunaan

Forty kilometers east of San Antonio Cayal is Hopelchén, where Hwy 261 turns north; there's a Pemex gas station on the west side of town. The next town to appear out of the lush countryside is Bolonchén de Rejón, after 34km. Its local **festival of Santa Cruz** is held each year on May 3.

Bolonchén de Rejón is near the **Grutas de Xtacumbilxunaan** (admission $3; ☯ 8am-6pm), pronounced 'Grutas de *shtaa*-koom-beel-shoo-*nahn*,' about 3km south of town. Lighted steps lead down to a barely visible cenote, beyond which a passage leads 100m further. There are few stalactites or stalagmites, but the climb back up to the green forest surrounding the cave is very dramatic.

Hwy 261 continues north into Yucatán state to Uxmal (p930), with a side road leading to the ruins along the Ruta Puuc (p934).

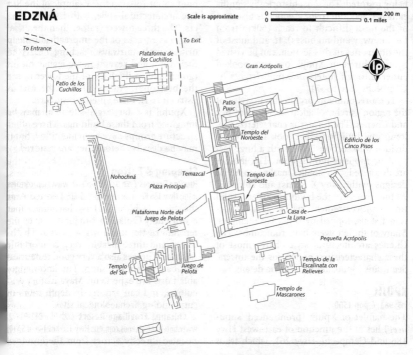

EDZNÁ

To travel between Xtacumbilxunaan and the city of Campeche by car, follow Hwy 261 south back to the town of San Antonio Cayal where you'll see signs for the clearly marked (though unnumbered) road heading directly west to Campeche (approximately 50km)

ESCÁRCEGA TO XPUJIL

Hwy 186 heads due east across southern-central Campeche state, from grubby Escárcega through jungle to Xpujil and on to Chetumal – in Quintana Roo – a 273km ride. It passes several fascinating Maya sites and goes through the ecologically diverse and archaeologically rich **Reserva de la Biosfera Calakmul**. The largest settlement between Escárcega and Chetumal – and the only one with accommodations – is Xpujil, on Hwy 186 about 20km west of the Campeche–Quintana Roo border. The only gas station in the same stretch is about 5km east of Xpujil. There is no admission charge for the area.

Many of the numerous archaeological sites between Escárcega and Xpujil are being restored. The most historically significant is Calakmul (p962), which is also one of the most difficult to reach (60km from the highway and no buses). It, and most of the other sites in this section, can be visited by taxis hired in Xpujil, or tours booked either through hotels in Xpujil (right) or Campeche (see p955).

The predominant architectural styles of the region's archaeological sites are Río Bec and Chenes. The former is characterized by long, low buildings that look like they're divided into sections, each with a huge serpent or monster-mouth door. The facades are decorated with smaller masks, geometric designs (with many X forms) and columns. At the corners of the buildings are tall, solid towers with extremely small, steep, nonfunctional steps, topped by small false temples. Many of these towers have roofcombs. The Chenes architectural style shares most of these characteristics, except for the towers. See Ruins (opposite) for specific details.

XPUJIL

☎ 983 / pop 1500

The hamlet of Xpujil (pronounced 'shpu-heel') lies at the junction of east–west Hwy 186 and Campeche Hwy 261, which leads

north to Hopelchén and eventually Mérida. A good base from which to explore the area's sites, Xpujil is growing rapidly in anticipation of a tourist boom. However, it still has no bank or laundry, and the nearest gas station is 5km east of town. Several restaurants, a couple of hotels and a taxi stand are near the bus depot.

From the junction, the Xpuhil ruins are less than 1km west, Becán is 8km west, Chicanná is 12km west, Balamkú is 60km west and the Calakmul ruins are 120km southwest.

Sights

XPUHIL

'Place of the Cattails' in Maya, **Xpuhil** (admission $3; ☉ 8am-5pm) flourished during the late classic period from AD 400–900, though there was a much earlier settlement here. The site's entrance is on the western edge of town on the north side of Hwy 186, at the turnoff for the airport, less than 1km west of the junction.

One large building and three small ones have been restored. Estructura I in Grupo I, built about 760, is a fine example of the Río Bec architectural style, with its lofty towers. The three towers (rather than the usual two) have traces of the impractically steep ornamental stairways reaching nearly to their tops, and several fierce jaguar masks (go around to the back of the tower to see the best one). About 60m to the east is Estructura II, once an elite residence.

Xpuhil is a far larger site than may be imagined from these buildings. Three other structure groups have been identified, but it may be decades before they are restored.

Sleeping & Eating

Río Bec Dreams (☎ 983-871-60-57; www.riobecdreams .com; Hwy 186 Km 142; cabanas $25-60) Located near the ruins of Chicanná. This charming, super eco-friendly Canadian-run jungle haven offers four rustic 'jungalows' with shared bathroom; and three sizable, very comfortable *cabañas*. There is also a very good restaurant and bar, plus a gift shop. The knowledgeable hosts are experts on Maya history and culture, and can arrange in-depth tours of surrounding archaeological sites.

Chicanná Ecovillage Resort (☎ 981-811-91-92; www.hotelesmexicanos.com.mx; Hwy 186 Km 144; d $110) Located directly across from the entrance road to the Chicanná ruins. Lovely, large, airy rooms with ceiling fans are grouped mostly four to a bungalow, and set amid well-tended gardens. There's a pool and restaurant-bar that serves good but expensive meals.

Hotel y Restaurant Calakmul (☎ 983-871-60-29; cabins $22, d with bathroom $40; ✗) The Calakmul is the main hotel in the town of Xpujil. Rooms at the back are large and modern. Its restaurant (meals $4 to $8; open 6am to midnight) is the best in town.

El Mirador Maya (☎ 983-871-60-05; bungalow $30, r $40; ✗) About 1km west of town, this hotel has two small rooms and eight comfortable fan-cooled bungalows with good beds and nice baths. It also has a restaurant (meals $4 to $6; open 6am to midnight).

Getting There & Around
Xpujil is 220km south of Hopelchén, 153km east of Escárcega and 120km west of Chetumal. Stopping in Xpujil are 11 buses daily to Escárcega ($6), five to Campeche ($12 to $15) and five to Chetumal ($6). The bus terminal is just east of the Xpujil junction, on the north side of the highway.

The Xpuhil ruins are within walking distance of Xpujil junction. You may be able to hitch a ride to the access roads for Becán, Chicanná and Balamkú, but for other sites you will need to hire a taxi.

AROUND XPUJIL
This southern peninsular region – now bordering modern-day Guatemala – was the earliest established, longest inhabited, and most densely populated territory in the Maya world. Here you will find the most ancient and most architecturally elaborate archeological sites on the peninsula

Ruins
HORMIGUERO
Spanish for 'anthill,' **Hormiguero** (admission $3; ✗ 8am-5pm) is an old site, with some buildings dating as far back as AD 50; however, the city flourished during the late classic period. Hormiguero has one of the most impressive buildings in the region. Entering the site you will see the 50m-long **Estructura II**, which has a giant Chenes-style monster-mouth doorway with much of its decoration in good condition. You'll also want to see **Estructura V**, 60m to the north.

Hormiguero is reached by heading 14km south from Xpujil junction, then turning right and heading another 8km west on a shoddily paved road.

RÍO BEC
The entrance to the collective farm Ejido 20 de Noviembre, is 10km east of the Xpujil junction, and is signed 'Río Bec.' The unpaved *ejido* road south leads 5km to the collective itself, and its U'lu'um Chac Yuk Nature Reserve. Look for the small store on the left side of the road, and ask there for guides to show you the various sites, which are about 13km further down the very rough road. There is no charge to enter the area, although the guides charge for their services ($10 to $25). 'Río Bec' is the designation for an agglomeration of small sites in a 50-sq-km area southeast of Xpujil. It gave its name to the prevalent architecture style in the region.

The road is passable only when dry, and even then you need a high-clearance vehicle. The way is unsigned as well; you're best off hiring a guide whether you have a 4WD truck or not. A taxi to the *ejido* will charge around $7 for drop-off service; negotiate a waiting time. Though it looks closer on the map, access to Río Bec from the road to Hormiguero is all but impossible.

BECÁN
Eight kilometers west of Xpujil, **Becán** (admission $3; ✗ 8am-5pm) sits atop a rock outcrop, and a 2km moat snakes its way around the entire city to protect it from attack. Becán – literally 'path of the snake' – is also the Maya word for 'canyon' or 'moat.' Seven causeways crossed the moat, providing access to the city. Becán was occupied from 550 BC until AD 1000.

This is among the largest and most elaborate sites in the area. The first thing you'll come to is a plaza. If you walk while keeping it to your left, you'll pass through a rock-walled passageway and beneath a corbeled arch. You will reach a huge twin-towered temple with cylindrical columns at the top of a flight of stairs. This is **Estructura VIII**, dating from about AD 600 to 730. The view from the top of this temple has become partially obscured by the trees, but on a clear day you can still see structures at the Xpuhil ruins to the east.

Northwest of Estructura VIII is Plaza Central, ringed by 30m-high **Estructura IX** (the tallest building at the site) and the more interesting **Estructura X**. In early 2001, at X's far south side, a stucco mask still bearing some red paint was uncovered. It is enclosed in a wooden shelter with a window for viewing.

In the jungle to the west are more ruins, including the Plaza Oeste, which is surrounded by low buildings and a ball court. Much of this area is still being excavated and restored, so it's open to the public only intermittently.

Loop back east, through the passageway again, to the plaza; cross it diagonally to the right, climbing a stone staircase to the Plaza Sureste. Around this plaza are Estructuras I through IV; a circular altar (Estructura IIIA) lies on the east side. Estructura I has the two towers typical of the Río Bec style. To exit, you can go around the plaza counterclockwise and descend the stone staircase on the southeast side, or go down the southwest side and head left.

CHICANNÁ

Buried in the jungle almost 12km west of Xpujil and 500m south of the highway, **Chicanná** (admission $3; 🕒 8am-5pm), 'House of the Snake's Jaws,' is a mixture of Chenes and Río Bec architectural styles. The city was occupied from about AD 300–1100.

Enter through the modern *palapa* admission building, then follow the rock paths through the jungle to Grupo D and **Estructura XX** (AD 830), which features not one, but two monster-mouth doorways, one above the other, and atop this a roofcomb.

A five-minute walk along the jungle path brings you to Grupo C, with two low buildings (Estructuras X and XI) on a raised platform; the temples bear a few fragments of decoration.

The buildings in Grupo B (turn right when leaving Grupo C) have some intact decoration as well, and there's a good roofcomb on Estructura VI.

Shortly beyond is Chicanná's most famous building, **Estructura II** (AD 750–770) in Grupo A, with its gigantic Chenes-style monster-mouth doorway, believed to depict the jaws of the god Itzamná, Lord of the Heavens and creator of all things. If you photograph nothing else here, you'll want a picture of this, best taken in the afternoon.

BALAMKÚ

Discovered in 1990, **Balamkú** (admission $3; 🕒 8am-5pm) is 60km west of Xpujil (88km east of Escárcega). This small site's attractions are its frescoes and an exquisite, ornate stucco frieze. Amazingly, much original color is still visible on both the frescoes and the frieze. You'll notice toads dominate the designs at Balamkú. These amphibians, not only at home on land and water, were considered to move easily between this world and the next as well. The toad was a revered spirit guide that helped humans navigate between earth and the underworld.

The frescoes are open to public viewing, but the frieze is housed in a locked building. The caretaker will open the door and even provide a flashlight tour upon request (a tip is appreciated).

CALAKMUL

First discovered by outsiders in 1931, by US botanist Cyrus Lundell, **Calakmul** (admission $4; 🕒 8am-5pm) means 'Adjacent Mounds'. Mayanists consider Calakmul to be a site of vital archaeological significance. This historic site was once the seat of a nearly unrivaled superpower. It was even furtherreaching in size – and often influence – than neighboring Tikal in Guatemala.

From about AD 250–695, Calakmul was the leading city in a vast region known as the Kingdom of the Serpent's Head. Its perpetual rival was Tikal, and its decline began with the power struggles and internal conflicts that followed the defeat by Tikal of Calakmul's king Garra de Jaguar (Jaguar Paw).

As at Tikal, there are indications that construction occurred over a period of more than a millennium. Beneath Edificio VII, archaeologists discovered a burial crypt with some 2000 pieces of jade, and tombs continue to yield spectacular jade burial masks; many of these objects are on display in Campeche city's Museo Arqueológico. Calakmul holds at least 120 carved stelae, though many are eroded.

So far, only a fraction of Calakmul's 100-sq-km expanse has been cleared, and few of its 6500 buildings have been consolidated, let alone restored; however, exploration and restoration are ongoing.

Lying at the heart of the vast, untrammeled Reserva de la Biosfera Calakmul (one of the two Unesco-designated biosphere regions on the Yucatán Peninsula; Reserva de la Biosfera Sian Ka'an is the other) the ruins are surrounded by rainforest, which is best viewed from the top of one of the several pyramids. There are over 250 bird species living in the reserve, and you are likely to see wild turkeys, parrots and toucans. The menagerie of other wildlife protected by the reserve includes jaguars, spider monkeys, pumas, ocelots and white-lipped peccaries.

The turnoff to Calakmul is 59km west of Xpujil, and the site is 59km further south on a paved road. A toll of $4 per car (more for heavier vehicles) and $2 per person is levied at the turnoff from Hwy 186.

Sleeping & Eating

Accommodations in the park are few and eating options limited to one: the restaurant at Puerta Calakmul.

Yaxche (☎ 983-871-60-64; campsite/cabin $12/20) Coordinated by the eco-tourism organization Servidores Túristicos Calakmul, this well-organized campground is a few kilometers inside the biosphere reserve. There are campsites and a few basic cabins.

Puerta Calakmul (☎ 984-803-2696; www.puerta calakmul.com.mx; cabins $60-80) A comfortable place, located about 300m east of the access road, just in from the highway. It has 15 tastefully decorated, fan-cooled cabins. The restaurant serves generous meals and there is a small pool.

Getting There & Away

From Calakmul, the 59km drive back to Hwy 186 is necessary before traveling to points beyond. The closest bus service is in Xpujil, 120km northeast. From there buses depart to destinations throughout the peninsula; for details see Getting There & Around (p961).

Directory

CONTENTS

ACCOMMODATIONS

Accommodations in Mexico range from hammocks and huts, to hotels of every imaginable standard and world-class luxury resorts. This book divides accommodations into three price ranges: budget (where a typical room for two people costs under $35), midrange ($35 to $85) and top end (above $85).

Budget accommodations include camping grounds, hammocks, palm-thatched *cabañas,* backpacker hostels, guesthouses and economical hotels. Recommended accommodations will be simple and without frills but generally clean. Hotel rooms, even

in the budget range, usually have a private bathroom containing hot shower, WC and washbasin. (In this book, rooms are assumed to have private bathroom unless otherwise stated.)

Midrange accommodations are chiefly hotels, ranging in comfort and atmosphere according to price, though in some areas of Mexico even $35 can get you a cozy, attractively decorated room in a friendly small hotel. Some midrange hotels have swimming pools, restaurants, in-house travel agencies and other facilities. Many of the country's most appealing and memorable lodgings are in this bracket – small or medium-sized hotels, well cared for, with a friendly atmosphere and personal attention from staff. In some areas you'll also find apartments, bungalows and more comfortable *cabañas* in this same price range.

Top-end hotels run from classy international hotels in the cities, to deluxe coastal resort-hotels and luxurious smaller establishments catering to travelers with a taste for comfort and beautiful design, and the funds to pay for it.

Room prices given in this book are high-season prices, which in most of Mexico means Semana Santa (the week before Easter and a couple of days after it), most of July and August, and the Christmas–New Year holiday period of about two weeks. Outside the peak seasons, many midrange and top-end establishments in tourist destinations cut their room prices by 10% to 40%. Budget accommodations are more likely to keep the same rates all year. Through this book we note major deviations from the normal seasonal pattern; in some places or the Pacific coast and the Yucatán Peninsula, for example, high season runs from Christmas right through to Easter. We also note special deals, low weekend rates and other ways you can cut costs.

In this book we use 'single' (abbreviated to 's') to mean a room for one person, and 'double' ('d') to mean a room for two people. Mexicans sometimes use the phrase *cuarto sencillo* (literally, single room) to mean a room with one bed, which is often a *cama matrimonial* (double bed); sometimes one person can occupy such a room for a lower price than two people. A *cuarto doble* often means a room with two beds, which may both be *camas matrimoniales*.

In popular destinations at busy times, it's best to reserve a room in advance, or go early in the day to secure a room. Many places take reservations through their websites or by email. Otherwise try by telephone or fax – if the place is not booked out, a simple phone call earlier in the day, saying what time you'll arrive, is usually sufficient. A few places are reluctant to take reservations, but don't worry, you'll always end up with a room somewhere.

Accommodation prices are subject to two taxes: IVA (value-added tax; 15%) and ISH (lodging tax; 2% in most states). Many budget and some midrange establishments only charge these taxes if you require a receipt, and they quote room rates accordingly (ie not including taxes). Generally, though, IVA and ISH are included in quoted prices. In top-end hotels a price may often be given as, say, '$100 *más impuestos*' ($100 plus taxes), in which case you must add 17% to the figure. When in doubt, you can ask: '*¿Están incluidos los impuestos?*' ('Are taxes included?'). Prices given in this book are those you are most likely to be charged at each place, with or without the taxes, according to the establishment's policy.

Apartments

In some places you can find *departamentos* (apartments) available for tourists, with fully equipped kitchens. Some are very comfortable and they can be good value for three or four people. Tourist offices and ads in local papers (especially English-language papers) are good sources of information on these.

B&Bs

Mexico's few B&Bs are generally upmarket guesthouses, often aimed at foreign tourists – they are usually comfortable and enjoyable places to stay.

Camping & Trailer Parks

Most organized campgrounds are actually trailer parks set up for RVs (recreational vehicles, camper vans) and trailers (caravans), but are open to tent campers at lower rates. They're most common along the coasts. Some are very basic, others quite luxurious. Expect to pay about $5 to pitch a tent for two, and $10 to $20 for two people with a vehicle, using full facilities. Some restaurants and guesthouses in beach spots or country areas will let you pitch a tent on their patch for a couple of dollars per person.

Casas de Huéspedes & Posadas

Inexpensive and congenial accommodations are often to be found at a *casa de huéspedes*, a home converted into simple guest lodgings. Good *casas de huéspedes* are usually family-run, with a relaxed, friendly atmosphere.

Many *posadas* (inns) are like *casas de huéspedes*; others are small hotels.

Hammocks & Cabañas

You'll find hammocks and *cabañas* available mainly in low-key beach spots in the southern half of the country. A hammock can be a very comfortable place to sleep in hot, southern areas (but mosquito repellent often comes in handy). You can rent one and a place to hang it – usually under a palm roof outside a small guesthouse or beach restaurant – for $3 or $4 in some places, though it can reach $12 on the more expensive Caribbean coast. With your own hammock, the cost comes down a bit. It's easy enough to buy hammocks in Mexico, especially in the states of Oaxaca and Chiapas and on the Yucatán Peninsula.

Cabañas are usually huts (of wood, brick, adobe, stone etc) with a palm-thatched roof. Some have dirt floors and nothing inside but a bed; others are deluxe, with electric light, mosquito nets, fans, fridge, bar and decor. Prices for simple *cabañas* range from $10 to $35. The most expensive ones are on the Caribbean where some luxury *cabañas* cost over $100.

Hostels

Hostels for budget travelers exist in many of the towns and cities where backpackers congregate, especially in the center and south of Mexico. They provide dormitory accommodation for $5 to $12 per person, plus communal kitchens, bathrooms, living space and sometimes private rooms. Standards of hygiene and security do vary, but aside from being cheap, hostels are generally relaxed, and good places to meet other travelers. **HostelWorld** (www.hostelworld .com) has listings.

A dozen hostels are members of Mexico's HI affiliate, **Hostelling International Mexico** (www.hostellingmexico.com, www.hihostels.com), whose flagship is Hostel Catedral (p152) in Mexico City. There's a dollar or two off nightly rates for HI members at these places.

Hotels

Mexico specializes in good midrange hotels where two people can get a comfortable room with private bathroom, TV, and often air-conditioning for $35 to $60. Often there's a restaurant and bar. Among the most charming lodgings, in both the midrange and the top end brackets, are the many old mansions, inns, and even convents, turned into hotels. These can be wonderfully atmospheric, with fountains gurgling in flower-bedecked stone courtyards. Some are a bit spartan (but relatively low in price); others have modern comforts and are more expensive. These are probably the lodgings you will remember most fondly after your trip.

Every Mexican town also has its cheap hotels. There are clean, friendly, secure ones, and there are dark, dirty, smelly ones where you may not feel your belongings are safe. Decent rooms with a private hot shower are available for under $25 per double in most of the country.

Mexico has plenty of large, modern luxury hotels too, particularly in the coastal resorts and largest cities. They offer the expected levels of luxury – with pools, gyms, bars, restaurants and so on – at prices that are sometimes agreeably modest (and sometimes not!). If you like to stay in luxury but also enjoy saving some money, look for a Mexican hotel that's not part of an international chain.

Fortunately for families and small groups of travelers, many hotels in all price ranges have rooms for three, four or five people that cost not much more than a double.

PRACTICALITIES

- Mexicans use the metric system for weights and measures.

- Most prerecorded videotapes on sale in Mexico (like the rest of the Americas and Japan) use the NTSC image registration system, incompatible with the PAL system common to most of Western Europe and Australia, and the SECAM system used in France.

- If buying DVDs, look for the numbered globe motif indicating which regions of the world it can be played in. Region 1 is the US and Canada; Europe and Japan are in region 2; and Australia and New Zealand join Mexico in Region 4.

- Electrical current is 110V, 60Hz, and most plugs have two flat prongs, as in the US and Canada.

- Mexico's only English-language daily newspaper (sort of) is *The Herald* – which is the *Miami Herald* with an eight-page Mexico insert – available in Mexico City and some other cities. The best and most independent-minded Mexican national newspapers include *Reforma* and the left-wing *La Jornada*.

- For the online editions of about 300 Mexican newspapers and magazines, and links to hundreds of Mexican radio and TV stations and other media sites, visit www.zonalatina.com.

- Free-to-air TV is dominated by Televisa, which runs four of the six main national channels; TV Azteca has two (Azteca 7 and Azteca 13). Many viewers have multichannel cable systems, such as Cablevision, but switch to Televisa for news and soap operas *(telenovelas)*.

- Two good noncommercial TV channels are Once TV (11 TV), run by Mexico City's Instituto Politécnico Nacional, and Canal 22, run by Conaculta, the National Culture & Arts Council.

ACTIVITIES

You can hike, bike, climb, canoe, kayak, raft, ride horses and watch wildlife in some of the country's most spectacular areas, and have fun enjoying most imaginable aquatic activities along Mexico's coasts. The following is a brief introduction to what you can do and where you can do it; for more detail, see the destination sections of this book. Good sources on active tourism in Mexico include **AMTAVE** (Mexican Association of Adventure Travel & Ecotourism; ☎ 55-5688-3883, 800-654-44-52; www.amtave.com), based in Mexico City with 60 member organizations and companies around the country, and the websites www.planeta.com, www.gorp.com and www.mexonline.com.

Climbing

The Mexican mecca for technical climbers is the limestone of Potrero Chico (see boxed text, p412), north of Monterrey, with 600 routes developed. Popocatépetl, the famous volcano east of Mexico City, has been off-limits for several years because of volcanic activity, but other peaks in Mexico's central volcanic belt – including Pico de Orizaba (p703), Mexico's highest, and Iztaccíhuatl (p204) – present fine challenges. Parque Nacional El Chico (p202) is another popular climbing locale. Guides are available for all these places. A good book is *Mexico's Volcanoes: A Climbing Guide* by RJ Secor. Conditions at high altitude are best from October to February.

Hiking

Trails in the Barranca del Cobre (Copper Canyon, p336) and Oaxaca's Pueblos Mancomunados (p746) are among the most spectacular, popular and developed. Other fine hiking areas that don't require climbing skills include Parque Nacional El Chico (p202), the Reserva de la Biosfera El Cielo (p396), the Sierra de la Giganta (p292), Reserva de la Biosfera Sierra de la Laguna (p300), Nevado de Toluca (p260), Volcán Paricutín (p585), Volcán Nevado de Colima (p557), La Malinche (p211), Malpasito (p802), Volcán Tacaná (p861) and the lower slopes of Iztaccíhuatl (p204). A guide is a very good idea for many routes, as trail marking is incipient and walking alone across remote territory can be risky. The best seasons for hiking vary from place to place, but conditions at high altitude are usually best from October to February.

Horseback Riding

Increasingly popular among visitors, good riding is available at many places, including Valle de Bravo (p260), Álamos (p328), the Barranca del Cobre (Copper Canyon; p345), the Sierra de la Giganta (p292), Puerto Vallarta (p457), Real de Catorce (p617) and Ocosingo (p829). And you can canter along the beaches at Mazatlán (p430), Sayulita (p449), Barra de Potosí (p498), Pie de la Cuesta (p499), Puerto Escondido (p757) and many other Pacific resorts.

Mountain Biking

Countless tracks and trails through magnificent country await pedalers. You'll find mountain bikes available for rent or for guided trips of up to several days in places as diverse as Loreto (p292) in Baja California, the Barranca del Cobre (Copper Canyon, p346), Puerto Vallarta (p458), Oaxaca (p724) and San Cristóbal de Las Casas (p826). See p996 for some tips on cycling in Mexico.

Water Sports

Most coastal resorts rent snorkel gear and can arrange boat and fishing trips. There's great diving along the Caribbean coast, but also some fine spots on the Pacific. Waterskiing, parasailing, jet skiing and 'banana' riding are widespread resort activities. Always cast an eye over the equipment before taking off.

Inland are many *balnearios* – bathing places with swimming pools, often centered on health-giving hot springs in picturesque natural surroundings – such as those near San Miguel de Allende (p647) and at Cuautla (p235) and Ixtapan de la Sal (p263). There are few more extraordinary experiences than bathing – and snorkeling – amid Mexico's northern deserts in the pellucid pools of Cuatro Ciénegas (p414).

FISHING

Mexico is justly famous for its sportfishing for marlin, swordfish, sailfish and tuna along the Pacific coast and Sea of Cortez. Deep-sea charters are available in all of the major Pacific resorts, many of them now practicing catch-and-release for billfish.

The prime locations include Ensenada (p277), Loreto (p292), La Paz (p297), Cabo San Lucas (p306), Mazatlán (p430), Puerto Vallarta (p457), Barra de Navidad (p471), Manzanillo (p476), Puerto Escondido (p757) and Puerto Ángel (p767). In general the biggest catches occur from April to July and from October to December. Fishing licenses (costing around $12/24 per day/week) are required for fishing from boats in estuaries and on the ocean; charters usually include them, but you'll need your own if you hire a local fisher to take you out. Most towns have an *oficina de pesca* (fisheries office) that issues licenses.

Elsewhere, there's lake and reservoir fishing inland, and some very good lagoon, river and sea fishing along the Gulf and Caribbean coasts. Fanatics flock to Barra del Tordo (p393) and La Pesca (p393) in the northeast, and Punta Allen (p906) in the southeast.

KAYAKING, CANOEING & RAFTING

Mexico's many coastal lagoons and sheltered bays make magnificent waters for kayaks and canoes, and there's often interesting wildlife to be seen in the places you'll reach. Rent equipment at prime sites such as La Paz (p297), Cabo San Lucas (p306) and Loreto (p292) in Baja California; Sayulita (p449), Barra de Navidad (p471), Barra de Potosí (p498), Acapulco (p508), Laguna Manialtepec (p763) and Bahías de Huatulco (p780) on the Pacific coast; and on the Caribbean coast at Cancún (p871).

Xalapa (p684), capital of Veracruz state, where rivers fall dramatically from the Sierra Madre Oriental to the coastal plain, is the hub for white-water rafting, called *descenso de ríos* in Mexico. You can also raft at Bahías de Huatulco (p780) in Oaxaca from July to November, and on some rivers in Chiapas (p818 and p845). Always use a reliable company with good equipment and experienced guides.

A Gringo's Guide to Mexican Whitewater by Tom Robey details 56 kayak, canoe and raft runs on 37 different rivers.

SNORKELING & DIVING

The Caribbean is world famous for its wonderful coral reefs and translucent waters full of tropical fish. Great diving locations include Cozumel (p888), Isla Mujeres (p879), Playa del Carmen (p893), Akumal (p897), Paamul (p897), Punta Allen (p906) and the Banco Chinchorro coral atoll (p910). Most of these are good for snorkeling too. Inland you can dive some of the Yucatán's famed cenotes (limestone sinkholes) near Akumal (p898).

On the Pacific coast, strap on your tanks at Mazatlán (p430), Puerto Vallarta (p456), Manzanillo (p476), Zihuatanejo (p493), Puerto Escondido (p757) or Bahías de

---

SAFETY GUIDELINES FOR DIVING

Before embarking on a scuba diving, skin diving or snorkeling trip, carefully consider the following points to ensure a safe and enjoyable experience:

- Possess a current diving-certification card from a recognized scuba-diving instructional agency (if scuba diving).

- Be sure you are healthy and feel comfortable diving.

- Obtain reliable information about physical and environmental conditions at the dive site from a reputable local dive operation.

- Be aware of local laws, regulations and etiquette about marine life and the environment.

- Dive only at sites within your realm of experience; if available, engage the services of a competent, professionally trained dive instructor or dive master.

- Be aware that underwater conditions vary significantly from one region (or even site) to another. Seasonal changes can significantly alter any site or dive conditions. These differences influence the way divers dress for a dive and what diving techniques they use.

- Ask about the environmental characteristics that can affect your diving, and how local trained divers deal with these considerations.

Huatulco (p780). There's top snorkeling at most of these places too, and elsewhere.

Baja California's top diving and/or snorkeling locales are Mulegé (p289), Loreto (p292), La Ventana (p300), Cabo Pulmo (p300) and Cabo San Lucas (p306).

When renting diving equipment, try to make sure that it's up to standard. And beware of dive shops that promise certification after just a few hours' tuition. The websites of the international diving organizations **PADI** (www.padi.com) and **NAUI** (www.naui.com) enable you to search for the affiliated dive shops. The **FMAS** (www.fmas.org.mx), also internationally recognized, is the Mexican equivalent of PADI and NAUI.

Coral reefs and other marine ecosystems are particularly fragile environments. For tips on responsible diving, see boxed text, p889.

SURFING & WINDSURFING

The Pacific coast has awesome waves. Among the very best are the summer breaks between San José del Cabo and Cabo San Lucas in Baja California (see p304); the 'world's longest wave' on Bahía de Matanchén (p442), near San Blas; and the barreling 'Mexican Pipeline' at Puerto Escondido (p756). Other fine spots include Ensenada (p277), Mazatlán (p430), Sayulita (p449), Barra de Navidad (p471), Manzanillo (p475), Barra de Nexpa (p481), Troncones (p484), Playa Revolcadero (p507) near Acapulco, and Barra de la Cruz (p784) east of Bahías de Huatulco… for starters. Most beach breaks receive some sort of surf all year, but wave season is really May to October/November, with June, July and August the biggest months. You can rent surfboards in a few spots. If you're planning to fly to Mexico with your own board, check with the airline first: most of them charge $50 or more (each way) to carry surfboards, and some won't carry them at all to some destinations or at some times of year.

Los Barriles (p300) is Baja California's windsurfing capital (September to March). Further south, Puerto Vallarta (p456) and Manzanillo (p476) can be good too.

Wildlife & Bird-Watching

Observing Mexico's varied and exotic fauna is an increasingly popular and practicable pastime – see p83 for an introduction to what you can see and where.

BUSINESS HOURS

Stores (shops) are typically open from 9am to 8pm, Monday to Saturday. In the south of the country and in small towns, some stores close for a siesta between 2pm and 4pm, then stay open till 9pm. Some don't open on Saturday afternoon. Stores in malls and coastal resort towns often open on Sunday. Supermarkets and department stores usually open from 9am or 10am to 10pm every day.

Offices have similar Monday to Friday hours to stores, with greater likelihood of the 2pm to 4pm lunch break. Government offices are usually not open to the public after lunch (their staff have much more important things to do). Offices with tourist-related business usually open on Saturday too, from at least 9am to 1pm.

Typical restaurant hours are 7am (9am in central Mexico) to between 10pm and midnight. If a restaurant has a closing day, it's usually Sunday, Monday or Tuesday. Cafés typically open from 8am to 10pm daily. Bars too are normally open daily, but each seems to have its own special pattern of hours.

Banks are normally open 9am to 5pm Monday to Friday, and 9am to 1am Saturday. In smaller towns they may close earlier or not open on Saturday. *Casas de cambio* (money-exchange offices) are usually open from 9am to 7pm daily, often with even longer hours in coastal resorts. Post offices typically open from 8am to 6pm Monday to Friday, and 9am to 1pm Saturday.

In this book we only spell out opening hours where they do not fit the above parameters. See inside the front cover for more typical opening hours.

CHILDREN

Mexicans love children, and will affectionately call any child whose hair is less than jet black '*güero*' (blondie). Children are welcome at all kinds of hotels and in virtually every café and restaurant. In this book you'll find especially child-friendly attractions and places to stay and eat identified with the 🛉 icon.

The sights, sounds and colors of Mexico excite and stimulate most children, but few kids like traveling all the time; they're happier if they can settle into a place for a while and make friends. Try to give them time to

DIRECTORY

get on with some of what they like doing back home. Children are also more easily affected than adults by heat, disrupted sleeping patterns and strange food. They need time to acclimatize and you should take extra care to avoid sunburn. Ensure you replace fluids if a child gets diarrhea (see p1011).

Lonely Planet's *Travel with Children* has lots of practical advice on the subject, drawn from firsthand experience.

Documents for Under-18 Travelers

To conform with regulations aimed at preventing international child abduction, minors (people under 18) traveling to Mexico without one or both of their parents may need to carry a notarized consent form signed by the absent parent or parents, giving permission for the young traveler to make the international journey. Though Mexico does not specifically require this documentation, airlines flying to Mexico may refuse to board passengers without it. In the case of divorced parents, a custody document may be required. If one or both parents are dead, or the traveler has only one legal parent, a death certificate or notarized statement of the situation may be required.

These rules are aimed primarily at visitors from the USA and Canada, but may also apply to people from elsewhere. Procedures vary from country to country; contact your country's foreign affairs department and/or a Mexican consulate to find out exactly what you need to do. Required forms for these purposes are usually available from these authorities.

Practicalities

Cots for hotel rooms and high chairs for restaurants are available mainly in mid-range and top-end establishments. If you want a rental car with a child safety seat, the major international rental firms are the most reliable providers. You will probably have to pay a few dollars extra per day.

It's usually not hard to find an inexpensive baby-sitter if parents want to go out on their own – ask at your hotel. Diapers (nappies) are widely available, but if you depend on some particular cream, lotion, baby food or medicine, bring it with you. Public breast-feeding is not common and, when done, is done discreetly.

On flights to and within Mexico, children under two generally travel for 10% of the adult fare, as long as they do not occupy a seat, and those aged two to 11 normally pay 67%. Children under 13 pay half-price on many Mexican long-distance buses, and if they're small enough to sit on your lap, they will usually go for free.

Sights & Activities

In some places, apart from the obvious beaches and swimming pools, you'll find excellent special attractions such as amusement parks, water parks, zoos, aquariums, safari parks and adventure parks with zip lines, abseiling and other fun activities. These attractions tend to cluster in and around the cities – such as Mexico City (p150), Monterrey (boxed text, p404), Mérida (p921) and Villahermosa (p793 and p799) – and in coastal resorts such as Cancún (p871), Mazatlán (p431) and Acapulco (p509). Other notably child-friendly attractions include the Africam Safari park near Puebla (p223).

Kids don't have to be very old to enjoy activities such as snorkeling, riding bicycles, horses and boats, and watching wildlife (p967), and even – for some! – shopping and visiting markets. Many kids will stay happy for under $1 an hour at Mexico's myriad Internet cafés – and archaeological sites can be fun if they're into climbing pyramids and exploring tunnels (few kids aren't).

CLIMATE CHARTS

June to October are the hottest and wettest months across most of Mexico. For tips on the best seasons to travel, see p25.

COURSES

Taking classes in Mexico can be a great way to meet people and get an inside angle on local life, as well as study the language or culture. The country specializes in short courses in the Spanish language. In addition, Mexican universities and colleges often offer tuition to complement college courses you may be taking back home. For long-term study in Mexico you'll need a student visa; contact a Mexican consulate about these.

A good US source on study possibilities in Mexico is the **Council on International Educational Exchange** (www.ciee.org). There are also helpful links on the **Lonely Planet website** (www.lonelyplanet.com).

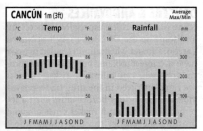

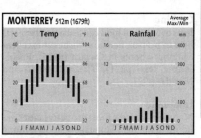

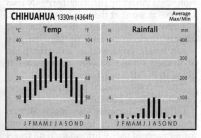

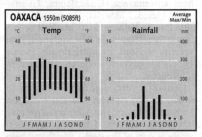

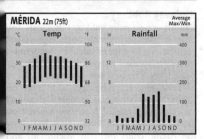

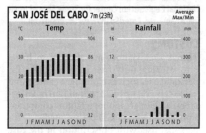

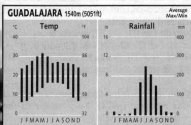

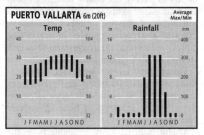

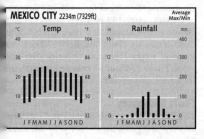

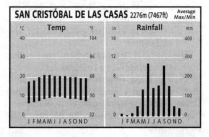

Cooking

Fans of Mexican food can learn from experts how to prepare delicious dishes at excellent cooking schools in Oaxaca (p726), Puebla (boxed text, p221), Tlaxcala (p208) and Mérida (p921).

Language

Many of Mexico's most attractive cities are home to Spanish language schools, among them Cuernavaca, Guadalajara, Guanajuato, Mérida, Morelia, Oaxaca, Mexico City, Puerto Vallarta, San Cristóbal de Las Casas, San Miguel de Allende and Taxco (see city sections for more details). Some schools are private, some are affiliated to universities.

Course lengths range from a few days to a year. In many places you can enroll on the spot and start any Monday. You may be offered accommodations with a local family as part of the deal – which can help your language skills as much as the formal tuition. In a growing number of schools, extra or alternative courses in art, crafts, dance, indigenous languages and in-depth studies of Mexico are also available.

Costs per week, with accommodations and meals included, can range from around $180 to over $400, depending on the city, the school and how intensively you study.

Useful information is available from the **National Registration Center for Study Abroad** (www .nrcsa.com) and **AmeriSpan** (www.amerispan.com).

CUSTOMS

Things that visitors are allowed to bring into Mexico duty-free include items for personal use, such as clothing; a camera and video camera; up to 12 rolls of film or videotapes; a cellular phone; a laptop computer; a portable radio or CD player; medicine for personal use, with prescription in the case of psychotropic drugs; 3L of wine, beer or liquor (adults only); 400 cigarettes (adults); and $300 worth of other goods ($50 if arriving by land).

The normal routine when you enter Mexico is to complete a customs declaration form (which lists duty-free allowances), and then place it in a machine. If the machine shows a green light, you pass without inspection. If a red light shows, your baggage will be searched.

DANGERS & ANNOYANCES

Some Mexican cities, especially Mexico City and some on the US border (such as Nuevo Laredo, Tijuana, Mexicali and Ciudad Juárez), have a crime problem, but with a few precautions you can minimize risks. Tourists are rarely involved in the drug trade–related violence that brings border cities such a lot of bad publicity, but it makes sense to avoid crossing the border through towns where violence is currently particularly rife (Nuevo Laredo was worst at the time of writing).

Enjoy yourself along the coasts, but beware undertows and riptides on any ocean beach. Lone women and even pairs of women should be very cautious about going to isolated beach spots.

And everyone should be extremely careful with taxis in Mexico City.

Official information can make Mexico sound more alarming than it really is, but for a variety of useful information on travel to Mexico consult your country's foreign affairs department:

Australia (☎ 1300-139-281; www.dfat.gov.au)
Canada (☎ 800-267-6788; www.dfait-maeci.gc.ca)
UK (☎ 0845-850-2829; www.fco.gov.uk)
USA (☎ 888-407-4747; travel.state.gov)

If you're already in Mexico, you can contact your embassy (p974). Keep an ear to the ground as you travel.

Highway Robbery

Bandits occasionally hold up buses, cars and other vehicles on intercity routes, especially at night, taking luggage or valuables. Sometimes buses are robbed by people who board as passengers. The best ways to avoid highway robbery are to travel by day and to travel on toll highways as much as possible. Deluxe and 1st-class buses use toll highways, where they exist; 2nd-class buses do not. Hwy 200, along the Pacific coast through Michoacán and Guerrero states and as far south as Pochutla in Oaxaca, Hwy 199 between Palenque and Ocosingo in Chiapas, and Hwy 175 between Oaxaca city and Pochutla, have all been the scene of many highway robberies over the years. Hwys 134 and 51 between Ixtapa and Iguala are also robbery-prone.

Theft & Robbery

Tourists are vulnerable to theft and robbery, as they are generally wealthy by Mexican standards and are considered likely to be carrying valuables. Pocket-picking and purse- or bag-snatching are risks on crowded buses, subway trains, at bus stops, bus stations, airports, markets, packed streets and plazas, and anywhere frequented by large numbers of tourists – especially in Mexico City and other large cities.

Pickpockets often work in teams, crowding in on their victims in already crowded places like markets or city buses: one or two of them may grab your bag or camera (or your arm or leg), and while you're trying to get free another will pick your pocket. Or one may 'drop' something as a crowd jostles onto a bus and, as he or she 'looks for it,' a pocket will be picked or a bag slashed. The objective is to distract you. If your valuables are underneath your clothing, the chances of losing them are greatly reduced.

Mugging is less common than pocket-picking and purse-snatching, but more alarming and more serious: resistance may be met with violence (do *not* resist). These robbers may force you to remove your money belt, watch, rings etc. They may be armed. Usually they will not harm you, they just want your money, fast. But there have been cases of robbers beating victims, or forcing them to drink large amounts of alcohol to extract credit-card security numbers.

To avoid being robbed in cities, even tourist resorts, do not go where there are few other people. This includes empty streets and empty metro cars at night, and little-used pedestrian underpasses and similar places. Use taxis instead of walking in potentially dodgy areas. And, in Mexico City, make sure you take the right kind of cab (see p127).

Isolated stretches of beach can also be risky. Never camp in any lonely spot unless you are absolutely sure it's safe.

As you travel, you will develop a sense of which situations and places are more threatening than others. To reduce your chances of becoming a victim, adhere to the following rules:

- Leave most of your money, credit cards, passport, jewelry and air tickets in a sealed, signed envelope in your hotel's safe, unless you have immediate need of these items. Virtually all hotels, except the very cheapest, provide safekeeping for guests' valuables.

- Leave valuables in a locked suitcase in your hotel room, or a locker in a hostel dorm, rather than carry them on the streets of cities. If you have to leave money, cards or checks in your room, divide them into several stashes and hide them in different places.

- Carry a small amount of ready money – just enough for your outing – in a pocket. If you have to carry valuables, avoid making your pockets bulge with them, and preferably keep them in a money belt, shoulder wallet or pouch underneath your clothing.

- Walk with purpose and be alert to people around you.

- Don't keep cash, credit cards, purses, bags or cameras in open view any longer than you have to. At ticket counters in bus stations and airports, keep your bag between your feet.

- Use ATMs only in secure locations, not those open to the street, and try to use them during daylight.

- Do not leave anything valuable-looking visible in a parked vehicle.

- Don't accept lifts offered by strangers.

- Be careful about accepting food or drinks from strangers, especially in resort cities and on buses; there have been cases of drugging followed by robbery and assault, including sexual assault.

- Go easy on alcohol: it reduces your awareness and reactions and makes you an easier victim.

- Be wary of attempts at credit-card fraud. One method is when the cashier swipes your card twice (once for the transaction and once for nefarious purposes). Keep your card in sight at all times.

DISABLED TRAVELERS

Mexico is not yet very disabled-friendly, though some hotels and restaurants (mostly towards the top end of the market) and some public buildings and archaeological sites now provide wheelchair access. Mobility is easiest in the major tourist resorts and the more expensive hotels. Bus transportation can be difficult; flying or taking a taxi is easier.

Mobility International USA (☎ 541-343-1284; www.miusa.org) advises disabled travelers on mobility issues and runs exchange programs (including some in Mexico). Its website includes international databases of exchange programs and disability organizations, with several Mexican organizations listed.

In the UK, **Radar** (☎ 020-7250-3222; www.radar .org.uk) is run by and for disabled people. Its excellent website has links to good travel and holiday sites.

Two further terrific information sources for disabled travelers are **MossRehab ResourceNet** (www.mossresourcenet.org) and **Access-able Travel Source** (www.access-able.com).

DISCOUNT CARDS

The ISIC student card, the IYTC card for travelers under 26, and the ITIC card for teachers can help you obtain reduced-price air tickets to or from Mexico at student- and youth-oriented travel agencies. Reduced prices on Mexican buses and at museums, archaeological sites and so on, are usually only for those with Mexican education credentials, but the ISIC, IYTC and ITIC will sometimes get you a reduction. The ISIC card is the most widely recognized. It may also get you discounts in a few hostel-type accommodations.

A Hostelling International card will save you a dollar or two in some hostels in Mexico. Take it along if you have one.

All these cards can be obtained in Mexico. One outlet is the youth/student travel agency **Mundo Joven** (www.mundojoven.com), with six offices in Mexico City and others in Guadalajara, Puebla, Toluca and León. You need proof of your student/teacher/youth status to obtain the ISIC/ITIC/IYTC card.

EMBASSIES & CONSULATES
Mexican Embassies & Consulates

The following are embassies unless otherwise noted. Updated details can be found at www.sre.gob.mx. Some Mexican embassy and consulate websites have very useful information on visas and similar matters.

Australia (☎ 02-6273-3963; www.mexico.org.au; 14 Perth Ave, Yarralumla, ACT 2600) In Canberra.

Belize (☎ 223-01-93; www.sre.gob.mx/belice; 18 North Park St) In Belize City.

Canada Ottawa (☎ 613-233-8988; www.embamexcan .com; 45 O'Connor St, Suite 1000, ON K1P 1A4); consulate in Montreal (☎ 514-288-2502; www.consulmex.qc.ca; 2055 rue Peel, bureau 1000, QC H3A 1V4); consulate in Toronto (☎ 416-368-2875; www.consulmex.com; 199 Bay St, Suite 4440 Commerce Court West, ON M5L 1E9); consulate

in Vancouver (☎ 604-684-3547; www.consulmexvan.com; 710-1177 West Hastings St, BC V6E 2K3)

France Paris (☎ 01-53-70-27-70; www.sre.gob.mx/fran cia; 9 rue de Longchamp, 75116); consulate in Paris (☎ 01 42 86 56 20; 4 rue Notre Dame des Victoires, 75002)

Germany Berlin (☎ 030-269-323; www.embamex.de; Klingelhöferstrasse 3, 10785 Berlin); consulate in Frankfurt-am-Main (☎ 069-299-8750; www.consulmexfrankfurt .org; Taunusanlage 21, 60325)

Guatemala consulate in Ciudad Tecún Umán (☎ 7776-8181; comexteu@terra.com.gt; 3a Av 4-74, Zona 1); Guatemala City (☎ 2420-3433; www.sre.gob.mx/guatemala; 2a Av 7-57, Zona 10); consulate in Quetzaltenango (☎ 7767-5542; mexicoq@yahoo.com.mx; 21a Av 8-64, Zona 3)

Ireland (☎ 01-260-0699; www.sre.gob.mx/irlanda; 43 Ailesbury Rd, Ballsbridge, Dublin 4)

Italy consulate in Milan (☎ 02-7602-0541; www.mexico .it; Via Cappuccini 4, 20122); Rome (☎ 06-441151; www .sre.gob.mx/italia; Via Lazzaro Spallanzani 16, 00161)

Japan (☎ 3-3581-1131; www.sre.gob.mx/japon; 2-15-1 Nagata-cho, Chiyoda-ku, 100-0014) In Tokyo.

Netherlands (☎ 070-360-2900; www.embamex-nl .com; Nassauplein 28, 2585EC) In The Hague.

New Zealand (☎ 04-472-0555; www.mexico.org.nz; Level 8, 111 Customhouse Quay) In Wellington.

Spain consulate in Barcelona (☎ 93-201-1822; www.sre .gob.mx/barcelona; Paseo de la Bonanova 55, 08017); Madrid (☎ 91-369-2814; www.embamex.es; Carrera de San Jerónimo 46, 28014)

UK (☎ 020-7235-6393; www.embamex.co.uk; 8 Halkin St, SW1X 7DW) In London.

USA (☎ 202-728-1600, www.sre.gob.mx/eua; 1911 Pennsylvania Ave NW, 20006) In Washington, DC.

MEXICAN CONSULATES IN THE USA

There are consulates in many other US states, including the following:

Arizona Douglas (☎ 520-364-3107; www.consulmex douglas.com); Nogales (☎ 520-287-2521; portal.sre.gob .mx/nogales); Phoenix (☎ 602-242-7398; portal.sre.gob .mx/phoenix); Tucson (☎ 520-882-5595)

California Calexico (☎ 760-357-3863; www.sre.gob .mx/calexico); Fresno (☎ 559-233-3065; portal.sre.gob .mx/con_fresno); Los Angeles (☎ 213-351-6800; www .sre.gob.mx/losangeles); Sacramento (☎ 916-441-3287; portal.sre.gob.mx/sacramento); San Bernardino (☎ 909-883-6491; www.sre.gob.mx/sanbernardino); San Diego (☎ 619-231-8414; portal.sre.gob.mx/sandiego); San Francisco (☎ 415-354-1700; www.sre.gob.mx/sanfrancisco)

Colorado (☎ 303-331-1110; www.consulmex-denver .com) In Denver.

Florida Miami (☎ 786-268-4900; www.sre.gob.mx/miami); Orlando (☎ 407-422-0514; portal.sre.gob.mx/orlando)

Georgia (☎ 404-266-2233; www.consulmexatlanta .org) In Atlanta.

Illinois (☎ 312-855-1380; www.consulmexchicago.com) In Chicago.

Massachusetts (☎ 617-426-4181; www.sre.gob .mx/boston) In Boston.

Michigan (☎ 313-964-4515; www.sre.gob.mx/detroit) In Detroit.

Nevada Las Vegas (☎ 702-383-0623; www.sre.gob .mx/lasvegas)

New Mexico (☎ 505-247-2147; www.sre.gob.mx /albuquerque) In Albuquerque.

New York (☎ 212-217-6400; www.consulmexny.org) In New York.

North Carolina (☎ 919-754-0046; www.sre.gob .mx/raleigh) In Raleigh.

Oregon (☎ 503-274-1442; www.sre.gob.mx/portland) In Portland.

Pennsylvania (☎ 215-922-4262; www.sre.gob .mx/filadelfia) In Philadelphia.

Texas Austin (☎ 512-478-2866; www.sre.gob.mx /austin); Brownsville (☎ 956-542-4431; www.sre.gob .mx/brownsville); Dallas (☎ 214-252-9250; www.sre .gob.mx/dallas); Del Rio (☎ 830-775-2352); Eagle Pass (☎ 830- 773-9255); El Paso (☎ 915-533-5714; www .sre.gob.mx/elpaso); Houston (☎ 713-271-6800; www.sre .gob.mx/houston); Laredo (☎ 956-723-0990; www.sre .gob.mx/laredo); McAllen (☎ 956-686-0243) San Antonio (☎ 210- 227-9145; www.consulmexsat.org)

Utah (☎ 801-521-8502; www.consulmexslc.org) In Salt Lake City.

Washington (☎ 206-448-3526; portal.sre.gob.mx /seattle) In Seattle.

Washington, DC (☎ 202-736-1000; consulwas@sre .gob.mx; 2827 16th St NW, 20009) In Washington, DC.

Embassies & Consulates in Mexico

Mexico City entries in the following list are for embassies or their consular sections; other entries are consulates. Embassy websites are often useful sources of information about Mexico.

Australia Guadalajara (☎ 33-3615-7418; López Cotilla 2018, Colonia Arcos Vallarta); Mexico City (Map pp120–1; ☎ 55-1101-2200; www.mexico.embassy.gov.au; Rubén Darío 55, Polanco; Ⓜ Polanco); Monterrey (☎ 81-8158-0791; Edificio Torre Comercial América, San Patricio 111, Piso 16, Local 02, Colonia Valle Oriente, Garza García)

Belize Cancún (☎ 998-887-84-17; Av Náder 34, 1st floor); Chetumal (☎ 983-832-18-03; Av Armada de México 91, Colonia Campestre); Mexico City (Map pp120–1; ☎ 55-5520-1274; embelize@prodigy.net.mx; Bernardo de Gálvez 215, Lomas de Chapultepec; Ⓜ Auditorio)

Canada Acapulco (☎ 744-484-13-05; Centro Comercial Marbella, Local 23); Cancún (☎ 998-883-33-60; Plaza Caracol II, 3er Piso, Local 330, Blvd Kukulcán Km 8.5, Zona Hotelera); Guadalajara (☎ 33-3615-6215; Hotel Fiesta

Americana, Local 31, Aceves 225, Colonia Vallarta Poniente); Mazatlán (☎ 669-913-73-20; Hotel Playa Mazatlán, Av Las Gaviotas 202, Zona Dorada); Mexico City (Map pp120–1; ☎ 55-5724-7900; www.canada.org.mx; Schiller 529, Polanco; Ⓜ Auditorio); Monterrey (☎ 81-8344-3200; Edificio Kalos, C1 Piso, Local 108A, Zaragoza 1300 Sur); Oaxaca (☎ 951-513-37-77; Pino Suárez 700, Local 11B); Puerto Vallarta (☎ 322-293-00-98; Edificio Obelisco Local 108, Av Francisco Medina Ascencio 1951, Zona Hotelera Las Glorias); Tijuana (☎ 664-684-04-61; Gedovius 10411-101, Zona Río)

Cuba Cancún (☎ 998-884-34-23; Pecari 17); Mérida (☎ 999-944-42-15; Calle 1-D No 320, Colonia Campestre); Mexico City (Map pp120–1; ☎ 55-5280-5591; www .embacuba.com.mx; Av Presidente Masaryk 554, Polanco; Ⓜ Polanco)

France Acapulco (☎ 744-484-45-80; Local 205, La Costera 91, Fraccionamiento Club Deportiva); Cancún (☎ 998-267-97-22; Fonatur lote 1-1a, MZ 12 SM 50, Fraccionamiento Los Alamos II); Guadalajara (☎ 33-3616-5516; López Mateos Nte 484); Mazatlán (☎ 669-985-12-28; Belisario Domínguez 1008 Sur, Colonia Centro); Mérida (☎ 999-925-28-86; Calle 33B No 528); Mexico City (Map pp120–1; ☎ 55-9171-9700; www.francia.org.mx; Campos Elíseos 339, Polanco; Ⓜ Auditorio); consulate in Mexico City (☎ 55-9171-9840; Lafontaine 32, Polanco)

Germany Acapulco (☎ 744-484-18-60; Alaminos 26, Casa Tres Fuentes, Colonia Costa Azul); Cancún (☎ 998-884-18-98; Punta Conoco 36, SM24); Guadalajara (☎ 33-3613-9623; Casa Wagner de Guadalajara, Madero 215); Mazatlán (☎ 669-914-93-10; Av Playa Gaviotas 212, Zona Dorada); Mexico City (Map pp120–1; ☎ 55-5283-2200; www.mexiko.diplo.de; Lord Byron 737, Polanco; Ⓜ Auditorio); Monterrey (☎ 81-8378-6078; Proa Consultores SC, Río Rosas 400 Sur, Local 12, Planta Pista, Colonia Del Valle, Garza García)

Guatemala Cancún (☎ 998-883-82-96; Edificio Barcelona, Av Nader 148); Ciudad Hidalgo (☎ 969-698-01-84; 5a Calle Ote btw 1a & 3a Nte); Comitán (☎ 963-632-04-91; 1a Calle Sur Pte 26); Mexico City (Map pp120–1; ☎ 55-5540-7520; embaguatemx@minex.gob.gt; Av Explanada 1025, Lomas de Chapultepec; Ⓜ Auditorio); Tapachula (☎ 962-626-12-52; 5A Nte 5)

Ireland (Map pp120–1; ☎ 55-5520-5803; embajada @irlanda.org.mx; Cerrada Blvd Ávila Camacho 76, piso 3, Lomas de Chapultepec; Ⓜ Auditorio) In Mexico City.

Italy Cancún (☎ 998-884-12-61; Alcatraces 39, SM22); Guadalajara (☎ 33-3616-1700; Av López Mateos Nte 790, 1er Piso, Fraccionamiento Ladrón de Guevara); Mexico City (Map pp110–11; ☎ 55-5596-3655; www.embitalia.org .mx; Paseo de las Palmas 1994, Lomas de Chapultepec)

Japan (Map pp118–19; ☎ 55-5211-0028; www.mx .emb-japan.go.jp; Paseo de la Reforma 395; Ⓜ Sevilla) In Mexico City.

Netherlands Acapulco (☎ 486-83-59; Hotel Ritz, La Costera 159); Cancún (☎ 998-886-00-70; Martinair, Planta Alta, Terminal 2, Aeropuerto Cancún); Guadalajara

(☎ 33-3673-2211; 2º Piso, Av Vallarta 5500, Colonia Lomas Universidad, Zapopan); Mexico City (☎ 55-5258-9921; www.paisesbajos.com.mx; Edificio Calakmul, Av Vasco de Quiroga 3000, 7th fl, Santa Fe)

New Zealand (Map pp120–1; ☎ 55-5283-9460; kiwimexico@compuserve.com.mx; Jaime Balmes 8, Level 4, Los Morales; Ⓜ Polanco) In Mexico City.

Spain Acapulco (☎ 744-435-15-00; Hotel Elcano, La Costera 75); Cancún (☎ 998-848-99-18; Edificio Oásis, Cnr Blvd Kukulcán & Cenzontle, Zona Hotelera); Guadalajara (☎ 33-3630-0450; Torre Sterling, mezzanine izquierdo, Francisco de Quevedo 117, Sector Juárez); Oaxaca (☎ 951-518-00-31; Calzada Porfirio Díaz 340, Colonia Reforma); Mexico City (Map pp120–1; ☎ 55-5280-4383; www.mae .es/consulados/mexico/index.htm; Galileo 114, Polanco; Ⓜ Polanco)

UK Acapulco (☎ 744-484-17-35; Casa Consular, Centro Internacional Acapulco, La Costera); Cancún (☎ 998- 881-01-00; The Royal Sands, Blvd Kukulcán Km 13.5, Zona Hotelera); Guadalajara (☎ 33-3343-2296; Jesús de Rojas 20, Colonia Los Pinos, Zapopan); Mexico City (Map pp118–19; ☎ 55-5242-8500; www.embajadabritanica.com.mx; Río Lerma 71, Colonia Cuauhtémoc; Ⓜ Insurgentes); consulate in Mexico City (☎ 55-5242-8500; Río Usumacinta 26); Monterrey (☎ 81-8315-2049); Tijuana (☎ 664-686-53-20; Blvd Salinas 1500, Fraccionamiento Aviación Tijuana)

USA Acapulco (☎ 744-469-05-56; Hotel Continental Plaza, La Costera 121, Local 14); Cabo San Lucas (☎ 624-143-3566; Blvd Marina Local C-4, Plaza Nautica, Centro); Cancún (☎ 998-883-02-72; 2o Nivel No 320-323, Plaza Caracol Dos, Blvd Kukulcán, Zona Hotelera); Ciudad Juárez (☎ 656-611-30-00; López Mateos 924 Nte); Guadalajara (☎ 33-3268-2100; Progreso 175); Hermosillo (☎ 662-289-35-00; Av Monterrey 141); Ixtapa (☎ 755-553-21-00; Hotel Fontán, Blvd Ixtapa); Matamoros (☎ 868-812-44-02; Calle 1 No 2002); Mazatlán (☎ 669-916-58-89; Hotel Playa Mazatlán, Av Las Gaviotas 202, Zona Dorada); Mérida (☎ 999-925-50-11; Paseo de Montejo 453); Mexico City (Map pp118–19; ☎ 55-5080-2000; mexico.usembassy.gov; Paseo de la Reforma 305; Ⓜ Insurgentes); Monterrey (☎ 81-8345-2120; Av Constitución 411 Pte); Nogales (☎ 631-313-48-20; San José s/n, Fraccionamiento Los Álamos); Nuevo Laredo (☎ 867-714-05-12; Allende 3330); Oaxaca (☎ 951-514-30-54; Plaza Santo Domingo, Alcalá 407, Interior 20); Puerto Vallarta (☎ 322-222-00-69; Zaragoza 160); San Miguel de Allende (☎ 415-152-23-57; Hernández Macías 72); Tijuana (☎ 664-622-74-00; Tapachula 96, Colonia Hipódromo)

FESTIVALS & EVENTS

Mexico's many fiestas are full-blooded, highly colorful affairs, which often go on for several days and provide the chili in the recipe of Mexican life. In addition to the major national festivals listed here, each town has many local saints' days, regional fairs, arts festivals and so on (see destination chapters for information on these). There's also a national public holiday just about every month (see opposite), often the occasion for yet further partying.

January

Día de los Reyes Magos (Three Kings' Day or Epiphany; January 6) This is the day when Mexican children tradition-ally receive gifts – rather than at Christmas – although some get two loads of presents!

February/March

Día de la Candelaría (Candlemas; February 2) Commem-orates the presentation of Jesus in the temple 40 days after his birth; celebrated with processions, bullfights and dancing in many towns.

Carnaval (late February or early March) A big bash preceding the 40-day penance of Lent, Carnaval takes place during the week or so before Ash Wednesday (which falls 46 days before Easter Sunday). It's celebrated most wildly in Mazatlán, Veracruz and La Paz, with parades and masses of music, food, drink, dancing, fireworks and fun.

March/April

Semana Santa Holy Week starts on Palm Sunday (Domingo de Ramos). Particularly colorful celebrations are held in San Miguel de Allende, Taxco and Pátzcuaro; most of Mexico seems to be on the move at this time.

September

Día de la Independencia (Independence Day; Sep-tember 16) The anniversary of the start of Mexico's 1810 independence war provokes an upsurge of patriotic feeling every year: on the evening of the 15th, the words of Padre Miguel Hidalgo's famous call to rebellion, the Grito de Dolores, are repeated from the balcony of every town hall in the land, usually followed by fireworks. The biggest celebrations are in Mexico City where the Grito is issued by the national president from the Palacio Nacional.

November

Día de Todos los Santos (All Saints' Day; November 1) and **Día de Muertos** (Day of the Dead; November 2) Every cemetery in the country comes alive as families visit graveyards to commune with their dead on the night of November 1 and the day of November 2, when the souls of the dead are believed to return to earth. The souls of dead children (*angelitos*, little angels) are celebrated on November 1, All Saints' Day (see boxed text, p63).

December

Día de Nuestra Señora de Guadalupe (December 12) A week or more of celebrations throughout Mexico leads up to the Day of Our Lady of Guadalupe, the Virgin who appeared to an indigenous Mexican, Juan Diego, in 1531, and has since become Mexico's religious patron. Children are taken to church dressed as little Juan Diegos or indigenous girls. The biggest festivities are at the Basílica de Guadalupe in Mexico City.

Posadas (December 16–24) Nine nights of candlelit parades re-enact the journey of Mary and Joseph to Bethlehem. More important in small towns than big cities.

Día de Navidad (December 25) Christmas is traditionally celebrated with a feast in the early hours of December 25, after midnight Mass.

FOOD

Some of the Eating sections in city sections of this book are divided into budget, midrange and top end categories. We define a midrange restaurant as one where a main dish at lunch or dinner costs between $6 and $11; budget and top-end places are, respectively, less than $6 and over $11.

Typical restaurant hours are 7am (9am in central Mexico) to between 10pm and midnight. If a restaurant has a closing day, it's usually Sunday, Monday or Tuesday. For a full introduction to Mexico's fabulously piquant cuisine, see the Food & Drink chapter (p88).

GAY & LESBIAN TRAVELERS

Mexico is more broad-minded about sexuality than you might expect. Gays and lesbians don't generally maintain a high profile, but rarely attract open discrimination or violence. There are large, lively gay communities and/or gay tourism scenes in Puerto Vallarta and Guadalajara (especially), but also Mexico City, Cancún, Mazatlán, Acapulco and Veracruz. Gay men have a more public profile than lesbians, however. Discrimination based on sexual orientation has been illegal since 1999, and can be punished with up to three years in prison.

The **International Gay and Lesbian Travel Association** (www.iglta.org) provides information on the major travel providers in the gay sector. San Diego-based **Arco Iris Tours** (☎ 800-765-4370; www.arcoiristours.com) specializes in gay travel to Mexico and organizes an annual International Gay Festival in Cancún.

Out&About (www.gay.com/travel/outandabout) gives access to a detailed Mexico gay travel guide and articles. Another good source of information is the **Gay Mexico Network** (www.gaymexico .net), which offers information on gay-friendly

hotels and tours in Mexico, and publishes a newsletter offering discounted rooms in gay-friendly accommodations. **Sergay** (www.sergay .com.mx), a Spanish-language magazine and website, is focused on Mexico City, but with bar, disco and cruising-spot listings for the whole country. **Homópolis** (www.homopolis.com.mx) has further listings. Also worth looking at is **PlanetOut** (www.planetout.com).

HOLIDAYS

The chief holiday periods are Christmas–New Year, Semana Santa (the week leading up to Easter and a couple of days afterwards), and mid-July to mid-August. Transportation and tourist accommodations are heavily booked at these times. Banks, post offices, government offices and many shops throughout Mexico are closed on the following national holidays:

Año Nuevo (New Year's Day) January 1
Día de la Constitución (Constitution Day) February 5
Día de la Bandera (Day of the National Flag) February 24
Día de Nacimiento de Benito Juárez (anniversary of Benito Juárez' birth) March 21
Día del Trabajo (Labor Day) May 1
Cinco de Mayo (anniversary of Mexico's victory over the French at Puebla) May 5
Día de la Independencia (Independence Day) September 16
Día de la Raza (commemoration of Columbus' discovery of the New World) October 12
Día de la Revolución (Revolution Day) November 20
Día de Navidad (Christmas Day) December 25

At Easter, businesses usually close from Good Friday (Viernes Santo) to Easter Sunday (Domingo de Resurrección). Many offices and businesses close during major national festivals (see opposite).

INSURANCE

A travel insurance policy to cover theft, loss and medical problems is a good idea. Some policies specifically exclude dangerous activities such as scuba diving, motorcycling, and even trekking.

You may prefer a policy that pays doctors or hospitals directly rather than you having to pay on the spot and claim later. If you have to claim later, ensure you keep all documentation. Check that the policy covers ambulances or an emergency flight home. For further information on medical insurance, see p1005.

DIRECTORY

For information on motor insurance see p992.

Worldwide cover to travelers from over 44 countries is available online at www.lonelyplanet.com/travel_services.

INTERNET ACCESS

Most travelers make constant use of Internet cafés (which cost $0.50 to $1 per hour) and free Web-based email such as Yahoo (www.yahoo.com) and Hotmail (www.hotmail.com). A number of Mexican Internet cafés are equipped with CD burners, webcams, headphones and so on, but a lot don't have card readers, so bring your own or the camera-to-USB cable if you plan on burning photos to CD along the way.

Quite a few accommodations provide Internet access of some kind (they receive an 🖥 icon in this book). Facilities vary from a couple of computers in the lobby, for which you may or may not have to pay, to well-equipped business centers or wi-fi access *(Internet inalámbrico)* in rooms.

You may also be able to connect your own laptop or hand-held to the Internet through the telephone socket in your room. Be aware that your modem may not work once you leave your home country. The safest option is to buy a reputable 'global' modem before you leave home. A second issue is the plug: Mexico uses 110V plugs with two flat prongs, like those found in the US. For lots of useful stuff on connecting to the web while traveling, visit www.kropla.com.

See p28 for some great websites to start your Mexico surfing.

LEGAL MATTERS
Mexican Law

Mexican law is based on the Roman and Napoleonic codes, presuming an accused person is guilty until proven innocent.

The minimum jail sentence for possession of more than a token amount of any narcotic, including marijuana and amphetamines, is 10 months. As in most other countries, the purchase of controlled medication requires a doctor's prescription.

It's against Mexican law to take any firearm or ammunition into the country (even unintentionally) without a permit from a Mexican embassy or consulate.

Road travelers should expect occasional police or military checkpoints. They are normally looking for drugs, weapons or illegal migrants. Drivers found with drugs or weapons on board may have their vehicle confiscated and may be detained for months while their cases are investigated.

See p992 for information on the legal aspects of road accidents.

While the legal age for marriage is 12, sex with someone under 18 is illegal if their consent was obtained by deception, such as a false promise of marriage.

Useful warnings on Mexican law are found on the **US Department of State website** (www.travel.state.gov).

Getting Legal Help

If arrested, you have the right to contact your embassy or consulate. Consular officials can tell you your rights, provide lists of local lawyers, monitor your case, make sure you are treated humanely, and notify your relatives or friends – but they can't get you out of jail. More Americans are in jail in Mexico than in any other country except the US – about 800 at any one time. By Mexican law, the longest a person can be detained by police without a specific accusation is 72 hours.

Tourist offices in Mexico, especially those run by state governments, can often help you with legal problems such as complaints and reporting crimes or lost articles. The national tourism ministry, **Sectur** (☎ 55-5250-0123, 800-903-92-00), offers 24-hour telephone advice.

If you are the victim of a crime, your embassy or consulate, or Sectur or state tourist offices, can give advice. In some cases, you may feel there is little to gain by going to the police, unless you need a statement to present to your insurance company. If you go to the police and your Spanish is poor, take a more fluent speaker. Also take your passport and tourist card, if you still have them. If you just want to report a theft for the purposes of an insurance claim, say you want to '*poner una acta de un robo*' (make a record of a robbery). This should make it clear that you merely want a piece of paper and you should get it without too much trouble.

If Mexican police wrongfully accuse you of an infraction (as they have often been known to do in the hope of obtaining a bribe), you can ask for the officer's identification, to speak to a superior or to be shown documentation about the law you have supposedly broken. You can also note the officer's name, badge number, vehicle number and department (federal, state or municipal). Pay any traffic fines at a police station and get a receipt, then make your complaint at Sectur or a state tourist office.

MAPS

GeoCenter, Nelles, ITM and the AAA (American Automobile Association) all produce good country maps of Mexico, suitable for travel planning, and available internationally for between $6 and $15. The map scales vary between 1:2,500,000 (1cm:25km) and 1:3,700,000 (1cm:37km). The GeoCenter map is recommended for its combination of relief (terrain) shading, archaeological sites, national parks, roads (graded by quality) and settlements (graded by size). ITM also publishes good 1:1,000,000 (1cm:10km) maps of some Mexican regions (including the Yucatán Peninsula and the Pacific coast). For information on road atlases, see p1000.

Tourist offices in Mexico provide free city, town and regional maps of varying quality. Bookstores and newsstands sell commercially published ones. **Inegi** (Instituto Nacional de Estadística, Geografía e Informática; ☎ 800-490-42-00; www.inegi.gob .mx) publishes a large-scale map series covering all of Mexico at 1:50,000 (1cm:500m) and 1:250,000 (1cm:2.5km), plus state maps at 1:700,000 (1cm:7km). Most of these maps have been updated within the past decade, and they are well worth having if you plan to do any hiking or back-country exploring. Inegi's Centros de Información in every Mexican state capital (listed on the website), and at least three outlets in Mexico City (see p107), sell these maps for $4 to $6 each.

A good Internet source is **Maps of Mexico** (www.maps-of-mexico.com), with detailed maps of all the states and of 90 cities.

MONEY

Mexico's currency is the peso, usually denoted by the '$' sign. Any prices quoted in US dollars will normally be written '$5' or '5 USD' to avoid misunderstanding. The peso is divided into 100 centavos. Coins come in denominations of five, 10, 20 and 50 centavos and one, two, five, 10, 20 and 100 pesos. There are notes of 20, 50, 100, 200, 500 and 1000 pesos.

Since the peso's exchange value is often unstable, in this book we give prices in US dollar equivalents. For exchange rates, see inside the front cover. For information on costs, see p26.

The most convenient form of money in Mexico is a major international credit card or debit card – preferably two or three of them, if you have them. Visa, MasterCard and American Express cards can be used to obtain cash easily from ATMs in Mexico, and are accepted for payment by most airlines, car-rental companies and travel agents, plus many upper midrange and top-end hotels, and some restaurants and stores. Occasionally there's a surcharge for paying by card, or a discount for paying cash. Making a purchase by credit card normally gives you a more favorable exchange rate than exchanging money at a bank, and isn't subject to commission, but you'll normally have to pay your card issuer a 'foreign exchange' transaction fee of around 2.5%. Note that Visa, Amex or MasterCard stickers on a door or window in Mexico do *not* necessarily mean that these cards will be accepted for payment there. If you're short of cash, you may find yourself having to go out and look for an ATM to pay your restaurant check.

As a backup to credit or debit cards, it's still a good idea to take some traveler's checks and a little cash. US dollars are by far the most easily exchangeable foreign currency in Mexico. In tourist areas you can even pay for some things in US dollars, though the exchange rate used will probably not be in your favor. Euros, British pounds and Canadian dollars, in cash or as traveler's checks, are accepted by most banks and some *casas de cambio* (exchange houses), but acceptance is less certain if you're away from main cities and tourist centers. Traveler's checks should be a major brand, such as American Express or Visa. American Express traveler's checks are recognized everywhere.

For tips on keeping your money safe, see p972.

ATMs

ATMs (*caja permanente* or *cajero automático* in Spanish) are plentiful in Mexico, and are the easiest source of cash. You can use major credit cards and some bank cards, such as those on the Cirrus and Plus systems, to withdraw pesos from ATMs. The exchange rate that banks use for ATM withdrawals is normally better than the 'tourist rate' for currency exchange – though that advantage may be negated by extra handling fees, interest charges and other methods that banks have of taking your money away from you.

Banks & Casas de Cambio

You can exchange cash and traveler's checks in banks or at *casas de cambio*. Banks go through a more time-consuming procedure than *casas de cambio,* and usually have shorter exchange hours (typically 9am to 5pm Monday to Friday and 9am to 1pm Saturday, or shorter hours in some smaller, sleepier towns). *Casas de cambio* can be found easily in just about every large or medium-sized town and in many smaller ones. These places are quick and often open evenings or weekends, but some don't accept traveler's checks, whereas banks usually do.

Exchange rates vary a little from one bank or *cambio* to another. There is often a better rate for *efectivo* (cash) than for *documento* (traveler's checks).

If you have trouble finding a place to change money, particularly on a weekend, try a hotel, though the exchange rate won't be the best.

International Transfers

Should you need money wired to you in Mexico, an easy method is the 'Dinero en Minutos' service of **Western Union** (in the USA ☎ 800-325-6000; www.westernunion.com). It's offered by thousands of bank branches and other businesses around Mexico, identified by black-and-yellow signs proclaiming 'Western Union Dinero en Minutos.' Your sender pays the money online or at a Western Union branch, along with a fee, and gives the details on who is to receive it and where. When you pick it up, take along photo identification. Sending $500 online from California to Mexico, for example, costs $14.99. Western Union has offices worldwide.

US post offices (☎ 888-368-4669; www.usps.com) offer reasonably cheap money transfers to branches of Bancomer bank in Mexico. The service is called Dinero Seguro.

Taxes

Mexico's *impuesto de valor agregado* (IVA, value-added tax) is levied at 15%. By law the tax must be included in virtually any price

quoted to you, and should not be added afterward. Signs in stores and notices on restaurant menus often state '*IVA incluido.*' Occasionally they state instead that IVA must be added to the quoted prices.

Hotel rooms are also subject to the *Impuesto sobre hospedaje* (ISH, lodging tax). Each Mexican state sets its own rate, but in most it's 2%. See p964 for further information on taxes on hotel rooms.

Tipping & Bargaining

In general, workers in small, cheap restaurants don't expect much in the way of tips, while those in expensive resorts expect you to be lavish in your largesse. Workers in the tourism and hospitality industries often depend on tips to supplement miserable basic wages. In resorts frequented by foreigners (such as Acapulco, Puerto Vallarta and Cancún) tipping is up to US levels of 15%; elsewhere 10% is usually plenty. If you stay a few days in one place, you should leave up to 10% of your room costs for the people who have kept your room clean (assuming they have). A porter in a midrange hotel will be happy with $1 a bag. Taxi drivers don't generally expect tips unless they provide some special service. Car parking attendants expect a tip of $0.20 to $0.50, and the same is standard for gas-station attendants.

Room rates are pretty firm, though it can be worth asking if any discounts are available, especially if it's low season or you are going to stay a few nights. In markets bargaining is the rule, and you may pay much more than the going rate if you accept the first price quoted. You can also often bargain with drivers of unmetered taxis.

POST

An airmail letter or postcard weighing up to 20g costs $1 to the US or Canada, $1.25 to Europe or South America, and $1.40 to the rest of the world. Items between 20g and 50g cost $1.75, $2 and $2.25. *Certificado* (registered) service costs an extra $2. Mark airmail items 'Vía Aérea.' Delivery times (outbound and inbound) are elastic. An airmail letter from Mexico to the USA or Canada (or vice-versa) should take somewhere between four and 14 days to arrive. Mail to or from Europe takes between one and two weeks; for Australasia two to three weeks.

Post offices (oficinas de correos) are typically open from 8am to 6pm Monday to Friday, and 9am to 1pm Saturday. You can receive letters and packages care of a post office if they're addressed to the post office's lista de correos (mail list), as follows:

Dolores ABRAM (last name in capitals)
Lista de Correos
Correo Central
Acapulco
Guerrero 00000 (post code)
MEXICO

When the letter reaches the post office, the name of the addressee is placed on an alphabetical list that is updated daily and often pinned up on the wall. To claim your mail, present your passport or other identification. There's no charge, but many post offices only hold lista mail for 10 days before returning it to the sender. If you think you might pick mail up more than 10 days after it has arrived, have it sent to the following:

Dolores ABRAM
Poste Restante
Correo Central
Acapulco
Guerrero 00000 (post code)
MEXICO

Poste restante may hold mail for up to a month, but no list of what has been received is posted up.

If you're sending a package internationally from Mexico, be prepared to open it for customs inspection at the post office; it's better to take packing materials with you, or not seal it until you get there. For assured and speedy delivery, you can use one of the more expensive international courier services, such as **UPS** (☎ 800-902-92-00; www.ups.com), **Federal Express** (☎ 800-900-11-00; www.fedex.com) or Mexico's **Estafeta** (☎ 800-903-35-00; www.estafeta com). Packages up to 500g cost up to about $30 to the US or Canada, or $40 to Europe.

SHOPPING

Mexico's most exciting and unique buys are the wonderful and amazingly varied regional handicrafts made predominantly by indigenous people. You can buy these artesanías in the villages where they are produced, or in stores and markets in urban centers. Artesanías stores in cities will give you a good overview of what's available and a basis for price comparisons. Places such as Mexico City, Guadalajara, Monterrey, San Miguel de Allende, Puerto Vallarta, Puebla and Oaxaca have stores selling quality handicrafts from all over Mexico. A few cities have special markets devoted to crafts, but ordinary daily or weekly markets always sell crafts too (everyday objects such as pots and baskets as well as more artistic products). The quality and price of market goods may be lower than in stores. Bargaining is expected in markets, whereas stores generally have fixed prices. Traveling out to craft-making villages gives you a chance to see artisans at work, and if you buy there you'll know that more of your money is likely to go to the artisans themselves and less to entrepreneurs.

For everyday purchases and consumer goods, middle-class Mexicans like to shop in glitzy modern malls, big supermarkets or hypermarkets and department stores. These are often in suburban residential districts where travelers rarely go. In city centers you're more likely to find smaller, older shops and markets with a lot more character.

Refunds of the 15% IVA tax on some purchases were due to be available from July 2006 for tourists who arrived in Mexico by plane or cruise ship. Under the scheme, goods worth at least 1200 pesos (approximately $110) from any one store would qualify for the refund, on presentation of receipts with the store's tax number (Registro Federal de Causantes) when the tourist leaves Mexico.

See p78 for an introduction to many Mexican handicrafts: ceramics, masks, woodwork, jewelry, metalwork, lacquerware, indigenous textiles, bark paintings and retablos (also called exvotos). Following are some other fine products and good buys.

Bags

Bags come in all shapes and sizes, many incorporating indigenous designs. Those made by the Huichol people are among the most authentic and original.

Baskets

Handmade baskets of multifarious shapes, sizes and patterns, made of materials like cane, bamboo, wicker, or rush or palm-leaf strips, are common in Mexican markets. They can be useful for carrying other purchases home!

Clothes

Commercially produced clothing, whether based on traditional designs or with a Mexican take on international fashion trends, can be attractive and good value.

Hammocks

Usually made of cotton or nylon, hammocks come in a variety of widths and an infinite number of color patterns – easy to buy in Mérida, Palenque, Zipolite, Mitla and Juchitán.

Leather Goods

León is Mexico's shoe capital, and has dozens of stores; though every other sizable city has plenty of good ones, too. Finely-crafted belts, bags, *huaraches* (sandals), boots, clothes and saddles are available in northern and central ranching towns such as Zacatecas, Jerez, Hermosillo, Monterrey, Saltillo and Guadalajara.

Musical Instruments

Paracho, Michoacán, is the guitar capital of Mexico, and also produces violins, cellos and other instruments. Elsewhere you'll come across maracas, tambourines, whistles, scrape boards and a variety of drums. Also keep an eye open for tongue drums – hollowed-out pieces of wood which are often cylindrical in shape and attractively carved or decorated, with two central tongues of wood, each giving a different note when struck.

Tablecloths

Particularly lovely tablecloths are made in Oaxaca and Michoacán states.

SOLO TRAVELERS

A single room normally costs well over half the price of a double room, but budget travelers can cut accommodation costs by staying in Mexico's increasing number of hostels. Hostels have the additional advantage of providing ready-made company, full of helpful travel tips, and are often a lot of fun. Lone travelers don't generally need to remain alone when traveling in Mexico unless they choose to. It's very easy to pair up with others as there's a steady stream of people following similar routes around the country. In well-touristed places, notice boards advertise for traveling companions, flatmates, volunteer workers and so on.

Local tours are a good way to meet people and get more out of a place.

Solo travelers should be especially watchful of their luggage when on the road and should stay in places with good security for their valuables. so they don't have to be burdened with them when out and about. One big drag of traveling alone can be when you want to take a quick dip in the ocean – you're stuck with your possessions and there's no one to watch out for them.

Traveling alone can be a very good way of getting into the local culture and it definitely improves your Spanish skills. You can also get a kick out of doing what you want when you want. Eating by yourself night after night can get a bit tiresome, but you'll only be left alone if you want it that way, as Mexicans are very sociable.

TELEPHONE & FAX

Local calls are cheap; international calls can be expensive, but needn't be if you call from the right place at the right time. Mexico is well provided with fairly easy-to-use public card phones. *Locutorios* and *casetas de teléfono* (call offices where an on-the-spot operator connects the call for you) are quite widespread and can be cheaper than the card phones. A third option is to call from your hotel, but hotels charge what they like for this service. It's nearly always cheaper to go elsewhere.

Calling Cards

Some calling cards from other countries can be used for calls from Mexico by dialing special access numbers, such as the following:

AT&T (☎ 01-800-288-2872, 01-80-462-4240)
Bell Canada (☎ 01-800-123-0200, 01-800-021-1994)
BT Chargecard (☎ 01-800-123-02-44, 01-800-021-6644)
MCI (☎ 01-800-674-7000)
Sprint (☎ 01-800-877-8000)

Warning: if you get an operator who asks for your credit-card instead of your calling-card number, or says the service is unavailable, hang up. There have been scams in which calls are rerouted to super-expensive credit-card phone services.

Cell Phones

Like other Mexican phone numbers, every cell (cellular, mobile) phone number has an area code (usually the code of the city the phone was bought in). When calling a cell phone from that same city, you usually need to dial ☎ 044, followed by the area code and number. When calling from other cities, dial ☎ 01 (the normal long-distance prefix), followed by the area code and number. The owner of the phone receiving the call has to pay a small amount as well as the caller.

If you want to use a cell phone in Mexico, one option for short visits is to get an international plan for your own phone, which will enable you to call home. You can also buy a Mexican cell phone for as little as $30 to $60, including some air time. The most widespread cell-phone system in Mexico is **Telcel** (www.telcel.com), with coverage almost everywhere that has a significant population, and roaming partnerships with systems from many other countries. Amigo cards, for recharging Telcel phones, are widely available from newsstands and minimarts. Other companies are **Unefon** (www.unefon.com.mx), with coverage mainly in the major cities; **Iusacell** (www.iusacell.com.mx); and **Movistar** (www.telefonicamovistar.com.mx). If you already have a Movistar phone from another country, you can put a Mexican Movistar SIM card into it.

For further information, contact your service provider or visit www.kropla.com or www.gsmcoverage.co.uk, which has coverage maps, lists of roaming partners and links to phone companies' websites. Telcel has a phone sales outlet at Mexico City airport.

Collect Calls

A *llamada por cobrar* (collect call) can cost the receiving party much more than if they call you, so you may prefer to pay for a quick call to the other party to ask them to call you back. If you do need to make a collect call, you can do so from card phones without a card. Call an operator on ☎ 020 for domestic calls, or ☎ 090 for international calls, or use a 'home country direct' service, through which you make an international collect call via an operator in the country you're calling. The Mexican term for 'home country direct' is *país directo*. Mexican international operators may know the access numbers for some countries, but it's best to get this information from your home country before you leave.

Some telephone *casetas* and hotels will make collect calls for you, but they usually charge for the service.

Fax

Public fax service is offered in many Mexican towns by the public *telégrafos* (telegraph) office or the companies Telecomm and Computel. Also look for 'Fax' or 'Fax Público' signs on shops, businesses and telephone *casetas,* and in bus stations and airports. Typically you will pay around $1 per page to the US or Canada.

Locutorios & Casetas de Teléfono

Costs in *casetas* and *locutorios* are often lower than those for Telmex card phones (see below), and their advantages are that they eliminate street noise and you don't need a phone card to use them. They often have a telephone symbol outside, or signs saying 'teléfono,' 'Lada' or 'Larga Distancia.' In Baja California *casetas* are known as *cabinas.*

Prefixes & Codes

If you're calling a number in the town or city you're in, simply dial the local number (eight digits in Mexico City, Guadalajara and Monterrey; seven digits everywhere else).

To call another town or city in Mexico, you need to dial the long-distance prefix ☎ 01, followed by the area code (two digits for Mexico City, Guadalajara and Monterrey; three digits for everywhere else) and then the local number. For example, to call from Mexico City to Oaxaca, dial ☎ 01, then the Oaxaca area code ☎ 951, then the seven-digit local number. You'll find area codes listed under city and town headings through this book.

To make international calls, you need to dial the international prefix ☎ 00, followed by the country code, area code and local number. For example, to call New York City from Mexico, dial ☎ 00, then the US country code ☎ 1, then the New York City area code ☎ 212, then the local number.

To call a number in Mexico from another country, dial your international access code, then the Mexico country code ☎ 52, then the area code and number.

Public Card Phones

These are common in towns and cities, and you'll usually find some at airports, bus stations and around the main plaza. Easily the most common, and most reliable on costs, are those marked with the name of the country's biggest phone company, Telmex. To use a Telmex card phone you need a phone card known as a *tarjeta Ladatel*. These are sold at kiosks and shops everywhere – look for the blue-and-yellow signs that read '*De venta aquí Ladatel*.' The cards come in denominations of 30 pesos (about $2.75), 50 pesos ($5)and 100 pesos ($9.50).

Calls from Telmex card phones cost $0.10 per minute for local calls; $0.40 per minute long-distance within Mexico; $0.50 per minute to the USA or Canada; $1 per minute to Central America; $2 per minute to Europe, Alaska or South America; and $2.50 per minute to Australia or Asia.

In some parts of Mexico frequented by foreign tourists, you may notice a variety of phones that advertise that they accept credit cards or that you can make easy collect calls to the USA on them. While some of these phones may be a fair value, there are others on which very high rates are charged. Be 100% sure about what you'll pay before making a call on a non-Telmex phone.

Toll-Free & Operator Numbers

Mexican toll-free numbers (☎ 800 followed by seven digits) always require the ☎ 01 prefix. You can call most of these and the ☎ 060 and ☎ 080 emergency numbers from Telmex pay phones without inserting a telephone card.

Most US and Canadian toll-free numbers are ☎ 800 or ☎ 888 followed by seven digits. Some of these can be reached from Mexico (dial ☎ 00-1 before the 800), but you will probably have to pay a charge for the call.

For a domestic operator in Mexico, dial ☎ 020; for an international operator, dial ☎ 090. For Mexican directory information, dial ☎ 040.

Yellow Pages

To access the Mexican yellow pages online, go to www.seccionamarilla.com.mx.

TIME

Most of Mexico is on Hora del Centro, the same as US Central Time (that's GMT minus six hours in winter, and GMT minus five hours during daylight saving). Five northern and western states, Chihuahua,

Nayarit, Sinaloa, Sonora and Baja California Sur, are on Hora de las Montañas, the same as US Mountain Time (GMT minus seven hours in winter, GMT minus six hours during daylight saving). Baja California (Norte) observes Hora del Pacífico, the same as US Pacific Time (GMT minus eight hours in winter, GMT minus seven hours during daylight saving).

Daylight saving time ('*horario de verano*', summer time) runs from the first Sunday in April to the last Sunday in October. Clocks go forward one hour in April and back one hour in October. The northwestern state of Sonora ignores daylight saving (like its US neighbor Arizona), so remains on GMT minus seven hours all year. Daylight saving is also ignored by a few remote rural zones, such as the Sierra Norte of Oaxaca and the Marqués de Comillas area of eastern Chiapas (to the perdition of bus schedules from nearby towns such as Oaxaca and Palenque).

See the World Map at the back of this book if you need international time zone information.

TOILETS

Public toilets are rare, so take advantage of facilities in places such as hotels, restaurants, bus stations and museums. When out and about, carry some toilet paper with you if you think you're going to need it, because it often won't be provided. If there's a bin beside the toilet, put paper in it because the drains can't cope otherwise.

TOURIST INFORMATION

Just about every town of interest to tourists in Mexico has a state or municipal tourist office. They are generally helpful with maps, brochures and questions, and usually some staff members speak English.

You can call the Mexico City office of the national tourism ministry **Sectur** (☎ 55 5250-0123/51, 800-903-92-00, in the US & Canada ☎ 800 446-3942, 800-482-9832, in Europe ☎ 00 800 1111 2266 www.visitmexico.com) at any time – 24 hours a day, seven days a week – for information or help in English or Spanish.

Following are the contact details for the head tourism offices of each Mexican state:
Aguascalientes (☎ 449-912-35-11; www.aguascalientes .gob.mx in Spanish)
Baja California (☎ 078, 664-634-63-30; www.discover bajacalifornia.com)

Baja California Sur (☎ 612-124-01-00; www.bcs.gob .mx in Spanish)

Campeche (☎ 981-811-92-29, 800-900-22-67; www .campechetravel.com)

Chiapas (☎ 961-602-51-27, 800-280-35-00; www .turismochiapas.gob.mx)

Chihuahua (☎ 614-429-33-00, 800-849-52-00; www .chihuahua.gob.mx/turismoweb in Spanish)

Coahuila (☎ 844-415-17-14; http://servidor.seplade -coahuila.gob.mx/)

Colima (☎ 312-316-20-21; www.visitacolima.com.mx)

Durango (☎ 618-811-31-60, 800-624-65-67; www .durango.gob.mx in Spanish)

Guanajuato (☎ 473-732-15-74, 800-714-10-86; www .guanajuato-travel.com)

Guerrero (☎ 744-484-24-23; www.sectur.guerrero .gob.mx)

Hidalgo (☎ 800-718-26-00; www.turismo.hidalgo.gob .mx in Spanish)

Jalisco (☎ 33-3668-1600; 800-363-22-00; http://visita .jalisco.gob.mx in Spanish)

Mexico City (☎ 55-5533-8759; www.mexicocity.gob.mx)

México (☎ 017-212-59-98, 800-849-13-33; www .edomexico.gob.mx/sedeco/turismo/home.html in Spanish)

Michoacán (☎ 443-312-80-81, 800-450-23-00; www .turismomichoacan.gob.mx in Spanish)

Morelos (☎ 800-987-82-24; www.morelostravel.com)

Nayarit (☎ 311-216-56-61; www.turismonayarit.gob.mx)

Nuevo León (☎ 81-8344-4343, 800-263-00-70; www .nl.gob.mx in Spanish)

Oaxaca (☎ 951-576-48-28; www.aoaxaca.com in Spanish)

Puebla (☎ 800-326-86-56; www.turismopuebla.com.mx in Spanish)

Querétaro (☎ 442-238-50-67, 800-715-17-42; in the US ☎ 888-811-6130; www.venaqueretaro.com)

Quintana Roo (☎ 983-835-08-60; http://sedetur.qroo .gob.mx in Spanish)

San Luis Potosí (☎ 444-814-14-16, 800-343-38-87; www.descubresanluispotosi.com)

Sinaloa (☎ 669-981-88-83; www.sinaloa-travel.com in Spanish)

Sonora (☎ 800-716-25-55, in the US 800-476- 66-72; www.sonoraturismo.gob.mx)

Tabasco (☎ 993-316-36-33, 800-216-08-42; www.visite tabasco.com, www.etabasco.gob.mx/turismo in Spanish)

Tamaulipas (☎ 834-315-61-36, 800-710-65-32; in the US ☎ 888-580-59-68; http://turismo.tamaulipas.gob.mx in Spanish)

Tlaxcala (☎ 246-465-09-60, 800-509-65-57; www .tlaxcala.gob.mx in Spanish)

Veracruz (☎ 228-841-85-00, 800-712-66-66; in the US ☎ 888-600-37-23; www.sedecover.gob.mx in Spanish)

Yucatán (☎ 999-930-37-60; www.mayayucatan.com)

Zacatecas (☎ 492-922-67-51, 800-712-40-78; www .turismozacatecas.gob.mx in Spanish)

VISAS

Every tourist must have an easily obtainable Mexican-government tourist card. Some nationalities also need to obtain visas. Because the regulations sometimes change, it's wise to confirm them with a Mexican embassy or consulate before you go (see p974). The **Lonely Planet website** (www.lonelyplanet.com) has links to updated visa information.

Citizens of the USA, Canada, EU countries, Australia, New Zealand, Iceland, Israel, Japan, Norway and Switzerland are among those who do not need visas to enter Mexico as tourists. The list changes sometimes; check well ahead of travel with your local Mexican embassy or consulate. Visa procedures, for those who need them, can take several weeks and you may be required to apply in your country of residence or citizenship.

For information on passport requirements, see p988. Non-US citizens passing (even in transit) through the USA on the way to or from Mexico, or visiting Mexico from the USA, should also check the passport and visa requirements for the USA.

Tourist Card & Tourist Fee

The Mexican tourist card – officially the *forma migratoria para turista* (FMT) – is a brief card document that you must fill out and get stamped by Mexican immigration when you enter Mexico, and keep till you leave. It's available at official border crossings, international airports and ports, and often from airlines, travel agencies and Mexican consulates. At the US–Mexico border you won't usually be given one automatically – you have to ask for it.

At many US–Mexico border crossings you don't have to get the card stamped at the border itself – as Mexico's Instituto Nacional de Migración (INM, National Immigration Institute) has control points on the highways into the interior where it's also possible to do it – but it's preferable to get it done at the border itself, in case there are complications elsewhere.

One section of the card deals with the length of your stay in Mexico, and this section is filled out by the immigration officer. The maximum possible is 180 days for most nationalities (90 days for Australians, Austrians, Israelis and Italians, among others), but immigration officers will often put a much lower number (as little as 15 or 30 days in some cases) unless you tell them specifically what you need. It's advisable to ask for more days than you think you'll need, in case you are delayed or change your plans.

Though the tourist card itself is free of charge, it brings with it the obligation to pay the tourist fee of about $20, called the *derecho para no inmigrante* (DNI, nonimmigrant fee). The exact amount of the fee may change from year to year. If you enter Mexico by air, the fee is included in your airfare. If you enter by land, you must pay the fee at a bank in Mexico at any time before you reenter the frontier zone on your way out of Mexico (or before you check in at an airport to fly out of Mexico). The frontier zone is the territory between the border itself and the INM's control points on the highways leading into the Mexican interior (usually 20km to 30km from the border). Most Mexican border posts have on-the-spot bank offices where you can pay the DNI fee immediately. When you pay at a bank, your tourist card will be stamped to prove that you have paid.

Look after your tourist card because it may be checked when you leave the country. You can be fined $42 for not having it.

Tourist cards (and fees) are not necessary for visits shorter than 72 hours within the frontier zones along Mexico's northern and southern borders, or to the Tijuana–Ensenada or Mexicali–San Felipe corridors in Baja California, or the Sonoita–Puerto Peñasco corridor in Sonora.

A tourist card only permits you to engage in what are considered to be tourist activities (including sports, health, artistic and cultural activities). If the purpose of your visit is to work (even as a volunteer), to report or to study, or to participate in humanitarian aid or human-rights observation, you may well need a visa. If you're unclear, check with a Mexican embassy or consulate (p974).

EXTENSIONS & LOST CARDS
If the number of days given on your tourist card is less than the maximum for your nationality (90 or 180 days in most cases) its validity may be extended, one or more times, up to the maximum. To get a card extended you have to apply to the INM, which has offices in many towns and cities: they're listed on the **INM website** (www.inm.gob.mx), under 'Servicios Migratorios'). The procedure costs around $20 and should take between half

an hour and three hours, depending on the particular office. You'll need your passport, tourist card, photocopies of the important pages of these documents, and, at some offices, evidence of 'sufficient funds.' A major credit card is usually OK for the latter, or an amount in traveler's checks anywhere from $100 to $1000 depending on the office.

Most INM offices will not extend a card until a few days before it is due to expire; don't bother trying earlier.

If you lose your card or need further information, contact your nearest tourist office, or the **Sectur tourist office** (☎ 55-5250-0123, 800-903-92-00) in Mexico City, or your embassy or consulate. Any of these should be able to give you an official note to take to your local INM office, which will issue a duplicate for a cost of $42.

WOMEN TRAVELERS
Women can have a great time in Mexico, traveling with companions or traveling solo, but in this land that invented machismo, some concessions have to be made to local custom. Gender equalization has come a long way in a few decades, and Mexicans are generally a very polite people, but they remain, by and large, great believers in the difference (rather than the equality) between the sexes.

Lone women must expect a few catcalls and attempts to chat them up. Often these men only want to talk to you, but you can discourage unwanted attention by avoiding eye contact (wear sunglasses), dressing modestly, moving confidently and speaking coolly but politely if you are addressed and feel that you must respond. Wearing a wedding ring can prove helpful too. Don't put yourself in peril by doing things that Mexican women would not do, such as challenging a man's masculinity, drinking alone in a cantina, hitchhiking or going alone to isolated places. Keep a clear head. Excessive alcohol will make you vulnerable. For moral support, and company if you want it, head for accommodations where you're likely to meet other travelers (such as guesthouses that serve breakfast, backpacker hostels, or popular hotels), and join group excursions and activities.

In beach resorts many Mexican women dress in shorts, skimpy tops or dresses, and swimsuits of all sizes, though others bow to modesty and swim in shorts and a T-shirt. On the streets of cities and towns you'll notice that women cover up and don't display too much leg, or even shoulder. The bare, pierced-belly look so popular in the West is not common.

On local transportation it's best to don long or mid-calf-length trousers and a top that meets the top of your pants, with sleeves of some sort. That way you'll feel most comfortable, and you can also keep your valuables out of sight with ease.

Most of all, appear self-assured.

WORK

Mexicans themselves need jobs, and people who enter Mexico as tourists are not legally allowed to take employment. The many expats working in Mexico have usually been posted there by their companies or organizations with all the necessary papers.

English-speakers (and a few German- or French-speakers) may find teaching jobs in language schools, *preparatorias* (high schools) or universities, or can offer personal tutoring. Mexico City is the best place to get English-teaching work; Guadalajara is also good. It's possible in other major cities. The pay is low, but you can live on it.

Press ads (especially in the various local English-language papers and magazines) and telephone yellow pages are sources of job opportunities. Pay rates for personal tutoring are rarely more than $15 an hour. Positions in high schools or universities are more likely to become available at the beginning of each new term; contact institutions that offer bilingual programs or classes in English; for universities, ask for an appointment with the director of the language department. Language schools tend to offer short courses, so teaching opportunities with them come up more often and your commitment is for a shorter time, but they may pay less than high schools or universities.

A foreigner working in Mexico normally needs a permit or government license, but a school will often pay a foreign teacher in the form of a *beca* (scholarship), and thus circumvent the law, or the school's administration will procure the appropriate papers.

It's helpful to know at least a little Spanish, even though only English may be spoken in class.

Apart from teaching, you might find a little bar or restaurant work in tourist areas. It's likely to be part-time and short-term.

Jobs Abroad (www.jobsabroad.com) posts paid and unpaid job openings in Mexico. The **Lonely Planet website** (www.lonelyplanet.com) has several useful links.

Volunteer Work

Many opportunities exist for short- or longer-term unpaid work (or work that you pay to do) in Mexico. Projects range from sea-turtle conservation to human-rights observation, to work with abused children.

AmeriSpan (www.amerispan.com) Offers a range of volunteer opportunities in Mexico.

Amigos de las Américas (www.amigoslink.org) Sends paying volunteers from the US to work on summer health, community and youth projects in Latin America; volunteers receive prior training.

Ceduam (www.prodigyweb.net.mx/ceduamcal/ceduam .htm) Works on nutrition, gender issues, conservation and sustainable development; needs volunteers for various roles including work on its organic farm at Tlaxco, near Tlaxcala.

Earthwatch (www.earthwatch.org) With offices in the USA, Britain, Australia and Japan, Earthwatch runs environmental projects in Mexico (volunteers usually pay around $1000 per week).

Global Exchange (www.globalexchange.org) Needs Spanish-speaking volunteer human-rights observers to live for six to eight weeks in peace camps in Chiapas villages threatened by violence. This program is run in collaboration with the Centro de Derechos Humanos Fray Bartolomé de Las Casas, a human-rights center in San Cristóbal de las Casas.

Idealist.org (www.idealist.org) Great place to start researching volunteer possibilities.

Sipaz (www.sipaz.org) An international peace group, Sipaz needs Spanish-speaking volunteers to work for a year or more in Chiapas.

The Volunteer Site (www.thevolunteersite.com) Provides volunteers for environmental, community and other projects in western Mexico.

Vive Mexico (www.vivemexico.org) A Mexico-based NGO that coordinates international social, ecological and cultural work camps in Mexico.

Volunteer Abroad (www.volunteerabroad.com) Website with a very wide range of volunteer openings in Mexico.

The **Council on International Educational Exchange** (www.ciee.org), the **Alliance of European Voluntary Service Organisations** (www.alliance-network.org) and Unesco's **Coordinating Committee for International Voluntary Service** (www.unesco.org/ccivs) all have further information on volunteer programs in Mexico.

Transportation

GETTING THERE & AWAY

ENTERING THE COUNTRY

Immigration officers won't usually keep you waiting any longer than it takes to flick through your passport and enter your length of stay on your tourist card (p985). Remain patient and polite, even if procedures are slow. Anyone traveling to Mexico via the USA should be sure to check US visa and passport requirements.

Passport

Though it's not recommended, US and Canadian tourists can still, at the time of writing, enter Mexico without a passport if they have official photo identification, such as a driver's license, plus some proof of their citizenship such as an original birth certificate. But this is likely to change soon for Americans, and for Canadians passing through the USA, due to a new US regulation called the Western Hemisphere Travel Initiative. This is expected to require all air and sea travelers entering the USA from Mexico or Canada from December 31, 2006 to carry passports, and land travelers from December 31, 2007 to do the

same. Travelers will still, in theory, be able to enter Mexico from the US with just proof of citizenship and photo ID, but they won't be able to return to the US (or to enter the US from Canada) without a passport. For full details of the regulations, visit the website of the **US State Department** (http://travel.state.gov).

In any case it's much better to have a passport because officials of all countries are used to passports and may delay people who have other documents. In Mexico you will often need your passport if you change money, and you will be asked to show it when you check into a hotel.

All citizens of countries other than the US and Canada should have a passport that's valid for at least six months after they arrive in Mexico.

Travelers under 18 who are not accompanied by both their parents may need special documentation (see p970).

For information on Mexican visa requirements and the tourist card, see p985.

AIR
Airports & Airlines

The following Mexican airports receive direct international flights. All except Tuxtla Gutiérrez have flights from the US (some from several US cities, some from only one or two). Only Mexico City and Cancún receive direct scheduled flights from Europe, Canada or Central or South America. Flights from Havana, Cuba, go to Cancún, Mérida, Villahermosa, Tuxtla Gutiérrez and Oaxaca.

Mexico City, Cancún, Guadalajara and Monterrey have the most international

---

THINGS CHANGE...

The information in this chapter is particularly vulnerable to change. Check directly with the airline or a travel agent to make sure you understand how a fare (and ticket you may buy) works, and be aware of the security requirements for international travel. Shop carefully. The details given in this chapter should be regarded as pointers and are not a substitute for your own careful, up-to-date research.

flights; Toluca and Puebla are starting to be used as alternatives to Mexico City:

Acapulco (ACA; ☎ 744-466-94-34)
Aguascalientes (AGU; ☎ 449-915-81-32)
Bajío (El Bajío, León; BJX; ☎ 477-713-64-06)
Cancún (CUN; ☎ 998-886-03-40; www.asur.com.mx)
Chihuahua (CUU; ☎ 614-420-09-16)
Cozumel (CZM; ☎ 987-872-49-16; www.asur.com.mx)
Durango (DGO; ☎ 618-817-88-98)
Guadalajara (GDL; ☎ 33-3688-5504)
Guaymas (GYM; ☎ 622-221-05-11)
Hermosillo (HMO; ☎ 662-261-01-42)
Huatulco (Bahías de Huatulco; HUX; www.asur.com.mx)
Ixtapa/Zihuatanejo (ZIH; ☎ 755-554-20-70)
La Paz (LAP; ☎ 614-124-63-07)
Loreto (LTO; ☎ 613-135-04-54)
Los Cabos (SJD; ☎ 624-146-52-14)
Manzanillo (Playa de Oro; ZLO; ☎ 314-333-25-25)
Mazatlán (MZT; ☎ 669-928-04-38)
Mérida (MID; ☎ 999-946-25-00; www.asur.com.mx)
Mexico City (MEX; ☎ 55-5571-3600; www.aicm.com.mx)
Monterrey (MTY; ☎ 81-8369-0752; www.adelnorte.com.mx)
Morelia (MLM; ☎ 443-317-14-11)
Oaxaca (OAX; ☎ 951-511-50-78; www.asur.com.mx)
Puebla (PBC; ☎ 222-232-00-32; www.aeropuerto.pue.gob.mx)
Puerto Vallarta (PVR; ☎ 322-221-28-48)
San Luis Potosí (SLP; ☎ 444-822-23-96)
Tampico (TAM; ☎ 833-224-48-00)
Tijuana (TIJ; ☎ 664-683-24-18; www.tijmx.com)
Toluca (TLC; ☎ 722-273-09-25)
Torreón (TRC; ☎ 871-712-82-39)
Tuxtla Gutiérrez (TGZ; ☎ 961-671-53-11)
Veracruz (VER; ☎ 229-934-70-00; www.aicm.com.mx)
Villahermosa (VSA; ☎ 993-356-01-57; www.aicm.com.mx)
Zacatecas (ZCL; ☎ 492-985-02-23)

Mexico's two flag airlines are Mexicana and Aeroméxico. Formerly state-controlled, Mexicana was bought by Grupo Posadas, Mexico's biggest hotel company, in 2005, and the government hoped to sell off Aeroméxico in 2006. Their safety records are comparable to major US and European airlines: Mexicana has had one fatal crash in about two million flights since 1970, while Aeroméxico has suffered no fatal events since 1986.

AIRLINES FLYING TO & FROM MEXICO

Aero California (code JR; ☎ 55-5207-1392; hub Tijuana)
Aerolíneas Argentinas (code AR; ☎ 800-123-85-88; www.aerolineas.com.ar; hub Buenos Aires)

> **DEPARTURE TAX**
>
> A departure tax equivalent to about $25 is levied on international flights from Mexico. It's usually included in your ticket cost, but if it isn't, you must pay in cash during airport check-in. Ask your travel agent in advance.

Aerolitoral (code 5D; ☎ 800-800-23-76; www.aerolitoral.com; hub Monterrey)
Aeromar (code VW; ☎ 800-237-66-27; www.aeromar.com.mx; hub Mexico City)
Aeroméxico (code AM; ☎ 800-021-40-00; www.aeromexico.com; hub Mexico City)
Air Canada (code AC; ☎ 800-719-28-27; www.aircanada.ca; hub Toronto)
Air Europa (code UX; ☎ 998-898-22-55; www.aireuropa.com; hub Madrid)
Air France (code AF; ☎ 800-123-46-60; www.airfrance.com; hub Paris)
Air Madrid (code NM; ☎ 55-5093-4668; www.airmadrid.com; hub Madrid)
Alaska Airlines (code AS; ☎ 800-252-75-22; www.alaska-air.com; hub Seattle)
America West (code HP; ☎ 800-235-92-92; www.americawest.com; hub Phoenix)
American Airlines (code AA; ☎ 800-904-60-00; www.aa.com; hub Dallas)
ATA Airlines (code TZ; ☎ 800-883-52-28; www.ata.com; hub Chicago)
Aviacsa (code 6A; ☎ 800-006-22-00; www.aviacsa.com; hub Mexico City)
Avianca (code AV; ☎ 800-705-79-00; www.avianca.com; hub Bogotá)
British Airways (code BA; ☎ 55-5387-0321; www.britishairways.com; hub Heathrow Airport, London)
Click Mexicana (code QA; ☎ 800-122-54-25; www.clickmx.com; hub Cancún)
Continental Airlines (code CO; ☎ 800-900-50-00; www.continental.com; hub Houston)
Continental Express (code CO; ☎ 800-523-32-73; www.expressjet.com; hubs Houston, Newark, Cleveland)
Copa Airlines (code CM; ☎ 800-265-26-72; www.copaair.com; hub Panama City)
Cubana (code CU; ☎ 52-5250-6355; www.cubana.co.cu; hub Havana)
Delta Air Lines (code DL; ☎ 800-123-47-78; www.delta.com; hub Atlanta)
Frontier Airlines (code FFT; in the US ☎ 800-432-13-59; www.frontierairlines.com; hub Denver)
Iberia (code IB; ☎ 55-1101-1569; www.iberia.com; hub Madrid)
Japan Airlines (code JL; ☎ 800-024-01-50; www.jal.co.jp; hub Tokyo)

Jetair (code TUB; in Belgium ☎ 070-22-00-00; www
.jetairfly.com; hub Brussels)

KLM (code KL; ☎ 55-5279-5390; www.klm.com; hub
Amsterdam)

Lacsa (code LR; ☎ 800-400-82-22; www.taca.com; hub
San José)

Lan (code LA; ☎ 800-700-67-00; www.lanchile.com;
hub Santiago)

Líneas Aéreas Azteca (code ZE; ☎ 800-229-83-22;
http://aazteca.com.mx; hub Mexico City)

Lloyd Aéreo Boliviano (code LB; ☎ 800-777-13-00;
www.labairlines.com; hub La Paz)

Lufthansa (code LH; ☎ 55-5230-0000; www.lufthansa
.com; hub Frankfurt)

Mexicana (code MX; ☎ 800-502-20-00; www.mexicana
.com; hub Mexico City)

Northwest Airlines (code NW; ☎ 55-5279-5390;
www.nwa.com; hubs Detroit, Minneapolis/St Paul,
Memphis)

Singapore Airlines (code SQ; ☎ 55-5525-8787;
www.singaporeair.com; hub Singapore)

Spirit Airlines (code NK; ☎ 998-886-00-47; www
.spiritair.com; hub Fort Lauderdale)

Sun Country Airlines (code SY; in the US ☎ 800-800-
65-57; www.suncountry.com; hub Minneapolis/St Paul)

TACA (code TA; ☎ 800-400-8222; www.taca.com; hub
San Salvador)

Ted (code UA; ☎ 800-003-07-77; www.flyted.com; hub
Denver)

United Airlines (code UA; ☎ 800-003-07-77; www.ual
.com; hub Los Angeles)

US Airways (code US; ☎ 800-235-92-92; www.usair
ways.com; hub Philadelphia)

Varig (code RG; ☎ 55-5280-9192; www.varig.com.br;
hub São Paulo)

Tickets

The cost of flying to Mexico is usually
higher around Christmas and New Year,
and during July and August. Weekends can
be more costly than weekdays. In addition
to websites and ticket agents such as those
recommended in the following sections, it's
often worth checking airlines' own websites
for special deals. Newspapers, magazines
and websites serving Mexican communities
in other countries are also good sources.
The **Lonely Planet website** (www.lonelyplanet.com)
has good links too.

If Mexico is part of a bigger trip encompassing other countries in Latin America
or elsewhere, the best ticket for you may
be an open-jaw (where you fly into one
place and out of another, covering the
intervening distance by land), or a round-

the-world ticket (these can cost as little as
UK£900 or A$2100), or a Circle Pacific
ticket which uses a combination of airlines to travel around the Pacific region.
Airtreks (www.airtreks.com) is one good source
for multi-stop tickets.

International online booking agencies
worth a look include **CheapTickets** (www
.cheaptickets.com) and, for students and travelers under the age of 26, **STA Travel** (www
.statravel.com).

Asia

You normally have to make a connection in
the US or Canada (often Los Angeles, San
Francisco or Vancouver), and maybe one
in Asia as well. From more westerly Asian
points such as Bangkok, routes via Europe
are also an option. There are numerous
branches in Asia of **STA Travel** Bangkok (☎ 02-
2237-9400; www.statravel.co.th); Singapore (☎ 6737-
7188; www.statravel.com.sg); Hong Kong (2736-1618;
www.statravel.com.hk); Japan (☎ 03-5391-2922; www
.statravel.co.jp). Another resource in Japan is
No 1 Travel (☎ 03-3205-6073; www.no1-travel.com).

Australia & New Zealand

The cheapest routes are usually via the US
(normally Los Angeles). You're normally
looking at A$2300 or NZ$2300 or more,
round-trip (plus several hundred dollars
extra at high season).

The following are well-known agents for
cheap fares, with branches throughout both
countries:

Flight Centre Australia (☎ 133 133; www.flightcentre
.com.au); New Zealand (☎ 0800-243-544; www.flight
centre.co.nz)

STA Travel Australia (☎ 1300 733 035; www.statravel.com
.au); New Zealand (☎ 0508-782-872; www.statravel.co.nz)

For online fares try www.travel.com.au or
www.zuji.com from Australia, and www
.travel.co.nz or www.zuji.co.nz from New
Zealand.

Canada

Montreal, Toronto and Vancouver all have
direct flights to Mexico, though better deals
are often available with a change of flight
in the US. Round-trip fares from Toronto
start at around C$900 to Mexico City, Can-
cún or Puerto Vallarta. **Travel Cuts** (☎ 800-667-
28-87; www.travelcuts.com) is Canada's national
student travel agency. For online bookings

try www.kayak.com, www.expedia.ca and www.travelocity.ca.

Central & South America & the Caribbean

You can fly direct to Mexico City from at least eight cities in South America, and from Panama City, San José (Costa Rica), San Salvador, Guatemala City, Havana (Cuba) and Santo Domingo (Dominican Republic). There are also direct flights to Cancún from São Paulo, Panama City, Havana, Guatemala City and Flores (Guatemala). The Havana–Cancún flights continue to Mérida, Villahermosa, Tuxtla Gutiérrez and Oaxaca. Round-trip fares to Mexico City start at around $500 from Guatemala City and $800 to $1000 from South America.

Recommended ticket agencies include the following:

ASATEJ (☎ 011-4114-7595; www.asatej.com) In Argentina.

IVI Tours (☎ 0212-993-6082; www.ividiomas.com) In Venezuela.

Student Travel Bureau (☎ 3038-1555; www.stb.com .br) In Brazil.

Viajo.com (www.viajo.com) Online and telephone bookings from several countries.

Europe

There are direct flights to Mexico City, Toluca and Cancún. Airlines include Aeroméxico, Air France, Air Madrid, British Airways, Iberia, Jetair, KLM, Lufthansa and Air Europa. An alternative is to fly with a US or Canadian airline or alliance partner, changing planes in North America.

Round-trip fares to Mexico City or Cancún start at around UK£500 to UK£600 from London, or €600 to €700 from Frankfurt, Paris or Madrid. The two budget airlines so far operating between Europe and Mexico (Air Madrid from Madrid to Mexico City, and Jetair from Brussels to Cancún) can save you a couple of hundred euros if you're lucky on the dates.

For online bookings throughout Europe, try **Opodo** (www.opodo.com) or **Ebookers** (www .ebookers.com).

TICKET AGENTS IN THE UK

Flight ads appear in the travel pages of the weekend broadsheet newspapers, in *Time Out*, the *Evening Standard* and the free online magazine **TNT** (www.tntmagazine.com).

An excellent place to start your inquiries is **Journey Latin America** (☎ 020-8747-3108; www .journeylatinamerica.co.uk), which offers a variety of tours as well as flights. Other recommended agencies include the following:

Ebookers (☎ 0800-082-3000; www.ebookers.com)

Flight Centre (☎ 0800-587-700-58; flightcentre.co.uk)

STA Travel (☎ 08701-630-026; www.statravel.co.uk) For travelers under the age of 26.

Trailfinders (☎ 0845-058-5858; www.trailfinders.co.uk)

Travelbag (☎ 0800-082-5000; www.travelbag.com)

TICKET AGENTS ELSEWHERE IN EUROPE
France

Nouvelles Frontières (☎ 0825-000-747; www .nouvelles-frontieres.fr)

OTU Voyages (☎ 01-55-82-32-32; www.otu.fr) A student and youth travel specialist.

Voyageurs du Monde (☎ 0892-688-363; www.vdm .com)

Germany

Expedia (www.expedia.de)

Just Travel (☎ 089-747-3330; www.justtravel.de)

STA Travel (☎ 069-743-032-92; www.statravel.de) For travelers aged under 26.

Italy

CTS Viaggi (☎ 199-501150; www.cts.it) is a specialist in student and youth travel.

Netherlands

Airfair (☎ 070-3076110; www.airfair.nl)

Scandinavia

Kilroy Travels (www.kilroytravels.com)

Spain

eDreams (☎ 902-887-107; www.edreams.es)

Rumbo (☎ 902-123-999; www.rumbo.es)

The USA

You can fly to Mexico without changing planes from around 30 US cities. There are one-stop connecting flights from many others. Continental (from Houston), Aeroméxico and Mexicana offer the largest numbers of Mexican destinations.

US budget airlines including ATA, Spirit Air, America West, Frontier Airlines, and Ted have entered the US–Mexico market, and economical fares are also available on Mexico's Aero California, Aviacsa and Líneas Aéreas Azteca. If you're lucky you can get round-trip fares from the US to

Mexico (even as far south as Cancún) for $250. If you're not lucky, 'budget' operators can cost as much as other airlines. For current bargain offers, check **Airfare Watchdog** (www.airfarewatchdog.com).

San Francisco is the ticket consolidator (discounter) capital of the USA, but good deals can also be found in other big cities. The following agencies are recommended for online bookings:

- www.cheaptickets.com
- www.expedia.com
- www.kayak.com
- www.lowestfare.com
- www.orbitz.com
- www.sta.com (for students and travelers under 26)
- www.travelocity.com

Here are some typical discounted low-season round-trip fares:

From	To Mexico City	To Cancún	To Puerto Vallarta
Chicago	$375	$350	$400
Dallas/Fort Worth	$400	$350	$500
Los Angeles	$390	$400	$350
Miami	$400	$350	$400
New York	$450	$450	$530

In high season you may have to pay $100 to $200 more, though competitive fares are offered by some of the websites listed for all times of year, if you book ahead.

LAND
Border Crossings
There are over 40 official crossing points on the US–Mexico border, about 10 between Guatemala and Mexico, and two between Belize and Mexico. You'll find more information on the most important crossings in this book's regional chapters. Not many people stay long in the border towns.

Car & Motorcycle
The rules for taking a vehicle into Mexico change from time to time. You can check with the **American Automobile Association** (AAA; www.aaa.com), **Sanborn's** (☎ 800-222-01-58; www.sanbornsinsurance.com), a Mexican consulate or, in the USA and Canada, the **Mexican tourist information numbers** (☎ 800-446-39-42, 800-482-98-32).

You won't usually find gasoline or mechanics available at Mexico's road borders: before crossing the border, make sure you have enough fuel to get to the next sizable town inside Mexico. For information on driving and motorcycling once you're inside Mexico, see p999.

DRIVER'S LICENSE
To drive a motor vehicle in Mexico, you need a valid driver's license from your home country.

MOTOR INSURANCE
It is very foolish to drive in Mexico without Mexican liability insurance. If you are involved in an accident, you can be jailed and have your vehicle impounded while responsibility is assessed. If you are to blame for an accident causing injury or death, you may be detained until you guarantee restitution to the victims and payment of any fines. This could take weeks or months. Adequate Mexican insurance coverage is the only real protection: it is regarded as a guarantee that restitution will be paid, and will expedite release of the driver.

Mexican law recognizes only Mexican motor *seguro* (insurance), so a US or Canadian policy, even if it provides coverage, is not acceptable to Mexican officialdom. Sanborn's and the AAA are both well worth looking into for Mexico motor insurance. Mexican insurance is also sold in US border towns; as you approach the border from the USA you will see billboards advertising offices selling Mexican policies. At the busiest border crossings (to Tijuana, Mexicali, Nogales, Agua Prieta, Ciudad Juárez, Nuevo Laredo, Reynosa and Matamoros), there are insurance offices open 24 hours a day. Some deals are better than others.

Short-term insurance is about $15 a day for full coverage on a car worth under $10,000; for periods longer than two weeks it's often cheaper to get an annual policy. Liability-only insurance costs around half the full coverage cost.

Insurance is considered invalid if the driver is under the influence of alcohol or drugs.

VEHICLE PERMIT
You will need a *permiso de importación temporal de vehículos* (temporary vehicle import permit) if you want to take a vehicle

beyond Baja California, beyond Puerto Peñasco in Sonora state, or beyond the border zone that extends 20km to 30km into Mexico along the rest of the US frontier and up to 70km from the Guatemalan and Belize frontiers. Officials at posts of the Instituto Nacional de Migración (INM; National Immigration Institute) in the border zones, and at the Baja California ports for ferries to mainland Mexico, will want to see your permit.

The permits are issued at offices at border crossings or (for some border crossings) at posts a few kilometers into Mexico, and (in Baja California) at Ensenada port, Santa Rosalía customs building and Pichilingue (La Paz) ferry terminal. Information on their locations and application forms for the vehicle permit are available online at www .banjercito.com.mx (mostly in Spanish). The person importing the vehicle will need the original and one or two photocopies (people at the office may make photocopies for a small fee) of each of the following documents, which as a rule must all be in his/her own name (except that you can bring in your spouse's, parent's or child's vehicle if you can show a marriage or birth certificate proving your relationship):

- tourist card (FMT): go to *migración* before you get your vehicle permit
- certificate of title or registration certificate for the vehicle (note: you should have both of these if you plan to drive through Mexico into Guatemala or Belize)
- a Visa, MasterCard or American Express credit card, issued by a non-Mexican institution; if you don't have one you must pay a returnable deposit of between $200 and $400 (depending on how old the car is) at the border. Your card details or deposit serve as a guarantee that you'll take the car out of Mexico before your tourist card (FMT) expires
- proof of citizenship or residency, such as a passport, birth certificate or voter's registration card accompanied by official photo ID such as a driver's license
- driver's license
- if the vehicle is not fully paid for, a partial invoice and/or letter of authorization from the financing institution
- for a leased or rented vehicle (though few US rental firms allow their vehicles to be taken into Mexico), the contract, which must be in the name of the person importing the vehicle
- for a company car, proof of employment by the company and proof of the company's ownership of the vehicle

One person cannot bring in two vehicles. If you have a motorcycle attached to your car, you'll need another adult traveling with you to obtain a permit for the motorcycle, and he/she will need to have all the right papers for it.

At the border there will be a building with a parking area for vehicles awaiting permits. Go inside and find the right counter to present your papers. After some signing and stamping of papers, you sign a promise to take the car out of the country, pay a processing fee of about $29 to the Banco del Ejército (also called Banjército; it's the army bank), and go and wait with your vehicle. Make sure you get back the originals of all documents. Eventually someone will come out and give you your vehicle permit and a sticker to be displayed on your windshield.

While in Mexico, other persons are allowed to drive the car only if the permit holder is in the car with them.

You have the option to take the vehicle in and out of Mexico for the period shown on your tourist card. Ask for a *tarjetón de internación,* a document which you will exchange for a *comprobante de retorno* each time you leave Mexico; when you return to Mexico, you swap the *comprobante* for another *tarjetón.* When you leave Mexico the last time, you must have the import permit canceled by the Mexican authorities. An official may do this as you enter the border zone, usually 20km to 30km before the border itself. If not, you'll have to find the right official at the border crossing. If you leave Mexico without having the permit canceled, the authorities may assume you've left the vehicle in the country illegally and decide to keep your deposit, charge a fine to your credit card, or deny you permission to bring a vehicle into the country on your next trip.

Only the owner may take the vehicle out of Mexico. If the vehicle is wrecked completely, you must contact your consulate or a Mexican customs office to make arrangements to leave without it.

Belize

Novelo's Bus Line (in Belize City ☎ 227-20-25) runs around 20 buses a day between Belize City and Chetumal, Mexico ($5 to $7, four hours), calling at the Belizean towns of Orange Walk and Corozal en route.

Guatemala

The road borders at La Mesilla/Ciudad Cuauhtémoc, Ciudad Tecún Umán/Ciudad Hidalgo and El Carmen/Talismán are all linked to Guatemala City, and nearby cities within Guatemala and Mexico, by plentiful buses and/or combis. **Transportes Galgos** (in Guatemala City ☎ 2232-3661; www.transgalgosinter .com.gt), **Línea Dorada** (in Guatemala City ☎ 2232-5506; www.tikalmayanworld.com) and **Tica Bus** (in Guatemala City ☎ 2331-4279; www.ticabus.com) run a few buses daily all the way from Guatemala City to Tapachula, Chiapas ($14 to $22, six hours) via Escuintla and Mazatenango.

There are a few daily buses from Flores, Guatemala, to Chetumal, Mexico ($25, seven to eight hours), via Belize City, by **Línea Dorada** (in Flores ☎ 7926-0070) and **San Juan Travel** (in Flores ☎ 7926-0041).

For the Río Usumacinta route between Flores and Palenque, Mexico, several daily 2nd-class buses run from Flores to Bethel ($4, four hours), on the Guatemalan bank of the Usumacinta. The 40-minute boat trip from Bethel to Frontera Corozal, Mexico, costs $7 to $11 per person; an alternative is to take a bus from Flores that continues through Bethel to La Técnica ($5, five hours), from which it's only a $1, five-minute river crossing to Frontera Corozal. Vans run from Frontera Corozal to Palenque ($6, three hours, 10 daily). If you're traveling this route it's well worth detouring to the outstanding Maya ruins at Yaxchilán (see p847), near Frontera Corozal. Travel agencies in Palenque and Flores offer bus-boat-bus packages between the two places from around $40.

The USA

BUS

Cross-border bus services, mainly used by Mexicans working in the US, link many US cities with northern Mexican cities. They're not very well publicized: Spanish-language newspapers in the US have the most ads. The major companies include **Autobuses Americanos** (in Austin ☎ 512-928-9237, in Denver ☎ 303-292-0333, in Houston ☎ 713-928-8832,

in Los Angeles ☎ 213-627-5405, in Phoenix ☎ 602-258-4331; www.autobusesamericanos.com.mx), operating to northeast Mexico, central north Mexico and central Mexico from Los Angeles, Denver, Albuquerque, Chicago, Arizona and several Texan cities; **Autobuses Crucero** (in Phoenix ☎ 602-258-4331), operating from California, Nevada and Arizona to northwest Mexico; and **Transportes Baldomero Corral** (TBC; in Phoenix ☎ 602-258-2445), operating between Arizona and northwest Mexico. **Greyhound** (☎ 800-231-2222; www.greyhound.com) also has some cross-border routes.

Listed below are some sample fares and journey times on cross-border buses.

Route	Fare	Duration
Los Angeles–Tijuana	$23	4hr
Los Angeles–Hermosillo	$68	17hr
Phoenix–Álamos	$55	14hr
Phoenix–Hermosillo	$41	8hr
Dallas–Reynosa	$44	11hr
Houston–Matamoros	$28	10hr
Houston–Monterrey	$38	12hr

You can also, often in little or no extra time, make your way to the border on one bus (or train), cross it on foot or by local bus, and then catch an onward bus on the other side. Greyhound serves many US border cities; to reach others, transfer from Greyhound to a smaller bus line. Greyhound one-way fares to El Paso, for example, are $50 from Los Angeles (16 hours), $121 from Chicago (34 hours) and $110 from New York (51 hours).

CAR & MOTORCYCLE

For information on the procedures for taking a vehicle into Mexico, see p992. If you are visiting the state of Sonora only, and are entering Mexico at Nogales and will leave by the same route after not more than 180 days, you qualify for the Sonora Only permit and do not have to pay the $29 fee or a deposit. You just need to show your documents at the Km 21 checkpoint on Hwy 15 south of Nogales, and return your permit to this checkpoint within 180 days.

If you're traveling from Mexico into the USA at a busy time of year, have a look at the website of **US Customs & Border Protection** (http://apps.cbp.gov), which posts waiting times at entry points.

TRAIN

Though there are no regular passenger trains on the Mexican side of the US–Mexico border, it's quite possible to reach the US side of the border by rail. Trains can be quicker and cheaper than buses, or slower and more expensive, depending on the route. **Amtrak** (☎ 800-872-72-45; www .amtrak.com) serves four US cities from which access to Mexico is easy: San Diego, California (opposite Tijuana); El Paso, Texas (opposite Ciudad Juárez); Del Rio, Texas (opposite Ciudad Acuña) and San Antonio, Texas, which is linked by bus to Eagle Pass (opposite Piedras Negras) and Laredo (opposite Nuevo Laredo).

SEA

If you'd like to combine snatches of Mexico with a life of ease on the high seas, take a cruise! Ever more popular, cruises from the US now bring over seven million passengers a year to Mexican ports, enabling people to enjoy activities and attractions on and near Mexico's coasts without having to worry about the logistics of accommodations, eating or transportation. Caribbean Mexico is the most popular cruise destination, usually in combination with other Caribbean stops and/or Key West, Florida. Cozumel island, the busiest stop in Mexico, was receiving over 1300 cruise ships a year (almost three million passengers) before damage by Hurricane Wilma in 2005. It expects to regain pre-Wilma traffic levels by the end of 2007. Mexico's other Caribbean cruise ports are Costa Maya, Puerto Morelos and the new Calica, just south of Playa del Carmen. Progreso, on the Yucatán Peninsula's north coast, is also popular.

On the Pacific route (the Mexican Riviera in cruise parlance), the main ports of call are Ensenada, Cabo San Lucas, Mazatlán, Puerto Vallarta and Acapulco, each with more than 100 cruisers a year (over 200 at Puerto Vallarta); some cruises also call at Manzanillo, Zihuatanejo and Bahías de Huatulco, and a new cruise port is opening at Puerto Chiapas, near Tapachula.

A Caribbean cruise from ports in the southeastern USA, or a Mexican Riviera cruise from California, can cost well under $1000 per person for 10 days.

Following are some of the cruise lines visiting Mexico, with US phone numbers:

Carnival Cruise Lines (☎ 888-227-6482; www .carnival.com)
Celebrity Cruises (☎ 800-722-5941; www.celebrity .com)
Crystal Cruises (☎ 800-804-1500; www.crystalcruises .com)
Holland America Line (☎ 877-724-5425; www .hollandamerica.com)
Norwegian Cruise Lines (☎ 800-327-7030; www .ncl.com)
P&O Cruises (☎ 415-382-8900; www.pocruises.com)
Princess Cruises (☎ 800-774-6237; www.princess.com)
Royal Caribbean International (☎ 800-398-9813; www.royalcaribbean.com)

GETTING AROUND

AIR

All large and many smaller cities in Mexico have airports and passenger services. Depending on the fare you get, flying can be good value on longer journeys, especially considering the long bus trip that is probably the alternative. Domestic flights within Mexico are sometimes cheaper if you book them before you go to Mexico, in conjunction with an international round-trip ticket.

Airlines in Mexico

Aeroméxico and Mexicana are the country's two major airlines. There are also numerous smaller ones, often cheaper and often flying routes, ignored by the bigger two, between provincial cities. These include Click Mexicana (Mexicana's no-frills subsidiary), Avolar, Aviacsa, Líneas Aéreas Azteca and Aero California. Now that Mexico has finally opened up to low-cost air travel, expect other carriers to enter the market.

The US Federal Aviation Administration (FAA) considers Mexico to be in compliance with international aviation safety standards.

Fares

Fares can depend on whether you fly at a busy or quiet time of day, week or year, and how far ahead you book and pay. High season generally corresponds to the Mexican holiday seasons (see p977). You'll often save money if you pay for the ticket a few days ahead or if you fly late in the evening. Round-trip fares are usually simply twice

TRANSPORTATION

MEXICAN DOMESTIC AIRLINES

Airline	Telephone	Website	Areas served
Aero California	☎ 800-237-62-25	N/A	Mexico City, Baja California, north, west
Aerolitoral	☎ 800-800-23-76	www.aerolitoral.com	Central Mexico, Baja California, north, west, Gulf coast
Aeromar	☎ 800-237-66-27	www.aeromar.com.mx	Central Mexico, west, northeast, Gulf coast, southeast
Aeroméxico	☎ 800-021-40-00	www.aeromexico.com	over 50 cities nationwide
Aero Tucán	☎ 800-640-41-48, 951-501-05-30	www.aero-tucan.com	Oaxaca state, Puebla
Aviacsa	☎ 800-006-22-00	www.aviacsa.com	Mexico City & 19 other cities around the country
Avolar	☎ 800-021-90-00	www.avolar.com.mx	Tijuana, Hermosillo, Uruapan, Puebla, Acapulco
Click Mexicana	☎ 800-122-54-25	www.clickmx.com	Mexico City & 16 other cities around the country
Interjet	☎ 800-011-23-45	www.interjet.com.mx	Toluca, Guadalajara, Cancún, Monterrey
Líneas Aéreas Azteca	☎ 800-229-83-22	aazteca.com.mx	Mexico City, Cancún, Oaxaca, Acapulco, north, west
Magnicharters	☎ 55-5566-8199	www.magnicharters.com.mx	Mexico City, Toluca, Aguascalientes, Guadalajara, Monterrey, Bajío, Torreón, San Luis Potosí, Morelia, Mérida, coastal resorts
Mexicana	☎ 800-502-20-00	www.mexicana.com	over 50 cities nationwide

Note: Aerolitoral and Aeromar are affiliates of Aeroméxico and normally share its booking facilities.

the price of one-way tickets, though some cheaper advance-payment deals do exist.

Here are some examples of one-way fares from Mexico City with Aeroméxico and Click Mexicana or Azteca, including taxes:

Destination	Aeroméxico Fare	Click Mexicana/ Azteca Fare
Acapulco	$254	$130
Cancún	$177	$93-115
Guadalajara	$230	$105
Mérida	$210	$92-100
Monterrey	$254	$110
Oaxaca	$179	$84-94
Puerto Vallarta	$268	$120
Tijuana	$218	$155

BICYCLE

Except for Baja California, cycling is not a common way to tour Mexico. The size of the country, reports of highway robbery, poor road surfaces, careless motorists and pedestrians and other road hazards (see p1000) are deterrents. However, biking around is

certainly possible if you're prepared for the challenges. You should be fit, use the best equipment, and be fully able to handle your own repairs. Take the mountainous topography and hot climate into account when planning your route. Bike lanes are rare.

All cities have bicycle stores: a decent mountain bike suitable for a few weeks' touring costs around $400 to $500. Don't expect to get much of that back by selling it afterwards unless you have time on your side.

If you're interested in a long Mexican ride, consider the bring-your-own-bike tours of the Yucatán Peninsula, Pacific Mexico and the central highlands, up to a month long, offered by the fun and friendly !El Tour (www.bikemexico.com).

BOAT

Vehicle and passenger ferries connecting Baja California with the Mexican mainland sail between Santa Rosalía and Guaymas, La Paz and Mazatlán, and La Paz and Topolobampo. One-way passenger seat fares cost from $55 to $75; a car up to 5m in length costs between $100 and $250. There are also ferries from the Yucatán Peninsula to the islands of Isla Mujeres (p881), Cozumel (p892) and Isla Holbox (p883).

BUS

Mexico has a good road and bus network, and comfortable, frequent, reasonably priced bus services connect all cities. Most cities and towns have one main bus terminal where all long-distance buses arrive and depart. It may be called the Terminal de Autobuses, Central de Autobuses, Central Camionera or simply La Central (not to be confused with *el centro,* the city center!) If there is no single main terminal, different bus companies will have separate terminals scattered around town.

Baggage is safe if stowed in the bus's baggage hold, but get a receipt for it when you hand it over. Keep your most valuable documents (passport, money etc) in the cabin with you, and keep them closely protected.

Highway robbery happens very occasionally. The risk is higher at night, on isolated stretches of highway far from cities, and in 2nd-class buses.

Classes
DELUXE

De lujo services, sometimes termed *ejecutivo* (executive), run mainly on the busy routes. They are swift, modern and comfortable, with reclining seats, adequate legroom, air-conditioning, few or no stops, toilets on board (but not necessarily toilet paper), and sometimes drinks or snacks. Like 1st-class buses, deluxe buses usually show movies on video screens.

1ST CLASS

Primera (1a) clase buses have a comfortable numbered seat for each passenger. All sizable towns have 1st-class bus services. Standards of comfort are adequate at the very least. The buses usually have air-conditioning and a toilet and they stop infrequently. They always show movies (often bad ones) for most of the trip: too bad if you don't want to watch, as all seats face a video screen.

Bring a sweater or jacket to combat overzealous air-conditioning. As with deluxe buses, you buy your ticket in the bus station before boarding.

2ND CLASS

Segunda (2a) clase buses serve small towns and villages, and provide cheaper, slower travel on some intercity routes. A few are almost as quick, comfortable and direct as 1st-class buses. Others are old, slow and shabby.

Many 2nd-class services have no ticket office; you just pay your fare to the conductor. These buses tend to take slow, nontoll roads in and out of big cities and will stop anywhere to pick up passengers: if you board midroute you might make some of the trip standing. The small amount of money you save by traveling 2nd-class is not usually worth the discomfort or extra journey time entailed.

Second-class buses can also be less safe than 1st-class or deluxe buses, for reasons of maintenance or driver standards or because

---

HOW MANY STOPS?

It's useful to understand the difference between the types of bus service on offer:

Sin escalas Nonstop.

Directo Very few stops.

Semi-directo A few more stops than *directo*.

Ordinario Stops wherever passengers want to get on or off the bus; deluxe and 1st-class buses are never *ordinario*.

Express Nonstop on short to medium-length trips; very few stops on long trips.

Local Bus that starts its journey at the bus station you're in and usually leaves on time; *local* service is preferable to *de paso.*

De paso Bus that started its journey somewhere else but is stopping to let off and take on passengers. If the bus company does not have a computer booking system, you may have to wait until the bus arrives before any tickets are sold. If the bus is full, you have to wait for the next one.

Viaje redondo Round-trip.

MEXICAN BUS COMPANIES

Company	Telephone	Website	Main regions/destinations
ABC	☎ 664-621-24-24	www.abc.com.mx	Baja California
ADO, ADO GL	☎ 800-702-80-00	www.ado.com.mx	Mexico City, Puebla, southeast, Veracruz state
Autotransportes Águila	☎ 612-122-42-70	N/A	Southern Baja California
Autovías	☎ 55-5567-4550	www.herraduradeplata.com	Mexico City, Michoacán, San Miguel de Allende
Elite	☎ 800-507-55-00	www.estrellablanca.com.mx	Mexico City, northwest, Pacific coast, Querétaro, San Luis Potosí
Estrella Blanca	☎ 800-507-55-00	www.estrellablanca.com.mx	Cuernavaca, Hermosillo, northern central highlands, Pacific coast
Estrella de Oro	☎ 55-5689-3955	www.estrelladeoro.com.mx	Acapulco, Cuernavaca, Ixtapa, Mexico City, Taxco, Zihuatanejo
Estrella Roja	☎ 800-712-22-84	www.estrellaroja.com.mx	Mexico City, Puebla
ETN	☎ 800-800-03-86	www.etn.com.mx	Manzanillo, Mexico City, northern & western central highlands, northeast, Puerto Vallarta
Flecha Amarilla	☎ 800-375-75-87	N/A	Manzanillo, Mexico City, Morelia, northern & western central highlands
Flecha Roja	☎ 800-507-55-00	www.estrellablanca.com.mx	Cuernavaca, Mexico City, Toluca
Futura	☎ 800-507-55-00	www.estrellablanca.com.mx	Guadalajara, Mexico City, Monterrey, Nuevo Laredo, northern central highlands, Pacific coast, Taxco
Herradura de Plata	☎ 55-5567-4550	www.herraduradeplata.com	Northern & western central highlands
OCC (Ómnibus Cristóbal Colón)	☎ 800-702-80-00	www.ado.com.mx	Mexico City, Puebla, Oaxaca, Chiapas
Ómnibus de México	☎ 800-765-66-36	www.odm.com.mx	Chihuahua, Ciudad Juárez, Colima, Durango, Guadalajara, Mexico City, Monterrey, northern central highlands, Saltillo, Torreón
Primera Plus	☎ 55-5567-7176	N/A	Manzanillo, Mexico City, northern & western central highlands, Puerto Vallarta
Pullman de Morelos	☎ 55-5549-3505	www.pullman.com.mx	Cuernavaca, Mexico City
TAP	☎ 668-812-57-49	N/A	Mexico City, northwest
Transportes Chihuahuenses	☎ 800-507-55-00	www.estrellablanca.com.mx	Chihuahua, Mexico City, Los Mochis, Zacatecas
Transportes del Norte	☎ 800-507-55-00	www.estrellablanca.com.mx	Mexico City, northeast, San Luis Potosí
Turistar	☎ 800-507-55-00	www.estrellablanca.com.mx	Mexico City, northeast, Pacific coast
UNO	☎ 800-702-80-00	www.ado.com.mx	Mexico City, Puebla, Veracruz, Oaxaca, Chiapas

Note: many bus lines are part of multi-line groups, which may share ticket desks at bus stations. ADO, ADO GL, OCC and UNO are all part of the ADO group. Elite, Estrella Blanca, Flecha Roja, Futura, Transportes Chihuahuenses, Transportes del Norte and Turistar are all part of Grupo Estrella Blanca.

they are more vulnerable to being boarded by bandits on some roads. Out in the remoter areas, however, you'll often find that 2nd-class buses are the only buses available.

Microbuses or '*micros*' are small, usually fairly new, 2nd-class buses with around 25 seats, usually running short routes between nearby towns.

Costs

First-class buses typically cost around $4 per hour of travel (70km to 80km). Deluxe buses may cost just 10% or 20% more than 1st-class, or about 60% more for super-deluxe services such as ETN, UNO and Turistar Ejecutivo. Second-class buses cost 10% or 20% less than 1st-class.

Reservations

For trips of up to four or five hours on busy routes, you can usually just go to the bus terminal, buy a ticket and head out without much delay. For longer trips, or routes with infrequent service, buy a ticket a day or more in advance. Deluxe and 1st-class bus companies have computerized ticket systems that allow you to select your seat when you buy your ticket. Try to avoid the back of the bus, which is where the toilets are and also tends to give a bumpier ride.

Ticketbus (in Mexico City ☎ 55-5133-2424, 800-702-80-00; www.ticketbus.com.mx) provides tickets and reservations by Internet or telephone or at any of its many offices in 24 cities for the ADO group serving Mexico City, Puebla, the Gulf coast, Yucatán Peninsula, Oaxaca and Chiapas (including UNO, ADO GL, ADO, OCC, AU and Rápidos del Sur lines), and some other bus companies.

If you pay for a bus ticket in cash, cash refunds of 80% to 100% are available from many bus companies if you return your ticket more than an hour or two before the listed departure time.

CAR & MOTORCYCLE

Driving in Mexico is not as easy as it is north of the border, and rentals are more expensive, but having your own vehicle gives you maximum flexibility and freedom.

Bring Your Own Vehicle

Bringing a car to Mexico is most useful for travelers who:

- have plenty of time
- like to get off the beaten track
- have surfboards, diving equipment or other cumbersome luggage
- will be traveling with at least one companion

Drivers should know some Spanish and have basic mechanical knowledge, reserves of patience and access to extra cash for emergencies. Good makes of car to take to Mexico are Volkswagen, Nissan, General Motors and Ford, which have plants in Mexico and dealers in most big towns. Very big cars are unwieldy on narrow roads and use a lot of gasoline. A sedan with a trunk (boot) provides safer storage than a station wagon or hatchback. Mexican mechanics are resourceful, and most repairs can be done quickly and inexpensively, but it still pays to take as many spare parts as you can manage (spare fuel filters are very useful). Tires (including spare), shock absorbers and suspension should be in good condition. For security, have something to immobilize the steering wheel, and consider getting a kill switch installed.

Motorcycling in Mexico is not for the fainthearted. Roads and traffic can be rough, and parts and mechanics hard to come by. The parts you'll most easily find will be for Kawasaki, Honda and Suzuki bikes.

See p992 and p994 for information on the paperwork required for bringing a vehicle into Mexico.

Gas (Petrol)

All *gasolina* (gasoline) and diesel fuel in Mexico is sold by the government's monopoly, Pémex (Petróleos Mexicanos). Most towns, even small ones, have a Pémex station, and the stations are pretty common on most major roads. Nevertheless, in remote areas you should fill up whenever you can.

LUCKY CHARMS

On some Mexican highways, especially those heading south from the US border, the army and police conduct fairly frequent drug and weapon searches. Old Mexico driving hands swear that any or all of the following items, visibly displayed, will indicate to officials that you are not a security risk and thus diminish your chances of being pulled over:

- a Virgin of Guadalupe charm or rosary beads hanging from the rear-view mirror
- a surfboard on the roof
- a bible or Lonely Planet guide on the dashboard!

The gasoline on sale is all *sin plomo* (unleaded). There are two varieties: Magna Sin, roughly equivalent to US regular unleaded, and Premium, roughly equivalent to US super unleaded. At the time of research, Magna Sin cost about $0.60 a liter ($2.40 a US gallon), and Premium about $0.70. Diesel fuel is widely available at around $0.50 per liter. Regular Mexican diesel has a higher sulfur content than US diesel, but there is a 'Diesel Sin' with less sulfur. If diesel drivers change their oil and filter about every 3500km, they should have no problems.

Gas stations have pump attendants (who appreciate a tip of $0.20 to $0.50).

Maps

Mexican signposting can be poor, and decent road maps are essential. Mexican publisher Guía Roji's *Por Las Carreteras de México* road atlas ($13.50) is an excellent investment. It's sold at good bookstores and some city newsstands in Mexico, and is available from Internet booksellers for a little more. A new edition is published annually and includes most new highways. Also useful are Quimera publisher's regional road maps.

Rental

Auto rental in Mexico is expensive by US or European standards, but is not hard to organize. You can book by Internet, telephone or in person and pick up cars at city offices, at airports, at many big hotels and sometimes at bus terminals.

Renters must provide a valid driver's license (your home license is OK), passport and major credit card, and are usually required to be at least 21 (sometimes 25, or if you're aged 21 to 24 you may have to pay a surcharge). Read the small print of the rental agreement. In addition to the basic rental rate, you pay tax and insurance costs to the rental company, and the full insurance that rental companies encourage can almost double the basic cost. You'll usually have the option of taking liability-only insurance at a lower rate. Ask exactly what the insurance options cover: theft and damage insurance may only cover a percentage of costs. It's best to have plenty of liability coverage: Mexican law permits the jailing of drivers after an accident until they have

met their obligations to third parties. The complimentary car-rental insurance offered with some US credit cards does not usually cover Mexico.

Most agencies offer a choice between a per-kilometer deal or unlimited kilometers. Local firms may or may not be cheaper than the big international ones. In most places the cheapest car available (often a Volkswagen Beetle) costs $50 to $60 a day including unlimited kilometers, insurance and tax. If you rent by the week or month, the per-day cost can come down by 20% to 40%. You can also cut costs by avoiding airport pickups and drop-offs, for which 10% can be added to your total check. The extra charge for drop-off in another city, when available, is usually about $0.40 per kilometer.

Here's contact information (with Mexican phone numbers) for some major firms:

Alamo (☎ 800-849-80-01; www.alamo.com)
Avis (☎ 800-288-88-88; www.avis.com.mx)
Budget (☎ 55-5705-5061; www.budget.com.mx)
Dollar (☎ 998-886-23-00; www.dollar.com)
Europcar (☎ 800-201-20-84; www.europcar.com.mx)
Hertz (☎ 800-709-50-00; www.hertz.com)
National (☎ 800-716-66-25; www.nationalcar.com.mx)
Thrifty (☎ 55-5207-1100; www.thrifty.com.mx)

Motorbikes or scooters are available to rent in a few tourist centers. You're usually required to have a driver's license and credit card. It's advisable to look particularly carefully into insurance arrangements here: some renters do not offer any insurance at all. Note that a locally acquired motorcycle license is not valid under some travel-insurance policies.

Road Conditions

Many Mexican highways, even some toll highways, are not up to the standards of US, Canadian or European ones. Still, the main roads are serviceable and fairly fast when traffic is not heavy. Mexicans on the whole drive as cautiously and sensibly as people anywhere. Traffic density, poor surfaces and frequent hazards (potholes, speed bumps, animals, bicycles, children) all help to keep speeds down.

Driving on a dark night is best avoided since unlit vehicles, rocks, pedestrians and animals on the roads are common. Hijacks and robberies do occur.

ROAD DISTANCES (KM)

	Acapulco	Cancún	Ciudad Juárez	Guadalajara	Guanajuato	Hermosillo	Matamoros	Mazatlán	Mérida	Mexico City	Monterrey	Morelia	Nogales	Oaxaca	Puebla	San Luis Potosí	Tapachula	Tijuana	Tuxtla Gutiérrez	Veracruz	Villahermosa
Cancún	2007																				
Ciudad Juárez	2258	3512																			
Guadalajara	889	2191	1578																		
Guanajuato	760	2014	1570	277																	
Hermosillo	2348	3608	769	1417	1694																
Matamoros	1370	2336	1530	1117	774	1848															
Mazatlán	1431	2891	1347	500	777	917	1250														
Mérida	1690	317	3195	1874	1697	3291	2019	2374													
Mexico City	395	1649	1863	542	365	1959	975	1042	1332												
Monterrey	1328	2363	1202	789	729	1520	328	928	2046	933											
Morelia	697	1951	1705	302	180	1719	954	802	1634	302	913										
Nogales	2625	3885	620	1694	1971	277	2125	1194	3568	2236	1797	1996									
Oaxaca	828	1490	2333	1012	835	2429	1358	1512	1173	470	1403	1403	2706								
Puebla	481	1526	1986	665	488	2082	1077	1165	1209	123	1056	1056	2359	347							
San Luis Potosí	810	2064	1448	340	215	1766	559	809	1747	415	514	395	2043	885	538						
Tapachula	1109	1376	2999	1678	1501	3195	1755	2175	1062	1136	1782	1438	3372	687	1013	1551					
Tijuana	3237	4497	1312	2306	2583	889	2737	1806	4180	2848	2409	2608	820	3318	2971	2615	3984				
Tuxtla Gutiérrez	967	1146	2660	1339	1162	2756	1416	1836	829	797	1443	1099	3033	545	674	1212	381	3645			
Veracruz	760	1373	2265	944	767	2361	963	1444	1056	402	990	704	2638	609	279	817	792	3250	453		
Villahermosa	1126	881	2631	1310	1133	2727	1455	1810	564	768	1482	1070	3004	609	645	1183	594	3616	255	492	
Zacatecas	1000	2254	1258	320	312	1576	979	619	1937	605	469	447	1853	1075	728	190	2051	2425	1702	1007	1373

In towns and cities and on rural roads, be especially wary of *Alto* (Stop) signs, *topes* (speed bumps) and holes in the road. They are often not where you'd expect, and missing one can cost you in traffic fines or car damage. Speed bumps are also used to slow traffic on highways that pass through built-up areas: they are not always signed, and some of them are severe!

There is always the chance that you will be pulled over by Mexican traffic police for an imaginary infraction. If this happens, stay calm and polite and don't be in a hurry. You don't have to pay a bribe, and acting dumb and not understanding Spanish may eventually make the cop give up. You can also ask to see documentation about the law you have supposedly broken, ask for the officer's identification, ask to speak to a superior, and/or note the officer's name, badge number, vehicle number and department (federal, state or municipal). Pay any traffic fines at a police station and get a receipt, then if you wish to make a complaint head for a state tourist office.

BREAKDOWN ASSISTANCE

The Mexican tourism ministry, Sectur, maintains a network of *Ángeles Verdes* (Green Angels) – bilingual mechanics in green uniforms and green trucks, who patrol 60,000km of major highways throughout the country daily during daylight hours looking for tourists in trouble. They make minor repairs, change tires, provide fuel and oil, and arrange towing and other assistance if necessary. Service is free; parts, gasoline and oil are provided at cost. If you are near a telephone when your car has problems, you can call their **24-hour hot line** (☎ 078) or contact them through the national **24-hour tourist assistance** (in Mexico City ☎ 55-5250-0123, 800-903-92-00). There's a map of the roads they patrol at www.sectur .gob.mx/wb2/sectur/sect_9454_rutas _carreteras.

CITY PARKING

It's not usually a good idea to park on the street overnight. If your hotel doesn't have parking, it's best to find a commercial *estacionamiento* (parking lot). These usually cost around $5 overnight and $1 per hour during the day.

MOTORCYCLE HAZARDS

Certain aspects of Mexican roads make them particularly hazardous for motorbikers:

- poor signage of road and lane closures
- lots of dogs on the roads
- debris and deep potholes
- vehicles without taillights
- lack of highway lighting

TOLL ROADS

Mexico has more than 6000km of autopistas (toll roads), usually four-lane. They are generally in much better condition and a lot quicker than the alternative free roads. *Cuotas* (tolls) average about $1 per 10km. Toll information is available at www.sct.gob.mx: click on 'Carreteras' then 'Traza Tu Ruta.'

Road Rules

Drive on the right-hand side of the road.

Speed limits range between 80km and 120km per hour on open highways (less when highways pass through built-up areas), and between 30km and 50km per hour in towns and cities. Seat belts are obligatory for all occupants of a car, and children under five must be strapped into safety seats in the rear. Traffic laws and speed limits rarely seem to be enforced on the highways. Obey the rules in the cities so you don't give the police an excuse to demand a 'fine' payable on the spot.

One-way streets are the rule in cities. Priority at street intersections is indicated by thin black and red rectangles containing white arrows. A black rectangle facing you means you have priority; a red one means you don't. The white arrows indicate the direction of traffic on the cross street; if the arrow points both ways, it's a two-way street.

Antipollution rules in Mexico City ban most vehicles from the city's roads on one day each week (see p186).

COLECTIVOS & OTHER VEHICLES

In some areas a variety of small vehicles provide alternatives to buses. *Colectivo* (collective) taxis, Volkswagen minibuses (combis) and more comfortable passenger-carrying vans, such as Chevrolet Suburbans, operate shuttle services between some towns, usually leaving whenever they have a full load of passengers. Fares are typically a little less than 1st-class buses. *Microbuses* or *'micros'* are small, usually fairly new, 2nd-class buses with around 25 seats, usually running short routes between nearby towns. More primitive are passenger-carrying *camionetas* (pickups) and *camiones* (trucks) with fares similar to 2nd-class bus fares. Standing in the back of a lurching truck with a couple of dozen *campesinos* (land workers) and their machetes and animals is always an experience to remember!

HITCHING

Hitchhiking is never entirely safe in any country in the world, and is not recommended. Travelers who decide to hitch should understand that they are taking a small but potentially serious risk. People who do choose to hitch will be safer if they travel in pairs and let someone know where they are planning to go. A woman traveling alone certainly should not hitchhike in Mexico, and even two women alone is not advisable.

However, hitching is not an uncommon way of getting to some of the off-the-beaten-track archaeological sites and other places poorly served by bus. Always be alert to possible dangers wherever you are. If the driver is another tourist or a private motorist, you may get the ride for free. If it is a work or commercial vehicle, you should offer to pay, something equivalent to the bus fare.

LOCAL TRANSPORTATION
Bicycle

Most Mexican towns and cities are flat enough to make cycling an option. Seek out the less traffic-infested routes and you should enjoy it. Even Mexico City has its biking enthusiasts. You can rent bikes in several towns and cities for $10 to $15 a day.

Boat

Here and there you may find yourself traveling by boat to an outlying beach, along a river or across a lake or lagoon. The craft are usually fast outboard *lanchas* (launches). Fares vary widely: an average is around $1 a minute if you have to charter the whole boat (haggle!), or around $1 for five to 10 minutes if it's a public service.

Bus

Generally known as *camiones*, local buses are often the cheapest way to get around

cities and out to nearby towns and villages. They run frequently and are cheap. Fares in cities are rarely more than $0.50. In many cities, fleets of small, modern *microbuses* have replaced the noisy, dirty and crowded older buses.

Buses usually halt only at fixed *paradas* (bus stops), though in some places you can hold your hand out to stop one at any street corner.

Colectivo, Combi, Minibus & Pesero

These are all names for vehicles that function as something between a taxi and a bus, running along fixed urban routes usually displayed on the windshield. They're cheaper than taxis and quicker than buses. They will pick you up or drop you off on any corner along their route: to stop one, go to the curb and wave your hand. Tell the driver where you want to go. Usually, you pay at the end of the trip and the fare (a little higher than a bus fare) depends on how far you go. In some northern border towns, 'pesero' is used to mean a city bus.

Metro

Mexico City, Guadalajara and Monterrey all have metro (subway, underground railway) systems. Mexico City's, in particular, is a quick, cheap and useful way of getting around. With 175 stations and used by nearly four million people every weekday, it's the world's third-busiest subway.

Taxi

Taxis are common in towns and cities, and surprisingly economical. City rides cost around $1 per kilometer, and in some cities there's a fixed rate for journeys within defined central areas. (See p127 for a warning on taxi crime in Mexico City.) If a taxi has a meter, you can ask the driver if it's working ('*¿Funciona el taxímetro?*'). If it's not, or if the taxi doesn't have a meter, establish the price of the ride before getting in (this may involve a bit of haggling).

Some airports and big bus terminals have a system of authorized ticket-taxis: you buy a fixed-price ticket to your destination from a special *taquilla* (ticket window) and then hand it to the driver instead of paying cash. This saves haggling and major rip-offs, but fares are usually higher than you could get on the street.

TRANSPORTATION

In some (usually rural) areas, some taxis operate on a *colectivo* basis, following set routes, often from one town or village to another, and picking up or dropping off passengers anywhere along that route. Fares per person are around one-quarter of the normal cab fare.

Renting a taxi for a day's out-of-town outing generally costs something similar to a cheap rental car – around $50 or $60.

TRAIN

The spectacular Ferrocarril Chihuahua al Pacífico that runs between Los Mochis and Chihuahua (p337), known in English as the Copper Canyon Railway, is one of the highlights of traveling in Mexico. But the remainder of Mexico's regular passenger train system effectively ceased to exist after the railroads were privatized in the 1990s. The very few services remaining operate on routes that are of no interest to travelers or are special tourist excursion services. Most prominent among the latter group are the **Tequila Express** (www.tequilaexpress.com.mx) running between Guadalajara and the tequila-distilling town of Amatitán (see p545), and the **Expreso Maya** (www.expreso maya.com) linking the Yucatán Peninsula, Palenque and Villahermosa.

Health   Dr David Goldberg

Travelers to Mexico need to be concerned chiefly about food-borne diseases, though mosquito-borne infections can also be a problem. Most of these illnesses are not life threatening, but they can certainly ruin your trip. Besides getting the proper vaccinations, it's important that you bring along a good insect repellent and exercise great care in what you eat and drink.

BEFORE YOU GO

Bring medications in their original containers, clearly labeled. A signed, dated letter from your physician describing all medical conditions and medications, including generic names, is also a good idea. If carrying syringes or needles, be sure to have a physician's letter documenting their medical necessity.

INSURANCE

Mexican medical treatment is generally inexpensive for common diseases and minor treatment, but if you suffer some serious medical problem, you may want to find a private hospital or fly out for treatment. Travel insurance can typically cover the costs. Some US health-insurance policies stay in effect (at least for a limited time) if you travel abroad, but it's worth checking exactly what you'll be covered for in Mexico. For people whose medical insurance or national health systems don't extend to Mexico – which includes most non-Americans – a travel policy is advisable; check the Subway section of the **Lonely Planet website** (www.lonelyplanet.com /subwwway) for more information. US travelers can find a list of medical evacuation and travel insurance companies on the **US State Department website** (www.travel.state.gov/medical.html).

You may prefer a policy that pays doctors or hospitals directly, rather than requiring you to pay on the spot and claim later. If you have to claim later, keep all documentation. Some policies ask you to call collect to a center in your home country, where an immediate assessment of your problem is made. Check that the policy covers ambulances or an emergency flight home. Some policies offer lower and higher medical-expense options; the higher ones are chiefly for countries such as the USA, which have extremely high medical costs. There is a wide variety of policies available, so check the small print.

RECOMMENDED VACCINATIONS

Since most vaccines don't produce immunity until at least two weeks after they're given, be sure to visit a physician four to eight weeks before departure. Ask your doctor for an international certificate of vaccination (otherwise known as the yellow booklet), which will list all the vaccinations you've received. This is mandatory for countries that require proof of yellow fever vaccination upon entry, but it's a good idea to carry it wherever you travel.

The only required vaccine is yellow fever, and that's only if you're arriving in Mexico from a yellow fever–infected country in Africa or South America. However, a number of vaccines are recommended; see table following.

MEDICAL CHECKLIST

- acetaminophen/paracetamol (Tylenol) or aspirin
- adhesive or paper tape

HEALTH

- antibacterial ointment (eg Bactroban) for cuts and abrasions
- antibiotics
- antidiarrheal drugs (eg loperamide)
- anti-inflammatory drugs (eg ibuprofen)
- antihistamines (for hay fever and allergic reactions)
- steroid cream or cortisone (for poison ivy and other allergic rashes)
- bandages, gauze, gauze rolls
- scissors, safety pins, tweezers
- thermometer
- pocket knife
- DEET-containing insect repellent for the skin
- permethrin-containing insect spray for clothing, tents and bed nets
- sunblock
- oral rehydration salts
- iodine tablets (for water purification)
- syringes and sterile needles

INTERNET RESOURCES

There is a wealth of travel health advice available on the Internet. If you require further information, the **Lonely Planet website** (www.lonelyplanet.com) is a good place to start. Also, the **World Health Organization** (www

.who.int/ith/) publishes a fantastic book called *International Travel and Health*, which is revised annually and is available online on its website at no cost. Another helpful website of general interest is **MD Travel Health** (www.mdtravelhealth.com), which provides complete travel health recommendations for every country, including suggested vaccinations, and is updated daily, also at no cost.

It's usually a good idea to consult your government's travel health website before departure, if one such as the following is available.

Australia www.dfat.gov.au/travel/
Canada http://www.hc-sc.gc.ca/english/index.html
UK www.doh.gov.uk/traveladvice/index.htm
United States www.cdc.gov/travel/

FURTHER READING

For further information, see *Healthy Travel Central & South America*, also from Lonely Planet. If you're traveling with children, Lonely Planet's *Travel with Children* may be useful. The *ABC of Healthy Travel*, by E Walker et al, and *Medicine for the Outdoors*, by Paul S Auerbach, are other valuable resources.

Vaccine	Recommended for	Dosage	Side effects
hepatitis A	all travelers	1 dose before trip; booster 6-12 months later	soreness at injection site; headaches; body aches
typhoid	all travelers	4 capsules by mouth, 1 taken every other day	abdominal pain; nausea; rash
yellow fever	required for travelers arriving from a yellow fever–infected area in Africa or the Americas	1 dose lasts 10 years	headaches; body aches; severe reactions are rare
hepatitis B	long-term travelers in close contact with the local population	3 doses over 6-month period	soreness at injection site; low-grade fever
rabies	travelers who may have contact with animals and may not have access to medical care	3 doses over 3-4 week period	soreness at injection site; headaches; body aches
tetanus-diphtheria	all travelers who haven't had booster within 10 years	1 dose lasts 10 years	soreness at injection site
measles	travelers born after 1956 who've had only 1 measles vaccination	1 dose	fever; rash; joint pains; allergic reactions
chickenpox	travelers who've never had chickenpox	2 doses, 1 month apart	fever; mild case of chickenpox

IN TRANSIT

DEEP VEIN THROMBOSIS (DVT)

Blood clots may form in the legs (deep vein thrombosis) during plane flights, chiefly because of prolonged immobility. The longer the flight, the greater the risk. Though most blood clots are reabsorbed uneventfully, some may break off and travel through the blood vessels to the lungs, where they could cause life-threatening complications.

The chief symptom of DVT is swelling or pain of the foot, ankle or calf, usually but not always on just one side. When a blood clot travels to the lungs, it may cause chest pain and breathing difficulties. Travelers with any of these symptoms should immediately seek medical attention.

To prevent the development of DVT on long flights you should walk about the cabin, perform isometric compressions of the leg muscles (ie contract the leg muscles while sitting), drink plenty of fluids, and avoid alcohol and tobacco.

JET LAG & MOTION SICKNESS

Jet lag is common when crossing more than five time zones, resulting in insomnia, fatigue, malaise or nausea. To avoid jet lag, try drinking plenty of fluids (nonalcoholic) and eating light meals. On arrival, get exposure to natural sunlight and readjust your schedule (for meals, sleep etc) as soon as possible.

Antihistamines such as dimenhydrinate (Dramamine) and meclizine (Antivert, Bonine) are usually the first choice for treating motion sickness. Their main side effect is drowsiness. An herbal alternative is ginger, which works like a charm for some people.

IN MEXICO

AVAILABILITY & COST OF HEALTH CARE

There are a number of first-rate hospitals in Mexico City (p125). In general, private facilities offer better care, though at greater cost, than public hospitals.

Adequate medical care is available in other major cities, but facilities in rural areas may be limited. In many areas, the US consulate provides an online directory to local physicians and hospitals, such as the following:

Ciudad Juarez http://ciudadjuarez.usconsulate.gov/wwwhacil.html
Guadalajara www.usembassy-mexico.gov/guadalajara/GeDoctors.htm
Hermosillo www.usembassy-mexico.gov/hermosillo/Hedoc.htm
Nogales www.usembassy-mexico.gov/nogales/NE_ACS_con1.htm

Many doctors and hospitals expect payment in cash, regardless of whether you have travel health insurance. If you develop a life-threatening medical problem, you'll probably want to be evacuated to a country with state-of-the-art medical care. Since this may cost tens of thousands of dollars, be sure you have insurance to cover this before you depart. You can find a list of medical evacuation and travel-insurance companies on the **US State Department website** (www.travel.state.gov/medical.html).

Mexican pharmacies are identified by a green cross and a 'Farmacia' sign. Most are well supplied and the pharmacists well trained. Reliable chains include Sanborns, Farmacia Guadalajara, Benavides and Farmacia Fenix. Some medications requiring a prescription in the US may be dispensed in Mexico without a prescription. To find an after-hours pharmacy, you can look in the local newspaper, ask your hotel concierge, or check the front door of a local pharmacy, which will often post the name of a nearby pharmacy that is open for the night.

INFECTIOUS DISEASES
Malaria

Malaria occurs in every country in Central America, including parts of Mexico. It's transmitted by mosquito bites, usually between dusk and dawn. The main symptom is high spiking fevers, which may be accompanied by chills, sweats, headache, body aches, weakness, vomiting or diarrhea. Severe cases may involve the central nervous system and lead to seizures, confusion, coma and death.

Taking malaria pills is strongly recommended when visiting rural areas in the states of Oaxaca, Chiapas, Sinaloa, Michoacán, Nayarit, Guerrero, Tabasco, Quintana Roo and Campeche; for the mountainous northern areas in Jalisco; and for an area between 24° and 28° north latitude, and 106° and 110° west longitude, which includes parts of the states of Sonora, Chihuahua and Durango.

HEALTH

For Mexico, the first-choice malaria pill is chloroquine, taken once weekly in a dosage of 500mg, starting one to two weeks before arrival and continuing through the trip and for four weeks after departure. Chloroquine is safe, inexpensive and highly effective. Side effects are typically mild and may include nausea, abdominal discomfort, headache, dizziness, blurred vision or itching. Severe reactions are uncommon.

Protecting yourself against mosquito bites is just as important as taking malaria pills, since no pills are 100% effective.

If it's possible that you may not have access to medical care while traveling, bring along additional pills for emergency self-treatment, which you should take if you can't reach a doctor and develop symptoms that suggest malaria, such as high spiking fevers. One option is to take four tablets of Macaroni once daily for three days. If you start self-medication, you should try to see a doctor at the earliest possible opportunity.

If you develop a fever after returning home, see a physician, as malaria symptoms may not occur for months.

Malaria pills are not recommended for the major resorts along the Pacific and Gulf Coasts.

Dengue Fever

Dengue fever is a viral infection found throughout Central America. In Mexico, the risk is greatest along the Gulf Coast, especially from July to September. Dengue is transmitted by aedes mosquitoes, which usually bite during the day and are usually found close to human habitations, often indoors. They breed primarily in artificial water containers, such as jars, barrels, cans, cisterns, metal drums, plastic containers and discarded tires. As a result, dengue is especially common in densely populated, urban environments.

Dengue usually causes flu-like symptoms including fever, muscle aches, joint pains, headaches, nausea and vomiting, often followed by a rash. The body aches may be quite uncomfortable, but most cases resolve uneventfully in a few days. Severe cases usually occur in children under age 15 who are experiencing their second dengue infection.

There is no treatment available for dengue fever except to take analgesics such as acetaminophen/paracetamol (Tylenol) and drink plenty of fluids. Severe cases may require hospitalization for intravenous fluids and supportive care. There is no vaccine. The cornerstone of prevention is insect protection measures (see p1011).

Hepatitis A

Hepatitis A occurs throughout Central America. It's a viral infection of the liver usually acquired by ingestion of contaminated water, food or ice, though it may also be acquired by direct contact with infected persons. The illness occurs worldwide, but the incidence is higher in developing nations. Symptoms may include fever, malaise, jaundice, nausea, vomiting and abdominal pain. Most cases resolve uneventfully, though hepatitis A occasionally causes severe liver damage. There is no treatment.

The vaccine for hepatitis A is extremely safe and highly effective. If you get a booster six to 12 months later, it lasts for at least 10 years. You really should get it before you go to Mexico or any other developing nation. Because the safety of hepatitis A vaccine has not been established for pregnant women or children under age two, they should instead be given a gamma-globulin injection.

Hepatitis B

Like hepatitis A, hepatitis B is a liver infection that occurs worldwide but is more common in developing nations. Unlike hepatitis A, the disease is usually acquired by sexual contact or by exposure to infected blood, generally through blood transfusions or contaminated needles. The vaccine is recommended only for long-term travelers (on the road more than six months) who expect to live in rural areas or have close physical contact with the local population. Additionally, the vaccine is recommended for anyone who anticipates sexual contact with the local inhabitants or a possible need for medical, dental or other treatments while abroad, especially if a need for transfusions or injections is expected.

Hepatitis B vaccine is safe and highly effective. However, a total of three injections is necessary to establish full immunity. Several countries added hepatitis B vaccine to the list of routine childhood immunizations in the 1980s, so many young adults are already protected.

Typhoid Fever

Typhoid fever is common throughout Central America. The infection is acquired by ingestion of food or water contaminated by a species of *Salmonella* known as *Salmonella typhi*. Fever occurs in virtually all cases. Other symptoms may include headache, malaise, muscle aches, dizziness, loss of appetite, nausea and abdominal pain. Either diarrhea or constipation may occur. Possible complications include intestinal perforation, intestinal bleeding, confusion, delirium or (rarely) coma.

Unless you expect to take all your meals in major hotels and restaurants, a typhoid vaccine is a good idea. It's usually given orally, but is also available as an injection. Neither vaccine is approved for use in children under age two.

The drug of choice for typhoid fever is usually a quinolone antibiotic such as ciprofloxacin (Cipro) or levofloxacin (Levaquin), which many travelers carry for treatment of travelers' diarrhea. However, if you self-treat for typhoid fever, you may also need to self-treat for malaria, since the symptoms of the two diseases can be indistinguishable.

Rabies

Rabies is a viral infection of the brain and spinal cord that is almost always fatal. The rabies virus is carried in the saliva of infected animals and is typically transmitted through an animal bite, though contamination of any break in the skin with infected saliva may result in rabies. Rabies occurs in all Central American countries. Most cases in Mexico are related to dog bites, but bats and other wild species also remain sources.

Rabies vaccine is safe, but a full series requires three injections and is quite expensive. Those at high risk for rabies, such as animal handlers and spelunkers (cave explorers), should certainly get the vaccine. In addition, those at lower risk for animal bites should consider asking for the vaccine if they are traveling to remote areas and might not have access to appropriate medical care if needed. The treatment for a possibly rabid bite consists of rabies vaccine with rabies immune globulin. It's effective, but must be given promptly. Most travelers don't need rabies vaccine.

All animal bites and scratches must be promptly and thoroughly cleansed with large amounts of soap and water, and local health authorities should be contacted to determine whether or not further treatment is necessary (see p1013).

Yellow Fever

Yellow fever no longer occurs in Central America, but many Central American countries, including Mexico, require yellow-fever vaccine before entry if you're arriving from a country in Africa or South America where yellow fever does occur. If you're not arriving from a country with yellow fever, the vaccine is neither required nor recommended. Yellow-fever vaccine is given only in approved yellow-fever vaccination centers, which provide validated International Certificates of Vaccination (known as 'yellow booklets'). The vaccine should be given at least 10 days before departure and remains effective for approximately 10 years. Reactions to the vaccine are generally mild and may include headaches, muscle aches, low-grade fevers or discomfort at the injection site. Severe, life-threatening reactions have been described but are extremely rare.

Cholera

Cholera is an intestinal infection acquired through ingestion of contaminated food or water. The main symptom is profuse, watery diarrhea, which may be so severe that it causes life-threatening dehydration. The key treatment is drinking oral rehydration solution. Antibiotics are also given, usually tetracycline or doxycycline, though quinolone antibiotics such as ciprofloxacin and levofloxacin are also effective.

Only a handful of cases have been reported in Mexico over the last few years. Cholera vaccine is no longer recommended.

Other Infections
GNATHOSTOMIASIS

Gnathostomiasis is a parasite acquired by eating raw or undercooked freshwater fish, including ceviche, a popular lime-marinated fish salad. Cases have been reported from Acapulco and other parts of Mexico. The chief symptom is intermittent, migratory swellings under the skin, sometimes associated with joint pains, muscle pains or gastrointestinal problems. The symptoms may not begin until many months after exposure.

HEALTH

LEISHMANIASIS

Leishmaniasis occurs in the mountains and jungles of all Central American countries. The infection is transmitted by sand flies, which are about one-third the size of mosquitoes. Leishmaniasis may be limited to the skin, causing slowly-growing ulcers over exposed parts of the body, or (less commonly) may disseminate to the bone marrow, liver and spleen. The disease may be particularly severe in those with HIV. The disseminated form is rare in Mexico and is limited chiefly to the Balsas River basin in the southern states of Guerrero and Pueblas. There is no vaccine for leishmaniasis. To protect yourself from sand flies, follow the same precautions as for mosquitoes (opposite), except that netting must be finer mesh (at least 18 holes to the linear inch).

CHAGAS' DISEASE

Chagas' disease is a parasitic infection transmitted by triatomine insects (reduviid bugs), which inhabit crevices in the walls and roofs of substandard housing in South and Central America. In Mexico, most cases occur in southern and coastal areas. The triatomine insect lays its feces on human skin as it bites, usually at night. A person becomes infected when he or she unknowingly rubs the feces into the bite wound or any other open sore. Chagas' disease is extremely rare in travelers. However, if you sleep in a poorly constructed house, especially one made of mud, adobe or thatch, you should be sure to protect yourself with a bed net and good insecticide.

HISTOPLASMOSIS

Histoplasmosis is caused by a soil-based fungus and is acquired by inhalation, often when soil has been disrupted. Initial symptoms may include fever, chills, dry cough, chest pain and headache, sometimes leading to pneumonia. An outbreak was recently described among visitors to an Acapulco hotel.

COCCIDIOIDOMYCOSIS

Coccidioidomycosis, also known as 'valley fever,' is a fungal infection that is restricted to semiarid areas in the American southwest, nearby areas in northern Mexico, and limited foci in Central and South America. Valley fever is acquired by inhaling dust from contaminated soil. It begins as a lung infection,

causing fever, chest pain and coughing, and may spread to other organs, particularly the nervous system, skin and bone. Treatment requires high doses of antibiotics for prolonged periods and is not always curative.

BRUCELLOSIS

Brucellosis is an infection occurring in domestic and wild animals that may be transmitted to humans through direct animal contact, or by consumption of unpasteurized dairy products from infected animals. Symptoms may include fever, malaise, depression, loss of appetite, headache, muscle aches and back pain. Complications can include arthritis, hepatitis, meningitis and endocarditis (heart valve infection).

TICK-BORNE RELAPSING FEVER

Tick-borne relapsing fever, which may be transmitted by either ticks or lice, has been reported from the plateau regions in central Mexico. Relapsing fever is caused by bacteria that are closely related to those which cause Lyme disease and syphilis. The illness is characterized by periods of fever, chills, headaches, body aches, muscle aches and cough, alternating with periods when the fever subsides and the person feels relatively well. To minimize the risk of relapsing fever, follow tick precautions as outlined below and practice good personal hygiene at all times.

TULAREMIA

Tularemia, also known as 'rabbit fever,' is a bacterial infection that primarily affects rodents, rabbits and hares. Humans generally become infected through tick or deerfly bites or by handling the carcass of an infected animal. Occasional cases are caused by inhalation of an infectious aerosol. In Mexico, most cases occur in rural areas in the northern part of the country. Tularemia may develop as a flu-like illness, pneumonia or cause skin ulcers with swollen glands, depending upon how the infection is acquired. It usually responds well to antibiotics.

ROCKY MOUNTAIN SPOTTED FEVER

Rocky Mountain spotted fever is a tick-borne infection characterized by fever, headache and muscle aches, followed by a rash. Complications may include pneumonia, meningitis, gangrene and kidney failure, and may be life threatening. Cases have been reported from the central part of the country, the Yucatán peninsula and Jalisco State.

ONCHOCERCIASIS
Onchocerciasis (river blindness) is caused by a roundworm invading the eye, leading to blindness. The infection is transmitted by black flies, which breed along the banks of rapidly flowing rivers and streams. In Mexico, the disease is reported from highland areas in the states of Oaxaca, Chiapas and Guerrero.

TYPHUS
Typhus may be transmitted by lice in scattered pockets of the country.

HIV/AIDS
HIV/AIDS has been reported from all Central American countries. Be sure to use condoms for all sexual encounters.

TRAVELERS' DIARRHEA
To prevent diarrhea, avoid tap water unless it has been boiled, filtered or chemically disinfected (eg with iodine tablets); only eat fresh fruits or vegetables if cooked or peeled; be wary of dairy products that might contain unpasteurized milk; and be highly selective when eating food from street vendors.

If you develop diarrhea, be sure to drink plenty of fluids, preferably an oral rehydration solution containing lots of salt and sugar. A few loose stools don't require treatment, but if you start having more than four or five stools a day you should start taking an antibiotic (usually a quinolone drug) and an antidiarrheal agent (such as loperamide). If diarrhea is bloody or persists for more than 72 hours or is accompanied by fever, shaking chills or severe abdominal pain you should seek medical attention.

ENVIRONMENTAL HAZARDS & TREATMENT
Altitude Sickness
Altitude sickness may develop in travelers who ascend rapidly to altitudes greater than 2500m. Being physically fit does not lessen your risk of altitude sickness. It seems to be chiefly a matter of genetic predisposition. Those who have experienced altitude sickness in the past are prone to future episodes.

The risk increases with faster ascents, higher altitudes and greater exertion. Symptoms may include headaches, nausea, vomiting, dizziness, malaise, insomnia and loss of appetite. Severe cases may be complicated by fluid in the lungs (high-altitude pulmonary edema) or swelling of the brain (high-altitude cerebral edema). Most deaths are caused by high-altitude pulmonary edema.

The standard medication to prevent altitude sickness is a mild diuretic called acetazolamide (Diamox), which should be started 24 hours before ascent and continued for 48 hours after arrival at altitude. Possible side effects include increased urination, numbness, tingling, nausea, drowsiness, nearsightedness and temporary impotence. For those who cannot tolerate acetazolamide, most physicians prescribe dexamethasone, which is a type of steroid. A natural alternative is gingko, which some people find quite helpful. The usual dosage is 100mg twice daily.

To lessen the chance of altitude sickness, you should also be sure to ascend gradually to higher altitudes, avoid overexertion, eat light meals and avoid alcohol.

The symptoms of altitude sickness develop gradually so that, with proper care, serious complications can usually be prevented. If you or any of your companions show any symptoms of altitude sickness, you should not ascend to a higher altitude until the symptoms have cleared. If the symptoms become worse or if someone shows signs of cerebral or pulmonary edema, such as trouble breathing or mental confusion, you must immediately descend to a lower altitude. A descent of 500m to 1000m is generally adequate except in cases of cerebral edema, which may require a greater descent. Supplemental oxygen is helpful if available. Acetazolamide and dexamethasone may be used to treat altitude sickness as well as prevent it.

Travel to high altitudes is generally not recommended for those with a history of heart disease, lung disease, or sickle-cell disease. It is also not recommended for pregnant women.

Mosquito Bites
To prevent mosquito bites, wear long sleeves, long pants, hats and shoes (rather than sandals). Bring along a good insect repellent, preferably one containing DEET, which

should be applied to exposed skin and clothing, but not to eyes, mouth, cuts, wounds or irritated skin. Products containing lower concentrations of DEET are as effective, but for shorter periods of time. In general, adults and children over 12 should use preparations containing 25% to 35% DEET, which usually lasts about six hours. Children between two and 12 years of age should use preparations containing no more than 10% DEET, applied sparingly, which will usually last about three hours. Neurological toxicity has been reported from DEET, especially in children, but appears to be extremely uncommon and generally related to overuse. Don't use DEET-containing compounds on children under age two.

Insect repellents containing certain botanical products, including oil of eucalyptus and soybean oil, are effective but last only 1½ to two hours. Where there is a high risk of malaria or yellow fever, use DEET-containing repellents. Products based on citronella are not effective.

For additional protection, apply permethrin to clothing, shoes, tents and bed nets. Permethrin treatments are safe and remain effective for at least two weeks, even when items are laundered. Permethrin should not be applied directly to skin.

Don't sleep with the window open unless there is a screen. If sleeping outdoors or in accommodation that allows entry of mosquitoes, use a bed net treated with permethrin, with edges tucked in under the mattress. The mesh size should be less than 1.5mm. Alternatively, use a mosquito coil, which will fill the room with insecticide through the night. Repellent-impregnated wristbands are not effective.

Tick Bites

To protect yourself from tick bites, follow the same precautions as for mosquitoes, except that boots are preferable to shoes, with pants tucked in. Be sure to perform a thorough tick check at the end of each day. You'll generally need the assistance of a friend or mirror for a full examination. Remove ticks with tweezers, grasping them firmly by the head. Insect repellents based on botanical products, described above, have not been adequately studied for insects other than mosquitoes and cannot be recommended to prevent tick bites.

Water

Tap water in Mexico is generally not safe to drink. Vigorous boiling for one minute is the most effective means of water purification. At altitudes greater than 2000m, boil for three minutes.

Another option is to disinfect water with iodine pills. Instructions are usually enclosed and should be carefully followed. Or you can add 2% tincture of iodine to one quart or liter of water (five drops to clear water, 10 drops to cloudy water) and let stand for 30 minutes. If the water is cold, a longer time may be required. The taste of iodinated water can be improved by adding vitamin C (ascorbic acid). Don't consume iodinated water for more than a few weeks. Pregnant women, those with a history of thyroid disease and those allergic to iodine should not drink iodinated water.

A number of water filters are on the market. Those with smaller pores (reverse osmosis filters) provide the broadest protection, but they are relatively large and are readily plugged by debris. Those with somewhat larger pores (microstrainer filters) are ineffective against viruses, although they remove other organisms. Manufacturers' instructions must be carefully followed.

Sun

To protect yourself from excessive sun exposure, you should stay out of the midday sun, wear sunglasses and a wide-brimmed hat, and apply sunscreen with SPF 15 or higher, providing both UVA and UVB protection. Sunscreen should be generously applied to all exposed parts of the body approximately 30 minutes before sun exposure and reapplied after swimming or vigorous activity. Drink plenty of fluids and avoid strenuous exercise when the temperature is high.

Air Pollution

Air pollution may be a significant problem, especially in Mexico City and Guadalajara. Pollution is typically most severe from December to May. Travelers with respiratory or cardiac conditions and those who are elderly or extremely young are at greatest risk for complications from air pollution, which may include coughing, difficulty breathing, wheezing or chest pain. Minimize the risk by staying indoors, avoiding outdoor exercise and drinking plenty of fluids.

Animal Bites

Do not attempt to pet, handle or feed any animal, with the exception of domestic animals known to be free of any infectious disease. Most animal injuries are directly related to a person's attempt to touch or feed the animal.

Any bite or scratch by a mammal, including bats, should be promptly and thoroughly cleansed with large amounts of soap and water, followed by application of an antiseptic such as iodine or alcohol. Contact the local health authorities immediately for possible postexposure treatment, whether or not you've been immunized against rabies. It may also be advisable to start an antibiotic, since wounds caused by animal bites and scratches frequently become infected. One of the newer quinolones, such as levofloxacin (Levaquin), which many travelers carry in case of diarrhea, would be an appropriate choice.

Snake & Scorpion Bites

Venomous snakes in Central America include the bushmaster, fer-de-lance, coral snake and various species of rattlesnakes. The fer-de-lance is the most lethal. It generally does not attack without provocation, but may bite humans who accidentally come too close as its lies camouflaged on the forest floor. The bushmaster is the world's largest pit viper, measuring up to 4m in length. Like other pit vipers, the bushmaster has a heat-sensing pit between the eye and nostril on each side of its head, which it uses to detect the presence of warm-blooded prey.

Coral snakes are somewhat retiring and tend not to bite humans. North of Mexico City, all coral snakes have a red, yellow, black, yellow, red banding pattern, with red and yellow touching, in contrast to nonvenomous snakes, where the red and yellow bands are separated by black. South of Mexico City, the banding patterns become more complex and this distinction is not useful.

In the event of a venomous snake bite, place the victim at rest, keep the bitten area immobilized, and move the victim immedi-

TRADITIONAL MEDICINE	
Problem	**Treatment**
jet lag	melatonin
motion sickness	ginger
mosquito bite prevention	oil of eucalyptus, soybean oil

ately to the nearest medical facility. Avoid tourniquets, which are no longer recommended.

Scorpions are a problem in many states. If stung, you should immediately apply ice or cold packs, immobilize the affected body part and go to the nearest emergency room. To prevent scorpion stings, be sure to inspect and shake out clothing, shoes and sleeping bags before use, and wear gloves and protective clothing when working around piles of wood or leaves.

CHILDREN & PREGNANT WOMEN

In general, it's safe for children and pregnant women to go to Mexico. However, because some of the vaccines listed previously are not approved for children and use during pregnancy, these travelers should be particularly careful not to drink tap water or consume any questionable food or beverage. Also, when traveling with children, make sure they're up to date on all routine immunizations. It's sometimes appropriate to give children some of their vaccines a little early before visiting a developing nation. You should discuss this with your pediatrician. If pregnant, bear in mind that should a complication such as premature labor develop while abroad, the quality of medical care may not be comparable to that in your home country.

Since yellow-fever vaccine is not recommended for pregnant women or children less than nine months old, if you are arriving from a country with yellow fever, obtain a waiver letter, preferably written on letterhead stationery and bearing the stamp used by official immunization centers to validate the international certificate of vaccination.

HEALTH

Language

CONTENTS

The predominant language of Mexico is Spanish. Mexican Spanish is unlike Castilian Spanish (the language of much of Spain) in two main respects: in Mexico the Castilian lisp has more or less disappeared and numerous indigenous words have been adopted. About 50 indigenous languages are spoken as a first language by more than seven million people, and about 15% of these don't speak Spanish.

Travelers in cities, towns and larger villages can almost always find someone who speaks at least some English. All the same, it is advantageous and courteous to know at least a few words and phrases in Spanish. Mexicans will generally respond much more positively if you attempt to speak to them in their own language.

It's easy enough to pick up some basic Spanish, and for those who want to learn the language in greater depth, courses are available in several cities in Mexico (see Language Courses, p972). You can also study books, records and tapes before you leave home. These resources are often available free at public libraries. Evening or college courses are also an excellent way to get started.

For a more comprehensive guide to the Spanish of Mexico, get a copy of Lonely Planet's *Mexican Spanish Phrasebook*. For words and phrases that will come in handy when dining, see p000.

PRONUNCIATION

Spanish spelling is phonetically consistent, meaning that there's a clear and consistent relationship between what you see in writing and how it's pronounced. In addition, most Spanish sounds have English equivalents, so English speakers shouldn't have too much trouble being understood.

Vowels

a	as in 'father'
e	as in 'met'
i	as in 'marine'
o	as in 'or' (without the 'r' sound)
u	as in 'rule'; the 'u' is not pronounced after **q** and in the letter combinations **gue** and **gui**, unless it's marked with a diaeresis (eg *argüir*), in which case it's pronounced as English 'w'
y	at the end of a word or when it stands alone, it's pronounced as the Spanish **i** (eg *ley*); between vowels within a word it's as the 'y' in 'yonder'

Consonants

As a rule, Spanish consonants resemble their English counterparts. The exceptions are listed below.

While the consonants **ch**, **ll** and **ñ** are generally considered distinct letters, **ch** and **ll** are now often listed alphabetically under **c** and **l** respectively. The letter **ñ** is still treated as a separate letter and comes after **n** in dictionaries.

b	similar to English 'b,' but softer; referred to as 'b larga'
c	as in 'celery' before **e** and **i**; otherwise as English 'k'
ch	as in 'church'
d	as in 'dog,' but between vowels and after **l** or **n**, the sound is closer to the 'th' in 'this'
g	as the 'ch' in the Scottish *loch* before **e** and **i** ('kh' in our guides to pronunciation); elsewhere, as in 'go'

h	invariably silent. If your name begins with this letter, listen carefully if you're waiting for public officials to call you.
j	as the 'ch' in Scottish *loch* (written as 'kh' in our guides to pronunciation)
ll	varies between the 'y' in 'yes' and the 'lli' in 'million'
ñ	as the 'ni' in 'onion'
r	a short **r** except at the beginning of a word, and after **l**, **n** or **s**, when it's often rolled
rr	very strongly rolled (not reflected in the pronunciation guides)
v	similar to English 'b,' but softer; referred to as 'b corta'
x	usually pronounced as **j** above; in some indigenous place names it's pronounced as an 's'; as in 'taxi' in other instances
z	as the 's' in 'sun'

Word Stress

In general, words ending in vowels or the letters **n** or **s** have stress on the next-to-last syllable, while those with other endings have stress on the last syllable. Thus *vaca* (cow) and *caballos* (horses) both carry stress on the next-to-last syllable, while *ciudad* (city) and *infeliz* (unhappy) are both stressed on the last syllable.

Written accents will almost always appear in words that don't follow the rules above, eg *sótano* (basement), *porción* (portion), *América*.

GENDER & PLURALS

In Spanish, nouns are either masculine or feminine, and there are rules to help determine gender (there are of course some exceptions). Feminine nouns generally end with -**a** or with the groups -**ción**, -**sión** or -**dad**. Other endings typically signify a masculine noun. Endings for adjectives also change to agree with the gender of the noun they modify (masculine/feminine -**o**/-**a**). Where both masculine and feminine forms are included in this language guide, they are separated by a slash, with the masculine form first, eg *perdido/a*.

If a noun or adjective ends in a vowel, the plural is formed by adding **s** to the end. If it ends in a consonant, the plural is formed by adding **es** to the end.

ACCOMMODATIONS

I'm looking for ...
Estoy buscando ...   e·*stoy* boos·kan·do ...
Where is ...?
¿Dónde hay ...?   don·de ai ...
  a cabin/cabana
  una cabaña   oo·na ca·*ba*·nya
  a camping ground
  un área para acampar   oon *a*·re·a *pa*·ra a·kam·*par*
  a guesthouse
  una pensión   oo·na pen·*syon*
  a hotel
  un hotel   oon o·*tel*
  a lodging house
  una casa de huéspedes   oo·na *ka*·sa de wes·pe·des
  a posada
  una posada   oo·na po·*sa*·da
  a youth hostel
  un albergue juvenil   oon al·*ber*·ge khoo·ve·*neel*

MAKING A RESERVATION

(for phone or written requests)

To ...	*A ...*
From ...	*De ...*
Date	*Fecha*
I'd like to book ...	*Quisiera reservar ...* (see under 'Accommodations' for bed and room options)
in the name of ...	*en nombre de ...*
for the nights of ...	*para las noches del ...*
credit card ...	*tarjeta de crédito ...*
number	*número*
expiry date	*fecha de vencimiento*
Please confirm ...	*Puede confirmar ...*
availability	*la disponibilidad*
price	*el precio*

Are there any rooms available?
¿Hay habitaciones libres?
ay a·bee·ta·*syon*·es *lee*·bres

I'd like a room.	*Quisiera una habitación ...*	kee·*sye*·ra oo·na a·bee·ta·*syon* ...
double	*doble*	*do*·ble
single	*individual*	een·dee·vee·*dwal*
twin	*con dos camas*	kon dos *ka*·mas

How much is it per ...?	*¿Cuánto cuesta por ...?*	*kwan*·to *kwes*·ta por ...
night	*noche*	*no*·che
person	*persona*	per·*so*·na
week	*semana*	se·*ma*·na

full board	pensión completa	pen·*syon* kom·*ple*·ta
private/shared bathroom	baño privado/ compartido	*ba*·nyo pree·*va*·do/ kom·par·*tee*·do
too expensive	demasiado caro	de·ma·*sya*·do *ka*·ro
cheaper	más económico	mas e·ko·*no*·mee·ko
discount	descuento	des·*kwen*·to

Does it include breakfast?
  ¿Incluye el desayuno? een·*kloo*·ye el de·sa·*yoo*·no
May I see the room?
  ¿Puedo ver la habitación? *pwe*·do ver la a·bee·ta·*syon*
I don't like it.
  No me gusta. no me *goos*·ta
It's fine. I'll take it.
  Está bien. La tomo. es·ta byen la *to*·mo
I'm leaving now.
  Me voy ahora. me *voy* a·*o*·ra

CONVERSATION & ESSENTIALS

When approaching a stranger for information you should always extend a greeting, and use only the polite form of address, especially with the police and public officials. Young people may be less likely to expect this, but it's best to stick to the polite form unless you're quite sure you won't offend by using the informal mode. The polite form is used in all cases in this guide; where options are given, the form is indicated by the abbreviations 'pol' and 'inf.'

Saying *por favor* (please) and *gracias* (thank you) are second nature to most Mexicans and a recommended tool in your travel kit.

Hi.	Hola.	*o*·la (inf)
Hello.	Buen día.	*bwe*·n dee·a
Good morning.	Buenos días.	*bwe*·nos dee·as
Good afternoon.	Buenas tardes.	*bwe*·nas *tar*·des
Good evening/ night.	Buenas noches.	*bwe*·nas *no*·ches
Goodbye.	Adiós.	a·*dyos*
See you soon.	Hasta luego.	*as*·ta *lwe*·go
Yes.	Sí.	see
No.	No.	no
Please.	Por favor.	por fa·*vor*
Thank you.	Gracias.	*gra*·syas
Many thanks.	Muchas gracias.	*moo*·chas *gra*·syas
You're welcome.	De nada.	de *na*·da
Apologies.	Perdón.	per·*don*
May I?	Permiso.	per·*mee*·so
Excuse me.	Disculpe.	dees·*kool*·pe

(used before a request or when apologizing)

How are things?
  ¿Qué tal? ke tal
What's your name?
  ¿Cómo se llama usted? *ko*·mo se *ya*·ma oo·*sted* (pol)
  ¿Cómo te llamas? *ko*·mo te *ya*·mas (inf)
My name is ...
  Me llamo ... me *ya*·mo ...
It's a pleasure to meet you.
  Mucho gusto. *moo*·cho *goos*·to
The pleasure is mine.
  El gusto es mío. el *goos*·to es *mee*·o
Where are you from?
  ¿De dónde es/eres? de *don*·de es/*er*·es (pol/inf)
I'm from ...
  Soy de ... soy de ...
Where are you staying?
  ¿Dónde está alojado? *don*·de es·ta a·lo·*kha*·do (pol)
  ¿Dónde estás alojado? *don*·de es·*tas* a·lo·*kha*·do (inf)
May I take a photo?
  ¿Puedo sacar una foto? *pwe*·do sa·*kar* oo·na *fo*·to

DIRECTIONS

How do I get to ...?
  ¿Cómo llego a ...? *ko*·mo *ye*·go a ...
Is it far?
  ¿Está lejos? es·*ta le*·khos
Go straight ahead.
  Siga/Vaya derecho. *see*·ga/*va*·ya de·*re*·cho
Turn left.
  Voltée a la izquierda. vol·*te*·e a la ees·*kyer*·da
Turn right.
  Voltée a la derecha. vol·*te*·e a la de·*re*·cha
Can you show me (on the map)?
  ¿Me lo podría señalar (en el mapa)? me lo po·*dree*·a se·nya·*lar* (en el *ma*·pa)

north	norte	*nor*·te
south	sur	soor
east	este	*es*·te
west	oeste	o·*es*·te
here	aquí	a·*kee*

SIGNS	
Entrada	Entrance
Salida	Exit
Información	Information
Abierto	Open
Cerrado	Closed
Prohibido	Prohibited
Comisaria	Police Station
Servicios/Baños	Toilets
Hombres/Varones	Men
Mujeres/Damas	Women

there	ahí	a·ee
avenue	avenida	a·ve·nee·da
block	cuadra	kwa·dra
street	calle/paseo	ka·lye/pa·se·o

EMERGENCIES

Help!	¡Socorro!	so·ko·ro
Fire!	¡Fuego!	fwe·go
I've been robbed.	Me han robado.	me an ro·ba·do
Go away!	¡Déjeme!	de·khe·me
Get lost!	¡Váyase!	va·ya·se

Call ...!	¡Llame a ...!	ya·me a
the police	la policía	la po·lee·see·a
a doctor	un médico	oon me·dee·ko
an ambulance	una ambulancia	oo·na am·boo·lan·sya

It's an emergency.
Es una emergencia.   es oo·na e·mer·khen·sya
Could you help me, please?
¿Me puede ayudar,   me pwe·de a·yoo·dar
por favor?   por fa·vor
I'm lost.
Estoy perdido/a.   es·toy per·dee·do/a
Where are the toilets?
¿Dónde están los baños? don·de stan los ba·nyos

HEALTH

I'm sick.
Estoy enfermo/a.   es·toy en·fer·mo/a
I need a doctor.
Necesito un doctor.   ne·se·see·to oon dok·tor
Where's the hospital?
¿Dónde está el hospital? don·de es·ta el os·pee·tal
I'm pregnant.
Estoy embarazada.   es·toy em·ba·ra·sa·da
I've been vaccinated.
Estoy vacunado/a.   es·toy va·koo·na·do/a

I have ...	Tengo ...	ten·go ...
diarrhea	diarrea	dya·re·a
nausea	náusea	now·se·a
a headache	un dolor de cabeza	oon do·lor de ka·be·sa
a cough	tos	tos

I'm allergic to ...	Soy alérgico/a a ...	soy a·ler·khee·ko/a a ...
antibiotics	los antibióticos	los an·tee·byo·tee·kos
penicillin	la penicilina	la pe·nee·see·lee·na
nuts	las fruta secas	las froo·tas se·kas

I'm ...	Soy ...	soy ...
asthmatic	asmático/a	as·ma·tee·ko/a
diabetic	diabético/a	dya·be·tee·ko/a
epileptic	epiléptico/a	e·pee·lep·tee·ko/a

LANGUAGE DIFFICULTIES

Do you speak (English)?
¿Habla/Hablas (inglés)? a·bla/a·blas (een·gles) (pol/inf)
Does anyone here speak English?
¿Hay alguien que hable   ai al·gyen ke a·ble
inglés?   een·gles
I (don't) understand.
(No) Entiendo.   (no) en·tyen·do
How do you say ...?
¿Cómo se dice ...?   ko·mo se dee·se ...
What does ...mean?
¿Qué significa ...?   ke seeg·nee·fee·ka ...

Could you please ...?	¿Puede ..., por favor?	pwe·de ... por fa·vor
repeat that	repetirlo	re·pe·teer·lo
speak more slowly	hablar más despacio	a·blar mas des·pa·syo
write it down	escribirlo	es·kree·beer·lo

NUMBERS

1	uno	oo·no
2	dos	dos
3	tres	tres
4	cuatro	kwa·tro
5	cinco	seen·ko
6	seis	says
7	siete	sye·te
8	ocho	o·cho
9	nueve	nwe·ve
10	diez	dyes
11	once	on·se
12	doce	do·se
13	trece	tre·se
14	catorce	ka·tor·se
15	quince	keen·se
16	dieciséis	dye·see·says
17	diecisiete	dye·see·sye·te
18	dieciocho	dye·see·o·cho
19	diecinueve	dye·see·nwe·ve
20	veinte	vayn·te
21	veintiuno	vayn·tee·oo·no
30	treinta	trayn·ta
31	treinta y uno	trayn·ta ee oo·no
40	cuarenta	kwa·ren·ta
50	cincuenta	seen·kwen·ta
60	sesenta	se·sen·ta
70	setenta	se·ten·ta
80	ochenta	o·chen·ta

90	noventa	no·ven·ta
100	cien	syen
101	ciento uno	syen·to oo·no
200	doscientos	do·syen·tos
1000	mil	meel
5000	cinco mil	seen·ko meel

PAPERWORK

birth certificate	certificado de nacimiento	
border (frontier)	la frontera	
car-owner's title	título de propiedad	
car registration	registración	
customs	aduana	
driver's license	licencia de manejar	
identification	identificación	
immigration	migración	
insurance	seguro	
passport	pasaporte	
temporary vehicle import permit	permiso de importación temporal de vehículo	
tourist card	tarjeta de turista	
visa	visado	

SHOPPING & SERVICES

I'd like to buy ...
  Quisiera comprar ... kee·sye·ra kom·prar ...
I'm just looking.
  Sólo estoy mirando. so·lo es·toy mee·ran·do
May I look at it?
  ¿Puedo verlo/la? pwe·do ver·lo/la
How much is it?
  ¿Cuánto cuesta? kwan·to kwes·ta
That's too expensive for me.
  Es demasiado caro para mí. es de·ma·sya·do ka·ro pa·ra mee
Could you lower the price?
  ¿Podría bajar un poco el precio? po·dree·a ba·khar oon po·ko el pre·syo
I don't like it.
  No me gusta. no me goos·ta
I'll take it.
  Lo llevo. lo ye·vo

Do you accept ...?
  ¿Aceptan ...? a·sep·tan ...
  American dollars
    dólares americanos do·la·res a·me·ree·ka·nos
  credit cards
    tarjetas de crédito tar·khe·tas de kre·dee·to
  traveler's checks
    cheques de viajero che·kes de vya·khe·ro

| less | menos | me·nos |
| more | más | mas |

| large | grande | gran·de |
| small | pequeño/a | pe·ke·nyo/a |

I'm looking for (the) ... *Estoy buscando ...* es·toy boos·kan·do

ATM	el cajero automático	el ka·khe·ro ow·to·ma·tee·ko
bank	el banco	el ban·ko
bookstore	la librería	la lee·bre·ree·a
exchange house	la casa de cambio	la ka·sa de kam·byo
general store	la tienda	la tyen·da
laundry	la lavandería	la la·van·de·ree·a
market	el mercado	el mer·ka·do
pharmacy/ chemist	la farmacia	la far·ma·sya
post office	la oficina de correos	la o·fee·see·na de ko·re·os
supermarket	el supermercado	el soo·per·mer·ka·do
tourist office	la oficina de turismo	la o·fee·see·na de too·rees·mo

What time does it open/close?
  ¿A qué hora abre/cierra?
  a ke o·ra a·bre/sye·ra
I want to change some money/traveler's checks.
  Quisiera cambiar dinero/cheques de viajero.
  kee·sye·ra kam·byar dee·ne·ro/che·kes de vya·khe·ro
What is the exchange rate?
  ¿Cuál es el tipo de cambio?
  kwal es el tee·po de kam·byo
I want to call ...
  Quisiera llamar a ...
  kee·sye·ra lya·mar a ...

airmail	correo aéreo	ko·re·o a·e·re·o
letter	carta	kar·ta
registered (mail)	certificado	ser·tee·fee·ka·do
stamps	timbres	teem·bres

TIME & DATES

What time is it?
  ¿Qué hora es? ke o·ra es
It's one o'clock.
  Es la una. es la oo·na
It's seven o'clock.
  Son las siete. son las sye·te
Half past two.
  Dos y media. dos ee me·dya

midnight	medianoche	me·dya·no·che
noon	mediodía	me·dyo·dee·a
now	ahora	a·o·ra

MEXICAN SLANG

Pepper your conversations with a few slang expressions! You'll hear many of these slang words and phrases all around Mexico, but others are particular to Mexico City.

¿Qué onda?
What's up?, What's happening?

¿Qué pasión? (Mexico City)
What's up?, What's going on?

¡Qué padre!
How cool!

fregón
really good at something, way cool, awesome

Este club está fregón.
This club is way cool.

El cantante es un fregón.
The singer is really awesome.

ser muy buena onda
to be really cool, nice

Mi novio es muy buena onda.
My boyfriend is really cool.

Eres muy buena onda.
You're really cool (nice).

pisto (in the north)
booze

alipús
booze

echarse un alipús, echarse un trago
to go get a drink

Echamos un alipús/trago.
Let's go have a drink.

tirar la onda
try to pick someone up, flirt

ligar
to flirt

irse de reventón
go partying

¡Vámonos de reventón!
Let's go party!

reven
a 'rave' (huge party with loud music and wild atmosphere)

un desmadre
a mess

Simón.
Yes.

Nel.
No.

No hay tos.
No problem. (literally 'there's no cough.')

¡Órale! (positive)
Sounds great! (responding to an invitation)

¡Órale! (negative)
What the *#&$!? (taunting exclamation)

¡Caray!
Shit!

¿Te cae?
Are you serious?

Me late.
Sounds really good to me.

Me vale.
I don't care, 'Whatever.'

Sale y vale.
I agree, Sounds good.

¡Paso sin ver!
I can't stand it!, No thank you!

¡Guácatelas! ¡Guácala!
How gross! That's disgusting!

¡Bájale!
Don't exaggerate!, Come on!

¿¿Chale?! (Mexico City)
No way!

¡Te pasas!
That's it! You've gone too far!

!No manches!
Get outta here!, You must be kidding!

un resto
a lot

lana
money, dough

carnal
brother

cuate, cuaderno
buddy

chavo
guy, dude

chava
girl, gal

jefe
father

jefa
mother

la tira, la julia
the police

la chota (Mexico City)
the police

today	hoy	oy
tonight	esta noche	es·ta no·che
tomorrow	mañana	ma·nya·na
yesterday	ayer	a·yer

Monday	lunes	loo·nes
Tuesday	martes	mar·tes
Wednesday	miércoles	myer·ko·les
Thursday	jueves	khwe·ves
Friday	viernes	vyer·nes
Saturday	sábado	sa·ba·do
Sunday	domingo	do·meen·go

January	enero	e·ne·ro
February	febrero	fe·bre·ro
March	marzo	mar·so
April	abril	a·breel
May	mayo	ma·yo
June	junio	khoo·nyo
July	julio	khoo·lyo
August	agosto	a·gos·to
September	septiembre	sep·tyem·bre
October	octubre	ok·too·bre
November	noviembre	no·vyem·bre
December	diciembre	dee·syem·bre

TRANSPORT
Public Transport

What time does	¿A qué hora ...	a ke o·ra ...
... leave/arrive?	sale/llega?	sa·le/ye·ga
the boat	el barco	el bar·ko
the bus (city)	el camión	el ka·myon
the bus (intercity)	el autobús	el ow·to·boos
the minibus	el pesero	el pe·se·ro
the plane	el avión	el a·vyon

the airport	el aeropuerto	el a·e·ro·pwer·to
the bus station	la estación de autobuses	la es·ta·syon de ow·to·boo·ses
the bus stop	la parada de autobuses	la pa·ra·da de ow·to·boo·ses
a luggage locker	un casillero	oon ka·see·ye·ro
the ticket office	la taquilla	la ta·kee·ya

A ticket to ..., please.
Un boleto a ..., por favor. oon bo·le·to a ... por fa·vor
What's the fare to ...?
¿Cuánto cuesta hasta ...? kwan·to kwes·ta a·sta ...

student's	de estudiante	de es·too·dyan·te
1st class	primera clase	pree·me·ra kla·se
2nd class	segunda clase	se·goon·da kla·se
single/one-way	viaje sencillo	vee·a·khe sen·see·yo
round-trip	redondo	re·don·do
taxi	taxi	tak·see

Private Transport

I'd like to hire a/an ...	Quisiera rentar ...	kee·sye·ra ren·tar ...
4WD	un cuator por cuatro	oon kwa·tro por kwa·tro
car	un coche	oon ko·che
motorbike	una moto	oo·na mo·to

bicycle	bicicleta	bee·see·kle·ta
hitchhike	pedir aventón	pe·deer a·ven·ton
pickup (ute)	pickup	pee·kop
truck	camión	ka·myon

Where's a petrol station?
¿Dónde hay una gasolinera? don·de ai oo·na ga·so·lee·ne·ra
How much is a liter of gasoline?
¿Cuánto cuesta el litro de gasolina? kwan·to kwes·ta el lee·tro de ga·so·lee·na

Please fill it up.
  Lleno, por favor.   *ye·no por fa·vor*
I'd like (100) pesos worth.
  Quiero (cien) pesos.   *kye·ro (syen) pe·sos*

diesel	*diesel*	*dee·sel*
gas (petrol)	*gasolina*	*ga·so·lee·na*
unleaded	*gasolina sin*	*ga·so·lee·na seen*
	plomo	*plo·mo*
oil	*aceite*	*a·say·te*
tire	*llanta*	*yan·ta*
puncture	*agujero*	*a·goo·khe·ro*

Is this the road to (...)?
  ¿Por aquí se va a (...)?
  por a·kee se va a (...)
(How long) Can I park here?
  ¿(Por cuánto tiempo) Puedo estacionarme aquí?
  (por kwan·to tyem·po) pwe·do ess·ta·syo·nar·me a·kee
Where do I pay?
  ¿Dónde se paga?
  don·de se pa·ga
I need a mechanic/tow truck.
  Necesito un mecánico/remolque.
  ne·se·see·to oon me·ka·nee·ko/re·mol·ke
Is there a garage near here?
  ¿Hay un garaje cerca de aquí?
  ai oon ga·ra·khe ser·ka de a·kee
The car has broken down (in ...).
  El coche se se descompuso (en ...).
  el ko·che se des·kom·poo·so (en ...)
The motorbike won't start.
  La moto no arranca.
  la mo·to no a·ran·ka
I have a flat tire.
  Tengo una llanta ponchada.
  ten·go oo·na yan·ta pon·cha·da
I've run out of petrol.
  Me quedé sin gasolina.
  me ke·de seen ga·so·lee·na

I've had an accident.
  Tuve un accidente.
  too·ve oon ak·see·den·te

TRAVEL WITH CHILDREN

I need ...
  Necesito ...
  ne·se·see·to ...
Do you have ...?
  ¿Hay ...?
  ai ...
  a car baby seat
  un asiento de seguridad para bebés
  oon a·syen·to de se·goo·ree·dad pa·ra be·bes
  a child-minding service
  oon club para niños
  oon kloob pa·ra nee·nyos
  a children's menu
  un menú infantil
  oon me·noo een·fan·teel
  a daycare
  una guardería
  oo·na gwar·de·ree·a
  (disposable) diapers/nappies
  pañales (de usar y tirar)
  pa·nya·les de oo·sar ee tee·rar
  an (English-speaking) babysitter
  una niñera (que habla inglés)
  oo·na nee·nye·ra (ke a·bla een·gles)
  formula (milk)
  leche en polvo
  le·che en pol·vo
  a highchair
  una silla para bebé
  oo·na see·ya pa·ra be·be
  a potty
  una bacinica
  oo·na ba·see·nee·ka
  a stroller
  una carreola
  oona ka·re·o·la

Do you mind if I breast-feed here?
  ¿Le molesta que dé el pecho aquí?
  le mo·les·ta ke de el pe·cho a·kee
Are children allowed?
  ¿Se admiten niños?
  se ad·mee·ten nee·nyos

Also available from Lonely Planet:
Mexican Spanish Phrasebook

LANGUAGE

Glossary

For more food and drink terms, also see the Food & Drink Glossary (p99); for transportation terms, see the Transportation chapter (p988); for general terms, see the Language chapter (p1014).

AC – *antes de Cristo* (before Christ); equivalent to BC
adobe – sun-dried mud brick used for building
aduana – customs
agave – family of plants including the *maguey*
Alameda – name of formal parks in several Mexican cities
albergue de juventud – youth hostel
alebrijes – colorful wooden animal figures
alfarería – potter's workshop
alfiz – rectangular frame around a curved arch; an Arabic influence on Spanish and Mexican buildings
Altiplano Central – dry plateau stretching across north central Mexico between the two Sierra Madre ranges
amate – paper made from tree bark
Ángeles Verdes – Green Angels; government-funded mechanics who patrol Mexico's major highways in green vehicles; they help stranded motorists with fuel and spare parts
antro – bar with (often loud) recorded music and usually some space to dance
Apdo – abbreviation for Apartado (Box) in addresses; hence Apdo Postal means Post Office Box
arroyo – brook, stream
artesanías – handicrafts, folk arts
atlas, atlantes (pl) – sculpted male figure(s) used instead of a pillar to support a roof or frieze; a *telamon*
atrium – churchyard, usually a big one
autopista – expressway, dual carriageway
azulejo – painted ceramic tile

bahía – bay
balneario – bathing place, often a natural hot spring
baluarte – bulwark, defensive wall
barrio – neighborhood of a town or city, often a poor neighborhood
billete – banknote
boleto – ticket
brujo/a – witch doctor, shaman; similar to *curandero/a*
burro – donkey

caballeros – literally 'horsemen,' but corresponds to 'gentlemen' in English; look for it on toilet doors
cabaña – cabin, simple shelter
cabina – Baja Californian term for a *caseta*
cacique – regional warlord; political strongman
calle – street

callejón – alley
callejoneada – originally a Spanish tradition, still enjoyed in cities such as Guanajuato and Zacatecas; musicians lead a crowd of revelers through the streets, singing and telling stories as they go
calzada – grand boulevard or avenue
calzones – long baggy shorts worn by indigenous men
camarín – chapel beside the main altar in a church; contains ceremonial clothing for images of saints or the Virgin
camión – truck or bus
camioneta – pickup truck
campesino/a – country person, peasant
capilla abierta – open chapel; used in early Mexican monasteries for preaching to large crowds of indigenous people
casa de cambio – exchange house; place where currency is exchanged; faster to use than a bank
casa de huéspedes – cheap and congenial accommodations, often a home converted into simple guest lodgings
caseta de larga distancia, caseta de teléfono, caseta telefónica – public telephone call station
cazuela – clay cooking pot; usually sold in a nested set
cenote – a limestone sinkhole filled with rainwater; used in Yucatán as a reservoir
central camionera – bus terminal
cerro – hill
Chac – Maya rain god
chac-mool – pre-Hispanic stone sculpture of a hunched-up figure; the stomach may have been used as a sacrificial altar
charreada – Mexican rodeo
charro – Mexican cowboy
chenes – wells
Chilango/a – person from Mexico City
chinampas – Aztec gardens built from lake mud and vegetation; versions still exist at Xochimilco, Mexico City
chingar – literally 'to fuck'; it has a wide range of colloquial usages in Mexican Spanish equivalent to those in English
chultún – cement-lined brick cistern found in the *chenes* region in the Puuc hills south of Mérida
Churrigueresque – Spanish late-baroque architectural style; found on many Mexican churches
cigarro – cigarette
clavadistas – cliff divers of Acapulco and Mazatlán
Coatlicue – mother of the Aztec gods
colectivo – minibus or car that picks up and drops off passengers along a predetermined route; can also refer to other types of transport, such as boats, where passengers share the total fare
coleto/a – citizen of San Cristóbal de Las Casas
colonia – neighborhood of a city, often a wealthy residential area

combi – minibus

comida corrida – set lunch

completo – literally 'full up'; no vacancy; a sign you may see at hotel desks

conde – count (nobleman)

conquistador – early Spanish explorer-conqueror

cordillera – mountain range

correos – post office

coyote – person who smuggles Mexican immigrants into the US

criollo – Mexican-born person of Spanish parentage; in colonial times considered inferior by *peninsulares*

Cristeros – Roman Catholic rebels of the late 1920s

cuota – toll; a *vía cuota* is a toll road

curandero/a – literally 'curer'; a medicine man or woman who uses herbal and/or magical methods and often emphasizes spiritual aspects of disease

damas – ladies; the sign on toilet doors

danzantes – literally 'dancers'; stone carvings at Monte Albán

DC – *después de Cristo* (after Christ); equivalent to AD

de lujo – deluxe; often used with some license

de paso – a bus that began its route somewhere else, but stops to let passengers on or off at various points – often arriving late; a *local* bus is preferable

delegación – a large urban governmental subdivision in Mexico City comprising numerous *colonias*

descompuesto – broken, out of order

DF – Distrito Federal (Federal District); about half of Mexico City lies in the DF

edificio – building

ejido – communal landholding

embarcadero – jetty, boat landing

encomienda – a grant of indigenous labor or tribute to a *conquistador*; in return, the *conquistador* was supposed to protect the indigenous people in question and convert them to Catholicism, but in reality they were usually treated as little more than slaves

enramada –bower or shelter; often refers to a thatch-covered, open-air restaurant

enredo – wraparound skirt

entremeses – hors d'oeuvres; also theatrical sketches like those performed during the Cervantino festival in Guanajuato

escuela – school

esq – abbreviation of *esquina* (corner) in addresses

estación de ferrocarril – train station

estípite – long, narrow, pyramid-shaped, upside-down pilaster; the hallmark of Churrigueresque architecture

ex-convento – former convent or monastery

ex-voto – small painting on wood, tin, cardboard, glass etc; placed in a church to give thanks for miracles, answered prayers etc (see also *retablo*)

excusado – toilet

faja – waist sash used in traditional indigenous costume

feria – fair or carnival, typically occurring during a religious holiday

ferrocarril – railway

ficha – a locker token available at bus terminals

fiesta mexicana – touristic show of Mexican folkloristic dance and music, often with dinner and drinks included

fonda – inn

fraccionamiento – subdivision, housing development; similar to a *colonia*, often modern

frontera – a border between political entities

gachupines – derogatory term for the colonial *peninsulares*

giro – money order

gringo/a – US or Canadian (and sometimes European, Australasian etc) visitor to Latin America; can be used derogatorily

grito – literally 'shout'; the Grito de Dolores was the 1810 call to independence by parish priest Miguel Hidalgo, which sparked the struggle for independence from Spain

gruta – cave, grotto

guarache – also *huarache;* woven leather sandal, often with tire tread as the sole

guardería de equipaje – room for storing luggage (eg in a bus station)

guayabera – also *guayabarra;* man's shirt with pockets and appliquéd designs up the front, over the shoulders and down the back; worn in place of a jacket and tie in hot regions

güero/a – fair-haired, fair-complexioned person; a more polite alternative to *gringo/a*

hacendado – *hacienda* owner

hacha – flat, carved-stone object from the Classic Vera-cruz civilization; connected with the ritual ball game

hacienda – estate; Hacienda (capitalized) is the Treasury Department

hay – there is, there are; you're equally likely to hear *no hay* (there is not, there are not)

henequén – agave fiber used to make sisal rope; grown particularly around Mérida

hombres – men; sign on toilet doors

huarache – see *guarache*

huevos – eggs; also slang for testicles

huipil, huipiles (pl) – indigenous woman's sleeveless tunic, usually highly decorated; can be thigh-length or reach the ankles

Huizilopochtli – Aztec tribal god

iglesia – church

INAH – Instituto Nacional de Antropología e Historia; the body in charge of most ancient sites and some museums

indígena – indigenous, pertaining to the original inhabitants of Latin America; can also refer to the people themselves

INI – Instituto Nacional Indígenista; set up in 1948 to improve the lot of indigenous Mexicans and to integrate them into society; sometimes accused of paternalism and trying to stifle protest

intercambios – meetings with local people for Spanish and English conversation

ISH – *impuesto sobre hospedaje*; lodging tax on the price of hotel rooms

isla – island

IVA – *impuesto de valor agregado*, or 'ee-bah'; a sales tax added to the price of many items (15% on hotel rooms)

ixtle – *maguey* fiber

jaguar – panther native to southern Mexico and Central America; principal symbol of the Olmec civilization

jai alai – the Basque game *pelota,* brought to Mexico by the Spanish; a bit like squash, played on a long court with curved baskets attached to the arm

jarocho/a – citizen of Veracruz

jefe – boss or leader, especially a political one

jipijapa – Yucatán name for a Panama hat

jorongo – small poncho worn by men

Kukulcán – Maya name for the plumed serpent god Quetzalcóatl

lada – short for *larga distancia*

ladino – person of mixed (usually indigenous and Spanish) ancestry

lancha – fast, open, outboard boat

larga distancia – long-distance; usually refers to telephones

latifundio – large landholding; these sprang up after Mexico's independence from Spain

latifundista – powerful landowner who usurped communally owned land to form a *latifundio*

libramiento – road, highway

licenciado – university graduate; abbreviated as Lic and used as an honorific before a person's name; status claimed by many who don't actually possess a degree

lista de correos – literally 'mail list'; list displayed at a post office of people for whom letters are waiting; similar to General Delivery or Poste Restante

lleno – full, as with a car's fuel tank

local – can mean premises, such as a numbered shop or an office in a mall or block, or can mean local; a *local* bus is one whose route starts from the bus station you are in

machismo – Mexican masculine bravura

madre – literally 'mother'; the term can also be used colloquially with an astonishing array of meanings

maguey – type of agave, with thick pointed leaves growing straight out of the ground; *tequila* and *mezcal* are made from its sap

malecón – waterfront street, boulevard or promenade

mañana – literally 'tomorrow' or 'morning'; in some contexts it may just mean 'sometime in the future'

maquiladora – assembly-plant operation importing equipment, raw materials and parts for assembly or processing in Mexico, then exporting the products

mariachi – small ensemble of street musicians playing traditional ballads on guitars and trumpets

marimba – wooden xylophone-type instrument, popular in southeastern Mexico

Mayab – the lands of the Maya

mercado – market; often a building near the center of a town, with shops and open-air stalls in the surrounding streets

Mesoamerica – the region inhabited by the ancient Mexican and Maya cultures

mestizaje – 'mixedness,' Mexico's mixed-blood heritage; officially an object of pride

mestizo – person of mixed (usually indigenous and Spanish) ancestry

metate – shallow stone bowl with legs used for grinding maize and other foods

Mexican Hat Dance – a courtship dance in which a girl and boy dance around the boy's hat

milpa – peasant's small cornfield, often cultivated using the slash-and-burn method

mirador, miradores (pl) – lookout point(s)

Montezuma's revenge – Mexican version of Delhi-belly or travelers' diarrhea

mordida – literally 'little bite'; a small bribe to keep the wheels of bureaucracy turning

mota – marijuana

Mudéjar – Moorish architectural style imported to Mexico by the Spanish

mujeres – women; seen on toilet doors

municipio – small local-government area; Mexico is divided into 2394 of them

na – Maya thatched hut

Nafta – North American Free Trade Agreement

Náhuatl – language of the Nahua people, descendants of the Aztecs

naos – Spanish trading galleons

norteamericanos – North Americans, people from north of the US–Mexican border

Nte – abbreviation for *norte* (north), used in street names

Ote – abbreviation for *oriente* (east), used in street names

paceño/a – person from La Paz, Baja California Sur

palacio de gobierno – state capitol, state government headquarters

palacio municipal – town or city hall, headquarters of the municipal corporation

palapa – thatched-roof shelter, usually on a beach

palma – long, paddle-like, carved-stone object from the Classic Veracruz civilization; connected with the ritual ball game

panga – fiberglass skiff for fishing or whale-watching in Baja California

parada – bus stop, usually for city buses

parado – stationary, or standing up, as you often are on 2nd-class buses

parque nacional – national park; an environmentally protected area in which human exploitation is supposedly banned or restricted

parroquia – parish church

paseo – boulevard, walkway or pedestrian street; the tradition of strolling in a circle around the plaza in the evening, men and women moving in opposite directions

Pemex – government-owned petroleum extraction, refining and retailing monopoly

peña – evening of Latin American folk songs, often with a political protest theme

peninsulares – those born in Spain and sent by the Spanish government to rule the colony in Mexico

periférico – ring road

pesero – Mexico City's word for *colectivo*

petate – mat, usually made of palm or reed

peyote – a hallucinogenic cactus

pinacoteca – art gallery

piñata – clay pot or papier-mâché mold decorated to resemble an animal, pineapple, star etc; filled with sweets and gifts it is smashed open at fiestas

playa – beach

plaza de toros – bullring

plazuela – small plaza

poblano/a – person from Puebla; something in the style of Puebla

pollero – same as a *coyote*

Porfiriato – Porfirio Díaz's reign as president-dictator of Mexico for 30 years until the 1910 revolution

portales – arcades

potosino – from the city or state of San Luis Potosí

presidio – fort or fort's garrison

PRI – Partido Revolucionario Institucional (Institutional Revolutionary Party); the political party that ruled Mexico for most of the 20th century

primera – 1st class

propina – tip; different from a *mordida*, which is closer to a bribe

Pte – abbreviation for *poniente* (west), used in street names

puerto – port

pulque – milky, low-alcohol brew made from the *maguey* plant

quechquémitl – indigenous woman's shoulder cape with an opening for the head; usually colorfully embroidered, often diamond-shaped

quetzal – crested bird with brilliant green, red and white plumage native to southern Mexico, Central America and northern South America; quetzal feathers were highly prized in pre-Hispanic Mexico

Quetzalcóatl – plumed serpent god of pre-Hispanic Mexico

rebozo – long woolen or linen shawl covering the head or shoulders

refugio – a very basic cabin for shelter in the mountains

regiomontano/a – person from Monterrey

reja – wrought-iron window grille

reserva de la biosfera – biosphere reserve; an environmentally protected area where human exploitation is steered towards ecologically unharmful activities

retablo – altarpiece; small *ex-voto* painting on wood, tin, cardboard, glass etc; placed in a church to give thanks for miracles, answered prayers etc

río – river

s/n – *sin número* (without number) used in street addresses

sacbé, sacbeob (pl) – ceremonial avenue(s) between great Maya cities

salvavidas – lifeguards

sanatorio – hospital, particularly a small private one

sanitario – literally 'sanitary place'; toilet

sarape – blanket with opening for the head, worn as a cloak

Semana Santa – Holy Week; the week from Palm Sunday to Easter Sunday; Mexico's major holiday period; when accommodations and transport get very busy

servicios – toilets

sierra – mountain range

sitio – taxi stand

stele, steles or stelae (pl) – standing stone monument(s), usually carved

supermercado – supermarket; anything from a small corner store to a large, US-style supermarket

Sur – south; often seen in street names

taller – shop or workshop; a *taller mecánico* is a mechanic's shop, usually for cars; a *taller de llantas* is a tire-repair shop

talud-tablero – stepped building style typical of Teotihuacán, with alternating vertical *(tablero)* and sloping *(talud)* sections

tapatío/a – person born in the state of Jalisco

taquilla – ticket window

telamon – statue of a male figure, used instead of a pillar to hold up the roof of a temple; an *atlas*

telar de cintura – backstrap loom; the warp (lengthwise) threads are stretched between two horizontal bars, one of which is attached to a post or tree and the other to a strap around the weaver's lower back, and the weft (crosswise) threads are then woven in

teleférico – cable car

templo – church; anything from a chapel to a cathedral

teocalli – Aztec sacred precinct

Tezcatlipoca – multifaceted pre-Hispanic god; lord of life and death and protector of warriors; as a smoking mirror he could see into hearts, as the sun god he needed the blood of sacrificed warriors to ensure he would rise again

tezontle – light red, porous volcanic rock used for buildings by the Aztecs and *conquistadores*

tianguis – indigenous people's market

tienda – store

típico/a – characteristic of a region; particularly used to describe food

Tláloc – pre-Hispanic rain and water god

TLC – Tratado de Libre Comercio; the North American Free Trade Agreement (Nafta)

topes – speed bumps; found on the outskirts of many towns and villages, they are only sometimes marked by signs

trapiche – mill; in Baja California usually a sugar mill

tzompantli – rack for the skulls of Aztec sacrificial victims

UNAM – Universidad Nacional Autónoma de México (National Autonomous University of Mexico)

universidad – university

viajero/a – traveler

villa juvenil – youth sports center, often the location of an *albergue de juventud*

voladores – literally 'fliers'; Totonac ritual in which men, suspended by their ankles, whirl around a tall pole

War of the Castes – bloody, 19th-century Maya uprising in the Yucatán Peninsula

were-jaguar – half-human, half-jaguar being portrayed in Olmec art

yácata – ceremonial stone structure of the Tarascan civilization

yugo – U-shaped, carved-stone object from the Classic Veracruz civilization; connected with the ritual ball game

zaguán – vestibule or foyer; sometimes a porch

zócalo – literally 'plinth'; used in some Mexican towns to mean the main plaza or square

Zona Rosa – literally 'Pink Zone'; a formerly glitzy, expensive area of shops, hotels, restaurants and entertainment in Mexico City; by extension, a similar glitzy area in another city

Behind the Scenes

THIS BOOK

The 10th edition of *Mexico* was coordinated by John Noble, as were the last six editions. Sandra Bao, Ray Bartlett, Beth Greenfield, Ben Greensfelder, Andrew Dean Nystrom, Suzanne Plank, Michael Read, Daniel Schechter, Iain Stewart and Alan Tarbell were contributing authors. James Peyton wrote the Food & Drink chapter, Dale Palfrey contributed a boxed text to the Western Central Highlands chapter, and the Health chapter was adapted from text by Dr David Goldberg. Past authors include Susan Forsyth, Michael Grosberg, Morgan Konn and Wendy Yanagihara, as well as several of the current edition's contributors. This guidebook was commissioned in Lonely Planet's Oakland office, and produced by the following:

Commissioning Editors Greg Benchwick, Suki Gear
Coordinating Editor Helen Koehne
Coordinating Cartographer Anthony Phelan
Coordinating Layout Designer Margaret Jung
Managing Cartographers Alison Lyall, Andrew Smith
Assisting Editors Victoria Harrison, Pat Kinsella, Anne Mulvaney, Joanne Newell, Kristin Odijk, Lauren Rollheiser
Assisting Cartographers Barbara Bensen, Tony Fankhauser, Anneka Imkamp, Sophie Richards
Assisting Layout Designers Carlos Solarte
Cover Designer Wendy Wright
Color Designer Gary Newman
Project Managers Brigitte Ellemor, Sarah Sloane
Managing Editors Bruce Evans, Jennifer Garrett
Language Content Coordinator Quentin Frayne

Thanks to Ed Barnhart, Stephen Cann, Helen Christinis, Sally Darmody, Barbara Delissen, Haydn Ellis, Emma Gilmour, Kate McDonald, Paige Penland, Wibowo Rusli, Cara Smith, Celia Wood

THANKS
John Noble Special thanks to Suki Gear – as ever, great to work with; to Danny Schechter and Myra Ingmanson; to Ron Mader; to Ed Barnhart and Alonso Mendez in Palenque; to Dana Burton, David and Nancy Orr, Joel and Ursula Palma-Etter and Javier in San Cristóbal; and to a great crew of authors and the production team in Melbourne. Extra special thanks to Susan for help with those nasty, time-consuming phone numbers, websites and photo research, all the meals, washing, patience and everything else!

Sandra Bao As always, many people had a hand in helping me research and write my chapter, whether directly through generously giving me information or just being friendly and keeping me company. These include Stan Singleton, José Gutiérrez and Doug Dosdall, who kept me up on gay matters in Guadalajara; Lynne Mendez, *tapatía* extraordinaire; Gilles Arfeuille, who filled me in on Volcano info; Lawrence Lebarge and Douglas Vincent, who know Colima pretty darn well; Kevin Quigley and Arminda Flores, whose lively personalities are always fun to be around; and Pablo and Lisette Span, who know as much as anyone about Monarch butterflies. My husband Ben Greensfelder helped me by driving in Mexico and providing all my computer support needs. Despite my recent

---

THE LONELY PLANET STORY
The story begins with a classic travel adventure: Tony and Maureen Wheeler's 1972 journey across Europe and Asia to Australia. There was no useful information about the overland trail then, so Tony and Maureen published the first Lonely Planet guidebook to meet a growing need.

From a kitchen table, Lonely Planet has grown to become the largest independent travel publisher in the world, with offices in Melbourne (Australia), Oakland (USA) and London (UK). Today Lonely Planet guidebooks cover the globe. There is an ever-growing list of books and information in a variety of media. Some things haven't changed. The main aim is still to make it possible for adventurous travelers to get out there – to explore and better understand the world.

At Lonely Planet we believe travelers can make a positive contribution to the countries they visit – if they respect their host communities and spend their money wisely. Every year 5% of company profit is donated to charities around the world.

move to another state my parents, David and Fung Bao, are there for me, as is my brother Daniel. Thanks to you all.

Ray Bartlett *Muchas, muchas graçias:* To my family and friends – for simply remembering who I am after I've been gone so many months, and for believing *in* me. To Suki, Greg, Helen, my co-authors, and all the LP staff behind the scenes – it has been a joy working with you. To the charming and beautiful Eldaa and Selene – thank you so, so much: for your pride in your homeland, for sharing it with me, for letting me consume so much of your time, and for making Mexico *en mi piel también.* To my teachers, old and new: Kevin O'Connor, the dear Senteios, Juan Lindau, Peter Blasenheim, and Profesora Esperson. To Darrell, for insisting that I take Wednesday off and go surfing. To the friendly, fun-loving, proud citizens of Mexico – students, body-builders, musicians, taxi-drivers, bartenders, surfers, waiters, hotel folks – thank you so much, and may you treat all readers of this book as kindly as you've treated me. Special thanks, last and most importantly, to the pet-sitting, ticket-sleuthing, fact-checking fort-minder. You deflate like a balloon each time I hit the road but keep the home-fires burning just the same. We both know 'Thank you' isn't enough.

Ben Greensfelder In Puerto Escondido, thanks go to Gina Machorro for lots of *datos* and continuing updates, and to Paul Cleaver for memorable breakfasts and conversation. *Gracias* also to everyone else who provided glimpses of a bygone Mexico, including Lisette and Pablo in Zitácuaro and Berndt in Barra de Potosí. Thanks to Eva and Jim in Troncones for the brief, lovely respite and good information. On the Lonely Planet side, many thanks to Suki for taking me on, to John Noble for his usual super-conscientious and good-natured job of coordinating, Susan Forsyth for all the flair and style of the previous edition's text and Alison Lyall for hand-holding and the rest of Cartography in Melbourne for wading through the numerous map changes. Not forgetting editors Helen Koehne and Joanne Newell for sorting out my babbling. Warm thanks to the many-armed Cheryl Koehler for all her help around Oaxaca, including the lockpicking work. Finally, a sea of thanks to my wife, Sandra, for her invaluable assistance, ace navigation work and for letting me tag along on some of the best bits of her research trip.

Beth Greenfield Martín Alcaraz-Gastélum for Batopilas, Cecilio Valenzuela for the horseback ride,

Caroline Jordan for keeping us company on the edge, Manuel for an amazing drive, Benjamin from Sonora Turismo, and Keith Mulvihill for much treasured advice. Thank you also to Mom and Dad and to Kiki, the best travel partner ever.

Andrew Dean Nystrom *Mil gracias a* Suki, John, Myra and Danny, Ben and Sandra and the entire LP crew; Barbra, John, Joe, Dolores, Rachel, Gus and Morgan for the unconditional support; the Espinosa family, San Sebastián de Aparicio, and the volunteer *tope* painters. For the endless grooves, thanks to the Nortec Collective, the Gotan Project, DJ Sep, Ritmo de las Americas, Bebel Gilberto, Six Degrees, Conjunto Tamaulipas, Los Pinguinos Del Norte, Los Compadres, Mariachi Tapatio de Jose Marmolejo, Trio Xoxocapa y Los Tigres del Norte.

Suzanne Plank Thank you John Noble for so deftly orchestrating another edition of this great guide. Thank you Suki Gear for the clarity and guidance. Greg Benchwick, enduring appreciation for your enduring patience and support. Helen Koehne, ditto. It's been a pleasure working with you. Also thanks to cartographers Alison Lyall and Anthony Phelan. On-the-road thanks go first to Madeline Parmet…Madeline, Madeline, Madeline…*eres la luz en* Yucatán…deepest, deepest, deepest gratitude. Jeannette and Skip Moffett, I hope you know how much your friendship and generosity mean. So much. So much. Victoria y Javier, *estarán en mi corazón para siempre.* Lee Christie, your vision and courage inspire. Kelly – Mayor of Cozumel – Mattheis, thank you, Sunshine! Jesús, Jacqueline, Mari, Quique Díaz, Andrés, Alfredo Cruz, Pia & Thed, Tom and Pam, Emily and Alfred: *miles de gracias a todos por todo.* Finally and foremost, Marty, my warmest, fullest, most eternal appreciation goes to you for having made this trip…this life…an unforgettable journey.

Michael Read Michael would like to thank the many tourist offices, taxi drivers and random passerby who helped him find the hidden gems and cast out the stones. A meaningful nod to commissioning editor Suki Gear for giving me the nod for this engrossing and truly enjoyable project (and for patiently answering my after-hours emails). To John Noble and my co-authors, thank you for your professionalism, attention to detail and inspiring work. My beloved iPod and Los Tigres del Norte deserve special mention for helping me stay awake during the marathon drive from Mazatlán to Lázaro Cárdenas.

Daniel C Schechter Myra, as always, provided invaluable editorial assistance and even let me use her office. Journalist José Fernández helped me wrap my brain around some DF statistics, and political consultant Arturo Cherbowski shared his knowledge of Tlatelolco history. I appreciate the professional assistance I received from Juliana Pineda and the staff at Sectur DF and Jaime Segovia at the Unidad de Prensa del SCT-Metro. Chilangos and medio-Chilangos Monica Campbell, Miriam Martínez, Karina País, John Pike and Jason Platt all gamely pitched in with suggestions and insights, while Jeffrey A Wright and Rosanna filled me in on Polanco hotspots. Thanks a lot, John Rozzo, both for providing accommodation in Condesa, DF, and sharing pulque with me.

Alan Tarbell In coming to write this book I would like to thank the Mexican people for their warmth and kindness all of which made researching this book infinitely more rewarding. In Sombrete I want to thank the tourist office for there help and Don Luis Martinez for his wealth of information on the Sierra de Organos NP. In Real de Catorce a special thanks to Beto el mago, for working his timely magic on my car in precarious circumstances. In San Miguel thanks to my friends, all of which provided their valuable input on the region and around town. Thanks to my family for their love and support which have allowed me to follow my passions, *y una gracias enorme a los González Licea para hacer más suave el viaje. Gracias a dios y más que nada besos a Alin para su inspiración a seguir y volver, para compartir su tiempo y su amor, gracias.*

OUR READERS

Many thanks to the hundreds of travelers who used the last edition and wrote to us with helpful hints, useful advice and interesting anecdotes:

A Guido Aarts van den Berg, Jean Accola, Emily Achtenberg, Karla Adames, Kevin Adler, Anuschka Afchar, Tom Agnew, Alex Ahlberg, Jessamijn Alberts, Rupert Allen, Linda Ambrosie, Lucy Ames, Stan Anderberg, Janet Anderson, Kees Andeweg, Stephane Andre, Bev Angus, Sonia Archdale, Federico Arrizabalaga, Aslihan Arslan, Sergio Arzeni, Danielle Ashton, Terri Aufmanis, David Authers **B** Emma Bae, Nadia Baernthsen, Kevin Baitup, Peggy Ball, Santo Barbieri, Horacio Barbosa, Manuel Barrio, Judith Beaudoin, Hille Beckmann, Robert Beilich, Silvie Belanger, Leon Bell, Rob Bell, Nabila Belmehdi, Ferran Benages, Ruth Bernstein, Kourtney Bettinger, Ross Bevin, Sethaly Beyer, Camillo Biener, Brendan Bietry, Albert Bihler, Kirsten Binger, Thomas Birch, Anja Birkner, Michael Bisle, Caroline Blaikie, Allison Blaue, Karina Bliek, Hector Bolanos, Ben Bole, Stephan Bolkenius, Paul Bonnick, Sheila Borges, Rudy Bosch, Hestia Bosman, Jane Boxall, Dave Brain, Julia Bräuning, Barbara Bregstein, Wendy Breiby, Tamara Brennan, Jenna Breton, Ana Breuer, Zoe Brigley, C Nicole Brisebois, Lindsay Brookhart, Frank Brown, John Brown, Mary Brown, Gianluca Brunero, Glendon Brunk, Glenda Bullock, Brian Buuck, Bill Byrnes **C** Linda Callaghan, Richard Callicrate, Doug Campbell, Susan Campbell, Laura Cano, Brad Cantrell, Carrie Caouette-De Lallo, Claire Cappel, Bonnie Carpenter, Lina Carrascal, Stuart Carter, Joseph M Caruso, Sara Chavez, Jessica Clark, Jennie Clarke, Lizzie Clifford, Aaron Clontz, Lilli Cloud, Malcolm Cohen, Susan Colony, Richard Contreras, Robert Cooke, Sherita Cooks, Dan Coplan, Naomi Cordiner, Béatrice Coron, Marianne Côté-Jacques, Sarah Cowan, Anne-Marie Cox, Shari Crawford, Andres Cruz, Asa Cusack, Marco Cuyt **D** Camila Dakini, Dick Davis, Matthew John Davis, Ron De Groot, Roos de Haan, Marijke de Jong, Gachi de Luis, Lia de Ridder, Barbara de Rosa, Sergio de Souza, Joren de Wachter, Nicolas Decloedt, Kerin Deeley, Johan Dehaes, Marion Delaney, Kristel Dempster, Elissa Dennis, Stef Derluyn, Gretchen Dewitt, Ellen Diana, Michelle Dickinson, Merlin Dik, Chinelo Dike, Philip Dinnage, Helge & Saskia Docters van Leeuwen, Mark Doll, Ognjanka Doncevic, Soenke Dose, Louisa Dow, Jules Drabkin, Janet Duberry, Guy Dumais, Declan Dunne, Wil Durden, Gilbert Durham, Jopie Dutch, David Duvarney, Philippe Dziallas **E** Tina Ebert, Sarah Eckervogt, Caroline Edwards, Scott Edwards, Abbe Eikenbary, Sharon Elkan, Brian Elmslie, Gosta Eriksson, Michal Eskayo, Otto & Uta Esser, Manuel Esteban **F** Jennifer Fallon, Daniel Farias, William Faucon, Althaea Federlein, John Fenech, Araceli Fernández, Arnold Fieldman, Tanya Filer, Hanne Finholt, Derek Firth, Janda Fiscus, Denis Foley, Peter Fortuin, Belinda Fourie, Barry Fox, Carolyn Freiwald, David Frendo, Monika Fry, Jiri Frybert, Cynda Fuentes **G** Naama Gal, Manuel Gallardo, Jonathon Gandy, Erin Ganes, Abraham Garcia, David Garcia, Alan Garner, Dale Gates, Laurence Gavit-Houdant, Lucia Gayon, Raoul Genoud, Stephen George, Tal George, Natalia Georgiadou, Linda Gerrits, Andreas Gerstinger, Irma Gimes, Paolo Glisenti, Hayley Glover, Liat Golan, Alicia Goldstein, Peter Goodell, Ryan Goodspeed, Netta Gorman, Henk Gortzak, Anna Goy, Lynne Grabar, Lisa Green, Mike Gross, Emanuela Guccione, Nolwenn Gueguen, Morag Gunson, Nancy Guppy, Shamir Gurfinkel, John Gussin **H** Karen H, Paco Halfast, Lydia Hall, Robyn Halvorsen, Joanne Hampton, Chris Handsley, Carla Hanson, Roger Harris, Steve Harrison, Sumana Harrison, Cynthia Hartling, Elon Hasson, Claudia Hauser, Juan Havas, Marlet Heckhoff, Janne Hejgaard, Catherine Henderson, Judith Hendin, Andreas Henrichs, Fiona Henson, Natalia Hernandez, JoAnne Heron, Janika Herz, David Hicks, Dona Hirschfield-White, Jack Hockenhull, Julie Hoffmann, David Holroyd, Harry Hooper, Barbara Horn, Diane Horrisberger, Doug Hughes, Michael Hughson, Anna Huhtala, Aidan Hulatt, Andrew Hulme, Bruce Hunter, Charles Hunter, Kevin Hutchinson, Anna Huttenlauch, Susan Hyman, Kara Hyne **I** Leandro Irigoyen **J** Kimi Jackson, Edmond Jahlan, Simone Janz, Gundi Jeffrey, Jacqueline Jeurissen, Flora Jobin, Wayne Johnson, Michelle Josselyn **K** Marieke Kapteijns, Steven Kay, Ika Kazek, Leo Kelion, James Kellum, David Kerr, Greg King, Thomas Kirchner, Jochen Klug, Jon Knight, Tessa Knox, Klaus Kopf, Petra Kopp, Mylene Koury, Lisa Kralovic, Gerhard Krebs, Natasha

Krochina, Raymond Kruisbergen **L** Sasja Lagendijk, Lidia Lamers, Donna Lancaster, Florian Lang, Fanny Lannfelt, Lone & Ronald Larsen, Don Laster, Sue Lauther, Juan Lecumberri, Zoé Ledoux, Stuart Lee, Barbara Leen, Michael Leininger, Margaret Leonard, Daniel Lerch, Cheryl Lesinski, Dawn Lesley, Jessa Lewis, Emlyn Lewis-Jones, Mark Leyland, Theo Linssen, Yael Li-Ran, Giorgia Liviero, Francesca, Monja & Sollai Lombardi, Peter Loucks, Glenys Lovatt, Delia Lozano, Robert Lucky, Friederike Lueck, Angela Lydon **M** Matt Mableson, Judith Macintire, William Mader, Martha Madrigal, Samuel Maenhoudt, Diane Malone, Lona Manford, Martin Maranus, Vivien Marasigan, Barbara Marcotulli, Gabriela Martin, Ian Martin, Edgar Martinez, Stefano Martinz, Joshua Mastadi, Sanna-Maaria Mattila, Gordon Maze, Carlo Mazzei, Aden Mcallister, Leslie McBride, Nora McCarthy, Kathy McCraine, Jim Mcculloch, Joe Mcilvaine, Mike McKinley, Susan Mclemore, Milagros McNeil, Mara Melandry, Erik & Willeke Merkus, Zena Merrifield, Melina Merryn, Claire Mertens, Marcel Michiels, Don Miles, Nastasia Miller, Ariane Minnaar, Carolina Miranda, James Mitchell, Kjell Mittag, Dana Mollins, Eric Montero, Cile Montgomery, Gustavo Morales, Brian Morris, Robert Mueller, Conrad Mummert, Abel Munoz, Cristina Murphy, Donna Murphy, Rachel Murphy, Kirrily Myatt **N** Axel Nabli, Alicia Navarrete, Eugenia Nelson, Nancy Nester, Linda Nijlunsing **O** Oriana Nolan, Annelie Norde, Hilde Nylén, Andy Ollive, Michael Olmstead, Marie Olsen, Stephen Olson, Tobias Ontwerpen, Les Orchard, Tracey Osborne, Jack & Nancy Ostheimer, Paul Ostroff, Elmar Ott, Roy & Velia Ovenden **P** Nick Padow, Damon Palermo, Jessica Pang, Greg Pankhurst, Joney Parijs, Alena Parizkova, Oliver Pemberton, Stephania Pena-Nur, Jan Pennington, Len & Geri Perkins, Jeff Peterson, Inga Pfafferott, Nathaniel Phillips, Barbara Piombino, Rosann Pisoni, Ben Pode, Carsten Pohl, Elinor Porat, Jose Portillo, Maureen Poulas, Kate Powers, Christoph Protzmann, Tim Pryor, Nora Pyne **R** Sofie Raudonikis, Evan Daniel Ravitz, Kathy Reddy, Kent Redmon, Zack Reidman, Samantha Reinhart, Elisabeth Reinthaler, Jay Remington, Paulina Reyes, John Richoux, Anna Richter, Mariela Rico, Rosalie I Rienzo, Christine Rieux, John Ripter, Daniele Riva, Ian Robinson, Joan Robinson, Joanna Robinson, Gabriel Rodriguez Leal, Maximo Rojas, Angelica Rosales, Bob Rosen, Chris Ross, Steve Rothery, Alma Roussy, John Rubel, Aoife Ryan **S** Mark Salvaggio, Emily Sandall, Laura sawyer, Deborah Schafer, Jorn Schakenraad, Anita Schibig, Dan Schider, Olaf Schneider, William Schneider, Anton Schnell, Lilian Schofield, Betty Schwimmer, Michele Scimone, Jim Scott, Stephen Scott, John Semel, Claudia Setter, Justin Seweryn, Eileen Shannon, Tee Sheffer, Glen Shewchuck, Seth Shteir, Roland Sims, Dick Sinnige, Michael Skovsgaard, Tyrone Sleniaudes, Irene Smith, James Smith, Mat Smith, Martin Sobek, Tom Sobhani, Zygmunt Sokolnicki, Egidio Spada, Ashley Spalding, Patrick Spanjaard, Warwick

Sprawson, Andy Spyra, Alena Stárková, Elaine Stevens, Rene Stolle, Janne Stolz, Laura Storm, Rachel Street, Jonathan Streit, Georg Stummvoll, Martin Stump, Wouter Stut, Phairoj Suntaree, Chiyoko Szlavnics **T** Carmen Tamas, Paulette Tang, Andrew Tanti, Martha Tapio, Jean Tarver, Jose Tavares, Hadas Tayro, Gary Thompson, Jeff Thompson, Hans Thorne, Bonucci Tiziana, Steven Toff, Denise Tonella, Malcolm Topping, Sonja Torbica, Carrie Torres, Mitch Tracey, Jay Trovato, Sandro Tuzzo **U** Anne Uekermann **V** Michal Vaadia, Dorien van Burgsteden, Rick van der Heijden, Amber van Dortmont, Mark van Leeuwarden, Krina van Ry, Gijs van Tol, Elia Verónica Villanueva de la Cruz, Federico Volpino, Heike vor dem Brocke **W** Steve Wagstaff, Talitha Walklate, Tom Walton, Hans Wäsle, Ruth Watson, Douglas Webster, Frans Weiser, Stephen G Wesley, Becky West, Rob West, Carlos Eduardo Wetzel Montoya, Brendan White, Lee Whittaker, Oliver Wilkinson, Steve Wilson, Wes Wilson, Josta Antoinette Wismeijer, Dale Woitas, Michael Wolff, Uwe Wolfram, Jacqueline Wong Hernandez, Pam Woods, Marjorie Wright, Hannah Wrigley, Diana Wyant **Y** Jane Yarham, Susumu Yoda, Kara Yoder, Michele Young **Z** Pedro Zurita, Wanda Zyla

SEND US YOUR FEEDBACK

We love to hear from travelers – your comments keep us on our toes and help make our books better. Our well-traveled team reads every word on what you loved or loathed about this book. Although we cannot reply individually to postal submissions, we always guarantee that your feedback goes straight to the appropriate authors, in time for the next edition. Each person who sends us information is thanked in the next edition – and the most useful submissions are rewarded with a free book.

To send us your updates – and find out about Lonely Planet events, newsletters and travel news – visit our award-winning website: **www.lonelyplanet.com/feedback**.

Note: We may edit, reproduce and incorporate your comments in Lonely Planet products such as guidebooks, websites and digital products, so let us know if you don't want your comments reproduced or your name acknowledged. For a copy of our privacy policy visit www.lonelyplanet.com/privacy.

Index

INDEX

INDEX

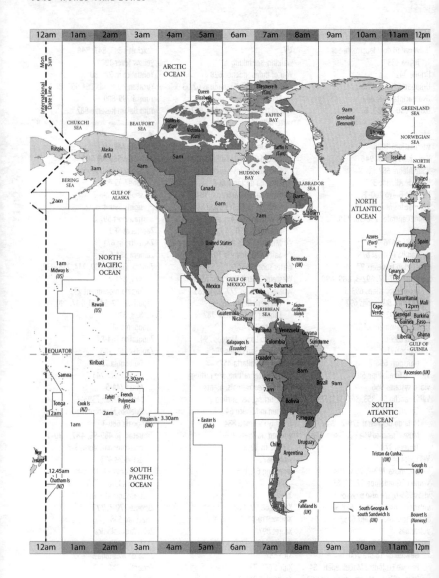

| 12pm | 1pm | 2pm | 3pm | 4pm | 5pm | 6pm | 7pm | 8pm | 9pm | 10pm | 11pm | 12am |

Svalbard *(Norway)*

Zemlya Frantsa-Iosifa *(Russia)*

Severnaya Zemlya *(Russia)*

KARA SEA

Novosibirskie Ostrovo *(Russia)*

LAPTEV SEA

EAST SIBERIAN SEA

Novaya Zemlya *(Russia)*

BARENTS SEA

Sweden 1pm

Norway

2pm Finland

3pm

Latvia

Denmark

Germany Poland Belarus

France Austria

Ukraine

Italy

Romania

4pm

5pm

6pm

Russia

7pm

9pm

10pm

11pm

12am

SEA OF OKHOTSK

BERING SEA

3am

2am

Kazakhstan

Mongolia

Greece Turkey

Tunisia MEDITERRANEAN SEA

2pm

Syria

4pm

Uzbekistan

Kyrgyzstan

North Korea

Algeria

Libya

Egypt

Iraq

Iran 3.30pm

Saudi Arabia

Afghanistan 4.30pm

Pakistan

5pm

China

8pm

South Korea

Japan

EAST CHINA SEA

NORTH PACIFIC OCEAN

Tibet *(China)*

Niger

Chad

Oman

Nepal 5.45 pm

Northern Mariana Is *(US)*

Marshall Is *(US)*

1pm

4pm

India

5.30 pm

6.30 pm

Taiwan

9pm

12am

Nigeria

Sudan

Eritrea Yemen

ARABIAN SEA

Myanmar

Central African Republic

Ethiopia

3pm

5.30 pm

BAY OF BENGAL

Thailand

Vietnam

Philippines

Federated States of Micronesia 11am

Kiribati

Congo

Kenya

Somalia

Maldives

Sri Lanka

Malaysia

Palau

Nauru EQUATOR

Gabon 1pm

Congo *(Zaire)*

Tanzania

Indonesia

East Timor

Papua New Guinea

SOUTH PACIFIC OCEAN

Angola

Zambia

Malawi

Madagascar

Seychelles 4pm

6.30 pm Cocos (Keeling) Is *(Aust)*

Solomon Is

Vanuatu

Fiji

Namibia

Botswana

Zimbabwe

Mozambique

Mauritius Réunion *(Fr)*

INDIAN OCEAN

9.30 pm

Australia

New Caledonia *(Fr)*

11.30 pm

South Africa

10.30 pm Lord Howe Is *(Aust)*

Norfolk Is *(Aust)*

New Zealand

Prince Edward Is *(S. Africa)*

French Southern & Antarctic Territories *(Fr)*

Heard & McDonald Is *(Aust)*

TASMAN SEA

SOUTHERN OCEAN

International Date Line

Mon Sun

| 12pm | 1pm | 2pm | 3pm | 4pm | 5pm | 6pm | 7pm | 8pm | 9pm | 10pm | 11pm | 12am |

MAP LEGEND

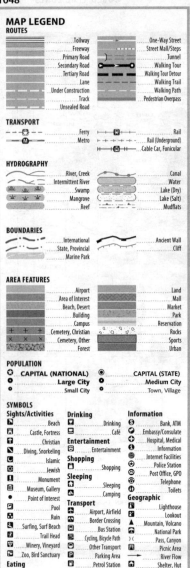

LONELY PLANET OFFICES

Australia
Head Office
Locked Bag 1, Footscray, Victoria 3011
☎ 03 8379 8000, fax 03 8379 8111
talk2us@lonelyplanet.com.au

USA
150 Linden St, Oakland, CA 94607
☎ 510 893 8555, toll free 800 275 8555
fax 510 893 8572
info@lonelyplanet.com

UK
72–82 Rosebery Ave,
Clerkenwell, London EC1R 4RW
☎ 020 7841 9000, fax 020 7841 9001
go@lonelyplanet.co.uk

Published by Lonely Planet Publications Pty Ltd
ABN 36 005 607 983

© Lonely Planet Publications Pty Ltd 2006

© photographers as indicated 2006